W9-ARK-227

TIME ALMANAC 2009

POWERED BY

ENCYCLOPÆDIA Britannica®

www.britannica.com

Jacob E. Safra, *Chairman of the Board*
Jorge Aguilar-Cauz, *President*

Chicago · London · New Delhi · Paris · Seoul · Sydney · Taipei · Tokyo

Year in Review

People

Awards

Nature, Science, Medicine, & Technology

United States

Business

Arts, Entertainment, & Leisure

Sport

ENCYCLOPÆDIA BRITANNICA, INC.

EDITORIAL
Thad King
Charles P. Trumbull
Patricia Bauer
Robert M. Lewis
Kenneth Pletcher
Barbara Schreiber
Melinda C. Shepherd
Karen Jacobs Sparks
Amy Tikkanen
Anita Wolff

PRODUCTION CONTROL
Marilyn L. Barton

WORLD DATA
Stephen Neher
Mary Kasprzak

CARTOGRAPHY
Michael Nutter

COPY
Sylvia Wallace
John M. Cunningham
Yvette Charboneau
Glenn Jenne

ART AND COMPOSITION
Steven N. Kapusta
Nicole DiGiacomo
Carol A. Gaines
Cate Nichols
Thomas J. Spanos

EDITORIAL LIBRARY
Henry Bolzon
Lars Mahinske

INFORMATION MANAGEMENT
Carmen-Maria Hetrea
Sheila Vasich
Mansur Abdullah

MANUFACTURING
Kim Gerber

MEDIA ASSET MANAGEMENT
Jeannine Deubel
Kimberly Cleary
Kurt Heintz

ENCYCLOPÆDIA BRITANNICA, INC.

Jacob E. Safra
Chairman of the Board

Jorge Aguilar-Cauz
President

Michael Ross
Senior Vice President, Corporate Development

Dale H. Hoiberg
Senior Vice President and Editor

Rosaline Jackson-Keys
Director, Almanac and World Data

Michael Levy
Executive Editor, Core Editorial

Marsha Mackenzie
Managing Editor and Director of Production

Time Inc.
HOME ENTERTAINMENT

CONTRIBUTING EDITOR
Kelly Knauer

DESIGN
Anthony Wing Kosner

PICTURES
Patricia Cadley

Richard Fraiman
Publisher

Steven Sandonato
General Manager

Carol Pittard
Executive Director, Marketing Services

Tom Mifsud
Director, Retail and Special Sales

Peter Harper
Director, New Product Development

Laura Adam
Assistant Director, Newsstand Marketing

Joy Butts
Assistant Director, Brand Marketing

Helen Wan
Associate Counsel

Holly Oakes
Senior Brand Manager, TWRS/M

Suzanne Janso
Book Production Manager

Anne-Michelle Gallero
Design and Prepress Manager

Michela Wilde
Associate Brand Manager

Special thanks to: Glenn Buonocore, Susan Chodakiewicz, Margaret Hess, Brynn Joyce, Robert Marasco, Brooke Reger, Mary Sarro-Waite, Ilene Schreider, Adriana Tierno, Alex Voznesenskiy

---

Cover photography credits: AP Images (12); Earth: NASA; Mars Phoenix probe: NASA; Heath Ledger as The Joker in *The Dark Knight*: copyright Warner Brothers Pictures 2008

ISBN-13: 978-1-60320-042-4 Hardcover
ISBN-13: 978-1-60320-793-5 Paperback
ISSN: 0073-7860

ENCYCLOPÆDIA BRITANNICA ALMANAC 2009

Britannica.com may be accessed on the Internet at http://www.britannica.com. For information on group and bulk sales, please send an e-mail to books@eb.com.

(Trademark Reg. U.S. Pat. Off.) Printed in U.S.A.

If you would like to order any of our hardcover Collector's Edition books, please call us at 1-800-327-6388 (Monday through Friday, 7:00 A.M.–8:00 P.M. or Saturday, 7:00 A.M.–6:00 P.M. Central Time).

Year in Review

Features

The Supreme Court's Group Hug 5
by Jeffrey Rosen, TIME

Libertarians: A (Not So) Lunatic Fringe. 6
by Nathan Thornburgh, TIME

Biofuels—The Next Great Source of Energy? 7
by Clarence Lehman

Subprime Mortgages: A Catalyst for Global Chaos 8
by Janet H. Clark

The Gulf States' Construction Boom 9
by John Duke Anthony

Chronology, July 2007–June 2008 Month by Month. 11

Disasters, July 2007–June 2008 Month by Month. 30

People

The TIME 100, 2008. 35

Celebrities and Newsmakers 37

Obituaries. 76

Awards

TIME's Top 100 Films 89

TIME's Person of the Year, 1927–2007 90

Nobel Prizes. 91

Special Achievement Awards 104

Science Honors 110

Nature, Science, Medicine, & Technology

Our Super-Sized Kids 117
by Jeffrey Kluger and Bryan Walsh, TIME

Time 119

The Universe 127

Cosmogony. 127
Constellations 129
Astronomical Phenomena for 2009 135

Measurements and Numbers 154

Applied Science. 165

Communications. 166

Aerospace Technology 167

Space Exploration 167
Space Exploration Firsts. 171

Air Travel. 172

Meteorology. 174

Geologic Disasters 178

Civil Engineering 180

Life on Earth 188

Animals. 188
Plants 189
Geology. 191

Preserving Nature 199

Health. 200

Diet and Exercise. 207

World

The Ghosts of the Balkans. 217
by Samantha Power, TIME columnist, and the TIME staff

Countries of the World 218

PHOTOS . . . . PLATES 1–16
FLAGS . . . . PLATES 17–22
MAPS . . . . PLATES 23–32

Rulers and Regimes 548

Populations 562

Languages of the World 564

Scholarship 565

Religion 567

The 2008 Annual Megacensus of Religions. 568

Law & Crime 574

Military Affairs. 577

United States

US Presidential Election of 2008. 579
by James Carney (McCain) and Michael Weiskopf (Obama)

History 581

United States Chronology 581
Important Documents in US History 584

Government. 596

The Presidency 596
The Supreme Court. 624
The Congress. 627
The Senate 627
The House of Representatives. 630

Military Affairs. 638

Population 645

The States and Other Areas. 653

State Government. 682

Cities. 687

Law and Crime. 689

Society 696

Family. 696
Education. 699

Business

The New President's Economy Problem 701
by Justin Fox, TIME

US Economy 703

Energy 705

Travel and Tourism 706

Employment 709

Consumer Prices 719

US Budget 721

US Taxes 724

Arts, Entertainment, & Leisure

Hollywood's 800-lb. Golden Gorilla 727
by Richard Corliss, TIME

Motion Pictures 729

Academy Awards 729

Television 746

Emmy Awards 746

Theater 749

Tony Awards 749
Encyclopædia Britannica's 25 Notable US Theater Companies 752

Music 752

Grammy Awards 752
Encyclopædia Britannica's 25 World-Class Orchestras 758
Encyclopædia Britannica's Top 25 Opera Companies 759

Pageants 759

Arts and Letters Awards 761

Pulitzer Prizes 761

Architecture Awards 781

Special Honors 782

Sport

Sporting Codes for Countries 783

The Olympic Games 785

Special Olympics 849

Automobile Racing 849

Baseball 851

Basketball 856

Billiard Games 860

Bowling 861

Chess 863

Cricket 864

Curling 865

Cycling 865

Football 868

US 869
Canadian 875
Australian 875
Rugby 875
Association Football (Soccer) 876

Golf 880

Horse Racing 886

Ice Hockey 895

Marathon 898

Rodeo 901

Skiing 902

Sled Dog Racing 906

Swimming 907

Tennis 912

Track & Field 927

Volleyball 936

Weight Lifting 936

INDEX 938

Year in Review

The Supreme Court's Group Hug

by Jeffrey Rosen, TIME

The biggest surprise from the Supreme Court term that just ended: Barack Obama hearts the Roberts court. At the end of June, the Democratic candidate praised Justice Antonin Scalia's 5–4 decision striking down the Washington ban on handgun possession, a ruling that recognizes the right to bear arms as an individual right. Two weeks earlier, from the other side of the ideological spectrum, Obama praised Justice Anthony Kennedy's 5–4 decision allowing enemy combatants to challenge their detentions in federal courts, a rebuke to the Bush administration's policies toward Guantánamo detainees. Obama's only major quarrel with the court was the 5–4 decision banning the execution of people who rape children: he said he has long believed that "the most egregious of crimes" deserve the death penalty. When a leading Democrat is criticizing the Supreme Court for not being conservative enough, it's time for liberals to breathe a sigh of relief.

It's true that there may be some election-year pandering in Obama's embrace of a court that many predicted would veer to the right under Chief Justice John Roberts. But by any measure, the term that just ended was hardly a disaster for liberals. On the contrary, liberals won several important victories—not only the Guantánamo and child-rape cases but also a series of employment-discrimination cases in which the court sided with workers rather than employers, by broad, bipartisan majorities.

Indeed, the court's term was something of a group hug between the liberal and conservative justices. The Supremes were far less divided than they seemed in 2007, when they sniped at one another in unusually personal terms. Despite some high-profile splits at the end, only 17% of the cases were decided by 5–4 votes—down sharply from the previous term, in which 33% of the cases were 5–4 splits. Cases upholding voter-ID requirements, execution by lethal injection, federal efforts to curb child pornography, and the detention of American citizens in Iraq were decided unanimously or by lopsided majorities.

So, what explains the new mood of bipartisan harmony on the Roberts court? At least some of the credit goes to Roberts's personality and leadership style.

He went out of his way to persuade his colleagues to turn down the volume and lighten up when they disagreed, even spicing up his dissent in a technical telecom dispute by borrowing playfully from Bob Dylan's "Like a Rolling Stone": "When you got nothing, you got nothing to lose."

According to Scalia, Roberts has used his power to assign opinions when he's in the majority to encourage his colleagues to write narrow decisions that Justices on both sides can accept. "The chief may say, 'Why don't you come along with a very narrow opinion? We can get seven votes for that, and it will look a lot better,'" Scalia said on *The Charlie Rose Show.* "You want to go along with the chief justice because...you want to make the institution work."

This, as it happens, is precisely what Roberts promised to do at the beginning of his tenure. In July 2006, Roberts told journalists that he was worried about "the personalization of judicial politics," whereby people identify the rule of law with the way individual justices vote in closely divided cases.

Embracing as a model his greatest predecessor, John Marshall, Roberts said he would use his power to assign majority opinions to promote narrow decisions agreed to by wide, bipartisan majorities rather than by polarizing 5–4 splits. On an evenly divided court, Roberts felt he could convince the liberal and conservative camps that converging on narrow opinions was in everyone's interest.

During his first term, which ended in 2006, Roberts managed to avoid 5–4 splits—for the most part, he said, because his colleagues were eager to be nice to the newcomer, like prospective in-laws meeting a fiancé for the first time at Thanksgiving. Then the honeymoon ended. When various justices were asked in 2007 whether they thought Roberts could rebuild an atmosphere of bipartisan harmony, they were hardly encouraging. Scalia scoffed, "Good luck!" Justice Stephen Breyer suggested Roberts could best foster comity by joining Breyer's opinions. Kennedy had a similar response: "Just let me write all the opinions!"

And yet, in his third term, Roberts has achieved what his colleagues had thought was nearly impossible. His success is a reminder of the importance of personality when it comes to leadership on the Supreme Court, in which the quirks and temperaments of individual justices are as important as judicial philosophy in shaping the law. Roberts told me that he thought much of Marshall's success was due to the fact that his colleagues liked and trusted him. Marshall persuaded the justices, at the beginning of the 19th century, to live in the same boarding house and discuss cases over glasses of his excellent Madeira.

Roberts's success is also a reminder of the chief justice's limited but real power: as the justice who speaks first at the court's private conference, he can frame the issues and influence the kinds of cases that the court agrees to hear in the first place. Under Roberts's leadership, the court has agreed to hear fewer polarizing constitutional cases and more cases of interest to business, which the justices are more inclined to resolve without dividing along ideological lines. Of the 15 cases in which the US Chamber of Commerce filed briefs this year, 80% were decided by 7–2 or higher, and a third were unanimous.

Roberts told me that he thinks that bipartisan agreement in the less-visible business cases can help develop a "culture and an ethos that says, 'It's good when we're all together.'" A sign of Roberts's success in putting his stamp on the court: he was in the majority in 90% of the cases this term, more frequently than any other justice.

How long will the changed mood last? The role of personality on the Supreme Court shouldn't be overstated. In cases in which they have strong, preexisting constitutional views on issues from abortion to guns to Guantánamo, the justices are unlikely to persuade one another. That's why, regardless of Roberts's current consensus building, the future of the court will be determined by the 2008 presidential election.

Libertarians: A (Not So) Lunatic Fringe

by Nathan Thornburgh, TIME

With his belly hiding his belt, with his red suspenders and white beard, Glen Parshall is a dead ringer for Santa Claus, except for the snub-nosed pistol he keeps tucked in his back pocket. Parshall spends his days behind the gun cage of Bargain Pawn, in a roughneck North Las Vegas neighborhood littered with homeless encampments, Catholic charities, and pawnshops. It's no Bellagio. But he is a gentle man who treats his customers with respect, whether hoodlum or homeowner. He knows everything there is to know about weapons and is a stickler for the byzantine rules of gun ownership—the waiting periods, the background checks, the ATF callbacks and information requests.

But just because he obeys the rules doesn't mean he likes them. Parshall is dissatisfied with a lot of what government does. He hates our gun laws. Hates the war in Iraq. He doesn't use drugs, but he sees the fight against them as another government power grab. Growing up as a Mormon in Salt Lake City, Parshall was a Barry Goldwater Republican. Now he's the kind of voter who should scare the GOP most—and he's not alone.

Maybe you haven't heard, but 2008 is the year of freedom. First there was the Ron Paul revolution, in which an avuncular 10-term representative from Brazoria county, Texas, raised more than US$34 million as a pseudo-Republican candidate, garnered more than a million primary votes, and outperformed Rudy Giuliani and Fred Thompson, all on the back of a get-government-off-my-back platform.

Now there's the Libertarian Party, which sold a little bit of its hard-line liberty-loving soul in exchange for the most respectable candidate it has ever had: recently converted former Republican congressman Bob Barr.

Since 2000, Libertarian candidates have peeled off enough votes from Republican congressional candidates to cost the party races in Washington, Nevada, Montana, and, most recently, Louisiana. But if anything, the GOP platform has grown more committed to foreign military intervention and domestic moralizing. The selection of John McCain was a final insult—most libertarians view him, fairly or not, as pro-war, anti-gun, pro-environmentalism, and anti-free speech (thanks to his advocacy for campaign-finance reform). In Nevada, McCain came in third in the GOP primary, behind Mitt Romney and Ron Paul. When the state GOP tried to crown McCain at its Reno convention in April, so many Paul supporters showed up that party leaders literally fled the hall, turned off the lights, and postponed the convention.

Land of Liberty. The central goal of libertarianism is hard to disagree with: freedom. Defining it is another matter. Party members I've met often speak of freedom as if it were a phantom limb: you're born with it, but it gets taken from you by the bureaucratic violence of the EPA, the ATF, the DOE, the DEA, the UN, NCLB, NAFTA, and—above all—the IRS. Freedom's restoration is the magic moment when the nanny state melts away and you can see the life you were supposed to live before the tax auditors and environmental regulators and drug warriors all came to rope, brand, and pen you in for life with their endless rule making and intrusions.

If the freedom that lives in the Libertarian imagination has an earthly home, it is the American West. If it has a temple, it is Nevada. It's not just the low taxes or the libertine veneer of Las Vegas; Nevada is free, I was told, in part because so much of it is populated by an unbroken and unbowed caste of ranchers, miners, and homesteaders who believe in the primacy of private property.

As you might guess, things that come between a Nevadan and his land don't sit well, and over the past decade, there's been nothing more disruptive than the environmental movement's good intentions. Nye county rancher Jim Berg, 68, doesn't call himself a libertarian, but he thinks the GOP has lost its will to keep the government from affecting his livelihood. He has plenty of war stories about his county's showdowns with the federal government, including a 1991 standoff when armed federales came to confiscate cattle belonging to a neighboring rancher who had let his herd graze on off-limits federal land. The Forest Service got some of Berg's cattle in the dragnet, auctioned them off, and kept the proceeds. "They wanted trouble that day," he says. "Why else would you gather another man's cattle with 25 to 30 armed men?"

There is a lot in the complaints in the libertarian heartland that sounds like nostalgia for an idealized American past. Jim Berg will tell you about grazing-rights grievances, but he's just as quick to lament the death of the ranching lifestyle. "My grandkids have scattered like quail," he says. "They've all gone city."

This sense that progress has gone too far and too fast unites a large swath of libertarians from coast to coast. To many, modernity just means having our daily lives ruled by mechanisms that have grown so complex that they are beyond comprehension or control. It's a notion that bonds anti-WTO progressives and anti-UN conservatives alike—and if the party has any real hope of becoming powerful, those seemingly disparate points on the political continuum will have to get closer.

It's tempting to think of libertarianism as nothing more than old-school Republicanism, but it's always been partially left-wing, drawing from a long history of American anarchism. The modern challenge is to unite those two wings—or, as magician (and stalwart libertarian) Penn Jillette told me, "Convince the dope guys that the gun guys are OK, and vice versa." And many libertarians believe the time is now. It helps that the US has been throttled for a century by two parties whose core differences are narrowing. For an electorate having a harder time distinguishing Coke from Pepsi, there's a thirst for something—anything—new.

The things libertarians care about—being able to gamble legally via their home computers, continuing to homeschool their kids without much interference, keeping taxes low—speak to a lot of Americans. If the old party was cobbled together from hard-line strains of voluntarianism, propertarianism, and paleolibertarianism, the new Libertarian Party is essentially suburbanarianism.

Voters alienated by our calcified party system may find in the Libertarians a party that's a lot like Glen Parshall—armed to the teeth but with a gentle logic and a contagious enthusiasm for freedom in all its forms. Libertarians are getting ready for the mainstream, and mainstream America may finally be ready for them.

Biofuels—The Next Great Source of Energy?

by Clarence Lehman

A boom in the production of biofuel was under way in 2007, especially in the United States, where in January about 75 refineries for producing the biofuel ethanol from corn (maize) were being built or expanded. This construction, not including additional facilities on the drawing board, was expected to double existing capacity, and the demand for corn pushed its price so high that American farmers planted more land with the crop than they had in a generation. Biofuel was perceived as a beneficial alternative to petroleum and other fossil fuels as the price of petroleum rose during the year to record levels and worldwide concern increased about how greenhouse-gas emissions from petroleum-derived fuels were contributing to climate change in the form of global warming. Despite its perceived economic and environmental benefits, however, many critics were expressing concerns about the scope of the expansion of certain biofuels because of their potential to create new problems.

Biofuels are fuels that are derived from biomass—that is, plant material or animal waste. Since such materials can be replenished readily, biofuels are a renewable source of energy, unlike fossil fuels, such as petroleum, coal, and natural gas. Some long-exploited biofuels, such as wood, can be used directly as a raw material that is burned to produce heat. The heat, in turn, can be used to run generators in a power plant to produce electricity. A number of existing power facilities burn grass, wood, or other kinds of biomass.

> ***"In March the US Department of Energy announced that it would be investing as much as US$385 million in six refineries for cellulosic ethanol."***

Liquid biofuels are of particular interest because of the vast infrastructure already in place to use them, especially for transportation. The liquid biofuel in greatest production is ethanol (an alcohol), which is made by fermenting starch or sugar. In the United States—the leading producer—ethanol biofuel is made primarily from corn grain, and it typically is blended with gasoline to produce a fuel that is 10% ethanol. In Brazil, which had been the leading producer until 2006, ethanol biofuel is made primarily from sugarcane, and it is commonly used as 100% ethanol fuel or in gasoline blends containing 85% ethanol. The second most common liquid biofuel is biodiesel, which is made primarily from oily plants (such as the soybean or oil palm) and to a lesser extent from other sources (such as cooking waste from restaurants). Biodiesel, which has found greatest acceptance in Europe, is used in diesel engines, usually blended with petroleum diesel in various percentages.

Other biofuels include methane gas, which can be derived from the decomposition of biomass in the absence of oxygen, and methanol, butanol, and dimethyl ether, which are in development. Much focus is on the development of methods to produce ethanol from biomass that has a high content of cellulose. This cellulosic ethanol could be produced from abundant low-value material, including wood chips, grasses, crop residues, and municipal waste. The mix of commercially used biofuels will undoubtedly shift as these fuels are developed, but the range of possibilities presently known could furnish power for transportation, heating, cooling, and electricity.

In evaluating the economic benefits of biofuels, the energy required for producing them has to be taken into account. For example, in growing corn to produce ethanol, fossil fuels are consumed in farming-equipment use, in fertilizer manufacturing, in corn transportation, and in ethanol distillation. In this respect ethanol made from corn represents a relatively small energy gain; the energy gain from sugarcane is greater and that from cellulosic ethanol could be even greater. Biofuels supply environmental benefits but, depending on their implementation, can also have serious drawbacks. As a renewable energy source, plant-based biofuels in principle make little net contribution to the greenhouse effect because the carbon dioxide (a major greenhouse gas) that enters the air during combustion will have been removed from the air earlier when the combustible material grew. Such a material is said to be carbon-neutral. In practice, however, the industrial production of agricultural biofuels can result in additional emissions of greenhouse gases that can offset the benefits of using a renewable fuel. These emissions include carbon dioxide from the burning of fossil fuels to produce the biofuel and nitrous oxide from soil that has been treated with nitrogen fertilizer. In this regard, cellulosic biomass is considered to be more beneficial.

Land use is also a major factor in evaluating the benefits of biofuels. Corn and soybeans are important foods, and their use in producing fuel can therefore affect the economics of food price and availability. In 2007 about one-fifth of US corn output was used for biofuel, and one study showed that even if all US corn land was used to produce ethanol, it could replace just 12% of gasoline consumption. Crops grown for biofuel can also compete for the world's natural habitats. For example, emphasis on ethanol derived from corn is shifting grasslands and brushlands to corn monocultures, and emphasis on biodiesel is bringing down ancient tropical forests to make way for palm plantations. Loss of natural habitat can change hydrology, increase erosion, and generally reduce biodiversity and wildlife areas. The clearing of land can also result in the sudden release of a large amount of carbon dioxide as the plant matter it contained decays.

Some of the disadvantages apply mainly to low-diversity biofuel sources—corn, soybeans, sugarcane, oil palms—which are traditional agricultural crops. An alternative recently proposed would use high-diversity mixtures of species, with the North American tall-grass prairie as a specific example. Converting degraded agricultural land presently out of production to such high-diversity biofuels could increase wildlife area, reduce erosion, cleanse waterborne pollutants, store carbon dioxide from the air as carbon compounds in the soil, and ultimately restore fertility to degraded lands. Such biofuels could be burned directly to generate electricity or converted to liquid fuels as technologies develop.

The proper way to grow biofuels to serve all needs simultaneously will continue to be a matter of much experimentation and debate, but the fast growth in biofuel production will likely continue. In the European Union, for example, 5.75% of transport fuels are to be biofuels by 2010, with 10% of its vehicles to run exclusively on biofuels by 2020. In December 2007 US Pres. George W. Bush signed into law the Energy Independence and Security Act, which mandated the use of 136 billion liters (36 billion gallons) of biofuels annually by 2020, more than a sixfold increase over 2006 production levels. The legislation required, with certain stipulations, that 79 billion liters (21 billion gallons) of the amount be biofuels other than corn-derived ethanol. In addition the law continued government subsidies and tax incentives for biofuel production. Some observers hoped that the law would encourage the commercialization of technology for producing cellulosic ethanol, for which there were a number of pilot plants in the United States.

The distinctive promise of biofuels not shared by other forms of renewable energy, such as solar power, is that in combination with an emerging technology called carbon capture and storage, biofuels are capable of perpetually removing carbon dioxide from the atmosphere. Under this vision biofuels would remove carbon dioxide from the air as they grew, energy facilities would capture that carbon dioxide when the biofuels were later burned for power, and then the captured carbon dioxide would be sequestered (stored) in long-term repositories such as geologic formations beneath the land, in sediments of the deep ocean, or conceivably as solids such as carbonates. With proper planning, therefore, biofuels have the potential to help create the conditions necessary for a sustainable world.

Clarence Lehman is an Adjunct Professor in the Department of Ecology, Evolution, and Behavior at the University of Minnesota.

Subprime Mortgages: A Catalyst for Global Chaos

by Janet H. Clark

One version of chaos theory opines that a butterfly flapping its wings in Beijing could produce a change in atmospheric pressure that in turn could cause a tornado in Kansas. This "butterfly effect" graphically demonstrates the theory whereby a small change in one area can cause a chain of events that leads to a major effect somewhere else. So it was in 2007 when losses in the subprime-mortgage sector in the US led to downturns in many housing markets around the world, followed by a widespread tightening of credit and turmoil in international financial markets.

> ***"In the financial sector, Countrywide Financial, the largest mortgage lender in the US, reported a third-quarter loss of US$1.2 billion, its first loss in 25 years."***

Early in the year, there was growing concern about the rise in mortgage defaults in the US housing market and fears of a US recession, which resulted in a global sell-off in equities in February. Over the past decade, strong economic growth, moderate inflation, and low interest rates had encouraged home ownership in the US and other developed countries, while the strong rise in house values made property an attractive investment to more people, including those with poor credit records and low incomes, who could not qualify for prime-rate loans from mainstream lenders. This led to an increase in the competitiveness and proliferation of subprime-mortgage lenders and brokers. Confidence among lenders was boosted by low funding costs and the widespread belief that if borrowers could not maintain loan repayments, the properties could be repossessed and resold at much higher prices. Credit standards were lowered, and many loans were made to high-risk borrowers, including those in low-income minority areas, who might otherwise have been excluded from the market. It was estimated that US$450 billion, or 30%, of outstanding subprime loans were adjustable-rate mortgages in which the repayment rate had been set for two years before being reset at higher interest rates (plus a margin) in 2007 and 2008. The rapid increase in interest rates by the Federal Reserve (Fed) from 1% in mid-2004 to 5.25% in mid-2006 meant that by midyear 2007 a rising number of the estimated six million subprime borrowers were defaulting on their mortgage payments, and their homes were being repossessed. Combined with an absence of new buyers (deterred by the higher interest rates), this led to a slump in the housing market. In August sales of new homes were down 21% over the year, and the decline was deepening. As the year progressed, it became increasingly clear that the US problem had global implications and could not be contained. This was because much of the mortgage debt had been rolled into bonds, called mortgage-backed securities, and then rebundled (together with lower-risk assets) by investment bankers in order to gain a higher credit-risk rating. The apparently less-risky bonds were then sold to other investors on the wholesale money market as collateralized debt obligations (CDOs). The market for CDOs was extremely buoyant, and banks, pension funds, hedge funds, and other investors all over the world bought them. Crucially, the complex structure of the market made it difficult to know who was holding the debt and where it was in the world financial system.

By midyear 2007, housing markets in many countries were beginning to falter and house prices to fall. House prices in many other Western industrial countries had risen faster than in the US (up 103%) over the previous decade, led by Ireland (up 253%), the UK (194%), Spain (173%), France (137%), Australia (135%), Sweden (124%), Denmark (115%), and New Zealand (105%). The supply of houses in 2005–06 had accelerated sharply compared with 10 years earlier; again it increased fastest in Ireland (up 210%), Spain (115%), Sweden (113%), and Denmark (76%). In the UK the number of mortgages approved for home buyers fell for the third straight month, and at just over 44,000 in October 2007, it reached a record low. The increased cost of mortgages—combined with the rejection of one in three mortgage applicants—contributed to a decline in the number of buyers for 11 straight months. The rate of repossessions in the UK was accelerating, with nearly 30,000 repossession orders in the third quarter of 2007.

In the UK, Northern Rock had to be bailed out by the Bank of England in September and was the focus of continuing attention. Northern Rock was the UK's eighth largest bank and fifth biggest mortgage lender, accounting for one in five UK mortgages. The bank had pioneered the securitization of mortgages in the UK, and though other lenders were more restrained, by the beginning of 2007 about half of all outstanding mortgages had been sold off in this way. By late November it was unclear what would happen to Northern Rock, which was being propped up by around £25 billion (nearly US$52 billion) in taxpayer money, with an additional £18 billion (about US$37 billion) in deposits being underwritten by the government.

In June the US investment bank Bear Stearns announced that two of its hedge funds, which invested in subprime-related debt, had registered large losses. In March 2008 the company was acquired by JPMorgan Chase for a fraction of its value in recent years. The Fed backed the deal with a US$30 billion dollar loan and by lowering its key discount rate of interest. Other funds, located as far away as Australia, also announced losses and froze redemptions. Securities backed by subprime mortgages were also being used as collateral for more borrowing and were putting additional pressure on financial markets. In July there were increasing worries about the exposure of several state-owned German banks to subprime debt, and in early August the French bank BNP Paribas announced that it was suspending funds invested in US subprime-related mortgages because of the difficulty of valuing the underlying assets. Markets were stunned on 9 August when the European Central Bank intervened with an unprecedented offer of unlimited short-term loans to the banking system. It injected €130 billion (about US$179 billion) in order to avert a potential liquidity crisis when overnight interest rates rose to 4.7%, exceeding the 4% cap. The Fed made a more modest intervention of US$24 billion. Further injections of funds continued, and in mid-December central banks gave a record US$530 billion to boost liquidity in credit markets.

Toward the end of the year, sharp declines in the value of the dollar against all major currencies raised concerns of inflation in the US, where the rate of consumer price increases was already accelerating. This limited the Fed's scope to raise interest rates for fear of the inflationary consequences. In December the Fed detailed plans that, if implemented, would give it more control over the US mortgage market and prevent another subprime crisis. In the UK politicians and financial regulators were planning banking-system reforms to reduce liquidity risk in the future.

Janet H. Clark is an editor, independent analyst, and writer on economic and financial topics.

The Gulf States' Construction Boom

by John Duke Anthony

In the early 21st century, virtually all six Gulf Cooperation Council (GCC) countries—Bahrain, Kuwait, Oman, Qatar, Saudi Arabia, and the United Arab Emirates (UAE)—showcased levels of economic development and infrastructure expansion not seen since the 1970s oil boom. Indeed, metaphorically speaking, the Gulf states, especially the UAE's largest emirates, Abu Dhabi and Dubai, had welcomed the return of an earlier era's most omnipresent bird: the building crane. In 2007 the mixed-use Burj ("Tower") Dubai, the final height of which was expected to exceed 800 m (2,640 ft), was officially designated the world's tallest structure, despite the fact that it was still under construction. Numerous factors and forces drove the boom: the vast public- and private-sector capital accumulation made possible by record-high oil and natural-gas revenues, the extension of what was already a sustained business-friendly environment, and the GCC region's stability and peace.

One result of this vast wealth and political stability was the large number of foreign firms with offices in the region; for example, according to the US Department of Commerce, over 750 American companies had established offices, acquired new business licenses, and/or entered into joint commercial ventures with local partners by 2007. The Texas-based oil-services firm Halliburton triggered widespread criticism when it announced in March 2007 that it was moving its international headquarters to Dubai. Accompanying these trends was an increase in the profusion of world-class banking institutions, together with a great concentration of Arab investment capital and liquidity. On 26 Sep 2005, trading began on the Dubai International Financial Exchange, the first international stock exchange in the Middle East.

Infrastructure projects were being financed on a scale not hitherto experienced. Many of these endeavors were associated with islands formed by land reclaimed from the sea. Nakheel ("The

Palms"), a Dubai property-development company with government ties, was adding thousands of kilometers of waterfront on reclaimed land. Nakheel claimed to have some US$30 billion in megaprojects under way in 2007, most notably a trilogy of palm-shaped man-made archipelagoes—Palm Jebel Ali, Palm Jumeirah, and Palm Deira—and the World, which comprised some 300 small man-made islands arranged to look from the air like a map of the world. Saadiyat Island, just off the coast of Abu Dhabi, was at the center of a reclaiming megaproject that would expand a natural island half the size of Bermuda into a much larger complex of hotels, golf courses, and other tourist amenities, three marinas, and private residences, as well as a 270-ha (670-ac) cultural district. Bahrain, Oman, and Qatar had similar islands under construction or in the planning stages.

On the tourism front, the region abounded with five-star hotels associated with the world's leading hoteliers. In addition to the dozens of luxury hotels planned for the new islands, hotels containing more than 7,000 rooms and suites opened in 2007, with plans to double the hotel "bed stock" in Dubai alone to at least 80,000 within a decade. Dubai already boasted the Burj Al Arab, a billion-dollar, 321-m (1,052-ft) sail-shaped "seven-star" hotel, and the US$500 million Hydropolis, under construction and planned to be the region's first underwater hotel. Not to be outdone, Abu Dhabi welcomed guests to its US$3 billion Emirates Palace Hotel.

An additional consequence, of special importance to Bahrain, Oman, and Saudi Arabia, was the proliferation of more diverse employment opportunities. These were generated by the associated local and foreign demands for travel guides, spas and swimming pools, ice-skating rinks, golf courses, and world-class entertainment, as well as expanded facilities for camel and horse racing.

"Ski Dubai, which opened in late 2005, was a winter wonderland in the desert, with "real" man-made snow, ski slopes of varying difficulty, and a snowboard quarterpipe."

One of the most remarkable projects was Dubailand, a massive complex of entertainment and tourist amenities that included the Mall of Emirates (the largest indoor shopping mall outside North America) and a 2.25-sq-km (about 1-sq-mi), 25-story-high indoor ski resort. The arts were not ignored, especially in Abu Dhabi, which announced that Saadiyat Island would include a performing arts center designed by architect Zaha Hadid, a Frank Gehry-designed Guggenheim Museum, and Louvre Abu Dhabi, the Paris icon's first international outpost.

Foreigners eager to benefit from the region's business opportunities had no choice but to establish themselves permanently on the ground. Vast numbers of foreign laborers were employed in the infrastructure projects. As a result all the Gulf countries were hard-pressed to accommodate the demand for increased housing and office space. In response, residential and commercial construction was also booming; Saadiyat Island was expected to house 150,000 full-time residents, while the three "Palms" would include residences for more than 250,000 people.

Despite the frenzied pace of development throughout much of the region, the implications of the boom for the interests and policies of individual Gulf countries and their foreign economic partners remained largely unnoticed by much of the outside world. What was long viewed as a subregion of vital significance to global economic growth mainly because of its energy sources had emerged as a center of abundant investment capital and almost unimaginably vast construction projects.

John Duke Anthony is the president and CEO of the National Council on US-Arab Relations and secretary of the US Gulf Cooperation Council Corporate Cooperation Committee.

Chronology, July 2007–June 2008

A day-by-day listing of important and interesting events, adapted from Britannica Book of the Year. *See also Disasters.*

July 2007

1 Jul Officials in Afghanistan say that NATO air strikes in a battle two days earlier in Helmand province killed 62 insurgents and 45 civilians.

▸ In Southern Pines NC, American golfer Cristie Kerr wins the US Women's Open; it is her first victory in one of the major golf tournaments.

2 Jul US Pres. George W. Bush commutes the 30-month prison sentence meted out to I. Lewis "Scooter" Libby, former chief of staff to the vice president, for perjury and obstruction of justice.

3 Jul Violence erupts between Pakistani security forces surrounding the Lal Masjid (Red Mosque) in Islamabad and students of two madrassas affiliated with the establishment; at least 10 people are killed.

▸ The 32nd America's Cup yacht competition is won for the second consecutive time by Switzerland's *Alinghi,* which sails across the finish line near Valencia, Spain, just one second ahead of Team New Zealand's vessel in race seven.

4 Jul The International Olympic Committee awards the 2014 Winter Games to Sochi, Russia.

▸ BBC reporter Alan Johnston, who was kidnapped on March 12 by a small Palestinian militant group in the Gaza Strip, is released to Hamas officials and then freed.

5 Jul The International Olympic Committee decides on the creation of a new Youth Olympics, for athletes aged 14–18; the first event is planned for summer 2010, with the venue to be decided in February 2008.

6 Jul UN health officials report that the number of people infected with HIV in India is 2.5 million, not 5.7 million as previously reported, and that India therefore ranks third in the world, not first, in number of infections, behind South Africa and Nigeria; the new tally was gleaned from a new and more accurate survey.

7 Jul A powerful truck bomb kills as many as 150 people in the Iraqi village of Amerli, a town of Turkmen Shi'ites; many are crushed to death by collapsing houses.

▸ American Venus Williams defeats Marion Bartoli of France to take the All-England (Wimbledon) women's tennis championship; the following day Roger Federer of Switzerland wins the men's title for a fifth consecutive year when he defeats Spaniard Rafael Nadal.

▸ Live Earth, a series of 11 concerts to promote environmental awareness and combat global warming, is broadcast on television, satellite radio, and the Internet.

8 Jul Israel's cabinet approves the early release of 250 Palestinian prisoners, most belonging to the Fatah party.

9 Jul Canadian Prime Minister Stephen Harper announces that the country will buy patrol ships to defend its claim to the Northwest Passage; many believe that continued global warming could make possible its being turned into a major shipping channel.

▸ The Chicago Board of Trade agrees to merge with its rival, the Chicago Mercantile Exchange, for US$11.9 billion; the combined exchange will be one of the world's largest.

10 Jul After seven days of fighting and a failed attempt to negotiate peace with the militants inside the Lal Masjid (Red Mosque), government forces storm the compound; eight members of the security forces and some 73 militants, including Abdul Rashid Ghazi, the mosque's leader, are killed.

▸ The Vatican issues a document that states that the Roman Catholic Church is the only true church established by Jesus Christ and that other denominations "suffer from defects."

▸ Zheng Xiaoyu, the former head of China's food and drug regulatory agency, is executed.

11 The movie *Harry Potter and the Order of the Phoenix* opens at midnight in theaters throughout the US, taking in a record US$12 million from these screenings alone and setting a single-day record for a Wednesday release.

12 Jul The annual Orange Order parades in Northern Ireland take place without incident and without the need for heavy policing to prevent violence between the Protestant marchers and Roman Catholics who disliked the processions' taking place near their neighborhoods.

13 Jul The International Atomic Energy Agency announces that Iran has agreed to allow the agency to inspect its heavy-water reactor in Arak before the end of the month.

14 Jul North Korea informs the US that it has shut down its nuclear reactor at Yongbyon and has admitted a team of inspectors from the International Atomic Energy Agency.

▸ Russian Pres. Vladimir Putin announces that his country will suspend its participation in the 1990 Conventional Forces in Europe Treaty; the move is in response to US plans to deploy missile-defense bases in Poland and the Czech Republic.

15 Jul Two suicide bombings in Pakistan's North-West Frontier Province leave at least 49 people dead.

▸ In Venezuela, Brazil defeats Argentina 3–0 to win its eighth Copa América, the South American championship in association football (soccer).

16 A magnitude-6.6 earthquake occurs in rural Niigata prefecture in Japan, killing at least 10 people and causing tremendous destruction, notably at the world's biggest nuclear power plant.

17 Jul A Brazilian TAM Airlines Airbus A320 airplane attempting to land at São Paulo's Congonhas Airport skids off a runway and into a building; at least 200 people are killed.

18 Jul The Dow Jones Industrial Average closes above 14,000 for the first time; also, the Standard & Poor's 500 closes at a record high of 1,553.08.

▸ Laotian-born American psychologist Jerry Yang uses his aggressive playing style to capture the 38th Annual World Series of Poker and earn US$8,250,000 in prize money.

19 Jul Some 115 wildfires are reported in southern Greece in the midst of a heat wave that is baking southern Europe.

▸ Pres. Idriss Déby of Chad agrees to allow a European Union (EU) force to help contain violence that has spread into the eastern part of the country from the Darfur region of The Sudan.

20 Jul Pakistan's Supreme Court rules that Pres. Pervez Musharraf's suspension of Iftikhar Muhammad Chaudhry as chief justice was illegal and reinstates Chaudhry, dismissing all charges against him.

QUOTE OF THE MONTH

> *Everyone thinks that there's no justice in the country, that only generals get to decide everything. But the court today was very brave.*
>
> —Ali Ahmed Kurd, an attorney for Iftikhar Muhammad Chaudhry, on a Pakistani Supreme Court ruling reinstating his client as chief justice, 20 July

▸ A US court of appeals rules that the government must make available to the court and to lawyers its information on detainees at Guantánamo Bay, Cuba, who are challenging decisions by military tribunals that they continue to be held, saying that meaningful review of the tribunals requires that information.

21 Jul Legislators in India choose Pratibha Patil as India's next president; she is the first woman named to the largely ceremonial position.

▸ The much-anticipated final volume of the Harry Potter saga, *Harry Potter and the Deathly Hallows,* is released worldwide at midnight, selling some 2.7 million copies and breaking book sales records over the next 24 hours in the UK.

▸ New Zealand wins the rugby union Tri-Nations trophy, defeating Australia 26–12 in the final.

22 Jul Padraig Harrington wins the British Open golf tournament at the Carnoustie Golf Club in Carnoustie, Scotland, defeating Sergio García of Spain in a four-hole play-off and becoming the first Irishman to win the tournament since 1947.

23 Jul Flooding of the Thames River in central England after a month of heavy rains causes widespread destruction and hardship; the area is experiencing its worst flooding in 60 years.

24 Jul After visits to Libyan leader Muammar al-Qaddafi by Cécilia Sarkozy, wife of French Pres. Nicolas Sarkozy, the five Bulgarian nurses and one Palestinian doctor who have been in a Libyan prison for the past eight years on charges of having injected hundreds of children with HIV are freed and flown to Bulgaria.

▸ In the US the minimum hourly wage is increased for the first time since September 1997, from US$5.15 to US$5.85; an additional raise is scheduled to take place each of the next two summers.

25 Jul After Iraq's association football (soccer) team defeats South Korea in a penalty shoot-out to win a semifinal match in the Asian Cup competition, jubilant Iraqis take to the streets in cities throughout the country in celebration; car bombs that explode among the revelers in Baghdad leave 50 dead.

26 Jul In Iraq, a car bomb in Baghdad sets a building on fire and kills at least 25 people, a car bomb kills at least 6 people in Kirkuk, and a suicide bomber near Mosul kills 7 people.

▸ Delegates from Iraq, Syria, Egypt, the Arab League, and the UN meeting in Amman, Jordan, to find ways to deal with the influx of some two million Iraqi refugees in the Middle East fail to arrive at solutions.

27 Jul Hundreds of Islamic extremists try to reoccupy the Lal Masjid (Red Mosque) in Islamabad, Pakistan, when the government reopens it for prayers, and a suicide bomber kills at least 13 people; the government regains control of the mosque and closes it indefinitely.

28 Jul In Gstaad, Switzerland, the US women's team of Misty May-Treanor and Kerri Walsh wins the beach volleyball world championship for the third consecutive year; the following day the US men's team of Todd Rogers and Phil Dalhausser also takes gold.

29 Jul Iraq defeats Saudi Arabia 1–0 to win the Asian Cup in association football (soccer) for the first time in tournament history.

▸ Spanish cyclist Alberto Contador wins the Tour de France, completing the race only 23 seconds faster than Cadel Evans of Australia.

30 Jul Legendary filmmakers Ingmar Bergman of Sweden and Michelangelo Antonioni of Italy both die.

31 Jul The Bancroft family, owners of Dow Jones & Co., which publishes *The Wall Street Journal,* agrees to sell the company to Rupert Murdoch's News Corp. for US$5 billion.

August 2007

1 Aug The American toy maker Mattel recalls 967,000 Chinese-manufactured toys that contain lead-based paint.

▸ Analysis shows that in July for the first time, sales of cars in the US made by foreign manufacturers overtook sales of cars from American automakers.

▸ An eight-lane bridge over the Mississippi River between Minneapolis and St. Paul in Minnesota collapses during the evening rush hour, dropping dozens of vehicles into the river and leaving 13 people dead.

2 Aug Russian explorers in minisubmarines plant a titanium Russian flag on the seafloor beneath the North Pole to underscore Russia's claim to the Arctic region.

▸ James H. Billington, the American librarian of Congress, names Charles Simic the country's 15th poet laureate, succeeding Donald Hall.

3 Aug The mortgage lender American Home Mortgage Investment goes out of business, citing difficulties in the secondary-mortgage market as well as the housing market.

4 Aug NASA launches the Phoenix Mars Lander; it is expected to land on 25 May 2008 in the north polar region of Mars, where it will collect and analyze soil samples.

▸ Ron Pierce, driving the trotter Donato Hanover, wins the Hambletonian harness race in New Jersey.

▸ The Pro Football Hall of Fame in Canton OH inducts tight end Charlie Sanders, wide receiver Michael Irvin, running back Thurman Thomas, offensive lineman Bruce Matthews, cornerback Roger Wehrli, and guard Gene Hickerson.

5 Aug US Pres. George W. Bush signs into law legislation that increases the government's authority to eavesdrop on electronic communications between Americans and people in other countries.

▸ Mexican golfer Lorena Ochoa wins the women's British Open golf tournament, the first women's professional golf tournament to be played at the St. Andrews Old Course in Scotland.

6 Aug Pres. José Ramos-Horta of East Timor names former president Xanana Gusmão prime minister.

▸ Prime Minister Ehud Olmert of Israel meets with Palestinian Authority Pres. Mahmoud Abbas in the West Bank city of Jericho; it is the first time since 2000 that an Israeli prime minister has been in Palestinian territory.

7 Aug Gela Bezhuashvili, the foreign minister of Georgia, contends that the previous day Russia fired a missile at the Georgian town of Tsitelubani; Russia denies the accusation.

▸ Barry Bonds of the San Francisco Giants hits his 756th home run to take over the Major League Baseball record of most career home runs from Hank Aaron, who had held the record since 1974.

8 Aug The *baiji,* or Yangtze River dolphin, is officially declared extinct in a report by a scientific expedition that engaged in an intensive and fruitless six-week search for the animal, which is considered the first cetacean species extinguished by human activity.

9 Aug The government of South Africa confirms that it has fired Nozizwe Madlala-Routledge, the deputy health minister, who had been internationally praised for her work to combat the AIDS pandemic in the country; she had clashed with the health minister, Manto Tshabalala-Msimang, who recommended the use of garlic and vitamins against the disease.

10 Aug Canadian Prime Minister Stephen Harper announces that the country will build two new military bases in Nunavut in order to protect its claims to the Northwest Passage.

QUOTE OF THE MONTH

> “*The first principle of Arctic sovereignty is use it or lose it.*”
>
> —Canadian Prime Minister Stephen Harper, announcing new military bases in the Arctic to guard the Northwest Passage, 10 August

▸ The UN Security Council passes a resolution increasing the scope of its mission in Iraq to promote reconciliation and consensus and to assist in border disputes.

11 Aug The governor of Al-Qadisiyah province in Iraq, together with the police chief and three bodyguards, is killed by a roadside bomb; the area is known to be a battleground between Shiʿite factions.

▸ The center span of the fourth bridge (the first three were built in 1591, 1854, and 1934) across the Grand Canal in Venice is put in place; the new bridge, designed by Santiago Calatrava, is scheduled to open in December.

12 Aug A team of Danish scientists begins an expedition to the Arctic region in an effort to map the underwater Lomonosov Ridge, seeking evidence that it is attached to Greenland, which could give Denmark sovereignty over the North Pole, together with possibly lucrative mineral and shipping rights.

▸ Tiger Woods defeats Woody Austin by two strokes to win the Professional Golfers' Association of America championship at the Southern Hills Country Club in Tulsa OK.

13 Aug Karl Rove, the closest aide of US Pres. George W. Bush, announces his resignation as deputy chief of staff.

14 Aug In the Iraqi villages of Qahtaniya and Jazeera, located in the Kurdish-speaking region near Syria, four truck bombs kill at least 500 people; most people in the area are members of the Yazidi religious sect.

15 Aug An earthquake measuring magnitude 8.0 strikes off the coast of southern Peru, destroying the city of Pisco; at least 540 people are killed and some 200,000 are made homeless.

16 Aug Jose Padilla, who was arrested as an enemy combatant in 2002 and then transferred to the civilian criminal court system in 2006, is found guilty by a US federal jury on charges of conspiracy to commit terrorism.

17 Aug Scientists at the National Snow and Ice Data Center report that the amount of sea ice in the Arctic has reached the lowest point ever measured, at 5.26 million sq km (2.02 million sq mi), and that melting is reportedly occurring more quickly than predicted by computer models.

18 Aug A referendum takes place in Maldives on the framework of a new constitution; voters choose a strong presidential system over a parliamentary one.

▸ Israel implements a controversial new rule to immediately deport all migrants who cross the border from Egypt into Israel, returning some 50 Africans, many of whom are believed to be refugees from the Darfur region of The Sudan, to Egypt.

19 Aug A referendum is held in Thailand on a new constitution that weakens the power of the executive and shifts power to the military; as expected, the document is approved.

▸ Hurricane Dean roars through the Caribbean, leaving a trail of destruction in Saint Lucia, Martinique, Dominica, Haiti, the Dominican Republic, and Jamaica; at least eight people die in the region.

20 Aug The governor of Iraq's Al-Muthanna province is killed by a roadside bomb; he was a member of the Supreme Islamic Iraqi Council, a Shiʿite political party that had clashed with the Mahdi Army, a Shiʿite militia loyal to the cleric Muqtada al-Sadr.

▸ Michael Vick, quarterback for the Atlanta Falcons, agrees to plead guilty to felony charges related to dogfighting; on 24 August he is suspended indefinitely by the National Football League.

21 Aug A US federal judge rules that the government has violated the federal law that mandates periodic studies by Washington on the impact of global warming; an assessment was due in 2004 and a research plan in 2006, and the judge requires a summary report by March 2008.

▸ In objection to the large military presence on campus that has been in place since January, students at the University of Dhaka, Bangladesh, engage in a second day of rioting, and violence spreads to other universities in the country.

22 Aug A US military Black Hawk helicopter crashes in northern Iraq, killing all 14 soldiers aboard; mechanical failure is blamed for the crash.

23 Aug Inmates take over a prison in Ponte Nova, Brazil, and 25 members of one gang are locked up and then burned to death.

▸ Pakistan's Supreme Court rules that Nawaz Sharif, whom Pres. Pervez Musharraf deposed as prime minister in 1999, has the legal right to return to the country and run for office.

24 Aug A bomb explodes outside a police barracks during the night in Durango, Spain; police believe it to be the work of the Basque separatist organization ETA.

25 Aug Two bombs, one at a laser show at an open-air auditorium and one at a popular restaurant, kill at least 42 people in Hyderabad, India.

▸ A national state of emergency is declared in Greece as the death toll from relentless wildfires rises to at least 46.

26 Aug The government of Iraq announces that an agreement has been reached to allow former members of the Ba'th Party to hold government posts; Ba'thists were banned from the government in 2003.

▸ With a walk-off solo home run by Dalton Carriker, the Warner Robins American team from Warner Robins GA defeats the Tokyo Kitasuna team from Japan 3–2 to win baseball's 61st Little League World Series.

▸ Official ceremonies are held in Samarkand, Uzbekistan, to celebrate the fabled city's 2,750th anniversary.

27 Aug US Attorney General Alberto Gonzales announces his resignation.

28 Aug Armed violence breaks out during a religious festival in Karbala, Iraq, between the Badr Organization and the Mahdi Army, both Shi'ite militias; at least 50 people are killed.

▸ On the third ballot, Turkey's legislature elects the controversial Abdullah Gul president.

29 Aug In Iraq the Shi'ite cleric Muqtada al-Sadr announces, to the surprise of observers, that the Mahdi Army's operations will be suspended for six months.

▸ China's official news source says that sandstorms are reducing to piles of dirt more than 59.5 km (37 mi) of the Great Wall in Gansu province.

30 Aug The International Atomic Energy Agency releases a report saying that Iran has been cooperative and forthcoming and that, though Tehran continues to expand its nuclear program, it is doing so at a much slower rate than had been expected.

▸ Italian police carry out a raid in San Luca, arresting 32 people in an effort to stop a feud between rival families in the 'Ndrangheta crime organization.

31 Aug Zimbabwe imposes a six-month freeze on increases in wages, rents, and fees in an attempt to stop runaway inflation; price controls have so far resulted in a burgeoning black market.

September 2007

1 Sep Sen. Larry Craig of Idaho announces his intention to resign after pleading guilty to a misdemeanor charge after he was accused of having solicited an undercover police officer for sex in a men's restroom in an airport; he later rescinds the resignation.

▸ In college football the lower-division Appalachian State Mountaineers of Boone NC defeat the number-five-ranked University of Michigan Wolverines 34–32 in what is believed to be one of the sport's biggest upsets.

2 Sep The Lebanese armed forces storm and seize control of the Nahr al-Bared Palestinian refugee camp after a standoff that started in May with Fatah al-Islam militants who had taken over the camp.

▸ China declares its intention to release information about its burgeoning military budget and to resume submitting data to the UN on its trade in conventional weapons; it had stopped sending such information in 1996.

3 Sep Khaleda Zia, a former prime minister of Bangladesh, is arrested on charges of corruption in Dhaka a few weeks after the arrest of another former prime minister, Sheikh Hasina Wazed.

▸ The ceremonial ground breaking of the project to expand the Panama Canal takes place at Paradise Hill; the project, which is expected to more than double the canal's capacity, is scheduled for completion in 2014.

▸ Aviator and adventurer Steve Fossett disappears in western Nevada after taking off in a single-engine plane; he was said to be looking for areas to practice driving his jet-powered race car.

4 Sep Two coordinated suicide bombings kill at least 25 people in Rawalpindi, Pakistan.

▸ Opposing factions of the recently bifurcated National Liberation Force engage in fierce fighting in Bujumbura, Burundi; at least 26 people are killed.

5 Sep The government of Germany announces that it has arrested three people who were in advanced stages of planning a major terrorist attack in Germany against American and German targets.

6 Sep Israel conducts air strikes against a target in Syria for the first time since 2003.

▸ A US federal judge rules unconstitutional a section of the USA PATRIOT Act that permits the government to demand customer records from communications companies and forbid the companies to reveal the existence of the demands.

▸ The online edition of the journal *Science* publishes research suggesting that a virus may be a major cause of the colony collapse disorder that has been afflicting honeybees in the US; about a quarter of American beekeepers have reported mass die-offs in their hives.

7 Sep Police in Portugal name Kate and Gerry McCann suspects in the May disappearance of their four-year-old daughter, Madeleine, from the British family's vacation rental in Praia da Luz; the highly publicized search for the child has engrossed the public in both Great Britain and Portugal.

8 Sep After holding presidential and legislative elections for the first time since 1996, Sierra Leone holds a runoff presidential election; the winner is opposition leader Ernest Bai Koroma.

▸ A van packed with explosives detonates in Dellys, Algeria, killing 34 coast guard officers.

▸ Justine Henin of Belgium defeats Svetlana Kuznetsova of Russia to win the women's US Open tennis championship; the following day Roger Federer of Switzerland defeats Novak Djokovic of Serbia to win the men's title for the fourth straight year.

9 Sep At the IAAF Grand Prix in Rieti, Italy, Asafa Powell of Jamaica sets a new 100-m record of 9.74 seconds.

▸ With his win over Scott Dixon of New Zealand in the Indy 300 race in Joliet IL, Scottish driver Dario Franchitti wins the overall IndyCar championship.

10 Sep Bombs set along four natural-gas pipelines and one oil pipeline in Mexico go off, creating major service disruptions; it is the third attack in three months against pipelines of the state oil company Pemex.

▸ A UN report is released saying that the number of suicide bombings in Afghanistan in the first eight months of 2007 increased by 69% over the same period in 2006.

11 Sep Pius Ncube resigns as Roman Catholic archbishop of Bulawayo, Zimbabwe, after having been accused of adultery; Ncube was an outspoken critic of Pres. Robert Mugabe.

12 Sep Mikhail Fradkov resigns as Russia's prime minister, and Pres. Vladimir Putin surprises observers by naming little-known Viktor A. Zubkov as Fradkov's replacement.

▸ A magnitude-8.4 earthquake with its epicenter undersea near Bengkulu on the Indonesian island of Sumatra leaves at least 10 people dead; a second earthquake, with a magnitude of 7.8, strikes early the next morning about 320 km (200 mi) northwest of the first, and a third major earthquake occurs later that day.

13 Sep Off Hammerfest, Norway, the first liquefied-natural-gas plant in Europe begins production at the Snøhvit oil field.

▸ UNICEF releases figures showing that worldwide mortality for children under the age of five has dropped to 9.7 million; it is the first time since records began in 1960 that the figure has dropped below 10 million.

14 Sep The European Space Agency reports that satellite images have revealed that for the first time in recorded history, the Northwest Passage briefly became open to navigation because of the record low amount of Arctic sea ice.

15 Sep The 2007 Albert Lasker Medical Research Awards are presented; winners are Ralph Steinman for his discovery of dendritic cells and their important role in the immune system, Alain Carpentier and Albert Starr for their development of prosthetic mitral and aortic heart valves, and Anthony Fauci for his role as architect of US AIDS and biodefense programs.

16 Sep The Emmy Awards are presented in Los Angeles; winners include the television shows *30 Rock* and *The Sopranos* and the actors Ricky Gervais, James Spader, America Ferrera, Sally Field, Jeremy Piven, Terry O'Quinn, Jaime Pressly, and Katherine Heigl.

▸ Tiger Woods wins the inaugural professional golf FedExCup by an astonishing eight strokes in the final game of the play-off series in Atlanta.

▸ The Phoenix Mercury defeats the Detroit Shock 108–92 to win its first Women's National Basketball Association championship.

17 Sep The government of Iraq announces that it has banned the American private security contractor Blackwater USA (now Blackwater Worldwide) from operating in the country the day after an incident in which Blackwater guards killed 17 Iraqi civilians.

18 Sep The giant retailer Wal-Mart announces plans to greatly improve the employee health care plan, mollifying many who had been critical of the company's parsimonious benefits.

19 Sep Israel declares the Gaza Strip a "hostile entity."

20 Sep The UN International Tribunal on the Law of the Sea rules that the maritime boundary between Guyana and Suriname should be equidistant from the two countries, giving Guyana the lion's share of the coastal waters, including an area where significant oil and gas exploration had been halted pending the tribunal's decision.

▸ Buddhist monks pray at the Shwedagon Pagoda, the holiest shrine in the country, and hundreds of them march through the streets of Yangon (Rangoon), Myanmar (Burma), for the third day in a row in protest against the country's military government.

QUOTE OF THE MONTH

“*The clergy boycotts the violent, mean, cruel, ruthless, pitiless kings, the great thieves who live by stealing from the national treasury.*”

—Public statement issued by Buddhist monks in Yangon (Rangoon), Myanmar (Burma), 20 September

▸ Some 10,000 protesters march in Jena LA to protest unduly harsh measures taken against six black local high-school students for a racial incident that took place in 2006.

▸ Floyd Landis is stripped of his title as winner of the 2006 Tour de France cycling race, and the Union Cycliste Internationale declares Oscar Pereiro, the second-place finisher, the official winner.

21 Sep Chile's Supreme Court agrees to the extradition of former Peruvian president Alberto Fujimori to Peru, where he is wanted on charges of human rights abuses and corruption.

22 Sep A delegation from Syria is received by a high-ranking government official in Pyongyang, North Korea.

23 Sep Yasuo Fukuda is elected to the presidency of the ruling Liberal Democratic Party in Japan; he is installed as prime minister of Japan on 26 September.

▸ The Movement for the Emancipation of the Niger Delta declares an end to its four-month cease-fire in Nigeria, saying that it will resume attacks on oil installations.

24 Sep After having failed to reach a labor agreement, 73,000 members of the United Auto Workers union go on strike against General Motors; it is the first strike against the manufacturer since 1970.

25 Sep A boycott by Hezbollah legislators prevents the Lebanese National Assembly from reaching a quorum, forcing it to postpone its selection of a new president.

26 Sep The management of the carmaker General Motors and the United Auto Workers union reach a tentative agreement on a contract that will shift the costs of health care for retirees to the union, ending a two-day strike.

27 Sep The military government of Myanmar (Burma) concludes two days of brutal suppression aimed at putting an end to antigovernment demonstrations; several people have been killed, among them a Japanese press photographer.

28 Sep Pakistan's Supreme Court dismisses two cases that challenge the constitutionality of Pres. Pervez Musharraf's candidacy for reelection as president while he is still head of the armed forces.

▸ Dominique Strauss-Kahn of France is named managing director of the IMF; he replaces Rodrigo de Rato of Spain.

29 Sep A rebel group invades a camp of African Union peacekeeping troops in the Darfur region of

The Sudan, killing 10 of the peacekeepers; it is believed that the rebels may have kidnapped others.

▸ In the Australian Football League Grand Final in Melbourne, the Geelong Cats defeat the Port Adelaide Power 24.19 (163) to 6.8 (44), a record-breaking margin of victory in the event.

30 Sep Haile Gebrselassie of Ethiopia wins the Berlin Marathon with a time of 2 hr 4 min 26 sec, a new world record for marathons, while his countrywoman Gete Wami is the fastest woman, with a time of 2 hr 23 min 17 sec; it is the second year in a row that the two have won the race.

October 2007

1 Oct Syria closes its borders to refugees from Iraq and imposes stringent new visa rules on Iraqis already in Syria.

▸ The Dow Jones Industrial Average closes at an all-time high of 14,087.55 points, while the Nasdaq composite index closes at 2740.99, its highest point since February 2001.

2 Oct South Korean Pres. Roh Moo Hyun steps across the border with North Korea for a summit meeting with North Korean leader Kim Jong Il; he is the first South Korean president to walk into North Korea.

3 Oct It is announced in Beijing that North Korea has agreed to disable all its nuclear facilities in return for 950,000 metric tons of fuel oil or other economic aid.

4 Oct The 50th anniversary of the Soviet Union's launch of Sputnik, the first man-made satellite, is observed; the launch kicked off the space race and led to the formation of NASA in the US.

5 Oct A US air strike on the Shi'ite town of Gizani al-Imam, Iraq, kills at least 25 Iraqis; the US military describes the dead as insurgents, while residents of the town say they were civilians.

▸ One of the largest makers of frozen beef patties in the US, Topps Meat Co., announces that it is going out of business in the wake of the recall of more than 9.8 million kg (21.7 million lb) of frozen beef products because of possible *E. coli* contamination.

▸ American track star Marion Jones pleads guilty to having lied to federal agents when she denied having used performance-enhancing steroids; three days later she relinquishes the three gold and two bronze medals she won at the Olympic Games in 2000.

6 Oct In Iraq rival Shi'ite leaders Muqtada al-Sadr and 'Abd al-Aziz al-Hakim forge a peace agreement.

7 Oct In Pakistan's North Waziristan region, Pakistani security forces attack militant bases, leaving at least 20 militants and 6 soldiers dead, while elsewhere in the region militants attack a military convoy, and 10 soldiers and 18 militants are killed in the ensuing battle.

▸ The Chicago Marathon is run on a day of unseasonable heat and humidity, causing hundreds to become ill and helping contribute to the death of one runner; the organizers cancel the run, but not before Patrick Ivuti of Kenya has won it by 0.05 sec with a time of 2 hr 11 min 11 sec and Berhane Adere of Ethiopia has crossed the finish line as the women's victor with a time of 2 hr 33 min 49 sec.

8 Oct British Prime Minister Gordon Brown announces his intention to withdraw half of the British troops in Iraq by the spring of 2008, citing progress in the training of Iraqi security forces and improvements in the situation in Basra, where British forces are based.

▸ The Nobel Prize for Physiology or Medicine is awarded to Americans Mario Capecchi and Oliver Smithies and Briton Martin Evans for their development of gene-targeting technology, in which particular genes in mice were silenced in order to learn the function of the gene.

9 Oct In Stockholm the Nobel Prize for Physics is awarded to Albert Fert of France and Peter Grünberg of Germany for their discovery of giant magnetoresistance, which was instrumental in the development of modern computer hard drives.

10 Oct The Nobel Prize for Chemistry is awarded to Gerhard Ertl of Germany for his work elucidating chemical reactions that occur when gas molecules meet with solid surfaces.

11 Oct The Nobel Prize for Literature is awarded to British writer Doris Lessing.

▸ The 10th annual Mark Twain Prize for American Humor is presented to comic Billy Crystal in a ceremony at the John F. Kennedy Center for the Performing Arts in Washington DC.

12 Oct The state media in China report that concerns over environmental damage, including the danger of landslides, in the area around the Three Gorges Dam have led to plans to relocate as many as four million people.

▸ The Nobel Peace Prize is awarded to American politician and environmentalist Al Gore and to the UN-sponsored Intergovernmental Panel on Climate Change.

13 Oct King Bhumibol Adulyadej of Thailand is hospitalized and diagnosed with cerebral ischemia.

14 Oct In Palm Desert CA, Lorena Ochoa of Mexico outscores Mi Hyun Kim of South Korea to secure the title of Ladies Professional Golf Association Player of the Year.

15 Oct Ukrainian Pres. Viktor Yushchenko's political party, Our Ukraine, reaches a coalition agreement with the Yuliya Tymoshenko Bloc, which would enable Tymoshenko to take office as prime minister.

▸ The Nobel Memorial Prize in Economic Sciences goes to Americans Leonid Hurwicz, Roger B. Myerson, and Eric S. Maskin for their development of and work using mechanism design theory, which explains interactions between individuals, markets, and institutions.

16 Oct A summit meeting of the five countries that border the Caspian Sea—Russia, Iran, Azerbaijan, Kazakhstan, and Turkmenistan—takes place in Tehran; they agree not to allow military strikes launched from any member country against any other member country.

▸ Libya, Vietnam, Burkina Faso, Costa Rica, and Croatia are chosen to replace the Republic of the Congo, Qatar, Ghana, Peru, and Slovakia as nonpermanent members of the UN Security Council.

▸ The Man Booker Prize for Fiction goes to Irish writer Anne Enright for her novel *The Gathering*.

17 Oct Despite strong objections from China, the Dalai Lama of Tibet is awarded a US Congressional Gold Medal in Washington DC.

▸ The *Journal of the American Medical Association* publishes a study by the US Centers for Disease Control and Prevention indicating that in 2005 some 19,000 people in the US died after infection with invasive methicillin-resistant *Staphylococcus aureus* (MRSA) bacteria, a much higher rate of infection than had been expected; most transmission was associated with hospitals and nursing homes.

18 Oct Former Pakistani prime minister Benazir Bhutto returns to Pakistan after eight years in exile, greeted by joyous crowds, but two bombs go off near the procession carrying her through Karachi, killing at least 140 people.

19 Oct Residents of Bolivia's wealthy Santa Cruz province retake control of Viru Viru International Airport, the country's busiest airport, a day after federal troops seized the airport from workers who were said to be demanding that landing fees and other payments be made to local officials rather than to the national airport authority.

20 Oct South Africa defeats England 15–6 in Paris to win the rugby union World Cup.

21 Oct Voters in Turkey approve several changes to the constitution, including one that would make the presidential term five years instead of seven and another that would require the popular rather than legislative election of the president.

▸ Finnish driver Kimi Räikkönen wins the Brazilian Grand Prix and with it the Formula 1 automobile racing drivers' championship.

22 Oct As massive wildfires driven by Santa Ana winds burn throughout southern California for a second day, some 250,000 residents of San Diego county are told to evacuate.

QUOTE OF THE MONTH

> *The house went up like a Roman candle....If we weren't here the whole neighborhood would go up.*
>
> —San Diego resident Tom Sollie, who ignored evacuation orders to help in attempts to save neighborhood houses from California wildfires, 22 October

▸ Joaquim Chissano, who was president of Mozambique in 1986–2005, wins the first Mo Ibrahim Prize for Achievement in African Leadership.

23 Oct The government of Somalia releases Idris Osman, the head of World Food Programme operations in Mogadishu, a week after he was seized in an attack on a UN compound.

24 Oct China launches the satellite Chang'e-1, which is expected to orbit the Moon for a year, returning images; it is China's first lunar probe and follows one launched by Japan in September.

25 Oct US Pres. George W. Bush visits southern California to view the devastation from wildfires, which have destroyed 1,800 homes and 202,000 ha (500,000 ac); at least seven deaths have resulted as well.

26 Oct The price of oil briefly passes US$92 a barrel before closing at a new record high of US$91.86.

27 Oct The Breeders' Cup Classic Thoroughbred horse race is won by Curlin in exceptionally sloppy conditions at Monmouth Park Racetrack in Oceanport NJ.

28 Oct Thousands of peasants who have marched for the past 26 days from Gwalior, India, arrive in New Delhi seeking enforceable rights to their land (much of Indian farmland is in small plots, and increasing industrialization has displaced growing numbers of peasants from their land); the following day the government sets up a panel to address the problem.

▸ The Boston Red Sox defeat the Colorado Rockies 4–3 in Denver in the fourth game of the World Series to win the Major League Baseball World Series in a sweep.

29 Oct Egyptian Pres. Hosni Mubarak announces that the country will build several nuclear reactors, reinstating a program that was halted some 20 years earlier.

▸ Authorities in Chad say that nine French workers with the aid organization Zoé's Ark will be charged with kidnapping and fraud after they were arrested in Abeche while trying to fly 103 children to Europe to be adopted.

30 Oct A major battle between Afghan and NATO forces and hundreds of Taliban fighters begins in the Arghandab district outside Kandahar, Afghanistan; Taliban forces had been ousted from the area in 2001, and this was their first reappearance.

31 Oct Russia invites only 70 of the usual 400 Organization for Security and Co-operation in Europe election observers to monitor the legislative elections scheduled for 2 December.

November 2007

1 Nov UN officials report that most of the 103 children that French aid organization Zoé's Ark was attempting to fly to Europe to be adopted were not orphans from The Sudan's war-torn Darfur region as claimed but rather children from Chad who were living with their families.

▸ In Nagoya, Japan, Chunichi Dragons pitcher Daisuke Yamai throws eight perfect innings in his team's 1–0 defeat of the Hokkaido Nippon Ham Fighters in game five of the best-of-seven Japan Series, resulting in the first baseball championship for the Dragons since 1954.

2 Nov S.P. Tamilselvan, the political leader of the Liberation Tigers of Tamil Eelam, is killed in an attack by Sri Lankan troops near Kilinochchi.

3 Nov Pakistani Pres. Pervez Musharraf declares a state of emergency, suspending the constitution and in effect imposing martial law; he fires Chief Justice Iftikhar Muhammad Chaudhry and the rest of the Supreme Court.

4 Nov Martin Lel of Kenya wins the New York City Marathon with a time of 2 hr 9 min 4 sec, while Britain's Paula Radcliffe is the fastest woman, with a time of 2 hr 23 min 9 sec.

5 Nov In a meeting in the White House with Turkish Prime Minister Recep Tayyip Erdogan, US Pres. George W. Bush promises American cooperation in intelligence in Turkey's fight against the Kurdistan Workers' Party (PKK).

▸ The Writers Guild of America, West, and the Writers Guild of America, East, go on strike against the movie and television industries, demanding a greater share of revenue from TV shows and movies distributed by DVD and online.

▸ US Pres. George W. Bush awards the Presidential Medal of Freedom to Americans Gary S. Becker, Francis S. Collins, Benjamin L. Hooks, Henry J. Hyde, Brian Lamb, and Harper Lee and to Oscar Elías Biscet of Cuba and Ellen Johnson-Sirleaf of Liberia.

6 Nov A suicide bomber attacks a delegation of legislators attending the opening of a sugar factory in Baghlan, Afghanistan; at least 72 people, including 6 legislators and 59 schoolchildren, are killed.

▸ Belgium passes its 149th day without a government following elections on 10 June; tension between leaders of the Flemish and the Walloon communities has caused the deadlock.

▸ British Queen Elizabeth II cuts the ribbon at the unveiling of the magnificently restored St. Pancras train station in London; beginning on November 14 the station will serve as the London terminus of the Eurostar, a high-speed train that connects London to continental Europe through the Channel Tunnel.

7 Nov After a day of violence between demonstrators and riot police in Tbilisi, Georgia, Pres. Mikheil Saakashvili declares a state of emergency.

▸ The US Consumer Product Safety Commission orders the recall of the Chinese-made toy Aqua Dots; the toy consists of plastic beads that when wetted stick together to form toys but when ingested release a poisonous chemical related to the date-rape drug GHB.

▸ The South Korean container ship *Cosco Busan* hits a stanchion of the Bay Bridge in San Francisco, causing an ecological disaster as it spills 220,000 liters (58,000 gal) of bunker oil in San Francisco Bay.

8 Nov The government of Brazil declares that huge new reserves, believed to contain five to eight billion barrels of recoverable light oil, have been found in the offshore Tupi oil field.

▸ At the Latin Grammy Awards in Las Vegas, Dominican singer and songwriter Juan Luis Guerra wins five awards, including album of the year for *La llave de mi corazón* and song of the year and record of the year for the album's title cut.

9 Nov The UN World Food Programme reports that about half of the children living in Laos are chronically malnourished and that government policies are partially to blame.

10 Nov Stagehands in New York City go on strike, and 27 Broadway shows go dark.

11 Nov A storm in the Black Sea causes at least 11 ships to sink, with some loss of life, and one tanker breaks apart in the Kerch Strait, spilling at least 1,000 tons of fuel oil and thus creating an environmental catastrophe.

▸ The drama series *Quarterlife*, produced by Marshall Herskovitz and Edward Zwick, makes its debut on MySpaceTV; it is the first television-style series to debut on the Internet.

12 Nov In South Korea the spokesmen for the former in-house lawyer for embattled electronics giant Samsung say that recipients of Samsung bribes included newly appointed prosecutor general Lim Chae Jin and top corruption investigators Lee Jong Baek and Lee Gui Nam.

13 Nov The 2007 Dorothy and Lillian Gish Prize is awarded to performance artist Laurie Anderson.

14 Nov The US National Medal of Arts is awarded to Morten Lauridsen, N. Scott Momaday, Roy R. Neuberger, Craig Noel, Les Paul, Henry Steinway, George Tooker, and Andrew Wyeth.

15 Nov Cyclone Sidr makes landfall on the southwestern coast of Bangladesh, devastating a large area and leaving at least 3,500 people dead.

▸ Major League Baseball player Barry Bonds, holder of the record for most career home runs, is indicted in San Francisco for perjury and obstruction of justice in an inquiry into the use of performance-enhancing drugs in baseball.

16 Nov Georgian Pres. Mikheil Saakashvili lifts the state of emergency and appoints Lado Gurgenidze to replace Zurab Nogaideli as prime minister.

▸ Donald Tusk is sworn in as prime minister of Poland.

17 Nov The Intergovernmental Panel on Climate Change releases its final report of 2007; it indicates that urgent action is needed to avert global climate disaster, which is likely to occur sooner than was once thought.

18 Nov The US military releases figures showing that the weekly number of attacks in Iraq has fallen to its lowest level since January 2006.

▸ A new pipeline that will carry natural gas originating in Azerbaijan to Greece from Turkey, bypassing Russia, is ceremonially inaugurated by the prime ministers of Greece and Turkey.

▸ After the final NASCAR race of the season, Jimmie Johnson is crowned winner of the Nextel Cup championship for the second year in a row.

▸ The Houston Dynamo wins the Major League Soccer title with a 2–1 victory over the New England Revolution in the MLS Cup in Washington DC.

19 Nov In Pakistan, Pres. Pervez Musharraf's now-handpicked Supreme Court dismisses the primary challenges to his reelection; the previous Supreme Court had been expected to rule in favor of the challenges.

20 Nov Online reports are published from two independent science teams, one in the US and one in Japan, both of which have developed a technique to reprogram human skin cells to make them behave like embryonic stem cells.

▸ The British government reveals that in October unencrypted computer disks containing detailed personal and financial information on 25 million people, 40% of the country's population, were lost; a government tax agency sent the disks unregistered to the National Audit Office, but they never arrived.

21 Nov The warship *Shenzhen* sails from China for the first port visit by the Chinese navy to Japan since World War II; the destroyer is to take part in military ceremonies with the Japanese navy.

22 Nov After close to three months of negotiations, Pres. Álvaro Uribe of Colombia withdraws his support for the involvement of Venezuelan Pres. Hugo Chávez in negotiations with the Revolutionary Armed Forces of Colombia (FARC) intended to lead to the release of dozens of hostages that FARC has held for several years.

23 Nov The cruise ship *Explorer* strikes an iceberg while traveling 96 km (60 mi) north of the Antarctic Peninsula and sinks; all 154 aboard are rescued, but the ship poses an ecological threat.

24 Nov In parliamentary elections in Australia, the ruling Liberal Party of Prime Minister John Howard loses to the Labor Party, whose leader, Kevin Rudd, becomes prime minister.

25 Nov The Saskatchewan Roughriders capture the 95th Canadian Football League Grey Cup, defeating the Winnipeg Blue Bombers 23–19.

26 Nov Youths and riot police engage in a second night of battles in Villiers-le-Bel, France, a suburb of Paris; the violence began after two teenagers on a motorbike were killed in a collision with a police car.

▸ Gillian Gibbons, a British teacher at a private school in The Sudan, is arrested and charged with having insulted Islam after it is learned that she permitted her students to give the name Muhammad to a teddy bear that was used in a school project.

27 Nov At a peace conference in Annapolis MD, Israeli Prime Minister Ehud Olmert and Palestinian Authority Pres. Mahmoud Abbas agree to negotiate a peace treaty by the end of 2008.

28 Nov A settlement to the stagehand strike that has kept Broadway shows closed for 19 days is announced in New York City.

29 Nov Pakistani Pres. Pervez Musharraf, who resigned his post as army chief the day before, is sworn in to a second term of office.

30 Nov Russian Pres. Vladimir Putin suspends the country's participation in the NATO Conventional Armed Forces in Europe treaty.

QUOTE OF THE MONTH

“*This was an extraordinary circumstance, ladies and gentlemen; it needed extraordinary measures to control. No half-hearted measures could have delivered.*”

—Pakistani Pres. Pervez Musharraf in a speech explaining his emergency rule, as he promises to lift it, 29 November

December 2007

1 Dec The Iraqi Accord Front, the largest Sunni bloc in Iraq's legislature, walks out to protest the detention of its leader, Adnan al-Dulaimi; in addition, al-Qaeda gunmen attack the village of Dwelah in Diyala province, killing 13 people.

2 Dec Voters go to the polls in Venezuela in a referendum on whether to accept 69 amendments to the constitution, some of which would increase the power of the president; in a major setback to Pres. Hugo Chávez, the amendments are defeated.

▶ The annual Kennedy Center Honors are presented in Washington DC to film director Martin Scorsese, comedian Steve Martin, and musicians Leon Fleisher, Brian Wilson, and Diana Ross.

3 Dec A new US National Intelligence Estimate is released that says that it is now believed that Iran stopped its nuclear weapons program in 2003 and has not restarted it, though the country is producing enough highly enriched uranium to be able to make a bomb in the next few years; this represents a dramatic reversal of a previous NIE assessment in 2005.

▶ Kevin Rudd is sworn in as prime minister of Australia; his first official act is to sign documents ratifying the Kyoto Protocol on climate change.

4 Dec Prime Minister Nikola Spiric of Bosnia and Herzegovina signs an accord with the enlargement commissioner of the EU in the first step toward the country's joining the EU.

5 Dec A man armed with a gun opens fire at a shopping mall in Omaha NE and kills eight people before turning the gun on himself.

6 Dec In Washington DC, Director of Central Intelligence Michael V. Hayden informs employees that in 2005 the CIA destroyed videotapes of the interrogations of two al-Qaeda operatives.

7 Dec Off the west coast of South Korea, a barge carrying a construction crane comes loose from its tugboat in heavy seas and hits the anchored oil tanker *Hebei Spirit,* punching three holes in the tanker's hull and causing a massive and disastrous oil spill.

▶ The Right Livelihood Awards are presented in Stockholm to Sri Lankan legal scholar Christopher Weeramantry, to Dekha Ibrahim Abdi of Kenya for her work in conflict resolution, to Percy and Louise Schmeiser of Canada for their work defending agricultural biodiversity, and to the Bangladeshi solar-energy company Grameen Shakti.

8 Dec University of Florida quarterback Tim Tebow wins the Heisman Trophy for best college football player; he is the first sophomore to win the award.

9 Dec The Banco del Sur, a Latin American regional-development bank intended as an alternative to the World Bank, is inaugurated in a ceremony in Buenos Aires attended by the presidents of Argentina, Bolivia, Brazil, Ecuador, Paraguay, and Venezuela.

10 Dec Russian Pres. Vladimir Putin endorses Dmitry Medvedev, a first deputy prime minister and the chairman of the oil monopoly Gazprom, to succeed him as president.

▶ The New York Philharmonic announces that it has accepted an invitation to play a concert in Pyongyang, North Korea, in February 2008; it will be the first major cultural visit from the US to North Korea.

11 Dec A car bomb goes off in front of a government building in Algiers, engulfing a bus carrying students to a university campus, and another car bomb explodes shortly thereafter at a UN building, destroying it; a minimum of 37 people are killed, at least 17 of them UN staff members.

▶ The United States Sentencing Commission votes unanimously to reduce the punishment for some crimes involving crack cocaine, which have been punished far more harshly than those related to powder cocaine, and to make the change retroactive; the change may affect some 19,500 prison inmates.

12 Dec UNESCO reports that Cyclone Sidr, which killed some 3,500 people in Bangladesh in November, also devastated the Sundarbans, a large mangrove forest on the Ganges delta that is a World Heritage site and a tiger preserve.

13 Dec Leaders of the member countries of the European Union sign the Lisbon Treaty, a new document delineating the governance of the organization; it includes a permanent president with a two-and-a-half-year term of office and provisions for decisions to be made by majority, rather than unanimous, vote; it must now be ratified by all 27 members.

▶ The long-awaited report on steroid abuse in professional baseball is released by its author, former senator George J. Mitchell; the report names 89 Major League Baseball players as having used illegal performance-enhancing substances.

14 Dec The World Bank reports that it has raised a record US$25.1 billion for its International Development Association; for the first time, the UK passed the US to become the organization's biggest donor.

15 Dec Pakistani Pres. Pervez Musharraf lifts the state of emergency and restores the constitution but with amendments and decrees that leave his hand-picked Supreme Court in place.

▸ Steer roper Trevor Brazile of Texas wins his fifth all-around cowboy world championship at the 49th annual Wrangler National Finals Rodeo in Las Vegas.

16 Dec British forces formally relinquish control of Basra province to Iraq's government; it is the most important province to have been handed back to Iraq since the 2003 invasion.

▸ In a National Football League game against the St. Louis Rams, Green Bay Packers quarterback Brett Favre sets a new all-time record as a 7-yd pass brings his career total to 61,405 passing yards; the previous record was Dan Marino's 61,361 yd.

17 Dec Guy Verhofstadt agrees to stay in office as prime minister of an interim government in Belgium pending the formation of a permanent government, which the country has lacked since elections in June; the interim government is formed on 19 December.

18 Dec The legislature of Ukraine approves the nomination of Yuliya Tymoshenko as prime minister.

▸ The US Congress passes legislation mandating higher fuel-economy standards for cars and trucks for the first time in 22 years, the production of renewable fuels, and higher efficiency requirements for household appliances and government buildings.

19 Dec A conservative politician, Lee Myung-bak, wins election as president of South Korea in a landslide; voters think he will be able to improve the country's economy.

20 Dec Thieves steal a painting by Pablo Picasso, *Portrait of Suzanne Bloch* (1904), and a painting by Brazilian artist Candido Portinari, *The Coffee Worker* (1939), from the Museum of Art in São Paulo; police believe the theft was ordered by a wealthy art collector.

21 Dec A bomb goes off in a mosque during Friday prayers and the celebration of 'Id al-Adha in Sherpao in northwestern Pakistan; at least 48 people are killed.

▸ The Czech Republic, Estonia, Hungary, Latvia, Lithuania, Malta, Poland, Slovakia, and Slovenia join the European Union's Schengen zone, the members of which do not require passports for travel within the zone.

22 Dec China's new National Center for the Performing Arts in Beijing, designed by French architect Paul Andreu, holds its first public concert; the building, a glass dome over a shallow lake, is entered via a passageway under the lake.

23 Dec Two 1,500-year-old terra-cotta statues of the Hindu god Vishnu disappear from the cargo area of the international airport in Dhaka, Bangladesh; the statues had been en route to the Guimet Museum in Paris for an exhibition.

24 Dec Near Aleg, Mauritania, four French tourists picnicking on the side of a road are shot and killed, and a fifth is injured; law enforcement comes to believe that the attack was connected to al-Qaeda.

25 Dec A suicide truck bomber rams his vehicle into a group of people waiting in line for cooking gas in Baiji, Iraq; at least 25 people are killed.

▸ At the San Francisco Zoo, a Siberian tiger escapes from its enclosure and attacks three people, killing one.

26 Dec The Serbian legislature overwhelmingly passes a resolution opposing independence for Kosovo and warning of international repercussions if the enclave should declare independence and other countries recognize it as independent.

27 Dec Former prime minister Benazir Bhutto is assassinated after leaving a political rally in Rawalpindi, Pakistan; moments later a suicide bomber detonates his weapon, killing at least 20 people in the crowd.

▸ Archaeologists report that an Aztec pyramid found in November in the Tlatelolco area of Mexico City may have been built as early as 1100, some 200 years before Aztec civilization in the area was thought to have begun.

28 Dec Nepal's legislature overwhelmingly votes to abolish the monarchy.

29 Dec Government officials in China announce that the first election in which Hong Kong voters may directly elect their leader will not take place until at least 2017; previously it had been thought that the elections in 2012 might be held democratically.

30 Dec In spite of evidence of fraud in the vote counts, Kenya's election commission declares that Mwai Kibaki has narrowly won reelection as president of Kenya, and he is immediately sworn in; the country erupts in violence.

QUOTE OF THE MONTH

> "*This is the saddest day in the history of democracy in this country. It is a coup d'état.*"
>
> —Koki Muli, cochairwoman of the Kenya Election Domestic Observation Forum, as Pres. Mwai Kibaki begins a second term as president of Kenya, 30 December

31 Dec The first legislative elections in Bhutan's history take place as voters choose members of the National Council, the legislature's future upper house.

January 2008

1 Jan A church in the village of Kiambaa, Kenya, where hundreds of Kikuyu people are taking refuge from the violence that broke out after the disputed election of 27 Dec 2007, is attacked by a mob and set on fire; some 50 people are burned to death.

▸ The euro replaces the Cypriot pound as Cyprus's currency and the Maltese lira as Malta's currency as the euro zone expands.

2 Jan The government of Sri Lanka formally annuls a cease-fire with the Liberation Tigers of Tamil Eelam that had been agreed to six years earlier; for practical purposes the agreement had not been observed since early 2006.

▸ The price of a barrel of light sweet crude oil for the first time reaches US$100 on the New York Mercantile Exchange.

3 Jan James H. Billington, the US librarian of Congress, announces the appointment of Jon Scieszka, author of *The Stinky Cheese Man and Other Fairly Stupid Tales* and *The True Story of the Three Little Pigs*, to the newly created position of ambassador for young people's literature.

4 Jan The movie studio Warner Brothers announces that in the future it will release its movies on Sony's Blu-ray discs rather than Toshiba's HD DVDs; industry insiders feel that this has decided which high-definition format will become the industry standard.

▸ The 30th annual Dakar Rally is canceled; organizers say that the French government had warned that terrorist organizations had made threats to disrupt the race.

5 Jan Presidential elections called by Pres. Mikheil Saakashvili after a brief state of emergency in November 2007 are held in Georgia; Saakashvili wins narrowly.

6 Jan The Arab League approves a plan for a new government in Lebanon, which has been without a president since November 2007.

7 Jan Louisiana State University defeats Ohio State University 38–24 in college football's Bowl Championship Series title game in New Orleans to win the NCAA Football Bowl Subdivision (formerly Division I-A) championship.

8 Jan Pres. Mwai Kibaki of Kenya announces his choices for half of the cabinet, and violence breaks out anew in several cities; some 500 people have been killed since violence erupted following the disputed election in 2007.

▸ Philippe de Montebello, who has been director of the Metropolitan Museum of Art in New York City for 30 years, announces his intention to retire at the end of the year.

9 Jan The legislature of the UN-administered Serbian province of Kosovo chooses the former leader of the Kosovo Liberation Army, Hashim Thaci, to be prime minister.

▸ The World Health Organization publishes a study that estimates the number of Iraqi civilians killed in the war from its inception in March 2003 until June 2006 at about 151,000.

10 Jan Members of the Revolutionary Armed Forces of Colombia (FARC) release to emissaries of Venezuelan Pres. Hugo Chávez two Colombian women: Consuelo González de Perdomo, a member of the legislature, and Clara Rojas, an aide to presidential candidate Ingrid Betancourt (herself still a captive).

11 Jan The Bank of America announces its planned purchase of troubled mortgage company Countrywide Financial Corp.

12 Jan Iraq's legislature passes a law to allow former Baʿthist officials to apply for positions in the government.

▸ Legislative elections in Taiwan are won by the Nationalist Party, which takes 81 of the 113 seats; Pres. Chen Shui-bian resigns as head of the Democratic Progressive Party.

13 Jan Jackie Selebi resigns as president of Interpol the day after he was put on leave as head of South Africa's police because of a corruption investigation.

14 Jan The spacecraft MESSENGER passes within 200 km (124 mi) of Mercury's surface, taking photographs and measurements of the planet, which was last visited by NASA's Mariner 10 in 1975.

▸ In the field of children's literature, the Newbery Medal is awarded to Laura Amy Schlitz for *Good Masters! Sweet Ladies! Voices from a Medieval Village,* a series of monologues and dialogues set in the Middle Ages, and Brian Selznick wins the Caldecott Medal for illustration for his novel *The Invention of Hugo Cabret.*

15 Jan At the Macworld Expo trade show in San Francisco, Apple CEO Steven P. Jobs introduces the ultralight MacBook Air laptop computer and the ability to rent movies by downloading them through iTunes.

16 Jan *The Proceedings of the Royal Society B* reports the discovery in Uruguay of fossil evidence of a rodent, named *Josephoartigasia monesi,* that was some 3 m (10 ft) long and weighed up to 1,100 kg (2,200 lb).

17 Jan Geoscientists report that a natural-gas black-shale reservoir in the northern Appalachians could hold as much as 15 trillion cu m (516 trillion cu ft) of gas; it would be a huge addition to US reserves.

18 Jan On the first day of the religious festival of ʿAshura, fighting between a millennial militia, the Soldiers of Heaven, and Iraqi government forces in several places in southern Iraq leaves at least 66 dead.

▸ Israel closes all border crossings between itself and the Gaza Strip, blocking, among other things, aid shipments, saying the step is intended to discourage rocket attacks from Gaza on Israel.

19 Jan Spain announces the arrest in Barcelona of 14 people of Pakistani and Indian origin who are believed to have been planning a terrorist attack on the city.

20 Jan It is reported that David D. Hiller, publisher of the *Los Angeles Times,* has removed James E. O'Shea as editor for refusing to make requested job cuts in the newsroom.

21 Jan Sudanese Pres. Omar al-Bashir defends his recent appointment of Musa Hilal as a senior government adviser; Hilal is generally believed to be a leader of the Janjawid militia forces.

▸ At Thoroughbred horse racing's 2007 Eclipse Awards, Curlin is named Horse of the Year.

22 Jan After an emergency meeting the US Federal Reserve lowers its benchmark lending rate three-quarters of a percentage point, to 3.5%, the largest single-day reduction it has ever made; stocks initially plummet but rally robustly.

▸ Iraq's legislature adopts a new flag, the same as the previous one except that the three stars that represent Baʿthist ideals have been removed.

23 Jan At the divided town of Rafah, members of Hamas break down a portion of the wall closing off Egypt from the Gaza Strip, and thousands of Palestinians pour across the border to purchase supplies.

▸ Prime Minister Kostas Karamanlis of Greece begins a three-day visit to Turkey; it is the first official visit to Turkey by a Greek prime minister since May 1959.

24 Jan The French banking giant Société Générale announces that a midlevel employee for the past year was a rogue trader and caused the bank to lose €4.9 billion (US$7.2 billion).

▸ Researchers at the J. Craig Venter Institute report that they have synthesized the genome of a small bacterium (*Mycoplasma genitalium*) by assembling about 100 DNA fragments in a major step toward creating a complete artificial organism.

25 Jan A dusk-to-dawn curfew is imposed in Nakuru, Kenya, in an attempt to contain ethnic violence that has broken out, contributing to a death toll of more than 650 people throughout the country since the disputed election.

26 Jan Russian Mariya Sharapova defeats Ana Ivanovic of Serbia to win her first Australian Open women's tennis championship; the following day Novak Djokovic of Serbia defeats Frenchman Jo-Wilfried Tsonga to win his first men's title.

▸ Top film awards at the annual Sundance Film Festival in Park City UT go to *Frozen River, Trouble the Water, The Wackness,* and *Fields of Fuel.*

27 Jan Indonesia's former president Suharto dies; a week of official mourning is declared.

28 Jan US Pres. George W. Bush delivers his final state of the union address; he asks the American people for patience on the Iraq War, discusses economic worries, and presents a modest domestic agenda.

QUOTE OF THE MONTH

> *As we meet tonight, our economy is undergoing a period of uncertainty.... At kitchen tables across our country, there is a concern about our economic future.*
>
> —US Pres. George W. Bush, in his final state of the union address, 28 January

▸ The ruling party in Turkey reaches an agreement on an amendment to the constitution that will allow women who wear head scarves for religious reasons to attend university; the measure must be approved by the legislature.

29 Jan King Bhumibol Adulyadej of Thailand ratifies the legislature's selection of Samak Sundaravej as the country's new prime minister.

30 Jan The US Federal Reserve Board cuts its benchmark interest rate a further half of a percentage point, to 3%.

31 Jan David Kimutai Too, an opposition lawmaker, is shot to death by a policeman in Eldoret, Kenya; though government officials say the killing was not politically motivated, violence throughout the country intensifies in response to the murder.

▸ The World Health Organization reports that programs in which mosquito nets and artemisinin, a new antimalarial medicine, were widely distributed in several African countries generally cut the number of deaths from malaria in half.

February 2008

1 Feb The American oil company Exxon Mobil Corp. reports that it earned US$40.6 billion last year, a new record for the highest profit ever recorded.

▸ Government officials in Japan say that at least 175 people have become ill after eating dumplings imported from China that were tainted with insecticide.

2 Feb Rebel troops attempting to overthrow Pres. Idriss Déby enter N'Djamena, the capital of Chad, and surround the presidential palace as Chad's armed forces resist.

3 Feb In Glendale AZ the New York Giants defeat the New England Patriots 17–14 to win the National Football League's Super Bowl XLII; the Patriots had an undefeated record going into the game.

4 Feb The US$250,000 A.M. Turing Award for excellence in computer science is granted to Edmund M. Clarke, E. Allen Emerson, and Joseph Sifakis for their development of an automated method to discover errors in the design of computer hardware and software.

▸ NASA transmits the Beatles song "Across the Universe" toward Polaris, the North Star, in celebration of the 50th anniversary of the agency and of its first satellite, Explorer I.

5 Feb The death toll from violence in Kenya since the presidential election in December 2007 passes 1,000 people as officials from the ruling and opposition parties begin negotiations on how to end the crisis.

6 Feb The vice president of Pakistan's Awami National Party is assassinated in Karachi, and rioting erupts.

7 Feb The Licey Tigers defeat the defending champions, the Cibao Eagles, 8–2 in the final game of the round-robin tournament in Santiago, Dominican Republic, to win baseball's Caribbean Series with a tournament record of 5–1; for the first time in the history of the event, both teams are from the host country.

8 Feb Dean Barrow is sworn in as the first black prime minister of Belize the day after his United Democratic Party won 81% of seats in a legislative election.

9 Feb A tentative agreement between the Writers Guild of America and movie and television production companies is reached, which indicates an end to the writers' strike that began in November 2007 and has stopped production of 63 TV shows; the strike formally ends on 12 February.

10 Feb At the Grammy Awards in Los Angeles, the top winner is British vocalist Amy Winehouse, who wins five awards, including both record of the year and song of the year for "Rehab" and the award for best new artist; the surprise choice for album of the year is *River: The Joni Letters* by jazz artist Herbie Hancock.

▸ In Ghana, Egypt defeats Cameroon 1–0 to win the African Cup of Nations in association football (soccer) for a record sixth time.

11 Feb Pres. José Ramos-Horta of East Timor is critically injured in an apparent assassination attempt; the country's prime minister, Xanana Gusmão, is also attacked, but he escapes injury.

▸ The drug company Baxter International announces its suspension of production of heparin, a blood thinner, because some 350 people have reacted badly to it, in some cases fatally.

12 Feb A report from a census of tigers in India is released; it finds that the number of tigers since the last census, in 2002, has fallen from 3,642 to only 1,411.

▸ K-Run's Park Me in First wins Best in Show at the Westminster Kennel Club's 132nd dog show; the popular beagle, known as Uno, is the first of its breed to win the top award at the premier American dog show.

13 Feb Iraq's legislature passes a package bill that includes a 2008 budget, an outline for defining provincial powers, and an amnesty for thousands of detainees; the amnesty is one of the benchmarks that the US government has expected from Iraq.

QUOTE OF THE MONTH

> *For the pain, suffering, and hurt of these Stolen Generations, their descendants, and for their families left behind, we say sorry....And for the indignity and degradation thus inflicted on a proud people and a proud culture, we say sorry.*
>
> —Australian Prime Minister Kevin Rudd, in his historic apology to the country's Aborigines, 13 February

▸ For the first time in the country's history, Prime Minister Kevin Rudd formally apologizes to Australia's Aborigines for the government's past mistreatment of them.

14 Feb A gunman enters a lecture hall at Northern Illinois University and begins shooting from the stage; he kills 5 students and wounds 16 others before killing himself.

▸ Kiribati declares a marine protected area that, at 425,300 sq km (164,200 sq mi), is the largest in the world; it preserves a rare oceanic coral archipelago ecosystem.

15 Feb Scottish cyclist Mark Beaumont breaks the world record for riding a bicycle around the world when he crosses the finish line in Paris 195 days after he began the 29,000-km (18,000-mi) journey.

16 Feb The Brazilian film *Tropa de elite* (*The Elite Squad*), directed by José Padilha, wins the Golden Bear at the Berlin International Film Festival.

17 Feb The UN-administered Serbian province of Kosovo unilaterally declares its independence; the following day the US, France, Germany, and Turkey, among others, recognize its sovereignty, but Russia, China, and Spain are among those that refuse recognition.

▸ In Daytona Beach FL, Ryan Newman wins the 50th running of the Daytona 500, the premier NASCAR race, by 0.092 second in an upset victory.

18 Feb Legislative elections in Pakistan result in a pronounced victory for the Pakistan People's Party (once led by Benazir Bhutto), with 120 seats, and the Pakistan Muslim League-N of Nawaz Sharif, with 90; Pres. Pervez Musharraf's party wins only 51 seats.

▸ The BBC transmits its final English-language shortwave radio broadcast in Europe; the service began 75 years earlier with an inaugural transmission by King George V.

19 Feb Fidel Castro announces his official retirement, saying he does not want another term as president of Cuba.

▸ Toshiba announces that it will phase out the production of HD DVD players and other products, leaving Sony's Blu-ray the sole new optical media format.

20 Feb A US missile interceptor successfully strikes a falling spy satellite, destroying its fuel tank as planned.

21 Feb Thousands of demonstrators angry about Kosovo's declaration of independence attack and set fire to the US embassy in Belgrade, Serbia.

▸ Brazil's central bank reveals that in January Brazil for the first time became a net creditor country.

22 Feb In Iraq the Shi'ite cleric Muqtada al-Sadr extends the cease-fire being observed by his Mahdi Army militia a further six months.

23 Feb The Ugandan government reaches a formal cease-fire agreement with the rebel group the Lord's Resistance Army.

24 Feb At the 80th Academy Awards presentation, hosted by Jon Stewart, Oscars are won by, among others, *No Country for Old Men* (best picture) and its directors, Joel and Ethan Coen, and actors Daniel Day-Lewis, Marion Cotillard, Javier Bardem, and Tilda Swinton.

25 Feb Flemish and Walloon leaders in Belgium agree on a series of reforms, including giving more powers to the regions, that should make it possible for a new government to be formed after close to nine months of disagreement.

▸ Lee Myung-bak is sworn in as president of South Korea.

26 Feb The Svalbard Global Seed Vault in the Norwegian Arctic is ceremonially opened with its first consignment of seeds; the depository is intended to safeguard samples of all known food crop seeds against any human or natural disaster.

▸ The New York Philharmonic plays a concert in Pyongyang, North Korea.

▸ A panel of judges in Nigeria upholds the election of Umaru Yar'Adua as president in a challenge brought after the April 2007 election.

27 Feb Former Thai prime minister Thaksin Shinawatra returns to Thailand after 17 months in exile; he is wanted on charges of corruption.

28 Feb Kenyan Pres. Mwai Kibaki and opposition leader Raila Odinga reach an agreement on a power-sharing government in which Kibaki remains president, Odinga becomes a powerful prime minister, and cabinet appointments are split between the parties.

▸ The Pew Center on the States releases a report showing that for the first time more than 1% of American adults are behind bars, with close to 2.3 million adults incarcerated at the beginning of 2008.

▸ The first 30,000 pages of the Web-based *Encyclopedia of Life* go live; the encyclopedia, which intends to catalog all living species by organizing information that is already available, is expected to grow to 1.77 million pages.

29 Feb Turkey ends its eight-day incursion into northern Iraq, withdrawing its troops to the Turkish side of the border.

▸ The government of India passes a budget that includes a provision to cancel all the debt owed by the country's small farmers.

March 2008

1 Mar Colombian armed forces attack a Revolutionary Armed Forces of Colombia (FARC) camp in Ecuador, killing 24 people, including the organization's second-in-command, Raúl Reyes.

2 Mar At a gathering of tribal elders who convened in Darra Adamkhel, Pakistan, to discuss forming a force to fight local militants, a bomb kills 42 people and injures 58.

▸ As expected, Dimitry Medvedev is elected president of Russia.

3 Mar The price of oil reaches US$103.95 a barrel, breaking the record set in August 1980 when that price, US$39.50, is adjusted for inflation.

▸ Ecuador breaks off diplomatic relations with Colombia in response to the raid Colombia made against FARC guerrillas in Ecuador.

4 Mar Ian Paisley announces that he will retire in May as first minister of Northern Ireland's power-sharing government and as head of the Democratic Unionist Party.

5 Mar The US Food and Drug Administration reports that heparin associated with bad reactions, including 19 deaths, was produced with ingredients made in China and contained a contaminant that effectively mimicked the active ingredient in genuine heparin.

6 Mar Two bombs explode in sequence in a shopping district in Baghdad; at least 68 people are killed.

▸ The US Federal Reserve Board reports that in the second quarter of 2007, for the first time since the board began tracking data in 1945, the percentage of equity Americans own in their homes fell below 50%.

▸ In New York City the winners of the National Book Critics Circle Awards are announced as Junot Díaz for *The Brief Wondrous Life of Oscar Wao* (fiction), Harriet Washington for *Medical Apartheid: The Dark History of Medical Experimentation on Black Americans from Colonial Times to the Present* (nonfiction), Tim Jeal for *Stanley: The Impossible Life of Africa's Greatest Explorer* (biography), Edwidge Danticat for *Brother, I'm Dying* (autobiography), Mary Jo Bang for *Elegy* (poetry), and Alex Ross for *The Rest Is Noise: Listening to the Twentieth Century* (criticism); Emilie Buchwald is granted the Ivan Sandrof Lifetime Achievement Award.

7 Mar At a summit meeting in the Dominican Republic, the leaders of Colombia, Ecuador, and Venezuela reach an agreement to end the spreading diplomatic crisis that was initiated by Colombia's military strike on the FARC encampment in Ecuador's territory.

8 Mar Pres. Boris Tadic of Serbia announces plans to call an early election as a result of dissension over Kosovo's declaration of independence from Serbia.

9 Mar In London, *Hairspray* wins four Laurence Olivier Awards—best new musical, best actor in a musical (Michael Ball), best actress in a musical (Leanne Jones), and best supporting performance in a musical (Tracie Bennett).

10 Mar Indian authorities block hundreds of Tibetan protesters near Dharmshala at the beginning of a six-month march to Tibet to protest China's hosting of the Olympic Games.

▸ In a ceremony in New York City, the Rock and Roll Hall of Fame, located in Cleveland, inducts musicians Leonard Cohen, Madonna, John Mellencamp, and Little Walter, the groups the Dave Clark Five and the Ventures, and the producers Kenny Gamble and Leon Huff.

11 Mar China announces a planned reorganization of its government that will create ministries to oversee environmental protection, social services, housing and construction, and industry and information.

▸ Two bombs in Lahore, Pakistan, the first at a Federal Investigation Agency office, kill at least 24 people.

12 Mar Michael Heller, a Polish cosmologist and philosopher, is named the winner of the Templeton Prize for Progress Toward Research or Discoveries About Spiritual Realities.

▸ Kate Christensen wins the PEN/Faulkner Award for fiction for her novel *The Great Man*.

▸ Lance Mackey wins the Iditarod Trail Sled Dog Race for the second consecutive year, crossing the Burled Arch in Nome AK after a journey of 9 days 11 hours 46 minutes 48 seconds.

13 Mar For the first time, Cuba allows ordinary citizens to purchase appliances and electronic devices such as computers and DVD players.

▸ It is reported that hundreds of monks in Tibet have been protesting China's rule over the province for the past few days.

14 Mar Violence breaks out in Lhasa, the capital of Tibet, between residents and Chinese security forces.

▸ A tornado roars through downtown Atlanta, injuring dozens and causing major damage to city landmarks.

15 Mar A munitions depot near Tirana, Albania, blows up, and the series of explosions as well as a strong shock wave leave 26 people dead and hundreds injured.

▸ A 19-story construction crane topples to the ground in New York City, destroying a town house and damaging several other buildings; six construction workers and a tourist are killed.

▸ With its 29–12 defeat of France, Wales wins the Six Nations Rugby Union championship, having achieved a won-lost record of 5–0.

16 Mar The bank JPMorgan Chase & Co. announces that with US$30 billion in funding from the Federal Reserve, it will buy the collapsing Wall Street investment bank Bear Stearns for only US$2 a share.

▸ The wreck of HMAS *Sydney*, which disappeared 66 years earlier, is found off Western Australia, where it sank with 645 aboard on 19 Nov 1941 after being torpedoed by the German raider *Kormoran;* the search vessel *Geosounder* finds the wreckage some 112 nautical miles from Denham.

17 Mar The World Glacier Monitoring Service releases a report charting changes in glaciers through 2006; it shows that the pace of melting appears to be accelerating.

▸ In Mitrovica, in northern Kosovo, Serbs attempting to force a partition of the northern part of Kosovo (which is populated heavily with ethnic Serbs) from the rest of Kosovo attack UN peacekeeping forces.

18 Mar Kenya's National Assembly approves a power-sharing plan intended to end the crisis set in motion by the presidential election.

▸ German Chancellor Angela Merkel addresses the Israeli Knesset (legislature); she is the first German chancellor to do so in Israel's 60-year history.

19 Mar US Pres. George W. Bush marks the fifth anniversary of the start of the Iraq War with a speech saying that going to war was the right thing to do and insisting that the war continue until the attainment of victory.

20 Mar Yves Leterme of the Flemish Christian Democratic Party is sworn in as prime minister of a coalition government in Belgium nine months after elections.

▸ A report is published in the journal *Science* saying that a study of a fossil thigh bone of the six-million-year-old protohuman species *Orrorin tugensis* found that the species was able to walk upright and that it may be more closely related to *Australopithecus* than to *Homo;* this is now the earliest-known example of bipedalism.

21 Mar The Republic of Cyprus's newly elected president, Demetris Christofias, meets with Turkish Cypriot leader Mehmet Ali Talat; they agree to resume talks aimed at reuniting the Greek and Turkish sides of the country.

22 Mar Ma Ying-jeou of the Nationalist Party is elected president of Taiwan; Ma campaigned on a platform of seeking closer economic ties with China.

▸ Asif Ali Zardari, head of the victorious Pakistan People's Party, names Yousaf Raza Gillani to become Pakistan's prime minister.

23 Mar A roadside bomb in Baghdad kills four US soldiers, bringing the number of American troops killed in the Iraq War to 4,000; at least 58 Iraqis are also killed in violence throughout the country.

24 Mar Voters in Bhutan choose the members of the National Assembly, the lower house of the country's new legislature, transforming the country into

QUOTE OF THE MONTH

“*First and foremost, you must vote. Every single person must exercise his or her franchise.*”

—King Jigme Khesar Namgyal Wangchuk of Bhutan, exhorting his subjects to vote in the following day's election that will end his absolute rule, 23 March

a parliamentary monarchy; 45 of the 47 seats are won by the Bhutan Peace and Prosperity Party, and turnout is close to 80%.

▸ Pakistan's newly named prime minister orders the release of the judges placed under house arrest in late 2007 by Pres. Pervez Musharraf.

▸ The Olympic torch is ceremonially lit in Olympia, Greece, though the ceremony is briefly interrupted by pro-Tibet protesters; until 8 August the torch is to travel around the world before arriving in Beijing for the Olympic Games.

25 Mar Military forces of the African Union and Comoros seize control of the autonomous island of Anjouan from Mohamed Bacar, who took power in a coup in 2001.

▸ Scientists report that a 415-sq-km (160-sq-mi) chunk of ice has fallen from the Wilkins ice shelf in western Antarctica; it is believed that the collapse can be attributed to global warming.

26 Mar Scientists report that the Cassini spacecraft has found that geysers on the Saturnian moon Enceladus contain molecules of water, methane, carbon dioxide, and carbon monoxide, all organic molecules.

▸ The sale of the Jaguar and Land Rover car brands from the Ford Motor Co. to the Indian car company Tata Motors, part of the Tata Group, is announced.

27 Mar Gov. Aníbal Acevedo Vilá of Puerto Rico is indicted on federal charges involving campaign finance violations.

▸ The Norwegian Academy of Science and Letters awards its annual Abel Prize for outstanding work in mathematics to American mathematician John Griggs Thompson and French mathematician Jacques Tits for their contributions to group theory.

28 Mar North Korea conducts test launches of short-range missiles off its western coast and threatens to slow down the disabling of its nuclear facilities.

29 Mar Presidential elections are held in Zimbabwe, and international observers are barred.

▸ Curlin, 2007 Horse of the Year, wins the Dubai World Cup, the world's richest horse race.

▸ Oxford defeats Cambridge in the 154th University Boat Race; Cambridge still leads the series, however, by 79–74.

30 Mar Shiʿite cleric Muqtada al-Sadr calls for his followers in Basra to cease fighting in return for concessions from the Iraqi government.

31 Mar The French liquor company Pernod Ricard announces its purchase of Vin & Sprit, the parent company of Absolut vodka.

▸ Prolific French architect Jean Nouvel is named winner of the 2008 Pritzker Architecture Prize; among his works are the Guthrie Theatre in Minneapolis MN, the Quai Branly Museum in Paris, and the Agbar Tower in Barcelona.

April 2008

1 Apr Intense fighting takes place between Chad's armed forces and rebel militias in the eastern part of the country.

▸ British Defense Minister Desmond Browne announces that a planned drawdown of troops in southern Iraq will be postponed until the security situation in Basra can be stabilized.

2 Apr Official returns from the 29 March legislative elections in Zimbabwe are released, showing that the opposition Movement for Democratic Change won 109 seats and the ruling ZANU-PF took 97; though the MDC releases figures showing that Morgan Tsvangirai won the presidential election, no official results are given.

▸ Irish Prime Minister Bertie Ahern announces that he will resign his post on 6 May.

3 Apr At a NATO summit meeting in Bucharest, Romania, leaders agree to endorse a proposed US missile defense system based in Europe and to increase the number of troops in Afghanistan but decline to offer the first step toward eventual membership to Georgia and Ukraine; in addition, Albania and Croatia are invited to full membership, but, on Greece's veto, Macedonia is not.

▸ Tony Hoagland is named the second winner of the US$50,000 Jackson Poetry Prize.

4 Apr Authorities in Texas raid the Yearning for Zion Ranch of the polygamous sect the Fundamentalist Church of Jesus Christ of Latter-day Saints in Eldorado and take 52 girls into protective custody; eventually more than 400 children are removed from the compound.

5 Apr In response to calls for a runoff presidential election in Zimbabwe, opposition presidential candidate Morgan Tsvangirai says that no such election is needed and petitions the High Court in an attempt to force a release of the official tally for the presidential vote.

6 Apr At the Olympic torch relay in London, pro-Tibet protesters attempting to seize or extinguish the torch to express their opposition to Chinese human rights abuses are engaged in a series of scuffles with police and prevented from achieving their goal.

7 Apr In New York City the winners of the 2008 Pulitzer Prizes are announced: six journalism awards go to the *Washington Post,* which wins for public service, breaking news reporting, national reporting, international reporting, feature writing, and commentary; winners in letters include Junot Díaz in fiction and Tracy Letts in drama.

▸ The National Collegiate Athletic Association championship in men's basketball is won by the University of Kansas, which defeats the University of Memphis 75–68; the following day the University of Tennessee defeats Stanford University 64–48 to win the women's NCAA title for the second consecutive year.

8 Apr The Orange Democratic Movement, headed by Raila Odinga, suspends peace talks with Pres. Mwai Kibaki of Kenya, insisting on the dismissal of the standing cabinet before negotiations can continue; rioting erupts in Nairobi and Kisumu.

▸ The petroleum companies BP and ConocoPhillips agree to build a pipeline to carry natural gas from Alaska's Prudhoe Bay into Canada and possibly as far as Chicago.

9 Apr Violence in reaction to an assault on a former cabinet minister breaks out in Karachi, with Pakistani Pres. Pervez Musharraf's followers battling supporters of the new government; at least seven people are killed.

▸ Kosovo's legislature adopts a constitution that makes the country a parliamentary democracy with a strong president; it will go into effect on 15 June.

10 Apr Voters in Nepal go to the polls to elect the Constituent Assembly that will write the country's new constitution; the Maoist party wins the largest number of seats.

11 Apr A new decree allows workers in Cuba who rent housing from their state employers to keep their homes after leaving their jobs, to gain title to their homes, and to pass their homes on to their children or other relatives.

12 Apr At the joint IMF–World Bank spring meeting in Washington DC, the World Bank president, Robert Zoellick, describes the skyrocketing price of food and its impact on poorer countries; there have been food riots in cities throughout the world.

▸ In Harbin, China, the US defeats Canada 4–3 to win the International Ice Hockey Federation world women's championship.

13 Apr The parties of Pres. Mwai Kibaki and opposition leader Raila Odinga agree on the composition of a new and much larger cabinet in Kenya.

▸ On a rainy day Martin Lel of Kenya wins the London Marathon for the second year in a row, with a time of 2 hr 5 min 15 sec, and Irina Mikitenko of Germany, in her first marathon, is the fastest woman in the race, with a time of 2 hr 24 min 14 sec.

14 Apr In two days of legislative elections in Italy, the largest percentage of votes goes to Silvio Berlusconi's People of Liberty alliance.

▸ For the first time since 1965, passenger train service between Kolkata (Calcutta), India, and Dhaka, Bangladesh, takes place, with one train departing from each city.

15 Apr The Prado Museum in Madrid opens the exhibition "Goya in Times of War," showcasing more than 200 paintings, drawings, and prints from the last 25 years of the career of artist Francisco de Goya; the show marks the 200th anniversary of the Spanish War of Independence.

16 Apr Russian Pres. Vladimir Putin orders that a number of Russian ministries establish direct relations with their counterparts in the de-facto governments of the separatist Georgian provinces of Abkhazia and South Ossetia.

▸ Government figures show that the rate of inflation in Zimbabwe reached 165,000% in February, up from 100,000% in January.

17 Apr Raila Odinga is sworn in as prime minister of Kenya; an agreement made in February gives him power that is equal to that of the president.

QUOTE OF THE MONTH

> "*We can now consign Kenya's past failures of grand corruption and grand tribalism to our history books.*"
>
> —Raila Odinga, upon being inaugurated as prime minister of Kenya, 17 April

18 Apr In Durban, South Africa, dockworkers refuse to unload a Chinese shipment of weapons that are intended to be delivered to Zimbabwe, and South Africa's High Court issues an order prohibiting the transport of the weapons across South Africa to Zimbabwe.

19 Apr Election officials in Zimbabwe begin a partial recount of the ballots from the general election at the request of the government; opposition leaders' legal challenge to stop the recount was unsuccessful.

▸ A Russian Soyuz space capsule carrying back from the space station former International Space Station commander Peggy A. Whitson of the US, Russian flight engineer Yury I. Malenchenko, and South Korea's first astronaut, Yi So-yeon, lands about 418 km (260 mi) off its mark in Kazakhstan.

20 Apr With his election to the presidency of Paraguay, former Roman Catholic bishop Fernando Lugo ends the rule of the Colorado Party, which had held power since 1946.

▸ American race-car driver Danica Patrick wins the Indy Japan 300 race, coming in six seconds ahead of Brazilian Helio Castroneves and becoming the first woman to win an IndyCar race.

21 Apr The 112th Boston Marathon is won for the third consecutive year by Robert K. Cheruiyot of Kenya, with a time of 2 hr 7 min 46 sec; the fastest woman is Dire Tune of Ethiopia, who crosses the finish line 2 seconds ahead of Alevtina Biktimirova of Russia and posts a time of 2 hr 25 min 25 sec.

22 Apr At a meeting convened in London by British Prime Minister Gordon Brown to discuss the rising price of food throughout the world, the World Food Programme's executive director, Josette Sheeran, likens the crisis to a "silent tsunami" in the poorest countries of the world.

▸ The European Synchrotron Radiation Facility in France reports that paintings found in the Bamiyan caves in Afghanistan have been proved to have been painted with drying oils centuries before the first oil paintings appeared in Europe.

23 Apr A major battle between government forces and the Liberation Tigers of Tamil Eelam takes place in northern Sri Lanka; some 90 combatants are killed.

▸ The US National Oceanic and Atmospheric Administration reports that atmospheric levels of carbon dioxide are increasing at an accelerating rate and that levels of methane are also beginning to rise.

24 Apr Pres. Gurbanguly Berdymukhammedov of Turkmenistan restores the standard month names and day names to the calendar, abolishing the calendar that the previous president had decreed to further his cult of personality.

25 Apr The government of China expresses its new willingness to meet with envoys of the Dalai Lama for discussions on Tibet.

▸ The banking company Wachovia Corp. agrees to pay up to US$144 million in fines and restitution to end an investigation into relationships the bank had with telemarketers that allowed them to steal millions of dollars from account holders.

26 Apr A running gun battle between rival groups of drug traffickers takes place in Tijuana, Mexico; 13 people are killed.

27 Apr At a military parade in Kabul staged to celebrate Afghanistan's national holiday, a coordinated attempt is made to assassinate Pres. Hamid Karzai, who escapes unharmed, though three people are killed, including a child caught in the cross fire.

▸ Austrian authorities divulge that a 73-year-old man in Amstetten has been discovered to have been keeping his daughter imprisoned in his basement for the past 24 years, during which time he fathered seven children with her, three of whom he forced her to keep in the basement, three of whom he adopted, and one of whom died.

28 Apr Mars, Inc., the maker of candies and other foodstuffs, announces its purchase of the Wrigley chewing gum company.

29 Apr In response to an offer by the Popular Revolutionary Army to suspend its attacks on oil and gas pipelines, the government of Mexico agrees to negotiations with the organization.

▸ Rockstar Games releases the fourth edition of its controversial video game series, *Grand Theft Auto IV;* this edition, which features a fully realized protagonist and complex plot lines, is greeted with critical acclaim.

30 Apr Turkey's legislature approves reforms to a law regulating free speech that restrict the opportunities for prosecution, reduce penalties, and change a prohibition against insults to "Turkishness" to one against insults to the "Turkish nation."

▸ Researchers report that DNA tests have confirmed that bone shards found in a forest near Yekaterinburg, Russia, in summer 2007 were those of Alexis and Maria, children of the last Romanov rulers of Russia, Nicholas and Alexandra; their fate had not been conclusively known heretofore.

May 2008

1 May Colorful Tory candidate Boris Johnson is elected mayor of London as the Labour incumbent, Ken Livingstone, is voted out.

▸ At the National Magazine Awards in New York City, *National Geographic* wins three awards, including one for general excellence; other winners include *The New Yorker, GQ, Backpacker, Mother Jones, Print,* and, in the online category, RunnersWorld.com.

2 May Cyclone Nargis makes landfall and churns up the southeast coast of Myanmar (Burma), causing enormous devastation, especially in the Irrawaddy River delta; the death toll is estimated to be at least 130,000.

▸ Zimbabwe's electoral commission releases official results of the 29 March presidential election, saying challenger Morgan Tsvangirai won 47.9% of the vote, to incumbent Robert Mugabe's 43.25%, necessitating a runoff; the Movement for Democratic Change maintains that Tsvangirai won 50.3% of the vote, an outright win.

▸ The Chaitén volcano in Chile's Patagonia region begins a massive eruption, burying an area of about 155 sq km (60 sq mi) in more than 38 cm (15 in) of ash; the volcano had not erupted for some 9,000 years.

3 May Big Brown wins the Kentucky Derby, the first race of Thoroughbred horse racing's US Triple Crown, but the event is marred when the filly Eight Belles, which finishes second, breaks both front ankles after crossing the finish line and is euthanized on the track.

4 May Residents of the Santa Cruz department of Bolivia overwhelmingly vote in a nonbinding referendum for the administrative subdivision to become autonomous.

5 May Iran suspends talks with the US on the security situation in Iraq.

▸ The Italian conductor Riccardo Muti, who resigned from the Teatro alla Scala in Milan in 2005, is announced as the new music director of the Chicago Symphony Orchestra.

6 May In Taiwan, in the midst of a scandal in which US$30 million of government money (intended to be given to Papua New Guinea if it switched its diplomatic relations from China to Taiwan) seems to have been stolen, Foreign Minister James Huang and Vice-Premier Chiou I-chen resign.

7 May A general strike against Lebanese government economic policies spirals into street fighting between Hezbollah supporters (who favor the strike and oppose a government move to shut down a private Hezbollah telephone network) and those who favor the government.

▸ Dmitry Medvedev takes office as president of Russia and names outgoing president Vladimir Putin prime minister.

8 May North Korea turns over to the US 18,000 pages of documentation on its plutonium program dating back to 1990.

▸ Edgar Millán Gómez, the acting chief of federal police in Mexico, is ambushed and killed by several men outside his home in Mexico City.

9 May Hezbollah fighters seize control of a large portion of western Beirut.

▸ As attacks against supporters of the opposition in Zimbabwe intensify, Pres. Thabo Mbeki of South Africa holds talks with Zimbabwean Pres. Robert Mugabe in Harare.

▸ Two shipments of food aid from the UN World Food Programme are confiscated by the Myanmar (Burma) government as it agrees to accept supplies but not personnel from outside sources, saying it will deliver the aid itself to victims of Cyclone Nargis.

QUOTE OF THE MONTH

> “*Myanmar is not in a position to receive rescue and information teams from foreign countries at the moment.*”
>
> Myanmar (Burma) Foreign Ministry statement one week after Cyclone Nargis devastated the country, 9 May

10 May A referendum on a new constitution that places a great deal of power in the hands of the military is held in Myanmar (Burma); 92.48% of voters are said to have approved the document.

▸ Shi'ite leaders of Iraq's legislature and representatives of Shi'ite cleric Muqtada al-Sadr reach an agreement on a truce to end the bloodshed in the Sadr City neighborhood of Baghdad.

11 May In legislative elections in Serbia, the coalition For a European Serbia wins 102 of the 250 seats, followed by 78 seats for the Serbian Radical Party.

12 May A magnitude-7.9 earthquake with its epicenter in Wenchuan causes devastation in the Chinese province of Sichuan as schools collapse, factories are destroyed, and whole villages are demolished; the initial death toll is about 10,000.

▸ The Pakistan Muslim League-N, led by Nawaz Sharif, withdraws from the cabinet because of the insistence of its coalition partner, the Pakistan People's Party, that judges appointed by Pres. Pervez Musharraf under emergency rule retain their seats even after the judges dismissed by Musharraf regain their seats.

13 May To the shock of environmentalists, Marina Silva resigns as Brazil's minister of the environment, citing a lack of government support for environmental goals; she is replaced by Carlos Minc.

▸ Carlos Ghosn, CEO of the car manufacturer Nissan Motor Co., announces that the company intends to bring an electric car to the American market by 2010.

14 May US Secretary of the Interior Dirk Kempthorne announces that the polar bear will be listed as an endangered species because the growing melting of sea ice threatens its survival.

▸ The Russian association football (soccer) club FC Zenit St. Petersburg defeats FC Rangers of Glasgow, Scotland, 2–0 to win the Union des Associations Européennes de Football (UEFA) Cup in Manchester, England.

15 May The California Supreme Court rules that state laws that limit marriage to opposite-sex couples are unconstitutional and that same-sex couples also have the right to marry.

16 May Zimbabwe's election commission schedules a runoff election between Pres. Robert Mugabe and opposition leader Morgan Tsvangirai for 27 June.

▸ Portugal's legislature adopts a spelling standardization agreement that will change the spelling of many words to match the Brazilian spelling.

▸ The government of Myanmar (Burma) raises the official death toll from Cyclone Nargis to 78,000, with a further 55,917 listed as missing.

17 May Trucks carrying men firing assault rifles roll into Villa Ahumada, Mexico; 6 people are killed, including the chief of police, and 10 others are kidnapped, prompting the entire surviving police force to flee and leaving the rest of the town terrorized.

▸ Kentucky Derby winner Big Brown decisively wins the Preakness Stakes, the second event in US Thoroughbred horse racing's Triple Crown.

18 May After a week of increasing and spreading anti-immigrant violence in and around Johannesburg in which at least 12 people were killed, South African Pres. Thabo Mbeki promises a commission to study the causes of the violence.

19 May Nelly Avila Moreno (nom de guerre Karina), a top commander in FARC (Revolutionary Armed Forces of Colombia), surrenders to the Colombian army.

20 May For the first time in 15 months, the foreign ministers of India and Pakistan engage in peace negotiations.

▸ A US federal court of appeals rules that the country's paper currency must be redesigned because the various denominations cannot be distinguished by the visually impaired.

21 May Israel and Syria announce that they are undertaking negotiations toward a peace treaty; the talks are taking place in Istanbul.

▸ In association football (soccer), Manchester United defeats another English team, Chelsea, on penalty kicks to win the UEFA Champions League championship in Moscow.

22 May The price of oil briefly reaches a record US$135.09 a barrel before closing at US$133.17.

▸ An appellate court in Texas rules that the state was wrong in removing more than 450 children from the custody of their parents at the polygamist Yearning for Zion ranch in April.

23 May Twelve countries in South America sign a treaty creating Unasur, a union intended to be similar to the European Union.

24 May UN Secretary-General Ban Ki-moon meets Chinese Premier Wen Jiabao in earthquake-ravaged Yingxiu and praises China's response to the disaster.

▸ In Belgrade, Serbia, the Russian pop star Dima Bilan wins the Eurovision Song Contest with his English-language rendition of "Believe," produced by American rap impresario Timbaland.

25 May NASA's Phoenix Mars Lander, launched on 4 Aug 2007, successfully makes a soft landing in the northern polar region of Mars, where it will analyze soil samples and search for proof of water.

▸ FARC confirms that its founder and chief, Manuel Marulanda, died on 26 March.

▸ The Sutong Bridge, between the Chinese cities of Suzhou and Nantong in Jiangsu province, opens to traffic; with a main span of 1,088 m (3,570 ft), the bridge is the world's longest cable-stayed bridge.

▸ The 92nd Indianapolis 500 automobile race is won by Scott Dixon of New Zealand.

26 May The International Atomic Energy Agency releases a report saying that Iran has failed to be forthcoming about its nuclear programs and that its nuclear capabilities are advancing.

27 May In the face of a military mutiny, Pres. Lansana Conté of Guinea fires Minister of Defense Bailo Diallo.

28 May Nepal's newly elected constituent assembly votes to transform the country from a monarchy to a republic, giving the royal family, which ruled the country for 240 years, 15 days to vacate the palace in Kathmandu.

▸ In Ilulissat, Greenland, the US, Russia, Canada, Denmark, and Norway sign an agreement to abide by the 1982 UN Convention on the Law of the Sea regarding territorial claims on the Arctic and to work cooperatively to limit environmental and other risks in any increased shipping and commerce in the region.

29 May The confirmed death toll in China's Sichuan earthquake is reported as 68,500 people, with a further 19,000 missing and presumed dead.

▸ *Science* publishes an online report describing DNA research on a swatch of Paleo-Eskimo hair from Greenland showing that the earliest known inhabitants of Greenland were not related to the later Thule people or American Indians but were related to people now living in the Komandor Islands off Russia's Kamchatka Peninsula.

▸ The Ruth Lilly Poetry Prize is presented in Chicago to Gary Snyder.

30 May Silverjet, a business-class-only airline based in London, ceases operations; it is the third airline of that type to shut down in six months.

31 May Zimbabwe's army chief of staff says that it is the duty of members of the country's armed forces to vote for Pres. Robert Mugabe in the upcoming runoff presidential election.

June 2008

1 Jun Parents in several cities in China's Sichuan province protest the shoddy construction of schools that collapsed in the earthquake three weeks earlier, crushing children, and China raises the official toll of the quake to 69,000 dead and 18,800 missing and presumed dead.

2 Jun Relief groups report that though the rulers of Myanmar (Burma) have increased openness somewhat, they are still severely limiting the access of foreign aid workers to the victims of Cyclone Nargis in the Irrawaddy delta.

▸ Georgia demands that Russia withdraw the peacekeeping forces and army troops that it sent to the separatist Abkhazia region of Georgia.

3 Jun A three-day conference on food security convened by the UN Food and Agriculture Organization and attended by top officials from some 150 countries opens in Rome.

4 Jun Rose Tremain wins the Orange Broadband Prize, an award for fiction written by women and published in the UK, for her novel *The Road Home.*

▸ The Detroit Red Wings defeat the Pittsburgh Penguins 3–2 to win the Stanley Cup, the National Hockey League championship trophy.

5 Jun The Constitutional Court of Turkey strikes down a new law that would allow women who cover their heads with scarves for religious reasons to attend public universities.

6 Jun In Seoul some 65,000 people demonstrate their opposition to a South Korean government plan to allow beef imports from the United States; such imports were banned in 2003.

7 Jun Ana Ivanovic of Serbia defeats Dinara Safina of Russia to win the women's French Open tennis title; the following day Rafael Nadal of Spain defeats Roger Federer of Switzerland to capture the men's championship for the fourth year in a row.

▸ The Derby, in its 229th year at Epsom Downs in Surrey, England, is won by New Approach, ridden by Kevin Manning.

▸ Long shot Da' Tara, with odds of 38–1, wins the Belmont Stakes, the last event in Thoroughbred horse racing's US Triple Crown; Big Brown, winner of the Kentucky Derby and the Preakness Stakes, comes in last.

8 Jun The i-LIMB, a bionic prosthetic hand that mimics both the form and the function of the human hand, wins the MacRobert Award for engineering excellence from the Royal Academy of Engineering in London.

▸ Yani Tseng of Taiwan wins the Ladies Professional Golf Association championship in a sudden-death play-off over Maria Hjorth of Sweden.

9 Jun A cache of cylinder seals dating from 3000–2000 BC that were looted from the National Museum of Iraq during the 2003 US-led invasion of the country are ceremonially returned to Iraq's Ministry of Antiquities in Baghdad; the seals were found by customs officials in Philadelphia in May 2008.

▸ Lake Delton, a centerpiece of the Wisconsin Dells resort area, breaches the highway after massive rainfalls and in less than two hours drains completely into the Wisconsin River.

10 Jun After a firefight against insurgents in Afghanistan just over the border from Pakistan, US forces make air and artillery strikes in Pakistan that kill 11 Pakistani paramilitary soldiers, outraging Pakistan's government.

▸ Armed battles break out on the border between Djibouti and Eritrea for the first time in 10 years.

11 Jun King Gyanendra of Nepal, bowing to the desires of the country's new government, gives up his crown and leaves the royal palace to take up life as an ordinary citizen.

▸ NASA launches the Gamma-ray Large Area Space Telescope (GLAST); the space telescope, which can detect an immense range of light, will examine gamma-ray bursts and, it is hoped, give scientists new information about the nature of the universe.

▸ Canadian Prime Minister Stephen Harper, in a speech before the House of Commons, apologizes for the country's policy of taking children of First Nations peoples and putting them in Christian boarding schools to assimilate them; some 100,000 children were placed in such schools beginning in the late 19th century, and abuse was rampant.

▸ The Belgian brewing giant InBev makes an unsolicited bid to buy American brewery Anheuser-Busch, headquartered in St. Louis MO.

12 Jun The US Supreme Court rules that in spite of the Military Commissions Act of 2006, prisoners at the US naval base at Guantánamo Bay, Cuba, have the right to challenge their detention in federal courts.

▸ China and Taiwan agree to establish offices in one another's capitals to facilitate discussions about closer relationships.

▸ As floodwaters roll down the Cedar River in Iowa, raising it 5 m (17 ft) above flood stage, torrential rains pound the area, and much of the town of Cedar Rapids is washed away.

13 Jun Thousands of people converge in Islamabad, Pakistan, to demand the reinstatement of judges dismissed in November 2007 by Pres. Pervez Musharraf.

14 Jun Pres. Robert Mugabe of Zimbabwe declares that he has no intention of ceding power, even if he should lose the runoff presidential election scheduled for 27 June.

15 Jun Kosovo's constitution officially goes into effect.

▸ The 62nd annual Tony Awards are presented in New York City; winners include the productions *August: Osage County, In the Heights, Boeing-Boeing,* and *South Pacific* and the actors Mark Rylance, Deanna Dunagan, Paulo Szot, and Patti LuPone.

▸ In the 76th running of the 24 Hours of Le Mans, the Audi team led by Tom Kristensen of Denmark takes the victory; it is Kristensen's record eighth victory in the classic endurance automobile race.

16 Jun When police attempt to break up a blockade of Peru's main road to Chile and to a major copper mine and smelter near Moquegua, Peru, protesters overcome them and force them to retreat; the demonstrators want more of the taxes paid by the copper company to be used in the region.

▸ Tiger Woods defeats Rocco Mediate in a thrilling sudden-death play-off to win the US Open golf tournament in San Diego CA.

▸ A ceremony is held in Takanezawa, Japan, as the first Honda FCX Clarity rolls off the assembly line; it is the first hydrogen-powered fuel-cell car capable of being mass-produced.

17 Jun Pres. Felipe Calderón of Mexico signs into law a constitutional amendment requiring that trials be openly argued before a judge with a presumption of innocence; the enormous changes entailed must be completed by 2016.

▸ The Boston Celtics defeat the Los Angeles Lakers 131–92 in game six of the best-of-seven tournament to secure the team's 17th National Basketball Association championship.

18 Jun Israel proposes holding peace talks with Lebanon, indicating that it is even willing to discuss the disposition of the disputed Shebaa Farms area on the border between the countries.

▸ China and Japan both announce that the countries

have reached an agreement to jointly develop gas fields in the East China Sea that lie in territory that both countries claim.

19 Jun A truce negotiated between Israel and the militant group Hamas, which controls the Gaza Strip, officially goes into effect.

20 Jun China unveils a plan to halve the number of cars on the road in and around Beijing from 20 July to 20 September and to prevent high-emission vehicles, such as trucks, from entering the city during the same period; the intent is to reduce both traffic and air pollution during the Olympics.

▸ The 2008 winners of the Kyoto Prize are announced: Richard M. Karp (advanced technology), Anthony J. Pawson (basic sciences), and Charles M. Taylor (arts and philosophy).

21 Jun Typhoon Fengshen roars through the Philippines, leaving at least 498 people dead, and the MV *Princess of the Stars,* a large ferry, capsizes and sinks in the storm off the Philippine island of Sibuyan; some 800 people are feared lost.

22 Jun Morgan Tsvangirai withdraws his candidacy in the presidential runoff election in Zimbabwe, citing the violence of the campaign being waged against his followers.

QUOTE OF THE MONTH

> “*We will no longer participate in the violent illegitimate sham of an election process.*”
>
> —Morgan Tsvangirai, announcing his withdrawal as a candidate in Zimbabwe's upcoming runoff presidential election, 22 June

23 Jun Fighting in Tripoli, Lebanon, between supporters of the government and partisans of Hezbollah continues for a second day; at least eight people have been killed.

24 Jun The United States Sugar Corp. reaches a tentative deal to sell 800 sq km (300 sq mi) of land in the Florida Everglades to the state of Florida; after six more years of sugarcane production, the land will be returned to its natural wetland condition.

▸ The retail giant Home Depot announces that all of its stores will accept old compact fluorescent light bulbs for recycling; because the bulbs contain mercury, they cannot be disposed of conventionally.

25 Jun The US Supreme Court rules that the punitive damages awarded in a lawsuit related to the 1989 *Exxon Valdez* oil disaster must be reduced to US$500 million, the amount that ExxonMobil has already paid out; in another ruling, the court bans the sentence of execution for the crime of child rape.

26 Jun In a landmark ruling, the US Supreme Court holds that the Second Amendment to the Constitution confers an individual rather than a collective right to gun ownership and that state and city governments may not forbid the owning of handguns.

▸ Girija Prasad Koirala resigns as prime minister of Nepal and asks the Maoist party to form a government.

▸ At its meeting in Paris, the Internet Corporation for Assigned Names and Numbers issues new guidelines allowing users to apply to use any domain name of their devising and permitting domain names to be registered in scripts other than the Roman alphabet.

▸ US Pres. George W. Bush announces that North Korea has been removed from the government's list of state sponsors of terrorism.

▸ The price of a barrel of light sweet crude oil briefly reaches a new record of US$140.39 a barrel before closing at a record US$139.64.

27 Jun In a runoff election in which he is unopposed, Pres. Robert Mugabe of Zimbabwe officially garners 85% of the vote; turnout is cited as 42.4%.

▸ North Korea publicly demolishes the cooling tower of its Yongbyon nuclear weapons plant.

28 Jun Pakistani security forces shell Taliban positions outside Peshawar, which has been increasingly threatened by the Taliban; it is the first military action taken against militants by the Pakistani government that took office in March.

29 Jun Israel agrees to trade the notorious Lebanese terrorist Samir Kuntar and four other Lebanese prisoners to the Lebanese militia Hezbollah in return for the bodies of the Israeli soldiers Ehud Goldwasser and Eldad Regev, whose 12 Jul 2006 kidnapping led to Israel's war with Hezbollah that year.

▸ Spain defeats Germany 1–0 in the final match to win Euro 2008; it is Spain's first major association football (soccer) title since it won the European championship in 1964.

30 Jun Officials in Lithuania report that over the weekend some 300 Web sites were defaced with Soviet symbols and anti-Lithuanian slogans by hackers; two weeks earlier Lithuania had banned the display of Soviet symbols.

▸ Iraq announces plans to open bidding on six major oil fields to 35 foreign companies.

Disasters

Listed here are major disasters between July 2007 and June 2008. The list includes natural and nonmilitary mechanical disasters that claimed 25 or more lives and/or resulted in significant damage to property.

July 2007

4 Jul Liaoning province, China. A karaoke bar full of university students is destroyed by an explosion; there are at least 25 fatalities.

5 Jul Culiacán, Mexico. A small cargo plane blows a tire during takeoff and crashes into a highway; three people aboard the plane, two soldiers guarding the airstrip, and four people in a car on the highway are killed.

8 Jul India. Government officials say the death toll from monsoon rains throughout the country has reached 660; hardest hit has been Maharashtra state.

16 Jul Near Lviv, Ukraine. A train carrying phosphorous from Kazakhstan to Poland derails and catches fire; the resultant cloud of toxic gas poisons at least 20 people and requires the evacuation of some 800 nearby residents.

17 Jul São Paulo. As a TAM Airlines Airbus 320 attempts to land at Congonhas Airport in the midst of a rainstorm, it skids off a runway, slides across a highway, and crashes into a building; at least 200 people, including some on the ground, are killed.

19 Jul Canary Islands. Off the coast of Tenerife, Spanish rescue crews spot a foundering wooden boat carrying African migrants; 48 migrants are saved, but some 50 more are feared drowned.

20 Jul Northwestern Pakistan. Landslides resulting from heavy rains leave more than 80 people dead in Dirbala district.

22 Jul France. Near the village of Vizille, a bus carrying Polish pilgrims from the shrine of Notre-Dame-de-la-Salette in the French Alps goes off the road, hitting a river bank and catching fire; 26 passengers are killed.

23 Jul Indonesia. Officials say flash floods and landslides that have inundated villages have left at least 30 people dead.

25 Jul Romania. Authorities report that an unremitting heat wave in southeastern Europe has killed 33 people in the country.

26 Jul Northern Syria. High temperatures cause a weapons depot near Aleppo to explode; at least 15 people are killed.

30 Jul China. The Xinhua news agency reports that unusually bad flooding from rain over the past few weeks has left some 650 people dead, including 17 in the past two days.

August 2007

1 Aug Democratic Republic of the Congo. The brakes fail on a freight train near Benaleka, and eight cars derail; about 100 people are reported to have perished.

3 Aug Sierra Leone. A boat traveling from Freetown to Rokupr capsizes in heavy rain at the mouth of the Great Scarcies River; the vast majority of the estimated 120 people aboard are believed to have drowned.

8 Aug India. Flooding in Gujarat state forces army personnel and helicopters to rescue and relocate people; so far this season some 290 people have died in flooding in the state.

10 Aug French Polynesia. A twin-engine turboprop Twin Otter plane carrying passengers on a seven-minute flight from the island of Moorea to the main island of Tahiti goes down in the ocean; all 20 passengers aboard perish.

11 Aug Indian-administered Kashmir. A fire breaks out at an ammunitions depot, causing explosions that continue for close to two days; at least 20 people, mostly firemen and soldiers, are killed.

13 Aug Off the shore of Mayotte. Officials in Mayotte, a French dependency in the Indian Ocean, report that a boat carrying migrants from Comoros capsized and at least 17 of the passengers drowned.

15 Aug Pisco, Peru. The city is destroyed by an offshore earthquake of magnitude 8.0 that leaves at least 540 people dead and some 200,000 in need of shelter.

16 Aug North Korea. After receiving permission from North Korea to examine flood-stricken regions after torrential rains, UN officials report 83 people dead and 60 missing as well as the destruction of 58,000 homes and 90,000 ha (222,400 ac) of farmland.

17 Aug Xintai, Shandong province, China. Excessive rainfall causes flash flooding from rivers into two coal mines, where 181 miners are trapped and drowned.

19 Aug Western Mexico. The waters of the Cuiztla River suddenly rise, sweeping away 15 members of the Universal Christian Church who were camping in Rancho Ixcamilpa.

20 Aug US. Authorities report that two violent storm systems, one in the upper Mississippi River states and one in Texas, have left at least 20 people dead.

22 Aug Northern Iraq. A US military Black Hawk helicopter crashes, killing all 14 soldiers aboard; mechanical failure is blamed for the crash.

23 Aug Mexico. The remnants of Hurricane Dean cause 8 deaths, bringing the death toll from the storm in the Caribbean and Mexico to 25.

24 Aug Greece. With high winds and high temperatures fueling them, dozens of wildfires have killed at least 15 people; by the time firefighters gain control over the flames on 29 August the death toll has risen to at least 64.

26 Aug Democratic Republic of the Congo. A cargo plane carrying tin ore crashes shortly after takeoff from Kongolo; 13 of the 15 people aboard are killed.

27 Aug Uganda. In the village of Kapchogo, a truck transporting army members and their families veers into a concrete barrier on the side of the road; 72 people perish.

28 Aug China. The minister of water resources reports that in spite of unusual extremes of weather in the country, the death toll (1,138) this year from floods is lower than last year's by nearly half because of better handling of disasters.

29 Aug Azerbaijan. A 16-story building under construction in Baku collapses, killing at least 19 people; the head of the construction company is arrested.

September 2007

4 Sep Nicaragua. Hurricane Felix makes landfall near Puerto Cabezas as a category 5 storm; more than 100 people are killed and a further 150 missing, with heavy damage to buildings and farmland in both Nicaragua and Honduras.

6 Sep Southern California. A week of unusually high temperatures comes to an end; some 20 people are believed to have perished in the heat wave.

7 Sep Rajasthan state, India. Near the village of Desuri Ki Naal, a truck loaded with pilgrims falls from the road into a gorge; at least 72 of those aboard perish.

9 Sep Mexico. In Coahuila state a truck loaded with mining explosives collides with another vehicle and after the arrival of emergency personnel and reporters the truck explodes; at least 37 people are incinerated.

15 Sep Mexico. A bus carrying tourists from Puerto Vallarta to Guadalajara goes off a mountain road into a ravine, killing at least 18 of the 35 passengers; most of the passengers had arrived on a flight from Phoenix that had been deflected to Puerto Vallarta from Guadalajara.

16 Sep Thailand. A passenger airliner crashes while attempting to land in heavy rain on the resort island of Phuket; at least 89 of those aboard, most of them tourists, are killed.

21 Sep Karachi, Pakistan. Police report that at least 22 people have died and many more been made ill as a result of drinking illegally brewed alcoholic beverages.

24 Sep Afghanistan. In Ghazni province, two passenger buses collide head-on; at least 40 people are killed.

26 Sep Vietnam. A 90-m (295-ft) section of the Can Tho Bridge being built over the Hau River in the southern Mekong delta collapses; at least 50 construction workers are crushed when the concrete section, poured only the previous day, falls.

October 2007

3 Oct Vietnam. Typhoon Lekima makes landfall, causing flooding and damage and leaving at least 32 people dead.

4 Oct Democratic Republic of the Congo. An Antonov-26 cargo plane crashes into the Kingasani neighborhood of Kinshasa, killing at least 51 people.

6 Oct Cuba. A bus and a train collide in a small town in Granma province; at least 28 people are killed.

9 Oct Africa. Agence France-Presse reports that over the past two months, flooding in much of the continent from unusually heavy summer rains has left at least 300 people dead.

10 Oct Brazil. A truck attempting to pass another truck on a mountainous curve hits a bus head-on, killing six passengers and the truck driver; after rescue workers arrive, another truck going down the hill plows into the scene, killing at least 21 of those present.

13 Oct Dnipropetrovsk, Ukraine. A natural gas explosion all but levels a 10-story apartment building; at least 23 people perish.

18 Oct Off Sulawesi, Indonesia. As the passenger ferry *Acita 003* nears shore, passengers climb to the upper deck in search of cell phone signals, causing the boat to capsize; at least 31 of the passengers drown.

19 Oct Near San Francisco del Mar, Mexico. The bodies of 24 people wash ashore; it is believed that they were attempting to migrate from Central America in a boat that capsized.

22 Oct Fujian province, China. In Putian a fire, reportedly caused by faulty wiring, kills at least 34 workers in a shoe factory.

23 Oct Gulf of Mexico. During a storm, large waves knock the Usumacinta drilling rig belonging to Pemex, the Mexican state oil company, into an adjacent platform, causing leaks of crude oil and natural gas; workers take to the sea in lifeboats to avoid suffocation, but at least 21 are killed.

26 Oct Senegal. A Spanish hospital ship returns a man to Dakar; the man was the only survivor of a group of African migrants that had set out by boat for the Canary Islands three weeks previously; some 50 others had perished.

29 Oct Ogun state, Nigeria. A fuel truck overturns and ignites; three commuter buses and four cars are engulfed in the flames, and at least 30 people are incinerated.

November 2007

1 Nov Caribbean. After devastating the Dominican Republic and Haiti, Tropical Storm Noel brings torrential rains and flooding to The Bahamas and Cuba; the overall death toll from the storm reaches 124.

3 Nov Mexico. After five days of record rainfall, much of the state of Tabasco suffers flooding, with some 80% of the city of Villahermosa under as much as 2.1 m (7 ft) of water; tens of thousands of residents have been displaced by the flooding.

4 Nov Argentina. A fire at a maximum security prison in the province of Santiago del Estero leaves at least 29 inmates dead.

6 Nov Atlantic Ocean. A Mauritanian patrol boat finds a boat that had left Senegal three weeks earlier loaded with African migrants attempting to reach the Canary Islands; some 100 survivors are on board, and they say that some 50 people perished on the journey and most were thrown overboard.

15 Nov Bangladesh. Cyclone Sidr lays waste to much of the southwestern coastal area of Bangladesh; some 3,500 people perish.

18 Nov Eastern Saudi Arabia. Workers are attempting to link a new pipeline to an existing oil pipeline when an explosion and subsequent fire occur; at least 28 people are killed.

21 Nov China. A landslide in the region of the Three Gorges Dam in China sweeps away a passenger bus, killing some 30 people; a few additional people are also killed by the landslide.

30 Nov Turkey. An Atlasjet MD-83 jetliner en route from Istanbul to Isparta crashes shortly before its destination; all 57 on board die.

December 2007

5 Dec Shanxi province, China. An explosion in the Xinyao coal mine in Linfen kills at least 105 miners.

11 Dec Dominican Republic. Tropical Storm Olga makes landfall, causing flooding and leaving at least 25 people dead, most killed by a release of water from a dam on the Yaque River that officials feared would otherwise collapse.

12 Dec Wenzhou, China. A fire in a 28-story apartment building leaves 21 people dead; it takes some 200 firefighters three hours to extinguish the blaze.

15 Dec Near Al-Irqah, Yemen. Doctors Without Borders finds the bodies of 56 Africans who drowned when their boat capsized; they had been trying to escape from Somalia and Ethiopia; later a Somali diplomat in Yemen says that the death toll is believed to be about 180.

18 Dec Pakistan. An express train traveling from Karachi to Lahore derails near Mehrabpur; at least 50 people lose their lives.

20 Dec Sierra Leone. An explosion, likely caused by a

gas leak, kills at least 17 people in downtown Freetown.

24 Dec US. State officials report that a storm involving freezing rain, snow, and high winds has over the past two days left many holiday travelers stranded throughout the Midwest; at least 19 people died in weather-related traffic accidents in Indiana, Kansas, Minnesota, Texas, Wisconsin, and Wyoming.

26 Dec Nigeria. As people attempt to siphon gas from a buried pipeline outside Lagos, the pipeline catches fire, incinerating at least 45 people.

31 Dec Beni Mzar, Egypt. When the driver of a pickup truck attempts to pass a passenger bus, the bus driver swerves to try to avoid an accident, and the vehicle falls into a canal that runs alongside the Nile River; 17 passengers and the drivers of both vehicles are killed.

January 2008

7 Jan Inch'on, South Korea. Fire breaks out at a newly built cold-storage facility; some 40 people are believed to have lost their lives.

9 Jan Iran. Authorities say that a disastrous blizzard in the Tehran area has resulted in the deaths of at least 28 people.

11 Jan Kazakhstan. An ArcelorMittal-owned coal mine suffers a gas explosion in which at least 30 miners are killed.

12 Jan Port Harcourt, Nigeria. A fuel tanker truck blows a tire and overturns; the fuel spills and ignites, incinerating at least 30 people.

16 Jan Morocco. An apartment building under construction in Kenitra collapses, killing 16 workers.

20 Jan India. Near the town of Nashik, an overloaded bus carrying pilgrims from a visit to Hindu shrines fails to negotiate a hairpin turn and plunges over a mountainside; at least 37 of the passengers are killed.

21 Jan Shanxi province, China. As miners attempt to reopen a shaft in a closed mine, an explosion takes place that kills at least 20 people.

23 Jan Poland. A transport plane carrying members of the Polish air force home from a conference on flight safety crashes near the town of Miroslawiec; all 20 aboard are killed.

26 Jan Near Jerash, Jordan. A passenger bus traveling from Irbid to Al-ʿAqabah collides with a water truck, and both vehicles fall off the road into the valley below; at least 20 people are killed and more than 30 injured.

29 Jan China. In Guizhou province, which is among those areas suffering prolonged severe winter storms, a bus goes off an ice-coated road; at least 25 passengers perish.

31 Jan Istanbul. An explosion, likely caused by fireworks, destroys a building, killing at least 22.

February 2008

3 Feb Africa. A series of earthquakes take place in the Great Lakes region, killing 40 people (34 in Rwanda and 6 in the Democratic Republic of the Congo) and injuring more than 400 others.

5 Feb US. An outbreak of tornadoes leaves a path of destruction in several southern states, particularly in Tennessee, where at least 30 people are killed, and Arkansas, which suffers a death toll of at least 13; a further 7 people are reported killed in Kentucky and 4 in Alabama.

7 Feb Egypt. Some 100 km (60 mi) south of Cairo, a bus collides with a minibus in heavy fog and some six more vehicles crash into them; at least 29 people are killed in the pileup.

8 Feb Indian-administered Kashmir. Heavy snowfall triggers avalanches that result in the deaths of at least 20 people.

10 Feb China. Officials say that power and transportation are beginning to be restored in some areas where the worst winter storms in 50 years have led to at least 60 deaths.

12 Feb Northern Bolivia. Pres. Evo Morales declares a national disaster because of flooding following heavy rains that has left at least 60 people dead.

16 Feb Afghanistan. Authorities say the harshest winter in 30 years has left 926 people dead, 462 of them in Herat province, and hundreds of thousands of cattle have also succumbed.

17 Feb Madagascar. A ferocious storm, Cyclone Ivan, makes landfall on the east coast, destroying the village of Ambodihazinina, leaving more than 80 people dead, and devastating the ripening rice crops.

21 Feb Near Itacoatiara, Brazil. The *Almirante Monteiro,* a ferry, collides with a barge in the Amazon River and sinks; some 20 people are feared lost.

28 Feb Near Dhaka, Bangladesh. A ferry collides with another vessel in the Buriganga River; at least 39 passengers are killed.

29 Feb Southern Guatemala. A greatly overloaded bus crashes on a dangerous corner near Jutiapa; at least 45 passengers perish.

March 2008

3 Mar Bay of Bengal. A wooden trawler carrying would-be migrants to Thailand or Malaysia from Bangladesh and Myanmar (Burma) is found drifting by the Sri Lankan navy; 20 of the more than 90 passengers have died of starvation and dehydration.

6 Mar Albania. A boat that is used to carry customers to and from a restaurant on Lake Farka near Tirana sinks; 16 people, most of whom had attended a birthday party at the restaurant, are drowned.

15 Mar Near Tirana, Albania. A series of strong explosions at a munitions depot kills 26 people and injures more than 300.

22 Mar Off Lantao Island, Hong Kong. A Ukrainian tugboat collides with a Chinese freighter and sinks; 18 crew members are feared lost.

25 Mar Western Honduras. A passenger bus goes off a highway in the mountains, rolling down a hillside; at least 26 of those aboard are killed.

26 Mar Xinjiang province, China. As authorities attempt to destroy illegal fireworks outside the city of

Turpan, an unplanned explosion occurs; 22 people are reported killed.

29 Mar Luanda, Angola. More than two dozen people are crushed to death when a seven-story building housing the headquarters of the police criminal-investigation department collapses.

April 2008

1 Apr Nigeria. In Kano state, a dugout canoe carrying a wedding party capsizes; at least 40 people, including the bride, drown.

3 Apr Suriname. A Blue Wings Airlines Antonov An-28 airliner crashes on its approach to the airport in Benzdorp; all 19 aboard lose their lives.

7 Apr Uganda. A fire in a dormitory for a girls' elementary school outside Kampala kills 19 schoolgirls and 2 adults; the cause is unclear, and reports indicate the doors may have been locked from the outside.

9 Apr Southern Thailand. In a truck carrying illegal Myanmarese (Burmese) migrant workers, 54 of the 121 crammed inside suffocate.

15 Apr Democratic Republic of the Congo. A plane taking off from the airport in Goma crashes into a neighborhood and bursts into flames; more than 40 people, most of them on the ground, are killed.

16 Apr Gujarat state, India. In Vadodara a state bus carrying schoolchildren goes off a bridge and falls some 18 m (60 ft) into a canal of the Narmada River; at least 44 children and 3 adults perish.

20 Apr Off the Bahamas. Rescue workers find the bodies of 20 drowned Haitians in the sea, as well as three survivors; the vessel that had been carrying them is not found.

23 Apr Rajasthan state, India. Northwest of Jodhpur, late at night, a truck and a crowded van collide; at least 24 of the van passengers lose their lives.

26 Apr Casablanca, Morocco. A four-story mattress factory goes up in flames; at least 55 people succumb to the smoke and fire.

28 Apr Black Sea. A Ukrainian Mi-8 helicopter falls into the water after its tail hits an offshore drilling platform; 19 of the 20 aboard die.

May 2008

2 May The Sudan. A Beechcraft 1900 airplane crashes near Rumbek, killing at least 23 people, including the southern Sudan's minister of defense, Dominic Dim.

2-3 May Myanmar (Burma). Cyclone Nargis, an extraordinarily strong tropical cyclone that formed in the Bay of Bengal and quickly strengthened to a category 4 storm, makes landfall and throughout the night churns up the densely populated rice-growing region of the Irrawaddy River delta, cutting a wide path of destruction augmented by a 4-m (12-ft) storm surge that obliterates coastal villages; tens of thousands of people perish.

4 May Brazil. The wooden ferry *Comandante Sales,* carrying some 80 partygoers, capsizes and sinks in the Solimões River; at least 41 people drown.

10 May United States. A violent storm system spawns tornadoes that lay waste to portions of Oklahoma, Missouri, and Georgia, leaving more than 23 people dead, at least 15 of them in Missouri.

12 May Bangladesh. A ferry on the Ghorautra River goes down quickly in bad weather; at least 44 people die.

12 May Sichuan province, China. A magnitude-7.9 earthquake devastates the area; at the epicenter, in Wenchuan, some 80% of the structures are flattened. At least 69,000 people lose their lives, and hundreds of thousands are made homeless.

14 May Uttar Pradesh state, India. A violent storm leaves at least 128 people dead and all but destroys the important mango crop.

15 May Nigeria. A fuel pipeline in a village near Lagos is ruptured by road construction equipment, engulfing much of the area in flames; some 100 people are killed.

19 May Democratic Republic of the Congo. An overloaded passenger boat sinks in a storm on Lake Tanganyika; dozens of people are lost.

20 May India. It is reported that at least 110 people have died after drinking illicit alcohol in the past few days in the Bengaluru (Bangalore) area; by 22 May the death toll has risen to 180.

27 May KwaZulu-Natal province, South Africa. A bus goes over a cliff and falls some 80 m (260 ft), landing upside-down in the river below; at least 30 people die.

29 May Southern India. A truck carrying at least 70 people to a wedding falls off a bridge after the driver swerves to avoid electrical wires on the road; at least 39 of the passengers perish.

29 May Panama. A helicopter carrying Chilean police officials visiting for a meeting of Latin American antiterrorism leaders crashes on top of a building; at least 15 people, including the head of Chile's national police force and at least 4 people on the ground, are killed.

June 2008

7 Jun Libya. A boat carrying would-be migrants to Italy capsizes shortly after departing from Zuwarah; at least 40 people are drowned, with a further 100 missing.

10 Jun Khartoum, Sudan. A Sudanese airliner bursts into flames after landing; at least 30 of the 214 people aboard are incinerated.

17 Jun Southern China. The death toll from flooding caused by incessant heavy rains rises to 171; more than a million people have been evacuated.

20 Jun India. Authorities say that the death toll from flooding resulting from heavy rain in eastern and northeastern areas of the county has risen past 50; thousands of villages are reportedly submerged.

21 Jun Philippines. Typhoon Fengshen smashes into the Philippines, and at least 498 residents perish; in addition, the MV *Princess of the Stars,* a large ferry, capsizes and sinks in the storm off the island of Sibuyan, and some 800 people perish.

People

The TIME 100, 2008

At the turn of the millennium in 2000, TIME selected 100 individuals as the most influential people of the 20th century. The resulting list provided such a revealing perspective on history that the magazine has now begun naming a TIME 100 each year, designating influential individuals in five categories. As with TIME's annual Person of the Year designation, the list includes both heroes and villains; inclusion reflects the power of an individual's impact on history, whether for good or for ill.

LEADERS & REVOLUTIONARIES

Michelle Bachelet Chile's president survived a brutal dictatorship to win worldwide respect.

Bartholomew I The Eastern Orthodox patriarch insisted that ecology and spirituality are one.

Ben Bernanke In a year of economic crisis, the Fed chief charted a bold and controversial course.

George W. Bush History will judge, but many still believe he responded to challenges courageously.

Hillary Clinton She proved her mettle and won the admiration of longtime enemies.

Dalai Lama Tibet's beacon of peace radiated calm compassion—even as Beijing cracked down on his long-suffering people.

Sonia Gandhi The Italian-born woman remains the power behind the throne of India's Congress Party.

Robert Gates Charged with heading an unpopular war, the US secretary of defense earned bipartisan respect for his intelligence and command.

Hu Jintao The host of the Olympics, and China's first leader who grew up in the aftermath of the 1949 communist revolution, has made his nation a looming presence on the world stage.

Anwar Ibrahim A global voice for moderate Islam is back in the center of Malaysian politics.

Ashfaq Kayani Pakistan's new top general kept the army out of the country's election.

Ma Ying-jeou Taiwan's rising political star hopes to resolve his nation's problems with China.

John McCain He defied the odds and stuck to his guns on Iraq to win the Republican nomination for president.

Baitullah Mehsud Pakistan's government identified him as the mastermind of the successful plot to kill Benazir Bhutto, proving he had forced his way into the top tier of terrorists.

Evo Morales Bolivia's low-key president moved quickly away from the neoliberal policies of the past to try to help his nation's most impoverished citizens.

Barack Obama He transformed American politics, attracting new voters to his call for change.

Vladimir Putin Russia's iron-willed leader passed on his mantle of rule but continued to rebuild his country as a great power—and an irritant to the West.

Kevin Rudd Australia's bold new prime minister got it right early, apologizing to native Aborigines.

Muqtada al-Sadr The firebrand Shi'ite cleric has become a major power broker in the new Iraq.

Jacob Zuma He fought charges of rape and corruption to remain the hero of South Africa's poor.

HEROES & PIONEERS

Andre Agassi With his charitable foundation, he proved that there is life beyond athletics.

Lance Armstrong The remarkable athlete inspires millions with his victory over cancer.

Daw Aung San Suu Kyi Burma's imprisoned Nobel Peace Prize recipient is today's Nelson Mandela.

Tony Blair Britain's successful former prime minister accepted a job as special envoy for the Quartet on the Middle East, where he is using the same diplomatic skills that brought peace to Northern Ireland.

Mia Farrow The actor and activist became a highly effective advocate for the people of Darfur.

Peter Gabriel The pop star cofounded the Elders to chart a new future for the global village.

Kaká Brazil's remarkable young soccer star is a tireless worker for the UN World Food Programme.

Sheikh Mohammed ibn Rashid al-Maktum The ruler of Dubai has made the UAE an internationally recognized symbol of success, becoming an unlikely poster boy for globalization.

George Mitchell He brought peace to Northern Ireland; now he is ridding baseball of illegal drugs.

Lorena Ochoa Mexico's great pro golfer is also a dedicated humanitarian.

Madeeha Hasan Odhaib Her business, employing some 100 women, is a quiet revolution in Iraqi life.

Randy Pausch The computer-science professor at Carnegie Mellon University, diagnosed with fatal pancreatic cancer, told a global audience to follow their dreams in a classroom lecture that became a YouTube sensation.

Oscar Pistorius South Africa's courageous double amputee—and world-class sprinter—has taught the world that seeming disabilities can be turned into abilities.

Brad Pitt and Angelina Jolie The star duo are now America's goodwill ambassadors to the world.

Yoani Sánchez The courageous Cuban, denied the chance to work as a philologist because of her anti-Castro views, has built her blog into a strong voice for freedom of speech.

Alexis Sinduhije The Burundian journalist founded Radio Publique Africaine to unify hostile tribes.

Oprah Winfrey The ebullient TV communicator continues to preach her gospel of responsibility.

Bob and Suzanne Wright The former CEO of NBC and his wife are leading the fight against autism.

SCIENTISTS & THINKERS

Paul Allen The Microsoft cofounder's Allen Institute for Brain Science mapped the mouse brain, illuminating how genes work, and then gave the results away for free online.

Isaac Berzin His goal is to turn algae into a biofuel that can reduce harmful carbon dioxide emissions.

Michael Bloomberg New York City's mayor succeeded in making his city more livable through sensible investments; now he hopes to make it a global model of sustainability.

Larry Brilliant The epidemiologist helped lead the World Health Organization's successful war on smallpox; now he is the head of Google's well-funded philanthropic efforts.

Nancy Brinker Her foundation fights breast cancer by encouraging millions to "Race for the Cure."
Eric Chivian and Richard Cizik The professor of psychiatry and the Evangelical Presbyterian minister joined in preaching the need for environmental stewardship.
Michael Griffin NASA's boss made it the openly communicative, inspired organization it used to be.
Jeff Han He led a revolution, introducing the concept of multitouch-sensing computer screens.
Mary Lou Jepsen Her One Laptop Per Child program gives cheap computers to kids everywhere.
Wendy Kopp The 5,000 teachers in her visionary program, Teach for America, reach 440,000 kids.
Harold McGee Four stars for his fine book *On Food and Cooking: The Science and Lore of the Kitchen.*
Mehmet Oz The Columbia University heart surgeon has informed millions with his illuminating, sensible health books; now he's taking his magic to TV.
Peter Pronovost His idea, a surgical checklist, has saved countless lives in the operating room.
Nicholas Schiff The neuroscientist's breakthrough technique, deep brain stimulation, helps reduce the symptoms of Parkinson disease and may help fight brain damage.
Susan Solomon She proved the peril of the thinning ozone layer; now she is tackling climate change.
Jill Bolte Taylor The afflicted neuroanatomist chronicled her fight to solve the mysteries of stroke.
J. Craig Venter The geneticist ruffles feathers, but in 2007 he created the first synthetic genome.
Shinya Yamanaka and James Thomson The researchers' breakthrough makes adult human cells act like embryonic stem cells, helping end a contentious moral debate.
Mark Zuckerberg The Facebook founder is helping transform the Internet into a vast social community.

ARTISTS & ENTERTAINERS

Judd Apatow The creator of hugely popular movie comedies is on a remarkable zeitgeist roll.
Mariah Carey With perseverance and a fantastic vocal range, she keeps reinventing her music.
George Clooney The actor is a respected advocate for causes ranging from Darfur to a free press.
Joel and Ethan Coen They won three Oscars in 2008, but their work isn't about garnering awards; their quirky films excel because they find a unique voice and eye, and stay true to both.
Miley Cyrus Disney's Hannah Montana is the rare teen star who knows she is a role model for fans.
Robert Downey, Jr. The actor came back from drug abuse to show his intelligence and charisma.
Peter Gelb The Metropolitan Opera's boss brought his company's artistry to millions of new fans.
Elizabeth Gilbert *Eat, Pray, Love,* her fine memoir of her postdivorce travels, touched countless lives.
Herbie Hancock The jazz pianist, now 68, has never lost his fearless inventiveness.
Khaled Hosseini With 2003's *The Kite Runner* and his new novel *A Thousand Splendid Suns,* he has helped his large audience look past stereotypes and see Afghans as real people.
Rem Koolhaas The Dutch-born architect-polemicist is helping architecture chart a path into the future.
Stephenie Meyer She mined a rich vein with her romantic vampire novels, the Twilight series.
Lorne Michaels *Saturday Night Live*'s creator has given America its sharpest political send-ups.
Takashi Murakami The Japanese pop artist playfully blurs the line between art and commerce.
Suze Orman The TV financial adviser made millions better informed on issues of dollars and sense.
Tyler Perry Madea's creator revolutionized the way Hollywood entertains urban audiences.
Alex Rigopulos and Eran Egozy The geeks behind *Guitar Hero* and *Rock Band* made us all stars.
Chris Rock The brilliant black comic takes on sex, racism, and marriage—and makes it all seem fun.
Tim Russert The late host of NBC's *Meet the Press* was an astute, discerning seeker of truth.
Bruce Springsteen The legendary troubadour continues to give voice to America's social conscience.
Tom Stoppard He challenges audiences with the intellect, scope, and verbiage of his plays.

BUILDERS & TITANS

Jay Adelson His Digg.com site, a user-driven ranking system for Internet content, attracts millions of viewers each month.
Prince al-Walid ibn Talal ibn Abdulaziz al-Saud The Saudi investor proves that good business can unite the most diverse of cultures and nations.
Michael Arrington With his TechCrunch blog, he is a leading authority on tech-biz culture.
Steve Ballmer Bill Gates's successor at Microsoft, he doesn't just throw fits at sales conferences and play the madman—he delivers results.
Jeff Bezos Amazon's visionary CEO unveiled Kindle, a paperback-sized, battery-powered digital book.
Lloyd Blankfein The CEO of Goldman Sachs wisely steered clear of mortgage-backed securities.
Cynthia Carroll Anglo American's CEO is helping revolutionize the global mining industry.
John Chambers With his new virtual-meeting system, TelePresence, Cisco's boss kept his Internet-systems company in the vanguard.
Jamie Dimon By leading JPMorgan Chase's purchase of the reeling investment firm Bear Stearns, he helped head off a financial-market meltdown.
Mo Ibrahim The cell-phone king is leading calls for democracy and good governance in Africa.
Jeffrey Immelt General Electric's boss is a polymath who is equally at home in a research lab, a turbine facility, or on the set of *Saturday Night Live.*
Lou Jiwei The former deputy finance minister is now controlling China's huge pool of investment dollars.
Steve Jobs Apple's boss is a countercultural icon and a brilliant businessman and marketer.
Neelie Kroes The Dutchwoman is the European Union's czar of competition—and a formidable voice for economic fairness and women's rights.
Karl Lagerfeld The visionary German designer showed that fashion can originate from the street, the media—anywhere.
Rupert Murdoch The new owner of *The Wall Street Journal,* the Australian-born press lord is the most influential newspaper publisher of his era.
Ali al-Naimi Saudi Arabia's thoughtful oil minister uses his influence well in global petropolitics.
Indra Nooyi PepsiCo's boss has made healthiness and sustainability part of the company's mission.
Radiohead The British rock band made their new album available online, dealing a death blow to music's old distribution models.
Carine Roitfeld The quintessentially Parisian editor of French *Vogue* energizes and defines the world of fashion by mixing street culture and high society.
Carlos Slim Helú The Mexican telecom superbillionaire is also a visionary and humanist.
Ratan Tata The Indian automotive mogul introduced an affordable car for India's masses.

Celebrities and Newsmakers

These mini-biographies are intended to provide background information about people in the news. See also the Obituaries (below) for recently deceased persons.

50 Cent (Curtis Jackson; 6 Jul 1976, Jamaica, Queens NY), American hardcore rapper.

Mahmoud (Ridha) Abbas (nom de guerre Abu Mazen; 26 Mar 1935, Zefat, British Palestine), Palestinian politician; secretary general of the PLO executive committee and cofounder (with Yasir Arafat) of the Fatah movement; he served as the first prime minister of the Palestine Authority and was its president from 2005.

Sidi Muhammad Ould Cheikh Abdallahi (1938), Mauritanian politician; president, 2007–08.

Mohamed Ould Abdel Aziz (1956, Akjoujt, Mauritania), Mauritanian military leader; chairman of the high council of state from 2008.

Paula (Julie) Abdul (19 Jun 1962, San Fernando CA), American pop singer, choreographer, and TV personality.

Abdullah (ʿAbdullah ibn ʿAbd al-ʿAziz al-Saʿud; 1923, Riyadh, Saudi Arabia), Saudi royal; king of Saudi Arabia from 2005.

Datuk Seri Abdullah Ahmad Badawi (26 Nov 1939, Penang state, Malaysia), Malaysian politician; prime minister from 2003.

Abdullah II (ʿAbd Allah ibn al-Husayn; 30 Jan 1962, Amman, Jordan), Jordanian royal, king from 1999.

Tuanku Mizan Zainal Abidin ibni al-Marhum Sultan Mahmud (22 Jan 1962, Kuala Terengganu, Malaysia), Malaysian politician; yang di-pertuan agong (head of state) in 2001 and again from 2006.

J(effrey) J(acob) Abrams (27 Jun 1966, New York NY), American TV producer whose credits include *Alias* (2001–06) and *Lost* (from 2004).

Aníbal (Salvador) Acevedo Vilá (13 Feb 1962, Hato Rey, Puerto Rico), American politician (Popular Democratic Party); governor of Puerto Rico from 2005.

Chinua Achebe (Albert Chinualumogu Achebe; 16 Nov 1930, Ogidi, Nigeria), Nigerian novelist and poet who won the second Man Booker International Prize for fiction in 2007.

Joe Ackermann (Josef Ackermann; 7 Feb 1948, Mels, Sankt Gallen, Switzerland), Swiss corporate executive; CEO of Deutsche Bank AG from 1997.

Valdas V. Adamkus (Valdas V. Adamkevicius; 3 Nov 1926, Kaunas, Lithuania), Lithuanian politician and president, 1998–2003 and again from 2004.

Amy (Lou) Adams (20 Aug 1974, Aviano, Italy), American stage and film actress.

Gerry Adams (Gerard Adams; Irish: Gearóid Mac Ádhaimh; 6 Oct 1948, West Belfast, Northern Ireland), Irish resistance leader; president of Sinn Féin, the political wing of the Irish Republican Army, from 1983.

John (Coolidge) Adams (15 Feb 1947, Worcester MA), American composer.

Scott Adams (8 Jun 1957, Windham NY), American cartoonist; creator of *Dilbert.*

Thomas Adès (27 Jun 1971, London, England), British composer, pianist, and conductor.

Chimamanda Ngozi Adichie (15 Sep 1977, Enugu, Nigeria), Nigerian novelist; winner of the 2007 Orange Broadband Prize for Fiction.

Ben(jamin Geza) Affleck (15 Aug 1972, Berkeley CA), American actor, director, and writer.

(Caleb) Casey Affleck (12 Aug 1975, Falmouth MA), American film actor.

Isaias Afwerki (2 Feb 1946, Asmara, Ethiopia [now in Eritrea]), Eritrean independence leader, secretary-general of the Provisional Government, and first president of Eritrea, from 1993.

Christina (Maria) Aguilera (18 Dec 1980, Staten Island NY), American pop singer.

Bertie Ahern (Bartholomew Patrick Ahern; 12 Sep 1951, Dublin, Ireland), Irish politician; prime minister (*taoiseach*) of Ireland, 1997–2008.

Mahmoud Ahmadinejad (28 Oct 1956, Garmsar, Iran), Iranian politician; president from 2005.

Abdullahi Yusuf Ahmed (15 Dec 1934, Galcaio, Somalia), Somali military officer; nominally president from 2004.

Iajuddin Ahmed (1 Feb 1931, Nayagaon, Bengal, British India [now in Bangladesh]), Bangladeshi scientist and educator; president of Bangladesh from 2002.

Akihito (original name Tsugu Akihito; era name Heisei; 23 Dec 1933, Tokyo, Japan), Japanese royal; emperor of Japan from 1989.

Akil Akilov (1944, Tajikistan?), Tajik politician; prime minister from 1999.

Peter Akinola (27 Jan 1944, Abeokuta, Nigeria), Nigerian Anglican churchman; archbishop of Nigeria from 2000.

Jessica (Marie) Alba (28 Apr 1981, Pomona CA), American TV and film actress.

Albert II (Albert Félix Humbert Théodore Christian Eugène Marie of Saxe-Coburg-Gotha; 6 Jun 1934, Brussels, Belgium), Belgian royal; king from 1993.

Albert II (Albert Alexandre Louis Pierre; 14 Mar 1958, Monaco), Monegasque prince and ruler of Monaco from 2005.

Karl Albrecht (1920, Germany), German business executive; cofounder (1946) of the Aldi supermarket chain.

Theo Albrecht (28 Mar 1922, Germany), German business executive; cofounder (1946) of the Aldi supermarket chain.

Alan Alda (Alphonso Joseph D'Abruzzo; 28 Jan 1936, New York NY), American film and TV actor.

Claribel Alegría (12 May 1924, Estelí, Nicaragua), Nicaraguan-born Salvadoran poet, essayist, and journalist; recipient of the 2006 Neustadt Prize.

Sherman J. Alexie, Jr. (7 Oct 1966, Wellpinit, Spokane Indian Reservation, Washington), American poet and novelist who writes of his Native American upbringing.

Alexis II (Aleksey Mikhaylovich Ridiger; 23 Feb 1929, Tallinn, Estonia), Russian religious leader; Orthodox Patriarch of Moscow and All Russia, the 15th primate of Russia, from 1990.

Monica Ali (20 Oct 1967, Dacca, Pakistan [now Dhaka, Bangladesh]), Bangladeshi-born British writer.

Muhammad Ali (Cassius Marcellus Clay, Jr.; 17 Jan 1942, Louisville KY), American boxer, the first to win the heavyweight championship three separate times.

Samuel A. Alito, Jr. (1 Apr 1950, Trenton NJ), American jurist; associate justice of the US Supreme Court from 2006.

Ilham Aliyev (Ilham Geidar ogly Aliev; 24 Dec 1961, Baku, USSR [now in Azerbaijan]), Azerbaijani politician; prime minister briefly in 2003 and president from October 2003.

Joan Allen (20 Aug 1956, Rochelle IL), American film and theater actress.

Paul G. Allen (21 Jan 1953, Mercer Island WA), American corporate executive; cofounder of Microsoft Corp. (1975) and owner of several professional sports teams.

Woody Allen (Allen Stewart Konigsberg; 1 Dec 1935, Brooklyn NY), American filmmaker, actor, and comedian.

Isabel Allende (2 Aug 1942, Lima, Peru), Chilean writer in the magic realist tradition.

Kirstie Alley (12 Jan 1951, Wichita KS), American film and TV actress.

Pedro Almodóvar (Caballero) (24 Sep 1949, Calzada de Calatrava, Spain), Spanish film director specializing in melodrama.

Prince Alois (Alois Philipp Maria Prince von und zu Liechtenstein; 11 Jun 1968, Zürich, Switzerland), Liechtenstein crown prince.

Marin Alsop (16 Oct 1956, New York NY), American conductor.

Amadou (Amadou Bagayoko; 24 Oct 1954, Bamako, French West Africa [now in Mali]), Malian guitarist (for Amadou and Mariam).

Pamela (Denise) Anderson (1 Jul 1967, Ladysmith, BC, Canada), Canadian-born model and actress.

Paul Thomas Anderson (26 Jun 1970, Studio City CA), American film director.

Wes Anderson (1 May 1969, Houston TX), American film director.

Tadao Ando (13 Sep 1941, Osaka, Japan), Japanese architect; recipient of the 1995 Pritzker Prize.

Marc Andreessen (July 1971, New Lisbon WI), American computer innovator; developer of Netscape.

Andrew (Andrew Albert Christian Edward; 19 Feb 1960, Buckingham Palace, London, England), British prince; second son of Queen Elizabeth II and Prince Philip, duke of Edinburgh; and duke of York.

Leif Ove Andsnes (7 Apr 1970, Karmøy, Norway), Norwegian pianist.

Criss Angel (Christopher Nicholas Sarantakos; 19 Dec 1967, Long Island NY), American magician and illusionist.

Maya Angelou (Marguerite Annie Johnson; 4 Apr 1928, St. Louis MO), American poet.

Jennifer Aniston (Jennifer Linn Anistassakis; 11 Feb 1969, Sherman Oaks CA), American TV and film actress.

Kofi (Atta) Annan (18 Apr 1938, Kumasi, Gold Coast [now Ghana]), Ghanaian diplomat; UN secretary-general, 1997–2006; corecipient, with the UN, of the 2001 Nobel Peace Prize.

Anne (Anne Elizabeth Alice Louise; 15 Aug 1950, Clarence House, London, England), British princess; daughter of Queen Elizabeth II and Prince Philip, duke of Edinburgh.

Andrus Ansip (1 Oct 1956, Tartu, USSR [now in Estonia]), Estonian politician; prime minister from 2005.

Carmelo Anthony (29 May 1984, New York NY), American pro basketball forward.

Marc Anthony (Marco Antonio Muñiz; 16 Sep 1968, Spanish Harlem, New York NY), American salsa singer.

Judd Apatow (6 Dec 1967, Syosset NY), American filmmaker.

Louise Arbour (10 Feb 1947, Montreal, QC, Canada), Canadian judge; UN High Commissioner for Human Rights from 2004.

Denys Arcand (25 Jun 1941, Deschambault, QC, Canada), Canadian film director and screenwriter.

Martha Argerich (5 Jun 1941, Buenos Aires, Argentina), Argentine concert pianist.

Óscar Arias Sánchez (13 Sep 1941, Heredia, Costa Rica), Costa Rican statesman; president of Costa Rica, 1986–90 and again from 2006; recipient of the 1987 Nobel Peace Prize.

Alan (Wolf) Arkin (26 Mar 1934, Brooklyn NY), American film and TV actor; recipient of the 2006 best supporting actor Academy Award.

Giorgio Armani (11 Jul 1934, Piacenza, Italy), Italian fashion designer.

Billie Joe Armstrong (17 Feb 1972, Rodeo CA), American punk rock vocalist and guitarist (for Green Day).

Lance Armstrong (18 Sep 1971, Plano TX), American cyclist who won the Tour de France seven years in succession, 1999–2005.

Gerald Arpino (14 Jan 1928, Staten Island NY), American ballet choreographer; cofounder (1956) of the Joffrey Ballet and its artistic director, 1988–2007.

Courteney Cox Arquette (Courteney Bass Cox; 15 Jun 1964, Birmingham AL), American TV and film actress.

Bashar al-Assad (11 Sep 1965, Damascus, Syria), Syrian politician; president from 2000.

Alaa Al Aswany (1957, Egypt), Egyptian dentist and popular writer.

Susan Athey (29 Nov 1970, Boston MA), American economist specializing in economic theory, empirical economics, and econometrics.

Kate Atkinson (1951, York, England), British author.

Abdul Rahman ibn Hamad al-Attiyah (1950, Qatar), Qatari international official; secretary-general of the Gulf Cooperation Council from 2002.

Margaret (Eleanor) Atwood (18 Nov 1939, Ottawa, ON, Canada), Canadian poet, novelist, and critic.

Robert John Aumann (8 Jun 1930, Frankfurt am Main, Germany), American Israeli mathematician; corecipient of the 2005 Nobel Prize for Economic Sciences.

Daw Aung San Suu Kyi (19 Jun 1945, Rangoon, Burma [now Yangon, Myanmar]), Burmese human rights activist; recipient in 1991 of the Nobel Peace Prize.

Hank Azaria (25 Apr 1964, Forest Hills NY), American actor best known for comic film roles and for providing voices for TV's The Simpsons.

(Verónica) Michelle Bachelet (Jeria) (29 Sep 1951, Santiago, Chile), Chilean politician (Socialist); president from 2006.

Bob Baffert (13 Jan 1953, Nogales AZ), American trainer of Thoroughbred racehorses.

Jerry D. Bailey (29 Aug 1957, Dallas TX), American jockey.

(Josiah) Voreque ("Frank") Bainimarama (27 Apr 1954, Kiuva, Fiji), Fijian military leader; self-appointed acting prime minister from 2007.

Kurmanbek Bakiyev (1 Aug 1949, Masadan, Kirghiz SSR, USSR [now Teyyit, Kyrgyzstan]), Kyrgyz politician; president of Kyrgyzstan from 2005.

John (Elias) Baldacci (30 Jan 1955, Bangor ME), American politician (Democrat); governor of Maine from 2003.

Alec Baldwin (Alexander Rae Baldwin III; 3 Apr 1958, Massapequa NY), American film and TV actor.

Christian (Charles Philip) Bale (30 Jan 1974, Haverfordwest, Pembrokeshire, Wales), British film actor.

Jan Peter Balkenende (7 May 1956, Kapelle, Netherlands), Dutch politician (Christian-Democratic Appeal); prime minister from 2002.

Steven A. Ballmer (24 Mar 1956, Detroit? MI), American corporate executive; CEO of Microsoft Corp. from 2000.

Ed(ward) Balls (25 Feb 1967, Norwich, England), British public official; secretary of state for children, schools, and families from 2007.

Ban Ki-moon (13 Jun 1944, Umsong, Japanese-occupied Korea [now in South Korea]), Korean government and international official; secretary-general of the United Nations from 2007.

Eric Bana (Eric Banadinovich; 9 Aug 1968, Melbourne, VIC, Australia), Australian actor.

(José) Antonio (Domínguez) Banderas (10 Oct 1960, Málaga, Spain), Spanish actor and director.

Russell Banks (28 Mar 1940, Newton MA), American novelist.

Tyra Banks (4 Dec 1973, Los Angeles CA), American model, actress, and TV show host.

Banksy (1974?, Bristol?, England), British graffiti artist.

Patricia Barber (8 Nov 1955, Lisle IL), American jazz singer and pianist.

Haley (Reeves) Barbour (22 Oct 1947, Yazoo City MS), American politician (Republican); governor of Mississippi from 2004.

Javier (Ángel Encinas) Bardem (1 Mar 1969, Las Palmas, Canary Islands, Spain), Spanish film actor; recipient of the 2007 best supporting actor Academy Award.

Daniel Barenboim (15 Nov 1942, Buenos Aires, Argentina), Israeli pianist and conductor; recipient of a Praemium Imperiale in 2007.

Julian Barnes (pseudonyms Edward Pygge and Dan Kavanagh; 19 Jan 1946, Leicester, Leicestershire, England), British author and TV critic.

Sacha (Noam) Baron Cohen (13 Oct 1971, Hammersmith, London, England), British comedian and actor.

José Manuel Durão Barroso (23 Mar 1956, Lisbon, Portugal), Portuguese politician; prime minister, 2002–04, and president of the European Commission from 2004.

Dean (Oliver) Barrow (2 Mar 1951, Belize City, British Honduras [now Belize]), Belizean politician (United Democratic Party); prime minister from 2008.

John D(avid) Barrow (29 Nov 1952, London, England), British cosmologist, a specialist in the anthropic principle; recipient of the 2006 Templeton Prize.

Dave Barry (3 Jul 1947, Armonk NY), American humorist, newspaper columnist, and author.

Drew Barrymore (Andrew Blythe Barrymore; 22 Feb 1975, Culver City CA), American film actress.

Frederick Barthelme (10 Oct 1943, Houston TX), American writer of short stories and novels.

Bartholomew I (Dimitrios Archontonis; 29 Feb 1940, Imbros [now Gökçeada], Turkey), Eastern Orthodox archbishop of Constantinople and ecumenical patriarch from 1991.

Richard Barton (2 Jun 1967, New Canaan CT), American Internet entrepreneur (Expedia.com, Zillow.com).

Mikhail (Nikolayevich) Baryshnikov (28 Jan 1948, Riga, USSR [now in Latvia]), Soviet-born American ballet dancer, director, and actor.

Traian Basescu (4 Nov 1951, Basarabi, Romania), Romanian politician; president from 2004.

Omar Hassan Ahmad al-Bashir (1944, Hosh Bannaga, Anglo-Egyptian Sudan), Sudanese military leader; president from 1989.

Pina Bausch (27 Jul 1940, Solingen, Germany), German choreographer and artistic director; recipient of a 1999 Praemium Imperiale and a 2007 Kyoto Prize.

Sanj(aagiyn) Bayar (1956, Ulaanbataar, Mongolia), Mongolian diplomat; prime minister from 2007.

Beatrix (31 Jan 1938, Soestdijk, Netherlands), Dutch royal; queen of The Netherlands from 1980.

Beck (Beck Hansen; 8 Jul 1970, Los Angeles CA), American singer and songwriter.

David (Robert) Beckham (2 May 1975, Leytonstone, East London, England), British association football (soccer) player.

Victoria Beckham (Victoria Caroline Adams; 7 Apr 1975, Goff's Oak, Hertfordshire, England), British pop singer ("Posh Spice" of the Spice Girls) and celebrity.

Kate Beckinsale (26 Jul 1973, London, England), British actress.

Mike Beebe (Michael Dale Beebe; 28 Dec 1946, Amagon AR), American politician (Democrat); governor of Arkansas from 2007.

Kenenisa Bekele (13 Jun 1982, near Bekoji, Ethiopia), Ethiopian cross-country runner.

Bill Belichick (William Stephen Belichick; 16 Apr 1952, Nashville TN), American football coach.

Joshua Bell (9 Dec 1967, Bloomington IN), American violinist.

Rob(ert) Bell (23 Aug 1970, Lansing MI), American evangelical pastor and author; founder of the Mars Hill Bible Church, Grandville MI.

Arden L. Bement, Jr. (22 May 1932, Pittsburgh PA), American materials scientist; director of the National Science Foundation from 2004.

Zine al-Abidine Ben Ali (3 Sep 1936, Hammam-Sousse, Tunisia), Tunisian politician and president from 1987.

Benedict XVI (Joseph Alois Ratzinger; 16 Apr 1927, Marktl am Inn, Bavaria, Germany), German Roman Catholic churchman; pope from 2005.

Alan Bennett (9 May 1934, Leeds, England), British dramatist and writer.

Gurbanguly Berdymukhammedov (29 Jun 1957, Bararab, USSR [now in Turkmenistan]), Turkmen politician; president from 2006.

Sali (Ram) Berisha (15 Oct 1944, Tropojë, Albania), Albanian cardiologist and politician (Democratic Party); president, 1992–97, and prime minister from 2005.

Silvio Berlusconi (29 Sep 1936, Milan, Italy), Italian businessman and politician; prime minister, 1994–95, 2001–06, and again from 2008.

Ben(jamin Shalom) Bernanke (13 Dec 1953, Augusta GA), American economist; chairman of the Board of Governors of the Federal Reserve System from 2006.

Tim(othy J.) Berners-Lee (8 Jun 1955, London, England), British inventor of the World Wide Web and director of the World Wide Web Consortium (W3C) from 1994.

Maxime Bernier (18 Jan 1963, Beauce, QC, Canada), Canadian insurance executive; foreign minister, 2007–08.

Halle (Maria) Berry (14 Aug 1968, Cleveland OH), American film actress and model.

Tarcisio Cardinal Bertone (2 Dec 1934, Romano Canavese, Italy), Italian Roman Catholic churchman; secretary of state of the Vatican from 2006.

Steve(n Lynn) Beshear (21 Sep 1944, Dawson Springs KY), American politician (Democrat); governor of Kentucky from 2007.

Beyoncé (Beyoncé Knowles; 4 Sep 1981, Houston TX), American R&B singer and actress.

Jeffrey P. Bezos (12 Jan 1964, Albuquerque NM), American corporate executive; founder and CEO of Amazon.com from 1995.

Bhumibol Adulyadej (Rama IX; 5 Dec 1927, Cambridge MA), Thai royal; king of Thailand from 1946.

Joseph (Robinette) Biden, Jr. (20 Nov 1942, Scranton PA), American politician (Democrat); senator from Delaware from 1973 and the Democratic nominee for vice president in 2008.

Jessica (Claire) Biel (3 Mar 1982, Ely MN), American TV and film actress.

Dima Bilan (Viktor Nikolayevich Belan; 24 Dec 1981, Maysky, Karachay-Cherkessk autonomous oblast, USSR [now Karachay-Cherkess Republic, Russia]), Russian pop singer; winner of the 2008 Eurovision Song Contest.

Osama bin Laden (also spelled Usamah ibn Ladin; 10 Mar 1957, Riyadh, Saudi Arabia), Saudi Arabian–born terrorist and leader of the al-Qaeda organization.

Juliette Binoche (9 Mar 1964, Paris, France), French film actress.

Harrison Birtwistle (15 Jul 1934, Accrington, Lancashire, England), British composer of operas, chamber music, and orchestral music.

Paul Biya (13 Feb 1933, Mvomeka'a, Cameroon), Cameroonian politician; president from 1982.

Jonas Björkman (23 Mar 1972, Växjö, Sweden), Swedish tennis player.

Jack Black (28 Aug 1969, Hermosa Beach CA), American film actor and comic rock musician.

Rubén Blades (16 Jul 1948, Panama City, Panama), Panamanian salsa singer and songwriter, actor, and politician.

Rod R. Blagojevich (Milorad R. Blagojevich; 10 Dec 1956, Chicago IL), American politician (Democrat); governor of Illinois from 2003.

Tony Blair (Anthony Charles Lynton Blair; 6 May 1953, Edinburgh, Scotland), British politician (Labour); prime minister of the UK, 1997–2007, and special envoy to the Middle East thereafter.

Cate Blanchett (Catherine Elise Blanchett; 14 May 1969, Melbourne, Australia), Australian film actress.

Kathleen Babineaux Blanco (15 Dec 1942, Coteau LA), American politician (Democrat); governor of Louisiana, 2004–08.

Mary J. Blige (11 Jan 1971, New York NY), American hip-hop soul singer.

Amy Bloom (1953, New York NY), American writer.

Harold (Irving) Bloom (11 Jul 1930, New York NY), American literary critic.

Orlando Bloom (13 Jan 1977, Canterbury, Kent, England), British film actor.

Michael R. Bloomberg (14 Feb 1942, Medford MA), American businessman, philanthropist, and politician (independent); mayor of New York City from 2002.

Matt(hew Roy) Blunt (20 Nov 1970, Springfield MO), American politician (Republican); governor of Missouri from 2005.

Andrea Bocelli (22 Sep 1958, Lajatico, Italy), Italian operatic tenor, blind from childhood.

Samuel (Wright) Bodman (26 Nov 1938, Chicago IL), American chemical engineer, corporate leader, and official; US secretary of energy from 2005.

Haji Hassanal Bolkiah Mu'izzadin Waddaulah (15 Jul 1946, Brunei Town [now Bandar Seri Begawan], Brunei), Bruneian royal; sultan from 1967.

Joshua B(rewster) Bolten (16 Aug 1954, Washington DC?), American international lawyer; director of the US Office of Management and Budget, 2003–06, and White House chief of staff from 2006.

Barry (Lamar) Bonds (24 Jul 1964, Riverside CA), American baseball player who broke the all-time home run record in 2007.

Omar Bongo Ondimba (Albert-Bernard Bongo; 30 Dec 1935, Lewai, Gabon), Gabonese politician; president from 1967.

(Thomas) Yayi Boni (1952, Tchaourou, French Dahomey [now Benin]), Beninese politician (independent); president from 2006.

Jon Bon Jovi (John Francis Bongiovi, Jr.; 2 Mar 1962, Perth Amboy NJ), American rock singer, musician, and songwriter.

Bono (Paul David Hewson; also known as Bono Vox; 10 May 1960, Dublin, Ireland), Irish rock vocalist (for U2) as well as a human rights activist and mediator.

Umberto Bossi (19 Sep 1941, Cassano Magnano, Italy), Italian politician and leader of the separatist Northern League from 1991.

Kate Bosworth (Catherine Anne Bosworth; 2 Jan 1983, Los Angeles CA), American film and TV actress.

Bouasone Bouphavanh (3 Jun 1954, Ban Tao Poun, Salavan province, French Indochina [now in Laos]), Laotian politician and prime minister from 2006.

Lucien Bouchard (22 Dec 1938, Saint-Coeur-de-Marie, QC, Canada), French Canadian politician, an advocate of the separation of Quebec from the rest of Canada.

Anthony (Michael) Bourdain (25 Jun 1956, New York NY), American chef, author, and TV personality.

Abdelaziz Bouteflika (2 Mar 1937, Tlemcen, Algeria), Algerian politician, diplomat, and president from 1999.

T. Coraghessan Boyle (Thomas John Boyle; 2 Dec 1948, Peekskill NY), American short-story writer and novelist.

François Bozizé (14 Oct 1946, Mouila, French Equatorial Africa [now in Gabon]), Central African Republic politician; president from 2003.

Tom Brady (Thomas Brady; 3 Aug 1977, San Mateo CA), American professional football quarterback.

Zach(ary Israel) Braff (6 Apr 1975, South Orange NJ), American TV and film actor.

Lakhdar Brahimi (1 Jan 1934, Algeria), Algerian statesman, diplomat, and international official.

Serge Brammertz (17 Feb 1962, Eupen, Belgium), Belgian jurist; deputy prosecutor for the International Criminal Court, 2003–07, and prosecutor for the International Tribunal for the Former Yugoslavia from 2008.

Richard (Charles Nicholas) Branson (18 Jul 1950, Shamley Green, Surrey, England), British entrepreneur who founded the Virgin empire in 1973.

Anthony Braxton (4 Jun 1945, Chicago IL), American avant-garde reed player and composer.

Phil(ip Norman) Bredesen (21 Nov 1943, Oceanport NJ), American politician (Democrat); governor of Tennessee from 2003.

Abigail (Kathleen) Breslin (14 Apr 1996, New York NY), American child actress.

Thierry Breton (15 Jan 1955, Paris, France), French businessman and politician; executive chairman of France Télécom, 2002–05, and French economic minister, 2005–07.

Stephen (Gerald) Breyer (15 Aug 1938, San Francisco CA), American jurist; associate justice of the US Supreme Court from 1994.

Sergey (Mikhaylovich) Brin (21 Aug 1973, Moscow, USSR [now in Russia]), Russian-born computer scientist and Internet entrepreneur who cofounded (1998) the Google Internet search engine.

Matthew Broderick (21 Mar 1962, New York NY), American comic actor.

Wallace S. Broecker (29 Nov 1931, Chicago IL), American geochemist, a specialist in climate change; recipient of a National Medal of Science in 1996 and a Crafoord Prize in 2006.

Josh (J.) Brolin (12 Feb 1968, Los Angeles CA), American film and TV actor.

Kix Brooks (Leon Eric Brooks; 12 May 1955, Shreveport LA), American country-and-western singer (for Brooks & Dunn).

(Troyal) Garth Brooks (7 Feb 1962, Tulsa OK), American country-and-western singer.

Pierce (Brendan) Brosnan (16 May 1953, Navan, County Meath, Ireland), Irish actor.

Dan Brown (22 Jun 1964, Exeter NH), American novelist.

Ewart (Frederick) Brown, Jr. (1946, Bermuda), Bermudan politician; prime minister from 2006.

(James) Gordon Brown (20 Feb 1951, Glasgow, Scotland), Scottish-born politician (Labour); chancellor of the Exchequer, 1997–2007, and prime minister from 2007.

Jerry Bruckheimer (21 Sep 1945, Detroit MI), American film and TV producer.

Kobe Bryant (23 Aug 1978, Philadelphia PA), American basketball player.

Bill Bryson (1951, Des Moines IA), American-born British journalist and travel writer.

Michael Bublé (9 Sep 1975, Burnaby, BC, Canada), Canadian pop singer.

Patrick J(oseph) Buchanan (2 Nov 1938, Washington DC), American conservative journalist.

Christopher (Taylor) Buckley (1952, New York NY), American satiric novelist and magazine editor.

Warren (Edward) Buffett (30 Aug 1930, Omaha NE), American investor; CEO of Berkshire Hathaway Inc. from 1965; named the world's richest person by *Forbes* in 2008.

Sandra (Annette) Bullock (26 Jul 1964, Arlington VA), American film actress.

Gisele (Caroline Nonnenmacher) Bündchen (20 Jul 1980, Horizontina, Rio Grande do Sul state, Brazil), Brazilian fashion model.

Daniel Buren (25 Mar 1938, Paris, France), French conceptual artist; recipient of a 2007 Praemium Imperiale.

Mark Burnett (17 Jul 1960, Myland, East London, England), English-born American reality-TV-show producer.

Ken(neth Lauren) Burns (29 Jul 1953, Brooklyn NY), American documentary filmmaker.

Gary Burton (23 Jan 1943, Anderson IN), American jazz vibraphonist and composer.

Tim(othy William) Burton (25 Aug 1958, Burbank CA), American film director and writer.

Steve Buscemi (13 Dec 1957, Brooklyn NY), American film actor.

Barbara Bush (Barbara Pierce; 8 Jun 1925, Rye NY), American first lady; wife of Pres. George H.W. Bush (married 6 Jan 1945).

Barbara Bush (25 Nov 1981, Dallas TX), American personality; daughter of Pres. George W. Bush.

George Herbert Walker Bush (12 Jun 1924, Milton MA), American statesman; vice president of the US, 1981–89, and 41st president, 1989–93; he is the father of Pres. George W. Bush.

George Walker Bush (6 Jul 1946, New Haven CT), American politician (Republican); 43rd president of the US, from 2001; he is the son of Pres. George H.W. Bush.

Jenna Bush (25 Nov 1981, Dallas TX), American personality; daughter of Pres. George W. Bush; she married Henry Hager on 10 May 2008.

Laura Bush (Laura Lane Welch; 4 Nov 1946, Midland TX), American first lady; wife of Pres. George W. Bush (married 5 Nov 1977).

Mangosuthu Gatsha Buthelezi (27 Aug 1928, Mahlabatini, Natal, Union of South Africa [now KwaZulu Natal province, South Africa]), South African Zulu chief, the founder (1975) and leader of the Inkatha Freedom Party.

A.S. Byatt (Antonia Susan Drabble; 24 Aug 1936, Sheffield, England), English literary critic and novelist.

Robert C(arlyle) Byrd (20 Nov 1917, North Wilkesboro NC), American politician (Democrat); senator from West Virginia from 1959 and president pro tempore of the Senate from 2007.

Nicolas Cage (Nicholas Kim Coppola; 7 Jan 1964, Long Beach CA), American film actor.

Cai Guo Qiang (8 Dec 1957, Quanzhou, Fujian province, China), Chinese installation artist.

Michael Caine (Maurice Joseph Micklewhite, Jr.; 14 Mar 1933, London, England), British actor.

Santiago Calatrava (28 Jul 1951, Valencia, Spain), Spanish architect.

Felipe (de Jesús) Calderón (Hinojosa) (18 Aug 1962, Morelia, Michoacán, Mexico), Mexican politician (National Action Party); president from 2006.

Felix Perez Camacho (30 Oct 1957, Camp Zama, Japan), American politician (Republican); governor of Guam from 2003.

David (William Donald) Cameron (9 Oct 1966, London, England), British politician and leader of the Conservative Party from 2005.

Camilla, duchess of Cornwall (Camilla Parker Bowles; Camilla Shand; 17 Jul 1947, London, England), English celebrity; wife of Charles, prince of Wales (married 9 Apr 2005).

Louis C. Camilleri (1955, Alexandria, Egypt), American corporate executive; president and CEO of Altria Group from 2002.

Gordon Campbell (12 Jan 1948, Vancouver, BC, Canada), Canadian politician (Liberal); premier of British Columbia from 2001.

John D. Campbell (8 Apr 1955, Ailsa Craig, ON, Canada), Canadian harness race driver; he was named 2006 Driver of the Year by the US Harness Writers Association.

Menzies Campbell (22 May 1941, Glasgow, Scotland), British politician; leader of the Liberal Democratic Party, 2006–07.

Naomi Campbell (22 May 1970, London, England), British runway and photographic model.

Fabio Cannavaro (13 Sep 1973, Naples, Italy), Italian association football (soccer) player.

Mario R. Capecchi (6 Oct 1937, Verona, Italy), Italian-born American biophysicist; corecipient of the 2007 Nobel Prize for Physiology or Medicine for developing a technique for introducing modified genes into mice.

Don(ald L.) Carcieri (16 Dec 1942, East Greenwich RI), American banker and politician (Republican); governor of Rhode Island from 2003.

Drew (Allison) Carey (23 May 1958, Cleveland OH), American comic TV actor and game-show host.

Mariah Carey (27 Mar 1970, Huntington, Long Island, NY), American pop singer.

Peter (Philip) Carey (7 May 1943, Bacchus Marsh, VIC, Australia), Australian author.

Carl XVI Gustaf (Carl Gustaf Folke Hubertus; 30 Apr 1946, Stockholm, Sweden), Swedish royal; king from 1973.

Lennart (Axel Edvard) Carleson (18 Mar 1928, Stockholm, Sweden), Swedish mathematician, a specialist in harmonic analysis; recipient of the 2006 Abel Prize.

Robert A. Caro (30 Oct 1935, New York NY), American biographer.

Caroline (Caroline Louise Margaret Grimaldi; 23 Jan 1957, Monte Carlo, Monaco), Monegasque princess, the elder daughter of Prince Rainier III and Princess Grace.

Alain (Frédéric) Carpentier (11 Aug 1933, Toulouse, France), French cardiovascular surgeon; recipient of a 2007 Lasker Medical Prize.

Steve(n John) Carrell (16 Aug 1962, Concord MA), American comic actor.

Jim Carrey (James Eugene Carrey; 17 Jan 1962, Newmarket, ON, Canada), Canadian-born American comic actor.

Edwin W. Carrington (1938, Tobago), Trinidadian international official; secretary-general of the Caribbean Community (CARICOM) from 1992.

Jimmy Carter (James Earl Carter, Jr.; 1 Oct 1924, Plains GA), American statesman; 39th president of the US, 1977–81, and recipient of the 2002 Nobel Peace Prize.

Marsh(all N.) Carter (1940, Washington DC?), American corporate executive; chairman of the New York Stock Exchange from 2005.

David Caruso (7 Jan 1956, Forest Hills NY), American actor.

James Carville, Jr. (25 Oct 1944, Carville LA), American political strategist and commentator.

George W. Casey, Jr. (22 Jul 1948, Sendai, Japan), American military officer; chief of staff of the US Army from 2007.

Fidel (Alejandro) Castro (Ruz) (13 Aug 1926, near Birán, Holguín province, Cuba), Cuban revolutionary; leader of Cuba, 1959–2008; he became a symbol of communist revolution in Latin America.

Raúl (Modesto) Castro (Ruz) (3 Jun 1931, near Birán, Holguín province, Cuba), Cuban revolutionary leader and politician; acting president of Cuba from 2006 following the illness of his brother, Fidel, and president from 2008.

Helio Castroneves (10 May 1975, São Paulo, Brazil), Brazilian race-car driver.

Kim Cattrall (21 Aug 1956, Liverpool, England), British-born film and TV actress.

Aníbal (António) Cavaco Silva (15 Jul 1939, Boliqueime, Algarve, Portugal), Portuguese politician; prime minister, 1985–95, and president from 2006.

Roberto Cavalli (15 Nov 1940, Florence, Italy), Italian fashion designer.

Vinton G(ray) Cerf (23 Jun 1943), American computer scientist known as the "father of the Internet"; recipient of a Japan Prize in 2008.

Michael Chabon (24 May 1963, Washington DC), American novelist and short-story writer.

Riccardo Chailly (20 Feb 1953, Milan, Italy), Italian orchestra conductor; music director of the Leipzig Opera, 2005–08, and Leipzig's Gewandhaus Orchestra from 2005.

John T. Chambers (23 Aug 1949, Cleveland OH), American corporate executive; president and CEO of Cisco Systems, Inc., from 1997.

Jackie Chan (Chan Kwong-Sang; 7 Apr 1954, Hong Kong), Chinese actor and director of martial arts films.

Margaret Chan (1947, Hong Kong), Hong Kong–born public health officer; director general of the World Health Organization from 2006.

Elaine L. Chao (26 Mar 1953, Taipei, Taiwan), American government official; secretary of labor from 2001.

Manu Chao (José-Manuel Thomas Arthur Chao; 21 Jun 1961, Paris, France), French-born Spanish rock musician.

Dave Chappelle (David Chappelle; 24 Aug 1973, Washington DC), American film and TV comedian and actor.

Jean Charest (John James Charest; 24 Jun 1958, Sherbrooke, QC, Canada), French Canadian politician; leader of the Quebec Liberal Party from 1998 and premier of Quebec from 2003.

Charles (Charles Philip Arthur George Windsor; 14 Nov 1948, Buckingham Palace, London, England), British prince of Wales; the eldest son of Queen Elizabeth II and Prince Philip, duke of Edinburgh; and heir apparent to the throne.

David Chase (David DeCesare; 22 Aug 1945, Mount Vernon NY), American TV writer, producer, and director.

Yves Chauvin (10 Oct 1930, Menin, Belgium), French chemist; corecipient of the 2005 Nobel Prize for Chemistry for the development of the metathesis method in organic synthesis.

Hugo Chávez Frías (28 Jul 1954, Sabaneta, Venezuela), Venezuelan military leader, politician, and president of Venezuela from 1999.

Don Cheadle (29 Nov 1964, Kansas City MO), American film and TV actor.

Chen Shui-bian (Pinyin: Ch'en Shui-pian; 18 Feb 1951, Hsichuang village, Tainan county, Taiwan), Taiwanese politician and president, 2000–08.

Dick Cheney (Richard Bruce Cheney; 30 Jan 1941, Lincoln NE), American politician (Republican); US secretary of defense, 1989–93, and vice president from 2001.

Taïeb Chérif (29 Dec 1941, Kasr El Boukhari, French Algeria), Algerian international official; secretary-general of the International Civil Aviation Organization from 2003.

Michael Chertoff (28 Nov 1953, Elizabeth NJ), American attorney; secretary of homeland security from 2005.

Robert Kipkoech Cheruiyot (26 Sep 1978, Eldoret, Kenya), Kenyan long-distance runner.

Kenny Chesney (26 Mar 1968, Luttrell TN), American country-and-western singer.

Judy Chicago (Judy Cohen; 20 Jul 1939, Chicago IL), American artist.

Dale Chihuly (20 Sep 1941, Tacoma WA), American glass artist.

Michael Chiklis (30 Aug 1963, Lowell MA), American TV actor.

Fujio Cho (1937, Tokyo, Japan), Japanese corporate executive; chairman of Toyota Motor Corp. from 2005.

Deepak Chopra (22 Oct 1946, New Delhi, British India), Indian-born American endocrinologist, alternative-medicine advocate, and best-selling author.

Choummaly Sayasone (6 Mar 1936, Attapu province, French Indochina [now in Laos]), Laotian political official; general secretary of the Lao People's Revolutionary Party from 2006, and president from 2006.

Chow Yun-Fat (Zhou Runfa; 18 May 1955, Lamma Island, Hong Kong), Hong Kong actor.

Julie (Frances) Christie (14 Apr 1941, Chukua, Assam, British India), British film actress.

Dimitris Christofias (29 Aug 1946, Kato Dhikomo, British Cyprus), Cypriot politician; president of Cyprus from 2008.

Ralph J(ohn) Cicerone (2 May 1943, New Castle PA), American electrical engineer and atmospheric scientist; president of the National Academy of Sciences from 2005.

Sandra Cisneros (20 Dec 1954, Chicago IL), American short-story writer and poet.

Tom Clancy (Thomas L. Clancy, Jr.; 12 Apr 1947, Baltimore MD), American best-selling novelist.

Eric Clapton (Eric Patrick Clapp; 30 Mar 1945, Ripley, Surrey, England), British guitarist, singer, and songwriter.

Helen Clark (26 Feb 1950, Hamilton, New Zealand), New Zealand politician (Labour); prime minister from 1999.

Victoria Clark (10 Oct 1959, Dallas TX), American stage actress.

Kelly Clarkson (24 Apr 1982, Burleson TX), American pop singer.

Patricia (Davies) Clarkson (29 Dec 1959, New Orleans LA), American stage, film, and TV actress.

John (Marwood) Cleese (27 Oct 1939, Weston-super-Mare, England), British comic actor.

Nick Clegg (Nicholas William Peter Clegg; 7 Jan 1967, Chalfont St. Giles, Buckinghamshire, England), British politician and MP; leader of the Liberal Democrats from 2007.

(William) Roger Clemens (4 Aug 1962, Dayton OH), American baseball pitcher.

Van Cliburn (Harvey Lavan Cliburn, Jr.; 12 Jul 1934, Shreveport LA), American pianist.

Lucille Clifton (27 Jun 1936, Depew NY), American poet; recipient of the 2007 Ruth Lilly Poetry Prize.

Bill Clinton (William Jefferson Blythe IV; 19 Aug 1946, Hope AR), American statesman; 42nd president of the US, 1993–2001.

Hillary Rodham Clinton (Hillary Diane Rodham; 26 Oct 1947, Chicago IL), American politician (Democrat); senator from New York from 2001 and candidate for president in 2008; wife of Pres. Bill Clinton.

George Clooney (6 May 1961, Lexington KY), American film and TV actor.

Chuck Close (Charles Thomas Close; 5 Jul 1940, Monroe WA), American Photo-realist painter.

Glenn Close (19 Mar 1947, Greenwich CT), American actress.

G. Wayne Clough (24 Sep 1941, Douglas GA), American educator and executive; secretary of the Smithsonian Institution from 2008.

Diablo Cody (Brooke Busey; 14 Jun 1978, Chicago IL), American stripper-turned-writer; author of the screenplay for the film *Juno*.

Paulo Coelho (24 Aug 1947, Rio de Janeiro, Brazil), Brazilian novelist.

Ethan Coen (21 Sep 1958, St. Louis Park MN), American filmmaker; winner of four Academy Awards, including three in 2007 for *No Country for Old Men*.

Joel Coen (29 Nov 1955, St. Louis Park MN), American filmmaker; winner of four Academy Awards, including three in 2007 for *No Country for Old Men*.

J(ohn) M(axwell) Coetzee (9 Feb 1940, Cape Town, Union of South Africa), South African novelist and critic; recipient of the 2003 Nobel Prize for Literature.

Leonard Cohen (21 Sep 1934, Montreal, QC, Canada), Canadian singer and songwriter.

Stephen Colbert (13 May 1964, Charleston SC), American TV commentator and satirist; host of *The Colbert Report* from 2005.

Ornette Coleman (9 Mar 1930, Fort Worth TX), American jazz saxophonist, composer, and bandleader; his *Sound Grammar* won the 2007 Pulitzer Prize for music.

Pierluigi Collina (13 Feb 1960, Bologna, Italy), Italian association football (soccer) referee.

Billy Collins (1941, New York NY), American poet; poet laureate of the US, 2001–03.

Marva Collins (Marva Delores Knight; 31 Aug 1936, Monroeville AL), American educator.

Alan Colmes (24 Sep 1950, Long Island NY), American liberal journalist and commentator on radio and TV.

Álvaro Colom Caballeros (15 Jun 1951, Guatemala City, Guatemala), Guatemalan politician (National Union for Hope); president from 2008.

Sean Combs (Puffy; Puff Daddy; P. Diddy; 4 Nov 1970, Harlem, New York NY), American rap artist, impresario, fashion mogul, and actor.

Common (Lonnie Rashid Lynn, Jr.; Common Sense; 13 Mar 1972, Chicago IL), American hip-hop artist and actor.

Blaise Compaoré (1951, Ziniane, Upper Volta [now Burkina Faso]), Burkinabe politician; president of Burkina Faso from 1987.

Bill Condon (22 Oct 1955, New York NY), American screenwriter and film director.

Jennifer Connelly (12 Dec 1970, Catskill Mountains NY), American fashion model and film actress.

(Thomas) Sean Connery (25 Aug 1930, Edinburgh, Scotland), Scottish film actor.

Lansana Conté (1934, Moussayah Loumbaya, French West Africa [now in Guinea]), Guinean military leader; president from 1984.

James T. Conway (26 Dec 1947, Walnut Ridge AR), American military officer; commandant of the US Marine Corps from 2006.

Dane (Jeffrey) Cook (18 Mar 1972, Boston MA), American comedian and actor.

Anderson (Hays) Cooper (3 Jun 1967, New York NY), American TV journalist.

Chris(topher W.) Cooper (9 Jul 1951, Kansas City MO), American film and TV actor.

Cynthia Cooper (14 Apr 1963, Chicago IL), American basketball player and coach.

Francis Ford Coppola (7 Apr 1939, Detroit MI), American film director, writer, and producer.

Sofia Coppola (14 May 1971, New York NY), American film director, writer, actress, and designer.

Chick Corea (Armando Anthony Corea; 12 Jun 1941, Chelsea MA), American jazz pianist, composer, and bandleader.

John Corigliano (16 Feb 1938, New York NY), American composer.

Patricia Cornwell (Patricia Daniels; 9 Jun 1956, Miami FL), American author of mystery novels.

Rafael (Vicente) Correa (Delgado) (6 Apr 1963, Guayaquil, Ecuador), Ecuadorian politician; president from 2007.

Carlos Correia (6 Nov 1933, Bissau, Portuguese Guinea), Guinea-Bissau politician; prime minister from 2008.

Jon (Stevens) Corzine (1 Jan 1947, Willey's Station IL), American politician (Democrat); senator from New Jersey, 2001–06, and governor from 2006.

Bill Cosby (William Henry Cosby, Jr.; 12 Jul 1937, Philadelphia PA), American comedian and actor.

Bob Costas (Robert Quinlan Costas; 22 Mar 1952, New York NY), American TV sportscaster and host.

Kevin (Michael) Costner (18 Jan 1955, Lynwood CA), American film actor and director.

Marion Cotillard (30 Sep 1975, Paris, France), French actress; recipient of the 2007 best actress Academy Award.

Pascal Couchepin (5 Apr 1942, Martigny, Switzerland), Swiss president, 2003 and again in 2008.

Tom Coughlin (Thomas Richard Coughlin; 31 Aug 1946, Waterloo NY), American football coach.

Ann (Hart) Coulter (8 Dec 1961, New Canaan CT), American attorney, political columnist, and author.

David Coulthard (27 Mar 1971, Twynholm, Scotland), British Formula 1 race-car driver.

Katie Couric (7 Jan 1957, Arlington VA), American TV talk-show host and news anchor.

Simon (Phillip) Cowell (7 Oct 1959, Brighton, East Sussex, England), British record producer and TV personality; a judge on the *American Idol* show (from 2002).

Brian Cowen (Irish: Brian Ó Comhain; 10 Jan 1960, Tullamore, County Offaly, Ireland), Irish politician (Fianna Fáil); prime minister from 2008.

Christopher Cox (16 Oct 1952, St. Paul MN), American politician (Republican); chairman of the US Securities and Exchange Commission from 2005.

Bantz John Craddock (1949, Doddridge county WV), American military official; Supreme Allied Commander, Europe (SACEUR) from 2006.

Tony Cragg (1949, Liverpool, England), British sculptor and installation artist; recipient of a Praemium Imperiale in 2007.

Daniel (Wroughton) Craig (2 Mar 1968, Chester, Cheshire, England), British stage and movie actor who played James Bond in films from 2006.

(John) Michael Crichton (23 Oct 1942, Chicago IL), American best-selling writer and director who specializes in novels on scientific themes.

Charlie Crist (Charles Joseph Crist, Jr.; 24 Jul 1956, Altoona PA), American politician (Republican); governor of Florida from 2007.

Stanley Crouch (14 Dec 1945, Los Angeles CA), American journalist and critic.

Sheryl Crow (11 Feb 1962, Kennett MO), American singer-songwriter.

Russell (Ira) Crowe (7 Apr 1964, Wellington, New Zealand), New Zealand–born Australian film actor.

Tom Cruise (Thomas Cruise Mapother IV; 3 Jul 1962, Syracuse NY), American actor.

Gastão Cruz (20 Jul 1941, Faro, Portugal), Portuguese poet and literary critic.

Nilo Cruz (1962?, Matanzas, Cuba), Cuban-born American playwright.

Penélope Cruz (Sánchez) (28 Apr 1974, Madrid, Spain), Spanish film actress.

Branko Crvenkovski (12 Oct 1962, Sarajevo, Yugoslavia [now in Bosnia and Herzegovina]), Macedonian politician; prime minister, 1992–98 and 2002–04, and president from 2004.

Jamie Cullum (20 Aug 1979, Essex, England), British pop, jazz, and rock pianist and vocalist.

Chet Culver (Chester John Culver; 25 Jan 1966, Washington DC), American politician (Democrat); governor of Iowa from 2007.

Joan Cusack (11 Oct 1962, New York NY), American film and TV actress.

John (Paul) Cusack (28 Jun 1966, Evanston IL), American film actor.

Mirko Cvetkovic (16 Aug 1950, Zajecar, Yugoslavia [now in Serbia]), Serbian politician; prime minister from 2008.

Miley Ray Cyrus (Destiny Hope Cyrus; 23 Nov 1992, Franklin TN), American TV actress (*Hannah Montana*) and singer.

Vincent (Phillip) D'Onofrio (30 Jul 1959, Brooklyn NY), American TV and film actor.

Paquito D'Rivera (Francisco Dejesus Rivera; 4 Jun 1948, Havana, Cuba), Cuban-born American jazz reed player and Afro-Cuban bandleader.

Willem Dafoe (William Dafoe, Jr.; 22 Jul 1955, Appleton WI), American film actor.

Dalai Lama (the 14th Dalai Lama, Tenzin Gyatso; original name Lhamo Dhondrub; 6 Jul 1935, Takster, Amdo province, Tibet [now Tsinghai province, China]), Tibetan spiritual leader (enthroned in 1940) and ruler-in-exile; head of the Tibetan Buddhists; recipient of the 1989 Nobel Peace Prize.

Richard M(ichael) Daley (24 Apr 1942, Chicago IL), American politician (Democrat); mayor of Chicago from 1989.

Matt(hew Page) Damon (8 Oct 1970, Cambridge MA), American film actor.

Claire (Catherine) Danes (12 Apr 1979, New York NY), American actress.

Mitch(ell Elais) Daniels, Jr. (7 Apr 1949, Monongahela PA), American businessman and politician (Republican); director of the US Office of Management and Budget, 2001–03, and governor of Indiana from 2005.

Edwidge Danticat (19 Jan 1969, Port-au-Prince, Haiti), Haitian-born American author.

Mahmoud Darwish (13 Mar 1942, Birwa, British Palestine), Palestinian nationalist poet.

Larry David (2 Jul 1947, Brooklyn NY), American actor and writer.

Mario Davidovsky (4 Mar 1934, Médanos, Buenos Aires, Argentina), Argentine-born American composer of electronic and electroacoustic works.

Terry Davis (Terence Anthony Gordon Davis; 5 Jan 1938, Stourbridge, West Midlands, England), British politician (Labour) and international executive; secretary-general of the Council of Europe from 2004.

Patrick Day (13 Oct 1953, Brush CO), American jockey.

Daniel (Michael Blake) Day-Lewis (29 Apr 1957, London, England), British film actor; recipient of the 1989 and 2007 Academy Awards for best actor.

Inge De Bruijn (24 Aug 1973, Barendrecht, Netherlands), Dutch swimmer.

Jaap de Hoop Scheffer (Jakob Gijsbert de Hoop Scheffer; 3 Apr 1948, Amsterdam, Netherlands), Dutch international official; secretary-general of NATO from 2004.

Danielle de Niese (1980, Melbourne, VIC, Australia), Australian-born American operatic soprano.

Robert De Niro (17 Aug 1943, New York NY), American film actor.

Howard (Brush) Dean III (17 Nov 1948, New York NY), American physician and politician (Democrat); governor of Vermont, 1991–2003, and chairman of the Democratic National Committee from 2005.

Idriss Déby Itno (1952, Fada, Chad, French Equatorial Africa [now in Chad]), Chadian politician; president from 1990.

Ellen DeGeneres (26 Jan 1958, Metairie LA), American comedian and TV personality.

John P. deJongh, Jr. (13 Nov 1957, St. Thomas, US Virgin Islands), American politician (Democrat); governor of the US Virgin Islands from 2007.

Benicio Del Toro (19 Feb 1967, San Turce, Puerto Rico), American film actor.

Bertrand Delanoë (30 May 1950, Tunis, French Tunisia), French politician (Socialist); mayor of Paris from 2001.

Don DeLillo (20 Nov 1936, New York NY), American postmodernist novelist.

Michael S. Dell (23 Feb 1965, Houston TX), American businessman; founder of Dell Computer Corp. and its CEO, 1984–2004 and again from 2007.

Yelena (Vyacheslavovna) Dementyeva (15 Oct 1981, Moscow, USSR [now in Russia]), Russian tennis player.

Patrick Dempsey (13 Jan 1966, Lewiston ME), American film and TV actor.

Judi Dench (Judith Olivia Dench; 9 Dec 1934, York, England), British stage, TV, and film actress.

Brian Dennehy (9 Jul 1938, Bridgeport CT), American TV, film, and stage actor.

Carl Dennis (17 Sep 1939, St. Louis MO), American poet.

Johnny Depp (John Christopher Depp II; 9 Jun 1963, Owensboro KY), American film actor.

Kiran Desai (3 Sep 1971, New Delhi, India), Indian-born American novelist; her *The Inheritance of Loss* won the 2006 Booker Prize.

Frankie Dettori (Lanfranco Dettori; 15 Dec 1970, Milan, Italy), Italian-born English jockey.

Cameron M. Diaz (30 Aug 1972, San Diego CA), American model and actress.

Junot Díaz (31 Dec 1968, Santo Domingo, Dominican Republic), Dominican-born American writer; his novel *The Brief Wondrous Life of Oscar Wao* won the 2008 Pulitzer Prize for fiction.

Kate DiCamillo (25 Mar 1965, Philadelphia PA), American author of children's books.

Leonardo (Wilhelm) DiCaprio (11 Nov 1974, Los Angeles CA), American film actor.

Joan Didion (5 Dec 1934, Sacramento CA), American author and journalist.

Vin Diesel (Mark Vincent; 18 Jul 1967, New York NY), American film actor.

Matt Dillon (18 Feb 1964, New Rochelle NY), American film actor.

Jamie Dimon (James Dimon; 13 Mar 1956, New York NY), American corporate executive; president (from 2004) and CEO (from 2005) of JPMorgan Chase & Co.

Fatou Diome (1968, Niodior island, Senegal), Senegalese French-language novelist.

Céline Dion (30 Mar 1968, Charlemagne, QC, Canada), French Canadian pop singer.

Stéphane Dion (28 Sep 1955, Quebec city, QC, Canada), Canadian politician; leader of the Liberal Party of Canada from 2007.

El Hadj Diouf (15 Jan 1981, Dakar, Senegal), Senegalese association football (soccer) star for French clubs and the Senegalese national team.

Jacques Diouf (1 Aug 1938, Saint-Louis, French West Africa [now in Senegal]), Senegalese international official; director-general of the Food and Agriculture Organization of the UN from 1994.

Waris Dirie (1967?, Somalia), Somali fashion model and women's rights activist.

Milo Djukanovic (15 Feb 1962, Niksic, Yugoslavia [now in Montenegro]), Montenegrin politician; president of Montenegro, 1998–2002, and prime minister, 2003–06 and again from 2008.

Lou Dobbs (24 Sep 1945, Childress TX), American business journalist and TV anchorman.

E(dgar) L(aurence) Doctorow (6 Jan 1931, New York NY), American novelist.

Christopher J(ohn) Dodd (27 May 1944, Willimantic CT), American politician (Democrat); senator from Connecticut from 1981.

Gary Doer (31 Mar 1948, Winnipeg, MB, Canada), Canadian politician (New Democratic Party); premier of Manitoba from 1999.

Domenico Dolce (13 Aug 1958, Polizzi Generosa, near Palermo, Italy), Italian fashion designer and partner of Stefano Gabbana.

Plácido Domingo (21 Jan 1941, Madrid, Spain), Spanish-born Mexican operatic tenor.

John (Joseph) Donahoe II (1960, US?), American corporate executive; president and CEO of eBay from 2008.

William Henry Donaldson (1931, Buffalo NY), American banker and corporate executive; chairman of the Security and Exchanges Commission, 2003–05.

José Eduardo dos Santos (28 Aug 1942, Luanda, Portuguese Angola), Angolan statesman and president from 1979.

Denzil L. Douglas (14 Jan 1953, St. Paul's, Saint Kitts and Nevis), West Indian politician; prime minister of Saint Kitts and Nevis from 1995.

James H. Douglas (21 Jun 1951, Springfield MA), American politician (Republican); governor of Vermont from 2003.

Michael Douglas (25 Sep 1944, New Brunswick NJ), American film actor and producer.

Rita (Frances) Dove (28 Aug 1952, Akron OH), American writer and teacher; poet laureate of the US, 1993–95.

Maureen Dowd (14 Jan 1952, Washington DC), American journalist and op-ed columnist for the *New York Times*.

Robert Downey, Jr. (4 Apr 1965, New York NY), American actor.

Jim Doyle (James Edward Doyle; 23 Nov 1945, Washington DC), American politician (Democrat); governor of Wisconsin from 2003.

Kimberly Dozier (6 Jul 1966, Honolulu HI), American TV journalist and foreign correspondent.

Dr. Dre (Andre Young; 18 Feb 1965, Los Angeles CA), American rap musician and impresario, considered a pioneer of gangsta rap.

Stacy Dragila (Stacy Mikaelson; 25 Mar 1971, Auburn CA), American pole vaulter.

E(rnest) Linn Draper, Jr. (6 Feb 1942, Houston TX), American energy engineer and corporate executive; chairman, president, and CEO of American Electric Power, Inc., 1992–2003.

Deborah Drattell (1956, Brooklyn NY), American composer of operas.

Dré (Andre Benjamin; Andre 3000; 27 May 1975, Atlanta GA), American hip-hop artist and actor.

Didier Drogba (11 Mar 1978, Abidjan, Côte d'Ivoire), Ivorian association football (soccer) player; he was voted African Footballer of the Year for 2006.

Matt Drudge (27 Oct 1967), American Internet journalist, editor of the Drudge Report.

Nicanor Duarte Frutos (11 Oct 1956, Coronel Oviedo, Paraguay), Paraguayan politician; president, 2003–08.

David (William) Duchovny (7 Aug 1960, New York NY), American TV and film actor.

Gustavo (Adolfo) Dudamel (Ramírez) (26 Jan 1981, Barquisimeto, Venezuela), Venezuelan conductor; music director of the Göteborg (Sweden) Symphony Orchestra from 2007 and tapped to take over the Los Angeles Philharmonic in 2009.

Hilary (Ann Lisa) Duff (28 Sep 1987, Houston TX), American TV and film actress and pop singer.

Sarah Dunant (8 Aug 1950, London, England), British crime and historical novelist, broadcaster, and critic.

Tim(othy Theodore) Duncan (25 Apr 1976, St. Croix, US Virgin Islands), American basketball player.

Ronnie Gene Dunn (1 Jun 1953, Coleman TX), American country-and-western singer (for Brooks & Dunn).

Kirsten (Caroline) Dunst (30 Apr 1982, Point Pleasant NJ), American film actress.

Robert Duvall (5 Jan 1931, San Diego CA), American actor, producer, and screenwriter.

Bob Dylan (Robert Allen Zimmerman; 24 May 1941, Duluth MN), American singer and songwriter; he received a special citation from the Pulitzer Prize committee in 2008.

Esther Dyson (14 Jul 1951, Zürich, Switzerland), American economist and journalist specializing in computer and cyberspace issues.

Freeman (John) Dyson (15 Dec 1923, Crowthorne, Berkshire, England), British-born American physicist and educator; recipient of the 2000 Templeton Prize.

Steve Earle (Stephen Fain Earle; 17 Jan 1955, Fort Monroe VA), American country singer, guitarist, and songwriter.

(Ralph) Dale Earnhardt, Jr. (10 Oct 1974, Concord NC), American NASCAR race-car driver.

Michael F(rancis) Easley (23 Mar 1950, Nash county NC), American politician (Democrat); governor of North Carolina from 2001.

Clint(on) Eastwood, Jr. (31 May 1930, San Francisco CA), American film actor and moviemaker.

Martin Eberhard (15 May 1960, Berkeley CA), American entrepreneur and cofounder of Tesla Motors.

Roger Ebert (18 Jun 1942, Urbana IL), American film critic.

Marcelo (Luis) Ebrard (Casaubon) (10 Oct 1959, Mexico City, Mexico), Mexican politician (Party of the Democratic Revolution); head of government of the Federal District (mayor of Mexico City) from 2006.

Umberto Eco (5 Jan 1932, Alessandria, Italy), Italian literary critic, novelist, and semiotician.

Marian Wright Edelman (6 Jun 1939, Bennettsville SC), American attorney and civil rights advocate who founded the Children's Defense Fund.

Edward (Edward Anthony Richard Louis; 10 Mar 1964, Buckingham Palace, London, England), British prince; third son of Queen Elizabeth II and Prince Philip, duke of Edinburgh; and earl of Wessex.

John Edwards (10 Jun 1953, Seneca SC), American politician (Democrat); senator from North Carolina, 1999–2005.

Tuiatua Tupua Tamasese Efi (1 Mar 1938, Samoa?), Samoan royal; O le Ao o le Malo (elective monarch) from 2007.

Edward Michael Cardinal Egan (2 Apr 1932, Oak Park IL), American Roman Catholic church leader; archbishop of New York from 2000 and cardinal from 2001.

Dave Eggers (8 Jan 1970, Chicago IL), American author and graphic artist; founder and editor of *McSweeney's*, a journal and Web site, from 1998.

Michael D(ammann) Eisner (7 Mar 1942, Mount Kisco NY), American corporate executive; CEO and chairman of the Walt Disney Co., 1984–2004.

Hicham El Guerrouj (14 Sep 1974, Berkane, Morocco), Moroccan distance runner, retired but still the holder of several world records.

Mohamed ElBaradei (Muhammad al-Baradei; 17 Jun 1942, Cairo, Egypt), Egyptian international official; director general of the International Atomic Energy Agency from 1997.

Carmen Electra (Tara Leigh Patrick; 20 Apr 1972, Sharonville OH), American model, TV actress, and celebrity.

Danny Elfman (29 May 1943, Los Angeles CA), American pop musician and composer of film and TV scores.

Olafur Eliasson (1967, Copenhagen, Denmark), Danish installation artist.

Elizabeth II (Elizabeth Alexandra Mary Windsor; 21 Apr 1926, London, England), British royal; queen of the United Kingdom of Great Britain and Northern Ireland from 1952.

George F(rancis) R(ayner) Ellis (11 Aug 1939, Johannesburg, Union of South Africa), South African applied mathematician and professor; recipient of the 2004 Templeton Prize.

Lawrence J(oseph) Ellison (17 Aug 1944, Chicago IL), American corporate executive; founder and CEO of Oracle Corp. from 1977.

James Ellroy (Lee Earle Ellroy; 4 Mar 1948, Los Angeles CA), American mystery writer.

Ernie Els (Theodore Ernest Els; 17 Oct 1969, Johannesburg, South Africa), South African golfer.

Eminem (Marshall Bruce Mathers III; 17 Oct 1973, St. Joseph MO), American hip-hop artist.

Emmanuel III Delly (Emmanuel-Karim Delly; 6 Oct 1927, Telkaif, Iraq), Iraqi churchman; patriarch of Babylonia and the Chaldeans (leader of the Chaldean Catholic Church) from 2003 and Roman Catholic cardinal from 2007.

Nambaryn Enhbayar (1 Jun 1958, Ulaanbaatar, Mongolia), Mongolian politician (People's Revolutionary Party); prime minister, 2000–04; and president of the Great Hural (parliament) from 2005.

Anne Enright (11 Oct 1962, Dublin, Ireland), Irish writer; her novel *The Gathering* was awarded the 2007 Man Booker Prize.

Enya (Eithne Ní Bhraonáin; 17 May 1961, Gweedore, County Donegal, Ireland), Irish New Age singer.

Recep Tayyip Erdogan (26 Feb 1954, Istanbul, Turkey), Turkish politician (Justice and Development Party); prime minister from 2003.

Gerhard (Ludwig) Ertl (10 Oct 1936, Bad Cannstadt, Germany), German physical chemist; recipient of the 2007 Nobel Prize for Chemistry for work on the reactions of gas molecules on solid surfaces.

Patricia Espinosa Cantellano (21 Oct 1958, Mexico City, Mexico), Mexican diplomat and government official; secretary of foreign affairs from 2006.

Gloria Estefan (Gloria Maria Milagrosa Fajardo; 1 Sep 1957, Havana, Cuba), Cuban-born American salsa singer and lyricist.

Melissa Etheridge (29 May 1961, Leavenworth KS), American rock singer and songwriter.

Robin Eubanks (25 Oct 1955, Philadelphia PA), American jazz trombone player.

Martin J. Evans (1 Jan 1941, Stroud, Gloucestershire, England), British biochemist; corecipient of the 2007 Nobel Prize for Physiology or Medicine for developing a technique for introducing modified genes into mice.

Eve (Eve Jihan Jeffers; "Eve of Destruction"; 10 Nov 1979, Philadelphia PA), American rapper.

Richard D. Fairbank (18 Sep 1950, Menlo Park CA), American corporate executive; founder, chairman, and CEO of Capital One Financial Corp. from 1988.

Edie Falco (Edith Falco; 5 Jul 1963, Brooklyn NY), American film and TV actress.

William J(oseph) Fallon (30 Dec 1944, East Orange NJ), American military leader; commander of the US Central Command, 2007–08.

(Hannah) Dakota Fanning (23 Feb 1994, Conyers GA), American child film actress.

Louis (Abdul) Farrakhan (Louis Eugene Walcott; 11 May 1933, Bronx NY), American leader of the Nation of Islam (Black Muslims) from 1978.

Colin (James) Farrell (31 May 1976, Dublin, Ireland), Irish actor.

Suzanne Farrell (Roberta Sue Ficker; 16 Aug 1945, Cincinnati OH), American ballet dancer.

Justin Fatica (c. 1980, Erie PA), American Catholic youth evangelist; founder (2002) of the Hard as Nails Ministry to bring students to Christ.

Anthony S(tephen) Fauci (24 Dec 1940, Brooklyn NY), American public-health physician and AIDS researcher; director of the National Institute of Allergy and Infectious Diseases from 1984; recipient of a Lasker Medical Award in 2007.

(Catharine) Drew Gilpin Faust (18 Sep 1947, New York NY), American educator and historian; president of Harvard University from 2007.

Brett (Lorenzo) Favre (10 Oct 1969, Kiln MS), American pro football quarterback.

Salam Fayyad (1952, near Tulkarm, Jordan [West Bank]), Palestinian politican (Third Way); prime minister of the Palestinian Authority from 2007.

Roger Federer (8 Aug 1981, Basel, Switzerland), Swiss tennis player.

Russ(ell Dana) Feingold (2 Mar 1953, Janesville WI), American politician (Democrat); senator from Wisconsin from 1993.

Felipe (Felipe de Borbón y Grecia; 30 Jan 1968, Madrid, Spain), Spanish royal, prince of Asturias, and heir to the Spanish throne.

Eddie Fenech Adami (7 Feb 1934, Birkirkara, Malta), Maltese politician; prime minister, 1987–96 and 1998–2004, and president from 2004.

Dennis Fentie (8 Nov 1950, Edmonton, AB, Canada), Canadian businessman and politician (Yukon Party); premier of the Yukon Territory from 2002.

Craig Ferguson (17 May 1962, Glasgow, Scotland), British film and TV actor; host of TV's *The Late Late Show* from 2005.

Sarah (Margaret) Ferguson (15 Oct 1959, London, England), British royal, duchess of York after her marriage (23 Jul 1986) to Prince Andrew; they divorced in 1996.

Cristina (Elisabet) Fernández (Wilhelm) de Kirchner (19 Feb 1953, La Plata, Argentina), Argentine politician; president, following her husband, Néstor Kirchner, from 2007.

Leonel Fernández (Reyna) (26 Dec 1953, Santo Domingo, Dominican Republic), Dominican politician; president, 1996–2000 and again from 2004.

Gil de Ferran (11 Nov 1967, Paris, France), French-born Brazilian race-car driver.

Will Ferrell (16 Jul 1967, Irvine CA), American comedian and actor.

America (Georgine) Ferrera (18 Apr 1984, Los Angeles CA), American film and TV actress.

Albert Fert (7 Mar 1938, Carcassonne, France), French physicist; corecipient of the 2007 Nobel Prize for Physics and a 2007 Japan Prize for work on magnetoresonance.

Tina Fey (Elizabeth Stamatina Fey; 18 May 1970, Upper Darby PA), American comedian and writer.

Robert Fico (15 Sep 1964, Topolcany, Czechoslovakia [now in Slovakia]), Slovak politician (Social Democrat); prime minister from 2006.

Sally Field (6 Nov 1946, Pasadena CA), American comic and dramatic actress.

Ralph (Nathaniel) Fiennes (22 Dec 1962, Suffolk, England), British dramatic actor.

Harvey (Forbes) Fierstein (6 Jun 1954, Brooklyn NY), American playwright and actor.

Luis (Filipe Madeira Caeiro) Figo (4 Nov 1972, Almada, Portugal), Portuguese association football (soccer) player; FIFA player of the year, 2001.

François Fillon (4 Mar 1954, LeMans, France), French politician; prime minister from 2007.

David (Leo) Fincher (28 Aug 1962, Denver CO), American film director.

Harvey V. Fineberg (15 Sep 1945, Pittsburgh PA), American public-health physician and medical administrator; president of the Institute of Medicine from 2002.

Carly Fiorina (Cara Carleton Sneed; 6 Sep 1954, Austin TX), American corporate executive and political adviser; president and CEO of Hewlett-Packard, 1999–2005, and chairman, 2000–05.

Heinz Fischer (9 Oct 1938, Graz, Austria), Austrian politician (Social Democrat); president from 2004.

Allison Fisher (24 Feb 1968, Cheshunt, Hertfordshire, England), British pocket-billiards champion.

Isla (Lang) Fisher (3 Feb 1976, Muscat, Oman), British film actress.

Benígno (Repeki) Fitial (27 Nov 1945, Saipan, Northern Mariana Islands), American politician (Covenant Party); governor of the Northern Mariana Islands from 2006.

Patrick Fitzgerald (22 Dec 1960, New York NY), American special prosecutor in a number of high-profile cases.

Tim Flannery (28 Jan 1956, Melbourne, VIC, Australia), Australian zoologist and environmentalist; he was named Australian of the Year for 2007.

Leon Fleisher (23 Jul 1928, San Francisco CA), American pianist; recipient of a 2007 Kennedy Center Honor.

Renée Fleming (14 Feb 1959, Indiana PA), American operatic soprano.

Ernie Fletcher (Ernest Lee Fletcher; 12 Nov 1952, Mount Sterling KY), American physician and politician (Republican); governor of Kentucky, 2003–07.

Juan Diego Flórez (13 Jan 1973, Lima, Peru), Peruvian bel canto tenor.

Carlisle Floyd (11 Jun 1926, Latta SC), American opera composer and librettist.

Ken Follett (pseudonyms Zachary Stone and Simon Myles; 5 Jun 1949, Cardiff, Wales), British author of political thrillers.

Phil Fontaine (Larry Phillip Fontaine; "Buddy"; 20 Sep 1944, Fort Alexander Reserve, MB, Canada), Canadian Ojibway First Nations activist; national chief of the Assembly of First Nations from 1997.

Harrison Ford (13 Jul 1942, Chicago IL), American film actor.

Richard Ford (16 Feb 1944, Jackson MS), American writer of novels and short stories.

Tom Ford (27 Aug 1961, Austin TX), American fashion designer.

William Clay Ford, Jr. (3 May 1957, Detroit MI), American corporate executive; chairman and CEO of Ford Motor Co. from 2001.

William Forsythe (1949, New York NY), American ballet dancer, choreographer, and director.

Jodie Foster (Alicia Christian Foster; 19 Nov 1962, Los Angeles CA), American film actress.

Norman (Robert) Foster (1 Jun 1935, near Manchester, England), British architect; recipient of the 1999 Pritzker Prize and a 2002 Praemium Imperiale.

Jamie Foxx (Eric Bishop; 13 Dec 1967, Terrell TX), American actor and comedian.

Don Francisco (Mario Kreutzberger; 28 Dec 1940, Talca, Chile), Chilean-born American TV personality; host of the popular show *Sábado Gigante*.

Al Franken (21 May 1951, New York NY), American comedian, writer, and congressional candidate in 2008.

Jonathan Franzen (17 Aug 1959, Western Springs IL), American author.

Charles Frazier (1950, Asheville NC), American novelist.

Frederik (Frederik André Henrik Christian; 26 May 1968, Copenhagen, Denmark), Danish crown prince.

Morgan Freeman (1 Jun 1937, Memphis TN), American theater and film actor.

Dawn French (11 Oct 1957, Holyhead, Wales), British actress, comedian, and writer.

Lucian Freud (8 Dec 1922, Berlin, Germany), German-born British painter.

Dave Freudenthal (David Duane Freudenthal; 12 Oct 1950, Thermopolis WY), American politician (Democrat); governor of Wyoming from 2003.

Saul Friedländer (11 Oct 1932, Prague, Czechoslovakia [now in the Czech Republic]), Czech-born French-Israeli historian and professor whose study *The Years of Extermination: Nazi Germany and the Jews, 1939–1945* won the 2008 Pulitzer Prize for general nonfiction.

Thomas L. Friedman (20 Jul 1953, Minneapolis MN), American journalist and author; foreign-affairs columnist for the *New York Times*.

Janus Friis (1976, Denmark), Danish Internet entrepreneur; codeveloper of Joost, a program to receive TV broadcasts on a personal computer.

Yasuo Fukuda (16 Jul 1936, Takasaki, Japan), Japanese politician (Liberal Democratic); prime minister from 2007.

Takeo Fukui (28 Nov 1944, Tokyo, Japan), Japanese corporate executive; president and CEO of Honda Motor Co. from 2003.

Richard S. Fuld, Jr. (26 Apr 1946), American corporate executive; CEO of Lehman Brothers Holdings from 1993.

Nelly (Kim) Furtado (2 Dec 1978, Victoria, BC, Canada), Canadian singer and songwriter.

Stefano Gabbana (14 Nov 1962, Milan, Italy), Italian fashion designer and partner of Domenico Dolce.

Neil (Richard) Gaiman (10 Nov 1960, Portchester, England), British graphic novelist.

Mary Gaitskill (11 Nov 1954, Lexington KY), American writer.

John Galliano (Juan Carlos Antonio Galliano Guillen; 28 Nov 1960, Gibraltar), British fashion designer and designer in chief at Christian Dior.

Sonia Gandhi (Sonia Maino; 9 Dec 1947, Turin, Italy), Italian-born Indian widow of Rajiv Gandhi and a political force in India.

James Gandolfini (18 Sep 1961, Westwood NJ), American TV and film actor.

Mario Garcia (1947?, Cuba), Cuban-born American newspaper designer.

Gael García Bernal (30 Oct 1978, Guadalajara, Jalisco, Mexico), Mexican actor.

Gabriel (José) García Márquez (6 Mar 1928, Aracataca, Colombia), Colombian novelist and short-story writer, a central figure in the magic realism movement in Latin American literature; recipient of the 1972 Neustadt Prize and the 1982 Nobel Prize for Literature.

Alan García Pérez (23 May 1949, Lima, Peru), Peruvian politician; president, 1985–90 and again from 2006.

Jennifer (Anne) Garner (17 Apr 1972, Houston TX), American TV and film actress.

Kevin (Maurice) Garnett (19 May 1976, Mauldin SC), American pro basketball player.

Kenny Garrett (9 Oct 1960, Detroit MI), American jazz alto saxophone player.

Ivan Gasparovic (27 Mar 1941, Poltar, Czechoslovakia [now in Slovakia]), Slovak politician; president from 2004.

Bill Gates (William Henry Gates III; 28 Oct 1955, Seattle WA), American computer programmer, businessman, philanthropist, and cofounder of the Microsoft Corp.; he is one of the richest people in the world.

Melinda Gates (Melinda French; 15 Aug 1964, Dallas TX), American philanthropist; cofounder of the Bill & Melinda Gates Foundation.

Robert M(ichael) Gates (25 Sep 1943, Wichita KS), American government official; CIA director, 1991–93, and secretary of defense from 2006.

Jean-Paul Gaultier (24 Apr 1952, Arcueil, France), French fashion designer.

Maumoon Abdul Gayoom (29 Dec 1937, Malé, Maldives), Maldive politician; president from 1978.

Laurent Gbagbo (31 May 1945, Gagnoa, French West Africa [now in Côte d'Ivoire]), Ivorian politician; president of Côte d'Ivoire from 2000.

Haile Gebrselassie (18 Apr 1973, Assela, Ethiopia), Ethiopian runner and world record holder in the 5,000-m and 10,000-m distances.

Frank Gehry (Frank Owen Goldberg; 28 Feb 1929, Toronto, ON, Canada), Canadian-born American architect and designer whose original, sculptural, often audacious work won him worldwide renown; recipient of the 1989 Pritzker Prize.

Bob Geldof (5 Oct 1954, Dublin, Ireland), Irish singer and songwriter and humanitarian.

Juan Gelman (3 May 1930, Buenos Aires, Argentina), Argentine poet; recipient of the 2007 Cervantes Prize.

Francis (Eugene) Cardinal George (16 Jan 1937, Chicago IL), American Roman Catholic churchman; archbishop of Chicago from 1997 and cardinal from 1998.

(Susan) Elizabeth George (26 Feb 1949, Warren OH), American mystery writer.

George Tupou V (Tupouto'a; 4 May 1948, Nuku'alofa, British Tonga), Tongan royal; king from 2006.

Leo W. Gerard (1947?, Sudbury, ON, Canada), Canadian labor leader; international president of the United Steelworkers International from 2001.

Richard (Tiffany) Gere (31 Aug 1949, Philadelphia PA), American film actor.

Valery (Abisalovich) Gergiev (2 May 1953, Moscow, USSR [now in Russia]), Russian conductor; director of the Kirov Opera from 1998.

Ricky (Dene) Gervais (25 Jun 1961, Reading, Berkshire, England), British comedian and actor.

Ron(ald Anthony) Gettelfinger (1 Aug 1944, near DePauw IN), American labor leader; president of the United Automobile Workers from 2002.

Mohamed Ghannouchi (18 Aug 1941, Al-Hamma, Tunisia), Tunisian politician and prime minister from 1999.

Jamal al-Ghitani (1945, Suhag, Egypt), Egyptian writer.

Robert Ghiz (21 Jan 1974, Charlottetown, PEI, Canada), Canadian politician (Liberal); premier of Prince Edward Island from 2007.

Paul (Edward Valentine) Giamatti (6 Jun 1967, New Haven CT), American film actor.

Frida Giannini (1972, Rome, Italy), Italian fashion designer; creative director at Gucci from 2006.

Jim Gibbons (James Arthur Gibbons; 16 Dec 1944, Sparks NV), American politician (Republican); governor of Nevada from 2007.

Charles (deWolf) Gibson (9 Mar 1943, Evanston IL), American TV journalist and anchorman.

Mel (Columcille Gerard) Gibson (3 Jan 1956, Peekskill NY), Australian American actor, producer, director.

Gilberto (Passos) Gil (Moreira) (26 Jun 1942, Salvador, Bahia state, Brazil), Brazilian pop singer and songwriter; minister of culture from 2003.

(Makhdoom Syed) Yousaf Raza Gilani (9 Jun 1952, Karachi, Pakistan), Pakistani politician (PPP); prime minister from 2008.

Melissa Gilbert (8 May 1964, Los Angeles CA), American film and TV actress; president of the Screen Actors Guild from 2002.

João Gilberto (do Prado Pereira de Oliveira) (10 Jun 1931, Juazeiro, Bahia state, Brazil), Brazilian bossa-nova singer, songwriter, and guitarist.

Vince Gill (Vincent Grant Gill; 12 Apr 1957, Norman OK), American country and progressive-bluegrass instrumentalist and singer.

Tony Gilroy (Anthony Joseph Gilroy; 11 Sep 1956, New York NY), American screenwriter.

Ruth Bader Ginsburg (15 Mar 1933, Brooklyn NY), American jurist; associate justice of the US Supreme Court from 1993.

Dana Gioia (24 Dec 1950, Los Angeles CA), American poet and critic; chairman of the US National Endowment for the Arts from 2003.

Nikki Giovanni (Yolande Cornelia Giovanni, Jr.; 7 Jun 1943, Knoxville TN), American poet.

Rudy Giuliani (Rudolph William Giuliani; 28 May 1944, Brooklyn NY), American politician (Republican); mayor of New York City, 1994–2002.

Ira Glass (3 Mar 1959, Baltimore MD), American radio broadcaster, creator (1995) and host of *This American Life* on public radio and later also on cable TV.

Philip Glass (31 Jan 1937, Baltimore MD), American minimalist composer.

Roy J. Glauber (1 Sep 1925, New York NY), American quantum physicist; corecipient of the 2005 Nobel Prize for Physics.

Savion Glover (19 Nov 1973, Newark NJ), American dancer and choreographer.

Louise (Elisabeth) Glück (22 Apr 1943, New York NY), American poet; US poet laureate, 2003–04.

Faure (Essozimna) Gnassingbé (Eyadéma) (6 Jun 1966, Afagnan, Togo), Togolese politician; president in February 2005 and again from May 2005.

Jean-Luc Godard (3 Dec 1930, Paris, France), French film director.

Ivars Godmanis (27 Nov 1951, Riga, USSR [now in Latvia]), Latvian politician; prime minister from 2007.

Whoopi Goldberg (Caryn Elaine Johnson; 13 Nov 1955, New York NY), American comedian and film actress.

(Orette) Bruce Golding (5 Dec 1947, Clarendon, Jamaica), Jamaican politician; prime minister from 2007.

Ralph E. Gonsalves (8 Aug 1946, Colonarie, Saint Vincent), West Indian politician; prime minister of Saint Vincent and the Grenadines from 2001.

Alejandro González Iñárritu (15 Aug 1963, Mexico City, Mexico), Mexican film director.

Lawrence Gonzi (1 Jul 1953, Valletta, Malta), Maltese politician (Nationalist); prime minister from 2004.

Roger Goodell (19 Feb 1959, Jamestown NY), American sports executive; commissioner of the National Football League from 2006.

Cuba Gooding, Jr. (2 Jan 1968, Bronx NY), American film actor.

Allegra Goodman (1967, Brooklyn NY), American writer, notably on Jewish themes.

Doris Kearns Goodwin (4 Jan 1943, Brooklyn NY), American historian, biographer, and TV commentator.

Al(bert Arnold) Gore, Jr. (31 Mar 1948, Washington DC), American statesman and environmental advocate; vice president of the US, 1993–2001, and corecipient of the 2007 Nobel Peace Prize.

Ryan (Thomas) Gosling (12 Nov 1980, London, ON, Canada), Canadian TV and film actor.

Jorie Graham (9 May 1951, New York NY), American poet.

Shawn Graham (22 Feb 1968, Rexton, NB, Canada), Canadian politician (Liberal); premier of New Brunswick from 2006.

(Allen) Kelsey Grammer (21 Feb 1955, St. Thomas, US Virgin Islands), American TV actor, writer, and producer.

Michael Grandage (2 May 1962, Yorkshire, England), British theater director; artistic director of London's Donmar Warehouse.

Jennifer Granholm (Jennifer Mulhern; 5 Feb 1959, Vancouver, BC, Canada), Canadian-born American attorney and politician (Democrat); governor of Michigan from 2003.

Hugh Grant (9 Sep 1960, London, England), British film actor.

Günter (Wilhelm) Grass (16 Oct 1927, Danzig, Germany [now Gdansk, Poland]), German poet, novelist, playwright, sculptor, and printmaker; recipient of the 1999 Nobel Prize for Literature.

Michael Graves (9 July 1934, Indianapolis IN), American postmodernist architect and housewares designer.

Zinaida Greceanii (7 Feb 1956, Tomsk oblast, USSR [now in Russia], Moldovan politician; prime minister from 2008.

Richard Greenberg (1958, Long Island NY), American playwright.

Brian Greene (9 Feb 1963, New York NY), American physicist and expert on string theory.

Paul Greengrass (13 Aug 1955, Cheam, Surrey, England), British film director.

Alan Greenspan (6 Mar 1926, New York NY), American monetary policymaker and chairman of the Board of Governors of the US Federal Reserve Bank, 1987–2006.

Christine Gregoire (Christine O'Grady; 24 Mar 1947, Auburn WA), American politician (Democrat); governor of Washington from 2005.

Grégoire III Laham (Lutfi Laham; 15 Dec 1933, Daraya, Syria), Syrian church leader; patriarch of Antioch in the Greek Melkite Catholic Church from 2000.

Philippa Gregory (9 Jan 1954, Nairobi, Kenya), British historical novelist.

Kate Grenville (14 Oct 1950, Sydney, Australia), Australian writer.

Brad Grey (1958?, Bronx NY), American talent agent, producer, and film executive; chairman and CEO of Paramount Motion Picture Group from 2005.

Michael (Douglas) Griffin (1 Nov 1949, Aberdeen MD), American aerospace engineer and businessman; administrator of NASA from 2005.

Ólafur Ragnar Grímsson (14 May 1943, Ísafjörður, Iceland), Icelandic politician; president from 1996.

John Grisham (8 Feb 1955, Jonesboro AR), American lawyer and best-selling novelist.

Josh(ua Winslow) Groban (27 Feb 1981, Los Angeles CA), American adult contemporary singer.

Matt(hew Abram) Groening (15 Feb 1954, Portland OR), American cartoonist and creator (1989) of TV's *The Simpsons*.

Dave Grohl (David Eric Grohl; 14 Jan 1969, Warren OH), American rock drummer, guitarist, and singer (for Nirvana and Foo Fighters).

Gilbert M. Grosvenor (5 May 1931, Washington DC), American executive; president of the National Geographic Society, 1980–96, and chairman of the board from 1987.

Andrew S. Grove (Andras Grof; 2 Sep 1936, Budapest, Hungary), Hungarian-born American corporate executive; CEO of Intel Corp. from 1997.

Robert H. Grubbs (27 Feb 1942, Calvert City KY), American chemical engineer; corecipient of the 2005 Nobel Prize for Chemistry.

Jon Gruden (17 Aug 1963, Sandusky OH), American professional football coach.

Nikola Gruevski (31 Aug 1970, Skopje, Yugoslavia [now in Macedonia]), Macedonian politician; prime minister from 2006.

Peter (Andreas) Grünberg (18 May 1939, Plzen, Czechoslovakia [now in the Czech Republic]), Czech-born German physicist; corecipient of the 2007 Nobel Prize for Physics and a 2007 Japan Prize for work on magnetoresonance.

Armando (Emílio) Guebuza (20 Jan 1943, Marrupula, Portuguese Mozambique), Mozambican politician; secretary-general of the Frelimo political party from 2002 and president from 2005.

Ismail Omar Guelleh (27 Nov 1947, Diré-Dawa, Ethiopia), Djiboutian politician; president from 1999.

Guillaume (Guillaume Jean Joseph Marie, Prince of Nassau and Bourbon-Parma; 11 Nov 1981, Château de Betzdorf, Luxembourg), Luxembourgian grand duke and heir to the throne.

Gilbert Guillaume (4 Dec 1930, Bois-Colombes, France), French jurist; president of the International Court of Justice, 2000–05.

Ozzie Guillen (Oswaldo José Guillen Barrios; 20 Jan 1964, Ocumare del Tuy, Venezuela), Venezuelan-born professional baseball manager.

Abdullah Gul (29 Oct 1950, Kayseri, Turkey), Turkish economist and politician; prime minister, 2002–03, and president from 2007.

Natalie (Anne) Gulbis (7 Jan 1983, Sacramento CA), American golfer.

James Edward Gunn (21 Oct 1938, Livingstone TX), American cosmologist; corecipient of the 2005 Crafoord Prize for research into the evolution of the universe.

José Ángel Gurría Treviño (8 May 1950, Tampico, Tamaulipas, Mexico), Mexican economist; secretary-general of the Organisation for Economic Co-operation and Development from 2006.

Alfred Gusenbauer (8 Feb 1960, Sankt-Pölten, Austria), Austrian politician (Social Democrat); chancellor from 2007.

Xanana Gusmão (José Alexandre Gusmão; 20 Jun 1946, Laleia, Portuguese Timor [now East Timor]), Timorese independence leader; first president of independent East Timor, 2002–07, and prime minister from 2007.

António (Manuel de Oliveira) Guterres (30 Apr 1949, Lisbon, Portugal), Portuguese politician (Socialist); prime minister, 1995–2002, and UN High Commissioner for Refugees from 2005.

Carlos M. Gutierrez (4 Nov 1953, Havana, Cuba), Cuban-born American corporate executive and government official; CEO of Kellogg Company, 2000–05, and US secretary of commerce from 2005.

Buddy Guy (George Guy; 30 Jul 1936, Lettsworth LA), American blues guitarist and singer.

Gyanendra Bir Bikram Shah Dev (7 Jul 1947, Kathmandu, Nepal), Nepalese king, 1950–51 and again from 2001–07.

Jake Gyllenhaal (Jacob Benjamin Gyllenhaal; 19 Dec 1980, Los Angeles CA), American film actor.

Ferenc Gyurcsány (4 Jun 1961, Pápa, Hungary), Hungarian politician; prime minister from 2004.

Haakon (Haakon Magnus; 20 Jul 1973, Oslo, Norway), Norwegian crown prince (heir to the throne).

Geir (Hilmar) Haarde (8 Apr 1951, Reykjavík, Iceland), Icelandic politician; prime minister from 2006.

Jürgen Habermas (18 Jun 1929, Düsseldorf, Germany), German philosopher, sociologist, and originator of the theory of communication ethics; he won a 2004 Kyoto Prize.

Charlie Haden (6 Aug 1937, Shenandoah IA), American jazz bass player.

Zaha Hadid (31 Oct 1950, Baghdad, Iraq), Iraqi-born architect; recipient of the 2004 Pritzker Prize.

Stephen (John) Hadley (13 Feb 1947, Toledo OH), American security official; US national security advisor from 2005.

Michael W. Hagee (1945, Hampton VA), American military officer; commandant of the US Marine Corps, 2003–06.

Ted (Arthur) Haggard (Pastor Ted; 27 Jun 1956, Delphi IN), American evangelical church leader who resigned from his church position amidst a sexual scandal in 2006.

Hilary Hahn (27 Nov 1979, Lexington VA), American violinist.

Jörg Haider (26 Jan 1950, Bad Giosern, Austria), Austrian ultra-right-wing politician.

Stelios Haji-Ioannou (14 Feb 1967, Athens, Greece), Greek entrepreneur and corporate executive (easyJet and easyGroup).

Donald (Andrew) Hall, Jr. (20 Sep 1928, New Haven CT), American poet, essayist, and critic; US poet laureate, 2006–07.

John L(ewis) Hall (21 Aug 1934, Denver CO), American physicist; corecipient of the 2005 Nobel Prize for Physics.

Tarja (Kaarina) Halonen (24 Dec 1943, Helsinki, Finland), Finnish politician; president from 2000.

Sam Hamill (1943, northern California?), American poet.

Jane Hamilton (13 Jul 1957, Oak Park IL), American novelist.

Han Zheng (April 1954, Cixi, Zhejiang province, China), Chinese politician (Communist); acting secretary of the Shanghai City Committee (mayor) and head of the Shanghai Communist Party Committee from 2006.

Herbie Hancock (Herbert Jeffrey Hancock; 12 Apr 1940, Chicago IL), American jazz keyboardist and composer.

Daniel Handler (pseudonym Lemony Snicket; 28 Feb 1970, San Francisco CA), American children's book author.

Ismail Haniya (1962, Shati refugee camp, Gaza, Egyptian-controlled Gaza Strip), Palestinian politician (Hamas); prime minister of the Palestine Authority, 2006–07.

Tom Hanks (Thomas Jeffrey Hanks; 9 Jul 1956, Concord CA), American film actor and director.

Sean (Patrick) Hannity (30 Dec 1961, New York NY), American conservative commentator and talk-show host.

Hans Adam II (14 Feb 1945, Vaduz, Liechtenstein), Liechtenstein royal; prince of Liechtenstein from 1989.

Theodor W(olfgang) Hänsch (30 Oct 1941, Heidelberg, Germany), German physicist; corecipient of the 2005 Nobel Prize for Physics for work in laser spectroscopy.

Harald V (21 Feb 1937, Skaugum, Norway), Norwegian royal; king from 1991.

Marcia Gay Harden (14 Aug 1959, La Jolla CA), American film actress.

Roy Hargrove (16 Oct 1969, Waco TX), American jazz trumpeter.

Joy Harjo (9 May 1951, Tulsa OK), American poet, musician, and Native American (Muskogee) activist.

Nikolaus Harnoncourt (6 Dec 1929, Berlin, Germany), Austrian conductor, cellist, and viol player; cofounder in the 1950s of the Concentus Musicus Wien, an early-music group.

Stephen (Joseph) Harper (30 Apr 1959, Toronto, ON, Canada), Canadian politician (Conservative); prime minister of Canada from 2006.

Padraig Harrington (31 Aug 1971, Dublin, Ireland), Irish golfer.

Ed(ward Allen) Harris (28 Nov 1950, Englewood NJ), American film and stage actor and director.

Mary Hart (Mary Johanna Harum; 8 Nov 1950, Madison SD), American actress and cohost of *Entertainment Tonight* on TV from 1982.

Harry (Henry Charles Albert David; 15 Sep 1984, London, England), British prince of Wales; son of Charles and Diana, prince and princess of Wales, and third in line to the British throne.

Dominik Hasek (29 Jan 1965, Pardubice, Czechoslovakia [now in the Czech Republic]), Czech ice-hockey goalie.

Robert Hass (1 Mar 1941, San Francisco CA), American poet; US poet laureate, 1995–97; his *Time and Materials* won a 2008 Pulitzer Prize in poetry.

Anne (Jacqueline) Hathaway (12 Nov 1982, Brooklyn NY), American TV and film actress.

Tony Hawk (Anthony Frank Hawk; 12 May 1968, San Diego CA), American professional skateboarder.

Stephen W. Hawking (8 Jan 1942, Oxford, Oxfordshire, England), British theoretical physicist, a specialist in cosmology and quantum gravity.

Issa Hayatou (9 Aug 1945, Garoua), Cameroonian association football (soccer) executive.

Michael (Vincent) Hayden (17 Mar 1945, Pittsburgh PA), American director of the National Security Agency, 1999–2005, and director of the CIA from 2006.

Salma Hayek (Jiménez) (2 Sep 1966, Coatzacoalcos, Veracruz, Mexico), Mexican-born actress.

Roy Haynes (13 Mar 1926, Roxbury, Boston MA), American jazz drummer and bandleader.

Todd Haynes (2 Jan 1961, Los Angeles CA), American film director, producer, and screenwriter.

Seamus (Justin) Heaney (13 Apr 1939, near Castledawson, County Londonderry, Northern Ireland), Irish poet; recipient of the 1995 Nobel Prize for Literature.

Chad Hedrick (17 Apr 1977, Spring TX), American champion inline and speed skater.

Hugh M. Hefner (9 Apr 1926, Chicago IL), American magazine publisher (*Playboy*).

Katherine (Marie) Heigl (24 Nov 1978, Washington DC), American model and film actress.

Dave Heineman (David Eugene Heineman; 12 May 1948, Falls City NE), American politician (Republican); governor of Nebraska from 2005.

Michael Heller (Michal Heller; 12 Mar 1936, Tarnow, Poland), Polish cosmologist and Roman Catholic priest; recipient of the 2008 Templeton Prize.

Justine Henin (1 Jun 1982, Liège, Belgium), Belgian tennis player who retired in 2008.

Henri (16 Apr 1955, Château de Betzdorf, Luxembourg), Luxembourgian grand duke of Luxembourg from 2000.

(Charles) Brad(ford) Henry (10 Jun 1963, Shawnee OK), American politician (Democrat); governor of Oklahoma from 2003.

Thierry (Daniel) Henry (17 Aug 1977, Châtillon, near Paris, France), French association football (soccer) player.

Seymour M(yron) Hersh (8 Apr 1937, Chicago IL), American investigative reporter and writer.

Mohamud Muse Hersi (?, ?), Somali general; president of the secessionist republic of Puntland from 2005.

Jacques Herzog (19 Apr 1950, Basel, Switzerland), Swiss architect; corecipient of the 2001 Pritzker Prize and of a Praemium Imperiale in 2007.

Lleyton Hewitt (24 Feb 1981, Adelaide, SA, Australia), Australian tennis player.

Rosalyn Higgins (Rosalyn Cohen; 2 Jun 1937, London, England), British jurist; president of the International Court of Justice from 2006.

Tommy Hilfiger (Thomas Jacob Hilfiger; 24 Mar 1951, Elmira NY), American fashion designer.

Faith Hill (Audrey Faith Perry; 21 Sep 1967, Jackson MS), American country singer.

Julia Butterfly Hill (18 Feb 1974, Mount Vernon MO), American environmental activist.

Tony Hillerman (27 May 1925, Sacred Heart OK), American mystery writer.

Rick Hillier (Richard J. Hillier; 1955, Campbellton, NF, Canada), Canadian general; chief of defense staff, 2005–08.

Paris Hilton (17 Feb 1981, New York NY), American heiress and socialite.

Sam(uel Archibald Anthony) Hinds (27 Dec 1943, Mahaicony, British Guiana [now Guyana]?), Guyanese politician; president in 1997 and prime minister, 1992–97, 1997–99, and again from 1999.

Emile (Davenport) Hirsch (13 Mar 1985, Palms CA), American film actor.

Damien Hirst (1965, Bristol, England), British artist.

Christopher Hitchens (26 Apr 1949, Portsmouth, England), American cultural and political critic and journalist.

Stanley Ho (Ho Hung-sun; 25 Nov 1921, Hong Kong), Macanese gaming magnate and multibillionaire.

Susan Hockfield (1951, Chicago IL), American neuroscientist; president of the Massachusetts Institute of Technology from 2004.

David Hockney (9 Jul 1937, Bradford, Yorkshire, England), British painter, draftsman, printmaker, photographer, and stage designer.

John (Henry) Hoeven III (13 Mar 1957, Bismarck ND), American politician (Republican); governor of North Dakota from 2000.

James P(hillip) Hoffa (19 May 1941, Detroit MI), American labor leader; president of the International Brotherhood of Teamsters from 1999.

Dustin Hoffman (8 Aug 1937, Los Angeles CA), American film and stage actor.

Philip Seymour Hoffman (23 Jul 1967, Fairport NY), American stage and film actor and theater director.

Hulk Hogan (Terry Gene Bollea; 11 Aug 1953, Augusta GA), American professional wrestler and actor.

Katie (Noelle) Holmes (18 Dec 1978, Toledo OH), American TV and film actress.

(Philip) Anthony Hopkins (31 Dec 1937, Margam, West Glamorgan, Wales), British film and stage actor.

Nick Hornby (17 Apr 1957, Redhill, Surrey, England), British novelist and journalist.

Khaled Hosseini (4 Mar 1965, Kabul, Afghanistan), Afghan-born American novelist.

Whitney (Elizabeth) Houston (9 Aug 1963, Newark NJ), American pop singer and film actress.

Ron Howard (1 Mar 1954, Duncan OK), American TV and film actor and director.

Terrence (Dashon) Howard (11 Mar 1969, Chicago IL), American TV and film actor.

Daniel Walker Howe (1937, Ogden UT), American historian and professor whose *What Hath God Wrought* won the 2008 Pulitzer Prize for history.

Hu Jintao (25 Dec 1942, Jixi, Anhui province, China), Chinese statesman; general secretary of the Communist Party of China, vice chairman of the Military Commission, and president of China from 2003.

Hu Shuli (1953, Beijing, China), Chinese journalist and editor; cofounder of *Caijin*, a business magazine.

Berthold Huber (15 Feb 1950, Ulm, West Germany [now in Germany]), German corporate executive; chairman of IG Metall from 2007.

Jan Huber (Johannes Huber; 1947?, The Netherlands), Dutch international official; executive secretary of the Antarctic Treaty system from 2004.

Mike Huckabee (Michael Dale Huckabee; 24 Aug 1955, Hope AR), American politician (Republican); governor of Arkansas, 1996–2007.

Jennifer (Kate) Hudson (12 Sep 1981, Chicago IL), American soul and gospel singer and film actress; recipient of the 2006 best supporting actress Academy Award.

Arianna Huffington (Ariana Stassinopoulos; 1950, Athens, Greece), Greek-born American political commentator, syndicated newspaper columnist, and author.

Felicity (Kendall) Huffman (9 Dec 1962, Bedford NY), American TV and film actress.

Robert (Studley Forrest) Hughes (28 Jul 1938, Sydney, Australia), Australian art critic and author.

Hun Sen (4 Apr 1951, Kompong Chom province, Cambodia), Cambodian politician and leader of the government from 1985.

Helen (Elizabeth) Hunt (15 Jun 1963, Culver City CA), American film and TV actress.

Holly Hunter (20 Mar 1958, Conyers GA), American film actress.

Jon M(eade) Huntsman, Jr. (26 Mar 1960, Palo Alto CA), American businessman (Huntsman Family Holdings), politician (Republican), and philanthropist; governor of Utah from 2005.

Lubomyr Cardinal Husar (26 Feb 1933, Lwow, Poland [now Lviv, Ukraine]), Ukrainian Greek Catholic Church leader; patriarch of Lviv from 2000 and cardinal from 2001.

Nicholas Hytner (7 May 1956, Didsbury, near Manchester, England), British theater director; artistic director of the National Theatre from 2003.

Ice Cube (O'Shea Jackson; 15 Jun 1969), American rapper, songwriter, and actor.

Ice-T (Tracy Morrow; 16 Feb 1958, Newark NJ), American hip-hop artist and actor.

Apisai Ielemia (19 Aug 1955, Vaitupu?, British Ellice Islands [now Tuvalu]), Tuvaluan politician; prime minister from 2006.

Ieronymos II (Ioannis Liapis; 1938, Oinofyta, Greece), Greek Orthodox churchman; archbishop of Athens and all Greece from 2008.

Ekmeleddin Ihsanoglu (26 Dec 1943, Cairo, Egypt), Turkish professor of history; secretary-general of the Organisation of the Islamic Conference from 2005.

Ratu Josefa Iloilo(vatu Uluivuda) (29 Dec 1920, Taveuni island, Fiji), Fijian politician; president from 2000.

Toomas Hendrik Ilves (26 Dec 1953, Stockholm, Sweden), Estonian diplomat; president from 2006.

Jeffrey R. Immelt (19 Feb 1956, Cincinnati OH), American corporate executive and CEO of the General Electric Co. from 2001.

Hubert (Alexander) Ingraham (4 Aug 1947, Pine Ridge, Bahamas), Bahamian politician; prime minister, 1992–2002 and again from 2007.

Hiroo Inokuchi (3 Feb 1927, Hiroshima, Japan), Japanese chemist, a specialist in the electrical conductivity of organic materials; recipient of a 2007 Kyoto Prize.

José Miguel Insulza (2 Jun 1943, Santiago, Chile), Chilean government official (Socialist); secretary-general of the Organization of American States from 2005.

Bill Irwin (11 Apr 1950, Santa Monica CA), American actor and choreographer.

Walter Isaacson (20 May 1952, New Orleans LA), American corporate executive; chairman and CEO of the Cable News Network (CNN), 2001–03, and president and CEO of the Aspen Institute from 2003.

Riduan Isamuddin (Encep Nurjaman; "Hambali"; 4 Apr 1966, Pamokolan, West Java, Indonesia), Indonesian militant and leader of the Jemaah Islamiya group.

Kazuo Ishiguro (8 Nov 1954, Nagasaki, Japan), Japanese-born British novelist.

Shintaro Ishihara (30 Sep 1932, Kobe, Japan), Japanese author and nationalist politician; governor of Tokyo from 1999.

Allen (Ezail) Iverson (7 Jun 1975, Hampton VA), American basketball player.

James (Francis) Ivory (7 Jun 1928, Berkeley CA), American film producer.

Hugh (Michael) Jackman (12 Oct 1968, Sydney, NSW, Australia), Australian film actor.

Alan (Eugene) Jackson (17 Oct 1958, Newnan GA), American country-and-western singer and guitarist.

Alphonso (Roy) Jackson (9 Sep 1945, Marshall TX), American politician; US secretary of housing and urban development, 2004–08.

Janet (Damita Jo) Jackson (16 May 1966, Gary IN), American singer and film and TV actress.

Jesse (Louis) Jackson (8 Oct 1941, Greenville SC), American civil rights leader, minister, and politician.

Michael (Joseph) Jackson (29 Aug 1958, Gary IN), American singer, songwriter, and dancer.

Peter Jackson (31 Oct 1961, Pukerua Bay, New Zealand), New Zealand film director and producer.

Phil(ip Douglas) Jackson (17 Sep 1945, Deer Lodge MT), American basketball player and coach.

Samuel L(eroy) Jackson (21 Dec 1948, Washington DC), American film actor.

Marc Jacobs (9 Apr 1963, New York NY), American fashion designer.

Bharrat Jagdeo (23 Jan 1964, Unity village, Demarara, Guyana), Guyanese politician; president from 1999.

Mick Jagger (Michael Philip Jagger; 26 Jul 1943, Dartford, Kent, England), British rock musician and lead singer for the Rolling Stones.

Helmut Jahn (4 Jan 1940, Nürnberg, Germany), German-born architect.

Zsuzsanna Jakab (17 May 1951, Hungary), Hungarian epidemiologist; the first director of the European Centre for Disease Prevention and Control (ECDC), from 2005.

LeBron James (30 Dec 1984, Akron OH), American professional basketball player.

Judith (Ann) Jamison (10 May 1944, Philadelphia PA), American dancer and choreographer (American Dance Theater).

Yahya Jammeh (Alphonse Jamus Jebulai Jammeh; 25 May 1965, Kanilai village, Gambia), Gambian politician; president from 1994.

Janez Jansa (Ivan Jansa; 17 Sep 1958, Ljubljana, Yugoslavia [now in Slovenia]), Slovenian defense official, politician (Social Democrat), and prime minister from 2004.

Mariss Jansons (14 Jan 1943, Riga, Latvia), Latvian-born American director; conductor of the Royal Concertgebouw Orchestra of Amsterdam from 2004.

Jim Jarmusch (22 Jan 1953, Akron OH), American avant-garde filmmaker.

Keith Jarrett (8 May 1945, Allentown PA), American jazz pianist, composer, and saxophonist.

Neeme Järvi (7 Jun 1937, Tallinn, Estonia), Estonian conductor; music director of the Detroit Symphony Orchestra, 1990–2005, and of the New Jersey Symphony Orchestra from 2005, and chief conductor of the Hague Philharmonic from 2005.

Jay-Z (Shawn Corey Carter; 4 Dec 1970, Brooklyn NY), American rapper.

Michaëlle Jean (6 Sep 1957, Port-au-Prince, Haiti), Haitian-born Canadian journalist; governor-general of Canada from 2005.

Katharine Jefferts Schori (26 Mar 1954, Pensacola FL), American church leader; presiding bishop of the US Episcopal Church from 2006.

(Philip) Michael Jeffery (12 Dec 1937, Wiluna, WA, Australia), Australian military officer; governor-general of Australia from 2003.

Derek (Sanderson) Jeter (26 Jun 1974, Pequannock NJ), American baseball player.

Ha Jin (Xuefei Jin; 21 Feb 1956, Jinzhou, Liaoning province, China), Chinese American novelist.

Bobby Jindal (Piyush Jindal; 10 Jun 1971, Baton Rouge LA), American politician (Republican); governor of Louisiana from 2008.

Steven (Paul) Jobs (24 Feb 1955, San Francisco CA), American inventor and corporate executive; cofounder of Apple Computer and CEO from 1997.

Scarlett Johansson (22 Nov 1984, New York NY), American film actress.

Elton John (Reginald Kenneth Dwight; 25 Mar 1947, Pinner, Middlesex, England), British singer, composer, and pianist.

Jasper Johns (15 May 1930, Augusta GA), American painter and graphic artist, a pioneer of Pop art.

Boris Johnson (Alexander Boris de Pfeffel Johnson; 19 Jun 1964, New York NY), American-born British journalist, editor (*Spectator*), and MP (Conservative); mayor of London from 2008.

Denis Johnson (1949, Munich, West Germany [now in Germany]), American novelist, short-story writer, and poet; his *Tree of Smoke* was a National Book Award winner in 2007.

Dwayne (Douglas) Johnson ("The Rock"; 2 May 1972, Hayward CA), American professional wrestler-turned-actor.

Robert L. Johnson (8 Apr 1946, Hickory MS), American entrepreneur; founder (1980) of BET (Black Entertainment Television) and owner of the Charlotte Bobcats NBA team and Charlotte Sting WNBA team.

Stephen L. Johnson (21 Mar 1951, Washington DC), American government official; director of the Environmental Protection Agency from 2005.

Ellen Johnson-Sirleaf (29 Oct 1938, Monrovia, Liberia), Liberian government and international official; president from 2006.

Angelina Jolie (Angelina Jolie Voight; 4 Jun 1975, Los Angeles CA), American film actress.

Bill T. Jones (William Tass Jones; 15 Feb 1952, Steuben county NY), American dancer, choreographer, and director.

Cherry Jones (21 Nov 1956, Paris TN), American stage actress.

Edward P(aul) Jones (5 Oct 1950, Washington DC), American short-story writer and novelist.

James Earl Jones (Todd Jones; 17 Jan 1931, Arkabutla MS), American actor.

Marion Jones (12 Oct 1975, Los Angeles CA), American sprinter and long jumper.

Norah Jones (30 Mar 1979, New York NY), American jazz-pop vocalist and pianist.

Quincy (Delight) Jones, Jr. (14 Mar 1933, Chicago IL), American jazz and pop arranger, composer, and producer.

Tommy Lee Jones (15 Sep 1946, San Saba TX), American actor.

Michael (Jeffrey) Jordan (17 Feb 1963, Brooklyn NY), American basketball player; he was voted ESPN's Athlete of the Century and is believed by many to be the best basketball player in history.

Juan Carlos I (Juan Carlos Alfonso Victor María de Borbón y Borbón; 5 Jan 1938, Rome, Italy), Spanish royal; king from 1975.

Juanes (Juan Estebán Aristizábal Vásquez; 9 Aug 1972, Medellín, Colombia), Colombian singer, songwriter, and guitarist.

Ashley Judd (Ashley Tyler Ciminella; 19 Apr 1968, Granada Hills CA), American film actress.

Anerood Jugnauth (29 Mar 1930, Mauritius), Mauritian politician; prime minister, 1982–95 and 2000–03, and president from 2003.

Jean-Claude Juncker (9 Dec 1954, Rédange-sur-Attert, Luxembourg), Luxembourgian politician; prime minister from 1995.

Joseph Kabila (4 Jun 1971, Sud-Kivu province, Democratic Republic of the Congo), Congolese politician; president of the Democratic Republic of the Congo from 2001.

Lech Kaczynski (18 Jun 1949, Warsaw, Poland), Polish politician (Law and Justice); president from 2005.

Ismail Kadare (28 Jan 1938, Gjirokastër, Albania), Albanian novelist and poet; recipient of the first Man Booker International Prize, in 2005.

Paul Kagame (23 Oct 1957, Gitarama, Ruanda-Urundi [now Rwanda]), Rwandan politician; president from 2000.

Dahir Riyale Kahin (1952), Somali president of the secessionist Republic of Somaliland from 2002.

Robert E(lliot) Kahn (23 Dec 1938, Brooklyn NY), American computer scientist, a key developer of the network that became the Internet; recipient of a Japan Prize in 2008.

Tim(othy Michael) Kaine (26 Feb 1958, St. Paul MN), American politician (Democrat); governor of Virginia from 2006.

Ingvar Kamprad (1926, Småland province, Sweden), Swedish businessman; founder of the home-furnishing company IKEA.

Hiroo Kanamori (17 Oct 1936, Tokyo, Japan), Japanese seismologist; recipient of a 2007 Kyoto Prize.

Radovan Karadzic (19 Jun 1945, Petnjica, Yugoslavia [now in Montenegro]), Bosnian Serb politician and president of Republika Srpska (Bosnia and Herzegovina), 1992–96; he was wanted as a war criminal and was arrested in 2008.

Kostas Karamanlis (Konstantinos Karamanlis; 14 Sep 1956, Athens, Greece), Greek politician (New Democracy); prime minister from 2004.

Donna Karan (Donna Faske; 2 Oct 1948, Forest Hills NY), American fashion designer.

Islam Karimov (30 Jan 1938, Samarkand, USSR [now in Uzbekistan]), Uzbek politician; president from 1990.

Mel(vin Alan) Karmazin (24 Aug 1943, New York NY), American media executive; CEO of Sirius XM Radio (formerly Sirius Satellite Radio) from 2004.

Hamid Karzai (24 Dec 1957, Karz, Afghanistan), Afghan statesman; president of Afghanistan from 2001.

Garry Kasparov (Garri Kimovich Kasparov; original name Garri or Harry Weinstein; 13 Apr 1963, Baku, USSR [now in Azerbaijan]), Azerbaijani-born Russian chess champion of the world, 1985–2000.

Jeffrey Katzenberg (21 Dec 1950, New York NY), American film producer and a cofounder (1994) of DreamWorks SKG.

Nobuhiko Kawamoto (3 Mar 1936, Tokyo, Japan), Japanese corporate executive; president of Honda Motor Co., Ltd., 1990–98.

Naomi Kawase (30 May 1969, Nara, Japan), Japanese film director.

Diane Keaton (Diane Hall; 5 Jan 1946, Los Angeles CA), American actress and director.

Keb' Mo' (Kevin Moore; 3 Oct 1951, Los Angeles CA), American blues musician.

Garrison Keillor (Gary Edward Keillor; 7 Aug 1942, Anoka MN), American humorist and writer best known for his long-running radio variety show, *A Prairie Home Companion.*

Toby Keith (Toby Keith Covel; 8 Jul 1961, Clinton OK), American country-and-western singer.

Bill Keller (18 Jan 1949), American journalist; managing editor of the *New York Times*, 1997–2001, and executive editor from 2003.

Tim(othy J.) Keller (1950, Pennsylvania), American churchman and author; founding pastor (1989) of Redeemer Presbyterian Church, New York City.

David E. Kelley (4 Apr 1956, Waterville ME), American TV producer and screenwriter.

Ellsworth Kelly (31 May 1923, Newburgh NY), American painter and sculptor.

R. Kelly (Robert S. Kelly; 8 Jan 1969, Chicago IL), American R&B performer.

William M. Kelso (30 Mar 1941, Chicago IL), American archaeologist; director of archaeology for the Jamestown Rediscovery Project.

Yashar Kemal (Kemal Sadik Gogceli; 1922, Hemite, Turkey), Turkish novelist of Kurdish descent.

Dirk (Arthur) Kempthorne (29 Oct 1951, San Diego CA), American politician (Republican); governor of Idaho, 1999–2006; US secretary of the interior from 2006.

Thomas (Michael) Keneally (pseudonym William Coyle; 7 Oct 1935, Sydney, Australia), Australian novelist.

Anthony (McCleod) Kennedy (23 Jul 1936, Sacramento CA), American jurist; associate justice of the US Supreme Court from 1988.

Edward M(oore) Kennedy (22 Feb 1932, Brookline MA), American politician (Democrat); senator from Massachusetts from 1962.

Lee Kernaghan (15 Apr 1964, Corryong, VIC, Australia), Australian country singer; he was named Australian of the Year for 2008.

John F(orbes) Kerry (11 Dec 1943, Fitzsimmons Army Hospital [now in Aurora CO]), American politician (Democrat) and senator from Massachusetts from 1985; the Democratic candidate for president in 2004.

Alan (Lee) Keyes (7 Aug 1950, New York NY), American diplomat, radio commentator, and conservative politician.

Alicia Keys (Alicia Augello Cook; 25 Jan 1981, New York NY), American R&B singer and pianist.

Cheb Khaled (Khaled Hadj Brahim; 29 Feb 1960, Sidi-El-Houri, near Oran, French Algeria), Algerian *rai* performer.

Hamad ibn Isa al-Khalifah (28 Jan 1950, Bahrain), Bahraini sheikh; emir and chief of state from 1999; he proclaimed himself king in 2002.

Zalmay (Mamozy) Khalilzad (22 Mar 1951, Mazar-i-Sharif, Afghanistan), Afghan-born American diplomat; ambassador to Afghanistan, 2003–05, to Iraq, 2005–07, and to the United Nations, 2007–08.

(Seretse Khama) Ian Khama (27 Feb 1953, Bechuanaland [now Botswana]), Botswanan military officer; president from 2008.

Hojatolislam Sayyed Ali Khamenei (15 Jul 1939, Meshed, Iran), Iranian Shiʿite clergyman and politician who served as president, 1981–89, and as that country's *rahbar*, or leader, from 1989.

Mikhail (Borisovich) Khodorkovsky (26 Jun 1963, Moscow, USSR [now in Russia]), Russian businessman, the imprisoned former billionaire head of Yukos Oil Co.

Abbas Kiarostami (22 Jun 1940, Tehran, Iran), Iranian film director.

Mwai Kibaki (15 Nov 1931, Gatuyaini village, Central province, Kenya), Kenyan politician; president from 2002.

Angelique Kidjo (14 Jul 1960, Ouidah, Dahomey [now Benin]), Beninese pop singer.

Nicole (Mary) Kidman (20 Jun 1967, Honolulu HI), American-born Australian actress.

Anselm Kiefer (8 Mar 1945, Donaueschingen, Germany), German Neo-Expressionist painter.

Jakaya (Mrisho) Kikwete (7 Oct 1950, Msoga, British Tanganyika [now in Tanzania]), Tanzanian military officer and government official; president from 2005.

Val (Edward) Kilmer (31 Dec 1959, Los Angeles CA), American film actor.

Jeong H. Kim (1961, Seoul, South Korea), Korean-born American electronics industry executive who was founder (1992) of Yurie Systems, Inc., and president of Alcatel-Lucent's Bell Labs from 2005.

Kim Jong Il (16 Feb 1941, near Khabarovsk, USSR [now in Russia]), North Korean leader and successor to his father, Kim Il-Sung, as general secretary of the Central Committee of the Worker's Party of Korea (North Korea) from 1997.

Jimmy Kimmel (13 Nov 1967, Brooklyn NY), American comedian and TV talk-show host.

Jamaica Kincaid (Elaine Potter Richardson; 25 May 1949, St. Johns, Antigua), Antiguan American writer.

B.B. King (Riley B. King; 16 Sep 1925, Itta Bena, near Indianola MS), American blues guitarist and singer.

Carole King (Carole Klein; 9 Feb 1942, Brooklyn NY), American pop singer and songwriter.

Larry King (Lawrence Harvey Zeiger; 19 Nov 1933, Brooklyn NY), American TV journalist.

Stephen (Edward) King (pseudonym Richard Bachman; 21 Sep 1947, Portland ME), American writer of novels combining horror, fantasy, and science fiction.

Stephenson King (13 Nov 1958, St. Lucia?), West Indian politician (United Workers Party); prime minister of Saint Lucia from 2007.

Galway Kinnell (1 Feb 1927, Providence RI), American poet.

Michael Kinsley (9 Mar 1951, Detroit MI), American political commentator and editor.

Gediminas Kirkilas (30 Aug 1951, Vilnius, USSR [now in Lithuania]), Lithuanian politician; prime minister from 2006.

Philippe Kirsch (1 Apr 1947, Namur, Belgium), Belgian-born Canadian jurist; president of the International Criminal Court from 2003.

Vaclav Klaus (19 Jun 1941, Prague, Czechoslovakia [now in the Czech Republic]), Czech politician who served as prime minister, 1992–97, and president for one month in 1993 and again from 2003.

Calvin (Richard) Klein (19 Nov 1942, Bronx NY), American fashion designer.

August Kleinzahler (1949, Jersey City NJ), American poet.

Carolina Evelyn Klüft (2 Feb 1983, Sandhult, Sweden), Swedish track and field athlete.

Heidi Klum (1 Jun 1973, Bergisch Gladbach, West Germany [now in Germany]), German supermodel.

Robbie Knievel (Robert Edward Knievel; "Kaptain"; 7 May 1962, Butte MT), American motorcycle stunt performer.

Bobby Knight (Robert Montgomery Knight; 25 Oct 1940, Massillon OH), American collegiate basketball coach who retired in 2008 as the men's coach with the most wins in history.

Gladys Knight (28 May 1944, Atlanta GA), American R&B singer.

Keira Knightley (26 Mar 1985, Teddington, London, England), British film actress.

Ko Un (1 Aug 1933, Kunsan, North Cholla province, Japanese-occupied Korea [now in South Korea]), Korean poet.

Samuel Kobia (20 Mar 1947, Miathene, British Kenya), Kenyan Methodist church leader; general secretary of the World Council of Churches from 2004.

Robert (Sedraki) Kocharyan (31 Aug 1954, Stepanakert, Nagorno-Karabakh, USSR [now in Azerbaijan]), Armenian politician; president, 1998–2008.

Horst Köhler (22 Feb 1943, Skierbieszow, Poland), German international economic official; president of Germany from 2004.

Girija Prasad Koirala (1925, Tadi, Bihar, British India), Nepalese prime minister, 1991–94, 1998–99, 2000–01, and 2006–08, and acting head of state, 2007–08.

Yusef Komunyakaa (29 Apr 1947, Bogalusa LA), American poet.

Masahiko Komura (3 Mar 1942, Yamaguchi prefecture, Japan), Japanese diplomat and politician; foreign minister, 1998–99 and again from 2007.

Alpha Oumar Konaré (2 Feb 1946, Kayes, French West Africa [now in Mali]), Malian statesman; president of Mali, 1992–2002, and chairman of the Commission of the African Union, 2003–08.

Maxim Kontsevich (25 Aug 1964, Khimki, USSR [now in Russia]), Russian mathematician, a specialist in algebraic geometry and algebraic topology; recipient of the Fields Medal in 1998 and a Crafoord Prize in 2008.

Joseph Kony (1964?, Odek, Uganda), Ugandan rebel commander; leader of the Lord's Resistance Army.

Tim Koogle (1951?, Alexandria VA), American corporate executive; CEO of Yahoo! Inc., 1995–2001.

Rem Koolhaas (17 Nov 1944, Rotterdam, Netherlands), Dutch architect; recipient of the 2000 Pritzker Prize.

Jeff Koons (21 Jan 1955, York PA), American Pop-art painter and sculptor.

Dean (Ray) Koontz (9 Jul 1945, Everett PA), American novelist.

Ted Kooser (Theodore Kooser; 25 Apr 1939, Ames IA), American poet; US poet laureate, 2004–06.

Ernest Bai Koroma (2 Oct 1953, Makeni, British Sierra Leone), Sierra Leonean politician; president from 2007.

Michael (David) Kors (Karl Anderson, Jr.; 1959, Merrick, Long Island NY), American fashion designer.

Vojislav Kostunica (24 Mar 1944, Belgrade, Yugoslavia [now in Serbia]), Serbian politician; president of Yugoslavia, 2000–03; prime minister of Serbia, 2004–08.

Bernard Kouchner (1 Nov 1939, Avignon, France), French foreign minister from 2007.

Lansana Kouyaté (15 Jul 1950, Koba, French West Africa [now in Guinea]), Guinean diplomat and statesman; prime minister, 2007–08.

Jon Krakauer (12 Apr 1954, Brookline MA), American author of nonfiction.

Vladimir (Borisovich) Kramnik (25 Jun 1975, Tuapse, USSR [now in Russia]), Russian chess grand master.

Alison Krauss (23 Jul 1971, Decatur IL), American bluegrass fiddle player and singer.

Lenny Kravitz (26 May 1964, Brooklyn NY), American rock musician.

Gidon Kremer (27 Feb 1947, Riga, USSR [now in Latvia]), Latvian-born violinist and conductor.

William Kristol (23 Dec 1952, New York NY), American editor and columnist.

Dennis J. Kucinich (8 Oct 1946, Cleveland OH), American politician (Democrat); mayor of Cleveland, 1977–79; congressman from Ohio from 1997.

John (Kofi Agyekum) Kufuor (8 Dec 1938, Kumisi, Gold Coast [now Ghana]), Ghanaian politician; president from 2001.

Ted Kulongoski (Theodore R. Kulongoski; 5 Nov 1940 Missouri), American politician (Democrat); governor of Oregon from 2003.

Yayoi Kusama (22 Mar 1929, Matsumoto city, Nagano prefecture, Japan), Japanese artist; recipient of a 2006 Praemium Imperiale.

Tony Kushner (16 Jul 1956, New York NY), American playwright.

Andrew Lack (16 May 1947, New York NY), American communications executive; chairman of Sony BMG Music Entertainment (formerly Sony Music Entertainment Corp.), 2003–06.

Christine Lagarde (1 Jan 1956, Paris, France), French lawyer; minister of finance from 2007.

Emeril (John) Lagasse (15 Oct 1959, Fall River MA), American TV chef, restaurateur, and media personality.

Karl Lagerfeld (10 Sep 1938, Hamburg, Germany), German-born French fashion designer.

Miroslav Lajcak (20 Mar 1963, Poprad, Czechoslovakia [now in Slovakia]), Slovak diplomat and government official; International High Representative in Bosnia and Herzegovina from 2007.

Guy Laliberté (1959, Quebec city, QC, Canada), Canadian circus performer and founder of Cirque de Soleil.

Edward S. Lampert (19 Jul 1962, Roslyn NY), American business executive and chairman of ESL Investments and Kmart Holding Corp.

Pascal Lamy (8 Apr 1947, Levallois-Perret, Paris, France), French financial and government official; EU trade commissioner, 1999–2004, and director-general of the World Trade Organization from 2005.

Floyd Landis (14 Oct 1975, Farmersville PA), American cyclist who won the 2006 Tour de France but was later disqualified.

Diane Lane (22 Jan 1965, New York NY), American film actress.

Nathan Lane (Joseph Lane; 3 Feb 1956, Jersey City NJ), American stage and film actor.

David Lang (8 Jan 1957, Los Angeles CA), American opera composer whose *The Little Match Girl Passion* won the 2008 Pulitzer Prize for music.

Helmut Lang (10 Mar 1956, Vienna, Austria), Austrian fashion designer.

André Lange (28 Jun 1983, Ilmenau, East Germany [now in Germany]), German bobsled driver.

Frank Langella (1 Jan 1940, Bayonne NJ), American film actor.

Sherry Lansing (Sherry Lee Heimann; 31 Jul 1944, Chicago IL), American actress and film executive.

Anthony M. LaPaglia (31 Jan 1959, Adelaide, SA, Australia), Australian film and TV actor.

Lewis H. Lapham (8 Jan 1935, San Francisco CA), American liberal political commentator and author; editor of *Harper's Magazine*, 1976–81 and 1983–2006.

Lyndon (Hermyle) LaRouche, Jr. (8 Sep 1922, Rochester NH), American economist, populist politician, and perennial presidential candidate.

Mark Latham (28 Feb 1961, Sydney, Australia), Australian politician (Labor) and party leader.

Matt(hew Todd) Lauer (30 Dec 1957, New York NY), American TV journalist and news anchor.

Ralph Lauren (Ralph Lipschitz; 14 Oct 1939, New York NY), American fashion designer.

Hugh Laurie (James Hugh Calum Laurie; 11 Jun 1959, Oxford, England), British TV and film actor.

Avril (Ramona) Lavigne (27 Sep 1984, Napanee, ON, Canada), Canadian pop singer.

Sergey (Viktorovich) Lavrov (21 Mar 1950, Moscow, USSR [now in Russia]), Russian politician; foreign minister from 2004.

Jude Law (29 Dec 1972, Blackheath, London, England), British stage and screen actor.

Martin Lawrence (16 Apr 1965, Frankfurt am Main, West Germany [now in Germany]), American TV actor and comedian.

Nigella (Lucy) Lawson (6 Jan 1960), British cook and author of food-related books.

John Le Carré (David John Moore Cornwell; 19 Oct 1931, Poole, Dorset, England), English spy novelist.

Ursula K(roeber) Le Guin (21 Oct 1929, Berkeley CA), American science-fiction and fantasy writer.

Meave Leakey (28 Jul 1942, London, England), British-born Kenyan paleoanthropologist.

Richard (Erskine Frere) Leakey (19 Dec 1944, Nairobi, Kenya), Kenyan physical anthropologist, paleontologist, conservationist, and politician.

Michael O. Leavitt (11 Feb 1951, Cedar City UT), American politician (Republican) and official; governor of Utah, 1993–2003, EPA director, 2003–05, and US secretary of heath and human services from 2005.

Matt LeBlanc (25 Jul 1967, Newton MA), American TV actor.

Ang Lee (23 Oct 1954, P'ing-Tung county, Taiwan), Taiwanese-born film director.

Jason (Michael) Lee (25 Apr 1970, Orange CA), American skateboarder and film and TV actor.

Spike Lee (Shelton Lee; 20 Mar 1957, Atlanta GA), American film director.

Stan Lee (Stanley Martin Lieber; 28 Dec 1922, New York NY), American comic-book artist; creator of Spider-Man and other superheroes.

Lee Hsien Loong (10 Feb 1952, Singapore), Singaporean politician and economic expert; prime minister from 2004.

Lee Kun Hee (9 Jan 1942, Uiryung, Japanese-occupied Korea [now in South Korea]), South Korean corporate executive; chairman of the Samsung Group, 1987–2008.

Lee Myung-bak (19 Dec 1941, Osaka, Japan), South Korean politician (Grand National Party); mayor of Seoul, 2002–06, and president of South Korea from 2008.

John Leguizamo (22 Jul 1964, Bogotá, Colombia), Colombian-born American comedian and actor.

Dennis Lehane (4 Aug 1966, Dorchester, Boston MA), American crime novelist.

Jim Lehrer (James C. Lehrer; 19 May 1934, Wichita KS), American TV journalist and author.

Annie Leibovitz (Anna-Lou Leibovitz; 2 Oct 1949, Westbury CT), American portrait photographer and photojournalist.

Jean Lemierre (6 Jun 1950, Sainte Adresse, France), French international banking executive and president of the European Bank for Reconstruction and Development from 2000.

Jay Leno (James Douglas Muir Leno; 28 Apr 1950, Short Hills NJ), American comedian and TV talk-show host.

Robert Lepage (12 Dec 1957, Quebec, QC, Canada), Canadian actor, director, and playwright.

Doris Lessing (Doris May Thaler; 22 Oct 1919, Kermanshah, Persia [now Bakhtaran, Iran]), British novelist and short-story writer; recipient of the 2007 Nobel Prize for Literature.

Yves (Camille Désiré) Leterme (6 Oct 1960, Werwik, Belgium), Belgian politician (Christian Democratic and Flemish); prime minister from 2008.

Jonathan (Allen) Lethem (19 Feb 1964, Brooklyn NY), American novelist, short-story writer, and essayist.

Letsie III (David Mohato; 17 Jul 1963, Morija, Basutoland [now Lesotho]), Lesotho royal; king of Lesotho, 1990–95 and again from 1996.

David (Michael) Letterman (12 Apr 1947, Indianapolis IN), American TV talk-show host.

Tracy Letts (4 Jul 1965, Tulsa OK), American playwright and actor whose *August: Osage County* won the 2008 Pulitzer Prize for drama.

Simon Asher Levin (22 Apr 1941, Baltimore MD), American biologist who specializes in the application of mathematics to problems in ecology.

James Levine (23 Jun 1943, Cincinnati OH), American conductor and pianist; principal conductor of the Boston Symphony Orchestra from 2004.

Bernard-Henri Lévy (5 Nov 1948, Béni-Saf, French Algeria), Algerian-born French media darling and author of best-selling "enhanced nonfiction" books.

Eugene Levy (17 Dec 1946, Hamilton, ON, Canada), Canadian comic actor and writer.

Kenneth D. Lewis (9 Apr 1947, Meridian MS), American corporate executive; CEO of the Bank of America Corp. from 1999.

Lennox (Claudius) Lewis (2 Sep 1965, West Ham, London, England), British heavyweight boxer.

(Diane) Monique Lhuillier (1971, Cebu, Philippines), American couturier.

Jet Li (Li Lian Jie; 26 Apr 1963, Beijing, China), Chinese-born *wushu* (acrobatic martial arts) champion and film actor.

Li Ka-shing (13 Jun 1928, Chaozhou, Guangdong province, China), Chinese (Hong Kong) corporate executive, chairman of Hutchison Whampoa Ltd. and Cheung Kong Holdings.

Li Ruigang (June 1969, Shanghai, China), Chinese business executive; president of Shanghai Media Group.

Daniel Libeskind (12 May 1946, Lodz, Poland), Polish-born Israeli-American architect.

Abu Yahya al-Libi (1963, Libya), Libyan militant Islamist leader associated with the Libyan Islamic Fighting Group and a top strategist for al-Qaeda.

Niklas (Erik) Lidström (28 Apr 1970, Västerås, Sweden), Swedish ice-hockey defenseman.

Joseph I. Lieberman (24 Feb 1942, Stamford CT), American politician (Independent Democrat); US senator from Connecticut from 1989.

Lil' Kim (Kimberly Denise Jones; 11 Jul 1975, Bedford-Stuyvesant, Brooklyn NY), American hip-hop performer.

Rush Limbaugh (12 Jan 1951, Cape Girardeau MO), American radio talk-show host and conservative commentator.

Linda Lingle (Linda Cutter; 4 Jun 1953, St. Louis MO), American politician (Republican); governor of Hawaii from 2002.

Laura Linney (5 Feb 1964, New York NY), American actress.

John Lithgow (19 Oct 1945, Rochester NY), American film and TV actor.

Liu Chao-shiuan (10 May 1943, Hengyang, Hunan province, China), Taiwanese politician; president of the Executive Yuan (premier) from 2008.

Lucy (Alexis) Liu (2 Dec 1968, Jackson Heights, Queens NY), American TV and film actress.

Nicholas (Joseph Orville) Liverpool (1934, Dominica?, Windward Islands, British West Indies), West Indian politician; president of Dominica from 2003.

Kenneth Livingstone (17 Jun 1945, Lambeth, London, England), British politician (Labour); mayor of London, 2000–08.

Tzipi Livni (Tzipora Malka Livni; 8 Jul 1958, Tel Aviv, Israel), Israeli politician (Kadima); foreign minister of Israel from 2006.

LL Cool J (James Todd Smith; 14 Jan 1968, Queens NY), American hip-hop artist and actor.

Andrew Lloyd Webber (22 Mar 1948, London, England), British composer of stage musicals; recipient of a Praemium Imperiale in 1995 and a 2006 Kennedy Center Honor.

Keith Alan Lockhart (7 Nov 1959, Poughkeepsie NY), American conductor of the Boston Pops from 1993.

Lindsay (Morgan) Lohan (2 Jul 1986, New York NY), American actress and film starlet.

Jonah Tali Lomu (12 May 1975, Auckland, New Zealand), New Zealand rugby winger.

Eva (Jacqueline) Longoria Parker (15 Mar 1975, Corpus Christi TX), American TV actress.

Jennifer Lopez (24 Jul 1970, Bronx NY), American pop singer, actress, and fashion designer.

Andrés Manuel López Obrador (13 Nov 1953, Tepetitán, Mexico), Mexican politician (Party of the Democratic Revolution); head of government of the Federal District (mayor of Mexico City), 2000–05; unsuccessful candidate for president in 2006.

Peter Löscher (17 Sep 1957, Villach, Austria), Austrian corporate executive; president and CEO of Siemens AG from 2007.

Trent Lott (9 Oct 1941, Grenada MS), American politician (Republican); senator from Mississippi, 1989–2007, Senate leader, 1996–2003, and Senate whip, 1995–96 and again in 2007.

Christian Louboutin (7 Jan 1963, Paris, France), French high-fashion shoe designer.

Joe Lovano (29 Dec 1952, Cleveland OH), American jazz tenor saxophone player, bandleader, and composer.

Henri Loyrette (31 May 1952, Neuilly-sur-Seine, France), French museum curator; director of the Louvre from 2001.

George (Walton) Lucas, Jr. (14 May 1944, Modesto CA), American film producer.

Susan Lucci (23 Dec 1947, Scarsdale NY), American TV soap opera star.

Fernando (Armindo) Lugo (Méndez) (30 May 1951, San Pedro del Paraná, Paraguay), Paraguayan Roman Catholic bishop and missionary; president from 2008.

Baz(mark Anthony) Luhrmann (17 Sep 1962, near Sydney, Australia), Australian film and stage director and producer.

Alyaksandr (Hrygorevich) Lukashenka (30 Aug 1954, Kopys, Vitebsk oblast, Belorussian SSR, USSR [now Belarus]), Belarusian politician; president from 1994.

Luiz Inácio Lula da Silva (27 Oct 1945, Garanhuns, Pernambuco state, Brazil), Brazilian labor leader and politician (Workers Party); president from 2003.

Sidney Lumet (25 Jun 1924, Philadelphia PA), American film, TV, and stage director.

Hilary Lunke (7 Jun 1979, Edina MN), American golfer.

Uri Lupolianski (1951, Haifa, Israel), Israeli politician (United Torah Judaism); mayor of Jerusalem from 2003.

Yury (Mikhaylovich) Luzhkov (21 Sep 1936, Moscow, USSR [now in Russia]), Russian politician (United Russia); mayor of Moscow from 1992.

John (H.) Lynch (25 Nov 1952, Waltham MA), American businessman and politician (Democrat); governor of New Hampshire from 2005.

Yo-Yo Ma (7 Oct 1955, Paris, France), American cellist.

Ma Ying-jeou (Pinyin: Ma Yingjiu; 13 Jul 1950, Hong Kong), Taiwanese politician and government official; mayor of Taipei, 1998–2006, and president from 2008.

Lorin Maazel (6 Mar 1930, Neuilly, France), French-born American conductor and violinist; music director of the New York Philharmonic from 2002.

Gloria (Macaraeg) Macapagal Arroyo (5 Apr 1947, San Juan, Philippines), Philippine politician; president from 2001.

Rodney (Joseph) MacDonald (2 Jan 1972, Inverness, NS, Canada), Canadian fiddle player and politician (Progressive Conservative); premier of Nova Scotia from 2006.

Alistair MacLeod (20 Jul 1936, North Batteford, SK, Canada), Canadian writer.

Madonna (Madonna Louise Veronica Ciccone; 16 Aug 1958, Bay City MI), American singer, songwriter, actress, and entrepreneur.

Tobey Maguire (Tobias Vincent Maguire; 27 Jun 1975, Santa Monica CA), American film actor.

Bill Maher (20 Jan 1956, New York NY), American TV comedian and personality.

Roger Michael Cardinal Mahony (27 Feb 1936, Hollywood CA), American Roman Catholic churchman; archbishop of Los Angeles from 1985 and cardinal from 1991.

Natalie Maines (14 Oct 1974, Lubbock TX), American country vocalist (for the Dixie Chicks).

Mohammed ibn Rashid al-Maktum (1949, Dubai, British Trucial States [now in United Arab Emirates]?), UAE sheikh; crown prince from 1995 and ruler of Dubai from 2006; he is also a noted horse breeder.

Tuilaepa Sailele Malielegaoi (14 Apr 1945, Lepa, Samoa), Samoan politician; prime minister of Samoa from 1998.

Nuri (Kamal) al-Maliki (Jawad al-Maliki; Abu Isra; 1 Jul 1950, near Karbala, Iraq), Iraqi politician (Shiʿite); prime minister of Iraq from 2006.

John (Gavin) Malkovich (9 Dec 1953, Christopher IL), American film actor and filmmaker.

David (George Joseph) Malouf (20 Mar 1934, Brisbane, QLD, Australia), Australian poet and novelist; recipient of the 2000 Neustadt Prize.

David (Alan) Mamet (30 Nov 1947, Chicago IL), American playwright, director, and screenwriter.

Joe Manchin (Joseph Manchin III; 24 Aug 1947, Farmington WV), American businessman and politician (Democrat); governor of West Virginia from 2005.

Nelson (Rolihlahla) Mandela (18 Jul 1918, Umtata, Cape of Good Hope, Union of South Africa), South African black nationalist leader and statesman; he was a political prisoner, 1962–90, president of South Africa (1994–99), and corecipient of the 1993 Nobel Peace Prize.

Winnie Madikizela Mandela (original name Nomzamo Nomandla Winifred Madikizela; original Xhosa name Nkosikazi Nobandle Nomzamo Madikizela; 26 Sep 1934/36, Bizana, Pondoland district, Cape of Good Hope, Union of South Africa), South African social worker and black nationalist leader; second wife of Nelson Mandela.

Peter (Benjamin) Mandelson (21 Oct 1953, London, England), British politician (Labour), cabinet minister, and international official; EU commissioner for trade from 2004.

Barry Manilow (Barry Alan Pincus; 17 Jun 1946, Brooklyn NY), American pop singer and songwriter.

Eli(sha Nelson) Manning (3 Jan 1981, New Orleans LA), American pro football quarterback.

Patrick (Augustus Merving) Manning (17 Aug 1946, San Fernando, Trinidad), Trinidadian politician; prime minister of Trinidad and Tobago, 1991–95 and again from 2001.

Peyton (Williams) Manning (24 Mar 1976, New Orleans LA), American pro football quarterback.

John H. Marburger III (1941?, Staten Island NY), American physicist; presidential science adviser and head of the Office of Science and Technology Policy from 2001.

Brice Marden (15 Oct 1938, Bronxville NY), American minimalist painter and printmaker.

Margrethe II (Margrethe Alexandrine Thorhildur Ingrid; 16 Apr 1940, Copenhagen, Denmark), Danish royal; queen from 1972.

Mariam (Mariam Doumbia; 15 Apr 1958), Malian singer (of Amadou and Mariam).

Mariza (Mariza Nunes; 1974?, Mozambique), Portuguese fado singer.

Mary Ellen Mark (20 Mar 1940, Philadelphia PA), American photojournalist.

Branford Marsalis (26 Aug 1960, Breaux Bridge LA), American jazz saxophonist, bandleader, and producer.

Wynton Marsalis (18 Oct 1961, New Orleans LA), American jazz trumpeter and composer.

Barry J. Marshall (30 Sep 1951, Kalgoorlie, WA, Australia), Australian clinician; corecipient of the 2005 Nobel Prize for Physiology or Medicine.

Yann Martel (25 Jun 1963, Salamanca, Spain), Spanish-born Canadian novelist; recipient of the 2002 Man Booker Prize.

Kevin Martin (14 Dec 1966, Charlotte NC), American politician and chairman of the Federal Communications Commission from 2005.

Steve Martin (14 Aug 1945, Waco TX), American comedic actor, screenwriter, playwright, and author; recipient of a 2007 Kennedy Center Honor.

Mel Martinez (Melquíades Rafael Martínez; 23 Oct 1946, Sagua la Grande, Cuba), Cuban-born American politican and official; US secretary of housing and urban development, 2001–03, senator (Republican) from Florida from 2005, and general chairman of the Republican National Committee in 2007.

Mary (Mary Donaldson; 5 Feb 1972, Hobart, TAS, Australia), Australian-born marketing executive and crown princess of Denmark; wife of Crown Prince Frederik (married 14 May 2004).

Masako (Masako Owada; 9 Dec 1963, Tokyo, Japan), Japanese royal; princess consort of Crown Prince Naruhito (married 9 Jun 1993).

Eric S. Maskin (12 Dec 1950, New York NY), American economist; corecipient of the 2007 Nobel Prize for Economic Sciences for work in mechanism design theory.

Master P (Percy Miller; 29 Apr 1970, New Orleans LA), American gangsta rap performer and producer.

Kalkot Mataskelekele (Mauliliu) (24 Apr 1949, Port Vila?, New Hebrides [now Vanuatu]), Vanuatuan lawyer and politician; president from 2004.

Mathilde (Mathilde d'Udekem d'Acoz; 21 Jan 1973, Uccle, Belgium), Belgian royal; princess consort of Prince Philippe (married 4 Dec 1999) and heir to the throne.

Hideki Matsui (12 Jun 1974, Ishikawa prefecture, Japan), Japanese baseball outfielder.

Koichiro Matsuura (29 Sep 1937, Tokyo, Japan), Japanese diplomat and international official; director-general of UNESCO from 1999.

Daisuke Matsuzaka (13 Sep 1980, Tokyo, Japan), Japanese baseball player.

Dave Matthews (David John Matthews; 9 Jan 1967, Johannesburg, South Africa), South African–born American rock musician (of the Dave Matthews Band).

Máxima (Máxima Zorreguieta Cerruti; 17 May 1971, Buenos Aires, Argentina), Argentine-born Dutch investment banker and princess consort of Crown Prince Willem-Alexander (married 2 Feb 2002).

John (Dayton) Mayer (1979, Fairfield CT), American singer and songwriter.

Thom Mayne (19 Jan 1944, Waterbury CT), American architect; recipient of the 2005 Pritzker Prize.

Floyd Mayweather, Jr. ("Pretty Boy"; 24 Feb 1977, Grand Rapids MI), American boxing champion in several weight classes, from lightweight to super welterweight.

Kiran Mazumdar-Shaw (1954?, Bangalore, India), Indian business executive; founder (1978) of Biocon India, India's first biotechnology company.

Thabo (Mvuyelwa) Mbeki (18 Jun 1942, Idutywa, Cape of Good Hope, Union of South Africa), South African politician; president from 1999.

Mary (Patricia) McAleese (27 Jun 1951, Belfast, Northern Ireland), Irish politician; president from 1997.

James (Andrew) McAvoy (21 Apr 1979, Glasgow, Scotland), British actor.

John (Sidney) McCain III (29 Aug 1936, Panama Canal Zone), American politician (Republican); senator from Arizona from 1987; candidate for president in 2008.

Cormac McCarthy (Charles McCarthy, Jr.; 20 Jul 1933, Providence RI), American novelist in the Southern gothic tradition.

(James) Paul McCartney (18 Jun 1942, Liverpool, England), British singer, songwriter, and former member of the Beatles.

Stella (Nina) McCartney (13 Sep 1971, London, England), British fashion designer.

Delbert McClinton (4 Nov 1940, Lubbock TX), American country-and-western singer and harmonica player.

Matthew McConaughey (4 Nov 1969, Uvalde TX), American film actor.

Mike McConnell (John Michael McConnell; 26 Jul 1943, Greenville SC), American military intelligence officer; director of the National Security Agency, 1992–96, and director of national intelligence from 2007.

David McCullough (7 Jul 1933, Pittsburgh PA), American biographer and historian.

Audra (Ann) McDonald (3 Jul 1970, West Berlin, West Germany [now in Germany]), American theater actress.

Frances McDormand (23 Jun 1957, Chicago IL), American film actress.

John (Patrick) McEnroe, Jr. (16 Feb 1959, Wiesbaden, West Germany [now in Germany]), American tennis player and TV sportscaster.

Reba McEntire (28 Mar 1954, McAlester OK), American country singer and TV and film actress.

Ian (Russell) McEwan (21 Jun 1948, Aldershot, England), British novelist.

Glenn (Donald) McGrath (9 Feb 1970, Dubbo, NSW, Australia), Australian cricket fast bowler.

Phil(lip C.) McGraw (1 Sep 1950, Vinita OK), American talk-show host, author, and psychologist-educator.

(Samuel) Tim(othy) McGraw (1 May 1967, Delhi LA), American country-and-western singer.

Dalton McGuinty (19 Jul 1955, Ottawa, ON, Canada), Canadian lawyer and politician (Liberal); premier of Ontario from 2003.

Kevin McKenzie (29 Apr 1954, Burlington VT), American ballet dancer, choreographer, and director.

Victor A(lmon) McKusick (21 Oct 1921, Parkman ME), American geneticist, a pioneer in the field of medical genetics; recipient of a Japan Prize in 2008.

Beverley McLachlin (7 Sep 1943, Pincher Creek, AB, Canada), Canadian Supreme Court justice from 1989 and chief justice from 2000.

Vince McMahon (Vincent Kennedy McMahon, Jr.; 24 Aug 1945, Pinehurst NC), American wrestling promoter; owner of World Wrestling Entertainment, Inc., from 1982.

Larry McMurtry (3 Jun 1936, Wichita Falls TX), American novelist.

W. James McNerney, Jr. (22 Aug 1949, Providence RI), American corporate executive; chairman of the board, president, and CEO of the Boeing Co. from 2005.

Marian McPartland (Margaret Marian Turner; 20 Mar 1918, Slough, England), English-born jazz pianist and composer.

James M. McPherson (11 Oct 1936, Valley City ND), American historian of slavery and the antislavery movement.

Ian McShane (29 Sep 1942, Blackburn, Lancashire, England), British film and TV actor.

Russell (Charles) Means (10 Nov 1939, Pine Ridge SD), American Lakota Sioux activist.

Dmitry (Anatolyevich) Medvedev (14 Sep 1965, Leningrad, USSR [now St. Petersburg, Russia]), Russian lawyer and politican; president of Russia from 2008.

Brad Mehldau (23 Aug 1970, Jacksonville FL), American jazz pianist and composer.

Zubin Mehta (29 Apr 1936, Bombay [now Mumbai], British India), Indian orchestral conductor; music director of the Israel Philharmonic from 1968; recipient of a 2006 Kennedy Center Honor.

Cildo Meireles (1948, Rio de Janeiro, Brazil), Brazilian installation artist and sculptor.

John Mellencamp (Johnny Cougar; John Cougar Mellencamp; 7 Oct 1951, Seymour IN), American singer and songwriter.

Eva Mendes (5 Mar 1974, Miami FL), American model and film actress.

Sam(uel Alexander) Mendes (1 Aug 1965, Reading, England), British film director.

Paulo Mendes da Rocha (25 Oct 1928, Vitória, Espírito Santo state, Brazil), Brazilian architect and professor; recipient of the 2006 Pritzker Prize.

Fradique de Menezes (1942), São Tomé and Príncipe politician; president, 2001–03 and again from 2003.

Angela Merkel (Angela Dorothea Kasner; 17 Jul 1954, Hamburg, West Germany [now in Germany]), German politician (Christian Democratic Union); chancellor of Germany from 2005.

W(illiam) S(tanley) Merwin (30 Sep 1927, New York NY), American poet and translator.

Stipe Mesic (Stjepan Mesic; 24 Dec 1934, Orahovica, Yugoslavia [now in Croatia]), Croatian politician; president from 2000.

Pat Metheny (12 Aug 1954, Lee's Summit MO), American jazz guitarist and bandleader.

Mette-Marit (Mette-Marit Tjessem Høiby; 19 Aug 1973, Kristiansand, Norway), Norwegian royal; princess consort of Crown Prince Haakon (married 25 Aug 2001).

Pierre de Meuron (8 May 1950, Basel, Switzerland), Swiss architect; corecipient of the 2001 Pritzker Prize and of a Praemium Imperiale in 2007.

Stephenie Meyer (24 Dec 1973, Hartford CT), American author of fiction for young adults.

Jonathan Rhys Meyers (Jonathan Michael Francis O'Keefe; 27 Jul 1977, Dublin, Ireland), Irish film actor.

Michael (Michael Hohenzollern-Sigmaringen; ruled as Mihai I; 25 Oct 1921, Sinaia, Romania), Romanian king, 1927–30 (under regency) and 1940–47.

Lorne Michaels (Lorne Michael Lipowitz; 17 Nov 1944, Toronto, ON, Canada), Canadian-born TV and film producer.

James (Alix) Michel (16 Aug 1944, Mahe Island, Seychelles), Seychelles politician; president from 2004.

Michiko (Michiko Shoda; 20 Oct 1934, Tokyo, Japan), Japanese royal; empress consort of Emperor Akihito (married 10 Apr 1959).

Bette Midler (1 Dec 1945, Honolulu HI), American comedian, singer, and actress.

Midori (Midori Goto; 25 Oct 1971, Osaka, Japan), Japanese-born American violinist.

David (Wright) Miliband (15 Jul 1965, London, England), British politician (Labour); foreign secretary from 2007.

David (Raymond) Miller (26 Dec 1958, San Francisco CA), American-born Canadian politician (independent); mayor of Toronto from 2003.

Dennis Miller (3 Nov 1953, Pittsburgh PA), American TV comedian and writer.

(Samuel) Bode Miller (12 Oct 1977, Easton NH), American Alpine skier.

Shannon (Lee) Miller (10 Mar 1977, Rolla MO), American gymnast.

Sienna (Rose) Miller (28 Dec 1981, New York NY), American-born British stage and film actress.

Sue Miller (29 Nov 1943, Chicago IL), American novelist.

Ming-Na (Ming-Na Wen; 20 Nov 1963, Macau), Macanese-born American TV actress.

Ruth Ann Minner (Ruth Ann Coverdale; 17 Jan 1935, Milford DE), American politician (Democrat); governor of Delaware from 2001.

Kylie (Ann) Minogue (28 May 1968, Melbourne, Australia), Australian actress and pop singer.

Helen Mirren (Ilyena Lydia Mironoff; 26 Jul 1945, Chiswick, London, England), British stage and film actress; recipient of the 2006 best actress Academy Award.

Joni Mitchell (Roberta Joan Anderson; 7 Nov 1943, Fort Macleod, AB, Canada), Canadian singer, songwriter, and painter.

Efthimios E. Mitropoulos (30 May 1939, Piraeus, Greece), Greek international official; secretary-general of the International Maritime Organization from 2004.

Lakshmi (Narayan) Mittal (15 Jun 1950, Sadulpur, Rajastan, India), Indian-born British steel magnate.

Satoshi Miura (3 Apr 1944, Japan?), Japanese corporate executive; CEO of Nippon Telephone & Telegraph from 2007.

Ratko Mladic (12 Mar 1943, Kalinovik village, Bosnia, Yugoslavia [now in Bosnia and Herzegovina]), Bosnian Serb military officer sought as a war criminal.

Phumzile Mlambo-Ngcuka (3 Nov 1955, Claremont, Natal, Union of South Africa [now KwaZulu Natal province, South Africa]), South African politician; deputy president from 2005.

Festus (Gontebanye) Mogae (21 Aug 1939, Serowe, Bechuanaland [now Botswana]), Botswanan politician; president, 1998–2008.

N(avarre) Scott Momaday (27 Feb 1934, Lawton OK), American writer of Kiowa heritage.

Thomas S(pencer) Monson (21 Aug 1927, Salt Lake City UT), American church leader; president of the Church of Jesus Christ of Latter-day Saints from 2008.

Alan Moore (18 Nov 1953), British author and creator of graphic novels.

Demi Moore (Demetria Gene Guynes; 11 Nov 1962, Roswell NM), American film actress.

Julianne Moore (Julie Anne Smith; 3 Dec 1960, Fayetteville NC), American film actress.

Lorrie Moore (Marie Lorena Moore; 13 Jan 1957, Glens Falls NY), American short-story writer and novelist.

Mandy Moore (Amanda Leigh Moore; 10 Apr 1984, Nashua NH), American pop singer and actress.

Michael Moore (23 Apr 1954, Davison MI), American film director and author.

(Juan) Evo Morales (Ayma) (26 Oct 1959, Orinoca, Bolivia), Bolivian farm-union leader; president from 2006.

Jason Moran (21 Jan 1975, Houston TX), American jazz pianist and bandleader.

Airto Moreira (5 Aug 1941, Itaiópolis, Santa Catarina state, Brazil), Brazilian jazz percussionist.

Luis Moreno Ocampo (4 Jun 1952, Buenos Aires, Argentina), Argentine lawyer; the first chief prosecutor of the International Criminal Court, from 2003.

Rhodri Morgan (29 Sep 1939, Cardiff, Wales), Welsh politician (Labour); first minister of Wales from 2000.

Manny Mori (Emanuel Mori; 1948, Chuuk state?, Micronesia), Micronesian politician; president from 2007.

Mark Morris (29 Aug 1956, Seattle WA), American dancer and choreographer.

Toni Morrison (Chloe Anthony Wofford; 18 Feb 1931, Lorain OH), American novelist; recipient of the 1993 Nobel Prize for Literature.

Viggo (Peter) Mortensen (20 Oct 1958, New York NY), American film actor.

Martin Mosebach (31 Jul 1951, Frankfurt am Main, West Germany [now in Germany]), German novelist; recipient of the 2007 Georg Büchner Prize.

Walter Mosley (12 Jan 1952, Los Angeles CA), American writer of science fiction and mystery novels.

Andrew Motion (26 Oct 1952, London, England), English poet, teacher, editor, and biographer; poet laureate of England from 1999.

Patrice (Tlhopane) Motsepe (28 Jan 1962, Johannesburg, South Africa), South African mining tycoon and sports club owner; founder (1997) and chairman of African Rainbow Minerals Ltd.

Markos Moulitsas (Zúniga) ("Kos"; 11 Sep 1971, Chicago IL), American populist journalist and blogger; founder and editor of the Daily Kos blog from 2002.

Amr Muhammad Moussa (3 Oct 1936, Cairo, Egypt), Egyptian secretary-general of the League of Arab States from 2001.

Bill Moyers (Billy Don Moyers; 5 Jun 1934, Hugo OK), American TV journalist, former government official, and author.

Mswati III (19 Apr 1968, Swaziland), Swazi royal; king of Swaziland from 1986.

(Muhammed) Hosni Mubarak (4 May 1928, Al-Minufiyah governorate, Egypt), Egyptian politician; president from 1981.

Daniel H. Mudd (1959, ?), American corporate executive; president and CEO of Fannie Mae from 2005.

Edward A. Mueller (1947, St. Louis MO), American corporate executive; chairman and CEO of Qwest Communications International Inc. from 2007.

Lisel Mueller (Lisel Neumann; 8 Feb 1924, Hamburg, Germany), German-born American poet.

Robert S(wan) Mueller III (7 Aug 1944, New York NY), American government official; FBI director from 2001.

Robert (Gabriel) Mugabe (21 Feb 1924, Kutama, Southern Rhodesia [now Zimbabwe]), Zimbabwean politician; the first prime minister (1980–87) of the reconstituted state of Zimbabwe and president from 1987.

Muhammad VI (Muhammad ibn al-Hassan; 21 Aug 1963, Rabat, Morocco), Moroccan royal; king from 1999.

Ali Muhammad Mujawar (1953, Shabwah, British-protected Aden [now in Yemen]), Yemeni politician; prime minister from 2007.

Michael (Bernard) Mukasey (28 Jul 1941, Bronx NY), American jurist; US attorney general from 2007.

Pranab Mukherjee (11 Dec 1935, Mirati village, West Bengal, British India), Indian politician (Indian National Congress); foreign minister, 1995–96 and again from 2006.

Paul Muldoon (20 Jun 1951, Portadown, Northern Ireland), Irish-born American poet.

Alice Munro (Alice Anne Laidlaw; 10 Jul 1931, Wingham, ON, Canada), Canadian short-story writer.

(Keith) Rupert Murdoch (11 Mar 1931, Melbourne, Australia), Australian-born British newspaper publisher and media entrepreneur; founder of the global media holding company News Corporation Ltd.

Eddie Murphy (3 Apr 1961, Brooklyn NY), American comedian and film actor.

Cormac Cardinal Murphy-O'Connor (24 Aug 1932, Reading, Berkshire, England), British church leader; archbishop of Westminster (leader of the Roman Catholic Church in the UK) from 2000 and cardinal from 2001.

Yoweri (Kaguta) Museveni (15 Aug 1944, Mbarra district, Uganda), Ugandan politician; president from 1986.

Pervez Musharraf (Pervez Musharraf Nish-i-Imtiaz; 11 Aug 1943, New Delhi, British India), Pakistani military leader and politician; head of Pakistan's government, 1999–2001, and president, 2001–08.

Bingu wa Mutharika (24 Feb 1934, Thyolo district, British Nyasaland [now Malawi]), Malawian politician (United Democratic Front); president from 2004.

Riccardo Muti (28 Jul 1941, Naples, Italy), Italian conductor; music director of La Scala Orchestra in Milan, 1986–2005; named to become music director of the Chicago Symphony Orchestra from 2010.

Halil Mutlu (Huben Hubenov; "Little Dynamo"; 14 Jul 1973, Postnik, Bulgaria), Bulgarian-born Turkish weight lifter.

Anne-Sophie Mutter (29 Jun 1963, Rheinfelden, West Germany [now in Germany]), German violinist.

Mike Myers (25 May 1963, Scarborough, ON, Canada), Canadian comedian and actor.

Roger B. Myerson (29 Mar 1951, Boston MA), American economist; corecipient of the 2007 Nobel Prize for Economic Sciences for work in mechanism design theory.

Youssou N'Dour (1 Oct 1959, Dakar, French West Africa [now in Senegal]), Senegalese singer and songwriter.

James Nachtwey (14 Mar 1948, Syracuse NY), American news photographer.

Rafael Nadal (Parera) (3 Jun 1986, Manacor, Mallorca, Spain), Spanish tennis player.

Ralph Nader (27 Feb 1934, Winsted CT), American social activist and politician; he was a presidential candidate in 2000, 2004, and 2008.

(Clarence) Ray Nagin, Jr. (11 Jun 1956, New Orleans LA), American politician (Democrat); mayor of New Orleans from 2002.

Parminder K. Nagra (5 Oct 1975, Leicester, Leicestershire, England), British film and TV actress.

Khalifah ibn Zayid Al Nahyan (c. 1948, Al-ʿAyn, Abu Dhabi, British Trucial States [now United Arab Emirates]), UAE sheikh; ruler of Abu Dhabi and president of the United Arab Emirates from 2004.

V(idiadhar) S(urajprasad) Naipaul (17 Aug 1932, Chaguanas, Trinidad), Trinidadian-born British writer; recipient of the 2001 Nobel Prize for Literature.

Mira Nair (15 Oct 1957, Bhubaneshwar, Orissa state, India), Indian film director and screenwriter.

Giorgio Napolitano (29 Jun 1925, Naples, Italy), Italian politician (Communist); president from 2006.

Janet Napolitano (29 Nov 1957, New York NY), American politician (Democrat); governor of Arizona from 2003.

Murthy Narayana (20 Aug 1946, Karnataka, British India), Indian international business executive and pioneer in India's high-tech industry; cofounder and CEO of Infosys Technologies Ltd., a technology and consulting firm.

Robert (Louis) Nardelli (17 May 1948, Old Forge PA), American corporate executive; CEO of the Home Depot, Inc., 2000–07, and of Chrysler Corp. thereafter.

Naruhito (23 Feb 1960, Tokyo, Japan), Japanese crown prince.

Nas (Nasir bin Olu Dara Jones; "Nasty Nas"; "Nas Escobar"; 14 Sep 1973, Queens NY), American hip-hop artist.

Milton Nascimento (26 Oct 1942, Rio de Janeiro, Brazil), Brazilian pop singer and songwriter.

Sayyed Hassan Nasrallah (31 Aug 1960, Borj Hammoud, Beirut, Lebanon), Lebanese Islamist military leader; secretary-general of Hezbollah from 1992.

Taslima Nasrin (25 Aug 1962, Mymensingh, Bangladesh), Bangladeshi Islamic feminist writer.

S(ellapan) R(amanathan) Nathan (3 Jul 1924, Singapore?), Singaporean politician; president from 1999.

Bruce Nauman (6 Nov 1941, Fort Wayne IN), American sculptor and installation and performance artist.

Nursultan Nazarbayev (6 Jul 1940, Chemolgan, USSR [now in Kazakhstan]), Kazakh politician; president from 1990.

Liam Neeson (William Neeson; 7 Jun 1952, Ballymena, Northern Ireland), British film actor.

Willie (Hugh) Nelson (30 Apr 1933, Fort Worth TX), American songwriter and guitarist.

Nerses Bedros XIX (Boutros Tarmouni; 17 Jan 1940, Cairo, Egypt), Armenian churchman; patriarch of the Catholic Armenians from 1999.

Randy Newman (Randall Stuart Newman; 28 Nov 1943, Los Angeles CA), American songwriter, singer, and pianist.

Marc Newson (1963, Sydney, NSW, Australia), Australian industrial designer.

Thandie Newton (Thandiwe Newton; 6 Nov 1972, Zambia), Zambian-born British TV and film actress.

Teodoro Obiang Nguema Mbasogo (1942, Acoacan, Río Muni [now Equatorial Guinea]), Equatorial Guinean politician; president of Equatorial Guinea from 1979.

Ngugi wa Thiong'o (James Thiong'o Ngugi; 5 Jan 1938, Limuru, Kenya), Kenyan novelist.

Nguyen Minh Triet (8 Oct 1942, Ben Cat district, French Indochina [now in Vietnam]), Vietnamese politician; president from 2006.

Nguyen Tan Dung (17 Nov 1949, Ca Mau, French Indochina [now in Vietnam]), Vietnamese politician; prime minister from 2006.

Mike Nichols (Michael Igor Peschkowsky; 6 Nov 1931, Berlin, Germany), American stage and film director.

Jack Nicholson (John Joseph Nicholson; 22 Apr 1937, Neptune NJ), American film actor.

Takashi Nishioka (1936?, Japan?), Japanese corporate executive; chairman and CEO of Mitsubishi Motors Corp. from 2005.

Uichiro Niwa (c. 1941, Aichi prefecture, Japan), Japanese corporate executive; CEO and president of Itochu Corp. from 1998.

Pierre Nkurunziza (18 Dec 1963, Ngozi province, Burundi), Burundian Hutu rebel leader; president from 2005.

Ronald K(enneth) Noble (1957?, New Jersey), American law professor and government official; secretary-general of Interpol from 2000.

Christopher (Jonathan James) Nolan (30 Jul 1970, London, England), British film director.

Indra Nooyi (28 Oct 1955, Madras [now Chennai], Tamil Nadu state, India), Indian-born American businesswoman; chairman and CEO of PepsiCo from 2007.

Norodom Sihamoni (14 May 1953, Phnom Penh, Cambodia), Cambodian royal; king from 2004.

Norodom Sihanouk (Preah Baht Samdach Preah Norodom Sihanuk Varman; 31 Oct 1922, Phnom Penh, Cambodia), Cambodian king, 1941–55 and 1993–2004; head of state, 1960–70 and 1991–93.

Richard C. Notebaert (1948?, Montreal, QC, Canada), Canadian-born corporate executive; chairman and CEO of Ameritech Corp., 1993–99, and of Qwest Communications International Inc., 2002–07.

Chris Noth (13 Nov 1954, Madison WI), American film and TV actor.

Lynn Nottage (1971?, Brooklyn NY), American playwright.

Jean Nouvel (12 Aug 1945, Fumel, France), French architect; recipient of a Praemium Imperiale in 2001 and the 2008 Pritzker Prize.

Robert Novak (26 Feb 1931, Joliet IL), American newspaper and TV journalist.

Jim Nussle (James Allen Nussle; 27 Jun 1960, Des Moines IA), American politician (Republican); director of the Office of Management and Budget from 2007.

Michael A(nthony) Nutter (29 Jun 1957, Philadelphia PA), American politician (Democrat); mayor of Philadelphia from 2008.

Conan O'Brien (18 Apr 1963, Brookline MA), American TV talk-show host.

Mark O'Connor (5 Aug 1961, Seattle WA), American country fiddle player.

Sandra Day O'Connor (26 Mar 1930, El Paso TX), American jurist; associate justice of the US Supreme Court, 1981–2005, the first woman appointed to the court.

Martin (Joseph) O'Malley (18 Jan 1963, Washington DC), American politician (Democrat); mayor of Baltimore, 1999–2007, and governor of Maryland from 2007.

Sean Patrick O'Malley (29 Jun 1944, Lakewood OH), American Roman Catholic churchman; archbishop of Boston from 2003; cardinal from 2006.

Shaquille (Rashaun) O'Neal (6 Mar 1972, Newark NJ), American basketball center.

Bill O'Reilly (William James O'Reilly, Jr.; 10 Sep 1949, New York NY), American TV journalist and talk-show host.

David J. O'Reilly (January 1947, Dublin, Ireland), Irish-born American corporate executive; chairman and CEO of ChevronTexaco Corp. from 2000.

Peter (Seamus) O'Toole (2 Aug 1932, Connemara, County Galway, Ireland), British stage and film actor.

Joyce Carol Oates (16 Jun 1938, Lockport NY), American novelist, short-story writer, and essayist.

Thoraya Obaid (2 Mar 1945, Baghdad, Iraq), Iraqi-born Saudi Arabian civil servant; executive director of the UN Population Fund from 2001.

Barack (Hussein) Obama, Jr. (4 Aug 1961, Honolulu HI), American politician (Democrat); senator from Illinois from 2005; candidate for president in 2008.

Lorena Ochoa (15 Nov 1981, Guadalajara, Jalisco, Mexico), Mexican golfer.

Piermaria J. Oddone (26 Mar 1944, Arequipa, Peru), Peruvian-born American experimental particle physicist and administrator; director of the Fermi National Accelerator Laboratory from 2005.

Raila (Amollo) Odinga (7 Jan 1945, Maseno, Nyanza province, British Kenya), Kenyan politician (Liberal Democratic); prime minister from 2008.

Nelson O. Oduber (7 Feb 1947), Aruban prime minister, 1989–94 and again from 2001.

Kenzaburo Oe (31 Jan 1935, Ose, Ehime prefecture, Japan), Japanese novelist; recipient of the 1994 Nobel Prize for Literature.

Sadaharu Oh (20 May 1940, Tokyo, Japan), Japanese baseball player.

Paul Okalik (26 May 1964, Pangnirtung, NT [now in NU], Canada), Canadian politican; premier of Nunavut from 1999.

Keith Olbermann (27 Jan 1959, New York NY), American TV sportscaster and commentator.

Claes (Thure) Oldenburg (28 Jan 1929, Stockholm, Sweden), Swedish-born Pop-art sculptor.

Sharon Olds (19 Nov 1942, San Francisco CA), American poet.

Jamie Oliver (27 May 1975, Essex, England), British chef and TV personality.

Ehud Olmert (30 Sep 1945, Binyamina, Palestine [now in Israel]), Israeli politician (Kadima); prime minister, 2006–08.

Ashley (Fuller) Olsen (13 Jun 1986, Sherman Oaks CA), American former child star and a marketing phenomenon in modeling, films, TV, and music videos.

Mary-Kate Olsen (13 Jun 1986, Sherman Oaks CA), American former child star and a marketing phenomenon in modeling, films, TV, and music videos.

(Philip) Michael Ondaatje (12 Sep 1943, Colombo, British Ceylon [now Sri Lanka]), Canadian novelist and poet.

Makoto Ooka (16 Feb 1931, Mishima, Shizuoka prefecture, Japan), Japanese poet and literary critic.

Suze Orman (5 Jun 1951, Chicago IL), American financial adviser and best-selling author.

Amancio Ortega Gaona (28 Mar 1936, León, Spain), Spanish textile magnate; founder (1985) and chairman of Inditex Group and of its subsidiary Zara España S.A., a retail and distribution company.

(José) Daniel Ortega (Saavedra) (11 Nov 1945, La Libertad, Nicaragua), Nicaraguan guerrilla leader and politician; president, 1984–90 and again from 2007.

Joel Osteen (5 Mar 1963, Houston TX), American evangelist; head of the Lakewood Church in Houston.

Butch Otter (Clement Leroy Otter; 3 May 1942, Caldwell ID), American politician (Republican); governor of Idaho from 2007.

Michael Ovitz (14 Dec 1946, Encino CA), American entertainment executive; cofounder (1975) of the Creative Artists Agency.

Clive Owen (3 Oct 1964, Keresley, Coventry, Warwickshire, England), British actor.

Amos Oz (4 May 1939, Jerusalem, British Palestine), Israeli novelist, short-story writer, and essayist.

Mehmet Oz (11 Jun 1960, Cleveland OH), American cardiac surgeon, professor, TV medical expert, and author.

Cynthia Ozick (17 Apr 1928, New York NY), American novelist, short-story writer, and playwright.

Makoto Ozone (25 Mar 1961, Kobe, Japan), Japanese jazz pianist.

Rajendra K. Pachauri (20 Aug 1940, Nainital, Uttar Pradesh [now in Uttarakhand state], British India), Indian businessman; head of the Intergovernmental Panel on Climate Change from 2002.

Al(fredo James) Pacino (25 Apr 1940, New York NY), American film actor.

Larry Page (Lawrence Edward Page; 1972, East Lansing MI), American computer scientist and Internet entrepreneur who cofounded (1998) the Google Internet search engine.

Ellen (Philpotts-) Page (21 Feb 1987, Halifax, NS, Canada), Canadian TV and film actress.

Brad Paisley (28 Oct 1972, Glen Dale WV), American contemporary country-and-western singer.

Ian (Richard Kyle) Paisley (6 Apr 1926, Armagh, County Armagh, Northern Ireland), Northern Irish Protestant leader and politician; first minister for Northern Ireland, 2007–08.

Sarah Palin (Sarah Heath; 11 Feb 1964, Sandpoint ID), American politician (Republican); governor of Alaska from 2006 and the Republican nominee for vice president in 2008.

Eddie Palmieri (15 Dec 1936, New York NY), American jazz-salsa pianist.

Samuel J. Palmisano (29 Jul 1951), American corporate executive; president and CEO of the International Business Machines (IBM) Corp. from 2002.

Gwyneth Paltrow (28 Sep 1972, Los Angeles CA), American film and stage actress.

Orhan Pamuk (7 Jun 1952, Istanbul, Turkey), Turkish novelist; recipient of the 2006 Nobel Prize for Literature.

Paola (Paola dei Principi Ruffo di Calabria; 11 Sep 1937, Forte dei Marmi, Italy), Italian-born Belgian royal; queen consort of King Albert II (married 2 Jul 1959).

Karolos Papoulias (4 Jun 1929, Ioannina, Greece), Greek politician; president from 2005.

Anna (Helene) Paquin (24 Jul 1982, Winnipeg, MB, Canada), New Zealand film actress.

Sara Paretsky (8 Jun 1947, Ames IA), American mystery writer.

Nick Park (Nicholas Wulstan Park; 6 Dec 1958, Preston, Lancashire, England), British film animator.

Alan (William) Parker (14 Feb 1944, Islington, London, England), British advertising copywriter and film director.

Mary-Louise Parker (2 Aug 1964, Fort Jackson SC), American actress on stage, in film, and on TV.

Sarah Jessica Parker (25 Mar 1965, Nelsonville OH), American TV and film actress.

Suzan-Lori Parks (10 May 1963, Fort Knox KY), American playwright.

Anja Pärson (25 Apr 1981, Umeå, Sweden), Swedish downhill skier.

Richard D(ean) Parsons (4 Apr 1949, Bedford-Stuyvesant, Brooklyn NY), American corporate executive; CEO of AOL Time Warner from 2002 and chairman from 2003.

Arvo Pärt (11 Sep 1935, Paide, Estonia), Estonian composer.

Dolly (Rebecca) Parton (19 Jan 1946, Locust Ridge TN), American country-and-western singer, songwriter, and actress; recipient of a 2006 Kennedy Center Honor.

Amy Pascal (1959, Los Angeles CA), American film executive; president of Turner Pictures from 1994 and, from Turner's merger in 1996 with Time Warner, president of Sony Corp.'s Columbia Pictures.

Ann Patchett (2 Dec 1963, Los Angeles CA), American novelist.

David A. Paterson (20 May 1954, Brooklyn NY), American politician (Democrat); governor of New York from 2008.

Pratibha Patil (19 Dec 1934, Jalgaon, British India), Indian politician; the country's first female president, from 2007.

Danica (Sue) Patrick (25 Mar 1982, Beloit WI), American race-car driver.

Deval (Laurdine) Patrick (31 Jul 1956, Chicago IL), American politician (Democrat); governor of Massachusetts from 2007.

Ron Paul (Ronald Ernest Paul; 20 Aug 1935, Pittsburgh PA), American physician and libertarian politician; congressman from Texas from 1997.

Henry M(erritt) Paulson, Jr. (28 Mar 1946, Palm Beach FL), American corporate executive and government official; CEO of Goldman Sachs Group, 1999–2006, and US secretary of the treasury from 2006.

Tim(othy James) Pawlenty (21 Nov 1960, St. Paul MN), American politician (Republican); governor of Minnesota from 2003.

James (Benjamin) Peake (18 Jun 1944, St. Louis MO), American army medical officer; secretary of veterans affairs from 2007.

P(hilip) James E(dward) Peebles (25 Apr 1935, Winnipeg, MB, Canada), Canadian-born cosmologist; recipient of the 1995 Bruce Gold Medal and corecipient of a 2005 Crafoord Prize.

Amanda Peet (11 Jan 1972, New York NY), American film and TV actress.

Harvey Pekar (1939, Cleveland OH), American file clerk and alternative comic-book artist.

Pelé (Edson Arantes do Nascimento; 23 Oct 1940, Três Corações, Minas Gerais state, Brazil), Brazilian association football (soccer) legend.

Cesar Pelli (12 Oct 1926, Tucumán, Argentina), Argentine architect.

Nancy Pelosi (Nancy D'Alesandro; 26 Mar 1940, Baltimore MD), American politician (Democrat); congresswoman from California from 1987, House Democratic leader, 2003–07, and speaker of the House from 2007.

Leonard Peltier (12 Sep 1944, Grand Forks ND), American Ojibwa and Lakota activist.

Sean (Justin) Penn (17 Aug 1960, Santa Monica CA), American film actor and director.

Murray Perahia (19 Apr 1947, New York NY), American concert pianist.

Sonny Perdue (George Ervin Perdue III; 20 Dec 1946, Perry GA), American agrobusinessman and politician (Republican); governor of Georgia from 2003.

Shimon Peres (Shimon Perski; 2 Aug 1923, Wolozyn, Poland [now Valozhyn, Belarus]), Israeli statesman, prime minister, 1984–86 and 1995–96, and president from 2007; he won the Nobel Peace Prize in 1994 for his efforts to work with the PLO.

Dana (Marie) Perino (9 May 1972, Evanston WY), American journalist and media official; White House press secretary from 2007.

Kieran Perkins (14 Aug 1973, Brisbane, QLD, Australia), Australian swimmer who held 12 world records in distance freestyle events.

Tom Perrotta (13 Aug 1961, Garwood NJ), American novelist.

Grayson Perry (24 Mar 1960, Chelmsford, Essex, England), British artist; recipient of the 2003 Turner Prize.

Rick Perry (James Richard Perry; 4 Mar 1950 West Texas), American politician (Republican); governor of Texas from 2000.

Bernadette Peters (Bernadette Lazzaro; 28 Feb 1948, Queens NY), American singer and actress.

Mary E. Peters (4 Dec 1948, Phoenix AZ), American transportation official; secretary of transportation from 2006.

David (Howell) Petraeus (7 Nov 1952, Cornwall-on-Hudson NY), American military leader; commander of Multinational Force Iraq (MNF-I), 2007–08, and of US Central Command from 2008.

Tom Petty (20 Oct 1953, Gainesville FL), American rock singer and songwriter.

Madeleine Peyroux (1973, Athens GA), American jazz singer.

Michelle Pfeiffer (29 Apr 1958, Santa Ana CA), American film actress.

Michael Phelps (30 Jun 1985, Baltimore MD), American swimmer.

Regis (Francis Xavier) Philbin (25 Aug 1934, New York NY), American TV personality.

Philip (Prince Philip of Greece and Denmark; 10 Jun 1921, Corfu, Greece), British duke of Edinburgh; prince consort of Queen Elizabeth II (married 20 November 1947).

Philippe (Philippe Leopold Louis Marie; 15 Apr 1960, Brussels, Belgium), Belgian royal; duke of Brabant and crown prince of Belgium.

(Matthew) Ryan Phillippe (10 Sep 1974, New Castle DE), American TV and film actor.

Stone Phillips (2 Dec 1954, Texas City TX), American TV host and anchorman.

Joaquin Phoenix (Joaquin Raphael Bottom; 28 Oct 1974, San Juan, Puerto Rico), American film actor.

Renzo Piano (14 Sep 1937, Genoa, Italy), Italian architect; winner of the 1998 Pritzker Prize and the 2002 UIA Gold Medal for Architecture.

T(homas) Boone Pickens (22 May 1928, Holdenville OK), American billionaire oilman; advocate of aggressive investment in alternative energy.

David Hyde Pierce (3 Apr 1959, Saratoga Springs NY), American comic actor.

Heinrich von Pierer (26 Jan 1941, Erlangen, Germany), German corporate executive; CEO of Siemens AG, 1992–05, and chairman, 2005–07.

DBC Pierre (Peter Warren Finlay; June 1961, Reynella, SA, Australia), Australian-born British novelist; winner of the 2003 Man Booker Prize.

François Pinault (21 Aug 1936, Les Champs-Géraux, Brittany, France), French corporate executive (Pinault-Printemps-Redoute) and art collector.

Laffit Pincay, Jr. (29 Dec 1946, Panama City, Panama), Panamanian-born American jockey.

Jean Ping (24 Nov 1942, Omboué, French Gabon), Gabonese statesman; UN General Assembly president, 2004, and chairman of the Commission of the African Union from 2008.

Pink (Alecia Beth Moore; 8 Sep 1979, Doylestown PA), American pop singer.

Jada Pinkett Smith (Jada Koren Pinkett; 18 Sep 1971, Baltimore MD), American actress, video director, and clothing designer.

Robert Pinsky (20 Oct 1940, Long Branch NJ), American poet and critic; poet laureate of the US, 1997–2000.

Harold Pinter (10 Oct 1930, London, England), English playwright and director; recipient of the 2005 Nobel Prize for Literature.

Pedro (Verona Rodrigues) Pires (April 1934, Ilha do Fogo, Cape Verde), Cape Verdean politician; president from 2001.

Surin Pitsuwan (28 Oct 1949, Nakhon Si Thammarat, Thailand), Thai intellectual and government official; secretary-general of the Association of Southeast Asian Nations from 2008.

(William) Brad(ley) Pitt (18 Dec 1963, Shawnee OK), American film actor.

Kira (Sergeyevna) Plastinina (1 Jun 1992, Moscow, Russia), Russian teenage fashion designer.

Yevgeny (Viktorovich) Plushchenko (also spelled Evgeni Plushenko; 3 Nov 1982, Solnechny, USSR [now in Russia]), Russian figure skater.

Amy Poehler (16 Sep 1971, Burlington MA), American actress and comedian on TV and in films.

Hifikepunye (Lucas) Pohamba (18 Aug 1935, Okanghudi, South West Africa [now Namibia]), Namibian independence leader and politician; president from 2005.

Sidney Poitier (20 Feb 1927?, Miami FL), Bahamian American stage and film actor and director.

Roman Polanski (Raimund Liebling; 18 Aug 1933, Paris, France), Polish film director, scriptwriter, and actor.

Judit Polgar (23 Jul 1976, Budapest, Hungary), Hungarian chess grand master.

Sigmar Polke (13 Feb 1941, Oels, Germany [now Olesnica, Poland]), German Pop-art painter of Capitalist Realism.

Calin (Constantin Anton) Popescu Tariceanu (14 Jan 1952, Bucharest, Romania), Romanian industrial engineer and politician (National Liberal Party); prime minister from 2004.

Gregg Popovich (28 Jan 1949, East Chicago IN), American professional basketball coach.

Natalie Portman (Natalie Hershlag; 9 Jun 1981, Jerusalem, Israel), Israeli-born American film actress.

Rob(ert Jones) Portman (19 Dec 1955, Cincinnati OH), American politician (Republican); director of the Office of Management and Budget, 2006–07.

Zac(hary E.) Posen (24 Oct 1980, Brooklyn NY), American fashion designer.

John E. Potter (1956, Bronx NY), American corporate executive; CEO and postmaster general of the US Postal Service from 2001.

Earl A. ("Rusty") Powell III (24 Oct 1943, Spartanburg SC), American museum official; director of the National Gallery of Art in Washington DC from 1992.

Samantha Power (1970, Ireland), Irish-born American writer and political adviser.

Velupillai Prabhakaran (26 Nov 1954, Jaffna, Sri Lanka), Sri Lankan secessionist, the founder and leader of the Liberation Tigers of Tamil Eelam (Tamil Tigers) from the early 1970s.

Miuccia Prada (1949, Milan, Italy), Italian fashion designer.

Azim Hasham Premji (24 Jul 1945, Bombay [now Mumbai], British India), Indian corporate executive; chairman of the Wipro Corp. of Bangalore from 1977.

Steve(n Clyde) Preston (1961?, Janesville WI?), American government official; US secretary of housing and urban development from 2008.

René (García) Préval (17 Jan 1943, Port-au-Prince, Haiti), Haitian politician; president from 2006.

André (George) Previn (6 Apr 1929, Berlin, Germany), German-born American pianist, composer, and conductor.

Richard Price (12 Oct 1949, Bronx NY), American novelist and screenwriter.

Prince (Prince Rogers Nelson; 7 Jun 1958, Minneapolis MN), American singer and songwriter.

Birgit Prinz (25 Oct 1977, Frankfurt am Main, West Germany [now in Germany]), German association football (soccer) player.

Romano Prodi (9 Aug 1939, Scandiano, Italy), Italian politician and prime minister, 1996–98 and 2006–08.

E(dna) Annie Proulx (22 Aug 1935, Norwich CT), American writer.

Georgi Purvanov (28 Jun 1957, Kovachevtsi, Bulgaria), Bulgarian politician; president from 2002.

Vladimir (Vladimirovich) Putin (7 Oct 1952, Leningrad, USSR [now St. Petersburg, Russia]), Russian intelligence officer; prime minister of Russia, 1999–2000, president, 1999–2008, and prime minister again from 2008.

(Sayyid) Qabus ibn Sa'id (18 Nov 1940, Salalah, Oman), Omani head of state; sultan of Oman from 1970 and prime minister from 1972.

Muammar al-Qaddafi (also spelled Muammar Khadafy, Moammar Gadhafi, or Mu'ammar al-Qadhdhafi; spring 1942, near Surt, Libya), Libyan military leader and Arab statesman; de facto chief of state from 1969.

Dennis Quaid (9 Apr 1954, Houston TX), American film actor.

Thomas Quasthoff (9 Nov 1959, Hildesheim, West Germany [now in Germany]), German bass-baritone.

Queen Latifah (Dana Elaine Owens; 18 Mar 1970, Newark NJ), American rap musician, film actress, and TV personality.

Anna (Marie) Quindlen (8 Jul 1953, Philadelphia PA), American political commentator and author.

Daniel Radcliffe (23 July 1989, Fulham, London, England), British film actor.

Paula Radcliffe (17 Dec 1973, Northwich, Cheshire, England), British marathon runner.

Aishwarya Rai (1 Nov 1973, Mangalore, Karnataka state, India), Indian beauty queen and film actress.

Sam(uel M.) Raimi (23 Oct 1959, Franklin MI), American cult filmmaker.

Rain (Jeong Ji-hoon; 25 Jun 1982, Seoul, South Korea), Korean pop singer and actor.

Bonnie Raitt (8 Nov 1949, Burbank CA), American blues and R&B singer and bottleneck guitarist.

Mahinda Rajapakse (18 Nov 1945, British Ceylon [now Sri Lanka]), Sri Lankan politician; prime minister, 2004–05, and president from 2005.

Imomali Rakhmonov (5 Oct 1952, Dangara, Tadzhik SSR, USSR [now Tajikistan]), Tajik politician; president from 1992.

Samuel Ramey (28 Mar 1942, Colby KS), American operatic bass.

José Ramos-Horta (26 Dec 1949, Dili, Portuguese Timor [now East Timor]), Timorese nationalist leader; prime minister, 2006–07, and president from 2007; corecipient of the 1996 Nobel Peace Prize.

Gordon (James) Ramsay (8 Nov 1966, Glasgow, Scotland), British chef and TV personality; proprietor of the London restaurants Aubergine (1993–98) and Gordon Ramsay Restaurant (from 1998).

Rania al-Abdullah (Rania al-Yaseen; 31 Aug 1970, Kuwait), Kuwaiti-born Jordanian royal; queen consort of King Abdullah II (married 10 Jun 1993).

Ian Rankin (28 Apr 1960, Cardenden, Fife, Scotland), British crime novelist.

Phylicia Rashad (Phylicia Ayers-Allen; 19 Jun 1948, Houston TX), American TV and stage actress.

Anders Fogh Rasmussen (26 Jan 1953, Ginnerup, Denmark), Danish politician; prime minister from 2001.

Aleksei (Osipovich) Ratmansky (27 Aug 1968, Leningrad, USSR [now St. Petersburg, Russia]), Russian dancer, choreographer, and director.

Simon (Denis) Rattle (19 Jan 1955, Liverpool, England), British orchestra conductor; principal conductor and artistic director of the Berlin Philharmonic from the 2002–03 season.

Marc Ravalomanana (1949, near Atananarivo, French Madagascar), Malagasy politician; president of Madagascar from 2002.

Rachael (Domenica) Ray (25 Aug 1968, Cape Cod MA), American TV cook and cookbook author.

(Charles) Robert Redford, Jr. (18 Aug 1937, Santa Monica CA), American film actor and director.

Lynn Redgrave (8 Mar 1943, London, England), British stage, screen, and TV actress.

Vanessa Redgrave (30 Jan 1937, London, England), British stage and screen actress and political activist.

Joshua Redman (1 Feb 1969, Berkeley CA), American jazz saxophone player.

Sumner Redstone (Sumner Murray Rothstein; 27 May 1923, Boston MA), American media executive.

David Rees (1973?), American comic artist.

Martin J(ohn) Rees (23 Jun 1942, Shropshire, England), British astronomer royal; recipient of the Crafoord Prize in 2005.

Keanu (Charles) Reeves (2 Sep 1964, Beirut, Lebanon), American actor.

Kathy Reichs (Kathleen Joan Toelle; 1950, Chicago IL), American anthropologist-turned-novelist.

Harry Reid (2 Dec 1939, Searchlight NV), American politician (Democrat); senator from Nevada from 1987, Senate whip, 1998–2005, and Senate leader from 2005.

John C(hristopher) Reilly (24 May 1965, Chicago IL), American stage and film actor.

Rob Reiner (6 Mar 1947, Bronx NY), American actor, director, writer, and producer.

(John) Fredrik Reinfeldt (4 Aug 1965, Österhaninge, Sweden), Swedish politician (Moderate Party); prime minister from 2006.

Jason Reitman (19 Oct 1977, Montreal, QC, Canada), Canadian actor, director, and writer.

M(argaret) Jodi Rell (Mary Carolyn Reavis; 16 Jun 1946, Norfolk VA), American politician (Republican); governor of Connecticut from 2004.

Thomas Esang Remengesau, Jr. (1956), Palauan politician; president from 2001.

Edward (Gene) Rendell (5 Jan 1944, New York NY), American politician (Democrat); mayor of Philadelphia, 1992–2000, and governor of Pennsylvania from 2003.

Ruth Rendell (Baroness Rendell of Babergh; pseudonym Barbara Vine; 17 Feb 1930, London, England), British mystery novelist.

Yasmina Reza (1 May 1959, Paris, France), French playwright.

Christina Ricci (12 Feb 1980, Santa Monica CA), American film actress.

Anne Rice (Howard Allen O'Brien; pseudonyms A.N. Roquelaure and Anne Rampling; 4 Oct 1941, New Orleans LA), American Gothic novelist.

Condoleezza Rice (14 Nov 1954, Birmingham AL), American academic and government official; national security advisor, 2001–05, and US secretary of state from 2005.

Adrienne (Cecile) Rich (16 May 1929, Baltimore MD), American poet.

Denise (Lee) Richards (17 Feb 1971, Downers Grove IL), American model and TV and film actress.

Keith Richards (18 Dec 1943, Dartford, Kent, England), British rock guitarist and singer (for the Rolling Stones).

(George) Maxwell Richards (1931, San Fernando, Trinidad), Trinidadian chemical engineer and university professor; president of Trinidad and Tobago from 2003.

Bill Richardson (William Blaine Richardson; 15 Nov 1947, Pasadena CA), American politician (Democrat); governor of New Mexico from 2003.

Nicole Richie (15 Sep 1981, Berkeley CA), American celebrity entertainer.

Gerhard Richter (9 Feb 1932, Dresden, Germany), German Capitalist Realist artist.

Kai-Uwe Ricke (29 Oct 1961, Krefeld, West Germany [now in Germany]), German corporate executive and CEO of Deutsche Telekom from 2002.

Sally K(risten) Ride (26 May 1951, Encino CA), American astronaut and astrophysicist.

Rihanna (Robyn Rihanna Fenty; 20 Feb 1988, Saint Michael parish, Barbados), West Indian pop singer.

Robert R. Riley (3 Oct 1944, Ashland AL), American politician (Republican); governor of Alabama from 2003.

LeAnn Rimes (28 Aug 1982, Jackson MS), American country-and-western singer.

Kelly Ripa (2 Oct 1970, Stratford NJ), American talk-show host and actress.

Bill Ritter (August William Ritter, Jr.; 6 Sep 1956, Denver CO), American politician (Democrat); governor of Colorado from 2007.

Rivaldo (Vitor Borba Ferreira; 19 Apr 1972, Recife, Brazil), Brazilian association football (soccer) player.

Geraldo (Miguel) Rivera (4 Jul 1943, Brooklyn NY), American TV journalist and talk-show host.

Tim Robbins (16 Oct 1958, West Covina CA), American actor.

Cecil E(dward) Roberts, Jr. (31 Oct 1946, Kayford WV), American labor leader; president of the United Mine Workers of America from 1995.

John G(lover) Roberts (27 Jan 1955, Buffalo NY), American jurist; chief justice of the US from 2005.

Julia Roberts (Julie Fiona Roberts; 28 Oct 1967, Smyrna GA), American film actress.

Nora Roberts (Eleanor Marie Robertson; 10 Oct 1950, Silver Spring MD), American novelist.

Peter (David) Robinson (29 Dec 1948, Belfast, Northern Ireland), Northern Irish Protestant loyalist politician; first minister of Northern Ireland from 2008.

Smokey Robinson (William Robinson, Jr.; 19 Feb 1940, Detroit MI), American R&B singer and songwriter; recipient of a 2006 Kennedy Center Honor.

Chris Rock (7 Feb 1966, Georgetown SC), American stand-up comedian and actor.

Kid Rock (Robert James Ritchie; 17 Jan 1971, Romeo MI), American rap-rock artist.

Andy Roddick (30 Aug 1982, Omaha NE), American tennis player.

Alex Rodriguez (27 Jul 1975, New York NY), American baseball shortstop and third baseman.

Narciso Rodríguez (January 1961, New Jersey), American fashion designer.

Robert (Anthony) Rodriguez (20 Jun 1968, San Antonio TX), Mexican American filmmaker.

Seth Rogen (15 Apr 1982, Vancouver, BC, Canada), Canadian film actor.

James E. Rogers (20 Sep 1947, Birmingham AL), American corporate executive; president and CEO (from 2006) and chairman of the board (from 2007) of Duke Energy.

Richard (George) Rogers (23 Jul 1933, Florence, Italy), British architect; recipient of a Praemium Imperiale in 2000 and the Pritzker Prize in 2007.

Jacques Rogge (2 May 1942, Ghent, Belgium), Belgian Olympic yachtsman, surgeon, and sports executive; president of the International Olympic Committee from 2001.

Roh Moo Hyun (6 Aug 1946, Kimbae, near Pusan, US-occupied Korea [now in South Korea]), Korean politician; president of South Korea, 2003–08.

Floyd Roland (23 Nov 1961, Inuvik, NT, Canada), Canadian politician; premier of the Northwest Territories from 2007.

Sonny Rollins (Theodore Walter Rollins; 7 Sep 1930, Harlem, New York NY), American jazz saxophonist.

Ray Romano (21 Dec 1957, Queens NY), American comic actor.

(Willard) Mitt Romney (12 Mar 1947, Bloomfield MI), American businessman, sports executive, and politician (Republican); governor of Massachusetts, 2003–07.

Tony Romo (21 Apr 1980, San Diego CA), American pro football quarterback.

Ronaldo (Ronaldo Luiz Nazario de Lima; 22 Sep 1976, Itaguai, Rio de Janeiro state, Brazil), Brazilian association football (soccer) player.

Charlie Rose (5 Jan 1942, Henderson NC), American TV journalist and interviewer.

Diana Ross (Diane Earle; 26 Mar 1944, Detroit MI), American R&B singer and actress; recipient of a 2007 Kennedy Center Honor.

Wilbur Ross (28 Nov 1937, North Bergen NJ), American financier and turnaround specialist; chairman of International Steel Group, Inc.

Philip (Milton) Roth (19 Mar 1933, Newark NJ), American novelist and short-story writer.

Mike Rounds (Marion Michael Rounds; 24 Oct 1954, Huron SD), American politician (Republican); governor of South Dakota from 2003.

Karl Rove (25 Dec 1950, Denver CO), American right-wing political operative and commentator; former chief strategist for Pres. George W. Bush.

J(oanne) K(athleen) Rowling (31 Jul 1965, Chipping Sodbury, near Bristol, Gloucestershire, England), British author, creator of the Harry Potter series.

Rick Rubin (Frederick Jay Rubin; 10 Mar 1963, Lido Beach NY), American record producer.

Kevin (Michael) Rudd (21 Sep 1957, Nambour, QLD, Australia), Australian politician (Labor); prime minister from 2007.

Erkki Ruoslahti (16 Feb 1940, Helsinki, Finland), Finnish-born American cell biologist and distinguished professor at the Burnham Institute, La Jolla CA; corecipient of the 2005 Japan Prize in Cell Biology.

Ed(ward Joseph) Ruscha (16 Dec 1937, Omaha NE), American Pop Art artist.

Geoffrey Rush (6 Jul 1951, Toowoomba, QLD, Australia), Australian film actor.

(Ahmed) Salman Rushdie (19 Jun 1947, Bombay [now Mumbai], British India), Anglo-Indian novelist.

Patricia F(iorello) Russo (12 Jun 1952, Trenton NJ), American business executive; CEO of Alcatel-Lucent from 2002.

Richard Russo (15 Jul 1949, Johnstown NY), American author; winner of the 2002 Pulitzer Prize for fiction.

Burt Rutan (Elbert L. Rutan; 17 Jun 1943, Portland OR), American test pilot, aerospace engineer, and designer of specialized aircraft.

John A. Ruthven (1927, Cincinnati OH), American wildlife artist.

John Rutter (24 Sep 1945, London, England), British composer and conductor; founder (1981) and leader of the Cambridge Singers.

Kay Ryan (11 Sep 1945, San Jose CA), American poet; recipient of the 2004 Ruth Lilly Poetry Prize and US poet laureate from 2008.

Meg Ryan (Margaret Mary Emily Anne Hyra; 19 Nov 1961, Fairfield CT), American film actress.

Winona Ryder (Winona Laura Horowitz; 29 Oct 1971, Winona MN), American film actress.

Mikhail Saakashvili (21 Dec 1967, Tbilisi, USSR [now in Georgia]), Georgian politician; president from 2004.

Charles Saatchi (9 Jun 1943, Baghdad, Iraq), Iraqi-born British advertising executive and art patron.

Sabah al-Ahmad al-Jabir Al Sabah (1929?, Kuwait city, Kuwait), Kuwaiti sheikh; emir from 2006.

Antonio (Elías) Saca (González) (9 Mar 1965, Usulután, El Salvador), Salvadoran politician (Nationalist Republican Alliance); president from 2004.

Jeffrey D(avid) Sachs (5 Nov 1954, Detroit MI), American economist.

Oliver (Wolf) Sacks (9 Jul 1933, London, England), British-born American neurologist and author of books on medical topics.

Muqtada al-Sadr (1974, Al-Najaf, Iraq), Iraqi Shiʿite Muslim cleric, a charismatic figure in the anti-American and anti-Western insurrection in Iraq following the US-led occupation of March 2003.

Sebastião (Ribeiro) Salgado (8 Feb 1944, Aimorés, Minas Gerais state, Brazil), Brazilian photographer.

ʿAli ʿAbdallah Salih (21 Mar 1942, Beit al-Ahmar, Yemen), Yemeni politician; president of Yemen (Sanʿa), 1978–90, and of the unified Yemen thereafter.

Alex(ander Elliot Anderson) Salmond (31 Dec 1954, Linlithgow, Scotland), Scottish politician (Scottish National Party); first minister of Scotland from 2007.

Esa-Pekka Salonen (30 Jun 1958, Helsinki, Finland), Finnish conductor and musical director of the Los Angeles Philharmonic from 1992.

Ahmed Abdallah Sambi (5 Jun 1958, Mutsamudu, Anjouan, French Comoro Islands), Comoran Muslim religious leader; president from 2006.

Ivo Sanader (8 Jun 1953, Split, Yugoslavia [now in Croatia]), Croatian scholar and politician; prime minister from 2003.

Adam Sandler (9 Sep 1966, Brooklyn NY), American comic actor.

Mark Sanford (Marshall Clement Sanford, Jr.; 15 Jan 1960, Fort Lauderdale FL), American politician (Republican); governor of South Carolina from 2003.

(Devadip) Carlos Santana (20 Jul 1947, Autlán de Navarro, Mexico), Mexican-born American guitarist and bandleader.

Johan (Alexander) Santana (Araque) (13 Mar 1979, Tovar, Venezuela), Venezuelan pro baseball left-handed starting pitcher.

Albert Pintat Santolària (23 Jun 1943, Sant Julià de Lòria, Andorra), Andorran chief executive from 2005.

Alejandro Sanz (Alejandro Sánchez Pizarro; 18 Dec 1968, Madrid, Spain), Spanish singer-songwriter and flamenco-pop artist.

Cristina Saralegui (29 Jan 1948, Havana, Cuba), Cuban-born American Spanish-language TV talk-show host.

José Saramago (16 Nov 1922, Azinhaga, Portugal), Portuguese novelist and man of letters; recipient of the 1998 Nobel Prize for Literature.

Susan Sarandon (Susan Abigail Tomalin; 4 Oct 1946, New York NY), American film actress.

Serzh (Azati) Sarkisyan (30 Jun 1954, Stepanakert, Nagorno-Karabakh autonomous oblast, USSR [now in Azerbaijan]), Armenian politician; prime minister, 2007–08, and president from April 2008.

Tigran Sarkisyan (29 Jan 1960, Kirovakan, USSR [now Vanadzor, Armenia]), Armenian economist and politician; prime minister from 2008.

Nicolas Sarkozy (Nicolas Paul-Stéphane Sarközy de Nagy-Bocsa; 28 Jan 1955, Paris, France), French conservative politician; interior minister, 2005–07, and president from 2007.

Mikio Sasaki (1937?), Japanese corporate executive; president and CEO of Mitsubishi Motors Corp., 1998–2004.

Denis Sassou-Nguesso (1943, Edou, French Equatorial Africa [now in the Republic of the Congo]), Congolese politician; president of the Republic of Congo, 1979–92 and again from 1997.

Marjane Satrapi (22 Nov 1969, Rasht, Iran), Iranian-born French graphic novelist; author of the Persepolis books, her memoirs of Iran during the last decades of the 20th century.

al-Walid ibn Talal ibn Abdulaziz al-Saud (1954, Riyadh, Saudi Arabia), Saudi prince and billionaire businessman.

Diane K. Sawyer (Lila Sawyer; 22 Dec 1945, Glasgow KY), American TV journalist.

Antonin Scalia (11 Mar 1936, Trenton NJ), American jurist; associate justice of the US Supreme Court from 1986.

Marjorie Scardino (Marjorie Morris; 25 Jan 1947, Flagstaff AZ), American-born British media executive; CEO of Pearson PLC from 1997.

Edward T(homas) Schafer (8 Aug 1946, Bismarck ND), American businessman and politician (Republican); US secretary of agriculture from 2008.

Eric E. Schmidt (1955?), American computer scientist and corporate executive; CTO of Sun Microsystems, Inc., 1983–97, chairman and CEO of Novell, Inc., 1997–2001, and chairman and CEO of Google, Inc., from 2001.

Julian Schnabel (26 Oct 1951, Brooklyn NY), American Neo-Expressionist artist and film director.

Peter J. Schoomaker (12 Feb 1946, Detroit MI), American military officer; chief of staff of the US Army, 2003–07.

Daniel Schorr (31 Aug 1916, New York NY), American TV and radio journalist and political commentator.

Richard Royce Schrock (4 Jan 1945, Berne IN), American chemist; corecipient of the 2005 Nobel Prize for Chemistry for the development of the metathesis method in organic synthesis.

Dieter Schulte (13 Jan 1940, Duisberg, Germany), German labor leader and head of the German Trade Union Federation from 1994.

Howard Schultz (19 Jul 1953, Brooklyn NY), American businessman; CEO of Starbucks Corp. from 1987, and principal owner of the Seattle SuperSonics professional basketball team, 2001–06.

Philip Schultz (1945, Rochester NY), American poet whose *Failure* won a 2008 Pulitzer Prize in poetry.

Michael Schumacher (3 Jan 1969, Hürth-Hermülheim, West Germany [now in Germany]), German Formula 1 race-car driver.

Wolfgang Schüssel (7 Jun 1945, Vienna, Austria), Austrian politician; chancellor, 2000–07.

Susan (Carol) Schwab (23 Mar 1955, Washington DC), American trade official; US trade representative from 2006.

Arnold (Alois) Schwarzenegger (30 Jul 1947, Thal bei Graz, Austria), Austrian-born American bodybuilder, film actor, and politician (Republican); governor of California from 2003.

Brian (David) Schweitzer (4 Sep 1955, Havre MT), American politician (Democrat); governor of Montana from 2005.

David Schwimmer (2 Nov 1966, Astoria, Queens NY), American TV and film actor.

Jon Scieszka (8 Sep 1954, Flint MI), American author of books for children.

John Scofield (26 Dec 1951, Dayton OH), American jazz electric guitarist, composer, and bandleader.

Martin Scorsese (17 Nov 1942, Flushing, Long Island NY), American film director, writer, and producer; recipient of an Academy Award as best director for 2006 and a 2007 Kennedy Center Honor.

H. Lee Scott, Jr. (1949?, Joplin MO), American corporate executive; president and CEO of Wal-Mart Stores from 2000.

Ridley Scott (30 Nov 1937, South Shields, Durham, England), British film director and producer.

Kristin Scott Thomas (24 May 1960, Redruth, Cornwall, England), British actress.

Vincent J(ames) Scully, Jr. (1930, New Haven CT), American architectural historian and critic.

Ryan (John) Seacrest (24 Dec 1974, Atlanta GA), American TV program host (*American Idol*).

Seal (Sealhenry Olusegun Olumide Samuel; 19 Feb 1963, Kilburn, London, England), British soul singer.

Sean Paul (Sean Paul Ryan Francis Henriques; 8 Jan 1973, St. Andrew, Jamaica), Jamaican reggae and rap musician.

Kathleen Sebelius (Kathleen Gilligan; 15 May 1948, Cincinnati OH), American politician (Democrat); governor of Kansas from 2003.

Alice Sebold (1963, Madison WI), American novelist.

Amy Sedaris (29 Mar 1961, Endicott NY), American comic actress and writer.

David Sedaris (26 Dec 1956, Johnson City NY), American writer and humorist.

Kyra (Minturn) Sedgwick (19 Aug 1965, New York NY), American film and TV actress.

Ivan G. Seidenberg (1947?, Bronx NY), American corporate executive; CEO of Verizon Communications from 2002.

Jerry Seinfeld (Jerome Seinfeld; 29 Apr 1954, Brooklyn NY), American comic and TV personality.

Fatmir Sejdiu (23 Oct 1951, Pakashtice, Yugoslavia [now in Kosovo]), Kosovar professor and politician; president of Kosovo from 2006.

Bud Selig (Allan H. Selig; 30 Jul 1934, Milwaukee WI), American sports executive; Major League Baseball commissioner from 1998.

Senait (Senait G. Mehari; 3 Dec 1976, Asmara, Ethiopia [now in Eritrea]), Eritrean-born German singer.

Paul Sereno (11 Oct 1957, Aurora IL), American paleontologist.

Marija Serifovic (14 Nov 1984, Kragujevac, Yugoslavia [now in Serbia]), Serbian pop singer; winner of the 2007 Eurovision Song Contest.

Richard Serra (2 Nov 1939, San Francisco CA), American minimalist sculptor of large outdoor works; recipient of a Praemium Imperiale in 1994.

Vikram Seth (20 Jun 1952, Calcutta [now Kolkata], India), Indian poet, novelist, and travel writer.

Nasrallah Pierre Cardinal Sfeir (Nasrallah Boutros Pierre Sfeir; 15 May 1920, Reyfoun, Lebanon), Lebanese (Maronite Catholic) patriarch of Antioch and all the East from 1986 and Roman Catholic cardinal from 1994.

Gil Shaham (19 Feb 1971, Champaign-Urbana IL), American violinist.

Shakira (Shakira Isabel Mebarak Ripoll; 2 Feb 1977, Barranquilla, Colombia), Colombian-born pop singer.

Tony Shalhoub (Anthony Marcus Shalhoub; 9 Oct 1953, Green Bay WI), American TV and film actor.

John Patrick Shanley (1950, Bronx NY), American screenwriter and playwright.

Mariya (Yuryevna) Sharapova (19 Apr 1987, Nyagan, USSR [now in Russia]), Russian tennis player.

Kamalesh Sharma (30 Sep 1941), Indian diplomat; secretary-general of the Commonwealth from 2008.

Al Sharpton (3 Oct 1954, New York NY), American politician (Democrat), political activist, and civil rights leader.

William Shatner (22 Mar 1931, Montreal, QC, Canada), Canadian TV actor.

Charlie Sheen (Carlos Irwin Estevez; 3 Sep 1965, New York NY), American film and TV actor.

Martin Sheen (Ramon Estevez; 3 Aug 1940, Dayton OH), American stage, film, and TV actor.

Judith Sheindlin (21 Oct 1942, Brooklyn NY), American TV judge (of *Judge Judy*).

Sam Shepard (Samuel Shepard Rogers; 5 Nov 1943, Fort Sheridan IL), American playwright and actor.

Cindy Sherman (Cynthia Morris Sherman; 19 Jan 1954, Glen Ridge NJ), American photographer.

Masaaki Shirakawa (27 Sep 1949, Kitakyushu, Japan), Japanese banker; governor of the Bank of Japan from 2008.

Vandana Shiva (5 Nov 1952, Dehra Dun, Uttar Pradesh [now in Uttarakhand] state, India), Indian biologist and social activist against the "biological theft" of the resources of poor countries by the richer ones.

Will Shortz (26 Aug 1952, Crawfordsville IN), American "enigmatologist" and "puzzlemaster"; crossword-puzzle editor at the *New York Times*.

Etsuhiko Shoyama (9 Mar 1936, Japan), Japanese corporate executive; CEO and chairman of Hitachi, Ltd., from 1999.

Than Shwe (2 Feb 1933, Kyaukse, Burma [now Myanmar]), Burmese military officer; head of government in Myanmar, 1992–2003, and chairman of the State Peace and Development Council (head of state) from 1992.

M(anoj) Night Shyamalan (6 Aug 1970, Pondicherry, India), Indian-born film director and screenwriter.

Malick Sidibé (1935/36, Soloba, French Sudan [now Mali]), Malian photographer.

(David) Derek Sikua (10 Sep 1959, Guadalcanal province, British-protected Solomon Islands), Solomon Islands politician; prime minister from 2007.

Haris Silajdzic (1 Oct 1945, Sarajevo, Yugoslavia [now in Bosnia and Herzegovina]), Bosnia and Herzegovinian Muslim political leader; prime minister or co-prime minister, 1993–2000, and chairman of the presidency of the republic from 2008.

Sarah (Kate) Silverman (1 Dec 1970, Bedford NH), American comedian, TV actress, and writer.

Silvia (Silvia Renate Sommerlath; 23 Dec 1943, Heidelberg, Germany), Swedish royal and social activist; queen consort of King Carl XVI Gustaf (married 19 Jun 1976).

Charles Simic (9 May 1938, Belgrade, Yugoslavia [now in Serbia]), Yugoslav-born American poet; US poet laureate, 2007–08.

Russell Simmons (4 Oct 1957, Queens NY), American hip-hop impresario and cofounder of Def Jam Records.

Jessica Simpson (10 Jul 1980, Dallas TX), American pop singer and actress.

Lorna Simpson (13 Aug 1960, Brooklyn NY), American multimedia artist.

Ashlee Simpson-Wentz (3 Oct 1984, Dallas TX), American actress and singer.

Hammerskjoeld Simwinga (17 Nov 1964, Isoka, Zambia), Zambian environmentalist; recipient of the 2007 Goldman Environmental Prize for Africa.

Kushal Pal Singh (15 Aug 1931, Bulandshahr, Uttar Pradesh, British India), Indian real-estate baron.

Manmohan Singh (26 Sep 1932, Gah, Punjab, British India [now in Pakistan]), Indian economist; prime minister from 2004.

Fouad Siniora (July 1943, Sidon, Lebanon), Lebanese banker and Sunni politician; prime minister from 2005 and acting president from 2007–08.

Gary Sinise (17 Mar 1955, Blue Island IL), American TV and film actor and director.

(Sayyid) Ali (Hussaini) al-Sistani (4 Aug 1930?, near Meshed, Iran), Iranian Shiʿite Muslim cleric.

Ricky Skaggs (18 Jul 1954, Cordell KY), American bluegrass and country musician.

Antonio Skármeta (7 Nov 1940, Antofagasta, Chile), Chilean novelist and screenwriter.

Jeffrey S. Skoll (16 Jan 1965, Montreal, QC, Canada), Canadian entrepreneur; cofounder of eBay and, from 1999, the president of the philanthropic Skoll Foundation.

Leonard (Edward) Slatkin (1 Sep 1944, Los Angeles CA), American conductor; music director of the National Symphony Orchestra from 1996.

Carlos Slim Helú (1940, Mexico?), Mexican investor; head of Grupo Carso, SA de CV, and longtime owner of the national telephone monopoly, Teléfonos de México (Telmex).

Lawrence M. Small (14 Sep 1941, New York NY), American businessman; president and COO of Fannie Mae, 1991–2000, and secretary of the Smithsonian Institution, 2000–07.

Tavis Smiley (13 Sep 1964, Gulfport MS), American advocacy journalist on radio and TV.

Alexander McCall Smith (24 Aug 1948, Bulawayo, Southern Rhodesia [now Zimbabwe]), British author of crime novels and works for children.

Anna Deavere Smith (18 Sep 1950, Baltimore MD), American playwright, actress, professor.

Marc (Kelly) Smith (195?, Chicago IL), American performance poet; originator of the poetry slam.

Michael W. Smith (7 Oct 1957, Kenova WV), American Christian singer.

Patti (Lee) Smith (30 Dec 1946, Chicago IL), American musician, poet, and visual artist.

Stephen Smith (12 Dec 1955, Narrogin, WA, Australia), Australian politician (Labor); foreign minister from 2007.

Will(ard Christopher) Smith, Jr. (25 Sep 1968, Philadelphia PA), American rapper and actor.

Zadie Smith (Sadie Smith; 27 Oct 1975, Willesden Green, London, England), British novelist.

Oliver Smithies (23 Jun 1925, Halifax, Yorkshire, England), British-born American biochemist; corecipient of the 2007 Nobel Prize for Physiology or Medicine for developing a technique for introducing modified genes into mice.

Wesley Snipes (31 Jul 1962, Orlando FL), American film actor.

Snoop Dogg (Calvin Broadus; 20 Oct 1972, Long Beach CA), American gangsta rap musician.

Gary (Sherman) Snyder (8 May 1930, San Francisco CA), American poet.

José Sócrates (José Sócrates Carvalho Pinto de Sousa; 6 Sep 1957, Vilar de Maçada, Portugal), Portuguese civil engineer and politician (Socialist); prime minister from 2005.

Steven Soderbergh (14 Jan 1963, Atlanta GA), American film director.

Sofia (Princess Sophie of Greece; Sofia de Grecia y Hannover; 2 Nov 1938, Athens, Greece), Spanish royal; queen consort of King Juan Carlos I (married 12 May 1962).

Javier Solana (Madariaga) (14 Jul 1942, Madrid, Spain), Spanish statesman; NATO secretary-general, 1995–99, and secretary-general of the Council of the European Union from 1999.

László Sólyom (3 Jan 1942, Pécs, Hungary), Hungarian jurist and politician; president from 2005.

Michael (Thomas) Somare (9 Apr 1936, Rabaul, Australian-mandated New Guinea [now Papua New Guinea]), Papua New Guinean politician; prime minister, 1975–80, 1982–85, and again from 2002.

Juan (Octavio) Somavia (21 Apr 1941, Chile), Chilean international official; director-general of the International Labour Organization from 1999.

Stephen (Joshua) Sondheim (22 Mar 1930, New York NY), American composer and lyricist for musical theater.

Sonja (Sonja Haraldsen; 4 Jul 1937, Oslo, Norway), Norwegian royal; queen consort of King Harald V (married 29 Aug 1968).

Sophie (Sophie Helen Rhys-Jones; 20 Jan 1965, Oxford, England), British royal; wife of Prince Edward (married 19 Jun 1999) and countess of Wessex.

Annika Sörenstam (9 Oct 1970, Stockholm, Sweden), Swedish golfer.

Aaron Sorkin (9 Jun 1961, Scarsdale NY), American screenwriter, playwright, and TV producer.

Guillaume Soro (8 May 1972, Kofiplé, Côte d'Ivoire), Ivorian politician; prime minister from 2007.

Ahmed Tidiane Souaré (1951, French West Africa?), Guinean economist and statesman; prime minister from 2008.

David H(ackett) Souter (17 Sep 1939, Melrose MA), American jurist; associate justice of the US Supreme Court from 1990.

Wole Soyinka (Akinwande Oluwole Soyinka; 13 Jul 1934, Abeokuta, Nigeria), Nigerian playwright, poet, novelist, and critic; recipient of the 1986 Nobel Prize for Literature.

Kevin Spacey (Kevin Matthew Fowler; 26 Jul 1959, South Orange NJ), American stage and film actor and artistic director of the Old Vic theater in London.

James (Todd) Spader (7 Feb 1960, Boston MA), American film and TV actor.

Nicholas Sparks (31 Dec 1965, Omaha NE), American novelist.

Britney (Jean) Spears (2 Dec 1981, Kentwood LA), American pop singer and celebrity.

Margaret Spellings (30 Nov 1957, Michigan), American political adviser, education expert, and secretary of education from 2005.

W(inston) Baldwin Spencer (8 Oct 1948), West Indian politician; prime minister of Antigua and Barbuda from 2004.

Steven Spielberg (18 Dec 1947, Cincinnati OH), American film director and producer; recipient of a 2006 Kennedy Center Honor.

Nikola Spiric (4 Sep 1956, Drvar, Yugoslavia [now in Bosnia and Herzegovina]), Bosnia and Herzegovinian politician; chairman of the Council of Ministers (prime minister) from 2007.

Eliot (Laurence) Spitzer (10 Jun 1959, Riverdale, Bronx NY), American attorney and politician (Democrat); governor of New York, 2007–08.

Bruce Springsteen (23 Sep 1949, Freehold NJ), American rock singer and songwriter.

(Michael) Sylvester (Enzio) Stallone ("Sly"; 6 Jul 1946, New York NY), American film actor and director.

Sergey (Dmitriyevich) Stanishev (5 May 1966, Kherson, USSR [now in Ukraine]), Bulgarian politician (Socialist); prime minister from 2005.

Mavis Staples (1940, Chicago IL), American gospel singer.

Albert Starr (1 Jun 1926, New York NY), American cardiovascular surgeon and inventor of an artificial heart valve; recipient of a 2007 Lasker Medical Prize.

Danielle (Fernande Schuelein-) Steel (14 Aug 1947, New York NY), American romance novelist.

Gwen Stefani (3 Oct 1969, Fullerton CA), American rock and pop vocalist.

Ralph M(arvin) Steinman (14 Jan 1943, Montreal, QC, Canada), American immunologist and specialist in immune response in cells; recipient of a 2007 Lasker Medical Prize.

Frank-Walter Steinmeier (5 Jan 1956, Detmold, West Germany [now in Germany]), German government official; foreign minister from 2005 and vice-chancellor from 2007.

Frank P(hilip) Stella (12 May 1936, Malden MA), American painter.

Ed Stelmach (11 May 1951, Lamont, AB, Canada), Canadian politician (Progressive Conservative); premier of Alberta from 2006.

Stephanie (Stéphanie Marie Elizabeth Grimaldi; 1 Feb 1965, Monaco), Monegasque princess; the youngest child of Prince Rainier III and Grace Kelly.

Stéphanos II (Amba Andraos Ghattas; Stéphanos Cardinal Ghattas; 16 Jan 1920, Cheikh Zein-el-Dine, Egypt), Egyptian churchman; patriarch of Alexandria of the Coptics from 1986; Roman Catholic cardinal from 2001.

Marcus Stephen (1 Oct 1969, Nauru?), Nauruan weight lifter and politician; president from 2007.

Howard Stern (12 Jan 1954, Roosevelt NY), American radio and TV personality.

John Paul Stevens (20 Apr 1920, Chicago IL), American jurist; associate justice of the US Supreme Court from 1975.

Ellen Stewart (7 Nov 1919, Chicago IL), American theater director and producer, the founder (1961) of La MaMa Experimental Theater Club in New York City; recipient of a Praemium Imperiale in 2007.

Jon Stewart (Jonathan Stewart Leibowitz; 28 Nov 1962, New York NY), American actor, writer, and comedian; anchor of TV's *The Daily Show* from 1999.

Patrick Stewart (13 Jul 1940, Mirfield, Yorkshire, England), British actor.

Rod(erick David) Stewart (10 Jan 1945, London, England), British singer and songwriter.

Julia (O'Hara) Stiles (28 Mar 1981, New York NY), American film actress.

Ben Stiller (30 Nov 1965, New York NY), American comedian, actor, and film director.

Sting (Gordon Matthew Sumner; 2 Oct 1951, Wallsend, Newcastle upon Tyne, England), British singer, songwriter, and actor.

Jens Stoltenberg (16 Mar 1959, Oslo, Norway), Norwegian economist and politician (Norwegian Labor Party); prime minister, 2000–01 and again from 2005.

Joss Stone (Joscelyn Eve Stoker; 11 Apr 1987, Dover, Kent, England), English soul singer.

Oliver (William) Stone (15 Sep 1946, New York NY), American director, writer, and producer.

Tom Stoppard (Tomas Straussler; 3 Jul 1937, Zlin, Moravia, Czechoslovakia [now in the Czech Republic]), Czech-born British playwright and screenwriter.

Mark Strand (11 Apr 1934, Summerside, PE, Canada), Canadian poet, writer of short fiction, and translator.

Dominique Strauss-Kahn (25 Apr 1949, Neuilly-sur-Seine), French politician (Socialist); chairman of the International Monetary Fund from 2007.

Jack Straw (John Whitaker Straw; 3 Aug 1946, Brentwood, Essex, England), British politician; home secretary, 1997–2001, foreign secretary, 2001–06, and secretary of state for justice and lord high chancellor from 2007.

Meryl Streep (Mary Louise Streep; 22 Jun 1949, Summit NJ), American film actress.

John F. Street (15 Oct 1943, Norristown PA), American politician (Democrat); mayor of Philadelphia, 2000–08.

Barbra Streisand (Barbara Joan Streisand; 24 Apr 1942, Brooklyn NY), American singer, actress, and film director.

Ted Strickland (4 Aug 1941, Lucasville OH), American politician (Democrat); governor of Ohio from 2007.

Howard Stringer (19 Feb 1942, Cardiff, Wales), Welsh-born business executive; chairman and CEO of Sony Corp. from 2005.

Susan Stroman (17 Oct 1954, Wilmington DE), American theater director.

(Christopher) Ruben Studdard (12 Sep 1978, Frankfurt am Main, West Germany [now in Germany]), American singer.

Juan Manuel Suárez del Toro Rivero (1952, Spain), Spanish international official; president of the International Federation of Red Cross and Red Crescent Societies from 2001.

Arthur Ochs Sulzberger, Jr. (22 Sep 1951, Mount Kisco NY), American newspaper executive, publisher of the *New York Times* from 1992 and CEO from 1997.

Pat Summitt (Patricia Head; 14 Jun 1952, Henrietta TN), American women's basketball coach.

Samak Sundaravej (13 Jun 1935, Bangkok, Siam [now Thailand]), Thai politician; prime minister from 2008.

Rashid Sunyaev (Rashid [Aliyevich] Syunyayev; 1 Mar 1943, Tashkent, USSR [now in Uzbekistan]), Uzbek-born Russian astrophysicist, a specialist in cosmological background radiation and black holes; director of the Max Planck Institute for Astrophysics from 1996; recipient of the 2000 Bruce Medal and a 2008 Crafoord Prize.

Kiefer Sutherland (William Frederick Dempsey George Sutherland; 21 Dec 1966, London, England), Canadian film and TV actor.

Ichiro Suzuki (22 Oct 1973, Kasugai, Aichi prefecture, Japan), Japanese baseball player.

Hilary Swank (30 Jul 1974, Lincoln NE), American film actress.

John J. Sweeney (5 May 1934, New York NY), American labor leader; president of the AFL-CIO from 1995.

Tilda Swinton (Katherine Matilda Swinton; 5 Nov 1960, London, England), British actress; recipient of the 2007 best supporting actress Academy Award.

Keiji Tachikawa (27 May 1939, Ogaki, Gifu prefecture, Japan), Japanese communications executive; president of DoCoMo, a wireless provider.

Boris Tadic (15 Jan 1958, Sarajevo, Yugoslavia [now in Bosnia and Herzegovina]), Serbian politician and government official; president of Serbia from 2004.

Masatoshi Takeichi (27 Nov 1943, Nagoya, Japan), Japanese developmental biologist, professor, and director of the RIKEN Center for Developmental Biology.

Jalal Talabani (1933, Kalkan, Iraq), Iraqi Kurdish politician; president of Iraq from 2005.

Mehmet Ali Talat (6 Jul 1952, Girne, British Cyprus), Turkish Cypriot politician; prime minister of the Turkish Republic of Northern Cyprus, 2004–05, and president from 2005.

Mamadou Tandja (1938, Maïné-Soroa, French West Africa [now in Niger]), Nigerois politician; president from 1999.

Quentin (Jerome) Tarantino (27 Mar 1963, Knoxville TN), American film director.

Marc Tarpenning (1 Jun 1964, Sacramento CA), American entrepreneur and cofounder of Tesla Motors.

Ratan (Naval) Tata (28 Dec 1937, Bombay [now Mumbai], British India), Indian corporate executive; chairman of the Tata Group and its several subsidiary companies in steel, motors, chemicals, hotels, etc.

Audrey Tautou (9 Aug 1978, Beaumont, France), French film actress.

John Tavener (28 Jan 1944, London, England), British composer.

Charles M(argrave) Taylor (5 Nov 1931, Montreal, QC, Canada), Canadian philosopher and professor; recipient of the 2007 Templeton Prize.

Elizabeth (Rosemond) Taylor (27 Feb 1932, London, England), American film actress.

Julie Taymor (15 Dec 1952, Newton MA), American theater and film director.

Mario Testino (1954, Lima, Peru), Peruvian fashion photographer.

Hashim Thaci (24 Apr 1969, Buroja, Yugoslavia [now in Kosovo]), Kosovar politician; prime minister from 2008.

Bal (Keshav) Thackeray (23 Jan 1927), Indian politician who established the Shiv Sena party.

John A. Thain (1955?), American financial official; CEO of the New York Stock Exchange, 2004–07, and CEO of Merrill Lynch from 2007.

Hamad ibn Khalifah al-Thani (1950, Doha, Qatar), Qatari sheikh; emir from 1995.

Twyla Tharp (1 Jul 1941, Portland IN), American dancer, director, and choreographer.

Charlize Theron (7 Aug 1975, Benoni, South Africa), South African actress.

Thich Nhat Hanh (11 Oct 1926, central Vietnam), Vietnamese Buddhist monk, pacifist, and teacher.

Lyonchen Jigme (Yoeser) Thinley (1952, Bumthang district, Bhutan), Bhutanese prime minister, 1998–99, 2003–04, and again from 2008.

Clarence Thomas (23 Jun 1948, Pinpoint community, near Savannah GA), American jurist; associate justice of the US Supreme Court from 1991.

Michael Tilson Thomas (21 Dec 1944, Hollywood CA), American conductor and composer; music director of the San Francisco Symphony from 1995.

Tillman (Joseph) Thomas (13 Jun 1945, Hermitage, St. Patrick, Grenada), West Indian politician; prime minister of Grenada from 2008.

David (John Howard) Thompson (December 1961, London, England), Barbadian politician; prime minister from 2008.

Emma Thompson (15 Apr 1959, London, England), British film actress.

Fred (Dalton) Thompson (19 Aug 1942, Sheffield AL), American film and TV actor and politician (Republican); senator from Tennessee, 1994–2003.

Jenny Thompson (26 Feb 1973, Danvers MA), American swimmer.

Robert Thomson (11 Mar 1961, Echuca, VIC, Australia), Australian journalist; editor of *The Times* of London from 2002.

Billy Bob Thornton (4 Aug 1955, Hot Springs AR), American director and actor.

Ian Thorpe (13 Oct 1982, Sydney, Australia), Australian swimmer.

Uma (Karuna) Thurman (29 Apr 1970, Boston MA), American film actress.

Rex W. Tillerson (23 Mar 1952, Wichita Falls TX), American petroleum company executive; president (from 2004) and CEO (from 2006) of Exxon Mobil Corp.

Timbaland (Timothy Z. Mosley; 10 Mar 1972, Norfolk VA), American R&B and rap composer, record producer, and performer.

Justin (Randall) Timberlake (31 Jan 1981, Memphis TN), American pop singer.

Claire Tomalin (Claire Delavenay; 20 Jun 1933, London, England), English biographer and author.

(Iroij) Litokwa Tomeing (14 Oct 1939, Wotje atoll, Japanese-mandated Marshall Islands), Marshallese politician; president of the Marshall Islands from 2008.

Anote Tong (1952), Kiribati politician; president from 2003.

Gaston Tong Sang (7 Aug 1949, Bora-Bora, Tahiti, French Polynesia), French Polynesian politician; president of French Polynesia, 2006–07 and again from 2008.

Bamir Topi (24 Apr 1957, Tiranë, Albania), Albanian biologist and politician; president from 2007.

Mirek Topolanek (15 May 1956, Vsetin, Moravia, Czechoslovakia [now in the Czech Republic]), Czech industrial engineer, businessman, and politician; prime minister from 2006.

Martín Torrijos Espino (18 Jul 1963, Panama City, Panama), Panamanian politician (Democratic Revolutionary Party); president from 2004.

Amadou Toumani Touré (4 Nov 1948, Mpoti, French Sudan [now in Mali]), Malian politician; president, 1991–92 and again from 2002.

Hamadoun Touré (3 Sep 1953, French Sudan [now Mali]), Malian international official; secretary-general of the International Telecommunication Union from 2007.

Avraham Trahtman (Avraam Trakhtman; 10 Feb 1944, Kalinovo, Sverdlovsk oblast, USSR [now Yekaterinburg, Russia]), Russian-born Israeli mathematician who published a proof of the road-coloring problem in 2007.

Randy Travis (Randy Traywick; 4 May 1959, Marshville NC), American country-and-western singer, songwriter, and actor.

John (Joseph) Travolta (18 Feb 1955, Englewood NJ), American TV and film actor.

Natasha Trethewey (26 Apr 1966, Gulfport MS), American poet whose *Native Guard* won the 2007 Pulitzer Prize for poetry.

Jean-Claude Trichet (20 Dec 1942, Lyons, France), French banker, governor of the Banque de France, 1993–2003, and president of the European Central Bank from 2003.

Libby Trickett (Lisbeth Lenton; 28 Jan 1985, Townsville, QLD, Australia), Australian freestyle swimmer.

Lars von Trier (30 Apr 1956, Copenhagen, Denmark), Danish film director and cinematographer.

Calvin Trillin (5 Dec 1935, Kansas City MO), American author, commentator, and occasional poet.

Travis Tritt (9 Feb 1963, Marietta GA), American country-and-western singer.

Robert L. Trivers (19 Feb 1943, Washington DC), American evolutionary biologist and sociobiologist; recipient of a 2007 Crafoord Prize "for his fundamental analysis of social evolution, conflict and cooperation."

Garry R. Trudeau (21 Jul 1948, New York NY), American cartoonist; creator of the durable *Doonesbury* syndicated comic strip.

Donald (John) Trump (14 Jun 1946, New York NY), American real-estate developer and reality-TV personality.

Ronald A. Tschetter (4 Oct 1941, Huron SD), American investment executive; director of the Peace Corps from 2006.

Morgan Tsvangirai (10 Mar 1952, Gutu, Southern Rhodesia [now Zimbabwe]), Zimbabwean labor leader and politician; head of the Movement for Democratic Change (from 1999), and main opposition leader to the regime of Pres. Robert Mugabe.

Togiola T(alalei) A. Tulafono (28 Feb 1947, Aunu'u Island, American Samoa), American politician (Democrat); governor of American Samoa from 2003.

Tommy Tune (28 Feb 1939, Wichita Falls TX), American musical-comedy dancer and actor.

Danilo Turk (19 Feb 1952, Maribor, Yugoslavia [now in Slovenia]), Slovenian law professor and diplomat; president from 2007.

Ted Turner (Robert Edward Turner III; 19 Nov 1938, Cincinnati OH), American TV executive, the founder of Turner Broadcasting System and owner of Cable News Network (CNN); sports club owner; yachtsman; and philanthropist.

John Turturro (27 Feb 1957, Brooklyn NY), American stage, film, and TV actor.

Donald (Franciszek) Tusk (22 Apr 1957, Gdansk, Poland), Polish politician (Civic Platform); prime minister from 2007.

Desmond (Mpilo) Tutu (7 Oct 1931, Klerksdorp, South Africa), South African Anglican cleric who in 1984 received the Nobel Peace Prize for his role in the opposition to apartheid in South Africa.

Cy Twombly (Edwin Parker Twombly, Jr.; 25 Apr 1928, Lexington VA), American abstract artist and sculptor.

Anne Tyler (25 Oct 1941, Minneapolis MN), American novelist and short-story writer.

Liv Tyler (Liv Rundgren; 1 Jul 1977, Portland ME), American actress and model.

Yuliya (Volodymyrivna) Tymoshenko (27 Nov 1960, Dnipropetrovsk, USSR [now in Ukraine]), Ukrainian businesswoman and politician (Yuliya Tymoshenko Bloc); prime minister in 2005 and again from 2007.

(Alfred) McCoy Tyner (Sulaimon Saud; 11 Dec 1938, Philadelphia PA), American jazz pianist and composer.

João Ubaldo (Osório Pimentel) Ribeiro (23 Jan 1941, Itaparica, Bahia state, Brazil), Brazilian novelist.

Robert J. Ulrich (1944?, Minneapolis MN), American corporate executive; CEO of Target Corp. from 1994.

Carrie Underwood (10 Mar 1983, Muskogee OK), American country singer.

John (Hoyer) Updike (18 Mar 1932, Shillington PA), American writer of novels, short stories, and poetry.

Keith (Lionel) Urban (26 Oct 1967, Whangerei, New Zealand), New Zealand-born Australian country singer.

Álvaro Uribe Vélez (4 Jul 1952, Medellín, Colombia), Colombian politician; president from 2002.

Usher (Usher Raymond IV; 14 Oct 1978, Chattanooga TN), American R&B singer.

Jørn Utzon (9 Apr 1918, Copenhagen, Denmark), Danish architect; recipient of the 2003 Pritzker Prize.

Jochem Uytdehaage (9 Jul 1976, Utrecht, Netherlands), Dutch speed skater.

Martine Van Hamel (16 Nov 1945, Brussels, Belgium), Belgian dancer and leading choreographer for the American Ballet Theatre.

Gus van Sant (24 Jul 1952, Louisville KY), American film director.

Matti Vanhanen (4 Nov 1955, Jyväskylä, Finland), Finnish politician; prime minister from 2003.

(Jorge) Mario (Pedro) Vargas Llosa (28 Mar 1936, Arequipa, Peru), Peruvian-born Spanish novelist.

Harold (Eliot) Varmus (18 Dec 1939, Oceanside NY), American virologist; corecipient of 1989 Nobel Prize for Physiology or Medicine; director of the National Institutes of Health, 1993–99, and president of Memorial Sloan-Kettering Cancer Center in New York City from 2000.

Alexander J. Varshavsky (1946, Russia, USSR), Russian-born American biochemist and cancer researcher; recipient of the first (2008) Gotham Prize.

Vince Vaughn (Vincent Anthony Vaughn; 28 Mar 1970, Minneapolis MN), American actor.

Tabaré (Ramón) Vázquez (Rosas) (17 Jan 1940, Barrio La Teja, Montevideo, Uruguay), Uruguayan physician and politician (Socialist); president from 2005.

Eddie Vedder (Edward Louis Severson III; 23 Dec 1964, Evanston IL), American rock vocalist and songwriter (for Pearl Jam).

Jeroen van der Veer (27 Oct 1947, Utrecht, Netherlands), Dutch corporate executive; CEO of Royal Dutch/Shell Group (The Netherlands).

Jaci Velasquez (Jacquelyn Davette Velasquez; 15 Oct 1979, Houston TX), American Latin and gospel singer.

Ann M. Veneman (29 Jun 1949, Modesto CA), American government official; US secretary of agriculture, 2001–05, and executive director of UNICEF from 2005.

(Runaldo) Ronald Venetiaan (18 Jun 1936, Paramaribo, Dutch Guiana [now Suriname]), Surinamese mathematician and politician; president, 1991–96 and again from 2000.

Maxim Vengerov (Maksim Aleksandrovich Vengerov; 20 Aug 1974, Novosibirsk, USSR [now in Russia]), Russian-born concert violinist.

J. Craig Venter (14 Oct 1946, Salt Lake City UT), American geneticist and researcher into the human genome; he was the founder of Celera Genomics.

Guy Verhofstadt (11 Apr 1953, Dendermonde, Belgium), Belgian politician (VLD); prime minister, 1999–2008.

Donatella Versace (2 May 1955, Reggio di Calabria, Italy), Italian fashion designer; creative director at the Versace design house from 1997.

Ben Verwaayen (February 1952), Dutch corporate executive; CEO of British Telecommunications PLC from 2002.

Charles M. Vest (9 Sep 1941, Morgantown WV), American scientist and educator; president of the Massachusetts Institute of Technology, 1990–2004, and president of the National Academy of Engineering from 2007.

Jack Vettriano (Jack Hoggan; 17 Nov 1951, St. Andrews, Fife, Scotland), British painter.

Victoria (Victoria Ingrid Alice Desirée; 14 Jul 1977, Stockholm, Sweden), Swedish crown princess and duchess of Västergötland.

João Bernardo Vieira (27 Apr 1939, Bissau, Portuguese Guinea [now Guinea-Bissau]), Guinea-Bissau politician; president, 1980–84, 1984–99, and again from 2005.

Antonio Villaraigosa (Antonio Ramón Villar, Jr.; 23 Jan 1953, East Los Angeles CA), American politician (Democrat); mayor of Los Angeles from 2005.

Diana Vishneva (Diana Viktorovna Vishnyova; 13 Jun 1976, Leningrad, USSR [now St. Petersburg, Russia]), Russian ballerina with the Mariinsky Ballet and, from 2003, the American Ballet Theatre.

Lindsey Vonn (Lindsey Kildow; 18 Oct 1984, St. Paul MN), American Alpine skier.

Vladimir Voronin (25 May 1941, Corjova, Moldavian SSR, USSR [now Moldova]), Moldovan politician; president from 2001.

Filip Vujanovic (1 Sep 1954, Belgrade, Yugoslavia [now in Serbia]), Montenegrin politician; president of the Republic of Montenegro, before and after its independence, 2002–03 (acting) and again from 2003.

Rem (Ivanovich) Vyakhirev (23 Aug 1934, Bolshaya Chernigovka, USSR [now in Russia]), Russian billionaire head (1992–2001) of Gazprom, the largest company in Russia, and chairman of Siberia Oil Co. from 1996.

Norio Wada (17 Nov 1949, Osaka, Japan), Japanese corporate executive; president and CEO of Nippon Telegraph & Telephone from 2002.

Abdoulaye Wade (29 May 1926, Kébémer, French West Africa [now in Senegal]), Senegalese politician; president from 2000.

G. Richard Wagoner, Jr. (9 Feb 1953, Wilmington DE), American corporate executive; CEO of General Motors Corp. from 2000.

Mark (Robert Michael) Wahlberg (5 Jun 1971, Dorchester, Boston MA), American actor.

Rufus Wainwright (22 Jul 1973, Rhinebeck NY), Canadian singer and songwriter.

Ted Waitt (18 Jan 1963, Sioux City IA), American computer executive and philanthropist; cofounder of Gateway Inc. in 1985 and chairman and CEO of the charitable Waitt Family Foundation from 1993.

Derek (Alton) Walcott (23 Jan 1930, Castries, Saint Lucia, British West Indies), West Indian poet and playwright; recipient of the 1992 Nobel Prize for Literature.

Jimmy (Donal) Wales (7 Aug 1966, Huntsville AL), American Internet publisher; founder of *Wikipedia*.

Alice (Malsenior) Walker (9 Feb 1944, Eatonton GA), American novelist, poet, and short-story writer.

David M(ichael) Walker (2 Oct 1951, Birmingham AL), American comptroller general (head of the Government Accountability Office), 1998–2008.

Brad Wall (24 Nov 1965, Swift Current, SK, Canada), Canadian businessman and politician (Progressive Conservative); premier of Saskatchewan from 2007.

Mike Wallace (Myron Leon Wallace; 9 May 1918, Brookline MA), American TV journalist, interviewer, and coeditor of CBS's *60 Minutes*.

Mark J. Walport (1953, England), British immunologist; director of the Wellcome Trust from 2003.

Barbara (Ann) Walters (25 Sep 1931, Boston MA), American broadcast journalist and TV interviewer.

John P. Walters (1951?), American civic and government official; director of national drug control policy ("drug czar") from 2001.

Alice L. Walton (c. 1949), American heiress of part of the Wal-Mart fortune.

Helen R. Walton (c. 1920), American heiress of part of the Wal-Mart fortune.

Jim C. Walton (c. 1948), American business executive; chairman and CEO of the Arvest Group.

Vera Wang (27 Jun 1949, New York NY), American fashion designer.

Jigme Khesar Namgyal Wangchuk (21 Feb 1980, Thimphu, Bhutan), Bhutanese royal; king from 2006.

Shane Keith Warne (13 Sep 1969, Ferntree Gully, VIC, Australia), Australian cricketer, a spin bowler named one of *Wisden*'s Five Cricketers of the Century.

J. Robin Warren (11 Jun 1937, Adelaide, SA, Australia), Australian pathologist; corecipient of the 2005 Nobel Prize for Physiology or Medicine.

Rick Warren (1954, San Jose CA), American evangelist minister.

Denzel Washington, Jr. (28 Dec 1954, Mount Vernon NY), American film and TV actor.

Kerry Washington (31 Jan 1977, Bronx NY), American film actress.

(Chaudhry) Wasim Akram (3 Jun 1966, Lahore, Pakistan), Pakistani cricket left-handed fast bowler.

Alice Waters (28 Apr 1944, Chatham NJ), American chef and restaurant owner (Chez Panisse, Berkeley CA).

John Waters (22 Apr 1946, Baltimore MD), American filmmaker.

Naomi Watts (28 Sep 1968, Shoreham, Kent, England), Australian film actress.

George (Manneh Oppong Ousman) Weah (1 Oct 1966, Monrovia, Liberia), Liberian-born association football (soccer) star, named in 1998 African Player of the Century.

Hugo Weaving (4 Apr 1960, Austin, Nigeria), Australian film actor.

Karrie Webb (21 Dec 1974, Ayr, QLD, Australia), Australian golfer.

Andrew (Thomas) Weil (8 Jun 1942, Philadelphia PA), American physician and champion of alternative medicine.

Bob Weinstein (1954, Queens NY), American film executive; cofounder of Miramax Films.

Harvey Weinstein (19 Mar 1952, Queens NY), American film executive; cofounder of Miramax Films.

Rachel Weisz (7 Mar 1971, London, England), British film actress.

Gillian Welch (2 Oct 1967, New York NY), American folk and country-and-western singer.

Wen Jiabao (September 1942, Tianjin, China), Chinese geologist and party and state official; premier from 2003.

Jann S. Wenner (7 Jan 1946, New York NY), American journalist; originator (1967) and publisher of *Rolling Stone* magazine.

Kanye West (8 Jun 1977, Atlanta GA), American rapper and music producer.

Randy Weston (Randolph Edward Weston; 6 Apr 1926, Brooklyn NY), American jazz pianist and composer.

Vivienne Westwood (Vivienne Swire; 8 Apr 1941, Tintwistle, Derbyshire, England), British fashion designer.

Christopher Wheeldon (22 Mar 1973, Yeovil, Somerset, England), British dancer and choreographer (with the New York City Ballet).

Forest (Steven) Whitaker (15 Jul 1961, Longview TX), American film actor and director; recipient of the 2006 best actor Academy Award.

Jack White (John Anthony Gillis; 9 Jul 1975, Detroit MI), American alternative-rock guitarist and vocalist (for the White Stripes and the Raconteurs) and record producer.

Shaun White (3 Sep 1986, San Diego CA), American snowboarder.

Meg Whitman (Margaret C. Whitman; 4 Aug 1956, Cold Spring Harbor NY), American corporate executive; president and CEO of eBay, 1998–2008.

Ratnasiri Wickremanayake (5 May 1933, British Ceylon [now Sri Lanka]), Sri Lankan politician; prime minister of Sri Lanka, 2000–01 and again from 2005.

John Edgar Wideman (14 Jun 1941, Washington DC), American novelist.

Richard (Purdy) Wilbur (1 Mar 1921, New York NY), American poet associated with the New Formalist movement; poet laureate of the US, 1987–88, and recipient of the 2006 Ruth Lilly Poetry Prize.

Tom Wilkinson (Thomas Jeffery Wilkinson, Jr.; 12 Dec 1948, Leeds, West Yorkshire, England), British character actor.

George F(rederick) Will (4 May 1941, Champaign IL), American conservative political commentator and columnist.

Willem-Alexander (27 Apr 1967, Utrecht, Netherlands), Dutch crown prince.

William (William Arthur Philip Louis Windsor; 21 Jun 1982, London, England), British prince of Wales; son of Charles and Diana, prince and princess of Wales, and second in line to the British throne.

Brian (Douglas) Williams (5 May 1959, Elmira NY), American TV newsman; anchor of *NBC Nightly News* from 2004.

C(harles) K(enneth) Williams (4 Nov 1936, Newark NJ), American poet.

Danny Williams (4 Aug 1950, St. John's, NF [now NL], Canada), Canadian lawyer and politician (Progressive Conservative); premier of Newfoundland from 2003.

John Williams (24 Apr 1941, Melbourne, Australia), Australian-born classical guitarist.

John (Towner) Williams (8 Feb 1932, Queens NY), American conductor and composer of movie sound tracks.

Lucinda Williams (26 Jan 1953, Lake Charles LA), American contemporary folk and country singer and songwriter.

Pharrell Williams ("Skateboard P"; 5 Apr 1973, Virginia Beach VA), American hip-hop artist, songwriter, and producer.

Robbie Williams (Robert Peter Maximillian Williams; 13 Feb 1974, Tunstall, Stoke-on-Trent, Staffordshire, England), British singer.

Robin Williams (21 Jul 1952, Chicago IL), American comedian and actor.

Rowan (Douglas) Williams (14 Jun 1950, Swansea, Wales), Welsh-born Anglican clergyman; archbishop of Canterbury from 2003.

Serena Williams (26 Sep 1981, Saginaw MI), American tennis player and clothing designer.

Vanessa (Lynn) Williams (18 Mar 1963, Tarrytown NY), American singer and actress.

Venus Williams (17 Jun 1980, Lynwood CA), American tennis player.

Bruce Willis (Walter Bruce Willison; 19 Mar 1955, Idar-Oberstein, West Germany [now in Germany]), American actor.

Brian Wilson (20 Jun 1942, Inglewood CA), American pop music songwriter and producer (for the Beach Boys); recipient of a 2007 Kennedy Center Honor.

Lanford Wilson (13 Apr 1937, Lebanon MO), American playwright.

Owen (Cunningham) Wilson (18 Nov 1968, Dallas TX), American actor.

Robert Wilson (4 Oct 1941, Waco TX), American avant-garde theater director.

Amy (Jade) Winehouse (14 Sep 1983, Enfield, Middlesex, England), British singer and songwriter.

Oprah Winfrey (29 Jan 1954, Kosciusko MS), American TV personality; host and producer of *The Oprah Winfrey Show* from 1985.

Kate Winslet (5 Oct 1975, Reading, England), British film actress.

Anna Wintour (3 Nov 1949, London, England), British-born fashion magazine editor, editor in chief of American *Vogue* from 1988.

(Laura Jean) Reese Witherspoon (22 Mar 1976, Baton Rouge LA), American film actress.

Edward Witten (26 Aug 1951, Baltimore MD), American mathematician and specialist in superstring theory; recipient of the 1990 Fields Medal and a 2008 Crafoord Prize.

Patricia A(nn) Woertz (17 Mar 1953, Pittsburgh PA), American corporate executive; CEO of Archer Daniels Midland from 2006.

Girma Wolde-Giorgis (December 1924, Addis Ababa, Ethiopia), Ethiopian military officer; president from 2001.

Nathan Wolfe (24 Aug 1970, Detroit MI), American virologist and professor, a specialist in the transfer of viruses from animals to humans.

Tom Wolfe (Thomas Kennerly Wolfe, Jr.; 2 Mar 1930, Richmond VA), American novelist, journalist, and social commentator.

Tobias (Jonathan Ansell) Wolff (19 Jun 1945, Birmingham AL), American writer.

Stevie Wonder (Steveland Judkins; Steveland Morris; 13 May 1950, Saginaw MI), American pop songwriter and singer.

Elijah (Jordan) Wood (28 Jan 1981, Cedar Rapids IA), American film actor.

Tiger Woods (Eldrick Woods; 30 Dec 1975, Cypress CA), American golfer.

Klaus Wowereit (1 Oct 1953, West Berlin, West Germany [now Berlin, Germany]), German politician (Social Democrat); mayor of Berlin from 2001.

Stephen Wozniak (11 Aug 1950, San Jose CA), American electrical engineer, cofounder of Apple Computer Corp., and youth leader.

Ram Baran Yadav (4 Feb 1948, Sapahi, Dhanukha, Nepal), Nepalese politician; the first president of Nepal, from 2008.

Aleksey (Konstantinovich) Yagudin (18 Mar 1980, Leningrad, USSR [now St. Petersburg, Russia]), Russian figure skater.

Shinya Yamanaka (4 Sep 1962, Osaka, Japan), Japanese physician and stem-cell researcher.

Yang Jiechi (May 1950, Shanghai, China), Chinese foreign minister from 2007.

Viktor (Fedorovych) Yanukovych (9 Jul 1950, Yenakiyevo, USSR [now in Ukraine]), Ukrainian politician; prime minister, 2002–05 and 2006–07.

Yao Ming (12 Sep 1980, Shanghai, China), Chinese basketball player.

Umaru Musa Yar'Adua (1951, Katsina, Nigeria), Nigerian politician; president from 2007.

Catherine Yass (1963, London, England), British photographic artist.

Trisha Yearwood (Patricia Lynn Yearwood; 19 Sep 1964, Monticello GA), American country singer.

Michelle Yeoh (Yang Zi Chong or Yeoh Chu-keng; 6 Aug 1962, Ipoh, Malaysia), Malaysian-born film actress.

Gloria Yerkovich (1942), American child-welfare advocate; founder of Child Find, an organization that helps locate missing children.

Frances Yip (Yip Lai Yee; 1948, Hong Kong), Hong Kong Chinese pop singer.

Banana Yoshimoto (Yoshimoto Mahoko; 24 Jul 1964, Tokyo, Japan), Japanese writer of best-selling fiction.

Will(iam Robert) Young (20 Jan 1979, Hungerford, Berkshire, England), British pop singer.

Susilo Bambang Yudhoyono (9 Sep 1949, Pacitan, East Java, Indonesia), Indonesian military officer; president from 2004.

Muhammad Yunus (28 Jun 1940, Chittagong, East Bengal, British India [now in Bangladesh]), Bangladeshi economist specializing in microcredit and founder of the Grameen Bank; corecipient of the 2006 Nobel Peace Prize.

Viktor (Andriyovych) Yushchenko (23 Feb 1954, Khoruzhivka, Sumy oblast, USSR [now in Ukraine]), Ukrainian banker and politician (Our Ukraine); prime minister, 1999–2001, and president from 2005.

Sadi Yusuf (1934, near Basra, Iraq), Iraqi-born poet.

Raúl Yzaguirre (22 Jul 1939, south Texas), American Hispanic rights activist.

Adam Zagajewski (21 Jun 1945, Lwow, Poland [now Lviv, Ukraine]), Polish poet, novelist, and essayist; recipient of the 2004 Neustadt Prize.

José Luis Rodríguez Zapatero (4 Aug 1960, Valladolid, Spain), Spanish politician (Socialist Workers Party); prime minister from 2004.

Asif Ali Zardari (21 Jul 1956, Nawabshah, Pakistan), Pakistani politician and widower of Benazir Bhutto; cochairman of the Pakistan Peoples Party from 2007.

Valdis Zatlers (22 Mar 1955), Latvian politician; president from 2007.

Ayman al-Zawahiri (19 Jun 1951, Maadi, Egypt), Egyptian-born physician and militant Islamist leader, the chief lieutenant of Osama bin Laden.

(José) Manuel Zelaya (Rosales) (20 Sep 1952, Catacamas, Honduras), Honduran politician (Liberal Party); president from 2006.

Sam Zell (Samuel Zielonka; 28 Sep 1941, Chicago IL), American real-estate tycoon.

Renée (Kathleen) Zellweger (25 Apr 1969, Katy TX), American actress.

Robert Zemeckis (14 May 1952, Chicago IL), American film director.

Meles Zenawi (8 May 1955, Adoua, Ethiopia), Ethiopian politician; prime minister from 1995.

Niklas Zennström (1966, Sweden), Swedish Internet entrepreneur; codeveloper of Joost, a program to receive TV broadcasts on a personal computer.

Elias (Adam) Zerhouni (1 Apr 1951, Nedroma, French Algeria), Algerian-born American radiologist and medical administrator; director of the National Institutes of Health from 2002.

Catherine Zeta-Jones (Catherine Jones; 25 Sep 1969, Swansea, West Glamorgan, Wales), Welsh-born American actress.

Zhang Yimou (14 Nov 1951, Xi'an, Shaanxi province, China), Chinese film director.

Zhang Ziyi (9 Feb 1979, Beijing, China), Chinese actress.

Zhou Guangzhao (May 1929, Changsha, Hunan province, China), Chinese mechanical engineer; president of the Chinese Academy of Sciences, 1987–97; chairman of the China Association of Science and Technology from 1996.

Mary (Alice) Zimmerman (23 Aug 1960, Lincoln NE), American stage director.

Slavoj Zizek (21 Mar 1949, Ljubljana, Yugoslavia [now in Slovenia]), Slovenian political philosopher and social critic.

Robert B. Zoellick (25 Jul 1953, Evergreen Park IL), American businessman and government official; US trade representative, 2001–05, deputy secretary of state, 2005–06, and president of the World Bank from 2007.

Mark Zuckerberg (14 May 1984, Dobbs Ferry NY), American Internet entrepreneur; founder and CEO of Facebook, a social networking Web site.

Mortimer B. Zuckerman (4 Jun 1937, Montreal, QC, Canada), Canadian-born American publisher, columnist, and editor in chief of *U.S. News & World Report*.

Jacob (Gedleyihlekisa) Zuma (12 Apr 1942, Inkandla, Natal, Union of South Africa [now in KwaZulu Natal province, South Africa]), South African politician; deputy president of South Africa, 1999–2005, and president of the African National Congress from 2007.

Obituaries

Death of notable people since 1 July 2007

Haidar Abdel Shafi (10 Jun 1919, Gaza, British-occupied Palestine—25 Sep 2007, Gaza, Emerging Palestinian Autonomous Area), Palestinian nationalist who was a founding member (1964–65) of the executive committee of the Palestine Liberation Organization and a longtime secular voice in negotiations with Israel for Palestinian self-rule.

Philip Burnett Franklin Agee (19 Jul 1935, Tacoma Park FL—7 Jan 2008, Havana, Cuba), American government official who was stripped of his US citizenship after publishing *Inside the Company: A CIA Diary* (1975), which divulged his disillusionment with the CIA, in which he served in the 1960s as an undercover officer; he also revealed the identities of some 250 CIA operatives working clandestinely, mainly in Latin America.

Baba Amte (Murlidhar Devidas Amte; 26 Dec 1914, Maharashtra district, British India—9 Feb 2008, Anandvan, Maharashtra, India), Indian lawyer and social activist who devoted his life to India's Harijan (untouchables) and especially to the care of those individuals who suffered from leprosy.

Jorge Isaac Anaya (27 Sep 1926, Bahía Blanca, Argentina—9 Jan 2008, Buenos Aires, Argentina), Argentine naval commander who led the failed attempt to invade and control the Falkland Islands (Islas Malvinas) in what became known as the 1982 Falkland Islands War with the UK.

Michelangelo Antonioni (29 Sep 1912, Ferrara, Italy—30 Jul 2007, Rome, Italy), Italian film director, cinematographer, and producer who eschewed "realistic" narrative and traditional plots in favor of character study and poetic visual imagery; his most successful motion picture was *Blowup* (1966), which won the Golden Palm at the Cannes Festival and came to epitomize "swinging '60s" London.

Art(hur) Eugene Arfons (3 Feb 1926, Akron OH—3 Dec 2007, Akron OH), American automotive racer who was a three-time holder of the world's land-speed record for wheeled vehicles; he designed a vehicle powered by a J-79 jet aircraft engine, which he drove 576.533 mph (927.64 km/hr) at Utah's Bonneville Salt Flats in 1965.

ʿAbd al-Rahman ʿArif (1916, Baghdad, Iraq—24 Aug 2007, Amman, Jordan), Iraqi army major general and politician who assumed the Iraqi presidency on 17 Apr 1966, four days after the death of his brother, Pres. ʿAbd al-Salam ʿArif; he was regarded as a weak president, however, and in July 1968 he was deposed in a Baʿthist coup.

Eddy Arnold (Richard Edward Arnold; "The Tennessee Plowboy"; 15 May 1918, Henderson TN—8 May 2008, Franklin TN), American singer and guitarist who ushered country music, which had been labeled as hillbilly music, into the mainstream; he sold more than 85 million recordings and reigned on the *Billboard* country charts, with the highest number of top 10 hits (92) and weeks at number one (145), and he was inducted into the Country Music Hall of Fame in 1966.

Neil Stanley Aspinall (13 Oct 1941, Prestatyn, Wales—24 Mar 2008, New York NY), British accountant and music company executive, who was often called "the Fifth Beatle" because of his distinctive clout as the road manager, trusted personal assistant, and, ultimately, corporate chief executive for the British rock group the Beatles as the head of the band's record company, Apple Corps Ltd., from 1973.

Brooke Russell Astor (Roberta Brooke Russell; 30 Mar 1902, Portsmouth NH—13 Aug 2007, Briarcliff Manor NY), American socialite, philanthropist, and writer who presided over the distribution of about US$195 million as president (1959–97) of the Vincent Astor Foundation, which she established with her husband (heir to the fortune of fur magnate and financier John Jacob Astor); in 1996 the New York Landmarks Conservancy named her a "Living Landmark."

Rafael Azcona (24 Oct 1926, Logroño, Spain—24 Mar 2008, Madrid, Spain), Spanish novelist and screenwriter who penned some 100 screenplays, notably for *La Grande Bouffe* (1973) and *Belle Epoque* (1992), which won the Academy Award for best foreign-language film; he was awarded an honorary Goya Award for lifetime achievement in 1998.

Raymond-Octave-Joseph Barre (12 Apr 1924, Saint-Denis, Réunion—25 Aug 2007, Paris, France), French economist and politician who, as minister of finance and economic affairs (1976–78) and prime minister (1976–81) of France, instituted austerity measures to reduce government expenditures and to control inflation and oversaw his country's entry (1979) into the European Monetary System; among his many honors was admission as a chevalier to the Legion of Honor.

Jeremy James Anthony Gibson Beadle (12 Apr 1948, London, England—30 Jan 2008, London, England), British television personality who hosted the hidden-camera television shows *Game for a Laugh* (1981–85) and *Beadle's About* (1987–96), in which practical jokes were played on members of the public; he was made OBE in 2001.

(Ernst) Ingmar Bergman (14 Jul 1918, Uppsala, Sweden—30 Jul 2007, Fårö, Sweden), Swedish writer-director who achieved worldwide fame for creating films that examine issues of morality by exploring man's relationship to himself, to others, and to God and were noted for their versatile camera work and fragmented narrative style; though Bergman never won an individual Academy Award (despite nine nominations), three of his movies won Oscars for best foreign language film—*Jungfrukällan* (1960; *The Virgin Spring*), *Såsom i en spegel* (1961; *Through a Glass Darkly*), and *Fanny och Alexander* (1983; *Fanny and Alexander*)—and in 1971 the Academy presented him with a lifetime achievement award; the trilogy he made in the 1960s—*Through a Glass Darkly, Nattsvardsgästerna* (1962; *Winter Light*), and *Tystnaden* (1963; *The Silence*)—is regarded by many as his crowning achievement. In 1977 he received the Swedish Academy of Letters Great Gold Medal, and in the following year the Swedish Film Institute established a prize in his name.

Benazir Bhutto (21 Jun 1953, Karachi, Pakistan—27 Dec 2007, Rawalpindi, Pakistan), Pakistani politician who, as the prime minister of Pakistan (1988–90 and 1993–96), was the first woman leader of a Muslim country in modern times; though she was admired by many as a progressive, pro-Western politician, her two administrations were both dismissed under accusations of corruption and economic mismanagement. The daughter of Pakistani leader Zulfikar Ali Bhutto, she became the titular head of his opposition Pakistan People's Party after his execution in 1979; in October 2007 Bhutto returned to Karachi from Dubai after eight years of self-imposed exile, and she was assassinated while campaigning for the upcoming national elections.

Joey Bishop (Joseph Abraham Gottlieb; 3 Feb 1918, New York NY—17 Oct 2007, Newport Beach CA), American comedian, remembered for his deadpan comic delivery, who was the last surviving member of the Hollywood clique known as the Rat Pack that included Frank Sinatra, Dean Martin, Sammy Davis, Jr., and Peter Lawford; Bishop appeared with the Rat Pack in the films *Ocean's Eleven* (1960) and *Sergeants Three* (1962), and he also hosted his own talk show.

Bert Richard Johannes Bolin (15 May 1925, Nyköping, Sweden—30 Dec 2007, Stockholm, Sweden), Swedish meteorologist who was the founding chairman (1988–97) of the UN Intergovernmental Panel on Climate Change, the corecipient (with former US vice president Al Gore) of the 2007 Nobel Prize for Peace; he was also the scientific director at the European Space Agency, and he did significant fundamental research into the carbon cycle in nature.

Philipp von Böselager (6 Sep 1917, Burg Heimerzheim, near Bonn, Germany—1 May 2008, Altenahr, Germany), German army officer who provided the plastic explosives for the briefcase bomb that was used in the assassination attempt on Adolf Hitler by German officers on 20 Jul 1944.

Christopher Bowman (30 Mar 1967, Los Angeles CA—10 Jan 2008, North Hills CA), American figure skater who was dubbed "Bowman the Showman" because of his flamboyance on the ice and his ability to thrill a crowd with his dynamic performances; he captured the US men's figure skating titles in 1989 and 1992 and took a silver (1989) and a bronze medal (1990) at the world championships.

Richard James Bradshaw (26 Apr 1944, Rugby, Warwickshire, England—15 Aug 2007, Toronto, ON, Canada), British-born Canadian conductor who raised the Canadian Opera Company (COC) to international stature and worked tirelessly to bring a purpose-built opera house to Toronto; as a result he was able to launch the COC's 2006–07 season in the new Four Seasons Centre for the Performing Arts.

Henry Dreyfuss Brant (15 Sep 1913, Montreal, QC, Canada—26 Apr 2008, Santa Barbara CA), American composer, a musical prodigy whose *Ice Field* (2001) won the Pulitzer Prize.

Angie Elisabeth Brooks-Randolph (4 Aug 1928, Virginia, Liberia—9 Sep 2007, Houston TX), Liberian jurist and diplomat who in 1969 became only the second woman president of the UN General Assembly; she was appointed to Liberia's mission to the UN in 1954, and she served for more than two decades; in 1977 she was appointed the first woman associate justice of the Liberian Supreme Court.

Bill Brown (William Alfred Brown; 31 Jul 1912, Toowoomba, QLD, Australia—16 Mar 2008, Brisbane, QLD, Australia), Australian cricketer who was the last pre-World War II Australian Test player and one of the last of the Invincibles of captain Don Bradman's 1948 touring side that was unbeaten in England.

William F(rank) Buckley, Jr. (24 Nov 1925, New York NY—27 Feb 2008, Stamford CT), American editor, commentator, and writer who became an important intellectual influence in politics as the founder (1955) and editor in chief of the journal *National Review*, which he used as a forum for conservative views and ideas; his column of political commentary, "On the Right," appeared regularly in more than 200 newspapers, and he wrote more than 50 books.

(Israel) Cachao (López) (14 Sep 1918, Havana, Cuba—22 Mar 2008, Coral Gables FL), Cuban-born bassist, composer, and bandleader who was credited, along with his brother, Orestes, with the creation of the mambo and salsa; his *Master Sessions I* (1994) received a Grammy Award, as did *¡Ahora Sí!* (2004).

Leopoldo Calvo Sotelo y Bustelo (14 Apr 1926, Madrid, Spain—3 May 2008, Pozuelo de Alarcón, near Madrid, Spain), Spanish politician who was the country's second prime minister (February 1981–December 1982) to preside over the country's difficult transition from Francisco Franco's military dictatorship to a modern constitutional monarchy; he was credited with instituting much-needed reforms in post-Franco Spain, negotiating the country's entry into NATO, and authorizing a degree of autonomy that temporarily quelled rebellion in the factious Basque region.

George (Denis Patrick) Carlin (12 May 1937, New York NY—22 Jun 2008, Santa Monica CA), American comedian who began working in the late 1950s as a low-key stand-up comedian known for such whimsical routines as "Wonderful WINO" and the "Hippy Dippy Weatherman"; beginning in the 1970s, however, he transformed himself into a provocative and incisive antiestablishment comic icon. Carlin was most closely identified with the monologue "Seven Words You Can Never Say on Television," in which he satirically analyzed the use and misuse of seven of the raunchiest obscenities in the English language; he was honored with the American Comedy Awards' Lifetime Achievement Award (2001) and the Mark Twain Prize for American Humor (2008), and in 2004 cable TV's Comedy Central network ranked Carlin second on its list of the "100 Greatest Stand-Ups of All Time," behind only actor-comedian Richard Pryor.

Cyd Charisse (Tula Ellice Finklea; 8 Mar 1921/22, Amarillo TX—17 Jun 2008, Los Angeles CA), American dancer and actress who won acclaim for her glamorous looks and sensual, technically flawless dancing in 1950s movie musicals, notably *The Band Wagon* (1953) and *Silk Stockings* (1957), both with Fred Astaire, and *Singin' in the Rain* (1952) and *Brigadoon* (1954), opposite Gene Kelly; she was awarded a National Medal of the Arts in 2006.

Christodoulos (Christos Paraskevaidis; 17 Jan 1939, Xanthi, Greece—28 Jan 2008, Psychiko, Greece), Greek religious figure who, as leader of the Greek Orthodox Church (archbishop of Athens and All Greece) from 1998, met with Pope John Paul II in 2001, in a step toward healing the rift between the Roman Catholic and the Orthodox churches.

Arthur Charles Clarke (16 Dec 1917, Minehead, Somerset, England—19 Mar 2008, Colombo, Sri Lanka), British author who was best known for such visionary science-fiction novels as *Rendezvous with Rama* (1973) and *The Fountains of Paradise* (1979)—both of which won Nebula and Hugo awards—as well as for his work on Stanley Kubrick's hugely successful motion picture *2001: A Space Odyssey* (1968), which was based on Clarke's short story "The Sentinel" (1951).

(Magdalena) Cecilia Colledge (28 Nov 1920, London, England—12 Apr 2008, Cambridge MA), British figure skater who competed in the 1932 Winter Olympics at age 11 years and 73 days, the youngest athlete ever to participate in the Winter

Games; she was the first woman to complete a double jump in competition (a double salchow) and was credited with inventing the camel spin, the layback spin, and the Colledge one-foot axel jump.

John George Melvin Compton (29 Apr 1925, Canouan island, British Windward Islands [now in Saint Vincent and the Grenadines]–7 Sep 2007, Castries, Saint Lucia), Saint Lucian politician who was instrumental in negotiating the independence of Saint Lucia from Britain (1979) and served three times as prime minister (1979, 1982–96, 2006–07), governing as a pro-Western conservative and supporting economic diversification and pan-Caribbean cooperation.

Pearl Cornioley (Cecile Pearl Witherington; 24 Jun 1914, Paris, France–24 Feb 2008, Loire Valley, France), British wartime agent who, as an operative of the British Special Operations Executive, parachuted into occupied France under the code name Pauline and by May 1944 was overseeing some 3,000 French Resistance fighters engaged in guerrilla warfare against German troops; she was made CBE in 2004 and was also a member of the French Legion of Honor.

Richard Gordon Darman (10 May 1943, Charlotte NC–25 Jan 2008, Washington DC), American government official who served in the cabinets of four US presidents (Richard Nixon, Gerald Ford, Ronald Reagan, and George H.W. Bush) but was best remembered for having advised President Bush to renege on his campaign promise "Read my lips, no new taxes," which action undermined voters' trust and was considered to have contributed to Bush's failure to win reelection in 1992.

Michael Ellis DeBakey (7 Sep 1908, Lake Charles LA–11 Jul 2008, Houston TX), American cardiovascular surgeon and educator who pioneered surgical procedures for the treatment of defects and diseases of the cardiovascular system; in 1932 he devised the "roller pump," an essential component that permitted open-heart surgery, and he also performed the first successful carotid endarterectomy for stroke (1953), the first successful coronary artery bypass (1964), and the first successful implantation of a ventricular assist device (1966); he was awarded the Congressional Gold Medal (2008), the highest civilian award given by the US Congress.

Norman Dello Joio (24 Jan 1913, New York NY–24 Jul 2008, East Hampton NY), American composer whose *Meditation on Ecclesiastes* for string orchestra won the Pulitzer Prize in music in 1957.

Bo Diddley (Otha Ellas Bates; Ellas McDaniel; 30 Dec 1928, McComb MS–2 Jun 2008, Archer FL), American singer, songwriter, and guitarist who was one of the most influential performers of rock music's early period. Raised mostly in Chicago by his adoptive family, he recorded for the legendary blues label Chess Records; though Diddley's songs hit the pop charts just five times and the top 20 only once, he was nevertheless one of rock's most innovative artists because he had developed his own beat, known as "hambone" or "shave-and-a-haircut-two-bits"; in 1987 he was inducted into the Rock and Roll Hall of Fame.

Giuseppe Di Stefano (24 Jul 1921, Motta Santa Anastasia, Sicily, Italy–3 Mar 2008, Santa Maria Hoe, near Milan, Italy), Italian lyric tenor who was hailed as one of the finest operatic tenors of his generation, performing memorably in such operas as *La traviata, Rigoletto, Faust, L'elisir d'amore, Un ballo in maschera,* and *Tosca.*

Dith Pran (27 Sep 1942, Siemreab, Cambodia–30 Mar 2008, New Brunswick NJ), Cambodian photojournalist and interpreter who was the model for the lead character in the film *The Killing Fields* (1984), based on the 1980 article "The Death and Life of Dith Pran" by *New York Times* correspondent Sydney Schanberg; Dith acted as Schanberg's assistant (1972–75) as they covered the Cambodian civil war, and when the Khmer Rouge seized power in 1975, he was taken prisoner, tortured, and put to work as a farm laborer, nearly starving in conditions of virtual slavery.

Janez Drnovsek (17 May 1950, Celje, Yugoslavia [now in Slovenia]–23 Feb 2008, Zaplana, Slovenia), Slovenian politician who helped lead Slovenia to a relatively peaceful independence from Yugoslavia and, as the new country's prime minister (14 May 1992–3 May 2000 and 17 Nov 2000–11 Dec 2002) and president (2002–07), led it to membership in NATO and the EU.

Will Elder (Wolf William Eisenberg; 22 Sep 1922, Bronx NY–14 May 2008, Rockleigh NJ), American illustrator who earned a reputation for his lavish, wildly irreverent drawings for such magazines as *Mad* and *Playboy.*

Albert Ellis (27 Sep 1913, Pittsburgh PA–24 Jul 2007, New York NY), American psychologist who developed the psychotherapeutic approach known as rational emotive behavior therapy; in 1982 an American Psychological Association ranked Ellis second only to Carl R. Rogers on a list of the most influential persons in their field.

Angus Fairhurst (4 Oct 1966, Pembury, Kent, England–29 Mar 2008, Bridge of Orchy, Argyll, Scotland), British artist who was a founding member (with Damien Hirst and Sarah Lucas) of the Young British Artists group that dominated British art in the 1990s; he was perhaps best known for a series of artworks featuring bronze representations of gorillas.

Clay Schuette Felker (2 Oct 1925, St. Louis MO–1 Jul 2008, New York NY), American magazine editor who was credited with the creation of a widely imitated magazine formula during his tenure as editor of *New York* magazine, which combined glossy pages and unique typography with thoughtful literary articles that targeted the city's intellectual elite.

Bobby Fischer (Robert James Fischer; 9 Mar 1943, Chicago IL–17 Jan 2008, Reykjavík, Iceland), American-born chess master who became the youngest grandmaster in history in 1958; he drew the attention of the American public to the game of chess, particularly when he defeated Boris Spassky of the Soviet Union in a highly publicized match held in Reykjavík in 1972 and became the first native-born American to hold the title of world champion; Fischer went into seclusion in 1992, in part because he had violated US restrictions on participating in events in Yugoslavia, and in 2004 he was detained in Tokyo after authorities discovered that his US passport had been revoked. In 2005 he was granted Icelandic citizenship, however, and within days of the decision he was flown to Reykjavík.

Dan(iel Grayling) Fogelberg (13 Aug 1951, Peoria IL–16 Dec 2007, Maine), American singer-songwriter who captured the essence of the mellow, folk-tinged pop music that emerged in America in the 1960s and '70s; his best-known songs include "Longer," "Hard To Say," "Same Old Lang Syne," and "Leader of the Band."

Steve Fossett (22 Apr 1944, Jackson TN–disappeared 3 Sep 2007, northern Nevada), American adventurer who set a number of world records in aviation and sailing; he became the first balloonist to circumnavigate the world alone in 2002, made the first nonstop solo global flight in an airplane in 2005, and undertook the longest nonstop airplane flight in 2006; reported missing after his single-engine plane disappeared, he was declared legally dead in February 2008.

Georgia Irwin Frontiere (21 Nov 1927, St. Louis MO—18 Jan 2008, Los Angeles CA), American sports executive who became the first female owner of an NFL team in 1979; enduring criticisms that a woman could not handle ownership of a professional football franchise, she watched her St. Louis Rams win the Super Bowl in 2000.

Estelle Getty (Estelle Scher Gettleman; 25 Jul 1923, New York NY—22 Jul 2008, Los Angeles CA), American actress who earned a legion of fans and seven straight Emmy Award nominations (1986–92; she won in 1988) for her portrayal of Sophia Petrillo, the sharp-tongued octogenarian in NBC television's situation comedy *The Golden Girls* (1985–92).

Abdul Rashid Ghazi (1964?, Pakistan?—9–10 Jul 2007, Islamabad, Pakistan), Pakistani Islamic militant who was the younger son of Maulana Abdullah, founder of the Lal Masjid (Red Mosque); he was among those killed in the fighting when Pakistani troops stormed the mosque compound after an eight-day standoff.

Ángel González (6 Sep 1925, Oviedo, Spain—12 Jan 2008, Madrid, Spain), Spanish poet who was a respected member of the "Generation of 1950"; his socially engaged poetic works were informed by his experience growing up during the Spanish Civil War and living during the subsequent rule of Gen. Francisco Franco; González was given the 1985 Prince of Asturias Award for Letters and served as a member of the Royal Spanish Academy from 1997.

Robert Gerard Goulet (26 Nov 1933, Lawrence MA—30 Oct 2007, Los Angeles CA), American singer and actor who possessed a rich baritone voice and matinee-idol good looks that fueled his rise to stardom as a recording artist and actor in musicals; he burst onto the American scene in 1960 when he played Sir Lancelot in the original Broadway production of *Camelot,* and in 1962 he won the Grammy Award for best new artist (he would place 16 albums on the charts by the end of the decade); he won an Emmy Award in 1966 for his work in *Brigadoon,* and a Tony Award came in 1968 for his performance in the Broadway musical *The Happy Time*.

Julien Gracq (Louis Poirier; 27 Jul 1910, Saint-Florent-le-Vieil, France—22 Dec 2007, Angers, France), French writer whose best-known novel, *Le Rivage des Syrtes* (1951), was awarded the Prix Goncourt, France's highest literary honor (though he declined it).

Simon (James Holliday) Gray (21 Oct 1936, Hayling Island, Hampshire, England—6 Aug 2008, London, England), British dramatist who wrote plays, often set in academia, that were noted for their challenging story lines, complex characterizations, and witty, highly literary dialogue; his best-known work—and first international success—was *Butley* (1971; filmed 1974), a play about a petulant university professor whose venomous wit masks an inner emptiness; Gray was made CBE in 2005.

Merv Griffin (Mervyn Edward Griffin; 6 Jul 1925, San Mateo CA—12 Aug 2007, Los Angeles CA), American television personality and producer who was the congenial host of *The Merv Griffin Show* (1962–63, 1965–86) and the creator of two of television's most successful game shows, *Jeopardy!* (1964–75, 1984–) and *Wheel of Fortune* (1975–); in 2005 he was honored with a Daytime Emmy Lifetime Achievement Award.

Ernest Gary Gygax (27 Jul 1938, Chicago IL—4 Mar 2008, Lake Geneva WI), American inventor who helped create the world's first role-playing fantasy game, Dungeons & Dragons (D&D), and ultimately paved the way for modern interactive video games online; in 1973 he cofounded the company Tactical Studies Rules (TSR), which produced the first edition of D&D the following year.

George Habash (1925/26, Lydda, Palestine [now Lod, Israel]—26 Jan 2008, Amman, Jordan), Palestinian militant who was the founder (1967–2000) of the Popular Front for the Liberation of Palestine.

Earle Harry Hagen (9 Jul 1919, Chicago IL—26 May 2008, Rancho Mirage CA), American musician and songwriter who composed some of the most memorable music for television, including the themes for *The Andy Griffith Show, The Dick Van Dyke Show, Gomer Pyle, U.S.M.C., Eight Is Enough, Make Room for Daddy,* and *The Dukes of Hazzard;* he won (1968) an Emmy Award for his creative musical arrangements for the espionage series *I Spy.*

Oakley Maxwell Hall (pseudonyms O.M. Hall and Jason Manor; 1 Jul 1920, San Diego CA—12 May 2008, Nevada City CA), American novelist who spun tales of the Old West in novels, notably *Warlock* (1958; filmed 1959), *The Bad Lands* (1978), and *Apaches* (1986).

Elizabeth Hardwick (27 Jul 1916, Lexington KY—2 Dec 2007, New York NY), American novelist, short-story writer, and essayist; as a novelist she was perhaps best known for *Sleepless Nights* (1979); she helped to found *The New York Review of Books* in 1963.

Yossi Harel (Yosef Hamburger), (4 Jan 1918?, Jerusalem, British Palestine [now in Israel]—26 Apr 2008, Tel Aviv, Israel), Israeli Zionist and intelligence officer who commanded the ship *Exodus 1947,* which carried more than 4,500 Jewish Holocaust survivors to Haifa, Palestine, where a blockade by the British prevented the refugees from landing; the incident was later dramatized in Leon Uris's novel *Exodus* (1958; filmed 1960).

René Reynaldo Harris (11 Nov 1947?, Nauru—5 Jul 2008, Nauru), Nauruan politician who served four times (27 Apr 1999–20 Apr 2000; 30 Mar 2001–9 Jan 2003; 17–18 Jan 2003; 8 Aug 2003–22 Jun 2004) as Nauru's president; his 31 years (1977–2008) as a member of the country's Parliament made him Nauru's longest-serving politician; in 2001 Harris and Australian Prime Minister John Howard negotiated the controversial "Pacific Solution," in which Nauru received millions of dollars in financial aid in exchange for maintaining detention centers for Australia-bound asylum seekers.

Bill Hartack (William John Hartack, Jr.; 9 Dec 1932, Ebensburg PA—26 Nov 2007, near Freer TX), American jockey who was the second jockey ever to win five Kentucky Derby races and the first to win US$2 million in a single year (in 1956), a record he broke the following year by earning US$3 million; he was the national champion jockey in 1955, 1956, 1957, and in 1960.

Isaac Lee Hayes, Jr. (20 Aug 1942, Covington TN—10 Aug 2008, East Memphis TN), American singer-songwriter, musician, and actor who was a pioneering figure in soul music whose recordings influenced the development of such musical genres as disco, rap, and urban contemporary; known for his shaved head, dark sunglasses, and smooth baritone voice, he was perhaps best remembered for his compelling sound track for the 1971 film *Shaft*, the title song of which, "Theme from Shaft," became a number one hit and earned Hayes an Academy Award for best original song. Hayes reached his greatest popularity in the late 1960s and '70s, placing (1969–76) 10 consecutive albums on the American pop and rhythm-and-blues charts; he was inducted in 2002 into the Rock and Roll Hall of Fame.

(Barton) Lee Hazlewood (9 Jul 1929, Mannford OK–4 Aug 2007, Henderson NV), American singer-songwriter and music producer who was a pioneer of country rock and achieved fame as the writer and producer of "These Boots Are Made for Walkin'," which became a number one hit in 1966 for singer Nancy Sinatra; he collaborated with her on nine albums and four top 10 singles.

Jeff Healey (Norman Jeffrey Healey; 25 Mar 1966, Toronto, ON, Canada–2 Mar 2008, Toronto, ON, Canada), blind Canadian musician who was a virtuoso guitarist who played the instrument positioned flat on his lap; he sold millions of records with his Jeff Healey Band and reached the apex of his career with the single "Angel Eyes," which scaled the *Billboard* Hot 100 chart to number 5 in 1989.

W(ilfred) C(harles) Heinz (11 Jan 1915, Mount Vernon NY–27 Feb 2008, Bennington VT), American journalist and novelist who helped usher in New Journalism, which combined traditional reporting with the techniques of fiction; among his novels is *MASH* (1968).

Jesse (Alexander) Helms (18 Oct 1921, Monroe NC–4 Jul 2008, Raleigh NC), American politician who, as a longtime member (1973–2003) of the US Senate, was a leading figure in the conservative movement. Nicknamed "Senator No," he maintained a staunchly right-wing stance on social issues, leading crusades against abortion and homosexuality, supporting prayer in public schools, and opposing the busing of students for racial integration, but he was perhaps best known for his vehement opposition to civil rights and gay rights. Portrayed by his critics as a demagogue, an extremist, and a bigot—he famously opposed the creation of a national holiday in honor of Martin Luther King, Jr.—Helms nevertheless displayed formidable skills as a politician and was reelected four times (1978, 1984, 1990, and 1996).

Leona Helmsley (Leona Mindy Rosenthal; 4 Jul 1920, Marbletown NY–20 Aug 2007, Greenwich CT), American hotel magnate who was dubbed "the queen of mean" as a result of her imperious manner and abusive treatment of employees of Helmsley Hotels, of which she became president in 1980; she added to her notoriety by leaving her pet Maltese a US$12 million trust fund in her will.

Luis Herrera Campíns (4 May 1925, Acarigua, Venezuela–9 Nov 2007, Caracas, Venezuela), Venezuelan politician who founded the moderate Social Christian Party in 1946 and served as president of Venezuela (1979–84) during a time when the country's economic boom stemming from high oil prices began to show serious defects; he lost the presidency when he failed to rein in inflation and the government's spiraling expenditures.

Charlton Heston (John Charlton Carter; 4 Oct 1924, Evanston IL–5 Apr 2008, Beverly Hills CA), American actor who possessed a commanding screen presence with his broad shoulders, chiseled features, and compelling speaking voice and became best known for his role as Moses in Cecil B. DeMille's *The Ten Commandments* (1956). Heston made his Broadway debut in *Antony and Cleopatra* (1947), and his first Hollywood film was *Dark City* (1950); among his numerous subsequent films were *Ben-Hur* (1959), which won 11 Academy Awards, including a best actor award for Heston, *El Cid* (1961), *The Agony and the Ecstasy* (1965), and *Planet of the Apes* (1968); he also served as president (1966–71) of the Screen Actors Guild, chairman (1973–83) of the American Film Institute, and president (1998–2003) of the National Rifle Association.

Oliver Hill (Oliver White; 1 May 1907, Richmond VA–5 Aug 2007, Richmond VA), prominent American civil rights attorney who battled against racial prejudice in numerous cases, most famously the 1954 landmark case *Brown* v. *Board of Education*, in which the US Supreme Court ruled that segregated public schools were unconstitutional; in 1999 Hill was awarded the Presidential Medal of Freedom.

Edmund Percival Hillary (20 Jul 1919, Auckland, New Zealand–11 Jan 2008, Auckland, New Zealand), New Zealand explorer who galvanized the world when, on 29 May 1953, he and Sherpa mountaineer Tenzing Norgay were the first to reach the summit of Mt. Everest, the highest mountain in the world; Hillary was knighted immediately after the expedition returned to London; through the Himalayan Trust, which he founded in 1960, Hillary built schools, hospitals, and airfields for the Himalayan peoples, especially the Sherpas, and in 2003 he was made an honorary citizen of Nepal.

Patrick John Hillery (2 May 1923, Milltown Malbay, County Clare, Ireland–12 Apr 2008, Dublin, Ireland), Irish politician who served (1976–90) as the sixth president of Ireland; when his first presidential term of office ended in 1983, he indicated that he did not intend to seek a second term but changed his mind when all three political parties pleaded with him to reconsider.

Albert Hofmann (11 Jan 1906, Baden, Switzerland–29 Apr 2008, Burg, Switzerland), Swiss chemist who discovered the psychedelic drug lysergic acid diethylamide (LSD), which he first synthesized in 1938 by isolating compounds found in the fungus ergot; he spent years investigating LSD's hallucinogenic properties in the belief that the drug would one day be useful in the therapeutic treatment of schizophrenics and other psychiatric patients.

Brendan Hughes ("The Dark"; 1948, Belfast, Northern Ireland–16 Feb 2008, Belfast, Northern Ireland), Irish militant who was a member of the Irish Republican Army (IRA); in the Maze prison, he led protests, including a 53-day hunger strike in 1980.

Rex Humbard (the Rev. Alpha Rex Emmanuel Humbard; 13 Aug 1919, Little Rock AR–21 Sep 2007, Lantana FL), American televangelist who used the medium of television to spread the gospel to people worldwide through his weekly program *Cathedral of Tomorrow*, which was broadcast in some 91 languages and at its peak of popularity attracted some 20 million viewers; the show featured revival preaching mixed with lively musical numbers, including songs performed by guest performers such as Johnny Cash and June Carter Cash.

Leonid Hurwicz (21 Aug 1917, Moscow, Russian Empire–24 Jun 2008, Minneapolis MN), Russian-born American economist who shared (with Eric S. Maskin and Roger B. Myerson) the 2007 Nobel Prize for Economics for his formulation of mechanism design theory.

Henry John Hyde (18 Apr 1924, Chicago IL—29 Nov 2007, Chicago IL), American politician who served in the US House of Representatives (1975–2007), where he was at the forefront of a group of Republicans who in 1998 monitored the impeachment hearings of Pres. Bill Clinton; he was the ranking Republican on the House Select Committee on Intelligence (1985–91), chairman of the House Judiciary Committee (1995–2001), and chairman of the House International Relations Committee (2001–07); he was awarded the Presidential Medal of Freedom in 2007.

Lady Bird Johnson (Claudia Alta Taylor; 22 Dec 1912, Karnack TX—11 Jul 2007, Austin TX), American first lady who was the wife of Lyndon B. Johnson, 36th president of the United States (1963–69), and was a noted environmentalist; she married Johnson on 17 Nov 1934, just a few months after their first meeting, and she gave birth to two daughters, Lynda Bird in 1944 and Luci Baines in 1947; following her husband's 1964 election she concentrated on Head Start, a program aimed at helping preschool children from disadvantaged backgrounds, but she was most closely identified with an environmental program, called "beautification," that sought to encourage people to make their surroundings more attractive, and she urged Congress to pass the Highway Beautification Bill, which was strenuously opposed by billboard advertisers. After the Johnsons retired to their ranch in Texas, she established the National Wildflower Research Center (now the Lady Bird Johnson Wildlife Center); in 1977 she was awarded the Medal of Freedom for her conservation efforts.

Tom (Thomas Christian) Johnson (18 Feb 1928, Baldur, MB, Canada—21 Nov 2007, Falmouth MA), Canadian ice hockey player and coach who played 15 seasons (1947–48, 1949–63) for the Montreal Canadiens, during which time he helped lead the team to six Stanley Cup titles (1953, 1956–60); he received the Norris Trophy in 1959 as the NHL's best defenseman, and he was inducted into the Hockey Hall of Fame in 1970.

Hamilton Jordan (William Hamilton McWhorter Jordan; 21 Sep 1944, Charlotte NC—20 May 2008, Atlanta GA), American political strategist and government official who was a highly influential adviser to Jimmy Carter during the latter's successful 1976 US presidential campaign and later served as chief of staff in the Carter administration.

Deborah Kerr (Deborah Jane Kerr-Trimmer; 30 Sep 1921, Helensburgh, Dunbartonshire, Scotland—16 Oct 2007, Suffolk, England), British actress who was known for her poise and serenity; she won the New York Film Critics' Circle Award for *Black Narcissus* (1947), *Heaven Knows, Mr. Allison* (1957) and *The Sundowners* (1960), and the scene from *From Here to Eternity* (1953) of Kerr and Burt Lancaster making love on the beach became a classic Hollywood image; she was awarded an honorary lifetime achievement Oscar in 1994 and was created CBE in 1997.

Mustafa Khalil (18 Nov 1920, Kalyoubieh, Egypt—7 Jun 2008, Cairo, Egypt), Egyptian politician who, as Egypt's prime minister (1978–80) and foreign minister (1979–80), helped to secure the Camp David Accords (1978) and subsequent peace treaty (1979) between his country and Israel, an action that set the framework for other Arab states to make peace with Israel.

Michael Kidd (Milton Greenwald; 12 Aug 1915, New York NY—23 Dec 2007, Los Angeles CA), American choreographer who collected five Tony Awards for his stage choreography—for *Finian's Rainbow* (1947), *Guys and Dolls* (1951), *Can-Can* (1953), *Li'l Abner* (1957), and *Destry Rides Again* (1959)—and was presented a special Academy Award in 1997.

Evel Knievel (Robert Craig Knievel; 17 Oct 1938, Butte MT—30 Nov 2007, Clearwater FL), American motorcycle daredevil who captivated audiences with more than 300 death-defying aerial stunts and horrified them with his bone-shattering crashes when he failed; perhaps his most famous stunts were a spectacular jump in 1968 over the fountains at Caesars Palace Hotel in Las Vegas in which he botched the landing and fractured his skull and a failed attempt in 1974 to soar over the Snake River Canyon in Idaho using a rocket-powered motorcycle.

Harvey Herschel Korman (15 Feb 1927, Chicago IL—29 May 2008, Los Angeles CA), American comedian who delighted television viewers with the screwball roles he created as part of the ensemble cast of *The Carol Burnett Show*—during Korman's 10 seasons (1967–77) with the program, he garnered four Emmy Awards and a Golden Globe Award; he later starred in *The Harvey Korman Show* (1978), *The Tim Conway Show* (1980–81), and *Mama's Family* (reprising the Burnett show character Ed Higgins).

Arthur Kornberg (3 Mar 1918, Brooklyn NY—26 Oct 2007, Stanford CA), American biochemist and physician who was corecipient (with Severo Ochoa) of the 1959 Nobel Prize for Physiology or Medicine for discovering the means by which DNA molecules are duplicated in the bacterial cell; his son Roger D. Kornberg won the 2006 Nobel Prize for Chemistry, and they became the sixth father-son tandem to win Nobel Prizes.

László Kovács (14 May 1933, Cece, Hungary—22 Jul 2007, Beverly Hills CA), Hungarian-born American cinematographer who photographed more than 70 notable films of the 1960s and '70s that represented the rise of a new independent cinema, beginning with *Easy Rider* (1969), in which he made the landscape a vital part of the movie; his most acclaimed work includes photography on director Bob Rafelson's *Five Easy Pieces* (1970) and Martin Scorsese's *New York, New York* (1977).

Willis Eugene Lamb, Jr. (12 Jul 1913, Los Angeles CA—15 May 2008, Tucson AZ), American physicist who was corecipient, with Polykarp Kusch, of the 1955 Nobel Prize for Physics for experimental work that spurred refinements in the quantum theories of electromagnetic phenomena.

Metropolitan Laurus (Vassily Mikhailovich Skurla; 1 Jan 1928, Ladomirovo, Czechoslovakia [now in Slovakia]—16 Mar 2008, Jordanville NY), Czech religious leader who was instrumental in reconciling the Russian Orthodox Church Outside of Russia and its parent church in Russia; in 2001 he was elected metropolitan of the Russian Orthodox Church Outside of Russia, and in 2007 he exchanged kisses with Alexis II, the patriarch of Moscow and All Russia, at a historic ceremony at which a reunification pact was signed.

Joshua Lederberg (23 May 1925, Montclair NJ—2 Feb 2008, New York NY), American geneticist who was a pioneer in the field of bacterial genetics and shared the 1958 Nobel Prize for Physiology or Medicine for discovering the mechanisms of genetic recombination in bacteria.

Heath Ledger (Heathcliff Andrew Ledger; 4 Apr 1979, Perth, WA, Australia—22 Jan 2008, New York NY), Australian actor who was renowned for his moving and intense performances in diverse motion-picture roles, in particular the taciturn and tormented cowboy Ennis Del Mar in *Brokeback Mountain* (2005), for which he won best actor honors from the Australian Film Institute and received a nomination in the Academy Awards, BAFTA Awards, and Golden Globes; he also won critical acclaim for his varied roles in *The Patriot* (2000), *Monster's Ball* (2001), *Lords of Dogtown* and *Casanova* (both 2005), and *Candy* (2006).

Sherman Emery Lee (19 Apr 1918, Seattle WA—9 Jul 2008, Chapel Hill NC), American museum director who elevated the Cleveland Museum of Art from a relatively obscure institution to an internationally renowned art museum.

Madeleine L'Engle (Madeleine L'Engle Camp; Madeleine Franklin; 29 Nov 1918, New York NY—6 Sep 2007, Litchfield CT), American author who wrote imaginative juvenile literature; in her best-known work, the 1963 Newbery Medal-winning *A Wrinkle in Time* (1962), L'Engle introduced a group of children who engage in a cosmic battle against a great evil that abhors individuality, and she continued the story in *A Wind in the Door* (1973), *A Swiftly Tilting Planet* (1978), and *Many Waters* (1986).

Ira Marvin Levin (27 Aug 1929, New York NY—12 Nov 2007, New York NY), American author who thrilled readers with his best-selling Gothic and suspense novels, most famously *A Kiss Before Dying* (1953), *Rosemary's Baby* (1967), and *The Stepford Wives* (1972), and also produced a number of plays, notably *Deathtrap*, which ran for nearly 1,800 performances on Broadway; in 2003 the Mystery Writers of America conferred on him the Grand Master Award.

Alfonso López Michelsen (30 Jun 1913, Bogotá, Colombia—11 Jul 2007, Bogotá, Colombia), Colombian politician who won election in 1974 as president in a landslide victory for the centrist Liberal Party and took immediate steps to curb inflation and raise taxes on high incomes; the elimination of price subsidies and a rise in unemployment, however, led to a surge in labor unrest, land seizures by peasants, and guerrilla activity, and in 1975 López Michelsen declared a state of siege.

Alfonso Cardinal López Trujillo (8 Nov 1935, Villahermosa, Colombia—19 Apr 2008, Rome, Italy), Colombian Roman Catholic prelate who exerted enormous influence as a conservative leader in the Latin American Bishops' Council and as president of the Pontifical Council for the Family; he was unwavering in his opposition to abortion, same-sex marriage, and condoms.

Kermit Ernest Hollingshead Love (7 Aug 1916, Spring Lake NJ—21 Jun 2008, Poughkeepsie NY), American costume designer who delighted children and adults alike with the puppets that he created for the American television program *Sesame Street*, especially the perennially six-year-old 2.5-m (8-ft 2-in) Big Bird, the woolly mammoth-like Mr. Snuffleupagus, Oscar the Grouch, and Cookie Monster.

Mildred Loving (Mildred Delores Jeter; 22 Jul 1939, Virginia—2 May 2008, Central Point VA), American civil-rights activist who was one of the plaintiffs in the landmark 1967 US Supreme Court case *Loving v. Virginia*, in which the court overturned long-standing miscegenation laws that had prohibited interracial marriages.

Jean-Marie Cardinal Lustiger (Aaron Lustiger; 17 Sep 1926, Paris, France—5 Aug 2007, Paris, France), French cleric who converted from Judaism to Roman Catholicism and went on to become archbishop of Paris (1981–2005), the head of the Roman Catholic Church in France; he worked throughout his career for Jewish-Christian reconciliation.

Bernie Mac (Bernard Jeffrey McCullough; 5 Oct 1957, Chicago IL—9 Aug 2008, Chicago IL), American comedian and actor who earned two Emmy nominations (2002 and 2003) for his portrayal of a high-strung comedian looking after his drug-addicted sister's three children on the television series *The Bernie Mac Show* (2001–06); he also achieved box-office success with roles in such films as *Ocean's Eleven* (2001) and its two sequels and *Charlie's Angels: Full Throttle* (2003).

Maharishi Mahesh Yogi (1917?, Jabalpur, British India—5 Feb 2008, Vlodrop, Netherlands), Hindu religious leader who introduced the practice of transcendental meditation to the West; his first world tour took place in 1959, and in the late 1960s, the English rock group the Beatles and other celebrities began to join his following; the principles of transcendental meditation are discussed in his books *The Science of Being and Art of Living* (1963) and *Meditations of Maharishi Mahesh Yogi* (1968).

Norman (Kingsley) Mailer (31 Jan 1923, Long Branch NJ—10 Nov 2007, New York NY), American novelist and journalist who was best known for New Journalism, which combines the imaginative subjectivity of literature with the more objective qualities of journalism; among his best works are *The Naked and the Dead* (1948), hailed as one of the finest American novels to come out of World War II, *The Armies of the Night* (1968), based on the Washington peace demonstrations of October 1967 and which won a Pulitzer Prize and a National Book Award, and *The Executioner's Song* (1979), a Pulitzer Prize-winning novel based on the life of convicted murderer Gary Gilmore.

Chris Mainwaring (27 Dec 1965, Geraldton, WA, Australia—1 Oct 2007, Perth, WA, Australia), Australian Rules Football player who was one of the most popular players in the Australian Football League (AFL); during his 13 seasons with the West Coast Eagles (1987–99), he scored 84 goals (including in premierships in 1992 and 1994), and he was a member of the AFL All-Australian squad in 1991 and 1996.

Anthony Joseph Mamo (9 Jan 1909, Birkirkara, Malta—1 May 2008, Mosta, Malta), Maltese jurist and statesman who was the first president (1974–76) of the independent Republic of Malta and came to be regarded as a symbol of the new country; he was made OBE in 1955, knighted in 1960, and created a Companion of Honour in the National Order of Merit in 1990.

Abby Mann (Abraham Goodman; 1 Dec 1927, Philadelphia PA—25 Mar 2008, Beverly Hills CA), American screenwriter who examined the Nazi war-crimes trials in the film *Judgment at Nuremberg* (1961), for which he won an Academy Award for best screenplay, and was the creator of the TV series *Kojak* (1973–78), inspired by his Emmy Award-winning *The Marcus-Nelson Murders* (1973).

Delbert Martin Mann, Jr. (30 Jan 1920, Lawrence KS—11 Nov 2007, Los Angeles CA), American film and television director who applied the low-budget intimacy of television to the big screen in film adaptations of such teleplays as *Marty* (1955), for which Mann received an Academy Award, and *The Bache-*

lor Party (1957), both classics created by playwright Paddy Chayefsky; Mann also served as president of the Directors Guild of America (1969–71).

Martin Ellyot Manulis (30 May 1915, New York NY—28 Sep 2007, Los Angeles CA), American television and film producer who was the creator and sole producer of more than 60 segments of *Playhouse 90* (1956–61), a 90-minute dramatic live anthology series that won six Emmy Awards in its first season and five Emmys in its second season.

Marcel Marceau (Marcel Mangel; 22 Mar 1923, Strasbourg, France—22 Sep 2007, Cahors, France), French mime who revived interest in the ancient art of mime through his silent portrayals executed with eloquence and balletic grace; his most celebrated characterization was the white-faced Pierrot-like Bip; worldwide acclaim came in the 1950s with his production of a "mimodrama" of Nikolay Gogol's "The Overcoat"; Marceau also acted in several movies, including *Silent Movie* (1976), in which he had the only spoken dialogue; the recipient of numerous honors, Marceau in 1970 was made an officer of the Legion of Honor.

Dick Martin (Thomas Richard Martin; 30 Jan 1922, Battle Creek MI—24 May 2008, Santa Monica CA), American comedian who was the cohost, with straight man Dan Rowan, of the hit television variety show *Rowan & Martin's Laugh-In* (1968–73).

Manuel Marulanda Vélez (Pedro Antonio Marín; "Tirofijo"; 12 May 1930?, Génova, Colombia—26 Mar 2008, unknown mountain encampment, Colombia), Colombian guerrilla leader who was a founder (1964) and commander of the Revolutionary Armed Forces of Colombia (FARC), estimated to possess some 10,000 to 15,000 armed soldiers and thousands of supporters; FARC supported a redistribution of assets from the wealthy to the poor and opposed the influence that multinational corporations and foreign governments (particularly the United States) had on Colombia.

Jim McKay (James Kenneth McManus; 24 Sep 1921, Philadelphia PA—7 Jun 2008, Monkton MD), American sportscaster and journalist who was a pioneer in American television sports coverage; as the sagacious and personable host (from 1961) of the groundbreaking ABC show *The Wide World of Sports,* he was one of the most recognizable faces on American TV, and in 1968 he became the first TV sports commentator to win an Emmy Award (he won 13 altogether, including a 1990 award for lifetime achievement). McKay gained international acclaim for his uninterrupted 16-hour coverage of the Israeli hostage crisis during the 1972 Summer Olympics in Munich; he covered 12 Olympics in all and also anchored TV coverage of the Indianapolis 500 for many years as well as numerous Triple Crown horse races and professional golf tournaments.

Pierre August Joseph Messmer (20 Mar 1916, Vincennes, France—29 Aug 2007, Paris, France), French Gaullist administrator and politician who was minister for the armed forces (1960–69) and prime minister (1972–74) of France; he helped quell an attempted coup by army officers in 1961 during Algeria's war for independence from France, and he also oversaw development of France's nuclear weapons program.

Tammy Faye Messner (Tammy Faye LaValley; Tammy Faye Bakker; 7 Mar 1942, International Falls MN—20 Jul 2007, near Kansas City MO), American televangelist who was best remembered as the diminutive wife of Jim Bakker and as his cohost on the televised *Jim and Tammy Show,* which was syndicated on the Praise the Lord Network, founded by the couple in 1974; the couple built a US$125 million empire that included Heritage USA, a religious theme park, and were often criticized for their lavish spending; in 1987 they lost their TV ministry following a series of sex and money scandals, and she and Bakker divorced after he was convicted in 1989 of having bilked followers of US$158 million.

James Walker Michaels (17 Jun 1921, Buffalo NY—2 Oct 2007, New York NY), American magazine editor who was credited with having transformed the reporting of business journalism during his tenure as editor of *Forbes* magazine (1961–99).

Buddy Miles (George Allen Miles, Jr.; 5 Sep 1947, Omaha NE—26 Feb 2008, Austin TX), American drummer and singer who was best known as the drummer in the Band of Gypsys (with Jimi Hendrix).

André Milongo (20 Oct 1935, Mankondi, French Equatorial Africa [now in the Republic of the Congo]—22–23 July 2007, Paris, France), Congolese politician who served as a key figure in his country's move to independence (1960) and was prime minister (1991–1992); he later joined the boards of governors of the African Development Bank and the World Bank.

Anthony Minghella (6 Jan 1954, Ryde, Isle of Wight—18 Mar 2008, London, England), British playwright, screenwriter, and director who was one of Britain's most gifted and admired filmmakers; he won the Academy Award for best director for his third movie, *The English Patient* (1996); he was named most promising playwright by the London Theatre Critics Circle in 1984 and won the best new play award two years later for *Made in Bangkok;* he also was made CBE in 2001 and was chairman (2003–08) of the British Film Institute.

Robert Gerald Mondavi (18 Jun 1913, Virginia MN—16 May 2008, Yountville CA), American winemaker who created American wines that rivaled European labels and helped generate the rebirth of California's wine industry; he was honored (2005) with the French Legion of Honor, and in 2007 he was inducted into the California Hall of Fame.

Norman Morrice (10 Sep 1931, Agua Dulce, Mexico—11 Jan 2008, London, England), British choreographer and dance director who incorporated elements of modern dance into ballet; he was artistic director of the Royal Ballet (1977–86).

Barry Morse (Herbert Morse; 10 Jun 1918, London, England—2 Feb 2008, London, England), British actor who appeared in some 3,000 stage and screen roles over a seven-decade (1935–2005) career, but his other achievements were overshadowed by his portrayal of Lieut. Philip Gerard, the tenacious police detective who relentlessly pursued the title character in the American television series *The Fugitive* (1963–67).

Bobby Ray Murcer (20 May 1946, Oklahoma City OK—12 Jul 2008, Oklahoma City OK), American baseball player and broadcaster who was a dependable center fielder and batter and was named to five consecutive All-Star teams (for the New York Yankees [1971–74] and the San Francisco Giants [1975]); during his 17 major league seasons, he slammed 252 home runs, had 1,043 runs batted in, and recorded a career batting average of .277.

Ken Nelson (Kenneth F. Nelson; 19 Jan 1911, Caledonia MN—6 Jan 2008, Somis CA), American record producer who helped define the smooth country-pop Nashville Sound and the twangy California-based Bakersfield Sound through his low-key approach in studio sessions; he cofounded (1958) the Country Music Association and was inducted into the Country Music Hall of Fame in 2001.

Larry David Norman (8 Apr 1947, Corpus Christi TX–24 Feb 2008, Salem OR), American singer-songwriter who is generally regarded as the father of Christian rock music—his *Upon This Rock* (1969) was hailed as the first Christian rock album—and in 2001 was inducted into the Gospel Music Hall of Fame.

Joe Nuxhall (Joseph Henry Nuxhall; 30 Jul 1928, Hamilton OH–15 Nov 2007, Fairfield OH), American baseball player and broadcaster who made his MLB debut in 1944 as a pitcher with the Cincinnati Reds at the age of 15 years 10 months 11 days, becoming the youngest player to appear in a game in the modern MLB era; he was named an All-Star in 1955 and 1956.

Joe O'Donnell (Joseph Roger O'Donnell; 7 May 1922, Johnstown PA–9 Aug 2007, Nashville TN), American photographer who documented the effects of the nuclear bombing in 1945 of the Japanese cities of Hiroshima and Nagasaki; his official photographs were taken for the US Marines, but he also amassed a private collection that was shown in Japan in 1995 and appeared in *Japan 1945: A US Marine's Photos from Ground Zero* (2005); he became an activist opposed to nuclear weapons.

Al(fred) Oerter (Jr.) (19 Sep 1936, Queens NY–1 Oct 2007, Fort Myers FL), American discus thrower who won four consecutive Olympic gold medals (1956, 1960, 1964, and 1968), setting an Olympic record each time; he also set world records four times (1962–64) during his career and won six national Amateur Athletic Union titles in college, and he was in the first class to be inducted into the US Olympic Hall of Fame (1983).

Norm O'Neill (Norman Clifford O'Neill; 19 Feb 1937, Carlton, near Sydney, Australia–3 Mar 2008, Sydney), Australian cricketer who was heralded as the new Don Bradman for his brilliant stroke making; he was perhaps best known for his score of 181 runs in the famous tied Test against West Indies in 1960.

Randy Pausch (Randolph Frederick Pausch; 23 Oct 1960, Baltimore MD–25 Jul 2008, Chesapeake VA), American computer scientist who delivered in September 2007 his celebrated "Last Lecture" on time management, an inspirational and uplifting testimonial, at Carnegie Mellon University, Pittsburgh; the speech became an international hit on the Internet and was the subject in 2008 of a best-selling nonfiction book (*The Last Lecture*, with Jeffrey Zaslow). Pausch, who in September 2006 was diagnosed with pancreatic cancer, discovered shortly before giving the lecture that he had only a few more months to live, and he prepared the speech titled "Really Achieving Your Childhood Dreams" as a type of time capsule for his three young children. In May 2008 he was named to *Time* magazine's list of the 100 Most Influential People in the World.

Luciano Pavarotti (12 Oct 1935, Modena, Italy–6 Sep 2007, Modena, Italy), Italian operatic lyric tenor who was considered one of the finest bel canto opera singers of his time; after winning the Concorso Internazionale, a singing competition, he made his professional operatic debut in Reggio Emilia, Italy, in 1961 and his debut at the Metropolitan Opera House in New York City in 1968. He toured the world, performing for as many as 500,000 fans at concerts as a solo performer or as one of the "Three Tenors" (with Plácido Domingo and José Carreras). Among Pavarotti's many prizes and awards were five Grammy Awards and a Kennedy Center Honor in 2001. His last public appearance was in the opening ceremony of the 2006 Winter Olympics in Turin, Italy, where he sang his signature aria, "Nessun dorma," from Giacomo Puccini's *Turandot*.

Suzanne Pleshette (31 Jan 1937, New York NY–19 Jan 2008, Los Angeles CA), American actress who was especially remembered for her role as sardonic Emily Hartley, the schoolteacher wife and foil to her husband, Bob, on the TV sitcom *The Bob Newhart Show* (1972–78); she also famously portrayed a teacher pecked to death by feathered killers in the Alfred Hitchcock classic *The Birds* (1963).

Geoffrey Paul Polites (5 Nov 1947?, Melbourne, Australia–20 Apr 2008, Melbourne, Australia), Australian automotive executive who rose through the ranks at Ford Motor Co. during a nearly 40-year career to become (2005) CEO of the US-based automaker's luxury Jaguar Land Rover division.

Sydney Irwin Pollack (1 Jul 1934, Lafayette IN–26 May 2008, Pacific Palisades CA), American director, producer, and actor who directed numerous television shows and more than a score of movies, including the epic romance *Out of Africa* (1985), a period piece set in colonial Kenya that earned him Academy Awards for best director and best picture. He directed actor Robert Redford in several films, including *The Way We Were* (1973), *Three Days of the Condor* (1975), *The Electric Horseman* (1979), and *Out of Africa*, but he was best remembered by many for his work on the comedy *Tootsie* (1982), which garnered him Oscar nominations for best director and best picture and won him a New York Film Critics Circle Award for best director; he directed more than 80 television programs, including a 1965 episode of *Bob Hope Presents the Chrysler Theatre* for which he won an Emmy Award.

Victor Rabinowitz (2 Jul 1911, Brooklyn NY–16 Nov 2007, New York NY), American lawyer who defended a pantheon of left-wing causes and such clients as Department of State official Alger Hiss and Cuban leader Fidel Castro; during US Sen. Joseph R. McCarthy's anticommunist crusade, Rabinowitz counted 225 suspected Communists, including novelist Dashiell Hammett, among his clients.

Dottie Rambo (Joyce Reba Luttrell; 2 Mar 1934, Madisonville KY–11 May 2008, Mount Vernon MO), American songwriter and singer who wrote more than 2,500 songs; her album *It's the Soul of Me* (1968) won a Grammy Award for Best Soul Gospel Performance, and she was inducted into the Gospel Music Association Hall of Fame as a solo singer in 1992 and the Nashville Songwriters Hall of Fame in 2007.

Paul Raymond (Geoffrey Anthony Quinn; 15 Nov 1925, Liverpool, England–2 Mar 2008, London, England), British entertainment mogul who, by opening (1958) the UK's first private striptease club, in London's Soho district, made himself a mainstay of the swinging London scene of the 1960s; his shrewd purchases of depressed properties made him one of Britain's wealthiest men.

Phil Rizzuto (Fiero Francis Rizzuto; "Scooter"; 25 Sep 1917, New York NY–13 Aug 2007, West Orange NJ), American baseball player and broadcaster who played an integral role in turning the Yankees into a dominating force, with eight World Series crowns (1941, 1943, 1947, and 1949–53); the consummate leadoff man, he won the American League's

Most Valuable Player award in 1950 and made five All-Star game appearances (1942, 1950–53), and he was elected to the Baseball Hall of Fame in 1994.

Holden Álvaro Roberto (12 Jan 1923, São Salvador [now M'banza Congo], Angola—2 Aug 2007, Luanda, Angola), Angolan independence leader who founded Angola's first nationalist movement in 1956—his National Liberation Front of Angola (FNLA) reached an agreement with Portugal in 1975 that led to the country's independence, but the FNLA, backed by several Western countries, was decisively defeated in 1976 by the Popular Movement for the Liberation of Angola, which was supported by the Soviet Union and Cuba.

Dame Anita Roddick (Anita Lucia Perella; 23 Oct 1942, Littlehampton, West Sussex, England—10 Sep 2007, Chichester, West Sussex, England), British entrepreneur who, as the founder of the Body Shop cosmetics chain, championed social issues such as environmental awareness, animal rights, and self-sufficiency for less-developed countries; she was made DBE in 2003.

John Roderick (15 Sep 1914, Waterville ME—11 Mar 2008, Honolulu HI), American journalist who was an illustrious foreign correspondent (1937–42 and 1945–84) for the Associated Press and won admiration for his reportage of the several months he spent living in caves (1945–47) with Chinese revolutionary leader Mao Zedong; he also witnessed the fall of the French garrison at Dien Bien Phu, Vietnam, during the First Indochina War (1946–54).

Grigory Vasilyevich Romanov (7 Feb 1923, Zikhnovo, USSR [now in Russia]—3 Jun 2008, Moscow, Russia), Soviet official who, as the Central Committee secretary for the military economy and the respected Communist Party boss (1970–83) of Leningrad (now St. Petersburg), was the major hard-line rival of Mikhail Gorbachev in the battle to lead the Soviet Union upon the death of Konstantin Chernenko in 1985.

Baron Elie Robert de Rothschild (29 May 1917, Paris, France—6 Aug 2007, near Scharnitz, Austria), French winemaker who took charge of the family wine estate Château Lafite Rothschild, which had been confiscated during the World War II Nazi occupation of France, and restored the château and its wine to their former grandeur, releasing acclaimed vintages in 1947, 1949, 1955, 1959, and 1961; he also held a share in the family banking interests under the direction of his cousin Baron Guy de Rothschild.

Tim(othy John) Russert (Jr.) (7 May 1950, Buffalo NY—13 Jun 2008, Washington DC), American journalist who, as the insightful moderator (1991–2008) of the television program *Meet the Press*—the long-running (since 1947) Sunday morning talk show that was a mainstay in American political discourse—established himself as a tough but evenhanded interviewer and became one of the most influential political commentators of his era. He was the recipient of numerous honors, including an Edward R. Murrow Award (2001) and an Emmy Award (2005), and he was also the author of two best-selling books.

Tony Ryan (Thomas Anthony Ryan; 2 Feb 1936, Thurles, County Tipperary, Ireland—3 Oct 2007, Celbridge, County Kildare, Ireland), Irish aviation entrepreneur who founded Ryanair (1985), which by 2007 was one of Europe's most successful budget airlines.

Sheikh Saad al-Abdullah al-Salim al-Sabah (1929?, British-protected Kuwait—13 May 2008, Kuwait city, Kuwait), Kuwaiti royal who, as a member of the ruling Sabah family, held a variety of government posts, including minister of the interior (1961–77), minister of defense (1965–77), and prime minister (1978–2003); as prime minister he headed a government-in-exile in Saudi Arabia during the 1990–91 Iraqi invasion of Kuwait.

Herbert Seymour Saffir (29 Mar 1917, New York NY—21 Nov 2007, Miami FL), American structural engineer who was an expert on hurricane damage to buildings and, with Robert H. Simpson, then director of the US National Hurricane Center, devised a five-category scale (the Saffir-Simpson scale) for ranking the destructive potential of hurricanes.

Yves Saint Laurent (Yves-Henri-Donat-Mathieu Saint Laurent; 1 Aug 1936, Oran, French Algeria—1 Jun 2008, Paris, France), French fashion designer who was regarded as one of the most influential designers in Paris and was especially noted for his popularization of women's trousers for all occasions. When a *Vogue* magazine executive showed Christian Dior some sketches by Saint Laurent, then aged 17, he was hired immediately as Dior's assistant, and the 21-year-old Saint Laurent was named the head of the House of Dior at Dior's death in 1957. In 1962 Saint Laurent opened his own fashion house; he was made a grand officer of the Legion of Honor in 2007.

Gene Savoy (Douglas Eugene Savoy; 11 May 1927, Bellingham WA—11 Sep 2007, Reno NV), American explorer and amateur archaeologist, dubbed "the real Indiana Jones" by the popular press because of his flamboyant style and Stetson hat, who was credited with establishing the theory (now widely supported) that Vilcabamba, rather than Machu Picchu, was the last refuge for Incas seeking to escape from the Spanish conquistadors.

Roy (Richard) Scheider (10 Nov 1932, Orange NJ—10 Feb 2008, Little Rock AR), American actor who was identified most closely with his role as the small-town police chief in the blockbuster *Jaws* films (1975 and 1978) but also earned Academy Award nominations for his supporting role in *The French Connection* (1971) and for his starring role in *All That Jazz* (1979).

(David) Paul Scofield (21 Jan 1922, Hurstpierpoint, Sussex, England—19 Mar 2008, West Sussex, England), British actor who delighted audiences with his sonorous voice and powerful performances in Shakespearean and other stage roles; he had his greatest success, however, as Sir Thomas More in Robert Bolt's *A Man for All Seasons* (1960–62), for which he won the Tony Award for best actor in a drama (1962) and the Academy Award for best actor for the film version (1967); he was made CBE in 1956 and was named a Companion of Honour in 2001.

Irena Sendler (Irena Krzyzanowska; 15 Feb 1910, Otwock, Russian Empire [now in Poland]—12 May 2008, Warsaw, Poland), Polish social worker who rescued some 2,500 Jewish children from the Warsaw ghetto during World War II; as a member of Zegota (Council to Aid the Jews), the Polish underground organization established to help save Jews from the Nazi occupiers, she used such creative means as coffins and ambulances to remove children to safety, supplied them with fake birth certificates with Aryan names, and buried jars containing lists of their real names for future reference; in 2007 she was nominated for the Nobel Prize for Peace.

Michel Serrault (24 Jan 1928, Brunnoy, France—29 Jul 2007, Honfleur, France), French actor who appeared in more than 130 motion pictures over a

50-year career but won the hearts of fans worldwide with his portrayal of the flamboyant but tenderhearted drag queen Albin/Zaza in *La Cage aux folles*—beginning with some 1,500 performances (1973–78) at the Théâtre du Palais Royal in Paris and then in the 1978 movie and its two sequels; he was appointed to the Legion of Honor in 1999.

P(ramod) K(aran) Sethi (28 Nov 1927, Benares, British India [now Varanasi, Uttar Pradesh, India]—6 Jan 2008, Jaipur, Rajasthan, India), Indian orthopedic surgeon who coinvented the Jaipur foot, a prosthetic foot that could be made cheaply, looked like a bare foot, and had sufficient flexibility and durability to allow users to walk on uneven terrain or climb trees.

Boris Anfiyanovich Shakhlin (27 Jan 1932, Ishim, USSR [now in Russia]—30 May 2008, Kiev, Ukraine), Siberian Soviet gymnast who set a career record of 10 individual titles in world championships and won gold medals at three successive Olympic Games (1956–64); his tally of 13 Olympic medals (7 gold, 4 silver, and 2 bronze) placed him among the most-decorated Olympians; he was inducted into the International Gymnastics Hall of Fame in 2002.

Chandra Shekhar (1 Jul 1927, Ibrahimpatti, Uttar Pradesh, British India—8 Jul 2007, New Delhi, India), Indian politician who served as prime minister of India from November 1990 to June 1991; he was a member of the Rajya Sabha (upper house of Parliament) from 1962 to 1967 and the Lok Sabha (lower house) from 1977 to 1984 and from 1989.

Dan Shomron (1937, Kibbutz Ashdot Ya'acov, British Palestine [now in Israel]—26 Feb 2008, Ra'anana, Israel), Israeli military leader who planned and led the daring rescue at the airport in Entebbe, Uganda, of more than 100 airline passengers who had been hijacked by Palestinian and German militants in 1976.

Kai Manne Börje Siegbahn (20 Apr 1918, Lund, Sweden—20 Jul 2007, Ängelholm, Sweden), Swedish physicist who was awarded one-half of the 1981 Nobel Prize for Physics (Nicolaas Bloembergen and Arthur Leonard Schawlow of the US shared the other half) for revolutionary work in spectroscopy, particularly the spectroscopic analysis of the interaction of electromagnetic radiation with matter; Siegbahn formulated the principles underlying the technique called ESCA (electron spectroscopy for chemical analysis).

Beverly Sills (Belle Miriam Silverman; 25 May 1929, Brooklyn NY—2 Jul 2007, New York NY), American operatic soprano and administrator who made her operatic debut in 1947 with the Philadelphia Civic Opera and in 1955 became a member of the New York City Opera; besides serving (1979–89) as director of that company, Sills was chairman of the board of New York's Lincoln Center (1994–2002) and of the Metropolitan Opera (2002–05).

Paul Sills (18 Nov 1927, Chicago IL—2 Jun 2008, Baileys Harbor WI), American theater director and teacher who established improvisational comedy and cofounded (1959) The Second City theater company in Chicago; his improvisation model for Second City and its spin-offs in other cities became the basis for the format used on *Saturday Night Live* and other comedy television programs.

G.P. Sippy (Gopaldas Parmanand Sippy; 14 Sep 1914, Hyderabad, British India—25 Dec 2007, Mumbai [Bombay], India), Indian filmmaker who was responsible for producing *Sholay* ("Flames," 1975), Bollywood's first "curry western" and the most commercially successful Bollywood film ever released (reportedly earning at least US$60 million); in 2000 he was honored with a Lifetime Achievement Award at the International Film Festival, Mumbai.

Ian Douglas Smith (8 Apr 1919, Selukwe, Rhodesia [now Shurugwi, Zimbabwe]—20 Nov 2007, Cape Town, South Africa), Rhodesian politician who was the first native-born prime minister of the British colony of Southern Rhodesia (1964–79) and was an ardent advocate of white rule; in 1965 he unilaterally declared Rhodesia's independence, but in the late 1970s he was compelled to negotiate a transfer of power to the black majority.

Mike Smith (Michael George Smith; 6 Dec 1943, Edmonton, Middlesex, England—28 Feb 2008, Aylesbury, Buckinghamshire, England), British singer and songwriter who was the lead singer and keyboardist for the Dave Clark Five (DC5), one of the most popular rock and roll bands of the British Invasion in the early 1960s; the band's hit songs include "Bits and Pieces," "Can't You See That She's Mine," "Catch Us if You Can," and "Over and Over;" he died less than two weeks before the DC5 was inducted into the Rock and Roll Hall of Fame.

Roger Bonham Smith (12 Jul 1925, Columbus OH—29 Nov 2007, near Detroit MI), American business executive who served as chairman and CEO of the General Motors Corp. (1981–90); he instituted vast changes in an attempt to return the company to profitability—implementing robotic technology in manufacturing, closing 11 assembly plants (including those in Flint MI, where some 30,000 jobs were lost—an act that inspired the Michael Moore documentary film *Roger & Me* [1989]), and launching the Saturn line of vehicles in 1990.

Tony Snow (Robert Anthony Snow; 1 Jun 1955, Berea KY—12 Jul 2008, Washington DC), American journalist who, during his 16-month stint (May 2006–September 2007) as White House press secretary, was appreciated for his good-natured banter with journalists, infusing energy into what many considered a lackluster position.

Tom Snyder (12 May 1936, Milwaukee WI—29 Jul 2007, San Francisco CA), American TV newsman who served as host of *The Tomorrow Show* (1973–82) and *The Late Late Show with Tom Snyder* (1995–99) and helped to establish the popularity of the late-night talk-show format; he was best known for his ability to connect with audiences and for his unusual questions and no-nonsense style of interviewing an array of guests.

Soe Win (1948, Burma [now Myanmar]—12 Oct 2007, Yangon [Rangoon], Myanmar), Myanmar military leader who was prime minister of Myanmar from 2004 and was associated with two bloody suppressions of the democracy movement—a violent crackdown in 1988 on a pro-democracy uprising in which some 3,000 protesters were believed to have been killed and an attack on the convoy of National League for Democracy leader Aung San Suu Kyi (briefly not under house arrest) in 2003, in which dozens of people were killed in Dipeyin, earning him the sobriquet "the butcher of Dipeyin."

Aleksandr Isayevich Solzhenitsyn (11 Dec 1918, Kislovodsk, Russia—3 Aug 2008, Troitse-Lykovo, near Moscow, Russia), Russian novelist and historian who was awarded the Nobel Prize for Literature in 1970. He submitted his short novel *Odin den iz zhizni Ivana Denisovicha* (1962; *One Day in the Life of Ivan Denisovich*) to the leading Soviet literary periodical *Novy Mir* ("New World"); the novel, based on Solzhenitsyn's own experiences, was noted for its simple, direct language and the obvious authority with which it treated the daily struggles and material hardships of life in a forced-labor camp during the Stalin era. After the publication of a collection of his short stories in 1963, however, he was denied further official publication of his work, and he resorted to samizdat ("self-published") literature—his most significant works of this period were *V kruge pervom* (1968; *The First Circle*) and *Avgust 1914* (1971; *August 1914*). In December 1973 the first parts of *Arkhipelag Gulag* (*The Gulag Archipelago*) were published in Paris after the KGB had seized a copy of the manuscript in the Soviet Union; the second and third volumes of *The Gulag Archipelago* were published in 1974–75. In 2007 he was awarded Russia's prestigious State Prize for his contribution to humanitarian causes.

John Coburn Stewart (5 Sep 1939, San Diego CA—19 Jan 2008, San Diego CA), American singer and songwriter who rose to fame when he wrote the chart-topping hit single "Daydream Believer" (1967) for the pop-rock group the Monkees; as a solo performer and member of bands such as the Kingston Trio, he wrote more than 600 songs, including the hit song "Gold," and released more than 50 albums.

William Huffman Stewart (19 May 1921, Minneapolis MN—23 Apr 2008, New Orleans LA), American government official and physician who was in the vanguard of US health policy while serving (1965–69) as the US surgeon general; he oversaw the implementation of Medicare and Medicaid, two US government programs created to guarantee health insurance for the elderly and the poor, respectively, and was the first surgeon general to issue health warnings on cigarette packs.

Suharto (8 Jun 1921, Kemusu Argamulja, Java, Dutch East Indies [now Indonesia]—27 Jan 2008, Jakarta, Indonesia), Indonesian army officer and political leader who pursued strongly anticommunist, pro-Western policies as president of Indonesia (1967–98); Suharto's three decades of uninterrupted rule gave his country much-needed political stability and sustained economic growth, but his authoritarian regime finally fell victim to an economic crisis and its own internal corruption. He fought in the guerrilla forces seeking independence (1950) from the Dutch and rose steadily through the ranks of the Indonesian army, and he took effective control of the government on 12 Mar 1966; in 1997, however, Indonesia became caught up in a currency crisis sweeping across Southeast Asia, during which the value of the rupiah plummeted, the economy went into recession, inflation skyrocketed, and living standards collapsed for the poor. Antigovernment demonstrations turned into rioting in May 1998, and Suharto was forced to resign on 21 May.

Fu'ad al-Takarli (1927, Baghdad, Iraq—11 Feb 2008, Amman, Jordan), Iraqi jurist and writer who was regarded as one of the best Iraqi writers of his generation.

John Marks Templeton (29 Nov 1912, Winchester TN—8 Jul 2008, Nassau, Bahamas), American-born British investor, mutual fund manager, and philanthropist who established (1972) the Templeton Prize for Progress in Religion (from 2003 the Templeton Prize for Progress Toward Research or Discoveries About Spiritual Realities), to be awarded annually to a living person who demonstrated "extraordinary originality in advancing humankind's understanding of God and/or spirituality"; Templeton, who took British citizenship in 1968, was knighted in 1987.

Teoctist (Toader Arapasu; 7 Feb 1915, Tocileni, Romania—30 Jul 2007, Bucharest, Romania), Romanian prelate who was patriarch of the Romanian Orthodox Church from 1986; he was also the first head of an Orthodox church to host the Roman Catholic pontiff (during Pope John Paul II's visit to Romania in 1999).

Hank Thompson (Henry William Thompson; 3 Sep 1925, Waco TX—6 Nov 2007, Keller TX), American singer and songwriter who created his own sound by blending western swing and honky-tonk; he sold more than 60 million records during a career that spanned six decades, and he had number one country songs with "The Wild Side of Life" and "It Wasn't God Who Made Honky-Tonk Angels"; he was elected to the Country Music Hall of Fame in 1989.

Gaston Egmond Thorn (3 Sep 1928, Luxembourg city, Luxembourg—26 Aug 2007, Luxembourg city, Luxembourg), Luxembourgian politician who pursued his longtime advocacy of European integration throughout a distinguished career that saw him named president of the UN General Assembly during the 1975–76 session and in 1981 president of the Commission of the European Economic Community.

Paul Warfield Tibbets, Jr. (23 Feb 1915, Quincy IL—1 Nov 2007, Columbus OH), brigadier general of the US Army Air Forces who piloted the B-29 bomber nicknamed the *Enola Gay,* which on 6 Aug 1945 dropped the world's first atomic bomb on Hiroshima, Japan; his awards included the Distinguished Service Cross, the Legion of Merit, and the Distinguished Flying Cross.

Margaret Truman (Mary Margaret Truman Daniel; 17 Feb 1924, Independence MO—29 Jan 2008, Chicago IL), American writer who was the illustrious only daughter of US Pres. Harry S. Truman and carved a literary niche for herself as her parents' biographer (*Harry S. Truman* [1973] and *Bess W. Truman* [1986]) and as the author of a number of best-selling mysteries.

Ike Turner (Izear Luster Turner, Jr.; 5 Nov 1931, Clarksdale MS—12 Dec 2007, San Marcos CA), American rhythm-and-blues artist who was best remembered as part of the singing duo of Ike and Tina Turner. The couple, who married in 1958, embraced the growing rock market in the late 1960s, most notably with John Fogerty's "Proud Mary" (1971); Tina alleged beatings, cocaine addiction, and infidelity, but after imprisonment for cocaine possession, Ike made a comeback, however, winning a Grammy Award in 2007 for the album *Risin' with the Blues;* Ike and Tina Turner were inducted into the Rock and Roll Hall of Fame in 1991.

Gene Upshaw (15 Aug 1945, Robstown, Texas—20 Aug 2008, near Lake Tahoe, California), American football player who was a standout offensive lineman for the Oakland Raiders—he led the team to three Super Bowls (1968, 1977, 1981) and was selected to play in seven Pro Bowls (1968, 1972–77); after his retirement he served as the executive director (1983–2008) of the National Football League Players Association; he was inducted into the Pro Football Hall of Fame in 1987.

Vo Van Kiet (Phan Van Hoa; 23 Nov 1922, Trung Hiep, French Indochina [now in Vietnam]—11 Jun 2008, Singapore), Vietnamese politician who, as Vietnam's prime minister (1991–97), strongly advocated *doi moi* (renovation), the economic plan that encouraged entrepreneurial initiative, foreign investment, and free-market reform; in 1995 he restored diplomatic relations between Vietnam and the US.

Porter Wayne Wagoner (12 Aug 1927, near West Plains MO—28 Oct 2007, Nashville TN), American singer who was a star of the Grand Ole Opry and helped to launch the career of Dolly Parton, with whom he recorded 14 top 10 songs; in 1960 he became the host of *The Porter Wagoner Show*, which ran for 21 years, and he won three Grammy Awards for gospel music he recorded with the Blackwood Brothers Quartet.

Bill Walsh (William Ernest Walsh; 30 Nov 1931, Los Angeles CA—30 Jul 2007, Woodside CA), American football coach who was the architect of the "West Coast offense," which featured short passes and quick slanting pass routes by receivers, and who helped build the San Francisco 49ers into a powerhouse NFL team—under Walsh the 49ers won Super Bowls XVI (1981), XIX (1985) and XXIII (1989) and registered a record of 102-63-1; he was inducted into the Pro Football Hall of Fame in 1993.

(Alice) Eileen Wearne (30 Jan 1912, Sydney, NSW, Australia—6 Jul 2007, Sydney, NSW, Australia), Australian athlete who was only the second woman to represent Australia in track and field in the Olympic Games, at the 1932 Los Angeles Olympics.

Jerry Wexler (10 Jan 1917, New York NY—15 Aug 2008, Sarasota FL), American record producer and music journalist who coined the phrase *rhythm and blues* in 1949; as an executive for Atlantic Records he guided the careers of such classic performers as Ray Charles, Wilson Pickett, Aretha Franklin, and the British group Led Zeppelin; he was inducted into the Rock and Roll Hall of Fame in 1987.

John Archibald Wheeler (9 Jul 1911, Jacksonville FL—13 Apr 2008, Hightstown NJ), American physicist who was the first American involved in the theoretical development of the atomic bomb; he helped develop (1949–51) the hydrogen bomb at Los Alamos NM, and he was director (1951–53) of Project Matterhorn, which was instituted to design thermonuclear weapons; he was awarded the Niels Bohr International Gold Medal in 1982.

Frank Yewell Whiteley, Jr. (1915?, Centreville MD—2 May 2008, Camden SC), American horse trainer who, in a 49-year (1936–84) career, conditioned such Thoroughbred champions as Damascas (winner of the Preakness Stakes, the Belmont Stakes, the Travers, and the Woodward and crowned 1967 Horse of the Year) and Ruffian (undefeated in 10 starts and winner of the filly Triple Crown); in 1978 Whiteley was inducted into the National Museum of Racing and Hall of Fame.

Phyllis Ayame Whitney (9 Sep 1903, Yokohama, Japan—8 Feb 2008, Faber VA), American author who wrote two novels—*The Mystery of the Haunted Pool* (1960) and *The Mystery of the Hidden Hand* (1963)—that won Edgar Allan Poe Awards from the Mystery Writers of America, of which she was president in 1975; in 1988 she received that organization's Grand Master Award for lifetime achievement.

Bill Willis (William Karnet Willis; 5 Oct 1921, Columbus OH—27 Nov 2007, Columbus OH), American football player who became one of the first African American players in professional football's modern era when he joined the Cleveland Browns of the newly formed All-America Football Conference (AAFC) in 1946; he earned all-league honors three times in the AAFC and four times in the NFL, and he was inducted into the Pro Football Hall of Fame in 1977 and was named to the NFL's 1940s All-Decade Team.

Stan Winston (Stanley Winston; 7 Apr 1946, Arlington VA—15 Jun 2008, Malibu CA), American special-effects artist who earned praise for his adeptness at combining makeup, animatronic creatures, and computer-generated images to produce incredibly realistic on-screen special effects; he won Academy Awards for *Aliens* (1986), *Terminator 2: Judgment Day* (1991), and *Jurassic Park* (1993); he also captured Emmy Awards for *Gargoyles* (1972) and *The Autobiography of Miss Jane Pittman* (1974).

Kathleen Woodiwiss (Kathleen Erin Hogg; 3 Jun 1939, Alexandria LA—6 Jul 2007, Princeton MN), American romance novelist who was the author of 14 popular romance novels; her paperbacks sold more than 35 million copies in 13 countries, and in 1988 Woodiwiss received the Romance Writers of America's lifetime achievement award.

John Youie Woodruff (5 Jul 1915, Connellsville PA—30 Oct 2007, Fountain Hills AZ), American track and field athlete who won gold in the 800-m race at the 1936 Berlin Olympic Games; his victory and those of Jesse Owens and other African American teammates embarrassed German leader Adolf Hitler; Woodruff won the Amateur Athletic Union 800-m championship in 1937 and the 880-yd NCAA title for three years (1937–39), and he was inducted into the National Track and Field Hall of Fame in 1978.

Jane Wyman (Sarah Jane Mayfield; Sarah Jane Fulks; 5 Jan 1917, St. Joseph MO—10 Sep 2007, Rancho Mirage CA), American actress who had a distinguished career in film and television but was perhaps equally well known as the first wife (1940–48) of US Pres. Ronald Reagan; she won the best actress Oscar for her portrayal of a deaf rape victim in *Johnny Belinda* (1948); she was also nominated for her roles in *The Yearling* (1946), *The Blue Veil* (1951), and *Magnificent Obsession* (1954).

Mohammad Zahir Shah (15 Oct 1914, Kabul, Afghanistan—23 Jul 2007, Kabul, Afghanistan), Afghan monarch who, as Afghanistan's last reigning king (1933–73), provided an era of stable government while maintaining a neutral position for his country in international politics; he established a constitutional monarchy, prohibited royal relatives from holding public office, and undertook a number of economic-development projects, including irrigation and highway construction, but in a bloodless coup on 17 Jul 1973, he was deposed, and he went into exile in Italy soon after; following the US overthrow of the Taliban, he returned to Afghanistan in 2002, and he was later given the honorary title Father of the Nation.

Hy Zaret (Hyman Harry Zaritsky; 21 Aug 1907, New York NY—2 Jul 2007, Westport CT), American lyricist who collaborated with composer Alex North to create the song "Unchained Melody" (1955), which became one of the most performed songs of all time.

Zhang Hanzhi (1935, Shanghai, China—26 Jan 2008, Beijing, China), Chinese diplomat and tutor who provided private English lessons to Chairman Mao Zedong in 1963; she interpreted for Prime Minister Zhou Enlai during US Secretary of State Henry Kissinger's confidential trip to China in 1971, and she also served as an interpreter for US Pres. Richard Nixon during his visit to China in 1972.

Awards

TIME's Top 100 Films

There's nothing like a list to stimulate a strong discussion, so in the hopes of striking a few sparks among movie lovers, TIME asked its longtime film critics Richard Corliss and Richard Schickel to compile a list of the 100 greatest films ever made. Of course, the discussions that followed between the two critics were entirely civil at all times. Below, the films and the year they were released.

A–C

Aguirre: The Wrath of God (1972)
The Apu Trilogy (1955, 1956, 1959)
The Awful Truth (1937)
Baby Face (1933)
Bande à part (1964)
Barry Lyndon (1975)
Berlin Alexanderplatz (1980)
Blade Runner (1982)
Bonnie and Clyde (1967)
Brazil (1985)
Bride of Frankenstein (1935)
Camille (1936)
Casablanca (1942)
Charade (1963)
Children of Paradise (1945)
Chinatown (1974)
Chungking Express (1994)
Citizen Kane (1941)
City Lights (1931)
City of God (2002)
Closely Watched Trains (1966)
The Crime of Monsieur Lange (1936)
The Crowd (1928)

D–F

Day for Night (1973)
The Decalogue (1989)
Detour (1945)
The Discreet Charm of the Bourgeoisie (1972)
Dodsworth (1936)
Double Indemnity (1944)
Dr. Strangelove or: How I Learned To Stop Worrying and Love the Bomb (1964)
Drunken Master II (1994)
E.T.: The Extra-Terrestrial (1982)
8 1/2 (1963)
The 400 Blows (1959)
Farewell My Concubine (1993)
Finding Nemo (2003)
The Fly (1986)

G–J

The Godfather, Parts I and II (1972, 1974)
The Good, the Bad, and the Ugly (1966)
Goodfellas (1990)
A Hard Day's Night (1964)
His Girl Friday (1940)
Ikiru (1952)
In a Lonely Place (1950)
Invasion of the Body Snatchers (1956)
It's a Gift (1934)
It's a Wonderful Life (1946)

K–M

Kandahar (2001)
Kind Hearts and Coronets (1949)
King Kong (1933)
The Lady Eve (1941)
The Last Command (1928)
Lawrence of Arabia (1962)
Léolo (1992)
The Lord of the Rings (2001, 2002, 2003)
The Man with a Camera (1929)
The Manchurian Candidate (1962)
Meet Me in St. Louis (1944)
Metropolis (1927)
Miller's Crossing (1990)
Mon oncle d'Amérique (1980)
Mouchette (1967)

N–P

Nayakan (1987)
Ninotchka (1939)
Notorious (1946)
Olympia, Parts 1 and 2 (1938)
On the Waterfront (1954)
Once upon a Time in the West (1968)
Out of the Past (1947)
Persona (1966)
Pinocchio (1940)
Psycho (1960)
Pulp Fiction (1994)
The Purple Rose of Cairo (1985)
Pyaasa (1957)

Q–S

Raging Bull (1980)
Schindler's List (1993)
The Searchers (1956)
Sherlock, Jr. (1924)
The Shop Around the Corner (1940)
Singin' in the Rain (1952)
The Singing Detective (1986)
Smiles of a Summer Night (1955)
Some Like It Hot (1959)
Star Wars (1977)
A Streetcar Named Desire (1951)
Sunrise (1927)
Sweet Smell of Success (1957)
Swing Time (1936)

T–Z

Talk to Her (2002)
Taxi Driver (1976)
Tokyo Story (1953)
A Touch of Zen (1971)
Ugetsu (1953)
Ulysses' Gaze (1995)
Umberto D (1952)
Unforgiven (1992)
White Heat (1949)
Wings of Desire (1987)
Yojimbo (1961)

TIME's Person of the Year, 1927–2007

Every year since 1927, TIME has named a Person of the Year, identifying the individual who has done the most to affect the news in the past twelve months. The designation is often mistaken for an honor, but the magazine has always pointed out that inclusion on the list is not a recognition of good works (like the Nobel Peace prize, for example), but rather a reflection of the sheer power of one's actions, whether for good or for ill. Hence, both Adolf Hitler and Ayatollah Ruhollah Khomeini were chosen Person of the Year at the time when their actions commanded the attention of the world. Below, the complete list of Persons of the Year.

1927	Charles Lindbergh
1928	Walter Chrysler
1929	Owen Young
1930	Mahatma Gandhi
1931	Pierre Laval
1932	Franklin Delano Roosevelt
1933	Hugh Johnson
1934	Franklin Delano Roosevelt
1935	Haile Selassie
1936	Wallis Simpson
1937	Chiang Kai-Shek and Soong Mei-ling
1938	Adolf Hitler
1939	Joseph Stalin
1940	Winston Churchill
1941	Franklin Delano Roosevelt
1942	Joseph Stalin
1943	George Marshall
1944	Dwight Eisenhower
1945	Harry Truman
1946	James F. Byrnes
1947	George Marshall
1948	Harry Truman
1949	Winston Churchill ("Man of the Half-Century")
1950	The American Fighting-Man (representing US troops fighting in the Korean War; first abstract chosen)
1951	Mohammed Mossadegh
1952	Queen Elizabeth II
1953	Konrad Adenauer
1954	John Foster Dulles
1955	Harlow Curtice
1956	Hungarian Freedom Fighter (representing the citizens' uprising against Soviet domination)
1957	Nikita Khrushchev
1958	Charles De Gaulle
1959	Dwight Eisenhower
1960	US Scientists (represented by Linus Pauling, Isidor Rabi, Edward Teller, Joshua Lederberg, Donald A. Glaser, Willard Libby, Robert Woodward, Charles Draper, William Shockley, Emilio Segrè, John Enders, Charles Townes, George Beadle, James Van Allen, and Edward Purcell)
1961	John F. Kennedy
1962	Pope John XXIII
1963	Martin Luther King, Jr.
1964	Lyndon Johnson
1965	William Westmoreland
1966	The Generation Twenty-Five and Under (representing American youth)
1967	Lyndon Johnson
1968	Apollo 8 astronauts Frank Borman, Jim Lovell, and William Anders
1969	The Middle Americans (representing the American electorate's turn to the right)
1970	Willy Brandt
1971	Richard Nixon
1972	Richard Nixon and Henry Kissinger
1973	John Sirica
1974	King Faisal
1975	American Women (represented by Betty Ford, Carla Hills, Ella Grasso, Barbara Jordan, Susie Sharp, Jill Conway, Billie Jean King, Susan Brownmiller, Addie Wyatt, Kathleen Byerly, Carol Sutton, and Alison Cheek)
1976	Jimmy Carter
1977	Anwar el-Sadat
1978	Deng Xiaoping
1979	Ayatollah Ruhollah Khomeini
1980	Ronald Reagan
1981	Lech Walensa
1982	The Computer (first non-human abstract chosen; termed "Machine of the Year")
1983	Ronald Reagan and Yuri Andropov
1984	Peter Ueberroth
1985	Deng Xiaoping
1986	Corazon Aquino
1987	Mikhail Gorbachev
1988	Endangered Earth ("Planet of the Year")
1989	Mikhail Gorbachev ("Man of the Decade")
1990	George H.W. Bush (termed "The Two George Bushes"; commended for his role in international affairs and criticized for his management of domestic affairs)
1991	Ted Turner
1992	Bill Clinton
1993	The Peacemakers (represented by Nelson Mandela and F.W. de Klerk of South Africa and Yasir Arafat and Yitzhak Rabin of the Middle East)
1994	Pope John Paul II
1995	Newt Gingrich
1996	David Ho
1997	Andy Grove
1998	Bill Clinton and Kenneth Starr
1999	Jeffrey P. Bezos
2000	George W. Bush
2001	Rudolph Giuliani
2002	The Whistleblowers (represented by Cynthia Cooper of Worldcom, Sherron Watkins of Enron, and Coleen Rowley of the FBI)
2003	The American Soldier (representing US troops fighting in Iraq and Afghanistan)
2004	George W. Bush
2005	The Good Samaritans (represented by Bono [Paul Hewson], Bill Gates, and Melinda Gates)
2006	You (representing the new age of user-generated Internet content)
2007	Vladimir Putin

Nobel Prizes

The Alfred B. Nobel Prizes are widely regarded as the world's most prestigious awards given for intellectual achievement. They are awarded annually from a fund bequeathed for that purpose by the Swedish inventor and industrialist Alfred Bernhard Nobel and administered by the Nobel Foundation. Nobel's 1895 will established five of the six prizes: those for physics, chemistry, literature, physiology or medicine, and peace. The prize for economic sciences was added in 1969. Each year thousands of invitations are sent out to members of scholarly academies, scientists, university professors, previous Nobel laureates, members of parliaments and other assemblies, and others, requesting nominations for the various prizes. The country given is the citizenship of the recipient at the time that the award was made. Prizes may be withheld or not awarded in years when no worthy recipient can be found or when the world situation (e.g., World Wars I and II) prevents the gathering of information needed to reach a decision. Prizes are announced in mid-October and awarded in December in Stockholm and Oslo. A cash award of SEK 10 million (about US$1,560,000), a personal diploma, and a commemorative medal are given for each prize category.

Nobel Foundation Web site: <http://nobelprize.org>.

Physics

YEAR	WINNER(S)	COUNTRY	ACHIEVEMENT
1901	Wilhelm Conrad Röntgen	Germany	discovery of X-rays
1902	Hendrik Antoon Lorentz	Neth.	investigation of the influence of magnetism on radiation
	Pieter Zeeman	Neth.	
1903	Henri Becquerel	France	discovery of spontaneous radioactivity
	Marie Curie	France	investigations of radiation phenomena discovered by Becquerel
	Pierre Curie	France	
1904	John William Strutt, 3rd Baron Rayleigh (of Terling Place)	UK	discovery of argon
1905	Philipp Lenard	Germany	research on cathode rays
1906	J.J. Thomson	UK	research into the electrical conductivity of gases
1907	A.A. Michelson	US	spectroscopic and metrological investigations
1908	Gabriel Lippmann	France	photographic reproduction of colors
1909	Ferdinand Braun	Germany	development of wireless telegraphy
	Guglielmo Marconi	Italy	
1910	Johannes Diederik van der Waals	Neth.	research concerning the equation of state of gases and liquids
1911	Wilhelm Wien	Germany	discoveries regarding laws governing heat radiation
1912	Nils Dalén	Sweden	invention of automatic regulators for lighting coastal beacons and light buoys
1913	Heike Kamerlingh Onnes	Neth.	investigation into the properties of matter at low temperatures; production of liquid helium
1914	Max von Laue	Germany	discovery of diffraction of X-rays by crystals
1915	Lawrence Bragg	UK	analysis of crystal structure by means of X-rays
	William Bragg	UK	
1917	Charles Glover Barkla	UK	discovery of the characteristic X-radiation of elements
1918	Max Planck	Germany	discovery of the elemental quanta
1919	Johannes Stark	Germany	discovery of the Doppler effect in positive ion rays and the division of spectral lines in the electric field
1920	Charles Édouard Guillaume	Switz.	discovery of anomalies in alloys
1921	Albert Einstein	Switz.	work in theoretical physics
1922	Niels Bohr	Denmark	investigation of atomic structure and radiation
1923	Robert Andrews Millikan	US	work on the elementary charge of electricity and on the photoelectric effect
1924	Karl Manne Georg Siegbahn	Sweden	work in X-ray spectroscopy
1925	James Franck	Germany	discovery of the laws governing the impact of an electron upon an atom
	Gustav Hertz	Germany	
1926	Jean Perrin	France	work on the discontinuous structure of matter
1927	Arthur Holly Compton	US	discovery of the wavelength change in diffused X-rays
	C.T.R. Wilson	UK	method of making visible the paths of electrically charged particles
1928	Owen Willans Richardson	UK	work on electron emission by hot metals
1929	Louis-Victor, 7e duc (duke) de Broglie	France	discovery of the wave nature of electrons
1930	Chandrasekhara Venkata Raman	India	work on light diffusion; discovery of Raman effect, light wavelength variation that occurs when a light beam is deflected by molecules

Physics (continued)

YEAR	WINNER(S)	COUNTRY	ACHIEVEMENT
1932	Werner Heisenberg	Germany	creation of quantum mechanics
1933	P.A.M. Dirac	UK	introduction of wave equations
	Erwin Schrödinger	Austria	in quantum mechanics
1935	James Chadwick	UK	discovery of the neutron
1936	Carl David Anderson	US	discovery of the positron
	Victor Francis Hess	Austria	discovery of cosmic radiation
1937	Clinton Joseph Davisson	US	experimental demonstration of the interference
	George Paget Thomson	UK	phenomenon in crystals irradiated by electrons
1938	Enrico Fermi	Italy	disclosure of artificial radioactive elements produced by neutron irradiation
1939	Ernest Orlando Lawrence	US	invention of the cyclotron
1943	Otto Stern	US	discovery of the magnetic moment of the proton
1944	Isidor Isaac Rabi	US	resonance method for the registration of various properties of atomic nuclei
1945	Wolfgang Pauli	Austria	discovery of the exclusion principle of electrons
1946	Percy Williams Bridgman	US	discoveries in the domain of high-pressure physics
1947	Edward V. Appleton	UK	discovery of the Appleton layer in the upper atmosphere
1948	Patrick M.S. Blackett	UK	discoveries in the domain of nuclear physics and cosmic radiation
1949	Hideki Yukawa	Japan	prediction of the existence of mesons
1950	Cecil Frank Powell	UK	photographic method of studying nuclear processes; discoveries concerning mesons
1951	John D. Cockcroft	UK	work on the transmutation of atomic nuclei
	Ernest T.S. Walton	Ireland	by accelerated particles
1952	Felix Bloch	US	discovery of nuclear magnetic
	E.M. Purcell	US	resonance in solids
1953	Frits Zernike	Neth.	method of phase-contrast microscopy
1954	Max Born	UK	statistical studies of atomic wave functions
	Walther Bothe	W.Ger.	invention of the coincidence method
1955	Polykarp Kusch	US	measurement of the magnetic moment of the electron
	Willis Eugene Lamb, Jr.	US	discoveries in the hydrogen spectrum
1956	John Bardeen	US	investigations on
	Walter H. Brattain	US	semiconductors and the
	William B. Shockley	US	invention of the transistor
1957	Tsung-Dao Lee	China	discovery of violations of the principle of parity, the
	Chen Ning Yang	China	symmetry between phenomena in coordinate systems
1958	Pavel Alexeyevich Cherenkov	USSR	discovery and interpretation of the Cherenkov effect, which indicates that electrons emit light as they
	Ilya Mikhaylovich Frank	USSR	pass through a transparent medium at a speed
	Igor Yevgenyevich Tamm	USSR	higher than the speed of light in that medium
1959	Owen Chamberlain	US	confirmation of the existence
	Emilio Segrè	US	of the antiproton
1960	Donald A. Glaser	US	development of the bubble chamber
1961	Robert Hofstadter	US	determination of the shape and size of atomic nucleons
	Rudolf Ludwig Mössbauer	W.Ger.	discovery of the Mössbauer effect, a nuclear process permitting the resonance absorption of gamma rays
1962	Lev Davidovich Landau	USSR	contributions to the understanding of condensed states of matter
1963	J. Hans D. Jensen	W.Ger.	development of the shell model theory of
	Maria Goeppert Mayer	US	the structure of the atomic nuclei
	Eugene Paul Wigner	US	principles governing the interaction of protons and neutrons in the nucleus
1964	Nikolay G. Basov	USSR	work in quantum electronics leading to the
	Aleksandr M. Prokhorov	USSR	construction of instruments based on
	Charles Hard Townes	US	maser-laser principles
1965	Richard P. Feynman	US	work in quantum electrodynamics, which
	Julian Seymour Schwinger	US	describes mathematically all interactions of light with
	Shin'ichiro Tomonaga	Japan	matter and of charged particles with one another
1966	Alfred Kastler	France	discovery of optical methods for studying Hertzian resonances in atoms
1967	Hans Albrecht Bethe	US	discoveries concerning the energy production of stars
1968	Luis W. Alvarez	US	work with elementary particles, in particular the discovery of resonance states
1969	Murray Gell-Mann	US	classification of elementary particles and their interactions
1970	Hannes Alfvén	Sweden	work in magnetohydrodynamics and
	Louis-Eugène-Félix Néel	France	in antiferromagnetism and ferrimagnetism
1971	Dennis Gabor	UK	invention of holography

Physics (continued)

YEAR	WINNER(S)	COUNTRY	ACHIEVEMENT
1972	John Bardeen	US	development of the theory of superconductivity, the disappearance of electrical resistance in various solids when they are cooled below certain temperatures
	Leon N. Cooper	US	
	John Robert Schrieffer	US	
1973	Leo Esaki	Japan	experimental discoveries in tunneling in semiconductors and superconductors
	Ivar Giaever	US	
	Brian D. Josephson	UK	predictions of supercurrent properties through a tunnel barrier
1974	Antony Hewish	UK	work in radio astronomy
	Martin Ryle	UK	
1975	Aage N. Bohr	Denmark	work on the atomic nucleus that paved the way for nuclear fusion
	Ben R. Mottelson	Denmark	
	James Rainwater	US	
1976	Burton Richter	US	discovery of new class of elementary particles (psi, or J)
	Samuel C.C. Ting	US	
1977	Philip W. Anderson	US	contributions to understanding the behavior of electrons in magnetic, noncrystalline solids
	Nevill F. Mott	UK	
	John H. Van Vleck	US	
1978	Pyotr L. Kapitsa	USSR	research in magnetism and low-temperature physics
	Arno Penzias	US	discovery of cosmic microwave background radiation, providing support for the big-bang theory
	Robert Woodrow Wilson	US	
1979	Sheldon Lee Glashow	US	contributions to the theory of the unified weak and electromagnetic interactions of subatomic particles
	Abdus Salam	Pakistan	
	Steven Weinberg	US	
1980	James Watson Cronin	US	demonstration of the simultaneous violation of both charge-conjugation and parity-inversion symmetries
	Val Logsdon Fitch	US	
1981	Nicolaas Bloembergen	US	applications of lasers in spectroscopy
	Arthur L. Schawlow	US	
	Kai M.B. Siegbahn	Sweden	development of electron spectroscopy
1982	Kenneth G. Wilson	US	analysis of continuous phase transitions
1983	Subrahmanyan Chandrasekhar	US	contributions to understanding the evolution and devolution of stars
	William A. Fowler	US	studies of nuclear reactions key to the formation of chemical elements
1984	Simon van der Meer	Neth.	discovery of subatomic particles W and Z, which supports the electroweak theory
	Carlo Rubbia	Italy	
1985	Klaus von Klitzing	W.Ger.	discovery of the quantized Hall effect, permitting exact measurements of electrical resistance
1986	Gerd Binnig	W.Ger.	development of the scanning tunneling electron microscope
	Heinrich Rohrer	Switz.	
	Ernst Ruska	W.Ger.	development of the electron microscope
1987	J. Georg Bednorz	W.Ger.	discoveries of superconductivity in ceramic materials
	Karl Alex Müller	Switz.	
1988	Leon Max Lederman	US	research in subatomic particles
	Melvin Schwartz	US	
	Jack Steinberger	US	
1989	Hans Georg Dehmelt	US	development of methods to isolate atoms and subatomic particles for study
	Wolfgang Paul	W.Ger.	
	Norman Foster Ramsey	US	development of the atomic clock
1990	Jerome Isaac Friedman	US	discovery of atomic quarks
	Henry Way Kendall	US	
	Richard E. Taylor	Canada	
1991	Pierre-Gilles de Gennes	France	discovery of general rules for behavior of molecules
1992	Georges Charpak	France	invention of a detector that traces subatomic particles
1993	Russell Alan Hulse	US	identification of binary pulsars
	Joseph H. Taylor, Jr.	US	
1994	Bertram N. Brockhouse	Canada	development of neutron-scattering techniques
	Clifford G. Shull	US	
1995	Martin Lewis Perl	US	discovery of the tau subatomic particle
	Frederick Reines	US	discovery of the neutrino subatomic particle
1996	David M. Lee	US	discovery of superfluidity in isotope helium-3
	Douglas D. Osheroff	US	
	Robert C. Richardson	US	
1997	Steven Chu	US	process of cooling and trapping atoms with laser light
	Claude Cohen-Tannoudji	France	
	William D. Phillips	US	
1998	Robert B. Laughlin	US	discovery of fractional quantum Hall effect, showing that electrons in a low-temperature magnetic field can form a quantum fluid with fractional electric charges
	Horst L. Störmer	US	
	Daniel C. Tsui	US	

Physics (continued)

YEAR	WINNER(S)	COUNTRY	ACHIEVEMENT
1999	Gerardus 't Hooft	Neth.	study of the quantum structure of electroweak interactions
	Martinus J.G. Veltman	Neth.	
2000	Zhores I. Alferov	Russia	development of fast semiconductors for use in microelectronics
	Herbert Kroemer	Germany	
	Jack S. Kilby	US	development of the integrated circuit (microchip)
2001	Eric A. Cornell	US	achievement of Bose-Einstein condensation in dilute gases of alkali atoms; early fundamental studies of the properties of the condensates
	Wolfgang Ketterle	Germany	
	Carl E. Wieman	US	
2002	Raymond Davis, Jr.	US	pioneering contributions to astrophysics, in particular the detection of cosmic neutrinos
	Masatoshi Koshiba	Japan	
	Riccardo Giacconi	US	pioneering contributions to astrophysics, which have led to the discovery of cosmic X-ray sources
2003	Alexei A. Abrikosov	US/Russia	pioneering contributions to the theory of superconductors and superfluids
	Vitaly L. Ginzburg	Russia	
	Anthony J. Leggett	UK/US	
2004	David J. Gross	US	discovery of asymptotic freedom in the theory of the strong interaction
	H. David Politzer	US	
	Frank Wilczek	US	
2005	Roy J. Glauber	US	contributions to quantum theory of optical coherence
	John L. Hall	US	contributions to the development of laser-based precision spectroscopy, including the optical frequency comb technique
	Theodor W. Hänsch	Germany	
2006	John C. Mather	US	discovery of the blackbody form and variability of cosmic microwave background radiation
	George F. Smoot	US	
2007	Albert Fert	France	discovery of Giant Magnetoresistance (large resistance changes in materials composed of alternating layers of various metallic elements), a nanotechnology application
	Peter Grünberg	Germany	

Chemistry

YEAR	WINNER(S)	COUNTRY	ACHIEVEMENT
1901	Jacobus H. van 't Hoff	Neth.	discovery of the laws of chemical dynamics and osmotic pressure
1902	Emil Fischer	Germany	work on sugar and purine syntheses
1903	Svante Arrhenius	Sweden	theory of electrolytic dissociation
1904	William Ramsay	UK	discovery of inert gas elements and their places in the periodic system
1905	Adolf von Baeyer	Germany	work on organic dyes and hydroaromatic compounds
1906	Henri Moissan	France	isolation of fluorine; introduction of the Moissan furnace
1907	Eduard Buchner	Germany	discovery of noncellular fermentation
1908	Ernest Rutherford	UK	investigations into the disintegration of elements and the chemistry of radioactive substances
1909	Wilhelm Ostwald	Germany	pioneer work on catalysis, chemical equilibrium, and reaction velocities
1910	Otto Wallach	Germany	pioneer work in alicyclic combinations
1911	Marie Curie	France	discovery of radium and polonium; isolation of radium
1912	Victor Grignard	France	discovery of the Grignard reagents
	Paul Sabatier	France	method of hydrogenating organic compounds
1913	Alfred Werner	Switz.	work on the linkage of atoms in molecules
1914	Theodore W. Richards	US	accurate determination of various atomic weights
1915	Richard Willstätter	Germany	research in plant pigments, especially chlorophyll
1918	Fritz Haber	Germany	synthesis of ammonia
1920	Walther Hermann Nernst	Germany	work in thermochemistry
1921	Frederick Soddy	UK	investigation into the chemistry of radioactive substances and the occurrence and nature of isotopes
1922	Francis William Aston	UK	work with mass spectrographs; formulation of the whole-number rule
1923	Fritz Pregl	Austria	method of microanalysis of organic substances
1925	Richard Zsigmondy	Austria	elucidation of the heterogeneous nature of colloidal solutions
1926	Theodor H.E. Svedberg	Sweden	work on disperse systems
1927	Heinrich Otto Wieland	Germany	research into the constitution of bile acids
1928	Adolf Windaus	Germany	research into the constitution of sterols and their connection with vitamins
1929	Hans von Euler-Chelpin	Sweden	investigations in the fermentation of sugars and the enzyme action involved
	Arthur Harden	UK	
1930	Hans Fischer	Germany	hemin, chlorophyll research; synthesis of hemin

Chemistry (continued)

YEAR	WINNER(S)	COUNTRY	ACHIEVEMENT
1931	Friedrich Bergius Carl Bosch	Germany Germany	invention and development of chemical high-pressure methods
1932	Irving Langmuir	US	discoveries and investigations in surface chemistry
1934	Harold C. Urey	US	discovery of heavy hydrogen
1935	Frédéric and Irène Joliot-Curie	France	synthesis of new radioactive elements
1936	Peter Debye	Neth.	work on dipole moments and diffraction of X-rays and electrons in gases
1937	Norman Haworth	UK	research on carbohydrates and vitamin C
	Paul Karrer	Switz.	research on carotenoids, flavins, and vitamins
1938	Richard Kuhn (declined)	Germany	carotenoid and vitamin research
1939	Adolf Butenandt (declined)	Germany	work on sexual hormones
	Leopold Ruzicka	Switz.	work on polymethylenes and higher terpenes
1943	Georg Charles von Hevesy	Hungary	use of isotopes as tracers in chemical research
1944	Otto Hahn	Germany	discovery of the fission of heavy nuclei
1945	Artturi Ilmari Virtanen	Finland	invention of the fodder preservation method
1946	John Howard Northrop Wendell M. Stanley	US US	preparation of enzymes and virus proteins in pure form
	James B. Sumner	US	discovery of enzyme crystallization
1947	Robert Robinson	UK	investigation of alkaloids and other plant products
1948	Arne Tiselius	Sweden	research on electrophoresis and adsorption analysis; discoveries concerning serum proteins
1949	William Francis Giauque	US	behavior of substances at extremely low temperatures
1950	Kurt Alder Otto Paul Hermann Diels	W.Ger. W.Ger.	discovery and development of diene synthesis
1951	Edwin M. McMillan Glenn T. Seaborg	US US	discovery of and research on transuranium elements
1952	A.J.P. Martin R.L.M. Synge	UK UK	development of partition chromatography
1953	Hermann Staudinger	W.Ger.	work on macromolecules
1954	Linus Pauling	US	study of the nature of the chemical bond
1955	Vincent du Vigneaud	US	first synthesis of a polypeptide hormone
1956	Cyril N. Hinshelwood Nikolay N. Semyonov	UK USSR	work on the kinetics of chemical reactions
1957	Alexander Robertus Todd, Baron Todd (of Trumpington)	UK	work on nucleotides and nucleotide coenzymes
1958	Frederick Sanger	UK	determination of the structure of the insulin molecule
1959	Jaroslav Heyrovsky	Czecho-slovakia	discovery and development of polarography
1960	Willard Frank Libby	US	development of radiocarbon dating
1961	Melvin Calvin	US	study of chemical steps that take place during photosynthesis
1962	John C. Kendrew Max Ferdinand Perutz	UK UK	determination of the structure of hemoproteins
1963	Giulio Natta Karl Ziegler	Italy W.Ger.	research into the structure and synthesis of polymers in the field of plastics
1964	Dorothy M.C. Hodgkin	UK	determination of the structure of biochemical compounds essential in combating pernicious anemia
1965	R.B. Woodward	US	synthesis of sterols, chlorophyll, and other substances
1966	Robert S. Mulliken	US	work concerning chemical bonds and the electronic structure of molecules
1967	Manfred Eigen	W.Ger.	studies of extremely fast chemical reactions
	Ronald G.W. Norrish George Porter	UK UK	studies of extremely fast chemical reactions
1968	Lars Onsager	US	work on the theory of thermodynamics of irreversible processes
1969	Derek H.R. Barton Odd Hassel	UK Norway	work in determining the actual three-dimensional shape of molecules
1970	Luis Federico Leloir	Argentina	discovery of sugar nucleotides and their role in the biosynthesis of carbohydrates
1971	Gerhard Herzberg	Canada	research in the structure of molecules
1972	Christian B. Anfinsen	US	fundamental contributions to enzyme chemistry
	Stanford Moore William H. Stein	US US	fundamental contributions to enzyme chemistry
1973	Ernst Otto Fischer Geoffrey Wilkinson	W.Ger. UK	organometallic chemistry

Chemistry (continued)

YEAR	WINNER(S)	COUNTRY	ACHIEVEMENT
1974	Paul J. Flory	US	studies of long-chain molecules
1975	John W. Cornforth	UK	work in stereochemistry
	Vladimir Prelog	Switz.	
1976	William N. Lipscomb, Jr.	US	studies on the structure of boranes
1977	Ilya Prigogine	Belgium	widening the scope of thermodynamics
1978	Peter Dennis Mitchell	UK	formulation of a theory of energy transfer processes in biological systems
1979	Herbert Charles Brown	US	introduction of compounds of boron and phosphorus in the synthesis of organic substances
	Georg Wittig	W.Ger.	introduction of compounds of boron and phosphorus in the synthesis of organic substances
1980	Paul Berg	US	first preparation of a hybrid DNA
	Walter Gilbert	US	development of chemical and biological analyses of DNA structure
	Frederick Sanger	UK	
1981	Kenichi Fukui	Japan	orbital symmetry interpretation of chemical reactions
	Roald Hoffmann	US	
1982	Aaron Klug	UK	determination of the structure of biological substances
1983	Henry Taube	US	study of electron transfer reactions
1984	Bruce Merrifield	US	development of a method of polypeptide synthesis
1985	Herbert A. Hauptman	US	development of a way to map the chemical structure of small molecules
	Jerome Karle	US	
1986	Dudley R. Herschbach	US	development of methods for analyzing basic chemical reactions
	Yuan T. Lee	US	
	John C. Polanyi	Canada	
1987	Donald J. Cram	US	development of molecules that can link with other molecules
	Jean-Marie Lehn	France	
	Charles J. Pedersen	US	
1988	Johann Deisenhofer	W.Ger.	discovery of structure proteins needed in photosynthesis
	Robert Huber	W.Ger.	
	Hartmut Michel	W.Ger.	
1989	Sidney Altman	US	discovery of certain basic properties of RNA
	Thomas Robert Cech	US	
1990	Elias James Corey	US	development of retrosynthetic analysis for synthesis of complex molecules
1991	Richard R. Ernst	Switz.	improvements in nuclear magnetic resonance spectroscopy
1992	Rudolph A. Marcus	US	explanation of how electrons transfer between molecules
1993	Kary B. Mullis	US	invention of techniques for gene study and manipulation
	Michael Smith	Canada	
1994	George A. Olah	US	development of techniques to study hydrocarbon molecules
1995	Paul Crutzen	Neth.	explanation of processes that deplete Earth's ozone layer
	Mario Molina	US	
	F. Sherwood Rowland	US	
1996	Robert F. Curl, Jr.	US	discovery of new carbon compounds called fullerenes
	Harold W. Kroto	UK	
	Richard E. Smalley	US	
1997	Paul D. Boyer	US	explanation of the enzymatic conversion of adenosine triphosphate
	John E. Walker	UK	
	Jens C. Skou	Denmark	discovery of sodium-potassium-activated adenosine triphosphatase
1998	Walter Kohn	US	development of the density-functional theory
	John A. Pople	UK	development of computational methods in quantum chemistry
1999	Ahmed H. Zewail	Egypt/US	study of the transition states of chemical reactions using femtosecond spectroscopy
2000	Alan J. Heeger	US	discovery of plastics that conduct electricity
	Alan G. MacDiarmid	US	
	Hideki Shirakawa	Japan	
2001	William S. Knowles	US	work on chirally catalyzed hydrogenation reactions
	Ryoji Noyori	Japan	
	K. Barry Sharpless	US	work on chirally catalyzed oxidation reactions
2002	John B. Fenn	US	development of soft desorption ionization methods for mass spectrometric analyses of biological macromolecules
	Koichi Tanaka	Japan	
	Kurt Wüthrich	Switz.	development of nuclear magnetic resonance spectroscopy for determining the three-dimensional structure of biological macromolecules in solution

Chemistry (continued)

YEAR	WINNER(S)	COUNTRY	ACHIEVEMENT
2003	Peter Agre	US	cell membrane channel discoveries
	Roderick MacKinnon	US	
2004	Aaron Ciechanover	Israel	discovery of ubiquitin-mediated protein degradation
	Avram Hershko	Israel	
	Irwin Rose	US	
2005	Yves Chauvin	France	development of the metathesis method in organic synthesis
	Robert H. Grubbs	US	
	Richard R. Schrock	US	
2006	Roger D. Kornberg	US	studies of the molecular basis of eukaryotic transcription
2007	Gerhard Ertl	Germany	studies of chemical processes on solid surfaces

Physiology or Medicine

YEAR	WINNER(S)	COUNTRY	ACHIEVEMENT
1901	Emil von Behring	Germany	work on serum therapy
1902	Ronald Ross	UK	discovery of how malaria enters an organism
1903	Niels Ryberg Finsen	Denmark	treatment of skin diseases with light
1904	Ivan Petrovich Pavlov	Russia	work on the physiology of digestion
1905	Robert Koch	Germany	tuberculosis research
1906	Camillo Golgi	Italy	work on the structure of the nervous system
	Santiago Ramón y Cajal	Spain	
1907	Alphonse Laveran	France	discovery of the role of protozoa in diseases
1908	Paul Ehrlich	Germany	work on immunity
	Élie Metchnikoff	Russia	
1909	Emil Theodor Kocher	Switz.	work on aspects of the thyroid gland
1910	Albrecht Kossel	Germany	researches in cellular chemistry
1911	Allvar Gullstrand	Sweden	work on dioptrics of the eye
1912	Alexis Carrel	France	work on the vascular suture; the transplantation of organs
1913	Charles Richet	France	work on anaphylaxis
1914	Robert Bárány	Austria-Hungary	work on vestibular apparatus
1919	Jules Bordet	Belgium	work on immunity factors in blood serum
1920	August Krogh	Denmark	discovery of the capillary motor-regulating mechanism
1922	A.V. Hill	UK	discoveries concerning heat production in muscles
	Otto Meyerhof	Germany	work on metabolism of lactic acid in muscles
1923	Frederick G. Banting	Canada	discovery of insulin
	J.J.R. Macleod	UK	
1924	Willem Einthoven	Neth.	discovery of the electrocardiogram mechanism
1926	Johannes Fibiger	Denmark	contributions to cancer research
1927	Julius Wagner-Jauregg	Austria	work on malaria inoculation in dementia paralytica
1928	Charles-Jules-Henri Nicolle	France	work on typhus
1929	Christiaan Eijkman	Neth.	discovery of the antineuritic vitamin
	Frederick Gowland Hopkins	UK	discovery of growth-stimulating vitamins
1930	Karl Landsteiner	US	discovery of human blood groups
1931	Otto Warburg	Germany	discovery of the nature and action of the respiratory enzyme
1932	Edgar Douglas Adrian, 1st Baron Adrian (of Cambridge)	UK	discoveries regarding the functions of neurons
	Charles Scott Sherrington	UK	
1933	Thomas Hunt Morgan	US	discoveries concerning chromosomal heredity functions
1934	George Richards Minot	US	discoveries concerning liver treatment for anemia
	William P. Murphy	US	
	George H. Whipple	US	
1935	Hans Spemann	Germany	discovery of the organizer effect in embryos
1936	Henry Dale	UK	work on the chemical transmission of nerve impulses
	Otto Loewi	Germany	
1937	Albert Szent-Gyorgyi	Hungary	work on biological combustion
1938	Corneille Heymans	Belgium	discovery of the role of sinus and aortic mechanisms in respiration regulation
1939	Gerhard Domagk (declined)	Germany	discovery of the antibacterial effect of Prontosil
1943	Henrik Dam	Denmark	discovery of vitamin K
	Edward Adelbert Doisy	US	discovery of the chemical nature of vitamin K

Physiology or Medicine (continued)

YEAR	WINNER(S)	COUNTRY	ACHIEVEMENT
1944	Joseph Erlanger	US	research on differentiated functions of nerve fibers
	Herbert S. Gasser	US	
1945	Ernst Boris Chain	UK	discovery of penicillin and its curative value
	Alexander Fleming	UK	
	Howard Walter Florey, Baron Florey	Australia	
1946	Hermann J. Muller	US	production of mutations by X-ray irradiation
1947	Carl and Gerty Cori	US	discovery of how glycogen is catalytically converted
	Bernardo A. Houssay	Argentina	discovery of the pituitary hormone function in sugar metabolism
1948	Paul Hermann Müller	Switz.	discovery of properties of DDT
1949	António Egas Moniz	Portugal	discovery of therapeutic value in leucotomy for psychoses
	Walter Rudolf Hess	Switz.	discovery of function of interbrain
1950	Philip Showalter Hench	US	research on adrenal cortex hormones, their structure, and their biological effects
	Edward Calvin Kendall	US	
	Tadeus Reichstein	Switz.	
1951	Max Theiler	South Africa	yellow fever discoveries
1952	Selman A. Waksman	US	discovery of streptomycin
1953	Hans Adolf Krebs	UK	discovery of the citric-acid cycle
	Fritz Albert Lipmann	US	discovery of coenzyme A metabolism
1954	John Franklin Enders	US	cultivation of the poliomyelitis virus in tissue cultures
	Frederick C. Robbins	US	
	Thomas H. Weller	US	
1955	Axel H.T. Theorell	Sweden	discoveries concerning oxidation enzymes
1956	André F. Cournand	US	discoveries concerning heart catheterization and circulatory changes
	Werner Forssmann	W.Ger.	
	Dickinson W. Richards	US	
1957	Daniel Bovet	Italy	production of synthetic curare
1958	George Wells Beadle	US	discovery of the genetic regulation of chemical processes
	Edward L. Tatum	US	
	Joshua Lederberg	US	discoveries concerning genetic recombination
1959	Arthur Kornberg	US	work on producing nucleic acids artificially
	Severo Ochoa	US	
1960	Macfarlane Burnet	Australia	discovery of acquired immunity to tissue transplants
	Peter B. Medawar	UK	
1961	Georg von Békésy	US	discovery of functions of the inner ear
1962	Francis H.C. Crick	UK	discoveries concerning the molecular structure of DNA
	James Dewey Watson	US	
	Maurice Wilkins	UK	
1963	John Carew Eccles	Australia	study of the transmission of impulses along a nerve fiber
	Alan Hodgkin	UK	
	Andrew F. Huxley	UK	
1964	Konrad Bloch	US	discoveries concerning cholesterol and fatty-acid metabolism
	Feodor Lynen	W.Ger.	
1965	François Jacob	France	discoveries concerning regulatory activities of the body cells
	André Lwoff	France	
	Jacques Monod	France	
1966	Charles B. Huggins	US	research on causes and treatment of cancer
	Peyton Rous	US	
1967	Ragnar Arthur Granit	Sweden	discoveries about chemical and physiological visual processes in the eye
	Haldan Keffer Hartline	US	
	George Wald	US	
1968	Robert William Holley	US	deciphering of the genetic code
	Har Gobind Khorana	US	
	Marshall W. Nirenberg	US	
1969	Max Delbrück	US	research and discoveries concerning viruses and viral diseases
	A.D. Hershey	US	
	Salvador Luria	US	
1970	Julius Axelrod	US	discoveries concerning the chemistry of nerve transmission
	Ulf von Euler	Sweden	
	Sir Bernard Katz	UK	
1971	Earl W. Sutherland, Jr.	US	discoveries concerning the action of hormones
1972	Gerald M. Edelman	US	research on the chemical structure of antibodies
	Rodney Robert Porter	UK	
1973	Karl von Frisch	Austria	discoveries in animal behavior patterns
	Konrad Lorenz	Austria	
	Nikolaas Tinbergen	UK	

Physiology or Medicine (continued)

YEAR	WINNER(S)	COUNTRY	ACHIEVEMENT
1974	Albert Claude	US	research on the structural
	Christian René de Duve	Belgium	and functional organization
	George E. Palade	US	of cells
1975	David Baltimore	US	discoveries concerning the interaction between
	Renato Dulbecco	US	tumor viruses and the genetic
	Howard Martin Temin	US	material of the cell
1976	Baruch S. Blumberg	US	studies of the origin and
	D. Carleton Gajdusek	US	spread of infectious diseases
1977	Roger C.L. Guillemin	US	research on pituitary
	Andrew Victor Schally	US	hormones
	Rosalyn S. Yalow	US	development of radioimmunoassay
1978	Werner Arber	Switz.	discovery and application
	Daniel Nathans	US	of enzymes that
	Hamilton O. Smith	US	fragment DNA
1979	Allan M. Cormack	US	development of
	Godfrey N. Hounsfield	UK	the CAT scan
1980	Baruj Benacerraf	US	investigations of genetic
	Jean Dausset	France	control of the response of the
	George Davis Snell	US	immune system to foreign substances
1981	David Hunter Hubel	US	discoveries concerning the processing of visual
	Torsten Nils Wiesel	Sweden	information by the brain
	Roger Wolcott Sperry	US	discoveries concerning cerebral hemisphere functions
1982	Sune K. Bergström	Sweden	discoveries concerning the biochemistry
	Bengt I. Samuelsson	Sweden	and physiology of
	John Robert Vane	UK	of prostaglandins
1983	Barbara McClintock	US	discovery of mobile plant genes that affect heredity
1984	Niels K. Jerne	Denmark	theory and development
	Georges J.F. Köhler	W.Ger.	of a technique
	César Milstein	UK/ Argentina	for producing monoclonal antibodies
1985	Michael S. Brown	US	discovery of cell receptors relating to
	Joseph L. Goldstein	US	cholesterol metabolism
1986	Stanley Cohen	US	discovery of chemical agents
	Rita Levi-Montalcini	Italy	that help regulate the growth of cells
1987	Susumu Tonegawa	Japan	study of genetic aspects of antibodies
1988	James Black	UK	development of new
	Gertrude Belle Elion	US	classes of drugs for
	George H. Hitchings	US	combating disease
1989	J. Michael Bishop	US	study of cancer-causing
	Harold Varmus	US	genes called oncogenes
1990	Joseph E. Murray	US	development of kidney and
	E. Donnall Thomas	US	bone-marrow transplants
1991	Erwin Neher	Germany	discovery of how cells
	Bert Sakmann	Germany	communicate, as related to diseases
1992	Edmond H. Fischer	US	discovery of a class of enzymes
	Edwin Gerhard Krebs	US	called protein kinases
1993	Richard J. Roberts	UK	discovery of "split," or
	Phillip A. Sharp	US	interrupted, genetic structure
1994	Alfred G. Gilman	US	discovery of cell signalers
	Martin Rodbell	US	called G-proteins
1995	Edward B. Lewis	US	identification of genes
	Christiane Nüsslein-Volhard	Germany	that control the body's early structural
	Eric F. Wieschaus	US	development
1996	Peter C. Doherty	Australia	discovery of how the immune
	Rolf M. Zinkernagel	Switz.	system recognizes virus-infected cells
1997	Stanley B. Prusiner	US	discovery of the prion, a type of disease-causing protein
1998	Robert F. Furchgott	US	discovery that nitric oxide
	Louis J. Ignarro	US	acts as a signaling molecule in
	Ferid Murad	US	the cardiovascular system
1999	Günter Blobel	US	discovery that proteins have signals governing cellular organization
2000	Arvid Carlsson	Sweden	discovery of how signals
	Paul Greengard	US	are transmitted between nerve
	Eric Kandel	US	cells in the brain
2001	Leland H. Hartwell	US	discovery of key
	R. Timothy Hunt	UK	regulators of
	Paul M. Nurse	UK	the cell cycle

Physiology or Medicine (continued)

YEAR	WINNER(S)	COUNTRY	ACHIEVEMENT
2002	Sydney Brenner	UK	discoveries concerning how genes regulate and program organ development and cell death
	H. Robert Horvitz	US	
	John E. Sulston	UK	
2003	Paul C. Lauterbur	US	discoveries concerning magnetic resonance imaging
	Peter Mansfield	UK	
2004	Richard Axel	US	discoveries of odorant receptors and the organization of the olfactory system
	Linda B. Buck	US	
2005	Barry J. Marshall	Australia	discovery of the bacterium *Helicobacter pylori* and its role in peptic ulcer disease and gastritis
	J. Robin Warren	Australia	
2006	Andrew Z. Fire	US	discovery of RNA interference: gene silencing by double-stranded RNA
	Craig C. Mello	US	
2007	Mario R. Capecchi	US	discoveries of principles for introducing specific gene modifications using embryonic stem cells
	Martin J. Evans	UK	
	Oliver Smithies	US	

Literature

YEAR	WINNER(S)	COUNTRY	FIELD
1901	Sully Prudhomme	France	poetry
1902	Theodor Mommsen	Germany	history
1903	Bjørnstjerne Martinus Bjørnson	Norway	prose fiction, poetry, drama
1904	José Echegaray y Eizaguirre	Spain	drama
	Frédéric Mistral	France	poetry
1905	Henryk Sienkiewicz	Poland	prose fiction
1906	Giosuè Carducci	Italy	poetry
1907	Rudyard Kipling	UK	poetry, prose fiction
1908	Rudolf Christoph Eucken	Germany	philosophy
1909	Selma Lagerlöf	Sweden	prose fiction
1910	Paul Johann Ludwig von Heyse	Germany	poetry, prose fiction, drama
1911	Maurice Maeterlinck	Belgium	drama
1912	Gerhart Hauptmann	Germany	drama
1913	Rabindranath Tagore	India	poetry
1915	Romain Rolland	France	prose fiction
1916	Verner von Heidenstam	Sweden	poetry
1917	Karl Gjellerup	Denmark	prose fiction
	Henrik Pontoppidan	Denmark	prose fiction
1918	Erik Axel Karlfeldt (declined)	Sweden	poetry
1919	Carl Spitteler	Switz.	poetry, prose fiction
1920	Knut Hamsun	Norway	prose fiction
1921	Anatole France	France	prose fiction
1922	Jacinto Benavente y Martínez	Spain	drama
1923	William Butler Yeats	Ireland	poetry
1924	Wladyslaw Stanislaw Reymont	Poland	prose fiction
1925	George Bernard Shaw	Ireland	drama
1926	Grazia Deledda	Italy	prose fiction
1927	Henri Bergson	France	philosophy
1928	Sigrid Undset	Norway	prose fiction
1929	Thomas Mann	Germany	prose fiction
1930	Sinclair Lewis	US	prose fiction
1931	Erik Axel Karlfeldt (posthumously)	Sweden	poetry
1932	John Galsworthy	UK	prose fiction
1933	Ivan Alekseyevich Bunin	USSR	poetry, prose fiction
1934	Luigi Pirandello	Italy	drama
1936	Eugene O'Neill	US	drama
1937	Roger Martin du Gard	France	prose fiction
1938	Pearl Buck	US	prose fiction
1939	Frans Eemil Sillanpää	Finland	prose fiction
1944	Johannes V. Jensen	Denmark	prose fiction
1945	Gabriela Mistral	Chile	poetry
1946	Hermann Hesse	Switz.	prose fiction
1947	André Gide	France	prose
1948	T.S. Eliot	UK	poetry, criticism
1949	William Faulkner	US	prose fiction
1950	Bertrand Russell	UK	philosophy
1951	Pär Lagerkvist	Sweden	prose fiction
1952	François Mauriac	France	poetry, prose fiction, drama
1953	Winston Churchill	UK	history, oration

Literature (continued)

1954	Ernest Hemingway	US	prose fiction
1955	Halldór Laxness	Iceland	prose fiction
1956	Juan Ramón Jiménez	Spain	poetry
1957	Albert Camus	France	prose fiction, drama
1958	Boris L. Pasternak (declined)	USSR	prose fiction, poetry
1959	Salvatore Quasimodo	Italy	poetry
1960	Saint-John Perse	France	poetry
1961	Ivo Andric	Yugoslavia	prose fiction
1962	John Steinbeck	US	prose fiction
1963	George Seferis	Greece	poetry
1964	Jean-Paul Sartre (declined)	France	philosophy, drama
1965	Mikhail A. Sholokhov	USSR	prose fiction
1966	S.Y. Agnon	Israel	prose fiction
	Nelly Sachs	Sweden	poetry
1967	Miguel Ángel Asturias	Guatemala	prose fiction
1968	Yasunari Kawabata	Japan	prose fiction
1969	Samuel Beckett	Ireland	prose fiction, drama
1970	Aleksandr I. Solzhenitsyn	USSR	prose fiction
1971	Pablo Neruda	Chile	poetry
1972	Heinrich Böll	W.Ger.	prose fiction
1973	Patrick White	Australia	prose fiction
1974	Eyvind Johnson	Sweden	prose fiction
	Harry Martinson	Sweden	prose fiction, poetry
1975	Eugenio Montale	Italy	poetry
1976	Saul Bellow	US	prose fiction
1977	Vicente Aleixandre	Spain	poetry
1978	Isaac Bashevis Singer	US	prose fiction
1979	Odysseus Elytis	Greece	poetry
1980	Czeslaw Milosz	US	poetry
1981	Elias Canetti	Bulgaria	prose
1982	Gabriel García Márquez	Colombia	prose fiction, journalism, social criticism
1983	William Golding	UK	prose fiction
1984	Jaroslav Seifert	Czechoslovakia	poetry
1985	Claude Simon	France	prose fiction
1986	Wole Soyinka	Nigeria	drama, poetry
1987	Joseph Brodsky	US	poetry, prose
1988	Naguib Mahfouz	Egypt	prose fiction
1989	Camilo José Cela	Spain	prose fiction
1990	Octavio Paz	Mexico	poetry, prose
1991	Nadine Gordimer	South Africa	prose fiction
1992	Derek Walcott	St. Lucia	poetry
1993	Toni Morrison	US	prose fiction
1994	Kenzaburo Oe	Japan	prose fiction
1995	Seamus Heaney	Ireland	poetry
1996	Wislawa Szymborska	Poland	poetry
1997	Dario Fo	Italy	drama
1998	José Saramago	Portugal	prose fiction
1999	Günter Grass	Germany	prose fiction
2000	Gao Xingjian	France	prose fiction, drama
2001	V.S. Naipaul	UK	prose fiction
2002	Imre Kertész	Hungary	prose fiction
2003	J.M. Coetzee	South Africa	prose fiction
2004	Elfriede Jelinek	Austria	prose fiction, drama
2005	Harold Pinter	UK	drama
2006	Orhan Pamuk	Turkey	prose fiction
2007	Doris Lessing	UK	prose fiction, social criticism

Peace

YEAR	WINNER(S)	COUNTRY
1901	Henri Dunant	Switzerland
	Frédéric Passy	France
1902	Élie Ducommun	Switzerland
	Charles-Albert Gobat	Switzerland
1903	Randal Cremer	UK
1904	Institute of International Law	(founded 1873)
1905	Bertha, Freifrau von Suttner	Austria-Hungary
1906	Theodore Roosevelt	US

Peace (continued)

YEAR	WINNER(S)	COUNTRY
1907	Ernesto Teodoro Moneta	Italy
	Louis Renault	France
1908	Klas Pontus Arnoldson	Sweden
	Fredrik Bajer	Denmark
1909	Auguste-Marie-François Beernaert	Belgium
	Paul-H.-B. d'Estournelles de Constant	France
1910	International Peace Bureau	(founded 1891)
1911	Tobias Michael Carel Asser	Netherlands
	Alfred Hermann Fried	Austria-Hungary
1912	Elihu Root	US
1913	Henri-Marie Lafontaine	Belgium
1917	International Committee of the Red Cross	(founded 1863)
1919	Woodrow Wilson	US
1920	Léon Bourgeois	France
1921	Karl Hjalmar Branting	Sweden
	Christian Lous Lange	Norway
1922	Fridtjof Nansen	Norway
1925	Austen Chamberlain	UK
	Charles G. Dawes	US
1926	Aristide Briand	France
	Gustav Stresemann	Germany
1927	Ferdinand-Édouard Buisson	France
	Ludwig Quidde	Germany
1929	Frank B. Kellogg	US
1930	Nathan Söderblom	Sweden
1931	Jane Addams	US
	Nicholas Murray Butler	US
1933	Norman Angell	UK
1934	Arthur Henderson	UK
1935	Carl von Ossietzky	Germany
1936	Carlos Saavedra Lamas	Argentina
1937	Robert Gascoyne-Cecil, 1st Viscount Cecil (of Chelwood)	UK
1938	Nansen International Office for Refugees	(founded 1931)
1944	International Committee of the Red Cross	(founded 1863)
1945	Cordell Hull	US
1946	Emily Greene Balch	US
	John R. Mott	US
1947	American Friends Service Committee	US
	Friends Service Council	UK
1949	John Boyd Orr, Baron Boyd-Orr of Brechin Mearns	UK
1950	Ralph Bunche	US
1951	Léon Jouhaux	France
1952	Albert Schweitzer	France
1953	George C. Marshall	US
1954	Office of the United Nations High Commissioner for Refugees	(founded 1951)
1957	Lester B. Pearson	Canada
1958	Dominique Pire	Belgium
1959	Philip John Noel-Baker, Baron Noel-Baker (of the City of Derby)	UK
1960	Albert John Luthuli	South Africa
1961	Dag Hammarskjöld	Sweden
1962	Linus Pauling	US
1963	International Committee of the Red Cross	(founded 1863)
	League of Red Cross Societies	(founded 1919)
1964	Martin Luther King, Jr.	US
1965	United Nations Children's Fund	(founded 1946)
1968	René Cassin	France
1969	International Labour Organisation	(founded 1919)
1970	Norman Ernest Borlaug	US
1971	Willy Brandt	West Germany
1973	Henry Kissinger	US
	Le Duc Tho (declined)	North Vietnam
1974	Seán MacBride	Ireland
	Eisaku Sato	Japan
1975	Andrey Dmitriyevich Sakharov	USSR
1976	Mairéad Corrigan	Northern Ireland
	Betty Williams	Northern Ireland
1977	Amnesty International	(founded 1961)
1978	Menachem Begin	Israel
	Anwar el-Sadat	Egypt
1979	Mother Teresa	India
1980	Adolfo Pérez Esquivel	Argentina
1981	Office of the United Nations High Commissioner for Refugees	(founded 1951)
1982	Alfonso García Robles	Mexico
	Alva Myrdal	Sweden
1983	Lech Walesa	Poland
1984	Desmond Tutu	South Africa
1985	International Physicians for the Prevention of Nuclear War	(founded 1980)
1986	Elie Wiesel	US
1987	Oscar Arias Sánchez	Costa Rica
1988	United Nations Peace-keeping Forces	
1989	Dalai Lama	Tibet
1990	Mikhail Gorbachev	USSR
1991	Aung San Suu Kyi	Myanmar
1992	Rigoberta Menchú	Guatemala
1993	F.W. de Klerk	South Africa
	Nelson Mandela	South Africa
1994	Yasir Arafat	Palestinian
	Shimon Peres	Israel
	Yitzhak Rabin	Israel
1995	Pugwash Conferences	(founded 1957)
	Joseph Rotblat	UK
1996	Carlos Filipe Ximenes Belo	East Timor
	José Ramos-Horta	East Timor
1997	International Campaign to Ban Landmines	(founded 1992)
	Jody Williams	US
1998	John Hume	Northern Ireland
	David Trimble	Northern Ireland
1999	Doctors Without Borders	(founded 1971)
2000	Kim Dae Jung	South Korea
2001	Kofi Annan	Ghana
	United Nations	(founded 1945)
2002	Jimmy Carter	US
2003	Shirin Ebadi	Iran
2004	Wangari Maathai	Kenya
2005	Mohamed ElBaradei	Egypt
	International Atomic Energy Agency	(founded 1957)

Peace (continued)

YEAR	WINNER(S)	COUNTRY
2006	Muhammad Yunus	Bangladesh
	Grameen Bank	(founded 1976)
2007	Intergovernmental Panel on Climate Change	(founded 1988)
	Albert Arnold (Al) Gore, Jr.	US

Economics

YEAR	WINNER(S)	COUNTRY	ACHIEVEMENT
1969	Ragnar Frisch Jan Tinbergen	Norway Neth.	work in econometrics
1970	Paul Samuelson	US	work in scientific analysis of economic theory
1971	Simon Kuznets	US	extensive research on the economic growth of nations
1972	Kenneth J. Arrow John R. Hicks	US UK	contributions to general economic equilibrium theory and welfare theory
1973	Wassily Leontief	US	development of input-output analysis
1974	Friedrich von Hayek Gunnar Myrdal	UK Sweden	pioneering analysis of the interdependence of economic, social, and institutional phenomena
1975	Leonid V. Kantorovich Tjalling C. Koopmans	USSR US	contributions to the theory of optimum allocation of resources
1976	Milton Friedman	US	work in consumption analysis, monetary theory, and economic stabilization
1977	James Edward Meade Bertil Ohlin	UK Sweden	contributions to the theory of international trade
1978	Herbert A. Simon	US	decision-making processes in economic organizations
1979	Arthur Lewis Theodore W. Schultz	UK US	analyses of economic processes in developing nations
1980	Lawrence Robert Klein	US	development and analysis of empirical models of business fluctuations
1981	James Tobin	US	portfolio-selection theory of investment
1982	George J. Stigler	US	studies of economic effects of governmental regulation
1983	Gerard Debreu	US	mathematical proof of the supply-and-demand theory
1984	Richard Stone	UK	development of national income accounting systems
1985	Franco Modigliani	US	analyses of household savings and financial markets
1986	James M. Buchanan	US	public-choice theory bridging economics and political science
1987	Robert Merton Solow	US	contributions to the theory of economic growth
1988	Maurice Allais	France	contributions to the theory of markets and efficient use of resources
1989	Trygve Haavelmo	Norway	development of statistical techniques for economic forecasting
1990	Harry M. Markowitz Merton H. Miller William F. Sharpe	US US US	study of financial markets and investment decision making
1991	Ronald Coase	US	application of economic principles to the study of law
1992	Gary S. Becker	US	application of economic theory to social sciences
1993	Robert William Fogel Douglass C. North	US US	contributions to economic history
1994	John C. Harsanyi John F. Nash Reinhard Selten	US US Germany	development of game theory
1995	Robert E. Lucas, Jr.	US	incorporation of rational expectations in macroeconomic theory
1996	James A. Mirrlees William Vickrey	UK US	contributions to the theory of incentives under conditions of asymmetric information
1997	Robert C. Merton Myron S. Scholes	US US	method for determining the value of stock options and other derivatives
1998	Amartya Sen	India	contribution to welfare economics
1999	Robert A. Mundell	Canada	analysis of optimum currency areas and of policy under different exchange-rate regimes
2000	James J. Heckman Daniel L. McFadden	US US	development of methods of statistical analysis of individual and household behavior
2001	George A. Akerlof A. Michael Spence Joseph E. Stiglitz	US US US	analyses of markets with asymmetric information
2002	Daniel Kahneman	US/Israel	integration of psychological research into economics, particularly concerning factors in decision making
	Vernon L. Smith	US	establishment of laboratory experiments for empirical economic analysis of alternative market mechanisms

Economics (continued)

YEAR	WINNER(S)	COUNTRY	ACHIEVEMENT
2003	Robert F. Engle	US	methods of analysis of economic time series with time-varying volatility
	Clive W.J. Granger	UK	methods of analysis of economic time series with common trends
2004	Finn E. Kydland	Norway	macroeconomic analysis of the time consistency of economic policy and the driving forces behind business cycles
	Edward C. Prescott	US	
2005	Robert J. Aumann	Israel/US	enhancement of the understanding of conflict and cooperation through game-theory analysis
	Thomas C. Schelling	US	
2006	Edmund S. Phelps	US	analysis of intertemporal tradeoffs in macroeconomic policy
2007	Leonid Hurwicz	US	research that laid the foundations of mechanism design theory
	Eric S. Maskin	US	
	Roger B. Myerson	US	

Special Achievement Awards

Templeton Prize

Formerly the Templeton Prize for Progress in Religion, the Templeton Prize for Progress Toward Research or Discoveries About Spiritual Realities was established in 1972 by American-born British businessman and philanthropist Sir John Templeton. It recognizes the diversity of and rewards advancement in the ideas and perceptions of divinity. Each year an international interfaith group of judges chooses a winner from any of the world's religions. Award amount: £820,000 (about US$1,665,000).

Templeton Prize Web site: <www.templetonprize.org>.

YEAR	NAME	FIELD
1973	Mother Teresa	founder, Missionaries of Charity
1974	Brother Roger	founder, Taizé Community
1975	Sir Sarvepalli Radhakrishnan	president of India, 1962–67
1976	Leon Joseph Cardinal Suenens	pioneer, Charismatic Renewal Movement
1977	Chiara Lubich	founder, Focolare Movement
1978	Thomas F. Torrance	educator, writer on religion and science
1979	Nikkyo Niwano	founder, Rissho Kosei-Kai
1980	Ralph Wendell Burhoe	founder and editor, *Zygon: Journal of Religion and Science*
1981	Dame Cicely Saunders	founder, Hospice and Palliative Care Movement
1982	Billy Graham	Christian evangelist
1983	Aleksandr Solzhenitsyn	writer, dissident
1984	Michael Bourdeaux	scholar, religious freedom activist
1985	Sir Alister Hardy	scientist, educator
1986	James McCord	chancellor, Center of Theological Inquiry; president, Princeton Theological Seminary
1987	Stanley L. Jaki	Benedictine monk, professor of astrophysics
1988	Inamullah Khan	interfaith peace activist; founder, Modern World Muslim Congress
1989	Lord George MacLeod	founder, Iona Community
	Carl Friedrich von Weizsäcker	physics and theology scholar
1990	Baba Amte	social activist, philanthropist
	L. Charles Birch	natural scientist
1991	Lord Immanuel Jakobovits	Chief Rabbi of Great Britain and the Commonwealth, 1967–91
1992	Kyung-Chik Han	founder, Young Nak Presbyterian Church
1993	Charles W. Colson	prison ministry founder
1994	Michael Novak	theologian, writer on theology and economics
1995	Paul Charles William Davies	mathematical physicist
1996	William R. Bright	founder, Campus Crusade for Christ
1997	Pandurang Shastri Athavale	founder, *swadhyaya* self-study
1998	Sir Sigmund Sternberg	philanthropist, businessman
1999	Ian Graeme Barbour	technology ethicist
2000	Freeman J. Dyson	physicist, social activist
2001	Arthur Peacocke	founder, Society of Ordained Scientists
2002	John C. Polkinghorne	Anglican priest, mathematical physicist
2003	Holmes Rolston III	Presbyterian minister, environmental ethicist
2004	George Ellis	cosmologist, scholar of the relationship between science and faith
2005	Charles Townes	physicist, proponent of exploring commonalities between science and religion

Templeton Prize (continued)

YEAR	NAME	FIELD
2006	John D. Barrow	cosmologist, scholar of multidisciplinary perspectives integrating astronomy, physics, mathematics, and philosophy
2007	Charles Taylor	philosopher, advocate for inclusion of spiritual considerations in public policy discussions and in the humanities and social sciences
2008	Michael Heller	cosmologist, philosopher of the "theology of science"

Congressional Gold Medal

Individuals, institutions, or events of distinguished achievement are honored by the Congressional Gold Medal. The medal was first awarded in 1776 and has since been given out 138 times. Until the mid-19th century, medals went primarily to military figures. Past recipients include George Washington, the Wright Brothers, Thomas Edison, Bob Hope, Frank Sinatra, Elie Wiesel, Nelson Mandela, Charles M. Schulz, and the Navajo code talkers of World War II. In 2008 Congress awarded the medal to Dr. Michael Ellis DeBakey, a pioneering heart surgeon and chancellor emeritus of Baylor College of Medicine.

Kennedy Center Honors

The Kennedy Center Honors are bestowed annually by the John F. Kennedy Center for the Performing Arts in Washington DC. First conferred in 1978, the honors salute five artists each year for lifetime achievement in the performing arts and are celebrated by a televised gala in December. **Web site:** <www.kennedy-center.org/programs/specialevents/honors/>.

YEAR	NAME	FIELD
1978	Marian Anderson	opera singer
	Fred Astaire	dancer, actor
	George Balanchine	choreographer
	Richard Rodgers	composer
	Arthur Rubenstein	pianist
1979	Aaron Copland	composer
	Ella Fitzgerald	singer
	Henry Fonda	actor
	Martha Graham	dancer, choreographer
	Tennessee Williams	playwright
1980	Leonard Bernstein	conductor
	James Cagney	actor
	Agnes de Mille	dancer, choreographer
	Lynn Fontanne	actress
	Leontyne Price	opera singer
1981	Count Basie	jazz pianist
	Cary Grant	actor
	Helen Hayes	actress
	Jerome Robbins	dancer, choreographer
	Rudolf Serkin	pianist
1982	George Abbott	theater producer, director, writer
	Lillian Gish	actress
	Benny Goodman	swing musician
	Gene Kelly	dancer, actor
	Eugene Ormandy	conductor
1983	Katherine Dunham	dancer, choreographer
	Elia Kazan	theater and film director
	Frank Sinatra	singer, actor
	James Stewart	actor
	Virgil Thomson	composer, music critic
1984	Lena Horne	singer, actress
	Danny Kaye	actor, comedian
	Gian Carlo Menotti	composer
	Arthur Miller	playwright
	Isaac Stern	violinist
1985	Merce Cunningham	dancer, choreographer
	Irene Dunne	actress
	Bob Hope	entertainer, actor
1985 (cont.)	Alan Jay Lerner	playwright, lyricist
	Frederick Loewe	composer
	Beverly Sills	opera singer
1986	Lucille Ball	actress
	Ray Charles	soul musician
	Hume Cronyn	actor
	Jessica Tandy	actress
	Yehudi Menuhin	violinist
	Antony Tudor	choreographer
1987	Perry Como	singer
	Bette Davis	actress
	Sammy Davis, Jr.	singer, dancer, entertainer
	Nathan Milstein	violinist
	Alwin Nikolais	choreographer
1988	Alvin Ailey	dancer, choreographer
	George Burns	actor, comedian
	Myrna Loy	actress
	Alexander Schneider	violinist, conductor
	Roger L. Stevens	arts administrator
1989	Harry Belafonte	folk singer, actor
	Claudette Colbert	actress
	Alexandra Danilova	ballet dancer
	Mary Martin	actress, singer
	William Schuman	composer
1990	Dizzy Gillespie	jazz musician
	Katharine Hepburn	actress
	Risë Stevens	opera singer
	Jule Styne	composer
	Billy Wilder	film director
1991	Roy Acuff	country musician
	Betty Comden	theater and film writer
	Adolph Green	theater and film writer
	Fayard Nicholas	dancer
	Harold Nicholas	dancer
	Gregory Peck	actor
	Robert Shaw	conductor
1992	Lionel Hampton	swing musician
	Paul Newman	actor
	Joanne Woodward	actress

Kennedy Center Honors (continued)

YEAR	NAME	FIELD
1992 (cont.)	Ginger Rogers	dancer, actress
	Mstislav Rostropovich	musician, conductor
	Paul Taylor	dancer, choreographer
1993	Johnny Carson	television entertainer
	Arthur Mitchell	dancer, choreographer
	George Solti	conductor
	Stephen Sondheim	composer, lyricist
	Marion Williams	gospel singer
1994	Kirk Douglas	actor
	Aretha Franklin	soul singer
	Morton Gould	composer
	Harold Prince	theater director, producer
	Pete Seeger	folk musician
1995	Jacques d'Amboise	dancer, choreographer
	Marilyn Horne	opera singer
	B.B. King	blues musician
	Sidney Poitier	actor
	Neil Simon	playwright
1996	Edward Albee	playwright
	Benny Carter	jazz musician
	Johnny Cash	country musician
	Jack Lemmon	actor
	Maria Tallchief	ballet dancer
1997	Lauren Bacall	actress
	Bob Dylan	singer, songwriter
	Charlton Heston	actor
	Jessye Norman	opera singer
	Edward Villella	dancer, choreographer
1998	Bill Cosby	actor, comedian
	Fred Ebb and John Kander	lyricist and composer
	Willie Nelson	country musician
	André Previn	pianist, composer, conductor
	Shirley Temple Black	actress, diplomat
1999	Victor Borge	pianist, comedian
	Sean Connery	actor
	Judith Jamison	dancer, choreographer
	Jason Robards	actor
	Stevie Wonder	musician
2000	Mikhail Baryshnikov	dancer
	Chuck Berry	musician
2000 (cont.)	Plácido Domingo	opera singer
	Clint Eastwood	actor, director
	Angela Lansbury	actress
2001	Julie Andrews	actress
	Van Cliburn	pianist
	Quincy Jones	music producer, composer
	Jack Nicholson	actor
	Luciano Pavarotti	opera singer
2002	James Earl Jones	actor
	James Levine	conductor
	Chita Rivera	musical theater performer
	Paul Simon	singer
	Elizabeth Taylor	actress
2003	James Brown	musician
	Carol Burnett	actress
	Loretta Lynn	musician
	Mike Nichols	director
	Itzhak Perlman	musician
2004	Warren Beatty	film actor, director
	Ossie Davis and Ruby Dee	actors, writers, producers
	Elton John	musician
	Joan Sutherland	opera singer
	John Williams	composer
2005	Tony Bennett	singer
	Suzanne Farrell	dancer, teacher
	Julie Harris	actress
	Robert Redford	film actor, director, producer
	Tina Turner	singer, actress
2006	Zubin Mehta	conductor
	Dolly Parton	singer, actress
	Andrew Lloyd Webber	composer
	Steven Spielberg	film director, producer
	William "Smokey" Robinson	singer
2007	Steve Martin	actor, writer
	Diana Ross	singer, actress
	Leon Fleisher	pianist, conductor
	Martin Scorsese	film director
	Brian Wilson	composer, singer

National Medal of Arts

The National Medal of Arts, awarded annually since 1985 by the National Endowment for the Arts (NEA) and the president of the United States, honors artists and art patrons for remarkable contributions to American arts. Both the NEA and the president choose candidates for the award, and the winners are selected by the president.

Web site: <www.nea.gov/honors/medals/medalists_year.html>.

YEAR	NAME	FIELD
1985	Elliott Carter, Jr.	composer
	Ralph Ellison	writer
	José Ferrer	actor
	Martha Graham	dancer, choreographer
	Louise Nevelson	sculptor
	Georgia O'Keeffe	painter
	Leontyne Price	opera singer
	Dorothy Buffum Chandler	patron
	Lincoln Kirstein	patron
	Paul Mellon	patron
	Alice Tully	patron
	Hallmark Cards, Inc.	patron
1986	Marian Anderson	opera singer
	Frank Capra	film director
	Aaron Copland	composer
	Willem de Kooning	painter
	Agnes de Mille	dancer, choreographer
	Eva Le Gallienne	actress, producer
	Alan Lomax	ethnomusicologist
	Lewis Mumford	architectural critic
	Eudora Welty	writer
	Dominique de Menil	patron
	Exxon Corporation	patron
	Seymour H. Knox	patron
1987	Romare Bearden	painter
	Ella Fitzgerald	singer

National Medal of Arts (continued)

YEAR	NAME	FIELD
1987 (cont.)	Howard Nemerov	writer, scholar
	Alwin Nikolais	choreographer
	Isamu Noguchi	sculptor
	William Schuman	composer
	Robert Penn Warren	writer
	J.W. Fisher	patron
	Armand Hammer	patron
	Sydney and Frances Lewis	patrons
1988	Saul Bellow	writer
	Helen Hayes	actress
	Gordon Parks	photographer, writer
	I.M. Pei	architect
	Jerome Robbins	dancer, choreographer
	Rudolf Serkin	pianist
	Virgil Thomson	composer, music critic
	Sydney J. Freedberg	art historian, curator
	Roger L. Stevens	arts administrator
	Brooke Astor	patron
	Francis Goelet	patron
	Obert C. Tanner	patron
1989	Leopold Adler	historic preservationist, civic leader
	Katherine Dunham	dancer, choreographer
	Alfred Eisenstaedt	photojournalist
	Martin Friedman	museum director
	Leigh Gerdine	civic leader, patron
	Dizzy Gillespie	jazz musician
	Walker K. Hancock	sculptor
	Vladimir Horowitz[1]	pianist
	Czeslaw Milosz	writer
	Robert Motherwell	painter
	John Updike	writer
	Dayton Hudson Corp.	patron
1990	George Abbott	theater producer, director, writer
	Hume Cronyn	actor, director
	Jessica Tandy	actress
	Merce Cunningham	dancer, choreographer
	Jasper Johns	painter, sculptor
	Jacob Lawrence	painter
	B.B. King	blues musician
	Beverly Sills	opera singer
	Ian McHarg	landscape architect
	Harris & Carroll Sterling Masterson	patrons
	David Lloyd Kreeger	patron
	Southeastern Bell Corporation	patron
1991	Maurice Abravanel	conductor, music director
	Roy Acuff	country musician
	Pietro Belluschi	architect
	J. Carter Brown	museum director
	Charles "Honi" Coles	tap dancer
	John O. Crosby	opera director, conductor
	Richard Diebenkorn	painter
	Isaac Stern	violinist
	Kitty Carlisle Hart	actress, singer
	R. Philip Hanes, Jr.	patron
	Pearl Primus	choreographer, anthropologist
	Texaco Inc.	patron
1992	Marilyn Horne	opera singer
	James Earl Jones	actor
	Allan Houser	sculptor
1992 (cont.)	Minnie Pearl	Grand Ole Opry performer
	Robert Saudek	television producer, museum director
	Earl Scruggs	banjo player
	Robert Shaw	conductor
	Billy Taylor	jazz pianist
	Robert Venturi and Denise Scott Brown	architects
	Robert Wise	film director
	AT&T	patron
	Lila Wallace–Reader's Digest Fund	patron
1993	Cabell "Cab" Calloway	jazz musician
	Ray Charles	soul musician
	Bess Lomax Hawes	folklorist, musician
	Stanley Kunitz	poet
	Robert Merrill	opera singer
	Arthur Miller	playwright
	Robert Rauschenberg	painter
	Lloyd Richards	theater director
	William Styron	writer
	Paul Taylor	dancer, choreographer
	Billy Wilder	film director, writer
	Walter and Leonore Annenberg	patrons
1994	Harry Belafonte	folksinger, actor
	Dave Brubeck	jazz musician
	Celia Cruz	salsa singer
	Dorothy DeLay	violin instructor
	Julie Harris	actress
	Erick Hawkins	dancer, choreographer
	Gene Kelly	dancer, actor
	Pete Seeger	folk musician
	Wayne Thiebaud	painter
	Richard Wilbur	poet
	Young Audiences	arts organization
	Catherine Filene Shouse	patron
1995	Licia Albanese	opera singer
	Gwendolyn Brooks	poet
	Ossie Davis and Ruby Dee	actors
	David Diamond	composer
	James Ingo Freed	architect
	Bob Hope	entertainer
	Roy Lichtenstein	painter
	Arthur Mitchell	dancer, choreographer
	William S. Monroe	bluegrass musician
	Urban Gateways	arts education organization
	B. Gerald and Iris Cantor	patrons
1996	Edward Albee	playwright
	Sarah Caldwell	opera conductor
	Harry Callahan	photographer
	Zelda Fichandler	theater founder, director
	Eduardo "Lalo" Guerrero	Chicano musician
	Lionel Hampton	swing musician
	Bella Lewitzky	dancer, choreographer
	Robert Redford	actor, film director
	Maurice Sendak	illustrator, writer
	Stephen Sondheim	composer, lyricist
	Boys Choir of Harlem	choir
	Vera List	patron

National Medal of Arts (continued)

YEAR	NAME	FIELD
1997	Louise Bourgeois	sculptor
	Betty Carter	jazz singer
	Daniel Urban Kiley	landscape architect
	Angela Lansbury	actress
	James Levine	opera conductor, pianist
	Tito Puente	jazz and mambo musician
	Jason Robards	actor
	Edward Villella	dancer, choreographer
	Doc Watson	folk and country musician
	MacDowell Colony	artists' colony
	Agnes Gund	patron
1998	Jacques d'Amboise	dancer, choreographer
	Antoine "Fats" Domino	rock-and-roll musician
	Ramblin' Jack Elliott	folk musician
	Frank O. Gehry	architect
	Agnes Martin	painter
	Gregory Peck	actor
	Roberta Peters	opera singer
	Philip Roth	writer
	Gwen Verdon	actress, dancer
	Steppenwolf Theatre Company	arts organization
	Sara Lee Corporation	patron
	Barbara Handman	patron
1999	Aretha Franklin	soul singer
	Michael Graves	architect, designer
	Odetta	folksinger
	Norman Lear	television producer, writer
	Rosetta LeNoire	actress, theater founder
	Harvey Lichtenstein	arts administrator
	Lydia Mendoza	Tejano musician
	George Segal	sculptor
	Maria Tallchief	ballet dancer
	The Juilliard School	performing arts school
	Irene Diamond	patron
2000	Maya Angelou	poet, writer
	Eddy Arnold	country musician
	Mikhail Baryshnikov	dancer, dance company director
	Benny Carter	jazz musician
	Chuck Close	painter
	Horton Foote	dramatist
	Claes Oldenburg	sculptor
	Itzhak Perlman	violinist
	Harold Prince	theater director, producer
	Barbra Streisand	singer, actress
	Lewis Manilow	patron
	NPR Cultural Programming Division	broadcaster
2001	Alvin Ailey Dance Foundation	modern dance company and school
	Rudolfo Anaya	writer
	Johnny Cash	country musician
	Kirk Douglas	actor
	Helen Frankenthaler	painter
	Judith Jamison	dancer, choreographer
	Yo-Yo Ma	cellist
	Mike Nichols	theater and film director
2002	Florence Knoll Bassett	designer, architect
	Trisha Brown	dancer, choreographer
	Philippe de Montebello	museum director
	Uta Hagen	actress, educator
	Lawrence Halprin	landscape architect
	Al Hirschfeld[1]	artist, caricaturist
	George Jones	singer, songwriter
	Ming Cho Lee	painter, stage designer
	William "Smokey" Robinson, Jr.	singer, songwriter
2003	*Austin City Limits*	television show
	Beverly Cleary	children's book author
	Rafe Esquith	arts educator
	Suzanne Farrell	dancer, artistic director, arts educator
	Buddy Guy	blues musician
	Ron Howard	actor, director, writer
	The Mormon Tabernacle Choir	choir
	Leonard Slatkin	conductor
	George Strait	singer, songwriter
	Tommy Tune	director, actor
2004	Andrew W. Mellon Foundation	patron
	Ray Bradbury	writer
	Carlisle Floyd	opera composer
	Frederick "Rick" Hart[1]	sculptor
	Anthony Hecht[1]	poet
	John Ruthven	painter
	Vincent Scully	architectural historian
	Twyla Tharp	dancer, choreographer
2005	Louis Auchincloss	writer
	James DePreist	conductor
	Paquito D'Rivera	musician
	Robert Duvall	actor
	Leonard Garment	arts advocate
	Ollie Johnston	animator, artist
	Wynton Marsalis	musician, educator
	Pennsylvania Academy of the Fine Arts	arts academy
	Tina Ramirez	dancer, choreographer
	Dolly Parton	singer, songwriter
2006	William Bolcom	composer
	Cyd Charisse	dancer
	Roy R. DeCarava	photographer
	Wilhelmina C. Holladay	patron
	Interlochen Center for the Arts	music school
	Erich Kunzel	conductor
	Preservation Hall Jazz Band	jazz ensemble
	Gregory Rabassa	translator
	Viktor Schreckengost	industrial designer
	Dr. Ralph Stanley	bluegrass musician
2007	Morten Lauridsen	composer
	N. Scott Momaday	author, poet
	Roy R. Neuberger	patron
	R. Craig Noel	theater director
	Les Paul	guitarist, inventor
	Henry Steinway	patron
	George Tooker	painter
	Lionel Hampton International Jazz Festival	music competition, festival
	Andrew Wyeth	painter

[1]*Awarded posthumously.*

American Academy of Arts and Letters

The American Academy of Arts and Letters is a 335-member organization founded in 1898. Members elected in 2008: ▸ **Art**: John Baldessari, Glenn Murcutt, Ursula von Rydingsvard; ▸ **Literature**: Kwame Anthony Appiah, Robert A. Caro, Stephen Greenblatt, Paul Muldoon, Salman Rushdie, Calvin Trillin, Joy Williams; ▸ **Music**: Louis Andriessen, Yo-Yo Ma. The academy confers 27 awards for excellence. The Academy Awards in each field are the most prestigious. Winners receive US$7,500; music winners receive an additional US$7,500 to be used for the recording of a musical piece. Recipients for 2008: ▸ **Architecture**: James Carpenter, Neil Denari, Kenneth Frampton, Jim Jennings; ▸ **Art**: Llyn Foulkes, Eric Holzman, Judith Linhares, Gordon Moore, Susan Smith; ▸ **Literature**: Dan Chiasson, Brian Doyle, Rikki Ducornet, Will Eno, Edith Grossman, Fanny Howe, Richard Nelson, Mona Simpson; ▸ **Music**: Virko Baley, Donal Fox, Pablo Ortiz, Anna Weesner.

Web site: <www.artsandletters.org>.

National Humanities Medal

The National Humanities Medal (originally known as the Charles Frankel Prize, 1988–96) is awarded by the National Endowment for the Humanities for notable contributions to Americans' understanding of and involvement with the humanities. The recipients for 2007 were Stephen Balch, scholar and advocate; Russell Freedman, author; Victor Davis Hanson, military historian; Roger Hertog, philanthropist; Cynthia Ozick, author; Richard Pipes, historian; Pauline L. Schultz, curator; Henry Snyder, scholar and innovator; Ruth Wisse, scholar and author; and the Monuments Men Foundation for the Preservation of Art.

Web site: <www.neh.gov/whoweare/awards.html>.

Spingarn Medal

The National Association for the Advancement of Colored People (NAACP) presents the medal for distinguished achievement among African Americans. The medal is named for early NAACP activist Joel E. Spingarn.

YEAR	NAME	FIELD
1915	Ernest Everett Just	zoologist, marine biologist
1916	Charles Young	army officer
1917	Harry Thacker Burleigh	singer, composer
1918	William Stanley Braithwaite	poet, literary critic
1919	Archibald Henry Grimké	lawyer, diplomat, social activist
1920	W.E.B. Du Bois (William Edward Burghardt Du Bois)	sociologist, social activist
1921	Charles S. Gilpin	actor
1922	Mary Burnett Talbert	civil rights activist
1923	George Washington Carver	agricultural chemist
1924	Roland Hayes	singer, composer
1925	James Weldon Johnson	diplomat, anthologist
1926	Carter G. Woodson	historian
1927	Anthony Overton	businessman
1928	Charles W. Chesnutt	writer
1929	Mordecai W. Johnson	minister, university president
1930	Henry Alexander Hunt	educator, government official
1931	Richard B. Harrison	actor
1932	Robert Russa Moton	educator, civil rights leader
1933	Max Yergan	civil rights leader
1934	William T.B. Williams	educator
1935	Mary McLeod Bethune	educator, social activist
1936	John Hope	educator
1937	Walter White	civil rights leader
1938	*no medal awarded*	
1939	Marian Anderson	opera singer
1940	Louis T. Wright	surgeon, civil rights leader
1941	Richard Wright	writer
1942	A. Philip Randolph	labor and civil rights leader
1943	William H. Hastie	lawyer, judge
1944	Charles Richard Drew	surgeon, research scientist
1945	Paul Robeson	actor, singer, social activist
1946	Thurgood Marshall	lawyer, US Supreme Court justice
1947	Percy L. Julian	chemist
1948	Channing H. Tobias	civil rights leader
1949	Ralph Bunche	diplomat, scholar
1950	Charles Hamilton Houston	lawyer
1951	Mabel Keaton Staupers	nurse, social activist
1952	Harry T. Moore	civil rights activist, educator
1953	Paul R. Williams	architect
1954	Theodore K. Lawless	dermatologist, philanthropist
1955	Carl Murphy	journalist, civil rights activist
1956	Jackie Robinson (Jack Roosevelt Robinson)	baseball player
1957	Martin Luther King, Jr.	civil rights leader
1958	Daisy Bates and the Little Rock Nine	school integration activists
1959	Duke Ellington (Edward Kennedy Ellington)	jazz musician
1960	Langston Hughes	writer
1961	Kenneth Bancroft Clark	educator
1962	Robert C. Weaver	economist, government official
1963	Medgar Evers	civil rights activist
1964	Roy Wilkins	civil rights leader
1965	Leontyne Price	opera singer
1966	John H. Johnson	publisher
1967	Edward W. Brooke III	lawyer, US senator
1968	Sammy Davis, Jr.	singer, dancer, entertainer
1969	Clarence M. Mitchell, Jr.	civil rights lobbyist
1970	Jacob Lawrence	painter

Spingarn Medal (continued)

YEAR	NAME	FIELD
1971	Leon H. Sullivan	minister, civil rights activist
1972	Gordon Parks	photographer, writer
1973	Wilson C. Riles	educator
1974	Damon Keith	lawyer, judge
1975	Hank Aaron	baseball player
1976	Alvin Ailey	dancer, choreographer
1977	Alex Haley	writer
1978	Andrew Young	civil rights leader
1979	Rosa Parks	civil rights activist
1980	Rayford W. Logan	educator, writer
1981	Coleman A. Young	labor activist, politician
1982	Benjamin E. Mays	educator, minister
1983	Lena Horne	singer, actress
1984	Thomas Bradley	politician
1985	Bill Cosby	actor, comedian
1986	Benjamin L. Hooks	civil rights leader, government official
1987	Percy Ellis Sutton	civil rights activist, politician
1988	Frederick Douglass Patterson	educator
1989	Jesse Jackson	minister, politician, civil rights leader
1990	L. Douglas Wilder	politician
1991	Colin Powell	army general, government official
1992	Barbara Jordan	lawyer, politician
1993	Dorothy I. Height	social activist
1994	Maya Angelou	poet
1995	John Hope Franklin	historian, educator
1996	A. Leon Higginbotham	lawyer, judge, scholar
1997	Carl T. Rowan	journalist, commentator
1998	Myrlie Evers-Williams	civil rights activist
1999	Earl G. Graves	publisher
2000	Oprah Winfrey	television host, media personality
2001	Vernon E. Jordan, Jr.	lawyer, civil rights activist
2002	John Lewis	politician, civil rights activist
2003	Constance Baker Motley	judge, lawyer, civil rights activist
2004	Robert L. Carter	judge, lawyer, civil rights activist
2005	Oliver W. Hill	lawyer, civil rights activist
2006	Benjamin S. Carson	physician
2007	John Conyers, Jr.	politician

Science Honors

Fields Medal

The Fields Medal, officially known as the International Medal for Outstanding Discoveries in Mathematics, is granted every four years to between two and four mathematicians for outstanding or groundbreaking research. It is traditionally given to mathematicians under the age of 40. Prize: Can$15,000 (about US$15,000).

YEAR	NAME	BIRTHPLACE	PRIMARY RESEARCH
1936	Lars Ahlfors	Helsinki, Finland	Riemann surfaces
	Jesse Douglas	New York NY	Plateau problem
1950	Laurent Schwartz	Paris, France	functional analysis
	Atle Selberg	Langesund, Norway	number theory
1954	Kunihiko Kodaira	Tokyo, Japan	algebraic geometry
	Jean-Pierre Serre	Bages, France	algebraic topology
1958	Klaus Roth	Breslau, Germany	number theory
	René Thom	Montbéliard, France	topology
1962	Lars Hörmander	Mjällby, Sweden	partial differential equations
	John Milnor	Orange NJ	differential topology
1966	Michael Atiyah	London, England	topology
	Paul Cohen	Long Branch NJ	set theory
	Alexandre Grothendieck	Berlin, Germany	algebraic geometry
	Stephen Smale	Flint MI	topology
1970	Alan Baker	London, England	number theory
	Heisuke Hironaka	Yamaguchi prefecture, Japan	algebraic geometry
	Sergey Novikov	Gorky, USSR (now in Russia)	topology
	John Thompson	Ottawa KS	group theory
1974	Enrico Bombieri	Milan, Italy	number theory
	David Mumford	Worth, Sussex, England	algebraic geometry
1978	Pierre Deligne	Brussels, Belgium	algebraic geometry
	Charles Fefferman	Washington DC	classical analysis
	Gregory Margulis	Moscow, USSR (now in Russia)	Lie groups
	Daniel Quillen	Orange NJ	algebraic *K*-theory
1983	Alain Connes	Darguignan, France	operator theory
	William Thurston	Washington DC	topology
	Shing-Tung Yau	Swatow, China	differential geometry

Fields Medal (continued)

YEAR	NAME	BIRTHPLACE	PRIMARY RESEARCH
1986	Simon Donaldson	Cambridge, England	topology
	Gerd Faltings	Gelsenkirchen, West Germany	Mordell conjecture
	Michael Freedman	Los Angeles CA	Poincaré conjecture
1990	Vladimir Drinfeld	Kharkov, USSR (now in Ukraine)	algebraic geometry
	Vaughan Jones	Gisborne, New Zealand	knot theory
	Shigefumi Mori	Nagoya, Japan	algebraic geometry
	Edward Witten	Baltimore MD	superstring theory
1994	Jean Bourgain	Ostend, Belgium	analysis
	Pierre-Louis Lions	Grasse, France	partial differential equations
	Jean-Christophe Yoccoz	France	dynamical systems
	Yefim Zelmanov	Khabarovsk, USSR (now in Russia)	group theory
1998	Richard Borcherds	Cape Town, South Africa	mathematical physics
	William Gowers	Marlborough, Wiltshire, England	functional analysis
	Maksim Kontsevich	Khimki, USSR (now in Russia)	mathematical physics
	Curt McMullen	Berkeley CA	chaos theory
2002	Laurent Lafforgue	Antony, France	number theory and analysis
	Vladimir Voevodsky	Moscow, USSR (now in Russia)	algebraic geometry
2006	Andrei Okounkov	Moscow, USSR (now in Russia)	algebraic geometry
	Grigory Perelman (declined)	Leningrad, USSR (now in Russia)	Ricci flow
	Terence Tao	Adelaide, SA, Australia	prime numbers, nonlinear equations
	Wendelin Werner	Cologne, West Germany	mathematics of critical phenomena

Japan Prize

The Science and Technology Foundation of Japan awards the Japan Prize annually to living individuals whose achievements in science and technology have advanced knowledge and promoted human peace and prosperity. A cash award of ¥50 million (about US$460,000), a certificate of merit, and a commemorative medal are given for each prize category. **Web site:** <www.japanprize.jp>.

YEAR	LAUREATE	COUNTRY	AREA OF ACHIEVEMENT
1985	John R. Pierce	US	electronics and communications technologies
	Ephraim Katchalski-Katzir	Israel	basic theory of immobilized enzymes
1986	David Turnbull	US	new materials technology such as amorphous solids
	Willem J. Kolff	US	artificial organs
1987	Henry M. Beachell	US	high-yield rice
	Gurdev S. Khush	India	hardy rice
	Theodore H. Maiman	US	lasers
1988	Georges Vendryes	France	fast-breeder reactor technology
	Donald A. Henderson	US	eradication of smallpox
	Isao Arita	Japan	eradication of smallpox
	Frank Fenner	Australia	eradication of smallpox
	Luc Montagnier	France	discovery of HIV
	Robert C. Gallo	US	isolation of HIV and development of AZT
1989	Frank Sherwood Rowland	US	stratospheric ozone depletion by chlorofluorocarbons
	Elias James Corey	US	syntheses of prostaglandins and related compounds
1990	Marvin Minsky	US	artificial intelligence
	William Jason Morgan	US	plate tectonics
	Dan Peter Mckenzie	UK	plate tectonics
	Xavier Le Pichon	France	plate tectonics
1991	Jacques-Louis Lions	France	analysis and control of distributed systems
	John Julian Wild	US	ultrasound imaging
1992	Gerhard Ertl	Germany	chemistry and physics of solid surfaces
	Ernest John Christopher Polge	UK	cryopreservation of semen and embryos in animals
1993	Frank Press	US	seismology and disaster science
	Kary B. Mullis	US	polymerase chain reaction
1994	William Hayward Pickering	US	space travel and unmanned space exploration
	Arvid Carlsson	Sweden	dopamine's role in mental and motor functions
1995	Nick Holonyak, Jr.	US	light-emitting diodes and lasers
	Edward F. Knipling	US	pest management
1996	Charles K. Kao	Hong Kong	wide-band, low-loss optical fiber communications
	Masao Ito	Japan	cerebellum function
1997	Takashi Sugimura	Japan	cancer
	Bruce N. Ames	US	cancer
	Joseph F. Engelberger	US	robotics
	Hiroyuki Yoshikawa	Japan	robotics

Japan Prize (continued)

YEAR	LAUREATE	COUNTRY	AREA OF ACHIEVEMENT
1998	Leo Esaki	Japan	man-made superlattice crystals
	Jozef S. Schell	Belgium	transgenic plants
	Marc C.E. Van Montagu	Belgium	
1999	W. Wesley Peterson	US	algebraic coding theory
	Jack L. Strominger	US	human histocompatibility
	Don C. Wiley	US	antigens and their peptides
2000	Ian L. McHarg	US	ecological city planning and land-use evaluation
	Kimishige Ishizaka	Japan	immunoglobulin E and IgE-mediated allergic reactions
2001	John B. Goodenough	US	environmentally benign electrode materials for rechargeable lithium batteries
	Timothy R. Parsons	Canada	fishery resources and marine environment conservation
2002	Timothy John Berners-Lee	UK	World Wide Web
	Anne McLaren	UK	study and manipulation of early-
	Andrzej K. Tarkowski	Poland	stage mammalian embryos
2003	Benoit B. Mandelbrot	France	fractals
	James A. Yorke	US	concept of chaos in complex systems
	Seiji Ogawa	Japan	magnetic resonance imaging
2004	Kenichi Honda	Japan	photochemical
	Akira Fujishima	Japan	catalysis
	Keith Sainsbury	New Zealand	sustainable usage of seabed-shelf ecosystems
	John H. Lawton	UK	conservation of biodiversity
2005	Makoto Nagao	Japan	natural language and intelligent image processing
	Masatoshi Takeichi	Japan	contributions to clarifying the molecular
	Erkki Ruoslahti	US	mechanisms of cell adhesion
2006	Sir John Houghton	UK	study of atmospheric structure using satellite technology and transglobal assessments of climate change
2007	Albert Fert	France	discovery of Giant Magneto-
	Peter Grünberg	Germany	Resistance (GMR)
	Peter Shaw Ashton	UK	conservation of tropical forests
2008	Vinton Gray Cerf	US	invention of the network concept that
	Robert Elliot Kahn	US	developed into the Internet
	Victor A. McKusick	US	establishment of many of the foundations of medical genetics

National Medal of Science

The National Medal of Science was established by Congress in 1959. Awarded annually since 1962 by the National Science Foundation, it recognizes notable achievements in mathematics, engineering, and the physical, natural, and social sciences. A presidentially appointed committee selects the winners from a pool of nominees.

National Science Foundation Web site: <www.nsf.gov/od/nms/medal.jsp>.

YEAR	NAME	FIELD
1962	Theodore von Karman	aerospace engineering
1963	Luis W. Alvarez	physics
	Vannevar Bush	electrical engineering
	John Robinson Pierce	communications engineering
	Cornelius Barnardus van Niel	biology
	Norbert Wiener	mathematics
1964	Roger Adams	chemistry
	Othmar Herman Ammann	civil engineering
	Theodosius Dobzhansky	genetics
	Charles Stark Draper	aerospace engineering
	Solomon Lefschetz	mathematics
	Neal Elgar Miller	psychology
	H. Marston Morse	mathematics
	Marshall Warren Nirenberg	biochemistry
	Julian Seymour Schwinger	physics
	Harold C. Urey	chemistry
	Robert Burns Woodward	chemistry
1965	John Bardeen	physics
	Peter J.W. Debye	physical chemistry
	Hugh L. Dryden	physics
	Clarence L. Johnson	aerospace engineering
	Leon M. Lederman	physics
	Warren K. Lewis	chemical engineering
	Francis Peyton Rous	pathology
	William W. Rubey	geology
	George Gaylord Simpson	paleontology
	Donald D. Van Slyke	chemistry
	Oscar Zariski	mathematics
1966	Jacob A.B. Bjerknes	meteorology
	Subrahmanyan Chandrasekhar	astrophysics
	Henry Eyring	chemistry
	Edward F. Knipling	entomology
	Fritz Albert Lipmann	biochemistry
	John Willard Milnor	mathematics
	William C. Rose	biochemistry
	Claude E. Shannon	mathematics, electrical engineering
	John H. Van Vleck	physics

National Medal of Science (continued)

YEAR	NAME	FIELD
1966 (cont.)	Sewall Wright	genetics
	Vladimir Kosma Zworykin	electrical engineering
1967	Jesse W. Beams	physics
	Francis Birch	geophysics
	Gregory Breit	physics
	Paul Joseph Cohen	mathematics
	Kenneth S. Cole	biophysics
	Louis P. Hammett	chemistry
	Harry F. Harlow	psychology
	Michael Heidelberger	immunology
	George B. Kistiakowsky	chemistry
	Edwin Herbert Land	physics
	Igor I. Sikorsky	aircraft design
	Alfred H. Sturtevant	genetics
1968	Horace A. Barker	biochemistry
	Paul D. Bartlett	chemistry
	Bernard B. Brodie	pharmacology
	Detlev W. Bronk	biophysics
	J. Presper Eckert, Jr.	engineering, computer science
	Herbert Friedman	astrophysics
	Jay L. Lush	livestock genetics
	Nathan M. Newmark	civil engineering
	Jerzy Neyman	statistics
	Lars Onsager	chemistry
	B.F. Skinner	psychology
	Eugene Paul Wigner	mathematical physics
1969	Herbert C. Brown	chemistry
	William Feller	mathematics
	Robert J. Huebner	virology
	Jack Kilby	electrical engineering
	Ernst Mayr	biology
	Wolfgang K.H. Panofsky	physics
1970	Richard Dagobert Brauer	mathematics
	Robert H. Dicke	physics
	Barbara McClintock	genetics
	George E. Mueller	physics
	Albert Bruce Sabin	medicine, vaccine development
	Allan R. Sandage	astronomy
	John C. Slater	physics
	John Archibald Wheeler	physics
	Saul Winstein	chemistry
1971	*no awards given*	
1972	*no awards given*	
1973	Daniel I. Arnon	biochemistry
	Carl Djerassi	chemistry
	Harold E. Edgerton	electrical engineering, photography
	Maurice Ewing	geophysics
	Arie Jan Haagen-Smit	biochemistry
	Vladimir Haensel	chemical engineering
	Frederick Seitz	physics
	Earl W. Sutherland, Jr.	biochemistry
	John Wilder Tukey	statistics
	Richard T. Whitcomb	aerospace engineering
	Robert Rathbun Wilson	particle physics
1974	Nicolaas Bloembergen	physics
	Britton Chance	biophysics
	Erwin Chargaff	biochemistry
	Paul J. Flory	physical chemistry
	William A. Fowler	nuclear astrophysics
1974 (cont.)	Kurt Gödel	mathematics
	Rudolf Kompfner	physics
	James Van Gundia Neel	genetics
	Linus Pauling	chemistry
	Ralph Brazelton Peck	geotechnical engineering
	Kenneth Sanborn Pitzer	physical chemistry
	James Augustine Shannon	physiology
	Abel Wolman	sanitary engineering
1975	John W. Backus	computer science
	Manson Benedict	nuclear engineering
	Hans Albrecht Bethe	theoretical physics
	Shiing-shen Chern	mathematics
	George B. Dantzig	mathematics
	Hallowell Davis	physiology
	Paul Gyorgy	medicine, vitamin research
	Sterling Brown Hendricks	chemistry
	Joseph O. Hirschfelder	chemistry
	William Hayward Pickering	physics
	Lewis H. Sarett	chemistry
	Frederick Emmons Terman	electrical engineering
	Orville Alvin Vogel	research agronomy
	Wernher von Braun	aerospace engineering
	E. Bright Wilson, Jr.	chemistry
	Chien-Shiung Wu	physics
1976	Morris Cohen	materials science
	Kurt Otto Friedrichs	mathematics
	Peter C. Goldmark	communications engineering
	Samuel Abraham Goudsmit	physics
	Roger Charles Louis Guillemin	physiology
	Herbert S. Gutowsky	chemistry
	Erwin W. Mueller	physics
	Keith Roberts Porter	cell biology
	Efraim Racker	biochemistry
	Frederick D. Rossini	chemistry
	Verner E. Suomi	meteorology
	Henry Taube	chemistry
	George Eugene Uhlenbeck	physics
	Hassler Whitney	mathematics
	Edward O. Wilson	biology
1977	*no awards given*	
1978	*no awards given*	
1979	Robert H. Burris	biochemistry
	Elizabeth C. Crosby	neuroanatomy
	Joseph L. Doob	mathematics
	Richard P. Feynman	theoretical physics
	Donald E. Knuth	computer science
	Arthur Kornberg	biochemistry
	Emmett N. Leith	electrical engineering
	Herman F. Mark	chemistry
	Raymond D. Mindlin	mechanical engineering
	Robert N. Noyce	computer science
	Severo Ochoa	biochemistry
	Earl R. Parker	materials science
	Edward M. Purcell	physics

National Medal of Science (continued)

YEAR	NAME	FIELD
1979 (cont.)	Simon Ramo	electrical engineering
	John H. Sinfelt	chemical engineering
	Lyman Spitzer, Jr.	astrophysics
	Earl Reece Stadtman	biochemistry
	George Ledyard Stebbins	botany, genetics
	Victor F. Weisskopf	physics
	Paul Alfred Weiss	biology
1980	*no awards given*	
1981	Philip Handler	biochemistry
1982	Philip W. Anderson	physics
	Seymour Benzer	molecular biology
	Glenn W. Burton	genetics
	Mildred Cohn	biochemistry
	F. Albert Cotton	chemistry
	Edward H. Heinemann	aerospace engineering
	Donald L. Katz	chemical engineering
	Yoichiro Nambu	theoretical physics
	Marshall H. Stone	mathematics
	Gilbert Stork	organic chemistry
	Edward Teller	nuclear physics
	Charles Hard Townes	physics
1983	Howard L. Bachrach	biochemistry
	Paul Berg	biochemistry
	E. Margaret Burbidge	astronomy
	Maurice Goldhaber	physics
	Herman H. Goldstine	computer science
	William R. Hewlett	electrical engineering
	Roald Hoffmann	chemistry
	Helmut E. Landsberg	climatology
	George M. Low	aerospace engineering
	Walter H. Munk	oceanography
	George C. Pimentel	chemistry
	Frederick Reines	physics
	Wendell L. Roelofs	chemistry, entomology
	Bruno B. Rossi	astrophysics
	Berta V. Scharrer	neuroscience
	John Robert Schrieffer	physics
	Isadore M. Singer	mathematics
	John G. Trump	electrical engineering
	Richard N. Zare	chemistry
1984	*no awards given*	
1985	*no awards given*	
1986	Solomon J. Buchsbaum	physics
	Stanley Cohen	biochemistry
	Horace R. Crane	physics
	Herman Feshbach	physics
	Harry Gray	chemistry
	Donald A. Henderson	medicine, public health
	Robert Hofstadter	physics
	Peter D. Lax	mathematics
	Yuan Tseh Lee	chemistry
	Hans Wolfgang Liepmann	aerospace engineering
	T.Y. Lin	civil engineering
	Carl S. Marvel	chemistry
	Vernon B. Mountcastle	neurophysiology
	Bernard M. Oliver	electrical engineering
	George Emil Palade	cell biology
	Herbert A. Simon	social science
	Joan A. Steitz	molecular biology
	Frank H. Westheimer	chemistry
	Chen Ning Yang	theoretical physics
	Antoni Zygmund	mathematics
1987	Philip Hauge Abelson	physical chemistry
	Anne Anastasi	psychology
	Robert Byron Bird	chemical engineering
	Raoul Bott	mathematics
	Michael E. DeBakey	heart surgery
	Theodor O. Diener	plant pathology
	Harry Eagle	cell biology
	Walter M. Elsasser	physics
	Michael H. Freedman	mathematics
	William S. Johnson	chemistry
	Har Gobind Khorana	biochemistry
	Paul C. Lauterbur	chemistry
	Rita Levi-Montalcini	neurology
	George E. Pake	research, physics
	H. Bolton Seed	civil engineering
	George J. Stigler	economics
	Walter H. Stockmayer	chemistry
	Max Tishler	chemistry
	James Alfred Van Allen	physics
	Ernst Weber	electrical engineering
1988	William O. Baker	chemistry
	Konrad E. Bloch	biochemistry
	David Allan Bromley	physics
	Michael S. Brown	molecular genetics
	Paul C.W. Chu	physics
	Stanley N. Cohen	genetics
	Elias James Corey	chemistry
	Daniel C. Drucker	engineering education
	Milton Friedman	economics
	Joseph L. Goldstein	molecular genetics
	Ralph E. Gomory	mathematics, research
	Willis M. Hawkins	aerospace engineering
	Maurice R. Hilleman	vaccine research
	George W. Housner	earthquake engineering
	Eric Kandel	neurobiology
	Joseph B. Keller	mathematics
	Walter Kohn	physics
	Norman Foster Ramsey	physics
	Jack Steinberger	physics
	Rosalyn S. Yalow	medical physics
1989	Arnold O. Beckman	chemistry
	Richard B. Bernstein	chemistry
	Melvin Calvin	biochemistry
	Harry G. Drickamer	chemistry, physics
	Katherine Esau	botany
	Herbert E. Grier	aerospace engineering
	Viktor Hamburger	biology
	Samuel Karlin	mathematics
	Philip Leder	genetics
	Joshua Lederberg	genetics
	Saunders Mac Lane	mathematics
	Rudolph A. Marcus	chemistry
	Harden M. McConnell	chemistry
	Eugene N. Parker	theoretical astrophysics
	Robert P. Sharp	geology
	Donald C. Spencer	mathematics
	Roger Wolcott Sperry	neurobiology
	Henry M. Stommel	oceanography
	Harland G. Wood	biochemistry

National Medal of Science (continued)

YEAR	NAME	FIELD
1990	Baruj Benacerraf	pathology, immunology
	Elkan R. Blout	chemistry
	Herbert W. Boyer	biochemistry, genetics
	George F. Carrier	mathematics
	Allan MacLeod Cormack	physics
	Mildred S. Dresselhaus	physics
	Karl August Folkers	chemistry
	Nick Holonyak, Jr.	electrical engineering
	Leonid Hurwicz	economics
	Stephen Cole Kleene	mathematics
	Daniel E. Koshland, Jr.	biochemistry
	Edward B. Lewis	developmental genetics
	John McCarthy	computer science
	Edwin Mattison McMillan	nuclear physics
	David G. Nathan	pediatrics
	Robert V. Pound	physics
	Roger R.D. Revelle	oceanography
	John D. Roberts	chemistry
	Patrick Suppes	philosophy, statistics education
	E. Donnall Thomas	medicine
1991	Mary Ellen Avery	pediatrics
	Ronald Breslow	chemistry
	Alberto P. Calderon	mathematics
	Gertrude B. Elion	pharmacology
	George H. Heilmeier	electrical engineering
	Dudley R. Herschbach	chemistry
	G. Evelyn Hutchinson	zoology
	Elvin A. Kabat	immunology
	Robert W. Kates	geography
	Luna B. Leopold	hydrology, geology
	Salvador Luria	biology
	Paul A. Marks	hematology, cancer research
	George A. Miller	psychology
	Arthur L. Schawlow	physics
	Glenn T. Seaborg	nuclear chemistry
	Folke K. Skoog	botany
	H. Guyford Stever	aerospace engineering
	Edward C. Stone	physics
	Steven Weinberg	nuclear physics
	Paul C. Zamecnik	molecular biology
1992	Eleanor J. Gibson	psychology
	Allen Newell	computer science
	Calvin F. Quate	electrical engineering
	Eugene M. Shoemaker	planetary geology
	Howard E. Simmons, Jr.	chemistry
	Maxine F. Singer	biochemistry, administration
	Howard Martin Temin	virology
	John Roy Whinnery	electrical engineering
1993	Alfred Y. Cho	electrical engineering
	Donald J. Cram	chemistry
	Val Logsdon Fitch	particle physics
	Norman Hackerman	chemistry
	Martin D. Kruskal	mathematics
	Daniel Nathans	microbiology
	Vera C. Rubin	astronomy
	Salome G. Waelsch	molecular genetics
1994	Ray W. Clough	civil engineering
	John Cocke	computer science
	Thomas Eisner	chemical ecology
1994 (cont.)	George S. Hammond	chemistry
	Robert K. Merton	sociology
	Elizabeth F. Neufeld	biochemistry
	Albert W. Overhauser	physics
	Frank Press	geophysics, administration
1995	Thomas Robert Cech	biochemistry
	Hans Georg Dehmelt	physics
	Peter M. Goldreich	astrophysics
	Hermann A. Haus	electrical engineering
	Isabella L. Karle	chemistry
	Louis Nirenberg	mathematics
	Alexander Rich	molecular biology
	Roger N. Shepard	psychology
1996	Wallace S. Broecker	geochemistry
	Norman Davidson	chemistry, molecular biology
	James L. Flanagan	electrical engineering
	Richard M. Karp	computer science
	C. Kumar N. Patel	electrical engineering
	Ruth Patrick	limnology
	Paul Samuelson	economics
	Stephen Smale	mathematics
1997	William K. Estes	psychology
	Darleane C. Hoffman	chemistry
	Harold S. Johnston	chemistry
	Marshall N. Rosenbluth	theoretical plasma physics
	Martin Schwarzschild	astrophysics
	James Dewey Watson	genetics, biophysics
	Robert A. Weinberg	biology, cancer research
	George W. Wetherill	planetary science
	Shing-Tung Yau	mathematics
1998	Bruce N. Ames	biochemistry, cancer research
	Don L. Anderson	geophysics
	John N. Bahcall	astrophysics
	John W. Cahn	materials science
	Cathleen Synge Morawetz	mathematics
	Janet D. Rowley	medicine, cancer research
	Eli Ruckenstein	chemical engineering
	George M. Whitesides	chemistry
	William Julius Wilson	sociology
1999	David Baltimore	virology, administration
	Felix E. Browder	mathematics
	Ronald R. Coifman	mathematics
	James Watson Cronin	particle physics
	Jared Diamond	physiology
	Leo P. Kadanoff	theoretical physics
	Lynn Margulis	microbiology
	Stuart A. Rice	chemistry
	John Ross	chemistry
	Susan Solomon	atmospheric science
	Robert M. Solow	economics
	Kenneth N. Stevens	electrical engineering, speech
2000	Nancy C. Andreasen	psychiatry
	John D. Baldeschwieler	chemistry
	Gary S. Becker	economics
	Yuan-Cheng B. Fung	bioengineering
	Ralph F. Hirschmann	chemistry
	Willis Eugene Lamb, Jr.	physics
	Jeremiah P. Ostriker	astrophysics

National Medal of Science (continued)

YEAR	NAME	FIELD
2000 (cont.)	Peter H. Raven	botany
	John Griggs Thompson	mathematics
	Karen K. Uhlenbeck	mathematics
	Gilbert F. White	geography
	Carl R. Woese	microbiology
2001	Andreas Acrivos	chemical engineering
	Francisco J. Ayala	molecular biology
	George F. Bass	nautical archaeology
	Mario R. Capecchi	genetics
	Marvin L. Cohen	materials science
	Ernest R. Davidson	chemistry
	Raymond Davis, Jr.	chemistry, astrophysics
	Ann M. Graybiel	neuroscience
	Charles D. Keeling	oceanography
	Gene E. Likens	ecology
	Victor A. McKusick	medical genetics
	Calyampudi R. Rao	mathematics, statistics
	Gabor A. Somorjai	chemistry
	Elias M. Stein	mathematics
	Harold Varmus	virology, administration
2002	Leo L. Beranek	engineering
	John I. Brauman	chemistry
	James E. Darnell	cell biology
	Richard L. Garwin	physics
	James G. Glimm	mathematics, statistics
	W. Jason Morgan	geophysics
	Evelyn M. Witkin	genetics
	Edward Witten	mathematical physics
2003	J. Michael Bishop	microbiology
	G. Brent Dalrymple	geology
	Carl R. de Boor	mathematics
	Riccardo Giacconi	astrophysics
	R. Duncan Luce	cognitive science
	John M. Prausnitz	chemical engineering
2003 (cont.)	Solomon H. Snyder	neuroscience
	Charles Yanofsky	molecular biology
2004	Kenneth J. Arrow	economics
	Norman E. Borlaug	agriculture
	Robert N. Clayton	geochemistry
	Edwin N. Lightfoot	engineering
	Stephen J. Lippard	chemistry
	Phillip A. Sharp	molecular biology, biochemistry
	Thomas E. Starzl	medicine
	Dennis P. Sullivan	mathematics
2005	Jan D. Achenbach	mechanical engineering
	Ralph A. Alpher	astronomy
	Gordon H. Bower	psychology
	Bradley Efron	statistics
	Anthony S. Fauci	immunology
	Tobin J. Marks	chemistry
	Lonnie G. Thompson	glaciology
	Torsten N. Wiesel	neurobiology
2006	Hyman Bass	mathematics
	Marvin H. Caruthers	genetic engineering
	Rita R. Colwell	marine microbiology
	Peter B. Dervan	organic chemistry
	Nina V. Fedoroff	molecular biology
	Daniel Kleppner	atomic physics
	Robert S. Langer	medical research
	Lubert Stryer	biochemistry
2007	Fay Ajzenberg-Selove	nuclear physics
	Mostafa A. El-Sayed	laser dynamics
	Leonard Kleinrock	Internet technology
	Robert J. Lefkowitz	receptor biology
	Bert W. O'Malley	molecular biology
	Charles P. Slichter	condensed-matter physics
	Andrew J. Viterbi	wireless communications
	David J. Wineland	ionic physics

National Inventor of the Year Award

The National Inventor of the Year Award is given by the Intellectual Property Owners Association, a trade organization established in 1972. Patented American inventions from the preceding four years are eligible for nomination annually; runners-up receive recognition as Distinguished Inventors. The winner for 2008 was scientist Ihor Lys, honored for his development of Powercore, a technological innovation in light emitting diode (LED) systems. LED systems can last as much as 50 times longer than traditional incandescent light bulbs, but they required an external power supply and cables. Powercore eliminates this need by integrating power supply and voltage conversion into the light fixture, resulting in increased efficiency, ease of installation, and lower overall cost. Award amount: US$25,000.

Intellectual Property Owners Association Web site: <www.ipo.org>.

Intel Science Talent Search

The Intel Science Talent Search encourages American high-school seniors to pursue careers in the sciences by awarding scholarships for outstanding science projects. Created in 1942 by Science Service, a nonprofit organization devoted to public appreciation of science, and Westinghouse Electric Corporation, the contest brings 40 finalists each year to exhibit their projects at the Science Talent Institute in Washington DC and compete for the top prizes. Since 1998 the talent search has been sponsored by Intel Corp. The highest-place winners for 2008 were **Shivani Sud** of Durham NC (first prize, US$100,000), **Graham William Wakefield Van Schaik** of Columbia SC (second prize, US$75,000), and **Brian Davis McCarthy** of Hillsboro OR (third prize, US$50,000).

Sud presented statistical analysis of a 50-gene model to attempt to predict recurrence of colon cancer in patients and to determine which drug combinations would be most effective in their treatment. Van Schaik studied the long-term effects of pyrethroids, found in pesticides, on human health. McCarthy created new types of solar cells using photosynthetic materials.

Intel Science Talent Search Web site: <www.sciserv.org/sts>.

Nature, Science, Medicine, & Technology

Our Super-Sized Kids

by Jeffrey Kluger and Bryan Walsh, TIME

Americans disagree about a lot of things, but we rarely quarrel when it comes to our food. For a nation built on grand democratic virtues, there is still nothing that defines us quite like our love of chow time. We have plenty of reasons to fetishize our food—not the least being that we've always had so much of it. Settlers fleeing the privations of the Old World landed in the new one and found themselves on a fat, juicy center cut of continent, big enough to baste its coasts in two different oceans. The prairies ran so dark with buffalo, you could practically net them like cod; the waters swam so thick with cod, you could bag them like slow-moving buffalo. The soil was the kind of rich stuff in which you could bury a brick and grow a house, and the pioneers grew plenty—fruits and vegetables and grains and gourds and legumes and tubers, in a variety and abundance they'd never seen before.

With all that, was it any wonder that when we had a chance to establish our first national holiday, it was Thanksgiving—a feast that doesn't merely accompany a celebration but in effect is the celebration? Is it any wonder that what might be our most evocative patriotic song is "America the Beautiful," in which an ideal like brotherhood doesn't even get mentioned until the second-to-last line, well after rhapsodic references to waves of grain and fruited plains?

"We've defined an American version of what it means to succeed," says neuroscientist Randy Seeley, associate director of the Obesity Research Center at the University of Cincinnati Medical School. "And a big part of that is access to an environment in which there is a lot of food to be consumed."

The problem is, all those calories come at a price. Humans, like most animals, are hardwired not just to eat but to gorge, since living in the wild means never knowing when the next famine is going to strike. Best to load up on calories when you can—even if that famine never comes. "We're not only programmed to eat a lot," says Sharman Apt Russell, author of *Hunger: An Unnatural History,* "but to prefer foods that are high in calories." What's more, the better we got at producing food, the easier it became. If you're a settler, you eat a lot of buffalo in part because you need a lot of buffalo—at least after burning so many calories hunting and killing it. But what happens when eating requires no sweat equity at all, when the grocery store is always nearby and always full?

What happens is, you get fat, and that's precisely what we've done. In 1900 the average weight of a college-age male in the US was 133 lb (60 kg); the average woman was 122 lb (55 kg). By 2000, men had plumped up to 166 lb (75 kg) and women to 144 lb (65 kg). And while the small increase in average height for men (women have remained the same) accounts for a bit of that, our eating habits are clearly responsible for most. Over the past 20 years in particular, we've stuffed ourselves like pâté geese. In 1985 there were only eight states in which more than 10% of the adult population was obese—though the data collection then was admittedly spottier than it is now. By 2006, there were no states left in which the obesity rates were that low, and in 23 states, the number exceeded 25%. Even those figures don't tell the whole story, since they include only full-blown obesity. Overall, about two-thirds of all Americans weigh more than they should. "Sit down on a bench in a park with a person on either side of you," says Penelope Slade-Royall, director of the US Office of Disease Prevention and Health Promotion. "If you're not overweight, statistically speaking, both of the other people sitting with you are."

The Kids Are Not Alright. If there was any fire wall against the fattening of American adults, it was American kids. The quick metabolism and prodigious growth spurts of childhood make it a challenge just to keep up with all the calories you need, never mind exceed them. But even the most active kids could not hold out forever against the storm of food coming at them every day. In 1971 only 4% of 6-to-11-year-old kids were obese; by 2004, the figure had leaped to 18.8%. In the same period, the number rose from 6.1% to 17.4% in the 12-to-19-year-old group and from 5% to 13.9% among kids ages just 2 to 5. And as with adults, that's just obesity. Include all overweight kids, and a whopping 32% of all American children now carry more pounds than they should. "There's no way to overestimate how scary numbers like this are," says Seeley.

Obese boys and girls are already starting to develop the illnesses of excess associated with people in their 40s and beyond: heart disease, liver disease, diabetes, gallstones, joint breakdown, and even brain damage as fluid accumulation inside the skull leads to headaches, vision problems, and possibly lower IQs. A staggering 90% of overweight kids already have at least one avoidable risk factor for heart disease, such as high cholesterol or hypertension. Type 2 diabetes is now being diagnosed in teens as young as 15. Health experts warn that the current generation of children may be the first in American history to have a shorter life expectancy than their parents'. "The more overweight you are, the worse all of these things will be for you," says acting US Surgeon General Steven Galson. And, warns Seeley, the worse they are likely to stay: "When you're talking about morbidly obese kids, zero percent will grow up to be normal-weight adults."

It's hardly a secret how American children have come to this sickly pass. In the era of the 64-oz soda, the 1,200-calorie burger, and the 700-calorie Frappuccino, food companies now produce enough each day for every American to consume a belt-popping 3,800 calories per day, never mind that even an adult needs only 2,350 to survive. Not only are adults and kids alike consuming far more calories than they can possibly use, but they're also doing less and less with them. The transformation of American homes into high-def, Web-enabled, TiVo-equipped entertainment centers means that children who come home after a largely sedentary day at a school desk spend an average of three more sedentary hours in front of some kind of screen. Schools have contributed, with shrinking budgets causing more and more of them to slash physical-education programs. In 1991, only 42% of high-school students participated in daily phys ed—already a troublingly low figure. Today that number is 25% or less.

It's Not Just Genetics. It's easy to forget that social factors play a significant role in America's epidemic of childhood obesity. The tide of obesity discriminates by race: according to the Centers for Disease Control and Protection's 2006 figures, 30.7% of white American kids are overweight or obese, compared with 34.9% of blacks and 38% of Mexican Americans. It discriminates by income: 22.4% of 10-to-17-year-olds living below the poverty line—less than US$21,200 for a family of four—are overweight or obese, compared with 9.1% of kids whose families earn at least four times that amount. It discriminates, perhaps most tellingly, by geography, with 16.5% of rural kids qualifying as obese, compared with 14.4% of urban kids, according to the 2003 National Survey of Children's Health. The poorest states of the South and Appalachia—Arkansas, West Virginia, Mississippi, and Kentucky—have the heaviest children. Adult obesity levels triple when you cross north of 96th Street in Manhattan, leaving the mostly white and well-off Upper East Side for the predominantly minority, poorer neighborhood of Spanish Harlem. Even in trim Colorado, there are obesity hot zones.

All that provides a new way to look at—and attack—obesity. We tend not to talk about a problem like body weight in the language of infectious disease, but scientists do, knowing that like any other epidemic, the US's obesity scourge hits some communities harder than others. The skyrocketing increase in childhood obesity—the percentage of 6-to-11-year-olds classified as obese has nearly tripled since 1980—may argue strongly that the American environment has changed in a way that makes gaining weight much less avoidable. But the uneven distribution of the problem argues that who you are, where you are, and how much your family has in the bank have a lot to do with whether your child will be claimed by the crisis or emerge unharmed.

"The environment makes it easier or harder for healthy choices to be the default choices," says Risa Lavizzo-Mourey, president of the Robert Wood Johnson Foundation, which last year pledged US$500 million to end the rise in childhood obesity by 2015. "And adults create the environment that kids live in." The geography of childhood obesity is largely the geography of poverty. There's no pretending that the problem—and resultant disparities in income, education, and opportunity—will be easy to address, but there's no denying that it's imperative that we try. "It's the poorest and most deprived neighborhoods that suffer the most," says Adam Drewnowski, director of the nutritional-science program at the University of Washington. "This has to be fixed."

The federal government, meanwhile, has dropped the ball when it comes to obesity. Seven years ago, Congress allocated US$125 million for a smart new health campaign, dubbed Verb, aimed at getting preteen kids to become more active. Boldface names such as teen star Miley Cyrus and quarterback Donovan McNabb headlined public-service ads, and volunteers set up booths at public events. In the program's first year, up to 80% of kids polled were aware of the Verb message, and communities began sponsoring their own Verb-based activities. But that success could not survive congressional budget cuts, and the program's funding was steadily slashed. By 2007, funds were shut off altogether, and Verb was past tense.

The government insists that the decision was a fiscally prudent one and that local and state programs, like the widely publicized fitness initiatives launched by California Gov. Arnold Schwarzenegger or the less publicized INShape program begun in 2005 by Indiana Gov. Mitch Daniels, are a more efficient way to get the message out. "Obesity is not the kind of problem that is going to respond to just the flow of federal funds," says Galson. The fact is, however, that in the case of Verb, responding was precisely what it was doing—even if only a little.

Looking Ahead. In all of this, there are flickers of hope. In May 2008, epidemiologists were thrilled when the *Journal of the American Medical Association* published a study of 8,165 children, which showed that for the first time in decades, the increase in US childhood obesity had leveled off. It's not certain if the plateau is a sign that public-awareness programs and improved menus in many school cafeterias are producing results or merely that some kind of saturation point has been reached, with most kids genetically susceptible to gaining too much weight having done so. "Whether this is meaningful data, we don't know yet," says Seeley. "But anyone who wants to stick a flag in this and declare victory is just crazy."

Clearly, nobody is going that far. Victory may indeed come, but it will be only after a long, multifront war, one that is at last being joined. Parents are fighting it in the home as they learn how to make healthier meals available to their families, set better examples with their own food choices, and manage the critical issues of self-esteem that can be so disabling for overweight kids.

Policy makers are fighting it as they study the growing body of research showing how everything from income to race to education plays a role in how much kids weigh and as they craft local solutions to solve these local problems.

Doctors are fighting it as they deal daily with the ills associated with childhood obesity and work to repair the damage that's been done. And perhaps most important, teachers, mentors, and public role models are fighting it as they help kids navigate a culture that fosters fat but idealizes thin and as they teach them that what truly counts is getting themselves as fit as their body type and genes allow—and then loving that body no matter what.

Do all these things—and do them right—and the national obesity epidemic just might be brought under control before some kids struggling with their weight today even reach middle age. "If we got this way over the last 30 years," says Galson, "it's not going to take us centuries to get back. We could reverse things at the same speed or even faster." Americans will continue to love good food; the trick will be to learn to love good health even more.

Time

Measuring Time

The measurement of time is an ancient science. The **Cro-Magnons** recorded the phases of the Moon some 30,000 years ago—but the first minutes were counted accurately only 400 years ago, and the atomic clocks that allow us to track time to the billionth of a second are less than 50 years old. Timekeeping has been both a lens through which humanity has observed the heavens and a mirror reflecting the progress of science and civilization. Our millennia-long struggle to **define and calibrate** time through calendars and clocks has meant trying to bring the register of human affairs in line with natural cycles—of the Earth, Sun, Moon, and stars, of the physics of matter—but always cycles. What vary are the cultural values and goals that dictate which cycles are significant.

With a religious culture dominated by gods of the Sun and sky and a civilization dependent on the annual cycle of a river, the **ancient Egyptians** were expert astronomers who studied the Sun's recurrent movements and their effects on the Earth very closely. By plotting the beginning of the Nile's flood each year, a reliable harbinger of seasonal change, they measured a cycle 365 days long—a reasonable approximation of the duration of the solar year. Observations of the star Sirius eventually allowed Egyptian astronomers to adjust the solar year to 365.25 days. Astronomic studies by the Mayan civilization of the first millennium AD underlay a complex calendrical system involving an accurately determined solar year (18 months of days, plus an unlucky 5-day period) and a sacred year of 260 days (13 cycles of 20 named days).

About 127 BC the **Greek astronomer Hipparchus** further refined the year. His adjustments centered on the equinoxes—which he discovered to be shifting to the west at the barely perceptible rate of two degrees in 150 years. Because of this discovery, Hipparchus realized that the solar year was slightly shorter than the accepted 365.25 days. His calculation of 365.242 days was remarkably close to the present calculation of 365.242199 days.

Unfortunately for people of the next 1,600 years, Hipparchus's discoveries were virtually ignored by calendar makers. **Julius Caesar**'s calendrical reforms in 46 BC left the calendar year at 365.25 days—more than 11 minutes too long. By the 1500s the Julian calendar was 10 days behind the solar year. The shortfall alarmed Christian religious leaders because it meant that holy days, including Easter, were being observed at the wrong times. In 1582 **Pope Gregory XIII** officially revised the accepted length of the year to 365.2422 days, adjusted the leap-year rule, and lopped off the 10 extra days, creating in the process the calendar in most widespread use today.

Meanwhile, the quest to measure time accurately on a much smaller scale was still in its early phases. The invention of the **weight-driven mechanical clock** some 200 years earlier had revolutionized timekeeping, making it possible to count equal units of time and radically changing the way people thought about time and the best ways to measure it.

Calendars are deemed accurate according to how well they accommodate the variations in larger celestial cycles. Clocks, on the other hand, have historically been judged accurate in relation to the average duration of the Earth's rotation around the Sun—that is, by how well they keep **"mean time."** While calendrical standards have remained fairly stable, the clock's units of measure have gradually shifted away from using the Earth-Sun relationship as a norm. With the introduction of mechanical clocks, clock time became increasingly removed from cyclical events in the sky, for the cycles on which mechanical clocks base their measures are independent of Earth and Sun. A **pendulum clock**, for example, measures only the beat of its pendulum, not any part of a "real" day.

The pendulum clock kicked off the modern search for the perfect clock, a timepiece governed by a naturally cycling period that operated free from mechanical friction and fatigue. In 1927 W.A. Marrison invented a clock that operated via a tiny **quartz crystal**. The crystal vibrated at an ultrasonic frequency when exposed to an electric field. These vibrations were constant and delivered a virtually frictionless beat to the counting mechanism of the clock. Accurate to thousandths of a second, quartz clocks led scientists to make the belated discovery that the Earth was not a reliable clock to begin with. Disparities between the measurements of quartz clocks and the rotation of the Earth revealed unpredictable irregularities in the rotation, which had to that point defined the duration of a second (1/86,400 of the mean solar day).

In 1967 the **definition of a second** was officially divorced from the Earth's rotation when the 13th General Conference of Weights and Measures redefined the second as "9,192,631,770 periods of the radiation corresponding to the transition between the two hyperfine levels of the ground state of the cesium-133 atom." **Cesium atoms** are superior to quartz crystals because they do not wear out and have cycles that comprise oscillations between precisely defined energy states that can oscillate forever without any distortion. Furthermore, each atom of cesium oscillates at exactly the same frequency as all others, making each one a perfect timekeeper. To keep solar time and atomic time from drifting too far apart, the two were combined in 1964 to form **Coordinated Universal Time**, which is based on the atomic second and kept within 0.9 second of solar time by adding a leap second as needed.

The liger is the offspring of a lion and a tigress, whereas the tigon is the result of mating a tiger with a lioness. Both are zoo-bred hybrids, and it is probable that neither occurs in the wild, as differences in the behavior and habitat of the lion and tiger make interbreeding unlikely. The liger and the tigon possess features of both parents, in variable proportions, but are generally larger and darker than either.

Time Zone Map

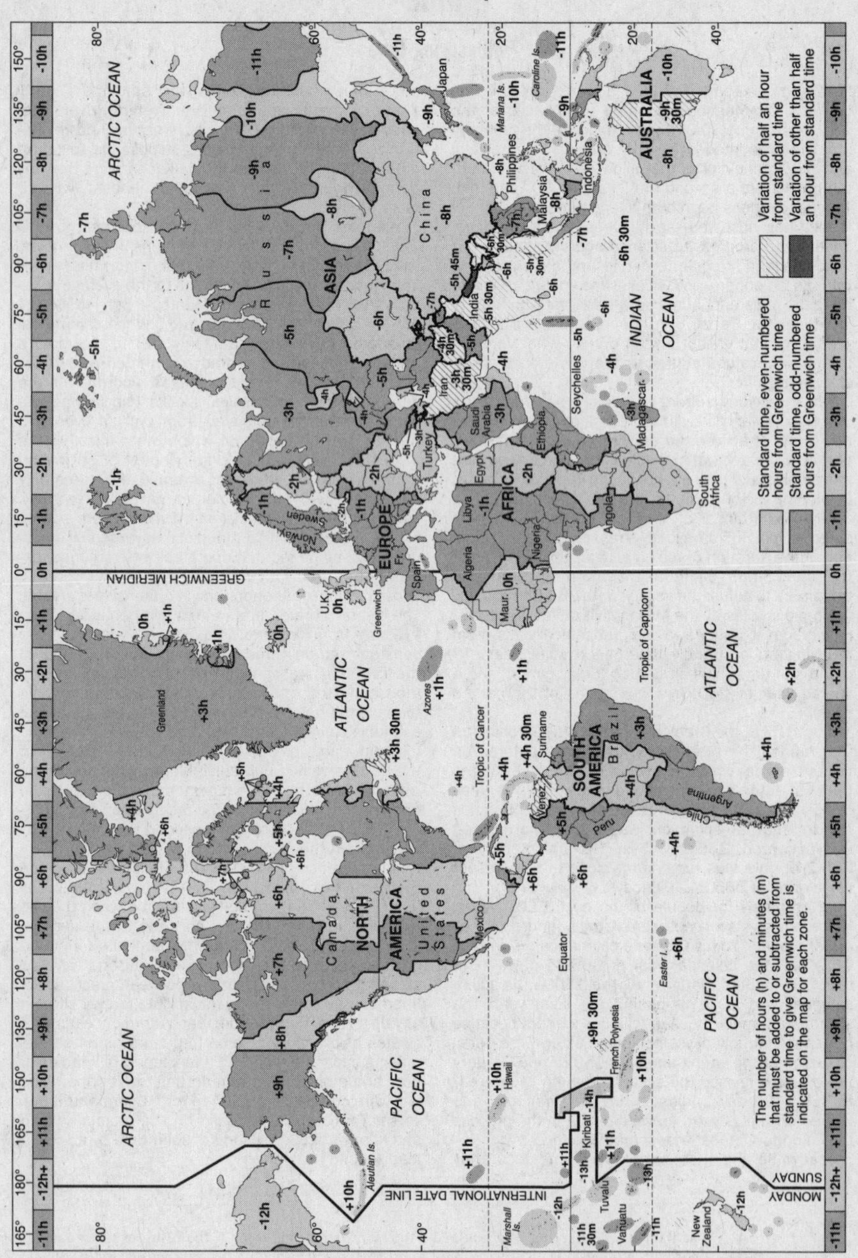

Based on data from the US Defense Mapping Agency Hydrographic/Topographic Center

Daylight Saving Time

Also called **summer time, daylight saving time** is a system for uniformly advancing clocks, especially in summer, so as to extend daylight hours during conventional waking time. In the Northern Hemisphere, clocks are usually set ahead one hour in late March or in April and are set back one hour in late September or in October; most Southern Hemisphere countries that observe daylight saving time set clocks ahead in October or November and reset them in March or April. Equatorial countries do not observe daylight saving time because daylight hours stay about the same from season to season in the lower latitudes.

The practice was first suggested in a whimsical essay by **Benjamin Franklin** in 1784. In 1907 an Englishman, William Willett, campaigned for setting the clock ahead by 80 minutes in four moves of 20 minutes each during the spring and summer months. In 1908 the British House of Commons rejected a bill to advance the clock by one hour in the spring and return to Greenwich Mean (standard) Time in the autumn.

Several countries, including Australia, Great Britain, Germany, and the United States, adopted **summer daylight saving time** during World War I to conserve fuel by reducing the need for artificial light. During World War II, clocks were kept continuously advanced by an hour in some nations—for instance, in the US from 9 Feb 1942 to 30 Sep 1945—and England used "double summer time" during part of the year, advancing clocks two hours from the standard time during the summer and one hour during the winter months.

In 2005 the US Congress changed the law governing daylight saving time, moving the start of daylight saving time from the first Sunday in April to the second Sunday in March, while moving the end date from the last Sunday in October to the first Sunday in November starting in 2007. In most of the countries of Western Europe, daylight saving time starts on the last Sunday in March and ends on the last Sunday in October.

Julian and Gregorian Calendars

The **Julian calendar**, also called the Old Style calendar, is a dating system established by Julius Caesar as a reform of the Roman republican calendar. Caesar, advised by the Alexandrian astronomer Sosigenes, made the new calendar solar, not lunar, and he took the length of the solar year as 365¼ days. The year was divided into 12 months, all of which had either 30 or 31 days except February, which contained 28 days in common (365-day) years and 29 in every fourth year (a leap year, of 366 days). Because of misunderstandings, the calendar was not established in smooth operation until AD 8. Further, Sosigenes had overestimated the length of the year by 11 minutes 14 seconds, and by the mid-1500s, the cumulative effect of this error had shifted the dates of the seasons by about 10 days from Caesar's time.

This inaccuracy led **Pope Gregory XIII** to reform the Julian calendar. His **Gregorian calendar**, also called the **New Style calendar**, is still in general use. Gregory's proclamation in 1582 restored the calendar to the seasonal dates of AD 325, an adjustment of 10 days. Although the amount of regression was some 14 days by Pope Gregory's time, Gregory based his reform on restoration of the vernal equinox, then falling on 11 March, to the date (21 March) it had in AD 325, the time of the Council of Nicaea. Advancing the calendar 10 days after 4 Oct 1582, the day following being reckoned as 15 October, effected the change.

The Gregorian calendar differs from the Julian only in that no century year is a leap year unless it is exactly divisible by 400 (e.g., 1600, 2000). A further refinement, the designation of years evenly divisible by 4,000 as common (not leap) years, will keep the Gregorian calendar accurate to within one day in 20,000 years.

Jewish Calendar

The **Jewish calendar** is **lunisolar**—i.e., regulated by the positions of both the Moon and the Sun. It consists usually of 12 alternating lunar months of 29 and 30 days each (except for Heshvan and Kislev, which sometimes have either 29 or 30 days), and totals 353, 354, or 355 days per year. The average lunar year (354 days) is adjusted to the solar year (365¼ days) by the periodic introduction of leap years in order to assure that the major festivals fall in their proper season. The leap year consists of an additional 30-day month called **First Adar**, which always precedes the month of (Second) Adar. (During leap year, the Adar holidays are postponed to Second Adar.) A leap year consists of either 383, 384, or 385 days and occurs seven times during every 19-year period (the so-called Metonic cycle). Among the consequences of the lunisolar structure are these: (1) The number of days in a year may vary considerably, from 353 to 385 days. (2) The first day of a month can fall on any day of the week, that day varying from year to year. Consequently, the days of the week upon which an annual Jewish festival falls vary from year to year despite the festival's fixed position in the Jewish month. The months of the Jewish calendar and their Gregorian equivalents are as follows:

JEWISH MONTH	GREGORIAN MONTH(S)	JEWISH MONTH	GREGORIAN MONTH(S)
Tishri	September–October	Nisan	March–April
Heshvan, or Marheshvan	October–November	Iyyar	April–May
Kislev	November–December	Sivan	May–June
Tevet	December–January	Tammuz	June–July
Shevat	January–February	Av	July–August
Adar	February–March	Elul	August–September

Muslim Calendar

The **Muslim calendar** (also called the **Islamic calendar**, or **Hijrah**) is a dating system used in the Muslim world that is based on a year of 12 months. Each month begins with the sighting of the crescent of the new moon as it emerges from eclipse. The **months** of the Muslim calendar are Muharram, Safar, Rabi I, Rabi II, Jumada I, Jumada II, Rajab, Sha'ban, Ramadan, Shawwal, Dhu al-Qa'dah, and Dhu al-Hijjah.

In the standard Muslim calendar the months are alternately 30 and 29 days long except for the 12th month, Dhu al-Hijjah, the length of which is varied in a 30-year cycle intended to keep the calendar in step with the true phases of the Moon. In 11 years of this cycle, Dhu al-Hijjah has 30 days, and in the other 19 years it has 29. Thus the year has either 354 or 355 days. No months are intercalated, so that the named months do not remain in the same seasons but retrogress through the entire solar, or seasonal, year (of about 365.25 days) every 32.5 solar years.

There are some exceptions to this calendar in the Muslim world. **Turkey** uses the Gregorian calendar, while the **Iranian Muslim calendar** is based on a solar year. The Iranian calendar still begins from the same dating point as other Muslim calendars—that is, some 10 years prior to the death of Muhammad in AD 632. Thus, the Gregorian year AD 2009 corresponds to the Hijrah years of AH 1430–31.

Chinese Calendar

The **Chinese calendar** is a dating system used concurrently with the Gregorian (Western) calendar in China and Taiwan and in neighboring countries (e.g., Japan). The calendar consists of 12 months of alternately 29 and 30 days, equal to 354 or 355 days, or approximately 12 full lunar cycles. Intercalary months have been inserted to keep the calendar year in step with the solar year of about 365 days. **Months** have no names but are instead referred to by numbers within a year and sometimes also by a series of 12 animal names that from ancient times have been attached to years and to hours of the day.

The calendar also incorporates a **meteorologic cycle** that contains 24 points, each beginning one of the periods named. The establishment of this cycle required a fair amount of astronomical understanding of the Earth as a celestial body. Modern scholars acknowledge the superiority of pre-Sung **Chinese astronomy** (at least until about the 13th century AD) over that of other, contemporary nations.

The **24 points** within the meteorologic cycle coincide with points 15° apart on the ecliptic (the plane of the Earth's yearly journey around the Sun or, if it is thought that the Sun turns around the Earth, the apparent journey of the Sun against the stars). It takes about 15.2 days for the Sun to travel from one of these points to another (because the ecliptic is a complete circle of 360°), and the Sun needs 365¼ days to finish its journey in this cycle. Supposedly, each of the 12 months of the year contains two points, but, because a lunar month has only 29½ days and the two points share about 30.4 days, there is always the chance that a lunar month will fail to contain both points, though the distance between any two given points is only 15°. If such an occasion occurs, the intercalation of an extra month takes place. For instance, one may find a year with two "Julys" or with two "Augusts" in the Chinese calendar. In fact, as mentioned above, the exact length of the month in the Chinese calendar is either 30 days or 29 days—a phenomenon that reflects its lunar origin.

SOLAR TERMS—CHINESE (ENGLISH EQUIVALENTS)	GREGORIAN DATE (APPROXIMATE)
Lichun (spring begins)	5 February
Yushui (rain water)	19 February
Jingzhe (excited insects)	5 March
Chunfen (vernal equinox)	20 March
Qingming (clear and bright)	5 April
Guyu (grain rains)	20 April
Lixia (summer begins)	5 May
Xiaoman (grain fills)	21 May
Mangzhong (grain in ear)	6 June
Xiazhi (summer solstice)	21 June
Xiaoshu (slight heat)	7 July
Dashu (great heat)	23 July
Liqiu (autumn begins)	7 August
Chushu (limit of heat)	23 August
Bailu (white dew)	8 September
Qiufen (autumn equinox)	23 September
Hanlu (cold dew)	8 October
Shuangjiang (hoar frost descends)	24 October
Lidong (winter begins)	8 November
Xiaoxue (little snow)	22 November
Daxue (heavy snow)	7 December
Dongzhi (winter solstice)	22 December
Xiaohan (little cold)	6 January
Dahan (severe cold)	20 January

LUNAR MONTH (CORRESPONDENCE OF LUNAR AND SOLAR MONTHS APPROXIMATE)
1—tiger
2—rabbit/hare
3—dragon
4—snake
5—horse
6—sheep/ram
7—monkey
8—chicken/rooster
9—dog
10—pig/boar
11—rat
12—cow/ox

Chinese Calendar (continued)

CHINESE NEW YEAR	GREGORIAN DATE	ANIMAL	CHINESE NEW YEAR	GREGORIAN DATE	ANIMAL
4700	12 Feb 2002	horse	4707	26 Jan 2009	cow/ox
4701	1 Feb 2003	sheep/ram	4708	14 Feb 2010	tiger
4702	22 Jan 2004	monkey	4709	3 Feb 2011	rabbit/hare
4703	9 Feb 2005	chicken/rooster	4710	23 Jan 2012	dragon
4704	29 Jan 2006	dog	4711	10 Feb 2013	snake
4705	18 Feb 2007	pig/boar	4712	31 Jan 2014	horse
4706	7 Feb 2008	rat	4713	19 Feb 2015	sheep/ram

Popcorn king Orville Redenbacher developed a hybrid popcorn with his partner, Charles Bowman. The hybrid produced plumper and more tender kernels, but no company would buy the product because it was so expensive to produce. Redenbacher went into business for himself, promoting his "gourmet" popcorn as "The World's Most Expensive," a marketing ploy that made Redenbacher's product an enormous success starting in the 1970s.

Religious and Traditional Holidays

The word holiday comes from "holy day," and it was originally a day of dedication to religious observance; in modern times a holiday may be of either religious or secular commemoration. All dates in this article are Gregorian.

Jewish holidays—The major holidays are the Pilgrim Festivals: **Pesach** (Passover), **Shavuot** (Feast of Weeks, or Pentecost), and **Sukkot** (Tabernacles); and the High Holidays: **Rosh Hashana** (New Year) and **Yom Kippur** (Day of Atonement).

Pesach commemorates the Exodus from Egypt and the servitude that preceded it. As such, it is the most significant of the commemorative holidays, for it celebrates the very inception of the Jewish people—i.e., the event that provided the basis for the covenant between God and Israel. The term Pesach refers originally to the paschal (Passover) lamb sacrificed on the eve of the Exodus, the blood of which marked the Jewish homes to be spared from God's plague. Leaven (*se'or*) and foods containing leaven (*hametz*) are neither to be owned nor consumed during Pesach. Aside from meats, fresh fruits, and vegetables, it is customary to consume only those foods prepared under rabbinic supervision and labeled "kosher for Passover." The unleavened bread (matzo) consists entirely of flour and water. On the eve of Pesach families partake of the Seder, an elaborate festival meal. The table is bedecked with an assortment of foods symbolizing the passage from slavery (e.g., bitter herbs) into freedom (e.g., wine). Pesach will begin at sundown on 8 April and end on 16 April in 2009. (All Jewish holidays begin at sundown.)

A distinctive **Rosh Hashana** observance is the sounding of the ram's horn (shofar) at the synagogue service. Symbolic ceremonies, such as eating bread and apples dipped in honey, accompanied by prayers for a "sweet" and propitious year, are performed at the festive meals. In 2009 Rosh Hashana will begin at sundown on 18 September and will end on 20 September. **Yom Kippur** is a day when sins are confessed and expiated and man and God are reconciled. It is the holiest and most solemn day of the Jewish year. It is marked by fasting, penitence, and prayer. Working, eating, drinking, washing, anointing one's body, engaging in sexual intercourse, and donning leather shoes are all forbidden. Yom Kippur begins at sundown on 27 September in 2009.

Though not as important theologically, the feast of **Hanukkah** has become socially significant, especially in Western cultures. Hanukkah commemorates the rededication (164 BCE) of the Second Temple of Jerusalem after its desecration three years earlier. Though modern Israel tends to emphasize the military victory of the general Judas Maccabeus, the distinctive rite of lighting the menorah also recalls the Talmud story of how the small supply of nondesecrated oil—enough for one day—miraculously burned in the Temple for eight full days until new oil could be obtained. During Hanukkah, in addition to the lighting of the ceremonial candles, gifts are exchanged and children play holiday games. The festival occurs 21 through 29 Dec 2008, subsequently spanning 11 through 19 Dec 2009.

Christian holidays—The major holidays celebrated by nearly all Christians are **Easter** and **Christmas.**

Easter celebrates the Resurrection of Jesus on the third day after his Crucifixion. In the Christian liturgical year, Easter is preceded by the period of **Lent**, the 40 days (not counting Sundays) before Easter, which traditionally were observed as a period of penance and fasting. Lent begins on **Ash Wednesday,** a day devoted to penitence. Holy Week precedes **Easter Sunday** and includes **Maundy Thursday**, the commemoration of Jesus' last supper with his disciples; **Good Friday**, the day of his Crucifixion; and **Holy Saturday**, the transition between Crucifixion and Resurrection. Easter shares with Christmas the presence of numerous customs, some of which have little to do with the Christian celebration of the resurrection but clearly derive from folk customs. In 2009 the Western churches (nearly all Christian denominations) will observe Ash Wednesday on 25 February and Easter on 12 April. For Eastern Orthodox Christians, Lent begins on 2 March and Easter will be observed on 19 Apr 2009.

Christmas commemorates the birth of Jesus Christ. Since the early part of the 20th century, Christmas has also become a secular family holiday, observed by non-Christians, devoid of Christian elements, and marked by an increasingly elaborate exchange of gifts. In this secular Christmas celebration, a mythical figure named Santa Claus plays the pivotal role. Christmas is held on 25 December in most Christian cultures but occurs on the following 7 January in some Eastern Orthodox churches.

Islamic holidays—**Ramadan** is the holy month of fasting for Muslims. The Islamic ordinance prescribes abstention from evil thoughts and deeds as well as from food, drink, and sexual intercourse from dawn until dusk throughout the month. The beginning and end of Ramadan are announced when one trustworthy witness testifies before the authorities that the new moon has been sighted; a cloudy sky may therefore delay or prolong the fast. The end of the fast is celebrated as the feast of **ʿId al-Fitr**. Ramadan begins on 21 August in 2009 and ʿId al-Fitr falls on 20 September of that year (all Islamic holidays begin at sundown). The Muslim New Year, **Hijra**, is on 17 December in 2009.

After ʿId al-Fitr, the second major Islamic festival is **ʿId al-Adha**. Throughout the Muslim world, all who are able sacrifice sheep, goats, camels, or cattle and then divide the flesh equally among themselves, the poor, and friends and neighbors to commemorate the ransom of Ishmael with a ram. This festival falls at the end of the hajj, the pilgrimage to the holy city of Mecca in Saudi Arabia, which every adult Muslim of either sex must make at least once in his or her lifetime. ʿId al-Adha will be observed on 27 November in 2009.

Ashura was originally designated in AD 622 by Muhammad as a day of fasting from sunset to sunset, probably patterned on the Jewish Day of Atonement, Yom Kippur. Among the Shiʿites, Ashura is a major festival that commemorates the death of Husayn (Hussein), son of Ali and grandson of Muhammad. It is a period of expressions of grief and of pilgrimage to Karbala (the site of Husayn's death, now in present-day Iraq). Ashura is on 6 January in 2009.

Buddhist holidays—Holidays practiced by a large number of Buddhists are ***uposatha*** days and days that commemorate events in the life of the Buddha.

The four monthly holy days of ancient Buddhism continue to be observed in the Theravada countries of Southeast Asia. These *uposatha* days—the new moon and full moon days of each lunar month and the eighth day following the new and full moons—have their origin, according to some scholars, in the fast days that preceded the Vedic soma sacrifices.

The three major events of the Buddha's life—his birth, Enlightenment, and entrance into final nirvana—are commemorated in all Buddhist countries but not everywhere on the same day. In the Theravada countries the three events are all observed together on **Vesak**, the full moon day of the sixth lunar month, which usually occurs in May. In Japan and other Mahayana countries, the three anniversaries of the Buddha are observed on separate days (in some countries the birth date is 8 April, the Enlightenment date is 8 December, and the death date is 15 February).

Chinese holidays—The **Chinese New Year** is celebrated with a big family meal, and presents of cash are given to children in red envelopes. In 2009 the Chinese New Year will be on 26 January.

During the **Chinese Moon Festival**, on the 15th day of the 8th month of the lunar calendar, people return to their homes to visit with their family. The traditional food is moon cakes, round pastries stuffed with food such as red bean paste. The Moon Festival will occur on 2 October in 2009.

Japanese holidays—The Japanese celebrate **7-5-3 day** (Shichi-go-san no hi), in which parents bring children of those ages to the Shinto shrine to pray for their continued health. This day is held on 15 November.

In mid-July (or mid-August, in some areas) the Japanese celebrate **Obon** (also known as Bon Matsuri, or Urabon). The festival honors the spirits of deceased householders and of the dead generally. Memorial stones are cleaned, community dances are performed, and paper lanterns and fires are lit to welcome the dead and to bid them farewell at the end of their visit. The Shinto New Year, **Gantan-sai**, is celebrated on 1–3 January.

Hindu holidays—**Dussehra** celebrates the victory of Rama over Ravana, the symbol of evil on earth. In 2009 Dussehra falls on 28 September. **Diwali** is a festival of lights devoted to Laksmi, the goddess of wealth. During the festival, small earthenware lamps filled with oil are lighted and placed in rows along the parapets of temples and houses and set adrift on rivers and streams. Diwali is on 17 October in 2009. **Sivaratri**, the most important sectarian festival of the year for devotees of the Hindu god Shiva, occurs on 23 February in 2009. **Holi** is a spring festival, probably of ancient origin. Participants throw colored waters and powders on one another, and, on this day, the usual restrictions of caste, sex, status, and age are disregarded. It will be on 11 March in 2009.

Sikh holidays—Sikhs observe all festivals celebrated by the Hindus of northern India. In addition, they celebrate the birthdays of the first and the last Gurus and the martyrdom of the fifth (Arjun) and the ninth (Tegh Bahadur). In 2009 **Guru Nanak Dev Sahib's birthday** is celebrated on 2 November, and that of **Guru Gobind Singh Sahib** is celebrated on 5 January. On 16 June **Arjun's martyrdom** is observed. *Kachi lassi* (sweetened milk) is offered to passersby to commemorate his death. On 24 November the **martyrdom of Tegh Bahadur** is observed.

Baha'i holidays—The Baha'i New Year (**Naw Ruz**) in 2009 will fall on 21 March (all Baha'i holidays begin at sundown). Other important observances include the **declaration of the Bab** on 22 May, the **Baha ʿUllah's birth** (11 November), and **Ascension** (28 May).

Zoroastrian holidays—**Noruz** (New Day) is on 21 March for 2009, and the 26th of that month is **Khordad Sal**, the birth of the prophet Zarathustra.

African American holiday—**Kwanzaa** (Swahili for "First Fruits") is celebrated each year from 26 December to 1 January and is patterned after various African harvest festivals. Maulana Karenga, a black-studies professor, created Kwanzaa in 1966 as a nonreligious celebration of family and social values. Each day of Kwanzaa is dedicated to one of seven principles: unity (*umoja*), self-determination (*kujichagulia*), collective responsibility (*ujima*), cooperative economics (*ujamaa*), purpose (*nia*), creativity (*kuumba*), and faith (*imani*).

Perpetual Calendar

The perpetual calendar is a type of dating system that makes it possible to find the correct day of the week for any date over a wide range of years. Aspects of the perpetual calendar can be found in the Jewish religious and the Julian calendars, and some form of it has appeared in many proposed calendar reforms.

To find the day of the week for any Gregorian or Julian date in the perpetual calendar provided in this table, first find the proper dominical letter (one of the letters A through G) for the year in the upper table. Leap years have two dominical letters, the first applicable to dates in January and February, the second to dates in the remaining months. Then find the same dominical letter in the lower table, in whichever column it appears opposite the month in question. The days then fall as given in the lowest section of the column.

YEAR				CENTURY											
				JULIAN CALENDAR							GREGORIAN CALENDAR				
				0 700 1400	100 800 1500*	200 900	300 1000	400 1100	500 1200	600 1300	1500**	1600 2000	1700 2100	1800 2200	1900 2300
0				DC	ED	FE	GF	AG	BA	CB	...	BA	C	E	G
1	29	57	85	B	C	D	E	F	G	A	F	G	B	D	F
2	30	58	86	A	B	C	D	E	F	G	E	F	A	C	E
3	31	59	87	G	A	B	C	D	E	F	D	E	G	B	D
4	32	60	88	FE	GF	AG	BA	CB	DC	ED	CB	DC	FE	AG	CB
5	33	61	89	D	E	F	G	A	B	C	A	B	D	F	A
6	34	62	90	C	D	E	F	G	A	B	G	A	C	E	G
7	35	63	91	B	C	D	E	F	G	A	F	G	B	D	F
8	36	64	92	AG	BA	CB	DC	ED	FE	GF	ED	FE	AG	CB	ED
9	37	65	93	F	G	A	B	C	D	E	C	D	F	A	C
10	38	66	94	E	F	G	A	B	C	D	B	C	E	G	B
11	39	67	95	D	E	F	G	A	B	C	A	B	D	F	A
12	40	68	96	CB	DC	ED	FE	GF	AG	BA	GF	AG	CB	ED	GF
13	41	69	97	A	B	C	D	E	F	G	E	F	A	C	E
14	42	70	98	G	A	B	C	D	E	F	D	E	G	B	D
15	43	71	99	F	G	A	B	C	D	E	C	D	F	A	C
16	44	72		ED	FE	GF	AG	BA	CB	DC	...	CB	ED	GF	BA
17	45	73		C	D	E	F	G	A	B	...	A	C	E	G
18	46	74		B	C	D	E	F	G	A	...	G	B	D	F
19	47	75		A	B	C	D	E	F	G	...	F	A	C	E
20	48	76		GF	AG	BA	CB	DC	ED	FE	...	ED	GF	BA	DC
21	49	77		E	F	G	A	B	C	D	...	C	E	G	B
22	50	78		D	E	F	G	A	B	C	...	B	D	F	A
23	51	79		C	D	E	F	G	A	B	...	A	C	E	G
24	52	80		BA	CB	DC	ED	FE	GF	AG	...	GF	BA	DC	FE
25	53	81		G	A	B	C	D	E	F	...	E	G	B	D
26	54	82		F	G	A	B	C	D	E	C	D	F	A	C
27	55	83		E	F	G	A	B	C	D	B	C	E	G	B
28	56	84		DC	ED	FE	GF	AG	BA	CB	AG	BA	DC	FE	AG

MONTH	DOMINICAL LETTER						
January, October	A	B	C	D	E	F	G
February, March, November	D	E	F	G	A	B	C
April, July	G	A	B	C	D	E	F
May	B	C	D	E	F	G	A
June	E	F	G	A	B	C	D
August	C	D	E	F	G	A	B
September, December	F	G	A	B	C	D	E
1 8 15 22 29	Sunday	Saturday	Friday	Thursday	Wednesday	Tuesday	Monday
2 9 16 23 30	Monday	Sunday	Saturday	Friday	Thursday	Wednesday	Tuesday
3 10 17 24 31	Tuesday	Monday	Sunday	Saturday	Friday	Thursday	Wednesday
4 11 18 25	Wednesday	Tuesday	Monday	Sunday	Saturday	Friday	Thursday
5 12 19 26	Thursday	Wednesday	Tuesday	Monday	Sunday	Saturday	Friday
6 13 20 27	Friday	Thursday	Wednesday	Tuesday	Monday	Sunday	Saturday
7 14 21 28	Saturday	Friday	Thursday	Wednesday	Tuesday	Monday	Sunday

**On and before 1582, 4 October only.* ***On and after 1582, 15 October only.*
Source: Smithsonian Physical Tables, *9th edition, rev. 1956.*

Civil Holidays

DAY	EVENT
1 January	New Year's Day, the first day of the modern calendar (various countries)
20 January	Inauguration Day, for quadrennial inauguration of US president
26 January	Australia Day, commemorates the establishment of the first British settlement in Australia
3rd Monday in January	Martin Luther King Day, for birth of US civil rights leader
2nd new moon after winter solstice (at the earliest 21 January and at the latest 19 February)	New Year, for Chinese lunar year, inaugurating a 15-day celebration
6 February	Waitangi Day, for Treaty of Waitangi, granting British sovereignty (New Zealand)
11 February	National Foundation Day, for founding by first emperor (Japan)
14 February	St. Valentine's Day, celebrating the exchange of love messages and named for either of two 3rd-century Christian martyrs (various)
3rd Monday in February	Presidents' Day, Washington-Lincoln Day, or Washington's Birthday, for birthdays of US Presidents George Washington and Abraham Lincoln
8 March	International Women's Day, celebration of the women's liberation movement
17 March	St. Patrick's Day, for patron saint of Ireland (Ireland and various)
21 or 22 March	Vernal Equinox Day, for beginning of spring (Japan)
25 March	Independence Day, for proclamation of independence from the Ottoman Empire (Greece)
4th Sunday in Lent	Mothering Day (UK)
1 April	April Fools' Day, or All Fools' Day, day for playing jokes, falling one week after the old New Year's Day of 25 March (various)
5 April	Qingming, for sweeping tombs and honoring the dead (China)
7 April	World Health Day, for founding of World Health Organization
22 April	Earth Day, for conservation and reclaiming of the natural environment (various)
25 April	ANZAC Day, for landing at Gallipoli (Australia/New Zealand/Samoa/Tonga)
29 April	Green Day, national holiday for environment and nature (Japan)
30 April	Queen's Birthday, for Queen Beatrix's investiture and former queen Juliana's birthday (The Netherlands)
1 May	May Day, celebrated as labor day or as festival of flowers (various)
3 May	Constitution Memorial Day, for establishment of democratic government (Japan)
5 May	Children's Day, honoring children (Japan/South Korea)
5 May	Cinco de Mayo, anniversary of Mexico's victory over France in the Battle of Puebla (Mexico)
8/9 May	V-E Day, or Liberation Day, for end of World War II in Europe (various)
2nd Sunday in May	Mother's Day, honoring mothers (US)
Monday on or preceding 25 May	Victoria Day, for Queen Victoria's birthday (Canada)
30 or last Monday in May	Memorial Day, or Decoration Day, in honor of the deceased, especially the war dead (US)
2 June	Anniversary of the Republic, for referendum establishing republic (Italy)
5 June	Constitution Day (Denmark)
6 June	National Day, for Gustav I Vasa's ascension to the throne and adoption of Constitution (Sweden)
10 June	Portugal's Day, or Camões Memorial Day, anniversary of Luis de Camões's death
14 June	Flag Day, honoring flag (US)
3rd Saturday in June	Queen's Official Birthday, for Queen Elizabeth II (UK/New Zealand)
3rd Sunday in June	Father's Day, honoring fathers (US)
23 June	National Day, for Grand Duke Jean's official birthday (Luxembourg)
23–24 June	Midsummer Eve and Midsummer Day, celebrating the return of summer (various European)
last Sunday in June	Gay and Lesbian Pride Day, final day of weeklong advocacy of rights of gay men and lesbians (international)
1 July	Canada Day (formerly Dominion Day), for establishment of dominion
4 July	Independence Day, for Declaration of Independence from Britain (US)
12 July	Orangemen's Day, or Orange Day, anniversary of the Battle of the Boyne (Northern Ireland)
14 July	Bastille Day, for fall of the Bastille and onset of French Revolution (France)
21 July	National Day, for separation from The Netherlands (Belgium)
1 August	National Day, anniversary of the founding of the Swiss Confederation (Switzerland)
6 August	Hiroshima Day, for dropping of atomic bomb (Japan)
full-moon day of 8th lunar month	Chusok, harvest festival (Korea)
1st Monday in September	Labor Day, tribute to workers (US/Canada)
15 September	Respect-for-the-Aged Day, for the elderly (Japan)
16 September	Independence Day, for independence from Spain (Mexico)
23 or 24 September	Autumnal Equinox Day, for beginning of autumn; in honor of ancestors (Japan)

Civil Holidays (continued)

DAY	EVENT
two weeks ending on 1st Sunday in October	Oktoberfest, festival of food and drink, formerly commemorating marriage of King Louis (Ludwig) I (Germany)
3 October	Day of German Unity, for reunification of Germany
5 October	Republic Day, for founding of the republic (Portugal)
12 or 2nd Monday in October	Hispanic Day, Columbus Day, Discovery Day, or Day of the Race, for Christopher Columbus's discovery of the New World on behalf of Spain (Spain and various)
2nd Monday in October	Thanksgiving Day, harvest festival (Canada)
24 October	United Nations Day, for effective date of UN Charter (international)
26 October	National Day, for end of postwar occupation and return of sovereignty (Austria)
31 October	Halloween, or All Hallows' Eve, festive celebration of ghosts and spirits, on eve of All Saints' Day (various)
5 November	Guy Fawkes Day, anniversary of the Gunpowder Plot to blow up the king and Parliament (UK)
11 November	Armistice Day, Remembrance Day, or Veterans Day, honoring participants in past wars and recalling the Armistice of World War I (various)
23 November	Labor Thanksgiving Day, honoring workers (Japan)
4th Thursday in November	Thanksgiving Day, harvest festival (US)
16 December	Day of Reconciliation, for promoting national unity (South Africa)
23 December	Emperor's Birthday, for birthday of Emperor Akihito (Japan)
26 December	Boxing Day, second day of Christmas, for giving presents to service people (various)
31 December	New Year's Eve, celebration ushering out the old year and in the new year (various)

The Universe

Cosmogony (Theories of the Origin of the Universe)

Three great ages of scientific thinking about the universe can be distinguished. The first began in Greece in the 6th century BC when the **Pythagoreans** introduced the concept of a **spherical Earth** and postulated a universe in which the motions of heavenly bodies were governed by natural laws. The **infinite atomist universe** of Leucippus and Democritus followed, wherein countless worlds, teeming with life, were the result of chance aggregations of atoms. The **geocentric Aristotelian universe** arose in the 4th century BC. It consisted of a central Earth surrounded by revolving, translucent spheres to which were attached the Sun and the planets; the outermost sphere supported the fixed stars.

The **Copernican revolution** ushered in the second great age. In the 16th century, Nicolaus Copernicus revived ancient ideas and proposed a heliocentric universe, which during the following century was transformed into the mechanistic, infinite **Newtonian universe** that flourished until the early 1900s. In the mid-18th century, Thomas Wright proposed the influential notion of a universe composed of numerous **galaxies**, and William Herschel, followed by many other astronomers, made rapid strides in the study of stars and of the Milky Way Galaxy, of which the Earth is a component.

The third great age began in the early years of the 20th century, with the discovery of **special relativity** and its development into **general relativity** by **Albert Einstein**. These years also saw momentous developments in astronomy: extragalactic redshifts were detected by Vesto Slipher; extragalactic nebulae were shown to be galaxies comparable with the Milky Way; and **Edwin Hubble** began to estimate the distances of these galactic systems. Such discoveries and the application of general relativity to cosmology eventually gave rise to the view that the **universe is expanding.** The basic premise of modern thinking on the universe is the principle that asserts that the universe is **homogeneous in space** (on the average all places are alike at any time) and that the laws of physics are everywhere the same.

Two theories of the origin of the universe have been the most influential during the last century—the steady state theory and the big bang theory. The **steady state theory** posits that the universe is always expanding but maintains a constant average density, matter being continuously created to form new stars and galaxies at the same rate that old ones become unobservable as a consequence of their increasing distance and velocity of recession. A steady-state universe has no beginning or end in time; and from any point within it the view on the grand scale—i.e., the average density and arrangement of galaxies—is the same. Galaxies of all possible ages are intermingled. Observations since the 1950s have produced much evidence contradictory to the steady-state picture and supportive of the big-bang model.

The essential feature of the widely-held **big bang theory** is the emergence of the universe from a state of extremely high temperature and density—the so-called big bang that occurred at least 10,000,000,000 years ago. Although this type of universe was proposed by Alexander Friedmann and Abbé Georges Lemaître in the 1920s, the modern version was developed by George Gamow and colleagues in the 1940s.

One current problem that scientists are studying is the **amount of matter in the universe.** Based upon such things as the rate of the motion of galaxies, scientists realized that there is some 90% more matter in the universe than can be seen. Scientists refer to the matter that can be observed as **"bright matter"** and this other 90% is called **"dark matter."** Whether dark matter is of a different and exotic nature from the matter with which we are familiar, or whether dark matter is just like luminous matter (and for some reason we cannot detect it), is something a large number of scientists are studying.

Astronomical Constants

QUANTITY	SYMBOL	VALUE

astronomical unit — AU — length of the semimajor axis of the Earth's orbit around the Sun—149,597,870 km (92,955,808 mi)
measures large distances in space; equals the average distance from the Earth to the Sun

parsec — pc — one parsec equals 3.26 light-years
measures the distance at which the radius of the Earth's orbit subtends an angle of one second of arc

light-year — ly — 9.46089×10^{12} km (5.8787×10^{12} mi)
measures the distance traveled by light moving in a vacuum in the course of one year

solar parallax — 8.79414 seconds of arc
quantifies the angular difference in direction of the Sun as seen from the Earth's center and a point one Earth radius away

lunar parallax — 57 minutes 02.608 seconds of arc
quantifies the angular difference in direction of the Moon as seen from the Earth's center and a point one Earth radius away

general precession — 50.29 seconds of arc per year
measures the cyclic wobbling in the orientation of the Earth's axis of rotation with a period of almost 26,000 years

constant of aberration — about 20.49 seconds of arc
the maximum amount of the apparent yearly aberrational displacement of a star or other celestial body, resulting from the Earth's orbital motion around the Sun

constant of nutation — 9.202 seconds of arc
a small irregularity in the Earth's axial precession of that occurs over a period of 18.6 years

speed of light (in a vacuum) — c — $2.99792458 \times 10^{10}$ cm per sec (186,282 mi per sec)

radius of the Sun — Sun $R_\odot$ — 6.96×10^{8} m (109 times the radius of Earth)

mass of the Sun — Sun $M_\odot$ — 1.989×10^{30} kg (330,000 times the mass of the Earth)

Earth's mean radius — 6,378 km (3,963 mi)

sidereal day (on Earth) — 23 h 56 min 4.10 sec of mean solar time
defined by the period between two successive passages of a star across the same meridian; it is the time required for the Earth to rotate once relative to the distant stars

mean solar day (on Earth) — 24 h 3 min 56.55 sec of mean sideral time
the interval between two successive passages of the Sun across the same meridian is a solar day; in practice, since the rate of the Sun's motion varies with the seasons, use is made of a fictitious Sun that always moves across the sky at an even rate

tropical (or solar) year (on Earth) — 365.242 days
the time required for the Earth's orbital motion to return the Sun's position to the spring equinoctial point

sidereal year (on Earth) — 365.256 days
the time required for the Earth in its orbit to return to the longitude of a distant star

synodic month (on Earth) — 29.53 days
the time required for the Moon to pass through one complete cycle of phases

sidereal month (on Earth) — 27.32 days
the time required for the Moon to return to the same place in relation to distant stars

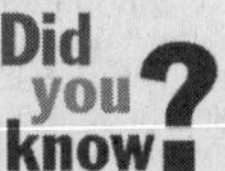

The speed of steamboats increased dramatically over the years; the run from New Orleans to Louisville KY, which took 25 days in 1816, required only 4 days by 1853. The average life span of a steamboat was only four to five years because of poor construction and maintenance, exploding boilers, and sinkings due to river construction. Spontaneous races were common and contributed greatly to the approximately 4,000 deaths in steamboat disasters between 1810 and 1850.

Definitions of Astronomical Positions

A **conjunction** is an apparent meeting or passing of two or more celestial bodies. For example, the Moon is in conjunction with the Sun at the phase of new Moon, when it moves between the Earth and Sun and the side turned toward the Earth is dark. Inferior planets—those with orbits smaller than the Earth's (namely, Venus and Mercury)—have two kinds of conjunctions with the Sun. An **inferior conjunction** occurs when the planet passes approximately between Earth and Sun; if it passes exactly between them, moving across the Sun's face as seen from Earth, it is said to be in transit (*see below*). A **superior conjunction** occurs when Earth and the other planet are on opposite sides of the Sun, but all three bodies are again nearly in a straight line. Superior planets, those having orbits larger than the Earth's can have only superior conjunctions with the Sun.

When celestial bodies appear in opposite directions in the sky they are said to be in **opposition**. The Moon, when full, is said to be in opposition to the Sun (the Earth is then approximately between them). A superior planet (one with an orbit farther from the Sun than Earth's) is in opposition when Earth passes between it and the Sun. The opposition of a planet is a good time to observe it, because the planet is then at its nearest point to the Earth and in its full phase. The inferior planets, Venus and Mercury, can never be in opposition to the Sun.

When a celestial body as seen from the Earth makes a right angle with the direction of the Sun it is said to be in **quadrature**. The Moon at first or last quarter is said to be at east or west quadrature, respectively. A superior planet is at west quadrature when its position is 90° west of the Sun.

The east-west coordinate by which the position of a celestial body is ordinarily measured is known as the **right ascension.** Right ascension in combination with **declination** defines the position of a celestial object. Declination is the angular distance of a body north or south of the celestial equator. North declination is considered positive and south, negative. Thus, +90° declination marks the north celestial pole, 0° the celestial equator, and –90° the south celestial pole. The symbol for right ascension is the Greek letter α (alpha) and for declination the lowercase Greek letter Δ (delta).

The angular distance in celestial longitude separating the Moon or a planet from the Sun is known as **elongation**. The greatest elongation possible for the two inferior planets is about 48° in the case of Venus and about 28° in that of Mercury. Elongation may also refer to the angular distance of any celestial body from another around which it revolves or from a particular point in the sky; e.g., the extreme east or west position of a star with reference to the north celestial pole.

The point at which a planet is closest to the Sun is called the **perihelion**, and the most distant point in that planet's orbit is the **aphelion**. The term helion refers specifically to the Sun as the primary body about which the planet is orbiting.

Occultation refers to the obscuring of the light of an astronomical body, most commonly a star, by another astronomical body, such as a planet or a satellite. Hence, a solar eclipse is the occultation of the Sun by the Moon. From occultations of stars by planets, asteroids, and satellites, astronomers are able to determine the precise sizes and shapes of the latter bodies in addition to the temperatures of planetary atmospheres. For example, astronomers unexpectedly discovered the rings of Uranus during a stellar occultation on 10 Mar 1977.

A complete or partial obscuring of a celestial body by another is an **eclipse**; these occur when three celestial objects become aligned. The Sun is eclipsed when the Moon comes between it and the Earth; the Moon is eclipsed when it moves into the shadow of the Earth cast by the Sun. Eclipses of natural or artificial satellites of a planet occur as the satellites move into the planet's shadow. When the apparent size of the eclipsed body is much smaller than that of the eclipsing body, the phenomenon is known as an **occultation** (*see above*). Examples are the disappearance of a star, nebula, or planet behind the Moon, or the vanishing of a natural satellite or space probe behind some body of the solar system. A **transit** (*see above*) occurs when, as viewed from the Earth, a relatively small body passes across the disk of a larger body, usually the Sun or a planet, eclipsing only a very small area: Mercury and Venus periodically transit the Sun, and a satellite may transit its planet.

When an object orbiting the Earth is at the point in its orbit that is the greatest distance from the center of the Earth, this point is known as **apogee**; the term is also used to describe the point farthest from a planet or a satellite (as the Moon) reached by an object orbiting it. **Perigee** is the opposite of apogee.

The difference in direction of a celestial object as seen by an observer from two widely separated points is termed **parallax**. The measurement of parallax is used directly to find the distance of the body from the Earth (geocentric parallax) and from the Sun (heliocentric parallax). The two positions of the observer and the position of the object form a triangle; if the base line between the two observing points is known and the direction of the object as seen from each has been measured, the apex angle (the parallax) and the distance of the object from the observer can be determined.

An **hour angle** is the angle between an observer's meridian (a great circle passing over his head and through the celestial poles) and the hour circle (any other great circle passing through the poles) on which some celestial body lies. This angle, when expressed in hours and minutes, is the time elapsed since the celestial body's last transit of the observer's meridian. The hour angle can also be expressed in degrees, 15° of arc being equal to one hour.

Constellations

Constellations are certain groupings of stars that were imagined—at least by those who named them—to form conspicuous configurations of objects or creatures in the sky. Constellations are useful in tracking artificial satellites and in assisting astronomers and navigators to locate certain stars.

From the earliest times the star groups known as constellations, the smaller groups (parts of constellations) known as **asterisms**, and, also, **individual stars** have received names connoting some meteorological phenomena or symbolizing religious or mythological beliefs. At one time it was held that the constellation

Constellations (continued)

names and myths were of Greek origin; this view has now been disproved. It is now thought that the Greek constellation system and the cognate legends are primarily of Semitic or even pre-Semitic origin and that they came to the Greeks through the Phoenicians.

The Alexandrian astronomer **Ptolemy** lists the names and orientation of the 48 constellations in his *Almagest,* and, with but few exceptions, they are identical with those used at the present time. The majority of the remaining 40 constellations that are now accepted were added by European astronomers in the 17th and 18th centuries. In the 20th century the delineation of precise boundaries for all the 88 constellations was undertaken by a committee of the International Astronomical Union. By 1930 it was possible to assign any star to a constellation.

NAME	GENITIVE	MEANING	NOTES
Constellations described by Ptolemy: the zodiac			(First-magnitude stars are given in italics in this column)
Aries	Arietis	Ram	
Taurus	Tauri	Bull	*Aldebaran* is the constellation's brightest star. Taurus also contains the Pleiades star cluster and the Crab Nebula.
Gemini	Geminorum	Twins	The brightest stars in Gemini are Castor and *Pollux.*
Cancer	Cancri	Crab	Cancer contains the well-known star cluster Praesepe.
Leo	Leonis	Lion	*Regulus* is the brightest star in Leo.
Virgo	Virginis	Virgin	*Spica* is the brightest star in Virgo.
Libra	Librae	Balance	
Scorpius	Scorpii	Scorpion	*Antares* is the brightest star of Scorpius, which also contains many star clusters.
Sagittarius	Sagittarii	Archer	The center of the Milky Way Galaxy lies in Sagittarius, with the densest star clouds of the galaxy.
Capricornus	Capricorni	Sea-goat	
Aquarius	Aquarii	Water-bearer	
Pisces	Piscium	Fishes	
Other Ptolemaic constellations			
Andromeda	Andromedae	Andromeda (an Ethiopian princess of Greek legend, daughter of Cepheus and Cassiopeia)	The constellation's most notable feature is the great spiral galaxy Andromeda (also called M31).
Aquila	Aquilae	Eagle	The brightest star in Aquila is *Altair.*
Ara	Arae	Altar	
Argo Navis	Argus Navis	the ship *Argo*	Argo Navis is now divided into smaller constellations that include Carina, Puppis, Pyxis, and Vela.
Auriga	Aurigae	Charioteer	The brightest star in Auriga is *Capella.* The constellation also contains open star clusters M36, M37, and M38.
Boötes	Boötis	Herdsman	*Arcturus* is the brightest star in Boötes.
Canis Major	Canis Majoris	Greater Dog	*Sirius* is the brightest star in Canis Major.
Canis Minor	Canis Minoris	Smaller Dog	*Procyon* is the brightest star in Canis Minor.
Cassiopeia	Cassiopeiae	Cassiopeia was a legendary queen of Ethiopia	Tycho's nova, one of the few recorded supernovae in the Galaxy, appeared in Cassiopeia in 1572.
Centaurus	Centauri	Centaur (possibly represents Chiron)	*Alpha Centauri* in Centaurus contains Proxima, the nearest star to the Sun.
Cepheus	Cephei	Cepheus (legendary king of Ethiopia)	Delta Cephei was the prototype for cepheid variables (a class of variable stars).
Cetus	Ceti	Whale	Mira Ceti was the first recognized variable star.
Corona Austrina	Coronae Austrinae	Southern Crown	
Corona Borealis	Coronae Borealis	Northern Crown	
Corvus	Corvi	Raven	
Crater	Crateris	Cup	
Cygnus	Cygni	Swan	Cygnus contains the asterism (grouping of stars) known as the Northern Cross; the constellation's brightest star is *Deneb.*
Delphinus	Delphini	Dolphin	Delphinus contains the asterism known as Job's Coffin.
Draco	Draconis	Dragon	Draco contains the star Thuban, which was the polestar in 3000 BC.

Constellations (continued)

NAME	GENITIVE	MEANING	NOTES
Other Ptolemaic constellations (continued)			
Equuleus	Equulei	Little Horse	
Eridanus	Eridani	River Eridanus or river god	*Achernar* is the brightest star in Eridanus.
Hercules	Herculis	Hercules (Greek hero)	Hercules contains the great globular star cluster M13.
Hydra	Hydrae	Water Snake	
Lepus	Leporis	Hare	
Lupus	Lupi	Wolf	
Lyra	Lyrae	Lyre	The brightest star in Lyra is *Vega*. In some 10,000 years, *Vega* will become the polestar. Lyra also contains the Ring Nebula (M57).
Ophiuchus	Ophiuchi	Serpent-bearer	When the Zodiac was conceived of, Ophiuchus was not in the Sun's path, but the Sun does now pass through Ophiuchus each December.
Orion	Orionis	Hunter	*Rigel* is the brightest star in Orion, followed closely by *Betelgeuse;* M42 (the Great Nebula) resides in Orion.
Pegasus	Pegasi	Pegasus (winged horse)	The constellation contains stars of the Great Square of Pegasus.
Perseus	Persei	Perseus (legendary Greek hero)	
Piscis Austrinus	Piscis Austrini	Southern Fish	The brightest star in Piscis Austrinus is *Fomalhaut*.
Sagitta	Sagittae	Arrow	
Serpens	Serpentis	Serpent	
Triangulum	Trianguli	Triangle	The constellation contains M33, a nearby spiral galaxy.
Ursa Major	Ursae Majoris	Great Bear	The seven brightest stars of this constellation are the Big Dipper (also called the Plough).
Ursa Minor	Ursae Minoris	Lesser Bear	Ursa Minor contains Polaris (the north polestar).
Southern constellations, added c. 1600			
Apus	Apodis	Bird of Paradise	
Chamaeleon	Chamaeleontis	Chameleon	
Dorado	Doradus	Swordfish	The most notable object in Dorado is the Large Magellanic Cloud.
Grus	Gruis	Crane	
Hydrus	Hydri	Water Snake	
Indus	Indi	Indian	
Musca	Muscae	Fly	
Pavo	Pavonis	Peacock	
Phoenix	Phoenicis	Phoenix (mythical bird)	
Triangulum Australe	Trianguli Australis	Southern Triangle	
Tucana	Tucanae	Toucan	The most notable object in Tucana is the Small Magellanic Cloud.
Volans	Volantis	Flying Fish	
Constellations of Bartsch, 1624			
Camelopardalis	Camelopardalis	Giraffe	
Columba	Columbae	Dove	The constellation was formed by Petrus Plancius in the early 1600s.
Monoceros	Monocerotis	Unicorn	
Constellations of Hevelius, 1687			
Canes Venatici	Canum Venaticorum	Hunting Dogs	The constellation contains M51 (the Whirlpool Galaxy).
Lacerta	Lacertae	Lizard	
Leo Minor	Leonis Minoris	Lesser Lion	
Lynx	Lyncis	Lynx	
Scutum	Scuti	Shield	Scutum contains the Scutim star cloud in the Milky Way.
Sextans	Sextantis	Sextant	
Vulpecula	Vulpeculae	Fox	Vulpecula contains M27 (the Dumbbell Nebula).

Constellations (continued)

NAME	GENITIVE	MEANING	NOTES
Ancient asterisms that are now separate constellations			
Carina	Carinae	Keel [of the legendary ship the *Argo*]	The brightest star in Carina is *Canopus*.
Coma Berenices	Comae Berenices	Berenice's Hair	The constellation contains both a coma (star cluster) and the north galactic pole (a point that lies perpendicular to the Milky Way).
Crux	Crucis	[Southern] Cross	
Puppis	Puppis	Stern [of the *Argo*]	
Pyxis	Pyxidis	Compass [of the *Argo*]	
Vela	Velorum	Sails [of the *Argo*]	
Southern constellations of Lacaille, c. 1750			
Antlia	Antliae	Pump	
Caelum	Caeli	[Sculptor's] Chisel	
Circinus	Circini	Drawing Compasses	
Fornax	Fornacis	[Chemical] Furnace	
Horologium	Horologii	Clock	
Mensa	Mensae	Table [Mountain]	
Microscopium	Microscopii	Microscope	
Norma	Normae	Square	
Octans	Octantis	Octant	Octans contains the south celestial pole.
Pictor	Pictoris	Painter's [Easel]	
Reticulum	Reticuli	Reticle	
Sculptor	Sculptoris	Sculptor's [Workshop]	Sculptor contains the south galactic pole.
Telescopium	Telescopii	Telescope	

Astrology: The Zodiac

Signs of the zodiac are popularly used for divination as well as for designation of constellations.

NAME	SYMBOL	DATES	SEX/NATURE	TRIPLICITY	HOUSE	EXALTATION
Aries the Ram	♈	21 Mar–19 Apr	masculine/moving	fire	Mars	Sun (19°)
Taurus the Bull	♉	20 Apr–20 May	feminine/fixed	earth	Venus	Moon (3°)
Gemini the Twins	♊	21 May–21 Jun	masculine/common	air	Mercury	
Cancer the Crab	♋	22 Jun–22 Jul	feminine/moving	water	Moon	Jupiter (15°)
Leo the Lion	♌	23 Jul–22 Aug	masculine/fixed	fire	Sun	
Virgo the Virgin	♍	23 Aug–22 Sep	feminine/common	earth	Mercury	Mercury (15°)
Libra the Balance	♎	23 Sep–23 Oct	masculine/moving	air	Venus	Saturn (21°)
Scorpius the Scorpion	♏	24 Oct–21 Nov	feminine/fixed	water	Mars	
Sagittarius the Archer	♐	22 Nov–21 Dec	masculine/common	fire	Jupiter	
Capricorn the Goat	♑	22 Dec–19 Jan	feminine/moving	earth	Saturn	Mars (28°)
Aquarius the Water Bearer	♒	20 Jan–18 Feb	masculine/fixed	air	Saturn	
Pisces the Fish	♓	19 Feb–20 Mar	feminine/common	water	Jupiter	Venus (27°)

Classification of Stars

The spectral sequence O–M represents stars of essentially the same chemical composition but of different temperatures and atmospheric pressures. Stars belonging to other, more rare types of spectral classifications differ in chemical composition from those stars classified under the O–M scheme.

Each spectral class is additionally subdivided into 10 spectral types. For example, spectral class A is subdivided into spectral types A0–A9 with 0 being the hottest and 9 the coolest. (Spectral class O is unusual in that it is subdivided into O4–O9.) Between two stars of the same spectral type, the more luminous star will also be larger in diameter. Thus the Yerkes system of luminosity also tells something of a star's radius, with Ia being the largest and V the smallest. Approximately 90% of all stars are main-sequence, or type V, stars.

Based upon these systems, the Sun would be a G2 V star (a yellow, relatively hot dwarf star).

SPECTRAL CLASS	COLOR	APPROXIMATE SURFACE TEMP (°C)	EXAMPLES
O	blue	30,000 or greater	these stars are relatively rare
B	blue-white	20,000 to 30,000	Rigel, Alpha Crucis, Beta Crucis
A	white	10,000 to 20,000	Sirius, Vega, Fomalhaut
F	yellow-white	7,000 to 10,000	Canopus, Procyon

Classification of Stars (continued)

SPECTRAL CLASS	COLOR	APPROXIMATE SURFACE TEMP (°C)	EXAMPLES
G	yellow	6,000 to 7,000	Sun
K	orange	4,500 to 6,000	Arcturus, Aldebaran
M	red	3,000 to 4,500	Betelgeuse, Antares

LUMINOSITY CLASSES (BASED UPON THE YERKES SYSTEM)	
Ia	most luminous supergiants
Ib	luminous supergiants
II	bright giants
III	normal giants
IV	subgiants
V	main-sequence stars (dwarfs)

The 20 Brightest Stars in the Night Sky

This table lists the stars in descending order from brightest to least bright, based on apparent visual magnitude. Formal names of stars, such as Alpha Carinae, refer to the constellation in which the star appears (Carina) and to which star appears the brightest in that constellation; the second highest would be designated Beta, etc. Some anomalies exist within the naming convention: Betelgeuse, for example, is the Alpha star of Orion, though Rigel appears brighter.

On the scale of brightness, negative magnitudes are brightest, and one magnitude difference corresponds to a difference in brightness of 2.5 times; e.g., a star of magnitude −1 is 10 times brighter than one of magnitude +1.5.

Apparent magnitude is a measure of how bright a star appears to a viewer on Earth. Absolute magnitude, another designation used by astronomers, represents the brightness one would perceive if all stars were located 10 parsecs (about 32.6 light-years; one light-year equals about 9.46×10^{12} km) from Earth. The Sun, for purposes of comparison with the stars in the table, has an apparent magnitude of −26.8; it is a yellow dwarf star that is 8.3 light-minutes (one light-minute equals about 18 million km) from Earth.

STAR	APPARENT VISUAL MAGNITUDE	DISTANCE FROM THE SOLAR SYSTEM (LIGHT-YEARS)	CONSTELLATION
Sirius (Alpha Canis Majoris, or Dog Star)	−1.44	8.6	Canis Major

Sirius is a blue-white dwarf with a white-dwarf companion; among the ancient Romans, the hottest part of the year was associated with the time in which the Dog Star rose just before dawn; this connection survives in the expression "dog days."

STAR	APPARENT VISUAL MAGNITUDE	DISTANCE FROM THE SOLAR SYSTEM (LIGHT-YEARS)	CONSTELLATION
Canopus (Alpha Carinae)	−0.73 (reported values vary)	312.0 (reported values vary)	Carina

A yellow-white supergiant, Canopus is sometimes used as a guide in the attitude control of spacecraft because of its angular distance from the Sun and the contrast of its brightness among nearby celestial objects.

STAR	APPARENT VISUAL MAGNITUDE	DISTANCE FROM THE SOLAR SYSTEM (LIGHT-YEARS)	CONSTELLATION
Arcturus (Alpha Boötis)	−0.05	36.7	Boötes

An orange-colored giant, Arcturus lies in an almost direct line with the tail of Ursa Major (the Great Bear), hence its name, derived from the Greek words for "bear guard."

STAR	APPARENT VISUAL MAGNITUDE	DISTANCE FROM THE SOLAR SYSTEM (LIGHT-YEARS)	CONSTELLATION
Alpha Centauri (Rigel Kentaurus)	0.00	4.4	Centaurus

Alpha Centauri is a triple star—a binary yellow dwarf circled by a red dwarf with a much smaller red dwarf; the faintest of Alpha Centauri's three stars, Proxima, is the star closest to the Sun.

STAR	APPARENT VISUAL MAGNITUDE	DISTANCE FROM THE SOLAR SYSTEM (LIGHT-YEARS)	CONSTELLATION
Vega (Alpha Lyrae)	+0.03	25.3	Lyra

A blue dwarf, Vega will become the northern polestar by about AD 14,000 because of the precession of the equinoxes.

STAR	APPARENT VISUAL MAGNITUDE	DISTANCE FROM THE SOLAR SYSTEM (LIGHT-YEARS)	CONSTELLATION
Capella (Alpha Aurigae)	+0.08	42.2	Auriga

Capella is actually four stars, two yellow giants and two red-dwarf companion stars. Scientists are studying Capella to determine why it emits more X-rays than other stars of its type.

STAR	APPARENT VISUAL MAGNITUDE	DISTANCE FROM THE SOLAR SYSTEM (LIGHT-YEARS)	CONSTELLATION
Rigel (Beta Orionis)	+0.18 (reported values vary)	773.0	Orion

Rigel is a blue-white supergiant with two smaller companion stars. The name Rigel derives from an Arabic term meaning "the left leg of the giant," referring to the figure of Orion.

The 20 Brightest Stars in the Night Sky (continued)

STAR	APPARENT VISUAL MAGNITUDE	DISTANCE FROM THE SOLAR SYSTEM (LIGHT-YEARS)	CONSTELLATION
Procyon (Alpha Canis Minoris)	+0.40	11.4	Canis Minor
Procyon is a yellow-white subgiant with a faint white-dwarf companion. The name Procyon apparently derives from Greek words for "before the dog," as in northern latitudes the star rises just before Sirius, the Dog Star.			
Achernar (Alpha Eridani)	+0.45	144.0	Eridanus
Achernar is a blue dwarf. The name Achernar probably derives from an Arabic phrase meaning "the end of the river," in which the river referred to is the constellation.			
Betelgeuse (Alpha Orionis)	+0.45 (reported values vary)	427.0	Orion
A red supergiant, Betelgeuse has a diameter that varies between 430 and 625 times the diameter of the Sun over a period of 5.8 years.			
Beta Centauri (Hadar)	+0.58	526.0	Centaurus
Beta Centauri is a blue-white supergiant with two smaller companion stars; the constellation Centaurus most likely is meant to represent the centaur Chiron. In Greek mythology Chiron was renowned for his wisdom and knowledge of medicine. He renounced his immortality to escape a painful wound, and Zeus placed him in the Southern sky.			
Altair (Alpha Aquilae)	+0.76	16.8	Aquila
A blue dwarf, Altair spins nearly 760,000 km/h (470,000 mph), as compared with Earth, which spins some 1,600 km/h (1,000 mph). This rapid spinning flattens Altair from a spherical into an oblate shape.			
Aldebaran (Alpha Tauri)	+0.87	65.1	Taurus
A red giant, Aldebaran has a name derived from the Arabic for "the follower," perhaps because it rises after the Pleiades cluster of stars.			
Spica (Alpha Virginis)	+0.98	262.0	Virgo
A binary blue-white dwarf with a nonvisible companion, Spica has a name derived from the Latin for "ear of wheat"; the star is said to represent the wheat being held by the Virgin/fertility goddess (for whom Virgo is named).			
Antares (Alpha Scorpii)	+1.06 (reported values vary)	604.0	Scorpio
Antares is a red supergiant. The name Antares seems to come from a Greek phrase meaning "rival of Ares" (i.e., rival of the planet Mars) and was probably given because of the star's color and brightness.			
Pollux (Beta Geminorum)	+1.16	96.7	Gemini
A red giant, Pollux is named for one of the twins of ancient Greek mythology (the other is Castor).			
Fomalhaut (Alpha Piscis Austrini)	+1.17	25.1	Piscis Austrinus
The blue-white dwarf Formalhaut's name is derived from the Arabic for "mouth of the fish."			
Becrux (Beta Crucis, or Mimosa)	+1.25	352.0	Crux (The Southern Cross)
A blue-white giant, Becrux forms the eastern tip of the Southern Cross.			
Deneb (Alpha Cygni)	+1.25	3,230.0	Cygnus
A blue-white supergiant, Deneb gained its name from an Arabic word meaning "tail," as it is considered the tail of the swan Cygnus.			
Acrux (Alpha Crucis)	+1.40	321.0	Crux (The Southern Cross)
Acrux is a double star that stands at the foot of the Southern Cross.			

**Data for apparent visual magnitudes taken from* Encyclopædia Britannica Online.

Astronomical Phenomena for 2009

Source: The Astronomical Almanac 2009.

MONTH	DAY	HOUR (GMT)	EVENT
January	1	20	Saturn stationary
	2	17	Uranus 5° S of Moon
	4	12	first quarter
	4	14	Mercury greatest elongation E (19°)
	4	15	Earth at perihelion
	10	11	Moon at perigee
	11	03	full moon
	11	07	Mercury stationary
	14	21	Venus greatest elongation E (47°)
	15	12	Saturn 6° N of Moon
	17	18	Ceres stationary
	18	03	last quarter
	18	22	Juno in conjunction with Sun
	20	16	Mercury in inferior conjunction
	21	13	Antares 0°02 S of Moon[1]
	21	13	Pallas stationary
	23	00	Moon at apogee
	23	16	Venus 1°4 N of Uranus
	24	06	Jupiter in conjunction with Sun
	26	08	new moon[2]
	27	18	Neptune 1°8 S of Moon
	30	01	Uranus 5° S of Moon
	30	12	Venus 3° S of Moon
February	1	02	Mercury stationary
	2	23	first quarter
	7	20	Moon at perigee
	9	15	full moon[3]
	11	20	Saturn 6° N of Moon
	12	13	Neptune in conjunction with Sun
	13	21	Mercury greatest elongation W (26°)
	16	22	last quarter
	17	10	Mars 0°6 S of Jupiter
	17	21	Antares 0°04 S of Moon[1]
	19	15	Venus greatest illuminated extent
	19	17	Moon at apogee
	22	22	Mercury 1°1 S of Moon[1]
	23	01	Jupiter 0°7 N of Moon[1]
	23	08	Mars 1°7 S of Moon
	24	03	Mercury 0°6 S of Jupiter
	25	02	new moon
	25	14	Ceres at opposition
	27	23	Venus 1°3 N of Moon[1]
March	1	20	Mercury 0°6 S of Mars
	4	08	first quarter
	5	01	Venus stationary
	7	15	Moon at perigee
	8	04	Mars 0°8 S of Neptune
	8	20	Saturn at opposition
	11	03	full moon
	11	03	Saturn 6° N of Moon
	13	01	Uranus in conjunction with Sun
	17	05	Antares 0°2 S of Moon[1]
	18	18	last quarter
	19	13	Moon at apogee
March	20	12	equinox
(continued)	22	21	Jupiter 1°5 S of Moon
	23	14	Neptune 2° S of Moon
	24	14	Mars 4° S of Moon
	26	16	new moon
	27	19	Venus in inferior conjunction
	31	03	Mercury in superior conjunction
April	2	02	Moon at perigee
	2	15	first quarter
	4	16	Pluto stationary
	7	07	Saturn 6° N of Moon
	9	15	full moon
	13	13	Antares 0°4 S of Moon[1]
	15	04	Mars 0°5 S of Uranus
	15	08	Venus stationary
	16	09	Moon at apogee
	17	14	last quarter
	17	15	Ceres stationary
	18	17	Venus 6° N of Mars
	19	16	Jupiter 2° S of Moon
	20	00	Neptune 2° S of Moon
	22	08	Uranus 5° S of Moon
	22	14	Venus 1°1 S of Moon[1]
	22	19	Mars 6° S of Moon
	25	03	new moon
	26	08	Mercury greatest elongation E (20°)
	26	16	Mercury 1°9 S of Moon
	28	06	Moon at perigee
May	1	21	first quarter
	2	15	Venus greatest illuminated extent
	4	11	Saturn 6° N of Moon
	7	16	Mercury stationary
	9	04	full moon
	10	21	Antares 0°6 S of Moon[1]
	14	03	Moon at apogee
	17	07	last quarter
	17	08	Jupiter 3° S of Moon
	17	09	Neptune 3° S of Moon
	17	19	Saturn stationary
	18	10	Mercury in inferior conjunction
	19	20	Uranus 5° S of Moon
	21	08	Venus 7° S of Moon
	21	20	Mars 7° S of Moon
	24	12	new moon
	25	13	Jupiter 0°4 S of Neptune
	26	04	Moon at perigee
	29	11	Neptune stationary
	30	16	Mercury stationary
	31	03	first quarter
	31	17	Saturn 6° N of Moon
June	5	21	Venus greatest elongation W (46°)
	7	04	Antares 0°6 S of Moon[1]
	7	18	full moon
	10	16	Moon at apogee
	13	12	Mercury greatest elongation W (23°)
	13	16	Neptune 3° S of Moon

Astronomical Phenomena for 2009 (continued)

MONTH	DAY	HOUR (GMT)	EVENT
June (continued)	13	18	Jupiter 3° S of Moon
	15	20	Jupiter stationary
	15	22	last quarter
	15	23	Juno 0°4 N of Moon[1]
	16	06	Uranus 6° S of Moon
	19	14	Venus 2° S of Mars
	19	17	Mars 6° S of Moon
	19	17	Venus 8° S of Moon
	21	06	solstice
	21	09	Mercury 7° S of Moon
	22	12	Vesta in conjunction with Sun
	22	14	Mercury 3° N of Aldebaran
	22	20	new moon
	23	08	Pluto at opposition
	23	11	Moon at perigee
	28	02	Saturn 7° N of Moon
	29	11	first quarter
July	1	16	Uranus stationary
	4	02	Earth at aphelion
	4	10	Antares 0°5 S of Moon[1]
	7	09	full moon[3]
	7	22	Moon at apogee
	10	22	Jupiter 4° S of Moon
	10	22	Neptune 3° S of Moon
	13	12	Uranus 6° S of Moon
	13	19	Jupiter 0°6 S of Neptune
	14	02	Mercury in superior conjunction
	14	18	Venus 3° N of Aldebaran
	15	10	last quarter
	18	12	Mars 5° S of Moon
	19	05	Venus 6° S of Moon
	21	20	Moon at perigee
	22	03	new moon[2]
	25	15	Saturn 7° N of Moon
	27	11	Mars 5° N of Aldebaran
	28	22	first quarter
	31	16	Antares 0°5 S of Moon[1]
August	2	19	Mercury 0°6 N of Regulus
	4	01	Moon at apogee
	6	01	full moon[3]
	6	22	Jupiter 3° S of Moon
	7	02	Neptune 3° S of Moon
	9	17	Uranus 6° S of Moon
	13	19	last quarter
	14	18	Jupiter at opposition
	15	18	Juno stationary
	16	03	Mars 3° S of Moon
	17	21	Neptune at opposition
	17	21	Venus 1°7 S of Moon
	18	07	Vesta 0°4 S of Moon[1]
	18	21	Mercury 3° S of Saturn
	19	05	Moon at perigee
	20	10	new moon
	22	04	Venus 7° S of Pollux
	22	06	Saturn 7° N of Moon
	22	12	Mercury 3° N of Moon
	24	16	Mercury greatest elongation E (27°)
	27	12	first quarter
	27	22	Antares 0°6 S of Moon[1]
	31	11	Moon at apogee
September	2	21	Jupiter 3° S of Moon
	3	07	Neptune 3° S of Moon
	4	16	full moon
	5	21	Uranus 6° S of Moon
	6	20	Mercury stationary
	11	16	Pluto stationary
	12	02	last quarter
	13	00	Pallas in conjunction with Sun
	13	16	Mars 1°1 S of Moon[1]
	16	08	Moon at perigee
	16	18	Venus 3° N of Moon
	17	10	Uranus at opposition
	17	18	Saturn in conjunction with Sun
	18	19	new moon
	20	10	Mercury in inferior conjunction
	20	10	Venus 0°5 N of Regulus
	21	08	Juno at opposition
	22	21	equinox
	24	06	Antares 0°8 S of Moon[1]
	26	05	first quarter
	28	04	Moon at apogee
	28	18	Mercury stationary
	30	00	Jupiter 3° S of Moon
	30	13	Neptune 3° S of Moon
October	3	02	Uranus 6° S of Moon
	4	06	full moon
	5	22	Mars 6° S of Pollux
	6	02	Mercury greatest elongation W (18°)
	8	09	Mercury 0°3 S of Saturn
	11	09	last quarter
	12	01	Mars 1°2 N of Moon[1]
	13	09	Jupiter stationary
	13	12	Moon at perigee
	13	16	Venus 0°6 S of Saturn
	16	13	Saturn 7° N of Moon
	16	19	Venus 7° N of Moon
	18	06	new moon
	21	15	Antares 1°0 S of Moon[1]
	25	23	Moon at apogee
	26	01	first quarter
	27	09	Jupiter 3° S of Moon
	27	21	Neptune 3° S of Moon
	30	09	Uranus 6° S of Moon
	31	10	Juno stationary
	31	15	Ceres in conjunction with Sun
November	2	02	Venus 4° N of Spica
	2	19	full moon
	4	19	Neptune stationary
	5	08	Mercury in superior conjunction
	7	07	Moon at perigee
	9	06	Mars 3° N of Moon
	9	16	last quarter
	13	01	Saturn 8° N of Moon
	16	19	new moon
	22	20	Moon at apogee
	23	22	Jupiter 4° S of Moon
	24	06	Neptune 3° S of Moon
	24	22	first quarter
	26	18	Uranus 6° S of Moon

Astronomical Phenomena for 2009 (continued)

MONTH	DAY	HOUR (GMT)	EVENT
December	2	05	Uranus stationary
	2	08	full moon
	4	14	Moon at perigee
	7	03	Mars 6° N of Moon
	9	00	last quarter
	10	11	Saturn 8° N of Moon
	16	12	new moon
	18	08	Mercury 1°.4 S of Moon
	18	17	Mercury greatest elongation E (20°)
	20	05	Jupiter 0°.6 S of Neptune
December (continued)	20	15	Moon at apogee
	21	15	Jupiter 4° S of Moon
	21	15	Neptune 4° S of Moon
	21	16	Mars stationary
	21	18	solstice
	24	02	Uranus 6° S of Moon
	24	18	first quarter
	24	18	Pluto in conjunction with Sun
	26	09	Mercury stationary
	31	19	full moon[2]

[1]*Occultation.* [2]*Eclipse.* [3]*Penumbral eclipse.*

Uranus was the first planet to be discovered with a telescope. The German-born astronomer William Herschel accidentally discovered the planet in 1781 during a routine sky survey at his observatory in Bath, England. At first he thought it was a comet. When astronomers concluded that the object was really a planet, the German astronomer J.E. Bode suggested that it be called Uranus, in honor of the ancient sky god who was the father of Saturn in Greco-Roman mythology.

Morning and Evening Stars

This table gives the morning and evening stars for autumn 2008 through 2009. The morning and evening stars are actually planets visible to the naked eye during the early morning and at evening twilight.

PLANET	MORNING STAR	EVENING STAR
Mercury	14 Oct–10 Nov 2008; 27 Jan–22 Mar, 28 May–6 Jul, 28 Sep–23 Oct 2009	8 Aug–30 Sep, 13–31 Dec 2008; 1–15 Jan, 9 Apr–9 May, 22 Jul– 14 Sep, 22 Nov–30 Dec 2009
Venus	1 Apr–1 Dec 2009	16 Jul–31 Dec 2008; 1 Jan–24 Mar 2009
Mars	1 Feb–31 Dec 2009	1 Jan–16 Oct 2008
Jupiter	7 Feb–14 Aug 2009	9 Jul–31 Dec 2008; 1–11 Jan, 14 Aug–31 Dec 2009
Saturn	22 Sep–31 Dec 2008; 1 Jan–8 Mar, 6 Oct–31 Dec 2009	24 Feb–17 Aug 2008; 8 Mar–31 Aug 2009
Uranus	late March–September 2008; early April–mid-December 2009	late December 2008–mid-February 2009, mid-December 2009
Neptune	early March–August 2008; early March–mid-November 2009	mid-November–31 Dec 2008; January 2009 mid-November–31 Dec 2009

Meteors, Meteorites, and Meteor Showers

A meteor (also called a **shooting star** or **falling star**) is a streak of light in the sky that results when a particle or small chunk of stony or metallic matter enters the Earth's atmosphere and vaporizes. The term is sometimes applied to the falling object itself, but the latter is properly called a **meteoroid.** The vast majority of meteoroids burn up in the upper atmosphere, but occasionally one of relatively large mass survives its fiery plunge and reaches the surface as a solid body. Such an object is known as a **meteorite.**

On any clear night in the countryside beyond the bright lights of cities, one can observe with the naked eye several meteors per hour as they streak through the sky. Quite often they vary in brightness along the path of their flight, appear to emit "sparks" or flares, and sometimes leave a luminous train that lingers after their flight has ended. These meteors are the result of the high-velocity collision of meteoroids with the Earth's atmosphere. Nearly all such interplanetary bodies are small fragments derived from comets or asteroids.

The brightest meteor (possibly of cometary origin) for which historical documentation exists—called the **Tunguska event**—struck on 30 Jun 1908 in central Siberia and rivaled the Sun in brightness. The energy delivered to the atmosphere by this impact was roughly equivalent to that of a 10-megaton thermonuclear explosion and caused the destruction of forest over an area of about 2,000 sq km (772.2 sq mi). The geologic record of cratering attests to the impact of much more massive meteoroids. Fortunately, impacts of this magnitude occur only once or twice every 100 million years. It is hypothesized that large impacts of this kind may have played a major role in determining the course of biological evolution by causing simultaneous **mass extinctions** of many species of organisms, possibly including the dinosaurs some 65 million years ago. If so, the replacement of reptiles by mammals as the dominant land animals, the eventual consequence of which was the rise of the human species, would be the result of a grand example of a phenomenon observable every clear night.

The **visibility of meteors** is a consequence of the high velocity of meteoroids in interplanetary space. Before entering the region of the Earth's gravitational influence, their **velocities** range from a few kilometers per second up to as high as 72 km (44.7 mi) per second. As they approach the Earth, the Earth's gravitational field accelerates them to even higher velocities. This great release of energy destroys meteoroids of small mass—particularly those with relatively high velocities—very quickly. Numerous meteors end their observed flight at altitudes above 80 km (49.7 mi), and penetration to as low as 50 km (31 mi) is unusual.

"**Showers**" of meteors have been known since ancient times. On rare occasions, these showers are very dramatic, with thousands of meteors falling per hour. More often, the background hourly rate of roughly 5 observed meteors increases up to about 10–50. Some of the best-known meteor showers are listed below, with their average date of maximum strength and associated comet, if known: **Quadrantid** (3 January); **Lyrid** (22 April; 1861 I [Thatcher]); **Eta Aquarid** (3 May; Halley); **S. Delta Aquarid** (29 July); **Capricornid** (30 July); **Perseid** (12 August; Swift-Tuttle); **Andromedid** (3 October; Biela); **Draconid** (9 October; Giacobini-Zinner); **Orionid** (21 October; Halley); **Taurid** (8 November; Encke); **Leonid** (17 November; Temple-Tuttle); **Germinid** (14 December; 3200 Phaeton [this body exhibits no cometary activity and may be of asteroidal rather than cometary origin]).

Auroras

Auroras are **luminous phenomena** of the upper atmosphere that occur primarily in high latitudes of both hemispheres; auroras in the Northern Hemisphere are called **aurora borealis**, or **northern lights**; in the Southern Hemisphere, **aurora australis**, or **southern lights.**

Auroras are caused by the interaction of energetic particles (electrons and protons) from outside the atmosphere with atoms of the upper atmosphere. Such interaction occurs in zones surrounding the Earth's magnetic poles. During periods of intense solar activity, auroras occasionally extend to the middle latitudes; for example, the aurora borealis has been seen at latitudes as far south as 40° in the US.

Auroras take many **forms,** including luminous curtains, arcs, bands, and patches. The uniform arc is the most stable form of aurora, sometimes persisting for hours without noticeable variation. In a great display, however, other forms appear, commonly undergoing dramatic variation. The lower edges of the arcs and folds are usually much more sharply defined than the upper parts. Greenish rays may cover most of the sky poleward of the magnetic zenith, ending in an arc that is usually folded and sometimes edged with a lower red border that may ripple like drapery. The display ends with a poleward retreat of the auroral forms, the rays gradually degenerating into diffuse areas of white light.

The **mechanisms** that produce auroral displays are not completely understood. It is known, however, that charged particles arriving in the vicinity of Earth as part of the solar wind are captured by the Earth's magnetic field and conducted downward toward the magnetic poles. They collide with oxygen and nitrogen atoms, knocking away electrons to leave ions in excited states. These ions emit radiation at various wavelengths, creating the characteristic colors (red or greenish blue) of the aurora.

Eclipses

An **eclipse** is a complete or partial obscuring of one celestial body by another; this event occurs when three celestial objects become aligned.

The Sun is eclipsed when the Moon comes between it and the Earth. (Hence, a **solar eclipse** can only occur during a new moon.) The Moon's shadow sweeps across the Earth, darkening the sky, while the Moon blocks out some portion of the view of the Sun. During a total eclipse of the Sun, the Moon's elliptical orbit brings the satellite closer to Earth and causes it to appear larger than the Sun. When the Moon's orbit places it at its farthest distance from Earth, the Moon appears smaller than the Sun and the eclipse will appear as a ring, or "annulus," of bright sunlight around the Moon.

A **lunar eclipse** occurs when the Moon moves into the shadow of the Earth cast by the Sun. A lunar eclipse can only occur during a full moon. Lunar eclipses can be penumbral, partial, or total. The first type is of interest to astronomers but is difficult to detect because the Moon's dimming is so slight. With the next two types either a portion of the Moon or the entire Moon passes through Earth's umbral shadow.

It is safe to watch a lunar eclipse, but solar eclipses must be viewed via a projection onto another surface or through protective filters designed specially for eclipses.

The eclipses for 2009 are given in the table below. Penumbral eclipses are not included.

	DATE	TYPE	VISIBLE IN
Solar eclipses	26 January	annular eclipse	southern Atlantic, southern Africa, Antarctica, southeastern Asia, and Australia
	21–22 July	total eclipse	southern and eastern Asia, western and central Pacific
Lunar eclipses	31 December	partial eclipse	Australia, Asia, Africa, Europe, the Arctic, northern Americas

Characteristics of Celestial Bodies

Mean orbital velocity *indicates the average speed with which a planet orbits the Sun unless otherwise specified.* ***Inclination of orbit to ecliptic*** *indicates the angle of tilt between a planet's orbit and the plane of the Earth's orbit (essentially the plane of the solar system).* ***Orbital period*** *indicates the planet's sidereal year (in Earth days except where noted).* ***Rotation period*** *indicates the planet's sidereal day (in Earth days except where noted).* ***Inclination of equator to orbit*** *indicates the angle of tilt between a planet's orbit and its equator.* ***Gravitational acceleration*** *is a measure of the body's gravitational pull on other objects.* ***Escape velocity*** *is the speed needed at the surface to escape the planet's gravitational pull.* ***Eccentricity of orbit*** *is a measure of the circularity or elongation of an orbit; 0 indicates circular orbits, and closer to 1 more elliptical ones.*

Sun
diameter (at equator): 1,390,000 km (863,705 mi)
mass (in 10^{20} kg): 19.8 billion
density (mass/volume, in kg/m^3): 1,408
mean orbital velocity: the Sun orbits the Milky Way's center at around 220 km/sec (136.7 mi/sec)
orbital period: the Sun takes approximately 250 million Earth years to complete its orbit around the Milky Way's center
rotation period: 25–36 Earth days
gravitational acceleration: 275 m/sec^2 (902.2 ft/sec^2)
escape velocity: 618.02 km/sec (384.01 mi/sec)
mean temperature at visible surface: 5,527 °C (9,980 °F)
probes and space missions: US—Pioneer 5–9, launched 1959–87; Skylab, launched 1973; Genesis, 2001; Japan—Yohkoh, 1991; US/European Space Agency (ESA)—Ulysses, 1990; SOHO, 1995.

Mercury
average distance from Sun: 58 million km (36 million mi)
diameter (at equator): 4,879 km (3,032 mi)
mass (in 10^{20} kg): 3,300
density (mass/volume, in kg/m^3): 5,427
eccentricity of orbit: 0.205
mean orbital velocity: 47.9 km/sec (29.7 mi/sec)
inclination of orbit to ecliptic: 7.0°
orbital period: 88 Earth days
rotation period: 58.6 Earth days
inclination of equator to orbit: probably 0°
gravitational acceleration: 3.7 m/sec^2 (12.1 ft/sec^2)
escape velocity: 4.3 km/sec (2.7 mi/sec)
mean temperature at surface†: 167 °C (333 °F)
satellites: none known
probes and space missions: US—Mariner 10, 1973; Messenger, 2004.

Venus
average distance from Sun: 108.2 million km (67.2 million mi)
diameter (at equator): 12,104 km (7,521 mi)
mass (in 10^{20} kg): 48,700
density (mass/volume, in kg/m^3): 5,243
eccentricity of orbit: 0.007
mean orbital velocity: 35.0 km/sec (21.8 mi/sec)
inclination of orbit to ecliptic: 3.4°
orbital period: 224.7 Earth days
rotation period: 243.0 Earth days (retrograde)
inclination of equator to orbit: 177.4°
gravitational acceleration: 8.9 m/sec^2 (29.1 ft/sec^2)
escape velocity: 10.4 km/sec (6.4 mi/sec)
mean temperature at surface†: 464 °C (867 °F)
satellites: none known
probes and space missions: USSR—Venera 1–16, 1961–83; Vega 1 and 2, 1984; US—Mariner 2, 5, and 10, 1962, 1967, and 1973; Pioneer Venus 1 and 2, 1978; Galileo, 1989; Magellan, 1989; Venus Express, 2005.

Earth
average distance from Sun: 149.6 million km (93 million mi)
diameter (at equator): 12,756 km (7,926 mi)
mass (in 10^{20} kg): 59,700
density (mass/volume, in kg/m^3): 5,515
eccentricity of orbit: 0.017
mean orbital velocity: 29.8 km/sec (18.5 mi/sec)
inclination of orbit to ecliptic: 0.00°
orbital period: 365.25 days
rotation period: 23 hours, 56 minutes, and 4 seconds of mean solar time
inclination of equator to orbit: 23.5°
gravitational acceleration: 9.8 m/sec^2 (32.1 ft/sec^2)
escape velocity: 11.2 km/sec (7.0 mi/sec)
mean temperature at surface†: 15 °C (59 °F)
satellites: 1 known—the Moon.

Moon (of Earth)
average distance from Earth: 384,401 km (238,855.7 mi)
diameter (at equator): 3,475 km (2,159 mi)
mass (in 10^{20} kg): 730
density (mass/volume, in kg/m^3): 3,340
eccentricity of orbit: orbital eccentricity of Moon around Earth is 0.055
mean orbital velocity: the Moon orbits Earth at 1.0 km/sec (0.64 mi/sec)
inclination of orbit to ecliptic: 5.1°
orbital period: the Moon revolves around the Earth in 27.32 Earth days
rotation period: the Moon rotates on its axis every 27.32 Earth days (synchronous with orbital period)
inclination of equator to orbit: 6.7°
gravitational acceleration: 1.6 m/sec^2 (5.3 ft/sec^2)
escape velocity: 2.4 km/sec (1.5 mi/sec)
mean temperature at surface†: daytime: 107 °C (224.6 °F); nighttime: −153 °C (−243.4 °F)
probes and space missions: USSR, US, ESA, Japan—collectively about 70 missions since 1959, including 9 manned missions by the US. On 20 Jul 1969 humans first set foot on the Moon, from NASA's Apollo 11.

Mars
average distance from Sun: 227.9 million km (141.6 million mi)
diameter (at equator): 6,794 km (4,222 mi)
mass (in 10^{20} kg): 6,420
density (mass/volume, in kg/m^3): 3,933
eccentricity of orbit: 0.094
mean orbital velocity: 24.1 km/sec (15 mi/sec)
inclination of orbit to ecliptic: 1.9°
orbital period: 687 Earth days (1.88 Earth years)
rotation period: 24.6 Earth hours
inclination of equator to orbit: 24.9°
gravitational acceleration: 3.7 m/sec^2 (12.1 ft/sec^2)
escape velocity: 5.0 km/sec (3.1 mi/sec)
mean temperature at surface†: −65 °C (−85 °F)
satellites: 2 known—Phobos and Deimos

probes and space missions: US—Mariner 4, 6, 7, and 9, 1964–71; Viking 1 and 2, 1975; Mars Global Surveyor, 1996; Mars Pathfinder, 1996; 2001 Mars Odyssey, 2001; Mars Exploration Rovers, 2003; USSR—Mars 2-7, 1971–73; Phobos 1 and 2, 1988; ESA—Mars Express, 2003; Mars Exploration Rovers, 2004; Phoenix, 2007.

asteroids

(several hundred thousand small rocky bodies, about 1,000 km [610 mi] or less in diameter, that orbit the Sun primarily between the orbits of Mars and Jupiter)
distance from Sun: between approximately 300 million km (190 million mi) and 600 million km (380 million mi), with notable outlyers
estimated mass: 2.3 x 10^{21} kg
probes and space missions: US—Galileo, 1989; Ulysses, 1990; NEAR Shoemaker, 1996; Deep Space 1, 1998; Stardust, 1999; US/ESA/Italy—Cassini-Huygens, 1997; ESA—Rosetta, 2004; Japan—Hayabusa, 2003.

Jupiter

average distance from Sun: 778.6 million km (483.8 million mi)
diameter (at equator): 142,984 km (88,846 mi)
mass (in 10^{20} kg): 18,990,000
density (mass/volume, in kg/m^3): 1,326
eccentricity of orbit: 0.049
mean orbital velocity: 13.1 km/sec (8.1 mi/sec)
inclination of orbit to ecliptic: 1.3°
orbital period: 11.86 Earth years
rotation period: 9.9 Earth hours
inclination of equator to orbit: 3.1°
gravitational acceleration: 23.1 m/sec^2 (75.9 ft/sec^2)
escape velocity: 59.5 km/sec (37.0 mi/sec)
mean temperature at surface†: −110 °C (−166 °F)
satellites: at least 63 moons—including Callisto, Ganymede, Europa, and Io—plus rings
probes and space missions: US—Pioneer 10 and 11, 1972–73; Voyager 1 and 2, 1977; Galileo, 1989; Ulysses, 1990; US/ESA/Italy—Cassini-Huygens, 1997.

Saturn

average distance from Sun: 1.433 billion km (890.8 million mi)
diameter (at equator): 120,536 km (74,897 mi)
mass (in 10^{20} kg): 5,680,000
density (mass/volume, in kg/m^3): 687
eccentricity of orbit: 0.057
mean orbital velocity: 9.7 km/sec (6 mi/sec)
inclination of orbit to ecliptic: 2.5°
orbital period: 29.43 Earth years
rotation period: 10.7 Earth hours
inclination of equator to orbit: 26.7°
gravitational acceleration: 9.0 m/sec^2 (29.4 ft/sec^2)
escape velocity: 35.5 km/sec (22.1 mi/sec)
mean temperature at surface†: −140 °C (−220 °F)
satellites: at least 60 moons—including Titan—plus rings
probes and space missions: US—Pioneer 11, 1973; Voyager 1 and 2, 1977; US/ESA/Italy—Cassini/Huygens, 1997.

Uranus

average distance from Sun: 2.872 billion km (1.784 billion miles)
diameter (at equator): 51,118 km (31,763 mi)
mass (in 10^{20} kg): 868,000
density (mass/volume, in kg/m^3): 1,270
eccentricity of orbit: 0.046
mean orbital velocity: 6.8 km/sec (4.2 mi/sec)
inclination of orbit to ecliptic: 0.8°
orbital period: 84.01 Earth years
rotation period: 17.2 Earth hours (retrograde)
inclination of equator to orbit: 97.8°
gravitational acceleration: 8.7 m/sec^2 (28.5 ft/sec^2)
escape velocity: 21.3 km/sec (13.2 mi/sec)
mean temperature at surface†: −195 °C (−320 °F)
satellites: at least 27 moons, plus rings
probes and space missions: US—Voyager 2, 1977.

Neptune

average distance from Sun: 4.495 billion km (2.793 billion mi)
diameter (at equator): 49,528 km (30,775 mi)
mass (in 10^{20} kg): 1,020,000
density (mass/volume, in kg/m^3): 1,638
eccentricity of orbit: 0.009
mean orbital velocity: 5.4 km/sec (3.4 mi/sec)
inclination of orbit to ecliptic: 1.8°
orbital period: 164.79 Earth years
rotation period: 16.1 Earth hours
inclination of equator to orbit: 28.3°
gravitational acceleration: 11.0 m/sec^2 (36.0 ft/sec^2)
escape velocity: 23.5 km/sec (14.6 mi/sec)
mean temperature at surface†: −200 °C (−330 °F)
satellites: at least 13 moons, plus rings
probes and space missions: US—Voyager 2, 1977.

Pluto

average distance from Sun: 5.910 billion km (3.67 billion mi); Pluto lies within the Kuiper belt and can be considered its largest known member
diameter (at equator): 2,344 km (1,485 mi)
mass (in 10^{20} kg): 125
density (mass/volume, in kg/m^3): about 2,000
eccentricity of orbit: 0.249
mean orbital velocity: 4.72 km/sec (2.93 mi/sec)
inclination of orbit to ecliptic: 17.2°
orbital period: 248 Earth years
rotation period: 6.4 Earth days (retrograde)
inclination of equator to orbit: 122.5°
gravitational acceleration: 0.6 m/sec^2 (1.9 ft/sec^2)
escape velocity: 1.1 km/sec (0.7 mi/sec)
mean temperature at surface†: −225 °C (−375 °F)
satellites: 3 known—including Charon
probes and space missions: US—New Horizons, 2006.

Charon (moon of Pluto)

average distance from Pluto: 19,600 km (12,178.8 mi)
diameter (at equator): 1,250 km (777 mi)
mass (in 10^{20} kg): 19
density (mass/volume, in kg/m^3): about 1,700
eccentricity of orbit: 0
mean orbital velocity: Charon orbits Pluto at 0.23 km/sec (0.142 mi/sec)
inclination of orbit to Pluto's equator: close to 0°
orbital period: 6.3873 Earth days
rotation period: 6.3873 Earth days
gravitational acceleration: 0.21 m/sec^2 (0.69 ft/sec^2)
escape velocity: 0.58 km/sec (0.36 mi/sec)
mean temperature at surface†: as low as −240 °C (−400 °F).

Comet 1P Halley
distance from Sun at closest point of orbit is 87.8 million km (54 million mi). Farthest distance from Sun is 5.2 billion km (3.2 billion mi).
diameter (at equator): 16 x 8 x 8 km (9.9 x 4.9 x 4.9 mi)
density (mass/volume, in kg/m^3): possibly as low as 200
eccentricity of orbit: 0.967
inclination of orbit to ecliptic: 18°
orbital period: 76.1 to 79.3 Earth years. The next appearance will be 2061. The comet's orbit is retrograde.
rotation period: 52 Earth hours
probes and space missions: ESA–Giotto, 1985; USSR–Vega 1 and 2, 1985; Japan–Sakigake and Suisei, 1985.

Comet 2P Encke
distance from Sun at closest point of orbit is 50 million km (31 million mi). Farthest distance from Sun is 658 million km (408 million mi).
eccentricity of orbit: 0.847
orbital period: 3.3 Earth years (shortest known for a comet); next closest pass of Sun is on 19 Apr 2007.

Comet 9P Tempel 1
distance from Sun at closest point of orbit is 225 million km (140 million mi). Farthest distance from Sun is 708 million km (440 million mi).
eccentricity of orbit: 0.52
orbital period: 5.52 Earth years; next closest pass of Sun is in January 2011.
rotation period: 41 Earth hours
probes and space missions: US–Deep Impact, 2005

Comet 81P Wild 2
distance from Sun at closest point of orbit is 236.8 million km (147.1 million mi). Farthest distance from Sun is 10 billion km (6.2 billion mi).
eccentricity of orbit: 0.54
orbital period: 6.39 Earth years; next closest pass of Sun is in February 2010.
probes and space missions: US–Stardust, 1999.

Comet Hale-Bopp
distance from Sun at closest point of orbit is 136 million km (84.5 million mi). Farthest distance from Sun is 74.7 billion km (46.4 billion mi).
eccentricity of orbit: 0.995
orbital period: 4,000 Earth years; last closest pass of Sun was on 31 Mar 1997.

Comet Hyakutake
distance from Sun at closest point of orbit is 34 million km (21 million mi). Farthest distance from Sun is 344 billion km (213 billion mi).
eccentricity of orbit: 0.9998
orbital period: about 40,000 Earth years; last closest pass of Sun was on 1 May 1996.

Kuiper belt
(a huge flat ring located beyond Neptune containing residual icy material from the formation of the outer planets)
average distance from Sun (main concentration): 4.5–7.5 billion km (2.8–4.7 billion mi)
mass: Scientists estimate there may be as many as 100,000 icy, cometlike bodies of a size greater than 100 km in the Kuiper belt; the belt is estimated to have a mass of 6,000 x 10^{20} kg.

Oort cloud
(an immense, roughly spherical cloud of icy, cometlike bodies inferred to orbit Sun at distances roughly 1,000 times that of the orbit of Pluto)
average distance from Sun: 3–7 trillion km (1.9–4.3 trillion mi)
mass: some trillions of the cloud's icy objects have an estimated total mass of at least 600,000 x 10^{20} kg (10 times the mass of Earth).

†*For celestial bodies with no surface, temperature given is at a level in the atmosphere equal to 1 bar of pressure.*

Solar System Superlatives

Largest planet in the solar system: Jupiter (142,984 km [88,846 mi] diameter); all of the other planets in the solar system could fit inside Jupiter.
Largest moon in the solar system: Jupiter's moon Ganymede (5,270 km [3,275 mi]).
Smallest planet in the solar system: Mercury (4,879 km [3,032 mi] diameter).
Smallest moons in the solar system: Saturn and Jupiter both have numerous satellites that are smaller than 10 km (6 mi) in diameter.
Planet closest to the Sun: Mercury (average distance from the Sun 58 million km [36 million mi]).
Planet farthest from the Sun: Neptune (average distance from the Sun 4.50 billion km [2.80 billion mi]); Pluto, demoted to the status of dwarf planet in 2006, was the farthest planet from the Sun for all but 20 years of its 248-year orbital period.
Planet with the most eccentric (least circular) orbit: Mercury (eccentricity of 0.206).
Moon with the most eccentric orbit: Neptune's moon Nereid (eccentricity of 0.75).
Planet with the least eccentric orbit: Venus (eccentricity of 0.007).
Moon with the least eccentric orbit: Saturn's moon Tethys (eccentricity of 0.00000).
Planet most tilted on its axis: Uranus (axial tilt of 98° from its orbital plane).
Planet with the most moons: Jupiter (at least 63).
Planets with the fewest moons: Mercury and Venus (no moons).
Planet with the longest day: Venus (1 day on Venus equals 243 Earth days).
Planet with the shortest day: Jupiter (1 day on Jupiter equals 9.9 hours).
Planet with the longest year: Neptune (1 year on Neptune equals 165 Earth years).
Planet with the shortest year: Mercury (1 year on Mercury equals 88 Earth days).

Fastest orbiting planet in the solar system: Mercury (47.9 km per second [29.7 mi per second] average orbital speed).

Slowest orbiting planet in the solar system: Neptune (5.48 km per second [3.40 mi per second] average orbital speed).

Hottest planet in the solar system: Venus (464 °C [867 °F] average temperature); although Mercury is closer to the Sun, Venus is hotter because Mercury has no atmosphere, whereas the atmosphere of Venus traps heat via a strong greenhouse effect.

Coldest planet in the solar system: Neptune (−220 °C [−364 °F] average temperature).

Brightest visible star in the night sky: Sirius (−1.46 apparent visual magnitude).

Brightest planet in the night sky: Venus (apparent visual magnitude −4.5 to −3.77).

Densest planet: Earth (density of 5,515 kg/m³).

Least dense planet: Saturn (density of 687 kg/m³); Saturn in theory would float in water.

Planet with strongest gravity: Jupiter (more than twice the gravitational force of Earth at an altitude at which 1 bar of atmospheric pressure is exerted).

Planet with weakest gravity: Mars (slightly more than ⅓ the gravitational force of Earth).

Planet with the largest mountain: Mars (Olympus Mons, an extinct volcano, stands some 21 km [13 mi] above the planet's mean radius and 540 km [335 mi] across).

Planet with the deepest valley: Mars (Valles Marineris, a system of canyons, is some 4,000 km [2,500 mi] long and from about 2 to 9 km [1 to 5.6 mi] deep).

Largest known impact crater: Valhalla, a crater on Jupiter's moon Callisto, has a bright central area that is about 600 km (370 mi) across, with sets of concentric ridges extending about 1,500 km (900 mi) from the center. For contrast, the largest crater on Earth believed to be of impact origin is the Vredefort ring structure in South Africa, which is about 300 km (190 mi) across.

The Sun

The Sun is the star around which the Earth and the other components of the solar system revolve. It is the dominant body of the system, constituting more than 99% of the system's entire mass. The Sun is the source of an enormous amount of energy, a portion of which provides the Earth with the light and heat necessary to support life. The geologic record of the Earth and Moon reveals that the Sun was formed about 4.5 billion years ago. The energy radiated by the Sun is produced during the conversion of hydrogen atoms to helium. The Sun is at least 90% hydrogen by number of atoms, so the fuel is readily available.

The Sun is classified as a G2 V star, where G2 stands for the second hottest stars of the yellow G class—of surface temperature about 5,500 °C (10,000 °F)—and V represents a main sequence, or dwarf, star, the typical star for this temperature class (see also "Classification of Stars"). The Sun exists in the outer part of the Milky Way Galaxy and was formed from material that had been processed inside other stars and supernovas.

The mass of the Sun is 743 times the total mass of all the planets in the solar system and 330,000 times that of the Earth. All the interesting planetary and interplanetary gravitational phenomena are negligible effects in comparison to the gravitational force exerted by the Sun. Under the force of gravity, the great mass of the Sun presses inward, and to keep the star from collapsing, the central pressure outward must be great enough to support its weight. The Sun's core, which occupies approximately 25% of the star's radius, has a density about 100 times that of water (roughly 6 times that at the center of the Earth), but the temperature at the core is at least 15 million °C (27 million °F), so the central pressure is at least 10,000 times greater than that at the center of the Earth. In this environment atoms are completely stripped of their electrons, and at this high temperature the bare nuclei collide to produce the nuclear reactions that are responsible for generating the energy vital to life on Earth.

The temperature of the Sun's surface is so high that no solid or liquid can exist; the constituent materials are predominantly gaseous atoms, with a very small number of molecules. As a result, there is no fixed surface. The surface viewed from Earth, the photosphere, is approximately 400 km (250 mi) thick and is the layer from which most of the radiation reaches us; the radiation from below the photosphere is absorbed and reradiated, while the emission from overlying layers drops sharply, by about a factor of six every 200 km (124 mi).

While the temperature of the Sun drops from 15 million °C (27 million °F) at the core to around 5,500 °C (10,000 °F) at the photosphere, a surprising reversal occurs above that point; the temperature begins to rise in the chromosphere, a layer several thousand kilometers thick. Temperatures there range from 4,200 °C (7,600 °F) to 100,000 °C (180,000 °F). Above the chromosphere is a comparatively dim, extended halo called the corona, which has a temperature of 1 million °C (1.8 million °F) and reaches far past the planets. Beyond a distance of around 3.5 million km (2.2 million mi) from the Sun, the corona flows outward at a speed (near the Earth) of 400 km/sec (250 mi/sec); this flow of charged particles is called the solar wind.

The Sun is a very stable source of energy. Superposed on this stability, however, is an interesting 11-year cycle of magnetic activity manifested by regions of transient strong magnetic fields called sunspots. The largest sunspots can be seen on the solar surface even without a telescope.

Mercury

Mercury is the planet closest to the Sun, revolving around it at an average distance of 58 million km (36 million mi). In Sumerian times, some 5,000 years ago, it was already known in the night sky. In classical Greece the planet was called Apollo when it appeared as a morning star and Hermes, for the Greek equivalent of the Roman god Mercury, when it appeared as an evening star.

Mercury's orbit lies inside the orbit of the Earth and is more elliptical than those of most of the other planets. At its closest approach (perihelion), Mercury is only 46 million km (28.5 million mi) from the Sun, while its greatest distance (aphelion) approaches 70 million km (43.5 million mi). Mercury orbits the Sun in 88 Earth days at an average speed of 48 km per second (29.8 mi per sec), allowing it to overtake and pass Earth every 116 Earth days (synodic period).

Because of its proximity to the Sun, the surface of Mercury can become extremely hot. High temperatures at "noon" may reach 400 °C (755 °F) while the "predawn" lowest temperature is −173 °C (−280 °F). Mercury's equator is almost exactly in its orbital plane (its spin-axis inclination is nearly zero), and thus Mercury does not have seasons as does the Earth. Because of its elliptical orbit and a peculiarity of its rotational period (see below), however, certain longitudes experience cyclical variations in temperatures on a "yearly" as well as on a "diurnal" basis.

Mercury is about 4,879 km (3,032 mi) in diameter, the smallest of the planets. Mercury is only a bit larger than the Moon. Its mass, as measured by the gravitational perturbation of the path of the Mariner 10 spacecraft during close flybys in 1974–75, is about one-eighteenth of the mass of the Earth. Escape velocity, the speed needed to escape from a planet's gravitational field, is about 4.3 km per second (2.7 mi per second)—compared with 11.2 km per sec (7 mi per sec) for the Earth.

The mean density of Mercury, calculated from its mass and radius, is about 5.43 grams per cubic cm, nearly the same as that of the Earth (5.52 grams per cubic cm).

Photographs relayed by the Mariner 10 spacecraft showed that Mercury spins on its axis (rotates) once every 58.646 Earth days, exactly two-thirds of the orbital period of 87.9694 Earth days. This observation confirmed that Mercury is in a 3:2 spin-orbit tidal resonance—i.e., that tides raised on Mercury by the Sun have forced it into a condition that causes it to rotate three times on its axis in the same time it takes to revolve around the Sun twice. The 3:2 spin-orbit coupling combines with Mercury's eccentric orbit to create very unusual temperature effects.

Although Mercury rotates on its axis once every 58.646 Earth days, one rotation does not bring the Sun back to the same part of the sky, because during that time Mercury has moved partway around the Sun. A solar day on Mercury (for example, from one sunrise to another, or one noon to another) is 176 Earth days (exactly two Mercurian years).

Mercury's low escape velocity and high surface temperatures do not permit it to retain a significant atmosphere.

In January 2008 the MESSENGER spacecraft flew by Mercury, revealing previously unseen details in photographs, and scientists approved dozens of new names for surface features such as craters.

Venus

Venus is the second planet from the Sun and the planet whose orbit is closest to that of the Earth. When visible, Venus is the brightest planet in the sky. Viewed through a telescope, it presents a brilliant, yellow-white, essentially featureless face to the observer. The obscured appearance results because the surface of the planet is hidden from sight by a continuous and permanent cover of clouds.

Venus's orbit is the most nearly circular of that of any planet, with a deviation from perfect circularity of only about 1 part in 150. The period of the orbit—that is, the length of the Venusian year—is 224.7 Earth days. The rotation of Venus is unusual in both its direction and speed. Most of the planets in the solar system rotate in a counterclockwise direction when viewed from above their north poles; Venus, however, rotates in the opposite, or retrograde, direction. Were it not for the planet's clouds, an observer on Venus's surface would see the Sun rise in the west and set in the east.

Venus spins on its axis slowly, taking 243 Earth days to complete one rotation. Venus's spin and orbital periods are nearly synchronized with the Earth's orbit such that Venus presents almost the same face toward the Earth when the two planets are at their closest.

Venus is nearly the Earth's twin in terms of size and mass. Venus's equatorial diameter is about 95% of the Earth's diameter, while its mass is 81.5% that of the Earth. The similarities to the Earth in size and mass also produce a similarity in density; Venus's density is 5.24 grams per cubic cm, as compared with 5.52 for the Earth.

In terms of its shape, Venus is more nearly a perfect sphere than are most planets. A planet's rotation generally causes a slight flattening at the poles and bulging at the equator, but Venus's very slow rotation rate allows it to maintain its highly spherical shape.

Venus has the most massive atmosphere of all the terrestrial planets (Mercury, Venus, Earth, and Mars). Its atmosphere is composed of 96.5% carbon dioxide and 3.5% nitrogen. The atmospheric pressure at the planet's surface varies with the surface elevation but averages about 90 bars, or 90 times the atmospheric pressure at the Earth's surface. This is the same pressure found at a depth of about one kilometer in the Earth's oceans. Temperatures range between a minimum temperature of −45 °C (−49 °F) and a maximum temperature of 500 °C (932 °F); the average temperature is 464 °C (867 °F).

Earth

The Earth is the third planet in distance outward from the Sun. It is the only planetary body in the solar system that has conditions suitable for life, at least as known to modern science.

The average distance of the Earth from the Sun—149.6 million km (93 million mi)—is designated as the distance of the unit of measurement known as the AU (astronomical unit). The Earth orbits the Sun at a speed of 29.8 km (18.5 mi) per second, making one complete revolution in 365.25 days. As it revolves around the Sun, the Earth spins on its axis and rotates completely once every 23 hr 56 min 4 sec. The Earth has a single natural satellite, the Moon.

The fifth largest planet of the solar system, the Earth has a total surface area of roughly 509.6 million sq km (197 million sq mi), of which about 29%, or 148 million square km (57 million square mi), is land. Oceans and smaller seas cover the balance of the surface. The Earth is the only planet known to have liquid water. Together with ice, the liquid water constitutes the hydrosphere. Seawater makes up more than 98% of the total mass of the hydrosphere and covers about 71% of the Earth's surface. Significantly, seawater constituted the environment of the earliest terrestrial life forms.

The Earth's atmosphere consists of a mixture of gases, chiefly nitrogen (78%) and oxygen (21%). Argon makes up much of the remainder of the gaseous envelope, with trace amounts of water vapor, carbon dioxide, and various other gases also present.

The Earth's structure consists of an inner core of nearly solid iron, surrounded by successive layers of molten metals and solid rock, and a thin layer at the surface comprising the continental crust.

The Earth is surrounded by a magnetosphere, a region dominated by the Earth's magnetic field and extending upward from about 140 km (90 mi) in the upper atmosphere. In the magnetosphere, the magnetic field of the Earth traps rapidly moving charged particles (mainly electrons and protons), the majority of which flow from the Sun (as solar wind). If it were not for this shielding effect, such particles would bombard the terrestrial surface and destroy life. High concentrations of the trapped particles make up two doughnut-shaped zones called the Van Allen radiation belts. These belts play a key role in certain geophysical phenomena, such as auroras.

The Moon

The Moon is the sole natural satellite of the Earth. It revolves around the planet from west to east at a mean distance of about 384,400 km (238,900 mi). The Moon is less than one-third the size of the Earth, having a diameter of only about 3,475 km (2,159 mi) at its equator. The Moon shines by reflecting sunlight, but its albedo—i.e., the fraction of light received that is reflected—is only 0.073.

The Moon rotates about its own axis in about 27.32 days, which is virtually identical to the time it takes to complete its orbit around the Earth. As a result, the Moon always presents nearly the same face to the Earth. The rate of actual rotation is uniform, but the arc through which the Moon moves from day to day varies somewhat, causing the lunar globe (as seen by a terrestrial observer) to oscillate slightly over a period nearly equal to that of revolution.

The surface of the Moon has been a subject of continuous telescopic study from the time of Galileo's first observation in 1609. The Italian Jesuit astronomer Giovanni B. Riccioli designated the dark areas on the Moon as seas (maria), with such fanciful names as Mare Imbrium ("Sea of Showers") and Mare Nectaris ("Sea of Nectar"). This nomenclature continues to be used even though it is now known that the Moon is completely devoid of surface water. During the centuries that followed the publication of these early studies, more detailed maps and, eventually, photographs were produced. A Soviet space probe photographed the side of the Moon facing away from the Earth in 1959. By the late 1960s the US Lunar Orbiter missions had yielded close-up photographs of the entire lunar surface. On 20 Jul 1969, Apollo 11 astronauts Neil Armstrong and Edwin ("Buzz") Aldrin set foot on the Moon.

The most striking formations on the Moon are its craters. These features, which measure up to about 200 km (320 mi) or more in diameter, are scattered over the surface in great profusion and often overlap one another. Meteorites hitting the lunar surface at high velocity produced most of the large craters. Many of the smaller ones—those measuring less than 1 km (0.6 mi) across—appear to have been formed by explosive volcanic activity, however. The Moon's maria have relatively few craters. These lava outpourings spread over vast areas after most of the craters had already been formed.

Various theories for the Moon's origin have been proposed. At the end of the 19th century, the English astronomer Sir George H. Darwin advanced a hypothesis stating that the Moon had been originally part of the Earth but had broken away as a result of tidal gravitational action and receded from the planet. This was proved unlikely in the 1930s. A theory that arose during the 1950s postulated that the Moon had formed elsewhere in the solar system and was then later captured by the Earth. This idea was also proved to be physically implausible and was dismissed. Today, most investigators favor an explanation known as the giant-impact hypothesis, which postulates that a Mars-sized body struck the proto-Earth early in the history of the solar system. As a result, a cloud of fragments from both bodies was ejected into orbit around the Earth, and this later accreted into the Moon.

Moon Phases, 2008–2009

As the Moon orbits the Earth, more or less of the half of the Moon illuminated by the Sun is visible on Earth. During the lunar month the Moon's appearance changes from dark (the new moon) to being illuminated more and more on the right side (waxing crescent, first quarter, and waxing gibbous) to the full disc being illuminated (the full moon). The phases of the Moon are completed by the Moon being illuminated less and less on the left side (waning gibbous, last quarter, and waning crescent) and end with another new moon. The cycle of the Moon takes place over a period of around 29 days; the time from new moon to new moon is referred to as a lunation.

The phases of the Moon are caused by the positions of the Sun in relationship to the Moon. Thus, when the Sun and Moon are close in the sky a dark new moon is the result (the Sun is lighting the half of the Moon not visible to Earth). When the Sun and Moon are at opposition (in opposite parts of the sky) the full moon occurs (the Sun illuminates fully the half of the Moon seen on Earth). When the Sun and Moon are at about a 90-degree angle, one sees either a first quarter or last quarter moon.

The dates for the new moon, first quarter, full moon, and last quarter for June 2008–December 2009 are given in the table below.

Moon Phases, 2008–2009 (continued)

	NEW MOON	FIRST QUARTER	FULL MOON	LAST QUARTER
June 2008	3	10	18	26
July 2008	3	10	18	25
August 2008	1	8	16	23
September 2008	(30 August)	7	15	22
October 2008	(29 September	7	14	21
November 2008	(28 October)	6	13	19
December 2008	(27 November)	5	12	19
January 2009	(27 Dec 2008)	4	11	18
February 2009	(26 January)	2	9	16
March 2009	(25 February)	4	11	18
April 2009	(26 March)	2	9	17
May 2009	(25 April)	1	9	17
June 2009	(24 May)	(31 May)	7	15
July 2009	(22 June)	(29 June)	7	15
August 2009	(22 July)	(28 July)	6	13
September 2009	(20 August)	(27 August)	4	12
October 2009	(18 September)	(26 September)	4	11
November 2009	(18 October)	(26 October)	2	9
December 2009	(16 November)	(24 November)	2	9
	16	24	31	

Moon's Apogee and Perigee, 2009

The distance between the centers of mass of the Earth and the Moon varies rather widely due to the combined gravity of the Earth, the Sun, and the planets. For example, during the period 1969–2000, apogee (when the Moon is at the greatest distance from Earth) varied from 404,063 to 406,711 km (251,073 to 252,719 mi), while perigee (when the Moon is closest to Earth) varied from 356,517 to 370,354 km (221,529 to 230,127 mi). Tidal interactions have braked the Moon's spin so that presently the same side always faces the Earth. Dates are Universal Time/GMT.

Moon at apogee

DATE	OCCURS
23 January	between last quarter and new moon
19 February	between last quarter and new moon
19 March	between full moon and last quarter
16 April	between full moon and last quarter
14 May	between full moon and last quarter
10 June	at full moon
7 July	between first quarter and full moon
4 August	between first quarter and full moon
31 August	between first quarter and full moon
28 September	at first quarter
25 October	between new moon and first quarter
22 November	between new moon and first quarter
20 December	between last quarter and new moon

Moon at perigee

DATE	OCCURS
10 January	between first quarter and full moon
7 February	at first quarter
7 March	between new moon and first quarter
2 April	between new moon and first quarter
28 April	between new moon and first quarter
26 May	at new moon
23 June	between last quarter and new moon
21 July	between last quarter and new moon
19 August	between last quarter and new moon
16 September	between full moon and last quarter
13 October	between full moon and last quarter
7 November	between full moon and last quarter
4 December	at full moon

Mars

Mars is the fourth planet in order of distance from the Sun and the seventh in order of diminishing size and mass. It orbits the Sun once in 687 Earth days and spins on its axis once every 24 hr 37 min.

Owing to its blood-red color, Mars has often been associated with warfare and slaughter. It is named for the Roman god of war; as far back as 3,000 years ago, Babylonian astronomer-astrologers called the planet Nergal for their god of death and pestilence. The Greeks called it Ares for their god of battle; the planet's two satellites, Phobos (Fear) and Deimos (Terror), were later named for the two sons of Ares and Aphrodite.

Mars moves around the Sun at a mean distance of approximately 1.52 times that of the Earth from the Sun. Because the orbit of Mars is relatively elongated, the distance between Mars and the Sun varies from 206.6 to 249.2 million km (128.4 to 154.8 million mi). Mars completes a single orbit in roughly the time in which the Earth completes two. At its closest approach, Mars is less than 56 million km (34.8 million mi) from the Earth, but it recedes to almost 400 million km (248.5 million mi). Mars is a small planet. Its equatorial radius is about half that of Earth, and its mass is only one-tenth the terrestrial value.

The axis of rotation is inclined to the orbital plane at an angle of 24.9°, and, as for the Earth, the tilt gives rise to the seasons on Mars. The Martian year consists of 668.6 Martian solar days (called sols). The orientation and eccentricity of the orbit (eccentricity denotes how much the orbit deviates from a perfect circle: the more elongated, the more eccentric) leads to seasons that are quite uneven in length.

The Martian atmosphere is composed mainly of carbon dioxide. It is very thin (less than 1% of the Earth's atmospheric pressure). Evidence suggests that the atmosphere was much denser in the remote past and that water was once much more abundant at the surface. Only small amounts of water are found in the lower atmosphere today, occasionally forming thin ice clouds at high altitudes and, in several localities, morning ice fogs. Mars's polar caps consist of frozen carbon dioxide and water ice. Intriguing spacecraft observations confirm that water ice also is present under large areas of the Martian surface and hint that liquid water may have flowed in geologically recent times.

The characteristic temperature in the lower atmosphere is about −70 °C (−100 °F). Unlike that of Earth, the total mass (and pressure) of the atmosphere experiences large seasonal variations, as carbon dioxide "snows out" at the winter pole.

The surface of Mars shows some of the most dramatic variation in the solar system: the massive extinct volcano Olympus Mons stands some 21 km (13 mi) above the planet's mean radius and is 540 km (335 mi) across, and Valles Marineris, a system of canyons, is some 4,000 km (2,500 mi) long and from about 2 to 9 km (1 to 5.6 mi) deep.

The two satellites of Mars—Phobos and Deimos—were discovered in 1877 by Asaph Hall of the United States Naval Observatory. Little was known about these bodies until observations were made by NASA's orbiting Mariner 9 spacecraft nearly a century later. The moons of Mars cannot be seen from all locations on the planet because of their small size, proximity to the planet, and near-equatorial orbits.

Two Mars Exploration Rovers—Spirit and Opportunity—landed on Mars in January 2004. In 2008 they continued to explore features of the planet, notably stratigraphy and volcanic activity, in their third Martian winter. In May 2008 the spacecraft Phoenix successfully landed on the planet and began its mission to be the first spacecraft to retrieve and study water (ice) from another planet. In late July it confirmed the presence of water on Mars.

Small Celestial Bodies

Small bodies are defined as all the natural objects in the solar system other than the Sun and the major planets and their satellites. The solar system is populated by vast numbers of these small bodies, which can be grouped as asteroids, comets, and meteoroids (at times, however, the distinctions between these groupings can be somewhat blurred).

Small bodies in stable orbits are found in several regions of the solar system. Most asteroids reside in a belt between Mars and Jupiter at approximately 300–600 million km (190–380 million mi). Others, called Trojan asteroids, are found at gravitationally stable points near the orbits of Mars and Jupiter.

The trans-Neptunian objects (considered comets) are located outside the orbit of Neptune, from around 4.5–7.5 billion km (2.8–4.7 billion mi) in the area known as the Kuiper belt. A spherical cloud known as the Oort cloud also contains comets at a distance of some 3–15 trillion km (1.8–9 trillion mi).

Other small bodies travel in unstable paths which cross planetary orbits. These include: all observed comets; near-Earth asteroids, whose orbits either cross or closely approach Earth's orbit; and other planet-crossing objects (a mixture of both asteroids and icy cometlike bodies). All objects on planet-crossing orbits will eventually collide with the Sun or a planet or be permanently ejected from the solar system, although some of these objects do survive for long periods of time due to stabilizing orbital resonances.

Comets originate, and most are still located, in the Kuiper belt and Oort cloud. Even though comets are brief visitors to the inner solar system, their population is constantly replenished through perturbations of the comets in these areas.

There are several characteristics that traditionally have distinguished asteroids, comets, and meteoroids. These are based upon origin, orbital, and physical differences. An object is classified as a comet when it displays a coma or tail (or any evidence of gas or dust coming from it). In addition, the icy objects found in the Kuiper belt (and the Oort cloud, though none of these are observable) are also considered to be comets. They do not display cometary activity because of their great distance from the Sun. Nevertheless, they are believed to be made up of the same volatile material—primarily water and carbon dioxide—as the nuclei of observed comets, and it is the presence of these volatiles on the surface that is responsible for cometary activity. Finally, objects on parabolic or hyperbolic (nonreturning) orbits are generally considered to be comets.

Meteoroids are defined as any small object in space, especially one less than a few tens of meters in size. When a meteoroid enters the Earth's atmosphere, the heat of friction creates a glowing trail of hot gases called a meteor. Should any part of a meteoroid reach the ground without being completely vaporized, that object is termed a meteorite. The term asteroid is traditionally reserved for the larger rocky bodies in solar orbit, which range up to nearly 1,000 km (600 mi) in size.

Asteroids and the Asteroid Belt

Asteroids are any of a host of small rocky bodies, about 1,000 km (600 mi) or less in diameter, that orbit the Sun. About 95% of the known asteroids move in orbits between those of Mars and Jupiter in an area known as the asteroid belt. The orbits of the asteroids, however, are not uniformly distributed within the asteroid belt, but exhibit "gaps." Known as Kirkwood gaps, these asteroid-less areas are maintained by the gravitational force exerted by Jupiter upon asteroids in certain orbits.

The vast majority of asteroids have orbital periods between three years and six years—i.e., between one-fourth and one-half of Jupiter's orbital period. These asteroids are said to be main-belt asteroids. Within the main belt are asteroids that share certain traits. Known as families, about 40% of all known asteroids belong to such groupings. Families are usually assigned the name of the lowest numbered (first discovered) asteroid in the family. The three largest families (Eos, Koronis, and Themis) have been determined to be compositionally homogeneous; each is thought to comprise fragments from a larger parent body that broke apart in a collision.

Besides the few asteroids in highly unusual orbits, there are a number of groups that fall outside the main belt. Those that have orbital periods greater than one-half that of Jupiter are called outer-belt asteroids. There are four such groups: the Cybeles, Hildas, Thule, and Trojan groups.

There is only one known group of inner-belt asteroids—namely, the Hungarias. The Hungaria asteroids have orbital periods that are less than one-fourth that of Jupiter. Finally, asteroids that pass inside the orbit of Mars are said to be near-Earth asteroids. There are two groups of near-Earth asteroids that deeply cross the Earth's orbit on an almost continuous basis. The first of these to be discovered were the Apollo asteroids. The other group of Earth-crossing asteroids is named Atens. A third group, the Amors, comprises part-time Earth crossers.

Asteroids are thought to be made of the same rocky (stony, metallic, and carbon-rich) material that formed the planets. Scientists believe that at the time the planets were forming the gravitational influence of what became Jupiter kept the asteroids from aggregating into a single planet. Since that time they have been evolving through ongoing collisions so that most of the present-day asteroids are remnants or fragments of larger bodies. As of 2008 astronomers had detected and numbered more than 90,000 asteroids.

Jupiter

Jupiter is the most massive of the planets and is fifth in distance from the Sun. When ancient astronomers named the planet Jupiter for the ruler of the gods in the Greco-Roman pantheon, they had no idea of the planet's true dimensions, but the name is appropriate, for Jupiter is larger than all the other planets combined. It has a narrow ring system and at least 63 known satellites, 3 larger than the Earth's Moon. Jupiter also has an internal heat source—i.e., it emits more energy than it receives from the Sun. This giant has the strongest magnetic field of any planet, with a magnetosphere so large that, if it could be seen from Earth, its apparent diameter would exceed that of the Moon. Jupiter's system is the source of intense bursts of radio noise, at some frequencies occasionally radiating more energy than the Sun.

Of special interest concerning Jupiter's physical properties is the low mean density of 1.33 grams per cubic cm—in contrast with Earth's 5.52 grams/cm^3—coupled with the large dimensions and mass and the short rotational period. The low density and large mass indicate that Jupiter's composition and structure are quite unlike those of the Earth and the other inner planets, a deduction that is supported by detailed investigations of the giant planet's atmosphere and interior.

Jupiter has no solid surface; the transition from the atmosphere to its highly compressed core occurs gradually at great depths. The close-up views of Jupiter from the Voyager spacecraft revealed a variety of cloud forms, with a predominance of elliptical features reminiscent of cyclonic and anticyclonic storm systems on the Earth. All these systems are in motion, appearing and disappearing on time scales dependent on their sizes and locations. Also observed to vary are the pastel shades of various colors present in the cloud layers—from the tawny yellow that seems to characterize the main layer, through browns and blue-grays, to the well-known salmon-colored Great Red Spot, Jupiter's largest, most prominent, and longest-lived feature.

Because Jupiter has no solid surface, it has no topographic features, and latitudinal currents dominate the planet's large-scale circulation. The lack of a solid surface with physical boundaries and regions with different heat capacities makes the persistence of these currents and their associated cloud patterns all the more remarkable. The Great Red Spot, for example, moves in longitude with respect to Jupiter's rotation, but it does not move in latitude.

The Voyager 1 spacecraft verified the existence of a ring system surrounding Jupiter when it crossed the planet's equatorial plane. Subsequently, images from the Galileo spacecraft revealed that the ring system consists principally of four concentric components whose boundaries are associated with the orbits of Jupiter's four innermost moons. The ring system is comprised of large numbers of micrometer-sized particles that produce strong forward scattering of incident sunlight. The presence of such small particles requires a source, and the association of the ring boundaries with the four moons makes the source clear. The particles are generated by impacts on these moons (and on still smaller bodies within the main part of the ring) by micrometeoroids, cometary debris, and possibly volcanically produced material from Jupiter's moon Io.

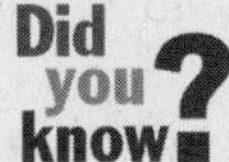

With the exception of snakes and bees, scorpions cause more deaths than any other non-parasitic group of animals. It is thought that more than 5,000 people die each year from scorpion stings. A long curved tail with a venomous stinger and grasping, fingerlike first appendages are typical scorpion features.

Jovian Moons

The satellites orbiting Jupiter are numerous; there are at least 63 Jovian moons and likely additional ones to be discovered.

The first objects in the solar system discovered by means of a telescope (by Galileo in 1610) were the four brightest moons of Jupiter. Now known as the Galilean satellites, they are (in order of increasing distance from Jupiter) Io, Europa, Ganymede, and Callisto. Each is a unique world in its own right. Callisto and Ganymede, for example, are as large or larger than the planet Mercury, but, while Callisto's icy surface is ancient and heavily cratered from impacts, Ganymede's appears to have been extensively modified by internal activity. Europa may still be geologically active and may harbor an ocean of liquid water, and possibly even life, beneath its frozen surface. Io is the most volcanically active body in the solar system; its surface is a vividly colored landcape of erupting vents, pools and solidified flows of lava, and sulfurous deposits.

Data for the first 16 known Jovian moons (discovered 1610–1979) are summarized below. The orbits of the inner eight satellites have low inclinations (they are not tilted relative to the planet's equator) and low eccentricities (their orbits are relatively circular). The orbits of the outer eight have much higher inclinations and eccentricities, and four of them are retrograde (they are opposite to Jupiter's spin and orbital motion around the Sun). The innermost four satellites are thought to be intimately associated with Jupiter's ring and are the sources of the fine particles within the ring itself.

Beginning in 1999 some 47 tiny moons (including one seen in 1975 and then lost) were discovered photographically in observations from Earth. All have high orbital eccentricities and inclinations and large orbital radii; nearly all of the orbits are retrograde. Rough size estimates based on their brightness place them between 2 and 8 km (1.2 and 5 mi) in diameter. They were assigned provisional numerical designations on discovery; many also have received official names.

In the table, "sync" denotes that the orbital period and rotational period are the same, or synchronous; hence, the moon always keeps the same face toward Jupiter. "R" following the orbital period indicates a retrograde orbit. Unspecified quantities are unknown.

NAME (DESIGNATION)	MEAN DISTANCE FROM JUPITER	DIAMETER	MASS (10^{20} KG)	ORBITAL PERIOD (EARTH DAYS)	ROTATIONAL PERIOD (EARTH DAYS)
Metis (JXVI)	128,000 km (79,500 mi)	40 km (25 mi)	0.001	0.295	sync
Adrastea (JXV)	129,000 km (80,000 mi)	20 km (12 mi)	0.0002	0.298	sync
Amalthea (JV)[1]	181,000 km (112,500 mi)	189 km (117 mi)	0.075	0.498	sync
Thebe (JXIV)	222,000 km (138,000 mi)	100 km (62 mi)	0.008	0.675	sync
Io (JI)[1]	422,000 km (262,000 mi)	3,630 km (2,256 mi)	893.2	1.769	sync
Europa (JII)[1]	671,000 km (417,000 mi)	3,130 km (1,945 mi)	480.0	3.551	sync
Ganymede (JIII)[1]	1,070,000 km (665,000 mi)	5,268 km (3,273 mi)	1,482.0	7.155	sync
Callisto (JIV)[1]	1,883,000 km (1,170,000 mi)	4,806 km (2,986 mi)	1,076.0	16.689	sync
Leda (JXIII)	11,127,000 km (6,914,000 mi)	10 km (6 mi)	0.00006	234	
Himalia (JVI)	11,480,000 km (7,133,000 mi)	170 km (106 mi)	0.095	251	0.4
Lysithea (JX)	11,686,000 km (7,261,300 mi)	24 km (15 mi)	0.0008	258	0.5
Elara (JVII)	11,737,000 km (7,293,000 mi)	80 km (50 mi)	0.008	256	0.5
Ananke (JXII)	21,269,000 km (13,216,000 mi)	20 km (12.5 mi)	0.0004	634 R	0.4
Carme (JXI)	23,350,000 km (14,509,000 mi)	30 km (18.6 mi)	0.001	729 R	0.4
Pasiphae (JVIII)	23,500,000 km (14,602,000 mi)	36 km (22.3 mi)	0.003	735 R	
Sinope (JIX)	23,700,000 km (14,726,500 mi)	28 km (17.3 mi)	0.0008	758 R	0.5

[1]Densities are known for these moons. They are: Amalthea (0.86 grams/cm^3), Io (3.53 grams/cm^3), Europa (3.01 grams/cm^3), Ganymede (1.94 grams/cm^3), Callisto (1.83 grams/cm^3).

Jovian Ring

Jupiter's complex ring was discovered and first studied by the twin Voyager spacecraft during their flybys of the giant planet in 1979. It is now known to consist of four main components: an outer gossamer ring, whose outer radius coincides with the orbital radius of the Jovian moon Thebe (222,000 km; 138,000 mi); an inner gossamer ring bounded on its outer edge by the orbit of Amalthea (181,000 km; 112,500 mi); the main ring, extending inward some 6,000 km (3,700 mi) from the orbits of Adrastea (129,000 km; 80,000 mi) and Metis (128,000 km; 79,500 mi); and a halo of particles with a thickness of 25,000 km (15,500 mi) that extends from the main ring inward to a radius of about 95,000 km (59,000 mi). For comparison, Jupiter's visible surface lies at a radius of about 71,500 km (44,400 mi) from its center. The four moons involved with the ring are believed to supply the fine particles that compose it.

Saturn

Saturn is the sixth planet in order of distance from the Sun and the second largest of the planets in mass and size. Its dimensions are almost equal to those of Jupiter, while its mass is about a third as large; it has the lowest mean density of any object in the solar system.

Both Saturn and Jupiter resemble stellar bodies in that the light gas hydrogen dominates their bulk **chemical composition.** Saturn's atmosphere is 91% hydrogen by mass and is thus the most hydrogen-rich atmosphere in the solar system. Saturn's structure and **evolutionary history,** however, differ significantly from those of its larger counterpart. Like the other giant planets—Jupiter, Uranus, and Neptune—Saturn has extensive satellite and ring systems, which may provide clues to its origin and evolution. The planet has at least 60 moons, including the second largest in the solar system. Saturn's dense and extended rings, which lie in its equatorial plane, are the most impressive in the solar system.

Saturn has no single **rotation period.** Cloud motions in its massive upper atmosphere can be used to trace out a variety of rotation periods, with periods as short as about 10 hours 10 minutes near the equator and increasing with some oscillation to about 30 minutes longer at latitudes higher than 40°. The rotation period of Saturn's deep interior can be determined from the rotation period of the magnetic field, which is presumed to be rooted in an outer core of hydrogen compressed to a metallic state. The "surface" of Saturn that is seen through telescopes and in spacecraft images is actually a complex layer of clouds.

The **atmosphere** of Saturn shows many smaller-scale time-variable features similar to those found in Jupiter, such as red, brown, and white spots, bands, eddies, and vortices. The atmosphere generally has a much blander appearance than Jupiter's, however, and is less active on a small scale. A spectacular exception occurred during September–November 1990, when a large white spot appeared near the equator, expanded to a size exceeding 20,000 km (12,400 mi), and eventually spread around the equator before fading.

Saturnian Moons

At least 60 natural satellites are known to circle the planet Saturn. Data for the first 18 Saturnian moons (discovered 1655–1990) are summarized below. As with the other giant planets, those satellites closest to Saturn are mostly regular, meaning that their orbits are fairly circular and not greatly inclined (tilted) with respect to the planet's equator. All of the satellites in the table except distant Phoebe are regular.

Titan is Saturn's largest moon and the only satellite in the solar system known to have clouds and a dense atmosphere (composed mostly of nitrogen and methane). The moon is also enveloped in a reddish haze, which is thought to be composed of complex organic compounds that are produced by the action of sunlight on its clouds and atmosphere. That organic molecules may have been settling out of the haze onto Titan's surface for much of its history has encouraged some scientists to speculate on the possibility that life may have evolved there. Observations by the Cassini-Huygens spacecraft showed Titan to have a varied surface sculpted by rains of hydrocarbon compounds, flowing liquids, wind, impacts, and possibly volcanic and tectonic activity. Saturn's second largest moon is **Rhea,** followed by **Iapetus** and **Dione.**

An unusual Saturnian satellite is **Hyperion.** Owing to its highly irregular shape and eccentric orbit, it does not rotate stably about a fixed axis. Unlike any other known object in the solar system, Hyperion rotates chaotically, alternating unpredictably between periods of tumbling and seemingly regular rotation.

Between 2000 and 2005 about 30 additional tiny moons occupying various (mostly distant) orbits were discovered. Like the numerous outer moons of Jupiter, nearly all of the recent finds around Saturn belong to the irregular class, meaning that their orbits are highly inclined and elliptical. More than half of them, plus Phoebe, are in retrograde orbits (they move opposite to Saturn's spin and orbital motion around the Sun).

In March 2008 it was announced that the Cassini spacecraft had taken images of Rhea in 2005 that appeared to show the first known ring around a moon.

In the table, "sync" denotes that the orbital period and rotational period are the same, or synchronous. Unspecified quantities are unknown.

NAME (DESIGNATION)	MEAN DISTANCE FROM SATURN	DIAMETER	MASS (10^{20} KG)	DENSITY (GRAMS/CM^3)	ORBITAL PERIOD (EARTH DAYS)	ROTATIONAL PERIOD (EARTH DAYS)
Pan (SXVIII)	133,580 km (83,000 mi)	20 km (12 mi)	0.00003	0.63	0.5750	
Atlas (SXV)	137,670 km (85,540 mi)	28 km (17 mi)	0.0001	0.63	0.6019	

Saturnian Moons (continued)

NAME (DESIGNATION)	MEAN DISTANCE FROM SATURN	DIAMETER	MASS (10^{20} KG)	DENSITY (GRAMS/CM³)	ORBITAL PERIOD (EARTH DAYS)	ROTATIONAL PERIOD (EARTH DAYS)
Prometheus (SXVI)	139,350 km (86,590 mi)	92 km (57 mi)	0.0033	0.63	0.6130	
Pandora (SXVII)	141,700 km (88,050 mi)	92 km (57 mi)	0.002	0.63	0.6285	
Epimetheus (SXI)	151,420 km (94,090 mi)	114 km (71 mi)	0.0054	0.60	0.6942	sync
Janus (SX)	151,470 km (94,120 mi)	178 km (111 mi)	0.0192	0.65	0.6945	sync
Mimas (SI)	185,520 km (115,280 mi)	392 km (244 mi)	0.375	1.14	0.94	sync
Enceladus (SII)	238,020 km (147,900 mi)	520 km (323 mi)	0.7	1.0	1.37	sync
Tethys (SIII)	294,660 km (183,090 mi)	1,060 km (659 mi)	6.27	1.0	1.88	sync
Telesto (SXIII)*	294,660 km (183,090 mi)	30 km (19 mi)	0.00007	1.0	1.88	
Calypso (SXIV)*	294,660 km (183,090 mi)	26 km (16 mi)	0.00004	1.0	1.88	
Dione (SIV)	377,400 km (234,510 mi)	1,120 km (696 mi)	11	1.5	2.73	sync
Helene (SXII)†	377,400 km (234,510 mi)	32 km (20 mi)	0.0003	1.5	2.73	
Rhea (SV)	527,040 km (327,490 mi)	1,530 km (951 mi)	23.1	1.24	4.51	sync
Titan (SVI)	1,221,830 km (759,210 mi)	5,150 km (3,200 mi)	1,350	1.881	15.94	sync
Hyperion (SVII)	1,481,100 km (920,310 mi)	286 km (178 mi)	0.2	1.50	21.27	chaotic
Iapetus (SVIII)	3,561,300 km (2,212,890 mi)	1,460 km (907 mi)	16	1.02	79.33	sync
Phoebe (SIX)	12,952,000 km (8,048,000 mi)	220 km (137 mi)	0.004	1.3	550.5 (retrograde)	0.4

**Telesto and Calypso occupy the same orbit as Tethys but about 60° ahead and behind, respectively.*
†Helene occupies the same orbit as Dione but about 60° behind.

Saturnian Rings

Saturn's rings rank among the most spectacular phenomena in the solar system. They have intrigued astronomers ever since they were discovered telescopically by Galileo in 1610, and their mysteries have only deepened since they were photographed and studied by Voyagers 1 and 2 in the early 1980s. The **particles** that make up the rings are composed primarily of water ice and range from dust specks to car- and house-sized chunks. The rings exhibit a great amount of structure on many scales, from the broad **A, B, and C rings** visible from Earth down to myriad narrow component ringlets. Odd structures resembling spokes, braids, and spiral waves are also present. Some of this detail is explained by gravitational interaction with a number of Saturn's 56 moons (the orbits of well more than a dozen known moons, from Pan to Dione and Helene, lie within the rings), but much of it remains unaccounted for.

Numerous divisions or **gaps** are seen in the major ring regions. A few of the more prominent ones are named for famous astronomers who were associated with studies of Saturn.

The major rings and gaps, listed outward from Saturn, are given below. For comparison, Saturn's visible surface lies at a radius of about 60,300 km (37,500 mi).

RING (OR DIVISION)	RADIUS OF RING'S INNER EDGE	WIDTH	COMMENTS
D ring	66,900 km (41,600 mi)	7,500 km (4,700 mi)	faint, visible only in reflected light
(Guerin division)			
C ring	74,500 km (46,300 mi)	17,500 km (10,900 mi)	also called Crepe ring
(Maxwell division)			
B ring	92,000 km (57,200 mi)	25,500 km (15,800 mi)	brightest ring
(Cassini division, Huygens gap)			Cassini division is the largest ring gap
A ring	122,200 km (75,900 mi)	14,600 km (9,100 mi)	the outermost ring visible from Earth

Saturnian Rings (continued)

RING (OR DIVISION)	RADIUS OF RING'S INNER EDGE	WIDTH	COMMENTS
(Encke division)			located within the A ring, near its outer edge
F ring	140,200 km (87,100 mi)	30–500 km (20–300 mi)	faint, narrowest major ring
G ring	165,800 km (103,000 mi)	8,000 km (5,000 mi)	faint
E ring	180,000 km (111,800 mi)	300,000 km (186,400 mi)	faint

Uranus

Uranus is the seventhth planet in order of distance from the Sun and the first found with the aid of a telescope. Its low density and large size place it among the four giant planets, all of which are composed primarily of hydrogen, helium, water, and other volatile compounds and which thus are without solid surfaces. Absorption of red light by methane gas gives the planet a blue-green color. The planet has at least 27 satellites, ranging up to 789 km (490 mi) in radius, and 13 narrow rings.

Uranus spins on its side; its **rotation axis** is tipped at an angle of 98° relative to its orbit axis. The 98° tilt is thought to have arisen during the final stages of planetary accretion when bodies comparable in size to the present planets collided in a series of violent events that knocked Uranus onto its side.

Although Uranus is nearly featureless, extreme contrast enhancement of images taken by the Voyager spacecraft reveals faint bands oriented parallel to circles of constant latitude. Apparently the rotation of the planet and not the distribution of absorbed sunlight controls the cloud patterns.

Wind is the motion of the atmosphere relative to the rotating planet. At high latitudes on Uranus, as on the Earth, this relative motion is in the direction of the planet's rotation. At low (that is, equatorial) latitudes, the relative motion is in the opposite direction. On the Earth these directions are called east and west, respectively, but the more general terms are prograde and retrograde. The winds that exist on Uranus are several times stronger than are those of the Earth. The wind is 200 m (656 ft) per second (prograde) at a latitude of 55° S and 110 m (360.8 ft) per second (retrograde) at the equator. Neptune's equatorial winds are also retrograde, although those of Jupiter and Saturn are prograde. No satisfactory theory exists to explain these differences.

Uranus has no large **spots** like the Great Red Spot of Jupiter or the Great Dark Spot of Neptune. Since the giant planets have no solid surfaces, the spots represent atmospheric storms. For reasons that are not clear, Uranus seems to have the smallest number of storms of any of the giant planets. Most of the mass of Uranus (roughly 80%) is in the form of a liquid core made primarily of icy materials (water, methane, and ammonia).

Uranus was discovered in 1781 by the English astronomer **William Herschel**, who had undertaken a survey of all stars down to eighth magnitude–i.e., those about five times fainter than stars visible to the naked eye. Herschel suggested naming the new planet the Georgian Planet after his patron, King George III of England, but the planet was eventually named according to the tradition of naming planets for the gods of Greek and Roman mythology; Uranus is the father of Saturn, who is in turn the father of Jupiter.

After the discovery, Herschel continued to observe the planet with larger and better telescopes and eventually discovered its two largest satellites, Titania and Oberon, in 1787. Two more satellites, Ariel and Umbriel, were discovered by the British astronomer William Lassell in 1851. The names of the four satellites come from English literature—they are characters in works by Shakespeare and Pope—and were proposed by Herschel's son, John Herschel. A fifth satellite, Miranda, was discovered by Gerard P. Kuiper in 1948. The tradition of naming the satellites after characters in Shakespeare's and Pope's works continues to the present.

Uranian Moons and Rings

Uranus has 27 known **satellites** forming three distinct groups: 13 small moons orbiting quite close to the planet, 5 large moons located somewhat farther out, and finally, another 9 small and much more distant moons. The members of the first two groups are in nearly circular orbits with low inclinations with respect to the planet.

The densities of the four largest satellites, **Ariel, Umbriel, Titania,** and **Oberon,** suggest that they are about half (or more) water ice and the rest rock. Oberon and Umbriel are heavily scarred with large impact craters dating back to the very early history of the solar system, evidence that their surfaces probably have been stable since their formation. In contrast, Titania and Ariel have far fewer large craters, indicating relatively young surfaces shaped over time by internal geological activity. **Miranda**, though small compared with the other major moons, has a unique jumbled patchwork of varied surface terrain revealing surprisingly extensive past activity. Data for the major satellites are summarized below.

The 5 major moons were **discovered** telescopically from Earth between 1787 and 1948. Eleven of the 13 innermost moons, with diameters of about 40–160 km (25–100 mi), were found in Voyager 2 images. The rest of the moons, with diameters of 10–200 km (6–120 mi), were detected in Earth-based observations between 1997 and 2003; the orbital motion of nearly all of the outermost moons is retrograde (opposite to the direction of Uranus's spin and revolution around the Sun).

Thirteen narrow rings are known to encircle Uranus, with radii from 39,600 to 97,700 km (24,600 to 60,700 mi), for the most part within the orbits of the innermost moons. For comparison, Uranus's visible surface lies at a radius of about 25,600 km (15,900 mi). The ring system was first detected in 1977 during Earth-based observations of Uranus. Subsequent observations from Earth and images from Voyager 2 and the Hubble Space Telescope clarified the number and other features of the rings.

Uranian Moons and Rings (continued)

NAME (DESIGNATION)	MEAN DISTANCE FROM URANUS	DIAMETER	MASS (10^{20} KG)	DENSITY (GRAMS/CM³)	ORBITAL PERIOD/ ROTATIONAL PERIOD (EARTH DAYS)*
Miranda (V)	129,390 km (80,400 mi)	472 km (293 mi)	0.66	1.2	1.41
Ariel (I)	191,020 km (118,690 mi)	1,158 km (720 mi)	13.5	1.67	2.52
Umbriel (II)	266,300 km (165,470 mi)	1,169 km (726 mi)	11.7	1.4	4.14
Titania (III)	435,910 km (270,860 mi)	1,578 km (981 mi)	35.3	1.71	8.71
Oberon (IV)	583,520 km (362,580 mi)	1,523 km (946 mi)	30.1	1.63	13.46

**The orbital period and rotational period are the same, or synchronous, for the listed moons.*

Neptune

Neptune is the eighth planet in average distance from the Sun. It was named for the Roman god of the sea. The sea god's trident serves as the planet's astronomical symbol.

Neptune's **distance** from the Sun varies between 29.8 and 30.4 astronomical units (AUs). Its **diameter** is about four times that of the Earth, but because of its great distance Neptune cannot be seen from the Earth without the aid of a telescope. Neptune's deep blue **color** is due to the absorption of red light by methane gas in its atmosphere. It receives less than half as much sunlight as Uranus, but heat escaping from its interior makes Neptune slightly warmer than the latter. The heat released may also be responsible for Neptune's stormier **atmosphere,** which exhibits the fastest winds seen on any planet in the solar system.

Neptune's **orbital period** is 164.8 Earth years. It has not completely circled the Sun since its discovery in 1846, so some refinements in calculations of its orbital size and shape are still expected. The planet's orbital eccentricity of 0.009 means that its orbit is very nearly circular; among the planets in the solar system, only Venus has a smaller eccentricity. Neptune's seasons (and the seasons of its moons) are therefore of nearly equal length, each about 41 Earth years in duration. The length of Neptune's day, as determined by Voyager 2, is 16.11 hours.

As with the other giant planets of the outer solar system, Neptune's atmosphere is composed predominantly of hydrogen and helium. The **temperature** of Neptune's atmosphere varies with altitude. A minimum temperature of about −223 °C (−369 °F) occurs at pressure near 0.1 bar. The temperature increases with altitude to about 477 °C (891 °F) at 2,000 km (1,240 mi, which corresponds to a pressure of 10^{-11} bar) and remains uniform above that altitude. It also increases with depth to about 6,730 °C (12,140 °F) near the center of the planet.

As with the other giant planets of the outer solar system, the **winds** on Neptune are constrained to blow generally along lines of constant latitude and are relatively invariable with time. Winds on Neptune vary from about 100 m/sec (328 ft/sec) in an easterly (prograde) direction near latitude 70° S to as high as 700 m/sec (2,300 ft/sec) in a westerly (retrograde) direction near latitude 20° S.

The high winds and relatively large contribution of escaping internal heat may be responsible for the observed turbulence in Neptune's visible atmosphere. Two large dark ovals are clearly visible in images of Neptune's southern hemisphere taken by Voyager 2 in 1989, although they are not present in Hubble Space Telescope images made 2 years later. The largest, called the **Great Dark Spot** because of its similarity in latitude and shape to Jupiter's Great Red Spot, is comparable to the entire Earth in size. It was near this feature that the highest wind speeds were measured. Atmospheric storms such as the Great Dark Spot may be centers where strong upwelling of gases from the interior takes place.

Neptune's mean **density** is about 30% of the Earth's; nevertheless, it is the densest of the giant planets. Neptune's greater density implies that a larger percentage of its interior is composed of melted ices and molten rocky materials than is the case for the other gas giants.

Neptunian Moons and Rings

Neptune has at least 13 natural satellites, but Earth-based observations had found only 2 of them, Triton in 1846 and Nereid in 1949, before Voyager 2 flew by the planet. The spacecraft observed 5 small moons orbiting close to Neptune and verified the existence of a 6th that had been detected from Earth in 1981. Data for these 8 moons are summarized in the table below. In 2002–03, 5 additional small moons (diameters roughly 30–60 km [20–40 mi]) were discovered telescopically from Earth; they all occupy highly inclined and elliptical orbits that are comparatively far from Neptune.

Triton is Neptune's only large moon and the only large satellite in the solar system to orbit its planet in the retrograde direction (opposite the planet's rotation and orbital motion around the Sun). Thus, as is also suspected of the solar system's other retrograde moons, Triton likely was captured by its planet rather than formed in orbit with its planet from the solar nebula. Its density (2 grams/cm³) suggests that it is about 25% water ice and the rest rock. Triton has a tenuous atmosphere, mostly of nitrogen. Its varied icy surface, imaged by Voyager 2, contains giant faults and dark markings that have been interpreted as the product of geyserlike

Neptunian Moons and Rings (continued)

"ice volcanoes" in which the eruptive material may be gaseous nitrogen and methane. Nereid has the most elliptical orbit of any planet or moon in the solar system; it also is probably a captured object.

Neptune's system of six faint rings, with radii from about 42,000 to 63,000 km (26,000–39,000 mi), straddles the orbits of its 4 innermost moons. (Neptune's visible surface lies at a radius of 24,800 km, or 15,400 mi.) The outermost ring, named Adams, is unusual in that it contains several clumps, or concentrations of material, that before Voyager 2's visit had been interpreted incorrectly as independent ring arcs. What created and has maintained this structure has not yet been fully explained; it has been suggested that the clumps resulted from the relatively recent breakup of a small moon and are being temporarily held together by the gravitational effects of the nearby moon Galatea.

NAME (DESIGNATION)	MEAN DISTANCE FROM NEPTUNE	DIAMETER	MASS (10^{20} KG)	ORBITAL PERIOD (EARTH DAYS)
Naiad (III)	48,230 km (29,970 mi)	58 km (36 mi)	0.002	0.294
Thalassa (IV)	50,070 km (31,110 mi)	80 km (50 mi)	0.004	0.311
Despina (V)	52,530 km (32,640 mi)	148 km (92 mi)	0.02	0.335
Galatea (VI)	61,950 km (38,490 mi)	158 km (98 mi)	0.04	0.429
Larissa (VII)	73,550 km (45,700 mi)	192 km (119 mi)	0.05	0.555
Proteus (VIII)	117,640 km (73,100 mi)	416 km (258 mi)	0.5	1.122
Triton (I)*	354,800 km (220,460 mi)	2,700 km (1,678 mi)	214	5.877 (retrograde)
Nereid (II)	5,509,100 km (3,423,200 mi)	340 km (211 mi)	0.2	359.632

**Among the rotational periods of Neptune's moons, only Triton's has been established; it is the same as (synchronous with) the orbital period.*

Pluto

Pluto is named for the god of the underworld in Roman mythology. It was long considered the planet normally farthest from the Sun, but on 24 Aug 2006, the International Astronomical Union announced that it was downgrading the status of Pluto to a dwarf planet. The key criterion in this classification was that Pluto, which orbits in the cluttered, icy Kuiper belt, had not cleared the neighborhood around its orbit. This was a controversial decision sure to be revisited.

Pluto has three natural satellites, Charon, Hydra, and Nix. Because Charon's diameter is more than half the size of Pluto's and they orbit around a common center of gravity, it was common to speak of the Pluto-Charon system as a double planet. Charon, named for the boatman in Greek mythology who carried the souls of the dead across the river Styx, was discovered in 1978, while Hydra and Nix were both first seen in 2005. The New Horizons spacecraft, launched in January 2006 and scheduled to arrive at Pluto in 2015, will search for yet more new satellites.

Pluto is so distant (its average **distance** from the Sun is 39.6 astronomical units, or AU) that sunlight traveling at 299,792 km/sec (186,282.1 mi/sec) takes more than five hours to reach it. An observer standing on the dwarf planet's surface would see the Sun as an extremely bright star in the dark sky, providing Pluto with only 1/1600 the amount of sunlight reaching the Earth.

Pluto has a **diameter** less than half that of Mercury; it is about two-thirds the size of the Moon. Pluto's physical characteristics are unlike those of any of the planets. Pluto resembles most closely Neptune's icy satellite Triton, which implies a similar origin for these two bodies. Most scientists now believe that Pluto and Charon are large icy planetesimals left over from the formation of the giant outer planets of the solar system. Accordingly, Pluto can be interpreted to be the largest known member of the Kuiper belt (which, as discussed, includes the outer part of Pluto's orbit). Observations of Pluto show that it appears slightly red, though not as red as Mars or Io. Thus, the surface of Pluto cannot be composed simply of pure ices. Its overall reflectivity, or albedo, ranges from 0.3 to 0.5, as compared with 0.1 for the Moon and 0.8 for Triton.

The surface **temperature** of Pluto has proved very difficult to measure. Observations made from the Infrared Astronomical Satellite suggest values in the range of −228 to −215 °C (−379 to −355 °F), whereas measurements at radio wavelengths imply a range of −238 to −223 °C (−397 to −370 °F). The temperature certainly must vary over the surface, depending on the local reflectivity and solar zenith angle. There is also expected to be a seasonal decrease in incident solar energy by a factor of roughly three as Pluto moves from perihelion to aphelion.

The detection of methane ice on Pluto's surface made scientists confident that it had an **atmosphere** before one was actually discovered. The atmosphere was finally detected in 1988 when Pluto passed in front of a star as observed from the Earth. The light of the star was dimmed before disappearing entirely behind Pluto during the occultation. This proved that a thin, greatly distended atmosphere was present. Because that atmosphere must consist of vapors in equilibrium with their ices, small changes in temperature will have a large effect on the amount of gas in the atmosphere.

Comets

Comets are a class of small bodies orbiting the Sun and developing diffuse gaseous envelopes. They also often form long luminous tails when near the Sun. The comet makes a transient appearance in the sky and is often said to have a "hairy" tail. In fact, the word comes from the Greek *kometes*, meaning "hairy one," a description that fits the bright comets noticed by the ancients.

Despite their name, many comets do not develop tails. Moreover, a comet is not surrounded by nebulosity during most of its lifetime. The only permanent feature of a comet is its **nucleus**, which is a small body that may be seen as a starlike object in large telescopes when tail and nebulosity do not exist, particularly when the comet is still far away from the Sun. Two characteristics differentiate the cometary nucleus from a rocky body such as an asteroid or meteoroid—its orbit and its chemical nature. A comet's **orbit** is more eccentric (less circular); therefore, its distance to the Sun varies considerably. Its material contains more volatile components, with water ice the predominant compound. They have been described as "dirty snowballs" or "icy mudballs." When far from the Sun, however, a comet remains in its pristine state for eons without losing any volatile components because of the deep cold of space. For this reason, astronomers believe that pristine cometary nuclei may represent the oldest and best-preserved material in the solar system.

During a close passage near the Sun, the nucleus of a comet loses water vapor and other more volatile compounds, as well as dust dragged away by the sublimating gases. It is then surrounded by a transient dusty "atmosphere" that is steadily lost to space. This feature is the **coma**, which gives a comet its nebulous appearance.

The astronomer **Edmond Halley**, a friend of Isaac Newton, endeavored to compute the orbits of 24 comets for which he had found fairly accurate historical documents. Applying a method Newton had developed, Halley predicted that the comet that now bears his name would return to Earth in 1758, and that proved correct. Since its prediction by astronomers and its appearance in 1758/59, Comet Halley has reappeared three times—in 1835, 1910, and 1986.

Each century, a score of comets brighter than Comet Halley have been discovered. Many are **periodic** (returning) **comets** like Comet Halley, but their periods are extremely long (millennia or even scores or hundreds of millennia), and they have not left any identifiable trace in prehistory. Bright Comet Bennett (1970) will return in 17 centuries, whereas the spectacular Comet West (1976) will reappear in about 500,000 years. Among the comets that can easily be seen with the unaided eye, Comet Halley is the only one that returns in a single lifetime. About 200 comets whose periods are between 3 and 200 years are known, however. Unfortunately, they are or have become too faint to be readily seen without the aid of telescopes.

For faraway objects that contain volatile ices, the distinction between **asteroids and comets** becomes a matter of semantics because many orbits are unstable; an asteroid that comes closer to the Sun than usual may become a comet by producing a transient atmosphere that gives it a fuzzy appearance and that may develop into a tail. Some objects have been reclassified as a result of such occurrences. For example, asteroid 1990 UL3, which crosses the orbit of Jupiter, was reclassified as Comet P/Shoemaker-Levy 2 late in 1990. Conversely, it is suspected that some of the Earth-approaching asteroids (Amors, Apollos, and Atens) could be the extinct nuclei of comets that have now lost most of their volatile ices.

Measurements and Numbers

The International System of Units (SI)

Rapid advances in science and technology in the 19th and 20th centuries fostered the development of several overlapping systems of units of measurements as scientists improvised to meet the practical needs of their disciplines. The **General Conference on Weights and Measures** was chartered by international convention in 1875 to produce standards of physical measurement based upon an earlier international standard, the meter-kilogram-second (MKS) system. The convention calls for regular General Conference meetings to consider improvements or modifications in standards, an International Committee of Weights and Measures elected by the Conference (meets annually), and several consultative committees. **The International Bureau of Weights and Measures** (Bureau International des Poids et Mesures) at Sèvres, France, serves as a depository for the primary international standards and as a laboratory for certification and intercomparison of national standard copies.

The 1960 **International System** (universally abbreviated as **SI**, from *système international*) builds upon the MKS system. Its **seven basic units**, from which other units are derived, are currently defined as follows: the **meter**, defined as the distance traveled by light in a vacuum in 1/299,792,458 second; the **kilogram** (about 2.2 pounds avoirdupois), which equals 1,000 grams as defined by the international prototype kilogram of platinum-iridium in the keeping of the International Bureau of Weights and Measures; the **second**, the duration of 9,192,631,770 periods of radiation associated with a specified transition of the cesium-133 atom; the **ampere**, which is the current that, if maintained in two wires placed one meter apart in a vacuum, would produce a force of 2×10^{-7} newton per meter of length; the **candela**, defined as the intensity in a given direction of a source emitting radiation of frequency 540×10^{12} hertz and that has a radiant intensity in that direction of 1/683 watt per steradian; the **mole**, defined as containing as many elementary entities of a substance as there are atoms in 0.012 kilogram of carbon-12; and the **kelvin**, which is 1/273.16 of the thermodynamic temperature of the triple point (equilibrium among the solid, liquid, and gaseous phases) of pure water.

International Bureau of Weights and Measures Web site: <www.bipm.fr>.

Elemental and Derived SI Units and Symbols

Quantity	SI Units		
	UNIT	FORMULA/EXPRESSION IN BASE UNITS	SYMBOL
elemental units			
length	meter	—	m
mass	kilogram	—	kg
time	second	—	s
electric current	ampere	—	A
luminous intensity	candela	—	cd
amount of substance	mole	—	mol
thermodynamic temperature	kelvin	—	K
derived units			
acceleration	meter/second squared	m/s^2	
area	square meter	m^2	
capacitance	farad	A × s/V	F
charge	coulomb	A × s	C
Celsius temperature	degree Celsius	K	°C
density	kilogram/cubic meter	kg/m^3	
electric field strength	volt/meter	V/m	
electrical potential	volt	W/A	V
energy	joule	N × m	J
force	newton	$kg \times m/s^2$	N
frequency	hertz	s^{-1}	Hz
illumination	lux	lm/m^2	lx
inductance	henry	V × s/A	H
kinematic viscosity	square meter/second	m^2/s	
luminance	candela/square meter	cd/m^2	
luminous flux	lumen	cd × sr	lm
magnetic field strength	ampere/meter	A/m	
magnetic flux	weber	V × s	Wb
magnetic flux density	tesla	Wb/m^2	T
plane angle	radian	$m \times m^{-1}=1$	rad
power	watt	J/s	W
pressure	pascal (newton/square meter)	N/m^2	Pa
resistance	ohm	V/A	Ω
solid angle	steradian	$m^2 \times m^{-2}=1$	sr
stress	pascal (newton/square meter)	N/m^2	Pa
velocity	meter/second	m/s	
viscosity	newton-second/square meter	$N \times s/m^2$	
volume	cubic meter	m^3	

Conversion of Metric Weights and Measures

The International System of Units is a decimal system of weights and measures derived from and extending the metric system of units. Adopted by the 11th General Conference on Weights and Measures in 1960, it is abbreviated "SI" in all languages. Below are common equivalents and conversion factors for US customary and SI systems.

approximate common equivalents		conversions accurate within 10 parts per million	
1 inch	= 25 millimeters	inches × 25.4[1]	= millimeters
1 foot	= 0.3 meter	feet × 0.3048[1]	= meters
1 yard	= 0.9 meter	yards × 0.9144[1]	= meters
1 mile	= 1.6 kilometers	miles × 1.60934	= kilometers
1 square inch	= 6.5 sq. centimeters	square inches × 6.4516[1]	= square centimeters
1 square foot	= 0.09 square meter	square feet × 0.0929030	= square meters
1 square yard	= 0.8 square meter	square yards × 0.836127	= square meters
1 acre	= 0.4 hectare[2]	acres × 0.404686	= hectares
1 cubic inch	= 16 cubic centimeters	cubic inches × 16.3871	= cubic centimeters
1 cubic foot	= 0.03 cubic meter	cubic feet × 0.0283168	= cubic meters
1 cubic yard	= 0.8 cubic meter	cubic yards × 0.764555	= cubic meters
1 quart (liq)	= 1 liter[2]	quarts (liquid) × 0.946353	= liters
1 gallon	= 0.004 cubic meter	gallons × 0.00378541	= cubic meters
1 ounce (avdp)[3]	= 28 grams	ounces (avdp)[3] × 28.3495	= grams
1 pound (avdp)[3]	= 0.45 kilogram	pounds (avdp)[3] × 0.453592	= kilograms
1 horsepower	= 0.75 kilowatt	horsepower × 0.745700	= kilowatts
1 millimeter	= 0.04 inch	millimeters × 0.0393701	= inches
1 meter	= 3.3 feet	meters × 3.28084	= feet

Conversion of Metric Weights and Measures (continued)

1 meter	= 1.1 yards	meters × 1.09361	= yards
1 kilometer	= 0.6 mile (statute)	kilometers × 0.621371	= miles (statute)
1 square centimeter	= 0.16 square inch	square centimeters × 0.155000	= square inches
1 square meter	= 11 square feet	square meters × 10.7639	= square feet
1 square meter	= 1.2 square yards	square meters × 1.19599	= square yards
1 hectare[2]	= 2.5 acres	hectares × 2.47105	= acres
1 cubic centimeter	= 0.06 cubic inch	cubic centimeters × 0.0610237	= cubic inches
1 cubic meter	= 35 cubic feet	cubic meters × 35.3147	= cubic feet
1 cubic meter	= 1.3 cubic yards	cubic meters × 1.30795	= cubic yards
1 liter[2]	= 1 quart (liq)	liters × 1.05669	= quarts (liq)
1 cubic meter	= 264 gallons	cubic meters × 264.172	= gallons
1 gram	= 0.035 ounce (avdp)[3]	grams × 0.0352740	= ounces (avdp)[3]
1 kilogram	= 2.2 pounds (avdp)[3]	kilograms × 2.20462	= pounds (avdp)[3]
1 kilowatt	= 1.3 horsepower	kilowatts × 1.34102	= horsepower

[1]*Exact.* [2]*Common term not used in SI.* [3]*avdp = avoirdupois.*
Source: National Institute of Standards and Technology.

Tables of Equivalents: Metric System Units and Prefixes

base unit[1]

QUANTITY	NAME OF UNIT	SYMBOL
length	meter	m
area	square meter	square m, or m^2
	are (100 square meters)	a
volume	cubic meter	cubic m, or m^3
	stere (1 cubic meter)	s
mass	gram	g
	metric ton (1,000,000 grams)	t
capacity	liter	l
temperature	degree Celsius	°C

prefixes designating multiples and submultiples

PREFIX	SYMBOL	FACTOR BY WHICH UNIT IS MULTIPLIED			EXAMPLES
exa-	E	10^{18}	=	1,000,000,000,000,000,000	
peta-	P	10^{15}	=	1,000,000,000,000,000	
tera-	T	10^{12}	=	1,000,000,000,000	
giga-	G	10^{9}	=	1,000,000,000	
mega-	M	10^{6}	=	1,000,000	megaton (Mt)
kilo-	k	10^{3}	=	1,000	kilometer (km)
hecto-, hect-	h	10^{2}	=	100	hectare (ha)
deca- dec- .	da	10	=	10	decastere (das)
				1	
deci-	d	10^{-1}	=	0.1	decigram (dg)
centi-, cent-	c	10^{-2}	=	0.01	centimeter (cm)
milli-	m	10^{-3}	=	0.001	milliliter (ml)
micro-, micr-	μ	10^{-6}	=	0.000001	microgram (μg)
nano-	n	10^{-9}	=	0.000000001	
pico-	p	10^{-12}	=	0.000000000001	
femto-	f	10^{-15}	=	0.000000000000001	
atto-	a	10^{-18}	=	0.000000000000000001	

[1]*The metric system of bases and prefixes has been applied to many other units, such as decibel (0.1 bel), kilowatt (1,000 watts), and microhm (one-millionth of an ohm).*

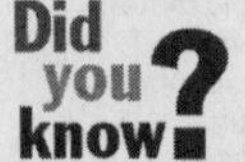

The US was an independent nation for 13 years before the Constitution was signed in 1789, the same year George Washington was elected the country's first president. In 1781, American Revolutionary leader John Hanson was elected by the Continental Congress "President of the United States in Congress Assembled." Hanson is thus referred to by some as the first US president, but he was a congressional presiding officer and had none of the presidential powers that would be granted under the Constitution.

British/US System (foot-pound-second, fps)

length				
1 statute mi	= 5,280 ft	= 1,760 yd	= 320 rods	= 8 furlongs
1 nautical mi	= 6,076 ft	= 1.151 mi		
1 furlong	= 660 ft	= 220 yd	= 40 rods	= 1/8 mi
1 chain (Gunter's)	= 66 ft	= 22 yd	= 100 links	= 4 rods
1 rod	= 16.5 ft	= 5.5 yd	= 25 links	
1 fathom	= 6 ft	= 72 in		
1 yd	= 3 ft	= 36 in		
1 ft	= 12 in			
1 link (Gunter's)	= 0.66 ft	= 7.92 in		
1 hand	= 4 in			
1 mil	= 0.001 in			

area				
1 sq mi	= 640 acres	= 102,400 sq rods	= 3,097,600 sq yd	= 27,878,400 sq ft
1 acre	= 10 sq chains	= 160 sq rods	= 4,840 sq yd	= 43,560 sq ft
1 sq ft	= 144 sq in			

volume			
1 cu ft	= 1/27 cu yd	= 12 board ft	= 1,728 cu in
1 cu in	= 1/46,656 cu yd	= 1/1,728 cu ft	
1 acre-ft	= 43,560 cu ft	= 1,613 cu yd	
1 board ft	= 144 cu in	= 1/12 cu ft	= 1 super ft (lumber)
1 cord (US)	= 128 cu ft		

capacity		
1 cu ft	= 7.481 gal (US)	= 6.229 gal (British)

liquid measure (US)				
1 barrel, oil	= 42 gal (US)	= 34.97 gal (British)		
1 gal	= 0.833 gal (British)	= 4 quarts	= 231.00 cu in	= 128 fl oz
1 quart	= 1/4 gal	= 2 pints	= 57.75 cu in	= 32 fl oz
1 pint	= 1/8 gal	= 1/2 quart	= 28.88 cu in	= 16 fl oz
1 gill	= 1/32 gal	= 1/4 pint	= 7.22 cu in	= 4 fl oz
1 fl oz	= 1/128 gal	= 1/16 pint	= 1.80 cu in	

dry measure (US)				
1 bushel	= 0.97 bushel (British)	= 4 pecks	= 2,150.4 cu in	= 1.24 cu ft
1 peck	= 1/4 bushel	= 8 quarts	= 537.6 cu in	= 0.31 cu ft
1 quart	= 1/32 bushel	= 2 pints	= 67.2 cu in	= 1/8 peck
1 pint	= 1/64 bushel	= 1/2 quart	= 33.6 cu in	

liquid and dry measure (British)					
1 bushel	= 1.03 bushels (US)	= 8 gal	= 4 pecks	= 2,219.36 cu in	= 1.284 cu ft
1 peck	= 0.25 bushel	= 2 gal	= 8 quarts	= 554.84 cu in	
1 gal	= 1.20 gal (US)	= 4 quarts		= 277.42 cu in	
1 quart	= 0.30 gal	= 2 pints	= 1/8 peck	= 69.36 cu in	
1 pint	= 4.80 gills (US)	= 4 gills		= 34.68 cu in	= 20 fl oz
1 gill	= 1.20 gills (US)			= 8.67 cu in	= 5 fl oz
1 fl oz	= 0.96 fl oz (US)			= 1.73 cu in	

weight			
1 short ton (US)	= 0.89 long ton	= 2,000 lbs	= 20 short cwt[1]
1 long ton (British)	= 1.12 short tons	= 2,240 lbs	= 22.4 short cwt[1]
1 short cwt[1] (US)	= 0.05 short ton	= 100 lbs	
1 long cwt[1] (British)	= 0.05 long ton	= 112 lbs	
1 stone (person)	= 0.14 short cwt[1]	= 14 lbs	
1 lb	= 0.07 stone (British)		
1 oz avoirdupois	= 437.50 grains	= 1/16 lb	= 0.911 oz troy
1 oz troy	= 480.00 grains	= 1/12 lb	= 1.097 oz
1 grain		= 0.0023 oz	= 0.0021 oz troy

[1]*cwt = hundredweight.*

Electrical Units

UNIT	SYMBOL	ATTRIBUTE MEASURED	EXPRESSION IN OTHER UNITS (S = SECOND)
ampere	A	current	C/s *or* V/Ω

the basic electrical unit of the International System of Units (SI), since 1948 defined by the International Bureau of Weights and Measures as the constant current which, if maintained in two straight parallel conductors of infinite length, of negligible circular cross section, and placed one meter apart in a vacuum, would produce between these conductors a force equal to 2×10^{-7} newton per meter of length. One ampere is equal to a flow of one coulomb of electricity per second; or, the flow produced in a conductor with a resistance of one ohm by a potential difference of one volt.

farad	F	capacitance (ability to hold a charge)	A × s/V *or* C/V

the ability of two parallel, oppositely charged plates (a capacitor) to hold an electric charge equals one farad when one coulomb of electricity changes the potential between the plates by one volt.

coulomb	C	charge	A × s

the quantity of electricity transported in one second by a current of one ampere. Approximately equal to 6.24×10^{18} electrons.

watt	W	power	J/s *or* V × A

one joule of work performed per second; or, the power dissipated in an electrical conductor carrying one ampere current between points at one volt potential difference.

ohm	Ω	resistance	V/A *or* W/A²

resistance of a circuit in which a potential difference of one volt produces a current of one ampere; or, the resistance in which one watt of power is dissipated when one ampere flows through it.

volt	V	potential	W/A *or* A × Ω

the difference in potential between two points in a conductor carrying one ampere current when the power dissipated between the points is one watt; or, the difference in potential between two points in a conductor across a resistance of one ohm when one ampere is flowing through it.

Temperature Equivalents

Instructions for converting °F into °C or K[1], and °C into °F: Find the figure you wish to convert in the second column. If this figure is in °F, the corresponding temperature in °C and K will be found in the third and fourth columns; if the figure is in °C, the corresponding temperature in °F will be found in the first column. To convert a temperature range between two scales, rather than finding equivalent temperatures, see the temperature conversion instructions, below.

°FAHRENHEIT (°F)	FIGURE TO BE CONVERTED	°CELSIUS (°CENTIGRADE) (°C)	KELVIN (K)
	−459.67	−273.15	0
	−400	−240.00	+33.15
	−300	−184.44	+88.71
−459.67	−273.15	−169.53	+103.62
−328.0	−200	−128.89	+144.26
−148.0	−100	−73.33	+199.82
−130.0	−90	−67.78	+205.37
−112.0	−80	−62.22	+210.93
−94.0	−70	−56.67	+216.48
−76.9	−60	−51.11	+222.04
−58.0	−50	−45.56	+227.59
−40.0	−40	−40.00	+233.15
−22.0	−30	−34.44	+238.71
−4.0	−20	−28.89	+244.26
+14.0	−10	−23.33	+249.82
+32.0	0	−17.78	+255.37
+33.8	+1	−17.22	+255.93
+35.6	+2	−16.67	+256.48
+37.4	+3	−16.11	+257.04
+39.2	+4	−15.56	+257.59
+41.0	+5	−15.00	+258.15
+42.8	+6	−14.44	+258.71
+44.6	+7	−13.89	+259.26
+46.4	+8	−13.33	+259.82
+48.2	+9	−12.78	+260.37
+50.0	+10	−12.22	+260.93
+68.0	+20	−6.67	+266.48
+86.0	+30	−1.11	+272.04
+89.6	+32	0.00	+273.15
+104.0	+40	+4.44	+277.59
+122.0	+50	+10.00	+283.15
+140.0	+60	+15.56	+288.71
+158.0	+70	+21.11	+294.26
+176.0	+80	+26.67	+299.82
+194.0	+90	+32.22	+305.37
+212.0	+100	+37.78	+310.93
+392.0	+200	+93.33	+366.48
+572.0	+300	+148.89	+422.04
+752.0	+400	+204.44	+477.59
+932.0	+500	+260.00	+533.15
+1112.0	+600	+315.56	+588.71
+1292.0	+700	+371.11	+644.26
+1472.0	+800	+426.67	+699.82
+1652.0	+900	+482.22	+755.37
+1832.0	+1000	+537.78	+810.93
+3632.0	+2000	+1093.33	+1366.45
+5432.0	+3000	+1648.89	+1922.05

Temperature Equivalents (continued)

All systems of measuring temperature in degrees or units (kelvins) on a scale are based on the interval between the freezing and boiling points of water and differ only in the number of degrees or units into which this interval is divided.

Fahrenheit: interval is divided into 180 degrees (32° to 212°); 0° is at 32° below the freezing point of water.

Rankine: degree is the same as the Fahrenheit degree; 0° is at absolute zero (the theoretical point at which a thermodynamic system has the lowest energy, –459.67 °F). Once common in engineering applications in the US, the Rankine scale is now rarely used.

Celsius: interval is divided into 100 degrees; 0° is at the freezing point of water.

Kelvin: interval is the same as the Celsius degree; 0 K is at absolute zero (the theoretical point at which a thermodynamic system has the lowest energy, –273.15 °C).

Réaumur: interval is divided into 80 degrees; 0° is at the freezing point of water. One of the earliest (1730) temperature scales in widespread use, the Réaumur scale had been supplanted by other scales by the late 19th century.

temperature conversion instructions: [2]

°Fahrenheit	into	°Celsius	subtract 32, divide by 1.8[2]
°Celsius	into	°Fahrenheit	multiply by 1.8, add 32[2]
°Celsius	into	kelvin	add 273.15

[1]*Because a kelvin is itself a unit of measurement, it is incorrect to use "degree" or the ° symbol with it, as is necessary with the units of the Rankine, Fahrenheit, Celsius, and Réaumur scales. One kelvin is equal to one degree Celsius.* [2]*Instructions are for finding equivalent temperatures; to find the equivalent number of degrees in a temperature range (e.g., tomorrow's temperature will be 11.0 °F, or 6.1°C, warmer than today's temperature), omit the step of adding or subtracting 32.*

Cooking Measurements

MEASURE	CONVENTIONAL EQUIVALENTS[1]	METRIC EQUIVALENT
drop	1⁄60 teaspoon	0.08 ml
dash	⅛ teaspoon	0.62 ml
teaspoon	8 dashes; ⅓ tablespoon; ⅙ fluid ounce	4.93 ml
tablespoon	3 teaspoons; ½ fluid ounce	14.79 ml
ounce (weight)	1⁄16 pound	28.35 g
fluid ounce (volume)	2 tablespoons	29.57 ml
cup	8 fluid ounces; 16 tablespoons; ½ pint	236.59 ml
pound	16 ounces	453.6 g
pint	16 fluid ounces; 2 cups; ½ quart	473.18 ml
quart	32 fluid ounces; 4 cups; 2 pints; ¼ gallon	946.36 ml
gallon	128 fluid ounces; 16 cups; 8 pints; 4 quarts	3.785 l
peck	2 gallons	7.57 l
bushel	8 gallons; 4 pecks	30.28 l

[1]*All ounce measurements are in US ounces or fluid ounces.*

OVEN TEMPERATURE EQUIVALENTS

°F	°C	AMERICAN OVEN TEMPERATURE TERMS	FRENCH OVEN TEMPERATURE TERMS AND THERMOSTAT SETTINGS	BRITISH "GAS MARK" OVEN THERMOSTAT SETTINGS
160	71		#1	
170	77			
200	93		très doux; étuve	
212	100			
221	105		#2	
225	107	very slow	doux	
230	110		#3	
250	121			#¼ (241 °F)
275	135			#½ (266 °F)
284	140	slow	moyen; modéré	#1 (291 °F)
300	149			
302	150		#4	
320	160			#2 (313 °F)
325	163			#3 (336 °F)
350	177	moderate	assez chaud; bon four	

Cooking Measurements (continued)

OVEN TEMPERATURE EQUIVALENTS (CONTINUED)

°F	°C	AMERICAN OVEN TEMPERATURE TERMS	FRENCH OVEN TEMPERATURE TERMS AND THERMOSTAT SETTINGS	BRITISH "GAS MARK" OVEN THERMOSTAT SETTINGS
356	180			#4 (358 °F)
375	190		#5	#5 (379 °F)
390	200			
400	205			#6 (403 °F)
410	210	hot	chaud	
425	218		#6	#7 (424 °F)
428	220			
437	225			
450	232			#8 (446 °F)
475	246	very hot	très chaud; vif	#9 (469 °F)
500	260		#7	
525	274		#8	
550	288		#9	

Spirits Measure

Many specific volumes have varied over time and from place to place, but the proportional relationships within families of measures have generally remained the same. All ounce measures are in US fluid ounces.

MEASURE	CONVENTIONAL EQUIVALENTS	METRIC EQUIVALENT
pony	0.75 oz = ¾ shot= ½ jigger	22.17 ml
shot/ounce/finger	1 oz = 1⅓ ponies = ⅔ jigger	29.57 ml
jigger	1.5 oz = 2 ponies = 1½ shots	44.36 ml
double	2 oz = 2 shots	59.15 ml
triple	3 oz = 3 shots	88.72 ml
noggin/imperial gill/drink (whiskey)	4.8 oz	142.1 ml
pint	16 oz = ⅝ fifth = ½ quart	473.2 ml
quarter yard	20 oz = 1¼ pints	591.5 ml
bottle (champagne or other wine)	about 25.5 oz or ⅙ imperial gallon	750 ml (industry standard)
fifth	25.6 oz = ⅘ quart = ⅕ gallon	757.1 ml
quart	32 oz = ½ magnum = ¼ gallon	946.3 ml
half yard	40 oz = 2½ pints	1.182 l
magnum	2 bottles (champagne or other wine)	1.5 l
magnum	64 oz = 2 quarts = ½ gallon	1.893 l
yard	80 oz = 5 pints	2.365 l
jeroboam	4 bottles (champagne or other wine)	3 l
gallon/double magnum	128 oz = 4 quarts = 5 fifths = 2 magnums	3.785 l
rehoboam	6 bottles (champagne or other wine)	4 l
imperial gallon	1.20 gallons = ⅖ barn gallon = ⅒ anker	4.546 l
ale/beer gallon	1.22 gallons	4.620 l
methuselah	8 bottles (champagne or other wine)	6 l
salmanazar	12 bottles (champagne or other wine)	9 l
barn gallon	2½ imperial gallons = ¼ anker	11.37 l
balthazar	16 bottles (champagne or other wine)	12 l
half keg	5 gallons (type varies)	varies
nebuchadnezzar	20 bottles (champagne or other wine)	15 l
firkin	9 gallons	34.07 l
keg	10 gallons (type varies)	varies
anker	60 bottles = 10 imperial gallons = 4 barn gallons	45.46 l
runlet/rundlet/rudlet	144 pints = 72 quarts = 18 gallons = 2 firkins	68.14 l
octave	15.75 imperial gallons = ⅛ butt (wine)	71.60 l
British bottle	126 bottles = 21 imperial gallons	95.47 l
aum	120 quarts = 30 gallons	113.6 l
barrel (wine)	126 quarts = 31½ gallons = ¾ tierce	119.2 l
barrel (ale/beer)	144 quarts = 36 gallons = ½ puncheon (ale/beer)	136.3 l
tierce	168 quarts = 42 gallons = ½ puncheon (wine)	159.0 l
British hogshead (ale/beer)	54 imperial gallons = ½ butt (ale/beer) = ¼ tun (ale/beer)	245.5 l
puncheon (ale/beer)	72 gallons = 2 barrels (ale/beer)	272.5 l
British hogshead (wine)	63 imperial gallons = ½ butt (wine) = ¼ tun (wine)	286.4 l
puncheon (wine)	84 gallons = 2 tierces	318.0 l
butt/pipe (ale/beer)	108 imperial gallons = ½ tun (ale/beer)	491.0 l
butt/pipe (wine)	126 imperial gallons = ½ tun (wine)	572.8 l
tun (ale/beer)	216 imperial gallons = 4 British hogsheads (ale/beer) = 2 butts (ale/beer)	982.0 l
tun (wine)	252 imperial gallons = 12 British bottles = 2 butts (wine)	1,146 l

Playing Cards and Dice Chances

Blackjack

Number of two-card combinations in a 52-card deck (where aces equal 1 or 11 and face cards equal 10) for each number between 13 and 21

TOTAL WITH TWO CARDS	POSSIBLE COMBINATIONS FROM 52 CARDS
21	64
20	136
19	80
18	86
17	96
16	86
15	96
14	102
13	118

Approximate chances of various hands reaching or exceeding 21

TOTAL IN HAND BEFORE DEAL (TWO OR MORE CARDS)	CHANCE OF REACHING A COUNT OF 17 TO 21 (%)	CHANCE OF EXCEEDING 21: ONE CARD (%)	CHANCE OF EXCEEDING 21: ANY NUMBER OF CARDS (%)
16	38	62	62
15	42	54	58
14	44	46	56
13	48	38	52

Poker

Number of ways to reach and odds of reaching various five-card combinations on a single deal (52-card deck, no wild cards)

HAND	NUMBER OF COMBINATIONS	ODDS OF RECEIVING ON A SINGLE DEAL
royal flush	4	1 in 649,740
straight flush	36	1 in 72,193
four of a kind	624	1 in 4,165
full house	3,744	1 in 694
flush	5,108	1 in 509
straight	10,200	1 in 255
three of a kind	54,912	1 in 47
two pairs	123,552	1 in 21
one pair	1,098,240	1 in 2

Dice

Probabilities of two-die totals

TWO-DIE TOTAL	NUMBER OF COMBINATIONS	PROBABILITY (%)	TWO-DIE TOTAL	NUMBER OF COMBINATIONS	PROBABILITY (%)
2	1	2.78	8	5	13.89
3	2	5.56	9	4	11.11
4	3	8.33	10	3	8.33
5	4	11.11	11	2	5.56
6	5	13.89	12	1	2.78
7	6	16.67	**total**	**36**	**100**[1]

[1] *Detail may not add to total given because of rounding.*

Ancient Measures

The standard unit of measure is listed first, with a rough modern equivalent in parentheses. Often, standard units varied over time, so a range is sometimes given. The subdivisions below relate to the standard unit of measure given first.

CULTURE	LENGTH	WEIGHT	LIQUID
Egyptian	cubit (524 mm; 20.62 in)	kite (4.5–29.9 g; 0.16–1.05 oz)	cubic cubit (0.14 cubic m; 37 gal)[1]
	digit (1⁄28 of a cubit)	deben (10 kites)	khar
	palm (4 digits)	sep (10 debens)	hekat
	hand (5 digits)		hin
	small span (12 digits, or 3 palms)		ro
	large span (14 digits, or ½ cubit)		
	small cubit (24 digits, or 6 palms)		
Babylonian	kus[2] (530 mm; 20.9 in)	mina (640–978 g; 23–34 oz)	ka (99–102 cubic mm; 3.9–4.0 cubic in)
	foot (⅔ kus)	shekel	gur (300 ka)
	shusi (1⁄30 kus)		
Hebrew[3]		sacred mina (60 shekels)	bat[4]
		sacred talent (3,000 shekels, or 50 sacred minas)	hin
			log

Ancient Measures (continued)

CULTURE	LENGTH	WEIGHT	LIQUID
Hebrew[3] (continued)		Talmudic mina (25 shekels) Talmudic talent (1,500 shekels, or 60 Talmudic minas)	
Greek	finger (19.3 mm; 0.76 in) foot (16 fingers) Olympic cubit (24 fingers)	talent (25.8 kg; 56.9 lb)	metretes (39.4 l; 10.4 gal)
Roman	foot (subdivided into the uncia [plural unciae]; 1⁄12 ft) pace, or double step (5 ft) mille passus (1,000 paces)	libra (327.45 g; 11.55 oz) uncia (1⁄12 lb)	sextarius (plural sextarii; 0.53 l; 0.14 gal) amphora (48 sextarii)
Chinese[5]	chih (25 cm; 9.8 in) chang (3 m; 9.8 ft)	shih, or tan (60 kg; 132 lb)	

[1]Measures given below the cubic cubit run from small to large. [2]Also called the Babylonian cubit. [3]The Hittites, Assyrians, Phoenicians, and Hebrews derived their systems from the Babylonians and Egyptians. Hebrew standards were based on the relationship between the mina, the talent (the basic unit), and the shekel. [4]Volumes are not definitely known but are listed from largest to smallest. [5]The Chinese system of measurement exhibited all the principal characteristics of the Western. It was, however, fundamentally chaotic in that there was no relationship between different types of units, such as those of length and those of volume. It also fluctuated from region to region. The first emperor of China, Shi Huangdi (221–210/09 BC), fixed the basic units given here.

Roman Numerals

Seven numeral-characters compose the Roman numeral system. When a numeral appears with a line above it, it represents the base value multiplied by 1,000. However, because Roman numerals are now seldom utilized for values beyond 4,999, this convention is no longer in use.

ARABIC	ROMAN	ARABIC	ROMAN	ARABIC	ROMAN	ARABIC	ROMAN
1	I	15	XV	70	LXX	1,000	M
2	II	16	XVI	80	LXXX	1,001	MI
3	III	17	XVII	90	XC	1,002	MII
4	IV	18	XVIII	100	C	1,003	MIII
5	V	19	XIX	101	CI	1,900	MCM
6	VI	20	XX	102	CII	2,000	MM
7	VII	21	XXI	200	CC	2,001	MMI
8	VIII	22	XXII	300	CCC	2,002	MMII
9	IX	23	XXIII	400	CD	2,100	MMC
10	X	24	XXIV	500	D	3,000	MMM
11	XI	30	XXX	600	DC	4,000	MMMM or M$\overline{V}$
12	XII	40	XL	700	DCC	5,000	$\overline{V}$
13	XIII	50	L	800	DCCC		
14	XIV	60	LX	900	CM		

Mathematical Formulas

The ratio of the circumference of a circle to its diameter is π (3.141592653589793238462643383279..., generally rounded to 22⁄7 or 3.1416). It occurs in various mathematical problems involving the lengths of arcs or other curves, the areas of surfaces, and the volumes of many solids.

	SHAPE	ACTION	FORMULA
circumference	circle	multiply diameter by π	πd
area	circle	multiply radius squared by π	πr^2
	rectangle	multiply height by length	hl
	sphere surface	multiply radius squared by π by 4	$4\pi r^2$
	square	length of one side squared	s^2
	trapezoid	parallel side length A + parallel side length B multiplied by height and divided by 2	$(A+B)h/2$
	triangle	multiply base by height and divide by 2	$hb/2$
volume	cone	multiply base radius squared by π by height and divide by 3	$br^2\pi h/3$
	cube	length of one edge cubed	a3
	cylinder	multiply base radius squared by π by height	$br^2\pi h$
	pyramid	multiply base area by height and divide by 3	$hb/3$
	sphere	multiply radius cubed by π by 4 and divide by 3	$4\pi r^3/3$

Large Numbers

The American system of numeration for denominations above one million was modeled on a French system, but subsequently the French system changed to correspond to the German and British systems. In recent years, British usage reflects widespread and increasing use of the values of the American system. In the American system each of the denominations above 1,000 millions (the American *billion*) is 1,000 times the preceding one (one trillion = 1,000 billions; one quadrillion = 1,000 trillions). In the British system the first denomination above 1,000 millions (the British *milliard*) is 1,000 times the preceding one, but each of the denominations above 1,000 milliards (the British *billion*) is 1,000,000 times the preceding one (one trillion = 1,000,000 billions; one quadrillion = 1,000,000 trillions).

Source: *Merriam-Webster's Collegiate Dictionary*, Eleventh Edition, Merriam-Webster, Inc., 2003.

AMERICAN NAME	VALUE IN POWERS OF TEN	NUMBER OF ZEROS
billion	10^{9}	9
trillion	10^{12}	12
quadrillion	10^{15}	15
quintillion	10^{18}	18
sextillion	10^{21}	21
septillion	10^{24}	24
octillion	10^{27}	27
nonillion	10^{30}	30
decillion	10^{33}	33
undecillion	10^{36}	36
duodecillion	10^{39}	39
tredecillion	10^{42}	42
quattuordecillion	10^{45}	45
quindecillion	10^{48}	48
sexdecillion	10^{51}	51
septendecillion	10^{54}	54
octodecillion	10^{57}	57
novemdecillion	10^{60}	60
vigintillion	10^{63}	63
googol	10^{100}	100
centillion	10^{303}	303

BRITISH NAME	VALUE IN POWERS OF TEN	NUMBER OF ZEROS
milliard	10^{9}	9
billion	10^{12}	12
trillion	10^{18}	18
quadrillion	10^{24}	24
quintillion	10^{30}	30
sextillion	10^{36}	36
septillion	10^{42}	42
octillion	10^{48}	48
nonillion	10^{54}	54
decillion	10^{60}	60
undecillion	10^{66}	66
duodecillion	10^{72}	72
tredecillion	10^{78}	78
quattuordecillion	10^{84}	84
quindecillion	10^{90}	90
sexdecillion	10^{96}	96
septendecillion	10^{102}	102
octodecillion	10^{108}	108
novemdecillion	10^{114}	114
vigintillion	10^{120}	120
centillion	10^{600}	600

Decimal Equivalents of Common Fractions

4THS	8THS	16THS	32NDS	DECIMAL
				0.015625
			1	0.03125
		1	2	0.0625
			3	0.09375
	1	2	4	0.125
			5	0.15625
		3	6	0.1875
			7	0.21875
1	2	4	8	0.25
			9	0.28125
		5	10	0.3125
			11	0.34375
	3	6	12	0.375
			13	0.40625
		7	14	0.4375
			15	0.46875
2	4	8	16	0.5
			17	0.53125
		9	18	0.5625
			19	0.59375
	5	10	20	0.625
			21	0.65625
		11	22	0.6875
			23	0.71875
3	6	12	24	0.75
			25	0.78125
		13	26	0.8125
			27	0.84375
	7	14	28	0.875
			29	0.90625
		15	30	0.9375
			31	0.96875
4	8	16	32	1

3RDS	6THS	12THS	DECIMAL
		1	0.833334
	1	2	0.166667
		3	0.25
1	2	4	0.333334
		5	0.416667
	3	6	0.5
		7	0.583333
2	4	8	0.666667
		9	0.75
	5	10	0.833333
		11	0.916667
	6	12	1

5THS	DECIMAL
1	0.2
2	0.4
3	0.6
4	0.8
5	1

7THS	DECIMAL
1	0.142857
2	0.285714
3	0.428571
4	0.571428
5	0.714285
6	0.857142
7	1

Periodic Table of the Elements

The periodic table arranges the elements into groups (vertically) of elements sharing common physical and chemical characteristics and into periods (horizontally) of sequentially increasing atomic number and electron-shell configuration. Elements 112–116 and 118 have been created experimentally and have temporary names. Atomic weights in parentheses indicate the number of the most stable isotope of a radioactive element.

1	2	3	4	5	6	7	8	9	10	11	12	13	14	15	16	17	18
1 H																	2 He
3 Li	4 Be											5 B	6 C	7 N	8 O	9 F	10 Ne
11 Na	12 Mg											13 Al	14 Si	15 P	16 S	17 Cl	18 Ar
19 K	20 Ca	21 Sc	22 Ti	23 V	24 Cr	25 Mn	26 Fe	27 Co	28 Ni	29 Cu	30 Zn	31 Ga	32 Ge	33 As	34 Se	35 Br	36 Kr
37 Rb	38 Sr	39 Y	40 Zr	41 Nb	42 Mo	43 Tc	44 Ru	45 Rh	46 Pd	47 Ag	48 Cd	49 In	50 Sn	51 Sb	52 Te	53 I	54 Xe
55 Cs	56 Ba	57 La	72 Hf	73 Ta	74 W	75 Re	76 Os	77 Ir	78 Pt	79 Au	80 Hg	81 Tl	82 Pb	83 Bi	84 Po	85 At	86 Rn
87 Fr	88 Ra	89 Ac	104 Rf	105 Db	106 Sg	107 Bh	108 Hs	109 Mt	110 Ds	111 Rg	112 Uub	113 Uut	114 Uuq	115 Uup	116 Uuh		118 Uuo

Lanthanide Series	58 Ce	59 Pr	60 Nd	61 Pm	62 Sm	63 Eu	64 Gd	65 Tb	66 Dy	67 Ho	68 Er	69 Tm	70 Yb	71 Lu
Actinide Series	90 Th	91 Pa	92 U	93 Np	94 Pu	95 Am	96 Cm	97 Bk	98 Cf	99 Es	100 Fm	101 Md	102 No	103 Lr

Element	Symbol	Atomic no.	Atomic weight	Element	Symbol	Atomic no.	Atomic weight
Actinium	Ac	89	(227)	Molybdenum	Mo	42	95.94
Aluminum	Al	13	26.98154	Neodymium	Nd	60	144.242
Americium	Am	95	(243)	Neon	Ne	10	20.1797
Antimony	Sb	51	121.760	Neptunium	Np	93	(237)
Argon	Ar	18	39.948	Nickel	Ni	28	58.6934
Arsenic	As	33	74.92160	Niobium	Nb	41	92.90638
Astatine	At	85	(210)	Nitrogen	N	7	14.0067
Barium	Ba	56	137.327	Nobelium	No	102	(259)
Berkelium	Bk	97	(247)	Osmium	Os	76	190.23
Beryllium	Be	4	9.01218	Oxygen	O	8	15.9994
Bismuth	Bi	83	208.98040	Palladium	Pd	46	106.42
Bohrium	Bh	107	(272)	Phosphorus	P	15	30.97376
Boron	B	5	10.811	Platinum	Pt	78	195.084
Bromine	Br	35	79.904	Plutonium	Pu	94	(244)
Cadmium	Cd	48	112.411	Polonium	Po	84	(209)
Calcium	Ca	20	40.078	Potassium	K	19	39.0983
Californium	Cf	98	(251)	Praseodymium	Pr	59	140.90765
Carbon	C	6	12.0107	Promethium	Pm	61	(145)
Cerium	Ce	58	140.116	Protactinium	Pa	91	231.03588
Cesium	Cs	55	132.90545	Radium	Ra	88	(226)
Chlorine	Cl	17	35.453	Radon	Rn	86	(222)
Chromium	Cr	24	51.9961	Rhenium	Re	75	186.207
Cobalt	Co	27	58.93320	Rhodium	Rh	45	102.90550
Copper	Cu	29	63.546	Roentgenium	Rg	111	(280)
Curium	Cm	96	(247)	Rubidium	Rb	37	85.4678
Darmstadtium	Ds	110	(281)	Ruthenium	Ru	44	101.07
Dubnium	Db	105	(268)	Rutherfordium	Rf	104	(267)
Dysprosium	Dy	66	162.500	Samarium	Sm	62	150.36
Einsteinium	Es	99	(252)	Scandium	Sc	21	44.9559
Erbium	Er	68	167.259	Seaborgium	Sg	106	(271)
Europium	Eu	63	151.964	Selenium	Se	34	78.96
Fermium	Fm	100	(257)	Silicon	Si	14	28.0855
Fluorine	F	9	18.99840	Silver	Ag	47	107.8682
Francium	Fr	87	(223)	Sodium	Na	11	22.98977
Gadolinium	Gd	64	157.25	Strontium	Sr	38	87.62
Gallium	Ga	31	69.723	Sulfur	S	16	32.065
Germanium	Ge	32	72.64	Tantalum	Ta	73	180.94788
Gold	Au	79	196.96657	Technetium	Tc	43	(98)
Hafnium	Hf	72	178.49	Tellurium	Te	52	127.60
Hassium	Hs	108	(270)	Terbium	Tb	65	158.92535
Helium	He	2	4.00260	Thallium	Tl	81	204.3833
Holmium	Ho	67	164.93032	Thorium	Th	90	232.03806
Hydrogen	H	1	1.00794	Thulium	Tm	69	168.93421
Indium	In	49	114.818	Tin	Sn	50	118.710
Iodine	I	53	126.90447	Titanium	Ti	22	47.867
Iridium	Ir	77	192.217	Tungsten (wolfram)	W	74	183.85
Iron	Fe	26	55.845	Ununbium	Uub	112	(285)
Krypton	Kr	36	83.798	Ununhexium	Uuh	116	(293)
Lanthanum	La	57	138.90547	Ununoctium	Uuo	118	(294)
Lawrencium	Lr	103	(262)	Ununpentium	Uup	115	(288)
Lead	Pb	82	207.2	Ununquadium	Uuq	114	(289)
Lithium	Li	3	6.941	Ununtrium	Uut	113	(284)
Lutetium	Lu	71	174.967	Uranium	U	92	238.02891
Magnesium	Mg	12	24.3050	Vanadium	V	23	50.9415
Manganese	Mn	25	54.93805	Xenon	Xe	54	131.293
Meitnerium	Mt	109	(276)	Ytterbium	Yb	70	173.04
Mendelevium	Md	101	(258)	Yttrium	Y	39	88.90585
Mercury	Hg	80	200.59	Zinc	Zn	30	65.409
				Zirconium	Zr	40	91.224

Applied Science

Chemistry

Chemistry is the science that deals with the properties, composition, and structure of substances (defined as elements and compounds), the transformations that they undergo, and the energy that is released or absorbed during these processes. Every substance, whether naturally occurring or artificially produced, consists of one or more of the hundred-odd species of atoms that have been identified as elements. Although these atoms, in turn, are composed of more elementary particles, they are the basic building blocks of chemical substances; there is no quantity of oxygen, mercury, or gold, for example, smaller than an atom of that substance. Chemistry, therefore, is concerned not with the subatomic domain but with the properties of atoms and the laws governing their combinations and with how the knowledge of these properties can be used to achieve specific purposes.

Common Alloys

ALLOY	COMPOSITION
brass	55% copper, 45% zinc
bronze	copper, tin
cast iron	iron, carbon, silicon, manganese, trace impurities
cupronickel	copper, nickel
pewter	tin, antimony, copper
solder	tin, lead
stainless steel	iron, carbon, chromium, nickel
steel	iron, carbon
sterling silver	silver, copper

Physics

Physics is the science that deals with the structure of matter and the interactions between the fundamental constituents of the observable universe. The basic physical science, its aim is the discovery and formulation of the fundamental laws of nature. In the broadest sense, physics (from the Greek *physikos*) is concerned with all aspects of nature on both the macroscopic and submicroscopic levels. Its scope of study encompasses not only the behavior of objects under the action of given forces but also the nature and origin of gravitational, electromagnetic, and nuclear force fields. Its ultimate objective is the formulation of a few comprehensive principles that bring together and explain all such disparate phenomena. Physics can, at base, be defined as the science of matter, motion, and energy. Its laws are typically expressed with economy and precision in the language of mathematics.

Weight, Mass, and Density

Mass, strictly defined, is the quantitative measure of inertia, the resistance a body offers to a change in its speed or position when force is applied to it. The greater the mass of a body, the smaller the change produced by an applied force. In more practical terms, it is the measure of the amount of material in an object, and in common usage is often expressed as weight. However, the mass of an object is constant regardless of its position, while weight varies according to gravitational pull.

In the International System of Units (SI; the metric system), the kilogram is the standard unit of mass, defined as equaling the mass of the international prototype of the kilogram, currently a platinum-iridium cylinder kept at Sèvres, near Paris, France; it is roughly equal to the mass of 1,000 cubic centimeters of pure water at the temperature of its maximum density. In the US customary system, the unit is the slug, defined as the mass which a one pound force can accelerate at a rate of one foot per second per second, which is the same as the mass of an object weighing 32.17 pounds on the earth's surface.

Weight is the gravitational force of attraction on an object, caused by the presence of a massive second object, such as the Earth or Moon. Weight is the product of an object's mass and the acceleration of gravity at the point where the object is located. A given object will have the same mass on the Earth's surface, on the Moon, or in the absence of gravity, while its weight on the Moon would be about one sixth of its weight on the Earth's surface, because of the Moon's smaller gravitational pull (due in turn to the Moon's smaller mass and radius), and in the absence of gravity the object would have no weight at all.

Weight is measured in units of force, not mass, though in practice units of mass (such as the kilogram) are often substituted because of mass's relatively constant relation to weight on the Earth's surface. The weight of a body can be obtained by multiplying the mass by the acceleration of gravity. In SI, weight is expressed in newtons, or the force required to impart an acceleration of one meter per second per second to a mass of one kilogram. In the US customary system, it is expressed in pounds.

Density is the mass per unit volume of a material substance. It offers a convenient means of obtaining the mass of a body from its volume, or vice versa; the mass is equal to the volume multiplied by the density, while the volume is equal to the mass divided by the density. In SI, density is expressed in kilograms per cubic meter.

Communications

Introduction to the Internet

The **Internet** is a dynamic collection of computer networks that has revolutionized communications and methods of commerce by enabling those networks around the world to interact with each other. Sometimes referred to as a "**network of networks**," the Internet was developed in the United States in the 1970s but was not widely used by the general public until the early 1990s. By early 2008 nearly 1.5 billion people, or roughly 22% of the world's population, were estimated to have access to the Internet. It is widely assumed that at least half of the world's population will have some form of Internet access by 2010 and that wireless access will play a growing role.

The Internet is so powerful and general that it can be used for almost any purpose that depends on the processing of information, and it is accessible by every individual who connects to one of its constituent networks. It supports human communication via **electronic mail** (e-mail), real-time "chat rooms," instant messaging (IM), newsgroups, and audio and video transmission and allows people to work collaboratively at many different locations. It supports access to information by many applications, including the **World Wide Web**, which uses text and graphical presentations. Publishing has been revolutionized, as whole novels and reference works are available on the Web, and periodicals, including data prepared daily for an individual subscriber (such as stock market reports or news summaries), are also common. The Internet has attracted a large and growing number of "e-businesses" (including subsidiaries of traditional "brick-and-mortar" companies) that carry out most of their sales and services over the Internet.

While the precise structure of the future Internet is not yet clear, many directions of growth seem apparent. One is the increased availability of wireless access, enabling better real-time use of Web-managed information. Another future development is toward higher backbone and network access speeds. Backbone data rates of 10 billion bits (10 gigabits) per second are readily available today, but data rates of 1 trillion bits (1 terabit) per second or higher will eventually become commercially feasible. At very high data rates, high-resolution video, for example, would occupy only a small fraction of available bandwidth, and remaining bandwidth could be used to transmit auxiliary information about the data being sent, which in turn would enable rapid customization of displays and prompt resolution of certain local queries.

Communications connectivity will be a key function of a future Internet as more machines and devices are interconnected. Since the Internet Engineering Task Force published its 128-bit IP address standard in 1998, the increased number of available addresses (2^{128}, as opposed to 2^{32} under the previous standard) allowed almost every electronic device imaginable to be assigned a unique address. Thus the expressions "wired" office, home, and car may all take on new meanings, even if the access is really wireless.

Growth of Internet Use

Sources: International Telecommunications Union, Yearbook of Statistics; *ICT Statistics Database.*

YEAR	US USERS	WORLD USERS	YEAR	US USERS	WORLD USERS
1996	45,000,000	70,000,000	2002	159,000,000	618,434,100
1997	60,000,000	116,000,000	2003	161,632,400	718,772,300
1998	84,587,000	171,587,000	2004	185,000,000	851,804,400
1999	102,000,000	275,518,600	2005	197,800,000	980,386,700
2000	124,000,000	390,251,600	2006	210,200,000	1,201,139,800
2001	142,823,000	489,924,200	2007	220,000,000	1,472,916,300

Worldwide Cellular Mobile Telephone Subscribers, 2007

Source: International Telecommunication Union, ICT Statistics Database.

COUNTRY	SUBSCRIBERS	SUBSCRIBERS PER 1,000 RESIDENTS	COUNTRY	SUBSCRIBERS	SUBSCRIBERS PER 1,000 RESIDENTS
China	547,286,000	412	Ukraine	55,240,400	1,196
United States	255,400,000	835	Thailand	51,376,800	804
India	233,620,000	200	Spain	48,813,000	1,102
Russia	170,000,000	1,193	South Korea	43,500,000	902
Brazil	120,980,100	631	Philippines	42,868,900[1]	508[1]
Japan	100,525,000	786	South Africa	42,300,000	871
Germany	97,151,000	1,176	Poland	41,388,800	1,087
Indonesia	81,834,600	353	Argentina	40,401,800	1,022
Pakistan	78,852,900	481	Nigeria	40,395,600	273
Italy	78,571,000[1]	1,351[1]	Bangladesh	34,370,000	217
United Kingdom	71,992,500	1,185	Colombia	33,941,100	735
Mexico	68,253,600	641	Egypt	30,047,000	398
Turkey	61,975,800	828	Iran	28,499,300	400
France	55,358,100	898	**World**	**3,280,751,500**	**493**

[1]*Data for 2006.*

Growth of Cell Phone Use in the US

Number of cellular mobile telephone subscribers in the US, 1996–2007. Source: CTIA-The Wireless Association's Annualized Wireless Industry Survey Results, December 1985–December 2007.

YEAR	SUBSCRIBERS	YEAR	SUBSCRIBERS	YEAR	SUBSCRIBERS	YEAR	SUBSCRIBERS
1996	44,042,992	1999	86,047,003	2002	140,766,842	2005	207,896,198
1997	55,312,293	2000	109,478,031	2003	158,721,981	2006	233,040,781
1998	69,209,321	2001	128,374,512	2004	182,140,362	2007	255,395,599

Aerospace Technology

Space Exploration

Three men were the first scientists to conceive pragmatically of spaceflight: the Russian **Konstantin Tsiolkovsky**, the American **Robert Goddard**, and the German **Hermann Oberth**. Technology in the early 20th century, however, was a long way from the level required for rocket-powered flight. Nonetheless, the theory and dynamics of such flights were rigorously studied. By the end of World War II, the German development of rocket propulsion for aircraft and guided missiles (notably the V-2) had reached a high level. With the German surrender in 1945, the US and its Allies fell heir to the technical knowledge of rocket power developed by the Germans. The technical director of the German missile effort, **Wernher von Braun**, and some 150 of his top aides surrendered to US troops. Most emigrated to the US, where they assembled and launched V-2 missiles that had been captured and shipped there. The USSR carried out an unpublicized but extensive and likely similar program; Britain and France conducted smaller programs.

In both the US and the USSR the development of **military missile technology** was essential to the achievement of satellite flight. Preparations for the International Geophysical Year (IGY, 1957–58) stimulated discussion of the possibility of launching **artificial Earth satellites** for scientific investigations. Both the US and the USSR became determined to prepare scientific satellites for launching during the IGY. While the US was still developing a space launch vehicle, the USSR startled the world by placing **Sputnik 1** in orbit on 4 Oct 1957. This was followed a month later by **Sputnik 2** carrying a live dog. The failure by the US to launch its small payload on 6 Dec 1957 heightened that nation's political discomfiture in view of its supposed advanced status in science. Following debates on the necessity of achieving parity, the US government established the **National Aeronautics and Space Administration (NASA)** in 1958. Since that time, NASA has conducted virtually all major aspects of the US space program.

The first successful US satellite, **Explorer 1**, was launched about 4 months after Sputnik 1. During the next decades the two nations participated in a space race, conducting thousands of successful launches of spacecraft of all varieties including scientific-research, communications, meteorological, remote-sensing, military-reconnaissance, early-warning, and navigation satellites, lunar and planetary probes, and manned craft. The USSR launched the first human, **Yury Gagarin**, into orbit around Earth on 12 Apr 1961. On 20 July 1969, the US landed two men, **Neil Armstrong** and **Edwin ("Buzz") Aldrin**, on the surface of the Moon as part of the **Apollo 11** mission. On 12 Apr 1981, the 20th anniversary of manned space flight, the US launched the first reusable manned space transportation system, the space shuttle. From the 1960s the European nations, Japan, India, and other countries have formed their own agencies for space exploration and development. The **European Space Agency (ESA)** consists of 15 member nations. Private corporations, too, offer space launches for communications and remote-sensing satellites.

In the post-Apollo decades, while the US focused much of its manned space program on the **shuttle**, the USSR concentrated on launching a series of increasingly sophisticated Earth-orbiting **space stations**, beginning with the world's first in 1971. Station crews, who were carried up in two- and three-person spacecraft, carried out mostly scientific missions while gaining experience in living and working for long periods in the space environment. After the USSR was dissolved in 1991, its space program was continued by Russia on a much smaller scale owing to economic constraints. The US launched a space station in 1973 using surplus Apollo hardware and conducted shuttle missions to a Russian station, Mir, in the 1990s. In 1998, at the head of a 16-nation consortium and with Russia as a major partner, it began in-orbit assembly of the **International Space Station (ISS)**, using the shuttle and Russian expendable launch vehicles to ferry the facility's modular components and crews into space. In addition to manned and unmanned lunar exploration, space exploration programs have included deep-space robotic missions to the planets, their moons, and smaller bodies such as comets and asteroids. Also important has been the development of unmanned space-based astronomical observatories, which allow observation of near and distant cosmic objects above the filtering and distorting effects of Earth's atmosphere.

Significant space programs and missions:

Sputnik (Russian for "fellow traveler")

Years launched: 1957–58. **Country or space agency:** USSR. **Designation:** 1 through 3 (first series). **Not manned. Events of note:** Sputnik 1 was the first satellite to be successfully launched into space; Sputnik 2 carried a small dog named Laika ("Barker"); Sputnik 3 became the first multipurpose space-science satellite.

Vanguard

Years launched: 1958–59. **Country or space agency:** US. **Designation:** 1 through 3. **Not manned. Events of note:** The first attempted Vanguard launch, hastily mounted in December 1957 after the USSR's Sputnik successes, failed with the launch vehicle's explosion.

Explorer

Years launched: 1958–75. **Country or space agency:** US. **Designation:** 1 through 55. **Not manned. Events of note: Explorer 1, the first successful US satellite, discovered Earth's inner radiation belt. Other Explorers in this long series conducted pioneering studies over a broad spectrum of Earth and space sciences.

Pioneer

Years launched: 1958–78. **Country or space agency:** US. **Designation:** 1 through 13. **Not manned. Events of note:** Pioneer 10 was the first spacecraft to travel through the asteroid belt, to fly by Jupiter, and to escape the solar system; Pioneer 11 was the first to visit Saturn. Complementary Pioneer 12 and 13 spacecraft (also called Pioneer Venus) explored Venus, one conducting radar mapping of the planet's cloud-shrouded surface from orbit while the other dropped atmospheric probes.

Luna (Russian for "Moon")

Years launched: 1959–76. **Country or space agency:** USSR. **Designation:** 1 through 24. **Not manned. Events of note:** Luna 2 was the first spacecaft to crash-land on the lunar surface; Luna 3 took the first photographs of the Moon's far side; three Lunas (16, 20, and 24) returned with samples of lunar soil.

Mercury

Years launched: 1961–63 (manned missions). **Country or space agency:** US. **Designation:** Mercury spacecraft had program designations, but they were better known by the individual names bestowed on them, such as *Freedom 7*, to honor the seven NASA astronauts chosen for the program. **Events of note:** Some 20 preliminary unmanned Mercury missions took place between 1959 and 1961. Of the six manned missions, *Freedom 7* was launched in 1961 with Alan Shepard (the first American in space) aboard; *Liberty Bell 7* in 1961 with Virgil "Gus" Grissom; *Friendship 7* in 1962 with John Glenn (the first American to orbit Earth); *Aurora 7* in 1962 with Scott Carpenter; *Sigma 7* in 1962 with Walter Schirra; and *Faith 7* in 1963 with Gordon Cooper.

Vostok (Russian for "east")

Years launched: 1961–63. **Country or space agency:** USSR. **Designation:** 1 through 6. **Manned. Events of note:** The first man in space and to orbit Earth was Soviet cosmonaut Yury Gagarin in Vostok 1, launched on 12 April 1961. Vostok 2 was launched with Gherman Titov in 1961, Vostok 3 with Andriyan Nikolayev in 1962, Vostok 4 with Pavel Popovich in 1962, Vostok 5 with Valery Bykovsky in 1963, and Vostok 6 with Valentina Tereshkova, the first woman in space, in 1963.

Venera (Russian for "Venus")

Years launched: 1961–83. **Country or space agency:** USSR. **Designation:** 1 through 16. **Not manned. Events of note:** Venera 1 carried out the first Venus flyby. Venera 3 was the first spacecraft to impact on another planet, and Venera 7 was the first to soft-land on another planet. Venera 9 and 10 sent back the first close-up pictures of Venus's surface.

Ranger

Years launched: 1961–65. **Country or space agency:** US. **Designation:** 1 through 9. **Not manned. Events of note:** Ranger 4 was the first US spacecraft to crash-land on the Moon; the last three Rangers returned thousands of images of the lunar surface before crashing on the lunar surface as planned.

Mariner

Years launched: 1962–73. **Country or space agency:** US. **Designation:** 1 through 10. **Not manned. Events of note:** Various Mariners in the program flew by Venus, Mercury, and Mars. Mariner 9 mapped Mars in detail from orbit, becoming the first spacecraft to orbit another planet. Mariner 10 is the only spacecraft to have visited the vicinity of Mercury.

Voskhod (Russian for "sunrise" or "ascent")

Years launched: 1964–65. **Country or space agency:** USSR. **Designation:** 1 and 2. **Manned. Events of note:** Voskhod 1 was the first spacecraft to carry more than one person; Aleksey Leonov performed the first space walk, from the Voskhod 2 spacecraft, on 18 Mar 1965.

Gemini

Years launched: 1965–66. **Country or space agency:** US. **Designation:** 1 through 12. **Manned. Events of note:** Ten two-person manned missions followed two unmanned test flights. Gemini 8 was the first spacecraft to dock with another craft, an unmanned launcher stage. The Gemini program showed that astronauts could carry out rendezvous and docking maneuvers and could live and work in space for the time needed for a round-trip to the Moon.

Lunar Orbiter

Years launched: 1966–67. **Country or space agency:** US. **Designation:** 1 through 5. **Not manned. Events of note:** Five consecutive spacecraft made detailed photographic surveys of most of the Moon's surface, providing the mapping essential for choosing landing sites for the manned Apollo missions.

Soyuz (Russian for "union")

Years launched: 1967–present. **Country or space agency:** USSR. **Designation:** 1 through 40 (first series). Three subsequent series of upgraded spacecraft received the additional suffix letters T, TM, or TMA and were renumbered from 1. **Manned. Events of note:** On 24 Apr 1967 cosmonaut Vladimir Komarov conducted the inaugural test flight (Soyuz 1) of this multiperson transport craft but died returning to Earth after the parachute system failed, becoming the first fatality during a spaceflight. Soyuz 11 ferried the crew of the first space station, Salyut 1. Soyuz TM-2 made the inaugural manned flight of this TM upgrade while transporting the second crew of the Mir space station. Soyuz TM-31 carried up the International Space Station's first three-man crew. An automated unmanned cargo ferry, called Progress, was derived from the Soyuz design. High-resolution remote observations of Earth were made possible in 2006 with the launch of the Resurs-DK1 satellite.

Apollo

Years launched: 1968–72. **Country or space agency:** US. **Designation:** 7 through 17. **Manned. Events of note:** Several unmanned test flights preceded 11 manned Apollo missions, including two in Earth orbit (7 and 9), two in lunar orbit (8 and 10), one lunar flyby (13), and six lunar landings (11, 12, and 14–17) in which a total of 12 astronauts walked on the Moon. Apollo 11, crewed by Neil Armstrong, Michael Collins, and Buzz Aldrin, was the first mission to land humans on the Moon, on 20 Jul 1969. Apollo 13, planned as a lunar landing mission, experienced an onboard explosion en route to the Moon; after a swing around the Moon, the crippled spacecraft made a harrowing but safe return journey to Earth with its crew, James Lovell, John Swigert, and Fred Haise. The six landing missions collectively returned almost 382 kg (842 lb) of lunar rocks and soil for study on Earth.

Salyut (Russian for "salute")
Years launched: 1971–82. **Country or space agency:** USSR. **Designation:** 1 through 7 (two designs). **Manned. Events of note:** Salyut 1, launched 19 Apr 1971, was the world's first space station; its crew, cosmonauts Georgy Dobrovolsky, Vladislav Volkov, and Viktor Patsayev, died returning to Earth when their Soyuz spacecraft depressurized. Salyut 6, the first of an improved design, operated as a highly successful scientific space platform, supporting a series of crews and international visitors over a four-year period.

Skylab
Year launched: 1973. **Country or space agency:** US. **Manned. Events of note:** Skylab, based on the outfitted and pressurized upper stage of a Saturn V Moon rocket, was the first US space station. Three successive astronaut crews carried out solar astronomy studies, materials-sciences research, and biomedical experiments on the effects of weightlessness.

Apollo-Soyuz
Year launched: 1975. **Countries or space agencies:** US and USSR. **Manned. Events of note:** As a sign of improved US-Soviet relations, an Apollo spacecraft carrying three astronauts docked in Earth orbit with a Soyuz vehicle carrying two cosmonauts. It was the first cooperative multinational space mission and the last use of an Apollo craft.

Viking
Year launched: 1975. **Country or space agency:** US. **Designation:** 1 and 2. **Not manned. Events of note:** Both space probes traveled to Mars, released landers, and took photographs of large expanses of Mars from orbit. The Viking 1 lander transmitted the first pictures from the Martian surface; both landers carried experiments designed to detect living organisms or life processes but found no convincing signs of life.

Voyager
Year launched: 1977. **Country or space agency:** US. **Designation:** 1 and 2. **Not manned. Events of note:** Both Voyager spacecraft flew past Jupiter and Saturn, transmitting measurements and photographs; Voyager 2 went on to Uranus in 1986 and then to Neptune. Both craft continued out of the solar system, with Voyager 1 overtaking Pioneer 10 in 1998 to become the most distant human-made object in space.

space shuttle (Space Transportation System, or STS)
Years launched: 1981–present. **Country or space agency:** US. **Designation:** Individual missions were designated STS with a number (and sometimes letter) suffix, although the orbiter spacecraft themselves were reused. **Manned. Events of note:** The first flight of a manned space shuttle, STS-1, was on 12 Apr 1981 with the orbiter *Columbia*. Other original operational orbiters included *Challenger, Discovery,* and *Atlantis.* During shuttle mission STS-51-L, *Challenger* exploded after liftoff on 28 Jan 1986, killing all seven astronauts aboard, including a private citizen, Christa McAuliffe; the orbiter *Endeavour* was built as a replacement vehicle. Space shuttle missions were used to deploy satellites, space observatories, and planetary probes; to carry out in-space repairs of orbiting spacecraft; and to take US astronauts to the Russian space station Mir. Beginning in 1998 a series of shuttle missions ferried components, supplies, and crews to the International Space Station during its assembly and operation. In 2003 the orbiter *Columbia* disintegrated while returning from a space mission, claiming the lives of its seven-person crew, including Ilan Ramon, the first Israeli astronaut to go into space.

Giotto
Year launched: 1985. **Countries or space agency:** ESA. **Not manned. Events of note:** This first deep-space probe launched by ESA made a close flyby of Halley's Comet, collecting data and transmitting images of the icy nucleus. It was then redirected to a second comet, using a gravity-assist flyby of Earth, the first time that a spacecraft coming back from deep space had made such a maneuver.

Mir (Russian for "peace" and "world")
Years launched: 1986–96. **Country or space agency:** USSR/Russia. **Manned. Events of note:** The core of this modular space station was launched on 20 Feb 1986; five additional modules were added over the next decade to create a large, versatile space laboratory. Although intended for a five-year life, it supported human habitation between 1986 and 2000, including an uninterrupted stretch of occupancy of almost 10 years, and it hosted a series of US astronauts as part of a Mir–space shuttle cooperative endeavor. In 1995 Mir cosmonaut Valery Polyakov set a space endurance record of nearly 438 days.

Magellan
Year launched: 1989. **Country or space agency:** US. **Not manned. Events of note:** Magellan was the first deep-space probe deployed by the space shuttle. During four years in orbit above Venus, it mapped some 98% of the surface of the cloud-covered planet with radar at high resolution. At the end of its mission, it was sent on a gradual dive into the Venusian atmosphere, where it measured various properties before burning up.

Galileo
Year launched: 1989. **Country or space agency:** US. **Not manned. Events of note:** En route to Jupiter, Galileo took the first detailed pictures of two asteroids and returned unique images of a comet as it impacted Jupiter's atmosphere. Near the Jovian system, it released an atmospheric probe and then went into orbit around Jupiter for an extended study of the giant planet and its Galilean moons. Among many discoveries, Galileo found evidence of a liquid-water ocean below the moon Europa's icy surface.

Ulysses
Year launched: 1990. **Countries or space agency:** US and ESA. **Not manned. Events of note:** Ulysses traveled first to Jupiter in order to use the giant planet's gravity to sling the probe out of the plane of the planets. Ulysses successively passed over the Sun's south and north poles, studying properties of the corona, solar wind, and interplanetary space at high solar latitudes.

Clementine
Year launched: 1994. **Country or space agency:** US. **Not manned. Events of note:** This probe was designed to test new imaging sensors in space for defense applications. It mapped the Moon in various wavelengths from lunar orbit, determining mineral content of the surface and producing tantalizing hints of the existence of frozen water in permanently shadowed craters near the Moon's south pole.

NEAR Shoemaker (Near Earth Asteroid Rendezvous Shoemaker)

Year launched: 1996. **Country or space agency:** US. **Not manned. Events of note:** This spacecraft was the first to orbit a small body (the Earth-approaching asteroid Eros) to touch down on its surface. It studied Eros for a year with cameras and instruments and then made a slow descent and a soft landing and transmitted gamma-ray data from the surface for more than two weeks.

Mars Global Surveyor (MGS)

Year launched: 1996. **Country or space agency:** US. **Not manned. Events of note:** MGS conducted long-term mapping from Martian orbit of the planet's entire surface and studies of its magnetic, atmospheric, and internal properties. Close-up images suggested, controversially, that liquid water may have flowed on or near the planet's surface in geologically recent times and still may exist in protected areas. They also showed that the "face on Mars" formation first photographed by Viking 1 was of natural origin and not a product of alien intelligence, as some had purported.

Mars Pathfinder

Year launched: 1996. **Country or space agency:** US. **Not manned. Events of note:** The first spacecraft to land on Mars since the 1976 Viking missions, Pathfinder descended to the Martian surface using a novel combination of parachutes, rockets, and air bags. The lander and its robotic surface rover, Sojourner, which together successfully collected 17,000 images and other data, added to evidence that ancient Mars was much more Earth-like than it is today.

Cassini-Huygens

Year launched: 1997. **Country or space agency:** US, ESA, and Italy. **Not manned. Events of note:** Consisting of an orbiter (Cassini) and a descent probe (Huygens), the spacecraft traveled seven years to the Saturnian system. En route it flew by Jupiter and returned detailed images. At Saturn, Cassini established an orbit around the planet for several years of studies, while the Huygens probe parachuted through the atmosphere of the moon Titan, transmitting pictures and other data for about three hours during its descent and once on the moon's surface.

Lunar Prospector

Year launched: 1998. **Country or space agency:** US. **Not manned. Events of note:** Equipped with radiation- and particle-measuring equipment to assay the geochemistry of the Moon's surface from orbit, the probe strengthened the evidence for water (first found by Clementine) in the south polar region. It later was deliberately crashed into a permanently shadowed crater at the south pole in an unsuccessful attempt to liberate water vapor, which could be detected from Earth.

International Space Station (ISS)

Years launched: 1998–present. **Countries or space agencies:** US, Russia, ESA, Canada, Japan, and Brazil. **Manned. Events of note:** A large modular complex of habitat modules and laboratories powered by solar arrays, the ISS continued to be assembled in Earth orbit by means of space-shuttle and Proton and Soyuz rocket flights that ferried components, crews, and supplies between Earth and the station. The first component, a US-funded, Russian-built module called Zarya, was launched on 20 Nov 1998. The ISS received its first resident crew on 2 Nov 2000.

Chandra X-Ray Observatory

Year launched: 1999. **Country or space agency:** US. **Not manned. Events of note:** The world's most powerful X-ray telescope, it revolves in an elliptical orbit around Earth, delivering roughly 1,000 observations annually of the universe. To scientists, the stunning images of the universe's outer limits (including images of black holes and distant galaxies) help clarify its origin and evolution.

2001 Mars Odyssey

Year launched: 2001. **Country or space agency:** US. **Not manned. Events of note:** This spacecraft was launched to study Mars from orbit and serve as a communications relay for future US and multinational landers. Its instruments mapped the distribution of various elements on or near the surface; some of its data suggested the presence of huge subsurface reservoirs of frozen water in both polar regions.

Mars Express

Year launched: 2003. **Country or space agency:** ESA. **Not manned. Events of note:** Carrying instruments to study the atmosphere, surface, and subsurface from Mars orbit, the spacecraft detected vast fields of water ice as well as carbon-dioxide ice at the planet's south pole. Its lander, Beagle 2, which was designed to examine the rocks and soil for signs of past or present life, failed to establish radio contact after presumably reaching the Martian surface.

Mars Exploration Rovers

Year launched: 2003. **Country or space agency:** US. **Designation:** Spirit and Opportunity. **Not manned. Events of note:** Twin six-wheeled robotic rovers, each equipped with cameras, a microscopic imager, a rock-grinding tool, and other instruments, landed on opposite sides of Mars. Both rovers found evidence of past water; particularly dramatic was the discovery by Opportunity of rocks that appeared to have been laid down at the shoreline of an ancient body of salty water.

Deep Impact

Year launched: 2005. **Country or space agency:** US. **Not manned. Events of note:** Deep Impact was the first spacecraft designed to study the interior composition of a comet. As it traveled past Comet Tempel 1, it released a 370-kg (820-lb) instrumented impactor into the path of the comet's icy nucleus. A high-resolution camera and other apparatuses on the flyby portion of the probe studied the impact and the resulting crater and excavated debris. The collision occurred at a relative speed of about 37,000 km/hr (23,000 mi/hr).

Mars Reconnaissance Orbiter

Year launched: 2005. **Country or space agency:** US. **Not manned. Events of note:** It carries the most powerful camera ever flown on a space mission. The Orbiter is expected to be an important communications link between other spacecraft, Mars, and Earth.

Phoenix

Year launched: 2007. **Country or space agency:** US. **Not manned. Events of note:** Phoenix was the first spacecraft designed to measure water (ice) on a planet other than Earth. It is equipped with robotic arms and sophisticated sensors to dig under the surface of Mars, collect soil samples, and analyze them. It landed on the surface of Mars on 25 May 2008 and quickly established communications with Earth.

Space Exploration Firsts

EVENT	DETAILS	COUNTRY OR AGENCY	DATE ACCOMPLISHED
earliest known person to write about spaceflight	Lucian, in *True History,* which includes a visit to the Moon	ancient Greece	2nd century AD
earliest appearance of rocket propulsion technology	recorded use of gunpowder-propelled arrows in battle	China	by 13th century
first person to study in detail the use of rockets for spaceflight	Konstantin Tsiolkovsky	Russia	late 19th–early 20th centuries
first launch of a liquid-fueled rocket	Robert Goddard	US	16 Mar 1926
first launch of the V-2 ballistic missile, the forerunner of modern space rockets	Wernher von Braun	Germany	3 Oct 1942
first artificial Earth satellite	Sputnik 1	USSR	4 Oct 1957
first animal launched into space	dog Laika aboard Sputnik 2	USSR	3 Nov 1957
first spacecraft to hard-land on another celestial object (the Moon)	Luna 2	USSR	14 Sep 1959
first pictures of the far side of the Moon	Luna 3	USSR	7 Oct 1959
first applications satellite launched	TIROS 1 (weather observation)	US	1 Apr 1960
first recovery of a payload from Earth orbit	*Discoverer 13* (part of Corona reconnaissance satellite program)	US	11 Aug 1960
first piloted spacecraft to orbit Earth	Yury Gagarin on Vostok 1	USSR	12 Apr 1961
first US citizen in space	Alan Shepard on *Freedom 7*	US	5 May 1961
first piloted US spacecraft to orbit Earth	John Glenn on *Friendship 7*	US	20 Feb 1962
first active communications satellite	Telstar 1	US	10 July 1962
first data transmitted to Earth from vicinity of another planet (Venus)	Mariner 2	US	14 Dec 1962
first woman in space	Valentina Tereshkova on Vostok 6	USSR	16 Jun 1963
first satellite to operate in geostationary orbit	Syncom 2 (telecommunications satellite)	US	26 Jul 1963
first space walk	Aleksey Leonov on Voskhod 2	USSR	18 Mar 1965
first spacecraft pictures of Mars	Mariner 4	US	14 Jul 1965
first spacecraft to soft-land on the Moon	Luna 9	USSR	3 Feb 1966
first death during a space mission	Vladimir Komarov on Soyuz 1	USSR	24 Apr 1967
first humans to orbit the Moon	Frank Borman, James Lovell, and William Anders on Apollo 8	US	24 Dec 1968
first human to walk on the Moon	Neil Armstrong on Apollo 11	US	20 Jul 1969
first unmanned spacecraft to carry lunar samples back to Earth	Luna 16	USSR	24 Sep 1970
first soft landing on another planet (Venus)	Venera 7	USSR	15 Dec 1970
first space station launched	Salyut 1	USSR	19 Apr 1971
first spacecraft to orbit another planet (Mars)	Mariner 9	US	13 Nov 1971
first spacecraft to soft-land on Mars	Mars 3	USSR	2 Dec 1971
first spacecraft to fly by Jupiter	Pioneer 10	US	3 Dec 1973
first international docking in space	Apollo and Soyuz spacecraft during Apollo-Soyuz Test Project	US/USSR	17 Jul 1975
first pictures transmitted from the surface of Mars	Viking 1	US	20 Jul 1976
first spacecraft to fly by Saturn	Pioneer 11	US	1 Sep 1979
first reusable spacecraft launched and returned from space	space shuttle *Columbia*	US	12–14 Apr 1981
first spacecraft to fly by Uranus	Voyager 2	US	24 Jan 1986
first spacecraft to make a close flyby of a comet's nucleus	Giotto at Halley's Comet	European Space Agency (ESA)	13 Mar 1986
first spacecraft to fly by Neptune	Voyager 2	US	24 Aug 1989
first large optical space telescope launched	Hubble Space Telescope	US/ESA	25 Apr 1990
first spacecraft to orbit Jupiter	Galileo	US	7 Dec 1995
first confirmed case of a large black hole outside of the nucleus of a galaxy	Chandra X-Ray Observatory	US	September 1999–12 Jun 2000
first resident crew to occupy the International Space Station	William Shepherd, Yury Gidzenko, and Sergey Krikalev	US/Russia	2 Nov 2000
first spacecraft to orbit and land on an asteroid	NEAR Shoemaker at the asteroid Eros	US	14 Feb 2000–12 Feb 2001
first piloted Chinese spacecraft to orbit Earth	Shenzhou 5, piloted by Yang Liwei	China	15 Oct 2003
first privately funded human spaceflight (to 100 km [62 mi])	*SpaceShipOne*, piloted by Michael W. Melvill	US (private venture)	21 Jun 2004
first spacecraft to strike a comet's nucleus and study its interior composition	Deep Impact at Comet Tempel 1	US	4 Jul 2005
first spacecraft designed to measure water (ice) on a planet other than Earth	Phoenix	US	5 Jun 2008

Air Travel

Flight History

Humanity has been fascinated with the possibility of flight for millennia. The history of flight began at least as early as about AD 400 with historical references to a Chinese kite that used a rotary wing as a source of lift. Other toys using the principle of the helicopter—in this case a rotary blade turned by the pull of a string—were known during the Middle Ages. During the latter part of the 15th century, Leonardo da Vinci made drawings pertaining to flight. In the 1700s experiments were made with the ornithopter, a machine with flapping wings.

The history of successful flight begins with the hot-air balloon. In southwestern France, two brothers, Joseph and Étienne Montgolfier, papermakers, experimented with a large cell contrived of paper in which they could collect heated air. On 19 Sep 1783 the Montgolfiers sent aloft a balloon with a rooster, a duck, and a sheep, and on 21 November the first manned flight was made. Balloons gained importance as their flights increased into hundreds of miles, but they were essentially unsteerable.

Count Ferdinand von Zeppelin, a former military man, spent much of his life after retiring in 1890 working with balloons, particularly on the steering problem. As his experimentation continued, hydrogen and illuminating gas were substituted for hot air, and a motor was mounted on a bag filled with gas that had been fitted with propellers and rudders. It was Zeppelin who first saw clearly that maintaining a steerable shape was essential, so he created a rigid but light frame. On 2 Jul 1900 Zeppelin undertook the first experimental flight of what he called an airship. The development of the dirigible went well until the docking procedure at Lakehurst NJ on 6 May 1937, when the *Hindenburg* burst into flames and exploded, with a loss of 36 lives. Public feeling about the craft made further development futile.

It should be remembered, however, that neither balloons nor dirigibles had produced true flight: what they had done was harness the dynamics of the atmosphere to lift a craft off the ground, using what power (if any) they supplied primarily to steer. The first scientific exposition of the principles that ultimately led to the successful flight with a heavier-than-air device came in 1843 from Sir George Cayley, who is also regarded by many as the father of fixed-wing flight. It was Cayley who built the successful man-carrying glider that came closest to permitting real flight. Cayley's work was built upon in the experiments and writings on gliders from the late 1800s by aviation pioneers Otto Lilienthal of Germany and Octave Chanute of the United States. The works of Cayley, Lilienthal, and Chanute would eventually inspire and form the basis of the Wright brothers' work.

The Americans Wilbur and Orville Wright by 1902 had developed a fully practical biplane glider that could be controlled in every direction. Fitting a small engine and two propellers to another biplane, the Wrights on 17 Dec 1903 made the world's first successful flight of a man-carrying, engine-powered, heavier-than-air craft at a site near Kitty Hawk NC.

The Wright brothers' success soon inspired successful aircraft designs and flights by others, and World War I (1914–18) further accelerated the expansion of aviation. Though initially used for aerial reconnaissance, aircraft were soon fitted with machine guns to shoot at other aircraft and with bombs to drop on ground targets; military aircraft with these types of missions and armaments became known, respectively, as fighters and bombers.

By the 1920s the first small commercial airlines had begun to carry mail, and the increased speed and range of aircraft made nonstop flights over the world's oceans, poles, and continents possible. In the 1930s more efficient monoplane aircraft with an all-metal fuselage and a retractable undercarriage became standard. Aircraft played a key role in World War II (1939–45), developing in size, weight, speed, power, range, and armament. The war marked the high point of piston-engined propeller craft while also introducing the first aircraft with jet engines, which could fly at higher speeds. Jet-engined craft became the norm for fighters in the late 1940s and proved their superiority as commercial transports beginning in the '50s. The high speeds and low operating costs of jet airliners led to a massive expansion of commercial air travel in the second half of the 20th century.

The next great aviation innovation after the jet engine was aircraft able to fly at supersonic speeds. The first was a Bell XS-1 rocket-powered research plane piloted by Maj. Charles E. Yeager of the US Air Force on 14 Oct 1947. The XS-1 broke the sound barrier at 1,066 km/hr (662 mph) and attained a top speed of 1,126 km/hr (700 mph). Thereafter many military aircraft capable of supersonic flight were built. The first supersonic passenger-carrying commercial airplane, the Concorde, was built jointly by aircraft manufacturers in Great Britain and France and was in regular commercial service between 1976 and 2003. In the 21st century aircraft manufacturers strove to produce larger planes. A huge new passenger airliner, the double-decker Airbus A380, with a passenger capacity of 555 (40% greater than the next largest airplane), began commercial flights in late October 2007.

Airlines in the US: Best On-Time Arrival Performance

Source: US Department of Transportation, June 2008.

	AIRLINE	% OF ALL FLIGHTS		AIRLINE	% OF ALL FLIGHTS		AIRLINE	% OF ALL FLIGHTS
1	Hawaiian Airlines	90.5	8	Pinnacle Airlines	80.4	14	Northwest Airlines	75.9
2	SkyWest Airlines	84.0	9	JetBlue Airways	77.0	15	Comair	75.3
3	Southwest Airlines	83.3	10	Atlantic Southeast Airlines	77.0	16	American Eagle Airlines	74.4
4	Frontier Airlines	82.1						
5	Alaska Airlines	81.6	11	Delta Air Lines	76.8	17	Mesa Airlines	73.2
6	US Airways	81.3	12	ExpressJet Airlines	76.5	18	United Airlines	72.8
7	AirTran Airways	81.1	13	Continental Airlines	76.5	19	American Airlines	65.3

US Aviation Safety, 1988–2007

2007 data are preliminary.
Source: US National Transportation Safety Board.

	US AIRLINES[1]				US GENERAL AVIATION			
YEAR	NO. OF ACCIDENTS	NO. OF ACCIDENTS WITH FATALITIES	TOTAL NO. OF DEATHS	HOURS FLOWN	ALL ACCIDENTS	FATAL ACCIDENTS	TOTAL FATALITIES	HOURS FLOWN
1988	30	3	285	11,140,548	2,388	460	797	27,446,000
1989	28	11	278	11,274,543	2,242	432	769	27,920,000
1990	24	6	39	12,150,116	2,242	444	770	28,510,000
1991	26	4	62	11,780,610	2,197	439	800	27,678,000
1992	18	4	33	12,359,715	2,111	451	867	24,780,000
1993	23	1	1	12,706,206	2,064	401	744	22,796,000
1994	23	4	239	13,124,315	2,021	404	730	22,235,000
1995	36	3	168	13,505,257	2,056	413	735	24,906,000
1996	37	5	380	13,746,112	1,908	361	636	24,881,000
1997	49	4	8	15,838,109	1,844	350	631	25,591,000
1998	50	1	1	16,816,555	1,905	365	625	25,518,000
1999	51	2	12	17,555,208	1,905	340	619	29,246,000
2000	56	3	92	18,299,257	1,837	345	596	27,838,000
2001	46	6	531	17,814,191	1,727	325	562	25,431,000
2002	41	0	0	17,290,198	1,715	345	581	25,545,000
2003	54	2	22	17,467,700	1,740	352	633	25,998,000
2004	30	2	14	18,882,503	1,617	314	559	24,888,000
2005	40	3	22	19,390,029	1,670	321	563	23,168,000
2006	33	2	50	19,263,209	1,518	306	703	23,963,000
2007	26	1	1	19,305,000	1,631	284	491	23,835,000

[1]*Scheduled and nonscheduled service.*

World's Busiest Airports

Ranked by total aircraft movement (takeoffs and landings), 2007.
Source: Airports Council International (preliminary statistics), <www.airports.org>.

RANK	AIRPORT	LOCATION	AIRPORT CODE	TOTAL MOVEMENTS
1	Hartsfield-Jackson Atlanta International Airport	Atlanta GA	ATL	994,346
2	O'Hare International Airport	Chicago IL	ORD	927,834
3	Dallas/Fort Worth International Airport	Dallas/Fort Worth TX	DFW	684,779
4	Los Angeles International Airport	Los Angeles CA	LAX	681,445
5	Denver International Airport	Denver CO	DEN	614,169
6	McCarran International Airport	Las Vegas NV	LAS	609,472
7	George Bush Intercontinental Airport	Houston TX	IAH	603,836
8	Paris Charles de Gaulle International Airport	Paris, France	CDG	552,721
9	Phoenix Sky Harbor International Airport	Phoenix AZ	PHX	538,063
10	Charlotte Douglas International Airport	Charlotte NC	CLT	522,541
11	Philadelphia International Airport	Philadelphia PA	PHL	498,963
12	Frankfurt Airport	Frankfurt, Germany	FRA	492,569
13	Madrid Barajas International Airport	Madrid, Spain	MAD	483,284
14	Heathrow Airport	London, UK	LHR	481,356
15	Detroit Metropolitan Wayne County Airport	Detroit MI	DTW	467,230
16	Amsterdam Airport Schiphol	Amsterdam, Netherlands	AMS	454,357
17	Minneapolis–St. Paul International Airport	Minneapolis/St. Paul MN	MSP	450,337
18	Newark Liberty International Airport	Newark NJ	EWR	443,952
19	John F. Kennedy International Airport	New York NY	JFK	443,004
20	Munich International Airport	Munich, Germany	MUC	431,815
21	Toronto Pearson International Airport	Toronto, ON, Canada	YYZ	425,513
22	Salt Lake City International Airport	Salt Lake City UT	SLC	414,395
23	Beijing Capital International Airport	Beijing, China	PEK	399,986
24	Boston Logan International Airport	Boston MA	BOS	399,537
25	Long Beach Airport	Long Beach CA	LGB	398,433
26	LaGuardia Airport	New York NY	LGA	389,492
27	Miami International Airport	Miami FL	MIA	386,981
28	Washington Dulles International Airport	Washington DC	IAD	382,907
29	San Francisco International Airport	San Francisco CA	SFO	379,500
30	Phoenix Deer Valley Airport	Phoenix AZ	DVT	378,349

Meteorology

Global Temperatures and Precipitation

Listed in alphabetical order by city. For more information see <www.weatherbase.com>.

CITY	AVERAGE TEMPERATURE °F (°C) JAN	APR	JUL	OCT	AVERAGE ANNUAL PRECIPITATION LEVELS IN INCHES (MM)
Ankara, Turkey	27 (−2)	49 (9)	69 (20)	52 (11)	13.6 (346)
Beijing, China	26 (−3)	57 (13)	79 (26)	57 (13)	25.1 (630)
Buenos Aires, Argentina	75 (23)	62 (16)	50 (10)	61 (16)	38.5 (970)
Cairo, Egypt	57 (13)	71 (21)	83 (28)	75 (23)	1 (25)
Casablanca, Morocco	55 (12)	60 (15)	73 (22)	66 (18)	16.1 (400)
Christchurch, New Zealand	63 (17)	54 (12)	44 (6)	53 (11)	25.5 (640)
Colombo, Sri Lanka	81 (27)	84 (28)	83 (28)	82 (27)	87.8 (2,230)
Doha, Qatar	63 (17)	80 (26)	96 (35)	85 (29)	3.2 (80)
Hanoi, Vietnam	62 (16)	76 (24)	86 (30)	78 (25)	66.2 (1,682)
Havana, Cuba	71 (21)	76 (24)	82 (27)	78 (25)	48.2 (1,225)
Jerusalem, Israel	46 (7)	59 (15)	73 (22)	66 (18)	23 (580)
Johannesburg, South Africa	69 (20)	61 (16)	52 (11)	64 (17)	28.7 (720)
Kandahar, Afghanistan	44 (6)	68 (19)	89 (31)	64 (17)	7.4 (180)
Lima, Peru	74 (23)	71 (21)	64 (17)	65 (18)	0.3 (7.6)
Lisbon, Portugal	51 (10)	58 (14)	73 (22)	64 (17)	27.9 (708)
London, UK	39 (3)	46 (7)	62 (16)	51 (10)	29.7 (750)
Mbarara, Uganda	69 (20)	69 (20)	68 (20)	69 (20)	35.3 (890)
Moscow, Russia	16 (−8)	42 (5)	63 (17)	39 (3)	23.6 (590)
Nice, France	48 (8)	55 (12)	74 (23)	62 (16)	32.4 (820)
Nuuk, Greenland	17 (−8)	25 (−3)	45 (7)	31 (0)	23.9 (600)
Pala, Chad	77 (25)	87 (31)	77 (25)	78 (26)	40.4 (1,027)
Reykjavík, Iceland	31 (0)	37 (2)	52 (11)	40 (4)	32.2 (810)
Rotterdam, The Netherlands	38 (3)	47 (8)	63 (17)	52 (11)	N/A
Santiago, Chile	70 (21)	59 (15)	47 (8)	58 (14)	13.4 (340)
São Paulo, Brazil	74 (23)	70 (21)	63 (17)	69 (20)	53.2 (1,350)
South Pole, Antarctica	−16 (−26)	−69 (−56)	−74 (−58)	−58 (−50)	0.1 (2.5)
Sydney, Australia	72 (22)	65 (18)	53 (11)	64 (17)	44.5 (1,130)
Tokyo, Japan	42 (5)	57 (13)	77 (25)	64 (17)	60.2 (1,520)
Toronto, ON, Canada	21 (−6)	44 (6)	70 (21)	48 (8)	30.1 (760)
Vilnius, Lithuania	23 (−5)	41 (5)	62 (17)	42 (6)	26.3 (669)

N/A: not available.

World Temperature Extremes

REGION	highest recorded air temperature: PLACE (ELEVATION)	°F	°C	lowest recorded air temperature: PLACE (ELEVATION)	°F	°C
Africa	Al-'Aziziyah, Libya (112 m [367 ft]; 13 Sep 1922)	136.0	57.8	Ifrane, Morocco (1,635 m [5,364 ft]; 11 Feb 1935)	−11.0	−23.9
Antarctica	Vanda Station, Scott Coast (15 m [49 ft]; 5 Jan 1974)	59.0	15.0	Vostok, 78° 27″ S, 106° 52″ E (3,420 m [11,220 ft]; 21 Jul 1983)	−129.0	−89.4
Asia	Tirat Zevi, Israel (−220 m [−722 ft]; 21 Jun 1942)	129.0	53.9	Oymyakon, Russia (806 m [2,625 ft]; 6 Feb 1933)	−90.0	−67.8
Australia	Cloncurry, Queensland (190 m [622 ft]; 16 Jan 1889)	128.0	53.3	Charlotte Pass, New South Wales (1,755 m [5,758 ft]; 29 Jun 1994)	−9.4	−23.0
Europe	Seville, Spain (8 m [26 ft]; 4 Aug 1881)	122.0	50.0	Ust-Shchuger, Russia (85 m [279 ft]; exact date unknown)	−67.0	−55.0
North America	Greenland Ranch, Death Valley, California (−54 m [−178 ft]; 10 Jul 1913)	134.0	56.7	Snag, Yukon (646 m [2,120 ft]; 3 Feb 1947)	−81.4	−63.0
South America	Rivadavia, Argentina (206 m [676 ft]; 11 Dec 1905)	120.0	48.9	Colonia, Sarmiento, Argentina (268 m [879 ft]; 1 Jun 1907)	−27.0	−32.8
Tropical Pacific	Tuguegarao, Philippines (22 m [72 ft]; 29 Apr 1912)	108.0	42.2	Haleakala, Hawaii (2,972 m [9,750 ft]; 17 May 1979)	12.0	−11.1

Normal Temperatures and Precipitation for Selected US Cities

Statistics from city airports, 1971–2000. Alphabetical by state.
Source: National Oceanic and Atmospheric Administration, National Climatic Data Center, Asheville NC.

CITY	MEAN TEMPERATURE (°F)				ANNUAL PRECIPITATION (IN)
	JAN	APR	JUL	OCT	
Montgomery AL	46.6	64.3	81.8	65.4	54.77
Anchorage AK	15.8	36.3	58.4	34.1	16.08
Phoenix AZ	54.2	70.2	92.8	74.6	8.29
Little Rock AR	40.1	61.4	82.4	63.3	50.93
Los Angeles CA	57.1	60.8	69.3	66.9	13.15
San Francisco CA	49.4	56.2	62.8	61.0	20.11
Denver CO	29.2	47.6	73.4	51.0	15.81
Hartford CT	25.7	48.9	73.7	51.9	46.16
Wilmington DE	31.5	52.4	76.6	55.8	42.81
Miami FL	68.1	75.7	83.7	78.8	58.53
Atlanta GA	42.7	61.6	80.0	62.8	50.20
Honolulu HI	73.0	75.6	80.8	80.2	18.29
Boise ID	30.2	50.6	74.7	52.8	12.19
Chicago IL[1]	22.0	47.8	73.3	52.1	36.27
Indianapolis IN	26.5	52.0	75.4	54.6	40.95
Des Moines IA	20.4	50.6	76.1	52.8	34.72
Topeka KS	27.2	54.5	78.4	56.6	35.64
Louisville KY	33.0	56.4	78.4	58.5	44.54
New Orleans LA	52.6	68.2	82.7	70.0	64.16
Portland ME	21.7	43.7	68.7	47.7	45.83
Baltimore MD	32.3	53.2	76.5	55.4	41.94
Boston MA	29.3	48.3	73.9	54.1	42.53
Detroit MI	24.5	48.1	73.5	51.9	32.89
Minneapolis MN	13.1	46.6	73.2	48.7	29.41
Jackson MS	45.0	63.4	81.4	64.4	55.95
St. Louis MO	29.6	56.6	80.2	58.3	38.75
Missoula MT	23.5	45.2	66.9	44.4	13.82
Lincoln NE	22.4	51.2	77.8	53.5	28.37
Las Vegas NV	47.0	66.0	91.2	68.7	4.49
Concord NH	20.1	44.6	70.0	47.8	37.60
Newark NJ	31.3	52.3	77.2	56.4	46.25
Albuquerque NM	35.7	55.6	78.5	57.3	9.47
New York NY[2]	31.8	50.1	74.8	56.5	42.46
Charlotte NC	41.7	60.9	80.3	61.7	43.51
Fargo ND	6.8	43.5	70.6	45.3	21.19
Cleveland OH	25.7	47.6	71.9	52.2	38.71
Tulsa OK	36.4	60.8	83.5	62.6	42.42
Portland OR	39.9	51.2	68.1	54.3	37.07
Philadelphia PA	32.3	53.1	77.6	57.2	42.05
Providence RI	28.7	48.6	73.3	53.0	46.45
Charleston SC	47.9	64.2	81.7	66.2	51.53
Rapid City SD	22.4	44.7	71.7	48.2	16.64
Memphis TN	39.9	62.1	82.5	63.8	54.65
Dallas TX[3]	44.1	65.0	85.0	67.2	34.73
Salt Lake City UT	29.2	50.0	77.0	52.5	16.50
Burlington VT	18.0	43.5	70.6	47.7	36.05
Richmond VA	36.4	57.1	77.9	58.3	43.91
Seattle WA	40.9	50.2	65.3	52.7	37.07
Charleston WV	33.4	54.3	73.9	55.1	44.05
Milwaukee WI	20.7	45.2	72.0	51.4	34.81
Casper WY	22.3	42.7	70.0	45.7	13.03

[1]Data from O'Hare International Airport. [2]Data from John F. Kennedy International Airport. [3]Data from Dallas/Fort Worth International Airport.

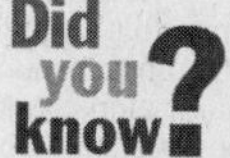

The oldest detected meteorite impact on Earth occurred 3.47 billion years ago. The meteor left geochemical evidence of its impact in southern Africa and Australia and is thought to have been about 20 km (12 mi) wide. It would have taken less than two seconds to pass through the atmosphere and slam into the surface of the planet, causing immense tsunamis and devastating erosion to the ocean floor and small continents.

Indexes

Wind Chill Index

The wind chill index is based upon a formula that determines how cold the atmosphere feels by combining the temperature and wind speed and applying other factors. For more information, see <www.nws.noaa.gov/om/windchill/index.shtml>.

		TEMPERATURE (°F)														
	CALM	40	35	30	25	20	15	10	5	0	-5	-10	-15	-20	-25	-30
	5	36	31	25	19	13	7	1	-5	-11	-16	-22	-28	-34	-40	-46
	10	34	27	21	15	9	3	-4	-10	-16	-22	-28	-35	-41	-47	-53
	15	32	25	19	13	6	0	-7	-13	-19	-26	-32	-39	-45	-51	-58
	20	30	24	17	11	4	-2	-9	-15	-22	-29	-35	-42	-48	-55	-61
WIND	25	29	23	16	9	3	-4	-11	-17	-24	-31	-37	-44	-51	-58	-64
SPEED	30	28	22	15	8	1	-5	-12	-19	-26	-33	-39	-46	-53	-60	-67
(MPH)	35	28	21	14	7	0	-7	-14	-21	-27	-34	-41	-48	-55	-62	-69
	40	27	20	13	6	-1	-8	-15	-22	-29	-36	-43	-50	-57	-64	-71
	45	26	19	12	5	-2	-9	-16	-23	-30	-37	-44	-51	-58	-65	-72
	50	26	19	12	4	-3	-10	-17	-24	-31	-38	-45	-52	-60	-67	-74
	55	25	18	11	4	-3	-11	-18	-25	-32	-39	-46	-54	-61	-69	-75
	60	25	17	10	3	-4	-11	-19	-26	-33	-40	-48	-55	-62	-69	-76

Heat Index

The Heat Index shows the effects of the combination of heat and humidity. Apparent temperature is the temperature as it feels to your body. For more information see <www.jeonet.com/heat.htm>.

	AIR TEMPERATURE (°F)										
relative humidity	70	75	80	85	90	95	100	105	110	115	120
	apparent temperature										
0%	64	69	73	78	83	87	91	95	99	103	107
10%	65	70	75	80	85	90	95	100	105	111	116
20%	66	72	77	82	87	93	99	105	112	120	130
30%	67	73	78	84	90	96	104	113	123	135	148
40%	68	74	79	86	93	101	110	123	137	151	
50%	69	75	81	88	96	107	120	135	150		
60%	70	76	82	90	100	114	132	149			
70%	70	77	85	93	106	124	144				
80%	71	78	86	97	113	136	157				
90%	71	79	88	102	122	150	170				
100%	72	80	91	108	133	166					

	HEAT INDEX/HEAT DISORDERS
Heat Index	Possible heat disorders for people in higher risk groups*
130°F or higher	Heatstroke/sunstroke highly likely with continued exposure.
105°-130°F	Sunstroke, heat cramps, or heat exhaustion likely, and heatstroke possible with prolonged exposure and/or physical activity.
90°-105°F	Sunstroke, heat cramps, and heat exhaustion possible with prolonged exposure and/or physical activity.
80°-90°F	Fatigue possible with prolonged exposure and/or physical activity.

**Small children, the elderly, the chronically ill, those on certain medications or drugs (especially tranquilizers and anticholinergics), and persons with weight and alcohol problems are particularly susceptible to heat reactions, especially during heat waves in areas where moderate climate usually prevails.*

Ultraviolet (UV) Index

The Ultraviolet (UV) Index predicts the intensity of the sun's ultraviolet rays. It was developed by the National Weather Service and the US Environmental Protection Agency to provide a daily forecast of the expected risk of overexposure to the sun. The Index is calculated on a next-day basis for dozens of cities across the US. Other local conditions, such as cloud cover, are taken into account in determining the UV Index number. UV Index numbers are: 0–2 (minimal exposure); 3–4 (low exposure); 5–6 (moderate exposure); 7–9 (high exposure); and 10 and over (very high exposure).

Some simple precautions can be taken to reduce the risk of sun-related illness: limit time in the sun between 10 AM and 4 PM, when rays are generally the strongest; seek shade whenever possible; use a broad spectrum sunscreen with an SPF of at least 15; wear a wide-brimmed hat and, if possible, tightly woven, full-length clothing; wear UV-protective sunglasses; avoid sunlamps and tanning salons; and watch for the UV Index daily. The UV Index should not be used by seriously sun-sensitive individuals, who should consult their doctors and take additional precautions regardless of the exposure level.

Hurricanes

Hurricane and Tornado Classifications

The Saffir/Simpson Hurricane Scale[1] is used to rank tropical cyclones in the North Atlantic Ocean and the eastern North Pacific.

Category 1. *Barometric pressure:* 28.91 in or more; *wind speed:* 74–95 mph; *storm surge:* 4–5 ft; *damage:* minimal.

Category 2. *Barometric pressure:* 28.50–28.91 in; *wind speed:* 96–110 mph; *storm surge:* 6–8 ft; *damage:* moderate.

Category 3. *Barometric pressure:* 27.91–28.47 in; *wind speed:* 111–130 mph; *storm surge:* 9–12 ft; *damage:* extensive.

Category 4. *Barometric pressure:* 27.17–27.88 in; *wind speed:* 131–155 mph; *storm surge:* 13–18 ft; *damage:* extreme.

Category 5. *Barometric pressure:* less than 27.17 in; *wind speed:* 155 mph or more; *storm surge:* 18 ft or more; *damage:* catastrophic.

Tornado classifications.
Tornado intensity is commonly estimated after the fact by analyzing damaged structures and then correlating the damage with the wind speeds known to produce various degrees of damage. Tornadoes are assigned specific values on the Fujita Scale, or F-Scale, of tornado intensity established by meteorologist T. Theodore Fujita.

Categories:

F0. *Wind speed:* 40–72 mph; *damage:* light.

F1. *Wind speed:* 73–112 mph; *damage:* moderate.

F2. *Wind speed:* 113–157 mph; *damage:* considerable.

F3. *Wind speed:* 158–206 mph; *damage:* severe.

F4. *Wind speed:* 207–260 mph; *damage:* devastating.

F5. *Wind speed:* 261–318 mph; *damage:* incredible.

[1]*Published by permission of Herbert Saffir, consulting engineer, and Robert Simpson, meteorologist.*

Hurricane Names

Source: National Hurricane Center.

In 1953, the National Hurricane Center developed a list of given names for Atlantic tropical storms. This list is now maintained by the World Meteorological Organization (WMO). Until 1979 only women's names were used, but since then men's and women's names have alternated. There are six lists currently in rotation, so names can be reused every six years. Any country affected by a hurricane, however, can request its name be retired for ten years. Also, if a storm has been particularly destructive, the WMO can remove it from the list and replace it with a different name.

Deadliest Hurricanes in the US

Listed below, in order of number of deaths, are the 30 deadliest hurricanes to hit the US or its territories in 1851–2006. Hurricane names are given in parentheses after the location, when applicable. Note: ranking numbers 10 and 20 on the list are repeated due to the equal number of fatalities in separate hurricanes. Source: National Hurricane Center. **Web site:** <www.nhc.noaa.gov/Deadliest_Costliest.shtml>.

	HURRICANE LOCATION	YEAR	CATEGORY	DEATHS
1	Galveston TX	1900	4	8,000[1]
2	NC; SC; Puerto Rico	1899	3	3,419
3	Lake Okeechobee, Florida	1928	4	2,500[2]
4	Cheniere Caminada LA	1893	4	2,000[3]
5	southeastern LA; MS; FL (Katrina)	2005	3	1,500
6	Sea Islands, South Carolina and Georgia	1893	3	1,000[4]
7	Puerto Rico; US Virgin Islands	1867	3	811
8	Puerto Rico	1852	1	800
9	GA; SC	1881	2	700
10	Last Island, Louisiana	1856	4	600[3]
	New Orleans LA	1915	4	600[3]
12	southwestern LA; northern TX (Audrey)	1957	4	416
13	Florida Keys	1935	5	408
14	northeastern US	1944	3	390[3]
15	FL; MS; AL	1926	4	372
16	Grand Isle LA	1909	3	350
17	Puerto Rico (San Felipe)	1928	5	312
18	southern TX; Florida Keys	1919	4	287
19	Galveston TX	1915	4	275
20	MS; southeastern LA; VA (Camille)	1969	5	256
	New England	1938	3	256
22	US Virgin Islands; Puerto Rico	1932	2	225
23	northeastern US (Diane)	1955	1	184
24	GA; SC; NC	1898	4	179
25	TX	1875	3	176
26	southeastern FL	1906	3	164
27	Indianola TX	1886	4	150
28	FL; MS; AL	1906	2	134
29	FL; GA; SC	1896	3	130
30	FL; northeastern US (Agnes)	1972	1	122

[1]*Death toll may have been as high as 12,000.* [2]*Death toll may have been as high as 3,000.* [3]*Including those lost at sea.* [4]*Death toll may have been as high as 2,000.*

Costliest Hurricanes in the US

Listed below, in order of the highest monetary damage figures in constant 2006 US dollars, are the 30 deadliest hurricanes to hit the US or its territories in 1900–2006. Locations of the damaged areas are given in parentheses after the hurricane name. Note that figures for Hurricane Hugo reflect the damage done by that storm both on the US mainland and on its Caribbean territories. Source: National Hurricane Center. <www.nhc.noaa.gov/Deadliest_Costliest.shtml>.

RANK	HURRICANE (LOCATION)	YEAR	CATEGORY	ESTIMATED DAMAGE (US$), NOT ADJUSTED	DAMAGE IN CONSTANT 2006 US DOLLARS
1	Katrina (LA; MS; FL)	2005	3	81,000,000,000	84,645,000,000
2	Andrew (southeastern FL; southeastern LA)	1992	5	26,500,000,000	48,058,000,000
3	Wilma (southern FL)	2005	3	20,600,000,000	21,527,000,000
4	Charley (southwestern FL)	2004	4	15,000,000,000	16,322,000,000
5	Ivan (northwestern FL; AL)	2004	3	14,200,000,000	15,541,000,000
6	Hugo (SC; US Virgin Islands; Puerto Rico)	1989	4	8,000,000,000	14,982,000,000
7	Agnes (FL; northeastern US)	1972	1	2,100,000,000	12,424,000,000
8	Betsy (southeastern FL; southeastern LA)	1965	3	1,420,500,000	11,883,000,000
9	Rita (LA; TX; FL)	2005	3	11,300,000,000	11,808,000,000
10	Camille (MS; southeastern LA; VA)	1969	5	1,420,700,000	9,781,000,000
11	Frances (FL)	2004	2	8,900,000,000	9,684,000,000
12	Diane (northeastern US)	1955	1	831,700,000	7,700,000,000
13	Jeanne (southeastern FL)	2004	3	6,900,000,000	7,508,000,000
14	Frederic (AL; MS)	1979	3	2,300,000,000	6,922,000,000
15	(New England)	1938	3	300,000,000	6,571,000,000
16	Allison (northern TX)	2001	TS[1]	5,000,000,000	6,414,000,000
17	Floyd (mid-Atlantic US; northeastern US)	1999	2	4,500,000,000	6,342,000,000
18	(northeastern US)	1944	3	100,000,000	5,927,000,000
19	Fran (NC)	1996	3	3,200,000,000	4,979,000,000
20	Alicia (northern TX)	1983	3	2,000,000,000	4,825,000,000
21	Opal (northwestern FL; AL)	1995	3	3,000,000,000	4,758,000,000
22	Carol (northeastern US)	1954	3	460,000,000	4,345,000,000
23	Isabel (NC; VA)	2003	2	3,370,000,000	3,985,000,000
24	Juan (LA)	1985	1	1,500,000,000	3,417,000,000
25	Donna (FL; eastern US)	1960	4	386,500,000	3,345,000,000
26	Celia (southern TX)	1970	3	453,800,000	3,038,000,000
27	Bob (NC; northeastern US)	1991	2	1,500,000,000	2,853,000,000
28	Elena (MS; AL; northwestern FL)	1985	3	1,250,000,000	2,848,000,000
29	Carla (northern and central TX)	1961	4	300,000,000	2,604,000,000
30	Iniki (Kauai, Hawaii)	1992	3–4	1,800,000,000	2,563,000,000

[1]*Of tropical storm intensity but included because of high damage.*

Geologic Disasters

Measuring Earthquakes

The seismologists Beno Gutenberg and Charles Francis Richter introduced measurement of the seismic energy released by earthquakes on a magnitude scale in 1935. Each increase of one unit on the scale represents a 10-fold increase in the magnitude of an earthquake. Seismographs are designed to measure different components of seismic waves, such as wave type, intensity, and duration. This table shows the typical effects of earthquakes in various magnitude ranges. For further information, see <www.seismo.unr.edu/ftp/pub/louie/class/100/magnitude.html>.

MAGNITUDE	EARTHQUAKE EFFECTS
Less than 3.5	Generally not felt, but recorded.
3.5–5.4	Often felt, but rarely causes damage.
Less than 6.0	At most, slight damage to well-designed buildings. Can cause major damage to poorly constructed buildings over small regions.
6.1–6.9	Can be destructive in areas up to about 100 km (61 mi) across where people live.
7.0–7.9	Major earthquake. Can cause serious damage over larger areas.
8 or greater	Great earthquake. Can cause serious damage in areas several hundred km across.

Major Historical Earthquakes

Magnitudes given for pre-20th-century events are generally estimations from intensity data. In cases where no magnitude was available, the earthquake's maximum intensity, written as a Roman numeral from I to XII, is given.

YEAR (AD)	AFFECTED AREA	MAGNITUDE OR INTENSITY	DEATHS
365	Knossos, Crete, Greece	XI	50,000
526	Antioch, Syria	unknown	250,000
844	Damascus, Syria	VIII	50,000
847	Damascus, Syria	X	70,000
847	Mosul, Iraq	unknown	50,000
856	Damghan, Iran	unknown	200,000
893	Daipur, India	unknown	180,000
893	Ardabil, Iran	unknown	150,000
893	Caucasus	unknown	82,000
1042	Palmyra, Syria	X	50,000
1138	Aleppo, Syria	unknown	230,000
1201	Upper Egypt or Syria	IX	1,100,000
1268	Cilicia, Anatolia, Turkey	unknown	60,000
1290	Chihli, China	unknown	100,000
1556	Shaanxi province, China	8.0	830,000
1667	Shemakha, Azerbaijan	unknown	80,000
1668	Shandong province, China	XII	50,000
1693	Sicily, Italy	7.5	60,000
1703	Jeddo, Japan	unknown	200,000
1727	Tabriz, Iran	unknown	77,000
1730	Hokkaido, Japan	unknown	137,000
1731	Beijing, China	unknown	100,000
1739	China	X	50,000
1755	Lisbon, Portugal; Spain; Morocco	8.7	70,000
1755	Kashan, Iran	unknown	40,000
1780	Tabriz, Iran	unknown	100,000
1783	Calabria, Italy	unknown	50,000
1811	New Madrid MO	8.6	unknown
1812	Caracas, Venezuela	7.7	26,000
1835	northern Japan	7.6	28,300
1857	Tejon Pass, California	7.9	1
1868	Arica, Chile	9.0	25,000
1868	Ecuador; Colombia	7.7	70,000
1883	Java, Indonesia	unknown	100,000
1896	Sanriku, Japan	8.5	27,000
1905	Calabria, Italy	7.9	557
1905	Kangra, India	7.5	19,000
1906	off the coast of Ecuador	8.8	1,000
1906	Valparaíso, Chile	8.2	20,000
1906	San Francisco CA	7.8	c. 3,000
1907	southwestern Tajikistan	8.0	12,000
1908	Messina, Italy	7.2	70,000
1912	Sea of Marmara, Turkey	7.8	2,800
1915	Avezzano, Italy	7.0	32,610
1920	Ningxia province, China	7.8	200,000
1923	Tokyo; Yokohama, Japan	7.9	143,000
1927	Qinghai province, China	7.6	40,900
1932	Gansu province, China	7.6	unknown
1933	Sanriku, Japan	8.4	2,990
1935	Quetta, Pakistan	7.5	30,000
1939	Erzincan, Turkey	7.8	32,700
1939	Chillán, Chile	7.8	28,000
1944	Tonankai, Japan	8.1	998
1944	San Juan, Argentina	7.4	c. 8,000
1945	off the coast of Pakistan	8.0	4,000
1946	Nankaido, Japan	8.1	1,362
1948	Ashgabat, Turkmenistan	7.3	110,000
1950	China-India border, near Myanmar (Burma)	8.6	1,526
1960	Puerto Montt, Chile	9.5	1,655
1960	Agadir, Morocco	5.7	10,000–15,000
1964	Prince William Sound, Alaska	9.2	128
1968	Khorasan, Iran	7.3	12,000
1970	northern Peru	7.9	66,000
1970	Yunnan province, China	7.5	10,000
1972	Fars, Iran	7.1	5,054
1972	Managua, Nicaragua	6.2	5,000
1974	Yunnan province, China	6.8	20,000
1974	North-West Frontier Province, Pakistan	6.2	5,300
1975	Liaoning province, China	7.0	2,000
1976	Mindanao, Philippines	7.9	8,000
1976	Tangshan, China	7.5	255,000–655,000
1976	Guatemala City, Guatemala	7.5	23,000
1976	Turkey-Iran border	7.3	5,000
1977	Bucharest, Romania	7.2	1,500
1978	Khorasan, Iran	7.8	15,000
1979	Colombia; Ecuador	7.9	579
1980	Ech-Cheliff (El-Asnam), Algeria	7.7	5,000
1980	southern Italy	6.5	3,114
1985	Michoacán, Mexico	8.0	9,500–35,000
1988	Gyumri (Leninakan), Armenia	6.8	25,000
1990	Luzon, Philippines	7.7	1,621
1990	Rasht, Iran	7.4	50,000
1991	northern India	6.8	2,000
1992	Flores Island, Indonesia	7.5	2,500
1993	Latur, India	6.2	9,748
1995	Sakhalin Island, Russia	7.1	1,989
1995	Kobe, Japan	6.9	5,502
1997	eastern Iran	7.3	1,567
1998	Feyzabad, Afghanistan	6.6	4,000
1999	Taiwan	7.6	2,400
1999	Golcuk, Turkey	7.6	17,118
2001	El Salvador	7.7	852
2001	Gujarat, India	7.6	20,023
2003	northern Algeria	6.8	2,266
2003	Bam, Iran	6.6	31,000
2004	off the western coast of northern Sumatra, Indonesia	9.1	227,898
2005	northern Sumatra, Indonesia	8.6	1,313
2005	Kashmir, Pakistan	7.6	c. 86,000
2006	Kuril Islands, Russia	8.3	unknown
2006	Tonga	7.9	unknown
2006	Bantul, Indonesia	6.3	5,749
2007	southern Sumatra, Indonesia	8.5	25
2007	Solomon Islands	8.1	54
2007	off the coast of central Peru	8.0	514
2008	eastern Sichuan province, China	7.9	69,000

Tsunami

A tsunami is a catastrophic ocean wave, usually caused by a submarine earthquake occurring less than 30 mi (50 km) beneath the seafloor, with a magnitude greater than 6.5. Underwater or coastal landslides or volcanic eruptions also may cause a tsunami. The often-used term tidal wave is a misnomer: the wave has no connection with the tides. After the earthquake or other generating impulse, a train of simple, progressive oscillatory waves is propagated great distances at the ocean surface in ever-widening circles, much like the waves produced by a pebble falling into a shallow pool. In deep water, the wavelengths are enormous, about 60 to 125 mi (100 to 200 km), and the wave heights are very small, only 1 to 2 ft (0.3 to 0.6 m). The resulting wave steepness is extremely low; coupled with the waves' long periods that vary from five minutes to an hour, this enables normal wind waves and swell to completely obscure the waves in deep water. Thus, a ship in the open ocean experiences the passage of a tsunami as an insignificant rise and fall. As the waves approach the continental coasts, friction with the increasingly shallow bottom reduces the velocity of the waves. The period must remain constant; consequently, as the velocity lessens, the wavelengths become shortened and the wave amplitudes increase, coastal waters rising as high as 100 feet (30 m) in 10 to 15 minutes. By a poorly understood process, the continental shelf waters begin to oscillate after the rise in sea level. Between three and five major oscillations generate most of the damage; the oscillations cease, however, only several days after they begin. Occasionally, the first arrival of a tsunami at a coast may be a trough, the water receding and exposing the shallow seafloor.

Deadly Volcano Eruptions

Casualty figures are approximate.

VOLCANO (LOCATION)	YEAR	CASUALTIES
Tambora (Indonesia)	1815	92,000[1]
Krakatoa (Indonesia)	1883	36,000[1]
Pelée (Martinique)	1902	30,000
Ruiz (Colombia)	1985	25,000[2]
Etna (Italy)	1669	20,000
Unzen (Japan)	1792	15,000
Kelud (Indonesia)	1586	10,000
Laki (Iceland)	1783	9,000
Kelud (Indonesia)	1919	5,000
Vesuvius (Italy)	79	3,360
Awu (Indonesia)	1711	3,200
Raung (Indonesia)	1638	3,000
Raung (Indonesia)	1730	3,000
Lamington (Papua New Guinea)	1951	3,000
Awu (Indonesia)	1856	2,800
Taal (Philippines)	1906	1,500
Taal (Philippines)	1911	1,300
Etna (Italy)	1536	1,000
Paricutín (Mexico)	1949	1,000
Purace (Colombia)	1949	1,000
Pinatubo (Philippines)	1991	350
El Chichón (Mexico)	1982	100
St. Helens (Washington)	1980	57

[1]*Includes tsunami triggered by eruption.* [2]*Includes mudflow triggered by eruption.*

Civil Engineering

The Seven Wonders of the Ancient World

The seven wonders of the ancient world were considered to be the preeminent architectural and sculptural achievements of the Mediterranean and Middle East. The best known are those of the 2nd-century-BC writer Antipater of Sidon. Some early lists included the Walls of Babylon or the Palace of King Cyrus of Persia, but the established list usually contained the following:

Pyramids of Giza. The oldest of the wonders and the only one substantially in existence today, the pyramids of Giza were erected c. 2575–c. 2465 BC on the west bank of the Nile River near Al-Jizah in northern Egypt. The designations of the pyramids—Khufu, Khafre, and Menkaure—correspond to the kings for whom they were built. Khufu (also called the Great Pyramid) is the largest of the three, the length of each side at the base averaging 230 m (755 ¾ ft). Its original height was 147 m (481.4 ft); none of the pyramids reach their original heights because they have been almost entirely stripped of their outer casings of smooth white limestone. According to Herodotus, the Great Pyramid took 20 years to construct and demanded the labor of 100,000 men.

Hanging Gardens of Babylon. A series of landscaped terraces ascribed to either Queen Sammu-ramat (810–783 BC) or King Nebuchadrezzar II (c. 605–c. 561 BC), the gardens were built within the walls of the royal palace at Babylon (in present-day southern Iraq). They did not actually "hang" but were instead "up in the air"—that is, they were roof gardens laid out on a series of ziggurat terraces that were irrigated by pumps from the Euphrates River. Although no traces of the Hanging Gardens have been found, classical authors related that the terraces were roofed with stone balconies on which were layered various materials, such as reeds, bitumen, and lead, so that the irrigation water would not seep through them.

Statue of Zeus. A large, ornate figure of Zeus on his throne, this wonder was made around 430 BC by Phidias of Athens. It was placed in the huge Temple of Zeus at Olympia in western Greece. The statue, almost 12 m (40 ft) high and plated with gold and ivory, represented the god sitting on an elaborate cedarwood throne ornamented with ebony, ivory, gold, and precious stones. On his outstretched right hand was a statue of Nike (Victory), and in the god's left hand was a scepter on which an eagle was perched. The statue, which took eight years to construct, may have been destroyed along with the temple in AD 426, or in a fire at Constantinople (Istanbul) about 50 years later.

Temple of Artemis. The great temple was built by Croesus, king of Lydia, in about 550 BC and was rebuilt after being burned by a madman named Herostratus in 356 BC. The artemesium was famous not only for its great size (over 110 by 55 m [350 by 80 ft]) but also for the magnificent works of art that adorned it. It was destroyed by invading Goths in AD 262 and was never rebuilt. Little remains of the temple, but excavation has revealed traces of it, and copies survive of the famous statue of Artemis. A mummylike figure, this early representation of the goddess stands stiffly straight, with her hands extended outward. The original statue was made of gold, ebony, silver, and black stone, the legs and hips covered by a garment decorated with reliefs of animals and bees and the head adorned with a high-pillared headdress.

Mausoleum of Halicarnassus. Monumental tomb of Mausolus, the tyrant of Caria in southwestern Asia Minor, the mausoleum was built between about 353 and 351 BC by Mausolus' sister and widow, Artemisia. The architect was Pythius (Pytheos), and the sculptures that adorned the building were the work of four leading Greek artists. According to the description of Pliny the Elder, the monument was almost square, with a total periphery of 125 m (411 ft). It was bounded by 36 columns, and the top formed a 24-step pyramid surmounted by a four-horse marble chariot. Fragments of the mausoleum's sculpture are preserved in the British Museum. The mausoleum was probably destroyed by an earthquake between the 11th and 15th century AD, and the stones were reused in local buildings.

Colossus of Rhodes. This huge bronze statue was built at the harbor of Rhodes in ancient Greece in commemoration of the raising of the siege of Rhodes (305–304 BC). The sculptor was Chares of Lyndus, and the statue was made of bronze, reinforced with iron, and weighted with stones. The Colossus was said to be 70 cubits (32 m [105 ft]) high and stood beside Mandrákion harbor. It is technically impossible that the statue could have straddled the harbor entrance, and the popular belief that it did so dates only from the Middle Ages. The Colossus took 12 years to build (c. 294–282 BC) and was toppled by an earthquake about 225 BC. The fallen Colossus was left in place until AD 654, when Arabian forces raided Rhodes and had the statue broken up and the bronze sold for scrap.

Pharos of Alexandria. The most famous lighthouse of the ancient world, it was built by Sostratus of Cnidus, perhaps for Ptolemy I Soter, but was finished during the reign of his son, Ptolemy II of Egypt, about 280 BC. The lighthouse stood on the island of Pharos off Alexandria and is said to have been more than 100 m (350 ft) high; the only taller man-made structures at the time would have been the pyramids of Giza. It was a technological triumph and is the archetype of all lighthouses since. According to ancient sources, a broad spiral ramp led to the top, where a fire burned at night. The lighthouse was destroyed by an earthquake in the 1300s. In 1994 a large amount of masonry blocks and statuary was found in the waters off Pharos.

Tallest Buildings in the World

Building height equals the distance from the sidewalk level of the main entrance to the structural top of the building, including spires but not including antennae, signage, or flag poles. Only buildings that have been completed are included here.
Source: Council on Tall Buildings and Urban Habitat.

RANK	BUILDING	CITY	YEAR COMPLETED	HEIGHT IN FT/M	STORIES
1	Taipei 101	Taipei, Taiwan	2004	1,670/509	101
2	Petronas Tower 1	Kuala Lumpur, Malaysia	1998	1,483/452	88
3	Petronas Tower 2	Kuala Lumpur, Malaysia	1998	1,483/452	88
4	Sears Tower	Chicago IL	1974	1,451/442	110
5	Jin Mao Building	Shanghai, China	1999	1,381/421	88
6	Two International Finance Centre	Hong Kong, China	2003	1,362/415	88
7	CITIC Plaza	Guangzhou, China	1996	1,283/391	80
8	Shun Hing Square	Shenzhen, China	1996	1,260/384	69
9	Empire State Building	New York NY	1931	1,250/381	102
10	Central Plaza	Hong Kong, China	1992	1,227/374	78
11	Bank of China	Hong Kong, China	1989	1,205/367	70
12	Emirates Tower One	Dubai, UAE	1999	1,165/355	54
13	Tuntex Sky Tower	Kaohsiung, Taiwan	1997	1,140/348	85
14	Aon Centre	Chicago IL	1973	1,136/346	83
15	The Center	Hong Kong, China	1998	1,135/346	73
16	John Hancock Center	Chicago IL	1969	1,127/344	100
17	Rose Rotana Tower	Dubai, UAE	2007	1,093/333	72
18	Shimao International Plaza	Shanghai, China	2006	1,093/333	60
19	Minsheng Bank Building	Wuhan, China	2008	1,087/331	68
20	Q1	Gold Coast, QLD, Australia	2005	1,058/323	78
21	Burj Al Arab	Dubai, UAE	1999	1,053/321	60
22	Nina Tower I	Hong Kong, China	2006	1,046/319	80
23	Chrysler Building	New York NY	1930	1,046/319	77
24	New York Times Tower	New York NY	2007	1,046/319	52
25	Bank of America Plaza	Atlanta GA	1993	1,039/317	55

Longest Span Structures in the World by Type

Bridges

SUSPENSION	LOCATION	YEAR OF COMPLETION	MAIN SPAN (M)
Akashi Kaikyo	Kobe–Awaji Island, Japan	1998	1,991
part of eastern link between islands of Honshu and Shikoku			
Store Baelt (Great Belt)	Zealand–Funen, Denmark	1998	1,624
part of link between Copenhagen and mainland Europe			
Nancha	Zhenjiang, China	2005	1,490
world's third longest suspension bridge			
Humber	near Hull, England	1981	1,410
crosses Humber estuary between Yorkshire and Lincolnshire			
Jiangyin	Jiangsu province, China	1999	1,385
crosses Chang Jiang (Yangtze River) near Shanghai			
Tsing Ma	Hong Kong, China	1997	1,377
connects Hong Kong city with airport on Landao Island			
Verrazano-Narrows	New York NY	1964	1,298
spans New York Harbor between Brooklyn and Staten Island			
Golden Gate	San Francisco CA	1937	1,280
spans entrance to San Francisco Bay			
Höga Kusten (High Coast)	Kramfors, Sweden	1997	1,210
crosses Angerman River on scenic coastal route in northern Sweden			
Mackinac	Mackinaw City–St. Ignace MI	1957	1,158
spans Mackinac Straits between upper and lower peninsulas of Michigan			
CABLE-STAYED (STEEL)			
Tatara	Onomichi–Imabari, Japan	1999	890
part of western link between islands of Honshu and Shikoku			
Normandie	near Le Havre, France	1995	856
crosses Seine estuary between upper and lower Normandy			
Nanjing Yangtze Sanqiao	Nanjing, China	2005	648
world's third longest cable-stayed bridge			
Nancha	Nanjing, China	2001	628
southern span of Second Nanjing Yangtze Bridge			
Wuhan Baishazhou	Hubei province, China	2000	618
provides third crossing of Chang Jiang (Yangtze River) in city of Wuhan			
Rion–Antirion	near Patrai, Greece (Gulf of Corinth)	2004	560
world's second largest cable-stayed bridge			
Millau Viaduct	Tarn Gorge, France	2004	342
world's highest bridge (270 m) and longest cable-stayed bridge (2,460 m)			
ARCH			
steel			
Lupu	Shanghai, China	2003	550
crosses Huangpujiang (Huang-p'u River) between central Shanghai and Pudong New District			
New River Gorge	Fayetteville WV	1977	518
provides road link through scenic New River Gorge National River area			
Bayonne	Bayonne NJ–New York NY	1931	504
spans the Kill Van Kull between New Jersey and Staten Island			
Sydney Harbour	Sydney, NSW, Australia	1932	503
links the City of Sydney with North Sydney			
concrete			
Wanxian	Sichuan province, China	1997	420
crosses Chang Jiang (Yangtze River) in Three Gorges area			
Krk I	Krk Island, Croatia	1980	390
links scenic Krk Island with mainland Croatia			
Jiangjiehe	Guizhou province, China	1995	330
spans gorge of Wujiang (Wu River)			
CANTILEVER			
steel truss			
Pont de Québec	Quebec City, QC, Canada	1917	549
provides rail crossing over St. Lawrence River			
Forth	Queensferry, Scotland	1890	2 spans, each 521
provides rail crossing over Firth of Forth			
Minato	Osaka–Amagasaki, Japan	1974	510
carries road traffic across Osaka's harbor			
Commodore John J. Barry	Bridgeport NJ–Chester PA	1974	501
provides road crossing over Delaware River			

Longest Span Structures in the World by Type (continued)

CANTILEVER (CONTINUED)	LOCATION	YEAR OF COMPLETION	MAIN SPAN (M)
prestressed concrete			
Shibanpo-2	Chongqing, China	2006	336
world's longest prestressed-concrete box girder bridge			
Stolmasundet	Austevoll, Norway	1998	301
links islands of Stolmen and Sjelbörn south of Bergen			
Raftsundet	Lofoten, Norway	1998	298
crosses Raft Sound in arctic Lofoten Islands			
Sundøy	Leirfjord, Norway	2003	298
links Alsten Island to mainland Norway			
BEAM			
steel truss			
Ikitsuki Ohashi	Nagasaki prefecture, Japan	1991	400
connects islands of Iki and Hirado off northwest Kyushu			
Astoria	Astoria OR	1966	376
carries Pacific Coast Highway across Columbia River between Oregon and Washington			
Francis Scott Key	Baltimore MD	1977	366
spans Patapsco River at Baltimore Harbor			
Oshima	Yamaguchi prefecture, Japan	1976	325
links Yanai City and Oshima Island			
steel plate and box girder			
Presidente Costa e Silva	Rio de Janeiro state, Brazil	1974	300
crosses Guanabara Bay between Rio de Janeiro and suburb of Niterói			
Neckartalbrücke-1	Weitingen, Germany	1978	263
carries highway across Neckar River Valley			
Brankova	Belgrade, Serbia	1956	261
provides road crossing of Sava River between Old and New Belgrade			
Ponte de Vitória-3	Espírito Santo state, Brazil	1989	260
provides road link to state capital on Vitória Island			
MOVABLE			
vertical lift			
Arthur Kill	Elizabeth NJ–New York NY	1959	170
provides rail link between port of Elizabeth and Staten Island			
Cape Cod Canal	Cape Cod MA	1935	166
provides rail crossing over waterway near Buzzard's Bay			
Delair	Delair NJ–Philadelphia PA	1960	165
provides rail link across Delaware River between Philadelphia and South Jersey shore			
Marine Parkway–Gil Hodges Memorial	New York NY	1937	165
carries road traffic over mouth of Jamaica Bay between Brooklyn and the Rockaways, Queens			
swing span			
Al-Firdan (El-Ferdan)	Suez Canal, Egypt	2001	340
provides road and rail link between Sinai Peninsula and eastern Nile Delta region			
Santa Fe	Fort Madison IA–Niota IL	1927	160
provides road and rail crossing of Mississippi River			
BASCULE			
South Capitol Street/Frederick Douglass Memorial	Washington DC	1949	118
carries road traffic over Anacostia River			
Sault Sainte Marie	Sault Sainte Marie MI–Ontario, Canada	1941	102
connects rail systems of United States and Canada			
Charles Berry	Lorain OH	1940	101
carries road traffic over Black River			
Market Street/Chief John Ross	Chattanooga TN	1917	94
carries road traffic over Tennessee River			
Causeways (fixed link over water only)			
Lake Pontchartrain-2	Metairie–Mandeville LA	1969	38,422
carries northbound road traffic from suburbs of New Orleans to north lakeshore			
Lake Pontchartrain-1	Mandeville–Metairie LA	1956	38,352
carries southbound road traffic from north lakeshore to suburbs of New Orleans			
King Fahd Causeway	Bahrain–Saudi Arabia	1986	24,950
carries road traffic across Gulf of Bahrain in Persian Gulf			
Confederation Bridge	Borden-Carleton, PE–Cape Jourimain, NB, Canada	1997	12,900
carries road traffic over Northumberland Strait			

Basic Types of Bridges

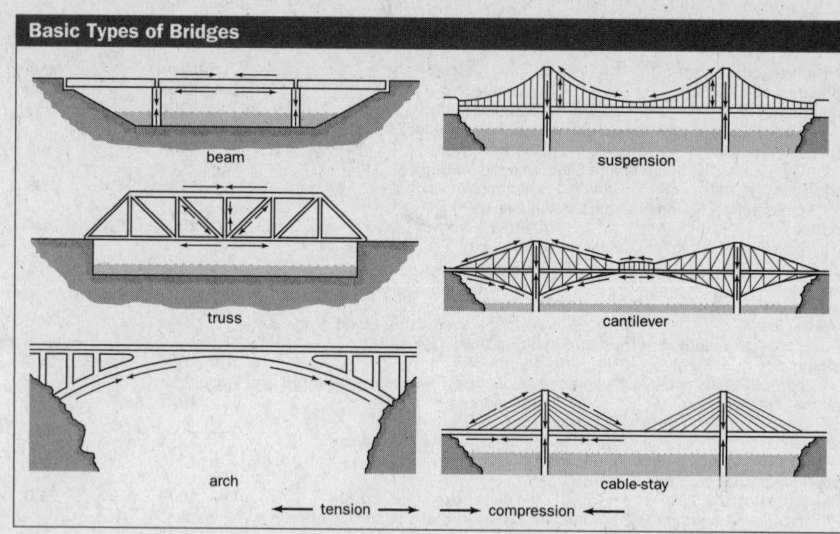

Longest Tunnels in the World

TUNNEL	LOCATION	LENGTH IN KM (MI)	COMPLETED	USE
Seikan	Japan	53.9 (33.5)	1988	railway
passes under the Tsugaru Strait between islands of Honshu and Hokkaido				
Channel Tunnel (Eurotunnel)	UK–France	50.5 (31.4)	1994	railway
passes under English Channel between Folkestone (UK) and Sangatte (France)				
Lötschberg Base	Switzerland	34.6 (21.5)	2007	railway
world's longest land tunnel (under Alps between Frutigen and Raron)				
Guadarrama	Spain	28.4 (17.6)	2007	railway
on high-speed rail line between Madrid and Valladolid				
Iwate-Ichinohe	Japan	25.8 (15.7)	2002	railway
carries Tohoku high-speed line through mountains between Tokyo and northern Honshu				
Lærdal	Norway	24.5 (15.3)	2000	highway
carries main cross-country highway through mountains in central Norway				
Dai-Shimizu	Japan	22.2 (13.8)	1982	railway
on Joetsu "Bullet" Line across Honshu between Tokyo and Niigata				
Wushaoling I and II (dual-bore)	China	21.0 (13.1)	2006	railway
between Lanzhou and Wuwei				
Simplon I	Italy–Switzerland	19.8 (12.3)	1906	railway
Simplon II	Italy–Switzerland	19.8 (12.3)	1922	railway
rail links under Simplon Pass, traditional divide between northern and southern Europe				
Vereina	Switzerland	19.1 (11.9)	1999	railway
rail link under Flüela Pass between upper Rhine and lower Engadin valleys				
Shin-Kanmon	Japan	18.7 (11.6)	1975	railway
carries Sanyo high-speed line under Kanmon Strait between islands of Honshu and Kyushu				
Great Apennine	Italy	18.5 (11.5)	1934	railway
rail link through mountains between Bologna and Florence				
Qinling	China	18.5 (11.5)	2001	railway
traverses Qinling (Tsinling) Mountains, historic barrier between northern and southern China				
Zhongnanshan	China	18.0 (11.2)	2007	highway
world's longest double-tube four-lane highway tunnel				
St. Gotthard	Switzerland	16.9 (10.5)	1980	highway
links Uri and Ticino cantons under St. Gotthard Pass				
Rokko	Japan	16.3 (10.1)	1972	railway
carries Sanyo high-speed line through Rokko Mountains near Kobe				
Furka	Switzerland	15.4 (9.6)	1982	railway
carries scenic Glacier Express Line under Furka Pass				
Haruna	Japan	15.4 (9.6)	1982	railway
on Joetsu "Bullet" Line across Honshu between Tokyo and Niigata				
Severomuyskiy	Russia	15.3 (9.5)	2001	railway
on the Baikal–Amur Line to the northeast of Lake Baikal				

Longest Tunnels in the World (continued)

TUNNEL	LOCATION	LENGTH IN KM (MI)	COMPLETED	USE
Gorigamine	Japan	15.2 (9.4)	1997	railway
on the Hokuriku high-speed line between Takasaki and Nagano				
Monte Santomarco	Italy	15.0 (9.3)	1987	railway
tunnel in Calabria between Paola and Cosenza				
St. Gotthard	Switzerland	15.0 (9.3)	1882	railway
carries Luzern–Milan line under St. Gotthard Pass between Uri and Ticino cantons				
Nakayama	Japan	14.9 (9.2)	1982	railway
on Joetsu "Bullet" Line across Honshu between Tokyo and Niigata				
Mount MacDonald	BC, Canada	14.7 (9.2)	1988	railway
longest tunnel in Western Hemisphere; in Canada's Glacier National Park				

Largest Dams in the World

Source: International Water Power and Dam Construction Yearbook *(1996).*

NAME	TYPE*	DATE OF COMPLETION	RIVER	COUNTRY	
by height					**height (m)**
Nurek	E	1980	Vakhsh	Tajikistan	300
Grand Dixence	G	1961	Dixence	Switzerland	285
Inguri	A	1980	Inguri	Georgia	272
Vaiont[1]	A	1961	Vaiont	Italy	262
Chicoasen	ER	1980	Grijalva	Mexico	261
Tehri	ER	2002[2]	Bhagirathi	India	261
Mauvoisin	A	1957	Drance de Bagnes	Switzerland	250
by volume					**volume ('000 cubic m)**
Syncrude Tailings	E	N/A	...[3]	Canada	540,000
New Cornelia Tailings	E	1973	Ten Mile Wash	US	209,500
Tarbela	ER	1976	Indus	Pakistan	106,000
Fort Peck	E	1937	Missouri	US	96,050
Lower Usuma	E	1990	Usuma	Nigeria	93,000
Tucurui	EGR	1984	Tocantins	Brazil	85,200
Ataturk	ER	1990	Euphrates	Turkey	84,500
by size of reservoir					**reservoir capacity ('000 cubic m)**
Owen Falls	G	1954	Victoria Nile	Uganda	2,700,000,000[4]
Kakhovsk	EG	1955	Dnieper	Ukraine	182,000,000
Kariba	A	1959	Zambezi	Zimbabwe–Zambia	180,600,000
Bratsk	EG	1964	Angara	Russia	169,270,000
Aswan High	ER	1970	Nile	Egypt	168,900,000
Akosombo	ER	1965	Volta	Ghana	153,000,000
Daniel Johnson	M	1968	Manicouagan	Canada	141,852,000
Guri (Raúl Leoni)	EGR	1986	Caroní	Venezuela	138,000,000
by power capacity					**power capacity (megawatts)**
Itaipú	EGR	1983	Paraná	Brazil–Paraguay	13,320
Guri (Raúl Leoni)	EGR	1986	Caroní	Venezuela	10,055
Grand Coulee	G	1942	Columbia	US	6,809
Sayano-Shushenskoye	GA	1989	Yenisey	Russia	6,400
Krasnoyarsk	G	1968	Yenisey	Russia	6,000
Churchill Falls	E	1971	Churchill	Canada	5,428
La Grande 2	R	1979	LaGrande	Canada	5,328
Three Gorges	G	2003	Yangtze	China	4,970

**Key: A, arch; B, buttress; E, earth fill; G, gravity; M, multi-arch; R, rock fill. N/A indicates "not available." [1]Vaiont Dam was the scene of a massive landslide and flood in 1963 and no longer operates. [2]Diversion tunnels closed and reservoir filling begun December 2002. [3]Near Fort McMurray AB. [4]Most of this reservoir is a natural lake.*

Notable Civil Engineering Projects (in progress or completed as of July 2008)

NAME	LOCATION		YEAR OF COMPLETION	NOTES
airports		**terminal area (sq m)**		
Beijing Capital (new Terminal 3)	northeast of Beijing	904,000	2008	Opened 29 Feb 2008; the world's largest building
Changi (new Terminal 3)	mostly on landfill at eastern tip of Singapore	380,000	2008	Opened 9 Jan 2008; new terminal in Asia's 6th busiest airport in passenger traffic
Heathrow (new Terminal 5 complex)	southwest of London	"70,000"	2008	Opened 14 Mar 2008; includes world's 1st personal rapid-transit system
bridges		**length (main span; m)**		
Manifa Causeway	in Persian Gulf offshore of Manifa, Saudi Arabia	41 km (total causeway length)	2011	Includes 20 km of laterals from main causeway to drilling islands; will enable massive oil-field redevelopment
Hangzhou Bay Transoceanic	near Jiaxing, China–near Cixi, China	36 km	2008	Opened 1 May 2008; S-shaped; world's longest transoceanic bridge/causeway
Sutong	Nantong, China (100 km from Yangtze mouth)	1,088	2008	Opened 25 May 2008; cable-stayed bridge; set world records for length of main span and height of main bridge tower
buildings		**height (m)**		
Burj ("Tower") Dubai	Dubai, UAE	643	2009	To be world's tallest building; world's tallest structure from 13 Sep 2007
Russia Tower	Moscow	612	2012	Construction began 18 Sep 2007; to be world's 2nd tallest building upon completion
Chicago Spire	Chicago	2,000 ft (609.6 m)	2011	Construction began 25 Jun 2007; will be North America's tallest structure and the world's tallest all-residential building
dams and hydrologic projects		**crest length (m)**		
St. Petersburg Flood Protection Barrier	Gulf of Finland embankment, Russia (Gorskaya–Bronka via Kotlin Island)	25,400	2008	To protect city from tidal storm surges; incorporates discharge sluices and navigation channels; begun 1980, halted 1987, resumed 2003
Three Gorges (3rd of 3 phases)	west of Yichang, China	2,309	2007	Final stage completed 21 Dec 2007; created world's largest reservoir (660 km long) and world's largest hydroelectric complex by power capacity
Sardar Sarovar (Narmada) Project	Narmada River, Madhya Pradesh, India	1,210	2009	Largest dam of controversial 30-dam project; drinking and irrigation water for Gujarat
highways		**length (km)**		
Interoceanic Highway	Iñapari–Ilo/Matarani/San Juan de Marcona, Peru	2,603	2009	To be paved road for Brazilian imports/exports from/to Asia via 3 Peruvian ports
East-West Economic Corridor	Danang, Vietnam–Moulmein, Myanmar (via Laos and Thailand)	1,450	2008	All-weather gravel road linking the Pacific and Indian oceans; economic development of remote areas expected
Highway 1	Kabul–Kandahar–Herat, Afghanistan	1,048	2008	Final, 556-km Kandahar–Herat section 81% completed by August 2007; remaining section stalled owing to security concerns

Notable Civil Engineering Projects (in progress or completed as of July 2008) (continued)

NAME	LOCATION		YEAR OF COMPLETION	NOTES
land reclamation, canal		**area (sq km)**		
Palm Jumeirah	in Persian Gulf, off Dubai, UAE	c. 25	2012	Phase I residence handover began 2006; land of 3 other Persian Gulf developments was partially to mostly reclaimed in late 2007
Panama Canal Expansion	between Panama City and Colón		2014	Will include new wider and longer 3-chamber locks
railways (heavy)		**length (km)**		
Benguela Railway (rehabilitation; closed 1975–2002)	Benguela–Luau, Angola (at Democratic Republic of the Congo border)	1,301	2010	Chinese-financed rehabilitation will enable resumption of copper exports from the Democratic Republic of the Congo and Zambia
Xinqiu–Bayan Ul Railway	Xinqiu, Liaoning–Bayan Ul, Inner Mongolia, China	487	2010	To be used for coal transport; future link to Mongolia planned
North-South Railway (in part)	Araguaína, Tocantins–Palmas, Tocantins, Brazil	361	2009	Rail exports of agriculture, forestry, and mineral products from vast area of interior north Brazil expected
railways (high speed)		**length (km)**		
Spanish high speed	Madrid to France (via Barcelona)	719	2009	Operational to Barcelona suburbs from mid-2007
Turkey high speed	Ankara–Istanbul	533	2010	To connect capital with largest city
Beijing–Tianjin high speed	Beijing–Tianjin, China	115	2008	Opened 1 Aug 2008; improves country's transportation system for 2008 Olympic Games
subways/metros/light rails		**length (km)**		
Delhi Metro (Phase II)	Delhi	118.6	2010	Many extensions/new lines under construction between 2007 and 2010
Shanghai Metro	Shanghai	96.0	2007	Distance is for length of 3 new lines and 2 extensions; all operational on 29 Dec 2007
Dubai Metro (Red/Green lines)	Dubai, UAE	69.7	2009/2010	To be world's longest driverless transport system
tunnels		**length (m)**		
Apennine Range tunnels (9)	Bologna–Florence (high-speed railway)	73,400	2008	Longest tunnel (Vaglia, 18.6 km); tunnels to cover 93% of line
Lötschberg #2	Frutigen–Raron, Switzerland	34,577	2007	Opened 15 Jun 2007 for freight traffic and 9 Dec 2007 for passengers; world's 3rd longest rail tunnel
Eiksund	Ørstan–Hareid, Norway	7,797	2007	Breakthrough 1 Feb 2007; world's deepest underwater tunnel (287 m under water surface)
miscellaneous		**length (km)**		
East Africa Submarine Cable System	western Indian Ocean between South Africa and The Sudan	13,700	2009	To be 1st underwater fiber-optic cable in Indian Ocean, providing Internet and communications services to 250 million people in Africa
Svalbard Global Seed Vault	near Longyearbyen, Spitsbergen, in the Norwegian Arctic	—	2008	Capable of storing 3 million seeds in perpetuity and guarding them against disease, war, and other catastrophes; opened 26 Feb 2008

1 m=3.28 ft; 1 km=0.62 mi

Life on Earth

Taxonomy

Taxonomy is the classification of living and extinct organisms. The term is derived from the Greek *taxis* ("arrangement") and *nomos* ("law") and refers to the methodology and principles of systematic botany and zoology by which the various kinds of plants and animals are arranged in hierarchies of superior and subordinate groups.

Popularly, classifications of living organisms arise according to need and are often superficial; for example, although the term fish is common to the names shellfish, crayfish, and starfish, there are more anatomical differences between a shellfish and a starfish than there are between a bony fish and a human. Also, vernacular names vary widely. Biologists have attempted to view all living organisms with equal thoroughness and thus have devised a formal classification. A formal classification supports a relatively uniform and internationally understood nomenclature, thereby simplifying cross-referencing and retrieval of information.

Carolus Linnaeus, who is usually regarded as the founder of modern taxonomy and whose books are considered the beginning of modern botanical and zoological nomenclature, drew up rules for assigning names to plants and animals and was the first to use binomial nomenclature consistently, beginning in 1758. Classification since Linnaeus has incorporated newly discovered information and more closely approaches a natural system, and the process of clarifying relationships continues to this day. The table below shows the seven ranks that are accepted as obligatory by zoologists and botanists and sample listings for animals and plants.

	ANIMALS	PLANTS
Kingdom	Animalia	Plantae
Phylum/Division	Chordata	Tracheophyta
Class	Mammalia	Pteropsida
Order	Primates	Coniferales
Family	Hominidae	Pinaceae
Genus	*Homo*	*Pinus*
Species	*Homo sapiens* (human)	*Pinus strobus* (white pine)

Animals

Period of Gestation and Longevity of Selected Mammals

ANIMAL	AVERAGE GESTATION (DAYS)	AVERAGE LONGEVITY (YEARS)
bear (black)	219	18
bear (grizzly)	225	25
bear (polar)	240	20
cat (domestic)	63	12
dog (domestic)	61	12
elephant (Asian)	645	40
fox (red)	52	7
guinea pig	68	4
hippopotamus	238	25–30
horse	330	20
human (worldwide)	266–70	Men: 64.7; Women: 68.9
monkey (rhesus)	164	15
mouse (domestic white)	19	3
pig (domestic)	112	10
rabbit (domestic)	31	5
sheep (domestic)	154	12
squirrel (gray)	44	9–10

Names of the Male, Female, Young, and Group of Animals

ANIMAL	MALE	FEMALE	YOUNG	GROUP
ape	male	female	baby	shrewdness
bear	boar	sow	cub	sleuth, sloth
camel	bull	cow	calf	flock
cattle	bull	cow	calf	drift, drove, herd, mob
chicken	rooster	hen	chick, pullet (hen), cockrell (rooster)	flock, brood (hens), clutch & peep (chicks)
deer	buck, stag	doe	fawn	herd
donkey	jack, jackass	jennet, jenny	colt, foal	drove, herd
elephant	bull	cow	calf	herd, parade
ferret	hob	jill	kit	business, fesynes
fox	reynard	vixen	kit, cub, pup	skulk, leash
giraffe	bull	doe	calf	herd, corps, tower, group
goat	buck, billy	doe, nanny	kid, billy	herd, tribe, trip
gorilla	male	female	infant	band

Names of the Male, Female, Young, and Group of Animals (continued)

ANIMAL	MALE	FEMALE	YOUNG	GROUP
hamster	buck	doe	pup	horde
hippopotamus	bull	cow	calf	herd, bloat
horse	stallion, stud	mare, dam	foal, colt (male), filly (female)	stable, harras, herd, team (working) string or field (racing)
human	man	woman	baby, infant, toddler	clan (related), crowd, family (closely related), community, gang, mob, tribe, etc.
lion	lion	lioness	cub	pride
louse	male	female	nymph	lice, colony, infestation
mouse	buck	doe	pup, pinkie, kitten	horde, mischief
ostrich	cock	hen	chick	flock
pig	boar	sow	piglet, shoat, farrow	drove, herd, litter (of pups), sounder
quail	cock	hen	chick	bevy, covey, drift
rhinoceros	bull	cow	calf	crash
seal	bull	cow	pup	herd, pod, rookery, harem
sheep	buck, ram	ewe, dam	lamb, lambkin, cosset	drift, drove, flock, herd, mob, trip
turkey	tom	hen	poult	rafter
turtle	male	female	hatchling	bale
whale	bull	cow	calf	gam, grind, herd, pod, school
wolf	dog	bitch	pup, whelp	pack, rout
zebra	stallion	mare	colt, foal	herd, crossing

Plants

Oldest Trees and Flowering Plants in the World

	MAXIMUM AGE IN YEARS		
	ESTIMATED	VERIFIED	LOCATION
trees			
Bristlecone pine		4,900	Wheeler Peak, Humboldt National Forest, Nevada
Sierra redwood	4,000	2,200–2,300	northern California
Swiss stone pine	1,200	750	Riffel Alp, Switzerland
common juniper	2,000	544	Kola Peninsula, northeastern Russia
European larch	700	417	Riffel Alp, Switzerland
Norway spruce	1,200	350–400	Eichstätt, Bavaria, Germany
flowering plants			
bo tree	2,000–3,000		Bodh Gaya, India; Anuradhapura, Sri Lanka
English oak	2,000	1,500	Hasbruch Forest, Lower Saxony, Germany
linden		815	Lithuania
European beech	900	250	Montigny, Normandy, France
English ivy	440		Ginac, near Montpellier, France
dragon tree	200		Tenerife, Canary Islands
dwarf birch		80	eastern Greenland

Forests of the World

This table shows the 25 countries or dependencies that lost the most forest area between 1990 and 2005 and those that gained the most, as well as forest losses or gains by continent. 1 hectare (ha) = x .01 sq km, .004 sq mi. Source: State of the World's Forests 2007. ***Web site:*** *<www.fao.org/forestry>.*

COUNTRY/AREA	LAND AREA ('000 HA)	TOTAL FOREST IN 1990 ('000 HA)	TOTAL FOREST IN 2005 ('000 HA)	PERCENTAGE OF LAND AREA IN 2005 (%)	% CHANGE 1990–2005
Kiribati	73	28	2	2.7	−92.86
Kazakhstan	269,970	9,758	3,337	1.2	−65.80
Comoros	186	12	5	2.7	−58.33
Togo	5,439	719	386	7.1	−46.31
Lesotho	3,035	14	8	0.3	−42.86
The Bahamas	1,001	842	515	51.5	−38.84
Brunei	527	452	278	52.8	−38.50
Mozambique	78,409	31,238	19,262	24.6	−38.34
Burundi	2,568	241	152	5.9	−36.93
Nigeria	91,077	17,501	11,089	12.2	−36.64
Afghanistan	65,209	1,351	867	1.3	−35.83

Forests of the World (continued)

COUNTRY/AREA	LAND AREA ('000 HA)	TOTAL FOREST IN 1990 ('000 HA)	TOTAL FOREST IN 2005 ('000 HA)	PERCENTAGE OF LAND AREA IN 2005 (%)	% CHANGE 1990–2005
Mauritania	102,522	415	267	0.3	−35.66
Niger	126,670	1,945	1,266	1.0	−34.91
Haiti	2,756	158	105	3.8	−33.54
Pakistan	77,088	2,755	1,902	2.5	−30.96
Libya	175,954	311	217	0.1	−30.23
Benin	11,062	3,349	2,351	21.3	−29.80
Uganda	19,710	5,103	3,627	18.4	−28.92
Ghana	22,754	7,535	5,517	24.2	−26.78
Albania	2,740	1,069	794	29.0	−25.72
Liberia	9,632	4,241	3,154	32.7	−25.63
Bangladesh	13,017	1,169	871	6.7	−25.49
Indonesia	181,157	118,110	88,495	48.8	−25.07
Paraguay	39,730	24,602	18,475	46.5	−24.90
Dem. People's Rep. of Korea	12,041	8,210	6,187	51.4	−24.64
Lebanon	1,023	37	136	13.3	267.57
Micronesia	70	24	63	90.6	162.50
Ethiopia	100,000	4,996	13,000	13.0	160.21
Cape Verde	403	35	84	20.8	140.00
Northern Mariana Islands	46	14	33	72.4	135.71
Mauritius	203	17	37	18.2	117.65
Tunisia	15,536	499	1,056	6.8	111.62
Kuwait	1,782	3	6	0.3	100.00
Oman	30,950	1	2	[1]	100.00
Sierra Leone	7,162	1,416	2,754	38.5	94.49
Uruguay	17,502	791	1,506	8.6	90.39
Iceland	10,025	25	46	0.5	84.00
Saudi Arabia	214,969	1,504	2,728	1.3	81.38
Puerto Rico	887	234	408	46.0	74.36
Uzbekistan	41,424	1,923	3,295	8.0	71.35
St. Vincent and the Grenadines	39	7	11	28.2	57.14
El Salvador	2,072	193	298	14.4	54.40
Iran	163,620	7,299	11,075	6.8	51.73
East Timor	1,487	541	798	53.7	47.50
Cyprus	924	119	174	18.9	46.22
Morocco	44,630	3,037	4,364	9.8	43.69
Vietnam	32,549	9,303	12,931	39.7	39.00
Ireland	6,889	489	669	9.7	36.81
United States of America	915,896	222,113	303,089	33.1	36.46
China	932,742	145,417	197,290	21.2	35.67
South America	1,753,646	922,731	831,540	47.4	−9.88
Africa	2,962,656	702,502	635,412	21.4	−9.55
Europe	2,260,180	1,030,475	1,001,394	44.3	−2.82
North and Central America	2,143,910	555,002	705,849	32.9	27.18
Asia	3,097,913	551,448	571,577	18.5	3.65
Oceania	849,116	201,271	206,254	24.3	2.48
World	13,067,421	3,963,429	3,952,025	30.2	−0.29

[1]*Negligible.*

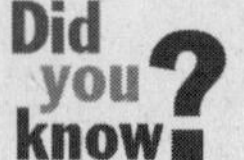

In 17th-century Holland a speculative frenzy erupted over the sale of tulip bulbs. Tulips had been introduced into Europe from Turkey shortly after 1550. Demand for new varieties soon exceeded the supply, and prices rose to astonishing heights. The craze, known as the tulip mania, reached its peak in Holland in 1633–37. Homes, estates, and industries were mortgaged so that bulbs could be purchased; bulbs of rare varieties sold for the equivalent of hundreds of dollars each. The crash came in 1637, when almost overnight the price structure collapsed, sweeping away fortunes and leaving behind financial ruin for many Dutch families.

Geology

The Continents

Figures given are approximate. Area and population as of 2007. Highest and lowest points listed are all given in relation to sea level.

CONTINENT	POPULATION	AREA	% OF TOTAL LAND AREA[1]	HIGHEST/LOWEST POINT
Africa	939,166,800	30,246,121 sq km 11,678,182 sq mi	20.2	Mt. Kilimanjaro (Tanzania): 5,895 m (19,340 ft) Lake Assal (Djibouti): −157 m (−515 ft)
Antarctica	N/A	14,200,000 sq km 5,500,000 sq mi	9.5	Vinson Massif: 4,892 m (16,050 ft) Bentley Subglacial Trench: −2,500 m (−8,200 ft)
Asia	3,976,028,000	31,699,257 sq km 12,239,181 sq mi	21.1	Mt. Everest (China/Nepal): 8,850 m (29,035 ft) Dead Sea (Israel/Jordan): −400 m (−1,312 ft)
Europe	732,578,400	23,039,279 sq km 8,895,468 sq mi	15.4	Mt. Elbrus (Russia): 5,642 m (18,510 ft) Caspian Sea (Russia): −27 m (−90 ft)
North America	523,775,400	24,393,585 sq km 9,418,416 sq mi	16.3	Mt. McKinley (Alaska): 6,194 m (20,320 ft) Death Valley (California): −86 m (−282 ft)
Australia (and Oceania)	34,375,070	8,515,144 sq km 3,287,717 sq mi	5.7	Jaya Peak (Indonesia): 5,030 m (16,500 ft) Lake Eyre (Australia): −15 m (−50 ft)
South America	376,055,500	17,824,370 sq km 6,882,027 sq mi	11.9	Mt. Aconcagua (Argentina/Chile): 6,959 m (22,834 ft) Valdés Peninsula (Argentina): −40 m (−131 ft)

[1]*Together, the continents make up about 29.2% of the Earth's surface.*

Earth's interior layers (depths below surface)

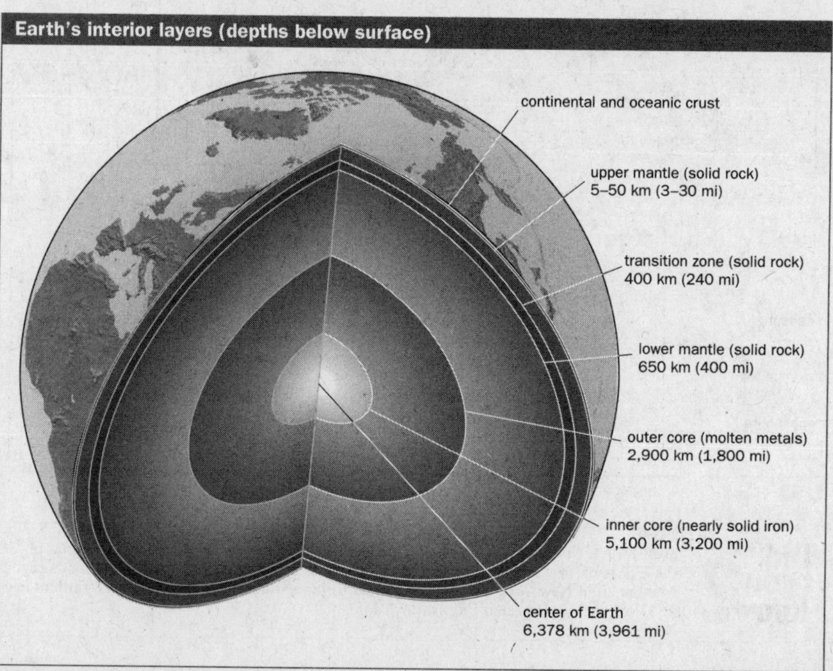

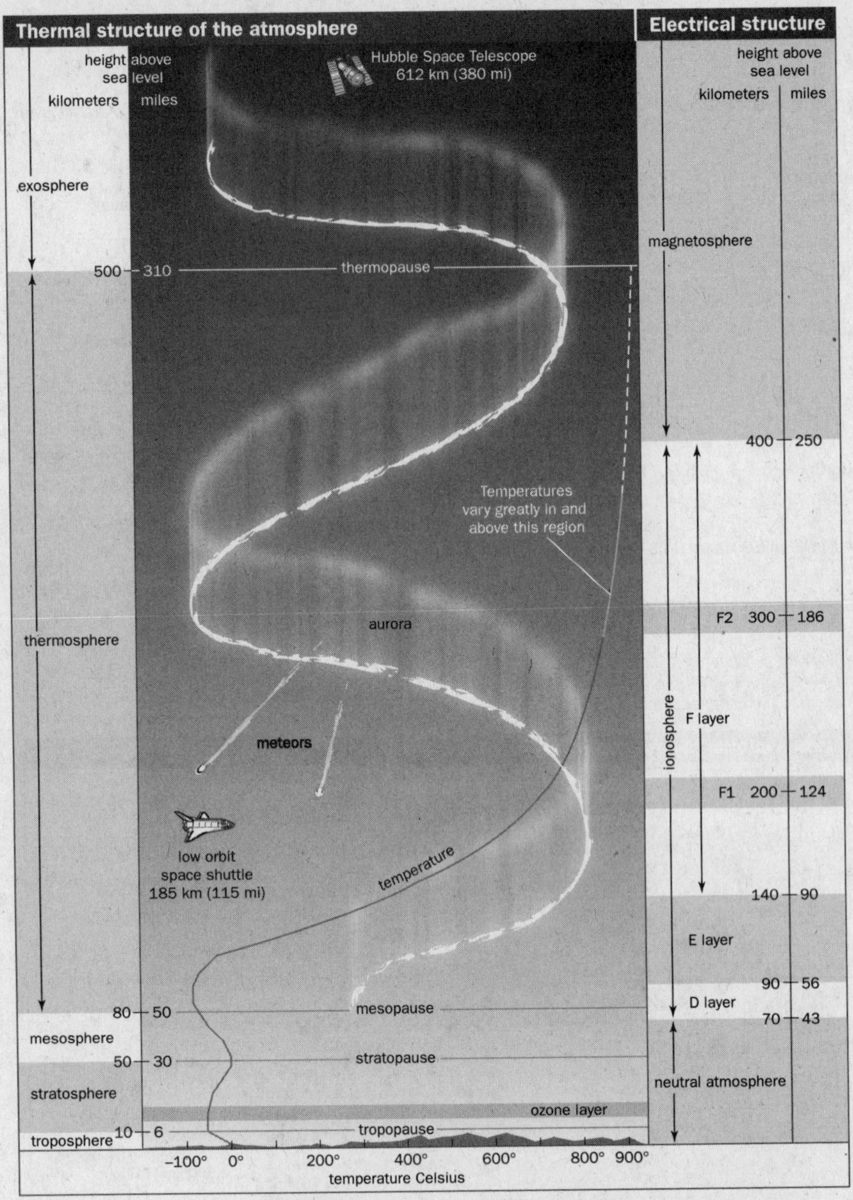

Thermal structure of the atmosphere

height above sea level
kilometers miles

Hubble Space Telescope
612 km (380 mi)

exosphere

500 – 310 thermopause

thermosphere

Temperatures vary greatly in and above this region

aurora

meteors

low orbit space shuttle
185 km (115 mi)

temperature

80 – 50 mesopause

mesosphere

50 – 30 stratopause

stratosphere

ozone layer

10 – 6 tropopause

troposphere

−100° 0° 200° 400° 600° 800° 900°
temperature Celsius

Electrical structure

height above sea level
kilometers miles

magnetosphere

400 – 250

F2 300 – 186

ionosphere

F layer

F1 200 – 124

140 – 90

E layer

90 – 56

D layer

70 – 43

neutral atmosphere

Wall Street, which was recognized even before the Civil War as the financial capital of the US, is narrow and short, extending only about seven blocks across part of southern Manhattan in New York City. It was named for an earthen wall built by Dutch settlers in 1653 to repel an expected English invasion.

Geologic Time Scale

Eon	Era	Period	Epoch	Age	mya[1]
Phanerozoic	Cenozoic	Neogene	Holocene		0.0117
			Pleistocene	Upper	0.126
				"Ionian"	0.781
				Calabrian	1.806
			Pliocene	Gelasian	2.588
				Piacenzian	3.600
				Zanclean	5.332
			Miocene	Messinian	7.246
				Tortonian	11.608
				Serravallian	13.82
				Langhian	15.97
				Burdigalian	20.43
				Aquitanian	23.03
		Paleogene	Oligocene	Chattian	28.4 ± 0.1
				Rupelian	33.9 ± 0.1
			Eocene	Priabonian	37.2 ± 0.1
				Bartonian	40.4 ± 0.2
				Lutetian	48.6 ± 0.2
				Ypresian	55.8 ± 0.2
			Paleocene	Thanetian	58.7 ± 0.2
				Selandian	~61.1
				Danian	65.5 ± 0.3
	Mesozoic	Cretaceous	Upper	Maastrichtian	70.6 ± 0.6
				Campanian	83.5 ± 0.7
				Santonian	85.8 ± 0.7
				Coniacian	~88.6
				Turonian	93.6 ± 0.8
				Cenomanian	99.6 ± 0.9
			Lower	Albian	112.0 ± 1.0
				Aptian	125.0 ± 1.0
				Barremian	130.0 ± 1.5
				Hauterivian	~133.9
				Valanginian	140.2 ± 3.0
				Berriasian	145.5 ± 4.0

Eon	Era	Period	Epoch	Age	mya[1]
Phanerozoic	Mesozoic	Jurassic	Upper	Tithonian	145.5 ± 4.0 150.8 ± 4.0
				Kimmeridgian	~155.6
				Oxfordian	161.2 ± 4.0
			Middle	Callovian	164.7 ± 4.0
				Bathonian	167.7 ± 3.5
				Bajocian	171.6 ± 3.0
				Aalenian	175.6 ± 2.0
			Lower	Toarcian	183.0 ± 1.5
				Pliensbachian	189.6 ± 1.5
				Sinemurian	196.5 ± 1.0
				Hettangian	199.6 ± 0.6
		Triassic	Upper	Rhaetian	203.6 ± 1.5
				Norian	216.5 ± 2.0
				Carnian	~228.7
			Middle	Ladinian	237.0 ± 2.0
				Anisian	~245.9
			Lower	Olenekian	~249.5
				Induan	251.0 ± 0.4
	Paleozoic	Permian	Lopingian	Changhsingian	253.8 ± 0.7
				Wuchiapingian	260.4 ± 0.7
			Guadalupian	Capitanian	265.8 ± 0.7
				Wordian	268.0 ± 0.7
				Roadian	270.6 ± 0.7
			Cisuralian	Kungurian	275.6 ± 0.7
				Artinskian	284.4 ± 0.7
				Sakmarian	294.6 ± 0.8
				Asselian	299.0 ± 0.8
		Carboniferous	Pennsylvanian[3] Upper	Gzhelian	303.4 ± 0.9
				Kasimovian	307.2 ± 1.0
			Pennsylvanian[3] Middle	Moscovian	311.7 ± 1.1
			Pennsylvanian[3] Lower	Bashkirian	318.1 ± 1.3
			Mississippian[3] Upper	Serpukhovian	328.3 ± 1.6
			Mississippian[3] Middle	Visean	345.3 ± 2.1
			Mississippian[3] Lower	Tournaisian	359.2 ± 2.5

Eon	Era	Period	Epoch	Age	mya[1]
Phanerozoic	Paleozoic	Devonian	Upper	Famennian	359.2 ± 2.5 374.5 ± 2.6
				Frasnian	385.3 ± 2.6
			Middle	Givetian	391.8 ± 2.7
				Eifelian	397.5 ± 2.7
			Lower	Emsian	407.0 ± 2.8
				Pragian	411.2 ± 2.8
				Lochkovian	416.0 ± 2.8
		Silurian	Pridoli		418.7 ± 2.7
			Ludlow	Ludfordian	421.3 ± 2.6
				Gorstian	422.9 ± 2.5
			Wenlock	Homerian	426.2 ± 2.4
				Sheinwoodian	428.2 ± 2.3
			Llandovery	Telychian	436.0 ± 1.9
				Aeronian	439.0 ± 1.8
				Rhuddanian	443.7 ± 1.5
		Ordovician	Upper	Hirnantian	445.6 ± 1.5
				Katian	455.8 ± 1.6
				Sandbian	460.9 ± 1.6
			Middle	Darriwilian	468.1 ± 1.6
				Dapingian	471.8 ± 1.6
			Lower	Floian	478.6 ± 1.7
				Tremadocian	488.3 ± 1.7
		Cambrian[2]	Furongian	Stage 10	~492.0
				Stage 9	~496.0
				Paibian	499.0
			Series 3	Guzhangian	~503.0
				Drumian	~506.5
				Stage 5	~510.0
			Series 2	Stage 4	~515.0
				Stage 3	~521.0
			Terreneuvian	Stage 2	~528.0
				Fortunian	542.0 ± 1.0

	Eon	Era	Period	mya[1]
Precambrian	Proterozoic	Neoproterozoic	Ediacaran	542.0 ~635.0
			Cryogenian	850.0
			Tonian	1,000.0
		Mesoproterozoic	Stenian	1,200.0
			Ectasian	1,400.0
			Calymmian	1,600.0
		Paleoproterozoic	Statherian	1,800.0
			Orosirian	2,050.0
			Rhyacian	2,300.0
			Siderian	2,500.0
	Archean	Neoarchean		2,800.0
		Mesoarchean		3,200.0
		Paleoarchean		3,600.0
		Eoarchean		4,000.0
		Hadean (informal)		

[1] Millions of years ago.
[2] Cambrian unit age boundaries are informal and are awaiting ratified definitions.
[3] Both the Mississippian and Pennsylvanian time units are formally designated as subperiods within the Carboniferous Period.

Published with permission from the International Commission on Stratigraphy (ICS). International chronostratigraphic units, ranks, names, and formal status are approved by the ICS and ratified by the International Union of Geological Sciences (IUGS). Source: 2008 International Stratigraphic Chart produced by the ICS.

Largest Islands of the World

NAME AND LOCATION	CONTINENT	AREA[1] SQ MI	SQ KM
Greenland	North America	822,700	2,130,800
New Guinea, Papua New Guinea/Indonesia	Australia (and Oceania)	309,000	800,000
Borneo, Indonesia/Malaysia/Brunei	Asia	292,000	755,000
Madagascar	Africa	226,662	587,051
Baffin, Nunavut, Canada	North America	195,928	507,451
Sumatra, Indonesia	Asia	186,253	482,393
Great Britain, UK	Europe	88,386	228,919
Honshu, Japan	Asia	87,992	227,898
Victoria, Northwest Territories/Nunavut, Canada	North America	83,896	217,291
Ellesmere, Nunavut, Canada	North America	75,767	196,236
Celebes, Indonesia	Asia	74,845	193,847
South Island, New Zealand	Australia (and Oceania)	58,776	152,229
Java, Indonesia	Asia	49,926	129,307
North Island, New Zealand	Australia (and Oceania)	44,872	116,219
Cuba	North America	42,804	110,861
Newfoundland, Canada	North America	42,031	108,860
Luzon, Philippines	Asia	40,420	104,688
Iceland	Europe	39,741	102,928
Mindanao, Philippines	Asia	36,537	94,630
Ireland, Ireland/UK	Europe	32,375	83,849
Hokkaido, Japan	Asia	30,107	77,978
Sakhalin, Russia	Asia	29,500	76,400
Hispaniola, Haiti/Dominican Republic	North America	29,418	76,192
Banks, Northwest Territories, Canada	North America	27,038	70,028
Tasmania, Australia	Australia	26,410	68,401
Sri Lanka	Asia	25,332	65,610
Devon, Nunavut, Canada	North America	21,331	55,247

[1]*Area given may include small adjoining islands. Conversions for rounded figures may be rounded to the nearest hundred.*

Highest Mountains of the World by Region

"I" in the name of a peak refers to the highest in a group of numbered peaks of the same name.

NAME AND LOCATION	HEIGHT IN M	HEIGHT IN FT	YEAR FIRST CLIMBED
Africa			
Kilimanjaro (Kibo peak), Tanzania	5,895	19,340	1889
Mt. Kenya (Batian peak), Kenya	5,199	17,058	1899
Margherita, Ruwenzori Range, Dem. Rep. of the Congo/Uganda	5,119	16,795	1906
Ras Dejen, Simen Mtns., Ethiopia	4,620	15,157	1841
Antarctica			
Vinson Massif, Sentinel Range, Ellsworth Mtns.	4,892	16,050	1966
Tyree, Sentinel Range, Ellsworth Mtns.	4,852	15,919	1967
Shinn, Sentinel Range, Ellsworth Mtns.	4,801	15,751	1966
Asia			
Everest (Chomolungma), Himalayas, Nepal/Tibet, China	8,850	29,035	1953
K2 (Godwin Austen) (Chogori), Karakoram Range, Pakistan/Xinjiang, China	8,611	28,251	1954
Kanchenjunga I, Himalayas, Nepal/India	8,586	28,169	1955
Lhotse I, Himalayas, Nepal/Tibet, China	8,501	27,890	1956
Makalu I, Himalayas, Nepal/Tibet, China	8,463	27,766	1955
Caucasus			
Elbrus, Russia	5,642	18,510	1874
Dykh-Tau, Russia	5,204	17,073	1888
Koshtan-Tau, Russia	5,151	16,900	1889
Shkhara, Russia/Georgia	5,068	16,627	1888
Europe			
Mont Blanc, Alps, France/Italy/Switzerland	4,807	15,771	1786
Dufourspitze, Monte Rosa Massif, Alps, Switzerland/Italy	4,634	15,203	1855

Highest Mountains of the World by Region (continued)

NAME AND LOCATION	HEIGHT IN M	HEIGHT IN FT	YEAR FIRST CLIMBED
Europe (continued)			
Dom (Mischabel), Alps, Switzerland	4,545	14,912	1858
Weisshorn, Alps, Switzerland	4,505	14,780	1861
North America			
McKinley, Alaska Range, Alaska	6,194	20,320	1913
Logan, St. Elias Mtns., Yukon, Canada	5,951	19,524	1925
Citlaltépetl (Orizaba), Cordillera Neo-Volcánica, Mexico	5,610	18,406	1848
St. Elias, St. Elias Mtns., Alaska/Canada	5,489	18,008	1897
Australia (and Oceania)			
Jaya (Sukarno) (Carstensz), Sudirman Range, Indonesia	5,030	16,500[1]	1962
Pilimsit (Idenburg), Sudirman Range, Indonesia	4,800	15,750[1]	1962
Trikora (Wilhelmina), Jayawijaya Mtns., Indonesia	4,750	15,580[1]	1912
Mandala (Juliana), Jayawijaya Mtns., Indonesia	4,700	15,420[1]	1959
South America			
Aconcagua, Andes, Argentina/Chile	6,959	22,831	1897
Ojos del Salado, Andes, Argentina/Chile	6,893	22,614	1937
Bonete, Andes, Argentina	6,872	22,546	1913
Mercedario, Andes, Argentina/Chile	6,770	22,211	1934

[1]*Conversions rounded to the nearest 10 ft.*

Major Caves and Cave Systems of the World by Continent

Source: Bob Gulden, National Speleological Society.

NAME AND LOCATION	DEPTH[1] FEET	M	LENGTH[2] MILES	KM
Africa				
Ambatoharanana, Madagascar	N/A	N/A	11.2	18.1
Boussouil, Algeria	2,641	805	2.0	3.2
Ifflis, Algeria	3,839	1,170	1.2	2.0
Sof ‘Umar, Ethiopia	49	15	9.4	15.1
Tafna (Bou Ma’za), Algeria	N/A	N/A	11.4	18.4
Asia				
Air Jernih, Malaysia	1,165	355	94.1	151.4
Boj-Bulok, Uzbekistan	4,642	1,415	8.9	14.3
Evren Gunay Dudeni, Turkey	4,688	1,429	1.9	3.1
Kap-Kutan/Promezhutochnaya, Turkmenistan	1,017	310	35.4	57.0
Oreshnaya, Russia	787	240	36.0	58.0
Australia (and Oceania)				
Atea, Papua New Guinea	1,148	350	21.4	34.5
Bullita, NT, Australia	75	23	68.1	109.6
Bulmer, New Zealand	2,457	749	32.4	52.1
Neide-Muruk, Papua New Guinea	4,127	1,258	10.6	17.0
Nettlebed, New Zealand	2,917	889	15.1	24.2
Europe				
Hölloch, Switzerland	3,079	939	120.7	194.2
Jean Bernard, France	5,256	1,602	12.8	20.5
Krubera, Georgia	7,188	2,191	8.2	13.2
Optimisticheskaya, Ukraine	49	15	133.6	215.0
Trave, Spain	4,728	1,441	5.7	9.2
North America				
Cuicateca, Mexico	4,869	1,484	16.3	26.2
Huautla, Mexico	4,839	1,475	38.6	62.1
Jewel, South Dakota	632	193	140.1	225.4
Mammoth–Flint Ridge, Kentucky	379	116	367.0	590.6
Wind, South Dakota	646	197	127.8	205.6

Major Caves and Cave Systems of the World (continued)

NAME AND LOCATION	DEPTH[1] FEET	DEPTH[1] M	LENGTH[2] MILES	LENGTH[2] KM
South America				
Aonda, Venezuela	1,188	362	N/A	N/A
Barriguda, Brazil	200	61	18.6	30.0
Boa Vista, Brazil	164	50	63.7	102.5
Kaukiran, Peru	1,335	407	1.3	2.1
São Mateus-Imbira, Brazil	N/A	N/A	12.7	20.5

[1]*Below highest entrance.* [2]*Explored portion of cave.*

Major Deserts of the World by Continent

DESERT (LOCATION)	AREA SQ KM	AREA SQ MI
Africa		
Sahara, northern Africa	8,600,000	3,320,000
Kalahari, southwestern Africa	930,000	360,000
Namib, southwestern Africa	135,000	52,000
Libyan, Libya, Egypt, and Sudan	N/A	N/A
Asia		
Arabia, southwestern Asia	2,330,000	900,000
Gobi, Mongolia and northeastern China	1,300,000	500,000
Rubʿ al-Khali, southern Arabian Peninsula	650,000	250,000
Karakum, Turkmenistan	350,000	135,000
Kyzylkum, Kazakhstan and Uzbekistan	300,000	115,000
Takla Makan, northern China	270,000	105,000
Kavir, central Iran	260,000	100,000
Syrian, Saudi Arabia, Jordan, Syria, and Iraq	260,000	100,000
Thar, India and Pakistan	200,000	77,000
Lut, eastern Iran	52,000	20,000
Australia		
Great Victoria, Western and South Australia	647,000	250,000
Great Sandy, northern Western Australia	400,000	150,000
Simpson, Northern Territory	145,000	56,000
Gibson, Western Australia	N/A	N/A
North America		
Great Basin, southwestern US	492,000	190,000
Chihuahuan, northern Mexico	450,000	175,000
Sonoran, southwestern US and Baja California	310,000	120,000
Mojave, southwestern US	65,000	25,000
Colorado, California and northern Mexico	N/A	N/A
Yuma, Arizona and Sonora, Mexico	N/A	N/A
South America		
Patagonian, southern Argentina	673,000	260,000
Atacama, northern Chile	140,000	54,000

Major Volcanoes of the World by Continent

VOLCANO, LOCATION	ELEVATION M	ELEVATION FT	FIRST RECORDED ERUPTION	MOST RECENT ERUPTION
Africa				
Kilimanjaro, Tanzania[1]	5,895	19,340	N/A	N/A
Cameroon, Cameroon	4,095	13,435	1650	2000
Teide (Tenerife), Canary Islands	3,715	12,188	N/A	1909
Nyiragongo, Dem. Rep. of the Congo	3,470	11,384	1884	2007
Nyamuragira, Dem. Rep. of the Congo	3,058	10,033	1882	2006
Antarctica				
Erebus, Ross Island	3,794	12,447	1841	2007
Darnley, Sandwich Islands	1,100	3,609	1823	N/A
Asia, Oceania, and the Pacific				
Klyuchevskaya, Kamchatka, Russia[2]	4,835	15,863	1697	2007
Mauna Kea, Hawaii	4,205	13,796	N/A	c. 2460 BC
Mauna Loa, Hawaii	4,170	13,681	1750	1984
Kerinci, Sumatra, Indonesia	3,800	12,467	1838	2008
Fuji, Honshu, Japan	3,776	12,388	1050 BC	1708
Rinjani, Lombok, Indonesia	3,726	12,224	1847	2004
Tolbachik, Kamchatka, Russia	3,682	12,080	1740	1976
Semeru, Java, Indonesia	3,676	12,060	1818	2007

Major Volcanoes of the World (continued)

VOLCANO, LOCATION	ELEVATION M	ELEVATION FT	FIRST RECORDED ERUPTION	MOST RECENT ERUPTION
Europe and the Atlantic				
Etna, Italy	3,350	10,991	N/A	2007
Askja, Iceland	1,516	4,974	1875	1961
Hekla, Iceland	1,491	4,892	1104	2000
Vesuvius, Italy	1,281	4,203	79	1944
Stromboli, Italy	924	3,031	N/A	2007
North America				
Citlaltépetl, Mexico	5,675	18,619	N/A	1846
Popocatépetl, Mexico	5,426	17,802	1347	2007
Rainier, Washington	4,392	14,409	N/A	1894
Shasta, California	4,317	14,163	1786	1786
Colima, Mexico	3,850	12,631	1576	2007
St. Helens, Washington	2,549	8,363	N/A	2007
South America				
Guallatiri, Chile	6,071	19,918	1825	1960
Tupungatito, Chile	6,000	19,685	1829	1987
Cotopaxi, Ecuador	5,911	19,393	1532	1940
Láscar, Chile	5,592	18,346	1848	2007
Nevado del Ruiz, Colombia	5,321	17,457	1595	1991

[1]*Includes three dormant volcanoes (Kibo, Mawensi, and Shira) that have not erupted in historic times.* [2]*Highest active volcano on the Kamchatka Peninsula.*

Oceans & Seas

	AREA SQ KM	AREA SQ MI	VOLUME CU KM	VOLUME CU MI
Pacific Ocean				
without marginal seas	165,250,000	63,800,000	707,600,000	169,900,000
with marginal seas	179,680,000	69,370,000	723,700,000	173,700,000
Atlantic Ocean				
without marginal seas	82,440,000	31,830,000	324,600,000	77,900,000
with marginal seas	106,460,000	41,100,000	354,700,000	85,200,000
Indian Ocean				
without marginal seas	73,440,000	28,360,000	291,000,000	69,900,000
with marginal seas	74,920,000	28,930,000	291,900,000	70,100,000
Arctic Ocean	14,090,000	5,440,000	17,000,000	4,100,000
Australasian Central Sea	8,140,000	3,140,000	9,900,000	2,400,000
Gulf of Mexico and Caribbean Sea	4,320,000	1,670,000	9,600,000	2,300,000
Mediterranean and Black Seas	2,970,000	1,150,000	4,200,000	100,000
Bering Sea	2,304,000	890,000	3,330,000	80,000
Sea of Okhotsk	1,583,000	611,000	1,300,000	30,000
Hudson Bay	1,230,000	470,000	160,000	40,000
North Sea	570,000	220,000	50,000	10,000
Baltic Sea	420,000	160,000	20,000	5,000
Irish Sea	100,000	40,000	6,000	1,000
English Channel	75,000	29,000	4,000	1,000

	AVERAGE DEPTH M	AVERAGE DEPTH FT	DEEPEST POINT
Pacific Ocean			
without marginal seas	4,280	14,040	Mariana Trench
with marginal seas	4,030	13,220	(11,034 m; 36,201 ft)
Atlantic Ocean			
without marginal seas	3,930	12,890	Puerto Rico Trench
with marginal seas	3,330	10,920	(8,380 m; 27,493 ft)
Indian Ocean			
without marginal seas	3,960	10,040	Sunda Deep of the Java
with marginal seas	3,900	12,790	Trench (7,450 m; 24,442 ft)
Arctic Ocean	1,205	3,950	(5,502 m; 18,050 ft)

Oceans & Seas (continued)

	AVERAGE DEPTH M	AVERAGE DEPTH FT	DEEPEST POINT
Australasian Central Sea	1,210	3,970	N/A
Gulf of Mexico and Caribbean Sea	2,220	7,280	Cayman Trench (7,686 m; 25,216 ft)
Mediterranean and Black Seas	1,430	4,690	Ionian Basin (4,900 m; 16,000 ft)
Bering Sea	1,440	4,720	Bowers Basin (4,097 m; 13,442 ft)
Sea of Okhotsk	838	2,750	Kuril Basin (2,499 m; 8,200 ft)
Hudson Bay	128	420	(867 m; 2,846 ft)
North Sea	94	310	Skagerrak (700 m; 2,300 ft)
Baltic Sea	55	180	Landsort Deep (459 m; 1,506 ft)
Irish Sea	60	200	Mull of Galloway (175 m; 576 ft)
English Channel	54	180	Hurd Deep (172 m; 565 ft)

Major Natural Lakes of the World

Conversions for figures may have been rounded, thousands to the nearest hundred and hundreds to the nearest ten.

NAME	LOCATION	AREA SQ MI	AREA SQ KM
Caspian Sea	Central Asia	149,200	386,400
Superior	Canada/US	31,700	82,100
Victoria	eastern Africa	26,828	69,484
Huron	Canada/US	23,000	59,600
Michigan	US	22,300	57,800
Tanganyika	eastern Africa	12,700	32,900
Great Bear	Northwest Territories, Canada	12,096	31,328
Nyasa (Malawi)	eastern Africa	11,430	29,604
Great Slave	Northwest Territories, Canada	11,030	28,568
Erie	Canada/US	9,910	25,667
Winnipeg	Manitoba, Canada	9,416	24,387
Ontario	Canada/US	7,340	19,010
Aral Sea[1]	Central Asia	6,711	17,382

[1]*Salt lake.*

Longest Rivers of the World by Continent

This list includes both rivers and river systems. Conversions of rounded figures may be rounded to the nearest 10 or 100 miles or kilometers.

NAME	OUTFLOW	LENGTH MI	LENGTH KM
Africa			
Nile	Mediterranean Sea	4,132	6,650
Congo	South Atlantic Ocean	2,900	4,700
Niger	Gulf of Guinea	2,600	4,200
Zambezi	Mozambique Channel	2,200	3,540
Kasai	Congo River	1,338	2,153
Asia			
Yangtze	East China Sea	3,915	6,300
Yenisey-Baikal-Selenga	Kara Sea	3,442	5,539
Huang He (Yellow)	Gulf of Chihli	3,395	5,464
Ob-Irtysh	Gulf of Ob	3,362	5,410
Amur-Argun	Sea of Okhotsk	2,762	4,444
Europe			
Volga	Caspian Sea	2,193	3,530
Danube	Black Sea	1,770	2,850
Ural	Caspian Sea	1,509	2,428
Dnieper	Black Sea	1,367	2,200
Don	Sea of Azov	1,162	1,870
North America			
Mississippi-Missouri-Jefferson	Gulf of Mexico	3,710	5,971
Mackenzie-Slave-Peace	Beaufort Sea	2,635	4,241
Missouri-Jefferson	Mississippi River	2,540	4,088
St. Lawrence–Great Lakes	Gulf of St. Lawrence	2,500	4,000
Mississippi	Gulf of Mexico	2,350	3,782

Longest Rivers of the World by Continent (continued)

NAME	OUTFLOW	LENGTH MI	LENGTH KM
Australia			
Darling	Murray River	1,702	2,739
Murray	Great Australian Bight	1,572	2,530
Murrumbidgee	Murray River	1,050	1,690
Lachlan	Murrumbidgee River	930	1,500
Cooper Creek	Lake Eyre	880	1,420
South America			
Amazon-Ucayali-Apurímac	South Atlantic Ocean	4,000	6,400
Paraná	Río de la Plata	3,032	4,880
Madeira-Mamoré-Guaporé	Amazon River	2,082	3,352
Juruá	Amazon River	2,040	3,283
Purus	Amazon River	1,995	3,211

Preserving Nature

US National Parks

Dates in parentheses indicate when the area was first designated a park, in most cases under a different name. ***Web site:*** *<www.nps.gov/parks.html>.*

PARK	LOCATION	DESIGNATION DATE	SQ MI	SQ KM
Acadia	Bar Harbor ME	1929 (1916)	74	192
American Samoa	American Samoa	1993 (1988)	14	36
Arches	Moab UT	1971 (1929)	120	311
Badlands	southwestern South Dakota	1978 (1939)	379	982
Big Bend	curve of the Rio Grande river, Texas	1944	1,252	3,243
Biscayne	near Miami FL	1980 (1968)	270	699
Black Canyon of the Gunnison	near Montrose CO	1999 (1933)	43	112
Bryce Canyon	Bryce Canyon, Utah	1928 (1923)	56	145
Canyonlands	near Moab UT	1964	527	1,366
Capitol Reef	near Torrey UT	1971 (1937)	379	982
Carlsbad Caverns	near Carlsbad NM	1930 (1923)	73	189
Channel Islands	Ventura CA	1980 (1938)	75	194
Congaree	Hopkins SC	2003	34	88
Crater Lake	Crater Lake OR	1902	286	741
Cuyahoga Valley	near Cleveland and Akron OH	2000 (1974)	51	133
Death Valley	Death Valley, California	1994 (1933)	5,219	13,518
Denali	central Alaska	1980 (1917)	9,492	24,584
Dry Tortugas	Key West FL	1992 (1935)	101	262
Everglades	southern Florida	1947	2,358	6,107
Gates of the Arctic	Bettles AK	1980 (1978)	13,238	34,287
Glacier	northwest Montana	1910	1,584	4,102
Glacier Bay	Gustavus AK	1980 (1925)	5,130	13,287
Grand Canyon	Grand Canyon, Arizona	1919 (1908)	1,902	4,927
Grand Teton	Moose WY	1950 (1929)	484	1,255
Great Basin	near Baker NV	1986 (1922)	121	313
Great Sand Dunes	Mosca CO	2000 (1932)	132	343
Great Smoky Mountains	Tennessee and North Carolina	1934	815	2,110
Guadalupe Mountains	Salt Flat TX	1972	135	350
Haleakala	Kula, Maui HI	1960 (1916)	47	121
Hawaii Volcanoes	near Hilo HI	1961 (1916)	328	849
Hot Springs	Hot Springs AR	1921 (1832)	9	22
Isle Royale	Houghton MI	1940 (1931)	893	2,314
Joshua Tree	near Palm Springs CA	1994 (1936)	1,591	4,120
Katmai	near King Salmon AK	1980 (1918)	7,385	19,128
Kenai Fjords	Seward AK	1980 (1978)	1,047	2,711
Kobuk Valley	Kotzebue AK	1980 (1978)	2,672	6,920
Lake Clark	Port Alsworth AK	1980 (1978)	6,297	16,309
Lassen Volcanic	Mineral CA	1916 (1907)	166	430
Mammoth Cave	Mammoth Cave, Kentucky	1941	83	214
Mesa Verde	near Cortez and Mancos CO	1906	81	211
Mount Rainier	near Ashford WA	1899	368	954
North Cascades	near Marblemount WA	1968	1,069	2,769
Olympic	near Port Angeles WA	1938	1,442	3,734

US National Parks (continued)

PARK	LOCATION	DESIGNATION DATE	SQ MI	SQ KM
Petrified Forest	Arizona	1962 (1906)	146	379
Redwood	Crescent City CA	1994	172	445
Rocky Mountain	near Estes Park and Grand Lake CO	1915	415	1,076
Saguaro	Tucson AZ	1994 (1933)	143	370
Sequoia & Kings Canyon	near Three Rivers CA	1940 (1890)	1,351	3,498
Shenandoah	near Luray VA	1935	311	805
Theodore Roosevelt	Medora ND (south unit); near Watford City ND (north unit)	1978 (1947)	110	285
Virgin Islands	St. John, US Virgin Islands	1956	23	59
Voyageurs	International Falls MN	1975	341	883
Wind Cave	near Hot Springs SD	1903	44	115
Wolf Trap	Vienna VA	2002 (1966)	130 acres	
Wrangell–St. Elias	near Copper Center AK	1980	20,587	53,320
Yellowstone	Idaho, Montana, and Wyoming	1872	3,468	8,983
Yosemite	in the Sierra Nevada, California	1890 (1864)	1,189	3,081
Zion	Springdale UT	1919 (1909)	229	593

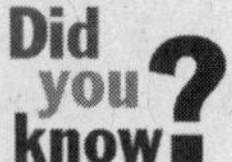

On 13 May 1864, a Confederate prisoner who died in a local hospital became the first soldier laid to rest at Arlington National Cemetery. Dead from every war in which the US has participated have since been buried there. More than 300,000 people are interred at Arlington, and the Fields of the Dead, with their seemingly endless lines of plain stones, follow a pattern adopted in 1872 for use in all national cemeteries.

Health

Worldwide Health Indicators

*Column data as follows: **Life expectancy** in 2005; **Doctors** = persons per doctor[1]; **Infant mortality** per 1,000 births in 2005; **Water** = percentage (%) of population with access to safe drinking water in 2004; **Food** = percentage (%) of the FAO recommended minimum in 2004[2].*

	LIFE EXPECTANCY			INFANT		
REGION/BLOC	MALE	FEMALE	DOCTORS	MORTALITY	WATER	FOOD
World	**66.0**	**70.0**	**730**	**38.3**	**83**	**118**
Africa	**51.8**	**53.8**	**2,560**	**78.4**	**64[3]**	**103**
Central Africa	49.8	50.2	12,890	96.1	46[3]	80
East Africa	46.9	48.2	13,620	86.7	50[3]	86
North Africa	67.2	71.0	890	39.2	91	125
Southern Africa	47.8	51.2	1,610	55.1	85[3]	119
West Africa	47.7	49.7	6,260	94.3	65[3]	109
Americas	**71.5**	**77.6**	**520**	**17.1**	**91[3]**	**129**
Anglo-America[4]	75.0	80.4	370	6.2	100[3]	140
Canada	76.7	83.6	540	4.8	100	136
United States	74.8	80.1	360	6.4	100	141
Latin America	69.4	76.0	690	23.6	91	123
Caribbean	67.5	71.6	380	29.4	79[3]	118
Central America	67.9	73.7	950	21.4	88[3]	106
Mexico	72.7	77.6	810	12.6	97	134
South America	68.9	76.2	710	26.3	86[3]	122
Andean Group	69.4	75.6	830	23.5	86[3]	108
Brazil	67.7	75.9	770	30.7	90	132
Other South America	72.1	79.4	410	17.5	82[3]	120
Asia	**67.2**	**70.3**	**970**	**39.6**	**81[3]**	**116**
Eastern Asia	71.2	75.0	610	22.3	78[5]	121
China	70.4	73.7	620	25.2	77	123
Japan	78.6	85.6	530	2.7	100	110
Republic of Korea	71.7	79.3	740	6.4	92	123
Other Eastern Asia	71.7	77.3	500	13.8	94[3]	93

Worldwide Health Indicators (continued)

REGION/BLOC	LIFE EXPECTANCY MALE	LIFE EXPECTANCY FEMALE	DOCTORS	INFANT MORTALITY	WATER	FOOD
Asia (continued)						
South Asia	63.3	64.6	2,100	60.5	85[6]	108
India	63.6	65.2	1,920	56.3	86	112
Pakistan	64.7	65.5	1,840	76.2	91	100
Other South Asia	60.4	60.5	5,080	71.0	85[3]	97
Southeast Asia	66.8	71.9	3,120	33.9	82	123
Southwest Asia	67.3	71.9	610	35.5	85[3]	118
Central Asia	61.0	68.9	330	54.0	82[3]	99
Gulf Cooperation Council	73.4	77.5	620	12.7	95[3]	117
Iran	68.6	71.4	1,200	41.6	94	131
Other Southwest Asia	67.6	71.9	690	31.6	82[3]	119
Europe	**71.0**	**79.1**	**300**	**7.2**	**98[3]**	**130**
European Union (EU)	75.5	81.8	290	4.8	100[3]	137
France	76.7	83.8	330	3.6	100	142
Germany	75.8	82.0	290	4.1	100	131
Italy	77.6	83.2	180	5.9	100[3]	151
Spain	76.7	83.2	240	4.4	100	138
United Kingdom	75.9	81.0	720	5.1	100	137
Other EU	73.6	80.3	320	5.2	100[3]	133
Non-EU[7]	78.5	83.5	480	3.8	100[3]	131
Eastern Europe	62.3	73.8	290	11.7	95[3]	119
Russia	59.9	73.3	240	11.5	97	117
Ukraine	62.2	74.0	330	10.0	96	120
Other Eastern Europe	67.3	74.7	370	13.4	84[3]	121
Australia	**78.5**	**83.3**	**400**	**4.7**	**100**	**116**
Oceania	**74.5**	**79.4**	**480**	**14.7**	**50[8]**	**117**
Pacific Ocean Islands	68.3	73.3	770	30.1	67[3]	118

[1]Latest data available for individual countries. [2]The Food and Agriculture Organization of the United Nations (FAO) calculates this percentage by dividing the caloric equivalent to the known average daily supply of foodstuffs for human consumption in a given country by its population, thus arriving at a minimum daily per capita caloric intake. The higher the percentage, the more calories consumed. [3]Data for 2000. [4]Includes Canada, the US, Greenland, Bermuda, and St. Pierre and Miquelon. [5]Does not include Japan. [6]Includes Iran. [7]Western Europe only; includes Andorra, Faroe Islands, Gibraltar, Guernsey, Iceland, Isle of Man, Jersey, Liechtenstein, Monaco, Norway, San Marino, and Switzerland. [8]Does not include New Zealand.

Causes of Death, Worldwide, by Sex

Global estimates for 2002 as published in the World Health Organization World Health Report 2003. *Data are percentages of total deaths in each category. Ranking is based on categories defined by the Inter*national Classification of Diseases, Tenth Revision. *All other causes of death (mostly residual) make up approximately 3.7 percent of all deaths.*

	LEADING CAUSES OF DEATH	ALL CATEGORIES (%)	MALES (%)	FEMALES (%)
1	Major cardiovascular diseases	29.2	27.0	31.7
	Ischemic heart diseases	*12.6*	*12.6*	*12.5*
	Cerebrovascular diseases	*9.6*	*8.5*	*10.9*
	Hypertensive heart disease	*1.6*	*1.4*	*1.8*
2	Infectious and parasitic diseases	19.5	19.9	19.0
	HIV/AIDS	*4.9*	*5.1*	*4.8*
	Diarrheal diseases	*3.1*	*3.1*	*3.1*
	Tuberculosis	*2.8*	*3.5*	*2.0*
	Childhood diseases	*2.4*	*2.3*	*2.5*
	Malaria	*2.1*	*2.0*	*2.4*
3	Malignant neoplasms	12.5	13.2	11.6
	Trachea, bronchus, and lung	*2.2*	*3.0*	*1.3*
	Stomach	*1.5*	*1.7*	*1.2*
	Colon, rectum, and anus	*1.1*	*1.1*	*1.1*
	Liver	*1.1*	*1.4*	*0.7*
4	Respiratory infections	6.7	6.4	7.1
5	Respiratory diseases	6.5	6.4	6.6
	Chronic obstructive pulmonary disease	*4.8*	*4.7*	*4.9*

Causes of Death, Worldwide, by Sex (continued)

	LEADING CAUSES OF DEATH	ALL CATEGORIES (%)	MALES (%)	FEMALES (%)
6	Accidents (unintentional injuries)	6.2	7.7	4.6
	Road traffic injuries	*2.1*	*2.9*	*1.2*
	Falls	*0.7*	*0.8*	*0.6*
7	Perinatal conditions	4.3	4.6	4.0
8	Digestive diseases	3.4	3.6	3.2
	Chronic liver disease and cirrhosis of the liver	*1.4*	*1.7*	*1.0*
9	Neuropsychiatric disorders	1.9	1.9	2.0
	Alzheimer and other dementias	*0.7*	*0.5*	*0.9*
10	Diabetes mellitus	1.7	1.5	2.0
11	Nephritis, nephrotic syndrome, and nephrosis	1.2	1.2	1.2
12	Intentional injuries	2.9	3.9	1.7
	Intentional self-harm (suicide)	*1.5*	*1.8*	*1.2*
	Violence (assault)	*1.0*	*1.5*	*0.4*

Causes of Death, Worldwide, by Region

Global estimates for 2002 as published in the World Health Organization (WHO) World Health Report 2004. *Regions are as defined by the WHO. Numbers are in thousands ('000).*

	LEADING CAUSES OF DEATH	ALL CATEGORIES (%)	ALL CATEGORIES	REGION: AFRICA	AMERICAS	EASTERN MEDITERRANEAN	EUROPE	SOUTHEAST ASIA	WESTERN PACIFIC
1	Ischemic heart disease	12.6	7,208	332	921	538	2,373	2,039	993
2	Cerebrovascular disease	9.7	5,509	359	452	227	1,447	1,059	1,957
3	Lower respiratory infections	6.8	3,884	1,104	223	348	280	1,453	471
4	HIV disease	4.9	2,777	2,095	103	44	36	436	61
5	Chronic obstructive pulmonary disease	4.8	2,748	117	241	95	261	656	1,375
6	Perinatal conditions	4.3	2,462	554	175	303	65	1,012	349
7	Diarrheal diseases	3.2	1,798	707	57	259	16	604	154
8	Tuberculosis	2.7	1,566	348	46	138	69	599	366
9	Malaria	2.2	1,272	1,136	1	59	0	65	11
10	Trachea, bronchus, and lung cancers	2.2	1,243	17	231	27	366	174	427
11	Road traffic accidents	2.1	1,192	195	135	133	127	296	304
12	Diabetes mellitus	1.7	988	80	253	55	142	263	192
13	Hypertensive heart disease	1.6	911	60	135	97	179	152	284
14	Self-inflicted injuries	1.5	873	34	63	34	163	246	331
15	Stomach cancer	1.5	850	34	74	21	157	63	500
16	Cirrhosis of the liver	1.4	786	54	105	67	171	204	185
17	Nephritis and nephrosis	1.2	677	99	102	65	76	169	165
18	Colon and rectum cancers	1.1	622	20	109	15	228	63	186
19	Liver cancer	1.1	618	45	37	15	66	61	394
20	Measles	1.1	611	311	0	70	6	196	28
21	Violence	1.0	559	134	146	26	73	113	66
22	Congenital anomalies	0.9	493	56	58	83	38	149	108
23	Breast cancer	0.8	477	35	89	27	150	93	82
24	Esophagus cancer	0.8	446	22	32	16	48	82	245
25	Inflammatory heart disease	0.7	404	42	67	37	101	76	81
26	Alzheimer/other dementias	0.7	397	7	118	11	105	88	66
27	Drowning	0.7	382	65	22	26	38	98	132
28	Poisoning	0.6	350	39	17	15	111	95	75
29	Lymphomas	0.6	334	33	68	20	75	96	42
30	Rheumatic heart disease	0.6	327	20	10	24	30	133	110
31	Mouth and oropharynx cancers	0.6	318	18	24	20	51	149	57
32	Pertussis	0.5	294	131	3	46	0	111	2
33	Prostate cancer	0.5	269	41	78	8	93	27	21
34	Leukemia	0.5	264	13	48	20	62	46	74
35	Peptic ulcer disease	0.5	264	15	20	12	39	99	79
36	Malnutrition	0.5	260	104	43	26	5	68	14
37	Asthma	0.4	240	26	18	16	43	97	42
38	Cervix uteri cancer	0.4	239	38	31	7	26	101	34
39	Pancreas cancer	0.4	231	8	52	5	88	19	58
40	Tetanus	0.4	214	84	0	36	0	82	11

Ten Leading Causes of Death in the US, by Age

Preliminary data for 2006. Numbers in thousands. Rates per 100,000 population. Numbers are based on weighted data rounded to the nearest individual, so category percentages and rates may not add to totals given.
Source: National Vital Statistics Report, <www.cdc.gov/nchs>.

CAUSE	NUMBER	RATE	%
1–4 YEARS			
1 Accidents	1,591	9.8	34.3%
Motor-vehicle accidents	586	3.6	12.6%
All other accidents	1,005	6.2	21.7%
2 Congenital malformations, deformations, and chromosomal abnormalities	501	3.1	10.8%
3 Malignant neoplasms	372	2.3	8.0%
4 Assault (homicide)	350	2.1	7.5%
5 Diseases of heart	160	1.0	3.5%
6 Influenza and pneumonia	114	0.7	2.5%
7 Septicemia	88	0.5	1.9%
8 Conditions of perinatal origin	67	0.4	1.4%
9 Nonmalignant/unknown neoplasms	63	0.4	1.4%
10 Cerebrovascular diseases	53	0.3	1.1%
All other causes	1,277	7.8	27.5%
All causes, 1–4 years	**4,636**	**28.5**	**100.0%**
5–14 YEARS			
1 Accidents	2,228	5.5	36.3%
Motor-vehicle accidents	1,323	3.3	21.6%
All other accidents	905	2.2	14.7%
2 Malignant neoplasms	916	2.3	14.9%
3 Assault (homicide)	387	1.0	6.3%
4 Congenital malformations, deformations, and chromosomal abnormalities	330	0.8	5.4%
5 Diseases of heart	242	0.6	3.9%
6 Intentional self-harm (suicide)	213	0.5	3.5%
7 Chronic lower respiratory diseases	113	0.3	1.8%
8 Cerebrovascular diseases	93	0.2	1.5%
9 Septicemia	78	0.2	1.3%
10 Nonmalignant/unknown neoplasms	76	0.2	1.2%
All other causes	1,460	3.6	23.8%
All causes, 5–14 years	**6,136**	**15.2**	**100.0%**
15–24 YEARS			
1 Accidents	15,859	37.4	45.8%
Motor-vehicle accidents	10,845	25.6	31.3%
All other accidents	5,014	11.8	14.5%
2 Assault (homicide)	5,596	13.2	16.2%
3 Intentional self-harm (suicide)	4,097	9.7	11.8%
4 Malignant neoplasms	1,643	3.9	4.7%
5 Diseases of heart	1,021	2.4	2.9%
6 Congenital malformations, deformations, and chromosomal abnormalities	456	1.1	1.3%
7 Cerebrovascular diseases	206	0.5	0.6%
8 HIV disease	198	0.5	0.6%
9 Influenza and pneumonia	180	0.4	0.5%
10 Pregnancy and childbirth	172	0.4	0.5%
All other causes	5,204	12.3	15.0%
All causes, 15–24 years	**34,632**	**81.6**	**100.0%**
25–44 YEARS			
1 Accidents	30,949	36.8	24.7%
Motor-vehicle accidents	13,779	16.4	11.0%
All other accidents	17,170	20.4	13.7%
2 Malignant neoplasms	17,604	20.9	14.1%
3 Diseases of heart	14,873	17.7	11.9%
4 Intentional self-harm (suicide)	11,240	13.4	9.0%
5 Assault (homicide)	7,525	8.9	6.0%
6 HIV disease	5,150	6.1	4.1%
7 Chronic liver disease and cirrhosis	2,805	3.3	2.2%
8 Diabetes mellitus	2,705	3.2	2.2%
9 Cerebrovascular diseases	2,703	3.2	2.2%
10 Septicemia	1,131	1.3	0.9%
All other causes	28,488	33.9	22.8%
All causes, 25–44 years	**125,173**	**148.9**	**100.0%**
45–64 YEARS			
1 Malignant neoplasms	151,654	202.6	32.7%
2 Diseases of heart	101,588	135.7	21.9%
3 Accidents	29,505	39.4	6.4%
Motor-vehicle accidents	10,939	14.6	2.4%
All other accidents	18,566	24.8	4.0%
4 Diabetes mellitus	17,012	22.7	3.7%
5 Cerebrovascular diseases	16,779	22.4	3.6%
6 Chronic lower respiratory diseases	16,181	21.6	3.5%
7 Chronic liver disease and cirrhosis	14,725	19.7	3.2%
8 Intentional self-harm (suicide)	11,492	15.4	2.5%
9 Nephritis, nephrotic syndrome, and nephrosis	6,495	8.7	1.4%
10 Septicemia	6,184	8.3	1.3%
All other causes	92,848	124.0	20.0%
All causes, 45–64 years	**464,463**	**620.4**	**100.0%**
65 YEARS AND OVER			
1 Diseases of heart	510,934	1,371.3	29.0%
2 Malignant neoplasms	387,828	1,040.9	22.0%
3 Cerebrovascular diseases	117,284	314.8	6.7%
4 Chronic lower respiratory diseases	107,058	287.3	6.1%
5 Alzheimer disease	72,135	193.6	4.1%
6 Diabetes mellitus	52,599	141.2	3.0%
7 Influenza and pneumonia	49,459	132.7	2.8%
8 Nephritis, nephrotic syndrome, and nephrosis	36,960	99.2	2.1%
9 Accidents	36,436	97.8	2.1%
Motor-vehicle accidents	6,953	18.7	0.4%
All other accidents	29,483	79.1	1.7%
10 Septicemia	26,125	70.1	1.5%
All other causes	365,186	980.1	20.7%
All causes, 65 years and over	**1,762,004**	**4,728.9**	**100.0%**

Twenty Leading Causes of Death in the US for All Ages

Data for 2006. Rates per 100,000 population. Source: National Vital Statistics Report, <*www.cdc.gov/nchs*>.

	CAUSE	NUMBER	RATE	TOTAL %	% MALE (RANK)[1]	% FEMALE (RANK)[1]
1	Diseases of heart	629,121	210.2	25.9	28.0 (1)	28.0 (1)
	Ischemic heart diseases	424,892	141.9	17.5	20.5	18.8
	Heart failure	60,315	20.1	2.5	1.9	2.8
2	Malignant neoplasms	560,102	187.1	23.1	24.0 (2)	21.6 (2)
	Neoplasms of the trachea, bronchus, and lung	158,525	52.9	6.5	7.5	5.5
	Neoplasms of the colon, rectum, and anus	53,465	17.9	2.2	2.3	2.2
	Neoplasms of the breast	41,223	13.8	1.7	0.03	3.3
3	Cerebrovascular diseases	137,265	45.8	5.7	5.1 (4)	7.7 (3)
4	Chronic lower respiratory diseases	124,614	41.6	5.1	5.1 (5)	5.3 (4)
	Emphysema	12,570	4.2	0.5	0.6	0.6
5	Accidents	117,748	39.3	4.9	5.9 (3)	3.1 (7)
	Motor-vehicle accidents	44,572	14.9	1.8	2.6	1.1
	Accidental poisoning and exposure to noxious substances	24,702	8.3	1.0	1.1	0.5
	Falls	20,533	6.9	0.8	0.7	0.7
6	Diabetes mellitus	72,507	24.2	3.0	2.9 (6)	3.1 (6)
7	Alzheimer disease	72,914	24.4	3.0	1.5 (10)	3.6 (5)
8	Pneumonia	55,387	18.5	2.3	2.3 (7)	2.8 (8)
9	Nephritis, nephrotic syndrome, and nephrosis	44,791	15.0	1.8	1.7 (9)	1.8 (9)
10	Septicemia	34,031	11.4	1.4	1.2 (12)	1.5 (10)
11	Intentional self-harm (suicide)	32,185	10.7	1.3	2.1 (8)	0.5 (17)
12	Chronic liver disease and cirrhosis	27,299	9.1	1.1	1.5 (11)	0.8 (12)
13	Essential (primary) hypertension and hypertensive renal disease	23,985	8.0	1.0	0.7 (18)	1.1 (11)
14	Parkinson disease	19,660	6.6	0.8	0.8 (14)	0.6 (15)
15	Assault (homicide)	18,029	6.0	0.7	1.2 (13)	0.3 (21)
16	Pneumonitis due to solids and liquids	16,961	5.7	0.7	0.7 (17)	0.7 (13)
17	Conditions of perinatal origin	14,384	4.8	0.6	0.7 (19)	0.5 (18)
18	Benign and in situ neoplasms	14,101	4.7	0.6	0.6 (20)	0.6 (16)
19	Aortic aneurysm and dissection	13,178	4.4	0.5	0.7 (16)	0.5 (19)
20	HIV disease	12,045	4.0	0.5	0.8 (15)	0.3 (22)

[1]*Percentages and rankings are for 2003.*

HIV/AIDS

Acquired Immunodeficiency Syndrome, or AIDS, is a fatal transmissable disorder of the immune system that is caused by the human immunodeficiency virus (HIV). HIV was first isolated in 1983. In most cases, HIV slowly attacks and destroys the **immune system**, leaving the infected individual vulnerable to malignancies and infections that eventually cause death. AIDS is the last stage of HIV infection, during which time these diseases arise. An average interval of 10 years exists between infection with HIV and development of the conditions typical of AIDS. **Pneumonia** and **Kaposi's sarcoma** are two of the most common diseases seen in AIDS patients.

HIV is contracted through semen, vaginal fluid, breast milk, blood, or other body fluids containing blood. Health care workers may come into contact with other body fluids that may transmit the HIV virus, including amniotic and synovial fluids. Although it is a transmissable virus, it is not contagious and it cannot be spread through coughing, sneezing, or casual physical contact. Other **STDs**, such as genital herpes, may increase the risk of contracting HIV through sexual contact.

The main **cellular target** of HIV is a special class of white blood cells critical to the immune system known as T4 helper cells. Once HIV has entered a helper T cell, it can cause the cell to function poorly or it can destroy the cell. A hallmark of the onset of AIDS is a drastic reduction in the number of helper T cells in the body. Two predominant strains of the virus, designated HIV-1 and HIV-2, are known. Worldwide the most common strain is HIV-1, with HIV-2 more common primarily in western Africa; the two strains act in a similar manner, but the latter causes a form of AIDS that progresses much more slowly.

Diagnosis is made on the basis of blood tests approved by the Centers for Disease Control and Prevention that may be administered by a doctor or at a local health department. Alternately, a home collection kit may be purchased at many pharmacies. No vaccine or cure has yet been developed that can prevent HIV infection. Several **drugs** are now used to slow the development of AIDS, including azidothymidine (AZT). **Protease inhibitors**, such as ritonavir and indinavir, have been shown to block the development of AIDS, at least temporarily. Protease inhibitors are most effective when used in conjunction with two different reverse transcriptase inhibitors—the so-called "triple-drug therapy."

HIV/AIDS is a major problem in developing countries, particularly sub-Saharan Africa. At the end of 2007, as many as 36.1 million people were estimated to be living with HIV. In 2007 alone, as many as 4.1 million contracted the disease and up to 2.4 million died of it.

For information on **prevention**, see Safer Sex Defined, below.

For confidential information on HIV/AIDS, call 1-800-342-AIDS.

Internet resources: <www.cdc.gov/hiv>.

Sexually Transmitted Diseases (STDs)

A sexually transmitted disease (STD) is usually passed from person to person by direct sexual contact. It may also be transmitted from a mother to her child before or at birth or, less frequently, may be passed from person to person in nonsexual contact. STDs usually initially affect the genitals, the reproductive tract, the urinary tract, the oral cavity, the anus, or the rectum but may mature in the body to attack various organs and systems. Following are some of the major STDs:

Syphilis was first widely reported by European writers in the 16th century, and a virtual epidemic swept Europe around the year 1500. Syphilis is spread through direct contact with a syphilis sore (chancre); development of this sore is the first stage of the disease. The second stage manifests itself as a rash on the palms and the bottoms of the feet. In the last stage, symptoms disappear, but the disease remains in the body and may damage internal organs and lead to paralysis, blindness, dementia, and even death. For individuals infected less than a year, a single dose of penicillin will cure the disease. Larger doses are needed for those who have had it for a longer period of time.

Gonorrhea, a form of urethritis (an infection and inflammation of the urethra), is one of the most common STDs. Although spread through sexual contact, the gonorrhea infection can also be spread to other parts of the body after touching the infected area. Men manifest symptoms, which include discharge and a burning sensation when urinating, more often than women. If gonorrhea is left untreated, women may develop pelvic inflammatory disease (PID) and men may become infertile. The disease can also spread to the blood or joints and is potentially life threatening.

Chlamydia, another form of urethritis, can be transmitted during vaginal, anal, or oral sex. Since there are frequently no symptoms, most infected individuals do not know they have the disease until complications develop. Untreated chlamydia can cause pain during urination or sex in men and PID in women. Antibiotics can successfully cure the disease.

Genital herpes, a disease that became especially widespread in the 1960s and 1970s, often presents minimal symptoms upon infection. The most common sign, however, is blistering in the genital area; outbreaks can occur over many years but generally decrease in severity and number. Genital herpes is caused by the herpes simplex viruses type 1 (HSV-1) and type 2 (HSV-2). The former causes infections on and around the mouth but may be spread through the saliva to the genitals; the latter is transmitted during sexual contact with someone who has a genital infection. The HSV-2 infection can cause problems for people with suppressed immune systems and for infants who contract the disease upon delivery. Herpes can also leave individuals more susceptible to HIV infection and make those carrying the disease more infectious. A variety of treatments, including antiviral medications, have been used to help manage genital herpes, but currently there is no cure for the disease.

Almost all STDs have reasonably effective drug cures. For information on STD **prevention,** see below, "Safer Sex Defined." For information on **HIV disease,** see individual entry.

Internet resources:
<www.cdc.gov/nchstp/od/nchstp.html>.

Safer Sex Defined

Defining risky sexual behavior. Any activity involving the exchange of body fluids—vaginal secretions, semen, or blood—could result in the transmission of AIDS and other STDs. Unprotected vaginal and anal intercourse present the highest risks for contraction of STDs. Women are at greater risk than men of developing an infection as a result of heterosexual intercourse, though many STDs present fewer symptoms in women than in men. Men and women of all sexual orientations should practice safer sex to reduce their risk of contracting an STD.

HIV testing. It can take years to develop symptoms of HIV disease, so it is important to be tested for HIV after any behavior that might have resulted in infection. The CDC recommends undergoing two separate HIV-antibody tests, six months apart. If the second test is negative, there is a reasonable certainty that HIV is not present.

STD testing. It is important to get checked for other STDs at least once a year. Do not assume that STD testing is part of a routine checkup.

Abstinence. Refraining from any sexual activity that would allow the exchange of body fluids is by far the most effective method of birth control and disease prevention.

Monogamous intercourse. Sexual intercourse with only one partner can be as effective as abstinence in preventing disease transmission, if both partners have been properly tested for AIDS and other STDs. Most health professionals, however, recommend continuing to practice safer sex, even in monogamous relationships, as there is no way to be sure a partner is being faithful.

Condoms. Using a latex or female condom correctly and consistently significantly reduces the chance of unplanned pregnancy. Condoms also reduce the risk of transmission of HIV, vaginitis, chlamydia, honeymoon cystitis, syphilis, pelvic inflammatory disease, chancroid, and gonorrhea. Condoms may be less effective in preventing genital warts, herpes, and hepatitis B. Male and female condoms should not be worn simultaneously.

Birth control. There are many methods of birth control that can help prevent unwanted pregnancy, including birth-control pills, Norplant, Depo-Provera, condoms, diaphragms, and cervical caps. However, of these, only condoms protect against STDs. Emergency contraception, including the "morning-after" pill, should be used only when necessary and not relied upon as a regular method of birth control. Withdrawal and family planning are not recommended forms of birth control.

Internet resources: <www.sexualhealth.com>.

Contraceptive Use by US Women

Percent distribution by age. Source: National Survey of Family Growth, *2002 (CDC/National Center for Health Statistics), the most recent survey published.*

	AGE	AGE					
	15–44	15–19	20–24	25–29	30–34	35–39	40–44
Using contraception							
Pill	19.0	16.7	31.8	25.6	21.8	13.2	7.6
Condom	11.1	8.5	14.0	14.0	11.8	11.1	8.0
Female sterilization	16.7	—	2.2	10.3	19.0	29.2	34.7
Male sterilization	5.7	—	0.5	2.8	6.4	10.0	12.7
Implant or patch[1]	0.8	0.4	0.9	1.7	0.9	0.5	0.2
Injectable[2]	3.3	4.4	6.1	4.4	2.9	1.5	1.1
Intrauterine device (IUD)	1.3	0.1	1.1	2.5	2.2	1.0	0.8
Diaphragm	0.2	—	0.1	0.3	0.1	—	0.4
Periodic abstinence (rhythm)	0.7	—	0.8	0.3	0.9	1.1	1.2
Natural family planning	0.2	—	—	0.4	0.2	0.3	0.4
Withdrawal	2.5	0.8	3.1	5.3	2.6	2.4	1.0
Other[3]	0.6	0.6	0.2	0.4	0.4	0.5	1.1
Total using contraception[4]	**61.9**	**31.5**	**60.7**	**68.0**	**69.2**	**70.8**	**69.1**
Not using contraception							
Surgically sterile female or male	1.5	—	...	0.4	0.9	2.1	4.9
Nonsurgically sterile female or male	1.6	0.7	0.7	0.9	1.4	1.2	4.4
Pregnant or postpartum	5.3	3.5	9.5	8.4	6.9	3.8	0.8
Seeking pregnancy	4.2	1.2	2.8	5.5	7.0	5.1	3.3
Other							
Never had intercourse	10.9	49.5	11.4	2.7	1.5	1.6	1.1
No intercourse in last 3 months	7.2	6.7	6.6	6.2	6.1	7.5	9.7
Had intercourse in last 3 months	7.4	6.9	8.4	8.0	7.0	7.7	6.7
Total not using contraception[4]	**38.1**	**68.5**	**39.3**	**32.0**	**30.8**	**29.2**	**30.9**

— None. ... Less than 0.05.

[1]Includes Lunelle™. [2]Depo-Provera™. [3]Includes female condom, cervical cap, Today™ sponge, and other methods. [4]Includes other categories not listed. Detail may not add to total given because of rounding.

US Health Expenditures, by Kind

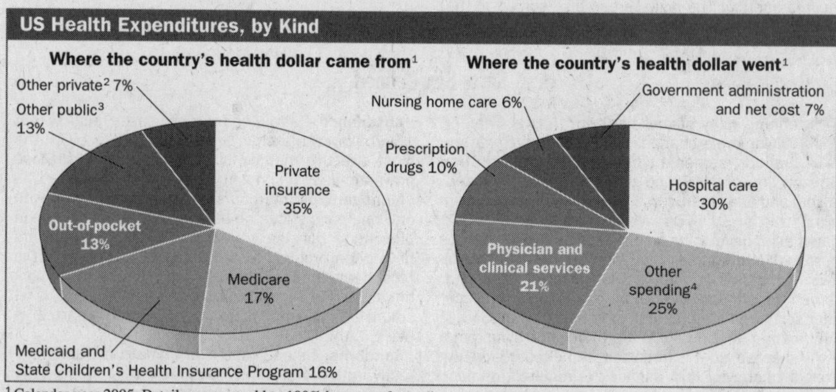

[1] Calendar year 2005. Details may not add to 100% because of rounding.
[2] Other private includes industrial in-plant, privately funded construction, and non-patient revenues, including philanthropy.
[3] Other public includes programs such as workers' compensation, public health activity, US Department of Defense, US Department of Veterans Affairs, Indian Health Service, state and local hospital subsidies, and school health.
[4] Other spending includes dentist and other professional services, home health care, durable medical equipment, other nondurable medical products, government public health activities, and research and construction.
Source: Centers for Medicare and Medicaid Services, Office of the Actuary, National Health Statistics Group.

Diet and Exercise

The Food and Drug Administration (FDA)

The FDA is a division of the US Department of Health and Human Services. ***FDA Web site:*** *<www.fda.gov>.*

Mission: To promote and protect the public health by helping safe and effective products reach the market in a timely way and monitoring products for continued safety after they are in use. **History:** The FDA celebrated its 100th anniversary in 2006, having been created by the passing of the Food and Drugs Act, or Wiley Act, in 1906. The Food, Drug, and Cosmetic Act of 1938 then brought cosmetics and medical devices under the authority of the FDA. The Food and Drug Administration Act of 1988 officially established the body as an agency of the Department of Health and Human Services, with a commissioner of food and drugs appointed by the president with the consent of the Senate. **Location:** Rockville MD (with a transfer to Silver Spring MD in progress and scheduled to be completed in 2012). **Commissioner of Food and Drugs:** Andrew C. von Eschenbach. **Budget:** FY 2009 (requested) US$2.4 billion. **Functions:** The FDA is the agency of the US federal government authorized by Congress to inspect, test, approve, and set safety standards for foods and food additives, drugs, chemicals, cosmetics, and household and medical devices. Generally, the FDA is empowered to prevent untested products from being sold and to take legal action to halt sale of undoubtedly harmful products or of products which involve a health or safety risk. Through court procedure, the FDA can seize products and prosecute the persons or firms responsible for legal violation. FDA authority is limited to interstate commerce. The agency cannot control prices nor directly regulate advertising except of prescription drugs and medical devices.

Vitamins, with Daily Recommendations

Vitamins are organic substances that are usually divided into two types: water-soluble and fat-soluble. Small quantities are necessary for normal health and growth in higher forms of animal life, as they work to regulate reactions that occur in metabolism (in contrast to macronutrients such as fats, carbohydrates, and proteins, which are the compounds utilized in the reactions regulated by vitamins). Absence of a vitamin blocks one or more specific metabolic reactions in a cell; thus, vitamin deficiency may result in specific diseases. As they generally cannot be synthesized by humans, vitamins must be obtained from the diet or from a synthetic source.

The name of each vitamin is followed by its alternative name and usual pharmaceutical preparation, respectively. Amounts shown indicate recommended daily consumption.

Abbreviations—mg: milligram; mcg: microgram; RAE: retinol activity equivalent; IU: international unit; N/A: not applicable.

Water-soluble vitamins

Thiamin (vitamin B_1; thiamine hydrochloride)

Purpose: energy metabolism and initiation of nerve impulses. **Dietary sources:** pork, nuts, peas. **Men over 13:** 1.2 mg; **women over 18:** 1.1 mg; **pregnant women:** 1.4 mg; **lactating women:** 1.4 mg.

Riboflavin (vitamin B_2; riboflavin)

Purpose: release of energy from carbohydrates, fats, and proteins; maintaining integrity of red blood cells. **Dietary sources:** milk, eggs, kidney, liver, peas, soybeans, leafy vegetables. **Men over 13:** 1.3 mg; **women over 18:** 1.1 mg; **pregnant women:** 1.4 mg; **lactating women:** 1.6 mg.

Niacin (nicotinic acid; nicotinamide or niacinamide)

Purpose: release of energy from carbohydrates and fats; red-blood-cell formation; metabolism of proteins. **Dietary sources:** cereal grains, nuts, green vegetables, liver, kidney. **Men over 13:** 16.0 mg; **women over 18:** 14.0 mg; **pregnant women:** 18.0 mg; **lactating women:** 17.0 mg.

Pantothenic acid (vitamin B_5; calcium pantothenate)

Purpose: metabolism of carbohydrates; synthesis and degradation of fats; synthesis of sterols and other compounds. **Dietary sources:** liver, kidney, eggs, avocados, bananas. **All adults:** 4.0–7.0 mg.

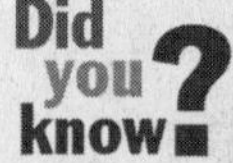

The celebrated "four-color map problem," framed in 1850 and publicized in 1878, bears little relation to cartography. The question is mathematical: how many colors are needed to color any map so that no two regions sharing a common border will have the same color? The proof, in 1977, that four colors are always sufficient occupied 170 pages of text and diagrams derived from more than 1,000 hours of calculations on a large computer.

Vitamins, with Daily Recommendations (continued)

Water-soluble vitamins (continued)

Vitamin B_6 (pyroxidine; pyroxidine hydrochloride)

Purpose: amino acid, carbohydrate, and fat metabolism. **Dietary sources:** bananas, cereal grains, fish, nuts, spinach. **Men 14–50:** 1.3 mg; **men over 50:** 1.7 mg; **women 19–50:** 1.3 mg; **women over 50:** 1.5 mg; **pregnant women:** 1.9 mg; **lactating women:** 2.0 mg.

Biotin (N/A; biotin)

Purpose: carbohydrate and fat metabolism. **Dietary sources:** beef liver, yeast, oatmeal. **Adults:** 30 mcg; **pregnant women:** 30 mcg; **lactating women:** 35 mcg.

Folate (folacin or vitamin B_9; folacin or folic acid)

Purpose: cellular metabolism, including synthesis of DNA components; normal red-blood-cell formation. **Dietary sources:** chicken, liver, green leafy vegetables, wheat bran and germ, citrus fruits, cereals, beans, asparagus. **Adults:** 400 mcg; **pregnant women:** 600 mcg; **lactating women:** 500 mcg.

Vitamin B_{12} (cobalamin; cyanocobalamin or hydroxocobalamin)

Purpose: proper functioning of many enzymes involved in carbohydrate, fat, and protein metabolism; synthesis of the insulating sheath around nerve cells; cell reproduction and normal growth; red-blood-cell formation. **Dietary sources:** eggs, meat, milk, nutritional yeast, fortified cereals. **Adults:** 2.4 mcg; **pregnant women:** 2.6 mcg; **lactating women:** 2.8 mcg.

Vitamin C (ascorbic acid; ascorbic acid)

Purpose: prevention of oxidative damage to DNA, membrane lipids, and proteins; synthesis of collagen, hormones, transmitters of the nervous sytem, lipids, and proteins; proper immune function. **Dietary sources:** citrus fruits, green peppers, broccoli, cantaloupe, green leafy vegetables. **Men over 18:** 90 mg; **women over 18:** 75 mg; **pregnant women:** 80–85 mg; **lactating women:** 115–120 mg.

Fat-soluble vitamins

Vitamin A (retinol; retinol)

Purpose: functioning of the retina; growth and maturation of epithelial cells; growth of bone; reproduction and embryonic development. **Dietary sources:** fish and fish-liver oils, liver, butter, orange vegetables and fruits, dark green leafy vegetables; tomatoes. **Men over 13:** 900 RAE; **women over 13:** 700 RAE; **pregnant women:** 750–770 RAE; **lactating women:** 1,200–1,300 RAE.

Vitamin D (vitamins D_2 and D_3; [ergo] calciferol)

Purpose: promotes formation of bone by increasing the blood levels of calcium and phosphorus. **Dietary sources:** fish-liver oils, eggs, milk enriched with Vitamin D. **All adults:** 200–600 IU.

Vitamin E (N/A; tocopherol)

Purpose: protection of cell membranes and prevention of damage to membrane-associated enzymes. **Dietary sources:** nuts, vegetable oils, margarine, cereal grains. **Adults:** 15 mg; **pregnant women:** 15 mg; **lactating women:** 19 mg.

Vitamin K (N/A; vitamin K_1)

Purpose: formation of several blood clotting factors. **Dietary sources:** green leafy vegetables, vegetable oils. **Men over 18:** 120 mcg; **women over 18:** 90 mcg; **pregnant women:** 75–90 mcg; **lactating women:** 75–90 mcg.

Fat Intake in US Diet

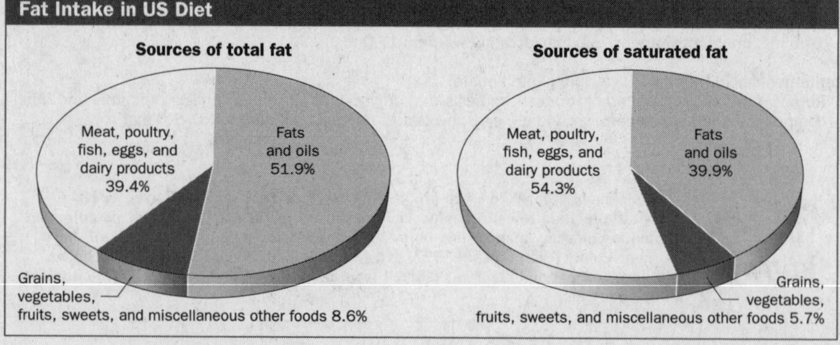

Food Guide Pyramid

In 2005 the USDA released an update of its food-pyramid guide to a healthy diet. It is designed to help individuals get proper nutrients while at the same time consuming the appropriate amount of calories necessary to maintain healthy weight. The 2005 pyramid also provides information about exercise and weight loss. Diets should be low in added sugars, salt, saturated fat and cholesterol and moderate in overall fat.

Find your balance between food and physical activity:

- Be sure to stay within your daily calorie needs.
- Be physically active for at least 30 minutes most days of the week.
- About 60 minutes a day of physical activity may be needed to prevent weight gain.
- For sustaining weight loss, at least 60 to 90 minutes a day of physical activity may be required.
- Children and teenagers should be physically active for 60 minutes every day or most days.

Recommended daily intake
These amounts are appropriate for individuals who get less than 30 minutes per day of moderate physical activity, beyond normal daily activities. Those who are more physically active may be able to consume more because they may have greater calorie needs.

	Grains	Vegetables	Fruits	Fats and Oils—limit your intake	Milk	Meat and Beans
Children 2–3 years old	3 ounce equivalents[1]	1 cup[2]	1 cup[3]		2 cups[4]	2 ounce equivalents[5]
Children 4–8 years old	4–5 ounce equivalents[1]	1.5 cups[2]	1–1.5 cups[3]		2 cups[4]	3–4 ounce equivalents[5]
Girls 9–13 years old	5 ounce equivalents[1]	2 cups[2]	1.5 cups[3]		3 cups[4]	5 ounce equivalents[5]
Boys 9–13 years old	6 ounce equivalents[1]	2.5 cups[2]	1.5 cups[3]		3 cups[4]	5 ounce equivalents[5]
Girls 14–18 years old	6 ounce equivalents[1]	2.5 cups[2]	1.5 cups[3]		3 cups[4]	5 ounce equivalents[5]
Boys 14–18 years old	7 ounce equivalents[1]	3 cups[2]	2 cups[3]		3 cups[4]	6 ounce equivalents[5]
Women 19–30 years old	6 ounce equivalents[1]	2.5 cups[2]	2 cups[3]		3 cups[4]	5.5 ounce equivalents[5]
Men 19–30 years old	8 ounce equivalents[1]	3 cups[2]	2 cups[3]		3 cups[4]	6.5 ounce equivalents[5]
Women 31–50 years old	6 ounce equivalents[1]	2.5 cups[2]	1.5 cups[3]		3 cups[4]	5 ounce equivalents[5]
Men 31–50 years old	7 ounce equivalents[1]	3 cups[2]	2 cups[3]		3 cups[4]	6 ounce equivalents[5]
Women 51+ years old	5 ounce equivalents[1]	2 cups[2]	1.5 cups[3]		3 cups[4]	5 ounce equivalents[5]
Men 51+ years old	6 ounce equivalents[1]	2.5 cups[2]	2 cups[3]		3 cups[4]	5.5 ounce equivalents[5]

[1] 1 slice of bread, 1 cup of ready-to-eat cereal, or $\frac{1}{2}$ cup of cooked rice, cooked pasta, or cooked cereal can be considered as 1 ounce equivalent from the grains group.
[2] 1 cup of raw or cooked vegetables or vegetable juice or 2 cups of raw leafy greens can be considered as 1 cup from the vegetable group.
[3] 1 cup of fruit or 100% fruit juice or $\frac{1}{2}$ cup of dried fruit can be considered as 1 cup from the fruit group.
[4] 1 cup of milk or yogurt, $1\frac{1}{2}$ ounces of natural cheese, or 2 ounces of processed cheese can be considered as 1 cup from the milk group.
[5] 1 ounce of meat, poultry, or fish, $\frac{1}{4}$ cup cooked dry beans, 1 egg, 1 tablespoon of peanut butter, or $\frac{1}{2}$ ounce of nuts or seeds can be considered as 1 ounce equivalent from the meat and beans group.

Source: USDA.

Individuals Meeting Dietary Guidelines

1977–78 and 1994–96.

Percentages of US population that meet or exceed the minimum dietary guidelines given in *Nutrition and Your Health: Dietary Guidelines for Americans*, 5th ed. (2000), a joint publication of the Departments of Health and Human Services and Agriculture. (The 2005 edition does not include this breakout.) To view the complete publication or to order a print copy, visit <www.health.gov/dietaryguidelines>.

AGE AND GENDER	CALORIES	TOTAL FAT	SATURATED FAT	CHOLESTEROL	SODIUM	FIBER	CALCIUM	IRON
1977–78								
Children (2–17)	33	14	N/A	N/A	N/A	N/A	37	39
Adults (18 and over)	23	13	N/A	N/A	N/A	N/A	15	43
Males 60 and over	29	12	N/A	N/A	N/A	N/A	11	66
Females 60 and over	18	17	N/A	N/A	N/A	N/A	4	40
All individuals 2 and over	**26**	**13**	**N/A**	**N/A**	**N/A**	**N/A**	**22**	**42**
1994–96								
Children (2–17)	38	37	31	77	39	39	37	59
Adults (18 and over)	27	37	43	69	34	20	21	60
Males 60 and over	28	36	43	65	30	26	16	77
Females 60 and over	18	41	49	79	54	35	6	56
All individuals 2 and over	**30**	**37**	**40**	**71**	**35**	**25**	**25**	**59**

N/A indicates data not available.

Nutrient Composition of Selected Fruits and Vegetables

Values shown are approximations for 100 grams (3.57 oz.). Foods are raw unless otherwise noted. Source: USDA Nutrient Data Laboratory. kcal: kilocalorie; g: gram; mg: milligram; IU: international unit.

	ENERGY (KCAL)	WATER (G)	CARBOHYDRATE (G)	PROTEIN (G)	FAT (G)	VITAMIN A (IU)	VITAMIN C (MG)	THIAMINE (MG)	RIBOFLAVIN (MG)	NIACIN (MG)
Fruits										
Apple	59	83.93	15.25	0.19	0.36	53	5.7	0.017	0.014	0.077
Apricot	48	86.35	11.12	1.40	0.39	2,612	10.0	0.030	0.040	0.600
Avocado	161	74.27	7.39	1.98	15.32	61	7.9	0.108	0.122	1.921
Banana	92	74.26	23.43	1.03	0.48	81	9.1	0.045	0.100	0.540
Blackberries	52	85.64	12.76	0.72	0.39	165	21.0	0.030	0.040	0.400
Blueberries	56	84.61	14.13	0.67	0.38	100	13.0	0.048	0.050	0.359
Cantaloupe	35	89.78	8.36	0.88	0.28	3,224	42.2	0.036	0.021	0.574
Cherries (sweet)	72	80.76	16.55	1.20	0.96	214	7.0	0.050	0.060	0.400
Grapes	67	81.30	17.15	0.63	0.35	100	4.0	0.092	0.057	0.300
Grapefruit	32	90.89	8.08	0.63	0.10	124	34.4	0.036	0.020	0.250
Kiwi	61	83.05	14.88	0.99	0.44	175	98.0	0.020	0.050	0.500
Lemon	29	88.98	9.32	1.10	0.30	29	53.0	0.040	0.020	0.100
Lime	30	88.26	10.54	0.70	0.20	10	29.1	0.030	0.020	0.200
Mango	65	81.71	17.00	0.51	0.27	3,894	27.7	0.058	0.057	0.584
Nectarine	49	86.28	11.78	0.94	0.46	736	5.4	0.017	0.041	0.990
Orange	47	86.75	11.75	0.94	0.12	205	53.2	0.087	0.040	0.282
Peach	43	87.66	11.10	0.70	0.09	535	6.6	0.017	0.041	0.990
Pear	59	83.81	15.11	0.39	0.40	20	4.0	0.020	0.040	0.100
Pineapple	49	86.50	12.39	0.39	0.43	23	15.4	0.092	0.036	0.420
Plum	55	85.20	13.01	0.79	0.62	323	9.5	0.043	0.096	0.500
Raspberries	49	86.57	11.57	0.91	0.55	130	25.0	0.030	0.090	0.900
Strawberries	30	91.57	7.02	0.61	0.37	27	56.7	0.020	0.066	0.230
Tangerine	44	87.60	11.19	0.63	0.19	920	30.8	0.105	0.022	0.160
Watermelon	32	91.51	7.18	0.62	0.43	366	9.6	0.080	0.020	0.200
Vegetables										
Artichoke[1]	50	83.97	11.18	3.48	0.16	177	10.0	0.065	0.066	1.001
Asparagus[1]	24	92.20	4.23	2.59	0.31	539	10.8	0.123	0.126	1.082
Beans (snap, green)	31	90.27	7.14	1.82	0.12	668	16.3	0.084	0.105	0.752
Beet	43	87.58	9.56	1.61	0.17	38	4.9	0.031	0.040	0.334
Broccoli	28	90.69	5.24	2.98	0.35	1,542	93.2	0.065	0.119	0.638
Brussels sprout	43	86.00	8.96	3.38	0.30	883	85.0	0.139	0.090	0.745
Cabbage	25	92.15	5.43	1.44	0.27	133	32.2	0.050	0.040	0.300
Carrot	43	87.79	10.14	1.03	0.19	28,129	9.3	0.097	0.059	0.928
Cauliflower	25	91.91	5.20	1.98	0.21	19	46.4	0.057	0.063	0.526

Nutrient Composition of Selected Fruits and Vegetables (continued)

	ENERGY (KCAL)	WATER (G)	CARBO-HYDRATE (G)	PROTEIN (G)	FAT (G)	VITAMIN A (IU)	VITAMIN C (MG)	THIAMINE (MG)	RIBO-FLAVIN (MG)	NIACIN (MG)
Vegetables (continued)										
Celery	16	94.64	3.65	0.75	0.14	134	7.0	0.046	0.045	0.323
Collards[1]	26	91.86	4.90	2.11	0.36	3,129	18.2	0.040	0.106	0.575
Corn (sweet, yellow)[1]	108	69.57	25.11	3.32	1.28	217	6.2	0.215	0.072	1.614
Cucumber	13	96.01	2.76	0.69	0.13	215	5.3	0.024	0.022	0.221
Eggplant[1]	28	91.77	6.64	0.83	0.23	64	1.3	0.076	0.020	0.600
Lettuce (iceberg)	12	95.89	2.09	1.01	0.19	330	3.9	0.046	0.030	0.187
Mushroom[1]	27	91.08	5.14	2.17	0.47	0	4.0	0.073	0.300	4.460
Okra[1]	32	89.91	7.21	1.87	0.17	575	16.3	0.132	0.055	0.871
Onion[1]	44	87.86	10.15	1.36	0.19	0	5.2	0.042	0.023	0.165
Pepper (sweet, green)	27	92.19	6.43	0.89	0.19	632	89.3	0.066	0.030	0.509
Pepper (sweet, red)	27	92.19	6.43	0.89	0.19	5,700	190.0	0.066	0.030	0.509
Potato[2]	93	75.42	21.56	1.96	0.10	0	12.8	0.105	0.021	1.395
Spinach	22	91.58	3.50	2.86	0.35	6,715	28.1	0.078	0.189	0.724
Sweet potato[2]	103	72.85	24.27	1.72	0.11	21,822	24.6	0.073	0.127	0.604
Tomato (red)	21	93.76	4.64	0.85	0.33	623	19.1	0.059	0.048	0.628

[1]*Boiled.* [2]*Baked.*

Nutritional Value of Selected Foods

Values shown are approximations. Source: Home and Garden Bulletin No. 72, *USDA. kcal: kilocalorie; g: gram; mg: milligram; oz: ounce; fl oz: fluid ounce.*

FOOD	AMOUNT	GRAMS	ENERGY (KCAL)	CARBO-HYDRATE (G)	PROTEIN (G)	TOTAL FAT (G)	SATU-RATED FAT (G)	CALCIUM (MG)	IRON (MG)	SODIUM (MG)
Beverages										
Beer	12 fl oz	360	150	13	1	0	0	14	0.1	18
Cola, regular	12 fl oz	369	160	41	0	0	0	11	0.2	18
Cola, diet (w/aspartame and saccharine)	12 fl oz	355	0	0	0	0	0	14	0.2	32
Coffee, brewed	6 fl oz	180	0	0	0	0	0	4	0	2
Orange juice, canned	8 fl oz	249	105	25	1	0	0	20	1.1	5
Tea, instant, prepared, unsweetened	8 fl oz	241	0	1	0	0	0	1	0	1
Wine, table, red	3.5 fl oz	102	75	3	0	0	0	8	0.4	5
Dairy										
Butter, salted	4 oz	113	810	0	1	92	57.1	27	0.2	933
Cheese, American (pasteurized, processed)	1 oz	28.35	105	0	6	9	5.6	174	0.1	406
Cheese, cheddar	1 oz	28.35	115	0	7	9	6	204	0.2	176
Cheese, mozzarella (whole milk)	1 oz	28.35	80	1	6	6	3.7	147	0.1	106
Cheese, swiss	1 oz	28.35	105	1	8	8	5	272	0	74
Cottage cheese, small curd	8 oz	210	215	6	26	9	6	126	0.3	850
Cream cheese	1 oz	28.35	100	1	2	10	6.2	23	0.3	84
Cream, half and half	0.5 oz	15	20	1	0	2	1.1	16	0	6
Cream, sour	8 oz	230	495	10	7	48	30	268	0.1	123
Eggs, cooked, fried	1 egg	46	90	1	6	7	1.9	25	0.7	162
Eggs, cooked, hard-cooked	1 egg	50	75	1	6	5	1.6	25	0.6	62
Eggs, cooked, scrambled	1 egg	61	100	1	7	7	2.2	44	0.7	171
Ice cream, vanilla, 11% fat	8 oz	133	270	32	5	14	8.9	176	0.1	116
Milk, whole, 3.3% fat	8 oz	244	150	11	8	8	5.1	291	0.1	120
Milk, low fat, 2% fat	8 oz	244	120	12	8	5	2.9	297	0.1	122
Milk, skim	8 oz	245	85	12	8	0	0.3	302	0.1	126
Milk, chocolate	8 oz	250	210	26	8	8	5.3	280	0.6	149
Yogurt, plain, low fat	8 oz	227	145	16	12	4	2.3	415	0.2	159
Fats, oils										
Lard	0.5 oz	13	115	0	0	13	5.1	0	0	0
Margarine, hard, 80% fat	0.5 oz	14	100	0	0	11	2.2	4	0	132

Nutritional Value of Selected Foods (continued)

FOOD	AMOUNT	GRAMS	ENERGY (KCAL)	CARBO-HYDRATE (G)	PROTEIN (G)	TOTAL FAT (G)	SATU-RATED FAT (G)	CALCIUM (MG)	IRON (MG)	SODIUM (MG)
Fats, oils (continued)										
Olive oil	0.5 oz	14	125	0	0	14	1.9	0	0	0
Vegetable shortening	0.5 oz	13	115	0	0	13	3.3	0	0	0
Fish										
Crabmeat, canned	8 oz	135	135	1	23	3	0.5	61	1.1	1350
Fish sticks, frozen	1 piece	28	70	4	6	3	0.8	11	0.3	53
Ocean perch, breaded, fried	1 piece	85	185	7	16	11	2.6	31	1.2	138
Oysters, raw	8 oz	240	160	8	20	4	1.4	226	15.6	175
Salmon, baked, red	3 oz	85	140	0	21	5	1.2	26	0.5	55
Shrimp, fried	3 oz	85	200	11	16	10	2.5	61	2	384
Trout, broiled, w/butter and lemon juice	3 oz	85	175	0	21	9	4.1	26	1	122
Tuna, canned, white, in water	3 oz	85	135	0	30	1	0.3	17	0.6	468
Fruits, fruit products										
Apples, peeled, sliced	8 oz	110	65	16	0	0	0.1	4	0.1	0
Applesauce, canned, sweetened	8 oz	255	195	51	0	0	0.1	10	0.9	8
Apricots	3 apricots	106	50	12	1	0	0	15	0.6	1
Bananas	1 banana	114	105	27	1	1	0.2	7	0.4	1
Blackberries	8 oz	144	75	18	1	1	0.2	46	0.8	0
Blueberries	8 oz	145	80	20	1	1	0	9	0.2	9
Grapefruit, pink	½ grapefruit	120	40	10	1	0	0	14	0.1	0
Grapes, European, Thompson	10 grapes	50	35	9	0	0	0.1	6	0.1	1
Oranges	1 orange	131	60	15	1	0	0	52	0.1	0
Peaches	1 peach	87	35	10	1	0	0	4	0.1	0
Pears, Bartlett	1 pear	166	100	25	1	1	0	18	0.4	0
Pineapple, canned, heavy syrup	8 oz	255	200	52	1	0	0	36	1	3
Plums, 2⅛-in. diam.	1 plum	66	35	9	1	0	0	3	0.1	0
Prunes, dried, large	5 prunes	49	115	31	1	0	0	25	1.2	2
Raisins	8 oz	145	435	115	5	1	0.2	71	3	17
Strawberries	8 oz	149	45	10	1	1	0	21	0.6	1
Watermelon	1 piece	482	155	35	3	2	0.3	39	0.8	10
Grains										
Bagels, plain	1 bagel	68	200	38	7	2	0.3	29	1.8	245
Bread, rye, light	1 slice	25	65	12	2	1	0.2	20	0.7	175
Bread, wheat	1 slice	25	65	12	2	1	0.2	32	0.9	138
Bread, white	1 slice	25	65	12	2	1	0.3	32	0.7	129
Bread, whole wheat	1 slice	28	70	13	3	1	0.4	20	1	180
Cereal, Cheerios	1 oz	28.35	110	20	4	2	0.3	48	4.5	307
Cereal, Kellogg's Corn Flakes	1 oz	28.35	110	24	2	0	0	1	1.8	351
Cereal, Lucky Charms	1 oz	28.35	110	23	3	1	0.2	32	4.5	201
Cereal, Post Raisin Bran	1 oz	28.35	85	21	3	1	0.1	13	4.5	185
Cake, white, w/white frosting, commercial	1 piece	71	260	42	3	9	2.1	33	1	176
Cheesecake	1 piece	92	280	26	5	18	9.9	52	0.4	204
Chocolate chip cookies, commercial	4 cookies	42	180	28	2	9	2.9	13	0.8	140
Cornmeal, whole-ground, dry	8 oz	122	435	90	11	5	0.5	24	2.2	1
Doughnuts, cake, plain	1 doughnut	50	210	24	3	12	2.8	22	1	192
English muffins, plain	1 muffin	57	140	27	5	1	0.3	96	1.7	378
Oatmeal, instant, cooked, w/salt	8 oz	234	145	25	6	2	0.4	19	1.6	374
Macaroni, cooked, firm	8 oz	130	190	39	7	1	0.1	14	2.1	1
Muffins, blueberry, commercial mix	1 muffin	45	140	22	3	5	1.4	15	0.9	225
Pancakes, plain, commercial mix	1 pancake	27	60	8	2	2	0.5	36	0.7	160
Pie, apple	1 piece	158	405	60	3	18	4.6	13	1.6	476

Nutritional Value of Selected Foods (continued)

FOOD	AMOUNT	GRAMS	ENERGY (KCAL)	CARBO-HYDRATE (G)	PROTEIN (G)	TOTAL FAT (G)	SATU-RATED FAT (G)	CALCIUM (MG)	IRON (MG)	SODIUM (MG)
Grains (continued)										
Popcorn, air-popped, unsalted	8 oz	8	30	6	1	0	0	1	0.2	0
Pretzels, stick	10 pieces	3	10	2	0	0	0	1	0.1	48
Rice, brown, cooked	8 oz	195	230	50	5	1	0.3	23	1	0
Rice, white, instant, cooked	8 oz	165	180	40	4	0	0.1	5	1.3	0
Saltines	4 pieces	12	50	9	1	1	0.5	3	0.5	165
Spaghetti, cooked, tender	8 oz	140	155	32	5	1	0.1	11	1.7	1
Waffles, from commercial mix	1 waffle	75	205	27	7	8	2.7	179	1.2	515
Meat, poultry										
Bacon, regular, cooked	3 slices	19	110	0	6	9	3.3	2	0.3	303
Beef, chuck, lean, cooked	2.2 oz	62	170	0	19	9	3.9	8	2.3	44
Chicken, breast, roasted	3 oz	86	140	0	27	3	0.9	13	0.9	64
Chicken, drumstick, floured, fried	1.7 oz	49	120	1	13	7	1.8	6	0.7	44
Ground beef, broiled	3 oz	85	245	0	20	18	6.9	9	2.1	70
Ham, roasted, lean and fat	3 oz	85	205	0	18	14	5.1	6	0.7	1009
Hamburger	4-oz patty	174	445	38	25	21	7.1	75	4.8	763
Lamb chops, braised, lean	1.7 oz	48	135	0	17	7	2.9	12	1.3	36
Turkey, roasted, light and dark	8 oz	140	240	0	41	7	2.3	35	2.5	98
Veal cutlet, med. fat, braised or broiled	3 oz	85	185	0	23	9	4.1	9	0.8	56
Nuts, legumes, seeds										
Mixed nuts w/peanuts, dry, salted	1 oz	28.35	170	7	5	15	2	20	1	190
Peanuts, oil-roasted, unsalted	8 oz	145	840	27	39	71	9.9	125	2.8	22
Peanut butter	0.5 oz	16	95	3	5	8	1.4	5	0.3	75
Pinto beans, dry, cooked	8 oz	180	265	49	15	1	0.1	86	5.4	3
Sunflower seeds	1 oz	28.35	160	5	6	14	1.5	33	1.9	1
Tofu	1 piece	120	85	3	9	5	0.7	108	2.3	8
Sauces, dressings, condiments										
Catsup	0.5 oz	15	15	4	0	0	0	3	0.1	156
Cheese sauce w/milk, from mix	8 fl oz	279	305	23	16	17	9.3	569	0.3	1565
Honey	0.5 oz	21	65	17	0	0	0	1	0.1	1
Jams/preserves	0.5 oz	20	55	14	0	0	0	4	0.2	2
Mayonnaise	0.5 oz	14	100	0	0	11	1.7	3	0.1	80
Mustard, yellow	0.17 oz	5	5	0	0	0	0	4	0.1	63
Salad dressing, French	0.5 oz	16	85	1	0	9	1.4	2	0	188
Salad dressing, Italian, low calorie	0.5 oz	15	5	2	0	0	0	1	0	136
Syrup, table	1 oz	42	122	32	0	0	0	1	0	19
Sugars, sweets, miscellaneous snacks										
Caramels, plain or chocolate	1 oz	28.35	115	22	1	3	2.2	42	0.4	64
Chocolate, milk, candy, w/almonds	1 oz	28.35	150	15	3	10	4.8	65	0.5	23
Chocolate, dark, sweet	1 oz	28.35	150	16	1	10	5.9	7	0.6	5
Gelatin dessert, prepared	4 oz	120	70	17	2	0	0	2	0	55
Hard candy	1 oz	28.35	110	28	0	0	0	0	0.1	7
Popsicle	1 popsicle	95	70	18	0	0	0	0	0	11
Potato chips	10 chips	20	105	10	1	7	1.8	5	0.2	94
Pudding, chocolate, instant	4 oz	130	155	27	4	4	2.3	130	0.3	440
Sugar, brown	8 oz	220	820	212	0	0	0	187	4.8	97
Sugar, white, granulated	8 oz	200	770	199	0	0	0	3	0.1	5
Vegetables										
Beans, snap, yellow, canned, no salt	8 oz	135	25	6	2	0	0	35	1.2	3
Broccoli	1 spear	151	40	8	4	1	0.1	72	1.3	41

Nutritional Value of Selected Foods (continued)

FOOD	AMOUNT	GRAMS	ENERGY (KCAL)	CARBO-HYDRATE (G)	PROTEIN (G)	TOTAL FAT (G)	SATU-RATED FAT (G)	CALCIUM (MG)	IRON (MG)	SODIUM (MG)
Vegetables (continued)										
Carrots, cooked from frozen	8 oz	146	55	12	2	0	0	41	0.7	86
Cauliflower, cooked from raw	8 oz	125	30	6	2	0	0	34	0.5	8
Celery, Pascal, raw	1 stalk	40	5	1	0	0	0	14	0.2	35
Corn, yellow, cooked from frozen	8 oz	165	135	34	5	0	0	3	0.5	8
Cucumber, w/peel	6 slices	28	5	1	0	0	0	4	0.1	1
Lettuce, crisphead	1 wedge	135	20	3	1	0	0	26	0.7	12
Mushrooms	8 oz	70	20	3	1	0	0	4	0.9	3
Onions, sliced	8 oz	115	40	8	1	0	0.1	29	0.4	2
Peas, green, cooked from frozen	8 oz	160	125	23	8	0	0.1	38	2.5	139
Potatos, boiled, peeled after	1 potato	136	120	27	3	0	0	7	0.4	5
Tomatoes, raw	1 tomato	123	25	5	1	0	0	9	0.6	10

Reading Food Labels

The FDA requires most food manufacturers to provide standardized information about certain nutrients. Within strict guidelines the nutritional labels are designed to **aid the consumer in making informed dietary decisions** as well as to **regulate claims made by manufacturers** about their products.

The percent daily value is based on a 2,000-calorie-per-day diet. Some larger packages will have listings for both 2,000-calorie and 2,500-calorie diets. For products that require additional preparation before eating, such as dry cake mixes, manufacturers often provide two columns of nutritional information, one with the values of the food as purchased, the other with the values of the food as prepared.

The FDA selects mandatory label components (see sample label at right) based on current understanding of nutrition concerns, and **component order on the label is consistent with the priority of dietary recommendations**. Components that may appear in addition to the mandatory components are limited to the following: calories from saturated fat, polyunsaturated fat, monounsaturated fat, potassium, soluble fiber, insoluble fiber, sugar alcohol (for example, the sugar substitutes xylitol, mannitol, and sorbitol), other carbohydrate (the difference between total carbohydrate and the sum of dietary fiber, sugars, and sugar alcohol if declared), percent of vitamin A present as beta-carotene, and other essential vitamins and minerals. Any of these optional components that form the basis of product claims, fortification, or enrichment must appear in the nutrition facts. In 2006 labels were required to specify amounts of trans fatty acids.

Certain key descriptions are also regulated by the FDA. They include the following, in amounts per serving:

Low fat: 3 g or less
Low saturated fat: 1 g or less
Low sodium: 140 mg or less
Low cholesterol: 20 mg or less and 2 g or less of saturated fat
Low calorie: 40 calories or less

Dietary Guidelines for Americans, 2005
Web site: <www.health.gov/dietaryguidelines>.

Nutrition Facts

Serving Size 1 cup (228g)
Servings Per Container 2

Amount Per Serving

Calories 250 — Calories from Fat 110

	%Daily Value*
Total Fat 12g	**18%**
Saturated Fat 3g	**15%**
Trans Fat 3g	
Cholesterol 30mg	**10%**
Sodium 470mg	**20%**
Potassium 700mg	**20%**
Total Carbohydrate 31g	**10%**
Dietary Fiber 0g	**0%**
Sugars 5g	
Protein 5g	
Vitamin A	**4%**
Vitamin C	**2%**
Calcium	**20%**
Iron	**4%**

* Percent Daily Values are based on a 2,000 calorie diet. Your Daily Values may be higher or lower depending on your calorie needs:

	Calories	2,000	2,500
Total Fat	Less than	65g	80g
Sat Fat	Less than	20g	25g
Cholesterol	Less than	300mg	300mg
Sodium	Less than	2,400mg	2,400mg
Total Carbohydrate		300g	375g
Dietary Fiber		25g	30g

Americans and Physical Activity

This table shows selected data illustrating the number of leisure-time periods of vigorous physical activity per week (lasting 10 minutes or longer) among persons 18 years of age and over. Numbers are in thousands ('000). Detail may not add to total given because of rounding. Source: Centers for Disease Control and Prevention, National Center for Health Statistics, National Health Interview Survey, 2006.

SELECTED CHARACTERISTIC	ALL PERSONS 18 YEARS OF AGE AND OVER	NEVER	LESS THAN 1	1–2	3–4	5 OR MORE
Total	**220,267**	**133,416**	**5,542**	**24,964**	**27,930**	**23,728**
Age						
18–44 years	110,391	57,327	3,408	15,639	17,602	13,825
45–64 years	74,203	46,898	1,805	7,931	8,291	7,731
65–74 years	19,081	14,764	193	917	1,392	1,447
75 years and over	16,593	14,427	137	478	645	725
Sex						
Male	106,252	59,079	3,084	13,753	14,432	13,260
Female	114,014	74,337	2,458	11,211	13,498	10,468
Ethnicity						
White	179,456	107,599	4,701	20,601	23,034	19,652
Black	26,223	16,920	514	2,847	3,093	2,257
Asian	10,066	6,045	237	1,044	1,260	1,285
Hispanic[1] or Latino	28,664	19,491	529	2,800	3,011	2,351
Education (respondents 25 and older)						
Less than a high-school diploma	31,750	25,879	362	1,839	1,229	1,844
High-school diploma or GED	54,586	38,435	1,195	4,915	4,395	4,640
Some college	51,159	30,246	1,322	6,483	6,757	5,380
Bachelor's degree or higher	51,863	23,164	1,709	7,771	10,679	7,504
Family income						
Less than US$20,000	38,472	27,839	715	3,218	2,986	3,084
US$20,000–US$34,999	30,921	21,540	709	2,832	2,768	2,686
US$35,000–US$54,999	33,488	20,559	810	3,950	3,983	3,706
US$55,000–US$74,999	23,782	12,991	753	3,618	3,187	2,978
US$75,000 or more	49,556	22,108	1,833	7,859	9,953	7,145
Marital status						
Married	124,727	75,533	3,316	14,570	15,889	12,891
Widowed	13,182	11,267	115	519	422	720
Divorced or separated	24,244	15,989	412	2,295	2,734	2,270
Never married	44,415	22,762	1,323	5,962	7,029	6,309
Living with a partner	12,860	7,324	377	1,596	1,799	1,513

[1] *Hispanics may be of any race.*

Ways To Burn 150 Calories

Values shown are approximations. Activities are listed from more to less vigorous—the more vigorous an activity, the less time it takes to burn a calorie. When specific distances are given, the activity must be performed in the time shown (for example, one must run 1.5 miles in 15 minutes to burn 150 calories).

ACTIVITY	DURATION (MINUTES)
Climbing stairs	15
Shoveling snow	15
Running 1.5 miles (10 minutes/mile)	15
Jumping rope	15
Bicycling 4 miles	15
Playing basketball	15–20
Playing wheelchair basketball	20
Swimming laps	20
Performing water aerobics	30
Walking 2 miles (15 minutes/mile)	30
Raking leaves	30
Pushing a stroller 1.5 miles	30
Dancing fast	30
Bicycling 5 miles	30
Shooting baskets	30
Walking 1.75 miles (20 minutes/mile)	35
Wheeling oneself in a wheelchair	30–40
Gardening (standing)	30–45
Playing touch football	30–45
Playing volleyball	45
Washing windows or floors	45–60
Washing and waxing a car or boat	45–60

Target Heart Rate Training Zones

Measuring **target heart rate** involves monitoring your pulse periodically as you exercise. To use the Target Heart Rate chart:

1. Calculate your maximum heart rate by subtracting your age from 220.
2. Determine your target heart rate zone (50–70% of your maximum heart rate).
3. While exercising, monitor your pulse regularly. Count the number of beats for 10 seconds, then multiply by 6 to determine in what zone you are working.

The American Heart Association recommends using the target heart rate scale when participating in more vigorous athletic activity, such as jogging or aerobics. If your activity is moderate or taking your pulse is too bothersome, a "talk test" can be used as a substitute. If you can converse with someone with minimal effort, you are not working too hard. Alternately, if you can sing without difficulty, you are not working hard enough.

Note: For optimal cardiovascular fitness, you should work toward the middle of your 50 and 70% zones. Always check with your physician before starting any fitness routine, especially if you have heart or respiratory concerns.

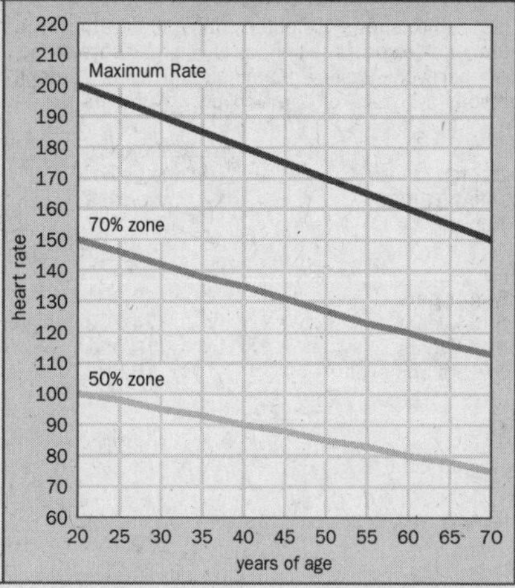

Body Mass Index (BMI)

The BMI is a measure expressing the relationship of weight to height determined by dividing body weight in kilograms by the square of height in meters (for convenience, the information has been converted to standard US measurements in the table below). It is more highly correlated with body fat than any other indicator of height and weight. The National Institutes of Health recommend using the BMI scale to help assess the risk of diseases and disabilities associated with an unhealthy weight. Individuals with a BMI below 18.5 are considered underweight; those with a BMI from 18.5 to 24.9 are considered normal; those with a BMI between 25.0 and 29.9 are considered overweight; and those with a BMI of 30.0 or more are considered obese. The BMI may overestimate body fat in athletes and others who have a muscular build, and it may underestimate body fat in older persons and others who have lost muscle mass.

Source: <www.nhlbi.nih.gov>.

HEIGHT (INCHES)	BODY WEIGHT (POUNDS)																				
58	91	96	100	105	110	115	119	124	129	134	138	143	148	153	158	162	167	172	177	181	186
59	94	99	104	109	114	119	124	128	133	138	143	148	153	158	163	168	173	178	183	188	193
60	97	102	107	112	118	123	128	133	138	143	148	153	158	163	168	174	179	184	189	194	199
61	100	106	111	116	122	127	132	137	143	148	153	158	164	169	174	180	185	190	195	201	206
62	104	109	115	120	126	131	136	142	147	153	158	164	169	175	180	186	191	196	202	207	213
63	107	113	118	124	130	135	141	146	152	158	163	169	175	180	186	191	197	203	208	214	220
64	110	116	122	128	134	140	145	151	157	163	169	174	180	186	192	197	204	209	215	221	227
65	114	120	126	132	138	144	150	156	162	168	174	180	186	192	198	204	210	216	222	228	234
66	118	124	130	136	142	148	155	161	167	173	179	186	192	198	204	210	216	223	229	235	241
67	121	127	134	140	146	153	159	166	172	178	185	191	198	204	211	217	223	230	236	242	249
68	125	131	138	144	151	158	164	171	177	184	190	197	203	210	216	223	230	236	243	249	256
69	128	135	142	149	155	162	169	176	182	189	196	203	209	216	223	230	236	243	250	257	263
70	132	139	146	153	160	167	174	181	188	195	202	209	216	222	229	236	243	250	257	264	271
71	136	143	150	157	165	172	179	186	193	200	208	215	222	229	236	243	250	257	265	272	279
72	140	147	154	162	169	177	184	191	199	206	213	221	228	235	242	250	258	265	272	279	287
73	144	151	159	166	174	182	189	197	204	212	219	227	235	242	250	257	265	272	280	288	295
74	148	155	163	171	179	186	194	202	210	218	225	233	241	249	256	264	272	280	287	295	303
75	152	160	168	176	184	192	200	208	216	224	232	240	248	256	264	272	279	287	295	303	311
76	156	164	172	180	189	197	205	213	221	230	238	246	254	263	271	279	287	295	304	312	320
BMI	**19**	**20**	**21**	**22**	**23**	**24**	**25**	**26**	**27**	**28**	**29**	**30**	**31**	**32**	**33**	**34**	**35**	**36**	**37**	**38**	**39**
	NORMAL						OVERWEIGHT					OBESE									

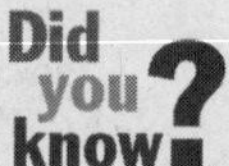

The colorful onion domes of Saint Basil the Blessed above Red Square are perhaps the most common vision Westerners conjure up in Moscow. The church was commissioned by Ivan the Terrible in honor of the Russian victory over the Tatars in Kazan and Astrakhan.

World

The Ghosts of the Balkans

by Samantha Power, TIME columnist, and the TIME staff

On 17 February, after almost a decade of legal limbo and two years of unsuccessful international mediation, Kosovo declared its independence from Serbia. The US moved swiftly to recognize the new country, and nearly 2 million ethnic Albanians celebrated their long-awaited freedom, dancing in city streets, releasing fireworks, and waving flags. Having bristled under Serbian rule and then UN administration, Kosovars were elated by the prospect of at last controlling their own affairs.

The Serbs weren't quite so thrilled. On 21 February, hundreds of thousands protested in Belgrade, chanting "Kosovo is Serbia" and holding placards that read, RUSSIA, HELP. Rioters set the US embassy on fire; Russian Pres. Vladimir Putin vowed never to recognize Kosovo and threatened to support secessionist movements in Georgia and Moldova—a threat the Russians would keep in August.

The US embassy was unguarded when several hundred demonstrators attacked it following the protest rally. At that event, the sharp divisions that typify Serbian politics were nowhere to be seen, as leaders from across the spectrum united in a massive show of force to protest Kosovo's secession. The protest turned deadly when several hundred hooded protesters broke away from that 500,000-strong crowd. The smaller group hurled rocks and Molotov cocktails at the Croatian and US embassies. Flames licked up to the second floor of the old brick building, which is located in the heart of the capital. Serbian paramilitary police, arriving in Humvees, dispersed the crowd using tear gas. Speaking at the United Nations, US Ambassador Zalmay Khalilzad condemned the attack, saying he would seek a UN resolution "reminding the Serb government of its responsibility to protect diplomatic facilities."

Not so long ago, the scenes of unrest would have inspired fears of the kind of ethnic violence that devastated the Balkans in the '90s. But these are different times. Kosovo's ethnic Albanian leaders belatedly tried to extend an olive branch to the province's aggrieved 120,000 Serbs. In addition to allowing Serbs in northern Kosovo to have their own police, schools, and hospitals, Kosovo's new prime minister, Hashim Thaci, did the unthinkable: he delivered part of his inauguration speech in the hated Serbian language. The gesture failed to quell the Serbs' discontent, but in reality, Serbia was in no position to cut ties with the West. The EU supplies 49% of Serbia's imports and buys 56% of its exports—a far more valuable trade relationship than Serbia enjoys with its primary ally, Russia.

Kosovo matters to America's future because it underscores three alarming features of the current international system. First, it exposes the chill in relations between the US and Russia. Putin, who stepped down from his leadership role in the Kremlin only three months after Kosovo's declaration of independence, used the standoff in Serbia as yet another excuse to flaunt his petro-powered invincibility, sending his anointed successor, Dmitry Medvedev, to Belgrade to sign a gas agreement. If a firm international response is to be mobilized toward Iran, The Sudan, or other trouble spots in the coming years, the US will have to find a way to persuade Russia to become a partner rather than a rival in improving collective security.

Second, the 27-country EU, which is bitterly divided over Kosovo, lacks an overarching defense or security vision. After Kosovo declared independence, Britain, France, and other countries offered recognition, while Spain, Romania, Greece, Cyprus, Bulgaria, and Slovakia refused to do so. Keeping peace in Kosovo will require European nations to put their citizens at risk. Unfortunately, the stated desire of many European countries to reduce their commitments to the NATO effort in Afghanistan does little to bolster confidence in Europe's eagerness to maintain international security.

Finally, the disagreements over Kosovo exposed the world's fickleness in determining which secessionist movements deserve international recognition. A claimant has a far stronger claim if, like Kosovo, it is relatively homogeneous and not yet self-governing, if it has been abused by the sovereign government, and if its quest for independence does not incite its kin in a neighboring country to make comparable demands. Not all secessionists can clear that bar. Iraq's Kurds, for instance, are clamoring for independence. But the Kurds are already exercising self-government, and their independence could have the destabilizing effect of causing the Kurdish population in Turkey to try to secede.

Taking Sides. The modern world isn't divided between capitalism and communism; it's divided in part between nations done dealing with their secessionists and those still fighting. When Kosovo declared its independence, Sri Lanka sided with Serbia, mindful of its Tamil rebels. Even Spain opposed Kosovo's claim as a precedent that could threaten Madrid's sovereignty by encouraging separatists.

In August separatist problems in the former Soviet republic of Georgia led to outright war. On 8 August, as the world's attention was focused on the opening of the Olympic Games in Beijing, Russian tanks rolled into Georgia's disputed territory of South Ossetia, which has long sought to break away from Georgia and become a province of Russia, after Georgian forces attempted to establish control there. On the 11th, Russian forces invaded Georgia through the disputed territory of Abkhazia in Georgia's west, opening a second front. Several weeks of fighting and Russian occupation ensued, and hundreds of civilians and troops were killed. Russian forces had largely withdrawn to the two separatist territories by the end of August. On 26 August Russia recognized the independence of South Ossetia and Abkhazia. US Pres. George W. Bush and other NATO leaders strongly denounced the incursion, but no troops were mustered. The world, once again, was taking sides. There's a reason they call it "Balkanization."

Countries of the World

The information about the countries of the world that follows has been assembled and analyzed by *Encyclopædia Britannica* editors from hundreds of private, national, and international sources. Included are all the sovereign states of the world as well as the major dependent, or nonsovereign, areas. The historical background sketches have been adapted, augmented, and updated from *Britannica Concise Encyclopedia* and the statistical sections from *Britannica World Data,* which is published annually in conjunction with *Britannica Book of the Year*. The section called Recent Developments also has been adapted from material appearing in recent issues of the yearbook, as well as from other sources inside and outside Britannica. The locator maps have been prepared by Britannica's Cartography Department. Several countries, including those with the largest economies, are given expanded coverage in this section.

All information is the latest available to Britannica. It must be understood that in many cases it takes several years for the various countries or agencies to gather and process statistics—the most current data available will normally be dated several years earlier.

A few definitions of terms used in the articles may be useful. **Gross domestic product** (GDP) is the total value of goods and services produced in a country during a given accounting period, usually a year. Unless otherwise noted, the value is given in current prices of the year indicated. **Gross national income** (GNI) is essentially GDP plus income from foreign transactions minus payments made outside the country. **Imports** are material goods legally entering a country (or customs area) and subject to customs regulations and exclude financial movements. The value of goods imported is given free on board (**f.o.b.**) unless otherwise specified; the value of goods exported and imported f.o.b. is calculated from the cost of production and excludes the cost of transport. The principal alternate basis for valuation of goods in international trade is that of cost, insurance, and freight (**c.i.f.**); its use is restricted to imports, as it comprises the principal charges needed to bring the goods to the customs house in the country of destination. **Exports** are material goods legally leaving a country and subject to customs regulations. Valuation of goods exported is also f.o.b. unless otherwise specified. The **FAO recommended minimum** daily per capita caloric intake varies by region and is calculated from age and sex distributions, average body weights, and environmental temperatures.

The symbol **$** is always given with its country identifier ("US," "A," etc.) to avoid confusion. **"CFA franc"** stands for Communauté Financière Africaine franc. A few helpful **conversions** for the statistical section are given at the foot of the left-hand pages.

Afghanistan

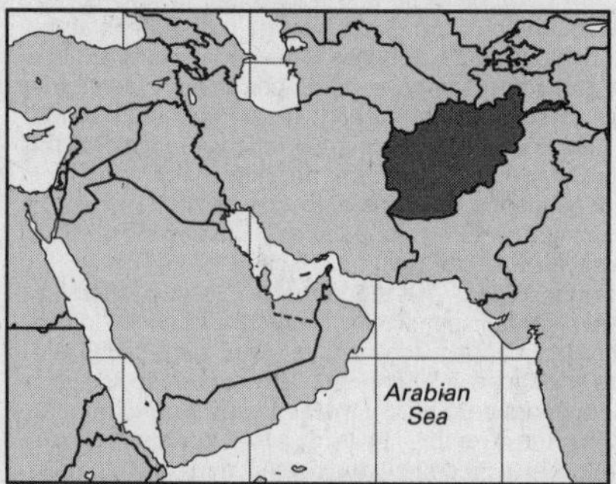

Official name: Islamic Republic of Afghanistan (Jomhuri-ye Eslami-ye Afghanestan [Dari (Persian)] Da Afghanestan Eslami Jamhuriyat [Pashto]). **Form of government:** Islamic republic with two legislative bodies (House of Elders [102]; House of the People [249]). **Chief of state and head of government:** President Hamid Karzai (from 2002). **Capital:** Kabul. **Official languages:** Dari (Persian); Pashto; six additional local languages have official status per the 2004 constitution. **Official religion:** Islam. **Monetary unit:** 1 (new) afghani (Af) = 100 puls (puli); valuation (1 Jul 2008) US$1 = Af 49.98.

Demography

Area: 249,347 sq mi, 645,807 sq km. **Population** (2007): 27,145,000. **Density** (2007): persons per sq mi 108.9, persons per sq km 42.0. **Urban** (2006): 21.5%. **Sex distribution** (2006): male 51.14%; female 48.86%. **Age breakdown** (2006): under 15, 44.6%; 15–29, 26.7%; 30–44, 16.0%; 45–59, 8.6%; 60–74, 3.5%; 75 and over 0.6%. **Ethnolinguistic composition** (2004): Pashtun 42%; Tajik 27%; Hazara 9%; Uzbek 9%; Chahar Aimak 4%; Turkmen 3%; other 6%. **Religious affiliation** (2004): Sunni Muslim 82%; Shiʿi Muslim 17%; other 1%. **Major cities** (2006): Kabul 2,536,300; Herat 349,000; Kandahar (Qandahar) 324,800; Mazar-e Sharif 300,600; Jalalabad 168,600. **Location:** southern Asia, bordering Uzbekistan, Tajikistan, China, Pakistan, Iran, and Turkmenistan.

Vital statistics

Birth rate per 1,000 population (2006): 46.6 (world avg. 20.3). **Death rate** per 1,000 population (2006): 20.3 (world avg. 8.6). **Total fertility rate** (avg. births per childbearing woman; 2006): 6.69. **Life expectancy** at birth (2006): male 43.2 years; female 43.5 years.

National economy

Budget (2005–06). *Revenue:* Af 67,531,000,000 (grants for development revenue 51.3%; grants for current revenue 24.8%; domestic revenue 23.9%, of which taxes 18.2%). *Expenditures:* Af 91,417,000,000 (development expenditure 64.0%; current expenditure 36.0%). **Gross national income** (2006): US$8,309,000,000 (US$319 per capita). **Public debt** (external, outstanding; 2004): US$8,000,000,000. **Production** (metric tons except as noted). *Agriculture, forestry, fishing* (2005): wheat

1 metric ton = about 1.1 short tons; 1 kilometer = 0.6 mi (statute); 1 metric ton-km cargo = about 0.68 short ton-mi cargo; c.i.f.: cost, insurance, and freight; f.o.b.: free on board

4,265,000, rice 470,000, grapes 350,000, opium poppy 4,100 (represents 87% of world production); livestock (number of live animals) 8,800,000 sheep, 7,300,000 goats, 180,000 camels; roundwood 3,226,629 cu m, of which fuelwood 45%; fisheries production (2004) 1,000. *Mining and quarrying* (2004): salt 38,000; gemstones (particularly lapis lazuli) n.a. *Manufacturing* (value added in Af '000,000; 2005–06): food 48,575; chemicals 1,206; cement, bricks, and ceramics 809. *Energy production (consumption):* electricity (kW-hr; 2004–05) 783,000,000 (623,000,000); coal (metric tons; 2004) 34,000 (34,000); petroleum products (metric tons; 2004) none (183,000); natural gas (cu m; 2004) 3,050,000 (3,050,000). **Households** (2003). Average household size 8.0; sources of income: wages and salaries 49%, self-employment 47%; expenditure (2004): food 60.6%, housing and energy 16.5%, clothing 9.1%. **Population economically active** (1994): total 5,557,000; activity rate of total population 29.4% (participation rates: female 9.0%; unemployed [2005] 8.5%). **Land use** as % of total land area (2003): in temporary crops 12.1%, in permanent crops 0.2%, in pasture 46.0%; overall forest area (2005) 1.3%. **Selected balance of payments data.** Receipts from (US$'000,000): tourism (1998) 1.0; foreign direct investment (2001–05 avg.) 20; official development assistance (2005) 2,775. Disbursements for (US$'000,000): tourism (1997) 1.0.

Foreign trade

Imports (2005–06; c.i.f.): US$2,471,000,000 (machinery and equipment 12.2%; base and fabricated metals 10.6%; fabrics, clothing, and footwear 10.3%; mineral fuels 10.0%; flour 5.1%). *Major import sources:* Japan 16.8%; Pakistan 15.9%; China 12.8%; Russia 9.2%; Uzbekistan 8.3%. **Exports** (2005–06; f.o.b.): US$384,000,000 (carpets and handicrafts 39.6%; dried fruits 33.4%; skins 8.4%; fresh fruits 8.4%). *Major export destinations:* Pakistan 77.6%; India 6.0%; Russia 3.4%; UAE 2.9%; Germany 1.8%.

Transport and communications

Transport. *Railroads* (2006): none. *Roads* (2005): total length 34,782 km (paved 7%). *Vehicles* (2004–05): passenger cars 197,449; trucks and buses 123,964. *Air transport* (2004–05): passenger-km 681,000,000; metric ton-km cargo 20,624,000. **Communications,** in total units (units per 1,000 persons). Televisions (2003): 312,000 (14); telephone landlines (2005): 100,000 (4); cellular telephone subscribers (2005): 1,200,000 (48); total Internet users (2005): 30,000 (1.3); broadband Internet subscribers (2005): 220 (0.01).

Education and health

Literacy (2006): total population age 15 and over literate 28.1%; males 43.1%; females 12.6%. **Health:** physicians (2005) 4,747 (1 per 5,000 persons); hospital beds (2004; public hospitals only) 9,667 (1 per 2,381 persons); infant mortality rate (2006) 160.2.

Military

Total active duty personnel (2006): 50,000 (army 100%); foreign troops (2007): NATO-sponsored security forces 35,000 (including 12,000 US troops); other US 14,000. **Military expenditure as percentage of GDP** (2005): 9.9%; per capita expenditure US$31.

The Karakoram Range is a great mountain system extending some 300 miles (500 km) from the easternmost extension of Afghanistan in a southeasterly direction along the watershed between Central and South Asia. Found there are the greatest concentration of high mountains in the world and the longest glaciers outside the high latitudes.

Background

The area was part of the Persian empire in the 6th century BC and was conquered by Alexander the Great in the 4th century BC. Hindu influence entered with the Hephthalites and Sasanians; Islam became entrenched during the rule of the Saffarids, c. AD 870. Afghanistan was divided between the Mughal empire of India and the Safavid empire of Persia until the 18th century, when other Persians under Nadir Shah took control. Great Britain and Russia fought several wars in the area in the 19th century. From the 1930s Afghanistan had a stable monarchy; it was overthrown in the 1970s. The rebels' intention was to institute Marxist reforms, but the reforms sparked rebellion, and troops from the USSR invaded to establish order. Afghan guerrillas prevailed, and the Soviet Union withdrew in 1988–89. In 1992 rebel factions overthrew the government and established an Islamic republic, but fighting among factions continued. In 1996 the government was taken over by the Taliban faction. A US-led coalition invaded Afghanistan and overthrew the Taliban government in late 2001.

Recent Developments

With only a small national army of its own in 2007, Afghanistan, supported by almost 50,000 NATO and US soldiers, faced a Taliban resistance that had refocused its tactics. There was an upsurge in suicide bombing, kidnapping, and other tactics similar to those used by insurgents in Iraq. As well, though Taliban leaders had disapproved of and greatly reduced opium cultivation while in power, in 2007 poppy growing provided significant monetary support for their cause and contributed almost one-third of Afghanistan's overall GDP; it was estimated that as much as 93% of the world's opium came from Afghanistan. Afghanistan's relations with the US, though extremely close, were complicated when it came to Pakistan and Iran. Pres. Hamid Karzai blamed Pakistan for not doing enough to cut off aid and shelter to the Taliban in Pakistan, and he saw the US as reluctant to push Pakistan on this point. US officials, for their part, repeatedly blamed Iran for supplying weapons to the Taliban, but several times during the year Karzai spoke of his country's close relations with Iran.

Internet resources: <www.afghan-web.com>.

Albania

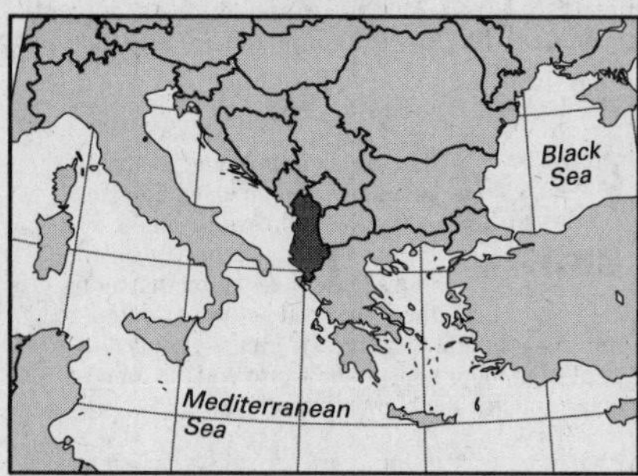

Official name: Republika e Shqipërisë (Republic of Albania). **Form of government:** unitary multiparty republic with one legislative house (Assembly [140]). **Chief of state:** President Bamir Topi (from 2007). **Head of government:** Prime Minister Sali Berisha (from 2005). **Capital:** Tirana (Tiranë). **Official language:** Albanian. **Official religion:** none. **Monetary unit:** 1 lek = 100 qindars; valuation (1 Jul 2008) US$1 = 77.27 leks.

Demography

Area: 11,082 sq mi, 28,703 sq km. **Population** (2007): 3,176,000. **Density** (2007): persons per sq mi 286.6, persons per sq km 110.7. **Urban** (2005): 44.5%. **Sex distribution** (2005): male 49.82%; female 50.18%. **Age breakdown** (2005): under 15, 26.9%; 15–29, 25.3%; 30–44, 19.8%; 45–59, 16.0%; 60–74, 9.3%; 75–84, 2.4%; 85 and over, 0.3%. **Ethnic composition** (2000): Albanian 91.7%; Vlach (Aromanian) 3.6%; Greek 2.3%; other 2.4%. **Traditional religious groups** (2005): Muslim 68%, of which Sunni 51%, Bektashi 17%; Orthodox 22%; Roman Catholic 10%. **Major cities** (2001): Tirana (Tiranë) 343,078; Durrës 99,546; Elbasan 87,797; Shkodër 82,455; Vlorë 77,691. **Location:** southeastern Europe, bordering Montenegro, Kosovo, Macedonia, Greece, and the Mediterranean Sea.

Vital statistics

Birth rate per 1,000 population (2004): 13.8 (world avg. 21.1). **Death rate** per 1,000 population (2004): 5.7 (world avg. 8.8). **Total fertility rate** (avg. births per childbearing woman; 2006): 2.03. **Life expectancy** at birth (2006): male 74.8 years; female 80.3 years.

National economy

Budget (2005). *Revenue:* 199,600,000,000 leks (tax revenue 91.3%, of which turnover tax/VAT 31.7%, social security contributions 18.4%, customs duties and excise taxes 17.0%, taxes on income and profits 11.8%; other revenue 8.7%). *Expenditures:* 245,100,000,000 leks (current expenditure 79.4%, of which social security and welfare 22.5%, wages and salaries 22.5%, debt service 12.2%; development expenditure 20.6%). **Gross national income** (2006): US$9,542,000,000 (US$3,008 per capita). **Public debt** (external, outstanding; 2005): US $1,375,000,000. **Production** (metric tons except as noted). *Agriculture, forestry, fishing* (2005): alfalfa for forage and silage 1,800,000, wheat 260,000, corn (maize) 219,900; livestock (number of live animals) 1,760,000 sheep, 941,000 goats, 655,000 cattle; roundwood 296,200 cu m, of which fuelwood 75%; fisheries production (2004) 5,132 (from aquaculture 31%). *Mining and quarrying* (2004): chromium ore 148,392. *Manufacturing* (value added in US$'000,000; 2004): base metals 31; textiles 29; leather (all forms) 29. *Energy production (consumption):* electricity (kW-hr; 2004) 5,559,000,000 (5,762,000,000); lignite (metric tons; 2004) 109,000 (118,000); crude petroleum (barrels; 2004) 2,769,000 (2,769,000); petroleum products (metric tons; 2004) 270,000 (1,183,000); natural gas (cu m; 2004) 16,299,000 (16,299,000). **Population economically active** (2005): total 1,085,000; activity rate of total population 34.5% (participation rates: ages 15–64, 57.8%; female 39.6%; unemployed [October 2005–September 2006] 14.0%). **Households** (2002). Average household size 4.3; average annual income per household: 401,928 leks (US$2,868); sources of income (2000; urban areas only): wages and salaries/self-employment 64.2%, transfers/pensions 14.8%, other 21.0%; expenditure: food, beverages, and tobacco 68.2%, energy 9.2%, transportation and communications 6.6%. **Selected balance of payments data.** Receipts from (US$'000,000): tourism (2005) 854; remittances (2006) 1,359; foreign direct investment (2001–05 avg.) 222; official development assistance (2005) 301 (commitments). Disbursements for (US$'000,000): tourism (2005) 786; remittances (2006) 27. **Land use** as % of total land area (2003): in temporary crops 21.1%, in permanent crops 4.4%, in pasture 15.4%; overall forest area (2005) 29.0%.

Foreign trade

Imports (2006): 299,134,000,000 leks (nonelectrical and electrical machinery 20.2%; food, beverages, and tobacco 17.9%; construction materials and base and fabricated metals 16.0%; mineral products 13.9%; textiles and footwear 11.7%). *Major import sources:* Italy 28.1%; Greece 15.7%; Turkey 7.6%; China 6.0%; Germany 5.7%. **Exports** (2006): 77,633,000,000 leks (textiles and footwear 54.7%; construction materials and base and fabricated metals 16.8%; food, beverages, and tobacco 7.9%). *Major export destinations:* Italy 72.6%; Greece 9.6%; Germany 3.2%; Macedonia 1.6%; Turkey 1.3%.

Transport and communications

Transport. *Railroads* (2004): length (2005) 447 km; passenger-km 89,000,000; metric ton-km cargo 32,000,000. *Roads* (2002): total length 18,000 km (paved 39%). *Vehicles* (2005): passenger cars 190,004; trucks and buses 71,875. *Air transport* (2005; Albanian Air only): passenger-km 152,000,-000. **Communications,** in total units (units per 1,000 persons). Daily newspaper circulation (2003): 76,000 (25); televisions (2003): 989,000 (318); telephone landlines (2004): 275,000 (88); cellular telephone subscribers (2004): 1,260,000 (403); per-

1 metric ton = about 1.1 short tons; 1 kilometer = 0.6 mi (statute); 1 metric ton-km cargo = about 0.68 short ton-mi cargo; c.i.f.: cost, insurance, and freight; f.o.b.: free on board

sonal computers (2002): 36,000 (12); total Internet users (2005): 188,000 (60).

Education and health

Educational attainment (2001). Population ages 20 and over having: no formal schooling/incomplete primary education 7.8%; primary 55.6%; lower secondary 2.7%; upper secondary 17.9%; vocational 8.8%; university 7.2%. **Literacy** (2006): total population ages 15 and over literate 98.7%; males 99.2%; females 98.3%. **Health:** physicians (2004) 3,699 (1 per 845 persons); hospital beds (2005) 9,284 (1 per 339 persons); infant mortality rate per 1,000 live births (2006) 20.8. **Food** (2005): daily per capita caloric intake 2,918 (vegetable products 70%, animal products 30%); 147% of FAO recommended minimum.

Military

Total active duty personnel (March 2006): 21,500 (army 74.4%, navy 9.3%, air force 16.3%). **Military expenditure as percentage of GDP** (2005): 1.4%; per capita expenditure US$37.

Albania is the poorest country on the continent of Europe, with an annual income in 1999 of only US$930 per person.

Background

The Albanians are descended from the Illyrians, an ancient Indo-European people who lived in central Europe and migrated south by the beginning of the Iron Age. Of the two major Illyrian migrating groups, the Ghegs settled in the north and the Tosks in the south, along with Greek colonizers. The area was under Roman rule by the 1st century BC; after AD 395 it was connected administratively to Constantinople. Turkish invasion began in the 14th century and continued into the 15th century; though the national hero, Skanderbeg, was able to resist them for a time, after his death (1468) the Turks consolidated their rule. The country achieved independence in 1912 and was admitted into the League of Nations in 1920. It was briefly a republic in 1925–28, then became a monarchy under Zog I, whose initial alliance with Benito Mussolini led to Italy's invasion of Albania in 1939. After the war a socialist government under Enver Hoxha was installed. Gradually Albania cut itself off from the nonsocialist international community and eventually from all nations, including China, its last political ally. By 1990 economic hardship had produced antigovernment demonstrations, and in 1992 a noncommunist government was elected and Albania's international isolation ended. In 1997 it plunged into chaos, brought on by the collapse of pyramid investment schemes. In 1999 it was overwhelmed by ethnic Albanians seeking refuge from Yugoslavia.

Recent Developments

Albania was affected by two major international events in 2008. Neighboring Kosovo, which as a UN-administered province of Serbia was more than 90% ethnic Albanian, declared its independence on 17 February. At the NATO summit in April in Bucharest, Romania, Albania was invited to begin the application process to join the defense organization, and days later it pledged 100 more troops for the NATO force in Afghanistan.

Internet resources: <www.albaniantourism.com>.

Algeria

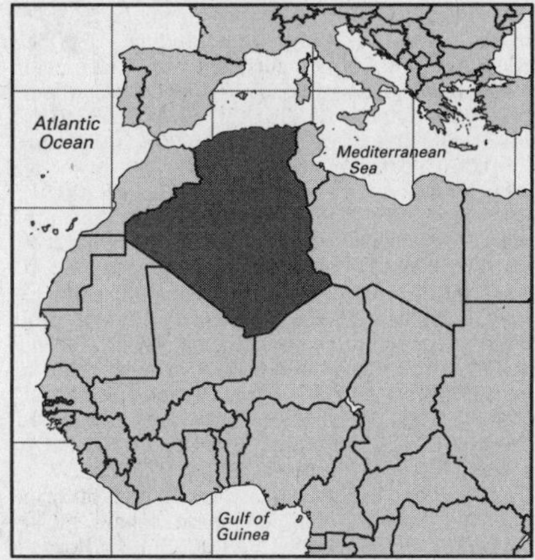

Official name: Al-Jumhuriyah al-Jazairiyah al-Dimuqratiyah al-Shaʿbiyah (Arabic) (People's Democratic Republic of Algeria). **Form of government:** multiparty republic with two legislative bodies (Council of the Nation [144; includes 48 nonelected seats appointed by the president]; National People's Assembly [389]). **Chief of state:** President Abdelaziz Bouteflika (from 1999). **Head of government:** Prime Minister Abdelaziz Belkhadem (from 2006). **Capital:** Algiers. **Official languages:** Arabic; Tamazight is designated as a national language. **Official religion:** Islam. **Monetary unit:** 1 Algerian dinar (DA) = 100 centimes; valuation (1 Jul 2008) US$1 = DA 62.72.

Demography

Area: 919,595 sq mi, 2,381,741 sq km. **Population** (2007): 33,858,000. **Density** (2007): persons per sq mi 36.8, persons per sq km 14.2. **Urban** (2005): 60.0%. **Sex distribution** (2005): male 50.46%; female 49.54%. **Age breakdown** (2005): under 15, 29.7%; 15–29, 32.1%; 30–44, 21.0%; 45–59, 10.8%; 60–74, 5.0%; 75–84, 1.2%; 85 and over, 0.2%. **Ethnic composition** (2000): Algerian Arab 59.1%; Berber 26.2%, of which Arabized Berber 3.0%; Bedouin Arab 14.5%; other 0.2%. **Religious affiliation** (2000): Muslim 99.7%, of which Sunni 99.1%, Ibadiyah 0.6%; Christian 0.3%. **Major cities** (1998): Algiers 1,519,570; Oran 692,516; Constantine 462,187; Annaba 348,554; Batna 242,514. **Location:** northern Africa, bordering the Mediterranean Sea, Tunisia, Libya, Niger, Mali, Mauritania, Western Sahara, and Morocco.

Vital statistics

Birth rate per 1,000 population (2006): 17.1 (world avg. 20.3). **Death rate** per 1,000 population (2006): 4.6 (world avg. 8.6). **Natural increase rate** per 1,000 population (2006): 12.5 (world avg. 11.7). **Total fer-**

tility rate (avg. births per childbearing woman; 2006): 1.89. **Life expectancy** at birth (2006): male 71.7 years; female 74.9 years.

National economy

Budget (2005). *Revenue:* DA 3,081,700,000,000 (hydrocarbon revenue 76.3%; nonhydrocarbon revenue 23.7%). *Expenditures:* DA 1,985,900,000,000 (current expenditure 65.1%; capital expenditure 34.9%). **Public debt** (external, outstanding; 2005): US$15,476,000,000. **Production** (metric tons except as noted). *Agriculture, forestry, fishing* (2005): wheat 2,415,000, potatoes 2,156,000, barley 1,033,000; livestock (number of live animals) 18,909,100 sheep, 3,590,000 goats; roundwood 7,742,000 cu m, of which fuelwood 99%; fisheries production (2004) 140,588. *Mining and quarrying* (2004): iron ore 1,414,000; phosphate rock 784,000; zinc (metal content; 2003) 5,201. *Manufacturing* (value added in US$'000,000; 1997): food products 463; cement, bricks, and tiles 393; iron and steel 118. *Energy production (consumption):* electricity (kW-hr; 2004) 31,250,000,000 (31,264,000,000); coal (metric tons; 2004) none (615,000); crude petroleum (barrels; 2004) 471,000,000 (146,000,000); petroleum products (metric tons; 2004) 39,061,000 (11,209,000); natural gas (cu m; 2004) 81,291,000,000 (21,173,000,000). **Land use** as % of total land area (2003): in temporary crops 3.2%, in permanent crops 0.2%, in pasture 13.3%; overall forest area (2005) 1.0%. **Households.** Average household size (2004) 6.2; disposable income per household (2002) US$5,700; sources of income (2004): self-employment 39.9%, wages and salaries 36.9%, transfers 23.2%. **Gross national income** (2006): US$111,547,000,000 (US$3,345 per capita). **Population economically active** (2006): total 10,109,600; activity rate of population 30% (participation rates: ages 15–64 [1998] 52.6%; female 16.9%; unemployed 12.3%). **Selected balance of payments data.** Receipts from (US$'000,000): tourism (2005) 184; remittances (2005) 1,950; foreign direct investment (2001–05 avg.) 955; official development assistance (2005) 511 (commitments). Disbursements for (US$'000,000): tourism (2005) 370.

Foreign trade

Imports (2004): US$17,954,000,000 (industrial equipment 37.2%; semifinished products 19.1%; food 18.9%; consumer goods 14.5%). *Major import sources:* France 22.6%; Italy 8.5%; Germany 6.5%; US 6.0%; China 5.0%. **Exports** (2004): US$32,220,000,000 (crude petroleum 39.0%; natural and manufactured gas 34.4%; condensate 15.1%; refined petroleum 9.4%). *Major export destinations:* US 23.6%; Italy 16.1%; France 11.4%; Spain 11.2%; The Netherlands 7.4%.

Transport and communications

Transport. *Railroads* (2004): route length 3,973 km; (2000) passenger-km 1,142,000,000; metric ton-km cargo 2,029,000,000. *Roads* (2004): total length 108,302 km (paved 70%). *Vehicles* (2001): passenger cars 1,692,148; trucks and buses 948,553. *Air transport* (2005; Air Algérie only): passenger-km 3,101,000,000; metric ton-km cargo 36,177,000.

Communications, in total units (units per 1,000 persons). Daily newspaper circulation (2004): 873,000 (27); televisions (2003): 3,633,000 (114); telephone landlines (2005): 3,200,000 (97); cellular telephone subscribers (2005): 13,661,000 (416); personal computers (2005): 1,920,000 (58); total Internet users (2005): 1,920,000 (58); broadband Internet subscribers (2005): 195,000 (5.9).

Education and health

Educational attainment (1998). Percentage of economically active population age 6 and over having: no formal schooling 30.1%; primary education 29.9%; lower secondary 20.7%; upper secondary 13.4%; higher 4.3%; other 1.6%. **Literacy** (2005): total population age 15 and over literate 72.1%; males literate 80.6%; females literate 63.4%. **Health:** physicians (2003) 36,347 (1 per 877 persons); hospital beds (1999) 57,796 (1 per 520 persons); infant mortality rate (2006) 29.9. **Food** (2005): daily per capita caloric intake 3,510 (vegetable products 90%, animal products 10%); 188% of FAO recommended minimum.

Military

Total active duty personnel (2006): 137,500 (army 87.3%, navy 5.4%, air force 7.3%). **Military expenditure as percentage of GDP** (2005): 2.9%; per capita expenditure US$89.

Background

Phoenician traders settled the area early in the 1st millennium BC; several centuries later the Romans invaded, and by AD 40 they had control of the Mediterranean coast. The fall of Rome in the 5th century led to invasion by the Vandals and later by Byzantium. The Islamic invasion began in the 7th century; by 711 all of northern Africa was under the control of the Umayyad caliphate. Several Islamic Berber empires followed, most prominently the Almoravid (c. 1054–1130), which extended its domain to Spain, and the Almohad (c. 1130–1269). The Barbary Coast pirates, operating in the area, had menaced Mediterranean trade for centuries, and France seized this pretext to enter Algeria in 1830. By 1847 France had established control in the region, and by the late 19th century it had instituted civil rule. Popular movements resulted in the bloody Algerian War (1954–62); independence was achieved following a referendum in 1962. In the 1990s Islamic fundamentalists opposing the military brought Algeria to a state of civil war.

Recent Developments

Attacks by the Salafist Group for Preaching and Combat, which claimed to have joined al-Qaeda in September 2006, increased in 2007. In April coordinated suicide bombings, the first in Algeria in many years, wrecked the offices of the prime minister and left 33 persons dead, while a suicide bomber killed 22 persons on 6 September. Two days later a naval barracks in Dellys was attacked by a car bomb, killing 34. In December two car bombs in Algiers, one at a UN compound, killed 37 people.

Internet resources: <www.algeria.com>.

1 metric ton = about 1.1 short tons; 1 kilometer = 0.6 mi (statute); 1 metric ton-km cargo = about 0.68 short ton-mi cargo; c.i.f.: cost, insurance, and freight; f.o.b.: free on board

American Samoa

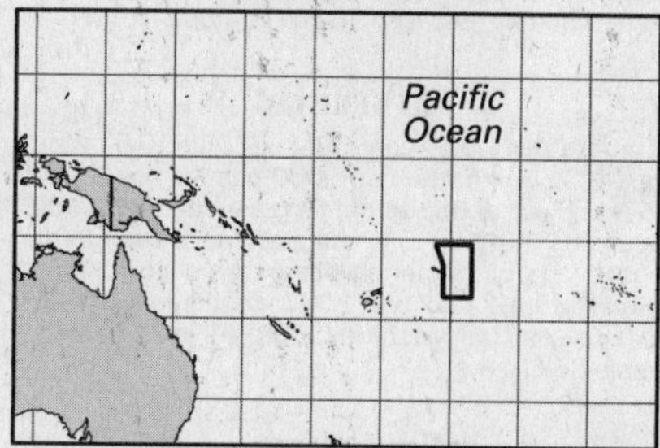

Official name: American Samoa (English); Amerika Samoa (Samoan). **Political status:** unincorporated and unorganized territory of the US with two legislative houses (Senate [18]; House of Representatives [20]). **Chief of state:** US President George W. Bush (from 2001). **Head of government:** Governor Togiola Tulafono (from 2003). **Capital:** Fagatogo (legislative and judicial) and Utulei (executive). **Official languages:** English; Samoan. **Official religion:** none. **Monetary unit:** 1 US dollar ($) = 100 cents.

Demography

Area: 77 sq mi, 200 sq km. **Population** (2007): 64,400. **Density** (2007): persons per sq mi 833.1, persons per sq km 321.7. **Urban** (2003): 54.0%. **Sex distribution** (2006): male 51.42%; female 48.58%. **Age breakdown** (2006): under 15, 34.7%; 15–29, 24.9%; 30–44, 22.4%; 45–59, 13.0%; 60–74, 4.1%; 75 and over, 0.9%. **Ethnic composition** (2000): Samoan 88.2%; Tongan 2.8%; Asian 2.8%; Caucasian 1.1%; other 5.1%. **Religious affiliation** (2005): Protestant 38%, of which Congregational 21%; Mormon 19%; Roman Catholic 15%; other (including nonreligious) 28%. **Major villages** (2000): Tafuna 8,406; Nu'uuli 5,154; Pago Pago 4,278 (urban agglomeration [2001] 15,000); Leone 3,568; Fagatogo 2,096. **Location:** group of islands in the South Pacific Ocean.

Vital statistics

Birth rate per 1,000 population (2005): 26.3 (world avg. 20.3); within marriage 65.9%. **Death rate** per 1,000 population (2005): 4.3 (world avg. 8.6). **Natural increase rate** per 1,000 population (2005): 22.0 (world avg. 11.7). **Total fertility rate** (avg. births per childbearing woman; 2006): 3.16. **Life expectancy** at birth (2006): male 72.5 years; female 79.8 years.

National economy

Budget (2004). *Revenue:* US$188,877,568 (US government grants 44.9%; taxes 29.0%; charges for services 4.1%; other 22.0%). *Expenditures:* US$192,421,535 (general government 32.1%; education and culture 27.9%; health and welfare 19.3%; public safety 6.7%). **Gross domestic product** (2002): US$559,000,000 (US$9,040 per capita). **Production** (metric tons except as noted). *Agriculture, forestry, fishing* (2005): coconuts 4,700, taros 1,500, bananas 750; livestock (number of live animals) 10,500 pigs, 38,000 chickens; fisheries production (2004) 4,043, of which tuna, bonitos, and billfish 4,025. *Manufacturing* (value of exports in US$; 2003): canned tuna 467,700,000; pet food 9,800,000; other manufactures include garments, handicrafts, soap, and alcoholic beverages. *Energy production (consumption):* electricity (kW-hr; 2005) 189,000,000 (167,000,000); petroleum products (metric tons; 2002) none (93,000). **Population economically active** (2000): total 17,664; activity rate of total population 30.8% (participation rates: ages 16 and over 52.0%; female 41.5%; unemployed 5.1%). **Households.** Average household size (2005) 5.7; income per household (2000): US$24,000; expenditure (1995): food and beverages 30.9%, housing and furnishings 25.8%, church donations 20.7%, transportation and communications 9.4%, clothing 2.9%, other 10.3%. **Selected balance of payments data.** Receipts from (US$'000,000): tourism (1998) 10. Disbursements for (US$'000,000): tourism (1996) 2.0. **Land use** as % of total land area (2003): in temporary crops 10%, in permanent crops 15%; overall forest area (2005) 90%.

Foreign trade

Imports (2005): US$506,200,000 (fish for cannery 43.9%; consumer goods 18.0%; other food 17.0%; mineral fuels 8.8%). *Major import sources* (2000): US 56.7%; Australia 14.9%; New Zealand 11.1%; Fiji 5.7%; Samoa 3.1%. **Exports** (2005): US$373,800,000 (canned tuna 94.1%; pet food 5.8%; fish meal 0.1%). *Major export destination* (2000): US 99.6%.

Transport and communications

Transport. *Roads* (1991): total length 350 km (paved 43%). *Vehicles* (2005): passenger cars 7,349; trucks and buses 657. *Air transport* (2005): passenger arrivals 64,211; passenger departures 64,908; incoming cargo 920 metric tons, outgoing cargo 379 metric tons. **Communications,** in total units (units per 1,000 persons). Daily newspaper circulation (2004): 6,300 (195); televisions (2000): 13,000 (211); telephone landlines (2005): 11,000 (163); cellular telephone subscribers (2005): 8,100 (123).

Education and health

Educational attainment (2005). Percentage of population ages 25 and over having: no formal schooling to some secondary education 31.2%; completed secondary 42.6%; some college 19.0%; bachelor's degree 5.0%; graduate degree 2.2%. **Literacy** (2000): total population ages 10 and over literate, virtually 100%. **Health** (2003): physicians 49 (1 per 1,253 persons); hospital beds 128 (1 per 480 persons); infant mortality rate per 1,000 live births (2005) 7.0.

Military

Military defense is the responsibility of the US.

Background

The Samoan islands were probably inhabited by Polynesians 2,500 years ago. Dutch explorers first arrived in 1722. A haven for runaway sailors and escaped convicts, the islands were ruled by native chiefs until c. 1860. The US gained the right to establish a naval station at Pago Pago in 1878, and the

US, Britain, and Germany administered a tripartite protectorate in 1889–99. The eastern islands were ceded to the US in 1904, and Swains Island was added in 1925. The first constitution was approved in 1960, and in 1977 the territory's first elected governor took office.

Recent Developments

American Samoa experienced labor shortages as US nationals returned to the US for job opportunities and local reservists departed for military service in 2007. Despite its population of 59,000, the territory had to look to independent Samoa for labor for its tuna-canning plants.

Internet resources: <www.americansamoa.gov>.

Andorra

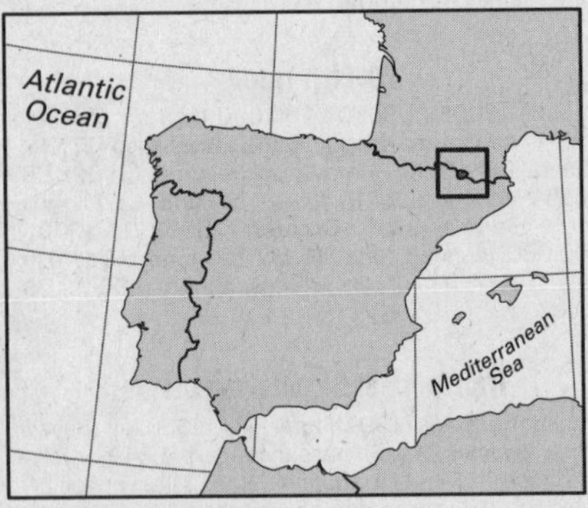

Official name: Principat d'Andorra (Principality of Andorra). **Form of government:** parliamentary coprincipality with one legislative house (General Council [28]). **Chiefs of state:** French President Nicolas Sarkozy (from 2007); Bishop of Urgell, Spain, Joan Enric Vives Sicília (from 2003). **Head of government:** Chief Executive Albert Pintat Santolària (from 2005). **Capital:** Andorra la Vella. **Official language:** Catalan. **Official religion:** none (Roman Catholicism enjoys special recognition in accordance with Andorran tradition). **Monetary unit:** 1 euro (€) = 100 cents; valuation (1 Jul 2008) US$1 = €0.63.

Demography

Area: 179 sq mi, 464 sq km. **Population** (2007): 82,600. **Density** (2007): persons per sq mi 461.5, persons per sq km 178.0. **Urban** (2003): 93%. **Sex distribution** (2005): male 52.16%; female 47.84%. **Age breakdown** (2005): under 15, 14.8%; 15–29, 19.4%; 30–44, 29.3%; 45–59, 20.2%; 60–74, 10.3%; 75–84, 4.2%; 85 and over, 1.8%. **Ethnic composition** (by nationality; 2005): Spanish 37.4%; Andorran 35.7%; Portuguese 13.0%; French 6.6%; British 1.3%; Moroccan 0.7%; Argentine 0.5%; other 4.8%. **Religious affiliation** (2000): Roman Catholic 89.1%; other Christian 4.3%; Muslim 0.6%; Hindu 0.5%; nonreligious 5.0%; other 0.5%. **Major urban areas** (2006): Andorra la Vella 24,211; Escaldes-Engordany 16,391; Encamp 13,685. **Location:** southwestern Europe, between France and Spain.

Vital statistics

Birth rate per 1,000 population (2005): 10.5 (world avg. 20.3). **Death rate** per 1,000 population (2005): 3.5 (world avg. 8.6). **Natural increase rate** per 1,000 population (2005): 7.0 (world avg. 11.7). **Total fertility rate** (avg. births per childbearing woman; 2006): 1.30. **Marriage rate** per 1,000 population (2005): 2.9. **Life expectancy** at birth (2006): male 80.6 years; female 86.6 years.

National economy

Budget (2005). *Revenue:* €308,500,000 (indirect taxes 70.9%; investment income 7.1%; taxes and other income 22.0%). *Expenditures:* €308,500,000 (current expenditures 52.6%; development expenditures 47.2%; financial operations 0.2%). **Public debt** (2004): US$278,000,000. **Production.** *Agriculture, forestry, fishing* (2005): tobacco 335 metric tons; other traditional crops include hay, potatoes, and grapes; livestock (number of live animals; 2004–05) 3,214 sheep, 1,572 cattle, 507 goats. *Quarrying:* small amounts of marble are quarried. *Manufacturing* (value of recorded exports in €'000; 2003): motor vehicles and parts 17,513; electrical machinery and apparatus 11,433; optical, photographic, and measuring apparatus 10,658. *Energy production (consumption):* electricity (kW-hr; 2005) 83,900,000 (568,000,000); petroleum products (metric tons; 1998) none (nearly 100,000). **Households** (2003). Average household size 2.8; expenditure per household €35,470 (US$40,034); expenditure: transportation 22.1%, food, beverages, and tobacco products 19.4%, housing and energy 16.1%, hotels and restaurants 7.8%, clothing and footwear 7.6%, recreation and culture 6.9%. **Population economically active** (2005): total 42,416; activity rate of total population 55% (participation rates: ages 15–64 [2003] 75.1%; female 45.8%). **Gross national income** (at 2006 market prices): US$3,337,000,000 (US$44,962 per capita). **Selected balance of payments data.** Disbursements for (US$'000,000; 2001–02): remittances 12. **Land use** as % of total land area (2000): in temporary and permanent crops 4%, in pasture 45%; overall forest area (2005) 36%.

Foreign trade

Imports (2005): €1,442,000,000 (food and beverages 16.6%; electrical machinery and apparatus 13.0%; motor vehicles 11.3%; clothing and knitwear 7.8%; perfumes, cosmetics, and soaps 7.4%; mineral fuels 4.6%). *Major import sources* (2005): Spain 53.2%; France 21.0%; Germany 5.6%; Japan 3.7%; Italy 3.2%. **Exports** (2005): €114,000,000 (food and beverages 28.7%; electrical machinery and apparatus 18.7%; motor vehicles 16.3%; optical equipment, photo equipment, and other professional goods 6.3%; perfumes, cosmetics, and soaps 3.0%). *Major export destinations* (2005): Spain 59.1%; France 17.0%; Germany 11.6%; UK 5.0%; Portugal 3.9%.

Transport and communications

Transport. *Roads* (1999): 269 km (paved 74%). *Vehicles* (2005): passenger cars 49,632; trucks and buses 4,621. **Communications,** in total units (units per 1,000 persons). Daily newspaper circulation (2004): 17,000 (232); televisions (2000): 36,000 (461); telephone landlines (2005): 35,000 (459); cellular telephone subscribers (2005): 65,000 (837); total Internet users (2005): 269,000 (284); broadband Internet subscribers (2005): 10,300 (134).

Education and health

Literacy: resident population is virtually 100% literate. **Health** (2003): physicians 244 (1 per 296 persons); hospital beds 233 (1 per 310 persons); infant mortality rate per 1,000 live births (2006) 4.0.

Military

Total active duty personnel: none. France and Spain are responsible for Andorra's external security; the police force is assisted in alternate years by either French gendarmerie or Barcelona police. Andorra has no defense budget.

Background

Andorra's independence is traditionally ascribed to Charlemagne, who recovered the region from the Muslims in 803. It was placed under the joint suzerainty of the French counts of Foix and the Spanish bishops of the See of Urgell in 1278, and it was subsequently governed jointly by the Spanish bishop of Urgell and the French head of state. This feudal system of government, the last in Europe, lasted until 1993, when a constitution was adopted that transferred most of the coprinces' powers to the Andorran General Council, a body elected by universal suffrage. Andorra has long had a strong affinity with Catalonia; its institutions are based in Catalonian law, and it is part of the diocese of the See of Urgell (Spain). The traditional economy was based on sheep raising, but tourism has been very important since the 1950s.

Recent Developments

No snow fell in Andorra until the middle of March 2007, and the skiing season was crippled. This was a blow to the tourism industry—the country's major source of revenue. It was feared that the number of visitors for 2007 would drop by at least 10%, but the actual number was about 2%.

Internet resources: <www.andorra.ad/en-US/>.

Angola

Official name: República de Angola (Republic of Angola). **Form of government:** unitary multiparty republic with one legislative house (National Assembly [220]). **Head of state and government:** President José Eduardo dos Santos (from 1979), assisted by Prime Minister Fernando da Piedade Dias dos Santos (from 2002). **Capital:** Luanda. **Official language:** Portuguese. **Official religion:** none. **Monetary unit:** 1 kwanza (AOA) = 100 lwei; valuation (1 Jul 2008) US$1 = refloated kwanza 75.01.

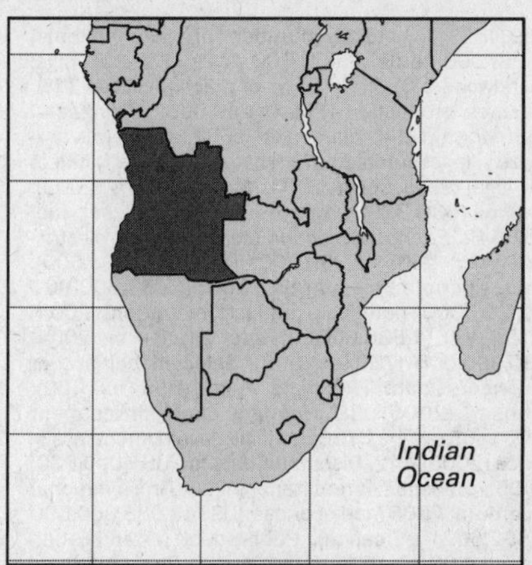

Demography

Area: 481,354 sq mi, 1,246,700 sq km. **Population** (2007): 12,264,000. **Density** (2007): persons per sq mi 25.5, persons per sq km 9.8. **Urban** (2005): 53.3%. **Sex distribution** (2005): male 50.48%; female 49.52%. **Age breakdown** (2005): under 15, 43.8%; 15–29, 26.5%; 30–44, 16.7%; 45–59, 8.5%; 60–74, 3.9%; 75 and over, 0.6%. **Ethnic composition** (2000): Ovimbundu 25.2%; Kimbundu 23.1%; Kongo 12.6%; Lwena (Luvale) 8.2%; Chokwe 5.0%; Kwanyama 4.1%; Nyaneka 3.9%; Luchazi 2.3%; Ambo (Ovambo) 2.0%; Mbwela 1.7%; Nyemba 1.7%; mixed race (Eurafrican) 1.0%; white 0.9%; other 8.3%. **Religious affiliation** (2001): Christian 94.1%, of which Roman Catholic 62.1%, Protestant 15.0%; traditional beliefs 5.0%; other 0.9%. **Major cities** (2004): Luanda (urban agglomeration; 2005) 2,766,000; Huambo 173,600; Lobito 137,400; Benguela 134,500; Namibe 132,900. **Location:** southern Africa, bordering the Democratic Republic of the Congo (DRC), Zambia, Namibia, and the Atlantic Ocean; the exclave of Cabinda on the Atlantic Ocean borders the Republic of the Congo and the DRC.

Vital statistics

Birth rate per 1,000 population (2006): 45.0 (world avg. 20.3). **Death rate** per 1,000 population (2006): 25.2 (world avg. 8.6). **Natural increase rate** per 1,000 population (2006): 19.8 (world avg. 11.7). **Total fertility rate** (avg. births per childbearing woman; 2006): 6.35. **Life expectancy** at birth (2006): male 36.5 years; female 38.2 years.

National economy

Budget (2004). *Revenue:* AOA 602,187,000,000 (tax revenue 99.1%, of which taxes on petroleum 77.9%; nontax revenue 0.9%). *Expenditures:* AOA 591,955,000,000 (current expenditure 87.6%; development expenditure 12.4%). **Households** (2002). Average household size 5.0; expenditure (Luanda only): food and nonalcoholic beverages 46.1%, housing and energy 12.3%, household furnishings 6.5%, transportation 6.5%. **Production** (metric tons except as noted). *Agriculture, forestry, fishing* (2005): cassava 8,606,210, corn (maize) 720,275, sweet potatoes

659,451; livestock (number of live animals) 4,150,000 cattle, 2,050,000 goats, 780,000 pigs; roundwood 4,670,000 cu m, of which fuelwood 77%; fisheries production (2004) 240,005. *Mining and quarrying* (2004): diamonds 6,631,000 carats (excludes illegal production estimated to be nearly half of the legal production in 2004). *Manufacturing* (2003): fuel oil 639,319; cement 500,620; diesel fuel 407,542. *Energy production (consumption):* electricity (kW-hr; 2004) 2,339,000,000 (2,339,000,000); crude petroleum (barrels; 2005) 453,300,000 (21,200,000); petroleum products (metric tons; 2004) 1,784,000 (1,836,000); natural gas (cu m; 2004) 730,000,000 (730,000,000). **Selected balance of payments data.** Receipts from (US$'000,000): tourism (2005) 88; foreign direct investment (2001–05 avg.) 1,750; official development assistance (2005) 442. Disbursements for (US$'000,000; 2005): tourism 74; remittances 215. **Gross national income** (at 2006 market prices): US$43,088,000,000 (US$2,602 per capita). **Public debt** (external, outstanding; 2005): US$9,428,000,000. **Population economically active** (1999): total 5,729,000; activity rate of total population 57.7% (participation rates: over age 10 [1991] 60.1%; female 38.4%; unemployed [2002] 70%). **Land use** as % of total land area (2003): in temporary crops 2.6%, in permanent crops 0.2%, in pasture 43.3%; overall forest area (2005) 47.4%.

Foreign trade

Imports (2005): US$8,353,000,000 (consumer goods 61.1%; capital goods 28.6%; intermediate goods 10.3%). *Major import sources:* South Korea 20.5%; Portugal 13.4%; US 12.5%; South Africa 7.4%; Brazil 7.0%. **Exports** (2005): US$24,109,400,000 (crude petroleum 93.7%; diamonds 4.5%; refined petroleum 1.0%). *Major export destinations:* US 39.8%; China 29.6%; France 7.8%; Chile 5.4%; Taiwan 4.4%.

Transport and communications

Transport. *Railroads* (2004): route length of lines in operation 850 km; (2001) passenger-km 3,722,300,000. *Roads* (2001): total length 51,429 km (paved 10%). *Vehicles* (2001): passenger cars 117,200; trucks and buses 118,300. *Air transport*: passenger-km (2001; TAAG airline only) 732,968,000; metric ton-km cargo (2004) 64,000,000. **Communications,** in total units (units per 1,000 persons). Daily newspaper circulation (2005): 51,000 (4.3); televisions (2003): 582,000 (52); telephone landlines (2005): 94,000 (7.9); cellular telephone subscribers (2005): 1,094,000 (92); personal computers (2004): 27,000 (2.3); total Internet users (2005): 176,000 (15).

Education and health

Literacy (2006): percentage of population ages 15 and over literate 67.4%; males literate 82.9%; females literate 54.2%. **Health:** physicians (2004) 1,165 (1 per 9,890 persons); hospital beds (2001) 13,810 (1 per 769 persons); infant mortality rate per 1,000 live births (2006) 186.6. **Food** (2005): daily per capita caloric intake 2,518 (vegetable products 92%, animal products 8%); 140% of FAO recommended minimum.

Military

Total active duty personnel (2006): 108,400 (army 92.3%, navy 2.2%, air force 5.5%). **Military expenditure as percentage of GDP** (2005): 5.7%; per capita expenditure US$140.

Background

An influx of Bantu-speaking peoples in the 1st millennium AD led to their dominance in the area by c. 1500. The most important Bantu kingdom was the Kongo; south of the Kongo was the Ndongo kingdom of the Mbundu people. Portuguese explorers arrived in 1483 and over time gradually extended their rule. Angola's frontiers were largely determined with other European nations in the 19th century, but not without severe resistance by the indigenous peoples. Its status as a Portuguese colony was changed to that of an overseas province in 1951. Resistance to colonial rule led to the outbreak of fighting in 1961, which led ultimately to independence in 1975. Rival factions continued fighting after independence; although a peace accord was reached in 1994, forces led by Jonas M. Savimbi continued to resist government control. The killing of Savimbi in February 2002 changed the political balance and led to the signing of a cease-fire agreement in Luanda in April that effectively ended the civil war.

Recent Developments

Angola made significant advances in 2007, significantly because of its status as the second largest producer of crude oil in Africa south of the Sahara. On 1 January the country became the 12th full member of OPEC, and Angola, already China's largest supplier of crude oil, began negotiating deals with Russia. In May the country was elected as a member of the UN Human Rights Council, and in the summer agreements on improving military relations and trade with South Africa were signed.

Internet resources: <www.angola.org>.

Antigua and Barbuda

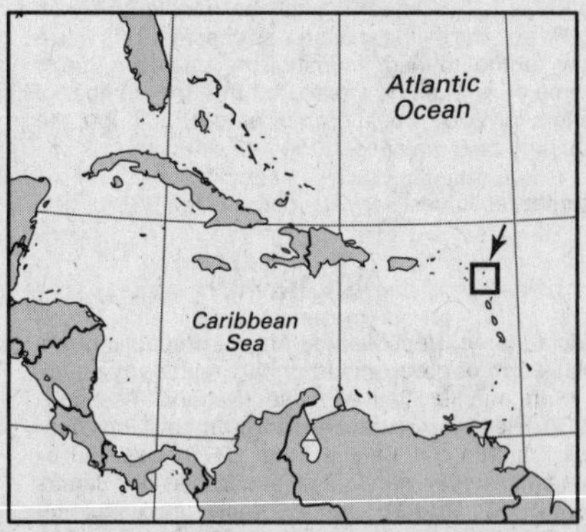

1 metric ton = about 1.1 short tons; 1 kilometer = 0.6 mi (statute); 1 metric ton-km cargo = about 0.68 short ton-mi cargo; c.i.f.: cost, insurance, and freight; f.o.b.: free on board

Official name: Antigua and Barbuda. **Form of government:** constitutional monarchy with two legislative houses (Senate [17]; House of Representatives [17]). **Chief of state:** British Queen Elizabeth II (from 1952), represented by Governor-General Louise Lake-Tack (from 2007). **Head of government:** Prime Minister Baldwin Spencer (from 2004). **Capital:** Saint John's. **Official language:** English. **Official religion:** none. **Monetary unit:** 1 Eastern Caribbean dollar (EC$) = 100 cents; valuation (1 Jul 2008) US$1 = EC$2.70.

Demography

Area: 171 sq mi, 442 sq km. **Population** (2007): 85,900. **Density** (2007): persons per sq mi 503.8, persons per sq km 194.5. **Urban** (2003): 37.7%. **Sex distribution** (2001): male 46.96%; female 53.04%. **Age breakdown** (2001): under 15, 28.3%; 15–29, 24.4%; 30–44, 25.0%; 45–59, 13.0%; 60–74, 6.2%; 75–84, 2.3%; 85 and over 0.8%. **Ethnic composition** (2000): black 82.4%; US white 12.0%; mulatto 3.5%; British 1.3%; other 0.8%. **Religious affiliation** (2001): Christian 74%, of which Anglican 23%, independent Christian 23%, other Protestant (including Methodist, Moravian, and Seventh-day Adventist) 28%; Rastafarian 2%; atheist/nonreligious 5%; other/unknown 19%. **Major towns** (2001): Saint John's (2004) 23,600; All Saints 3,412; Liberta 2,239; Potters Village 2,067; Codrington 980. **Location:** eastern Caribbean Sea.

Vital statistics

Birth rate per 1,000 population (2006): 16.9 (world avg. 20.3); (2001) within marriage 25.7%. **Death rate** per 1,000 population (2006): 5.4 (world avg. 8.6). **Natural increase rate** per 1,000 population (2006): 11.5 (world avg. 11.7). **Total fertility rate** (avg. births per childbearing woman; 2006): 2.24. **Life expectancy** at birth (2006): male 69.8 years; female 74.7 years.

National economy

Budget (2005). *Revenue:* EC$1,080,000,000 (tax revenue 42.1%, of which taxes on international transactions 25.9%, income taxes 5.9%; current nontax revenue 3.6%; development revenue 1.7%; grants 52.6%). *Expenditures:* EC$657,500,000 (current expenditures 85.7%, of which interest payments 13.6%; development expenditures 14.3%). **Production** (metric tons except as noted). *Agriculture, forestry, fishing* (2005): tropical fruit (including papayas, guavas, soursops, and oranges) 7,900, mangoes 1,430, melons 840, "Antiguan Black" pineapples 210; livestock (number of live animals) 19,000 sheep, 14,300 cattle; fisheries production (2004) 2,527. *Mining and quarrying:* crushed stone for local use. *Manufacturing:* manufactures include cement, handicrafts, and furniture, as well as electronic components for export. *Energy production (consumption):* electricity (kW-hr; 2004) 109,000,000 (109,000,000); petroleum products (metric tons; 2004) none (135,000). **Population economically active** (2001): total 39,564; activity rate of total population 51.5% (participation rates: ages 15–64, 77.0%; female 50.0%; unemployed 8.4%). **Households** (2001). Average household size 3.1; expenditure: housing 21.8%, food 21.4%, transportation and communications 15.4%, household furnishings 12.6%, clothing and footwear 11.1%. **Gross national income** (2005): US$885,000,000 (US$10,920 per capita). **Public debt** (external, outstanding; 2004): US$519,900,000. **Land use** as % of total land area (2003): in temporary crops 18%, in permanent crops 5%, in pasture 9%; overall forest area (2005) 21%. **Selected balance of payments data.** Receipts from (US$'000,000): tourism (2005) 327; remittances (2005) 11; foreign direct investment (2001–05 avg.) 118. Disbursements for (US$'000,000; 2005): tourism 40.

Foreign trade

Imports (1999): US$356,000,000 (machinery and equipment 32.2%; agricultural products 24.7%; basic manufactures 15.4%; petroleum products 10.5%). *Major import sources* (2004): US 21.6%; Singapore 17.1%; China 9.7%; Trinidad and Tobago 6.0%; Poland 5.4%. **Exports** (1999): US$37,800,000 (reexports [significantly, petroleum products reexported to neighboring islands] 60.3%, domestic exports 39.7%). *Major export destinations* (2004): Germany 49.3%; UK 29.1%; France 3.4%; Bermuda 2.9%; US 2.3%.

Transport and communications

Transport. *Roads* (2002): total length 1,165 km (paved 33%). *Vehicles:* passenger cars (1998) 24,000; trucks and buses (1995) 1,342. *Air transport* (2001): passenger-km 304,000,000; metric ton-km cargo 200,000. **Communications,** in total units (units per 1,000 persons). Televisions (2001): 34,000 (449); telephone landlines (2004): 38,000 (494); cellular telephone subscribers (2004): 54,000 (701); total Internet users (2005): 29,000 (373).

Education and health

Educational attainment (2001). Percentage of population ages 25 and over having: no formal schooling 0.6%; incomplete primary education 2.6%; complete primary 27.9%; secondary 43.6%; higher 25.3%. **Literacy** (2003): percentage of total population ages 15 and over literate 85.8%. **Health:** physicians (1999) 76 (1 per 867 persons); hospital beds (1996) 255 (1 per 269 persons); infant mortality rate per 1,000 live births (2006) 18.9. **Food** (2005): daily per capita caloric intake 2,045 (vegetable products 67%, animal products 33%).

Military

Total active duty personnel (2006): a 170-member defense force (army 73.5%, navy 26.5%) is part of the eastern Caribbean Regional Security System. **Military expenditure as percentage of GDP** (2004): 0.6%; per capita expenditure US$57.

Background

Christopher Columbus visited Antigua in 1493 and named it after a church in Seville, Spain. It was colonized in 1632 by English settlers, who imported African slaves to grow tobacco and sugarcane. Barbuda was colonized by the English in 1678. In 1834 its slaves were emancipated. Antigua (with Barbuda) was part of the British colony of the Leeward Islands from 1871 until that colony was defederated in 1956. The islands achieved full independence in 1981.

Recent Developments

The World Trade Organization (WTO) ruled in favor of Antigua and Barbuda in March 2007 in its case against the US for not complying with the WTO's 2005 ruling to cease blocking foreign Internet gambling operations from operating inside the US, and in May Antigua and Barbuda called on other WTO members to support its demand for compensation from the US. Meanwhile, Antigua and Barbuda continued to take steps to ensure that the country's financial system was not used for money laundering.

Internet resources: <www.antigua-barbuda.org>.

Argentina

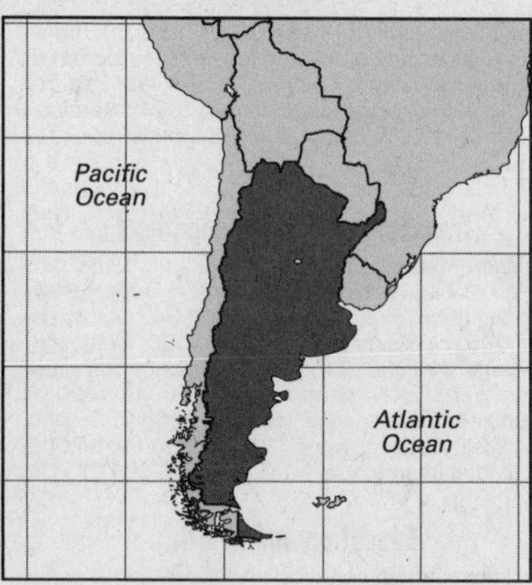

Official name: República Argentina (Argentine Republic). **Form of government:** federal republic with two legislative houses (Senate [72]; Chamber of Deputies [257]). **Head of state and government:** President Cristina Fernández de Kirchner (from 2007), assisted by Cabinet Chief Alberto Fernández (from 2003). **Capital:** Buenos Aires. **Official language:** Spanish. **Official religion:** Roman Catholicism. **Monetary unit:** 1 peso (ARS) = 100 centavos; valuation (1 Jul 2008) US$1 = ARS 3.02.

Demography

Area: 1,073,519 sq mi, 2,780,403 sq km. **Population** (2007): 39,531,000. **Density** (2007): persons per sq mi 36.8, persons per sq km 14.2. **Urban** (2003): 90.1%. **Sex distribution** (2005): male 48.90%; female 51.10%. **Age breakdown** (2005): under 15, 26.4%; 15–29, 25.5%; 30–44, 19.1%; 45–59, 15.0%; 60–74, 9.6%; 75–84, 3.5%; 85 and over, 0.9%. **Ethnic composition** (2000): European extraction 86.4%; mestizo 6.5%; Amerindian 3.4%; Arab 3.3%; other 0.4%. **Religious affiliation** (2000): Roman Catholic 79.8%; Protestant 5.4%; Muslim 1.9%; Jewish 1.3%; other 11.6%. **Major cities** (2001): Buenos Aires 2,776,138 (metropolitan area 11,460,575); Córdoba 1,267,521; San Justo 1,253,921; Rosario 908,163; La Plata 563,943. **Location:** southern South America, bordering Bolivia, Paraguay, Brazil, Uruguay, the South Atlantic Ocean, and Chile.

Vital statistics

Birth rate per 1,000 population (2004): 19.3 (world avg. 20.3). **Death rate** per 1,000 population (2004): 7.7 (world avg. 8.6). **Natural increase rate** per 1,000 population (2004): 11.6 (world avg. 11.7). **Total fertility rate** (avg. births per childbearing woman; 2006): 2.16. **Life expectancy** at birth (2006): male 72.4 years; female 80.1 years.

National economy

Budget (2005). *Revenue:* ARS 82,106,000,000 (tax revenue 77.4%; social security contributions 16.2%; nontax revenue 2.3%; other 4.1%). *Expenditures:* ARS 77,531,000,000 (current expenditure 88.2%, of which interest on debt 13.0%; capital expenditure 11.8%). **Public debt** (external, outstanding; 2005): US$61,952,000,000. **Gross national income** (at 2006 market prices): US$208,992,000,000 (US$5,340 per capita). **Production** (metric tons except as noted). *Agriculture, forestry, fishing* (2005): alfalfa (2004) 38,783,000, soybeans 38,300,000, corn (maize) 19,500,000, sugarcane 19,300,000, wheat 16,000,000; livestock (number of live animals; 2004) 50,768,000 cattle, 12,450,000 sheep, 3,655,000 horses; roundwood 14,917,000 cu m, of which fuelwood 37%; fisheries production 933,902. *Mining and quarrying* (2005): copper (metal content) 187,317; silver 263,766 kg; gold 27,904 kg. *Manufacturing* (value added in US$'000,000; 2002): food products 10,152; base metals 4,031; industrial and agricultural chemicals 2,770; refined petroleum products 2,514. *Energy production (consumption):* electricity (kW-hr; 2004) 100,260,000,000 (103,729,000,000); coal (metric tons; 2004) 51,000 (937,000); crude petroleum (barrels; 2005) 246,000,000 (161,000,000); petroleum products (metric tons; 2004) 25,224,000 (19,470,000); natural gas (cu m; 2004) 52,390,000,000 (43,459,000,000). **Selected balance of payments data.** Receipts from (US$'000,000): tourism (2005) 2,753; remittances (2005) 413; foreign direct investment (2001–05 avg.) 2,981; official development assistance (2005) 115 (commitments). Disbursements for (US$'000,000): tourism (2005) 2,817; remittances (2005) 279; foreign direct investment (2001–05 avg.) 381. **Population economically active** (2001): total 15,264,783; activity rate of total population 42.1% (participation rates: ages 14 and over 57.2%; female 40.9%; unemployed [October 2004–September 2005] 12.1%). **Households.** Average household size (2001) 3.6; average annual income per household (1996–97): ARS 12,972 (US$12,978); expenditure (1996–97): food products 26.8%, transportation and communications 15.0%, housing and energy 13.4%, health 10.2%. **Land use** as % of total land area (2000): in temporary crops 12.2%, in permanent crops 0.5%, in pasture 51.9%; overall forest area 12.7%.

Foreign trade

Imports (2005; f.o.b. in balance of trade and c.i.f. in commodities and trading partners): US$28,689,-

000,000 (electrical machinery and equipment 29.7%; transportation equipment 17.0%; chemicals 16.2%; plastic and rubber products 7.2%). *Major import sources:* Brazil 35.5%; US 14.1%; China 9.3%; Germany 4.5%; Mexico 2.8%. **Exports** (2005): US$40,106,000,000 (minerals 18.5%; vegetables 16.0%; food products 14.8%; fats and oils 8.2%; live animals 7.5%; transport equipment 7.4%; chemical products 6.1%). *Major export destinations:* Brazil 15.8%; US 11.4%; Chile 11.2%; China 9.1%; Spain 3.9%.

Transport and communications

Transport. *Railroads:* route length (2003) 35,753 km; passenger-km (2004) 7,526,000,000; metric ton-km cargo (2001) 11,603,000,000. *Roads* (2003): total length 233,000 km (paved 31%). *Vehicles*: passenger cars (2000) 5,386,700; commercial vehicles and buses (1998) 1,496,567. *Air transport* (2003): passenger-km 12,485,000,000; metric ton-km cargo 113,400,000. **Communications,** in total units (units per 1,000 persons). Daily newspaper circulation (2000): 1,471,000 (40); televisions (2004): 12,500,000 (323); telephone landlines (2006): 9,460,000 (242); cellular telephone subscribers (2006): 31,510,000 (805); personal computers (2005): 3,500,000 (90); total Internet users (2006): 8,184,000 (209); broadband Internet subscribers (2006): 1,568,000 (40).

Education and health

Educational attainment (2001). Percentage of population ages 15 and over having: no formal schooling 3.7%; incomplete primary education 14.2%; complete primary 28.0%; secondary 37.1%; some higher 8.3%; complete higher 8.7%. **Literacy** (2001): percentage of total population ages 10 and over literate 97.4%; males literate 97.4%; females literate 97.4%. **Health:** physicians (2004) 122,706 (1 per 312 persons); hospital beds (2000) 150,813 (1 per 244 persons); infant mortality rate (2006) 14.7. **Food** (2005): daily per capita caloric intake 2,854 (vegetable products 72%, animal products 28%); 122% of FAO recommended minimum.

Military

Total active duty personnel (2006): 71,400 (army 58.0%, navy 24.5%, air force 17.5%). **Military expenditure as percentage of GDP** (2005): 1.0%; per capita expenditure US$50.

Background

Little is known of Argentina's indigenous population before the Europeans' arrival. The area was explored for Spain by Sebastian Cabot in 1526–30; by 1580, Asunción, Santa Fe, and Buenos Aires had been settled. At first attached to the Viceroyalty of Peru (1620), it was later included with regions of modern Uruguay, Paraguay, and Bolivia in the Viceroyalty of the Río de la Plata, or Buenos Aires (1776). With the establishment of the United Provinces of the Río de la Plata in 1816, Argentina achieved its independence from Spain, but its boundaries were not set until the early 20th century. In 1943 the government was overthrown by the military; Col. Juan Perón took control in 1946. He in turn was overthrown in 1955. He returned to power in 1973 after two decades of turmoil. His second wife, Isabel, became president on his death in 1974 but lost power after a military coup in 1976. The military government tried to take the Falkland Islands (Islas Malvinas) in 1982 but was defeated by the British, with the result that the government returned to civilian rule in 1983. The government of Raúl Alfonsín worked to end the human rights abuses that characterized the former regimes. Hyperinflation led to public riots and Alfonsín's electoral defeat in 1989; his Peronist successor, Carlos Menem, instituted laissez-faire economic policies. In 1999 Fernando de la Rúa of the Alliance coalition was elected president, and his administration struggled with rising unemployment, foreign debt, and government corruption until the collapse of the government late in 2001.

Recent Developments

In October 2007 Cristina Fernández de Kirchner (see Biographies) became the first woman in Argentina's history to be directly elected president, following the decision by her husband, Néstor Kirchner, not to seek reelection. Elections to renew 130 of the 257 seats in the Chamber of Deputies and 24 of the 72 seats in the Senate were held as well, and the Front for Victory and allied parties supporting the candidacy of Fernández de Kirchner won 83 Chamber and 16 Senate seats, leading to coalition majorities in both. Fernández de Kirchner thus was expected to have little difficulty in passing her initial legislative program. The economy experienced robust growth during the year, with GDP increasing by 8%. Optimism was tempered by an inflation rate estimated at approximately 20%.

Internet resources: <www.sectur.gov.ar>.

Armenia

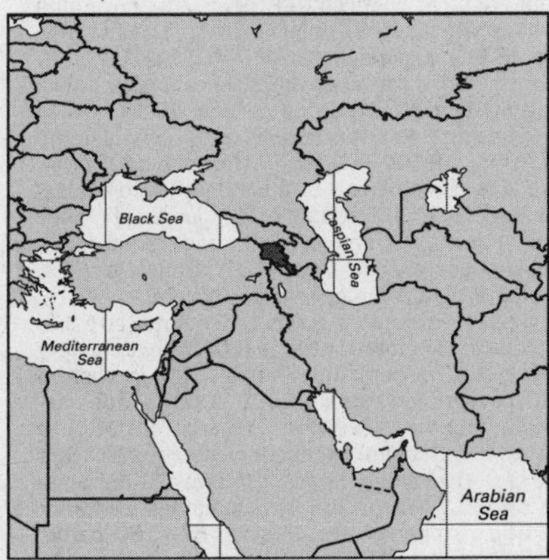

Official name: Hayastani Hanrapetut'yun (Republic of Armenia). **Form of government:** unitary multiparty republic with a single legislative body (National Assembly [131]). **Head of state:** President Robert Kocharyan (from 1998). **Head of government:** Prime Minister Serzh Sarkisyan (from 2007). **Capital:** Yerevan. **Official language:** Armenian. **Official religion:** none, but the Armenian Apostolic Church (Armenian Orthodox Church) has special status per 1991 religious law. **Monetary unit:** 1 dram (AMD) = 100 lumas; valuation (1 Jul 2008) US$1 = 303.00 drams.

Demography

Area: 11,484 sq mi, 29,743 sq km; in addition, about 16% of neighboring Azerbaijan (including the 1,700-sq mi [4,400-sq km] geographic region of Nagorno-Karabakh [Armenian: Artsakh]) has been occupied by Armenian forces since 1993. **Population** (2007): 3,002,000. **Density** (2007): persons per sq mi 261.4, persons per sq km 100.9. **Urban** (2006): 64.1%. **Sex distribution** (2006): male 48.28%; female 51.72%. **Age breakdown** (2005): under 15, 20.9%; 15–29, 27.2%; 30–44, 19.5%; 45–59, 17.9%; 60–74, 10.2%; 75–84, 3.8%; 85 and over, 0.5%. **Ethnic composition** (2001): Armenian 97.9%; Kurdish 1.3%; Russian 0.5%; other 0.3%. **Religious affiliation** (2005): Armenian Apostolic (Orthodox) 72.9%; Roman Catholic 4.0%; Sunni Muslim 2.4%; other Christian 1.3%; Yazidi 1.3%; other/nonreligious 18.1%. **Major cities** (2006): Yerevan 1,103,800; Gyumri 148,300; Vanadzor 105,500; Vagharshapat 56,700; Hrazdan 52,800. **Location:** southwestern Asia, bordering Georgia, Azerbaijan, Iran, and Turkey.

Vital statistics

Birth rate per 1,000 population (2005): 11.7 (world avg. 20.3); within marriage 88.5%. **Death rate** per 1,000 population (2005): 8.2 (world avg. 8.6). **Natural increase rate** per 1,000 population (2005): 3.5 (world avg. 11.7). **Total fertility rate** (avg. births per childbearing woman; 2006): 1.33. **Life expectancy** at birth (2005): male 70.3 years; female 76.5 years.

National economy

Budget (2005). *Revenue:* AMD 374,746,900,000 (tax revenue 81.2%, of which VAT 39.2%, tax on profits 12.4%, excise tax 10.3%, income tax 7.1%; nontax revenue 18.8%). *Expenditures:* AMD 417,505,900,000 (defense 15.4%; education and science 14.6%; public administration 10.6%; social security 10.6%; police 8.4%; health 7.4%). **Public debt** (external, outstanding; 2005): US$923,000,000. **Households** (2005). Average household size 3.8; money income per household AMD 1,720,195 (US$3,758); sources of money income: rent, self-employment, and remittances 38.9%, wages and salaries 34.5%, transfers 7.1%, other 19.5%; expenditure: food and beverages 56.6%, services 24.0%, nonfood goods 14.3%, tobacco 5.1%. **Land use** as % of total land area (2003): in temporary crops 17.6%, in permanent crops 2.1%, in pasture 29.6%; overall forest area (2005) 10.0%. **Gross national income** (2006): US$6,152,000,000 (US$2,040 per capita). **Production** (metric tons except as noted). *Agriculture, forestry, fishing* (2005): potatoes 564,211, wheat 258,361, tomatoes 234,948; livestock (number of live animals) 573,260 cattle, 556,597 sheep, 4,590,000 chickens; roundwood 41,000 cu m, of which fuelwood 10%; fisheries production (2004) 1,031 (from aquaculture 79%). *Mining and quarrying* (2004): copper concentrate (metal content) 17,600; molybdenum (metal content) 3,000; gold (metal content) 2,100 kg. *Manufacturing* (value of production in AMD '000,000; 2005): base and fabricated metals 259,305; food products and beverages 202,057; construction materials 23,648; 320,000 carats of cut diamonds were processed in 2004. *Energy production (consumption):* electricity (kW-hr; 2006) 5,941,000,000 ([2005] 5,503,000,000); petroleum products (metric tons; 2004) none (300,000); natural gas (cu m; 2004) none (1,300,000,000). **Population economically active:** total (2004) 1,196,500; activity rate of total population (2001) 49.5% (participation rates: ages 15–64 [2001] 72.1%; female [2004] 48.2%; officially unemployed [2006] 7.4%). **Selected balance of payments data.** Receipts from (US$'000,000): tourism (2005) 141; remittances (2006) 1,175; foreign direct investment (2001–05) 165; official development assistance (2005) 312 (commitments). Disbursements for (US$'000,000): tourism (2005) 117; remittances (2006) 148.

Foreign trade

Imports (2005): US$1,801,735,900 (precious and semiprecious stones [mostly rough diamonds] 19.3%; food products 15.1%; mineral fuels 14.7%; machinery and apparatus 8.7%; motor vehicles 8.1%). *Major import sources:* Russia 13.5%; Belgium 8.0%; Germany 7.8%; Ukraine 7.0%; Turkmenistan 6.3%. **Exports** (2005): US$973,920,500 (base and fabricated metals 34.7%; precious and semiprecious stones [nearly all cut diamonds] 34.5%; beverages [nearly all wine and grape brandy] 8.7%; metal ores and scrap 5.3%). *Major export destinations:* Germany 15.6%; The Netherlands 13.7%; Belgium 12.8%; Russia 12.2%; Israel 11.5%.

Transport and communications

Transport (2005). *Railroads:* length 732 km; passenger-km 26,600,000; metric ton-km cargo 654,100,000. *Roads:* length 7,515 km (paved 69%). *Air transport:* passenger-km 959,500,000; metric ton-km cargo 10,700,000. **Communications,** in total units (units per 1,000 persons). Daily newspaper circulation (2004): 27,000 (9); televisions (2003): 687,000 (229); telephone landlines (2005): 537,000 (180); cellular telephone subscribers (2005): 320,000 (107); personal computers (2004): 200,000 (67); total Internet users (2005): 161,000 (54); broadband Internet subscribers (2004): 1,000 (0.3).

Education and health

Educational attainment (2001). Percentage of population ages 25 and over having: no formal schooling 0.7%; primary education 13.0%; completed secondary and some postsecondary 66.0%; higher 20.3%. **Literacy** (2006): total population ages 15 and over literate, virtually 100%. **Health** (2005): physicians 12,307 (1 per 242 persons); hospital beds 14,353 (1 per 208 persons); infant mortality rate per 1,000 live births 12.3. **Food** (2005): daily per capita caloric intake 2,379 (vegetable products 80%, animal products 20%); 120% of FAO recommended minimum.

Military

Total active duty personnel (2006): 48,160 (army 93.4%, air force 6.6%); Russian troops (2006) 3,500. **Military expenditure as percentage of GDP** (2005): 2.7%; per capita expenditure US$46.

Background

Armenia is a successor state to a historical region in southwestern Asia. Historical Armenia's boundaries have varied considerably, but the region extended over what is now northeastern Turkey and the Republic of Armenia. The area was later conquered by the Medes and the Macedonians and still later allied with the Roman Empire. Armenia adopted Christianity as its national religion in AD 303. It came under the rule of the Ottoman Turks in 1514. Over the next centuries, as parts were ceded to other rulers, nationalism arose among the scattered Armenians; by the late 19th century it was causing widespread disruption. Fighting between Turks and Russians escalated when part of Armenia was ceded to Russia in 1878, and it continued through World War I, leading to Armenian deaths on a genocidal scale. With the Turkish defeat, the Russian-controlled part of Armenia was set up as a Soviet republic in 1921. Armenia became a constituent republic of the USSR in 1936. With the latter's dissolution in the late 1980s, Armenia declared its independence in 1990. It fought Azerbaijan for control over Nagorno-Karabakh until a cease-fire in 1994. About one-fifth of the population left the country beginning in 1993 because of an energy crisis. Political tension escalated, and in 1999 the prime minister and some legislators were killed in a terrorist attack on the legislature.

Recent Developments

The strong economic growth of recent years continued in Armenia as GDP increased by 13.8% in 2007. On 19 March Pres. Robert Kocharyan and Iranian Pres. Mahmoud Ahmadinejad inaugurated the first section of a pipeline that provided Armenia with Iranian natural gas. The 19 January murder in Istanbul of Armenian author Hrant Dink triggered widespread outrage in Armenia. Armenian officials nonetheless continued trying to persuade Turkey to open its border as a prelude to establishing diplomatic relations.

Internet resources: <www.armeniaemb.org>.

Aruba

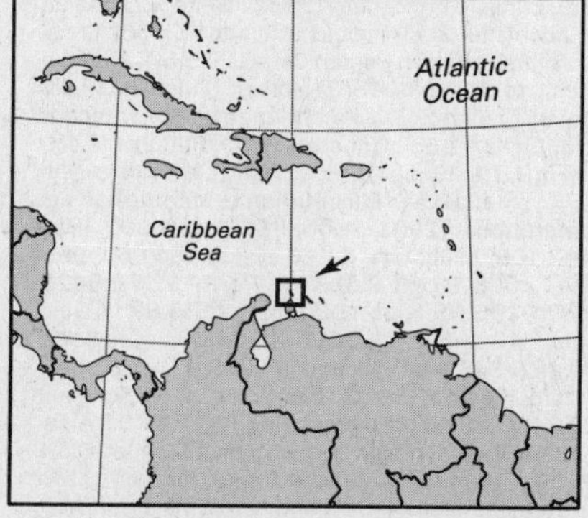

Official name: Aruba. **Political status:** nonmetropolitan territory of The Netherlands with one legislative house (States of Aruba [21]). **Chief of state:** Dutch Queen Beatrix (from 1980), represented by Governor Fredis Refunjol (from 2004). **Head of government:** Prime Minister Nelson O. Oduber (from 2001). **Capital:** Oranjestad. **Official language:** Dutch. **Official religion:** none. **Monetary unit:** 1 Aruban florin (Af.) = 100 cents; pegged to the US dollar at a fixed rate of Af. 1.79 = $1.

Demography

Area: 75 sq mi, 193 sq km. **Population** (2007): 105,000. **Density** (2007): persons per sq mi 1,400.0, persons per sq km 544.0. **Urban** (2003): 45.4%. **Sex distribution** (2005): male 47.72%; female 52.28%. **Age breakdown** (2005): under 15, 21.2%; 15–29, 18.9%; 30–44, 26.1%; 45–59, 21.3%; 60–74, 9.6%; 75–84, 2.2%; 85 and over, 0.7%. **Linguistic composition** (2000): Papiamento 69.4%; Spanish 13.2%; English 8.1%; Dutch 6.1%; Portuguese 0.3%; other 2.0%; unknown 0.9%. **Religious affiliation** (2005): Roman Catholic 82.7%, Protestant 10.2%, other/nonreligious 7.1%. **Major urban areas** (2000): Oranjestad 26,355; San Nicolas 15,848. **Location:** southern Caribbean Sea, north of Venezuela.

Vital statistics

Birth rate per 1,000 population (2005): 12.3 (world avg. 20.3); within marriage 50.8%. **Death rate** per 1,000 population (2005): 4.8 (world avg. 8.6). **Total fertility rate** (avg. births per childbearing woman; 2006): 1.79. **Life expectancy** at birth (2006): male 76.0 years; female 82.8 years.

National economy

Budget (2005). *Revenue:* Af. 907,300,000 (tax revenue 85.7%, of which taxes on income and profits 40.0%, sales tax 29.2%; nontax revenue 11.2%; grants 3.1%). *Expenditures:* Af. 1,032,200,000 (wages 29.5%; goods and services 14.8%; social security contributions 13.1%; interest 8.1%). **Production** (metric tons except as noted). *Agriculture, forestry, fishing:* aloes are cultivated for export; small amounts of tomatoes, beans, cucumbers, gherkins, watermelons, and lettuce are grown on hydroponic farms; divi-divi pods, sour orange fruit, sorghum, and peanuts (groundnuts) are nonhydroponic crops of limited value; fisheries production (2004) 162. *Mining and quarrying:* excavation of sand for local use. *Manufacturing:* refined petroleum, rum, cigarettes, aloe products, and soaps. *Energy production (consumption):* electricity (kW-hr; 2004) 816,000,000 (816,000,000); crude petroleum (barrels; 2004) 880,000 (3,335,000); petroleum products (metric tons; 2004) none (247,000). **Gross national income** (2006): US$2,244,000,000 (US$21,625 per capita). **Population economically active** (2004): total 41,500; activity rate of total population 42.6% (participation rates: ages 15–64 [2000] 70.9%; female [2000] 46.6%; unemployed [2005] 6.9%). **Public debt** (external, outstanding; 2005): US$478,700,000. **Households.** Average household size (2000) 3.1; average annual income per household (1999) Af. 39,000 (US$21,800); expenditure (2000): housing 23.0%, transportation and communications 19.7%, food 14.7%, clothing and footwear 10.9%, household furnishings 10.0%, recreation and education 8.0%. **Land use** as % of total land area (2003): in temporary crops 11%; overall forest area (2005) 2%.

Selected balance of payments data. Receipts from (US$'000,000): tourism (2005) 1,096; remittances (2006) 13; foreign direct investment (2001–05 avg.) 98. Disbursements for (US$'000,000): tourism (2005) 241; remittances (2006) 69.

Foreign trade

Imports (2005): Af. 7,614,000,000 (crude petroleum 77.6%; electrical and nonelectrical machinery 4.1%; food products 2.3%). *Major import sources* (excluding petroleum): US 60.4%; The Netherlands 11.7%; Venezuela 2.8%; Netherlands Antilles 2.8%. **Exports** (2005): Af. 7,830,000,000 (refined petroleum 99.4%). *Major export destinations* (excluding petroleum): US 48.5%; Netherlands Antilles 21.3%; The Netherlands 15.4%; Venezuela 4.1%.

Transport and communications

Transport. *Roads* (1995): total length 800 km (paved 64%). *Vehicles* (2005): passenger cars 49,521; trucks and buses 1,207. *Air transport* (2001; Air Aruba only): passenger-km 800,000,000. **Communications,** in total units (units per 1,000 persons). Daily newspaper circulation (2004): 33,900 (348); televisions (2001): 20,000 (218); telephone landlines (2002): 37,000 (397); cellular telephone subscribers (2004): 98,000 (1,002); total Internet users (2002): 24,000 (257).

Education and health

Educational attainment (2000). Percentage of population ages 25 and over having: no formal schooling or incomplete primary education 9.7%; primary education 33.9%; secondary/vocational 39.2%; advanced vocational/higher 16.2%. **Literacy** (2000): percentage of total population ages 13 and over literate 97.3%. **Health** (2005): physicians 144 (1 per 699 persons); hospital beds 310 (1 per 330 persons); infant mortality rate per 1,000 live births (2003–05) 6.0.

Military

Total active duty personnel (2005): more than 1,000 Dutch naval personnel (including 400 marines) are stationed in the Aruba/Netherlands Antilles vicinity.

Background

Aruba's earliest inhabitants were Arawak Indians, whose cave drawings can still be seen. Though the Dutch took possession of Aruba in 1636, they did not begin to develop it aggressively until 1816. In 1986 Aruba seceded from the Federation of the Netherlands Antilles in an initial step toward independence.

Recent Developments

Aruba received high marks in September 2007 from American ratings agency Fitch, which commented favorably on the island's market-friendly institutional environment, high per capita income, and political and social stability. In December officials on Aruba closed their investigation into the disappearance of American teenager Natalee Holloway, missing since 2005, but a secretly taped confession led them to reopen the case in early 2008.

Internet resources: <www.aruba.com>.

Australia

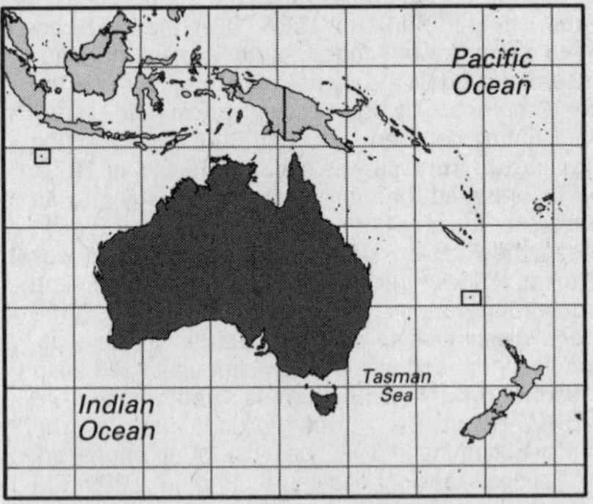

Official name: Commonwealth of Australia. **Form of government:** federal parliamentary state (formally a constitutional monarchy) with two legislative houses (Senate [76]; House of Representatives [150]). **Chief of state:** British Queen Elizabeth II (from 1952), represented by Governor-General Michael Jeffery (from 2003). **Head of government:** Prime Minister Kevin Rudd (from 2007). **Capital:** Canberra. **Official language:** English. **Official religion:** none. **Monetary unit:** 1 Australian dollar ($A) = 100 cents; valuation (1 Jul 2008) US$1 = $A 1.05.

Demography

Area: 2,969,978 sq mi, 7,692,208 sq km. **Population** (2007): 20,857,000. **Density** (2007): persons per sq mi 7.0, persons per sq km 2.7. **Urban** (2005): 88.2%. **Sex distribution** (2006): male 49.78%; female 50.22%. **Age breakdown** (2006): under 15, 19.8%; 15–29, 20.1%; 30–44, 21.9%; 45–59, 20.1%; 60–74, 11.7%; 75–84, 4.8%; 85 and over, 1.6%. **Ethnic composition** (2001): white 92%; Asian 6%; aboriginal 2%. **Religious affiliation** (2006): Christian 63.9%, of which Roman Catholic 25.6%, Anglican Church of Australia 18.7%, other Christian 19.6% (Uniting Church 5.7%, Presbyterian 2.9%, Orthodox 2.6%, Baptist 1.6%, Lutheran 1.3%); Buddhist 2.1%; Muslim 1.7%; Hindu 0.7%; Jewish 0.4%; no religion 18.7%; other 12.5%. **Major urban centers/urban agglomerations** (2001/2006): Sydney 3,502,301/4,293,105; Melbourne 3,160,171/3,684,461; Brisbane 1,508,161/1,820,375; Perth 1,176,542/-1,507,949; Adelaide 1,002,127/138,833; Gold Coast 421,557/ (2005) 482,000; Canberra 339,727/328,441; Newcastle 279,975/512,131; Gosford (Central Coast) 255,429/n.a.; Wollongong 228,846/276,155. **Place of birth** (2006): 70.9% native-born; 29.1% foreign-born, of which Europe 10.5% (UK 5.2%, Italy 1.0%, Greece 0.6%, Germany 0.5%, The Netherlands 0.4%, Poland 0.3%), Asia and Mid-

1 metric ton = about 1.1 short tons; 1 kilometer = 0.6 mi (statute); 1 metric ton-km cargo = about 0.68 short ton-mi cargo; c.i.f.: cost, insurance, and freight; f.o.b.: free on board

dle East 7.3% (China [including Hong Kong] 1.4%, Vietnam 0.8%, India 0.7%), New Zealand 2.0%, Africa, the Americas, and other 9.3%. **Location**: Oceania, continent between the Indian Ocean and the South Pacific Ocean. **Mobility** (1999). Population ages 15 and over living in the same residence as in 1998: 84.4%; different residence between states, regions, and neighborhoods 15.6%. **Households** (2006). Total number of households 8,058,248. Average household size 2.6; 1 person (2003–04) 25.4%, 2 persons (2003–04) 33.9%, 3 or more persons (2003–04) 40.7%. Family households 5,665,000 (70.3%); nonfamily 2,393,000 (29.7%), of which 1-person 26.5%. **Immigration** (2004–05): permanent immigrants admitted 123,400, from UK 14.7%, New Zealand 14.0%, China 9.0%, India 7.6%, Sudan 4.6%, South Africa 3.7%, Philippines 3.4%, Malaysia 2.4%, Singapore 2.4%, Sri Lanka 1.9%, Vietnam 1.8%, Iraq 1.5%. Refugee arrivals 13,200. Emigration 59,200.

Vital statistics

Birth rate per 1,000 population (2006): 12.8 (world avg. 20.3); (2005) within marriage 67.8%. **Death rate** per 1,000 population (2006): 6.5 (world avg. 8.6). **Natural increase rate** per 1,000 population (2006): 6.3 (world avg. 11.7). **Total fertility rate** (avg. births per childbearing woman; 2005): 1.81. **Life expectancy** at birth (2005): male 78.5 years; female 83.3 years.

Social indicators

Quality of working life. Average workweek (2005) 34.7 hours. Working 50 hours a week or more (2003) 28.8%. Annual rate per 100,000 workers for: accidental injury and industrial disease (2004) 1,220; death (2004) 1.0. Proportion of employed persons insured for damages or income loss resulting from: injury 100%; permanent disability 100%; death 100%. Working days lost to industrial disputes per 1,000 employees (2006) 22. Means of transportation to work (2003): private automobile 74.5%; public transportation 12.0%; motorcycle, bicycle, and foot 5.7%. Discouraged job seekers (2006) 52,900 (0.5% of labor force). **Educational attainment** (2005). Percentage of population ages 15–64 having: no formal schooling through incomplete secondary education 48.5%; complete secondary through postsecondary, technical, or other certificate/diploma 28.9%; bachelor's degree 14.2%; incomplete graduate and graduate degree or diploma 5.4%; unknown 3.0%. **Social participation.** Eligible voters participating in last national election (2007) 94%; voting is compulsory. Trade union membership in total workforce (2006) 20%. **Social deviance** (2005). Offense rate per 100,000 population for: murder 1.3; sexual assault (2003) 92; assault (2003) 798; auto theft 419; burglary and housebreaking (2004) 1,534; robbery 69. Incidence per 100,000 in general population of: prisoners 124; suicide 10.3. **Material well-being** (2005). Households possessing: automobile (1995) 85.0%; refrigerator 99.9%; washing machine 96.4%; dishwasher 41.5%.

National economy

Gross national income (2006): US$747,304,-000,000 (US$36,400 per capita). **Budget** (2005–06). *Revenue:* $A 225,513,000,000 (tax revenue 91.6%, of which individual 50.7%, corporate 21.7%, excise duties and sales tax 15.3%; nontax revenue 8.4%). *Expenditures:* $A 209,797,000,000 (social security and welfare 41.2%; health 17.9%; economic services 8.0%; public services 8.0%; education 7.9%; defense 7.5%; interest on public debt 2.6%; other 6.6%). **Public debt** (2002–03): $A 69,926,000,000. **Production** (gross value in $A '000 except as noted). *Agriculture, forestry, fishing* (2004–05): livestock (slaughtered value) 12,030,200 (cattle 7,828,800, sheep and lambs 1,949,000, poultry 1,303,700, pigs 906,000); wheat 4,316,500, wool 2,195,500, grapes 1,508,200, barley 1,233,300, sugarcane 979,500, seed cotton 945,100, apples 529,000, canola 503,000, potatoes 434,000, bananas 327,000, oranges 310,000, sorghum 270,000, oats 171,800, carrots 166,000; livestock (number of live animals; 2005) 101,125,000 sheep, 27,782,000 cattle, 2,538,000 pigs, 78,187,000 poultry; roundwood (2005) 30,529,000 cu m, of which fuelwood 10%; fisheries production (2005) 293,022 (from aquaculture 16%); aquatic plants production 14,167. *Mining and quarrying* (metric tons except as noted; 2005): iron ore (metal content) 280,000,000 (world rank: 3); bauxite 58,000,000 (world rank: 1); zinc (metal content) 1,400,000 (world rank: 2); ilmenite 1,140,000 (world rank: 1); copper (metal content) 930,000 (world rank: 5); lead (metal content) 760,000 (world rank: 2); nickel (metal content) 210,000 (world rank: 2); rutile 160,000 (world rank: 1); cobalt (metal content) 6,600 (world rank: 3); opal (value of production; 2003) $A 65,000,000 (world rank: 1); diamonds 22,700,000 carats (world rank by volume: 1); gold 254,000 kg (world rank: 2). *Manufacturing* (gross value added in $A '000,000; 2004–05): food, beverages, and tobacco 19,076; machinery and apparatus 18,185; fabricated metal products 17,483; mineral fuels 12,817; printing and publishing 10,095; wood and paper products 6,924; cement, bricks, and ceramics 4,852; textiles and wearing apparel 2,621. *Energy production (consumption):* electricity (kW-hr; 2006) 228,918,000,000 ([2004] 230,497,-000,000); hard coal (metric tons; 2006) 400,000,000 ([2004] 32,900,000); lignite (metric tons; 2005–06) 71,000,000 ([2004] 100,700,000); crude petroleum (barrels; 2006–07) 171,900,000 ([2005] 320,200,000); petroleum products (metric tons; 2004) 33,302,000 (34,264,000); natural gas (cu m; 2006) 38,883,000,000 ([2004] 28,399,000,000). **Population economically active** (July 2007): total 10,952,000; activity rate of total population 52.5% (participation rates: ages 15 and over 65.0%; female [2006] 45.0%; unemployed 4.3%). **Households** (2003–04). Average household size (2006) 2.6; average annual disposable income per household $A 47,528 (US$33,745); sources of income: wages and salaries 57.5%, transfer payments 27.7%, self-employment 6.0%, other 8.8%; expenditure: food and nonalcoholic beverages 17.1%, housing 16.1%, transportation and communications 15.6%, recreation 12.8%, household services and operation 6.1%. **Selected balance of payments data.** Receipts from (US$'000,000): tourism (2005) 14,940; remittances (2006) 3,064; foreign direct investment (FDI) (2001–05 avg.) 8,715. Disbursements for (US$'000,000): tourism (2005) 11,282; remittances (2006) 2,681; FDI (2001–05 avg.) 2,536. **Land use** as % of total land area (2003): in temporary crops 6.1%, in permanent crops 0.04%, in pasture 51.0%; overall forest area (2005) 21.3%.

Foreign trade

Imports (2005–06; f.o.b.): $A 167,603,000,000 (machinery and apparatus 29.3%, of which telecommunications equipment 5.8%, office machines and automatic data-processing equipment 5.3%, electrical machinery 4.8%; transportation equipment 15.8%, of which motor vehicles 12.2%; crude and refined petroleum 12.7%; chemicals and related products 6.1%, of which medicines and pharmaceuticals 4.3%; textiles and wearing apparel 3.9%). *Major import sources* (2006–07): China 15.0%; US 13.8%; Malaysia 3.7%; Japan 9.6%; Singapore 5.6%; Germany 5.1%; UK 4.1%; Thailand 4.0%; South Korea 3.3%; New Zealand 3.1%. **Exports** (2005–06; f.o.b.): $A 151,792,000,000 (mineral fuels 24.9%, of which coal [all forms] 16.0%, petroleum products and natural gas 8.9%; food and beverages 12.0%, of which meat and meat preparations 4.4%, cereals and cereal preparations 3.2%; iron ore 8.2%; aluminum and aluminum ore 6.9%; gold 4.8%; machinery and apparatus 4.1%; transportation equipment 3.5%). *Major export destinations* (2006–07): Japan 19.4%; China 13.6%; South Korea 7.8%; US 5.8%; New Zealand 5.6%; UK 3.7%; Taiwan 3.7%; Singapore 2.7%; Indonesia 2.5%; Thailand 2.5%.

Transport and communications

Transport. *Railroads* (2006): route length 38,550 km; passenger-km (2004–05) 11,200,000,000; metric ton-km cargo (2004–05) 182,990,000,000. *Roads* (2004): total length 810,641 km (paved 42%). *Vehicles* (2006): passenger cars 11,189,000; trucks and buses 2,665,000. *Air transport* (2006; domestic carriers only): passenger-km 88,173,000,000; metric ton-km cargo 2,633,000,000. **Communications**, in total units (units per 1,000 persons). Daily newspaper circulation (2004): 2,934,000 (146); televisions (2003): 14,371,000 (722); telephone landlines (2006): 9,940,000 (483); cellular telephone subscribers (2006): 19,760,000 (960); personal computers (2005): 14,007,000 (689); total Internet users (2006): 15,300,000 (743); broadband Internet subscribers (2006): 3,900,000 (189).

Education and health

Literacy (2006): total population literate, virtually 100%. **Health** (2005–06): physicians 63,300 (1 per 322 persons); hospital beds (2005) 83,349 (1 per 244 persons); infant mortality rate per 1,000 live births 5.0. **Food** (2005): daily per capita caloric intake 3,101 (vegetable products 68%, animal products 32%).

Military

Total active duty personnel (2006): 51,610 (army 48.9%, navy 24.6%, air force 26.5%). **Military expenditure as percentage of GDP** (2005): 1.8%; per capita expenditure US$645.

Background

Australia has long been inhabited by Aborigines, who arrived on the continent 40,000–60,000 years ago. Estimates of the population at the time of European settlement in 1788 range from 300,000 to more than 1,000,000. Widespread European knowledge of Australia began with 17th-century explorations. The Dutch landed in 1616 and the British in 1688, but the first large-scale expedition was that of James Cook in 1770, which established Britain's claim to Australia. The first English settlement, at Port Jackson (1788), consisted mainly of convicts and seamen; convicts were to make up a large proportion of the incoming settlers. By 1859 the colonial nuclei of all Australia's states had been formed, but with devastating effects on the Aborigines, whose population declined sharply with the introduction of European diseases and weaponry. Britain granted its colonies limited self-government in the mid-19th century, and Australia achieved federation in 1901. Australia fought alongside the British in World War I, notably at Gallipoli, and again in World War II, preventing the occupation of Australia by the Japanese. It joined the US in the Korean and Vietnam wars. Since the 1960s the government has sought to deal more fairly with the Aborigines, and a loosening of immigration restrictions has led to a more heterogeneous population. Constitutional links allowing British interference in government were formally abolished in 1968, and Australia has assumed a leading role in Asian and Pacific affairs. During the 1990s it experienced several debates about giving up its British ties and becoming a republic.

Recent Developments

Australia's Prime Minister John Howard was defeated in an election in November 2007, bringing an end to more than a decade of conservative government. Opposition leader Kevin Rudd of the Australian Labor Party won handily, and Howard lost not only the premiership but also his own seat in Parliament. Rudd announced major changes to Australian domestic and international policies. Immediately after taking his oath as prime minister, he fulfilled one of his campaign promises by ratifying the Kyoto Protocol, which Howard had vehemently opposed. Rudd also began the promised withdrawal of Australian combat troops from Iraq in June 2008. His new cabinet featured seven women, including Deputy Prime Minister Julia Gillard. Public opinion during the year was deeply affected by the plight of Aboriginal children in remote communities, and many people demanded that the government take measures to end domestic violence and sexual assaults. In August laws were passed allowing federal intervention in Aboriginal communities, and the government promised to spend more than $A 587 million (about US$470 million) in a wide-ranging reform program that involved banning alcohol and pornography and acquiring control of townships through five-year leases. The Australian economy remained strong. Strong company tax receipts and less expenditure on welfare provided a surplus of $A 17.3 billion (about US$14 billion) in 2007. GDP growth that year was 3.9%, and by midyear 2008 unemployment had fallen to 4.1%. The Howard government announced in 2007 that it intended to sell uranium to India for peaceful purposes. Howard also decided to canvass possible sales of uranium to Russia and signed a deal with Russian Pres. Vladimir Putin when Putin visited Australia during the Asia-Pacific Economic Cooperation

1 metric ton = about 1.1 short tons; 1 kilometer = 0.6 mi (statute); 1 metric ton-km cargo = about 0.68 short ton-mi cargo; c.i.f.: cost, insurance, and freight; f.o.b.: free on board

(APEC) meeting in September. The APEC summit, which was held in Sydney, was the largest gathering of international world leaders ever hosted by Australia. During the summit threats of demonstrations against US Pres. George W. Bush overshadowed more pressing concerns of global warming and climate change.

Internet resources: <www.australia.com>.

Austria

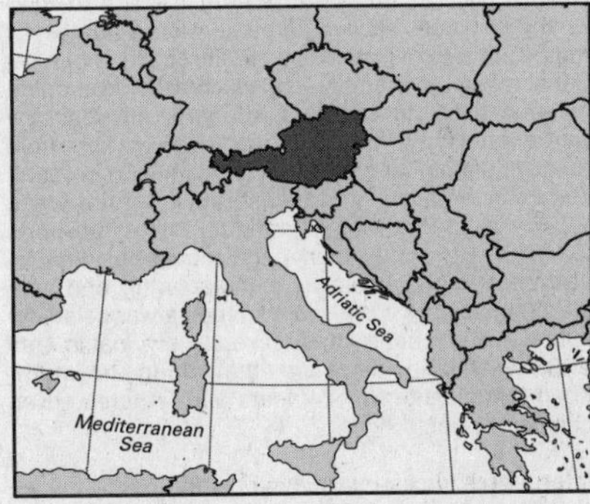

Official name: Republik Österreich (Republic of Austria). **Form of government:** federal state with two legislative houses (Federal Council [64]; National Council [183]). **Chief of state:** President Heinz Fischer (from 2004). **Head of government:** Chancellor Alfred Gusenbauer (from 2007). **Capital:** Vienna. **Official language:** German. **Official religion:** none. **Monetary unit:** 1 euro (€) = 100 cents; valuation (1 Jul 2008) US$1 = €0.63.

Demography

Area: 32,383 sq mi, 83,871 sq km. **Population** (2007): 8,319,000. **Density** (2007): persons per sq mi 256.9, persons per sq km 99.2. **Urban** (2003): 65.8%. **Sex distribution** (2005): male 48.61%; female 51.39%. **Age breakdown** (2005): under 15, 16.0%; 15–29, 18.5%; 30–44, 24.1%; 45–59, 19.4%; 60–74, 14.3%; 75–84, 6.1%; 85 and over, 1.6%. **Ethnic composition** (2000): Austrian 86.5%; German Swiss 4.0%; German 3.5%; Bosniac 0.9%; Turkish 0.9%; Polish 0.5%; other 3.7%. **Religious affiliation** (2001): Christian 81.5%, of which Roman Catholic 73.7%, Protestant (mostly Lutheran) 4.7%, Orthodox 2.2%; Muslim 4.2%; nonreligious 12.0%; other 0.3%; unknown 2.0%. **Major cities** (2006): Vienna 1,651,437; Graz 244,604; Linz 188,362; Salzburg 148,473; Innsbruck 116,851. **Location:** central Europe, bordering the Czech Republic, Slovakia, Hungary, Slovenia, Italy, Switzerland, Liechtenstein, and Germany.

Vital statistics

Birth rate per 1,000 population (2005): 9.5 (world avg. 20.3); within marriage 63.5%. **Death rate** per 1,000 population (2005): 9.1 (world avg. 8.6). **Natural increase rate** per 1,000 population (2005): 0.4 (world avg. 11.7). **Total fertility rate** (avg. births per childbearing woman; 2005): 1.41. **Life expectancy** at birth (2005): male 76.7 years; female 82.2 years.

National economy

Budget (2004). *Revenue:* €59,237,000,000 (tax revenue 97.3%, of which turnover tax 32.0%, individual income taxes 29.2%, corporate income tax 7.3%, other taxes 28.8%; nontax revenue 2.7%). *Expenditures:* €62,667,000,000 (social security, health, and welfare 34.4%; education 14.3%; interest 13.3%; transportation 9.6%; public safety 3.8%; defense 2.8%). **Public debt** (December 2006): US$194,118,000,000. **Production** (metric tons except as noted). *Agriculture, forestry, fishing* (2005): sugar beets 3,084,000, corn (maize) 1,725,000, wheat 1,453,000; livestock (number of live animals) 3,125,400 pigs, 2,051,000 cattle; roundwood (2004) 16,483,000 cu m, of which fuelwood 21%; fisheries production (2004) 2,667 (from aquaculture 85%). *Mining and quarrying* (2005): iron ore (metal content) 655,000; manganese (metal content) 16,000. Manufacturing (value added in €'000,000; 2004): nonelectrical machinery and apparatus 5,034; electrical machinery and electronics 4,060; fabricated metals 3,979. *Energy production (consumption):* electricity (kW-hr; 2004) 64,125,000,000 (67,207,000,000); hard coal (metric tons; 2004) none (4,252,000); lignite (metric tons; 2004) 235,000 (1,228,000); crude petroleum (barrels; 2005) 6,200,000 ([2004] 59,800,000); petroleum products (metric tons; 2004) 7,200,000 (12,029,000); natural gas (cu m; 2004) 2,142,000,000 (9,792,000,000). **Population economically active** (2005): total 4,032,200; activity rate of total population 49.7% (participation rates: ages 15–64, 72.4%; female 45.4%; unemployed 7.2%). **Gross national income** (2006): US$318,478,000,000 (US$38,244 per capita). **Households.** Average household size (2005) 2.3; average annual disposable income per household (2003) €28,709 (US$32,403); sources of income (1995): wages and salaries 54.8%, transfer payments 25.9%; expenditure (2004–05): housing and energy 22.3%, transportation 16.1%, recreation and culture 12.6%, food 11.7%. **Land use** as % of total land area (2003): in temporary crops 16.8%, in permanent crops 0.9%, in pasture 23.3%; overall forest area (2005) 46.7%. **Selected balance of payments data.** Receipts from (US$'000,000): tourism (2005) 15,589; remittances (2006) 2,941; foreign direct investment (FDI) (2001–05 avg.) 5,205. Disbursements for (US$'000,000): tourism (2005) 10,994; remittances (2006) 2,543; FDI (2001–05 avg.) 6,552.

Foreign trade

Imports (2005; c.i.f.): €96,499,000,000 (machinery and transport equipment 36.8%, of which nonelectrical machinery and apparatus 11.5%, road vehicles 11.5%; mineral fuels 12.2%; chemicals and related products 10.9%; food products 5.2%). *Major import sources:* Germany 42.2%; Italy 6.6%; France 4.0%; Switzerland 3.3%; Czech Republic 3.3%. **Exports** (2005; f.o.b.): €94,705,000,000 (machinery and transport equipment 41.6%, of which nonelectrical machinery and apparatus 17.2%, road vehicles 11.8%, electrical machinery and apparatus 7.3%; chemicals and chemical products 9.8%; iron and steel 5.7%). *Major export destinations:* Germany

31.8%; Italy 8.6%; US 5.6%; Switzerland 4.5%; France 4.2%.

Transport and communications

Transport. *Railroads* (2004; federal railways only): route length 5,629 km; passenger-km (2003) 8,248,700,000; metric ton-km cargo 17,931,100,000. *Roads* (2003): total length 133,718 km (paved 100%). *Vehicles* (2004): passenger cars 4,109,129; trucks and buses 342,384. *Air transport* (2005; Austrian Airlines Group only): passenger-km 22,894,000,000; metric ton-km cargo 561,882,000. **Communications,** in total units (units per 1,000 persons). Daily newspaper circulation (2004): 2,570,000 (3159); televisions (2002): 2,570,000 (315); telephone landlines (2006): 3,564,000 (434); cellular telephone subscribers (2006): 9,255,000 (1,128); personal computers (2005): 4,000,000 (489); total Internet users (2006): 4,200,000 (512); broadband Internet subscribers (2006): 1,428,000 (172).

Education and health

Educational attainment (2002). Percentage of population ages 25 and over having: no formal schooling through lower-secondary education 22%; upper secondary/higher vocational 63%; university 14%. **Literacy**: virtually 100%. **Health**: physicians (2006) 39,750 (1 per 208 persons); hospital beds (2005) 65,053 (1 per 133 persons); infant mortality rate per 1,000 live births (2005) 4.2. **Food** (2005): daily per capita caloric intake 4,023 (vegetable products 71%; animal products 29%).

Military

Total active duty personnel (2006): 39,900 (army 83.2%; air force 16.8%). **Military expenditure as percentage of GDP** (2005): 0.9%; per capita expenditure US$329.

Background

Settlement in Austria goes back some 3,000 years, when Illyrians were probably the main inhabitants. The Celts invaded c. 400 BC and established Noricum. The Romans arrived after 200 BC and established the provinces of Raetia, Noricum, and Pannonia; prosperity followed and the population became Romanized. With the fall of Rome in the 5th century AD, many tribes invaded, including the Slavs; they were eventually subdued by Charlemagne, and the area became ethnically Germanic. The distinct political entity that would become Austria emerged in 976 with Leopold I of Babenberg as margrave. In 1278 Rudolf I of the Holy Roman Empire (formerly Rudolf IV of Habsburg) conquered the area; Habsburg rule lasted until 1918. While in power the Habsburgs created a kingdom centered on Austria, Bohemia, and Hungary. The Napoleonic Wars brought about the creation of the Austrian Empire (1804) and the end of the Holy Roman Empire (1806). Count von Metternich tried to assure Austrian supremacy among Germanic states, but war with Prussia led Austria to divide the empire into the Dual Monarchy of Austria-Hungary. Nationalist sentiment plagued the kingdom, and the assassination of Francis Ferdinand by a Serbian nationalist in 1914 triggered World War I, which destroyed the Austrian empire. In the postwar carving up of Austria-Hungary, Austria became an independent republic. It was annexed by Nazi Germany in 1938 and joined the Axis powers in World War II. The republic was restored in 1955 after 10 years of Allied occupation. Austria became a member of the European Union in 1995.

Recent Developments

Despite political tensions in Austria in 2007, the governing coalition reached agreement on a number of important reforms, including the introduction of a national minimum monthly wage, increased investment in education and transport infrastructure, and the partial opening of the labor market to workers from the 10 EU member states that joined the EU in 2004. The economy grew at its fastest rate in eight years in 2007, driven by strong demand for Austrian exports (particularly from Germany) and robust business investment in the booming manufacturing and construction sectors. Household spending was relatively subdued. The country was rocked by scandal in April 2008 when it was discovered that a man had imprisoned his daughter for 24 years and fathered seven children by her.

Internet resources: <www.austria.info>.

Azerbaijan

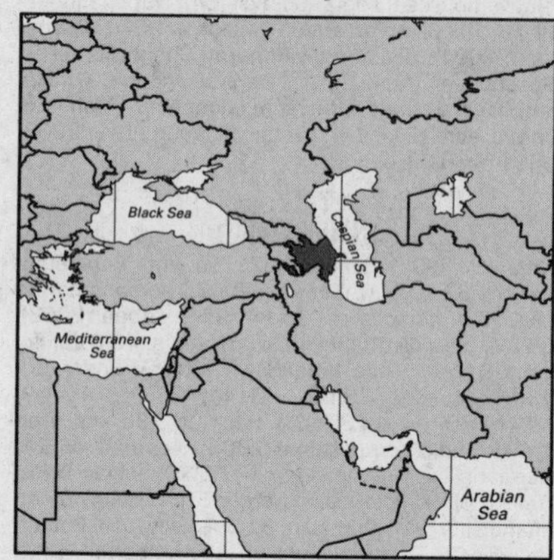

Official name: Azerbaycan Respublikasi (Republic of Azerbaijan). **Form of government:** unitary multiparty republic with a single legislative body (National Assembly [124]). **Head of state and government:** President Ilham Aliyev (from 2003), assisted by Prime Minister Artur Rasizade (from 2003). **Capital:** Baku. **Official language:** Azerbaijani. **Official religion:** none. **Monetary unit:** The (new) manat was introduced on 1 Jan 2006, at a rate of 4,500 (old) manats (AZM) to 1 (new) manat (AZN). 1 new manat (AZN) = 100 gopik; valuation (1 Jul 2008) free rate, US$1 = AZN 0.81.

1 metric ton = about 1.1 short tons; 1 kilometer = 0.6 mi (statute); 1 metric ton-km cargo = about 0.68 short ton-mi cargo; c.i.f.: cost, insurance, and freight; f.o.b.: free on board

Demography

Area: 33,400 sq mi, 86,600 sq km. **Population** (2007): 8,120,000. **Density** (2007): persons per sq mi 242.9, persons per sq km 93.8. **Urban** (2006): 51.6%. **Sex distribution** (2006): male 49.16%; female 50.84%. **Age breakdown** (2006): under 15, 26.3%; 15–29, 27.9%; 30–44, 22.7%; 45–59, 14.1%; 60–74, 6.7%; 75–84, 1.9%; 85 and over, 0.4%. **Ethnic composition** (1999): Azerbaijani 90.6%; Lezgian (Dagestani) 2.2%; Russian 1.8%; Armenian 1.5%; other 3.9%. **Religious affiliation** (2005): Muslim 87.0%, of which Shi'i 52.8%, Sunni 34.2%; nonreligious/other 13.0%. **Major cities** (2006): Baku 1,132,800 (urban agglomeration [2005] 1,856,000); Ganca 305,600; Sumqayit (Sumgait) 266,600; Mingacevir (Mingechaur) 95,300. **Location:** eastern Transcaucasia, bordering Russia, the Caspian Sea, Iran, Turkey, Armenia, and Georgia.

Vital statistics

Birth rate per 1,000 population (2005): 17.2 (world avg. 20.3); within marriage 81.6%. **Death rate** per 1,000 population (2005): 6.3 (world avg. 8.6). **Total fertility rate** (avg. births per childbearing woman; 2005): 2.33. **Life expectancy** at birth (2005): male 69.6 years; female 75.2 years.

National economy

Budget (2005). *Revenue:* AZN 2,055,200,000 (tax revenue 86.0%, of which VAT 29.2%, taxes on profits 17.3%, personal income tax 15.5%, taxes on international trade 10.0%; nontax revenue 14.0%). *Expenditures:* AZN 2,140,700,000 (national economy 21.6%; education 18.1%; social security/welfare 14.8%; defense/police 10.0%; health 5.6%). **Production** (metric tons except as noted). *Agriculture, forestry, fishing* (2005): wheat 1,527,000, vegetables 1,491,000, potatoes 1,083,100; livestock (number of live animals) 6,887,000 sheep, 2,007,000 cattle; roundwood 13,500 cu m, of which fuelwood 47%; fisheries production (2004) 9,296. *Mining and quarrying* (2004): limestone 800,000. *Manufacturing* (value added in US$'000,000; 2005): food, beverages, and tobacco products 301; petroleum products 251; base metals, fabricated metals, and machinery 126. *Energy production (consumption):* electricity (kW-hr; 2005) 22,600,000,000 ([2004] 20,600,000,000); crude petroleum (barrels; 2005) 164,000,000 (55,200,000); petroleum products (metric tons; 2004) 5,875,000 (3,583,000); natural gas (cu m; 2005) 5,676,000,000 (9,449,000,000). **Households** (2003). Average household size 4.4; annual income per household AZM 2,254,450 (US$459); sources of income: wages and salaries 30.5%, self-employment 22.8%, agriculture 15.5%; expenditure: food 54.7%, household furnishings 7.1%, clothing 6.8%. **Population economically active** (2005): total 3,906,500; activity rate of total population 46.3% (participation rates: ages 15–61 [male], 15–56 [female] 71.8%; female 47.7%; officially unemployed 1.4%). **Gross national income** (at 2006 market prices): US$18,676,000,000 (US$2,222 per capita). **Public debt** (external, outstanding; 2005): US$1,344,000,000. **Selected balance of payments data.** Receipts from (US$'000,000): tourism (2005) 78; remittances (2006) 813; foreign direct investment (FDI) (2001–05 avg.) 2,028; official development assistance (2005) 396 (commitments). Disbursements for (US$'000,000): tourism (2005) 164; remittances (2006) 301; FDI (2001–05 avg.) 739. **Land use** as % of total land area (2003): in temporary crops 22.2%, in permanent crops 2.7%, in pasture 32.5%; overall forest area (2005) 11.3%.

Foreign trade

Imports (2005): US$4,211,000,000 (machinery and equipment 33.3%; mineral fuels 15.2%; base and fabricated metals 11.6%; food and agricultural products 10.6%). *Major import sources:* Russia 17.0%; UK 9.1%; Singapore 9.1%; Turkey 7.4%; Germany 6.1%. **Exports** (2005): US$4,347,000,000 (mineral fuels [mostly crude petroleum] 76.8%, of which diesel fuel 17.1%; transport equipment 6.3%; vegetables 4.5%; aluminum oxide 2.3%). *Major export destinations:* Italy 30.3%; France 9.4%; Russia 6.6%; Turkmenistan 6.3%; Turkey 6.3%.

Transport and communications

Transport. *Railroads* (2005): length 2,122 km; passenger-km 881,000,000; metric ton-km cargo 9,524,000,000. *Roads* (2004): total length 59,141 km (paved 49%). *Vehicles* (2005): passenger cars 479,447; trucks and buses 117,587. *Air transport* (2005): passenger-km 1,587,000,000; metric ton-km cargo 313,000,000. **Communications,** in total units (units per 1,000 persons). Daily newspaper circulation (2001): 132,000 (16); televisions (2003): 2,750,000 (334); telephone landlines (2006): 1,189,000 (140); cellular telephone subscribers (2006): 3,323,000 (392); personal computers (2005): 195,000 (23); total Internet users (2006): 829,000 (98); broadband Internet subscribers (2006): 2,200 (0.3).

Education and health

Educational attainment (1999). Percentage of population ages 25 and over having: primary education 4.1%; some secondary 9.3%; secondary 50.1%; vocational 4.2%; some higher 0.9%; higher 13.3%. **Literacy** (1999): 98.8%. **Health** (2006): physicians 30,300 (1 per 265 persons); hospital beds 68,800 (1 per 117 persons); infant mortality rate per 1,000 live births (2005) 9.2. **Food** (2005): daily per capita caloric intake 2,744 (vegetable products 85%, animal products 15%); 141% of FAO recommended minimum.

Military

Total active duty personnel (2006): 66,740 (army 85.2%, navy 3.0%, air force 11.8%). **Military expenditure as percentage of GDP** (2005): 2.5%; per capita expenditure US$37.

Background

Azerbaijan adjoins the Iranian region of the same name, and the origin of their respective inhabitants is the same. By the 9th century AD the area had come under Turkish influence, and in ensuing centuries it was fought over by Arabs, Mongols, Turks, and Iranians. Russia acquired the territory of what is now independent Azerbaijan in the early 19th century. After the Russian Revolution of 1917, Azerbaijan declared its independence; it was subdued by the Red Army in 1920 and became a Soviet Socialist Republic. It declared independence from the collapsing Soviet Union in 1991. Azerbaijan has two geographic peculiarities.

The exclave Nakhichevan is separated from the rest of Azerbaijan by Armenian territory. Nagorno-Karabakh, which lies within Azerbaijan and is administered by it, has a Christian Armenian majority. Azerbaijan and Armenia went to war over both territories in the 1990s, causing great economic disruption. Though a cease-fire was declared in 1994, the political situation remained unresolved.

Recent Developments

Economic growth continued in Azerbaijan in 2007, with an estimated 35% increase in GDP. Annual inflation reached 20%, however, and the consortium developing the huge Shah Deniz natural-gas field in the Caspian Sea warned of possible delays. In August a high-rise building under construction in Baku collapsed, killing 19 persons. During the recent building boom, many contractors had failed to secure official permits, and safety measures were being skirted. President Aliyev met in June in St. Petersburg with Armenian Pres. Robert Kocharyan to continue talks on how to resolve the Nagorno-Karabakh conflict, though no marked progress was made.

Internet resources: <http://azerbaijan.tourism.az>.

The Bahamas

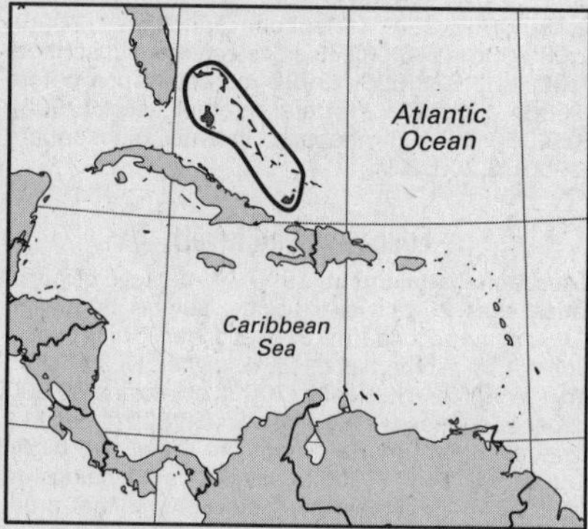

Official name: The Commonwealth of The Bahamas. **Form of government:** constitutional monarchy with two legislative houses (Senate [16]; House of Assembly [41]). **Chief of state:** British Queen Elizabeth II (from 1952), represented by Governor-General Arthur Dion Hanna (from 2006). **Head of government:** Prime Minister Hubert Ingraham (from 2007). **Capital:** Nassau. **Official language:** English. **Official religion:** none. **Monetary unit:** 1 Bahamian dollar (B$) = 100 cents; valuation (1 Jul 2008) US$1 = B$1.00.

Demography

Area: 5,382 sq mi, 13,939 sq km. **Population** (2007): 331,000. **Density** (2006): persons per sq mi 85.1, persons per sq km 32.9. **Urban** (2003): 89.5%. **Sex distribution** (2006): male 48.90%; female 51.10%. **Age breakdown** (2006): under 15, 27.6%; 15–29, 26.0%; 30–44, 22.2%; 45–59, 14.9%; 60–74, 7.1%; 75 and over, 2.2%. **Ethnic composition** (2000): local black 67.5%; mulatto 14.2%; British 12.0%; Haitian black 3.0%; US white 2.4%; other 0.9%. **Religious affiliation** (2000): Baptist 35.4%; Anglican 15.1%; Roman Catholic 13.5%; other Protestant/independent Christian 32.3%; other/nonreligious 3.7%. **Major cities** (2002): Nassau 179,300; Freeport 42,600; West End 7,800; Cooper's Town 5,700; Marsh Harbour 3,600. **Location:** chain of islands in the Caribbean Sea, southeast of Florida.

Vital statistics

Birth rate per 1,000 population (2006): 17.6 (world avg. 20.3); (2000) within marriage 43.2%. **Death rate** per 1,000 population (2006): 9.1 (world avg. 8.6). **Natural increase rate** per 1,000 population (2006): 8.5 (world avg. 11.7). **Total fertility rate** (avg. births per childbearing woman; 2006): 2.18. **Life expectancy** at birth (2006): male 62.2 years; female 69.0 years.

National economy

Budget (2004–05). *Revenue:* B$1,039,376,000 (tax revenue 89.0%, of which import taxes 39.7%, stamp taxes from imports 10.8%, departure taxes 6.7%, business and professional licenses 5.8%; nontax revenue 11.0%). *Expenditures:* B$1,143,469,000 (education 18.7%; health 16.9%; public order 12.3%; interest on public debt 10.3%; tourism 6.0%; defense 3.1%). **Public debt** (external, outstanding; 2005): US$334,600,000. **Production** (metric tons except as noted). *Agriculture, forestry, fishing* (2005): sugarcane 55,500, citrus fruits 21,700; livestock (number of live animals) 3,000,000 chickens; roundwood 17,000 cu m; fisheries production (2004) 11,357 (mainly lobsters, crayfish, and conch). *Mining and quarrying* (2004): salt 1,269,209; aragonite 19,918. *Manufacturing* (value of export production in B$'000; 2004): rum 31,344; chemical products (2001) 13,842. *Energy production (consumption):* electricity (kW-hr; 2004) 2,087,000,000 (2,087,000,000); petroleum products (metric tons; 2004) none (652,000). **Households.** Average household size (2000) 3.5; income per household (2004) B$39,626 (US$39,626); expenditure (1995): housing 32.8%, transportation and communications 14.8%, food and beverages 13.8%, household furnishings 8.9%. **Land use** as % of total land area (2003): in temporary crops 0.8%, in permanent crops 0.4%, in pasture 0.2%; overall forest area (2005) 51.5%. **Gross national income** (2006): US$6,077,000,000 (US$18,570 per capita). **Population economically active** (2004): total 176,330; activity rate of total population 55.6% (participation rates: ages 15–64 [2000] 76.6%; female 48.8%; unemployed [2005] 10.2%). **Selected balance of payments data.** Receipts from (US$'000,000): tourism (2005) 2,072; foreign direct investment (2001–05 avg.) 216. Disbursements for (US$'000,000): tourism (2005) 344; remittances (2006) 144.

Foreign trade

Imports (2005; c.i.f.): B$2,567,000,000 (machinery and transport equipment 22.1%; mineral fuels 19.8%; food products 13.2%; chemicals and chemical products 7.0%). *Major import sources* (2005): US

83.9%; Curaçao 7.1%; Puerto Rico 1.9%; Japan 1.2%. **Exports** (2005; f.o.b.): B$450,800,000 (domestic exports 60.1%, of which plastics 25.7%, fish, crustaceans, and mollusks [mainly crayfish] 17.2%, alcoholic beverages [mainly rum] 3.7%; reexports 39.9%, of which petroleum 9.0%, nonelectrical machinery 5.1%). *Major export destinations* (2005): US 68.9%; France 8.3%; Germany 7.0%; UK 4.6%; Canada 4.5%.

Transport and communications

Transport. *Roads* (2000): total length 2,693 km (paved 57%). *Vehicles* (2001): passenger cars 80,000; trucks and buses 25,000. *Air transport* (2001; Bahamasair only): passenger-km 374,000,000; metric ton-km cargo 1,764,000. **Communications,** in total units (units per 1,000 persons). Daily newspaper circulation (2004): 39,000 (122); televisions (2001): 77,000 (247); telephone landlines (2005): 133,000 (412); cellular telephone subscribers (2005): 228,000 (705); total Internet users (2005): 103,000 (319); broadband Internet subscribers (2004): 13,000 (40).

Education and health

Educational attainment (2000). Percentage of population ages 15 and over having: no formal schooling 1.5%; primary education 8.7%; incomplete secondary 19.9%; complete secondary 53.7%; incomplete higher 8.1%; complete higher 7.1%; not stated 1.0%. **Literacy** (2005): total percentage ages 15 and over literate 95.8%; males literate 95.0%; females literate 96.7%. **Health** (2001): physicians 458 (1 per 672 persons); hospital beds 1,540 (1 per 200 persons); infant mortality rate per 1,000 live births (2006) 24.7. **Food** (2005): daily per capita caloric intake 2,520 (vegetable products 68%, animal products 32%); 130% of FAO recommended minimum.

Military

Total active duty personnel (2006): 860 (paramilitary coast guard 100%). **Military expenditure as percentage of GDP** (2005): 0.7%; per capita expenditure US$121.

Background

The islands were inhabited by Lucayan Indians when Christopher Columbus sighted them on 12 Oct 1492. He is thought to have landed on San Salvador (Watling) Island. The Spaniards made no attempt to settle but carried out slave raids that depopulated the islands; when English settlers arrived in 1648 from Bermuda, the islands were uninhabited. They became a haunt of pirates, and few of the ensuing settlements prospered. The islands enjoyed some prosperity following the American Revolution, when Loyalists fled the US and established cotton plantations. The islands were a center for blockade runners during the American Civil War. Not until the development of tourism after World War II did permanent economic prosperity arrive. The Bahamas was granted internal self-government in 1964 and became independent in 1973.

Recent Developments

The Free National Movement (FNM) party, led by Hubert Ingraham, defied the pundits and won the general election in The Bahamas in May 2007 by a relatively comfortable margin, and in his first policy statement, Prime Minister Ingraham announced the privatization of Bahamasair, the money-losing government-owned airline.

Internet resources: <www.bahamas.com>.

Bahrain

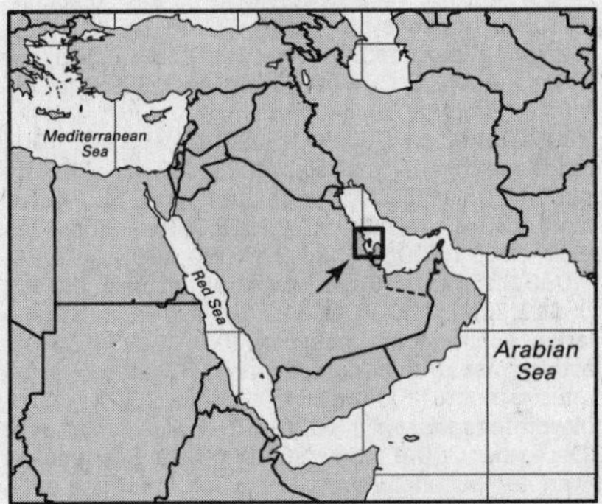

Official name: Mamlakat al-Bahrayn (Kingdom of Bahrain). **Form of government:** constitutional monarchy (declared 14 Feb 2002) with two legislative houses (Council of Representatives [40] and Shura Council [40]). **Chief of state:** King Hamad ibn ʿIsa al-Khalifah (from 2002). **Head of Government:** Prime Minister Sheikh Khalifah ibn Sulman al-Khalifah (from 1970). **Capital:** Manama. **Official language:** Arabic. **Official religion:** Islam. **Monetary unit:** 1 Bahrain dinar (BD) = 1,000 fils; valuation (1 Jul 2008) US$1 = BD 0.38.

Demography

Area: 278 sq mi, 720 sq km. **Population** (2007): 749,000. **Density** (2007): persons per sq mi 2,665.5, persons per sq km 1,028.8. **Urban** (2005): 96.4%. **Sex distribution** (2005): male 57.52%; female 42.48%. **Age breakdown** (2005): under 15, 27.2%; 15–29, 23.2%; 30–44, 29.9%; 45–59, 15.2%; 60–74, 3.6%; 75–84, 0.8%; 85 and over, 0.1%. **Ethnic composition** (2000): Bahraini Arab 63.9%; Indo-Pakistani 14.8%, of which Urdu 4.5%, Malayali 3.5%; Persian 13.0%; Filipino 4.5%; British 2.1%; other 1.7%. **Religious affiliation** (2000): Muslim 82.4%, of which Shiʿi 58.0%, Sunni 24.0%; Christian 10.5%; Hindu 6.3%; other 0.8%. **Major urban areas** (2001): Manama 143,035; Muharraq 91,307; Ar-Rifaʿ 79,550; Madinat Hamad 52,718; Al-ʿAli 47,529. **Location:** the Middle East, archipelago in the Persian Gulf, east of Saudi Arabia.

Vital statistics

Birth rate per 1,000 population (2005): 18.1 (world avg. 20.3). **Death rate** per 1,000 population (2005): 4.1 (world avg. 8.6). **Natural increase rate** per 1,000 population (2005): 14.0 (world avg. 11.7). **Total fertility rate** (avg. births per childbearing woman; 2005): 2.63. **Life expectancy** at birth (2005): male 71.7 years; female 76.8 years.

National economy

Budget (2005). *Revenue:* BD 1,671,400,000 (petroleum and natural gas revenue 75.7%; other 24.3%). *Expenditures:* BD 1,289,200,000 (current expenditure 79.4%; development expenditure 20.6%). **Production** (metric tons except as noted). *Agriculture, forestry, fishing* (2005): dates 15,000, vegetables 7,703 (of which tomatoes 2,100, onions 1,149), fruit (excluding dates) 5,010; livestock (number of live animals) 40,000 sheep, 26,000 goats, chickens 470,000; fisheries production (2004) 14,267. *Manufacturing* (barrels; 2005): jet fuel 19,956,000; distillate fuel oil 19,278,000; gasoline 7,309,000. *Energy production (consumption):* electricity (kW-hr; 2005–06) 9,567,000,000 ([2004] 7,198,000,000); crude petroleum (barrels; 2005–06) 66,400,000 ([2004] 93,100,000); petroleum products (metric tons; 2004) 10,939,000 (1,018,000); natural gas (cu m; 2005) 10,278,000,000 ([2004] 7,030,000,000). **Gross national income** (2006): US$15,229,000,000 (US$20,609 per capita). **Population economically active** (2005): total 350,000; activity rate of total population 48.3% (participation rates: ages 15 and over 67%; female 23.2%; unemployed [citizens only; 2006] 16–18%). **Public debt** (December 2004): US$3,866,000,000. **Households.** Average household size (2001) 5.9. **Land use** as % of total land area (2003): in temporary crops 3%, in permanent crops 6%, in pasture 6%; overall forest area (2005) 1%. **Selected balance of payments data.** Receipts from (US$'000,000): tourism (2005) 920; foreign direct investment (FDI) (2001–05 avg.) 546. Disbursements for (US$'000,000): tourism (2005) 414; remittances (2006) 1,531; FDI (2001–05 avg.) 661.

Foreign trade

Imports (2005; c.i.f.): BD 2,988,000,000 (crude and refined petroleum 52.5%; machinery and apparatus 9.0%; transport equipment 7.3%; chemicals and chemical products 6.4%). *Major import sources* (2004): Saudi Arabia 47.7%; Japan 6.2%; UK 3.7%; Germany 3.6%; France 3.6%. **Exports** (2005; f.o.b.): BD 3,769,000,000 (crude and refined petroleum 77.6%; base and fabricated metals, including aluminum [all forms] 12.9%; chemicals and chemical products 2.6%). *Major export destinations* (2004): unknown destinations for petroleum exports 76.5%; Saudi Arabia 6.4%; US 3.2%; Taiwan 2.7%.

Transport and communications

Transport. *Roads* (2003): total length 3,498 km (paved 79%). *Vehicles* (2005): passenger cars 241,813; trucks and buses 44,811. *Air transport* (2005; Gulf Air, the national airline of both Bahrain and Oman, only): passenger-km 17,467,000,000; metric ton-km cargo 674,000,000. **Communications,** in total units (units per 1,000 persons). Daily newspaper circulation (2004): 198,000 (284); televisions (2002): 273,000 (411); telephone landlines (2006): 190,000 (262); cellular telephone subscribers (2006): 835,000 (1,148); personal computers (2004): 121,000 (164); total Internet users (2006): 157,000 (230); broadband Internet subscribers (2006): 39,000 (52).

Education and health

Educational attainment (2001). Percentage of population ages 15 and over having: no formal education 24.0%; primary education 37.1%; secondary 26.4%; higher 12.5%. **Literacy** (2005): percentage of population ages 15 and over literate 90.0%; males literate 92.6%; females literate 86.4%. **Health** (2005): physicians 1,973 (1 per 362 persons); hospital beds 2,033 (1 per 352 persons); infant mortality rate per 1,000 live births 17.3.

Military

Total active duty personnel (2006): 11,200 (army 75.9%, navy 10.7%, air force 13.4%); US troops (2006) 3,000. **Military expenditure as percentage of GDP** (2005): 3.6%; per capita expenditure US$675.

Background

The area has long been an important trading center and is mentioned in Persian, Greek, and Roman references. It was ruled by Arabs from the 7th century AD but was then occupied by the Portuguese in 1521–1602. Since 1783 it has been ruled by the Khalifah family, though through a series of treaties its defense remained a British responsibility from 1820 to 1971. After Britain withdrew its forces from the Persian Gulf (1968), Bahrain declared its independence in 1971. It served as a center for the allies in the Persian Gulf War (1990–91). Since 1994 it has experienced bouts of political unrest, mainly by Shi'ites, who attempted to get the government to restore the parliament (abolished in 1975).

Recent Developments

Some progress was made in Bahrain in the realm of women's affairs in 2007. On 28 March Bahraini diplomat Haya Rashid Al-Khalifa, president of the 61st session of the UN General Assembly, became the first woman to deliver a speech at the Arab League summit conference, which was held in conservative Saudi Arabia.

Internet resources: <www.bahrain-tourism.com>.

Bangladesh

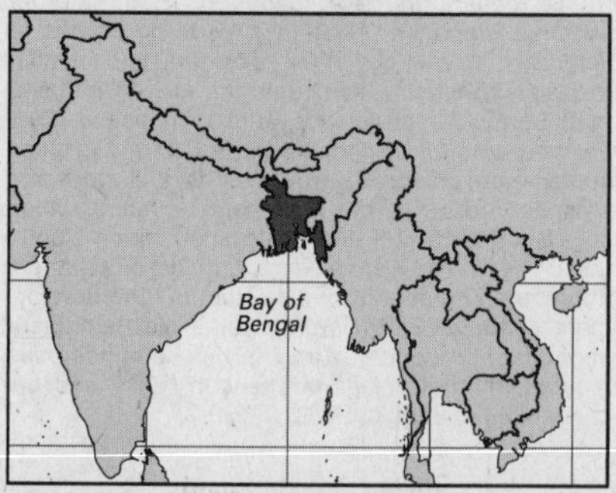

1 metric ton = about 1.1 short tons; 1 kilometer = 0.6 mi (statute); 1 metric ton-km cargo = about 0.68 short ton-mi cargo; c.i.f.: cost, insurance, and freight; f.o.b.: free on board

Official name: Gana Prajatantri Bangladesh (People's Republic of Bangladesh). **Form of government:** unitary multiparty republic with one legislative house (Parliament [300]). **Chief of state:** President Iajuddin Ahmed (from 2002). **Head of government:** Chief Adviser Fakhruddin Ahmed (from 2007). **Capital:** Dhaka. **Official language:** Bengali. **Official religion:** Islam. **Monetary unit:** 1 Bangladesh taka (Tk) = 100 paisa; valuation (1 Jul 2008) US$1 = Tk 68.52.

Demography

Area: 56,977 sq mi, 147,570 sq km. **Population** (2007): 140,661,000. **Density** (2007): persons per sq mi 2,614.7, persons per sq km 1,009.5. **Urban** (2003): 24.2%. **Sex distribution** (2005): male 51.09%; female 48.91%. **Age breakdown** (2005): under 15, 35.5%; 15–29, 28.6%; 30–44, 19.5%; 45–59, 10.8%; 60–74, 4.6%; 75–84, 0.9%; 85 and over, 0.1%. **Ethnic composition** (1997): Bengali 97.7%; tribal 1.9%, of which Chakma 0.4%, Saontal 0.2%, Marma 0.1%; other 0.4%. **Religious affiliation** (2005): Muslim (nearly all Sunni) 88.3%; Hindu 10.5%; Christian 0.3%; Buddhist 0.6%; other 0.3%. **Major urban areas** (2004): Dhaka 10,550,000; Chittagong 2,640,000; Khulna 1,230,000; Rajshahi 725,200; Narayanganj 363,600. **Location:** South Asia, bordering India, Myanmar (Burma), and the Bay of Bengal.

Vital statistics

Birth rate per 1,000 population (2006): 29.8 (world avg. 20.3). **Death rate** per 1,000 population (2006): 8.3 (world avg. 8.6). **Natural increase rate** per 1,000 population (2006): 21.5 (world avg. 11.7). **Total fertility rate** (avg. births per childbearing woman; 2006): 3.11. **Life expectancy** at birth (2006): male 61.9 years; female 59.7 years.

National economy

Budget (2005–06). *Revenue:* Tk 448,700,000,000 (tax revenue 80.6%, of which VAT 27.6%, import duties 18.4%, taxes on income and profits 15.5%; nontax revenue 19.4%). *Expenditures:* Tk 610,600,000,000 (current expenditure 57.0%, of which education 10.4%, domestic interest payments 10.2%, defense 5.5%, health 3.3%; development expenditure 35.2%; other 7.8%). **Production** (metric tons except as noted). *Agriculture, forestry, fishing* (2005): paddy rice 41,104,000, sugarcane 6,500,000, potatoes 4,855,000; livestock (number of live animals) 36,900,000 goats, 24,500,000 cattle, 142,000,000 chickens; roundwood 27,944,000 cu m, of which fuelwood 99%; fisheries production (2004) 2,102,026 (from aquaculture 43%). *Mining and quarrying* (2004–05): marine salt 350,000; kaolin 8,400. *Manufacturing* (value added in US$'000,000; 1998): wearing apparel 839; tobacco products 634; textiles 567. *Energy production (consumption):* electricity (kW-hr; 2004) 21,466,000,000 (21,466,000,000); coal (metric tons; 2004) n.a. (700,000); crude petroleum (barrels; 2005) 1,900,000 ([2004] 9,600,000); petroleum products (metric tons; 2004) 842,000 (3,209,000); natural gas (cu m; 2004) 13,300,000,000 (13,300,000,000). **Households.** Average household size (2004) 5.3; average annual income per household (2000) Tk 70,103 (US$1,344); sources of income: self-employment 56.9%, wages and salaries 28.1%, transfer payments 9.1%, other 5.9%; expenditure (2000): food and beverages 54.6%, housing 9.0%, energy 6.8%, clothing and footwear 6.3%. **Population economically active** (2002–03): total 46,324,000; activity rate of total population 34.7% (participation rates: ages 15–64, 58.6%; female 22.3%; officially unemployed 4.3%). **Public debt** (external, outstanding; 2006): US$17,938,000,000. **Gross national income** (2006): US$72,050,000,000 (US$462 per capita). **Land use** as % of total land area (2003): in temporary crops 61.3%, in permanent crops 3.4%, in pasture 4.6%; overall forest area (2005) 6.7%. **Selected balance of payments data.** Receipts from (US$'000,000): tourism (2005) 70; remittances (2006) 5,922; foreign direct investment (2001–05 avg.) 437; official development assistance (2005) 1,321. Disbursements for (US$'000,000): tourism (2005) 132; remittances (2005) 6.

Foreign trade

Imports (2005–06; f.o.b. in balance of trade and c.i.f. in commodities and trading partners): US$14,746,000,000 (textile yarn, fabrics, and made-up articles 15.1%; capital machinery 10.4%; imports for export processing zone 7.2%; base metals 6.6%; cotton 5.0%). *Major import sources* (2004): India 18.5%; China 13.1%; Singapore 10.5%; Japan 5.4%; Hong Kong 5.0%. **Exports** (2005–06): US$10,526,300,000 (woven garments 38.8%; hosiery and knitwear 36.3%; frozen fish and shrimp 4.4%; jute manufactures 3.4%). *Major export destinations* (2004): US 25.6%; Germany 17.6%; UK 12.0%; France 7.5%; Italy 4.6%.

Transport and communications

Transport. *Railroads* (2002): route length 2,768 km; passenger-km 3,970,000,000; metric ton-km cargo 908,000,000. *Roads* (2003): total length 239,226 km (paved 10%). *Vehicles* (2004): passenger cars 185,000; trucks and buses 88,000. *Air transport* (2005; Biman Bangladesh only): passenger-km 5,163,000,000; metric ton-km cargo 181,034,000. **Communications**, in total units (units per 1,000 persons). Daily newspaper circulation (2004): 913,000 (6.8); televisions (2004): 11,531,000 (85); telephone landlines (2006): 1,134,000 (7.9); cellular telephone subscribers (2006): 19,131,000 (133); personal computers (2004): 1,650,000 (12); total Internet users (2006): 450,000 (3.1).

Education and health

Educational attainment (2004; estimated). Percentage of population ages 25 and over having: no formal schooling 48.8%; incomplete primary education 17.9%; complete primary 7.7%; incomplete secondary 15.1%; complete secondary or higher 10.5%. **Literacy** (2002): total population ages 15 and over literate 41.1%; males literate 50.3%; females literate 31.4%. **Health** (2002): physicians 32,498 (1 per 4,049 persons); hospital beds 45,607 (1 per 2,886 persons); infant mortality rate per 1,000 live births (2006) 60.8. **Food** (2005): daily per capita caloric intake 2,388 (vegetable products 98%, animal products 2%); 130% of FAO recommended minimum.

Military

Total active duty personnel (2006): 125,500 (army 87.6%, navy 7.2%, air force 5.2%). **Military expendi-**

ture as percentage of GDP (2005): 1.0%; per capita expenditure US$5.

Background

In its early years Bangladesh was known as Bengal. When the British left the subcontinent in 1947, the area that was East Bengal became the part of Pakistan called East Pakistan. Bengali nationalist sentiment increased after the creation of an independent Pakistan. In 1971 violence erupted; some one million Bengalis were killed, and millions more fled to India, which finally entered the war on the side of the Bengalis, ensuring West Pakistan's defeat. East Pakistan became the independent nation of Bangladesh. Little of the devastation caused by the war has been repaired, and political instability, including the assassination of two presidents, has continued. In addition, the low-lying country has been repeatedly battered by natural disasters, notably tropical storms and flooding.

Recent Developments

The volatility of the situation in Bangladesh was highlighted in August 2007 when a brawl between university students and soldiers turned into countrywide violence. The country also faced economic challenges. Officially, in June inflation stood at 9.2%, but steeper price hikes were reported for food items, and the ready-made-garment sector faced an order dearth. In addition back-to-back floods caused more than 1,000 fatalities, along with huge losses to infrastructure and crops. Thousands more deaths were caused by a cyclone that struck southern Bangladesh in mid-November. (See Disasters.)

Internet resources: <www.bangladeshtourism.-gov.bd>.

Barbados

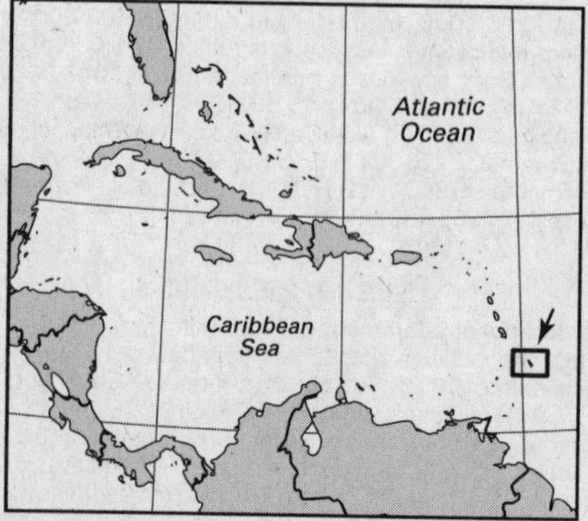

Official name: Barbados. **Form of government:** constitutional monarchy with two legislative houses (Senate [21]; House of Assembly [30]). **Chief of state:** British Queen Elizabeth II (from 1952), represented by Governor-General Sir Clifford Husbands (from 1996). **Head of government:** Prime Minister David Thompson (from 2008). **Capital:** Bridgetown. **Official language:** English. **Official religion:** none. **Monetary unit:** 1 Barbados dollar (BDS$) = 100 cents; valuation (1 Jul 2008) US$1 = BDS$2.00.

Demography

Area: 166 sq mi, 430 sq km. **Population** (2007): 294,000. **Density** (2007): persons per sq mi 1,771, persons per sq km 683.7. **Urban** (2005): 52.6%. **Sex distribution** (2005): male 48.26%; female 51.74%. **Age breakdown** (2005): under 15, 19.0%; 15–29, 22.8%; 30–44, 26.1%; 45–59, 19.0%; 60–74, 8.2%; 75–84, 3.8%; 85 and over, 1.1%. **Ethnic composition** (2000): local black 87.1%; mulatto 6.0%; British expatriates 4.3%; US white 1.2%; Indo-Pakistani 1.1%; other 0.3%. **Religious affiliation** (2000): Christian 72.5%, of which Anglican 28.3%, Pentecostal 18.7%, Adventist 5.5%, Methodist 5.1%; Rastafarian 1.1%; Muslim 0.7%; Hindu 0.3%; nonreligious 17.3%; other/unknown 8.1%. **Major urban areas** (2004): Bridgetown 99,100; Speightstown 3,600; Oistins (2000) 1,203; Holetown (2000) 1,087. **Location:** northeast of Venezuela at the eastern edge of the Caribbean Sea where it adjoins the North Atlantic Ocean.

Vital statistics

Birth rate per 1,000 population (2006): 12.7 (world avg. 20.3). **Death rate** per 1,000 population (2006): 8.7 (world avg. 8.6). **Natural increase rate** per 1,000 population (2006): 4.0 (world avg. 11.7). **Total fertility rate** (avg. births per childbearing woman; 2006): 1.65. **Life expectancy** at birth (2006): male 70.8 years; female 74.8 years.

National economy

Budget (2005–06). *Revenue:* BDS$2,145,000,000 (tax revenue 95.2%, of which VAT 31.8%, corporate taxes 16.8%, personal income taxes 14.3%; nontax revenue 4.8%). *Expenditures:* BDS$2,328,500,000 (current expenditure 85.2%, of which education 18.3%, general public service 14.6%, debt payments 12.8%, health 11.3%, defense 2.2%; development expenditure 14.8%). **Public debt** (external, outstanding; December 2005): US$763,500,000. **Production** (metric tons except as noted). *Agriculture, forestry, fishing* (2005): raw sugar 38,240, sweet potatoes 2,000, coconuts 1,950; livestock (number of live animals) 19,000 pigs, 10,800 sheep, 3,400,000 chickens; roundwood 6,000 cu m; fisheries production (2004) 2,500. Manufacturing (value added in US$'000,000; 1997): industrial chemicals 87; food products 63; beverages (significantly rum and beer) 58. *Energy production (consumption):* electricity (kW-hr; 2005) 793,000,000 (793,000,000); crude petroleum (barrels; 2004) 612,000 (negligible); petroleum products (metric tons; 2004) 1,000 (346,000); natural gas (cu m; 2004) 25,000,000 (25,000,000). **Households.** Average household size (2004) 2.8; expenditure (2001): food 33.8%, medical and personal care 17.0%, housing 12.3%, household furnishings and operations 10.1%, education and recreation 7.4%, energy 6.3%. **Population economically active** (December 2005): total 145,800; activity rate of total population 53.1% (participation rates: ages 15 and over, 69.0%; female 49.5%; unemployed [March 2006] 8.1%). **Gross national income** (2006): US$3,307,000,000 (US$11,291 per capita). **Selected balance of payments data.** Receipts from (US$'000,000): tourism (2005) 897; remittances (2005) 140; foreign direct investment (2001–05 avg.) 48. Disbursements for (US$'000,000): tourism (2005) 96; remittances (2005) 40. **Land use** as % of total land area (2003): in temporary crops 37%, in permanent crops 2%, in pasture 5%; overall forest area (2005) 4%.

Foreign trade

Imports (2005; c.i.f.): BDS$3,209,000,000 (machinery 17.0%; food and beverages 13.8%; mineral fuels 11.7%; construction materials 7.5%). *Major import sources:* US 36.5%; Trinidad and Tobago 22.0%; UK 5.5%; Canada 3.6%. **Exports** (2005; f.o.b.): BDS$719,000,000 (domestic exports 58.6%, of which manufactured goods [other than rum] 27.6%, rum 7.1%, sugar 6.2%; reexports 41.4%). *Major export destinations:* Caricom (Caribbean Community and Common Market) 37.8%, of which Trinidad and Tobago 9.3%, Jamaica 4.8%; US 12.8%; UK 8.7%.

Transport and communications

Transport. *Roads* (2004): total length 1,600 km (paved 100%). *Vehicles* (2004): passenger cars 92,195; trucks and buses 8,597. *Air transport* (2003): metric ton-km cargo 200,000. **Communications**, in total units (units per 1,000 persons). Daily newspaper circulation (2004): 35,000 (130); televisions (2004): 78,000 (291); telephone landlines (2005): 135,000 (501); cellular telephone subscribers (2005): 206,000 (766); personal computers (2005): 40,000 (148); total Internet users (2005): 160,000 (593); broadband Internet subscribers (2005): 32,000 (118).

Education and health

Educational attainment (2003). Percentage of employed labor force having: no formal schooling 0.5%; primary education 14.9%; secondary 58.7%; technical/vocational 5.4%; university 19.6%; other/unknown 0.9%. **Literacy** (2002): total population ages 15 and over literate 99.7%. **Health** (2002): physicians 376 (1 per 721 persons); hospital beds 501 (1 per 541 persons); infant mortality rate per 1,000 live births (2006) 11.8. **Food** (2005): daily per capita caloric intake 2,727 (vegetable products 83%, animal products 17%); 151% of FAO recommended minimum.

Military

Total active duty personnel (2006): 610 (army 82.0%, navy 18.0%). **Military expenditure as percentage of GDP** (2005): 0.5%; per capita expenditure US$52.

Background

The island of Barbados was probably inhabited by Arawak Indians who originally came from South America. Spaniards may have landed by 1518, and by 1536 they had apparently wiped out the Indian population. Barbados was settled by the English in the 1620s. Slaves were brought in to work the sugar plantations, which were especially prosperous in the 17th–18th centuries. The British Empire abolished slavery in 1834, and all the slaves in Barbados were freed by 1838. In 1958 Barbados joined the West Indies Federation. When the latter dissolved in 1962, Barbados sought independence from Britain; it achieved it and joined the Commonwealth in 1966.

Recent Developments

Barbadian officials announced in May 2007 that Barbados would import natural gas by pipeline from Trinidad and Tobago and in June launched an open-bid round for offshore exploration.

Internet resources: <www.barbados.org>.

Belarus

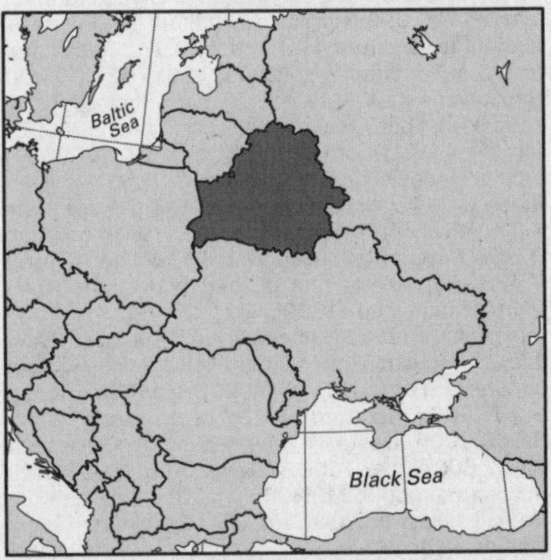

Official name: Respublika Belarus (Republic of Belarus). **Form of government:** republic with two legislative bodies (Council of the Republic [64]; House of Representatives [110]). **Head of state and government:** President Alyaksandr H. Lukashenka (from 1994), assisted by Prime Minister Syarhey Sidorski (from 2003). **Capital:** Minsk. **Official languages:** Belarusian; Russian. **Official religion:** none. **Monetary unit:** Belarusian ruble (Br); valuation (1 Jul 2008) US$1 = Br 2,125.50; ruble re-denominated 1 Jan 2000; as of that date 1,000 (old) rubles = 1 (new) ruble.

Demography

Area: 80,153 sq mi, 207,595 sq km. **Population** (2007): 9,692,000. **Density** (2007): persons per sq mi 120.8, persons per sq km 46.7. **Urban** (2007): 72.8%. **Sex distribution** (2007): male 46.69%; female 53.31%. **Age breakdown** (2005): under 15, 15.2%; 15–29, 24.1%; 30–44, 22.0%; 45–59, 20.2%; 60–74, 12.8%; 75–84, 5.0%; 85 and over, 0.7%. **Ethnic composition** (1999): Belarusian 81.2%; Russian 11.4%; Polish 3.9%; Ukrainian 2.4%; Jewish 0.3%; other 0.8%. **Religious affiliation** (2000): Belarusian Orthodox 48.7%; Roman Catholic 13.2%; unaffiliated Christian 5.9%; other Christian 2.4%; Jewish 0.6%; Muslim 0.3%; nonreligious 24.0%; atheist 4.9%. **Major cities** (2005): Minsk 1,765,800; Homyel 481,200; Mahilyow 366,900; Vitsyebsk 342,700; Hrodna 316,700. **Location:** eastern Europe, bordering Latvia, Russia, Ukraine, Poland, and Lithuania.

Vital statistics

Birth rate per 1,000 population (2005): 9.2 (world avg. 20.3); within marriage 75.9%. **Death rate** per 1,000 population (2005): 14.5 (world avg. 8.6). **Natural increase rate** per 1,000 population (2005): −5.3 (world avg. 11.7). **Total fertility rate** (avg. births per childbearing woman; 2005): 1.21. **Life expectancy** at birth (2005): male 62.9 years; female 75.1 years.

National economy

Budget (2004). *Revenue:* Br 17,417,000,000 (tax revenue 72.7%, of which VAT 21.9%, tax on profits 9.3%, personal income tax 8.1%, excise tax 6.4%; nontax revenue 5.7%; other 21.6%). *Expenditures:* Br 17,595,000,000 (current expenditure 75.1%; development expenditure 4.6%; other 20.3%). **Public debt** (external, outstanding; 2005): US$783,000,000. **Households** (2004). Average household size 3.1; sources of money income: wages and salaries 49.2%, transfers 18.1%, other 32.7%; expenditure (2001): food and nonalcoholic beverages 53.6%, clothing and footwear 9.4%, housing and energy 7.2%, transport 6.3%, alcoholic beverages and tobacco products 5.9%. **Population economically active** (2005): 4,426,300; activity rate of total population 45.4% (participation rate [1999]: ages 15–64, 69.7%; female 53.1%; officially unemployed [December 2006] 1.2%). **Production** (metric tons except as noted). *Agriculture, forestry, fishing* (2005): maize for forage 9,227,000, potatoes 8,185,000, sugar beets 3,065,000; livestock (number of live animals) 3,962,600 cattle, 3,406,800 pigs, 24,600,000 chickens; roundwood 7,542,800 cu m, of which fuelwood 15%; fisheries production (2004) 5,040 (from aquaculture 82%). *Mining and quarrying* (2004): potash 4,650,000; peat 2,100,000. *Manufacturing* (2006): fertilizers 5,469,000; cement 3,495,000; steel (2002) 1,607,000. *Energy production (consumption):* electricity (kW-hr; 2006) 31,800,000,000 ([2005] 34,999,000,000); coal (2004) none (234,000); crude petroleum (barrels; 2005) 13,100,000 (145,400,000); petroleum products (2004) 15,200,000 (5,049,000); natural gas (cu m; 2005) 228,000,000 (20,407,000,000). **Gross national income** (2006): US$36,838,000,000 (US$3,781 per capita). **Land use** as % of total land area (2003): in temporary crops 26.8%, in permanent crops 0.6%, in pasture 15.4%; overall forest area (2005) 38.0%. **Selected balance of payments data.** Receipts from (US$'000,000): tourism (2005) 253; remittances (2005) 370; foreign direct investment (2001–05 avg.) 197. Disbursements for (US$'000,000): tourism (2005) 604; remittances (2005) 94.

Foreign trade

Imports (2006; c.i.f.): US$22,323,000,000 (mineral products 33.4%; machinery, equipment, and vehicles 24.1%; chemicals and chemical products 12.6%; food and beverages 9.4%). *Major import sources* (2004): Russia 68.2%; Germany 6.6%; Ukraine 3.3%; Poland 2.9%; Italy 1.8%. **Exports** (2006; f.o.b.): US$19,739,000,000 (mineral products [significantly refined petroleum] 38.8%; machinery, equipment, and vehicles 20.0%; chemicals and chemical products 14.4%; food and beverages 7.5%). *Major export destinations* (2004): Russia 47.0%; UK 8.3%; The Netherlands 6.7%; Poland 5.3%; Ukraine 3.9%.

Transport and communications

Transport. *Railroads* (2006): length (2002) 5,533 km; passenger-km 9,968,000,000; metric ton-km cargo 45,723,000,000. *Roads* (2004): total length 93,310 km (paved 87%). *Vehicles*: passenger cars (2004) 1,707,888; trucks and buses (2001) 85,791. *Air transport* (2006): passenger-km 754,000,000; metric ton-km cargo 92,000,000. **Communications,** in total units (units per 1,000 persons). Daily newspaper circulation (2004): 887,000 (90); televisions (2003): 3,809,000 (386); telephone landlines (2006): 3,368,000 (347); cellular telephone subscribers (2006): 5,960,000 (614); total Internet users (2006): 4,200,000 (512); broadband Internet subscribers (2006): 11,000 (1.2).

Education and health

Literacy (2001): total population ages 15 and over literate, virtually 100%. **Health** (2005): physicians 45,600 (1 per 214 persons); hospital beds 108,800 (1 per 90 persons); infant mortality rate per 1,000 live births 6.3. **Food** (2005): daily per capita caloric intake 2,885 (vegetable products 72%, animal products 28%); 146% of FAO recommended minimum.

Military

Total active duty personnel (2006): 72,940 (army 40.6%, air force and air defense 24.9%, centrally controlled units 34.5%). **Military expenditure as percentage of GDP** (2005): 7.2%; per capita expenditure US$38.

Background

While Belarusians share a distinct identity and language, they did not enjoy political sovereignty until the late 20th century. The territory that is now Belarus underwent partition and changed hands often; as a result its history is entwined with those of its neighbors. In medieval times the region was ruled by Lithuanians and Poles. Following the Third Partition of Poland, it was ruled by Russia. After World War I, the western part was assigned to Poland, and the eastern part became Soviet Russian territory. After World War II, the Soviets expanded what had been the Belorussian SSR by annexing more of Poland. Much of the area suffered contamination from the Chernobyl accident in 1986, forcing many to evacuate. Belarus declared its independence in 1991 and later joined the Commonwealth of Independent States. Amid increasing political turmoil in the 1990s, it proposed a union with Russia in 1997 that was still being debated at the start of the 21st century.

Recent Developments

In 2007 Belarus resolved two fractious disputes with Russia over natural gas prices and petroleum. Belarus agreed to pay US$100 per 1,000 cu m for im-

1 metric ton = about 1.1 short tons; 1 kilometer = 0.6 mi (statute); 1 metric ton-km cargo = about 0.68 short ton-mi cargo; c.i.f.: cost, insurance, and freight; f.o.b.: free on board

ported Russian gas, more than double the 2006 rate, and to increase the price each year to reach the European rate (at that time about US$265) by 2011. Minsk and Moscow also signed an agreement on oil transit. The tax Belarus was paying on oil imported from Russia was reduced from US$180 to US$53 per ton, though it was to pay an additional tariff on exports of Belarusian products that were produced from imported Russian oil. Despite the energy problems, economic performance was positive. Official estimates put GDP growth at 21% in 2007. Industrial output rose by 8.2% and consumer goods by 7.3%.

Internet resources: <www.belarusembassy.org>.

Belgium

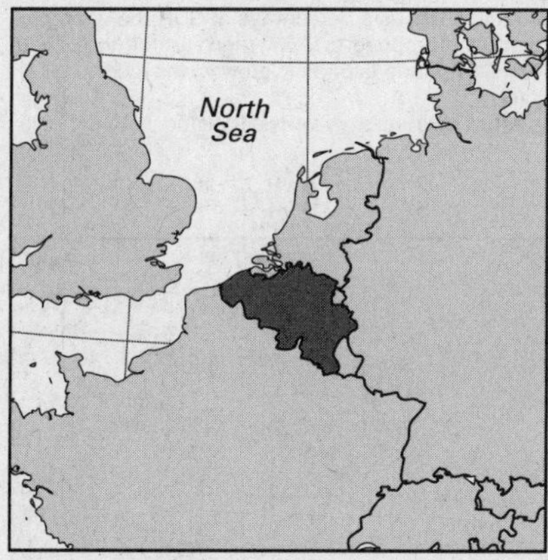

Official name: Koninkrijk België (Dutch); Royaume de Belgique (French) (Kingdom of Belgium). **Form of government:** federal constitutional monarchy with two legislative chambers (Senate [71]; House of Representatives [150]). **Chief of state:** King Albert II (from 1993). **Head of government:** Prime Minister Yves Leterme (from 2008). **Capital:** Brussels. **Official languages:** Dutch; French; German. **Official religion:** none. **Monetary unit:** 1 euro (€) = 100 cents; US$1 = €0.63 (1 Jul 2008).

Demography

Area: 11,787 sq mi, 30,528 sq km. **Population** (2007): 10,597,000. **Density** (2007): persons per sq mi 899.0, persons per sq km 347.1. **Urban** (2005): 97.2%. **Sex distribution** (2005): male 48.94%; female 51.06%. **Age breakdown** (2005): under 15, 16.8%; 15–29, 18.1%; 30–44, 21.9%; 45–59, 20.8%; 60–74, 14.1%; 75–84, 6.5%; 85 and over, 1.8%. **Ethnic composition** (2000): Flemish 53.7%; Walloon (French) 31.6%; Italian 2.6%; French 2.0%; Arab 1.8%; German 1.5%; Berber 0.9%; other 5.9%. **Religious affiliation** (2001): self-identified Roman Catholic 46.7%; other Christian 2.6%; Muslim 3.9%; nonreligious/secular/other 46.8%. **Major cities** (2006): Brussels (population of capital region) 1,024,492; Antwerp 464,038; Ghent 233,925; Charleroi 201,456; Liège 187,432. **Location:** western Europe, bordering The Netherlands, Germany, Luxembourg, France, and the North Sea.

Vital statistics

Birth rate per 1,000 population (2005): 11.2 (world avg. 20.3); within marriage 73.1%. **Death rate** per 1,000 population (2005): 9.8 (world avg. 8.6). **Total fertility rate** (avg. births per childbearing woman; 2005): 1.72. **Life expectancy** at birth (2005): male 76.7 years; female 82.4 years.

National economy

Budget (2005). *Revenue:* €149,218,000,000 (social security contributions 28.2%; personal income tax 24.3%; taxes on goods and services 23.0%). *Expenditures:* €149,504,000,000 (social insurance benefits 46.3%, of which health 12.6%; wages 24.1%; interest on debt 9.1%; capital expenditure 5.4%). **Public debt** (December 2006): US$357,000,000,000. **Production** (metric tons except as noted). *Agriculture, forestry, fishing* (2005): sugar beets 5,606,000, potatoes 2,654,000, wheat 1,768,000; livestock (number of live animals) 6,332,000 pigs, 2,695,000 cattle; roundwood 4,950,000 cu m, of which fuelwood 13%; fisheries production (2004) 27,775 (from aquaculture 4%). *Mining and quarrying* (2005): Belgian bluestone 1,200,000 cu m. *Manufacturing* (value added in €'000,000; 2005): chemicals and chemical products 8,903; base and fabricated metals 7,116; food/beverages/tobacco 6,046; value of traded polished diamonds handled in Antwerp (2005) US$15,900,000,000. *Energy production (consumption):* electricity (kW-hr; 2004–05) 82,665,000,000 ([2004] 85,643,000,000); coal (metric tons; 2004) none (8,244,000); crude petroleum (barrels; 2004) none (252,000,000); petroleum products (metric tons; 2004) 30,086,000 (17,694,000); natural gas (cu m; 2004) negligible (21,300,000,000). **Households.** Avg. household size (2005) 2.4; average net income per household (2003) €24,455 (US$27,602); sources of income (2003): wages and transfer payments 69.3%, property income 11.1%; expenditure (2004): housing 21.0%, food, beverages, tobacco 15.8%, transportation 13.4%, recreation and culture 8.6%. **Land use** as % of total land area (2003): in temporary crops 27.6%, in permanent crops 0.8%, in pasture 17.7%; overall forest area (2005) 22.0%. **Population economically active** (2004): total 4,797,000; activity rate 46.1% (participation rates: ages 15–64, 70.3%; female [2002] 43.0%; unemployed [2006] 8.1%). **Gross national income** (2006): US$395,886,000,000 (US$37,955 per capita). **Selected balance of payments data.** Receipts from (US$'000,000): tourism (2005) 9,845; remittances (2006) 7,154; foreign direct investment (FDI) (2001–05 avg.) 23,072. Disbursements for (US$'000,000): tourism (2005) 14,787; remittances (2006) 2,548; FDI (2001–05 avg.) 21,525.

Foreign trade

Imports (2003; c.i.f.): €208,539,000,000 (machinery and apparatus 16.0%; road vehicles 12.6%; medicine and pharmaceuticals 10.1%; food 7.1%). *Major import sources* (2005–06): The Netherlands 23.0%; Germany 15.8%; France 12.9%; UK 7.6%; US 4.5%. **Exports** (2003; f.o.b.): €226,196,000,000 (road vehicles 14.0%; machinery and apparatus 13.4%; pharmaceuticals 10.0%; food 7.6%; organic chemicals 6.6%; diamonds 4.6%). *Major export destinations* (2005–06): France 17.8%; Germany 16.7%; The Netherlands 12.7%; UK 8.1%; Italy 5.1%.

Transport and communications

Transport. *Railroads* (2005): route length 3,536 km; passenger-km 9,117,000,000; metric ton-km cargo 8,130,000,000. *Roads* (2004): total length 150,567 km (paved 78%). *Vehicles* (2006): passenger cars 4,976,286; trucks and buses 638,579. *Air transport* (2005; SN Brussels, European Air Transport, and TNT Airways S.A. only): passenger-km 4,918,000,000; metric ton-km cargo 705,130,000. **Communications,** in total units (units per 1,000 persons). Daily newspaper circulation (2004): 1,706,000 (164); televisions (2004): 5,800,000 (557); telephone landlines (2006): 4,719,000 (452); cellular telephone subscribers (2006): 9,660,000 (926); personal computers (2004): 3,627,000 (351); total Internet users (2005): 4,800,000 (458); broadband Internet subscribers (2005): 2,005,000 (191).

Education and health

Educational attainment (2002). Percentage of population ages 25 and over having: no formal schooling through lower-secondary education 39%; upper secondary/higher vocational 33%; university 28%. **Health:** physicians (2005) 42,176 (1 per 248 persons); hospital beds (2004) 70,865 (1 per 147 persons); infant mortality rate (2005) 4.4. **Food** (2005): daily per capita caloric intake 3,109 (vegetable products 63%, animal products 37%).

Military

Total active duty personnel (2006): 37,000 (army 67.0%, navy 6.9%, air force 17.2%, medical service 4.9%, other 4.0%). **Military expenditure as percentage of GDP** (2005): 1.1%; per capita expenditure US$403.

Background

Inhabited in ancient times by the Belgae, a Celtic people, the area was conquered by Caesar in 57 BC; under Augustus it became the Roman province of Gallia Belgica. Conquered by the Franks, it later broke up into semi-independent territories, including Brabant and Luxembourg. By the late 15th century AD, the territories of The Netherlands, of which the future Belgium was a part, had gradually united and passed to the Habsburgs. In the 16th century, it was a center for European commerce. The basis of modern Belgium was laid in the southern Catholic provinces that split from the northern provinces after the Union of Utrecht in 1579. Overrun by the French and incorporated into France in 1801, it was reunited to Holland and with it became the independent Kingdom of The Netherlands in 1815. After the revolt of its citizens in 1830, it became the independent Kingdom of Belgium. Under Léopold II it acquired vast lands in Africa. Overrun by the Germans in World Wars I and II, Belgium was the scene of the Battle of the Bulge. Internal discord led to legislation in the 1970s and 1980s that created three nearly autonomous regions in accordance with language distribution: Flemish Flanders, French Wallonia, and bilingual Brussels. In 1993 it became a federation comprising the three regions. It is a member of the European Union.

Recent Developments

Belgium experienced its most serious political crisis in decades following the country's general election in June 2007, as political parties struggled to form a government. In Dutch-speaking Flanders there were major gains for the Christian Democrats, while in Francophone Wallonia the Christian Democrats made modest gains and the Liberals emerged as the largest political force. The clear winner was Yves Leterme, the leader of the Flemish Christian Democrats. His demands for wide-ranging constitutional reforms and increased autonomy for the regions, notably Flanders, met firm opposition from potential French-speaking partners, however, and stalled the formation of a coalition. After nine months of stalemate, Leterme was made prime minister in March 2008. The economy was strong in 2007. Public debt was declining as a percentage of GDP, the unemployment rate dropped to 7.5% (and further, to 6.7% by May 2008), and economic growth was 4.5%.

Internet resources: <www.visitbelgium.com>.

Belize

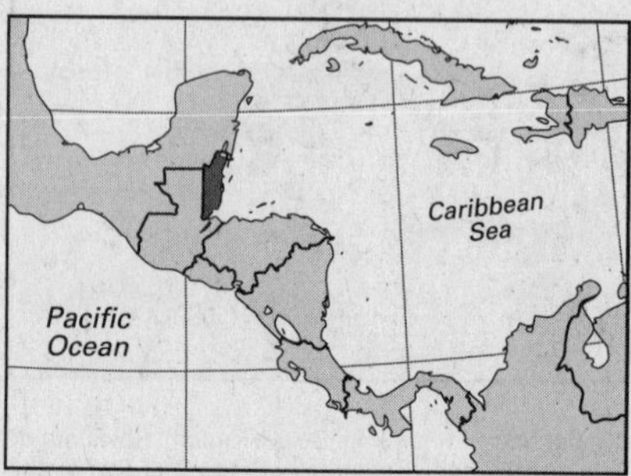

Official name: Belize. **Form of government:** constitutional monarchy with two legislative houses (Senate [12]; House of Representatives [32]). **Chief of state:** British Queen Elizabeth II (from 1952), represented by Governor-General Sir Colville Young (from 1993). **Head of government:** Prime Minister Dean Barrow (from 2008). **Capital:** Belmopan. **Official language:** English. **Official religion:** none. **Monetary unit:** 1 Belize dollar (BZ$) = 100 cents; valuation (1 Jul 2008) US$1 = BZ$1.97 (pegged to the US dollar).

Demography

Area: 8,867 sq mi, 22,965 sq km. **Population** (2007): 306,000. **Density** (2007): persons per sq mi 34.5, persons per sq km 13.3. **Urban** (2005): 50.2%. **Sex distribution** (2005): male 50.51%; female 49.49%. **Age breakdown** (2005): under 15, 41.0%; 15–29, 27.7%; 30–44, 17.4%; 45–59, 8.1%; 60–74, 4.2%; 75–84, 1.2%; 85 and over, 0.4%. **Ethnic composition** (2000): mestizo (Spanish-Indian) 48.7%; Creole (predominantly black) 24.9%; Mayan Indian 10.6%; Garifuna (black–Carib Indian) 6.1%; white 4.3%; East Indian 3.0%; other or not stated 2.4%. **Religious affiliation** (2000): Roman Catholic

49.6%; Protestant 31.8%, of which Pentecostal 7.4%, Anglican 5.3%, Seventh-day Adventist 5.2%, Mennonite 4.1%; other Christian 1.9%; nonreligious 9.4%; other 7.3%. **Major cities** (2005): Belize City 60,800; San Ignacio/Santa Elena 16,800; Orange Walk 15,300; Belmopan 13,500; Dangriga 10,800. **Location:** Central America, bordering Mexico, the Caribbean Sea, and Guatemala.

Vital statistics

Birth rate per 1,000 population (2005): 29.3 (world avg. 20.3); (1997) within marriage 40.3%. **Death rate** per 1,000 population (2005): 5.7 (world avg. 8.6). **Natural increase rate** per 1,000 population (2005): 23.7 (world avg. 11.7). **Total fertility rate** (avg. births per childbearing woman; 2005): 3.68. **Life expectancy** at birth (2005): male 66.5 years; female 70.4 years.

National economy

Budget (2006–07). *Revenue:* BZ$598,048,000 (tax revenue 85.9%, of which taxes on goods and services 33.8%, taxes on international trade 28.5%, taxes on income and profits 22.6%; other revenue 14.1%). *Expenditures:* BZ$667,943,000 (current expenditure 84.1%; capital expenditure 15.9%). **Production** (metric tons except as noted). *Agriculture, forestry, fishing* (2005): sugarcane (2006) 1,188,000, oranges 213,400, bananas (2006) 69,600; livestock (number of live animals) 57,800 cattle, 1,600,000 chickens; roundwood 187,600 cu m, of which fuelwood 67%; fisheries production (2004) 14,335 (from aquaculture 80%). *Mining and quarrying* (2004): limestone 571,000; sand and gravel 162,000. *Manufacturing* (value added in US$'000,000; 2004): food products and beverages (significantly citrus concentrate, flour, sugar, and beer) 69.2; textiles, clothing, and footwear 7.2; other (including cigarettes) 11.5. *Energy production (consumption):* electricity (kW-hr; 2004) 169,000,000 (194,000,000); crude petroleum (barrels; 2006) 810,000 (n.a.); petroleum products (metric tons; 2004) none (292,000). **Households.** Average household size (2004) 4.4; average annual income of employed head of household (1993) BZ$6,450 (US$3,225); expenditure: food, beverages, and tobacco 34.7%, transportation 17.0%, housing and energy 16.8%, clothing and footwear 9.2%. **Land use** as % of total land area (2003): in temporary crops 3.1%, in permanent crops 1.4%, in pasture 2.2%; overall forest area (2005) 72.5%. **Population economically active** (2005): total 110,786; activity rate of total population 38.2% (participation rates: ages 14 and over 59.4%; female 36.7%; unemployed 11.0%). **Gross national income** (2006): US$1,003,000,000 (US$3,560 per capita). **Public debt** (external, outstanding; September 2006): US$929,600,000. **Selected balance of payments data.** Receipts from (US$'000,000): tourism (2005) 208; remittances (2006) 96; foreign direct investment (2001–05 avg.) 34; official development assistance (2005) 23 (commitments). Disbursements for (US$'000,000): tourism (2005) 42; remittances (2005) 20.

Foreign trade

Imports (2005; f.o.b. in balance of trade and c.i.f. in commodities and trading partners): BZ$1,226,200,000 (mineral fuels and electricity 19.2%; machinery and transport equipment 16.3%; direct imports to commercial free zone 15.0%; food and live animals 9.8%; chemicals and chemical products 7.2%). *Major import sources:* US 39%; Central American countries 19%; Mexico 9%; EU 7%; Caricom (Caribbean Community and Common Market) 2%. **Exports** (2005): BZ$643,800,000 (domestic exports 60.4%, of which seafood products [significantly shrimp] 14.1%, citrus [mostly oranges] concentrate 11.9%, raw sugar 10.8%, bananas 7.9%, garments 5.3%; reexports [principally to Mexico] 39.6%). *Major export destinations* (domestic exports only): US 52%; UK 22%; other EU 7%; Caricom 11%; Mexico 4%.

Transport and communications

Transport. *Roads* (2000): total length 2,984 km (paved 14%). *Vehicles* (2003): passenger cars 36,952; trucks and buses 7,380. *Air transport* (2001; Belize international airport only): passenger arrivals 256,564, passenger departures 240,900; cargo loaded 186 metric tons, cargo unloaded 1,272 metric tons. **Communications,** in total units (units per 1,000 persons). Televisions (2003): 52,000 (190); telephone landlines (2006): 34,000 (137); cellular telephone subscribers (2006): 118,000 (430); personal computers (2002): 35,000 (132); total Internet users (2006): 34,000 (124); broadband Internet subscribers (2006): 5,600 (19).

Education and health

Educational attainment (2000). Percentage of population ages 25 and over having: no formal schooling 36.6%; primary education 40.9%; secondary 11.7%; postsecondary/advanced vocational 6.4%; university 3.8%; other/unknown 0.6%. **Literacy** (2001): total population ages 14 and over literate 93.4%; males 93.6%; females 93.3%. **Health** (2004): physicians 221 (1 per 1,279 persons); hospital beds 650 (1 per 435 persons); infant mortality rate per 1,000 live births (2005) 25.4. **Food** (2005): daily per capita caloric intake 2,921 (vegetable products 80%, animal products 20%); 161% of FAO recommended minimum.

Military

Total active duty personnel (2006): 1,050 (army 100%); foreign forces (2006): British army 30. **Military expenditure as percentage of GDP** (2004): 1.4%; per capita expenditure US$55.

Background

The area was inhabited by the Maya c. 300 BC–AD 900; the ruins of their ceremonial centers, including Caracol and Xunantunich, can still be seen. The Spanish claimed sovereignty from the 16th century but never tried to settle Belize, though they regarded as interlopers the British who did. British logwood cutters arrived in the mid-17th century; Spanish opposition was finally overcome in 1798. When settlers began to penetrate the interior they met with Indian resistance. In 1871 British Honduras became a crown colony, but an unfulfilled provision of an 1859 British-Guatemalan treaty led Guatemala to claim the territory. The situation had not been resolved when Belize was granted its independence in 1981. A British force, stationed there to ensure the new nation's security, was withdrawn after Guatemala officially recognized the territory's independence in 1991.

Recent Developments

The government of Belize addressed its unsustainable debt burden in 2007. Most of its creditors agreed to exchange their claims for new bonds, with a face value of US$546.8 million, that would mature in 2019. Unfortunately, the devastation inflicted in August by Hurricane Dean resulted in an estimated US$98.6 million loss, about one-third of the government revenues for the April 2007–March 2008 period.

Internet resources: <www.belizetourism.org>.

Benin

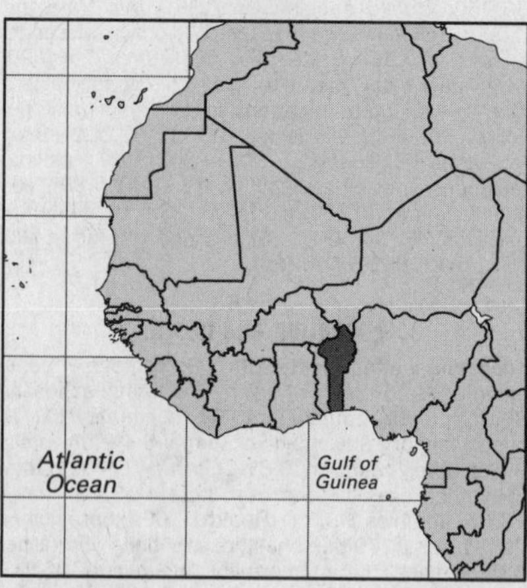

Official name: République du Bénin (Republic of Benin). **Form of government:** multiparty republic with one legislative house (National Assembly [83]). **Head of state and government:** President Yayi Boni (from 2006). **Capital:** Porto-Novo (official capital and seat of legislature; administrative seat in Cotonou). **Official language:** French. **Official religion:** none. **Monetary unit:** 1 CFA franc (CFAF) = 100 centimes; valuation (1 Jul 2008) US$1 = CFAF 414.60 (pegged since 1 Jan 2002 to the euro (€) at €1 = CFAF 655.96).

Demography

Area: 43,484 sq mi, 112,622 sq km. **Population** (2007): 8,079,000. **Density** (2007): persons per sq mi 185.8, persons per sq km 71.7. **Urban** (2005): 38.8%. **Sex distribution** (2002): male 48.51%; female 51.49%. **Age breakdown** (2005): under 15, 44.5%; 15–29, 28.5%; 30–44, 15.6%; 45–59, 7.5%; 60–74, 3.3%; 75 and over, 0.6%. **Ethnic composition** (2002): Fon 39.2%; Adjara 15.2%; Yoruba (Nago) 12.3%; Bariba 9.2%; Fulani 7.0%; Somba (Otomary) 6.1%; Yoa-Lokpa 4.0%; other 7.0%. **Religious affiliation** (2002): Christian 42.8%, of which Roman Catholic 27.1%, Protestant 5.4%, indigenous Christian 5.3%; Muslim 24.4%; traditional beliefs 23.3%, of which voodoo 17.3%; nonreligious 6.5%; other 3.0%. **Major cities** (2004): Cotonou 818,100; Porto-Novo 234,300; Parakou 227,900; Djougou 206,500; Abomey 126,800. **Location:** western Africa, bordering Burkina Faso, Niger, Nigeria, the Atlantic Ocean, and Togo.

Vital statistics

Birth rate per 1,000 population (2006): 38.8 (world avg. 20.3). **Death rate** per 1,000 population (2006): 12.2 (world avg. 8.6). **Natural increase rate** per 1,000 population (2006): 26.6 (world avg. 11.7). **Total fertility rate** (avg. births per childbearing woman; 2006): 5.20. **Life expectancy** at birth (2006): male 51.9 years; female 54.2 years.

National economy

Budget (2005). *Revenue:* CFAF 422,100,000,000 (tax revenue 79.2%; nontax revenue 11.7%; grants 9.1%). *Expenditures:* CFAF 455,300,000,000 (current expenditures 73.4%, of which interest on public debt 1.5%; development expenditure 26.8%; net lending −0.2%). **Public debt** (external, outstanding; 2005): US$1,762,000,000. **Gross national income** (2006): US$4,649,000,000 (US$531 per capita). **Production** (metric tons except as noted). *Agriculture, forestry, fishing* (2005): cassava 2,861,000, yams 2,084,000, corn (maize) 865,000; livestock (number of live animals) 1,800,000 cattle, 1,380,000 goats, 750,000 sheep; roundwood 6,393,188 cu m, of which fuelwood 95%; fisheries production (2004) 39,995. *Mining* (2005): insignificant production of clay and gold. *Manufacturing* (value added in US$'000,000; 1999): food products 74; textiles 42; beverages 36. *Energy production (consumption):* electricity (kW-hr; 2004) 81,000,000 (659,000,000); crude petroleum (barrels; 2004) 137,000 (negligible); petroleum products (metric tons; 2004) none (737,000). **Population economically active** (2002): total 2,830,900; activity rate of total population 41.4% (participation rates: ages 15–64 [1997] 84.3%; female [1998] 50.8%; unemployed in Cotonou [April 2003] 6.8%). **Households.** Average household size (2002) 5.6; expenditure (1996): food and nonalcoholic beverages 38.2%, transportation 10.1%, expenditures in cafés and hotels 9.8%, housing and energy 9.5%, clothing and footwear 6.9%. **Land use** as % of total land area (2003): in temporary crops 24.0%, in permanent crops 2.4%, in pasture 5.0%; overall forest area (2005) 21.3%. **Selected balance of payments data.** Receipts from (US$'000,000): tourism (2005) 106; remittances (2005) 63; foreign direct investment (2001–05 avg.) 38; official development assistance (2005) 349. Disbursements for (US$'000,000): tourism (2004) 29; remittances (2005) 7.

Foreign trade

Imports (2005): CFAF 454,600,000,000 (food products 31.2%; petroleum products 14.7%; machinery and transport equipment 13.6%). *Major import sources* (2004): China 32%; France 13%; Thailand 7%; Côte d'Ivoire 5%. **Exports** (2005): CFAF 300,000,000,000 (domestic exports 59.5%, of which cotton 30.4%; reexports 40.5%). *Major export* *destinations* (2004): China 30%; India 19%; Ghana 6%; Niger 6%; Nigeria 4%.

Transport and communications

Transport. *Railroads* (2002): length (2004) 578 km; passenger-km 62,194,000; metric ton-km cargo 88,832,000. *Roads* (2004): total length 19,000 km (paved 9.5%). *Vehicles* (1996): passenger cars 37,772; trucks and buses 8,058. *Air transport* (2003): passengers carried 46,000; metric ton-km cargo 7,000,000. **Communications,** in total units (units per 1,000 persons). Daily newspaper circulation (2004): 16,000 (2.2); televisions (2004): 431,000 (59); telephone landlines (2006): 77,000 (8.9); cellular telephone subscribers (2006): 1,056,000 (121); personal computers (2005): 32,000 (4.2); total Internet users (2006): 700,000 (80); broadband Internet subscribers (2006): 100 (0.03).

Education and health

Educational attainment (2002). Percentage of population ages 15 and over having: no formal schooling 63.5%; primary education 18.7%; secondary 15.9%; postsecondary 1.9%. **Literacy** (2005): total percentage of population ages 15 and over literate 43.2%; males literate 58.8%; females literate 28.4%. **Health** (2001): physicians 923 (1 per 7,183 persons); hospital beds 590 (1 per 11,238 persons); infant mortality rate per 1,000 live births (2006) 79.6. **Food** (2005): daily per capita caloric intake 2,437 (vegetable products 95%, animal products 5%); 135% of FAO recommended minimum.

Military

Total active duty personnel (2006): 4,550 (army 94.5%, navy 2.2%, air force 3.3%). **Military expenditure as percentage of GNP** (2005): 1.7%; per capita expenditure US$10.

Background

In southern Benin, the Dahomey, or Fon, established the Abomey kingdom in 1625. In the 18th century, the kingdom became known as Dahomey when it expanded to include Allada and Ouidah, where French forts had been established in the 17th century. In 1857 the French reestablished themselves in the area, and eventually fighting ensued. In 1894 Dahomey became a French protectorate; it was incorporated into the federation of French West Africa in 1904. It achieved independence in 1960. The area called Dahomey was renamed Benin in 1975. At the end of the 20th century, its chronically weak economy produced tension between laborers and the government.

Recent Developments

Pres. Thomas Yayi Boni organized a "march against corruption" in July 2007, and he later vowed to fulfill his election promises by wiping it out. In June it was announced that the Benin scientist Jérôme Fagla Médégan had been granted a patent for his new treatment for a strain of sickle-cell anemia, marking the first time that an African had been given a patent for a new drug.

Internet resources: <http://benintourisme.com>.

Bermuda

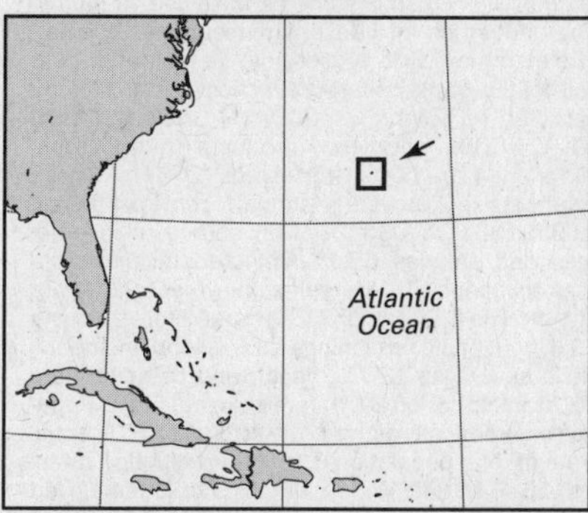

Official name: Bermuda. **Political status:** overseas territory of the UK with two legislative houses (Senate [11]; House of Assembly [36]). **Chief of state:** British Queen Elizabeth II (from 1952), represented by Governor Sir Richard Gozney (from 2007). **Head of government:** Premier Ewart Brown (from 2006). **Capital:** Hamilton. **Official language:** English. **Official religion:** none. **Monetary unit:** 1 Bermuda dollar (Bd$) = 100 cents; valuation (1 Jul 2008) US$1 = Bd$1.00.

Demography

Area: 20.5 sq mi, 53.1 sq km. **Population** (2007): 64,900. **Density** (2007): persons per sq mi 3,166, persons per sq km 1,222. **Urban** (2005): 100%. **Sex distribution** (2006): male 47.81%; female 52.19%. **Age breakdown** (2006): under 15, 18.1%; 15–29, 17.6%; 30–44, 24.8%; 45–59, 22.7%; 60–74, 11.9%; 75–84, 3.9%; 85 and over, 1.0%. **Ethnic composition** (2000): black 50.4%; British expatriates 29.0%; mulatto 10.0%; US white 6.0%; Portuguese 4.5%; other 0.1%. **Religious affiliation** (2000): Protestant 64.3%, of which Anglican 22.6%, Methodist 14.9%; Roman Catholic 14.9%; nonreligious 13.8%; other 6.0%; unknown 1.0%. **Major cities** (2000): St. George 1,752; Hamilton 969. **Location:** North Atlantic Ocean, east of North Carolina (US).

Vital statistics

Birth rate per 1,000 population (2004): 13.1 (world avg. 21.1); (2002) within marriage 64.2%. **Death rate** per 1,000 population (2004): 7.2 (world avg. 8.8). **Natural increase rate** per 1,000 population (2004): 5.9 (world avg. 12.3). **Total fertility rate** (avg. births per childbearing woman; 2006): 1.89. **Life expectancy** at birth (2006): male 75.8 years; female 80.1 years.

National economy

Budget (2004–05). *Revenue:* Bd$782,500,000 (payroll taxes 31.6%; customs duties 27.1%; taxes on international companies 6.3%; stamp duties 6.1%; taxes on land 5.4%; other 23.5%). *Expenditures:* Bd$809,000,000 (current expenditure 89.3%; development expenditure 10.7%). **Public debt** (2004–05): US$128,000,000. **Production** (value in Bd$'000 except as noted). *Agriculture, forestry, fishing* (2005): vegetables 4,709, fruits 334, flowers 228; livestock (number of live animals) 900 horses, 600 cattle,

45,000 chickens; fisheries production 379. *Mining and quarrying:* crushed stone for local use. *Manufacturing:* industries include pharmaceuticals, cosmetics, electronics, fish processing, handicrafts, and small boat building. *Energy production (consumption):* electricity (kW-hr; 2004) 661,000,000 (661,000,000); petroleum products (metric tons; 2004) none (198,000). **Households** (2004). Average household size 2.3; average annual income per household Bd$106,233 (US$106,233); sources of income: wages and salaries 65.1%, imputed income from owner occupancy 14.4%, self-employment 9.2%, net rental income 4.1%, other 7.2%; expenditure: housing 33.3%, household furnishings 13.8%, food and nonalcoholic beverages 13.7%, health and personal care 8.7%, transportation 8.0%, foreign travel 5.4%. **Population economically active** (2000): total 37,879; activity rate of total population 61.0% (participation rates: ages 16–64, 84.8%; female 48.3%; unemployed [2005] 2.1%). **Gross national income** (at 2005 market prices): US$5,056,000,000 (US$78,538 per capita). **Selected balance of payments data.** Receipts from (US$'000,000): tourism (2005–06) 453; foreign direct investment (2001–05 avg.) 8,620. Disbursements for (US$'000,000): tourism (1997) 148. **Land use** as % of total land area (2003): in temporary crops 2%; overall forest area (2005) 20%.

Foreign trade

Imports (2002): Bd$746,000,000 (food, beverages, and tobacco 20.2%; machinery 16.5%; chemicals and chemical products 13.9%; mineral fuels 7.8%; transport equipment 6.0%). *Major import sources:* US 76%; Canada 5%; UK 5%; Caribbean countries (mostly Netherlands Antilles) 3%. **Exports** (2002): Bd$57,000,000 (nearly all reexports [including sales of fuel to aircraft and ships and pharmaceuticals]; diamond market was established in 1990s). *Major export destinations:* mostly US, UK, Norway, and Spain.

Transport and communications

Transport. *Roads* (2002): total length 225 km (paved 100%). *Vehicles* (2005): passenger cars 21,978; trucks and buses 4,873. *Air transport*: passenger arrivals and departures (2005) 900,000; cargo loaded (2001) 909 metric tons, cargo unloaded (2001) 4,862 metric tons. **Communications,** in total units (units per 1,000 persons). Daily newspaper circulation (2003): 17,000 (268); televisions (2001): 68,000 (1,077); telephone landlines (2006): 58,000 (889); cellular telephone subscribers (2006): 60,000 (916); personal computers (2002): 34,000 (535); total Internet users (2005): 42,000 (646); broadband Internet subscribers (2006): 24,000 (360).

Education and health

Educational attainment (2000). Percentage of total population ages 15 and over having: no formal schooling 0.4%; primary education 7.0%; secondary 39.3%; postsecondary technical 25.7%; higher 26.8%; not stated 0.8%. **Literacy** (1997): total population ages 15 and over literate 98%. **Health:** physicians (2005) 135 (1 per 482 persons); hospital beds (2005–06) 351 (1 per 186 persons); infant mortality rate per 1,000 live births (2001–03) 2.0. **Food** (2005): daily per capita caloric intake 3,083 (vegetable products 81%, animal products 19%).

Military

Total active duty personnel (2006): 530; part-time defense force assists police and is drawn from Bermudian conscripts.

Background

The Bermuda archipelago was named for Juan de Bermúdez, who may have visited the islands in 1503. Colonized by the English in 1612, Bermuda became a crown colony in 1684 and a British overseas territory in 2002. Its economy is based on tourism and international finance; its per capita gross national product is among the world's highest.

Recent Developments

In the local elections on Bermuda on 18 December 2007, Premier Ewart Brown's Progressive Liberal Party (PLP) won 52.35% of the vote and 22 seats, compared with 47.25% and 14 seats for the United Bermuda Party. It was the PLP's third successive election victory and left the balance of parliamentary power unchanged.

Internet resources: <www.bermudatourism.org>.

Bhutan

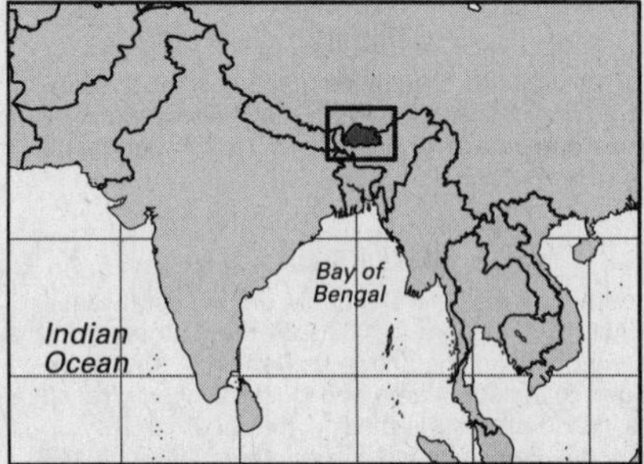

Official name: Druk-Yul (Kingdom of Bhutan). **Form of government:** constitutional monarchy with two legislative houses (National Council [25]; National Assembly [47]). **Chief of state:** King Jigme Khesar Namgyal Wangchuk (from 2006). **Head of government:** Prime Minister Lyonchen Jigme Thinley (from 2008). **Capital:** Thimphu. **Official language:** Dzongkha (a Tibetan dialect). **Official religion:** Mahayana Buddhism. **Monetary unit:** 1 ngultrum (Nu) = 100 chetrum; valuation (1 Jul 2008) US$1 = Nu 43.35; the Indian rupee is also accepted legal tender.

Demography

Area: 14,824 sq mi, 38,394 sq km. **Population** (2007): 658,000. **Density** (2007): persons per sq mi

44.4, persons per sq km 17.1. **Urban** (2005): 30.9%. **Sex distribution** (2005): male 54.20%; female 45.80%. **Age breakdown** (2005): under 15, 33.2%; 15-29, 32.1%; 30-44, 17.6%; 45-59, 10.4%; 60-74, 5.5%; 75-84, 1.1%; 85 and over, 0.1%. **Ethnic composition** (2005): Bhutia (Ngalops) 50%; Nepalese (Gurung) 35%; Sharchops 15%. **Religious affiliation** (2005): Buddhist 74%; Hindu 25%; Christian 1%. **Major towns** (2001): Thimphu 50,510; Phuentsholing 13,292; Gedu 7,826; Gelaphu 6,384; Samtse 3,703. **Location:** southern Asia, bordering China and India.

Vital statistics

Birth rate per 1,000 population (2005): 20.5 (world avg. 20.3). **Death rate** per 1,000 population (2005): 7.5 (world avg. 8.6). **Natural increase rate** per 1,000 population (2005): 13.0 (world avg. 11.7). **Total fertility rate** (avg. births per childbearing woman; 2005): 2.55. **Life expectancy** at birth (2005): male 62.9 years; female 66.4 years.

National economy

Budget (2005-06). *Revenue:* Nu 13,534,000,000 (grants 47.2%; tax revenue 27.8%; nontax revenue 22.5%; other 2.5%). *Expenditures:* Nu 16,151,000,000 (capital expenditures 55.1%; current expenditures 44.9%). **Public debt** (external, outstanding; September 2006): US$691,100,000. **Production** (metric tons except as noted). *Agriculture, forestry, fishing* (2005): corn (maize) 70,000, potatoes 47,000, rice 45,000; livestock (number of live animals) 372,000 cattle, 41,000 pigs, 28,000 horses; roundwood 4,679,000 cu m, of which fuelwood 97%; fisheries production (2004) 300. *Mining and quarrying* (2005): limestone 536,000; dolomite 388,700; gypsum 150,600. *Manufacturing* (value of sales in Nu '000,000; 2005): chemical products 857; cement 807; ferroalloys 651. *Energy production (consumption):* electricity (kW-hr; 2005) 2,355,000,000 (739,000,000); coal (metric tons; 2005) 85,300 ([2004] 65,000); petroleum products (metric tons; 2004) none (51,000). **Households.** Average household size (2005) 4.6; expenditure (2003): food 36%, housing 27%, clothing 10%, education 3%, health care 1%. **Population economically active** (2005): total 257,000; activity rate of total population 38.2% (officially unemployed 3.1%). **Gross national income** (2006): US$921,000,000 (US$1,420 per capita). **Land use** as % of total land area (2003): in temporary crops 3.2%, in permanent crops 0.4%, in pasture 8.8%; overall forest area (2005) 68.0%. **Selected balance of payments data.** Receipts from (US$'000,000): tourism (2005-06) 21; remittances (2005) 1.5; foreign direct investment (2001-05 avg.) 38; official development assistance (2005) 90.

Foreign trade

Imports (2005; c.i.f.): Nu 17,035,000,000 (machinery, transport equipment, and base and fabricated metals 45.5%; mineral fuels 16.1%; food and beverages 14.9%; textiles 4.2%). *Major import sources:* India 75.1%; Japan 3.8%; Singapore 2.6%; Thailand 1.6%; South Korea 1.5%. **Exports** (2005; f.o.b.): Nu 11,386,000,000 (electricity 30.2%; copper wire and cable 9.6%; calcium carbide 6.2%; ferroalloys 6.0%; cement 5.4%; polyester yarn 4.2%). *Major export destinations:* India 87.6%; Hong Kong 6.0%; Bangladesh 4.9%.

Transport and communications

Transport. *Roads* (2004): total length 4,153 km (paved 59%). *Vehicles* (2003): passenger cars 10,574; trucks and buses 3,852. *Air transport* (2002): passenger-km 61,000,000; metric ton-km cargo 5,700,000. **Communications**, in total units (units per 1,000 persons). Televisions (2004): 25,000 (33); telephone landlines (2006): 32,000 (49); cellular telephone subscribers (2006): 82,000 (128); personal computers (2005): 13,000 (16); total Internet users (2006): 30,000 (47).

Education and health

Literacy (2005): total population ages 6 and over literate 59.5%; males literate 69.1%; females literate 48.7%. **Health** (2003): physicians 140 (1 per 5,245 persons); hospital beds 1,093 (1 per 672 persons); infant mortality rate per 1,000 live births (2005) 48.8.

Military

Total active duty personnel (2002): about 6,000 (army 100%). **Military expenditure as percentage of GDP** (2005): 1.0%; per capita expenditure US$11.

Background

Bhutan's mountains and forests long made it inaccessible to the outside world, and its feudal rulers banned foreigners until well into the 20th century. It nevertheless became the object of foreign invasions; in 1865 it came under British influence, and in 1910 it agreed to be guided by Britain in its foreign affairs. It later became oriented toward British-ruled India, though much of its trade was with Tibet. India took over Britain's role in 1949, and China's 1950 occupation of neighboring Tibet further strengthened Bhutan's ties with India. The apparent Chinese threat made Bhutan's rulers aware of the need to modernize, and it embarked on a program to build roads and hospitals and to create a system of secular education.

Recent Developments

In 2008 Bhutan transitioned from an absolute monarchy to a multiparty democracy. Bhutan's first general elections were held in March, resulting in the election of Lyonpo Jigme Thinley as prime minister with real executive powers. The fate of more than 100,000 Bhutanese refugees staying in UN High Commissioner for Refugees-administered camps in eastern Nepal remained uncertain. Following the completion in 2007 of the Tala Hydroelectric Project, which supplied India with power, plans were approved for work to begin in 2008 on the Punatsangchu-I project.

Internet resources: <www.kingdomofbhutan.com>.

Bolivia

Official name: República de Bolivia (Republic of Bolivia). **Form of government:** unitary multiparty republic with two legislative houses (Chamber of Senators

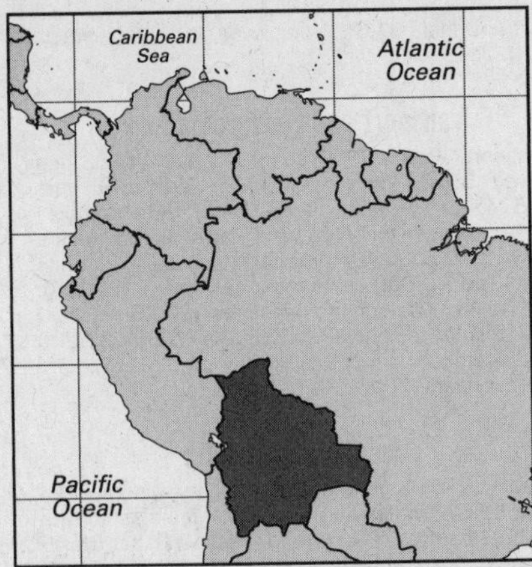

[27]; Chamber of Deputies [130]). **Head of state and government:** President Evo Morales (from 2006). **Capitals:** La Paz (administrative); Sucre (judicial). **Official languages:** Spanish; Aymara; Quechua. **Official religion:** Roman Catholicism. **Monetary unit:** 1 boliviano (Bs) = 100 centavos; valuation (1 Jul 2008) US$1 = Bs 7.20.

Demography

Area: 424,164 sq mi, 1,098,581 sq km. **Population** (2007): 9,525,000. **Density** (2007): persons per sq mi 22.5, persons per sq km 8.7. **Urban** (2005): 64.2%. **Sex distribution** (2006): male 49.85%; female 50.15%. **Age breakdown** (2005): under 15, 38.1%; 15–29, 27.1%; 30–44, 17.6%; 45–59, 10.4%; 60–74, 5.3%; 75–84, 1.3%; 85 and over, 0.2%. **Ethnic composition** (2001): Amerindian 62%, of which Quechua 31%, Aymara 25%; mestizo 28%; white 10%, of which German 3%. **Religious affiliation** (2001): Roman Catholic 78%; Protestant/independent Christian 16%; other Christian 3%, of which Mormon 1.8%; nonreligious 2.5%; other 0.5%. **Major cities** (2001): Santa Cruz 1,116,059 (urban agglomeration [2005] 1,320,000); La Paz 789,585 (urban agglomeration [2005] 1,527,000); El Alto (within La Paz urban agglomeration) 647,350; Cochabamba 516,683; Oruro 201,230. **Location:** central South America, bordering Brazil, Paraguay, Argentina, Chile, and Peru.

Vital statistics

Birth rate per 1,000 population (2006): 23.3 (world avg. 20.3). **Death rate** per 1,000 population (2006): 7.5 (world avg. 8.6). **Natural increase rate** per 1,000 population (2006): 15.8 (world avg. 11.7). **Total fertility rate** (avg. births per childbearing woman; 2006): 2.85. **Life expectancy** at birth (2006): male 63.2 years; female 68.6 years.

National economy

Budget (2006). *Revenue:* Bs 30,071,900,000 (taxes on hydrocarbons 35.4%; other tax income 49.5%; other 15.1%). *Expenditures:* Bs 26,876,500,000 (current expenditure 65.3%; capital expenditure 34.7%). **Public debt** (external, outstanding; 2005): US$4,664,000,000. **Production** (metric tons except as noted). *Agriculture, forestry, fishing* (2005): sugarcane 5,112,000, soybeans 1,689,000, corn (maize) 816,700 (Bolivia was the third largest producer of coca in the world in 2005); livestock (number of live animals) 8,550,000 sheep, 6,822,200 cattle, 2,984,000 pigs, (2004) 1,900,000 llamas and alpacas; roundwood 3,061,337 cu m, of which fuelwood 74%; fisheries production (2004) 7,196 (from aquaculture 6%). *Mining and quarrying* (metal content; 2005): zinc 157,019; tin 18,694; silver 420. *Manufacturing* (value added in Bs '000,000; 2004, in 1990 prices): food products 1,545; beverages and tobacco products 581; petroleum products 497. *Energy production (consumption):* electricity (kW-hr; 2005) 4,778,000,000 ([2004] 4,547,000,000); crude petroleum (barrels; 2004) 15,300,000 (10,700,000); petroleum products (metric tons; 2004) 1,618,000 (1,454,000); natural gas (cu m; 2004) 9,544,000,000 (1,732,000,000). **Population economically active** (2000): total 3,823,937; activity rate of total population 46.2% (participation rates: ages 15–64, 71.8%; female 44.6%; unemployed [2006] 8% in urban areas). **Gross national income** (2006): US$10,163,000,000 (US$1,087 per capita). **Households.** Average household size (2004) 4.3; annual income per household (1999): Bs 16,980 (US$2,920); expenditure (2000): food 28.6%, transportation and communications 23.1%, rent and energy 10.3%, expenditures in cafés and hotels 9.5%, recreation and culture 7.1%, household furnishings 6.3%. **Selected balance of payments data.** Receipts from (US$'000,000): tourism (2005) 239; remittances (2006) 1,030; foreign direct investment (2001–05 avg.) 274; official development assistance (2005) 547 (commitments). Disbursements for (US$'000,000): tourism (2005) 186; remittances (2005) 66. **Land use** as % of total land area (2003): in temporary crops 2.8%, in permanent crops 0.2%, in pasture 31.2%; overall forest area (2005) 54.2%.

Foreign trade

Imports (2005; c.i.f.): US$2,343,300,000 (machinery and apparatus 20.1%; chemicals and chemical products 14.6%; base and fabricated metals 11.0%; mineral products 10.9%; transport equipment 10.1%). *Major import sources:* Brazil 21.9%; Argentina 16.7%; US 13.8%; Chile 6.9%; Peru 6.5%. **Exports** (2005; f.o.b.): US$2,810,400,000 (natural gas 35.0%; soybeans 13.3%; petroleum 12.7%; zinc 7.1%; tin 4.5%; silver 2.8%). *Major export destinations:* Brazil 36.8%; US 14.0%; Argentina 9.5%; Colombia 6.6%; Venezuela 5.8%.

Transport and communications

Transport. *Railroads* (2004): route length 3,519 km; (1997) passenger-km 224,900,000; (1997) metric ton-km cargo 838,900,000. *Roads* (2004): total length 62,479 km (paved 7%). *Vehicles* (2004): passenger cars 171,642; trucks and buses 173,864. *Air transport* (2003): passenger-km 1,704,000,000; metric ton-km cargo 24,348,000. **Communications,** in total units (units per 1,000 persons). Daily news-

1 metric ton = about 1.1 short tons; 1 kilometer = 0.6 mi (statute); 1 metric ton-km cargo = about 0.68 short ton-mi cargo; c.i.f.: cost, insurance, and freight; f.o.b.: free on board

paper circulation (2004): 139,000 (16); televisions (2004): 1,210,000 (134); telephone landlines (2006): 667,000 (71); cellular telephone subscribers (2006): 2,698,000 (289); personal computers (2004): 210,000 (23); total Internet users (2006): 580,000 (62); broadband Internet subscribers (2005): 11,000 (1.2).

Education and health

Educational attainment (2003). Percentage of population ages 19 and over having: no formal schooling/unknown 14.8%; primary education 44.9%; secondary 24.8%; higher 15.5%. **Literacy** (2003): total population ages 15 and over literate 87.2%; males literate 93.1%; females literate 81.6%. **Health**: physicians (2002) 2,987 (1 per 2,827 persons); hospital beds (2005) 9,886 (1 per 954 persons); infant mortality rate (2006) 51.8. **Food** (2005): daily per capita caloric intake 2,128 (vegetable products 81%, animal products 19%); 118% of FAO recommended minimum.

Military

Total active duty personnel (2006): 33,000 (army 75.8%, navy 15.1%, air force 9.1%). **Military expenditure as percentage of GDP** (2005): 1.6%; per capita expenditure US$16.

Background

The Bolivian highlands were the location of the advanced Tiwanaku culture in the 7th–11th centuries and, with its passing, became the home of the Aymara, an Indian group conquered by the Incas in the 15th century. The Incas were overrun by the invading Spanish under Francisco Pizarro in the 1530s. By 1600 Spain had established the cities of Charcas (now Sucre), La Paz, Santa Cruz, and what would become Cochabamba, and had begun to exploit the silver wealth of Potosí. Bolivia flourished in the 17th century, and for a time Potosí was the largest city in the Americas. By the end of the century, the mineral wealth had dried up. Talk of independence began as early as 1809, but not until 1825 were Spanish forces finally defeated. Bolivia shrank in size when it lost Atacama province to Chile in 1884 at the end of the War of the Pacific and again in 1939 when it lost most of Gran Chaco to Paraguay. One of South America's poorest countries, it was plagued by governmental instability for much of the 20th century. By the 1990s Bolivia had become one of the world's largest producers of coca, from which cocaine is derived. The government subsequently instituted a largely successful program to eradicate the crop, although such efforts were resisted by the many poor farmers who depended on coca.

Recent Developments

As South America's first Indian president, Bolivia's Evo Morales forged ahead in 2007 with bold attempts to restructure Bolivia on terms more favorable to its impoverished Indian majority. He scored some successes, significantly boosting the government's share of revenue from natural gas and mineral resources. The constituent assembly made little progress in drafting a new constitution, however, and tension increased between the Indian-dominated western highlands and the resource-rich eastern lowlands. The rivalry between the regions was further aggravated by a proposal to transfer the political capital back to Sucre (the sole capital until 1899), sparking massive protests in La Paz.

Internet resources: <www.ine.gov.bo>.

Bosnia and Herzegovina

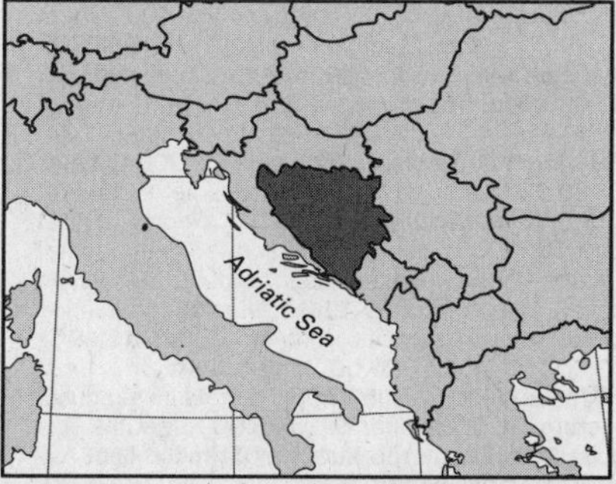

Official name: Bosna i Hercegovina (Bosnia and Herzegovina). **Form of government:** federal multiparty republic with bicameral legislature (House of Peoples [15]; House of Representatives [42]). **Chiefs of state:** Tripartite presidency with 8-month-long rotating chairmanship (final authority rests with International High Representative Christian Schwarz-Schilling [from 2008]). **Head of government:** Prime Minister Nikola Spiric (from 2007). **Capital:** Sarajevo. **Official language:** Bosnian (Serbo-Croatian). **Official religion:** none. **Monetary unit:** 1 marka (KM) = 100 fenning; valuation (1 Jul 2008) US$1 = KM 1.24 (pegged to the euro from 1 Jan 2002; the euro also circulates as semiofficial legal tender).

Demography

Area: 19,772 sq mi, 51,209 sq km. **Population** (2007): 3,855,000. **Density** (2007): persons per sq mi 195.0, persons per sq km 75.3. **Urban** (2005): 45.7%. **Sex distribution** (2005): male 48.63%; female 51.37%. **Age breakdown** (2005): under 15, 17.6%; 15–29, 21.6%; 30–44, 22.8%; 45–59, 18.9%; 60–74, 15.5%; 75–84, 3.3%; 85 and over, 0.3%. **Ethnic composition** (1999): Bosniac 44.0%; Serb 31.0%; Croat 17.0%; other 8.0%. **Religious affiliation** (2002): Sunni Muslim 40%; Serbian Orthodox 31%; Roman Catholic 15%; Protestant 4%; nonreligious/other 10%. **Major cities** (2005): Sarajevo 380,000 (urban agglomeration [2004] 602,500); Banja Luka 165,100; Zenica 84,300; Tuzla 84,100; Mostar 63,500. **Location:** southeastern Europe, bordered by Croatia, Serbia, Montenegro, and the Adriatic Sea.

Vital statistics

Birth rate per 1,000 population (2005): 9.0 (world avg. 20.3); within marriage 88.8%. **Death rate** per 1,000 population (2005): 8.9 (world avg. 8.6). **Natural increase rate** per 1,000 population (2005): 0.1 (world avg. 11.7). **Total fertility rate** (avg. births per childbearing woman; 2005): 1.19. **Life expectancy** at birth (2005): male 71 years; female 77 years.

National economy

Budget (2004). *Revenue:* KM 6,191,000,000 (indirect taxes 42.1%; social security contributions 30.1%; taxes on trade 8.1%; other 19.7%). *Expenditures:* KM 6,601,000,000 (current expenditures 87.3%; development expenditures 12.3%). **Gross national income** (2006): US$11,566,000,000 (US$2,946 per capita). **Production** (metric tons except as noted). *Agriculture, forestry, fishing* (2005): corn (maize) 1,004,000, potatoes 458,600, wheat 248,300; livestock (number of live animals) 902,700 sheep, 653,300 pigs, 459,800 cattle (in addition, 259,600 beehives); roundwood 3,806,000 cu m, of which fuelwood 36%; fisheries production (2004) 8,394 (from aquaculture 76%). *Mining* (2004): bauxite 480,000; lime 81,000; iron ore (metal content) 64,000. *Manufacturing* (value of exports in KM '000,000; 2003): base metals and fabricated metal products 498.3; wood and wood products 398.9; machinery and apparatus 286.1. *Energy production (consumption):* electricity (kW-hr; 2004) 12,599,000,000 (10,517,000,000); lignite (metric tons; 2004) 8,578,000 (8,953,000); petroleum products (metric tons; 2004) none (1,088,000); natural gas (cu m; 2004) none (366,000,000). **Public debt** (external, outstanding; 2005): US$2,560,000,000. **Population economically active** (2006): total 1,177,000; activity rate of total population 30.6% (participation rates: ages 15–64, 51.3%; female 36%; unemployed 31.1%). **Households.** Average household size (2004) 3.6; sources of income (1990): wages 53.2%, transfers 18.2%, self-employment 12.0%, other 16.6%. **Selected balance of payments data.** Receipts from (US$'000,000): tourism (2005) 565; remittances (2005) 1,844; foreign direct investment (2001–05 avg.) 334; official development assistance (2005) 384 (commitments). Disbursements for (US$'000,000): tourism (2005) 123; remittances (2005) 26. **Land use** as % of total land area (2003): in temporary crops 19.6%, in permanent crops 1.9%, in pasture 20.4%; overall forest area (2005) 43.1%.

Foreign trade

Imports (2005): KM 10,990,000,000 (food products 18.0%; machinery and apparatus 16.2%; mineral fuels 14.5%; base metals and fabricated metal products 9.7%). *Major import sources:* Croatia 16.1%; Germany 12.1%; Serbia and Montenegro 10.0%; Italy 8.7%; Slovenia 6.0%. **Exports** (2005): KM 3,533,000,000 (base metals and fabricated metal products 26.4%; mineral fuels 14.2%; wood products 10.7%; machinery and apparatus 9.2%). *Major export destinations:* Croatia 21.7%; Serbia and Montenegro 16.5%; Italy 14.0%; Slovenia 10.3%; Germany 9.2%.

Transport and communications

Transport. *Railroads* (2005): length (2004) 1,021 km; passenger-km 51,396,000; metric ton-km cargo 1,159,000,000. *Roads* (2005): total length 22,419 km (paved [2001] 64%). *Vehicles* (1996): passenger cars 96,182; trucks and buses 10,919. *Air transport* (2001): passenger-km 44,000,000; metric ton-km (2003) 1,000,000. **Communications,** in total units (units per 1,000 persons). Daily newspaper circulation (2004): 106,000 (28); televisions (2002): 950,000 (248); telephone landlines (2006): 989,000 (253); cellular telephone subscribers (2006): 1,888,000 (483); total Internet users (2006): 950,000 (243); broadband Internet subscribers (2006): 40,000 (3.6).

Education and health

Educational attainment (2004; Federation of Bosnia and Herzegovina only). Percentage of population ages 18 and over having: no formal schooling 8.0%; some to complete primary education 31.9%; lower secondary 24.4%; upper secondary 26.6%; higher 4.9%; advanced 4.2%. **Literacy** (2002): total population ages 15 and over literate 94.6%; males literate 98.4%; females literate 91.1%. **Health:** physicians (2004) 5,004 (1 per 769 persons); hospital beds (2003) 11,981 (1 per 322 persons); infant mortality rate per 1,000 live births (2005) 6.7. **Food** (2005): daily per capita caloric intake 3,068 (vegetable products 87%, animal products 13%); 153% of FAO recommended minimum.

Military

Total active duty personnel (2006): 11,865 (army virtually 100%); EU-sponsored peacekeeping troops (EUFOR) (November 2007) 2,450. **Military expenditure as percentage of GDP** (2005): 1.9%; per capita expenditure US$46.

Background

Habitation long predates the era of Roman rule, when much of the country was included in the province of Dalmatia. Slav settlement began in the 6th century AD. For the next several centuries, parts of the region fell under the rule of Serbs, Croats, Hungarians, Venetians, and Byzantines. The Ottoman Turks invaded Bosnia in the 14th century, and after many battles it became a Turkish province in 1463. Herzegovina, then known as Hum, was taken in 1482. In the 16th–17th century the area was an important Turkish outpost, constantly at war with the Habsburgs and Venice. During this period much of the native population converted to Islam. At the Congress of Berlin after the Russo-Turkish War of 1877–78, Bosnia and Herzegovina was assigned to Austria-Hungary, and it was fully annexed in 1908. Growing Serb nationalism resulted in the 1914 assassination of the Austrian archduke Francis Ferdinand at Sarajevo by a Bosnian Serb, an event that precipitated World War I. After the war the area was annexed to Serbia. Following World War II the twin territory became a republic of communist Yugoslavia. With the collapse of communist regimes in Eastern Europe, Bosnia and Herzegovina declared its independence in 1992; its Serb population objected, and conflict ensued among Serbs, Croats, and Muslims. The 1995 peace accord established a loosely federated government roughly divided between a Muslim-Croat Federation and a Serb Republic (Republika Srpska). In 1996 a NATO peacekeeping force was installed there.

Recent Developments

In April 2008 the parliament of Bosnia and Herzegovina adopted reforms of the country's police forces required by the European Union enlargement commissioner, and in June a stabilization and association agreement was signed, paving the way for eventual membership in the EU. However, local media and government watchdog activists criticized the government for widespread corruption, extensive waste, and poor economic conditions—at least 29% of labor force was unemployed, and nearly half of the population lived at or below the poverty level.

Internet resources: <www.bhtourism.ba/eng>.

Botswana

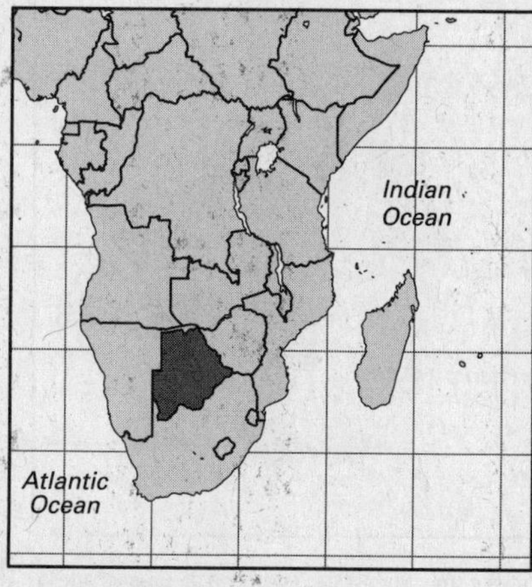

Official name: Republic of Botswana. **Form of government:** multiparty republic with one legislative body (National Assembly [63]). **Head of state and government:** President Festus Mogae (from 1998). **Capital:** Gaborone. **Official language:** English (Tswana is the national language). **Official religion:** none. **Monetary unit:** 1 pula (P) = 100 thebe; valuation (1 Jul 2008) US$1 = P 6.53.

Demography

Area: 224,848 sq mi, 582,356 sq km. **Population** (2007): 1,882,000. **Density** (2007): persons per sq mi 8.4, persons per sq km 3.2. **Urban** (2005): 53.6%. **Sex distribution** (2005): male 49.12%; female 50.88%. **Age breakdown** (2005): under 15, 37.6%; 15–29, 32.8%; 30–44, 14.9%; 45–59, 9.6%; 60–74, 4.1%; 75–84, 0.9%; 85 and over, 0.1%. **Ethnic composition** (2000): Tswana 66.8%; Kalanga 14.8%; Ndebele 1.7%; Herero 1.4%; San (Bushman) 1.3%; Afrikaner 1.3%; other 12.7%. **Religious affiliation** (2005): independent Christian 41.7%; traditional beliefs 35.0%; Protestant 12.8%; Muslim 0.3%; Hindu 0.2%; other 10.0%. **Major cities** (2004): Gaborone 199,600; Francistown 89,100; Molepolole 58,600; Selebi-Pikwe 53,500; Maun 47,000. **Location:** southern Africa, bordered by Namibia, Zimbabwe, and South Africa.

Vital statistics

Birth rate per 1,000 population (2005): 25.5 (world avg. 20.3). **Death rate** per 1,000 population (2005): 15.2 (world avg. 8.6). **Natural increase rate** per 1,000 population (2005): 10.2 (world avg. 11.7). **Total fertility rate** (avg. births per childbearing woman; 2005): 3.04. **Life expectancy** at birth (2005): male 48.1 years; female 49.0 years.

National economy

Budget (2005–06). *Revenue:* P 21,697,300,000 (tax revenue 88.2%, of which mineral royalties 50.2%, customs duties and excise tax 16.1%, general sales tax 8.9%; nontax revenue 10.8%, of which property income 2.6%; grants 1.0%). *Expenditures:* P 20,122,200,000 (general government services including defense 27.7%, education 24.5%, economic services 15.4%, health 12.4%, transfers 9.0%). **Population economically active** (2001): total 587,882; activity rate of total population 35.0% (participation rates: ages 15–64, 57.6%; female 43.8%; unemployed [2004] more than 20%). **Production** (metric tons except as noted). *Agriculture, forestry, fishing* (2005): roots and tubers 93,000, sorghum 32,000, pulses 17,500; livestock (number of live animals) 3,100,000 cattle, 1,950,000 goats, 300,000 sheep; roundwood 765,750 cu m, of which fuelwood 86%; fisheries production (2004) 161. *Mining and quarrying* (2005): soda ash 279,085; nickel ore (metal content) 39,305; copper ore (metal content) 31,300; diamonds 31,890,000 carats (Botswana is the world's leading producer of diamonds by value). *Manufacturing* (value added in US$'000,000; 2004): beverages 50; motor vehicles (1997) 33; textiles 12. *Energy production (consumption):* electricity (kW-hr; 2004) 891,000,000 (2,641,000,000); coal (metric tons; 2004) 916,000 (916,000). **Land use** as % of total land area (2003): in temporary crops 0.7%, in permanent crops 0.01%, in pasture 45.2%; overall forest area (2005) 21.1%. **Gross national income** (2006): US$8,153,000,000 (US$4,387 per capita). **Public debt** (external, outstanding; 2005): US$438,000,000. **Households** (2002–03). Average household size (2004) 4.3; average annual disposable income per household P 29,095 (US$5,320), of which cash income P 25,519 (US$4,670); expenditure: food and nonalcoholic beverages 23.7%, transportation 15.6%, housing and energy 12.9%, alcoholic beverages and tobacco 9.6%, household furnishings 8.0%. **Selected balance of payments data.** Receipts from (US$'000,000): tourism (2005) 562; remittances (2005) 125; foreign direct investment (FDI) (2001–05 avg.) 318; official development assistance (2005) 117 (commitments). Disbursements for (US$'000,000): tourism (2005) 282; remittances (2005) 123; FDI (2001–05 avg.) 129.

Foreign trade

Imports (2005; c.i.f.): US$3,247,000,000 (machinery and apparatus 16.3%; food, beverages, and tobacco 13.7%; mineral fuels 13.3%; transport equipment 12.5%; chemical and rubber products 11.9%). *Major import sources:* Customs Union of Southern Africa (CUSA) 85.1%; Europe 6.5%, of which UK 1.3%; Zimbabwe 1.5%; US 1.2%. **Exports** (2005; f.o.b.): US$4,395,000,000 (diamonds 75.1%; copper-nickel matte 10.3%; textiles 5.0%; meat products 1.7%). *Major export destinations:* Europe 77.0%, of which UK 75.7%; CUSA 9.0%; Zimbabwe 4.1%.

Transport and communications

Transport. *Railroads* (2002): route length 888 km; (2001) passenger-km 106,000,000; (2001) metric ton-km cargo 747,000,000. *Roads* (2003): total length 25,233 km (paved 35%). *Vehicles* (2005): passenger cars 82,056; trucks and buses 74,387. *Air transport* (2002; Air Botswana only): passenger-km 96,000,000; metric ton-km cargo 300,000. **Communications,** in total units (units per 1,000 persons). Daily newspaper circulation (2004): 80,000 (45); televisions (2003): 78,000 (44); telephone landlines (2006): 137,000 (78); cellular telephone subscribers (2006): 980,000 (557); personal computers (2005): 86,000 (49); total Internet users (2005): 60,000 (34); broadband Internet subscribers (2005): 1,600.

Education and health

Educational attainment (1993). Percentage of population ages 25 and over having: no formal schooling 34.7%; primary education 44.1%; some secondary 19.8%; postsecondary 1.4%. **Literacy** (2005): total population over age 15 literate 81.4%; males literate 78.6%; females literate 84.1%. **Health** (2006): physicians 526 (1 per 3,346 persons); hospital beds 3,911 (1 per 450 persons); infant mortality rate per 1,000 live births (2005) 52.7. **Food** (2004): daily per capita caloric intake 2,084 (vegetable products 82%, animal products 18%); 112% of FAO recommended minimum.

Military

Total active duty personnel (2006): 9,000 (army 94.4%, air force 5.6%). **Military expenditure as percentage of GDP** (2005): 3.0%; per capita expenditure US$177.

Background

The region's earliest inhabitants were the Khoekhoe and San (Bushmen). Sites were settled as early as AD 190 during the southerly migration of Bantu-speaking farmers. Tswana dynasties, which developed in the western Transvaal in the 13th–14th century, moved into Botswana in the 18th century and established several powerful states. European missionaries arrived in the early 19th century, but it was the discovery of gold in 1867 that excited European interest. In 1885 the area became the British Bechuanaland Protectorate. The next year the region south of the Molopo River became a crown colony, and it was annexed by the Cape Colony 10 years later. Bechuanaland itself continued as a British protectorate until the 1960s. In 1966 the Republic of Bechuanaland (later Botswana) was proclaimed an independent member of the British Commonwealth. Independent Botswana tried to maintain a delicate balance between its economic dependence on South Africa and its relations with the surrounding black countries; the independence of Namibia in 1990 and South Africa's rejection of apartheid eased tensions.

Recent Developments

Controversy in Botswana continued in 2007 over the eviction of Bushmen from the Central Kalahari Game Reserve and the transfer of sales and distribution of Botswana's diamonds from London to Gaborone. The De Beers Group's Diamond Trading Co. neared completion of a US$450 million sorting center near Gaborone's international airport. New foreign-owned diamond-cutting and polishing workshops, however, came into conflict with local unions over issues related to minimum wages.

Internet resources: <www.botswana-tourism.gov.bw>.

Brazil

Official name: República Federativa do Brasil (Federative Republic of Brazil). **Form of government:** multiparty federal republic with two legislative houses (Federal Senate [81]; Chamber of Deputies [513]). **Chief of state and government:** President Luiz Inácio Lula da Silva (from 2003). **Capital:** Brasília. **Official language:** Portuguese. **Official religion:** none. **Monetary unit:** 1 real (R$) = 100 centavos; valuation (1 Jul 2008) US$1 = 1.61 reais.

Demography

Area: 3,287,612 sq mi, 8,514,877 sq km. **Population** (2007): 189,335,000. **Density** (2007): persons per sq mi 57.6, persons per sq km 22.2. **Urban** (2005): 82.8%. **Sex distribution** (2005): male 49.34%; female 50.66%. **Age breakdown** (2005): under 15, 27.8%; 15–29, 27.6%; 30–44, 21.7%; 45–59, 14.1%; 60–74, 6.5%; 75–84, 1.8%; 85 and over, 0.5%. **Racial composition** (2000): white 53.7%; mulatto and mestizo 39.1%; black and black/Amerindian 6.2%; Asian 0.5%; Amerindian 0.4%. **Religious affiliation** (2005): Roman Catholic 65.1%; Protestant 12.7%, of which Assemblies of God 9.2%; independent Christian 10.7%, of which Universal Church of the Kingdom of God 2.2%; Spiritist (Kardecist) 1.3%; Jehovah's Witness 0.7%; African and syncretic religions 0.4%; Muslim 0.4%; nonreligious/other 8.7%. **Major cities (metropolitan areas)** (2005): São Paulo 10,277,500 (19,037,487); Rio de Janeiro 6,094,200 (11,570,524); Belo Horizonte 2,375,300 (5,391,284); Porto Alegre 1,386,900 (3,978,263); Recife 1,501,000 (3,599,181); Brasília 2,231,100 (3,454,961); Salvador 2,672,500 (3,350,523); Fortaleza 2,374,900 (3,349,826); Curitiba 1,757,900 (3,141,366); Campinas 1,028,300 (2,633,938); Belém 1,396,800 (2,042,530); Goiânia 1,193,100 (1,897,961); Manaus 1,634,100 (1,644,690); Santos 416,100 (1,637,565). **Location:** eastern South America, bordered by Venezuela, Guyana, Suriname, French Guiana, Uruguay, Argentina, Paraguay, Bolivia, Peru, and Colombia. **Families.** Average family size (2005) 3.2; 1–2 persons (1996) 25.2%, 3 persons 20.3%, 4 persons 22.2%, 5–6 persons 23.3%, 7 or more persons 9.0%. **Emigration** (2000): Brazilian emigrants living abroad 1,887,895; in the US 42.3%, in Paraguay 23.4%, in Japan 12.0%. **Immigration** (2000): foreign-born immigrants living in Brazil 683,830; from Europe 56.3%, of which Portugal 31.2%; South/Central America 21.0%; Asia 17.8%, of which Japan 10.4%.

Vital statistics

Birth rate per 1,000 population (2005): 20.4 (world avg. 20.3). **Death rate** per 1,000 population (2005): 6.3 (world avg. 8.6). **Natural increase rate** per 1,000 population (2005): 14.1 (world avg. 11.7). **Total fertility rate** (avg. births per childbearing woman; 2005): 2.30. **Life expectancy** at birth (2005): male 68.1 years; female 75.8 years.

Social indicators

Educational attainment (2005). Percentage of population ages 25 and over having: no formal schooling through less than one year of primary education 15.0%; 1 to 3 years of primary education 13.7%; complete primary/incomplete secondary 40.2%; complete secondary 18.8%; 1 to 3 years of higher education 3.8%; 4 years or more of higher education 8.0%; unknown 0.5%. **Quality of working life.** Proportion of employed population receiving minimum wage (2002) 53.5%. Number and percentage of children (age 5–17) working 5,400,000 (12.6% of age group). **Access to services** (1999). Proportion of households having access to: electricity (2002) 96.0%, of which urban households having access 98.8%, rural households having access 73.2%; safe public (piped) water supply 79.8%, of which urban households having access 92.3%, rural households having access 24.9%; public (piped) sewage system 43.6%, of which urban households having access 52.5%, rural households having access 4.5%; no sewage disposal 8.5%, of which urban households having no disposal 2.9%, rural households having no disposal 32.9%. **Social participation.** Voter turnout at last (October 2006) national legislative election 83.3%. Trade union membership in total workforce (2001) 19,500,000. Practicing Roman Catholic population in total affiliated Roman Catholic population (2000): large cities 10–15%; towns and rural areas 60–70%. **Social deviance.** Annual murder rate per 100,000 population (2002): 28; Rio de Janeiro only, 56; São Paulo only, 54. **Material well-being** (2003). Households possessing: television receiver 89.9%, of which urban 94.5%, rural 69.4%; refrigerator 86.7%, of which urban 91.7%, rural 60.0%; washing machine 34.0%, of which urban 38.1%, rural 10.0%.

National economy

Gross national income (at current market prices; 2006): US$1,041,609,000,000 (US$5,502 per capita). **Budget** (2004). *Revenue:* R$422,450,000,000 (tax revenue 76.4%, of which income tax 24.3%, social security contributions 18.2%, VAT 5.4%; social welfare contributions 22.2%; other 1.4%). *Expenditures:* R$372,730,000,000 (social security and welfare 33.8%; personnel 23.5%; transfers to state and local governments 18.1%; other 24.6%). **Public debt** (external, outstanding; 2005): US$94,497,000,000. **Production** ('000 metric tons except as noted). *Agriculture, forestry, fishing* (2005): sugarcane 420,121, soybeans 50,195, corn (maize) 34,860, cassava 26,645, oranges 17,805, rice 13,141, bananas 6,703, wheat 5,201, seed cotton 3,727, tomatoes 3,304, dry beans 3,076, coconuts 3,034, potatoes 2,950, coffee 2,179, papayas 1,650, cashew apples 1,610, sorghum 1,530, pineapples 1,418, grapes 1,209, dry onions 1,059, lemons and limes 1,000, tobacco 879, mangoes 850, apples 844, maté 560, oil palm fruit 550, peanuts (groundnuts) 292, cashews 251, cacao beans 214, sisal 213, natural rubber 97, garlic 88, Brazil nuts 29; livestock (number of live animals) 207,000,000 cattle, 33,200,000 pigs, 15,200,000 sheep, 5,700,000 horses; roundwood (2004) 255,880,000 cu m, of which fuelwood 54%; fisheries production (2004) 1,015,916 (from aquaculture 27%). *Mining and quarrying* (metric tons; 2004): iron ore (metal content) 169,300,000 (world rank: 1); columbium (niobium) 39,741 of pyrochlore in concentrates (world rank: 1); bauxite 19,700,000 (world rank: 2); manganese (metal content in concentrate) 3,143,000 (world rank: 2); tantalum 277 (world rank: 2); asbestos fibre 231,115 (world rank: 4); tin (mine output; metal content) 12,468 (world rank: 5); kaolin (marketable product) 2,148,000; copper (metal content) 103,153; nickel (metal content in ore) 51,886; gold 47,596 kg; diamonds 300,000 carats. *Energy production (consumption):* electricity (kW-hr; 2004) 383,200,000,000 (391,700,000,000); coal (metric tons; 2004) 6,000,000 (21,300,000); crude petroleum (barrels; 2005) 603,700,000 ([2004] 624,000,000); petroleum products (metric tons; 2004) 78,984,000 (72,211,000); natural gas (cu m; 2004) 9,600,000,000 (17,300,000,000); ethanol production (barrels; 2005) 102,900,000, of which exported to US 2,600,000. **Land use** as % of total land area (2003): in temporary crops 7.0%, in permanent crops 0.9%, in pasture 23.3%; overall forest area (2005) 57.2%. **Population economically active** (2004): total 92,860,100; activity rate of total population 51.1% (participation rates: ages 15–64, 73.2%; female 43.1%; unemployed [February 2006–January 2007] 10.0%). **Selected balance of payments data.** Receipts from (US$'000,000): tourism (2005) 3,861; remittances (2006) 7,373; foreign direct investment (FDI) (2001–05) 16,481. Disbursements for (US$'000,000): tourism (2005) 4,720; remittances (2005) 498; FDI (2001–05) 2,559. **Households.** Average household size (2005) 3.5. *Family/household income and expenditure.* Average family size (2000) 3.5; average annual income per household (2000) R$14,065 (US$7,686), median annual income per household (2000) R$6,744 (US$3,685); expenditure (1995–96; urban areas only): housing, energy, and household furnishings 28.8%, food and beverages 23.4%, transportation and communications 13.8%, health care 9.2%, education and recreation 8.4%.

Foreign trade

Imports (2005): US$73,500,000,000 (mineral fuels 18.3%; mechanical equipment 15.8%; electrical equipment 14.2%; chemicals and chemical products 7.3%; motor vehicles 5.8%). *Major import sources* (2006): US 16.2%; African countries 8.9%; Argentina 8.8%; China 8.7%; Germany 7.1%; Japan 4.2%; South Korea 3.4%; Chile 3.2%; France 3.1%. **Exports** (2005): US$118,300,000,000 (food products 22.1%, of which soy 8.6%, meat 6.8%, sugar 4.0%, coffee 2.4%; transportation equipment 16.2%; metal products 10.7%; mineral metals 6.8%; chemicals and chemical products 6.3%; machinery and apparatus 5.9%). *Major export destinations* (2006): US 18.0%; Argentina 8.5%; China 6.1%; African countries 5.4%; The Netherlands 4.2%; Germany 4.1%; Mexico 3.2%; Japan 2.8%; Italy 2.8%; Chile 2.8%.

Transport and communications

Transport. *Railroads* (2005): route length 29,605 km; passenger-km 5,852,000,000; metric ton-km cargo 154,870,000,000. *Roads* (2004): total length 1,751,868 km (paved [2000] 6%). *Vehicles* (2004): passenger cars 24,936,541; trucks and buses 6,294,502. *Air transport* (2005): passenger-km 50,689,000,000; metric ton-km cargo 1,530,700,000. **Communications,** in total units (units per 1,000 persons). Daily newspaper circulation (2004): 6,522,000 (36); televisions (2003): 65,949,000 (369); telephone landlines (2006): 38,800,000 (205); cellular telephone subscribers (2006): 99,919,000 (529); personal computers (2005): 32,130,000 (174); total Internet users (2006): 42,600,000 (226); broadband Internet subscribers (2005): 3,304,000 (18).

Education and health

Literacy (2005): total population ages 15 and over literate/functionally literate 89.0%/76.5%; males literate/functionally literate 88.7%/75.9%; females literate/functionally literate 89.2%/77.0%. **Health:** physicians (2001) 357,888 (1 per 485 persons); hospital beds (2005) 443,210 (1 per 416 persons); infant mortality rate per 1,000 live births (2005) 25.4. **Food** (2005): daily per capita caloric intake 3,244 (vegetable products 79%, animal products 21%); 171% of FAO recommended minimum.

Military

Total active duty personnel (2006): 287,159 (army 65.8%, navy 11.4%, air force 22.7%). **Military expenditure as percentage of GDP** (2005): 1.6%; per capita expenditure US$68.

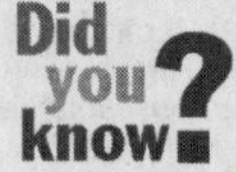

The city of Rio de Janeiro lies on a strip of Brazil's Atlantic coast, close to the Tropic of Capricorn, where the shoreline is oriented east-west, the city facing south. It was founded on an inlet of this stretch of the coast, Guanabara Bay, at the entrance to which is the landmark peak called Sugar Loaf.

Background

Little is known about Brazil's early indigenous inhabitants. Though the area was theoretically allotted to Portugal by the 1494 Treaty of Tordesillas, it was not formally claimed by discovery until Pedro Álvares Cabral accidentally touched land in 1500. It was first settled by the Portuguese in the early 1530s on the southeastern coast and at São Vicente (near modern São Paulo); the French and Dutch created small settlements over the next century. A viceroyalty was established in 1640, and Rio de Janeiro became the capital in 1763. In 1808 Brazil became the refuge and seat of the government of John VI of Portugal when Napoleon invaded Portugal; ultimately the Kingdom of Portugal, Brazil, and the Algarves was proclaimed, and John ruled from Brazil in 1815–21. On John's return to Portugal, his son Pedro I proclaimed Brazilian independence. In 1889 his successor, Pedro II, was deposed, and a constitution mandating a federal republic was adopted. The 20th century saw increased immigration and growth in manufacturing along with frequent military coups and suspensions of civil liberties. Construction of a new capital at Brasília, intended to spur development of the country's interior, worsened the inflation rate. After 1979 the military government began a gradual return to democratic practices, and in 1989 the first popular presidential election in 29 years was held.

Recent Developments

Brazil confirmed its spot among world energy giants in recent years. In 2007 the country was completely self-sufficient with respect to energy, largely because of its development and use of sugarcane biofuel, which that year passed hydroelectricity as the country's second largest energy source (after petroleum). A number of stunning discoveries had international impacts as well. In November 2007 Brazil announced an offshore oil field, named Tupi, that could potentially almost double the country's petroleum reserves. This was followed in January 2008 by the discovery of an offshore natural-gas field, nicknamed Jupiter, that was estimated to be as large as Tupi. Finally, in April the government announced the discovery of an offshore oil field that, if confirmed in volume, would amount to the world's third largest known oil reserve. While these discoveries would take years to confirm and exploit, their announcements nonetheless moved Brazil into the spotlight as a potential world supplier of oil and natural gas. The economy showed signs of strengthening. GDP growth in 2007 was 9.7%, and urban unemployment had fallen to 8.6% in March 2008.

Internet resources: <www.braziltour.com/site/en/-home/index.php>.

Brunei

Official name: Negara Brunei Darussalam (State of Brunei, Abode of Peace). **Form of government:** monarchy (sultanate) with one advisory body (Legislative Council [29]). **Head of state and government:** Sultan Haji Hassanal Bolkiah Muʿizzadin Waddaulah

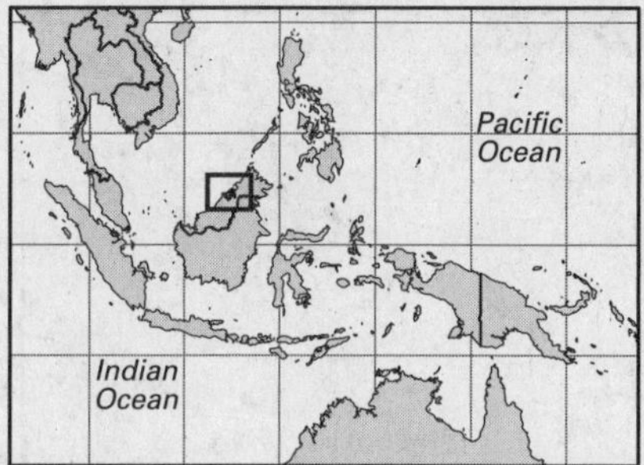

(from 1967). **Capital:** Bandar Seri Begawan. **Official language:** Malay. **Official religion:** Islam. **Monetary unit:** 1 Brunei dollar (B$) = 100 cents; valuation (1 Jul 2008) US$1 = B$1.36.

Demography

Area: 2,226 sq mi, 5,765 sq km. **Population** (2007): 393,000. **Density** (2007): persons per sq mi 176.5, persons per sq km 68.2. **Urban** (2005): urban 73.5%. **Sex distribution** (2005): male 52.77%; female 47.23%. **Age breakdown** (2005): under 15, 29.5%; 15–29, 28.4%; 30–44, 24.1%; 45–59, 13.2%; 60–74, 4.0%; 75 and over, 0.8%. **Ethnic composition** (2003): Malay 66.6%; Chinese 10.9%; other indigenous 3.6%; other 18.9%. **Religious affiliation** (2004): Muslim 67%; Buddhist 13%; Christian 10%; traditional beliefs/other 10%. **Major cities** (2004): Bandar Seri Begawan (urban agglomeration) 81,500; Kuala Belait 28,400; Seria 23,500. **Location:** southeastern Asia, bordering the South China Sea and Malaysia.

Vital statistics

Birth rate per 1,000 population (2005): 19.9 (world avg. 20.3). **Death rate** per 1,000 population (2005): 2.8 (world avg. 8.6). **Natural increase rate** per 1,000 population (2005): 17.1 (world avg. 11.7). **Total fertility rate** (avg. births per childbearing woman; 2005): 2.10. **Life expectancy** at birth (2005): male 74.6 years; female 77.5 years.

National economy

Budget (2005–06). *Revenue:* B$8,441,000,000 (tax revenue 62.2%, of which taxes on petroleum and natural gas companies 59.1%; nontax revenue 37.8%, of which dividends paid by petroleum companies 22.9%, petroleum and natural gas royalties 10.0%). *Expenditures:* B$5,086,000,000 (current expenditure 80.1%; capital expenditure 19.9%). **Production** (metric tons except as noted). *Agriculture, forestry, fishing* (2005): vegetables 10,500; fruits 5,565, of which pineapples 990, bananas 680; cassava 1,800; livestock (number of live animals) 5,000 buffalo, 13,000,000 chickens; roundwood 228,637 cu m, of which fuelwood 5%; fisheries production (2004) 3,136 (from aquaculture 23%). *Mining and quarrying:* petroleum, natural gas, sand and gravel for construction. *Manufacturing* (value added in B$'000,000; 2005): liquefied natural gas 1,672; textiles and apparel 197; other manufactures 83. *Energy production (consumption):* electricity (kW-hr; 2005) 2,913,000,000 ([2004] 2,726,000,000); crude petroleum (barrels; 2005) 68,300,000 ([2004] 650,000); petroleum products (metric tons; 2004) 1,189,000 (1,187,000); natural gas (cu m; 2005) 12,200,000,000 ([2004] 1,457,000,000). **Gross national income** (at 2006 market prices): US$11,481,000,000 (US$30,058 per capita). **Population economically active** (2001): total 157,594 (foreign workers accounted for 70% of the 160,500 economically active in 2004); activity rate of total population 45.2% (participation rates: ages 15–64, 65.9%; female 41.2%; unemployed [2005] 4.3%). **Public debt** (external, outstanding; 2005): none. **Households.** Average household size (2002) 5.6; expenditure (2002): food and nonalcoholic beverages 28.8%, transportation 22.5%, housing and energy 8.8%, household furnishings 8.6%, recreation and entertainment 8.1%, clothing and footwear 5.6%, communications 5.5%. **Land use** as % of total land area (2003): in temporary crops 2.5%, in permanent crops 0.9%, in pasture 1.1%; overall forest area (2005) 52.8%. **Selected balance of payments data.** Receipts from (US$'000,000): tourism (1998) 37; foreign direct investment (2001–05 avg.) 1,085. Disbursements for (US$'000,000): remittances (2003) 139.

Foreign trade

Imports (2005; c.i.f.): US$1,491,000,000 (machinery and transport equipment 32.1%; basic manufactures 24.6%; food and live animals 17.4%; chemicals and chemical products 9.3%). *Major import sources:* Malaysia 24.4%; Singapore 18.7%; US 9.7%; Japan 9.1%; China 6.3%. **Exports** (2005; f.o.b.): US$6,249,000,000 (crude petroleum 62.8%; liquefied natural gas 31.3%; machinery and transport equipment 2.0%). *Major export destinations:* Japan 36.7%; Indonesia 18.6%; South Korea 12.6%; Australia 9.6%; US 7.5%.

Transport and communications

Transport. *Railroads* (2004; privately owned only): length 19 km. *Roads* (2004): total length 3,560 km (paved 78%). *Vehicles* (2003): passenger cars 212,000; trucks and buses (2002) 20,000. *Air transport* (2005; Royal Brunei Airlines only): passenger-km 3,767,000,000; metric ton-km cargo 134,127,000. **Communications,** in total units (units per 1,000 persons). Daily newspaper circulation (2005): 35,000 (95); televisions (2001): 215,000 (648); telephone landlines (2006): 80,000 (210); cellular telephone subscribers (2006): 254,000 (665); personal computers (2004): 31,000 (87); total Internet users (2006): 166,000 (434); broadband Internet subscribers (2006): 11,000 (28).

Education and health

Educational attainment (1991). Percentage of population ages 25 and over having: no formal schooling/unknown 17.5%; primary education 43.3%; secondary 26.3%; postsecondary and higher 12.9%. **Literacy** (2002): percentage of total population ages 15 and over literate 93.9%; males literate 96.3%; females literate 91.4%. **Health** (2004): physicians 463 (1 per 773 persons); hospital beds 943 (1 per 379 persons); infant mortality rate per 1,000 live births (2005) 8.8. **Food** (2005): daily per capita caloric intake 2,610 (vegetable products 77%, animal products 23%); 137% of FAO recommended minimum.

Military

Total active duty personnel (2006): 7,000 (army 70.0%, navy 14.3%, air force 15.7%); British troops (a Gurkha batallion) 1,120; Singaporean troops 500. **Military expenditure as percentage of GDP** (2005): 3.9%; per capita expenditure US$684.

Background

Brunei traded with China in the 6th century AD. Through allegiance to the Javanese Majapahit kingdom (13th–15th century), it came under Hindu influence. In the early 15th century, with the decline of the Majapahit kingdom, many people converted to Islam, and Brunei became an independent sultanate. When Ferdinand Magellan's ships visited in 1521, the sultan of Brunei controlled almost all of Borneo and its neighboring islands. Beginning in the late 16th century, Brunei lost power because of the Portuguese, Dutch, and, later, British activities in the region. By the 19th century, the sultanate of Brunei included Sarawak (present-day Brunei) and part of North Borneo (now part of Sabah). In 1841 a revolt took place against the sultan, and a British soldier, James Brooke, helped put it down; he was later proclaimed governor. In 1847 the sultanate entered into a treaty with Great Britain and by 1906 had yielded all administration to a British resident. Brunei rejected membership in the Federation of Malaysia in 1963, negotiated a new treaty with Britain in 1979, and achieved independence in 1984, with membership in the Commonwealth.

Recent Developments

Brunei made efforts in 2007 to diversify the economy. The government launched a landmark project to build the country's first petrochemical production plant, a US$400 million methanol plant that was being constructed in a joint venture with Japan's Mitsubishi Gas Chemical Co. and Itochu Corp. Brunei and Malaysia reached a tentative agreement in resolving maritime border issues during the August visit to Bandar Seri Begawan of Malaysian Prime Minister Abdullah Ahmad Badawi, who met with Sultan Haji Hassanal Bolkiah Mu'izzaddin Waddaulah. The new parliament building in the capital neared completion.

Internet resources: <www.tourismbrunei.com>.

Bulgaria

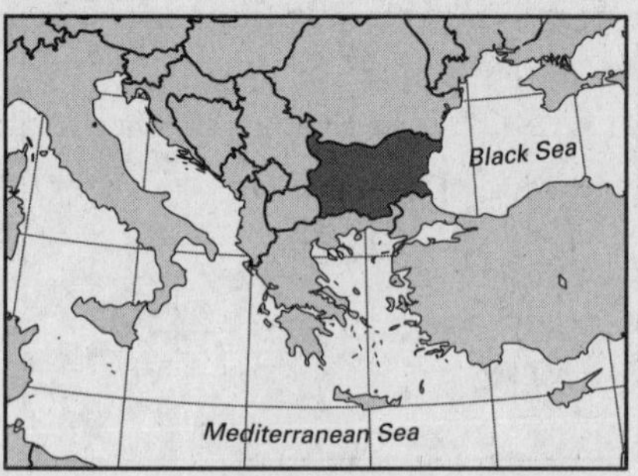

Official name: Republika Bulgariya (Republic of Bulgaria). **Form of government:** unitary multiparty republic with one legislative body (National Assembly [240]). **Chief of state:** President Georgi Purvanov (from 2002). **Head of government:** Prime Minister Sergey Stanishev (from 2005). **Capital:** Sofia. **Official language:** Bulgarian. **Official religion:** none. **Monetary unit:** 1 lev (Lw; plural leva) = 100 stotinki; valuation (1 Jul 2008) US$1 = 1.24 leva.

Demography

Area: 42,858.1 sq mi, 111,002 sq km. **Population** (2007): 7,645,000. **Density** (2007): persons per sq mi 178.4, persons per sq km 68.9. **Urban** (2005): 70.0%. **Sex distribution** (2005): male 48.55%; female 51.45%. **Age breakdown** (2005): under 15, 13.8%; 15–29, 21.2%; 30–44, 20.9%; 45–59, 21.3%; 60–74, 15.9%; 75–84, 6.0%; 85 and over, 0.9%. **Ethnic composition** (2001): Bulgarian 83.9%; Turkish 9.4%; Rom (Gypsy) 4.7%; other 2.0%. **Religious affiliation** (2005): Bulgarian Orthodox 81%; Sunni Muslim 12%; Evangelical Protestant 2%; Catholic 1%; other 4%. **Major cities** (2005): Sofia 1,138,950; Plovdiv 341,464; Varna 312,026; Burgas 189,529; Ruse 158,201. **Location:** southeastern Europe, bordering Romania, the Black Sea, Turkey, Greece, Macedonia, and Serbia.

Vital statistics

Birth rate per 1,000 population (2005): 9.2 (world avg. 20.3); within marriage 51.0%. **Death rate** per 1,000 population (2005): 14.6 (world avg. 8.6). **Total fertility rate** (avg. births per childbearing woman; 2005): 1.31. **Life expectancy** at birth (2005): male 69.0 years; female 76.3 years.

National economy

Budget (2005). *Revenue:* 17,030,000,000 leva (tax revenue 79.7%, of which VAT 28.2%, social insurance 20.6%; nontax revenue 20.3%). *Expenditures:* 17,008,000,000 leva (social insurance 33.1%; economic services 14.4%; defense and security 12.2%; health 11.8%; education 10.7%). **Public debt** (external, outstanding; 2007): US$7,253,300,000. **Gross national income** (2006): US$30,782,000,000 (US$4,002 per capita). **Production** (metric tons except as noted). *Agriculture, forestry, fishing* (2005): wheat 3,478,000, corn (maize) 1,586,000, sunflower seeds 934,900; livestock (number of live animals) 1,692,507 sheep, 931,402 pigs, 671,579 cattle; roundwood 5,862,000 cu m, of which fuelwood 46%; fisheries production (2004) 10,739 (from aquaculture 23%). *Mining and quarrying* (2004): copper (metal content) 107,000; iron (metal content) 27,000; gold 2,431 kg. *Manufacturing* (value added in US$'000,000; 2004): refined petroleum products, n.a.; wearing apparel 359; food products 320; nonelectrical machinery and apparatus 278. *Energy production (consumption):* electricity (kW-hr; 2005) 44,196,000,000 ([2004] 35,742,000,000); hard coal (metric tons; 2004) 33,000 (4,265,000); lignite (metric tons; 2004) 26,452,000 (26,292,000); crude petroleum (barrels; 2004) 220,000 (38,757,000); petroleum products (metric tons; 2004) 4,669,000 (3,563,000); natural gas (cu m; 2004) 354,000,000 (3,301,000,000). **Households** (2006). Average household size (2004) 2.7; income per household 5,204 leva (US$3,167); sources of income: wages and salaries 51.8%, transfers 29.9%, self-employment 8.1%; expenditure: food and nonalcoholic beverages 36.9%, housing and energy 16.0%, communications 5.8%, health 5.5%, transportation 5.0%. **Population economically active** (2005): total 3,314,200; activity rate of total population 49.7% (participation rates: ages 15-64 [2003] 60.9%; female 44.4%; unemployed [January 2006] 10.7%). **Land use** as % of total land area (2003): in temporary crops 30.0%, in permanent crops 1.9%, in pasture 16.2%; overall forest area (2005) 32.8%. **Selected balance of payments data.** Receipts from (US$'000,000): tourism (2005) 2,383; remittances (2006) 1,695; foreign direct investment (2001–05 avg.) 1,919. Disbursements for (US$'000,000): tourism (2005) 1,293; remittances (2006) 47.

Foreign trade

Imports (2006; f.o.b. in balance of trade and c.i.f. for commodities and trading partners): €18,375,-000,000 (crude petroleum and natural gas 17.4%; transport equipment and parts 13.8%; machinery and apparatus 12.1%; textiles 7.7%; base and other metals 6.6%). *Major import sources:* Russia 17.3%; Germany 12.4%; Italy 8.7%; Turkey 6.0%; Greece 4.9%. **Exports** (2006): €11,982,600,000 (base and fabricated metals 21.6%, of which iron and steel 7.4%; mineral fuels 15.5%, of which petroleum products 13.3%; machinery and transport equipment 14.3%; clothing and footwear 13.4%). *Major export destinations:* Turkey 11.4%; Italy 10.1%; Germany 9.6%; Greece 8.9%; Belgium 6.5%.

Transport and communications

Transport. *Railroads* (2004): track length 6,238 km; passenger-km 2,404,000,000; metric ton-km cargo 5,212,000,000. *Roads* (2004): length 44,033 km (paved 99%). *Vehicles* (2004): cars 2,438,383; trucks and buses 353,681. *Air transport* (2003): passenger-km 3,005,000,000; metric ton-km cargo 21,000,000. **Communications**, in total units (units per 1,000 persons). Daily newspaper circulation (2005): 961,000 (124); televisions (2002): 3,620,000 (453); telephone landlines (2006): 2,399,000 (313); cellular telephone subscribers (2006): 8,253,000 (1,076); personal computers (2004): 461,000 (59); total Internet users (2006): 1,870,000 (244); broadband Internet subscribers (2006): 384,000 (50).

Education and health

Educational attainment (2004). Percentage of population ages 25–64 having: no formal schooling to complete primary education 28%; secondary 50%; higher 22%. **Literacy** (2003): total population ages 15 and over literate 98.6%; males 99.1%; females 98.2%. **Health** (2006): physicians 28,030 (1 per 274 persons); hospital beds 50,688 (1 per 152 persons); infant mortality rate per 1,000 live births (2005) 10.4. **Food** (2005): daily per capita caloric intake 2,839 (vegetable products 77%, animal products 23%); 143% of FAO recommended minimum.

Military

Total active duty personnel (2006): 51,000 (army 49.0%, navy 8.6%, air force 25.7%, other 16.7%). **Military expenditure as percentage of GDP** (2005): 2.4%; per capita expenditure US$74.

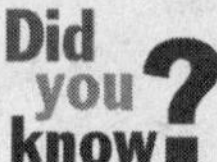

The historical, cultural, transport, industrial, and tourist center of Bulgaria is the town of Veliko Tarnovo, which served as the medieval capital of Bulgaria. During its heyday in the 12th-14th centuries, European royal circles glorified it as "the third Rome and the second Constantinople."

Background

Evidence of human habitation in Bulgaria dates from prehistoric times. Thracians were its first recorded inhabitants, dating from c. 3500 BC, and their first state dates from about the 5th century BC; the area was subdued by the Romans, who divided it into the provinces of Moesia and Thrace. In the 7th century AD the Bulgars took the region to the south of the Danube. The Byzantine Empire in 681 formally recognized Bulgar control over the area between the Balkans and the Danube. In the second half of the 14th century, Bulgaria fell to the Turks and ultimately lost its independence. At the end of the Russo-Turkish War (1877–78), Bulgaria rebelled. The ensuing Treaty of San Stefano was unacceptable to the Great Powers, and the Congress of Berlin (1878) resulted. In 1908 the Bulgarian ruler, Ferdinand, declared Bulgaria's independence. After its involvement in the Balkan Wars (1912–13), Bulgaria lost territory. It sided with the Central Powers in World War I and with Germany in World War II. A communist coalition seized power in 1944, and in 1946 a people's republic was declared. Like other eastern European countries in the late 1980s, Bulgaria experienced political unrest; its communist leader resigned in 1989. A new constitution proclaiming a republic was implemented in 1991. The rest of the decade brought economic turmoil.

Recent Developments

Bulgaria joined the the European Union in January 2007. Foreign investment poured into the country, and though the rate of unemployment plummeted from 9.1% in 2006 to 6.9% in 2007, Bulgarian wages stayed low, while prices continued to increase rapidly. Major contributors to the rises were the 7.8% increase in energy prices and an average 3.9% price hike in food items; the latter rise was worsened by prolonged drought and a negative outlook for the fall harvest. Real-estate prices saw rapid growth of 15.0% for the first six months of the year. Overall price pressure prompted educators to stage protest strikes in their quest for higher salaries, and the government agreed to partially satisfy their demands.

Internet resources: <www.bulgariatravel.org/eng>.

Burkina Faso

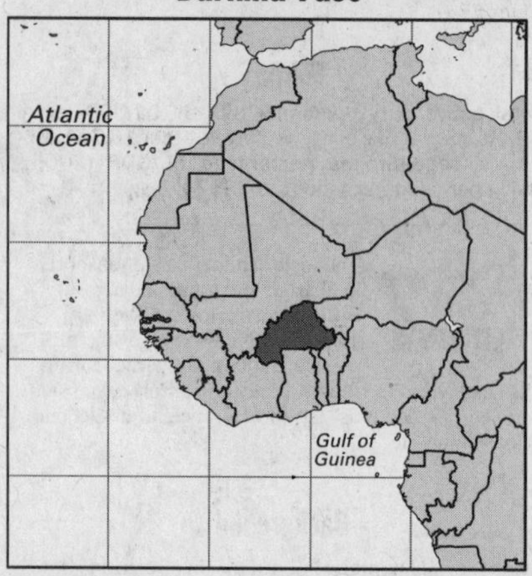

Official name: Burkina Faso. **Form of government:** multiparty republic with one legislative body (National Assembly [111]). **Chief of state:** President Blaise Compaoré (from 1987). **Head of government:** Prime Minister Tertius Zongo (from 2007). **Capital:** Ouagadougou. **Official language:** French. **Official religion:** none. **Monetary unit:** 1 CFA franc (CFAF) = 100 centimes; valuation (1 Jul 2008) US$1 = CFAF 414.60 (pegged since 1 Jan 2002 to the euro [€] at €1 = CFAF 655.96).

Demography

Area: 103,456 sq mi, 267,950 sq km. **Population** (2007): 14,326,000. **Density** (2007): persons per sq mi 138.5, persons per sq km 53.5. **Urban** (2005): 18.3%. **Sex distribution** (2006): male 49.78%; female 50.22%. **Age breakdown** (2006): under 15, 46.7%; 15–29, 28.0%; 30–44, 14.8%; 45–59, 6.5%; 60–74, 3.3%; 75 and over, 0.7%. **Ethnic composition** (1995): Mossi 47.9%; Fulani 10.3%; Lobi 6.9%; Bobo 6.9%; Mande 6.7%; Senufo 5.3%; Grosi 5.0%; Gurma 4.8%; Tuareg 3.1%. **Religious affiliation** (2005): Muslim 48%; traditional beliefs 32%; Roman Catholic 12%; Protestant/independent Christian 8%. **Major cities** (2005): Ouagadougou 1,488,176; Bobo-Dioulasso 452,349; Koudougou 142,360; Tenkodogo 130,084; Solenzo 123,488. **Location:** western Africa, bordering Mali, Niger, Benin, Togo, Ghana, and Côte d'Ivoire.

Vital statistics

Birth rate per 1,000 population (2006): 45.6 (world avg. 20.3). **Death rate** per 1,000 population (2006): 15.6 (world avg. 8.6). **Natural increase rate** per 1,000 population (2006): 30.0 (world avg. 11.7). **Total fertility rate** (avg. births per childbearing woman; 2006): 6.47. **Life expectancy** at birth (2006): male 47.3 years; female 50.4 years.

National economy

Budget (2006). *Revenue:* CFAF 793,000,000,000 (tax revenue 52.3%, of which taxes on goods and services 29.3%; loans 23.2%; grants 18.5%; nontax revenue 3.6%; other 2.4%). *Expenditures:* CFAF 892,100,000,000 (current expenditure 50.1%; development expenditure 49.9%). **Public debt** (external; 2005): US$1,920,000,000. **Households.** Average household size (2003) 6.3; expenditure (2003): food, beverages, and tobacco 48.8%, housing and energy 17.8%, transportation 7.0%, clothing 6.8%, health 4.4%, recreation and culture 4.1%. **Production** (metric tons except as noted). *Agriculture, forestry, fishing* (2005): sorghum 1,552,911, millet 1,196,253, corn (maize) 799,052; livestock (number of live animals) 10,708,992 goats, 8,010,158 cattle, 7,009,407 sheep; roundwood 13,067,000 cu m, of which fuelwood 91%; fisheries production (2004) 9,005. *Mining and quarrying* (2005): gold 1,397 kg. *Manufacturing* (value added in CFAF '000,000; 1999): food products, beverages, and tobacco 126,125; textiles 46,217; chemicals and chemical products 9,335. *Energy production (consumption):* electricity (kW-hr; 2005) 516,000,000 ([2004] 400,000,000); petroleum products (metric tons; 2004) none (352,000). **Population economically active** (1996): total 5,075,615; activity rate 49.2% (participation rates: over age 10, 70.0%; female 48.2%). **Gross national income** (2006): US$6,226,000,000 (US$434 per capita). **Land use** as % of total land area (2003): in temporary crops 17.7%, in permanent crops 0.2%, in pasture 21.9%; overall forest area (2005) 29.0%. **Selected balance of payments data.** Receipts from (US$'000,000): tourism (2005) 19; remittances (2005) 50; foreign direct investment (2001–05 avg.) 17; official development assistance (2005) 660. Disbursements for (US$'000,000): tourism (2001) 22; remittances (2005) 44.

Foreign trade

Imports (2005): CFAF 619,000,000,000 (mineral fuels 24.6%; machinery and apparatus 14.3%; chemicals and chemical products 14.1%; transport equipment 9.1%). *Major import sources:* France 18.7%; Côte d'Ivoire 18.0%; Togo 11.4%; Benin 6.8%; Ghana 5.9%. **Exports** (2005): CFAF 175,000,000,000 (raw cotton 74.5%; sesame 2.9%; cigarettes 2.1%; sugar 1.5%). *Major export destinations:* Togo 41.1%; Ghana 16.7%; Côte d'Ivoire 10.5%; France 9.8%; Switzerland 9.4%.

Transport and communications

Transport. *Railroads:* route length (2004) 622 km; passenger-km (2003) 9,980,000; metric ton-km cargo (2005) 674,900,000. *Roads* (2006): total length 15,272 km (paved 17%). *Vehicles* (2005): passenger cars 84,161; trucks and buses 38,261. *Air transport* (2005; combined data for Ouagadougou and Bobo-Dioulasso airports only): passenger arrivals 134,247, passenger departures 137,373; cargo unloaded 2,837 metric tons, cargo loaded 1,347 metric tons. **Communications,** in total units (units per 1,000 persons). Daily newspaper circulation (2004): 12,000 (0.9); televisions (2004): 156,000 (12); telephone landlines (2006): 95,000 (7); cellular telephone subscribers (2006): 1,017,000 (75); personal computers (2005): 31,000 (2.4); total Internet users (2006): 80,000 (5.9); broadband Internet subscribers (2006): 1,700 (0.1).

1 metric ton = about 1.1 short tons; 1 kilometer = 0.6 mi (statute); 1 metric ton-km cargo = about 0.68 short ton-mi cargo; c.i.f.: cost, insurance, and freight; f.o.b.: free on board

Education and health

Educational attainment (2003). Percentage of population ages 25 and over having: no formal schooling/unknown 85.4%; incomplete to complete primary education 7.9%; incomplete to complete secondary 5.5%; higher 1.2%. **Literacy** (2003): percentage of total population ages 15 and over literate 26.6%; males literate 36.8%; females literate 16.6%. **Health:** physicians (2004) 369 (1 per 35,439 persons); hospital beds (2001) 15,801 (1 per 735 persons); infant mortality rate per 1,000 live births (2006) 91.4. **Food** (2005): daily per capita caloric intake 2,593 (vegetable products 93%, animal products 7%); 144% of FAO recommended minimum.

Military

Total active duty personnel (2006): 10,800 (army 98.1%, air force 1.9%). **Military expenditure as percentage of GDP** (2005): 1.3%; per capita expenditure US$6.

Background

Probably in the 14th century, the Mossi and Gurma peoples established themselves in eastern and central areas of what is now Burkina Faso. The Mossi kingdoms of Yatenga and Ouagadougou existed into the early 20th century. A French protectorate was established over the region (1895–97), and its southern boundary was demarcated through an Anglo-French agreement. It was part of the Upper Senegal–Niger colony and then became a separate colony in 1919. Named Upper Volta, it was constituted an overseas territory within the French Union in 1947, became an autonomous republic within the French Community in 1958, and achieved total independence in 1960. Since then, the country has been ruled primarily by the military and has experienced several coups; following one in 1983, the country received its present name. A new constitution, adopted in 1991, restored multiparty rule.

Recent Developments

Burkina Faso Pres. Blaise Compaoré expanded his role in international affairs with his election in 2007 as head of both the Economic Community of West African States and the West African Economic and Monetary Union. Results of the December 2006 census published in April showed a total population of 13,730,258, an increase of almost 3.5 million people in 10 years. Despite years of internationally funded aid programs, Burkina Faso remained among the poorest countries in the world, with nearly half the population living on less than US$1 daily. A deadly meningitis epidemic, low cotton prices, and severe summer flooding added to Burkina Faso's economic woes.

Internet resources: <www.burkinaembassy-usa.org>.

Burundi

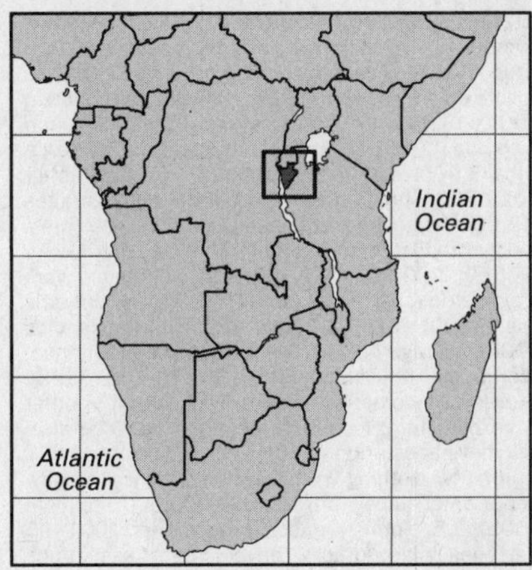

Official name: Republika y'u Burundi (Rundi); République du Burundi (French) (Republic of Burundi). **Form of government:** republic with two legislative bodies (Senate [49]; National Assembly [100]). **Head of state and government:** President Pierre Nkurunziza (from 2005), assisted by Vice President Yves Sahinguvu (from 2007). **Capital:** Bujumbura. **Official languages:** Rundi; French. **Official religion:** none. **Monetary unit:** 1 Burundi franc (FBu) = 100 centimes; valuation (1 Jul 2008) US$1 = FBu 1,194.46.

Demography

Area: 10,740 sq mi, 27,816 sq km. **Population** (2007): 8,391,000. **Density** (2007): persons per sq mi 837.4, persons per sq km 323.4. **Urban** (2005): 10.0%. **Sex distribution** (2005): male 48.82%; female 51.18%. **Age breakdown** (2005): under 15, 45.1%; 15–29, 29.0%; 30–44, 13.7%; 45–59, 8.2%; 60–74, 3.2%; 75–84, 0.7%; 85 and over, 0.1%. **Ethnic composition** (2000): Hutu 80.9%; Tutsi 15.6%; Lingala 1.6%; Twa Pygmy 1.0%; other 0.9%. **Religious affiliation** (2004): Christian 67%, of which Roman Catholic 62%, Protestant 5%; traditional beliefs 23%; Muslim 10%. **Major cities** (2004): Bujumbura 340,300; Gitega 46,900; Muyinga 45,300; Ngozi 40,200; Ruyigi 36,800. **Location:** central Africa, bordering Rwanda, Tanzania, Lake Tanganyika, and the Democratic Republic of the Congo.

Vital statistics

Birth rate per 1,000 population (2005): 45.6 (world avg. 20.3). **Death rate** per 1,000 population (2005): 16.1 (world avg. 8.6). **Natural increase rate** per 1,000 population (2005): 29.5 (world avg. 11.7). **Total fertility rate** (avg. births per childbearing woman; 2005): 6.80. **Life expectancy** at birth (2005): male 47.0 years; female 49.8 years.

National economy

Budget (2006). *Revenue:* FBu 220,170,000,000 (tax revenue 71.3%, of which sales tax 37.8%, taxes on international trade 11.7%, corporate income tax 11.1%, personal income tax 8.7%; grants 18.8%; nontax revenue 6.9%; other 3.0%). *Expenditures:* FBu 319,061,000,000 (current expenditure 70.1%, of which debt service 6.4%; capital expenditure 27.9%; other 2.0%). **Public debt** (external, outstanding; September 2006): US$1,227,000,000. **Production** (metric tons except as noted). *Agriculture, forestry, fishing* (2005): bananas 1,600,000, sweet potatoes 835,000, cassava 710,000; livestock (number of live animals) 750,000 goats, 396,000 cattle, 243,000 sheep; roundwood 13,067,000 cu m, of which fuelwood 91%; fisheries production (2004) 13,631 (from aquaculture 1%). *Mining and quarrying* (2005): columbite-tantalite ore 42,592 kg; gold 3,905 kg. *Manufacturing* (2005): beer 1,012,500 hectolitres; carbonated beverages 143,600 hectolitres; cottonseed oil 135,900 litres. *Energy production (consumption):* electricity (kW-hr; 2005) 99,200,000 (119,800,000); petroleum products (metric tons; 2004) none (70,000); peat (metric tons; 2005) 4,700 ([2000] 12,000). **Households** (2004). Average household size 5.6; average annual income per household FBu 168,000 (US $153); sources of income: agriculture/livestock 91%, other 9%; expenditure: food 46%, debt service 14%, alcoholic beverages and tobacco 8%, transportation 6%, health 5%, clothing 4%. **Selected balance of payments data.** Receipts from (US$'000,000): tourism (2005) 1.5; foreign direct investment (2001–05 avg.) negligible; official development assistance (2005) 365. Disbursements for (US$'000,000): tourism (2005) 60; remittances (2005) 1.0. **Gross national income** (2006): US$903,000,000 (US$110 per capita). **Population economically active** (2003): total 3,464,000; activity rate of total population 49.2% (participation rates: ages 15–64, 92.2%; female 52.1%). **Land use** as % of total land area (2003): in temporary crops 38.6%, in permanent crops 14.2%, in pasture 38.6%; overall forest area (2005) 5.9%.

Foreign trade

Imports (2006): FBu 442,500,000,000 (machinery and apparatus 21.3%; transportation equipment 15.7%; mineral fuels 13.4%; fabricated metals 7.2%; pharmaceuticals 6.6%). *Major import sources:* Saudi Arabia 12.6%; Belgium/Luxembourg 11.7%; Kenya 8.2%; Japan 7.8%; Russia 4.7%. **Exports** (2006): FBu 60,400,000,000 (coffee 67.7%; tea 17.0%; hides and skins 2.6%; cotton fabric 1.9%). *Major export destinations:* Switzerland 34.4%; UK 12.3%; Pakistan 7.8%; Rwanda 5.1%; other EU 24.6%.

Transport and communications

Transport. *Roads* (2004): total length 12,322 km (paved 7%). *Vehicles* (2002): passenger cars 19,800; trucks and buses 14,400. *Air transport* (2005; figures for Bujumbura airport only): passenger arrivals 73,072, passenger departures 63,908; cargo unloaded 3,093 metric tons, cargo loaded 188 metric tons. **Communications,** in total units (units per 1,000 persons). Daily newspaper circulation (2004): 2,500 (0.3); televisions (2004): 280,000 (37); telephone landlines (2005): 31,000 (4.1); cellular telephone subscribers (2005): 153,000 (20); personal computers (2004): 34,000 (4.8); total Internet users (2006): 60,000 (7.7).

Education and health

Literacy (2003): percentage of total population ages 15 and over literate 51.6%; males literate 58.5%; females literate 45.2%. **Health** (2004): physicians 200 (1 per 37,581 persons); hospital beds (1999) 3,380 (1 per 1,657 persons); infant mortality rate per 1,000 live births (2005) 64.4. **Food** (2005): daily per capita caloric intake 1,693 (vegetable products 98%, animal products 2%); 94% of FAO recommended minimum.

Military

Total active duty personnel (2006): 50,500 (army 89.1%, gendarmerie 10.9%). **Military expenditure as percentage of GDP** (2005): 6.2%; per capita expenditure US$6.

Background

Original settlement by the Twa people was followed by Hutu settlement, which occurred gradually and was completed by the 11th century. The Tutsi arrived 300–400 years later; though a minority, they established the kingdom of Burundi in the 16th century. In the 19th century the area came within the German sphere of influence, but the Tutsi remained in power. Following World War I the Belgians took control of the area, which became a UN trusteeship after World War II. Colonial-period conditions had intensified Hutu-Tutsi ethnic animosities, and as independence neared, hostilities flared. Independence was granted in 1962 in the form of a kingdom ruled by the Tutsi. In 1965 the Hutu rebelled but were brutally repressed. The rest of the 20th century saw violent clashes between the two groups, leading to charges of genocide in the 1990s. The very unstable government that existed in these surroundings was overthrown by the military in 1996.

Recent Developments

Progress toward reconciliation made in 2006 between the government of Burundi and the last remaining rebel group was reversed in 2007. The original cease-fire deal, signed by Pres. Pierre Nkurunziza and the National Liberation Forces (FNL) leader Agathon Rwasa, was never implemented owing to unresolved issues, namely the release of FNL prisoners. Violence in Bujumbura increased significantly during the summer of 2007, and in September the FNL turned down calls by the UN for a return to the negotiating table.

Internet resources: <www.burundi.gov.bi>.

Cambodia

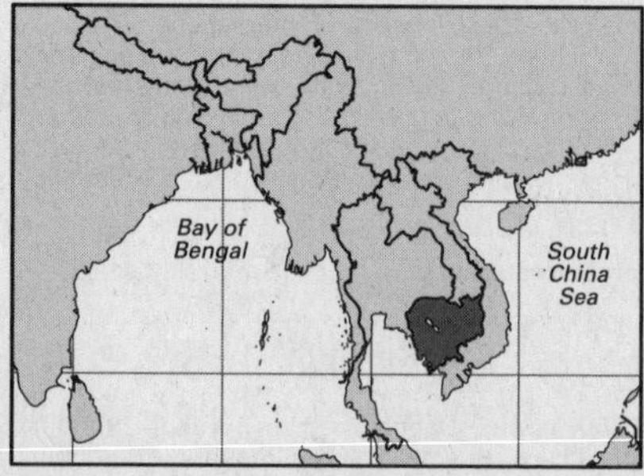

1 metric ton = about 1.1 short tons; 1 kilometer = 0.6 mi (statute); 1 metric ton-km cargo = about 0.68 short ton-mi cargo; c.i.f.: cost, insurance, and freight; f.o.b.: free on board

Official name: Preah Reach Ana Pak Kampuchea (Kingdom of Cambodia). **Form of government:** constitutional monarchy with two legislative houses (Senate [61]; National Assembly [123]). **Chief of state:** King Norodom Sihamoni (from 2004). **Head of government:** Prime Minister Hun Sen (from 1998). **Capital:** Phnom Penh. **Official language:** Khmer. **Official religion:** Buddhism. **Monetary unit:** 1 riel = 100 sen; valuation (1 Jul 2008) US$1 = 4,106.00 riels.

Demography

Area: 69,898 sq mi, 181,035 sq km. **Population** (2007): 13,893,000. **Density** (2007): persons per sq mi 202.1, persons per sq km 78.0. **Urban** (2004): 15.0%. **Sex distribution** (2005): male 48.75%; female 51.25%. **Age breakdown** (2005): under 15, 36.6%; 15–29, 30.5%; 30–44, 18.4%; 45–59, 9.4%; 60–74, 4.1%; 75–84, 0.9%; 85 and over, 0.1%. **Ethnic composition** (2000): Khmer 85.2%; Chinese 6.4%; Vietnamese 3.0%; Cham 2.5%; Lao 0.6%; other 2.3%. **Religious affiliation** (2000): Buddhist 84.7%; Chinese folk religionist 4.7%; traditional beliefs 4.3%; Muslim 2.3%; Christian 1.1%; other 2.9%. **Major urban areas** (1998): Phnom Penh (2005) 1,364,000; Battambang 124,290; Sisophon 85,382; Siemreap 83,715; Sihanoukville 66,723. **Location:** southeastern Asia, bordering Thailand, Laos, Vietnam, and the Gulf of Thailand.

Vital statistics

Birth rate per 1,000 population (2006): 26.9 (world avg. 20.3). **Death rate** per 1,000 population (2006): 9.1 (world avg. 8.6). **Total fertility rate** (avg. births per childbearing woman; 2006): 3.37. **Life expectancy** at birth (2006): male 57.4 years; female 61.3 years.

National economy

Budget (2005). *Revenue:* 3,280,300,000,000 riels (tax revenue 58.3%; nontax revenue 17.2%; grants 20.0%; other 4.5%). *Expenditures:* 3,294,700,000,000 riels (current expenditure 59.7%; development expenditure 40.3%). **Production** (metric tons except as noted). *Agriculture, forestry, fishing* (2005): rice 5,986,000, cassava 535,600, corn (maize) 247,800; livestock (number of live animals) 3,100,000 cattle, 2,500,000 pigs, 650,000 buffalo, 120,000 crocodiles; roundwood 9,334,000 cu m, of which fuelwood 99%; fisheries production (2004) 326,652 (from aquaculture 6%); aquatic plants production 16,840 (from aquaculture 100%). *Mining and quarrying* (2005): gold, n.a.; gemstones, n.a.; crude stones 600,000. *Manufacturing* (value added in '000,000,000 riels; 2002): wearing apparel 1,808; food products 392; base and fabricated metals 120. *Energy production (consumption):* electricity (kW-hr; 2004) 130,000,000 (130,000,000); petroleum products (metric tons; 2004) negligible (174,000). **Households.** Average household size (2004) 5.1; average annual extrapolated monetary and nonmonetary income (1993–94): 2,031,000 riels (US$787); sources of income (1993–94): monetary 67.4%, of which nonagricultural (mostly self-employment) 36.8%, agricultural 18.1%, wages and salaries 9.1%; nonmonetary 32.6%, of which agricultural 11.4%; household expenditure (2002): food, beverages, and tobacco 62.6%, housing and energy 19.7%, health 6.0%, transportation and communications 3.4%. **Selected balance of payments data.** Receipts from (US$'000,000): tourism (2005) 840; remittances (2005) 200; foreign direct investment (2001–05 avg.) 178; official development assistance (2005) 538. Disbursements for (US$'000,000): tourism (2005) 97; remittances (2005) 144. **Gross national income** (2006): US$6,177,000,000 (US$435 per capita). **Public debt** (external, outstanding; 2005): US$3,155,000,000. **Population economically active** (2004): total 7,557,600; activity rate of total population 55% (participation rates: ages 15–64, 82.6%; female 49.4%; unemployed [2001] 1.8%). **Land use** as % of total land area (2003): in temporary crops 21.0%, in permanent crops 0.8%, in pasture 8.5%; overall forest area (2005) 59.2%.

Foreign trade

Imports (2005; c.i.f.): US$4,254,000,000 (retained imports 97.3%; imports for reexport 2.7%). *Major import sources* (2004): Thailand 23.9%; Hong Kong 15.0%; China 13.5%; Singapore 11.5%; Vietnam 7.6%. **Exports** (2005; f.o.b.): US$2,910,000,000 (domestic exports 95.3%, of which garments 77.7%, rice 6.1%, rubber 4.1%, fish 2.6%, sawn timber and logs 0.5%; reexports 4.7%). *Major export destinations* (2004): US 56.2%; Germany 11.5%; UK 7.0%; Canada 4.3%; Vietnam 3.7%.

Transport and communications

Transport. *Railroads* (2004): length 602 km; passenger-km (2000) 45,000,000; metric ton-km (1999) 76,171,000. *Roads* (2004): total length 38,257 km (paved 6%). *Vehicles* (2004): passenger cars 235,298; trucks and buses 35,448. *Air transport* (2005–06): passenger-km 198,000,000; metric ton-km cargo 1,214,000. **Communications,** in total units (units per 1,000 persons). Daily newspaper circulation (2004): 36,000 (2.7); televisions (2003): 103,000 (8); telephone landlines (2006): 33,000 (2.3); cellular telephone subscribers (2006): 1,140,000 (79); personal computers (2004): 38,000 (2.6); total Internet users (2005): 44,000 (3.1); broadband Internet subscribers (2005): 1,000 (0.1).

Education and health

Educational attainment (2004). Percentage of literate population ages 25 and over having: no formal schooling/unknown 4.6%; incomplete primary education 54.0%; complete primary 23.7%; incomplete secondary 11.3%; secondary/vocational 5.3%; higher 1.1%. **Literacy** (2004): percentage of total population ages 15 and over literate 74.4%; males literate 82.1%; females literate 67.4%. **Health:** physicians (2004) 2,122 (1 per 6,169 persons); hospital beds (2002) 9,800 (1 per 1,405 persons); infant mortality rate per 1,000 live births (2006) 68.8. **Food** (2005): daily per capita caloric intake 2,370 (vegetable products 92%, animal products 8%); 134% of FAO recommended minimum.

Military

Total active duty personnel (2006): 124,300 (army 60.3%, navy 2.3%, air force 1.2%, provincial forces 36.2%). **Military expenditure as percentage of GDP** (2005): 1.8%; per capita expenditure US$8.

Did you know? The Kizuna bridge became the first bridge ever to span the Mekong River when it opened to the public on 4 Dec 2001. The Mekong flows through Cambodia for about 500 km (300 mi) and is considered the country's most important river.

Background

In the early Christian era, what is now Cambodia was under Hindu and, to a lesser extent, Buddhist influence. The Khmer state gradually spread in the early 7th century and reached its height under Jayavarman II and his successors in the 9th–12th centuries, when it ruled the Mekong Valley and the tributary Shan states and built Angkor. Widespread adoption of Buddhism occurred in the 13th century, resulting in a script change from Sanskrit to Pali. From the 13th century Cambodia was attacked by Annam and Siamese city-states and was alternately a province of one or the other. The area became a French protectorate in 1863. It was occupied by the Japanese in World War II and became independent in 1954. Cambodia's borders were the scene of fighting in the Vietnam War from 1961, and in 1970 its northeastern and eastern areas were occupied by the North Vietnamese and penetrated by US and South Vietnamese forces. An indiscriminate US bombing campaign alienated much of the population, enabling the communist Khmer Rouge under Pol Pot to seize power in 1975. Their regime of terror resulted in the deaths of at least one million Cambodians. Vietnam invaded in 1979 and drove the Khmer Rouge into the western hinterlands, but it was unable to effect reconstruction of the country, and Cambodian infighting continued. A peace accord was reached by most Cambodian factions under UN auspices in 1991, and elections were held in 1993. In 2004 King Norodom Sihanouk abdicated, and his son Sihamoni was named his successor.

Recent Developments

In Cambodia in 2007 the Khmer Rouge Tribunal continued to move forward in a slow, almost tortuous process. In July prosecutors recommended that five senior Khmer Rouge leaders be tried for genocide and crimes against humanity committed during the Pol Pot regime (1975–79). Although only two were officially charged, the Cambodian press speculated that others named internally might include Khieu Samphan, head of state during the regime. New reports predicted that Cambodian offshore oil fields might yield more than initially expected. A September IMF study indicated that Cambodia could begin generating approximately US$174 million in oil income by 2011, with production peaking at US$1.7 billion in 2021—significant revenue in relation to the Cambodian economy. The country was expanding its navy to protect the offshore sites.

Internet resources: <www.tourismcambodia.com>.

Cameroon

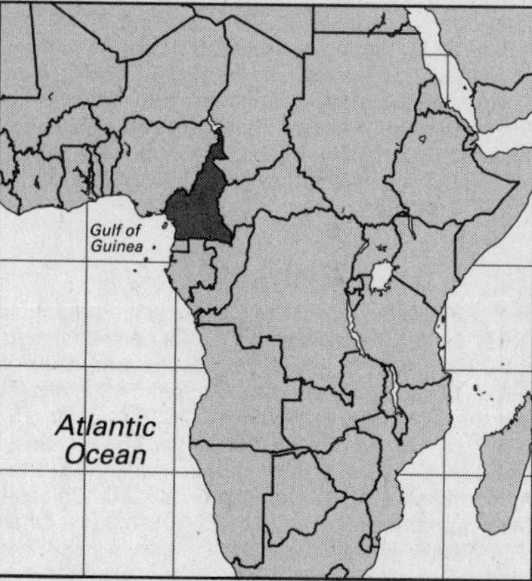

Official name: République du Cameroun (French); Republic of Cameroon (English). **Form of government:** unitary multiparty republic with one legislative house (National Assembly [180]). **Chief of state:** President Paul Biya (from 1982). **Head of government:** Prime Minister Ephraïm Inoni (from 2004). **Capital:** Yaoundé. **Official languages:** French; English. **Official religion:** none. **Monetary unit:** 1 CFA franc (CFAF) = 100 centimes; valuation (1 Jul 2008) US$1 = CFAF 414.60 (pegged to the euro [€] at the rate of €1 = CFAF 655.96).

Demography

Area: 183,569 sq mi, 475,442 sq km. **Population** (2007): 18,060,000. **Density** (2007): persons per sq mi 100.4, persons per sq km 38.8. **Urban** (2004): 53.4%. **Sex distribution** (2006): male 50.15%; female 49.85%. **Age breakdown** (2006): under 15, 41.5%; 15–29, 29.0%; 30–44, 15.7%; 45–59, 8.8%; 60–74, 4.1%; 75–84, 0.8%; 85 and over, 0.1%. **Ethnic composition** (1983): Fang 19.6%; Bamileke and Bamum 18.5%; Duala, Luanda, and Basa 14.7%; Fulani 9.6%; Tikar 7.4%; Mandara 5.7%; Maka 4.9%; Chamba 2.4%; Mbum 1.3%; Hausa 1.2%; French 0.2%; other 14.5%. **Religious affiliation** (2005): Roman Catholic 27.4%; traditional beliefs 22.2%; Protestant 20.2%; Sunni Muslim 20.0%; nonreligious/other 10.2%. **Major urban areas** (2004): Douala 1,532,800; Yaoundé 1,434,700; Garoua 409,000; Kousséri 332,900; Bamenda 298,500. **Location:** western Africa, bordering Chad, the Central African Republic, the Republic of the Congo, Gabon, Equatorial Guinea, the Bight of Biafra, and Nigeria.

Vital statistics

Birth rate per 1,000 population (2006): 35.6 (world avg. 20.3). **Death rate** per 1,000 population (2006): 13.0 (world avg. 8.6). **Natural increase rate** per 1,000 population (2006): 22.6 (world avg. 11.7). **Total fertility rate** (avg. births per childbearing woman; 2006):

1 metric ton = about 1.1 short tons; 1 kilometer = 0.6 mi (statute); 1 metric ton-km cargo = about 0.68 short ton-mi cargo; c.i.f.: cost, insurance, and freight; f.o.b.: free on board

4.58. **Life expectancy** at birth (2006): male 51.7 years; female 53.0 years.

National economy

Budget (2005). *Revenue:* CFAF 1,590,000,000,000 (non-oil revenue 69.4%, of which VAT 22.0%, direct taxes 16.5%, customs duties 11.9%, nontax revenue 7.9%; oil revenue 27.6%; grants 3.0%). *Expenditures:* CFAF 1,278,000,000,000 (current expenditure 82.6%, of which interest on public debt 10.1%; capital expenditure 16.1%; other 1.3%). **Gross national income** (2006): US$17,707,000,000 (US$974 per capita). **Households.** Average household size (2004) 4.8; expenditure (1993): food 49.1%, housing 18.0%, transportation and communications 13.0%, health 8.6%, clothing 7.6%, recreation 2.4%. **Population economically active** (2003): total 6,093,000; activity rate of total population 38.7% (participation rates: ages 15–64, 68.4%; female 39.6%). **Public debt** (external, outstanding; 2005): US$5,521,000,000. **Production** (metric tons except as noted). *Agriculture, forestry, fishing* (2005): cassava 2,139,000, sugarcane 1,450,000, plantains 1,356,000; livestock (number of live animals) 6,000,000 cattle, 4,400,000 goats, 3,800,000 sheep; roundwood 11,285,000 cu m, of which fuelwood 84%; fisheries production (2004) 108,330. *Mining and quarrying* (2005): pozzolana 600,000; limestone 130,000; gold 1,500 kg. *Manufacturing* (value added in US$'000,000; 2002): food products 97; refined petroleum 88; beverages 78. *Energy production (consumption):* electricity (kW-hr; 2005) 4,004,000,000 (3,264,000,000); crude petroleum (barrels; 2005) 21,900,000 ([2004] 14,043,000); petroleum products (metric tons; 2004) 1,752,000 (917,000). **Land use** as % of total land area (2003): in temporary crops 12.8%, in permanent crops 2.6%, in pasture 4.3%; overall forest area (2005) 45.6%. **Selected balance of payments data.** Receipts from (US$'000,000): tourism (2005) 36; remittances (2005) 31; foreign direct investment (FDI) (2001–05 avg.) 4.0; official development assistance (2005) 358 (commitments). Disbursements for (US$'000,000): tourism (2003) 212; remittances (2005) 63; FDI (2001–03 avg.) 24.

Foreign trade

Imports (2005): CFAF 1,524,200,000,000 (crude petroleum 27.8%; machinery and apparatus 11.6%; chemicals and chemical products 11.1%; cereals 7.4%; motor vehicles 6.1%). *Major import sources:* Nigeria 21.0%; France 17.7%; China 5.0%; US 4.6%; Japan 3.9%. **Exports** (2005): CFAF 1,476,000,000,000 (crude petroleum 44.8%; fuels and lubricants 12.2%; sawn wood 12.0%; cocoa beans 7.5%; aluminum 4.7%; raw cotton 4.7%; bananas 2.4%; coffee 2.3%). *Major export destinations:* Spain 19.7%; France 12.7%; Italy 11.7%; The Netherlands 7.6%; US 6.7%.

Transport and communications

Transport. *Railroads* (2005): route length 1,016 km; passenger-km 323,000,000; metric ton-km cargo 1,119,000,000. *Roads* (2004): total length 50,000 km (paved 10%). *Vehicles* (2005): passenger cars 175,981; trucks and buses 59,399. *Air transport* (2001): passenger-km 796,567,000; metric ton-km cargo 23,255,000. **Communications**, in total units (units per 1,000 persons). Daily newspaper circulation (2005): 59,000 (3.5); televisions (2004): 720,000 (43); telephone landlines (2005): 100,000 (6.1); cellular telephone subscribers (2005): 2,252,000 (133); personal computers (2005): 200,000 (12); total Internet users (2006): 370,000 (22).

Education and health

Educational attainment (2004): Percentage of population ages 25 and over having: no formal schooling 32.9%; primary education 35.3%; secondary 26.2%; higher 4.2%; other/unknown 1.4%. **Literacy** (2003): percentage of total population ages 15 and over literate 74.6%; males literate 81.5%; females literate 67.9%. **Health** (2004): physicians 2,966 (1 per 5,609 persons); hospital beds 38,067 (1 per 437 persons); infant mortality rate per 1,000 live births (2006) 67.2. **Food** (2005): daily per capita caloric intake 2,634 (vegetable products 94%, animal products 6%); 142% of FAO recommended minimum.

Military

Total active duty personnel (2006): 14,100 (army 88.7%, navy 9.2%; air force 2.1%). **Military expenditure as percentage of GDP** (2005): 1.3%; per capita expenditure US$13.

Background

The Cameroon area had long been inhabited before European colonization. Bantu speakers from equatorial Africa settled in the south, followed by Muslim Fulani from the Niger River basin, who settled in the north. Portuguese explorers visited in the late 15th century and established a foothold, but they lost control to the Dutch in the 17th century. In 1884 the Germans took control and extended their protectorate over Cameroon. In World War I joint French-British action forced the Germans to retreat, and after the war the region was divided into French and British administrative zones. After World War II the two areas became UN trusteeships. In 1960 the French trust territory became an independent republic. In 1961 the southern part of the British trust territory voted for union with the new republic of Cameroon, and the northern part voted for union with Nigeria. In recent decades economic problems have produced unrest in the country.

Recent Developments

Teachers complained in 2007 that Franglais (a mixture of English, French, and the creole language) was having a profound effect on how students spoke and wrote French and English, Cameroon's two official languages. In January, Chinese Pres. Hu Jintao paid a state visit to Yaoundé. Presidents Hu and Paul Biya signed a series of cooperative agreements and concessionary loans, including an interest-free US$3.86 million loan for projects to be determined at a future date by the Cameroonian government.

Internet resources:
<http://www.statistics-cameroon.org/>.

Canada

Official name: Canada. **Form of government:** federal multiparty parliamentary state with two legislative houses (Senate [105]; House of Commons [308]). **Chief of state:** British Queen Elizabeth II (from 1952),

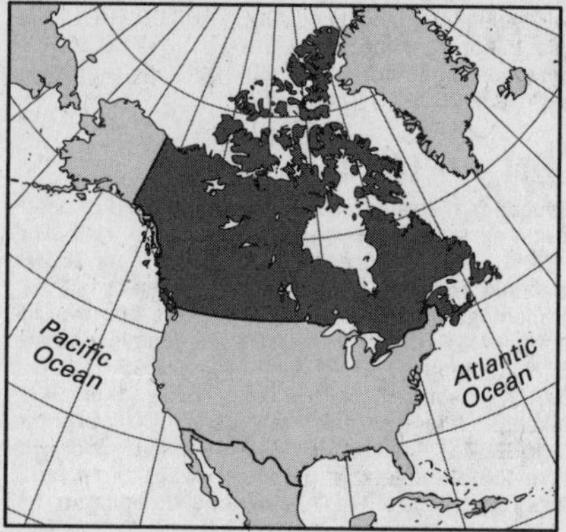

represented by Governor-General Michaëlle Jean (from 2005). **Head of government:** Prime Minister Stephen Harper (from 2006). **Capital:** Ottawa. **Official languages:** English; French. **Official religion:** none. **Monetary unit:** 1 Canadian dollar (Can$) = 100 cents; valuation (1 Jul 2008) US$1 = Can$1.02.

Demography

Area: 3,855,103 sq mi, 9,984,670 sq km. **Population** (2007): 32,945,000. **Density** (2007): persons per sq mi 9.4, persons per sq km 3.6. **Urban** (2003): 80.4%. **Sex distribution** (2006): male 49.52%; female 50.48%. **Age breakdown** (2006): under 15, 17.3%; 15–29, 20.4%; 30–44, 22.3%; 45–59, 21.9%; 60–74, 11.8%; 75–84, 4.7%; 85 and over, 1.6%. **Ethnic origin** (2000): Anglo-Canadian 45.5%; French-Canadian 23.5%; Chinese 3.4%; British expatriates 3.3%; Indo-Pakistani 2.6%, of which Punjabi 2.3%; German 2.4%; Italian 2.2%; US white 1.8%; Métis (part Indian) 1.8%; Indian 1.5%, of which detribalized 0.5%; Jewish 1.4%; Arab 1.3%; Ukrainian 1.2%; Eskimo (Inuit) 0.1%; other 8.0%. **Religious affiliation** (2001): Christian 77.1%, of which Roman Catholic 43.2%, Protestant 28.3%, unspecified Christian 2.6%, Orthodox 1.7%, other Christian 1.3%; Muslim 2.0%; Jewish 1.1%; Hindu 1.0%; Buddhist 1.0%; Sikh 0.9%; nonreligious 16.5%; other 0.4%. **Major metropolitan areas** (2006): Toronto 5,113,149; Montreal 3,635,571; Vancouver 2,116,581; Ottawa-Hull 1,130,761; Calgary 1,079,310; Edmonton 1,034,945; Quebec 715,515; Winnipeg 694,668; Hamilton 692,911; London 457,720. **Location:** northern North America, bordering the Arctic Ocean, the North Atlantic Ocean, the US, and the North Pacific Ocean. **Place of birth** (2001): 81.6% native-born; 18.4% foreign-born, of which in the UK 2.0%, elsewhere in Europe 5.7%, Asia 5.8%, US 0.8%, other 4.1%. **Mobility** (2001). Population living in the same residence as in 1996: 58.1%; different residence, same municipality 22.4%; same province, different municipality 3.3%; different province 12.7%; different country 3.5%. **Households.** Total number of households (2004) 11,952,550. Average household size (2004) 2.7; 1 person (1997) 25.2%, 2 persons 33.0%, 3 persons 16.7%, 4 persons 16.3%, 5 or more persons 8.8%. Family households (2001): 8,371,020 (72.4%), nonfamily 3,191,955 (27.6%, of which 1 person 75.6%). **Immigration** (2004): permanent immigrants admitted 235,824; from Asia 48.6%, of which China 15.4%, India 10.8%, Philippines 5.6%; Europe 17.8%, of which UK 2.6%, France 2.1%; US 3.2%; refugee arrivals 26,526; overall refugee population (2004) 141,398.

Vital statistics

Birth rate per 1,000 population (2005–06): 10.6 (world avg. 20.3); (1997) within marriage 72.3%. **Death rate** per 1,000 population (2005–06): 7.2 (world avg. 8.6). **Natural increase rate** per 1,000 population (2005–06): 3.4 (world avg. 11.7). **Total fertility rate** (avg. births per childbearing woman; 2006): 1.61. **Life expectancy** at birth (2006): male 76.9 years; female 83.7 years.

Social indicators

Educational attainment (2004). Percentage of population ages 15 and over having: incomplete primary and complete primary education 8.8%; incomplete secondary 15.7%; complete secondary 19.3%; some university/higher vocational 39.0%; bachelor's degree or higher 17.2%. **Quality of working life.** Average workweek (2005): 35.2 hours. Annual rate per 100,000 workers for (2005): injury, accident, or industrial illness 2,090; death 6.8. Average days lost to labor stoppages per 1,000 employee-workdays (2001): 0.7. Average commuting distance (2001): 7.2 km; mode of transportation: automobile 80.7%, public transportation 10.5%, walking 6.6%, other 2.2%. Labor force covered by a pension plan (2001): 33.6%. **Access to services.** Proportion of households having access to: electricity (2002) 100%; public water supply (1996) 99.8%; public sewage collection (1996) 99.3%. **Social participation.** Eligible voters participating in last national election (January 2006): 64.9%. Population over 18 years of age participating in voluntary work (2000): 26.7%. Union membership as percentage of civilian labor force (2003) 25.0%. Attendance at religious services on a weekly basis (2006): 17%. **Social deviance** (2004). Offense rate per 100,000 population for: violent crime 946.1, of which assault 731.8, sexual assault 73.7, homicide 2.0; property crime 3,990.9, of which auto theft 530.7, breaking and entering 859.9. **Material well-being** (2003). Households possessing: automobile 62.4%; telephone 96.3%; cellular phone 53.9%; color television 99.0%; central air conditioner 39.3%; cable television 65.1%; home computers 66.8%; Internet access 56.9%.

National economy

Gross national income (at current market prices; 2006): US$1,249,635,000,000 (US$38,360 per capita). **Budget** (2005–06). *Revenue:* Can$229,660,000,000 (income tax 62.9%; sales tax 15.4%; contributions to social security 9.6%; other 12.1%). *Expenditures:* Can$216,156,000,000 (social services and welfare 37.1%; defense and social protection 11.2%; health 10.0%; public debt interest 9.9%; resource conservation and industrial development 3.8%; education 2.3%). **Public debt** (January 2007): US$582,601,000,000. **Production** (metric tons except as noted). *Agriculture, forestry, fishing* (2005):

1 metric ton = about 1.1 short tons; 1 kilometer = 0.6 mi (statute); 1 metric ton-km cargo = about 0.68 short ton-mi cargo; c.i.f.: cost, insurance, and freight; f.o.b.: free on board

wheat 26,775,000, barley 12,481,200, rapeseed 9,660,200, corn (maize) 9,460,800, potatoes 4,386,500, oats 3,432,300, soybeans 3,161,300, dry peas 3,099,800, lentils 1,277,900, linseed 1,082,000, tomatoes 839,250, apples 394,100, canary seed 227,200, mustard seed 201,400, cranberries and blueberries 139,099, mushrooms 80,000; livestock (number of live animals; 2006) 14,329,000 pigs, 14,315,000 cattle, 590,500 sheep; roundwood 199,345,000 cu m, of which fuelwood 1%; fisheries production 1,255,821 (from aquaculture 12%). *Mining and quarrying* (value of production in Can$'000,000; 2005): nickel 3,302 (world rank: 3); potash 2,839 (world rank: 1); copper 2,455 (world rank: 8); gold 2,041 (world rank: 8); diamonds (gemstones) 1,684 (world rank: 4); iron ore 1,496 (world rank: 9); sand and gravel 1,165; stone 1,133; zinc 998 (world rank: 4); salt 420 (world rank: 5); silver 299 (world rank: 6); lime 262; gypsum 100 (world rank: 3); cobalt 91 (world rank: 4). *Manufacturing* (value added in Can$'000,000,000 of 1997; 2005): transportation equipment 28.1; food 17.6; chemicals 17.2; fabricated metal products 14.2; wood industries 13.7; machinery 12.5; primary metals 12.3; paper products 11.4; rubber and plastic products 10.3; computers and electronic products 10.3. *Energy production (consumption):* electricity (kW-hr; 2004) 567,600,000,000 (556,600,000,000); hard coal (metric tons; 2004) 29,261,000 (18,057,000); lignite (metric tons; 2004) 36,700,000 (40,804,000); crude petroleum (barrels; 2004) 1,146,000,000 (840,000,000); petroleum products (metric tons; 2004) 117,367,000 (107,573,000); natural gas (cu m; 2004) 180,000,000,000 (93,300,000,000). **Population economically active** (2006): total 17,825,800; activity rate of total population 55.6% (participation rates: ages 15 and over 67.5%; female 46.7%; unemployed [February 2007] 6.1%). **Households.** Average household size (2004) 2.7; average annual income per family (2003) Can$72,700 (US$51,888); sources of income (2001): wages, salaries, and self-employment 71.8%, transfer payments 14.0%, other 14.2%; expenditure (2004): housing 26.9%, transportation 19.0%, food 15.2%, recreation 9.3%, household operations 6.4%, clothing 5.5%, household furnishings 4.1%, health 3.7%, alcoholic beverages and tobacco 3.3%, education 2.4%, other 4.2%. **Land use** as % of total land area (2003): in temporary crops 5.0%, in permanent crops 0.7%, in pasture 1.7%; overall forest area (2005) 33.6%. **Selected balance of payments data.** Receipts from (US$'000,000): tourism (2005) 13,584; foreign direct investment (FDI; 2001–05 avg.) 18,558. Disbursements for (US$'000,000): tourism (2005) 18,341; FDI (2001–05 avg.) 32,331.

Foreign trade

Imports (2006): Can$404,535,000,000 (machinery and apparatus 24.7%; transport equipment 23.4%, of which road vehicles and parts 19.7%; chemicals and chemical products 7.3%; base metals 6.9%; food products 5.8%; crude petroleum 5.6%). *Major import sources* (2006): US 65.5%; Japan 2.9%; UK 2.4%; other EU 8.0%. **Exports** (2006): Can$458,166,-900,000 (transport equipment 22.7%, of which road vehicles and parts 18.1%; machinery and apparatus 16.4%; base metals and alloys 9.9%; crude petroleum 8.4%; food products 6.9%; chemicals and chemical products 6.8%; natural gas 6.0%; wood and wood pulp 4.9%; paper and paperboard 2.4%). *Major export destinations* (2006): US 78.9%; UK 2.6%; Japan 2.3%; other EU 4.7%.

Transport and communications

Transport. *Railroads* (2005): length 72,168 km; passenger-km 1,472,781,000; metric ton-km cargo 352,133,000,000. *Roads* (2004): total length 1,408,900 km (paved 35%). *Vehicles* (2005): passenger cars 18,123,885; trucks and buses 785,649. *Air transport* (2003): passenger-km 90,136,000,000; metric ton-km cargo 1,880,000,000. **Communications,** in total units (units per 1,000 persons). Daily newspaper circulation (2004): 5,350,000 (167); televisions (2003): 22,384,000 (707); telephone landlines (2005): 20,780,000 (501); cellular telephone subscribers (2005): 17,017,000 (525); personal computers (2004): 22,390,000 (701); total Internet users (2005): 20,000,000 (620); broadband Internet subscribers (2006): 7,676,000 (236).

Education and health

Literacy (2005): total population ages 15 and over literate virtually 100%. **Health:** physicians (2004) 67,087 (1 per 476 persons); hospital beds (2002–03) 115,120 (1 per 274 persons); infant mortality rate (2005) 4.8. **Food** (2005): daily per capita caloric intake 3,486 (vegetable products 72%, animal products 28%).

Military

Total active duty personnel (2006): 62,100 (army 53.2%, navy 19.3%, air force 27.5%). **Military expenditure as percentage of GDP** (2005): 1.1%; per capita expenditure US$403.

Background

Originally inhabited by American Indians and Inuit, Canada was visited c. AD 1000 by Scandinavian explorers, whose discovery is confirmed by archaeological evidence from Newfoundland. Fishing expeditions off Newfoundland by the English, French, Spanish, and Portuguese began as early as 1500. The French claim to Canada was made in 1534 when Jacques Cartier entered the Gulf of St. Lawrence. A small settlement was made in Nova Scotia (Acadia) in 1605, and in 1608 Samuel de Champlain founded Quebec. Fur trading was the impetus behind the early colonizing efforts. In response to French activity, the English in 1670 formed the Hudson's Bay Company.

The British-French rivalry for the interior of upper North America lasted almost a century. The first French loss occurred in 1713 at the conclusion of Queen Anne's War (War of the Spanish Succession) when Nova Scotia and Newfoundland were ceded to the British. The Seven Years' War (French and Indian War) resulted in France's expulsion from continental North America in 1763. After the US War of Independence, the population was augmented by Loyalists fleeing the US, and the increasing number arriving in Quebec led the British to divide the colony into Upper and Lower Canada in 1791. The British reunited the two provinces in 1841. Canadian expansionism resulted in the confederation movement of the mid-19th century, and in 1867 the Dominion of Canada, comprising Nova Scotia, New Brunswick, Quebec, and Ontario, came into existence. After confederation, Canada entered a period of westward expansion.

The prosperity that accompanied Canada into the 20th century was marred by continuing conflict between the English and French communities. Through the Statute of Westminster (1931), Canada was recognized as an equal of Great Britain. With the Constitution Act of 1982, the British gave Canada total control over its constitution and severed the remaining legal connections between the two countries. French Canadian unrest continued to be a major concern, with a movement growing for Quebec separatism in the late 20th century. Referendums for more political autonomy for Quebec were rejected in 1992 and 1995, but the issue remained unresolved. In 1999 Canada formed the new territory of Nunavut, and in December 2001 Newfoundland was renamed Newfoundland and Labrador.

Recent Developments

Canadian Defense Minister Gordon O'Connor found himself embroiled in a scandal in April 2007 when the media reported claims of torture from prisoners who were detained by Canadian troops and were being held by Afghan security forces. O'Connor had stated in the House of Commons in May 2006 that the International Committee of the Red Cross had signed an agreement with Canada to examine prison conditions and to report any inhumane or illegal treatment. In March 2007, however, the Red Cross disputed that such a deal had ever existed. O'Connor apologized for misleading Parliament and announced that a new deal with the Afghan government had been signed, but in August he was demoted to minister of national revenue in a cabinet shuffle. In the speech from the throne to open Parliament, Prime Minister Stephen Harper announced plans for new legislation to toughen crime statutes and to enhance initiatives to assert the country's claims to Arctic sovereignty. The speech also indicated that Canada would not meet its Kyoto Protocol carbon-emissions-reduction targets. Canada demanded in early 2008 that its NATO allies provide more helicopters and unmanned drones and 1,000 extra troops in Afghanistan, warning that failure to do so would lead to the withdrawal of Canadian troops after the scheduled end of their deployment in February 2009. After these demands were met at the NATO summit in Bucharest, Romania, in April 2008, Canada announced that it was extending the mandate for its force in Afghanistan, numbering about 2,500 troops, through 2011. Quebec garnered many national headlines in 2007. In September a special commission investigating the issue of tolerance for multiculturalism and "reasonable accommodation" for minority groups in the province began to hold hearings. The commission, called by Premier Jean Charest, was the result of several widely reported incidents in which Quebecers revealed deep concerns about some religious and ethnic minorities. Early in the year the small rural town of Hérouxville adopted a code of "norms" for prospective immigrants. Although the town had only a single immigrant family among its 1,338 residents, concerns about new cultural groups in larger centers prompted a code that prohibited stoning or burning women with acid, wearing face-covering garments, or carrying ceremonial weapons (such as the Sikh *kirpan*). The overall economy performed exceptionally well in 2007. The Canadian dollar, which had soared in value since 2002, in September closed above the US dollar for the first time since November 1976. In October the country's unemployment rate reached its lowest level since November 1974, falling to 5.8% (though by April 2008 it had risen to 6.1%). Sovereignty over the Arctic was a growing international issue in 2007 as global warming reduced the ice pack and opened the possibility of future access to Arctic natural resources and shipping routes. The government in July announced plans to build up to eight new ships to patrol the Northwest Passage and other Arctic waterways. In August, barely a week after Russian scientists planted a flag on the seabed under the North Pole, Prime Minister Harper spoke at the end of a three-day trip to the Canadian Arctic. He reiterated Canadian sovereignty over the region and announced the construction in Nunavut of new facilities on Resolute Bay and of a port at Nanisivik to bolster Canada's jurisdiction over its northern coast.

Internet resources: <www.travelcanada.ca>.

Cape Verde

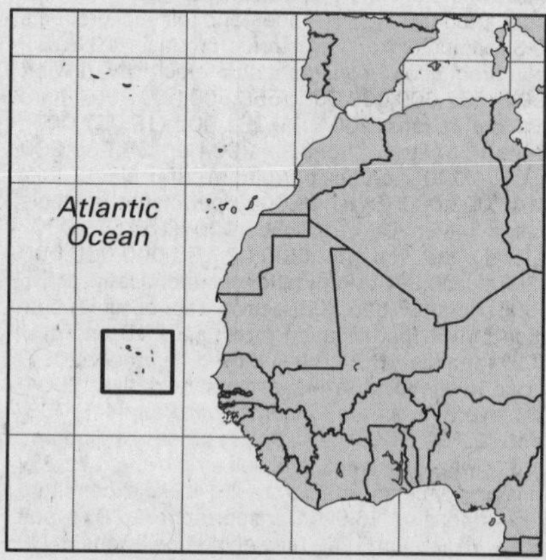

Official name: República de Cabo Verde (Republic of Cape Verde). **Form of government:** multiparty republic with one legislative house (National Assembly [72]). **Chief of state:** President Pedro Pires (from 2001). **Head of government:** Prime Minister José Maria Neves (from 2001). **Capital:** Praia. **Official language:** Portuguese. **Official religion:** none. **Monetary unit:** 1 escudo (C.V.Esc.) = 100 centavos; valuation (1 Jul 2008) US$1 = C.V.Esc. 69.90 (pegged to the euro [€] at the rate of €1 = C.V.Esc. 110.27).

Demography

Area: 1,557 sq mi, 4,033 sq km. **Population** (2007): 496,000. **Density** (2007): persons per sq mi 318.6, persons per sq km 123.0. **Urban** (2003): 55.9%. **Sex distribution** (2005): male 48.47%; female 51.53%. **Age breakdown** (2005): under 15, 39.4%; 15–29, 31.0%; 30–44, 16.6%; 45–59, 7.5%; 60–74, 4.1%; 75–84, 1.2%; 85 and over, 0.2%. **Ethnic composition** (2000): Cape Verdean *mestiço* (black-white admixture) 69.6%; Fulani 12.2%; Balanta 10.0%; Mandyako

4.6%; Portuguese white 2.0%; other 1.6%. **Religious affiliation** (2000): Christian 95.1%, of which Roman Catholic 88.1%, Protestant 3.3%, independent Christian 2.7%; Muslim 2.8%; other 2.1%. **Major cities** (2005): Praia 111,500; Mindelo 70,000; Santa Maria (2000) 13,220; Assomada 11,900; Pedra Badejo 10,700. **Location:** off the coast of western Africa; consists of 10 islands in the North Atlantic Ocean.

Vital statistics

Birth rate per 1,000 population (2006): 24.9 (world avg. 20.3). **Death rate** per 1,000 population (2006): 6.6 (world avg. 8.6). **Natural increase rate** per 1,000 population (2006): 18.3 (world avg. 11.7). **Total fertility rate** (avg. births per childbearing woman; 2005): 2.90. **Life expectancy** at birth (2006): male 68.3 years; female 76.1 years.

National economy

Budget (2006). *Revenue:* C.V.Esc. 34,603,000,000 (tax revenue 68.1%, of which consumption taxes 28.6%, taxes on income and profits 22.0%; grants 20.2%; nontax revenue 11.0%; net lending 0.7%). *Expenditures:* C.V.Esc. 36,309,000,000 (current expenditure 59.7%; capital expenditure 34.8%; other 5.5%). **Public debt** (external, outstanding; 2005): US$545,800,000. **Gross national income** (2006): US$1,089,000,000 (US$2,099 per capita). **Production** (metric tons except as noted). *Agriculture, forestry, fishing* (2005): sugarcane 14,000, fruits 9,000, pulses 7,000; livestock (number of live animals) 205,000 pigs, 112,500 goats; roundwood 1,542 cu m, of which fuelwood 100%; fisheries production (2004) 8,446. *Mining and quarrying* (2005): salt 1,600. *Manufacturing* (1999): flour 15,901; soap 1,371; frozen fish (2002) 900. *Energy production (consumption):* electricity (kW-hr; 2004) 220,000,000 (220,000,000); petroleum products (metric tons; 2004) none (89,000). **Population economically active** (2003): total 157,000; activity rate of total population 32.5% (participation rates: ages 15–64 58%; female 34%; unemployed [2006] 21.1%). **Households.** Average household size (2006) 4.9; expenditure (1997): food 38.7%, transportation 13.6%, alcoholic beverages 10.1%, housing 7.7%, household furnishings 6.0%, energy 5.0%. **Land use** as % of total land area (2003): in temporary crops 11.4%, in permanent crops 0.7%, in pasture 6.2%; overall forest area (2005) 20.7%. **Selected balance of payments data.** Receipts from (US$'000,000): tourism (2005) 122; remittances (2006) 123; foreign direct investment (2001–05 avg.) 15; official development assistance (2005) 161. Disbursements for (US$'000,000): tourism (2005) 67; remittances (2004) 1.0.

Foreign trade

Imports (2006): C.V.Esc. 47,578,000,000 (food and agricultural products 27.2%; machinery and apparatus 10.7%; mineral fuels 8.6%; transport equipment 5.4%; iron and steel 5.2%; cement 4.5%). *Major import sources:* Portugal 30.9%; The Netherlands and Belgium 13.3%; US 12.8%; Spain 7.6%; Brazil 5.4%. **Exports** (2006): C.V.Esc. 7,286,000,000 (reexports [significantly, resold fuel (bunkering) to passing ships and aircraft] 75.9%; domestic exports 18.2%, of which fresh fish 10.5%, clothing 6.7%, footwear 3.3%). *Major export destinations* (domestic exports only): Portugal 49.8%; Spain 27.3%.

Transport and communications

Transport. *Roads* (2001): total length 1,400 km (paved [2000] 69%). *Vehicles* (2003): passenger cars 23,811; trucks and buses 5,032. *Air transport* (2002): passenger-km 279,000,000. **Communications,** in total units (units per 1,000 persons). Daily newspaper circulation (2005): 5,000 (11); televisions (2003): 48,000 (105); telephone landlines (2006): 72,000 (138); cellular telephone subscribers (2006): 109,000 (210); personal computers (2004): 48,000 (102); total Internet users (2005): 25,000 (53); broadband Internet subscribers (2006): 1,800 (3.7).

Education and health

Educational attainment (1990). Percentage of population ages 25 and over having: no formal schooling 47.9%; primary 40.9%; incomplete secondary 3.9%; complete secondary 1.4%; higher 1.5%; unknown 4.4%. **Literacy** (2006): total population ages 15 and over literate 78.9%; males literate 86.5%; females literate 71.9%. **Health** (2005): physicians 241 (1 per 1,976 persons); hospital beds 950 (1 per 501 persons); infant mortality rate per 1,000 live births 30.0. **Food** (2005): daily per capita caloric intake 2,875 (vegetable products 84%, animal products 16%).

Military

Total active duty personnel (2006): 1,200 (army 83.3%, air force 8.3%, coast guard 8.4%). **Military expenditure as percentage of GDP** (2004): 0.7%; per capita expenditure US$15.

Background

When visited by the Portuguese in 1456–60, the islands were uninhabited. In 1460 Diogo Gomes sighted and named Maio and São Tiago, and in 1462 the first settlers landed on São Tiago, founding the city of Ribeira Grande. The city's importance grew with the development of the slave trade, but its wealth attracted pirates so often that it was abandoned after 1712. The prosperity of the Portuguese-controlled islands vanished with the decline of the slave trade in the 19th century but later improved because of their position on the great trade routes between Europe, South America, and southern Africa. In 1951 the colony became an overseas province of Portugal. Many islanders preferred outright independence, and it was finally granted in 1975. At one time associated politically with Guinea-Bissau, Cape Verde split from it in 1981.

Recent Developments

Cape Verde enjoyed political stability and a tourism boom in 2007. New direct flights brought Europeans from Portugal and Britain, and new international airports were being built on two of the islands. Few of the more than 500,000 Cape Verdeans living abroad (half of them in the US) returned, however, and they continued to outnumber those living on the islands. The large sums in remittances sent home, along with donor money from the European Development Fund, Japan, and others, continued to keep Cape Verde afloat.

Internet resources: <www.ine.cv>.

Central African Republic

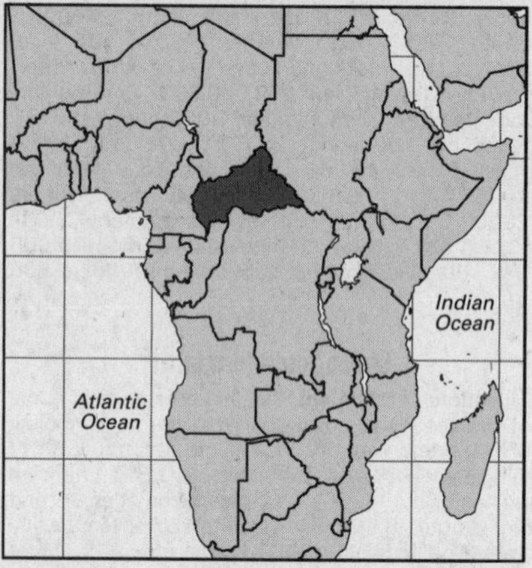

Official name: République Centrafricaine (Central African Republic). **Form of government:** multiparty republic with one legislative body (National Assembly [105]). **Chief of state:** President François Bozizé (from 2003). **Head of government:** Prime Minister Faustin Archange Touadéra (from 2008). **Capital:** Bangui. **Official languages:** French; Sango. **Official religion:** none. **Monetary unit:** 1 CFA franc (CFAF) = 100 centimes; valuation (1 Jul 2008) US$1 = CFAF 414.60 (pegged to the euro [€] at the rate of €1 = CFAF 655.96).

Demography

Area: 240,324 sq mi, 622,436 sq km. **Population** (2007): 4,343,000. **Density** (2007): persons per sq mi 18.1, persons per sq km 7.0. **Urban** (2005): 38.0%. **Sex distribution** (2005): male 48.72%; female 51.28%. **Age breakdown** (2005): under 15, 42.7%; 15–29, 28.1%; 30–44, 14.7%; 45–59, 8.8%; 60–74, 4.6%; 75–84, 1.0%; 85 and over, 0.1%. **Ethnolinguistic composition** (2004): Gbaya (Baya) 33%; Banda 27%; Mandjia 13%; Sara 10%; Mbum 7%; Ngbaka 4%; other 6%. **Religious affiliation** (2005): independent Christian 20.2%; Roman Catholic 19.8%; traditional beliefs 19.5%; Protestant 16.4%; Sunni Muslim 14.5%; nonreligious/other 9.6%. **Major cities** (2003): Bangui 622,771; Bimbo 124,176; Berbérati 76,918; Carnot 45,421; Bambari 41,356. **Location:** central Africa, bordering Chad, The Sudan, the Democratic Republic of the Congo, the Republic of the Congo, and Cameroon.

Vital statistics

Birth rate per 1,000 population (2006): 33.9 (world avg. 20.3). **Death rate** per 1,000 population (2006): 18.7 (world avg. 8.6). **Natural increase rate** per 1,000 population (2006): 15.1 (world avg. 11.7). **Total fertility rate** (avg. births per childbearing woman; 2006): 4.41. **Life expectancy** at birth (2006): male 43.5 years; female 43.6 years.

National economy

Budget (2005). *Revenue:* CFAF 88,000,000,000 (taxes 57.5%, of which indirect domestic taxes 30.0%, direct taxes on income and profits 16.7%, taxes on international trade 10.8%; grants 33.5%; nontax revenue 9.0%). *Expenditures:* CFAF 120,400,000,000 (current expenditure 62.6%; development expenditure 31.9%; interest payments 5.5%). **Public debt** (external, outstanding; 2005): US$871,000,000. **Production** (metric tons except as noted). *Agriculture, forestry, fishing* (2005): cassava 563,000, yams 350,000, peanuts (groundnuts) 140,000; livestock (number of live animals) 3,423,000 cattle, 3,087,000 goats, 805,000 pigs; roundwood 2,832,000 cu m, of which fuelwood 71%; fisheries production (2004) 15,000. *Mining and quarrying* (2005): diamonds 380,000 carats (official figure; a roughly equal amount was smuggled out of the country in 2004). *Manufacturing* (2002): refined sugar 10,570; palm oil 2,743; soap 1,625. *Energy production (consumption):* electricity (kW-hr; 2004) 110,000,000 (110,000,000); petroleum products (metric tons; 2004) none (82,000). **Households.** Average household size (2004) 5.3; average annual income per household (1988) CFAF 91,985 (US$435); expenditure (1991): food 70.5%, clothing 8.5%, energy 7.3%. **Gross national income** (at 2006 market prices): US$1,416,000,000 (US$332 per capita). **Population economically active** (2003): total 1,786,000; activity rate of total population 45.4% (participation rates: ages 15–64, 80.4%; female 46.2%; unemployed [Bangui only; 2001] 23%). **Selected balance of payments data.** Receipts from (US$'000,000): tourism (2005) 4.0; foreign direct investment (2001–05 avg.) 1.0; official development assistance (2005) 95. Disbursements for (US$'000,000): tourism (2004) 32. **Land use** as % of total land area (2003): in temporary crops 3.1%, in permanent crops 0.2%, in pasture 5.0%; overall forest area (2005) 36.5%.

Foreign trade

Imports (2005): CFAF 90,300,000,000 (petroleum products 19.6%; unspecified 80.4%). *Major import sources:* France 17%; The Netherlands 10%; Cameroon 10%; US 7%. **Exports** (2005): CFAF 67,400,000,000 (diamonds 48.7%; wood and wood products 38.3%; cotton 1.6%; coffee 1.3%). *Major export destinations:* Belgium 35%; France 10%; Spain 9%; Italy 8%; China 7%.

Transport and communications

Transport. *Roads* (2005): total length (national roads only; much of the 15,600-km local road network is unusable) 10,000 km (paved 7%). *Vehicles* (2001): passenger cars 5,300; trucks and buses 6,300. *Air transport* (2003): passenger arrivals (departures) (Bangui airport only) 19,250 (19,107); metric ton-km cargo 7,000,000. **Communications**, in total units (units per 1,000 persons). Daily newspaper circulation (2005): 4,000 (1); televisions (2004): 24,000 (6.1); telephone landlines (2005): 10,000 (2.5); cellular telephone subscribers (2005): 100,000 (25); personal computers (2005): 12,000 (3); total Internet users (2006): 13,000 (3.2).

1 metric ton = about 1.1 short tons; 1 kilometer = 0.6 mi (statute); 1 metric ton-km cargo = about 0.68 short ton-mi cargo; c.i.f.: cost, insurance, and freight; f.o.b.: free on board

Education and health

Educational attainment (1994–95). Percentage of population ages 25 and over having: no formal schooling/unknown 55.1%; at least some primary education 30.5%; at least some secondary education 14.4%. **Literacy** (2003): total population ages 15 and over literate 42.7%; males literate 53.8%; females literate 32.0%. **Health:** physicians (2004) 331 (1 per 11,867 persons); hospital beds (2001) 4,365 (1 per 879 persons); infant mortality rate (2006) 85.6. **Food** (2005): daily per capita caloric intake 2,104 (vegetable products 86%, animal products 14%); 117% of FAO recommended minimum.

Military

Total active duty personnel (2006): 2,550 (army 54.9%; air force 5.9%; paramilitary [gendarmerie] 39.2%); French troops (2006) 200. **Military expenditure as percentage of GDP** (2005): 1.1%; per capita expenditure US$2.

Background

For several centuries before the arrival of Europeans, the territory was subjected to slave traders. The French explored and claimed central Africa and in 1889 established a post at Bangui. In 1898 they partitioned the colony among commercial concessionaires. United with Chad in 1906 to form the French colony of Ubangi-Shari, it later became part of French Equatorial Africa. It was separated from Chad in 1920 and became an overseas territory in 1946. Named an autonomous republic within the French Community in 1958, the country achieved independence in 1960. In 1966 the military overthrew a civilian government and installed Jean-Bédel Bokassa, who in 1976 declared himself Emperor Bokassa I and renamed the country the Central African Empire. He was overthrown in 1979, but the military again seized power in the 1980s. Elections in 1993 led to the installation of a civilian government.

Recent Developments

The crisis in the northern Central African Republic (CAR) worsened during 2007, with tens of thousands of civilians forced to flee as fighting between dissident groups and the army intensified. Relief agencies estimated that at least one million people were in need of basic provisions. An agreement signed between the governments of Chad and the CAR to allow their military forces to cross each other's border to pursue rebels wreaked further misery upon civilians caught in the cross fire. Two volunteer health workers were abducted in May by rebels, and Doctors Without Borders reported the fatal shooting in June of one of its workers. The following day all aid agencies in the north of the country suspended operations.

Internet resources:
<http://www.stat-centrafrique.com/>.

Chad

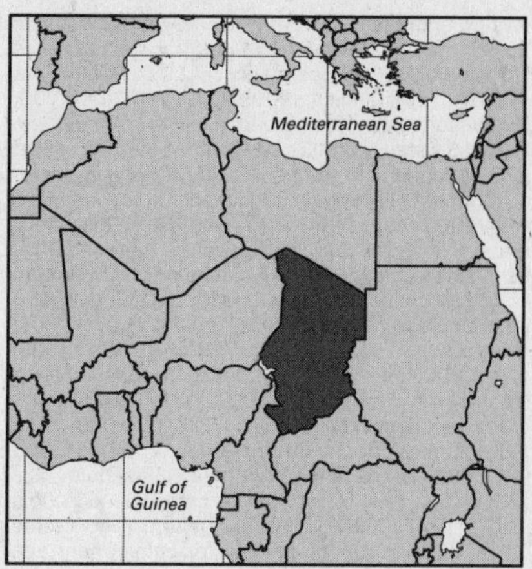

Official name: Jumhuriyah Tshad (Arabic); République du Tchad (French) (Republic of Chad). **Form of government:** unitary republic with one legislative body (National Assembly [155]). **Chief of state:** President Idriss Déby (from 1990). **Head of government:** Prime Minister Delwa Kassire Koumakoye (from 2007). **Capital:** N'Djamena. **Official languages:** Arabic; French. **Official religion:** none. **Monetary unit:** 1 CFA franc (CFAF) = 100 centimes; valuation (1 Jul 2008) US$1 = CFAF 414.60 (pegged to the euro [€] at the rate of €1 = CFAF 655.96).

Demography

Area: 495,755 sq mi, 1,284,000 sq km. **Population** (2007): 10,239,000. **Density** (2007): persons per sq mi 20.7, persons per sq km 8.0. **Urban** (2005): 25.3%. **Sex distribution** (2005): male 48.82%; female 51.18%. **Age breakdown** (2005): under 15, 48.0%; 15–29, 26.7%; 30–44, 13.7%; 45–59, 7.3%; 60–74, 3.5%; 75 and over, 0.8%. **Ethnolinguistic composition** (1993): Sara 27.7%; Sudanic Arab 12.3%; Mayo-Kebbi peoples 11.5%; Kanem-Bornu peoples 9.0%; Ouaddaï peoples 8.7%; Hadjeray (Hadjaraï) 6.7%; Tangale (Tandjilé) peoples 6.5%; Gorane peoples 6.3%; Fitri-Batha peoples 4.7%; Fulani (Peul) 2.4%; other 4.2%. **Religious affiliation** (2005): Sunni Muslim 57.0%; animist 18.8%; Protestant 10.5%; other (significantly Roman Catholic and nonreligious) 13.7%. **Major cities** (2000): N'Djamena (urban agglomeration; 2005) 888,000; Moundou 108,728; Sarh 95,050; Abéché 63,165; Kelo 36,643. **Location:** central Africa, bordered by Libya, The Sudan, the Central African Republic, Cameroon, Nigeria, and Niger.

Vital statistics

Birth rate per 1,000 population (2005): 46.2 (world avg. 20.3). **Death rate** per 1,000 population (2005): 16.7 (world avg. 8.6). **Natural increase rate** per 1,000 population (2005): 29.5 (world avg. 11.7). **Total fertility rate** (avg. births per childbearing woman; 2005): 6.32. **Life expectancy** at birth (2005): male 45.6 years; female 48.9 years.

National economy

Budget (2005). *Revenue:* CFAF 311,100,000,000 (tax revenue 45.9%; petroleum revenue 43.7%; nontax revenue 10.4%). *Expenditures:* CFAF 482,000,000,000 (capital expenditure 61.9%; current expenditure 38.1%, of which wages and salaries 13.9%, materials and supply 7.8%, transfer payments 7.1%, defense 6.3%, debt service 2.9%). **Public debt** (external, outstanding; 2005): US$1,537,000,000. **Production** (metric tons except as noted). *Agriculture, forestry, fishing* (2005): sorghum 582,600, millet 578,300, peanuts (groundnuts) 450,000, gum arabic (2006) 20,000; livestock (number of live animals) 6,540,000 cattle, 5,843,000 goats, 740,000 camels; roundwood 7,249,000 cu m, of which fuelwood 90%; fisheries production (2004) 70,000. *Mining and quarrying* (2005): natron 12,000; salt 10,000; gold 150 kg. *Manufacturing* (2004–05): cotton fiber 88,158; refined sugar 51,823; woven cotton fabrics (2000) 1,000,000 meters. *Energy production (consumption):* electricity (kW-hr; 2004) 99,000,000 (99,000,000); crude petroleum (barrels; 2006) 62,000,000 (n.a.); petroleum products (metric tons; 2004) 59,000 (41,000). **Households.** Average household size (2004) 5.0; average annual income per household (1993) CFAF 96,806 (US$458); sources of income (1995–96; urban): informal-sector employment and entrepreneurship 36.7%, transfers 24.8%, wages 23.6%, ownership of real estate 8.6%. **Selected balance of payments data.** Receipts from (US$'000,000): tourism (2005) 14; foreign direct investment (2001–05 avg.) 656; official development assistance (2005) 380. Disbursements for (US$'000,000): tourism (2002) 80. **Population economically active** (2003): total 3,385,000; activity rate of total population 37.1% (participation rates: ages 15–64, 70.2%; female 47.3%). **Gross national product** (2006): US$3,509,000,000 (US$335 per capita). **Land use** as % of total land area (2003): in temporary crops 2.9%, in permanent crops 0.02%, in pasture 35.7%; overall forest area (2005) 9.5%.

Foreign trade

Imports (2005): CFAF 323,500,000,000 (nonpetroleum private sector 42.7%; public sector 19.3%; petroleum sector 15.6%). *Major import sources:* France 21%; Cameroon 15%; US 12%; Belgium 7%; Portugal 5%. **Exports** (2004): CFAF 1,152,300,000,000 (crude petroleum 84.5%; live cattle 10.4%; cotton 3.3%). *Major export destinations:* US 78%; China 10%; Taiwan 4%.

Transport and communications

Transport. *Roads* (2002): total length 33,400 km (paved 1%). *Vehicles* (2002): passenger cars 8,900; trucks and buses 12,400. *Air transport*: passenger-km (2001) 130,000,000; metric ton-km cargo (2004) 7,000,000. **Communications,** in total units (units per 1,000 persons). Televisions (2004): 55,000 (5.9); telephone landlines (2006): 13,000 (1.3); cellular telephone subscribers (2006): 466,000 (47); personal computers (2004): 15,000 (1.6); total Internet users (2006): 60,000 (6).

Education and health

Educational attainment (2003). Percentage of population ages 25 and over having: no formal schooling 74.5%; primary education 17.4%; secondary education 6.8%; higher education 1.3%. **Literacy** (2003): percentage of total population ages 15 and over literate 47.5%; males 56.0%; females 39.3%. **Health:** physicians (2004) 345 (1 per 27,180 persons); hospital beds (1998) 4,105 (1 per 1,908 persons); infant mortality rate (2005) 93.1. **Food** (2005): daily per capita caloric intake 2,190 (vegetable products 93%, animal products 7%); 120% of FAO recommended minimum.

Military

Total active duty personnel (2006): 25,350 (army 78.9%; air force 1.4%; other 19.7%); French peacekeeping troops (November 2006) 1,550. **Military expenditure as percentage of GDP** (2005): 1.0%; per capita expenditure US$6.

Did you know?

Mount Koussi, the highest summit in the Sahara (11,204 feet [3,415 metres]), is situated 109 miles (176 km) north-northwest of Faya in the Tibesti massif of northwestern Chad. It is an extinct volcano with a crater approximately 12 miles (19 km) wide and 4,000 feet (1,200 metres) deep.

Background

About AD 800 the kingdom of Kanem was founded in north-central Africa, and by the early 1200s its borders had expanded to form a new kingdom, Kanem-Bornu, in the northern regions of the area. Its power peaked in the 16th century with its command of the southern terminus of the trans-Sahara trade route to Tripoli. Around this time the rival kingdoms of Baguirmi and Wadai evolved in the south. In the years 1883–93 all three kingdoms fell to the Sudanese adventurer Rabih al-Zubayr, who was in turn pushed out by the French in 1900. Extending their power, the French in 1910 made Chad a part of French Equatorial Africa. Chad became a separate colony in 1920 and was made an overseas territory in 1946. The country achieved independence in 1960. This was followed by decades of civil war and frequent intervention by France and Libya.

Recent Developments

Chad continued to be affected in 2007 by both the conflict across its border in the Darfur region of The Sudan and the ongoing low-intensity warfare between various rebel factions and the government of Pres. Idriss Déby. At the beginning of 2008 there were an estimated 233,000 Sudanese refugees from Darfur in camps in eastern Chad, and more than 100,000 Chadians in the east had been forced from their homes. As raids by mounted armed men from Darfur continued, UN Secretary-General Ban Ki-moon and the French government called for a UN–European Union peacekeeping force to be established in eastern Chad to protect the camps. This force, initially of 1,800 soldiers, was deployed in March 2008. In its 2007 report, Transparency International once again found Chad to be one of the most corrupt countries in the world.

Internet resources: <www.inseed-tchad.org>.

Chile

Official name: República de Chile (Republic of Chile). **Form of government:** multiparty republic with two legislative houses (Senate [38]; Chamber of Deputies [120]). **Head of state and government:** President Michelle Bachelet (from 2006). **Capital:** Santiago (legislative bodies meet in Valparaíso). **Official language:** Spanish. **Official religion:** none. **Monetary unit:** 1 peso (Ch$) = 100 centavos; valuation (1 Jul 2008) US$1 = Ch$528.00.

Demography

Area: 291,930 sq mi, 756,096 sq km. **Population** (2007): 16,598,000. **Density** (2007): persons per sq mi 56.9, persons per sq km 22.0. **Urban** (2003): 87.0%. **Sex distribution** (2005): male 49.47%; female 50.53%. **Age breakdown** (2005): under 15, 24.9%; 15–29, 24.3%; 30–44, 23.0%; 45–59, 16.2%; 60–74, 8.3%; 75–84, 2.5%; 85 and over, 0.8%. **Ethnic composition** (2002): mestizo 72%; white 22%; Amerindian 5%, of which Araucanian (Mapuche) 4%; other 1%. **Religious affiliation** (2002): Roman Catholic 70.0%; Protestant/independent Christian 15.1%; other Christian 2.0%; atheist/nonreligious 8.3%. **Major urban agglomerations** (2002): Santiago 5,428,590; Valparaíso/Viña del Mar 803,683; Concepción 666,381; La Serena/Coquimbo 296,253; Antofagasta 285,255. **Location:** southern South America, bordering Peru, Bolivia, Argentina, the South Atlantic Ocean, and the South Pacific Ocean.

Vital statistics

Birth rate per 1,000 population (2006): 15.2 (world avg. 20.3). **Death rate** per 1,000 population (2006): 5.8 (world avg. 8.6). **Total fertility rate** (avg. births per childbearing woman; 2006): 2.00. **Life expectancy** at birth (2006): male 73.5 years; female 80.2 years.

National economy

Budget (2005). *Revenue:* Ch$15,680,877,000,000 (tax revenue 71.3%; copper revenue 15.6%; other 13.1%). *Expenditures:* Ch$10,582,361,000,000 (subsidies and grants 31.0%; pension payments 28.7%; wages and salaries 23.8%; goods and services 11.1%). **Public debt** (external, outstanding; 2005): US$9,096,000,000. **Population economically active** (2005): total 6,345,400; activity rate of total population 39.2% (participation rates: ages 15–64, 59.3%; female 35.6%; unemployed [2006] 7.8%). **Production** (metric tons except as noted). *Agriculture, forestry, fishing* (2005): sugar beets 2,800,000, grapes 2,250,000, wheat 1,852,000; livestock (number of live animals) 4,200,000 cattle, 3,450,000 pigs, 3,400,000 sheep; roundwood 46,051,000 cu m, of which fuelwood 29%; fisheries production 5,028,539 (from aquaculture 14%); aquatic plants production 425,343 (from aquaculture 4%). *Mining* (2004): copper (metal content; 2005) 5,320,500; iron ore (metal content) 4,477,000; lithium carbonate 41,667. *Manufacturing* (value added in US$'000,000; 2003): food products 2,041; nonferrous base metals 1,877; beverages 962; refined petroleum 845. *Energy production (consumption):* electricity (kW-hr; 2005) 51,575,000,000 ([2004] 49,100,000,000); hard coal (metric tons; 2004) 188,000 (4,435,000); crude petroleum (barrels; 2006) 1,210,000 ([2005] 86,900,000); petroleum products (metric tons; 2004) 10,118,000 (10,641,000); natural gas (cu m; 2004) 1,967,000,000 (8,436,000,000). **Land use** as % of total land area (2003): in temporary crops 2.6%, in permanent crops 0.4%, in pasture 17.3%; overall forest area (2005) 21.5%. **Gross national income** (2006): US$126,436,000,000 (US$7,679 per capita). **Households.** Average household size (2004) 3,4; average annual income per household (2001) Ch$6,804,000 (US$9,530); sources of income (2001): wages and salaries 39.5%, transfer payments 19.7%, rent on property 14.5%, self-employment 9.8%, other 16.5%. **Selected balance of payments data.** Receipts from (US$'000,000): tourism (2005) 1,256; remittances (2006) 3; foreign direct investment (FDI) (2001–05 avg.) 4,979. Disbursements for (US$'000,000): tourism (2005) 1,057; remittances (2006) 6; FDI (2001–05 avg.) 1,446.

Foreign trade

Imports (2005; f.o.b. in balance of trade and c.i.f. in commodities and trading partners): US$32,021,400,000 (capital goods 22.3%; consumer goods 14.7%; crude petroleum 11.8%; free zone imports 5.1%). *Major import sources* (2004): Argentina 18.5%; US 15.1%; Brazil 12.4%; China 8.3%. **Exports** (2005): US$39,881,400,000 (copper 45.9%; foodstuffs 12.0%, of which salmon and trout 4.2%; fruits 5.3%; wood and wooden furniture 4.5%; paper and paper products 4.2%). *Major export destinations* (2004): US 14.8%; Japan 12.0%; China 10.4%; South Korea 5.8%; The Netherlands 5.4%.

Transport and communications

Transport. *Railroads* (2002): route length 8,707 km; passenger-km (2004) 830,259,000; metric ton-km cargo 3,899,000,000. *Roads* (2003): total length 80,505 km (paved 22%). *Vehicles* (2005): passenger cars 1,406,796; trucks and buses 681,974. *Air transport* (2005; LAN Chile Group, Aerolineas Del Sur, Aerovías DAP, and Sky Service only): passenger-km 18,977,000,000; metric ton-km cargo 1,757,000,000. **Communications,** in total units (units per 1,000 persons). Daily newspaper circulation (2004): 816,000 (52); televisions (2004):

4,305,000 (268); telephone landlines (2006): 3,326,000 (202); cellular telephone subscribers (2006): 12,451,000 (756); personal computers (2005): 2,800,000 (172); total Internet users (2006): 4,156,000 (252); broadband Internet subscribers (2006): 978,000 (60).

Education and health

Educational attainment (2002). Percentage of population ages 25 and over having: no formal schooling/other 5.4%; incomplete primary education 24.6%; complete primary 8.7%; secondary 43.9%; higher technical 4.9%; university 12.5%. **Literacy** (2002): total population ages 15 and over literate 95.7%; males literate 95.8%; females literate 95.6%. **Health:** physicians (2004) 20,726 (1 per 778 persons); hospital beds (2003) 39,782 (1 per 401 persons); infant mortality rate (2006) 8.6. **Food** (2005): daily per capita caloric intake 3,079 (vegetable products 74%, animal products 26%); 160% of FAO recommended minimum.

Military

Total active duty personnel (2006): 78,098 (army 61.1%, navy 24.8%, air force 14.1%). **Military expenditure as percentage of GDP** (2005): 3.8%; per capita expenditure US$270.

Background

Originally inhabited by native peoples, including the Mapuche, the Chilean coast was invaded by the Spanish in 1536. A settlement begun at Santiago in 1541 was governed under the Viceroyalty of Peru but became a separate captaincy general in 1778. It revolted against Spanish rule in 1810; its independence was finally assured by the victory of José de San Martín in 1818, and the area was then governed by Bernardo O'Higgins to 1823. In the War of the Pacific against Peru and Bolivia, it won the rich nitrate fields on the coast of Bolivia, effectively forcing that country into a landlocked position. Chile remained neutral in World War I and in World War II but severed diplomatic ties with the Axis in 1943. In 1970 Salvador Allende was elected president, becoming the first avowed Marxist to be elected chief of state in Latin America. Following economic upheaval, he was ousted in 1973 in a coup led by Gen. Augusto Pinochet, whose military junta for many years harshly suppressed all internal opposition. A national referendum in 1988 rejected Pinochet, and elections held in 1989 returned the country to civilian rule.

Recent Developments

A series of problems eroded Chilean Pres. Michelle Bachelet's popularity in 2007. Among these was the disastrous implementation of Transantiago, a plan to reorganize and better integrate Santiago's bus and subway system, and a large number of student disturbances and labor mobilizations. There was also some positive news, however. In the realm of human rights, arrests and trials continued of those who had committed offenses during the military dictatorship. A key Bachelet promise to help women was realized with the establishment of more preschools and women's domestic-violence shelters. The economic picture continued to be strong. The price of copper, Chile's largest single export, reached its highest level in more than 40 years, and there were both a large budget surplus and a positive trade balance. Economic growth, though slower than in the preceding year, ran at close to 5%. The Bachelet government approved the development of alternative energy, including nuclear power and additional dams for hydroelectric generation, both of which were opposed by environmentalists.

Internet resources: <www.visit-chile.org>.

China

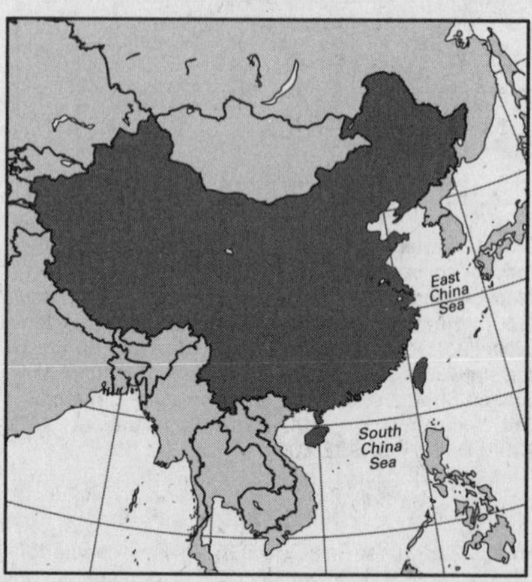

Official name: Zhonghua Renmin Gongheguo (People's Republic of China). **Form of government:** single-party people's republic with one legislative house (National People's Congress [2,980]). **Chief of state:** President Hu Jintao (from 2003). **Head of government:** Premier Wen Jiabao (from 2003). **Capital:** Beijing (Peking). **Official language:** Mandarin Chinese. **Official religion:** none. **Monetary unit:** 1 Renminbi (yuan) (Y) = 10 jiao = 100 fen; valuation (1 Jul 2008) US$1 = Y 6.86.

Demography

Area: 3,696,100 sq mi, 9,572,900 sq km. **Population** (2007): 1,317,925,000. **Density** (2007): persons per sq mi 356.6, persons per sq km 137.7. **Urban** (2006): 43.9%. **Sex distribution** (2006): male 51.52%; female 48.48%. **Age breakdown** (2004): under 15, 19.3%; 15–29, 22.1%; 30–44, 27.2%; 45–59, 19.0%; 60–74, 9.6%; 75–84, 2.4%; 85 and over, 0.4%. **Ethnic composition** (2000): Han (Chinese) 91.53%; Chuang 1.30%; Manchu 0.86%; Hui 0.79%; Miao 0.72%; Uighur 0.68%; Tuchia 0.65%; Yi 0.62%; Mongolian 0.47%; Tibetan 0.44%; Puyi 0.24%; Tung 0.24%; Yao 0.21%; Korean 0.15%; Pai 0.15%; Hani 0.12%; Kazakh 0.10%; Li 0.10%; Tai 0.09%; other 0.54%. **Religious affiliation** (2005): nonreligious 39.2%; Chinese folk-religionist 28.7%;

Christian 10.0%, of which unregistered Protestant 7.7%, registered Protestant 1.2%, unregistered Roman Catholic 0.5%, registered Roman Catholic 0.4%; Buddhist 8.4%; atheist 7.8%; traditional beliefs 4.4%; Muslim 1.5%. **Major urban agglomerations** (2005): Shanghai 14,503,000; Beijing 10,717,000; Guangzhou 8,425,000; Shenzhen 7,233,000; Wuhan 7,093,000; Tianjin 7,040,000; Chongqing 6,363,000; Shenyang 4,720,000; Dongguan 4,320,000; Chengdu 4,065,000; Xi'an 3,926,000; Harbin 3,695,000; Nanjing 3,621,000; Guiyang 3,447,000; Dalian 3,073,000; Changchun 3,046,000; Zibo 2,982,000; Kunming 2,837,000; Hangzhou 2,831,000; Qingdao 2,817,000; Taiyuan 2,794,000; Jinan 2,743,000; Zhengzhou 2,590,000; Fuzhou 2,453,000; Changsha 2,451,000; Lanzhou 2,411,000. **Location:** eastern Asia, bordering Mongolia, Russia, North Korea, the Yellow Sea, the East China Sea, the South China Sea, Vietnam, Laos, Myanmar (Burma), India, Bhutan, Nepal, Pakistan, Afghanistan, Tajikistan, Kyrgyzstan, and Kazakhstan. **Households.** Average household size (2004) 3.6, of which urban households 3.0, rural households 4.1; 1 person 7.8%, 2 persons 19.6%, 3 persons 31.4%, 4 persons 21.8%, 5 persons 12.4%, 6 or more persons 7.0%; non-family households 0.8%. **Mobility** (2004). Population residing in registered enumeration area 91.3%; population not residing in registered enumeration area for more than 6 months 7.4%; remainder 1.3%.

Vital statistics

Birth rate per 1,000 population (2006): 12.1 (world avg. 20.3). **Death rate** per 1,000 population (2006): 6.8 (world avg. 8.6). **Natural increase rate** per 1,000 population (2006): 5.3 (world avg. 11.7). **Total fertility rate** (avg. births per childbearing woman; 2005): 1.72. **Life expectancy** at birth (2005): male 70.9 years; female 74.3 years.

Social indicators

Educational attainment (2000). Percentage of population ages 15 and over having: no schooling and incomplete primary 15.6%; completed primary 35.7%; some secondary 34.0%; complete secondary 11.1%; some postsecondary through advanced degree 3.6%. **Quality of working life.** Average workweek (1998) 40 hours. Annual rate per 100,000 workers of death in mining, industrial, or commercial enterprises (2006) 3.33. Death toll from work accidents (2006) 112,822. **Access to services.** Percentage of population having access to electricity (2003) 97.7%. Percentage of total (urban, rural) population with safe public water supply (2002) 83.6% (94.0%, 73.0%). Sewage system (1999): total (urban, rural) households with flush apparatus 20.7% (50.0%, 4.3%), with pit latrines 69.3% (33.6%, 86.7%), with no latrine 5.3% (7.8%, 4.1%). **Social participation.** Trade union membership in total labor force (2004) 18%. **Social deviance.** Annual reported arrest rate per 100,000 population (2004) for: thievery 197; robbery 23. **Material well-being.** Urban households possessing (number per household; 2004): bicycles 1.4; color televisions 1.3; washing machines 1.0; refrigerators 0.9; air conditioners 0.7; cameras 0.5. Rural families possessing (number per household; 2004): bicycles 1.2; color televisions 0.8; washing machines 0.4; refrigerators 0.2; air conditioners 0.05; cameras 0.04.

National economy

Gross national income (2006): US$2,641,846,000,000 (US$2,035 per capita). **Budget** (2004). *Revenue:* Y 2,639,647,000,000 (tax revenue 91.5%, of which VAT 34.2%, corporate income taxes 15.0%, business tax 13.6%, consumption tax 5.7%; nontax revenue 8.5%). *Expenditures:* Y 2,848,689,000,000 (economic development 27.8%, of which agriculture 8.3%; social, cultural, and educational development 26.3%; administration 19.4%; defense 7.7%; other 18.8%). **Public debt** (external, outstanding; 2005): US$82,853,000,000. **Production** (metric tons except as noted). *Agriculture, forestry, fishing* (2005): grains—rice 184,254,000, corn (maize) 131,145,000, wheat 96,160,250, barley 3,200,000; oilseeds—soybeans 16,900,300, peanuts (groundnuts) 14,638,500, rapeseed 11,300,010, sunflower seeds 1,850,000; fruits and nuts—watermelons 69,315,000, apples 25,006,500, citrus 16,019,500, cantaloupes 15,138,000, pears 11,625,000, bananas 6,390,000; other—sweet potatoes 107,676,100, sugarcane 92,130,000, potatoes 73,776,500, cabbage 34,101,000, tomatoes 31,644,040, cucumbers 26,559,600, onions 19,047,000, eggplants 17,030,300, seed cotton 16,305,000, chilies and peppers 12,531,000, garlic 11,093,500, asparagus 5,906,000, spinach 4,494,000, tobacco leaves 2,505,500, tea 900,500, silkworm cocoons (2003) 667,000; livestock (number of live animals) 488,809,978 pigs, 195,758,954 goats, 170,882,215 sheep, 115,229,500 cattle, 22,745,250 water buffalo, 4,360,243,000 chickens, 725,018,000 ducks; roundwood 286,103,000 cu m, of which fuelwood 67%; fisheries production 49,467,309 (from aquaculture 66%); aquatic plants production 11,103,395 (from aquaculture 97%). *Mining and quarrying* (2005): metal content of mine output—iron ore 138,000,000 (world rank: 3), zinc 2,450,000 (world rank: 1), manganese 1,100,000 (world rank: 5), lead 1,000,000 (world rank: 1), copper 740,000 (world rank: 7), antimony 120,000 (world rank: 1), tin 110,000 (world rank: 1), tungsten 61,000 (world rank: 1), silver 2,500 (world rank: 3), gold 225 (world rank: 2); metal ores—bauxite 18,000,000 (world rank: 3), vanadium 17,000 (world rank: 1); nonmetals—salt 44,547,000 (world rank: 2), phosphate rock 9,130,000 (world rank: 2), magnesite 4,700,000 (world rank: 1), barite 4,200,000 (world rank: 1), talc 3,000,000 (world rank: 1), fluorspar 2,700,000 (world rank: 1), asbestos 520,000 (world rank: 2), strontium 140,000 (world rank: 2). *Manufacturing* (value added in US$'000,000; 2003): electrical machinery 66,521; industrial chemicals, paints, and soaps 45,727; transport equipment 35,000; iron and steel 34,119; nonelectrical machinery 31,395; food products 25,776; textiles 23,036; tobacco products 19,010; cement, bricks, and tiles 16,334; refined petroleum 15,554; fabricated metal products 11,731; wearing apparel 11,073; nonferrous base metals 10,899. Distribution of industrial production (percentage of total value added by sector; 2004): directly state-owned and state-controlled enterprises 42.4%; private enterprises 15.1%; collectives 5.3%; remainder 37.2%. *Energy production (consumption):* electricity (kW-hr; 2006) 2,834,400,000,000 ([2004] 2,178,000,000,000); coal (metric tons; 2006) 2,380,000,000 (2,370,000,000); crude petroleum (barrels; 2006) 1,347,000,000 (2,346,000,000); petroleum products (metric tons; 2004) 212,352,000

(244,178,000); natural gas (cu m; 2006) 58,550,000,000 (55,600,000,000). **Population economically active** (2003): total 766,430,000; activity rate of total population 59.0% (participation rates: ages 15–64, 82.4%; female 44.6%; registered unemployed in urban areas [2005] 4.2%). **Households.** Average annual per capita disposable income of household (2006): rural households Y 3,587 (US$450), urban households Y 11,579 (US$1,452). Sources of income (2004): rural households–income from household businesses 59.5%, wages 34.0%, transfers and property 6.5%; urban households–wages 70.6%, transfers 22.9%, business income 4.9%, property 1.6%. Expenditure: rural (urban) households–food 47.2% (37.8%), housing and energy 14.8% (10.2%), education and recreation 11.3% (14.4%), transportation and communications 8.8% (11.7%), clothing 5.5% (9.6%), medicine and medical service 6.0% (7.4%), household furnishings 4.1% (5.7%). **Selected balance of payments data.** Receipts from (US$'000,000): tourism (2006) 33,950; remittances (2005) 22,492; foreign direct investment (FDI) (2001–05 avg.) 57,232; official development assistance (2005) 1,962 (commitments). Disbursements for (US$'000,000): tourism (2005) 21,800; remittances (2005) 2,602; FDI (2001–05 avg.) 4,472. **Land use** as % of total land area (2004): in temporary crops or permanent crops 13.5%, in pasture 41.5%; overall forest area (2005) 21.2%.

Foreign trade

Imports (2004; c.i.f.): US$561,229,000,000 (machinery and apparatus 41.7%; mineral fuels 8.6%; professional and scientific equipment 7.4%; plastics and related products 5.0%; organic chemicals 4.2%; iron and steel 4.2%). *Major import sources:* Japan 16.8%; Taiwan 11.5%; South Korea 11.1%; US 8.0%; Germany 5.4%; Malaysia 3.2%; Singapore 2.5%; Russia 2.2%; Hong Kong 2.1%; Australia 2.1%. **Exports** (2004; f.o.b.): US$593,326,000,000 (machinery and apparatus 41.8%; wearing apparel and accessories 11.3%; iron and steel [including finished products] 4.2%; chemicals and chemical products 4.1%; transport equipment 3.5%). *Major export destinations:* US 21.1%; Hong Kong 17.0%; Japan 12.4%; South Korea 4.7%; Germany 4.0%; The Netherlands 3.1%; UK 2.5%; Taiwan 2.3%; Singapore 2.1%; France 1.7%.

Transport and communications

Transport. *Railroads* (2005): route length (2004) 74,400 km; passenger-km 662,200,000,000; metric ton-km cargo 2,195,400,000,000. *Roads* (2004): total length 1,870,661 km (paved 81%). *Vehicles* (2004): passenger cars 17,359,100; trucks 8,930,000. *Air transport* (2006): passenger-km 236,990,000,000; metric ton-km cargo 9,430,000,000. **Communications,** in total units (units per 1,000 persons). Daily newspaper circulation (2005): 96,600,000 (74); televisions (2003): 493,902,000 (381); telephone landlines (2007): 367,810,000 (279); cellular telephone subscribers (2007): 461,080,000 (350); personal computers (2004): 52,990,000 (40); total Internet users (2006): 137,000 (104); broadband Internet subscribers (2006): 50,916,000 (39).

Education and health

Literacy (2000): total population ages 15 and over literate 90.9%; males literate 95.1%; females literate 86.5%. **Health** (2006): physicians 1,970,000 (1 per 668 persons); hospital beds 3,216,000 (1 per 409 persons); infant mortality rate per 1,000 live births (2005) 24.4. **Food** (2003): daily per capita caloric intake 2,740 (vegetable products 82%, animal products 18%); 142% of FAO recommended minimum.

Military

Total active duty personnel (2006): 2,255,000 (army 71.0%, navy 11.3%, air force 17.7%). **Military expenditure as percentage of GDP** (2005): 2.0%; per capita expenditure US$34.

Background

The discovery of Peking man (Homo erectus) in 1927 dated the advent of early humans in what is now China to the Middle Pleistocene, about 900,000 to 130,000 years ago. Chinese civilization probably spread from the Huang He (Yellow River) valley, where it existed c. 3000 BC. The first dynasty for which there is definite historical material is the Shang (c. 16th century BC), which had a writing system and a calendar. The Zhou, a subject state of the Shang, overthrew its Shang rulers in the 11th century BC and ruled until the 3rd century BC. Taoism and Confucianism were founded in this era.

A time of conflict, called the Warring States period, lasted from the 5th century BC until 221 BC, when the Qin (Ch'in) dynasty (from whose name China is derived) was established after its rulers had conquered rival states and created a unified empire. The Han dynasty was established in 206 BC and ruled until AD 220. A time of turbulence followed, and Chinese reunification was not achieved until the Sui dynasty was established in 581.

After the founding of the Song dynasty in 960, the capital was moved to the south because of northern invasions. In 1279 this dynasty was overthrown and Mongol (Yuan) domination began. During this time Marco Polo visited Kublai Khan. The Ming dynasty followed the period of Mongol rule and lasted from 1368 to 1644, cultivating antiforeign feelings to the point that China closed itself off from the rest of the world.

Peoples from Manchuria overran China in 1644 and established the Qing (Manchu) dynasty. Ever-increasing incursions by Western and Japanese interests led in the 19th century to the Opium Wars, the Taiping Rebellion, and the Sino-Japanese War, all of which weakened the Manchus.

The dynasty fell in 1911, and a republic was proclaimed in 1912 by Sun Yat-sen. The power struggles of warlords weakened the republic. Under Sun's successor, Chiang Kai-shek, some national unification was achieved in the 1920s, but Chiang soon broke with the Communists, who then formed their own armies. Japan invaded northern China in 1937; its occupation lasted until 1945. The Communists gained support after the Long March (1934–35), in which Mao Zedong emerged as their leader.

Upon Japan's surrender at the end of World War II, a fierce civil war began; in 1949 the Nationalists fled to Taiwan and the Communists proclaimed the People's

1 metric ton = about 1.1 short tons; 1 kilometer = 0.6 mi (statute); 1 metric ton-km cargo = about 0.68 short ton-mi cargo; c.i.f.: cost, insurance, and freight; f.o.b.: free on board

Republic of China. The Communists undertook extensive reforms, but pragmatic policies alternated with periods of revolutionary upheaval, most notably in the Great Leap Forward and the Cultural Revolution. The chaos of the latter led, after Mao's death in 1976, to a turn to moderation under Deng Xiaoping, who undertook economic reforms and renewed China's ties to the West. The government established diplomatic ties with the US in 1979. It suppressed the Tiananmen Square student demonstration in 1989. The economy has been in transition since the late 1970s, moving from central planning and state-run industries to a mixture of state-owned and private enterprises in manufacturing and services. The death of Deng in 1997 marked the end of a political era, but power passed peacefully to Jiang Zemin. In 1997 Hong Kong reverted to Chinese rule, as did Macao in 1999.

Recent Developments

China's economy continued its recent meteoric rise. GDP grew by almost 12% and the trade surplus approached US$260 billion in 2007; foreign-exchange reserves were up a spectacular US$153.9 billion in the first quarter of 2008 from year's end 2007; and the Chinese renminbi continued to appreciate against the US dollar at an annual rate of about 5%. Massive trade surpluses boosted the country's currency reserves to a record US$1.33 trillion in September 2007.

Chinese exporters struggled to redeem their image after a succession of product recalls of tainted goods. Early in 2007 toy manufacturer Mattel recalled nearly 20 million Chinese-made products, most of which contained lead-tainted paint. In July the former head of China's State Food and Drug Administration was executed for having taken bribes from pharmaceutical companies and having approved fake drugs.

The environmental consequences of China's economic boom came under increased government scrutiny. Reports emerged showing that just 1% of China's approximately 560 million urban residents were breathing air considered safe by the EU, and some 500 million people lacked access to clean drinking water. Meanwhile, it was reported in 2008 that China had become the global leader in greenhouse-gas emissions in 2006.

There were signs in 2007 that China was moderating its foreign policy—possibly ahead of the Beijing Olympic Games in 2008. China opposed international sanctions against the Sudanese government but supported the deployment of peacekeepers to The Sudan and helped persuade the government to accept them. (China imported 7% of its oil from The Sudan, and in a sign of close relations Pres. Hu Jintao visited the country in February 2007.) Relations with the US got off to a rocky start after China shot down a weather satellite during an unannounced test, demonstrating the country's military-space capabilities. Continuing trade tensions led US lawmakers to introduce legislation intended to force China to revalue its currency.

In May 2008 a 7.9-magnitude earthquake struck in China's Sichuan province. More than 6,900 schools were destroyed, and engineers feared that serious damage had been inflicted on hundreds of dams in the area. As many as 5,000,000 people were made homeless, and more than 68,000 people perished.

Internet resources: <www.cnto.org>.

Colombia

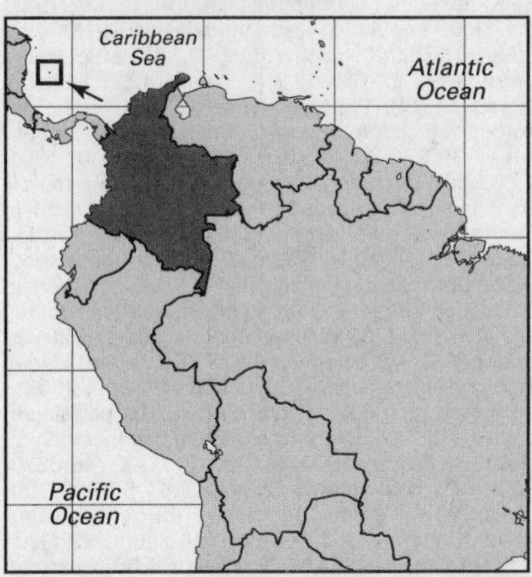

Official name: República de Colombia (Republic of Colombia). **Form of government:** unitary multiparty republic with two legislative houses (Senate [102]; House of Representatives [166]). **Head of state and government:** President Álvaro Uribe Vélez (from 2002). **Capital:** Bogotá. **Official language:** Spanish. **Official religion:** none. **Monetary unit:** 1 peso (Col$) = 100 centavos; valuation (1 Jul 2008) US$1 = Col$1,905.60.

Demography

Area: 440,762 sq mi, 1,141,568 sq km. **Population** (2007): 42,870,000. **Density** (2007): persons per sq mi 97.2, persons per sq km 37.5. **Urban** (2005): 72.7%. **Sex distribution** (2005): male 49.25%; female 50.75%. **Age breakdown** (2005): under 15, 30.3%; 15–29, 27.1%; 30–44, 21.6%; 45–59, 13.4%; 60–74, 5.6%; 75–84, 1.6%; 85 and over, 0.4%. **Ethnic composition** (2000): mestizo 47.3%; mulatto 23.0%; white 20.0%; black 6.0%; black-Amerindian 1.0%; Amerindian/other 2.7%. **Religious affiliation** (2005): Roman Catholic 92.5%; Protestant 2.8%; independent Christian 2.4%; Mormon 0.3%; Muslim 0.2%; other 1.8%. **Major cities** (2005): Bogotá 6,763,325; Medellín 2,187,356; Cali 2,039,626; Barranquilla 1,109,067; Cartagena 845,801. **Location:** northern South America, bordering the Caribbean Sea, Venezuela, Brazil, Peru, Ecuador, the Pacific Ocean, and Panama.

Vital statistics

Birth rate per 1,000 population (2006): 20.5 (world avg. 20.3). **Death rate** per 1,000 population (2006): 5.6 (world avg. 8.6). **Natural increase rate** per 1,000 population (2006): 14.9 (world avg. 11.7). **Total fertility rate** (avg. births per childbearing woman; 2006): 2.54. **Life expectancy** at birth (2006): male 68.2 years; female 76.0 years.

National economy

Budget (2003–04). *Revenue:* Col$39,951,400,000,000 (tax revenue 92.0%; nontax revenue 8.0%). *Expenditures:* Col$53,934,600,000,000 (transfers

53.1%; debt service 19.0%; other 27.9%). **Public debt** (external, outstanding; 2005): US$22,491,000,000. **Population economically active** (2005): total 20,575,200; activity rate 46.1% (participation rates: ages 12–55, 65.7%; female 42.1%; unemployed 11.8%). **Production** (metric tons except as noted). *Agriculture, forestry, fishing* (2005): sugarcane 39,850,000, plantains 3,457,000, rice 2,502,000 (also major producer of cut flowers; export value [2006] US$1,000,000,000); livestock (number of live animals) 25,699,000 cattle, 3,332,993 sheep, 2,553,621 horses; roundwood 9,658,000 cu m, of which fuelwood 83%; fisheries production 181,074 (from aquaculture 33%). *Mining and quarrying* (2004): nickel (metal content) 75,032; gold 37,739 kg; emeralds 9,825,000 carats. *Manufacturing* (value added in Col$'000,000,000; 2003): processed food 6,471; chemicals 5,737; petroleum products 3,712. *Energy production (consumption):* electricity (kW-hr; 2004) 50,291,000,000 (48,657,000,000); coal (metric tons; 2004) 53,700,000 (3,144,000); crude petroleum (barrels; 2004) 189,200,000 (112,400,000); petroleum products (metric tons; 2004) 14,106,000 (9,164,000); natural gas (cu m; 2004) 6,354,000,000 (6,219,000,000). **Land use** as % of total land area (2003): in temporary crops 2.0%, in permanent crops 1.3%, in pasture 34.5%; overall forest area (2005) 58.5%. **Gross national income** (2006): US$125,898,000,000 (US$2,763 per capita). **Households.** Average household size (2004) 3.8; sources of income (2002): wages 42.6%, self-employment 38.9%; expenditure (1992): food 34.2%, transportation 18.5%, housing 7.8%, health care 6.4%. **Selected balance of payments data.** Receipts from (US$'000,000): tourism (2005) 1,218; remittances (2006) 4,200; foreign direct investment (FDI) (2001–05 avg.) 3,946; official development assistance (2005) 838 (commitments). Disbursements for (US$'000,000): tourism (2005) 1,127; remittances (2006) 66; FDI (2001–05 avg.) 1,315.

Foreign trade

Imports (2006; f.o.b. in balance of trade and c.i.f. in commodities and trading partners): US$26,162,000,000 (chemicals and chemical products 20.2%; transportation equipment 15.3%; nonelectrical machinery 11.2%; telecommunications equipment 8.6%). *Major import sources:* US 26.5%; Mexico 8.8%; China 8.5%; Brazil 7.2%; Venezuela 5.7%. **Exports** (2006): US$24,391,000,000 (crude and refined petroleum 26.0%; coal 11.9%; chemicals and chemical products 7.4%; base metals 6.6%; food, beverages, and tobacco 6.5%; coffee 6.0%; textiles and clothing 5.4%). *Major export destinations:* US 39.6%; EU 13.7%; Venezuela 11.1%; Ecuador 5.1%; Peru 2.8%.

Transport and communications

Transport. *Railroads:* route length (2004) 3,304 km; metric ton-km cargo (1999) 473,000,000. *Roads* (2000): total length 112,998 km (paved 23%). *Vehicles* (1999): cars 1,803,201; trucks 319,294. *Air transport* (2005): passenger-km 7,764,000,000; metric ton-km cargo 252,852,000. **Communications,** in total units (units per 1,000 persons). Daily newspaper circulation (2005): 1,294,000 (30); televisions (2004): 11,358,000 (268); telephone landlines (2006): 7,865,000 (170); cellular telephone subscribers (2006): 29,763,000 (643); personal computers (2005): 1,892,000 (44); total Internet users (2006): 6,705,000 (145); broadband Internet subscribers (2006): 628,000 (14).

Education and health

Educational attainment (2005). Percentage of population ages 25 and over having: no schooling/unknown 10.2%; primary education 40.1%; secondary 34.2%; higher 15.5%. **Literacy** (2003): population ages 15 and over literate 92.5%; males literate 92.4%; females literate 92.6%. **Health** (2004): physicians 59,235 (1 per 714 persons); hospital beds 50,773 (1 per 833 persons); infant mortality rate (2006) 20.4. **Food** (2005): daily per capita caloric intake 2,744 (vegetable products 83%, animal products 17%); 150% of FAO recommended minimum.

Military

Total active duty personnel (2006): 207,000 (army 86.0%, navy 10.6%, air force 3.4%). **Military expenditure as percentage of GDP** (2005): 3.7%; per capita expenditure US$106.

Background

The Spanish arrived in what is now Colombia c. 1500 and by 1538 had defeated the area's Chibchan-speaking Indians and made the area subject to the Viceroyalty of Peru. After 1740 authority was transferred to the newly created Viceroyalty of New Granada. Parts of Colombia threw off Spanish jurisdiction in 1810, and full independence came after Spain's defeat by Simón Bolívar in 1819. Civil war in 1840 checked development. Conflict between the Liberal and Conservative parties led to the War of a Thousand Days (1899–1903). Years of relative peace followed, but hostility erupted again in 1948; the two parties agreed in 1958 to a scheme for alternating governments. A new constitution was adopted in 1991, but democratic power remained threatened by civil unrest. Many leftist rebels and right-wing paramilitary groups funded their activities through kidnappings and narcotics trafficking.

Recent Developments

Problems continued in Colombia stemming from the presence of right-wing paramilitaries—the United Self-Defense Forces of Colombia—and those on the left—the Revolutionary Armed Forces of Colombia (FARC) and the National Liberation Army. FARC continued to demand a demilitarized zone before it would begin to discuss a prisoner exchange, and the government continued to refuse to cede territory to the group. The 11 provincial legislators held by FARC since 2002 were killed when the guerrillas came under attack from what the FARC said was an "unidentified group." Colombian troops raided a FARC base in Ecuador and killed the group's second in command, Raúl Reyes, in March 2008. Ecuador and Venezuela both massed troops on their borders with Colombia, but peace was reestablished at a summit in the Dominican Republic later that month. In July 2008, former member of

1 metric ton = about 1.1 short tons; 1 kilometer = 0.6 mi (statute); 1 metric ton-km cargo = about 0.68 short ton-mi cargo; c.i.f.: cost, insurance, and freight; f.o.b.: free on board

congress and presidential candidate Ingrid Betancourt, along with 14 other hostages, was freed from FARC captivity in a daring Colombian army raid.

Internet resources: <www.turiscolombia.andes.com/colombia_eng.htm>.

Comoros

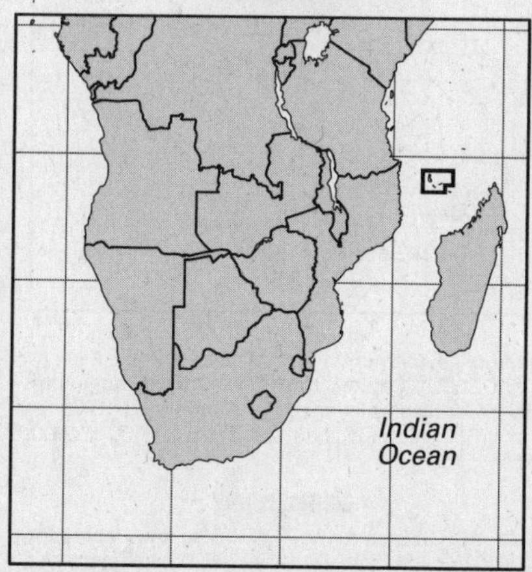

Official name: Udzima wa Komori (Comorian); L'Union des Comores (French) (Union of the Comoros). **Form of government:** federal republic with one legislative house (Federal Assembly [33]). **Head of state and government:** President Ahmed Abdallah Mohamed Sambi (from 2006). **Capital:** Moroni. **Official languages:** Comorian (Shikomor); Arabic; French. **Official religion:** Islam. **Monetary unit:** 1 Comorian franc (CF; pegged to the euro [€] at the rate of €1 = CF 491.97) = 100 centimes; valuation (1 Jul 2008) US$1 = CF 312.27.

Demography

Area: 719 sq mi, 1,862 sq km. **Population** (2007): 629,000. **Density** (2007): persons per sq mi 874.8, persons per sq km 337.8. **Urban** (2003): 35.0%. **Sex distribution** (2006): male 49.61%; female 50.39%. **Age breakdown** (2006): under 15, 42.7%; 15–29, 26.6%; 30–44, 17.8%; 45–59, 8.2%; 60–74, 3.9%; 75 and over, 0.8%. **Ethnic composition** (2000): Comorian (a mixture of Bantu, Arab, Malay, and Malagasy peoples) 97.1%; Makua 1.6%; French 0.4%; Arab 0.1%; other 0.8%. **Religious affiliation** (2005): Muslim (nearly all Sunni) 98.4%; other 1.6%. **Major cities** (2002): Moroni (urban agglomeration [2003]) 53,000; Mutsamudu 21,558; Domoni 13,254; Fomboni 13,053; Tsémbéhou 10,552. **Location:** western Indian Ocean, lying between Madagascar and Mozambique.

Vital statistics

Birth rate per 1,000 population (2006): 36.9 (world avg. 20.3). **Death rate** per 1,000 population (2006): 8.2 (world avg. 8.6). **Natural increase rate** per 1,000 population (2006): 28.7 (world avg. 11.7). **Total fertility rate** (avg. births per childbearing woman; 2006): 5.03. **Life expectancy** at birth (2006): male 60.0 years; female 64.7 years.

National economy

Budget (2005). *Revenue:* CF 30,509,000,000 (tax revenue 58.3%, of which taxes on international trade 31.0%, income and profit taxes 20.3%; grants 21.4%; nontax revenue 20.3%). *Expenditures:* CF 30,425,000,000 (current expenditures 77.3%, of which education 25.1%, health 15.6%, interest on debt 3.9%; development expenditures 22.7%). **Public debt** (external, outstanding; 2004): US$301,-000,000. **Production** (metric tons except as noted). *Agriculture, forestry, fishing* (2005): coconuts 77,000, bananas 65,000, cassava 58,000; livestock (number of live animals) 115,000 goats, 45,000 cattle, 21,000 sheep; roundwood 8,650; fisheries production 15,070. *Mining and quarrying:* sand, gravel, and crushed stone from coral mining for local construction. *Manufacturing:* products of small-scale industries include processed vanilla and ylang-ylang, cement, handicrafts, soaps, soft drinks, woodwork, and clothing. *Energy production (consumption):* electricity (kW-hr; 2005) 36,000,000 (35,900,000); petroleum products (metric tons; 2004) none (29,000). **Population economically active** (2000): total 287,000; activity rate of total population 41.0% (participation rates: ages 15–64, 73.2%; female 40.4%; unemployed [2005] 13.3%). **Households.** Average household size (2004) 5.8; average annual income per household (2004) CF 699,000 (US$1,764); sources of income (2004): wages/self-employment 36.9%, value of self-produced food 27.7%, value of principal dwelling 23.9%; expenditure (1999): food, beverages, and tobacco products 68.0%, housing and energy 15.5%, clothing and footwear 4.7%, education 4.2%. **Gross national income** (2006): US$397,000,000 (US$485 per capita). **Selected balance of payments data.** Receipts from (US$'000,000): tourism (2005) 14; remittances (2005) 12; foreign direct investment (2001–05 avg.) 1.0; official development assistance (2005) 25. Disbursements for (US$'000,000): tourism (1998) 3.0. **Land use** as % of total land area (2003): in temporary crops 36%, in permanent crops 23%, in pasture 7%; overall forest area (2005) 2.9%.

Foreign trade

Imports (2004; c.i.f.): CF 33,917,000,000 (food products 30.3%, of which rice 14.3%, meat 8.9%; petroleum products 20.9%; vehicles 11.5%; cement 5.1%). *Major import sources:* France 23%; South Africa 11%; United Arab Emirates 7%; Kenya 7%; Mauritius 6%. **Exports** (2004; f.o.b.): CF 5,777,000,000 (cloves 49.9%; vanilla 30.8%; ylang-ylang 14.7%). *Major export destinations:* US 42%; France 18%; Singapore 16%; Turkey 5%; Germany 4%.

Transport and communications

Transport. *Roads* (2004): total length 793 km (paved 70%). *Vehicles* (1996): passenger cars 9,100; trucks and buses 4,950. *Air transport* (2001): passengers arriving/departing Moroni 108,000. **Communications**, in total units (units per 1,000 persons). Televisions (2002): 13,000 (23); telephone landlines (2005): 17,000 (28); cellular telephone subscribers (2005): 16,000 (26); personal computers (2004): 5,000 (6.3); total Internet users (2006): 21,000 (26).

Education and health

Educational attainment (1996). Percentage of population ages 25 and over having: no formal schooling 72.7%; primary education 11.0%; secondary 15.1%; unknown 1.2%. **Literacy** (2005): total population ages 15 and over literate 56.8%; males literate 63.9%; females literate 49.7%. **Health** (2004): physicians 48 (1 per 12,417 persons); hospital beds (1995) 1,450 (1 per 342 persons); infant mortality rate per 1,000 live births (2006) 72.9. **Food** (2005): daily per capita caloric intake 1,766 (vegetable products 93%, animal products 7%); 97% of FAO recommended minimum.

Military

Total active duty personnel (2006): the Comoros small standing army is not necessarily accepted by each of the islands; each island also has its own armed security. France provides training for military personnel. **Military expenditure as percentage of GDP** (2005): 3.5%; per capita expenditure US$21.

Background

The Comoros islands were known to European navigators from the 16th century. In 1843 France officially took possession of Mayotte and in 1886 placed the other three islands under protection. Subordinated to Madagascar in 1912, the Comoros became an overseas territory of France in 1947. In 1961 they were granted autonomy. In 1974 majorities on three of the islands voted for independence, which was granted in 1975. The following decade saw several coup attempts, which culminated in the assassination of the president in 1989. French intervention permitted multiparty elections in 1990, but the country remained in a state of chronic instability. Anjouan and Mohéli seceded from the Comoros federation in 1997. The army took control of the government in 1999. A referendum at the end of 2001 renamed the country the Union of the Comoros and granted the three main islands partially autonomous status.

Recent Developments

Comoros endured serious political crisis in 2007. Although the three autonomous islands each chose local presidents every five years, Anjouan Pres. Col. Mohamed Bacar, elected to the office in 2002 after having seized power a year earlier in a coup, defied federal orders to step down in 2007. The government postponed the Anjouan elections, but Bacar claimed victory in elections that he staged. Comoran troops, backed by African Union forces, invaded Anjouan in March 2008, and Bacar was captured and transported to Réunion to face charges.

Internet resources: <www.bancecom.com>.

Democratic Republic of the Congo

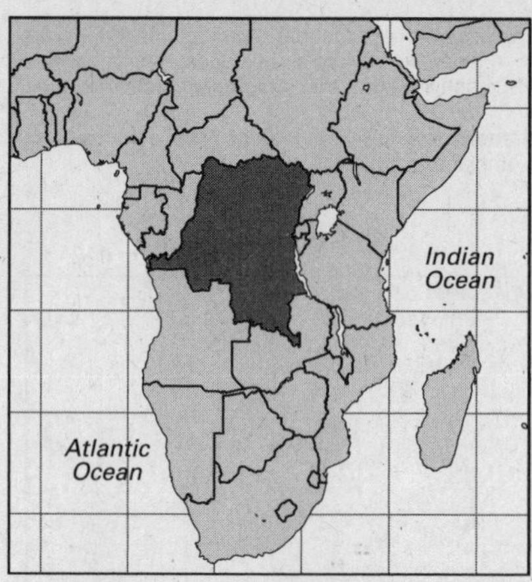

Official name: République Democratique du Congo (Democratic Republic of the Congo). **Form of government:** unitary multiparty republic with two legislative bodies (Senate [108]; National Assembly [500]). **Chief of state:** President Joseph Kabila (from 2001). **Head of government:** Prime Minister Antoine Gizenga (from 2006). **Capital:** Kinshasa. **Official languages:** French. **Official religion:** none. **Monetary unit:** Congo franc (FC); valuation (1 Jul 2008) US$1 = FC 552.00.

Demography

Area: 905,355 sq mi, 2,344,858 sq km. **Population** (2007): 62,636,000. **Density** (2007): persons per sq mi 69.2, persons per sq km 26.7. **Urban** (2005): 32.1%. **Sex distribution** (2005): male 49.48%; female 50.52%. **Age breakdown** (2005): under 15, 47.2%; 15–29, 27.1%; 30–44, 14.2%; 45–59, 7.4%; 60–74, 3.4%; 75–84, 0.6%; 85 and over, 0.1%. **Ethnic composition** (1983): Luba 18.0%; Kongo 16.1%; Mongo 13.5%; Rwanda 10.3%; Azande 6.1%; Bangi and Ngale 5.8%; Rundi 3.8%; Teke 2.7%; Boa 2.3%; Chokwe 1.8%; Lugbara 1.6%; Banda 1.4%; other 16.6%. **Religious affiliation** (2004): Roman Catholic 50%; Protestant 20%; Kimbanguist (indigenous Christian) 10%; Muslim 10%; traditional beliefs and syncretic sects 10%. **Major urban areas** (2004): Kinshasa 7,273,947; Lubumbashi 1,283,380; Mbuji-Mayi 1,213,726; Kananga 720,362; Kisangani 682,599. **Location:** central Africa, bordering the Central African Republic, The Sudan, Uganda, Rwanda, Burundi, Tanzania, Zambia, Angola, the South Atlantic Ocean, and the Republic of the Congo.

Vital statistics

Birth rate per 1,000 population (2005): 49.6 (world avg. 20.3). **Death rate** per 1,000 population (2005): 18.7 (world avg. 8.6). **Natural increase rate** per 1,000 population (2005): 30.9 (world avg. 11.7). **Total fertility rate** (avg. births per childbearing woman; 2005): 6.70. **Life expectancy** at birth (2005): male 44.3 years; female 47.0 years.

National economy

Budget (2005). *Revenue:* FC 564,900,000,000 (grants 31.1%; customs and excise taxes 25.7%; direct and indirect taxes 19.7%; petroleum royalties and taxes 17.4%). *Expenditures:* FC 655,500,000,000 (current expenditure 65.3%, of which interest on external debt 14.8%; capital expenditure 17.4%; expenditure on demobilization and reintegration 14.8%). **Public debt** (external, outstanding; 2005): US$10,822,000,000. **Production** (metric tons except as noted). *Agriculture, forestry, fishing* (2005): cassava 14,975,000, sugarcane 1,800,000, plantains 1,193,000; livestock (number of live animals) 4,022,000 goats, 959,000 pigs, game meat 88,735 metric tons; roundwood (2005) 74,719,000 cu m, of which fuelwood 95%; fisheries production 222,965 (from aquaculture 1%). *Mining and quarrying* (2005): copper (metal content) 92,000; cobalt (metal content) 22,000; silver 53,553 kg. *Manufacturing* (2004): cement 402,500; flour 199,000; steel 130,000. *Energy production (consumption):* electricity (kW-hr; 2004) 6,852,000,000 (5,402,000,000); coal (metric tons; 2004) 108,000 (153,000); crude petroleum (barrels; 2005) 10,000,000 (negligible); petroleum products (metric tons; 2004) none (376,000). **Households.** Expenditure (1995): food 61.4%, housing and energy 13.9%, clothing and footwear 4.8%, other 19.9%. **Gross national income** (2006): US$7,784,000,000 (US$128 per capita). **Population economically active** (2003): total 21,718,000; activity rate 40.0% (participation rates: ages 15–64, 77.1%; female 41.1%). **Selected balance of payments data.** Receipts from (US$'000,000): tourism (2005) 1.0; foreign direct investment (2001–05 avg.) 343; official development assistance (2005) 1,828. Disbursements for (US$'000,000): tourism (1997) 7.0. **Land use** as % of total land area (2003): in temporary crops 3.0%, in permanent crops 0.5%, in pasture 6.6%; overall forest area (2005) 58.9%.

Foreign trade

Imports (2005): US$2,465,000,000 (aid-related imports 22.9%; other imports 77.1%). *Major import sources* (2004): South Africa 18.5%; Belgium 15.6%; France 10.9%; US 6.2%; Germany 5.9%. **Exports** (2005): US$2,042,000,000 (diamonds 48.4%; crude petroleum 20.0%; cobalt [2004] 15.0%; copper [2004] 3.3%). *Major export destinations:* Belgium 42.5%; Finland 17.8%; Zimbabwe 12.2%; US 9.2%; China 6.5%.

Transport and communications

Transport. *Railroads* (2003): length (2004) 5,138 km; passenger-km 152,930,000; metric ton-km cargo 506,010,000. *Roads* (2004): total length 153,497 km (paved 2%). *Vehicles* (1999): passenger cars 172,600; trucks and buses 34,600. *Air transport* (1999): passenger-km 263,000,000; metric ton-km cargo 39,000,000. **Communications,** in total units (units per 1,000 persons). Televisions (2003): 146,000 (2.7); telephone landlines (2006): 9,700 (0.2); cellular telephone subscribers (2006): 4,416,000 (74); total Internet users (2006): 180,000 (3); broadband Internet subscribers (2006): 1,500 (0.03).

Education and health

Literacy (2003): percentage of total population ages 15 and over literate 65.5%; males literate 76.2%; females literate 55.1%. **Health:** physicians (2004) 5,827 (1 per 9,585 persons); infant mortality rate per 1,000 live births (2005) 116.5. **Food** (2005): daily per capita caloric intake 1,398 (vegetable products 97%, animal products 3%); 76% of FAO recommended minimum.

Military

Total active duty personnel (2006): 64,800 (army 92.6%, air force 4.6%, navy 2.8%); UN peacekeepers (June 2007): 16,600 troops; 1,000 police. **Military expenditure as percentage of GDP** (2005): 2.4%; per capita expenditure US$2.

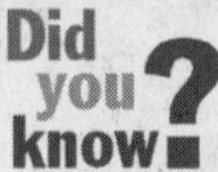

Congo was known as Zaire, an attempt by then-ruler Mobutu Sese Seko to return to the source of the nation's identity and authenticity. After Mobutu's overthrow in 1997, however, the name of the country before 1971, the Democratic Republic of the Congo, was restored.

Background

Prior to European colonization, several native kingdoms had emerged in the Congo region, including the 16th-century Luba kingdom and the Kuba federation, which reached its peak in the 18th century. European development began late in the 19th century when King Léopold II of Belgium financed Henry Morton Stanley's exploration of the Congo River. The 1884–85 Berlin West Africa Conference recognized the Congo Free State with Léopold as its sovereign. The growing demand for rubber helped finance the exploitation of the Congo, but abuses against native peoples outraged Western nations and forced Léopold to grant the Free State a colonial charter as the Belgian Congo (1908). Independence was granted in 1960, and the country's name was changed to Zaire in 1971. The post-independence period was marked by unrest, culminating in a military coup that brought Gen. Mobutu Sese Seko to power in 1965. Mismanagement, corruption, and increasing violence devastated the infrastructure and economy. Mobutu was deposed in 1997 by Laurent Kabila, who restored the country's name to Democratic Republic of the Congo. Regional instability and desire for Congo's mineral wealth led to military involvement by numerous African countries. Kabila was assassinated in 2001 and succeeded by his son Joseph.

Recent Developments

Fighting broke out in the Democratic Republic of the Congo (DRC) in March 2007 between supporters of the the victorious Pres. Joseph Kabila and his opponent in the 2006 presidential election, Jean-Pierre Bemba. After several hundred people were killed, the violence was brought to an end by the intervention of the peacekeeping UN Organization Mission in the Democratic Republic of the Congo and the EU. Troubles in North Kivu province on the eastern frontier proved less easy to settle. Although government troops inflicted heavy casualties there on Rwandan rebel militia fighters, the rebels continued to harass the civilian population and forced some 650,000 people to flee their homes. Relations with Uganda were also strained. Uganda threatened in March to send troops to the DRC to deal with rebels, who, Kampala claimed, were threatening the southwestern border from the Ituri district, and expanded the threats in August, accusing the Congolese authorities of encroaching upon Uganda's exploration for oil near Lake Albert.

Internet resources: <www.bcc.cd/go.html>.

Republic of the Congo

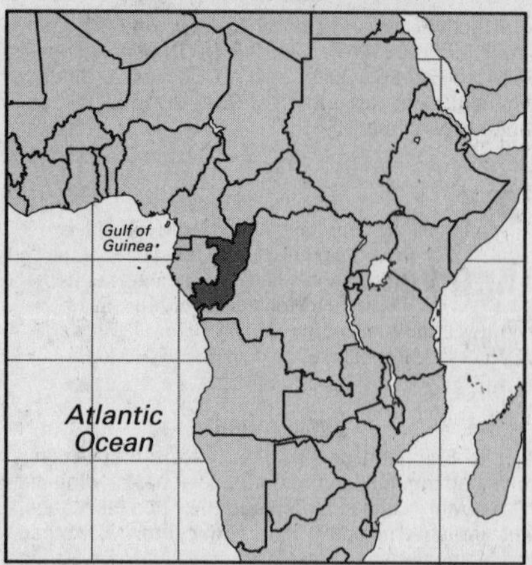

Official name: République du Congo (Republic of the Congo). **Form of government:** republic with two legislative houses (Senate [66]; National Assembly [137]). **Chief of state:** President Denis Sassou-Nguesso (from 1997). **Head of government:** Prime Minister Isidore Mvouba (from 2005). **Capital:** Brazzaville. **Official language:** French. **Official religion:** none. **Monetary unit:** 1 CFA franc (CFAF) = 100 centimes; valuation (1 Jul 2008) US$1 = CFAF 414.60 (pegged to the euro [€] at the rate of €1 = CFAF 655.96).

Demography

Area: 132,047 sq mi, 342,000 sq km. **Population** (2007): 3,768,000. **Density** (2007): persons per sq mi 28.5, persons per sq km 11.0. **Urban** (2005): 53.3%. **Sex distribution** (2006): male 49.68%; female 50.32%. **Age breakdown** (2006): under 15, 46.4%; 15–29, 27.1%; 30–44, 14.9%; 45–59, 7.3%; 60–74, 3.5%; 75 and over, 0.8%. **Ethnic composition** (2000): Kongo 21.2%; Yombe 11.5%; Teke 10.7%; Kougni 8.0%; Mboshi 5.4%; Ngala 4.2%; Sundi 4.0%; other 35.0%. **Religious affiliation** (2005): Roman Catholic 49%; independent Christian 13%; Protestant 11%; Muslim 2%; other (mostly traditional beliefs and nonreligious) 25%. **Major cities** (2005): Brazzaville 1,174,005; Pointe-Noire 663,359; Dolisie 106,262; Nkayi 56,686; Ouesso 24,322. **Location:** west-central Africa, bordering Cameroon, the Central African Republic, the Democratic Republic of the Congo, Angola, the South Atlantic Ocean, and Gabon.

Vital statistics

Birth rate per 1,000 population (2006): 42.6 (world avg. 20.3). **Death rate** per 1,000 population (2006): 12.9 (world avg. 8.6). **Natural increase rate** per 1,000 population (2006): 29.6 (world avg. 11.7). **Total fertility rate** (avg. births per childbearing woman; 2006): 6.07. **Life expectancy** at birth (2006): male 51.7 years; female 54.0 years.

National economy

Budget (2005). *Revenue:* CFAF 1,300,100,000,000 (petroleum revenue 80.6%; nonpetroleum receipts 16.9%; grants 2.5%). *Expenditures:* CFAF 736,400,-000,000 (current expenditure 77.0%, of which interest 20.4%, wages and salaries 17.7%; capital expenditure 23.0%). **Public debt** (external, outstanding; 2005): US$5,161,000,000. **Households.** Average household size (2000) 5.9. **Gross national income** (2006): US$5,787,000,000 (US$1,569 per capita). **Production** (metric tons except as noted). *Agriculture, forestry, fishing* (2005): cassava 900,000, sugarcane 460,000, oil palm fruit 90,000; livestock (number of live animals) 295,000 goats, 115,000 cattle, 99,000 sheep; roundwood 2,265,000 cu m, of which fuelwood 60%; fisheries production 58,448. *Mining and quarrying* (2005): gold 20 kg; diamonds 50,000 carats. *Manufacturing* (2000): residual fuel oil 206,000; refined sugar (2001) 71,814; distillate fuel oils 62,000. *Energy production (consumption):* electricity (kW-hr; 2004) 399,000,000 (802,000,000); crude petroleum (barrels; 2005) 82,900,000 ([2004] 5,944,000); petroleum products (metric tons; 2004) 535,000 (288,000); natural gas (cu m; 2004) 124,700,000 (124,700,000). **Population economically active** (2000): total 1,232,000; activity rate of total population 35.7% (participation rates: ages 15–64, 60.3%; female [1997] 43.4%). **Selected balance of payments data.** Receipts from (US$'000,000): tourism (2005) 34; remittances (2004) 1; foreign direct investment (2001–05 avg.) 321; official development assistance (2005) 1,557 (commitments). Disbursements for (US$'000,000): tourism (2005) 103; remittances (2003) 24. **Land use** as % of total land area (2003): in temporary crops 1.4%, in permanent crops 0.2%, in pasture 29.3%; overall forest area (2005) 65.8%.

Foreign trade

Imports (2005): CFAF 746,400,000,000 (nonpetroleum sector 85.9%; petroleum sector 14.1%). *Major import sources* (2002): France 26%; US 11%; Italy 8%; Lebanon 6%; The Netherlands 5%. **Exports** (2005): CFAF 2,484,300,000,000 (crude petroleum 92.5%; wood and wood products 4.6%; refined petroleum 1.2%). *Major export destinations* (2002): Taiwan 27%; North Korea 11%; US 10%; South Korea 7%; France 7%.

Transport and communications

Transport. *Railroads* (1998): length 894 km; passenger-km 242,000,000; metric ton-km cargo 135,000,000. *Roads* (2004): total length 17,289 km (paved 5%). *Vehicles* (1997): passenger cars 37,240; trucks and buses 15,500. *Air transport* (2002): passenger-km 27,000,000; metric ton-km cargo 3,000,000. **Communications,** in total units (units per 1,000 persons). Televisions (2002): 40,000 (12); telephone landlines (2005): 16,000 (4); cellular telephone subscribers (2005): 490,000 (136); personal computers (2005): 19,000 (4.8); total Internet users (2006): 70,000 (17).

Education and health

Educational attainment (1984). Percentage of population ages 25 and over having: no formal schooling

58.7%; primary education 21.4%; secondary education 16.9%; postsecondary 3.0%. **Literacy** (2005): total population ages 15 and over literate 85.8%; males literate 91.2%; females literate 80.8%. **Health:** physicians (2000) 540 (1 per 5,745 persons); hospital beds (2001) 5,195 (1 per 623 persons); infant mortality rate per 1,000 live births (2006) 85.3. **Food** (2005): daily per capita caloric intake 2,026 (vegetable products 92%, animal products 8%); 111% of FAO recommended minimum.

Military

Total active duty personnel (2006): 10,000 (army 80.0%, navy 8.0%, air force 12.0%). **Military expenditure as percentage of GDP** (2005): 1.4%; per capita expenditure US$22.

Background

In precolonial days the Congo area was home to several thriving kingdoms, including the Kongo, which had its beginnings in the 1st millennium AD. The slave trade began in the 15th century with the arrival of the Portuguese; it supported the local kingdoms and dominated the area until its suppression in the 19th century. The French arrived in the mid-19th century and established treaties with two of the kingdoms, placing them under French protection prior to their becoming part of the colony of French Congo. In 1910 the French possessions were renamed French Equatorial Africa, and Congo became known as Middle (Moyen) Congo. In 1946 Middle Congo became a French overseas territory and in 1958 voted to become an autonomous republic within the French Community. Full independence came two years later. The area has suffered from political instability since independence. Congo's first president was ousted in 1963. A Marxist party, the Congolese Labor Party, gained strength, and in 1968 another coup, led by Maj. Marien Ngouabi, created the People's Republic of the Congo. Ngouabi was assassinated in 1977. A series of military rulers followed, at first militantly socialist but later oriented toward social democracy. Fighting between local militias that began in 1997 badly disrupted the economy.

Recent Developments

Congolese health authorities blamed poor hygiene for the severe cholera outbreak (about 6,500 cases were reported) in Pointe-Noire in January 2007; at least 62 people died. In July the Ministry of Health announced that 400,000 children under the age of five had been vaccinated against polio, despite a continuing shortage of trained medical staff. Sponsored by the government and UNICEF, a special train left Pointe-Noire in August, carrying 300,000 insecticide-treated antimalaria mosquito nets for delivery to remote medical clinics along the southwestern coast.

Internet resources: <www.cnsee.org>.

Costa Rica

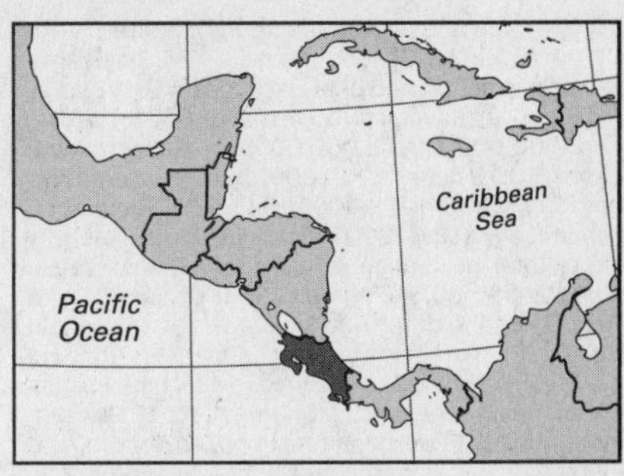

Official name: República de Costa Rica (Republic of Costa Rica). **Form of government:** unitary multiparty republic with one legislative house (Legislative Assembly [57]). **Head of state and government:** President Óscar Arias Sánchez (from 2006). **Capital:** San José. **Official language:** Spanish. **Official religion:** Roman Catholicism. **Monetary unit:** 1 Costa Rican colón (₡) = 100 céntimos; valuation (1 Jul 2008) US$1 = ₡519.64.

Demography

Area: 19,730 sq mi, 51,100 sq km. **Population** (2007): 4,445,000. **Density** (2007): persons per sq mi 225.3, persons per sq km 87.0. **Urban** (2003): 60.6%. **Sex distribution** (2006): male 50.76%; female 49.24%. **Age breakdown** (2005): under 15, 28.4%; 15–29, 28.1%; 30–44, 21.5%; 45–59, 13.7%; 60–74, 5.9%; 75–84, 1.8%; 85 and over, 0.6%. **Ethnic composition** (2000): white 77.0%; mestizo 17.0%; black/mulatto 3.0%; East Asian (mostly Chinese) 2.0%; Amerindian 1.0%. **Religious affiliation** (2004): Roman Catholic (practicing) 47%; Roman Catholic (nonpracticing) 25%; Evangelical Protestant 13%; nonreligious 10%; other 5%. **Major cities** (district population; 2006): San José (urban agglomeration; 2003) 1,085,000; Limón 68,215; Alajuela 49,376; San Isidro de El General 46,490; San Francisco 45,972. **Location:** Central America, bordering Nicaragua, the Caribbean Sea, Panama, and the North Pacific Ocean.

Vital statistics

Birth rate per 1,000 population (2006): 16.2 (world avg. 20.3); within marriage 38.4%. **Death rate** per 1,000 population (2006): 3.8 (world avg. 8.6). **Natural increase rate** per 1,000 population (2006): 12.4 (world avg. 11.7). **Total fertility rate** (avg. births per childbearing woman; 2006): 1.97. **Life expectancy** at birth (2006): male 77.0 years; female 81.4 years.

National economy

Budget (2004). *Revenue:* ₡1,860,988,000,000 (taxes on goods and services 38.5%; social security contributions 27.2%; income tax 14.4%; import duties 5.0%; grants 3.7%). *Expenditures:* ₡1,951,392,000,000 (current expenditures 92.9%, of which wages 37.7%, transfers 25.8%, interest on debt 17.2%; development expenditures 7.1%). **Public debt** (external, outstanding; February 2006): US$3,893,400,000. **Gross national income** (2006): US$21,367,000,000 (US$4,857 per capita). **Production** (metric tons except as noted). *Agriculture, forestry, fishing* (2005): sugarcane 3,615,582, bananas 2,220,000, pineapples 1,605,237; livestock (number of live animals) 1,000,000 cattle, 550,000 pigs, 19,500,000 chickens; roundwood 4,636,000 cu m, of which fuelwood 74%; fisheries production 46,378 (from aquaculture 52%). *Mining and quarrying* (2004): limestone

920,000; gold 500 kg. *Manufacturing* (value added in US$'000,000; 2003): food products 734; beverages 188; paints, soaps, and pharmaceuticals 169. *Energy production (consumption):* electricity (kW-hr; 2004) 8,210,000,000 (7,972,000,000); crude petroleum (barrels; 2004) none (3,900,000); petroleum products (metric tons; 2004) 288,000 (1,541,000). **Population economically active** (2005): total 1,903,068; activity rate of total population 44.6% (participation rates: ages 12–59, 60.8%; female 36.2%; unemployed 6.6%). **Households** (2004–05). Average household size 3.7; average annual household income ₡4,225,680 (US$9,214); sources of income: wages and salaries 67.9%, rent 11.0%, transfers 10.9%, self-employment 8.1%; expenditure: food, beverages, and tobacco 21.9%, housing and energy 19.3%, transportation 14.8%, recreation and culture 7.9%, wearing apparel 6.9%. **Selected balance of payments data.** Receipts from (US$'000,000): tourism (2005) 1,666; remittances (2006) 520; foreign direct investment (2001–05 avg.) 593. Disbursements for (US$'000,000): tourism (2005) 470; remittances (2006) 246. **Land use** as % of total land area (2003): in temporary crops 4.4%, in permanent crops 5.9%, in pasture 45.8%; overall forest area (2005) 46.8%.

Foreign trade

Imports (2005; c.i.f.): US$9,640,100,000 (machinery and apparatus 34.2%; chemicals and chemical products 11.0%; mineral fuels 10.5%; plastics 7.0%; fabricated metal products 6.8%). *Major import sources:* US 40.1%; Japan 5.8%; Mexico 5.0%; Venezuela 4.9%; Ireland 4.5%. **Exports** (2005; f.o.b.): US$7,150,690,000 (machinery and apparatus 29.8%; food products 24.8%, of which bananas 6.8%, pineapples 4.6%, coffee 3.7%; professional and scientific equipment 8.1%; textiles 7.5%; chemicals and chemical products 6.0%). *Major export destinations:* US 40.2%; Hong Kong 6.8%; The Netherlands 6.3%; Guatemala 4.0%; Nicaragua 3.9%.

Transport and communications

Transport. *Railroads* (2004): 278 km. *Roads* (2004): total length 35,330 km (paved 24%). *Vehicles* (2004): passenger cars 620,992; trucks and buses 220,456. *Air transport* (2005; Lacsa [Costa Rican Airlines] only): passenger-km 2,284,000,000; metric ton-km cargo 10,351,000. **Communications,** in total units (units per 1,000 persons). Daily newspaper circulation (2004): 477,000 (115); televisions (2004): 1,068,000 (257); telephone landlines (2006): 1,351,000 (307); cellular telephone subscribers (2006): 1,444,000 (328); personal computers (2005): 1,000,000 (233); total Internet users (2006): 1,214,000 (276); broadband Internet subscribers (2006): 59,000 (14).

Education and health

Educational attainment (2004). Percentage of population ages 5 and over having: no formal schooling/unknown 12.8%; incomplete primary education 23.3%; complete primary 24.5%; incomplete secondary 18.2%; complete secondary 8.5%; higher 12.7%. **Literacy** (2003): total population ages 15 and over literate 96.0%; males literate 95.9%; females literate 96.1%. **Health** (2004): physicians 6,600 (1 per 644 persons); hospital beds (2003) 5,908 (1 per 714 persons); infant mortality rate per 1,000 live births (2006) 9.7. **Food** (2005): daily per capita caloric intake 2,618 (vegetable products 80%, animal products 20%); 136% of FAO recommended minimum.

Military

Paramilitary expenditure as percentage of GDP (2005): 0.4%; per capita expenditure US$24. The army was officially abolished in 1948. Paramilitary (police) forces had 8,400 members in 2006.

Background

Christopher Columbus landed in Costa Rica in 1502 in an area inhabited by a number of small, independent Indian tribes. These peoples were not easily dominated, and it took almost 60 years for the Spanish to establish a permanent settlement. Ignored by the Spanish crown because of its lack of mineral wealth, the colony grew slowly. Coffee exports and the construction of a rail line improved its economy in the 19th century. It joined the short-lived Mexican Empire in 1821, was a member of the United Provinces of Central America, 1823–38, and adopted a constitution in 1871. In 1890 Costa Ricans held what is considered to be the first free and honest election in Central America, beginning a tradition of democracy for which Costa Rica is renowned. In 1987 then president Óscar Arias Sánchez was awarded the Nobel Peace Prize. During the 1990s Costa Rica struggled with its economic policies. It suffered severe damage from a hurricane in 1996.

Recent Developments

In Costa Rica's first-ever national referendum, held on 7 October 2007, citizens voted in favor of the Central America–Dominican Republic Free Trade Agreement (CAFTA–DR) with the United States. Pres. Óscar Arias Sánchez, who spent much of his term trying to secure passage of the agreement, said that the treaty would bring long-term economic growth. In June Costa Rica established diplomatic relations with China in an effort to promote trade and economic cooperation, meanwhile breaking off 60 years of formal ties with Taiwan. Economic growth remained strong, hovering near 7%. In October, Costa Rica was elected to serve as a member of the UN Security Council in 2008–09.

Internet resources: <www.inec.go.cr/>.

Côte d'Ivoire

Official name: République de Côte d'Ivoire (Republic of Côte d'Ivoire). **Form of government:** transitional regime with one legislative house (National Assembly [223]). **Chief of state and government:** President Laurent Gbagbo (from 2000), assisted by Prime Minister Guillaume Soro (from 2007). **Capital:** Abidjan. **Official language:** French. **Official religion:** none. **Monetary unit:** 1 CFA franc (CFAF) = 100 centimes; valuation (1 Jul 2008) US$1 = CFAF 414.60 (pegged to the euro [€] at the rate of €1 = CFAF 655.96).

1 metric ton = about 1.1 short tons; 1 kilometer = 0.6 mi (statute); 1 metric ton-km cargo = about 0.68 short ton-mi cargo; c.i.f.: cost, insurance, and freight; f.o.b.: free on board

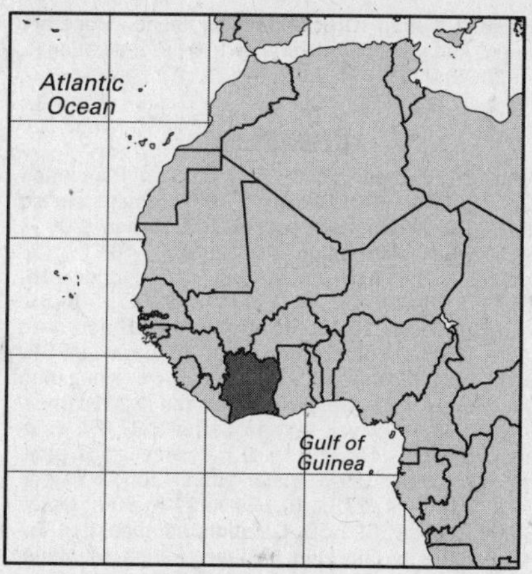

Demography

Area: 123,863 sq mi, 320,803 sq km. **Population** (2007): 19,262,000. **Density** (2007): persons per sq mi 155.5, persons per sq km 60.0. **Urban** (2005): 45.0%. **Sex distribution** (2005): male 50.82%; female 49.18%. **Age breakdown** (2005): under 15, 41.7%; 15-29, 29.4%; 30-44, 14.7%; 45-59, 9.1%; 60-74, 4.3%; 75-84, 0.7%; 85 and over, 0.1%. **Ethnolinguistic composition** (1998): Akan 42.1%; Mande 26.5%; other 31.4%. **Religious affiliation** (2005): traditional beliefs 37%; Christian 32%, of which Roman Catholic 17%, Protestant 8%, independent Christian 7%; Muslim 28%; other 3%. **Major cities** (2005): Abidjan (agglomeration) 3,576,000; Bouaké 573,700; Daloa 215,100; Yamoussoukro (2003) 185,600; Korhogo (2003) 115,000. **Location:** western Africa, bordering Mali, Burkina Faso, Ghana, the Atlantic Ocean, Liberia, and Guinea.

Vital statistics

Birth rate per 1,000 population (2005): 36.2 (world avg. 20.3). **Death rate** per 1,000 population (2005): 16.0 (world avg. 8.6). **Total fertility rate** (avg. births per childbearing woman; 2005): 4.76. **Life expectancy** at birth (2005): male 46.7 years; female 48.6 years.

National economy

Budget (2005). *Revenue:* CFAF 1,566,000,000,000 (tax revenue 79.9%; nontax revenue 14.1%; grants 6.0%). *Expenditures:* CFAF 1,536,600,000,000 (current expenditure 78.4%; interest on public debt 11.5%; remainder 10.1%). **Public debt** (external, outstanding; 2005): US$9,007,000,000. **Production** (metric tons except as noted). *Agriculture, forestry, fishing* (2005): yams 3,000,000, oil palm fruit 1,882,000, cassava 1,500,000; livestock (number of live animals) 1,523,000 sheep, 1,500,000 cattle; roundwood 10,047,000 cu m, of which fuelwood 87%; fisheries production 55,866 (from aquaculture 2%). *Mining and quarrying* (2005): gold 1,638 kg; diamonds 300,000 carats (A UN embargo on rough diamond exports was rescinded in November 2007). *Manufacturing* (value added in CFAF '000,000,000; 1997): food 156.6, of which cocoa and chocolate 72.4, vegetable oils 62.7; chemicals 60.2. *Energy production (consumption):* electricity (kW-hr; 2004) 5,370,000,000 (2,973,800,000); crude petroleum (barrels; 2004) 9,485,000 (26,400,000); petroleum products (metric tons; 2004) 3,248,000 (906,000); natural gas (cu m; 2005) 2,200,000,000 ([2004] 1,000,000,000). **Population economically active** (2003): total 6,544,000; activity rate of total population 37.2% (participation rates: ages 15-64, 65.5%; female 28.9%). **Households.** Average household size (2004) 8.0; expenditure (1996): food 32.2%, housing and energy 13.9%, hotels and restaurants 12.3%, transportation 9.6%, clothing 7.4%, household equipment 5.7%. **Selected balance of payments data.** Receipts from (US$'000,000): tourism (2003) 50; remittances (2005) 160; foreign direct investment (2001-05 avg.) 225; official development assistance (2005) 236 (commitments). Disbursements for (US$'000,000): tourism (2001) 192; remittances (2005) 592. **Gross national income** (2006): US$17,052,000,000 (US$902 per capita). **Land use** as % of total land area (2003): in temporary crops 10.4%, in permanent crops 11.3%, in pasture 40.9%; overall forest area (2005) 32.7%.

Foreign trade

Imports (2005): CFAF 2,687,000,000,000 (machinery and transport equipment 40.1%; crude and refined petroleum 32.3%; food products 17.0%). *Major import sources* (2004): France 24.3%; Nigeria 19.2%; UK 4.0%; China 4.0%; Italy 3.8%. **Exports** (2005): CFAF 3,950,000,000,000 (cocoa beans and products 27.5%; crude petroleum and petroleum products 26.9%; wood and wood products 3.8%; coffee 2.1%). *Major export destinations* (2004): US 11.6%; The Netherlands 10.3%; France 9.5%; Italy 5.5%; Belgium 4.7%.

Transport and communications

Transport. *Railroads* (1999): route length (2004) 660 km; passenger-km 93,100,000; metric ton-km cargo 537,600,000. *Roads* (2004): total length 80,000 km (paved 8%). *Vehicles* (2001): passenger cars 113,900; trucks and buses 54,900. *Air transport* (2002; Abidjan airport only): passenger arrivals and departures 821,400; cargo unloaded and loaded 16,699 metric tons. **Communications,** in total units (units per 1,000 persons). Daily newspaper circulation (2005): 83,000 (4.7); televisions (2004): 880,000 (52); telephone landlines (2006): 261,000 (14); cellular telephone subscribers (2006): 4,065,000 (220); personal computers (2004): 262,000 (16); total Internet users (2006): 300,000 (16); broadband Internet subscribers (2005): 1,200 (0.07).

Education and health

Educational attainment (1998-99). Percentage of population ages 25 and over having: no formal schooling/unknown 63.0%; primary education 19.4%; secondary 14.3%; higher 3.3%. **Literacy** (2003): percentage of population ages 15 and over literate 50.9%; males literate 57.9%; females literate 43.6%. **Health:** physicians (2004) 2,081 (1 per 8,143 persons); hospital beds (2001) 5,981 (1 per 2,660 persons); infant mortality rate (2005) 119.4. **Food** (2005): daily per capita caloric intake 2,268 (vegetable products 95%, animal products 5%); 123% of FAO recommended minimum.

Military

Total active duty personnel (2006): 17,050 (army 38.1%, navy 5.3%, air force 4.1%, presidential guard 7.9%, gendarmerie 44.6%); Peacekeeping troops (June 2007): UN 7,900, French 3,500. **Military expenditure as percentage of GDP** (2005): 1.2%; per capita expenditure US$11.

Background

Europeans came to the area to trade in ivory and slaves beginning in the 15th century, and local kingdoms gave way to French influence in the 19th century. The French colony of Côte d'Ivoire was founded in 1893, and full occupation took place during 1908–18. In 1946 it became a territory in the French Union. Côte d'Ivoire achieved independence in 1960, when Félix Houphouët-Boigny was elected president. The country's first multiparty presidential elections were held in 1990. In 2002 the country began to fracture politically into north and south, and civil war ensued.

Recent Developments

Promising steps were taken in 2007 toward unifying Côte d'Ivoire, which had been divided by nearly five years of civil war. On 4 March at a meeting in Ouagadougou, Burkina Faso, Ivoirian Pres. Laurent Gbagbo and New Forces leader Guillaume Soro signed a peace agreement calling for a new transitional government. Weeks later the president also created a new military command to be composed equally of government and rebel soldiers, with the objective to disarm all militias. Soro took office as prime minister in April. A general amnesty was declared in April for all crimes committed during the civil war. The government announced plans to issue new identity papers for millions of undocumented Ivoirians.

Internet resources: <www.ins.ci>.

Croatia

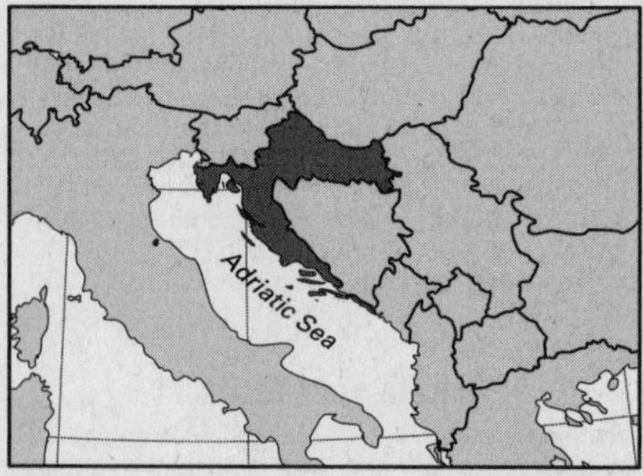

Official name: Republika Hrvatska (Republic of Croatia). **Form of government:** multiparty republic with one legislative house (House of Representatives [153]). **Head of state:** President Stipe Mesic (from 2000). **Head of government:** Prime Minister Ivo Sanader (from 2003). **Capital:** Zagreb. **Official language:** Croatian. **Official religion:** none. **Monetary unit:** 1 kuna (kn; plural kune) = 100 lipa; valuation (1 Jul 2008) US$1 = kn 4.58.

Demography

Area: 21,851 sq mi, 56,594 sq km. **Population** (2007): 4,440,000. **Density** (2007): persons per sq mi 203.2, persons per sq km 78.5. **Urban** (2005): 56.5%. **Sex distribution** (2006): male 48.17%; female 51.83%. **Age breakdown** (2004): under 15, 16.1%; 15–29, 20.2%; 30–44, 20.9%; 45–59, 20.7%; 60–74, 15.9%; 75–84, 5.3%; 85 and over, 0.9%. **Ethnic composition** (2001): Croat 89.6%; Serb 4.5%; Bosniac 0.5%; Italian 0.4%; Hungarian 0.4%; other 4.6%. **Religious affiliation** (2001): Christian 92.6%, of which Roman Catholic 87.8%, Eastern Orthodox 4.4%; Muslim 1.3%; nonreligious/atheist 5.2%; other 0.9%. **Major cities** (2001): Zagreb 691,724; Split 175,140; Rijeka 143,800; Osijek 90,411; Zadar 69,556. **Location:** southeastern Europe, bordering Slovenia, Hungary, Serbia, Montenegro, Bosnia and Herzegovina, and the Adriatic Sea.

Vital statistics

Birth rate per 1,000 population (2006): 9.5 (world avg. 20.3); (2005) within marriage 89.5%. **Death rate** per 1,000 population (2006): 11.5 (world avg. 8.6). **Natural increase rate** per 1,000 population (2006): −2.0 (world avg. 11.7). **Total fertility rate** (avg. births per childbearing woman; 2005): 1.42. **Life expectancy** at birth (2005): male 71.8 years; female 78.8 years.

National economy

Budget (2006). *Revenue:* kn 95,236,000,000 (tax revenue 61.4%, of which VAT 36.7%, excise taxes 12.1%; social security contributions 35.6%; nontax revenue 2.8%; grants 0.2%). *Expenditures:* kn 95,948,000,000 (social security and welfare 43.5%; compensation of employees 25.3%; interest payments 4.9%). **Population economically active** (2005): total 1,802,000; activity rate 40.5% (participation rates: ages 15–64, 58.3%; female 45.5%; unemployed [July 2005–June 2006] 12.7%). **Production** (metric tons except as noted). *Agriculture, forestry, fishing* (2005): corn (maize) 2,100,000, sugar beets 1,000,000, wheat 850,000; livestock (number of live animals) 1,205,000 pigs, 796,000 sheep, 471,000 cattle; roundwood 4,018,000 cu m, of which fuelwood 23%; fisheries production 48,465 (from aquaculture 28%). *Mining and quarrying* (2004): ceramic clay 637,000; ornamental stone 1,000,000 sq m. *Manufacturing* (value added in kn '000,000; 2004): food products and beverages 7,112; refined petroleum 4,005; chemicals and chemical products 2,774. *Energy production (consumption):* electricity (kW-hr; 2005) 12,722,000,000 ([2004] 14,163,000,000); coal (metric tons; 2004) negligible (1,106,000); crude petroleum (barrels; 2005) 7,740,000 ([2004] 37,200,000); petroleum products (metric tons; 2004) 4,824,000 (4,218,000); natural gas (cu m; 2004) 2,198,000,000 (2,934,000,000). **Gross national income** (2006): US$40,251,000,000 (US$8,835 per capita). **Public debt** (external, outstanding; December 2006): US$8,350,000,000. **Households** (2005). Average household size (2001) 3.0; average annual income per household kn 69,180 (US$11,629); sources: wages 51.0%, pensions 17.9%, self-employment 16.5%; expenditure: food and nonalcoholic beverages 33.2%, housing and energy 13.6%, transportation 10.9%, clothing and footwear 7.7%, recreation and culture 6.2%. **Selected balance of payments data.** Receipts from (US$'000,000): tourism (2005) 7,460; remittances (2006) 1,234; foreign direct investment (FDI) (2001–05 avg.) 1,528. Disbursements for (US$'000,000): tourism (2005) 751; remittances (2006) 274; FDI (2001–05 avg.) 267. **Land use** as % of total land area (2003): in temporary crops 26.1%, in permanent crops 2.2%, in pasture 27.8%; overall forest area (2005) 38.2%.

Foreign trade

Imports (2004): US$16,589,000,000 (machinery and apparatus 21.4%; chemicals and chemical products 11.2%; road vehicles 10.0%; crude and refined petroleum 8.9%; food and live animals 7.2%). *Major import sources:* Italy 17.0%; Germany 15.5%; Russia 7.3%; Slovenia 7.1%; Austria 6.8%. **Exports** (2002): US$4,899,000,000 (machinery and apparatus 17.0%; ships and tankers 13.5%; clothing 7.9%; petroleum products 7.9%; food products 6.3%; pharmaceuticals 3.1%). *Major export destinations:* Italy 22.9%; Bosnia and Herzegovina 14.4%; Germany 11.2%; Austria 9.4%; Slovenia 7.5%.

Transport and communications

Transport. *Railroads* (2006): length (2004) 2,726 km; passenger-km 1,339,000,000; metric ton-km cargo 3,183,000,000. *Roads:* total length (2004) 28,472 km (paved [2003] 85%). *Vehicles* (2006): passenger cars 1,435,781; trucks and buses 174,612. *Air transport* (2006): passenger-km 1,857,000,000; metric ton-km cargo 4,000,000. **Communications,** in total units (units per 1,000 persons). Daily newspaper circulation (2004): 382,000 (85); televisions (2003): 1,401,000 (315); telephone landlines (2006): 1,832,000 (402); cellular telephone subscribers (2006): 3,650,000 (821); personal computers (2004): 842,000 (191); total Internet users (2006): 1,576,000 (346); broadband Internet subscribers (2006): 252,000 (57).

Education and health

Educational attainment (2001). Percentage of population ages 15 and over having: no schooling/unknown 3.5%; incomplete primary education 15.8%; primary 21.7%; secondary 47.1%; postsecondary and higher 11.9%. **Literacy** (2003): population ages 15 and over literate 98.5%; males literate 99.4%; females literate 97.8%. **Health** (2005): physicians 8,216 (1 per 541 persons); hospital beds 24,000 (1 per 185 persons); infant mortality rate per 1,000 live births 5.7. **Food** (2005): daily per capita caloric intake 2,811 (vegetable products 78%, animal products 22%); 140% of FAO recommended minimum.

Military

Total active duty personnel (2006): 20,800 (army 67.5%, navy 12.0%, air force and air defense 11.1%, headquarters staff 9.4%). **Military expenditure as percentage of GDP** (2005): 1.6%; per capita expenditure US$138.

Background

The Croats, a southern Slavic people, arrived in the area in the 7th century AD and in the 8th century came under Charlemagne's rule. They converted to Christianity soon afterward and formed a kingdom in the 10th century. Most of Croatia was taken by the Turks in 1526; the rest voted to accept Austrian rule. In 1867 it became part of Austria-Hungary, with Dalmatia and Istria ruled by Vienna and Croatia-Slavonia a Hungarian crown land. In 1918, after the defeat of Austria-Hungary in World War I, it joined other south Slavic territories to form the Kingdom of Serbs, Croats, and Slovenes, renamed Yugoslavia in 1929. During World War II an independent state of Croatia was established by Germany and Italy, embracing Croatia-Slavonia, part of Dalmatia, and Bosnia and Herzegovina; after the war Croatia was rejoined to Yugoslavia as a people's republic. It declared its independence in 1991, sparking insurrections by Croatian Serbs, who carved out autonomous regions with Serbian-led Yugoslav army help; Croatia had taken back most of these regions by 1995. With some stability returning, Croatia's economy began to revive in the late 1990s.

Recent Developments

Croatia continued in 2007 to redress problems stemming from its war of national liberation during the 1990s, bringing to trial several suspected war criminals. In June retired generals Mirko Norac and Rahim Ademi were charged with the unlawful killing in 1993 of at least 29 Serbian civilians. In October, Branimir Glavas faced trial for having tortured and murdered Serb civilians in 1991 as war commander in the besieged city of Osijek. Croatian GDP growth for 2007 was an estimated 9.8%; inflation held steady at 2.9%; unemployment dropped to 9.5%; and the budget deficit was trimmed to 3.0% of GDP. Tourism, meanwhile, grew an estimated 8.0% year-on-year and generated more than US$10.5 billion in revenue, a record. In April 2008 Croatia was invited to begin negotiations for eventual membership in NATO.

Internet resources:
<www.croatia.hr/English/Home/Naslovna.aspx>.

Cuba

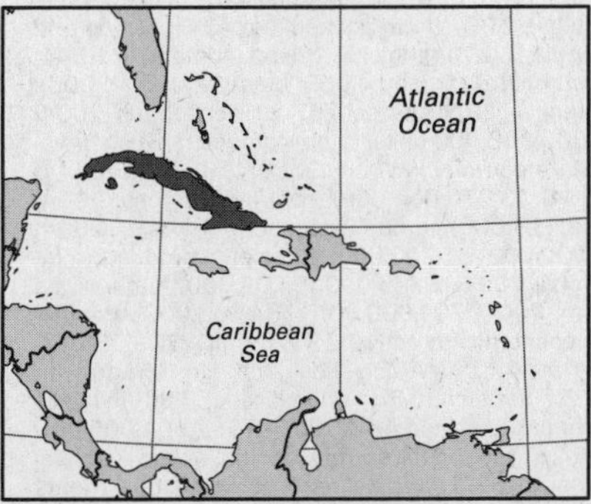

Official name: República de Cuba (Republic of Cuba). **Form of government:** unitary socialist republic with one legislative house (National Assembly of the People's Power [609]). **Head of state and government:** President Raúl Castro Ruz (from 2008). **Capital:** Havana. **Official language:** Spanish. **Official religion:** none. **Monetary unit:** 1 Cuban peso (CUP) = 100 centavos; valuation (1 Jul 2008) US$1 = 1.00 CUP.

Demography

Area: 42,804 sq mi, 110,861 sq km. **Population** (2007): 11,238,000. **Density** (2007): persons per sq mi 264.9, persons per sq km 102.3. **Urban** (2005): 75.5%. **Sex distribution** (2006): male 50.08%; female 49.92%. **Age breakdown** (2005): under 15, 19.2%; 15–29, 20.5%; 30–44, 27.6%; 45–59, 17.0%; 60–74, 10.8%; 75–84, 3.6%; 85 and over, 1.3%. **Ethnic composition** (1994): mixed 51.0%; white 37.0%; black 11.0%; other 1.0%. **Religious affiliation** (2005): Roman Catholic 47%; Protestant 5%; nonreligious 22%; other 26% (up to 70% of the population also practices Santería). **Major cities** (2002): Havana 2,201,610; Santiago de Cuba 423,392; Camagüey 301,574; Holguín 269,618; Santa Clara 210,220. **Location:** island southeast of Florida (US), between the North Atlantic Ocean and the Caribbean Sea.

Vital statistics

Birth rate per 1,000 population (2006): 9.9 (world avg. 20.3). **Death rate** per 1,000 population (2006): 7.2 (world avg. 8.6). **Natural increase rate** per 1,000 population (2006): 2.7 (world avg. 11.7). **Total fertility rate** (avg. births per childbearing woman; 2006): 1.40. **Life expectancy** at birth (2006): male 75.1 years; female 79.0 years.

National economy

Budget (2006). *Revenue:* CUP 30,012,400,000 (tax revenue 73.6%; nontax revenue 26.4%). *Expenditures:* CUP 31,742,400,000 (current revenue 84.2%, of which education 14.8%, social security contributions 11.2%, health 9.7%, housing and community services 7.2%; capital expenditure 15.8%). **Public debt** (external, outstanding; 2004): US$12,000,000,000. **Production** (metric tons except as noted). *Agriculture, forestry, fishing* (2005): raw sugar (2006) 1,300,000, tomatoes 802,600, plantains 770,000; livestock (number of live animals) 3,950,000 cattle, 2,361,000 sheep, 1,626,000 pigs; roundwood 2,579,000 (2005) cu m, of which fuelwood 70%; fisheries production 52,387 (from aquaculture 43%). *Mining and quarrying* (2004): nickel (metal content) 71,944; cobalt (metal content) 4,055. *Manufacturing* (2006): cement 1,713,900; steel 257,200; cigarettes (2004) 12,800,000,000 units. *Energy production (consumption):* electricity (kW-hr; 2006) 16,468,500,000 ([2004] 13,270,000,000); coal (metric tons; 2004) none (13,000); crude petroleum (barrels; 2004) 24,500,000 (31,300,000); petroleum products (metric tons; 2004) 1,896,000 (5,104,000); natural gas (cu m; 2004) 704,000,000 (704,000,000). **Population economically active** (2004): total 4,729,386; activity rate 42.1% (participation rates: ages 15 and over, 52.3%; female 36.5%; unemployed [2006] 1.9%). **Gross national income** (2006): US$51,504,000,000 (US$4,571 per capita). **Households.** Average household size (2002) 3.2. **Selected balance of payments data.** Receipts from (US$'000,000): tourism (2005) 1,920; remittances (2003) 1,200; official development assistance (2005) 83 (commitments). **Land use** as % of total land area (2003): in temporary crops 27.9%, in permanent crops 6.6%, in pasture 26.1%; overall forest area (2005) 24.7%.

Foreign trade

Imports (2001; f.o.b. in trading partners and c.i.f. for balance of trade and commodities): US$4,838,700,000 (machinery and transport equipment 25.5%, of which motor vehicles and parts 5.0%; food and live animals 15.7%, of which cereals 6.5%; refined petroleum 13.1%; crude petroleum 6.6%). *Major import sources* (2004): Spain 15.4%; Venezuela 13.7%; US 11.5%; China 8.0%; Canada 6.6%. **Exports** (2001): US$1,660,600,000 (raw sugar 32.6%; nickel [all forms] 27.8%; raw tobacco and tobacco products 15.8%; fresh and frozen fish 4.6%; medicinal and pharmaceutical products 2.4%). *Major export destinations* (2004): The Netherlands 23.5%; Canada 21.9%; China 8.3%; Russia 7.8%; Spain 6.6%.

Transport and communications

Transport. *Railroads* (2003; Cuban Railways only; length of railways exclusively for the transport of sugar equals 7,742 km): length 4,226 km; passenger-km (2001) 1,766,600; metric ton-km cargo 806,900,000. *Roads* (1999): total length 60,858 km (paved 49%). *Vehicles* (1998): passenger cars 172,574; trucks and buses 185,495. *Air transport* (2003; Cubana only): passenger-km 2,044,000,000; metric ton-km cargo 40,933,000. **Communications,** in total units (units per 1,000 persons). Daily newspaper circulation (2004): 400,000 (36); televisions (2004): 3,000,000 (267); telephone landlines (2006): 983,000 (101); cellular telephone subscribers (2006): 153,000 (14); personal computers (2005): 377,000 (33); total Internet users (2006): 240,000 (21).

Education and health

Educational attainment (2002): Percentage of population ages 25 and over having: no formal schooling 14.1%; primary education 17.2%; secondary 26.6%; vocational/technical/teacher training 32.8%; university 9.3%. **Literacy** (2004): total population ages 15 and over literate 96.9%; males literate 97.0%; females literate 96.8%. **Health** (2006): physicians 70,594 (1 per 160 persons); hospital beds (2004) 70,079 (1 per 160 persons); infant mortality rate per 1,000 live births 5.3. **Food** (2005): daily per capita caloric intake 3,547 (vegetable products 88%, animal products 12%); 183% of FAO recommended minimum.

Military

Total active duty personnel (2006): 49,000 (army 77.6%, navy 6.1%, air force 16.3%); US military forces at Naval Base Guantanamo Bay (2005) 950. **Military expenditure as percentage of GDP** (2005): 3.8%; per capita expenditure US$151.

Background

Several Indian groups, including the Ciboney, the Taino, and the Arawak, inhabited Cuba at the time of

1 metric ton = about 1.1 short tons; 1 kilometer = 0.6 mi (statute); 1 metric ton-km cargo = about 0.68 short ton-mi cargo; c.i.f.: cost, insurance, and freight; f.o.b.: free on board

the first Spanish contact. Christopher Columbus claimed the island for Spain in 1492, and the Spanish conquest began in 1511, when the settlement of Baracoa was founded. The native Indians were eradicated over the succeeding centuries, and African slaves, from the 18th century until slavery was abolished in 1886, were imported to work the sugar plantations. Cuba revolted unsuccessfully against Spain in the Ten Years' War (1868–78); a second war of independence began in 1895. In 1898 the US entered the war; Spain relinquished its claim to Cuba, which was occupied by the US for three years before gaining its independence in 1902. The US invested heavily in the Cuban sugar industry in the first half of the 20th century, and this, combined with tourism and gambling, caused the economy to prosper. Inequalities in the distribution of wealth persisted, however, as did political corruption. In 1958–59 the communist revolutionary Fidel Castro overthrew Cuba's longtime dictator, Fulgencio Batista, and established a socialist state aligned with the Soviet Union, abolishing capitalism and nationalizing foreign-owned enterprises. Relations with the US deteriorated, reaching a low point with the 1961 Bay of Pigs invasion and the 1962 Cuban missile crisis. In 1980 about 125,000 Cubans, including many that their government officially labeled "undesirables," were shipped to the US in the so-called "Mariel boat lift." When communism collapsed in the USSR, Cuba lost important financial backing and its economy suffered greatly. The latter gradually improved in the 1990s with the encouragement of tourism, though diplomatic relations with the US were not resumed.

Recent Developments

Following a severe stomach illness, longtime Cuban leader Fidel Castro had stepped down from power in July 2006, and in February 2008 he was officially succeeded as president by his brother Raúl Castro, who had been acting president. Cuba's relations with Venezuelan Pres. Hugo Chávez continued to deepen. Chávez met with Fidel several times, and in February 2007 the two countries signed agreements for US$1.5 billion in projects, including the development of 11 ethanol plants. In August the Venezuelan state oil company announced that it would explore for offshore oil in Cuban waters. Honduras named its first full ambassador to Cuba in 45 years, and in April Spain's foreign minister became the highest-level Spanish official to have visited Cuba in nearly a decade. Top Chinese officials also met with Raúl to pledge continuing political and economic cooperation, and Russia announced in November that it was restructuring Cuba's US$166 million debt. US-Cuban relations remained frozen, however. In the US Congress, a new Democratic majority introduced several proposals to repeal trade and travel sanctions, but none were passed.

Internet resources: <www.cubatravel.cu>.

Cyprus

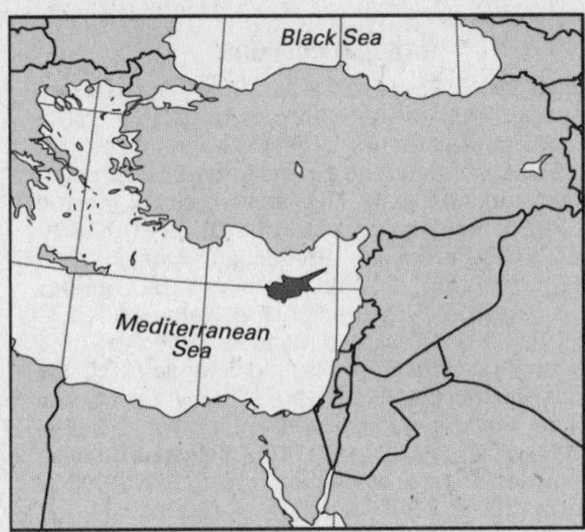

Two de facto states currently exist on the island of Cyprus: the Republic of Cyprus (ROC), predominantly Greek in character, occupying the southern two-thirds of the island, which is the original and still the internationally recognized de jure government of the whole island; and the Turkish Republic of Northern Cyprus (TRNC), proclaimed unilaterally 15 Nov 1983, on territory originally secured for the Turkish Cypriot population by the 20 Jul 1974 intervention of Turkey. Only Turkey recognizes the TRNC, and the two ethnic communities have failed to reestablish a single state. Provision of separate data below does not imply recognition of either state's claims but is necessitated by the lack of unified data.

Area: 3,572 sq mi, 9,251 sq km. **Population** (2007): 1,047,000; includes 150,000–160,000 "settlers" from Turkey; excludes 3,300 British military in the Sovereign Base Areas (SBA) in the ROC and 850 UN peacekeeping forces. **Location:** the Middle East, island in the Mediterranean Sea, south of Turkey.

Republic of Cyprus

Official name: Kipriakí Dhimokratía (Greek); Kibris Cumhuriyeti (Turkish) (Republic of Cyprus). **Form of government:** unitary multiparty republic with a unicameral legislature (House of Representatives [80]). **Head of state and government:** President Dimitris Christofias (from 2008). **Capital:** Lefkosia (Nicosia). **Official languages:** Greek; Turkish. **Monetary unit:** 1 euro (€) = 100 cents; valuation (1 Jul 2008) US$1 = €0.63.

Demography

Area (includes 99 sq mi [256 sq km] of British military SBA and 107 sq mi (278 sq km) of the UN Buffer Zone): 2,276 sq mi, 5,896 sq km. **Population** (2007): 781,000. **Age breakdown** (2005): under 15, 18.4%; 15–29, 23.9%; 30–44, 21.8%; 45–59, 19.2%; 60–74, 11.7%; 75–84, 3.9%; 85 and over, 1.1%. **Ethnic composition** (2000): Greek Cypriot 91.8%; Armenian 3.3%; Arab 2.9%, of which Lebanese 2.5%; British 1.4%; other 0.6%. **Religious affiliation** (2001): Greek Orthodox 94.8%; Roman Catholic 2.1%, of which Maronite 0.6%; Anglican 1.0%; Muslim 0.6%; other 1.5%. **Urban areas** (2004): Lefkosia (ROC only) 219,200; Limassol 172,500; Larnaca 77,000.

Vital statistics

Birth rate per 1,000 population (2006): 11.2 (world avg. 20.3). **Death rate** per 1,000 population (2006): 6.8 (world avg. 8.6). **Total fertility rate** (avg. births per childbearing woman; 2005) 1.42. **Life expectancy** at birth (2004–05): male 77.0 years; female 81.7 years.

National economy

Budget (2005). *Revenue:* £C 3,273,700,000 (excises and import duties 41.4%; income tax 22.3%; social security contributions 19.9%). *Expenditures:* £C 3,459,300,000 (current expenditures 91.3%; development expenditures 8.7%). **Gross national income** (at 2006 market prices): US$18,191,000,000 (US$23,735 per capita). **Production.** *Agriculture* (in '000 metric tons; 2005): potatoes 116.0, grapes 80.9, olives 27.5. *Manufacturing* (value added in US$'000,000; 2005): food products, beverages, and tobacco 281; cement, bricks, and ceramics 98; base metals and fabricated metal products 67. *Energy production (consumption):* electricity (kW-hr; 2005) 4,338,000,000 (3,931,000,000). **Selected balance of payments data.** Receipts from (US$'000,000): tourism (2006) 2,240; remittances (2006) 154; foreign direct investment (FDI) (2001–05 avg.) 1,027. Disbursements for (US$'000,000): tourism (2005) 932; remittances (2006) 278; FDI (2001–05 avg.) 450. **Land use** as % of total land area (2003): in temporary crops 12.4%, in permanent crops 4.4%, in pasture 0.4%; overall forest area (2005) 18.9%.

Foreign trade

Imports (2005; c.i.f.): £C 2,967,000,000 (consumer goods 33.0%; fuels and lubricants 16.2%; motor vehicles 10.2%; capital goods 9.1%). *Major import sources:* Greece 17.1%; Italy 10.1%; UK 8.8%; Germany 8.3%; Israel 7.0%. **Exports** (2005; f.o.b.): £C 672,000,000 (reexports 49.1%; domestic exports 35.7%, of which fresh vegetables, fruits, and nuts 8.1%, pharmaceuticals 7.5%; ships' stores 15.2%). *Major export destinations:* France 16.9%; UK 16.8%; Greece 11.4%; Germany 5.3%; UAE 2.6%.

Transport and communications

Transport. *Roads* (2004): total length 12,059 km (paved 65%). *Vehicles* (2004): cars 335,634; trucks and buses 121,024. *Air transport* (2005; Cyprus Airways only): passenger-km 3,187,000,000; metric ton-km cargo 46,607,000. **Communications,** in total units (units per 1,000 persons). Daily newspaper circulation (2004): 77,000 (104); televisions (2003): 276,000 (384); telephone landlines (2006): 408,000 (483); cellular telephone subscribers (2006): 778,000 (921); personal computers (2004): 249,000 (309); total Internet users (2006): 357,000 (422); broadband Internet subscribers (2006): 50,000 (59).

Education and health

Educational attainment (2004). Percentage of population ages 20 and over having: no formal schooling/incomplete primary education 10%; complete primary 20%; secondary 45%; higher education 25%. **Health** (2004): physicians 1,965 (1 per 375 persons); hospital beds 3,075 (1 per 240 persons); infant mortality rate per 1,000 live births (2005) 4.6.

Military

Total active duty personnel (2006): 10,000 (national guard 100%); Greek troops 950. **Military expenditure** as percentage of GDP (2005): 1.4%; per capita expenditure US$241.

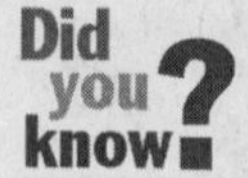

The city of Nicosia is the capital of the Republic of Cyprus. It lies along the Pedieos River, in the center of the Mesaoria Plain between the Kyrenia Mountains (north) and the Troodos range (south).

Turkish Republic of Northern Cyprus

Official name: Kuzey Kibris Türk Cumhuriyeti (Turkish Republic of Northern Cyprus). **Capital:** Lefkosa (Nicosia). **Official language:** Turkish. **Monetary unit:** 1 new Turkish lira (YTL) = 100 kurush; valuation (1 Jul 2008) US$1 = YTL 1.25. **Population** (2007; includes 150,000–160,000 "settlers" from Turkey; excludes 3,300 British military in the Sovereign Base Areas (SBA) in the ROC and 850 UN peacekeeping forces): 266,000 (Lefkosa [TRNC only; 2006] 49,237; Magusa [Famagusta; 2006] 34,803; Girne [Kyrenia; 2006] 24,122; Guzelyurt [Morphou; 2006] 12,425). **Ethnic composition** (2006): Turkish Cypriot/Turkish 96.8%; other 3.2%. **Budget** (2004). *Revenue:* US$885,187,000 (indirect taxes 21.4%; direct taxes 18.8%; foreign aid 13.9%; loans 11.8%). *Expenditures:* US$885,187,000 (wages 29.7%; social transfers 22.9%; investments 10.3%; defense 6.2%). **Imports** (2004; c.i.f.): US$853,100,000 (machinery and transport equipment 35.7%; food 9.4%). *Major import sources:* Turkey 60.1%; UK 10.7%. **Exports** (2004; f.o.b.): US$62,000,000 (citrus fruits 32.4%; clothing 18.9%). *Major export destinations:* Turkey 46.3%; UK 21.8%. **Health** (2004): physicians 422 (1 per 573 persons); hospital beds 1,291 (1 per 186 persons); infant mortality rate per 1,000 live births 10.0.

Background

Cyprus was inhabited by the early Neolithic Age; by the late Bronze Age it had been visited and settled by Mycenaeans and Achaeans, who introduced Greek culture and language, and it became a trading center. By 800 BC Phoenicians had begun to settle there. Ruled over the centuries by the Assyrian, Persian, and Ptolemaic empires, it was annexed by Rome in 58 BC. It was part of the Byzantine empire in the 4th–12th centuries AD. Cyprus was conquered by the English king Richard I in 1191. A part of the Venetian empire from 1489, it was taken by Ottoman Turks in 1571. In 1878 the British assumed control, and Cyprus became a British crown colony in 1925. It gained independence in 1960. Conflict between Greek and Turkish Cypriots led to the establishment of a UN peacekeeping mission in 1964. In 1974, fearing a movement to unite Cyprus with Greece, Turkish soldiers occupied the northern third of the country, and Turkish Cypriots established a functioning government, which obtained recognition only from Turkey. Conflict has continued to the present, and the UN peacekeeping mission has remained in place. Reunification talks have remained deadlocked.

1 metric ton = about 1.1 short tons; 1 kilometer = 0.6 mi (statute); 1 metric ton-km cargo = about 0.68 short ton-mi cargo; c.i.f.: cost, insurance, and freight; f.o.b.: free on board

Recent Developments

Cypriots from both sides routinely crossed the border to shop and work in 2007, though the UN's peacekeeping operations there remained. The Turkish Cypriots removed a controversial footbridge, and the Cyprus government dismantled a wall in Nicosia—both removals signifying a step toward establishing a pedestrian buffer zone—and in April 2008 officials opened a popular street in the capital as another border crossing. Problems persisted, however; title to confiscated real estate remained vexatious, for instance, and Turkish Cypriots protested the shipping of goods out of Greek Cypriot ports. European Union membership enhanced prosperity and provided economic stimulus to both zones, however, and tourism revenue increased on both sides.

Internet resources: <www.visitcyprus.com>.

Czech Republic

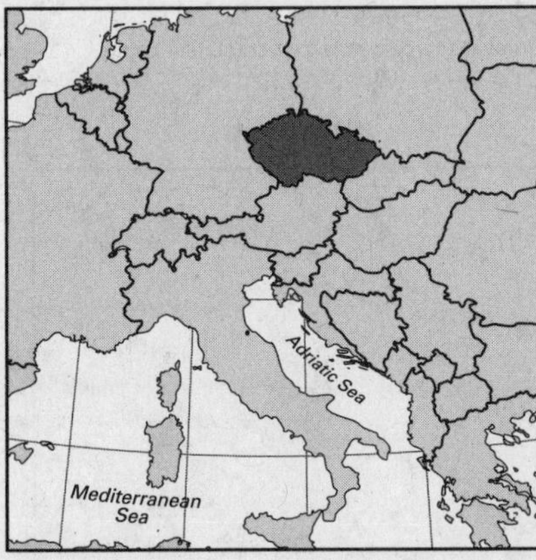

Official name: Ceska Republika (Czech Republic). **Form of government:** unitary multiparty republic with two legislative houses (Senate [81]; Chamber of Deputies [200]). **Chief of state:** President Vaclav Klaus (from 2003). **Head of government:** Prime Minister Mirek Topolanek (from 2006). **Capital:** Prague. **Official language:** Czech. **Official religion:** none. **Monetary unit:** 1 koruna (Kc) = 100 halura; valuation (1 Jul 2008) US$1 = 15.06 Kc.

Demography

Area: 30,450 sq mi, 78,866 sq km. **Population** (2007): 10,302,000. **Density** (2007): persons per sq mi 338.3, persons per sq km 130.6. **Urban** (2003): 74.3%. **Sex distribution** (2006): male 48.83%; female 51.17%. **Age breakdown** (2004): under 15, 14.9%; 15–29, 22.1%; 30–44, 21.3%; 45–59, 22.0%; 60–74, 13.6%; 75–84, 5.2%; 85 and over, 0.9%. **Ethnic composition** (2001): Czech 90.4%; Moravian 3.7%; Slovak 1.9%; Polish 0.5%; German 0.4%; Silesian 0.1%; Rom (Gypsy) 0.1%; other 2.9%. **Religious affiliation** (2000): Christian 63.0%, of which Roman Catholic 40.4%, unaffiliated Christian 16.0%, Protestant (mostly Lutheran) 3.1%, independent Christian (mostly independent Catholic [Hussite Church of the Czech Republic]) 2.6%; atheist 5.0%; Jewish 0.1%; nonreligious 31.9%. **Major cities** (2005): Prague 1,181,610; Brno 366,757; Ostrava 310,078; Plzen 162,759; Olomouc 100,381. **Location:** central Europe, bordering Germany, Poland, Slovakia, and Austria.

Vital statistics

Birth rate per 1,000 population (2006): 10.3 (world avg. 20.3); (2005) within marriage 68.3%. **Death rate** per 1,000 population (2006): 10.2 (world avg. 8.6). **Natural increase rate** per 1,000 population (2006): 0.1 (world avg. 11.7). **Total fertility rate** (avg. births per childbearing woman; 2005): 1.28. **Life expectancy** at birth (2005): male 72.9 years; female 79.1 years.

National economy

Budget (2005). *Revenue:* Kc 1,279,628,000,000 (tax revenue 82.8%, of which social security contributions 32.5%, taxes on goods and services 26.8%, taxes on income and profits 22.4%; nontax revenue 4.5%; grants 2.5%; other 10.2%). *Expenditures:* Kc 1,279,054,000,000 (social security and welfare 29.1%; health 14.5%; transportation and communications 9.8%; education 9.6%; defense 4.4%). **Production** (metric tons except as noted). *Agriculture, forestry, fishing* (2005): wheat 4,145,000, sugar beets 3,496,000, barley 2,195,000; livestock (number of live animals) 2,877,000 pigs, 1,397,000 cattle; roundwood 15,510,000 cu m, of which fuelwood 8%; fisheries production 24,697 (from aquaculture 83%). *Mining and quarrying* (2004): kaolin 4,100,000; feldspar 400,000. *Manufacturing* (value added in Kc '000,000; 2003): base and fabricated metals 93,380; food, beverages, and tobacco products 81,440; electrical and optical equipment 70,800. *Energy production (consumption):* electricity (kW-hr; 2004) 84,333,000,000 (57,118,-000,000); hard coal (metric tons; 2005) 13,248,000 ([2004] 9,860,000); lignite (metric tons; 2005) 48,780,000 ([2004] 48,430,000); crude petroleum (barrels; 2004) 2,074,000 (45,500,000); petroleum products (metric tons; 2004) 4,806,000 (6,578,000); natural gas (cu m; 2005) 202,000,000 ([2004] 10,969,000,000). **Households** (2004). Average household size 2.5; average annual income per household Kc 295,011 (US$11,479); sources of income: wages and salaries 66.7%, transfer payments 20.6%, self-employment 8.8%, other 3.9%; expenditure: food and nonalcoholic beverages 21.3%, housing and energy 19.3%, transportation 11.0%, recreation and culture 10.9%, household furnishings 6.5%. **Population economically active** (2005): total 5,174,000; activity rate of total population 50.6% (participation rates: ages 15–64, 70.4%; female 44.1%; unemployed [2006] 7.1%). **Public debt** (external, outstanding; 2004): US$12,020,000,000. **Gross national income** (2006): US$134,001,000,000 (US$13,152 per capita). **Selected balance of payments data.** Receipts from (US$'000,000): tourism (2005) 4,631; remittances (2006) 1,058; foreign direct investment (FDI) (2001–05 avg.) 6,438. Disbursements for (US$'000,000): tourism (2005) 2,405; remittances (2006) 2,645; FDI (2001–05 avg.) 490. **Land use** as % of total land area (2003): in temporary crops 39.6%, in permanent crops 3.1%, in pasture 12.6%; overall forest area (2005) 34.3%.

Foreign trade

Imports (2004): Kc 1,746,671,000,000 (machinery and apparatus 31.1%; chemicals and chemical products 10.4%; motor vehicles 9.8%; base metals 7.6%; fabricated metals 4.5%). *Major import sources:* Germany 31.7%; Slovakia 5.4%; Italy 5.3%; China 5.2%; Poland 4.8%. **Exports** (2004): Kc 1,723,731,000,000 (machinery and apparatus 34.1%, of which telecommunications equipment 6.6%, office machinery and computers 6.1%; motor vehicles 15.7%; fabricated metal products 6.6%; base metals 6.4%). *Major export destinations:* Germany 36.2%; Slovakia 8.5%; Austria 6.0%; Poland 5.3%; UK 4.7%.

Transport and communications

Transport. *Railroads* (2005): route length (2004) 9,441 km; passenger-km 6,667,000; metric ton-km cargo 14,866,000,000. *Roads* (2003): total length 127,672 km (paved 100%). *Vehicles* (2005): passenger cars 3,958,708; trucks and buses 435,235. *Air transport* (2005): passenger-km 9,735,710,000; metric ton-km cargo 44,668,000. **Communications,** in total units (units per 1,000 persons). Daily newspaper circulation (2004): 1,861,000 (182); televisions (2003): 5,488,000 (538); telephone landlines (2006): 3,541,000 (345); cellular telephone subscribers (2006): 12,150,000 (1,190); personal computers (2004): 5,100,000 (500); total Internet users (2006): 3,541,000 (347); broadband Internet subscribers (2006): 1,087,000 (106).

Education and health

Educational attainment (2001). Percentage of population ages 15 and over having: no formal schooling 0.2%; primary education 21.6%; secondary 68.7%; higher 9.5%. **Literacy** (2001): 99.8%. **Health** (2005): physicians 36,381 (1 per 282 persons); hospital beds 65,022 (1 per 158 persons); infant mortality rate per 1,000 live births (2006) 3.3. **Food** (2005): daily per capita caloric intake 3,303 (vegetable products 75%, animal products 25%); 163% of FAO recommended minimum.

Military

Total active duty personnel (2006): 22,272 (army 74.8%, air force 25.2%). **Military expenditure as percentage of GDP** (2005): 1.8%; per capita expenditure US$216.

Background

Until 1918 the history of what is now the Czech Republic was largely that of Bohemia. In that year the independent republic of Czechoslovakia was born through the union of Bohemia and Moravia with Slovakia. Czechoslovakia came under the domination of the Soviet Union after World War II, and from 1948 to 1989 it was ruled by a communist government. Its growing political liberalization was suppressed by a Soviet invasion in 1968. After communist rule collapsed in 1989–90, separatist sentiments emerged among the Slovaks, and in 1992 the Czechs and Slovaks agreed to break up their federated state. On 1 Jan 1993 the Czechoslovakian republic was peacefully dissolved and replaced by two new countries, the Czech Republic and Slovakia, with the region of Moravia remaining in the former. In 1999 the Czech Republic entered NATO and in 2004 the EU.

Recent Developments

Public finance reform was the most important policy issue in the Czech Republic in 2007. The government's proposed fiscal package included a shift to a flat tax on personal income, a reduction in corporate tax rates, and the introduction of fees for health care services. Critics emerged on both ends of the spectrum; while the left argued that the reforms would help only the rich, the right claimed that the measures failed to simplify the taxation system. In the end, however, the package was approved. From an international perspective, an incredibly controversial issue was the decision by the US to build a radar base in the Czech Republic as part of a missile-defense shield, an action most Czechs opposed. In April 2008 NATO approved the shield, setting in motion plans to begin construction, though Russia vehemently protested.

Internet resources: <www.czechtourism.com>.

Denmark

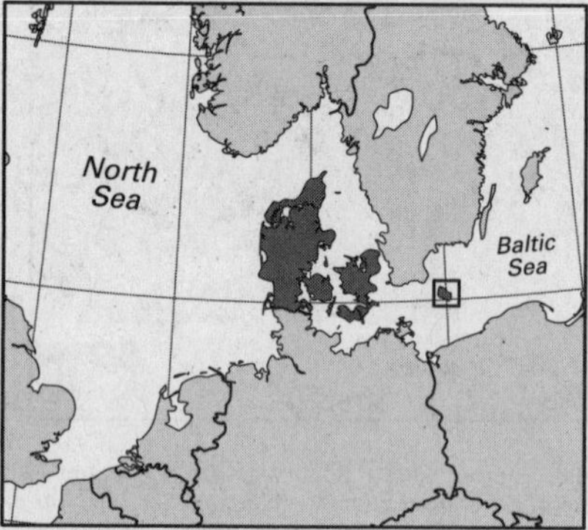

Official name: Kongeriget Danmark (Kingdom of Denmark). **Form of government:** constitutional monarchy with one legislative house (Folketing [179]). **Chief of state:** Queen Margrethe II (from 1972). **Head of government:** Prime Minister Anders Fogh Rasmussen (from 2001). **Capital:** Copenhagen. **Official language:** Danish. **Official religion:** Evangelical Lutheran. **Monetary unit:** 1 Danish krone (DKK; plural kroner) = 100 øre; valuation (1 Jul 2008) US$1 = DKK 4.72.

Demography

Area: 16,640 sq mi, 43,098 sq km (excludes the Faroe Islands and Greenland). **Population** (2007): 5,454,000. **Density** (2007): persons per sq mi 327.8, persons per sq km 126.5. **Urban** (2004): 85.4%. **Sex distribution** (2006): male 49.51%; female 50.49%. **Age breakdown** (2006): under 15,

1 metric ton = about 1.1 short tons; 1 kilometer = 0.6 mi (statute); 1 metric ton-km cargo = about 0.68 short ton-mi cargo; c.i.f.: cost, insurance, and freight; f.o.b.: free on board

18.6%; 15–29, 17.3%; 30–44, 21.9%; 45–59, 20.2%; 60–74, 15.0%; 75–84, 5.1%; 85 and over, 1.9%. **Ethnic composition** (2006): Danish 91.9%; Turkish 0.6%; German 0.5%; Iraqi 0.4%; Swedish 0.4%; Norwegian 0.3%; Bosnian 0.3%; other 5.6%. **Religious affiliation** (2006): Evangelical Lutheran 83.0%; other Christian 1.3%; Muslim 3.7%; nonreligious 5.4%; atheist 1.5%; other 5.1%. **Major urban areas** (2005): Greater Copenhagen 1,084,855; Århus 228,764; Odense 152,060; Ålborg 100,617; Frederiksberg 92,234. **Location:** northern Europe, bordering the North Sea, the Baltic Sea, and Germany.

Vital statistics

Birth rate per 1,000 population (2006): 12.0 (world avg. 20.3); (2005) within marriage 54.3%. **Death rate** per 1,000 population (2006): 10.3 (world avg. 8.6). **Natural increase rate** per 1,000 population (2006): 1.7 (world avg. 11.7). **Total fertility rate** (avg. births per childbearing woman; 2005): 1.80. **Life expectancy** at birth (2005): male 75.6 years; female 80.2 years.

National economy

Budget (2005). *Revenue:* DKK 882,940,000,000 (income/wealth taxes 54.4%; import/production taxes 31.0%; other 14.6%). *Expenditures:* DKK 821,539,000,000 (social protection 41.9%; education 15.2%; health 13.4%; economic affairs 6.6%; defense 2.9%). **National debt** (December 2006): US$57,887,000,000. **Population economically active** (2005): total 2,876,100; activity rate of total population 53.1% (participation rates: ages 15–64, 80.2%; female 47.0%; unemployed [July 2005–June 2006] 5.0%). **Households.** Average household size (2005) 2.2; average annual disposable income per household (2003) DKK 270,176 (US$41,010); sources of gross income (2003): wages and salaries 63.8%, transfers 24.6%, property income 6.8%, self-employment 3.9%; expenditure (2003): housing 22.5%, transportation and communications 15.7%, food 11.1%, recreation and entertainment 11.1%, energy 7.5%. **Production** (metric tons except as noted). *Agriculture, forestry, fishing* (2005): wheat 4,826,000, barley 3,730,000, sugar beets 2,800,000; livestock (number of live animals) 13,466,000 pigs, 1,544,000 cattle; roundwood 2,285,000 cu m, of which fuelwood 55%; fisheries production 949,625 (from aquaculture 4%). *Mining and quarrying* (2005): sand and gravel 29,000,000 cu m; chalk 1,950,000. *Manufacturing* (value of sales in DKK '000,000; 2005): food products 121,040; nonelectrical machinery and apparatus 66,050; computer and telecommunications equipment 49,078. *Energy production (consumption):* electricity (kW-hr; 2004) 40,260,000,000 (68,616,000,000); coal (metric tons; 2006) none (9,436,000); crude petroleum (barrels; 2006) 129,000,000 ([2005] 59,300,000); petroleum products (metric tons; 2004) 7,948,000 (7,050,000); natural gas (cu m; 2006) 10,358,000,000 (4,918,000,000). **Gross national income** (2006): US$278,800,000,000 (US$51,344 per capita). **Selected balance of payments data.** Receipts from (US$'000,000): tourism (2005) 4,493; remittances (2006) 869; foreign direct investment (FDI; 2001–05 avg.) 3,067. Disbursements for (US$'000,000): tourism (2005) 5,690; remittances (2006) 1,792; FDI (2001–05 avg.) 3,830. **Land use** as % of total land area (2003): in temporary crops 53.4%, in permanent crops 0.2%, in pasture 9.1%; overall forest area (2005) 11.8%.

Foreign trade

Imports (2005; c.i.f.): DKK 452,304,000,000 (machinery and apparatus [including parts] 23.1%; transport equipment and parts 16.9%; food, beverages, and tobacco 8.6%; chemical products 6.6%; fuels 6.6%; clothing and footwear 4.3%). *Major import sources:* Germany 20.7%; Sweden 13.7%; The Netherlands 6.6%; UK 6.0%; China 4.8%. **Exports** (2005; f.o.b.): DKK 506,920,000,000 (machinery and apparatus 26.4%; agricultural products 16.7%, of which swine meat 4.6%; mineral fuels and lubricants 10.3%; pharmaceuticals 7.6%; textiles and clothing 5.0%; furniture 3.2%). *Major export destinations:* Germany 17.3%; Sweden 13.3%; UK 9.0%; US 6.5%; Norway 5.3%.

Transport and communications

Transport. *Railroads* (2004): route length 2,644 km; passenger-km 6,132,000,000; metric ton-km cargo 1,976,000,000. *Roads* (2006): total length 72,362 km (paved 100%). *Vehicles* (2006): passenger cars 2,020,013; trucks and buses 508,788. *Air transport* (Danish share of Scandinavian Airlines System only): passenger-km (2005) 5,940,000,000; metric ton-km cargo (2004) 170,352,000. **Communications,** in total units (units per 1,000 persons). Daily newspaper circulation (2004): 1,328,000 (246); televisions (2003): 5,264,000 (977); telephone landlines (2006): 3,098,000 (569); cellular telephone subscribers (2006): 5,841,000 (1,073); personal computers (2004): 3,543,000 (659); total Internet users (2006): 3,171,000 (582); broadband Internet subscribers (2006): 1,728,000 (317).

Education and health

Educational attainment (2004). Percentage of population ages 25–69 having: complete lower secondary/unknown 30.3%; complete upper secondary or vocational 43.9%; undergraduate 19.6%; graduate 6.2%. **Literacy:** 100%. **Health:** physicians (2002) 15,692 (1 per 342 persons); hospital beds (2004) 20,638 (1 per 262 persons); infant mortality rate per 1,000 live births (2005) 4.4. **Food** (2005): daily per capita caloric intake 3,494 (vegetable products 67%, animal products 33%).

Military

Total active duty personnel (2006): 21,180 (army 59.0%, air force 19.8%, navy 18.0%, other 3.2%). **Military expenditure as percentage of GDP** (2005): 1.8%; per capita expenditure US$640.

Background

The Danes, a Scandinavian branch of the Teutons, settled the area c. the 6th century AD. During the Viking period the Danes expanded their territory, and by the 11th century the united Danish kingdom included parts of what are now Germany, Sweden, England, and Norway. Scandinavia was united under Danish rule from 1397 until 1523, when Sweden became independent; a series of debilitating wars with Sweden in the 17th century resulted in the Treaty of

Copenhagen (1660), which established the modern Scandinavian frontiers. Denmark gained and lost various other territories, including Norway, in the 19th and 20th centuries; it went through three constitutions between 1849 and 1915 and was occupied by Nazi Germany in 1940–45. A founding member of NATO (1949), Denmark adopted its current constitution in 1953. It became a member of the European Community in 1973 and modified its membership during the 1990s. The island of Zealand, on which Copenhagen stands, was connected to the central island of Funen by a rail tunnel and bridge in 1997. This ended more than 100 years of ferry service and cut the crossing time from an hour to under 10 minutes.

Recent Developments

With polls showing persistent opposition among Danes to their country's continued presence in Iraq, Denmark in August 2007 withdrew its 460-strong military force from southern Iraq, where it had been operating since 2003 under British command, and the remaining 55 troops in the Basra province were removed in late December 2007. However, the country enlarged its contingent in Afghanistan to 662 soldiers by early 2008 (most in the turbulent Helmand province). International disapproval of Denmark's tight immigration policy continued, with the Council of Europe challenging the government to soften its contentious stipulations for family reunification, drop stiff bank guarantees for immigrants, and call off cuts in welfare benefits for newly arrived immigrants. Meanwhile, Denmark enjoyed a robust economy, with almost four years of uninterrupted growth, the lowest unemployment in 33 years (about 3%), no foreign debt, and a budget surplus in excess of 3% of GDP.

Internet resources: <www.denmark.dk>.

Djibouti

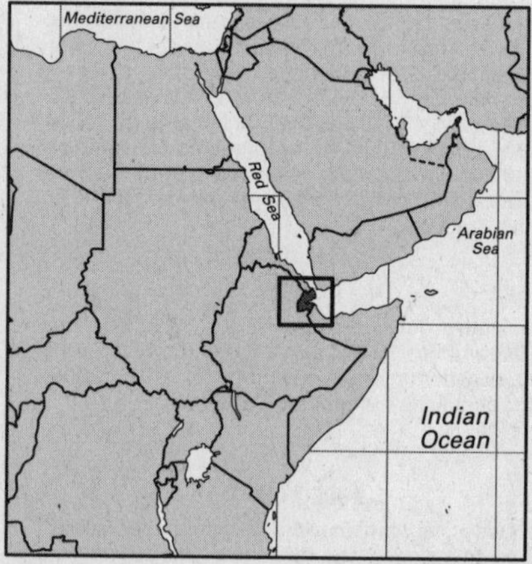

Official name: Jumhuriyah Jibuti (Arabic); République de Djibouti (French) (Republic of Djibouti). **Form of government:** multiparty republic with one legislative house (National Assembly [65]). **Chief of state and head of government:** President Ismail Omar Guelleh (from 1999), assisted by Prime Minister Dileita Muhammad Dileita (from 2001). **Capital:** Djibouti. **Official languages:** Arabic; French. **Official religion:** none. **Monetary unit:** 1 Djibouti franc (FDJ) = 100 centimes; valuation (1 Jul 2008) US$1 = FDJ 177.72.

Demography

Area: 8,950 sq mi, 23,200 sq km. **Population** (2007): 496,000. **Density** (2007): persons per sq mi 55.4, persons per sq km 21.4. **Urban** (2005): 86.1%. **Sex distribution** (2006): male 51.19%; female 48.81%. **Age breakdown** (2006): under 15, 43.3%; 15–29, 28.0%; 30–44, 13.7%; 45–59, 9.2%; 60–74, 5.1%; 75 and over, 0.7%. **Ethnic composition** (2000): Somali 46.0%; Afar 35.4%; Arab 11.0%; mixed African and European 3.0%; French 1.6%; other/unspecified 3.0%. **Religious affiliation** (2000): Muslim (nearly all Sunni) 94.1%; Christian 4.5%, of which Orthodox 3.0%, Roman Catholic 1.4%; nonreligious 1.3%; other 0.1%. **Major city and towns:** Djibouti (2006) 325,000; Dikhil (1991) 20,480; ʻAli Sabih (1991) 16,423; Tadjoura (1991) 7,309. **Location:** eastern Africa, bordering Eritrea, the Red Sea, the Gulf of Aden, Somalia, and Ethiopia.

Vital statistics

Birth rate per 1,000 population (2006): 39.5 (world avg. 20.3). **Death rate** per 1,000 population (2006): 19.3 (world avg. 8.6). **Natural increase rate** per 1,000 population (2006): 20.2 (world avg. 11.7). **Total fertility rate** (avg. births per childbearing woman; 2006): 5.31. **Life expectancy** at birth (2006): male 41.9 years; female 44.5 years.

National economy

Budget (2005). *Revenue:* FDJ 46,710,000,000 (tax revenue 65.8%, of which indirect taxes 26.3%, direct taxes 24.8%, transit taxes, harbor dues and other registration fees 14.7%; nontax revenue 17.5%; grants 16.7%). *Expenditures:* FDJ 46,378,000,000 (current expenditures 74.7%; capital expenditures 25.3%). **Public debt** (external, outstanding; February 2006): US$474,000,000. **Production** (metric tons except as noted). *Agriculture, forestry, fishing* (2005): lemons and limes 1,800, dry beans 1,500, tomatoes 1,283; livestock (number of live animals) 512,000 goats, 466,000 sheep, 69,000 camels; fisheries production 260. *Mining and quarrying*: mineral production limited to locally used construction materials such as basalt and evaporated salt. *Manufacturing* (2003): products of limited value include furniture, nonalcoholic beverages, meat and hides, light electromechanical goods, and mineral water. *Energy production (consumption):* electricity (kW-hr; 2005) 303,000,000 (220,000,000); petroleum products (metric tons; 2004) none (119,000); natural gas (cu m; 2004) none (4,380,000); geothermal, wind, and solar resources are substantial but largely undeveloped. **Population economically active** (2003): total 299,000; activity rate of total population 39.1% (participation rates: ages 15–64, 69.0%; female 39.5%; unemployed [2006] 60%). **Households.** Average household size (2004) 6.4; expenditure (1999; Djibouti city only): food 36.2%, housing and energy 18.1%, tobacco and related products 14.4%, transportation 8.8%, household furnishings 7.7%. **Gross national income** (2006): US$792,000,000 (US$968 per capita). **Selected balance of payments data.** Receipts from (US$'000,000): tourism (2005) 7.1; foreign direct investment (2001–05 avg.) 17; official development assistance (2005) 79. Disbursements for (US$'000,000): tourism (2005) 2.8. **Land use** as % of total land area (2003): in temporary crops 0.4%, in pasture 73.3%; overall forest area (2005) 0.2%.

Foreign trade

Imports (1999): US$152,700,000 (food and beverages 25.0%; machinery and electric appliances 12.5%; khat 12.2%; petroleum products 10.9%; transport equipment 10.3%). *Major import sources* (2004): Saudi Arabia 21.9%; India 18.7%; China 10.2%; Ethiopia 4.8%; France 4.7%. **Exports** (2001): US$10,200,000 (aircraft parts 24.5%; hides and skins of cattle, sheep, goats, and camels 20.6%; leather 7.8%; live animals 6.9%). *Major export destinations* (2005): Somalia 66.4%; Ethiopia 21.5%; Yemen 3.4%.

Transport and communications

Transport. *Railroads:* length (2006) 100 km; passenger-km (1999) 81,000,000; metric ton-km cargo (2002) 201,000,000. *Roads* (2002): total length 2,890 km (paved 13%). *Vehicles* (2002): passenger cars 15,700; trucks and buses 3,200. *Air transport* (2005): passenger arrivals and departures 219,119; metric tons of freight loaded and unloaded 10,973. **Communications,** in total units (units per 1,000 persons). Televisions (2004): 53,000 (114); telephone landlines (2005): 11,000 (23); cellular telephone subscribers (2005): 44,000 (94); personal computers (2005): 19,000 (41); total Internet users (2006): 11,000 (23); broadband Internet subscribers (2005): 40 (0.09).

Education and health

Literacy (2003): percentage of population ages 15 and over literate 68.0%; males literate 78.2%; females literate 58.6%. **Health:** physicians (2004) 129 (1 per 3,619 persons); hospital beds (2000) 694 (1 per 621 persons); infant mortality rate per 1,000 live births (2006) 102.4. **Food** (2005): daily per capita caloric intake 2,674 (vegetable products 90%, animal products 10%); 151% of FAO recommended minimum.

Military

Total active duty personnel (2006): 9,850 (army 81.3%, navy 2.0%, air force 2.5%, paramilitary 14.2%); foreign troops: French (2007) 2,700; US and German military personnel at Camp Lemonier (2006) 1,729 and 320, respectively. **Military expenditure as percentage of GDP** (2004): 4.0%; per capita expenditure US$52.

Background

Settled around the 3rd century BC by the Arab ancestors of the Afars, Djibouti was later populated by Somali Issas. In AD 825 Islam was brought to the area by missionaries. Arabs controlled the trade in this region until the 16th century; it became the French protectorate of French Somaliland in 1888. In 1946 it became a French overseas territory, and in 1977 it gained its independence. In the late 20th century, the country received refugees from the Ethiopian-Somali war and from civil conflicts in Eritrea. In the 1990s it suffered from political unrest.

Recent Developments

In January 2007 the United States military launched air raids on suspected al-Qaeda hideouts in southern Somalia from the Combined Joint Task Force–Horn of Africa, which was based at Camp Lemonier in Djibouti, the only official US military presence in Africa. Djibouti Pres. Ismail Omar Guelleh condemned the raids as being counterproductive to the diplomatic efforts being made to end the clashes in Somalia. An estimated 53,000 Djiboutians faced malnutrition and hunger when in April and May the UN World Food Programme halted its feeding programs due to a shortfall in funding.

Internet resources: <www.office-tourisme.dj>.

Dominica

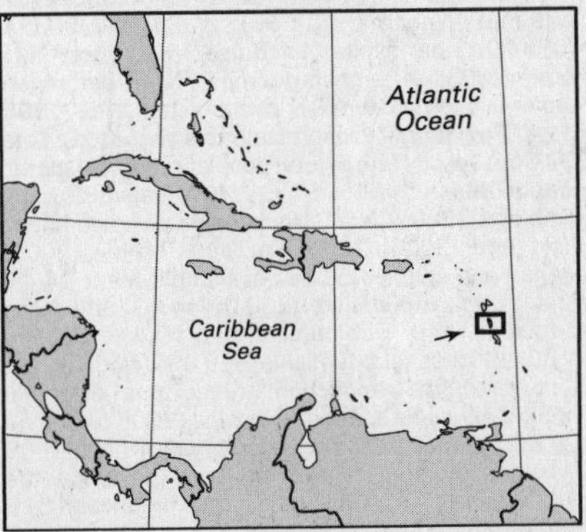

Official name: Commonwealth of Dominica. **Form of government:** multiparty republic with one legislative house (House of Assembly [31]). **Chief of state:** President Nicholas Liverpool (from 2003). **Head of government:** Prime Minister Roosevelt Skerrit (from 2004). **Capital:** Roseau. **Official language:** English. **Official religion:** none. **Monetary unit:** 1 East Caribbean dollar (EC$) = 100 cents; valuation (1 Jul 2008) US$1 = EC$2.70.

Demography

Area: 290 sq mi, 750 sq km. **Population** (2007): 70,600. **Density** (2007): persons per sq mi 243.4, persons per sq km 94.1. **Urban** (2003): 72.0%. **Sex distribution** (2006): male 50.34%; female 49.66%. **Age breakdown** (2006): under 15, 26.1%; 15–29, 23.8%; 30–44, 27.4%; 45–59, 12.4%; 60–74, 7.0%; 75 and over, 3.3%. **Ethnic composition** (2000): black 88.3%; mulatto 7.3%; black-Amerindian 1.7%; British expatriates 1.0%; Indo-Pakistani 1.0%; other 0.7%. **Religious affiliation** (2001): Roman Catholic 61%; four largest Protestant groups (including Seventh-day Adventist, Pentecostal groups, and Methodist) 28%;

nonreligious 6%; other 5%. **Major towns** (2004): Roseau 20,200; Berekua 4,000; Portsmouth 3,600; Marigot 2,900; Atkinson (1991) 2,518. **Location:** island in the southern Caribbean Sea, south of Guadeloupe and north of Martinique.

Vital statistics

Birth rate per 1,000 population (2006): 15.3 (world avg. 20.3); (1991) within marriage 24.1%. **Death rate** per 1,000 population (2006): 6.7 (world avg. 8.6). **Natural increase rate** per 1,000 population (2006): 8.5 (world avg. 11.7). **Total fertility rate** (avg. births per childbearing woman; 2006): 1.94. **Life expectancy** at birth (2006): male 72.0 years; female 77.9 years.

National economy

Budget (2005–06). *Revenue:* EC$325,000,000 (tax revenue 73.7%, of which taxes on international trade and transactions 29.8%, taxes on goods and services 25.3%; grants 18.6%; nontax revenue 7.3%; development revenue 0.4%). *Expenditures:* EC$315,300,000 (current expenditures 76.2%, of which wages 33.4%, transfers 14.7%, debt payment 13.6%; development expenditures and net lending 23.8%). **Public debt** (external, outstanding; 2004): US$186,700,000. **Gross national income** (2006): US$287,000,000 (US$4,242 per capita). **Land use** as % of total land area (2003): in temporary crops 7%, in permanent crops 21%, in pasture 3%; overall forest area (2005) 61%. **Population economically active** (2001): total 27,865; activity rate of total population 40.0% (participation rates: ages 15–64, 64.7%; female 38.9%; unemployed [2002] 25%). **Households.** Average household size (2003) 3.0; sources of income (2001): wages and salaries 68.2%, self-employment 24.4%, other 7.4%; expenditure (2001): food 32.9%, transportation and communications 19.4%, housing 11.2%, household furnishings 9.4%, clothing and footwear 8.2%. **Production** (metric tons except as noted). *Agriculture, forestry, fishing* (2005): bananas 29,000, grapefruit and pomelos 17,000, taro 11,200; livestock (number of live animals) 13,400 cattle, 9,700 goats, 7,600 sheep; fisheries production 579. *Mining and quarrying:* pumice, limestone, and sand and gravel are quarried primarily for local consumption. *Manufacturing* (value of production in EC$'000; 2004): toilet and laundry soap 24,588; toothpaste 8,774; crude coconut oil (2001) 1,758. *Energy production (consumption):* electricity (kW-hr; 2004) 79,000,000 (79,000,000); petroleum products (metric tons; 2004) none (35,000). **Selected balance of payments data.** Receipts from (US$'000,000): tourism (2005) 56; remittances (2005) 4; foreign direct investment (2001–05 avg.) 24; official development assistance (2005) 37 (commitments). Disbursements for (US$'000,000): tourism (2005) 10.

Foreign trade

Imports (2004; f.o.b. in balance of trade and c.i.f. in commodities and trading partners): US$144,200,000 (machinery and apparatus 25.1%; food, beverages, and tobacco 19.1%; mineral fuels 11.1%; telecommunications equipment 7.3%). *Major import sources* (2003): Japan 21.6%; US 15.1%; China 14.8%; Trinidad and Tobago 12.0%; South Korea 7.7%. **Exports** (2004): US$42,200,000 (agricultural exports 31.8%, of which bananas 17.2%; manufactured exports 61.8%, of which coconut-based soaps 26.4%; reexports 4.0%). *Major export destinations* (2003): Japan 27.1%; UK 16.4%; Jamaica 15.1%; US 6.6%; Antigua and Barbuda 6.2%.

Transport and communications

Transport. *Roads* (1999): total length 780 km (paved 50%). *Vehicles* (1998): passenger cars 8,700; trucks and buses 3,400. *Air transport* (1997): passenger arrivals and departures 74,100; cargo loaded and unloaded 938 metric tons. **Communications,** in total units (units per 1,000 persons). Televisions (2000): 16,000 (220); telephone landlines (2004): 21,000 (295); cellular telephone subscribers (2004): 42,000 (589); personal computers (2004): 13,000 (182); total Internet users (2005): 26,000 (372); broadband Internet subscribers (2004): 3,300 (46).

Education and health

Educational attainment (2002). Percentage of population ages 15 and over having: primary education 62%; secondary 31%; vocational/university 7%. **Literacy** (1996): total population ages 15 and over literate, 94.0%. **Health** (2004): physicians 38 (1 per 1,824 persons); hospital beds (2002) 270 (1 per 257 persons); infant mortality rate per 1,000 live births (2006) 13.7. **Food** (2005): daily per capita caloric intake 3,083 (vegetable products 78%, animal products 22%); 160% of FAO recommended minimum.

Military

Total active duty personnel (2003): none.

Background

At the time of the arrival of Christopher Columbus in 1493, Dominica was inhabited by the Caribs. With its steep coastal cliffs and inaccessible mountains, it was one of the last islands to be explored by Europeans, and the Caribs remained in possession until the 18th century; it was then settled by the French and ultimately taken by Britain in 1783. Subsequent hostilities between the settlers and the native inhabitants resulted in the Caribs' near extinction. Incorporated with the Leeward Islands in 1883 and with the Windward Islands in 1940, it became a member of the West Indies Federation in 1958. Dominica became independent in 1978.

Recent Developments

Dominica began talks in early 2007 with Venezuela concerning the building by Caracas of an $80 million, 1,600 bbl-per-day refinery in the country. The project would be funded under the PetroCaribe oil-assistance program introduced by Venezuelan Pres. Hugo Chávez to help Caribbean territories hard hit by rising oil costs. The political opposition insisted, however, that the government did not have a mandate to establish a refinery in Dominica.

Internet resources: <www.ndcdominica.dm>.

1 metric ton = about 1.1 short tons; 1 kilometer = 0.6 mi (statute); 1 metric ton-km cargo = about 0.68 short ton-mi cargo; c.i.f.: cost, insurance, and freight; f.o.b.: free on board

Dominican Republic

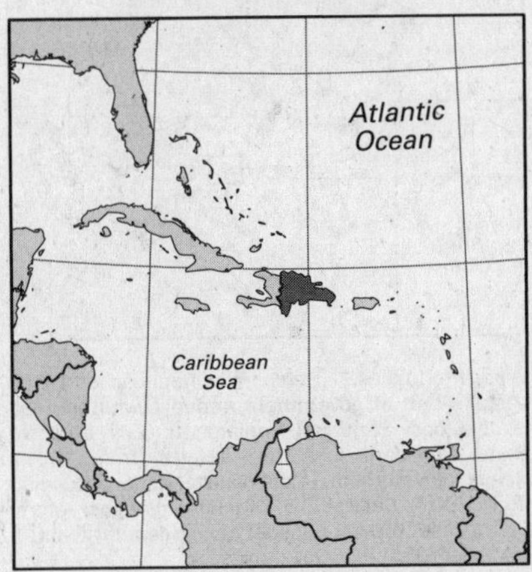

Official name: República Dominicana (Dominican Republic). **Form of government:** multiparty republic with two legislative houses (Senate [32]; Chamber of Deputies [178]). **Head of state and government:** President Leonel Fernández Reyna (from 2004). **Capital:** Santo Domingo. **Official language:** Spanish. **Official religion:** none (Roman Catholicism is the state religion per concordat with Vatican City). **Monetary unit:** 1 Dominican peso (RD$) = 100 centavos; valuation (1 Jul 2008) US$1 = RD$34.15.

Demography

Area: 18,792 sq mi, 48,671 sq km. **Population** (2007): 9,366,000. **Density** (2007): persons per sq mi 498.4, persons per sq km 192.4. **Urban** (2005): 66.8%. **Sex distribution** (2005): male 50.18%; female 49.82%. **Age breakdown** (2002): under 15, 33.5%; 15–29, 26.6%; 30–44, 20.2%; 45–59, 11.7%; 60–74, 5.9%; 75–84, 1.6%; 85 and over, 0.5%. **Ethnic composition** (2003): mulatto 73%; white 16%; black 11%. **Religious affiliation** (2004): Roman Catholic 64.4%; other Christian 11.4%; nonreligious 22.5%; other 1.7%. **Major urban centres** (2002): Santo Domingo 1,887,586; Santiago 507,418; San Pedro de Macorís 193,713; La Romana 191,303; San Cristóbal 137,422. **Location:** eastern two-thirds of the island of Hispaniola, bordered by the North Atlantic Ocean, the Caribbean Sea, and Haiti.

Vital statistics

Birth rate per 1,000 population (2006): 23.2 (world avg. 20.3). **Death rate** per 1,000 population (2006): 5.4 (world avg. 8.6). **Total fertility rate** (avg. births per childbearing woman; 2006): 2.83. **Marriage/divorce rates** per 1,000 population (2001): 2.8/1.0. **Life expectancy** at birth (2006): male 71.0 years; female 74.5 years.

National economy

Budget (2005). *Revenue:* RD$157,585,000,000 (tax revenue 94.2%, of which taxes on goods and services 49.0%, import duties 24.0%, income taxes 18.8%; nontax revenue 5.8%). *Expenditures:* RD$161,612,000,000 (current expenditures 75.7%; development expenditures 24.3%). **Public debt** (external, outstanding; 2005): US$6,093,000,000. **Gross national income** (2006): US$29,890,000,000 (US$3,109 per capita). **Households** (1997–98). Average household size (2002) 3.9; average annual household income RD$130,394 (US$8,745); sources of income: wages and salaries 32.1%, self-employment 31.0%, nonmonetary income 22.8%, transfers 12.0%; expenditure: food, beverages, and tobacco 33.2%, transportation 16.0%, housing 9.3%, clothing and footwear 7.9%. **Production** (metric tons except as noted). *Agriculture, forestry, fishing* (2005): sugarcane 4,950,000, rice 566,000, bananas 500,000; livestock (number of live animals) 2,200,000 cattle, 47,500,000 chickens; roundwood 562,300 cu m, of which fuelwood 99%; fisheries production 12,086 (from aquaculture 8%). *Mining* (2005): nickel (metal content) 47,000; marble 10,384 cu m. *Manufacturing* (2005): cement 2,779,000; refined sugar 139,203; beer 4,541,000 hectolitres. *Energy production (consumption):* electricity (kW-hr; 2004) 13,760,000,000 (13,760,000,000); coal (metric tons; 2004) none (777,000); crude petroleum (barrels; 2004) none (33,500,000); petroleum products (metric tons; 2004) 1,993,000 (5,151,000); natural gas (cu m; 2004) none (5,305,000). **Population economically active** (2004): total 3,701,804; activity rate of total population 43.1% (participation rates: ages 10 and over, 55.1%; female 38.7%; unemployed [2006] 16.2%). **Selected balance of payments data.** Receipts from (US$'000,000): tourism (2006) 3,792; remittances (2006) 2,911; foreign direct investment (2001–05 avg.) 853. Disbursements for (US$'000,000): tourism (2005) 352; remittances (2005) 26. **Land use** as % of total land area (2003): in temporary crops 22.7%, in permanent crops 10.3%, in pasture 43.4%; overall forest area (2005) 28.4%.

Foreign trade

Imports (2006): US$8,745,000,000 (consumer goods 50.7%, of which refined petroleum 21.0%, food products 5.8%; capital goods 15.4%; crude petroleum 10.9%). *Major import sources* (2005): US 50.0%; Colombia 6.2%; Mexico 5.8%. **Exports** (2006): US$6,440,000,000 (reexports from free zones 70.0%, of which assembled clothing 24.8%, electronics 10.3%, jewelry 9.8%; ferronickel 11.0%; fuels 5.6%; raw sugar 1.6%): *Major export destinations* (2005): US 78.9%; The Netherlands 2.4%; Mexico 1.9%.

Transport and communications

Transport. *Railroads* (2004): route length 615 km (includes 240 km of track that is privately owned and serves the sugar industry only). *Roads* (2002): total length 19,705 km (paved 51%). *Vehicles* (2001): passenger cars 561,300; trucks and buses 284,700. *Air transport*: passenger-km (1999) 4,900,000; metric ton-km cargo (2003) 200,000. **Communications,** in total units (units per 1,000 persons). Daily newspaper circulation (2005): 283,000 (30); televisions (2004): 1,950,000 (209); telephone landlines (2006): 897,000 (99); cellular telephone subscribers (2006): 4,606,000 (511); personal computers (2005): 206,000 (22); total Internet users (2006): 2,000,000 (222); broadband Internet subscribers (2006): 67,000 (7.1).

Education and health

Educational attainment (2002). Percentage of population ages 25 and older having: no formal education/unknown 4.1%; incomplete/complete primary education 53.1%; secondary 25.9%; undergraduate 15.9%; graduate 1.0%. **Literacy** (2003): total population ages 15 and over literate 84.7%. **Health:** physicians (2005; public sector only) 12,966 (1 per 730 persons); hospital beds (2005) 9,640 (1 per 982 persons); infant mortality rate (2006) 29.0. **Food** (2005): daily per capita caloric intake 2,673 (vegetable products 84%, animal products 16%); 139% of FAO recommended minimum.

Military

Total active duty personnel (2006): 24,500 (army 61.2%, navy 16.3%, air force 22.5%). **Military expenditure as percentage of GDP** (2005): 0.5%; per capita expenditure US$20.

Background

The Dominican Republic was originally part of the Spanish colony of Hispaniola. In 1697 the western third of the island, which later became Haiti, was ceded to France; the remainder of the island passed to France in 1795. The eastern two-thirds of the island was returned to Spain in 1809, and the colony declared its independence in 1821. Within a matter of weeks it was overrun by Haitian troops and occupied until 1844. Since then the country has been under the rule of a succession of dictators, except for short interludes of democratic government, and the US has frequently been involved in its affairs. The termination of the dictatorship of Rafael Trujillo in 1961 led to civil war in 1965 and US military intervention. The country suffered from severe hurricanes in 1979 and 1998.

Recent Developments

In 2007 the Dominican Republic remained a country of economic and social contrasts. The burgeoning economy of the previous three years continued with an increase of 8.3% in GDP (one of the highest in Latin America), an improved fiscal regulatory system, better tax collection, and a manageable inflation rate of 6%. Business confidence was strengthened with the implementation in March of the Central America–Dominican Republic Free Trade Agreement (CAFTA–DR) with the US. However, the Dominican Republic ranked 79th out of 177 countries in the 2007–08 UN Human Development Report and 26th out of 108 less-developed countries on the UN Poverty Index. The quality of public education and public health remained poor, and the government invested more in the capital's subway project than in both of those sectors combined. Little discernible headway was made against corruption.

Internet resources:
<www.godominicanrepublic.com>.

East Timor

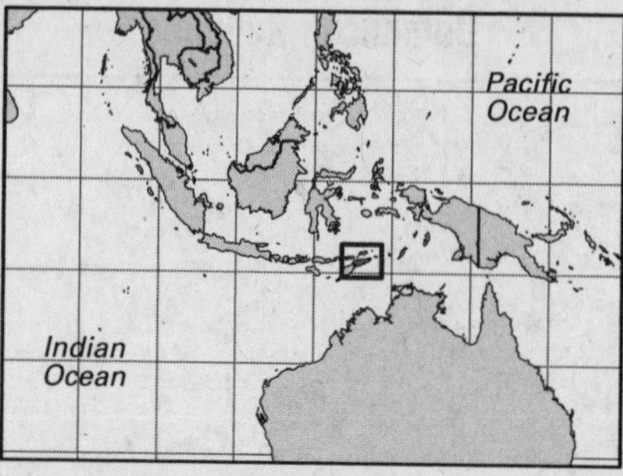

Official name: Repúblika Demokrátika Timor Lorosa'e (Tetum); República Democrática de Timor-Leste (Portuguese) (Democratic Republic of Timor-Leste). **Form of government:** republic with one legislative body (National Parliament [65]). **Chief of State:** President José Ramos-Horta (from 2007). **Head of government:** Prime Minister Xanana Gusmão (from 2007). **Capital:** Dili. **Official languages:** Tetum; Portuguese. **Official religion:** none. **Monetary unit:** 1 US dollar (US$) = 100 centavos.

Demography

Area: 5,760 sq mi, 14,919 sq km. **Population** (2007): 1,155,000. **Density** (2007): persons per sq mi 200.5, persons per sq km 77.4. **Urban** (2005): 7.8%. **Sex distribution** (2006): male 50.86%; female 49.14%. **Age breakdown** (2006): under 15, 36.3%; 15–29, 28.9%; 30–44, 18.4%; 45–59, 11.2%; 60–74, 4.4%; 75 and over, 0.8%. **Ethnic composition** (1999): East Timorese 80%; other (nearly all Indonesian, and particularly West Timorese) 20%. **Religious affiliation** (2005): Roman Catholic 98%; Protestant 1%; Muslim 1%. **Major urban areas** (2004): Dili 151,026; Los Palos (Lospalos) 12,612; Same 9,966; Pante Macassar 9,754; Maliana 9,721. **Location:** southeast Asia, eastern end of the island of Timor plus an exclave on the western end, bordering the Timor Sea and Indonesia.

Vital statistics

Birth rate per 1,000 population (2006): 27.0 (world avg. 20.3). **Death rate** per 1,000 population (2006): 6.2 (world avg. 8.6). **Natural increase rate** per 1,000 population (2006): 20.8 (world avg. 11.7). **Total fertility rate** (avg. births per childbearing woman; 2006): 3.53. **Life expectancy** at birth (2006): male 64.0 years; female 68.7 years.

National economy

Budget (2005–06). *Revenue:* US$485,000,000 (oil and gas revenue 93.1%, of which taxes 74.8%, royalties 15.5%; domestic revenue 6.9%). *Expenditures:* US$93,000,000 (current expenditure 71.3%; capital expenditure 16.9%; previous year spending 11.8%). **Production** (metric tons except as noted). *Agriculture, forestry, fishing* (2005): corn (maize) 80,000, rice 65,000, cassava 41,500; livestock (number of live animals) 346,000 pigs, 110,000 buffalo, 20,000 beehives; fisheries production 350. *Mining and quarrying* (2005): commercial quantities of marble are exported. *Manufacturing* (2001): principally the production of textiles, garments, handicrafts, bottled water, and processed coffee. *Energy production (consumption):* electricity (kW-hr; 2004) 300,000,000 (300,000,000); crude petroleum (barrels; 2004) 990,000 (negligible); petroleum products (metric tons; 2004) 6,700,000 (57,000). **Households.** Average household size (2004) 4.7. **Population economically active** (2001): total 232,000; activity rate of total population 28% (participation rates: ages 15–64, 57%; unemployed 50%). **Gross national income** (2006): US$847,000,000 (US$761 per capita). **Selected balance of payments data.** Receipts from (US$'000,000): foreign direct investment (2001–05 avg.) 19; official development assistance (2005) 185. **Land use** as % of total land area (2003): in temporary crops 8.2%, in permanent crops 4.6%, in pasture 10.1%; overall forest area (2005) 53.7%.

Foreign trade

Imports (2004): US$146,100,000 (mineral fuels and oils 25.2%; vehicles and vehicle parts 10.1%; electrical machinery and equipment 6.7%; cereals 5.6%). *Major import sources:* Indonesia 42.8%; Australia 17.1%; Singapore 11.2%; Vietnam 3.6%; Portugal 3.0%. **Exports** (2004): US$6,972,000 (coffee 86.1%). *Major export destinations:* Australia 41.7%; Japan 22.8%; Portugal 13.0%; US 4.1%.

Transport and communications

Transport. *Roads* (2005): total length 5,000 km (paved 50%). *Vehicles* (1998): passenger cars 3,156; trucks and buses 7,140. **Communications,** in total units (units per 1,000 persons). Daily newspaper circulation (2004): 600 (0.7); telephone landlines (1996): 6,600 (8); total Internet users (2004): 1,000 (1.1).

Education and health

Educational attainment (2002). Percentage of population ages 15 and over having: no formal education 54.3%; some primary education 14.4%; complete primary 6.2%; lower secondary 10.4%; upper secondary and higher 14.7%. **Literacy** (2005): percentage of population ages 15 and over literate 49%; males literate 54%; females literate 45%. **Health:** physicians (2002) 47 (1 per 17,355 persons); hospital beds (1999) 560 (1 per 1,277 persons); infant mortality rate per 1,000 live births (2006) 45.9.

Military

Total active duty personnel (2006): 1,250 (army 100%); UN peacekeeping personnel were withdrawn in May 2005, and 600 police personnel were reintroduced in August 2006. **Military expenditure as percentage of GDP** (2003): 1.3%; per capita expenditure US$5.

Background

The Portuguese first settled on the island of Timor in 1520 and were granted rule over Timor's eastern half in 1860. The Timor political party Fretilin declared East Timor independent in 1975 after Portugal withdrew its troops. It was invaded by Indonesian forces and was incorporated as a province of Indonesia in 1976. The takeover, which resulted in thousands of East Timorese deaths during the next two decades, was disputed by the UN. In 1999 an independence referendum won overwhelmingly; civilian militias, armed by the military and led by local supporters of integration, then rampaged through the province, killing 1,000–2,000 people. The Indonesian parliament rescinded Indonesia's annexation of the territory, and East Timor was returned to its preannexation status as a non-self-governing territory, though this time under UN supervision. Preparation for independence got under way in 2001, with East Timorese voting by universal suffrage in August for a Constituent Assembly of 88 members. Independence was declared on 20 May 2002 and was followed by the swearing in of Xanana Gusmão as the first president of the country.

Recent Developments

Prime Minister José Ramos-Horta, corecipient of the 1996 Nobel Prize for Peace, won East Timor's presidential runoff election in May 2007. Ramos-Horta swore in former president Xanana Gusmão as prime minister in August, even though Gusmão's party had won fewer seats than the ruling party in parliamentary elections in June. Two days of rioting followed in which hundreds of buildings and cars were set on fire. In February 2008 Ramos-Horta was seriously wounded in an assassination attempt.

Internet resources:
<www.turismotimorleste.com/en>.

Ecuador

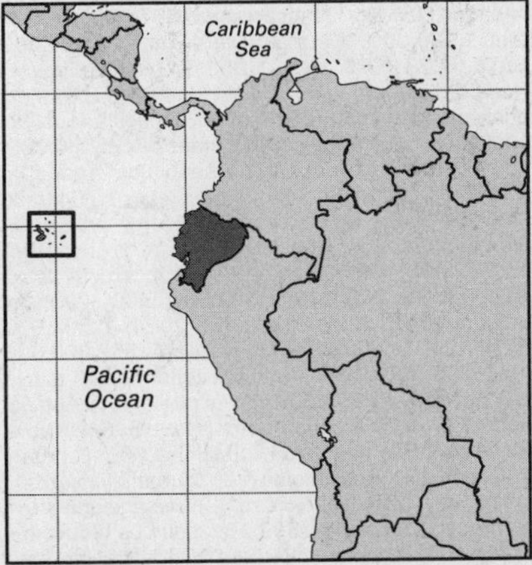

Official name: República del Ecuador (Republic of Ecuador). **Form of government:** unitary multiparty republic with one legislative house (National Congress [100]). **Head of state and government:** President Rafael Correa Delgado (from 2007). **Capital:** Quito. **Official language:** Spanish (Quechua and Shuar are also official languages for the indigenous peoples). **Official religion:** none. **Monetary unit:** 1 US dollar (US$) = 100 cents.

Demography

Area: 105,037 sq mi, 272,045 sq km. **Population** (2007): 13,341,000. **Density** (2007): persons per sq mi 127.0, persons per sq km 49.0. **Urban** (2005):

62.8% **Sex distribution** (2005): male 50.15%; female 49.85%. **Age breakdown** (2005): under 15, 32.6%; 15–29, 27.4%; 30–44, 19.5%; 45–59, 12.1%; 60–74, 6.1%; 75–84, 1.8%; 85 and over, 0.5%. **Ethnic composition** (2000): mestizo 42.0%; Amerindian 40.8%; white 10.6%; black 5.0%; other 1.6%. **Religious affiliation** (2005): Roman Catholic (practicing) 35%; Roman Catholic (nonpracticing) 50%; other (significantly Evangelical Protestant) 15%. **Major cities** (2003): Guayaquil (urban agglomeration) 2,387,000; Quito (urban agglomeration) 1,514,000; Cuenca 303,994; Machala 217,266; Santo Domingo de los Colorados 211,689. **Location:** northwestern South America, bordering Colombia, Peru, and the Pacific Ocean.

Vital statistics

Birth rate per 1,000 population (2005): 22.1 (world avg. 20.3). **Death rate** per 1,000 population (2005): 5.0 (world avg. 8.6). **Total fertility rate** (avg. births per childbearing woman; 2005): 2.70. **Life expectancy** at birth (2005): male 71.7 years; female 77.6 years.

National economy

Budget (2006). *Revenue:* US$6,895,000,000 (nonpetroleum revenue 75.1%, of which value-added tax 32.3%, income tax 15.5%, customs duties 9.0%; petroleum export revenue 24.9%). *Expenditures:* US$7,011,000,000 (current expenditure 76.2%; capital expenditure 23.8%). **Production** (metric tons except as noted). *Agriculture, forestry, fishing* (2005): bananas 5,878,000, sugarcane 5,657,000, oil palm fruit 1,930,000; livestock (live animals) 4,971,000 cattle, 1,281,000 pigs, 1,053,000 sheep; roundwood 6,638,000 cu m, of which fuelwood 82%; fisheries production 486,023 (from aquaculture 16%). *Mining and quarrying* (2004): limestone 5,160,000; gold 5,300 kg. *Manufacturing* (value added in US$'000,000; 2004): refined petroleum 1,794; food products 870; beverages 845. *Energy production (consumption):* electricity (kW-hr; 2004) 11,702,000,000 (13,344,000,000); crude petroleum (barrels; 2006) 197,000,000 (55,000,000); petroleum products (metric tons; 2004) 6,594,000 (5,777,000); natural gas (cu m; 2004) 352,000,000 (352,000,000). **Population economically active** (2005): total 4,225,400; activity rate of total population 47.9% (participation rates: ages 15–64, 70.6%; female 41.5%; unemployed [March 2006–February 2007] 10.1%). **Households** (2003; urban households only). Average household size 4.2; average annual income per household US$8,161; sources of income: wages 47.0%, self-employment 25.6%, transfer payments 15.7%, rent 11.7%; expenditure: food, beverages, and tobacco 23.8%, housing and energy 19.1%, transportation and communications 12.9%, restaurants and hotels 10.4%, clothing 8.1%. **Public debt** (external, outstanding; December 2006): US$10,215,000,000. **Gross national income** (2006): US$36,796,000,000 (US$2,787 per capita). **Selected balance of payments data.** Receipts from (US$'000,000): tourism (2006) 497; remittances (2006) 2,916; foreign direct investment (2001–05 avg.) 1,447; official development assistance (2005) 271 (commitments). Disbursements for (US$'000,000): tourism (2006) 466; remittances (2005) 38. **Land use** as % of total land area (2003): in temporary crops 4.7%, in permanent crops 4.3%, in pasture 17.2%; overall forest area (2005) 39.2%.

Foreign trade

Imports (2004; f.o.b. in balance of trade and c.i.f. for commodities and trading partners): US$7,861,000,000 (machinery and apparatus 24.3%; road vehicles 10.6%; mineral fuels and lubricants 10.2%; food and live animals 7.4%). *Major import sources* (2004): US 16.8%; Colombia 14.1%; China 9.0%; Venezuela 7.1%; Brazil 6.5%. **Exports** (2006): US$12,658,000,000 (crude petroleum 54.8%; bananas and plantains 9.6%; refined petroleum 4.8%; shrimp 4.6%; cut flowers 3.5%). *Major export destinations* (2006): US 53.6%; Peru 8.2%; Colombia 5.6%; Chile 4.4%; Italy 3.3%.

Transport and communications

Transport. *Railroads* (2004): route length (2005) 965 km; passenger-km 3,000,000; metric ton-km cargo 2,000. *Roads* (2004): total length 43,197 km (paved 15%). *Vehicles* (2004): passenger cars 413,432; trucks and buses 310,009. *Air transport* (2005): passenger-km 867,100,000; metric ton-km cargo 5,400,000. **Communications,** in total units (units per 1,000 persons). Daily newspaper circulation (2005): 901,000 (68); televisions (2004): 3,298,000 (253); telephone landlines (2006): 1,754,000 (131); cellular telephone subscribers (2006): 8,485,000 (632); personal computers (2005): 866,000 (65); total Internet users (2006): 1,549,000 (115); broadband Internet subscribers (2005): 27,000 (2).

Education and health

Educational attainment (1995). Percentage of population ages 25 and over having: no formal schooling/incomplete primary education 18.8%; complete primary/incomplete secondary 47.2%; complete secondary 16.1%; higher 17.9%. **Literacy** (2003): total population ages 15 and over literate 92.5%; males literate 94.0%; females literate 91.0%. **Health:** physicians (2004) 21,625 (1 per 603 persons); hospital beds (2004) 21,200 (1 per 615 persons); infant mortality rate (2005) 23.0. **Food** (2005): daily per capita caloric intake 2,770 (vegetable products 83%, animal products 17%); 152% of FAO recommended minimum.

Military

Total active duty personnel (2006): 46,500 (army 79.6%, navy 11.8%, air force 8.6%). **Military expenditure as percentage of GDP** (2005): 2.6%; per capita expenditure US$66.

Background

Ecuador was conquered by the Incas in AD 1450 and came under Spanish control in 1534. Under the Spaniards it was a part of the Viceroyalty of Peru until 1740, when it became a part of the Viceroyalty of New Granada. It gained its independence from Spain in 1822 as part of the republic of Gran Colombia, and in 1830 it became a sovereign state. A succession of

1 metric ton = about 1.1 short tons; 1 kilometer = 0.6 mi (statute); 1 metric ton-km cargo = about 0.68 short ton-mi cargo; c.i.f.: cost, insurance, and freight; f.o.b.: free on board

authoritarian governments ruled into the mid-20th century, and economic hardship and social unrest prompted the military to take a strong role. Border disputes led to war between Peru and Ecuador in 1941; the two fought periodically until agreeing to a final demarcation in 1998. The economy, booming in the 1970s with petroleum profits, was depressed in the 1980s by reduced oil prices and earthquake damage. A new constitution was adopted in 1979. In the 1990s social unrest caused political instability and several changes of heads of state. In a controversial move to help stabilize the economy, the US dollar replaced the sucre as the national currency in 2000.

Recent Developments

The inauguration of Pres. Rafael Correa in January 2007 added Ecuador to the list of South American countries in which elected leftist leaders sought to implement major political, economic, and social change. His administration appeared to favor political reform as a priority over economic nationalism, and it moved swiftly to overhaul the constitution and Ecuador's discredited political institutions. He said that he would disavow debts contracted corruptly or illegally and that the government would renegotiate agreements with private oil companies to increase its share of revenues. He spoke in favor of US legislation extending the Andean Trade Promotion and Drug Eradication Act (which gave trade preferences to Ecuador in exchange for antinarcotic aid) but opposed a bilateral free-trade agreement between Ecuador and the US.

Internet resources: <www.ecuador.com>.

Egypt

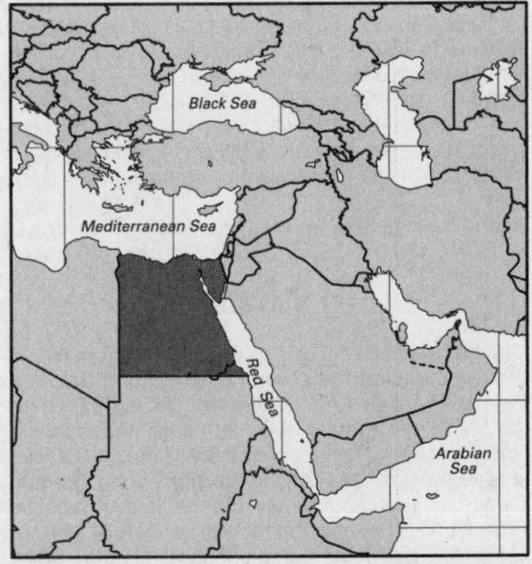

Official name: Jumhuriah Misr al-ʿArabiyah (Arab Republic of Egypt). **Form of government:** republic with one legislative house (People's Assembly [454]). **Chief of state:** President Hosni Mubarak (from 1981). **Head of government:** Prime Minister Ahmed Nazif (from 2004). **Capital:** Cairo. **Official language:** Arabic. **Official religion:** Islam. **Monetary unit:** 1 Egyptian pound (£E) = 100 piastres; valuation (1 Jul 2008) US$1 = £E 5.33.

Demography

Area: 385,229 sq mi, 997,739 sq km. **Population** (2007): 73,358,000. **Density** (2007): persons per sq mi 190.4, persons per sq km 73.5. **Urban** (2006): 42.6%. **Sex distribution** (2006): male 51.11%; female 48.89%. **Age breakdown** (2005): under 15, 33.0%; 15–29, 28.0%; 30–44, 19.8%; 45–59, 12.3%; 60–74, 5.7%; 75 and over, 1.2%. **Ethnic composition** (2000): Egyptian Arab 84.1%; Sudanese Arab 5.5%; Arabized Berber 2.0%; Bedouin 2.0%; Rom (Gypsy) 1.6%; other 4.8%. **Religious affiliation** (2000): Muslim (nearly all Sunni) 84.4%; Christian 15.1%, of which Orthodox 13.6%; nonreligious 0.5%. **Major cities** ('000; 2006): Cairo 7,787 ([2005 urban agglomeration] 11,128); Alexandria 4,110; Al-Jizah 2,950; Shubra al-Khaymah (1996) 871; Port Said (1996) 470. **Location:** northern Africa, bordering the Mediterranean Sea, the Gaza Strip, Israel, the Red Sea, The Sudan, and Libya.

Vital statistics

Birth rate per 1,000 population (2005): 25.5 (world avg. 20.3). **Death rate** per 1,000 population (2005): 6.4 (world avg. 8.6). **Total fertility rate** (avg. births per childbearing woman; 2006): 2.83. **Life expectancy** at birth (2006): male 69.2 years; female 73.6 years.

National economy

Budget (2003–04). *Revenue:* £E 116,490,000,000 (income and profits taxes 28.3%; sales taxes 19.4%; customs duties 13.0%; Suez Canal fees 4.4%; petroleum revenue 3.5%). *Expenditures:* £E 159,600,000,000 (current expenditure 76.6%; capital expenditure 23.4%). **Population economically active** (2005): total 22,310,000; activity rate 31.3% (participation rates: ages 15–64 [2001] 46.9%; female 23.3%; unemployed [2006] 9.3%). **Production** ('000; metric tons except as noted). *Agriculture, forestry, fishing* (2005): sugarcane 16,335, wheat 8,185, corn (maize) 7,698; livestock ('000; number of live animals) 5,150 sheep, 4,500 cattle, 120 camels; roundwood 17,060,000 cu m, of which fuelwood 80%; fisheries production 889,302 (from aquaculture 61%). *Mining and quarrying* (2005): phosphate rock 2,730; iron ore 2,600; salt 1,400. *Manufacturing* (value added in US$'000,000; 2002): chemicals (all forms) 2,823; food products 1,016; textiles and wearing apparel 618. *Energy production (consumption):* electricity ('000,000 kW-hr; 2004–05) 101,300 ([2004] 100,600); coal ('000 metric tons; 2004) 33 (1,850); crude petroleum ('000 barrels; 2004) 253,000 (240,000); petroleum products ('000 metric tons; 2004) 32,600 (28,000); natural gas ('000,000 cu m; 2003) 33,000 (29,400). **Households.** Average household size (2006) 4.2. **Gross national income** (2006): US$111,348,000,000 (US$1,501 per capita). **Public debt** (external, outstanding; 2006): US$28,000,000,000. **Land use** as % of total land area (2003): in temporary crops 2.9%, in permanent crops 0.5%; overall forest area (2005) 0.1%. **Selected balance of payments data.** Receipts from (US$'000,000): tourism (2005) 6,851; remittances (2005–06) 5,034; foreign direct investment (2001–05 avg.) 1,785; official development assistance (2005) 987 (commitments). Disbursements for (US$'000,000): tourism (2005) 1,629; remittances (2005) 57.

Foreign trade

Imports (2005–06; c.i.f.): US$30,441,000,000 (petroleum 17.6%; machinery and apparatus 10.9%; food products 9.7%; metal products 7.3%; chemicals and chemical products 6.0%). *Major import sources* (2004): free zones 11.3%; US 10.3%; Germany 6.6%; China 5.1%; Italy 4.9%. **Exports** (2005–06; f.o.b.): US$18,455,100,000 (petroleum 55.4%, of which crude petroleum 17.4%; finished goods 28.0%; semimanufactured goods 6.4%). *Major export destinations* (2004): Italy 12.5%; bunkers and ships' stores 9.8%; US 7.4%; free zones 5.7%; Spain 5.5%.

Transport and communications

Transport. *Railroads* (2005): length 9,525 km; passenger-km 54,853,000,000; metric ton-km cargo 4,234,000,000. *Roads* (2004): length 92,370 km (paved 81%). *Vehicles* (2002): passenger cars 1,847,000; trucks and buses 650,000. *Inland water* (2006): Suez Canal, number of transits 18,664; cargo 742,708,000 metric tons. *Air transport* (2005; EgyptAir only): passenger-km 10,048,000,000; metric ton-km cargo 287,561,000. **Communications,** in total units (units per 1,000 persons). Daily newspaper circulation (2005): 3,577,000 (51); televisions (2004): 17,500,000 (253); telephone landlines (2006): 10,808,000 (143); cellular telephone subscribers (2006): 18,001,000 (239); personal computers (2005): 2,800,000 (40); total Internet users (2006): 6,000,000 (80); broadband Internet subscribers (2006): 206,000 (2.9).

Education and health

Educational attainment (2006). Percentage of population ages 10 and over having: no formal schooling 42.9%; incomplete primary 19.4%; complete primary 24.9%; secondary 3.2%; higher 9.6%. **Literacy** (2001): total population ages 15 and over literate 56.1%; males literate 67.2%; females literate 44.8%. **Health** (2006): physicians 161,000 (1 per 451 persons); hospital beds (2007) 185,000 (1 per 393 persons); infant mortality rate (2005) 20.5. **Food** (2005): daily per capita caloric intake 3,274 (vegetable products 92%, animal products 8%); 172% of FAO recommended minimum.

Military

Total active duty personnel (2006): 468,500 (army 72.6%, navy 3.9%, air force [including air defense] 23.5%). **Military expenditure as percentage of GDP** (2005): 2.8%; per capita expenditure US$37.

Background

Egypt is home to one of the world's oldest continuous civilizations. Upper and Lower Egypt were united c. 3000 BC, beginning a period of cultural achievement and a line of native rulers that lasted nearly 3,000 years. Egypt's ancient history is divided into the Old, Middle, and New Kingdoms, spanning 31 dynasties and lasting to 332 BC. The pyramids date from the Old Kingdom; the cult of Osiris and the refinement of sculpture, from the Middle Kingdom; and the era of empire and the Exodus of the Jews, from the New Kingdom. An Assyrian invasion occurred in the 7th century BC, and the Persian Achaemenids established a dynasty in 525 BC. The invasion by Alexander the Great in 332 BC inaugurated the Macedonian Ptolemaic period and the ascendancy of Alexandria. The Romans held Egypt from 30 BC to AD 395; later it was placed under the control of Constantinople. Constantine's granting of tolerance in 313 to the Christians began the development of a formal Egyptian (Coptic) church. Egypt came under Arab control in 642 and ultimately was transformed into an Arabic-speaking state, with Islam as the dominant religion. Held by the Umayyad and Abbasid dynasties, in 969 it became the center of the Fatimid dynasty. In 1250 the Mamluks established a dynasty that lasted until 1517, when Egypt fell to the Ottoman Turks. An economic decline ensued, and with it a decline in Egyptian culture. Egypt became a British protectorate in 1914 and received nominal independence in 1922, when a constitutional monarchy was established. A coup overthrew the monarchy in 1952, with Gamal Abdel Nasser taking power. Following three wars with Israel, Egypt, under Nasser's successor, Anwar el-Sadat, ultimately played a leading role in Middle East peace talks. Sadat was succeeded by Hosni Mubarak, who followed Sadat's peace initiatives and in 1982 regained Egyptian sovereignty (lost in 1967) over the Sinai Peninsula. Although Egypt took part in the coalition against Iraq during the Persian Gulf War (1991), it later made peace overtures to Iraq and other countries in the region.

Recent Developments

Egypt's government intensified its campaign in 2007 to contain political dissent led by the banned Muslim Brotherhood. A number of amendments were passed, including a new antiterrorism law, which would provide the police with increased powers of arrest and surveillance; a new election law that would eliminate the need for judicial monitoring of each ballot box; and a ban on the creation of political parties based on religion. Though there was an estimated US$5 billion surplus and a decline in unemployment (from 9.5% in 2005–06 to 9.1% in 2006–07) and the rate of inflation (from 12.8% in March to 8.5% in August), there was a 10.5% rise in the cost of living. Nonetheless, 14 million Egyptians were classified as poor.

Internet resources: <www.egypt.travel>.

El Salvador

Official name: República de El Salvador (Republic of El Salvador). **Form of government:** republic with one legislative house (Legislative Assembly [84]). **Chief of state and government:** President Elías Antonio Saca González (from 2004). **Capital:** San Salvador. **Official language:** Spanish. **Official religion:** none (Roman Catholicism, although not official, enjoys special recognition in the constitution). **Monetary unit:** 1 colón (₡) = 100 centavos; valuation (1 Jul 2008) US$1 = ₡8.75 (the US dollar [US$] has also been legal tender since 1 Jan 2001; the colón is rarely in use).

Demography

Area: 8,124 sq mi, 21,041 sq km. **Population** (2007): 6,857,000. **Density** (2007): persons per sq mi 844.0,

1 metric ton = about 1.1 short tons; 1 kilometer = 0.6 mi (statute); 1 metric ton-km cargo = about 0.68 short ton-mi cargo; c.i.f.: cost, insurance, and freight; f.o.b.: free on board

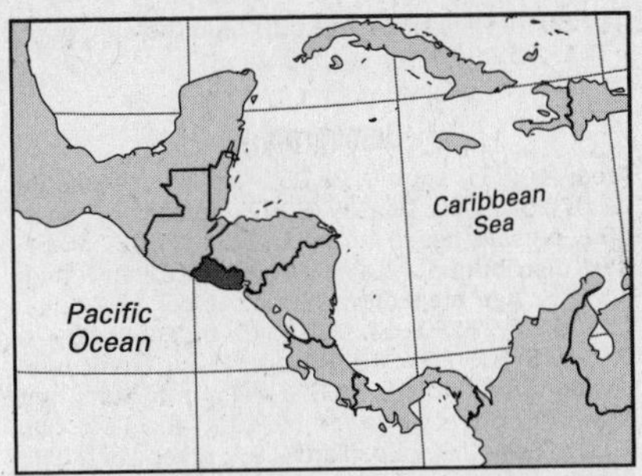

persons per sq km 325.9. **Urban** (2005): 59.8%. **Sex distribution** (2005): male 49.17%; female 50.83%. **Age breakdown** (2005): under 15, 34.0%; 15–29, 28.8%; 30–44, 19.1%; 45–59, 10.5%; 60–74, 5.6%; 75–84, 1.6%; 85 and over, 0.4%. **Ethnic composition** (2000): mestizo 88.3%; Amerindian 9.1%, of which Pipil 4.0%; white 1.6%; other/unknown 1.0%. **Religious affiliation** (2005): Roman Catholic 71%; independent Christian 11%; Protestant 10%; Jehovah's Witness 2%; other 6%. **Major cities** (2005): San Salvador 507,700 (urban agglomeration 2,232,300); Soyapango 294,600; Mejicanos 188,700; San Miguel 183,200; Santa Ana 178,600. **Location:** Central America, bordering Guatemala, Honduras, and the North Pacific Ocean.

Vital statistics

Birth rate per 1,000 population (2005): 16.3 (world avg. 20.3); (1998) within marriage 27.2%. **Death rate** per 1,000 population (2005): 4.5 (world avg. 8.6). **Total fertility rate** (avg. births per childbearing woman; 2006): 3.12. **Life expectancy** at birth (2006): male 67.9 years; female 75.3 years.

National economy

Budget. Revenue (2005): US$2,307,500,000 (VAT 47.8%; individual income taxes 29.0%; import duties 7.8%; nontax revenue 5.5%). *Expenditures:* $2,484,600,000 (education 18.6%; defense and public security 11.4%; public health and welfare 9.8%; public works 6.3%; other 53.9%). **Public debt** (external, outstanding; 2005): US$4,760,000,000. **Production** (metric tons except as noted). *Agriculture, forestry, fishing* (2005): sugarcane 4,405,000, corn (maize) 727,607, sorghum 141,400; livestock (number of live animals) 1,256,517 cattle, 355,991 pigs, 13,437 chickens; roundwood 4,855,000 cu m, of which fuelwood 86%; fisheries production 43,317 (from aquaculture 5%). *Mining and quarrying* (2004): limestone 1,161,000. *Manufacturing* (value added in US$'000,000; 2004): food products 875; textiles and wearing apparel 262; chemicals and chemical products 262; refined petroleum 234. *Energy production (consumption):* electricity (kW-hr; 2006) 5,293,000,000 (5,204,000,000); crude petroleum (barrels; 2004) none (7,100,000); petroleum products (metric tons; 2004) 989,000 (1,851,000). **Households.** Average household size (2004) 4.2; average income per household (2004) US$5,016; expenditure (2005): food, beverages, and tobacco 36.4%, housing and energy 16.8%, transportation and communications 10.2%, household furnishings 8.4%. **Land use** as % of total land area (2003): in temporary crops 31.9%, in permanent crops 12.1%, in pasture 38.3%; overall forest area (2005) 14.4%. **Population economically active** (2004): total 2,710,237; activity rate of total population 40.1% (participation rates: ages 15–64, 63.2%; female 39.6%; unemployed [2005] 7.2%). **Gross national income** (2006): US$15,553,000,000 (US$2,300 per capita). **Selected balance of payments data.** Receipts from (US$'000,000): tourism (2005) 543; remittances (2006) 3,316; foreign direct investment (2001–05 avg.) 357; official development assistance (2005) 234 (commitments). Disbursements for (US$'000,000): tourism (2005) 347; remittances (2005) 24.

Foreign trade

Imports (2004; c.i.f.): US$6,268,754,000 (imports for reexport 22.0%; machinery and apparatus 12.3%; food 11.3%; petroleum [all forms] 10.2%; chemicals and chemical products 9.6%). *Major import sources* (2006): US 40.5%; Guatemala 8.0%; Costa Rica 2.9%; Honduras 2.3%; Japan 2.0%. **Exports** (2004; f.o.b.): US$3,295,258,000 (reexports [mostly clothing] 55.2%; yarn, fabrics, and made-up articles 6.8%; chemicals and chemical products 4.8%). *Major export destinations* (2006): US 57.1%; Guatemala 13.0%; Honduras 8.0%; Nicaragua 4.8%; Costa Rica 3.4%.

Transport and communications

Transport. *Railroads* (2007): length 562 km. *Roads* (2002): total length 11,458 km (paved 23%). *Vehicles* (2000): passenger cars 148,000; trucks and buses 250,800. *Air transport* (2005; TACA International Airlines only): passenger-km 8,117,465,000; metric ton-km cargo 37,883,000. **Communications,** in total units (units per 1,000 persons). Daily newspaper circulation (2004): 250,000 (37); televisions (2004): 1,560,000 (233); telephone landlines (2006): 1,037,000 (148); cellular telephone subscribers (2006): 3,852,000 (551); personal computers (2005): 350,000 (51); total Internet users (2005): 637,000 (93); broadband Internet subscribers (2005): 42,000 (6.2).

Education and health

Educational attainment (2004). Percentage of population ages 26 and over having: no formal schooling 22.0%; primary education 39.0%; secondary 28.5%; higher 10.5%. **Literacy** (2004): total population ages 10 and over literate 84.5%; males literate 87.0%; females literate 82.3%. **Health** (2003): physicians 4,100 (1 per 1,620 persons); hospital beds 4,625 (1 per 1,436 persons); infant mortality rate per 1,000 live births (2004) 10.5. **Food** (2005): daily per capita caloric intake 2,680 (vegetable products 89%, animal products 11%); 149% of FAO recommended minimum.

Military

Total active duty personnel (2006): 15,500 (army 89.4%, navy 4.5%, air force 6.1%). **Military expenditure as percentage of GDP** (2005): 0.6%; per capita expenditure US$16.

Background

The Spanish arrived in the area in 1524 and subjugated the Pipil Indian kingdom of Cuzcatlán by 1539. The country was divided into two districts, San Salvador and Sonsonate, both attached to Guatemala. When independence came in 1821, San Salvador was incorporated into the Mexican Empire; upon its collapse in 1823, Sonsonate and San Salvador combined to form the new state of El Salvador within the United Provinces of Central America. From its founding, El Salvador experienced a high degree of political turmoil and was under military rule from 1931 to 1979, when the government was ousted in a coup. Elections held in 1982 set up a new government, and in 1983 a new constitution was adopted, but civil war continued through the 1980s. An accord in 1992 brought an uneasy truce.

Recent Developments

A close ally of the US, El Salvador continued to boycott Cuba in 2007 and was the only Latin American country to keep troops in Iraq, despite widespread opposition. The US rewarded Salvadoran support with leniency regarding the deportation of illegal immigrants back to El Salvador. Nearly one-third of native-born Salvadorans lived in the US, and their remittances of about US$2.5 billion annually aided El Salvador's weak economy. El Salvador enjoyed a rise in exports to the US, including the reexport of Brazilian ethanol, which was made possible under the Central America–Dominican Republic Free Trade Agreement (CAFTA–DR) with the US, but American corn-produced ethanol drove up grain prices in El Salvador.

Internet resources: <www.elsalvador.travel>.

Equatorial Guinea

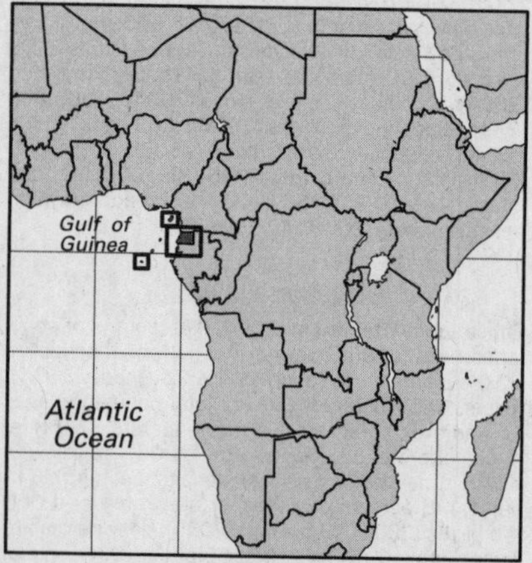

Official name: República de Guinea Ecuatorial (Spanish); République du Guinée Équatoriale (French) (Republic of Equatorial Guinea). **Form of government:** republic with one legislative house (House of Representatives of the People [100]). **Chief of state:** President Teodoro Obiang Nguema Mbasogo (from 1979). **Head of government:** Prime Minister Ricardo Mangue Obama Nfubea (from 2006). **Capital:** Malabo. **Official languages:** Spanish; French. **Official religion:** none. **Monetary unit:** 1 CFA franc (CFAF) = 100 centimes; valuation (1 Jul 2008) US$1 = CFAF 414.60 (pegged since 1 Jan 2002 to the euro at €1 = CFAF 655.96).

Demography

Area: 10,831 sq mi, 28,051 sq km. **Population** (2007): 507,000. **Density** (2007): persons per sq mi 46.8, persons per sq km 18.1. **Urban** (2006): 50.9%. **Sex distribution** (2005): male 48.82%; female 51.18%. **Age breakdown** (2005): under 15, 42.4%; 15–29, 26.2%; 30–44, 15.5%; 45–59, 9.5%; 60–74, 5.0%; 75–84, 1.2%; 85 and over 0.2%. **Ethnic composition** (2000): Fang 56.6%; migrant laborers from Nigeria 12.5%, of which Yoruba 8.0%, Igbo 4.0%; Bubi 10.0%; Seke 2.9%; Spaniard 2.8%; other 15.2%. **Religious affiliation** (2000): Roman Catholic 79.9%; Sunni Muslim 4.1%; independent Christian 3.7%; Protestant 3.2%; traditional beliefs 2.1%; nonreligious/atheist 4.9%; other 2.1%. **Major cities** (2003): Malabo 92,900; Bata 66,800; Mbini 11,600; Ebebiyin 9,100; Luba 6,800. **Location:** western Africa, the mainland portion bordering Cameroon, Gabon, and the Bight of Biafra (inlet of the Atlantic Ocean).

Vital statistics

Birth rate per 1,000 population (2005): 39.1 (world avg. 20.3). **Death rate** per 1,000 population (2005): 15.6 (world avg. 8.6). **Natural increase rate** per 1,000 population (2005): 23.5 (world avg. 11.7). **Total fertility rate** (avg. births per childbearing woman; 2005): 5.50. **Life expectancy** at birth (2005): male 49.2 years; female 51.7 years.

National economy

Budget (2005). *Revenue:* CFAF 1,528,825,000,000 (oil revenue 94.3%, of which profit sharing 32.1%, royalties 30.1%; non-oil revenue 5.6%, of which tax revenue 3.8%, nontax revenue 1.8%; grants 0.1%). *Expenditures:* CFAF 697,948,000,000 (capital expenditure 63.9%; current expenditure 22.8%; net lending 13.3%). **Public debt** (external, outstanding; 2005): US$4,760,000,000. **Gross national income** (at 2006 market prices): US$3,023,000,000 (US$2,300 per capita). **Production** (metric tons except as noted). *Agriculture, forestry, fishing* (2005): cassava 45,000, sweet potatoes 36,000, oil palm fruit 35,000; livestock (number of live animals) 37,600 sheep, 9,000 goats, 6,100 pigs; roundwood 866,000 cu m, of which fuelwood 52%; fisheries production (2004) 3,500. *Mining and quarrying*: gold (2005) 200 kg. *Manufacturing* (2004): methanol 1,027,300; processed timber 31,200 cu m. *Energy production (consumption):* electricity (kW-hr; 2004) 83,000,000 (51,000,000); crude petroleum (barrels; 2005) 153,000,000 ([2004] negligible); petroleum products (metric tons; 2004) none (47,000); natural gas (cu m; 2005) 2,300,000,000 ([2004] 480,000,000). **Population economically active** (1997): total 177,000; activity rate of total population 40.0% (participation rates: ages 15–64, 74.7%; female 35.4%; unemployed [1998] 30%). **Households.** Expenditure (2000): food and beverages 60.4%, clothing 14.7%, household furnishings 8.6%. **Land use** as % of total land area (2003): in temporary crops 4.6%, in permanent crops 3.6%, in pasture 3.7%; overall forest area (2005) 58.2%. **Selected bal-**

ance of payments data. Receipts from (US$'000,-000): tourism (2005) 5; foreign direct investment (2001–05 avg.) 1,245; official development assistance (2005) 39.

Foreign trade

Imports (2005): CFAF 1,112,500,000,000 (for petroleum sector 55.8%; for public sector 33.0%; petroleum products 4.5%). *Major import sources:* US 26.8%; Côte d'Ivoire 21.4%; Spain 13.6%; France 8.8%; UK 7.8%. **Exports** (2005): CFAF 3,764,200,000,000 (crude petroleum 92.1%; methanol 6.9%; timber 0.7%). *Major export destinations* (2003): US 33.2%; Spain 25.4% China 14.2%; Canada 12.7%; Italy 6.3%.

Transport and communications

Transport. *Roads* (1999): total length 2,880 km (paved 13%). *Vehicles* (2002): passenger cars 8,380; trucks and buses 6,618. **Communications,** in total units (units per 1,000 persons). Televisions (2002): 55,000 (116); telephone landlines (2005): 10,000 (20); cellular telephone subscribers (2005): 97,000 (193); personal computers (2004): 7,000 (3.3); total Internet users (2006): 8,000 (16).

Education and health

Literacy (2006): percentage of total population ages 15 and over literate 87.0%; males literate 93.4%; females literate 80.5%. **Health:** physicians (2004) 101 (1 per 5,020 persons); hospital beds (1998) 907 (1 per 472 persons); infant mortality rate per 1,000 live births (2005) 96.5.

Military

Total active duty personnel (2006): 1,320 (army 83.3%, navy 9.1%, air force 7.6%). **Military expenditure as percentage of GDP** (2005): 0.1%; per capita expenditure US$14.

Background

The first inhabitants of the mainland region appear to have been Pygmies. The now-prominent Fang and Bubi reached the mainland region in the 17th-century Bantu migrations. Equatorial Guinea was ceded by the Portuguese to the Spanish in the late 18th century; it was frequented by slave traders, as well as by British, German, Dutch, and French merchants. Bioko was administered by British authorities (1827–58) before the official takeover by the Spanish. The mainland (Río Muni) was not effectively occupied by the Spanish until 1926. Independence was declared in 1968, followed by a reign of terror and economic chaos under the dictatorial president Macías Nguema, who was overthrown by a military coup in 1979 and later executed. A new constitution was adopted in 1982, but political unrest persisted.

Recent Developments

Equatorial Guinea continued in 2007 to have one of the highest GDP growth rates in the world, estimated at more than 20%. The country was one of the members that participated in the 2006 inaugural meeting of the Gulf of Guinea Commission, which aimed to ensure that the energy resources of the region led to development and that Malabo's long-standing dispute with neighboring Gabon over the status of the islands in Corsico Bay would at last be settled. In May it was announced that there would be a delay in the awarding of further offshore exploration blocks because the bids were not satisfactory, but in September seven new oil blocks were granted to foreign companies. Relations with Zimbabwe, which had become close since 2004 when Zimbabwe intercepted mercenaries bound for Equatorial Guinea to stage a coup, remained warm. Zimbabwe extradited Simon Mann, the leader of the mercenaries, to Equatorial Guinea in February 2008 to face charges there.

Internet resources: <http://guinea-equatorial.com>.

Eritrea

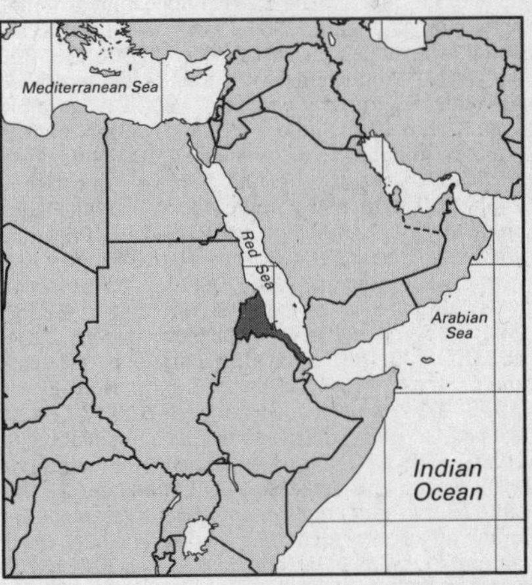

Official name: State of Eritrea. **Form of government:** transitional regime with one interim legislative body (Transitional National Assembly [150]). Constitution adopted in May 1997 was still not implemented in early 2008. **Head of state and government:** President Isaias Afwerki (from 1993). **Capital:** Asmara. **Official language:** none. **Official religion:** none. **Monetary unit:** 1 nakfa (Nfa) = 100 cents; valuation (1 Jul 2008) US$1 = Nfa 15.00.

Demography

Area: 46,774 sq mi, 121,144 sq km. **Population** (2007): 4,907,000. **Density** (2007): persons per sq mi 125.5, persons per sq km 48.6. **Urban** (2006): 21.3%. **Sex distribution** (2006): male 49.84%; female 50.16%. **Age breakdown** (2006): under 15, 44.0%; 15–29, 27.9%; 30–44, 14.3%; 45–59, 8.2%; 60–74, 4.5%; 75 and over, 1.1%. **Ethnolinguistic composition** (2004): Tigrinya (Tigray) 50.0%; Tigré 31.4%; Afar 5.0%; Saho 5.0%; Beja 2.5%; Bilen 2.1%; other 4.0%. **Religious affiliation** (2004): Muslim (virtually all Sunni) 50%; Christian 48%, of which Eritrean Orthodox 40%, Roman Catholic 5%, Protestant 2%; traditional beliefs 2%. **Major cities** (2003): Asmara 435,000; Keren 57,000; Assab 28,000; Mendefera 25,000; Massawa 25,000. **Location:** the Horn of Africa, bordering The Sudan, the Red Sea, Djibouti, and Ethiopia.

Vital statistics

Birth rate per 1,000 population (2006): 34.3 (world avg. 20.3). **Death rate** per 1,000 population (2006): 9.6 (world avg. 8.6). **Natural increase rate** per 1,000 population (2006): 24.7 (world avg. 11.7). **Total fertility rate** (avg. births per childbearing woman; 2006): 5.08. **Life expectancy** at birth (2006): male 57.4 years; female 60.7 years.

National economy

Budget (2002). *Revenue:* Nfa 3,409,800,000 (tax revenue 45.1%, of which import duties 18.1%, sales tax 10.8%, corporate tax 9.9%; grants 32.8%; nontax revenue 21.2%; extraordinary revenue 0.9%). *Expenditures:* Nfa 6,138,200,000 (defense 34.3%; health 9.6%; humanitarian assistance 7.9%; education 7.6%; transportation, construction, and communications 6.5%; debt service 5.7%). **Public debt** (external, outstanding; 2005): US$723,000,000. **Gross national income** (2006): US$1,360,000,000 (US$290 per capita). **Production** (metric tons except as noted). *Agriculture, forestry, fishing* (2005): sorghum 114,300, roots and tubers 102,500, pulses 35,200; livestock (number of live animals) 2,100,000 sheep, 1,950,000 cattle, 75,000 camels; roundwood 2,449,000 cu m, of which fuelwood 99.9%; fisheries production 4,027. *Mining and quarrying* (2005): granite 350,280; basalt 184,027; coral 91,348. *Manufacturing* (value added in US$'000,000; 2004): beverages 31; tobacco products 8; furniture 7. *Energy production (consumption):* electricity (kW-hr; 2004) 283,000,000 (283,000,000); petroleum products (metric tons; 2004) none (239,000). **Households** (1996–97). Average household size (2004) 5.0; average annual disposable income per household: Nfa 10,967 (US$1,707); sources of income (urban areas only): wages and salaries 34.0%, transfers 29.3%, rent 19.8%, self-employment 16.9%; expenditure (urban areas only): food 36.2%, housing 30.2%, clothing and footwear 9.3%, energy 6.8%, household furnishings 4.6%, transportation and communications 4.1%. **Population economically active** (2000): total 1,451,000; activity rate of total population 40.8% (participation rates: ages 15–64, 75.4%; female 41.5%). **Selected balance of payments data.** Receipts from (US$'000,000): tourism (2005) 66; remittances (2003) 150; foreign direct investment (2001–05 avg.) 11; official development assistance (2005) 355. Disbursements for (US$'000,000): remittances (2000) 1. **Land use** as % of total land area (2003): in temporary crops 5.6%, in permanent crops 0.03%, in pasture 69.0%; overall forest area (2005) 15.4%.

Foreign trade

Imports (2003; c.i.f.): US$432,800,000 (food and live animals 40.5%, of which cereals 25.5%; machinery and apparatus 14.8%; road vehicles 7.3%; chemicals and chemical products 6.1%). *Major import sources* (2005): Italy 31.4%; US 11.9%; Belarus 5.9%; France 5.1%; Germany 4.6%. **Exports** (2003; f.o.b.): US$6,600,000 (food and live animals 36.4%, of which fresh fish 22.7%; leather 10.6%; corals and shells 9.1%). *Major export destinations* (2005): Italy 15.1%; France 11.8%; US 9.5%; Germany 8.6%; Taiwan 7.4%.

Transport and communications

Transport. *Railroads* (2005): route length 306 km. *Roads* (2004): total length 4,000 km (paved 20%). *Vehicles* (1996): automobiles 5,940. *Air transport* (2001; Asmara airport only): passenger arrivals 39,266, passenger departures 46,448; freight loaded 202 metric tons, freight unloaded 1,548 metric tons. **Communications,** in total units (units per 1,000 persons). Daily newspaper circulation (2005): 49,000 (10); televisions (2004): 250,000 (58); telephone landlines (2006): 38,000 (8.2); cellular telephone subscribers (2006): 62,000 (14); personal computers (2005): 35,000 (7.5); total Internet users (2006): 100,000 (22).

Education and health

Educational attainment (2002). Percentage of population ages 25 and over having: no formal education/unknown 67.6%; incomplete primary education 16.6%; complete primary 1.3%; incomplete secondary 5.8%; complete secondary 5.7%; higher 3.0%. **Literacy** (2006): total population ages 15 and over literate 61.4%; males literate 72.3%; females literate 50.7%. **Health:** physicians (2004) 215 (1 per 20,791 persons); hospital beds (2000) 3,126 (1 per 1,187 persons); infant mortality rate per 1,000 live births (2006) 46.3. **Food** (2003): daily per capita caloric intake 1,519 (vegetable 94%, animal products 6%); 88% of FAO recommended minimum.

Military

Total active duty personnel (2006): 201,750 (army 99.1%, navy 0.7%, air force 0.2%); UN peacekeeping force along Eritrean-Ethiopian border (July 2007) 1,470 troops. **Military expenditure as percentage of GDP** (2003): 24.1%; per capita expenditure US$49.

Background

As the site of the main ports of the Aksumite empire, Eritrea was linked to the beginnings of the Ethiopian kingdom, but it retained much of its independence until it came under Ottoman rule in the 16th century. From the 17th to the 19th century, control of the territory was disputed among Ethiopia, the Ottomans, the kingdom of Tigray, Egypt, and Italy; it became an Italian colony in 1890. Eritrea was used as the main base for the Italian invasions of Ethiopia (1896 and 1935–36) and in 1936 became part of Italian East Africa. It was captured by the British in 1941, federated to Ethiopia in 1952, and made a province of Ethiopia in 1962. Thirty years of guerrilla warfare by Eritrean secessionist groups ensued. A provisional Eritrean government was established in 1991 after the overthrow of the Ethiopian government, and independence came in 1993. A new constitution was ratified in 1997.

Recent Developments

Eritrea's enmity with neighboring Ethiopia continued to dominate the 2007 agenda of the country, sapping energy required for improving relations with the West and resolving the dire economic and social needs of its people. In January a proxy war exploded when both countries lent support to opposing sides in a conflict

1 metric ton = about 1.1 short tons; 1 kilometer = 0.6 mi (statute); 1 metric ton-km cargo = about 0.68 short ton-mi cargo; c.i.f.: cost, insurance, and freight; f.o.b.: free on board

in Somalia, which reached a climax when Somalia's Transitional Federal Government, backed by Ethiopian troops, routed the Islamic Courts Union, supported by Eritrea. As Eritrea's relations with Western countries worsened, Asmara strengthened its ties with China, which in January cancelled a portion of Eritrea's foreign debt. In July the countries signed economic pacts, and in October Eritrea granted mineral exploration rights to two Chinese firms.

Internet resources: <http://www.shabait.com>.

Estonia

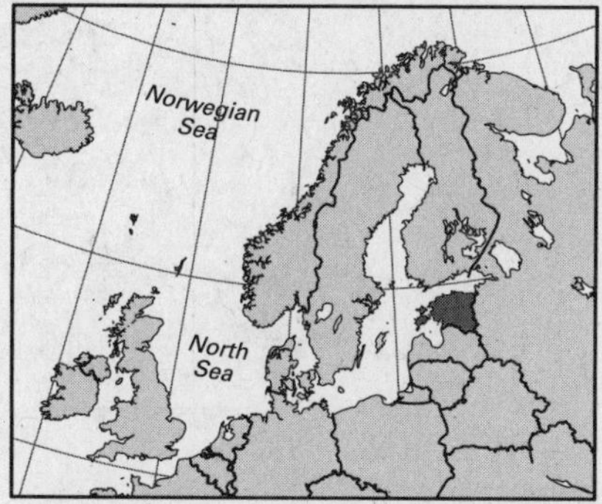

Official name: Eesti Vabariik (Republic of Estonia). **Form of government:** unitary multiparty republic with a single legislative body (Riigikogu [101]). **Chief of state:** President Toomas Hendrik Ilves (from 2006). **Head of government:** Prime Minister Andrus Ansip (from 2005). **Capital:** Tallinn. **Official language:** Estonian. **Official religion:** none. **Monetary unit:** 1 kroon (KR) = 100 senti; valuation (1 Jul 2008) US$1 = KR 9.90.

Demography

Area: 17,462 sq mi, 45,227 sq km. **Population** (2007): 1,338,000. **Density** (2006): persons per sq mi 81.8, persons per sq km 31.6. **Urban** (2005): 69.3%. **Sex distribution** (2005): male 46.06%; female 53.94%. **Age breakdown** (2005): under 15, 15.1%; 15–29, 22.7%; 30–44, 20.5%; 45–59, 20.2%; 60–74, 14.7%; 75–84, 5.7%; 85 and over, 1.1%. **Ethnic composition** (2005): Estonian 68.6%; Russian 25.7%; Ukrainian 2.1%; Belarusian 1.2%; Finnish 0.8%; other 1.6%. **Religious affiliation** (2000): Christian 63.5%, of which unaffiliated Christian 25.6%, Protestant (mostly Lutheran) 17.2%, Orthodox 16.5%, independent Christian 3.3%; nonreligious 25.1%; atheist 10.9%; other 0.5%. **Major cities** (2006): Tallinn 396,852; Tartu 101,965; Narva 66,712; Kohtla-Järve 45,399; Pärnu 44,074. **Location:** eastern Europe, bordering the Gulf of Finland, Russia, Latvia, the Gulf of Riga, and the Baltic Sea.

Vital statistics

Birth rate per 1,000 population (2006): 11.0 (world avg. 20.3); (2005) within marriage 41.5%. **Death rate** per 1,000 population (2006): 13.0 (world avg. 8.6). **Natural increase rate** per 1,000 population (2006): −2.0 (world avg. 11.7). **Total fertility rate** (avg. births per childbearing woman; 2005): 1.50. **Life expectancy** at birth (2005): male 67.3 years; female 78.1 years.

National economy

Budget (2004). *Revenue:* KR 54,836,300,000 (tax revenue 82.3%, of which social security contributions 28.3%, VAT 20.6%, personal income taxes 17.4%, excise taxes 9.6%; nontax revenue 11.8%; grants 5.9%). *Expenditures:* KR 52,429,100,000 (current expenditure 90.9%, of which social benefits 29.6%; capital expenditure 7.8%; other 1.3%). **Production** (metric tons except as noted). *Agriculture, forestry, fishing* (2005): barley 366,700, wheat 263,400, potatoes 209,800; livestock (number of live animals) 340,100 pigs, 249,800 cattle; roundwood 6,800,000 cu m, of which fuelwood 19%; fisheries production 100,136. *Mining and quarrying* (2005): oil shale 11,500,000; peat 800,000. *Manufacturing* (value added in US$'000,000; 2004): food products 163; fabricated metal products 150; wood products (excluding furniture) 138. *Energy production (consumption):* electricity (kW-hr; 2005) 10,184,000,000 (7,494,000,000); hard coal (metric tons; 2004) none (58,000); lignite (metric tons; 2004) 13,993,000 (15,503,000); petroleum products (metric tons; 2004) none (862,000); natural gas (cu m; 2005) none (997,000,000). **Population economically active** (2005): total 659,600; activity rate of total population 48.8% (participation rates: ages 15–64, 69.6%; female 50.1%; unemployed [2006] 5.9%). **Households** (2005). Average household size (2004) 2.5; average annual disposable income per household member KR 41,176 (US$3,272); sources of income: wages and salaries 66.1%, transfers 25.6%, self-employment 3.3%; expenditure: food and beverages 28.3%, transportation and communications 16.8%, housing 15.0%, recreation and culture 7.6%. **Public debt** (external, outstanding; January 2005): US$435,000,000. **Gross national income** (2006): US$15,183,000,000 (US$11,331 per capita). **Selected balance of payments data.** Receipts from (US$'000,000): tourism (2005) 948; remittances (2006) 402; foreign direct investment (FDI; 2001–05 avg.) 1,129. Disbursements for (US$'000,000): tourism (2005) 448; remittances (2006) 75; FDI (2001–05 avg.) 272. **Land use** as % of total land area (2003): in temporary crops 12.9%, in permanent crops 0.4%, in pasture 6.3%; overall forest area (2005) 53.9%.

Foreign trade

Imports (2006; c.i.f.): KR 165,298,500,000 (mineral fuels 16.1%; electrical machinery and equipment 15.9%; vehicles and transport equipment 12.1%; chemicals and chemical products 6.5%; textiles and apparel 5.1%). *Major import sources:* Finland 18.2%; Russia 13.1%; Germany 12.4%; Sweden 9.0%; Lithuania 6.5%. **Exports** (2006; f.o.b.): KR 119,519,700,000 (electrical machinery and equipment 19.4%; mineral fuels 15.9%; wood and paper products 11.6%; vehicles and transport equipment 6.7%; textiles and apparel 5.2%). *Major export destinations:* Finland 18.2%; Sweden 12.3%; Latvia 8.7%; Russia 7.9%; Germany 5.0%.

Transport and communications

Transport. *Railroads* (2005): route length (2004) 958 km; passenger-km 246,951,000; metric ton-km cargo 10,629,398,000. *Roads* (2004): total length

56,856 km (paved 24%). *Vehicles* (2005): passenger cars 493,800; trucks and buses 91,400. *Air transport* (2006; Estonian Air only): passenger-km 1,132,997,000; metric ton-km cargo 2,796,200. **Communications,** in total units (units per 1,000 persons). Daily newspaper circulation (2004): 257,000 (192); televisions (2003): 686,000 (507); telephone landlines (2006): 542,000 (409); cellular telephone subscribers (2006): 1,659,000 (1,252); personal computers (2005): 650,000 (483); total Internet users (2006): 760,000 (574); broadband Internet subscribers (2006): 228,000 (170).

Education and health

Educational attainment (2000). Percentage of population ages 10 and over having: no formal schooling/incomplete primary education 6.7%; complete primary/lower secondary 31.6%; complete secondary 29.2%; higher vocational 17.5%; undergraduate 12.3%; advanced degree 0.4%; unknown 2.3%. **Literacy** (2003): virtually 100%. **Health:** physicians (2003) 4,277 (1 per 316 persons); hospital beds (2004) 7,850 (1 per 172 persons); infant mortality rate per 1,000 live births (2005) 5.5. **Food** (2005): daily per capita caloric intake 2,744 (vegetable products 72%, animal products 28%); 140% of FAO recommended minimum.

Military

Total active duty personnel (2006): 4,934 (army 89.4%, navy 6.7%, air force 3.9%). **Military expenditure as percentage of GDP** (2005): 1.7%; per capita expenditure US$152.

Background

The lands on the eastern shores of the Baltic Sea were invaded by Vikings in the 9th century AD and later by Danes, Swedes, and Russians, but the Estonians were able to withstand the assaults until the Danes took control in 1219. In 1346 the Danes sold their sovereignty to the Teutonic Order, which was then in possession of Livonia (southern Estonia and Latvia). In the mid-16th century Estonia was once again divided, with northern Estonia capitulating to Sweden and Poland gaining Livonia, which it surrendered to Sweden in 1629. Russia acquired Livonia and Estonia in 1721. Nearly a century later, serfdom was abolished, and from 1881 Estonia underwent intensive Russification. In 1918 Estonia obtained independence from Russia, which lasted until the Soviet Union occupied the country in 1940 and forcibly incorporated it into the USSR. Germany held the region (1941–44) during World War II, but the Soviet regime was restored in 1944, after which Estonia's economy was collectivized and integrated into that of the Soviet Union. In 1991, along with other parts of the former USSR, it proclaimed its independence and subsequently held elections. Estonia continued negotiations with Russia to settle their common border.

Recent Developments

Controversy surrounded Estonia's removal of a Soviet-era World War II monument—the *Bronze Soldier*—from central Tallinn to a remote military cemetery in 2007. In April two days of riots broke out, resulting in one death and scores of injuries, and a wave of cyber attacks against Estonian government, media, and banking Web sites, thought by many to be the work of Russian hackers, followed.

Internet resources: <http://visitestonia.com>.

Ethiopia

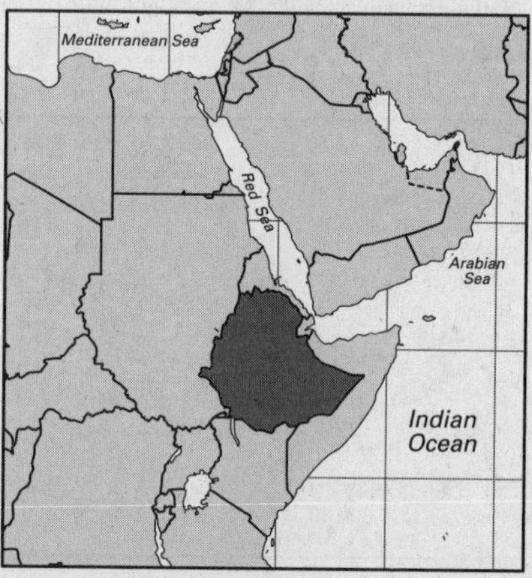

Official name: Federal Democratic Republic of Ethiopia. **Form of government:** federal republic with two legislative houses (House of the Federation [112]; House of People's Representatives [547]). **Chief of state:** President Girma Wolde-Giorgis (from 2001). **Head of government:** Prime Minister Meles Zenawi (from 1995). **Capital:** Addis Ababa. **Official language:** none. **Official religion:** none. **Monetary unit:** 1 birr (Br) = 100 cents; valuation (1 Jul 2008) US$1 = Br 9.66.

Demography

Area: 435,186 sq mi, 1,127,127 sq km. **Population** (2007): 76,512,000. **Density** (2007): persons per sq mi 175.8, persons per sq km 67.9. **Urban** (2006): 16.2%. **Sex distribution** (2006): male 49.88%; female 50.12%. **Age breakdown** (2006): under 15, 43.7%; 15–29, 28.1%; 30–44, 15.3%; 45–59, 8.5%; 60–74, 3.7%; 75 and over, 0.7%. **Ethnolinguistic composition** (2000): Oromo 35.8%; Amharic 31.0%; Tigrinya 6.1%; Gurage 4.9%; Sidamo 3.8%; Welaita 2.1%; Somali 1.4%; other 14.9%. **Religious affiliation** (2005): Muslim 33.7%; Ethiopian Orthodox 33.4%; Protestant 16.3%; traditional beliefs 10.4%; other 6.2%. **Major cities** (2006): Addis Ababa 2,973,000; Dire Dawa 281,750; Nazret 228,623; Gonder 194,773; Dese 169,104. **Location:** the Horn of Africa, bordering Eritrea, Djibouti, Somalia, Kenya, and The Sudan.

Vital statistics

Birth rate per 1,000 population (2006): 38.0 (world avg. 20.3). **Death rate** per 1,000 population (2006):

14.9 (world avg. 8.6). **Total fertility rate** (avg. births per childbearing woman; 2006): 5.22. **Life expectancy** at birth (2006): male 47.9 years; female 50.2 years.

National economy

Budget (2004–05). *Revenue:* Br 20,032,000,000 (tax revenue 61.2%, of which import duties 28.7%, income and profits tax 17.8%, sales tax 9.3%; grants 22.8%; nontax revenue 16.0%). *Expenditures:* Br 24,551,000,000 (current expenditure 53.1%, of which defense 11.9%, education 11.8%; capital expenditure 46.9%, of which economic development 31.6%). **Public debt** (external, outstanding; 2005): US$5,897,000,000. **Gross national income** (2006): US$13,278,000,000 (US$164 per capita). **Production** (metric tons except as noted). *Agriculture, forestry, fishing* (2005): corn (maize) 3,342,892, wheat 2,306,862, sorghum 2,200,241; leading producer of beeswax, honey, cut flowers, and khat; livestock (number of live animals) 38,500,000 cattle, 17,000,000 sheep, (2004) 468,390 camels, (1998) 3,037 civets; roundwood 97,409,000 cu m, of which fuelwood 97%; fisheries production 9,450. *Mining and quarrying* (2005): rock salt 200,000; tantalum 45,000 kg; niobium 7,100 kg. *Manufacturing* (value added in US$'000,000; 2004): food products 157; beverages 118; bricks, cement, and ceramics 69. *Energy production (consumption):* electricity (kW-hr; 2004) 2,547,000,000 (2,547,000,000); crude petroleum (barrels; 2004) none (5,600,000); petroleum products (metric tons; 2004) 3,000 (1,624,000). **Land use** as % of total land area (2003): in temporary crops 11.1%, in permanent crops 0.7%, in pasture 20.0%; overall forest area (2005) 11.9%. **Population economically active** (2005): total 32,158,392; activity rate of total population 50.9% (participation rates: ages 10 and over 78.4%; female [1999] 45.5%; unemployed 5.0%). **Households** (1999–2000). Average household size (2004) 5.3; sources of income: self-employment 70.9% (of which agriculture-based 57.6%), wages and salaries 10.9%, salvaging 6.6%, rent 3.9%, other 7.7%; expenditure: food and beverages 52.8%, housing and energy 14.4%, household operations 13.9%, clothing and footwear 7.9%. **Selected balance of payments data.** Receipts from (US$'000,000): tourism (2005) 168; remittances (2006) 172; foreign direct investment (2001–05 avg.) 364; official development assistance (2005) 1,937. Disbursements for (US$'000, 000): tourism (2005) 77; remittances (2006) 14.

Foreign trade

Imports (2003–04): US$2,587,400,000 ([2002] machinery and apparatus 20.2%; chemicals and chemical products 12.8%; road vehicles 12.0%; refined petroleum 11.7%; iron and steel 6.4%). *Major import sources* (2004–05): Saudi Arabia 17.0%; China 11.2%; US 10.5%; India 6.1%; Italy 4.2%. **Exports** (2003–04): US$600,700,000 (coffee 37.2%; khat 14.7%; sesame seeds 13.8%; nonmonetary gold 8.1%; leather 7.5%). *Major export destinations* (2004–05): Germany 15.1%; Djibouti 13.4%; Japan 7.8%; Saudi Arabia 5.9%; US 5.5%.

Transport and communications

Transport. *Railroads:* length (2003) 781 km; passenger-km (1998–99) 151,000,000; metric ton-km cargo (1998–99) 90,000,000. *Roads* (2004): total length 36,469 km (paved 19%). *Vehicles* (2003): passenger cars 71,311; trucks and buses 65,557. *Air transport* (2005; Ethiopian Airlines only): passenger-km 5,418,376; metric ton-km cargo 132,601,000. **Communications,** in total units (units per 1,000 persons). Daily newspaper circulation (2005): 83,000 (1.1); televisions (2003): 547,000 (7.9); telephone landlines (2006): 725,000 (9.1); cellular telephone subscribers (2006): 867,000 (11); personal computers (2004): 113,000 (1.7); total Internet users (2005): 164,000 (2.2).

Education and health

Educational attainment (2000). Percentage of population ages 15 and over having: no formal schooling 63.8%; incomplete primary education 21.6%; primary 2.6%; incomplete secondary 8.1%; secondary 2.5%; post-secondary 1.4%. **Literacy** (2006): total population ages 15 and over literate 46.3%; males literate 53.3%; females literate 39.3%. **Health** (2004–05): physicians 1,077 (1 per 66,236 persons); hospital beds 13,851 (1 per 5,150 persons); infant mortality rate (2006) 93.6. **Food** (2005): daily per capita caloric intake 1,582 (vegetable products 94%, animal products 6%); 92% of FAO recommended minimum.

Military

Total active duty personnel (2006): 182,500 (army 98.6%, air force 1.4%); UN peacekeeping personnel along Ethiopian-Eritrean border (July 2007): 1,470 troops. **Military expenditure as percentage of GDP** (2005): 3.9%; per capita expenditure US$5.

Background

Ethiopia, the Biblical land of Cush, was inhabited from earliest antiquity and was once under ancient Egyptian rule. Ge'ez-speaking agriculturalists established the kingdom of Da'amat in the 2nd millennium BC. After 300 BC they were superseded by the kingdom of Aksum, whose King Menilek I, according to legend, was the son of King Solomon and the Queen of Sheba. Christianity was introduced in the 4th century AD and became widespread. Ethiopia's prosperous Mediterranean trade was cut off by the Muslim Arabs in the 7th and 8th centuries, and the area's interests were directed eastward. Contact with Europe resumed in the late 15th century with the arrival of the Portuguese. Modern Ethiopia began with the reign of Tewodros II, who began the consolidation of the country. In the wake of European encroachment, the coastal region was made an Italian colony in 1890, but under Emperor Menilek II the Italians were defeated and ousted in 1896. Ethiopia prospered under his rule, and his modernization programs were continued by Emperor Haile Selassie in the 1930s. In 1936 Italy again gained control of the country, and it was held as part of Italian East Africa until 1941, when it was liberated by the British. Ethiopia incorporated Eritrea in 1952. In 1974 Haile Selassie was deposed, and a Marxist government, plagued by civil wars and famine, controlled the country until 1991. In 1993 Eritrea gained its independence, but border conflicts with Ethiopia and neighboring Somalia continued in the 1990s.

Recent Developments

The release in July 2007 of many of Ethiopia's high-profile political detainees signaled the possible return to normal politics, though thousands of others remained incarcerated throughout the country. Inflation and ballooning consumer prices put a strain on efforts to meet demands for economic development—price increases on basic consumer products were nearly 100% in some cases. The Ethiopian economy grew at a rate of 6.3% in 2007, up from 5.9% in 2006, but despite generally good harvests and improvements in markets and infrastructure, at least 7.3 million Ethiopians were considered in need of food assistance. Ethiopia and Eritrea supported opposing sides in the war in Somalia, feeding speculation that a regional war was possible.

Internet resources: <http://tourismethiopia.org>.

Faroe Islands

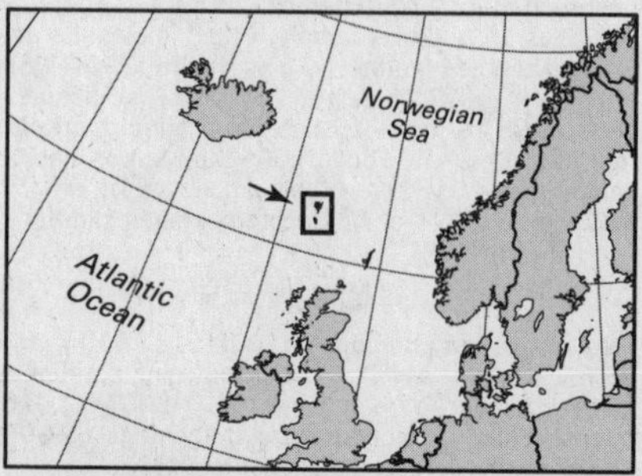

Official name: Føroyar (Faroese); Færøerne (Danish) (Faroe Islands; alternative spelling is Faeroe Islands). **Political status:** self-governing region of the Danish realm with a single legislative body (Lagting [32]). **Chief of state:** Danish Queen Margrethe II (from 1972), represented by High Commissioner Dan M. Knudsen (from 2008). **Head of home government:** Prime Minister Jóannes Eidesgaard (from 2004). **Capital:** Tórshavn (Thorshavn). **Official languages:** Faroese; Danish. **Official religion:** Faroese Lutheran. **Monetary unit:** 1 Faroese króna (plural krónur); valuation (1 Jul 2008) US$1 = Faroese krónur 4.72 (the Faroese króna is equivalent in value to the Danish krone [DKK]).

Demography

Area: 540.1 sq mi, 1,398.8 sq km. **Population** (2007): 48,400. **Density** (2007): persons per sq mi 89.6, persons per sq km 34.6. **Urban** (2003): 38.8%. **Sex distribution** (2006): male 51.99%; female 48.01%. **Age breakdown** (2006): under 15, 22.4%; 15–29, 19.3%; 30–44, 20.6%; 45–59, 18.9%; 60–74, 12.2%; 75–84, 4.9%; 85 and over, 1.7%. **Ethnic composition** (2000): Faroese 97.0%; Danish 2.5%; other Scandinavian 0.4%; other 0.1%. **Religious affiliation** (2005): Protestant 91%, of which Lutheran 79%, Plymouth Brethren 10%; other 9%. **Major municipalities** (2005): Tórshavn 19,314; Klaksvík 4,889; Runavík 3,642; Tvøroyri 1,814. **Location:** island group north of the British Isles between the Norwegian Sea and the North Atlantic Ocean.

Vital statistics

Birth rate per 1,000 population (2006): 14.7 (world avg. 20.3); (1998) within marriage 62.0%. **Death rate** per 1,000 population (2006): 8.6 (world avg. 8.6). **Natural increase rate** per 1,000 population (2006): 5.1 (world avg. 11.7). **Total fertility rate** (avg. births per childbearing woman; 2004): 1.80. **Life expectancy** at birth (2006): male 75.9 years; female 82.8 years.

National economy

Budget (2003). *Revenue:* DKK 5,737,000,000 (tax revenue 78.6%, of which income taxes 47.6%, VAT 18.5%; transfers from the Danish government 14.8%; other 6.6%). *Expenditures:* DKK 5,329,000,000 (social welfare 34.7%, education 15.3%, health 14.5%, debt service 4.0%, agriculture, fishing, and hunting 2.8%). **Gross national income** (at current market prices; 2003): US$1,472,000,000 (US$30,680 per capita). **Production** (metric tons except as noted). *Agriculture, forestry, fishing* (2005): potatoes 1,500, other vegetables, grass, hay, and silage are produced; livestock (number of live animals) 68,100 sheep, 2,000 cattle; fisheries production 588,715 (including blue whiting 267,447, pollock 75,971, cod 35,755, and capelin 19,752; from aquaculture 4%). *Manufacturing* (value added in DKK '000,000; 1999): processed fish 393; all other manufacturing 351 (important products include handicrafts and woolen textiles and clothing). *Energy production (consumption):* electricity (kW-hr; 2006) 259,000,000 ([2004] 290,000,000); petroleum products (metric tons; 2004) none (215,000). **Population economically active** (2006): total 29,400; activity rate of total population 61% (participation rates: ages 16–74, 85.8%; female 44.8%; unemployed 2.7%). **Public debt** (external, outstanding; including Danish debt; 2004): US$155,000,000. **Households.** Expenditure (1998): food and beverages 25.1%, transportation and communications 17.7%, housing 12.5%, recreation 11.9%, energy 7.7%. **Selected balance of payments data.** Receipts from (US$'000,000): tourism (2005) 25; remittances (2003) 44. Disbursements for (US$'000,000): remittances (2003) 5. **Land use** as % of total land area (2003): in temporary crops 2.1%, in pasture 93%; overall forest area (2005) 0.1%.

Foreign trade

Imports (2006): DKK 4,649,488,600 (goods for household consumption 27.7%; fuels, lubricants, and electric current 18.5%; machinery and apparatus 10.8%; goods for the construction industry 9.7%; road vehicles 7.9%). *Major import sources* (2005): Denmark 26.7%; Sweden 17.4%; Spain 6.7%; Germany 6.6%; Finland 5.4%. **Exports** (2006): DKK 3,744,957,600 (chilled and frozen fish 64.9%; salted fish 12.8%; dried fish 12.7%; smoked, canned, and other conserved fish 3.5%). *Major export destinations* (2005): UK 28.6%; Denmark 14.4%; Spain 9.7%; France and Monaco 8.2%; Norway 5.9%.

Transport and communications

Transport. *Roads* (2006): total length 464 km. *Vehicles* (2006): passenger cars 19,110; trucks, vans, and buses 4,452. *Air transport* (2005): passenger arrivals 89,190, passenger departures 89,101. **Communications,** in total units (units per 1,000 persons). Daily newspaper circulation (2003): 18,000 (375); televisions (2000): 47,000 (1,022); telephone landlines (2006): 23,000 (478); cellular telephone subscribers (2006): 50,000 (1,040); total Internet users (2005): 32,000 (645); broadband Internet subscribers (2006): 10,000 (208).

Education and health

Health (2005): physicians 57 (1 per 849 persons); hospital beds 295 (1 per 164 persons); infant mortality rate per 1,000 live births (2004) 6.4.

Military

Defense responsibility lies with Denmark.

Background

First settled by Irish monks (c. 700), the islands were colonized by the Vikings (c. 800) and were ruled by Norway from the 11th century until 1380, when they passed to Denmark. They unsuccessfully sought independence in 1946 but received self-government in 1948.

Recent Developments

In 2007 the Faroe Islands and Iceland signed agreements that would increase trade and that defined the maritime boundary between the two countries, officially establishing the valuable fishing rights of both and the limits of each country's continental shelf claim, which would prove extremely important in the event of the future discovery of offshore petroleum fields.

Internet resources:
<www.tourist.fo/default.asp?l=EN>.

Fiji

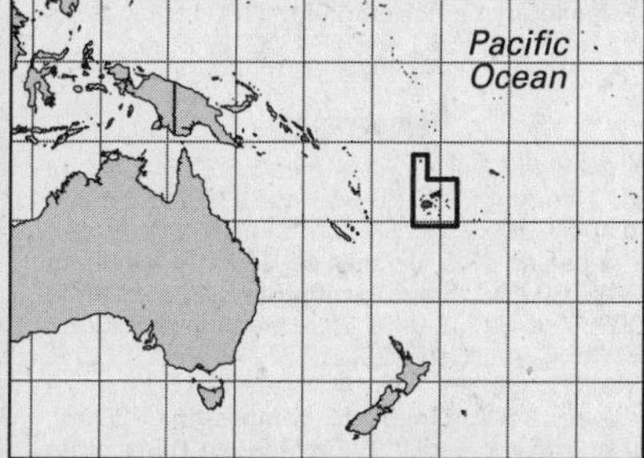

Official name: Republic of the Fiji Islands; Kai Vakarairai ni Fiji (Fijian). **Form of government:** military regime. **Chief of state:** President Ratu Josefa Iloilo (from 2000). **Head of government:** Prime Minister Voreque Bainimarama (from 2007). **Capital:** Suva. **Official languages:** English, Fijian, and Hindustani have equal status per constitution. **Official religion:** none. **Monetary unit:** 1 Fiji dollar (F$) = 100 cents; valuation (1 Jul 2008) US$1 = F$1.49.

Demography

Area: 7,055 sq mi, 18,272 sq km. **Population** (2007): 839,000. **Density** (2007): persons per sq mi 118.9, persons per sq km 45.9. **Urban** (2007): 50.9%. **Sex distribution** (2006): male 50.17%; female 49.83%. **Age breakdown** (2006): under 15, 31.1%; 15–29, 28.6%; 30–44, 19.7%; 45–59, 13.6%; 60–74, 6.1%; 75 and over, 0.9%. **Ethnic composition** (2007): Fijian 57.3%; Indian 37.6%; other 5.1%. **Religious affiliation** (2005): Protestant (mostly Methodist) 35%; Hindu 33%; independent Christian 11%, Roman Catholic 8%; Muslim 7%; other 6%. **Major urban areas** (2007): Suva 86,178 (urban agglomeration, 219,759); Lautoka 52,742; Nausori 46,811; Nadi 42,712. **Location:** archipelago in the South Pacific Ocean, between Hawaii (US) and New Zealand.

Vital statistics

Birth rate per 1,000 population (2006): 22.6 (world avg. 20.3). **Death rate** per 1,000 population (2006): 5.7 (world avg. 8.6). **Natural increase rate** per 1,000 population (2006): 16.9 (world avg. 11.7). **Total fertility rate** (avg. births per childbearing woman; 2006): 2.73. **Life expectancy** at birth (2006): male 67.3 years; female 72.5 years.

National economy

Budget (2005). *Revenue:* F$1,218,332,000 (customs duties and port dues 59.4%; income taxes 28.9%; fees and royalties 4.7%; other 7.0%). *Expenditures:* F$1,231,556,000 (department expenditures 70.7%, charges on public debt 26.3%, other 3.0%). **Public debt** (external, outstanding; September 2005): US$96,200,000. **Production** (metric tons except as noted). *Agriculture, forestry, fishing* (2005): sugarcane 2,952,000, coconuts 140,000, taro 38,000; livestock (number of live animals) 310,000 cattle, 260,000 goats, 140,000 pigs; roundwood 509,000 cu m, of which fuelwood 7%; fisheries production 41,596. *Mining and quarrying* (2005): gold 3,800 kg; silver 1,500 kg. *Manufacturing* (value added in F$'000,000; 2001): food products 94.6; textiles and clothing 92.4; beverages and tobacco 88.3. *Energy production (consumption):* electricity (kW-hr; 2004) 540,000,000 (540,000,000); coal (metric tons; 2004) none (13,000); petroleum products (metric tons; 2004) none (321,000). **Population economically active** (2000): total 341,700; activity rate of total population 42.2% (participation rates: ages 15–64 [1996] 60.6%; female 32.2%; unemployed [2002] 14.1%). **Gross national income** (at 2006 market prices): US$2,929,000,000 (US$3,515 per capita). **Households.** Average household size (2007) 4.7; average annual income per household (2002) F$15,757 (US$12,784); sources of income (2002): wages and salaries 64.3%, transfers 8.4%, self-employment 7.2%; expenditure (2002): food, beverages, and tobacco 31.2%, housing and energy 18.5%, transportation and communications 17.9%. **Selected balance of payments data.** Receipts from (US$'000,000): tourism (2005) 431; remittances (2006) 216; foreign direct investment (2001–05 avg.) 36; official development assistance (2005) 43 (commitments). Disbursements for (US$'000,000): tourism (2005) 106; remittances (2005) 40. **Land use** as % of total land area (2003): in temporary crops 10.9%, in permanent crops 4.7%, in pasture 9.6%; overall forest area (2005) 54.7%.

Foreign trade

Imports (2006; c.i.f.): F$3,119,920,000 (mineral products 33.4%; machinery and apparatus 14.9%; transport equipment 7.1%; chemicals and chemical products 5.3%; textiles and clothing 5.0%). *Major import sources* (2005): Singapore 29.9%; Australia 24.5%; New Zealand 18.0%; Japan 4.2%; US 3.8%. **Exports** (2006; f.o.b.): F$1,175,206,000 (reexports [mostly petroleum products] 29.4%; sugar 18.3%; fish 8.3%; clothing 8.1%; mineral water 7.4%). *Major export destinations* (2005): Australia 20.4%; Singapore 20.3%; US 15.5%; UK 15.1%; New Zealand 5.1%.

Transport and communications

Transport. *Railroads* (2003; owned by the Fiji Sugar Corporation): length 597 km. *Roads* (1999): total length 3,440 km (paved 49%). *Vehicles* (2005): passenger cars 76,273; trucks and buses 42,311. *Air transport* (2004–05; Air Pacific only): passenger-km 2,360,000,000; metric ton-km cargo 92,108,000. **Communications**, in total units (units per 1,000 persons). Daily newspaper circulation (2001): 49,000 (60); televisions (2003): 98,000 (118); telephone landlines (2005): 113,000 (133); cellular telephone subscribers (2005): 205,000 (242); personal computers (2004): 44,000 (52); total Internet users (2006): 80,000 (94).

Education and health

Educational attainment (1996). Percentage of population ages 25 and over having: no formal schooling 4.4%; some education 22.3%; incomplete secondary 47.7%; complete secondary 17.0%; some higher 6.7%; university degree 1.9%. **Literacy** (2003): total population ages 15 and over literate 93.7%; males literate 95.5%; females literate 91.9%. **Health** (2005): physicians 361 (1 per 2,343 persons); hospital beds 1,810 (1 per 467 persons); infant mortality rate per 1,000 live births (2006) 12.3. **Food** (2005): daily per capita caloric intake 3,197 (vegetable products 82%, animal products 18%); 166% of FAO recommended minimum.

Military

Total active duty personnel (2006): 3,500 (army 91.4%, navy 8.6%). **Military expenditure as percentage of GDP** (2004): 1.2%; per capita expenditure US$36.

Background

Archaeological evidence shows that the islands of Fiji were occupied in the late 2nd millennium BC and that the inhabitants had developed pottery by c. 1300 BC. The first European sighting was by the Dutch in the 17th century; in 1774 the islands were visited by Capt. James Cook, who found a mixed Melanesian-Polynesian population with a complex society. Traders and the first missionaries arrived in 1835. In 1857 a British consul was appointed, and in 1874 Fiji was proclaimed a crown colony. It became independent as a member of the Commonwealth in 1970 and was declared a republic in 1987 following a military coup. Elections in 1992 restored civilian rule. A new constitution was approved in 1997.

Recent Developments

In early 2007 Fiji military commander Voreque ("Frank") Bainimarama declared himself interim prime minister. Within the country short-lived opposition to the coup reflected both the military's efficiency and some public support for its determination to eliminate corruption. Opposition from international aid partners was more intense and sustained. Fiji was suspended from the Commonwealth of Nations, and aid was withheld until the country established a program for a return to civilian government. Donors also imposed "smart sanctions," designed to limit the mobility of coup leaders (and their families) without imposing further hardship on Fiji's poor.

Internet resources: <www.bulafiji.com/>.

Finland

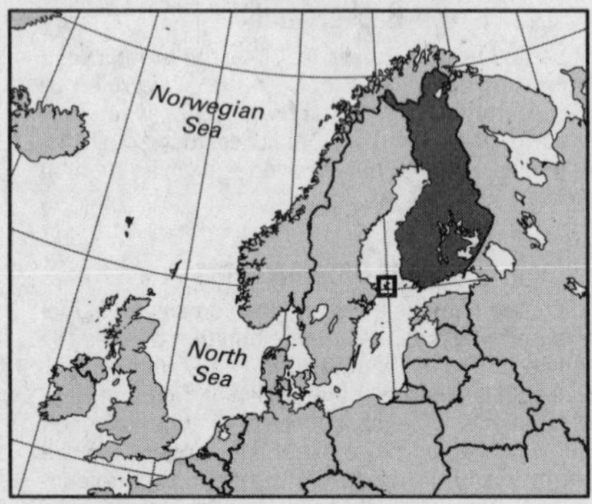

Official names: Suomen Tasavalta (Finnish); Republiken Finland (Swedish) (Republic of Finland). **Form of government:** multiparty republic with one legislative house (Parliament [200]). **Chief of state:** President Tarja Halonen (from 2000). **Head of government:** Prime Minister Matti Vanhanen (from 2003). **Capital:** Helsinki. **Official languages:** none. **Official religion:** none. **Monetary unit:** 1 euro (€) = 100 cents; valuation (1 Jul 2008) US$1 = €0.63.

Demography

Area (includes inland water area of 13,001 sq mi [33,672 sq km]): 130,559 sq mi; 338,145 sq km. **Population** (2007): 5,286,000. **Density** (2007): persons per sq mi 45.0, persons per sq km 17.4. **Urban** (2004): 62.1%. **Sex distribution** (2006): male 48.96%; female 51.04%. **Age breakdown** (2006): under 15, 17.1%; 15–29, 18.7%; 30–44, 19.5%; 45–59, 22.3%; 60–74, 14.7%; 75–84, 5.9%; 85 and over, 1.8%. **Linguistic composition** (2006): Finnish 91.5%; Swedish 5.5%; Russian 0.8%; other 2.2%. **Religious affiliation** (2005): Evangelical Lutheran 83.1%; nonreligious 14.7%; Finnish (Greek) Orthodox 1.1%; Muslim 0.4%; other 0.7%. **Major cities** (2006): Helsinki 564,521 (urban agglomeration [2003] 1,075,000); Espoo 235,019; Tampere 206,368; Vantaa 189,711; Turku 175,354. **Location:** northern Europe, bordering Norway, Russia, the

1 metric ton = about 1.1 short tons; 1 kilometer = 0.6 mi (statute); 1 metric ton-km cargo = about 0.68 short ton-mi cargo; c.i.f.: cost, insurance, and freight; f.o.b.: free on board

Gulf of Finland, the Baltic Sea, the Gulf of Bothnia, and Sweden.

Vital statistics

Birth rate per 1,000 population (2006): 11.2 (world avg. 20.3); within marriage (2004) 59.2%. **Death rate** per 1,000 population (2006): 9.1 (world avg. 8.6). **Natural increase rate** per 1,000 population (2006): 2.0 (world avg. 11.7). **Total fertility rate** (avg. births per childbearing woman; 2004): 1.80. **Life expectancy** at birth (2006): male 75.8 years; female 82.8 years.

National economy

Budget (2006). *Revenue:* €39,582,000,000 (VAT 33.3%; income and property taxes 32.4%; excise duties 11.7%). *Expenditures:* €39,582,000,000 (social security and health 28.6%; education 16.3%; agriculture and forestry 6.8%; defense 5.7%). **Public debt** (2006): US$73,898,000,000. **Production** (metric tons except as noted). *Agriculture, forestry, fishing* (2006): barley 1,972,000, oats 1,029,000, sugar beets 952,000; livestock (number of live animals) 1,436,000 pigs, 949,000 cattle, 198,000 reindeer; roundwood 51,599,000 cu m, of which fuelwood 9%; fisheries production (2005) 146,096 (from aquaculture 10%). *Mining and quarrying* (2005): chromite 326,000; zinc (metal content) 72,474; gold 3,747 kg. *Manufacturing* (value added in €'000,000; 2005): electrical and optical equipment (largely telephone apparatus) 7,187; nonelectrical machinery and apparatus 3,744; chemicals and chemical products 3,615. *Energy production (consumption):* electricity (kW-hr; 2005) 67,862,000,000 (84,851,000,000); hard coal (metric tons; 2004) none (8,082,000); crude petroleum (barrels; 2004) none (79,300,000); petroleum products (metric tons; 2004) 12,459,000 (10,242,000); natural gas (cu m; 2004) none ([2005] 3,863,000,000). **Population economically active** (2006): total 2,648,000; activity rate of total population 50.3% (participation rates: ages 15–64 [2004] 73.8%; female [2004] 48.1%; unemployed 7.7%). **Households** (2004). Average household size 2.2; disposable income per household €31,706 (US$39,367); sources of gross income (2003): wages and salaries 74.4%, rent 18.0%, self-employment 7.1%; expenditure: housing 25.6%, food, beverages, and tobacco 17.7%, transportation and communications 16.0%, recreation, culture, and education 11.7%. **Gross national income** (2006): US$210,516,000,000 (US$40,013 per capita). **Selected balance of payments data.** Receipts from (US$'000,000): tourism (2006) 2,357; remittances (2006) 698; foreign direct investment (FDI; 2001–05 avg.) 4,614. Disbursements for (US$'000,000): tourism (2006) 3,417; remittances (2006) 251; FDI (2001–05 avg.) 3,069. **Land use** as % of total land area (2003): in temporary crops 7.3%, in permanent crops 0.03%, in pasture 0.09%; overall forest area (2005) 73.9%.

Foreign trade

Imports (2004; c.i.f.): €40,729,700,000 (electrical machinery and apparatus 15.0%; nonelectrical machinery and apparatus 12.4%; mineral fuels 12.2%; automobiles and bicycles 9.2%). *Major import sources* (2006): Russia 14.1%; Germany 13.9%; Sweden 9.8%; China 7.4%; UK 4.8%. **Exports** (2004; f.o.b.): €48,917,000,000 (electrical machinery and apparatus 21.5%, of which telecommunications equipment 15.3%; paper and paper products 16.8%; nonelectrical machinery and apparatus 12.0%; base metals 6.8%; wood and wood products [excluding furniture] 5.1%). *Major export destinations* (2006): Germany 11.3%; Sweden 10.5%; Russia 10.1%; UK 6.5%; US 6.5%.

Transport and communications

Transport. *Railroads* (2006): route length 5,905 km; passenger-km 3,600,000,000; metric ton-km cargo 11,100,000,000. *Roads* (2004): total length 78,168 km (paved 65%). *Vehicles* (2005): passenger cars 2,430,345; trucks and buses 363,644. *Air transport* (2005; Finnair only): passenger-km 16,735,000,000; metric ton-km cargo 340,000,000. **Communications,** in total units (units per 1,000 persons). Daily newspaper circulation (2004): 2,255,000 (431); televisions (2003): 3,540,000 (679); telephone landlines (2006): 1,920,000 (365); cellular telephone subscribers (2006): 5,670,000 (1,078); personal computers (2004): 2,515,000 (482); total Internet users (2006): 2,925,000 (556); broadband Internet subscribers (2006): 1,428,000 (271).

Education and health

Educational attainment (2003). Percentage of population ages 25 and over having: incomplete upper-secondary education 35.6%; complete upper secondary or vocational 35.8%; higher 28.6%. **Literacy**: virtually 100%. **Health** (2004): physicians (2006) 18,507 (1 per 285 persons); hospital beds 36,082 (1 per 145 persons); infant mortality rate per 1,000 live births 3.3. **Food** (2005): daily per capita caloric intake 3,387 (vegetable products 68%, animal products 32%).

Military

Total active duty personnel (2006): 28,300 (army 72.4%, navy 17.7%, air force 9.9%). **Military expenditure as percentage of GDP** (2005): 1.4%; per capita expenditure US$515.

Background

Recent archaeological discoveries have led some to suggest that human habitation in Finland dates back at least 100,000 years. Ancestors of the Sami apparently were present in Finland by about 7000 BC. The ancestors of the present-day Finns came from the southern shore of the Gulf of Finland in the 1st millennium BC. The area was gradually Christianized from the 11th century. From the 12th century Sweden and Russia contested for supremacy in Finland, but by 1323 Sweden ruled most of the country. Russia was ceded part of Finnish territory in 1721; in 1808 Alexander I of Russia invaded Finland, which in 1809 was formally ceded to Russia. The subsequent period saw the growth of Finnish nationalism. Russia's losses in World War I and the Russian Revolution of 1917 set the stage for Finland's independence in 1917. It was defeated by the Soviet Union in the Russo-Finnish War (1939–40) but then sided with Nazi Germany against the Soviets during World War II and regained the territory it had lost. Facing defeat again by the advancing Soviets in 1944, it reached a peace agreement with the USSR, ceding territory and paying reparations. Finland's economy recovered after World War II. It joined the EU in 1995.

Recent Developments

A leading theme of the opposition in elections to the Finnish parliament in March 2007 was the purportedly low wages of nurses. Agreement was reached with nurses' unions in November to provide raises of 22–28% over four years and a 2007 year-end (Christmas) bonus of €270 (about US$400). Finnish cellular phone giant Nokia agreed in October to buy the American company Navteq, a maker of digital maps for mobile systems, for €5.7 billion (about US$8.1 billion). The move was seen as the cell phone behemoth's effort to evolve with the times by providing content (and advertising space).

Internet resources: <www.visitfinland.com>.

France

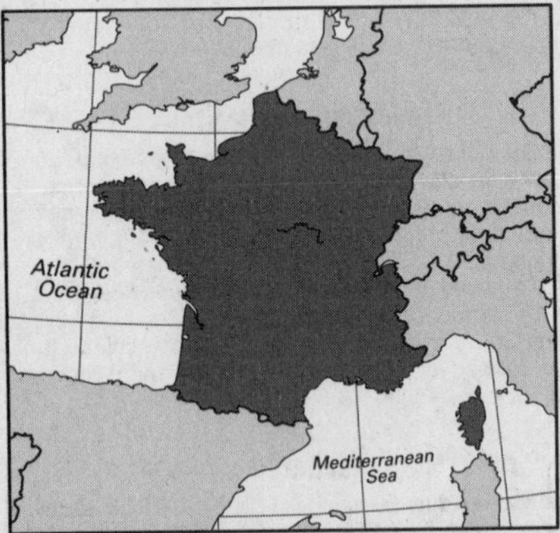

Official name: République Française (French Republic). **Form of government:** republic with two legislative houses (Senate [331], National Assembly [577]). **Chief of state:** President Nicolas Sarkozy (from 2007). **Head of government:** Prime Minister François Fillon (from 2007). **Capital:** Paris. **Official language:** French. **Official religion:** none. **Monetary unit:** 1 euro (€) = 100 cents; valuation (1 Jul 2008) US$1 = €0.63.

Demography

Area: 210,026 sq mi, 543,965 sq km. **Population** (2007): 61,709,000. **Density** (2007): persons per sq mi 293.8, persons per sq km 113.4. **Urban** (2003): 76.3%. **Sex distribution** (2006): male 48.60%; female 51.40%. **Age breakdown** (2005): under 15, 18.4%; 15–29, 19.1%; 30–44, 21.1%; 45–59, 20.4%; 60–74, 12.7%; 75–84, 6.3%; 85 and over, 2.0%. **Ethnic composition** (2000): French 76.9%; Algerian and Moroccan Berber 2.2%; Italian 1.9%; Portuguese 1.5%; Moroccan Arab 1.5%; Fleming 1.4%; Algerian Arab 1.3%; Basque 1.3%; Jewish 1.2%; German 1.2%; Vietnamese 1.0%; Catalan 0.5%; other 8.1%. **Religious affiliation** (2004): Roman Catholic 64.3%, of which practicing 8%; nonreligious/atheist 27%; Muslim 4.3%; Protestant 1.9%; Buddhist 1%; Jewish 0.6%; Jehovah's Witness 0.4%; Orthodox 0.2%; other 0.3%. **Major cities** (urban agglomeration; 2005): Paris 2,153,600 (9,854,000); Marseille 820,900 (1,384,000); Lyon 466,400 (1,408,000); Toulouse 435,000 (839,000); Nice 347,900 (915,000); Nantes 281,800; Strasbourg 272,700; Montpellier 244,300; Bordeaux 230,600 (794,000); Lille 225,100 (1,031,000); Rennes 209,900; Reims 184,800; Le Havre 183,900; Saint-Étienne 175,700; Toulon 166,800. **Location:** western Europe, bordering the North Atlantic Ocean, Belgium, Luxembourg, Germany, Switzerland, Italy, the Mediterranean Sea, Spain, and Andorra. **Dependent territories:** French Guiana, French Polynesia, Guadeloupe, Martinique, Mayotte, New Caledonia, Réunion, Saint Pierre and Miquelon, and Wallis and Futuna. **Households** (2004). Average household size 2.4; 1 person 32.8%, 2 persons 32.5%, 3 persons 15.1%, 4 persons 12.8%, 5 persons or more 6.8%. Individual households 14,320,000 (56.0%); collective households 11,232,000 (44.0%). **Immigration:** total immigrant population (2004) 4,850,000; immigrants admitted (2002) 205,707, of which North African 30.7%, EU 20.8%, sub-Saharan African 15.2%, Asian 14.1%, other European 11.8%.

Vital statistics

Birth rate per 1,000 population (2006): 13.1 (world avg. 20.3); (2005) within marriage 52.6%. **Death rate** per 1,000 population (2006): 8.4 (world avg. 8.6). **Total fertility rate** (avg. births per childbearing woman; 2006): 2.00. **Life expectancy** at birth (2006): male 77.2 years; female 84.1 years.

Social indicators

Educational attainment (2002). Percentage of population ages 25–64 having: no formal schooling through lower-secondary education 35%; upper secondary/higher vocational 41%; university 24%. **Quality of working life.** Legally worked week for full-time employees (2005) 36.0 hours. Rate of fatal injuries per 100,000 insured workers (2004) 3.7. Average days lost to labor stoppages per 1,000 workers (2004) 13. Trade union membership (2003) 1,900,000 (8% of labor force). **Access to services** (2004). Proportion of principal residences having: electricity 97.4%; indoor toilet 94.6%; indoor kitchen with sink 94.2%; hot water 60.3%; air conditioner 15.4%. **Social participation.** Eligible voters participating in last (May 2007) national election 84.0%. Population over 15 years of age participating in voluntary associations (1997) 28.0%. **Social deviance.** Offense rate per 100,000 population (2006) for: murder 1.5, rape 16.0, other assault 269.2; theft (including burglary and housebreaking) 3,403.8. Incidence per 100,000 in general population (2001) of: homicide 0.8; suicide 16.1. **Leisure.** Members of sports federations (2004) 15,226,000, of which football (soccer) 2,147,000, tennis 1,066,000. Movie tickets sold (2005) 174,200,000. Average daily hours of television viewing for population age 4 and over (2005) 3.43. **Material well-being** (2004).

Households possessing: automobile 81%; color television 95%; personal computer 45%; washing machine 92%; microwave 74%; dishwasher (2001) 39%.

National economy

Gross national income (2006): US$2,256,465,-000,000 (US$35,725 per capita). **Budget** (2004). *Revenue:* €330,140,000,000 (VAT 47.1%; direct taxes 38.3%; other taxes 14.6%). *Expenditures:* €355,470,000,000 (current civil expenditure 86.0%; military expenditure 8.7%; development expenditure 5.3%). **Public debt** (2005): US$1,375,000,000,000. **Production** (metric tons except as noted). *Agriculture, forestry, fishing* (2005): corn (maize) for forage and silage 43,600,000, wheat 36,840,806, sugar beets 31,242,506, corn (maize) 13,849,729, barley 10,317,062, grapes 6,793,249, potatoes 6,680,817, rapeseed 4,533,841, apples 2,246,351, triticale 1,793,974, sunflower seeds 1,502,106, dry peas 1,330,640, tomatoes 790,049, carrots 659,313, oats 505,652, lettuce 488,736, peaches and nectarines 430,619, green peas 428,000, cauliflower 377,056, string beans 359,608, leeks 182,910, chicory roots 181,198, mushrooms 165,000, flax fibre and tow 90,000; livestock (number of live animals) 19,383,000 cattle, 15,020,198 pigs, 9,185,475 sheep, 189,998,000 chickens, 30,820,000 turkeys, 22,406,000 ducks; roundwood 34,420,000 cu m, of which fuelwood 8%; fisheries production 832,805 (from aquaculture 31%); aquatic plants production 76,678. *Mining and quarrying* (2005): gypsum 3,500,000; crude talc 340,000; kaolin 316,000; gold (2004) 1,312 kg. *Manufacturing* (value added in US$'000,000; 2003): food products 27,023; pharmaceuticals, soaps, and paints 22,675; motor vehicles, trailers, and motor vehicle parts 20,269; fabricated metal products 14,264; general purpose machinery 10,595; plastic products 8,754; medical, measuring, and testing appliances 7,551; aircraft and spacecraft 7,476; publishing 6,911; special purpose machinery 6,605; bricks, cement, and ceramics 5,922; basic chemicals 5,843; base metals 5,547, of which basic iron and steel 4,117; paper and paper products 5,532; beverages 5,509; furniture 4,218. *Energy production (consumption):* electricity (kW-hr; 2004) 572,241,000,000 (510,201,000,000); hard coal (metric tons; 2004) 872,000 (20,780,000); lignite (metric tons; 2004) none (40,000); crude petroleum (barrels; 2005) 7,800,000 ([2004] 631,000,000); petroleum products (metric tons; 2004) 74,910,000 (74,274,000); natural gas (cu m; 2004) 1,374,000,000 (49,845,000,000). *Retail trade* (value of sales in €'000,000; 2004): large food stores 162,600; large nonfood stores 136,400; auto repair shops 120,400; pharmacies and stores selling orthopedic equipment 32,600; shops selling bread, pastries, or meat 31,800; small food stores and boutiques 15,300. **Population economically active** (2005): total 27,637,000; activity rate of total population 45.5% (participation rates: ages 15–64, 69.1%; female 46.4%; unemployed [April 2007] 8.2%). **Households.** Average household size (2004) 2.4; average disposable income per household (2004) €28,340 (US$35,187); sources of income (2004): wages and salaries 66%, transfers 23%, self-employment 7%, other 4%; expenditure (2005): housing and energy 24.7%, transportation 14.9%, food and nonalcoholic beverages 13.9%, recreation and culture 9.3%, restaurants and hotels 6.2%, household furnishings 5.8%. **Selected balance of payments data.** Receipts from (US$'000,000): tourism (2005) 42,283; remittances (2006) 12,554; foreign direct investment (FDI; 2001–05 avg.) 47,391. Disbursements for (US$'000,000): tourism (2005) 31,180; remittances (2006) 4,268; FDI (2001–05 avg.) 72,600. **Land use** as % of total land area (2003): in temporary crops 33.5%, in permanent crops 2.0%, in pasture 18.4%; overall forest area (2005) 28.3%.

Foreign trade

Imports (2004; c.i.f.): US$431,005,000,000 (machinery and apparatus 24.0%, of which electrical machinery and electronic microcircuits 6.2%, industrial machinery 4.5%; chemicals and chemical products 13.9%; road vehicles 11.7%; crude petroleum and refined petroleum 8.5%; food products 7.2%). *Major import sources:* Germany 17.4%; Italy 9.0%; Spain 7.4%; Belgium 7.3%; UK 6.5%; US 6.4%; China 4.7%; The Netherlands 4.4%; Japan 3.1%; Switzerland 2.3%. **Exports** (2004; f.o.b.): US$410,700,000,000 (machinery and apparatus 22.1%, of which electrical machinery and electronic microcircuits 6.3%, industrial machinery 4.6%; transport equipment 20.6%, of which road vehicles and parts 14.7%, aircraft, spacecraft, and related parts 5.3%; chemicals and chemical products 16.9%, of which pharmaceuticals 5.0%; food 8.0%; iron and steel 3.4%; perfumes, cosmetics, and toiletries 3.0%; alcoholic beverages 2.4%). *Major export destinations:* Germany 15.0%; Spain 10.0%; UK 9.3%; Italy 9.3%; Belgium 7.7%; US 6.9%; The Netherlands 4.0%; Switzerland 3.1%; Japan 1.6%; China 1.6%.

Transport and communications

Transport. *Railroads:* route length (in operation; 2004) 29,085 km; passenger-km (2003) 53,080,000,000; metric ton-km cargo (2003) 46,840,000,000. *Roads* (2004): total length 951,220 km (paved 100%). *Vehicles* (2004): passenger cars 29,900,000; trucks and buses 6,139,000. *Air transport* (2005): passenger-km 115,116,000,000; metric ton-km cargo 5,526,-000,000. **Communications,** in total units (units per 1,000 persons). Daily newspaper circulation (2004): 7,934,000 (131); televisions (2004): 23,723,000 (391); telephone landlines (2006): 33,897,000 (558); cellular telephone subscribers (2006): 51,662,000 (851); personal computers (2005): 35,000,000 (573); total Internet users (2006): 30,100,000 (496); broadband Internet subscribers (2006): 12,699,000 (208).

Education and health

Health (2003): physicians 203,487 (1 per 296 persons); hospital beds 457,132 (1 per 132 persons); infant mortality rate (2006) 3.7. **Food** (2005): daily per capita caloric intake 3,681 (vegetable products 67%, animal products 33%).

Military

Total active duty personnel (2006): 254,895 (army 52.4%, navy 17.3%, air force 24.9%, headquarters staff 2.0%, health services 3.4%). **Military expenditure as percentage of GDP** (2005): 2.5%; per capita expenditure US$871.

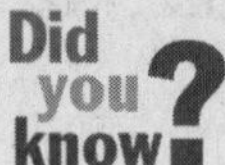

Also called the Maid of Orléans, Joan of Arc was a peasant girl who, believing that she was acting under divine guidance, led the French army in a momentous victory at Orléans that repulsed an English attempt to conquer France during the Hundred Years' War (1337–1453).

Background

Archaeological excavations in France indicate continuous settlement from Paleolithic times. About 1200 BC the Gauls migrated into the area, and in 600 BC Ionian Greeks established several settlements, including one at Marseille. Julius Caesar completed the Roman conquest of Gaul in 50 BC. During the 6th century AD, the Salian Franks ruled; by the 8th century power had passed to the Carolingians, the greatest of whom was Charlemagne. The Hundred Years' War (1337–1453) resulted in the return to France of land that had been held by the British; by the end of the 15th century, France approximated its modern boundaries. The 16th century was marked by the Wars of Religion between Protestants (Huguenots) and Roman Catholics. Henry IV's Edict of Nantes (1598) granted substantial religious toleration, but this was revoked in 1685 by Louis XIV, who helped to raise monarchical absolutism to new heights. In 1789 the French Revolution proclaimed the rights of the individual and destroyed the ancient regime. Napoleon ruled from 1799 to 1814, after which a limited monarchy was restored until 1871, when the Third Republic was created. World War I (1914–18) ravaged the northern part of France. After Nazi Germany's invasion during World War II, the collaborationist Vichy regime governed. Liberated by Allied and Free French forces in 1944, France restored parliamentary democracy under the Fourth Republic. A costly war in Indochina and rising nationalism in French colonies during the 1950s overwhelmed the Fourth Republic. The Fifth Republic was established in 1958 under Charles de Gaulle, who presided over the dissolution of most of France's overseas colonies. In 1981 François Mitterrand became France's first elected Socialist president. During the 1990s the French government, balancing right- and left-wing forces, moved toward solidifying European unity.

Recent Developments

In the 6 May 2007 runoff presidential election, French voters chose Nicolas Sarkozy of the center-right Union for a Popular Movement over the Socialist candidate, Ségolène Royal, to succeed Pres. Jacques Chirac. While maintaining Europe as the prime focus of his foreign policy, Sarkozy was relatively pro-American compared with his predecessors. He created a coalition government, which influenced his decision not to scrap the famous law that placed a 35-hour maximum on the standard workweek (a landmark Socialist law) but rather to use tax relief on overtime pay to moderate the law's rigidity. To the relief of many European Union partners, Sarkozy agreed to put forward a revamped EU treaty for ratification by the French parliament and not by referendum (as Chirac had tried and failed to do in 2005). Sarkozy also took a pragmatic approach to the issue of Turkey's application for EU membership, which he opposed. He gave a green light to negotiations compatible with Turkey's becoming an associate, but not a member, of the EU. Meanwhile, he promoted the idea of a union of Mediterranean rim countries and went to Libya in July and Algeria in December. Visiting Beijing on the eve of a European Union–China summit, Sarkozy bluntly complained about China's surplus with the EU and the undervaluation of the Chinese currency, which was effectively pegged to the dollar. He also warned that the EU might penalize imports from carbon-emitting countries such as China that did not do enough on climate change. Sarkozy made his first official visit as president to the US in early November. He stressed that France would continue to support the fight against terrorism, including keeping French troops in Afghanistan, and endorsed a strong joint stand against Iran's nuclear program. In April 2008 at the NATO summit in Bucharest, Romania, France pledged an additional 700–800 troops to its 1,500-strong contingent in Afghanistan.

Internet resources: <http://us.franceguide.com>.

French Guiana

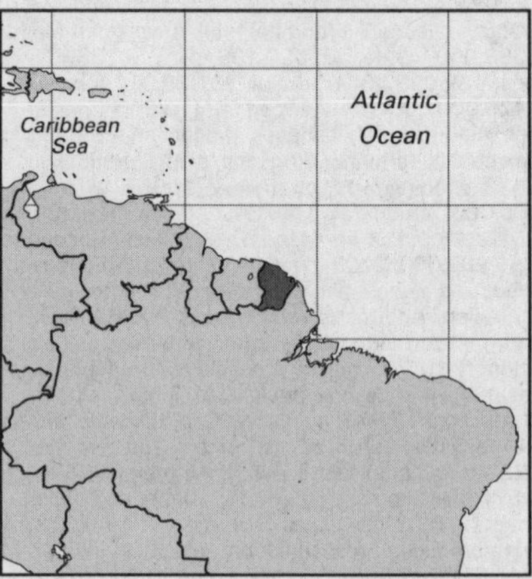

Official name: Département de la Guyane française (Department of French Guiana). **Political status:** overseas department of France with two legislative houses (General Council [19]; Regional Council [31]). **Chief of state:** French President Nicolas Sarkozy (from 2007). **Heads of government:** Prefect Jean-Pierre Laflaquière (from 2006), President Pierre Désert of the General Council (from 2004), and President Antoine Karam of the Regional Council (from 1992). **Capital:** Cayenne. **Official language:** French. **Official religion:** none. **Monetary unit:** 1 euro (€) = 100 cents; valuation (1 Jul 2008) US$1 = €0.63.

Demography

Area: 32,253 sq mi, 83,534 sq km. **Population** (2007): 211,000. **Density** (2007): persons per sq mi

6.5, persons per sq km 2.5. **Urban** (2003): 75.4%. **Sex distribution** (2005): male 50.58%; female 49.42%. **Age breakdown** (2005): under 15, 29.3%; 15–29, 22.8%; 30–44, 21.1%; 45–59, 17.4%; 60–74, 7.2%; 75 and over, 2.2%. **Ethnic composition** (2000): Guianese Mulatto 37.9%; French 8.0%; Haitian 8.0%; Surinamese 6.0%; Antillean 5.0%; Chinese 5.0%; Brazilian 4.9%; East Indian 4.0%; other (other West Indian, Hmong, other South American) 21.2%. **Religious affiliation** (2000): Christian 84.6%, of which Roman Catholic 80.0%, Protestant 3.9%; Chinese folk-religionist 3.6%; Spiritist 3.5%; nonreligious/atheist 3.0%; traditional beliefs 1.9%; Hindu 1.6%; Muslim 0.9%; other 0.9%. **Major cities** (1999; commune population): Cayenne (2003) 60,500 (urban agglomeration 84,181); Saint-Laurent-du-Maroni 19,211; Kourou 19,107; Matoury 18,032; Rémire-Montjoly 15,555. **Location:** northern South America, bordering the Atlantic Ocean, Brazil, and Suriname.

Vital statistics

Birth rate per 1,000 population (2005): 30.9 (world avg. 20.3); (2005) within marriage 10%. **Death rate** per 1,000 population (2005): 4.0 (world avg. 8.6). **Total fertility rate** (avg. births per childbearing woman; 2005): 4.10. **Life expectancy** at birth (2006): male 74.0 years; female 80.8 years.

National economy

Budget (2002). *Revenue:* €145,000,000 (direct taxes 33.1%; indirect taxes 31.7%; revenue from French central government 20.7%). *Expenditures:* €145,000,000 (current expenditures 83.4%; capital expenditures 16.6%). **Production** (metric tons except as noted). *Agriculture, forestry, fishing* (2005): rice 17,774, cassava 10,400, cabbages 6,350; livestock (number of live animals) 10,500 pigs, 9,200 cattle; roundwood 160,373 cu m, of which fuelwood 63%; fisheries production 5,302. *Mining and quarrying* (2004): stone, sand, and gravel 3,000; gold 2,564 kg; tantalum 1,500 kg. *Manufacturing* (2001): pork 1,245; chicken meat 560; rum (2004) 3,786 hectolitres; other products include leather goods, clothing, rosewood essence, yogurt, and beer. Number of satellites launched from the Kourou Space Centre (2005) 5 (in 2004 the European Space Agency, which uses Kourou, accounted for 26% of GDP and employed 8,300). *Energy production (consumption):* electricity (kW-hr; 2004) 430,000,000 (430,000,000); petroleum products (metric tons; 2004) none (317,000). **Households.** Average household size (1999) 3.3; income per household (2000) €30,542 (US$28,139); sources of income (2000): wages and salaries 55.4%, self-employment 17.6%, transfer payments 14.4%; expenditure (2005): food and beverages 21.7%, housing and energy 20.8%, transportation and communications 15.4%, restaurants and hotels 7.9%, household furnishings 7.3%. **Land use** as % of total land area (2003): in temporary crops 0.14%, in permanent crops 0.05%, in pasture 0.08%; overall forest area (2005) 91.8%. **Gross national income** (at 2003 market prices): US$1,610,000,000 (US$9,040 per capita). **Population economically active** (2005): total 60,012; activity rate of total population 30.3% (participation rates: ages 15 and over 65.0%; female 44.7%; unemployed [2006] 29.1%). **Selected balance of payments data.** Receipts from (US$'000,000): tourism (2005) 45.

Foreign trade

Imports (2004): €672,000,000 (machinery and apparatus 18.3%; transportation equipment 16.7%; food products, beverages, and tobacco 13.1%; mineral fuels [mostly refined petroleum] 10.7%; chemicals and chemical products 9.7%). *Major import sources:* France 47.2%; Trinidad and Tobago 9.4%; Japan 2.3%; Martinique 1.8%; US 1.5%. **Exports** (2004): €91,000,000 (nonferrous metals [nearly all gold] 49.7%; live animals and food products [mostly fish, shrimp, and rice] 13.3%; transportation equipment [mostly parts for air and space vehicles] 9.9%; machinery and apparatus 9.9%). *Major export destinations:* France 62.0%; Switzerland 17.1%; Martinique 5.9%; Guadeloupe 3.3%; Italy 2.7%.

Transport and communications

Transport. *Roads* (1996): total length 1,245 km. *Vehicles* (1999): passenger cars 32,900; trucks and buses 11,900. *Air transport* (2005): passengers carried 375,844; cargo carried (2004) 4,400 metric tons. **Communications,** in total units (units per 1,000 persons). Daily newspaper circulation (2005): 9,000 (46); televisions (1998): 37,000 (202); telephone landlines (2001): 51,000 (301); cellular telephone subscribers (2004): 98,000 (536); personal computers (2004): 33,000 (180); total Internet users (2005): 42,000 (216).

Education and health

Educational attainment (1999). Percentage of population ages 20 and over having: no formal education/unknown through lower secondary education 60.9%; vocational 17.5%; upper secondary 9.3%; incomplete higher 5.6%; completed higher 6.7%. **Health** (2005): physicians 342 (1 per 580 persons); hospital beds 697 (1 per 284 persons); infant mortality rate per 1,000 live births 12.1.

Military

Total active duty personnel (2006): French troops 1,470 (army 88.4%, navy 11.6%).

Background

Originally settled by the Spanish, French, and Dutch, the territory of French Guiana was awarded to France in 1667, and the inhabitants were made French citizens after 1877. By 1852 the French began using the territory as a penal colony with one locale, on Devils Island, being especially notorious. It became an overseas territory of France in 1946; the penal colonies were closed by 1939.

Recent Developments

Authorities cracked down on environmentally harmful gold mining in 2008 in French Guiana. Neighboring Suriname expected an influx of gold miners entering the country after French authorities announced new restrictions. Additionally, the establishment of a gold mine by a Canadian company, which environmentalists feared would wreak havoc on the ecosystem, was blocked.

Internet resources: <www.insee.fr/fr/insee_regions/guyane/home/home_page.asp>.

French Polynesia

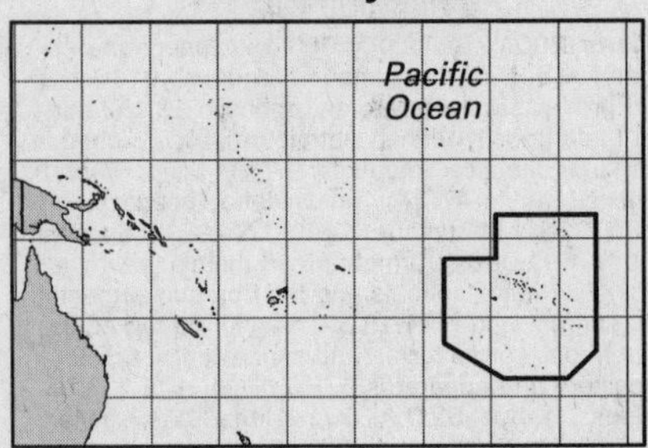

Official name: Polynésie française (French); Polynesia Farani (Tahitian) (French Polynesia). **Political status:** overseas country of France with one legislative house (Assembly [57]). **Chief of state:** French President Nicolas Sarkozy (from 2007), represented by High Commissioner Anne Boquet (from 2005). **Head of government:** President Gaston Flosse (from 2008). **Capital:** Papeete. **Official languages:** French; Tahitian. **Official religion:** none. **Monetary unit:** 1 franc de la Comptoirs française du pacifique (CFPF) = 100 centimes; valuation (1 Jul 2008) US$1 = CFPF 75.59 (pegged to the euro [€] at €1 = CFPF 119.25).

Demography

Area: 1,544 sq mi, 4,000 sq km. **Population** (2007): 261,000. **Density** (2007): persons per sq mi 192.1, persons per sq km 74.1. **Urban** (2005): 51.9%. **Sex distribution** (2005): male 51.64%; female 48.36%. **Age breakdown** (2005): under 15, 26.8%; 15–29, 27.5%; 30–44, 22.9%; 45–59, 14.0%; 60–74, 6.9%; 75 and over, 1.9%. **Ethnic composition** (2000): Polynesian 58.4%, of which Tahitian 41.0%, Tuamotuan 8.5%; mixed European-Polynesian 17.0%; Han Chinese 11.3%; French 11.0%; other 2.3%. **Religious affiliation** (2005): Protestant 36%, of which Maohi Protestant Church (Presbyterian) 33%; Roman Catholic 31%; other Christian 11%, of which Mormon 6%; Chinese folk-religionist, nonreligious, and other 22%. **Major communes** (2007): Faaa 29,851; Papeete 26,017 (urban agglomeration 131,695); Punaauia 25,441; Moorea-Maiao 14,550; Pirae 14,475. **Location:** Oceania, archipelago in the South Pacific Ocean, about midway between South America and Australia.

Vital statistics

Birth rate per 1,000 population (2006): 17.8 (world avg. 20.3); (2004) within marriage 26%. **Death rate** per 1,000 population (2006): 4.4 (world avg. 8.6). **Total fertility rate** (avg. births per childbearing woman; 2006): 2.20. **Life expectancy** at birth (2006): male 73.0 years; female 76.9 years.

National economy

Budget (2005). *Revenue:* CFPF 100,343,000,000 (indirect taxes 70.7%; direct taxes and nontax revenue 29.3%). *Expenditures:* CFPF 148,618,000,000 (current expenditure 68.7%; capital expenditure 31.3%). **Production** (metric tons except as noted). *Agriculture, forestry, fishing* (2005): coconuts 87,000, copra 8,000, cassava 4,300; livestock (number of live animals) 27,000 pigs, 16,500 goats, 12,000 cattle; fisheries production 15,105 (from aquaculture 20%); export production of black pearls (2004) 9,015 kg. *Manufacturing* (2004): copra (metric tons sold) 4,143; coconut oil (2001) 5,000; other manufactures include *monoï* oil (primarily refined coconut and sandalwood oils), beer, printed cloth, and sandals. *Energy production (consumption):* electricity (kW-hr; 2005) 607,100,000 ([2004] 485,000,000); petroleum products (metric tons; 2004) none (218,000). **Population economically active** (2002): total 99,498; activity rate of total population 40.6% (participation rates: ages 15–64, 61.7%; female 40.0%; unemployed 11.7%). **Selected balance of payments data.** Receipts from (US$'000,000): tourism (2005) 550; foreign direct investment (2001–05 avg.) 20. Disbursements for (US$'000,000): tourism (2005) 303. **Gross national income** (2006): US$5,643,000,000 (US$21,766 per capita). **Public debt** (external, outstanding; 1999): US$542,000,000. **Households.** Average household size (2007) 3.8; sources of income (1993): salaries 61.9%, self-employment 21.5%, transfer payments 16.6%; expenditure (2000–01): food and beverages 21.9%, housing 19.2%, transportation 16.7%, hotel and café expenditures 7.7%, culture and recreation 6.9%, household furnishings 5.8%. **Land use** as % of total land area (2003): in temporary crops 0.8%, in permanent crops 6.0%, in pasture 5.5%; overall forest area (2005) 28.7%.

Foreign trade

Imports (2006; c.i.f.): CFPF 157,489,000,000 (machinery and apparatus 16.9%; mineral fuels 12.7%; motor vehicles and parts 10.0%; pharmaceutical products 4.1%). *Major import sources:* France 30.6%; Singapore 12.4%; US 10.3%; China 6.6%; New Zealand 6.5%. **Exports** (2006; f.o.b.): CFPF 22,380,000,000 (pearl products [mostly black cultured pearls] 56.2%; transportation [including aerospace] equipment 8.3%; *noni* fruit 5.2%; fish 1.9%; coconut oil 1.1%; vanilla 0.9%; *monoï* oil 0.9%). *Major export destinations:* Hong Kong 26.8%; Japan 23.1%; France 11.0%; US 10.1%; New Caledonia 1.7%.

Transport and communications

Transport. *Roads* (1999): total length 2,590 km (paved 67%). Motor vehicles: passenger cars (1996) 47,300; trucks and buses (1993) 15,300. *Air transport* (Air Tahiti and Air Tahiti Nui only): passenger-km (2005) 4,023,700,000; metric ton-km cargo (2004) 96,492,000. **Communications,** in total units (units per 1,000 persons). Daily newspaper circulation (2005): 27,000 (106); televisions (2004): 56,000 (223); telephone landlines (2004): 53,000 (216); cellular telephone subscribers (2004): 73,000 (289); personal computers (2005): 28,000 (109); total Internet users (2005): 55,000 (216); broadband Internet subscribers (2005): 11,000 (43).

Education and health

Educational attainment (2002). Percentage of population ages 25 and over having: no formal schooling 4.9%; less than lower-secondary education 46.2%;

1 metric ton = about 1.1 short tons; 1 kilometer = 0.6 mi (statute); 1 metric ton-km cargo = about 0.68 short ton-mi cargo; c.i.f.: cost, insurance, and freight; f.o.b.: free on board

lower secondary 10.9%; upper secondary 11.7%; vocational 15.8%; higher 10.5%. **Literacy** (2000): total population ages 15 and over literate, virtually 100%. **Health:** physicians (2004) 447 (1 per 561 persons); hospital beds (2003) 971 (1 per 256 persons); infant mortality rate per 1,000 live births (2006) 6.8. **Food** (2005): daily per capita caloric intake 3,202 (vegetable products 70%, animal products 30%); 166% of FAO recommended minimum.

Military

Total active duty personnel (2006): 1,510 French military personnel (army 53.0%, navy 47.0%).

Background

European contact with the islands of French Polynesia was gradual. Portuguese navigator Ferdinand Magellan sighted Pukapuka in the Tuamotu group in 1521. The southern Marquesas Islands were discovered in 1595. Dutch explorer Jacob Roggeveen in 1722 discovered Makatea, Bora-Bora, and Maupiti. Captain Samuel Wallis in 1767 discovered Tahiti, Moorea, and Maiao Iti. The Society Islands were named after the Royal Society, which had sponsored the expedition under Capt. James Cook that observed from Tahiti the 1769 transit of the planet Venus. Tubuai was discovered on Cook's last voyage, in 1777. The islands became French protectorates in the 1840s, and in the 1880s the French colony of Oceania was established. French Polynesia became an overseas territory of France after World War II and was granted partial autonomy in 1977.

Recent Developments

French Polynesia had another tumultuous year in 2007 after the pro-independence government of Pres. Oscar Temaru was deposed in December 2006. Pres. Gaston Tong Sang, whose coalition advocated autonomy, announced that the territory would secede from France. Tong Sang was soon deposed by members of his own party, however, and Temaru returned in September to win election as president for the third time in three years. France, seeking a solution to the ongoing instability, proposed to shorten the local assembly's term and to change the electoral system.

Internet resources:
<www.polynesianislands.com/fp>.

Gabon

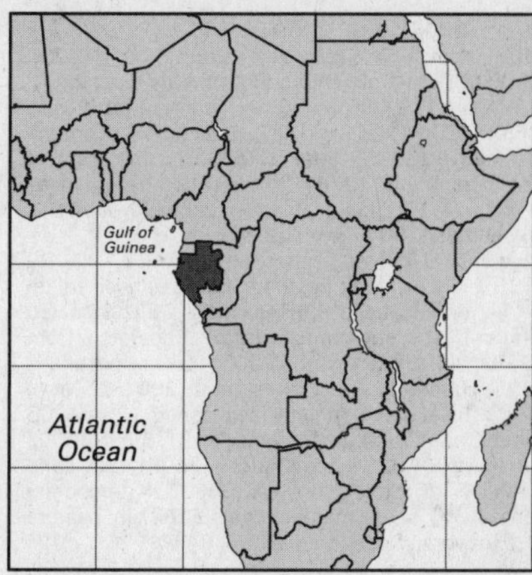

Official name: République Gabonaise (Gabonese Republic). **Form of government:** unitary multiparty republic with two legislative houses (Senate [91]; National Assembly [120]). **Chief of state:** President Omar Bongo Ondimba (from 1967). **Head of government:** Prime Minister Jean Eyeghe Ndong (from 2006). **Capital:** Libreville. **Official language:** French. **Official religion:** none. **Monetary unit:** 1 CFA franc (CFAF) = 100 centimes; valuation (1 Jul 2008) US$1 = CFAF 414.60.

Demography

Area: 103,347 sq mi, 267,667 sq km. **Population** (2007): 1,331,000. **Density** (2007): persons per sq mi 12.9, persons per sq km 5.0. **Urban** (2006): 85.7%. **Sex distribution** (2006): male 49.67%; female 50.33%. **Age breakdown** (2005): under 15, 40.0%; 15–29, 28.3%; 30–44, 16.1%; 45–59, 9.3%; 60–74, 4.6%; 75–84, 1.4%; 85 and over, 0.3%. **Ethnic composition** (2000): Fang 28.6%; Punu 10.2%; Nzebi 8.9%; French 6.7%; Mpongwe 4.1%; Teke 4.0%; other 37.5%. **Religious affiliation** (2005): Christian 73%, of which Roman Catholic 45%, Protestant/independent Christian 28%; Muslim 12%; traditional beliefs 10%; nonreligious 5%. **Major urban areas** (2003): Libreville 661,600; Port-Gentil 116,200; Franceville 41,300; Lambaréné 9,000. **Location:** western Africa, bordering Cameroon, the Republic of the Congo, the South Atlantic Ocean, and Equatorial Guinea.

Vital statistics

Birth rate per 1,000 population (2006): 36.2 (world avg. 20.3). **Death rate** per 1,000 population (2006): 12.3 (world avg. 8.6). **Natural increase rate** per 1,000 population (2006): 23.9 (world avg. 11.7). **Total fertility rate** (avg. births per childbearing woman; 2006): 4.74. **Life expectancy** at birth (2006): male 53.2 years; female 55.8 years.

National economy

Budget (2005). *Revenue:* CFAF 1,432,200,000,000 (oil revenues 63.3%; taxes on international trade 15.0%, of which VAT 5.6%; direct taxes 9.7%; indirect taxes 7.9%; other revenues 4.1%). *Expenditures:* CFAF 872,400,000,000 (current expenditure 82.2%, of which wages and salaries 26.1%, transfers 23.8%, debt service 14.8%; capital expenditure 17.8%). **Public debt** (external, outstanding; 2005): US$3,582,-000,000. **Gross national income** (2006): US$6,828,-000,000 (US$5,209 per capita). **Production** (metric tons except as noted). *Agriculture, forestry, fishing* (2005): plantains 270,000, sugarcane 235,000, cassava 230,000; livestock (number of live animals) 300,000 rabbits, 212,000 pigs, 195,000 sheep; roundwood 3,728,000 cu m, of which fuelwood 14%; fisheries production 43,941. *Mining and quarrying* (2005): manganese ore 2,859,000; gold 300 kg. *Manufacturing* (value added in CFAF '000,000,000; 2004): agricultural products 48.0; wood products (excluding furniture) 31.3; refined petroleum products 18.1. *Energy production (consumption):* electricity (kW-hr; 2004) 1,537,000,000 (1,537,000,000); crude petroleum (barrels; 2004) 78,000,000 (5,000,000); petroleum products (metric tons; 2004) 713,000 (412,000); natural gas (cu m; 2004) 126,000,000 (126,000,000). **Population economically active** (2003): total 570,000; activity rate of total population 42.5% (participation rates: ages 15–64, 74.1%; female 43.0%; unemployed 21%). **Households** (2004). Average household size 5.0; average annual income per household CFAF 1,730,000 (US$3,275); expenditure: food 85.3%, transportation and communications 3.6%, clothing 1.8%. **Selected balance of payments data.** Receipts from (US$'000,000): tourism (2005) 15; remittances (2005) 6; foreign direct investment (2001–05 avg.) 154; official development assistance (2005) 65 (commitments). Disbursements for (US$'000, 000): tourism (2004) 214; remittances (2005) 110. **Land use** as % of total land area (2003): in temporary crops 1.3%, in permanent crops 0.7%, in pasture 18.1%; overall forest area (2005) 84.5%.

Foreign trade

Imports (2005): CFAF 722,600,000,000 (for petroleum sector 27.3%; unspecified 72.7%). *Major import sources* (2003): France 50%; US 5%; UK 5%; The Netherlands 4%; Cameroon 4%. **Exports** (2005): CFAF 2,882,000,000,000 (crude petroleum and petroleum products 83.2%; manganese ore and concentrate 6.4%). *Major export destinations* (2003): US 52%; France 9%; China 8%; Japan 4%; Trinidad and Tobago 3%.

Transport and communications

Transport. *Railroads* (2002): route length (2005) 814 km; passenger-km 97,500,000; metric ton-km cargo 1,553,000,000. *Roads* (2004): total length 9,170 km (paved 10%). *Vehicles* (1997): passenger cars 24,750; trucks and buses 16,490. *Air transport* (2002): passenger-km 643,000,000. **Communications,** in total units (units per 1,000 persons). Daily newspaper circulation (2005): 48,000 (35); televisions (2004): 220,000 (173); telephone landlines (2006): 37,000 (26); cellular telephone subscribers (2006): 765,000 (544); personal computers (2005): 45,000 (33); total Internet users (2006): 81,000 (58); broadband Internet subscribers (2006): 1,200 (0.9).

Education and health

Educational attainment (2000): no formal schooling 6.2%; incomplete primary and complete primary education 32.7%; lower secondary 41.3%; upper secondary 14.2%; higher 5.6%. **Literacy** (2000): total population ages 15 and over literate 71%; males literate 80%; females literate 62%. **Health** (2003–04): physicians 270 (1 per 5,006 persons); hospital beds 4,460 (1 per 303 persons); infant mortality rate per 1,000 live births (2006) 54.5. **Food** (2005): daily per capita caloric intake 2,705 (vegetable products 87%, animal products 13%); 146% of FAO recommended minimum.

Military

Total active duty personnel (2006): 4,700 (army 68.1%, navy 10.6%, air force 21.3%); French troops (2006) 2,260. **Military expenditure as percentage of GDP** (2005): 1.5%; per capita expenditure US$79.

Background

Artifacts dating from late Paleolithic and early Neolithic times have been found in Gabon, but it is not known when the Bantu speakers who established Gabon's ethnic composition arrived. Pygmies were probably the original inhabitants. The Fang arrived in the late 18th century and were followed by the Portuguese and by French, Dutch, and English traders. The slave trade dominated commerce in the 18th and much of the 19th century. The French then took control, and Gabon was administered (1843–86) with French West Africa. In 1886 the colony of French Congo was established to include both Gabon and the Congo; in 1910 Gabon became a separate colony within French Equatorial Africa. An overseas territory of France from 1946, it became an autonomous republic within the French Community in 1958 and declared its independence in 1960. Rule by a sole political party was established in the 1960s, but discontent with it led to riots in Libreville in 1990. Legalization of opposition parties led to new elections in 1990. Peace negotiations with Chadian rebels and with the Republic of the Congo were ongoing in the 1990s.

Recent Developments

China in January 2007 agreed to send 44 agricultural experts to assist small farmers in Gabon. The government promised in March to supply free electricity and water to the country's poorest households to offset the impact of a 25% increase in the price of foodstuffs and fuel, and in an attempt to control surging inflation, price ceilings on basic commodities were put in place in September for a six-month period.

Internet resources:
<www.legabon.org/uk/home.php>.

The Gambia

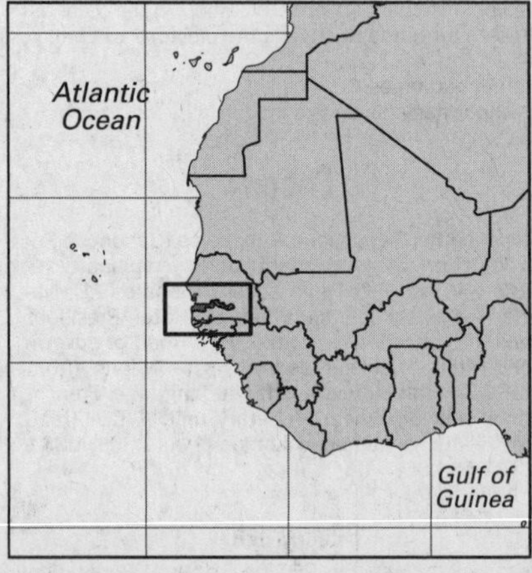

1 metric ton = about 1.1 short tons; 1 kilometer = 0.6 mi (statute); 1 metric ton-km cargo = about 0.68 short ton-mi cargo; c.i.f.: cost, insurance, and freight; f.o.b.: free on board

Official name: The Republic of The Gambia. **Form of government:** multiparty republic with one legislative house (National Assembly [53]). **Head of state and government:** President Col. Yahya Jammeh (from 1994). **Capital:** Banjul. **Official language:** English. **Official religion:** none. **Monetary unit:** 1 dalasi (D) = 100 butut; valuation (1 Jul 2008) US$1 = D 20.90.

Demography

Area (including inland water area of 802 sq mi [2,077 sq km]): 4,127 sq mi, 10,689 sq km. **Population** (2007): 1,709,000. **Density** (2007): persons per sq mi 514.0, persons per sq km 198.4. **Urban** (2006): 26.2%. **Sex distribution** (2003): male 49.59%; female 50.41%. **Age breakdown** (2005): under 15, 40.1%; 15–29, 26.4%; 30–44, 17.3%; 45–59, 10.2%; 60–74, 5.0%; 75–84, 0.9%; 85 and over, 0.1%. **Ethnic composition** (2003): Malinke 42%; Fulani 18%; Wolof 16%; Diola 10%; Soninke 9%; other 5%. **Religious affiliation** (2005): Muslim 90%; Christian (mostly Roman Catholic) 9%; traditional beliefs/other 1%. **Major cities** (2004): Serekunda 225,500; Brikama 81,400; Bakau 74,700; Banjul 36,100 (Greater Banjul [2003] 523,589); Farafenni 31,600. **Location:** western Africa, bordering Senegal and the North Atlantic Ocean.

Vital statistics

Birth rate per 1,000 population (2006): 39.4 (world avg. 20.3). **Death rate** per 1,000 population (2006): 12.3 (world avg. 8.6). **Natural increase rate** per 1,000 population (2006): 27.1 (world avg. 11.7). **Total fertility rate** (avg. births per childbearing woman; 2003): 5.13. **Life expectancy** at birth (2006): male 52.3 years; female 56.0 years.

National economy

Budget (2005). *Revenue:* D 2,823,500,000 (tax revenue 80.2%, of which taxes on international trade 42.7%, corporate taxes 14.4%; nontax revenue 12.0%; grants 7.8%). *Expenditures:* D 3,961,100,000 (current expenditure 61.1%, of which interest payments 28.6%; capital expenditure 38.9%). **Production** (metric tons except as noted). *Agriculture, forestry, fishing* (2005): millet 127,600, peanuts (groundnuts) 100,000, oil palm fruit 35,000; livestock (number of live animals) 330,000 cattle, 270,000 goats, 148,000 sheep; roundwood 760,000 cu m, of which fuelwood 85%; fisheries production 32,000. *Mining and quarrying*: sand, clay ([2005] 13,700), and gravel are excavated for local use. *Manufacturing* (value added in US$; 1995): food products and beverages 6,000,000; textiles, clothing, and footwear 750,000; wood products 550,000. *Energy production (consumption):* electricity (kW-hr; 2005) 156,000,000 (156,000,000); petroleum products (metric tons; 2004) none (93,000). **Population economically active** (2003): total 730,000; activity rate of total population 52.2% (participation rates: female 44.2%; unemployed [2004] extremely high). **Households.** Average household size (2003) 8.6; expenditure (1991; low-income population in Banjul and Kanifing only): food and beverages 58.0%, clothing and footwear 17.5%, energy and water 5.4%, housing 5.1%. **Public debt** (external, outstanding; 2005): US$626,000,000. **Gross national income** (at 2006 market prices): US$485,000,000 (US$292 per capita). **Selected balance of payments data.** Receipts from (US$'000,000): tourism (2005) 56; remittances (2005) 58; foreign direct investment (FDI; 2001–05 avg.) 21; official development assistance (2005) 58. Disbursements for (US$'000,000): tourism (2005) 5; remittances (2005) 1; FDI (2001–05 avg.) 8. **Land use** as % of total land area (2003): in temporary crops 31.5%, in permanent crops 0.5%, in pasture 45.9%; overall forest area (2005) 41.7%.

Foreign trade

Imports (2004; c.i.f.): US$236,600,000 (food and live animals 27.3%; machinery and transport equipment 18.1%; mineral fuels 10.1%; chemicals and chemical products 7.4%). *Major import sources*: China 24.6%; Brazil 16.8%; Senegal 10.4%; UK 5.8%; The Netherlands 4.5%. **Exports** (2004; f.o.b.): US$127,000,000 (reexports 79.7%; peanuts [groundnuts] 13.3%; fruits and vegetables 4.1%). *Major export destinations*: Thailand 16.5%; UK 15.4%; France 14.0%; India 12.8%; Germany 9.1%.

Transport and communications

Transport. *Roads* (2004): total length 3,742 km (paved 19%). *Vehicles* (2004): passenger cars 8,109; trucks and buses 2,961. *Air transport* (2001; Yumdum International Airport at Banjul only): passenger arrivals 300,000, passenger departures 300,000; cargo loaded and unloaded 2,700 metric tons. **Communications,** in total units (units per 1,000 persons). Televisions (2003): 20,000 (13); telephone landlines (2006): 53,000 (32); cellular telephone subscribers (2006): 404,000 (243); personal computers (2004): 23,000 (16); total Internet users (2005): 58,000 (36); broadband Internet subscribers (2005): 100 (0.06).

Education and health

Literacy (2006): total population ages 15 and over literate 43.7%; males literate 51.1%; females literate 36.6%. **Health** (2003): physicians 156 (1 per 9,769 persons); hospital beds (2000) 1,140 (1 per 1,199 persons); infant mortality rate per 1,000 live births (2006) 71.6. **Food** (2005): daily per capita caloric intake 2,537 (vegetable products 93%, animal products 7%); 137% of FAO recommended minimum.

Military

Total active duty personnel (2006): 800 (army 100%). **Military expenditure as percentage of GDP** (2005): 0.5%; per capita expenditure US$2.

Background

Beginning about the 13th century AD, the Wolof, Malinke, and Fulani peoples settled in different parts of what is now The Gambia and established villages and then kingdoms in the region. European exploration began when the Portuguese sighted the Gambia River in 1455. Britain and France both settled in the area in the 17th century. The British Fort James, on an island about 20 mi (32 km) from the river's mouth, was an important collection point for the slave trade. In 1783 the Treaty of Versailles reserved the Gambia River for Britain. After the British abolished slavery in 1807, they built a fort at the mouth of the river to block the continuing slave trade. In 1889 The Gambia's boundaries were agreed upon by Britain and France; the

British declared a protectorate over the area in 1894. Independence was proclaimed in 1965, and The Gambia became a republic within the Commonwealth in 1970. It formed a limited confederation with Senegal in 1982 that was dissolved in 1989. During the 1990s the government was in turmoil.

Recent Developments

Pres. Yahya Jammeh of The Gambia made international news in January 2007 when he announced that on particular days of the week, he could cure HIV, using herbs and bananas and spiritual methods. He also resisted pressure from China to drop his country's support for Taiwan. In early 2008 Jammeh announced that significant amounts of uranium had been discovered in the country and would be exploited.

Internet resources: <www.visitthegambia.gm>.

Georgia

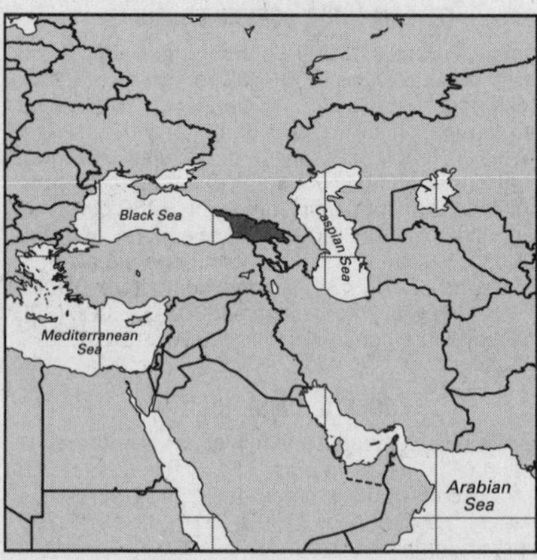

Official name: Sak'art'velo (Georgia). **Form of government:** unitary multiparty republic with a single legislative body (Parliament [235]). **Head of state and government:** President Mikheil Saakashvili (from 2008), assisted by Prime Minister Lado Gurgenidze (from 2007). **Capital:** Tbilisi. **Official language:** Georgian (locally Abkhazian, in Abkhazia). **Official religion:** none (special recognition is given to the Georgian Orthodox Church). **Monetary unit:** 1 Georgian lari (GEL) = 100 tetri; valuation (1 Jul 2008) US$1 = 1.42 lari.

Demography

Area: 27,086 sq mi, 70,152 sq km. **Population** (2007): 4,613,000. **Density** (2007): persons per sq mi 170.3, persons per sq km 65.8. **Urban** (2004): 52.3%. **Sex distribution** (2005): male 47.50%; female 52.50%. **Age breakdown** (2005): under 15, 17.9%; 15–29, 24.2%; 30–44, 21.5%; 45–59, 18.9%; 60 and over, 17.5%. **Ethnic composition** (2002): Georgian 83.8%; Azerbaijani 6.5%; Armenian 5.7%; Russian 1.5%; Ossetian 0.9%; other 1.6%. **Religious affiliation** (2005): Georgian Orthodox 54.8%; Sunni Muslim 14.5%; Shi'i Muslim 5.0%; Armenian Apostolic (Orthodox) 3.9%; Catholic 0.8%; Yazidi 0.4%; Protestant 0.4%; nonreligious 13.0%; other 7.2%. **Major cities** (2006): Tbilisi 1,103,300; K'ut'aisi 190,100; Bat'umi 122,100; Rust'avi 118,200; Sokhumi (2002) 45,000. **Location:** Caucasus region of southwestern Asia, bordering Russia, Azerbaijan, Armenia, Turkey, and the Black Sea.

Vital statistics

Birth rate per 1,000 population (2005): 10.7 (world avg. 20.3); within marriage 50.3%. **Death rate** per 1,000 population (2005): 9.9 (world avg. 8.6). **Total fertility rate** (avg. births per childbearing woman; 2005): 1.35. **Life expectancy** at birth (2005): male 69.3 years; female 76.7 years.

National economy

Budget (2005). *Revenue:* GEL 3,257,200,000 (tax revenue 74.0%, of which VAT 30.3%, income tax 8.9%, excise tax 8.8%, taxes on corporate profits 6.5%; nontax revenue 23.0%; grants 3.0%). *Expenditures:* GEL 3,280,800,000 (social security and welfare 19.1%; defense 12.1%; general public service 10.8%; education 8.8%; public order 8.7%). **Public debt** (external, outstanding; March 2006): US$1,642,850,000. **Population economically active** (2005): total 2,023,900; activity rate of total population 44.1% (participation rates: ages 15–64, 68.4%; female 46.9%; unemployed 13.8%). **Production** (metric tons except as noted). *Agriculture, forestry, fishing* (2005): potatoes 432,202, corn (maize) 421,347, grapes 250,294; livestock (number of live animals) 1,250,672 cattle, 804,900 sheep and goats; roundwood 615,900, of which fuelwood 74%; fisheries production 3,072 (from aquaculture 2%). *Mining and quarrying* (2004): manganese ore 218,700. *Manufacturing* (value of production in GEL '000,000; 2005): food products and beverages 799.6, basic metals 205.7, nonmetallic mineral products 131.2. *Energy production (consumption):* electricity (kW-hr; 2004) 6,920,000,000 ([2005] 9,800,000,000); crude petroleum (barrels; 2004) 718,000 (271,000); petroleum products (metric tons; 2004) 16,000 (508,000); natural gas (cu m; 2004) 11,000,000 ([2005] 1,500,000,000). **Households** (2005). Average household size (2004) 3.7; average annual income per household GEL 3,642 (US$2,009); sources of income: wages and salaries 28.8%, self-employment 13.0%, remittances 12.0%, agricultural income 10.6%, non-cash income 26.1%, other 9.5%; expenditure: food, beverages, and tobacco 38.9%, transportation 7.8%, energy 7.6%, health 5.7%, clothing and footwear 4.3%. **Gross national income** (2006): US$8,296,000,000 (US$1,871 per capita). **Selected balance of payments data.** Receipts from (US$'000,000): tourism (2005) 242; remittances (2006) 545; foreign direct investment (2001–05 avg.) 318; official development assistance (2005) 258 (commitments). Disbursements for (US$'000,000): tourism (2005) 169; remittances (2006) 131. **Land use** as % of total land area (2003): in temporary crops 11.5%, in permanent crops 3.8%, in pasture 27.9%; overall forest area (2005) 39.7%.

Foreign trade

Imports (2006; c.i.f.): US$3,681,230,000 (mineral fuels 17.8%; food products and beverages 15.4%; motor vehicles 9.1%; nonelectrical machinery 9.1%; chemicals and chemical products 8.2%). *Major import sources* (2005): Russia 15.4%; Turkey 11.4%; Azerbaijan 9.4%; Ukraine 8.8%; Germany 8.3%. **Exports** (2006; f.o.b.): US$993,054,000 (food and beverages [including wine] 23.3%; iron and steel 16.6%; transportation equipment 14.1%; chemicals and chemical products 7.8%). *Major export destinations* (2005): Russia 17.8%; Turkey 14.1%; Azerbaijan 9.6%; Turkmenistan 8.7%; Bulgaria 4.9%.

Transport and communications

Transport. *Railroads* (2005): 1,559 km; passenger-km 719,500,000; metric ton-km cargo 6,127,100,000. *Roads* (2005): 20,329 km (paved [2004] 40%). *Vehicles* (2004): passenger cars 255,200; trucks and buses 68,600. *Air transport* (2005): passenger-km 510,800,000; metric ton-km cargo 3,600,000. **Communications,** in total units (units per 1,000 persons). Daily newspaper circulation (2001): 23,000 (5); televisions (2003): 1,627,000 (357); telephone landlines (2006): 553,000 (119); cellular telephone subscribers (2006): 1,704,000 (368); personal computers (2004): 192,000 (42); total Internet users (2006): 332,000 (72); broadband Internet subscribers (2006): 27,000 (5.8).

Education and health

Educational attainment (2004). Percentage of population ages 15 and over having: no formal education/unknown 1.6%; primary education 4.1%; incomplete secondary 10.5%; secondary 48.2%; incomplete higher 12.3%; higher 23.3%. **Literacy** (2004): virtually 100%. **Health** (2005): physicians 20,311 (1 per 226 persons); hospital beds 17,100 (1 per 268 persons); infant mortality rate per 1,000 live births 19.7. **Food** (2005): daily per capita caloric intake 1,797 (vegetable products 72%, animal products 28%); 92% of FAO recommended minimum.

Military

Total active duty personnel (2006): 11,320 (army 62.2%, national guard 14.0%, navy 11.9%, air force 11.9%); UN peacekeeping troops (September 2007): 120 observers and 17 police; the final withdrawal of Russian troops (in Georgia since the collapse of the USSR in 1991) occurred in November 2007. **Military expenditure as percentage of GDP** (2005): 3.5%; per capita expenditure US$51.

Background

Ancient Georgia was the site of the kingdoms of Iberia and Colchis, whose fabled wealth was known to the ancient Greeks. The area was part of the Roman empire by 65 BC and became Christian in AD 337. For the next three centuries it was involved in the conflicts between the Byzantine and Persian empires; after 654 it was controlled by Arab caliphs, who established an emirate in Tbilisi. It was controlled by the Bagratids from the 8th to the 12th century, and the zenith of Georgia's power was reached in the reign of Queen Tamara, whose realm stretched from Azerbaijan to Circassia, forming a pan-Caucasian empire. Invasions by Mongols and Turks in the 13th and 14th centuries disintegrated the kingdom, and the fall of Constantinople (now Istanbul) to the Ottoman Turks in 1453 isolated it from western Christendom. The next three centuries saw repeated invasions by the Armenians, Turks, and Persians. Georgia sought Russian protection in 1783, and in 1801 it was annexed to Russia. After the Russian Revolution of 1917, the area was briefly independent; in 1921 a Soviet regime was installed, and in 1936 Georgia became the Georgian SSR, a full member of the Soviet Union. In 1990 a noncommunist coalition came to power in the first free elections ever held in Soviet Georgia, and in 1991 Georgia declared independence. In the 1990s, while Pres. Eduard Shevardnadze tried to steer a middle course, internal dissension resulted in conflicts with the northwestern republic of Abkhazia, and external distrust of Russian motives in the area grew. In 1992 Abkhazia reinstated its 1925 constitution and declared independence, which Georgia refused to recognize.

Recent Developments

The Georgian parliament in May 2007 endorsed a proposal to create a temporary administration for the breakaway republic of South Ossetia. Dmitry Sanakoyev, who was elected alternative South Ossetian "president" in November 2006, was named to head that administration. Two unidentified aircraft entered Georgian air space in August 2007 and dropped a missile that failed to explode. International experts tentatively concluded that the aircraft were Russian. Georgian special forces killed two Russian military instructors in Abkhazia in September and took seven Abkhaz border guards prisoner. In August 2008, Georgian troops entered South Ossetia, and Russia responded by invading. Several weeks of fighting and Russian occupation ensued, leaving hundreds dead. Russia withdrew most of its forces to the two separatist regions by the end of the month, but on 26 August Moscow recognized the independence of both.

Internet resources: <www.tourism.gov.ge>.

Germany

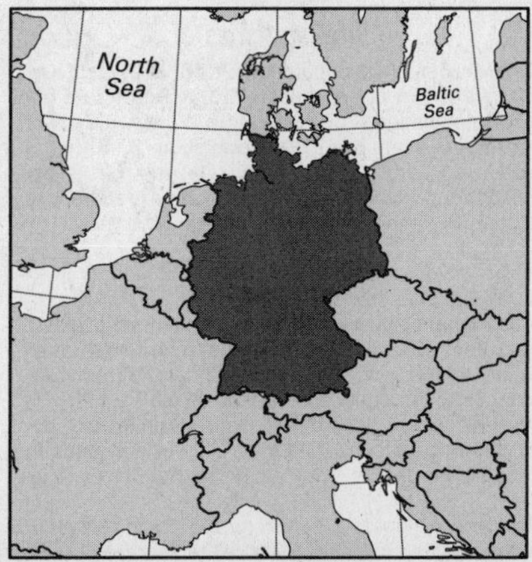

Official name: Bundesrepublik Deutschland (Federal Republic of Germany). **Form of government:** federal multiparty republic with two legislative houses (Federal Council [69]; Federal Diet [614]). **Chief of state:** President Horst Köhler (from 2004). **Head of government:** Chancellor Angela Merkel (from 2005). **Capital:** Berlin; some ministries remain in West Germany's previous capital, Bonn. **Official language:** German. **Official religion:** none. **Monetary unit:** 1 euro (€) = 100 cents; valuation (1 Jul 2008) US$1 = €0.63.

Demography

Area: 137,856 sq mi, 357,046 sq km. **Population** (2007): 82,249,000. **Density** (2007): persons per sq mi 596.6, persons per sq km 230.4. **Urban** (2003): 88.1%. **Major cities (urban agglomerations)** (2005): Berlin 3,395,189 (4,200,072); Hamburg 1,743,627 (2,549,339); Munich 1,259,677 (7,940,477); Cologne 983,347 (1,846,241); Frankfurt am Main 651,899 (1,915,002); Stuttgart 592,569 (2,625,690); Dortmund 588,168 (5,746,018); Essen 585,430 (5,746,018); Düsseldorf 574,514 (1,318,512); Bremen 546,852 (858,488); Hannover 515,729 (1,001,580); Leipzig 502,651 (580,050); Duisburg 501,564 (5,746,018); Nuremberg (Nürnberg) 499,237 (1,030,168). **Location:** central Europe, bordering Denmark, the Baltic Sea, Poland, the Czech Republic, Austria, Switzerland, France, Luxembourg, Belgium, The Netherlands, and the North Sea. **Sex distribution** (2006): male 48.96%; female 51.04%. **Ethnic composition** (by nationality; 2000): German 88.2%; Turkish 3.4% (including Kurdish 0.7%); Italian 1.0%; Greek 0.7%; Serb 0.6%; Russian 0.6%; Polish 0.4%; other 5.1%. **Households** (2005). Number of households 39,178,000; average household size 2.1; 1 person 37.5%, 2 persons 33.9%, 3 persons 14.0%, 4 persons 10.7%, 5 or more persons 3.9%. **Age breakdown** (2003): under 15, 14.7%; 15–29, 17.4%; 30–44, 23.9%; 45–59, 19.3%; 60–74, 16.9%; 75–84, 6.1%; 85 and over, 1.7%. **Religious affiliation** (2005): Protestant 35.0%, of which Lutheran/Reformed churches 34%; Roman Catholic 32.5%; Sunni Muslim 4.3%; Orthodox 1.7%; New Apostolic (an independent Christian group) 0.5%; Buddhist 0.3%; Jewish 0.2%; nonreligious 18.0%; atheist 2.0%; other 5.5%. **Immigration** (2003): immigrant arrivals 601,759, from Poland 14.6%, Turkey 8.0%, Russia 5.2%, Romania 3.9%.

Vital statistics

Birth rate per 1,000 population (2006): 8.2 (world avg. 20.3); (2004) within marriage 72.0%. **Death rate** per 1,000 population (2006): 10.0 (world avg. 8.6). **Natural increase rate** per 1,000 population (2006): −1.8 (world avg. 11.7). **Total fertility rate** (avg. births per childbearing woman; 2006): 1.39. **Life expectancy** at birth (2006): male 75.8 years; female 82.0 years.

Social indicators

Educational attainment (2002). Percentage of population ages 25–64 having: no formal schooling through lower secondary 17%; upper secondary/higher vocational 60%; university 23%. **Quality of working life.** Average workweek (2005) 38.2 hours. Annual rate per 100,000 workers (2002) for: injuries or accidents at work 3,554; deaths 2.9. Proportion of labor force insured for damages of income loss resulting from: injury, virtually 100%; permanent disability, virtually 100%; death, virtually 100%. Average days lost to labor stoppages per 1,000 workers (2005) 0.5. **Access to services.** Proportion of dwellings (2002) having: electricity, virtually 100%; piped water supply, virtually 100%; flush sewage disposal (1993) 98.4%; public fire protection, virtually 100%. **Social participation.** Eligible voters participating in last (September 2005) national election 77.7%. Trade union membership in total workforce (2003) 18%. **Social deviance** (2000). Offense rate per 100,000 population for: murder and manslaughter 3.8; sexual abuse 37.0, of which rape and forcible sexual assault 11.7, child molestation 10.2; assault and battery 153.2; theft 754.2. **Material well-being** (2005). Households possessing: automobile 76.8%; telephone (2006) 95.2%; mobile telephone (2006) 80.6%; refrigerator 99.1%; television (2004) 95.0%; DVD player 50.1%; washing machine (2004) 95.5%; clothes dryer 39.3%; personal computer (2006) 71.6%; dishwasher 59.1%; microwave oven 67.0%; Internet access (2006) 57.9%; MP3 player 14.7%.

National economy

Budget (2004). *Revenue:* €639,220,000,000 (social security contributions 58.3%; tax revenue 37.6%, of which individual income taxes 13.7%, taxes on goods and services 10.2%, excise taxes 10.2%; nontax revenue 2.2%; other 1.9%). *Expenditures:* €691,480,-000,000 (social benefits 71.4%; grants 7.9%; interest 5.7%; compensation of employees 5.5%). **Total public debt** (2004): US$1,732,000,000,000. **Production** (metric tons except as noted; 2005). *Agriculture, forestry, fishing:* sugar beets 25,284,700, wheat 23,692,700, potatoes 11,624,000, barley 11,613,800, rapeseed 5,051,700, grapes 1,014,700, apples 852,600, cabbages 721,500, currants 148,000, gooseberries 38,000, hops 34,500; livestock (number of live animals) 26,857,800 pigs, 13,034,500 cattle, 2,642,400 sheep, 107,267,000 chickens; roundwood 56,946,000 cu m, of which fuelwood 11%; fisheries production 330,353 (from aquaculture 14%). *Mining and quarrying:* potash (potassium oxide content) 3,664,000; feldspar 500,000. *Manufacturing* (value added in US$'000,000; 2003): transportation equipment 80,003, of which motor vehicles 46,854, motor vehicle parts 20,655; nonelectrical machinery and apparatus 64,943; electrical machinery and electronics 47,403, of which electricity distribution and control apparatus 18,799; fabricated metal products 41,855; food and food products 31,727; paints, soaps, and pharmaceuticals 26,172; industrial chemicals 20,211; printing and publishing 19,829; professional and scientific equipment 19,045, of which medical, measuring, and testing appliances 16,737; plastic products 17,333; cement, bricks, and ceramics 10,736. *Energy production (consumption):* electricity (kW-hr; 2004) 533,268,000,000 (616,785,000,000); hard coal (metric tons; 2004) 29,200,000 (57,900,000); lignite (metric tons; 2004) 181,900,000 (182,000,000); crude petroleum (barrels; 2004) 25,100,000 (810,600,000); petroleum products (metric tons; 2004) 103,600,000 (99,900,000); natural gas (cu m; 2004) 29,100,000,000 (120,600,000,000). **Gross na-**

1 metric ton = about 1.1 short tons; 1 kilometer = 0.6 mi (statute); 1 metric ton-km cargo = about 0.68 short ton-mi cargo; c.i.f.: cost, insurance, and freight; f.o.b.: free on board

tional income (2006): US$2,901,482,000,000 (US$35,110 per capita). **Households.** Average annual disposable income per household (2003) €33,840 (US$38,194); sources of take-home income (1997): wages 77.6%, self-employment 12.0%, transfer payments 10.4%; expenditure (2003): housing and energy 32.5%, transportation 14.4%, food, beverages, and tobacco 14.0%, recreation and culture 11.8%, household furnishings 5.7%, clothing and footwear 5.0%, restaurants and hotels 4.3%. **Population economically active** (2005): total 41,150,000; activity rate of total population 49.9% (participation rates: ages 15–64, 73.7%; female 44.8%; unemployed [2006] 8.1%). **Selected balance of payments data.** Receipts from (US$'000,000): tourism (2005) 29,151; remittances (2006) 6,667; foreign direct investment (FDI) (2001–05 avg.) 25,337. Disbursements for (US$'000,000): tourism (2005) 72,488; remittances (2006) 12,344; FDI (2001–05 avg.) 22,464. **Land use** as % of total land area (2003): in temporary crops 33.9%, in permanent crops 0.6%, in pasture 14.2%; overall forest area (2005) 31.7%.

Foreign trade

Imports (2005; c.i.f.): €625,632,000,000 (machinery and equipment 21.7%, of which televisions, telecommunications equipment, and electronic components 6.4%, office machinery and computers 4.6%; transport equipment 14.2%, of which road vehicles 10.2%; chemicals and chemical products 11.3%; crude petroleum and natural gas 8.3%; base metals 6.0%; food products and beverages 4.5%; wearing apparel 2.6%). *Major import sources* (2006): France 8.7%; The Netherlands 8.3%; China 6.7%; US 6.6%; UK 5.9%; Italy 5.5%; Belgium 4.9%; Russia 4.1%; Austria 4.1%; Switzerland 3.4%. **Exports** (2005; f.o.b.): €786,186,000,000 (machinery and equipment 26.5%, of which televisions, telecommunications equipment, and electronic components 4.7%; transport equipment 22.6%, of which road vehicles 19.2%; chemicals and chemical products 13.1%; base metals 5.2%; medical and precision instruments and watches and clocks 4.2%). *Major export destinations* (2006): France 9.6%; US 8.7%; UK 7.3%; Italy 6.7%; The Netherlands 6.2%; Belgium 5.5%; Austria 5.5%; Spain 4.7%; Switzerland 3.9%; Poland 3.2%.

Transport and communications

Transport. *Railroads* (2001): length 85,653 km; passenger-km (2003) 71,292,000,000; metric ton-km cargo (2004) 86,400,000,000. *Roads* (2004): total length 231,420 km (paved 100%). *Vehicles* (2006): passenger cars 46,090,300; trucks and buses 2,573,100. *Air transport* (2005): passenger-km 137,364,000,000; metric ton-km cargo 7,680,396,000. **Communications,** in total units (units per 1,000 persons). Daily newspaper circulation (2004): 22,095,000 (268); televisions (2003): 55,758,000 (675); telephone landlines (2006): 54,200,000 (658); cellular telephone subscribers (2006): 84,300,000 (1,023); personal computers (2004): 46,300,000 (561); total Internet users (2006): 38,600,000 (469); broadband Internet subscribers (2006): 14,085,000 (171).

Education and health

Health (2004): physicians 306,000 (1 per 270 persons); hospital beds 531,333 (1 per 155 persons); infant mortality rate per 1,000 live births (2006) 4.1. **Food** (2005): daily per capita caloric intake 3,472 (vegetable products 68%, animal products 32%).

Military

Total active duty personnel (2006): 284,500 (army 67.3%, navy 9.0%, air force 23.7%); German peacekeeping troops abroad (April 2006) more than 7,500; US troops in Germany (2005) 66,000; British troops (2005) 22,000; French troops (2005) 2,800; Dutch troops (2005) 2,300. **Military expenditure as percentage of GDP** (2005): 1.4%; per capita expenditure US$462.

Did you know? The Berlin Wall surrounded West Berlin and prevented access to it from East Berlin and adjacent areas of East Germany during the period from 1961 to 1989 (28 years).

Background

Germanic tribes entered the region about the 2nd century BC, displacing the Celts. The Romans failed to conquer the region, which became a political entity only with the division of the Carolingian Empire in the 9th century AD. The monarchy's control was weak, and power increasingly devolved upon the nobility, organized in feudal states. The monarchy was restored under Saxon rule in the 10th century, and the Holy Roman Empire, centering on Germany and northern Italy, was revived. Continuing conflict between the Holy Roman emperors and the Roman Catholic popes undermined the empire, and its dissolution was accelerated by Martin Luther's revolt in 1517, which divided Germany, and ultimately Europe, into Protestant and Roman Catholic camps, culminating in the Thirty Years' War (1618–48). Germany's population and borders were greatly reduced, and its numerous feudal princes gained virtually full sovereignty. In 1862 Otto von Bismarck came to power in Prussia and over the next decade reunited Germany in the German Empire. It was dissolved in 1918 after the German defeat in World War I. Germany was stripped of much of its territory and all of its colonies. In 1933 Adolf Hitler became chancellor and established a totalitarian state, the Third Reich, dominated by the Nazi Party. Hitler's invasion of Poland in 1939 plunged the world into World War II. Following its defeat in 1945, Germany was divided by the Allied Powers into four zones of occupation. Disagreement with the USSR over the reunification of the zones led to the creation in 1949 of the Federal Republic of Germany (West Germany) and the German Democratic Republic (East Germany). Berlin, the former capital, remained divided. West Germany became a prosperous parliamentary democracy, East Germany a one-party state under Soviet control. The East German Communist government was brought down peacefully in 1989, and Germany was reunited in 1990. After the initial euphoria over unity, the former West Germany sought to incorporate the former East Germany both politically and economically, resulting in heavy financial burdens for the wealthier western Germans. The country continued to move toward deeper political and economic integration with Western Europe through its membership in the European Union.

Recent Developments

Energy security in Germany in 2007 was very much bound up with the topic of nuclear energy. The idea of potentially having to increase the use of nuclear energy, or even build a new nuclear energy reactor, seemed inconceivable to many Germans—even though this might be the only way to reach the country's ambitious emission goals (a reduction of 40% by 2020, relative to 1990). The renewable-energy sector showed a large upswing in the economy. The overall economy posted a positive trend. Unemployment decreased to some 3.5 million (with a slight cyclical increase of unemployment in the summer), and in the year ending March 2008 the unemployment rate had dropped almost a full percent, to 8.0%. Germany's GDP grew by 4.4%. The population growth rate in 2007 was estimated at −0.033%. As Germans had fewer children, the resulting decrease in the number of taxpayers—along with an increasing number of retirees—was likely to cause economic problems. In June 2008 Germany agreed to send an additional 1,000 troops to its force in Afghanistan.

Internet resources: <www.germany-tourism.de>.

Ghana

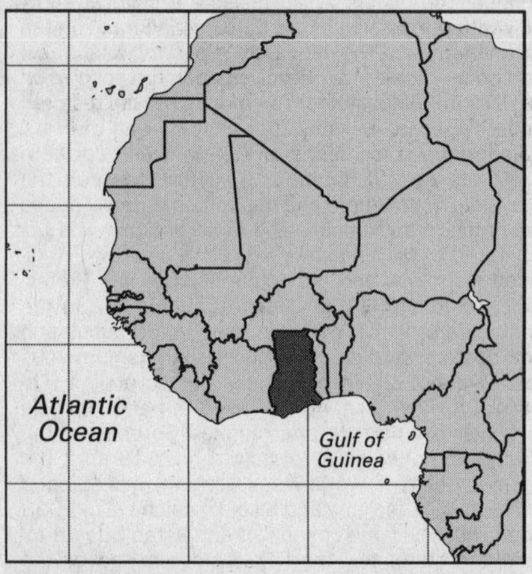

Official name: Republic of Ghana. **Form of government:** unitary multiparty republic with one legislative house (House of Parliament [230]). **Head of state and government:** President John Agyekum Kufuor (from 2001). **Capital:** Accra. **Official language:** English. **Official religion:** none. **Monetary unit:** 1 Ghana cedi (GH¢) = 100 pesewas; valuation (1 Jul 2008) US$1 = GH¢ 10,945.00 (the Ghana cedi replaced the cedi [₵] 1 Jul 2007, at the rate of 1 GH¢ = ₵10,000).

Demography

Area: 92,098 sq mi, 238,533 sq km. **Population** (2007): 22,931,000. **Density** (2007): persons per sq mi 249.0, persons per sq km 96.1. **Urban** (2006): 46.8%. **Sex distribution** (2006): male 50.05%; female 49.95%. **Age breakdown** (2006): under 15, 38.7%; 15–29, 29.0%; 30–44, 18.1%; 45–59, 8.9%; 60–74, 4.2%; 75–84, 1.0%; 85 and over, 0.1%. **Ethnic composition** (2000): Akan 41.6%; Mossi 23.0%; Ewe 10.0%; Ga-Adangme 7.2%; Gurma 3.4%; Nzima 1.8%; Yoruba 1.6%; other 11.4%. **Religious affiliation** (2005): Protestant 23.7%; traditional beliefs 21.5%; Sunni Muslim 20.1%; independent Christian 15.9%; Roman Catholic 12.2%; other 6.6%. **Major cities** (2001): Accra (2003) 1,847,432; Kumasi 627,600; Tamale 269,200; Tema 237,700; Obuasi 122,600. **Location:** western Africa, bordering Burkina Faso, Togo, the Atlantic Ocean, and Côte d'Ivoire.

Vital statistics

Birth rate per 1,000 population (2006): 30.5 (world avg. 20.3). **Death rate** per 1,000 population (2006): 9.7 (world avg. 8.6). **Natural increase rate** per 1,000 population (2006): 20.8 (world avg. 11.7). **Total fertility rate** (avg. births per childbearing woman; 2006): 3.99. **Life expectancy** at birth (2006): male 58.0 years; female 59.6 years.

National economy

Budget (2006). *Revenue:* ₵31,917,680,000,000 (tax revenue 77.2%, of which VAT 18.4%, trade tax 17.0%, petroleum tax 12.8%, income tax 9.7%, corporate tax 9.4%; grants 19.9%; nontax revenue 2.9%). *Expenditures:* ₵38,734,730,000,000 (current expenditure 63.9%, of which transfers 14.7%, debt service 10.2%; capital expenditure 36.1%). **Public debt** (external, outstanding; 2005): US$5,734,000,000. **Households** (1999). Average household size (2003) 3.9; mean annual household income ₵2,267,000 (US$849); sources of income: income from agriculture 37.0%, other self-employment 31.3%, wages and salaries 22.8%, remittances 4.8%; expenditure: food and nonalcoholic beverages 53.6%, clothing and footwear 10.0%, household operations 8.8%, education 6.1%, transportation and communications 5.6%. **Gross national income** (2006): US$12,000,000,000 (US$522 per capita). **Production** (metric tons except as noted). *Agriculture, forestry, fishing* (2005): cassava 9,739,000, yams 3,892,000, plantains 2,381,000; livestock (number of live animals) 3,631,600 goats, 3,211,100 sheep, 1,385,000 cattle; roundwood 22,028,000 cu m, of which fuelwood 94%; fisheries production 393,428. *Mining and quarrying* (2005): bauxite 726,000; manganese (metal content) 600,000; gold 66,852 kg. *Manufacturing* (value added in US$'000,000; 2003): processed wood and wood products 157; chemicals and chemical products 115; food products 108. *Energy production (consumption):* electricity (kW-hr; 2004) 6,044,000,000 (6,044,000,000); crude petroleum (barrels; 2005) 350,000 ([2004] 13,200,000); petroleum products (metric tons; 2004) 1,646,000 (1,898,000). **Population economically active** (2000): total 9,039,318; activity rate of total population 47.8% (participation rates: ages 15–64, 76.2%; female 54.1%; unemployed [2001] 20.3%). **Selected balance of payments data.** Receipts from (US$'000,000): tourism (2005) 796; remittances (2005) 99; foreign direct investment (2001–05 avg.) 116; official development assistance (2005) 1,184 (commitments). Disbursements for (US$'000,000):

tourism (2005) 303; remittances (2005) 6. **Land use** as % of total land area (2003): in temporary crops 18.4%, in permanent crops 9.7%, in pasture 36.7%; overall forest area (2005) 24.2%.

Foreign trade

Imports (2005): US$5,279,810,000 (crude and refined petroleum 19.8%; nonpetroleum imports 80.2%). *Major import sources* (2004): Nigeria 12.8%; China 10.1%; UK 7.0%; US 6.7%; France 5.3%. **Exports** (2005): US$2,736,610,000 (gold 34.6%; cocoa beans and products 30.8%; sawn wood 8.3%). *Major export destinations* (2004): The Netherlands 11.1%; UK 10.9%; France 6.9%; US 6.0%; Belgium 4.8%.

Transport and communications

Transport. *Railroads* (2002): route length (2005) 953 km; passenger-km 238,000,000; metric ton-km cargo 168,000,000. *Roads* (2003): total length 47,787 km (paved 18%). *Vehicles* (2002): passenger cars 463,000; trucks and buses 56,000. *Air transport* (2003; Ghana Airways only, which subsequently ceased operations in July 2004): passenger-km 906,000,000; metric ton-km cargo 16,630,000. **Communications,** in total units (units per 1,000 persons). Daily newspaper circulation (2005): 190,000 (8.7); televisions (2003): 1,114,000 (53); telephone landlines (2006): 356,000 (16); cellular telephone subscribers (2006): 5,207,000 (232); personal computers (2004): 112,000 (5.2); total Internet users (2006): 610,000 (27); broadband Internet subscribers (2006): 13,000 (0.6).

Education and health

Educational attainment (2003). Percentage of population ages 25 and over having: no formal schooling/unknown 41.8%; incomplete primary education 9.6%; primary 3.6%; incomplete secondary 35.0%; secondary 5.4%; higher 4.6%. **Literacy** (2005): total population ages 15 and over literate 77.0%; males literate 84.2%; females literate 70.0%. **Health:** physicians (2004) 3,240 (1 per 6,631 persons); hospital beds (2001) 18,448 (1 per 1,089 persons); infant mortality rate per 1,000 live births (2006) 54.9. **Food** (2005): daily per capita caloric intake 3,098 (vegetable products 96%, animal products 4%); 167% of FAO recommended minimum.

Military

Total active duty personnel (2006): 7,000 (army 71.4%, navy 14.3%, air force 14.3%). **Military expenditure as percentage of GDP** (2005): 0.7%; per capita expenditure US$4.

Background

The modern state of Ghana is named after the ancient Ghana empire that flourished until the 13th century AD in the western Sudan, about 500 mi (800 km) northwest of the modern state. The Akan peoples then founded their first states in modern Ghana. Gold-seeking Mande traders arrived by the 14th century, and Hausa merchants arrived by the 16th century. During the 15th century the Mande founded the states of Dagomba and Mamprussi in the northern half of the region. The Ashanti, an Akan people, originated in the central forest region and formed a strongly centralized empire that was at its height in the 18th and 19th centuries. European exploration of the region began early in the 15th century, when the Portuguese landed on the Gold Coast; they later established a settlement at Elmina as headquarters for the slave trade. By the mid-18th century the Gold Coast was dominated by numerous forts controlled by Dutch, British, and Danish merchants. Britain made the Gold Coast a crown colony in 1874, and British protectorates over the Ashanti and the northern territories were established in 1901. In 1957 the Gold Coast became the independent state of Ghana.

Recent Developments

In June 2007 the British firm Tullow Oil announced the discovery of a major new oil field offshore from Ghana, with reserves estimated at 600 million bbl. Company officials cautioned that it would take up to seven years before the oil field was operational. Nevertheless, Pres. John Kufuor enthused that this find would transform the country into an "African tiger." For those who feared that Ghana would mismanage its future oil wealth, Kufuor assured them that Accra's economy would remain robust even without oil revenue.

Internet resources: <www.touringghana.com>.

Greece

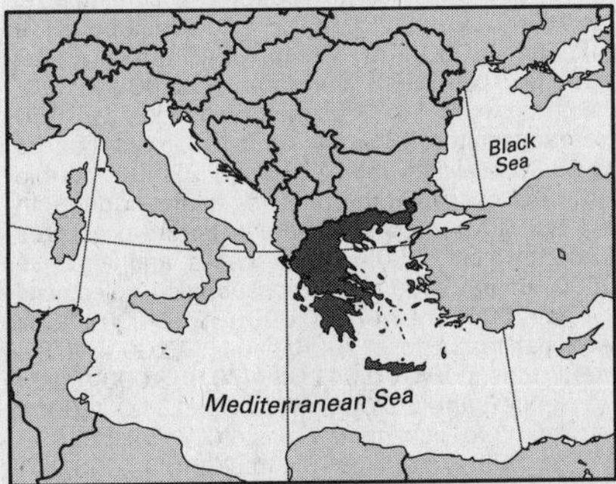

Official name: Elliniki Dhimokratia (Hellenic Republic). **Form of government:** unitary multiparty republic with one legislative house (Hellenic Parliament [300]). **Chief of state:** President Karolos Papoulias (from 2005). **Head of government:** Prime Minister Konstantinos (Kostas) Karamanlis (from 2004). **Capital:** Athens. **Official language:** Greek. **Official religion:** Eastern Orthodox. **Monetary unit:** 1 euro (€) = 100 cents; valuation (1 Jul 2008) US$1 = €0.63 (the euro replaced the drachma [Dr] 1 Jan 2002, at the rate of €1 = Dr 340.75).

Demography

Area: 50,949 sq mi, 131,957 sq km. **Population** (2007): 11,190,000. **Density** (2007): persons per sq mi 219.6, persons per sq km 84.8. **Urban** (2003): 60.8%. **Sex distribution** (2005): male 49.41%; female 50.59%. **Age breakdown** (2005): under 15, 14.3%; 15–29, 20.3%; 30–44, 23.0%; 45–59, 19.4%; 60–74, 15.3%; 75–84, 6.2%; 85 and over, 1.5%. **Ethnic composition** (2000; unofficial source; government states that there are no ethnic divisions in

Greece): Greek 90.4%; Macedonian 1.8%; Albanian 1.5%; Turkish 1.4%; Pomak 0.9%; Rom (Gypsy) 0.9%; other 3.1%. **Religious affiliation** (2005): Orthodox 90%; Sunni Muslim 5%; Roman Catholic 2%; other 3%. **Major cities** (2001): Athens 745,514 (urban agglomeration 3,187,734); Thessaloniki 363,987 (urban agglomeration 800,764); Piraeus (Piraievs) 175,697; Patrai 161,114; Peristerion 137,918. **Location:** southern Europe, bordering Albania, Macedonia, Bulgaria, Turkey, and the Mediterranean Sea.

Vital statistics

Birth rate per 1,000 population (2005): 9.7 (world avg. 20.3); within marriage 94.9%. **Death rate** per 1,000 population (2005): 9.5 (world avg. 8.6). **Total fertility rate** (avg. births per childbearing woman; 2005): 1.28. **Life expectancy** at birth (2005): male 76.6 years; female 81.5 years.

National economy

Budget (2006). *Revenue:* €48,600,000,000 (tax revenue 92.2%, of which VAT 32.6%, income taxes 30.4%; nontax revenue 7.8%). *Expenditures:* €50,413,-000,000 (pensions and salaries 38.8%; interest payments 18.9%; health and social insurance 17.2%; operating expenditure 17.0%). **Public debt** (consolidated, general; 2005): US$305,300,000,000. **Production** (metric tons except as noted). *Agriculture, forestry, fishing* (2005): sugar beets 2,573,400, corn (maize) 2,300,000, olives 2,200,000; livestock (number of live animals) 9,000,000 sheep, 5,400,000 goats, 1,300,000 beehives; roundwood 1,523,000 cu m, of which fuelwood 66%; fisheries production 198,950 (from aquaculture 53%). *Mining and quarrying*: bauxite 3,315,300; nickel (metal content) 22,000; marble 230,000 cu m. *Manufacturing* (value added in US$'000,000; 2005): food products and beverages 5,300; textiles 1,950; cement, bricks, and ceramics 1,600. *Energy production (consumption):* electricity (kW-hr; 2004) 59,344,000,000 (62,164,000,000); hard coal (metric tons; 2004) none (776,000); lignite (metric tons; 2004) 70,041,000 (70,855,000); crude petroleum (barrels; 2004) 847,000 (134,000,000); petroleum products (metric tons; 2004) 19,115,000 (17,915,000); natural gas (cu m; 2004) 34,000,000 (2,657,000,000). **Households** (1998–99). Average household size (2004) 3.1; income per family Dr 6,429,000 (US$21,390); sources of income: wages and salaries 21.8%, transfer payments 21.7%, income from agriculture, forestry, and fishing 15.6%, self-employment 11.9%, other 29.0%; expenditure (2004–05): food 17.1%, transportation 12.6%, housing and energy 10.7%, café/hotel expenditures 9.6%, clothing and footwear 8.4%. **Population economically active** (2006): total 4,891,200; activity rate of total population 43.9% (participation rates: ages 15–64, 66.9%; female 40.8%; unemployed [January–March 2007] 9.1%). **Gross national income** (2006): US$307,364,000,000 (US$27,634 per capita). **Selected balance of payments data.** Receipts from (US$'000,000): tourism (2005) 13,578; remittances (2006) 1,543; foreign direct investment (FDI) (2001–05 avg.) 1,240. Disbursements for (US$'000,000): tourism (2005) 3,039; remittances (2006) 982; FDI (2001–05 avg.) 833. **Land use** as % of total land area (2003): in temporary crops 20.9%, in permanent crops 8.8%, in pasture 35.7%; overall forest area (2005) 29.1%.

Foreign trade

Imports (2003; f.o.b. in balance of trade and c.i.f. in commodities and trading partners): US$44,856,-000,000 (machinery and apparatus 15.1%; chemicals and chemical products 12.5%; crude petroleum 9.2%; food products 9.2%; road vehicles 8.8%; ships and boats 8.2%). *Major import sources* (2004): Germany 13.4%; Italy 12.9%; France 6.4%; The Netherlands 5.6%; Russia 5.4%. **Exports** (2003): US$13,671,000,000 (food 14.4%, of which fruits and nuts 5.0%; clothing and apparel 13.3%; machinery and apparatus 10.2%; refined petroleum 6.4%). *Major export destinations* (2004): Germany 13.2%; Italy 10.1%; UK 7.6%; Bulgaria 6.3%; US 5.3%.

Transport and communications

Transport. *Railroads* (2002): length 2,383 km; passenger-km 1,836,000,000; metric ton-km cargo 327,000,000. *Roads* (2004): total length 114,931 km (paved [1999] 92%). *Vehicles* (2004): passenger cars 4,073,511; trucks and buses 1,185,917. *Air transport* (2005): passenger-km 7,332,000,000; metric ton-km cargo 58,464,000. **Communications,** in total units (units per 1,000 persons). Daily newspaper circulation (2005): 878,000 (79); televisions (2003): 6,152,000 (558); telephone landlines (2006): 6,185,000 (555); cellular telephone subscribers (2006): 11,098,000 (996); personal computers (2004): 1,476,000 (150); total Internet users (2006): 2,048,000 (184); broadband Internet subscribers (2006): 488,000 (44).

Education and health

Educational attainment (2001). Percentage of population ages 25 and over having: no formal schooling 12.7%; primary education 34.3%; lower secondary 8.5%; upper secondary 25.7%; higher 18.8%. **Literacy** (2001): total population ages 15 and over literate 97.3%; males literate 98.5%; females literate 96.1%. **Health:** physicians (2001) 47,944 (1 per 229 persons); hospital beds (2001) 52,276 (1 per 210 persons); infant mortality rate (2005) 3.8. **Food** (2005): daily per capita caloric intake 3,706 (vegetable products 76%, animal products 24%).

Military

Total active duty personnel (2006): 163,850 (army 67.1%, navy 11.8%, air force 14.0%, joint staff 7.1%); Greek troops in Cyprus (2006) 1,150. **Military expenditure as percentage of GDP** (2005): 4.1%; per capita expenditure US$833.

Background

The earliest urban society in Greece was the palace-centered Minoan civilization, which reached its height on Crete c. 2000 BC. It was succeeded by the mainland Mycenaean civilization, which arose c. 1600 BC following a wave of Indo-European invasions. About 1200 BC a second wave of invasions destroyed the Bronze Age cultures, and a dark age followed, known mostly through the epics of Homer. At the end of this time, classical Greece began to emerge (c. 750 BC) as a collection of independent city-states, including Sparta in the Peloponnese and Athens in Attica. The civilization reached its zenith after repelling the Persians at the beginning of the 5th century BC and began to decline after the civil strife of the Peloponnesian War at the century's end. In 338 BC the Greek city-states were taken over by Philip II of Macedon, and Greek culture was spread by Philip's son Alexander the Great throughout his empire. The Romans, themselves heavily influenced by Greek culture, conquered the Greek states in the 2nd century BC. After the fall of Rome, Greece remained part of the Byzantine empire until the mid-15th century, when it became part of the expanding Ottoman Empire; it gained its independence in 1832. It was occupied by Nazi Germany during World War II. Civil war followed and lasted until 1949, when communist forces were defeated. In 1952 Greece joined NATO. A military junta ruled the country from 1967 to 1974, when democracy was restored and a referendum declared an end to the Greek monarchy. In 1981 Greece joined the European Community, the first Eastern European country to do so. Upheavals in the Balkans in the 1990s strained Greece's relations with some neighboring states, notably the former Yugoslav entity that took the name Republic of Macedonia.

Recent Developments

In the summer of 2007, Greece was hit hard by the most devastating series of forest fires in decades. The fires claimed at least 64 lives and also threatened the site of ancient Olympia. Partly as a consequence of the inadequate response to the fires, Prime Minister Konstantinos (Kostas) Karamanlis merged the Public Order Ministry with the Interior Ministry, though he did not establish a separate Environment Ministry, as many demanded. The Greek economy continued to perform well. The gross domestic product grew by about 6.7% in 2007. Unemployment dropped to 8.0% in January 2008 (from 8.6% in January 2007), and inflation hovered under 4.0%. The tourism sector remained strong despite the weakening dollar, bringing in some €15 billion in 2007.

Internet resources: <www.gnto.gr>.

Greenland

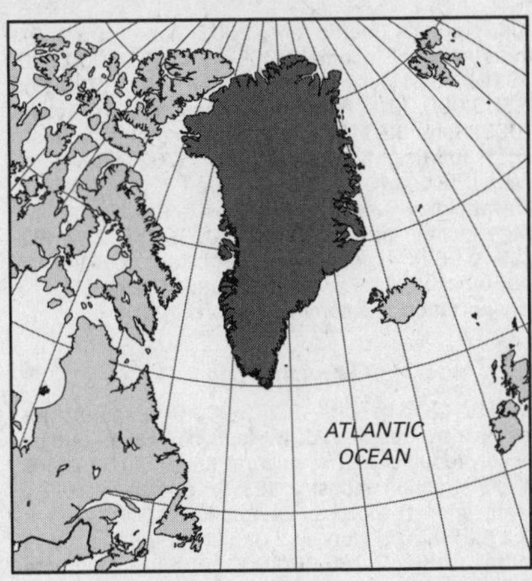

Official name: Kalaallit Nunaat (Greenlandic); Grønland (Danish) (Greenland). **Political status:** integral part of the Danish realm with one legislative house (Parliament [31]). **Chief of state:** Danish Queen Margrethe II (from 1972). **Heads of government:** High Commissioner (for Denmark) Søren Hald Møller (from 2005); Prime Minister (for Greenland) Hans Enoksen (from 2002). **Capital:** Nuuk (Godthåb). **Official languages:** Greenlandic; Danish. **Official religion:** Evangelical Lutheran (Lutheran Church of Greenland). **Monetary unit:** 1 Danish krone (DKK) = 100 øre; valuation (1 Jul 2008) US$1 = DKK 4.72.

Demography

Area: 836,330 sq mi, 2,166,086 sq km. **Population** (2007): 57,000. **Density** (2007): persons per sq mi 0.36, persons per sq km 0.14. **Urban** (2005): 82.7%. **Sex distribution** (2005): male 53.04%; female 46.96%. **Age breakdown** (2006): under 15, 23.9%; 15–29, 21.1%; 30–44, 24.3%; 45–59, 19.4%; 60–74, 8.8%; 75–84, 1.7%; 85 and over, 0.8%. **Ethnic composition** (2000): Greenland Eskimo 79.1%; Danish 13.6%; other 7.3%. **Religious affiliation** (2000): Protestant 69.2%, of which Evangelical Lutheran 64.2%, Pentecostal 2.8%; other Christian 27.4%; other/nonreligious 3.4%. **Major towns** (2005): Nuuk (Godthåb) 14,501; Sisimiut (Holsteinsborg) 5,350; Ilulissat (Jakobshavn) 4,533; Qaqortoq (Julianehåb) 3,144. **Location:** North Atlantic Ocean, east of northern Canada.

Vital statistics

Birth rate per 1,000 population (2006): 16.0 (world avg. 20.3); (1993) within marriage 29.2%. **Death rate** per 1,000 population (2006): 7.9 (world avg. 8.6). **Natural increase rate** per 1,000 population (2006): 8.1 (world avg. 11.7). **Total fertility rate** (avg. births per childbearing woman; 2006): 2.40. **Life expectancy** at birth (2006): male 66.4 years; female 73.6 years.

National economy

Budget (2005). *Revenue:* DKK 8,031,552,000 (block grant from Danish government 45.4%; income tax 32.3%; import duties 6.9%). *Expenditures:* DKK 7,466,650,000 (social welfare 25.4%, education 17.9%, health 12.0%, public order 3.2%, defense 3.0%). **Tourism** (2006): number of overnight stays at hotels 245,432, of which visitors from within Greenland 104,012, from Denmark 101,387, from the US 9,536. **Land use** as % of total land area (2003): in temporary crops, negligible, in permanent crops, none, in pasture 0.6%; overall forest area (2005) negligible. **Production** (metric tons except as noted). *Fishing, animal products:* fish catch (2003) 340,200 (by local boats 196,500, of which prawn 98,900, halibut 28,900, cod 8,500, crab 6,900; by foreign boats 143,700; whales 2,767); livestock (number of live animals; 2003) 19,259 sheep, 3,100 tame reindeer; animal products (value of external sales in DKK '000; 2004) sealskins 23,026, polar bear skins (1998) 579 (164 polar bears killed by trophy hunters in 2004). *Manufacturing:* principally handicrafts and fish processing. *Energy production (consumption):* electricity (kW-hr; 2004) 295,000,000 (274,000,000); petroleum products (metric tons; 2003) none (185,000). **Gross national income** (2006): US$1,618,000,000 (US$27,991 per capita). **Public debt** (2000): US$53,000,000. **Population economically active** (2003): total 32,119; activity rate of total population 56.5% (participation rates: ages 15–62, 83.5%; female [2002] 45.7%; unemployed [2006] 8.6%). **Households.** Average household size (2005) 2.5; average income per household (2003) DKK 269,992 (US$40,982); expenditure (1994): food, beverages, and tobacco 41.6%, housing and energy 22.4%, transportation and communications 10.2%.

Foreign trade

Imports (2004): DKK 3,279,000,000 (goods for trades and industries 21.4%; food, beverages, and tobacco products 21.2%; mineral fuels 13.6%; goods for construction industry 12.6%; machinery 6.7%). *Major import sources:* Denmark 59.2%; Sweden 14.1%; US 2.0%; Norway 2.0%; China 1.8%. **Exports** (2004): DKK 2,285,000,000 (marine products 86.8%, of which shrimp 50.6%, halibut 19.9%, cod 3.1%). *Major export destinations:* Denmark 88.0%; Spain 5.7%; US 1.6%; Iceland 1.0%.

Transport and communications

Transport. *Roads* (1998): total length 150 km (paved 60%). *Vehicles* (2004): passenger cars 2,861; trucks and buses 1,531. *Air transport* (2006; Air Greenland A/S only): passenger-km 441,422,000; metric ton-km cargo 49,485,000. **Communications,** in total units (units per 1,000 persons). Telephone landlines (2005): 24,000 (421); cellular telephone subscribers (2005): 46,000 (808); total Internet users (2005): 38,000 (666).

Education and health

Educational attainment (2002). Two-thirds of labor force has no formal education. **Literacy** (2001): virtually 100%. **Health:** physicians (2004) 91 (1 per 626 persons); hospital beds (2001) 406 (1 per 139 persons); infant mortality rate per 1,000 live births (2006) 15.4.

Military

Total active duty personnel. Denmark is responsible for Greenland's defense. Greenlanders are not liable for military service. US troops (2006): 146.

Background

The Inuit probably crossed to northwestern Greenland from North America, along the islands of the Canadian Arctic, from 4000 BC to AD 1000. The Norwegian Erik the Red visited Greenland in 982; his son, Leif Eriksson, introduced Christianity in the 11th century. Greenland came under joint Danish-Norwegian rule in the late 14th century. The original Norse settlements became extinct in the 15th century, but Greenland was recolonized by Denmark in 1721. In 1776 Denmark closed the Greenland coast to foreign trade; it was not reopened until 1950. Greenland became part of the kingdom of Denmark in 1953. Home rule was established in 1979.

Recent Developments

Greenland remained prominent in the international debate over global warming, and residents experienced longer growing and fishing seasons. In July 2007 researchers reported in *Science* magazine that DNA extracted from the 3-km- (1.9-mi)-long Greenland Ice Core Project confirmed that some 450,000–800,000 years ago the southernmost part of the island was covered by boreal forests. Offshore tests indicated that massive reserves of petroleum may exist off of Greenland's coasts, though commercial production remained years away.

Internet resources: <www.greenland.com>.

Grenada

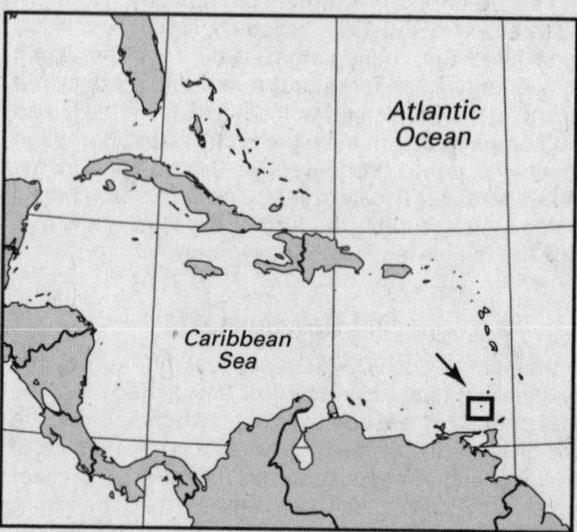

Official name: Grenada. **Form of government:** constitutional monarchy with two legislative houses (Senate [13]; House of Representatives [15]). **Chief of state:** British Queen Elizabeth II (from 1952), represented by Governor-General Sir Daniel Williams (from 1996). **Head of government:** Prime Minister Tillman Thomas (from 2008). **Capital:** St. George's. **Official language:** English. **Official religion:** none. **Monetary unit:** 1 East Caribbean dollar (EC$) = 100 cents; valuation (1 Jul 2008) US$1 = EC$2.70.

Demography

Area: 133 sq mi, 344 sq km. **Population** (2007): 108,000. **Density** (2007): persons per sq mi 812.0, persons per sq km 314.0. **Urban** (2004): 41.5%. **Sex distribution** (2001): male 49.19%; female 50.81%. **Age breakdown** (2001): under 15, 35.1%; 15–29, 28.1%; 30–44, 17.6%; 45–59, 9.0%; 60 and over, 10.2%. **Ethnic composition** (2000): black 51.7%; mixed 40.0%; Indo-Pakistani 4.0%; white 0.9%; other 3.4%. **Religious affiliation** (2005): Roman Catholic 41%; Protestant (of which significantly Anglican and Seventh-day Adventist) 30%; Rastafarian 5%; nonreligious/other 24%. **Major localities** (2004): St. George's 4,300 (urban agglomeration [2001] 35,559); Gouyave 3,200; Grenville 2,300; Victoria 2,100. **Location:** island between the Caribbean Sea and the Atlantic Ocean, north of Trinidad and Tobago.

1 metric ton = about 1.1 short tons; 1 kilometer = 0.6 mi (statute); 1 metric ton-km cargo = about 0.68 short ton-mi cargo; c.i.f.: cost, insurance, and freight; f.o.b.: free on board

Vital statistics

Birth rate per 1,000 population (2006): 22.1 (world avg. 20.3). **Death rate** per 1,000 population (2006): 6.9 (world avg. 8.6). **Natural increase rate** per 1,000 population (2006): 15.2 (world avg. 11.7). **Total fertility rate** (avg. births per childbearing woman; 2006): 2.34. **Life expectancy** at birth (2006): male 63.1 years; female 66.7 years.

National economy

Budget (2006). *Revenue:* EC$490,800,000 (tax revenue 73.3%, of which tax on international trade 43.3%, income taxes 11.4%; grants 21.3%; nontax revenue 5.4%). *Expenditures:* EC$588,800,000 (current expenditure 53.9%, of which wages 26.2%, transfers 11.6%, debt service 4.9%; capital expenditure 46.1%). **Public debt** (external, outstanding; 2005): US$337,800,000. **Gross national income** (at 2006 market prices): US$419,000,000 (US$3,971 per capita). **Production** (metric tons except as noted). *Agriculture, forestry, fishing* (2005): sugarcane 7,080, coconuts 6,014, nutmeg 2,965; livestock (number of live animals) 13,200 sheep, 7,200 goats, 2,650 pigs; fisheries production 2,050. *Mining and quarrying*: excavation of limestone, sand, and gravel for local use. *Manufacturing* (value of production in EC$'000; 1997): wheat flour 13,390; soft drinks 9,798; beer 7,072. *Energy production (consumption):* electricity (kW-hr; 2004) 157,000,000 (157,000,000); petroleum products (metric tons; 2004) none (72,000). **Households.** Average household size (2003) 3.3; income per capita (2000) EC$8,922 (US$3,400); expenditure (2001): food, beverages, and tobacco 38.6%, transportation and communications 15.7%, housing 10.2%, clothing and footwear 9.8%. **Population economically active** (2004): total 37,000; activity rate of total population 35% (participation rate: ages 15–64 [1998] 78%; female [1998] 43.5%; unemployed [2002] 12.2%). **Selected balance of payments data.** Receipts from (US$'000,000): tourism (2005) 71; remittances (2005) 22; foreign direct investment (2001–05 avg.) 59; official development assistance (2005) 62 (commitments). Disbursements for (US$'000,000): tourism (2005) 11; remittances (2005) 2. **Land use** as % of total land area (2003): in temporary crops 6%, in permanent crops 29%, in pasture 3%; overall forest area (2005) 12%.

Foreign trade

Imports (2004; f.o.b. in balance of trade and c.i.f. for commodities and trading partners): US$263,100,000 (food and live animals 21.2%; machinery and transport equipment 17.9%; mineral fuels 9.6%; chemicals and chemical products 6.7%). *Major import sources:* US 27.7%; Trinidad and Tobago 25.4%; UK 5.2%. **Exports** (2004): US$31,000,000 (domestic exports 78.7%, of which nutmeg 31.6%, fish 9.7%, flour 8.7%, paper products 6.8%, cocoa beans 6.5%; reexports 21.3%). *Major export destinations:* Saint Lucia 11.8%; US 11.6%; The Netherlands 8.1%; Antigua and Barbuda 8.0%; Germany 7.7%.

Transport and communications

Transport. *Roads* (1999): total length 1,040 km (paved 61%). *Vehicles* (2001): passenger cars 15,800; trucks and buses 4,200. *Air transport* (2001; Point Salines airport only): passengers 331,000; cargo 2,747 metric tons. **Communications,** in total units (units per 1,000 persons). Televisions (2001): 38,000 (375); telephone landlines (2006): 28,000 (262); cellular telephone subscribers (2006): 46,000 (431); personal computers (2004): 16,000 (155); total Internet users (2004): 8,000 (76); broadband Internet subscribers (2006): 5,500 (52).

Education and health

Educational attainment (2001). Percentage of population ages 18 and over having: no formal schooling/unknown 7.6%; primary education 65.1%; secondary 21.7%; higher 5.6%, of which university 1.5%. **Literacy** (2004): total population ages 15 and over literate 98.0%. **Health** (2003): physicians 127 (1 per 803 persons); hospital beds 330 (1 per 309 persons); infant mortality rate per 1,000 live births (2006) 14.3. **Food** (2005): daily per capita caloric intake 2,425 (vegetable products 74%, animal products 26%); 127% of FAO recommended minimum.

Military

Total active duty personnel (2001) none (a 755-member police force includes an 80-member paramilitary unit and a 40-member coast guard unit).

Grenada is widely known as "Spice Island" because of its extensive export of spices. It is especially famous for its production of nutmeg.

Background

The warlike Carib Indians dominated Grenada when Christopher Columbus sighted the island in 1498 and named it Concepción; they ruled it for the next 150 years. In 1674 it became subject to the French crown and remained so until 1762, when British forces captured it. In 1833 the island's black slaves were freed. Grenada was the headquarters of the government of the British Windward Islands, 1885–1958, and a member of the West Indies Federation, 1958–62. It became a self-governing state in association with Britain in 1967 and gained its independence in 1974. In 1979 a left-wing government took control in a bloodless coup. Relations with its US-oriented Latin American neighbors became strained as Grenada leaned toward Cuba and the Soviet bloc. In order to counteract this trend, the US invaded the island in 1983; democratic self-government was reestablished in 1984. Its relations with Cuba, once suspended, were restored in 1997.

Recent Developments

In June 2007 the Grenada High Court ordered the immediate release of 3 of the remaining 13 imprisoned leaders of the 1983 insurrection against then prime minister Maurice Bishop, who, together with four cabinet ministers and six supporters, was murdered by a firing squad.

Internet resources: <www.grenadagrenadines.com>.

Guadeloupe

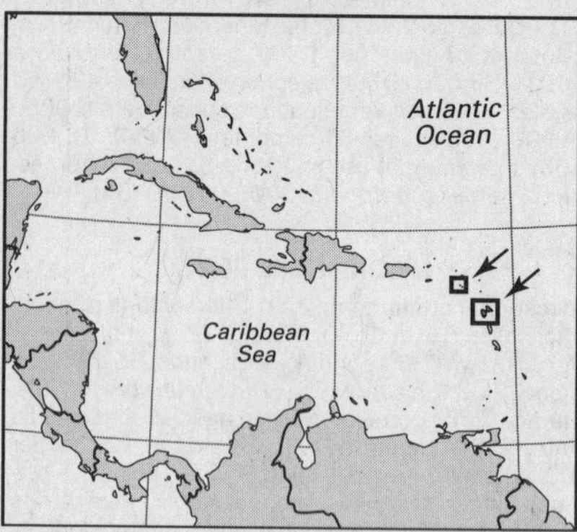

Official name: Département de la Guadeloupe (Department of Guadeloupe). **Political status:** overseas department of France with two legislative houses (General Council [42]; Regional Council [41]). **Chief of state:** French President Nicolas Sarkozy (from 2007). **Heads of government:** Prefect Emmanuel Berthier (from 2007); President of the General Council Jacques Gillot (from 2001); President of the Regional Council Victorin Lurel (from 2004). **Capital:** Basse-Terre. **Official language:** French. **Official religion:** none. **Monetary unit:** 1 euro (€) = 100 cents; valuation (1 Jul 2008) US$1 = €0.63.

Demography

Area: 658 sq mi, 1,705 sq km. **Population** (2007): 451,300. **Density** (2007): persons per sq mi 656.6, persons per sq km 253.4. **Urban** (2005): 99.8%. **Sex distribution** (2005): male 49.25%; female 50.75%. **Age breakdown** (2005): under 15, 24.0%; 15–29, 22.7%; 30–44, 26.2%; 45–59, 14.6%; 60–74, 8.4%; 75 and over, 4.1%. **Ethnic composition** (2000): Creole (mulatto) 76.7%; black 10.0%; Guadeloupe mestizo (French–East Asian) 10.0%; white 2.0%; other 1.3%. **Religious affiliation** (2000): Roman Catholic 86.4%; Protestant 4.5%; Jehovah's Witness 3.9%; nonreligious/atheist 3.1%; other 2.1%. **Major communes** (1999): Les Abymes (2003) 65,700; Saint-Martin (Marigot) 29,078; Le Gosier 25,360; Pointe-à-Pitre 20,948 (urban agglomeration 171,773); Basse-Terre (2003) 12,900 (urban agglomeration 54,076). **Location:** islands in the eastern Caribbean Sea, southeast of Puerto Rico.

Vital statistics

Birth rate per 1,000 population (2005): 15.4 (world avg. 20.3); (1999) within marriage 34.7%. **Death rate** per 1,000 population (2005): 6.1 (world avg. 8.6). **Total fertility rate** (avg. births per childbearing woman; 2005): 1.91. **Life expectancy** at birth (2005): male 75.2 years; female 82.0 years.

National economy

Budget (2004). *Revenue:* €312,400,000 (direct tax revenues 46.7%; transfers from France 36.9%; loans 16.0%; other 0.4%). *Expenditures:* €312,400,000 (current expenditures 62.3%; capital expenditures 37.7%). **Production** (metric tons except as noted). *Agriculture, forestry, fishing* (2005): sugarcane 841,000, bananas 62,000, yams 10,750; livestock (number of live animals) 77,800 cattle, 36,550 goats, 24,400 pigs; roundwood (2004) 15,300 cu m, of which fuelwood 98%; fisheries production 10,100 (from aquaculture 31). *Mining and quarrying* (2002): pumice 210,000. *Manufacturing* (2005): cement 266,121; raw sugar 73,000; rum 59,000 hectolitres. *Energy production (consumption):* electricity (kW-hr; 2005) 1,564,000,000 (1,564,000,000); petroleum products (metric tons; 2003) none (520,000). **Land use** as % of total land area (2003): in temporary crops 12%, in permanent crops 3%, in pasture 12%; overall forest area 47%. **Population economically active** (2006): total 219,000; activity rate of total population 48.5% (participation rates: ages 15–59, 74.8%; female 50.5%; unemployed [December 2005] 23.3%). **Gross domestic product** (at 2005 market prices): US$9,131,000,000 (US$20,040 per capita). **Households** (2000). Average household size 2.3; disposable income per household €25,441 (US$23,439); sources of income: wages and salaries 81.5%, transfer payments 17.2%, property 1.3%; expenditure (1994–95): housing 26.2%, food and beverages 21.4%, transportation and communications 14.1%, household durables 6.0%. **Selected balance of payments data.** Receipts from (US$'000,000): tourism (2005) 246.

Foreign trade

Imports (2004): €1,831,000,000 (food and agricultural products 20.0%; machinery and equipment 13.8%; motor vehicles 13.2%; mineral fuels 10.6%; pharmaceuticals 8.5%). *Major import sources:* France 63.2%; Germany 3.8%; Trinidad and Tobago 3.4%; Italy 2.9%; Martinique 2.6%. **Exports** (2004): €139,000,000 (food and agricultural products 67.7% [including bananas, sugar, rum, melons, eggplant, and flowers]; electrical equipment 7.2%). *Major export destinations:* France 66.9%; Martinique 18.0%; French Guiana 2.9%; US 1.4%.

Transport and communications

Transport. *Roads* (1998): total length 3,415 km (paved [1986] 80%). *Vehicles* (2001): passenger cars 117,700; trucks and buses 31,400. *Air transport* (2005): passenger arrivals and departures 1,825,144; cargo unloaded 6,931 metric tons. **Communications,** in total units (units per 1,000 persons). Daily newspaper circulation (2005): 50,000 (110); televisions (2001): 125,000 (289); telephone landlines (2000): 205,000 (480); cellular telephone subscribers (2005): 315,000 (710); personal computers (2005): 90,000 (200); total Internet users (2005): 85,000 (187).

Education and health

Educational attainment (1999). Percentage of population ages 20 and over having: unknown through lower secondary education 63.5%; upper secondary 10.1%; vocational 16.6%; higher 9.8%. **Literacy** (1992): total population ages 15 and over literate

90.1%; males literate 89.7%; females literate 90.5%. **Health** (2003): physicians 956 (1 per 463 persons); hospital beds 2,330 (1 per 190 persons); infant mortality rate per 1,000 live births (2005) 8.6.

Military

Total active duty personnel (2006): French troops in Antilles (Guadeloupe and Martinique) 1,250 (army 64.0%, navy 36.0%).

Background

The Carib Indians held off the Spanish and French for a number of years before the islands of Guadeloupe became part of France in 1674. The British occupied Guadeloupe for short periods in the 18th and 19th centuries; the islands became officially French in 1816. In 1946 Guadeloupe was made an overseas territory of France. Tourism has benefited the economy in recent decades.

Recent Developments

Guadeloupe had administered Saint-Martin (the French part of the island of Saint Martin; Dutch Sint Maarten occupies the other part) and Saint-Barthélemy, but in a referendum in 2003 both voted to become independent overseas collectivities of France. On 21 Feb 2007, both achieved this status and separated from Guadeloupe.

Internet resources: <www.lesilesdeguadeloupe.com/2/Home-guadeloupe.htm>.

Guam

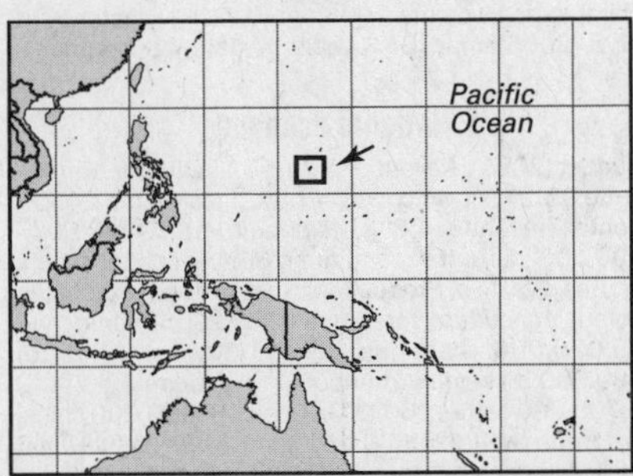

Official name: Teritorion Guam (Chamorro); Territory of Guam (English). **Political status:** self-governing, organized, unincorporated territory of the US with one legislative house (Guam Legislature [15]). **Chief of state:** US President George W. Bush (from 2001). **Head of government:** Governor Felix Camacho (from 2003). **Capital:** Hagatna (Agana). **Official languages:** Chamorro; English. **Official religion:** none. **Monetary unit:** 1 US dollar (US$) = 100 cents.

Demography

Area: 209 sq mi, 541 sq km. **Population** (2007): 173,000. **Density** (2007): persons per sq mi 827.8, persons per sq km 319.8. **Urban** (2003): 93.7%. **Sex distribution** (2006): male 50.94%; female 49.06%. **Age breakdown** (2006): under 15, 29.0%; 15–29, 23.0%; 30–44, 22.2%; 45–59, 16.1%; 60–74, 7.4%; 75 and over, 2.3%. **Ethnic composition** (2000): Pacific Islander 44.6%, of which Chamorro 37.0%; Asian 32.5%, of which Filipino 26.3%, Korean 2.5%; white 6.8%; black 1.0%; mixed 13.9%; other 1.2%. **Religious affiliation** (2005): Roman Catholic 72%; Protestant 12%; nonreligious/other 16%. **Major populated places** (2000): Tamuning 10,833; Mangilao 7,794; Yigo 6,391; Astumbo 5,207; Hagatna 1,122. **Location:** Oceania, island in the North Pacific Ocean, south of the Northern Mariana Islands.

Vital statistics

Birth rate per 1,000 population (2006): 18.8 (world avg. 20.3); (2004) within marriage 42.8%. **Death rate** per 1,000 population (2006): 4.5 (world avg. 8.6). **Total fertility rate** (avg. births per childbearing woman; 2006): 2.58. **Life expectancy** at birth (2006): male 75.5 years; female 81.8 years.

National economy

Budget (2003). *Revenue:* US$426,276,454 (local taxes 81.8%; federal contributions 15.3%; other 2.9%). *Expenditures:* US$342,550,414 (education 46.1%; public order 16.0%; health 3.9%). **Production** (metric tons except as noted). *Agriculture, forestry, fishing* (2005): coconuts 57,400, watermelons 2,470, nuts 422; livestock (number of live animals) 205,000 poultry, 5,100 pigs, 680 goats; fisheries production 162. *Mining and quarrying*: sand and gravel. *Manufacturing* (value of sales in US$'000; 2002): food processing 26,733; printing and publishing 7,382; fabricated metal products 4,052. *Energy production (consumption):* electricity (kW-hr; 2004) 1,589,-000,000 (1,589,000,000); petroleum products (metric tons; 2002) none (1,333,000). **Households.** Average household size (2003) 3.7; annual mean (median) household income (2003) US$41,196 (US$33,457); expenditure (1995): housing, energy, and household furnishings 37.0%, food and beverages 25.2%, transportation 13.7%. **Selected balance of payments data.** Receipts from (US$'000,000): tourism (2005) 1,149. **Gross domestic product** (at 2002 market prices): US$3,428,000,000 (US$21,120 per capita). **Population economically active** (2005): total 64,130; activity rate of total population 38% (participation rates: over age 15, 61.1%; female [2004] 43.3%; unemployed 7.0%). **Land use** as % of total land area (2003): in temporary crops 4%, in permanent crops 18%, in pasture 15%; overall forest area (2005) 47%.

Foreign trade

Imports (2005): US$532,687,000 (food products and nonalcoholic beverages 31%; transportation equipment 21%; leather luggage and handbags 14%). *Major import sources:* significantly US and Japan. **Exports** (2005): US$51,844,521 (transportation equipment 33.5%; food products 14.5%, of which fish 13.0%; aluminum scrap metal 8.4%; tobacco products 7.5%). *Major export destinations* (2005): Finland 20.9%; Japan 19.5%; Federated States of Micronesia 18.4%; China 9.7%; Hong Kong 8.5%.

Transport and communications

Transport. *Roads* (1999): total length 885 km (paved 76%). *Vehicles* (2005): passenger cars 63,631; trucks and buses 25,615. *Air transport* (2006; Continental Micronesia only): passenger-km 4,762,-000,000; metric ton-km cargo 102,000,000. **Communications**, in total units (units per 1,000 persons). Daily newspaper circulation (2005): 29,000 (171); televisions (1997): 106,000 (668); telephone landlines (2004): 70,000 (420); cellular telephone subscribers (2004): 98,000 (594); total Internet users (2005): 65,000 (385).

Education and health

Educational attainment (2000). Percentage of population ages 25 and over having: unknown to some secondary education 23.7%; complete secondary 31.9%; some higher 24.5%; undergraduate 15.3%; advanced degree 4.6%. **Literacy**: virtually 100%. **Health**: physicians (2005) 93 (1 per 1,828 persons); hospital beds (2005; Guam Memorial Hospital only) 187 (1 per 903 persons); infant mortality rate per 1,000 live births (2006) 6.8.

Military

Total active duty US personnel (2005): 2,931 (army 1.4%; navy 42.3%; air force 56.3%); 8,000 US Marines based in Japan are to be moved to Guam by 2014 per 2006 agreement.

Background

Possibly visited by Ferdinand Magellan in 1521, Guam was formally claimed by Spain in 1565. It remained Spanish until it was ceded to the US after the Spanish-American War in 1898. During World War II the Japanese occupied the island (1941–44). It subsequently became a major US air and naval base. In 1950 it was made a US territory.

Recent Developments

US remilitarization of the Pacific in 2007 led to an increase in the number of American soldiers in Guam. In August, as 22,000 US troops were involved in exercises off Guam, Russia deployed two strategic bombers to the area for the first time since the Cold War. In February 2008 a US$1 billion B-2 stealth bomber crashed in Guam, the first to do so since the aircraft's introduction in 1988.

Internet resources: <www.visitguam.org/>.

Guatemala

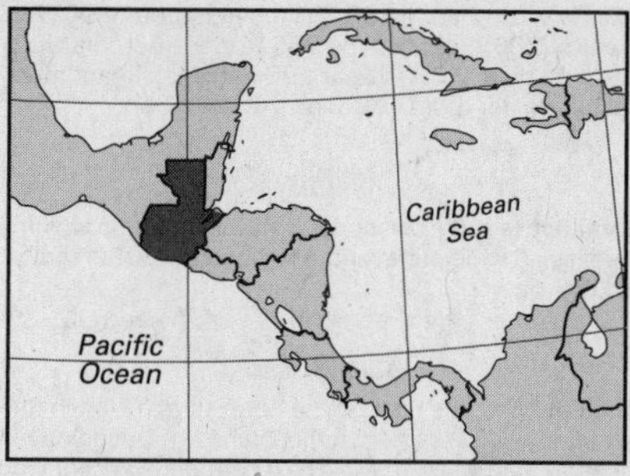

Official name: República de Guatemala (Republic of Guatemala). **Form of government:** republic with one legislative house (Congress of the Republic [158]). **Head of state and government:** President Álvaro Colom Caballeros (from 2008). **Capital:** Guatemala City. **Official language:** Spanish. **Official religion:** none. **Monetary unit:** 1 quetzal (Q) = 100 centavos; valuation (1 Jul 2008) US$1 = Q 7.52.

Demography

Area: 42,130 sq mi, 109,117 sq km. **Population** (2007): 12,728,000. **Density** (2007): persons per sq mi 302.1, persons per sq km 116.6. **Urban** (2005): 47.2%. **Sex distribution** (2006): male 49.35%; female 50.65%. **Age breakdown** (2006): under 15, 41.5%; 15–29, 28.6%; 30–44, 14.7%; 45–59, 9.6%; 60–74, 4.4%; 75–84, 1.1%; 85 and over, 0.1%. **Ethnic composition** (2000): mestizo 63.7%; Amerindian (virtually all Mayan) 33.1%; black 2.0%; white 1.0%; other 0.2%. **Religious affiliation** (2005): Roman Catholic 57%; Protestant/independent Christian 40%; traditional Mayan religions 1%; other 2%. **Major cities** (2002; urban populations of municipios): Guatemala City 942,348 (urban agglomeration [2001] 3,366,000); Mixco 277,400; Villa Nueva 187,700; Quetzaltenango 106,700; Escuintla 65,400. **Location:** Central America, bordering Mexico, Belize, the Caribbean Sea, Honduras, El Salvador, and the Pacific Ocean.

Vital statistics

Birth rate per 1,000 population (2006): 29.6 (world avg. 20.3). **Death rate** per 1,000 population (2006): 5.4 (world avg. 8.6). **Total fertility rate** (avg. births per childbearing woman; 2005): 4.30. **Life expectancy** at birth (2005): male 64.3 years; female 71.6 years.

National economy

Budget (2005). *Revenue:* Q 24,521,300,000 (tax revenue 95.2%, of which VAT 43.8%, income tax 24.7%; nontax revenue 4.8%). *Expenditures:* Q 28,500,-500,000 (current expenditures 66.4%; capital expenditures 33.6%). **Production** (metric tons except as noted). *Agriculture, forestry, fishing* (2005): sugarcane 19,070,000, bananas 1,071,000, corn (maize) 989,600; livestock (number of live animals; 2006) 2,796,000 cattle, 260,000 sheep, 27,000,000 chickens; roundwood 16,670,211 cu m, of which fuelwood 98%; fisheries production 16,756 (from aquaculture 27%). *Mining and quarrying* (2004): gypsum 106,140; gold 2,000 kg; marble 33 cu m. *Manufacturing* (value added in Q '000,000 at 1958 prices; 2005): food products 213; textiles and wearing apparel 126; beverages 98. *Energy production (consumption):* electricity (kW-hr; 2004) 7,009,000,000 (6,586,000,000); coal (metric tons; 2004) none (461,000); crude petroleum (barrels; 2004) 7,260,000 (2,180,000); petroleum products (metric tons; 2004) 22,000 (3,032,000). **Households.** Average household size (2002) 4.4; income per household (1989) Q 4,306 (US$1,529); expenditure (2000): food and beverages 32.9%, household furnishings 14.7%, clothing 11.8%, recreation and culture 9.2%, health 7.3%. **Land use** as % of total land area (2003): in temporary crops 13.3%, in permanent crops 5.6%, in pasture 24.0%; overall forest area (2005) 36.3%. **Gross national income** (at 2006 market prices): US$30,030,000,000 (US$2,305 per capita). **Public debt** (external, outstanding; April 2007): US$4,162,600,000. **Population economically active** (2004): total 5,059,800; activity rate of total population 40.5% (participation rates: ages 15–64, 64.7%; female 34.9%; unemployed [2003] 7.5%). **Selected balance of payments data.** Receipts from (US$'000,000): tourism (2005) 846; remittances (2006) 3,610; foreign direct investment (2001–05 avg.) 212; official development assistance (2005) 311 (commitments). Disbursements for (US$'000,000): tourism (2005) 444; remittances (2006) 35.

Foreign trade

Imports (2005; f.o.b. in balance of trade and c.i.f. for commodities and trading partners): US$8,812,297,-500 (mineral fuels 18.9%; machinery and apparatus 16.9%; chemical products 13.6%; transportation equipment 9.6%). *Major import sources:* US 39.4%; Mexico 8.5%; El Salvador 5.5%; Panama 4.6%; Costa Rica 3.8%. **Exports** (2005): US$3,378,459,100 (chemical products [2002] 17.7%; coffee 13.7%; bananas 7.0%; sugar 7.0%; crude petroleum 6.7%; cardamom 2.1%). *Major export destinations:* US 31.0%; El Salvador 18.3%; Honduras 11.2%; Nicaragua 6.1%; Costa Rica 6.0%.

Transport and communications

Transport. *Railroads* (2004): route length 886 km. *Roads* (2002): total length 14,044 km (paved 39%). *Vehicles* (2004): passenger cars 1,328,100; trucks and buses (2000) 53,236. *Air transport* (1999): passenger-km 341,700,000; metric ton-km cargo (2003) 200,000. **Communications,** in total units (units per 1,000 persons). Daily newspaper circulation (2001): 377,000 (33); televisions (2004): 2,000,000 (167); telephone landlines (2006): 1,355,000 (105); cellular telephone subscribers (2006): 7,179,000 (556); personal computers (2005): 262,000 (21); total Internet users (2006): 1,320,000 (102); broadband Internet subscribers (2005): 27,000 (2.1).

Education and health

Educational attainment (2002). Percentage of heads of households having: no formal schooling 33.3%; primary education 46.1%; secondary 15.0%; higher 5.6%. **Literacy** (2005): total population ages 15 and over literate 71.8%; males literate 79.1%; females literate 64.6%. **Health** (2003): physicians 11,700 (1 per 1,053 persons); hospital beds 6,118 (1 per 1,961 persons); infant mortality rate per 1,000 live births (2006) 30.8. **Food** (2005): daily per capita caloric intake 2,298 (vegetable products 90%, animal products 10%); 131% of FAO recommended minimum.

Military

Total active duty personnel (2006): 29,200 (army 92.5%, navy 5.1%, air force 2.4%). **Military expenditure as percentage of GDP** (2005): 0.3%; per capita expenditure US$8.

Background

From simple farming villages dating to 2500 BC, the Maya of Guatemala and the Yucatan developed an impressive civilization. The civilization of the Maya declined after AD 900, and the Spanish began the subjugation of their descendants in 1523. The Central American colonies declared independence from Spain in Guatemala City in 1821, and Guatemala became part of the Mexican Empire until its collapse in 1823. In 1839 Guatemala became an independent republic under the first of a series of dictators who held power almost continuously for the next century. In 1945 a liberal-democratic coalition came to power and instituted sweeping reforms. Attempts to expropriate land belonging to American business interests prompted the US government in 1954 to sponsor an invasion. In the following years Guatemala's social revolution came to an end and most of the reforms were reversed. Chronic political instability and violence thenceforth marked Guatemalan politics; most of the 200,000 deaths that resulted were blamed on government forces. In 1991 the country abandoned its long-standing claims of sovereignty over Belize, and the two established diplomatic relations. It continued to experience violence as guerrillas sought to seize power. A peace treaty was signed in 1996, and the country started slowly to recover from its civil war.

Recent Developments

US Pres. George W. Bush visited Guatemala in March 2007 to promote trade under the Central America–Dominican Republic Free Trade Agreement (CAFTA–DR) and encourage Guatemala to increase its production of ethanol from sugarcane (the country would soon have five sugarcane-based ethanol plants in operation). The heightened security for the visit disrupted commerce, prompting Guatemalans to complain that their country had been violated by Bush's "security invasion force." Under CAFTA–DR Guatemalan imports had increased much more than exports, and living standards had not improved as expected; 51% of the population lived on less than US$50 monthly, and 15% earned less than US$21 per month.

Internet resources:
<www.visitguatemala.com/nuevo/mainE.asp>.

Guernsey

Official name: Bailiwick of Guernsey. **Political status:** crown dependency of the UK with one legislative house (States of Deliberation [51]); Alderney and Sark have their own parliaments. **Chief of state:** British Queen Elizabeth II (from 1952), represented by Lieutenant Governor Sir Fabian Malbon (from 2005). **Head of government:** Chief Minister Mike Torode (from 2007). **Capital:** St. Peter Port. **Official language:** English. **Monetary unit:** 1 Guernsey pound (£G) = 100 pence; valuation (1 Jul 2008) US$1 = £G 0.50 (the Guernsey pound is equivalent in value to the British pound sterling [£]).

Demography

Area: 30.2 sq mi, 78.1 sq km. **Population** (2007): 63,700. **Density** (2007): persons per sq mi 2,109.3, persons per sq km 815.6. **Urban** (2003): 30.5%. **Sex distribution** (2004): male 49.42%; female 50.58%. **Age breakdown** (2001): under 15, 17.2%; 15–29, 18.8%; 30–44, 23.1%; 45–59, 20.0%; 60–74, 13.4%; 75–84, 5.4%; 85 and over, 2.1%. **Population**

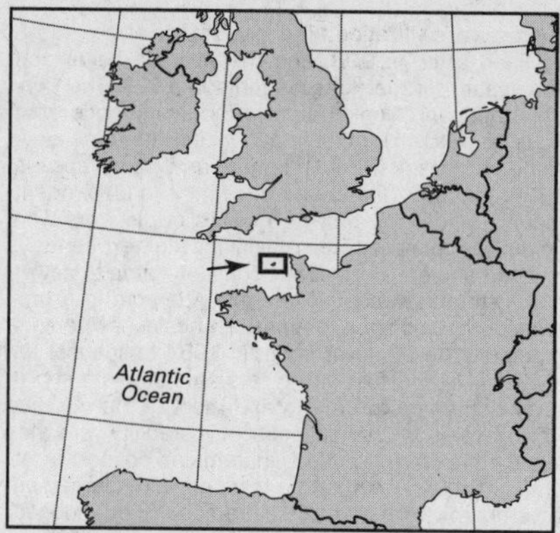

by place of birth (2001): Guernsey 64.3%; UK 27.4%; Portugal 1.9%; Jersey 0.7%; Ireland 0.7%; Alderney 0.2%; Sark 0.1%; other Europe 3.2%; other 1.5%. **Religious affiliation** (2000): Protestant 51.0%, of which Anglican 44.1%; unaffiliated Christian 20.1%; Roman Catholic 14.6%; nonreligious 12.4%; other 1.9%. **Major cities** (2001; parish populations): St. Peter Port 16,488; Vale 9,573; Castel 8,975; St. Sampson 8,592; St. Martin 6,267. **Location:** western Europe, island in the English Channel, northwest of France.

Vital statistics

Birth rate per 1,000 population (2005): 10.5 (world avg. 20.3); (2000) within marriage 65.2%. **Death rate** per 1,000 population (2005): 8.7 (world avg. 8.6). **Total fertility rate** (avg. births per childbearing woman; 2005): 1.38. **Life expectancy** at birth (2005): male 77.3 years; female 83.4 years.

National economy

Budget (2005). *Revenue:* £310,000,000 (income tax 82.8%; document duties 5.8%; customs duties and excise taxes 5.6%; automobile taxes 1.9%). *Expenditures:* £292,000,000 (2004; health 28.9%; education 23.2%; social security and welfare 22.4%; law and order 5.1%). **Production** (metric tons except as noted). *Agriculture, forestry, fishing* (1999): flowers 1,154,000 boxes, of which roses 288,000 boxes, freesia 184,000 boxes, carnations 161,000 boxes; livestock (number of live animals) 3,262 cattle; fisheries production (2003): 4,210 (from aquaculture 16%), of which crustaceans 2,032 (sea spiders and crabs 1,814), mollusks 1,239, marine fish 939. *Manufacturing* (value of exports in £'000,000; 2001): plants 20.3; cut flowers 11.7. *Energy production (consumption):* electricity (kW-hr; 2004) n.a. (317,000,000). **Population economically active** (2007): total 31,664; activity rate of total population 49.7% (participation rates: ages 15–64 [2001] 79.1%; female [2001] 45.2%; unemployed 0.8%). **Gross national income** (2005): US$2,885,711,000 (US$45,370 per capita). **Households.** Average household size (2001) 2.6; expenditure (1998–99): housing 21.6%, food 12.7%, household furnishings and services 11.2%, recreation services 9.2%. **Selected balance of payments data.** Receipts from (US$'000,000): tourism (1996) 275. **Land use** as % of total land area (1999): in pasture 37%; overall forest area (2005) 4.1%.

Foreign trade

Imports (1999): petroleum products are important. *Major import sources* (2005): mostly UK. **Exports** (1998): £93,000,000 (light industry 50.5%; flowers 36.6%; vegetables 5.4%). *Major export destinations* (2005): mostly UK.

Transport and communications

Transport. *Vehicles* (2005): passenger cars 40,163; trucks and buses 7,713. *Air transport* (2001; Guernsey airport only): passenger arrivals 429,076, passenger departures 430,254; cargo loaded 969 metric tons, cargo unloaded 3,557 metric tons. **Communications,** in total units (units per 1,000 persons). Daily newspaper circulation (2005): 16,000 (255); telephone landlines (2005): 45,100 (810); cellular telephone subscribers (2005): 43,800 (790); total Internet users (2005): 39,000 (613).

Education and health

Literacy (2002): virtually 100%. **Health** (2004): physicians 96 (1 per 656 persons); hospital beds (Princess Elizabeth and King Edward VII hospitals only) 310 (1 per 204 persons); infant mortality rate per 1,000 live births (2005) 4.7. **Food** (2004): daily per capita caloric intake 3,481 (vegetable products 73%, animal products 27%).

Military

Total active duty personnel*:* The UK is responsible for defense.

Guinea

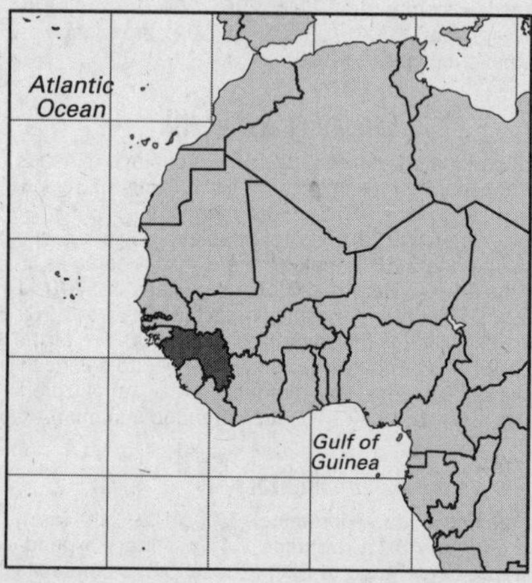

Official name: République de Guinée (Republic of Guinea). **Form of government:** unitary multiparty republic with one legislative house (National Assembly [114 seats]). **Head of state and government:** President Lansana Conté (from 1984), assisted by Prime Minister Ahmed Tidiane Souaré (from 2008). **Capital:** Conakry. **Official language:** French. **Official religion:** none. **Monetary unit:** 1 Guinean franc (FG) = 100 cauris; valuation (1 Jul 2008) US$1 = FG 4,447.00.

Demography

Area: 94,918 sq mi, 245,836 sq km. **Population** (2007): 9,370,000. **Density** (2007): persons per sq mi 98.7, persons per sq km 38.1. **Urban** (2004): 29.6%. **Sex distribution** (2005): male 50.00%; female 50.00%. **Age breakdown** (2005): under 15, 44.4%; 15–29, 26.5%; 30–44, 15.4%; 45–59, 8.7%; 60–74, 4.1%; 75 and over, 0.9%. **Ethnic composition** (2000): Fulani 38.3%; Malinke 25.6%; Susu 12.2%; Kpelle 5.2%; Kisi 4.8%; other 13.9%. **Religious affiliation** (2005): Muslim (nearly all Sunni) 85%; Christian 8%; traditional beliefs 7%. **Major cities** (2004): Conakry 1,851,800; Kankan 113,900; Labé (2001) 64,500; Kindia (2001) 56,000; Nzérékoré (2001) 55,000. **Location:** western Africa, bordering Guinea-Bissau, Senegal, Mali, Côte d'Ivoire, Liberia, Sierra Leone, and the North Atlantic Ocean.

Vital statistics

Birth rate per 1,000 population (2005): 42.0 (world avg. 20.3). **Death rate** per 1,000 population (2005): 15.6 (world avg. 8.6). **Natural increase rate** per 1,000 population (2005): 26.4 (world avg. 11.7). **Total fertility rate** (avg. births per childbearing woman; 2005): 5.83. **Life expectancy** at birth (2005): male 48.2 years; female 50.6 years.

National economy

Budget (January–November 2005). *Revenue:* FG 1,449,530,000,000 (current revenue 94.2%, of which VAT 34.3%, mining sector revenue 22.7%, tax on trade 19.5%; grants 5.8%). *Expenditures:* FG 1,545,690,000,000 (current expenditure 71.7%, of which wages and salaries 20.5%, interest on debt 18.6%; capital expenditure 28.3%). **Public debt** (external, outstanding; 2005): US$2,931,000,000. **Production** (metric tons except as noted). *Agriculture, forestry, fishing* (2005): cassava 1,303,760, rice 951,900, oil palm fruit 896,300; livestock (number of live animals) 3,756,300 cattle, 1,396,000 goats, 1,169,000 sheep; roundwood 12,338,298 cu m, of which fuelwood 95%; fisheries production 96,571. *Mining and quarrying* (2006): bauxite 16,956,200; gold 25,100 kg; diamonds 444,000 carats. *Manufacturing* (2006): cement 151,500; flour 54,600; paints 1,362. *Energy production (consumption):* electricity (kW-hr; 2006) 583,400,000 ([2004] 801,000,000); petroleum products (metric tons; 2004) none (378,000). **Households** (1994–95). Average household size (2004) 6.6; average annual household income FG 1,905,899 (US$1,952); sources of income: agriculture 49.3%, self-employment 22.2%, wages and salaries 15.7%; expenditure: food 50.0%; housing 14.0%; health 12.3%. **Population economically active** (2003): total 4,247,000; activity rate of total population 49.0% (participation rates: ages 15–64, 86.2%; female 46.3%). **Gross national income** (2006): US$3,732,000,000 (US$410 per capita). **Selected balance of payments data.** Receipts from (US$'000,000): tourism (2005) 30; remittances (2005) 42; foreign direct investment (2001–05 avg.) 63; official development assistance (2005) 182. Disbursements for (US$'000,000): tourism (2004) 25; remittances (2005) 48. **Land use** as % of total land area (2003): in temporary crops 4.5%, in permanent crops 2.6%, in pasture 43.5%; overall forest area (2005) 27.4%.

Foreign trade

Imports (2004): US$569,320,000 (machinery and apparatus 28.0%; food 20.6%; refined petroleum 18.9%). *Major import sources:* France 14.6%; China 9.6%; The Netherlands 6.8%; Belgium 6.0%; US 5.9%. **Exports** (2004): US$772,820,000 (bauxite 39.0%; alumina 20.3%; gold 18.9%; diamonds 6.5%; cotton 5.6%). *Major export destinations:* South Korea 15.6%; Russia 13.1%; Spain 12.3%; Ireland 9.1%; US 7.5%.

Transport and communications

Transport. *Railroads* (2004): route length (mostly for bauxite transport) 837 km; metric ton-km cargo (1993) 710,000,000. *Roads* (2003): total length 44,348 km (paved 10%). *Vehicles* (2003): passenger cars 47,524; trucks and buses 26,467. *Air transport* (1999): passenger-km 94,000,000; metric ton-km cargo 10,000,000. **Communications,** in total units (units per 1,000 persons). Televisions (2004): 140,000 (16); telephone landlines (2005): 26,000 (3.3); cellular telephone subscribers (2005): 189,000 (24); personal computers (2005): 45,000 (5.6); total Internet users (2006): 50,000 (5.4).

Education and health

Educational attainment (1999). Percentage of population ages 25 and over having: no formal schooling/unknown 81.4%; primary 7.8%; secondary 6.8%; higher 4.0%. **Literacy** (2000): percentage of total population ages 15 and over literate 41.0%; males literate 55.0%; females literate 27.0%. **Health** (2004): physicians 987 (1 per 9,323 persons); hospital beds 2,990 (1 per 3,078 persons); infant mortality rate per 1,000 live births (2005) 91.5. **Food** (2005): daily per capita caloric intake 2,612 (vegetable products 96%, animal products 4%); 142% of FAO recommended minimum.

Military

Total active duty personnel (2006): 9,700 (army 87.7%, navy 4.1%, air force 8.2%). **Military expenditure as percentage of GDP** (2005): 2.8%; per capita expenditure US$8.

Background

About AD 900 successive migrations of the Susu swept down from the desert and pushed the original inhabitants of Guinea, the Baga, to the Atlantic coast. Small kingdoms of the Susu rose in importance in the 13th century and later extended their rule to the coast. In the mid-15th century the Portuguese visited the coast and developed a slave trade. In the 16th century the Fulani established domination over the Fouta Djallon region; they ruled into the 19th century. In the early 19th century the French arrived and in 1849 proclaimed the coastal region a French protectorate. In 1895 French Guinea became part of the federation of French West Africa. In 1946 it was made an overseas territory of France, and in 1958 it achieved independence. Following a military coup in

1984, Guinea began implementing Westernized government systems. A new constitution was adopted in 1991, and the first multiparty elections were held in 1993. During the 1990s Guinea accommodated several hundred thousand war refugees from neighboring Liberia and Sierra Leone.

Recent Developments

In January 2007 unions called a strike, the third in 12 months, and demanded the resignation of Guinean Pres. Lansana Conté. The following week thousands of demonstrators battled with police throughout the capital, leaving at least 50 dead and hundreds injured. Conté, who had ruled Guinea since a 1984 coup, agreed to yield some powers to the prime minister. In August the government announced the discovery of substantial uranium deposits.

Internet resources: <www.mirinet.net.gn/ont>.

Guinea-Bissau

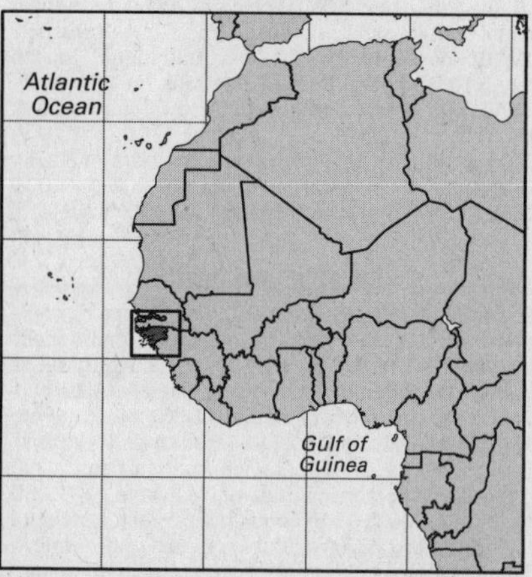

Official name: Républica da Guiné-Bissau (Republic of Guinea-Bissau). **Form of government:** republic with one legislative house (National People's Assembly [102]). **Chief of state:** President João Bernardo Vieira (from 2005). **Head of government:** Prime Minister Carlos Correia (from 2008). **Capital:** Bissau. **Official language:** Portuguese. **Official religion:** none. **Monetary unit:** 1 CFA franc (CFAF) = 100 centimes; valuation (1 Jul 2008) US$1 = CFAF 414.60 (pegged to the euro at €1 = CFAF 655.96).

Demography

Area: 13,948 sq mi, 36,125 sq km. **Population** (2007): 1,472,000. **Density** (2006): persons per sq mi 135.6, persons per sq km 52.3. **Urban** (2003): 34.0%. **Sex distribution** (2005): male 48.53%; female 51.47%. **Age breakdown** (2005): under 15, 41.6%; 15–29, 28.1%; 30–44, 16.1%; 45–59, 9.4%; 60–74, 4.1%; 75 and over, 0.7%. **Ethnic composition** (1996): Balante 30%; Fulani 20%; Mandyako 14%; Malinke 13%; Pepel 7%; nonindigenous Cape Verdean mulatto 2%; other 14%. **Religious affiliation** (2005): traditional beliefs 49%; Muslim 42%; Christian/other 9%. **Major cities** (2004): Bissau 305,700; Bafatá 15,000; Cacheu 14,000; Gabú 10,000. **Location:** western Africa, bordering Senegal, Guinea, and the North Atlantic Ocean.

Vital statistics

Birth rate per 1,000 population (2005): 37.6 (world avg. 20.3). **Death rate** per 1,000 population (2005): 16.7 (world avg. 8.6). **Natural increase rate** per 1,000 population (2005): 20.9 (world avg. 11.7). **Total fertility rate** (avg. births per childbearing woman; 2005): 4.93. **Life expectancy** at birth (2005): male 44.8 years; female 48.5 years.

National economy

Budget (2005). *Revenue:* CFAF 41,378,000,000 (tax revenue 44.3%, of which taxes on international trade 15.5%, sales tax 13.6%; grants 32.4%; nontax revenue 23.3%, of which fishing licenses 18.2%). *Expenditures:* CFAF 60,524,000,000 (current expenditures 72.7%, of which wages and salaries 35.1%, interest payments 11.1%; capital expenditures 27.3%). **Production** (metric tons except as noted). *Agriculture, forestry, fishing* (2004): rice 89,000, cashews 81,000, oil palm fruit 80,000; livestock (number of live animals) 520,000 cattle, 360,000 pigs, 330,000 goats; roundwood (2005) 592,000 cu m, of which fuelwood 71%; fisheries production (2005) 6,200. *Mining and quarrying:* extraction of construction materials only. *Manufacturing* (2003): processed wood 11,000; bakery products 7,900; wood products 4,400. *Energy production (consumption):* electricity (kW-hr; 2004) 61,000,000 (61,000,000); petroleum products (metric tons; 2004) none (88,000). **Selected balance of payments data.** Receipts from (US$'000,000): tourism (2005) 2; remittances (2005) 28; foreign direct investment (2001–05 avg.) 4; official development assistance (2005) 79. Disbursements for (US$'000,000): tourism (2004) 13; remittances (2005) 5. **Population economically active** (2003): total 643,000; activity rate of total population 47.2% (participation rates [1995]: over age 10, 65.5%; female 39.9%). **Public debt** (external, outstanding; 2005): US$671,000,000. **Households.** Average household size (1996) 6.9; expenditure (2001–02; Bissau only): food and nonalcoholic beverages 59.7%, housing and energy 13.6%, clothing and footwear 7.6%. **Gross national income** (at 2006 market prices): US$306,000,000 (US$186 per capita). **Land use** as % of total land area (2003): in temporary crops 10.7%, in permanent crops 8.9%, in pasture 38.4%; overall forest area (2005) 73.5%.

Foreign trade

Imports (2005): US$119,100,000 (construction material 17.3%; petroleum products 13.3%; foodstuffs 12.6%, of which rice 9.1%; transportation equipment 11.1%; equipment and machinery 10.1%). *Major import sources:* Senegal 34.6%; Italy 20.4%; Portugal 12.7%; The Netherlands 3.0%; France 2.5%. **Exports** (2005): US$100,800,000 (cashew nuts 89.5%; cotton 1.4%; wood products 1.4%). *Major export desti-*

nations: India 67.4%; Nigeria 19.0%; Senegal 1.5%; Portugal 1.1%.

Transport and communications

Transport. *Roads* (2003): total length 2,755 km (paved 28%). *Vehicles* (1996): passenger cars 7,120; trucks and buses 5,640. *Air transport* (1998): passenger-km 10,000,000. **Communications,** in total units (units per 1,000 persons). Daily newspaper circulation (2005): 6,000 (4.2); televisions (2001): 47,000 (36); telephone landlines (2005): 10,000 (7.6); cellular telephone subscribers (2005): 95,000 (71); total Internet users (2006): 37,000 (26).

Education and health

Literacy (2003): total population ages 15 and over literate 32.2%; males literate (2001) 55.2%; females literate (2001) 24.7%. **Health:** physicians (2004) 188 (1 per 7,374 persons); hospital beds (2001) 1,448 (1 per 902 persons); infant mortality rate per 1,000 live births (2005) 107.2. **Food** (2005): daily per capita caloric intake 1,902 (vegetable products 93%, animal products 7%); 106% of FAO recommended minimum.

Military

Total active duty personnel (2005): 9,250 (army 73.5%, navy 3.8%, air force 1.1%, paramilitary [gendarmerie] 21.6%). **Military expenditure as percentage of GDP** (2005): 4.0%; per capita expenditure US$6.

Background

More than 1,000 years ago the coast of Guinea-Bissau was occupied by iron-using agriculturists. They grew irrigated and dry rice and were also the major suppliers of marine salt to the western Sudan. At about the same time, the region came under the influence of the Mali empire and became a tributary kingdom known as Gabú. After 1546 Gabú was virtually autonomous; vestiges of the kingdom lasted until 1867. The earliest overseas contacts came in the 15th century with the Portuguese, who imported slaves from the Guinea area to the offshore Cape Verde Islands. Portuguese control of Guinea-Bissau was marginal despite claims to sovereignty there. The end of the slave trade forced the Portuguese inland in search of new profits. Their subjugation of the interior was slow and sometimes violent; it was not effectively achieved until 1915, though sporadic resistance continued until 1936. Guerrilla warfare in the 1960s led to the country's independence in 1974, but political turmoil continued and the government was overthrown by a military coup in 1980. A new constitution was adopted in 1984, and the first multiparty elections were held in 1994. A destructive civil war in 1998 was followed by a military coup in 1999 and another in 2003.

Recent Developments

Underscoring the instability in 2007 in Guinea-Bissau (one of the world's 10 poorest countries), Pres. João Bernardo Vieira's supporters in parliament began defecting to other parties, and street demonstrators called for a new government. Vieira's appointment in April of a new prime minister, Martinho Ndafa Kabi, restored a measure of stability. Kabi, who promised to work for fiscal discipline, reduced the price of cashews (the country's main export) and called for a "relentless" fight against drug trafficking. The UN's 2007 World Drug Report named Guinea-Bissau as a key staging post for cocaine moving from Latin America to Europe.

Internet resources: <www.guineabissau-government.com/english/index-english.php>.

Guyana

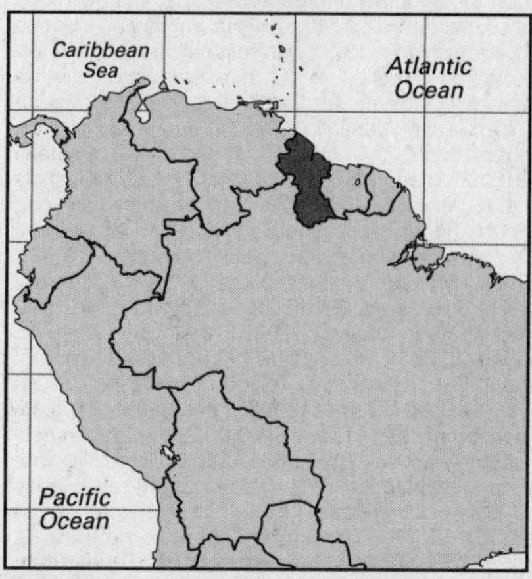

Official name: Co-operative Republic of Guyana. **Form of government:** unitary multiparty republic with one legislative house (National Assembly [65]). **Chief of state:** President Bharrat Jagdeo (from 1999). **Head of government:** Prime Minister Sam Hinds (from 1999). **Capital:** Georgetown. **Official language:** English. **Official religion:** none. **Monetary unit:** 1 Guyana dollar (G$) = 100 cents; valuation (1 Jul 2008) US$1 = G$204.70.

Demography

Area: 83,012 sq mi, 214,999 sq km. **Population** (2007): 738,000. **Density** (2007): persons per sq mi 9.7, persons per sq km 3.7. **Urban** (2005): 38.5%. **Sex distribution** (2006): male 50.06%; female 49.94%. **Age breakdown** (2005): under 15, 26.5%; 15–29, 29.7%; 30–44, 23.0%; 45–59, 13.3%; 60–74, 5.6%; 75 and over, 1.9%. **Ethnic composition** (2002): East Indian 43.5%; black 30.2%; mixed race 16.7%; Amerindian 9.2%; other 0.4%. **Religious affiliation** (2002): Christian 57.3%, of which Protestant/independent Christian 48.2% (including Anglican 6.9%), Roman Catholic 8.0%, Jehovah's Witness 1.1%; Hindu 28.4%; Muslim 7.2%; Rastafarian 0.5%; nonreligious 4.3%; other/unknown 2.3%. **Major cities** (2002): Georgetown 35,440 (urban agglomeration 137,520); Linden 29,502; New Amsterdam 15,997; Anna Regina 12,448; Corriverton 11,536. **Location:** northern South America, bordering the North Atlantic Ocean, Suriname, Brazil, and Venezuela.

Vital statistics

Birth rate per 1,000 population (2005): 18.5 (world avg. 20.3). **Death rate** per 1,000 population (2005): 8.3 (world avg. 8.6). **Total fertility rate** (avg. births per childbearing woman; 2005): 2.05. **Life expectancy** at birth (2005): male 62.9 years; female 68.3 years.

National economy

Budget (2005): *Revenue:* G$69,414,800,000 (tax revenue 76.2%, of which income taxes 34.2%, consumption taxes 31.0%, taxes on international trade 6.9%; nontax revenue 4.6%; grants 11.4%; other revenue 7.8%). *Expenditures:* G$88,861,400,000 (current expenditure 60.5%, of which wages and salaries 20.9%, transfers 13.3%, interest payments 4.9%; development expenditure 39.5%). **Production** (metric tons except as noted). *Agriculture, forestry, fishing* (2005): sugar cane 3,016,000, rice 273,300, coconuts 66,100; livestock (number of live animals) 130,000 sheep, 110,000 cattle, 20,000,000 chickens; roundwood 1,276,009 cu m, of which fuelwood 68%; fisheries production 53,980 (from aquaculture 1%); catch of shrimps and prawns equaled 15,573 metric tons. *Mining and quarrying* (2006): bauxite 1,374,000; gold 6,406 kg; diamonds 340,500 carats. *Manufacturing* (2006): flour 37,400; margarine 2,265; rum 119,000 hectolitres. *Energy production (consumption):* electricity (kW-hr; 2004) 835,000,000 (835,000,000); petroleum products (metric tons; 2004) none (470,000). **Population economically active** (2006): total 279,100; activity rate of total population 37% (participation rates: ages 15–65, 60%; female [2002] 34.1%; unemployed [2002] 11.7%). **Gross national income** (2006): US$857,000,000 (US$1,159 per capita). **Public debt** (external, outstanding; 2006): US$920,550,000. **Households.** Average household size (2002) 4.1. **Selected balance of payments data.** Receipts from (US$'000,000): tourism (2005) 35; remittances (2006) 270; foreign direct investment (2001–05 avg.) 47; official development assistance (2005) 92 (commitments). Disbursements for (US$'000,000): tourism (2005) 40; remittances (2005) 55. **Land use** as % of total land area (2003): in temporary crops 2.4%, in permanent crops 0.2%, in pasture 6.2%; overall forest area (2005) 76.7%.

Foreign trade

Imports (2005; c.i.f.): US$785,500,000 (fuels and lubricants 28.1%; consumer goods 24.9%; capital goods 19.7%). *Major import sources* (2004): Trinidad and Tobago 24.8%; US 24.5%; Cuba 6.8%; UK 5.4%. **Exports** (2005; f.o.b.): US$551,000,000 (sugar 21.4%; gold 20.3%; bauxite 11.4%; shrimp 11.3%; timber 9.0%; reexports 2.8%). *Major export destinations* (2004): Canada 23.2%; US 19.2%; UK 10.9%; Portugal 9.0%; Belgium 6.4%.

Transport and communications

Transport. *Railroads* (2001): 187 km (entirely devoted to transportation of ore). *Roads* (1999): total length 7,970 km (paved 7%). *Vehicles* (2001): passenger cars 61,300; trucks and buses 15,500. *Air transport* (2001): passenger-km 174,800,000; metric ton-km cargo 1,600,000. **Communications,** in total units (units per 1,000 persons). Daily newspaper circulation (2005): 67,000 (88); televisions (2003): 125,000 (169); telephone landlines (2005): 110,000 (146); cellular telephone subscribers (2005): 281,000 (375); personal computers (2005): 29,000 (39); total Internet users (2005): 160,000 (212); broadband Internet subscribers (2005): 2,000 (2.6).

Education and health

Educational attainment (1992). Percentage of employed persons having: no formal schooling 1.6%; incomplete primary education 9.3%; complete primary 54.7%; secondary 30.0%; higher 4.4%. **Literacy** (2005): total population ages 15 and over literate 99.0%; males literate 99.2%; females literate 98.7%. **Health** (2005): physicians 323 (1 per 2,325 persons); hospital beds 3,267 (1 per 230 persons); infant mortality rate per 1,000 live births 33.3. **Food** (2005): daily per capita caloric intake 2,784 (vegetable products 83%, animal products 17%); 148% of FAO recommended minimum.

Military

Total active duty personnel (2006): 1,100 (army 81.8%, navy 9.1%, air force 9.1%). **Military expenditure as percentage of GDP** (2004): 1.8%; per capita expenditure US$19.

Background

Guyana was colonized by the Dutch in the 17th century. During the Napoleonic Wars the British occupied the territory and afterward purchased the colonies of Demerara, Berbice, and Essequibo, united in 1831 as British Guiana. The slave trade was abolished in 1807, but emancipation of the 100,000 slaves in the colonies was not completed until 1838. From the 1840s East Indian and Chinese indentured servants were brought to work the plantations; by 1917 almost 240,000 East Indians had migrated to British Guiana. It was made a crown colony in 1928 and granted home rule in 1953. Political parties began to emerge, developing on racial lines as the People's Progressive Party (largely East Indian) and the People's National Congress (largely black). The PNC formed a coalition government and led the country into independence as Guyana in 1966. In 1970 Guyana became a republic within the Commonwealth; in 1980 it adopted a new constitution. Venezuela has long claimed land west of the Essequibo River, and the UN has continued to arbitrate the issue.

Recent Developments

The UN International Tribunal for the Law of the Sea's decision in September 2007 on the maritime boundary dispute between Guyana and Suriname gave Georgetown the far-larger share of the Guyana-Suriname Basin in contention, and Guyana was expected to vigorously resume offshore oil exploration.

Internet resources: <www.guyana-tourism.com>.

Haiti

Official name: Repiblik Dayti (Haitian Creole); République d'Haïti (French) (Republic of Haiti). **Form of government:** republic with two legislative

1 metric ton = about 1.1 short tons; 1 kilometer = 0.6 mi (statute); 1 metric ton-km cargo = about 0.68 short ton-mi cargo; c.i.f.: cost, insurance, and freight; f.o.b.: free on board

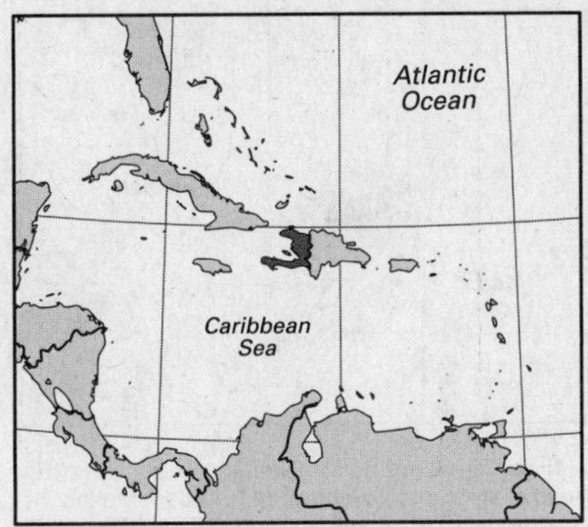

houses (Senate [30]; Chamber of Deputies [99]). **Chief of state:** President René Préval (from 2006). **Head of government:** Prime Minister Michèle Pierre-Louis (from 2008). **Capital:** Port-au-Prince. **Official languages:** Haitian Creole; French. **Official religions:** Roman Catholicism has special recognition per concordat with the Vatican; voodoo became officially sanctioned per governmental decree of April 2003. **Monetary unit:** 1 gourde (G) = 100 centimes; valuation (1 Jul 2008) US$1 = G 38.75.

Demography

Area: 10,695 sq mi, 27,700 sq km. **Population** (2007): 9,598,000. **Density** (2007): persons per sq mi 897.4, persons per sq km 346.5. **Urban** (2003): 40.8%. **Sex distribution** (2005): male 49.29%; female 50.71%. **Age breakdown** (2005): under 15, 42.6%; 15–29, 30.5%; 30–44, 14.2%; 45–59, 7.5%; 60–74, 4.2%; 75 and over, 1.0%. **Ethnic composition** (2000): black 94.2%; mulatto 5.4%; other 0.4%. **Religious affiliation** (2003): Roman Catholic 54.7% (about 80% of all Roman Catholics also practice voodoo); Protestant/independent Christian 28.5%, of which Baptist 15.4%, Pentecostal 7.9%; voodoo 2.1%; nonreligious/other 14.7%. **Major cities** (2003): Port-au-Prince 703,023 (metropolitan area 1,977,036); Carrefour (1999) 336,222; Delmas (1999) 284,079; Cap-Haïtien 111,094; Gonaïves 104,825. **Location:** western third of the island of Hispaniola, bordered by the North Atlantic Ocean, the Caribbean Sea, and the Dominican Republic.

Vital statistics

Birth rate per 1,000 population (2005): 36.6 (world avg. 20.3). **Death rate** per 1,000 population (2005): 12.3 (world avg. 8.6). **Total fertility rate** (avg. births per childbearing woman; 2005): 5.02. **Life expectancy** at birth (2005): male 51.6 years; female 54.3 years.

National economy

Budget (2003–04). *Revenue:* G 12,473,800,000 (customs duties 28.3%; sales tax 27.7%; individual taxes on income and profits 22.3%). *Expenditures:* G 17,164,900,000 (current expenditure 78.7%, of which wages 24.1%, transfers 6.0%, interest on public debt 5.0%; capital expenditure 21.3%). **Production** (metric tons except as noted). *Agriculture, forestry, fishing* (2005): sugarcane 1,080,000, cassava (manioc) 326,800, bananas 321,800; livestock (number of live animals) 1,900,000 goats, 1,456,000 cattle, 500,000 horses; roundwood 2,239,070 cu m, of which fuelwood 89%; fisheries production 8,300. *Mining and quarrying* (2002): sand 2,000,000 cu m. *Manufacturing* (value added in G '000,000, at prices of 1986–87; 2002): food and beverages 484.5; textiles, wearing apparel, and footwear 195.7; chemical and rubber products 63.8. *Energy production (consumption):* electricity (kW-hr; 2004) 547,000,000 (547,000,000); petroleum products (metric tons; 2004) none (523,000). **Gross national income** (2006): US$4,619,000,000 (US$489 per capita). **Population economically active** (2003): total 3,467,000; activity rate of total population 41.8% (participation rates: ages 15–64, 69.5%; female 41.5%; unemployed 32.7% [unofficial estimate is 70%]). **Public debt** (external, outstanding; 2005): US$1,276,000,000. **Households.** Average household size (2000) 4.7; sources of income (2001): self-employment 37%, transfers 25%, wages 20%; expenditure (1996): food, beverages, and tobacco 49.4%, housing and energy 9.1%, transportation 8.7%, clothing and footwear 8.5%. **Selected balance of payments data.** Receipts from (US$'000,000): tourism (2005) 110; remittances (2006) 1,650; foreign direct investment (2001–05 avg.) 8.0; official development assistance (2005) 515. Disbursements for (US$'000,000): tourism (2005) 54; remittances (2005) 59. **Land use** as % of total land area (2003): in temporary crops 28.3%, in permanent crops 11.6%, in pasture 17.8%; overall forest area (2005) 3.8%.

Foreign trade

Imports (2003): US$1,115,800,000 (food and live animals 24.0%; basic manufactures 22.4%; petroleum and derivatives 17.6%; machinery and transport equipment 14.8%). *Major import sources* (2004): US 52.9%; Dominican Republic 6.0%; Japan 2.9%. **Exports** (2003): US$333,160,000 (reexports to US 83.5%, of which clothing and apparel 82.1%; cacao 1.8%; essential oils 1.5%). *Major export destinations* (2004): US 81.8%; Dominican Republic 7.2%; Canada 4.2%.

Transport and communications

Transport. *Roads* (1999): total length 4,160 km (paved 24%). *Vehicles* (1999): passenger cars 93,000; trucks and buses 61,600. **Communications,** in total units (units per 1,000 persons). Daily newspaper circulation (2005): 11,000 (1.3); televisions (2003): 60,000 (7.2); telephone landlines (2005): 145,000 (17); cellular telephone subscribers (2005): 500,000 (59); personal computers (2005): 16,000 (1.9); total Internet users (2006): 650,000 (69).

Education and health

Educational attainment (2000). Percentage of population ages 25 and over having: no formal schooling/unknown 46.1%; incomplete primary education 28.9%; primary 5.3%; incomplete secondary 15.6%; secondary 1.8%; higher 2.3%. **Literacy** (2005): total population ages 15 and over literate 54.8%; males literate 56.5%; females literate 52.3%. **Health:** physicians (1999) 1,910 (1 per 4,000 persons); hospital beds (2000) 6,431 (1 per 1,234 persons); infant mortality rate per 1,000 live births (2005) 73.5. **Food** (2005): daily per capita caloric intake 1,863 (vegetable products 91%, animal products 9%); 96% of FAO recommended minimum.

Military

Total active duty personnel: The Haitian army was disbanded in 1995. The national police force had 5,000 personnel in mid-2006. UN peacekeeping troops (June 2007) 7,065.

Background

Haiti gained its independence when the former slaves of the island, initially led by Toussaint Louverture, and later by Jean-Jacques Dessalines, rebelled against French rule in 1791–1804. The new republic encompassed the entire island of Hispaniola, but the eastern portion was restored to Spain in 1809. The island was reunited under Haitian Pres. Jean-Pierre Boyer (1818–43); after his overthrow the eastern portion revolted and formed the Dominican Republic. Haiti's government was marked by instability, with frequent coups and assassinations. It was occupied by the US in 1915–34. In 1957 the dictator François ("Papa Doc") Duvalier came to power. Despite an economic decline and civil unrest, Duvalier ruled until his death in 1971. He was succeeded by his son, Jean-Claude ("Baby Doc") Duvalier, who was forced into exile in 1986. Haiti's first free presidential elections, held in 1990, were won by Jean-Bertrand Aristide. He was deposed by a military coup in 1991, after which tens of thousands of Haitians attempted to flee to the US in small boats. The military government stepped down in 1994, and Aristide returned from exile and resumed the presidency.

Recent Developments

A sense of optimism enveloped Haiti during 2007 as the country continued to creep away from its past of political conflict, insecurity, and economic decline. Fueling optimism were the continuing efforts of Pres. René Préval to include opposition groups within his coalition government and the government's success, supported by the UN Stabilization Mission in Haiti (MINUSTAH), in eliminating most of the gang violence and kidnapping that had paralyzed much of the country. MINUSTAH's mandate, extended until 15 Oct 2008, was reconfigured toward shifting its presence to unsecured border and coastal locations to target arms and drug smuggling. Haiti's poor majority voiced frustration with the lack of tangible, sustained economic improvement in their lives. However, inflation fell from 40.0% to an estimated 8%, and GDP rose to a forecast growth of 3.2%. Significant amounts of previously pledged international aid flowed into Haiti, with much of it allocated to short-term job-creation programs. Cash transfers from Haitians living overseas (an estimated US$1.6 billion annually) continued to serve as a mechanism for bridging the gap between survival and growth.

Internet resources: <www.haititourisme.org>.

Honduras

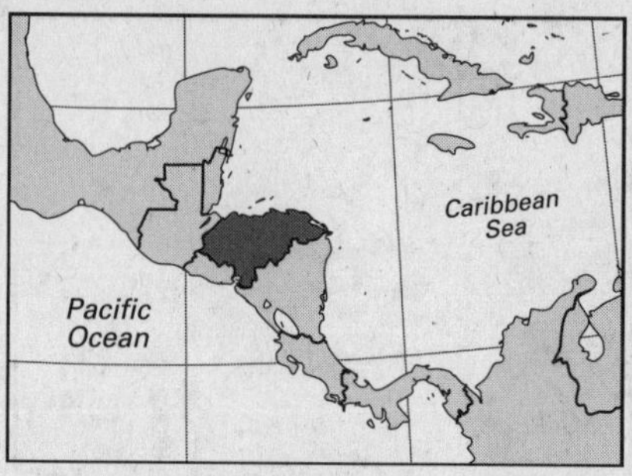

Official name: República de Honduras (Republic of Honduras). **Form of government:** multiparty republic with one legislative house (National Assembly [128]). **Head of state and government:** President Manuel Zelaya (from 2006). **Capital:** Tegucigalpa. **Official language:** Spanish. **Official religion:** none. **Monetary unit:** 1 Honduran lempira (L) = 100 centavos; valuation (1 Jul 2008) US$1 = L 18.90.

Demography

Area: 43,433 sq mi, 112,492 sq km. **Population** (2007): 7,484,000. **Density** (2007): persons per sq mi 172.3, persons per sq km 66.5. **Urban** (2006): 45.5%. **Sex distribution** (2006): male 48.47%; female 51.53%. **Age breakdown** (2005): under 15, 40.5%; 15–29, 29.2%; 30–44, 16.7%; 45–59, 8.6%; 60–74, 3.9%; 75 and over, 1.1%. **Ethnic composition** (2000): mestizo 86.6%; Amerindian 5.5%; black (including Black Carib) 4.3%; white 2.3%; other 1.3%. **Religious affiliation** (2002): Roman Catholic 63%; Evangelical Protestant 23%; other 14%. **Major cities** (2005): Tegucigalpa 900,400; San Pedro Sula 558,200; Choloma 177,400; La Ceiba 150,400; El Progreso 107,400. **Location:** Central America, bordering the Caribbean Sea, Nicaragua, the North Pacific Ocean, El Salvador, and Guatemala.

Vital statistics

Birth rate per 1,000 population (2005): 28.5 (world avg. 20.3). **Death rate** per 1,000 population (2005): 6.0 (world avg. 8.6). **Natural increase rate** per 1,000 population (2005): 22.5 (world avg. 11.7). **Total fertility rate** (avg. births per childbearing woman; 2005): 3.50. **Life expectancy** at birth (2005): male 66.5 years; female 70.7 years.

National economy

Budget (2005). *Revenue:* L 32,305,100,000 (tax revenue 82.7%; nontax revenue 5.8%; transfers 11.5%). *Expenditures:* L 37,017,900,000 (current expenditure 78.6%; capital expenditure 21.4%). **Public debt** (external, outstanding; March 2006): US$4,327,-500,000. **Production** (metric tons except as noted). *Agriculture, forestry, fishing* (2005): sugarcane 5,625,000, oil palm fruit 1,233,000, bananas 887,100; livestock (number of live animals) 2,500,000 cattle, 490,000 pigs, 18,700,000 chickens; roundwood 9,632,614 cu m, of which fuelwood 90%; fisheries production 48,580 (from aquaculture 60%). *Mining and quarrying* (2004): gypsum 60,000; zinc (metal content) 46,500; silver 48,000 kg. *Manu-*

facturing (value added in L '000,000; 1996): food products 1,937; wearing apparel 1,266 (important product of the maquiladora sector; garment assembly employed 110,000 in 2001); beverages 700. *Energy production (consumption):* electricity (kW-hr; 2005) 5,551,300,000 (5,551,300,000); coal (metric tons; 2004) none (174,000); petroleum products (metric tons; 2004) none (2,038,000). **Land use** as % of total land area (2003): in temporary crops 9.5%, in permanent crops 3.2%, in pasture 13.5%; overall forest area (2005) 41.5%. **Population economically active** (2005): total 2,651,300; activity rate of total population 36.5% (participation rates: ages 15 and over 57.7%; female 32.4%; unemployed [2006] unofficially 27.9%). **Gross national income** (2006): US$8,989,-000,000 (US$1,290 per capita). **Households** (2004). Average household size (2006) 4.8; average annual income per household L 85,860 (US$4,716); sources of income: wages and salaries 51%, self-employment 34%, remittances 8%, other 7%; expenditure (1999): food and nonalcoholic beverages 32%, housing and energy 19%, transportation 9%, clothing and footwear 8%, household furnishings 7%. **Selected balance of payments data.** Receipts from (US$'000,000): tourism (2005) 472; remittances (2006) 2,359; foreign direct investment (2001–05 avg.) 243; official development assistance (2005) 1,318 (commitments). Disbursements for (US$'000,000): tourism (2005) 248; remittances (2005) 1.

Foreign trade

Imports (2006; f.o.b. in balance of trade and c.i.f. in commodities and trading partners): US$5,417,-800,000 (mineral fuels and lubricants 20.6%; food products and live animals 16.6%; machinery and electrical equipment 15.6%; chemicals and chemical products 12.9%; fabricated metal products 7.6%). *Major import sources* (2005): US 37.5%; Guatemala 9.0%; El Salvador 5.9%; Costa Rica 5.5%; Mexico 5.3%. **Exports** (2006): US$1,929,500,000 (coffee 20.9%; bananas 13.0%; shrimp 9.4%; zinc 5.8%; gold 4.1%; wood and wood products 3.4%). *Major export destinations* (2005): US 36.8%; El Salvador 10.5%; Germany 8.5%; Guatemala 7.9%; Belgium 5.4%.

Transport and communications

Transport. *Railroads* (2005): serviceable lines 253 km. *Roads* (2005): total length 13,720 km (paved 22%). *Vehicles* (2003): passenger cars 386,468; trucks and buses 113,744. *Air transport* (1995): passenger-km 341,000,000; metric ton-km cargo 33,000,000. **Communications,** in total units (units per 1,000 persons). Daily newspaper circulation (2005): 198,000 (28); televisions (2004): 1,000,000 (143); telephone landlines (2006): 708,000 (97); cellular telephone subscribers (2006): 2,241,000 (306); personal computers (2005): 120,000 (17); total Internet users (2006): 337,000 (46).

Education and health

Educational attainment (1988). Percentage of population ages 10 and over having: no formal schooling 33.4%; primary education 50.1%; secondary education 13.4%; higher 3.1%. **Literacy** (2005): total population ages 15 and over literate 78.0%; males literate 77.6%; females literate 78.3%. **Health:** physicians (2001) 5,681 (1 per 1,149 persons); hospital beds (2005) 5,546 (1 per 1,292 persons); infant mortality rate (2005) 26.5. **Food** (2005): daily per capita caloric intake 2,752 (vegetable products 75%, animal products 25%); 155% of FAO recommended minimum.

Military

Total active duty personnel (2006): 12,000 (army 69.2%, navy 11.7%, air force 19.1%); US troops (2005) 438. **Military expenditure as percentage of GDP** (2005): 0.6%; per capita expenditure US$7.

Background

Early residents of Honduras were part of the Maya civilization that flourished in the 1st millennium AD. Christopher Columbus reached Honduras in 1502, and permanent settlement followed. A major war between the Spanish and the Indians broke out in 1537, culminating in the decimation of the Indian population through disease and enslavement. After 1570 Honduras was part of the captaincy general of Guatemala until Central American independence in 1821. Part of the United Provinces of Central America, Honduras withdrew in 1838 and declared its independence. In the 20th century, under military rule, there was constant civil war and some intervention by the US. A civilian government assumed office in 1982. The military remained in the background, however, as the activity of leftist guerrillas increased.

Recent Developments

The US government in May 2007 extended for 18 months the Temporary Protected Status (TPS) that allowed 78,000 Hondurans to work legally in the US because of environmental disasters in Honduras. TPS worker remittances, in addition to remittances from undocumented workers, accounted for approximately 25% of the country's GDP.

Internet resources: <www.honduras.com>.

Hong Kong

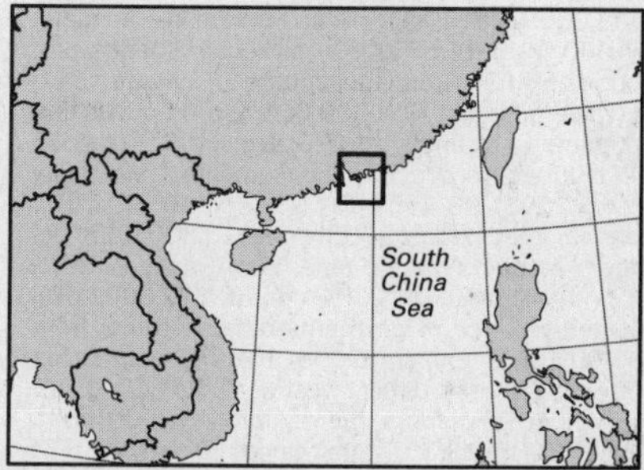

Official name: Xianggang Tebie Xingzhengqu (Chinese); Hong Kong Special Administrative Region (English). **Political status:** special administrative region (People's Republic of China) with one legislative house (Legislative Council [60]). **Chief of state:** Chinese President Hu Jintao (from 2003). **Head of government:** Chief Executive Donald Tsang (from 2005). **Official languages:** Chinese; English. **Official religion:** none. **Monetary unit:** 1 Hong Kong dollar (HK$) = 100 cents; valuation (1 Jul 2008) US$1 = HK$7.80.

Demography

Area: 426 sq mi, 1,104 sq km. **Population** (2007): 6,924,000. **Density** (2007): persons per sq mi 16,254, persons per sq km 6,272. **Urban** (2003): 100%. **Sex distribution** (2006): male 47.68%; female 52.32%. **Age breakdown** (2005): under 15, 14.2%; 15–29, 19.9%; 30–44, 27.0%; 45–59, 23.3%; 60–74, 10.2%; 75–84, 4.2%; 85 and over, 1.2%. **Ethnic composition** (2006): Chinese 95.0%; Filipino 1.6%; Indonesian 1.3%; assorted Caucasian 0.5%; Indian 0.3%; Nepalese 0.2%; other 1.1%. **Religious affiliation** (2002): nonreligious/non-practitioner of religion 57%; participant of religious practice 43%, of which Protestant 4.5%, Roman Catholic 3.5%, Muslim 1.5%, other (mostly Buddhist, Taoist, or Confucianist) 33.5%. **Major built-up areas** (2005): Kowloon 2,070,000; Victoria 986,800; Tuen Mun 473,100; Sha Tin 432,600; Tseung Kwan O 344,500. **Location:** east Asia, bordering China and the South China Sea.

Vital statistics

Birth rate per 1,000 population (2006): 9.6 (world avg. 20.3). **Death rate** per 1,000 population (2006): 5.4 (world avg. 8.6). **Natural increase rate** per 1,000 population (2006): 4.2 (world avg. 11.7). **Total fertility rate** (avg. births per childbearing woman; 2005): 0.97. **Life expectancy** at birth (2006): male 79.5 years; female 85.6 years.

National economy

Budget (2005–06). *Revenue:* HK$247,035,000,000 (earnings and profits taxes 45.6%; indirect taxes 20.4%; capital revenue 17.3%; other 16.7%). *Expenditures:* HK$245,000,000,000 (education 22.0%; social welfare 13.6%; health 12.9%; police 10.1%; housing 6.2%; economic services 5.3%). **Public debt** (external, outstanding; 2005): US$1,589,700,000. **Gross national income** (2006): US$190,196,-000,000 (US$26,667 per capita). **Production** (metric tons except as noted). *Agriculture, forestry, fishing* (2005): vegetables 24,600, fruits 350, eggs 2,008,000 units; livestock (number of live animals) 377,000 pigs, 11,676,000 chickens; fisheries production 158,995 (from aquaculture 2%). *Manufacturing* (value added in HK$'000,000; 2004): publishing and printed materials 11,270; textiles 6,067; food 5,031. *Energy production (consumption):* electricity (kW-hr; 2005) 38,448,000,000 (44,545,000,000); hard coal (metric tons; 2005) none (10,800,000); petroleum products (metric tons; 2004) none (4,207,-000); natural gas (cu m; 2004) none (2,132,000,000). **Selected balance of payments data.** Receipts from (US$'000,000): tourism (2005) 10,179; remittances (2006) 297; foreign direct investment (FDI) (2001–05 avg.) 23,402. Disbursements for (US$'000,000): tourism (2005) 13,307; remittances (2006) 365; FDI (2001–05 avg.) 22,515. **Population economically active** (2004): total 3,529,000; activity rate of total population 52.0% (participation rates: ages 15–64, 70.2%; female 44.2%; unemployed [January–March 2007] 4.3%). **Households.** Average household size (2006) 2.8; median annual income per household (2001) HK$224,500 (US$28,800); expenditure (2001): housing and energy 22.2%, clothing and footwear 15.2%, food and nonalcoholic beverages 13.5%, household furnishings 12.6%, transportation 11.0%. **Land use** as % of total land area (2000): in temporary and permanent crops 5.4%, in pasture 29.3%; overall forest area 18.0%.

Foreign trade

Imports (2006; c.i.f.): HK$2,599,800,000,000 (capital goods 29.6%; consumer goods 26.8%; mineral fuels and lubricants 2.8%; foodstuffs 2.5%). *Major import sources:* China 45.9%; Japan 10.3%; Taiwan 7.5%; Singapore 6.3%; US 4.8%. **Exports** (2006; f.o.b.): HK$2,461,000,000,000 (reexports 94.5%, of which consumer goods 30.6%, capital goods 29.2%; domestic exports 3.3%, of which clothing accessories and apparel 2.1%). *Major export destinations:* China 47.0%; US 15.1%; Japan 4.9%; Germany 3.1%; UK 3.0%.

Transport and communications

Transport. *Railroads* (2003): route length 64 km; passenger-km 4,256,000,000. *Roads* (2006): total length 1,984 km (paved 100%). *Vehicles* (2006): passenger cars 378,000; trucks and buses 131,000. *Air transport* (2005; Cathay Pacific and Dragonair only): passenger-km 71,595,000,000; metric ton-km cargo 8,026,729,000. **Communications,** in total units (units per 1,000 persons). Daily newspaper circulation (2005): 2,468,000 (356); televisions (2003): 3,467,000 (507); telephone landlines (2006): 3,836,000 (556); cellular telephone subscribers (2006): 9,356,000 (1,364); personal computers (2005): 4,172,000 (602); total Internet users (2006): 3,770,000 (550); broadband Internet subscribers (2006): 1,796,000 (262).

Education and health

Educational attainment (2005). Percentage of population ages 15 and over having: no formal schooling 6.5%; primary education 19.5%; secondary 45.9%; matriculation 5.2%; nondegree higher 7.9%; higher degree 15.1%. **Literacy** (2000): total population ages 15 and over literate 93.5%; males literate 96.5%; females literate 90.2%. **Health** (2005): physicians 11,775 (1 per 588 persons; there were an additional 4,848 practitioners of traditional Chinese medicine in Hong Kong at the beginning of 2006); hospital beds 33,939 (1 per 204 persons); infant mortality rate per 1,000 live births (2006) 1.8. **Food** (2001): daily per capita caloric intake 3,104 (vegetable products 68%, animal products 32%); 136% of FAO recommended minimum.

Military

Total active duty personnel (2003): 4,000 troops of Chinese military (including elements of army, navy, and air force); Hong Kong residents are exempted from military service.

Background

The island of Hong Kong and adjacent islets were ceded by China to the British in 1842, and the Kowloon Peninsula and the New Territories were later leased by

1 metric ton = about 1.1 short tons; 1 kilometer = 0.6 mi (statute); 1 metric ton-km cargo = about 0.68 short ton-mi cargo; c.i.f.: cost, insurance, and freight; f.o.b.: free on board

the British from China for 99 years (1898–1997). A joint Chinese-British declaration, signed on 19 Dec 1984, paved the way for the entire territory to be returned to China, which occurred on 1 Jul 1997.

Recent Developments

Hong Kong was the scene of an international diplomatic incident in 2007. The aircraft carrier USS *Kitty Hawk* was due to stop in Hong Kong over Thanksgiving but was refused entry by Chinese authorities, leaving thousands of sailors' relatives unable to celebrate the holiday with their loved ones. Although the *Kitty Hawk* eventually did stop in Hong Kong (in April 2008), no adequate explanation was ever publicly given by the Chinese.

Internet resources: <www.discoverhongkong.com>.

Hungary

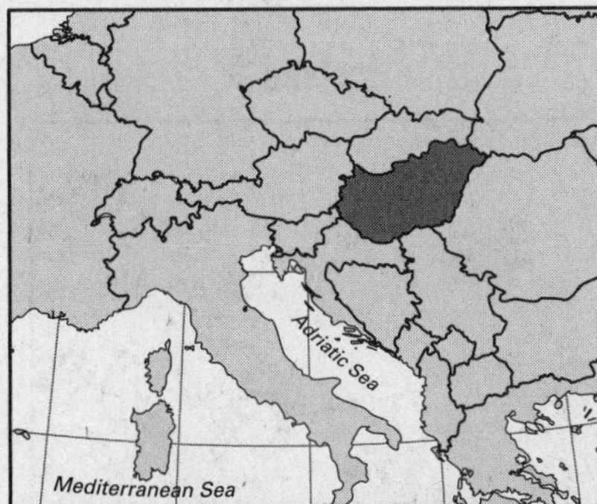

Official name: Magyar Köztársaság (Republic of Hungary). **Form of government:** unitary multiparty republic with one legislative house (National Assembly [386]). **Chief of state:** President László Sólyom (from 2005). **Head of government:** Prime Minister Ferenc Gyurcsány (from 2004). **Capital:** Budapest. **Official language:** Hungarian. **Official religion:** none. **Monetary unit:** 1 forint (Ft) = 100 filler; valuation (1 Jul 2008) US$1 = Ft 149.56.

Demography

Area: 35,919 sq mi, 93,030 sq km. **Population** (2007): 10,055,000. **Density** (2007): persons per sq mi 279.9, persons per sq km 108.1. **Urban** (2004): 64.8%. **Sex distribution** (2005): male 47.47%; female 52.53%. **Age breakdown** (2005): under 15, 15.6%; 15–29, 21.3%; 30–44, 20.4%; 45–59, 21.3%; 60–74, 14.7%; 75–84, 5.6%; 85 and over, 1.1%. **Ethnic composition** (2000): Hungarian 84.4%; Rom 5.3%; Ruthenian 2.9%; German 2.4%; Romanian 1.0%; Slovak 0.9%; Jewish 0.6%; other 2.5%. **Religious affiliation** (2001): Roman Catholic 51.9%; Reformed 15.9%; Lutheran 3.0%; Greek Catholic 2.6%; Jewish 0.1%; nonreligious 14.5%; other/unknown 12.0%. **Major cities** (2004): Budapest 1,697,343; Debrecen 204,297; Miskolc 175,701; Szeged 162,889; Pécs 156,567. **Location:** central Europe, bordering Slovakia, Ukraine, Romania, Serbia, Croatia, Slovenia, and Austria.

Vital statistics

Birth rate per 1,000 population (2006): 9.9 (world avg. 20.3); (2004) within marriage 66.0%. **Death rate** per 1,000 population (2006): 13.1 (world avg. 8.6). **Total fertility rate** (avg. births per childbearing woman; 2006): 1.35. **Life expectancy** at birth (2006): male 69.0 years; female 77.4 years.

National economy

Budget (2005). *Revenue:* Ft 6,458,391,000,000 (VAT 27.6%; personal income taxes 15.5%; corporate taxes 15.5%; excise taxes 11.4%). *Expenditures:* Ft 7,003,392,000,000 (general administration 47.6%; public debt 13.1%; family benefits 7.1%). **Production** (metric tons except as noted). *Agriculture, forestry, fishing* (2005): corn (maize) 9,050,000, wheat 5,088,000, sugar beets 3,516,000, Hungarian red paprika 49,380; livestock (number of live animals) 4,913,000 pigs, 739,000 cattle, 2,127,000 geese; roundwood 5,940,000 cu m, of which fuelwood 53%; fisheries production 21,270 (from aquaculture 64%). *Mining and quarrying* (2004): bauxite 647,000. *Manufacturing* (value added in US$'000,000; 2002): electrical machinery and apparatus 1,885; motor vehicles and parts 1,176; chemical products 1,113. *Energy production (consumption):* electricity (kW-hr; 2004) 33,708,000,000 (41,176,000,000); hard coal (metric tons; 2004) none (1,299,000); lignite (metric tons; 2004) 11,242,000 (12,173,000); crude petroleum (barrels; 2004) 7,205,000 (42,635,000); petroleum products (metric tons; 2004–05) 6,540,000 ([2004] 5,354,000); natural gas (cu m; 2004–05) 2,935,000,000 ([2004] 15,021,000,000). **Selected balance of payments data.** Receipts from (US$'000,000): tourism (2005) 4,279; remittances (2006) 363; foreign direct investment (FDI) (2001–05 avg.) 4,085. Disbursements for (US$'000,000): tourism (2005) 2,925; remittances (2006) 189; FDI (2001–05 avg.) 952. **Population economically active** (2006): total 4,246,900; activity rate of total population 42.2% (participation rates: ages 15–64, 62.0%; female [2004] 45.7%; unemployed 7.5%). **Gross national income** (2006): US$104,036,000,000 (US$10,343 per capita). **Public debt** (external, outstanding; 2005): US$21,216,000,000. **Households.** Average household size (2005) 2.6; income per household (2001) Ft 2,898,000 (US$10,300); sources of income (2001): wages 48.3%, transfers 25.7%, self-employment 16.3%; expenditure (2005): food products 22.8%, transportation and communications 20.1%, housing and energy 19.1%, recreation 8.1%. **Land use** as % of total land area (2003): in temporary crops 51.3%, in permanent crops 2.3%, in pasture 11.9%; overall forest area (2005) 21.5%.

Foreign trade

Imports (2003; c.i.f.): Ft 10,469,000,000,000 (electrical machinery 16.6%; nonelectrical machinery 15.7%; road vehicles 8.4%; telecommunications equipment 7.1%; mineral fuels 5.8%). *Major import sources* (2006): Germany 27.4%; Russia 8.2%; Austria 6.2%; China 5.1%; France 4.7%. **Exports** (2003; f.o.b.): Ft 9,646,000,000,000 (telecommunications equipment 12.6%; electrical machinery 11.9%; motor vehicle engines 8.7%; road vehicles 8.2%; office machines and computers 7.0%). *Major export destinations* (2006): Germany 29.4%; Italy 5.4%; Austria 4.8%; France 4.6%; UK 4.5%.

Transport and communications

Transport. *Railroads* (2003): route length 7,898 km; passenger-km (2004) 10,544,000,000; metric ton-km cargo 8,878,000,000. *Roads* (2003): total length 159,568 km (paved 44%). *Vehicles*: passenger cars (2005) 2,888,735; trucks and buses (2003) 395,000. *Air transport* (2006; Malév Hungarian Airlines only): passenger-km 4,099,000,000; metric ton-km cargo 25,000,000. **Communications,** in total units (units per 1,000 persons). Daily newspaper circulation (2004): 1,820,000 (181); televisions (2003): 4,810,000 (475); telephone landlines (2006): 3,350,000 (333); cellular telephone subscribers (2006): 9,965,000 (990); personal computers (2005): 1,504,000 (149); total Internet users (2006): 3,500,000 (348); broadband Internet subscribers (2006): 977,000 (97).

Education and health

Educational attainment (2002). Population ages 25–64 having: no formal schooling through lower-secondary education 29%; upper secondary/higher vocational 57%; university 14%. **Health** (2004): physicians 38,877 (1 per 260 persons); hospital beds 79,610 (1 per 127 persons); infant mortality rate per 1,000 live births (2006) 5.7. **Food** (2005): daily per capita caloric intake 3,438 (vegetable products 72%, animal products 28%); 172% of FAO recommended minimum.

Military

Total active duty personnel (2006): 32,300 (army 74.2%, air force 23.2%, headquarters staff 2.6%). **Military expenditure as percentage of GDP** (2005): 1.5%; per capita expenditure US$158.

Background

The western part of Hungary was incorporated into the Roman Empire in 14 BC. The Magyars, a nomadic people, occupied the middle basin of the Danube River in the late 9th century AD. Stephen I, crowned in 1000, Christianized the country and organized it into a strong and independent state. Invasions by the Mongols in the 13th century and by the Ottoman Turks in the 14th century devastated the country, and by 1568 the territory of modern Hungary had been divided into three parts: Royal Hungary went to the Habsburgs; Transylvania gained autonomy in 1566 under the Turks; and the central plain remained under Turkish control until the late 17th century, when the Austrian Habsburgs took over. Hungary declared its independence from Austria in 1849, and in 1867 the dual monarchy of Austria-Hungary was established. Its defeat in World War I resulted in the dismemberment of Hungary, leaving it only those areas in which Magyars predominated. In an attempt to regain some of this lost territory, Hungary cooperated with the Germans against the Soviet Union during World War II. After the war, a pro-Soviet provisional government was established, and in 1949 the Hungarian People's Republic was formed. Opposition to this Stalinist regime broke out in 1956 but was suppressed. Nevertheless, from 1956 to 1988 communist Hungary grew to become the most tolerant of the Soviet-bloc nations of Eastern Europe. It gained its independence in 1989 and soon attracted the largest amount of direct foreign investment in east-central Europe. In 1999 it joined NATO and in 2004 the European Union (EU).

Recent Developments

During 2007 the popularity of Socialist Prime Minister Ferenc Gyurcsány's government plummeted in the wake of a strict austerity program that was designed to reduce the Hungarian government's soaring budget deficit and bring macroeconomic indicators in line with EU requirements to join the euro zone. The most controversial element in the package, which included reforms of the public administration sector and cuts in energy subsidies to the public, was a radical overhaul of the debt-ridden health sector, including closures and mergers, a 10% cut in hospital beds, and the introduction of a patient "visit fee." A particularly controversial provision opened up the sector to profit-making health insurance funds and privatized hospitals.

Internet resources: <www.hungary.com>.

Iceland

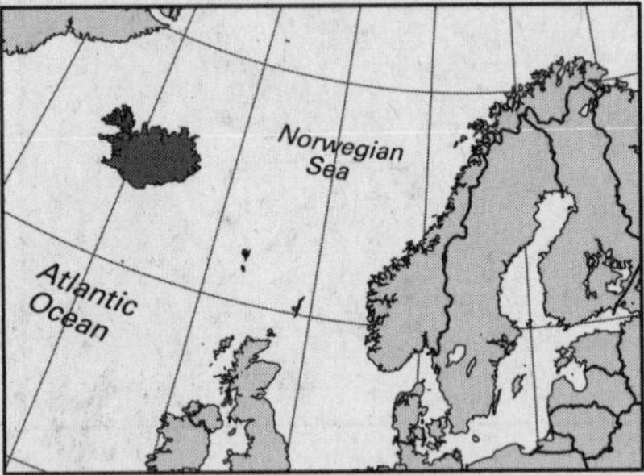

Official name: Lýdhveldidh Ísland (Republic of Iceland). **Form of government:** unitary multiparty republic with one legislative house (Althingi [63]). **Chief of state:** President Ólafur Ragnar Grímsson (from 1996). **Head of government:** Prime Minister Geir H. Haarde (from 2006). **Capital:** Reykjavík. **Official language:** Icelandic. **Official religion:** Evangelical Lutheran. **Monetary unit:** 1 króna (ISK; plural krónur) = 100 aurar; valuation (1 Jul 2008) US$1 = ISK 79.33.

Demography

Area: 39,741 sq mi, 102,928 sq km. **Population** (2007): 310,000. **Density** (2007): persons per sq mi 33.7, persons per sq km 13.0. **Urban** (2004): 94.0%. **Sex distribution** (2005): male 50.42%; female 49.58%. **Age breakdown** (2005): under 15, 21.8%; 15–29, 21.9%; 30–44, 21.5%; 45–59, 18.9%; 60–74, 10.2%; 75–84, 4.3%; 85 and over, 1.4%. **Ethnic composition** (2006; by citizenship): Icelandic 94.0%; European 4.0%, of which Polish 1.9%, Nordic 0.5%; Asian 0.9%; other 1.1%. **Religious affiliation** (2004): Evangelical Lutheran 85.4%; other Lutheran 4.5%; Roman Catholic 2.0%; other Christian 1.9%; other/not specified 6.2%. **Major cities** (2006): Reykjavík 116,642 (urban area [2005] 187,426); Kó-

1 metric ton = about 1.1 short tons; 1 kilometer = 0.6 mi (statute); 1 metric ton-km cargo = about 0.68 short ton-mi cargo; c.i.f.: cost, insurance, and freight; f.o.b.: free on board

pavogur 27,525; Hafnarfjördhur 23,751; Akureyri 16,887; Gar abær 9,556. **Location:** northern Europe, island between the Greenland Sea, the Norwegian Sea, and the North Atlantic Ocean.

Vital statistics

Birth rate per 1,000 population (2006): 14.5 (world avg. 20.3); within marriage 34.4%. **Death rate** per 1,000 population (2006): 6.2 (world avg. 8.6). **Natural increase rate** per 1,000 population (2006): 8.3 (world avg. 11.7). **Total fertility rate** (avg. births per childbearing woman; 2006): 2.07. **Life expectancy** at birth (2006): male 79.4 years; female 83.0 years.

National economy

Budget (2004). *Revenue:* ISK 279,425,000,000 (tax revenue 90.3%, of which VAT 30.8%, individual income tax 26.4%, social security contribution 10.4%; nontax revenue 9.7%). *Expenditures:* ISK 273,035,000,000 (social security and health 40.4%; education 11.8%; social affairs 8.4%; interest payment 5.5%). **Production** (metric tons except as noted). *Agriculture, forestry, fishing* (2005): potatoes 13,800, cereals 9,773, tomatoes 1,508; livestock (number of live animals) 454,950 sheep, 74,820 horses, 65,979 cattle; fisheries production (value in ISK '000,000; 2005) 67,920, of which cod 24,924, haddock 8,881, redfish 5,461, herring 5,161, capelin 5,031, halibut 3,035, blue whiting 1,489; fisheries production by tonnage 1,669,578 (from aquaculture 1%). *Mining and quarrying* (2005): diatomite 3,236. *Manufacturing* (value of sales in ISK '000,000; 2004): food products and beverages (mainly preserved and processed fish) 179,749; base metals 42,067; chemicals and chemical products 20,504. *Energy production (consumption):* electricity (kW-hr; 2004) 8,619,000,000 (8,619,000,000); coal (metric tons; 2004) none (104,000); petroleum products (metric tons; 2004) none (729,000). **Selected balance of payments data.** Receipts from (US$'000,000): tourism (2005) 409; remittances (2006) 87; foreign direct investment (FDI) (2001–05 avg.) 711. Disbursements for (US$'000,000): tourism (2005) 975; remittances (2006) 80; FDI (2001–05 avg.) 2,058. **Population economically active** (2006): total 174,300; activity rate of total population 57.4% (participation rates: ages 16–74, 82.1%; female 45.4%; unemployed 2.5%). **Gross national income** (2006): US$15,096,000,000 (US$50,586 per capita). **Public debt** (December 2005): US$4,222,000,000. **Households.** Average household size (2004) 2.5; annual employment income per household (2003) ISK 2,428,000 (US$31,700); sources of income (2001): wages and salaries 78.6%, pension 10.3%, self-employment 2.0%, other 9.1%; expenditure (2005): housing and energy 25.5%, transportation and communications 16.3%, food 14.4%, recreation, education, and culture 13.3%. **Land use** as % of total land area (2003): in temporary crops 0.07%, in permanent crops, none, in pasture 22.7%; overall forest area (2005) 0.5%.

Foreign trade

Imports (2005; f.o.b. in balance of trade and c.i.f. in commodities and trading partners): ISK 313,854,600,000 (machinery and apparatus 23.7%; transport equipment 18.2%; crude petroleum and petroleum products 8.8%; metal and metal products 8.7%; chemicals and chemical products 7.8%). *Major import sources:* Germany 13.8%; US 9.3%; Norway 8.4%; Denmark 7.1%; UK 7.0%. **Exports** (2005): ISK 194,355,300,000 (marine products 56.7%, of which cod 21.6%, haddock 6.0%, redfish 4.1%, shrimp 4.1%; aluminum 18.0%; transport equipment 5.5%). *Major export destinations:* UK 17.8%; Germany 15.8%; The Netherlands 12.5%; US 8.8%; Spain 7.4%.

Transport and communications

Transport. *Roads* (2006): total length 13,038 km (paved 33%). *Vehicles* (2005): passenger cars 187,442; trucks and buses 27,443. *Air transport* (2006; Icelandair only): passenger-km 4,248,000,000; metric ton-km cargo [2005] 121,591,000. **Communications,** in total units (units per 1,000 persons). Daily newspaper circulation (2005): 170,000 (573); televisions (2004): 101,000 (345); telephone landlines (2006): 194,000 (652); cellular telephone subscribers (2006): 329,000 (1,106); personal computers (2005): 142,000 (481); total Internet users (2006): 194,000 (653); broadband Internet subscribers (2006): 88,000 (290).

Education and health

Educational attainment (2002): Percentage of population ages 25–64 having: primary through some secondary education 34.4%; secondary 45.7%; higher 19.9%. **Literacy:** virtually 100%. **Health:** physicians (2004) 1,056 (1 per 277 persons); hospital beds (2002) 2,432 (1 per 118 persons); infant mortality rate per 1,000 live births (2005) 2.3. **Food** (2005): daily per capita caloric intake 3,245 (vegetable products 60%, animal products 40%).

Military

Total active duty personnel (2005): 130 coast guard personnel; NATO-sponsored US-manned Iceland Defense Force 1,250. **Coast guard expenditure as percentage of GDP** (2005): 0.3%; per capita expenditure US$140.

Background

Iceland was settled by Norwegian seafarers in the 9th century and was Christianized by 1000. Its legislature, the Althing, was founded in 930, making it one of the oldest legislative assemblies in the world. Iceland united with Norway in 1262. It became an independent state of Denmark in 1918 but severed those ties to become an independent republic in 1944. Vigdís Finnbogadóttir became the world's first female elected president in 1980.

Recent Developments

Iceland's economy began to slow down in 2007, following the vigorous growth of the previous several years. The Kárahnjúkar 690-MW hydropower station in the northeastern part of the country was completed and began supplying power to the Alcoa aluminum plant at Reyðarfjörður. The construction of the power station provoked a bitter debate on damage to the environment and the future plans for additional power projects and aluminum plants. The stock of codfish in Icelandic waters had diminished over the years, despite stringent efforts to manage the catch by limiting the annual catch to 130,000 tons.

Internet resources: <www.icetourist.is>.

India

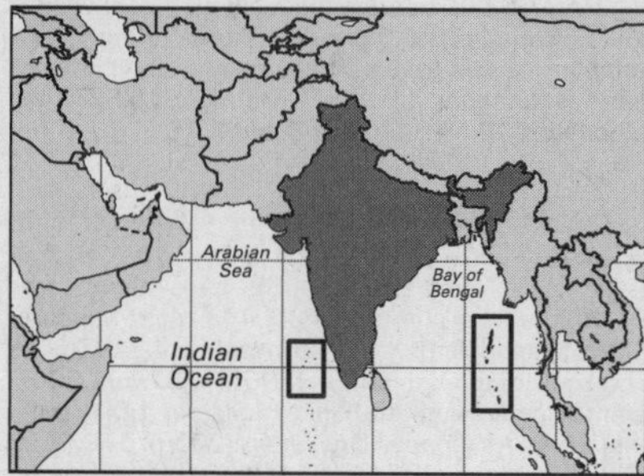

Official name: Bharat (Hindi); Republic of India (English). **Form of government:** multiparty federal republic with two legislative houses (Council of States [245], House of the People [545]). **Chief of state:** President Pratibha Patil (from 2007). **Head of government:** Prime Minister Manmohan Singh (from 2004). **Capital:** New Delhi. **Official languages:** Hindi; English. **Official religion:** none. **Monetary unit:** 1 Indian rupee (Re, plural Rs) = 100 paise; valuation (1 Jul 2008) US$1 = Rs 43.35.

Demography

Area: 1,222,559 sq mi, 3,166,414 sq km (excludes 46,660 sq mi [120,849 sq km] of territory claimed by India as part of Jammu and Kashmir but occupied by Pakistan or China). **Population** (2007): 1,129,-866,000. **Density** (2007): persons per sq mi 924.2, persons per sq km 356.8. **Urban** (2004): 28.5%. **Sex distribution** (2005): male 51.57%; female 48.43%. **Age breakdown** (2005): under 15, 32.1%; 15–29, 27.1%; 30–44, 20.2%; 45–59, 12.7%; 60–74, 6.2%; 75–84, 1.4%; 85 and over, 0.3%. **Major cities** (2001; urban agglomerations): Greater Mumbai (Greater Bombay) 11,978,450 (16,434,386); Delhi 9,879,172 (12,877,470); Kolkata (Calcutta) 4,580,546 (13,205,697); Chennai (Madras) 4,343,645 (6,560,242); Bengaluru (Bangalore) 4,301,326 (5,701,446); Hyderabad 3,637,483 (5,742,036); Ahmadabad 3,520,085 (4,525,013); Kanpur 2,551,337 (2,715,555); Pune (Poona) 2,538,473 (3,760,636); Surat 2,433,835 (2,811,614); Jaipur 2,322,575 (2,322,575); New Delhi 302,363. **Location:** southern Asia, bordering Pakistan, China, Nepal, Bhutan, Myanmar (Burma), Bangladesh, and the Indian Ocean. **Linguistic composition** (1991): Hindi 27.58% (including associated languages and dialects, 38.58%); Bengali 8.22%; Telugu 7.80%; Marathi 7.38%; Tamil 6.26%; Urdu 5.13%; Gujarati 4.81%; Kannada 3.87%; Malayalam 3.59%; Oriya 3.32%; Punjabi 2.76%; Assamese 1.55%; Bhili/Bhilodi 0.66%; Santhali 0.62%; Kashmiri 0.47%; Gondi 0.25%; Sindhi 0.25%; Nepali 0.25%; Konkani 0.21%; Tulu 0.18%; Kurukh 0.17%; Manipuri 0.15%; Bodo 0.14%; Khandeshi 0.12%; other 3.26%. Hindi (66.00%) and English (19.00%) are also spoken as lingua francas. **Castes/tribes** (2001): number of scheduled castes (formerly referred to as "untouchables") 166,635,700; number of scheduled tribes (aboriginal peoples) 84,326,240. **Religious affiliation** (2005): Hindu 72.04%; Muslim 12.26%, of which Sunni 8.06%, Shiʿi 4.20%; Christian 6.81%, of which Independent 3.23%, Protestant 1.74%, Roman Catholic 1.62%, Orthodox 0.22%; traditional beliefs 3.83%; Sikh 1.87%; Buddhist 0.67%; Jain 0.51%; Baha'i 0.17%; Zoroastrian (Parsi) 0.02%; nonreligious 1.22%; atheist 0.17%; remainder 0.43%. **Households** (2001). Total number of households 193,579,954. Average household size 5.30. Type of household: permanent 51.8%; semipermanent 30.0%; temporary 18.2%. Average number of rooms per household 2.2; 1 room 38.4%, 2 rooms 30.0%, 3 rooms 14.3%, 4 rooms 7.5%, 5 rooms 2.9%, 6 or more rooms 3.7%, unspecified number of rooms 3.2%.

Vital statistics

Birth rate per 1,000 population (2005): 22.3 (world avg. 20.3). **Death rate** per 1,000 population (2005): 8.3 (world avg. 8.6). **Total fertility rate** (avg. births per childbearing woman; 2005): 2.78. **Life expectancy** at birth (2005): male 63.6 years; female 65.2 years.

Social indicators

Educational attainment (2001). Percentage of population ages 25 and over having: no formal schooling 48.1%; incomplete primary education 9.0%; complete primary 22.1%; secondary 13.7%; higher 7.1%. **Quality of working life.** Average workweek (2006) 50 hours. Rate of fatal injuries per 100,000 employees (2004) 28. Agricultural workers in servitude to creditors (early 1990s) 10–20%. Children ages 5–14 working as child laborers (2003) 35,000,000 (14% of age group). **Access to services** (2001). Percentage of total (urban, rural) households having access to: electricity for lighting purposes (2003) 61.5% (90.8%, 51.6%), kerosene for lighting purposes 36.9% (8.3%, 46.6%), water closets 18.0% (46.1%, 7.1%), pit latrines 11.5% (14.6%, 10.3%), no latrines 63.6% (26.3%, 78.1%), closed drainage for waste water 12.5% (34.5%, 3.9%), open drainage for waste water 33.9% (43.4%, 30.3%), no drainage for waste water 53.6% (22.1%, 65.8%). Type of fuel used for cooking in households (2003): firewood 61.1% (20.0%, 74.9%), LPG (liquefied petroleum gas) 20.8% (55.4%, 9.1%), cow dung 7.4% (1.8%, 9.3%), kerosene 4.7% (13.0%, 1.9%), coal 1.5% (3.3%, 0.9%), other 4.6% (6.6%, 3.9%). Source of drinking water: hand pump or tube well 41.3% (21.3%, 48.9%), piped water 36.7% (68.7%, 24.3%), well 18.2% (7.7%, 22.2%), river, canal, spring, public tank, pond, or lake 2.7% (0.7%, 3.5%). **Social participation.** Eligible voters participating in April–May 2004 national election 58.1%. Trade union membership (1998) 16,000,000 (primarily in the public sector). **Social deviance** (2003). Offense rate per 100,000 population for: murder 3.1; rape 1.5; dacoity (gang robbery) 0.5; theft 23.0; riots 5.4. Rate of suicide per 100,000 population (2002) 11.2. **Material well-being** (2001). Total (urban, rural) households possessing: television receivers 31.6% (64.3%, 18.9%), telephones 9.1% (23.0%, 3.8%), scooters, motorcycles, or mopeds 11.7% (24.7%, 6.7%), cars, jeeps, or vans 2.5% (5.6%, 1.3%). Households availing banking services 35.5% (49.5%, 30.1%).

National economy

Gross national income (at current market prices; 2006): US$887,483,000,000 (US$771 per capita).

Budget (2004). *Revenue:* Rs 3,941,400,000,000 (tax revenue 80.6%, of which taxes on income and profits 35.4%, excise taxes 27.7%; nontax revenue 18.1%; other 1.3%). *Expenditures:* Rs 5,104,800,000,000 (general public services 59.3%, of which public debt payments 24.6%; economic affairs 17.7%; defense 15.1%; housing 4.2%; education 2.2%; health 1.5%). **Public debt** (external, outstanding; 2005): US$80,281,000,000. **Production** (in '000 metric tons except as noted). *Agriculture, forestry, fishing* (2005): cereals 242,284 (of which rice 136,574, wheat 72,000, corn [maize] 14,710, millet 10,300, sorghum 7,500), sugarcane 232,300, fruits 43,035 (of which bananas 11,710, mangoes 11,140, oranges 3,469, lemons and limes 1,618, apples 1,353, pineapples 1,305), oilseeds 29,784 (of which peanuts [groundnuts] 7,200, rapeseed 6,800, soybeans 6,300, sunflower seeds 1,500, castor beans 870, sesame 680), potatoes 23,631, pulses 13,760 (of which chickpeas 5,470, dry beans 2,660, pigeon peas 2,350), eggplants 9,802, coconuts 9,534, seed cotton 7,500, cauliflower 5,363, okra 3,550, jute 2,100, allspice and pimiento 1,100, tea 831, natural rubber 780, garlic 646, tobacco 598, betel 453, ginger 349; livestock (number of live animals) 185,000,000 cattle, 120,000,000 goats, 98,000,000 water buffalo, 62,500,000 sheep, 14,300,000 pigs, 635,000 camels; roundwood 328,677,000 cu m, of which fuelwood 93%; fisheries production 6,319 (from aquaculture 41%). *Mining and quarrying* (2005): mica 1.6 (world rank: 1); iron ore (metal content) 90,000 (world rank: 4); bauxite 11,957; chromium 3,255; barite 1,000; manganese (metal content) 640; zinc (metal content) 200; lead (metal content) 42.0; copper (metal content) 26.9; gold 3,200 kg; gem diamonds 16,000 carats. *Manufacturing* (value added in US$'000,000; 2003): refined petroleum 5,955; iron and steel 5,834; paints, soaps, varnishes, drugs, and medicines 4,891; industrial chemicals 4,105; food products 3,467; textiles 3,432; motor vehicles and parts 3,193; nonelectrical machinery and apparatus 2,333; cements, bricks, and tiles 2,029. *Energy production (consumption):* electricity (kW-hr; 2005–06) 697,300,000,000 ([2004] 667,568,000,000); hard coal (metric tons; 2005–06) 407,040,000 ([2004] 404,691,000); lignite (metric tons; 2005–06) 30,060,000 ([2004] 30,028,000); crude petroleum (barrels; 2004–05) 257,900,000 ([2004] 970,900,000); petroleum products (metric tons; 2004–05) 111,970,000 ([2004] 84,734,000); natural gas (cu m; 2004–05) 31,763,000,000 ([2004] 30,654,000,000). **Land use** as % of total land area (2003): in temporary crops 53.6%, in permanent crops 3.4%, in pasture 3.6%; overall forest area (2005) 22.8%. **Population economically active** (2001): total 402,234,724; activity rate of total population 39.1% (participation rates: ages 15–69, 60.2%; female 31.6%; unemployed [2005] 9.9%). **Households.** Average household size (2004) 5.40; expenditure (2003): food and nonalcoholic beverages 50.0%, housing and energy 11.2%, clothing and footwear 7.8%, health 6.7%, transportation 4.1%, tobacco and intoxicants 2.3%. **Service enterprises** (net value added in Rs '000,000,000; 1998–99): wholesale and retail trade 1,562; finance, real estate, and insurance 1,310; transport and storage 804; community, social, and personal services 763; construction 545. **Selected balance of payments data.** Receipts from (US$'000,000): tourism (2003) 3,887; remittances (2006) 26,900; foreign direct investment (FDI) (2001–05 avg.) 5,551; official development assistance (2005) 2,819 (commitments). Disbursements for (US$'000,000): tourism (2003) 3,510; remittances (2005) 1,008; FDI (2001–05 avg.) 1,558.

Foreign trade

Imports (2004–05): US$107,066,100,000 (crude petroleum and petroleum products 27.9%; gold and silver 10.1%; electronic goods [including computer software] 9.7%; precious and semiprecious stones 8.8%; nonelectrical machinery and apparatus 6.1%; organic and inorganic chemicals 5.0%). *Major import sources:* China 6.3%; US 5.9%; Switzerland 5.4%; UAE 4.3%; Belgium 4.3%; Australia 3.3%; UK 3.2%; South Korea 3.0%; Japan 2.8%. **Exports** (2004–05): US$79,247,000,000 (engineering goods 20.7%; gems and jewelry 17.3%; chemicals and chemical products 15.0%; food and agricultural products 10.1%; petroleum products 8.6%; ready-made garments 7.6%; cotton yarn, fabrics, and thread 4.0%). *Major export destinations:* US 16.7%; UAE 9.0%; China 5.8%; Singapore 4.8%; Hong Kong 4.6%; UK 4.5%; Germany 3.3%; Belgium 3.1%; Italy 2.7%; Japan 2.5%.

Transport and communications

Transport. *Railroads* (2002): length 144,647 km; passenger-km 936,037,000,000; metric ton-km cargo 541,783,000,000. *Roads* (2002): total length 3,319,644 km (paved 46%). *Vehicles* (2003): passenger cars 8,619,000; trucks and buses 4,215,000. *Air transport* (2004–05): passenger-km 42,444,000,000; metric ton-km cargo 759,000,000. **Communications,** in total units (units per 1,000 persons). Daily newspaper circulation (2005): 78,700,000 (71); televisions (2003): 88,876,000 (83); telephone landlines (2006): 40,770,000 (36); cellular telephone subscribers (2006): 166,050,000 (148); personal computers (2005): 17,000,000 (15); total Internet users (2005): 60,000,000 (54); broadband Internet subscribers (2006): 2,300,000 (2.1).

Education and health

Literacy (2003): percentage of total population ages 15 and over literate 59.5%; males literate 70.2%; females literate 48.3%. **Health:** physicians (2005) 767,500 (1 per 1,425 persons); hospital beds (2003) 963,720 (1 per 1,111 persons); infant mortality rate per 1,000 live births (2005) 56.3. **Food** (2005): daily per capita caloric intake 2,529 (vegetable products 92%, animal products 8%); 139% of FAO recommended minimum.

Military

Total active duty personnel (2006): 1,325,000 (army 83.0%, navy 4.2%, air force 12.8%); personnel in paramilitary forces 1,089,700. **Military expenditure as percentage of GDP** (2005): 2.8%; per capita expenditure US$20.

Background

India has been inhabited for thousands of years. Agriculture dates back to at least the 7th millennium BC, and an urban civilization, that of the Indus Valley, was established by 2600 BC. Buddhism and Jainism arose in the 6th century BC in reaction to the caste-based society created by the Vedic religion and its successor, Hinduism. Muslim invasions began c. AD 1000, establishing the long-lived Delhi sultanate in 1206 and the Mughal dynasty in 1526. Vasco da Gama's voyage to India in 1498 initiated several centuries of commercial rivalry among the Portuguese, Dutch, English, and French. British conquests in the 18th and 19th centuries led to the rule of the British East India Co., and direct administration by the British Empire began in 1858. After Mohandas K. Gandhi helped end British rule in 1947, Jawaharlal Nehru became India's first prime minister, and he, Indira Gandhi (his daughter), and Rajiv Gandhi (his grandson) guided the nation's destiny for all but a few years until 1989. The subcontinent was partitioned into two countries—India, with a Hindu majority, and Pakistan, with a Muslim majority—in 1947. A later clash with Pakistan resulted in the creation of Bangladesh in 1971. In the 1980s and '90s, Sikhs sought to establish an independent state in Punjab, and ethnic and religious conflicts took place in other parts of the country as well.

Recent Developments

India continued to face the problem of terrorists operating in neighboring countries as well as domestic extremists. Pakistan, Bangladesh, Nepal, Myanmar (Burma), and Sri Lanka continued to grapple with civil unrest and conflict. Several terrorist attacks in India during the year were traced to groups in Bangladesh, and other major terror attacks in various cities continued to cause concern.

Despite political uncertainty and social tensions, the Indian economy continued to perform robustly, establishing an unprecedented record of five continuous years of nearly 9% annual growth. The main worries for India's macroeconomic managers were inflation and the strengthening of the Indian rupee vis-à-vis the US dollar. Negotiating the civil nuclear-energy cooperation agreement with the US and securing the support of all 45 member countries of the Nuclear Suppliers' Group were the government's main foreign-policy concerns. While the US Congress took an important step forward in passing the Hyde Act, which enabled the US to negotiate the so-called 123 Agreement with India to resume cooperation in civil nuclear energy, various provisions of the act came under attack in both countries. Both governments, however, remained firmly committed to the agreement. In mid-2008, however, Indian government officials announced that an Indo-US civilian nuclear agreement was unlikely during the tenure of US Pres. George W. Bush.

Internet resources: <www.tourisminindia.com>.

Indonesia

Official name: Republik Indonesia (Republic of Indonesia). **Form of government:** multiparty republic with two legislative houses (Regional Representatives Council [128]; House of Representatives [500]). **Head of state and government:** President Susilo Bambang Yudhoyono (from 2004). **Capital:** Jakarta. **Official language:** Indonesian (Bahasa Indonesia). **Official religion:** monotheism. **Monetary unit:** 1 Indonesian rupiah (Rp) = 100 sen; valuation (1 Jul 2008) US$1 = Rp 9,220.00.

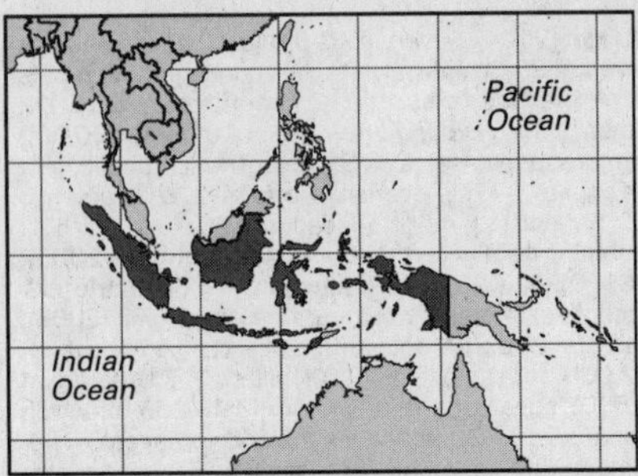

Demography

Area: 718,289 sq mi, 1,860,360 sq km. **Population** (2007): 231,627,000. **Density** (2007): persons per sq mi 322.5, persons per sq km 124.5. **Urban** (2003): 45.6%. **Sex distribution** (2006): male 50.01%; female 49.99%. **Age breakdown** (2006): under 15, 29.1%; 15–29, 27.0%; 30–44, 22.2%; 45–59, 13.5%; 60–74, 6.7%; 75–84, 1.4%; 85 and over, 0.1%. **Ethnic composition** (2000): Javanese 36.4%; Sundanese 13.7%; Malay 9.4%; Madurese 7.2%; Han Chinese 4.0%; Minangkabau 3.6%; other 25.7%. **Religious affiliation** (2005): Muslim (excluding syncretists) 55.8%; Neoreligionists (syncretists) 21.2%; Christian 13.2%; Hindu 3.2%; traditional beliefs 2.6%; nonreligious 1.8%; other 2.2%. **Major municipalities** (2003): Jakarta 8,603,349 (urban agglomeration 12,300,000); Surabaya 2,660,381; Bandung 2,229,706; Medan 1,979,340; Bekasi 1,845,245. **Location:** archipelago in southeast Asia, bordering Malaysia, the Pacific Ocean, Papua New Guinea, and the Indian Ocean.

Vital statistics

Birth rate per 1,000 population (2006): 20.1 (world avg. 20.3). **Death rate** per 1,000 population (2006): 6.3 (world avg. 8.6). **Total fertility rate** (avg. births per childbearing woman; 2006): 2.41. **Life expectancy** at birth (2006): male 67.4 years; female 72.4 years.

National economy

Budget (2005). *Revenue:* Rp 495,444,000,000,000 (tax revenue 70.0%, of which income tax 35.4%, VAT 20.4%; nontax revenue 30.0%, of which revenue from petroleum 14.7%). *Expenditures:* Rp 509,419,000,000,000 (current expenditure 58.5%; regional expenditure 29.5%; developmental expenditure 12.0%). **Public debt** (external, outstanding; December 2006): US$75,809,000,000. **Population economically active** (2006): total 106,388,935; activity rate 46.5% (participation rates: over age 15, 66.2%; unemployed 10.3%). **Households.** Average household size (2004) 4.0. **Production** (metric tons except as noted). *Agriculture, forestry, fishing* (2005): rice 53,984,592, sugarcane 29,300,000, cassava 19,460,000; livestock (number of live animals) 13,182,100 goats, 11,500,000 cattle, 8,306,930 sheep; roundwood 106,216,000 cu m, of which fuelwood 69%; fisheries production 5,578,369 (from aquaculture 21%); aquatic plants production 918,366 (from aquaculture 99%). *Mining and quarrying* (2005): bauxite 1,081,700; copper (metal content; 2004) 840,318; nickel (metal content; 2004) 133,000. *Manufacturing* (value added in US$'000,000; 2003): textiles, clothing, and footwear 5,011; tobacco products 4,584; transport equipment 4,189. *Energy production (consumption):* electricity (kW-hr; 2004) 120,200,000,000 (94,111,000,000); coal (metric tons; 2005) 98,600,000 ([2004] 14,167,000); crude petroleum (barrels; 2005) 387,300,000 ([2004] 381,600,000); petroleum products (metric tons; 2004) 47,906,000 (58,131,000); natural gas (cu m; 2005) 83,400,000,000 (22,500,000,000). **Gross national income** (2006): US$308,964,000,000 (US$1,350 per capita). **Selected balance of payments data.** Receipts from (US$'000,000): tourism (2005) 4,522; remittances (2005) 1,865; foreign direct investment (FDI) (2001–05 avg.) 745; official development assistance (2005) 3,866 (commitments). Disbursements for (US$'000,000): tourism (2005) 3,584; remittances (2005) 1,200; FDI (2001–05 avg.) 1,359. **Land use** as % of total land area (2003): in temporary crops 12.7%, in permanent crops 7.4%, in pasture 6.2%; overall forest area (2005) 48.8%.

Foreign trade

Imports (2005–06; c.i.f. in balance of trade and commodities and f.o.b. in trading partners): US$65,712,154,000 (petroleum and natural gas 23.7%; machinery and apparatus 16.8%; chemicals and chemical products 10.4%; base metals 8.8%; transport equipment 6.5%). *Major import sources* (2004): Japan 13.1%; Singapore 13.1%; China 8.8%; US 7.0%; Thailand 6.0%. **Exports** (2005–06): US$78,740,892,000 (petroleum and natural gas 27.4%; rubber products 15.7%; machinery and apparatus 14.5%; textiles 10.8%; base metals 7.0%). *Major export destinations* (2004): Japan 22.3%; US 12.3%; Singapore 8.4%; South Korea 6.8%; China 6.4%.

Transport and communications

Transport. *Railroads* (2004): route length 6,458 km; passenger-km 15,077,000,000; metric ton-km cargo 4,698,000,000. *Roads* (2005): length 391,009 km (paved 55%). *Vehicles* (2005): passenger cars 5,494,034; trucks and buses 4,105,746. *Air transport* (2005): passenger-km 22,986,000,000; metric ton-km cargo (2004) 248,000,000. **Communications,** in total units (units per 1,000 persons). Daily newspaper circulation (2004): 4,866,000 (22); televisions (2003): 33,255,000 (153); telephone landlines (2006): 14,821,000 (66); cellular telephone subscribers (2006): 63,803,000 (283); personal computers (2005): 3,285,000 (15); total Internet users (2005): 16,000,000 (73); broadband Internet subscribers (2005): 108,000 (0.5).

Education and health

Educational attainment (2002–03). Percentage of population ages 15–64 having: no schooling or incomplete primary education 19.3%; primary and some secondary 57.2%; complete secondary 19.3%; higher 4.2%. **Literacy** (2003): total population ages 15 and over literate 88.4%; males literate 92.8%; females literate 84.1%. **Health:** physicians (2003) 29,499 (1 per 7,368 persons); hospital beds (2001) 124,834 (1 per 1,697 persons); infant mortality rate (2006) 33.3. **Food** (2005): daily per capita caloric intake 2,972 (vegetable products 95%, animal products 5%); 162% of FAO recommended minimum.

Military

Total active duty personnel (2006): 302,000 (army 77.2%, navy 14.9%, air force 7.9%). **Military expenditure as percentage of GDP** (2005): 1.2%; per capita expenditure US$38.

Background

Proto-Malay peoples migrated to Indonesia from mainland Asia before 1000 BC. Commercial relations were established with China in about the 5th century AD, and Hindu and Buddhist cultural influences from India began to take hold. Arab traders brought Islam to the islands in the 13th century; the religion took hold throughout the islands, except for Bali, which retained its Hindu religion and culture. European influence began in the 16th century, and the Dutch ruled Indonesia from the late 17th century until 1942, when the Japanese invaded. Independence leader Sukarno declared Indonesia's independence in 1945, which the Dutch granted, with nominal union to The Netherlands, in 1949; Indonesia dissolved this union in 1954. The suppression of an alleged coup attempt in 1965 resulted in the deaths of more than 300,000 people the government claimed to be communists, and by 1968 Gen. Suharto had taken power. His government forcibly incorporated East Timor into Indonesia in 1975–76, with much loss of life (the country became independent in 2002). In the 1990s the country was beset by political, economic, and environmental problems, and Suharto was deposed in 1998.

Recent Developments

Indonesia continued its democratic and economic consolidation in 2007. The economy continued to perform well, with 6.3% growth during the year. Investment also increased at a healthy 6.9% in the same period. Even the high poverty and unemployment levels, for which the government had been sharply criticized, fell modestly. Approximately 37 million people, or 16.6% of the population, were classed as living below the poverty line in 2007, compared with 39 million the previous year; during the same period, unemployment declined from 10.4% to 9.8%. Also, most of the country remained peaceful, despite a succession of natural disasters and continuing local direct elections. The December 2006 Aceh election, which went off largely without incident, was particularly important, as it was the culmination of the peace agreement signed in 2005, bringing an end to decades of bloody conflict between pro-independence insurgents and the Indonesian military. Finally, the government's anticorruption campaign led to hundreds of high-profile figures being prosecuted for malfeasance. Some of the most important cases were those of former maritime and fisheries minister Rokhmin Dahuri, who stood accused of dispersing millions of dollars in bribes and inducements, and former president Suharto's son Tommy, who was under renewed investigation over graft allegations.

Internet resources: <www.indonesia-tourism.com>.

Iran

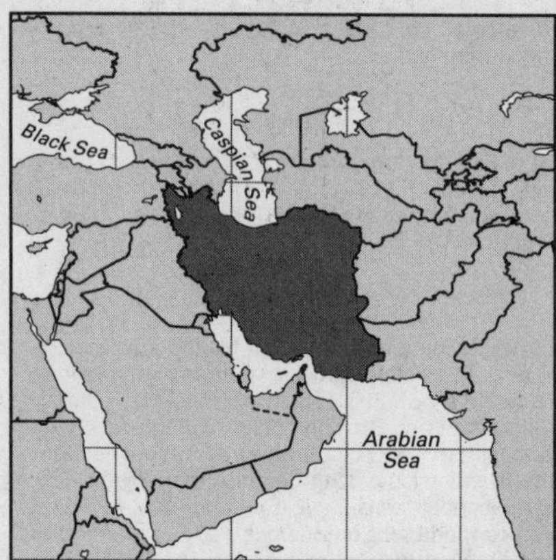

Official name: Jomhuri-ye Eslami-ye Iran (Islamic Republic of Iran). **Form of government:** unitary Islamic republic with one legislative house (Islamic Consultative Assembly [290]). **Supreme political/religious authority:** *Rahbar* (Spiritual Leader) Ayatollah Sayyed Ali Khamenei (from 1989). **Head of state and government:** President Mahmoud Ahmadinejad (from 2005). **Capital:** Tehran. **Official language:** Farsi (Persian). **Official religion:** Islam. **Monetary unit:** 1 rial (Rls); valuation (1 Jul 2008) US$1 = Rls 9,210.00.

Demography

Area (land area only): 628,789 sq mi, 1,628,554 sq km. **Population** (2007): 71,243,000. **Density** (2007): persons per sq mi 112.0, persons per sq km 43.2. **Urban** (2006): 68.5%. **Sex distribution** (2005): male 50.96%; female 49.04%. **Age breakdown** (2005): under 15, 27.1%; 15–29, 35.0%; 30–44, 20.4%; 45–59, 10.7%; 60–74, 5.0%; 75 and over, 1.8%. **Ethnic composition** (2000): Persian 34.9%; Azerbaijani 15.9%; Kurd 13.0%; Luri 7.2%; Gilaki 5.1%; Mazandarani 5.1%; Afghan 2.8%; Arab 2.5%; other 13.5%. **Religious affiliation** (2005): Muslim 98.2%, of which Shi'i 86.1%, Sunni 10.1%, other 2.0%; Baha'i 0.5%; Christian 0.4%; Zoroastrian 0.1%; other 0.8%. **Major cities** (2006): Tehran 7,797,520; Mashhad 2,427,316; Esfahan 1,602,110; Tabriz 1,398,060; Shiraz 1,227,331. **Location:** the Middle East, bordering the Caspian Sea, Turkmenistan, Afghanistan, Pakistan, the Gulf of Oman, the Persian Gulf, Iraq, Turkey, Azerbaijan, and Armenia.

Vital statistics

Birth rate per 1,000 population (2005–06): 17.7 (world avg. 20.3). **Death rate** per 1,000 population (2005–06): 5.2 (world avg. 8.6). **Total fertility rate** (avg. births per childbearing woman; 2005): 1.82. **Life expectancy** at birth (2005): male 68.6 years; female 71.4 years.

National economy

Budget (2004–05). *Revenue:* Rls 428,872,000,000,000 (petroleum and natural gas revenue 61.7%; taxes 19.7%, of which import duties 7.1%, corporate 6.1%; other 18.6%). *Expenditures:* Rls 433,670,000,000,000 (current expenditure 60.5%; development expenditures 17.7%; other 21.8%). **Public debt** (external, outstanding; 2005): US$10,493,000,000. **Gross national income** (2006): US$238,669,000,000 (US$3,396 per capita). **Production** (metric tons except as noted). *Agriculture, forestry, fishing* (2005): wheat 14,500,000, tomatoes 4,781,000, potatoes 4,200,000; livestock (number of live animals) 54,000,000 sheep, 26,500,000 goats, 8,800,000 cattle; roundwood 774,000 cu m, of which fuelwood 9%; fisheries production 527,912 (from aquaculture 22%). *Mining and quarrying* (2004–05): iron ore (metal content) 9,000,000; chromite 223,563; copper ore (metal content) 190,000. *Manufacturing* (value added in US$'000,000; 2003): motor vehicles and parts 2,900; refined petroleum products 1,864; iron and steel 1,749. *Energy production (consumption):* electricity (kW-hr; 2005–06) 176,342,000,000 (134,238,000,000); coal (metric tons; 2004) 1,246,000 (1,707,000); crude petroleum (barrels; 2005) 1,477,885,000 (605,535,000); petroleum products (metric tons; 2004) 76,128,000 (65,105,000); natural gas (cu m; 2004–05) 148,738,000,000 ([2003–04] 115,400,000,000). **Population economically active** (2005): total 22,317,000; activity rate of total population 33.3% (participation rates: ages 15–64, 48.3%; female 20.5%; unemployed 11.5%). **Households** (2004–05). Average household size (2005) 4.2; annual average monetary income per urban household Rls 41,697,965 (US$4,742); sources of urban monetary income: wages 40.8%, self-employment 35.0%, other 24.2%; expenditure: housing and energy 26.8%, food, beverages, and tobacco 25.3%, transportation and communications 16.5%. **Selected balance of payments data.** Receipts from (US$'000,000): tourism (2005) 992; remittances (2005) 1,032; foreign direct investment (2001–05 avg.) 244. Disbursements for (US$'000,000): tourism (2005) 4,380. **Land use** as % of total land area (2003): in temporary crops 10.3%, in permanent crops 1.3%, in pasture 26.9%; overall forest area (2005) 6.8%.

Foreign trade

Imports (2005–06; c.i.f.): US$40,969,000,000 (nonelectrical machinery and apparatus 23.5%; iron and steel 13.8%; road vehicles 13.0%; chemicals and chemical products 10.7%). *Major import sources:* UAE 19.7%; Germany 13.1%; France 6.8%; Italy 6.0%; China 5.5%. **Exports** (2005–06; f.o.b.): US$60,013,000,000 (crude petroleum 73.1%; chemicals and chemical products 5.2%; fruits and nuts 2.2%, of which pistachios 1.4%; wool carpets 0.8%). *Major export destinations:* Japan 16.9%; China 11.9%; Turkey 5.8%; Italy 5.7%; South Korea 5.7%.

Transport and communications

Transport. *Railroads* (2004–05): route length 7,584 km; passenger-km 10,012,000,000; metric ton-km cargo 18,182,000,000. *Roads* (2005–06): length

1 metric ton = about 1.1 short tons; 1 kilometer = 0.6 mi (statute); 1 metric ton-km cargo = about 0.68 short ton-mi cargo; c.i.f.: cost, insurance, and freight; f.o.b.: free on board

71,711 km (paved 90%). *Vehicles* (2003–04): passenger cars 634,482; trucks and buses 85,473. *Air transport* (2005; Iran Air): passenger-km 7,347,795,000; metric ton-km cargo 83,396,000. **Communications,** in total units (units per 1,000 persons). Daily newspaper circulation (2005): 1,205,000 (17); televisions (2003): 11,566,000 (173); telephone landlines (2006): 21,981,000 (312); cellular telephone subscribers (2006): 13,659,000 (194); personal computers (2005): 8,694,000 (125); total Internet users (2006): 18,000,000 (255); broadband Internet subscribers (2006): 465,000 (6.7).

Education and health

Literacy (2003): total population ages 15 and over literate 79.4%; males literate 85.6%; females literate 73.0%. **Health** (2005–06): physicians (public sector only) 26,564 (1 per 2,618 persons); hospital beds (2004–05) 203,666 (1 per 340 persons); infant mortality rate per 1,000 live births (2005) 41.6. **Food** (2005): daily per capita caloric intake 3,425 (vegetable products 91%, animal products 9%); 185% of FAO recommended minimum.

Military

Total active duty personnel (2006): 545,000 (revolutionary guard corps 22.9%, army 64.2%, navy 3.3%, air force 9.6%). **Military expenditure as percentage of GDP** (2005): 5.8%; per capita expenditure US$130.

Background

Habitation in Iran dates to c. 100,000 BC, but recorded history began with the Elamites c. 3000 BC. The Medes flourished from c. 728 BC but were overthrown (550 BC) by the Persians, who were in turn conquered by Alexander the Great in the 4th century BC. The Parthians created a Greek-speaking empire that lasted from 247 BC to AD 226, when control passed to the Sasanians. Arab Muslims conquered them in 640 and ruled Iran for 850 years. In 1502 the Safavids established a dynasty that lasted until 1736. The Qajars ruled from 1779, but in the 19th century the country was controlled economically by the Russian and British empires. Reza Khan seized power in a coup (1921). His son Mohammad Reza Shah Pahlavi alienated religious leaders with a program of modernization and Westernization and was overthrown in 1979; Shiʿite cleric Ruhollah Khomeini then set up a fundamentalist Islamic republic, and Western influence was suppressed. The destructive Iran-Iraq War of the 1980s ended in a stalemate. During the 1990s the government gradually moved to a more liberal conduct of state affairs.

Recent Developments

The year 2007 was an apparent triumph for Iranian Pres. Mahmoud Ahmadinejad, who successfully managed the development of Iran's atomic-energy program, against the wishes of the US and the EU, and sustained the country's position as a leader in the Islamic world. He was popular at home for his robust resistance to the US, but he was under great pressure from the Iranian hierarchy to reach a compromise with the EU on the nuclear issue and thereby preempt economic or military moves against Iran. The EU was concerned that Iran already had the capacity to manufacture medium-range missiles but, like the US, was constrained by its inability to persuade Russia and China to permit more than minor UN sanctions against Iran. Although national economic performance was good—oil-export earnings totaled more than US$33 billion during the Iranian year 2006–07—government policies were criticized because there were fuel shortages at home, and Iran was required to import US$5 billion in products to avoid popular discontent. In an open letter in June to Ahmadinejad signed by 57 Iranian economists, the president was berated for neglecting the domestic economy and for damaging foreign policy at a time when opportunities were ideal for using expanded oil income. The signatories urged investment in productive assets and capital projects.

Internet resources: <www.itto.org>.

Iraq

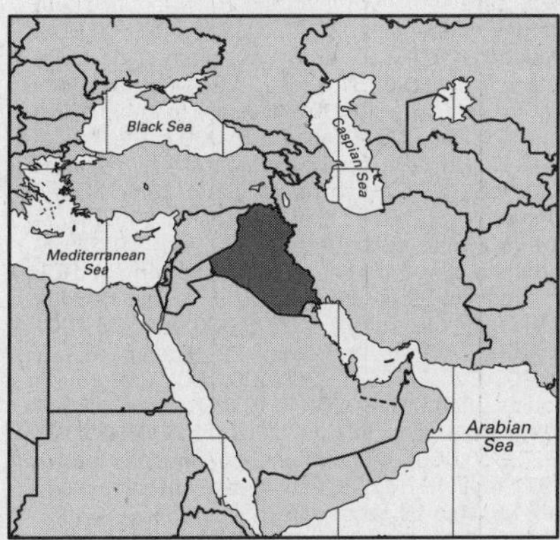

Official name: Al-Jumhuriyah al-Iraqiyah (Republic of Iraq). **Form of government:** multiparty republic with one legislative house (Council of Representatives [275]). **Head of state:** President Jalal Talabani (from 2005). **Head of government:** Prime Minister Nuri al-Maliki (from 2006). **Capital:** Baghdad. **Official languages:** Arabic; Kurdish. **Official religion:** Islam. **Monetary unit:** 1 Iraqi dinar (ID); valuation (1 Jul 2008) US$1 = ID 1,194.00.

Demography

Area: 167,618 sq mi, 434,128 sq km. **Population** (2007): 28,993,000 (including 1,400,000 Iraqi refugees in Syria, 750,000 Iraqi refugees in Jordan, and nearly 300,000 elsewhere; about 2 million Iraqis were internally displaced as of mid-2007). **Density** (2007): persons per sq mi 173.0, persons per sq km 66.8. **Urban** (2004): 65.0%. **Sex distribution** (2004): male 49.95%; female 50.05%. **Age breakdown** (2004): under 15, 39.5%; 15–29, 29.8%; 30–44, 16.6%; 45–59, 9.2%; 60–74, 3.8%; 75 and over, 1.1%. **Ethnic composition** (2000): Arab 64.7%; Kurd 23.0%; Azerbaijani 5.6%; Turkmen 1.2%; Persian 1.1%; other 4.4%. **Religious affiliation** (2000): Shiʿi Muslim 62.0%; Sunni Muslim 34.0%; Christian (primarily Chaldean rite and Syrian rite Catholic and Nestorian) 3.2%; other (primarily Yazidi syncretist) 0.8%. **Major cities** (2005): Baghdad 5,904,000;

Mosul 1,234,000; Irbil (2003) 850,000; Al-Basrah 837,000; Karkuk (2003) 750,000. **Location:** the Middle East, bordering Turkey, Iran, the Persian Gulf, Kuwait, Saudi Arabia, Jordan, and Syria.

Vital statistics

Birth rate per 1,000 population (2005): 32.5 (world avg. 20.3). **Death rate** per 1,000 population (2005): 5.5 (world avg. 8.6). **Natural increase rate** per 1,000 population (2005): 27.0 (world avg. 11.7). **Total fertility rate** (avg. births per childbearing woman; 2005): 4.28. **Life expectancy** at birth (2005): male 67.5 years; female 70.0 years.

National economy

Budget (2006). *Revenue:* ID 61,650,000,000,000 (petroleum revenue 79.9%; grants 20.1%). *Expenditures:* ID 53,480,000,000,000 (current expenditure 79.8%; development expenditure 20.2%). **Public debt** (external, outstanding; 2006): US$81,480,000,000. **Production** (metric tons except as noted). *Agriculture, forestry, fishing* (2005): wheat 2,228,000, tomatoes 939,000, potatoes 808,000; livestock (number of live animals) 6,200,000 sheep, 1,500,000 cattle; roundwood 115,427 cu m, of which fuelwood 49%; fisheries production 32,970 (from aquaculture 39%). *Mining and quarrying* (2005): phosphate rock 1,000. *Manufacturing* (value added in US$'000,000; 1995): refined petroleum 143; bricks, tiles, and cement 103; food products 59. *Energy production (consumption):* electricity (kW-hr; 2004) 32,600,000,000 (33,700,-000,000); crude petroleum (barrels; 2006) 584,000,000 ([2004] 173,500,000); petroleum products (metric tons; 2004) 19,617,000 (20,850,-000); natural gas (cu m; 2004) 2,600,000,000 (2,600,000,000). **Population economically active** (1997): total 4,757,000; activity rate of total population 24.8% (participation rates: ages 15–59, 42.9%; female 10.5%; unemployed [2004] 28%). **Households** (2004). Average household size 6.4; median annual household income ID 2,230,000 (US$1,517); expenditure (1993): food 62%, housing 12%, clothing 10%. **Gross national income** (2005): US$46,917,000,000 (US$1,646 per capita). **Selected balance of payments data.** Receipts from (US$'000,000): tourism (2002) 45; foreign direct investment (FDI) (2001–05 avg.) 76; official development assistance (2005) 19,107 (commitments). Disbursements for (US$'000,000): tourism (2002) 26. **Land use** as % of total land area (2003): in temporary crops 13.1%, in permanent crops 0.6%, in pasture 9.1%; overall forest area (2005) 1.9%.

Foreign trade

Imports (2004; c.i.f. in balance of trade and commodities and f.o.b. in trading partners): US$21,302,-000,000 (government imports 58.2%, of which capital goods 19.2%, UN oil-for-food program 17.0%; private sector imports 26.2%, of which capital goods 19.6%; refined petroleum 9.9%). *Major import sources:* Turkey 25.0%; US 11.1%; Jordan 10.0%; Vietnam 7.7%; Germany 5.6%. **Exports** (2004): US$17,810,000,000 (crude petroleum 98.0%; refined petroleum 1.4%; remainder 0.6%). *Major export destinations:* US 55.8%; Spain 8.0%; Japan 7.3%; Italy 6.5%; Canada 5.8%.

Transport and communications

Transport. *Railroads* (2006): route length 580 km. *Roads* (2002): total length 45,550 km (paved 84%). *Vehicles* (2001): passenger cars 754,066; trucks and buses 372,241. **Communications,** in total units (units per 1,000 persons). Televisions (2001): 472,000 (19); telephone landlines (2004): 1,034,000 (40); cellular telephone subscribers (2004): 574,000 (22); personal computers (2002): 212,000 (8.3); total Internet users (2004): 36,000 (1.3).

Education and health

Educational attainment (2004). Percentage of population ages 25 and over having: no formal schooling 28%; incomplete primary education 12%; primary 36%; secondary 9%; higher 15%. **Literacy** (2003): total population ages 15 and over literate 40.4%; males literate 55.9%; females literate 24.4%. **Health** (2003): physicians 16,594 (1 per 1,587 persons); hospital beds 34,505 (1 per 763 persons); infant mortality rate per 1,000 live births (2005) 50.3.

Military

Total active duty personnel (2006): 117,400; US/allied coalition forces (2007): 168,000/13,000.

Background

Called Mesopotamia in classical times, the region gave rise to the world's earliest civilizations, including those of Sumer, Akkad, and Babylon. Conquered by Alexander the Great in 330 BC, the area later became a battleground between Romans and Parthians and then between Sasanians and Byzantines. Arab Muslims conquered it in the 7th century AD and ruled until the Mongols took over in 1258. The Ottomans took control in the 16th century and ruled until 1917. The British occupied the country during World War I and created the kingdom of Iraq in 1921. The British occupied Iraq again during World War II. A king was restored following the war, but a revolution ended the monarchy in 1958. Following a series of military coups, the socialist Ba'th Party, led by Saddam Hussein, took control and established totalitarian rule in 1968. The Iran-Iraq War of the 1980s and the Persian Gulf War (precipitated by the Iraqi invasion of Kuwait in 1990) brought heavy casualties and disrupted the economy. The 1990s were dominated by economic and political turmoil. In response to increasingly willful and autocratic behavior by Saddam Hussein and the contention that Iraq was in possession of weapons of mass destruction (none were ever found), on 19 March 2003 air attacks on Baghdad began, and soon afterward US and British ground forces invaded southern Iraq from Kuwait; within a month most of the country was under the control of coalition forces. Saddam was taken into custody in December. In July US authorities established an Iraqi Governing Council, and a new interim constitution was agreed upon in late February 2004. Almost immediately after the occupation began, however, various forms of Iraqi opposition arose, and resistance attacks grew in frequency and violence in the years that followed.

1 metric ton = about 1.1 short tons; 1 kilometer = 0.6 mi (statute); 1 metric ton-km cargo = about 0.68 short ton-mi cargo; c.i.f.: cost, insurance, and freight; f.o.b.: free on board

Recent Developments

Divisions in Iraq in 2007 remained evident, with armed confrontations between sects and between militias of the majority Shiʿites. The most significant intra-Shiʿite confrontation took place in August in Karbala between the Mahdi Army of Muqtada al-Sadr and forces belonging to the Islamic Supreme Council of Iraq, which left over 50 people dead. The main Sunni group in the government, the Iraqi Accord Front, announced in August that it was withdrawing its six ministers to protest, among other things, an alleged "genocide campaign" against Sunni, though they rejoined the government in April 2008. Key legislation remained hostage to protracted negotiations in an unwieldy parliament that could barely muster a quorum. Acts of violence by Sunni insurgents, al-Qaeda operatives, and Shiʿite militias against the US and Iraqi government forces continued throughout the year. The most spectacular act of violence since the US-led invasion in 2003 occurred on 14 August, when a series of truck bombs struck two villages in northern Iraq inhabited by members of the ancient Yazidi sect. The incident left at least 500 people dead and 1,000 wounded. Some success was achieved in reducing violence in Al-Anbar province, a Sunni Arab stronghold in western Iraq where local forces, with the backing of the US, had formed a unified front called the Anbar Salvation Council; its aim was to use local tribesmen to fight insurgents. In September 2007 US Pres. George W. Bush visited the province and met with members of the council. Success in Al-Anbar encouraged the US to expand the model to other provinces, including the Shiʿite areas of central and southern Iraq. Early in the year, the US decided to increase the number of its troops in Iraq, in a "surge" of 30,000 additional US forces designed to pacify Baghdad and other parts of Iraq. By year's end there was a decrease in the number of attacks and casualties in Baghdad and western Iraq, but fighting continued between Shiʿite and Sunni militias. This had led to massive internal migration; it was estimated that some two and a half million Iraqis were displaced internally. Iraqis also continued to flee to neighboring countries, mainly Syria (1.4 million) and Jordan (750,000).

Early in September the British government reduced its troop levels and began to withdraw those that remained from the city of Basra to bases outside the city. Iraqi security forces took over positions previously held by the British. In August Turkey and Iraq agreed to clear Turkish Kurdish rebels from northern Iraq. Although initially encountering resistance from the US and Iraq, in 2008 Turkey made a number of incursions in force across the border with Iraq, with the US providing intelligence to Turkish commanders.

Internet resources: <www.cbiraq.org/cb1.htm>.

Ireland

Official name: Éire (Irish); Ireland (English). **Form of government:** unitary multiparty republic with two legislative houses (Senate [60]; House of Representatives [166]). **Chief of state:** President Mary McAleese (from 1997). **Head of government:** Prime Minister Brian Cowen (from 2008). **Capital:** Dublin. **Official languages:** Irish; English. **Official religion:** none. **Monetary unit:** 1 euro (€) = 100 cents; valuation (1 Jul 2008) US$1 = €0.63 (the euro replaced the Irish pound [£Ir] 1 Jan 2002, at the rate of 1€ = £Ir 0.79).

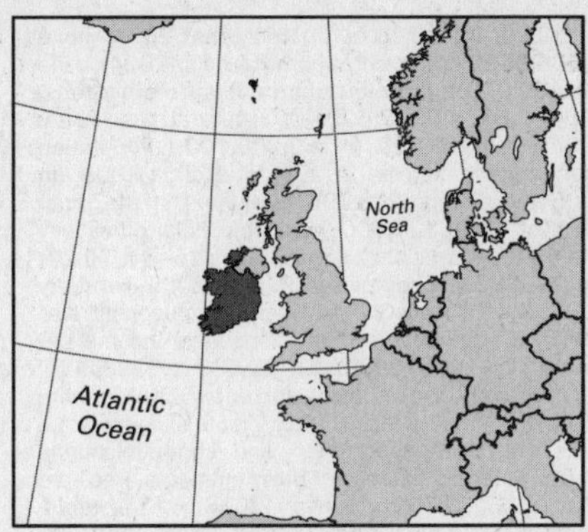

Demography

Area: 27,133 sq mi, 70,273 sq km. **Population** (2007): 4,330,000. **Density** (2007): persons per sq mi 159.6, persons per sq km 61.6. **Urban** (2005): 60.5%. **Sex distribution** (2006): male 50.03%; female 49.97%. **Age breakdown** (2006): under 15, 20.4%; 15–29, 23.7%; 30–44, 23.0%; 45–59, 17.6%; 60–74, 10.5%; 75–84, 3.7%; 85 and over, 1.1%. **Ethnic composition** (2000): Irish 95.0%; British 1.7%, of which English 1.4%; Ulster Irish 1.0%; US white 0.8%; other 1.5%. **Religious affiliation** (2006): Roman Catholic 86.8%; Church of Ireland (Anglican) 3.0%; other Christian 2.7%; nonreligious 4.4%; other 3.1%. **Major cities** (2006): Dublin 506,211 (urban agglomeration 1,186,159); Cork 119,418; Galway 72,414; Limerick 52,539; Waterford 45,748. **Location:** western Europe, bordering the UK (Northern Ireland), the Irish Sea, the Celtic Sea, and the North Atlantic Ocean.

Vital statistics

Birth rate per 1,000 population (2006): 15.0 (world avg. 20.3); within marriage 66.8%. **Death rate** per 1,000 population (2006): 7.0 (world avg. 8.6). **Total fertility rate** (avg. births per childbearing woman; 2005): 1.88. **Life expectancy** at birth (2005): male 75.0 years; female 80.3 years.

National economy

Budget (2005). *Revenue:* €39,849,000,000 (VAT 30.3%; income taxes 28.3%; corporate taxes 13.5%). *Expenditures:* €33,496,000,000 (current expenditure 88.4%; capital expenditure 11.6%). **Total public debt** (December 2005): US$50,288,000,000. **Gross national income** (2006): US$185,955,000,000 (US$44,052 per capita). **Production** (metric tons except as noted). *Agriculture, forestry, fishing* (2005): sugar beets 1,395,000, barley 1,025,000, wheat 798,100; livestock (number of live animals) 6,888,000 cattle, 4,556,700 sheep, 1,681,000 pigs; roundwood 2,648,000 cu m, of which fuelwood 1%; fisheries production 322,582 (from aquaculture 19%). *Mining and quarrying* (2005): zinc ore (metal content) 428,596; lead ore (metal content) 63,810. *Manufacturing* (gross value added in €'000,000; 2003): chemicals and chemical products 15,988; food, beverages, and tobacco 9,111; electrical and optical equipment 6,677. *Energy production (consumption):* electricity (kW-hr; 2004) 25,627,000,000

(27,191,000,000); coal (metric tons; 2004) none (2,638,000); crude petroleum (barrels; 2004) none (21,400,000); petroleum products (metric tons; 2004) 2,874,000 (7,627,000); natural gas (cu m; 2004) 805,000,000 (4,263,000,000). **Population economically active** (2005): total 2,014,800 (in 2005 there were 243,000 foreigners in the labor force, of which 120,000 were from Poland); activity rate 48.8% (participation rates: ages 15–64, 70.2%; female 42.3%; unemployed [March 2005–February 2006] 4.4%). **Households.** Average household size (2006) 2.8; average annual disposable income per household (1999–2000): £Ir 22,589 (US$28,800); expenditure (2004): housing and energy 20.7%, food, beverages, and tobacco 14.9%, hotels and restaurants 14.2%, transportation and communications 14.0%. **Selected balance of payments data.** Receipts from (US$'000,000): tourism (2006) 6,677; remittances (2006) 600; foreign direct investment (FDI) (2001–05 avg.) 10,028. Disbursements for (US$'000,000): tourism (2005) 6,056; remittances (2006) 1,173; FDI (2001–05 avg.) 9,876. **Land use** as % of total land area (2003): in temporary crops 17.2%, in permanent crops 0.03%, in pasture 46.2%; overall forest area (2005) 9.7%.

Foreign trade

Imports (2006; c.i.f.): €60,665,000,000 (machinery 33.0%, of which office machines and parts 17.2%, electrical machinery 6.3%; chemicals and chemical products 13.2%; transportation equipment 9.0%; mineral fuels 7.7%). *Major import sources* (2004): UK 30.7%; US 13.9%; Germany 7.5%; China 5.7%; France 4.5%. **Exports** (2006; f.o.b.): €86,861,000,000 (organic chemicals 19.6%; medicinal and pharmaceutical products 16.4%; office machines and parts 16.2%; food 8.1%). *Major export destinations* (2005): US 19.7%; UK 17.7%; Belgium 14.7%; Germany 7.7%; France 6.0%.

Transport and communications

Transport. *Railroads* (2004): route length 3,312 km; passenger-km 1,581,698,000; metric ton-km cargo 343,747,000. *Roads* (2003): length 96,602 km (paved 100%). *Vehicles* (2003): passenger cars 1,507,106; trucks and buses 251,130. *Air transport* (2006; Aer Lingus only): passenger-km 13,363,000,000; metric ton-km cargo (2004) 124,156,000. **Communications,** in total units (units per 1,000 persons). Daily newspaper circulation (2004): 742,000 (183); televisions (2002): 2,707,000 (694); telephone landlines (2006): 2,097,000 (431); cellular telephone subscribers (2006): 4,690,000 (1,114); personal computers (2005): 2,198,000 (530); total Internet users (2006): 1,437,000 (341); broadband Internet subscribers (2006): 517,000 (122).

Education and health

Educational attainment (2005). Percentage of population ages 25–64 having: no formal schooling through primary education 16.8%; lower secondary 17.7%; upper secondary/higher vocational 34.7%; some higher 10.4%; complete higher 17.9%; unknown 2.5%. **Health:** physicians (2004) 11,141 (1 per 365 persons); hospital beds (2004) 12,377 (1 per 330 persons); infant mortality rate per 1,000 live births (2004–05) 4.7. **Food** (2005): daily per capita caloric intake 3,503 (vegetable products 66%, animal products 34%).

Military

Total active duty personnel (2006): 10,460 (army 81.3%, navy 10.5%, air force 8.2%). **Military expenditure as percentage of GDP** (2005): 0.6%; per capita expenditure US$275.

Mary Robinson was president of Ireland from 1990 to 1997. Nominated by the Labour Party and supported by the Green Party and the Workers' Party, she became Ireland's first woman president by mobilizing a liberal constituency and merging it with a more conservative constituency opposed to the Fianna Fail party.

Background

Human settlement in Ireland began c. 6000 BC, and Celtic migration dates from c. 300 BC. St. Patrick is credited with Christianizing the country in the 5th century AD. Norse domination began in 795 and ended in 1014, when the Norse were defeated by Brian Boru. Gaelic Ireland's independence ended in 1171 when English King Henry II proclaimed himself overlord of the island. Beginning in the 16th century, Irish Catholic landowners fled religious persecution by the English and were replaced by English and Scottish Protestant migrants. The United Kingdom of Great Britain and Ireland was established in 1801. The Great Famine of the 1840s led over two million people to emigrate and built momentum for Irish Home Rule. The Easter Rising (1916) was followed by civil war (1919–21) between the Catholic majority in southern Ireland, who favored complete independence, and the Protestant majority in the north, who preferred continued union with Britain. Southern Ireland was granted dominion status and became the Irish Free State in 1921, and in 1937 it adopted the name Éire and became a sovereign independent nation. It remained neutral during World War II. Britain recognized the status of Ireland in 1949 but declared that cession of the northern six counties could not occur without the consent of the Parliament of Northern Ireland. In 1973 Ireland joined the European Economic Community (later the European Community) and is now a member of the EU. The late 20th century was dominated by sectarian hostilities between the island's Catholics and Protestants.

Recent Developments

The historic deal in 2007 between unionist and nationalist politicians to share power in a new government for Northern Ireland cemented the peace process that Irish Prime Minister Bertie Ahern had pursued since he was first elected in 1997. Unionist leader Ian Paisley and Sinn Féin leader Gerry Adams reached agreement in March, and on 8 May Paisley and Martin McGuinness, a former leader of the illegal

1 metric ton = about 1.1 short tons; 1 kilometer = 0.6 mi (statute); 1 metric ton-km cargo = about 0.68 short ton-mi cargo; c.i.f.: cost, insurance, and freight; f.o.b.: free on board

Irish Republican Army, were appointed first minister and deputy first minister, respectively, ending almost 40 years of conflict in the six northern counties of Ireland under British jurisdiction that left more than 3,700 people dead. Ahern was invited to become the first Irish prime minister to address the joint houses of the British Parliament. However, Ahern announced that he would resign in May 2008 as a result of investigations into political corruption.

Internet resources: <www.discoverireland.ie>.

Isle of Man

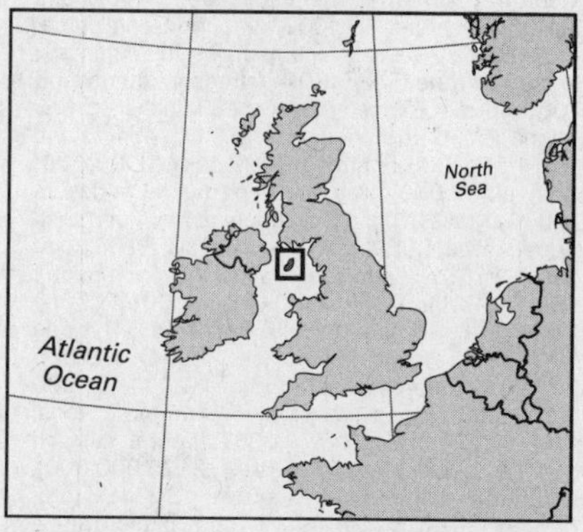

Official name: Isle of Man (Manx Gaelic: Ellan Vannin). **Political status:** crown dependency of the UK with two legislative bodies (collectively named Tynwald; Legislative Council [11]; House of Keys [24]). **Chief of state:** British Queen Elizabeth II (from 1952), represented by Lieutenant Governor Sir Paul Haddacks (from 2005). **Head of government:** Chief Minister Tony Brown (from 2006). **Capital:** Douglas. **Official language:** English. **Official religion:** none. **Monetary unit:** 1 Manx pound (£M) = 100 new pence; valuation (1 Jul 2008) US$1 = £M 0.50 (the Manx pound is equivalent in value to the British pound sterling [£]).

Demography

Area: 220.9 sq mi, 572.0 km. **Population** (2007): 81,000. **Density** (2007): persons per sq mi 366.7, persons per sq km 141.6. **Urban** (2006): 71.6%. **Sex distribution** (2006): male 49.37%; female 50.63%. **Age breakdown** (2006): under 15, 16.9%; 15–29, 17.2%; 30–44, 22.0%; 45–59, 21.1%; 60–74, 14.4%; 75–84, 6.0%; 85 and over, 2.4%. **Religious affiliation** (2000): Christian 63.7%, of which Anglican 40.5%, Methodist 9.9%, Roman Catholic 8.2%; other (mostly nonreligious) 36.3%. **Major towns** (2006): Douglas 26,218; Onchan 9,172; Ramsey 7,309; Peel 4,280; Port Erin 3,575. **Location:** Irish Sea, midway between Ireland and Great Britain.

Vital statistics

Birth rate per 1,000 population (2006): 11.3 (world avg. 20.3); (2004) within marriage 63.9%. **Death rate** per 1,000 population (2006): 9.6 (world avg. 8.6). **Natural increase rate** per 1,000 population (2006): 1.7 (world avg. 11.7). **Total fertility rate** (avg. births per childbearing woman; 2006): 1.65. **Life expectancy** at birth (2006): male 75.3 years; female 81.2 years.

National economy

Budget (2005–06). *Revenue:* £494,410,400 (customs duties and excise taxes 67.8%; income taxes 31.5%, of which resident 28.4%, nonresident 3.1%; nontax revenue 0.7%). *Expenditures:* £518,356,000 (health and social security 39.4%; education 17.5%; transportation 6.8%; home affairs 6.1%). **Production.** *Agriculture, forestry, fishing:* main crops include hay, oats, barley, wheat, and orchard crops; livestock (number of live animals; 2006) 136,751 sheep, 20,654 cattle, 601 pigs; fish catch (value of principal catch in £; 2006): 3,053,961, of which scallops 1,505,919, queen scallops 803,205, crab 372,656, lobster 328,618; fisheries production by tonnage (2005) 2,566 metric tons. *Mining and quarrying:* sand and gravel. *Manufacturing* (value added in US$; 2001–02): electrical and nonelectrical machinery/apparatus, textiles, and other 76,100,000; food and beverages 21,900,000. *Energy production (consumption):* electricity (kW-hr; 2006) n.a. (379,200,000). **Households.** Average household size (2006) 2.4; income per household (1995–96) £24,180 (US$37,965); sources of income (1995–96): wages and salaries 63.0%, transfer payments 16.0%, self-employment 10.0%, property income 8.0%, other 3.0%; expenditure (1995–96): food and nonalcoholic beverages 18.0%, housing 16.0%, transportation 13.0%, recreation and culture 13.0%, energy 7.0%. **Gross national income** (at current market prices; 2004–2005): US$2,719,000,000 (US$33,960 per capita). **Population economically active** (2006): total 41,793; activity rate of total population 52.2% (participation rates: ages 16–64, 79.9%; female 45.8%; unemployed [June 2007] 1.4%). **Selected balance of payments data.** Receipts from (US$'000,000): tourism (2006) 211. **Land use** as % of total land area (2003): in temporary crops 7.4%, in permanent crops 0.9%, in pasture 71.7%; overall forest area (2005) 6.1%.

Foreign trade

Imports: n.a. *Major import sources:* mostly the UK. **Exports:** traditional exports include scallops, herring, beef, lambs, and tweeds. *Major export destinations:* mostly the UK.

Transport and communications

Transport. *Railroads* (2006): route length 65 km. *Roads* (2006): total length 800 km (paved, virtually 100%). *Vehicles* (2003): passenger cars 50,596; trucks and buses 11,637. *Air transport* (1998; Manx Airlines only): passenger-km 846,775,000; metric ton-km cargo 168,000. **Communications,** in total units (units per 1,000 persons). Televisions (2000): 29,000 (355); telephone landlines (2001): 56,000 (741); cellular telephone subscribers (2001): 32,000 (424).

Education and health

Health: physicians (2006) 130 (1 per 616 persons); hospital beds (2006) 355 (combined total for Noble's Hospital and Ramsey and District Cottage Hospital; 1 per 225 persons); infant mortality rate per 1,000 live births (2004–05) 2.3. **Food** (2003): daily per capita caloric intake 3,450 (vegetable products 69%, animal products 31%).

Military

Total active duty personnel: The UK is responsible for defense.

Israel

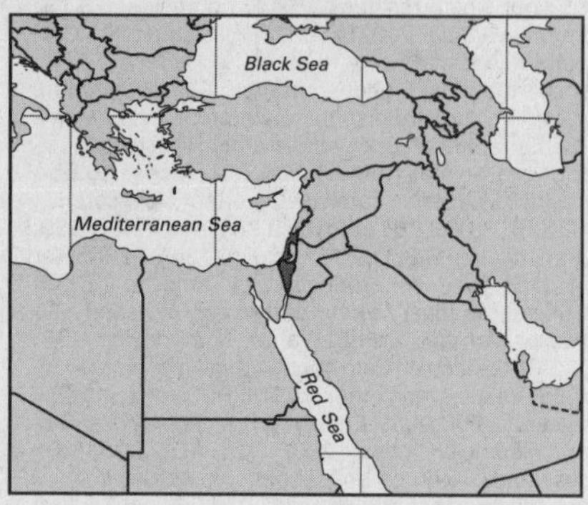

Official name: Medinat Yisrael (Hebrew); Israil (Arabic) (State of Israel). **Form of government:** multiparty republic with one legislative house (Knesset [120]). **Chief of state:** President Shimon Peres (from 2007). **Head of government:** Prime Minister Ehud Olmert (from 2006). **Capital:** Jerusalem is the proclaimed capital of Israel and the actual seat of government, but recognition of its status as capital by the international community has largely been withheld. **Official languages:** Hebrew; Arabic. **Official religion:** none. **Monetary unit:** 1 new (Israeli) sheqel (NIS) = 100 agorot; valuation (1 Jul 2008) US$1 = NIS 3.30.

Demography

Area: 8,357 sq mi, 21,643 sq km (excludes the West Bank and the Gaza Strip; includes the Golan Heights and East Jerusalem). **Population** (2007): 6,900,000. **Density** (2007): persons per sq mi 825.7, persons per sq km 318.8. **Urban** (2004): 91.5%. **Sex distribution** (2005): male 49.39%; female 50.61%. **Age breakdown** (2005): under 15, 28.3%; 15–29, 24.2%; 30–44, 19.0%; 45–59, 15.6%; 60–74, 8.3%; 75–84, 3.6%; 85 and over, 1.0%. **Ethnic composition** (2005): Jewish 76.2%; Arab and other 23.8%. **Religious affiliation** (2005): Jewish 76.3%, of which "secular" 33%, "traditionally observant" 30%, Orthodox 7%, ultra-Orthodox 6%; Muslim 16.1%; Christian 2.1%; Druze 1.6%; other 3.9%. **Major cities** (2006): Jerusalem 729,100; Tel Aviv–Yafo 382,500 (metro area 3,040,400); Haifa 267,000 (metro area 996,000); Rishon LeZiyyon 221,500. **Location:** Middle East, bordering Lebanon, Syria, Jordan, the West Bank, Egypt, the Gaza Strip, and the Mediterranean Sea.

Vital statistics

Birth rate per 1,000 population (2005): 20.8 (world avg. 20.3). **Death rate** per 1,000 population (2005): 5.6 (world avg. 8.6). **Total fertility rate** (avg. births per childbearing woman; 2005): 2.84. **Life expectancy** at birth (2005): male 78.3 years; female 82.3 years.

National economy

Budget (2005). *Revenue:* NIS 262,954,000,000 (tax revenue 67.3%; social contributions 15.5%; nontax revenue 13.2%; grants 4.0%). *Expenditures:* NIS 276,000,000,000 (social security and welfare 24.4%; defense 17.2%; education 15.2%; interest on loans 11.2%; health 10.5%). **Public debt** (2004): US$121,839,000,000. **Gross national income** (2006): US$138,986,000,000 (US$20,410 per capita). **Production** (metric tons except as noted). *Agriculture, forestry, fishing* (2005): potatoes 550,000, tomatoes 405,000, grapefruit and pomelos 250,000; livestock (number of live animals) 400,000 cattle, 390,000 sheep; roundwood 27,000 cu m, of which fuelwood 8%; fisheries production 26,555 (from aquaculture 84%). *Mining and quarrying* (2005): phosphate rock 3,000,000; potash 2,260,000. *Manufacturing* (value added in US$'000,000; 2003): medical, measuring, and testing appliances 1,959; fabricated metals 1,766; food products 1,661. *Energy production (consumption):* electricity (kW-hr; 2004) 49,025,000,000 (47,566,-000,000); hard coal (metric tons; 2004) none (12,875,000); lignite (metric tons; 2004) 439,000 (439,000); crude petroleum (barrels; 2004) 14,000 (78,847,000); petroleum products (metric tons; 2004) 10,024,000 (10,779,000); natural gas (cu m; 2005) 1,655,000,000 ([2004] 1,125,000,000). **Population economically active** (2004): total 2,678,500; activity rate 40.8% (participation rates: ages 15 and over, 54.9%; female 49.6%; unemployed [April 2006–March 2007] 8.2%). **Households.** Average household size (2005) 3.3; gross annual income per household (2004) NIS 125,280 (US$27,952); sources of income (2003): salaries and wages 66.1%, self-employment 10.5%; expenditure: housing 21.9%, transport and communications 20.4%, food and beverages 16.3%, education and entertainment 13.5%. **Selected balance of payments data.** Receipts from (US$'000,000): tourism (2005) 2,842; remittances (2006) 1,063; foreign direct investment (FDI) (2001–05 avg.) 3,335. Disbursements for (US$'000,000): tourism (2005) 2,895; remittances (2006) 2,400; FDI (2001–05 avg.) 2,153. **Land use** as % of total land area (2003): in temporary crops 15.6%, in permanent crops 4.0%, in pasture 5.9%; overall forest area (2005) 8.3%.

Foreign trade

Imports (2004; f.o.b. in balance of trade and c.i.f. in commodities and trading partners): US$40,968,-700,000 (diamonds 22.4%; machinery and apparatus 22.2%; chemicals and chemical products 10.5%; crude petroleum and refined petroleum 9.7%). *Major import sources:* US 14.9%; Belgium 10.1%; Germany 7.5%; Switzerland 6.5%; UK 6.1%. **Exports** (2004): US$38,618,300,000 (cut diamonds 27.4%; chemicals and chemical products 14.7%; rough diamonds 8.7%; telecommunications equipment 7.5%; electronic microcircuits 4.4%). *Major export destinations:* US 36.7%; Belgium 7.5%; Hong Kong 4.9%; UK 3.7%.

1 metric ton = about 1.1 short tons; 1 kilometer = 0.6 mi (statute); 1 metric ton-km cargo = about 0.68 short ton-mi cargo; c.i.f.: cost, insurance, and freight; f.o.b.: free on board

Transport and communications

Transport. *Railroads* (2005): route length 643 km; passenger-km 1,618,000,000, metric ton-km cargo 1,149,000,000. *Roads* (2005): total length 17,364 km (paved 100%). *Vehicles* (2006): passenger cars 1,626,388; trucks and buses 362,915. *Air transport* (2006; El Al only): passenger-km 16,054,000,000; metric ton-km cargo 904,000,000. **Communications,** in total units (units per 1,000 persons). Daily newspaper circulation (2005): 972,000 (145); televisions (2003): 2,136,000 (330); telephone landlines (2006): 3,005,000 (439); cellular telephone subscribers (2006): 8,404,000 (1,227); personal computers (2004): 5,037,000 (734); total Internet users (2006): 1,899,000 (277); broadband Internet subscribers (2006): 1,421,000 (209).

Education and health

Educational attainment (2004). Percentage of population ages 25 and over having: no formal schooling/unknown 3.7%; primary 12.5%; secondary 37.9%; postsecondary, vocational, and higher 45.9%. **Literacy** (2003): total population ages 15 and over literate 95.4%; males literate 97.3%; females literate 93.6%. **Health** (2005): physicians 25,058 (1 per 266 persons); hospital beds 42,632 (1 per 157 persons); infant mortality rate per 1,000 live births (2005) 4.3. **Food** (2005): daily per capita caloric intake 3,831 (vegetable products 79%, animal products 21%).

Military

Total active duty personnel (2006): 168,300 (army 74.3%, navy 4.9%, air force 20.8%). **Military expenditure as percentage of GDP** (2005): 9.7%; per capita expenditure US$1,875.

Background

The record of human habitation in Israel is at least 100,000 years old. Efforts by Jews to establish a national state there began in the late 19th century. Britain supported Zionism and in 1922 assumed political responsibility for what was Palestine. Migration of Jews there during Nazi persecution led to deteriorating relations with Arabs. In 1947 the UN voted to partition the region into separate Jewish and Arab states, a decision opposed by neighboring Arab countries. The State of Israel was proclaimed in 1948, and Egypt, Transjordan, Syria, Lebanon, and Iraq immediately declared war on it. Israel won this war as well as the 1967 Six-Day War, in which it claimed the West Bank from Jordan and the Gaza Strip from Egypt. Another war with its Arab neighbors followed in 1973, but the Camp David Accords led to the signing of a peace treaty between Israel and Egypt in 1979. Israel invaded Lebanon to quell the Palestine Liberation Organization (PLO) in 1982, and in the late 1980s a Palestinian resistance movement arose in the occupied territories. Peace negotiations between Israel and the Arab states and Palestinians began in 1991. Israel and the PLO agreed in 1993 upon a five-year extension of self-government to the Palestinians of the West Bank and the Gaza Strip. Israel signed a full peace treaty with Jordan in 1994. Israeli soldiers and Lebanon's Hezbollah forces clashed in 1997. Following numerous contentious talks between Israel and Lebanon, Israeli troops abruptly withdrew from Lebanon in 2000.

Recent Developments

As Israel celebrated the 60th anniversary of its independence in May 2008, it looked back on a year that saw a renewal of the Israeli-Palestinian peace process. The new US-led drive for accommodation was made possible by a split in Palestinian ranks between the moderate, largely secular Fatah and the radical Hamas. The seminal event for Israeli-Palestinian ties in 2007 was a bitter showdown in Gaza in June between Fatah and Hamas. During a week that saw often brutal fighting, disorganized Fatah forces collapsed in the face of a well-coordinated onslaught by Hamas, who seized power in Gaza. However, though Hamas had won a national election in January 2006 and was in sole control in Gaza, in the wake of the fighting Palestinian Pres. Mahmoud Abbas of Fatah invoked his constitutional authority to dismiss Hamas Prime Minister Ismail Haniyeh and form a new Fatah-led administration under Salam Fayad, a highly respected economist. This government was immediately recognized by most of the international community, including Israel. All the key players were quick to recognize the peacemaking potential in the new situation, and a US-sponsored regional conference was set for the fall. At the peace conference, held in Annapolis MD on 27 November and attended by 16 Arab countries, Israel and the Palestinians agreed on a joint statement only under heavy American pressure and by avoiding specific reference to any of the core issues. Nevertheless, Israel and the Palestinians hoped to negotiate a final peace deal by the end of 2008. Relations between Israel and Syria were also strained. Tensions came to a head on 6 September when Israeli planes crossed into Syria and bombed a military building. In April 2008 US officials provided video evidence that they claimed proved that the facility was in fact a nuclear-weapons lab and that North Korea had provided technical expertise for its construction.

Internet resources:
<www.goisrael.com/tourism_eng>.

Italy

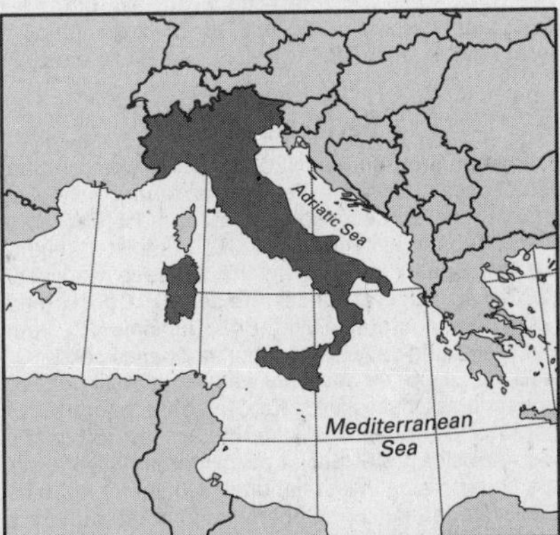

Official name: Repubblica Italiana (Italian Republic). **Form of government:** republic with two legislative houses (Senate [321]; Chamber of Deputies [630]). **Chief of state:** President Giorgio Napolitano (from

2006). **Head of government:** Prime Minister Silvio Berlusconi (from 2008). **Capital:** Rome. **Official language:** Italian. **Official religion:** none. **Monetary unit:** 1 euro (€) = 100 cents; valuation (1 Jul 2008) US$1 = €0.63.

Demography

Area: 116,346 sq mi, 301,336 sq km. **Population** (2007): 59,051,000. **Density** (2007): persons per sq mi 507.5, persons per sq km 196.0. **Urban** (2003): 67.4%. **Sex distribution** (2004): male 48.54%; female 51.46%. **Age breakdown** (2005): under 15, 14.0%; 15–29, 16.5%; 30–44, 23.8%; 45–59, 20.1%; 60–74, 16.3%; 75–84, 7.2%; 85 and over, 2.1%. **Ethnolinguistic composition** (2000): Italian 96.0%; North African Arab 0.9%; Italo-Albanian 0.8%; Albanian 0.5%; German 0.4%; Austrian 0.4%; other 1.0%. **Religious affiliation** (2005): Roman Catholic 83%, of which practicing 28%; Muslim 2%; nonreligious/atheist 14%; other 1%. **Major cities** (2007): Rome 2,705,603; Milan 1,303,347; Naples 975,139; Turin 900,569; Palermo 666,552; Genoa 615,686; Bologna 373,026; Florence 365,966; Bari 325,052; Catania 301,564; Venice 268,934; Verona 260,718; Messina 245,159; Padua 210,301. **Location:** southern Europe, bordering Switzerland, Austria, Slovenia, the Mediterranean Sea, and France. **Households.** Average household size (2004) 2.5; composition of households (2001): 1 person 24.9%, 2 persons 27.1%, 3 persons 21.6%, 4 persons 19.0%, 5 or more persons 7.4%. Family households (2001): 21,810,676, of which couple with children 41.5%, single family 24.9%, couple without children 20.8%, mother with children 7.3%, father with children 1.6%. **Immigration** (1997): immigrants 162,857, from Europe 41.1%, of which EU countries 14.2%; Africa 25.5%; Asia 19.0%; Western Hemisphere 14.0%.

Vital statistics

Birth rate per 1,000 population (2006): 9.5 (world avg. 20.3); (2004) within marriage 85.1%. **Death rate** per 1,000 population (2006): 9.4 (world avg. 8.6). **Natural increase rate** per 1,000 population (2006): 0.1 (world avg. 11.7). **Total fertility rate** (avg. births per childbearing woman; 2006): 1.35. **Life expectancy** at birth (2006): male 78.6 years; female 84.0 years.

Social indicators

Educational attainment (2002). Percentage of labor force ages 25 to 64 having: no formal schooling through lower secondary education 55.6%; completed upper secondary 34.0%; completed higher 10.4%. **Quality of working life.** Average workweek (2004) 39.7 hours. Annual rate per 100,000 workers (2005) for: nonfatal injury 2,848; fatal injury 5. Number of working days lost to labor stoppages per 1,000 workers (2005) 40. **Material well-being.** Rate per 100 households possessing (2006): mobile phone 82.3; personal computer 46.1; Internet access 35.6; satellite television 25.0. **Social participation.** Eligible voters participating in last national election (April 2006) 83%. Trade union membership in total workforce (2004) 30%. **Social deviance** (2003). Offense rate per 100,000 population for: murder 1.2; rape 4.8; theft 2,306; robbery 72.5; drug trafficking 64.7; suicide (2002) 7.0. **Access to services** (2002). Nearly 100% of dwellings have access to electricity, a safe water supply, and toilet facilities.

National economy

Gross national income (at current market prices; 2006): US$1,843,325,000,000 (US$31,360 per capita). **Budget** (2006). *Revenue:* €680,054,000,000 (current revenue 99.3%, of which indirect taxes 32.1%, direct taxes 31.4%, social security contributions 28.2%; capital revenue 0.7%). *Expenditures:* €745,558,000,000 (current expenditure 88.1%, of which social assistance benefits 39.5%, wages and salaries 21.9%, interest payments 9.1%; capital expenditure 11.9%). **Public debt** (2005): US$1,771,919,000,000. **Production** (metric tons except as noted). *Agriculture, forestry, fishing* (2005): sugar beets 14,160,000, corn (maize) 10,510,000, grapes 8,554,000, wheat 7,717,000, tomatoes 7,187,000, olives 3,716,000; livestock (number of live animals) 9,200,000 pigs, 7,954,000 sheep, 6,255,000 cattle; roundwood 8,049,000 cu m, of which fuelwood 67%; fisheries production 479,316 (from aquaculture 38%). *Mining and quarrying* (2005): limestone 120,000,000; marble 5,600,000; feldspar 3,000,000; pumice 600,000. *Manufacturing* (value added in US$'000,000; 2003): nonelectrical machinery and apparatus 31,422; fabricated metal products 30,311; paints, soaps, pharmaceuticals 13,975; food products 13,203; bricks, cement, ceramics 11,749. *Energy production (consumption):* electricity (kW-hr; 2004) 303,347,000,000 (348,982,000,000); coal (metric tons; 2004) 98,000 (24,280,000); crude petroleum (barrels; 2005) 41,900,000 (668,000,000); petroleum products (metric tons; 2004) 88,757,000 (79,452,000); natural gas (cu m; 2004) 12,527,000,000 (80,637,000,000). **Population economically active** (2005): total 24,451,400; activity rate of total population 42.1% (participation rates: ages 15–64, 62.4%; female 40.1%; unemployed [2006] 6.8%). **Households.** Average household size (2004) 2.5; average annual disposable income per household (2000) €28,100 (US$25,900); sources of income (1996): salaries and wages 38.8%, property income and self-employment 38.5%, transfer payments 22.0%; expenditure (2004): housing and energy 30.1%, food and beverages 19.0%, transportation and communications 16.3%, clothing 6.6%, household operations 6.3%. **Selected balance of payments data.** Receipts from (US$'000,000): tourism (2005) 35,319; remittances (2006) 2,398; foreign direct investment (FDI) (2001–05 avg.) 16,523. Disbursements for (US$'000,000): tourism (2005) 22,371; remittances (2006) 5,815; FDI (2001–05 avg.) 21,320. **Land use** as % of total land area (2003): in temporary crops 27.1%, in permanent crops 9.3%, in pasture 14.9%; overall forest area (2005) 33.9%.

Foreign trade

Imports (2004; c.i.f. in balance of trade and commodities and f.o.b. in trading partners): US$350,391,000,000 (transport equipment 14.2%; chemical products 13.5%; electrical equipment 13.1%; fuels 10.4%; fabricated metals 10.4%). *Major import sources* (2005): Germany 17.2%; France 9.9%; The Nether-

1 metric ton = about 1.1 short tons; 1 kilometer = 0.6 mi (statute); 1 metric ton-km cargo = about 0.68 short ton-mi cargo; c.i.f.: cost, insurance, and freight; f.o.b.: free on board

lands 5.6%; China 4.6%; Belgium 4.5%; Spain 4.2%; UK 4.0%. **Exports** (2004): US$348,513,000,000 (machinery and apparatus 20.4%; transport equipment 11.2%; chemical products 9.7%; fabricated metals 9.6%; textiles and wearing apparel 9.2%; electrical equipment 9.1%). *Major export destinations* (2005): Germany 13.1%; France 12.2%; US 8.1%; Spain 7.4%; UK 6.4%; Switzerland 3.9%.

Transport and communications

Transport. *Railroads* (2003): length (2004) 19,319 km; passenger-km 45,221,000,000; metric ton-km cargo 22,457,000,000. *Roads* (2003): total length 484,688 km (paved 100%). *Vehicles* (2004): passenger cars 33,973,147; trucks and buses 4,108,486. *Air transport* (2006; Alitalia and Alitalia Express only): passenger-km 39,502,000,000; metric ton-km cargo 1,473,000,000. **Communications,** in total units (units per 1,000 persons). Daily newspaper circulation (2004): 7,737,000 (134); televisions (2001): 28,153,000 (494); telephone landlines (2005): 25,049,000 (431); cellular telephone subscribers (2005): 71,535,000 (1,231); personal computers (2005): 21,486,000 (370); total Internet users (2006): 28,855,000 (496); broadband Internet subscribers (2006): 8,639,000 (146).

Education and health

Literacy (2003): total population ages 15 and over literate 98.6%; males literate 99.0%; females literate 98.3%. **Health:** physicians (2002) 353,692 (1 per 162 persons); hospital beds (2003) 237,216 (1 per 243 persons); infant mortality rate (2004) 6.1. **Food** (2005): daily per capita caloric intake 3,754 (vegetable products 73%, animal products 27%).

Military

Total active duty personnel (2006): 191,152 (army 58.6%, navy 17.8%, air force 23.6%); US military forces (2005) 11,400. **Military expenditure as percentage of GDP** (2005): 1.9%; per capita expenditure US$578.

The Po River is the longest river in Italy, rising in the Monte Viso group of the Cottian Alps on Italy's western frontier and emptying into the Adriatic Sea in the east after a course of 405 miles (652 km). Its drainage basin covers 27,062 square miles (70,091 square km), forming Italy's widest and most fertile plain.

Background

The Etruscan civilization arose in the 9th century BC and was overthrown by the Romans in the 4th–3rd centuries BC. Barbarian invasions of the 4th and 5th centuries AD destroyed the western Roman empire. Italy's political fragmentation lasted for centuries but did not diminish its impact on European culture, notably during the Renaissance. From the 15th to the 18th century, Italian lands were ruled by France, the Holy Roman Empire, Spain, and Austria. When Napoleonic rule ended in 1815, Italy was again a grouping of independent states. The Risorgimento successfully united most of Italy, including Sicily and Sardinia, by 1861, and the unification of peninsular Italy was completed by 1870. Italy joined the Allies during World War I, but social unrest in the 1920s brought to power the Fascist movement of Benito Mussolini, and Italy allied itself with Nazi Germany in World War II. Defeated by the Allies in 1943, Italy proclaimed itself a republic in 1946. It was a charter member of NATO (1949) and of the European Community. It completed the process of setting up regional legislatures with limited autonomy in the 1970s. Since World War II it has experienced rapid changes of government but has remained socially stable. It worked with other European countries to establish the European Union.

Recent Developments

Relations between Italy and the US suffered in February 2007 after the Italian Senate unexpectedly voted down a nonbinding foreign-policy resolution that pledged to maintain Italy's 2,360-strong Afghanistan troop contingent and to allow the US to expand its military presence at a vital NATO base in Vicenza. Relations got another jolt in February when a Milan judge ruled that 26 Americans and 7 Italians, mostly current or former intelligence agents, should stand trial in connection with the 2003 kidnapping of the Muslim cleric Osama Moustafa Hassan Nasr (known as Abu Omar), who was abducted from a Milan street by the CIA in conjunction with Italian secret services and flown to Egypt, where he was imprisoned for four years on terrorism charges. In April 2008 former premier Silvio Berlusconi was reelected to the post, and he quickly reaffirmed Italy's commitment to the Afghan mission.

Internet resources: <www.italiantourism.com>.

Jamaica

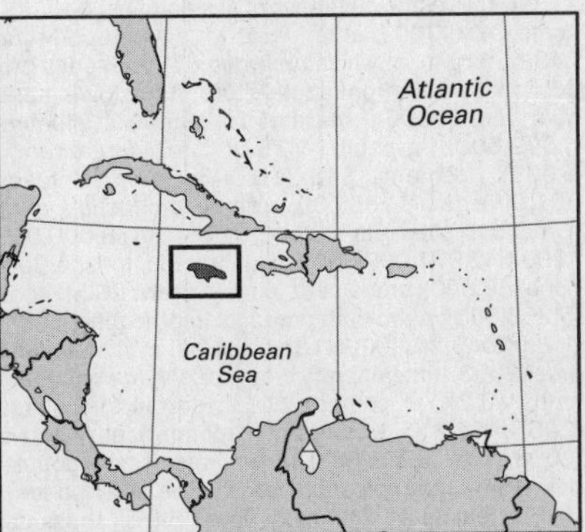

Official name: Jamaica. **Form of government:** constitutional monarchy with two legislative houses (Senate [21]; House of Representatives [60]). **Chief of state:** British Queen Elizabeth II (from 1952), represented by Governor-General Kenneth Hall (from 2006). **Head of government:** Prime Minister Bruce Golding (from 2007). **Capital:** Kingston. **Official language:** English. **Official religion:** none. **Monetary unit:** 1 Jamaica dollar (J$) = 100 cents; valuation (1 Jul 2008) US$1 = J$72.00.

Demography

Area: 4,244 sq mi, 10,991 sq km. **Population** (2007): 2,680,000. **Density** (2007): persons per sq mi 631.5, persons per sq km 243.8. **Urban** (2005): 52.2%. **Sex distribution** (2005): male 49.41%; female 50.59%. **Age breakdown** (2005): under 15, 33.7%; 15–29, 29.4%; 30–44, 17.6%; 45–59, 9.5%; 60–74, 6.7%; 75 and over, 3.1%. **Ethnic composition** (2001): black 91.6%; mixed race 6.2%; East Indian 0.9%; Chinese 0.2%; white 0.2%; other/unknown 0.9%. **Religious affiliation** (2001): Protestant 61.2%, of which Church of God 23.8%, Seventh-day Adventist 10.8%, Pentecostal 9.5%; Roman Catholic 2.6%; other Christian 1.7%; Rastafarian 0.9%; nonreligious 20.9%; other 12.7%. **Major cities** (2004): Kingston 594,500; Spanish Town 134,900; Portmore 102,000; Montego Bay 89,200; May Pen 49,900. **Location:** island in the Caribbean Sea, south of Cuba.

Vital statistics

Birth rate per 1,000 population (2006): 17.0 (world avg. 20.3). **Death rate** per 1,000 population (2006): 5.7 (world avg. 8.6). **Total fertility rate** (avg. births per childbearing woman; 2005): 2.50. **Life expectancy** at birth (2005): male 69.2 years; female 72.7 years.

National economy

Budget (2005). *Revenue:* J$177,986,900,000 (tax revenue 88.4%, of which income taxes 35.2%, taxes on goods and services 27.5%, customs duties 8.6%; nontax revenue 6.4%; other 5.2%). *Expenditures:* J$204,513,700,000 (public debt 42.4%; wages and salaries 30.8%; capital expenditures 8.1%). **Public debt** (external, outstanding; April 2007): US$6,065,200,000. **Production** (metric tons except as noted). *Agriculture, forestry, fishing* (2005): sugarcane 1,900,000, coconuts 198,700, oranges 172,300; livestock (number of live animals) 440,000 goats, 430,000 cattle, 85,000 pigs; roundwood 845,559 cu m, of which fuelwood 67%; fisheries production 18,766 (from aquaculture 30%). *Mining and quarrying* (2006): bauxite 14,865,400; alumina 4,099,500; gypsum 375,000. *Manufacturing* (2005): cement 848,365,000; animal feeds 367,600; flour 135,000. *Energy production (consumption):* electricity (kW-hr; 2005) 3,878,000,000 ([2004] 2,974,000,000); coal (metric tons; 2004) none (66,000); crude petroleum (barrels; 2004) none (5,358,000); petroleum products (metric tons; 2004) 668,000 (3,264,000). **Land use** as % of total land area (2003): in temporary crops 16.1%, in permanent crops 10.2%, in pasture 21.1%; overall forest area (2005) 31.3%. **Population economically active** (2006): total 1,251,600; activity rate of total population 46.9% (participation rates: ages 14 and over 64.6%; female 44.2%; unemployed 8.9%). **Gross national income** (2006): US$9,448,000,000 (US$3,501 per capita). **Households.** Average household size (2004) 3.5; expenditure (1988): food and beverages 48.2%, housing 7.9%, household furnishings 7.6%, meals away from home 7.4%, transportation 6.4%. **Selected balance of payments data.** Receipts from (US$'000,000): tourism (2005) 1,545; remittances (2006) 1,770; foreign direct investment (2001–05 avg.) 604. Disbursements for (US$'000,000): tourism (2005) 250; remittances (2005) 394.

Foreign trade

Imports (2005; f.o.b. in balance of trade and c.i.f. in commodities and trading partners): US$4,867,-280,000 (mineral fuels 27.9%; machinery and transport equipment 17.9%; manufactured goods 13.1%; food 12.4%; chemicals 11.4%). *Major import sources* (2003): US 44.4%; Caricom (Caribbean Community and Common Market) 12.8%; Latin American countries 10.6%; EU 10.5%, of which UK 4.1%. **Exports** (2005): US$1,658,650,000 (alumina 55.5%; nontraditional exports [including chemical products and mineral fuels] 20.6%; free zone exports [mostly clothing] 7.7%; bauxite 6.0%; refined sugar 4.6%). *Major export destinations* (2003): US 28.8%; Canada 16.1%; UK 12.8%; Norway 3.7%.

Transport and communications

Transport. *Railroads* (2004): route length 201 km. *Roads* (2004): total length 20,996 km (paved 73%). *Vehicles* (2004): passenger cars 357,660; trucks and buses 128,239. *Air transport* (2005; Air Jamaica only): passenger-km 3,854,519,000; metric ton-km cargo 15,823,000. **Communications,** in total units (units per 1,000 persons). Daily newspaper circulation (2005): 95,000 (36); televisions (2003): 1,006,000 (374); telephone landlines (2005): 342,000 (125); cellular telephone subscribers (2005): 2,804,000 (1,058); personal computers (2005): 179,000 (68); total Internet users (2005): 1,232,000 (465).

Education and health

Educational attainment (2001). Percentage of population ages 15 and over having: no formal schooling/unknown 6.7%; primary education 25.5%; secondary 55.5%; higher 12.3%, of which university 4.2%. **Literacy** (2005): population ages 15 and over literate 88.7%; males literate 85.0%; females literate 92.3%. **Health:** physicians (2003) 2,253 (1 per 1,193 persons); hospital beds (2004) 4,882 (1 per 556 persons); infant mortality rate per 1,000 live births (2005) 19.2. **Food** (2005): daily per capita caloric intake 3,075 (vegetable products 88%, animal products 12%); 159% of FAO recommended minimum.

Military

Total active duty personnel (2006): 2,830 (army 88.3%, coast guard 6.7%, air force 5.0%). **Military expenditure as percentage of GDP** (2005): 0.6%; per capita expenditure US$20.

Background

The island of Jamaica was settled by Arawak Indians c. AD 600. It was sighted by Christopher Columbus in 1494; Spain colonized it in the early 16th century but neglected it because it lacked gold reserves. Britain gained control in 1655, and by the end of the 18th century Jamaica had become a prized colonial possession due to the volume of sugar produced by slave laborers. Slavery was abolished in the late 1830s,

1 metric ton = about 1.1 short tons; 1 kilometer = 0.6 mi (statute); 1 metric ton-km cargo = about 0.68 short ton-mi cargo; c.i.f.: cost, insurance, and freight; f.o.b.: free on board

and the plantation system collapsed. Jamaica gained full internal self-government in 1959 and became an independent country within the British Commonwealth in 1962.

Recent Developments

The 2007 Cricket World Cup tournament, the biggest sporting event ever held in the Caribbean, suffered a setback on the Jamaica leg in March when the coach of the Pakistani team, Englishman Bob Woolmer, was found dead in his hotel room. Local investigators pursued the case as a murder inquiry, but pathologists later confirmed that Woolmer had, in fact, died from a sudden heart attack.

Internet resources: <www.visitjamaica.com>.

Japan

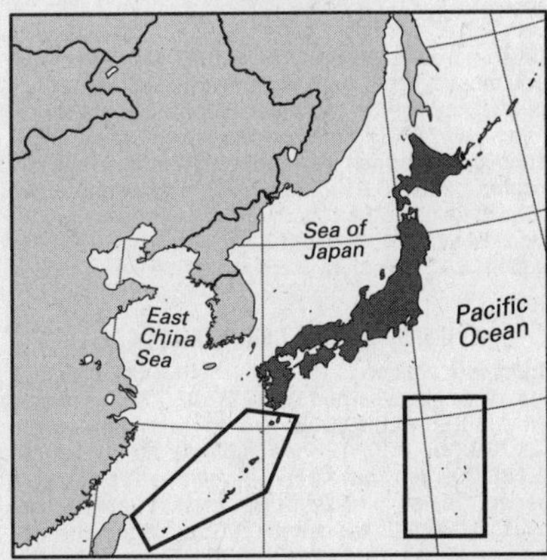

Official name: Nihon (Japan). **Form of government:** constitutional monarchy with a national Diet consisting of two legislative houses (House of Councillors [247]; House of Representatives [480]). **Symbol of state:** Emperor Akihito (from 1989). **Head of government:** Prime Minister Yasuo Fukuda (from 2007). **Capital:** Tokyo. **Official language:** Japanese. **Official religion:** none. **Monetary unit:** 1 yen (¥) = 100 sen; valuation (1 Jul 2008) US$1 = ¥105.54.

Demography

Area: 145,898 sq mi, 377,873 sq km. **Population** (2007): 127,770,000. **Density** (2007): persons per sq mi 875.7, persons per sq km 338.1. **Urban** (2003): 65.4%. **Sex distribution** (2006): male 48.78%; female 51.22%. **Age breakdown** (2006): under 15, 13.7%; 15–29, 17.4%; 30–44, 20.9%; 45–59, 21.1%; 60–74, 17.5%; 75–84, 7.0%; 85 and over, 2.4%. **Composition by nationality** (2004): Japanese 98.5%; Korean 0.5%; Chinese 0.4%; Brazilian 0.2%; other 0.4%. **Immigration/emigration** (2004): permanent immigrants/registered aliens in Japan 1,973,747, from North and South Korea 30.8%, Taiwan, Hong Kong, and China 24.7%, Brazil 14.5%, Philippines 10.1%, Peru 2.8%, US 2.5%, other 14.6%. Japanese living abroad 961,307, in the US 35.3%, in China 10.3%, in Brazil 7.2%, in the UK 5.3%, in Australia 5.1%, in other 36.8%. **Major cities** (2006): Tokyo 8,535,792; Yokohama 3,602,758; Osaka 2,635,420; Nagoya 2,223,148; Sapporo 1,888,953; Kobe 1,528,687; Kyoto 1,472,511; Fukuoka 1,414,417; Kawasaki 1,342,262; Saitama 1,182,744; Hiroshima 1,157,846; Sendai 1,027,329; Kita-Kyushu 990,585. **Location:** eastern Asia, island chain between the North Pacific Ocean and the Sea of Japan. **Religious affiliation** (2003): Shinto and related beliefs 84.2%; Buddhism and related beliefs 73.6%; Christian 1.7%; Muslim 0.1%; other 7.8%. **Households** (2005). Total households 50,382,000; average household size 2.6; 1 person 27.6%, 2 persons 27.6%, 3 persons 18.5%, 4 persons 16.5%, 5 persons 6.7%, 6 or more persons 3.1%. Family households (2004) 32,573,000 (70.3%); nonfamily 13,751,000 (29.7%). **Mobility** (2004). Percentage of total population moving: within a prefecture 2.5%; between prefectures 2.1%.

Vital statistics

Birth rate per 1,000 population (2005): 8.4 (world avg. 20.3). **Death rate** per 1,000 population (2005): 8.6 (world avg. 8.6). **Natural increase rate** per 1,000 population (2005): −0.2 (world avg. 11.7). **Total fertility rate** (avg. births per childbearing woman; 2005): 1.25. **Life expectancy** at birth (2005): male 78.5 years; female 85.5 years.

Social indicators

Educational attainment (2003). Percentage of population ages 25–64 having: no formal schooling through lower secondary education 16%; upper secondary/higher vocational 47%; university 37%. **Quality of working life.** Average hours worked per month (2005) 152.4. Annual rate of industrial deaths per 100,000 workers (2001) 2.7. Proportion of labor force insured for damages or income loss resulting from injury, permanent disability, and death (2005) 53.1%. Average man-days lost to labor stoppages per 1,000 workdays (2003) 6.7. Average duration of journey to work (2003) 34.2 minutes. Rate per 1,000 workers of discouraged workers (unemployed no longer seeking work: 1997) 89.4. **Access to services** (2004). Proportion of households having access to: safe public water supply 96.9%; public sewage system 65%. **Social participation.** Adult population working as volunteers at least once in the year (2006) 26.2%. Trade union membership in total workforce (2004) 16.3%. **Social deviance** (2005). Offense rate per 100,000 population for: homicide 1.0; robbery 3.0; larceny and theft 151.6. Incidence in general population of drug and substance abuse 0.1. Rate of suicide per 100,000 population 22.0. **Material well-being** (2003–04). Households possessing: automobile 81.6%; air conditioner (2002) 87.2%; personal computer 77.5%; cellular phone 91.1%; Internet connection (2004) 86.8%.

National economy

Gross national income (at current market prices; 2006): US$4,520,998,000,000 (US$35,333 per capita). **Budget** (2003–04). *Revenue:* ¥86,878,703,-000,000 (government bonds 42.1%; income tax 16.2%; corporation tax 12.6%; VAT 11.2%). *Expenditures:* ¥86,878,703,000,000 (social security 23.5%; debt service 21.0%; public works 10.2%; education and science 7.2%; national defense 5.7%). **Public debt** (March 2006): US$7,038,635,000,000. **Households.** Average household size (2005) 2.6; average annual income per household (2004) ¥6,380,280 (US$58,970); sources of income (1994): wages and salaries 59.0%, transfer payments 20.5%, self-employment 12.8%, other 7.3%; expenditure (2005): food 22.9%, transportation and communications 12.9%, recreation 10.3%, fuel, light, and water charges 7.1%, housing 6.5%, clothing and footwear 4.5%, medical care 4.3%, education 4.2%. *Energy production (consumption):* electricity (kW-hr; 2004) 1,080,124,000,000 (1,080,124,000,000); coal (metric tons; 2004) none (production ceased in 2002) (180,807,000); crude petroleum (barrels; 2005) 1,800,000 ([2004] 1,466,000,000); petroleum products (metric tons; 2004) 174,149,000, of which (by volume [1998]) diesel 32.8%, heavy fuel oil 21.7%, gasoline 21.7%, kerosene and jet fuel 12.0% (186,112,000); natural gas (cu m; 2004) 5,228,000,000 (81,950,000,000). Composition of energy supply by source (2002): crude oil and petroleum products 49.7%, coal 19.5%, natural gas 13.5%, nuclear power 11.6%, hydroelectric power 3.2%, solar power and other new energy supplies 2.4%, geothermal 0.1%. Domestic energy demand by end use (1998): mining and manufacturing 46.3%, residential and commercial 26.3%, transportation 25.2%, other 2.2%. **Population economically active** (2006): total 66,570,000; activity rate of total population 52.1% (participation rates: ages 15 and over, 60.4%; female 41.6%; unemployed [June 2007] 3.7%). **Production** (metric tons except as noted). *Agriculture, forestry, fishing* (2005): rice 11,342,000, sugar beets 4,201,000, potatoes 2,752,000, cabbages 2,287,000, sugarcane 1,214,000, tangerines and mandarin oranges 1,132,000, dry onions 1,083,000, sweet potatoes 1,053,000, wheat 875,000, apples 818,900, carrots 762,100, tomatoes 758,100, cucumbers 674,700, green onions 554,000, lettuce 551,600, eggplant 395,400, pears 394,600, spinach 297,900, persimmons 285,400, cantaloupes 270,000, pumpkins 234,100, soybeans 225,000, yams 204,100, strawberries 196,200, taro 184,600, peaches 174,000, cauliflower 130,600, tea 100,000, plums 90,000, buckwheat 31,200, chestnuts 21,800; livestock (number of live animals) 9,600,000 pigs, 4,402,000 cattle, 265,200,000 chickens; roundwood 16,276,000 cu m, of which fuelwood 1%; fisheries production 4,819,116 (including mackerel 811,728, anchovy 348,647, skipjack tuna 293,087, Yesso scallop 287,486; from aquaculture 15% [including Pacific oyster 218,896, Yesso scallop 203,352]); aquatic plants 612,635 (from aquaculture [mostly seaweed] 83%); (2003) 830 whales caught; pearls 29 metric tons. *Mining and quarrying* (2005): limestone 165,240,000; silica sand 4,700,000; dolomite (2004) 3,727,000; pyrophyllite 351,111; zinc 41,452; lead 3,437; copper (2001) 744; silver 54,098 kg; gold 8,318 kg. *Manufacturing* (value added in US$'000,000; 2003): machinery and apparatus 225,282, of which nonelectrical machinery 89,580, electronics, televisions, and radios 81,109, electrical machinery 54,593; transportation equipment 123,083; chemicals and chemical products 96,800; food and food products 75,123; fabricated metal products 51,583; rubber products and plastic products 47,089, of which plastic products 35,565; iron and steel 36,772; cement, bricks, and ceramics 32,192; printing and publishing 29,052; beverages and tobacco 26,542; paper and paper products 22,936; textiles, wearing apparel, and footwear 19,175; professional and scientific equipment and watches 13,439. **Selected balance of payments data.** Receipts from (US$'000,000): tourism (2005) 12,430; remittances (2006) 1,380; foreign direct investment (FDI) (2001–05 avg.) 6,479. Disbursements for (US$'000,000): tourism (2005) 37,565; remittances (2006) 3,476; FDI (2001–05 avg.) 35,229. **Land use** as % of total land area (2003): in temporary crops 12.1%, in permanent crops 0.9%; overall forest area (2005) 68.2%.

Foreign trade

Imports (2005; c.i.f.): ¥56,949,400,000,000 (crude and refined petroleum 25.6%; electrical equipment [significantly computers and office machinery] 11.5%; nonelectrical machinery 10.0%; food products 9.6%; chemicals and chemical products 7.2%; base and fabricated metals 4.0%). *Major import sources:* China 21.0%; US 12.4%; Saudi Arabia 5.6%; UAE 4.9%; Australia 4.8%; South Korea 4.7%; Indonesia 4.0%; Taiwan 3.5%; Germany 3.5%; Thailand 3.0%. **Exports** (2005; f.o.b.): ¥65,656,500,000,000 (electrical equipment [significantly electronic microcircuits, computers, and office machinery] 20.6%; nonelectrical machinery 20.3%; transportation equipment 9.3%; chemicals and chemical products 8.7%; base and fabricated metals 5.9%). *Major export destinations:* US 22.5%; China 13.5%; South Korea 7.8%; Taiwan 7.3%; Hong Kong 6.0%; Thailand 3.8%; Indonesia 3.5%; Singapore 3.1%; Germany 3.1%; UK 2.5%.

Transport and communications

Transport. *Railroads* (2005): length (2004) 23,577 km; passengers carried 21,893,000,000; passenger-km 390,697,000,000; metric ton-km cargo 22,779,000,000. *Roads* (2004): total length 1,188,000 km (paved 80%). *Vehicles* (2005): passenger cars 57,092,000; trucks and buses 17,116,000. *Air transport* (2005): passengers carried (2004) 112,000,000; passenger-km 166,216,000,000; metric ton-km cargo 8,587,000,000. *Urban transport* (2000): passengers carried 57,719,000, of which by rail 34,020,000, by road 19,466,000, by subway 4,233,000. **Communications**, in total units (units per 1,000 persons). Daily newspaper circulation (2005): 69,700,000 (546); televisions (2003): 107,527,000 (842); telephone landlines (2006): 55,153,000 (430); cellular telephone subscribers (2006): 101,698,000 (793); personal computers (2005): 86,389,000 (675); total Internet users (2006): 87,540,000 (683); broadband Internet subscribers (2006): 25,755,000 (202). *Radio and television broadcasting* (2003): total radio stations 1,612, of which commercial 723; total television stations 15,021, of which commercial 8,276. Commercial broadcasting hours (by percentage of programs): reports–radio 12.3%, television 19.8%; education–radio 2.4%, television 12.3%; culture–radio 13.3%, television 25.1%; entertainment–radio 69.3%, television 37.5%. Advertisements (daily average): radio 149, television 445.

Education and health

Literacy: total population ages 15 and over literate: virtually 100%. **Health** (2004): physicians 267,943 (1

1 metric ton = about 1.1 short tons; 1 kilometer = 0.6 mi (statute); 1 metric ton-km cargo = about 0.68 short ton-mi cargo; c.i.f.: cost, insurance, and freight; f.o.b.: free on board

per 477 persons); dentists 94,022 (1 per 1,359 persons); nurses 799,416 (1 per 160 persons); pharmacists 241,369 (1 per 529 persons); midwives 25,257 (1 per 5,059 persons); hospital beds 1,631,553 (1 per 78 persons); infant mortality rate per 1,000 live births (2005) 2.8. **Food** (2005): daily per capita caloric intake 2,838 (vegetable products 77%, animal products 23%).

Military

Total active duty personnel (2006): 248,000 (army 59.7%, navy 21.9%, air force 18.4%); US troops (2006) 35,400. **Military expenditure as percentage of GDP** (2005): 1.0%; per capita expenditure US$345.

The conflict between Japan and China (1894–95) marked the emergence of Japan as a major world power and demonstrated the weakness of the Chinese empire. The war grew out of conflict between the two countries for supremacy in Korea.

Background

Japan's history began with the accession of the legendary first emperor, Jimmu, in 660 BC. The Yamato court established the first unified Japanese state in the 4th–5th century AD; during this period Buddhism arrived in Japan by way of Korea. For centuries Japan borrowed heavily from Chinese culture, but it began to sever its links with the mainland by the 9th century. In 1192 Minamoto Yoritomo established Japan's first *bakufu,* or shogunate. Unification was achieved in the late 1500s under the leadership of Oda Nobunaga, Toyotomi Hideyoshi, and Tokugawa Ieyasu. During the Tokugawa shogunate, beginning in 1603, the government imposed a policy of isolation. Under the leadership of Emperor Meiji (1868–1912), it adopted a constitution (1889) and began a program of modernization and Westernization. Japanese imperialism led to war with China (1894–95) and Russia (1904–05) as well as to the annexation of Korea (1910) and Manchuria (1931). During World War II Japan attacked US forces in Hawaii and the Philippines (December 1941) and occupied European colonial possessions in South Asia. In 1945 the US dropped atomic bombs on Hiroshima and Nagasaki, and Japan surrendered to the Allied powers. US postwar occupation of Japan led to a new democratic constitution in 1947. In rebuilding Japan's ruined industrial plant, new technology was used in every major industry. A tremendous economic recovery followed, and it was able to maintain a favorable balance of trade into the 1990s.

Recent Developments

In elections held in July 2007, Japan's ruling Liberal Democratic Party (LDP) lost control of the upper house of the Diet (parliament) for the first time since the party's establishment in 1955, and Prime Minister Shinzo Abe stepped down in September. The LDP selected Yasuo Fukuda, a moderate conservative, to lead the party, and he formally took office on 26 September.

Japan's economy grew by 2.1% in 2007, while the unemployment rate settled at 4.1% in February 2008. The government viewed a contraction in Japan's economic output in the second quarter of 2007 as a temporary drop in Japan's sixth year of continuing growth, the longest expansion since 1945. Many Japanese analysts worried about a possible economic slowdown in the US, one of Japan's largest export markets. In spite of a softening in export sales to the US, Japan's overall trade surplus expanded to about ¥11.7 trillion (about US$104 million) in fiscal year 2007. Weaker American demand for Japanese goods was offset by growth in shipments to Europe and to other Asian countries, particularly China. It was reported in April that China had replaced the US as Japan's largest trading partner.

Chinese Premier Wen Jiabao's three-day visit to Japan in April—the first by a Chinese premier in seven years—was intended to help nurture relations between the two Asian giants. In August Prime Minister Abe visited India, where he met with Prime Minister Manmohan Singh and signed a series of bilateral trade agreements. Also in August Japan reached a preliminary free-trade agreement with ASEAN (Association of Southeast Asian Nations) intended to boost economic integration in East Asia. No progress, however, occurred between Japan and North Korea in their attempts to establish diplomatic relations. Japan's effort to seek full information about Pyongyang's kidnappings of Japanese citizens in the 1970s and '80s remained stymied. Tensions over North Korea also crept into US-Japanese relations as the Japanese feared that the US would remove North Korea from its list of countries that sponsored terrorism, even if North Korea refused to settle the kidnapping issue with Japan. Tensions also flared between the US and Japan over the passage by the US House of Representatives of a nonbinding resolution urging Japan to formally apologize for its military's coercion of Asian women into sexual slavery during World War II. Japan announced that it was canceling aid to Myanmar (Burma) in response to Yangon's (Rangoon's) violent suppression of monk-led pro-democracy demonstrations in September. During those demonstrations a Japanese video journalist covering the protests was shot and killed as government troops opened fire on the participants.

Internet resources: <www.jnto.go.jp/eng>.

Jersey

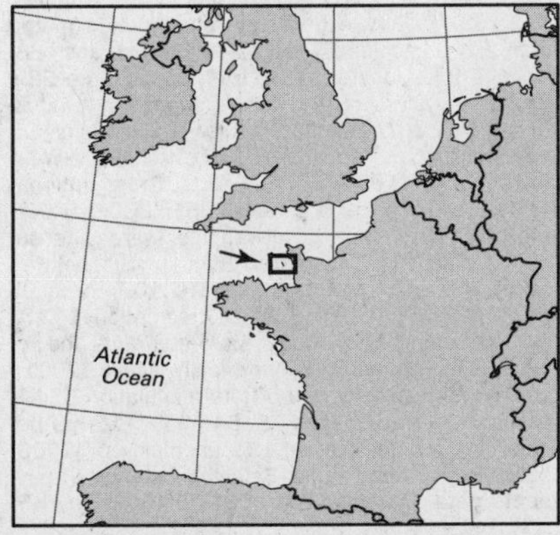

Official name: Bailiwick of Jersey. **Political status:** crown dependency (UK) with one legislative house

(States of Jersey [58]). **Chief of state:** British Queen Elizabeth II (from 1952), represented by Lieutenant Governor Andrew Ridgway (from 2006). **Head of government:** Chief Minister Frank Walker (from 2005). **Capital:** Saint Helier. **Official language:** English (Jèrriais, a Norman-French dialect, is spoken by a small number of residents). **Official religion:** none. **Monetary unit:** 1 Jersey pound (£J) = 100 pence; valuation (1 Jul 2008) US$1 = £J 0.50 (the Jersey pound is equivalent in value to the British pound sterling [£]).

Demography

Area: 45.6 sq mi, 118.2 sq km. **Population** (2007): 89,500. **Density** (2007): persons per sq mi 1,962.7, persons per sq km 757.2. **Urban** (2001): 28.9%. **Sex distribution** (2005): male 49.22%; female 50.78%. **Age breakdown** (2005): under 15, 17.5%; 15–29, 15.1%; 30–44, 25.1%; 45–59, 21.6%; 60–74, 13.7%; 75–84, 5.0%; 85 and over, 2.0%. **Population by place of birth** (2001): Jersey 52.6%; UK, Guernsey, or Isle of Man 35.8%; Portugal 5.9%; France 1.2%; other 4.5%. **Religious affiliation** (2000): Christian 86.0%, of which Anglican 44.1%, Roman Catholic 14.6%, other Protestant 6.9%, unaffiliated Christian 20.1%; nonreligious/atheist 13.4%; other 0.6%. **Major cities** (2001; population of parishes): St. Helier 28,310; St. Saviour 12,491; St. Brelade 10,134. **Location:** western Europe, island in the English Channel.

Vital statistics

Birth rate per 1,000 population (2006): 10.6 (world avg. 20.3). **Death rate** per 1,000 population (2006): 8.5 (world avg. 8.6). **Total fertility rate** (avg. births per childbearing woman; 2005): 1.57. **Life expectancy** at birth (2005): male 76.8 years; female 81.9 years.

National economy

Budget (2005). *Revenue:* £J 446,000,000 (income tax 81.4%; import duties 11.2%; stamp duties 3.4%; other 4.0%). *Expenditures:* £J 466,000,000 (current expenditure 90.8%, of which health 27.4%, education 19.5%, social security 17.7%, public services 5.8%; capital expenditure 9.2%). **Production.** *Agriculture, forestry, fishing* (value of export crops in £J '000; 2005): potatoes 19,700, tomatoes 4,700, flowers (2004) 900; livestock (number of live animals; 2002) 3,970 dairy cattle; fisheries production (metric tons) 2,260 (including whelks 442, brown crabs 438, scallops 231, lobsters 139; from aquaculture 28% [including oysters 580]). *Manufacturing:* light industry, mainly electrical goods, textiles, and clothing. *Energy production (consumption):* electricity (kW-hr; 2001) 153,000,000 (567,000,000). **Gross national income** (at 2005 market prices): US$5,800,000,000 (US$66,000 per capita). **Households.** Average household size (2001) 2.4; median annual household income (2004–05) £J 34,000 (US$62,100); expenditure (2004–05): housing 29.2%, recreation 14.2%, transportation 11.6%, food 9.8%, restaurants and hotels 5.8%. **Population economically active** (2001): total 48,105; activity rate of total population 55.2% (participation rates: ages 15–64 [male], 15–59 [female] 81.7%; female 44.1%; unemployed [2006] 2.3%). **Public debt:** none. **Selected balance of payments data.** Receipts from (US$'000,000): tourism (2005) 379. **Land use** as % of total land area (1997): in temporary and permanent crops 29%, in pasture 22%; overall forest area (2005) 4.1%.

Foreign trade

Imports: n.a. *Major import sources* (2001): mostly the UK. **Exports:** agricultural and marine exports (2001) £J 40,626,000 (potatoes 67.4%; greenhouse tomatoes 19.1%; flowers 3.3%; zucchini 3.0%; crustaceans 2.0%; mollusks 2.0%). *Major export destinations:* mostly the UK.

Transport and communications

Transport. *Roads* (1995): total length 557 km (paved 100%). *Vehicles* (2002): passenger cars 74,007; trucks and buses 12,957. **Communications,** in total units (units per 1,000 persons). Daily newspaper circulation (2005): 22,000 (250); telephone landlines (2006): 72,000 (804); cellular telephone subscribers (2006): 102,000 (1,148); total Internet users (2004): 27,000 (308).

Education and health

Educational attainment (2001). Percentage of population ages 16–64 (male) and 16–59 (female) having: no formal degree 34.1%; undergraduate 7.1%; graduate (advanced degree) 4.1%. **Literacy** (2002): 100%. **Health:** physicians (2001) 174 (1 per 500 persons); hospital beds (2000) 651 (1 per 133 persons); infant mortality rate per 1,000 live births (2005) 2.4.

Military

Total active duty personnel (2006): none; defense is the responsibility of the UK.

Jordan

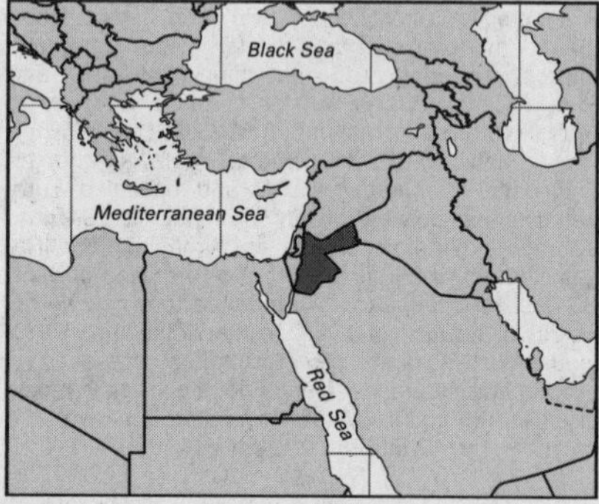

Official name: Al-Mamlakah al-Urdunniyah al-Hashimiyah (Al-Urdun) (Hashemite Kingdom of Jordan). **Form of government:** constitutional monarchy with two legislative houses (Senate [55]; House of Representatives [110]). **Head of state and government:** King Abdullah II (from 1999), assisted by Prime Minister Nader Dahabi (from 2007). **Capital:** Amman.

1 metric ton = about 1.1 short tons; 1 kilometer = 0.6 mi (statute); 1 metric ton-km cargo = about 0.68 short ton-mi cargo; c.i.f.: cost, insurance, and freight; f.o.b.: free on board

Official language: Arabic. **Official religion:** Islam. **Monetary unit:** 1 Jordan dinar (JD) = 1,000 fils; valuation (1 Jul 2008) US$1 = JD 0.71.

Demography

Area: 34,277 sq mi, 88,778 sq km. **Population** (2007): 5,924,000. **Density** (2007): persons per sq mi 172.8, persons per sq km 66.7. **Urban** (2004): 78.3%. **Sex distribution** (2004): male 51.46%; female 48.54%. **Age breakdown** (2005): under 15, 37.2%; 15–29, 28.9%; 30–44, 20.7%; 45–59, 8.2%; 60–74, 4.2%; 75–84, 0.7%; 85 and over, 0.1%. **Ethnic composition** (2000): Arab 97.8%, of which Jordanian 32.4%, Palestinian 32.2%, Iraqi 14.0%, Bedouin 12.8%; Circassian 1.2%; other 1.0%. **Religious affiliation** (2005): Sunni Muslim 95%; Christian 3%; other (mostly Shi'i Muslim and Druze) 2%. **Major cities** (2004): Amman 1,036,330; Al-Zarqa 395,227; Irbid 250,645; Al-Rusayfah 227,735; Al-Quwaysimah 135,500. **Location:** the Middle East, bordering Syria, Iraq, Saudi Arabia, the Gulf of Aqaba, Israel, and parts of the emerging Palestinian Autonomous Areas.

Vital statistics

Birth rate per 1,000 population (2005): 27.5 (world avg. 20.3). **Death rate** per 1,000 population (2005): 3.2 (world avg. 8.6). **Natural increase rate** per 1,000 population (2005): 24.3 (world avg. 11.7). **Total fertility rate** (avg. births per childbearing woman; 2005): 2.71. **Life expectancy** at birth (2003): male 70.6 years; female 72.4 years.

National economy

Budget (2004). *Revenue:* JD 2,949,800,000 (tax revenue 48.4%, of which sales tax 28.0%, custom duties 8.8%, income and profits taxes 7.4%; foreign grants 27.5%; nontax revenue 22.0%, of which licenses and fees 12.4%; repayments 2.1%). *Expenditures:* JD 3,102,100,000 (current expenditure 75.0%, of which defense 21.1%, wages 15.0%, social security and pensions 12.9%, oil subsidies 8.4%, interest payments 7.4%; capital expenditure 25.0%). **Production** (metric tons except as noted). *Agriculture, forestry, fishing* (2005): tomatoes 598,900, potatoes 172,100, cucumbers 166,200; livestock (number of live animals) 1,890,440 sheep, 516,140 goats, 25,000,000 chickens; roundwood 265,771 cu m, of which fuelwood 98%; fisheries production 1,071 (from aquaculture 52%). *Mining and quarrying* (2005): phosphate ore 6,375,000; potash 1,830,000. *Manufacturing* (value added in US$'000,000; 2004): chemicals and chemical products 347; bricks, cement, and ceramics 287; food products 232. *Energy production (consumption):* electricity (kW-hr; 2004) 8,967,000,000 (9,792,000,000); crude petroleum (barrels; 2004) 8,480 (30,087,000); petroleum products (metric tons; 2004) 3,817,000 (4,426,000); natural gas (cu m; 2004) 266,521,000 (266,521,000). **Selected balance of payments data.** Receipts from (US$'000,000): tourism (2005) 1,441; remittances (2005) 2,500; foreign direct investment (2001–05 avg.) 566; official development assistance (2005) 636 (commitments). Disbursements for (US$'000,000): tourism (2005) 585; remittances (2005) 349. **Population economically active** (2003): total 1,293,000; activity rate of total population 23.6% (participation rates: over age 15, 37.9%; female 14.9%; unemployed 14.5%). **Gross national income** (2006): US$14,595,000,000 (US$2,548 per capita). **Public debt** (external, outstanding; 2005): US$6,878,000,000. **Households.** Average household size (2005) 5.4; income per household (2002–03) JD 5,590 (US$7,880); sources of income (2002–03): wages and salaries 45.3%, rent and property income 23.0%, transfer payments 19.9%, self-employment 11.8%; expenditure (2002–03): food and beverages 36.2%, housing and energy 26.4%, transportation and communications 13.2%, education 6.2%, clothing and footwear 4.8%. **Land use** as % of total land area (2003): in temporary crops 2.0%, in permanent crops 0.9%, in pasture 8.4%; overall forest area (2005) 0.9%.

Foreign trade

Imports (2004; c.i.f.): JD 5,799,200,000 (machinery and apparatus 22.7%, of which transport equipment 9.1%; crude petroleum 13.2%; food products 13.1%; chemicals and chemical products 9.8%; textile yarn and fabric 7.9%). *Major import sources:* Saudi Arabia 19.8%; China 8.4%; Germany 6.8%; US 6.8%; Italy 3.8%. **Exports** (2004; f.o.b.): JD 2,753,000,000 (domestic exports 83.8%, of which clothing 25.8%, chemicals and chemical products 18.2% [including medicines and pharmaceuticals 5.8%], potash 5.9%, vegetables 4.6%, phosphates 4.3%; reexports 16.2%). *Major export destinations:* US 31.5%; Iraq 15.7%; India 7.7%; Saudi Arabia 6.0%; Syria 4.2%.

Transport and communications

Transport. *Railroads* (2003): length 788 km; passenger-km 2,100,000; metric ton-km cargo 348,000,000. *Roads* (2004): total length 7,500 km (paved 100%). *Vehicles* (2004): passenger cars 387,565; trucks and buses 190,188. *Air transport* (2006; Royal Jordanian airlines only): passenger-km 5,521,000,000; metric ton-km cargo 210,000,000. **Communications,** in total units (units per 1,000 persons). Daily newspaper circulation (2005): 265,000 (49); televisions (2004): 1,065,000 (198); telephone landlines (2006): 614,000 (105); cellular telephone subscribers (2006): 4,343,000 (744); personal computers (2005): 355,000 (62); total Internet users (2006): 797,000 (137); broadband Internet subscribers (2006): 49,000 (8.8).

Education and health

Educational attainment (2004). Percentage of population ages 25 and over having: no formal schooling: illiterate 14.0%, literate 4.8%; primary/lower secondary education 36.6%; upper secondary 19.4%; some higher 25.1%, of which advanced degree 2.1%; unknown 0.1%. **Literacy** (2005): percentage of population ages 15 and over literate 91.1%; males literate 95.2%; females literate 87.0%. **Health:** physicians (2005) 17,569 (1 per 316 persons); hospital beds (2005) 10,141 (1 per 539 persons); infant mortality rate per 1,000 live births (2005) 24.0. **Food** (2005): daily per capita caloric intake 3,299 (vegetable products 91%, animal products 9%); 182% of FAO recommended minimum.

Military

Total active duty personnel (2005): 100,500 (army 84.6%, navy 0.5%, air force 14.9%). **Military expenditure as percentage of GDP** (2005): 5.3%; per capita expenditure US$130.

Background

Jordan shares much of its history with Israel, since both occupied the area known historically as Palestine. Much of present-day eastern Jordan was incorporated into Israel under Kings David and Solomon c. 1000 BC. It fell to the Seleucids in 330 BC and to Muslim Arabs in the 7th century AD. The Crusaders extended the kingdom of Jerusalem east of the Jordan River in 1099. Jordan submitted to Ottoman Turkish rule during the 16th century. In 1920 the area comprising Jordan (then known as the Transjordan) was established within the British mandate of Palestine. Transjordan became an independent state in 1927, although the British mandate did not end until 1948. After hostilities with the new state of Israel ceased in 1949, Jordan annexed the West Bank of the Jordan River, administering the territory until Israel gained control of it in the Six-Day War of 1967. In 1970–71 Jordan was wracked by fighting between the government and guerrillas of the Palestine Liberation Organization (PLO), a struggle that ended in the expulsion of the PLO from Jordan. In 1988 King Hussein renounced all Jordanian claims to the West Bank in favor of the PLO. In 1994 Jordan and Israel signed a full peace agreement. Upon the death of King Hussein in 1999, his son Abdullah took over the throne.

Recent Developments

The Jordanian economy grew in 2007 but was brought in check somewhat by a growing foreign trade deficit and decreased foreign direct investment. Jordan's central bank reported that GDP growth was 6.0% over data from 2006 and that the rate of inflation fell from 6.25% to 5.40%. As well, public debt grew by little more than 1%. The trade deficit grew by 25.0% in 2007, however, as the value of the country's imports was more than double that of its exports. Foreign direct investment dropped 75.4%, though compared to 2005 data it grew by 3.5%.

Internet resources: <www.visitjordan.com>.

Kazakhstan

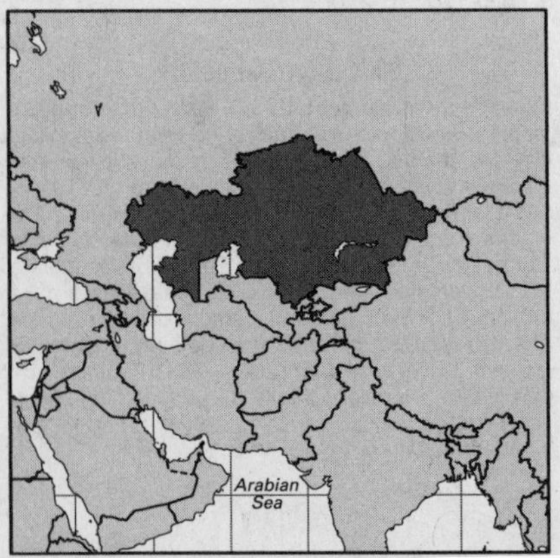

Official name: Qazaqstan Respublikasy (Republic of Kazakhstan). **Form of government:** unitary republic with a parliament consisting of two chambers (Senate [47] and Assembly [107]). **Head of state and government:** President Nursultan Nazarbayev (from 1990), assisted by Prime Minister Karim Masimov (from 2007). **Capital:** Astana. **Official language:** Kazakh (Russian commands equal status at state-owned organizations and local government bodies). **Official religion:** none. **Monetary unit:** 1 tenge (T) = 100 tiyn; valuation (1 Jul 2008) US$1 = 120.62 tenge.

Demography

Area: 1,052,100 sq mi, 2,724,900 sq km. **Population** (2007): 15,472,000. **Density** (2007): persons per sq mi 14.7, persons per sq km 5.7. **Urban** (2006): 57.4%. **Sex distribution** (2005): male 48.30%; female 51.70%. **Age breakdown** (2005): under 15, 23.7%; 15–29, 28.7%; 30–44, 20.7%; 45–59, 16.4%; 60–74, 7.9%; 75–84, 2.3%; 85 and over, 0.3%. **Ethnic composition** (2003): Kazakh 57.2%; Russian 27.2%; Ukrainian 3.1%; Uzbek 2.7%; German 1.6%; Tatar 1.6%; Uighur 1.5%; other 5.1%. **Religious affiliation** (2000): Muslim (mostly Sunni) 42.7%; nonreligious 29.3%; Christian 16.7%, of which Orthodox 8.6%; atheist 10.9%; other 0.4%. **Major cities** (2004): Almaty 1,175,208; Shymkent (Chimkent) 513,110; Astana 510,533; Qaraghandy (Karaganda) 428,867; Taraz 327,911. **Location:** central Asia, bordering Russia, China, Kyrgyzstan, Uzbekistan, the Aral Sea, Turkmenistan, and the Caspian Sea.

Vital statistics

Birth rate per 1,000 population (2006): 19.7 (world avg. 20.3); (2000) within marriage 76.1%. **Death rate** per 1,000 population (2006): 10.3 (world avg. 8.6). **Total fertility rate** (avg. births per childbearing woman; 2005): 1.90. **Life expectancy** at birth (2006): male 60.6 years; female 72.0 years.

National economy

Budget (2004). *Revenue:* T 1,441,000,000,000 (tax revenue 90.7%, of which corporate taxes 33.8%, VAT 16.9%, social security 11.7%, petroleum taxes 10.0%; nontax revenue 9.3%). *Expenditures:* T 1,289,300,000,000 (social security 21.1%; education 14.8%; health 10.2%; public order 9.2%). **Public debt** (external, outstanding; 2005): US$2,184,000,000. **Population economically active** (2006): total 8,028,900; activity rate of total population 52.4% (participation rates: ages 15–64 [2004] 76.6%; female [2004] 49.0%; unemployed 7.8%). **Production** (metric tons except as noted). *Agriculture, forestry, fishing* (2005): wheat 9,970,000, potatoes 2,521,000, barley 1,546,000; livestock (number of live animals) 11,410,000 sheep, 5,204,000 cattle, 2,000,000 goats; roundwood 300,800 cu m, of which fuelwood 57%; fisheries production 31,589 (from aquaculture 2%). *Mining and quarrying* (2004): iron ore 20,300,000; bauxite 4,705,600; chromite 3,267,000. *Manufacturing* (value of production in T '000,000; 2004): base metals 600,000; food and food products 356,000; coke, refined petroleum products, and nuclear fuel 134,000. *Energy production (consumption):* electricity (kW-hr; 2005)

66,500,000,000 (59,200,000,000); hard coal (metric tons; 2004) 86,800,000 (60,277,000); lignite (metric tons; 2004) 3,945,000 (3,673,000); crude petroleum (barrels; 2005) 471,000,000 ([2004] 90,000,000); petroleum products (metric tons; 2004) 10,305,000 (8,906,000); natural gas (cu m; 2004) 21,855,000,000 (16,472,000,000). **Gross national income** (2006): US$72,388,000,000 (US$4,727 per capita). **Households** (2001). Average household size (2004) 3.8; sources of income: salaries and wages 72.1%, social benefits 9.2%; expenditure: food and beverages 56.0%, housing 11.7%. **Selected balance of payments data.** Receipts from (US$'000,000): tourism (2005) 701; remittances (2006) 187; foreign direct investment (2001–05 avg.) 2,674; official development assistance (2005) 141 (commitments). Disbursements for (US$'000,000): tourism (2005) 753; remittances (2006) 3,036. **Land use** as % of total land area (2003): in temporary crops 8.4%, in permanent crops 0.05%, in pasture 68.6%; overall forest area (2005) 1.2%.

Foreign trade

Imports (2004; c.i.f.): US$12,781,250,000 (machinery and apparatus 26.8%; mineral fuels and lubricants 14.7%; transportation equipment 13.9%; base metals 13.0%; chemicals and chemical products 8.8%). *Major import sources* (2006): Russia 35.7%; China 20.0%; Germany 7.6%; France 3.5%; Italy 3.3%. **Exports** (2004; f.o.b.): US$20,096,230,000 (mineral fuels 68.3%; base metals 19.4%; agricultural products [mostly cereals] 3.2%). *Major export destinations* (2006): Germany 12.5%; Russia 11.3%; China 11.0%; Italy 10.6%; France 7.5%.

Transport and communications

Transport. *Railroads* (2006): route length (2004) 13,700 km; passenger-km 12,705,000,000; metric ton-km cargo 191,000,000,000. *Roads* (2004): total length 90,018 km (paved 93%). *Vehicles* (2004): passenger cars 1,204,118; trucks and buses 287,766. *Air transport* (2006): passenger-km 3,716,000,000; metric ton-km cargo (2003) 94,000,000. **Communications,** in total units (units per 1,000 persons). Televisions (2003): 5,106,000 (338); telephone landlines (2006): 2,928,000 (191); cellular telephone subscribers (2006): 7,834,000 (512); total Internet users (2006): 1,247,000 (81); broadband Internet subscribers (2006): 31,000 (2.1).

Education and health

Educational attainment (1999). Population ages 25 and over having: no formal schooling/some primary education 9.1%; primary education 23.1%; secondary/some postsecondary 57.8%; higher 10.0%. **Literacy** (2003): percentage of total population ages 15 and over literate 99.5%; males literate 99.8%; females literate 99.3%. **Health** (2006): physicians 57,500 (1 per 266 persons); hospital beds 119,000 (1 per 129 persons); infant mortality rate per 1,000 live births 13.9. **Food** (2005): daily per capita caloric intake 3,027 (vegetable products 74%, animal products 26%); 155% of FAO recommended minimum.

Military

Total active duty personnel (2006): 65,800 (army 71.1%, air force 28.9%). **Military expenditure as percentage of GDP** (2005): 1.1%; per capita expenditure US$39.

The Aral Sea was once a large, shallow saltwater lake, straddling the boundary between Kazakhstan to the north and Uzbekistan to the south, that ranked as the world's fourth largest body of inland water. It nestles in the climatically inhospitable heart of Central Asia, to the east of the Caspian Sea.

Background

Named for its earliest inhabitants, the Kazakhs, the area came under Mongol rule in the 13th century. The Kazakhs consolidated a nomadic empire in the 15th–16th centuries. Under Russian rule by the mid-19th century, it became part of the Kirgiz Autonomous Republic formed by the Soviets in 1920, and in 1925 its name was changed to the Kazakh Autonomous Soviet Socialist Republic. Kazakhstan obtained its independence in 1991, and during the 1990s it attempted to stabilize its economy.

Recent Developments

In 2007 Kazakhstan continued to have one of the strongest economies in the Commonwealth of Independent States, thanks largely to its oil revenues, though backsliding on democratization was increasingly evident. Kazakhstan became the first state in Central Asia to become a donor to the economic development of its neighbors, promising US$100 million in April to aid the Kyrgyz economy. In addition, a number of Kazakh firms announced plans to invest in industries in Tajikistan. In February, Minister of Environmental Protection Nurlan Iskakov warned that foreign oil firms working in Kazakhstan would face suspension of their activities for alleged failure to observe environmental regulations.

Internet resources: <www.kazakhembus.com>.

Kenya

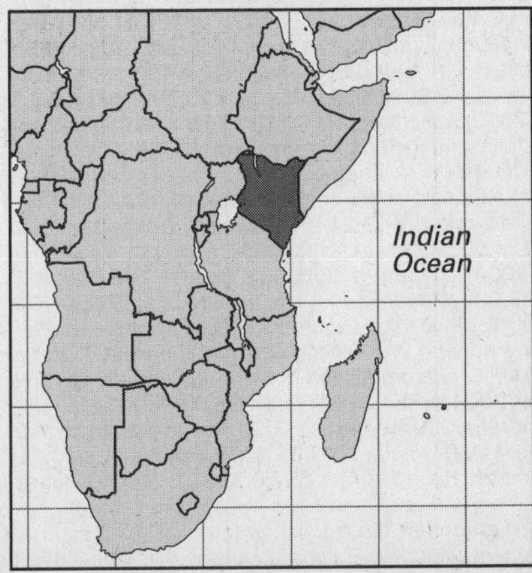

Official name: Jamhuri ya Kenya (Swahili); Republic of Kenya (English). **Form of government:** unitary multiparty republic with one legislative house (National Assembly [224]). **Head of state and government:** President Mwai Kibaki (from 2002), assisted by Prime Minister Raila Odinga (from 2008). **Capital:** Nairobi. **Official languages:** Swahili; English. **Official religion:** none. **Monetary unit:** 1 Kenya shilling (K Sh) = 100 cents; valuation (1 Jul 2008) US$1 = K Sh 65.31.

Demography

Area: 224,961 sq mi, 582,646 sq km. **Population** (2007): 36,914,000. **Density** (2007): persons per sq mi 164.1, persons per sq km 63.4. **Urban** (2005): 20.7%. **Sex distribution** (2006): male 48.90%; female 51.10%. **Age breakdown** (2006): under 15, 43.1%; 15–29, 30.2%; 30–44, 15.2%; 45–59, 7.0%; 60–74, 3.5%; 75 and over, 1.0%. **Ethnic composition** (2004): Kikuyu 21%; Luhya 14%; Luo 13%; Kalenjin 11%; Kamba 11%; Gusii 6%; Meru 5%; other 19%. **Religious affiliation** (2006): Protestant/independent Christian 66%; Roman Catholic 23%; Muslim 8%; nonreligious 2%; traditional beliefs 1%. **Major cities** (2004): Nairobi 2,504,400; Mombasa 777,100; Nakuru 256,300; Kisumu 227,100; Eldoret 195,200. **Location:** eastern Africa, bordering Ethiopia, Somalia, the Indian Ocean, Tanzania, Uganda, and The Sudan.

Vital statistics

Birth rate per 1,000 population (2005): 40.1 (world avg. 20.3). **Death rate** per 1,000 population (2005): 14.7 (world avg. 8.6). **Natural increase rate** per 1,000 population (2005): 25.5 (world avg. 11.7). **Total fertility rate** (avg. births per childbearing woman; 2005): 4.96. **Life expectancy** at birth (2006): male 54.3 years; female 59.1 years.

National economy

Budget (2004–05). *Revenue:* K Sh 304,705,000,000 (tax revenue 79.7%, of which income and profit taxes 32.6%, VAT 24.9%, excise tax 14.5%; nontax revenue 15.4%; grants 4.9%). *Expenditures:* K Sh 303,705,000,000 (recurrent expenditure 85.0%, of which wages and salaries 34.3%, interest payments 10.0%; development expenditure 15.0%). **Public debt** (external, outstanding; 2005): US$5,520,000,000. **Production** (metric tons except as noted). *Agriculture, forestry, fishing* (2005): sugarcane 4,801,000, corn (maize) 2,906,000, potatoes 980,000, cut flowers (2002) largest supplier to EU (25% of total market); livestock (number of live animals) 13,883,000 goats, 13,019,000 cattle, 10,033,000 sheep; roundwood 22,356,000 cu m, of which fuelwood 92%; fisheries production 143,274, of which freshwater fish 124,621 (from aquaculture 1%). *Mining and quarrying* (2004): soda ash 355,380; fluorite 108,000; salt 22,000. *Manufacturing* (value added in US$'000,000; 2002): food and food products 400; textiles and wearing apparel 245; chemicals and chemical products 142. *Energy production (consumption):* electricity (kW-hr; 2004) 4,864,000,000 (5,035,000,000); coal (metric tons; 2004) none (108,000); crude petroleum (barrels; 2004) none (14,983,000); petroleum products (metric tons; 2004) 1,657,000 (2,703,000). **Households.** Average household size (2004) 4.5; expenditure (1993–94): food 42.4%, housing and energy 24.1%, clothing and footwear 9.1%, transportation 6.4%, other 18.0%. **Population economically active** (2001): total 12,952,000; activity rate of total population 42.1% (participation rates [1998–99]: ages 15–64, 73.6%; female [1997] 46.1%; unemployed 14.6%). **Gross national income** (2006): US$23,564,000,000 (US$645 per capita). **Selected balance of payments data.** Receipts from (US$'000,000): tourism (2005) 579; remittances (2004) 464; foreign direct investment (2001–05 avg.) 36; official development assistance (2005) 995 (commitments). Disbursements for (US$'000,000): tourism (2005) 124. **Land use** as % of total land area (2000): in temporary crops 7.9%, in permanent crops 1.0%, in pasture 37.4%; overall forest area 30.0%.

Foreign trade

Imports (2006; c.i.f.): K Sh 526,870,000,000 (machinery and transport equipment 30.7%; petroleum and petroleum products 23.9%; chemicals and chemical products 13.7%; food and live animals 5.2%). *Major import sources:* UAE 14.7%; India 7.1%; UK 6.5%; South Africa 6.4%; Japan 5.6%. **Exports** (2006): K Sh 267,900,000,000 (soda ash 35.6%; food 22.4%, of which tea 17.3%, coffee 3.6%; cut flowers 15.7%; petroleum products 2.7%). *Major export destinations:* Uganda 10.4%; UK 10.1%; The Netherlands 7.3%; Tanzania 6.8%; US 6.6%.

Transport and communications

Transport. *Railroads* (2000): route length 2,700 km; passenger-km 302,000,000; metric ton-km cargo 1,557,000,000. *Roads* (2000): total length 63,942 km (paved 12%). *Vehicles* (2000): passenger cars 244,836; trucks and buses 96,726. *Air transport* (2004; Kenya Airways only): passenger-km 5,283,000,000; metric ton-km cargo 193,430,000. **Communications,** in total units (units per 1,000 persons). Daily newspaper circulation (2005): 310,000 (8.8); televisions (2000): 758,000 (25); telephone landlines (2006): 293,000 (8.4); cellular telephone subscribers (2006): 6,485,000 (185); personal computers (2004): 330,000 (9.5); total Internet users (2006): 2,770,000 (79).

Education and health

Educational attainment (1998–99). Percentage of population ages 6 and over having: no formal schooling/unknown 20.2%; primary education 59.0%; secondary 19.7%; university 1.1%. **Literacy** (2002): total population ages 16 and over literate 84.3%; males literate 90.0%; females literate 78.5%. **Health:** physicians (2006) 5,889 (1 per 6,268 persons); hospital beds (2004) 65,971 (1 per 485 persons); infant mortality rate per 1,000 live births (2005) 61.5. **Food** (2003): daily per capita caloric intake 1,974 (vegetable products 87%, animal products 13%); 85% of FAO recommended minimum.

Military

Total active duty personnel (2006): 24,120 (army 82.9%, navy 6.7%, air force 10.4%). **Military expendi-**

1 metric ton = about 1.1 short tons; 1 kilometer = 0.6 mi (statute); 1 metric ton-km cargo = about 0.68 short ton-mi cargo; c.i.f.: cost, insurance, and freight; f.o.b.: free on board

ture as percentage of GDP (2005): 1.6%; per capita expenditure US$9.

Jomo Kenyatta, an African statesman and nationalist, was the first prime minister (1963–64) and then president (1964–78) of independent Kenya. As president, he encouraged foreign investment from Western and other countries. Largely as a result of his policies, Kenya's gross national product grew almost fivefold from 1971 to 1981, and its rate of economic growth was among the highest on the continent in the first two decades after independence.

Background

The coastal region of East Africa was dominated by Arabs until it was seized by the Portuguese in the 16th century. The Masai people held sway in the north and moved into central Kenya in the 18th century, while the Kikuyu expanded from their home region in south-central Kenya. The interior was explored by European missionaries in the 19th century. After the British took control, Kenya was established as a British protectorate (1890) and a crown colony (1920). The Mau Mau rebellion of the 1950s was directed against European colonialism. In 1963 the country became fully independent, and a year later a republican government under Jomo Kenyatta was elected. In 1992 Kenyan Pres. Daniel arap Moi allowed the country's first multiparty elections in three decades, though the balloting was marred by violence and fraud. Political turmoil occurred over the following years.

Recent Developments

The main preoccupation of politicians in Kenya remained the presidential and parliamentary elections that were held in late December 2007. The last session of the parliament, which opened in March, provided Pres. Mwai Kibaki with the opportunity to emphasize the government's achievements in the field of primary education and in the allocation of funds to support regional projects. In the final count Kibaki emerged the winner, claiming roughly 47% of the vote to the 44% taken by his opponent, Raila Odinga. Kibaki was immediately sworn in for a second term in office, while opposition leaders expressed outrage and deadly riots erupted, particularly in the shantytowns around Nairobi. In the ensuing violence throughout the first part of 2008, more than 1,500 people were killed. Odinga and Kibaki agreed to a power-sharing deal to end the violence.

Internet resources: <www.magicalkenya.com>.

Kiribati

Official name: Republic of Kiribati. **Form of government:** unitary republic with a unicameral legislature (House of Assembly [42]). **Head of state and government:** President Anote Tong (from 2003). **Capital:** Bairiki, on Tarawa Atoll. **Official language:** English. **Official religion:** none. **Monetary unit:** 1 Australian dollar ($A) = 100 cents; valuation (1 Jul 2008) US$1 = $A 1.05.

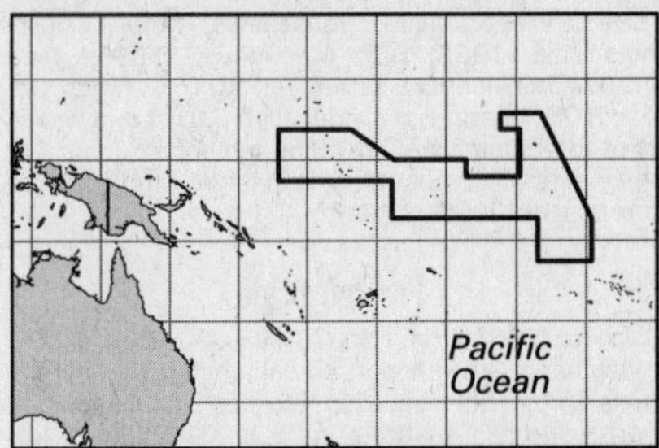

Demography

Area: 312.9 sq mi, 810.5 sq km. **Population** (2007): 95,500. **Density** (2007): persons per sq mi 341.1, persons per sq km 131.5. **Urban** (2005): urban 47.5%. **Sex distribution** (2005): male 49.29%; female 50.71%. **Age breakdown** (2005): under 15, 36.9%; 15–29, 28.3%; 30–44, 18.7%; 45–59, 10.7%; 60–74, 4.5%; 75 and over, 0.9%. **Ethnic composition** (2000): Micronesian 98.8%; Polynesian 0.7%; European 0.2%; other 0.3%. **Religious affiliation** (2005): Roman Catholic 55.3%; Kiribati Protestant (Congregational) 35.7%; Mormon 3.1%; Baha'i 2.2%; other/nonreligious 3.7%. **Major villages** (2005): Betio 12,509; Bikenibeu 6,170; Teaoraereke 3,939; Bairiki 2,766. **Location:** western Pacific Ocean, south of the Hawaiian Islands (US).

Vital statistics

Birth rate per 1,000 population (2005): 30.9 (world avg. 20.3). **Death rate** per 1,000 population (2005): 8.4 (world avg. 8.6). **Natural increase rate** per 1,000 population (2005): 22.5 (world avg. 11.7). **Total fertility rate** (avg. births per childbearing woman; 2005): 4.20. **Life expectancy** at birth (2005): male 58.7 years; female 64.9 years.

National economy

Budget (2005). *Revenue:* $A 182,369,000 (nontax revenue 35.7%; tax revenue 16.7%; grants 47.6%). *Expenditures:* $A 78,560,000 (education 25.3%; health 16.7%; economic services 15.6%; defense 7.3%). **Public debt** (external, outstanding; 2002): US$3,900,000. **Production** (metric tons except as noted). *Agriculture, forestry, fishing* (2005): coconuts 109,800, bananas 4,939, taro 2,000; livestock (number of live animals) 12,400 pigs, 460,000 chickens; fisheries production 34,012; aquatic plants (all seaweed) production 3,904 (from aquaculture 100%). *Manufacturing:* copra (6,194 metric tons produced in 2005), processed fish, clothing, and handicrafts. *Energy production (consumption):* electricity (kW-hr; 2004) 10,000,000 (10,000,000); petroleum products (metric tons; 2004) none (9,000). **Selected balance of payments data.** Receipts from (US$'000,000): tourism (2001) 3.2; remittances (2005) 11; foreign direct investment (2001–05 avg.) 16; official development assistance (2005) 28. Disbursements for (US$'000,000): tourism (1999) 2.0. **Population economically active** (2005): total 36,970; activity rate of total population 40% (participation rates: ages 16 and over [1995] 84.0%; female [1995] 47.8%; unemployed 6.1%). **Gross national income** (2006): US$130,000,000

(US$1,391 per capita). **Households.** Average household size (1995) 6.5; expenditure (1996): food 45.0%, nonalcoholic beverages 10.0%, transportation 8.0%, energy 8.0%, education 8.0%. **Land use** as % of total land area (2003): in temporary crops 3%, in permanent crops 48%, in pasture, none; overall forest area (2005) 30%.

Foreign trade

Imports (2003; c.i.f.): $A 79,495,000 (food 30.6%; machinery and transport equipment 16.1%; mineral fuels 13.1%; beverages and tobacco 9.8%). *Major import sources:* Australia 47.8%; Fiji 22.1%; New Zealand 11.1%; Japan 6.0%; China 3.0%. **Exports** (2003; f.o.b.): $A 4,470,000 (domestic exports 82.2%, of which copra 47.3%, shark fins 10.5%, seaweed 8.6%, aquarium fish 7.2%, trepang 5.7%; reexports 17.8%). *Major export destinations* (2001): Japan 45.8%; Thailand 24.8%; South Korea 10.7%; Bangladesh 5.5%; Brazil 3.0%.

Transport and communications

Transport. *Roads* (1999): total length 670 km (paved [1996] 5%). *Vehicles* (2004; South Tarawa only): passenger cars 610; trucks and buses 808. *Air transport* (1998): passenger-km 11,000,000; metric ton-km cargo 2,000,000. **Communications,** in total units (units per 1,000 persons). Televisions (2003): 4,000 (44); telephone landlines (2004): 5,000 (50); cellular telephone subscribers (2004): 600 (6.7); personal computers (2004): 1,000 (11); total Internet users (2006): 2,000 (21).

Education and health

Educational attainment (2000). Percentage of population ages 5 and over having: no schooling/preprimary education 11%; incomplete primary 23%; complete primary 34%; incomplete secondary 18%; complete secondary 13%; higher 1%. **Literacy** (2001): population ages 15 and over literate 94.0%; males literate 93.0%; females literate 95.0%. **Health** (2004): physicians 20 (1 per 4,455 persons); hospital beds 140 (1 per 680 persons); infant mortality rate per 1,000 live births (2005) 48.5. **Food** (2005): daily per capita caloric intake 2,818 (vegetable products 85%, animal products 15%); 156% of FAO recommended minimum.

Military

Total active duty personnel (2006): none; defense assistance is provided by Australia and New Zealand.

Background

The islands were settled by Austronesian-speaking peoples before the 1st century AD. In 1765 the British discovered the island of Nikunau; the first permanent European settlers arrived in 1837. In 1916 the Gilbert and Ellice islands and Banaba became a crown colony of Britain; they were later joined by the Phoenix and Line islands. The Ellice Islands declared independence (as Tuvalu) in 1978, and in 1979 the remaining islands became the nation of Kiribati.

Recent Developments

Kiribati experienced economic and environmental pressure in 2007 from annual population growth rates of 2.25%, particularly on South Tarawa, where about half of the population resided. Kiribati had a well-managed Revenue Equalization Reserve Fund, which invested globally, but the fund faced declining returns as the impact of failures in the American subprime mortgage market was felt. The government hoped that a joint venture to build high-value fiberglass pleasure craft for the Australian market would be lucrative and long lasting.

Internet resources: <www.visit-kiribati.com>.

North Korea

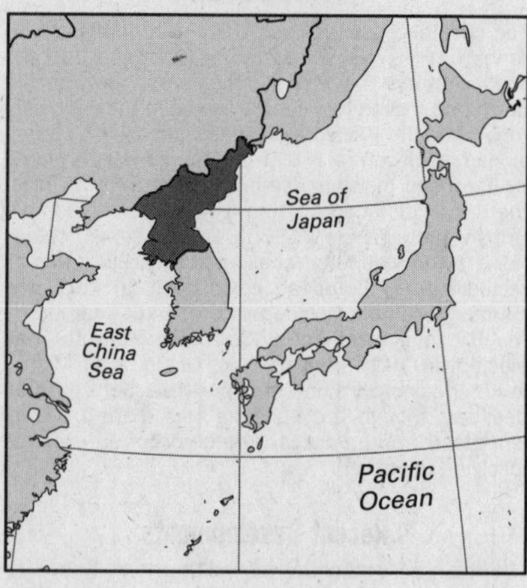

Official name: Choson Minjujuui In'min Konghwaguk (Democratic People's Republic of Korea). **Form of government:** unitary single-party republic with one legislative house (Supreme People's Assembly [687]). **Head of state and government:** Chairman of the National Defense Commission Kim Jong Il (from 1998). **Capital:** P'yongyang. **Official language:** Korean. **Official religion:** none. **Monetary unit:** 1 (North Korean) won (W) = 100 chon; valuation (1 Jul 2008) US$1 = 140.00 won.

Demography

Area: 47,399 sq mi, 122,762 sq km. **Population** (2007): 23,790,000. **Density** (2007): persons per sq mi 501.9, persons per sq km 193.8. **Urban** (2005): 61.6%. **Sex distribution** (2005): male 48.49%; female 51.51%. **Age breakdown** (2005): under 15, 24.2%; 15–29, 22.8%; 30–44, 25.5%; 45–59, 15.0%; 60–74, 10.5%; 75 and over, 2.0%. **Ethnic composition** (1999): Korean 99.8%; Chinese 0.2%. **Religious affiliation** (2005): mostly nonreligious/atheist; autonomous religious activities almost nonexistent. **Major cities** (2005): P'yongyang (urban agglomeration) 3,351,000; Namp'o (urban agglomeration) 1,102,000; Hamhung (urban agglomeration)

1 metric ton = about 1.1 short tons; 1 kilometer = 0.6 mi (statute); 1 metric ton-km cargo = about 0.68 short ton-mi cargo; c.i.f.: cost, insurance, and freight; f.o.b.: free on board

804,000; Ch'ongjin (1993) 582,480; Kaesong (1993) 334,433. **Location:** eastern Asia, bordering China, Russia, the Sea of Japan (East Sea), South Korea, and the Yellow Sea.

Vital statistics

Birth rate per 1,000 population (2005): 16.1 (world avg. 20.3). **Death rate** per 1,000 population (2005): 7.1 (world avg. 8.6). **Natural increase rate** per 1,000 population (2005): 9.0 (world avg. 11.7). **Total fertility rate** (avg. births per childbearing woman; 2005): 2.15. **Life expectancy** at birth (2005): male 68.7 years; female 74.2 years.

National economy

Budget (1999). *Revenue:* W 19,801,000,000 (turnover tax and profits from state enterprises). *Expenditures:* W 20,018,200,000 ([1994] national economy 67.8%, social and cultural affairs 19.0%, defense 11.6%). **Population economically active** (2003): total 10,708,000; activity rate of total population 48.1% (participation rates: ages 15–64, 67.4%; female 39.4%; unemployed [2000] 24.1%). **Production** (metric tons except as noted). *Agriculture, forestry, fishing* (2005): rice 2,582,000, potatoes 2,070,000, corn (maize) 2,062,000; livestock (number of live animals) 3,200,000 pigs, 2,740,000 goats, 570,000 cattle; roundwood 7,297,000 cu m, of which fuelwood 79%; fisheries production (2003) 268,700 (from aquaculture 24%). *Mining and quarrying* (2005): iron ore (metal content) 1,400,000; magnesite 1,200,000; phosphate rock 300,000. *Manufacturing* (2006): cement 6,155,000; steel semimanufactures (1994) 2,700,000; coke 2,000,000. *Energy production (consumption):* electricity (kW-hr; 2004) 21,974,000,000 (21,974,000,000); hard coal (metric tons; 2004) 22,800,000 (22,666,000); lignite (metric tons; 2004) 7,340,000 (7,340,000); crude petroleum (barrels; 2004) none (4,200,000); petroleum products (metric tons; 2004) 545,000 (1,091,000). **Households.** Average household size (1999) 4.6. **Public debt** (external, outstanding; 2000): US$12,500,000,000. **Gross national income** (2006): US$25,600,000,000 (US$1,108 per capita). **Selected balance of payments data.** Receipts from (US$'000,000): foreign direct investment (FDI) (2001–05 avg.) 90; official development assistance (2005) 62. Disbursements for (US$'000,000): FDI (2001–04 avg.) 1.0. **Land use** as % of total land area (2003): in temporary crops 22.4%, in permanent crops 1.7%, in pasture 0.4%; overall forest area (2005) 51.4%.

Foreign trade

Imports (2005): US$2,718,472,000 ([2002; excludes trade with South Korea] food, beverages, and other agricultural products 19.3%; mineral fuels and lubricants 15.5%; machinery and apparatus 15.4%; textiles and clothing 10.4%). *Major import sources:* China 39.8%; South Korea 26.3%; Russia 8.2%; Thailand 7.6%; Singapore 2.7%. **Exports** (2005): US$1,338,281,000 ([2002; excludes trade with South Korea] live animals and agricultural products 39.3%; textiles and wearing apparel 16.7%; machinery and apparatus 11.6; mineral fuels and lubricants 9.5%). *Major export destinations:* China 37.3%; South Korea 25.4%; Japan 9.8%; Thailand 9.3%; Russia 0.6%.

Transport and communications

Transport. *Railroads* (2006): length 5,235 km. *Roads* (2004): total length 25,185 km (paved 12%). *Vehicles* (1990): passenger cars 248,000. *Air transport* (2004): passenger-km (2002) 35,000,000; metric ton-km cargo 2,000,000. **Communications,** in total units (units per 1,000 persons). Televisions (2003): 3,563,000 (160); telephone landlines (2004): 980,000 (44).

Education and health

Educational attainment (1987–88). Percentage of population ages 16 and over having attended or graduated from postsecondary-level school 13.7%. **Literacy** (1997): 95%. **Health:** physicians (2003) 74,597 (1 per 299 persons); hospital beds (2002) 292,340 (1 per 76 persons); infant mortality rate per 1,000 live births (2005) 24.0. **Food** (2005): daily per capita caloric intake 2,419 (vegetable products 94%, animal products 6%); 127% of FAO recommended minimum.

Military

Total active duty personnel (2006): 1,106,000 (army 85.9%, navy 4.2%, air force 9.9%). **Military expenditure as percentage of GNI** (2004): 8.1%; per capita expenditure US$80.

Background

According to tradition, the ancient kingdom of Choson was established in the northern part of the Korean Peninsula, probably by peoples from northern China, in the 3rd millennium BC and was conquered by China in 108 BC. The kingdom was ruled by the Yi dynasty from 1392 to 1910. That year Korea was formally annexed by Japan. It was freed from Japanese control in 1945, at which time the USSR occupied the area north of latitude 38° N and the US occupied the area south of it. The Democratic People's Republic of Korea (DPRK) was established as a communist state in 1948. North Korea launched an invasion of South Korea in 1950, initiating the Korean War, which ended with an armistice in 1953. Under Kim Il-sung, North Korea became one of the most harshly regimented societies in the world, with a state-owned economy that failed to produce adequate food. In the late 1990s, under Kim Il-sung's successor, Kim Jong Il, the country endured a serious famine; as many as a million Koreans may have died.

Recent Developments

North Korea showed signs in 2007 that it might be willing to give up its nuclear programs if the price was right. The first breakthrough came in February when North Korea agreed to shut down its decrepit light-water nuclear reactor in exchange for a modest package of economic assistance. A second breakthrough came in October when the North agreed to disable the reactor and submit a list of all remaining nuclear programs by the end of the year. However, North Korean negotiators hinted that they might not reveal how many weapons the North had and also refused to admit to having a uranium-enrichment program. Furthermore, in September 2007 Israeli warplanes bombed a site deep in Syrian territory that Israel later claimed was a nuclear-weapons facility. In April 2008 US officials released video evidence that they claimed proved both the facility's illicit purpose (the Syrians had claimed that it was an unused military warehouse) and that the technology in it had come directly from North Korea, further heightening tensions. North Korea had failed to meet the 31 December deadline but appeared to comply in May 2008 after the video release.

Internet resources: <www.kcna.co.jp/index-e.htm>.

South Korea

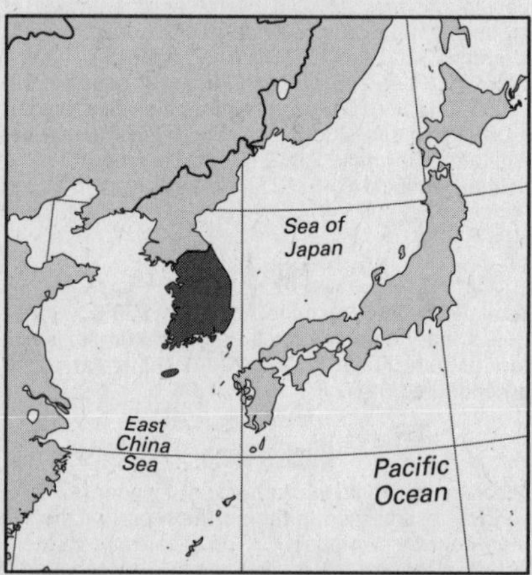

Official name: Taehan Min'guk (Republic of Korea). **Form of government:** unitary multiparty republic with one legislative house (National Assembly [299]). **Head of state and government:** President Lee Myung Bak (from 2008), assisted by Prime Minister Han Seung Soo (from 2008). **Capital:** Seoul. **Official language:** Korean. **Official religion:** none. **Monetary unit:** 1 South Korean won (W) = 100 chon; valuation (1 Jul 2008) US$1 = W 1,050.33.

Demography

Area: 38,486 sq mi, 99,678 sq km. **Population** (2007): 48,456,000. **Density** (2007): persons per sq mi 1,259.1, persons per sq km 486.1. **Urban** (2005): 81.5%. **Sex distribution** (2005): male 49.97%; female 50.03%. **Age breakdown** (2005): under 15, 18.6%; 15–29, 22.5%; 30–44, 26.0%; 45–59, 19.2%; 60–74, 10.7%; 75–84, 2.5%; 85 and over, 0.5%. **Ethnic composition** (2000): Korean 97.7%; Japanese 2.0%; US white 0.1%; Han Chinese 0.1%; other 0.1%. **Religious affiliation** (2005): Christian 43%, of which Protestant 17%, independent Christian 16%, Roman Catholic 9%; traditional beliefs 15%; Buddhist 14%; New Religionist 14%; Confucianist 10%; other 4%. **Major cities** (2005): Seoul 9,820,171; Pusan 3,523,582; Inch'on 2,531,280; Taegu 2,464,547; Taejon 1,442,856. **Location:** northeast Asia, bordering North Korea, the Sea of Japan (East Sea), and the Yellow Sea.

Vital statistics

Birth rate per 1,000 population (2005): 9.0 (world avg. 20.3). **Death rate** per 1,000 population (2005): 5.0 (world avg. 8.6). **Natural increase rate** per 1,000 population (2005): 4.0 (world avg. 11.7). **Total fertility rate** (avg. births per childbearing woman; 2006): 1.13. **Life expectancy** at birth (2005): male 75.1 years; female 81.9 years.

National economy

Budget (2005). *Revenue:* W 191,447,000,000,000 (current revenue 99.3%, of which tax revenue 79.6%, nontax revenue 19.7%; capital revenue 0.7%). *Expenditures:* W 184,922,000,000,000 (current expenditure 86.7%; capital expenditure 13.3%). **Public debt** (2005): US$240,000,000,000. **Production** (metric tons except as noted). *Agriculture, forestry, fishing* (2006): rice 6,305,000, cabbages 3,068,000, tangerines, mandarins, and satsumas 620,300, green onions 543,000, pears 431,464; livestock (number of live animals) 9,382,000 pigs, 2,484,000 cattle, 119,181,000 chickens; roundwood 4,877,000 cu m, of which fuelwood 51%; fisheries production (2005) 2,075,301 (from aquaculture 21%); aquatic plants production (2005) 636,366 (from aquaculture 98%). *Mining and quarrying* (2005): feldspar 508,644; iron ore (metal content) 131,000. *Manufacturing* (value added in US$'000,000; 2001): electrical machinery and apparatus 31,583, of which televisions, radios, telecommunications equipment, and electronic parts 25,223; transportation equipment 26,027, of which automobiles 12,660, ship and boat construction 6,050, automobile parts 5,938; chemicals and chemical products 16,296, of which paints, soaps, and pharmaceuticals 8,040, industrial chemicals 7,131; textiles, wearing apparel, and footwear 11,646, of which textiles 6,878. *Energy production (consumption):* electricity (kW-hr; 2004) 371,011,000,000 (371,011,000,000); coal (metric tons; 2004) 3,191,000 (82,116,000); crude petroleum (barrels; 2005) none ([2004] 828,000,000); petroleum products (metric tons; 2004) 90,627,000 (60,701,000); natural gas (cu m; 2004) none (29,611,000,000). **Households** (2001). Average household size (2005) 2.9; annual income per household (2006) W 32,303,000 (US$33,800); sources of income: wages 84.2%, other 15.8%; expenditure: food and beverages 26.3%, transportation and communications 16.3%, education 11.3%. **Gross national income** (at 2006 market prices): US$871,992,000,000 (US$18,147 per capita). **Population economically active** (2005): total 23,743,000; activity rate of total population 49.3% (participation rates: ages 15–64, 66.4%; female 41.5%; unemployed [July 2007] 3.2%). **Selected balance of payments data.** Receipts from (US$'000,000): tourism (2005) 5,660; remittances (2006) 917; foreign direct investment (FDI) (2001–05 avg.) 5,145. Disbursements for (US$'000,000): tourism (2005) 15,314; remittances (2006) 4,245; FDI (2001–05 avg.) 3,487. **Land use** as % of total land area (2003): in temporary crops 16.7%, in permanent crops 2.0%, in pasture 0.6%; overall forest area (2005) 63.5%.

Foreign trade

Imports (2003; c.i.f.): US$178,827,000,000 (electric and electronic products 17.5%; nonelectrical ma-

1 metric ton = about 1.1 short tons; 1 kilometer = 0.6 mi (statute); 1 metric ton-km cargo = about 0.68 short ton-mi cargo; c.i.f.: cost, insurance, and freight; f.o.b.: free on board

chinery and transport equipment 17.5%; crude petroleum 12.9%; chemicals and chemical products 9.2%; food and live animals 4.7%). *Major import sources:* Japan 20.3%; US 13.9%; China 12.3%; Saudi Arabia 5.2%; Germany 3.8%. **Exports** (2003; f.o.b.): US$193,817,000,000 (machinery and apparatus 44.7%; transport equipment 17.8%; chemicals and chemical products 9.2%; textile yarn, fabrics 5.6%). *Major export destinations:* China 18.1%; US 17.7%; Japan 8.9%; Hong Kong 7.6%; Taiwan 3.6%.

Transport and communications

Transport. *Railroads* (2005): length (2001) 6,819 km; passenger-km 31,004,200,000; metric ton-km cargo 9,336,000,000. *Roads* (2004): total length 100,279 km (paved 87%). *Vehicles* (2004): passenger cars 10,464,827; trucks and buses 4,041,527. *Air transport* (2005): passenger-km 69,276,000,000; metric ton-km cargo 7,433,000,000. **Communications,** in total units (units per 1,000 persons). Daily newspaper circulation (2000): 18,500,000 (396); televisions (2004): 22,915,000 (477); telephone landlines (2006): 26,866,000 (556); cellular telephone subscribers (2006): 40,197,000 (832); personal computers (2005): 25,685,000 (532); total Internet users (2006): 34,120,000 (706); broadband Internet subscribers (2006): 14,043,000 (291).

Education and health

Educational attainment (2002). Percentage of population ages 25–64 having: no formal schooling through lower secondary 29%; upper secondary/higher vocational 45%; university 26%. **Literacy** (2001): total population ages 15 and over literate 97.9%; males literate 99.2%; females literate 96.6%. **Health** (2005): physicians 85,369 (1 per 564 persons); hospital beds (2004) 353,289 (1 per 136 persons); infant mortality rate per 1,000 live births (2003) 7.3. **Food** (2005): daily per capita caloric intake 3,040 (vegetable products 83%, animal products 17%); 157% of FAO recommended minimum.

Military

Total active duty personnel (2006): 687,000 (army 81.5%, navy 9.2%, air force 9.3%); US military forces (2006) 29,500. **Military expenditure as percentage of GDP** (2005): 2.6%; per capita expenditure US$430.

The Unification Church is a religious movement founded in Pusan, South Korea, by the Reverend Sun Myung Moon in 1954. Known for its mass weddings, the church teaches a unique Christian theology.

Background

Civilization in the Korean Peninsula dates to the 3rd millennium BC (see background of Democratic People's Republic of Korea, above). The Republic of Korea was established in 1948 in the southern portion of the Korean peninsula. In 1950 North Korean troops invaded South Korea, precipitating the Korean War. UN forces intervened on the side of South Korea, while Chinese troops backed North Korea in the war, which ended with an armistice in 1953. The devastated country was rebuilt with US aid, and South Korea prospered in the postwar era, developing a strong export-oriented economy. It experienced an economic downturn in the mid-1990s that affected many economies in the area.

Recent Developments

South Korea was anything but the "Land of the Morning Calm" as voters went to the polls in December 2007 to elect their first CEO president, Lee Myung-bak. Despite questions concerning Lee's involvement in a financial scandal, Koreans showed a preference for pragmatism over populism by overwhelmingly voting for the former Hyundai executive and mayor of Seoul. This election focused less on anxieties over North Korea and more on economic issues such as creating jobs and making home prices more affordable. Pres. Roh Moo Hyun traveled to Pyongyang in early October to meet with his Northern counterpart, Chairman Kim Jong Il, a full seven years after the first North-South summit. Aside from a vague pledge to replace the armistice agreement with a peace treaty to formally bring the Korean War to an end, the summit did little to reduce military tensions, but it did underscore the fact that North-South economic cooperation had skyrocketed in recent years. In the Kaesong Industrial Complex in North Korea, just across the demilitarized zone, more than 20,000 North Koreans were working for South Korean companies. In August the North-South railway line was reconnected for the first time since the division of the Korean peninsula in 1945.

Internet resources: <www.korea.net>.

Kosovo

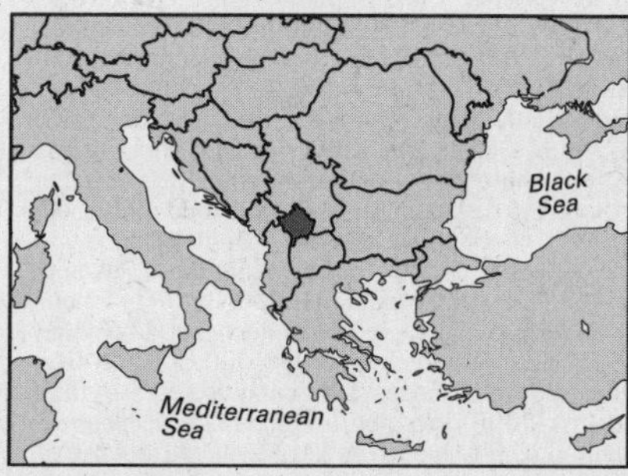

Official name: Republika e Kosovës (Albanian); Republika Kosovo (Serbian) (Republic of Kosovo). **Form of government:** multiparty transitional republic with one legislative house (Assembly of the Republic [120]). **Chief of state:** President Fatmir Sejdiu (from 2008; final authority rests with UN Interim Administrator Lamberto Zannier [from 2008]). **Head of government:** Prime Minister Hashim Thaçi (from 2008). **Capital:** Pristina. **Official languages:** Albanian; Serbian. **Official religion:** none. **Monetary unit:** 1 euro (€) = 100 cents; US$1 = €0.63 (1 Jul 2008).

Demography

Area: 4,212 sq mi, 10,908 sq km. **Population** (2008): 2,143,000. **Density** (2008): persons per sq mi 508.8, persons per sq km 196.5. **Urban** (2006): 37.0%. **Sex**

distribution (2006): male 50.90%; female 49.10%. **Age breakdown** (2003): under 15, 32.2%; 15–59, 58.7%; 60 and over 9.1%. **Ethnic composition** (2008): Albanian 92.0%; Serb 5.3%; other 2.7%. **Religious affiliation** (2006): Muslim 91.0%; Orthodox 5.5%; Roman Catholic 3.0%, Protestant 0.5%. **Major cities** (2003): Pristina 165,844; Prizren 107,614; Ferizaj 71,758; Mitrovicë 68,929; Gjakovë 68,645. **Location:** southeastern Europe, bordering Serbia, Macedonia, Albania, and Montenegro.

Vital statistics

Birth rate per 1,000 population (2006): 16.3 (world avg. 20.3); (2005) within marriage 53.1%. **Death rate** per 1,000 population (2006): 3.6 (world avg. 8.6). **Total fertility rate** (avg. births per childbearing woman; 2003): 3.00. **Life expectancy** at birth (2004; Albanian population only): male 69.8 years; female 71.4 years.

National economy

Budget (2005). *Revenue:* €758,000,000 (varied taxes on imported goods at border [including customs and VAT] 69.0%; donor assistance 16.0%; other internal revenue [mostly income tax] 9.0%). *Expenditures:* €717,000,000 (current expenditure 73.2%; development expenditure 26.8%). **Population economically active** (2006): total 680,000 (participation rates: ages 15–64, 33.0%; female 33.0%; unemployed 44.1%). **Production** (metric tons except as noted). *Agriculture, forestry, fishing* (2005): wheat 273,377, hay 186,959, corn (maize) 142,140; livestock (number of live animals) 351,800 cattle, 151,200 sheep, 2,386,000 chickens; roundwood 400,000 cu m, of which fuelwood 98%. *Manufacturing* (2006): cement, bricks, and tiles for reconstruction of housing; food; beverages. *Energy production (consumption):* electricity (kW-hr; 2006) 3,971,000,000 (2,155,000,000); lignite (metric tons; 2006) 6,530,000 (n.a.). **Gross national income** (2005): US$3,364,000,000 (US$1,640 per capita). **Households.** Average household size (2003) 6.5; sources of income (2005): wages and salaries 58.0%, remittances 13.0%, self-employment 9.0%, pensions 8.0%; expenditures (2002): food 42.5%, energy 9.5%, clothing and footwear 8.3%, transportation 8.1%. **Selected balance of payments data.** Receipts from (US$'000,000): tourism (2006) 32; remittances (2006) 586; foreign direct investment (2004–06 avg.) 488. Disbursements for (US$'000,000; 2006): tourism 78; remittances 126. **Land use** as % of total land area (2005): in temporary crops 12.9%, in permanent crops 0.5%, in pasture 11.2%; overall forest area 41.7%.

Foreign trade

Imports (2006; c.i.f.): €1,305,900,000 (food and live animals 17.5%; mineral fuels 16.6%; machinery and apparatus 12.5%; iron and steel [all forms] 7.5%; motor vehicles 5.8%). *Major import sources:* Macedonia 19.7%; Serbia 14.6%; Germany 9.4%; Turkey 7.4%; China 5.7%. **Exports** (2006; f.o.b.): €110,800,000 (iron and steel [all forms] 30.2%; other base and fabricated metals 17.8%; mineral fuels 7.7%; food and live animals 7.7%). *Major export destinations:* Serbia 18.9%; Bulgaria 12.2%; Italy 11.4%; Albania 11.4%; Macedonia 8.8%.

Transport and communications

Transport. *Railroads* (2005): route length 430 km. *Roads* (2005): total length 1,924 km (paved 87%). *Air transport* (2005; Pristina airport only): passenger arrivals 452,362, passenger departures 478,258. **Communications,** in total units (units per 1,000 persons). Telephone landlines (2006): 135,000 (65); cellular telephone subscribers (2006): 540,000 (259); total Internet users (2006): 50,000 (24); broadband Internet subscribers (2005): 4,700 (2.3).

Education and health

Educational attainment (2003). Percentage of population ages 25–49 having: no formal schooling 3.5%; incomplete/complete primary education 46.0%; incomplete/complete secondary 45.0%; higher 5.5%. **Literacy** (2000): population ages 15 and over literate 93.5%; males literate 97.7%; females literate 89.9%. **Health** (2005): physicians 2,500 (1 per 822 persons); hospital beds 5,308 (1 per 387 persons); infant mortality rate per 1,000 live births (2006) 12.0.

Military

Total active duty personnel (February 2008): NATO-led Kosovo Force 15,900.

Background

The Kingdom of the Serbs, Croats, and Slovenes was created after the collapse of Austria-Hungary at the end of World War I. The country signed treaties with Czechoslovakia and Romania in 1920–21, marking the beginning of the Little Entente. In 1929 an absolute monarchy was established, the country's name was changed to Yugoslavia, and it was divided into regions without regard to ethnic boundaries. Axis powers invaded Yugoslavia in 1941, and German, Italian, Hungarian, and Bulgarian troops occupied it for the rest of World War II. In 1945 the Socialist Federal Republic of Yugoslavia was established; it included the republics of Bosnia and Herzegovina, Croatia, Macedonia, Montenegro, Serbia, and Slovenia. Its independent form of communism under Josip Broz Tito's leadership provoked the USSR. Internal ethnic tensions flared up in the 1980s, causing the country's ultimate collapse. In 1991–92 independence was declared by Croatia, Slovenia, Macedonia, and Bosnia and Herzegovina; the new Federal Republic of Yugoslavia (containing roughly 45% of the population and 40% of the area of its predecessor) was proclaimed by Serbia and Montenegro. Still fueled by long-standing ethnic tensions, hostilities continued into the 1990s. Despite the approval of the Dayton Peace Agreement (1995), sporadic fighting continued and was followed in 1998–99 by Serbian repression and expulsion of ethnic populations in the province of Kosovo. In September–October 2000, the battered nation of Yugoslavia ended the autocratic rule of Pres. Slobodan Milosevic. In April 2001 he was arrested and in June extradited to The Hague to stand trial for war crimes, genocide, and crimes against humanity committed during the fighting in Kosovo. In February 2003 both houses of the Yugoslav federal legislature voted to accept a new state charter and change the name of the country from Yugoslavia to Serbia and Montenegro. Henceforth, defense, international political and economic relations, and human rights matters would be handled centrally, while all other functions would be run from the republican capitals, Belgrade and Podgorica, respectively. The move was seen as an acknowledgment that Serbia and Montenegro had little in common, and a provision was included for both states to vote on independence after three years; Serbia declared its independence in June 2006, shortly after Montenegro severed its federal union with Serbia. From 1999 an autonomous region administrered by the UN, Kosovo declared its independence from Serbia on 17 Feb 2008.

Recent Developments

The independence declaration was obviously the major news of 2008 in Kosovo. The country was immediately recognized by the US, Turkey, and most of the members of the EU, including the UK, France, and Germany. However, in addition to Serbia, the list of countries that refused to recognize Kosovo included Russia, China, Spain, Greece, and Cyprus. Kosovo's economic and social situation was mixed in 2007. The Central Banking Authority of Kosovo reported that GDP grew 4.6% and that there was a budget surplus, while inflation rose only 2.0%. According to the World Bank, however, 37% of Kosovo's population were considered poor, and 15% lived in extreme poverty. A UN report showed that 57% of those living in extreme poverty were under the age of 25, and unemployment for those under 25 was 40%.

Internet resources:
<www.visitkosova.org/english/index.htm>.

Kuwait

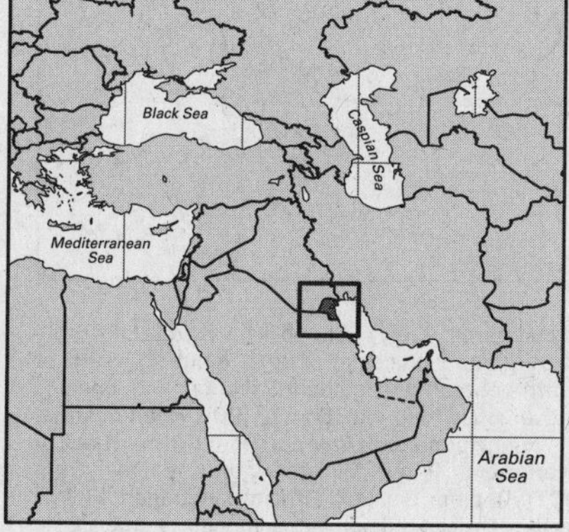

Official name: Dawlat al-Kuwayt (State of Kuwait). **Form of government:** constitutional monarchy with one legislative body (National Assembly [50]). **Head of state and government:** Emir Sheikh Sabah al-Ahmad al-Jabir al-Sabah (from 2006), assisted by Prime Minister Sheikh Nassar Muhammad al-Ahmad al-Sabah (from 2006). **Capital:** Kuwait (city). **Official language:** Arabic. **Official religion:** Islam. **Monetary unit:** 1 Kuwaiti dinar (KD) = 1,000 fils; valuation (1 Jul 2008) US$1 = KD 0.26.

Demography

Area: 6,880 sq mi, 17,818 sq km. **Population** (2007): 3,294,000. **Density** (2007): persons per sq mi 478.8, persons per sq km 184.9. **Urban** (2005): 98.3%. **Sex distribution** (2005): male 62.69%; female 37.31%. **Age breakdown** (2005): under 15, 24.3%; 15–29, 26.8%; 30–44, 34.2%; 45–59, 11.6%; 60–74, 2.7%; 75–84, 0.3%; 85 and over, 0.1%. **Ethnic composition** (2005): Arab 57%, of which Kuwaiti 35%; Bedouin 4%; non-Arab (primarily Asian) 39%. **Religious affiliation** (2005): Muslim 74%, of which Sunni 59%, Shiʿi 15%; Christian 13%, of which Roman Catholic 9%; Hindu 10%; Buddhist 3%. **Major cities** (2005): Qalib al-Shuyukh 179,264; Al-Salimiyah 145,328; Hawalli 106,992; Kuwait (city) 32,403 (urban agglomeration 1,810,000). **Location:** the Middle East, bordering Iraq, the Persian Gulf, and Saudi Arabia.

Vital statistics

Birth rate per 1,000 population (2005): 20.7 (world avg. 20.3). **Death rate** per 1,000 population (2005): 1.9 (world avg. 8.6). **Total fertility rate** (avg. births per childbearing woman; 2004): 3.00. **Life expectancy** at birth (2004): male 75.9 years; female 77.9 years.

National economy

Budget (2004–05). *Revenue:* KD 12,346,700,000 (oil revenue 93.8%). *Expenditures:* KD 6,315,200,000 (defense 20.9%; transfers 18.5%; public utilities 14.0%; education 8.0%). **Public debt** (external, outstanding; 2004): US$668,000,000. **Gross national income** (2006): US$111,464,000,000 (US$40,114 per capita). **Production** (metric tons except as noted). *Agriculture, forestry, fishing* (2005): tomatoes 55,750, cucumbers and gherkins 37,260, potatoes 20,740; livestock (number of live animals) 900,000 sheep, 150,000 goats, 5,000 camels; fisheries production 5,222 (from aquaculture 6%). *Mining and quarrying* (2005): sulfur 700,000; lime 49,800. *Manufacturing* (value added in US$'000,000; 2004): refined petroleum products 2,701; chemicals and chemical products 533; fabricated metal products 319. *Energy production (consumption):* electricity (kW-hr; 2004) 41,256,000,000 (41,256,000,000); crude petroleum (barrels; 2006) 927,100,000 ([2004] 320,700,000); petroleum products (metric tons; 2004) 35,425,000 (12,683,000); natural gas (cu m; 2004) 9,700,000,000 (9,700,000,000). **Population economically active** (2004): total 1,634,315, of which Kuwaiti 18.3%, non-Kuwaiti 81.7%; activity rate of total population 59.4% (participation rates: ages 15 and over 76.4%; female [2002] 25.7%; unemployed 2.2%). **Households.** Average Kuwaiti household size (2004) 4.8; average non-Kuwaiti household size (2004) 5.0; sources of income (1986): wages and salaries 53.8%, self-employment 20.8%, other 25.4%; expenditure (2000): housing and energy 26.8%, food 18.3%, transportation and communications 16.1%, household furnishings 14.7%, clothing and footwear 8.9%. **Selected balance of payments data.** Receipts from (US$'000,000): tourism (2005) 165; foreign direct investment (FDI) (2001–05 avg.) 20. Disbursements for (US$'000,000): tourism (2005) 4,277; remittances (2006) 2,648; FDI (2001–05 avg.) 57. **Land use** as % of total land area (2003): in temporary crops 0.8%, in permanent crops 0.2%, in pasture 7.6%; overall forest area (2005) 0.3%.

Foreign trade

Imports (2004; c.i.f.): KD 3,722,234,000 (transport equipment 23.1%; machinery and apparatus 16.9%; food 12.4%; chemicals and chemical products 8.7%). *Major import sources:* Germany 11.5%; US 10.8%; Saudi Arabia 7.9%; China 6.8%; Japan 6.4%. **Exports** (2004; f.o.b.): KD 8,428,100,000 (crude petroleum and petroleum products 93.3%; chemicals and chemical products 3.8%; reexports 1.7%). *Major export destinations:* Japan 20.0%; South Korea 14.0%; US 12.0%; Singapore 11.0%; Taiwan 10.0%.

Transport and communications

Transport. *Roads* (2004): total length 5,720 km (paved [1999] 81%). *Vehicles* (2004): passenger cars 848,590; trucks and buses 172,219. *Air transport* (2003–04): passenger-km 6,681,000,000; metric ton-km cargo 223,514,000. **Communications,** in total units (units per 1,000 persons). Daily newspaper circulation (2005): 482,000 (168); televisions (2004): 1,040,000 (392); telephone landlines (2005): 510,000 (190); cellular telephone subscribers (2005): 2,380,000 (886); personal computers (2005): 600,000 (223); total Internet users (2006): 817,000 (295); broadband Internet subscribers (2005): 25,000 (8.1).

Education and health

Educational attainment (2005). Percentage of population ages 10 and over having: no formal schooling: illiterate 6.2%, literate 37.9%; primary education 12.7%; lower secondary 20.8%; upper secondary 11.7%; higher 10.7%. **Literacy** (2005): total population ages 15 and over literate 84.4%; males literate 85.7%; females literate 82.8%. **Health** (2003): physicians 4,718 (1 per 526 persons); hospital beds 5,215 (1 per 476 persons); infant mortality rate per 1,000 live births (2005) 8.2. **Food** (2005): daily per capita caloric intake 3,420 (vegetable products 81%, animal products 19%); 172% of FAO recommended minimum.

Military

Total active duty personnel (2006): 15,500 (army 71.0%, navy 12.9%, air force 16.1%); US troops for Iraqi support (2007) 10,000–20,000. **Military expenditure as percentage of GDP** (2005): 4.8%; per capita expenditure US$1,370.

Background

Faylakah Island, in Kuwait Bay, had a civilization dating back to the 3rd millennium BC that flourished until 1200 BC. Greek colonists resettled the island in the 4th century BC. Abd Rahim of the Sabah dynasty became sheikh in 1756, the first of a family that continues to rule Kuwait. In 1899, to thwart German and Ottoman influences, Kuwait gave Britain control of its foreign affairs. Following the outbreak of war in 1914, Britain established a protectorate there. In 1961, after Kuwait became independent, Iraq laid claim to it. British troops defended Kuwait, the Arab League recognized its independence, and Iraq dropped its claim. Iraqi forces invaded and occupied Kuwait in 1990, and a US-led military coalition drove them out in 1991. The destruction of many of Kuwait's oil wells complicated reconstruction efforts.

Recent Developments

The year 2007 was marked by tensions in the Kuwaiti government. Having increased in importance after playing a pivotal role in January 2006 in removing the ailing emir and replacing him with Emir Sabah al-Ahmad al-Jabir al-Sabah, the parliament attempted to play a greater role in government and function as an elected body. There were even unsuccessful calls for a constitutional monarchy. Kuwaiti social and economic concerns were focused on revision of the educational system; improved health, water, and electricity services; and implementation of long-term planning in the fields of housing and employment. The government began a campaign to encourage Kuwaitis to work in the private sector—in 2008, foreign workers made up an estimated 97% of the total private-sector labor force. Planning continued for the construction of a new US$19 billion oil refinery, the largest of its kind in the Middle East.

Internet resources: <www.cbk.gov.kw>.

Kyrgyzstan

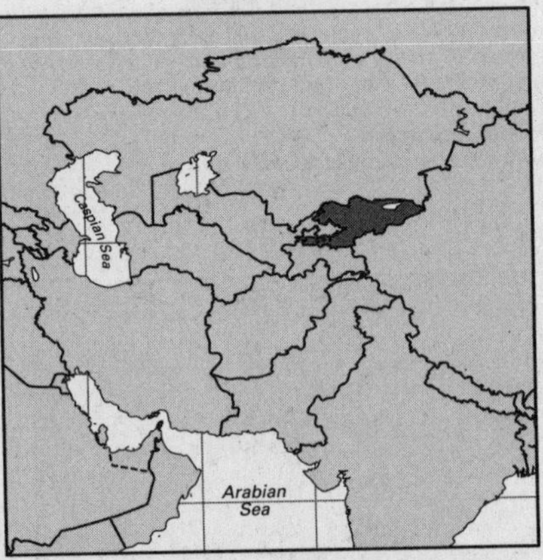

Official name: Kyrgyz Respublikasy (Kyrgyz); Respublika Kirgizstan (Russian) (Kyrgyz Republic). **Form of government:** unitary multiparty republic with one legislative house (Supreme Council [90]). **Head of state:** President Kurmanbek Bakiyev (from 2005). **Head of government:** Prime Minister Igor Chudinov (from 2007). **Capital:** Bishkek. **Official languages:** Kyrgyz; Russian. **Official religion:** none. **Monetary unit:** 1 som (KGS) = 100 tyiyn; valuation (1 Jul 2008) US$1 = KGS 36.43.

Demography

Area: 76,641 sq mi, 198,500 sq km. **Population** (2007): 5,317,000. **Density** (2007): persons per sq mi 69.4, persons per sq km 26.8. **Urban** (2003):

1 metric ton = about 1.1 short tons; 1 kilometer = 0.6 mi (statute); 1 metric ton-km cargo = about 0.68 short ton-mi cargo; c.i.f.: cost, insurance, and freight; f.o.b.: free on board

33.9%. **Sex distribution** (2005): male 49.03%; female 50.97%. **Age breakdown** (2005): under 15, 31.5%; 15–29, 29.8%; 30–44, 18.8%; 45–59, 12.0%; 60–74, 5.7%; 75–84, 1.9%; 85 and over, 0.3%. **Ethnic composition** (2005): Kyrgyz 67.4%; Uzbek 14.2%; Russian 10.3%; Hui 1.1%; Uighur 1.0%; other 6.0%. **Religious affiliation** (2000): Muslim (mostly Sunni) 60.8%; Christian 10.4%, of which Russian Orthodox 7.7%; nonreligious 21.6%; atheist 6.3%; other 0.9%. **Major cities** (1999): Bishkek 750,327; Osh 208,520; Jalal-Abad 70,401; Tokmok 59,409; Kara-Kol 47,159. **Location:** central Asia, bordering Kazakhstan, China, Tajikistan, and Uzbekistan.

Vital statistics

Birth rate per 1,000 population (2006): 23.3 (world avg. 20.3); (1994) within marriage 83.2%. **Death rate** per 1,000 population (2006): 7.4 (world avg. 8.6). **Total fertility rate** (avg. births per childbearing woman; 2005): 2.69. **Life expectancy** at birth (2006): male 63.5 years; female 72.1 years.

National economy

Budget (2005). *Revenue:* KGS 20,368,100,000 (tax revenue 80.3%, of which VAT 34.8%, income tax 8.6%, profit tax 6.3%; nontax revenue 17.7%; grants 2.0%). *Expenditures:* KGS 20,143,700,000 (administration, defense, and police 30.5%; education 24.4%; social security 14.2%; health 11.3%). **Public debt** (external, outstanding; 2005): US$1,670,-000,000. **Population economically active** (2005): total 2,260,600; activity rate of total population 43.4% (participation rates: ages 15–64 [2002] 68.7%; female 42.9%; unemployed 8.1%). **Production** (metric tons except as noted). *Agriculture, forestry, fishing* (2005): potatoes 1,141,000, wheat 950,100, corn (maize) 437,300; livestock (number of live animals) 2,965,220 sheep, 1,034,890 cattle, 347,178 horses; roundwood (2005) 27,300 cu m, of which fuelwood 66%; fisheries production 27 (from aquaculture 74%). *Mining and quarrying* (2004): mercury 488; antimony 20; gold 22,000 kg. *Manufacturing* (value of production in KGS '000,000; 2004): base and fabricated metal products 24,330; food and tobacco products 6,811; cement, bricks, and ceramics 3,574. *Energy production (consumption):* electricity (kW-hr; 2004) 15,145,000,000 (11,817,000,000); hard coal (metric tons; 2004) 64,000 (961,000); lignite (metric tons; 2004) 397,000 (475,000); crude petroleum (barrels; 2004) 542,000 (667,000); petroleum products (metric tons; 2004) 88,000 (541,000); natural gas (cu m; 2004) 29,000,000 (798,000,000). **Households.** Average household size (2004) 4.3; income per capita of household (2003) KGS 9,270 (US$212); sources of income (1999): wages and salaries 29.2%, self-employment 25.6%, other 45.2%; expenditure (1990): food and clothing 48.0%, health care 13.1%, housing 5.9%. **Gross national income** (2006): US$2,712,000,000 (US$516 per capita). **Selected balance of payments data.** Receipts from (US$'000,000): tourism (2005) 73; remittances (2005) 322; foreign direct investment (2001–05 avg.) 56; official development assistance (2005) 193 (commitments). Disbursements for (US$'000,000): tourism (2005) 58; remittances (2005) 122. **Land use** as % of total land area (2003): in temporary crops 7.0%, in permanent crops 0.3%, in pasture 49.2%; overall forest area (2005) 4.5%.

Foreign trade

Imports (2003; c.i.f.): US$717,000,000 (mineral fuels 25.3%, of which refined petroleum 17.3%; chemicals and chemical products 14.2%; machinery and apparatus 12.9%; food products 7.9%). *Major import sources* (2006): Russia 38.0%; China 14.4%; Kazakhstan 11.6%; US 5.7%; Uzbekistan 3.8%. **Exports** (2003; f.o.b.): US$581,700,000 (gold 44.6%; refined petroleum 8.2%; raw cotton 7.3%; food 6.4%). *Major export destinations* (2006): Switzerland 26.2%; Kazakhstan 20.5%; Russia 19.4%; Afghanistan 9.4%; China 4.8%.

Transport and communications

Transport. *Railroads* (2004): length (2000) 424 km; passenger-km 45,300,000; metric ton-km cargo 714,900,000. *Roads* (1999): total length 18,500 km (paved 91%). *Vehicles* (2004): passenger cars 196,339. *Air transport* (2005; Kyrghyzstan Airlines, Altyn Air Airlines, and Itek Air only): passenger-km 368,080,000; metric ton-km cargo 2,014,000. **Communications,** in total units (units per 1,000 persons). Daily newspaper circulation (2005): 68,000 (13); televisions (2004): 955,000 (185); telephone landlines (2005): 440,000 (84); cellular telephone subscribers (2005): 541,000 (103); personal computers (2005): 100,000 (19); total Internet users (2006): 298,000 (56); broadband Internet subscribers (2005): 2,500 (0.5).

Education and health

Educational attainment (1999). Percentage of population ages 15 and over having: primary education 6.3%; some secondary 18.3%; completed secondary 50.0%; some postsecondary 14.9%; higher 10.5%. **Literacy** (2003): total population ages 15 and over literate 98.7%; males literate 99.3%; females literate 98.1%. **Health:** physicians (2004) 13,996 (1 per 363 persons); hospital beds (2004) 26,040 (1 per 195 persons); infant mortality rate per 1,000 live births (2006) 29.2. **Food** (2005): daily per capita caloric intake 3,027 (vegetable products 81%, animal products 19%); 157% of FAO recommended minimum.

Military

Total active duty personnel (2006): 12,500 (army 68.0%, air force 32.0%); US troops (2006) 1,600; Russian troops (2006) 1,000. **Military expenditure as percentage of GDP** (2005): 3.1%; per capita expenditure US$15.

Background

The Kyrgyz, a nomadic people of Central Asia, settled in the Tian Shan region in ancient times. They were conquered by Genghis Khan's son Jochi in 1207. The area became part of the Qing empire of China in the mid-18th century. The region came under Russian control in the 19th century, and its rebellion against Russia in 1916 resulted in a long period of brutal repression. Kirgiziya became an autonomous province of the USSR in 1924 and was made the Kirghiz Soviet Socialist Republic in 1936. Kyrgyzstan gained independence in 1991. In the 1990s it struggled with its democratization process and with establishing a thriving economy.

Recent Developments

The political situation in Kyrgyzstan continued to worsen in 2007, and there was general agreement that the 2005 "Tulip Revolution" had been a failure. Frequent demonstrations called for Pres. Kurmanbek Bakiyev's resignation, usually on grounds of corruption and favoritism. Another reason for disenchantment was continuing economic stagnation, and increasing numbers of Kyrgyz citizens were forced to find work abroad. In January Bakiyev signed constitutional amendments that expanded the powers of the president. In September the Constitutional Court declared the amendments unconstitutional on the grounds that they had not been confirmed by popular referendum. Official results of the October referendum showed 80% of voters approved the new amendments, but observers from NGOs reported numerous cases of ballot-box stuffing.

Internet resources:
<www.stat.kg/English/index.html>.

Laos

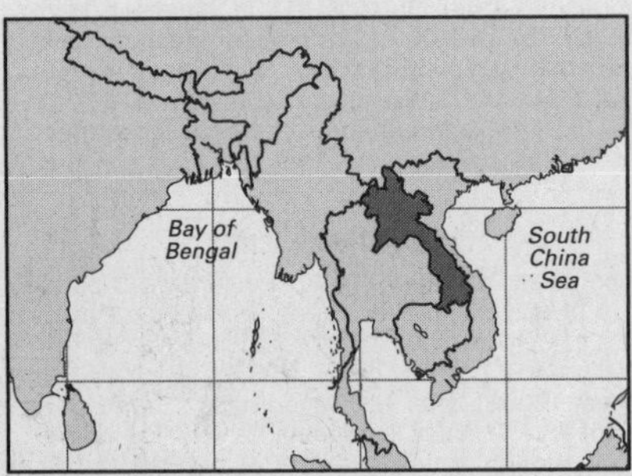

Official name: Sathalanalat Paxathipatai Paxaxon Lao (Lao People's Democratic Republic). **Form of government:** unitary single-party people's republic with one legislative house (National Assembly [115]). **Chief of state:** President Choummaly Sayasone (from 2006). **Head of government:** Prime Minister Bouasone Bouphavanh (from 2006). **Capital:** Vientiane (Viangchan). **Official language:** Lao. **Official religion:** none. **Monetary unit:** 1 kip (KN) = 100 at; valuation (1 Jul 2008) US$1 = KN 8,675.00.

Demography

Area: 91,429 sq mi, 236,800 sq km. **Population** (2007): 5,859,000. **Density** (2007): persons per sq mi 64.1, persons per sq km 24.7. **Urban** (2005): 27.1%. **Sex distribution** (2005): male 49.81%; female 50.19%. **Age breakdown** (2005): under 15, 39.4%; 15–29, 28.3%; 30–44, 17.0%; 45–59, 9.5%; 60–74, 4.4%; 75 and over, 1.4%. **Ethnic composition** (2005): Lao 54.6%; Khmou 10.9%; Hmong 8.0%; Tai 3.8%; Phu Tai (Phouthay) 3.3%; Lue 2.2%; Katang 2.1%; Makong 2.1%; other 13.0%. **Religious affiliation** (2005): traditional beliefs 49%; Buddhist 43%; Christian 2%; nonreligious/other 6%. **Major cities** (2003): Vientiane 194,200 (urban agglomeration [2005] 702,000); Savannakhet 58,200; Pakxe 50,100; Xam Nua 40,700; Muang Khammouan 27,300. **Location:** southeastern Asia, bordering China, Vietnam, Cambodia, Thailand, and Myanmar (Burma).

Vital statistics

Birth rate per 1,000 population (2005): 34.7 (world avg. 20.3). **Death rate** per 1,000 population (2005): 9.8 (world avg. 8.6). **Natural increase rate** per 1,000 population (2005): 24.9 (world avg. 11.7). **Total fertility rate** (avg. births per childbearing woman; 2005): 4.77. **Life expectancy** at birth (2005): male 53.1 years; female 57.2 years.

National economy

Budget (2003–04). *Revenue:* KN 3,282,000,000,000 (tax revenue 72.5%, of which sales tax 18.9%, excise tax 13.6%; grants 14.2%; nontax revenue 13.3%). *Expenditures:* KN 4,261,000,000,000 (capital expenditure 51.1%, of which foreign-financed 34.2%; current expenditure 48.9%). **Public debt** (external, outstanding; 2005): US$1,971,000,000. **Population economically active** (2005): total 2,778,000; activity rate of total population 66.6% (participation rates: ages 15–64, 81.3%; female 50.2%; unofficially unemployed [2004] 7.0%). **Production** (metric tons except as noted). *Agriculture, forestry, fishing* (2005): rice 2,350,000, sweet potatoes 248,000, sugarcane 230,000, ramie 1,800; livestock (number of live animals) 1,827,000 pigs, 1,272,000 cattle, 1,097,000 water buffalo; roundwood 6,335,968 cu m, of which fuelwood 94%; fisheries production 107,800 (from aquaculture 72%). *Mining and quarrying* (2005): limestone 560,000; gypsum 250,000; refined copper 30,480. *Manufacturing* (value added in US$'000,000; 1999): food and food products 22; wearing apparel 14; tobacco products 8. *Energy production (consumption):* electricity (kW-hr; 2005) 3,430,000,000 ([2004] 762,000,000); hard coal (metric tons; 2004) 290,000 (290,000); petroleum products (metric tons; 2004) none (126,000). **Gross national income** (2006): US$3,270,000,000 (US$568 per capita). **Households.** Average household size (2005) 5.9; average annual income per household (1995) KN 3,710 (US$371); expenditure (1990): food and nonalcoholic beverages 46.2%, transportation and communications 17.9%, household furnishings 8.1%, alcoholic beverages and tobacco 6.4%. **Selected balance of payments data.** Receipts from (US$'000,000): tourism (2005) 146; remittances (2005) 1.0; foreign direct investment (FDI; 2001–05 avg.) 23; official development assistance (2005) 296. Disbursements for (US$'000,000): tourism (2001) 0.1; remittances (2005) 1.0. **Land use** as % of total land area (2003): in temporary crops 4.2%, in permanent crops 0.4%, in pasture 3.8%; overall forest area (2005) 69.9%.

Foreign trade

Imports (2004; c.i.f.): US$505,900,000 ([2003] consumption goods 49.2%; construction and electrical equipment 12.0%; materials for garment assembly 10.6%; machinery and apparatus 10.2%; mineral fuels 10.2%). *Major import sources:* Thailand 60%; China 9%; Vietnam 9%; Singapore 4%; Germany 3%. **Exports** (2004; f.o.b.): US$361,100,000 (garments

1 metric ton = about 1.1 short tons; 1 kilometer = 0.6 mi (statute); 1 metric ton-km cargo = about 0.68 short ton-mi cargo; c.i.f.: cost, insurance, and freight; f.o.b.: free on board

26.9%; electricity 26.9%; wood products [mostly logs and timber] 18.6%). *Major export destinations:* Thailand 19.0%; Vietnam 17.0%; France 8.0%; Germany 6.0%; UK 5.0%.

Transport and communications

Transport. *Roads* (2004): total length 24,000 km (paved 16%). *Vehicles* (1996): passenger cars 16,320; trucks and buses 4,200. *Air transport* (2004): passenger-km 216,300,000; metric ton-km cargo 2,000,000. **Communications,** in total units (units per 1,000 persons). Daily newspaper circulation (2005): 33,000 (5.8); televisions (2003): 321,000 (59); telephone landlines (2005): 75,000 (13); cellular telephone subscribers (2005): 638,000 (108); personal computers (2005): 100,000 (17); total Internet users (2005): 26,000 (4.6); broadband Internet subscribers (2005): 200 (0.03).

Education and health

Educational attainment (2005). Percentage of population ages 25 and over having: no formal schooling 32.8%; incomplete primary education 21.6%; complete primary 18.2%; lower secondary 11.4%; upper secondary 6.2%; higher 9.8%. **Literacy** (2005): total population ages 15 and over literate 72.7%; males literate 82.5%; females literate 63.2%. **Health** (2005): physicians 5,000 (1 per 1,129 persons); hospital beds 6,736 (1 per 838 persons); infant mortality rate per 1,000 live births 85.2.

Military

Total active duty personnel (2006): 29,100 (army 88.0%, air force 12.0%). **Military expenditure as percentage of GDP** (2004): 0.4%; per capita expenditure US$2.

Background

The Lao people migrated into Laos from southern China after the 8th century AD, displacing indigenous tribes. In the 14th century Fa Ngum founded the first Laotian state, Lan Xang. Except for a period of rule by Burma (1574–1637), the Lan Xang kingdom ruled Laos until 1713, when it split into three kingdoms. France gained control of the region in 1893. In 1945 Japan seized it and declared Laos independent. The area reverted to French rule after World War II. The Geneva Conference of 1954 unified and granted independence to Laos. Communist forces took control in 1975, establishing the Lao People's Democratic Republic. Laos held its first election in 1989 and promulgated a new constitution in 1991. Although its economy was adversely affected by the mid-1990s Asian monetary crises, it realized a longtime goal in 1997 when it joined the Association of Southeast Asian Nations.

Recent Developments

The economy of Laos continued to grow steadily in 2007, with a growth rate of about 6.8%. This expansion was driven to a large extent by foreign direct investment, particularly in the natural resource and industry sectors through the ongoing construction of a number of large hydropower dams (Nam Theun 2, Nam Ngum 2, and Se Kaman 3) and the development of mining activities. Without these large hydropower and mining projects, Laos's GDP growth rate would have averaged nearly 2 points lower between 2003 and 2006. The continued rapid growth of the mining industry was expected; in its five-year plan (2006–11), the Ministry of Trade and Handicrafts envisioned annual growth of nearly 11.5% in mineral production. The negative social and environmental impacts of these projects remained concerning, however.

Internet resources: <www.visit-laos.com>.

Latvia

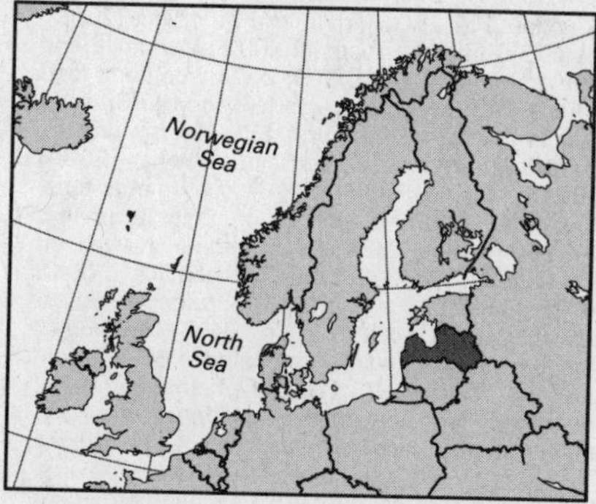

Official name: Latvijas Republika (Republic of Latvia). **Form of government:** unitary multiparty republic with a single legislative body (Parliament, or Saeima [100]). **Chief of state:** President Valdis Zatlers (from 2007). **Head of government:** Prime Minister Ivars Godmanis (from 2007). **Capital:** Riga. **Official language:** Latvian. **Official religion:** none. **Monetary unit:** 1 lats (Ls; plural lati) = 100 santimi; valuation (1 Jul 2008) US$1 = 0.45 Ls.

Demography

Area: 24,938 sq mi, 64,589 sq km. **Population** (2007): 2,274,000. **Density** (2007): persons per sq mi 91.2, persons per sq km 35.2. **Urban** (2004): 68.0%. **Sex distribution** (2004): male 46.08%; female 53.92%. **Age breakdown** (2004): under 15, 14.8%; 15–29, 22.5%; 30–44, 21.2%; 45–59, 19.3%; 60–74, 15.6%; 75–84, 5.5%; 85 and over, 1.1%. **Ethnic composition** (2004): Latvian 58.8%; Russian 28.6%; Belarusian 3.8%; Ukrainian 2.6%; Polish 2.5%; Lithuanian 1.4%; other 2.3%. **Religious affiliation** (2005): Orthodox 29%, of which Russian 16%, Latvian 13%; Roman Catholic 19%; Lutheran 14%; nonreligious 26%; atheist/other 12%. **Major cities** (2006): Riga 722,485; Daugavpils 108,091; Liepaja 85,477; Jelgava 66,051; Jurmala 55,408. **Location:** eastern Europe, bordering Estonia, Russia, Belarus, Lithuania, and the Baltic Sea.

Vital statistics

Birth rate per 1,000 population (2006): 9.7 (world avg. 20.3); within marriage 56.6%. **Death rate** per 1,000 population (2006): 14.5 (world avg. 8.6). **Natural increase rate** per 1,000 population (2006): −4.8 (world avg. 11.7). **Total fertility rate** (avg. births per childbearing woman; 2005): 1.29. **Life expectancy** at birth (2006): male 65.9 years; female 76.8 years.

National economy

Budget (2004). *Revenue:* Ls 2,522,202,000 (social security contributions 25.4%; VAT 19.3%; nontax revenue 19.0%; income taxes 17.3%; excises 9.4%). *Expenditures:* Ls 2,600,612,000 (social security and welfare 28.1%; education 16.5%; health 9.4%; police 6.3%). **Public debt** (external, outstanding; March 2007): US$1,224,000,000. **Production** (metric tons except as noted). *Agriculture, forestry, fishing* (2005): wheat 676,500, potatoes 658,200, sugar beets 519,900; livestock (number of live animals) 435,700 pigs, 371,100 cattle; roundwood 12,842,600 cu m, of which fuelwood 7%; fisheries production 151,160. *Mining and quarrying* (2005): peat 675,866; limestone 420,000. *Manufacturing* (value added in US$'000,000; 2004): food and food products 245; sawed and planed wood 206; wood products (excluding furniture) 130. *Energy production (consumption):* electricity (kW-hr; 2004) 4,680,000,000 (6,786,000,000); coal (metric tons; 2004) none (98,000); petroleum products (metric tons; 2004) none (1,240,000); natural gas (cu m; 2004) none (1,663,000,000). **Households** (2004). Average household size (2006) 2.5; annual disposable income per household Ls 3,037 (US$5,624); sources of income: wages and salaries 64.7%, pensions and transfers 25.1%, self-employment 9.4%; expenditure: food, beverages, and tobacco 34.1%, transportation and communications 18.5%, housing and energy 12.6%. **Land use** as % of total land area (2003): in temporary crops 15.4%, in permanent crops 0.2%, in pasture 9.8%; overall forest area (2005) 47.4%. **Gross national income** (2006): US$19,531,000,000 (US$8,532 per capita). **Population economically active** (2005): total 1,135,000; activity rate of total population 49.2% (participation rates: ages 15–64, 69.5%; female 48.3%; unemployed [October 2006–June 2007] 6.7%). **Selected balance of payments data.** Receipts from (US$'000,000): tourism (2005) 341; remittances (2006) 481; foreign direct investment (FDI) (2001–05 avg.) 402. Disbursements for (US$'000,000): tourism (2005) 584; remittances (2006) 30; FDI (2001–05 avg.) 59.

Foreign trade

Imports (2005; c.i.f.): Ls 4,834,713,000 (machinery and apparatus 19.7%; mineral fuels 15.6%; food and food products 11.7%; transport vehicles 10.8%; base and fabricated metals 9.2%; chemicals and chemical products 8.3%). *Major import sources:* Germany 13.8%; Lithuania 13.7%; Russia 8.6%; Estonia 7.9%; Poland 6.3%. **Exports** (2005; f.o.b.): Ls 2,871,401,000 (wood and wood products [mostly sawn wood] 26.9%; base and fabricated metals [mostly iron and steel] 13.2%; food and food products 12.2%; textiles and clothing 9.0%). *Major export destinations:* Lithuania 10.8%; Estonia 10.8%; Germany 10.3%; UK 10.1%; Russia 8.0%.

Transport and communications

Transport. *Railroads* (2005): length (2005) 2,270 km; passenger-km 892,000,000; metric ton-km cargo 19,779,000,000. *Roads* (2005): total length 51,759 km (paved 39%). *Vehicles* (2005): passenger cars 742,447; trucks and buses 123,757. *Air transport* (2005): passenger-km 1,478,000,000; metric ton-km cargo 31,000,000. **Communications,** in total units (units per 1,000 persons). Daily newspaper circulation (2005): 228,000 (99); televisions (2003): 1,992,000 (857); telephone landlines (2006): 657,000 (287); cellular telephone subscribers (2006): 2,184,000 (955); personal computers (2005): 566,000 (245); total Internet users (2006): 1,071,000 (468); broadband Internet subscribers (2006): 110,000 (48).

Education and health

Educational attainment (2004; employed population only). Percentage of population ages 15–74 having: none/unknown through complete primary education 12.3%; secondary 25.0%; vocational 40.0%; higher 22.7%. **Literacy** (2003): total population ages 15 and over literate, virtually 100%. **Health** (2006): physicians 8,341 (1 per 273 persons); hospital beds 20,728 (1 per 110 persons); infant mortality rate per 1,000 live births 7.6. **Food** (2005): daily per capita caloric intake 2,875 (vegetable products 72%, animal products 28%); 147% of FAO recommended minimum.

Military

Total active duty personnel (2006): 5,238 (army 34.7%, navy 13.1%, air force 4.9%, headquarters/administrative 47.3%). **Military expenditure as percentage of GDP** (2005): 1.7%; per capita expenditure US$119.

Background

Latvia was settled by the Balts in ancient times. It was conquered by the Vikings in the 9th century and later dominated by its German-speaking neighbors, who Christianized the people in the 12th–13th centuries. By 1230 German rule was established. From the mid-16th to the early 18th century, the region was split between Poland and Sweden, but by the end of the 18th century all of Latvia had been annexed by Russia. Latvia declared its independence after the Russian Revolution of 1917, but in 1940 the Soviet Red Army invaded. Held by Nazi Germany in 1941–44, the country was recaptured by the Soviets and incorporated into the Soviet Union. Latvia gained its independence in 1991 with the breakup of the Soviet Union; throughout the 1990s it sought to privatize the economy and build ties with Western Europe.

Recent Developments

Latvia's foreign relations in 2007 developed along anticipated lines. The EU extended the Schengen passport-free travel zone to Latvia, and Canada permitted Latvians visa-free travel. Given the unpopularity of the war in Iraq, in late June the Latvian unit returned home, but 260 peacekeepers were later sent to join the 100 already in Afghanistan. Agreement was reached in March on a border treaty with Russia, though it remained controversial in Latvia because it affirmed the borders imposed by the Soviet regime and accepted the seizure of Latvian border counties by the USSR. Domestically, Latvia experienced an

1 metric ton = about 1.1 short tons; 1 kilometer = 0.6 mi (statute); 1 metric ton-km cargo = about 0.68 short ton-mi cargo; c.i.f.: cost, insurance, and freight; f.o.b.: free on board

overheated economy. Though gross domestic product grew by an estimated 25%, the growth was offset somewhat by 13% inflation.

Internet resources: <www.latviatourism.lv>.

Lebanon

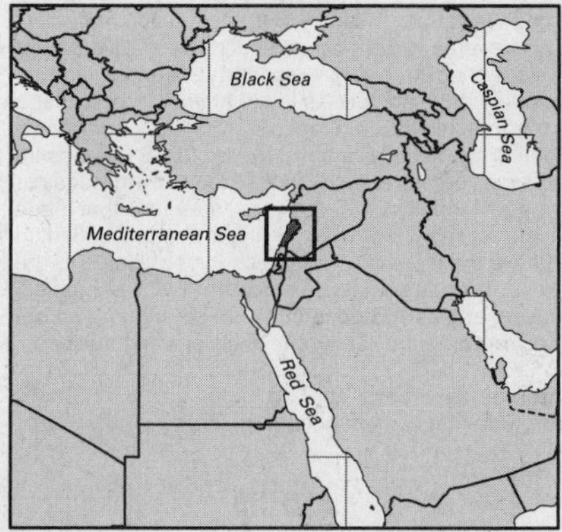

Official name: Al-Jumhuriyah al-Lubnaniyah (Lebanese Republic). **Form of government:** unitary multiparty republic with one legislative house (National Assembly [128]). **Chief of state:** President Michel Suleiman (from 2008). **Head of government:** Prime Minister Fouad Siniora (from 2005). **Capital:** Beirut. **Official language:** Arabic. **Official religion:** none. **Monetary unit:** 1 Lebanese pound (LBP) = 100 piastres; valuation (1 Jul 2008) US$1 = LBP 1,506.50.

Demography

Area: 4,016 sq mi, 10,400 sq km. **Population** (2007): 4,099,000. **Density** (2007): persons per sq mi 1,021, persons per sq km 394.1. **Urban** (2005): 86.6%. **Sex distribution** (2005): male 48.99%; female 51.01%. **Age breakdown** (2005): under 15, 28.6%; 15–29, 26.2%; 30–44, 21.2%; 45–59, 13.7%; 60–74, 7.9%; 75–84, 2.1%; 85 and over, 0.3%. **Ethnic composition** (2000): Arab 84.5%, of which Lebanese 71.2%, Palestinian 12.1%; Armenian 6.8%; Kurd 6.1%; other 2.6%. **Religious affiliation** (1995): Muslim 55.3%, of which Shi'i 34.0%, Sunni 21.3%; Christian 37.6%, of which Catholic 25.1% (Maronite 19.0%, Greek Catholic or Melchite 4.6%), Orthodox 11.7% (Greek Orthodox 6.0%, Armenian Apostolic 5.2%), Protestant 0.5%; Druze 7.1%. **Major cities** (2003): Beirut (urban agglomeration; 2005) 1,777,000; Tripoli 212,900; Sidon 149,000; Tyre (Sur) 117,100; Al-Nabatiyah 89,400. **Location:** the Middle East, bordering Syria, Israel, and the Mediterranean Sea.

Vital statistics

Birth rate per 1,000 population (2006): 18.0 (world avg. 20.3). **Death rate** per 1,000 population (2006): 4.6 (world avg. 8.6). **Total fertility rate** (avg. births per childbearing woman; 2005): 1.92. **Life expectancy** at birth (2005): male 70.2 years; female 75.2 years.

National economy

Budget (2005). *Revenue:* LBP 6,984,200,000,000 (tax revenue 69.7%, of which VAT revenues 24.2%, customs and excise revenues 18.1%; nontax revenue 30.3%). *Expenditures:* LBP 7,802,200,000,000 (general expenditures 54.7%; interest expenditures 45.3%, of which foreign 25.7%, domestic 19.6%). **Public debt** (external, outstanding; April 2007): US$20,417,000,000. **Gross national income** (2006): US$21,662,000,000 (US$5,342 per capita). **Production** (metric tons except as noted). *Agriculture, forestry, fishing* (2005): potatoes 511,400, tomatoes 277,000, oranges 235,600; livestock (number of live animals) 430,000 goats, 340,000 sheep, 90,000 cattle; roundwood 88,504 cu m, of which fuelwood 92%; fisheries production 4,601 (from aquaculture 18%). *Mining and quarrying* (2005): lime 14,000; salt 3,500; gypsum 1,700. *Manufacturing* (value added in US$'000,000; 1998): food and food products 345; cement, bricks, and ceramics 212; wood and wood products 188, of which furniture (including metal furniture) 135. *Energy production (consumption):* electricity (kW-hr; 2005) 9,183,000,000 (10,581,000,000); coal (metric tons; 2004) none (200,000); petroleum products (metric tons; 2005) none (4,309,000). **Population economically active** (2004): total 1,170,800; activity rate of total population 30% (participation rates: ages 15–64 [1997] 49.2%; female 21.2%; unemployed 8.2%). **Households.** Average household size (2004) 4.3; average annual income per household (1994; Beirut only) LBP 2,400,000 (US$1,430); expenditure (2002): food, beverages, and tobacco 28.3%, health and education 17.2%, housing and energy 16.7%, household furnishings 7.4%, transportation and communications 7.0%. **Selected balance of payments data.** Receipts from (US$'000,000): tourism (2005) 5,432; remittances (2005) 4,924; foreign direct investment (FDI) (2001–05 avg.) 2,024; official development assistance (2005) 248 (commitments). Disbursements for (US$'000,000): tourism (2005) 2,878; remittances (2005) 4,233; FDI (2001–05 avg.) 431. **Land use** as % of total land area (2003): in temporary crops 16.6%, in permanent crops 14.0%, in pasture 1.6%; overall forest area (2005) 13.3%.

Foreign trade

Imports (2005; c.i.f.): US$9,339,900,000 (mineral products 23.8%; electrical equipment 11.4%; food and live animals 10.3%; chemicals and chemical products 8.8%; transportation equipment 8.7%). *Major import sources:* Italy 10.4%; France 8.4%; China 7.9%; Germany 7.0%; US 5.9%. **Exports** (2005): US$1,879,800,000 (electrical equipment 16.7%; base metals 14.7%; precious metal jewelry and stones [significantly gold and pearls] 11.9%; food and live animals 10.7%; chemicals and chemical products 8.7%). *Major export destinations:* Syria 10.0%; Iraq 9.5%; UAE 8.2%; Saudi Arabia 7.4%; Switzerland 6.7%.

Transport and communications

Transport. *Roads* (2004): total length 7,300 km (paved 85%). *Vehicles* (2001): passenger cars 1,370,897; trucks and buses 102,394. *Air transport* (2006; Middle East Airlines only): passenger-km 1,940,000,000; metric ton-km cargo 29,000,000. **Communications,** in total units (units per 1,000 persons). Daily newspaper circulation (2005): 634,000 (158); televisions (2004): 1,269,000 (320); telephone landlines (2006): 681,000 (178); cellular telephone subscribers (2006): 1,103,000 (288); personal computers (2005): 409,000 (102); total Internet users (2006): 950,000 (248); broadband Internet subscribers (2006): 170,000 (44).

Education and health

Educational attainment (2004). Percentage of population ages 4 and over having: no formal education/unknown 13.7%; incomplete primary education 3.2%; primary 54.2%; secondary/vocational 15.5%; upper vocational 1.7%; higher 11.7%. **Literacy** (2005): total population ages 15 and over literate 88.3%; males literate 93.6%; females literate 83.4%. **Health** (2004): physicians 10,304 (1 per 364 persons); hospital beds (2006) 9,786 (1 per 414 persons); infant mortality rate per 1,000 live births (2005) 24.5. **Food** (2005): daily per capita caloric intake 2,916 (vegetable products 80%, animal products 20%); 152% of FAO recommended minimum.

Military

Total active duty personnel (2006): 72,100 (army 97.1%, navy 1.5%, air force 1.4%); UN peacekeeping troops (June 2007) 13,300; Syrian troops ended 29-year presence in April 2005. **Military expenditure as percentage of GDP** (2005): 4.5%; per capita expenditure US$280.

Background

Much of present-day Lebanon corresponds to ancient Phoenicia, which was settled c. 3000 BC. In the 6th century AD, Christians fleeing Syrian persecution settled in what is now northern Lebanon and founded the Maronite Church. Arab tribesmen settled in southern Lebanon and by the 11th century had founded the Druze faith. Lebanon was later ruled by the Mamluks. In 1516 the Ottoman Turks seized control; the Turks ended the local rule of the Druze Shihab princes in 1842. After the massacre of Maronites by Druze in 1860, France forced the Ottomans to form an autonomous province for the Christian area, known as Mount Lebanon. Following World War I, it was administered by the French military, but by late 1946 it was fully independent. After the Arab-Israeli War of 1948–49, Palestinian refugees settled in southern Lebanon. In 1970 the Palestine Liberation Organization (PLO) moved its headquarters there and began raids into northern Israel. The Christian-dominated Lebanese government tried to curb them, and in response the PLO sided with Lebanon's Muslims in their conflict with Christians, sparking a civil war by 1975. In 1982 Israeli forces invaded in an effort to drive Palestinian forces out of southern Lebanon. Israeli troops withdrew from most of Lebanon in 1985, leaving the conflict unresolved, but later returned. A cease-fire, agreed to in 1996, was broken in 1997 when Israeli soldiers and Lebanon's Hezbollah forces clashed.

Recent Developments

Political problems associated with choosing a new president for Lebanon arose in 2007. Bickering continued between the parliamentary majority, which insisted on an independent president, and the minority, which was pushing for a pro-Syrian president. On 24 November Gen. Émile Lahoud's nine-year extended term as president came to an end, but no one was elected to replace him, and Prime Minister Fouad Siniora was made acting president. In the thick of continuing political conflict, two parliamentary deputies were killed. In September deputy Antoine Ghanem of the Christian Phalange Party was killed in a car bombing in Beirut; his death came just a few months after another car bomb had killed Walid Eido, a deputy of the Sunni-dominated Future Movement. Both belonged to the pro-government majority bloc in the parliament and were against the imposition of Syrian policies in Lebanon. In December a car bomb killed Gen. François al-Hajj, the operations chief of the Lebanese army. In May 2008 the Muslim extremist organization Hezbollah took up arms against the government in protest against decisions that made its private telephone network illegal and that sought to remove the head of airport security for his ties to the group. The worst violence since the civil war ensued, leaving at least 65 dead in a week of fighting before the government reversed the decisions in question.

Internet resources:
<www.destinationlebanon.gov.lb/eng>.

Lesotho

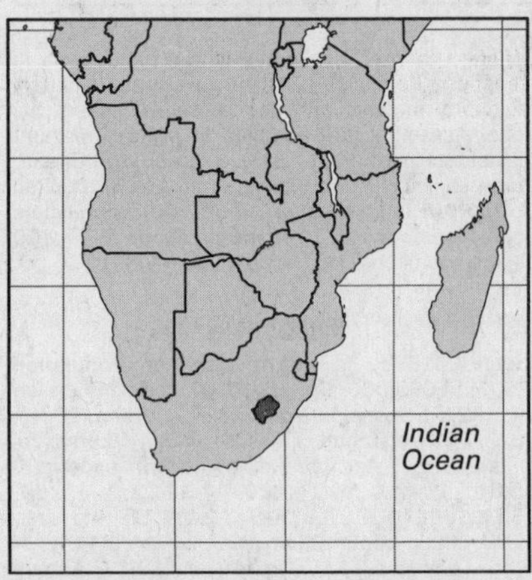

Official name: Lesotho (Sotho); Kingdom of Lesotho (English). **Form of government:** constitutional monarchy with two legislative houses (Senate [33]; National Assembly [120]). **Chief of state:** King Letsie III (from 1996). **Head of government:** Prime Minister Bethuel Pakalitha Mosisili (from 1998). **Capital:** Maseru. **Official languages:** Sotho; English. **Official religion:** Christianity. **Monetary unit:** 1 loti (plural maloti [M]) = 100 lisente; valuation (1 Jul 2008) US$1 = M 7.92 (the South African rand is accepted as legal tender within Lesotho).

Demography

Area: 11,720 sq mi, 30,355 sq km. **Population** (2007): 2,008,000. **Density** (2007): persons per sq mi 171.3, persons per sq km 66.2. **Urban** (2006): 23.7%. **Sex distribution** (2006): male 48.69%; female 51.31%. **Age breakdown** (2001): under 15, 35.8%; 15–29, 31.2%; 30–44, 14.7%; 45–59, 10.0%; 60–74, 6.0%; 75 and over, 2.1%; unknown 0.2%. **Ethnic composition** (2000): Sotho 80.3%; Zulu 14.4%; other 5.3%. **Religious affiliation** (2000): Christian 91.0%, of which Roman Catholic 37.5%, unaffiliated Christian 23.9%, Protestant (mostly Reformed and Anglican) 17.7%, independent Christian 11.8%; traditional beliefs 7.7%; other 1.3%. **Major urban centers** (2004): Maseru 178,300; Maputsoe 36,200; Mafeteng 36,000; Teyateyaneng 23,700; Hlotse 23,400. **Location:** southern Africa, surrounded by South Africa.

Vital statistics

Birth rate per 1,000 population (2006): 25.1 (world avg. 20.3). **Death rate** per 1,000 population (2006): 22.7 (world avg. 8.6). **Natural increase rate** per 1,000 population (2006): 2.4 (world avg. 11.7). **Total fertility rate** (avg. births per childbearing woman; 2006): 3.28. **Life expectancy** at birth (2006): male 40.4 years; female 39.1 years.

National economy

Budget (2004–05). *Revenue:* M 4,080,300,000 (tax revenue 82.7%, of which customs receipts 49.3%, income and profit tax 17.9%, sales tax 13.3%; nontax revenue 11.8%; grants 5.5%). *Expenditures:* M 3,762,300,000 (education and community services 29.9%; health and social security 12.8%; public order 10.1%; defense 5.6%; interest payments 4.2%). **Public debt** (external, outstanding; 2005): US$647,000,000. **Production** (metric tons except as noted). *Agriculture, forestry, fishing* (2005): potatoes 98,770, corn (maize) 76,090, sorghum 15,828; livestock (number of live animals; 2006) 1,000,000 sheep, 790,000 goats, 650,000 cattle; roundwood 2,053,000 cu m, of which fuelwood 100%; fisheries production 46 (from aquaculture 2%). *Mining and quarrying* (2005): diamonds 37,000 carats. *Manufacturing* (value of manufactured exports; US$'000,000; 2002): apparel and clothing accessories 233.7; footwear 23.9; television receivers 13.8. *Energy production (consumption):* electricity (kW-hr; 2004) 250,000,000 (244,500,000); petroleum products (metric tons; 2003) none (100,000). **Population economically active** (2003): total 640,000; activity rate of total population 35.5% (participation rates: ages 15–64, 60.8%; female 45.0%; unemployed [2005] 50%). **Households.** Average household size (2004) 4.1; expenditure (2000): food and nonalcoholic beverages 39.9%, household furnishings 17.0%, clothing and footwear 15.6%, transportation 7.8%. **Gross national income** (at 2006 market prices): US$1,748,000,000 (US$876 per capita). **Selected balance of payments data.** Receipts from (US$'000,000): tourism (2005) 30; remittances (2005) 327; foreign direct investment (2001–05 avg.) 39; official development assistance (2005) 69. Disbursements for (US$'000,000): tourism (2005) 27; remittances (2005) 17. **Land use** as % of total land area (2003): in temporary crops 10.9%, in permanent crops 0.1%, in pasture 65.9%; overall forest area (2005) 0.3%.

Foreign trade

Imports (2004; f.o.b. in balance of trade and c.i.f. in commodities and trading partners): M 9,236,000,000 (1999; food products 15.3%; unspecified commodities 84.7%). *Major import sources* (2004): Customs Union of Southern Africa (CUSA; mostly South Africa) 73.4%; Asian countries 23.6%. **Exports** (2004): M 4,652,000,000 (clothing 74.4%; telecommunications equipment 3.3%; footwear 2.8%). *Major export destinations* (2004): North America (mostly the US) 74%; EU 16%; CUSA (mostly South Africa) 9%.

Transport and communications

Transport. *Railroads* (2001): length 2.6 km. *Roads* (1999): total length 5,940 km (paved 18%). *Vehicles* (1996): passenger cars 12,610; trucks and buses 25,000. **Communications,** in total units (units per 1,000 persons). Televisions (2003): 80,000 (41); telephone landlines (2005): 48,000 (24); cellular telephone subscribers (2005): 298,000 (150); personal computers (2005): 1,000 (0.5); total Internet users (2005): 52,000 (26); broadband Internet subscribers (2005): 50 (0.02).

Education and health

Educational attainment (2001). Percentage of population ages 25 and over having: no formal education 22%; incomplete primary 40%; complete primary 17%; secondary and higher 21%. **Literacy** (2000–04): total population ages 15 and over literate 81.4%; males literate 73.7%; females literate 90.3%. **Health** (2003): physicians 140 (1 per 16,298 persons); hospital beds 1,025 (1 per 2,226 persons); infant mortality rate per 1,000 live births (2006) 81.3.

Military

Total active duty personnel (2006): 2,000 (army 100%). **Military expenditure as percentage of GDP** (2005): 2.3%; per capita expenditure US$17.

Background

Bantu-speaking farmers began to settle the area in the 16th century, and a number of chiefdoms arose. The most powerful organized the Basotho in 1824 and obtained British protection in 1843, as tension between the Basotho and the South African Boers increased. The area became a British territory in 1868 and was annexed to the Cape Colony in 1871. The colony's effort to disarm the Basotho resulted in revolt in 1880, and four years later it separated from the colony and became a British High Commission Territory. In 1966 it declared its independence. A new constitution (1993) ended seven years of military rule. In the late 20th century, Lesotho suffered from internal political problems and a deteriorating economy.

Recent Developments

An estimated one in five people faced the prospect of food shortages in Lesotho in late 2007. Planting of crops had declined because of a lack of resources, and the HIV/AIDS pandemic reduced available labor, but the main cause of the food crisis was the drought (the country's worst in 30 years), which early in the year ravaged the low-lying areas west of the mountains, where most crops were grown.

Internet resources: <www.lesotho.gov.ls>.

Liberia

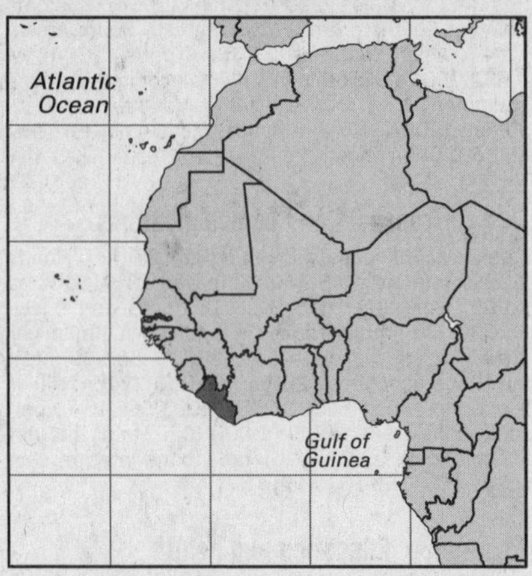

Official name: Republic of Liberia. **Form of government:** multiparty republic with two legislative bodies (Senate [30]; House of Representatives [64]). **Head of state and government:** President Ellen Johnson-Sirleaf (from 2006). **Capital:** Monrovia. **Official language:** English. **Official religion:** none. **Monetary unit:** 1 Liberian dollar (L$) = 100 cents; valuation (1 Jul 2008) US$1 = L$63.50.

Demography

Area: 37,743 sq mi, 97,754 sq km. **Population** (2007): 3,750,000. **Density** (2007): persons per sq mi 99.4, persons per sq km 38.4. **Urban** (2005): 58.1%. **Sex distribution** (2005): male 49.72%; female 50.28%. **Age breakdown** (2005): under 15, 42.7%; 15–29, 28.4%; 30–44, 15.3%; 45–59, 9.0%; 60–74, 3.9%; 75 and over, 0.7%. **Ethnic composition** (2000): Kpelle 18.9%; Bassa 13.1%; Grebo 10.3%; Gio (Dan) 7.4%; Kru 6.9%; Mano 6.1%; Loma 5.3%; Kissi 3.8%; Krahn 3.7%; Americo-Liberian 2.4% (descendant from freed US slaves); other 22.1%. **Religious affiliation** (2005): traditional beliefs 40%; Christian (mostly Protestant/independent Christian) 40%; Muslim 20%. **Major cities** (2003): Monrovia 550,200 (urban agglomeration [2005] 936,000); Zwedru 35,300; Buchanan 27,300; Yekepa 22,900; Harper 20,000. **Location:** western Africa, bordering Guinea, Côte d'Ivoire, the North Atlantic Ocean, and Sierra Leone.

Vital statistics

Birth rate per 1,000 population (2006): 44.8 (world avg. 20.3). **Death rate** per 1,000 population (2006): 23.1 (world avg. 8.6). **Natural increase rate** per 1,000 population (2006): 21.7 (world avg. 11.7). **Total fertility rate** (avg. births per childbearing woman; 2006): 6.02. **Life expectancy** at birth (2006): male 38.0 years; female 41.3 years.

National economy

Budget (2005). *Revenue:* US$83,300,000 (tax revenue 87.2%, of which import duties 34.7%, income and profit taxes 34.7%, maritime revenue 10.7%, taxes on goods and services 6.6%; nontax revenue 8.0%; grants 4.8%). *Expenditures:* US$81,400,000 (current expenditures 88.3%, of which wages 48.5%, goods and services 28.4%, interest on debt 2.2%; development expenditures 11.7%). **Public debt** (external, outstanding; 2005): US$1,115,000,000. **Population economically active** (2003): total 1,182,000; activity rate 36.7% (participation rates: ages 15–64, 70.0%; female 39.8%; unemployed [2006] 85%). **Production** (metric tons except as noted). *Agriculture, forestry, fishing* (2005): cassava 483,440, sugarcane 255,000, oil palm fruit 183,000; livestock (number of live animals) 220,000 goats, 210,000 sheep, 130,000 pigs; roundwood 6,141,423 cu m, of which fuelwood 95%; fisheries production 10,000. *Mining and quarrying* (2005): diamonds 10,000 carats (UN sanctions on exports of rough diamonds from 2001 ended in April 2007); gold 16 kg. *International maritime licensing* (registration fees earned; 2006): more than US$8,000,000. *Manufacturing* (value of sales in L$'000; January–June 2005): cement 417,224; beer 328,207; carbonated beverages 205,564. *Energy production (consumption):* electricity (kW-hr; 2004) 330,000,000 (330,000,000); petroleum products (metric tons; 2004) negligible (146,000). **Households.** Average household size (2004) 5.1; expenditure (1998): food 34.4%, housing 14.9%, clothing 13.8%, household furnishings 6.1%. **Gross national income** (2006): US$546,000,000 (US$153 per capita). **Selected balance of payments data.** Receipts from (US$'000,000): remittances (2005) 620; foreign direct investment (FDI) (2001–05 avg.) 157; official development assistance (2005) 236. Disbursements for (US$'000,000): remittances (2005) 598; FDI (2001–05 avg.) 66. **Land use** as % of total land area (2003): in temporary crops 4.0%, in permanent crops 2.3%, in pasture 20.8%; overall forest area (2005) 32.7%.

Foreign trade

Imports (2005): US$273,600,000 (petroleum and petroleum products 33.2%; food, beverages, and tobacco 21.2%, of which rice 9.0%; machinery and transportation equipment 16.4%). *Major import sources* (2004): South Korea 38.1%; Japan 21.9%; Singapore 12.6%; Croatia 4.8%. **Exports** (2005): US$112,200,000 (rubber 88.0%; cocoa beans 5.1%). *Major export destinations* (2004): US 61.4%; Belgium 29.5%; China 5.3%; France 1.6%.

Transport and communications

Transport. *Railroads* (2007): route length 78 km. *Roads* (2003): total length 10,600 km (paved 6%). *Vehicles* (2002): passenger cars 17,100; trucks and buses 12,800. **Communications,** in total units (units per 1,000 persons). Daily newspaper circulation (2004): 2,100 (0.7); televisions (2001): 69,000 (25); telephone landlines (2002): 6,900 (2.5); cellular telephone subscribers (2006): 160,000 (53).

1 metric ton = about 1.1 short tons; 1 kilometer = 0.6 mi (statute); 1 metric ton-km cargo = about 0.68 short ton-mi cargo; c.i.f.: cost, insurance, and freight; f.o.b.: free on board

Education and health

Literacy (2005): total population ages 15 and over literate 58.9%; males literate 75.2%; females literate 42.7%. **Health:** physicians (2004) 103 (1 per 27,255 persons); hospital beds (2001) 2,751 (1 per 1,003 persons); infant mortality rate per 1,000 live births (2006) 155.8. **Food** (2005): daily per capita caloric intake 2,078 (vegetable products 96%, animal products 4%); 114% of FAO recommended minimum.

Military

Total active duty personnel (2006): 2,400; UN peacekeeping troops (August 2007) 13,900. **Military expenditure as percentage of GDP** (2003): 11%; per capita expenditure US$16.

Background

Africa's oldest republic, Liberia was established as a home for freed American slaves under the American Colonization Society, which founded a colony at Cape Mesurado in 1821. In 1822 Jehudi Ashmun, a Methodist minister, became the director of the settlement and Liberia's real founder. Joseph Jenkins Roberts, Liberia's first nonwhite governor, proclaimed Liberian independence in 1847 and expanded its boundaries, which were officially established in 1892. In 1980 a coup led by Samuel K. Doe marked the end of the Americo-Liberians' long political dominance over the descendants of indigenous Africans. A rebellion in 1989 escalated into a destructive civil war in the 1990s. A peace agreement was reached in 1996, and elections were held in 1997.

Recent Developments

Former Liberian president Charles Taylor's war-crimes trial for murder, rape, and enlistment of child soldiers began in June 2007 in The Netherlands. It was expected that testimony would incriminate important members of the political class. The trial continued in 2008 with sensational testimony, including the assertion from one of Taylor's aides that African peacekeepers and UN personnel were killed and eaten on Taylor's orders. Although the UN Security Council extended the mandate of its peacekeeping force until September 2008, it cut the mission's strength by 20% and also reduced the size of its police force. Economic conditions improved slightly. In April 2007 the Security Council lifted its ban on Liberian diamond exports, imposed in 2001 to reduce the export of illegal "blood diamonds" that had helped finance the civil war.

Internet resources: <www.cbl.org.lr>.

Libya

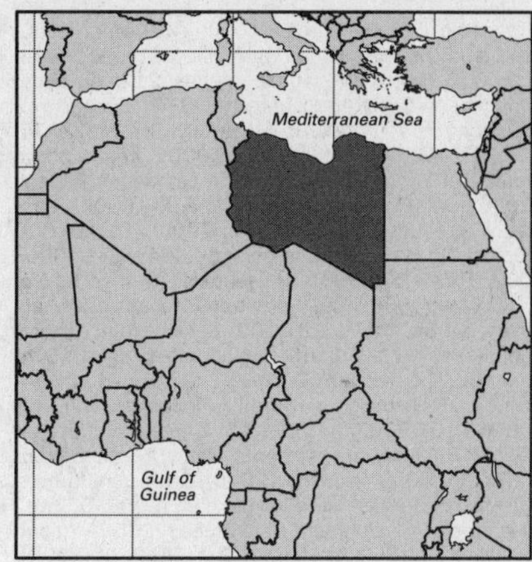

Official name: Al-Jamahiriyah al-'Arabiyah al-Libiyah al-Sha'biyah al-Ishtirakiyah al-'Uzma (Socialist People's Libyan Arab Jamahiriya). **Form of government:** authoritarian state with one policy-making body (General People's Congress [468]). **Chief of state:** Muammar al-Qaddafi (de facto; from 1969); Secretary of the General People's Congress Zentani Muhammad al-Zentani (de jure; from 1992). **Head of government:** Secretary of the General People's Committee (Prime Minister) Al-Baghdadi Ali al-Mahmudi (from 2006). **Capital:** Tripoli. **Official language:** Arabic. **Official religion:** Islam. **Monetary unit:** 1 Libyan dinar (LD) = 1,000 dirhams; valuation (1 Jul 2008) US$1 = LD 1.18.

Demography

Area: 679,362 sq mi, 1,759,540 sq km. **Population** (2007): 6,342,000. **Density** (2007): persons per sq mi 9.3, persons per sq km 3.6. **Urban** (2005): 84.8%. **Sex distribution** (2006): male 51.93%; female 48.07%. **Age breakdown** (2005): under 15, 30.1%; 15 -29, 32.2%; 30–44, 19.8%; 45–59, 11.4%; 60–74, 5.3%; 75–84, 1.0%; 85 and over, 0.2%. **Ethnic composition** (2000): Arab 87.1%, of which Libyan 57.2%, Bedouin 13.8%, Egyptian 7.7%, Sudanese 3.5%, Tunisian 2.9%; Amazigh (Berber) 6.8%, of which Arabized 4.2%; other 6.1%. **Religious affiliation** (2000): Muslim (nearly all Sunni) 96.1%; Orthodox 1.9%; Roman Catholic 0.8%; other 1.2%. **Major cities** (2005): Tripoli 911,643 (urban agglomeration 2,098,000); Banghazi 685,367 (urban agglomeration 1,114,000); Misratah (2003) 121,669. **Location:** northern Africa, bordering the Mediterranean Sea, Egypt, The Sudan, Chad, Niger, Algeria, and Tunisia.

Vital statistics

Birth rate per 1,000 population (2005): 26.8 (world avg. 20.3). **Death rate** per 1,000 population (2005): 3.5 (world avg. 8.6). **Natural increase rate** per 1,000 population (2005): 23.3 (world avg. 11.7). **Total fertility rate** (avg. births per childbearing woman; 2005): 3.34. **Life expectancy** at birth (2005): male 74.3 years; female 78.8 years.

National economy

Budget (2005). *Revenue:* LD 37,433,000,000 (oil revenues 92.9%). *Expenditures:* LD 18,319,000,000 (development expenditures 54.0%; current expenditures 46.0%, of which wages and salaries 24.3%). **Public debt** (external, outstanding; 2005): US$3,-900,000,000. **Production** (metric tons except as noted). *Agriculture, forestry, fishing* (2005): tomatoes 212,800, olives 211,300, potatoes 195,000; livestock (number of live animals) 4,500,000 sheep, 1,265,000 goats, 47,000 camels; roundwood 652,000 cu m, of which fuelwood 82%; fisheries production 46,339 (from aquaculture 1%). *Mining and* *quarrying* (2005): lime 250,000; gypsum 175,000; salt 40,000. *Manufacturing* (value of production in LD '000,000; 1996): base metals 212; electrical equipment 208; petrochemicals 175. *Energy production (consumption):* electricity (kW-hr; 2004) 20,202,000,000 (20,202,000,000); coal (metric tons; 2002) none (4,000); crude petroleum (barrels; 2006) 642,800,000 ([2004] 125,900,000); petroleum products (metric tons; 2005) 16,419,000 (9,288,000); natural gas (cu m; 2004) 6,816,000,000 (5,746,000,000). **Households.** Average household size (2006) 5.9. **Population economically active** (2003): total 2,137,000; activity rate of total population 37.9% (participation rates: ages 15 to 64, 56.7%; female 24.7%; unemployed [2004] 30.0%). **Gross national income** (2006): US$50,107,000,000 (US$8,298 per capita). **Selected balance of payments data.** Receipts from (US$'000,000): tourism (2005) 250; remittances (2005) 15; foreign direct investment (2001–05 avg.) 12; official development assistance (2005) 14 (commitments). Disbursements for (US$'000,000): tourism (2005) 680; remittances (2005) 914. **Land use** as % of total land area (2003): in temporary crops 1.0%, in permanent crops 0.2%, in pasture 7.6%; overall forest area (2005) 0.1%.

Foreign trade

Imports (2004): US$8,768,000,000 (machinery and transport equipment 48.0%; food and live animals 14.1%; chemicals and chemical products 4.0%). *Major import sources:* Europe 63.1%, of which Italy 18.3%, Germany 12.0%, UK 4.1%; Japan 8.3%; Arab countries 6.1%. **Exports** (2004): US$20,600,000,000 (hydrocarbons [mostly crude petroleum] 95.7%). *Major export destinations:* Europe 90.5%, of which Italy 39.3%, Germany 18.3%, Spain 13.3%, Turkey 8.3%; Asian countries 4.1%.

Transport and communications

Transport. *Roads* (1999): total length 83,200 km (paved 57%). *Vehicles* (2001): passenger cars 552,700; trucks and buses 195,500. *Air transport* (2003): passenger-km 825,000,000; metric ton-km cargo (2001) 259,000. **Communications,** in total units (units per 1,000 persons). Televisions (2000): 717,000 (133); telephone landlines (2006): 483,000 (81); cellular telephone subscribers (2006): 3,928,000 (658); personal computers (2005): 130,000 (21); total Internet users (2005): 232,000 (40).

Education and health

Literacy (2005): percentage of total population ages 15 and over literate 84.1%; males literate 93.4%; females literate 74.2%. **Health:** physicians (2004) 7,405 (1 per 775 persons); hospital beds (2002) 21,400 (1 per 256 persons); infant mortality rate per 1,000 live births (2005) 24.6. **Food** (2005): daily per capita caloric intake 2,885 (vegetable products 88%, animal products 12%); 152% of FAO recommended minimum.

Military

Total active duty personnel (2006): 76,000 (army 59.2%, navy 10.5%, air force 30.3%). **Military expenditure as percentage of GDP** (2005): 2.0%; per capita expenditure US$128.

The Qattara Depression is an arid Libyan Desert (Eastern Saharan) basin in northwestern Egypt. It covers about 7,000 sq mi (18,100 sq km) of salt lakes and marshes and descends to 435 ft (133 m) below sea level. During World War II, because it was impassable to military traffic, the depression formed a natural anchor at the southern end of the British defense lines at El-Alamein against the final advance of Field Marshal Erwin Rommel's German army in July 1942. In the late 1970s oil deposits were discovered in the southern part of the depression.

Background

Greeks and Phoenicians settled the area in the 7th century BC. It was conquered by Rome in the 1st century BC and by Arabs in the 7th century AD. In the 16th century the Ottoman Turks combined Libya's three regions under one regency in Tripoli. In 1911 Italy claimed control of Libya, and by the outbreak of World War II, 150,000 Italians lived there. It became an independent state in 1951. The discovery of oil in 1959 brought wealth to Libya. A decade later a group of army officers led by Muammar al-Qaddafi deposed the king and made the country an Islamic republic. Under Qaddafi's rule it supported the Palestinian Liberation Organization and terrorist groups, bringing protests from many countries, particularly the US. Intermittent warfare with Chad during the 1970s and '80s ended with Chad's defeat of Libya in 1987. International relations in the 1990s were dominated by the consequences of the 1988 bombing of an American airliner over Lockerbie, Scotland; the US accused Libyan nationalists of the deed and imposed a trade embargo on Libya, endorsed by the UN in 1992.

Recent Developments

After nearly eight years of political and legal squabbles, in 2007 the case was settled involving five Bulgarian nurses and one Palestinian doctor who had been sentenced to death by Libyan courts on charges of having infected 426 Libyan children with HIV/AIDS. In July all six, who said that they were tortured to give false confessions, were released and flown to Bulgaria, where Bulgarian Pres. Georgi Purvanov immediately issued them a general pardon. Independent experts maintained that the charges were unfounded, and Saif ul-Islam al-Qaddafi, the son of Libyan leader Muammar al-Qaddafi, later disclosed in a TV interview that the case was "contrived" and that the police investigation involved "manipulation" of information. In October Libya was elected as a nonpermanent member of the UN Security Council for a period of two years. Also in October, Libya's conciliatory initiative to bring all of the parties involved in the Darfur crisis in The Sudan to the negotiating table faltered as key rebel figures refused to attend. It was announced that 12 concessions would be awarded to foreign companies for offshore gas prospecting, and

1 metric ton = about 1.1 short tons; 1 kilometer = 0.6 mi (statute); 1 metric ton-km cargo = about 0.68 short ton-mi cargo; c.i.f.: cost, insurance, and freight; f.o.b.: free on board

in May Libya signed a US$900 million contract with British Petroleum to drill for oil and gas—an indication that rapprochement between Libya and the West was continuing.

Internet resources:
<www.libyan-tourism.org/index?ID=2>.

Liechtenstein

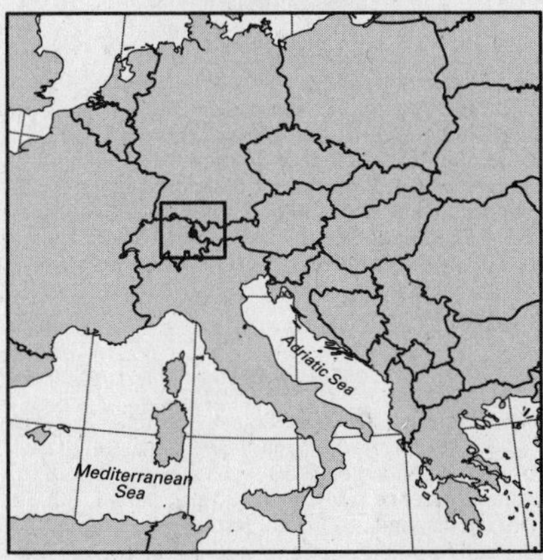

Official name: Fürstentum Liechtenstein (Principality of Liechtenstein). **Form of government:** constitutional monarchy with one legislative house (Diet [25]). **Chief of state:** Prince Hans Adam II (from 1989). **Head of government:** Otmar Hasler (from 2001). **Capital:** Vaduz. **Official language:** German. **Official religion:** none. **Monetary unit:** 1 Swiss franc (CHF) = 100 centimes; valuation (1 Jul 2008) US$1 = CHF 1.02.

Demography

Area: 62.0 sq mi, 160.5 sq km. **Population** (2007): 35,300. **Density** (2007): persons per sq mi 569.4, persons per sq km 219.9. **Urban** (2003): 21.6%. **Sex distribution** (2005): male 49.29%; female 50.71%. **Age breakdown** (2004): under 15, 17.6%; 15–29, 18.9%; 30–44, 25.3%; 45–59, 21.7%; 60–74, 11.5%; 75–84, 3.9%; 85 and over, 1.1%. **Ethnic composition** (2004): Liechtensteiner 65.7%; Swiss 10.4%; Austrian 5.9%; Italian 3.5%; German 3.4%; Turkish 2.6%; other 8.5%. **Religious affiliation** (2002): Christian 83.9%, of which Roman Catholic 76.0%, Protestant 7.0%, Orthodox 0.8%; Muslim 4.1%; nonreligious/other/unknown 12.0%. **Major cities** (2005): Schaan 5,811; Vaduz 5,047; Triesen 4,643; Balzers 4,436; Eschen 4,076. **Location:** central Europe, between Austria and Switzerland.

Vital statistics

Birth rate per 1,000 population (2006): 10.0 (world avg. 20.3); (2005) within marriage 81.1%. **Death rate** per 1,000 population (2006): 6.6 (world avg. 8.6). **Natural increase rate** per 1,000 population (2006): 3.5 (world avg. 11.7). **Total fertility rate** (avg. births per childbearing woman; 2005): 1.51. **Life expectancy** at birth (2005): male 77.7 years; female 83.1 years.

National economy

Budget (2004). *Revenue:* CHF 1,068,400,000 (current revenue 72.0%, of which taxes and duties 55.4%, investment income 10.9%, charges and fees 3.8%; capital revenue 28.0%). *Expenditures:* CHF 1,048,500,000 (current expenditure 74.5%, of which financial affairs 21.7%, social welfare 17.3%, education 12.3%, general administration 7.7%, public safety 4.5%, transportation 3.0%; capital expenditure 25.5%). **Public debt**: none. **Population economically active** (2005): total 15,667; activity rate of total population 44.8% (participation rates: ages 15 and over, 54.3%; female [2003] 41.4%; unemployed [2004] 2.4%). **Households.** Average household size (2003) 2.5. **Production** (metric tons except as noted). *Agriculture, forestry, fishing* (2005): grapes 157; significantly market gardening, other crops include cereals and apples; livestock (number of live animals) 6,000 cattle, 3,000 pigs, 2,900 sheep; roundwood 22,167 cu m, of which fuelwood 19%. *Manufacturing* (2004): small-scale precision manufacturing includes optical lenses, electron microscopes, electronic equipment, and high-vacuum pumps. *Energy production (consumption):* electricity (kW-hr; 2005) 67,800,000 (353,000,000); coal (metric tons; 2004) none ([2003] 13); petroleum products (metric tons; 2004) none (50,000). **Gross national income** (2006): US$2,893,000,000 (US$82,826 per capita). **Land use** as % of total land area (2003): in temporary crops 25%, in pasture 31%; overall forest area (2005) 43%.

Foreign trade

Imports (2005): CHF 1,909,000,000 (machinery and apparatus 31.4%; fabricated metals 15.2%; glass [all forms] and ceramics 6.5%; iron and steel 5.6%; chemicals and chemical products 5.1%). *Major direct import sources:* Germany 42.1%; Austria 32.5%; Italy 5.4%; US 3.8%; France 2.7%. **Exports** (2005): CHF 3,227,000,000 (machinery and apparatus [mostly electronic products and precision tools] 31.1%; fabricated metals 15.7%; motor vehicles and parts 10.3%; chemicals and chemical products 8.4%; glass and ceramic products [including lead crystal and specialized dental products] 8.3%). *Major direct export destinations:* Germany 21.2%; US 16.2%; France 11.6%; Austria 10.2%; Italy 7.3%.

Transport and communications

Transport. *Railroads* (2006): length 18.5 km. *Roads* (2006): total length 250 km (paved 100%). *Vehicles*: passenger cars (2006) 24,293; trucks and buses (2003) 2,560. *Air transport*: the nearest scheduled airport service is through Zürich, Switzerland. **Communications,** in total units (units per 1,000 persons). Daily newspaper circulation (2004): 18,000 (517); televisions (2002): 17,000 (510); telephone landlines (2006): 20,000 (575); cellular telephone subscribers (2006): 29,000 (820); total Internet users (2006): 22,000 (627); broadband Internet subscribers (2006): 10,000 (285).

Education and health

Educational attainment (2000). Percentage of population ages 25 and over having: incomplete compulsory education (schooling to age 16) 3.0%; complete compulsory 22.9%; lower vocational 44.5%; higher vocational/teacher training 13.8%; university 6.6%; unknown 9.2%. **Literacy:** virtually 100%. **Health:** physicians (2005) 79 (1 per 441 persons); hospital beds (1997) 108 (1 per 288 persons); infant mortality rate per 1,000 live births (2005) 4.7.

Military

Total active duty personnel: none; Liechtenstein has had no standing army since 1868; defense is the responsibility of Switzerland.

Background

The Rhine plain was occupied for centuries by two independent lordships of the Holy Roman Empire, Vaduz and Schellenberg. The principality of Liechtenstein, consisting of these two lordships, was founded in 1719 and remained part of the Holy Roman Empire. It was included in the German Confederation (1815–66). In 1866 it became independent, recognizing Vaduz and Schellenberg as unique regions forming separate electoral districts. An almost 60-year ruling coalition dissolved in 1997, and the prince urged adoption of constitutional reforms.

Recent Developments

Liechtenstein in August 2007 began work on modernizing its justice system. There was particular concern about the placement of detainees waiting to be deported, as Liechtenstein had to address several issues to come into compliance with the European Convention on Human Rights. Although Liechtenstein had made progress in the area, it remained on the Organisation for Economic Co-operation and Development blacklist of uncooperative tax havens.

Internet resources: <www.liechtenstein.li/en/>.

Lithuania

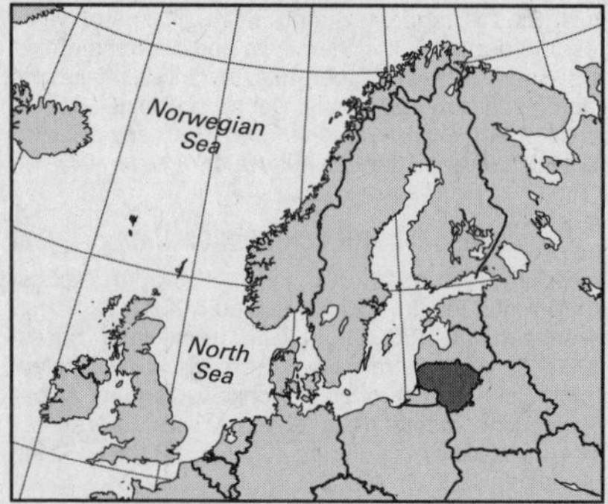

Official name: Lietuvos Respublika (Republic of Lithuania). **Form of government:** unitary multiparty republic with a single legislative body (the Seimas [141]). **Head of state:** President Valdas Adamkus (from 2004). **Head of government:** Prime Minister Gediminas Kirkilas (from 2006). **Capital:** Vilnius. **Official language:** Lithuanian. **Official religion:** none. **Monetary unit:** 1 litas (LTL; plural litai) = 100 centai; valuation (1 Jul 2008) US$1 = LTL 2.18.

Demography

Area: 25,212 sq mi, 65,300 sq km. **Population** (2007): 3,375,000. **Density** (2007): persons per sq mi 133.9, persons per sq km 51.7. **Urban** (2006): 66.8%. **Sex distribution** (2006): male 46.59%; female 53.41%. **Age breakdown** (2005): under 15, 16.7%; 15–29, 22.1%; 30–44, 22.4%; 45–59, 18.2%; 60–74, 14.2%; 75–84, 5.3%; 85 and over, 1.1%. **Ethnic composition** (2001): Lithuanian 83.5%; Polish 6.7%; Russian 6.3%; Belarusian 1.2%; Ukrainian 0.7%; other 1.6%. **Religious affiliation** (2001): Roman Catholic 79.0%; Orthodox 4.8%, of which Old Believers 0.8%; Protestant 1.0%; nonreligious 9.5%; unknown/other 5.7% **Major cities** (2006): Vilnius 554,400; Kaunas 358,100; Klaipeda 185,900; Siauliai 128,400; Panevezys 114,600. **Location:** eastern Europe, bordering Latvia, Belarus, Poland, Russia, and the Baltic Sea.

Vital statistics

Birth rate per 1,000 population (2006): 9.2 (world avg. 20.3); (2005) within marriage 71.5%. **Death rate** per 1,000 population (2006): 13.2 (world avg. 8.6). **Natural increase rate** per 1,000 population (2006): −4.0 (world avg. 11.7). **Total fertility rate** (avg. births per childbearing woman; 2005): 1.26. **Life expectancy** at birth (2005): male 65.4 years; female 77.4 years.

National economy

Budget (2004). *Revenue:* LTL 17,960,900,000 (tax revenue 59.2%, of which VAT 36.4%, income tax 22.2%; social security contributions 32.0%; other [including grants] 8.8%). *Expenditures:* LTL 17,817,400,000 (social security and welfare 40.4%; wages and salaries 18.3%; grants and subsidies 17.3%). **Gross national income** (2006): US$28,630,-000,000 (US$8,400 per capita). **Production** (metric tons except as noted). *Agriculture, forestry, fishing* (2005): wheat 1,379,400, barley 948,300, potatoes 894,688; livestock (number of live animals) 1,114,700 pigs, 800,300 cattle; roundwood 6,045,000 cu m, of which fuelwood 19%; fisheries production 141,798 (from aquaculture 1%). *Mining and quarrying* (2005): limestone 1,242,200; peat 535,000; sulfur 74,277. *Manufacturing* (value added in LTL '000,000; 2005): food and beverages 2,569; refined petroleum products 2,077; textiles 1,395. *Energy production (consumption):* electricity (kW-hr; 2004) 18,912,000,000 (12,079, 000,000); coal (metric tons; 2004) none (263,000); crude petroleum (barrels; 2004) 2,200,000 (63,500,000); petroleum products (metric tons; 2003) 6,715,000 (1,942,000); natural gas (cu m; 2004) none (2,929,000,000). **Public debt** (external outstanding; March 2006): US$3,156,000,000. **Population economically active** (2006): total 1,588,300; activity rate of total population 46.7% (participation rates: ages 15–64, 67.4%; female 49.5%; registered unemployed 5.6%). **Households** (2005). Average household size (2004) 2.5; average annual per capita disposable household income: LTL 6,956 (US$2,508); sources of income: wages and salaries 56.6%, transfers 22.6%, self-employment 13.7%; expenditure: food and beverages 39.1%, transportation and communications 13.9%, housing and energy 12.0%, clothing and footwear 8.6%. **Selected balance of payments data.** Receipts from (US$'000,000): tourism (2005) 921; remittances (2006) 622; foreign direct investment (FDI) (2001–05 avg.) 628. Disbursements for (US$'000,000): tourism (2005) 744; remittances (2006) 54; FDI (2001–05 avg.) 131. **Land use** as % of total land area (2003): in temporary crops 24.3%, in permanent crops 0.7%, in pasture 15.5%; overall forest area (2005) 33.5%.

Foreign trade

Imports (2005; c.i.f.): LTL 42,974,600,000 (mineral fuels [mostly crude petroleum] 25.6%; machinery and apparatus 17.9%; transport equipment 11.7%; agricultural and food products 8.1%; chemicals and chemical products 7.8%). *Major import sources:* Russia 27.8%; Germany 15.2%; Poland 8.3%; Latvia 3.9%; The Netherlands 3.7%. **Exports** (2005; f.o.b.): LTL 32,807,300,000 (mineral fuels [mostly refined petroleum] 27.5%; agricultural and food products 12.6%; machinery and apparatus 12.4%; textiles and clothing 9.4%; transport equipment [mostly auto components] 8.3%). *Major export destinations:* Russia 10.4%; Latvia 10.3%; Germany 9.4%; France 7.0%; Estonia 5.9%.

Transport and communications

Transport. *Railroads* (2006): route length 1,771 km; passenger-km 430,500,000; metric ton-km cargo 12,896,000,000. *Roads* (2005): total length 79,497 km (paved 89%). *Vehicles* (2005): passenger cars 1,455,276; trucks and buses 121,086. *Air transport* (2006): passenger-km 1,200,000,000; metric ton-km cargo 4,682,000. **Communications**, in total units (units per 1,000 persons). Daily newspaper circulation (2004): 371,000 (108); televisions (2004): 1,785,000 (519); telephone landlines (2006): 792,000 (232); cellular telephone subscribers (2006): 4,718,000 (1,381); personal computers (2005): 616,000 (180); total Internet users (2006): 1,083,000 (317); broadband Internet subscribers (2006): 369,000 (109).

Education and health

Educational attainment (2005). Percentage of population ages 15 and over having: no schooling through complete primary education 14.7%; lower secondary 18.0%; higher secondary 28.2%; vocational/technical 19.3%; higher 19.8%. **Literacy** (2003): total population ages 15 and over literate: virtually 100%. **Health** (2006): physicians 13,510 (1 per 251 persons); hospital beds 27,114 (1 per 125 persons); infant mortality rate per 1,000 live births (2006) 6.8. **Food** (2005): daily per capita caloric intake 3,530 (vegetable products 74%, animal products 26%); 178% of FAO recommended minimum.

Military

Total active duty personnel (2006): 13,510 (army 74.8%, navy 5.2%, air force 8.9%, active reserve 11.1%). **Military expenditure as percentage of GDP** (2005): 1.2%; per capita expenditure US$90.

Background

Lithuanian tribes united in the mid-13th century to oppose the Teutonic knights. Gediminas, one of the grand dukes, expanded Lithuania into an empire that dominated much of Eastern Europe in the 14th through 16th centuries. In 1386 the Lithuanian grand duke became the king of Poland, and the two countries remained closely associated until Lithuania was acquired by Russia in the Third Partition of Poland in 1795. Occupied by Germany during World War I, it declared its independence in 1918. In 1940 the Red Army gained control of Lithuania. Germany occupied it again in 1941–44, but the USSR regained control in 1944. With the breakup of the USSR, Lithuania became independent in 1991. It signed a border treaty with Russia in 1997, and it joined the European Union and NATO in 2004.

Recent Developments

In an effort to reduce Lithuania's dependency on Russian energy resources, Vilnius encouraged closer energy collaboration in Europe in 2007. In February the Baltic states and Poland agreed to build a new nuclear power station in Lithuania. In Vilnius in October, the Baltic states and Black Sea regions were encouraged to bypass Russia and secure a reliable supply route for Caspian Sea oil. The GDP grew 18.1% in 2007, largely due to the significant increase in foreign direct investment (FDI) in Lithuania. By the beginning of 2008, FDI had reached more than US$73 billion.

Internet resources: <www.tourism.lt/en>.

Luxembourg

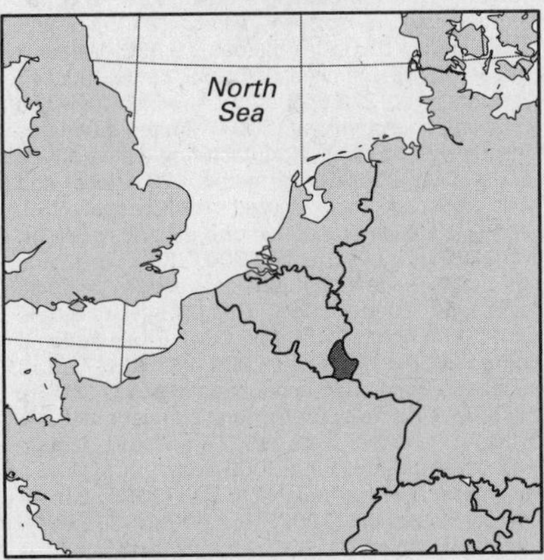

Official name: Groussherzogtum Lëtzebuerg (Luxembourgian); Grand-Duché de Luxembourg (French); Grossherzogtum Luxemburg (German) (Grand Duchy of Luxembourg). **Form of government:** constitutional monarchy with one legislative body (Chamber of Deputies [60]). **Chief of state:** Grand Duke Henri (from 2000). **Head of government:** Prime Minister Jean-Claude Juncker (from 1995). **Capital:** Luxembourg. **Official language:** none; Luxembourgian (national); French (used for most official purposes); German (lingua franca). **Official religion:** none. **Monetary**

unit: 1 euro (€) = 100 cents; valuation (1 Jul 2008) US$1 = €0.63.

Demography

Area: 999 sq mi, 2,586 sq km. **Population** (2007): 467,000. **Density** (2007): persons per sq mi 467.5, persons per sq km 180.6. **Urban** (2005): 82.8%. **Sex distribution** (2006): male 49.52%; female 50.48%. **Age breakdown** (2005): under 15, 18.6%; 15–29, 17.9%; 30–44, 24.4%; 45–59, 20.2%; 60–74, 12.4%; 75–84, 5.2%; 85 and over, 1.3%. **Ethnic composition** (nationality; 2005): Luxembourger 60.4%; Portuguese 14.8%; French 5.0%; Italian 4.1%; Belgian 3.5%; German 2.3%; English 1.0%; other 8.9%. **Religious affiliation** (2005): Roman Catholic 90%; Protestant 3%; Muslim 2%; Orthodox 1%; other 4%. **Major cities** (2001): Luxembourg 76,688; Esch-sur-Alzette 27,146; Dudelange 17,320; Differdange 10,248; Schifflange 7,849. **Location:** western Europe, bordering Belgium, Germany, and France.

Vital statistics

Birth rate per 1,000 population (2006): 12.1 (world avg. 20.3); (2005) within marriage 72.8%. **Death rate** per 1,000 population (2006): 7.7 (world avg. 8.6). **Total fertility rate** (avg. births per childbearing woman; 2005): 1.70. **Life expectancy** at birth (2005): male 76.2 years; female 82.3 years.

National economy

Budget (2004). *Revenue:* €6,392,568,500 (indirect taxes 48.6%; direct taxes 46.2%; other 5.2%). *Expenditures:* €6,476,725,500 (current expenditure 89.7%; development expenditure 10.3%). **Public debt** (2006): negligible. **Production** (metric tons except as noted). *Agriculture, forestry, fishing* (2005): wheat 71,750, barley 52,850, potatoes 19,330; livestock (number of live animals) 185,235 cattle, 90,147 pigs; roundwood 276,618 cu m, of which fuelwood 5%. *Mining and quarrying* (2004): limited quantities of limestone and slate. *Manufacturing* (value added in €'000,000; 2004): base metals 420; rubber and plastic products 324; fabricated metal products 232. *Energy production (consumption):* electricity (kW-hr; 2005) 3,203,000,000 (6,140,000,000); coal (metric tons; 2004) none (129,000); petroleum products (metric tons; 2004) none (2,533,000); natural gas (cu m; 2004) none (1,430,000,000). **Gross national income** (2006): US$32,911,000,000 (US$71,336 per capita). **Population economically active** (2005): total 202,700; activity rate of total population 45.1% (participation rates: ages 15–64, 66.6%; female 42.4%; unemployed [June 2005–May 2006] 4.4%). **Households.** Average household size (2005) 2.5; income per household (2002) €61,800 (US$55,600); sources of income (1992): wages and salaries 67.1%, transfer payments 28.1%, self-employment 4.8%; expenditure (2004): food, beverages, and tobacco 21.4%, housing and energy 21.0%, transportation and communications 20.0%, entertainment and culture 8.1%, household goods and furniture 8.0%. **Selected balance of payments data.** Receipts from (US$'000,000): tourism (2005) 3,614; remittances (2006) 1,292; foreign direct investment (FDI) (2002–05 avg.) 3,895. Disbursements for (US$'000,000): tourism (2005) 2,976; remittances (2006) 7,533; FDI (2002–05 avg.) 4,106. **Land use** as % of total land area (2003): in temporary crops 23.9%, in permanent crops 0.4%, in pasture 25.1%; overall forest area (2005) 33.5%.

Foreign trade

Imports (2005; c.i.f.): €14,140,200,000 (machinery and apparatus 17.4%; transport equipment 14.5%; mineral fuels 12.3%; base and fabricated metals 10.6%; chemicals and chemical products 10.0%). *Major import sources:* Belgium 34.8%; Germany 27.0%; France 11.9%; The Netherlands 6.3%; Italy 3.0%. **Exports** (2005; f.o.b.): €10,175,600,000 (base and fabricated metals [mostly iron and steel] 28.8%; machinery and apparatus 19.6%; chemicals and chemical products 6.6%; transport equipment 6.3%). *Major export destinations:* Germany 26.1%; France 17.3%; Belgium 11.4%; Italy 6.4%; UK 5.2%.

Transport and communications

Transport. *Railroads* (2005): route length 275 km; passenger-km 272,000,000; metric ton-km cargo 420,000,000. *Roads* (2005): total length 2,894 km (paved 100%). *Vehicles* (2005): passenger cars 307,265; trucks and buses 26,203. *Air transport* (2006; Luxair only): passenger-km 516,000,000. **Communications,** in total units (units per 1,000 persons). Daily newspaper circulation (2004): 115,000 (253); televisions (2003): 70,000 (156); telephone landlines (2006): 247,000 (524); cellular telephone subscribers (2006): 714,000 (1,516); personal computers (2005): 290,000 (634); total Internet users (2006): 339,000 (720); broadband Internet subscribers (2006): 93,000 (202).

Education and health

Educational attainment (2003). Percentage of population ages 25–64 having: no formal schooling through primary education 19%; lower secondary 10%; upper secondary/higher vocational 56%; higher 15%. **Literacy** (2005): virtually 100%. **Health** (2004): physicians 1,591 (1 per 285 persons); hospital beds 3,045 (1 per 149 persons); infant mortality rate per 1,000 live births (2005) 2.6. **Food** (2005): daily per capita caloric intake 4,713 (vegetable products 65%, animal products 35%).

Military

Total active duty personnel (2006): 900 (army 100%). **Military expenditure as percentage of GDP** (2005): 0.8%; per capita expenditure US$584.

Background

At the time of Roman conquest (57–50 BC), Luxembourg was inhabited by a Belgic tribe. After AD 400, Germanic tribes invaded the region. Made a duchy in 1354, it was ceded to the house of Burgundy in 1443 and to the Habsburgs in 1477. In the mid-16th century it became part of the Spanish Netherlands. It was made a grand duchy in 1815. After an uprising in 1830, its western portion became part of Belgium, while the remainder was held by The Netherlands. In

1 metric ton = about 1.1 short tons; 1 kilometer = 0.6 mi (statute); 1 metric ton-km cargo = about 0.68 short ton-mi cargo; c.i.f.: cost, insurance, and freight; f.o.b.: free on board

1867 the European powers guaranteed the neutrality and independence of Luxembourg. In the late 19th century it exploited its extensive iron-ore deposits. It was invaded and occupied by Germany in both world wars. It abandoned its neutrality by joining NATO in 1949; it had joined the Benelux Economic Union in 1944. A member of the European Union, its economy has continued to expand. On 7 Oct 2000, Grand Duke Jean abdicated power in favor of his son, Crown Prince Henri, after 36 years on the throne.

Recent Developments

Luxembourg's economy was ranked the fourth most competitive in the world in 2007. While more than 80% of goods produced in Luxembourg were exported to the EU, the country was working actively to diversify its trade internationally. Luxembourg continued to work to develop its infrastructure and housing stock, and a new airport terminal was opened in May 2008.

Internet resources: <www.ont.lu>.

Macau

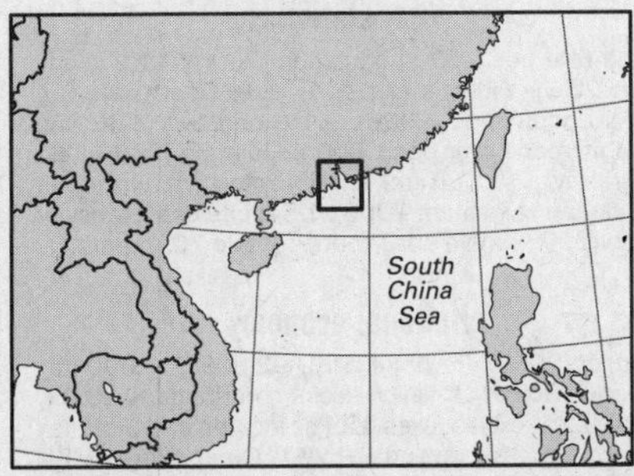

Official name: Aomen Tebie Xingzhengqu (Chinese); Região Administrativa Especial de Macau (Portuguese) (Macau Special Administrative Region). **Political status:** special administrative region (China) with one legislative house (Legislative Council [29]). **Chief of state:** President Hu Jintao of China (from 2003). **Head of government:** Chief Executive Edmund Ho Hau-wah (from 1999). **Capital:** Macau. **Official languages:** Chinese; Portuguese. **Official religion:** none. **Monetary unit:** 1 pataca (MOP) = 100 avos; valuation (1 Jul 2008) US$1 = MOP 8.03.

Demography

Area: 11.1 sq mi, 28.6 sq km. **Population** (2007): 527,000. **Density** (2007): persons per sq mi 47,477, persons per sq km 18,427. **Urban** (2006): virtually 100%. **Sex distribution** (2006): male 48.82%; female 51.18%. **Age breakdown** (2006): under 15, 15.2%; 15–29, 25.6%; 30–44, 26.3%; 45–59, 23.0%; 60–74, 6.6%; 75–84, 2.6%; 85 and over, 0.7%. **Ethnic composition** (by place of birth; 2006): mainland China 47.1%; Macau 42.5%; Hong Kong 3.7%; Philippines 2.0%; Portugal 0.3%; other 4.4%. **Religious affiliation** (1996): nonreligious 60.9%; Buddhist 16.8%; Buddhist/Taoist/Confucianist 13.9%; Roman Catholic 6.7%; Protestant 1.7%. **Major city** (2006): Macau 502,133. **Location:** eastern Asia, bordering China and the South China Sea.

Vital statistics

Birth rate per 1,000 population (2006): 8.1 (world avg. 20.3); (2004) within marriage 82.7%. **Death rate** per 1,000 population (2006): 3.1 (world avg. 8.6). **Total fertility rate** (avg. births per childbearing woman; 2005): 1.00. **Life expectancy** at birth (2001–04): male 77.5 years; female 82.1 years.

National economy

Budget (2004). *Revenue:* MOP 19,345,000,000 (revenue from gambling tax 78.8%; stamp duties 3.8%; property income tax 3.8%). *Expenditures:* MOP 17,703,000,000 (current expenditure 52.4%; specific accounts 25.5%; capital expenditure 22.1%). **Land use** as % of total land area (2004): "green area" 21.6%. **Gross national income** (at 2006 market prices): US$14,902,000,000 (US$31,207 per capita). **Production** (metric tons except as noted). *Agriculture, forestry, fishing* (2003): eggs 1,100,000; livestock (number of live animals; 2004) 700,000 chickens; fisheries production (2005) 1,500. *Quarrying* (value added in MOP '000; 2003): 17,139. *Manufacturing* (value added in US$'000,000; 2004): wearing apparel 240; textiles 56; furniture 35. *Energy production (consumption):* electricity (kW-hr; 2006) 1,668,000,000 ([2004] 2,124,000,000); petroleum products (metric tons; 2004) none (719,000). **Public debt** (long-term, external; 2004): US$3,100,000,000. **Population economically active** (2006): total 275,500; activity rate of total population 56.6% (participation rates: ages 14–64, 70.8%; female 46.6%; unemployed [January–March 2007] 3.2%). **Selected balance of payments data.** Receipts from (US$'000,000): tourism (2005) 7,757; remittances (2004) 72; foreign direct investment (2001–05 avg.) 443. Disbursements for (US$'000,000): remittances (2004) 132. **Households** (2002–03). Average household size (2006) 3.0; annual income per household MOP 183,648 (US$22,862); expenditure: food and nonalcoholic beverages 31.4%, housing and energy 29.9%, education, health, and other services 19.2%, transportation and communications 9.8%.

Foreign trade

Imports (2005): MOP 31,340,300,000 (consumer goods 38.2%; capital goods 18.5%; mineral fuels 9.7%). *Major import sources:* China 43.1%; EU 13.1%; Japan 10.9%; Hong Kong 10.0%; US 4.1%. **Exports** (2005): MOP 19,823,300,000 (domestic exports 72.5%, of which machine-knitted clothing 40.4%, machine-woven clothing 25.7%; reexports 27.5%). *Major export destinations:* US 48.7%; EU 17.1%, of which Germany 5.9%; China 14.9%; Hong Kong 9.8%.

Transport and communications

Transport. *Roads* (2004): total length 362 km (paved 100%). *Vehicles* (2006): passenger cars 67,384; trucks and buses 5,780. *Air transport* (2006; Air Macau only): passenger-km 3,039,000,000; metric ton-km cargo 193,000,000. **Communications,** in total units (units per 1,000 persons). Daily newspaper circulation (2005): 164,000 (347); televisions (2003): 130,000 (292); telephone landlines (2006): 177,000 (381); cellular telephone subscribers (2006): 636,000 (1,374); personal computers (2005): 160,000 (338); total Internet users (2006): 200,000 (432); broadband Internet subscribers (2006): 92,000 (183).

Education and health

Educational attainment (2006). Population ages 25 and over having: no formal schooling 6.2%; incomplete primary education 10.7%; completed primary 22.5%; incomplete secondary 24.9%; completed secondary 21.4%; higher technical 1.7%; university 12.6%. **Literacy** (2003): percentage of population ages 15 and over literate 94.5%; males literate 97.2%; females literate 92.0%. **Health** (2005): physicians 1,032 (1 per 473 persons); hospital beds 984 (1 per 496 persons); infant mortality rate per 1,000 live births (2006) 2.7.

Military

Total active duty personnel (2004): up to 1,000 Chinese troops; Macau residents are prohibited from entering military service.

Background

Portuguese traders first arrived in Macau in 1513, and it soon became the chief market center for the trade between China and Japan. It was declared a Portuguese colony in 1849 and an overseas territory in 1951. In December 1999 Portugal returned Macau to Chinese rule.

Recent Developments

Development in the gaming industry continued in Macau with the opening in August 2007 of the Venetian Macao, the world's largest casino, and in February 2008 of the Ponte 16 resort, which brought the number of casinos in Macau to 29. Gaming revenue for 2008 was projected to exceed US$10 billion, slightly lower than the US$10.4 billion earned in 2007.

Internet resources:
<www.macautourism.gov.mo/en>.

Macedonia

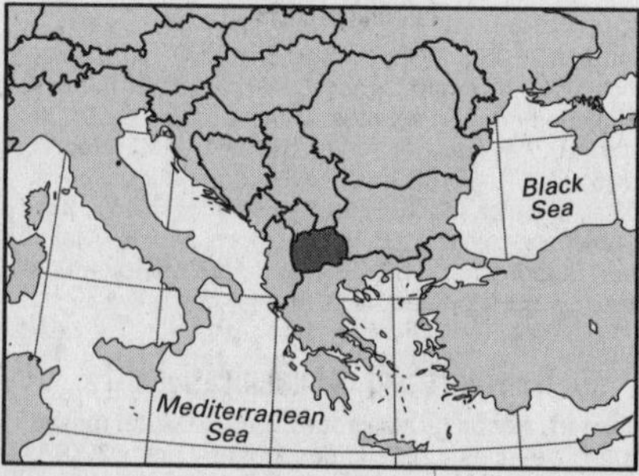

Official name: Republika Makedonija (Macedonian); Republika e Maqedonisë (Albanian) (Republic of Macedonia [member of the UN under the name The Former Yugoslav Republic of Macedonia]). **Form of government:** unitary multiparty republic with a unicameral legislature (Assembly [120]). **Head of state:** President Branko Crvenkovski (from 2004). **Head of government:** Prime Minister Nikola Gruevski (from 2006). **Capital:** Skopje. **Official languages:** Macedonian; Albanian. **Official religion:** none. **Monetary unit:** denar (MKD); valuation (1 Jul 2008) US$1 = 39.16 MKD.

Demography

Area: 9,928 sq mi, 25,713 sq km. **Population** (2007): 2,044,000. **Density** (2007): persons per sq mi 205.9, persons per sq km 79.5. **Urban** (2005): 68.9%. **Sex distribution** (2005): male 49.95%; female 50.05%. **Age breakdown** (2005): under 15, 20.5%; 15–29, 23.8%; 30–44, 21.8%; 45–59, 18.8%; 60–74, 11.5%; 75–84, 3.2%; 85 and over, 0.4%. **Ethnic composition** (2002): Macedonian 64.2%; Albanian 25.2%; Turkish 3.9%; Rom (Gypsy) 2.7%; Serbian 1.8%; Bosniac 0.8%; other 1.4%. **Religious affiliation** (2005): Orthodox 65%; Sunni Muslim 32%; Roman Catholic 1%; other (mostly Protestant) 2%. **Major municipalities** (2002): Skopje 467,257; Kumanovo 103,025; Bitola 86,408; Prilep 73,351; Tetovo 70,841. **Location:** southeastern Europe, bordering Kosovo, Serbia, Bulgaria, Greece, and Albania.

Vital statistics

Birth rate per 1,000 population (2006): 11.2 (world avg. 20.3); within marriage 87.5%. **Death rate** per 1,000 population (2006): 9.1 (world avg. 8.6). **Natural increase rate** per 1,000 population (2006): 2.1 (world avg. 11.7). **Total fertility rate** (avg. births per childbearing woman; 2005): 1.57. **Life expectancy** at birth (2005): male 71.3 years; female 76.4 years.

National economy

Budget (2005). *Revenue:* MKD 92,805,000,000 (tax revenue 90.8%, of which social contributions 30.8%, VAT 29.2%, excise taxes 12.7%, income and profit tax 11.8%; nontax revenue 9.2%). *Expenditure:* MKD 92,228,000,000 (transfers 55.0%, wages and salaries 24.0%). **Public debt** (external, outstanding; 2005): US$1,613,000,000. **Production** (metric tons except as noted). *Agriculture, forestry, fishing* (2005): wheat 333,900, grapes 265,700, potatoes 186,700; livestock (number of live animals) 1,200,000 sheep, 265,000 cattle; roundwood 822,000 cu m, of which fuelwood 81%; fisheries production 1,114 (from aquaculture 78%). *Mining and quarrying* (2005): copper (metal content) 21,800. *Manufacturing* (value added in US$'000,000; 2001): food products 186; textiles 89; glass and glass products 57. *Energy production (consumption):* electricity (kW-hr; 2005) 6,271,000,000 (7,933,000,000); hard coal (metric tons; 2004) none (9,000); lignite (metric tons; 2004) 7,245,000 (7,551,000); crude petroleum (barrels; 2004) none (6,090,000); petroleum products (metric tons; 2004) 807,000 (821,000); natural gas (cu m; 2004) none (70,000,000). **Households.** Average household size (2002) 3.6; sources of income (2000): wages and salaries 54.2%, transfers 22.6%; expenditure: food 38.4%, transportation and communications 9.7%, fuel 8.2%, beverages and tobacco 7.6%. **Population economically active** (2006): total 891,679; activity rate 55.1% (participation rates: ages 15–64, 61.4%; female 39.5%; unemployed 36.0%). **Gross national income** (2006): US$6,251,000,000 (US$3,070 per capita). **Selected balance of payments data.** Receipts from (US$'000,000): tourism (2005) 84; remittances (2005) 226; foreign direct investment (2001–05 avg.) 174; official development assistance (2005) 185 (commitments). Disbursements for (US$'000,000): tourism (2005) 60; remittances (2005) 16. **Land use** as % of total land area (2003): in temporary crops 22.3%, in permanent crops 1.8%, in pasture 24.8%; overall forest area (2005) 35.8%.

Foreign trade

Imports (2005; c.i.f.): US$3,228,000,000 (mineral fuels 19.2%; machinery and transport equipment 17.4%; food and live animals 10.6%; chemicals and chemical products 10.3%). *Major import sources:* Russia 13.2%; Germany 10.4%; Greece 9.2%; Serbia and Montenegro 8.2%; Bulgaria 7.3%. **Exports** (2005; f.o.b.): US$2,041,270,000 (clothing and accessories 27.3%; iron and steel 26.2%; food and live animals 8.2%; mineral fuels 8.0%; tobacco [all forms] 5.0%). *Major export destinations:* Serbia and Montenegro 22.5%; Germany 17.8%; Greece 15.3%; Italy 8.3%; Croatia 4.0%.

Transport and communications

Transport. *Railroads* (2005): length (2004) 699 km; passenger-km 94,000,000; metric ton-km cargo 531,000,000. *Roads* (2000): length 12,522 km (paved 58%). *Vehicles* (2002): passenger cars 307,581; trucks and buses 33,002. *Air transport* (2005; Macedonian Airlines only): passenger-km 266,000,000; metric ton-km cargo 111,000. **Communications,** in total units (units per 1,000 persons). Daily newspaper circulation (2004): 189,000 (93); televisions (2003): 507,000 (250); telephone landlines (2006): 491,000 (241); cellular telephone subscribers (2006): 1,417,000 (696); personal computers (2005): 451,000 (221); total Internet users (2006): 268,000 (132); broadband Internet subscribers (2006): 37,000 (18).

Education and health

Educational attainment (2002). Percentage of population ages 15 and over having: less than full primary education 18.1%; primary 35.0%; secondary 36.9%; postsecondary and higher 10.0%. **Literacy** (2003): total population ages 10 and over literate 96.1%; males literate 98.2%; females literate 94.1%. **Health:** physicians (2001) 4,459 (1 per 452 persons); hospital beds (2002) 9,757 (1 per 207 persons); infant mortality rate per 1,000 live births (2006) 8.9. **Food** (2005): daily per capita caloric intake 2,955 (vegetable products 79%, animal products 21%); 149% of FAO recommended minimum.

Military

Total active duty personnel (2006): 10,890 (army 89.6%, air force 10.4%). **Military expenditure as percentage of GDP** (2005): 2.2%; per capita expenditure US$62.

Background

Macedonia has been inhabited since before 7000 BC. Part of it was incorporated into a Roman province in AD 29. It was settled by Slavic tribes by the mid-6th century AD. Seized by the Bulgarians in 1185, it was ruled by the Ottoman Empire from 1371 to 1912. The north and center of the region were annexed by Serbia in 1913 and in 1918 became part of what was later known as Yugoslavia. When Yugoslavia was partitioned by the Axis powers in 1941, Yugoslav Macedonia was occupied principally by Bulgaria. Macedonia again became part of Yugoslavia in 1946. After Croatia and Slovenia seceded from Yugoslavia, fear of Serbian dominance drove Macedonia to declare its independence in 1991. Because of Greek objections to the new state using the name of an ancient Greek province, it entered the UN as "the Former Yugoslav Republic of Macedonia."

Recent Developments

The disagreement with Greece over Macedonia's name remained unresolved, though diplomats of both countries agreed in May 2007 to start a fresh round of talks. The European Union, disappointed at the slow pace of reform in the country, declined to set a date for the start of accession talks with Macedonia, though in April 2008, EU officials stated that the naming controversy should not be an impediment to Macedonian membership. Earlier in the month, however, Greece vetoed Macedonia's bid to join NATO over the dispute.

Internet resources: <www.exploringmacedonia.com>.

Madagascar

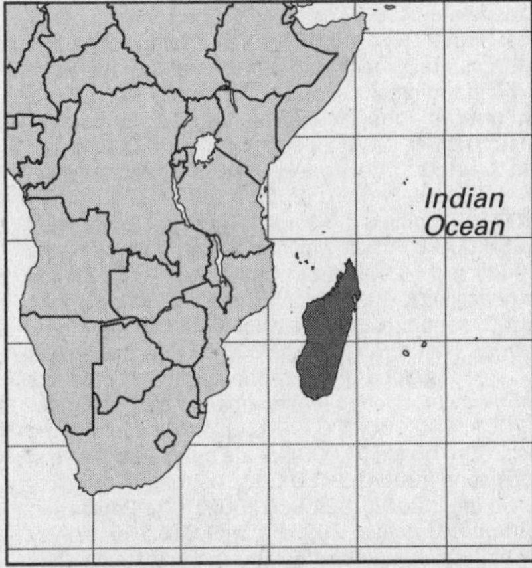

Official name: Repoblikan'i Madagasikara (Malagasy); République de Madagascar (French) (Republic of Madagascar). **Form of government:** multiparty republic with two legislative houses (Senate [90]; National Assembly [127]). **Heads of state and government:** President Marc Ravalomanana (from 2002), assisted by Prime Minister Charles Rabemananjara (from 2007). **Capital:** Antananarivo. **Official languages:** French; English; Malagasy is the national language. **Official religion:** none. **Monetary unit:** 1 ariary (MGA) = 100 centimes; valuation (1 Jul 2008) US$1 = MGA 1,592.00.

Demography

Area: 226,662 sq mi, 587,051 sq km. **Population** (2007): 19,683,000. **Density** (2007): persons per sq mi 86.8, persons per sq km 33.5. **Urban** (2006):

27.3%. **Sex distribution** (2005): male 49.72%; female 50.28%. **Age breakdown** (2006): under 15, 44.1%; 15–29, 27.1%; 30–44, 15.7%; 45–59, 8.4%; 60–74, 3.7%; 75–84, 0.9%; 85 and over, 0.1%. **Ethnic composition** (2000): Malagasy 95.9%, of which Merina 24.0%, Betsi-misaraka 13.4%, Betsileo 11.3%, Tsimihety 7.0%, Sakalava 5.9%; Makua 1.1%; French 0.6%; Comorian 0.5%; Reunionese 0.4%; other 1.5%. **Religious affiliation** (2005): traditional beliefs 42%; Protestant (significantly Lutheran) 27%; Roman Catholic 20%; Sunni Muslim 2%; other 9%. **Major cities** (2001): Antananarivo 1,403,449; Toamasina 179,045; Antsirabe 160,356; Fianarantsoa 144,225; Mahajanga 135,660. **Location:** island in the Indian Ocean, east of the mainland of southern Africa.

Vital statistics

Birth rate per 1,000 population (2006): 38.8 (world avg. 20.3). **Death rate** per 1,000 population (2006): 8.7 (world avg. 8.6). **Natural increase rate** per 1,000 population (2006): 30.1 (world avg. 11.7). **Total fertility rate** (avg. births per childbearing woman; 2006): 5.29. **Life expectancy** at birth (2006): male 59.9 years; female 63.7 years.

National economy

Budget (2004). *Revenue:* MGA 1,653,000,000,000 (tax revenue 53.7%, of which import duties 26.9%, VAT 10.5%; grants 40.6%; nontax revenue 5.7%). *Expenditures:* MGA 2,045,000,000,000 (current expenditure 50.2%; capital expenditure 49.8%). **Public debt** (external, outstanding; 2005): US$3,178,000,000. **Production** (metric tons except as noted). *Agriculture, forestry, fishing* (2005): paddy rice 3,400,000, sugarcane 2,446,000, cassava 2,144,000; livestock (number of live animals; 2006) 9,687,300 cattle, 1,600,000 pigs, 3,000,000 geese; roundwood 11,238,000 cu m, of which fuelwood 98%; fisheries production 144,900 (from aquaculture 6%). *Mining and quarrying* (2005): chromite ore 105,000; graphite 15,000; sapphires (export volume) 4,700 kg. *Manufacturing* (value in US$'000,000; 2004): beverages 107; wearing apparel 57; fabricated metal products 35. *Energy production (consumption):* electricity (kW-hr; 2004) 990,000,000 (990,000,000); coal (metric tons; 2004) none (10,000); crude petroleum (barrels; 2005) none ([2004] 3,480,000); petroleum products (metric tons; 2004) 321,000 (602,000). **Population economically active** (2005): total 9,844,100; activity rate of total population 52.8% (participation rates: ages 15–64, 88.1%; female 49.6%; unemployed 2.8%). **Selected balance of payments data.** Receipts from (US$'000,000): tourism (2005) 62; remittances (2005) 3; foreign direct investment (2001–05 avg.) 59; official development assistance (2005) 929. Disbursements for (US$'000,000): tourism (2005) 25; remittances (2005) 8. **Households.** Average household size (2003–04) 4.6; expenditure (2000): food, beverages, and tobacco 50.1%, housing and energy 18.2%, transportation 8.0%. **Gross national income** (at current market prices; 2006): US$5,414,000,000 (US$283 per capita). **Land use** as % of total land area (2003): in temporary crops 5.1%, in permanent crops 1.0%, in pasture 41.3%; overall forest area (2005) 22.1%.

Foreign trade

Imports (2006; c.i.f.): US$1,760,300,000 (petroleum [all forms] 18.3%; textiles 17.9%; food and live animals 11.4%; chemical products 8.6%). *Major import sources:* China 17.8%; Bahrain 16.4%; France 13.2%; South Africa 5.7%; US 3.6%. **Exports** (2006): US$1,008,200,000 (textiles and wearing apparel 25.0%; shellfish 13.4%; petroleum [all forms] 8.0%; vanilla 4.7%; cloves 2.7%). *Major export destinations:* France 39.5%; US 15.0%; Germany 6.0%; Italy 4.2%; UK 3.0%.

Transport and communications

Transport. *Railroads:* route length (2003) 901 km; (2000) passenger-km 24,471,000; (2000) metric ton-km cargo 27,200,000. *Roads* (1999): total length 49,827 km (paved 12%). *Vehicles* (1998): passenger cars 64,000; trucks and buses 9,100. *Air transport* (2005; Air Madagascar only): passenger-km 1,177,875,000; metric ton-km cargo 15,365,000. **Communications,** in total units (units per 1,000 persons). Daily newspaper circulation (2005): 141,000 (7.6); televisions (2002): 410,000 (25); telephone landlines (2006): 130,000 (6.8); cellular telephone subscribers (2006): 1,046,000 (55); personal computers (2005): 102,000 (5.5); total Internet users (2006): 110,000 (5.8).

Education and health

Educational attainment (2003–04). Percentage of population ages 25–59 (male) and 25–49 (female) having: no formal schooling 20.4%; incomplete primary education 33.6%; complete primary 13.2%; incomplete secondary 23.0%; complete secondary 6.4%; higher 3.4%. **Literacy** (2006): percentage of total population ages 15 and over literate 70.7%; males literate 76.5%; females literate 65.3%. **Health** (2004): physicians 1,861 (1 per 9,998 persons); hospital beds 9,303 (1 per 2,000 persons); infant mortality rate (2006) 58.5. **Food** (2005): daily per capita caloric intake 2,046 (vegetable products 91%, animal products 9%); 136% of FAO recommended minimum.

Military

Total active duty personnel (2006): 13,500 (army 92.6%, navy 3.7%, air force 3.7%). **Military expenditure as percentage of GDP** (2005): 1.1%; per capita expenditure US$3.

Background

Indonesians migrated to Madagascar about AD 700. The first European to visit the island was Portuguese navigator Diogo Dias in 1500. Trade in arms and slaves allowed the development of Malagasy kingdoms at the beginning of the 17th century. The Merina kingdom became dominant in the 18th century and in 1868 signed a treaty granting France control over the northwestern coast. In 1895 French troops took the island, and Madagascar became a French overseas territory in 1946. As the Malagasy Republic, it gained independence in 1960. It severed ties with France in the 1970s, taking its present name in

1 metric ton = about 1.1 short tons; 1 kilometer = 0.6 mi (statute); 1 metric ton-km cargo = about 0.68 short ton-mi cargo; c.i.f.: cost, insurance, and freight; f.o.b.: free on board

1975. A new constitution was adopted in 1992. The country has since been both politically and economically unstable.

Recent Developments

After winning election to a second five-year term in office in December 2006, Pres. Marc Ravalomanana pushed through a number of amendments to the Madagascar constitution in 2007. They included reducing the size of the National Assembly from 160 to 127 seats, ending the autonomy of Madagascar's provinces, and giving the president increased powers, including authority to make laws directly if a state of emergency were declared. More than 70% of those who voted in a national referendum held in April supported the constitutional changes, though the parliamentary opposition called for a boycott.

Internet resources: <www.wildmadagascar.org/>.

Malawi

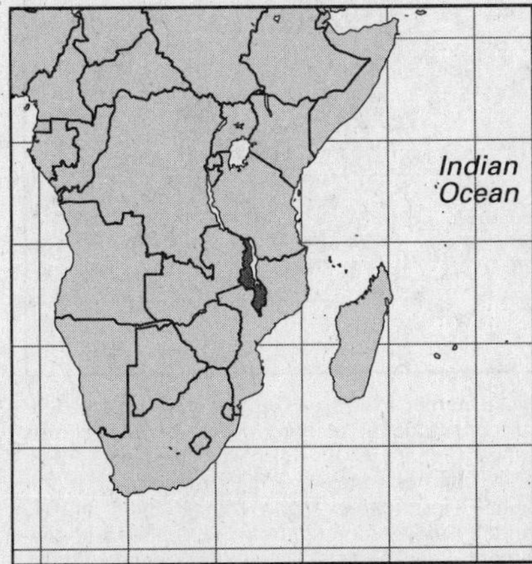

Official name: Republic of Malawi. **Form of government:** multiparty republic with one legislative house (National Assembly [193]). **Head of state and government:** President Bingu wa Mutharika (from 2004). **Capital:** Lilongwe. **Official language:** none. **Official religion:** none. **Monetary unit:** 1 Malawi kwacha (MK) = 100 tambala; valuation (1 Jul 2008) US$1 = MK 140.51.

Demography

Area: 45,747 sq mi, 118,484 sq km. **Population** (2007): 13,603,000. **Density** (2007): persons per sq mi 373.7, persons per sq km 144.3. **Urban** (2005): 17.2%. **Sex distribution** (2005): male 49.65%; female 50.35%. **Age breakdown** (2005): under 15, 47.3%; 15–29, 27.6%; 30–44, 12.9%; 45–59, 7.5%; 60–74, 3.8%; 75–84, 0.8%; 85 and over, 0.1%. **Ethnic composition** (2000): Chewa 34.7%; Maravi 12.2%; Ngoni 9.0%; Yao 7.9%; Tumbuka 7.9%; Lomwe 7.7%; Ngonde 3.5%; other 17.1%. **Religious affiliation** (2005): Protestant/independent Christian 55%; Roman Catholic 20%; Muslim 20%; traditional beliefs 3%; other 2%. **Major cities** (2006): Blantyre 744,734; Lilongwe 706,322; Mzuzu 142,128; Zomba 107,195; Karonga (1998) 27,811. **Location:** southeastern Africa, bordering Tanzania, Mozambique, and Zambia.

Vital statistics

Birth rate per 1,000 population (2006): 42.4 (world avg. 20.3). **Death rate** per 1,000 population (2006): 18.7 (world avg. 8.6). **Natural increase rate** per 1,000 population (2006): 23.7 (world avg. 11.7). **Total fertility rate** (avg. births per childbearing woman; 2006): 5.82. **Life expectancy** at birth (2006): male 42.8 years; female 41.9 years.

National economy

Budget (2005). *Revenue:* MK 103,298,600,000 (tax revenue 52.9%, of which VAT 16.7%, income tax 11.7%, excises 7.3%, import tax 6.4%; grants 38.7%; nontax revenue 8.4%). *Expenditures:* MK 110,943,700,000 (current expenditure 76.3%; capital expenditure 21.0%; other 2.7%). **Production** (metric tons except as noted). *Agriculture, forestry, fishing* (2006): sugarcane 2,100,000, cassava 2,075,000, potatoes 1,800,000; livestock (number of live animals) 1,900,000 goats, 750,000 cattle, 456,300 pigs; roundwood (2005) 5,661,000 cu m, of which fuelwood 91%; fisheries production (2005) 59,595 (from aquaculture 1%). *Mining and quarrying* (2005): limestone 28,000; gemstones (including rubies and sapphires) 1,400 kg. *Manufacturing* (value added in US$'000,000; 2001): food products 62; beverages 28; chemicals and chemical products 11. *Energy production (consumption):* electricity (kW-hr; 2004) 1,270,000,000 (1,262,000,000); hard coal (metric tons; 2004) 70,000 (57,000); petroleum products (metric tons; 2004) none (275,000). **Land use** as % of total land area (2003): in temporary crops 26.0%, in permanent crops 1.5%, in pasture 19.7%; overall forest area (2005) 36.2%. **Population economically active** (2003): total 5,707,000; activity rate of total population 46.3% (participation rates: ages 15–64, 88.0%; female 49.7%). **Households** (2004–05). Average household size 4.5; average annual household income MK 50,904 (US$467); expenditure: food 55.6%, housing and energy 20.6%, transportation and communications 6.6%. **Gross national income** (2006): US$2,194,000,000 (US$162 per capita). **Public debt** (external, outstanding; 2006): US$496,600,000. **Selected balance of payments data.** Receipts from (US$'000,000): tourism (2005) 23; remittances (2005) 1.0; foreign direct investment (2001–05 avg.) 9.2; official development assistance (2005) 575. Disbursements for (US$'000,000): tourism (2005) 47; remittances (2005) 1.0.

Foreign trade

Imports (2003; f.o.b. in balance of trade and c.i.f. in commodities and trading partners): MK 70,500,000,000 (chemicals and chemical products 16.6%; machinery and apparatus 15.4%; refined petroleum products 11.3%; road vehicles 10.5%; food 7.9%). *Major import sources* (2004): South Africa 40.4%; India 7.9%; Tanzania 4.9%; Zambia 4.4%; US 3.6%. **Exports** (2004): MK 52,627,000,000 (tobacco 42.3%; sugar 15.0%; tea 9.8%; cotton 4.2%; reexports 4.0%). *Major export destinations* (2004): South Africa 13.4%; US 12.2%; Germany 11.9%; Egypt 8.6%; UK 6.8%.

Transport and communications

Transport. *Railroads* (2004): route length 797 km; passenger-km 29,523,000; metric ton-km cargo 26,055,000. *Roads* (2003): total length 15,451 km (paved 45%). *Vehicles* (2001): passenger cars 22,500; trucks and buses 57,600. *Air transport* (2005; Air Malawi only): passenger-km 201,000,000; metric ton-km cargo 1,364,000. **Communications,** in total units (units per 1,000 persons). Daily newspaper circulation (2005): 22,000 (1.7); televisions (2003): 65,000 (5.2); telephone landlines (2005): 103,000 (7.9); cellular telephone subscribers (2005): 532,000 (41); personal computers (2005): 25,000 (1.9); total Internet users (2006): 60,000 (4.5); broadband Internet subscribers (2005): 400 (0.03).

Education and health

Educational attainment (2004). Percentage of population ages 25 and over having: no formal education/unknown 33.5%; incomplete primary education 24.2%; complete primary 27.9%; secondary and university 14.4%. **Literacy** (2005): total population ages 15 and over literate 64.3%; males literate 77.1%; females literate 51.9%. **Health:** physicians (2004) 266 (1 per 46,644 persons); hospital beds (1998) 14,087 (1 per 735 persons); infant mortality rate per 1,000 live births (2006) 93.7. **Food** (2005): daily per capita caloric intake 2,231 (vegetable products 97%, animal products 3%); 125% of FAO recommended minimum.

Military

Total active duty personnel (2006): 5,300 (army 100%). **Military expenditure as percentage of GDP** (2005): 0.7%; per capita expenditure US$1.

Cape Maclear Beach, located at the southern tip of Lake Malawi (in Lake Malawi National Park), is a favorite vacation spot in Africa because of its 3 mi (5 km) of beaches and its fine restaurants.

Background

Inhabited since at least 8000 BC, the region was settled by Bantu-speaking peoples between the 1st and the 4th century AD. About 1480 they founded the Maravi Confederacy, which encompassed most of central and southern Malawi. In northern Malawi the Ngonde people established a kingdom about 1600. The slave trade flourished during the 18th–19th centuries. Britain established colonial authority in 1891, and the area became known as Nyasaland in 1907. The colonies of Northern and Southern Rhodesia and Nyasaland formed a federation (1951–53), which was dissolved in 1963. The next year Malawi achieved independence. In 1966 it became a republic, with Hastings Banda as president. In 1971 Banda was designated president for life, and he ruled until he was defeated in multiparty elections in 1994. A new constitution was adopted in 1995.

Recent Developments

A bumper corn (maize) harvest for the second consecutive year helped Malawi's recovery in 2007 from long periods of drought and made it possible in May to supply Zimbabwe with US$120 million of the cereal. In August an additional 10,000 tons were provided for drought-stricken Lesotho and Swaziland. The granting in April of a mining license to a subsidiary of an Australian company to develop uranium deposits near Lake Malawi was viewed as a positive economic development, though critics were concerned about its impact on the environment and public health.

Internet resources: <www.malawi-tourism-association.org.mw>.

Malaysia

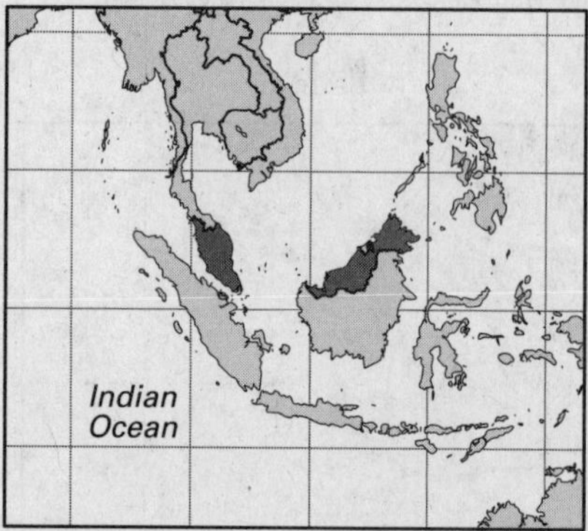

Official name: Malaysia. **Form of government:** federal constitutional monarchy with two legislative houses (Senate [70]; House of Representatives [219]). **Chief of state:** Yang di-Pertuan Agong (Paramount Ruler) Tuanku Mizan Zainal Abidin ibni al-Marhum Sultan Mahmud (from 2006). **Head of government:** Prime Minister Datuk Seri Abdullah Ahmad Badawi (from 2003). **Capital:** transferring from Kuala Lumpur to Putrajaya between 1999 and 2012. **Official language:** Malay. **Official religion:** Islam. **Monetary unit:** 1 ringgit, or Malaysian dollar (RM) = 100 cents; valuation (1 Jul 2008) US$1 = RM 3.27.

Demography

Area: 127,366 sq mi, 329,876 sq km. **Population** (2007): 26,572,000. **Density** (2007): persons per sq mi 208.6, persons per sq km 80.6. **Urban** (2005): 67.3%. **Sex distribution** (2005): male 50.75%; female 49.25%. **Age breakdown** (2005): under 15, 32.4%; 15–29, 26.2%; 30–44, 20.6%; 45–59, 13.8%; 60–74, 5.6%; 75–84, 1.2%; 85 and over, 0.2%. **Ethnic composition** (2005): Malay 50.5%; other indigenous 11.0%; Chinese 23.5%; Indian 7.0%; other citizen 1.2%; noncitizen 6.8%. **Religious affiliation** (2000): Muslim 60.4%; Buddhist 19.2%; Christian 9.1%; Hindu 6.3%; Chinese folk religionist 2.6%; animist 0.8%; other 1.6%. **Major cities** (2000): Kuala Lumpur 1,297,526; Ipoh 566,211; Klang 563,173;

Petaling Jaya 438,084; Johor Bahru 384,613; Putrajaya (2006) 55,000. **Location:** southeastern Asia, on the Malay Peninsula and the northern third of the island of Borneo, bordering Thailand, the South China Sea, Brunei, and Indonesia.

Vital statistics

Birth rate per 1,000 population (2006): 18.7 (world avg. 20.3). **Death rate** per 1,000 population (2006): 4.5 (world avg. 8.6). **Total fertility rate** (avg. births per childbearing woman; 2005): 3.07. **Life expectancy** at birth (2006): male 71.8 years; female 76.3 years.

National economy

Budget (2005). *Revenue:* RM 105,856,000,000 (income tax revenue 71.2%, of which corporate taxes 19.4%, taxes on petroleum 15.9%, personal income taxes 9.4%, excises 7.9%; nontax revenue 28.8%). *Expenditures:* RM 128,755,000,000 (current expenditure 76.3%; development expenditure 23.7%). **Population economically active** (2004): total 10,353,600; activity rate of total population 40.5% (participation rates: ages 15–64 [2000] 65.5%; female 47.3%; unemployed [April 2006–March 2007] 3.2%). **Production** (metric tons except as noted). *Agriculture, forestry, fishing* (2006): oil palm fruit 75,650,000, rice 2,154,000, natural rubber 1,283,600; livestock (number of live animals) 2,168,000 pigs, 185,000,000 chickens; roundwood 28,237,000 cu m, of which fuelwood 11%; fisheries production (2005) 1,390,000 (from aquaculture 13%). *Mining and quarrying* (2004): iron ore 663,732; tin (metal content) 2,745; gold 4,221 kg. *Manufacturing* (value added in RM '000,000; 2004): electrical machinery/electronics 39,790; chemical products 16,468; petroleum and coal products 16,183. *Energy production (consumption):* electricity (kW-hr; 2004) 82,282,000,000 (81,759,000,000); coal (metric tons; 2005) 792,000 ([2004] 13,275,000); crude petroleum (barrels; 2006) 250,500,000 ([2004] 200,800,000); petroleum products (metric tons; 2004) 20,450,000 (21,244,000); natural gas (cu m; May 2006–April 2007) 60,360,000,000 ([2004] 30,045,000,000). **Gross national income** (2006): US$141,751,000,000 (US$5,428 per capita). **Public debt** (external, outstanding; 2005): US$22,449,000,000. **Households.** Average household size (2004) 4.6; annual gross income per household (2002) RM 36,132 (US$9,508); expenditure (2003): food and nonalcoholic beverages 26.0%, housing and energy 22.1%, transportation 20.8%, restaurants and hotels 6.1%. **Selected balance of payments data.** Receipts from (US$'000,000): tourism (2005) 8,846; remittances (2006) 1,492; foreign direct investment (FDI) (2001–05 avg.) 2,964; official development assistance (2005) 798 (commitments). Disbursements for (US$'000,000): tourism (2005) 3,711; remittances (2006) 5,527; FDI (2001–05 avg.) 1,715. **Land use** as % of total land area (2003): in temporary crops 5.5%, in permanent crops 17.6%, in pasture 0.9%; overall forest area (2005) 63.6%.

Foreign trade

Imports (2004; c.i.f.): RM 400,076,800,000 (microcircuits, transistors, and valves 25.7%; computers/office machines 5.9%; petroleum products 5.3%; telecommunications equipment 3.6%). *Major import sources* (2006): Japan 13.2%; US 12.5%; China 12.1%; Singapore 11.7%; Thailand 5.5%. **Exports** (2006; f.o.b.): RM 588,965,000,000 (semiconductors/office machines 37.6%; crude and refined petroleum 8.8%; telecommunications equipment 5.9%; natural gas 4.0%; palm oil 3.7%). *Major export destinations* (2006): US 18.8%; Singapore 15.4%; Japan 8.9%; China 7.2%; Thailand 5.3%.

Transport and communications

Transport. *Railroads* (2004): route length 1,949 km; passenger-km 1,152,139,000; metric ton-km cargo 1,016,730,000. *Roads* (2004): total length 77,695 km (paved 76%). *Vehicles* (2004): passenger cars 5,987,421; trucks and buses 827,215. *Air transport* (2006; Malaysia Airlines only): passenger-km 41,100,000,000; metric ton-km cargo 2,598,000,000. **Communications**, in total units (units per 1,000 persons). Daily newspaper circulation (2005): 2,435,000 (93); televisions (2003): 5,480,000 (222); telephone landlines (2006): 4,342,000 (163); cellular telephone subscribers (2006): 19,464,000 (731); personal computers (2005): 5,600,000 (218); total Internet users (2006): 11,292,000 (424); broadband Internet subscribers (2006): 897,000 (34).

Education and health

Educational attainment (2002). Percentage of population ages 25–64 having: no formal schooling/unknown 8.4%; primary education 28.7%; lower secondary 20.7%; upper secondary 31.1%; higher 11.1%. **Literacy** (2004): total population ages 15 and over literate 94.4%; males literate 95.6%; females literate 93.2%. **Health** (2004): physicians 18,246 (1 per 1,402 persons); hospital beds 47,822 (1 per 535 persons); infant mortality rate per 1,000 live births (2006) 6.6. **Food** (2005): daily per capita caloric intake 3,035 (vegetable products 84%, animal products 16%); 164% of FAO recommended minimum.

Military

Total active duty personnel (2006): 109,000 (army 73.4%, navy 12.8%, air force 13.8%). **Military expenditure as percentage of GDP** (2005): 2.4%; per capita expenditure US$119.

Background

Malaya has been inhabited for 6,000–8,000 years, and small kingdoms existed in the 2nd–3rd century AD, when adventurers from India first arrived. Sumatran exiles founded the city-state of Malacca about 1400, and it flourished as a trading and Islamic religious center until its capture by the Portuguese in 1511. Malacca passed to the Dutch in 1641. The British founded a settlement on Singapore Island in 1819, and by 1867 they had established the Straits Settlements, including Malacca, Singapore, and Penang. During the late 19th century the Chinese began to migrate to Malaya. Japan invaded in 1941. Opposition to British rule led to the creation of the United Malays National Organization (UNMO) in 1946, and in 1948 the peninsula was federated with Penang. Malaya gained independence in 1957, and the Federation of Malaysia was established in 1963. Its economy expanded greatly from the late 1970s, but it suffered from the economic slump that struck the area in the mid-1990s.

Recent Developments

Malaysia's economy remained robust in 2007, with GDP growth of 6.3% for the year. The country enjoyed a large trade surplus, but with plantations in Johor damaged by flooding, exports of palm oil (Malaysia's most valuable agricultural export, contributing about 13% of the value of GDP in 2007) dropped by about 10%. One year after its launch in September 2006, Malaysia's biotechnology initiative had attracted about 40 companies and investments of 1 billion ringgit (about US$300 million). In February Malaysia, Indonesia, and Brunei pledged to protect 200,000 sq km (124,000 sq mi) of rainforest on the island of Borneo, where palm-oil plantations and logging had destroyed vast tracts of rainforest. In June the US added Malaysia to a list of countries that it said were not doing enough to stop human trafficking, a charge the government denied. Free-trade negotiations with the United States broke down and showed no signs of starting again in 2008.

Internet resources: <www.motour.gov.my>.

Maldives

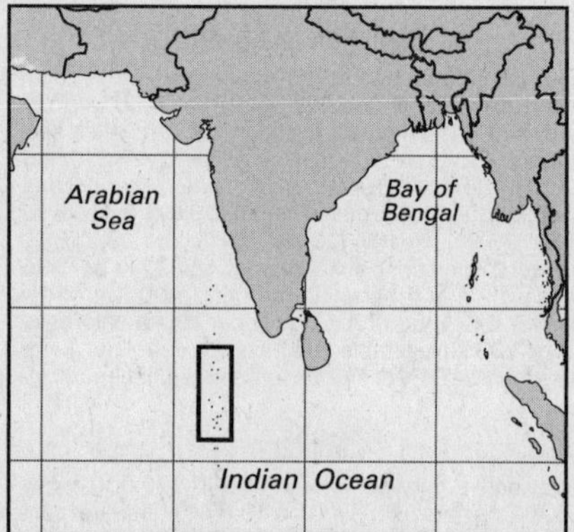

Official name: Dhivehi Raajjeyge Jumhooriyyaa (Republic of Maldives). **Form of government:** multiparty republic with one legislative house (Majlis [50]). **Head of state and government:** President Maumoon Abdul Gayoom (from 1978). **Capital:** Male. **Official language:** Divehi. **Official religion:** Islam. **Monetary unit:** 1 Maldivian rufiyaa (Rf) = 100 laari; valuation (1 Jul 2008) US$1 = Rf 12.80.

Demography

Area: 115 sq mi, 298 sq km. **Population** (2007): 305,000. **Density** (2007): persons per sq mi 6,763, persons per sq km 2,611. **Urban** (2006): 34.7%. **Sex distribution** (2006): male 50.66%; female 49.34%. **Age breakdown** (2006): under 15, 31.1%; 15–29, 33.2%; 30–44, 18.3%; 45–59, 9.2%; 60–74, 5.2%; 75–84, 1.1%; 85 and over, 0.2%; unknown 1.7%. **Ethnic composition** (2000): Maldivian 98.5%; Sinhalese 0.7%; other 0.8%. **Religious affiliation:** virtually 100% Sunni Muslim. **Major islets** (2006): Male (capital island) 103,693; Hithadhoo 9,465; Fuvammulah 7,636; Kulhudhuffushi 6,998; Thinadhoo 4,442. **Location:** islands in the Indian Ocean, south of India.

Vital statistics

Birth rate per 1,000 population (2005): 18.7 (world avg. 20.3). **Death rate** per 1,000 population (2005): 3.4 (world avg. 8.6). **Total fertility rate** (avg. births per childbearing woman; 2005): 2.72. **Life expectancy** at birth (2005): male 71.7 years; female 72.7 years.

National economy

Budget (2006). *Revenue:* Rf 6,548,800,000 (nontax revenue 41.3%, of which resort lease rent 19.2%; tax revenue 32.2%, of which import duties 23.2%; grants 25.9%; other 0.6%). *Expenditures:* Rf 8,644,700,000 (community programs 25.7%; economic services 18.0%; general administration 17.6%; education 13.0%; police/security 10.4%; health 8.9%). **Production** (metric tons except as noted). *Agriculture, forestry, fishing* (2005): coconuts 15,827, bananas 3,930; fisheries production 185,980, of which skipjack 132,100, yellowfin tuna 24,600. *Mining and quarrying:* coral for construction materials. *Manufacturing:* major industries include boat building and repairing, coir yarn and mat weaving, coconut and fish processing, lacquerwork, garment manufacturing, and handicrafts. *Energy production (consumption):* electricity (kW-hr; 2004) 160,000,000 (160,000,000); petroleum products (metric tons; 2004) none (236,000). **Selected balance of payments data.** Receipts from (US$'000,000): tourism (2005) 287; remittances (2006) 2; foreign direct investment (2001–05 avg.) 13; official development assistance (2005) 67. Disbursements for (US$'000,000): tourism (2005) 70; remittances (2006) 84. **Population economically active** (2006): total 128,836; activity rate of total population 43.1% (participation rates: ages 15–64, 65.8%; female 41.3%; unemployed 14.4%). **Households** (2002–03). Average household size (2006) 6.5; average annual income per household Rf 188,743 (US$14,746); sources of income: self-employment 34.5%, wages and salaries 31.5%, rent 13.4%; expenditure: housing and energy 35.8%, food, beverages, and tobacco 29.9%, transportation and communications 7.8%. **Land use** as % of total land area (2003): in temporary crops 13%, in permanent crops 30%, in pasture 3%; overall forest area (2005) 3%. **Gross national income** (at 2006 market prices): US$870,000,000 (US$2,897 per capita). **Public debt** (external, outstanding; December 2006): US$267,300,000.

Foreign trade

Imports (2006; c.i.f.): US$644,700,000 (consumer goods 34.2%, of which food products 15.2%; petroleum products 19.6%; construction-related goods 13.1%; transport equipment 8.2%). *Major import sources:* Singapore 23.9%; UAE 21.1%; India 9.4%; Malaysia 6.6%; Sri Lanka 6.1%. **Exports** (2006; f.o.b.): US$225,200,000 (domestic exports 60.0%, of which chilled or frozen tuna 44.8%, dried fish 5.6%, canned fish 5.1%; reexports [mostly jet fuel] 40.0%). *Major export destinations:* Thailand 26.1%; Japan 15.0%; Sri Lanka 12.8%; UK 9.7%; France 5.1%.

1 metric ton = about 1.1 short tons; 1 kilometer = 0.6 mi (statute); 1 metric ton-km cargo = about 0.68 short ton-mi cargo; c.i.f.: cost, insurance, and freight; f.o.b.: free on board

Transport and communications

Transport. *Vehicles:* passenger cars (2007) 3,393; trucks and buses (2005) 1,573. *Air transport* (2005; Male airport only): passenger arrivals 773,845, passenger departures 761,922; cargo unloaded 17,336 metric tons, cargo loaded 10,923 metric tons. **Communications,** in total units (units per 1,000 persons). Daily newspaper circulation (2005): 8,000 (25); televisions (2003): 41,000 (144); telephone landlines (2006): 33,000 (110); cellular telephone subscribers (2006): 263,000 (876); personal computers (2005): 45,000 (152); total Internet users (2005): 20,000 (68); broadband Internet subscribers (2006): 4,700 (16).

Education and health

Educational attainment (2000). Population ages 25 and over 71,937, of which percentage with university education 0.4%. **Literacy** (2003): total population ages 15 and over literate 97.4%; males literate 97.4%; females literate 97.3%. **Health** (2005): physicians 380 (1 per 775 persons); hospital beds 765 (1 per 384 persons); infant mortality rate per 1,000 live births 12.1. **Food** (2005): daily per capita caloric intake 3,327 (vegetable products 80%, animal products 20%); 181% of FAO recommended minimum.

Military

Total active duty personnel (2006): n.a.; the national security service (paramilitary police force) includes an air element and coast guard. **Military expenditure as percentage of GDP** (2005): 5.5%; per capita expenditure US$169.

Background

The archipelago was settled in the 5th century BC by Buddhists from Sri Lanka and southern India, and Islam was adopted there in 1153. The Portuguese held sway in Male in 1558–73. The islands were a sultanate under the Dutch rulers of Ceylon (now Sri Lanka) during the 17th century. After the British gained control of Ceylon in 1796, the area became a British protectorate, a status formalized in 1887. The islands won full independence from Britain in 1965, and in 1968 a republic was founded. During the 1990s its economy gradually developed.

Recent Developments

In the wake of the first-ever bomb explosion in Male targeting foreign tourists, the government remained seriously concerned over the growing threat of Islamic extremism. As a countermeasure, it began to crack down on religious groups advocating Islamic fundamentalism and militancy. Among other steps, the government declared that bearded mullahs or clerics were barred from entering the country unless invited by the authorities. The political reform process continued at a snail's pace in 2007. An August referendum on the nature of the political system resulted in an overwhelming number of voters choosing a presidential system over a parliamentary one. In August 2008, however, a new constitution, providing for multiparty elections, was signed and adopted.

Internet resources: <www.visitmaldives.com>.

Mali

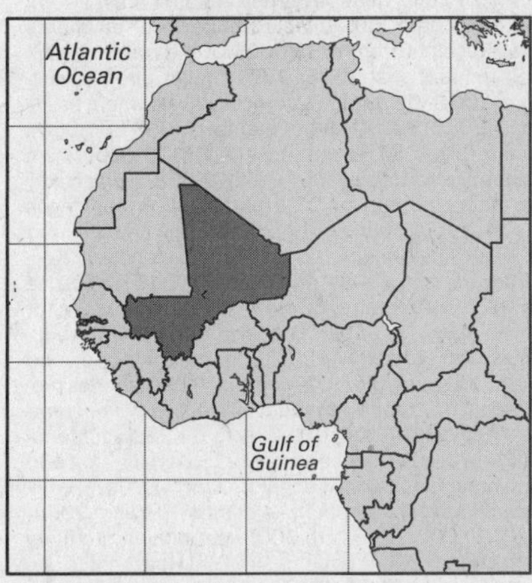

Official name: République du Mali (Republic of Mali). **Form of government:** multiparty republic with one legislative house (National Assembly [147]). **Chief of state:** President Amadou Toumani Touré (from 2002). **Head of government:** Prime Minister Modibo Sidibé (from 2007). **Capital:** Bamako. **Official language:** French. **Official religion:** none. **Monetary unit:** 1 CFA franc (CFAF) = 100 centimes; valuation (1 Jul 2008) US$1 = CFAF 414.60.

Demography

Area: 482,077 sq mi, 1,248,574 sq km. **Population** (2007): 11,995,000. **Density** (2007): persons per sq mi 24.9, persons per sq km 9.6. **Urban** (2005): 30.5%. **Sex distribution** (2006): male 49.67%; female 50.33%. **Age breakdown** (2006): under 15, 48.1%; 15–29, 27.7%; 30–44, 12.9%; 45–59, 6.4%; 60–74, 4.1%; 75–84, 0.7%; 85 and over, 0.1%. **Ethnic composition** (2000): Bambara 30.6%; Senufo 10.5%; Fula Macina (Niafunke) 9.6%; Soninke 7.4%; Tuareg 7.0%; Maninka 6.6%; Songhai 6.3%; Dogon 4.3%; Bobo 3.5%; other 14.2%. **Religious affiliation** (2005): Muslim (nearly all Sunni) 90%; Christian (mostly Roman Catholic) 5%; traditional beliefs/nonreligious 5%. **Major cities** (1998): Bamako (2005; urban agglomeration) 1,368,000; Sikasso 113,803; Ségou 90,898; Mopti 79,840; Koutiala 74,153. **Location:** western Africa, bordering Algeria, Niger, Burkina Faso, Côte d'Ivoire, Guinea, Senegal, and Mauritania.

Vital statistics

Birth rate per 1,000 population (2006): 49.9 (world avg. 20.3). **Death rate** per 1,000 population (2006): 16.9 (world avg. 8.6). **Natural increase rate** per 1,000 population (2006): 33.0 (world avg. 11.7). **Total fertility rate** (avg. births per childbearing woman; 2006): 7.42. **Life expectancy** at birth (2006): male 47.2 years; female 51.0 years.

National economy

Budget (2006). *Revenue:* CFAF 694,300,000,000 (tax revenue 66.1%; grants 23.4%; nontax revenue 4.3%; other 6.2%). *Expenditures:* CFAF 795,100,000,000 (current expenditure 56.8%; capital expenditure 43.2%). **Public debt** (external, outstanding; 2005): US$2,843,000,000. **Selected balance of payments data.** Receipts from (US$'000,000): tourism (2005) 148; remittances (2006) 177; foreign direct investment (2001–05 avg.) 152; official development assistance (2005) 691. Disbursements for (US$'000,000): tourism (2005) 77; remittances (2006) 70. **Population economically active** (2004): total 2,598,200; activity rate of total population 23% (participation rates: ages 15–64, 51.1%; female 42.5%; officially unemployed 8.8%). **Production** (metric tons except as noted). *Agriculture, forestry, fishing* (2005): millet 1,157,810, rice 945,823, corn (maize) 634,464; livestock (number of live animals) 12,050,000 goats, 8,370,000 sheep, 7,700,000 cattle, 472,000 camels; roundwood 5,440,000 cu m, of which fuelwood 92%; fisheries production 101,008 (from aquaculture 1%). *Mining and quarrying* (2005): salt 6,000; gold 44,230 kg. *Manufacturing* (2001): beef and veal 215,000; mutton and lamb meat 66,000; raw sugar (2003) 34,000. *Energy production (consumption):* electricity (kW-hr; 2004) 455,000,000 (455,000,000); petroleum products (metric tons; 2004) none (184,000). **Households.** Average household size (2004) 6.0. **Gross national income** (2006): US$5,704,000,000 (US$477 per capita). **Land use** as % of total land area (2003): in temporary crops 3.9%, in permanent crops, 0.03%, in pasture 28.4%; overall forest area (2005) 10.3%.

Foreign trade

Imports (2005): CFAF 669,000,000,000 (petroleum products 32.5%; machinery and apparatus 24.1%; food products 21.2%). *Major import sources* (2004): African countries 49.3%, of which Senegal 9.8%, Côte d'Ivoire 7.6%; France 14.5%; Germany 4.0%. **Exports** (2005): CFAF 598,900,000,000 (gold 65.0%; raw cotton and cotton products 24.2%). *Major export destinations* (2004): China 31.6%; Thailand 6.9%; Italy 6.9%; Germany 5.1%.

Transport and communications

Transport. *Railroads* (2002): route length (2004) 729 km; passenger-km 196,000,000; metric ton-km cargo 188,000,000. *Roads* (2004): total length 18,709 km (paved 18%). *Vehicles* (2001): passenger cars 18,900; trucks and buses 31,700. **Communications,** in total units (units per 1,000 persons). Daily newspaper circulation (2005): 34,000 (3.1); televisions (2004): 400,000 (36); telephone landlines (2006): 83,000 (5.9); cellular telephone subscribers (2006): 1,513,000 (129); personal computers (2005): 45,000 (4.1); total Internet users (2006): 70,000 (5.0); broadband Internet subscribers (2006): 2,900 (0.2).

Education and health

Educational attainment (2001). Population ages 25 and over having: no formal schooling/unknown 82.1%; incomplete primary education 7.7%; complete primary 2.0%; secondary 6.5%; higher 1.7%. **Literacy** (2005): percentage of total population ages 15 and over literate 29.5%; males literate 40.0%; females literate 19.4%. **Health:** physicians (2004) 1,053 (1 per 10,566 persons); hospital beds (2001) 1,664 (1 per 6,203 persons); infant mortality rate per 1,000 live births (2006) 107.5.

Military

Total active duty personnel (2006): 7,350 (army 100%). **Military expenditure as percentage of GDP** (2005): 2.3%; per capita expenditure US$10.

Background

Inhabited since prehistoric times, the region was situated on a caravan route across the Sahara. In the 12th century the Malinke empire of Mali was founded on the Upper and Middle Niger. In the 15th century the Songhai empire in the Timbuktu-Gao region gained control. In 1591 Morocco invaded the area, and Timbuktu remained under the Moors for two centuries. In the mid-19th century the French conquered the area, which became a part of French West Africa known as the French Sudan. In 1946 it became an overseas territory of the French Union. It was proclaimed the Sudanese Republic in 1958, briefly joined with Senegal (1959–60) to form the Mali Federation, and became the Republic of Mali in 1960. The government was overthrown by military coups in 1968 and 1991. Elections were held in 1992 and 1997, but political instability continued.

Recent Developments

In late August 2007 members of a dissident Tuareg group, allied with the Niger Movement for Justice, launched two attacks on military targets in northern Mali. The rebels had refused to accept a 2006 peace settlement. At least 35 soldiers were kidnapped, while 11 civilians were reported killed by land mines. In September seven Tuaregs and one soldier died in a skirmish near Tinzaouatène, in northeastern Mali.

Internet resources: <www.malitourisme.com>.

Malta

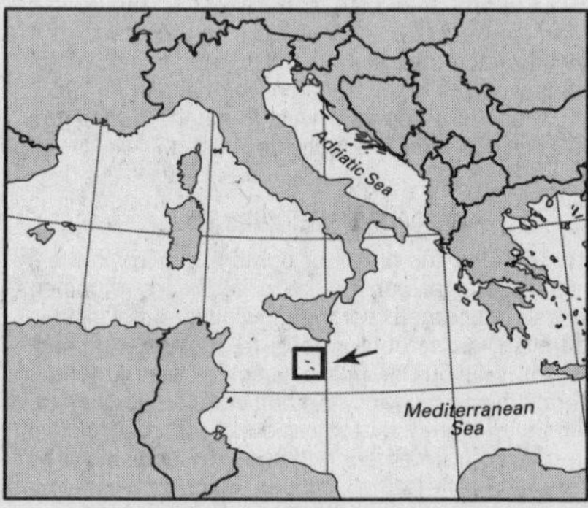

Official name: Repubblikka ta' Malta (Maltese); Republic of Malta (English). **Form of government:** unitary multiparty republic with one legislative house (House of Representatives [65]). **Chief of state:** President Eddie Fenech Adami (from 2004). **Head of government:** Prime Minister Lawrence Gonzi (from 2004). **Capital:** Valletta. **Official languages:** Maltese; English. **Official religion:** Roman Catholicism. **Monetary unit:** 1 euro (€) = 100 cents valuation (1 Jul 2008) US$1 = €0.63.

Demography

Area: 121.9 sq mi, 315.6 sq km. **Population** (2007): 409,000. **Density** (2007): persons per sq mi 3,355, persons per sq km 1,296. **Urban** (2005): 95.3%. **Sex distribution** (2005): male 49.59%; female 50.41%. **Age breakdown** (2005): under 15, 17.2%; 15–29, 21.7%; 30–44, 19.7%; 45–59, 22.3%; 60–74, 13.5%; 75–84, 4.5%; 85 and over, 1.1%. **Ethnic composition** (2005): Maltese 97.0%; other European 23.7%, of which British 1.2%; other 0.7%. **Religious affiliation** (2004): Roman Catholic 95%; other Christian 0.5%; Muslim 0.7%; nonreligious/atheist 2%; other 1.8%. **Major localities** (2005): Birkirkara 21,858; Mosta 18,735; Qormi 16,559; Zabbar 14,671; Valletta 6,300 (urban agglomeration 81,047). **Location:** islands in the Mediterranean Sea, south of Sicily (Italy).

Vital statistics

Birth rate per 1,000 population (2006): 9.4 (world avg. 20.3); (2005) within marriage 80.0%. **Death rate** per 1,000 population (2006): 7.5 (world avg. 8.6). **Natural increase rate** per 1,000 population (2006): 1.8 (world avg. 11.7). **Total fertility rate** (avg. births per childbearing woman; 2005): 1.37. **Life expectancy** at birth (2005): male 77.7 years; female 81.4 years.

National economy

Budget (2005). *Revenue:* Lm 1,032,046,000 (social security 21.5%; income tax 19.0%; grants and loans 17.1%; VAT 16.3%). *Expenditures:* Lm 985,552,000 (recurrent expenditures 76.7%, of which social security 22.4%, education 5.2%; capital expenditure 13.3%; public debt service 9.0%). **Public debt** (2006): US$731,600,000. **Production** (metric tons except where noted). *Agriculture, forestry, fishing* (2006): potatoes 22,000, melons 17,680, tomatoes 15,910; livestock (number of live animals) 73,025 pigs, 19,742 cattle, 14,642 sheep; fisheries production (2005) 2,171 (from aquaculture 34%). *Mining and quarrying* (2006): limestone 1,200,000 cu m; small quantities of salt. *Manufacturing* (value added in US$'000,000; 2004): telecommunications equipment and electronics 171; food products 78; printing and publishing 59. *Energy production (consumption):* electricity (kW-hr; 2004) 2,216,000,000 (2,216,-000,000); petroleum products (metric tons; 2004) none (799,000). **Population economically active** (2006): total 164,400; activity rate of total population 40.5% (participation rates: ages 15–64, 59.1%; female 32.1%; unemployed [March 2007] 6.8%). **Households.** Average household size (2005) 2.9; average annual income per household (2000) Lm 7,945 (US$18,155); sources of income (1993): wages and salaries 63.8%, professional and unincorporated enterprises 19.3%, rents, dividends, and interest 16.9%; expenditure (2000): food and beverages 36.6%, transportation and communications 23.4%, recreation, entertainment, and education 9.4%. **Gross national income** (2006): US$5,899,-000,000 (US$14,575 per capita). **Selected balance of payments data.** Receipts from (US$'000,000): tourism (2005) 754; remittances (2006) 34; foreign direct investment (FDI) (2001–05 avg.) 326. Disbursements for (US$'000,000): tourism (2005) 268; remittances (2006) 32; FDI (2001–05 avg.) 101. **Land use** as % of total land area (2003): in temporary crops 31%, in permanent crops 3%; overall forest area (2005) 1%.

Foreign trade

Imports (2004; c.i.f.): Lm 1,316,900,000 (machinery and transport equipment 47.4%; food 9.2%; chemicals and chemical products 8.4%; mineral fuels 8.0%). *Major import sources:* Italy 17.9%; France 17.7%; UK 9.6%; Germany 9.1%; Singapore 6.9%. **Exports** (2004; f.o.b.): Lm 909,300,000 (machinery and transport equipment [mostly electronic microcircuits] 63.9%; basic manufactures 18.8%; refined petroleum 4.4%). *Major export destinations:* Singapore 15.2%; US 11.6%; France 10.9%; UK 10.0%; Germany 8.9%.

Transport and communications

Transport. *Roads* (2004): total length 2,254 km (paved 88%). *Vehicles* (2005): passenger cars 207,055; trucks and buses 45,054. *Air transport* (2006; Air Malta only): passenger-km 2,376,-000,000; metric ton-km cargo 11,000,000. **Communications,** in total units (units per 1,000 persons). Daily newspaper circulation (2004): 68,000 (169); televisions (2004): 222,000 (553); telephone landlines (2006): 202,000 (502); cellular telephone subscribers (2006): 347,000 (860); personal computers (2005): 67,000 (166); total Internet users (2005): 127,000 (315); broadband Internet subscribers (2006): 42,000 (104).

Education and health

Educational attainment (2005). Percentage of population ages 15 and over having: no formal schooling 2.4%; special education for disabled 0.3%; primary education 25.9%; secondary 45.3%; some postsecondary 16.5%; undergraduate or professional qualification 7.2%; graduate 2.4%. **Literacy** (2005): total population ages 10 and over literate 92.8%; males literate 91.7%; females literate 93.9%. **Health** (2002): physicians 1,084 (1 per 365 persons); hospital beds 1,932 (1 per 205 persons); infant mortality rate per 1,000 live births (2005) 6.0. **Food** (2005): daily per capita caloric intake 3,762 (vegetable products 74%, animal products 26%).

Military

Total active duty personnel (2006): 2,237 (armed forces includes air and marine elements). **Military expenditure as percentage of GDP** (2005): 0.7%; per capita expenditure US$101.

Background

Inhabited as early as 3800 BC, Malta was ruled by the Carthaginians from the 6th century BC until it came under Roman control in 218 BC. In AD 60 the apostle Paul converted the inhabitants to Christianity. It was under Byzantine rule until the Arabs seized control in 870. In 1091 the Normans defeated the Arabs, and

Malta was ruled by feudal lords until it came under the Knights of Malta in 1530. Napoleon seized control in 1798, the British took it in 1800, and it was returned to the Knights in 1802. The Maltese protested and acknowledged the British as sovereign, an arrangement ratified in 1814. It became self-governing in 1921 but reverted to a colonial regime in 1936. Malta was severely bombed by Germany and Italy during World War II, and in 1942 it received the George Cross, Britain's highest civilian decoration. In 1964 it gained independence within the Commonwealth and in 1974 became a republic. When its alliance with Britain ended in 1979, Malta proclaimed its neutral status.

Recent Developments

In 2007 patrols run by the EU border agency Frontex turned back from Malta more than 700 would-be illegal immigrants from Africa. In April an agreement to set up a SmartCity in Malta was signed, and in September the master plan and model of the project, the biggest foreign investment Malta had ever seen, was unveiled in Dubai. Tourism to Malta was the best since 2001, while GDP was expected to rise 4%. Malta joined the euro zone on 1 Jan 2008.

Internet resources: <www.mol.net.mt>.

Marshall Islands

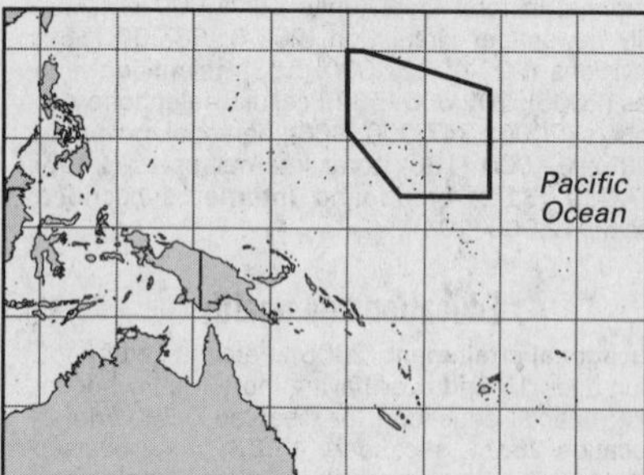

Official name: Majol (Marshallese); Republic of the Marshall Islands (English). **Form of government:** unitary republic with one legislative house (Nitijela [33]). **Head of state and government:** President Litokwa Tomeing (from 2008). **Capital:** Majuro (Rita). **Official languages:** Marshallese (Kajin-Majol); English. **Official religion:** none. **Monetary unit:** 1 US dollar (US$) = 100 cents.

Demography

Area: 70.05 sq mi, 181.43 sq km. **Population** (2007): 56,600. **Density** (2007): persons per sq mi 808.0, persons per sq km 312.0. **Urban** (2005): 66.1%. **Sex distribution** (2006): male 51.02%; female 48.98%. **Age breakdown** (2006): under 15, 38.1%; 15–29, 30.8%; 30–44, 16.5%; 45–59, 10.3%; 60–74, 3.4%; 75–84, 0.8%; 85 and over, 0.1%. **Ethnic composition** (nationality; 2000): Marshallese 88.5%; US white 6.5%; other Pacific Islander and East Asian 5.0%. **Religious affiliation** (1999): Protestant 85.0%, of which United Church of Christ 54.8%, Assemblies of God 25.8%; Roman Catholic 8.4%; Mormon 2.1%; nonreligious 1.5%; other/unknown 3.0%. **Major towns** (1999): Majuro (2004) 20,800; Ebeye 9,345; Laura 2,256; Ajeltake 1,170; Enewetak 823. **Location:** Oceania, group of atolls and reefs in the North Pacific Ocean, halfway between Hawaii (US) and Papua New Guinea.

Vital statistics

Birth rate per 1,000 population (2006): 33.0 (world avg. 20.3). **Death rate** per 1,000 population (2006): 4.7 (world avg. 8.6). **Natural increase rate** per 1,000 population (2006): 28.3 (world avg. 11.7). **Total fertility rate** (avg. births per childbearing woman; 2006): 3.84. **Life expectancy** at birth (2006): male 68.3 years; female 72.3 years.

National economy

Budget (2005). *Revenue:* US$83,900,000 (US government grants 63.9%; tax revenue 26.4%, of which income tax 11.7%, import duties 9.3%; nontax revenue 9.7%). *Expenditures:* US$86,900,000 (current expenditure 80.2%; capital expenditure 19.8%). **Public debt** (external, outstanding; 2004–05): US$100,800,000. **Production** (metric tons except as noted). *Agriculture, forestry, fishing* (2002–03): breadfruit 4,536, coconuts 885, bananas 161; livestock (number of live animals) 12,900 pigs, 86,000 chickens; fisheries production (2005) 56,664, of which skipjack (2004) 36,810. *Mining and quarrying:* for local construction only. *Manufacturing* (2005): copra 5,194; coconut oil and chilled or frozen fish are important products; the manufacture of handicrafts and personal items (clothing, mats, boats, etc.) by individuals is also significant. *Energy production (consumption):* electricity (kW-hr; 2005) 81,000,000 (81,000,000). **Population economically active** (1999): total 14,677; activity rate of total population 28.9% (participation rates: ages 15–64, 52.1%; female 34.1%; unemployed [2004] 33.6%). **Households.** Average household size (2006) 7.9; average annual income per household (2005) US$17,482; sources of income (2002): wages and salaries 89.3%, rent and investments 2.4%, social security 2.2%; expenditure (2003): food 35.9%, housing and energy 17.1%, transportation 13.7%, education and communication 6.6%. **Gross national income** (2006): US$191,000,000 (US$3,295 per capita). **Selected balance of payments data.** Receipts from (US$'000,000): tourism (2004–05) 5.5; remittances (2005) 0.4; foreign direct investment (2001–05 avg.) 125; official development assistance (2005) 52 (commitments). **Land use** as % of total land area (2003): in temporary crops 6%, in permanent crops 44%, in pasture 22%.

Foreign trade

Imports (2000; f.o.b. in balance of trade and c.i.f. in commodities and trading partners): US$68,200,000 (mineral fuels and lubricants 43.6%; machinery and transport equipment 16.9%; food, beverages, and tobacco 10.9%). *Major import sources* (2003): US 54.1%; Australia 13.4%; Japan 4.9%; New Zealand

3.4%; Hong Kong 3.3%. **Exports** (2005): US$16,400,000 (reexports of diesel fuel 80.9%; crude coconut oil 15.4%). *Major export destinations* (2000): US 71%.

Transport and communications

Transport. *Roads* (2002): only Majuro and Kwajalein have paved roads (64.5 km). *Vehicles* (2004): passenger cars 1,694; trucks and buses 602. *Air transport* (2005; Air Marshall Islands only): passenger-km 36,000,000; metric ton-km cargo 327,000. **Communications,** in total units (units per 1,000 persons). Telephone landlines (2004): 4,500 (82); cellular telephone subscribers (2004): 600 (12); personal computers (2004): 5,000 (92); total Internet users (2006): 2,200 (36).

Education and health

Educational attainment (2006). Percentage of population ages 25 and over having: no formal schooling 2.1%; elementary education 28.0%; secondary 55.8%; some higher 7.9%; undergraduate degree 5.1%; advanced degree 1.1%. **Literacy** (2000): total population ages 15 and over literate 92.0%; males literate 92.0%; females literate 92.0%. **Health** (2004): physicians 33 (1 per 1,744 persons); hospital beds 140 (1 per 411 persons); infant mortality rate per 1,000 live births (2006) 28.3.

Military

The US provides for the defense of the Republic of the Marshall Islands under the 1984 and 2003 compacts of free association (the US Army's premier ballistic-missile test site is at Kwajalein).

Background

The islands were sighted in 1529 by the Spanish navigator Álvaro Saavedra. Germany purchased them from Spain in 1899, and Japan seized them in 1914. During World War II the US took Kwajalein and Enewetak, and the Marshall Islands were made part of a UN trust territory under US jurisdiction in 1947. Bikini and Enewetak atolls served as testing grounds for US nuclear weapons from 1946 to 1958. The country became an internally self-governing republic in 1979. In 1986 it became fully self-governing when it entered into a Compact of Free Association with the US, which was renewed in 2003.

Recent Developments

Tension arose in the Marshall Islands over the Nuclear Claims Tribunal, which awarded US$1 billion to Marshall Islanders exposed to fallout during the 1954 hydrogen bomb test at Bikini Atoll. The award brought an end to an action initiated 15 years earlier, but the plaintiffs were unlikely to receive compensation because the tribunal had virtually no funds.

Internet resources:
<www.visitmarshallislands.com/travel.htm>.

Martinique

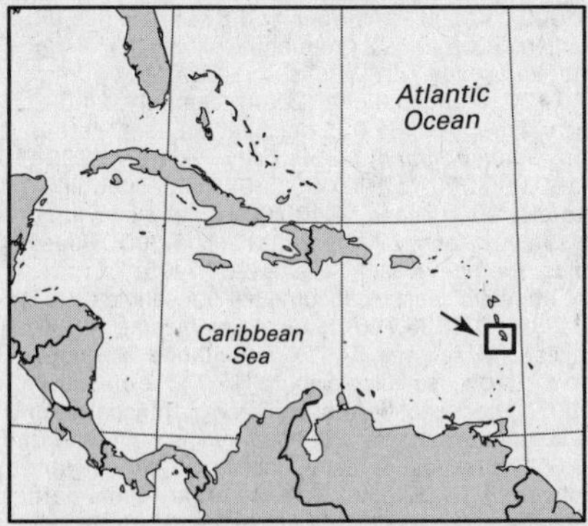

Official name: Département de la Martinique (Department of Martinique). **Political status:** overseas department of France with two legislative houses (General Council [45]; Regional Council [41]). **Chief of state:** French President Nicolas Sarkozy (from 2007). **Head of government:** Prefect (for France) Ange Mancini (from 2007); President of the General Council (for Martinique) Claude Lise (from 1992). **Capital:** Fort-de-France. **Official language:** French. **Official religion:** none. **Monetary unit:** 1 euro (€) = 100 cents; valuation (1 Jul 2008) US$1 = €0.63.

Demography

Area: 436 sq mi, 1,128 sq km. **Population** (2007): 401,000. **Density** (2007): persons per sq mi 919.7, persons per sq km 355.5. **Urban** (2005): 98.0%. **Sex distribution** (2004): male 47.01%; female 52.99%. **Age breakdown** (2005): under 15, 21.4%; 15–29, 19.4%; 30–44, 23.7%; 45–59, 18.4%; 60–74, 11.1%; 75–84, 4.3%; 85 and over, 1.7%. **Ethnic composition** (2000): mixed race (black/white/Asian) 93.4%; French (metropolitan and Martinique white) 3.0%; East Indian 1.9%; other 1.7%. **Religious affiliation** (2000): Roman Catholic 86.0%; Protestant 5.6% (mostly Seventh-day Adventist); other Christian 5.4%; other 3.0%. **Major communes** (2003): Fort-de-France 96,400; Le Lamentin 36,400; Schœlcher 21,400; Le Robert (1999) 21,201; Sainte-Marie 20,600. **Location:** island in the Atlantic Ocean and the Caribbean Sea, between Dominica and Saint Lucia.

Vital statistics

Birth rate per 1,000 population (2005): 13.3 (world avg. 20.3); (1997) within marriage 31.8%. **Death rate** per 1,000 population (2005): 7.0 (world avg. 8.6). **Total fertility rate** (avg. births per childbearing woman; 2005): 1.90. **Life expectancy** at birth (2005): male 75.9 years; female 82.0 years.

National economy

Budget (2004). *Revenue:* €599,000,000 (current revenue 75.3%, of which tax revenue 46.1%, aid from France 25.7%; capital revenue 24.7%). *Expenditures:* €599,000,000 (current expenditure 70.8%, of which transfers 51.1%, wages and salaries 13.2%; capital expenditure 29.2%). **Public debt** (1994): US$186,700,000. **Production** (metric tons except as noted). *Agriculture, forestry, fishing* (2006): bananas 300,000, sugarcane 211,000, plantains 18,030; livestock (number of live animals) 25,000 cattle, 20,000 pigs, 18,000 sheep; roundwood (2005)

12,000 cu m, of which fuelwood 83%; fisheries production (2005) 5,592 (from aquaculture 2%). *Mining and quarrying* (2005): salt 200,000; pumice 130,000. *Manufacturing* (2004): cement 224,090; sugar 4,140; rum 81,091 hectolitres. *Energy production (consumption):* electricity (kW-hr; 2004) 1,190,000,000 (1,190,000,000); crude petroleum (barrels; 2004) none (4,400,000); petroleum products (metric tons; 2004) 820,000 (605,000). **Households.** Average household size (2004–05) 2.6; average annual disposable income per household (2001) €32,859 (US$36,720); sources of income (2000): wages and salaries 54.7%, inheritance or endowment 14.0%, self-employment 12.7%; expenditure (1993): food and beverages 32.1%, transportation and communications 20.7%, housing and energy 10.6%, household durable goods 9.4%, clothing and footwear 8.0%. **Selected balance of payments data.** Receipts from (US$'000,000): tourism (2005) 280. **Population economically active** (2003): total 183,000; activity rate of total population 46.7% (participation rates: ages 15–64, 70.4%; female 49.7%; unemployed [2005] 21.8%). **Gross national income** (2003): US$5,780,000,000 (US$14,730 per capita). **Land use** as % of total land area (2003): in temporary crops 9%, in permanent crops 10%, in pasture 10%; overall forest area (2005) 44%.

Foreign trade

Imports (2002; c.i.f.): €1,855,000,000 (products for agricultural industry and food 18.5%; automobiles 12.2%; mineral fuels 9.7%; chemicals and chemical products 7.9%). *Major import sources:* France 64.5%; Venezuela 5.9%; Netherlands Antilles 3.8%; Germany 3.3%; Italy 2.7%. **Exports** (2002; f.o.b.): €325,000,000 (agricultural products [significantly bananas] 42.8%; refined petroleum 20.0%; processed foods and beverages [significantly rum] 19.1%). *Major export destinations:* France 68.9%; Guadeloupe 19.1%; French Guiana 4.0%.

Transport and communications

Transport. *Roads* (2000): total length 2,105 km (paved [1988] 75%). *Vehicles* (1998): passenger cars 147,589; trucks and buses 35,615. *Air transport* (2004): passengers 1,614,876; cargo 13,003 metric tons. **Communications,** in total units (units per 1,000 persons). Daily newspaper circulation (2005): 30,000 (75); televisions (2001): 66,000 (169); telephone landlines (2001): 172,000 (417); cellular telephone subscribers (2004): 295,000 (745); personal computers (2004): 82,000 (207); total Internet users (2005): 130,000 (326).

Education and health

Educational attainment (1999). Percentage of population ages 20 and over having: unknown/no formal education through lower secondary education 63.6%; vocational 16.7%; upper secondary 9.2%; incomplete higher 5.0%; complete higher 5.5%. **Literacy** (2005): percentage of total population ages 15 and over literate 98.0%; males literate 97.6%; females literate 98.3%. **Health** (2004): physicians 986 (1 per 403 persons); hospital beds 2,036 (1 per 195 persons); infant mortality rate per 1,000 live births 7.3.

Military

Total active duty personnel (2005): 1,250 French troops (including troops stationed in Guadeloupe, excluding gendarmerie).

Background

Carib Indians, who had ousted earlier Arawak inhabitants, resided on the island when Christopher Columbus visited it in 1502. In 1635 the French established a colony there. The British captured and held the island in 1762–63 and again during the Napoleonic Wars, but each time it was returned to France. Made a department of France in 1946, Martinique remains under French rule despite a 1970s independence movement.

Recent Developments

Martinique was affected by two natural disasters in 2007. In August Hurricane Dean swept over the island. Though the tourism industry was largely unaffected, the storm destroyed the entire banana crop. In November a 7.4-magnitude earthquake struck off the coast of Martinique, causing property damage and knocking out power to half of the island.

Internet resources: <www.martinique.org>.

Mauritania

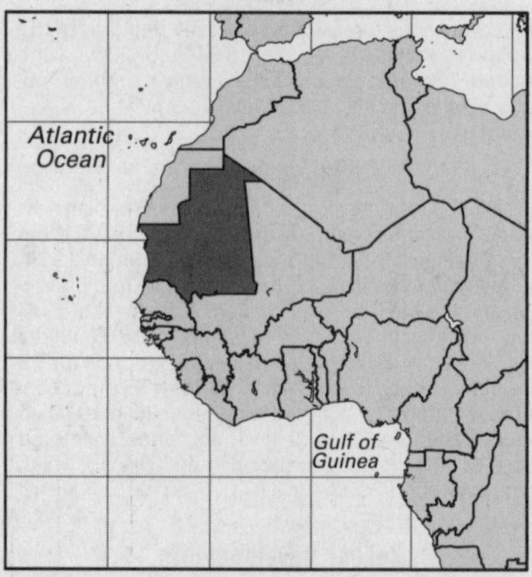

Official name: Al-Jumhuriyah al-Islamiyah al-Muritaniyah (Islamic Republic of Mauritania). **Form of government:** multiparty republic with two legislative houses (Senate [56]; National Assembly [95]). **Head of state and government:** Chairman of the High Council of State Mohamed Ould Abdel Aziz (from 2008), assisted by Prime Minister Moulaye Ould Mohamed Laghdaf (from 2008). **Capital:** Nouakchott. **Official language:** Arabic (Arabic, Fulani, Soninke, and Wolof are national languages). **Official religion:** Islam. **Monetary unit:** 1 ouguiya (UM) = 5 khoums; valuation (1 Jul 2008) US$1 = UM 235.96.

1 metric ton = about 1.1 short tons; 1 kilometer = 0.6 mi (statute); 1 metric ton-km cargo = about 0.68 short ton-mi cargo; c.i.f.: cost, insurance, and freight; f.o.b.: free on board

Demography

Area: 398,000 sq mi, 1,030,700 sq km. **Population** (2007): 3,124,000. **Density** (2007): persons per sq mi 7.8, persons per sq km 3.0. **Urban** (2006): 65.5%. **Sex distribution** (2006): male 49.50%; female 50.50%. **Age breakdown** (2006): under 15, 45.6%; 15–29, 27.2%; 30–44, 15.6%; 45–59, 8.0%; 60–74, 3.1%; 75 and over, 0.5%. **Ethnic composition** (2003): black African-Arab-Berber (Black Moor) 40%; Arab-Berber (White Moor) 30%; black African (mostly Wolof, Tukulor, Soninke, and Fulani) 30%. **Religious affiliation** (2000): Sunni Muslim 99.1%; traditional beliefs 0.5%; Christian 0.3%; other 0.1%. **Major cities** (2005): Nouakchott 743,500; Nouadhibou 94,700; Rosso (2000) 48,922; Boghé (2000) 37,531; Adel Bagrou (2000) 36,007. **Location:** northern Africa, bordering Western Sahara (annexed by Morocco), Algeria, Mali, Senegal, and the North Atlantic Ocean.

Vital statistics

Birth rate per 1,000 population (2006): 41.0 (world avg. 20.3). **Death rate** per 1,000 population (2006): 12.2 (world avg. 8.6). **Total fertility rate** (avg. births per childbearing woman; 2006): 5.86. **Life expectancy** at birth (2006): male 50.9 years; female 55.4 years.

National economy

Budget (2005). *Revenue:* UM 131,300,000,000 (tax revenue 57.9%, of which VAT 20.3%, corporate taxes 17.0%, import taxes 8.2%; nontax revenue 34.3%, of which fishing royalties 26.9%; grants 7.8%). *Expenditures:* UM 166,100,000,000 (current expenditure 76.2%, of which goods and services 36.5%, wages and salaries 13.5%, defense 10.7%; capital expenditure 23.8%). **Land use** as % of total land area (2003): in temporary crops 0.5%, in permanent crops 0.01%, in pasture 38.3%; overall forest area (2005) 0.3%. **Production** (metric tons except as noted). *Agriculture, forestry, fishing* (2006): sorghum 83,800, rice 70,462, dates 22,000; livestock (number of live animals; 2005) 7,363,000 sheep, 5,600,000 goats, 1,651,000 camels; roundwood (2005) 1,629,000 cu m, of which fuelwood 99.6%; fisheries production 491,877, of which octopuses 19,023. *Mining and quarrying* (gross weight; 2006–07): iron ore 11,439,000; gypsum (2005) 39,000; copper 5,000. *Manufacturing* (value added in US$'000,000; 1997): food, beverages, and tobacco products 5.2; machinery, transport equipment, and fabricated metals 3.8; bricks, tiles, and cement 1.6. *Energy production (consumption):* electricity (kW-hr; 2006–07) 404,000,000 (290,000,000); coal (metric tons; 2004) none (7,000); crude petroleum (barrels; 2006–07) 9,600,000 ([2004] 8,830,000); petroleum products (metric tons; 2006–07) none (431,000). **Selected balance of payments data.** Receipts from (US$'000,000): tourism (2005) 11; remittances (2006) 2; foreign direct investment (FDI) (2001–05 avg.) 109; official development assistance (2005) 190. Disbursements for (US$'000,000): tourism (1999) 55. **Population economically active** (2006): total 1,238,000; activity rate of total population 39.2% (participation rates: over age 15, 68.8%; female 40.4%; unemployed [2005] 32.5%). **Households.** Average household size (2004): 5.8; expenditure (2002–03): food and beverages 53.1%, housing and energy 13.7%, transportation and communications 12.1%. **Gross national income** (2006): US$2,830,000,000 (US$930 per capita). **Public debt** (external, outstanding; 2006): US$2,300,000,000.

Foreign trade

Imports (2006): US$1,167,000,000 (petroleum exploration equipment 37.2%; petroleum products 19.5%). *Major import sources:* France 11.9%; China 8.2%; US 6.8%; Belgium 6.7%; Italy 5.9%. **Exports** (2006): US$1,366,600,000 (petroleum 47.0%; iron ore 34.2%; fish 14.7%). *Major export destinations:* China 26.3%; Italy 11.8%; France 10.2%; Belgium 6.8%; Spain 6.7%.

Transport and communications

Transport. *Railroads:* route length (2005) 697 km; metric ton-km cargo (2000)7,766,000,000. *Roads* (2005): total length 9,144 km (paved 30%). *Vehicles* (2001): passenger cars 12,200; trucks and buses 18,200. *Air transport* (2002): passenger-km 45,000,000; metric ton-km cargo 4,000,000. **Communications**, in total units (units per 1,000 persons). Televisions (2003): 123,000 (44); telephone landlines (2006): 34,000 (11); cellular telephone subscribers (2006): 1,060,000 (348); personal computers (2005): 42,000 (14); total Internet users (2006): 100,000 (33); broadband Internet subscribers (2006): 700 (0.2).

Education and health

Educational attainment (2000). Percentage of population ages 6 and over having: no formal schooling 43.9%; no formal schooling but literate 2.5%; Islamic schooling 18.4%; primary education 23.2%; lower secondary 5.3%; upper secondary 4.6%; higher technical 0.4%; higher 1.7%. **Literacy** (2006): percentage of total population ages 15 and over literate 51.2%; males literate 59.5%; females literate 43.4%. **Health** (2006): physicians (2005) 477 (1 per 6,212 persons); hospital beds 1,826 (1 per 1,667 persons); infant mortality rate per 1,000 live births 69.5. **Food** (2003): daily per capita caloric intake 2,786 (vegetable products 82%, animal products 18%); 121% of FAO recommended minimum.

Military

Total active duty personnel (2006): 15,870 (army 94.5%, navy 3.9%, air force 1.6%). **Military expenditure as percentage of GDP** (2005): 3.6%; per capita expenditure US$24.

Background

Inhabited in ancient times by Sanhadja Berbers, in the 11th and 12th centuries Mauritania was the center of the Berber Almoravid movement, which imposed Islam. Arab tribes arrived in the 15th century and formed powerful confederations; the Portuguese also arrived then. France gained control of the coast in 1817 and in 1903 made the territory a protectorate. In 1904 it was added to French West Africa, and later it became a colony. In 1960 Mauritania achieved independence. Its first president was ousted in a 1978 military coup. After a series of military rulers, in 1991 a new constitution was adopted, and multiparty elections were held in 1992. During the 1990s relations between the government and opposition groups deteriorated, even as there was some success in liberalizing the economy.

Recent Developments

Voters went to the polls in March 2007 to elect a new president for Mauritania. Sidi Mohamed Ould Cheikh Abdallahi took 53% of the vote in the second round of balloting that marked Mauritania's first truly democratic presidential election since independence in 1960. The African Union indicated its approval by lifting its suspension of Mauritania. However, in August 2008 the government, accused of being soft on terrorism, was overthrown in a military coup.

Internet resources: <www.ons.mr>.

Mauritius

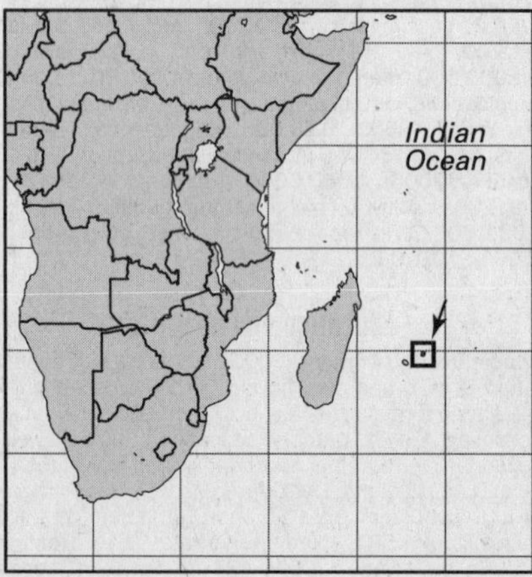

Official name: Republic of Mauritius. **Form of government:** republic with one legislative house (National Assembly [70]). **Chief of state:** President Sir Anerood Jugnauth (from 2003). **Head of government:** Prime Minister Navin Ramgoolam (from 2005). **Capital:** Port Louis. **Official language:** English. **Official religion:** none. **Monetary unit:** 1 Mauritian rupee (Mau Re; plural Mau Rs) = 100 cents; valuation (1 Jul 2008) US$1 = Mau Rs 27.25.

Demography

Area: 788 sq mi, 2,040 sq km. **Population** (2007): 1,263,000. **Density** (2007): persons per sq mi 1,603, persons per sq km 619.1. **Urban** (2006): 42.1%. **Sex distribution** (2006): male 49.43%; female 50.57%. **Age breakdown** (2006): under 15, 23.9%; 15–29, 24.9%; 30–44, 23.4%; 45–59, 18.0%; 60–74, 7.2%; 75–84, 2.1%; 85 and over, 0.5%. **Ethnic composition** (2000): Indo-Pakistani 67.0%; Creole (mixed Caucasian, Indo-Pakistani, and African) 27.4%; Chinese 3.0%; other 2.6%. **Religious affiliation** (2000): Hindu 49.6%; Christian 32.2%, of which Roman Catholic 23.6%; Muslim 16.6%; Buddhist 0.4%; other 1.2%. **Major urban areas** (2006): Port Louis 148,878; Beau Bassin–Rose Hill 109,182; Vacoas-Phoenix 106,255; Curepipe 83,375; Quatre Bornes 80,325. **Location:** island in the Indian Ocean, east of Madagascar.

Vital statistics

Birth rate per 1,000 population (2006): 14.1 (world avg. 20.3). **Death rate** per 1,000 population (2006): 7.3 (world avg. 8.6). **Total fertility rate** (avg. births per childbearing woman; 2006): 1.73. **Life expectancy** at birth (2006): male 68.9 years; female 75.8 years.

National economy

Budget (2005–06). *Revenue:* Mau Rs 39,220,000,000 (tax revenue 90.2%, of which taxes on goods and services 47.8%, taxes on trade 18.3%, corporate income tax 12.0%; nontax revenue/grants 9.8%). *Expenditures:* Mau Rs 48,875,000,000 (social security 21.1%; interest on debt 15.0%; education 14.0%; police/defense 8.8%; health 8.6%). **Public debt** (external, outstanding; 2005): US$731,000,000. **Gross national income** (2006): US$6,460,000,000 (US$5,160 per capita). **Production** (metric tons except as noted). *Agriculture, forestry, fishing* (2005): sugarcane 4,984,000, tomatoes 12,840, potatoes 12,780; livestock (number of live animals) 28,000 cattle; roundwood 12,500 cu m, of which fuelwood 40%; fisheries production 10,448 (from aquaculture 4%). *Mining* (2005): basalt, n.a.; marine salt 7,900. *Manufacturing* (value added in Mau Rs '000,000; 2004): apparel 10,734; food products 3,887; beverages and tobacco 2,224. *Energy production (consumption):* electricity (kW-hr; 2004) 2,165,000,000 (2,165,000,000); coal (metric tons; 2004) none (289,000); petroleum products (metric tons; 2004) none (791,000). **Population economically active** (2004): total 549,600; activity rate of total population 44.5% (participation rates: ages 15 and over, 59.2%; female 35.0%; unemployed [2006] 8.9%). **Households.** Average household size (2004) 3.9; annual income per household (2001–02) Mau Rs 170,784 (US$5,780); expenditure (2001–02): food and nonalcoholic beverages 31.9%, transportation 12.7%, housing and energy 9.4%, alcohol and tobacco 9.1%. **Selected balance of payments data.** Receipts from (US$'000,000): tourism (2005) 871; remittances (2006) 215; foreign direct investment (FDI) (2001–05 avg.) 21; official development assistance (2005) 47 (commitments). Disbursements for (US$'000,000): tourism (2005) 275; remittances (2006) 11; FDI (2001–05 avg.) 17. **Land use** as % of total land area (2003): in temporary crops 49%, in permanent crops 3%, in pasture 3%; overall forest area (2005) 18%.

Foreign trade

Imports (2005; c.i.f.): Mau Rs 93,282,000,000 (machinery and apparatus 22.9%; food and live animals 14.8%; refined petroleum 14.4%; fabrics and yarn 8.0%; transport equipment 5.1%). *Major import sources:* China 9.8%; South Africa 8.6%; France 7.5%; India 6.9%; Bahrain 5.5%. **Exports** (2005; f.o.b.): Mau Rs 63,219,000,000 (domestic exports 66.6%, of which clothing 30.9%, sugar 16.7%, fish and fish preparations 5.0%; reexports 26.9%, of which machinery and transport equipment 14.5%).

1 metric ton = about 1.1 short tons; 1 kilometer = 0.6 mi (statute); 1 metric ton-km cargo = about 0.68 short ton-mi cargo; c.i.f.: cost, insurance, and freight; f.o.b.: free on board

Major export destinations: UK 29.9%; France 13.3%; US 9.0%; UAE 8.0%; Madagascar 5.3%.

Transport and communications

Transport. *Roads* (2005): total length 2,020 km (paved 98%). *Vehicles* (2005): passenger cars 84,818; trucks and buses 38,596. *Air transport* (2005; Air Mauritius only): passenger-km 6,274,000,000; metric ton-km cargo 211,716,000. **Communications**, in total units (units per 1,000 persons). Daily newspaper circulation (2004): 60,000 (48); televisions (2004): 260,000 (209); telephone landlines (2006): 357,000 (285); cellular telephone subscribers (2006): 772,000 (615); personal computers (2005): 210,000 (169); total Internet users (2005): 300,000 (241); broadband Internet subscribers (2006): 22,000 (17).

Education and health

Educational attainment (2000). Percentage of population ages 25 and over having: no formal education/unknown 12.8%; primary 44.1%; lower secondary 23.2%; upper secondary/some higher 17.3%; complete higher 2.6%. **Literacy** (2000): percentage of total population ages 12 and over literate 85.1%; males literate 88.7%; females literate 81.6%. **Health** (2006): physicians 1,400 (1 per 895 persons); hospital beds 3,727 (1 per 336 persons); infant mortality rate per 1,000 live births 14.1. **Food** (2005): daily per capita caloric intake 2,945 (vegetable products 85%, animal products 15%); 154% of FAO recommended minimum.

Military

Total active duty personnel (2006): none; a 2,000-person paramilitary force includes a coast guard unit. **Paramilitary expenditure as percentage of GDP** (2005): 0.2%; per capita expenditure US$9.

Background

The island was visited by the Portuguese in the early 16th century. The Dutch took possession in 1598 and made attempts to settle it (1638–58 and 1664–1710) before abandoning it to pirates. The French East India Company occupied Mauritius in 1721 and administered it until the French government took over in 1767. Sugar production allowed the colony to prosper. The British captured the island in 1810 and were granted formal control in 1814. In the late 19th century, competition from beet sugar and the opening of the Suez Canal caused an economic decline. After World War II, Mauritius adopted political and economic reforms, and in 1968 it became an independent state within the Commonwealth. In 1992 it became a republic. It experienced political unrest during the 1990s.

Recent Developments

Prompted by a downturn in two key industries, sugar production and textiles (following price cuts and the imposition of global trade quotas), Mauritius attempted in 2007 to bolster its economy through trade agreements with China and Pakistan. In mid-May the High Court in London rejected an appeal to block the right of exiled Chagos islanders (who had been removed from Diego Garcia, the largest of the islands, to allow the US to build a military base there) to return to the Chagos Archipelago (British-controlled territory claimed by Mauritius).

Internet resources: <www.mauritius.net>.

Mayotte

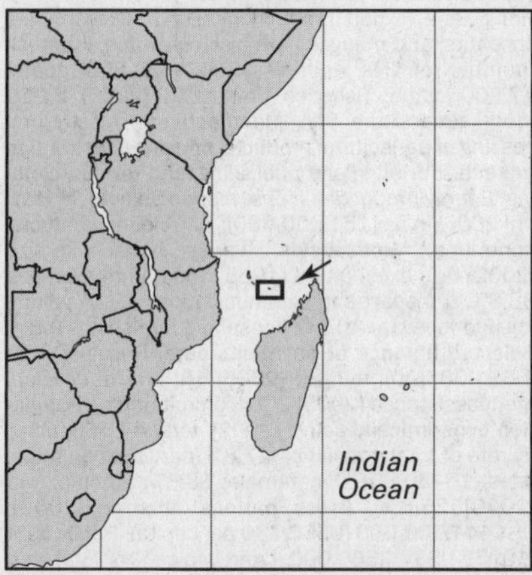

Official name: Collectivité Départementale de Mayotte (Departmental Collectivity of Mayotte); known as Mahoré or Maore in Shimaoré, the local Swahili-based language. **Political status:** overseas dependency of France with one legislative house (General Council [19]); claimed by Comoros since 1975. **Chief of state:** French President Nicolas Sarkozy (from 2007). **Head of government:** President of the General Council Said Omar Oili (from 2004). **Capital:** Mamoudzou. **Official language:** French. **Official religion:** none. **Monetary unit:** 1 euro (€) = 100 cents; valuation (1 Jul 2008) US$1 = €0.63.

Demography

Area: 144.1 sq mi, 373.3 sq km. **Population** (2007): 194,000. **Density** (2007): persons per sq mi 1,346, persons per sq km 519.7. **Sex distribution** (2006): male 52.27%; female 47.73%. **Age breakdown** (2006): under 15, 45.9%; 15–29, 24.6%; 30–44, 18.1%; 45–59, 8.4%; 60–74, 2.5%; 75–84, 0.4%; 85 and over, 0.1%. **Ethnic composition** (2000): Comorian 92.3%; Swahili 3.2%; white (French) 1.8%; Makua 1.0%; other 1.7%. **Religious affiliation** (2000): Sunni Muslim 96.5%; Christian, principally Roman Catholic, 2.2%; other 1.3%. **Major communes** (2002): Mamoudzou 45,485; Koungou 15,383; Dzaoudzi 12,308. **Location:** island in the Indian Ocean, between the northern tip of Madagascar and the African mainland.

Vital statistics

Birth rate per 1,000 population (2006): 41.0 (world avg. 20.3). **Death rate** per 1,000 population (2006): 7.7 (world avg. 8.6). **Natural increase rate** per 1,000 population (2006): 33.3 (world avg. 11.7). **Total fertility rate** (avg. births per childbearing woman; 2006): 5.79. **Life expectancy** at birth (2006): male 59.6; female 64.0.

National economy

Budget (2005; Mayotte is largely dependent on French aid). *Revenue:* €269,400,000 (current revenue 81.0%, of which taxes including customs duties 44.8%; development revenue 19.0%). *Expenditures:* €252,000,000 (current expenditure 78.9%, development expenditure 21.1%). **Production** (metric tons except as noted). *Agriculture, forestry, fishing* (2006): ylang-ylang (export production) 8,057 kg; bananas, coconuts, and mangoes are also cultivated; livestock (number of live animals; 2003) 22,800 goats, 17,200 cattle; fisheries production (2005) 2,050 (from aquaculture 8%). *Manufacturing:* mostly processing of agricultural products, housing construction materials, printing and publishing, and textiles/clothing. *Energy production (consumption):* electricity (kW-hr; 2006) n.a. (151,000,000); petroleum products, none (n.a.). **Households.** Average household size (2002) 4.3; expenditure (1995): food and beverages 38.8%, transport and communications 13.1%, clothing and footwear 10.7%, household furnishings 9.8%. **Selected balance of payments data.** Receipts from (US$'000,000): tourism (2005) 18; official development assistance (2005) 208 (commitments). **Population economically active** (2002): total 44,558; activity rate of total population 27.8% (participation rates: ages 15–60, 50.0%; female 38.6%; unemployed [2006] 25.6%). **Gross national income** (2002): US$444,000,000 (US$2,780 per capita). **Public debt** (1997): US$74,600,000. **Land use** as % of total land area (2005): overall forest area 14.7%.

Foreign trade

Imports (2005; c.i.f.): €218,200,000 (food products 25.5%; machinery and apparatus 16.7%; transport equipment 14.0%; chemicals and chemical products 8.9%). *Major import sources:* France 49.3%; Seychelles 9.0%; China 4.2%; South Africa 2.9%; Brazil 2.8%. **Exports** (2005; f.o.b.): €5,200,000 (transport equipment and parts 27.0%; machinery and apparatus 23.1%; food products 19.4%, of which fish 10.7%; ylang-ylang 8.8%). *Major export destinations:* France 42.6%; Comoros 36.1%; Réunion 14.9%; Madagascar 3.1%.

Transport and communications

Transport. *Roads* (2006): total length 232 km (paved 100%). *Vehicles* (2004): passenger cars 2,279; trucks and buses 1,453. *Air transport* (2005): passenger arrivals and departures 200,389; cargo unloaded and loaded 1,395 metric tons. **Communications,** in total units (units per 1,000 persons). Telephone landlines (2002): 10,000 (63); cellular telephone subscribers (2004): 48,000 (277).

Education and health

Educational attainment (2002). Percentage of population ages 15 and over having: no formal education 37.6%; participating in formal education 17.8%; primary education 20.8%; lower secondary 13.4%; upper secondary 6.3%; higher 4.1%. **Literacy** (1997): 86.1%. **Health** (2006): physicians 120 (1 per 1,587 persons); hospital beds 245 (1 per 780 persons); infant mortality rate per 1,000 live births 61.2.

Military

Total active duty personnel (2006): n.a.; a detachment of the French Foreign Legion and French naval personnel is stationed at Dzaoudzi.

Background

Originally inhabited by descendants of Bantu and Malayo-Indonesian peoples, Mayotte was converted to Islam by Arab invaders in the 15th century. Taken by a Malagasy tribe from Madagascar at the end of the 18th century, it came under French control in 1843. Together with the other Comoros islands and Madagascar, it became part of a single French overseas territory in the early 20th century. It has been administered separately since 1975, when the three northernmost islands of the Comoros declared independence.

Recent Developments

Illegal immigrants continued to drown while attempting to cross from the Comoros islands to the relatively prosperous island of Mayotte. In one incident in August 2007, at least 17 people were confirmed dead and another 19 were missing after a primitive wooden vessel capsized in rough waters off the coast. In March 2008 Mohamed Bacar, the self-declared rebel president of the Comoran island of Anjouan, was arrested after having fled to Mayotte.

Internet resources: <www.mayotte-tourisme.com>.

Mexico

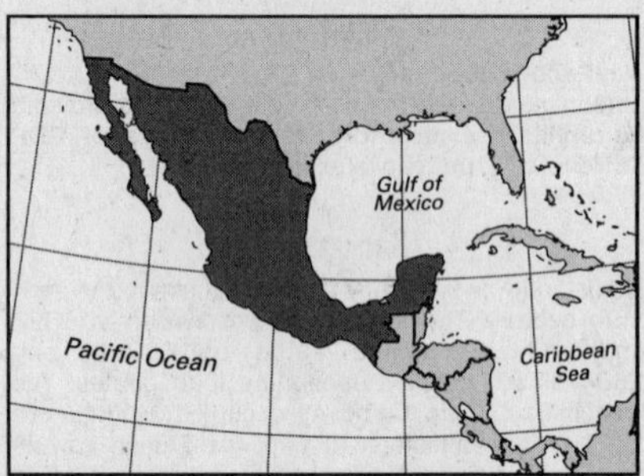

Official name: Estados Unidos Mexicanos (United Mexican States). **Form of government:** federal republic with two legislative houses (Senate [128]; Chamber of Deputies [500]). **Head of state and government:** President Felipe Calderón Hinojosa (from 2006). **Capital:** Mexico City. **Official language:** Spanish. **Official religion:** none. **Monetary unit:** 1 Mexican peso (Mex$) = 100 centavos; valuation (1 Jul 2008) US$1 = Mex$10.41.

Demography

Area: 758,450 sq mi, 1,964,375 sq km. **Population** (2007): 106,535,000. **Density** (2007): persons per sq mi 140.8, persons per sq km 54.4. **Urban** (2005): 76.0%. **Sex distribution** (2005): male 48.66%; female

1 metric ton = about 1.1 short tons; 1 kilometer = 0.6 mi (statute); 1 metric ton-km cargo = about 0.68 short ton-mi cargo; c.i.f.: cost, insurance, and freight; f.o.b.: free on board

51.34%. **Age breakdown** (2005): under 15, 30.7%; 15–29, 26.3%; 30–44, 20.4%; 45–59, 11.8%; 60–74, 5.9%; 75–84, 1.7%; 85 and over, 0.5%; unknown 2.7%. **Ethnic composition** (2000): mestizo 64.3%; Amerindian 18.0%, of which detribalized 10.5%; Mexican white 15.0%; Arab 1.0%; Mexican black 0.5%; Spaniard 0.3%; US white 0.2%; other 0.7%. **Religious affiliation** (2000): Christian 96.3%, of which Roman Catholic 87.0%, Protestant 3.2%, independent Christian 2.7%, unaffiliated Christian 1.4%, other Christian (mostly Mormon and Jehovah's Witness) 2.0%; Muslim 0.3%; nonreligious 3.1%; other 0.3%. **Major cities (urban agglomerations)** (2005): Mexico City 8,463,906 (19,411,000); Ecatepec 1,687,549; Guadalajara 1,600,894 (3,968,000); Puebla 1,399,519 (1,824,000); Juárez 1,301,452 (1,540,000); Tijuana 1,286,187 (1,649,000); León 1,137,465 (1,481,000); Ciudad Netzahualcóyotl 1,136,300; Monterrey 1,133,070 (3,596,000); Zapopan 1,026,492. **Location:** middle America, bordering the US, the Gulf of Mexico, the Caribbean Sea, Belize, Guatemala, and the North Pacific Ocean. **Households** (2000). Total number of households 21,954,733; distribution by size: 1 person 6.0%, 2 persons 12.3%, 3 persons 17.2%, 4 persons 21.8%, 5 persons 17.7%, 6 persons 10.9%, 7 or more persons 14.1%. **Migration.** Legal Mexican immigrants entering the US in 2004: 173,664; total number of illegal Mexican immigrants in US (2006) 6,500,000.

Vital statistics

Birth rate per 1,000 population (2006): 19.0 (world avg. 20.3). **Death rate** per 1,000 population (2006): 4.8 (world avg. 8.6). **Total fertility rate** (avg. births per childbearing woman; 2005): 2.45. **Life expectancy** at birth (2006): male 72.4 years; female 77.2 years.

Social indicators

Educational attainment (2005). Percentage of population ages 15 and over having: no formal schooling/unknown 10.9%; incomplete primary education 14.3%; complete primary 17.6%; incomplete/complete secondary 25.2%; vocational/professional 31.3%; advanced university (masters or doctorate degree) 0.7%. **Access to services** (2005). Proportion of dwellings having: electricity 96.6%; piped water supply 87.8%; piped sewage 84.8%. **Material well-being.** Percentage of households possessing (2005): television 91.0%; refrigerator 79.0%; washing machine 62.7%; computer 19.6%. **Quality of working life.** Average workweek (2004) 43.5 hours. Annual rate per 100,000 insured workers for (2004) injury 2,922; death 11. Labor stoppages (2001) 35, involving 23,234 workers. **Social participation.** Eligible voters participating in last national election (July 2006) 58.6%. Trade union membership in total workforce (2000) less than 20%. Practicing religious population (1995–97): percentage of adult population attending church services at least once per week 46%. **Social deviance** (2000). Offense rate per 100,000 population for: murder 14.1; rape 13.3; major assault 185.0; automobile theft 162.0. Incidence per 100,000 in general population of: alcoholism 7.6; suicide (2001) 3.1.

National economy

Gross national income (2006): US$816,892,000,000 (US$7,775 per capita). **Budget** (2004). *Revenue:* Mex$1,774,200,000,000 (tax revenue 43.4%, of which income tax 19.5%; nontax revenue 28.2%; revenue from PEMEX state oil company 10.9%; other 17.5%). *Expenditures:* Mex$1,797,500,000,000 (current expenditure 58.3%; capital expenditure 15.2%; extra-budgetary expenditure 26.5%). **Public debt** (external, outstanding; 2005): US$108,786,000,000. **Production** (metric tons except as noted). *Agriculture, forestry, fishing* (2006): sugarcane 50,600,000, corn (maize) 21,760,000, sorghum 5,487,000, oranges 3,980,000, wheat 3,336,000, tomatoes 2,878,000, bananas 2,197,000, guavas and mangoes 2,050,000, lemons and limes 1,866,000, chilies and green peppers 1,681,000, potatoes 1,543,000, dry beans 1,375,000, green onions 1,151,000, avocados 1,137,000, papayas 805,700, blue agave 778,000, pineapples 627,800, grapefruit and pomelos 379,700, coffee (green) 287,600, nuts 176,200, safflower seeds 72,370, vanilla 306; livestock (number of live animals) 28,648,787 cattle, 15,370,386 pigs, 8,897,182 goats, 7,484,118 sheep, 6,540,000 asses, mules, and hinnies, 6,260,000 horses, 289,663,000 chickens; roundwood (2005) 44,646,877 cu m, of which fuelwood 86%; fisheries production (2005) 1,422,344 (from aquaculture 8%). *Mining and quarrying* (2005): fluorite 876,000 (world rank: 2); bismuth (metal content) 970 (world rank: 2); silver (metal content) 2,894,161 kg (world rank: 2); celestite 110,833 (world rank: 3); lead 134,388 (metal content) (world rank: 5); cadmium (metal content) 1,627 (world rank: 5); gypsum 6,251,969 (world rank: 6); zinc (metal content) 476,307 (world rank: 6); sulfur 1,590,000; copper (metal content) 429,042; iron ore (metal content) 7,012,000; gold 30,356 kg. *Manufacturing* (value added in US$'000,000; 2000): motor vehicles and parts 10,718; food products 8,883; paints, soaps, pharmaceuticals 7,044; beverages 5,422; bricks, cement, ceramics 3,580; iron and steel 2,891; paper and paper products 2,243; basic chemicals 1,682; fabricated metal products 1,518. **Households.** Average household size (2005) 4.2; average annual income per household (2004) Mex$28,177 (US$2,497); sources of income (2004): wages and salaries 53.7%, nonmonetary income 19.0%, self-employment 14.0%, transfers 9.6%; expenditure (2000): food, beverages, and tobacco 29.9%, transportation and communications 17.8%, education 17.3%, housing (includes household furnishings) 16.5%. *Energy production (consumption):* electricity (kW-hr; 2004) 224,077,000,000 (223,118,000,000); hard coal (metric tons; 2004) 1,735,000 (1,765,000); lignite (metric tons; 2004) 8,147,000 (11,681,000); crude petroleum (barrels; 2005) 1,216,000,000 (743,000,000); petroleum products (metric tons; 2004) 66,539,000 (71,195,000); natural gas (cu m; 2005) 49,797,000,000 ([2004] 50,450,000,000). **Population economically active** (2006): total 43,575,500; activity rate of total population 41.6% (participation rates: ages 15–64, 63.0%; female 37.1%; unemployed 3.2%). **Selected balance of payments data.** Receipts from (US$'000,000): tourism (2005) 11,803; remittances (2006) 24,732; foreign direct investment (FDI) (2001–05 avg.) 19,268; official development assistance (2005) 305 (commitments). Disbursements for (US$'000,000): tourism (2005) 7,600; FDI (2001–05 avg.) 3,430. **Land use** as % of total land area (2003): in temporary crops 13.0%, in permanent crops 1.3%, in pasture 41.9%; overall forest area (2005) 33.7%.

Foreign trade

Imports (2005): US$221,269,800,000 (nonmaquiladora sector 66.0%, of which machinery and apparatus 18.7%, transport and communications equipment 11.9%, chemicals and chemical products 5.9%, processed food, beverages, and tobacco 3.6%; maquiladora sector 34.0%, of which electrical machinery, apparatus, and electronics 14.9%, nonelectrical machinery and apparatus 7.7%). *Major import sources:* US 53.4%; China 8.0%; Japan 5.9%; Germany 3.9%; South Korea 3.0%; Canada 2.8%; Brazil 2.4%. **Exports** (2005): US$213,711,200,000 (nonmaquiladora sector 54.7%, of which road vehicles and parts 14.8%, crude petroleum 13.3%, machinery and apparatus 7.4%; maquiladora sector 45.3%, of which electrical machinery, apparatus, and electronics 19.1%, nonelectrical machinery and apparatus 8.5%). *Major export destinations:* US 85.7%; Canada 2.0%; Spain 1.4%; Germany 1.1%; Colombia 0.7%; Japan 0.7%; UK 0.6%.

Transport and communications

Transport. *Railroads* (2006): route length 26,662 km; passenger-km 73,000,000; metric ton-km cargo 55,113,000,000. *Roads* (2005): total length 355,796 km (paved 34%). *Vehicles* (2004): passenger cars 14,713,085; trucks and buses 7,158,105. *Air transport* (2005): passenger-km 27,864,000,000; metric ton-km cargo 177,048,000. **Communications,** in total units (units per 1,000 persons). Daily newspaper circulation (2000): 9,850,000 (98); televisions (2003): 29,400,000 (282); telephone landlines (2006): 19,861,000 (183); cellular telephone subscribers (2006): 57,016,000 (526); personal computers (2005): 14,000,000 (131); total Internet users (2005): 18,623,000 (181); broadband Internet subscribers (2006): 3,728,000 (36).

Education and health

Literacy (2000): total population ages 15 and over literate (2005) 91.6%; males literate 93.4%; females literate 89.5%. **Health** (2005): physicians 134,157 (1 per 777 persons); hospital beds 76,420 (1 per 1,364 persons); infant mortality rate per 1,000 live births (2006) 16.2. **Food** (2005): daily per capita caloric intake 3,252 (vegetable products 80%, animal products 20%); 171% of FAO recommended minimum.

Military

Total active duty personnel (2006): 192,770 (army 74.7%, navy 19.2%, air force 6.1%). **Military expenditure as percentage of GDP** (2005): 0.4%; per capita expenditure US$29.

Background

Inhabited for more than 20,000 years, Mexico produced great civilizations in AD 100–900, including the Olmec, Toltec, Mayan, and Aztec. The Aztec were conquered in 1521 by Spanish explorer Hernán Cortés, who established Mexico City on the site of the Aztec capital, Tenochtitlán. Francisco de Montejo conquered the remnants of Maya civilization in the mid-16th century, and Mexico became part of the Viceroyalty of New Spain. In 1821 rebels negotiated a status quo independence from Spain, and in 1823 a new congress declared Mexico a republic. In 1845 the US voted to annex Texas, initiating the Mexican War. Under the Treaty of Guadalupe Hidalgo in 1848, Mexico ceded a vast territory in what is now the western and southwestern US. The Mexican government endured several rebellions and civil wars in the late 19th and early 20th centuries. During World War II it declared war on the Axis powers (1942), and in the postwar era it was a founding member of the UN (1945) and the Organization of American States (1948). In 1993 it ratified the North American Free Trade Agreement. The election of Vicente Fox to the presidency in 2000 ended 71 years of rule by the Institutional Revolutionary Party.

Recent Developments

Mexican Pres. Felipe Calderón began his term with a high-visibility militarized offensive against drug-trafficking cartels. By early 2007 he had deployed 30,000 army troops and federal police in such operations in nine different states. Human rights advocates voiced concerns about the extensive use of the armed forces for this purpose because military operations of this kind had often produced serious human rights violations. On balance, though, public opinion polls indicated strong public support for Calderón's actions. The fact that Mexico experienced an unprecedented surge in drug-related killings, kidnappings, and gruesome violence (including beheadings) did suggest, however, that any progress against drug cartels would be slow, and this was confirmed in May 2008 when gunmen assassinated the acting chief of federal police in Mexico. Between the start of Calderón's offensive and mid-2008 more than 200 policemen were killed. In foreign affairs the Calderón administration worked hard to repair diplomatic relations with Cuba and Venezuela, which had been severely strained during the previous administration. Within North America the Mexican government pursued discussions with Canada and the United States concerning a "Security and Prosperity Partnership" designed to deepen cooperation between the three countries. Mexico demonstrated its commitment to cooperation with the US government in the battle against organized drug trafficking by extraditing several major traffickers to the US. It also conducted extensive negotiations with the US over greatly expanded US financial and technical assistance to combat drug-related organized crime. However, the US government's failure to enact a progressive immigration-reform bill and continuing US efforts to tighten border security to block Mexican migrants remained significant irritants in bilateral relations. Mexico's GDP rose by 3.0% during 2007. The annual rate of inflation was 4.0%. The US economic slowdown, especially in industries such as home construction, also affected the volume of cash remittances that emigrants sent back to Mexico (US$24 billion in 2007). Remittances in January 2008 fell at the fastest pace in 13 years.

Internet resources: <www.visitmexico.com>.

1 metric ton = about 1.1 short tons; 1 kilometer = 0.6 mi (statute); 1 metric ton-km cargo = about 0.68 short ton-mi cargo; c.i.f.: cost, insurance, and freight; f.o.b.: free on board

Federated States of Micronesia

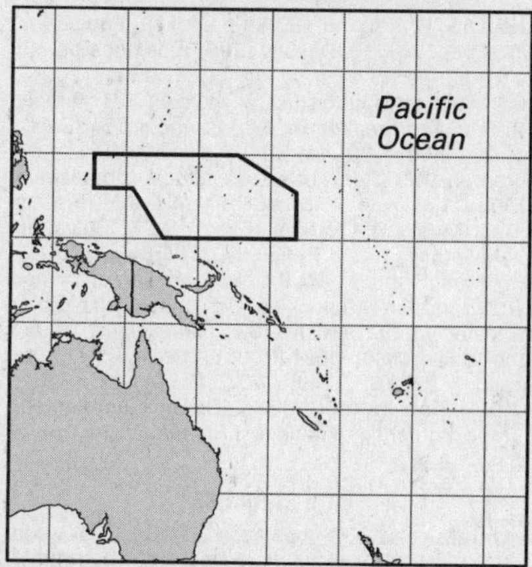

Official name: Federated States of Micronesia. **Form of government:** federal nonparty republic in free association with the US with one legislative house (Congress [14]). **Head of state and government:** President Emanuel Mori (from 2007). **Capital:** Palikir. **Official language:** none. **Official religion:** none. **Monetary unit:** 1 US dollar (US$) = 100 cents.

Demography

Area: 270.8 sq mi, 701.4 sq km. **Population** (2007): 111,000. **Density** (2007): persons per sq mi 409.9, persons per sq km 158.3. **Urban** (2005): 22.5%. **Sex distribution** (2007): male 50.37%; female 49.63%. **Age breakdown** (2005): under 15, 37.1%; 15–29, 29.6%; 30–44, 17.2%; 45–59, 11.7%; 60–74, 3.5%; 75 and over, 0.9%. **Ethnic composition** (2000): Chuukese/Mortlockese 33.6%; Pohnpeian 24.9%; Yapese 10.6%; Kosraean 5.2%; US white 4.5%; Asian 1.3%; other 19.9%. **Religious affiliation** (2005): Roman Catholic 50%; Protestant 47%; other 3%. **Major towns** (2000): Weno 13,802; Palikir 6,444; Nett 6,158; Kolonia 5,681; Colonia 3,216. **Location:** Oceania, island group in the North Pacific Ocean, northeast of New Guinea.

Vital statistics

Birth rate per 1,000 population (2005): 27.8 (world avg. 20.3); (2003) within marriage 78.9%. **Death rate** per 1,000 population (2005): 6.2 (world avg. 8.6). **Natural increase rate** per 1,000 population (2005): 21.6 (world avg. 11.7). **Life expectancy** at birth (2005): male 67.3 years; female 68.8 years.

National economy

Budget (2004–05). *Revenue:* US$134,100,000 (external grants 63.0%; tax revenue 21.7%; nontax revenue 15.3%, of which fishing access revenue 9.8%). *Expenditures:* US$146,900,000 (current expenditures 90.8%; capital expenditure 9.2%). **Public debt** (external, outstanding; 2005): US$60,800,000. **Population economically active** (2000): total 37,414; activity rate of total population 35.0% (participation rates: ages 15–64, 60.7%; female 42.9%; unemployed 22.0%). **Production** (metric tons except as noted). *Agriculture, forestry, fishing* (2005): coconuts 40,000, cassava 11,800, sweet potatoes 3,000; livestock (number of live animals) 32,000 pigs, 13,900 cattle; fisheries production 29,336, of which (2004) skipjack tuna 22,998. *Mining and quarrying:* quarrying of sand and aggregate for local construction only. *Manufacturing:* n.a.; however, copra and coconut oil, traditionally important products, are being displaced by garment production; the manufacture of handicrafts and personal items (clothing, mats, boats, etc.) by individuals is also important. *Energy production (consumption):* electricity (kW-hr; 2005) 74,400,000 (n.a.); petroleum products, none (n.a.). **Households** (2004). Average household size 7.0; annual income per household (2000) US$8,944 (median income: US$4,618); sources of income (1994): wages and salaries 51.8%, operating surplus 23.0%, social security 2.1%; expenditure (1998): food 45.5%, services (includes taxi fares) 16.5%, alcohol, tobacco, kava (sakau), and betel nut 8.5%. **Gross national income** (at 2006 market prices): US$256,000,000 (US$2,317 per capita). **Selected balance of payments data.** Receipts from (US$'000,000): tourism (2005) 17; remittances (2005) 6.0. Disbursements for (US$'000,000): tourism (2005) 5.7. **Land use** as % of total land area (2003): in temporary crops 6%, in permanent crops 46%, in pasture 16%; overall forest area 91%.

Foreign trade

Imports (2006; c.i.f.): US$137,993,000 (food and beverages 32.1%; mineral fuels 22.4%; machinery and apparatus 10.6%; transport equipment 6.0%). *Major import sources:* US 39.7%; Japan 8.8%; South Korea 5.8%; Singapore 4.6%; Philippines 4.4%. **Exports** (2004; f.o.b.): US$14,003,000 (marine products [mostly fish] 73.5%; garment products 20.7%; betel nuts 2.5%; copra 1.2%; kava [sakau] 0.9%). *Major export destinations:* Japan 21.4%; US 20.9%; Guam 3.4%; Northern Marianas 1.0%; unspecified 53.0%.

Transport and communications

Transport. *Roads* (1999): total length 240 km (paved 18%). *Vehicles* (2004): passenger cars 4,601; trucks and buses 3,770. *Air transport* (2004): passengers 17,473; freight 1,713,086 metric tons. **Communications,** in total units (units per 1,000 persons). Televisions (2004): 2,800 (26); telephone landlines (2005): 12,000 (109); cellular telephone subscribers (2005): 14,000 (127); personal computers (2005): 6,000 (55); total Internet users (2006): 16,000 (144).

Education and health

Educational attainment (2000). Percentage of population ages 25 and over having: no formal schooling 12.3%; primary education 37.0%; some secondary 18.3%; secondary 12.9%; some college 18.4%. **Literacy** (2000): total population ages 10 and over literate 92.4%; males literate 92.9%; females literate 91.9%. **Health** (2005): physicians 62 (1 per 1,774 persons); hospital beds 365 (1 per 301 persons); infant mortality rate per 1,000 live births 36.0.

Military

External security is provided by the US.

Background

The islands of Micronesia were probably settled by people from eastern Melanesia some 3,500 years ago. Europeans first landed on the islands in the 16th century. Spain took control of the islands in 1886 and then sold them to Germany in 1899. The islands came under Japanese rule after World War I. They were captured by US forces during World War II, and in 1947 they became a UN trust territory administered by the US. The group of islands centered on the Caroline Islands became an internally self-governing federation in 1979. In 1986 Micronesia entered into a Compact of Free Association with the US, which was amended in 2003. In the late 1990s the republic was struggling to solve its economic difficulties.

Recent Developments

Some of the weaknesses of the loose federal structure of the Federated States of Micronesia (FSM) became apparent in 2007. Some US$100 million in funds from the US Compact of Free Association, along with an additional US$36 million in grants, flowed annually through the FSM government to the governments of the four semiautonomous states, yet two states, Chuuk and Kosrae, found themselves in serious budgetary difficulties. Of serious concern also was the threat of rising sea levels inundating the low-lying islands.

Internet resources: <www.visit-fsm.org>.

Moldova

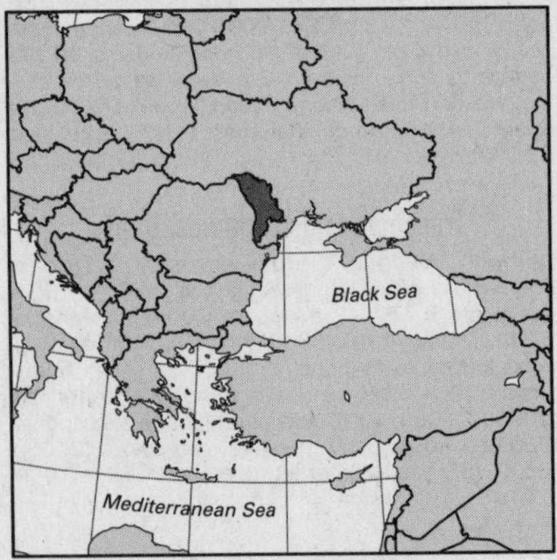

Official name: Republica Moldova (Republic of Moldova). **Form of government:** unitary parliamentary republic with a single legislative body (Parliament [101]). **Head of state:** President Vladimir Voronin (from 2001). **Head of government:** Prime Minister Zinaida Greceanii (from 2008). **Capital:** Chisinau. **Official language:** Romanian (constitutionally designated as Moldovan). **Official religion:** none. **Monetary unit:** 1 Moldovan leu (plural lei) = 100 bani; valuation (1 Jul 2008) free rate, US$1 = 9.83 Moldovan lei.

Demography

Area: 13,067 sq mi, 33,843 sq km. **Population** (2007): 3,794,000. **Density** (2007): persons per sq mi 290.3, persons per sq km 112.1. **Urban** (2006): 40.9%. **Sex distribution** (2006): male 47.89%; female 52.11%. **Age breakdown** (2004): under 15, 19.1%; 15–29, 26.3%; 30–44, 20.9%; 45–59, 19.1%; 60 and over, 14.3%; unknown 0.3%. **Ethnic composition** (2004): Moldovan 75.8%; Ukrainian 8.4%; Russian 5.9%; Gagauz 4.4%; Rom (Gypsy) 2.2%; Bulgarian 1.9%; other 1.4%. **Religious affiliation** (2005): Moldovan Orthodox 31.8%; Bessarabian Orthodox 16.1%; Russian Orthodox 15.4%; Sunni Muslim 5.5%; Protestant 1.7%; Jewish 0.6%; nonreligious 19.9%; other 9.0%. **Major cities** (2006): Chisinau 593,800; Tiraspol 159,163; Balti 122,700; Tighina (2004) 97,027; Râbnita (2004) 53,648. **Location:** eastern Europe, bordering Ukraine and Romania.

Vital statistics

Birth rate per 1,000 population (2006): 10.5 (world avg. 20.3); (2005) within marriage 76.1%. **Death rate** per 1,000 population (2006): 12.0 (world avg. 8.6). **Total fertility rate** (avg. births per childbearing woman; 2005): 1.81. **Life expectancy** at birth (2006): male 64.6 years; female 72.2 years.

National economy

Budget (2004). *Revenue:* 11,324,000,000 Moldovan lei (tax revenue 84.3%, of which VAT 30.3%, social fund contributions 22.0%, excise taxes 8.0%, personal income tax 7.0%; nontax and extra budgetary revenue 14.6%; grants 1.1%). *Expenditures:* 11,092,000,000 Moldovan lei (current expenditures 95.5%, of which social fund expenditures 25.0%, education 15.2%, health 10.4%%; capital expenditure 4.5%). **Public debt** (external, outstanding; end of 2006): US$718,000,000. **Production** (metric tons except as noted). *Agriculture, forestry, fishing* (2006): corn (maize) 1,322,000, sugar beets 1,177,000, wheat 691,500; livestock (number of live animals) 818,300 sheep, 460,678 pigs, 310,476 cattle; roundwood (2005) 56,800 cu m, of which fuelwood 52%; fisheries production (2005) 5,001 (from aquaculture 89%). *Mining and quarrying* (2004): gypsum 491,000. *Manufacturing* (value of production in '000,000 Moldovan lei; 2004): alcoholic beverages 4,013, of which wine 3,098; food products 3,461, of which dairy products 624; nonmetallic mineral products 1,273. *Energy production (consumption):* electricity (kW-hr; 2004) 3,617,000,000 (6,554,000,000); coal (metric tons; 2004) none (186,000); petroleum products (metric tons; 2004) none (621,000); natural gas (cu m; 2004) none (2,773,000,000). **Population economically active** (2005): total 1,422,300; activity rate of total de facto population 39.5% (participation rates: ages 15–64, 53.2%; female 51.5%; unemployed [2006] 7.4%). **Gross national income** (2006): US$3,356,000,000 (US$876 per capita). **Households.** Average household size (2004) 3.2; annual average income per household (2002) US$1,200; sources of income (1994): wages and salaries 41.2%, social benefits 15.3%, agricultural income 10.4%; expenditure (2001): food and drink 40.4%, housing 13.5%, utilities 10.5%, transportation 8.9%. **Selected balance of payments data.** Receipts from (US$'000,000): tourism (2005) 128; remittances (2006) 1,182; foreign direct investment (FDI) (2001–05 avg.) 138; official development assistance (2005) 172 (commitments). Disbursements for (US$'000,000): tourism (2005) 167; remittances (2006) 85. **Land use** as % of total land area (2003): in temporary crops 56.4%, in permanent crops 9.1%, in pasture 11.5%; overall forest area (2005) 10.0%.

Foreign trade

Imports (2004): US$1,774,000,000 (mineral fuels 21.7%; machinery and apparatus 13.5%; chemicals and chemical products 9.1%; textiles and wearing apparel 8.6%). *Major import sources* (2005): Ukraine 23.3%; Romania 15.8%; Russia 13.2%; Germany 7.6%; Italy 5.4%. **Exports** (2004): US$986,000,000 (processed food, beverages [significantly wine], and tobacco products 35.1%; textiles and wearing apparel 17.3%; vegetables, fruits, seeds, and nuts 12.2%). *Major export destinations* (2005): Russia 31.9%; Italy 12.2%; Romania 10.2%; Ukraine 9.1%; Belarus 6.5%.

Transport and communications

Transport. *Railroads* (2006): length 1,154 km; passenger-km 471,000,000; metric ton-km cargo 3,673,000,000. *Roads* (2006): total length 9,467 km (paved 94%). *Vehicles* (2003): passenger cars 252,490; trucks and buses 77,534. *Air transport* (2006): passenger-km 481,000,000; metric ton-km cargo 1,300,000. **Communications**, in total units (units per 1,000 persons). Daily newspaper circulation (2004): 75,000 (18); televisions (2003): 1,300,000 (327); telephone landlines (2006): 1,018,000 (243); cellular telephone subscribers (2006): 1,358,000 (324); personal computers (2005): 348,000 (83); total Internet users (2006): 728,000 (174); broadband Internet subscribers (2006): 22,000 (5.2).

Education and health

Literacy (2003): total population ages 15 and over literate 99.1%; males literate 99.6%; females literate 98.7%. **Health** (2006): physicians 12,674 (1 per 283 persons); hospital beds 22,471 (1 per 160 persons); infant mortality rate (2005) 12.5. **Food** (2005): daily per capita caloric intake 3,295 (vegetable products 84%, animal products 16%); 167% of FAO recommended minimum.

Military

Total active duty personnel (2006): 6,750 (army 84.6%, air force 15.4%); opposition forces (excluding Russian troops) in Transdniestria (2006) 7,500; Russian troops in Transdniestria (2006) 500. **Military expenditure as percentage of GDP** (2005): 0.3%; per capita expenditure US$6.

Background

Moldova, once part of the principality of Moldavia, was founded by the Vlachs in the 14th century. In the mid-16th century it was under Ottoman rule. In 1774 it came under Russian control and lost portions of its territory. In 1859 it joined with the principality of Walachia to form the state of Romania, and in 1918 some of the territory it had ceded earlier also joined Romania. Romania was compelled to cede some of the Moldavian area to Russia in 1940, and that area combined with what Russia already controlled to become the Moldavian SSR. In 1991 Moldavia declared independence from the Soviet Union. It adopted the Romanian spelling of Moldova after having legitimized (1989) the use of the Roman rather than the Cyrillic alphabet. During the 1990s the country struggled to find economic equilibrium.

Recent Developments

In July 2007 Moldovan Pres. Vladimir Voronin confirmed that he had been negotiating with the Kremlin in an effort to secure an end to the secession of Transdniestria, where much of the country's industry was located. In recent years Voronin had engaged in a balancing game between the West and Russia, and this move suggested that he was tilting toward Russia. He had been especially shaken in 2006 by the imposition of an embargo on Moldovan wine by Russia, a major consumer. However, a poll in May showed that 72% of Moldovans would vote to join the European Union. Igor Smirnov, the leader of Transdniestria, cracked down sharply on opposition after his parliament in January annulled a decision that left open the prospect of a confederation between the pro-Russian breakaway territory and Moldova.

Internet resources: <www.turism.md/eng>.

Monaco

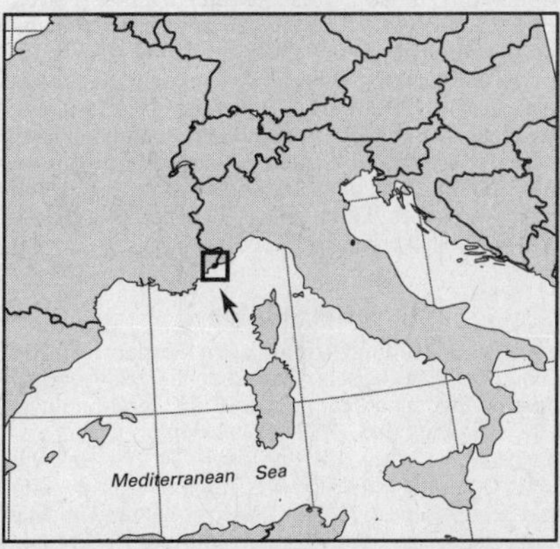

Official name: Principauté de Monaco (Principality of Monaco). **Form of government:** constitutional monarchy with one legislative body (National Council [24]). **Chief of state:** Prince Albert II (from 2005). **Head of government:** Minister of State Jean-Paul Proust (from 2005). **Capital:** no separate area is distinguished as such. **Official language:** French. **Official religion:** Roman Catholicism. **Monetary unit:** 1 euro (€) = 100 centimes; valuation (1 Jul 2008) US$1 = €0.63.

Demography

Area: 0.76 sq mi, 1.97 sq km. **Population** (2007): 34,000. **Density** (2007): persons per sq mi 44,737, persons per sq km 17,259. **Urban** (2005): 100%. **Sex distribution** (2005): male 47.65%; female 52.35%. **Age breakdown** (2005): under 15, 15.4%; 15–29, 13.9%; 30–44, 20.2%; 45–59, 21.3%; 60–74,

17.3%; 75–84, 8.7%; 85 and over, 3.2%. **Ethnic composition** (2007): French 47%; Italian 16%; Monegasque 16%; other 21%. **Religious affiliation** (2000): Christian 93.2%, of which Roman Catholic 89.3%; Jewish 1.7%; nonreligious and other 5.1%. **Location:** western Europe, bordering the Mediterranean Sea and France.

Vital statistics

Birth rate per 1,000 population (2005): 26.8 (world avg. 20.3); within marriage 61.4%. **Death rate** per 1,000 population (2005): 18.2 (world avg. 8.6). **Total fertility rate** (avg. births per childbearing woman; 2005): 1.70. **Life expectancy** at birth (2005): male 74.7 years; female 83.6 years.

National economy

Budget (2006). *Revenue:* €727,936,000 (taxes on commerce 51.8%; state-run monopolies 11.4%; property taxes 8.7%). *Expenditures:* €789,132,000 (current expenditure 65.8%; capital expenditure 34.2%). **Production.** *Agriculture, forestry, fishing:* some horticulture and greenhouse cultivation; fisheries production (metric tons; 2005) 2. *Manufacturing* (value of sales in €'000; 2006): chemicals, cosmetics, perfumery, and pharmaceuticals 361,392; plastic products 265,783; light electronics and precision instruments 83,612. *Energy production (consumption):* electricity (kW-hr; 2001) n.a. (475,000,000 [imported from France]). **Gross national income** (2006): US$1,165,000,000 (US$35,725 per capita). **Population economically active** (2005): total 40,289; activity rate of total population 58.4% (participation rates: ages 17–64 [2000] 61.1%; female 41.4%; unemployed [2000] 3.6%). **Households.** Average household size (2004) 2.3. **Selected balance of payments data** (2006): tourism: 2,555 hotel rooms, 313,070 overnight visitors. **Land use** as % of total land area (2000): public gardens 20%.

Foreign trade

Imports (excluding trade with France; 2006): €752,000,000 (nonelectrical machinery and apparatus 36.0%; consumer goods 15.9%; food products 9.8%; automobiles 6.5%). *Major import sources:* China 27.3%; Italy 19.1%; Japan 10.2%; Belgium 6.7%; Germany 5.4%. **Exports** (excluding trade with France; 2006): €679,000,000 (rubber and plastic products, glass, construction materials, organic chemicals, and paper and paper products 35.9%; products of automobile industry 13.6%; pharmaceuticals, perfumes, clothing, and publishing 12.2%). *Major export destinations:* Germany 17.2%; Italy 10.3%; Spain 10.1%; UK 9.1%; Japan 4.2%.

Transport and communications

Transport. *Railroads* (2001): length 1.7 km; passengers 2,171,100; cargo 3,357 tons. *Roads* (2001): total length 50 km (paved 100%). *Vehicles* (1997): passenger cars 21,120; trucks and buses 2,770. *Air transport* (2004; charter service of Monacair) passenger-km 414,000. **Communications,** in total units (units per 1,000 persons). Televisions (2004): 25,000 (758); telephone landlines (2005): 34,000 (1,019); cellular telephone subscribers (2005): 17,000 (510); total Internet users (2006): 20,000 (593); broadband Internet subscribers (2005): 9,400 (282).

Education and health

Educational attainment (2000). Percentage of population ages 17 and over having: primary/lower secondary education 24.7%; upper secondary 27.6%; vocational 12.7%; university 35.0%. **Literacy:** virtually 100%. **Health** (2002): physicians 156 (1 per 207 persons); hospital beds 521 (1 per 62 persons); infant mortality rate pe. 1,000 live births (2005) 5.4.

Military

Defense responsibility lies with France according to the terms of the Versailles Treaty of 1919.

Background

Inhabited since prehistoric times, Monaco was known to the Phoenicians, Greeks, Carthaginians, and Romans. In 1191 the Genoese took possession of it; in 1297 the reign of the Grimaldi family began. The Grimaldis allied themselves with France except for the period 1524–1641, when they were under the protection of Spain. France annexed Monaco in 1793, and it remained under French control until the fall of Napoleon, when the Grimaldis returned. In 1815 it was put under the protection of Sardinia. A treaty in 1861 called for the sale of the towns of Menton and Roquebrune to France and the establishment of Monaco's independence. Monaco is one of Europe's most luxurious resorts. In 1997 the 700-year rule of the Grimaldis, then under Prince Rainier III, was celebrated.

Recent Developments

Planning continued in 2007 on Monaco's expansion of its territory into the Mediterranean. The new district would be built on the surface of the water in order to avoid disturbing the marine life below and would increase Monaco's current land surface by about 5%.

Internet resources: <www.visitmonaco.com>.

Mongolia

Official name: Mongol Uls (Mongolia). **Form of government:** unitary multiparty republic with one legislative house (State Great Hural [76]). **Chief of state:** President Nambaryn Enkhbayar (from 2005). **Head of government:** Prime Minister Sanj Bayar (from 2007). **Capital:** Ulaanbaatar (Ulan Bator). **Official language:** Khalkha Mongolian. **Official religion:** none. **Monetary unit:** 1 tugrik (Tug) = 100 mongo; valuation (1 Jul 2008) US$1 = Tug 1,158.25.00.

Demography

Area: 603,930 sq mi, 1,564,160 sq km. **Population** (2007): 2,609,000. **Density** (2007): persons per sq mi 4.3, persons per sq km 1.7. **Urban** (2006): 60.9%.

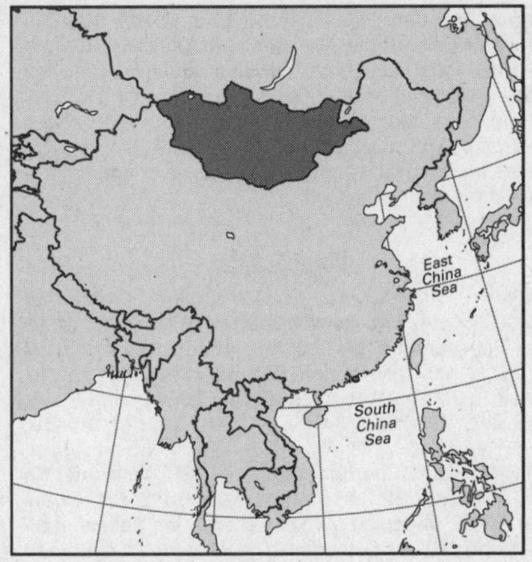

Sex distribution (2004): male 49.60%; female 50.40%. **Age breakdown** (2005): under 15, 28.9%; 15–29, 32.3%; 30–44, 22.6%; 45–59, 10.3%; 60–74, 4.5%; 75–84, 1.1%; 85 and over, 0.3%. **Ethnic composition** (2000): Khalkha Mongol 81.5%; Kazakh 4.3%; Dörbed Mongol 2.8%; Bayad 2.1%; Buryat Mongol 1.7%; Dariganga Mongol 1.3%; Zakhchin 1.3%; Tuvan (Uriankhai) 1.1%; other 3.9%. **Religious affiliation** (2005): traditional beliefs (shamanism) 32%; Buddhist (Lamaism) 23%; Muslim 5%; Christian 1%; nonreligious 30%; atheist/other 9%. **Major cities** (2000): Ulaanbaatar (Ulan Bator [2004]) 942,747; Erdenet 68,310; Darhan 65,791; Choybalsan 41,714; Ulaangom 26,319. **Location:** north-central Asia, bordering Russia and China.

Vital statistics

Birth rate per 1,000 population (2006): 18.3 (world avg. 20.3); (2001) within marriage 82.2%. **Death rate** per 1,000 population (2006): 6.0 (world avg. 8.6). **Total fertility rate** (avg. births per childbearing woman; 2005): 1.97. **Life expectancy** at birth (2004): male 61.6 years; female 67.8 years.

National economy

Budget (2006). *Revenue:* Tug 1,360,400,000,000 (tax revenue 83.0%, of which income taxes 35.0%, taxes on goods and services 25.9%; nontax revenue 16.6%; other 0.4%). *Expenditures:* Tug 1,237,000,000,000 (economic services 26.1%; social security 20.8%; general administration 19.6%; education 15.6%; health 8.0%). **Population economically active** (2004): total 986,100; activity rate of total population 39.3% (participation rates: ages 16–59, 63.7%; female 51.0%; unemployed [2006] 3.2%). **Production** (metric tons except as noted). *Agriculture, forestry, fishing* (2006): hay (2005) 830,700, wheat 127,757, potatoes 109,070; livestock (number of live animals) 13,267,000 goats, 12,884,500 sheep, 2,029,100 horses, 254,200 camels; roundwood (2005) 631,000 cu m, of which fuelwood 29%; fisheries production (2005) 366. *Mining and quarrying* (2005): fluorspar 367,000; copper (metal content) 126,547; molybdenum (metal content) 1,188. *Manufacturing* (value of production in Tug '000,000; 2006): textiles 93,475; base metals 74,879; food products 71,428. *Energy production (consumption):* electricity (kW-hr; 2004) 3,303,000,000 (3,466,000,000); hard coal (metric tons; 2004) 1,120,000 (1,120,000); lignite (metric tons; 2004) 5,745,000 (4,185,000); crude petroleum (barrels; 2005) 201,000 (n.a.); petroleum products (metric tons; 2004) none (562,000). **Gross national income** (2006): US$2,916,000,000 (US$1,120 per capita). **Public debt** (external; 2005): US$1,267,000,000. **Households:** Average household size (2004) 4.2; annual income per household (2005) Tug 1,629,600 (US$1,350); sources of income (2005): wages 35.2%, self-employment 31.3%, transfer payments 10.6%; expenditure (2005): food and nonalcoholic beverages 42.2%, housing and energy 10.5%, clothing and footwear 10.1%, transportation 9.5%. **Selected balance of payments data.** Receipts from (US$'000,000): tourism (2005) 201; remittances (2006) 177; foreign direct investment (2001–05 avg.) 106; official development assistance (2005) 133 (commitments). Disbursements for (US$'000,000): tourism (2005) 205; remittances (2006) 40. **Land use** as % of total land area (2003): in temporary crops 0.8%, in pasture 82.5%; overall forest area (2005) 6.5%.

Foreign trade

Imports (2006; c.i.f.): US$1,489,200,000 (mineral fuels 30.0%; machinery and apparatus 18.2%; food and agricultural products 12.4%; transportation equipment 10.3%). *Major import sources:* Russia 36.6%; China 27.5%; Japan 6.8%; South Korea 5.6%; Kazakhstan 3.5%. **Exports** (2006; f.o.b.): US$1,528,800,000 (copper concentrate 42.7%; gold 18.1%; refined copper 7.2%; combed goat down 5.3%; raw [greasy] cashmere 4.2%). *Major export destinations:* China 68.1%; Canada 11.2%; US 7.8%; Russia 2.9%; UK 2.5%.

Transport and communications

Transport. *Railroads* (2006): route length 1,810 km; passenger-km 1,287,000,000; metric ton-km cargo 10,513,000,000. *Roads* (2002): total length 49,250 km (paved 4%). *Vehicles* (2006): passenger cars 95,115; trucks and buses 41,234. *Air transport* (2006): passenger-km 835,800,000; metric ton-km cargo 86,400,000. **Communications,** in total units (units per 1,000 persons). Daily newspaper circulation (2004): 50,000 (20); televisions (2003): 220,000 (88); telephone landlines (2005): 156,000 (59); cellular telephone subscribers (2005): 557,000 (211); personal computers (2005): 340,000 (133); total Internet users (2005): 268,000 (105); broadband Internet subscribers (2005): 1,800 (0.7).

Education and health

Educational attainment (2000). Percentage of population ages 10 and over having: no formal education 11.6%; primary education 23.5%; secondary 46.1%; vocational secondary 11.2%; higher 7.6%. **Literacy** (2004): percentage of total population ages 15 and over literate 97.8%; males literate 98.0%; females literate 97.5%. **Health** (2004): physicians 6,590 (1 per 384 persons); hospital beds 18,400 (1 per 138 persons); infant mortality rate per 1,000 live births (2006) 19.8. **Food** (2005): daily per capita caloric intake 1,954 (vegetable products 65%, animal products 35%); 105% of FAO recommended minimum.

Military

Total active duty personnel (2006): 8,600 (army 87.2%, air force 9.3%, unspecified 3.5%). **Military expenditure as percentage of GDP** (2005): 1.6%; per capita expenditure US$12.

Background

In Neolithic times Mongolia was inhabited by small groups of nomads. During the 3rd century BC it became the center of the Xiongnu empire. Turkic-speaking peoples held sway in the 4th–10th centuries AD. In the early 13th century Genghis Khan united the Mongol tribes and conquered central Asia. His successor, Ogodei, conquered the Chin dynasty of China in 1234. Kublai Khan established the Yuan, or Mongol, dynasty in China in 1279. After the 14th century the Ming dynasty of China confined the Mongols to their homeland in the steppes; later they became part of the Chinese Ch'ing dynasty. Inner Mongolia was incorporated into China in 1644. After the fall of the Ch'ing dynasty in 1911, Mongol princes declared Mongolia's independence from China, and in 1921 Russian forces helped drive off the Chinese. The Mongolian People's Republic was established in 1924 and recognized by China in 1946. The nation adopted a new constitution in 1992 and shortened its name to Mongolia.

Recent Developments

The renegotiation of a contract with Ivanhoe Mines (Rio Tinto) for exploitation of Mongolia's prime gold and copper deposit at Oyuu Tolgoy was delayed into 2008 following public protests and government indecision. Several regions suffered problems that were caused by gangs of unlicensed miners, pollution, and environmental damage. Mongolia's GDP grew 9.9% in 2007 and was projected to grow significantly in 2008. Although minerals such as copper and gold made up two-thirds of exports in 2007, the value of total reported gold production dropped for the year, suggesting a rise in smuggling.

Internet resources: <www.mongoliatourism.gov.mn>.

Montenegro

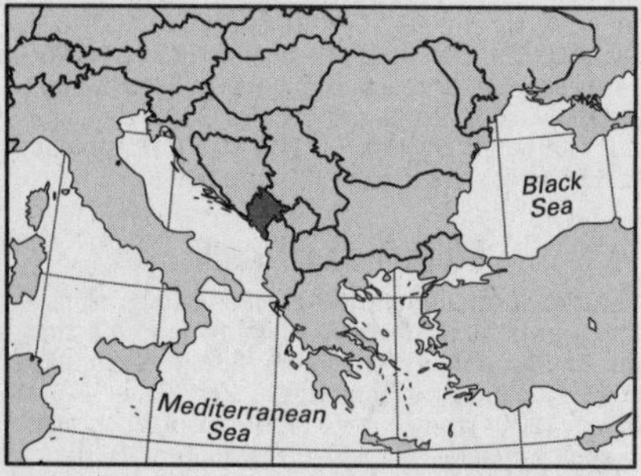

Official name: Republika Crna Gora (Republic of Montenegro). **Form of government:** multiparty republic with one legislative house (Parliament [81]). **Chief of state:** President Filip Vujanovic (from 2003). **Head of government:** Prime Minister Milo Djukanovic (from 2008). **Capital:** Cetinje. **Administrative center:** Podgorica. **Official language:** Montenegrin. **Official religion:** none. **Monetary unit:** 1 euro (€) = 100 cents; valuation (1 Jul 2008) US$1 = €0.63; Montenegro uses the euro as its official currency, even though it is not a member of the EU.

Demography

Area: 5,333 sq mi, 13,812 sq km. **Population** (2007): 624,000. **Density** (2007): persons per sq mi 117.0, persons per sq km 45.2. **Urban** (2005): 52.2%. **Sex distribution** (2006): male 49.23%; female 50.77%. **Age breakdown** (2005): under 15, 19.6%; 15–29, 23.6%; 30–44, 19.8%; 45–59, 19.1%; 60–74, 12.8%; 75–84, 4.3%; 85 and over, 0.8%. **Ethnic composition** (2003): Montenegrin 43.2%; Serb 32.0%; Bosniac/Muslim 11.8%; Albanian 5.0%; undeclared 4.0%; other 4.0%. **Religious affiliation** (2003): Orthodox 70%; Muslim 21%; Roman Catholic 4%; other 5%. **Major cities** (2005): Podgorica 173,000; Niksic 75,000; Bijelo Polje 50,000; Bar 41,000; Berane 35,000. **Location:** southeastern Europe, bordering Croatia, Bosnia and Herzegovina, Serbia, Kosovo, Albania, and the Mediterranean Sea.

Vital statistics

Birth rate per 1,000 population (2005): 11.8 (world avg. 20.3); within marriage 79.1%. **Death rate** per 1,000 population (2005): 9.4 (world avg. 8.6). **Natural increase rate** per 1,000 population (2005): 2.4 (world avg. 11.7). **Total fertility rate** (avg. births per childbearing woman; 2005): 1.60. **Life expectancy** at birth (2004): male 71 years; female 75 years.

National economy

Budget (2006). *Revenue:* €582,258,287 (tax revenue 85.8%, of which VAT 44.5%, income tax 12.5%, excise tax 12.4%, taxes on international trade 9.7%; nontax revenue 14.2%). *Expenditures:* €579,780,129 (wages and salaries 27.4%; transfers 20.7%; debt service 20.0%). **Public debt** (external, outstanding; January 2007): US$655,056,000. **Production** (metric tons except as noted). *Agriculture, forestry, fishing* (2006): potatoes 126,000, grapes 50,000, tomatoes 21,600; livestock (number of live animals) 254,898 sheep, 117,842 cattle, 10,697 pigs; roundwood (2005; state forests only) 279,228 cu m, of which fuelwood 13%; fisheries production (2005) 1,236. *Mining and quarrying* (2006): bauxite 659,370; sea salt 5,000. *Manufacturing* (gross value added in €'000; 2004): base and fabricated metal products (mostly of aluminum) 58,718; food products, beverages, and tobacco 56,846; paper products, publishing, and printing 6,647. *Energy production (consumption):* electricity (kW-hr; 2006) 2,952,000,000 ([2004] 19,000,000); hard coal (metric tons; 2005) n.a. (66,900); lignite (metric tons; 2006) 1,500,000 ([2005] 1,230,000); crude petroleum (barrels; 2004) n.a. (164,000). **Land use** as % of total land area (2005): in temporary crops 3.3%, in permanent crops 1.1%, in pasture 32.8%; overall forest area 44.7%. **Population economically active** (2005): total 256,569; activity rate 40.4% (participation rates: ages 16 and over, 49.9%; female

44.2%; unemployed 30.3%). **Gross national income** (2006): US$2,251,000,000 (US$3,745 per capita). **Households** (2006). Average household size 3.5; average annual income per household €5,328 (US$6,684); sources of income: wages and salaries 62.5%, transfer payments 19.7%, agriculture 9.0%; expenditure: food and nonalcoholic beverages 42.5%, housing and energy 12.5%, transportation 8.7%, clothing and footwear 7.9%. **Selected balance of payments data.** Receipts from (US$'000,000): tourism (2006) 340; remittances (2006) 100; foreign direct investment (FDI) (2002–05 avg.) 139. Disbursements for (US$'000,000): FDI (2006) 223.

Foreign trade

Imports (2005): €940,344,000 (machinery and transportation equipment 22.3%, of which motor vehicles 6.1%; mineral fuels and lubricants 15.6%; food and live animals 15.6%; household equipment 15.1%; chemicals and chemical products 8.7%). *Major import sources:* Serbia and Kosovo 34.8%; Italy 9.2%; Slovenia 7.1%; Croatia 7.0%; Greece 5.6%. **Exports** (2005): €434,458,000 (aluminum 42.9%; machinery and transportation equipment 11.7%; food and live animals 8.3%; beverages and tobacco 7.1%; wood and wood products 4.1%). *Major export destinations:* Serbia and Kosovo 36.8%; Italy 27.3%; Greece 9.1%; Slovenia 6.8%; Bosnia and Herzegovina 5.3%.

Transport and communications

Transport. *Railroads* (2006): length 250 km; passenger-km 131,500,000; metric ton-km cargo 182,163,000. *Roads* (2006): total length 7,368 km (paved [2005] 58%). *Vehicles* (2005): passenger cars 118,930. *Air transport* (2006): passengers 833,715. **Communications,** in total units (units per 1,000 persons). Daily newspaper circulation (2004): 73,000 (118); telephone landlines (2006): 176,000 (282); cellular telephone subscribers (2006): 703,000 (1,126); personal computers (2004): 389,000 (359); total Internet users (2006): 266,000 (426); broadband Internet subscribers (2006): 26,000 (42).

Education and health

Educational attainment (2005). Percentage of population ages 15 and over having: no formal education 3.2%; incomplete primary education 6.8%; complete primary 22.5%; secondary 55.0%; higher 12.5%. **Literacy** (2003): total population ages 20 and over literate 97.3%; males literate 99.2%; females literate 95.5%. **Health** (2005): physicians 1,257 (1 per 496 persons); hospital beds 4,065 (1 per 153 persons); infant mortality rate per 1,000 live births 9.5.

Military

Total active duty personnel (2006): 7,300 (army 54.8%, navy 45.2%).

Background

The Kingdom of the Serbs, Croats, and Slovenes was created after the collapse of Austria-Hungary at the end of World War I. The country signed treaties with Czechoslovakia and Romania in 1920–21, marking the beginning of the Little Entente. In 1929 an absolute monarchy was established, the country's name was changed to Yugoslavia, and it was divided into regions without regard to ethnic boundaries. Axis powers invaded Yugoslavia in 1941, and German, Italian, Hungarian, and Bulgarian troops occupied it for the rest of World War II. In 1945 the Socialist Federal Republic of Yugoslavia was established; it included the republics of Bosnia and Herzegovina, Croatia, Macedonia, Montenegro, Serbia, and Slovenia. Its independent form of communism under Josip Broz Tito's leadership provoked the USSR. Internal ethnic tensions flared up in the 1980s, causing the country's ultimate collapse. In 1991–92 independence was declared by Croatia, Slovenia, Macedonia, and Bosnia and Herzegovina; the new Federal Republic of Yugoslavia (containing roughly 45% of the population and 40% of the area of its predecessor) was proclaimed by Serbia and Montenegro. Still fueled by long-standing ethnic tensions, hostilities continued into the 1990s. Despite the approval of the Dayton Peace Agreement (1995), sporadic fighting continued and was followed in 1998–99 by Serbian repression and expulsion of ethnic populations in the province of Kosovo. In September–October 2000, the battered nation of Yugoslavia ended the autocratic rule of Pres. Slobodan Milosevic. In April 2001 he was arrested and in June extradited to The Hague to stand trial for war crimes, genocide, and crimes against humanity committed during the fighting in Kosovo. In February 2003 both houses of the Yugoslav federal legislature voted to accept a new state charter and change the name of the country from Yugoslavia to Serbia and Montenegro. Henceforth, defense, international political and economic relations, and human rights matters would be handled centrally, while all other functions would be run from the republican capitals, Belgrade and Podgorica, respectively. A provision was included for both states to vote on independence after three years, and in June 2006 Montenegro's parliament declared the republic's independence, severing some 88 years of union with Serbia.

Recent Developments

In October 2007 Montenegro's parliament adopted the country's first constitution after gaining independence from Serbia in June 2006. The country took steps toward EU membership by joining the Council of Europe and by signing the Stabilization and Association Agreement with NATO. The governing coalition unveiled a judiciary-reform program to combat corruption, pledged to cooperate with the International Criminal Tribunal for the Former Yugoslavia on any war crimes committed in Montenegro, prepared draft laws on national security, and began the planned reduction of its armed forces. Montenegro agreed to bolster ties with Serbia and Bosnia and Herzegovina and underscored the country's neutral stance regarding the final status of Kosovo. Foreign direct investment topped €1 billion (almost US$1.5 billion) for the year, a 56% increase from 2006. The budget showed a surplus and inflation was under 10%. Real wages rose 15.0% in 2007, while the cost of living increased only 4.2%. Unemployment was estimated at 19.3% for the year, however.

Internet resources: <www.visit-montenegro.com>.

Morocco

Official name: Al-Mamlakah al-Maghribiyah (Kingdom of Morocco). **Form of government:** constitutional monarchy with two legislative houses (House of Coun-

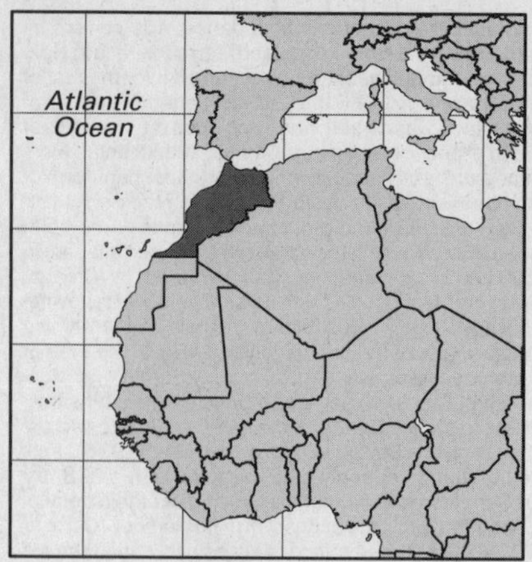

cillors [270]; House of Representatives [325]). **Chief of state and head of government:** King Muhammad VI (from 1999), assisted by Prime Minister Abbas El Fassi (from 2007). **Capital:** Rabat. **Official language:** Arabic. **Official religion:** Islam. **Monetary unit:** 1 Moroccan dirham (DH) = 100 Moroccan francs; valuation (1 Jul 2008) US$1 = DH 7.28.

Demography

Area (includes Western Sahara): 274,461 sq mi, 710,850 sq km. **Population** (includes Western Sahara; 2007): 31,704,000. **Density** (includes Western Sahara; 2007): persons per sq mi 115.5, persons per sq km 44.6. **Urban** (2004): 55.1%. **Sex distribution** (2004): male 49.33%; female 50.67%. **Age breakdown** (2004): under 15, 31.2%; 15–29, 28.9%; 30–44, 20.1%; 45–59, 11.7%; 60–74, 6.0%; 75 and over, 2.0%; unknown 0.1%. **Ethnic composition** (2000): Amazigh (Berber) 45%, of which Arabized 24%; Arab 44%; Moors originally from Mauritania 10%; other 1%. **Religious affiliation** (2004): Muslim, more than 99%, of which Sunni 97%, Shiʿi 2%; other, less than 1%. **Major cities** (2004): Casablanca 2,933,684; Rabat 1,622,860; Fès 946,815; Marrakech 823,154; Agadir 678,596; Tangier 669,685. **Location:** northern Africa, bordering the Mediterranean Sea, the Spanish exclaves of Ceuta and Melilla, Algeria, Mauritania, and the North Atlantic Ocean.

Vital statistics

Birth rate per 1,000 population (2005): 22.3 (world avg. 20.3). **Death rate** per 1,000 population (2005): 5.6 (world avg. 8.6). **Total fertility rate** (avg. births per childbearing woman; 2005): 2.73. **Life expectancy** at birth (2005): male 68.4 years; female 73.1 years.

National economy

Budget. *Revenue* (2005): DH 131,436,000,000 (VAT 24.8%; income tax 17.3%; corporate taxes 14.7%; excises 11.9%). *Expenditures* (2005): DH 151,693,000,000 (current expenditure 83.6%; capital expenditure 13.2%; other 3.2%). **Public debt** (external, outstanding; 2005): US$13,113,000,000. **Households.** Average household size (2004) 5.3; expenditure (2001): food 41.3%, housing and energy 22.1%, health 7.6%. **Population economically active** (2006): total 10,990,000; activity rate 36.0% (participation rates: ages 15 and over, 51.3%; female [2005] 27.5%; unemployed 9.7%). **Production** (metric tons except as noted). *Agriculture, forestry, fishing* (2006): wheat 6,300,000, sugar beets 2,252,000, potatoes 1,569,000; livestock (number of live animals) 16,872,000 sheep, 5,331,600 goats, 2,721,700 cattle; roundwood (2005) 957,000 cu m, of which fuelwood 40%; fisheries production (2005) 934,961, of which sardines 629,496 (roughly 60% of Morocco's fisheries production comes from Atlantic waters off of Western Sahara). *Mining and quarrying* (2005): phosphate rock 27,254,000; barite 475,700; zinc (metal content) 77,100. *Manufacturing* (value added in US$'000,000; 2004): food products 1,130; wearing apparel 733; tobacco products 595. *Energy production (consumption):* electricity (kW-hr; 2005) 18,701,000,000 (16,968,000,000); coal (metric tons; 2004) none ([2005] 5,938,000); crude petroleum (barrels; 2004) 246,000 (47,204,000); petroleum products (metric tons; 2005) 6,352,000 (7,454,000); natural gas (cu m; 2004) 50,665,000 ([2005] 40,000,000). **Land use** as % of total land area (2003): in temporary crops 19.0%, in permanent crops 2.0%, in pasture 47.1%; overall forest area (2005) 9.8%. **Gross national income** (2006): US$64,066,000,000 (US$2,046 per capita). **Selected balance of payments data.** Receipts from (US$'000,000): tourism (2005) 4,610; remittances (2006) 5,048; foreign direct investment (2001–05 avg.) 1,968. Disbursements for (US$'000,000): tourism (2005) 612; remittances (2006) 40.

Foreign trade

Imports (2005; c.i.f.): DH 180,294,000,000 (mineral fuels 21.8%, of which crude petroleum 13.3%, refined petroleum products 6.4%; machinery and apparatus 19.7%; food, beverages, and tobacco 8.6%). *Major import sources:* France 18.2%; Spain 11.0%; Saudi Arabia 6.8%; Italy 6.1%; China 5.2%. **Exports** (2005; f.o.b.): DH 94,358,000,000 (food, beverages, and tobacco products 19.8%, of which fisheries products 9.8%; garments 18.7%; phosphoric acid 8.1%; knitwear 7.2%; cannabis is an important illegal export; estimated production [2004] 88,900 metric tons). *Major export destinations:* France 31.3%; Spain 16.3%; UK 7.1%; Italy 4.3%; US 3.6%.

Transport and communications

Transport. *Railroads* (2004): route length 1,907 km; passenger-km 2,645,000,000; metric ton-km cargo 5,563,000,000. *Roads* (2004): total length 56,987 km (paved 61%). *Vehicles*: passenger cars (2002) 1,326,108; trucks and buses (2000) 415,700. *Air transport* (2006; Royal Air Maroc only): passenger-km 8,643,000,000; metric ton-km cargo 72,000,000. **Communications**, in total units (units per 1,000 persons). Daily newspaper circulation (2005): 411,000 (14); televisions (2004): 5,010,000 (164); telephone landlines (2006): 1,266,000 (41); cellular telephone

1 metric ton = about 1.1 short tons; 1 kilometer = 0.6 mi (statute); 1 metric ton-km cargo = about 0.68 short ton-mi cargo; c.i.f.: cost, insurance, and freight; f.o.b.: free on board

subscribers (2006): 16,005,000 (521); personal computers (2005): 740,000 (24); total Internet users (2006): 6,100,000 (199); broadband Internet subscribers (2006): 391,000 (13).

Education and health

Educational attainment (2004). Percentage of population ages 10 and over having: no formal education through incomplete primary education 45.5%; complete primary 40.8%; secondary 8.7%; higher 5.0%. **Literacy** (2005): total population ages 16 and over literate 53.5%; males literate 65.5%; females literate 41.5%. **Health** (2004): physicians 16,775 (1 per 1,778 persons); hospital beds (public hospitals only) 26,136 (1 per 1,141 persons); infant mortality rate per 1,000 live births (2005) 41.6. **Food** (2005): daily per capita caloric intake 3,492 (vegetable products 93%, animal products 7%); 187% of FAO recommended minimum.

Military

Total active duty personnel (2006): 200,800 (army 89.6%, navy 3.9%, air force 6.5%). **Military expenditure as percentage of GDP** (2005): 4.5%; per capita expenditure US$77.

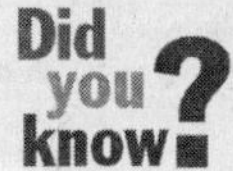

Marrakech is the chief city of central Morocco. The first of Morocco's four imperial cities, it lies in the center of the fertile, irrigated Haouz Plain, south of the Wadi Tennsift. The ancient section of the city, known as the medinah, was designated a UNESCO World Heritage site in 1985.

Background

The Berbers entered Morocco near the end of the 2nd millennium BC. Phoenicians established trading posts along the Mediterranean during the 12th century BC, and Carthage had settlements along the Atlantic in the 5th century BC. After the fall of Carthage, Morocco became a loyal ally of Rome, and in AD 42 it was annexed by Rome as part of the province of Mauretania. It was invaded by Muslims in the 7th century. Beginning in the mid-11th century, the Almoravids, Almohads, and Marinids ruled successively. After the fall of the Marinids in the mid-15th century, the Sa'dis ruled for a century after 1550. The French fought Morocco over the Algerian boundary in the 1840s, and the Spanish seized part of Moroccan territory in 1859. It was a French protectorate from 1912 until its independence in 1956. In the mid-1970s it reasserted claim to the Western Sahara, and in 1976 Spanish troops left there. Conflicts with Mauritania and Algeria over the region continued into the 1990s. As the decade wore on, the UN tried to solve the dispute. King Hassan II died in July 1999 after 38 years on the throne and was succeeded by his eldest son, Sidi Muhammad, who took the name Muhammad VI.

Recent Developments

In 2007 violence flared once again in Morocco. In early March a young man from a poverty-stricken district in Casablanca blew himself up in an Internet café after an altercation with the owner, and in April three suicide bombers blew themselves up in Casablanca and a fourth was shot by police. Days later the US consulate and a US cultural center came under attack when two suicide bombers detonated their explosives near the buildings. Police later apprehended three suspected accomplices and were able to connect all the perpetrators in the March–April bombings.

Internet resources: <www.tourisme-marocain.com/onmt_en/Marches/INS/index.aspx>.

Mozambique

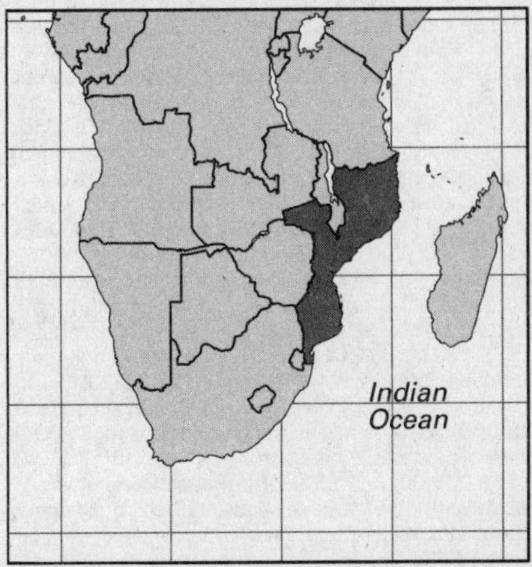

Official name: República de Moçambique (Republic of Mozambique). **Form of government:** multiparty republic with a single legislative house (Assembly of the Republic [250]). **Head of state and government:** President Armando Guebuza (from 2005), assisted by Prime Minister Luisa Diogo (from 2004). **Capital:** Maputo. **Official language:** Portuguese. **Official religion:** none. **Monetary unit:** 1 (new) metical (MTn; plural meticais) = 100 centavos; valuation (1 Jul 2008) US$1 = MTn 23.99 (the [new] metical replaced the [old] metical [MT] on 1 Jul 2006, at the rate of 1 MTn = MT 1,000).

Demography

Area: 308,642 sq mi, 799,379 sq km. **Population** (2007): 20,906,000. **Density** (2007): persons per sq mi 67.7, persons per sq km 26.2. **Urban** (2006): 39.1%. **Sex distribution** (2005): male 49.05%; female 50.95%. **Age breakdown** (2005): under 15, 43.1%; 15–29, 26.8%; 30–44, 16.5%; 45–59, 9.0%; 60–74, 3.9%; 75 and over, 0.7%. **Ethnic composition** (2000): Makuana 15.3%; Makua 14.5%; Tsonga 8.6%; Sena 8.0%; Lomwe 7.1%; Tswa 5.7%; Chwabo 5.5%; other 35.3%. **Religious affiliation** (2005): traditional beliefs 46%; Christian 37%, of which Roman Catholic 19%, Protestant 11%; Muslim 9%; other 8%. **Major cities** (2004): Maputo 1,140,400; Matola 520,500; Beira 487,100; Nampula 371,800; Chimoio 209,700. **Location:** southern Africa, bordering Tanzania, the Indian Ocean, South Africa, Swaziland, Zimbabwe, Zambia, and Malawi.

Vital statistics

Birth rate per 1,000 population (2006): 39.0 (world avg. 20.3). **Death rate** per 1,000 population (2006): 20.7 (world avg. 8.6). **Total fertility rate** (avg. births per childbearing woman; 2006): 5.35. **Life expectancy** at birth (2006): male 41.2 years; female 40.4 years.

National economy

Budget (2004). *Revenue:* MT 26,891,000,000,000 (tax revenue 58.0%, of which VAT 23.9%, personal income tax 9.0%, taxes on international trade 8.5%; grants 37.4%; nontax revenue 4.6%). *Expenditures:* MT 32,602,000,000,000 (current expenditures 58.3%; capital expenditures 38.5%; net lending 3.2%). **Public debt** (external, outstanding; 2005): US$3,727,000,000. **Production** (metric tons except as noted). *Agriculture, forestry, fishing* (2006): cassava 11,460,000, sugarcane 2,650,000, corn (maize) 1,300,000; livestock (number of live animals) 1,320,000 cattle, 392,000 goats, 28,000,000 chickens; roundwood (2005) 18,028,000 cu m, of which fuelwood 93%; fisheries production (2005) 43,695 (from aquaculture 3%). *Mining and quarrying* (2005): limestone 654,179; bauxite 9,518; tantalite 281,212 kg. *Manufacturing* (value added in MT '000,000,000; 2003): aluminum 19,067; beverages 4,773; food products 2,577. *Energy production (consumption):* electricity (kW-hr; 2004) 11,714,000,000 (10,579,000,000); coal (metric tons; 2004) 38,000 (23,000); petroleum products (metric tons; 2004) none (624,000); natural gas (cu m; 2004) 1,341,000,000 (3,152,000). **Households.** Average household size (2004) 4.2; source of income (1992–93): wages and salaries 51.6%, self-employment 12.5%, barter 11.5%; expenditure (1998): food, beverages, and tobacco 63.5%, firewood and furniture 17.0%, transportation and communications 4.6%, clothing and footwear 4.6%. **Population economically active** (2003): total 8,981,000; activity rate of total population 47.1% (participation rates: ages 15–64, 84.4%; female 53.8%). **Gross national income** (2006): US$6,790,000,000 (US$324 per capita). **Selected balance of payments data.** Receipts from (US$'000,000): tourism (2005) 130; remittances (2006) 80; foreign direct investment (FDI) (2001–05 avg.) 258; official development assistance (2005) 1,286. Disbursements for (US$'000,000): tourism (2005) 176; remittances (2006) 26. **Land use** as % of total land area (2003): in temporary crops 5.5%, in permanent crops 0.3%, in pasture 56.1%; overall forest area (2005) 24.6%.

Foreign trade

Imports (2003; f.o.b. in balance of trade and c.i.f. for commodities and trading partners): US$1,753,000,000 (mineral fuels 16.5%; machinery and apparatus 16.2%; food products 12.3%, of which cereals 7.2%; transport equipment 9.0%). *Major import sources* (2004): South Africa 41.4%; The Netherlands 11.0%; Portugal 3.3%; US 2.4%. **Exports** (2003): US$1,044,000,000 (aluminum 54.4%; electricity 10.9%; prawns 7.3%; cotton 3.1%). *Major export destinations* (2004): The Netherlands 60.9%; South Africa 12.9%; Malawi 3.3%; Portugal 2.8%; Spain 2.5%.

Transport and communications

Transport. *Railroads* (2003): route length (2002) 3,123 km; passenger-km 167,000,000; metric ton-km cargo 1,362,000,000. *Roads* (1999): total length 30,400 km (paved 19%). *Vehicles* (2001): passenger cars 81,600; trucks and buses 76,000. *Air transport* (2006; LAM [Linhas Aéreas de Moçambique] only): passenger-km 462,000,000; metric ton-km cargo 5,000,000. **Communications,** in total units (units per 1,000 persons). Daily newspaper circulation (2004): 16,000 (0.8); televisions (2003): 391,000 (20); telephone landlines (2006): 67,000 (3.3); cellular telephone subscribers (2006): 2,339,000 (116); personal computers (2005): 283,000 (14); total Internet users (2005): 178,000 (9).

Education and health

Educational attainment (1997). Percentage of population ages 15 and over having: no formal schooling/unknown 79.0%; primary education 18.4%; secondary 2.0%; technical 0.4%; higher 0.2%. **Literacy** (2005): percentage of total population ages 15 and over literate 50.4%; males literate 65.7%; females literate 35.6%. **Health:** physicians (2003) 635 (1 per 30,525 persons); hospital beds (2003) 16,493 (1 per 1,175 persons); infant mortality rate per 1,000 live births (2006) 112.1. **Food** (2005): daily per capita caloric intake 2,287 (vegetable products 98%, animal products 2%); 121% of FAO recommended minimum.

Military

Total active duty personnel (2006): 11,200 (army 89%, navy 2%, air force 9%). **Military expenditure as percentage of GDP** (2005): 0.9%; per capita expenditure US$3.

Background

Inhabited in prehistoric times, Mozambique was settled by Bantu peoples about the 3rd century AD. Arab traders occupied the coastal region from the 14th century, and the Portuguese controlled the area from the early 16th century. The slave trade later became an important part of the economy. In the late 19th century private trading companies began to administer parts of the inland areas. It became an overseas province of Portugal in 1951. After years of war beginning in the 1960s, the country was granted independence in 1975. It was wracked by civil war in the 1970s and '80s. In 1990 a new constitution was promulgated, and a peace treaty was signed with the rebels in 1992.

Recent Developments

Mozambique's stability and security, together with the government's efforts to wipe out corruption and to increase food production, continued to impress foreign donors in 2007. In May donors and funding agencies announced their support for the 2008 budget by offering US$385.8 million, while the US Millennium Challenge Cooperation promised an additional US$506.9 million over the next five years. Two oil refineries were planned as well, costing over

1 metric ton = about 1.1 short tons; 1 kilometer = 0.6 mi (statute); 1 metric ton-km cargo = about 0.68 short ton-mi cargo; c.i.f.: cost, insurance, and freight; f.o.b.: free on board

US$12 billion and with output capacities of 650,000 bbl per day.

Internet resources: <www.moztour.com/mozambique.htm>.

Myanmar (Burma)

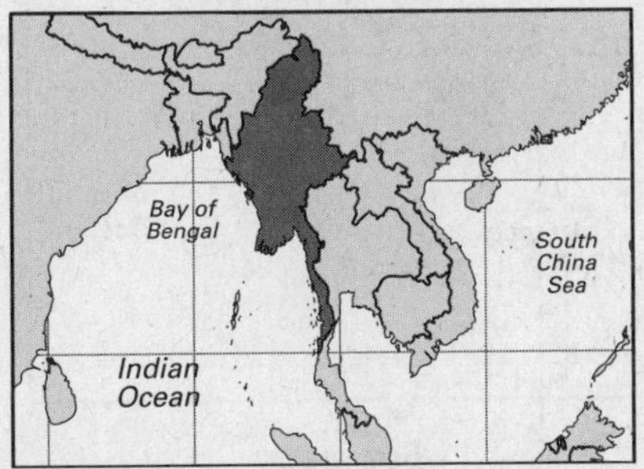

Official name: Pyidaungzu Myanma Naingngandaw (Union of Myanmar). **Form of government:** military regime. **Head of state and government:** Chairman of the State Peace and Development Council Gen. Than Shwe (from 1997), assisted by Prime Minister Thein Sein (from 2007). **Capital:** Naypyidaw. **Official language:** Burmese. **Official religion:** none. **Monetary unit:** 1 Myanmar kyat (K) = 100 pyas; valuation (1 Jul 2008) US$1 = K 6.42.

Demography

Area: 261,228 sq mi, 676,577 sq km. **Population** (2007): 47,374,000. **Density** (2007): persons per sq mi 181.4, persons per sq km 70.0. **Urban** (2005): 30.6%. **Sex distribution** (2006): male 49.48%; female 50.52%. **Age breakdown** (2006): under 15, 26.5%; 15–29, 29.2%; 30–44, 23.1%; 45–59, 13.5%; 60–74, 6.1%; 75–84, 1.4%; 85 and over, 0.2%. **Ethnic composition** (2000): Burman 55.9%; Karen 9.5%; Shan 6.5%; Han Chinese 2.5%; Mon 2.3%; Yangbye 2.2%; Kachin 1.5%; other 19.6%. **Religious affiliation** (2005): Buddhist 74%; Protestant 6%; Muslim 3%; Hindu 2%; traditional beliefs 11%; other 4%. **Major cities** (2004): Yangon (Rangoon; 2005) 4,107,000; Mandalay (2005) 924,000; Moulmein (Mawlamyine) 405,800; Bassein (Pathein) 215,600; Pegu (Bago) 200,900. **Location:** southeastern Asia, bordering China, Laos, Thailand, the Andaman Sea, the Bay of Bengal, Bangladesh, and India.

Vital statistics

Birth rate per 1,000 population (2006): 17.7 (world avg. 20.3). **Death rate** per 1,000 population (2006): 9.4 (world avg. 8.6). **Total fertility rate** (avg. births per childbearing woman; 2006): 1.98. **Life expectancy** at birth (2006): male 59.9 years; female 64.4 years.

National economy

Budget (2002–03). *Revenue:* K 279,377,000,000 (nontax revenue 59.6%; tax revenue 40.3%, of which taxes on goods and services 22.1%, taxes on individual income 16.3%; foreign grants 0.1%). *Expenditures:* K 353,389,000,000 (economic affairs 31.4%, of which transport 18.4%; public services 23.4%; defense 21.5%; education 14.6%). **Public debt** (external, outstanding; 2005): US$5,196,000,000. **Production** (metric tons except as noted). *Agriculture, forestry, fishing* (2005): rice 25,364,000, sugarcane 7,187,000, dry beans (2006) 1,700,000; livestock (number of live animals) 12,123,000 cattle, 5,677,000 pigs, 81,518,000 chickens; roundwood 42,548,000 cu m, of which fuelwood 90%; fisheries production 1,743,000 (from aquaculture 27%). *Mining and quarrying* (2006): copper (metal content; 2005) 34,500; jade 20,647,000 kg; rubies 1,685,000 carats. *Manufacturing* (value added in US$'000,000; 2003): tobacco products (2002) 1,320; nonelectrical machinery and apparatus 728; transportation equipment 483. *Energy production (consumption):* electricity (kW-hr; 2004) 6,437,000,000 (6,437,000,000); hard coal (metric tons; 2004) 831,000 (117,000); lignite (metric tons; 2004) 182,000 (68,000); crude petroleum (barrels; 2006) 7,675,000 ([2004] 7,509,000); petroleum products (metric tons; 2004) 917,000 (1,808,000); natural gas (cu m; 2006) 12,502,000,000 ([2004] 1,650,000,000). **Selected balance of payments data.** Receipts from (US$'000,000): tourism (2004) 84; remittances (2006) 117; foreign direct investment (2001–05 avg.) 245; official development assistance (2005) 145. Disbursements for (US$'000,000): tourism (2004) 29; remittances (2006) 25. **Households.** Average household size (2004) 5.0; expenditure (1997): food and nonalcoholic beverages 70.4%, fuel and lighting 6.6%, transportation 3.3%. **Gross national income** (2006): US$13,611,000,000 (US$280 per capita). **Population economically active** (2003): total 26,361,000; activity rate of total population 53.3% (participation rates: ages 15–64, 78.7%; female 44.9%; unemployed [2006] 10.2%). **Land use** as % of total land area (2003): in temporary crops 15.3%, in permanent crops 1.4%, in pasture 0.5%; overall forest area (2005) 49.0%.

Foreign trade

Imports (2006–07; c.i.f.): K 15,440,000,000 (mineral fuels 24.8%; nonelectrical machinery and transport equipment 15.9%; base and fabricated metals 7.0%; synthetic fabrics 6.5%). *Major import sources:* Singapore 36.5%; China 24.4%; Thailand 10.3%; India 5.3%; Japan 4.9%. **Exports** (2006–07; f.o.b.): K 27,381,000,000 (natural gas 42.6%; pulses [mostly beans] 11.1%; hardwood 10.0%, of which teak 6.0%; garments 5.3%). *Major export destinations:* Thailand 48.9%; India 13.7%; Hong Kong 8.2%; China 7.9%; Singapore 3.5%.

Transport and communications

Transport. *Railroads* (2006): route length (2004) 3,955 km; passenger-km 5,263,000,000; metric ton-km cargo 829,000,000. *Roads* (1999): total length 27,966 km (paved 11%). *Vehicles* (2006): passenger cars 203,441; trucks and buses 74,037. *Air transport* (2006): passenger-km 124,697,000; metric ton-km cargo 245,000,000. **Communications,** in total units (units per 1,000 persons). Daily newspaper circulation (2004): 501,000 (11); televisions (2004): 373,000 (8.1); telephone landlines (2005): 504,000 (9.3); cellular telephone subscribers (2006): 214,000 (4.2); personal computers (2005): 400,000 (8.6); total Internet users (2006): 94,000 (1.8); broadband Internet subscribers (2006): 800.

Education and health

Literacy (2003): total population ages 15 and over literate 89.7%; males literate 93.7%; females literate 86.2%. **Health** (2004–05): physicians 17,564 (1 per 2,660 persons); hospital beds 34,654 (1 per 1,350 persons); infant mortality rate per 1,000 live births (2006) 52.3. **Food** (2005): daily per capita caloric intake 3,620 (vegetable products 95%, animal products 5%); 199% of FAO recommended minimum.

Military

Total active duty personnel (2006): 482,750 (army 72.5%, navy 2.8%, air force 2.5%, paramilitary [people's militia and people's police] 22.2%). **Military expenditure as percentage of GDP** (2004): 7.6%.

Background

Myanmar, until 1989 known as Burma, has long been inhabited, with the Mon and Pyu states dominant between the 1st century BC and the 9th century AD. It was united in the 11th century under a Burmese dynasty that was overthrown by the Mongols in the 13th century. The Portuguese, Dutch, and English traded there in the 16th–17th centuries. The modern Burmese state was founded in the 18th century. It fell to the British in 1885 and became a province of India. It was occupied by Japan in World War II and became independent in 1948. A military coup took power in 1962 and nationalized major economic sectors. Civilian unrest in the 1980s led to antigovernment rioting. In 1990 opposition parties won in national elections, but the army remained in control. Trying to negotiate for a freer government amid the unrest, Aung San Suu Kyi, the National League for Democracy leader, was awarded the Nobel Peace Prize in 1991. She spent extended periods of the 1990s under house arrest.

Recent Developments

In May 2008 Myanmar was struck by Cyclone Nargis. Billions of dollars of damage was done by the winds and accompanying sea surge. As many as 2.5 million people were in need of food and shelter, and officials feared that the death toll would top 100,000. Thousands of livestock were lost and much of the country's rice crop was wiped out. The ruling junta was criticized for delaying the distribution of humanitarian aid, and there were reports of continuing exports of the country's rice and the distribution of rotting food to storm survivors.

Internet resources: <www.myanmar-tourism.com>.

Namibia

Official name: Republic of Namibia. **Form of government:** republic with two legislative houses (National Council [26]; National Assembly [72]). **Head of state and government:** President Hifikepunye Pohamba (from 2005), assisted by Prime Minister Nahas Angula (from 2005). **Capital:** Windhoek. **Official language:** English. **Official religion:** none. **Monetary unit:** 1 Namibian dollar (N$) = 100 cents; valuation (1 Jul 2008) US$1 = N$7.92.

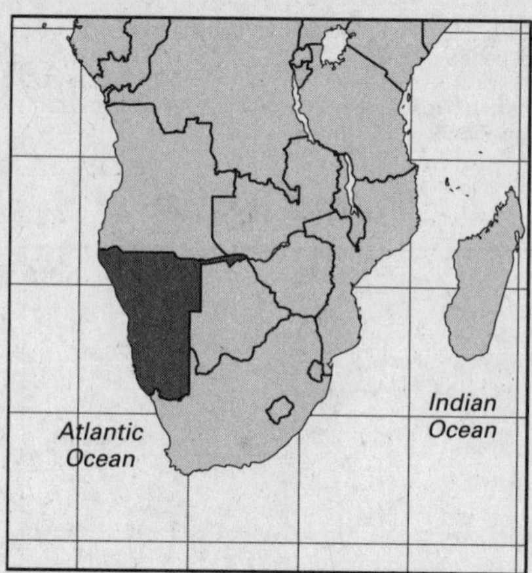

Demography

Area: 318,193 sq mi, 824,116 sq km. **Population** (2007): 2,074,000. **Density** (2007): persons per sq mi 6.5, persons per sq km 2.5. **Urban** (2006): 34.0%. **Sex distribution** (2006): male 50.13%; female 49.87%. **Age breakdown** (2006): under 15, 38.2%; 15–29, 31.3%; 30–44, 15.6%; 45–59, 9.2%; 60–74, 4.5%; 75 and over, 1.2%. **Ethnic composition** (2000): Ovambo 34.4%; mixed race (black/white) 14.5%; Kavango 9.1%; Afrikaner 8.1%; San (Bushmen) and Bergdama 7.0%; Herero 5.5%; Nama 4.4%; Kwambi 3.7%; German 2.8%; other 10.5%. **Religious affiliation** (2000): Protestant (mostly Lutheran) 49.3%; Roman Catholic 17.7%; unaffiliated Christian 14.1%; independent Christian 10.8%; traditional beliefs 6.0%; other 2.1%. **Major urban localities** (2001): Windhoek 233,529; Rundu 44,413; Walvis Bay 42,015; Oshakati 28,255; Katima Mulilo 22,694. **Location:** southwestern Africa, bordering Angola, Zambia, Botswana, South Africa, and the Atlantic Ocean.

Vital statistics

Birth rate per 1,000 population (2006): 24.3 (world avg. 20.3). **Death rate** per 1,000 population (2006): 18.9 (world avg. 8.6). **Total fertility rate** (avg. births per childbearing woman; 2006): 3.06. **Life expectancy** at birth (2006): male 44.5 years; female 42.3 years.

National economy

Budget (2006–07). *Revenue:* N$16,209,000,000 (tax revenue 90.0%, of which customs duties and excises 39.9%, income tax 28.9%, VAT 19.7%; nontax revenue and grants 10.0%). *Expenditures:* N$15,287,800,000 (current expenditure 82.0%, of which wages and salaries 40.2%; capital expenditure 18.0%). **Production** (metric tons except as noted). *Agriculture, forestry, fishing* (2006): roots and tubers 295,000, corn (maize) 60,853, millet 49,000; livestock (number of live animals) 2,660,252 sheep, 2,383,960 cattle, 2,061,403 goats; fisheries production (2005) 552,745. *Mining and quarrying* (2005):

salt 573,248; fluorspar 84,211; zinc (metal content) 68,000. *Manufacturing* (value added in N$'000,000; 2006): food and food products 2,633 (of which fish processing 620, meat processing 101); other manufactures include fur products (from Karakul sheep), textiles, carved wood products, and refined metals. *Energy production (consumption):* electricity (kW-hr; 2004) 1,397,000,000 (2,819,000,000). **Households** (2003–04). Average household size 4.9; average annual income per household N$43,520 (US$6,554); sources of income: wages and salaries 46.4%, farming 29.6%, transfer payments 10.2%, self-employment 7.1%; expenditure (2001): food and nonalcoholic beverages 29.6%, housing and energy 20.6%, transportation 14.8%, education 7.6%. **Selected balance of payments data.** Receipts from (US$'000,000): tourism (2005) 348; remittances (2006) 16; foreign direct investment (2001–05 avg.) 254; official development assistance (2005) 119 (commitments). Disbursements for (US$'000,000): tourism (2005) 108; remittances (2006) 17; foreign direct disinvestment (2001–05 avg.) −12. **Population economically active** (2006): total 656,000; activity rate of total population 32.0% (participation rates: over age 15, 54.0%; female 43.4%; officially unemployed 5.3%). **Public debt** (external, outstanding; 2004–05): US$317,015,000. **Gross national income** (2006): US$6,428,000,000 (US$3,141 per capita). **Land use** as % of total land area (2003): in temporary crops 1.0%, in permanent crops 0.01%, in pasture 46.2%; overall forest area (2005) 9.3%.

Foreign trade

Imports (2006; c.i.f. for commodities and trading partners): N$21,719,000,000 (refined petroleum products 18.3%; transport equipment 16.0%; chemicals, rubber, and plastics 12.1%; food, beverages, and tobacco 11.5%; machinery and apparatus 9.8%). *Major import sources* (2004): South Africa 85.4%; UK 2.6%; Germany 1.9%; China 1.2%; Zimbabwe 0.8%. **Exports** (2006): N$20,605,000,000 (diamonds 33.0%; fish 18.2%; other minerals [mainly gold, zinc, copper, lead, and silver] 12.4%; refined zinc 12.2%; meat preparations [mostly beef] 7.8%). *Major export destinations* (2004): South Africa 27.8%; UK 14.9%; Angola 13.8%; US 11.0%; Spain 9.6%.

Transport and communications

Transport. *Railroads:* route length (2006) 2,382 km; passenger-km (1995–96) 48,300,000; metric ton-km (2003–04) 1,247,400. *Roads* (2004): total length 42,237 km (paved 13%). *Vehicles* (2002): passenger cars 82,580; trucks and buses 81,002. *Air transport* (2005; Air Namibia only): passenger-km 1,012,000,000; metric ton-km cargo 60,429,000. **Communications,** in total units (units per 1,000 persons). Daily newspaper circulation (2005): 47,000 (23); televisions (2003): 509,000 (259); telephone landlines (2005): 139,000 (69); cellular telephone subscribers (2005): 495,000 (245); personal computers (2004): 220,000 (109); total Internet users (2005): 81,000 (40).

Education and health

Educational attainment (2000). Percentage of population ages 25 and over having: no formal schooling/unknown 26.5%; incomplete primary education 25.5%; complete primary 8.0%; incomplete secondary 24.9%; complete secondary 11.4%; higher 3.7%. **Literacy** (2006): total population ages 15 and over literate 85.0%; males literate 86.8%; females literate 83.5%. **Health:** physicians (2004) 598 (1 per 3,201 persons); hospital beds (2004–05; public sector only) 6,811 (1 per 283 persons); infant mortality rate (2006) 48.1. **Food** (2005): daily per capita caloric intake 1,996 (vegetable products 80%, animal products 20%); 109% of FAO recommended minimum.

Military

Total active duty personnel (2006): 9,200 (army 97.8%, navy 2.2%). **Military expenditure as percentage of GDP** (2005): 3.2%; per capita expenditure US$92.

Background

Long inhabited by indigenous peoples, Namibia was explored by the Portuguese in the late 15th century. In 1884 it was annexed by Germany as German South West Africa. It was captured in World War I by South Africa, which received it as a mandate from the League of Nations in 1920 and refused to give it up after World War II. A UN resolution in 1966 ending the mandate was challenged by South Africa in the 1970s and '80s. Through long negotiations involving many factions and interests, Namibia achieved independence in 1990.

Recent Developments

Namibia's international standing suffered somewhat in 2007. By September six senior police officers were facing charges or were under investigation for alleged corruption. Namibia also continued to support the regime of Pres. Robert Mugabe in Zimbabwe and invited him to make a state visit. The government was, however, able to persuade the De Beers diamond-mining company to sell it a larger share of its seafloor mining and to establish the Namibia Diamond Trading Company as a joint venture to sell some of Namibia's diamonds to local cutting and polishing companies. As a result of the increase in the price of uranium oxide, the Rossing uranium mine announced plans for large-scale expansion.

Internet resources: <www.namibiatourism.com.na>.

Nauru

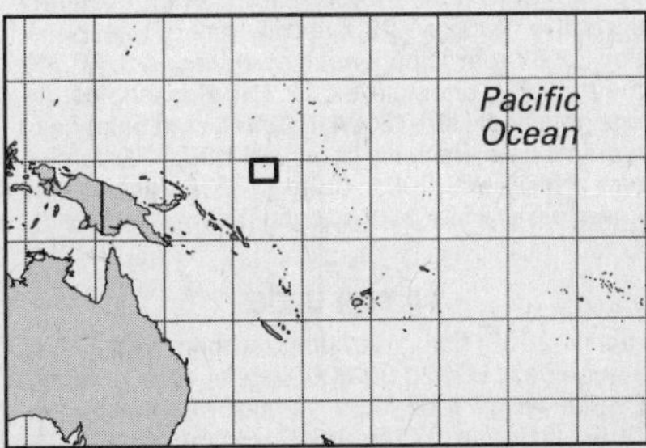

Official name: Naoero (Republic of Nauru). **Form of government:** republic with one legislative house (Parliament [18]). **Head of state and government:** President Marcus Stephen (from 2007). **Capital:** government offices are located in Yaren district. **Official language:** none; Nauruan is the national language; English is the language of business and government. **Official religion:** none. **Monetary unit:** 1 Nauruan dollar ($N) = 1 Australian dollar ($A) = 100 Nauruan and Australian cents; valuation (1 Jul 2008) US$1 = $A 1.05.

Demography

Area: 8.2 sq mi, 21.2 sq km. **Population** (2007): 10,200. **Density** (2007): persons per sq mi 1,244, persons per sq km 481.1. **Urban** (2005): 100%. **Sex distribution** (2005): male 50.11%; female 49.89%. **Age breakdown** (2005): under 15, 37.5%; 15–29, 29.5%; 30–44, 17.8%; 45–59, 11.8%; 60–74, 3.1%; 75 and over, 0.3%. **Ethnic composition** (2000): Nauruan 48.0%; Kiribertese (Gilbertese) 19.3%; Chinese 13.0%; Tuvaluan 6.9%; Australian white 6.2%; other 6.6%. **Religious affiliation** (2005): Protestant 49%, of which Congregational 29%; Roman Catholic 24%; Chinese folk-religionist 10%; other 17%. **Major cities:** none; population of Yaren urban area (2007) 4,616. **Location:** western Pacific Ocean, near the equator east of Papua New Guinea.

Vital statistics

Birth rate per 1,000 population (2005): 25.1 (world avg. 20.3). **Death rate** per 1,000 population (2005): 6.8 (world avg. 8.6). **Total fertility rate** (avg. births per childbearing woman; 2005): 3.19. **Life expectancy** at birth (2005): male 59.2 years; female 66.5 years.

National economy

Budget (2006). *Revenue:* $A 27,000,000 (largely from fishing license fees). *Expenditures:* $A 26,400,000. **Public debt** (2005): US$33,300,000. **Gross national income** (at current market prices; 2006): US$79,000,000 (US$7,840 per capita). **Production** (metric tons except as noted). *Agriculture, forestry, fishing* (2006): coconuts 1,600, tropical fruit (including mangoes) 275; coffee, almonds, figs, and pandanus (screw pine) are also cultivated; livestock (number of live animals) 2,800 pigs, 5,000 chickens; fisheries production (2005) 39. *Mining and quarrying* (2005): phosphate rock (gross weight including basic slag and guano) 11,000. *Manufacturing:* none. *Energy production (consumption):* electricity (kW-hr; 2004) 32,000,000 (32,000,000); petroleum products (metric tons; 2004) none (46,000). **Population economically active** (2002): 3,280; activity rate of total population 32.6% (participation rates: over age 15, 76.7%; female 45.5%; unemployed 22.7%). **Households.** Average household size (2004) 6.1. **Selected balance of payments data.** Receipts from (US$'000,000): foreign direct investment (2001–05 avg.) 1.0; official development assistance (2005) 16 (commitments).

Foreign trade

Imports (2003; f.o.b. in trading partners and c.i.f. in commodities): US$20,000,000 (agricultural products 8.0%, of which food 6.5%). *Major import sources* (2005): Australia 57.4%; US 9.6%; Germany 8.0%; Indonesia 7.4%; Fiji 3.7%. **Exports** (1999): US$40,000,000 (phosphate, virtually 100%). *Major export destinations* (2005): South Africa 56.9%; India 15.7%; Canada 5.9%; South Korea 3.3%; Germany 2.0%.

Transport and communications

Transport. *Railroads* (2001): length 5 km. *Roads* (2004): total length 40 km (paved 73%). *Vehicles* (1989): passenger cars, trucks, and buses 1,448. *Air transport* (2001): passenger-km 287,000,000; metric ton-km cargo 29,000,000. **Communications,** in total units (units per 1,000 persons). Televisions (2002): 800 (77); telephone landlines (2003): 1,600 (160); cellular telephone subscribers (2003): 1,300 (130).

Education and health

Educational attainment (1992). Percentage of population ages 5 and over having: primary education or less 77.4%; secondary education 12.9%; higher 4.1%; not stated 5.6%. **Literacy** (2004): total population ages 15 and over literate 97%. **Health** (2004): physicians 5 (1 per 2,012 persons); hospital beds 60 (1 per 168 persons); infant mortality rate per 1,000 live births (2005) 10.0.

Military

Total active duty personnel (2006): Nauru does not have any military establishment. The defense is assured by Australia, though no formal agreement exists.

Background

Nauru was inhabited by Pacific islanders when British explorers arrived in 1798 and named it Pleasant Island for the friendly welcome they received. Annexed by Germany in 1888, it was occupied by Australia at the start of World War I, and in 1919 it was placed under a joint mandate of Britain, Australia, and New Zealand. During World War II it was occupied by the Japanese. Made a UN trust territory under Australian administration in 1947, it gained independence in 1968. During the mid-1990s Nauru suffered political unrest.

Recent Developments

In March 2008 the detention center on Nauru set up to hold people seeking asylum in Australia was closed, dealing a severe blow to the island's economy (as much as 10% of the population was estimated to have been supported by the center in some capacity). A positive economic note, however, was that the country's flagging phosphate industry, once the mainstay of the economy and a source of great riches, was revived, with new mining methods and new deposits that some thought could last 30 more years.

Internet resources: <www.discovernauru.com>.

Nepal

Official name: Nepal (Federal Democratic Republic of Nepal). **Form of government:** multiparty republic with interim legislature (Constituent Assembly [statutory number, 601]). **Chief of state and government:** Prime

1 metric ton = about 1.1 short tons; 1 kilometer = 0.6 mi (statute); 1 metric ton-km cargo = about 0.68 short ton-mi cargo; c.i.f.: cost, insurance, and freight; f.o.b.: free on board

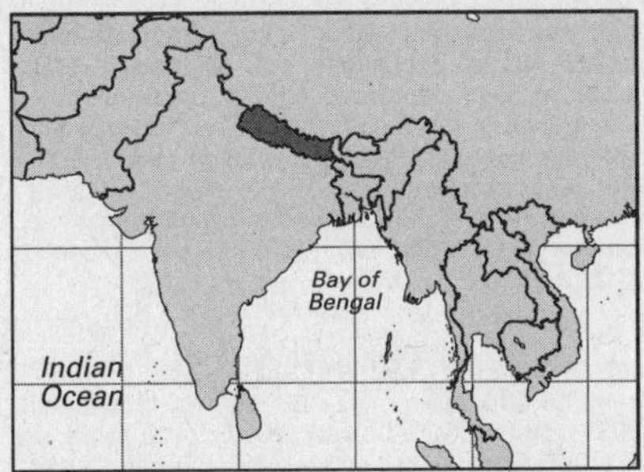

Minister Pushpa Kamal Dahal (from 2008). **Capital:** Kathmandu. **Official language:** Nepali. **Official religion:** none. **Monetary unit:** 1 Nepalese rupee (NR; plural NRs) = 100 paisa (pice); valuation (1 Jul 2008) US$1 = NRs 68.30.

Demography

Area: 56,827 sq mi, 147,181 sq km. **Population** (2007): 28,196,000. **Density** (2007): persons per sq mi 496.2, persons per sq km 191.6. **Urban** (2005): 15.8%. **Sex distribution** (2005): male 49.56%; female 50.44%. **Age breakdown** (2005): under 15, 39.0%; 15–29, 27.9%; 30–44, 17.2%; 45–59, 10.2%; 60–74, 4.7%; 75–84, 0.9%; 85 and over, 0.1%. **Ethnic composition** (2000): Nepalese 55.8%; Maithili 10.8%; Bhojpuri 7.9%; Tharu 4.4%; Tamang 3.6%; Newar 3.0%; Awadhi 2.7%; Magar 2.5%; Gurkha 1.7%; other 7.6%. **Religious affiliation** (2001): Hindu 80.6%; Buddhist 10.7%; Muslim 4.2%; Kirat (local traditional belief) 3.6%; Christian 0.5%; other 0.4%. **Major cities** (2001): Kathmandu 671,846; Biratnagar 166,674; Lalitpur 162,991; Pokhara 156,312; Birganj 112,484. **Location:** south-central Asia, bordering China and India.

Vital statistics

Birth rate per 1,000 population (2005): 29.1 (world avg. 20.3). **Death rate** per 1,000 population (2005): 8.2 (world avg. 8.6). **Natural increase rate** per 1,000 population (2005): 20.9 (world avg. 11.7). **Total fertility rate** (avg. births per childbearing woman; 2005): 3.48. **Life expectancy** at birth (2005): male 62.1 years; female 62.9 years.

National economy

Budget (2005–06). *Revenue:* NRs 86,800,000,000 (tax revenue 69.1%; grants 15.9%; nontax revenue 15.0%). *Expenditures:* NRs 97,900,000,000 (economic services 24.1%; education 19.5%; general public services 14.9%; defense 11.7%). **Public debt** (external, outstanding; 2005): US$3,217,000,000. **Production** (metric tons except as noted). *Agriculture, forestry, fishing* (2005): rice 4,290,000, sugarcane 2,376,103, potatoes 1,738,840; livestock (number of live animals) 7,154,000 goats, 6,994,000 cattle, 4,081,000 buffalo; roundwood 13,952,000 cu m, of which fuelwood 91%; fisheries production 42,463 (from aquaculture 53%). *Mining and quarrying* (2005): limestone 263,701; marble 23,850 sq m; talc 5,832. *Manufacturing* (value added in US$'000,000; 2002): food products 83; textiles and wearing apparel 73; tobacco products 55. *Energy production (consumption):* electricity (kW-hr; 2005) 2,401,000,000 (1,964,000,000); coal (metric tons; 2005) 9,298 (257,000); petroleum products (metric tons; 2004) none (685,000). **Gross national income** (at 2006 market prices): US$7,476,000,000 (US$270 per capita). **Population economically active** (2003): total 9,981,000; activity rate of total population 38.3% (participation rates: ages 15–64, 66.3%; female 41.0%; unofficially unemployed [2004] 42%). **Households** (2003–04). Average household size 5.3; income per household NRs 80,111 (US$1,084); sources of income: self-employment 47%, wages and salaries 28%; expenditure: food and beverages 59.0%, housing 9.5%, education 2.8%. **Selected balance of payments data.** Receipts from (US$'000,000): tourism (2005) 131; remittances (2006) 1,211; foreign direct investment (2001–05 avg.) 7.0; official development assistance (2005) 428. Disbursements for (US$'000,000): tourism (2005) 163; remittances (2006) 65. **Land use** as % of total land area (2003): in temporary crops 16.5%, in permanent crops 0.9%, in pasture 12.1%; overall forest area (2005) 25.4%.

Foreign trade

Imports (2005–06; c.i.f.): NRs 175,108,000,000 (basic manufactures [including fabrics, yarns, and made-up articles] 24.3%; mineral fuels [mostly refined petroleum] 20.8%; machinery and transport equipment 15.0%; chemicals and chemical products 14.2%). *Major import sources* (2006): India 48%; China 13%; UAE 12%; Saudi Arabia 5%; Kuwait 4%. **Exports** (2005–06; f.o.b.): NRs 61,167,000,000 (agricultural products 14.5%, of which vegetable ghee 6.6%; ready-made garments 12.2%; carpets 9.7%; jute goods 4.4%; pashminas 3.0%). *Major export destinations* (2006): India 58%; US 14%; Germany 6%; UK 3%; France 2%.

Transport and communications

Transport. *Railroads* (2004): route length 53 km; passengers carried (2002) 1,600,000; freight handled 22,000 metric tons. *Roads* (2004): total length 17,281 km (paved 31%). *Vehicles* (2003): passenger cars 66,395; trucks and buses 40,267. *Air transport* (2003): passenger-km 652,000,000. **Communications,** in total units (units per 1,000 persons). Daily newspaper circulation (2005): 486,000 (18); televisions (2003): 249,000 (9.6); telephone landlines (2006): 596,000 (22); cellular telephone subscribers (2006): 1,042,000 (38); personal computers (2005): 132,000 (4.9); total Internet users (2006): 249,000 (9).

Education and health

Educational attainment (2001). Percentage of population ages 6 and over having: no formal schooling/unknown 9.9%; primary education 41.9%; incomplete secondary 30.6%; complete secondary and higher 17.6%. **Literacy** (2003–04): total population ages 15 and over literate 48.0%; males literate 64.5%; females literate 33.8%. **Health** (2005–06): physicians 1,259 (1 per 21,737 persons); hospital beds 6,796 (1 per 4,027 persons); infant mortality rate per 1,000 live births (2005) 59.2. **Food** (2005): daily per capita caloric intake 2,503 (vegetable products 93%, animal products 7%); 138% of FAO recommended minimum.

Military

Total active duty personnel (2006): 69,000 (army 100.0%). **Military expenditure as percentage of GDP** (2005): 2.1%; per capita expenditure US$6.

Background

Nepal developed under early Buddhist influence, and dynastic rule dates from about the 4th century AD. It was formed into a single kingdom in 1769 and fought border wars with China, Tibet, and British India in the 18th–19th centuries. Its independence was recognized by Britain in 1923. A new constitution in 1990 restricted royal authority and accepted a democratically elected parliamentary government. The Maoist Communist Party of Nepal began an armed insurgency in 1996. Nepal signed trade agreements with India in 1997. On 1 Jun 2001, King Birendra, the queen, and seven other members of the royal family were fatally shot by Crown Prince Dipendra, who then turned the gun on himself.

Recent Developments

With the signing of a comprehensive peace accord between the government and Maoist rebels in November 2006, Nepal's 11-year-long Maoist insurgency came to an end. With the promulgation of an interim constitution in January 2007, Nepal turned from a Hindu kingdom into a secular state, with the role of the monarchy suspended. In December 2007 the legislature agreed to Maoist demands and voted to end the monarchy, and the Maoists, who had left the government over the issue, rejoined it. In April 2008 legislative elections the Maoists won the largest number of seats, and in late May the monarchy was abolished.

Internet resources: <www.welcomenepal.com>.

The Netherlands

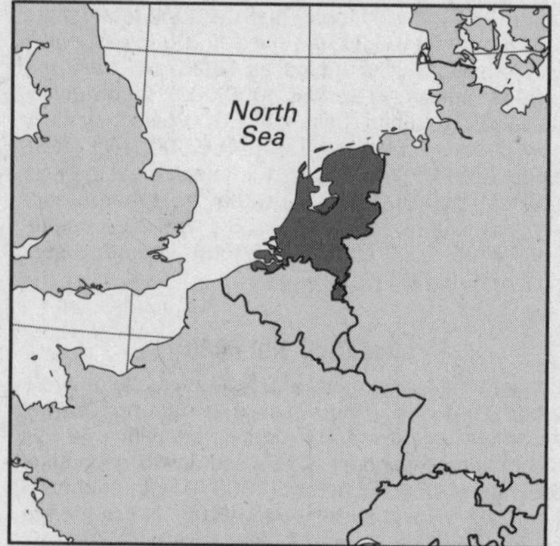

Official name: Koninkrijk der Nederlanden (Kingdom of The Netherlands). **Form of government:** constitutional monarchy with a parliament (States General) comprising two legislative houses (Senate [75]; House of Representatives [150]). **Chief of state:** Queen Beatrix (from 1980). **Head of government:** Prime Minister Jan Peter Balkenende (from 2002). **Seat of government:** The Hague. **Capital:** Amsterdam. **Official language:** Dutch. **Official religion:** none. **Monetary unit:** 1 euro (€) = 100 cents; valuation (1 Jul 2008) US$1 = €0.63.

Demography

Area: 16,034 sq mi, 41,528 sq km. **Population** (2007): 16,371,000. **Density** (2007): persons per sq mi 1,255, persons per sq km 484.6. **Urban** (2005): 80.2%. **Sex distribution** (2006): male 49.45%; female 50.55%. **Age breakdown** (2005): under 15, 18.3%; 15–29, 18.1%; 30–44, 23.0%; 45–59, 21.3%; 60–74, 12.9%; 75–84, 4.9%; 85 and over, 1.5%. **Ethnic composition** (by place of origin [including 2nd generation]; 2005): Netherlander 80.7%; Indonesian 2.4%; Turkish 2.2%; Surinamese 2.0%; Moroccan 2.0%; other 10.7%. **Religious affiliation** (2004): Roman Catholic 30%; Reformed/Lutheran tradition 20%; Muslim 6%; nonreligious/atheist 40%; other 4%. **Major urban agglomerations** (2005): Amsterdam 1,465,405; Rotterdam 1,176,869; The Hague 990,463; Utrecht 577,389; Haarlem 405,430. **Location:** northwestern Europe, bordering the North Sea, Germany, and Belgium.

Vital statistics

Birth rate per 1,000 population (2006): 11.3 (world avg. 20.3); within marriage 62.9%. **Death rate** per 1,000 population (2006): 8.3 (world avg. 8.6). **Total fertility rate** (avg. births per childbearing woman; 2006): 1.72. **Life expectancy** at birth (2006): male 77.6 years; female 81.9 years.

National economy

Budget (2004). *Revenue:* €192,220,000,000 (social security contributions 35.7%; VAT 19.8%; income tax 15.3%; corporate taxes 7.8%; nontax revenue 7.5%). *Expenditures:* €200,270,000,000 (social security and welfare 41.9%; education 11.1%; health 10.4%; economic affairs 6.6%; defense 3.6%). **National debt** (2006): US$322,400,000,000. **Production** (metric tons except as noted). *Agriculture, forestry, fishing* (2006): potatoes 6,240,000, sugar beets 5,414,000, wheat 1,184,000, flowering bulbs and tubers 79,000 acres (32,000 hectares), of which tulips 24,700 acres (10,000 hectares), cut flowers/plants under glass 12,400 acres (5,000 hectares); livestock (number of live animals) 11,356,000 pigs, 3,749,000 cattle, 1,376,000 sheep; roundwood (2005) 1,110,000 cu m, of which fuelwood 26%; fisheries production (2005) 617,383 (from aquaculture 11%). *Manufacturing* (value added in €'000,000; 2002): food, beverages, and tobacco 12,936; chemicals and chemical products 7,542; printing and publishing 5,743; electric/electronic machinery 5,050. *Energy production (consumption):* electricity (kW-hr; 2005) 96,366,000,000 (95,556,000,000); coal (metric tons; 2004) negligible (13,551,000); crude petroleum (barrels; 2005) 15,500,000 ([2004] 361,900,000); petroleum products (metric tons; 2004) 65,801,000 (28,801,000); natural gas (cu m; 2005) 82,920,000,000 ([2004] 54,010,000,000). **Households** (2005). Average household size (2006) 2.3; disposable income per household €34,321 (US$42,683); sources of income (1996): wages 48.4%, transfers 28.5%, self-employment 11.3%; expenditure: housing and energy 22.2%, transportation and communications 15.9%, food and beverages 13.6%, recreation and culture 10.1%. **Land use** as % of total land area (2003): in temporary crops 26.7%, in permanent crops 0.9%, in pasture 29.1%; overall forest area (2005) 10.8%. **Gross national income** (2006): US$670,483,000,000 (US$40,940 per capita). **Population economically active** (2005): total 8,308,000; activity rate of total population 51% (participation rates: ages 15–64, 75.1%; female 45.1%; unemployed [April 2005–March 2006] 6.3%). **Selected balance of payments data.** Receipts from (US$'000,000): tourism (2005) 10,383; remittances (2006) 2,424; foreign direct investment (FDI) (2001–05 avg.) 28,556. Disbursements for (US$'000,000): tourism (2005) 16,082; remittances (2006) 6,662; FDI (2001–05 avg.) 52,706.

Foreign trade

Imports (2005; c.i.f.): €248,827,000,000 (mineral fuels 14.7%, of which crude petroleum 7.5%; chemicals and chemical products 13.1%; computers and related equipment 11.7%; food 7.6%; road vehicles 5.7%). *Major import sources:* Germany 19.0%; Belgium/Luxembourg 10.7%; US 8.0%; China 7.7%; UK 6.3%. **Exports** (2005; f.o.b.): €280,743,000,000 (chemicals and chemical products 17.0%; food 11.6%; mineral fuels 11.0%; computers and related equipment 10.6%). *Major export destinations:* Germany 23.6%; Belgium/Luxembourg 11.9%; UK 9.3%; France 9.2%; Italy 5.7%.

Transport and communications

Transport. *Railroads:* length (2006) 2,797 km; passenger-km (2004) 14,097,000,000; metric ton-km cargo (2001) 4,293,000,000. *Roads* (2006): total length 134,981 km (paved 90%). *Vehicles* (2006): passenger cars 7,230,178; trucks and buses 1,064,846. *Air transport* (2005): passenger-km 68,316,000,000; metric ton-km cargo 4,650,500,000. **Communications**, in total units (units per 1,000 persons). Daily newspaper circulation (2004): 4,712,000 (289); televisions (2003): 10,514,000 (648); telephone landlines (2005): 7,600,000 (466); cellular telephone subscribers (2005): 15,834,000 (971); personal computers (2005): 12,060,000 (740); total Internet users (2006): 14,544,000 (889); broadband Internet subscribers (2006): 5,192,000 (318).

Education and health

Educational attainment (2004). Percentage of population ages 15–64 having: primary education 9.5%; lower secondary 9.6%; upper secondary 10.7%; vocational 44.0%; higher 25.4%, of which university 9.2%; unknown 0.8%. **Health:** physicians (2003) 50,854 (1 per 319 persons); hospital beds (2003) 81,125 (1 per 200 persons); infant mortality rate (2006) 4.4. **Food** (2005): daily per capita caloric intake 3,479 (vegetable products 70%, animal products 30%).

Military

Total active duty personnel (2006): 53,130 (army 43.6%, navy 22.8%, air force 20.8%, paramilitary 12.8%). **Military expenditure as percentage of GDP** (2005): 1.5%; per capita expenditure US$523.

Background

Celtic and Germanic tribes inhabited The Netherlands at the time of the Roman conquest. Under the Romans, trade and industry flourished, but by the mid-3rd century AD Roman power had waned, eroded by resurgent German tribes and the encroachment of the sea. A Germanic invasion (406–07) ended Roman control. The Merovingian dynasty followed the Romans but was supplanted in the 7th century by the Carolingian dynasty, which converted the area to Christianity. After Charlemagne's death in 814, the area was increasingly the target of Viking attacks. It became part of the kingdom of Lotharingia, which established an Imperial Church. In the 12th–14th centuries dike building occurred on a large scale. The dukes of Burgundy gained control in the late 14th century. By the early 16th century the Low Countries were ruled by the Spanish Habsburgs. In 1581 the seven northern provinces, led by Calvinists, declared their independence from Spain, and in 1648, following the Thirty Years' War, Spain recognized Dutch independence. The 17th century was the golden age of Dutch civilization. The Dutch East India Company secured Asian colonies, and the country's standard of living soared. In the 18th century the region was conquered by the French and became the kingdom of Holland under Napoleon (1806). It remained neutral in World War I and declared neutrality in World War II but was occupied by Germany. It joined NATO in 1949, was a founding member of what is now the European Community, and is part of the EU.

Recent Developments

Immigration and integration remained important topics of discussion in The Netherlands in 2007. Ayaan Hirsi Ali, a Somali-born former MP and controversial opponent of radical Islam, returned to The Netherlands in October from her work at the American Enterprise Institute in Washington DC when the Dutch government ended funding for her security detail abroad. There were political discussions about the presumed loyalty of dual citizens, as well as lively debate in response to a speech by Argentine-born Dutch Crown Princess Máxima, champion of integration in The Netherlands, in which she described Dutch identity as not "static" but rather multidimensional and fluid. The Dutch economy grew 4.7% in 2007. The government, which anticipated a budget surplus in 2008, announced plans to reemploy many of the long-term unemployed. It also reported its goal of giving priority to improvements in energy, water quality and water control, health care for citizens, and education. In an effort to continue to attract international business and innovative research, the government formulated plans to improve access to the country in order to admit talented foreigners to work in The Netherlands and to study at Dutch universities. In November the government extended the mandate to 2010 for some 1,700 Dutch soldiers stationed in southern Afghanistan.

Internet resources: <www.holland.com>.

Netherlands Antilles

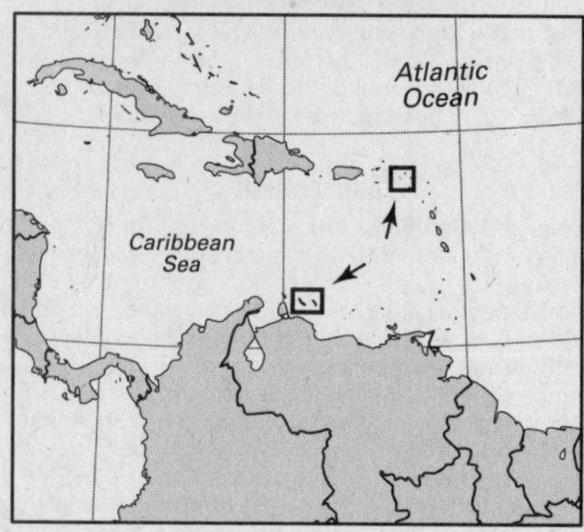

Official name: Nederlandse Antillen (Netherlands Antilles). **Political status:** nonmetropolitan territory of The Netherlands with one legislative house (Island Council of Curaçao [21]). **Chief of state:** Dutch Queen Beatrix (from 1980), represented by Governor Frits Goedgedrag (from 2002). **Head of government:** Prime Minister Emily de Jongh-Elhage (from 2006). **Capital:** Willemstad. **Official language:** Dutch. **Official religion:** none. **Monetary unit:** 1 Netherlands Antillean guilder (NAf.) = 100 cents; valuation (1 Jul 2008) US$1 = NAf. 1.79.

Demography

Area: 308 sq mi, 800 sq km. **Population** (2007): 192,000. **Density** (2007): persons per sq mi 623.4, persons per sq km 240.0. **Urban** (2003): 70.5%. **Sex distribution** (2006): male 46.53%; female 53.47%. **Age breakdown** (2006): under 15, 22.7%; 15–29, 18.6%; 30–44, 23.9%; 45–59, 20.8%; 60–74, 10.3%; 75–84, 2.8%; 85 and over, 0.9%. **Ethnic composition** (2000): local black-other (Antillean Creole) 81.1%; Dutch 5.3%; Surinamese 2.9%; other (significantly West Indian black) 10.7%. **Religious affiliation** (2001): Roman Catholic 72.0%; Protestant 16.0%; Spiritist 0.9%; Buddhist 0.5%; Jewish 0.4%; Baha'i 0.3%; Hindu 0.2%; Muslim 0.2%; other/unknown 9.5%. **Major locales** (2001): Willemstad 93,599; Kralendijk 3,179; Philipsburg 1,227; Oranjestad 1,003; The Bottom 462. **Location:** two separate island groups in the Caribbean Sea, one just north of Venezuela, the other east of Puerto Rico.

Vital statistics

Birth rate per 1,000 population (2006): 14.8 (world avg. 20.3). **Death rate** per 1,000 population (2006): 6.3 (world avg. 8.6). **Total fertility rate** (avg. births per childbearing woman; 2006): 1.99. **Life expectancy** at birth (2006): male 73.8 years; female 78.4 years.

National economy

Budget (2006). *Revenue:* NAf. 822,600,000 (tax revenue 78.9%, of which sales tax 40.0%, import duties 17.4%; grants 10.9%; nontax revenue 10.2%). *Expenditures:* NAf. 910,600,000 (current expenditures 99.8%, of which transfers 38.2%, wages 32.5%, interest payments 16.1%; development expenditures 0.2%). **Production** (metric tons except as noted). *Agriculture, forestry, fishing* (2005): mostly tomatoes, beans, cucumbers, gherkins, melons, and lettuce grown on hydroponic farms; livestock (number of live animals) 13,500 goats, 9,000 sheep, 2,600 asses; fisheries production 2,422. *Mining and quarrying* (2003): salt 500,000; sulfur byproduct (2002) 30,000. *Manufacturing* (2002): residual fuel oil 5,200,000; gas-diesel oils 2,620,000; asphalt 1,030,000; other manufactures include electronic parts, cigarettes, textiles, rum, and Curaçao liqueur. *Energy production (consumption):* electricity (kW-hr; 2005) 1,248,000,000 ([2004] 1,065,000,000); crude petroleum (barrels; 2004) none (79,800,000); petroleum products (metric tons; 2004) 9,081,000 (2,176,000). **Selected balance of payments data.** Receipts from (US$'000,000): tourism (2005) 988; remittances (2005) 5; foreign direct disinvestment (2001–05 avg.) −11. Disbursements for (US$'000,000): tourism (2005) 109; remittances (2004) 52; foreign direct investment (2001–05 avg.) 5.0. **Households.** Average household size (2005) 2.8; expenditure (1996): housing 26.5%, transportation and communications 19.9%, food 14.7%, household furnishings 8.8%, recreation and education 8.2%. **Population economically active** (2006): total 91,178; activity rate of total population 48.5% (participation rates [2001]: ages 15–64, 68.7%; female 49.0%; unemployed [2006] 13.2%). **Gross national income** (at current market prices; 2006): US$3,341,000,000 (US$17,691 per capita). **Public debt** (external outstanding; 2006): US$459,200,000. **Land use** as % of total land area (2003): in temporary crops 10.0%; overall forest area (2005) 1.5%.

Foreign trade

Imports (2002; c.i.f.): US$2,268,500,000 (crude petroleum 59.7%; refined petroleum 8.7%; food 6.4%). *Major import sources* (2004): Venezuela 51.1%; US 21.9%; The Netherlands 5.0%. **Exports** (2002; f.o.b.): US$1,699,200,000 (refined petroleum 94.7%; food 1.2%). *Major export destinations* (2004): US 20.4%; Panama 11.2%; Guatemala 8.8%; Haiti 7.1%; The Bahamas 5.6%.

Transport and communications

Transport. *Roads* (2003): total length 600 km (paved 50%). *Vehicles* (2004): passenger cars 64,947; trucks and buses 15,335. *Air transport* (2001; Curaçao and Sint Maarten airports only): passenger arrivals and departures 2,131,000; freight loaded and unloaded 18,900 metric tons. **Communications,** in total units (units per 1,000 persons). Daily newspaper circulation (2004): 66,000 (349); televisions (1999): 71,000 (390); telephone landlines (2004): 80,000 (437); cellular telephone subscribers (2004): 200,000 (1,092); total Internet users (1999): 2,000 (11).

Education and health

Educational attainment (2001). Percentage of population ages 25 and over having: no formal schooling/unknown 4.8%; primary education 24.2%; lower

1 metric ton = about 1.1 short tons; 1 kilometer = 0.6 mi (statute); 1 metric ton-km cargo = about 0.68 short ton-mi cargo; c.i.f.: cost, insurance, and freight; f.o.b.: free on board

secondary 42.8%; upper secondary 16.8%; higher 11.4%. **Literacy** (2005): total population ages 15 and over literate 96.9%; males literate 96.9%; females literate 97.0%. **Health:** physicians (2001) 333 (1 per 520 persons); hospital beds (2002) 1,264 (1 per 138 persons); infant mortality rate per 1,000 live births (2006) 9.9. **Food** (2004): daily per capita caloric intake 2,464 (vegetable products 85%, animal products 15%); 128% of FAO recommended minimum.

Military

Total active duty personnel (2005): more than 1,000 Dutch naval personnel are stationed in the Netherlands Antilles and Aruba.

Background

The islands of the Netherlands Antilles were sighted by Christopher Columbus in 1493 and claimed for Spain. In the 17th century the Dutch gained control, and in 1845 the islands became the Netherlands Antilles. In 1954 they became an integral part of The Netherlands, with full autonomy in domestic affairs. Aruba seceded from the group in 1986.

Recent Developments

The Netherlands Antillean islands of Bonaire, Sint Eustatius, and Saba were due to achieve the status of Dutch local authorities in January 2010 following agreement on a new constitution (which also conferred local autonomy on Curaçao and Sint Maarten). In December 2007 The Netherlands agreed to write off some €2.5 billion (about US$3.7 billion) of the islands' debt, a key development that the local governments had desired.

Internet resources: <www.cbs.an>.

New Caledonia

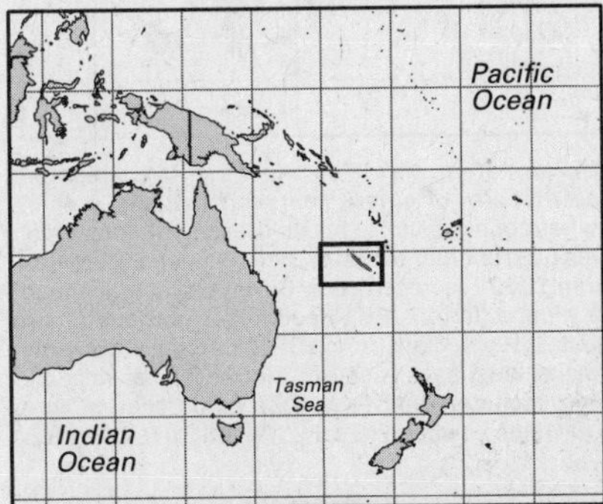

Official name: Nouvelle-Calédonie (New Caledonia). **Political status:** overseas collectivity of France with one legislative house (Congress [54]). **Chief of state:** French President Nicolas Sarkozy (from 2007), represented by High Commissioner Yves Dassonville (from 2007). **Head of government:** President Harold Martin (from 2007). **Capital:** Nouméa. **Official language:** none; Kanak languages and French have special recognition per the Nouméa Accord. **Official religion:** none. **Monetary unit:** 1 franc de la Comptoirs français du Pacifique franc (CFPF) = 100 centimes; valuation (1 Jul 2008) US$1 = CFPF 75.59.

Demography

Area: 7,172 sq mi, 18,575 sq km. **Population** (2007): 242,000. **Density** (2007): persons per sq mi 33.7, persons per sq km 13.0. **Urban** (2005): 63.7%. **Sex distribution** (2004): male 50.47%; female 49.53%. **Age breakdown** (2004): under 15, 28.0%; 15–29, 24.3%; 30–44, 23.4%; 45–59, 14.9%; 60–74, 7.2%; 75–84, 1.7%; 85 and over, 0.5%. **Ethnic composition** (1996): Melanesian 45.3%, of which local (Kanak) 44.1%, Vanuatuan 1.2%; European 34.1%; Wallisian or Futunan 9.0%; Indonesian 2.6%; Tahitian 2.6%; Vietnamese 1.4%; other 5.0%. **Religious affiliation** (2000): Roman Catholic 54.2%; Protestant 14.0%; unaffiliated/other Christian 18.8%; Muslim 2.7%; nonreligious 5.8%; other 4.5%. **Major communes** (2004): Nouméa 91,386 (urban agglomeration 146,245); Mont-Dore 24,195; Dumbéa 18,602; Païta 12,062; Poindimié 4,824. **Location:** South Pacific Ocean, east of Australia.

Vital statistics

Birth rate per 1,000 population (2006): 17.7 (world avg. 20.3); (2005) within marriage 32.0%. **Death rate** per 1,000 population (2006): 4.7 (world avg. 8.6). **Total fertility rate** (avg. births per childbearing woman; 2005): 2.20. **Life expectancy** at birth (2005): male 71.9 years; female 78.6 years.

National economy

Budget (2005). *Revenue:* CFPF 116,323,000,000 (tax revenue 71.4%, of which indirect taxes 35.8%, direct taxes 35.6%; nontax revenue 28.6%). *Expenditures:* CFPF 108,085,000,000 (current expenditure 95.8%; development expenditure 4.2%). **Public debt** (external, outstanding; 1998): US$79,000,000. **Production** (metric tons except as noted). *Agriculture, forestry, fishing* (2005): coconuts 16,350, yams 11,080, corn (maize) 5,669; livestock (number of live animals) 111,000 cattle, 27,000 pigs, 600,000 chickens; roundwood 4,800 cu m; fisheries production 5,848, of which tuna 2,450, shrimp 2,440 (from aquaculture 43%). *Mining and quarrying* (2006): nickel ore 6,150,000, of which nickel content 105,000; cobalt 1,100 (recovered). *Manufacturing* (2006): cement (2004) 114,762; ferronickel (metal content) 48,723; nickel matte (metal content) 13,655; other manufactures include beer, copra cake, and soap. *Energy production (consumption):* electricity (kW-hr; 2006) 1,873,000,000 ([2005] 1,826,000,000); coal (metric tons; 2004) none (281,000); petroleum products (metric tons; 2004) none (580,000). **Population economically active** (2004): total 96,406; activity rate of total population 41.8% (participation rates: ages 15 and over 57.1%; female [1996] 39.7%; registered unemployed [2005] 15.8%). **Gross national income** (2006): US$4,743,000,000 (US$19,935 per capita). **Households** (1991). Average household size (2004) 3.6; average annual income per household: CFPF 3,361,233 (US$32,879); sources of income: wages and salaries 68.2%, transfer payments 13.7%; expenditure: food and beverages 25.9%, housing 20.4%, transportation and communications 16.1%, recreation 4.8%. **Selected balance of payments data.** Receipts from (US$'000,000): tourism (2005) 253; foreign direct investment (FDI) (2001–05 avg.) 65. Disbursements for

(US$'000,000): tourism (2005) 171; FDI (2001–05 avg.) 8.0. **Land use** as % of total land area (2003): in temporary crops 0.3%, in permanent crops 0.2%, in pasture 13.1%; overall forest area (2005) 39.2%.

Foreign trade

Imports (2005; c.i.f.): CFPF 170,692,000,000 (machinery and apparatus 20.4%; mineral products [mostly coal and refined petroleum] 16.4%; transportation equipment 14.8%; food 13.4%; chemicals and chemical products 7.7%). *Major import sources:* EU 47.2%, of which France 32.3%; Singapore 15.0%; Australia 9.2%; New Zealand 5.5%. **Exports** (2005; f.o.b.): CFPF 104,047,000,000 (ferronickel 62.1%; nickel ore 15.3%; nickel matte 13.1%; shrimp 2.3%). *Major export destinations:* EU 34.5%, of which France 16.0%; Japan 18.8%; South Korea 13.5%; Taiwan 12.2%; China 5.7%.

Transport and communications

Transport. *Roads* (2000): total length 5,432 km (paved [1993] 52%). *Vehicles:* passenger cars (2005) 105,159; trucks and buses (1997) 23,000. *Air transport* (2006; Air Calédonie only): passenger-km 1,432,076,000; metric ton-km cargo 20,181,000. **Communications,** in total units (units per 1,000 persons). Daily newspaper circulation (2005): 19,000 (79); televisions (2004): 115,000 (498); telephone landlines (2005): 55,000 (236); cellular telephone subscribers (2005): 134,000 (573); personal computers (2005): 6,000 (25); total Internet users (2006): 80,000 (332); broadband Internet subscribers (2005): 9,600 (41).

Education and health

Educational attainment (2004). Percentage of population ages 25 and over having: no formal schooling through some primary education 38.1%; primary 9.5%; lower secondary 6.4%; upper secondary 11.8%; vocational 19.8%; higher 14.4%. **Literacy** (2002): total population ages 15 and over literate 91.0%; males literate 92.0%; females literate 90.0%. **Health:** physicians (2004) 485 (1 per 476 persons); hospital beds (2004) 727 (1 per 317 persons); infant mortality rate per 1,000 live births (2006) 5.7.

Military

Total active duty personnel (2006): 1,540 French troops.

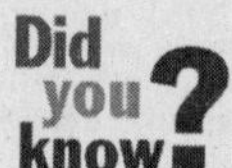

Between July 1772 and July 1775 James Cook made what ranks as one of the greatest sailing ship voyages, with a small former Whitby ship, the *Resolution*, and a consort ship, the *Adventure*. He found no trace of Terra Australis, though he sailed beyond latitude 70 deg S in the Antarctic, but he successfully completed the first west-east circumnavigation in high latitudes, charted Tonga and Easter Island during the winters, and discovered New Caledonia in the Pacific and the South Sandwich Islands and South Georgia Island in the Atlantic Ocean.

Background

Excavations indicate an Austronesian presence in New Caledonia about 2000–1000 BC. The islands were visited by James Cook in 1774 and by various navigators and traders in the 18th–19th centuries. They were occupied by France in 1853 and were a penal colony from 1864 to 1897. During World War II the islands were the site of Allied bases. They became a French overseas territory in 1946. In 1987 residents voted by referendum to remain part of France.

Recent Developments

After temporary setbacks, two nickel-mining plants in New Caledonia were scheduled to go ahead. The US$3.2 billion Goro nickel-cobalt project, which was stalled after cost blowouts of 72%, was due to commence production by the end of 2008. Construction of the US$3.8 billion Koniambo project in the Northern Province was scheduled to begin in 2010.

Internet resources: <www.newcaledoniatourism-south.com>.

New Zealand

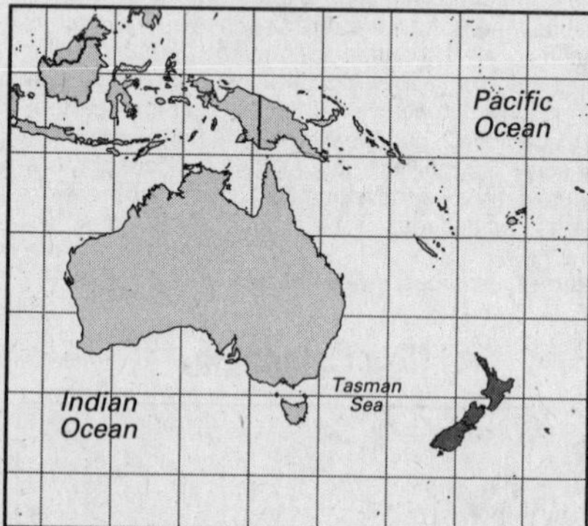

Official name: New Zealand (English); Aotearoa (Maori). **Form of government:** constitutional monarchy with one legislative house (House of Representatives [121]). **Chief of state:** British Queen Elizabeth II (from 1952), represented by Governor-General Anand Satyanand (from 2006). **Head of government:** Prime Minister Helen Clark (from 1999). **Capital:** Wellington. **Official languages:** English; Maori. **Official religion:** none. **Monetary unit:** 1 New Zealand dollar (NZ$) = 100 cents; valuation (1 Jul 2008) US$1 = NZ$ 1.32.

Demography

Area: 104,515 sq mi, 270,692 sq km. **Population** (2007): 4,184,000. **Density** (2007): persons per sq mi 40.0, persons per sq km 15.5. **Urban** (2005): 86.2%. **Sex distribution** (2006): male 49.22%; female 50.78%. **Age breakdown** (2006): under 15, 21.1%; 15–29, 20.5%; 30–44, 22.0%; 45–59, 19.4%; 60–74, 11.4%; 75–84, 4.3%; 85 and over,

1 metric ton = about 1.1 short tons; 1 kilometer = 0.6 mi (statute); 1 metric ton-km cargo = about 0.68 short ton-mi cargo; c.i.f.: cost, insurance, and freight; f.o.b.: free on board

1.3%. **Ethnic composition** (2006): European 67.6%, of which NZ European 59.1%; Maori (local Polynesian) 14.6%; Asian 9.2%, of which Chinese 3.7%; other Pacific peoples (mostly other Polynesian) 6.9%; other 1.7%. **Religious affiliation** (2006): Christian 51.1%, of which Anglican 13.3%, Roman Catholic 12.2%, Presbyterian 9.2%, Methodist 2.9%, Maori (indigenous) Christian 1.6%; Hindu 1.6%; Buddhist 1.3%; Muslim 1.0%; nonreligious 31.1%; unknown 12.9%; other 1.0%. **Major urban agglomerations** (2006): Auckland 1,208,091; Wellington 397,974; Christchurch 360,768; Hamilton 184,838; Napier 118,404. **Location:** between the South Pacific Ocean and the Tasman Sea, southeast of Australia.

Vital statistics

Birth rate per 1,000 population (2006–07): 14.8 (world avg. 20.3); (2005) within marriage 54.8%. **Death rate** per 1,000 population (2006–07): 6.8 (world avg. 8.6). **Total fertility rate** (avg. births per childbearing woman; 2006–07): 2.14. **Life expectancy** at birth (2004–06): male 77.9 years; female 81.9 years.

National economy

Budget (2004–05). *Revenue:* NZ$51,489,000,000 (tax revenue 91.8%, of which individual income taxes 45.7%, taxes on goods and services 26.7%; nontax revenue 8.0%; grants 0.2%). *Expenditures:* NZ$44,099,000,000 (social protection 35.0%; health 20.0%; education 17.9%; defense 3.0%). **Production** (metric tons except as noted). *Agriculture, forestry, fishing* (2005): apples 524,000, potatoes 500,000, kiwifruit 318,000, greasy wool 209,250; livestock (number of live animals) 39,928,000 sheep, 9,501,000 cattle; roundwood 19,143,000 cu m, of which fuelwood, none; fisheries production 640,695 (from aquaculture 16%). *Mining and quarrying* (2004): limestone/marl 5,226,000; silver 43,003 kg; gold 10,583 kg. *Manufacturing* (value added in US$'000,000; 2005): food products 4,175; fabricated metals 1,350; printing and publishing 1,250. *Energy production (consumption):* electricity (kW-hr; 2006) 40,034,000,000 ([2004] 41,813,000,000); hard coal (metric tons; 2004) 2,527,000 (198,000); lignite (metric tons; 2004) 2,629,000 (3,576,000); crude petroleum (barrels; 2006) 5,900,000 ([2004] 37,856,000); petroleum products (metric tons; 2004) 5,067,000 (6,214,000); natural gas (cu m; 2006) 3,773,000,000 ([2004] 3,766, 000,000). **Population economically active** (2005): total 2,152,200; activity rate of total population 52.5% (participation rates: ages 15–64, 77.0%; female 46.2%; unemployed [2006] 3.8%). **Households** (2003–04). Average household size (2004) 2.6; annual gross income per household (2006) NZ$68,500 (US$41,500); sources of income: wages and salaries 69.9%, transfer payments 12.8%, self-employment 9.1%; expenditure: housing 24.4%, food 16.1%, transportation 16.0%, household goods 12.6%. **Gross national income** (2006): US$98,383,000,000 (US$23,780 per capita). **Selected balance of payments data.** Receipts from (US$'000,000): tourism (2005) 4,984; remittances (2006) 650; foreign direct investment (2001–05 avg.) 2,091. Disbursements for (US$'000,000): tourism (2005) 2,657; remittances (2006) 865; foreign direct disinvestment (2001–05 avg.) −475. **Land use** as % of total land area (2003): in temporary crops 5.6%, in permanent crops 7.0%, in pasture 51.7%; overall forest area (2005) 31.0%.

Foreign trade

Imports (2006; c.i.f. in commodities and trading partners): NZ$40,774,000,000 (machinery and apparatus 21.4%; mineral fuels 14.9%; vehicles 11.7%; aircraft 4.2%; plastics 3.8%). *Major import sources:* Australia 20.1%; China 12.2%; US 12.1%; Japan 9.1%; Germany 4.4%. **Exports** (2006): NZ$34,619,000,000 (dairy products 20.6%; beef and sheep meat 12.1%; wood and paper [all forms] 9.4%; machinery and apparatus 8.6%; aluminum 4.3%; fish 3.7%). *Major export destinations:* Australia 20.5%; US 13.1%; Japan 10.3%; China 5.4%; UK 4.9%.

Transport and communications

Transport. *Railroads:* route length (2003) 3,898 km; metric ton-km cargo (1999–2000) 4,040,000,000. *Roads* (2003): total length 92,931 km (paved 64%). *Vehicles* (2004): passenger cars 2,402,207; trucks and buses 444,909. *Air transport* (2005; Air New Zealand only): passenger-km 26,093,000,000; metric ton-km cargo 781,000,000. **Communications**, in total units (units per 1,000 persons). Daily newspaper circulation (2005): 746,000 (182); televisions (2004): 2,338,000 (576); telephone landlines (2005): 1,729,000 (422); cellular telephone subscribers (2005): 3,530,000 (876); personal computers (2005): 2,077,000 (507); total Internet users (2006): 3,200,000 (788); broadband Internet subscribers (2006): 576,000 (139).

Education and health

Educational attainment (2005). Percentage of population ages 25–64 having: no formal schooling to incomplete secondary 24.5%; completed secondary 57.4%; completed undergraduate 18.1%. **Literacy:** virtually 100%. **Health:** physicians (2003) 8,790 (1 per 455 persons); hospital beds (2002) 23,825 (1 per 165 persons); infant mortality rate per 1,000 live births (2006–07) 5.0. **Food** (2005): daily per capita caloric intake 3,394 (vegetable products 70%, animal products 30%).

Military

Total active duty personnel (2006): 8,660 (army 51.1%, air force 26.0%, navy 22.9%). **Military expenditure as percentage of GDP** (2005): 1.0%; per capita expenditure US$269.

Background

Polynesian occupation of New Zealand dates to about AD 1000. First sighted by Dutch explorer Abel Janszoon Tasman in 1642, the main islands were charted by Capt. James Cook in 1769. Named a British crown colony in 1840, the area was the scene of warfare between colonists and native Maori through the 1860s. In 1907 the colony became the Dominion of New Zealand. It administered Western Samoa during 1919–62 and participated in both world wars. When Britain joined what is now the European Union in the early 1970s, its influence led New Zealand to expand its export markets and diversify its economy.

Recent Developments

In her formal address to the House of Representatives in February 2007, New Zealand Prime Minister Helen Clark declared plans for a carbon-neutral public service from 2012, a single government procurement policy for sustainably produced goods and services, a low-emission state vehicle fleet, improved waste management, and a program that would enable businesses to label themselves as carbon neutral. A guaranteed minimum wage for disabled workers was enacted in March, along with sick pay and leave entitlements. Free part-time preschool education for three- and four-year-olds was introduced in July, in addition to subsidized medical consultations and prescription medicines for those aged 25–44. Permits authorizing oil and gas exploration in the Great South Basin of the Southern Ocean over the next five years were granted in July to two international consortia. Bottom trawling and dredging was banned over 30% of the seabed in New Zealand's 200-nautical-mile exclusive economic zone. Government officials signed a free-trade agreement with China in April 2008 and began talks for similar agreements with Japan and South Korea in May.

Internet resources: <www.newzealand.com>.

Nicaragua

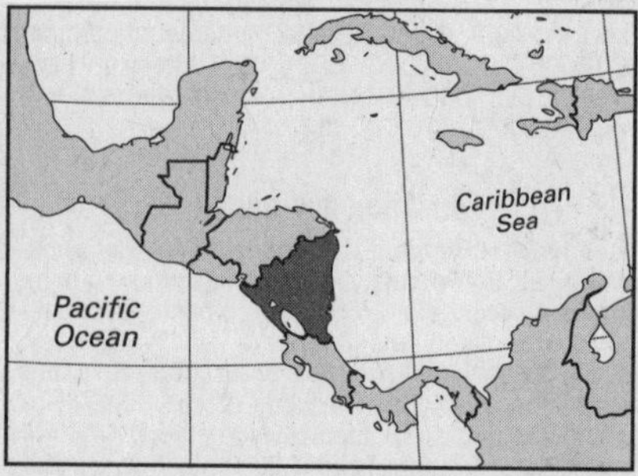

Official name: República de Nicaragua (Republic of Nicaragua). **Form of government:** unitary multiparty republic with one legislative house (National Assembly [92]). **Head of state and government:** President Daniel Ortega (from 2007). **Capital:** Managua. **Official language:** Spanish. **Official religion:** none. **Monetary unit:** 1 córdoba oro (C$) = 100 centavos; valuation (1 Jul 2008) US$1 = C$19.37.

Demography

Area: 50,337 sq mi, 130,373 sq km; land area alone equals 46,464 sq mi, 120,340 sq km. **Population** (2007): 5,602,000. **Density** (2007): persons per sq mi 120.6, persons per sq km 46.6. **Urban** (2005): 55.9%. **Sex distribution** (2005): male 49.29%; female 50.71%. **Age breakdown** (2005): under 15, 37.6%; 15–29, 29.9%; 30–44, 17.1%; 45–59, 9.3%; 60–74, 4.3%; 75–84, 1.3%; 85 and over, 0.5%. **Ethnic composition** (2000): mestizo (Spanish/Indian) 63.1%; white 14.0%; black 8.0%; multiple ethnicities 5.0%; other 9.9%. **Religious affiliation** (2005): Roman Catholic 58.5%; Protestant/independent Christian 23.2%, of which Evangelical 21.6%, Moravian 1.6%; nonreligious 15.7%; other 2.6%. **Major cities** (2005; populations of urban areas of *municipios*): Managua 908,892; León 139,433; Chinandega 95,614; Masaya 92,598; Estelí 90,294. **Location:** Central America, bordering Honduras, the Caribbean Sea, Costa Rica, and the North Pacific Ocean.

Vital statistics

Birth rate per 1,000 population (2005): 24.9 (world avg. 20.3). **Death rate** per 1,000 population (2005): 4.5 (world avg. 8.6). **Natural increase rate** per 1,000 population (2005): 20.4 (world avg. 11.7). **Total fertility rate** (avg. births per childbearing woman; 2005): 2.94. **Life expectancy** at birth (2005): male 68.3 years; female 74.4 years.

National economy

Budget (2004). *Revenue:* C$12,250,700,000 (tax revenue 96.3%, of which sales tax 38.2%, import duties 27.8%, tax on income and profits 25.9%; nontax revenue 3.7%). *Expenditures:* C$16,697,800,000 (current expenditure 58.4%; development expenditure 41.6%). **Production** (metric tons except as noted). *Agriculture, forestry, fishing* (2006): sugarcane 4,682,000, corn (maize) 504,100, rice 312,100; livestock (number of live animals) 3,500,000 cattle, 268,000 horses; roundwood (2005) 6,042,000 cu m, of which fuelwood 98%; fisheries production (2005) 29,500, of which lobster 8,800 (from aquaculture 29%). *Mining and quarrying* (2004–05): gold 123,600 troy oz. *Manufacturing* (value added in C$'000,000 at prices of 1994; 2003): food 1,917; textiles and wearing apparel 969; beverages 713. *Energy production (consumption):* electricity (kW-hr; 2004) 2,822,000,000 (2,823,000,000); crude petroleum (barrels; 2004) none (6,443,000); petroleum products (metric tons; 2004) 820,000 (1,308,000). **Households.** Average household size (2005) 4.9; expenditure (1999): food and beverages 41.8%, education 9.8%, housing 9.8%, transportation 8.5%. **Land use** as % of total land area (2003): in temporary crops 15.9%, in permanent crops 1.9%, in pasture 39.7%; overall forest area (2005) 42.7%. **Population economically active** (2006): total 2,204,300; activity rate of total population 39.9% (participation rates: ages 10 and over [2005] 55.0%; female [2005] 35.2%; officially unemployed 5.2%). **Gross national income** (2006): US$5,233,000,000 (US$946 per capita). **Public debt** (external, outstanding; 2005): US$4,113,-000,000. **Selected balance of payments data.** Receipts from (US$'000,000): tourism (2005) 207; remittances (2006) 656; foreign direct investment (FDI; 2001–05 avg.) 209; official development assistance (2005) 741 (commitments). Disbursements for (US$'000,000): tourism (2005) 90; FDI (2001–03 avg.) 12.

Foreign trade

Imports (2005; c.i.f. in commodities and trading partners): US$2,595,100,000 (nondurable consumer goods 24.4%; mineral fuels 20.8%; capital goods for industry 11.0%; transport equipment 7.3%). *Major* *import sources:* US 20.1%; Venezuela 11.9%; Costa Rica 8.9%; Mexico 8.3%; Guatemala 7.0%. **Exports** (2005): US$857,900,000 (coffee 14.5%; meat 13.9%; sugar 7.0%; shrimp 5.6%; gold 5.0%; chemical products 4.2%; lobster 3.9%). *Major export destinations:* US 32.1%; El Salvador 14.3%; Honduras 7.9%; Costa Rica 6.1%; Mexico 5.1%.

Transport and communications

Transport. *Roads* (2004): total length 18,669 km (paved [2002] 11%). *Vehicles* (2004): passenger cars 94,998; trucks and buses 152,813. *Air transport* (2000): passenger-km 72,200,000; metric ton-km cargo (2003) 200,000. **Communications,** in total units (units per 1,000 persons). Daily newspaper circulation (2004): 91,000 (18); televisions (2003): 648,000 (123); telephone landlines (2006): 248,000 (44); cellular telephone subscribers (2006): 1,830,000 (327); personal computers (2005): 220,000 (43); total Internet users (2006): 155,000 (28); broadband Internet subscribers (2006): 19,000 (3.6).

Education and health

Educational attainment (2005). Percentage of population ages 10 and over having: no formal schooling/unknown 20.5%; 1–3 years 16.6%; 4–6 years 27.0%; 7–9 years 16.1%; 10–12 years 10.5%; vocational 2.3%; incomplete university 2.6%; complete university 4.4%. **Literacy** (2005): total population ages 15 and over literate 78.0%; males literate 78.1%; females literate 77.9%. **Health** (2003): physicians 2,076 (1 per 2,538 persons); hospital beds 5,030 (1 per 1,047 persons); infant mortality rate per 1,000 live births (2005) 26.4. **Food** (2005): daily per capita caloric intake 2,542 (vegetable products 90%, animal products 10%); 140% of FAO recommended minimum.

Military

Total active duty personnel (2006): 14,000 (army 85.7%, navy 5.7%, air force 8.6%). **Military expenditure as percentage of GDP** (2005): 0.7%; per capita expenditure US$6.

Background

Nicaragua has been inhabited for thousands of years, most notably by the Maya. Christopher Columbus arrived in 1502, and Spanish explorers discovered Lake Nicaragua soon thereafter. Nicaragua was governed by Spain until 1821, when it declared its independence. It was part of Mexico and then the United Provinces of Central America until 1838, when full independence was achieved. The US intervened in political affairs by maintaining troops there in 1912–33. Ruled by the dictatorial Somoza dynasty from 1936 to 1979, it was taken over by the Sandinistas after a popular revolt. They were opposed by armed insurgents, the US-backed contras, from 1981. The Sandinista government nationalized several sectors of the economy but lost the national elections in 1990. The new government returned many economic activities to private control, but unrest continued through the 1990s.

Recent Developments

Nicaragua's nearly US$1 billion debt with the Inter-American Development Bank was canceled in 2007. The government signed cooperation agreements with Venezuela, Brazil, and Iran. Venezuela agreed to fund social programs, provide low-cost fuel, and build an oil refinery. Sweden, however, announced that it would soon withdraw all development assistance. Nicaraguan police seized ExxonMobil storage tanks by court order in August, citing unpaid customs duties. Although a settlement was later reached that allowed temporary usage of the tanks to store Venezuelan fuel, barriers to distribution caused prices to rise. Nicaragua's projected economic growth rate was 3.9%, with a 10% inflation rate. On 4 September Hurricane Felix struck north of Puerto Cabezas as a Category 5 storm, killing more than 100 people and leaving about 150 missing. (*See* Disasters.)

Internet resources: <www.intur.gob.ni>.

Niger

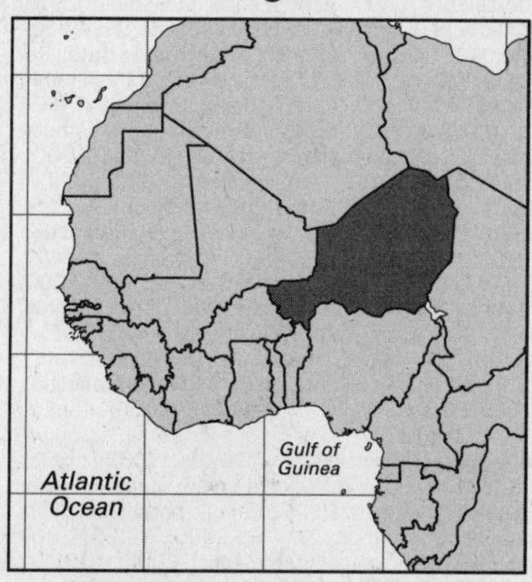

Official name: République du Niger (Republic of Niger). **Form of government:** multiparty republic with one legislative house (National Assembly [113]). **Head of state and government:** President Mamadou Tandja (from 1999), assisted by Prime Minister Seyni Oumarou (from 2007). **Capital:** Niamey. **Official language:** French. **Official religion:** none. **Monetary unit:** 1 CFA franc (CFAF) = 100 centimes; valuation (1 Jul 2008) US$1 = CFAF 414.60.

Demography

Area: 459,286 sq mi, 1,189,546 sq km. **Population** (2007): 14,226,000. **Density** (2007): persons per sq mi 31.0, persons per sq km 12.0. **Urban** (2006): 16.6%. **Sex distribution** (2005): male 50.69%; female 49.31%. **Age breakdown** (2005): under 15, 47.9%; 15–29, 24.1%; 30–44, 14.7%; 45–59, 8.5%; 60–74, 3.6%; 75–84, 0.9%; 85 and over, 0.3%. **Ethnolinguistic composition** (2001): Hausa 55.4%; Zarma-Songhai-Dendi 21.0%; Tuareg 9.3%; Fulani (Peul) 8.5%; Kanuri 4.7%; other 1.1%. **Religious affiliation** (2005): Muslim 90%, of which Sunni 85%, Shiʿi 5%; traditional beliefs 9%; other 1%. **Major cities** (2001): Niamey 707,951 (urban agglomeration [2005] 850,000); Zinder 170,575; Maradi 148,017; Agadez 78,289; Tahoua 73,002. **Location:** western

Africa, bordering Algeria, Libya, Chad, Nigeria, Benin, Burkina Faso, and Mali.

Vital statistics

Birth rate per 1,000 population (2006): 50.7 (world avg. 20.3). **Death rate** per 1,000 population (2006): 20.9 (world avg. 8.6). **Natural increase rate** per 1,000 population (2006): 29.8 (world avg. 11.7). **Total fertility rate** (avg. births per childbearing woman; 2006): 7.46. **Life expectancy** at birth (2006): male 43.8 years; female 43.7 years.

National economy

Budget (2006). *Revenue:* CFAF 365,000,000,000 (taxes 55.8%, of which import duties 26.2%; external aid and grants 32.3%; nontax revenue 11.9%). *Expenditures:* CFAF 359,600,000,000 (capital expenditures 50.8%; current expenditures 46.3%, of which wages and salaries 18.9%, debt service 3.0%; other 2.9%). **Public debt** (external, outstanding; 2006): US$1,800,-000,000. **Selected balance of payments data.** Receipts from (US$'000,000): tourism (2005) 34; remittances (2006) 60; foreign direct investment (FDI) (2001–05 avg.) 14; official development assistance (2005) 515. Disbursements for (US$'000,000): tourism (2005) 32; remittances (2006) 25; FDI (2001–05 avg.) 1.0. **Gross national income** (2006): US$3,361,000,000 (US$245 per capita). **Production** (metric tons except as noted). *Agriculture, forestry, fishing* (2006): millet 3,200,000, sorghum 800,000, cowpeas 690,584; livestock (number of live animals) 7,700,000 goats, 4,900,000 sheep, 2,430,000 cattle, 439,000 camels; roundwood (2005) 9,217,477 cu m, of which fuelwood 96%; fisheries production (2005) 50,058. *Mining and quarrying* (2006): uranium 3,431; salt (2004) 2,000; gold 2,615 kg. *Manufacturing* (value added in CFAF '000,000; 2002): textiles 1,876; food and food products 1,695; soaps and other chemical products 1,302. *Energy production (consumption):* electricity (kW-hr; 2005) 403,000,000 (461,000,000); coal (metric tons; 2006) 176,000 ([2005] 173,000); petroleum products (metric tons; 2004) none (233,000). **Population economically active** (2006): total 6,139,000; activity rate of total population 42.6% (participation rates: ages 16 and over 83.5%; female 41.9%; registered unemployed [2001] 1.6%). **Households.** Average household size (2004) 6.2; expenditure (2005; Niamey only): food, beverages, and tobacco products 53.7%, housing and rent 10.3%, transportation 9.9%, clothing and footwear 5.3%. **Land use** as % of total land area (2003): in temporary crops 11.4%, in permanent crops 0.01%, in pasture 18.9%; overall forest area (2005) 1.0%.

Foreign trade

Imports (2005; c.i.f.): CFAF 361,037,000,000 (live animals, food products, and beverages 33.4%; mineral fuels 14.8%; mechanical apparatus and machinery 12.8%; transportation equipment 7.5%). *Major import sources:* France 16.8%; Côte d'Ivoire 9.3%; Nigeria 5.9%; China 5.4%; Togo 5.2%. **Exports** (2005; f.o.b.): CFAF 163,508,000,000 (uranium 48.0%; gold 22.6%; onions 6.8%; cattle 6.3%; other live animals 5.5%). *Major export destinations:* France 34.4%; Nigeria 14.4%; Japan 13.2%; Ghana 4.2%; Spain 3.2%.

Transport and communications

Transport. *Roads* (2005): total length 18,423 km (paved 21%). *Vehicles* (2005): passenger cars 21,360. *Air transport* (2005; Niamey airport only): passenger arrivals 50,002, passenger departures 59,824; cargo unloaded 3,085 metric tons, cargo loaded 140 metric tons. **Communications,** in total units (units per 1,000 persons). Daily newspaper circulation (2006): 5,000 (0.3); televisions (2004): 150,000 (13); telephone landlines (2005): 24,000 (1.9); cellular telephone subscribers (2006): 324,000 (25); personal computers (2005): 10,000 (0.8); total Internet users (2006): 40,000 (3.1); broadband Internet subscribers (2005): 200 (0.02).

Education and health

Educational attainment (2006). Percentage of population ages 25 and over having: no formal schooling/unknown 86.2%; incomplete primary education 6.9%; complete primary 1.0%; incomplete secondary 3.7%; complete secondary 0.4%; higher 0.9%. **Literacy** (2006): total population ages 15 and over literate 28.7%; males literate 42.9%; females literate 15.1%. **Health** (2005): physicians 452 (1 per 27,599 persons); hospital beds 1,865 (1 per 6,689 persons); infant mortality rate per 1,000 live births (2006) 118.2. **Food** (2005): daily per capita caloric intake 2,060 (vegetable products 95%, animal products 5%); 114% of FAO recommended minimum.

Military

Total active duty personnel (2006): 5,300 (army 98.1%, air force 1.9%). **Military expenditure as percentage of GDP** (2004): 1.2%; per capita expenditure US$3.

Background

In the territory of Niger, there is evidence of Neolithic culture, and several kingdoms existed there before the colonialists arrived. First explored by Europeans in the late 18th century, it became a French colony in 1922. It became an overseas territory of France in 1946 and gained independence in 1960. The first multiparty elections were held in 1993.

Recent Developments

The government's control over northern Niger in 2007 was threatened as Tuaregs belonging to the Movement of Nigerians for Justice (MNJ) launched a series of deadly raids throughout the region. A uranium mine was hit in April, and in June the MNJ struck a Saharan garrison post, killing 15 and taking 72 hostages. The MNJ also claimed to have killed 17 soldiers in August when it attacked a convoy near Gougaram.

Internet resources: <www.niger-tourisme.com/accueil_gb.php>.

Nigeria

Official name: Federal Republic of Nigeria. **Form of government:** federal republic with two legislative bod-

1 metric ton = about 1.1 short tons; 1 kilometer = 0.6 mi (statute); 1 metric ton-km cargo = about 0.68 short ton-mi cargo; c.i.f.: cost, insurance, and freight; f.o.b.: free on board

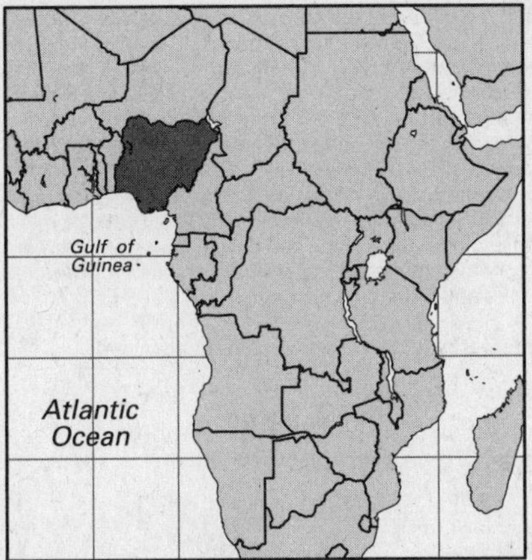

ies (Senate [109]; House of Representatives [360]). **Head of state and government:** President Umaru Yar'Adua (from 2007). **Capital:** Abuja. **Official language:** English. **Official religion:** none. **Monetary unit:** 1 Nigerian naira (N) = 100 kobo; valuation (1 Jul 2008) US$1 = N117.80.

Demography

Area: 356,669 sq mi, 923,768 sq km. **Population** (2007): 144,077,000. **Density** (2007): persons per sq mi 404.0, persons per sq km 156.0. **Urban** (2005): 48.2%. **Sex distribution** (2006): male 51.22%; female 48.78%. **Age breakdown** (2005): under 15, 44.4%; 15–29, 27.7%; 30–44, 15.0%; 45–59, 8.3%; 60–74, 3.8%; 75–84, 0.7%; 85 and over, 0.1%. **Ethnic composition** (2000): Yoruba 17.5%; Hausa 17.2%; Igbo (Ibo) 13.3%; Fulani 10.7%; Ibibio 4.1%; Kanuri 3.6%; Egba 2.9%; Tiv 2.6%; Igbira 1.1%; Nupe 1.0%; Edo 1.0%; Ijo 0.8%; detribalized 0.9%; other 23.3%. **Religious affiliation** (2003): Muslim 50.5%; Christian 48.2%, of which Protestant 15.0%, Roman Catholic 13.7%, other (mostly independent Christian) 19.5%; other 1.3%. **Major urban agglomerations** (2005): Lagos (2006) 9,013,534; Kano 2,993,000; Ibadan 2,437,000; Kaduna 1,375,000; Benin City 1,055,000. **Location:** western Africa, bordering Niger, Chad, Cameroon, the Gulf of Guinea, and Benin.

Vital statistics

Birth rate per 1,000 population (2005): 41.3 (world avg. 20.3). **Death rate** per 1,000 population (2005): 17.2 (world avg. 8.6). **Natural increase rate** per 1,000 population (2005): 24.1 (world avg. 11.7). **Total fertility rate** (avg. births per childbearing woman; 2005): 5.58. **Life expectancy** at birth (2005): male 46.7 years; female 47.3 years.

National economy

Budget (2005). *Revenue:* N5,621,000,000,000 (oil and gas revenue 84.7%, of which crude oil export proceeds 34.5%, oil profits tax 23.3%, crude oil sales to domestic refineries 13.7%; non-oil revenue 15.3%). *Expenditures:* N4,234,000,000,000 (state and local governments 46.3%; current expenditure 44.4%; capital expenditure 8.1%; other 1.2%). **Public debt** (external, outstanding; 2005): US$20,342,000,000. **Production** (metric tons except as noted). *Agriculture, forestry, fishing* (2005): cassava 41,565,000, yams 34,000,000, sorghum 9,178,000, millet 7,168,000, corn (maize) 5,957,000; livestock (number of live animals) 28,000,000 goats, 15,875,000 cattle; roundwood 70,692,260 cu m, of which fuelwood 87%; fisheries production 579,500 (from aquaculture 10%). *Mining and quarrying* (2005): granite 2,000,000; marble 149,000. *Manufacturing* (value added in N'000,000; 2005): refined petroleum 29,037; cement 8,502; other unspecified (particularly food, beverages, and textiles) 375,167. *Energy production (consumption):* electricity (kW-hr; 2005) 20,636,000,000 ([2004] 20,224,000,000); coal (metric tons; 2004) 3,000 (3,000); crude petroleum (barrels; 2006) 814,000,000 ([2004] 38,000,000); petroleum products (metric tons; 2004) 4,363,000,000 (9,985,000,000); natural gas (cu m; 2004) 22,388,000,000 (9,668,000,000). **Households.** Average household size (2003): 4.9; expenditures (2003): food 63.8%, housing/energy 18.1%, transportation 4.2%. **Gross national income** (at current market prices; 2006): US$116,374,000,000 (US$800 per capita). **Population economically active** (2003): total 45,165,000; activity rate of total population 35.9% (participation rates: ages 15–64, 65.9%; female 35.1%; officially unemployed [December 2005] 11.9%). **Selected balance of payments data.** Receipts from (US$'000,000): tourism (2005) 18; remittances (2006) 3,329; foreign direct investment (FDI) (2001–05 avg.) 2,204; official development assistance (2005) 5,989 (commitments). Disbursements for (US$'000,000): tourism (2005) 1,109; remittances (2006) 18; FDI (2001–05 avg.) 179. **Land use** as % of total land area (2003): in temporary crops 33.5%, in permanent crops 3.2%, in pasture 43.0%; overall forest area (2005) 12.2%.

Foreign trade

Imports (2003; c.i.f.): US$14,892,000,000 (machinery and apparatus 25.6%; mineral fuels 16.0%; food 14.0%; chemical products 10.3%; ships and boats 6.4%). *Major import sources* (2003): US 15.6%; UK 9.5%; Germany 7.3%; China 7.2%; Italy 4.3%; unspecified 15.0%. **Exports** (2006; f.o.b.): US$45,116,000,000 (crude petroleum 95.9%). *Major export destinations* (2005): US 52%; Spain 8%; Brazil 6%; France 3%; Côte d'Ivoire 3%.

Transport and communications

Transport. *Railroads* (2005): length 3,505 km; passenger-km 75,170,000. *Roads* (2005): total length 34,403 km (paved 64%). *Vehicles* (2004): passenger cars 2,176,000. *Air transport* (2006; Virgin Nigeria Airways only): passenger-km 969,900,000. **Communications,** in total units (units per 1,000 persons). Daily newspaper circulation (2000): 2,770,000 (23); televisions (2003): 8,393,000 (64); telephone landlines (2006): 1,688,000 (12); cellular telephone subscribers (2006): 32,322,000 (229); personal computers (2005): 1,200,000 (8.7); total Internet users (2006): 8,000,000 (57); broadband Internet subscribers (2005): 500.

Education and health

Educational attainment (2003). Percentage of population ages 25 and over having: no formal schooling/unknown 50.4%; primary education 20.4%; secondary 20.1%; higher 9.1%. **Literacy** (2006): total population ages 15 and over literate 76.3%; males literate 84.2%; females literate 68.4%. **Health** (2005): physicians 42,563 (1 per 3,234 persons); hospital beds 85,523 (1 per 1,609 persons); infant mortality rate per 1,000 live births 112.5. **Food** (2005): daily per capita caloric intake 2,731 (vegetable products 96%, animal products 4%); 149% of FAO recommended minimum.

Military

Total active duty personnel (2006): 85,000 (army 78.8%, navy 9.4%, air force 11.8%). **Military expenditure as percentage of GDP** (2005): 0.7%; per capita expenditure US$5.

Background

Inhabited for thousands of years, Nigeria was the center of the Nok culture from 500 BC to AD 200 and of several precolonial empires, including the state of Kanem-Bornu and the Songhai, Hausa, and Fulani kingdoms. Visited in the 15th century by Europeans, it became a center for the slave trade. The area began to come under British control in 1861; by 1903 British rule was total. Nigeria gained independence in 1960 and became a republic in 1963. Ethnic strife soon led to military coups, and military groups ruled the country from 1966 to 1979 and from 1983 to 1999. A civil war between the central government and the former Eastern Region—which seceded and called itself Biafra—began in 1967 and ended in 1970 with Biafra's surrender after widespread starvation and civilian deaths. In 1991 the capital was moved from Lagos to Abuja. The government's execution of environmental activist Ken Saro-Wiwa in 1995 led to international sanctions, and civilian rule was finally reestablished in 1999. By far the most populous nation in Africa, Nigeria suffers from rapid population increase, political instability, foreign debt, slow economic growth, a high rate of violent crime, and rampant government corruption.

Recent Developments

In May 2007 a milestone was reached in Nigeria's history when outgoing Pres. Olusegun Obasanjo handed over power to Umaru Musa Yar'Adua, marking the first time that a civilian head of state had been succeeded by another civilian. Yar'Adua had won the country's presidential election in a landslide with 24.6 million votes. In the Niger Delta, the source of 90% of Nigeria's wealth, the security situation deteriorated. Armed militia, backed by local inhabitants, edged dangerously closer to turning into an insurgency. In February the Movement for the Emancipation of the Niger Delta, a coalition of militant groups, released a proclamation threatening war. Kidnappings of foreign oil workers accelerated, with a new dimension of random abductions in the center of Port Harcourt. After the elections militants in various places, claiming that victorious politicians had reneged on promised payments for their services as party thugs, seized 11 Ondo state officials and a number of relatives of politicians, including children and the elderly mothers of two governors. Meanwhile, their truce with the government fell apart in August when fighting broke out among rival gangs in Port Harcourt, and many were killed or wounded. To restore order the government mobilized the Joint Task Force into the region to round up the militants and destroy their strongholds; this was followed in October by a federal army operation on the Port Harcourt waterfront. Residents, however, were skeptical of a military solution and urged the development of effective economic reforms and poverty alleviation. The attacks and kidnappings continued in 2008.

Internet resources: <www.nigeriatourism.net>.

Norway

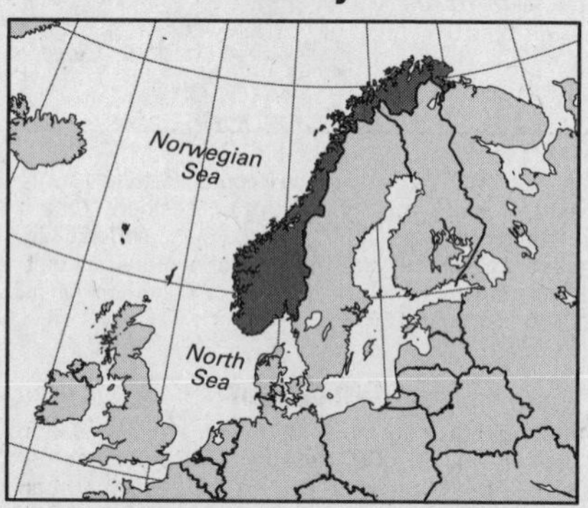

Official name: Kongeriket Norge (Kingdom of Norway). **Form of government:** constitutional monarchy with one legislative house (Parliament [169]). **Chief of state:** Norwegian King Harald V (from 1991). **Head of government:** Prime Minister Jens Stoltenberg (from 2005). **Capital:** Oslo. **Official language:** Norwegian. **Official religion:** Evangelical Lutheran. **Monetary unit:** 1 Norwegian krone (NOK) = 100 øre; valuation (1 Jul 2008) US$1 = NOK 5.06.

Demography

Area: 148,726 sq mi, 385,199 sq km. **Population** (2007): 4,702,000. **Density** (2007): persons per sq mi 37.1, persons per sq km 14.3. **Urban** (2005): 77.4%. **Sex distribution** (2004): male 49.59%; female 50.41%. **Age breakdown** (2006): under 15, 19.4%; 15–29, 18.7%; 30–44, 22.0%; 45–59, 19.7%; 60–74, 12.6%; 75–84, 5.4%; 85 and over, 2.2%. **Ethnic composition** (2000): Norwegian 93.8%; Vietnamese 2.4%; Swedish 0.5%; Punjabi 0.4%; Urdu 0.3%; US white 0.3%; Lapp 0.3%; other 2.0%. **Religious affiliation** (2003): Evangelical Lutheran 85.7%; other Christian 4.5%; Muslim 1.8%; other/nonreligious 8.0%. **Major cities** (2006; populations of municipalities): Oslo 548,617 (urban agglomeration 839,423); Bergen 236,590; Trondheim 154,530; Stavanger 115,087; Bærum 105,574. **Location:** northern Europe, bordering the Barents Sea, Russia, Finland, Sweden, the North Sea, and the Norwegian Sea.

Vital statistics

Birth rate per 1,000 population (2006): 12.6 (world avg. 20.3); (2005) within marriage 48.2%. **Death rate** per 1,000 population (2006): 8.9 (world avg. 8.6). **Natural increase rate** per 1,000 population (2006): 3.7 (world avg. 11.7). **Total fertility rate** (avg. births per childbearing woman; 2005): 1.84. **Life expectancy** at birth (2006): male 78.1 years; female 82.7 years.

National economy

Budget (2005). *Revenue:* NOK 1,066,860,000,000 (tax on income 41.1%; social security 16.2%; VAT 14.8%). *Expenditures:* NOK 763,318,000,000 (social security and welfare 40.5%; health 17.2%; education 14.0%; general public service 9.7%). **Production** (metric tons except as noted). *Agriculture, forestry, fishing* (2005): barley 619,000, wheat 410,000, oats 359,000; livestock (number of live animals) 2,417,000 sheep, 920,300 cattle; roundwood 9,667,000 cu m, of which fuelwood 12%; fisheries production 3,049,570 (from aquaculture 21%); aquatic plants production 148,322. *Mining and quarrying* (2004): ilmenite concentrate 860,000, iron ore (metal content) 408,000, cobalt (refined metal) 4,670. *Manufacturing* (value added in US$'000,000; 2001): food products 2,353; ships and oil platforms 1,543; nonelectrical machinery 1,257. *Energy production (consumption):* electricity (kW-hr; 2005) 138,073,000,000 (126,029,000,000); coal (metric tons; 2004) 2,900,000 (1,360,000); crude petroleum (barrels; 2005) 1,019,000,000 ([2004] 108,270,000); petroleum products (metric tons; 2004) 19,001,000 (10,022,000); natural gas (cu m; 2005) 87,563,000,000 ([2004] 5,107,000,000). **Selected balance of payments data.** Receipts from (US$'000,000): tourism (2005) 3,278; remittances (2005) 429; foreign direct investment (FDI) (2001–05 avg.) 2,427. Disbursements for (US$'000,000): tourism (2005) 9,753; remittances (2005) 953; FDI (2001–05 avg.) 12,085. **Population economically active** (2006): total 2,446,000; activity rate of total population 52.5% (participation rates: ages 15–64, 80.8%; female 47.1%; unemployed 3.4%). **Gross national income** (2006): US$335,314,000,000 (US$71,822 per capita). **Public debt** (2003): US$79,880,000,000. **Households.** Average household size (2001) 2.3; average annual net income per household (2004) NOK 359,300 (US$53,302); sources of income (2004): wages and salaries 63.3%, transfers 22.1%, self-employment 6.0%; expenditure (2003–05): housing 20.7%, transportation 18.1%, recreation and culture 12.3%, food 10.5%.

Foreign trade

Imports (2005; c.i.f.): NOK 357,750,300,000 (machinery and transport equipment 43.2%, of which road vehicles 9.7%, ships 1.6%; metals and metal products 10.4%; food products 6.0%; petroleum products 4.3%). *Major import sources* (2004): Sweden 15.7%; Germany 13.6%; Denmark 7.3%; UK 6.5%; US 4.9%. **Exports** (2005; f.o.b.): NOK 668,949,200,000 (crude petroleum 43.3%; natural gas 15.4%; metals and metal products 8.1%; machinery and transport equipment 7.4%; fish 4.7%). *Major export destinations* (2004): UK 22.6%; Germany 13.2%; The Netherlands 10.2%; France 8.8%; US 7.7%.

Transport and communications

Transport. *Railroads* (2005): route length 4,087 km; passenger-km 2,723,000,000; metric ton-km cargo (2001) 2,449,000,000. *Roads* (2005): total length 92,864 km (paved [2002] 78%). *Vehicles* (2005): passenger cars 2,028,909; trucks and buses 431,257. *Air transport* (2004; SAS [Norwegian part], Braathens, Norwegian, and Widerøe only): passenger-km 13,229,000,000; metric ton-km cargo 177,522,000. **Communications,** in total units (units per 1,000 persons). Daily newspaper circulation (2004): 2,405,000 (524); televisions (2003): 7,110,000 (1,557); telephone landlines (2006): 2,055,000 (443); cellular telephone subscribers (2006): 5,041,000 (1,086); personal computers (2004): 2,630,000 (578); total Internet users (2005): 3,400,000 (736); broadband Internet subscribers (2005): 991,000 (215).

Education and health

Educational attainment (2000). Percentage of population ages 16 and over having: primary and lower secondary education 21.5%; higher secondary 55.0%; higher 21.3%; unknown 2.2%. **Literacy** (2000): virtually 100%. **Health** (2006): physicians 15,443 (1 per 302 persons); hospital beds 16,303 (1 per 286 persons); infant mortality rate 3.2. **Food** (2005): daily per capita caloric intake 3,447 (vegetable products 69%, animal products 31%).

Military

Total active duty personnel (2006): 25,800 (army 57.0%, navy 20.6%, air force 19.4%, other 3.0%). **Military expenditure as percentage of GDP** (2005): 1.7%; per capita expenditure US$1,058.

Background

Several principalities were united into the kingdom of Norway in the 11th century. From 1380 it had the same king as Denmark until it was ceded to Sweden in 1814. The union with Sweden was dissolved in 1905, and Norway's economy grew rapidly. The country remained neutral during World War I, although its shipping industry played a vital role in the conflict. It declared its neutrality in World War II but was invaded and occupied by German troops. Norway is a member of NATO but turned down membership in the EU in 1994. Its economy grew consistently during the 1990s.

Recent Developments

Norway's economy continued to be strong in 2007. Only 2.5% of the workforce was unemployed, and GDP grew by 3.5%. Exports of oil, natural gas, fish, and industrial products—combined with the importation of cheap industrial products from China and other low-cost countries—gave Norway a trade surplus of some NOK 377 billion (about US$70 billion). The Norwegian Government Pension Fund reached NOK 1.94 trillion (about US$357 billion). The government promised to make Norway carbon neutral by 2050, partly by buying carbon quotas from less-developed countries and partly through domestic efforts, including investment in new offshore technology that could pump carbon gas back into former reservoirs of oil and gas.

Internet resources: <www.visitnorway.com>.

Oman

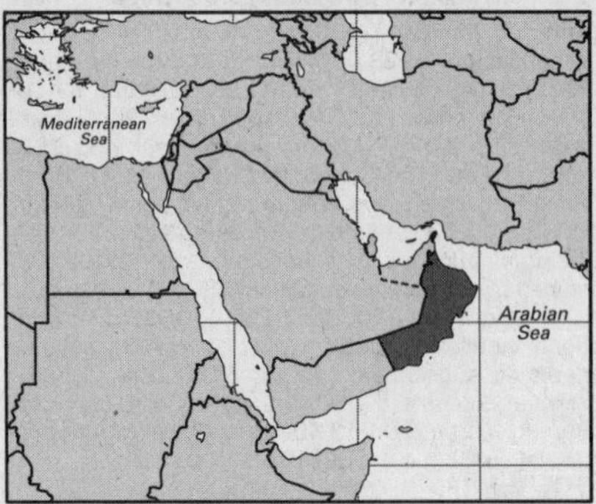

Official name: Saltanat ʿUman (Sultanate of Oman). **Form of government:** monarchy with two advisory bodies (State Council [70]; Consultative Council [84]). **Head of state and government:** Sultan (from 1970) and Prime Minister (from 1972) Qabus ibn Saʿid. **Capital:** Muscat. **Official language:** Arabic. **Official religion:** Islam. **Monetary unit:** 1 rial Omani (RO) = 1,000 baizas; valuation (1 Jul 2008) US$1 = RO 0.39.

Demography

Area: 119,500 sq mi, 309,500 sq km. **Population** (2007): 2,595,000. **Density** (2007): persons per sq mi 21.7, persons per sq km 8.4. **Urban** (2005): 71.5%. **Sex distribution** (2004): male 56.34%; female 43.66%. **Age breakdown** (2003): under 15, 33.9%; 15–29, 32.2%; 30–44, 20.8%; 45–59, 8.9%; 60–74, 3.2%; 75–84, 0.7%; 85 and over, 0.3%. **Ethnic composition** (2000): Omani Arab 48.1%; Indo-Pakistani 31.7%, of which Balochi 15.0%, Bengali 4.4%, Tamil 2.5%; other Arab 7.2%; Persian 2.8%; Zanzibari (blacks originally from Zanzibar) 2.5%; other 7.7%. **Religious affiliation** (2005): Muslim 89%, of which Ibadiyah 75%, Sunni 8%, Shiʿi 6%; Hindu 5%; Christian 5%; other 1%. **Major cities** (2005; populations of districts): As-Sib 242,363; Matrah 173,483; Salalah 171,074; Bawshar 168,025; Suhar 110,917; Muscat 26,668 (urban agglomeration 695,435). **Location:** the Middle East, bordering the Gulf of Oman, the Arabian Sea, Yemen, Saudi Arabia, and the UAE; the Ruʿus al-Jibal enclave occupies the northern tip of the Musandam Peninsula and borders the UAE, the Persian Gulf, and the Strait of Hormuz.

Vital statistics

Birth rate per 1,000 population (2005): 24.8 (world avg. 20.3). **Death rate** per 1,000 population (2005): 2.5 (world avg. 8.6). **Natural increase rate** per 1,000 population (2005): 22.3 (world avg. 11.7). **Total fertility rate** (avg. births per childbearing woman; 2005): 5.84. **Life expectancy** at birth (2005): male 73.2 years; female 75.4 years.

National economy

Budget (2006). *Revenue:* RO 5,027,200,000 (oil revenue 64.2%; natural gas revenue 12.2%; tax revenue 7.2%; other 16.4%). *Expenditures:* RO 4,936,100,000 (current expenditure 71.5%, of which defense 31.4%, education 11.3%, social security and welfare 6.8%; capital expenditure 24.3%; other 4.2%). **Public debt** (external, outstanding; 2005): US$842,000,000. **Gross national income** (2006): US$28,710,000,000 (US$11,275 per capita). **Households.** Average household size (2003) 6.8; expenditure (2000): food and nonalcoholic beverages 29.9%, transportation and communications 22.2%, housing 15.3%. **Production** (metric tons except as noted). *Agriculture, forestry, fishing* (2006): dates 258,700, tomatoes 40,440, bananas 25,960; livestock (number of live animals) 1,598,250 goats, 358,050 sheep, 307,580 cattle, 119,650 camels; fisheries production (2005) 150,744. *Mining and quarrying* (2005): marble 140,000; gypsum 60,000; chromite (gross weight) 19,000. *Manufacturing* (value added in US$'000,000; 2004): petroleum products 1,168; cement, bricks, and ceramics 232; food products 152. *Energy production (consumption):* electricity (kW-hr; 2005) 12,648,000,000 (12,023,000,000); crude petroleum (barrels; 2006) 269,000,000 ([2004] 27,300,000); petroleum products (metric tons; 2005) 4,306,000 ([2004] 3,300,000); natural gas (cu m; 2004) 18,096,000,000 (8,019,000,000). **Population economically active** (2003): total 736,624; activity rate of total population 31.5% (participation rates: female 15.4%; unemployed [2004] 15%). **Selected balance of payments data.** Receipts from (US$'000,000): tourism (2005) 481; remittances (2006) 39; foreign direct investment (FDI) (2001–05 avg.) 304. Disbursements for (US$'000,000): tourism (2005) 643; remittances (2006) 2,257; FDI (2003–05 avg.) 149. **Land use** as % of total land area (2003): in temporary crops 0.1%, in permanent crops 0.1%, in pasture 3.2%; overall forest area (2005) 0.01%.

Foreign trade

Imports (2005; c.i.f. for commodities and trading partners): RO 3,394,000,000 (motor vehicles and parts 26.6%; electrical machinery and equipment 21.6%; base and fabricated metals 11.3%; food and live animals 7.9%; chemical products 6.4%). *Major import sources:* UAE 26.5%; Japan 15.7%; Germany 6.9%; US 6.2%; India 4.5%. **Exports** (2005): RO 7,186,900,000 (domestic exports 91.9%, of which crude and refined petroleum 71.8%, natural gas 12.4%, food and live animals 1.8%; reexports 8.1%, of which motor vehicles and parts 6.1%). *Major export destinations:* China 22.7%; Thailand 11.9%; Japan 11.6%; South Korea 11.1%; UAE 7.1%.

Transport and communications

Transport. *Roads* (2004): total length 40,116 km (paved 37%). *Vehicles* (2003): passenger cars 324,085; trucks and buses 116,438. *Air transport* (2006; Oman Air only): passenger-km 1,749,000,000; metric ton-km cargo 11,000,000. **Communications,** in total units (units per 1,000 persons). Daily newspaper circulation (2004): 108,000 (45); televisions (2003): 1,557,000 (633); telephone landlines (2006): 278,000 (107); cellular telephone subscribers (2006): 1,818,000 (696); personal computers (2005): 130,000 (51); total Internet users

1 metric ton = about 1.1 short tons; 1 kilometer = 0.6 mi (statute); 1 metric ton-km cargo = about 0.68 short ton-mi cargo; c.i.f.: cost, insurance, and freight; f.o.b.: free on board

(2006): 319,000 (122); broadband Internet subscribers (2006): 152,000 (60).

Education and health

Educational attainment (2003). Percentage of population ages 10 and over having: no formal schooling (illiterate) 15.9%; no formal schooling (literate) 22.3%; primary 35.3%; secondary 17.0%; higher technical 3.3%; higher undergraduate 5.2%; higher graduate 0.7%; other 0.3%. **Literacy** (2003): percentage of total population ages 15 and over literate 75.8%; males literate 83.0%; females literate 67.2%. **Health** (2005): physicians 4,093 (1 per 602 persons); hospital beds 5,178 (1 per 476 persons); infant mortality rate per 1,000 live births 10.3.

Military

Total active duty personnel (2006): 41,700 (army 60.0%, navy 10.1%, air force 9.8%, royal household/foreign troops 20.1%). **Military expenditure as percentage of GDP** (2005): 11.9%; per capita expenditure US$1,516.

Background

Oman has been inhabited for at least 10,000 years. Arabs began migrating there in the 9th century BC. Tribal warfare was endemic until the conversion to Islam in the 7th century AD. It was ruled by Ibadi imams until 1154, when a royal dynasty was established. The Portuguese controlled the coastal areas from about 1507 to 1650, when they were expelled. The Al Bu Saʿid dynasty, founded in the mid-18th century, still rules Oman. Oil was discovered in 1964. In 1970 the sultan was deposed by his son, who began a policy of modernization, and under him the country joined the Arab League and the UN. In the Persian Gulf War, Oman cooperated with the allied forces against Iraq. In the 1990s it continued to expand its foreign relations.

Recent Developments

Record-high oil prices continued to fuel Oman's robust economic growth in 2007. Highlights included the addition of a third train of liquefied natural gas exports, the use of new technology to enhance recovery of oil from existing fields, and the accelerated development of Oman's newest port and aluminum facility at Sohar, located outside the Hormuz Strait. In addition the expansion of transportation and tourism services further diversified the economy and increased employment opportunities for the country's burgeoning population.

Internet resources: <www.omantourism.gov.om>.

Pakistan

Official name: Islam-i Jamhuriya-e Pakistan (Islamic Republic of Pakistan). **Form of government:** military-backed constitutional regime with two legislative houses (Senate [100]; National Assembly [342]). **Chief of state and government:** President Asif Ali Zardari (from 2008), assisted by Prime Minister Yousaf Raza Gilani (from 2008). **Capital:** Islamabad. **Official language:** Urdu. **Official religion:** Islam. **Monetary unit:** 1 Pakistan rupee (PKR) = 100 paisa; valuation (1 Jul 2008) US$1 = PKR 68.40.

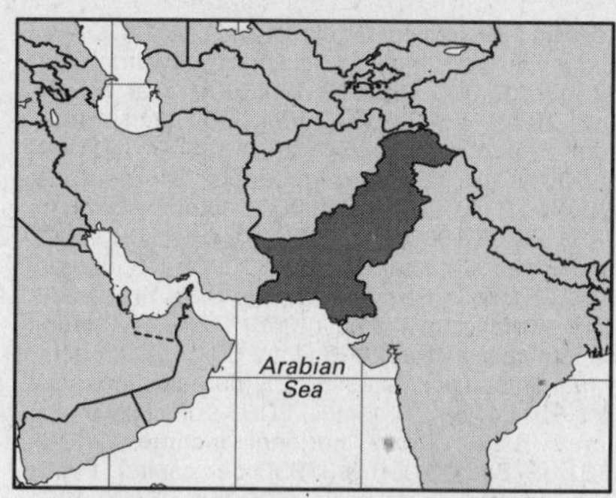

Demography

Demographic information, except ethnic and religious data, excludes Afghan refugees and the 2007 populations of Azad Kashmir (3,527,000) and the Northern Areas (1,096,000); area and density data exclude 33,136-sq-mi (85,823-sq-km) area of Pakistani-administered Jammu and Kashmir (comprising both Azad Kashmir and the Northern Areas). **Area:** 307,374 sq mi, 796,096 sq km. **Population** (2007): 159,060,000. **Density** (2007): persons per sq mi 517.5, persons per sq km 199.8. **Urban** (2006): 34.5%. **Sex distribution** (2005): male 51.44%; female 48.56%. **Age breakdown** (2005): under 15, 37.2%; 15–29, 29.9%; 30–44, 16.8%; 45–59, 10.2%; 60–74, 4.7%; 75–84, 1.0%; 85 and over, 0.2%. **Ethnic composition** (2000): Punjabi 52.6%; Pashtun 13.2%; Sindhi 11.7%; Urdu-speaking muhajirs 7.5%; Balochi 4.3%; other 10.7%. **Religious affiliation** (2000): Muslim 96.1%; Christian 2.5%; Hindu 1.2%; others (including Ahmadiyah) 0.2%. **Major urban agglomerations** (2005): Karachi 11,608,000; Lahore 6,289,000; Faisalabad 2,494,000; Rawalpindi 1,770,000; Multan 1,452,000. **Location:** southern Asia, bordering China, India, the Arabian Sea, Iran, and Afghanistan.

Vital statistics

Birth rate per 1,000 population (2006): 26.1 (world avg. 20.3). **Death rate** per 1,000 population (2006): 8.2 (world avg. 8.6). **Total fertility rate** (avg. births per childbearing woman; 2006): 3.28. **Life expectancy** at birth (2006): male 63.9 years; female 63.8 years.

National economy

Budget (2005–06). *Revenue:* PKR 1,022,704,-000,000 (tax revenue 70.0%, of which sales tax 28.0%, income/corporate profits 21.1%, customs 13.3%; nontax revenue 25.9%; other 4.1%). *Expenditures:* PKR 1,072,225,000 (general public service 61.4%, of which debt servicing 28.4%; defense 22.4%). **Production** (metric tons except as noted). *Agriculture, forestry, fishing* (2005): sugarcane 47,244,000, wheat 21,612,000, rice 8,321,000; livestock (number of live animals) 56,700,000 goats, 26,300,000 buffalo, 24,900,000 sheep; roundwood 29,270,000 cu m, of which fuelwood 91%; fisheries production 515,095 (from aquaculture 16%). *Mining and quarrying* (2005): limestone 14,857,000; gypsum 552,496. *Manufacturing* (value of production in PKR '000,000,000; 2000–01): textiles 321; food products 189; refined petroleum and coke 94. *Energy production (consumption):* electricity (kW-hr; 2004) 85,699,000,000 (85,699,000,000); coal (metric tons; 2004) 4,587,000 (7,894,000); crude petroleum (barrels; 2005) 24,000,000 ([2004] 85,000,000); petroleum products (metric tons; 2004) 10,031,000 (14,748,000); natural gas (cu m; 2005) 38,089,000,000 ([2004] 32,162,000,000). **Land use** as % of total land area (2003): in temporary crops 28.0%, in permanent crops 0.8%, in pasture 6.5%; overall forest area (2005) 2.5%. **Population economically active** (2006): total 50,055,000; activity rate of total population 32.2% (participation rates: ages 15–64, 54.2%; female 20.1%; officially unemployed 6.2%). **Gross national income** (2006): US$149,784,000,000 (US$930 per capita). **Public debt** (external, outstanding; 2005): US$29,490,000,000. **Selected balance of payments data.** Receipts from (US$'000,000): tourism (2005) 181; remittances (2006–07 avg.) 5,491; foreign direct investment (2001–05 avg.) 1,008; official development assistance (2005) 1,917 (commitments). Disbursements for (US$'000,000): tourism (2005) 1,275; remittances (2006) 3.0. **Households** (2001–02). Average household size (2005) 6.8; income PKR 86,102 (US$1,416); sources of income: self-employment 41.3%, wages and salaries 33.5%, transfer payments 11.6%; expenditure: food 48.3%, housing 13.2%.

Foreign trade

Imports (2006–07): US$26,652,000,000 (machinery and apparatus 19.1%; chemicals and chemical products 15.0%; refined petroleum 14.9%; crude petroleum 12.7%; food 9.1%). *Major import sources:* Saudi Arabia 12.2%; UAE 11.7%; China 8.7%; Kuwait 6.7%; Japan 5.5%. **Exports** (2006–07): US$16,924,000,000 (textiles 59.2%, of which woven cotton fabric 13.7%, knitwear 12.4%, bedding 8.2%, ready-made garments 6.5%; cotton yarn 6.4%; rice 6.7%; petroleum products 5.2%). *Major export destinations:* US 22.7%; UAE 7.5%; UK 5.9%; Hong Kong 4.4%; Germany 4.0%.

Transport and communications

Transport. *Railroads* (2004–05): length 11,515 km; passenger-km 24,238,000,000; metric ton-km cargo 5,013,540,000. *Roads* (2006–07): total length 259,197 km (paved 67%). *Vehicles* (2004): passenger cars 1,559,824; trucks and buses 507,945. *Air transport* (2006; Pakistan International Airlines only): passenger-km 15,110,000,000; metric ton-km cargo 426,991,000. **Communications,** in total units (units per 1,000 persons). Daily newspaper circulation (2003): 6,246,000 (42); televisions (2003): 12,223,000 (82); telephone landlines (2006): 5,240,000 (33); cellular telephone subscribers (2006): 34,507,000 (220); personal computers (2005): 803,000 (5.2); total Internet users (2006): 12,000,000 (76); broadband Internet subscribers (2006): 57,000 (0.4).

Education and health

Literacy (2005–06): total population ages 10 and over literate 54%; males literate 65%; females literate 42%. **Health** (2005): physicians 122,798 (1 per 1,263 persons); hospital beds 101,490 (1 per 1,517 persons); infant mortality rate per 1,000 live births 76.7. **Food** (2005): daily per capita caloric intake 2,422 (vegetable products 81%, animal products 19%); 137% of FAO recommended minimum.

Military

Total active duty personnel (2006): 619,000 (army 88.8%, navy 3.9%, air force 7.3%). **Military expenditure as percentage of GDP** (2005): 3.5%; per capita expenditure US$29.

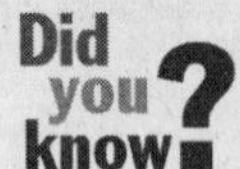

Harappa lies on the left bank of a now dry course of the Ravi River, west-southwest of the town of Sahiwal, in the Punjab of eastern Pakistan. The village stands on an extensive series of mounds in which excavations since 1921 have disclosed the remains of a large city of the Indus civilization, second in size to Mohenjo-daro, which lies about 400 miles (644 km) to the southwest.

Background

Pakistan has been inhabited since about 3500 BC. From the 3rd century BC to the 2nd century AD, it was part of the Mauryan and Kushan kingdoms. The first Muslim conquests were in the 8th century AD. The British East India Company subdued the reigning Mughal dynasty in 1757. During the period of British colonial rule, what is now Pakistan was part of India. When the British withdrew in 1947, the new state of Pakistan came into existence by act of the British Parliament. Kashmir remained a disputed territory between Pakistan and India, resulting in military clashes and full-scale war in 1965. Civil war between East Pakistan (now Bangladesh) and West Pakistan resulted in independence for Bangladesh in 1971. Many Afghan refugees migrated to Pakistan during the Soviet-Afghan War in the 1980s. Pakistan elected Benazir Bhutto, the first woman to head a modern Islamic state, in 1988. She was ousted in 1990 on charges of corruption and incompetence. During the 1990s border flare-ups with India continued, and Pakistan conducted nuclear tests.

Recent Developments

The assassination of former prime minister Benazir Bhutto on 27 Dec 2007, only days after the lifting of a state of emergency imposed by Pres. Pervez Musharraf in early November, plunged Pakistan into its deepest domestic crisis since the 1971 civil war. It is uncertain whether she was shot or struck her head, but a suicide bomber also blew himself up near her vehicle, killing more than 20. Her tragic passing framed the events of 2007. Musharraf, who had been reelected to another five-year term as Pakistan's president in a controversial election in October, placed the country on red alert and ordered all military and police to quell the riots that paralyzed many sectors of society. Bhutto's death and its aftermath placed the national and provincial elections scheduled for 2008 in question, but the elections were carried out in February 2008 and resulted in victory for the Pakistan People's Party (PPP), which had campaign platforms of defeating extremism and bringing modernity and democracy to the country. The cochairman of the PPP was Asif Ali Zardari, widower of Benazir Bhutto. The Pakistan Muslim League-N, led by former prime minister Nawaz Sharif, polled second. Yousaf Raza Gilani, a longtime ally of Bhutto, was sworn in as prime minister in March 2008. One of his first acts was to free the former chief justice, who had been placed under house arrest by Musharraf in 2007 for having challenged his October reelection. In August 2008 Musharraf resigned the presidency.

Internet resources: <www.tourism.gov.pk>.

Palau

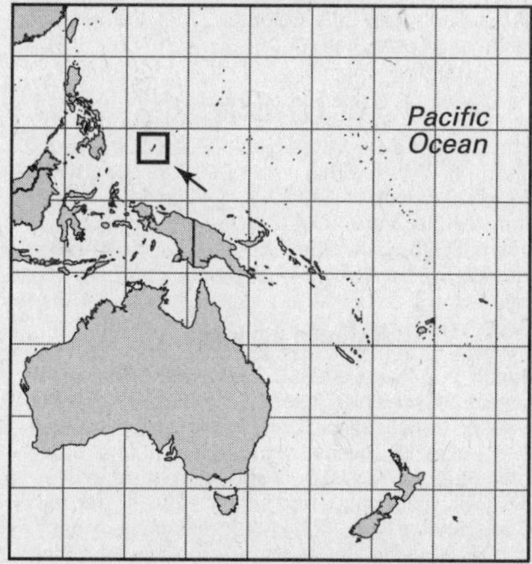

Official name: Belu'u er a Belau (Palauan); Republic of Palau (English). **Form of government:** nonparty republic with two legislative houses (Senate [9]; House of Delegates [16]). **Head of state and government:** President Tommy Remengesau, Jr. (from 2001). **Capital:** Melekeok. **Official languages:** Palauan; English; Sonsorolese-Tobian. **Official religion:** none. **Monetary unit:** 1 US dollar (US$) = 100 cents.

Demography

Area: 188 sq mi, 488 sq km. **Population** (2007): 20,200. **Density** (2007): persons per sq mi 107.4, persons per sq km 41.4. **Urban** (2005): 70.0%. **Sex distribution** (2006): male 53.72%; female 46.28%. **Age breakdown** (2006): under 15, 23.4%; 15–29, 21.6%; 30–44, 28.4%; 45–59, 18.3%; 60–74, 5.9%; 75 and over, 2.4%. **Ethnic composition** (2005; population ages 18 and over only): Palauan 65.2%; Asian 30.3%, of which Filipino 21.6%, Vietnamese 2.3%; other Micronesian 3.1%; white 1.1%; other 0.3%. **Religious affiliation** (2005; population ages 18 and over only): Roman Catholic 51.0%; Protestant 26.7%; Modekngei (marginal Christian sect) 8.9%; other Christian 1.8%; other 11.6%. **Major cities** (2005): Koror 10,743; Meyuns 1,153; Kloulklubed 680. **Location:** island group in the North Pacific Ocean, east of the Philippines.

Vital statistics

Birth rate per 1,000 population (2006): 12.9 (world avg. 20.3). **Death rate** per 1,000 population (2006): 7.2 (world avg. 8.6). **Life expectancy** at birth (2005): male 68.0 years; female 72.0 years.

National economy

Budget (2005–06). *Revenue:* US$83,671,000 (grants from the US 53.7%; tax revenue 34.9%; nontax revenue 7.9%; trust fund revenue 3.5%). *Expenditures:* US$87,586,000 (current expenditure 74.1%; capital expenditure 25.9%). **Public debt** (gross external debt; 2002–03): US$19,429,000. **Production** (metric tons except as noted). *Agriculture, forestry, fishing* (value of sales in US$; 2001): eggs (2003) 638,750, cabbages 116,948, cucumbers 44,009; livestock (number of live animals; 2001) 702 pigs, 21,189 poultry; fisheries production (2005) 937 (from aquaculture 1%). *Manufacturing:* includes handicrafts. *Energy production (consumption):* electricity (kW-hr; 2004) 171,000,000 ([2006] 114,000,000); petroleum products (metric tons; 2004) none (78,000). **Selected balance of payments data.** Receipts from (US$'000,000): tourism (2004) 97; foreign direct investment (2001–05 avg.) 4.8; official development assistance (2005) 29 (commitments). Disbursements for (US$'000,000): tourism (2004) 2.0. **Land use** as % of total land area (2003): in temporary crops 9%, in permanent crops 4%, in pasture 7%; overall forest area (2005) 88%. **Population economically active** (2005): total 10,203; activity rate of total population 51.3% (participation rates: over age 15, 69.1%; female 39.1%; unemployed 4.2%). **Gross national income** (2006): US$162,000,000 (US$8,011 per capita). **Households.** Average household size (2005) 3.9; annual average income per household (2005) US$20,422; expenditure (1997): food 42.2%, beverages and tobacco 14.8%, entertainment 13.1%.

Foreign trade

Imports (2001): US$95,700,000 (machinery and transport equipment 24.2%; food and live animals 15.2%; mineral fuels and lubricants 10.4%; beverages and tobacco products 8.3%; chemicals and chemical products 7.4%). *Major import sources* (2003): South Korea 56.4%; Japan 18.7%; Germany 11.3%; Indonesia 3.6%; Australia 3.0%. **Exports** (2001): US$9,000,000 (mostly high-grade tuna and garments). *Major export destinations* (2003): Japan 86.7%; Vietnam 5.9%; Zambia 4.6%.

Transport and communications

Transport. *Roads* (2004): total length 61 km (paved 59%). *Vehicles* (2004): passenger cars and trucks 7,247. *Air transport* (2003): passenger arrivals 80,017, passenger departures 78,608. **Communications,** in total units (units per 1,000 persons). Telephone landlines (2006): 8,000 (399); cellular telephone subscribers (2006): 8,300 (414); total Internet users (2003): 3,150 (160).

Education and health

Educational attainment (2005). Percentage of population ages 25 and over having: no formal schooling 1.9%; incomplete primary education 9.0%; complete primary 3.9%; incomplete secondary 14.9%; complete secondary 42.2%; postsecondary/vocational 14.1%; higher 14.0%. **Literacy** (2005): virtually 100%. **Health** (2004): physicians 21 (1 per 942 persons); hospital beds 135 (1 per 147 persons); infant mortality rate per 1,000 live births (2006) 7.7.

Military

The US is responsible for the external security of Palau, as specified in the Compact of Free Association of 1 Oct 1994.

Background

Palau's inhabitants began arriving 3,000 years ago in successive waves from the Indonesian and Philippine archipelagos and from Polynesia. The islands had been under nominal Spanish ownership for more than three centuries when they were sold to Germany in 1899. They were seized by Japan in 1914 and taken by Allied forces in 1944 during World War II. Palau became part of the UN Trust Territory of the Pacific Islands in 1947 and became a sovereign state in 1994; the US provides economic assistance and maintains a military presence in the islands.

Recent Developments

Palau vowed to join the United States and Russia in the fight against nuclear terrorism in 2007. In February Palau approved the statutory documents of the Global Initiative to Combat Nuclear Terrorism, which US Pres. George W. Bush and Russian Pres. Vladimir Putin had created.

Internet resources: <www.visit-palau.com>.

Panama

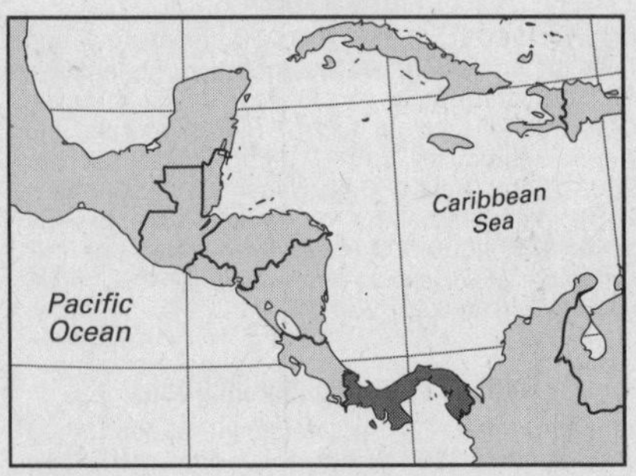

Official name: República de Panamá (Republic of Panama). **Form of government:** multiparty republic with one legislative house (Legislative Assembly [78]). **Head of state and government:** President Martín Torrijos (from 2004). **Capital:** Panama City. **Official language:** Spanish. **Official religion:** none. **Monetary unit:** 1 balboa (B) = 100 cents; valuation (1 Jul 2008) US$1 = B 1.00.

Demography

Area: 28,973 sq mi, 75,040 sq km. **Population** (2007): 3,343,000. **Density** (2007): persons per sq mi 115.4, persons per sq km 44.5. **Urban** (2005): 70.8%. **Sex distribution** (2005): male 50.54%; female 49.46%. **Age breakdown** (2005): under 15, 30.5%; 15–29, 26.3%; 30–44, 21.4%; 45–59, 12.8%; 60–74, 6.6%; 75 and over, 2.4%. **Ethnic composition** (2000): mestizo 58.1%; black and mulatto 14.0%; white 8.6%; Amerindian 6.7%; Asian 5.5%; other 7.1%. **Religious affiliation** (2000): Roman Catholic 70.6%; Protestant/independent Christian 14.0%; Muslim 4.4%; Baha'i 1.2%; Buddhist 0.8%; traditional beliefs 0.7%; nonreligious 2.5%; other 5.8%. **Major cities** (2000): Panama City 415,964 (urban agglomeration [2005] 1,216,000); San Miguelito 293,745; David (population of *cabecera*) 77,734; Arraiján (population of *cabecera*) 63,753; La Chorrera 55,871. **Location:** Central America, bordering the Caribbean Sea, Colombia, the North Pacific Ocean, and Costa Rica.

Vital statistics

Birth rate per 1,000 population (2006): 20.0 (world avg. 20.3); (2006) within marriage 17.3%. **Death rate** per 1,000 population (2006): 4.4 (world avg. 8.6). **Total fertility rate** (avg. births per childbearing woman; 2006): 2.40. **Life expectancy** at birth (2005): male 72.7 years; female 77.9 years.

National economy

Budget (2004). *Revenue:* B 2,042,000,000 (tax revenue 59.2%, of which income taxes 23.9%, taxes on domestic transactions 20.9%; other current revenue 39.9%, of which revenue from Panama Canal 9.0%). *Expenditures:* B 2,810,000,000 (current expenditure 83.8%, of which wages and salaries 27.2%, transfers 26.3%, debt service 21.1%; development expenditure 16.2%). **Public debt** (external, outstanding; 2005): US$7,514,000,000. **Production** (metric tons except as noted). *Agriculture, forestry, fishing* (2006): sugarcane 1,766,000, bananas 439,200, rice 280,000; livestock (number of live animals) 1,564,000 cattle, 286,000 pigs, 180,000 horses; roundwood (2005) 1,298,218 cu m, of which fuelwood 93%; fisheries production (2005) 222,756 (from aquaculture 4%). *Mining and quarrying* (2005): limestone 270,000. *Manufacturing* (value added in B '000,000; 2004): food products 410; beverages 167; cement, bricks, and ceramics 70. *Energy production (consumption):* electricity (kW-hr; 2004) 5,475,-000,000 (4,495,000,000); crude petroleum, none (negligible); petroleum products (metric tons; 2004) none (1,710,000). **Households.** Average household size (2004) 4.1; average annual income per household (1990) B 5,450 (US$5,450); expenditure (2001): food 22%, energy 18%, health care 14%. **Land use** as % of total land area (2003): in temporary crops 7.4%, in permanent crops 2.0%, in pasture 20.6%; overall forest area (2005) 57.7%. **Population economically active** (2006): total 1,332,059; activity rate of total population 39.8% (participation rates: ages 15–64, 66.9%; female 37.1%; unemployed 9.1%). **Gross national income** (2006): US$15,536,-000,000 (US$4,726 per capita). **Selected balance of**

payments data. Receipts from (US$'000,000): tourism (2005) 780; remittances (2006) 149; foreign direct investment (FDI) (2001–05 avg.) 605. Disbursements for (US$'000,000): tourism (2005) 271; remittances (2006) 121; FDI (2001–05 avg.) 1,777.

Foreign trade

Imports (2003; c.i.f.): B 3,122,000,000 (machinery and apparatus 18.7%; mineral fuels 13.0%; chemical products 12.4%; transport equipment 11.1%). *Major import sources* (2006): US 26.8%; direct imports from Colón Free Zone 11.9%; Curaçao 10.1%; Costa Rica 5.1%; Japan 4.7%. **Exports** (2003; f.o.b.): B 799,000,000 (marine products 42.3%, of which tuna 16.4%, shrimp and lobster 9.6%, salmon 7.0%; bananas 13.2%; melons 5.9%). *Major export destinations* (2006): US 38.5%; Spain 8.2%; The Netherlands 6.7%; Sweden 5.6%; Costa Rica 4.5%.

Transport and communications

Transport. *Railroads* (2002): route length (2005) 355 km; passenger-km (data for Panama Canal Railway and National Railway of Chiriquí) 35,693,000,000; metric ton-km cargo (data for Panama Canal Railway) 20,665,000,000. *Roads* (2005): total length 11,984 km (paved 72%). *Vehicles* (2005): passenger cars 269,704; trucks and buses 78,699. Panama Canal traffic (2005–06): oceangoing transits 12,764; cargo 205,058,000 metric tons. *Air transport* (2006; COPA only): passenger-km 6,560,000,000; metric ton-km cargo (2005) 37,226,000. **Communications,** in total units (units per 1,000 persons). Daily newspaper circulation (2005): 164,000 (52); televisions (2004): 620,000 (195); telephone landlines (2006): 433,000 (132); cellular telephone subscribers (2005): 1,694,000 (525); personal computers (2005): 147,000 (47); total Internet users (2006): 220,000 (67); broadband Internet subscribers (2005): 18,000 (5.6).

Education and health

Educational attainment (2000). Percentage of population ages 25 and over having: no formal schooling/unknown 13.8%; primary 36.4%; secondary 33.9%; undergraduate 14.4%; graduate 1.5%. **Literacy** (2005): total population ages 15 and over literate 93.0%; males literate 93.6%; females literate 92.4%. **Health** (2004): physicians 4,321 (1 per 715 persons); hospital beds 7,564 (1 per 408 persons); infant mortality rate per 1,000 live births (2006) 14.8. **Food** (2005): daily per capita caloric intake 2,627 (vegetable products 82%, animal products 18%); 144% of FAO recommended minimum.

Military

Total active duty personnel (2006): none. **Paramilitary expenditure as percentage of GDP** (2005): 1.1%; per capita expenditure US$50.

Background

Panama was inhabited by Native Americans when the Spanish arrived in 1501. The first successful Spanish settlement was founded by Vasco Núñez de Balboa in 1510. Panama was part of the viceroyalty of New Granada until it declared its independence from Spain in 1821 to join the Gran Colombia union. In 1903 it revolted against Colombia and was recognized by the US, to which it ceded the Canal Zone. The completed Panama Canal was opened in 1914; its jurisdiction reverted from the US to Panama in 1999. An invasion by US troops in 1989 overthrew the de facto ruler, Gen. Manuel Noriega.

Recent Developments

In June 2007 Panama's free-trade agreement with the US was signed by government representatives, and the National Assembly quickly ratified the treaty. On 3 September Pres. Martín Torrijos presided over the official opening of the US$5.25 billion expansion of the Panama Canal. The project involved constructing a third set of locks and new access channels and widening and deepening existing channels. The expansion was expected to increase the canal's capacity significantly, allowing cargo ships that currently are too large to pass through the canal, and extend its role in global maritime trade.

Internet resources:
<www.visitpanama.com/?id=&lang=en>.

Papua New Guinea

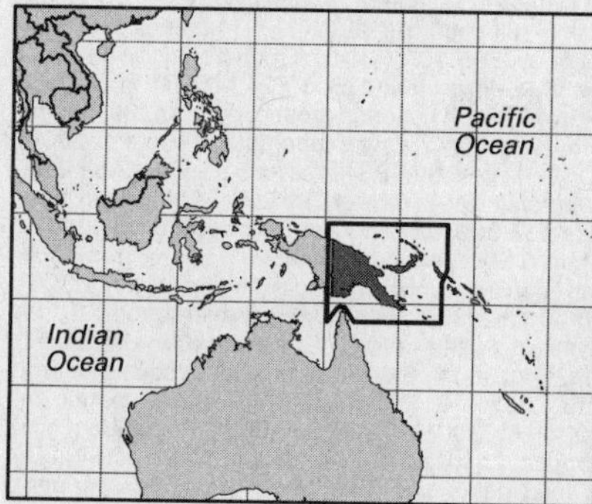

Official name: Independent State of Papua New Guinea. **Form of government:** constitutional monarchy with one legislative house (National Parliament [109]). **Chief of state:** British Queen Elizabeth II (from 1952), represented by Governor-General Sir Paulias Matane (from 2004). **Head of government:** Prime Minister Sir Michael Somare (from 2002). **Capital:** Port Moresby. **Official language:** English; English, Motu, and Tok Pisin (English Creole) are national languages. **Official religion:** none. **Monetary unit:** 1 Papua New Guinea kina (K) = 100 toea; valuation (1 Jul 2008) US$1 = K 2.60.

Demography

Area: 178,704 sq mi, 462,840 sq km. **Population** (2007): 6,331,000. **Density** (2007): persons per sq mi 35.4, persons per sq km 13.7. **Urban** (2005): 13.4%. **Sex distribution** (2005): male 50.79%; female 49.21%. **Age breakdown** (2005): under 15, 40.6%; 15–29, 27.3%; 30–44, 18.9%; 45–59, 9.3%; 60–74, 3.3%; 75–84, 0.5%; 85 and over, 0.1%. **Ethnic composition** (1983): New Guinea Papuan 84.0%; New Guinea Melanesian 15.0%; other 1.0%. **Religious affiliation** (2005): Protestant/independent

Christian 44%; Roman Catholic 22%; traditional beliefs 34%. **Major cities** (2004): Port Moresby 337,900; Lae 109,800; Madang 36,000; Wewak 28,600; Arawa 20,800. **Location:** group of islands, including the eastern half of the island of New Guinea, in the South Pacific Ocean near the Equator, bordering Indonesia and to the north of Australia.

Vital statistics

Birth rate per 1,000 population (2005): 31.8 (world avg. 20.3). **Death rate** per 1,000 population (2005): 9.8 (world avg. 8.6). **Natural increase rate** per 1,000 population (2005): 22.0 (world avg. 11.7). **Total fertility rate** (avg. births per childbearing woman; 2005): 4.05. **Life expectancy** at birth (2005): male 54.3 years; female 60.2 years.

National economy

Budget (2005). *Revenue:* K 5,243,000,000 (tax revenue 71.4%, of which taxes on minerals and petroleum 20.5%, indirect taxes 18.6%, income tax 16.0%; grants 23.3%; nontax revenue 5.3%). *Expenditures:* K 4,104,000,000 (current expenditure 69.0%; development expenditure 31.0%). **Public debt** (external, outstanding; March 2007): US$1,170,000,000. **Production** (metric tons except as noted). *Agriculture, forestry, fishing* (2005): oil palm fruit 1,300,000, bananas 919,800, coconuts 795,100; livestock (number of live animals) 1,750,000 pigs; roundwood 7,241,000 cu m, of which fuelwood 76%; fisheries production 250,280. *Mining and quarrying* (2005): copper (metal content; 2006) 194,355; gold 68,483 kg; silver 51,125 kg. *Manufacturing* (value of exports in US$'000; 2005): forest products 153,000; palm oil 126,100; coconut oil 30,200; copra 5,600; refined petroleum, n.a. *Energy production (consumption):* electricity (kW-hr; 2004) 1,399,000,000 (1,399,000,000); coal (metric tons; 2004) none (1,000); crude petroleum (barrels; 2004) 18,300,000 (476,000); petroleum products (metric tons; 2004) 46,000 (712,000); natural gas (cu m; 2004) 85,300,000 (85,300,000). **Population economically active** (2000): total 2,413,357; activity rate of total population 46.5% (participation rates: ages 15–64, 73.2%; female 47.9%). **Gross national income** (2006): US$5,523,000,000 (US$890 per capita). **Selected balance of payments data.** Receipts from (US$'000,000): tourism (2005) 3.6; remittances (2006) 13; foreign direct investment (FDI) (2001–05 avg.) 48; official development assistance (2005) 233 (commitments). Disbursements for (US$'000,000): tourism (2005) 56; remittances (2006) 135; FDI (2001–05 avg.) 11. **Land use** as % of total land area (2003): in temporary crops 0.5%, in permanent crops 1.4%, in pasture 0.4%; overall forest area (2005) 65.0%.

Foreign trade

Imports (2003; f.o.b. in trading partners and c.i.f. in commodities): K 4,628,000,000 (nonelectrical machinery 18.5%; food products 14.8%; refined petroleum 12.9%; transport equipment 8.8%; chemical products 8.4%). *Major import sources* (2006): Australia 34.2%; US 21.0%; Singapore 19.2%; Japan 5.0%; New Zealand 2.8%. **Exports** (2006): K 12,731,000,000 (copper 34.0%; gold 24.3%; crude petroleum 23.5%; logs 3.9%; palm oil 2.4%). *Major export destinations* (2006): Australia 40.7%; Japan 14.3%; Philippines 9.7%; Germany 4.5%; South Korea 4.4%.

Transport and communications

Transport. *Roads* (1999): total length 19,600 km (paved 4%). *Vehicles* (2002): passenger cars 24,900; trucks and buses 87,800. *Air transport* (2006; Air Niugini only): passenger-km 748,000,000; metric ton-km cargo 22,000,000. **Communications,** in total units (units per 1,000 persons). Daily newspaper circulation (2004): 51,000 (8.6); televisions (2003): 130,000 (22); telephone landlines (2005): 64,000 (11); cellular telephone subscribers (2005): 75,000 (13); personal computers (2005): 391,000 (64); total Internet users (2006): 110,000 (18).

Education and health

Educational attainment (1990). Percentage of population ages 25 and over having: no formal schooling 82.6%; some primary education 8.2%; completed primary 5.0%; some secondary 4.2%. **Literacy** (2003): total population ages 15 and over literate 57.3%; males literate 63.4%; females literate 50.9%. **Health** (2005): physicians 750 (1 per 7,849 persons); hospital beds (2000) 14,516 (1 per 371 persons); infant mortality rate per 1,000 live births 63.0.

Military

Total active duty personnel (2006): 3,100 (army 80.6%, maritime element [coastal patrol] 12.9%, air force 6.5%). **Military expenditure as percentage of GDP** (2005): 0.6%; per capita expenditure US$5.

Background

Papua New Guinea has been inhabited since prehistoric times. The Portuguese sighted the coast of New Guinea in 1512, and in 1545 the Spanish claimed the island. The first colony was founded in 1793 by the British. In 1828 the Dutch claimed the western half as part of the Dutch East Indies. In 1884 Britain annexed the southeastern part and Germany took over the northeastern sector. The British part became the Territory of Papua in 1906 and passed to Australia, which also governed the German sector after World War I. After World War II, Australia governed both sectors as the Territory of Papua and New Guinea. Dutch New Guinea was annexed to Indonesia in 1969. Papua New Guinea achieved independence in 1975 and joined the British Commonwealth. It moved to resolve its war with Bougainville independence fighters in 1997. The decadelong war on the island of Bougainville ended when final terms for peace were negotiated on 1 Jun 2001.

Recent Developments

Papua New Guinea Prime Minister Michael Somare, reelected in August 2007 to a second term, was forced to defend himself in 2008 from opposition accusations of financial impropriety. At issue was the government's attempts to block investigation into Somare's personal taxes. As well, he was linked to a scandal involving a

1 metric ton = about 1.1 short tons; 1 kilometer = 0.6 mi (statute); 1 metric ton-km cargo = about 0.68 short ton-mi cargo; c.i.f.: cost, insurance, and freight; f.o.b.: free on board

proposal for the country to recognize Taiwan, allegedly for a payment of almost US$30 million.

Internet resources: <www.pngtourism.org.pg>.

Paraguay

Official name: República del Paraguay (Spanish); Tetã Paraguáype (Guaraní) (Republic of Paraguay). **Form of government:** multiparty republic with two legislative houses (Chamber of Senators [45]; Chamber of Deputies [80]). **Head of state and government:** President Fernando Lugo (from 2008). **Capital:** Asunción. **Official languages:** Spanish; Guaraní. **Official religion:** none (Roman Catholicism enjoys special recognition in the 1992 constitution). **Monetary unit:** 1 guaraní (plural guaranies; ₲) = 100 céntimos; valuation (1 Jul 2008) US$1 = ₲ 3,950.00.

Demography

Area: 157,048 sq mi, 406,752 sq km. **Population** (2007): 6,127,000. **Density** (2007): persons per sq mi 39.0, persons per sq km 15.1. **Urban** (2006): 58.1%. **Sex distribution** (2006): male 49.57%; female 50.43%. **Age breakdown** (2005): under 15, 35.9%; 15–29, 28.6%; 30–44, 17.4%; 45–59, 11.2%; 60–74, 5.2%; 75 and over, 1.7%. **Ethnic composition** (2000): mixed (white/Amerindian) 85.6%; white 9.3%, of which German 4.4%, Latin American 3.4%; Amerindian 1.8%; other 3.3%. **Religious affiliation** (2002): Roman Catholic 89.6%; Protestant (including all Evangelicals) 6.2%; other Christian 1.1%; nonreligious/atheist 1.1%; traditional beliefs 0.6%; other/unknown 1.4%. **Major urban areas** (2002): Asunción (2006) 519,661 (urban agglomeration [2005] 1,858,000); Ciudad del Este 222,274; San Lorenzo 204,356; Luque 170,986; Capiatá 154,274. **Location:** central South America, bordering Brazil, Argentina, and Bolivia.

Vital statistics

Birth rate per 1,000 population (2005): 25.8 (world avg. 20.3). **Death rate** per 1,000 population (2005): 5.7 (world avg. 8.6). **Natural increase rate** per 1,000 population (2005): 20.1 (world avg. 11.7). **Total fertility rate** (avg. births per childbearing woman; 2005): 3.30. **Life expectancy** at birth (2005): male 69.2 years; female 73.4 years.

National economy

Budget (2006–07): *Revenue:* ₲10,174,723,000,000 (tax revenue 65.2%, of which VAT 28.5%, income tax 10.9%, taxes on international trade 8.5%; nontax revenue 34.8%). *Expenditures:* ₲9,682,282,000,000 (current expenditure 77.3%, of which wages and salaries 42.9%; capital expenditure 22.7%). **Public debt** (external, outstanding; August 2007): US$2,151,725,000. **Population economically active** (2006): total 2,735,646; activity rate 46.0% (participation rates: ages 15–64 [2002], 61.4%; female 38.5%; unemployed 11.1%). **Production** (metric tons except as noted). *Agriculture, forestry, fishing* (2006–07): soybeans 6,250,000, cassava 4,800,000, sugarcane 4,100,000, maté (2004–05) 74,000; livestock (number of live animals; 2006) 9,982,932 cattle, 1,600,000 pigs, 17,000,000 chickens; roundwood (2005) 10,090,794 cu m, of which fuelwood 60%; fisheries production (2005) 23,100 (from aquaculture 9%). *Mining and quarrying* (2005): kaolin 66,600. *Manufacturing* (value added in US$'000,000; 2001): food products 325; beverages 114; chemical products 77. *Energy production (consumption):* electricity (kW-hr; 2004) 51,921,000,000 (Paraguay is the world's second largest net exporter of electricity) (6,925,000,000); crude petroleum (barrels; 2004) none (491,000); petroleum products (metric tons; 2004) 64,000 (1,254,000). **Gross national income** (2006): US$9,281,000,000 (US$1,543 per capita). **Households.** Average household size (2005) 4.3. **Selected balance of payments data.** Receipts from (US$'000,000): tourism (2005) 76; remittances (2006) 268; foreign direct investment (FDI) (2001–05 avg.) 74; official development assistance (2005) 81 (commitments). Disbursements for (US$'000,000): tourism (2005) 79; FDI (2001–05 avg.) 5.0. **Land use** as % of total land area (2003): in temporary crops 7.2%, in permanent crops 0.2%, in pasture 54.6%; overall forest area (2005) 46.5%.

Foreign trade

Imports (2006): US$5,254,271,000 (machinery and apparatus 35.9%; mineral fuels 13.2%; transport equipment 11.5%; chemical products 6.3%; food, beverages, and tobacco products 6.1%). *Major import sources:* China 27.0%; Brazil 20.0%; Argentina 13.6%; Japan 8.3%; US 6.4%. **Exports** (2006): US$1,906,367,000 (soybeans 23.0%; meat 22.3%; cereals 11.4%; flour 7.5%; vegetable oils 6.2%). *Major export destinations:* Uruguay 22.0%; Brazil 17.2%; Russia 11.9%; Argentina 8.8%; Chile 6.9%.

Transport and communications

Transport. *Railroads* (2006): operational route length 36 km. *Roads* (1999): total length 29,500 km (paved 51%). *Vehicles* (2005): passenger cars 360,070; trucks 81,207. *Air transport* (2005; Transportes Aéreos del Mercosur only): passenger-km 501,000,000. **Communications,** in total units (units per 1,000 persons). Daily newspaper circulation (2004): 145,000 (25); televisions (2004): 1,300,000 (224); telephone landlines (2006): 331,000 (55); cellular telephone subscribers (2006): 3,233,000

(537); personal computers (2005): 460,000 (78); total Internet users (2006): 260,000 (43); broadband Internet subscribers (2006): 16,000 (2.7).

Education and health

Educational attainment (2003). Percentage of population ages 15 and over having: no formal schooling 4.1%; incomplete primary education 30.2%; complete primary 30.8%; secondary 26.9%; higher 8.0%. **Literacy** (2005): percentage of total population ages 15 and over literate 94.9%; males literate 95.9%; females literate 93.9%. **Health** (2005): physicians 5,517 (1 per 873 persons); hospital beds 5,843 (1 per 1,010 persons); infant mortality rate per 1,000 live births 33.8. **Food** (2005): daily per capita caloric intake 2,563 (vegetable products 78%, animal products 22%); 139% of FAO recommended minimum.

Military

Total active duty personnel (2006): 10,100 (army 75.2%, navy 13.9%, air force 10.9%). **Military expenditure as percentage of GDP** (2005): 0.7%; per capita expenditure US$9.

Background

Seminomadic tribes speaking Guaraní were in Paraguay long before it was settled by Spain in the 16th and 17th centuries. Paraguay was part of the Viceroyalty of the Río de la Plata until it became independent in 1811. It suffered from dictatorial governments in the 19th century and from the 1865 war with Brazil, Argentina, and Uruguay. The Chaco War with Bolivia over disputed territory was settled primarily in Paraguay's favor by the peace treaty of 1938. Military governments, including that of Alfredo Stroessner, predominated in the mid-20th century until the election of a civilian president, Juan Carlos Wasmosy, in 1993. Paraguay suffered a financial crisis in the late 1990s, and democratic government was in jeopardy.

Recent Developments

Political maneuvering in advance of the April 2008 presidential elections dominated Paraguay's attention during 2007, even as the country was hit by a series of corruption scandals. In December 2006 Fernando Lugo, the popular Roman Catholic bishop of San Pedro, resigned to run for the presidency, since Paraguay's constitution prohibited members of the clergy from holding office. Pres. Nicanor Duarte Frutos, after unsuccessfully seeking a constitutional amendment permitting him to run for a second term, began grooming his education minister, Blanca Ovelar, as his successor. Although Duarte took office on an anticorruption platform, allegations of corruption, bribery, and embezzlement by various government figures dogged his administration—including a case involving Education Ministry officials (serving under Ovelar) accused of having embezzled nearly US$6 million from a school meals program. In July 2007 the six leading opposition parties announced that they had forged an alliance behind Lugo, and in April 2008 he was elected, defeating Ovelar, whose Colorado Party had retained power in Paraguay since 1947.

Internet resources: <www.paraguay.com>.

Peru

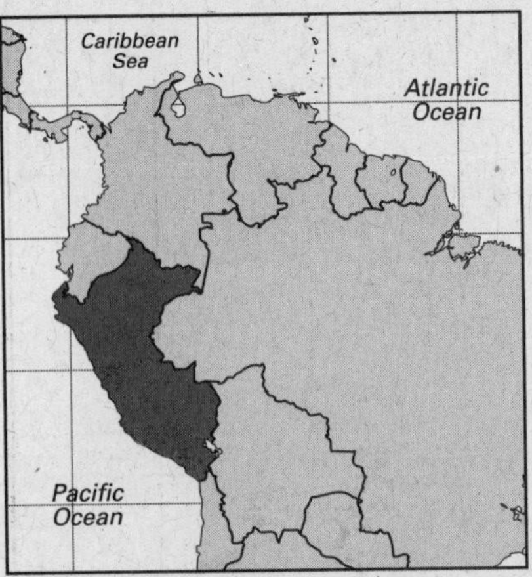

Official name: República del Perú (Spanish) (Republic of Peru). **Form of government:** unitary multiparty republic with one legislative house (Congress [120]). **Head of state and government:** President Alan García (from 2006), assisted by Prime Minister Jorge del Castillo (from 2006). **Capital:** Lima. **Official languages:** Spanish; Quechua; Aymara. **Official religion:** Roman Catholicism. **Monetary unit:** 1 nuevo sol (S/.) = 100 céntimos; valuation (1 Jul 2008) US$1 = S/. 2.96.

Demography

Area: 496,218 sq mi, 1,285,198 sq km. **Population** (2007): 27,903,000. **Density** (2007): persons per sq mi 56.2, persons per sq km 21.7. **Urban** (2005): 72.6%. **Sex distribution** (2005): male 49.94%; female 50.06%. **Age breakdown** (2005): under 15, 31.1%; 15–29, 28.0%; 30–44, 20.0%; 45–59, 12.1%; 60–74, 6.3%; 75–84, 1.9%; 85 and over, 0.6%. **Ethnic composition** (2000): Quechua 47.0%; mestizo 31.9%; white 12.0%; Aymara 5.4%; Japanese 0.5%; other 3.2%. **Religious affiliation** (2005): Roman Catholic 85%; Protestant 7%; independent Christian 4%; other 4%. **Major cities** (2005): metropolitan Lima 7,753,439; Arequipa 783,000; Trujillo 644,547; Chiclayo 495,415; Piura 361,832. **Location:** western South America, bordering Ecuador, Colombia, Brazil, Bolivia, Chile, and the South Pacific Ocean.

Vital statistics

Birth rate per 1,000 population (2005): 20.9 (world avg. 20.3). **Death rate** per 1,000 population (2005): 6.3 (world avg. 8.6). **Total fertility rate** (avg. births per childbearing woman; 2005): 2.56. **Life expectancy** at birth (2005): male 67.8 years; female 71.4 years.

National economy

Budget (2005). *Revenue:* S/. 41,432,000,000 (tax revenue 85.8%, of which VAT 44.6%, corporate taxes 14.8%; nontax revenue 14.2%). *Expenditures:* S/. 43,534,000,000 (current expenditure 77.1%, of which transfers 30.1%; debt service 11.7%; capital expenditure 11.2%). **Production** (metric tons except as noted). *Agriculture, forestry, fishing* (2006): sugarcane 7,600,000, alfalfa 5,606,000, potatoes 3,290,000 (in 2006 Peru ranked second in the world in coca production [114,100 metric tons produced]); livestock (number of live animals) 14,822,226 sheep, 5,241,298 cattle, (2005) 4,500,000 llamas and alpacas; roundwood (2005) 9,142,000 cu m, of which fuelwood 81%; fisheries production (2005) 9,416,130. *Mining and quarrying* (2005; metal content): iron ore 4,638,027; zinc 1,028,418; copper 790,198. *Manufacturing* (value in S/. '000,000; 2005): food products 11,854; textiles and clothing 5,310; chemical products 4,212. *Energy production (consumption):* electricity (kW-hr; 2005) 23,822,-000,000 (21,100,000,000); coal (metric tons; 2004) 16,000 (963,000); crude petroleum (barrels; 2005) 40,600,000 ([2004] 60,011,000); petroleum products (metric tons; 2004) 8,286,000 (7,233,000); natural gas (cu m; 2005) 4,956,000,000 (561,000,000). **Households.** Average household size (2005) 4.3; income per household (1988) US$2,173; sources of income (1991): self-employment 67.1%, wages 23.3%, transfers 7.6%; expenditure (1990): food 29.4%, recreation and education 13.2%, household durables 10.1%. **Selected balance of payments data.** Receipts from (US$'000,000): tourism (2005) 1,241; remittances (2006) 1,825; foreign direct investment (2001–05 avg.) 1,763. Disbursements for (US$'000,000): tourism (2005) 680; remittances (2006) 133. **Population economically active** (2002): total 12,892,000; activity rate of total population 48.2% (participation rates: ages 15–64, 72.6%; female 42.0%; urban unemployed [2005] 9.6%). **Gross national income** (2006): US$86,579,000,000 (US$3,138 per capita). **Public debt** (external, outstanding; 2005): US$22,222,000,000. **Land use** as % of total land area (2003): in temporary crops 2.9%, in permanent crops 0.5%, in pasture 13.2%; overall forest area (2005) 53.7%.

Foreign trade

Imports (2005): US$12,076,000,000 (consumer goods 19.2%; mineral fuels 19.2%; capital goods 17.5%; food products 6.2%). *Major import sources* (2006): US 16.5%; China 10.3%; Brazil 10.3%; Ecuador 7.2%; Colombia 6.1%. **Exports** (2005): US$17,336,000,000 (copper 19.4%; gold 18.3%; crude and refined petroleum 8.8%; textiles and clothing 7.4%; fishmeal 6.6%; molybdenum 6.6%). *Major export destinations* (2006): US 24.0%; China 9.6%; Switzerland 7.1%; Canada 6.8%; Chile 6.0%.

Transport and communications

Transport. *Railroads* (2002): length (2005) 3,462 km; passenger-km 98,000,000; metric ton-km cargo 1,008,000,000. *Roads* (2004): total length 78,829 km (paved 14%). *Vehicles* (2004): passenger cars 824,613; trucks and buses 462,803. *Air transport* (2006): passenger-km 4,440,000,000; metric ton-km cargo 100,092,000. **Communications,** in total units (units per 1,000 persons). Daily newspaper circulation (2005): 946,000 (35); televisions (2002): 4,592,000 (172); telephone landlines (2006): 2,332,000 (82); cellular telephone subscribers (2006): 8,500,000 (300); personal computers (2005): 2,800,000 (103); total Internet users (2006): 6,100,000 (215); broadband Internet subscribers (2006): 485,000 (17).

Education and health

Educational attainment (2005). Percentage of population ages 15 and over having: no formal schooling 11.8%; incomplete primary education 24.3%; complete primary 11.5%; incomplete secondary 15.3%; complete secondary 19.0%; higher 18.1%. **Literacy** (2005): total population ages 15 and over literate 91.6%; males literate 95.6%; females literate 87.7%. **Health** (2004): physicians 41,266 (1 per 651 persons); hospital beds (2005) 42,159 (1 per 647 persons); infant mortality rate per 1,000 live births (2005) 31.9. **Food** (2005): daily per capita caloric intake 2,583 (vegetable products 88%, animal products 12%); 141% of FAO recommended minimum.

Military

Total active duty personnel (2006): 80,000 (army 50.0%, navy 31.3%, air force 18.7%). **Military expenditure as percentage of GDP** (2005): 1.4%; per capita expenditure US$39.

Background

Peru was the center of the Inca empire, which was established about 1230 with its capital at Cuzco. In 1533 it was conquered by Francisco Pizarro, and it was dominated by Spain for almost 300 years as the Viceroyalty of Peru. It declared its independence in 1821, and freedom was achieved in 1824. Peru was defeated in the War of the Pacific with Chile (1879–83). A boundary dispute with Ecuador erupted into war in 1941 and gave Peru control over a larger part of the Amazon basin; further disputes ensued until the border was demarcated again in 1998. The government was overthrown by a military junta in 1968, and civilian rule was restored in 1980. The government of Alberto Fujimori dissolved the legislature in 1992 and promulgated a new constitution the following year. It later successfully combated the Sendero Luminoso (Shining Path) and Tupac Amarú rebel movements. Fujimori won a second term in 1995 and a controversial third term in 2000, but he left office and the country late that year amid allegations of corruption.

Recent Developments

Probably the most notable event in Peru in 2007 was the magnitude-8.0 earthquake that on 15 August struck the southern coast near the city of Ica. The final death toll was about 540, with some 200,000 in need of shelter. Macroeconomic indicators were strong throughout the year; economic growth surpassed 7.0% and there were substantial government revenues, significant trade surpluses, and large foreign reserves. Inflation stayed low (at about 2.5%). However, extreme disparities remained between Peru's wealthy and its poor. One of Peru's economic mainstays—mining—showed signs of trouble. Numerous mining communities protested against low wages and such environmental ills as water pollution and mercury spills. The city of La Oroya, a mining town with a refinery in the central Andean highlands, was reportedly one of the 10 worst polluted places in the world; more than 90% of children in the area had high levels of lead in their blood. Pres. Alan García supported a free-trade agreement with the US, and the Peru Trade Promotion Agreement was approved in November by the US House of Representatives and in December by the US Senate.

Internet resources: <www.peru.info/perueng.asp>.

Philippines

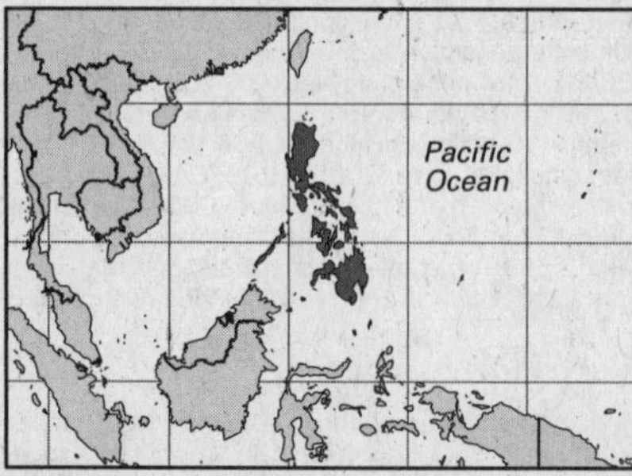

Official name: Republika ng Pilipinas (Filipino); Republic of the Philippines (English). **Form of government:** unitary republic with two legislative houses (Senate [24]; House of Representatives [240]). **Chief of state and head of government:** President Gloria Macapagal-Arroyo (from 2001). **Capital:** Quezon City/Manila. **Official languages:** Filipino; English. **Official religion:** none. **Monetary unit:** 1 Philippine peso (P) = 100 centavos; valuation (1 Jul 2008) US$1 = P 45.08.

Demography

Area: 122,121 sq mi, 316,294 sq km. **Population** (2007): 87,960,000. **Density** (2006): persons per sq mi 759.4, persons per sq km 293.2. **Urban** (2003): 61.0%. **Sex distribution** (2005): male 50.35%; female 49.65%. **Age breakdown** (2005): under 15, 35.1%; 15–29, 28.8%; 30–44, 19.0%; 45–59, 11.0%; 60–74, 5.0%; 75–84, 1.0%; 85 and over, 0.1%. **Ethnic composition** (2000): Tagalog 20.9%; Visayan (Cebu) 19.0%; Ilocano 11.1%; Hiligaynon (Visaya) 9.4%; Waray-Waray (Binisaya) 4.7%; Central Bikol (Naga) 4.6%; Filipino mestizo 3.5%; Pampango 3.1%; other 23.7%. **Religious affiliation** (2005): Roman Catholic 64.9%; independent Christian 17.7%; Muslim 5.1%; Protestant 5.0%; traditional beliefs 2.2%; other 5.1%. **Major cities** (2000): Quezon City 2,173,831; Manila 1,581,082 (Metro Manila [2003] 10,352,249); Caloocan 1,177,604; Davao 1,147,116; Cebu 718,821. **Location:** southeastern Asia, archipelago between the Philippine Sea and the South China Sea, east of Vietnam.

Vital statistics

Birth rate per 1,000 population (2005): 24.1 (world avg. 20.3). **Death rate** per 1,000 population (2005): 5.6 (world avg. 8.6). **Total fertility rate** (avg. births per childbearing woman; 2005): 3.41. **Life expectancy** at birth (2005): male 67.0 years; female 72.9 years.

National economy

Budget (2004). *Revenue:* P 757,945,000,000 (income taxes 42.1%; international duties 17.5%; sales tax 14.4%; nontax revenues 10.6%). *Expenditures:* P 899,990,000,000 (debt service 33.5%; economic affairs 17.7%; education 15.1%; transportation and communications 6.1%). **Production** (metric tons except as noted). *Agriculture, forestry, fishing* (2006): sugarcane 24,350,000, rice 15,330,000, coconuts 14,960,000; livestock (number of live animals) 13,046,680 pigs, 3,735,816 goats, 3,357,956 buffalo; roundwood (2005) 15,819,034 cu m, of which fuelwood 82%; fisheries production (2005) 2,803,603 (from aquaculture 20%); aquatic plants production 1,338,859 (from aquaculture 100%). *Mining and quarrying* (2005): chromite 36,070; nickel (metal content) 22,560; copper (metal content) 16,320. *Manufacturing* (value added in US$'000,000; 2003): petroleum products 1,980; electronic products 1,696; food products 1,338. *Energy production (consumption):* electricity (kW-hr; 2004) 55,957,000,000 (55,957,-000,000); hard coal (metric tons; 2004) 2,482,000 (9,456,000); crude petroleum (barrels; 2004) 1,000,000 (816,000,000); petroleum products (metric tons; 2004) 9,345,000 (14,427,000); natural gas (cu m; 2004) 2,479,000,000 (2,479,000,000). **Households** (2000). Average household size (2004) 5.0; income per family (2003) P 148,616 (US$2,742); sources of income: wages 52.1%, self-employment 25.1%, remittances 11.1%; expenditure: food, beverages, and tobacco 45.4%, housing 14.2%, transportation 6.8%. **Land use** as % of total land area (2003): in temporary crops 19.1%, in permanent crops 16.8%, in pasture 5.0%; overall forest area (2005) 24.0%. **Gross national income** (2006): US$127,832,000,000 (US$1,482 per capita). **Public debt** (external, outstanding; 2005): US$35,233,000,000. **Population economically active** (2007): total 36,434,000; activity rate of total population 41% (participation rates: ages 15 and over 63.6%; female [2006] 39.4%; unemployed [July 2007] 7.8%). **Selected balance of payments data.** Receipts from (US$'000,000): tourism (2005) 2,130; remittances (2006) 14,923; foreign direct investment (2001–05 avg.) 810. Disbursements for (US$'000,000): tourism (2005) 1,279; remittances (2006) 15.

Foreign trade

Imports (2006): US$51,774,000,000 (electronic products 47.2%; mineral fuels 15.4%; machinery and transport equipment 7.7%). *Major import sources* (2004): Japan 20.6%; US 16.0%; Singapore 8.4%; China 7.4%; Taiwan 7.3%. **Exports** (2006): US$47,410,000,000 (electronic products 62.6%; clothing 5.6%; copper cathodes 2.6%). *Major export destinations* (2004): US 17.4%; Japan 15.8%; China 11.4%; Hong Kong 8.3%; Singapore 7.7%.

Transport and communications

Transport. *Railroads* (2004): route length 897 km; passenger-km 83,400,000; metric ton-km cargo (2000) 660,000,000. *Roads* (2003): total length

1 metric ton = about 1.1 short tons; 1 kilometer = 0.6 mi (statute); 1 metric ton-km cargo = about 0.68 short ton-mi cargo; c.i.f.: cost, insurance, and freight; f.o.b.: free on board

200,037 km (paved 10%). *Vehicles* (2006): passenger cars 767,000; trucks and buses 240,000. *Air transport* (2006; Philippines Airlines only): passenger-km 13,513,000,000; metric ton-km cargo 257,000,000. **Communications,** in total units (units per 1,000 persons). Daily newspaper circulation (2003): 5,902,000 (73); televisions (2003): 14,770,000 (182); telephone landlines (2006): 3,633,000 (43); cellular telephone subscribers (2006): 42,869,000 (508); personal computers (2005): 4,521,000 (54); total Internet users (2005): 4,615,000 (55).

Education and health

Educational attainment (2000). Percentage of population ages 25 and over having: no formal schooling/unknown 6.1%; primary education 38.5%; incomplete secondary 12.5%; complete secondary 17.2%; technical 5.9%; incomplete undergraduate 11.8%; complete undergraduate 7.3%; graduate 0.7%. **Literacy** (2003): total population ages 15 and over literate 92.6%. **Health:** physicians (2005) 98,210 (1 per 857 persons); hospital beds (2004) 82,775 (1 per 999 persons); infant mortality rate per 1,000 live births (2004) 24.2. **Food** (2005): daily per capita caloric intake 2,474 (vegetable products 84%, animal products 16%); 137% of FAO recommended minimum.

Military

Total active duty personnel (2006): 106,000 (army 62.3%, navy 22.6%, air force 15.1%). **Military expenditure as percentage of GDP** (2005): 0.9%; per capita expenditure US$10.

Background

In ancient times, the inhabitants of the Philippines were a diverse agglomeration of peoples who arrived in various waves of immigrants from the Asian mainland. Ferdinand Magellan arrived in 1521. The islands were colonized by the Spanish, who retained control until the islands were ceded to the US in 1898 following the Spanish-American War. The Commonwealth of the Philippines was established in 1935 to prepare the country for political and economic independence, which was delayed by World War II and the Japanese invasion. The islands were liberated by US forces during 1944–45, and the Republic of the Philippines was proclaimed in 1946, with a government patterned on that of the US. In 1965 Ferdinand Marcos was elected president. He declared martial law in 1972, and it lasted until 1981. After 20 years of dictatorial rule, he was driven from power in 1986. Corazon Aquino became president and instituted a period of democratic rule that continued with the 1992 election of Fidel Ramos. Through the 1990s the government tried to come to terms with independence fighters in the southern islands.

Recent Developments

Opponents of Philippine Pres. Gloria Macapagal Arroyo asked voters to treat the national elections held in May 2007 as a referendum on her administration. In the elections, which were marred by violence that claimed at least 126 lives, Arroyo's supporters won more than 200 of the 219 seats that were contested in the House of Representatives to maintain their control there for another three years, though her opponents claimed 7 of the 12 Senate seats contested, enough to give them control of the 24-seat upper chamber. This contributed to a highly partisan situation that slowed or obstructed legislation recommended by Arroyo. In the southern Philippines in 2007, the heaviest fighting in three years disrupted a government cease-fire with the terrorist groups Abu Sayyaf and the Moro Islamic Liberation Front, extremists seeking a separate Muslim state. In December the two groups reached a tentative accord, but talks between the separatists and the government stalled and fighting continued in 2008. The Philippine economy grew 10.3% in 2007, and the unemployment rate fell to 7.4%. The economy benefited from remittances estimated at more than US$13 billion a year from some eight million Filipinos working abroad.

Internet resources: <www.tourism.gov.ph>.

Poland

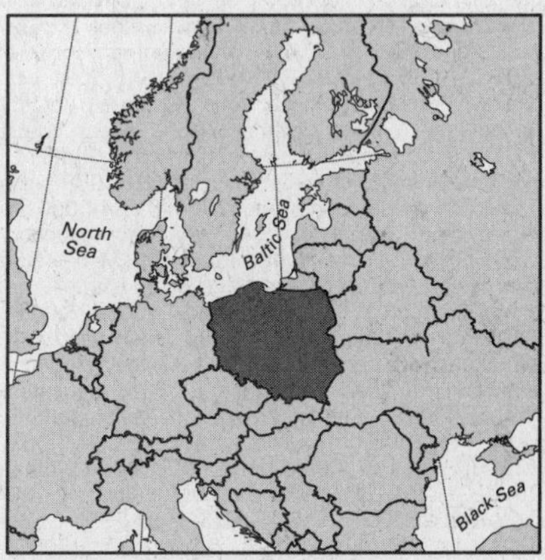

Official name: Rzeczpospolita Polska (Republic of Poland). **Form of government:** unitary multiparty republic with two legislative houses (Senate [100]; Sejm [460]). **Chief of state:** President Lech Kaczynski (from 2005). **Head of government:** Prime Minister Donald Tusk (from 2007). **Capital:** Warsaw. **Official language:** Polish. **Official religion:** none (Roman Catholicism has special recognition per 1997 concordat with Vatican City). **Monetary unit:** 1 zloty (Zl) = 100 groszy; valuation (1 Jul 2008) US$1 = Zl 2.12.

Demography

Area: 120,726 sq mi, 312,679 sq km. **Population** (2007): 38,110,000. **Density** (2007): persons per sq mi 315.7, persons per sq km 121.9. **Urban** (2006): 61.3%. **Sex distribution** (2006): male 48.33%; female 51.67%. **Age breakdown** (2006): under 15, 15.8%; 15–29, 24.1%; 30–44, 20.2%; 45–59, 22.3%; 60–74, 11.8%; 75–84, 4.8%; 85 and over, 1.0%. **Ethnic composition** (2000): Polish 90.0%; Ukrainian 4.0%; German 4.0%; Belarusian 0.5%; Kashubian 0.4%; other 1.1%. **Religious affiliation** (2005): Roman Catholic 89.6%; other Catholic 0.3%; Polish Orthodox 1.3%; Protestant 0.4%; Jehovah's Witness 0.3%; other (mostly nonreligious) 8.1%.

Major cities (2006): Warsaw 1,702,139; Lódz 760,251; Kraków 756,267; Wroclaw 634,630; Poznan 564,951. **Location:** central Europe, bordering the Baltic Sea, Russia (exclave of Kaliningrad), Lithuania, Belarus, Ukraine, Slovakia, Czech Republic, and Germany.

Vital statistics

Birth rate per 1,000 population (2006): 9.8 (world avg. 20.3); (2005) within marriage 81.5%. **Death rate** per 1,000 population (2006): 9.7 (world avg. 8.6). **Natural increase rate** per 1,000 population (2006): 0.1 (world avg. 11.7). **Total fertility rate** (avg. births per childbearing woman; 2006): 1.27. **Life expectancy** at birth (2006): male 70.9 years; female 79.6 years.

National economy

Budget (2006). *Revenue:* Zl 197,640,000,000 (VAT 42.7%; excise tax 21.3%; income tax 14.2%). *Expenditures:* Zl 222,703,000,000 (social security and welfare 22.6%; transfers 15.5%; public debt 12.5%; wages and salaries 10.4%). **Gross national income** (2006): US$324,482,000,000 (US$8,508 per capita). **Production** (metric tons except as noted). *Agriculture, forestry, fishing* (2006): sugar beets 11,474,820, potatoes 8,981,976, wheat 7,059,671; livestock (number of live animals) 18,813,000 pigs, 5,281,000 cattle; roundwood (2005) 31,944,000 cu m, of which fuelwood 11%; fisheries production (2005) 192,854 (from aquaculture 19%). *Mining and quarrying* (2005): sulfur 1,262,000; copper ore (metal content of concentrate) 614,800; silver (recoverable metal content) 1,344. *Manufacturing* (value of sales in Zl '000,000; 2006): food products 137,089; transport equipment 84,568; fabricated metals 49,106. *Energy production (consumption):* electricity ('000,000 kW-hr; 2006–07) 156,065 ([2005] 131,186); hard coal ('000 metric tons; 2006–07) 93,135 ([2004] 83,915); lignite ('000 metric tons; 2006) 60,844 ([2005] 61,589); crude petroleum (barrels; 2006) 5,900,000 ([2005] 134,900,000); petroleum products (metric tons; 2005) 23,153,000 (16,000,000); natural gas (cu m; 2006) 5,650,000,000 ([2005] 16,304,000,000). **Public debt** (external, outstanding; 2006): US$43,360,000,000. **Population economically active** (2006): total 16,938,000; activity rate of total population 44.4% (participation rates: ages 15–64, 64.3%; female 45.2%; unemployed [September 2006–August 2007] 14.0%). **Households** (2006). Average household size 3.1; average disposable annual income Zl 9,629 (US$3,103); sources of income: wages 49.4%, transfers 34.9%, self-employment 8.8%; expenditure: food, beverages, and tobacco 29.8%, housing and energy 19.7%, transportation and communications 13.9%, recreation 7.1%. **Selected balance of payments data.** Receipts from (US$'000,000): tourism (2005) 6,274; remittances (2006) 4,364; foreign direct investment (FDI) (2001–05 avg.) 7,006. Disbursements for (US$'000,000): tourism (2005) 4,341; remittances (2006) 785; FDI (2001–05 avg.) 539. **Land use** as % of total land area (2003): in temporary crops 41.1%, in permanent crops 1.0%, in pasture 10.7%; overall forest area (2005) 30.0%.

Foreign trade

Imports (2006; c.i.f.): Zl 394,030,015,000 (electrical equipment 14.8%; chemical products 12.6%; transportation equipment 12.4%; base and fabricated metals 12.0%; machinery and apparatus 10.7%; mineral fuels 10.2%). *Major import sources:* Germany 24.0%; Russia 9.7%; Italy 6.8%; China 6.1%; France 5.5%. **Exports** (2006; f.ob.): Zl 343,778,977,000 (transportation equipment 20.9%; base and fabricated metals 13.7%; electrical equipment 12.1%; machinery and apparatus 8.6%; food products 8.3%; chemical products 6.4%). *Major export destinations:* Germany 27.2%; Italy 6.5%; France 6.2%; UK 5.7%; Czech Republic 5.5%.

Transport and communications

Transport. *Railroads* (2006): length (2006) 20,176 km; passenger-km 18,552,100,000; metric ton-km cargo 53,622,500,000. *Roads* (2006; public roads only): total length 382,615 km (paved 67%). *Vehicles* (2006): passenger cars 13,384,299; trucks and buses 2,477,167. *Air transport* (2006): passenger-km 11,640,600,000; metric ton-km cargo 109,700,000. **Communications,** in total units (units per 1,000 persons). Daily newspaper circulation (2004): 4,333,000 (113); televisions (2007): 7,820,000 (205); telephone landlines (2007): 11,284,000 (296); cellular telephone subscribers (2007): 36,758,000 (964); personal computers (2004): 7,362,000 (191); total Internet users (2006): 11,000,000 (288); broadband Internet subscribers (2006): 2,640,000 (69).

Education and health

Educational attainment (2005). Percentage of population ages 13 and over having: no formal schooling/incomplete primary education 2.5%; complete primary 21.8%; lower secondary/vocational 28.5%; upper secondary and postsecondary 33.0%; university 14.2%. **Literacy** (2003): virtually 100%. **Health** (2005): physicians 76,046 (1 per 458 persons); hospital beds 236,980 (1 per 162 persons); infant mortality rate per 1,000 live births (2006) 6.0. **Food** (2005): daily per capita caloric intake 3,503 (vegetable products 74%, animal products 26%); 174% of FAO recommended minimum.

Military

Total active duty personnel (2006): 141,500 (army 62.9%, navy 10.1%, air force 21.2%, centrally controlled staff 5.8%). **Military expenditure as percentage of GDP** (2005): 1.9%; per capita expenditure US$154.

Background

Established as a kingdom in 922 under Mieszko I, Poland was united with Lithuania in 1386 under the Jagiellon Dynasty (1386–1572) to become the dominant power in east-central Europe. In 1466 it wrested western and eastern Prussia from the Teutonic Order, and its lands eventually stretched to the Black Sea. Wars with Sweden and Russia in the late 17th century led to the loss of considerable territory. In 1697

1 metric ton = about 1.1 short tons; 1 kilometer = 0.6 mi (statute); 1 metric ton-km cargo = about 0.68 short ton-mi cargo; c.i.f.: cost, insurance, and freight; f.o.b.: free on board

the electors of Saxony became kings of Poland, virtually ending Polish independence. In the late 18th century Poland was divided among Prussia, Russia, and Austria and ceased to exist. After 1815 the former Polish lands came under Russian domination, and from 1863 Poland was a Russian province. After World War I an independent Poland was established by the Allies. The invasion of Poland in 1939 by the USSR and Germany precipitated World War II, during which the Nazis sought to purge its culture and its large Jewish population. Reoccupied by Soviet forces in 1945, it was controlled by a Soviet-dominated government from 1947. In the 1980s the Solidarity labor movement achieved major political reforms, and free elections were held in 1989. An economic austerity program instituted in 1990 sped the transition to a market economy. In 2004 Poland joined the EU.

Recent Developments

Donald Tusk, the chairman of the pro-European Civic Platform, took office as prime minister in November 2007, vowing that Poland would be a more cooperative member of the EU and try to repair ties with Germany and defuse tensions with Russia. He wanted Polish troops to be pulled out of Iraq in 2008, the Polish military contribution in Afghanistan to be strengthened, and 350 troops to be sent in an EU mission to Chad. Tough negotiations led in August 2008 to an agreement to deploy US antimissile interceptors in Poland, a controversial move that angered Russia. Poland's economic growth in 2007 was vibrant. GDP grew 9.7%, the unemployment rate dropped from 15.2% in 2006 to 12.4%, inflation was held in check at 3.5%, and the budget deficit was low at 3.0%.

Internet resources: <www.polandtour.org>.

Portugal

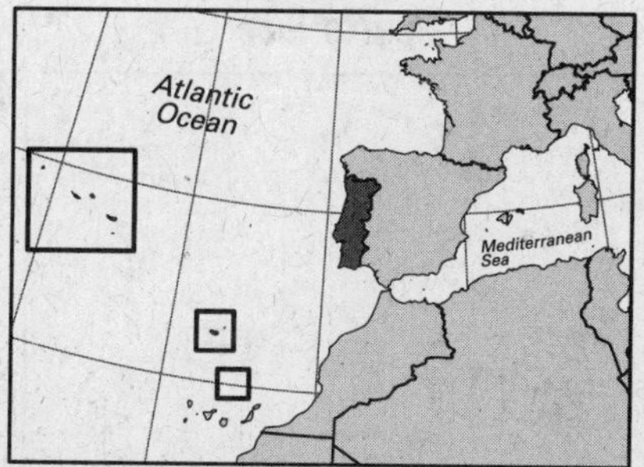

Official name: República Portuguesa (Portuguese Republic). **Form of government:** republic with one legislative house (Assembly of the Republic [230]). **Chief of state:** President Aníbal Cavaco Silva (from 2006). **Head of government:** Prime Minister José Sócrates (from 2005). **Capital:** Lisbon. **Official language:** Portuguese. **Official religion:** none. **Monetary unit:** 1 euro (€) = 100 cents; valuation (1 Jul 2008) US$1 = €0.63.

Demography

Area: 35,556 sq mi, 92,090 sq km. **Population** (2007): 10,629,000. **Density** (2007): persons per sq mi 298.9, persons per sq km 115.4. **Urban** (2005): urban 57.6%. **Sex distribution** (2005): male 48.40%; female 51.60%. **Age breakdown** (2005): under 15, 15.7%; 15–29, 20.4%; 30–44, 22.6%; 45–59, 19.2%; 60–74, 14.8%; 75–84, 5.9%; 85 and over, 1.4%. **Ethnic composition** (2000): Portuguese 91.9%; mixed-race people from Angola, Mozambique, and Cape Verde 1.6%; Brazilian 1.4%; Marrano 1.2%; other European 1.2%; Han Chinese 0.9%; other 1.8%. **Religious affiliation** (2000): Christian 92.4%, of which Roman Catholic 87.4%, independent Christian 2.7%, Protestant 1.3%, other Christian 1.0%; nonreligious/atheist 6.5%; Buddhist 0.6%; other 0.5%. **Major cities** (2001): Lisbon 564,657 (urban agglomeration [2005] 2,761,000); Porto 263,131 (urban agglomeration [2005] 1,309,000); Braga 164,192; Coimbra 148,443; Funchal 103,961. **Location:** southwestern Europe, bordering Spain and the North Atlantic Ocean.

Vital statistics

Birth rate per 1,000 population (2005): 10.4 (world avg. 20.3); (2004) within marriage 70.9%. **Death rate** per 1,000 population (2005): 10.2 (world avg. 8.6). **Natural increase rate** per 1,000 population (2005): 0.2 (world avg. 11.7). **Total fertility rate** (avg. births per childbearing woman; 2004): 1.42. **Life expectancy** at birth (2004–05): male 74.9 years; female 81.4 years.

National economy

Budget (2004). *Revenue:* €59,636,000,000 (social contributions 30.9%; indirect taxes 28.4%; direct taxes 21.0%). *Expenditures:* €63,511,000,000 (current expenditure 90.0%; development expenditure 10.0%). **Public debt** (2006): US$25,000,000,000. **Production** (metric tons except as noted). *Agriculture, forestry, fishing* (2006): grapes 973,400, tomatoes 922,000, potatoes 577,000, cork (2004) 120,000; livestock (number of live animals) 3,583,000 sheep, 2,344,000 pigs, 1,441,000 cattle; roundwood (2005) 11,106,000 cu m, of which fuelwood 5%; fisheries production (2005) 218,242 (from aquaculture 3%). *Mining and quarrying* (2005): marble 800,000; kaolin 160,000; copper (metal content) 89,541. *Manufacturing* (value added in US$000,000; 2003): food products 2,148; cement, tiles, and ceramics 1,611; fabricated metals 1,536. *Energy production (consumption):* electricity (kW-hr; 2004) 45,105,000,000 (51,586,000,000); coal (metric tons; 2004) none (5,514,000); crude petroleum (barrels; 2004) none (93,100,000); petroleum products (metric tons; 2004) 11,369,000 (12,377,000); natural gas (cu m; 2004) none (3,938,000,000). **Population economically active** (2006): total 5,587,300; activity rate of total population 52.5% (participation rates: ages 15–64, 73.9%; female 46.6%; unemployed 7.7%). **Gross national income** (at current market prices; 2006): US$188,263,000,000 (US$17,800 per capita). **Households.** Average household size (2004) 3.0; average annual household income (2001): €15,512 (US$13,881); sources of income (1995): wages and salaries 44.4%, self-employment 23.4%, transfers 22.2%; expenditure (2003): food and nonalcoholic beverages 18.7%, transportation 16.3%, housing and energy 10.7%, restaurants and hotels 10.0%, clothing and footwear 7.1%. **Selected balance of payments data.** Receipts from (US$'000,000): tourism (2005) 7,893; remittances (2006) 3,329; foreign direct investment (FDI) (2001–05 avg.) 4,421. Disbursements for (US$'000,000): tourism (2005)

3,073; remittances (2006) 1,386; FDI (2001–05 avg.) 4,649. **Land use** as % of total land area (2003): in temporary crops 17.6%, in permanent crops 8.4%, in pasture 15.6%; overall forest area (2005) 41.3%.

Foreign trade

Imports (2004): €40,293,000,000 (machinery and apparatus 20.0%; road vehicles 12.4%; chemical products 11.4%; food products 10.0%; crude petroleum 6.8%). *Major import sources:* Spain 29.3%; Germany 14.3%; France 9.3%; Italy 6.1%; UK 4.6%. **Exports** (2004): €26,220,000,000 (machinery and apparatus 18.5%; road vehicles and parts 13.9%; apparel and accessories 9.7%; chemical products 6.7%; fabrics and made-up articles 5.3%; footwear 4.6%). *Major export destinations:* Spain 24.9%; France 14.0%; Germany 13.5%; UK 9.6%; US 6.1%.

Transport and communications

Transport. *Railroads* (2004): length 2,836 km; passenger-km 3,217,000,000; metric ton-km cargo 2,588,000,000. *Roads* (2004): total length 78,470 km (paved [1999] 86%). *Vehicles* (2003): passenger cars 4,918,310; trucks and buses 372,179. *Air transport* (2006; TAP, Portugália, and SATA domestic and international airlines only): passenger-km 18,688,000,000; metric ton-km cargo 293,549,000. **Communications**, in total units (units per 1,000 persons). Daily newspaper circulation (2004): 680,000 (65); televisions (2003): 4,312,000 (413); telephone landlines (2006): 4,231,000 (401); cellular telephone subscribers (2006): 12,226,000 (1,160); personal computers (2005): 1,406,000 (133); total Internet users (2006): 3,213,000 (305); broadband Internet subscribers (2006): 1,460,000 (137).

Education and health

Educational attainment (2002). Percentage of population ages 25–64 having: no formal schooling through complete primary 67%; complete lower secondary 13%; complete upper secondary 11%; higher 9%. **Literacy** (2002): total population ages 15 and over literate 92.5%; males literate 95.2%; females literate 90.3%. **Health**: physicians (2004) 35,312 (1 per 297 persons); hospital beds (2005) 37,330 (1 per 283 persons); infant mortality rate per 1,000 live births (2006) 3.3. **Food** (2005): daily per capita caloric intake 3,635 (vegetable products 72%, animal products 28%).

Military

Total active duty personnel (2006): 43,960 (army 60.7%, navy 22.8%, air force 16.5%); US troops (2006) 940. **Military expenditure as percentage of GDP** (2005): 2.3%; per capita expenditure US$398.

Background

Celtic peoples settled the Iberian peninsula in the 1st millennium BC. They were conquered about 140 BC by the Romans, who ruled until the 5th century AD, when the area was invaded by Germanic tribes. A Muslim invasion in 711 left only the northern part of Portugal in Christian hands. In 1139 it became the kingdom of Portugal and expanded as it reconquered the Muslim-held sectors. The boundaries of modern continental Portugal were completed in 1270 under King Afonso III. In the 15th and 16th centuries the monarchy encouraged exploration that took Portuguese navigators to Africa, India, Indonesia, China, the Middle East, and South America, where colonies were established. António de Oliveira Salazar ruled Portugal as a dictator in the mid-20th century; he died in office in 1970, and his successor was ousted in a coup in 1974. A new constitution was adopted in 1976 (revised 1982), and civilian rule resumed. Portugal was a charter member of NATO and is a member of the European Union.

Recent Developments

Portugal saw modest economic growth in 2007, and efforts continued to rein in spending and reduce the swollen budget deficit. GDP grew by 4.9% for the year, held back a bit by rising interest rates and market turmoil in the US and in some other EU countries. Inflation was relatively cool at 2.5%, though unemployment had crept up to a multiyear high of 8.0%. Portugal also focused on alternative- and renewable-energy projects, with the aim to put Portugal at the forefront of the EU in reducing carbon-dioxide emissions. In March the world's largest photovoltaic generating site, with a capacity of some 11 MW, opened near Serpa in the sunny Alentejo region, and plans were afoot to build more solar facilities, expand the country's wind farms, and launch a prototype wave-power facility off the Atlantic coast. In May 2008 Portugal's parliament voted to approve a radical, controversial set of changes to the Portuguese language to reflect the spellings of the hundreds of millions of Portuguese speakers in Brazil, Angola, and elsewhere.

Internet resources: <www.portugal.org>.

Puerto Rico

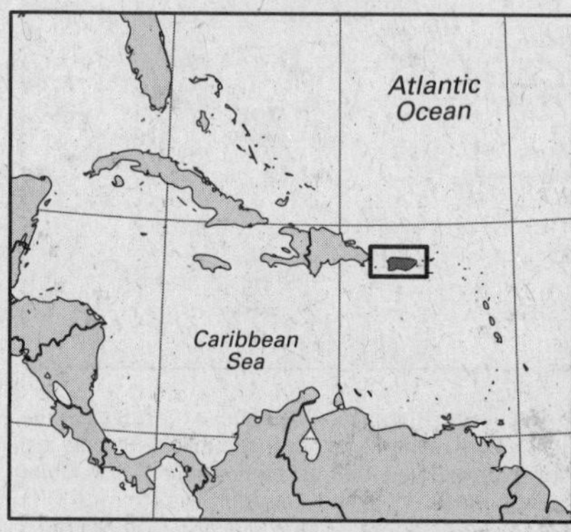

Official name: Estado Libre Asociado de Puerto Rico (Spanish); Commonwealth of Puerto Rico (English). **Political status:** self-governing commonwealth in association with the US, with two legislative houses (Senate [27]; House of Representatives [51]). **Chief of state:** US President George W. Bush (from 2001).

1 metric ton = about 1.1 short tons; 1 kilometer = 0.6 mi (statute); 1 metric ton-km cargo = about 0.68 short ton-mi cargo; c.i.f.: cost, insurance, and freight; f.o.b.: free on board

Head of government: Governor Aníbal Acevedo Vilá (from 2005). **Capital:** San Juan. **Official languages:** Spanish; English. **Monetary unit:** 1 US dollar (US$) = 100 cents.

Demography

Area: 3,515 sq mi, 9,104 sq km. **Population** (2007): 3,967,000. **Density** (2007): persons per sq mi 1,129, persons per sq km 435.7. **Urban** (2003): 96.7%. **Sex distribution** (2005): male 48.04%; female 51.96%. **Age breakdown** (2005): under 15, 22.0%; 15–29, 22.8%; 30–44, 20.1%; 45–59, 17.8%; 60–74, 11.9%; 75–84, 4.0%; 85 and over, 1.4%. **Ethnic composition** (2000): local white 72.1%; black 15.0%; mulatto 10.0%; US white 2.2%; other 0.7%. **Religious affiliation** (2000): Roman Catholic 74%; Protestant 13%; independent Christian 6%; Jehovah's Witness 2%; nonreligious/atheist 2%; Spiritist 1%; other 2%. **Major metropolitan areas** (2006): San Juan 2,590,824; Aguadilla 333,408; Ponce 263,799; San Germán 144,595; Yauco 123,441. **Location:** island in the Caribbean Sea, east of Cuba.

Vital statistics

Birth rate per 1,000 population (2006): 12.8 (world avg. 20.3). **Death rate** per 1,000 population (2006): 7.7 (world avg. 8.6). **Total fertility rate** (avg. births per childbearing woman; 2005): 1.91. **Life expectancy** at birth (2006): male 74.5 years; female 82.5 years.

National economy

Budget. Revenue (2005): US$12,444,000,000 (tax revenue 60.8%, of which income taxes 44.2%, excise taxes 14.7%; federal grants 26.7%; nontax revenue 12.5%). *Expenditures* (2002): US$10,556,400,000 (2001; welfare 22.3%; education 22.3%; public safety 15.7%; debt service 9.8%; health 9.2%). **Public debt** (December 2005): US$42,449,000,000. **Production** (in metric tons except as noted). *Agriculture, forestry, fishing* (2006): plantains 76,350, bananas 52,200, oranges 18,770; livestock (number of live animals) 376,925 cattle, 48,679 pigs; fisheries production (2005) 2,968 (from aquaculture 14%). *Mining* (2004): crushed stone 8,660. *Manufacturing* (value added in US$'000,000; 2001): chemicals, pharmaceuticals, and allied products 17,365; nonelectrical machinery 3,320; professional and scientific equipment 1,874. *Energy production (consumption):* electricity (kW-hr; 2006) 24,900,000,000 (20,600,000,000); coal (metric tons; 2002) none (176,000); crude petroleum (barrels; 2005) none (70,809,000); petroleum products (metric tons; 2002) 3,001,000 (6,610,000); natural gas (cu m; 2004) none (680,000,000). **Gross national income** (2006): US$58,418,000,000 (US$14,720 per capita). **Population economically active** (2006): total 1,420,000; activity rate of total population 35.9% (participation rates: ages 16 and over 47.8%; female [2002] 42.6%; unemployed [August 2007] 11.9%). **Households** (2002). Average family size 3.6; average annual income per family (2005) US$41,258; sources of income: wages and salaries 49.7%, transfers 30.6%, rent 7.7%, self-employment 6.1%; expenditure (2005): food and beverages 17.1%, health care 16.7%, housing 15.3%, transportation 13.4%, household furnishings 11.5%. **Selected balance of payments data.** Receipts from (US$'000,000): tourism (2006) 3,369. Disbursements for (US$'000,000): tourism (2005) 1,143. **Land use** as % of total land area (2003): in temporary crops 7.8%, in permanent crops 4.7%, in pasture 12.6%; overall forest area (2005) 46.0%.

Foreign trade

Imports (2004–05): US$38,905,200,000 (chemicals 43.9%; electronics 9.4%; petroleum and coal products 7.5%; transport equipment 7.2%). *Major import sources* (2006): US 50.4%; Ireland 18.6%; Japan 4.3%. **Exports** (2004–05): US$56,543,200,000 (pharmaceutical and chemical products 65.7%; electronic and electrical products 12.5%). *Major export destinations* (2006): US 82.6%; The Netherlands 3.9%; Belgium 2.4%.

Transport and communications

Transport. *Railroads* (2004): length 96 km (privately owned railway for sugarcane transport only). *Roads* (2005): total length 25,735 km (paved 95%). *Vehicles*: passenger cars (2001) 2,064,100; trucks and buses (1999) 306,600. *Air transport* (2001): passenger arrivals and departures 9,396,306; cargo loaded and unloaded (Luis Muñoz Marín International Airport only) 215,603 metric tons. **Communications**, in total units (units per 1,000 persons). Daily newspaper circulation (2004): 541,000 (139); televisions (2000): 1,290,000 (338); telephone landlines (2005): 1,038,000 (262); cellular telephone subscribers (2005): 3,354,000 (848); personal computers (2005): 33,000 (8.3); total Internet users (2005): 916,000 (232).

Education and health

Educational attainment (2000). Percentage of population ages 25 and over having: no formal schooling to lower secondary education 25.4%; some upper secondary to some higher 56.3%; undergraduate or graduate degree 18.3%. **Literacy** (2002): total population ages 15 and over literate 94.1%. **Health:** physicians (2001) 7,623 (1 per 504 persons); hospital beds (2002) 12,351 (1 per 312 persons); infant mortality rate (2006) 9.1.

Military

Total active duty US personnel (2006): 198.

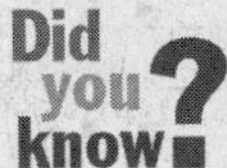

Puerto Rico is a commonwealth in free association with the United States; its residents are US citizens. According to the constitution of 1952, executive power resides in the governor, who is elected directly for a term of four years.

Background

Puerto Rico was inhabited by Arawak Indians when it was settled by the Spanish in the early 16th century. It remained largely undeveloped economically until the late 18th century. After 1830 it gradually developed a plantation economy based on the export crops of sugarcane, coffee, and tobacco. The independence movement began in the late 19th century, and Spain ceded the island to the US in 1898, after the Spanish-American War. In 1917 Puerto Ricans were granted US citizenship, and in 1952 the island became a commonwealth with autonomy in internal affairs. The question of Puerto Rican statehood has been a political issue, with commonwealth status approved by voters in 1967, 1993, and 1998.

Recent Developments

Puerto Rican Gov. Anibal Acevedo Vila was indicted in March 2008 on 19 counts stemming from financial dealings in three political campaigns. He denied the charges of illegal fundraising and election fraud.

Internet resources: <www.gotopuertorico.com>.

Qatar

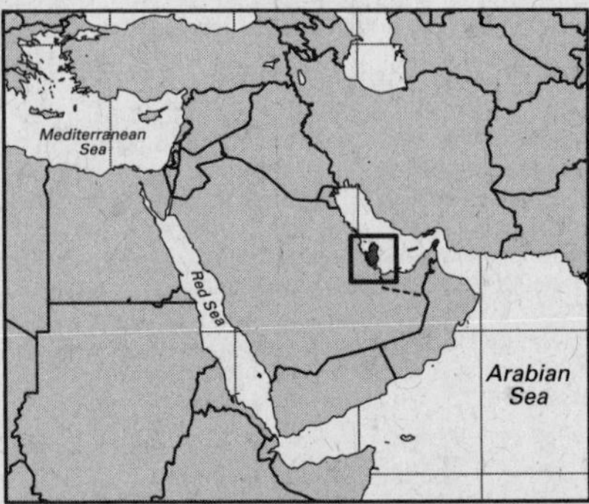

Official name: Dawlat Qatar (State of Qatar). **Form of government:** constitutional emirate; Islamic law is the basis of legislation in the state. **Head of state and government:** Emir Sheikh Hamad ibn Khalifah al-Thani (from 1995), assisted by Prime Minister Sheikh Hamad ibn Jassim ibn Jabr al-Thani (from 2007). **Capital:** Doha. **Official language:** Arabic. **Official religion:** Islam. **Monetary unit:** 1 riyal (QR) = 100 dirhams; valuation (1 Jul 2008) US$1 = QR 3.64.

Demography

Area: 4,184 sq mi, 10,836 sq km. **Population** (2007): 841,000. **Density** (2007): persons per sq mi 201.0, persons per sq km 77.6. **Urban** (2005): 95.4%. **Sex distribution** (2005): male 67.15%; female 32.85%. **Age breakdown** (2005): under 15, 21.8%; 15–29, 25.5%; 30–44, 33.7%; 45–59, 16.3%; 60–74, 2.4%; 75 and over, 0.3%. **Ethnic composition** (2000): Arab 52.5%, of which Palestinian 13.4%, Qatari 13.3%, Lebanese 10.4%, Syrian 9.4%; Persian 16.5%; Indo-Pakistani 15.2%; black African 9.5%; other 6.3%. **Religious affiliation** (2000): Muslim 83%, of which Sunni 73%, Shi'i 10%; Christian 10%, of which Roman Catholic 6%; Hindu 3%; Buddhist 2%; nonreligious 2%. **Major cities** (2004): Al-Dawhah (Doha) 339,847; Al-Rayyan 258,193; Al-Wakrah 26,993; Umm Salal Muhammad 25,413; Al-Khawr 18,036. **Location:** the Middle East, bordering the Persian Gulf and Saudi Arabia.

Vital statistics

Birth rate per 1,000 population (2005): 18.0 (world avg. 20.3). **Death rate** per 1,000 population (2005): 2.1 (world avg. 8.6). **Total fertility rate** (avg. births per childbearing woman; 2005): 2.80. **Life expectancy** at birth (2005): male 74.4 years; female 75.8 years.

National economy

Budget (2005–06). *Revenue:* QR 64,984,000,000 (oil and natural gas revenue 67.1%; investment income 21.9%; other 11.0%). *Expenditures:* QR 50,833,000,000 (current expenditure 64.4%; capital expenditure 35.6%). **Production** (metric tons except as noted). *Agriculture, forestry, fishing* (2005): dates 19,844, tomatoes 5,328, cantaloupes and other melons 4,909; livestock (number of live animals) 152,700 goats, 111,500 sheep, 13,800 camels; fisheries production 13,946. *Mining and quarrying* (2005): limestone 1,000,000; gypsum, sand and gravel, and clay are also produced. *Manufacturing* (value added in QR '000,000; 2005): refined petroleum products 4,502; chemical products 2,168; base metals 1,959. *Energy production (consumption):* electricity (kW-hr; 2005) 14,396,000,000 ([2004] 13,233,000,000); crude petroleum (barrels; 2006) 272,600,000 ([2004] 33,585,000); petroleum products (metric tons; 2004) 11,286,000 (6,131,000); natural gas (cu m; 2005) 43,500,000,000 ([2004] 16,872,000,000). **Households.** Average household size (2004) 7.4; expenditure (2001): housing 17.8%, food and beverages 16.3%, transportation 15.8%, household furnishings 8.6%, clothing and footwear 7.1%. **Population economically active** (2004): total 444,133; activity rate of total population 59.7% (participation rates: ages 15 and over, 77.1%; female 15.1%; unemployed 1.5%). **Gross national income** (2006): US$54,259,000,000 (US$66,060 per capita). **Selected balance of payments data.** Receipts from (US$'000,000): tourism (2005) 760; foreign direct investment (FDI) (2001–05 avg.) 843. Disbursements for (US$'000,000): tourism (2005) 1,759; remittances (2006–07) 5,000; FDI (2001–05 avg.) 108. **Land use** as % of total land area (2003): in temporary crops 1.6%, in permanent crops 0.3%, in pasture 4.5%.

Foreign trade

Imports (2005; c.i.f.): QR 36,621,000,000 (nonelectrical machinery and apparatus 22.3%; road vehicles 14.0%; electrical machinery and apparatus 11.2%; iron and steel 11.0%; chemical products 6.7%). *Major import sources* (2006): Japan 12.0%; US 9.9%; Germany 9.3%; Italy 9.3%; UAE 6.0%. **Exports** (2005): QR 92,234,000,000 (crude petroleum and refined petroleum 55.9%; natural gas 34.4%; manufactured fertilizers 2.7%; plastics 2.4%). *Major export destinations* (2006): Japan 42.0%; South Korea 14.1%; Singapore 9.5%; India 4.9%; UAE 3.9%.

Transport and communications

Transport. *Roads* (1999): total length 1,230 km (paved 90%). *Vehicles* (2004): passenger cars 265,609; trucks and buses 114,115. *Air transport* (2006; Qatar Airways only): passenger-km 24,032,000,000; metric ton-km cargo 888,498,000.

1 metric ton = about 1.1 short tons; 1 kilometer = 0.6 mi (statute); 1 metric ton-km cargo = about 0.68 short ton-mi cargo; c.i.f.: cost, insurance, and freight; f.o.b.: free on board

Communications, in total units (units per 1,000 persons). Daily newspaper circulation (2005): 143,000 (180); televisions (2004): 315,000 (412); telephone landlines (2006): 228,000 (272); cellular telephone subscribers (2006): 920,000 (1,096); personal computers (2005): 145,000 (182); total Internet users (2006): 290,000 (346); broadband Internet subscribers (2006): 47,000 (56).

Education and health

Educational attainment (2004). Percentage of population ages 10 and over having: no formal education/unknown 34.9%, of which illiterate 10.2%; primary 13.0%; preparatory (lower secondary) 16.2%; secondary 20.0%; postsecondary 15.9%. **Literacy** (2004): total population ages 15 and over literate 89.0%; males literate 89.1%; females literate 88.6%. **Health** (2005): physicians (public sector only) 1,657 (1 per 480 persons); hospital beds (public sector only) 1,567 (1 per 508 persons); infant mortality rate per 1,000 live births 9.0.

Military

Total active duty personnel (2006): 12,400 (army 68.6%, navy 14.5%, air force 16.9%); US troops (2006) 430. **Military expenditure as percentage of GDP** (2005): 6.2%; per capita expenditure US$2,751.

Background

Qatar was partly controlled by Bahrain in the 18th and 19th centuries and was part of the Ottoman Empire until World War I. In 1916 it became a British protectorate. Oil was discovered in 1939, and the country rapidly modernized. Qatar declared independence in 1971, when the British protectorate ended. In 1991 it served as a base for air strikes against Iraq in the Persian Gulf War.

Recent Developments

Economic highlights in Qatar in 2007 included the ongoing success of state-owned Qatar Airways, which garnered international awards for superior service, and Qatar National Bank, which again received the highest possible credit rating from the world's leading rating institutions. Qatar's continued meteoric expansion as one of the world's most important producers and exporters of liquefied natural gas and gas-to-liquids fuels, combined with record-high oil revenues, underscored the country's expanded role as a major center of international modernization and project financing, and, increasingly, industrialization and economic integration in the Persian Gulf.

Internet resources: <www.experienceqatar.com>.

Réunion

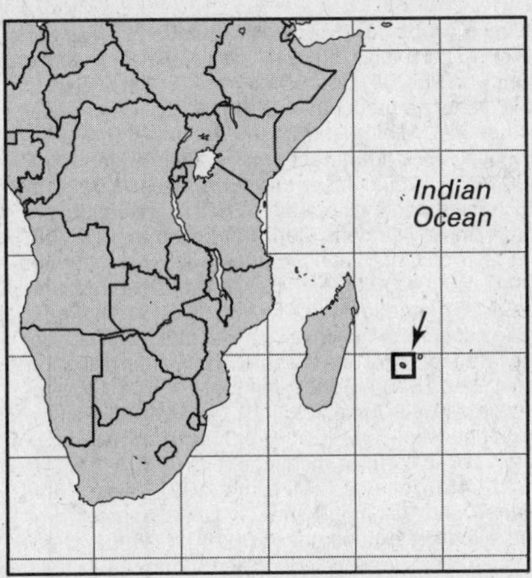

Official name: Département de la Réunion (Department of Réunion). **Political status:** overseas department of France with two legislative houses (General Council [49]; Regional Council [45]). **Chief of state:** French President Nicolas Sarkozy (from 2007). **Head of government:** Prefect Pierre-Henry Maccioni (from 2006). **Capital:** Saint-Denis. **Official language:** French. **Official religion:** none. **Monetary unit:** 1 euro (€) = 100 cents; valuation (1 Jul 2008) US$1 = €0.63 (the euro replaced the French franc [F] 1 Jan 2002, at the rate of €1 = 6.56 F).

Demography

Area: 968 sq mi, 2,507 sq km. **Population** (2007): 799,000. **Density** (2007): persons per sq mi 825.4, persons per sq km 318.7. **Urban** (2005): 92.4%. **Sex distribution** (2003): male 49.12%; female 50.88%. **Age breakdown** (2005): under 15, 27.3%; 15–29, 23.7%; 30–44, 24.1%; 45–59, 15.1%; 60–74, 7.3%; 75–84, 2.0%; 85 and over, 0.5%. **Ethnic composition** (2000): mixed race (black–white–South Asian) 42.6%; local white 25.6%; South Asian 23.0%, of which Tamil 20.0%; Chinese 3.4%; East African 3.4%; Malagasy 1.4%; other 0.6%. **Religious affiliation** (2000): Christian 87.8%, of which Roman Catholic 81.8%, Pentecostal 4.2%; Hindu 4.5%; Muslim 4.2%; nonreligious 1.7%; other 1.8%. **Major cities** (2004; population of commune): Saint-Denis 133,600 (urban agglomeration [2003] 178,000); Saint-Paul 92,500; Saint-Pierre 74,000 (urban agglomeration 140,600); Le Tampon 66,600; Saint-Louis (1999) 43,519. **Location:** island in the western Indian Ocean, east of Madagascar and near Mauritius.

Vital statistics

Birth rate per 1,000 population (2005): 19.0 (world avg. 20.3); within marriage 33.0%. **Death rate** per 1,000 population (2005): 5.6 (world avg. 8.6). **Total fertility rate** (avg. births per childbearing woman; 2005): 2.42. **Life expectancy** at birth (2005): male 72.3 years; female 80.1 years.

National economy

Budget (2003). *Revenue:* €750,000,000 (receipts from the French central government and local administrative bodies 50.0%; indirect taxes 20.0%; direct taxes 9.2%; loans 7.3%). *Expenditures:* €729,000,000 (current expenditures 68.6%; development expenditures 31.4%). **Gross domestic product** (2005): US$14,910,000,000 (US$19,130 per capita). **Production** (metric tons except as noted). *Agriculture, forestry, fishing* (2006): sugarcane 2,000,000, corn (maize) 11,700, pineapples 10,550, geranium essence (2005) 1.9; livestock (number of live animals) 77,118 pigs, 36,210 cattle, 36,141 goats; roundwood (2005) 36,100 cu m, of which fuelwood 86%; fisheries production (2005) 4,757 (from aquaculture 3%). *Mining and quarrying:* gravel and sand for local use. *Manufacturing* (value added in F '000,000; 1997): food and beverages 1,019, of which meat and milk products 268; construction materials (mostly cement) 394; fabricated metals 258. *Energy production (consumption):* electricity (kW-hr; 2004) 1,620,000,000 (1,620,000,000); petroleum products (metric tons; 2005) none (721,000). **Population economically active** (2006): total 321,700; activity rate of total population 40.8% (participation rates: ages 15–64, 60.9%; female [2005] 43.4%; unemployed [April–June 2006] 29.1%). **Households.** Average household size (2004) 3.0; average annual income per capita of household (2003) €11,446 (US$14,456); sources of income (1997): wages and salaries and self-employment 41.8%, transfer payments 41.3%; expenditure (2001): housing and energy 24.0%, transportation and communications 20.0%, food and beverages 17.0%, recreation and culture 10.0%. **Selected balance of payments data.** Receipts from (US$'000,000): tourism (2005) 384. **Land use** as % of total land area (2003): in temporary crops 14%, in permanent crops 2%, in pasture 5%; overall forest area (2005) 34%.

Foreign trade

Imports (2006): €3,911,679,000 (machinery and equipment 18.4%; food and agricultural products 16.2%; transport equipment 13.2%; mineral fuels 12.1%; chemicals and chemical products 10.9%). *Major import sources:* France 42.2%; Singapore 8.6%; China 4.0%; Germany 3.8%; Italy 3.2%. **Exports** (2006): €238,039,000 (food products 69.8%, of which sugar 41.0%; machinery and apparatus 9.3%; transportation equipment and parts 7.6%). *Major export destinations:* France 59.6%; Mayotte 8.0%; Japan 5.3%; Madagascar 5.2%; Mauritius 3.0%.

Transport and communications

Transport. *Roads* (2001): total length 1,214 km (paved [1991] 79%). *Vehicles* (1999): passenger cars 190,300; trucks and buses 44,300. *Air transport* (Air Austral only): passenger-km (2006) 2,859,000,000; metric ton-km cargo (2005) 48,547,000. **Communications,** in total units (units per 1,000 persons). Daily newspaper circulation (2005): 74,000 (95); televisions (2002): 138,000 (185); telephone landlines (2001): 300,000 (410); cellular telephone subscribers (2004): 579,000 (753); personal computers (2004): 278,000 (351); total Internet users (2005): 220,000 (282); broadband Internet subscribers (2004): 57,000 (74).

Education and health

Educational attainment (1999). Percentage of population ages 25 and over having: no formal schooling through incomplete secondary education 83.0%; complete secondary 7.4%; some higher 3.9%; complete higher 5.7%. **Literacy** (2003): total population ages 15 and over literate 88.9%; males literate 87.0%; females literate 90.8%. **Health** (2005): physicians 1,902 (1 per 413 persons); hospital beds 2,674 (1 per 295 persons); infant mortality rate per 1,000 live births (2004) 6.8.

Military

Total active duty personnel (2004): 3,600 French army and navy personnel.

Background

The island of Réunion was settled in the 17th century by the French, who brought slaves from eastern Africa to work on coffee and sugar plantations there. It was a French colony until 1946, when it became an overseas territory of France. Its economy is based almost entirely on the export of sugar.

Recent Developments

Réunion's economy rebounded in 2007 from the effects of an outbreak of chikungunya, a usually nonfatal viral disease spread by mosquitoes. In 2007, 380,500 tourists visited the island, a 36.5% increase from the year before.

Internet resources: <www.la-reunion-tourisme.com>.

Romania

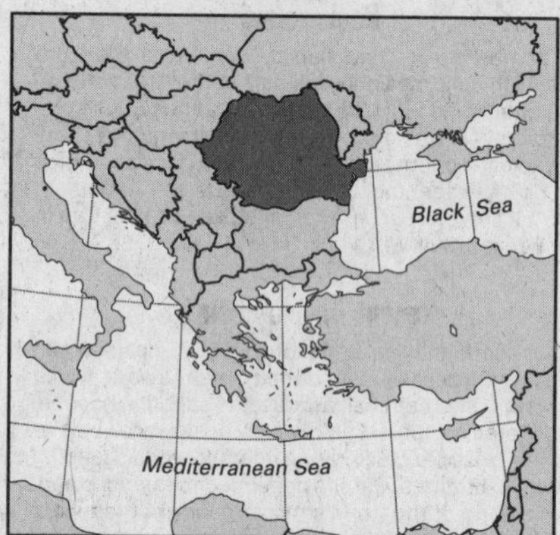

Official name: Romania. **Form of government:** unitary republic with two legislative houses (Senate [137]; Assembly of Deputies [332]). **Chief of state:** President Traian Basescu (from 2004). **Head of government:** Prime Minister Calin Popescu Tariceanu (from 2004). **Capital:** Bucharest. **Official language:** Romanian. **Official religion:** none. **Monetary unit:** 1 Romanian (new) leu (plural lei) = 100 bani; valuation (1 Jul 2008) US$1 = 2.30 (new) lei (the leu was re-denominated 1 Jul 2005, at the rate of 1 [new] leu [RON] = 10,000 [old] lei [ROL]).

Demography

Area: 92,043 sq mi, 238,391 sq km. **Population** (2007): 21,549,000. **Density** (2007): persons per sq mi 234.1, persons per sq km 90.4. **Urban** (2005): 53.7%. **Sex distribution** (2005): male 48.71%; female 51.29%. **Age breakdown** (2005): under 15, 15.7%; 15–29, 23.8%; 30–44, 21.5%; 45–59, 19.7%; 60–74, 13.8%; 75–84, 4.8%; 85 and over, 0.7%. **Ethnic composition** (2002): Romanian 89.5%; Hungarian 6.6%; Rom (Gypsy) 2.5%; Ukrainian 0.3%; German 0.3%; other 0.8%. **Religious affiliation** (2002): Romanian Orthodox 86.7%; Protestant 6.3%; Roman Catholic 4.7%; Greek Catholic 0.9%; Muslim 0.3%; other 1.1%. **Major cities** (2004): Bucharest 1,927,559; Iasi 317,812; Constanta 307,447; Timisoara 307,265; Galati 298,941. **Location:** southeastern Europe, bordering Ukraine, Moldova, the Black Sea, Bulgaria, Serbia, and Hungary.

Vital statistics

Birth rate per 1,000 population (2006): 10.2 (world avg. 20.3); (2005) within marriage 71.5%. **Death rate** per 1,000 population (2006): 12.0 (world avg. 8.6). **Total fertility rate** (avg. births per childbearing woman; 2005): 1.32. **Life expectancy** at birth (2005): male 68.2 years; female 75.4 years.

National economy

Budget (in ROL '000,000,000,000; 2004). *Revenue:* 322.0 (VAT 35.0%; excise tax 24.7%; tax on profits 20.0%). *Expenditures:* 340.7 (economic affairs 26.7%; social assistance 14.0%; police 11.9%; defense 10.5%). **Public debt** (external, outstanding; 2005): US$13,341,000,000. **Population economically active** (2006): total 10,041,600; activity rate of total population 46.5% (participation rates: ages 15–64, 63.7%; female 45.0%; unemployed 7.3%). **Households.** Average household size (2003) 2.8; average annual income per household (2004) ROL 130,295,388 (US$3,992); sources of income (2003): wages and salaries 44.8%, nonmonetary equivalent for consumption of own agricultural produce 23.4%, transfers 19.2%; expenditure (2004): food and nonalcoholic beverages 46.4%; housing and energy 14.7%; clothing and footwear 6.3%. **Production** (metric tons). *Agriculture* (2005): corn (maize) 10,388,000, wheat 7,341,000, potatoes 3,739,000, sunflower seed 1,341,000; livestock (number of live animals) 7,425,000 sheep, 6,495,000 pigs, 2,808,000 cattle; roundwood 14,501,000 cu m, of which fuelwood 20%; fisheries production 13,352 (from aquaculture 55%). *Mining* (2005): copper (metal content) 14,868; zinc (metal content) 13,784; lead (metal content) 11,610. *Manufacturing* (value added in US$'000,000; 2004): wearing apparel 1,015; iron and steel 883; food products 782. *Energy production (consumption):* electricity (kW-hr; 2006) 61,829,000,000 ([2004] 55,321,000,000); hard coal (metric tons; 2004) negligible (3,025,000); lignite (metric tons; 2006) 32,400,000 ([2004] 32,600,000); crude petroleum (barrels; 2006) 35,900,000 ([2004] 94,100,000); petroleum products (metric tons; 2004) 11,512,000 (8,705,000); natural gas (cu m; 2006) 10,231,000,000 ([2004] 16,269,000,000). **Gross national income** (2006): US$118,368,000,000 (US$5,500 per capita). **Selected balance of payments data.** Receipts from (US$'000,000): tourism (2005) 1,044; remittances (2006) 4,733; foreign direct investment (FDI) (2001–05 avg.) 3,484. Disbursements for (US$'000,000): tourism (2005) 878; remittances (2006) 34; FDI (2001–05 avg.) 19. **Land use** as % of total land area (2003): in temporary crops 40.8%, in permanent crops 2.0%, in pasture 21.6%; overall forest area (2005) 27.7%.

Foreign trade

Imports (2004; f.o.b. in trading partners and c.i.f. in commodities): US$32,664,000,000 (chemicals and chemical products 10.4%; textile yarn and fabrics 10.2%; nonelectrical machinery 10.0%; road vehicles 8.0%; electrical machinery 7.8%; petroleum [all forms] 7.2%). *Major import sources* (2005): Italy 15.5%; Germany 14.0%; Russia 8.3%; France 6.8%; Turkey 4.9%. **Exports** (2004): US$23,485,000,000 (clothing and accessories 20.1%; iron and steel 9.2%; electrical machinery and parts 7.9%; nonelectrical machinery and parts 7.1%; footwear 6.4%; petroleum products 6.1%). *Major export destinations* (2005): Italy 19.4%; Germany 14.0%; Turkey 7.9%; France 7.4%; UK 5.5%.

Transport and communications

Transport. *Railroads* (2004): route length (2003) 11,053 km; passenger-km 8,638,000,000; metric ton-km cargo 17,022,000,000. *Roads* (2004; public roads only): length 79,454 km (paved 26%). *Vehicles* (2004): cars 3,225,367; trucks and buses 525,617. *Air transport* (2006; TAROM, Carpatair, Blue Air, and Romavia airlines only): passenger-km 2,306,000,000; metric ton-km cargo 4,981,000. **Communications,** in total units (units per 1,000 persons). Daily newspaper circulation (2004): 1,148,000 (53); televisions (2003): 15,150,000 (697); telephone landlines (2006): 4,204,000 (195); cellular telephone subscribers (2006): 17,400,000 (806); personal computers (2005): 2,800,000 (129); total Internet users (2006): 7,000,000 (324); broadband Internet subscribers (2006): 1,769,000 (82).

Education and health

Educational attainment (2002). Percentage of population ages 10 and over having: no formal schooling 5.5%; primary education 20.1%; lower secondary 27.6%; upper secondary/vocational 36.7%; higher vocational 3.0%; university 7.1%. **Literacy** (2004): total population ages 15 and over literate 97.3%; males literate 98.4%; females literate 96.3%. **Health** (2004): physicians 48,150 (1 per 450 persons); hospital beds 142,029 (1 per 153 persons); infant mortality rate per 1,000 live births (2005) 15.0.

Military

Total active duty personnel (2006): 69,600 (army 59.3%, navy 10.5%, air force 15.1%, other 15.1%). **Military expenditure as percentage of GDP** (2005): 2.0%; per capita expenditure US$90.

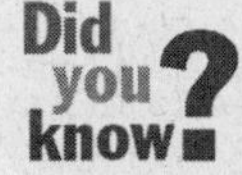

The Transylvanian Alps are a mountainous region of south-central Romania. It consists of that section of the Carpathian Mountain arc from the Prahova River valley (east) to the gap in which flow the Timis and Cerna rivers.

Background

Romania was formed in 1862 by the unification of the principalities Moldavia and Walachia, which had once been part of the ancient country of Dacia. During World War I, Romania sided with the Allies and doubled its territory in 1918 with the addition of Transylvania, Bukovina, and Bessarabia. Allied with Germany in World War II, it was occupied by Soviet troops in 1944 and became a satellite country of the USSR in 1948. During the 1960s Romania's foreign policy was frequently independent of the Soviet Union's. The communist regime of Nicolae Ceausescu was overthrown in 1989, and free elections were held in 1990. Throughout the 1990s Romania struggled with rampant corruption and organized crime as it tried to stabilize its economy.

Recent Developments

Romania joined the European Union on 1 Jan 2007. With its membership came both benefits and difficulties. The country's GDP grew 17.5% in 2007, and its industrial output increased by 5.4%. The rate of registered unemployment dropped from 5.2% in 2006 to 4.1%, and the average monthly wage increased as well. Relations with neighboring Moldova, the poorest country in Europe and until World War II a part of Romania, remained strained. After Romania's entrance into the EU, hundreds of thousands of Moldovans, eager for better financial opportunities, took advantage of existing Romanian laws to apply for joint Romanian-Moldovan citizenship. Moldova accused Romania of attempting to undermine its national security by luring away its people, while Romania, which itself was the poorest member of the EU, struggled with the social and economic costs of an influx in population.

Internet resources: <www.romaniatourism.com>.

Russia

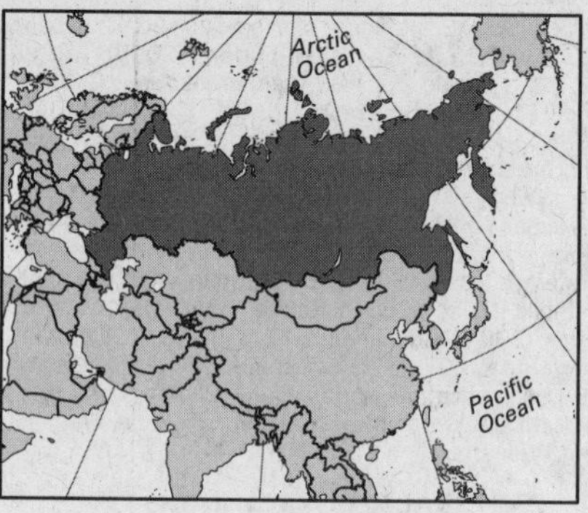

Official name: Rossiyskaya Federatsiya (Russian Federation). **Form of government:** federal multiparty republic with two legislative houses (Federation Council [172]; State Duma [450]). **Head of state:** President Dmitry Medvedev (from 2008). **Head of government:** Prime Minister Vladimir Putin (from 2008). **Capital:** Moscow. **Official language:** Russian. **Official religion:** none. **Monetary unit:** 1 ruble (RUB) = 100 kopecks; valuation (1 Jul 2008) market rate, US$1 = RUB 23.42.

Demography

Area: 6,592,800 sq mi, 17,075,400 sq km. **Population** (2007): 141,378,000. **Density** (2007): persons per sq mi 21.4, persons per sq km 8.3. **Urban** (2006): urban 73.0%. **Sex distribution** (2004): male 46.49%; female 53.51%. **Age breakdown** (2005): under 15, 14.9%; 15–29, 24.7%; 30–44, 21.5%; 45–59, 21.9%; 60–69, 8.4%; 70 and over, 8.6%. **Ethnic composition** (2002): Russian 79.82%; Tatar 3.83%; Ukrainian 2.03%; Bashkir 1.15%; Chuvash 1.13%; Chechen 0.94%; Armenian 0.78%; Mordvin 0.58%; Belarusian 0.56%; Avar 0.52%; Kazakh 0.45%; Udmurt 0.44%; Azerbaijani 0.43%; Mari 0.42%; German 0.41%; Kabardinian 0.36%; Ossetian 0.35%; Dargin 0.35%; Buryat 0.31%; Sakha 0.31%; other 4.83%. **Religious affiliation** (2005): Christian 58.4%, of which Russian Orthodox 53.1%, Roman Catholic 1.0%, Ukrainian Orthodox 0.9%, Protestant 0.9%; Muslim 8.2%; traditional beliefs 0.8%; Jewish 0.6%; nonreligious 25.8%; atheist 5.0%; other 1.2%. **Major cities** (2005): Moscow 10,425,075; St. Petersburg 4,580,620; Novosibirsk 1,397,015; Yekaterinburg 1,308,441; Nizhny Novgorod 1,283,553; Samara 1,143,346; Omsk 1,138,822; Kazan 1,112,673; Chelyabinsk 1,092,958; Rostov-na-Donu 1,054,865. **Location:** eastern Europe and northern Asia, bordering the Arctic Ocean, the Pacific Ocean, North Korea, China, Mongolia, Kazakhstan, the Caspian Sea, Azerbaijan, Georgia, the Black Sea, Ukraine, Belarus, Latvia, Estonia, Finland, and Norway; the exclave of Kaliningrad on the Baltic Sea borders Lithuania and Poland. **Migration** (2006): immigrants 186,380; emigrants 54,061. **Refugees** (2002): 828,784, of which from Kazakhstan 301,137, Uzbekistan 106,299, Tajikistan 86,041, Georgia 62,868. **Households** (2004). Total households 51,209,000; average household size 2.8; distribution by size (1995): 1 person 19.2%; 2 persons 26.2%; 3 persons 22.6%; 4 persons 20.5%; 5 persons or more 11.5%.

Vital statistics

Birth rate per 1,000 population (2006): 10.3 (world avg. 20.3); (2005) within marriage 70.0%. **Death rate** per 1,000 population (2006): 15.2 (world avg. 8.6). **Natural increase rate** per 1,000 population (2006): −4.9 (world avg. 11.7). **Total fertility rate** (avg. births per childbearing woman; 2006): 1.38. **Life expectancy** at birth (2005): male 58.9 years; female 72.4 years.

Social indicators

Educational attainment (2002). Percentage of population ages 15 and over having: no formal schooling 2.1%; primary education 7.7%; some secondary 18.1%; complete secondary/basic vocational 53.0%; incomplete higher 3.1%; complete higher 16.0%, of which advanced degrees 0.3%. **Quality of working**

life (2006). Average workweek (2004) 40 hours. Annual rate per 100,000 workers of: injury or accident 290; industrial illness 16.0; death 11.8. Average working days lost to labor strikes per 1,000 employees 0.2. **Social participation.** Trade union membership in total workforce (2003) 45%. **Social deviance.** Offense rate per 100,000 population (2006) for: murder and attempted murder 19.4; rape and attempted rape 6.3; serious injury 36.2; theft 1,180.4. Incidence per 100,000 population of: alcoholism (1992) 1,727.5; substance abuse (2000) 25.6; suicide (2006) 30.0. **Material well-being** (2002). Durable goods possessed per 100 households: automobiles 27; personal computers 7; television receivers 126; refrigerators and freezers 113; washing machines 93; VCRs 50; motorcycles 26; bicycles 71.

National economy

Public debt (external, outstanding; 2005): US$75,359,000,000. **Budget** (2006). *Revenue:* RUB 6,276,300,000,000 (VAT 24.1%; taxes on natural resources 17.8%; corporate taxes 8.1%; single social tax 5.0%). *Expenditures:* RUB 4,281,300,000,000 (transfers 21.4%; defense 15.9%; social and cultural services 14.4%; law enforcement 12.9%; debt service 3.9%). **Gross national income** (2006): US$956,557,000,000 (US$6,679 per capita). **Production** (metric tons except as noted). *Agriculture, forestry, fishing* (2006): wheat 45,006,300, potatoes 38,572,640, sugar beets 30,861,230, barley 18,153,550, sunflower seeds 6,752,860, oats 4,880,270, cabbages 4,073,240, corn (maize) 3,668,560, rye 2,965,060, tomatoes 2,414,860, carrots and turnips 1,918,370, onions 1,788,750, apples 1,617,000, cucumbers 1,423,210, peas 1,157,640; livestock (number of live animals) 21,473,926 cattle, 16,074,449 sheep, 13,454,876 pigs; roundwood (2005) 186,500,000 cu m, of which fuelwood 25%; fisheries production (2005) 3,305,698 (from aquaculture 3%); aquatic plants production (2005) 50,507. *Mining and quarrying* (2005): nickel (metal content) 315,000 (world rank: 1); mica 101,500 (world rank: 1); platinum-group metals 123,000 (world rank: 2); gem diamonds 21,400,000 carats (world rank: 2); industrial diamonds 10,400,000 carats (world rank: 3); vanadium (metal content) 9,000 (world rank: 3); iron ore (metal content; 2004) 56,200,000 (world rank: 5); cobalt 5,000 (world rank: 5); copper ore (metal content) 675,000 (world rank: 6); gold 165,000 kg (world rank: 6); tin (metal content) 3,000 (world rank: 7); molybdenum (metal content) 3,000 (world rank: 7). *Manufacturing* (value added in US$'000,000; 2004): refined petroleum products 14,329; iron and steel 11,801; food products 8,933; chemicals and chemical products 7,709; nonferrous base metals 7,600; beverages 4,446; transportation equipment 4,255; general purpose machinery 3,369; cement, bricks, and ceramics 3,266; fabricated metal products 1,949; wood products (excluding furniture) 1,922; printing and publishing 1,648; paper products 1,508; textiles and wearing apparel 1,374; rubber products 1,359; electrical equipment 1,165; tobacco products 1,055. *Energy production (consumption):* electricity (kW-hr; 2006–07) 989,017,000,000 ([2005] 940,000,000,000); hard coal (metric tons; 2006–07) 237,700,000 ([2004] 144,978,000); lignite (metric tons; 2006–07) 70,300,000 ([2004] 75,460,000); crude petroleum (barrels; 2006–07) 3,482,900,000 ([2005] 1,022,000,000); petroleum products (metric tons; 2004) 175,486,000 (94,312,000); natural gas (cu m; 2006–07) 865,524,000,000 ([2005] 402,100,000,000). **Population economically active** (2006): total 74,146,000; activity rate of total population 52.0% (participation rates: ages 15–64, 73.0%; female 49.4%; unemployed 7.2%). **Land use** as % of total land area (2003): in temporary crops 7.5%, in permanent crops 0.1%, in pasture 5.6%; overall forest area (2005) 47.9%. **Households.** Average household size (2004) 2.8; income per household: RUB 52,400 (US$1,692); sources of monetary income (2006): wages 66.4%, transfers 13.2%, self-employment 11.2%, property income 7.2%; expenditure (2002): food 41.7%, clothing 13.3%, housing 6.2%, furniture and household appliances 5.7%, alcohol and tobacco 3.2%. **Selected balance of payments data.** Receipts from (US$'000,000): tourism (2005) 5,466; remittances (2006) 3,308; foreign direct investment (FDI) (2001–05 avg.) 8,842. Disbursements for (US$'000,000): tourism (2005) 17,804; remittances (2006) 11,438; FDI (2001–05 avg.) 8,541.

Foreign trade

Imports (2006; c.i.f.): US$137,548,000,000 (machinery, apparatus, and transportation equipment 47.7%; chemicals and chemical products 15.8%; food, beverages, and tobacco 15.7%; nonferrous metals and iron and steel 7.7%). *Major import sources:* Germany 13.4%; China 9.4%; Ukraine 6.7%; Japan 5.7%; Belarus 5.0%; US 4.7%; France 4.3%; Italy 4.2%; Kazakhstan 2.8%. **Exports** (2006; f.o.b.): US$301,976,000,000 (fuels and lubricants 65.9%; nonferrous metals and iron and steel 16.4%; machinery, apparatus, and transportation equipment 5.8%; chemicals and chemical products 5.6%). *Major export destinations:* The Netherlands 11.9%; Italy 8.3%; Germany 8.1%; China 5.2%; Ukraine 5.0%; Turkey 4.8%; Belarus 4.3%; Switzerland 4.0%; Poland 3.8%; UK 3.4%.

Transport and communications

Transport. *Railroads* (2005): length (2006) 85,000 km; passenger-km 171,600,000,000; metric ton-km cargo 1,858,000,000,000. *Roads* (2006): total length 854,000 km (paved 85%). *Vehicles* (2002): passenger cars 22,342,000; trucks and buses (1999) 5,021,000. *Air transport* (2006–07): passenger-km 97,510,000,000; metric ton-km cargo 2,980,000,000. **Communications,** in total units (units per 1,000 persons). Daily newspaper circulation (2004): 15,075,000 (105); televisions (2003): 50,599,000 (351); telephone landlines (2005): 40,100,000 (281); cellular telephone subscribers (2005): 120,000,000 (840); personal computers (2005): 17,400,000 (121); total Internet users (2006): 25,689,000 (181); broadband Internet subscribers (2006): 2,900,000 (20).

Education and health

Health (2005): physicians 690,000 (1 per 206 persons); hospital beds 1,575,000 (1 per 90 persons); infant mortality rate per 1,000 live births (2006) 10.2. **Food** (2005): daily per capita caloric intake 3,363 (vegetable products 79%, animal products 21%); 170% of FAO recommended minimum.

Military

Total active duty personnel (2006): 1,027,000 (army 38.5%, navy 13.8%, air force 15.6%, strategic deterrent forces 7.8%, command and support 24.3%); an additional 415,000 personnel in paramilitary forces include railway troops, special construction troops, federal border guards, interior troops, and other federal guard units. **Military expenditure as percentage of GDP** (2005): 4.1%; per capita expenditure US$217.

Background

The region between the Dniester and Volga rivers was inhabited from ancient times by various peoples, including the Slavs. The area was overrun from the 8th century BC to the 6th century AD by successive nomadic peoples, including the Sythians, Sarmatians, Goths, Huns, and Avars. Kievan Rus, a confederation of principalities ruled from Kiev, emerged c. the 10th century. It lost supremacy in the 11th and 12th centuries to independent principalities, including Novgorod and Vladimir. Novgorod ascended in the north and was the only Russian principality to escape the domination of the Mongol Golden Horde in the 13th century. In the 14th–15th centuries the princes of Moscow gradually overthrew the Mongols. Under Ivan IV, Russia began to expand. The Romanov dynasty arose in 1613. Expansion continued under Peter I (the Great) and Catherine II (the Great). The area was invaded by Napoleon in 1812; after his defeat, Russia received most of the grand duchy of Warsaw (1815). Russia annexed Georgia, Armenia, and other Caucasus territories in the 19th century. The Russian southward advance against the Ottoman Empire was of key importance to Europe. Russia was defeated in the Crimean War. It sold Alaska to the US in 1867. Russia's defeat in the Russo-Japanese War led to an unsuccessful uprising in 1905. In World War I it fought against the Central Powers.

The Russian Revolution that overthrew the czarist regime in 1917 marked the beginning of a government of soviets (councils). The Bolsheviks brought the main part of the former empire under communist control and organized it as the Russian Soviet Federated Socialist Republic (RSFSR; coextensive with present-day Russia). The Russian SFSR joined other soviet republics in 1922 to form the USSR. Although it fought with the Allies in World War II, after the war tensions with the West led to the decades-long Cold War.

Upon the dissolution of the USSR in 1991, the Russian SFSR was renamed Russia and became the leading member of the Commonwealth of Independent States. It adopted a new constitution in 1993. During the 1990s it struggled on several fronts, beset with economic difficulties, political corruption, and independence movements. Vladimir Putin was elected president in 2000, with economic reform, governmental reorganization, cutbacks in the military, and rooting out corruption and favoritism as his chief goals.

Recent Developments

Russian Pres. Vladimir Putin, *Time* magazine's 2007 Person of the Year, was constitutionally barred from running for a third consecutive presidential term in 2008. However, in March 2008 First Deputy Prime Minister Dmitry Medvedev, a Putin protégé, won election to succeed him and immediately asked Putin to take the post of prime minister. Many feared that this spelled the continuation of Putin's hold on power in Russia.

Russia in 2007 recorded its ninth year of strong economic growth. The economy grew 8.1% in 2007, and there were large budget surpluses accompanied by high and rising foreign-exchange reserves. Russia's overall foreign debt remained modest. High world oil prices and a relatively cheap ruble played key roles in this economic resurgence. Living standards improved, wages rose, and both unemployment and the population living below the official poverty line declined.

International concern grew over the reliability of Russia, which held massive petroleum reserves and one-third of the world's natural gas reserves, as an energy supplier. In early 2007 Russia briefly suspended crude oil deliveries to Belarus after a dispute in which Gazprom, the state natural gas company, insisted Belarus accept a large increase in the price of Russian gas. In October Gazprom also threatened to cut gas supplies to Ukraine in what some interpreted as a political move following the return to power in Kiev of a Western-leaning administration, and in March 2008 it briefly did cut deliveries before the two sides agreed on a debt-repayment plan.

Relations between Russia and the US grew increasingly strained as the year wore on. Russia strongly objected to US plans to install antimissile defenses in Poland and the Czech Republic, arguing that the installations would undermine Russian national security. In August 2008, Georgian troops entered South Ossetia, and Russia responded by invading. Several weeks of fighting and Russian occupation ensued, leaving hundreds dead. Russia withdrew most of its forces to the two separatist regions of South Ossetia and Abkhazia by the end of the month, but on 26 August Moscow recognized the independence of both.

Internet resources: <www.russia-tourism.ru>.

Rwanda

Official name: Repubulika y'u Rwanda (Rwanda); République Rwandaise (French); Republic of Rwanda (English). **Form of government:** multiparty republic with two legislative bodies (Senate [26]; Chamber of Deputies [80]). **Head of state and government:** President Maj. Gen. Paul Kagame (from 2000), assisted by Prime Minister Bernard Makuza (from 2000). **Capital:** Kigali. **Official languages:** Rwanda; French; English. **Official religion:** none. **Monetary unit:** 1 Rwanda franc (RF); valuation (1 Jul 2008) US$1 = RF 540.61.

Demography

Area: 10,185 sq mi, 26,379 sq km. **Population** (2007): 9,725,000. **Density** (2007): persons per sq mi 995.0, persons per sq km 384.2. **Urban** (2006): 23.6%. **Sex distribution** (2005): male 48.16%; female 51.84%. **Age breakdown** (2005): under 15, 43.5%; 15–29, 32.0%; 30–44, 13.4%; 45–59, 7.4%; 60–74, 2.9%; 75–84, 0.7%; 85 and over, 0.1%. **Ethnic composition** (2002): Hutu 85%; Tutsi 14%; Twa 1%. **Religious affiliation** (2005): Roman Catholic 44%; Protestant 25%; Muslim 13%; other 18%. **Major cities** (2002): Kigali (2003) 656,153; Gitarama 84,669; Butare 77,449; Ruhengeri 71,511; Gisenyi

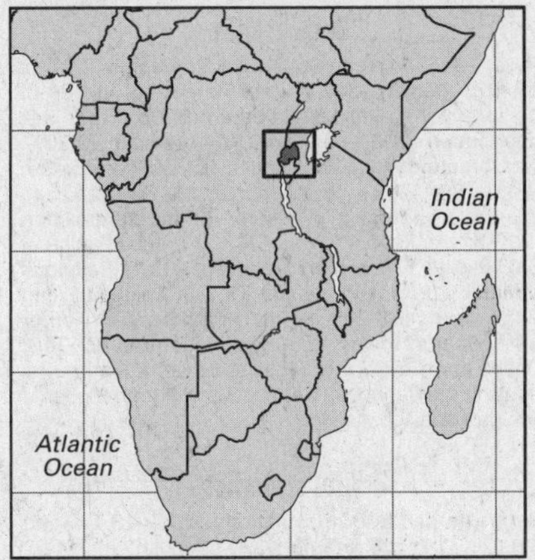

67,766. **Location:** east-central Africa, bordering Uganda, Tanzania, Burundi, and the Democratic Republic of the Congo.

Vital statistics

Birth rate per 1,000 population (2006): 40.3 (world avg. 20.3). **Death rate** per 1,000 population (2006): 15.4 (world avg. 8.6). **Natural increase rate** per 1,000 population (2006): 24.9 (world avg. 11.7). **Total fertility rate** (avg. births per childbearing woman; 2006): 5.43. **Life expectancy** at birth (2006): male 47.2 years; female 49.3 years.

National economy

Budget (2004). *Revenue:* RF 271,900,000,000 (grants 46.2%; taxes on goods and services 25.8%; income tax 13.5%; import and export duties 9.7%). *Expenditures:* RF 253,300,000,000 (current expenditures 64.7%, of which wages 13.1%, defense 9.4%, debt payment 4.7%; capital expenditure 35.3%). **Public debt** (external, outstanding; 2005): US$1,420,000,000. **Production** (metric tons except as noted). *Agriculture, forestry, fishing* (2006): plantains 2,653,000, potatoes 1,285,000, sweet potatoes 777,000; livestock (number of live animals) 1,339,740 goats, 1,004,100 cattle, 464,330 sheep; roundwood (2005) 5,495,000 cu m, of which fuelwood 91%; fisheries production (2005) 8,186 (from aquaculture 5%). *Mining and quarrying* (2005): cassiterite (tin content) 700; tungsten (wolframite content) 200; niobium 80,000 kg. *Manufacturing* (value added in RF '000,000; 2002): food products, beverages, and tobacco products 61,073; cement, bricks, and ceramics 4,326; chemicals and chemical products 3,201. *Energy production (consumption):* electricity (kW-hr; 2004) 173,000,000 (283,000,000); petroleum products (metric tons; 2004) none (169,000); natural gas (cu m; 2004) 179,000 (179,000). **Population economically active** (2002): total 3,418,047; activity rate of total population 42.0% (participation rates: ages 6 and over 52.1%; female 55.2%; officially unemployed 0.9%). **Land use** as % of total land area (2003): in temporary crops 48.6%, in permanent crops 10.9%, in pasture 18.8%; overall forest area (2005) 19.5%. **Households.** Average household size (2004) 3.4; expenditure (2003): food and nonalcoholic beverages 37.1%, housing and energy 15.8%, transportation 9.9%, household furnishings 7.6%. **Gross national income** (2006): US$2,295,000,000 (US$242 per capita). **Selected balance of payments data.** Receipts from (US$'000,000): tourism (2004) 44; remittances (2006) 21; foreign direct investment (2001–05 avg.) 5.6; official development assistance (2005) 576. Disbursements for (US$'000,000): tourism (2004) 31; remittances (2006) 35.

Foreign trade

Imports (2005): US$354,180,000 (intermediate goods 31.4%; capital goods 31.0%; energy products 22.1%; food 10.0%). *Major import sources* (2002): Kenya 21.9%; Germany 8.4%; Belgium 7.9%; Israel 4.3%; US 3.5%. **Exports** (2005): US$124,980,000 (coffee 30.6%; tea 19.5%; pyrethrum extract 16.2%; tin 14.3%; tantalite 13.5%; gold 3.8%). *Major export destinations* (2002): Indonesia 30.8%; Germany 14.6%; Hong Kong 8.9%; South Africa 5.5%.

Transport and communications

Transport. *Roads* (2004): total length 14,008 km (paved 19%). *Vehicles* (2000): passenger cars 10,726; trucks 15,828. *Air transport* (2000; Kigali airport only): passengers embarked and disembarked 101,000; cargo loaded and unloaded 4,300 metric tons. **Communications,** in total units (units per 1,000 persons). Televisions (2004): 70,000 (7.4); telephone landlines (2006): 17,000 (1.8); cellular telephone subscribers (2006): 314,000 (34); personal computers (2005): 19,000 (2.1); total Internet users (2006): 65,000 (7); broadband Internet subscribers (2006): 1,700 (0.2).

Education and health

Educational attainment (2000). Percentage of population ages 25 and over having: no formal education/unknown 45.5%; incomplete primary education 30.1%; complete primary 14.4%; secondary 9.1%; higher 0.9%. **Literacy** (2006): percentage of total population ages 15 and over literate 64.9%; males literate 71.4%; females literate 59.8%. **Health:** physicians (2005) 450 (1 per 19,054 persons); infant mortality rate per 1,000 live births (2006) 87.2. **Food** (2005): daily per capita caloric intake 1,936 (vegetable products 96%, animal products 4%); 111% of FAO recommended minimum.

Military

Total active duty personnel (2006): 35,000 (army 91.4%, air force 2.9%, national police 5.7%). **Military expenditure as percentage of GDP** (2005): 2.9%; per capita expenditure US$7.

Background

Originally inhabited by the Twa, a Pygmy people, Rwanda became home to the Hutu, who were well established there when the Tutsi appeared in the 14th century. The Tutsi conquered the Hutu and in the 15th century founded a kingdom near Kigali. The Belgians occupied Rwanda in 1916, and the League of Nations created Ruanda-Urundi as a Belgian mandate in 1923. The Tutsi retained their dominance until shortly before Rwanda reached independence in 1962, when the Hutu took control of the government and stripped the Tutsi of much of their land. Many Tutsi fled Rwanda, and the Hutu dominated the country's political system, waging sporadic civil wars until mid-1994, when the death of the country's leader in a plane crash—apparently shot down—led to massive violence. The Tutsi-led Rwandan Patriotic Front (FPR) took over the country by force after the massacre of almost 500,000 Tutsi by Hutu. Two million refugees, mostly Hutu, fled to neighboring countries after the FPR's victory.

Recent Developments

Genocide and its aftermath continued to dominate Rwandan domestic and foreign policy in 2007. In February about 8,000 prisoners accused of war crimes, many of them sick or elderly, were released because of prison congestion and calls for greater efforts toward reconciliation. In April Pres. Paul Kagame pardoned former president Pasteur Bizimungu, who had served just under 3 years of his 15-year prison sentence for setting up a militia, inciting ethnic violence, and committing financial fraud. In June the parliament abolished the death penalty, an important step in the country's efforts to extradite genocide suspects from European countries that had hitherto refused such requests because they objected to capital punishment.

Internet resources: <www.rwandatourism.com>.

Saint Kitts and Nevis

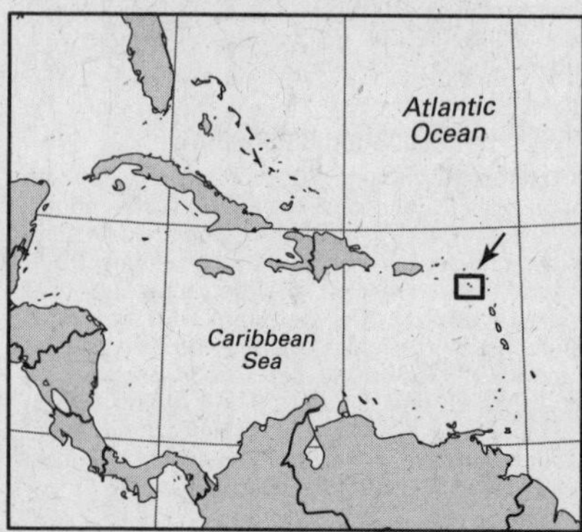

Official name: Federation of Saint Kitts and Nevis. **Form of government:** federated constitutional monarchy with one legislative house (National Assembly [15]). **Chief of state:** British Queen Elizabeth II (from 1952), represented by Governor-General Sir Cuthbert Sebastian (from 1996). **Head of government:** Prime Minister Denzil Douglas (from 1995). **Capital:** Basseterre. **Official language:** English. **Official religion:** none. **Monetary unit:** 1 Eastern Caribbean dollar (EC$) = 100 cents; valuation (1 Jul 2008) US$1 = EC$2.70.

Demography

Area: 104.0 sq mi, 269.4 sq km. **Population** (2007): 50,400. **Density** (2007): persons per sq mi 484.6, persons per sq km 187.1. **Urban** (2005): 33%. **Sex distribution** (2001): male 49.70%; female 50.30%. **Age breakdown** (2000): under 15, 30.7%; 15–29, 26.5%; 30–44, 21.1%; 45–59, 10.8%; 60–74, 6.1%; 75–84, 2.9%; 85 and over, 1.9%. **Ethnic composition** (2000): black 90.4%; mulatto 5.0%; Indo-Pakistani 3.0%; white 1.0%; other/unspecified 0.6%. **Religious affiliation** (2005): Protestant 75%, of which Anglican 24%, Methodist 23%; Roman Catholic 11%; other 14%. **Major towns** (2006): Basseterre 12,900; Charlestown 1,500; St. Paul's 1,200. **Location:** islands in the Caribbean Sea, between Puerto Rico and Trinidad and Tobago.

Vital statistics

Birth rate per 1,000 population (2005): 18.1 (world avg. 20.3). **Death rate** per 1,000 population (2005): 8.5 (world avg. 8.6). **Total fertility rate** (avg. births per childbearing woman; 2005): 2.33. **Life expectancy** at birth (2005): male 69.3 years; female 75.2 years.

National economy

Budget (2006). *Revenue:* EC$524,600,000 (tax revenue 71.3%, of which taxes on international trade 33.6%, taxes on domestic goods and services 17.3%, company taxes 12.7%; nontax revenue 22.4%; grants 5.2%; other 1.1%). *Expenditures:* EC$551,200,000 (current expenditure 86.0%, of which interest payments 19.1%; development expenditure 14.0%). **Production** (metric tons except as noted). *Agriculture, forestry, fishing* (2005): sugarcane 100,000, tropical fruit 1,300, coconuts 1,000; livestock (number of live animals) 16,000 goats, 12,500 sheep, 4,800 cattle; fisheries production 450. *Mining and quarrying:* excavation of sand and crushed stone for local use. *Manufacturing* (2003): raw sugar 22,000; carbonated beverages (2002) 32,000 hectoliters; beer (2002) 20,000 hectoliters; other manufactures include electronic components, garments, and cement. *Energy production (consumption):* electricity (kW-hr; 2004) 130,000,000 (130,000,000); petroleum products (metric tons; 2004) none (41,000). **Gross national income** (2006): US$453,000,000 (US$9,110 per capita). **Households.** Average household size (2001) 2.9; average annual income per wage earner (1994) EC$9,940 (US$3,681); expenditure (2001): food, beverages, and tobacco 28.8%, education 19.3%, health 14.1%, housing 13.0%, clothing and footwear 9.3%, fuel and light 4.4%. **Public debt** (external, outstanding; 2005): US$299,300,000. **Population economically active** (1995): total 18,170; activity rate of total population 41.7% (participation rates [1991]: ages 15–64, 70.5%; female 44.4%). **Selected balance of payments data.** Receipts from (US$'000,000): tourism (2005) 107; remittances (2006) 3; foreign direct investment (2001–05 avg.) 70; official development assistance (2005) 12 (commitments). Disbursements for (US$'000,000): tourism (2005) 11; remittances (2006) 2. **Land use** as % of total land area (2003): in temporary crops

19%, in permanent crops 3%, in pasture 6%; overall forest area (2005) 15%.

Foreign trade

Imports (2003; c.i.f.): US$204,800,000 (machinery and apparatus 22.0%; food 13.6%; refined petroleum 8.1%; chemicals and chemical products 6.9%; transport equipment 6.6%). *Major import sources:* US 53.3%; Trinidad and Tobago 12.9%; Canada 9.2%; UK 9.1%; Japan 3.2%. **Exports** (2003): US$48,300,000 (electrical switches and capacitors 73.1%; raw sugar 14.9%). *Major export destinations:* US 78.5%; UK 17.0%; Netherlands Antilles 1.2%.

Transport and communications

Transport. *Railroads* (2003): length 58 km. *Roads* (2002): total length 383 km (paved [2001] 44%). *Vehicles* (2002): passenger cars 6,900; trucks and buses 2,500. *Air transport* (2001; Saint Kitts airport only): passenger arrivals 135,237, passenger departures 134,937; cargo handled 1,802 metric tons. **Communications,** in total units (units per 1,000 persons). Televisions (2001): 11,000 (239); telephone landlines (2004): 25,000 (513); cellular telephone subscribers (2004): 10,000 (205); personal computers (2004): 11,000 (226); total Internet users (2002): 10,000 (214); broadband Internet subscribers (2002): 500 (11).

Education and health

Educational attainment (1991). Percentage of population ages 25 and over having: no formal schooling/unknown 6.8%; primary education 45.9%; secondary 38.4%; higher 8.9%. **Literacy** (2004): total population ages 15 and over literate 97.8%. **Health** (2005): physicians 62 (1 per 796 persons); hospital beds 247 (1 per 200 persons); infant mortality rate per 1,000 live births 14.5.

Military

Total active duty personnel: the defense force includes coast guard and police units.

Background

Saint Kitts became the first British colony in the West Indies in 1623. Anglo-French rivalry grew in the 17th century and lasted more than a century. In 1783, by the Treaty of Versailles, the islands became wholly British possessions. They were united with Anguilla from 1882 to 1980 but became an independent federation within the British Commonwealth in 1983. In 1997 Nevis considered becoming independent.

Recent Developments

Foreign citizenship held by members of the Saint Kitts and Nevis government became an issue in August 2007 when it was alleged that those who fell into that category were in violation of the constitution. At least four members of the National Assembly, including Dwyer Astaphan, the national security minister, were identified as having dual citizenship.

Internet resources: <www.stkittstourism.com>.

Saint Lucia

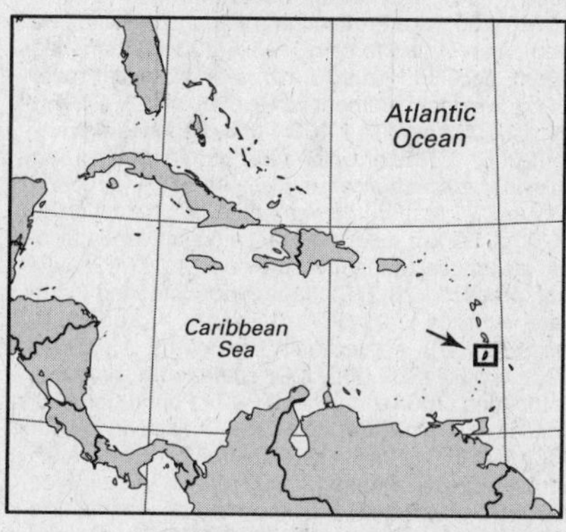

Official name: Saint Lucia. **Form of government:** constitutional monarchy with two legislative houses (Senate [11]; House of Assembly [17]). **Chief of state:** British Queen Elizabeth II (from 1952), represented by Governor-General Dame Pearlette Louisy (from 1997). **Head of government:** Prime Minister Stephenson King (from 2007). **Capital:** Castries. **Official language:** English. **Official religion:** none. **Monetary unit:** 1 Eastern Caribbean dollar (EC$) = 100 cents; valuation (1 Jul 2008) US$1 = EC$2.70.

Demography

Area: 238 sq mi, 617 sq km. **Population** (2007): 168,000. **Density** (2007): persons per sq mi 705.9, persons per sq km 272.3. **Urban** (2005): 28.0%. **Sex distribution** (2005): male 48.91%; female 51.09%. **Age breakdown** (2005): under 15, 28.4%; 15–29, 28.4%; 30–44, 21.5%; 45–59, 12.3%; 60–74, 6.5%; 75 and over, 2.9%. **Ethnic composition** (2000): black 50%; mulatto 44%; East Indian 3%; white 1%; other 2%. **Religious affiliation** (2001): Roman Catholic 67.5%; Protestant 22.0%, of which Seventh-day Adventist 8.4%, Pentecostal 5.6%; Rastafarian 2.1%; nonreligious 4.5%; other/unknown 3.9%. **Major towns** (2004): Castries (2001) 10,634 (urban area 37,962); Vieux Fort 4,900; Micoud 4,000; Soufrière 3,600. **Location:** island between the Caribbean Sea and North Atlantic Ocean, north of Trinidad and Tobago.

Vital statistics

Birth rate per 1,000 population (2005): 15.1 (world avg. 20.3); within marriage 15.0%. **Death rate** per 1,000 population (2005): 7.2 (world avg. 8.6). **Total fertility rate** (avg. births per childbearing woman; 2005): 2.21. **Life expectancy** at birth (2005): male 70.0 years; female 77.4 years.

National economy

Budget (2005). *Revenue:* EC$575,700,000 (tax revenue 93.9%, of which taxes, duties, and service charges on imports 47.7%, taxes on domestic goods and services 15.5%, taxes on company profits 10.5%; nontax revenue 6.1%). *Expenditures:* EC$663,200,000 (current expenditures 74.9%, of which interest payments 10.6%; development expenditures 25.1%). **Public debt** (external, outstanding; 2005): US$248,900,000. **Production** (metric tons except as noted). *Agriculture, forestry, fishing* (2004): bananas 42,326, coconuts 14,000, citrus and tropical fruits 7,500; livestock (number of live animals) 14,950 pigs, 12,500 sheep, 12,400 cattle; fisheries production (2005) 1,386, of which tuna 33.6%. *Mining and quarrying:* excavation of sand for local construction and pumice. *Manufacturing* (value of production in EC$'000; 2005): food, beverages (significantly alcoholic beverages), and tobacco products 78,002; electrical products 28,279; paper products and cardboard boxes 21,567. *Energy production (consumption):* electricity (kW-hr; 2004) 309,000,000 (309,000,000); petroleum products (metric tons; 2004) none (119,000). **Population economically active** (2004): total 80,600; activity rate of total population 49.7% (participation rates: ages 15 and over 68.6%; female [2000] 47.2%; unemployed [2005] 17.0%). **Households.** Average household size (2001) 3.2; expenditure (1984): food 46.8%; housing 13.5%; clothing and footwear 6.5%; transportation and communication 6.3%. **Gross national income** (2006): US$872,000,000 (US$5,349 per capita). **Selected balance of payments data.** Receipts from (US$'000,000): tourism (2005) 345; remittances (2004) 26; foreign direct investment (2001–05 avg.) 86; official development assistance (2005) 36 (commitments). Disbursements for (US$'000,000): tourism (2005) 40; remittances (2004) 3.6. **Land use** as % of total land area (2000): in temporary crops 7%, in permanent crops 23%, in pasture 3%; overall forest area 15%.

Foreign trade

Imports (2004; c.i.f.): US$430,800,000 (machinery and transport equipment 19.3%; food 18.8%; mineral fuels 17.2%; chemicals and chemical products 7.5%). *Major import sources:* US 35.1%; Trinidad and Tobago 14.2%; UK 7.7%; Japan 3.3%; Barbados 3.3%. **Exports** (2004): US$103,145,000 (reexports 46.0%, of which mineral fuels 30.6%; domestic exports 43.8%, of which bananas 19.5%, beverages (significantly beer) and tobacco products 11.4%; ships' stores and bunkers 10.2%). *Major export destinations:* UK 46.0%; Trinidad and Tobago 11.8%; Barbados 10.4%; US 9.2%; Dominica 8.4%.

Transport and communications

Transport. *Roads* (1999): total length 1,210 km (paved 5%). *Vehicles* (2001): passenger cars 22,453; trucks and buses 8,972. *Air transport* (2001; Castries and Vieux Fort airports only): passenger arrivals and departures 679,000; cargo unloaded and loaded 3,500 metric tons. **Communications,** in total units (units per 1,000 persons). Televisions (2001): 46,000 (291); telephone landlines (2002): 51,000 (336); cellular telephone subscribers (2005): 106,000 (657); personal computers (2004): 26,000 (173); total Internet users (2004): 55,000 (339).

Education and health

Educational attainment (2004). Percentage of population ages 15 and over having: no formal schooling/unknown 9.8%; incomplete primary education 7.4%; complete primary 45.0%; secondary 28.6%; higher vocational 6.2%; university 3.0%. **Literacy** (2000): 90.2%. **Health** (2002): physicians 92 (1 per 1,740 persons); hospital beds 285 (1 per 562 persons); infant mortality rate per 1,000 live births (2005) 18.9.

Military

Total active duty personnel (2004): a 300-member police force includes a specially trained paramilitary unit and a coast guard unit.

Background

Caribs replaced early Arawak inhabitants on the island c. AD 800–1300. Settled by the French in 1650, it was ceded to Great Britain in 1814 and became one of the Windward Islands in 1871. It became fully independent as Saint Lucia in 1979. The economy is based on agriculture and tourism.

Recent Developments

The United Workers Party (UWP) government in April 2007 made the controversial decision to reestablish diplomatic relations with Taiwan, much to the annoyance of China. The former Saint Lucia Labour Party government had switched diplomatic recognition to China in the mid-1990s, after a postindependence period during which Taiwan was the preferred choice. The UWP insisted that it could recognize both Beijing and Taiwan, but a Chinese spokesman rejected this option.

Internet resources: <www.stlucia.org>.

Saint Vincent and the Grenadines

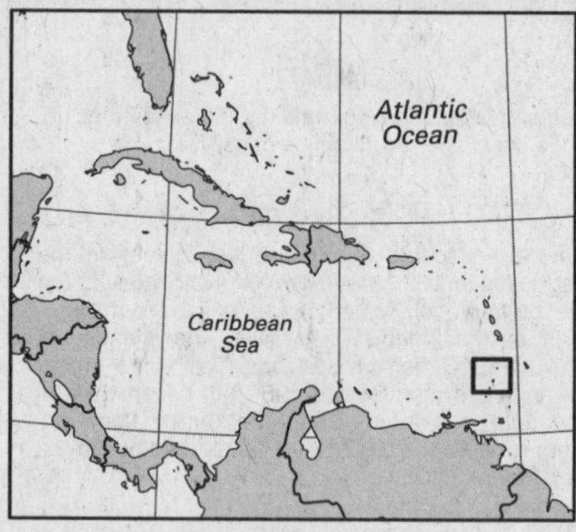

Official name: Saint Vincent and the Grenadines. **Form of government:** constitutional monarchy with one legislative house (House of Assembly [22]). **Chief of state:** British Queen Elizabeth II (from 1952), represented by Governor-General Sir Frederick Ballantyne (from 2002). **Head of government:** Prime Minister Ralph Gonsalves (from 2001). **Capital:** Kingstown.

1 metric ton = about 1.1 short tons; 1 kilometer = 0.6 mi (statute); 1 metric ton-km cargo = about 0.68 short ton-mi cargo; c.i.f.: cost, insurance, and freight; f.o.b.: free on board

Official language: English. **Official religion:** none. **Monetary unit:** 1 Eastern Caribbean dollar (EC$) = 100 cents; valuation (1 Jul 2008) US$1 = EC$2.70.

Demography

Area: 150.3 sq mi, 389.3 sq km. **Population** (2007): 106,000. **Density** (2007): persons per sq mi 705.3, persons per sq km 272.3. **Urban** (2006): 46.3%. **Sex distribution** (2005): male 50.85%; female 49.15%. **Age breakdown** (2005): under 15, 27.1%; 15–29, 30.0%; 30–44, 22.1%; 45–59, 12.1%; 60–74, 5.8%; 75 and over, 2.9%. **Ethnic composition** (1999): black 65.5%; mulatto 23.5%; Indo-Pakistani 5.5%; white 3.5%; black-Amerindian 2.0%. **Religious affiliation** (2000): Protestant 47.0%; unaffiliated Christian 20.3%; independent Christian 11.7%; Roman Catholic 8.8%; Hindu 3.4%; Spiritist 1.8%; Muslim 1.5%; nonreligious 2.3%; other 3.2%. **Major cities** (2004): Kingstown 13,044; Georgetown 1,700; Byera 1,400; Barrouallie 1,400. **Location:** islands in the Caribbean Sea, north of Trinidad and Tobago.

Vital statistics

Birth rate per 1,000 population (2006): 20.0 (world avg. 20.3); (2003) within marriage 15.6%. **Death rate** per 1,000 population (2006): 6.7 (world avg. 8.6). **Total fertility rate** (avg. births per childbearing woman; 2006): 2.20. **Life expectancy** at birth (2006): male 69.0 years; female 74.6 years.

National economy

Budget (2006). *Revenue:* EC$399,240,000 (tax revenue 90.6%, of which taxes on international trade and transactions 40.6%, income tax 12.4%, corporate taxes 10.9%, stamp duty 9.6%; nontax revenue 9.4%). *Expenditures:* EC$456,740,000 (current expenditure 77.8%, of which wages and salaries 37.5%; development expenditure 22.2%). **Production** (metric tons except as noted). *Agriculture, forestry, fishing* (2005): bananas 50,000, sugarcane 20,000, starchy roots and tubers (significantly eddoes and dasheens) 13,945; livestock (number of live animals) 12,000 sheep, 9,150 pigs, 7,200 goats; fisheries production 2,745. *Mining and quarrying:* sand and gravel for local use. *Manufacturing* (value added in EC$'000,000; 2000): beverages and tobacco products 17.4; food 15.6; paper products and publishing 3.6. *Energy production (consumption):* electricity (kW-hr; 2005) 132,000,000 ([2004] 110,000,000); petroleum products (metric tons; 2004) none (65,000). **Selected balance of payments data.** Receipts from (US$'000,000): tourism (2006) 113; remittances (2006) 5.0; foreign direct investment (2001–05 avg.) 42; official development assistance (2005) 7.4 (commitments). Disbursements for (US$'000,000): tourism (2005) 14; remittances (2006) 2.0. **Gross national income** (2006): US$424,000,000 (US$3,537 per capita). **Public debt** (external, outstanding; 2005): US$248,300,000. **Population economically active** (2006): total 58,000; activity rate of total population 48.3% (participation rates: ages 15–64, 75.3%; female 41.4%; unemployed [2004] 12.0%). **Households.** Average household size (1991) 3.9; income per household (1988) EC$4,579 (US$1,696); expenditure (2001): food and beverages 53.6%; housing and energy 12.8%; clothing and footwear 8.9%. **Land use** as % of total land area (2003): in temporary crops 18%, in permanent crops 18%, in pasture 5%; overall forest area (2005) 27%.

Foreign trade

Imports (2004; c.i.f.): US$226,290,000 (machinery and transport equipment 22.7%; food products 18.8%; mineral fuels 11.4%; chemicals and chemical products 8.4%). *Major import sources:* US 36.5%; Caricom (Caribbean Community and Common Market) countries 28.9%, of which Trinidad and Tobago 21.7%, Barbados 3.9%; UK 10.4%; Japan 3.7%. **Exports** (2004; f.o.b.): US$36,030,000 (domestic exports 90.3%, of which bananas 36.2%, packaged flour 13.6%, packaged rice 7.5%, eddoes and dasheens 6.1%; reexports 9.7%). *Major export destinations:* Caricom countries 58.5%, of which Barbados 13.3%, St. Lucia 11.7%, Trinidad and Tobago 10.0%; UK 34.1%; US 5.1%.

Transport and communications

Transport. *Roads* (2004): total length 829 km (paved 70%). *Vehicles* (2003): passenger cars 12,196; trucks and buses 4,447. *Air transport* (2003): passenger arrivals 133,769; passenger departures 137,899. **Communications,** in total units (units per 1,000 persons). Televisions (2000): 50,000 (446); telephone landlines (2006): 23,000 (218); cellular telephone subscribers (2006): 88,000 (834); personal computers (2005): 16,000 (152); total Internet users (2005): 10,000 (102); broadband Internet subscribers (2006): 5,600 (53).

Education and health

Educational attainment (2001). Percentage of employed population having: no formal schooling/unknown 1.7%; primary education 55.6%; secondary 27.3%; higher vocational 15.1%; university 0.3%. **Literacy** (2004): total population ages 15 and over literate 88.1%. **Health** (2005): physicians 72 (1 per 1,458 persons); hospital beds 472 (1 per 222 persons); infant mortality rate per 1,000 live births 15.7. **Food** (2005): daily per capita caloric intake 2,623 (vegetable products 79%, animal products 21%); 138% of FAO recommended minimum.

Military

Total active duty personnel (2006): no regular military forces; the paramilitary includes coast guard and police units.

Background

The French and the British contested for control of Saint Vincent and the Grenadines until 1763, when it was ceded to England by the Treaty of Paris. The original inhabitants, the Caribs, recognized British sovereignty but revolted in 1795. Most of the Caribs were deported; many who remained were killed in volcanic eruptions in 1812 and 1902. In 1969 Saint Vincent and the Grenadines became a self-governing state in association with the United Kingdom, and in 1979 it achieved full independence.

Recent Developments

In June 2007 Prime Minister Ralph Gonsalves defended the growing assistance provided by Cuba and Venezuela. He stressed that Saint Vincent and the Grenadines was also pursuing closer relations with Taiwan, Turkey, and Brazil and insisted that a small state had to take advantage of all opportunities for links with larger countries.

Internet resources: <www.svgtourism.com>.

Samoa

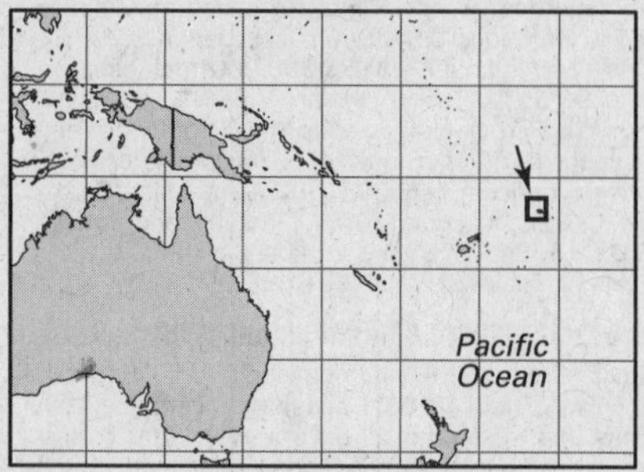

Official name: Malo Sa'oloto Tuto'atasi o Samoa (Samoan); Independent State of Samoa (English). **Form of government:** mix of parliamentary democracy and constitutional monarchy with one legislative house (Legislative Assembly [49]). **Chief of state:** Head of State Tuiatua Tupua Tamasese Efi (from 2007). **Head of government:** Prime Minister Tuila'epa Sa'ilele Malielegaoi (from 1998). **Capital:** Apia. **Official languages:** Samoan; English. **Official religion:** none. **Monetary unit:** 1 tala (plural tala; SAT) = 100 sene; valuation (1 Jul 2008) US$1 = SAT 2.51.

Demography

Area: 1,093 sq mi, 2,831 sq km. **Population** (2007): 180,000. **Density** (2007): persons per sq mi 164.7, persons per sq km 63.6. **Urban** (2006): 20.8%. **Sex distribution** (2006): male 51.88%; female 48.12%. **Age breakdown** (2001): under 15, 40.7%; 15–29, 25.5%; 30–44, 17.8%; 45–59, 9.3%; 60–74, 5.0%; 75–84, 1.3%; 85 and over, 0.2%; unknown 0.2%. **Ethnic composition** (2000): Samoan (Polynesian) 88.1%; Euronesian (European and Polynesian) 10.1%; European and US white 1.2%; other 0.6%. **Religious affiliation** (2001): Congregational 34.8%; Roman Catholic 19.6%; Methodist 15.0%; Mormon 12.7%; Assemblies of God 6.6%; other Christian 9.6%; other/unknown 1.7%. **Major towns** (2006): Apia 37,237 (urban agglomeration 60,702); Vaitele 6,294; Faleasi'u 3,548; Vailele 3,174; Le'auva'a 3,015. **Location:** group of islands in the South Pacific Ocean, about halfway between Hawaii (US) and New Zealand.

Vital statistics

Birth rate per 1,000 population (2005): 27.1 (world avg. 20.3). **Death rate** per 1,000 population (2005): 5.6 (world avg. 8.6). **Natural increase rate** per 1,000 population (2005): 21.5 (world avg. 11.7). **Total fertility rate** (avg. births per childbearing woman; 2005): 4.17. **Life expectancy** at birth (2005): male 67.8 years; female 74.2 years.

National economy

Budget (2005–06). *Revenue:* SAT 387,200,000 (tax revenue 70.5%, of which VAT 28.0%, excise taxes 17.8%, income tax 12.2%; grants 18.6%; nontax revenue 10.9%). *Expenditures:* SAT 391,700,000 (current expenditure 72.0%, of which general services 22.9%, economic services 14.4%, education 14.1%, health 12.1%; development expenditure 22.0%; net lending 6.0%). **Production** (metric tons except as noted). *Agriculture, forestry, fishing* (2005): coconuts 152,826, bananas 24,275, taro 17,000; livestock (number of live animals) 201,000 pigs, 29,000 cattle, 450,000 chickens; roundwood 131,000 cu m, of which fuelwood 53%; fisheries production 4,501. *Manufacturing* (value of manufactured exports in SAT '000; 2006–07): beer 3,520; noni (fruit known locally as *nonu;* also known as Indian mulberry) juice 3,130; coconut cream 2,130. *Energy production (consumption):* electricity (kW-hr; 2006) 113,000,000 (90,000,000); petroleum products (metric tons; 2004) none (49,000). **Households.** Average household size (2004) 7.2; sources of income (1997): wages and salaries 44%, other 56%; expenditure (2002): food 50.3%, transportation and communications 14.4%, alcohol and tobacco products 12.2%, household furnishings and operation 11.1%. **Population economically active** (2003): total 64,000; activity rate of total population 35% (participation rates: ages 15–64, 63%; female 32%). **Public debt** (external, outstanding; 2005): US$177,000,000. **Gross national income** (2006): US$409,000,000 (US$2,210 per capita). **Selected balance of payments data.** Receipts from (US$'000,000): tourism (2006–07) 86; remittances (2006–07) 119; foreign direct disinvestment (2001–05 avg.) −2.6; official development assistance (2005) 44. Disbursements for (US$'000,000): tourism (2005) 13; remittances (2005) 11. **Land use** as % of total land area (2003): in temporary crops 21.2%, in permanent crops 24.4%, in pasture 0.7%; overall forest area (2005) 60.4%.

Foreign trade

Imports (2005–06; c.i.f.): SAT 549,500,000 (petroleum products 19.0%; unspecified 81.0%). *Major import sources:* New Zealand 29.3%; Australia 18.8%; US 10.6%; Fiji 7.0%; China 5.3%. **Exports** (2005–06; f.o.b.): SAT 29,600,000 (fresh fish 42.8%; beer 14.6%; coconut cream 7.6%; taro 2.0%). *Major export destinations:* American Samoa 49.1%; US 32.6%; New Zealand 9.4%; Australia 3.4%; Japan 3.1%.

Transport and communications

Transport. *Roads* (2001): total length 2,337 km (paved 14%). *Vehicles* (2005): passenger cars 4,638; trucks and buses 4,894. *Air transport* (2004; Polynesian Airlines only): passenger-km 326,090,000; metric ton-km cargo 2,709,000. **Communications,** in total units (units per 1,000 persons). Daily newspaper circulation (2005): 4,500 (25); televisions (2003): 27,000 (152); telephone landlines (2005): 19,000 (106); cellular telephone subscribers (2005): 24,000 (134); personal computers (2005): 4,000 (22); total Internet users (2006): 8,000 (45); broadband Internet subscribers (2005): 100 (0.5).

1 metric ton = about 1.1 short tons; 1 kilometer = 0.6 mi (statute); 1 metric ton-km cargo = about 0.68 short ton-mi cargo; c.i.f.: cost, insurance, and freight; f.o.b.: free on board

Education and health

Educational attainment (2002). Percentage of population ages 25 and over having: no formal schooling 1.8%; incomplete/complete primary education 32.4%; incomplete/complete secondary 55.4%; higher 10.4%. **Literacy** (2003): total population ages 16 and over literate: virtually 100%. **Health** (2005): physicians 50 (1 per 3,570 persons); hospital beds 229 (1 per 780 persons); infant mortality rate per 1,000 live births 27.7. **Food** (2005): daily per capita caloric intake 3,605 (vegetable products 76%, animal products 24%); 193% of FAO recommended minimum.

Military

No military forces are maintained; informal defense ties exist with New Zealand per 1962 Treaty of Friendship.

Background

Polynesians inhabited the islands of the Samoan archipelago for thousands of years before they were visited by Europeans in the 18th century. Control of the islands was contested by the US, Britain, and Germany until 1899, when they were divided between the US and Germany. In 1914 Western Samoa was occupied by New Zealand, which received it as a League of Nations mandate in 1920. After World War II, it became a UN trust territory administered by New Zealand, and it achieved independence in 1962. In 1997 the word Western was dropped from the country's name.

Recent Developments

The Samoan government continued its economic and institutional restructuring programs and was rewarded with low inflation and stable external debt in 2007. The economy grew about 6%, due in part to increased returns from fishing, agriculture, tourism, and manufacturing. The UN Economic and Social Council removed Samoa from its list of least developed countries. The government remained dependent, however, on remittances from some 200,000 Samoans living abroad.

Internet resources: <www.visitsamoa.ws>.

San Marino

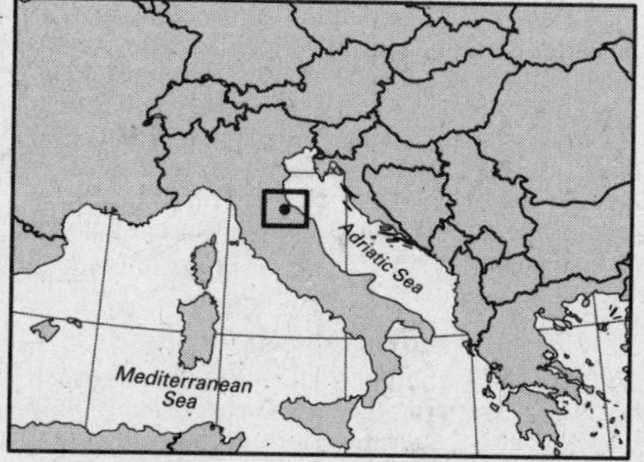

Official name: Repubblica di San Marino (Republic of San Marino). **Form of government:** unitary multiparty republic with one legislative house (Great and General Council [60]). **Heads of state and government:** two captains-regent who serve six-month terms beginning in April and October. **Capital:** San Marino. **Official language:** Italian. **Official religion:** none. **Monetary unit:** 1 euro (€) = 100 cents; valuation (1 Jul 2008) US$1 = €0.63.

Demography

Area: 23.63 sq mi, 61.20 sq km. **Population** (2007): 30,500. **Density** (2007): persons per sq mi 1,291, persons per sq km 498.4. **Urban** (2005): 96%. **Sex distribution** (2007): male 49.16%; female 50.84%. **Age breakdown** (2004): under 15, 15.3%; 15–29, 16.1%; 30–44, 27.3%; 45–59, 19.6%; 60–74, 14.1%; 75–84, 6.0%; 85 and over, 1.6%. **Ethnic composition** (2002): Sammarinesi 85.7%; Italian 13.0%; other 1.3%. **Religious affiliation** (2000): Roman Catholic 88.7%; other Christian 3.5%; nonreligious 5.1%; other 2.7%. **Major municipalities** (2007): Serravalle 9,908; Borgo Maggiore 6,082; San Marino 4,402. **Location:** southern Europe, completely surrounded by Italy.

Vital statistics

Birth rate per 1,000 population (2005): 9.5 (world avg. 20.3); within marriage 90.1%. **Death rate** per 1,000 population (2005): 7.3 (world avg. 8.6). **Natural increase rate** per 1,000 population (2005): 2.2 (world avg. 11.7). **Total fertility rate** (avg. births per childbearing woman; 2005): 1.11. **Life expectancy** at birth (2006): male 79.4 years; female 85.1 years.

National economy

Budget (2003). *Revenue:* €288,000,000 (direct taxes 34.7%; import taxes 33.0%; nontax revenue 22.0%). *Expenditures:* €272,400,000 (current expenditures 92.0%; capital expenditures 8.0%). **Public debt** (2003): US$52,900,000. **Tourism:** number of tourist arrivals (2006) 2,135,589. **Population economically active** (2006): total 21,272; activity rate of total population 70.4% (participation rates: ages 15–64 [2002] 72.1%; female 42.1%; unemployed 3.3%). **Households.** Average household size (2002) 2.5; expenditure (2004): food and beverages 22.0%, housing 13.8%, transportation 10.6%, vacation and recreation 10.1%, restaurants 9.3%. **Production** (metric tons except as noted). *Agriculture, forestry, fishing* (2005): small amounts of wheat, grapes, and barley; livestock (number of live animals) 991 cattle, 91 sheep, 32 pigs. *Quarrying:* building stone is an important export product. *Manufacturing* (2005): processed meats 283,674 kg, of which beef 270,616 kg, veal 8,549 kg, pork 3,615 kg; cheese 56,610 kg; butter 8,110 kg; other major products include electrical appliances, musical instruments, printing ink, paint, cosmetics, furniture, floor tiles, gold and silver jewelry, clothing, and postage stamps. *Energy production (consumption):* all electrical power is imported via electrical grid from Italy (kW-hr; consumption [2004] 212,000,000); natural gas (cu m; 2004) none (56,000,000). **Gross national income** (at 2006 market prices): US$1,257,000,000 (US$41,044 per capita). **Land use** as % of total land area (2003): in temporary crops 17%; overall forest (2005) 2%.

Foreign trade

Imports (2005): US$2,582,000,000 (manufactured goods of all kinds, petroleum products, natural gas, electricity, and gold). *Major import source* (2004): significantly Italy. **Exports** (2005): US$2,531,000,000 (goods include electronics, postage stamps, leather products, ceramics, wine, wood products, and building stone). *Major export destinations* (2004): Italy 90%.

Transport and communications

Transport. *Roads* (2001): total length 252 km. *Vehicles* (2005): passenger cars 32,263; trucks and buses 3,262. *Air transport:* a heliport provides passenger and cargo service between San Marino and Rimini, Italy, during the summer months. **Communications,** in total units (units per 1,000 persons). Televisions (2003): 25,000 (893); telephone landlines (2006): 21,000 (696); cellular telephone subscribers (2006): 17,000 (576); personal computers (2003): 23,000 (819); total Internet users (2006): 15,000 (510); broadband Internet subscribers (2006): 1,500 (50).

Education and health

Educational attainment (2002). Percentage of population ages 14 and over having: basic literacy or primary education 41.0%; some secondary 25.0%; secondary 27.0%; higher degree 7.0%. **Literacy** (2001): total population ages 15 and over literate 98.7%; males literate 98.9%; females literate 98.4%. **Health** (2002): physicians 117 (1 per 230 persons); hospital beds 134 (1 per 191 persons); infant mortality rate per 1,000 live births (2004) 3.4.

Military

Total active duty personnel (2006): defense is the responsibility of Italy.

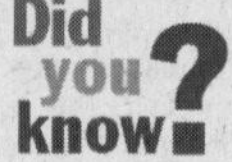

San Marino is a small republic situated on the slopes of Mount Titano, on the Adriatic side of central Italy between the Romagna and the Marche regions and surrounded on all sides by Italy.

Background

According to tradition, San Marino was founded in the early 4th century AD by St. Marinus. By the 12th century it had developed into a commune and remained independent despite challenges from neighboring rulers, including the Malatesta family in nearby Rimini, Italy. San Marino survived the Renaissance as a relic of the self-governing Italian city-state and remained an independent republic after the unification of Italy in 1861. It is one of the smallest republics in the world, and it may be the oldest one in Europe.

Recent Developments

The economy of San Marino was strong overall; the IMF reported in April 2007 that GDP growth in 2006 was about 5%, with unemployment hovering at about 2%. Some economic experts suggested further growth potential because San Marino would make an attractive location for the head offices of multinational enterprises, which could be enticed to relocate through tax incentives and improved financial services.

Internet resources: <www.visitsanmarino.com/default.asp?id=297>.

São Tomé and Príncipe

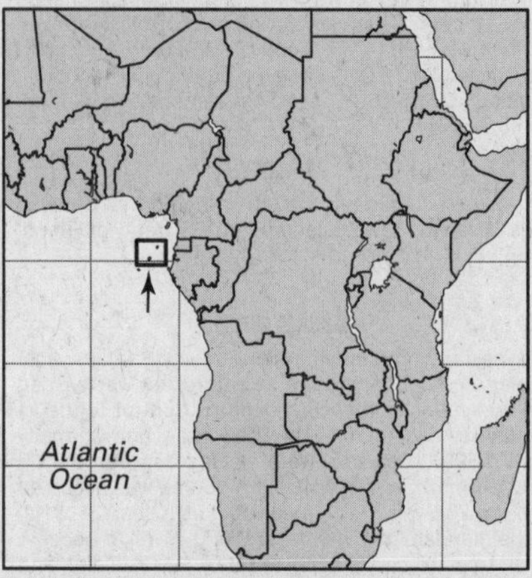

Official name: República Democrática de São Tomé e Príncipe (Democratic Republic of São Tomé and Príncipe). **Form of government:** multiparty republic with one legislative house (National Assembly [55]). **Chief of state:** President Fradique de Menezes (from 2003). **Head of government:** Prime Minister Patrice Trovoada (from 2008). **Capital:** São Tomé. **Official language:** Portuguese. **Official religion:** none. **Monetary unit:** 1 dobra (Db) = 100 cêntimos; valuation (1 Jul 2008) US$1 = Db 14,650.99.

Demography

Area: 386 sq mi, 1,001 sq km. **Population** (2007): 158,000. **Density** (2007): persons per sq mi 409.3, persons per sq km 157.8. **Urban** (2004): 37.9%. **Sex distribution** (2005): male 49.34%, female 50.66%. **Age breakdown** (2001): under 15, 42.1%; 15–29, 30.3%; 30–44, 14.4%; 45–59, 6.9%; 60–74, 4.7%; 75–84, 1.3%; 85 and over, 0.3%. **Ethnic composition** (2000): black-white admixture 79.5%; Fang 10.0%; Angolares (descendants of former Angolan slaves) 7.6%; Portuguese 1.9%; other 1.0%. **Religious affiliation** (2005): Roman Catholic 80%; Protestant 15%; Muslim 3%; other 2%. **Major urban areas** (2001): São Tomé 49,957; Neves 6,635; Santana 6,228; Trindade 6,049; Santo António 1,010. **Location:** islands in the Gulf of Guinea, straddling the Equator west of Gabon.

Vital statistics

Birth rate per 1,000 population (2005): 40.8 (world avg. 20.3). **Death rate** per 1,000 population (2005): 6.7 (world avg. 8.6). **Natural increase rate** per 1,000 population (2005): 34.1 (world avg. 11.7). **Total fer-**

tility rate (avg. births per childbearing woman; 2005): 5.71. **Life expectancy** at birth (2005): male 65.4 years; female 68.6 years.

National economy

Budget (2005). *Revenue:* Db 972,100,000,000 (petroleum exploration bonuses 57.8%; grants 18.9%; taxes 18.9%, of which consumption taxes 7.1%; nontax revenue 4.4%). *Expenditures:* Db 545,500,000,000 (current expenditure 58.7%; capital expenditure 35.5%; other 5.8%). **Public debt** (external, outstanding; 2005): US$293,700,000. **Production** (metric tons except as noted). *Agriculture, forestry, fishing* (2006): oil palm fruit 43,460, taro 28,000, bananas 27,000; livestock (number of live animals) 5,000 goats, 4,600 cattle, 3,000 sheep; roundwood (2005) 9,000 cu m; fisheries production (2005) 3,600. *Mining and quarrying:* some quarrying to support local construction industry. *Manufacturing* (value in Db; 1995): beer 880,000; clothing 679,000; lumber 369,000. *Energy production (consumption):* electricity (kW-hr; 2004) 37,200,000 (25,600,000); petroleum products (metric tons; 2004) none (30,000). **Households.** Average household size (2004) 5.5; expenditure (1995): food, beverages, and tobacco 71.9%, housing and energy 10.2%, transportation and communications 6.4%. **Population economically active** (2006): total 53,266; activity rate of total population 35.1% (participation rates: ages 10 and over (2001) 43.7%; female 41.6%; unemployed 30%). **Gross national income** (2006): US$55,000,000 (US$356 per capita). **Selected balance of payments data.** Receipts from (US$'000,000): tourism (2005) 14; remittances (2006) 1; foreign direct investment (2001–05 avg.) 2.4; official development assistance (2005) 32. Disbursements for (US$'000,000): tourism (2002) 0.6; remittances (2006) 1. **Land use** as % of total land area (2003): in temporary crops 8%, in permanent crops 49%, in pasture 1%; overall forest area (2005) 28%.

Foreign trade

Imports (2006): US$70,853,000 (food and beverages 30.1%; petroleum products 20.4%; machinery and equipment 13.5%; construction materials 8.7%; transportation equipment 8.2%). *Major import sources:* Portugal 63.6%; Angola 18.3%; Belgium 4.6%; Gabon 3.5%. **Exports** (2006): US$3,820,000 (cocoa beans 64.9%; coffee 24.2%; remainder 10.9%). *Major export destinations:* Portugal 33.3%; The Netherlands 27.1%; Belgium 14.3%; France 8.9%; US 5.3%.

Transport and communications

Transport. *Roads* (2000): total length 320 km (paved 68%). *Vehicles* (1996): passenger cars 4,040; trucks and buses 1,540. *Air transport* (2001): passenger-km 7,000,000. **Communications,** in total units (units per 1,000 persons). Televisions (2003): 19,000 (128); telephone landlines (2006): 7,600 (47); cellular telephone subscribers (2006): 18,000 (115); personal computers (2005): 6,000 (38); total Internet users (2006): 29,000 (181).

Education and health

Educational attainment (2001). Percentage of population ages 25 and over having: no formal schooling/unknown 22.9%; primary education 41.4%; lower secondary 25.0%; upper secondary/vocational 8.8%; higher 1.9%. **Literacy** (2006): total population ages 15 and over literate 85%; males literate 92%; females literate 78%. **Health:** physicians (2004) 81 (1 per 1,803 persons); hospital beds (1991) 532 (1 per 211 persons); infant mortality rate per 1,000 live births (2005) 43.1. **Food** (2005): daily per capita caloric intake 3,418 (vegetable products 95%, animal products 5%); 193% of FAO recommended minimum.

Military

Total active duty personnel (2005): 460 (army/coast guard 65.2%; presidential guard 34.8%). **Military expenditure as percentage of GDP** (2005): 1.2%; per capita expenditure US$4.

Background

First visited by European navigators in the 1470s, the islands of São Tomé and Príncipe were colonized by the Portuguese in the 16th century and were used in the trade and transshipment of slaves. Sugarcane and cacao were the main cash crops. The islands became an overseas province of Portugal in 1951 and achieved independence in 1975. During recent decades the country's economy was heavily dependent on international assistance.

Recent Developments

While São Tomé and Príncipe waited for the bonanza promised by the discovery of oil in its offshore waters, it was rewarded for its good governance and stable economy by the IMF, which offered debt relief in March 2008 under its Heavily Indebted Poor Countries initiative. Though no oil had yet been pumped from the country's waters, an estimated US$80 million had been earned for prospecting rights, and most of that money had been invested (on international advice) in interest-bearing securities.

Internet resources: <www.saotome.st>.

Saudi Arabia

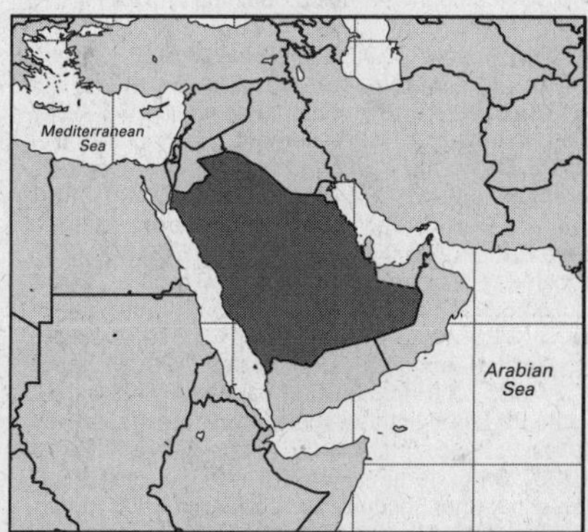

Official name: Al-Mamlakah al-ʿArabiyah al-Saʿudiyah (Kingdom of Saudi Arabia). **Form of government:** monarchy (assisted by the Consultative Council consisting of 150 appointed members). **Head of state**

and government: King Abdullah (from 2005). **Capital:** Riyadh. **Official language:** Arabic. **Official religion:** Islam. **Monetary unit:** 1 Saudi riyal (SR) = 100 halalah; valuation (1 Jul 2008) US$1 = SR 3.75.

Demography

Area: 830,000 sq mi, 2,149,690 sq km. **Population** (2007): 24,209,000. **Density** (2007): persons per sq mi 29.2, persons per sq km 11.3. **Urban** (2005): 81.0%. **Sex distribution** (2006): male 54.64%; female 45.36%. **Age breakdown** (2006): under 15, 38.2%; 15–29, 29.5%; 30–44, 22.9%; 45–59, 5.9%; 60–74, 2.7%; 75 and over, 0.8%. **Ethnic composition** (2005): Saudi Arab 74%; expatriates 26%, of which Indian 5%, Bangladeshi 3.5%, Pakistani 3.5%, Filipino 3%, Egyptian 3%, Palestinian 1%, other 7%. **Religious affiliation** (2000): Muslim 94%, of which Sunni 84%, Shi'i 10%; Christian 3.5%, of which Roman Catholic 3%; Hindu 1%; nonreligious/other 1.5%. **Major cities** (2005; urban agglomerations): Riyadh 4,193,000; Jiddah 2,860,000; Mecca 1,319,000; Medina 944,000; Al-Dammam 766,000. **Location:** the Middle East, bordering Iraq, Kuwait, the Persian Gulf, Qatar, the UAE, Oman, Yemen, the Red Sea, the Gulf of Aqaba, and Jordan.

Vital statistics

Birth rate per 1,000 population (2006): 29.3 (world avg. 20.3). **Death rate** per 1,000 population (2006): 2.6 (world avg. 8.6). **Natural increase rate** per 1,000 population (2006): 26.7 (world avg. 11.7). **Total fertility rate** (avg. births per childbearing woman; 2006): 4.00. **Life expectancy** at birth (2006): male 73.7 years; female 77.8 years.

National economy

Budget (2006). *Revenue:* SR 673,682,000,000 (oil revenues 89.7%). *Expenditures:* SR 393,322,000,000 (current expenditures 82.0%; capital expenditures 18.0%). **National debt** (domestic only; end of 2004): US$150,000,000,000. **Production** (metric tons except as noted). *Agriculture, forestry, fishing* (2006): wheat 2,400,000, alfalfa 1,644,661, dates 970,488; livestock (number of live animals) 7,000,000 sheep, 2,200,000 goats, 352,000 cattle, 260,000 camels; fisheries production (2005) 74,778 (from aquaculture 19%). *Mining and quarrying* (2005): gypsum 713,000; silver 13,501 kg; gold 7,456 kg. *Manufacturing* (value added in US$'000,000; 1998): industrial chemicals 3,349; refined petroleum 1,806; cement, bricks, and tiles 1,505. *Energy production (consumption):* electricity (kW-hr; 2005) 176,124,000,000 ([2006] 163,151,000,000); crude petroleum (barrels; 2006–07) 3,286,000,000 ([2004] 609,600,000); petroleum products (metric tons; 2004) 112,228,000 (67,300,000); natural gas (cu m; 2005) 81,350,000,000 ([2004] 65,679,000,000). **Population economically active** (2006): total 8,024,885, of which 3,900,591 Saudi workers and 4,124,294 foreign nationals; activity rate of total population 33.9% (participation rates: ages 15–64 [2003] 54%; female 15.5%; unemployed 6.3%). **Gross national income** (at current market prices; 2006): US$365,786,000,000 (US$15,131 per capita). **Households.** Average household size (2004) 5.7; expenditure (1998–99): food and nonalcoholic beverages 37.3%, transportation 18.9%, housing and energy 15.7%, household furnishings 9.7%. **Selected balance of payments data.** Receipts from (US$'000,000): tourism (2005) 5,181; foreign direct investment (FDI) (2001–05 avg.) 1,661; official development assistance (2005) 13 (commitments). Disbursements for (US$'000,000): tourism (2005) 4,764; remittances (2006) 14,318; FDI (2001–05 avg.) 301. **Land use** as % of total land area (2003): in temporary crops 1.7%, in permanent crops 0.1%, in pasture 79.1%; overall forest area (2005) 1.3%.

Foreign trade

Imports (2005; c.i.f.): SR 222,985,000,000 (machinery and apparatus 24.6%; transport equipment 20.7%; food and live animals 13.6%; base and fabricated metals 10.6%; chemicals and chemical products 9.7%). *Major import sources:* US 14.8%; Japan 9.0%; Germany 8.2%; China 7.4%; UK 4.7%. **Exports** (2005; f.o.b.): SR 677,144,000,000 (crude and refined petroleum 86.2%; other mineral fuels [mostly natural gas] 3.3%; organic chemicals 2.6%). *Major export destinations:* Japan 15.6%; US 15.5%; South Korea 8.5%; China 6.0%; India 5.9%.

Transport and communications

Transport. *Railroads* (2003): route length (2006) 1,392 km; passenger-km 232,000,000; metric ton-km cargo 778,000,000. *Roads* (2006): total length 174,429 km (paved 100%). *Vehicles* (2001): passenger cars 4,452,793; trucks and buses 4,110,271. *Air transport* (2006; Saudi Arabian Airlines only): passenger-km 28,722,000,000; metric ton-km cargo 1,092,000,000. **Communications,** in total units (units per 1,000 persons). Daily newspaper circulation (2004): 1,093,000 (48); televisions (2004): 6,576,000 (292); telephone landlines (2006): 3,951,000 (167); cellular telephone subscribers (2006): 19,663,000 (830); personal computers (2005): 8,184,000 (354); total Internet users (2006): 4,700,000 (198); broadband Internet subscribers (2006): 218,000 (9.2).

Education and health

Educational attainment (2000). Percentage of Saudi (non-Saudi) population ages 10 and over who: are illiterate 19.9% (12.1%); are literate/have primary education 39.5% (40.6%); have some/completed secondary 34.2% (36.0%); have at least begun university 6.4% (11.3%). **Literacy** (2005): percentage of total population ages 15 and over literate 80.4%; males literate 85.8%; females literate 73.3%. **Health** (2005): physicians 43,348 (1 per 533 persons); hospital beds 53,192 (1 per 435 persons); infant mortality rate per 1,000 live births (2006) 12.8. **Food** (2005): daily per capita caloric intake 3,527 (vegetable products 86%, animal products 14%); 190% of FAO recommended minimum.

Military

Total active duty personnel (2006): 124,500 (army 60.2%, navy 12.4%, air force 14.5%, air defense forces 12.9%); US troops (2007) 274. **Military expen-**

1 metric ton = about 1.1 short tons; 1 kilometer = 0.6 mi (statute); 1 metric ton-km cargo = about 0.68 short ton-mi cargo; c.i.f.: cost, insurance, and freight; f.o.b.: free on board

diture as percentage of GDP (2005): 8.2%; per capita expenditure US$1,092.

Background

Saudi Arabia is the historical home of Islam, founded by Muhammad in Medina in 622. During medieval times, local and foreign rulers fought for control of the Arabian Peninsula; in 1517 the Ottomans prevailed. In the 18th–19th centuries Islamic leaders supporting religious reform struggled to regain Saudi territory, all of which was restored by 1904. The British held Saudi lands as a protectorate from 1915 to 1927; then they acknowledged the sovereignty of the Kingdom of the Hejaz and Najd. The two kingdoms were unified as the Kingdom of Saudi Arabia in 1932. Since World War II, it has supported the Palestinian cause in the Middle East and maintained close ties with the US.

Recent Developments

Saudi liberals welcomed a royal decree in October 2007 overhauling the kingdom's judicial system—the reforms would preserve the centrality of the Shariʿah (Islamic law) but would take away many powers exercised by the Supreme Judicial Council, which was controlled by conservative clerics. In late September Saudi Arabia's grand mufti, Sheikh ʿAbd al-Aziz al-Sheikh, issued a fatwa (religious edict) prohibiting Saudi youth from traveling abroad under the pretext of jihad. It was understood that the fatwa was aimed at discouraging young Saudis from going to Iraq to fight US and other foreign forces there. The Saudi Arabian economy continued to perform extremely well, especially since the price of crude oil remained robust and, by mid-2008, had soared to over US$125 per barrel. The country enjoyed a massive trade surplus, and GDP grew by 7.1% in 2007. Saudi Arabia was to be the largest purchaser in a US$20 billion arms deal that was reached between the US and the Arab Gulf states, and in September Saudi Arabia signed a US$8.8 billion deal with the UK to buy and service 72 Eurofighter aircraft.

Internet resources: <www.sct.gov.sa>.

Senegal

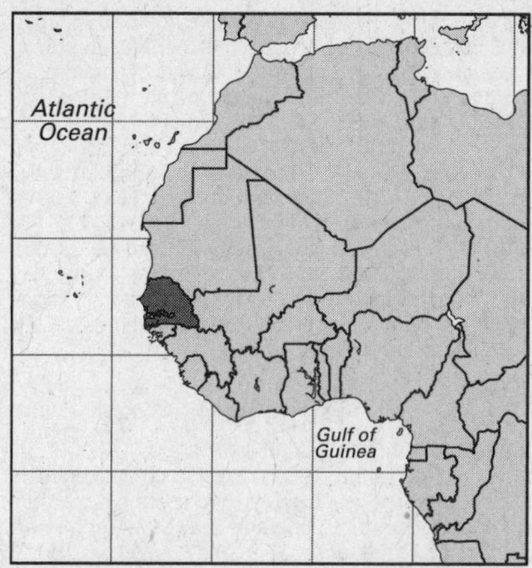

Official name: République du Sénégal (Republic of Senegal). **Form of government:** multiparty republic with two legislative houses (Senate [100]; National Assembly [150]). **Head of state and government:** President Abdoulaye Wade (from 2000), assisted by Prime Minister Cheikh Hadjibou Soumaré (from 2007). **Capital:** Dakar. **Official language:** French. **Official religion:** none. **Monetary unit:** 1 CFA franc (CFAF) = 100 centimes; valuation (1 Jul 2008) US$1 = CFAF 414.60.

Demography

Area: 75,955 sq mi, 197,021 sq km. **Population** (2007): 12,522,000. **Density** (2007): persons per sq mi 164.9, persons per sq km 63.7. **Urban** (2005): 41.6%. **Sex distribution** (2006): male 49.99%; female 50.01%. **Age breakdown** (2006): under 15, 42.2%; 15–29, 28.4%; 30–44, 16.0%; 45–59, 8.7%; 60–74, 3.9%; 75–84, 0.7%; 85 and over, 0.1%. **Ethnic composition** (2000): Wolof 34.6%; Peul (Fulani) and Tukulor 27.1%; Serer 12.0%; Malinke (Mandingo) 9.7%; other 16.6%. **Religious affiliation** (2005): Muslim 94%, of which Shiʿi 5%; Christian (mostly Roman Catholic) 4%; other 2%. **Major cities** (2007): Dakar 2,243,400; Touba 529,200; Thiès 263,500; Kaolack 186,000; Mbour 181,800. **Location:** western Africa, bordering Mauritania, Mali, Guinea, Guinea-Bissau, the North Atlantic Ocean, and The Gambia.

Vital statistics

Birth rate per 1,000 population (2006): 38.3 (world avg. 20.3). **Death rate** per 1,000 population (2006): 11.2 (world avg. 8.6). **Natural increase rate** per 1,000 population (2006): 27.1 (world avg. 11.7). **Total fertility rate** (avg. births per childbearing woman; 2006): 5.13. **Life expectancy** at birth (2006): male 55.0 years; female 57.7 years.

National economy

Budget (2005). *Revenue:* CFAF 955,800,000,000 (tax revenue 89.0%, of which taxes on domestic goods and services 28.7%, income taxes 21.4%, taxes on imports 19.7%; grants 7.9%; nontax revenue 3.1%). *Expenditures:* CFAF 1,084,400,000,000 (current expenditures 58.0%, of which public debt interest payments 4.3%; development expenditure 42.0%). **Public debt** (external, outstanding; 2005): US$3,467,000,000. **Production** (metric tons except as noted). *Agriculture, forestry, fishing* (2005): sugarcane (2006) 829,500, peanuts (groundnuts) 703,400, millet 608,600; livestock (number of live animals) 4,863,000 sheep, 4,144,000 goats, 3,091,000 cattle; roundwood 6,070,000 cu m, of which fuelwood 87%; fisheries production 405,263. *Mining and quarrying:* calcium phosphate (crude rock; 2005) 1,451,000. *Manufacturing* (value added in US$'000,000; 2002): food and food products 108; industrial chemicals 70; cement, bricks, and ceramics 31. *Energy production (consumption):* electricity (kW-hr; 2004) 2,351,000,000 (2,351,000,000); crude petroleum (barrels; 2004) negligible (8,583,000); petroleum products (metric tons; 2004) 1,127,000 (1,309,000); natural gas (cu m; 2005) 13,000,000 ([2004] 13,000,000). **Population economically active** (2003): total 4,383,000; activity rate of total population 39.4% (participation rates: ages 15–64, 71.5%; female 42.0%; unemployed [2005] 40%). **Households.** Average household size (2005) 8.7; sources of income (1997–2000):

agricultural 45%; other 55%; expenditure (2005): food and nonalcoholic beverages 54.8%, household furnishings 6.9%, housing and energy 6.3%, communications 6.0%. **Selected balance of payments data.** Receipts from (US$'000,000): tourism (2004) 212; remittances (2006) 633; foreign direct investment (FDI) (2001–05 avg.) 59; official development assistance (2005) 689. Disbursements for (US$'000,000): tourism (2004) 57; remittances (2006) 77; FDI (2001–05 avg.) 15. **Gross national income** (2006): US$9,335,000,000 (US$770 per capita). **Land use** as % of total land area (2003): in temporary crops 12.8%, in permanent crops 0.2%, in pasture 29.3%; overall forest area (2005) 40.0%.

Foreign trade

Imports (2005; c.i.f.): CFAF 1,697,000,000,000 (petroleum [all forms] 19.2%; food and live animals 19.2%, of which rice 7.8%; machinery and apparatus 12.4%; transport equipment 8.5%). *Major import sources* (2005): France 22.8%; Nigeria 11.4%; Brazil 4.5%; Thailand 4.2%; US 4.2%. **Exports** (2004): CFAF 697,000,000,000 (petroleum [all forms] 19.3%; phosphorous pentoxide and phosphoric acids 13.6%; fresh fish 12.6%; crustaceans and mollusks 9.0%; manufactured fertilizers 4.7%). *Major export destinations* (2005): Mali 16.9%; India 13.1%; France 9.5%; Spain 6.1%; Italy 5.5%.

Transport and communications

Transport. *Railroads* (2004): route length (2005) 906 km; passenger-km 122,000,000; metric ton-km cargo 358,000,000. *Roads* (2003): total length 13,576 km (paved 29%). *Vehicles* (2004): passenger cars 147,000; trucks and buses 46,000. *Air transport* (2006; Air Sénégal International only): passenger-km 937,000,000. **Communications,** in total units (units per 1,000 persons). Daily newspaper circulation (2005): 70,000 (6.5); televisions (2003): 869,000 (77); telephone landlines (2006): 283,000 (23); cellular telephone subscribers (2006): 2,983,000 (245); personal computers (2005): 250,000 (21); total Internet users (2006): 650,000 (53); broadband Internet subscribers (2006): 29,000 (2.4).

Education and health

Educational attainment (2005). Percentage of population ages 25 and over having: no formal schooling/unknown 70.0%; incomplete primary education 13.0%; complete primary 3.7%; incomplete secondary 9.5%; complete secondary 1.4%; higher 2.4%. **Literacy** (2003): percentage of total population ages 15 and over literate 40.2%; males literate 49.9%; females literate 30.8%. **Health:** physicians (2005) 693 (1 per 17,115 persons); hospital beds (1998) 3,582 (1 per 2,500 persons); infant mortality rate per 1,000 live births (2006) 61.4. **Food** (2005): daily per capita caloric intake 2,513 (vegetable products 92%, animal products 8%); 136% of FAO recommended minimum.

Military

Total active duty personnel (2006): 13,620 (army 87.4%, navy 7.0%, air force 5.6%); French troops (2006) 840. **Military expenditure as percentage of GDP** (2005): 1.5%; per capita expenditure US$11.

Background

Links between the peoples of Senegal and North Africa were established in the 10th century AD. Islam was introduced in the 11th century, although animism retained a hold on the country into the 19th century. The Portuguese explored the coast in 1445, and in 1638 the French established a trading post at the mouth of the Senegal River. Throughout the 17th and 18th centuries, Europeans exported slaves, ivory, and gold from Senegal. The French gained control over the coast in the early 19th century and moved inland, checking the expansion of the Tukulor empire; in 1895 Senegal became part of French West Africa. Its inhabitants were made French citizens in 1946, and it became an overseas territory of France. It became an autonomous republic in 1958 and was federated with Mali in 1959–60. It became an independent state in 1960. In 1982 it entered a confederation with The Gambia, called Senegambia, which was dissolved in 1989.

Recent Developments

The government of Senegal threatened in early 2007 to withdraw its 500 men from the African Union (AU) peacekeeping force in the Darfur region of The Sudan after 5 of them were killed there in April. In August, however, after a series of meetings with AU and UN authorities, the government committed Senegal to tripling the size of its contingent.

Internet resources: <www.senegal-tourism.com>.

Serbia

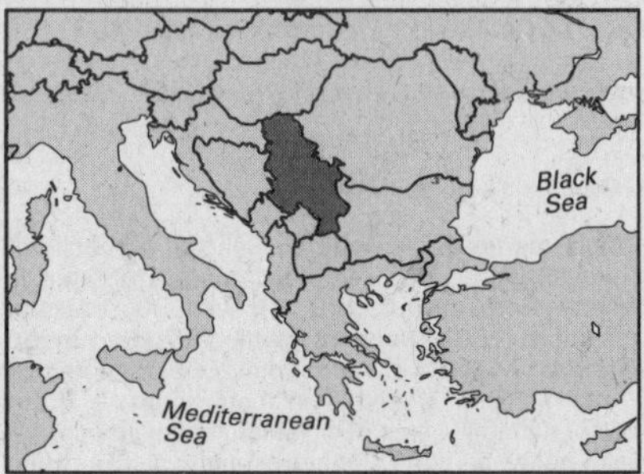

Many of these statistics include Kosovo, which declared its independence in February 2008. **Official name:** Republika Srbija (Republic of Serbia). **Form of government:** republic with National Assembly (250). **Chief of state:** President Boris Tadic (from 2004). **Head of government:** Prime Minister Mirko Cvetkovic (from 2008). **Capital:** Belgrade. **Official language:** Serbian. **Official religion:** none. **Monetary unit:** 1 Serbian dinar (CSD) = 100 paras; valuation (1 Jul 2008) $1 = 49.97 CSD.

1 metric ton = about 1.1 short tons; 1 kilometer = 0.6 mi (statute); 1 metric ton-km cargo = about 0.68 short ton-mi cargo; c.i.f.: cost, insurance, and freight; f.o.b.: free on board

Demography

Area: 34,128 sq mi, 88,391 sq km. **Population** (2007): 7,402,000. **Density** (2007): persons per sq mi 247.4, persons per sq km 95.5. **Urban** (2002): 56.4%. **Sex distribution** (2005): male 48.62%; female 51.38%. **Age breakdown** (2002): under 15, 15.7%; 15-29, 20.2%; 30-44, 19.9%; 45-59, 21.1%; 60-74, 17.2%; 75-84, 4.7%; 85 and over, 0.6%; unknown 0.6%. **Ethnic composition** (2002): Serb 82.9%; Hungarian 3.9%; Bosniac 1.8%; Rom (Gypsy) 1.4%; Yugoslav 1.1%; Croat 0.9%; Montenegrin 0.9%; other 7.1%. **Religious affiliation** (2002): Orthodox 85.0%; Roman Catholic 5.5%; Muslim 3.2%; Protestant 1.1%; other/unknown 5.2%. **Major cities** (2002): Belgrade 1,120,092; Novi Sad 191,405; Nis 173,724; Kragujevac 146,373. **Location:** southeastern Europe, bordering Romania, Bulgaria, Macedonia, Kosovo, Montenegro, Bosnia and Herzegovina, Croatia, and Hungary.

Vital statistics

Birth rate per 1,000 population (2005): 9.7 (world avg. 20.3); within marriage 77.8%. **Death rate** per 1,000 population (2005): 14.3 (world avg. 8.6). **Total fertility rate** (avg. births per childbearing woman; 2004): 1.60. **Life expectancy** at birth (2005): male 69.9 years; female 75.4 years.

National economy

Budget (2005). *Revenue:* CSD 701,200,000,000 (tax revenue 91.2%, of which VAT 30.8%, excises and customs duties 15.7%, personal and corporate income tax 14.9%; nontax revenue 8.8%). *Expenditures:* CSD 669,600,000,000 (current expenditure 95.1%; capital expenditure 4.9%). **Population economically active** (2006): total 3,323,716; activity rate of total population 44.0% (participation rates: ages 15-64, 63.6%; female 43.0%; unemployed 20.9%). **Production** (metric tons except as noted). *Agriculture, forestry, fishing* (2006): corn (maize) 6,017,000, sugar beets 3,189,000, wheat 1,875,000; livestock (number of live animals) 3,211,597 pigs, 1,609,239 sheep, 1,096,185 cattle; roundwood (data for Serbia and Montenegro; 2005) 3,170,000 cu m, of which fuelwood 58%; fisheries production (data for Serbia and Montenegro; 2005) 7,022 (from aquaculture 65%). *Mining and quarrying* (2005): copper (metal content) 27,000; lead (metal content) 2,000. *Manufacturing* (value added in CSD '000,000 in constant prices of 2002; 2004): food products and beverages 48,970; chemicals and chemical products 21,862; cement, bricks, and ceramics 11,445. *Energy production (consumption):* electricity (kW-hr; 2004) 33,874,000,000 (22,911,000,000); coal (metric tons; 2004) 424,000 (303,000); lignite (metric tons; 2004) 34,400,000 (30,900,000); crude petroleum (barrels; 2004) 4,840,000 (29,419,000; data for Serbia and Montenegro); petroleum products (metric tons; data for Serbia and Montenegro; 2004) 3,150,000 (3,150,000); natural gas (cu m; 2004) 317,000,000 (794,000,000). **Gross national income** (2006): US$34,927,000,000 (US$4,700 per capita). **Public debt** (external, outstanding; August 2007): US$8,697,300,000. **Households.** Average household size (2006) 3.2; average annual income per household CSD 394,740 (US$5,620); sources of income: wages and salaries 47.7%, transfers 26.5%, self-employment 5.5%; expenditure: food and nonalcoholic beverages 35.1%, housing and energy 18.9%, transportation 11.2%. **Selected balance of payments data.** Receipts from (US$'000,000): tourism (2004) 220; remittances (2005) 2,400; foreign direct investment (2001-05 avg.) 822 (data for Serbia and Montenegro); official development assistance (2005) 1,260 (data for Serbia and Montenegro; commitments). **Land use** as % of total land area (2002): in temporary crops 43.3%, in permanent crops 4.1%, in pasture 18.2%; overall forest area 25.2%.

Foreign trade

Imports (2005; c.i.f.): US$10,575,700,000 (mineral fuels 18.9%; chemicals and chemical products 13.6%; machinery and apparatus 10.3%; transportation equipment 8.2%; base metals 7.6%). *Major import sources:* Russia 15.9%; Germany 10.3%; Italy 8.6%; China 4.8%; US 3.6%. **Exports** (2005): US$4,553,-400,000 (base metals 15.4%; food and food products 14.7%; chemicals and chemical products 8.8%; rubber and plastic products 6.4%). *Major export destinations:* Bosnia and Herzegovina 16.4%; Italy 14.4%; Germany 9.8%; Macedonia 5.8%; Russia 5.0%.

Transport and communications

Transport. *Railroads* (2006): route length (2004) 3,809 km; passenger-km 684,000,000; metric ton-km cargo 4,232,000,000. *Roads* (2004): total length 38,507 km (paved 62%). *Vehicles* (2005): passenger cars 1,497,418; trucks and buses 257,642. *Air transport* (2006): passenger-km 1,252,000,000; metric ton-km cargo 5,470,000. **Communications,** in total units (units per 1,000 persons). Daily newspaper circulation (2002): 1,015,000 (95); televisions (2000): 2,980,000 (279); telephone landlines (2006): 2,719,000 (259); cellular telephone subscribers (2006): 6,644,000 (633); personal computers (2005): 446,000 (55); total Internet users (2006): 1,400,000 (133); broadband Internet subscribers (2006): 122,000 (16).

Education and health

Educational attainment (2002). Percentage of population ages 15 and over having: no formal education/unknown 7.8%; incomplete primary education 16.2%; complete primary 23.9%; secondary 41.1%; higher 11.0%. **Literacy** (2002): total population ages 10 and over literate 96.6%. **Health** (2004): physicians (2003) 19,900 (1 per 379 persons); hospital beds 45,283 (1 per 166 persons); infant mortality rate per 1,000 live births (2005) 8.0.

Military

Total active duty personnel (2006): 39,686 (army 83.6%, air force 16.4%). **Military expenditure as percentage of GDP** (2006) 2.3%; per capita expenditure US$99.

Background

The Kingdom of the Serbs, Croats, and Slovenes was created after the collapse of Austria-Hungary at the end of World War I. The country signed treaties with Czechoslovakia and Romania in 1920-21, marking the beginning of the Little Entente. In 1929 an absolute monarchy was established, the country's name was changed to Yugoslavia, and it was divided into regions without regard to ethnic boundaries. Axis powers invaded Yugoslavia in 1941, and German, Italian, Hungarian, and Bulgarian troops occupied it for the rest of World War II. In 1945 the Socialist Federal Republic of Yugoslavia was established; it included the republics of Bosnia and Herzegovina, Croatia, Macedonia, Montenegro, Serbia, and Slovenia. Its independent form of communism under Josip Broz Tito's leadership provoked the USSR. Internal ethnic tensions flared up in the 1980s, causing the country's ultimate collapse. In 1991–92 independence was declared by Croatia, Slovenia, Macedonia, and Bosnia and Herzegovina; the new Federal Republic of Yugoslavia (containing roughly 45% of the population and 40% of the area of its predecessor) was proclaimed by Serbia and Montenegro. Still fueled by long-standing ethnic tensions, hostilities continued into the 1990s. Despite the approval of the Dayton Peace Agreement (1995), sporadic fighting continued and was followed in 1998–99 by Serbian repression and expulsion of ethnic populations in the province of Kosovo. In September–October 2000, the battered nation of Yugoslavia ended the autocratic rule of Pres. Slobodan Milosevic. In April 2001 he was arrested and in June extradited to The Hague to stand trial for war crimes, genocide, and crimes against humanity committed during the fighting in Kosovo. In February 2003 both houses of the Yugoslav federal legislature voted to accept a new state charter and change the name of the country from Yugoslavia to Serbia and Montenegro. Henceforth, defense, international political and economic relations, and human rights matters would be handled centrally, while all other functions would be run from the republican capitals, Belgrade and Podgorica, respectively. The move was seen as an acknowledgment that Serbia and Montenegro had little in common, and a provision was included for both states to vote on independence after three years; Serbia declared its independence in June 2006, shortly after Montenegro severed its federal union with Serbia.

Recent Developments

Serbia's restive province of Kosovo declared its independence on 17 Feb 2008. Serbia's parliament had passed a resolution condemning any such attempt while rejecting any role the EU planned to take in Kosovo if the EU recognized the province's independence, and Prime Minister Vojislav Kostunica had suggested Hong Kong's "two systems, one state" arrangement with China as a model for relations between Serbia and Kosovo. The Kosovar declaration was backed by the US, Turkey, and most EU member states, including the UK, France, and Germany. It was rejected by several states that experienced their own struggles with independence movements, however, including Russia, China, Greece, Spain, Cyprus, and, obviously, Serbia. Economic growth was 7.5% in 2007, while inflation stood at 8.5%. In July 2008 Radovan Karadzic, former president of Bosnia, was captured in Serbia. He had been wanted to stand trial on charges of war crimes for more than a decade, stemming from atrocities committed by Bosnian Serb forces in the mid-1990s.

Internet resources: <www.serbia.travel>.

Seychelles

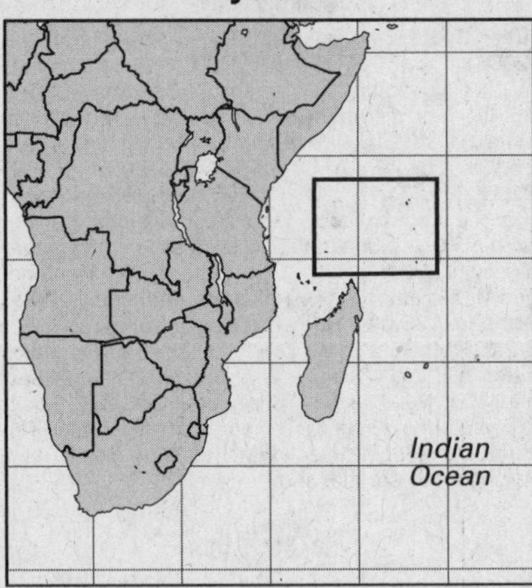

Official name: Repiblik Sesel (Creole); Republic of Seychelles (English); République des Seychelles (French). **Form of government:** multiparty republic with one legislative house (National Assembly [34]). **Head of state and government:** President James Michel (from 2004). **Capital:** Victoria. **Official languages:** none; Creole, English, and French are national languages. **Official religion:** none. **Monetary unit:** 1 Seychelles rupee (SR) = 100 cents; valuation (1 Jul 2008) US$1 = SR 8.00.

Demography

Area: 176 sq mi, 455 sq km. **Population** (2007): 84,300. **Density** (2007): persons per sq mi 479.8, persons per sq km 185.3. **Urban** (2005): 53%. **Sex distribution** (2006): male 50.68%; female 49.32%. **Age breakdown** (2006): under 15, 23.8%; 15–29, 26.4%; 30–44, 24.4%; 45–59, 15.1%; 60–74, 7.0%; 75 and over, 3.3%. **Ethnic composition** (2000): Seychellois Creole (mixture of Asian, African, and European) 93.2%; British 3.0%; French 1.8%; Chinese 0.5%; Indian 0.3%; other unspecified 1.2%. **Religious affiliation** (2002): Roman Catholic 82.3%; Anglican 6.4%; other Christian 4.5%; Hindu 2.1%; Muslim 1.1%; other 2.1%; unknown 1.5%. **Major towns** (2004): Victoria 23,200; Anse Royale 3,800. **Location:** group of islands in the Indian Ocean, northeast of Madagascar.

Vital statistics

Birth rate per 1,000 population (2006): 17.3 (world avg. 20.3); (2005) within marriage 23.6%. **Death rate** per 1,000 population (2006): 7.8 (world avg. 8.6). **Total fertility rate** (avg. births per childbearing woman; 2006): 2.11. **Life expectancy** at birth (2006): male 68.9 years; female 75.7 years.

National economy

Budget (2006). *Revenue:* SR 2,476,000,000 (current revenue 97.1%, of which dividends and interest 14.0%, income and business tax 12.0%, indirect taxes on services 9.5%, trades tax 9.1%; grants 2.9%). *Expenditures:* SR 2,302,000,000 (current expenditure 82.5%, of which public debt interest charges 17.6%, education 8.6%, health 8.4%; development expenditure 17.5%). **Public debt** (2006): US$1,035,000,000. **Gross national income** (2006): US$659,000,000 (US$7,660 per capita). **Production** (metric tons except as noted). *Agriculture, forestry, fishing* (2006): coconuts 2,529, bananas 2,046, tea 189; livestock (number of live animals) 18,500 pigs, 5,150 goats, 570,000 chickens; fisheries production 107,327 (from aquaculture 1%). *Mining and quarrying* (2006): granite 93,000. *Manufacturing* (2006): canned tuna 40,222; fish meal 14,821; copra 253. *Energy production (consumption):* electricity (kW-hr; 2006) 251,000,000 ([2004] 220,000,000); petroleum products (metric tons; 2004) none (178,000). **Population economically active** (2002): total 43,859; activity rate of total population 53.6% (participation rates: ages 15–64, 80.1%; female [1997] 47.6%; unemployed [2006] 2.6%). **Selected balance of payments data.** Receipts from (US$'000,000): tourism (2006) 227; remittances (2006) 11; foreign direct investment (FDI) (2001–05 avg.) 58; official development assistance (2005) 10 (commitments). Disbursements for (US$'000,000): tourism (2005) 39; remittances (2006) 10; FDI (2001–05 avg.) 8.4. **Households.** Average household size (2004) 3.5; sources of income (1997): wages and salaries 77.2%, self-employment 3.8%, transfer payments 3.2%; expenditure (2001): food 25.5%, housing and energy 14.8%, beverages 13.3% (of which alcoholic 10.7%), clothing and footwear 6.7%. **Land use** as % of total land area (2003): in temporary crops 2%, in permanent crops 13%; overall forest area (2005) 89%.

Foreign trade

Imports (2006; c.i.f.): SR 4,180,000,000 (mineral fuels 26.7%; food and beverages 24.1%, of which fish, crustaceans, and mollusks 12.6%; machinery and apparatus 11.0%; iron and steel 5.5%; vehicles 4.3%). *Major import sources:* Saudi Arabia 26.4%; Singapore 11.3%; France 8.0%; Spain 8.0%; South Africa 7.3%. **Exports** (2006; f.o.b.): SR 2,100,000,000 (domestic exports 56.5%, of which canned tuna 49.5%, medicaments and medical appliances 3.9%, crustaceans 1.2%, fish meal 1.2%; reexports 43.5%, of which petroleum products to ships and aircraft 42.4%). *Major export destinations* (domestic exports only): UK 42.0%; France 26.1%; Italy 18.0%; Germany 3.7%.

Transport and communications

Transport. *Roads* (2006): total length 502 km (paved 96%). *Vehicles* (2006): passenger cars 7,070; trucks and buses 2,796. *Air transport* (2006; Air Seychelles only): passenger-km 1,089,000,000; metric ton-km cargo 22,502,000. **Communications**, in total units (units per 1,000 persons). Daily newspaper circulation (2004): 3,500 (42); televisions (2003): 22,000 (266); telephone landlines (2006): 22,000 (260); cellular telephone subscribers (2006): 72,000 (851); personal computers (2005): 16,000 (193); total Internet users (2006): 29,000 (343); broadband Internet subscribers (2006): 1,300 (15).

Education and health

Educational attainment (2003). Percentage of population ages 12 and over having: less than primary or primary education 23.2%; secondary 73.4%; higher 3.4%. **Literacy** (2005): total population ages 12 and over literate 96.0%; males literate 96.0%; females literate 96.0%. **Health** (2006): physicians 83 (1 per 1,019 persons); hospital beds 417 (1 per 203 persons); infant mortality rate per 1,000 live births 9.5. **Food** (2005): daily per capita caloric intake 2,547 (vegetable products 81%, animal products 19%); 141% of FAO recommended minimum.

Military

Total active duty personnel (2006): 200 (army 100%). **Military expenditure as percentage of GDP** (2005): 1.8%; per capita expenditure US$157.

Background

The first recorded landing on the uninhabited Seychelles was made in 1609 by an expedition of the British East India Co. The archipelago was claimed by the French in 1756 and surrendered to the British in 1810. Seychelles became a British crown colony in 1903 and a republic within the Commonwealth in 1976. A one-party socialist state since 1979, Seychelles began moving toward democracy in the 1990s; it adopted a new constitution in 1993.

Recent Developments

In 2007 Seychelles continued efforts to strengthen its economy (one of the strongest in Africa) by forging foreign-trade agreements. In February Chinese Pres. Hu Jintao concluded his eight-country African tour in Victoria, where he met with Pres. James Michel, signed a number of cooperation agreements, canceled a debt, and pledged US$12 million in aid.

Internet resources: <www.seychelles.com>.

Sierra Leone

Official name: Republic of Sierra Leone. **Form of government:** republic with one legislative body (Parliament [124]). **Head of state and government:** President Ernest Bai Koroma (from 2007). **Capital:** Freetown. **Official language:** English. **Official religion:** none. **Monetary unit:** 1 leone (Le) = 100 cents; valuation (1 Jul 2008) US$1 = Le 2,969.80.

Demography

Area: 27,699 sq mi, 71,740 sq km. **Population** (2007): 5,866,000. **Density** (2007): persons per sq mi 211.8, persons per sq km 81.8. **Urban** (2005): 40.7%. **Sex distribution** (2005): male 49.23%; female 50.77%. **Age breakdown** (2005): under 15, 42.8%; 15–29, 26.1%; 30–44, 16.0%; 45–59, 9.6%; 60–74, 4.7%; 75–84, 0.7%; 85 and over, 0.1%. **Ethnic composition** (2000): Mende 26.0%; Temne 24.6%; Limba 7.1%; Kuranko 5.5%; Kono 4.2%; Fulani 3.8%; Bullom-Sherbro 3.5%; other 25.3%. **Religious affiliation** (2005): Muslim 65%; Christian 25%; traditional beliefs/other 10%. **Major cities** (2004): Freetown 772,873; Bo 149,957; Kenema 128,402; Yoni 87,627; Makeni 82,840. **Location:** western Africa, bordering Guinea, Liberia, and the North Atlantic Ocean.

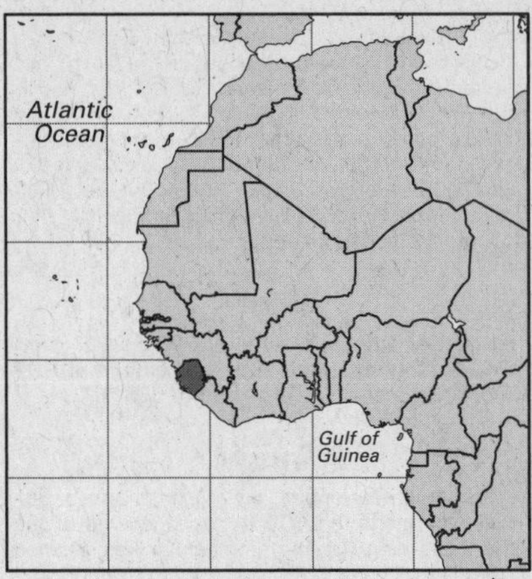

Vital statistics

Birth rate per 1,000 population (2005): 46.1 (world avg. 20.3). **Death rate** per 1,000 population (2005): 23.4 (world avg. 8.6). **Natural increase rate** per 1,000 population (2005): 22.7 (world avg. 11.7). **Total fertility rate** (avg. births per childbearing woman; 2005): 6.15. **Life expectancy** at birth (2005): male 37.7 years; female 42.1 years.

National economy

Budget (2005). *Revenue:* Le 765,762,000,000 (grants 46.0%; import taxes 22.4%; corporate taxes 8.1%). *Expenditures:* Le 830,410,000,000 (current expenditures 75.2%, of which wages and salaries 27.6%, goods and services 24.8%, debt service 15.1%; capital expenditures 24.8%). **Gross national income** (2006): US$1,791,000,000 (US$312 per capita). **Production** (metric tons except as noted). *Agriculture, forestry, fishing* (2006): rice 1,062,000, cassava 350,000, oil palm fruit 166,100; livestock (number of live animals) 540,000 goats, 470,000 sheep, 350,000 cattle; roundwood (2005) 5,546,391 cu m, of which fuelwood 98%; fisheries production 145,993. *Mining and quarrying* (2006): bauxite 1,071,140; rutile 73,600; diamonds 582,330 carats. *Manufacturing* (2006): soap 467,360; cement 234,440; paint 142,730 gallons. *Energy production (consumption):* electricity (kW-hr; 2004) 244,000,000 (244,000,000); crude petroleum (barrels; 2004) none (1,942,000); petroleum products (metric tons; 2004) 178,000 (248,000). **Households.** Average household size (2004) 6.0. **Public debt** (external, outstanding; January 2006): US$1,467,100,000. **Population economically active** (2003–04): total 2,005,900; activity rate of total population 40.0% (participation rates: ages 15–64, 68.2%; female 53.6%). **Selected balance of payments data.** Receipts from (US$'000,000): tourism (2005) 64; remittances (2006) 2; foreign direct investment (2001–05 avg.) 14; official development assistance (2005) 343. Disbursements for (US$'000,000): tourism (2005) 32; remittances (2006) 2. **Land use** as % of total land area (2003): in temporary crops 8.0%, in permanent crops 1.0%, in pasture 30.7%; overall forest area (2005) 38.5%.

Foreign trade

Imports (2006; c.i.f.): Le 1,169,446,800,000 (fuels 37.3%; machinery and transport equipment 17.5%; food and live animals 14.2%; chemicals and chemical products 6.1%). *Major import sources:* Côte d'Ivoire 9.7%; US 8.1%; China 8.0%; UK 7.0%; The Netherlands 5.8%. **Exports** (2006; f.o.b.): Le 684,311,100,000 (diamonds 54.1%; rutile 12.3%; bauxite 10.2%; cacao 5.0%; reexports 12.3%). *Major export destinations:* Belgium 51.7%; US 19.0%; The Netherlands 6.7%.

Transport and communications

Transport. *Railroads* (2002; Marampa Mineral Railway; there are no passenger railways): length 84 km. *Roads* (2002): total length 11,300 km (paved 8%). *Vehicles* (2003): passenger cars 17,439; trucks and buses 12,428. *Air transport:* passenger-km (2001) 73,000,000; metric ton-km cargo (2004) 8,000,000. **Communications**, in total units (units per 1,000 persons). Daily newspaper circulation (2004): 16,000 (3.3); televisions (2003): 63,000 (13); telephone landlines (2002): 24,000 (4.8); cellular telephone subscribers (2003): 113,000 (23); personal computers (1999): 100; total Internet users (2004): 10,000 (2).

Education and health

Educational attainment (2004): percentage of total population having: no formal schooling 62.2%; incomplete/complete primary 24.6%; lower secondary 6.4%; upper secondary 4.2%; vocational 2.0%; incomplete/complete higher 0.6%. **Literacy** (2004): total population ages 10 and over literate 39%; males literate 49%; females literate 29%. **Health:** physicians (2004) 162 (1 per 30,384 persons); hospital beds (2001) 2,770 (1 per 1,680 persons); infant mortality rate per 1,000 live births (2005) 162.6. **Food** (2005): daily per capita caloric intake 1,875 (vegetable products 95%, animal products 5%); 102% of FAO recommended minimum.

Military

Total active duty personnel (2006): 12,500 (army 98%, navy 2%). **Military expenditure as percentage of GDP** (2005): 1.0%; per capita expenditure US$2.

Background

The earliest inhabitants of Sierra Leone were probably the Buloms; the Mende and Temne peoples arrived in the 15th century. The coastal region was visited by the Portuguese in the 15th century, and by 1495 there was a Portuguese fort on the site of modern Freetown. European ships visited the coast regularly to trade for slaves and ivory, and the English built trading posts on offshore islands in the 17th century. British abolitionists and philanthropists founded Freetown in 1787 as a private venture for freed and runaway slaves. In 1808 the coastal settlement became a British colony. The region became a British

1 metric ton = about 1.1 short tons; 1 kilometer = 0.6 mi (statute); 1 metric ton-km cargo = about 0.68 short ton-mi cargo; c.i.f.: cost, insurance, and freight; f.o.b.: free on board

Aug 2008, Beijing, China: The 2008 Olympic Games commenced with a spectacular opening ceremony

9 Aug 2008, Vladikavkaz, Russia: Tanks roll toward former Soviet republic Georgia as Russia aided the Moscow-leaning breakaway provinces of Abkhazia and South Ossetia. More than 1,500 people died before a cease-fire took hold. At right, a Georgian couple mourn their son's death.

17 Feb 2008, Pristina, Kosovo: Young Kosovars celebrate as the Serb province declared its independence. The new nation was recognized by the US and most Western powers, but both Russia and Serbia opposed and denounced the breakaway.

14 Mar 2008, India: After Tibetans proteste against Chinese rule, a monk in Dharmshala, India, joined the cause

23 Jan 2008, Gaza Strip: Defying an Israe blockade, thousands of Palestinians crossed freely into Egypt from Rafah in the southern Gaza Strip after an Israeli security wall wa breached by Palestinian

.6 Jul 2008, Beirut, Lebanon: Militants :heer after five Hezbollah prisoners were 'eleased by Israel in exchange for the remains of Israeli soldiers.

7 Jul 2008, Kabul, Afghanistan: Afghan police guard the Indian embassy after a car bomb killed more than 40 people. Resurgent Taliban forces in Afghanistan forced US troops to abandon a base in mid-July.

.0 Mar 2008, Baghdad, Iraq: US soldiers inspect the site of a car bombing in the Shaab section of the city 2008 saw a decline in US casualties in Iraq, as the "surge" strategy that sent 27,000 more US troops to the ation, as well as a reduction of internal political tensions, helped restore order.

18 Aug 2008, Islamabad, Pakistan: Under threat of impeachment by a new government, Pakistan's Pres. Pervez Musharraf announced he would step down.

30 Jun 2008, Sharm el-Sheikh, Egypt: Zimbabwe's Pres. Robert Mugabe, here at a meeting abroad, refused to step down after he appeared to have lost the popular vote in a March election.

26 Jul 2008, Diyala province, Iraq: Gen. David Petraeus, the top US commander in Iraq and author of the US "surge" strategy, speaks to local leaders at a marketplace.

2 Jul 2008, Bogotá, Colombia: Former hostage Ingrid Betancourt rejoices after being freed in a surprise operation in the Colombian jungle.

21 May 2008, Tel Aviv, Israel: Prime minister Ehud Olmert, shown here discussing peace talks with Syria, said in July he would step down in

23 Jul 2008, Gorki, Russia: New Pres. Dmitry Med vedev meets with former President and new Prime Minister Vladimir Putin outside Moscow. Putin steppe down in May but was widel seen to be running Russia through his handpicked successor. On 9 August, Putin left the Olympics in Beijing and flew home to direct generals heading up the invasion of Russia's neighbor, Georgia.

18 Jul 2008, Belgrade, Serbia: Former Bosnian Serb leader and longtime fugitive Radovan Karadzic wa arrested in Serbia's capital. At left, Karadzic is shown in 1996; at right, he is seen in his adopted role as a health guru, which had allowed him to escape detection for years Karadzic will stand trial for wa crimes before a UN tribunal.

14 Jul 2008, Paris, France: Pres. Nikolas Sarkoz and his wife, onetime super model Carla Bruni, observe Bastille Day. Energetic and controversial, Sarkozy vowe to restore France's leadership role in global affairs. H welcomed former hostage Ingrid Betancourt to France earlier in July and flew to Moscow to argue for a peac deal after Russia invaded Georgia in August

28 Aug 2008, Denver CO: Democratic presidential candidate Sen. Barack Obama and running mate Sen. Joe Biden are hailed by delegates after Obama's acceptance address at the party's national convention. In choosing the long-serving Biden, chairman of the Senate Committee on Foreign Affairs, Obama sought to counter Republican charges that he lacked experience in foreign policy.

[illegible] Sep 2008, St. Paul MN: Republican presidential candidate Sen. John McCain and his running mate, Alaska Gov. Sarah Palin, are cheered at the GOP national convention. McCain's surprise choice of Palin, a strong social conservative, shook up the campaign, rallying the party's conservative base even as Democrat [illegible]

3 Jun 2008, New York NY: Democratic Sen. Hillary Clinton speaks, days before quitting the presidential race.

13 Jun 2008, Houston TX: Former Arkansas governor Mike Huckabee speaks at the Republican Texas convention.

2 May 2008, Augusta ME: Former Massachusetts governor Mitt Romney speaks at the Maine GOP convention.

18 Feb 2008, Tijuana, Mexico: Two Mexican men gaze into the US from behind a border fence on the beach. New sections of the long border wall between the two nations were built in Arizona and California in 2008.

12 Mar 2008, New York NY: Democrat Eliot Spitzer stepped down as governor of New York state after federal agents identified him as a patron of a high-end prostitution ring.

21 May 2008, Boston MA: Sen. Ted Kennedy leaves the hospital after a brain tumor diagnosis.

14 Apr 2008, Eldoraco TX: Female members of a 700-person fundamentalist Mormon community, the Yearning for Zion Ranch, gather after Texas authorities raided the compound and removed 462 minors upon allegations that they had been sexually abused. On 22 May a state appeals court ordered the children released, stating there was insufficient evidence to warrant their removal.

14 Jun 2008, Cedar Rapids IA: Cities and towns in Iowa and Missouri were flooded after heavy spring and early-summer rains raised the level of the Mississippi River. At least 24,000 people were forced from their homes in Cedar Rapids.

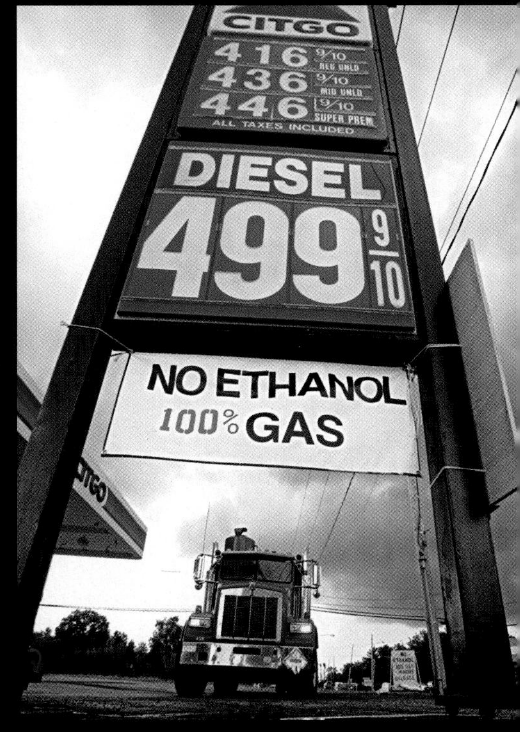

22 Apr 2008, Moreno Valley CA: As the US "housing bubble" collapsed, eal-estate values sank and the nation was nit with a wave of foreclosures that affected ederal mortgage giants Fannie Mae and Freddie Mac. In July Congress passed a plan to help both homeowners and the ederal lenders.

18 Jun 2008, Moreau NY: Oil prices soared to more than US$140 a barrel in he summer, causing price hikes across he US economy.

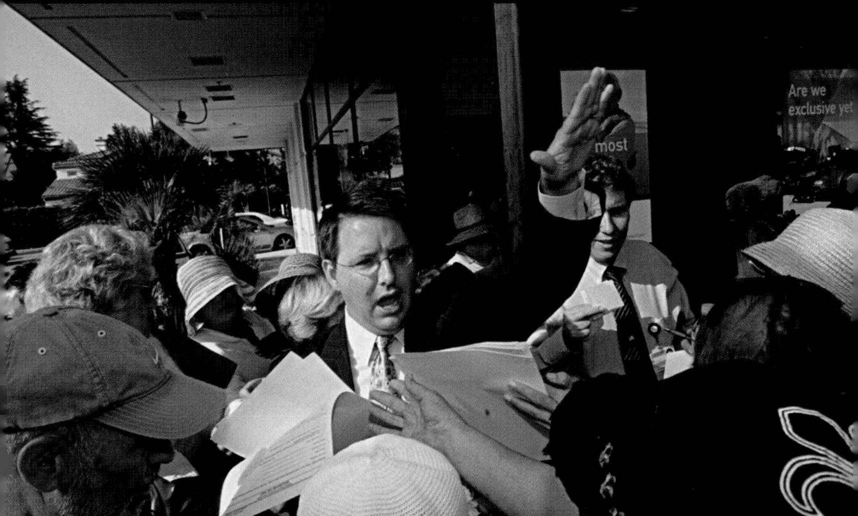

.5 Jul 2008, Encino CA: As the US economy faltered, the IndyMac Bank, a major mortgage lender, failed or 1 July. Here, depositors gather to remove money from their accounts.

18 May 2008, Mianzhu City, China: An aerial view shows massive damage six days after an earthquake measured at 7.9 on the moment-magnitude scale by the United States Geological Survey struck in China's Sichuan province. Official estimates placed the death toll at close to 70,000. The number of homeless was estimated at as many as 11 million people.

NASA

10 Jun 2008, Mars: NASA's Phoenix probe landed in the northern hemisphere of Mars via parachute on 25 May. The geological explorer's robot arm took soil samples from beneath the planet's surface, confirming the presence of water ice. But NASA officials said the tests showed the planet is neither as Earth-like nor as life-friendly as some had proposed in the past.

16 Aug 2008, Beijing, China: Jamaican sprinter Usain Bolt set a new world record of 9.69 seconds in winning the 100-m race. He later won the 200-m race, also in world record time.

21 Aug 2008, Beijing, China: Misty May-Treanor and Kerri Walsh of the US beat a Chinese team to win gold medals in the beach volleyball competition.

11 Aug 2008, Beijing, China: US swimmer Michael Phelps exults after the US men's team placed first in the 4x100-m freestyle relay event at the Beijing Games. Phelps made history when he won 8 gold medals at the Games, breaking US swimmer Mark Spitz's record of 7 golds at the 1972 Munich Games. Phelps broke 7 world records in Beijing and now holds 14 gold medals, the most won by a single athlete in Olympic history.

6 Jun 2008, San Diego CA: Popular journeyman Rocco Mediate, left, joins Tiger Woods after the two men dueled in an 18-hole play-off round at the US Open. Woods won, bringing his total number of wins in golf's four major events to 14, but days later he said he would undergo leg surgery and would not play again in 2008.

6 Jul 2008, Wimbledon, England: After years of dominating men's professional tennis, Swiss Roger Federer, left, yielded his No. 1 position to Spain's Rafael Nadal, right. Nadal beat Federer at the French Open in Paris and for the first time, at Wimbledon, where he ended Federer's streak of British championships at five straight. In August Nadal also won the men's gold medal at the Olympic tennis tournament in Beijing.

17 Jun 2008, Boston MA: From left, Celtics Kevin Garnett, Ray Allen, and Paul Pierce beat the LA Lakers to become NBA champs.

20 Jul 2008, Southport, England: Ireland's Padraig Harrington won both the British Open and the PGA Championship in 2008.

5 Jul 2008, Wimbledon, England: Sisters Venus and Serena Williams faced off in Wimbledon tennis final: older sister Venus won.

3 Feb 2008, Glendale AZ: New York Giants linebacker Zak DeOssie cheers after the Giants beat the favored New England Patriots 17–14 to win Super Bowl XLII.

29 Jun 2008, Vienna, Austria: Spain's Iker Casillas exults after Spain beat Germany 1–0 to

4 Jul 2008, New York NY: Lights illuminate a waterfall on the Manhattan side
as 4th of July fireworks burst behind. Danish-Icelandic environmental artist Olafur
waterfalls around New York Harbor in the summer of 2008.

18 Jul 2008, Hollywood CA: Australian actor Heath Ledger starred as the Joke
latest in the long-running Batman series. The film topped the US box office for fou
become one of the most financially successful films in history. Ledger, 28, was fo

26 Feb 2008, Pyongyang, North Korea: The New York Philharmonic plays at the East Pyongyang Grand Theater in North Korea's capital city. It was the first significant cultural visit by an American performing arts company to the communist nation since the end of the Korean War in the early 1950s.

24 Feb 2008, Hollywood CA: Non-Americans swept the acting honors at the Oscar Awards. From left, Britons Daniel Day-Lewis and Tilda Swinton, France's Marion Cotillard, and Spain's Javier Bardem.

15 Jun 2008, New York NY: Actress Kelli O'Hara performs a song from *South Pacific* at the Tony Awards. The revival of the 1949 Rodgers and Hammerstein musical won 7 Tonys.

OBITUARIES

Tim Russert: The widely respected, veteran NBC-TV journalist, host of *Meet the Press* and writer of the popular 2004 memoir *Big Russ and Me,* about his father, died on 13 June at 58 of a heart attack.

Jesse Helms: The longtime senator from North Carolina, admired by many for his conservative views but also denounced as a white supremacist, died on 4 July at 86.

Benazir Bhutto: The former prime minister of Pakistan was murdered in Rawalpindi on 27 Dec 2007, at 54, while campaigning in the nation's parliamentary elections. Bhutto was targeted by gunfire and a car bomb also exploded, killing some 20 spectators.

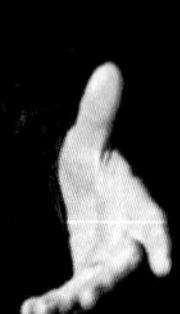

Aleksandr Solzhenitsyn: The Nobel Prize-winning writer who chronicled the Soviet gulag died at 89 on 3 August in Moscow. Expelled from the Soviet Union in 1974, he lived in the US until he returned to Russia in 1994.

George Carlin: The stand-up comic, known for his defiance of convention and witty musings on language, died at 71 on 22 June in California.

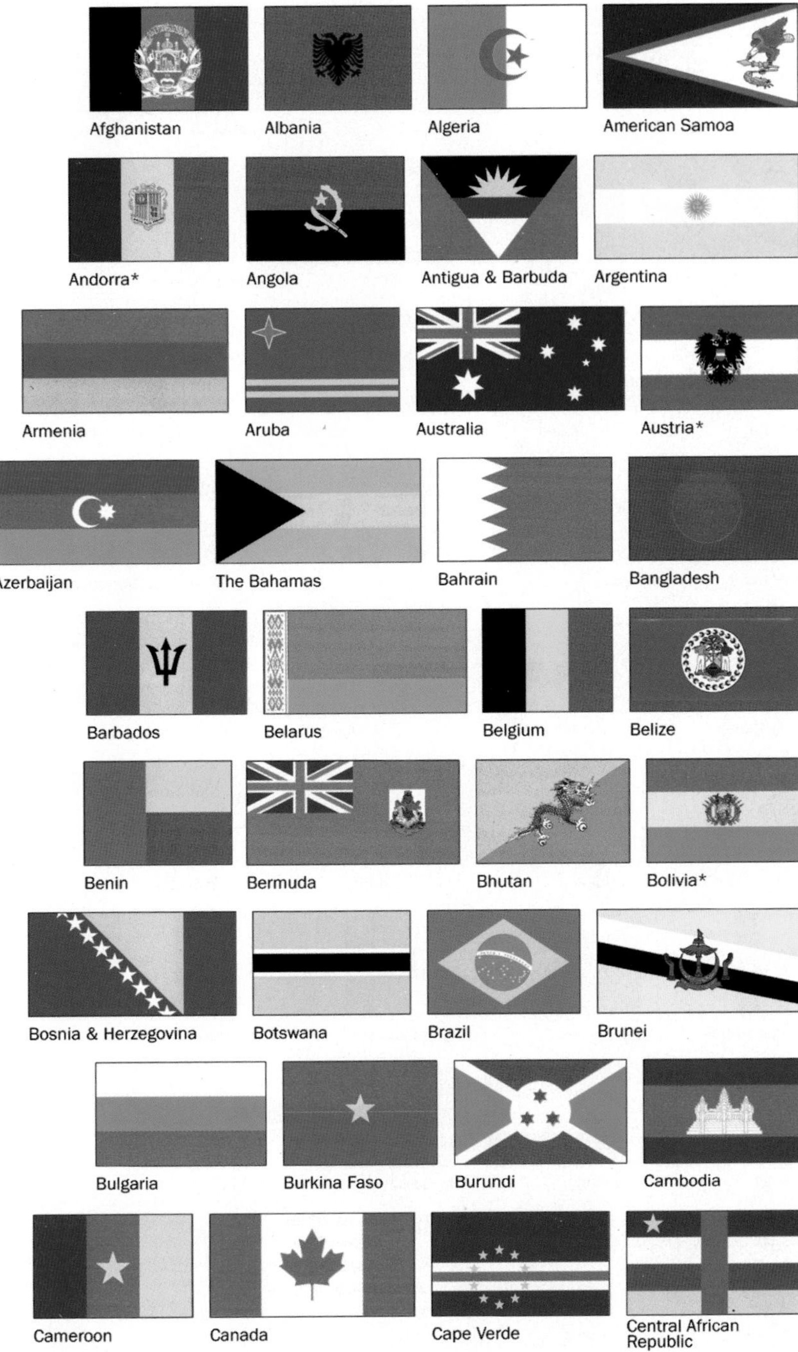

Civil flags are shown except where marked thus (*); in these cases, government flags are shown in order to illustrate emblems. Both styles are official national flags.

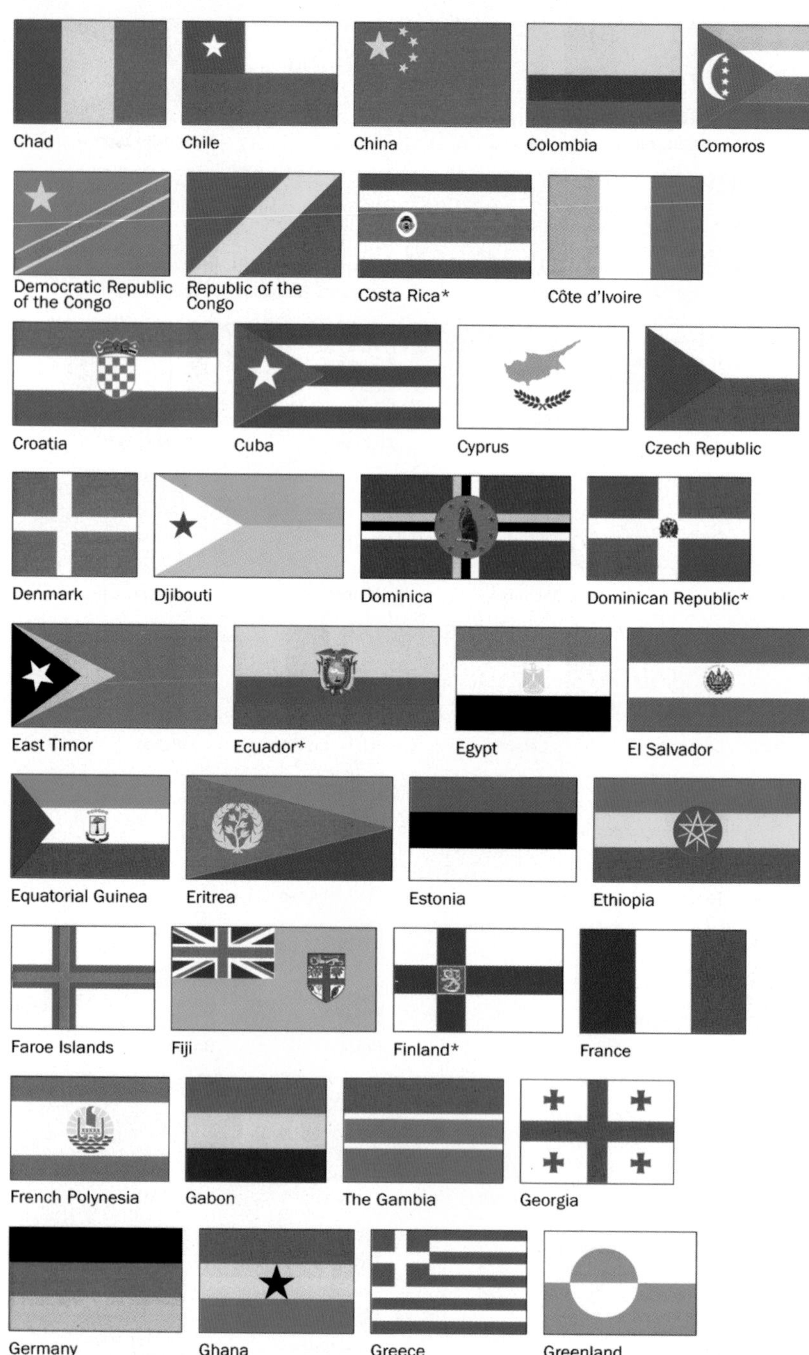

Chad Chile China Colombia Comoros

Democratic Republic of the Congo Republic of the Congo Costa Rica* Côte d'Ivoire

Croatia Cuba Cyprus Czech Republic

Denmark Djibouti Dominica Dominican Republic*

East Timor Ecuador* Egypt El Salvador

Equatorial Guinea Eritrea Estonia Ethiopia

Faroe Islands Fiji Finland* France

French Polynesia Gabon The Gambia Georgia

Germany Ghana Greece Greenland

Civil flags are shown except where marked thus (*); in these cases, government flags are shown in order to illustrate emblems. Both styles are official national flags.

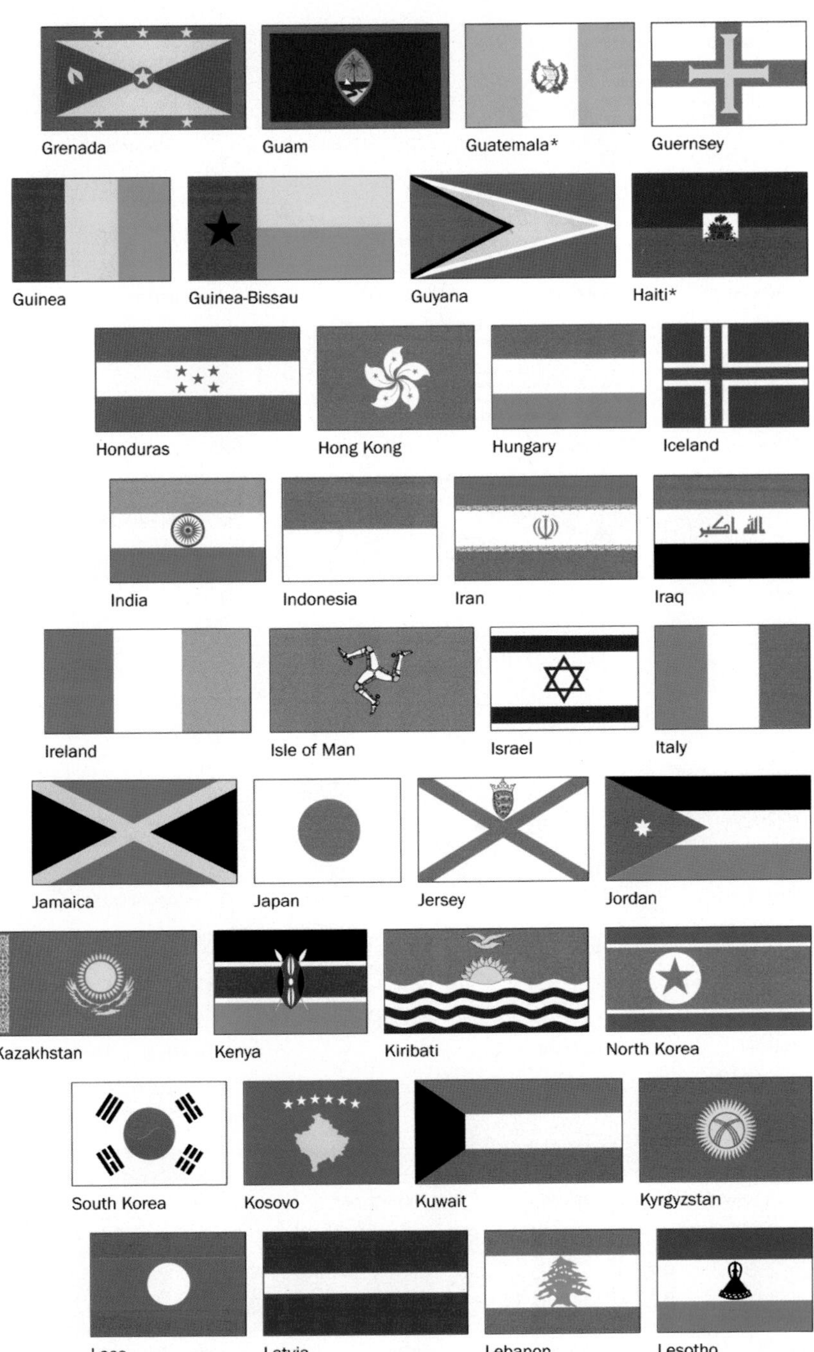

Civil flags are shown except where marked thus (*); in these cases, government flags are shown in order to illustrate emblems. Both styles are official national flags.

Liberia 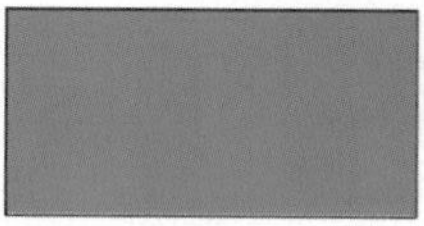 Libya  Liechtenstein  Lithuania

Luxembourg  Macau  Macedonia Madagascar

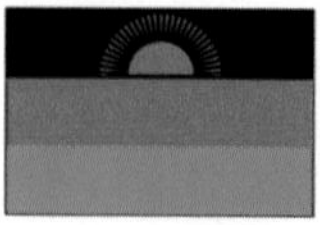

Malawi  Malaysia  Maldives  Mali

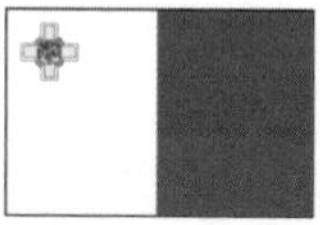

Malta  Marshall Islands  Mauritania  Mauritius

Mexico  Federated States of Micronesia  Moldova 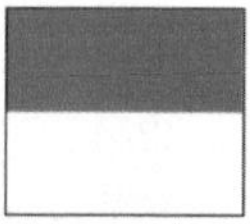 Monaco

Mongolia  Montenegro  Morocco  Mozambique

Myanmar  Namibia  Nauru  Nepal  The Netherlands

Netherlands Antilles  New Zealand  Nicaragua*  Niger

Nigeria

Norway

Oman

Pakistan

Civil flags are shown except where marked thus (*); in these cases, government flags are shown in order to illustrate emblems. Both styles are official national flags.

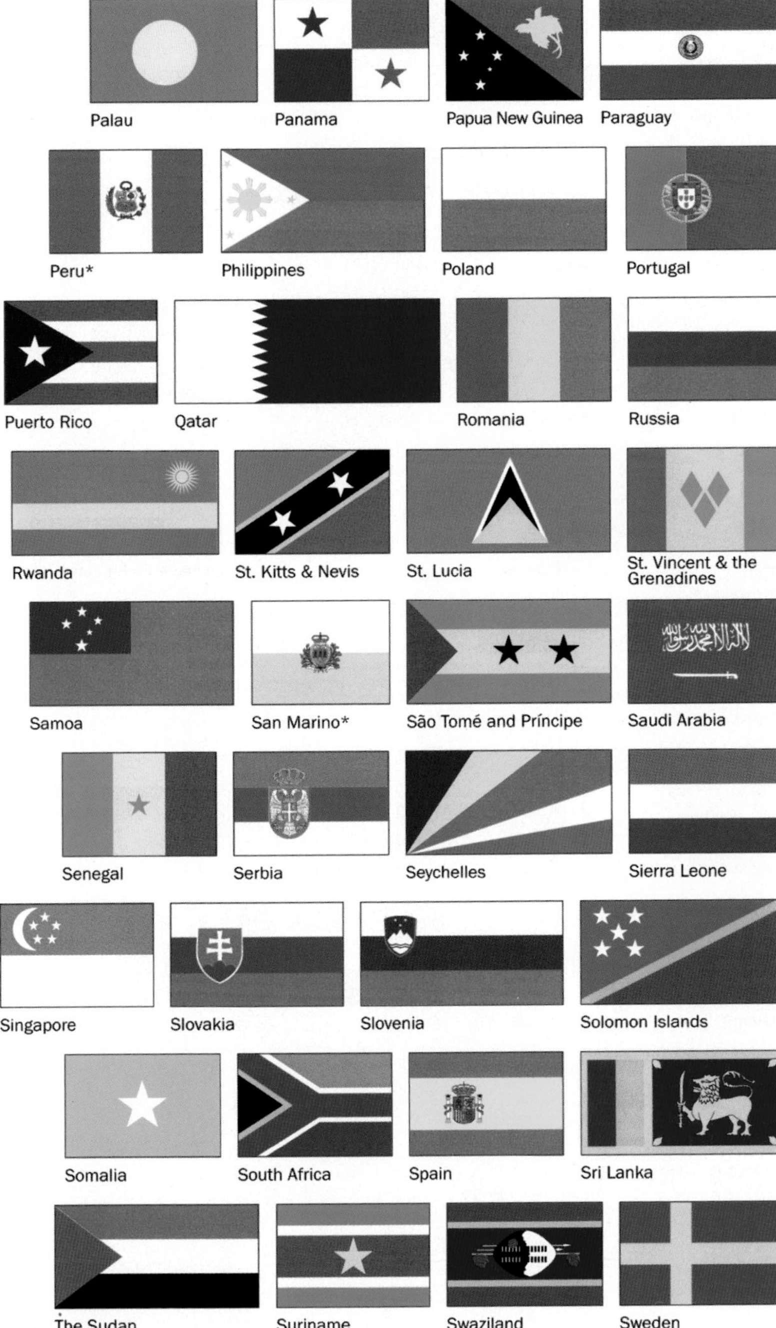

Civil flags are shown except where marked thus (*); in these cases, government flags are shown in order to illustrate emblems. Both styles are official national flags.

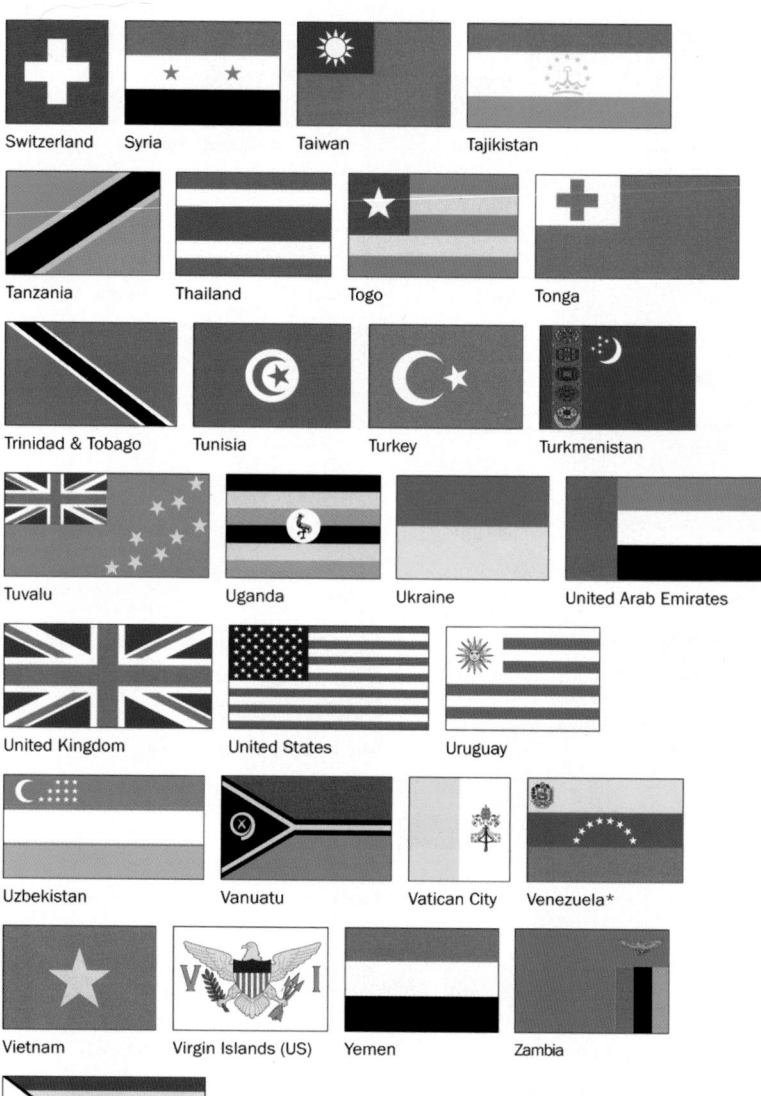

Switzerland Syria Taiwan Tajikistan

Tanzania Thailand Togo Tonga

Trinidad & Tobago Tunisia Turkey Turkmenistan

Tuvalu Uganda Ukraine United Arab Emirates

United Kingdom United States Uruguay

Uzbekistan Vanuatu Vatican City Venezuela*

Vietnam Virgin Islands (US) Yemen Zambia

Zimbabwe

Civil flags are shown except where marked thus (*); in these cases, government flags are shown in order to illustrate emblems. Both styles are official national flags.

World Religions

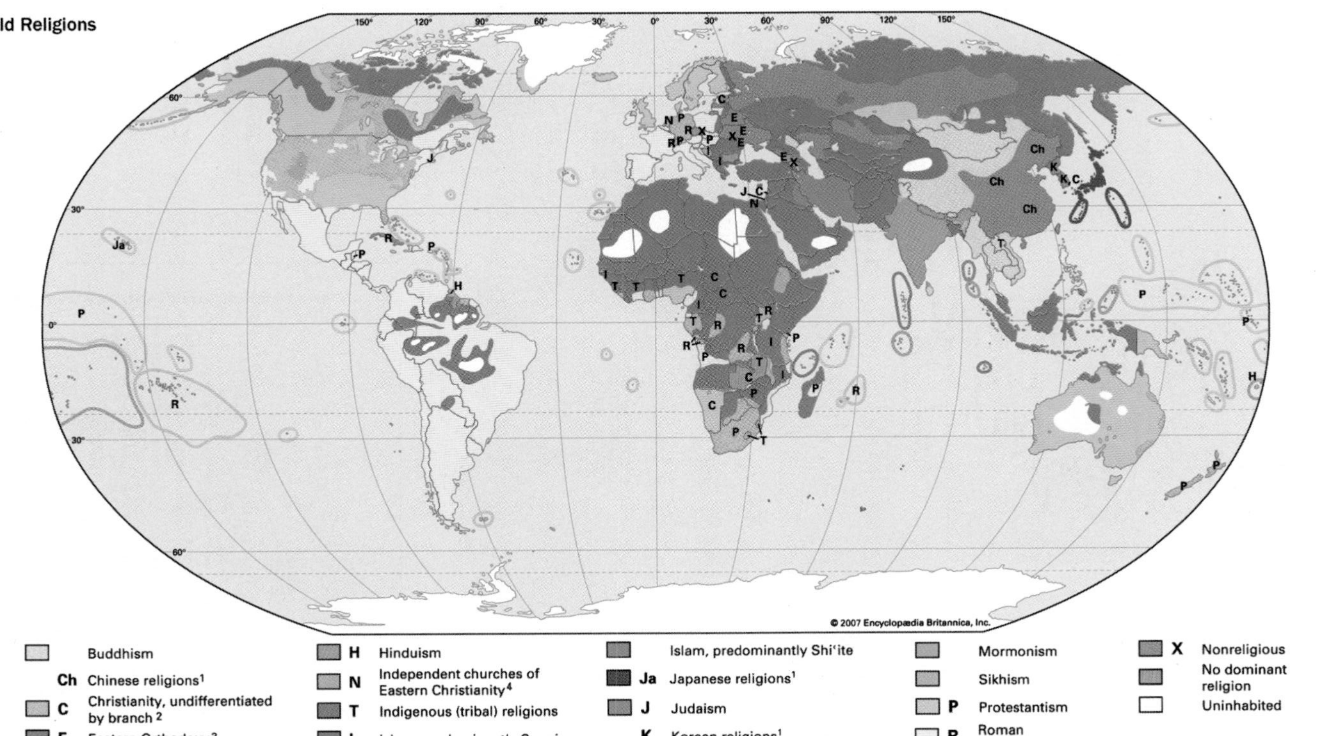

Footnotes:

[1] In certain eastern Asian areas, many of the people have plural religious affiliations. Religions in China and Korea include Buddhism, Taoism, Confucianism, and folk cults. The Japanese religions include Shintō and Buddhism.

[2] Chiefly mingled Protestantism and Roman Catholicism, neither predominant.

[3] Including Greek and Russian Orthodox Christianity.

[4] Including Armenian, Coptic, Ethiopian, East and West Syrian.

Note:

The majority of the inhabitants in each of the areas colored on the map share the religious tradition indicated. Letter symbols show religious traditions shared by at least 25 percent of the inhabitants within areas no smaller than 1,000 square miles. Therefore minority religions of city dwellers have generally not been represented.

RUSSIA
ARCTIC OCEAN
North Pole
Arctic Circle
GREENLAND (DEN.)
CANADA
ALEUTIAN ISLANDS
UNITED STATES
150°
120°
90°
60°
30°
QUEEN ELIZABETH ISLANDS
CHUKCHI SEA
BEAUFORT SEA
VICTORIA I.
BAFFIN I.
Baffin Bay
GREENLAND (DEN.)
Nuuk
Reykjavík
BROOKS RANGE
ALASKA (U.S.)
Fairbanks
Yukon
Mackenzie
Great Bear L.
BERING SEA
ALASKA RANGE
Mt. McKinley
Anchorage
Great Slave L.
Hudson Bay
LABRADOR SEA
Gulf of Alaska
Peace
C A N A D A
ROCKY MOUNTAINS
GREAT PLAINS
Edmonton
Saskatoon
Vancouver
Calgary
Winnipeg
L. Superior
Quebec
NEWFOUNDLAND
St. John's
Seattle
Montreal
Ottawa
Minneapolis
L. Huron
Portland
Snake
Michigan
Toronto
Halifax
Gulf of St. Lawrence
Chicago
Detroit
Boston
Missouri
U N I T E D   S T A T E S
New York City
Philadelphia
Washington, D.C.
APPALACHIAN MTS.
San Francisco
Las Vegas
Denver
Kansas City
Ohio
St. Louis
Colorado
Arkansas
Memphis
ATLANTIC OCEAN
AZORES (PORTUGAL)
Los Angeles
Phoenix
Oklahoma City
Dallas
Atlanta
Mississippi
San Diego
Ciudad Juárez
Rio Grande
BERMUDA (U.K.)
MADEIRA IS. (PORTUGAL)
30°
MIDWAY IS. (U.S.)
Baja California
SIERRA MADRE OCCIDENTAL
MEXICO
Houston
Gulf of Mexico
CANARY IS. (SPAIN)
El Aaiún
WESTERN SAHARA (occupied by Morocco)
Tropic of Cancer
Monterrey
THE BAHAMAS
HAWAII (U.S.)
Bay of Campeche
CUBA
DOMINICAN REPUBLIC
Guadalajara
Mexico City
Belmopan
BELIZE
HAITI
JAMAICA
Nouakchott
CAPE VERDE
Praia
THE GAMBIA
Dakar
Banjul
Bissau
GUINEA-BISSAU
Conakry
Freetown
SIERRA LEONE
Monrovia
Yamoussoukro
Guatemala City
GUATEMALA
San Salvador
EL SALVADOR
HONDURAS
Tegucigalpa
NICARAGUA
Managua
CARIBBEAN SEA
PACIFIC OCEAN
COSTA RICA
PANAMA
VENEZUELA
LLANOS
Orinoco
GUYANA
SURINAME
Georgetown
Paramaribo
Cayenne
FRENCH GUIANA (FR.)
PALMYRA ATOLL (U.S.)
Bogotá
Cali
COLOMBIA
GUIANA HIGHLANDS
Equator
0°
GALAPAGOS IS. (ECUADOR)
Quito
ECUADOR
Guayaquil
Manaus
Amazon
Belém
Fortaleza
KIRIBATI
Iquitos
Madeira
Tapajós
Xingu
Recife
PERU
ANDES
B R A Z I L
Tocantins
São Francisco
COOK IS. (N.Z.)
SAMOA
AMERICAN SAMOA (U.S.)
Lima
Ucayali
FRENCH POLYNESIA (FR.)
L. Titicaca
La Paz
BRAZILIAN HIGHLANDS
Brasília
Salvador
Arequipa
BOLIVIA
Sucre
TONGA
Belo Horizonte
Tropic of Capricorn
PARAGUAY
Paraná
Rio de Janeiro
São Paulo
ATLANTIC OCEAN
Antofagasta
ATACAMA DESERT
GRAN CHACO
Asunción
EASTER I. (CHILE)
SAN FÉLIX I.
SAN AMBROSIO I. (CHILE)
30°
Pôrto Alegre
Córdoba
MOUNTAINS
PAMPAS
Mt. Aconcagua
Valparaíso
Rosario
URUGUAY
Montevideo
JUAN FERNÁNDEZ ISLANDS (CHILE)
Santiago
Buenos Aires
Concepción
ARGENTINA
CHILE
CHILOÉ I.
PATAGONIA
FALKLAND IS. (ISLAS MALVINAS) (administered by U.K., claimed by ARG.)
SOUTH GEORGIA (U.K.)
Argentina, Australia, Chile, France, New Zealand, Norway, and the United Kingdom claim portions of Antarctica; all claims in Antarctica are in abeyance under the terms of the Antarctic Treaty effective in 1961.
TIERRA DEL FUEGO
Cape Horn

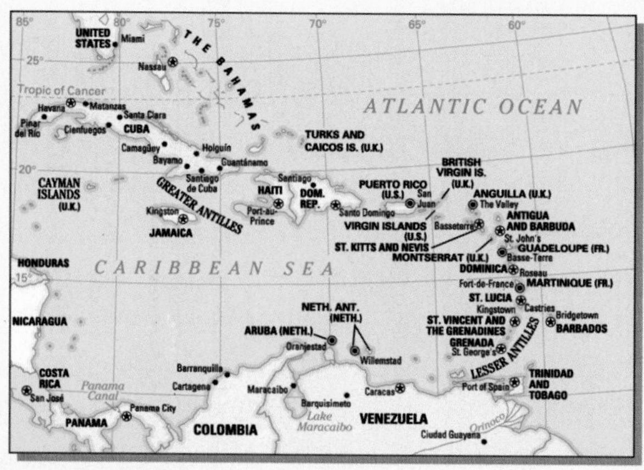

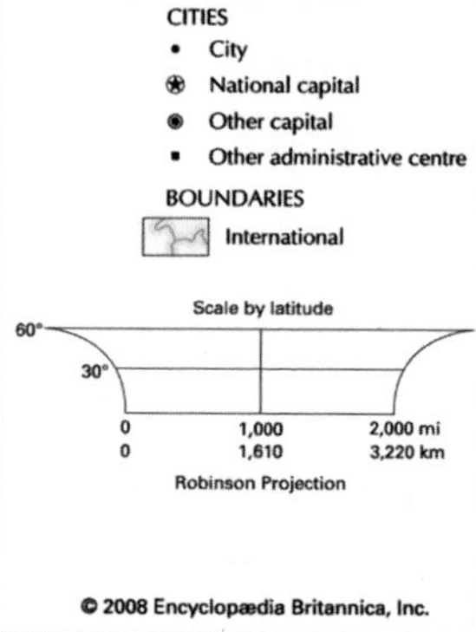

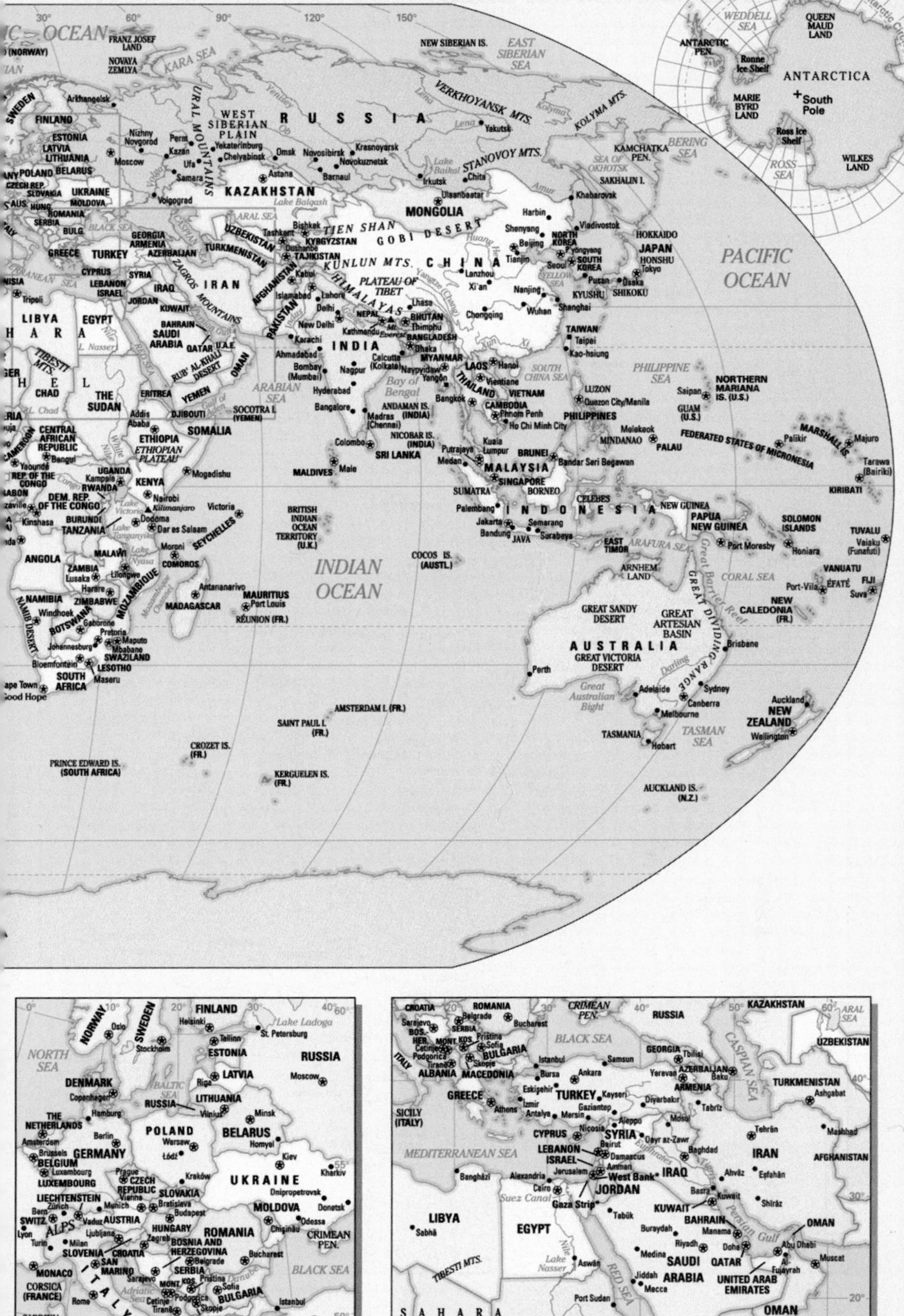

30°
60°
90°
120°
150°
FRANZ JOSEF LAND
(NORWAY)
NOVAYA ZEMLYA
KARA SEA
NEW SIBERIAN IS.
EAST SIBERIAN SEA
SWEDEN
FINLAND
Arkhangelsk
URAL MOUNTAINS
WEST SIBERIAN PLAIN
R U S S I A
VERKHOYANSK MTS.
KOLYMA MTS.
Yakutsk
ESTONIA
LATVIA
LITHUANIA
POLAND
BELARUS
CZECH REP.
SLOVAKIA
UKRAINE
MOLDOVA
AUS.
HUNG.
ROMANIA
SERBIA
BULG.
Nizhny Novgorod
Moscow
Perm
Kazan
Ufa
Samara
Yekaterinburg
Chelyabinsk
Omsk
Novosibirsk
Krasnoyarsk
Novokuznetsk
Barnaul
Irkutsk
Chita
STANOVOY MTS.
Lake Baikal
KAMCHATKA PEN.
BERING SEA
SEA OF OKHOTSK
SAKHALIN I.
Astana
KAZAKHSTAN
Volgograd
Lake Balqash
Ulaanbaatar
MONGOLIA
Khabarovsk
Harbin
Vladivostok
ARAL SEA
BLACK SEA
GEORGIA
ARMENIA
AZERBAIJAN
UZBEKISTAN
TURKMENISTAN
Bishkek
Tashkent
KYRGYZSTAN
Dushanbe
TAJIKISTAN
TIEN SHAN
GOBI DESERT
Shenyang
Beijing
Tianjin
NORTH KOREA
P'yongyang
Seoul
SOUTH KOREA
HOKKAIDO
JAPAN
HONSHU
Tokyo
Osaka
SHIKOKU
KYUSHU
Pusan
YELLOW SEA
GREECE
TURKEY
CYPRUS
SYRIA
LEBANON
ISRAEL
JORDAN
IRAQ
IRAN
ZAGROS MOUNTAINS
AFGHANISTAN
Kabul
Islamabad
Lahore
KUNLUN MTS.
C H I N A
Lanzhou
Xi'an
PLATEAU OF TIBET
HIMALAYAS
Lhasa
Nanjing
Wuhan
Shanghai
Chongqing
PACIFIC OCEAN
Tripoli
LIBYA
EGYPT
KUWAIT
BAHRAIN
SAUDI ARABIA
QATAR
U.A.E.
PAKISTAN
Delhi
New Delhi
NEPAL
Kathmandu
Mt. Everest
BHUTAN
Thimphu
BANGLADESH
Dhaka
TAIWAN
Taipei
Kao-hsiung
TIBESTI MTS.
L. Nasser
RED SEA
RUB' AL-KHALI DESERT
OMAN
Karachi
Ahmadabad
INDIA
Calcutta (Kolkata)
MYANMAR
Nay Pyi Taw
Yangon
LAOS
Hanoi
Vientiane
THAILAND
Bangkok
SOUTH CHINA SEA
PHILIPPINE SEA
NORTHERN MARIANA IS. (U.S.)
Saipan
CHAD
THE SUDAN
ERITREA
YEMEN
Gulf of Aden
DJIBOUTI
ARABIAN SEA
Bombay (Mumbai)
Nagpur
Hyderabad
Bangalore
Madras (Chennai)
Bay of Bengal
ANDAMAN IS. (INDIA)
CAMBODIA
Phnom Penh
VIETNAM
Ho Chi Minh City
LUZON
Quezon City/Manila
PHILIPPINES
GUAM (U.S.)
L. Chad
Addis Ababa
ETHIOPIA
SOCOTRA I. (YEMEN)
SOMALIA
CENTRAL AFRICAN REPUBLIC
Bangui
CAMEROON
Yaoundé
ETHIOPIAN PLATEAU
Colombo
SRI LANKA
NICOBAR IS. (INDIA)
Putrajaya
Kuala Lumpur
Medan
BRUNEI
Bandar Seri Begawan
MINDANAO
Melekeok
PALAU
FEDERATED STATES OF MICRONESIA
Palikir
MARSHALL IS.
Majuro
REP. OF THE CONGO
UGANDA
Kampala
KENYA
Mogadishu
MALDIVES
Male
MALAYSIA
SINGAPORE
Tarawa (Bairiki)
KIRIBATI
DEM. REP. OF THE CONGO
RWANDA
BURUNDI
Nairobi
Lake Victoria
Kilimanjaro
Victoria
SEYCHELLES
SUMATRA
BORNEO
CELEBES
Kinshasa
TANZANIA
Dodoma
Dar es Salaam
Lake Tanganyika
BRITISH INDIAN OCEAN TERRITORY (U.K.)
Palembang
I N D O N E S I A
NEW GUINEA
PAPUA NEW GUINEA
Port Moresby
SOLOMON ISLANDS
Honiara
TUVALU
Vaiaku (Funafuti)
Jakarta
Bandung
JAVA
Semarang
Surabaya
EAST TIMOR
ARAFURA SEA
ANGOLA
MALAWI
Lake Nyasa
Lilongwe
ZAMBIA
Lusaka
Moroni
COMOROS
COCOS IS. (AUSTL.)
INDIAN OCEAN
ARNHEM LAND
CORAL SEA
VANUATU
Port-Vila
ÉFATÉ
FIJI
Suva
Harare
ZIMBABWE
MOZAMBIQUE
Mozambique Channel
Antananarivo
MAURITIUS
Port Louis
MADAGASCAR
RÉUNION (FR.)
NAMIBIA
Windhoek
NAMIB DESERT
BOTSWANA
Gaborone
Pretoria
Maputo
Mbabane
Johannesburg
SWAZILAND
Bloemfontein
LESOTHO
Maseru
SOUTH AFRICA
Cape Town
Good Hope
GREAT SANDY DESERT
GREAT ARTESIAN BASIN
GREAT DIVIDING RANGE
Great Barrier Reef
NEW CALEDONIA (FR.)
A U S T R A L I A
GREAT VICTORIA DESERT
Brisbane
Perth
Darling
Great Australian Bight
Adelaide
Sydney
Canberra
Melbourne
TASMANIA
Hobart
TASMAN SEA
Auckland
NEW ZEALAND
Wellington
AMSTERDAM I. (FR.)
SAINT PAUL I. (FR.)
CROZET IS. (FR.)
PRINCE EDWARD IS. (SOUTH AFRICA)
KERGUELEN IS. (FR.)
AUCKLAND IS. (N.Z.)
WEDDELL SEA
QUEEN MAUD LAND
Antarctic Circle
ANTARCTIC PEN.
Ronne Ice Shelf
ANTARCTICA
MARIE BYRD LAND
South Pole
Ross Ice Shelf
ROSS SEA
WILKES LAND
0°
10°
20°
30°
40°
60°
55°
50°
NORWAY
Oslo
SWEDEN
Stockholm
FINLAND
Helsinki
Lake Ladoga
St. Petersburg
Tallinn
ESTONIA
NORTH SEA
Riga
LATVIA
RUSSIA
Moscow
DENMARK
Copenhagen
BALTIC SEA
LITHUANIA
Vilnius
Minsk
THE NETHERLANDS
Hamburg
Amsterdam
Berlin
POLAND
Warsaw
Łódź
BELARUS
Homyel
Brussels
BELGIUM
GERMANY
Luxembourg
LUXEMBOURG
Prague
CZECH REPUBLIC
Kraków
Kiev
UKRAINE
Kharkiv
LIECHTENSTEIN
Zürich
Bern
Vaduz
Munich
Vienna
AUSTRIA
Bratislava
SLOVAKIA
Budapest
Dnipropetrovsk
Donetsk
MOLDOVA
Odessa
Chişinău
SWITZ.
ALPS
Milan
Lyon
Turin
Ljubljana
SLOVENIA
CROATIA
Zagreb
HUNGARY
BOSNIA AND HERZEGOVINA
ROMANIA
Bucharest
CRIMEAN PEN.
MONACO
SAN MARINO
Sarajevo
SERBIA
Belgrade
Danube
BLACK SEA
CORSICA (FRANCE)
I T A L Y
MONT.
KOS.
Pristina
Sofia
BULGARIA
Adriatic Sea
Cetinje
Podgorica
Skopje
Rome
Tirana
Istanbul
SARDINIA (ITALY)
ALBANIA
MACEDONIA
Ankara
TURKEY
GREECE
Athens
İzmir
SICILY (ITALY)
MALTA
MEDITERRANEAN SEA
CYPRUS
CROATIA
ROMANIA
Belgrade
Bucharest
CRIMEAN PEN.
RUSSIA
KAZAKHSTAN
ARAL SEA
Sarajevo
BOS. HER.
SERBIA
MONT.
KOS.
Pristina
Sofia
Cetinje
Podgorica
Skopje
Tirana
BULGARIA
ITALY
ALBANIA
MACEDONIA
BLACK SEA
GEORGIA
Tbilisi
CASPIAN SEA
UZBEKISTAN
Istanbul
Samsun
Bursa
Ankara
Yerevan
AZERBAIJAN
Baku
ARMENIA
TURKMENISTAN
Ashgabat
GREECE
Eskişehir
TURKEY
Kayseri
Izmir
Antalya
Mersin
Gaziantep
Diyarbakır
Tabrīz
Athens
SICILY (ITALY)
CYPRUS
Nicosia
Aleppo
SYRIA
Mosul
Tehrān
Mashhad
Dayr az-Zawr
LEBANON
Beirut
Euphrates
MEDITERRANEAN SEA
ISRAEL
Damascus
Baghdad
IRAN
AFGHANISTAN
Amman
Banghāzī
Alexandria
Jerusalem
West Bank*
IRAQ
Ahvāz
Eşfahān
Cairo
JORDAN
Suez Canal
Gaza Strip*
Basra
Kuwait
Tabūk
KUWAIT
Shīrāz
LIBYA
Sabhā
EGYPT
Buraydah
BAHRAIN
Manama
OMAN
Riyadh
Doha
Persian Gulf
Abu Dhabi
Lake Nasser
Nile
Aswān
Medina
SAUDI ARABIA
QATAR
Muscat
Al-Fujayrah
TIBESTI MTS.
Jiddah
Mecca
UNITED ARAB EMIRATES
RED SEA
Port Sudan
S A H A R A
OMAN
Largeau
ERITREA
Asmara
ARABIAN SEA
Khartoum
YEMEN
Sanaa
Al-Mukallā
CHAD
Lake Chad
THE SUDAN
Ta'izz
Gulf of Aden
DJIBOUTI
Djibouti
N'Djamena
ETHIOPIA
* Final status to be determined.

Africa

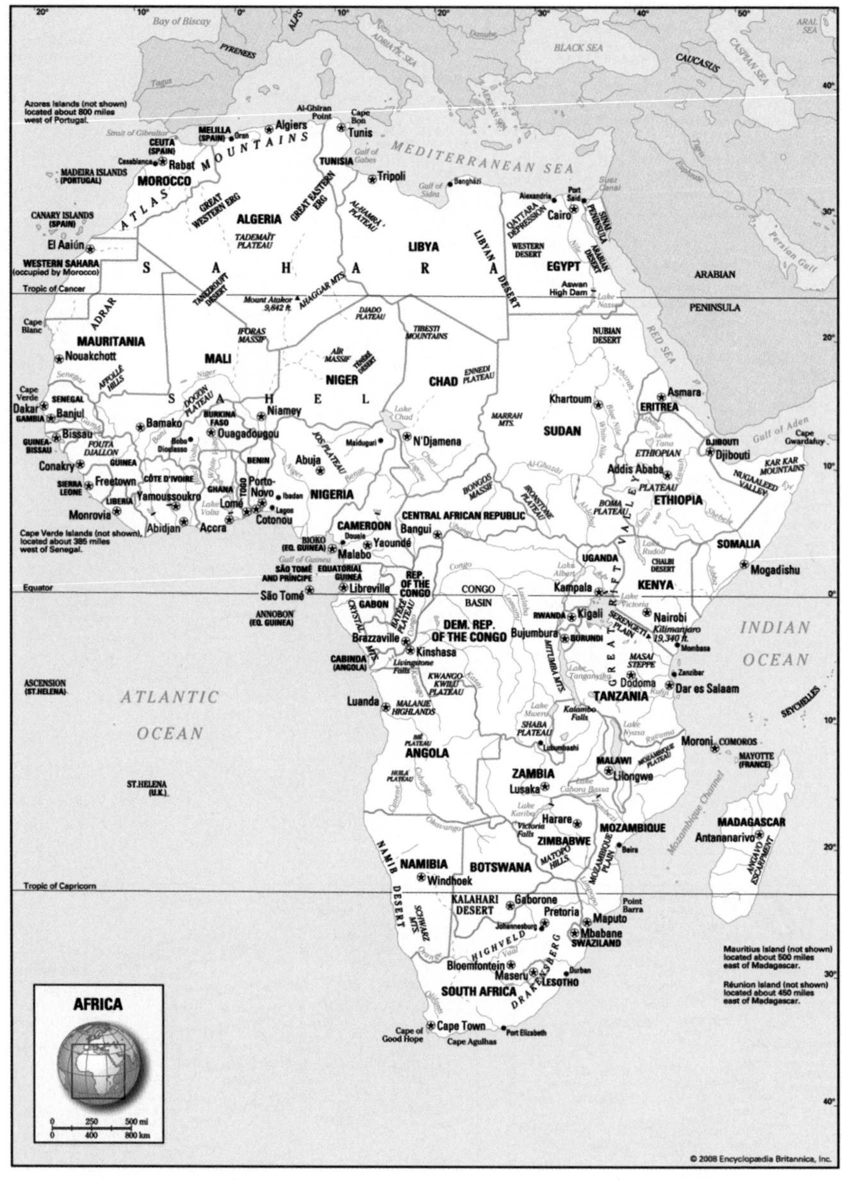

Bay of Biscay
PYRENEES
ALPS
ADRIATIC SEA
Danube
BLACK SEA
CAUCASUS
CASPIAN SEA
ARAL SEA
Tagus
Azores Islands (not shown) located about 800 miles west of Portugal.
Strait of Gibraltar
Al-Ghiran Point
Cape Bon
MELILLA (SPAIN)
Oran
Algiers
Tunis
CEUTA (SPAIN)
Casablanca
Rabat
ATLAS MOUNTAINS
TUNISIA
Gulf of Gabes
MEDITERRANEAN SEA
MADEIRA ISLANDS (PORTUGAL)
MOROCCO
Tripoli
Gulf of Sidra
Benghazi
Suez Canal
Tigris
Euphrates
CANARY ISLANDS (SPAIN)
GREAT WESTERN ERG
GREAT EASTERN ERG
ALGERIA
AL-HAMRA' PLATEAU
Alexandria
Port Said
Cairo
QATTARA DEPRESSION
SINAI PENINSULA
TADEMAÏT PLATEAU
LIBYA
LIBYAN DESERT
WESTERN DESERT
EGYPT
ARABIAN DESERT
Persian Gulf
El Aaiún
WESTERN SAHARA (occupied by Morocco)
S A H A R A
TANEZROUFT DESERT
AHAGGAR MTS.
Mount Atakor 9,642 ft.
Aswan High Dam
Lake Nasser
ARABIAN PENINSULA
Tropic of Cancer
ADRAR
Cape Blanc
MAURITANIA
Nouakchott
IFORAS MASSIF
DJADO PLATEAU
TIBESTI MOUNTAINS
NUBIAN DESERT
RED SEA
MALI
AÏR MASSIF
TÉNÉRÉ DESERT
NIGER
CHAD
ENNEDI PLATEAU
APPOLLÉ HILLS
Senegal
Niger
DOGON PLATEAU
S A H E L
Khartoum
Asmara
ERITREA
Cape Verde
Dakar
SENEGAL
Banjul
GAMBIA
Bamako
BURKINA FASO
Niamey
Lake Chad
MARRAH MTS.
SUDAN
Gulf of Aden
Cape Gwardafuy
GUINEA-BISSAU
Bissau
FOUTA DJALLON
Bobo-Dioulasso
Ouagadougou
JOS PLATEAU
Maiduguri
N'Djamena
Lake Tana
ETHIOPIAN PLATEAU
DJIBOUTI
Djibouti
Conakry
GUINEA
BENIN
Abuja
Al-Ghazal
Addis Ababa
KAR KAR MOUNTAINS
NUGAALEED VALLEY
SIERRA LEONE
Freetown
CÔTE D'IVOIRE
GHANA
TOGO
Porto-Novo
Ibadan
NIGERIA
BONGOS MASSIF
IRONSTONE PLATEAU
BOMA PLATEAU
ETHIOPIA
LIBERIA
Yamoussoukro
Lomé
Lagos
Monrovia
Lake Volta
Cotonou
Accra
Abidjan
CAMEROON
CENTRAL AFRICAN REPUBLIC
Bangui
Ubangi
Cape Verde Islands (not shown), located about 385 miles west of Senegal.
BIOKO (EQ. GUINEA)
Douala
Yaoundé
Malabo
Gulf of Guinea
Lake Rudolf
CHALBI DESERT
SOMALIA
SÃO TOMÉ AND PRÍNCIPE
EQUATORIAL GUINEA
UGANDA
Mogadishu
Lake Albert
Congo
REP. OF THE CONGO
KENYA
Equator
São Tomé
Libreville
CONGO BASIN
Kampala
Lake Victoria
GABON
GREAT RIFT VALLEY
ANNOBON (EQ. GUINEA)
CRYSTAL MTS.
BATÉKÉ PLATEAU
DEM. REP. OF THE CONGO
RWANDA
Kigali
Nairobi
SERENGETI PLAIN
Kilimanjaro 19,340 ft.
INDIAN OCEAN
Brazzaville
Kinshasa
Bujumbura
BURUNDI
Mombasa
CABINDA (ANGOLA)
Livingstone Falls
KWANGO-KWILU PLATEAU
MITUMBA MTS.
Lake Tanganyika
MASAI STEPPE
Zanzibar
ASCENSION (ST. HELENA)
ATLANTIC OCEAN
Dodoma
Dar es Salaam
TANZANIA
Kasai
Luanda
MALANJE HIGHLANDS
SEYCHELLES
Lake Mweru
Kalambo Falls
SHABA PLATEAU
Lake Nyasa
Lubumbashi
Moroni
COMOROS
ANGOLA
MALAWI
MOZAMBIQUE PLATEAU
MAYOTTE (FRANCE)
ST. HELENA (U.K.)
HUILA PLATEAU
ZAMBIA
Lilongwe
Lusaka
Lake Cahora Bassa
Mozambique Channel
Lake Kariba
Harare
MOZAMBIQUE
MADAGASCAR
Okavango
Victoria Falls
ZIMBABWE
Antananarivo
NAMIB DESERT
MATOPO HILLS
MOZAMBIQUE PLAIN
Beira
ANGAVO ESCARPMENT
NAMIBIA
BOTSWANA
Windhoek
Tropic of Capricorn
KALAHARI DESERT
Gaborone
Point Barra
Pretoria
Maputo
SCHWARZ MTS.
Johannesburg
Mbabane
SWAZILAND
HIGHVELD
Vaal
Orange
Mauritius Island (not shown) located about 500 miles east of Madagascar.
Bloemfontein
Maseru
DRAKENSBERG
Durban
LESOTHO
Réunion Island (not shown) located about 450 miles east of Madagascar.
SOUTH AFRICA
AFRICA
Cape of Good Hope
Cape Town
Cape Agulhas
Port Elizabeth
0 250 500 mi
0 400 800 km

Asia

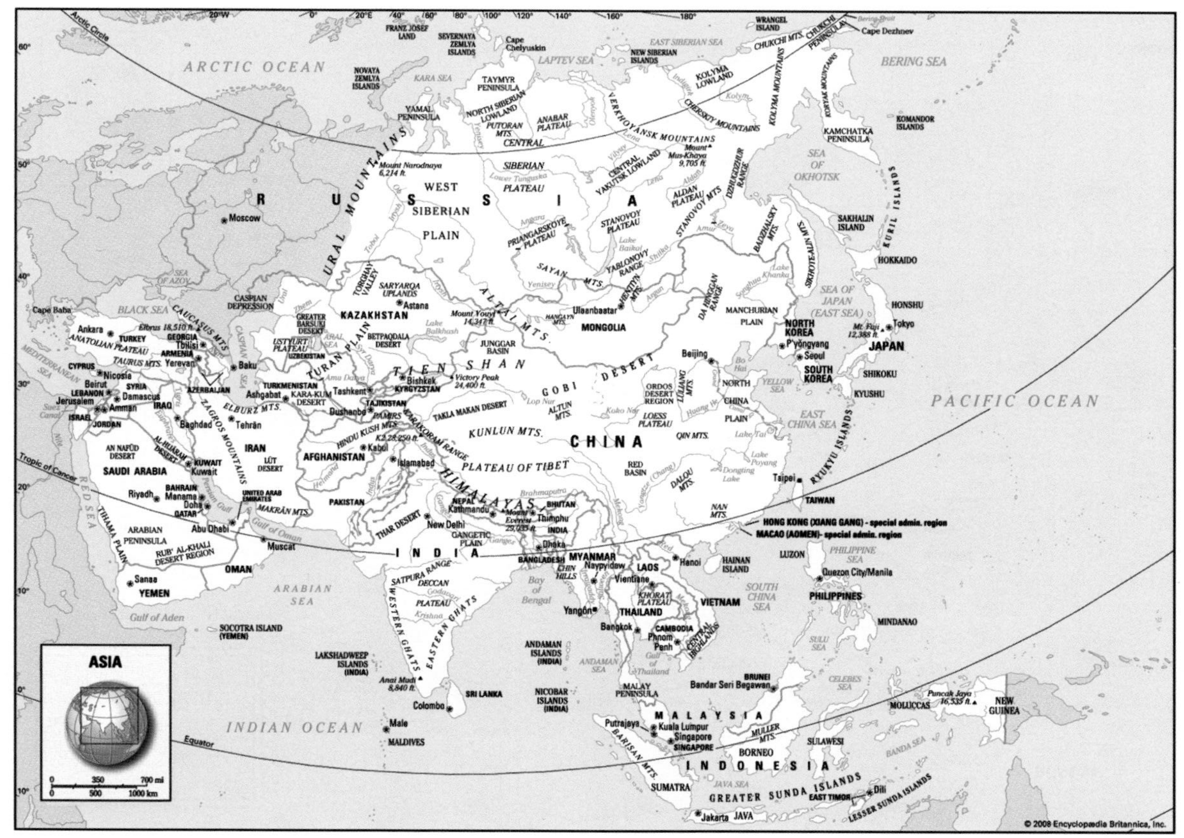
ASIA
ARCTIC OCEAN
PACIFIC OCEAN
INDIAN OCEAN
ARABIAN SEA
BERING SEA
SEA OF OKHOTSK
SEA OF JAPAN (EAST SEA)
SOUTH CHINA SEA
EAST CHINA SEA
YELLOW SEA
RED SEA
CASPIAN SEA
BLACK SEA
SEA OF AZOV
KARA SEA
LAPTEV SEA
EAST SIBERIAN SEA
PHILIPPINE SEA
SULU SEA
CELEBES SEA
BANDA SEA
Bay of Bengal
ANDAMAN SEA
JAVA SEA
Gulf of Aden
Gulf of Oman
Persian Gulf
Gulf of Thailand
RUSSIA
KAZAKHSTAN
MONGOLIA
CHINA
INDIA
JAPAN
NORTH KOREA
SOUTH KOREA
TAIWAN
VIETNAM
THAILAND
LAOS
CAMBODIA
MYANMAR
BANGLADESH
NEPAL
BHUTAN
SRI LANKA
MALDIVES
PAKISTAN
AFGHANISTAN
IRAN
IRAQ
SAUDI ARABIA
YEMEN
OMAN
TURKMENISTAN
UZBEKISTAN
KYRGYZSTAN
TAJIKISTAN
TURKEY
SYRIA
JORDAN
ISRAEL
LEBANON
CYPRUS
GEORGIA
ARMENIA
AZERBAIJAN
KUWAIT
QATAR
BAHRAIN
UNITED ARAB EMIRATES
PHILIPPINES
MALAYSIA
INDONESIA
BRUNEI
SINGAPORE
EAST TIMOR
NEW GUINEA
WEST SIBERIAN PLAIN
CENTRAL SIBERIAN PLATEAU
PLATEAU OF TIBET
GOBI DESERT
TAKLA MAKAN DESERT
HIMALAYAS
KUNLUN MTS.
TIEN SHAN
ALTAI MTS.
SAYAN MTS.
URAL MOUNTAINS
CAUCASUS MTS.
ZAGROS MOUNTAINS
ELBURZ MTS.
HINDU KUSH MTS.
KARAKORAM RANGE
PAMIRS
VERKHOYANSK MOUNTAINS
CHERSKIY MOUNTAINS
KOLYMA MOUNTAINS
CHUKCHI MTS.
KORYAK MOUNTAINS
STANOVOY MTS.
DA HINGGAN RANGE
WESTERN GHATS
EASTERN GHATS
DECCAN PLATEAU
ARABIAN PENINSULA
RUB' AL-KHALI DESERT REGION
AN NAFŪD DESERT
THAR DESERT
KAMCHATKA PENINSULA
TAYMYR PENINSULA
YAMAL PENINSULA
SAKHALIN ISLAND
KURIL ISLANDS
RYUKYU ISLANDS
HOKKAIDO
HONSHU
SHIKOKU
KYUSHU
LUZON
MINDANAO
BORNEO
SUMATRA
JAVA
SULAWESI
MOLUCCAS
HAINAN ISLAND
GREATER SUNDA ISLANDS
LESSER SUNDA ISLANDS
ANDAMAN ISLANDS (INDIA)
NICOBAR ISLANDS (INDIA)
LAKSHADWEEP ISLANDS (INDIA)
SOCOTRA ISLAND (YEMEN)
NOVAYA ZEMLYA ISLANDS
SEVERNAYA ZEMLYA ISLANDS
NEW SIBERIAN ISLANDS
WRANGEL ISLAND
FRANZ JOSEF LAND
KOMANDOR ISLANDS
Cape Dezhnev
Cape Chelyuskin
Cape Baba
Moscow
Beijing
Tokyo
Seoul
P'yongyang
Ulaanbaatar
Astana
Tashkent
Bishkek
Dushanbe
Kabul
Islamabad
New Delhi
Kathmandu
Thimphu
Dhaka
Colombo
Male
Yangon
Naypyidaw
Vientiane
Hanoi
Bangkok
Phnom Penh
Kuala Lumpur
Putrajaya
Singapore
Jakarta
Dili
Bandar Seri Begawan
Quezon City/Manila
Taipei
Tehrān
Baghdad
Kuwait
Riyadh
Manama
Doha
Abu Dhabi
Muscat
Sanaa
Damascus
Amman
Jerusalem
Beirut
Nicosia
Ankara
Tbilisi
Yerevan
Baku
Ashgabat
HONG KONG (XIANG GANG) - special admin. region
MACAO (AOMEN)- special admin. region
Mount Narodnaya 6,214 ft.
Mount Mus-Khaya 9,705 ft.
Mount Youyi 14,347 ft.
Mount Everest 29,035 ft.
K2 28,250 ft.
Mt. Fuji 12,388 ft.
Elbrus 18,510 ft.
Victory Peak 24,400 ft.
Anai Mudi 8,840 ft.
Puncak Jaya 16,535 ft.
Arctic Circle
Tropic of Cancer
Equator
0 350 700 mi
0 500 1000 km
© 2008 Encyclopædia Britannica, Inc.

Europe

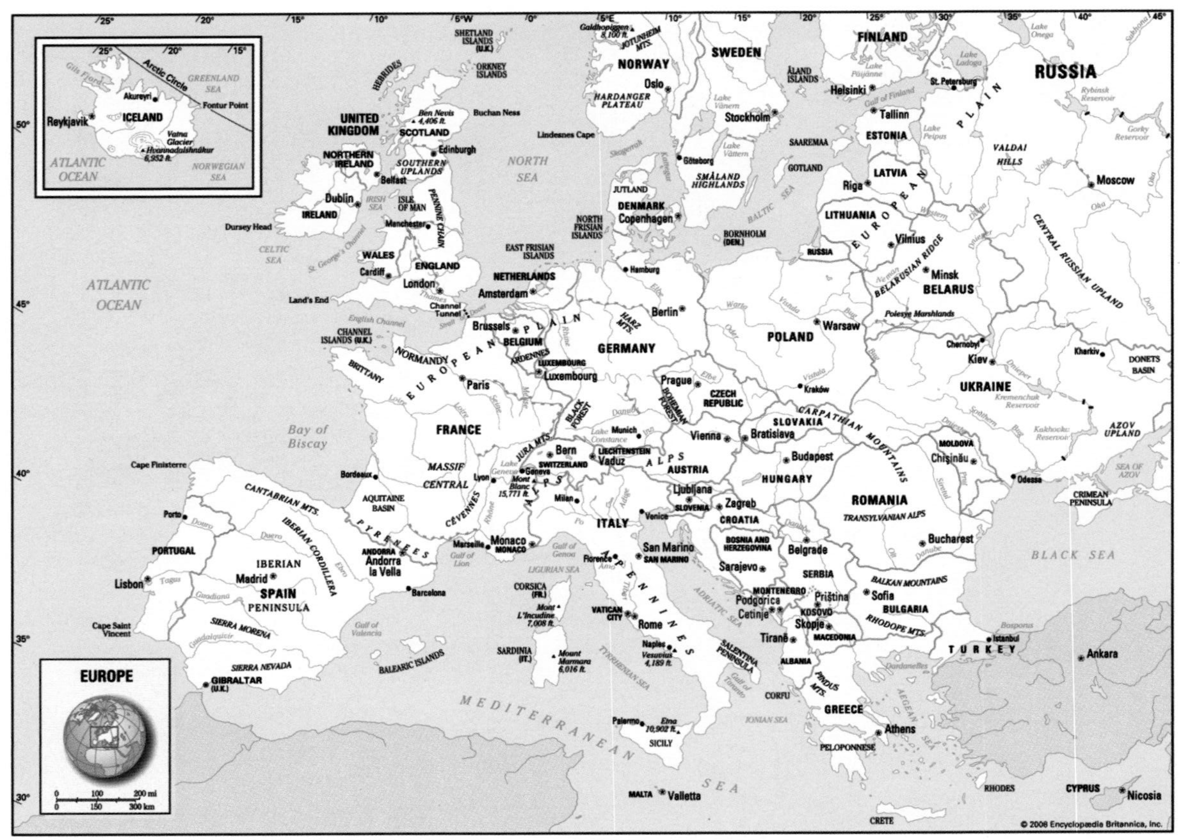

RUSSIA
Moscow
St. Petersburg
VALDAI HILLS
CENTRAL RUSSIAN UPLAND
FINLAND
Helsinki
ÅLAND ISLANDS
ESTONIA
Tallinn
SAAREMAA
LATVIA
Riga
LITHUANIA
Vilnius
RUSSIA
BELARUS
Minsk
BELARUSIAN RIDGE
Polesye Marshlands
UKRAINE
Kiev
Chernobyl
Kharkiv
DONETS BASIN
Odessa
AZOV UPLAND
SEA OF AZOV
CRIMEAN PENINSULA
POLAND
Warsaw
Kraków
SWEDEN
Stockholm
Göteborg
SMÅLAND HIGHLANDS
GOTLAND
NORWAY
Oslo
HARDANGER PLATEAU
JOTUNHEIM MTS.
Galdhøpiggen 8,100 ft.
Lindesnes Cape
DENMARK
Copenhagen
JUTLAND
BORNHOLM (DEN.)
NORTH FRISIAN ISLANDS
EAST FRISIAN ISLANDS
GERMANY
Berlin
Hamburg
Munich
HARZ MTS.
BLACK FOREST
CZECH REPUBLIC
Prague
BOHEMIAN FOREST
SLOVAKIA
Bratislava
CARPATHIAN MOUNTAINS
AUSTRIA
Vienna
HUNGARY
Budapest
ROMANIA
Bucharest
TRANSYLVANIAN ALPS
MOLDOVA
Chişinău
BULGARIA
Sofia
BALKAN MOUNTAINS
RHODOPE MTS.
SERBIA
Belgrade
CROATIA
Zagreb
SLOVENIA
Ljubljana
BOSNIA AND HERZEGOVINA
Sarajevo
MONTENEGRO
Podgorica
Cetinje
KOSOVO
Priština
MACEDONIA
Skopje
ALBANIA
Tiranë
GREECE
Athens
PINDUS MTS.
PELOPONNESE
CORFU
CRETE
RHODES
TURKEY
Istanbul
Ankara
Bosporus
Dardanelles
CYPRUS
Nicosia
ITALY
Rome
Milan
Venice
Florence
Naples
Vesuvius 4,189 ft.
Palermo
Etna 10,902 ft.
SICILY
SARDINIA (IT.)
Mount Marmora 6,016 ft.
CORSICA (FR.)
Mont L'Incudine 7,008 ft.
APENNINES
SALENTINA PENINSULA
SAN MARINO
San Marino
VATICAN CITY
MALTA
Valletta
SWITZERLAND
Bern
Geneva
Mont Blanc 15,771 ft.
JURA MTS.
ALPS
LIECHTENSTEIN
Vaduz
FRANCE
Paris
Lyon
Marseille
Bordeaux
NORMANDY
BRITTANY
MASSIF CENTRAL
CÉVENNES
AQUITAINE BASIN
MONACO
Monaco
LUXEMBOURG
Luxembourg
ARDENNES
BELGIUM
Brussels
NETHERLANDS
Amsterdam
EUROPEAN PLAIN
UNITED KINGDOM
ENGLAND
London
Manchester
PENNINE CHAIN
SCOTLAND
Edinburgh
SOUTHERN UPLANDS
Ben Nevis 4,406 ft.
WALES
Cardiff
NORTHERN IRELAND
Belfast
ISLE OF MAN
HEBRIDES
ORKNEY ISLANDS
SHETLAND ISLANDS (U.K.)
Buchan Ness
Land's End
Channel Tunnel
CHANNEL ISLANDS (U.K.)
IRELAND
Dublin
Dursey Head
SPAIN
Madrid
Barcelona
IBERIAN PENINSULA
IBERIAN CORDILLERA
CANTABRIAN MTS.
SIERRA MORENA
SIERRA NEVADA
BALEARIC ISLANDS
PORTUGAL
Lisbon
Porto
Cape Finisterre
Cape Saint Vincent
ANDORRA
Andorra la Vella
PYRENEES
GIBRALTAR (U.K.)
ICELAND
Reykjavík
Akureyri
Vatna Glacier
Hvannadalshnúkur 6,952 ft.
Fontur Point
Arctic Circle
GREENLAND SEA
NORWEGIAN SEA
ATLANTIC OCEAN
NORTH SEA
BALTIC SEA
CELTIC SEA
IRISH SEA
English Channel
Bay of Biscay
Gulf of Lion
LIGURIAN SEA
TYRRHENIAN SEA
ADRIATIC SEA
IONIAN SEA
AEGEAN SEA
MEDITERRANEAN SEA
BLACK SEA
EUROPE
0 100 200 mi
0 150 300 km
© 2008 Encyclopædia Britannica, Inc.

North America

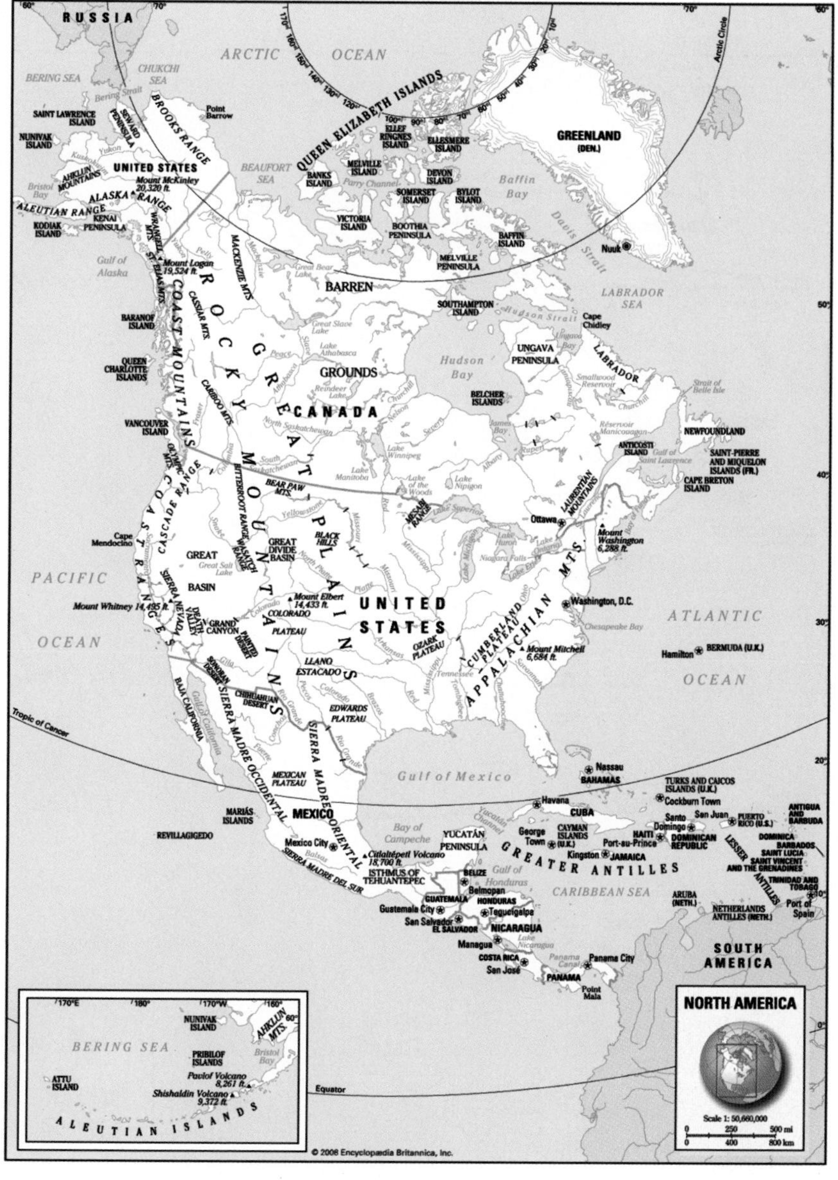

South America

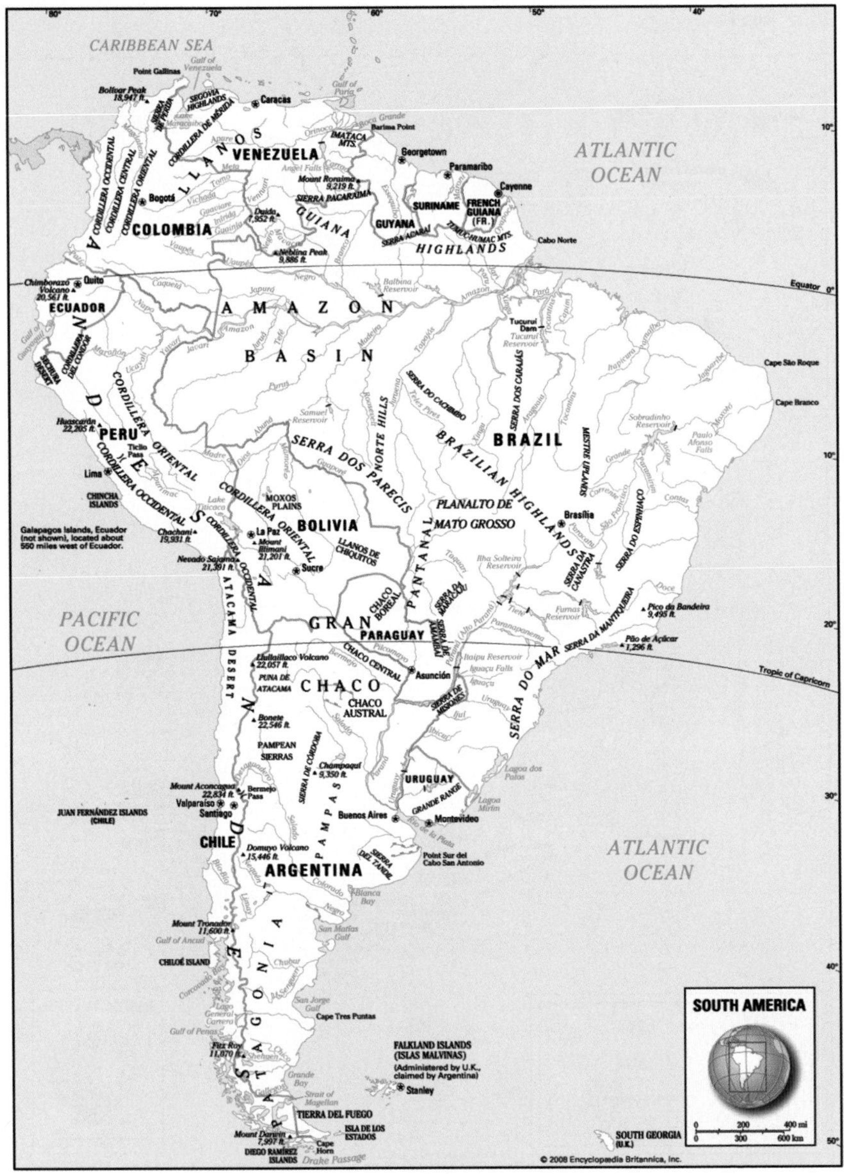

Australia

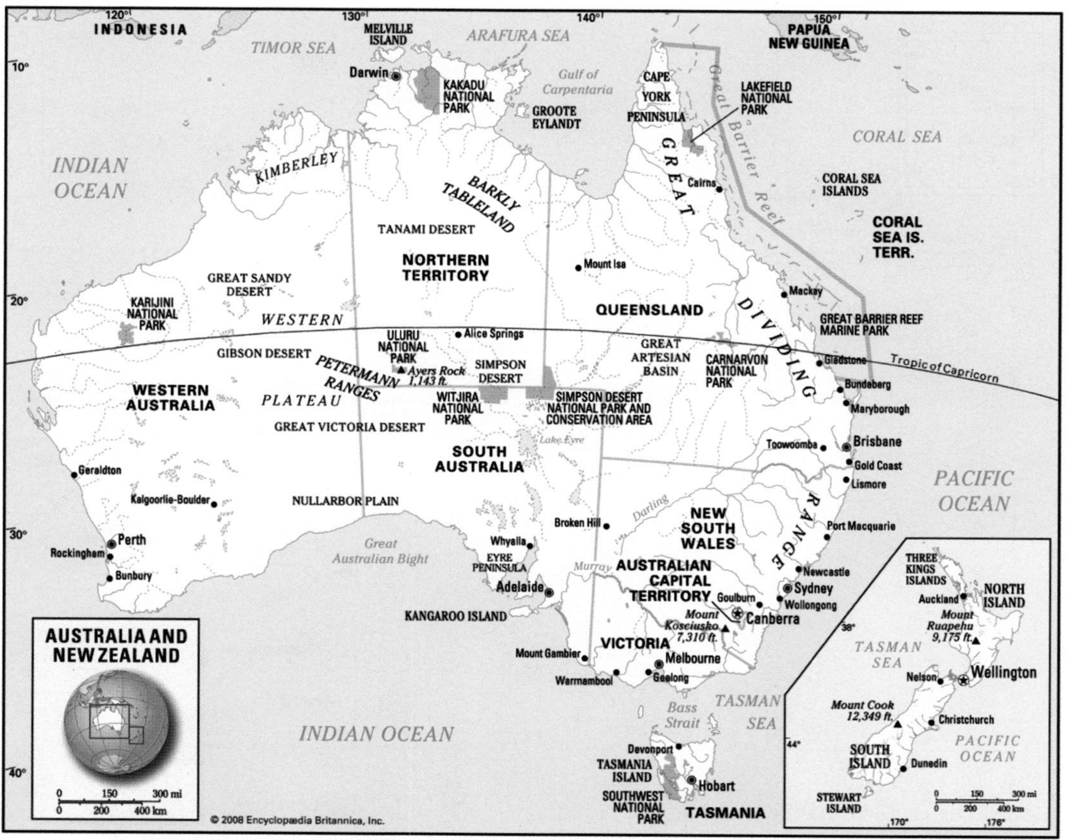
AUSTRALIA AND NEW ZEALAND
INDONESIA
PAPUA NEW GUINEA
TIMOR SEA
ARAFURA SEA
CORAL SEA
CORAL SEA ISLANDS
CORAL SEA IS. TERR.
Great Barrier Reef
GREAT BARRIER REEF MARINE PARK
PACIFIC OCEAN
INDIAN OCEAN
TASMAN SEA
Gulf of Carpentaria
Great Australian Bight
Bass Strait
Tropic of Capricorn
MELVILLE ISLAND
Darwin
KAKADU NATIONAL PARK
GROOTE EYLANDT
CAPE YORK PENINSULA
LAKEFIELD NATIONAL PARK
Cairns
GREAT DIVIDING RANGE
Mackay
Gladstone
Bundaberg
Maryborough
Brisbane
Gold Coast
Lismore
Toowoomba
Port Macquarie
Newcastle
Sydney
Wollongong
Canberra
Goulburn
Mount Kosciusko 7,310 ft.
Melbourne
Geelong
Warrnambool
Mount Gambier
Adelaide
KANGAROO ISLAND
EYRE PENINSULA
Whyalla
Broken Hill
Mount Isa
Alice Springs
Ayers Rock 1,143 ft.
ULURU NATIONAL PARK
SIMPSON DESERT
SIMPSON DESERT NATIONAL PARK AND CONSERVATION AREA
WITJIRA NATIONAL PARK
Lake Eyre
CARNARVON NATIONAL PARK
GREAT ARTESIAN BASIN
QUEENSLAND
NORTHERN TERRITORY
BARKLY TABLELAND
TANAMI DESERT
KIMBERLEY
GREAT SANDY DESERT
WESTERN PLATEAU
GIBSON DESERT
PETERMANN RANGES
GREAT VICTORIA DESERT
NULLARBOR PLAIN
WESTERN AUSTRALIA
SOUTH AUSTRALIA
NEW SOUTH WALES
AUSTRALIAN CAPITAL TERRITORY
VICTORIA
Darling
Murray
KARIJINI NATIONAL PARK
Kalgoorlie-Boulder
Geraldton
Perth
Rockingham
Bunbury
TASMANIA
TASMANIA ISLAND
Devonport
Hobart
SOUTHWEST NATIONAL PARK
NORTH ISLAND
THREE KINGS ISLANDS
Auckland
Mount Ruapehu 9,175 ft.
Wellington
Nelson
Christchurch
Mount Cook 12,349 ft.
Dunedin
SOUTH ISLAND
STEWART ISLAND
© 2008 Encyclopædia Britannica, Inc.

Oceania/Pacific Islands

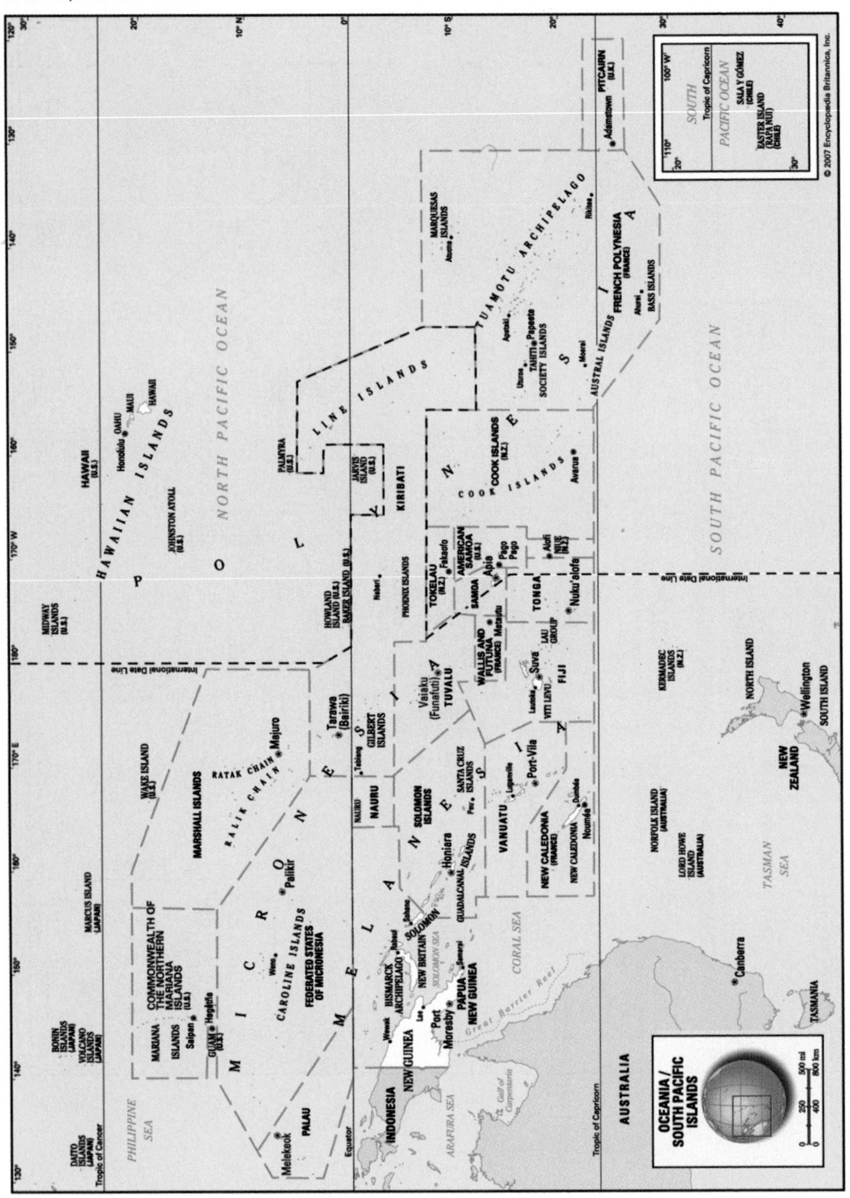

torate in 1896. It achieved independence in 1961 and became a republic in 1971. It was marked by political and economic turmoil in the late 20th century as successive military regimes tried to assume power. UN peacekeeping forces were stationed there but were ineffectual in preventing bloodletting and atrocities.

Recent Developments

Six years after the end of a decadelong civil war, the increasingly disillusioned people of Sierra Leone yearned for the implementation of an effective policy to end poverty in their mineral-rich country, which ranked last out of 177 countries in the United Nations Development Programme's human development index for 2007–08. Major priorities for the new regime of businessman Ernest Bai Koroma, inaugurated as Sierra Leone's president in September 2007, were to defuse ethnic tensions, stem unemployment, restore electricity, and continue the crackdown on the "blood diamonds" trade that had disrupted international trade and investment.

Internet resources: <www.visitsierraleone.org>.

Singapore

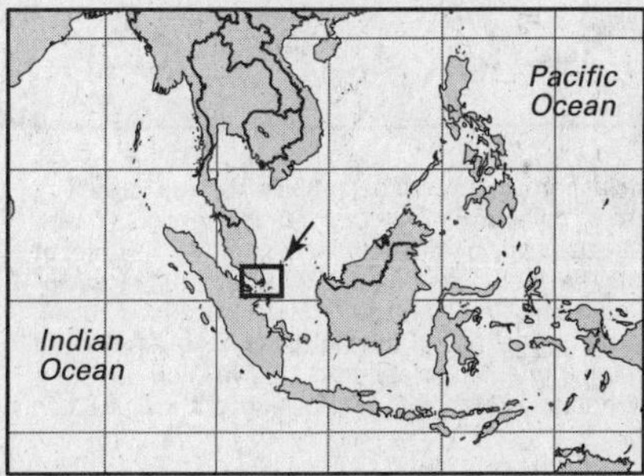

Official name: Xinjiapo Gongheguo (Chinese); Republik Singapura (Malay); Cingkappur Kudiyarasu (Tamil); Republic of Singapore (English). **Form of government:** unitary multiparty republic with one legislative house (Parliament [94]). **Head of state:** President Sellapan Rama (S.R.) Nathan (from 1999). **Head of state government:** Prime Minister Lee Hsien Loong (from 2004). **Capital:** Singapore. **Official languages:** Chinese; Malay; Tamil; English. **Official religion:** none. **Monetary unit:** 1 Singapore dollar (S$) = 100 cents; valuation (1 Jul 2008) US$1 = S$1.36.

Demography

Area: 271.8 sq mi, 704.0 sq km. **Population** (2007): 4,564,000. **Density** (2007): persons per sq mi 16,792, persons per sq km 6,483. **Urban:** 100%. **Sex distribution** (2007): male 49.48%; female 50.52%. **Age breakdown** (2007): under 15, 18.9%; 15–29, 20.2%; 30–44, 25.8%; 45–59, 22.7%; 60–74, 9.1%; 75–84, 2.6%; 85 and over, 0.7%. **Ethnic composition** (2007): Chinese 74.8%; Malay 13.5%; Indian 9.0%; other 2.7%. **Religious affiliation** (2000): Buddhist/Taoist/Chinese folk-religionist 51.0%; Muslim 14.9%; Christian 14.6%; Hindu 4.0%; traditional beliefs 0.6%; nonreligious 14.9%. **Location:** southeastern Asia, islands between Malaysia and Indonesia.

Vital statistics

Birth rate per 1,000 population (2006): 10.1 (world avg. 20.3). **Death rate** per 1,000 population (2006): 4.3 (world avg. 8.6). **Total fertility rate** (avg. births per childbearing woman; 2006): 1.26. **Life expectancy** at birth (2006): male 78.0 years; female 81.8 years.

National economy

Budget (2006). *Revenue:* S$31,072,000,000 (income tax 48.1%; goods and services tax 12.7%; fees and charges 6.8%; assets taxes 6.6%; customs and excise duties 6.3%). *Expenditures:* S$29,875,-000,000 (security and external relations 42.8%; education 21.3%; transportation 6.8%; health 6.2%; trade and industry 5.6%). **Public debt** (2006): US$122,000,000,000. **Production** (metric tons except as noted). *Agriculture, forestry, fishing* (2005): vegetables 5,800,orchids (15% of the world market) and other ornamental plants are cultivated for export; livestock (number of live animals) 250,000 pigs, 2,000,000 chickens; fisheries production 7,837 (from aquaculture 76%); aquarium fish farming is also an important economic pursuit; Singapore produces 30% of the world's ornamental fish. *Manufacturing* (value added in S$'000,000; 2005): pharmaceuticals 8,204; semiconductors 7,636; computer-related electronics 7,218. *Energy production (consumption):* electricity (kW-hr; 2005) 38,213,000,000 (34,761,000,000); crude petroleum (barrels; 2004) none (324,000,000); petroleum products (metric tons; 2004) 31,094,000 (8,794,000); natural gas (cu m; 2004) none (6,303,000,000). **Gross national income** (2006): US$127,980,000,000 (US$29,210 per capita). **Households** (2003). Average household size 3.6; income per household S$58,404 (US$33,523); sources of income: wages and salaries 82.5%, self-employment 12.3%; expenditure: housing costs and furnishings 22.4%, transportation and communications 21.4%, food 21.3%, education 7.8%. **Population economically active** (2006): total 1,880,800; activity rate of total population 52.1% (participation rates: ages 15–64, 71.3%; female 42.5%; unemployed 3.6%). **Selected balance of payments data.** Receipts from (US$'000,000): tourism (2005) 5,736; foreign direct investment (FDI) (2001–05 avg.) 13,653. Disbursements for (US$'000,000): tourism (2005) 9,853; FDI (2001–05 avg.) 7,926. **Land use** as % of total land area (2003): in temporary crops 0.9%, in permanent crops 0.3%; overall forest area (2005) 3.4%.

Foreign trade

Imports (2006; c.i.f.): S$378,924,000,000 (machinery and apparatus [including parts] and transport equipment 54.7%; crude and refined petroleum 19.7%; chemicals and chemical products 6.0%). *Major import sources* (2005): Malaysia 14.4%; US 12.4%; China 10.8%; Japan 10.1%; Indonesia 5.5%. **Exports** (2006; f.o.b.): S$431,559,000,000 (domestic exports 52.7%, of which electronics 18.2%, petroleum [all forms] 13.8%, chemicals and chemical products 9.2%; reexports 47.3%, of which electronics, nonelectrical machinery and transport equipment 34.6%). *Major export destinations* (2005): Malaysia 14.7%; US 11.5%; Indonesia 10.7%; Hong Kong 10.4%; China 9.5%.

Transport and communications

Transport. *Railroads* (2006): length 39 km. *Roads* (2005): total length 3,234 km (paved [2004] 99%). *Vehicles* (2006): passenger cars 476,333; trucks and buses 158,586. *Air transport* (2006; Singapore Airlines, Singapore Airlines Cargo, and SilkAir only): passenger-km 90,288,000,000; metric ton-km cargo 12,809,000,000. **Communications,** in total units (units per 1,000 persons). Daily newspaper circulation (2004): 1,624,000 (383); televisions (2005): 1,847,000 (425); telephone landlines (2006): 1,854,000 (413); cellular telephone subscribers (2006): 4,789,000 (1,068); personal computers (2005): 2,960,000 (682); total Internet users (2006): 1,717,000 (383); broadband Internet subscribers (2006): 797,000 (178).

Education and health

Educational attainment (2005). Percentage of population ages 15 and over having: no schooling 16.4%; primary education 22.0%; lower secondary 21.3%; upper secondary 15.1%; technical 8.2%; university 17.0%. **Literacy** (2004): 94.6% **Health** (2006): physicians 6,931 (1 per 647 persons); hospital beds 11,545 (1 per 388 persons); infant mortality rate per 1,000 live births 2.6.

Military

Total active duty personnel (2006): 72,500 (army 69.0%, navy 12.4%, air force 18.6%). **Military expenditure as percentage of GDP** (2005): 4.7%; per capita expenditure US$1,274.

Background

Long inhabited by fishermen and pirates, Singapore was an outpost of the Sumatran empire of Srivijaya until the 14th century, when it passed to Java and then Siam. It became part of the Malacca empire in the 15th century. In the 16th century the Portuguese controlled the area; they were followed by the Dutch in the 17th century. In 1819 Singapore was ceded to the British East India Co., becoming part of the Straits Settlements and the center of British colonial activity in Southeast Asia. The Japanese occupied the islands in 1942–45. In 1946 it became a crown colony. It achieved full internal self-government in 1959, became a part of Malaysia in 1963, and gained independence in 1965. It is influential in the affairs of the Association of Southeast Asian Nations. The country's dominant voice in politics for 30 years after independence was Lee Kuan Yew.

Recent Developments

In Singapore in 2007 the property market finally awoke—with a vengeance—from a five-year slumber. Lured by the prospect of becoming millionaires overnight, many property owners put their buildings on the market for collective sale. Proceeds from these collective sales were estimated to hit S$6 billion (about US$4.1 billion) in 2008. Even as the property market surged in 2007 (private housing prices increased 31.2% for the year), so too did inflation, which was projected to rise to as much as 5.5% in 2008, on the back of higher oil and food prices. The overall economy grew by 7.8% in 2007.

Internet resources: <www.sg>.

Slovakia

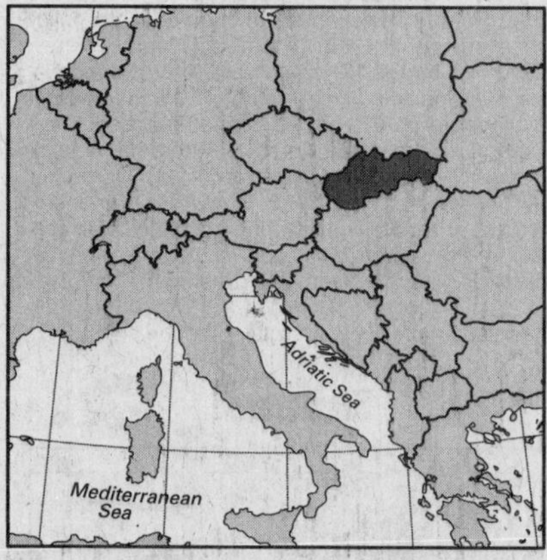

Official name: Slovenska Republika (Slovak Republic). **Form of government:** unitary multiparty republic with one legislative house (National Council [150]). **Chief of state:** President Ivan Gasparovic (from 2004). **Head of government:** Prime Minister Robert Fico (from 2006). **Capital:** Bratislava. **Official language:** Slovak. **Official religion:** none. **Monetary unit:** 1 Slovak koruna (Sk) = 100 halura; valuation (1 Jul 2008) US$1 = Sk 19.15.

Demography

Area: 18,933 sq mi, 49,035 sq km. **Population** (2007): 5,396,000. **Density** (2007): persons per sq mi 285.0, persons per sq km 110.0. **Urban** (2006): 55.4%. **Sex distribution** (2005): male 48.54%; female 51.46%. **Age breakdown** (2005): under 15, 16.7%; 15–29, 24.5%; 30–44, 21.8%; 45–59, 20.7%; 60–74, 11.3%; 75–84, 4.2%; 85 and over, 0.8%. **Ethnic composition** (2001): Slovak 85.8%; Hungarian 9.7%; Rom (Gypsy) 1.7%; Czech 0.8%; Ruthenian and Ukrainian 0.7%; other 1.3%. **Religious affiliation** (2001): Roman Catholic 68.9%; Protestant 9.2%, of which Lutheran 6.9%, Reformed Christian 2.0%; Greek Catholic 4.1%; Eastern Orthodox 0.9%; nonreligious 13.0%; other/unknown 3.9%. **Major cities** (2004): Bratislava 425,155; Kosice 235,006; Presov 91,767; Nitra 85,742; Zilina 85,268. **Location:** central Europe, bordering Poland, Ukraine, Hungary, Austria, and the Czech Republic.

Vital statistics

Birth rate per 1,000 population (2006): 10.0 (world avg. 20.3); (2004) within marriage 75.2%. **Death rate**

per 1,000 population (2006): 9.9 (world avg. 8.6). **Natural increase rate** per 1,000 population (2006): 0.1 (world avg. 11.7). **Total fertility rate** (avg. births per childbearing woman; 2004): 1.25. **Life expectancy** at birth (2006): male 70.1 years; female 77.9 years.

National economy

Budget (2005). *Revenue:* Sk 466,400,000,000 (tax revenue 46.6%, of which taxes on goods and services 37.2%; social security contributions 39.9%; nontax revenue 10.4%; grants 3.1%). *Expenditures:* Sk 515,900,000,000 (social protection 32.4%; general administration 21.8%; health 18.5%). **Production** (metric tons except as noted). *Agriculture, forestry, fishing* (2006): sugar beets 1,370,908, wheat 1,342,693, corn (maize) 838,000; livestock (number of live animals) 1,108,265 pigs, 527,889 cattle; roundwood (2005) 9,302,000 cu m, of which fuelwood 3%; fisheries production (2005) 2,648 (from aquaculture 36%). *Mining and quarrying* (2005): magnesite 447,700; iron ore (metal content) 300,000; kaolin 85,000. *Manufacturing* (value added in Sk '000,000; 2004): base and fabricated metals 54,558; transportation equipment 26,251; electrical equipment 26,146. *Energy production (consumption):* electricity (kW-hr; 2004) 30,567,000,000 (28,705,000,000); hard coal (metric tons; 2004) none (5,151,000); lignite (metric tons; 2005) 2,511,000 ([2004] 3,589,000); crude petroleum (barrels; 2004) 279,000 (41,876,000); petroleum products (metric tons; 2004) 5,569,000 (2,337,000); natural gas (cu m; 2004) 169,000,000 (6,555,000,000). **Population economically active** (2006): total 2,654,800; activity rate of total population 49.2% (participation rates: ages 15–64, 68.9%; female 45.8%; unemployed [March 2006–February 2007] 10.0%). **Households** (2003). Average household size 2.9; average annual gross income per household Sk 288,388 (US$7,842); sources of income: wages and salaries 73.9%, transfers 19.6%; expenditure: food and nonalcoholic beverages 25.7%, energy 18.8%, transportation 9.0%, recreation 7.5%, clothing and footwear 7.3%. **Public debt** (external, outstanding; 2005): US$3,340,000,000. **Gross national income** (2006): US$52,921,000,000 (US$9,820 per capita). **Selected balance of payments data.** Receipts from (US$'000,000): tourism (2005) 1,210; remittances (2006) 424; foreign direct investment (2001–05 avg.) 1,921. Disbursements for (US$'000,000): tourism (2005) 486; remittances (2006) 16. **Land use** as % of total land area (2003): in temporary crops 29.4%, in permanent crops 0.6%, in pasture 16.5%; overall forest area (2005) 40.1%.

Foreign trade

Imports (2005): US$34,292,000,000 (machinery and apparatus 25.8%; mineral fuels 15.4%; road vehicles 12.3%; base and fabricated metals 10.0%). *Major import sources:* Germany 25.1%; Czech Republic 19.3%; Russia 10.5%; Austria 6.1%; Poland 4.7%. **Exports** (2004): US$27,603,000,000 (machinery, apparatus, and parts 21.2%; passenger vehicles 15.4%; iron and steel 9.1%; parts and accessories of passenger vehicles 7.5%; chemicals and chemical products 5.4%; refined petroleum 5.2%). *Major export destinations* (2005): Germany 26.2%; Czech Republic 14.1%; Austria 7.1%; Italy 6.7%; Poland 6.3%.

Transport and communications

Transport. *Railroads* (2005): length 3,658 km; passenger-km 2,181,000,000; metric ton-km cargo 9,463,000,000. *Roads* (2004): total length 43,000 km (paved 87%). *Vehicles* (2004): passenger cars 1,337,425; trucks and buses 179,412. *Air transport* (2006; SkyEurope and Slovak airlines only): passenger-km 2,596,207,000; metric ton-km cargo 29,000. **Communications,** in total units (units per 1,000 persons). Daily newspaper circulation (2005): 894,000 (166); televisions (2004): 2,285,000 (425); telephone landlines (2006): 1,167,000 (216); cellular telephone subscribers (2006): 4,893,000 (908); personal computers (2005): 1,929,000 (358); total Internet users (2006): 2,256,000 (418); broadband Internet subscribers (2006): 317,000 (59).

Education and health

Educational attainment (2002). Percentage of population ages 25–64 having: primary education 1%; complete lower secondary 13%; complete upper secondary 75%; higher 11%. **Literacy** (2001): total population ages 15 and over literate: virtually 100%. **Health** (2005): physicians 20,158 (1 per 267 persons); hospital beds 48,622 (1 per 111 persons); infant mortality rate per 1,000 live births 6.4. **Food** (2005): daily per capita caloric intake 2,592 (vegetable products 73%, animal products 27%); 128% of FAO recommended minimum.

Military

Total active duty personnel (2006): 15,223 (army 39.7%, air force 24.0%, headquarters staff 17.2%, support/training 19.1%). **Military expenditure as percentage of GDP** (2005): 1.7%; per capita expenditure US$153.

Background

Slovakia was inhabited in the first centuries AD by Illyrian, Celtic, and Germanic tribes. Slovaks settled there around the 6th century. It became part of Great Moravia in the 9th century but was conquered by the Magyars c. 907. It remained in the kingdom of Hungary until the end of World War I, when the Slovaks joined the Czechs to form the new state of Czechoslovakia in 1918. In 1938 Slovakia was declared an autonomous unit within Czechoslovakia; it was nominally independent under German protection in 1939–45. After the expulsion of the Germans, Slovakia joined a reconstituted Czechoslovakia, which came under Soviet domination in 1948. In 1969 a partnership between the Czechs and Slovaks established the Slovak Socialist Republic. The fall of the communist regime in 1989 led to a revival of interest in autonomy, and Slovakia became an independent nation in 1993.

Recent Developments

The Slovak economy surged at a record pace in 2007 (GDP grew 13.2% during the year) as strong foreign demand contributed to a sharp narrowing of external deficits. Moreover, productivity gains continued to outpace real wage growth (though average monthly wages rose by 7.4%), keeping concerns about economic overheating to a minimum. The value of construction in the country grew by 9.8%. By the standards of Eurostat's Harmonized Index of Consumer Prices, Slovakia's inflation fell to about 2%, well within the Maastricht Treaty limit for entry to the euro zone. Thus, Slovakia appeared to be on track to adopt the euro in January 2009. On the downside, Slovakia recorded the highest unemployment rate (11.0%) in the EU during the year, falling behind Poland.

Internet resources: <www.slovakia.travel>.

Slovenia

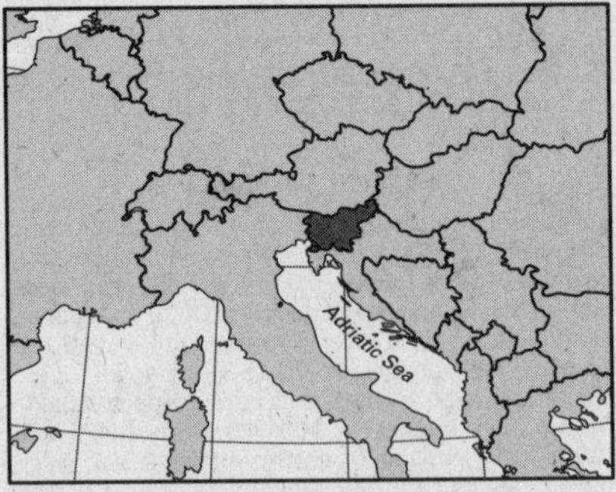

Official name: Republika Slovenija (Republic of Slovenia). **Form of government:** unitary multiparty republic with two legislative houses (National Council [40]; National Assembly [90]). **Head of state:** President Danilo Turk (from 2007). **Head of government:** Prime Minister Janez Jansa (from 2004). **Capital:** Ljubljana. **Official language:** Slovene. **Official religion:** none. **Monetary unit:** 1 euro (€) = 100 cents; valuation (1 Jul 2008) US$1 = €0.63 (the euro replaced the Slovenian tolar [SIT] 1 Jan 2007, at the rate of €1 = SIT 239.64).

Demography

Area: 7,827 sq mi, 20,273 sq km. **Population** (2007): 2,011,000. **Density** (2007): persons per sq mi 256.9, persons per sq km 99.2. **Urban** (2005): 51.0%. **Sex distribution** (2006): male 49.09%; female 50.91%. **Age breakdown** (2006): under 15, 14.0%; 15–29, 20.3%; 30–44, 22.5%; 45–59, 22.3%; 60–74, 14.1%; 75–84, 5.6%; 85 and over, 1.2%. **Ethnic composition** (2002): Slovene 91.2%; Serb 2.2%; Croat 2.0%; Bosniac (ethnic Muslim) 1.8%; other 2.8%. **Religious affiliation** (2002): Roman Catholic 57.8%; Muslim 2.4%; Orthodox 2.3%; Protestant 0.8%; nonreligious/atheist 10.2%; other/unknown/unspecified 26.5%. **Major cities** (2005; populations of municipalities): Ljubljana 266,941; Maribor 111,073; Kranj 52,938; Koper 49,479; Celje 48,607. **Location:** southeastern Europe, bordering Austria, Hungary, Croatia, the Adriatic Sea, and Italy.

Vital statistics

Birth rate per 1,000 population (2006): 9.4 (world avg. 20.3); within marriage 52.8%. **Death rate** per 1,000 population (2006): 9.1 (world avg. 8.6). **Natural increase rate** per 1,000 population (2005): 0.3 (world avg. 11.7). **Total fertility rate** (avg. births per childbearing woman; 2006): 1.31. **Life expectancy** at birth (2006): male 74.8 years; female 81.9 years.

National economy

Budget (2005). *Revenue:* SIT 2,739,000,000,000 (tax revenue 51.7%, of which taxes on goods and services 33.1%, personal income tax 9.4%; social security contributions 38.3%; nontax revenue 7.4%; grants 2.6%). *Expenditures:* SIT 2,846,000,000,000 (social protection 40.8%; health 14.6%; general administration 12.6%; education 12.6%). **Public debt** (2006): US$9,900,000,000. **Production** (metric tons except as noted). *Agriculture, forestry, fishing* (2006): corn (maize) 276,106, sugar beets 262,031, wheat 134,449; livestock (number of live animals) 547,430 pigs, 452,517 cattle; roundwood (2005) 2,732,822 cu m, of which fuelwood 35%; fisheries production (2005) 2,759 (from aquaculture 56%). *Mining and quarrying* (2005): sand and gravel 11,000,000; salt 125,000. *Manufacturing* (value added in SIT '000,000; 2005): chemicals and chemical products 189,495; fabricated metal products 177,195; nonelectrical machinery 153,770. *Energy production (consumption):* electricity (kW-hr; 2006) 14,117,000,000 (13,298,000,000); hard coal (metric tons; 2004) none (45,000); lignite (metric tons; 2006) 4,522,000 ([2004] 5,329,000); crude petroleum (barrels; 2005) 2,200 ([2004] negligible); petroleum products (metric tons; 2006) none (2,269,000); natural gas (cu m; 2006) 4,000,000 (1,105,000,000). **Land use** as % of total land area (2003): in temporary crops 8.6%, in permanent crops 1.4%, in pasture 15.3%; overall forest area (2005) 62.8%. **Households** (2005). Average household size 2.7; average annual income per household SIT 4,151,377 (US$21,542); sources of income: wages and salaries 53.4%, transfers 27.9%, self-employment 5.1%; expenditure: housing and energy 20.1%, transportation 16.2%, food and nonalcoholic beverages 15.9%, recreation and culture 9.2%. **Gross national income** (at current market prices; 2006): US$38,197,000,000 (US$19,020 per capita). **Population economically active** (2006): total 1,030,000; activity rate of total population 51.4% (participation rates: ages 15–64, 71.3%; female 46.7%; unemployed [April 2006–March 2007] 5.6%). **Selected balance of payments data.** Receipts from (US$'000,000): tourism (2005) 1,894; remittances (2006) 282; foreign direct investment (FDI) (2001–05 avg.) 732. Disbursements for (US$'000,000): tourism (2005) 1,019; remittances (2006) 119; FDI (2001–05 avg.) 377.

Foreign trade

Imports (2006; c.i.f.): €18,341,000,000 (machinery and transport equipment 32.5%, of which road vehicles 11.2%; chemicals and chemical products 12.2%; mineral fuels 11.2%, of which petroleum and petroleum products 7.0%; iron and steel 5.7%). *Major import sources:* Germany 20.4%; Italy 18.6%; Austria 12.2%; France 6.2%; Croatia 4.0%. **Exports** (2006; f.o.b.): €16,757,000,000 (machinery and transport equipment 38.2%, of which road vehicles 13.6%, electrical machinery and apparatus 9.9%; chemicals and chemical products 13.7%, of which medicines and pharmaceuticals 6.9%; furniture and parts 5.1%). *Major export destinations:* Germany 19.7%; Italy 12.9%; Croatia 8.7%; Austria 8.7%; France 6.8%.

Transport and communications

Transport. *Railroads* (2006): length 1,228 km; passenger-km 793,000,000; metric ton-km cargo 3,373,000,000. *Roads* (2006): total length 38,562 km (paved 100%). *Vehicles* (2006): passenger cars 980,261; trucks and buses 72,409. *Air transport* (2006): passenger-km 1,043,000,000; metric ton-km cargo 3,436,000. **Communications,** in total units (units per 1,000 persons). Daily newspaper circulation (2004): 362,000 (181); televisions (2005): 559,000 (279); telephone landlines (2006): 837,000 (417); cellular telephone subscribers (2006): 1,820,000 (907); personal computers (2005): 808,000 (404); total Internet users (2006): 1,251,000 (623); broadband Internet subscribers (2006): 264,000 (132).

Education and health

Educational attainment (2004). Percentage of population ages 15 and over having: no formal schooling 0.6%; incomplete and complete primary education 28.6%; secondary 6.0%; vocational 50.2%; some higher 5.0%; undergraduate 8.7%; advanced degree 0.9%. **Literacy** (2006): virtually 100%. **Health:** physicians (2005) 4,620 (1 per 433 persons); hospital beds (2004) 9,584 (1 per 208 persons); infant mortality rate per 1,000 live births (2006) 3.4. **Food** (2005): daily per capita caloric intake 2,756 (vegetable products 65%, animal products 35%); 139% of FAO recommended minimum.

Military

Total active duty personnel (2006): 6,550 (army 100%). **Military expenditure as percentage of GNI** (2005): 1.5%; per capita expenditure US$257.

Background

The Slovenes settled the region in the 6th century AD. In the 8th century it was incorporated into the Frankish empire of Charlemagne, and in the 10th century it came under Germany as part of the Holy Roman Empire. Except for 1809–14, when Napoleon ruled the area, most of the lands belonged to Austria until the formation of the Kingdom of Serbs, Croats, and Slovenes in 1918. It became a constituent republic of Yugoslavia in 1946 and received a section of the former Italian Adriatic coastline in 1947. In 1990 Slovenia held the first contested multiparty elections in Yugoslavia since before World War II. In 1991 it seceded from Yugoslavia; its independence was internationally recognized in 1992.

Recent Developments

Slovenia in 2007 became the 13th country in the European Union to adopt the euro as its currency, replacing the tolar. The country assumed the presidency of the European Union during the first half of 2008. Thus, Slovenia, the first of the 10 states that joined the EU in 2004 to adopt the euro, was also the first of that group to accede to the EU rotating presidency. A third major step came in December 2007, when extension of the Schengen Agreement abolished Slovenia's border controls with fellow members Italy, Austria, and Hungary and made Slovenia's border with Croatia an external border of the EU.

Internet resources: <www.slovenia.info>.

Solomon Islands

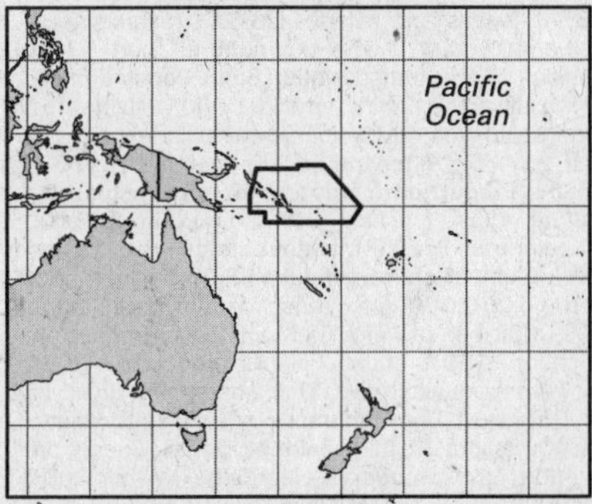

Official name: Solomon Islands. **Form of government:** constitutional monarchy with one legislative house (National Parliament [50]). **Chief of state:** British Queen Elizabeth II (from 1952), represented by Governor-General Sir Nathaniel Waena (from 2004). **Head of government:** Prime Minister Derek Sikua (from 2007). **Capital:** Honiara. **Official language:** English. **Official religion:** none. **Monetary unit:** 1 Solomon Islands dollar (SI$) = 100 cents; valuation (1 Jul 2008) US$1 = SI$7.72.

Demography

Area: 10,954 sq mi, 28,370 sq km. **Population** (2007): 495,000. **Density** (2007): persons per sq mi 45.2, persons per sq km 17.4. **Urban** (2005–06): 16.0%. **Sex distribution** (2006): male 51.53%; female 48.47%. **Age breakdown** (2006): under 15, 40.0%; 15–29, 28.7%; 30–44, 17.9%; 45–59, 8.5%; 60–74, 3.9%; 75 and over, 1.0%. **Ethnic composition** (2002): Melanesian 93.0%; Polynesian 4.0%; Micronesian 1.5%; other 1.5%. **Religious affiliation** (2005): Protestant 70%, of which Anglican 32%, Adventist 10%; Roman Catholic 18%; traditional beliefs 5%; other 7%. **Major towns** (2004): Honiara 57,600; Gizo 6,200; Auki 4,700; Buala 2,900. **Location:** southwestern Pacific Ocean, east of Papua New Guinea.

Vital statistics

Birth rate per 1,000 population (2006): 30.0 (world avg. 20.3). **Death rate** per 1,000 population (2006): 3.9 (world avg. 8.6). **Natural increase rate** per 1,000 population (2006): 26.1 (world avg. 11.7). **Total fertility rate** (avg. births per childbearing woman; 2006): 3.78. **Life expectancy** at birth (2006): male 70.4 years; female 75.5 years.

National economy

Budget (2006). *Revenue:* SI$946,200,000 (tax revenue 73.0%, of which VAT 17.9%, logging duties 13.6%, import duties 9.3%, corporate tax 8.2%; nontax revenue 13.9%; grants 13.1%). *Expenditures:* SI$911,100,000 (current expenditure 90.5%, of which wages 27.3%, debt service 13.9%; capital expenditure 9.5%). **Public debt** (external, outstanding; 2005): US$148,100,000. **Gross national income** (at current market prices; 2006): US$411,000,000 (US$849 per capita). **Households** (2005–06). Average household size 6.2; average annual income per household US$3,129; sources of income: home production (mostly food preparations and handicrafts) 36.9%, wages and salaries 26.6%, transfers 8.8%, self-employment 7.8%; expenditure: food 53.5%, housing 15.8%, transportation 6.8%. **Population economically active** (2006): total 201,000; activity rate of total population 41.0% (participation rates: ages 15 and over 68.8%; female 38.3%; unemployed [2003] 15.2%). **Production** (metric tons except as noted). *Agriculture, forestry, fishing* (2006): coconuts 276,000, oil palm fruit 162,290, sweet potatoes 88,723; livestock (number of live animals) 53,000 pigs, 13,500 cattle, 230,000 chickens; roundwood (2005) 692,000 cu m, of which fuelwood 20%; fisheries production 29,597; aquatic plants production (2005) 120 (from aquaculture 100%). *Mining and quarrying* (2005): gold 10 kg. *Manufacturing* (2006): coconut oil 59,000, copra 21,214, palm oil 5,427. *Energy production (consumption):* electricity (kW-hr; 2006) 68,000,000 (55,000,000); petroleum products (metric tons; 2004) none (57,000). **Selected balance of payments data.** Receipts from (US$'000,000): tourism (2005) 2.0; remittances (2006) 2.0; foreign direct disinvestment (2001–05 avg.) −3.0; official development assistance (2005) 198. Disbursements for (US$'000,000): tourism (2005) 5.0; remittances (2006) 6.0. **Land use** as % of total land area (2003): in temporary crops 0.6%, in permanent crops 2.1%, in pasture 1.4%; overall forest area (2005) 77.6%.

Foreign trade

Imports (2006; c.i.f.): US$250,613,000 (machinery and transport equipment 24.7%; petroleum [all forms] 21.7%; food 14.1%; construction materials 10.0%). *Major import sources:* Australia 25.3%; Singapore 23.4%; Japan 7.8%; New Zealand 5.0%; Fiji 4.2%. **Exports** (2006; f.o.b.): US$120,393,000 (timber 70.2%; fish products 15.9%; palm oil 3.3%; cacao beans 3.3%). *Major export destinations:* China 45.7%; South Korea 14.0%; Japan 8.5%; Thailand 4.4%; Philippines 4.0%.

Transport and communications

Transport. *Roads* (2007): total length 1,500 km (paved 2.7%). *Vehicles* (1993): passenger cars 2,052; trucks and buses 2,574. *Air transport* (2004; Solomon Airlines only): passenger-km 76,733,000; metric ton-km cargo 2,259,000. **Communications,** in total units (units per 1,000 persons). Daily newspaper circulation (2006): 4,000 (8.3); televisions (2004): 5,300 (11); telephone landlines (2005): 7,400 (16); cellular telephone subscribers (2005): 6,000 (13); personal computers (2005): 22,000 (47); total Internet users (2006): 8,000 (17); broadband Internet subscribers (2005): 400 (0.8).

Education and health

Educational attainment (2005–06). Percentage of population ages 15 and over having: no schooling/unknown 15.6%; primary education 46.7%; secondary 32.8%; vocational 4.0%; higher 0.9%. **Literacy** (2004): total population ages 15 and over literate 76.6%. **Health** (2005): physicians 89 (1 per 5,293 persons); hospital beds 691 (1 per 682 persons); infant mortality rate per 1,000 live births (2006) 20.6. **Food** (2005): daily per capita caloric intake 2,056 (vegetable products 90%, animal products 10%); 116% of FAO recommended minimum.

Military

Total active duty personnel (2007): none; 200–300 military troops and police in an Australian-led multinational regional intervention force (from mid-2003) maintain civil and political order.

Background

The Solomon Islands were probably settled c. 2000 BC by Austronesian people. Visited by the Spanish in 1568, the islands were subsequently explored and charted by the Dutch, French, and British. They came under British protection in 1893 and became the British Solomon Islands. During World War II, the Japanese invasion of 1942 ignited three years of the most bitter fighting in the Pacific, particularly on Guadalcanal. The protectorate became self-governing in 1975 and fully independent in 1978. (Another island group named Solomon Islands, which includes Bougainville, is part of Papua New Guinea.)

Recent Developments

In 2007 there was continuing tension between Prime Minister Manasseh Sogavare and the Australian-led Regional Assistance Mission to the Solomon Islands (RAMSI), which had been invited to the Solomons in 2003 to restore order and to rebuild government institutions. The economy was growing very quickly, but it was heavily dependent on unsustainable levels of logging, which had been growing at 6–12% annually. Natural forests were likely to be depleted in six years.

Internet resources: <www.visitsolomons.com.sb>.

Somalia

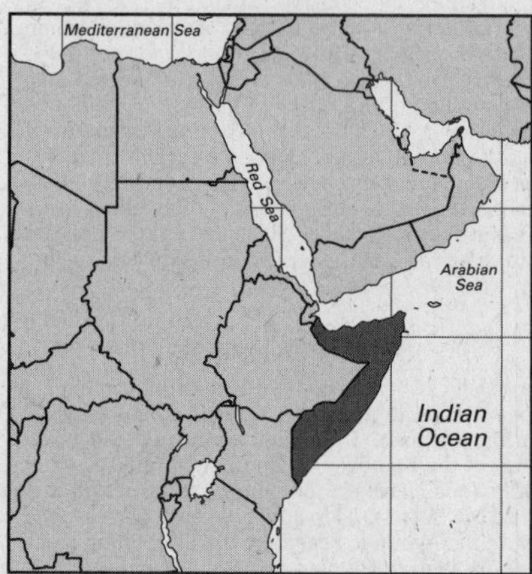

Proclamation of the "Republic of Somaliland" in May 1991 on territory corresponding to the former British

1 metric ton = about 1.1 short tons; 1 kilometer = 0.6 mi (statute); 1 metric ton-km cargo = about 0.68 short ton-mi cargo; c.i.f.: cost, insurance, and freight; f.o.b.: free on board

Somaliland had not received international recognition as of early 2008. This entity represented about a quarter of Somalia's territory. **Official name:** Soomaaliya (Somali); Al-Sumal (Arabic) (Somalia). **Form of government:** transitional regime (the "new transitional government" from October 2004 lacked effective control in early 2008) with one legislative body (Transitional Federal Parliament [275]). At present Somalia is divided into three autonomous regions: Somaliland in the northwest, Puntland in the northeast, and Somalia in the south. **Head of state and government:** President Abdullahi Yusuf Ahmed (from 2004), assisted by Prime Minister Nur Hassan Hussein (from 2007). **Capital:** Mogadishu. **Official languages:** Somali; Arabic. **Official religion:** Islam. **Monetary unit:** 1 Somali shilling (So.Sh.) = 100 cents; valuation (1 Jul 2008) US$1 = So.Sh. 1,392.00 (in early 2007 the black-market value was about 23,000 So.Sh. = US$1).

Demography

Area: 246,000 sq mi, 637,000 sq km. **Population** (2007): 8,699,000. **Density** (2007): persons per sq mi 35.4, persons per sq km 13.7. **Urban** (2006): 36.5%. **Sex distribution** (2002): male 51.47%; female 48.53%. **Age breakdown** (2005): under 15, 44.1%; 15–29, 27.1%; 30–44, 16.1%; 45–59, 8.5%; 60–74, 3.5%; 75–84, 0.6%; 85 and over, 0.1%. **Ethnic composition** (2000): Somali 92.4%; Arab 2.2%; Afar 1.3%; other 4.1%. **Religious affiliation** (2005): Muslim (nearly all Sunni) 99%; other 1%. **Major cities** (1990): Mogadishu (urban agglomeration; 2005) 1,320,000; Hargeysa (1997) 300,000; Kismaayo 90,000; Berbera 70,000; Marka 62,000. **Location:** eastern Africa, bordering Djibouti, the Gulf of Aden, the Indian Ocean, Kenya, and Ethiopia.

Vital statistics

Birth rate per 1,000 population (2005): 45.6 (world avg. 20.3). **Death rate** per 1,000 population (2005): 17.0 (world avg. 8.6). **Natural increase rate** per 1,000 population (2005): 28.6 (world avg. 11.7). **Total fertility rate** (avg. births per childbearing woman; 2005): 6.84. **Life expectancy** at birth (2005): male 46.4 years; female 49.9 years.

National economy

Budget (1991). *Revenue:* So.Sh. 151,453,000,000 (domestic revenue sources [principally indirect taxes and import duties] 60.4%; external grants and transfers 39.6%). *Expenditures:* So.Sh. 141,141,000,000 (general services 46.9%; economic and social services 31.2%; debt service 7.0%). **Public debt** (external, outstanding; 2005): US$1,882,000,000. **Production** (metric tons except as noted). *Agriculture, forestry, fishing* (2005): sugarcane 200,000, corn (maize) 190,000, sorghum 150,000, other tree/bush products include khat, frankincense, and myrrh; livestock (number of live animals) 13,100,000 sheep, 12,700,000 goats, 7,000,000 camels; roundwood 10,912,897 cu m, of which fuelwood 99%; fisheries production 30,000. *Mining and quarrying* (2004): gypsum 1,500; salt 1,000; garnet and opal are mined in Somaliland. *Manufacturing* (value added in So.Sh. '000,000; 1988): food 794; cigarettes and matches 562; hides and skins 420. *Energy production (consumption):* electricity (kW-hr; 2004) 286,000,000 (286,000,000). **Population economically active** (2001–02): total 3,906,000; activity rate of total population 52.6% (participation rates: ages 15–64, 56.4%; unemployed 47.4%). **Households** (2001–02). Average household size 5.8; income per household US$226; sources of income: self-employment 50%, remittances 22.5%, wages 14%, rent/aid 13.5%. **Gross national income** (2006): US$2,313,000,000 (US$274 per capita). **Selected balance of payments data.** Receipts from (US$'000,000): remittances (2005) 1,000; foreign direct investment (2001–05 avg.) 8.8; official development assistance (2005) 236. **Land use** as % of total land area (2003): in temporary crops 1.7%, in permanent crops 0.04%, in pasture 68.5%; overall forest area (2005) 11.4%.

Foreign trade

Imports (2003; c.i.f.): US$397,000,000 (agricultural products 26.5%, of which sugar 13.5%, cereals 6.4%; unspecified 73.5%). *Major import sources* (2004): Djibouti 31%; Kenya 14%; India 10%; Brazil 6%; Oman 5%. **Exports** (2003; f.o.b.): US$95,000,000 (agricultural products 45.1%, of which goats and sheep 25.6%, bovines 7.8%; unspecified 54.9%). *Major export destinations* (2004): Thailand 29%; UAE 24%; Yemen 15%; India 8%; Oman 6%.

Transport and communications

Transport. *Roads* (2003): total length 22,000 km (paved 12%). *Air transport* (2003; four Somaliland airports only): passenger arrivals 50,096, passenger departures 41,979; cargo unloaded 3,817 metric tons, cargo loaded 152 metric tons. **Communications,** in total units (units per 1,000 persons). Daily newspaper circulation (2005): 4,500 (0.5); televisions (2003): 108,000 (14); telephone landlines (2005): 100,000 (12); cellular telephone subscribers (2005): 500,000 (61); personal computers (2005): 75,000 (9.1); total Internet users (2006): 94,000 (11).

Education and health

Literacy (2002): percentage of total population ages 15 and over literate 19.2%; males literate 25.1%; females literate 13.1%. **Health** (1997): physicians 265 (1 per 25,032 persons); hospital beds 2,786 (1 per 2,381 persons); infant mortality rate per 1,000 live births (2005) 116.7.

Military

Total active duty personnel: no national army from 1991. African Union peacekeeping troops (September 2007) 1,600 (of planned 7,000).

Background

Muslim Arabs and Persians first established trading posts along the coasts of Somalia in the 7th–10th centuries. By the 10th century Somali nomads occupied the area inland from the Gulf of Aden, and the south and west were inhabited by various groups of pastoral Oromo peoples. Intensive European exploration began after the British occupation of Aden in 1839, and in the late 19th century Britain and Italy set up protectorates in the region. During World War II the Italians invaded British Somaliland (1940); a year later British troops retook the area, and Britain administered the region until 1950, when Italian Somaliland became a UN trust territory. In 1960 it was united with the former British Somaliland, and the two became the independent Republic of Somalia. Since then it has suffered political and civil strife, including military dictatorship, civil war, drought, and famine. In the 1990s no effective central government existed. In 1991 a proclamation of a Republic of Somaliland, on territory corresponding to the former British Somaliland, was issued by a breakaway group, but it did not receive international recognition. A multinational force intervened from 1992 to 1994 in an unsuccessful attempt to stabilize the region. The country remained in turmoil.

Recent Developments

Fierce fighting continued between forces from Ethiopia and from Somalia's Transitional Federal Government and soldiers of the Islamic Courts Union (ICU), an Islamic fundamentalist movement that had controlled most of the country in 2006. In January 2007, as fleeing ICU fighters became sandwiched between Ethiopian forces, the Kenyan border, and the Somali coastline, US gunships mounted a pair of air raids that were reportedly aimed at three high-ranking al-Qaeda operatives. Ethiopian troops in Mogadishu were joined by a contingent of some 1,500 African Union peacekeepers from Uganda. In March violence there reached its worst levels in more than a decade, with battles so intense that bodies were left lying in the streets for days, and fighting continued in 2008. The number of internally displaced people in Somalia approached one million, and more than 400,000 were refugees in neighboring countries.

Internet resources: <www.unsomalia.net>.

South Africa

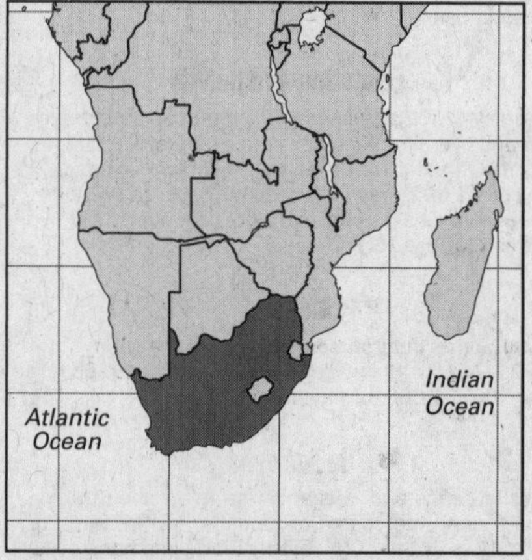

Official name: Republic of South Africa. **Form of government:** multiparty republic with two legislative houses (National Council of Provinces [90]; National Assembly [400]). **Head of state and government:** President Thabo Mbeki (from 1999). **Capitals** (de facto): Pretoria/Tshwane (executive); Bloemfontein/Mangaung (judicial); Cape Town (legislative). **Official languages:** Afrikaans; English; Ndebele; Pedi; Sotho; Swazi; Tsonga; Tswana; Venda; Xhosa; Zulu. **Official religion:** none. **Monetary unit:** 1 rand (R) = 100 cents; valuation (1 Jul 2008) US$1 = R 7.92.

Demography

Area: 470,693 sq mi, 1,219,090 sq km. **Population** (2007): 47,851,000. **Density** (2007): persons per sq mi 101.6, persons per sq km 39.2. **Urban** (2005): 59.3%. **Sex distribution** (2007): male 49.24%; female 50.76%. **Age breakdown** (2007): under 15, 31.9%; 15–29, 29.2%; 30–44, 19.3%; 45–59, 11.7%; 60–74, 6.3%; 75 and over, 1.6%. **Ethnic composition** (2001): black 78.4%, of which Zulu 23.8%, Xhosa 17.6%, Pedi 9.4%, Tswana 8.2%, Sotho 7.9%, Tsonga 4.4%, Swazi 2.7%, other black 4.4%; white 9.6%; mixed white/black 8.9%; Asian 2.5%; other 0.6%. **Religious affiliation** (2005): independent Christian 37.1%, of which Zion Christian 9.5%; Protestant 26.1%; traditional beliefs 8.9%; Roman Catholic 6.7%; Muslim 2.5%; Hindu 2.4%; nonreligious 3.0%; other/unknown 13.3%. **Major urban agglomerations** (2005): Johannesburg 3,288,000; Cape Town 3,103,000; Ekurhuleni (East Rand) 3,043,000; Ethekwini (Durban) 2,643,000; Tshwane (Pretoria) 1,282,000. **Location:** southern Africa, bordering Namibia, Botswana, Zimbabwe, Mozambique, Swaziland, and the southern Atlantic and western Indian oceans; wholly contained within South Africa is the country of Lesotho.

Vital statistics

Birth rate per 1,000 population (2005): 18.5 (world avg. 20.3). **Death rate** per 1,000 population (2005): 21.3 (world avg. 8.6). **Total fertility rate** (avg. births per childbearing woman; 2007): 2.69. **Life expectancy** at birth (2006): male 49.0 years; female 52.5 years.

National economy

Budget (2005–06). *Revenue:* R 411,085,100,000 (personal income taxes 30.6%; VAT 28.0%; company income taxes 23.5%). *Expenditures:* R 417,819,200,000 (transfer to provinces 36.0%; debt payments 12.7%; police and prisons 9.0%; defense 5.4%; education 3.0%). **Public debt** (external, outstanding; 2005): US$11,662,000,000. **Production** (in metric tons except as noted). *Agriculture, forestry, fishing* (2006): sugarcane 20,275,400, corn (maize) 6,935,000, wheat 2,105,000; livestock (number of live animals) 24,983,000 sheep, 13,790,000 cattle; roundwood (2005) 33,071,100 cu m, of which fuelwood 36%; fisheries production (2005) 820,750; aquatic plants production (2005) 9,619 (from aquaculture 30%). *Mining and quarrying* (value of sales in R '000,000,000; 2005): platinum-group metals 38.4; coal 35.6; gold 24.6. *Manufacturing* (value of sales in R '000,000; 2005): food products and beverages 153,496; transport equipment 137,870; chemicals 81,240. *Energy production* (consumption; 2004 data include Botswana, Lesotho, Namibia, and Swaziland): electricity (kW-hr; 2005) 244,920,000,000 (223,257,000,000); coal (metric tons; 2005) 244,500,000 ([2004] 180,287,000); crude petroleum (barrels; 2004) 4,800,000 (206,900,000); petroleum products (metric tons; 2004) 23,825,000

(19,750,000); natural gas (cu m; 2004) 1,978,000,000 (1,978,000,000). **Population economically active** (2005): total 16,788,000; activity rate of total population 35.8% (participation rates: ages 15–64, 56.5%; female 45.7%; unemployed 26.7%). **Households.** Average household size (2004) 4.0; expenditure (2005): food, beverages, and tobacco 25.8%, transportation and communications 16.9%, household furnishings 9.7%, housing 9.6%. **Gross national income** (2006): US$241,635,000,000 (US$5,005 per capita). **Selected balance of payments data.** Receipts from (US$'000,000): tourism (2005) 7,335; remittances (2006) 735. Disbursements for (US$'000,000): tourism (2005) 3,374; remittances (2006) 1,067. **Land use** as % of total land area (2003): in temporary crops 12.1%, in permanent crops 0.8%, in pasture 69.1%; overall forest area (2005) 7.6%.

Foreign trade

Imports (2003; c.i.f.): US$34,543,000,000 (nonelectrical machinery 13.8%; chemical products 10.7%; crude petroleum 10.4%; road vehicles 7.1%; telecommunications equipment 5.0%). *Major import sources* (2005): Germany 14.9%; US 7.0%; China 6.9%; UK 6.8%; Saudi Arabia 6.5%. **Exports** (2003): US$36,230,000,000 (gold 12.7%; iron and steel 10.7%; platinum-group metals 8.8%; road vehicles 8.6%; food 6.6%; nonelectrical machinery 6.5%). *Major export destinations* (2005): UK 11.1%; US 9.1%; Japan 8.3%; Germany 6.3%; China 5.2%.

Transport and communications

Transport. *Railroads* (2001): route length (2005) 20,872 km; passenger-km 3,930,000,000; metric ton-km cargo 106,786,000,000. *Roads* (2002): length 362,099 km (paved 20%). *Vehicles* (2005): passenger cars 4,574,972; trucks and buses 2,112,601. *Air transport* (2006; SAA only): passenger-km 25,501,000,000; metric ton-km cargo 1,228,000,000. **Communications,** in total units (units per 1,000 persons). Daily newspaper circulation (2004): 1,408,000 (30); televisions (2003): 9,134,000 (199); telephone landlines (2005): 4,729,000 (101); cellular telephone subscribers (2005): 33,960,000 (724); personal computers (2005): 3,966,000 (85); total Internet users (2005): 5,100,000 (109); broadband Internet subscribers (2005): 165,000 (3.5).

Education and health

Educational attainment (2006). Percentage of population ages 20 and over having: no formal schooling 10.4%; some primary education 21.1%; complete primary/some secondary 34.0%; complete secondary 24.9%; higher 9.1%. **Literacy** (2005): total population ages 15 and over literate 87.1%. **Health:** physicians (2006) 33,220 (1 per 1,427 persons); hospital beds (2004) 153,465 (1 per 303 persons); infant mortality rate per 1,000 live births (2007) 45.2. **Food** (2005): daily per capita caloric intake 2,933 (vegetable products 87%, animal products 13%).

Military

Total active duty personnel (2006): 62,334 (army 66.3%, navy 9.3%, air force 14.7%, military health service 9.7%). **Military expenditure as percentage of GDP** (2005): 1.5%; per capita expenditure US$76.

Background

San and Khoikhoi peoples roamed southern Africa as hunters and gatherers in the Stone Age, and the latter had developed a pastoralist culture by the time of European contact. By the 14th century, Bantu-speaking peoples had settled in the area and developed gold and copper mining and an active East African trade. In 1652 the Dutch established a colony at the Cape of Good Hope; the Dutch settlers became known as Boers and later as Afrikaners, after their Afrikaans language. In 1795 British forces captured the Cape, and in the 1830s, to escape British rule, Dutch settlers began the Great Trek northward and established the independent Boer republics of Orange Free State and the South African Republic (later the Transvaal region), which the British annexed as colonies by 1902 after the 30-month-long Boer War. In 1910 the British colonies of Cape Colony, Transvaal, Natal, and Orange River were unified into the new Union of South Africa. It became independent and withdrew from the Commonwealth in 1961. Throughout the 20th century South African politics were dominated by the issue of maintaining white supremacy over the country's black majority, and in 1948 South Africa formally instituted apartheid. Faced by increasing worldwide condemnation, it began dismantling the policy in the 1980s and ended it in 1990. In free elections in 1994, Nelson Mandela became the country's first black president. South Africa also rejoined the Commonwealth in 1994.

Recent Developments

A one-month public-service strike in June 2007 in South Africa involving up to one million workers was settled with a 7.5% pay increase. That strike and numerous others by midyear had accounted for more than 11 million lost working days, the highest ever recorded. GDP growth in 2007 was recorded at 14.5%. Inflation remained below the reserve bank's target of 6% for much of the year, but by year's end it had reached 7.1%. Growth boosted the current-account deficit in 2006 to 6.4% of GDP; the deficit for 2007 was estimated at 7.1%. Though unemployment had dropped somewhat during the year, by September 2007 it was still at 23.0%. In the 2006–07 financial year, there was an unprecedented budget surplus of 5 billion rand (about US$700 million).

Internet resources: <www.southafrica.net>.

Spain

Official name: Reino de España (Kingdom of Spain). **Form of government:** constitutional monarchy with two legislative houses (Senate [259]; Congress of Deputies [350]). **Chief of state:** King Juan Carlos I (from 1975). **Head of government:** Prime Minister José Luis Rodríguez Zapatero (from 2004). **Capital:** Madrid. **Official language:** Castilian Spanish; per constitution, Euskera (Basque), Catalan, Galician, and all other Spanish languages are also official in their autonomous communities). **Official religion:** none. **Monetary unit:** 1 euro (€) = 100 cents; valuation (1 Jul 2008) US$1 = €0.63.

Demography

Area: 194,845 sq mi, 504,645 sq km. **Population** (2007): 45,321,000. **Density** (2007): persons per sq mi 232.6, persons per sq km 89.8. **Urban** (2005):

76.7%. **Sex distribution** (2006): male 49.42%; female 50.58%. **Age breakdown** (2006): under 15, 14.3%; 15–29, 19.7%; 30–44, 25.3%; 45–59, 18.9%; 60–74, 13.6%; 75–84, 6.2%; 85 and over, 2.0%. **Ethnic composition** (2000): Spaniard 44.9%; Catalonian 28.0%; Galician 8.2%; Basque 5.5%; Aragonese 5.0%; Rom (Gypsy) 2.0%; other 6.4%. **Religious affiliation** (2006): Roman Catholic 77%; Muslim 2.5%; Protestant 1%; other (mostly nonreligious) 19.5%. **Major cities** (2006): Madrid 3,128,600 (urban agglomeration 6,008,183); Barcelona 1,605,602 (urban agglomeration 5,309,404); Valencia 805,304; Seville 704,414; Zaragoza 649,181. **Location**: southwestern Europe, bordering France, Andorra, the Mediterranean Sea, Gibraltar, the Atlantic Ocean, and Portugal; the North African exclaves of Ceuta and Melilla border Morocco.

Vital statistics

Birth rate per 1,000 population (2006): 10.7 (world avg. 20.3); (2005) within marriage 73.4%. **Death rate** per 1,000 population (2006): 8.3 (world avg. 8.6). **Total fertility rate** (avg. births per childbearing woman; 2005): 1.35. **Life expectancy** at birth (2005): male 80.0 years; female 83.5 years.

National economy

Budget (2006). *Revenue:* €129,546,000,000 (direct taxes 55.6%; indirect taxes 34.8%; transfers 4.3%; other 5.3%). *Expenditures:* €174,976,000,000 (current expenditures 64.9%, of which wages and salaries 12.6%, debt service 10.0%; capital expenditures 10.0%, of which transfers 4.6%; other 25.1%). **Gross national income** (2006): US$1,208,184,000,000 (US$27,530 per capita). **Land use** as % of total land area (2003): in temporary crops 27.3%, in permanent crops 9.9%, in pasture 21.2%; overall forest area (2005) 35.9%. **Production** (metric tons except as noted). *Agriculture, forestry, fishing* (2006): alfalfa 11,000,000, barley 8,318,400, grapes 6,401,500; livestock (number of live animals) 25,131,000 pigs, 22,513,970 sheep, 6,464,000 cattle; roundwood 15,531,798 cu m, of which fuelwood 14%; fisheries production (2005) 1,070,730 (from aquaculture 21%). *Mining and quarrying* (2005): slate 1,200,000; sepiolite 800,000; fluorspar 133,495. *Manufacturing* (value added in US$'000,000; 2003): food products 13,909; chemicals and chemical products 10,881; motor vehicles and parts 10,009. *Energy production (consumption):* electricity (kW-hr; 2006) 275,575,000,000 (256,120,000,000); hard coal (metric tons; 2006) 11,572,000 (37,552,000); lignite (metric tons; 2006) 6,820,000 (6,820,000); crude petroleum (barrels; 2006–07) 863,190,000 (457,438,000); petroleum products (metric tons; 2006–07) 56,376,000 ([2004] 58,547,000); natural gas (cu m; 2006) 80,376,000 (35,739,000,000). **Public debt** (December 2005): US$355,341,000,000. **Population economically active** (2006): total 21,584,800; activity rate of total population 49.2% (participation rates: ages 16–64, 71.9%; female 41.9%; unemployed 8.5%). **Selected balance of payments data.** Receipts from (US$'000,000): tourism (2006–07) 54,435; remittances (2006) 8,863; foreign direct investment (FDI) (2001–05 avg.) 28,246. Disbursements for (US$'000,000): tourism (2006–07) 18,043; remittances (2006) 11,004; FDI (2001–05 avg.) 38,531. **Households** (2005). Average household size 2.9; average annual net income per household (2004) €21,551 (US$26,758); expenditure: housing 26.5%, food 17.8%, household expenses 7.5%, clothing/footwear 6.5%.

Foreign trade

Imports (2004; c.i.f.): €208,410,703,600 (road vehicles 17.0%; nonelectrical machinery 12.0%; mineral fuels 11.2%; chemicals and chemical products 9.8%; electrical machinery 8.9%). *Major import sources:* Germany 16.0%; France 15.3%; Italy 9.1%; UK 6.1%; China 4.1%. **Exports** (2004; f.o.b.): €146,924,722,500 (road vehicles 23.3%; food 11.8%, of which fruits and vegetables 6.0%; chemicals and chemical products 8.5%; nonelectrical machinery 8.1%). *Major export destinations:* France 19.4%; Germany 11.6%; Portugal 9.8%; Italy 9.0%; UK 9.0%.

Transport and communications

Transport. *Railroads* (2006): route length 15,212 km; passenger-km 22,105,000,000; metric ton-km cargo 11,599,000,000. *Roads* (2003): length 677,646 km (paved 99%). *Vehicles* (2006): cars 20,909,000; trucks, vans, and buses 4,945,000. *Air transport* (2006–07): passenger-km 78,501,000,000; metric ton-km cargo 1,124,499. **Communications,** in total units (units per 1,000 persons). Daily newspaper circulation (2004): 4,240,000 (97); televisions (2003): 24,228,000 (564); telephone landlines (2006): 18,385,000 (409); cellular telephone subscribers (2006): 46,152,000 (1,028); personal computers (2005): 12,000,000 (269); total Internet users (2006): 18,578,000 (414); broadband Internet subscribers (2006): 6,655,000 (148).

Education and health

Educational attainment (2003). Percentage of population ages 16 and over having: no formal schooling 12.2%; primary education 26.1%; secondary 47.8%; undergraduate degree 6.5%; graduate degree 7.4%. **Literacy** (2003): total population ages 15 and over literate 97.9%; males literate 98.7%; females literate 97.2%. **Health** (2005): physicians 199,123 (1 per 223 persons); hospital beds 159,215 (1 per 282 persons); infant mortality rate (2006) 3.8. **Food** (2005): daily per capita caloric intake 3,169 (vegetable products 67%, animal products 33%).

1 metric ton = about 1.1 short tons; 1 kilometer = 0.6 mi (statute); 1 metric ton-km cargo = about 0.68 short ton-mi cargo; c.i.f.: cost, insurance, and freight; f.o.b.: free on board

Military

Total active duty personnel (2006): 147,255 (army 64.9%, navy 13.2%, air force 15.5%, other 6.4%). **Military expenditure as percentage of GDP** (2005): 1.1%; per capita expenditure US$268.

Background

Remains of Stone Age populations dating back some 35,000 years have been found in Spain. Celtic peoples arrived in the 9th century BC, followed by the Romans, who dominated Spain from c. 200 BC until the Visigoth invasion in the early 5th century. In the early 8th century most of the peninsula fell to Muslims (Moors) from North Africa and remained under their control until it was gradually reconquered by the Christian kingdoms of Castile, Aragon, and Portugal. Spain was reunited in 1479 following the marriage of Ferdinand II (of Aragon) and Isabella I (of Castile). The last Muslim kingdom, Granada, was reconquered in 1492, and around this time Spain also established a colonial empire in the Americas. In 1516 the throne passed to the Habsburgs, whose rule ended in 1700 when Philip V became the first Bourbon king of Spain. His ascendancy caused the War of the Spanish Succession, which resulted in the loss of numerous European possessions and sparked revolution in most of Spain's American colonies. Spain lost its remaining overseas possessions to the US in the Spanish-American War (1898). It became a republic in 1931. The Spanish Civil War (1936–39) ended in victory for the Nationalists under Gen. Francisco Franco, who ruled as dictator until his death in 1975. His successor as head of state, King Juan Carlos I, restored the monarchy; a new constitution in 1978 established a parliamentary monarchy. Spain joined NATO in 1982 and the European Community in 1986.

Recent Developments

In economic terms Spain continued to outperform most of its European Union partners, with growth of 7.0% in GDP in 2007. In the second half of the year, however, the slowdown in the all-important construction industry was accompanied by evidence of reduced consumer spending and export growth as well as a worrying rise in inflation. In December 2007 the Organisation for Economic Co-operation and Development cut its prediction for 2008 growth to 2.5%, and by March 2008 the unemployment rate stood at 9.6%. The most worrying development for the Socialist government of Prime Minister José Luis Rodríguez Zapatero came in June 2007, when the Basque separatist organization Euskadi Ta Askatasuna (ETA) broke off its 15-month cease-fire, dashing hopes of an end to the organization's 40-year armed struggle. In March hundreds of thousands of flag-waving demonstrators protested the early release of an ETA hunger striker who was allowed to serve out his sentence under house arrest. On 1 December two Civil Guard officers were shot and killed after a chance encounter with three ETA members. In March 2008 ETA was blamed for the murder of a former Socialist party official. At the NATO summit in Bucharest, Romania, in April 2008, Spain agreed to add a few hundred extra troops to its contingent in Afghanistan, which at the beginning of the month was 770 strong.

Internet resources: <www.tourspain.es/en/HOME>.

Sri Lanka

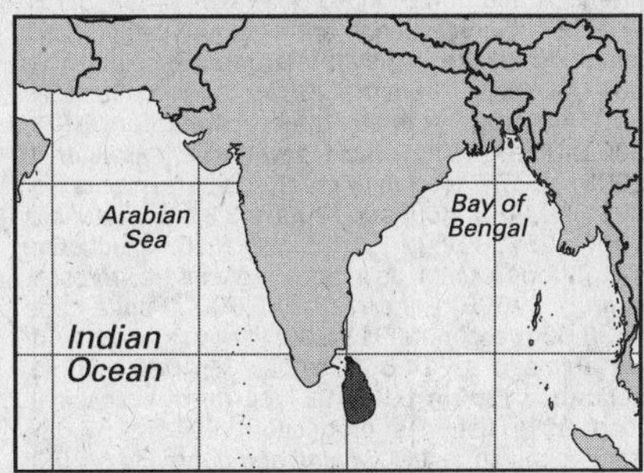

Official name: Sri Lanka Prajatantrika Samajavadi Janarajaya (Sinhala); Ilangai Jananayaka Socialisa Kudiarasu (Tamil) (Democratic Socialist Republic of Sri Lanka). **Form of government:** unitary multiparty republic with one legislative house (Parliament [225]). **Head of state and government:** President Mahinda Rajapakse (from 2005), assisted by Prime Minister Ratnasiri Wickremanayake (from 2005). **Capitals:** Colombo (executive and judicial); Sri Jayewardenepura Kotte (Colombo suburb; legislative). **Official languages:** Sinhala; Tamil. **Official religion:** none. **Monetary unit:** 1 Sri Lanka rupee (LKR) = 100 cents; valuation (1 Jul 2008) US$1 = LKR 107.69.

Demography

Area: 25,332 sq mi, 65,610 sq km. **Population** (2007): 20,102,000. **Density** (2007): persons per sq mi 793.5, persons per sq km 306.4. **Urban** (2005): 15.1%. **Sex distribution** (2005): male 50.82%; female 49.18%. **Age breakdown** (2005): under 15, 24.1%; 15–29, 26.6%; 30–44, 22.6%; 45–59, 16.0%; 60–74, 8.0%; 75–84, 2.3%; 85 and over, 0.4%. **Ethnic composition** (2000): Sinhalese 72.4%; Tamil 17.8%; Sri Lankan Moor 7.4%; other 2.4%. **Religious affiliation** (2005): Buddhist 70%; Hindu 15%; Christian (mostly Roman Catholic) 8%; Muslim (nearly all Sunni) 7%. **Major cities** (2004): Colombo 669,700 (greater Colombo 2,490,300); Dehiwala-Mount Lavinia 218,800; Moratuwa 184,800; Jaffna 172,300; Negombo 127,200. **Location:** island in the northern Indian Ocean, southeast of India.

Vital statistics

Birth rate per 1,000 population (2006): 18.7 (world avg. 20.3). **Death rate** per 1,000 population (2006): 5.8 (world avg. 8.6). **Total fertility rate** (avg. births per childbearing woman; 2005): 2.11. **Life expectancy** at birth (2005): male 72.5 years; female 76.5 years.

National economy

Budget (2005). *Revenue:* LKR 584,783,000,000 (tax revenue 57.6%, of which VAT 23.7%, excises 13.2%; domestic borrowings 21.2%; foreign loans/grants 13.8%; nontax revenue 7.4%). *Expenditures:* LKR 584,783,000,000 (interest payments 20.5%; welfare 15.9%; education 10.9%; defense 10.5%; health 7.7%; tsunami expenditure 4.1%). **Households** (2002). Average household size (2003–04) 4.3; average annual income per household: LKR 153,636 (US$1,606); sources of income: wages 42.0%, nonmonetary income 18.9%, agriculture 7.8%; expenditure: food and nonalcoholic beverages 44.5%, housing 12.6%, transportation and communication 7.1%. **Selected balance of payments data.** Receipts from (US$'000,000): tourism (2005) 429; remittances (2005) 1,908; foreign direct investment (FDI) (2001–05 avg.) 221; official development assistance (2005) 1,378 (commitments). Disbursements for (US$'000,000): tourism (2005) 315; remittances (2006) 257; FDI (2001–05 avg.) 16. **Production** (metric tons except as noted). *Agriculture, forestry, fishing* (2006): rice 3,342,000, sugarcane 1,136,600, coconuts 913,000; livestock (number of live animals) 1,214,650 cattle, 314,080 buffalo; roundwood (2005) 6,277,917 cu m, of which fuelwood 89%; fisheries production (2005) 163,684 (from aquaculture 1%). *Mining and quarrying* (2006): kaolin 9,500; graphite 3,200; sapphires 790,000 carats; diamonds, n.a. *Manufacturing* (value added in LKR '000,000; 2004): textiles and apparel 91,308; food, beverages, and tobacco 72,636; petrochemicals 26,179. *Energy production (consumption):* electricity (kW-hr; 2005) 8,766,000,000 (7,254,000,000); coal (metric tons; 2004) none (95,000); crude petroleum (barrels; 2004) none (16,300,000); petroleum products (metric tons; 2004) 2,085,000 (3,550,000). **Gross national income** (2006): US$27,026,000,000 (US$1,407 per capita). **Public debt** (external, outstanding; 2005): US$9,812,000,000. **Population economically active** (2006): total 7,602,000; activity rate 38.2% (participation rates: ages 15–59 [2000] 60.6%; female 36.3%; unemployed 6.5%). **Land use** as % of total land area (2003): in temporary crops 14.2%, in permanent crops 15.5%, in pasture 6.8%; overall forest area (2005) 29.9%.

Foreign trade

Imports (2005; c.i.f.): LKR 891,359,000,000 (petroleum 18.7%; textiles [mostly yarns and fabrics] 17.3%; machinery and equipment 9.7%; food and beverages 8.5%; building materials 5.7%). *Major import sources* (2004): India 18.0%; Singapore 8.7%; Hong Kong 7.7%; China 5.7%; Iran 5.2%. **Exports** (2005; f.o.b.): LKR 638,276,000,000 (textiles, clothing, and accessories 45.6%; tea 12.8%; sapphires, other precious and semiprecious stones, and jewelry 6.3%). *Major export destinations* (2004): US 32.4%; UK 13.5%; India 6.8%; Belgium/Luxembourg 5.1%; Germany 4.7%.

Transport and communications

Transport. *Railroads* (2004): route length 1,449 km; passenger-km 4,684,000,000; metric ton-km cargo 134,000,000. *Roads* (2003): total length 97,286 km (paved 81%). *Vehicles* (2004): passenger cars 293,747; trucks and buses 453,610. *Air transport* (2006): passenger-km 8,796,000,000; metric ton-km cargo 325,416,000. **Communications,** in total units (units per 1,000 persons). Daily newspaper circulation (2005): 591,000 (30); televisions (2003): 2,400,000 (117); telephone landlines (2006): 1,884,000 (90); cellular telephone subscribers (2006): 5,413,000 (259); personal computers (2005): 734,000 (35); total Internet users (2006): 428,000 (21); broadband Internet subscribers (2006): 29,000 (1.5).

Education and health

Literacy (2003–04): total population ages 5 and over literate 93.0%; males literate 94.9%; females literate 91.3%. **Health** (2004): physicians 8,749 (1 per 2,351 persons); hospital beds 60,328 (1 per 341 persons); infant mortality rate per 1,000 live births (2003) 11.2. **Food** (2005): daily per capita caloric intake 2,559 (vegetable products 94%, animal products 6%); 138% of FAO recommended minimum.

Military

Total active duty personnel (2006): 150,900 (army 78.1%, navy 9.9%, air force 12.0%). **Military expenditure as percentage of GDP** (2005): 2.6%; per capita expenditure US$30.

Background

The Sinhalese people of Sri Lanka (Ceylon) probably originated with the blending of aboriginal inhabitants and migrating Indo-Aryans from India c. the 5th century BC. The Tamils were later immigrants from Dravidian India, migrating over a period from the early centuries AD to c. 1200. Buddhism was introduced during the 3rd century BC. As Buddhism spread, the Sinhalese kingdom extended its political control over Ceylon but lost it to invaders from southern India in the 10th century AD. Between 1200 and 1505 Sinhalese power gravitated to southwestern Ceylon, while a southern Indian dynasty seized power in the north and established the Tamil kingdom in the 14th century. Foreign invasions from India, China, and Malaya occurred in the 13th–15th centuries. In 1505 the Portuguese arrived, and by 1619 they controlled most of the island. The Sinhalese enlisted the Dutch to help oust the Portuguese and eventually came under the control of the Dutch East India Co., which relinquished power in 1796 to the British. In 1802 Ceylon became a crown colony, gaining independence in 1948. It became the Republic of Sri Lanka in 1972 and was renamed the Democratic Socialist Republic of Sri Lanka in 1978. Civil strife between Tamil and Sinhalese groups has beset the country in recent years, with the Tamils demanding a separate autonomous state in northern Sri Lanka.

Recent Developments

The civil war between the government of Sri Lanka and the Liberation Tigers of Tamil Eelam (LTTE) that had continued at varying levels of intensity since 1983 flared up again in the form of fighting, suicide bombings, assassinations, and abductions. In November 2007 the government killed S.P. Thamilselvan, the leader of the LTTE's political wing. Reportedly, 350,000 people had been displaced and 5,000 had died in the latest fighting, bringing cumulative deaths since 1983 to more than 67,000. In addition, more than 1,000 individuals were abducted in 2007. Economic growth slowed to approximately 6% in 2007, though the garment sector continued to thrive and worker remittances provided valuable foreign exchange.

Internet resources: <www.srilankatourism.org>.

1 metric ton = about 1.1 short tons; 1 kilometer = 0.6 mi (statute); 1 metric ton-km cargo = about 0.68 short ton-mi cargo; c.i.f.: cost, insurance, and freight; f.o.b.: free on board

The Sudan

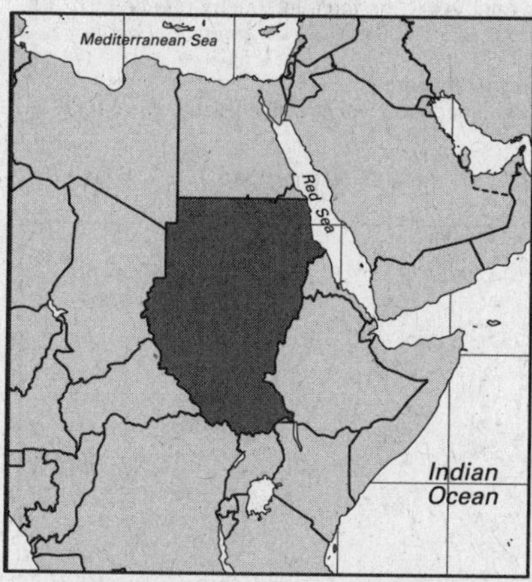

Official name: Jumhuriyat al-Sudan (Republic of the Sudan). **Form of government:** military-backed interim regime with two legislative houses (Council of States [50]; National Assembly [450]). **Head of state and government:** President Omar Hassan Ahmad al-Bashir (from 1989). **Capitals:** Khartoum (executive); Omdurman (legislative). **Official language:** Arabic; English has been designated the "principal" language in southern Sudan. **Official religion:** Islamic law and custom are sources of national law per 1998 constitution. **Monetary unit:** 1 Sudanese pound (SDG); valuation (1 Jul 2008) US$1 = SDG 2.06 (the Sudanese pound replaced the Sudanese dinar [SDD] 10 Jan 2007, at the rate of 1 SDG = 100 SDD).

Demography

Area: 967,499 sq mi, 2,505,810 sq km. **Population** (2007): 39,379,000. **Density** (2007): persons per sq mi 40.7, persons per sq km 15.7. **Urban** (2006): 37.6%. **Sex distribution** (2006): male 50.69%; female 49.31%. **Age breakdown** (2006): under 15, 42.1%; 15–29, 28.4%; 30–44, 16.9%; 45–59, 8.4%; 60–74, 3.6%; 75–84, 0.5%; 85 and over, 0.1%. **Ethnic composition** (2003): black 52%; Arab 39%; Beja 6%; other 3%. **Religious affiliation** (2005): Sunni Muslim 68.4%; traditional beliefs 10.8%; Roman Catholic 9.5%; Protestant 8.8%, of which Anglican 5.4%; other 2.5%. **Major cities** (1993): Omdurman 1,271,403; Khartoum 947,483 (urban agglomeration [2006] 6,700,000, including 2,000,000 internally displaced persons); Khartoum North 700,887; Port Sudan 308,195; Kassala 234,622. **Location:** northeastern Africa, bordering Egypt, the Red Sea, Eritrea, Ethiopia, Kenya, Uganda, the Democratic Republic of the Congo, the Central African Republic, Chad, and Libya.

Vital statistics

Birth rate per 1,000 population (2006): 35.3 (world avg. 20.3). **Death rate** per 1,000 population (2006): 15.2 (world avg. 8.6). **Total fertility rate** (avg. births per childbearing woman; 2006): 4.79. **Life expectancy** at birth (2006): male 47.1 years; female 48.8 years.

National economy

Budget (2006). *Revenue:* SDD 1,507,500,000,000 (nontax revenue 61.0%, of which government receipts for crude petroleum 50.3%; tax revenue 39.0%, of which customs and excise duties 20.9%). *Expenditures:* SDD 1,825,300,000,000 (federal government 64.1%; transfers to: northern states 19.7%; southern Sudan 16.2%). **Public debt** (external, outstanding; 2005): US$11,163,000,000. **Gross national income** (2006): US$33,882,000,000 (US$900 per capita). **Production** (metric tons except as noted). *Agriculture, forestry, fishing* (2005): sugarcane 7,186,000, sorghum 4,275,000, millet 745,000; livestock (number of live animals) 49,797,000 sheep, 42,526,000 goats, 40,468,000 cattle, 3,908,000 camels; roundwood 19,871,000 cu m, of which fuelwood 89%; fisheries production 63,600 (from aquaculture 3%). *Mining and quarrying* (2006): marble 11,470 cu m; gold 3,246 kg. *Manufacturing* (2006): diesel 1,817,000; flour 1,200,000; benzene 1,139,000. *Energy production (consumption):* electricity (kW-hr; 2006) 4,521,000,000 (3,458,000,000); crude petroleum (barrels; 2006) 132,700,000 (34,300,000); petroleum products (metric tons; 2006) 3,912,000 (3,623,000). **Population economically active** (2000): total 12,207,000; activity rate of total population 37.8% (participation rate: female 29.9%). **Households.** Average household size (2004) 6.2. **Selected balance of payments data.** Receipts from (US$'000,000): tourism (2006) 189; remittances (2006) 1,016; foreign direct investment (2001–05 avg.) 1,290; official development assistance (2005) 1,829. Disbursements for (US$'000,000): tourism (2005) 668; remittances (2006) 2. **Land use** as % of total land area (2003): in temporary crops 7.2%, in permanent crops 0.2%, in pasture 49.3%; overall forest area (2005) 28.4%.

Foreign trade

Imports (2006; c.i.f.): US$8,074,000,000 (machinery and equipment 34.8%; manufactured goods 20.3%; transport equipment 18.5%; foodstuffs 9.4%, of which wheat and wheat flour 5.1%). *Major import sources:* China 20.8%; EU 17.2%; Saudi Arabia 8.0%; Japan 7.4%; India 6.6%. **Exports** (2006; f.o.b.): US$5,657,000,000 (crude petroleum 83.2%; benzene 6.3%; sesame seeds 3.0%; livestock [mainly sheep and camels] 2.2%; cotton 1.5%). *Major export destinations:* China 75.0%; Japan 9.2%; UAE 4.0%; Saudi Arabia 2.2%; Egypt 1.7%.

Transport and communications

Transport. *Railroads* (2006): route length 4,578 km; passenger-km 49,000,000; metric ton-km cargo 893,000,000. *Roads* (2000): total length 11,900 km (paved 36%). *Vehicles* (2002): passenger cars 47,300; trucks and buses 62,500. *Air transport*: passenger-km (2003) 659,000,000; metric ton-km cargo (2001) 54,542,000. **Communications,** in total units (units per 1,000 persons). Televisions (2003): 12,886,000 (352); telephone landlines (2006): 637,000 (17); cellular telephone subscribers (2006): 4,683,000 (121); total Internet users (2006): 3,500,000 (91); broadband Internet subscribers (2006): 2,100 (0.05).

Education and health

Literacy (2003): total population ages 15 and over literate 60.9%; males literate 71.6%; females literate

50.4%. **Health** (2006): physicians 8,799 (1 per 4,384 persons); hospital beds 26,577 (1 per 1,451 persons); infant mortality rate per 1,000 live births 96.8. **Food** (2005): daily per capita caloric intake 2,351 (vegetable products 82%, animal products 18%); 128% of FAO recommended minimum.

Military

Total active duty personnel (2006): 104,800 (army 95.4%, navy 1.7%, air force 2.9%); foreign troops (September 2007): southern Sudan–UN peacekeeping 8,800; Darfur–African Union/UN peacekeeping 9,500. **Military expenditure as percentage of GDP** (2005): 1.8%; per capita expenditure US$13.

Background

From the end of the 4th millennium BC Nubia (now the northern Sudan) periodically came under Egyptian rule, and it was part of the kingdom of Cush from the 11th century BC to the 4th century AD. Christian missionaries converted The Sudan's three principal kingdoms during the 6th century AD; these black Christian kingdoms coexisted with their Muslim Arab neighbors in Egypt for centuries, until the influx of Arab immigrants brought about their collapse in the 13th–15th centuries. Egypt had conquered all of The Sudan by 1874 and encouraged British interference in the region; this aroused Muslim opposition and led to the revolt of al-Mahdi, who captured Khartoum in 1885 and established a Muslim theocracy in The Sudan that lasted until 1898, when his forces were defeated by the British. The British ruled the country, generally in partnership with Egypt, until The Sudan achieved independence in 1956. Since then the country has fluctuated between ineffective parliamentary government and unstable military rule. The non-Muslim population of the south has engaged in ongoing rebellion against the Muslim-controlled government of the north, leading to famines and the displacement of some four million people. Arab militias known as Janjaweed responded by killing as many as 400,000 people beginning in 2003 and causing a massive humanitarian disaster.

Recent Developments

Benefiting from high oil prices, The Sudan in 2007 recorded one of Africa's fastest-growing economies, estimated at nearly 10%. Foreign investment, spurred mainly by China, had quadrupled over the past decade. In October the Sudan People's Liberation Movement, the ruling party in southern Sudan, suspended its participation in the Government of National Unity, claiming that its northern counterpart (the National Congress Party) was causing delays in the compilation of a census, general elections, and the distribution of oil revenues from the disputed border region. Meanwhile, the rebellion in the western province of Darfur remained the focus of international attention. The UN Security Council in June declared that it had secured an unconditional agreement with the Sudanese government to deploy a joint African Union–UN peacekeeping force for Darfur, which would consist of nearly 20,000 troops and more than 6,000 police. Almost immediately the chief of the AU commission, reflecting the concerns of other African countries, stated that non-African troops would not be necessary because African countries had offered adequate reinforcements, but by April 2008 the force in country numbered 7,300 troops and 1,700 police from around the world.

Internet resources:
<www.sudan-tourism.gov.sd/english>.

Suriname

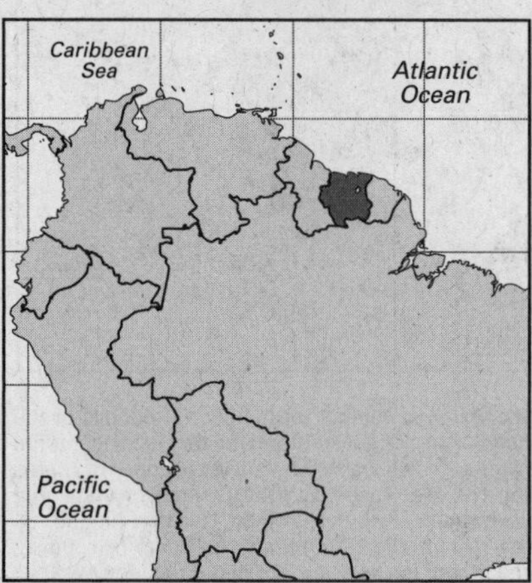

Official name: Republiek Suriname (Republic of Suriname). **Form of government:** multiparty republic with one legislative house (National Assembly [51]). **Head of state and government:** President Ronald Venetiaan (from 2000), assisted by Vice President Ram Sardjoe (from 2005). **Capital:** Paramaribo. **Official language:** Dutch. **Official religion:** none. **Monetary unit:** 1 Suriname dollar (SRD) = 100 cents; valuation (1 Jul 2008) US$1 = SRD 2.75 (the Suriname dollar replaced the Suriname guilder [SRG] 1 Jan 2004, at the rate of 1 SRD = SRG 1,000).

Demography

Area: 63,251 sq mi, 163,820 sq km. **Population** (2007): 510,000. **Density** (2007): persons per sq mi 8.1, persons per sq km 3.1. **Urban** (2005): 73.9%. **Sex distribution** (2006): male 49.71%; female 50.29%. **Age breakdown** (2006): under 15, 28.5%; 15–29, 26.8%; 30–44, 24.3%; 45–59, 12.0%; 60–74, 6.2%; 75 and over, 2.2%. **Ethnic composition** (2004): Indo-Pakistani ("Hindustani") 27.4%; Suriname Creole ("Afro-Surinamese") 17.7%; Maroon (descendants of runaway slaves living in the interior) 14.7%; Javanese ("Indonesian") 14.6%; mixed race 12.5%; Amerindian 1.5%; other/unknown 11.6%. **Religious affiliation** (2004): Christian (mostly Roman Catholic and Moravian) 40.7%; Hindu 19.9%; Muslim 13.5%; nonreligious 4.4%; traditional beliefs 3.3%; other 2.5%; unknown 15.7%. **Major cities** (1996/97): Paramaribo 222,800; Lelydorp 15,600; Nieuw Nickerie 11,100; Mungo (Moengo) 6,800; Meerzorg 6,600. **Location:** northern South America, bordering the North Atlantic Ocean, French Guiana, Brazil, and Guyana.

Vital statistics

Birth rate per 1,000 population (2006): 17.6 (world avg. 20.3). **Death rate** per 1,000 population (2006): 5.5 (world avg. 8.6). **Total fertility rate** (avg. births per childbearing woman; 2006): 2.05. **Life expectancy** at birth (2006): male 70.3 years; female 75.8 years.

National economy

Budget (2006). *Revenue:* SRD 1,665,800,000 (tax revenue 77.1%, of which taxes on international trade 23.3%, corporate taxes 18.3%, income tax 16.2%; nontax revenue 18.0%; grants 4.9%). *Expenditures:* SRD 1,660,500,000 (current expenditures 87.4%, of which wages and salaries 36.6%; capital expenditures 11.9%; other 0.7%). **Public debt** (external, outstanding; 2005): US$504,300,000. **Production** (metric tons except as noted). *Agriculture, forestry, fishing* (2006): rice 195,000, sugarcane 120,000, bananas 17,488; livestock (number of live animals) 137,000 cattle, 24,500 pigs, 3,800,000 chickens; roundwood (2005) 226,846 cu m, of which fuelwood 20%; fisheries production (2005) 40,191 (from aquaculture 1%). *Mining and quarrying* (2006): bauxite 4,945,000; alumina 2,133,000; gold (2005) 10,619 kg (recorded production). *Manufacturing* (value of production at factor cost in SRG; 1993): food products 992,000,000; beverages 558,000,000; tobacco 369,000,000. *Energy production (consumption):* electricity (kW-hr; 2006) 805,800,000 ([2004] 1,509,000,000); crude petroleum (barrels; 2006) 4,800,000 ([2004] 3,248,000); petroleum products (metric tons; 2004) 374,000 (583,000). **Population economically active** (2004): total 173,130; activity rate of total population 35.1% (participation rates: ages 15–64, 56.0%; female 36.7%; unemployed 9.5%). **Gross national income** (2006): US$2,039,000,000 (US$4,478 per capita). **Households** (2004). Average household size 4.0; average disposable income per household SRD 32,150 (US$11,760); expenditure (2000): food and beverages 40.0%, housing, energy, and household furnishings 23.6%, clothing and footwear 11.0%. **Selected balance of payments data.** Receipts from (US$'000,000): tourism (2005) 45; remittances (2006) 4.0; foreign direct disinvestment (2001–05 avg.) −35; official development assistance (2005) 51 (commitments). Disbursements for (US$'000,000): tourism (2005) 17; remittances (2006) 9.0. **Land use** as % of total land area (2003): in temporary crops 0.4%, in permanent crops 0.06%, in pasture 0.1%; overall forest area (2005) 94.7%.

Foreign trade

Imports (2005; c.i.f.): US$1,099,900,000 (machinery and transport equipment 26.8%, mineral fuels 15.6%, food products 9.1%, chemical products 6.9%). *Major import sources:* US 24.4%; The Netherlands 14.5%; Trinidad and Tobago 10.5%; China 5.4%; Japan 4.3%. **Exports** (2005): US$929,100,000 (alumina 48.1%; gold 36.4%; shrimp and fish 6.1%; crude petroleum 5.8%). *Major export destinations:* Norway 23.9%; US 16.8%; Canada 16.4%; France 8.1%; Iceland 2.9%.

Transport and communications

Transport. *Railroads* (2003): length 157 km. *Roads* (2003): total length 4,304 km (paved 26%). *Vehicles* (2000): passenger cars 61,365; trucks and buses 23,220. *Air transport* (2005): passenger-km 1,745,800,000; metric ton-km cargo 27,100,000. **Communications,** in total units (units per 1,000 persons). Televisions (2003): 118,000 (243); telephone landlines (2006): 82,000 (162); cellular telephone subscribers (2006): 320,000 (634); personal computers (2001): 20,000 (45); total Internet users (2005): 32,000 (64); broadband Internet subscribers (2006): 2,700 (5.3).

Education and health

Literacy (2004): total population ages 15 and over literate 89.6%; males literate 92.0%; females literate 87.2%. **Health:** physicians (2001) 236 (1 per 2,000 persons); hospital beds (2005) 1,797 (1 per 278 persons); infant mortality rate per 1,000 live births (2006) 20.8. **Food** (2005): daily per capita caloric intake 2,973 (vegetable products 88%, animal products 12%); 156% of FAO recommended minimum.

Military

Total active duty personnel (2006): 1,840 (all personnel are technically part of the army; army 76.1%, navy 13.0%, air force 10.9%). **Military expenditure as percentage of GDP** (2005): 1.6%; per capita expenditure US$43.

Background

Suriname was inhabited by various native peoples prior to European settlement. Spanish explorers claimed it in 1593, but the Dutch began to settle there in 1602, followed by the English in 1651. It was ceded to the Dutch in 1667, and in 1682 the Dutch West India Co. introduced coffee and sugarcane plantations and African slaves to cultivate them. Slavery was abolished in 1863, and indentured servants were brought from China, Java, and India to work the plantations, adding to the population mix. Except for brief interludes of British rule (1799–1802, 1804–15), it remained a Dutch colony. It gained internal autonomy in 1954 and independence in 1975. A military coup in 1980 ended civilian control until the electorate approved a new constitution in 1987. Military control resumed after a coup in 1990. Elections were held in 1991, followed by a resumption of democratic government.

Recent Developments

In September 2007 Suriname received the verdict of the UN International Tribunal for the Law of the Sea with dismay, as it awarded neighboring Guyana 65% of the contested maritime area, containing potentially valuable oil and natural gas deposits. Otherwise, Suriname enjoyed progress on several fronts, with improvements in its credit rating, tax revenue, and trade surplus and GDP growth of just above 5%.

Internet resources: <www.surinametourism.com>.

Swaziland

Official name: Umbuso weSwatini (Swazi); Kingdom of Swaziland (English). **Form of government:** constitutional monarchy with two legislative houses (Senate [30]; House of Assembly [65]). **Head of state and government:** King Mswati III (from 1986), assisted by Prime Minister Absalom Themba Dlamini (from 2003). **Capi-**

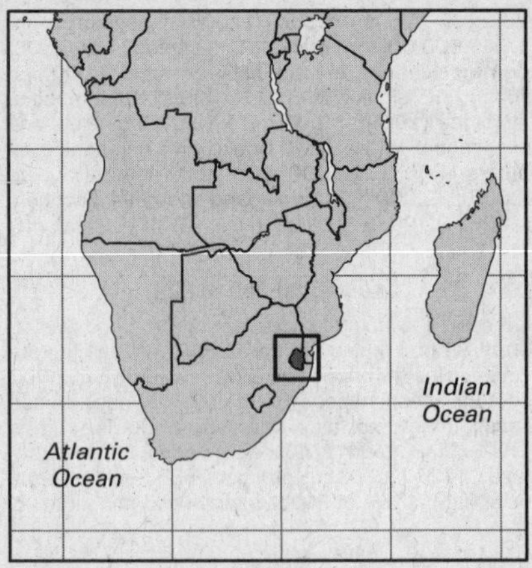

tals: Mbabane (administrative and judicial); Lozitha and Ludzidzini (royal); Lobamba (legislative). **Official languages:** Swati (Swazi); English. **Official religion:** none. **Monetary unit:** 1 lilangeni (plural emalangeni [E]) = 100 cents; valuation (1 Jul 2008) US$1 = E 7.92.

Demography

Area: 6,704 sq mi, 17,364 sq km. **Population** (2007): 1,141,000. **Density** (2007): persons per sq mi 170.2, persons per sq km 65.7. **Urban** (2006): 24.1%. **Sex distribution** (2005): male 48.26%; female 51.74%. **Age breakdown** (2005): under 15, 41.0%; 15–29, 33.7%; 30–44, 11.6%; 45–59, 8.3%; 60–74, 4.4%; 75–84, 0.9%; 85 and over, 0.1%. **Ethnic composition** (2000): Swazi 82.3%; Zulu 9.6%; Tsonga 2.3%; Afrikaner 1.4%; mixed (black-white) 1.0%; other 3.4%. **Religious affiliation** (2000): Christian 87%, of which African indigenous 43%, unaffiliated Christian 19%, Protestant 18%, Roman Catholic 5%; traditional beliefs 11%; Muslim 1%; nonreligious 1%. **Major cities** (1997): Mbabane 57,992; Manzini 25,571 (urban agglomeration 78,734); Big Bend 9,374; Mhlume 7,661; Malkerns 7,400. **Location:** southern Africa, bordering South Africa and Mozambique.

Vital statistics

Birth rate per 1,000 population (2005): 27.9 (world avg. 20.3). **Death rate** per 1,000 population (2005): 28.8 (world avg. 8.6). **Natural increase rate** per 1,000 population (2005): −0.9 (world avg. 11.7). **Total fertility rate** (avg. births per childbearing woman; 2005): 3.62. **Life expectancy** at birth (2005): male 32.5 years; female 34.0 years.

National economy

Budget (2004–05). *Revenue:* E 4,842,000,000 (receipts from Customs Union of Southern Africa 57.3%; individual income taxes 14.6%; sales taxes 11.3%; taxes on companies 8.4%). *Expenditures:* E 5,554,500,000 (general administration 26.2%; education 20.1%; police/defense 15.2%; transportation and communications 10.6%; health 8.0%). **Gross national income** (2006): US$2,775,000,000 (US$2,448 per capita). **Population economically active** (2001): total 392,000; activity rate of total population 39.3% (unemployed [2004] 31%). **Public debt** (external, outstanding; 2005): US$451,000,000. **Land use** as % of total land area (2003): in temporary crops 10.3%, in permanent crops 0.8%, in pasture 69.8%; overall forest area (2005) 31.5%. **Production** (metric tons except as noted). *Agriculture, forestry, fishing* (2006): sugarcane 5,000,000, oranges 35,900, grapefruit and pomelo 34,040; livestock (number of live animals) 580,000 cattle, 3,200,000 chickens; roundwood (2005) 890,000 cu m, of which fuelwood 63%; fisheries production 70. *Mining and quarrying* (2005): ferrovanadium 345; crushed stone 566,771 cu m. *Manufacturing* (value of exports in US$'000; 2002): apparel and clothing accessories 173,500; unbleached wood pulp 56,100; preserved fruit (significantly pineapples) 17,400. *Energy production (consumption):* electricity (kW-hr; 2005) 156,300,000 (1,123,000,000); coal (metric tons; 2005) 221,700 ([2003] 372,000). **Households.** Average household size (2004) 6.4; average annual income per household (2002) US$1,540; expenditure (1996): food 24.5%, housing 15.9%, household furnishings and operation 13.2%, clothing and footwear 11.0%, transportation and communications 8.2%. **Selected balance of payments data.** Receipts from (US$'000,000): tourism (2005) 69; remittances (2006) 81; foreign direct investment (2001–05 avg.) 25; official development assistance (2005) 53 (commitments). Disbursements for (US$'000,000): tourism (2005) 15; remittances (2006) 11; foreign direct disinvestment (2001–05 avg.) −1.4.

Foreign trade

Imports (2002; c.i.f.): US$879,400,000 (food and live animals 15.0%; machinery and apparatus 14.5%; chemicals and chemical products 10.8%; refined petroleum 10.6%; textile yarn, fabrics, and made-up articles 8.6%; road vehicles 8.4%). *Major import sources* (2004): South Africa 95.6%; EU 0.9%; Japan 0.9%. **Exports** (2003): US$1,484,000,000 (soft drink [including sugar and fruit juice] concentrates 51.3%; cottonseed and lint 14.8%; wood pulp 12.0%; sugar 8.0%; reexports 6.7%). *Major export destinations* (2004): South Africa 59.7%; US 8.8%; EU 8.8%; Mozambique 6.2%.

Transport and communications

Transport. *Railroads* (2005): route length 301 km; metric ton-km cargo (2001) 746,000,000. *Roads* (2002): total length 3,594 km (paved 30%). *Vehicles* (2003): passenger cars 44,113; trucks and buses 47,761. *Air transport:* (2000) passenger-km 68,000,000. **Communications,** in total units (units per 1,000 persons). Daily newspaper circulation (2004): 29,000 (28); televisions (2003): 38,000 (34); telephone landlines (2006): 44,000 (43); cellular telephone subscribers (2006): 250,000 (243); personal computers (2005): 42,000 (41); total Internet users (2005): 42,000 (40).

Education and health

Literacy (2006): total population ages 15 and over literate 79.6%; males literate 80.9%; females liter-

1 metric ton = about 1.1 short tons; 1 kilometer = 0.6 mi (statute); 1 metric ton-km cargo = about 0.68 short ton-mi cargo; c.i.f.: cost, insurance, and freight; f.o.b.: free on board

ate 78.3%. **Health:** physicians (2004) 171 (1 per 6,047 persons); hospital beds (2000) 1,570 (1 per 665 persons); infant mortality rate per 1,000 live births (2005) 71.8. **Food** (2005): daily per capita caloric intake 1,664 (vegetable products 86%, animal products 14%); 90% of FAO recommended minimum.

Military

Total active duty personnel (2006): 3,000 troops. **Military expenditure as percentage of GDP** (2004): 1.8%; per capita expenditure US$39.

Background

Stone tools and rock paintings indicate prehistoric habitation in the region, but it was not settled until the Bantu-speaking Swazi people migrated there in the 18th century and established the nucleus of the Swazi nation. The British gained control in the 19th century after the Swazi king sought their aid against the Zulus. Following the South African War, the British governor of Transvaal administered Swaziland; his powers were transferred to the British high commissioner in 1906. In 1949 the British rejected the Union of South Africa's request to control Swaziland. The country gained limited self-government in 1963 and achieved independence in 1968. In the 1970s new constitutions were framed based on the supreme authority of the king and traditional tribal government. During the 1990s forces demanding democracy arose, but the kingdom remained in place. In 2005 a new constitution was signed that contained a bill of rights, but it retained the ban on opposition political parties.

Recent Developments

The economic and social uncertainty that had dominated Swaziland during the previous year remained in 2007, though the budget showed a 2.8% surplus and GDP stood at US$2.3 billion. Corruption continued to be a problem in both government and the private sector, and in February the Prevention of Corruption Act was promulgated. The number of those living below the poverty line rose to 70%, from 69% in 2006. The prevalence of HIV/AIDS dropped sharply from 39.2% to 26% among those sexually active and to 19% overall.

Internet resources:
<www.welcometoswaziland.com>.

Sweden

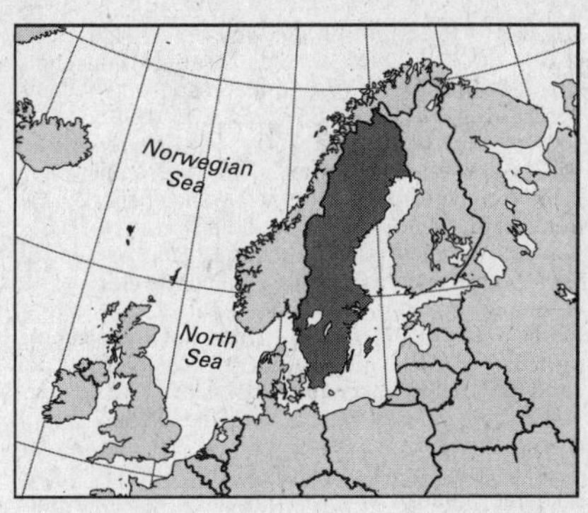

Official name: Konungariket Sverige (Kingdom of Sweden). **Form of government:** constitutional monarchy with one legislative house (Parliament [349]). **Chief of state:** King Carl XVI Gustaf (from 1973). **Head of government:** Prime Minister Fredrik Reinfeldt (from 2006). **Capital:** Stockholm. **Official language:** Swedish. **Official religion:** none. **Monetary unit:** 1 Swedish krona (SEK) = 100 ore; valuation (1 Jul 2008) US$1 = SEK 5.98.

Demography

Area: 173,860 sq mi, 450,295 sq km. **Population** (2007): 9,142,000. **Density** (2007): persons per sq mi 57.7, persons per sq km 22.3. **Urban** (2005): 84.4%. **Sex distribution** (2006): male 49.64%; female 50.36%. **Age breakdown** (2006): under 15, 17.0%; 15–29, 18.8%; 30–44, 20.7%; 45–59, 19.5%; 60–74, 15.2%; 75–84, 6.2%; 85 and over, 2.6%. **Ethnic composition** (2005): Swedish 83.8%; other European 10.1%, of which Finnish 2.9%, pre-1991 Yugoslav 2.2%; Asian 4.1%; other 2.0%. **Religious affiliation** (2005): Church of Sweden 77%; other Protestant 4.5%; Muslim 4%; Roman Catholic 1.6%; Orthodox 1.1%; other 11.8%. **Major cities** (2006): Stockholm 782,885; Göteborg 489,757; Malmö 276,244; Uppsala 185,187; Linköping 138,580. **Location:** northern Europe, bordering Finland, the Gulf of Bothnia, the Baltic Sea, and Norway.

Vital statistics

Birth rate per 1,000 population (2006): 11.6 (world avg. 20.3); (2005) within marriage 44.5%. **Death rate** per 1,000 population (2006): 10.0 (world avg. 8.6). **Total fertility rate** (avg. births per childbearing woman; 2005): 1.77. **Life expectancy** at birth (2006): male 78.7 years; female 82.9 years.

National economy

Budget (2005). *Revenue:* SEK 718,249,000,000 (taxes on goods and services 45.6%; statutory social security fees 37.9%; income/profits/capital gains taxes 9.5%). *Expenditures:* SEK 750,965,000,000 (social insurance 40.0%; defense 5.9%; education 5.8%; health 5.1%; debt service 4.7%). **Public debt** (September 2007): US$175,055,000,000. **Production** (metric tons except as noted). *Agriculture, forestry, fishing* (2006): sugar beets 2,189,000, wheat 2,001,400, barley 1,112,400; livestock (number of live animals) 1,681,000 pigs, 1,590,000 cattle, 480,000 sheep, (2004) 250,500 reindeer; roundwood (2005) 98,700,000 cu m, of which fuelwood 7%; fisheries production (2005) 262,239 (from aquaculture 2%). *Mining and quarrying* (2005): iron ore (metal content) 15,300,000; zinc (metal content) 214,600; copper (metal content) 97,800. *Manufacturing* (value added in SEK '000,000 at constant prices of 2000; 2005): electrical machinery, telecommunications equipment, and electronics 108,909; road vehicles/parts 65,211; chemicals and chemical products 62,320. *Energy production (consumption):* electricity (kW-hr; 2005) 154,981,000,000 (147,587,000,000); coal (metric tons; 2004) none (3,329,000); crude petroleum (barrels; 2004) none (150,600,000); petroleum products (metric tons; 2004) 18,360,000

(11,691,000); natural gas (cu m; 2004) none (1,054,000,000). **Households.** Average household size (2005) 2.1; average annual disposable income per household (2004) SEK 258,900 (US$35,230); sources of gross income (2004): wages and salaries 60.2%, transfer payments 30.7%, self-employment 2.8%; expenditure (2005): housing and energy 20.7%, transportation 16.6%, recreation and culture 15.5%, food and nonalcoholic beverages 13.3%. **Land use** as % of total land area (2003): in temporary crops 6.5%, in permanent crops 0.01%, in pasture 12.0%; overall forest area (2005) 66.9%. **Gross national income** (2006): US$381,786,000,000 (US$42,030 per capita). **Population economically active** (2006): total 4,586,000; activity rate of total population 50.5% (participation rates: ages 16–64, 78.7%; female 47.6%; unemployed [July 2006–June 2007] 4.9%). **Selected balance of payments data.** Receipts from (US$'000,000): tourism (2005) 7,361; remittances (2006) 630; foreign direct investment (FDI) (2001–05 avg.) 10,812. Disbursements for (US$'000,000): tourism (2005) 10,776; remittances (2006) 611; FDI (2001–05 avg.) 17,187.

Foreign trade

Imports (2006; c.i.f.): SEK 724,200,000,000 (road vehicles 10.9%; crude and refined petroleum 10.8%; nonelectrical machinery and apparatus 10.1%; office machines/telecommunications equipment 9.9%; base metals 6.8%). *Major import sources:* Germany 17.9%; Denmark 9.4%; Norway 8.7%; The Netherlands 6.3%; UK 6.2%. **Exports** (2006; f.o.b.): SEK 851,200,000,000 (nonelectrical machinery and apparatus 14.4%; road vehicles 13.6%; telecommunications equipment 8.5%; paper and paper products 6.8%; medicines and pharmaceuticals 6.0%; iron and steel 5.7%). *Major export destinations:* Germany 9.9%; US 9.4%; Norway 9.3%; UK 7.2%; Denmark 7.0%.

Transport and communications

Transport. *Railroads* (2004): length 11,050 km; passenger-km (2005) 8,922,000,000; metric ton-km cargo 21,675,000,000. *Roads* (2005): total length 425,383 km (paved 31%). *Vehicles* (2005): passenger cars 4,154,000; trucks and buses 474,000. *Air transport* (2006; includes SAS international and domestic traffic applicable to Sweden only): passenger-km 4,404,000,000; (2005) metric ton-km cargo 2,784,000. **Communications**, in total units (units per 1,000 persons). Daily newspaper circulation (2004): 4,312,000 (480); televisions (2003): 8,645,000 (965); telephone landlines (2006): 5,399,000 (594); cellular telephone subscribers (2006): 9,607,000 (1,058); personal computers (2005): 7,548,000 (836); total Internet users (2006): 6,981,000 (769); broadband Internet subscribers (2006): 2,346,000 (258).

Education and health

Educational attainment (2005). Percentage of population ages 15–74 having: incomplete or complete primary education 24.1%; incomplete or complete secondary 50.4%; incomplete or complete higher 23.9%; unknown 1.6%. **Health** (2005): physicians 27,600 (1 per 327 persons); hospital beds 26,540 (1 per 340 persons); infant mortality rate per 1,000 live births 2.4.

Military

Total active duty personnel (2006): 27,600 (army 50.0%, navy 28.6%, air force 21.4%). **Military expenditure as percentage of GDP** (2005): 1.5%; per capita expenditure US$612.

Background

The first inhabitants of Sweden were apparently hunters who crossed the land bridge from Europe c. 9000 BC. During the Viking era (9th–10th centuries) the Swedes controlled river trade in eastern Europe between the Baltic Sea and the Black Sea and also raided western European lands. Sweden was loosely united and Christianized in the 11th–12th centuries. It conquered the Finns in the 12th century and in the 14th united with Norway and Denmark under a single monarchy. It broke away in 1523 under Gustav I Vasa. In the 17th century it emerged as a great European power in the Baltic region, but its dominance declined after its defeat in the Second Northern War (1700–21). Sweden became a constitutional monarchy in 1809 and united with Norway 1814–1905; it acknowledged Norwegian independence in 1905. It maintained its neutrality during both world wars. It was a charter member of the UN but abstained from membership in the European Union until the 1990s and in NATO altogether. A new constitution drafted in 1975 reduced the monarch's role to that of ceremonial head of state. In 1997 it decided to begin the controversial shutdown of its nuclear power industry.

Recent Developments

The Swedish economy in 2007 grew 6.6%. Economic development included a rapid drop in the percentage of unemployed (from 4.9% in September 2006 to 4.2% a year later, though by March 2008 it had risen to 6.3%) and a sizable increase in the active workforce (which added 131,000 more jobs in the same period), though there was also a drop in productivity. Combined with generous wage agreements in the private sector, however, this situation was expected to have inflationary effects in the years to come.

Internet resources: <www.visit-sweden.com>.

Switzerland

Official name: Confédération Suisse (French); Schweizerische Eidgenossenschaft (German); Confederazione Svizzera (Italian); Confederaziun Svizra (Romansh) (Swiss Confederation). **Form of government:** federal state with two legislative houses (Council of States [46]; National Council [200]). **Head of state and government:** President Pascal Couchepin (from 2008). **Capitals:** Bern (administrative); Lausanne (judicial). **Official languages:** French; German; Italian; Romansh (locally). **Official religion:**

1 metric ton = about 1.1 short tons; 1 kilometer = 0.6 mi (statute); 1 metric ton-km cargo = about 0.68 short ton-mi cargo; c.i.f.: cost, insurance, and freight; f.o.b.: free on board

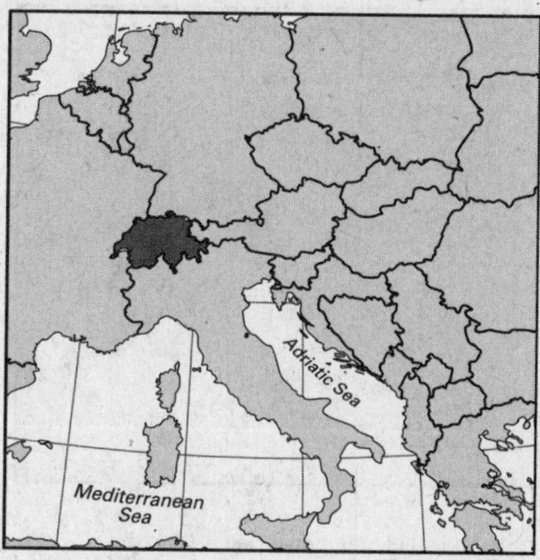

none. **Monetary unit:** 1 Swiss franc (CHF) = 100 centimes; valuation (1 Jul 2008) US$1 = CHF 1.02.

Demography

Area: 15,940 sq mi, 41,284 sq km. **Population** (2007): 7,607,000. **Density** (2007): persons per sq mi 477.2, persons per sq km 184.3. **Urban** (2005): 75.2%. **Sex distribution** (2005): male 48.97%; female 51.03%. **Age breakdown** (2005): under 15, 16.0%; 15–29, 18.1%; 30–44, 23.6%; 45–59, 20.6%; 60–74, 13.9%; 75–84, 5.7%; 85 and over, 2.1%. **National composition** (2004): Swiss 79.4%; pre-1991 Yugoslav 4.7%; Italian 4.1%; Portuguese 2.2%; German 2.0%; Turkish 1.0%; other 6.6%. **Religious affiliation** (2000): Roman Catholic 41.8%; Protestant 33.0%; Muslim 4.3%; Orthodox 1.8%; Jewish 0.2%; other Christian 2.7%; nonreligious 11.1%; other 0.8%; unknown 4.3%. **Major urban agglomerations** (2005): Zürich 1,101,710; Geneva 493,445; Basel 486,146; Bern 343,789; Lausanne 310,028. **Location:** central Europe, bordering Germany, Austria, Liechtenstein, Italy, and France.

Vital statistics

Birth rate per 1,000 population (2006): 9.7 (world avg. 20.3); (2005) within marriage 86.3%. **Death rate** per 1,000 population (2006): 8.1 (world avg. 8.6). **Natural increase rate** per 1,000 population (2006): 1.6 (world avg. 11.7). **Total fertility rate** (avg. births per childbearing woman; 2005): 1.42. **Life expectancy** at birth (2005): male 78.7 years; female 83.9 years.

National economy

Budget (2004). *Revenue:* CHF 165,097,000,000 (tax revenue 59.1%, of which taxes on income and wealth 39.6%; nontax revenue 22.2%; social security obligations 18.7%). *Expenditures:* CHF 170,738,000,000 (social security 19.0%; social welfare 16.2%; education 16.2%; health 11.3%; transportation 8.4%; defense 2.9%). **Production** (metric tons except as noted). *Agriculture, forestry, fishing* (2006): sugar beets 1,243,000, wheat 540,700, potatoes 392,000; livestock (number of live animals) 1,652,000 pigs, 1,554,700 cattle; roundwood (2005) 5,044,061 cu m, of which fuelwood 21%; fisheries production (2005) 2,689 (from aquaculture 45%). *Mining* (2006): salt 560,000 (polished diamond exports [2006]: US$661,000,000). *Manufacturing* (value added in CHF '000,000; 2002): chemicals and chemical products 14,771; professional and scientific equipment 10,892; food products, beverages, and tobacco 8,907. *Energy production (consumption):* electricity (kW-hr; 2004) 65,299,000,000 (64,596,000,000); coal (metric tons; 2004) none (177,000); crude petroleum (barrels; 2004) none (37,000,000); petroleum products (metric tons; 2004) 5,034,000 (10,527,000); natural gas (cu m; 2005) none (3,058,000,000). **Population economically active** (2006): total 4,220,000; activity rate of total population 55.8% (participation rates: ages 15–64, 81.2%; female 45.7%; unemployed 4.0%). **Households** (2004). Average household size 2.3; average gross income per household CHF 102,072 (US$82,084); sources of income: wages and salaries 64.7%, transfers 24.0%; expenditure: housing and energy 27.5%, food and nonalcoholic beverages 12.9%, transportation 12.0%, recreation 10.8%, restaurants and hotels 10.2%. **Gross national income** (2006): US$394,522,000,000 (US$52,922 per capita). **Public debt** (end of year; 2004): US$111,952,100,000. **Selected balance of payments data.** Receipts from (US$'000,000): tourism (2005) 11,063; remittances (2006) 1,946; foreign direct investment (FDI) (2001–05 avg.) 7,636. Disbursements for (US$'000,000): tourism (2005) 9,262; remittances (2006) 13,871; FDI (2001–05 avg.) 22,332. **Land use** as % of total land area (2003): in temporary crops 10.2%, in permanent crops 0.6%, in pasture 27.3%; overall forest area (2005) 30.9%.

Foreign trade

Imports (2005; c.i.f.): CHF 149,094,300,000 (chemicals 22.0%; machinery 20.1%; vehicles 9.6%; precision instruments, watches, and jewelry 7.2%). *Major import sources* (2006): Germany 33.3%; Italy 11.2%; France 10.3%; The Netherlands 5.0%; US 5.0%. **Exports** (2005; f.o.b.): CHF 156,977,300,000 (chemicals 34.9%; machinery 22.4%; watches 7.9%; fabricated metals 7.4%; precision instruments 7.3%). *Major export destinations* (2006): Germany 20.2%; US 10.3%; Italy 8.9%; France 8.6%; UK 4.7%.

Transport and communications

Transport. *Railroads* (2003): length (2004) 5,024 km; passenger-km 15,400,000,000; metric ton-km cargo 9,534,000,000. *Roads* (2005): total length 71,296 km. *Vehicles* (2005): passenger cars 3,863,807; trucks and buses 307,264. *Air transport* (2006): passenger-km 22,788,000,000; metric ton-km cargo 1,039,032,000. **Communications,** in total units (units per 1,000 persons). Daily newspaper circulation (2004): 2,486,000 (333); televisions (2004): 4,300,000 (576); telephone landlines (2006): 5,040,000 (694); cellular telephone subscribers (2006): 7,418,000 (1,021); personal computers (2005): 6,430,000 (857); total Internet users (2006): 4,360,000 (600); broadband Internet subscribers (2006): 2,140,000 (283).

Education and health

Educational attainment (2006). Percentage of resident population ages 25–64 having: compulsory education 17.9%; secondary 52.2%; higher 29.9%.

Health (2005): physicians 28,251 (1 per 266 persons); hospital beds (2004) 42,417 (1 per 176 persons); infant mortality rate per 1,000 live births 4.2. **Food** (2005): daily per capita caloric intake 3,085 (vegetable products 63%, animal products 37%).

Military

Total active duty personnel (2006): 4,200. **Military expenditure as percentage of GDP** (2005): 1.0%; per capita expenditure US$464.

Background

The original inhabitants of Switzerland were the Helvetians, who were conquered by the Romans in the 1st century BC. Germanic tribes penetrated the region from the 3rd to the 6th century AD, and Muslim and Magyar raiders ventured in during the 10th century. It came under the Holy Roman Empire in the 11th century. In 1291 three cantons formed an anti-Habsburg league that became the nucleus of the Swiss Confederation. It was a center of the Reformation, which divided the confederation and led to a period of political and religious conflict. The French organized Switzerland as the Helvetic Republic in 1798. In 1815 the Congress of Vienna recognized Swiss independence and guaranteed its neutrality. A new federal state was formed in 1848 with Bern as the capital. It remained neutral in both world wars and continued to guard this stance. With the formation of the European Union, it took steps toward provisional association with the European economic area.

Recent Developments

Switzerland showed no sign of wanting to join the EU, but its role as a transport hub at the heart of Europe was cemented with the opening in June 2007 of the transalpine Lötschberg Base Tunnel. The world's longest overland tunnel—a 34.6-km (21.5-mi) rail link—took eight years to build, and when full rail service began in December, it slashed the train journey between Germany and Italy from less than four hours to less than two. An even more ambitious project—the 57-km (35-mi) Gotthard Base Tunnel—was scheduled for completion by 2017 in a bid to move heavy trucks off the road and onto the rails. Swiss economic growth was forecast at a better-than-expected 2.6%. Unemployment fell for the third straight year, to 2.8%, and the government budget showed a surplus for the second year in a row. A government expert panel, however, warned that prospects for 2008 were highly uncertain. The crisis in the subprime mortgage sector in the US and the rising cost of foodstuffs and commodities were factors contributing to the dampening of expectations.

Internet resources: <www.myswitzerland.com>.

Syria

Official name: Al-Jumhuriyah al-ʿArabiyah al-Suriyah (Syrian Arab Republic). **Form of government:** unitary multiparty republic with one legislative house (People's Assembly [250]). **Head of state and government:** President Bashar al-Assad (from 2000), assisted by

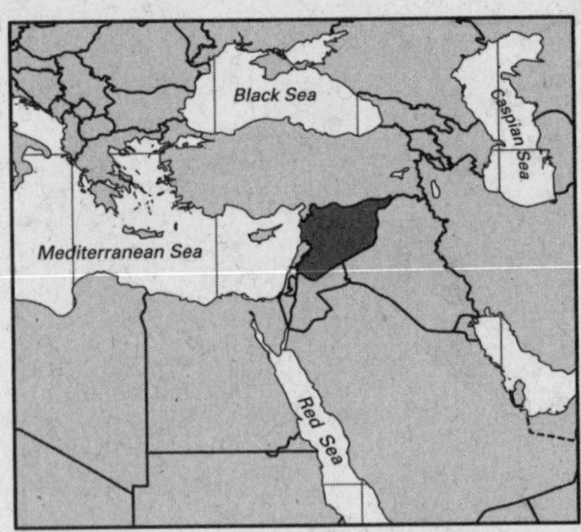

Prime Minister Muhammad Naji al-Otari (from 2003). **Capital:** Damascus. **Official language:** Arabic. **Official religion:** none, although Islam is the required religion of the head of state and is the basis of the legal system. **Monetary unit:** 1 Syrian pound (S.P) = 100 piastres; valuation (1 Jul 2008) US$1 = S.P 50.95.

Demography

Area: 71,498 sq mi, 185,180 sq km. **Population** (2007): 19,048,000. **Density** (2007): persons per sq mi 266.4, persons per sq km 102.9. **Urban** (2005): 50.6%. **Sex distribution** (2006): male 51.21%; female 48.79%. **Age breakdown** (2006): under 15, 37.0%; 15–29, 31.1%; 30–44, 18.7%; 45–59, 8.4%; 60–74, 3.7%; 75 and over, 1.1%. **Ethnic composition** (2000): Syrian Arab 74.9%; Bedouin Arab 7.4%; Kurd 7.3%; Palestinian Arab 3.9%; Armenian 2.7%; other 3.8%. **Religious affiliation** (2000): Muslim 86%, of which Sunni 74%, Alawite (Shiʿi) 11%; Christian 8%, of which Orthodox 5%, Roman Catholic 2%; Druze 3%; nonreligious/atheist 3%. **Major cities** (2004): Aleppo 1,975,200; Damascus 1,614,500; Homs (Hims) 800,400; Latakia 468,700; Hamah 366,800. **Location:** the Middle East, bordering Turkey, Iraq, Jordan, Israel, Lebanon, and the Mediterranean Sea.

Vital statistics

Birth rate per 1,000 population (2006): 27.8 (world avg. 20.3). **Death rate** per 1,000 population (2006): 4.8 (world avg. 8.6). **Total fertility rate** (avg. births per childbearing woman; 2006): 3.40. **Life expectancy** at birth (2006): male 69.0 years; female 71.7 years.

National economy

Budget (2005). *Revenue:* S.P 377,100,000,000 (petroleum royalties and taxes 33.2%; nonpetroleum nontax revenues 27.0%; nonpetroleum tax on income and profits 13.5%; taxes on international trade 6.7%). *Expenditures:* S.P 436,500,000,000 (current expenditures 61.4%, capital expenditures 38.6%). **Public debt** (external, outstanding; 2005): US$5,640,000,000. **Gross national income** (2006): US$28,697,000,000 (US$1,479 per capita). **Production** (metric tons except as noted). *Agriculture, forestry, fishing* (2006): wheat 4,668,750, sugar beets 1,096,291, seed cotton 1,021,996; livestock (number of live animals) 19,651,051 sheep, 1,295,725 goats, 1,082,623 cattle; roundwood (2005) 58,100 cu m, of which fuelwood 31%; fisheries production (2005) 16,980 (from aquaculture 50%). *Mining and quarrying* (2005): phosphate rock 3,850,000; gypsum 440,000. *Manufacturing* (value added in S.P '000,000; 2002): food, beverages, and tobacco 23,788; textiles and clothing 20,344; fabricated metals 15,462. *Energy production (consumption):* electricity (kW-hr; 2005) 34,900,000,000 (34,000,000,000); crude petroleum (barrels; 2006) 147,825,000 (83,950,000); petroleum products (metric tons; 2004) 10,756,000 (10,651,000); natural gas (cu m; 2006) 8,500,000,000 (5,100,000,000). **Population economically active** (2006): total 7,880,000; activity rate of total population 40.4% (participation rates: ages 15–64, 66.8%; female 30.9%; unemployed 8.5%). **Households.** Average household size (2004): 5.2; sources of income (2003–04): wages 49.2%, self-employment 39.8%. **Selected balance of payments data.** Receipts from (US$'000,000): tourism (2005) 2,175; remittances (2006) 823; foreign direct investment (2001–05 avg.) 236; official development assistance (2005) 78. Disbursements for (US$'000,000): tourism (2005) 550; remittances (2006) 40. **Land use** as % of total land area (2003): in temporary crops 25.4%, in permanent crops 4.5%, in pasture 45.4%; overall forest area (2005) 2.5%.

Foreign trade

Imports (2005; c.i.f.): S.P 481,406,000,000 (mineral fuels 25.7%; base and fabricated metals 13.2%; machinery and equipment 12.7%; foodstuffs 12.4%; transport equipment 8.0%). *Major import sources* (2004): Turkey 9.4%; Ukraine 8.7%; China 7.8%; Russia 5.4%; Saudi Arabia 5.2%. **Exports** (2005; f.o.b.): S.P 307,750,000,000 (crude petroleum 58.1%; textiles 5.8%; live animals and meat 3.4%; cotton fiber 2.7%). *Major export destinations* (2004): Italy 22.7%; France 18.0%; Turkey 12.9%; Iraq 9.0%; Saudi Arabia 6.2%.

Transport and communications

Transport. *Railroads* (2006): route length 2,711 km; passenger-km (2004) 691,916,000; metric ton-km cargo 1,922,829,000. *Roads* (2004): total length 48,767 km (paved 20%). *Vehicles* (2004): passenger cars 227,639; trucks and buses 441,579. *Air transport* (2006; SyrianAir only): passenger-km 2,340,000,000; metric ton-km cargo 16,000,000. **Communications,** in total units (units per 1,000 persons). Daily newspaper circulation (2006): 175,000 (9.4); televisions (2003): 3,093,000 (178); telephone landlines (2006): 3,243,000 (175); cellular telephone subscribers (2006): 4,675,000 (252); personal computers (2005): 800,000 (44); total Internet users (2006): 1,500,000 (81); broadband Internet subscribers (2006): 5,600 (0.03).

Education and health

Educational attainment (2003–04). Percentage of population having: no formal education (illiterate) 14.3%; no formal education (literate) 9.9%; primary education 45.8%; secondary 22.5%; incomplete higher 3.9%; higher 3.6%. **Literacy** (2005): total population ages 15 and over literate 78.4%; males literate 90.6%; females literate 66.1%. **Health** (2004): physicians 25,890 (1 per 685 persons); hospital beds 22,282 (1 per 760 persons); infant mortality rate per 1,000 live births (2006) 28.6. **Food** (2005): daily per capita caloric intake 3,058 (vegetable products 86%, animal products 14%); 166% of FAO recommended minimum.

Military

Total active duty personnel (2006): 307,600 (army 65.0%, navy 2.5%, air force 13.0%, air defense 19.5%); UN peacekeeping troops in Golan Heights (September 2007) 1,043. **Military expenditure as percentage of GDP** (2005): 7.2%; per capita expenditure US$80.

Background

Syria has been inhabited for several thousand years. From the 3rd millennium BC it was under the control variously of Sumerians, Akkadians, Amorites, Egyptians, Hittites, Assyrians, and Babylonians. In the 6th century BC it became part of the Persian Achaemenian dynasty, which fell to Alexander the Great in 330 BC. Seleucid rulers governed it from 301 BC to c. 164 BC; then Parthians and Nabataean Arabs divided the region. It flourished as a Roman province (64 BC–AD 300) and as part of the Byzantine Empire (300–634) until Muslims invaded and established control. It came under the Ottoman Empire in 1516, which held it, except for brief rules by Egypt, until the British invaded in World War I. After the war it became a French mandate; it achieved independence in 1945. It united with Egypt in the United Arab Republic (1958–61). During the Six-Day War (1967), it lost the Golan Heights to Israel. Syrian troops frequently clashed with Israeli troops in Lebanon during the 1980s and '90s. Hafez al-Assad's long and harsh regime was marked also by antagonism toward Syria's neighbors Turkey and Iraq.

Recent Developments

Syria's relations with Israel were the most newsworthy in 2007. In February an elite Israeli unit carried out exercises in the Golan Heights for the first time in five years, and the commander of the UN Disengagement Observer Force warned in late September that Israel was engaged in a dangerous troop buildup along the Golan front. Syrian officials told Egyptian journalists that "Syria wants the Golan back, whether peacefully or through a war." In September Israeli warplanes bombed a remote site outside Dair al-Zur. Some observers claimed that the strike destroyed a secret facility for the production or storage of chemical agents or nuclear material. Suspicions that the site was an illicit nuclear-weapons facility were strengthened by the lack of vigorous response from Syria or its allies, though the government did complain to the UN a week later. In April 2008 the US government released video evidence that it claimed showed that the facility was indeed to be a nuclear reactor for non-peaceful use, and that North Korea had assisted in its construction. However, that same month Turkey's government confirmed that it had been an intermediary between Israel and Syria in secret peace talks since April 2007.

Internet resources: <www.syriatourism.org>.

Taiwan

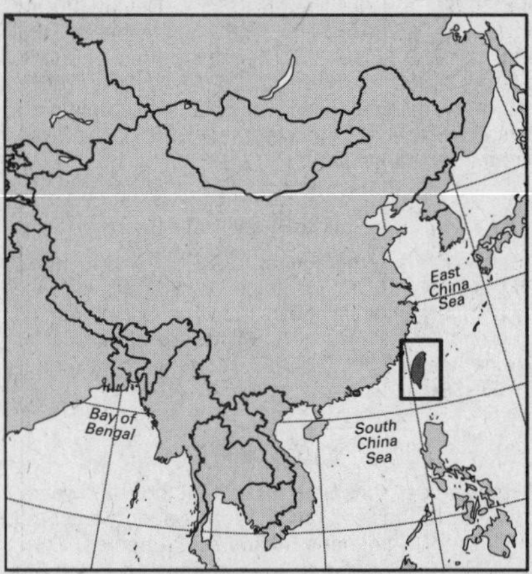

Official name: Chung-hua Min-kuo (Republic of China) **Form of government:** multiparty republic with one legislative body (Legislative Yuan [113]). **Chief of state:** President Ma Ying-jeou (from 2008). **Head of government:** Premier Liu Chao-shiuan (from 2008). **Administrative center:** Taipei. **Official language:** Mandarin Chinese. **Official religion:** none. **Monetary unit:** 1 New Taiwan dollar (NT$) = 100 cents; valuation (1 Jul 2008) US$1 = NT$30.37.

Demography

Area: 13,972 sq mi, 36,188 sq km. **Population** (2007): 22,902,000. **Density** (2006): persons per sq mi 1,639, persons per sq km 632.9. **Urban** (2000): 80.0%. **Sex distribution** (2006): male 50.67%; female 49.33%. **Age breakdown** (2006): under 15, 18.1%; 15–29, 23.5%; 30–44, 24.6%; 45–59, 20.5%; 60–74, 9.1%; 75–84, 3.4%; 85 and over, 0.8%. **Ethnic composition** (2003): Taiwanese 84.0%; mainland Chinese 14.0%; indigenous tribal peoples 2.0%, of which Ami 0.6%. **Religious affiliation** (2002): Buddhism 23.8%; Taoism 19.7%; Christian 4.5%, of which Protestant 2.6%, Roman Catholic 1.3%; I-kuan Tao 3.7% (syncretistic religion); Muslim 0.6%; other (mostly Chinese folk-religionist or nonreligious) 47.7%. **Major cities** (2006): Taipei 2,632,242; Kaohsiung 1,514,706; T'ai-chung 1,044,392; T'ai-nan 760,037; Pan-ch-'iao 544,292. **Location:** island between the East China Sea, the Philippine Sea, and the South China Sea, north of the Philippines and southeast of mainland China.

Vital statistics

Birth rate per 1,000 population (2006): 8.9 (world avg. 20.3); within marriage 95.8%. **Death rate** per 1,000 population (2006): 5.9 (world avg. 8.6). **Natural increase rate** per 1,000 population (2006): 3.0 (world avg. 11.7). **Total fertility rate** (avg. births per childbearing woman; 2006): 1.11. **Life expectancy** at birth (2005): male 74.5 years; female 80.8 years.

National economy

Budget (2005). *Revenue:* NT$2,115,227,000,000 (tax revenue 72.4%, of which income taxes 30.6%, corporate tax 11.2%, customs tax 3.8%). *Expenditures:* NT$2,309,564,000,000 (social security 27.4%; education, science, and culture 20.4%; economic development 20.2%). **Population economically active** (2006): total 10,522,000; activity rate of total population 46.3% (participation rates: ages 15–64, 57.9%; female 42.4%; unemployed 3.9%). **Production** (metric tons except as noted). *Agriculture, forestry, fishing* (2006): rice 1,262,000, sugarcane 651,000, citrus fruits 548,991; livestock (number of live animals) 7,068,621 pigs, 134,793 cattle; timber 30,372 cu m; fisheries production 1,282,279 (from aquaculture 25%). *Mining and quarrying* (2006): marble 25,493,000. *Manufacturing* (value added in NT$'000,000,000; 2003): electronic parts and components 452; computers, telecommunications, video electronics 232; refined petroleum products 223. *Energy production (consumption):* electricity (kW-hr; 2004) 181,245,000,000 (167,478,000,000); coal (metric tons; 2002) none (50,600,000); crude petroleum (barrels; 2004) 280,000 ([2003] 327,000,000); natural gas (cu m; 2004) 796,000,000 ([2002] 8,127,000,000). **Gross national income** (2005): US$354,900,000,000 (US$16,630 per capita). **Households** (2004). Average household size (2006) 3.1; average annual disposable income per household NT$891,249 (US$26,673); sources of income: wages and salaries 55.3%, transfers 15.2%, self-employment 15.1%; expenditure: food, beverages, and tobacco 23.7%, housing and energy 23.1%, education, recreation, and culture 13.3%, health care 12.9%, transportation and communication 12.5%. **Selected balance of payments data.** Receipts from (US$'000,000): tourism (2005) 5,040; remittances (2005) 323; foreign direct investment (FDI) (2001–05 avg.) 1,906. Disbursements for (US$'000,000): tourism (2005) 8,682; remittances (2005) 1,342; FDI (2001–05 avg.), 5,844. **Land use** as % of total land area (2001): in temporary crops 16.1%, in permanent crops 6.6%, in pasture 0.3%; overall forest area 58.1%.

Foreign trade

Imports (2006; c.i.f.): US$202,698,135,000 (minerals 19.1%; electronic machinery 18.1%; metals and metal products 11.4%; chemicals 11.1%; nonelectrical machinery 8.8%). *Major import sources:* Japan 22.8%; China 12.2%; US 11.2%; South Korea 7.4%; Saudi Arabia 4.8%. **Exports** (2006; f.o.b.): US$224,017,271,000 (nonelectrical machinery, electrical machinery, and electronics 49.8%; metal products 10.7%; clocks, precision instruments, watches, and musical instruments 8.2%; plastic articles 7.1%). *Major export destinations:* China 23.1%; Hong Kong 16.7%; US 14.4%; Japan 7.3%; Singapore 4.1%.

Transport and communications

Transport. *Railroads* (2006; Taiwan Railway Administration only): route length 1,118 km; passenger-km 12,352,000,000; metric ton-km cargo 997,000,000. *Roads* (2006): total length 39,286 km. *Vehicles* (2006): passenger cars 5,698,000; trucks and buses 1,000,000. *Air transport* (2006; China Airlines, EVA,

1 metric ton = about 1.1 short tons; 1 kilometer = 0.6 mi (statute); 1 metric ton-km cargo = about 0.68 short ton-mi cargo; c.i.f.: cost, insurance, and freight; f.o.b.: free on board

and Far Eastern Air transport only): passenger-km 59,108,000,000; metric ton-km cargo 11,470,000,000. **Communications**, in total units (units per 1,000 persons). Daily newspaper circulation (2003): 6,530,000 (289); televisions (1999): 9,200,000 (418); telephone landlines (2006): 14,497,000 (636); cellular telephone subscribers (2006): 23,249,000 (1,020); personal computers (2005): 13,098,000 (575); total Internet users (2006): 14,520,000 (637); broadband Internet subscribers (2006): 4,506,000 (197).

Education and health

Educational attainment (2003). Percentage of population ages 15 and over having: no formal schooling 4.6%; primary 19.8%; vocational 23.7%; secondary 26.8%; some college 12.0%; higher 13.1%. **Literacy** (1999): total population ages 15 and over literate 94.6%; males literate 97.6%; females literate 91.4%. **Health** (2006): physicians 34,899 (1 per 654 persons); hospital beds 148,962 (1 per 153 persons); infant mortality rate per 1,000 live births (2004) 5.9.

Military

Total active duty personnel (2006): 290,000 (army 69.0%, navy 15.5%, air force 15.5%). **Military expenditure as percentage of GDP** (2005): 2.2%; per capita expenditure US$324.

Background

Known to the Chinese as early as the 7th century, Taiwan was widely settled by them early in the 17th century. In 1646 the Dutch seized control of the island, only to be ousted in 1661 by a large influx of Chinese refugees from the Ming dynasty. Taiwan fell to the Manchus in 1683 and was not open to Europeans again until 1858. In 1895 it was ceded to Japan following the Sino-Japanese War. A Japanese military center in World War II, it was frequently bombed by US planes. After Japan's defeat it was returned to China, which was then governed by the Nationalists. When the Communists took over mainland China in 1949, the Nationalist government fled to Taiwan and made it their seat of government, with Gen. Chiang Kai-shek as president. In 1954 he and the US signed a mutual defense treaty, and Taiwan received US support for almost three decades, developing its economy in spectacular fashion. It was recognized by many noncommunist countries as the representative of all China until 1971, when it was replaced in the UN by the People's Republic of China. Martial law was lifted in Taiwan in 1987 and travel restrictions with mainland China in 1988. In 1989 opposition parties were legalized. The relationship with the mainland became increasingly close in the 1990s.

Recent Developments

Taiwan's politics were focused on the presidential elections scheduled for March 2008. The Kuomintang (KMT), or Nationalist Party, and the Democratic Progressive Party (DPP) were locked in an ideological struggle over the status of Taiwan—the DPP regarded Taiwan as an already independent country, while the KMT wanted to see Taiwan more closely integrated with China economically over the short term and ultimately united. The DPP's Frank Hsieh won his party's presidential nomination in May 2007 and called for a new constitution and name for the country. Hsieh's KMT opponent, Ma Ying-jeou, attempted to focus his campaign on the state of Taiwan's economy, promising that if elected he would restore economic growth by opening direct air and shipping links with China and by dropping a restriction on Taiwanese companies that capped their Chinese investments at 40% of their net assets. Both candidates proposed referenda to join the UN, increasingly straining relations with the US, which saw them as steps toward formal independence. The refusal to drop the proposals led senior US diplomat Thomas Christensen to abandon the US's policy of strategic ambiguity on the status of Taiwan by saying that the US does "not recognize Taiwan as an independent state." In March 2008 Ma won the election and both referenda were rejected, leading many to hope that Taiwan's ties with China, and the US, would improve.

Internet resources: <www.taiwantourism.org>.

Tajikistan

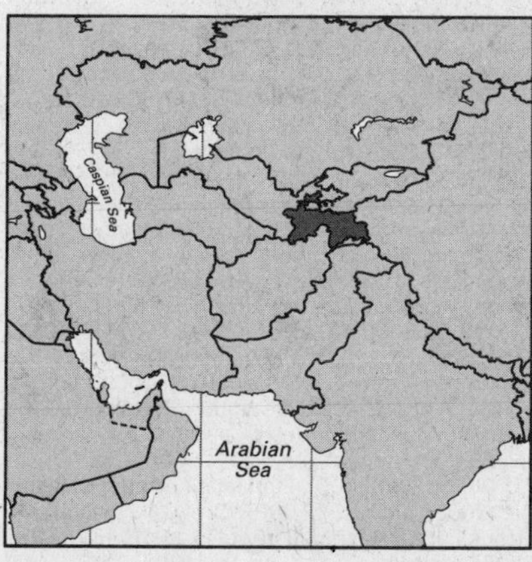

Official name: Jumhurii Tojikiston (Republic of Tajikistan). **Form of government:** parliamentary republic with two legislative houses (National Assembly [34]; House of Representatives [63]). **Chief of state:** President Imomalii Rakhmon (from 1994). **Head of government:** Prime Minister Akil Akilov (from 1999). **Capital:** Dushanbe. **Official language:** Tajik (Tojik). **Official religion:** none. **Monetary unit:** 1 somoni (TJS) = 100 dirams; valuation (1 Jul 2008) US$1 = TJS 3.43.

Demography

Area: 55,300 sq mi, 143,100 sq km **Population** (2007): 6,736,000. **Density** (2007): persons per sq mi 121.8, persons per sq km 47.1. **Urban** (2006): 26.3%. **Sex distribution** (2006): male 49.74%; female 50.26%. **Age breakdown** (2006): under 15, 35.6%; 15–29, 31.2%; 30–44, 18.8%; 45–59, 9.2%; 60–74, 4.0%; 75 and over, 1.2%. **Ethnic composition** (2000): Tajik 80.0%; Uzbek 15.3%; Russian 1.1%; Tatar 0.3%; other 3.3%. **Religious affiliation** (2005): Sunni Muslim 78%; Shi'i Muslim 6%; nonreligious 12%; other (mostly Christian) 4%. **Major cities** (2001): Dushanbe 575,900; Khujand 147,400; Kulyab 79,500; Kurgan-Tyube 61,200; Ura-Tyube 51,700.

Location: central Asia, bordering Kyrgyzstan, China, Afghanistan, and Uzbekistan.

Vital statistics

Birth rate per 1,000 population (2006): 27.4 (world avg. 20.3); (1994) within marriage 90.8%. **Death rate** per 1,000 population (2006): 7.2 (world avg. 8.6). **Natural increase rate** per 1,000 population (2006): 20.2 (world avg. 11.7). **Total fertility rate** (avg. births per childbearing woman; 2006): 3.14. **Life expectancy** at birth (2006): male 61.2 years; female 67.4 years.

National economy

Budget (2006). *Revenue:* TJS 1,566,000,000 (tax revenue 87.7%, of which taxes on goods and services 46.5%, customs duties 16.1%, payroll tax 11.0%; nontax revenue 9.8%; grants 2.3%). *Expenditures:* TJS 1,944,000,000 (education 17.3%; defense 12.3%; social security and welfare 12.2%; general administrative services 9.5%; health 5.5%). **Public debt** (external, outstanding; 2005): US$785,000,000. **Production** (metric tons except as noted). *Agriculture, forestry, fishing* (2006): potatoes 573,700, wheat 570,850, raw seed cotton 440,245; livestock (number of live animals) 1,893,000 sheep, 1,377,000 cattle, 1,160,000 goats, 42,000 camels; fisheries production (2005) 210 (from aquaculture 12%). *Mining and quarrying* (2004): antimony (metal content) 2,000; silver 5,000 kg; gold 3,000 kg. *Manufacturing* (value of production in TJS '000,000, at 1998 constant prices; 2001): nonferrous metals (nearly all aluminum) 442,000; food 138,000; textiles 104,000. *Energy production (consumption):* electricity (kW-hr; 2006–07) 19,198,800,000 ([2005] 17,321,000,000); hard coal (metric tons; 2006) 102,000 ([2004] 138,000); lignite (metric tons; 2004) 15,000 (15,000); crude petroleum (barrels; 2006) 161,000 ([2004] 110,000); petroleum products (metric tons; 2004) none (1,283,000); natural gas (cu m; 2006) 20,000,000 ([2004] 563,500,000). **Population economically active** (2003): total 1,932,000; activity rate of total population 29.1% (participation rates: ages 15–62 [male], 15–57 [female] 51.7%; female [1996] 46.5%; officially unemployed [September 2006–August 2007] 2.4%). **Gross national income** (2006): US$3,478,000,000 (US$524 per capita). **Land use** as % of total land area (2003): in temporary crops 6.6%, in permanent crops 0.9%, in pasture 22.8%; overall forest area (2005) 2.9%. **Selected balance of payments data.** Receipts from (US$'000,000): tourism (2004) 1.0; remittances (2006) 1,019; foreign direct investment (2001–05 avg.) 77; official development assistance (2005) 189 (commitments). Disbursements for (US$'000,000): tourism (2004) 3.0; remittances (2006) 393. **Households** (2005). Average household size (2004) 5.2; average disposable income per household TJS 3,462 (US$1,111); sources of income: wages and salaries 45.5%, self-employment 28.9%, transfers 7.0%; expenditure: food 72.1%, clothing 8.2%, transportation and communications 4.5%.

Foreign trade

Imports (2004): US$1,247,000,000 (alumina 26.8%; petroleum products 8.2%; electricity 5.3%; grain and flour 4.3%; natural gas 2.7%). *Major import sources* (2005): Russia 19.3%; Kazakhstan 12.7%; Uzbekistan 11.5%; Azerbaijan 8.6%; China 7.0%. **Exports** (2004): US$915,000,000 (aluminum 62.6%; cotton fiber 17.7%; electricity 6.6%). *Major export destinations* (2005): The Netherlands 46.6%; Turkey 15.8%; Russia 9.1%; Uzbekistan 7.3%; Latvia 4.9%.

Transport and communications

Transport. *Railroads* (2003): length (2006) 482 km; passenger-km 50,000,000; metric ton-km cargo 1,087,000,000. *Roads* (2000): total length 27,767 km (paved [1996] 83%). *Air transport* (2005; Tajikistan Airlines only): passenger-km 1,030,000,000; metric ton-km cargo 7,031,000. **Communications,** in total units (units per 1,000 persons). Televisions (2003): 2,350,000 (357); telephone landlines (2005): 280,000 (43); cellular telephone subscribers (2005): 265,000 (40); total Internet users (2005): 20,000 (3.1); broadband Internet subscribers (2003): 10,000 (1.6).

Education and health

Educational attainment (1989). Percentage of population ages 25 and over having: primary education or no formal schooling 16.3%; some secondary 21.1%; completed secondary and some postsecondary 55.1%; higher 7.5%. **Literacy** (2006): virtually 100%. **Health** (2006): physicians 13,300 (1 per 506 persons); hospital beds 40,300 (1 per 167 persons); infant mortality rate per 1,000 live births (2006) 45.0. **Food** (2004): daily per capita caloric intake 1,963 (vegetable products 89%, animal products 11%); 77% of FAO recommended minimum.

Military

Total active duty personnel (2006): 7,600 (army 100%); Russian troops (2007) 7,000. **Military expenditure as percentage of GDP** (2004): 2.2%; per capita expenditure US$7.

Background

Settled by the Persians c. the 6th century BC, Tajikistan was part of the empires of the Persians and of Alexander the Great and his successors. In the 7th–8th centuries AD it was conquered by the Arabs, who introduced Islam. The Uzbeks controlled the region in the 15th–18th centuries. In the 1860s Russia took over much of Tajikistan. In 1924 it became an autonomous republic under the administration of the Uzbek Soviet Socialist Republic, and it gained republic status in 1929. It achieved independence with the collapse of the Soviet Union in 1991. Civil war raged through much of the 1990s between government forces and an opposition of mostly Islamic forces. Peace was reached in 1997.

Recent Developments

The drift toward authoritarianism in Tajikistan continued in 2007 as Pres. Imomalii Rakhmon's extended family and personal clique made up most of the appointees to high government posts. He announced in

March that he was dropping the Russian suffix (-ov) from his surname and urged his countrymen to join in "Tajikization" of their names. The year began with Tajikistan in the midst of a severe power shortage caused by extremely low water levels in the reservoirs behind the country's power dams and Uzbekistan failing to fulfill its commitment to supply Tajikistan with power in winter. The disastrous winter intensified the Tajik government's efforts to find foreign investors to develop the country's hydroelectric potential.

Internet resources: <www.traveltajikistan.com>.

Tanzania

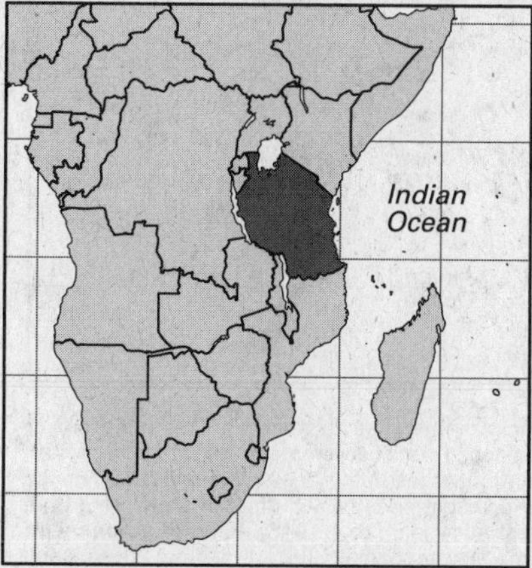

Official name: Jamhuri ya Muungano wa Tanzania (Swahili); United Republic of Tanzania (English). **Form of government:** unitary multiparty republic with one legislative house (National Assembly [274]). **Head of state and government:** President Jakaya Kikwete (from 2005), assisted by Prime Minister Mizengo Pinda (from 2008). **Capital:** Dar es Salaam (Dodoma is the capital designate). **Official languages:** Swahili; English. **Official religion:** none. **Monetary unit:** 1 Tanzania shilling (TZS) = 100 cents; valuation (1 Jul 2008) US$1 = TZS 1,169.50.

Demography

Area: 364,901 sq mi, 945,090 sq km. **Population** (2007): 39,384,000. **Density** (2007): persons per sq mi 107.9, persons per sq km 41.7. **Urban** (2006): 38.5%. **Sex distribution** (2006): male 49.46%; female 50.54%. **Age breakdown** (2006): under 15, 44.3%; 15–29, 29.1%; 30–44, 14.6%; 45–59, 7.6%; 60–74, 3.6%; 75–84, 0.7%; 85 and over, 0.1%. **Ethnolinguistic composition** (2000): 130 different Bantu tribes 95%, of which Sukuma 9.5%, Hehe and Bena 4.5%, Gogo 4.4%, Haya 4.2%, Nyamwezi 3.6%, Makonde 3.3%, Chagga 3.0%, Ha 2.9%; other 5%. **Religious affiliation** (2005): Muslim 35%, of which Sunni 30%, Shi'i 5%; Christian 35%; other (significantly traditional beliefs) 30%; Zanzibar only is 99% Muslim. **Major urban areas** (2002): Dar es Salaam 2,339,910; Arusha 270,485; Mbeya 232,596; Mwanza 209,806; Morogoro 209,058. **Location:** eastern Africa, bordering Kenya, the Indian Ocean, Mozambique, Malawi, Zambia, the Democratic Republic of the Congo, Burundi, Rwanda, and Uganda.

Vital statistics

Birth rate per 1,000 population (2006): 36.8 (world avg. 20.3). **Death rate** per 1,000 population (2006): 14.0 (world avg. 8.6). **Total fertility rate** (avg. births per childbearing woman; 2006): 4.93. **Life expectancy** at birth (2006): male 48.5 years; female 50.9 years.

National economy

Budget (2003–04). *Revenue:* TZS 1,447,500,000,000 (VAT 34.2%; income tax 24.9%; excise tax 15.0%; import duties 9.0%). *Expenditures:* TZS 2,531,500,000,000 (current expenditure 74.5%, of which wages 18.3%, education 17.7%, health 8.4%; capital expenditure 25.5%). **Gross national income** (2006): US$12,743,000,000 (US$332 per capita). **Public debt** (external, outstanding; 2005): US$6,183,000,000. **Production** (metric tons except as noted). *Agriculture, forestry, fishing* (2006): cassava 6,500,000, corn (maize) 3,373,000, sweet potatoes 1,056,000; livestock (number of live animals) 17,719,091 cattle, 12,550,000 goats, 3,521,000 sheep; roundwood (2005) 24,025,852 cu m, of which fuelwood 90%; fisheries production (2005) 347,811. *Mining and quarrying* (2005): gold 52,236 kg; garnets 7,400 kg; rubies 3,400 kg. *Manufacturing* (2005): cement 1,281,000; wheat flour 347,296; sugar 202,200; konyagi (a Tanzanian liquor) 41,050 hectoliters. *Energy production (consumption):* electricity (kW-hr; 2004) 2,478,000,000 (2,591, 000,000); coal (metric tons; 2004) 65,000 (65,000); petroleum products (metric tons; 2004) none (1,074,000). **Population economically active** (2002): total 14,841,000; activity rate of total population 43.1% (participation rates: ages 10 and over 64.9%; female 48.0%; officially unemployed 3.7%). **Households.** Average household size (2004) 5.0; annual income per household (2000–01) TZS 1,055,000 (US$1,310); sources of income (2000–01): agricultural income 51.4%, self-employment 20.6%, wages and salaries 12.0%; expenditure (2001): food 55.9%, transportation 9.7%, energy 8.5%. **Selected balance of payments data.** Receipts from (US$'000,000): tourism (2005) 824; remittances (2006) 16; foreign direct investment (FDI) (2001–05 avg.) 473; official development assistance (2005) 1,505. Disbursements for (US$'000,000): tourism (2005) 554; remittances (2006) 41. **Land use** as % of total land area (2003): in temporary crops 4.5%, in permanent crops 1.2%, in pasture 48.7%; overall forest area (2005) 39.9%.

Foreign trade

Imports (2005; c.i.f.): TZS 3,125,000,000,000 (machinery and apparatus 22.5%; transport equipment 12.1%; crude and refined petroleum 11.5%; construction materials 10.5%; food and beverages 7.5%). *Major import sources* (2006): South Africa 12.7%; UAE 11.6%; China 7.2%; Saudi Arabia 5.9%; Japan 5.8%. **Exports** (2005): TZS 1,608,000,000 (gold 40.7%; cotton 7.9%; coffee 5.2%; cashews 3.4%; diamonds 1.8%; cloves 0.6%). *Major export destinations* (2006): UK 18.1%; Switzerland 13.9%; South Africa 9.2%; China 6.9%; Germany 5.8%.

Transport and communications

Transport. *Railroads* (2003): length (2001) 3,690 km; passenger-km 1,305,000,000; metric ton-km cargo 4,461,000,000. *Roads* (2006): length 85,000 km (paved 5%). *Vehicles:* passenger cars (2000) 36,000; trucks and buses (1999) 98,800. *Air transport* (2005; Air Tanzania only): passenger-km 246,000,000; metric ton-km 2,364,000. **Communications,** in total units (units per 1,000 persons). Daily newspaper circulation (2004): 105,000 (2.9); televisions (2003): 1,500,000 (41); telephone landlines (2006): 157,000 (4); cellular telephone subscribers (2006): 5,767,000 (148); personal computers (2005): 356,000 (9.3); total Internet users (2005): 384,000 (10).

Education and health

Educational attainment (2002). Percentage of population ages 25 and over having: no formal schooling/unknown 49.6%; incomplete/complete primary education 44.0%; incomplete/complete secondary 5.5%; postsecondary 0.9%, of which university 0.4%. **Literacy** (2006): total percentage of population ages 15 and over literate 69.4%; males literate 77.5%; females literate 62.2%. **Health** (2002): physicians 822 (1 per 42,085 persons); hospital beds 36,853 (1 per 939 persons); infant mortality rate per 1,000 live births (2006) 73.0. **Food** (2005): daily per capita caloric intake 2,230 (vegetable products 94%, animal products 6%); 123% of FAO recommended minimum.

Military

Total active duty personnel (2006): 27,000 (army 85.2%, navy 3.7%, air force 11.1%). **Military expenditure as percentage of GDP** (2005): 1.1%; per capita expenditure US$4.

Background

Inhabited from the 1st millennium BC, Tanzania was occupied by Arab and Indian traders and Bantu-speaking peoples by the 10th century AD. The Portuguese gained control of the coastline in the late 15th century, but they were driven out by the Arabs of Oman and Zanzibar in the late 18th century. German colonists entered the area in the 1880s, and in 1891 the Germans declared the region a protectorate as German East Africa. In World War I Britain captured the German holdings, which became a British mandate (1920) under the name Tanganyika. Britain retained control of the region after World War II when it became a UN trust territory (1947). Tanganyika gained independence in 1961 and became a republic in 1962. In 1964 it united with Zanzibar under the name Tanzania.

Recent Developments

In 2007 the government of Tanzania announced a number of measures that were aimed at encouraging both foreign and local investors. These included a plan with Kuwait to create a deep-water harbor at Tanga to provide an alternative port to handle heavy goods. In May the Nile Basin Initiative launched a project to construct a US$200 million hydroelectric plant on the Kagera River on Tanzania's northwestern border with Uganda. A US$2.6 billion contract to build an oil refinery was controversially awarded to an international consortium in which a company owned by the ruling Chama Cha Mapinduzi party had a share. On a visit to Burundi in June, Pres. Jakaya Mrisho Kikwete announced that with peace restored in Burundi, the refugee camps in the northwest—long-standing drains on the country's resources—would close by year's end.

Internet resources: <www.tanzania.go.tz>.

Thailand

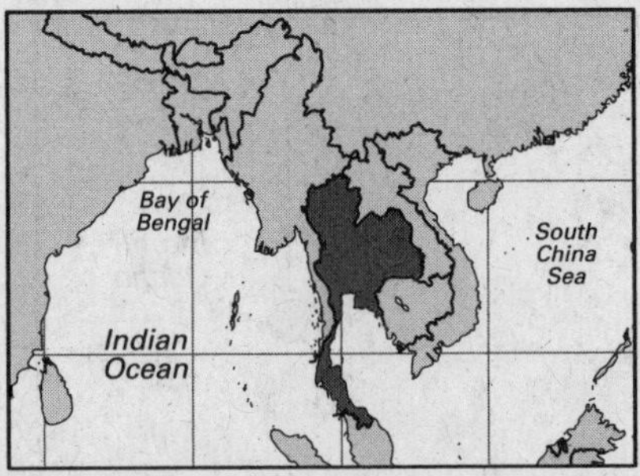

Official name: Ratcha Anachak Thai (Kingdom of Thailand). **Form of government:** constitutional monarchy with two legislative houses (Senate [150]; House of Representatives [480]). **Chief of state:** King Bhumibol Adulyadej (from 1946). **Head of government:** Prime Minister Samak Sundaravej (from 2008). **Capital:** Bangkok. **Official language:** Thai. **Official religion:** none. **Monetary unit:** 1 Thai baht (THB) = 100 stangs; valuation (1 Jul 2008) US$1 = THB 33.49.

Demography

Area: 198,117 sq mi, 513,120 sq km. **Population** (2007): 63,884,000. **Density** (2007): persons per sq mi 322.5, persons per sq km 124.5. **Urban** (2006): 29.9%. **Sex distribution** (2005): male 48.79%; female 51.21%. **Age breakdown** (2005): under 15, 21.7%; 15–29, 24.1%; 30–44, 24.1%; 45–59, 18.8%; 60–74, 8.6%; 75–84, 2.2%; 85 and over, 0.5%. **Ethnic composition** (2000): Tai peoples 81.4%, of which Thai (Siamese) 34.9%, Lao 26.5%; Han Chinese 10.6%; Malay 3.7%; Khmer 1.9%; other 2.4%. **Religious affiliation** (2005): Buddhist 83%; Muslim (nearly all Sunni) 9%; traditional beliefs 2.5%; nonreligious 2%; other (significantly Christian) 3.5%. **Major cities** (2000): Bangkok 6,355,144; Samut Prakan 378,741; Nonthaburi 291,555; Udon Thani 222,425; Nakhon Ratchasima 204,641. **Location:** southeastern Asia, bordering Laos, Cambodia, the Gulf of Thailand, Malaysia, and Myanmar (Burma).

Vital statistics

Birth rate per 1,000 population (2006): 13.9 (world avg. 20.3). **Death rate** per 1,000 population (2006): 7.0 (world avg. 8.6). **Total fertility rate** (avg. births per childbearing woman; 2005): 1.84. **Life expectancy** at birth (2006): male 69.9 years; female 74.7 years.

National economy

Budget (2005). *Revenue:* THB 1,490,900,000,000 (tax revenue, 81.8%, of which taxes on goods and services 40.0%, corporate taxes 23.7%, income tax 9.3%; nontax revenue 13.4%; social contributions 4.8%). *Expenditures:* THB 1,316,800,000,000 (economic affairs 30.3%; education 20.0%; general public services 17.6%; health 8.4%). **Public debt** (external, outstanding; 2005): US$13,483,000,000. **Production** (metric tons except as noted). *Agriculture, forestry, fishing* (2005): sugarcane 49,586,000, rice 30,292,000, cassava 16,938,000; livestock (number of live animals) 8,023,000 pigs, 5,610,000 cattle, 187,400,000 chickens; roundwood 28,566,000 cu m, of which fuelwood 70%; fisheries production 3,743,000 (from aquaculture 31%). *Mining and quarrying* (2005): gypsum 6,920,000; feldspar 1,000,000; dolomite 950,000. *Manufacturing* (value added in US$'000,000; 2000): textiles and wearing apparel 1,905; electronics 1,817; food products 1,311. *Energy production (consumption):* electricity (kW-hr; 2006) 136,767,000,000 (133,572,000,000); hard coal (metric tons; 2004) negligible (7,536,000); lignite (metric tons; 2006) 18,991,000 ([2004] 20,547,000); crude petroleum (barrels; 2006) 69,900,000 ([2004] 315,000,000); petroleum products (metric tons; 2004) 44,725,000 (39,643,000); natural gas (cu m; 2005) 24,807,000,000 ([2004] 27,295,000,000). **Land use** as % of total land area (2003): in temporary crops 27.7%, in permanent crops 7.0%, in pasture 1.6%; overall forest area (2005) 28.4%. **Population economically active** (2006): total 36,867,200; activity rate of total population 56.4% (participation rates: ages 15–59, 78.5%; female 46.0%; unemployed 1.2%). **Gross national income** (2006): US$202,098,000,000 (US$3,190 per capita). **Households** (2006). Average household size (2004) 3.5; average annual income per household THB 213,444 (US$5,634); sources of income: wages and salaries 39.9%, self-employment 32.6%, nonmonetary income 16.2%, transfers 9.4%; expenditure: food and nonalcoholic beverages 33.2%, housing, energy, and household furnishings 24.6%, transportation and communications 24.3%. **Selected balance of payments data.** Receipts from (US$'000,000): tourism (2005) 10,104; remittances (2006) 1,333; foreign direct investment (FDI) (2001–05 avg.) 2,377; official development assistance (2005) 607 (commitments). Disbursements for (US$'000,000): tourism (2005) 4,995; FDI (2001–05 avg.) 262.

Foreign trade

Imports (2006; c.i.f.): THB 4,871,000,000,000 (electrical machinery 19.6%, of which electronic integrated circuits 4.2%; crude petroleum 15.6%; nonelectrical machinery and parts 14.1%; base and fabricated metals 13.4%, of which iron and steel 8.2%). *Major import sources:* Japan 20.1%; China 10.6%; US 6.7%; Malaysia 6.6%; Singapore 4.5%. **Exports** (2006; f.o.b.): THB 4,931,500,000,000 (nonelectrical machinery 18.3%; electrical machinery 17.8%, of which electronic integrated circuits 4.9%; food products 11.0%; road vehicles 7.7%; rubber [all forms] 6.7%; plastics [all forms] 5.0%). *Major export destinations:* US 15.0%; Japan 12.7%; China 9.0%; Singapore 6.4%; Hong Kong 5.5%; Malaysia 5.1%.

Transport and communications

Transport. *Railroads* (2003): route length (2006) 4,071 km; passenger-km 10,251,000,000; metric ton-km cargo 3,987,000,000. *Roads* (2004): total length 57,403 km (paved 99%). *Vehicles* (2006): passenger cars 3,312,941; trucks and buses 4,568,895. *Air transport* (2006; Thai Airways and Bangkok Airways only): passenger-km 56,891,000,000; metric ton-km cargo 2,107,000,000. **Communications,** in total units (units per 1,000 persons). Daily newspaper circulation (2005): 3,957,000 (63); televisions (2003): 17,971,000 (289); telephone landlines (2006): 7,073,000 (111); cellular telephone subscribers (2006): 40,816,000 (643); personal computers (2005): 4,408,000 (70); total Internet users (2006): 8,466,000 (133).

Education and health

Educational attainment (2006). Percentage of employed population having: no formal schooling/unknown 4.1%; incomplete primary education 33.9%; complete primary 21.5%; lower secondary 14.4%; upper secondary 12.0%; some to complete higher 14.1%. **Literacy** (2003): total population ages 15 and over literate 92.5%; males literate 94.9%; females literate 90.5%. **Health** (2005): physicians (2004) 18,918 (1 per 3,307 persons); hospital beds 134,016 (1 per 470 persons); infant mortality rate per 1,000 live births 11.3. **Food** (2005): daily per capita caloric intake 3,042 (vegetable products 90%, animal products 10%); 163% of FAO recommended minimum.

Military

Total active duty personnel (2006): 306,600 (army 62.0%, navy 23.0%, air force 15.0%). **Military expenditure as percentage of GDP** (2005): 1.1%; per capita expenditure US$31.

Background

The region of Thailand has been occupied continuously for 20,000 years. It was part of the Mon and Khmer kingdoms from the 9th century AD. Thai-speaking peoples emigrated from China c. the 10th century. During the 13th century two Thai states emerged: the Sukhothai kingdom, founded c. 1220 after a successful revolt against the Khmer, and Chiang Mai, founded in 1296 after the defeat of the Mon. In 1350 the Thai kingdom of Ayutthaya succeeded Sukhothai. The Burmese were its most powerful rivals, occupying it briefly in the 16th century and destroying the kingdom in 1767. The Chakri dynasty came to power in 1782, moving the capital to Bangkok and extending the empire along the Malay Peninsula and into Laos and Cambodia. The country was named Siam in 1856. Though Western influence increased during the 19th century, Siam's rulers avoided colonization by granting concessions to European countries; it was the only Southeast Asian nation able to do so. In 1917 it entered World War I on the side of the Allies. It became a constitutional monarchy following a military coup in 1932 and was officially renamed Thailand in 1939. It was occupied by Japan in World War II. It participated in the Korean War as a UN forces member and was allied with South Vietnam in the Vietnam War. Along with other Southeast Asian nations, it suffered from the 1990s regional financial crisis.

Recent Developments

In May 2007 the military junta in Thailand—in power since ousting then prime minister Thaksin Shinawatra in a September 2006 coup—dissolved Thaksin's Thai Rak Thai (TRT) party and barred Thaksin and more than 100 top-ranking TRT members from politics for five years. Other TRT members formed or joined new parties, including the People Power Party (PPP). In August a referendum was held on a new constitution drafted by the junta's appointees. Approved by nearly 58% of referendum voters, the charter contained several undemocratic clauses that allowed the government to appoint half of the members of the Senate and to pardon the junta for its unconstitutional usurpation of power in 2006. Many Thais voted for the referendum because the junta threatened to postpone the general election if the referendum was rejected. Held on 23 December, the election saw the pro-Thaksin PPP gain the most parliamentary seats and Samak Sundaravej, a Thaksin ally, named the first democratically elected prime minister since the 2006 coup.

Internet resources: <www.tourismthailand.org>.

Togo

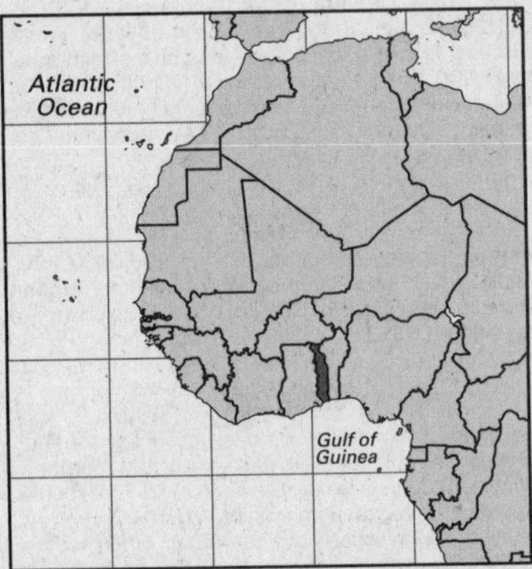

Official name: République Togolaise (Togolese Republic). **Form of government:** republic with one legislative body (National Assembly [81]). **Chief of state:** President Faure Gnassingbé (from 2005). **Head of government:** Prime Minister Komlan Mally (from 2007). **Capital:** Lomé. **Official language:** French. **Official religion:** none. **Monetary unit:** 1 CFA franc (CFAF) = 100 centimes; valuation (1 Jul 2008) US$1 = CFAF 414.60.

Demography

Area: 21,925 sq mi, 56,785 sq km. **Population** (2007): 6,585,000. **Density** (2007): persons per sq mi 300.3, persons per sq km 116.0. **Urban** (2005): 40.1%. **Sex distribution** (2005): male 49.07%; female 50.93%. **Age breakdown** (2005): under 15, 42.3%; 15–29, 29.9%; 30–44, 15.6%; 45–59, 8.0%; 60–74, 3.5%; 75 and over, 0.7%. **Ethnic composition** (2000): Ewe 22.2%; Kabre 13.4%; Wachi 10.0%; Mina 5.6%; Kotokoli 5.6%; Bimoba 5.2%; Losso 4.0%; Gurma 3.4%; Lamba 3.2%; Adja 3.0%; other 24.4%. **Religious affiliation** (2004): Christian 47.2%, of which Roman Catholic 27.8%, Protestant 9.5%, independent and other Christian 9.9%; traditional beliefs 33.0%; Muslim 13.7%; nonreligious 4.9%; other 1.2%. **Major cities** (2003): Lomé 676,400 (urban agglomeration [2005] 1,337,000); Sokodé 84,200; Kpalimé 75,200; Atakpamé 64,300; Kara 49,800. **Location:** western Africa, bordering Burkina Faso, Benin, the Atlantic Ocean, and Ghana.

Vital statistics

Birth rate per 1,000 population (2005): 37.2 (world avg. 20.3). **Death rate** per 1,000 population (2005): 10.0 (world avg. 8.6). **Total fertility rate** (avg. births per childbearing woman; 2005): 5.01. **Life expectancy** at birth (2005): male 55.0 years; female 59.1 years.

National economy

Budget (2005). *Revenue:* CFAF 175,600,000,000 (tax revenue 87.0%, of which taxes on international trade 41.5%; nontax revenue 7.0%; grants 6.0%). *Expenditures:* CFAF 168,400,000,000 (current expenditure 80.0%; capital expenditure 20.0%). **Production** (metric tons except as noted). *Agriculture, forestry, fishing* (2006): cassava 767,400, yams 621,100, corn (maize) 543,300; livestock (number of live animals) 1,850,000 sheep, 1,480,000 goats; roundwood (2005) 5,927,873 cu m, of which fuelwood 97%; fisheries production (2005) 29,267 (from aquaculture 5%). *Mining and quarrying* (2005): limestone 2,400,000; phosphate rock 1,020,870; diamonds 41,000 carats. *Manufacturing* (value added in CFAF '000,000; 2006): food products, beverages, and tobacco products 33,800; bricks, cement, and ceramics 19,300; base and fabricated metals 10,800. *Energy production (consumption):* electricity (kW-hr; 2004) 262,000,000 (610,000,000); petroleum products (metric tons; 2004) none (622,000). **Households** (2004). Average household size 6.0; expenditure: food products 36.1%, hotels and restaurants 12.9%, housing and energy 12.4%, transportation 8.5%, clothing and footwear 6.0%. **Population economically active** (2003): total 2,295,000; activity rate of total population 38.9% (participation rates: ages 16 and over 70.2%; female 37.0%; unemployed [2004] 32%). **Gross national income** (at current market prices; 2006): US$2,254,000,000 (US$352 per capita). **Public debt** (external, outstanding; 2005): US$1,469,000,000. **Selected balance of payments data.** Receipts from (US$'000,000): tourism (2004) 19; remittances (2006) 179; foreign direct investment (2001–05 avg.) 52; official development assistance (2005) 87. Disbursements for (US$'000,000): tourism (2004) 8; remittances (2006) 34. **Land use** as % of total land area (2003): in temporary crops 46.1%, in permanent crops 2.2%, in pasture 18.4%; overall forest area (2005) 7.1%.

Foreign trade

Imports (2004; c.i.f.; trade data breakdown is estimated): US$548,100,000 (mineral fuels 23.0%; food products 9.7%; iron and steel 8.1%; construction materials 7.4%; machinery and apparatus 6.9%; road vehicles 6.4%). *Major import sources:* France 19.5%; China 8.3%; Côte d'Ivoire 6.1%; Belgium 4.8%; Italy 3.7%. **Exports** (2004; trade data breakdown is estimated): US$384,400,000 (food products 19.1%, of which cocoa beans 6.4%; portland cement 17.3%; cotton 15.3%; phosphates 13.6%; iron and steel 11.7%). *Major export destinations:* Burkina Faso 13.1%; Benin 12.2%; Ghana 11.9%; Mali 11.2%; China 4.4%.

Transport and communications

Transport. *Railroads* (2001): route length (2004) 568 km; passenger-km 44,000,000; metric ton-km cargo 440,000,000. *Roads* (2001): total length 7,500 km (paved 24%). *Vehicles* (2002): passenger cars 51,400; trucks and buses 24,500. *Air transport*: passenger-km (2001) 130,000,000; metric ton-km cargo (2003) 7,000,000. **Communications**, in total units (units per 1,000 persons). Daily newspaper circulation (2004): 8,000 (1.5); televisions (2004): 650,000 (107); telephone landlines (2006): 82,000 (13); cellular telephone subscribers (2006): 708,000 (112); personal computers (2005): 185,000 (34); total Internet users (2006): 320,000 (51).

Education and health

Educational attainment (1998). Percentage of population ages 25 and over having: no formal education 56.3%; primary education 24.5%; secondary and higher 18.3%; unknown 0.9%. **Literacy** (2006): total population ages 15 and over literate 53.2%; males literate 68.7%; females literate 38.5%. **Health:** physicians (2004) 225 (1 per 23,357 persons); hospital beds (2002) 4,991 (1 per 997 persons); infant mortality rate (2005) 62.2. **Food** (2005): daily per capita caloric intake 2,123 (vegetable products 97%, animal products 3%); 116% of FAO recommended minimum.

Military

Total active duty personnel (2006): 8,550 (army 94.7%, navy 2.3%, air force 3.0%). **Military expenditure as percentage of GDP** (2005): 1.5%; per capita expenditure US$5.

Background

Until 1884 what is now Togo was an intermediate zone between the black African military states of Ashanti and Dahomey, and its various ethnic groups lived in general isolation from each other. In 1884 it became part of the Togoland German protectorate, which was occupied by British and French forces in 1914. In 1922 the League of Nations assigned eastern Togoland to France and the western portion to Britain. In 1946 the British and French governments placed the territories under UN trusteeship. Ten years later British Togoland was incorporated into the Gold Coast, and French Togoland became an autonomous republic within the French Union. Togo gained independence in 1960. It suspended its constitution in 1967–80. A multiparty constitution was approved in 1992, but the political situation remained unstable.

Recent Developments

In May 2007 the UN High Commissioner for Refugees (UNHCR) announced that it would close the camps that had been established in neighboring countries to care for the estimated 25,000 refugees who in 2005 had fled violence in Togo in the aftermath of the disputed presidential election. The UNHCR advised the refugees to return home, but the extent to which they were doing so was unclear. In August the severe floods that hit much of West Africa left more than 20,000 homeless in Togo. As a result, the opening of the school year was postponed for several weeks because many of the classrooms were requisitioned as shelters. The European Union pledged €2 million (about US$2.7 million) to assist flood victims in Togo, Ghana, and Burkina Faso.

Internet resources: <www.stat-togo.org>.

Tonga

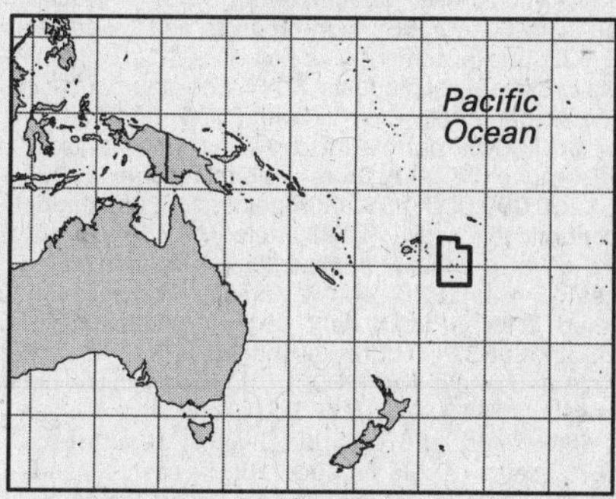

Official name: Pule'anga Fakatu'i 'o Tonga (Tongan); Kingdom of Tonga (English). **Form of government:** constitutional monarchy with one legislative house (Legislative Assembly [34]). **Head of state and government:** King Siaosi (George) Tupou V (from 2006), assisted by Prime Minister of the Privy Council Feleti Sevele (from 2006). **Capital:** Nuku'alofa. **Official languages:** Tongan; English. **Official religion:** none. **Monetary unit:** 1 pa'anga (T$) = 100 seniti; valuation (1 Jul 2008) US$1 = T$1.80.

Demography

Area: 289.5 sq mi, 749.9 sq km. **Population** (2007): 101,000. **Density** (2007): persons per sq mi 363.2, persons per sq km 140.2. **Urban** (2005): 23.5%. **Sex distribution** (2006): male 50.62%; female 49.38%. **Age breakdown** (2006): under 15, 37.4%; 15–29, 29.8%; 30–44, 14.6%; 45–59, 9.4%; 60–74, 6.7%; 75 and over, 2.1%. **Ethnic composition** (2000): Tongan 95.2%; mixed-race (Euronesian) 0.7%; British or Australian expatriates 0.5%; other 3.6%. **Religious affiliation** (2005): Mormon 35%; Protestant 30%, of which Methodist 25%; independent Christian (mostly local Methodist) 16%; Roman Catholic 12%; Baha'i 5%; other 2%. **Major towns** (2006): Nuku'alofa 23,438 (urban agglomeration 34,058); Neiafu 4,108; Havelolото 3,384; Tofoa-Koloua 3,193; Pangai 2,523. **Location:** archipelago in the South Pacific Ocean between Hawaii (US) and New Zealand.

Vital statistics

Birth rate per 1,000 population (2005): 25.2 (world avg. 20.3). **Death rate** per 1,000 population (2005):

5.4 (world avg. 8.6). **Total fertility rate** (avg. births per childbearing woman; 2006): 3.30. **Life expectancy** at birth (2006): male 71.0 years; female 74.0 years.

National economy

Budget (2005–06). *Revenue:* T$172,446,000 (tax revenue 72.9%; grants 15.1%; nontax revenue 12.0%). *Expenditures:* T$166,031,000 (current expenditure 93.0%; development expenditure 7.0%). **Production** (metric tons except as noted). *Agriculture, forestry, fishing* (2005): coconuts 58,000, pumpkins, squash, and gourds 20,000, cassava 9,000; livestock (number of live animals) 81,000 pigs, 12,500 goats, 11,400 horses; roundwood 2,100 cu m, of which fuelwood, none; fisheries production (2005) 1,901; aquatic plants production (2005) 887 (from aquaculture 9%). *Mining and quarrying:* coral and sand for local use. *Manufacturing* (value of production in T$'000; 2005): food products and beverages 19,722; bricks, cement, and ceramics 4,109; chemicals and chemical products 2,044. *Energy production (consumption):* electricity (kW-hr; 2006) 54,000,000 (47,000,000); petroleum products (metric tons; 2004) none (38,000). **Gross national income** (2006): US$230,000,000 (US$2,304 per capita). **Population economically active** (2003): total 36,450; activity rate of total population 34.1% (participation rates: ages 15–64 [1996] 60.4%; female 41.9%; unemployed 5.2%). **Public debt** (external, outstanding; 2005): US$83,200,000. **Households** (2000–01). Average household size (2006) 5.7; cash income per household T$12,871 (US$6,511); sources of cash income: wages and salaries 35.6%, remittances 19.7%, sales of own produce 16.1%; cash expenditure (2002): food and nonalcoholic beverages 44.4%, transportation 14.2%, alcoholic beverages, kava, and tobacco 12.3%, household furnishings and operation 12.0%. **Selected balance of payments data.** Receipts from (US$'000,000): tourism (2006–07) 13; remittances (2006) 66; foreign direct investment (2001–05 avg.) 4.0; official development assistance (2005) 16 (commitments). Disbursements for (US$'000,000): tourism (2002) 3.0; remittances (2006) 16. **Land use** as % of total land area (2003): in temporary crops 21%, in permanent crops 15%, in pasture 6%; overall forest area (2005) 5%.

Foreign trade

Imports (2005–06; c.i.f.): US$113,075,000 (mineral fuels and chemical products 31.7%; food and beverages 28.0%; machinery and transport equipment 12.9%). *Major import sources:* New Zealand 35.0%; Fiji 27.0%; Australia 10.7%; US 9.1%; Japan 3.6%. **Exports** (2005–06): US$9,225,000 (squash 43.7%; fish 34.7%; root crops 7.9%; manufactured goods 6.8%; kava 3.2%). *Major export destinations:* Japan 53.7%; New Zealand 11.6%; US 10.5%; Australia 2.1%; Fiji 1.1%.

Transport and communications

Transport. *Roads* (1999): total length 680 km (paved 27%). *Vehicles* (2004): passenger cars 7,705; trucks and buses 5,297. *Air transport* (2002): passenger-km 14,000,000; metric ton-km cargo 1,000,000. **Communications,** in total units (units per 1,000 persons). Televisions (2003): 7,100 (70); telephone landlines (2005): 14,000 (139); cellular telephone subscribers (2005): 30,000 (298); personal computers (2005): 5,000 (50); total Internet users (2006): 3,100 (31); broadband Internet subscribers (2005): 600 (0.6).

Education and health

Educational attainment (1996). Percentage of population ages 25 and over having: primary education 26%; lower secondary 58%; upper secondary 8%; higher 6%; unknown 2%. **Literacy** (2006): 99%. **Health** (2004): physicians 41 (1 per 2,447 persons); hospital beds 296 (1 per 332 persons); infant mortality rate per 1,000 live births (2006) 20.0. **Food** (1992): daily per capita caloric intake 2,946 (vegetable products 82%, animal products 18%); 129% of FAO recommended minimum.

Military

Total active duty personnel (2007): 450-member force includes air and coast guard elements. Tonga has defense cooperation agreements with both Australia and New Zealand. **Military expenditure as percentage of GDP** (2004): 1.0%; per capita expenditure US$23.

Background

Tonga was inhabited at least 3,000 years ago by people of the Lapita culture. The Tongans developed a stratified social system headed by a paramount ruler whose dominion by the 13th century extended as far as the Hawaiian Islands. The Dutch visited the islands in the 17th century; in 1773 Capt. James Cook arrived and named the archipelago the Friendly Islands. The modern kingdom was established during the reign (1845–93) of King George Tupou I. It became a British protectorate in 1900. This was dissolved in 1970, when Tonga, the only ancient kingdom surviving from the pre-European period in Polynesia, achieved complete independence within the Commonwealth.

Recent Developments

In 2007 Tonga still suffered from the aftermath of the November 2006 rioting that had caused some US$200 million in damages and destroyed about 80% of the capital's central business district. The parliament convened in May 2007, but little progress was made on political reform, and popular discontent was rising. Although international aid donors, including Australia and New Zealand, contributed to the reconstruction in Nuku'alofa, civil servants were told by the government that anticipated salary increases could not be afforded.

Internet resources: <www.tongaholiday.com>.

Trinidad and Tobago

Official name: Republic of Trinidad and Tobago. **Form of government:** multiparty republic with two legislative houses (Senate [31]; House of Representatives [41]). **Chief of state:** President George Maxwell Richards (from 2003). **Head of government:** Prime

1 metric ton = about 1.1 short tons; 1 kilometer = 0.6 mi (statute); 1 metric ton-km cargo = about 0.68 short ton-mi cargo; c.i.f.: cost, insurance, and freight; f.o.b.: free on board

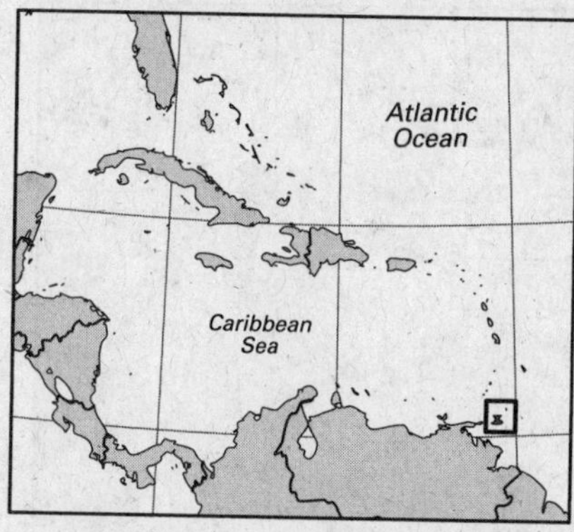

Minister Patrick Manning (from 2001). **Capital:** Port of Spain. **Official language:** English. **Official religion:** none. **Monetary unit:** 1 Trinidad and Tobago dollar (TT$) = 100 cents; valuation (1 Jul 2008) US$1 = TT$6.19.

Demography

Area: 1,990 sq mi, 5,155 sq km. **Population** (2007): 1,303,000. **Density** (2007): persons per sq mi 654.8, persons per sq km 252.8. **Urban** (2005): 12.2%. **Sex distribution** (2005): male 49.17%; female 50.83%. **Age breakdown** (2005): under 15, 22.3%; 15–29, 30.2%; 30–44, 22.6%; 45–59, 15.4%; 60–74, 7.0%; 75–84, 2.0%; 85 and over, 0.5%. **Ethnic composition** (2000): black 39.2%; East Indian 38.6%; mixed 16.3%; Chinese 1.6%; white 1.0%; other/not stated 3.3%. **Religious affiliation** (2005): Roman Catholic 29%; Hindu 24%; Protestant 19%; independent and other Christian 7%; Muslim 7%; nonreligious 2%; other/unknown 12%. **Major cities/built-up areas** (2000): Chaguanas 67,433; San Fernando 55,149; Port of Spain 49,031 (greater Port of Spain [2004] 264,000); Arima 32,278; Point Fortin 19,056. **Location:** islands northeast of Venezuela, between the North Atlantic Ocean and the Caribbean Sea.

Vital statistics

Birth rate per 1,000 population (2006): 13.7 (world avg. 20.3). **Death rate** per 1,000 population (2006): 7.7 (world avg. 8.6). **Total fertility rate** (avg. births per childbearing woman; 2005): 1.63. **Life expectancy** at birth (2005): male 67.3 years; female 71.4 years.

National economy

Budget (2005–06). *Revenue:* TT$38,489,000,000 (taxes on oil/natural gas corporations 45.7%; VAT 10.6%; nonoil corporate taxes 10.4%; other oil revenue 9.8%). *Expenditures:* TT$31,062,000,000 (current expenditures 85.4%; development expenditures and net lending 14.6%). **Production** (metric tons except as noted). *Agriculture, forestry, fishing* (2006): sugarcane 503,000, fruits 68,685, coconuts 10,560; livestock (number of live animals) 59,300 goats, 43,000 pigs, 28,200,000 chickens; roundwood (2005) 99,467 cu m, of which fuelwood 35%; fisheries production (2005) 13,414. *Mining and quarrying* (2005): limestone 850,000; natural asphalt 16,200. *Manufacturing* (2006): methanol 6,015,600; anhydrous ammonia 5,110,500; cement 883,000. *Energy production (consumption):* electricity (kW-hr; 2004) 6,430,000,000 (6,430,000,000); crude petroleum (barrels; 2006) 52,100,000 ([2004] 47,800,000); petroleum products (metric tons; 2004) 7,013,000 (601,000); natural gas (cu m; 2006) 37,973,000,000 ([2004] 12,528,000,000). **Households.** Average household size (2004) 3.8; average income per household (2002): TT$53,015 (US$8,484); expenditure (2003): housing 20.4%, food and nonalcoholic beverages 18.0%, transportation 16.7%, recreation and culture 8.5%. **Selected balance of payments data.** Receipts from (US$'000,000): tourism (2005) 453; remittances (2006) 87; foreign direct investment (FDI) (2001–05 avg.) 907. Disbursements for (US$'000,000): tourism (2005) 222; FDI (2001–05 avg.) 108. **Land use** as % of total land area (2003): in temporary crops 14.6%, in permanent crops 9.2%, in pasture 2.1%; overall forest area (2005) 44.1%. **Gross national income** (at current market prices; 2006): US$17,542,000,000 (US$13,520 per capita). **Population economically active** (2005): total 623,700; activity rate of total population 48.2% (participation rates: ages 15–64, 70.1%; female 41.9%; unemployed [2006] 6.2%). **Public debt** (external, outstanding; 2005): US$1,197,000,000.

Foreign trade

Imports (2006; c.i.f.): TT$40,934,000,000 (mineral fuels 35.0%; machinery 19.7%; chemicals and chemical products 8.1%; transport equipment 7.0%). *Major import sources* (2005): US 27.2%; Venezuela 13.1%; Brazil 13.1%; Japan 5.4%; Canada 4.1%. **Exports** (2006; f.o.b.): TT$89,298,000,000 (crude and refined petroleum 39.8%; natural gas [all forms] 34.4%; chemicals [including ammonia, methanol, and urea] 15.1%). *Major export destinations* (2005): US 68.6%; Jamaica 5.4%; Barbados 2.9%; Mexico 2.4%; France 2.2%.

Transport and communications

Transport. *Roads* (2000): total length 8,320 km (paved 51%). *Vehicles* (2001): passenger cars 261,087; trucks and buses 54,843. *Air transport* (2005; BWIA only): passenger-km 3,101,000,000; metric ton-km cargo 47,883,000. **Communications,** in total units (units per 1,000 persons). Daily newspaper circulation (2004): 159,000 (123); televisions (2003): 461,000 (359); telephone landlines (2006): 325,000 (250); cellular telephone subscribers (2006): 1,655,000 (1,275); personal computers (2005): 129,000 (100); total Internet users (2005): 163,000 (126); broadband Internet subscribers (2006): 21,000 (16).

Education and health

Educational attainment (2000). Percentage of population ages 15 and over having: no formal schooling/unknown 8.0%; primary education 35.4%; secondary 52.0%; university 4.6%. **Literacy** (2002): total population ages 15 and over literate 98.5%; males literate 99.0%; females literate 97.9%. **Health** (2004): physicians 1,293 (1 per 998 persons); hospital beds 4,553 (1 per 283 persons); infant mortality rate per 1,000 live births (2005) 13.8. **Food** (2005): daily per capita caloric intake 2,946 (vegetable products 83%, animal products 17%); 151% of FAO recommended minimum.

Military

Total active duty personnel (2006): 2,700 (army 74.1%, coast guard 25.9%). **Military expenditure as percentage of GNP** (2005): 0.2%; per capita expenditure US$25.

Background

When Christopher Columbus visited Trinidad in 1498, it was inhabited by the Arawak Indians; Caribs inhabited Tobago. The islands were settled by the Spanish in the 16th century. In the 17th and 18th centuries African slaves were imported for plantation labor to replace the original Indian population, which had been worked to death by the Spanish. Trinidad was surrendered to the British in 1797. The British attempted to settle Tobago in 1721, but the French captured the island in 1781 and transformed it into a sugar-producing colony; the British acquired it in 1802. After slavery ended in the islands in 1834–38, immigrants from India were brought in to work the plantations. The islands of Trinidad and Tobago were administratively combined in 1889. Granted limited self-government in 1925, the islands became an independent state within the Commonwealth in 1962 and a republic in 1976. Political unrest was followed in 1990 by an attempted Muslim fundamentalist coup against the government.

Recent Developments

The Ministry of Energy and Energy Industries confirmed in May 2007 that cross-border natural gas in reservoirs straddling blocks located in Trinidad and Tobago and Venezuela could amount to about 283 billion cu m (10 trillion cu ft), 27% of which was on the Trinidad and Tobago side—the commercialization of natural gas had led to the country's rapid industrial development in recent years.

Internet resources:
<www.gotrinidadandtobago.com>.

Tunisia

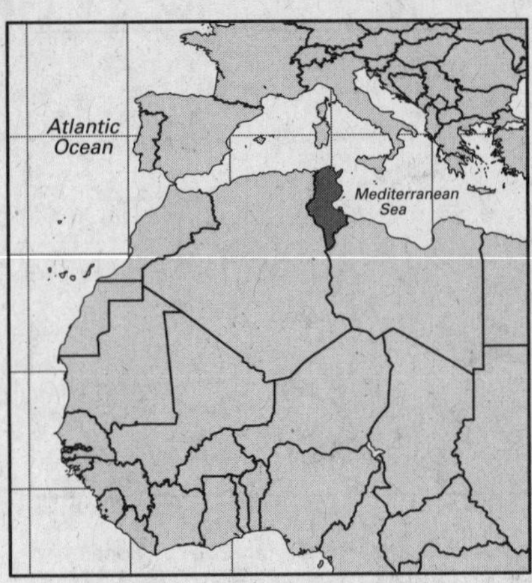

Official name: Al-Jumhuriyah al-Tunisiyah (Tunisian Republic). **Form of government:** multiparty republic with two legislative houses (Chamber of Councilors [126]; Chamber of Deputies [189]). **Chief of state:** President Zine al-Abidine Ben Ali (from 1987). **Head of government:** Prime Minister Mohamed Ghannouchi (from 1999). **Capital:** Tunis. **Official language:** Arabic. **Official religion:** Islam. **Monetary unit:** 1 dinar (TND) = 1,000 millimes; valuation (1 Jul 2008) US$1= TND 1.16.

Demography

Area: 63,170 sq mi, 163,610 sq km. **Population** (2007): 10,226,000. **Density** (2007): persons per sq mi 161.9, persons per sq km 62.5. **Urban** (2005): 65.3%. **Sex distribution** (2005): male 50.39%; female 49.61%. **Age breakdown** (2005): under 15, 25.9%; 15–29, 30.1%; 30–44, 22.1%; 45–59, 13.2%; 60–74, 6.6%; 75–84, 1.8%; 85 and over, 0.3%. **Ethnic composition** (2000): Tunisian Arab 67.2%; Bedouin Arab 26.6%; Algerian Arab 2.4%; Amazigh (Berber) 1.4%; other 2.4%. **Religious affiliation** (2005): Muslim 99%, of which Sunni 97%, Shi'i 2%; other 1%. **Major cities** (2004): Tunis 728,453 (urban agglomeration [2003] 1,996,000); Safaqis 265,131; Al-Arianah 240,749; Susah 173,047; Ettadhamen 118,487. **Location:** northern Africa, bordering the Mediterranean Sea, Libya, and Algeria.

Vital statistics

Birth rate per 1,000 population (2005): 17.1 (world avg. 20.3). **Death rate** per 1,000 population (2005): 5.9 (world avg. 8.6). **Total fertility rate** (avg. births per childbearing woman; 2005): 2.04. **Life expectancy** at birth (2005): male 71.6 years; female 75.5 years.

National economy

Budget (2005). *Revenue:* TND 12,279,600,000 (tax revenue 64.5%, of which VAT 18.7%, income tax 12.4%, social security 11.1%; grants and loans 24.3%; nontax revenue 11.2%). *Expenditures:* TND 13,024,500,000 (current expenditure 78.7%; development expenditure 21.3%). **Public debt** (external, outstanding; 2005): US$12,982,000,000. **Production** (metric tons except as noted). *Agriculture, forestry, fishing* (2006): wheat 1,251,000, olives 1,000,000, tomatoes 850,000; livestock (live animals) 7,213,390 sheep, 1,426,640 goats, 686,320 cattle, 231,000 camels; roundwood (2005) 2,366,704 cu m, of which fuelwood 91%; fisheries production (2005) 111,782 (from aquaculture 2%). *Mining and quarrying* (2005): phosphate rock 8,204,000; iron ore 206,000; zinc (metal content) 29,200. *Manufacturing* (value added in TND '000,000; 2005): textiles, leather, and wearing apparel 1,948; refined petroleum and petroleum products 1,478; food products 1,210. *Energy production (consumption):* electricity (kW-hr; 2005) 13,006,-000,000 (11,239,000,000); coal (metric tons; 2002) none (1,000); crude petroleum (barrels; 2005) 26,200,000 ([2004] 11,964,000); petroleum products (metric tons; 2005) 1,811,000 (3,922,000); natural gas (cu m; 2005) 2,344,000,000 (3,642,-000,000). **Households** (2000). Average household size (2004) 4.5; income per household TND 6,450 (US$4,640); expenditure: food and beverages 38.0%, housing and energy 21.5%, household durables 11.1%, health and personal care 10.0%, transportation 9.7%. **Gross national income** (2006): US$28,905,000,000 (US$2,830 per capita). **Population economically active** (2006): total 3,503,400; activity rate of total population 34.6% (participation rates: ages 15 and over 46.6%; female 25.0%; unemployed 14.3%). **Selected balance of payments data.** Receipts from (US$'000,000): tourism (2005) 2,124; remittances (2006) 1,499; foreign direct investment (FDI) (2001–05 avg.) 662. Disbursements for (US$'000,000): tourism (2005) 365; remittances (2006) 15; FDI (2001–05 avg.) 7.0. **Land use** as % of total land area (2003): in temporary crops 18.0%, in permanent crops 13.8%, in pasture 31.2%; overall forest area (2005) 6.8%.

Foreign trade

Imports (2005; c.i.f.): TND 17,101,500,000 (textiles 17.3%; crude and refined petroleum 12.5%; machinery and apparatus 10.8%; electrical machinery 10.7%; motor vehicles 6.7%; food products 5.5%). *Major import sources:* France 23.5%; Italy 20.9%; Germany 8.2%; Spain 5.1%; Libya 3.9%. **Exports** (2005; f.o.b.): TND 13,607,700,000 (textiles 32.7%; electrical machinery 14.5%; crude and refined petroleum 12.9%; leather products 5.0%; phosphates and phosphate derivatives 4.4%; olive oil 3.5%). *Major export destinations:* France 32.9%; Italy 24.0%; Germany 8.4%; Spain 5.5%; Libya 4.5%.

Transport and communications

Transport. *Railroads* (2005): route length 2,153 km; passenger-km 1,317,000,000; metric ton-km cargo 2,068,200,000. *Roads* (2004): total length 19,232 km (paved 66%). *Vehicles* (2004): passenger cars 825,990; trucks and buses 119,064. *Air transport* (2006): passenger-km 2,976,000,000; metric ton-km cargo 17,916,000. **Communications**, in total units (units per 1,000 persons). Daily newspaper circulation (2005): 272,000 (27); televisions (2004): 2,150,000 (217); telephone landlines (2006): 1,269,000 (124); cellular telephone subscribers (2006): 7,339,000 (719); personal computers (2005): 568,000 (56); total Internet users (2006): 1,295,000 (127); broadband Internet subscribers (2005): 16,000 (1.6).

Education and health

Educational attainment (2005). Percentage of population ages 10 and over having: no formal schooling 22.0%; primary education 36.5%; secondary 33.1%; higher 8.4%. **Literacy** (2006): total population ages 10 and over literate 74.3%; males literate 83.4%; females literate 65.3%. **Health:** physicians (2005) 9,422 (1 per 1,036 persons); hospital beds (2004) 17,269 (1 per 576 persons); infant mortality rate per 1,000 live births (2005) 20.3. **Food** (2005): daily per capita caloric intake 3,408 (vegetable products 90%, animal products 10%); 180% of FAO recommended minimum.

Military

Total active duty personnel (2006): 35,300 (army 76.5%, navy 13.6%, air force 9.9%). **Military expenditure as percentage of GDP** (2005): 1.6%; per capita expenditure US$29.

Background

From the 12th century BC the Phoenicians had a series of trading posts on the northern African coast. By the 6th century BC the Carthaginian kingdom encompassed most of present-day Tunisia. The Romans ruled from 146 BC until the Muslim Arab invasions in the mid-7th century AD. The area was fought over, won, and lost by many, including the Abbasids, the Almohads, the Spanish, and the Ottoman Turks, who finally conquered it in 1574 and held it until the late 19th century. For a time it maintained autonomy as the French, British, and Italians contended for the region. In 1881 Tunisia became a French protectorate. In World War II US and British forces captured it (1943) to end a brief German occupation. In 1956 France granted it full independence; Habib Bourguiba assumed power and remained in office until 1987.

Recent Developments

The Tunisian cereal harvest in 2007 reached two million tons and, despite both budget and current-account deficits, GDP growth reached 8.9% for the year. The country was still coping with corruption, however, and was tied for 61st out of 179 countries in Transparency International's annual Corruption Perceptions Index. The regime continued its repressive policies and targeted persons whom the government suspected of having sympathies for political Islam, as well as others, particularly journalists and human rights organizations that sought to create awareness of human rights abuses. In January 2007 about two dozen Islamic extremists who had apparently intended to attack US consular facilities in Tunis were intercepted by security forces in Grombalia, south of the capital. At least 12 people were killed, and 15 others were arrested.

Internet resources: <www.tourismtunisia.com>.

Turkey

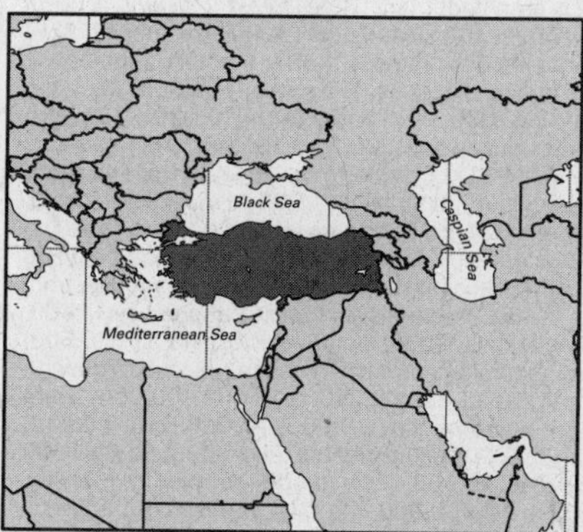

Official name: Turkiye Cumhuriyeti (Republic of Turkey). **Form of government:** multiparty republic with one legislative house (Grand National Assembly of Turkey [550]). **Chief of state:** President Abdullah Gul (from 2007). **Head of government:** Prime Minister

Recep Tayyip Erdogan (from 2003). **Capital:** Ankara. **Official language:** Turkish. **Official religion:** none. **Monetary unit:** 1 new Turkish lira (YTL) = 100 kurush; valuation (1 Jul 2008) US$1 = YTL 1.25 (the new Turkish lira replaced the [old] Turkish lira [TL] 1 Jan 2005, at the rate of 1 YTL = TL 1,000,000).

Demography

Area: 302,535 sq mi, 783,562 sq km. **Population** (2007): 73,884,000. **Density** (2007): persons per sq mi 244.2, persons per sq km 94.3. **Urban** (2006): 62.5%. **Sex distribution** (2005): male 50.44%; female 49.56%. **Age breakdown** (2005): under 15, 28.3%; 15–29, 27.7%; 30–44, 22.4%; 45–59, 13.4%; 60–74, 6.5%; 75–84, 1.5%; 85 and over, 0.2%. **Ethnic composition** (2000): Turk 65.1%; Kurd 18.9%; Crimean Tatar 7.2%; Arab 1.8%; Azerbaijani 1.0%; Yoruk 1.0%; other 5.0%. **Religious affiliation** (2005): Muslim 97.5%, of which Sunni 82.5%, Shiʿi (mostly nonorthodox Alevi) 15.0%; nonreligious 2.0%; other (mostly Christian) 0.5%. **Major urban agglomerations** (2005): Istanbul 9,712,000; Ankara 3,573,000; Izmir 2,487,000; Bursa 1,414,000; Adana 1,245,000; Gaziantep 992,000. **Location:** southwestern Asia and southeastern Europe, bordering the Black Sea, Georgia, Armenia, Azerbaijan, Iran, Iraq, Syria, the Mediterranean Sea, Greece, and Bulgaria.

Vital statistics

Birth rate per 1,000 population (2006): 18.7 (world avg. 20.3). **Death rate** per 1,000 population (2006): 6.3 (world avg. 8.6). **Total fertility rate** (avg. births per childbearing woman; 2006): 2.18. **Life expectancy** at birth (2006): male 69.1 years; female 74.0 years.

National economy

Budget (2005). *Revenue:* YTL 134,819,231,000 (tax revenue 79.3%, of which income tax 22.5%; nontax revenue 17.2%; grants and other revenue 3.5%). *Expenditures:* YTL 141,020,860,000 (finances 51.8%; education 10.5%; labor and social security 10.2%; defense 7.2%). **Production** (in '000 metric tons except as noted). *Agriculture, forestry, fishing* (2006): wheat 20,010, sugar beets 14,452, tomatoes 9,855, barley 9,551, potatoes 4,397; livestock (number of live animals) 25,304,000 sheep, 10,526,000 cattle, 317,000,000 chickens, (2004) 230,037 angora goats; roundwood (2005) 16,185,000 cu m, of which fuelwood 31%; fisheries production (2005) 546 (from aquaculture 22%). *Mining* (2005): magnesite 3,400; refined borates 800; chromite 700. *Manufacturing* (value added in US$'000,000; 2005): food products 8,800; telecommunications equipment and electronics 7,450; chemicals and chemical products 7,400; base metals 7,000; motor vehicles and parts 6,500. *Energy production (consumption):* electricity (kW-hr; 2005) 161,983,000,000 (118,768,000,000); hard coal (metric tons; 2005) 3,010,000 ([2004] 18,900,000); lignite (metric tons; 2005) 55,600,000 ([2004] 45,500,000); crude petroleum (barrels; 2006) 15,900,000 ([2004] 185,800,000); petroleum products (metric tons; 2005) 23,724,000 ([2004] 24,972,000); natural gas (cu m; 2004) 708,000,000 (23,372,000,000). **Population economically active** (2006): total 24,775,000; activity rate of total population 34.2% (participation rates: ages 15–64, 51.1%; female 26.1%; unemployed [May 2006–April 2007] 9.7%). **Households.** Average household size (2004) 4.1; average annual income per household (2003) TL 10,767,998,904 (US$7,174); sources of income (2004): wages and salaries 38.7%, self-employment 31.8%, transfers 21.2%; expenditure (2005): housing 25.9%, food and nonalcoholic beverages 24.9%, transportation 12.6%; household furnishings 6.8%. **Gross national income** (2006): US$397,699,000,000 (US$5,380 per capita). **Public debt** (external, outstanding; June 2007): US$65,310,000,000. **Selected balance of payments data.** Receipts from (US$'000,000): tourism (2005) 18,152; remittances (2006) 851; foreign direct investment (FDI) (2001–05 avg.) 3,752; official development assistance (2005) 1,668 (commitments). Disbursements for (US$'000,000): tourism (2005) 2,872; FDI (2001–05 avg.) 622. **Land use** as % of total land area (2003): in temporary crops 30.4%, in permanent crops 3.4%, in pasture 19.0%; overall forest area (2005) 13.2%.

Foreign trade

Imports (2006; c.i.f.): US$137,449,000,000 (machinery and apparatus 21.5%; mineral fuels 21.5%; base and fabricated metals 13.7%; transport equipment 9.1%; chemicals and chemical products 9.0%). *Major import sources:* EU 42.5%, of which Germany 10.6%, Italy 6.2%, France 5.2%; Russia 12.8%; China 6.9%; US 4.5%. **Exports** (2006; f.o.b.): US$85,309,000,000 (textiles and wearing apparel 23.1%; transport equipment 15.9%; machinery and apparatus 15.0%; base and fabricated metals 14.2%; mineral fuels 6.1%). *Major export destinations:* EU 56.0%, of which Germany 11.3%, UK 8.0%, Italy 7.9%, France 5.4%; US 5.9%; Russia 3.8%.

Transport and communications

Transport. *Railroads* (2005): length 8,697 km; passenger-km 5,036,000; metric ton-km cargo 9,152,000,000. *Roads* (2004): total length 347,553 km (paved 45%). *Vehicles* (2005): passenger cars 5,730,320; trucks and buses 2,624,259. *Air transport* (2006; Atlasjet, Turkish, Pegasus, and Sun Express airlines only): passenger-km 37,512,000,000; metric ton-km cargo 391,831,000. **Communications,** in total units (units per 1,000 persons). Daily newspaper circulation (2004): 4,948,000 (70); televisions (2002): 29,440,000 (424); telephone landlines (2006): 18,832,000 (258); cellular telephone subscribers (2006): 52,663,000 (722); personal computers (2005): 4,073,000 (57); total Internet users (2006): 12,283,000 (168); broadband Internet subscribers (2006): 2,774,000 (38).

Education and health

Educational attainment (2003). Percentage of population ages 25–64 having: no formal schooling through primary education 64%; lower secondary 10%; upper secondary/higher vocational 17%; university 9%. **Literacy** (2006): total population ages 15 and over literate 88.1%; males literate 96.0%; females literate 80.4%. **Health:** physicians (2004) 104,226 (1 per 683 persons); hospital beds (2006)

1 metric ton = about 1.1 short tons; 1 kilometer = 0.6 mi (statute); 1 metric ton-km cargo = about 0.68 short ton-mi cargo; c.i.f.: cost, insurance, and freight; f.o.b.: free on board

180,767 (1 per 404 persons); infant mortality rate per 1,000 live births (2006) 22.6. **Food** (2005): daily per capita caloric intake 3,416 (vegetable products 88%, animal products 12%); 173% of FAO recommended minimum.

Military

Total active duty personnel (2006): 514,850 (army 78.1%, navy 10.2%, air force 11.7%); US troops in Turkey (June 2007) 1,650. **Military expenditure as percentage of GDP** (2005): 2.8%; per capita expenditure US$143.

Background

Turkey's early history corresponds to that of Asia Minor, the Byzantine Empire, and the Ottoman Empire. Byzantine rule emerged when Constantine the Great made Constantinople (now Istanbul) his capital. The Ottoman Empire, begun in the 12th century, dominated for more than 600 years; it ended in 1918 after the Young Turk revolt precipitated its demise. Under the leadership of Mustafa Kemal Ataturk, a republic was proclaimed in 1923, and the caliphate was abolished in 1924. Turkey remained neutral throughout most of World War II, siding with the Allies in 1945. Since the war it has alternated between civil and military governments and has had several conflicts with Greece over Cyprus. The 1990s saw political and civic turmoil between fundamentalist Muslims and secularists.

Recent Developments

Militants of the radical nationalist Kurdistan Workers Party (PKK), which had its chief operational base in northern Iraq, mounted hit-and-run raids on Turkish security forces in 2007, while other PKK terrorists set off bombs in metropolitan areas. These attacks cost the lives of some 150 people during the year. A convention on the prevention of terrorism signed with Iraq in September had little effect. Prime Minister Recep Tayyip Erdogan asked the parliament to authorize the deployment of Turkish forces outside the country's boundaries. Attempts by the US administration to dissuade Turkey from an incursion into northern Iraq were hampered by a vote in October by the Foreign Affairs Committee of the US House of Representatives to recognize the massacres that attended the deportation of Armenians in the Ottoman Empire in 1915 as an act of genocide. US-Turkish relations improved, however, after Erdogan visited Pres. George W. Bush in Washington in early November. Following an agreement to share intelligence on the PKK, the US opened Iraqi airspace prior to a series of Turkish raids on PKK camps in December, and attacks by both sides continued in 2008. Progress on EU membership for Turkey, meanwhile, was stalled.

Internet resources: <www.tourismturkey.org>.

Turkmenistan

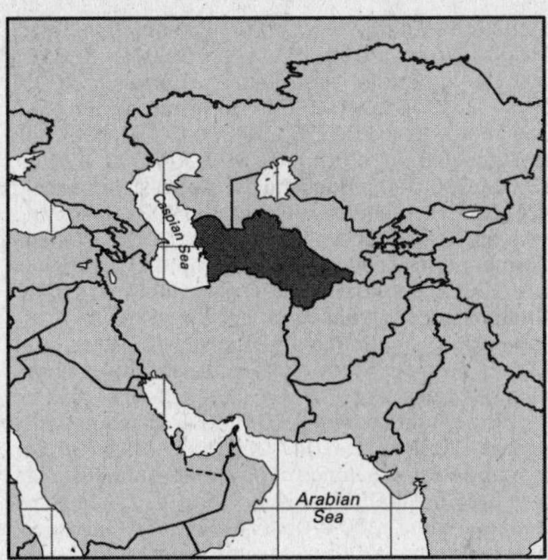

Official name: Turkmenistan. **Form of government:** unitary single-party republic with one legislative body (Majlis [Parliament; 50]). **Head of state and government:** President Gurbanguly Berdymukhammedov (from 2006). **Capital:** Ashgabat. **Official language:** Turkmen. **Official religion:** none. **Monetary unit:** manat (m); valuation (1 Jul 2008) US$1 = m 14,250.00 (in mid-2006 the black market value was about m 24,000 = US$1).

Demography

Area: 188,500 sq mi, 488,100 sq km. **Population** (2007): 5,097,000. **Density** (2007): persons per sq mi 27.0, persons per sq km 10.4. **Urban** (2005): 46.2%. **Sex distribution** (2005): male 49.24%; female 50.76%. **Age breakdown** (2005): under 15, 31.8%; 15–29, 30.0%; 30–44, 20.6%; 45–59, 11.4%; 60–74, 4.6%; 75–84, 1.4%; 85 and over, 0.2%. **Ethnic composition** (2000): Turkmen 79.2%; Uzbek 9.0%; Russian 3.0%; Kazakh 2.5%; Tatar 1.1%; other 5.2%. **Religious affiliation** (2000): Muslim (mostly Sunni) 87.2%; Russian Orthodox 1.7%; nonreligious 9.0%; other 2.1%. **Major cities** (1999): Ashgabat (2002) 743,000; Turkmenabat 203,000; Dasoguz 165,000; Mary 123,000; Balkanabat 108,000. **Location:** central Asia, bordering Kazakhstan, Uzbekistan, Afghanistan, Iran, and the Caspian Sea.

Vital statistics

Birth rate per 1,000 population (2006): 25.6 (world avg. 20.3); (1998) within marriage 96.2%. **Death rate** per 1,000 population (2006): 6.3 (world avg. 8.6). **Total fertility rate** (avg. births per childbearing woman; 2006): 3.19. **Life expectancy** at birth (2006): male 64.9 years; female 71.3 years.

National economy

Budget (2004). *Revenue:* m 14,262,000,000,000 (tax revenue 94.3%; nontax revenue 5.7%). *Expenditures:* m 14,251,000,000,000 (current expenditure 94.8%; development expenditure 5.2%). **Public debt** (external, outstanding; 2005): US$912,000,000. **Production** (metric tons except as noted). *Agriculture, forestry, fishing* (2006): wheat 3,260,000, seed cotton 700,000, tomatoes 282,000; livestock (number of live animals) 15,694,000 sheep, 2,065,000 cattle, 904,000 goats; roundwood (2005) 3,400 cu m, of which fuelwood 100%; fisheries production (2005) 15,016. *Mining and quarrying* (2004): iodine 250,000, salt 215,000, gypsum 100,000. *Manufacturing* (2001): residual fuel oils 2,681,000; distillate fuel (gas-diesel oil; 2003) 1,750,000; motor spirits

1,283,000. *Energy production (consumption):* electricity (kW-hr; 2004) 11,470,000,000 (9,816,-000,000); crude petroleum (barrels; 2005) 69,600,000 ([2004] 46,600,000); petroleum products (metric tons; 2004) 6,230,000 (3,407,000); natural gas (cu m; 2005) 63,000,000,000 ([2004] 13,691,000,000). **Households.** Average household size (2002) 5.7; sources of income (1998): wages and salaries 70.6%, pensions and grants 20.9%, self-employment (mainly agricultural income) 2.3%; expenditure (1998): food 45.2%, clothing and footwear 16.8%, furniture 13.3%, transportation 7.6%, health 7.0%. **Population economically active** (2003): total 2,073,000; activity rate of total population 44.1% (participation rates: ages 15–64, 70.7%; female 46.8%; unofficially unemployed [2004] 60%). **Gross national income** (2006): US$6,047,000,000 (US$1,234 per capita). **Selected balance of payments data.** Receipts from (US$'000,000): tourism (1998) 192; foreign direct investment (2001–05 avg.) 83; official development assistance (2005) 24 (commitments). Disbursements for (US$'000,000): tourism (1997) 125. **Land use** as % of total land area (2003): in temporary crops 4.7%, in permanent crops 0.1%, in pasture 65.3%; overall forest area (2005) 8.8%.

Foreign trade

Imports (2003; c.i.f.): US$2,450,000,000 (machinery and transport equipment 45.9%; basic manufactures 19.9%; chemicals and chemical products 11.1%; food products 5.3%). *Major import sources* (2006): UAE 13.9%; Azerbaijan 11.3%; Turkey 9.9%; Russia 8.0%; Ukraine 7.8%. **Exports** (2003; f.o.b.): US$3,720,-000,000 (natural gas 49.7%; petrochemicals 18.3%; crude petroleum 8.9%; cotton fiber 3.2%). *Major export destinations* (2006): Ukraine 46.3%; Iran 16.8%; Azerbaijan 4.2%; UAE 3.2%; Italy 3.1%.

Transport and communications

Transport. *Railroads* (1999): length (2005) 2,440 km; passenger-km 701,000,000; metric ton-km cargo 7,337,000,000. *Roads* (2001): total length 22,000 km (paved 82%). *Vehicles* (1995): passenger cars 220,000; trucks and buses 58,200. *Air transport* (2005; Turkmenistan Airlines only): passenger-km 1,913,000,000; metric ton-km cargo 25,997,000. **Communications,** in total units (units per 1,000 persons). Daily newspaper circulation (2004): 57,000 (12); televisions (2003): 855,000 (182); telephone landlines (2005): 398,000 (82); cellular telephone subscribers (2005): 105,000 (22); personal computers (2005): 348,000 (72); total Internet users (2006): 65,000 (13).

Education and health

Educational attainment (2000). Percentage of population ages 25 and over having: no formal schooling/unknown 3.2%; incomplete primary to complete standard secondary education 60.1%; vocational secondary 23.5%; higher 13.2%. **Literacy** (1995): total population ages 15 and over literate 98.8%; males literate 99.3%; females literate 98.3%. **Health:** physicians (2002) 20,032 (1 per 231 persons); hospital beds (1997) 33,000 (1 per 131 persons); infant mortality rate per 1,000 live births (2006) 55.2. **Food** (2005): daily per capita caloric intake 3,217 (vegetable products 81%, animal products 19%); 167% of FAO recommended minimum.

Military

Total active duty personnel (2006): 26,000 (army 80.8%, navy 2.7%, air force 16.5%). **Military expenditure as percentage of GDP** (2005): 3.7%; per capita expenditure US$93.

Background

The earliest traces of human settlement in central Asia, dating back to Paleolithic times, have been found in Turkmenistan. The nomadic, tribal Turkmen probably entered the area in the 11th century AD. They were conquered by the Russians in the early 1880s, and the region became part of Russian Turkistan. It was organized as the Turkmen Soviet Socialist Republic in 1924 and became a constituent republic of the USSR in 1925. The country gained full independence from the USSR in 1991 under the name Turkmenistan. From 1990 to 2006 the country was ruled by the ever more autocratic and mercurial strongman Saparmurad Niyazov.

Recent Developments

Following his election in February 2007, Gurbanguly Berdymukhammedov carried out a reform of the educational system, restoring the 10th year of basic education and the 5th year of university, and restored pensions that his predecessor had canceled. He promised to make Internet access available to all, and Internet cafés began to open early in the year, but access to sites outside the country was restricted. In June the Turkmen government granted permission to the American oil firm Chevron and to British Petroleum to open offices in Ashgabat, and the projected gas pipeline supplying Turkmen natural gas to Pakistan via Afghanistan came closer to realization in August when the American firm International Oil announced its decision to undertake the construction. In early October Indian Ambassador Mohammad Afzal informed Berdymukhammedov that India also wanted to take part in the trans-Afghan pipeline project. In return Berdymukhammedov raised the possibility of cooperation with India's information-technology sector.

Internet resources:
<www.turkmenistanembassy.org>.

Tuvalu

Official name: Tuvalu. **Form of government:** constitutional monarchy with one legislative house (Parliament [15]). **Chief of state:** British Queen Elizabeth II (from 1952), represented by Governor-General Filoimea Telito (from 2005). **Head of government:** Prime Minister Apisai Ielemia (from 2006). **Capital:** government offices are at Vaiaku, on Funafuti atoll. **Official language:** none. **Official religion:** none. **Monetary units:** 1 Tuvaluan dollar ($T) = 1 Australian dollar ($A) = 100 Tuvaluan and Australian cents; valuation (1 Jul 2008) US$1 = $A 1.05.

1 metric ton = about 1.1 short tons; 1 kilometer = 0.6 mi (statute); 1 metric ton-km cargo = about 0.68 short ton-mi cargo; c.i.f.: cost, insurance, and freight; f.o.b.: free on board

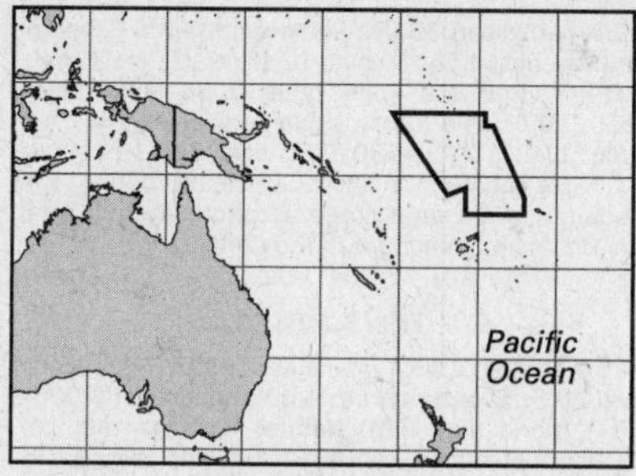

Demography

Area: 9.90 sq mi, 25.63 sq km. **Population** (2007): 9,700. **Density** (2007): persons per sq mi 979.8, persons per sq km 378.5. **Urban** (2004): 55.2%. **Sex distribution** (2006): male 48.79%; female 51.21%. **Age breakdown** (2006): under 15, 30.3%; 15–29, 27.5%; 30–44, 20.7%; 45–59, 14.1%; 60–74, 5.8%; 75 and over, 1.6%. **Ethnic composition** (2002): Tuvaluan (Polynesian) 93.6%; mixed (Tuvaluan/other) 4.6%; other Pacific 1.5%; other 0.3%. **Religious affiliation** (2002): Christian 97.0%, of which Church of Tuvalu (Congregational) 91.0%, Seventh-day Adventist 2.0%, Roman Catholic 1.0%; Baha'i 1.9%; other 1.1%. **Major locality** (2002): Fongafale islet of Funafuti atoll 4,492. **Location:** western Pacific Ocean, east of Papua New Guinea near the Equator.

Vital statistics

Birth rate per 1,000 population (2006): 22.2 (world avg. 20.3); (2005) within marriage 92.7%. **Death rate** per 1,000 population (2006): 7.1 (world avg. 8.6). **Total fertility rate** (avg. births per childbearing woman; 2006): 2.98. **Life expectancy** at birth (2006): male 66.1 years; female 70.7 years.

National economy

Budget (2005). *Revenue:* $A 25,539,000 (tax revenue 23.9%; nontax revenue [includes remittances from phosphate miners in Nauru and seafarers on German ships; rentals of fishing resources to Japan, Taiwan, and the US; and the leasing of the country's Internet domain, ".tv"] 38.0%; grants 38.1%). *Expenditures:* $A 22,323,000 (current expenditure 95.4%; development expenditure 4.6%). **Public debt** (external; 2002): US$5,000,000. **Gross national income** (2006): US$26,000,000 (US$2,441 per capita). **Production** (metric tons except as noted). *Agriculture, forestry, fishing* (2006): coconuts (2005) 1,139, fruits 749, bananas (2005) 284, other agricultural products include breadfruit, *pulaka* (taro), pandanus fruit, sweet potatoes, and pawpaws; livestock (number of live animals; 2005) 13,500 pigs, 15,000 ducks, 45,000 chickens; fisheries production (2005) 2,561. *Manufacturing* (value added in $A '000; 2002): cigarettes 755, cottage industries (including handicrafts and garments) 158. *Energy production (consumption):* electricity (kW-hr; 2005) n.a. (4,200,000); petroleum products, none (none). **Population economically active** (2002): total 3,463; activity rate of total population 36.2% (participation rates: ages 15 and over, 58.2%; female 43.4%; unemployed 6.5%). **Households** (2004–05). Average household size 5.3; average annual net income per household $A 13,007 (US$9,746); sources of income: wages and salaries 47.0%, rents, interest, bonuses, and other 28.7%, self-employment 12.1%, overseas remittances 9.1%; expenditure: food and nonalcoholic beverages 48.9%, housing 18.8%, household furnishings and energy 12.2%, education, health, and recreation 9.5%. **Selected balance of payments data.** Receipts from (US$'000,000): tourism (1998) 0.2; remittances (2006) 3.0; foreign direct investment (2001–05 avg.) 6.8; official development assistance (2005) 9.0. **Land use** as % of total land area (2003): in permanent crops 67%; overall forest area (2005) 33%.

Foreign trade

Imports (2005): $A 16,908,333 (food products [including live animals] 33.4%; mineral fuels 21.7%; machinery and apparatus 13.7%; transport equipment 5.2%; textiles 4.5%). *Major import sources:* Australia 33.7%; Fiji 19.7%; Singapore 17.5%; New Zealand 9.9%; China 5.1%. **Exports** (2005): $A 80,403 (precision instruments 18.6%; machinery and apparatus 17.4%; base and fabricated metals 15.4%; wood and wood products 12.5%; transportation equipment 11.6%). *Major export destinations:* Germany 60.5%; Italy 20.2%; Fiji 6.8%; Australia 2.7%; Ghana 1.5%.

Transport and communications

Transport. *Roads* (2002): total length 8 km (paved 100%). *Vehicles* (2003): passenger cars 102; trucks and buses 33. **Communications**, in total units (units per 1,000 persons). Telephone landlines (2005): 900 (93); cellular telephone subscribers (2005): 1,300 (135); total Internet users (2005): 1,700 (177).

Education and health

Educational attainment (2004–05). Percentage of population ages 15 and over having: no formal education/unknown 8.8%; primary education 52.4%; secondary 29.8%; higher 9.0%. **Literacy** (2004): total population literate 95%. **Health:** physicians (2003) 4 (1 per 2,393 persons); hospital beds (2001) 56 (1 per 170 persons); infant mortality rate per 1,000 live births (2006) 19.5.

Military

Total active duty personnel (2006): none; Tuvalu has nonformal security arrangements with Australia and New Zealand.

Background

The original Polynesian settlers of Tuvalu probably came mainly from Samoa or Tonga. The islands were sighted by the Spanish in the 16th century. Europeans settled there in the 19th century and intermarried with Tuvaluans. During this period Peruvian slave traders, known as "blackbirders," decimated the population. In 1856 the US claimed the four southern islands for guano mining. Missionaries from Europe arrived in 1865 and rapidly converted the islanders to Christianity. In 1892 Tuvalu joined the British Gilbert Islands, a protectorate that became the Gilbert and Ellice Islands Colony in 1916. Tuvaluans voted in 1974 for separation from the Gilberts (now Kiribati), whose people are Micronesian. Tuvalu gained independence in 1978, and in 1979 the US relinquished its claims. Elections were held in 1981, and a revised constitution was adopted in

1986. In recent decades, the government has tried to find overseas job opportunities for its citizens.

Recent Developments

Tuvalu's well-managed Tuvalu Trust Fund, which invested in major economies and funded a significant part of the government budget, suffered from global credit problems that emerged late in the year. Sea levels around Tuvalu were rising at a rate of almost an inch annually, as well, causing accelerated coastal degradation, and underground water supplies were deteriorating. The prospect that Tuvalu's nine atolls might be submerged by as early as 2040 had already raised questions concerning where the population might be relocated.

Internet resources: <www.timelesstuvalu.com>.

Uganda

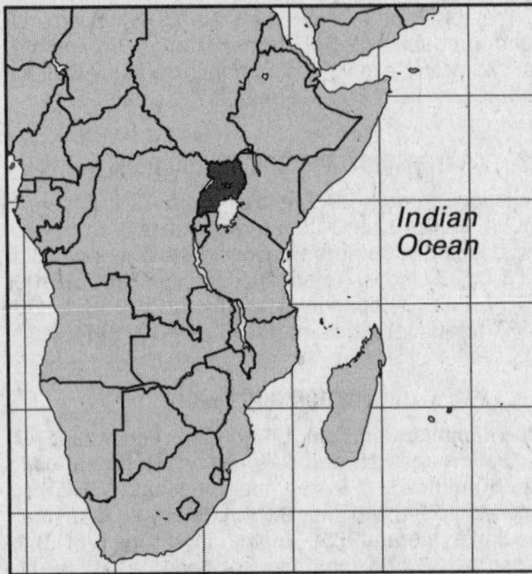

Official name: Republic of Uganda. **Form of government:** multiparty republic with one legislative house (Parliament [333]). **Head of state and government:** President Yoweri Museveni (from 1986), assisted by Prime Minister Apolo Nsibambi (from 1999). **Capital:** Kampala. **Official language:** English; Swahili. **Official religion:** none. **Monetary unit:** 1 Uganda shilling (UGX) = 100 cents; valuation (1 Jul 2008) US$1 = UGX 1,600.00.

Demography

Area: 93,263 sq mi, 241,551 sq km. **Population** (2007): 30,263,000. **Density** (2007): persons per sq mi 396.7, persons per sq km 153.2. **Urban** (2006): 13.1%. **Sex distribution** (2006): male 50.08%; female 49.92%. **Age breakdown** (2006): under 15, 50.3%; 15–29, 27.7%; 30–44, 12.9%; 45–59, 5.7%; 60–74, 2.7%; 75–84, 0.6%; 85 and over, 0.1%. **Ethnolinguistic composition** (2002): Ganda 17.3%; Nkole 9.8%; Soga 8.6%; Kiga 7.0%; Teso 6.6%; Lango 6.2%; Acholi 4.8%; Gisu 4.7%. **Religious affiliation** (2002): Christian 85.3%, of which Roman Catholic 41.9%, Anglican 35.9%, Pentecostal 4.6%, Seventh-day Adventist 1.5%; Muslim 12.1%; traditional beliefs 1.0%; nonreligious 0.9%; other 0.7%. **Major cities** (2002): Kampala (urban agglomeration) 1,208,544; Gulu 119,430; Lira 80,879; Jinja 71,213; Mbale 71,130. **Location:** eastern Africa, bordering The Sudan, Kenya, Lake Victoria, Tanzania, Rwanda, and the Democratic Republic of the Congo.

Vital statistics

Birth rate per 1,000 population (2006): 48.1 (world avg. 20.3). **Death rate** per 1,000 population (2006): 13.0 (world avg. 8.6). **Natural increase rate** per 1,000 population (2006): 35.1 (world avg. 11.7). **Total fertility rate** (avg. births per childbearing woman; 2006): 6.88. **Life expectancy** at birth (2006): male 50.2 years; female 51.9 years.

National economy

Budget (2003–04). *Revenue:* UGX 2,939,000,000,000 (tax revenue 52.7%, of which VAT 18.1%, petroleum taxes 9.2%, income tax 6.8%, tax on international trade 4.6%; grants 43.2%; nontax revenue 4.1%). *Expenditures:* UGX 3,170,000,000,000 (current expenditures 58.8%, of which education 13.8%, public administration 11.0%, defense 10.3%; capital expenditures 41.2%). **Production** (metric tons except as noted). *Agriculture, forestry, fishing* (2006): plantains 9,054,000, cassava 4,926,000, sweet potatoes 2,628,000; livestock (number of live animals) 8,034,000 goats, 6,973,000 cattle, 2,000,000 pigs; roundwood (2005) 39,972,000 cu m, of which fuelwood 92%; fisheries production (2005) 427,575 (from aquaculture 3%). *Mining and quarrying* (2005): cobalt 638; columbite-tantalite (ore and concentrate) 273 kg. *Manufacturing* (2005): cement 692,709; sugar 182,906; soap 127,589. *Energy production (consumption):* electricity (kW-hr; 2005) 1,858,000,000 ([2004] 1,726,000,000); petroleum products (metric tons; 2004) none (504,000). **Land use** as % of total land area (2003): in temporary crops 26.4%, in permanent crops 10.9%, in pasture 25.9%; overall forest area (2005) 18.4%. **Gross national income** (2006): US$9,702,000,000 (US$324 per capita). **Population economically active** (2002–03): total 9,773,000; activity rate of total population 37.7% (participation rates [2001]: ages 15–64, 78.9%; female 35.2%; officially unemployed 3.5%). **Public debt** (external, outstanding; 2005): US$4,250,000,000. **Households.** Average household size (2004) 4.7; income per household (1999–2000) UGX 141,000 (US$91); sources of income (1999–2000): wages and self-employment 78.0%, transfers 13.0%, rent 9.0%; expenditure (2002–03): food and nonalcoholic beverages 41.3%, rent, energy, and services 19.9%, education 8.0%, transportation 6.2%. **Selected balance of payments data.** Receipts from (US$'000,000): tourism (2005) 355; remittances (2006) 845; foreign direct investment (2001–05 avg.) 204; official development assistance (2005) 1,198. Disbursements for (US$'000,000): tourism (2005) 133; remittances (2006) 360.

Foreign trade

Imports (2005; c.i.f.): US$2,054,137,000 (petroleum products 16.7%; chemicals and chemical products

13.1%; food, beverages, and tobacco products 11.4%, of which cereals 6.9%; transport equipment 9.8%; base and fabricated metals 8.2%). *Major import sources:* Kenya 25.3%; Japan 7.1%; South Africa 7.0%; UAE 6.7%; India 6.4%. **Exports** (2005): US$812,-857,000 (coffee 21.3%; fish and fish products 17.6%; gold 9.0%; tea 4.2%; petroleum products 3.9%; to-bacco 3.9%; cotton 3.5%; in 2005 the estimated value of the unreported illegal export trade in diamonds from the Democratic Republic of the Congo via Uganda was US$200,000,000). *Major export destinations:* The Netherlands 10.5%; UAE 10.4%; Switzerland 9.2%; Kenya 8.9%; Democratic Republic of the Congo 7.4%.

Transport and communications

Transport. *Railroads* (2005): route length 1,244 km; metric ton-km cargo 185,559,000. *Roads* (2003): total length 70,746 km (paved 23%). *Vehicles* (2005): passenger cars 65,472; trucks and buses 100,323. *Air transport:* passenger-km (2003) 237,000,000; metric ton-km cargo (2004) 27,000,000. **Communications**, in total units (units per 1,000 persons). Daily newspaper circulation (2004): 89,000 (3.4); televisions (2003): 450,000 (17); telephone landlines (2006): 108,000 (3.6); cel-lular telephone subscribers (2006): 2,009,000 (67); personal computers (2005): 300,000 (10); total In-ternet users (2006): 750,000 (25).

Education and health

Educational attainment (2002). Percentage of popu-lation ages 25 and over having: no formal schooling 34.4%; incomplete primary education 36.0%; com-plete primary 11.1%; incomplete secondary 12.0%; complete secondary (some higher) 1.8%; complete higher (including vocational) 4.7%. **Literacy** (2006): total population ages 15 and over literate 66.8%; males literate 76.8%; females literate 57.7%. **Health** (2004): physicians 2,209 (1 per 11,947 persons); hospital beds 26,772 (1 per 986 persons); infant mortality rate per 1,000 live births (2006) 68.5. **Food** (2005): daily per capita caloric intake 2,333 (veg-etable products 95%, animal products 5%); 132% of FAO recommended minimum.

Military

Total active duty personnel (2006): 45,000 (army 100%). **Military expenditure as percentage of GDP** (2005): 2.3%; per capita expenditure US$7.

Background

By the 19th century the region around Uganda com-prised several separate kingdoms inhabited by vari-ous peoples, including Bantu- and Nilotic-speaking tribes. Arab traders reached the area in the 1840s. The native kingdom of Buganda was visited by the first European explorers in 1862. Protestant and Roman Catholic missionaries arrived in the 1870s, and the development of religious factions led to persecution and civil strife. In 1894 Buganda was formally pro-claimed a British protectorate. As Uganda, it gained its independence in 1962, and in 1967 it adopted a re-publican constitution. The civilian government was overthrown in 1971 and replaced by a military regime under Idi Amin. His invasion of Tanzania in late 1978 resulted in the collapse of his regime. In 1985 the civil-ian government was again deposed by the military, which in turn was overthrown in 1986. A constituent assembly enacted a new constitution in 1995.

Recent Developments

At the end of 2007 there were more than 1,250,000 internally displaced persons in Uganda, many dis-placed by the Lord's Resistance Army's (LRA's) rebel-lion. A precarious cease-fire prevailed, and intermit-tent negotiations took place into 2008 between the government and the LRA under rebel leader Joseph Kony. In Karamoja district, in the northeast, there was an acute shortage of food throughout the year, and cattle rustling remained endemic. In the less-turbu-lent central region, continuous heavy rains starting in July led to serious flooding, which displaced thou-sands of people. Along the western border, news of oil reserves remained good, but in August there was a dispute with the Democratic Republic of the Congo over a joint border. Even the more prosperous south had its problems. A venture there to build a third dam on the Nile River north of two existing dams located where the river leaves Lake Victoria proved con-tentious. The aim was to remedy Uganda's chronic need for more electricity, but critics pointed out that the dangerously low water level in Lake Victoria was already due as much to the excessive demands of the existing generators as to the persistent drought.

Internet resources: <www.visituganda.com>.

Ukraine

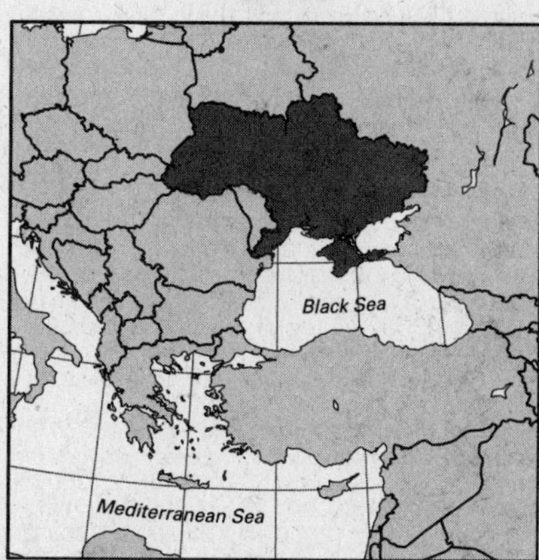

Official name: Ukrayina (Ukraine). **Form of govern-ment:** unitary multiparty republic with a single leg-islative body (Parliament [450]). **Head of state:** Presi-dent Viktor Yushchenko (from 2005). **Head of government:** Prime Minister Yuliya Tymoshenko (from 2007). **Capital:** Kiev (Kyyiv). **Official language:** Ukrain-ian. **Official religion:** none. **Monetary unit:** hryvnya (UAH); valuation (1 Jul 2008) US$1 = UAH 4.51.

Demography

Area: 233,062 sq mi, 603,628 sq km. **Population** (2007): 46,457,000. **Density** (2007): persons per sq mi 199.3, persons per sq km 77.0. **Urban** (2006): 68.0%. **Sex distribution** (2005): male 45.97%; female 54.03%. **Age breakdown** (2006): under 15, 14.3%; 15–29, 23.0%; 30–44, 21.1%; 45–59, 21.2%; 60–74, 14.1%; 75–84, 5.5%; 85 and over, 0.8%. **Ethnic composition** (2001): Ukrainian 77.8%; Russian 17.3%; Belarusian 0.6%; Moldovan 0.5%; Crimean Tatar 0.5%; other 3.3%. **Religious affiliation** (2004): Ukrainian Orthodox, of which "Kiev patriarchy" 19%, "no particular patriarchy" 16%, "Moscow patriarchy" 9%, Ukrainian Autocephalous Orthodox 2%; Ukrainian Catholic 6%; Protestant 2%; Latin Catholic 2%; Muslim 1%; Jewish 0.5%; nonreligious/atheist/other 42.5%. **Major cities** (2005): Kiev 2,718,000; Kharkiv 1,461,000; Dnipropetrovsk 1,039,000; Odesa (Odessa) 1,001,000; Donetsk (2005) 999,975. **Location:** eastern Europe, bordering Belarus, Russia, the Black Sea, Romania, Moldova, Hungary, Slovakia, and Poland.

Vital statistics

Birth rate per 1,000 population (2006): 9.8 (world avg. 20.3); (2005) within marriage 78.6%. **Death rate** per 1,000 population (2006): 16.2 (world avg. 8.6). **Total fertility rate** (avg. births per childbearing woman; 2005): 1.21. **Life expectancy** at birth (2006): male 62.1 years; female 73.6 years.

National economy

Budget (2006). *Revenue:* UAH 133,464,000,000 (tax revenue 71.0%, of which VAT 37.8%, corporate taxes 19.4%, excise tax 6.4%; nontax revenue 26.8%; other 2.2%). *Expenditures:* UAH 137,063,000,000 (social security 22.1%; education and health 12.8%; transportation and communications 4.9%; agriculture 4.8%; energy and construction 4.1%). **Public debt** (external; April 2007): US$12,400,000,000. **Production** (metric tons except as noted). *Agriculture, forestry, fishing* (2006): sugar beets 22,421,000, potatoes 19,467,000, wheat 14,000,000, sour cherries 120,000; livestock (number of live animals) 7,053,000 pigs, 6,514,000 cattle, 140,500,000 chickens; roundwood (2005) 14,606,300 cu m, of which fuelwood 56%; fisheries production (2005) 273,688 (from aquaculture 11%). *Mining and quarrying* (2005): iron ore (metal content) 37,700,000; manganese (metal content) 770,000; ilmenite concentrate (2004) 370,000. *Manufacturing* (value of production in UAH '000,000,000; 2005): base and fabricated metals 103.4; food and beverages 76.3; machinery and apparatus 59.7. *Energy production (consumption):* electricity (kW-hr; 2006) 192,204,000,000 ([2004] 76,831,000,000); hard coal (metric tons; 2006) 61,200,000 ([2004] 64,500,000); lignite (metric tons; 2006) 278,000 ([2004] 634,000); crude petroleum (barrels; 2006) 32,200,000 ([2004] 177,900,000); petroleum products (metric tons; 2004) 20,576,000 (11,938,000); natural gas (cu m; 2006) 17,733,000,000 ([2004] 78,531,000,000). **Households** (2005). Average household size 2.6; average annual disposable income per household UAH 16,527 (US$3,225); sources of income: wages and salaries 46.0%, transfers 30.9%, self-employment 4.9%; expenditure: food 61.0%. **Population economically active** (2005): total 22,280,800; activity rate of total population 47% (participation rates [2003]: ages 15–64, 65.8%; female 48.9%; unemployed [2006] 7.4%). **Gross national income** (2006): US$105,253,000,000 (US$2,260 per capita). **Selected balance of payments data.** Receipts from (US$'000,000): tourism (2005) 3,125; remittances (2006) 595; foreign direct investment (2001–05 avg.) 2,486; official development assistance (2005) 608 (commitments). Disbursements for (US$'000,000): tourism (2005) 2,805; remittances (2006) 34. **Land use** as % of total land area (2003): in temporary crops 56.1%, in permanent crops 1.6%, in pasture 13.8%; overall forest area (2005) 16.5%.

Foreign trade

Imports (2006): US$45,039,000,000 (mineral fuels 28.2%, of which natural gas 10.6%, crude petroleum 9.8%; machinery and apparatus 17.5%; road vehicles 10.9%; base and fabricated metals 7.4%). *Major import sources* (2005): Russia 35.5%; Germany 9.4%; Turkmenistan 7.4%; China 5.0%. **Exports** (2006): US$38,368,000,000 (base and fabricated metals 42.8%, of which iron and steel 34.0%; agricultural products 12.3%; chemical products 8.8%; machinery 8.7%). *Major export destinations* (2005): Russia 22.1%; Turkey 6.0%; Italy 5.6%; Germany 3.8%; Poland 3.0%.

Transport and communications

Transport. *Railroads* (2005): length 21,870 km; passenger-km 52,400,000,000; metric ton-km cargo 223,400,000,000. *Roads* (2005): total length 169,104 km (paved 98%). *Vehicles:* passenger cars (2005) 5,538,972; trucks and buses (2004) 1,093,372. *Air transport* (2006): passenger-km 4,393,000,000; metric ton-km cargo 40,692,000,000. **Communications,** in total units (units per 1,000 persons). Daily newspaper circulation (2004): 2,466,000 (52); telephone landlines (2006): 12,341,000 (264); cellular telephone subscribers (2006): 49,076,000 (1,049); personal computers (2005): 1,810,000 (38); total Internet users (2006): 5,545,000 (119).

Education and health

Literacy (2004): virtually 100%. **Health** (2006): physicians 225,000 (1 per 208 persons); hospital beds 444,000 (1 per 105 persons); infant mortality rate per 1,000 live births 9.8. **Food** (2005): daily per capita caloric intake 3,289 (vegetable products 81%, animal products 19%); 167% of FAO recommended minimum.

Military

Total active duty personnel (2006): 272,500 (army 45.9%, air force/air defense 18.0%, navy 5.0%, paramilitary 31.1%); Russian naval forces (2006) 1,100. **Military expenditure as percentage of GDP** (2005): 2.4%; per capita expenditure US$42.

Background

The area around Ukraine was invaded and occupied in the first millennium BC by the Cimmerians, Scythians, and Sarmatians and in the first millennium AD by the Goths, Huns, Bulgars, Avars, Khazars, and

Magyars. Slavic tribes settled there after the 4th century. Kiev was the chief town of Kievan Rus. The Mongol conquest in the mid-13th century decisively ended Kievan power. Ruled by Lithuania in the 14th century and Poland in the 16th century, it fell to Russian rule in the 18th century. The Ukrainian National Republic, established in 1917, declared its independence from Soviet Russia in 1918 but was reconquered in 1919; it was made the Ukrainian Soviet Socialist Republic of the USSR in 1922. The northwestern region was held by Poland from 1919 to 1939. Ukraine suffered a severe famine in 1932–33 under Soviet leader Joseph Stalin; over five million Ukrainians died of starvation in an unprecedented peacetime catastrophe. Overrun by Axis armies in 1941 in World War II, it was further devastated before being retaken by the Soviets in 1944. It was the site of the 1986 accident in Chernobyl, at a Soviet-built nuclear power plant. Ukraine declared independence in 1991. In recent years it has struggled economically as well as politically.

Recent Developments

Ukraine in 2007 was dominated by early parliamentary elections, which were held on 30 September. The election was notable for the sweeping gains made by the opposition party led by former prime minister Yuliya Tymoshenko. On 18 December she returned to the prime ministership after having gained the 226-vote majority needed for approval in the 450-member assembly by a single vote. According to government figures, GDP grew 32.6% in 2007, and industrial output increased by 10.2%, though agricultural output fell by 5.6% and consumer prices increased 16.6%. In April 2008 official unemployment stood at only 2.3%. In June 2007 Ukraine and Russia signed a new protocol on regulations for gas whereby Russia agreed to raise the volume of gas transported through Ukraine by 30 billion cu m by 2030. In 2007 Ukraine paid US$130 per 1,000 cu m of Russian gas, compared with US$95 in 2006. In October Ukraine's energy minister, Yury Boyko, signed an agreement with the head of the Russian energy company Gazprom to clear an outstanding debt of more than US$1.3 billion by cash payments and through the return of US$1.2 billion in gas owned by the Ukrainian energy company RosUkrEnergo to Gazprom Eksport. Though the EU did not accept Ukraine's request for membership, it had earlier promised US$647 million in aid to the country over the next four years. It also lifted visa restrictions, allowing free travel from Ukraine to the EU for those Ukrainians under the age of 18 or of retirement age.

Internet resources: <www.ukraine.com>.

United Arab Emirates

Official name: Al-Imarat al-ʿArabiyah al-Muttahidah (United Arab Emirates). **Form of government:** federation of seven emirates with one advisory body (Federal National Council [40]). **Chief of state:** President Sheikh Khalifah ibn Zayid al-Nahyan (from 2004). **Head of government:** Prime Minister Sheikh Muhammad ibn Rashid al-Maktum (from 2006). **Capital:** Abu Dhabi. **Official language:** Arabic. **Official religion:** Islam. **Monetary unit:** 1 UAE dirham (AED) = 100 fils; valuation (1 Jul 2008) US$1 = AED 3.67.

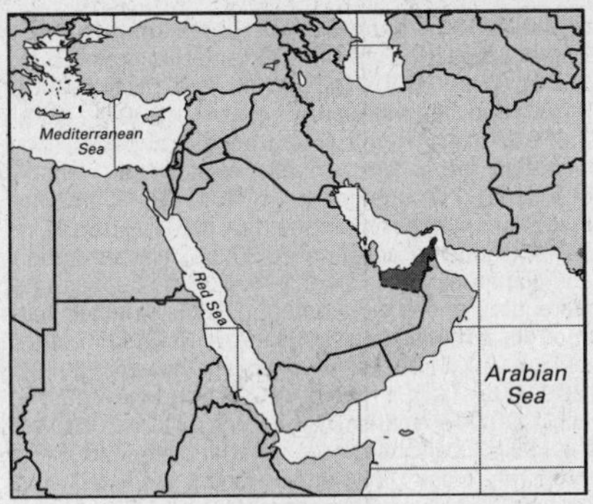

Demography

Area: 32,280 sq mi, 83,600 sq km. **Population** (2007): 4,444,000. **Density** (2007): persons per sq mi 137.7, persons per sq km 53.2. **Urban** (2005): 76.7%. **Sex distribution** (2006): male 68.61%; female 31.39%. **Age breakdown** (2006): under 15, 20.8%; 15–29, 29.3%; 30–44, 36.9%; 45–59, 11.3%; 60–74, 1.5%; 75–84, 0.2%; 85 and over, negligible. **Ethnic composition** (2000): Arab 48.1%, of which UAE Arab 12.2%, UAE Bedouin 9.4%, Egyptian Arab 6.2%, Omani Arab 4.1%, Saudi Arab 4.0%; South Asian 35.7%, of which Pashtun 7.1%, Balochi 7.1%, Malayali 7.1%; Persian 5.0%; Filipino 3.4%; white 2.4%; other 5.4%. **Religious affiliation** (2005): Muslim 62% (mostly Sunni); Hindu 21%; Christian 9%; Buddhist 4%; other 4%. **Major cities** (2007): Dubai 1,225,137; Abu Dhabi 633,136; Sharjah 584,286; Al-ʿAyn 444,331; ʿAjman 250,808 **Location:** the Middle East, bordering the Persian Gulf, the Gulf of Oman, Oman, and Saudi Arabia.

Vital statistics

Birth rate per 1,000 population (2006): 16.1 (world avg. 20.3). **Death rate** per 1,000 population (2006): 2.2 (world avg. 8.6). **Total fertility rate** (avg. births per childbearing woman; 2006): 2.44. **Life expectancy** at birth (2006): male 73.0 years; female 78.1 years.

National economy

Budget (2006). *Revenue:* AED 200,704,000,000 (royalties on hydrocarbons 80.5%; tax revenue 4.2%; other 15.3%). *Expenditures:* AED 128,238,000,000 (current expenditures 78.5%; development expenditure 13.1%; loans, net equity, and foreign grants 8.4%). **Gross national income** (2006): US$174,536,000,000 (US$41,082 per capita). **Public debt** (2005): US$20,000,000,000. **Production** (metric tons except as noted). *Agriculture, forestry, fishing* (2005): dates 760,000, tomatoes 240,000, eggplants 20,000; livestock (number of live animals) 1,520,000 goats, 580,000 sheep, 250,000 camels; fisheries production 90,570 (from aquaculture 1%). *Mining and quarrying* (2005): gypsum 100,000; lime 50,000. *Manufacturing* (value added in AED '000,000; 2002): chemical products (including refined petroleum) 18,467; textiles and wearing apparel 4,281; fabricated metal products and machinery 3,695. *Energy production (consumption):* electricity (kW-hr; 2005) 60,698,000,000 (53,874,000,000); crude petroleum (barrels; 2006–07) 942,585,000 ([2005]

153,000,000); petroleum products (metric tons; 2004) 22,655,000 (9,667,000); natural gas (cu m; 2006) 47,000,000,000 ([2004] 38,753,000,000). **Population economically active** (2004): total 2,459,145; activity rate of total population 56.9% (participation rates: ages 15 and over 76.2%; female [2001] 11.7%; unemployed [2001] 2.4%). **Households.** Average household size (2004) 6.4; expenditure (2000): housing and energy 36.1%, transportation and communications 14.9%, food 14.4%, education, recreation, and entertainment 10.3%. **Selected balance of payments data.** Receipts from (US$'000,000): tourism (2005) 2,233; foreign direct investment (FDI) (2001–05 avg.) 5,421. Disbursements for (US$'000,000): tourism (2005) 5,300; FDI (2001–05 avg.) 1,853. **Land use** as % of total land area (2003): in temporary crops 0.8%, in permanent crops 2.3%, in pasture 3.6%; overall forest area (2005) 3.7%.

Foreign trade

Imports (2006; c.i.f.): AED 316,280,000,000 (emirate imports 78.7%; free zone imports 21.3%). *Major import sources:* US 11.4%; China 11.0%; India 9.8%; Germany 6.2%; Japan 5.8%. **Exports** (2006): AED 523,350,000,000 (crude petroleum 40.8%; reexports 32.3%; free zone exports 14.4%; natural gas 5.0%). *Major export destinations:* Japan 25.9%; South Korea 10.3%; Thailand 5.9%; India 4.5%; Iran 3.6%.

Transport and communications

Transport. *Roads* (2003): total length, n.a. (paved roads only, 4,030 km). *Vehicles* (2003): passenger cars 684,092; trucks and buses 92,965. *Air transport* (2006): passenger-km 73,893,000,000; metric ton-km cargo 5,027,339,000. **Communications,** in total units (units per 1,000 persons). Daily newspaper circulation (2006): 706,000 (165); televisions (2004): 843,000 (216); telephone landlines (2006): 1,310,000 (307); cellular telephone subscribers (2006): 5,519,000 (1,294); personal computers (2005): 850,000 (208); total Internet users (2006): 1,709,000 (401); broadband Internet subscribers (2006): 241,000 (56).

Education and health

Educational attainment (2005). Percentage of population ages 10 and over having: no formal schooling (illiterate) 9.1%, (literate) 13.3%; primary education 14.5%; incomplete/complete secondary 42.0%; postsecondary 4.2%; undergraduate 15.1%; graduate 1.8%. **Literacy** (2005): total population ages 10 and over literate 90.9%; males literate 90.4%; females literate 92.2%. **Health** (2004): physicians 4,864 (public sector only; 1 per 779 persons); hospital beds 7,775 (1 per 487 persons); infant mortality rate per 1,000 live births (2006) 13.9. **Food** (2004): daily per capita caloric intake 3,280 (vegetable products 74%, animal products 26%); 162% of FAO recommended minimum.

Military

Total active duty personnel (2006): 50,500 (army 87.1%, navy 5.0%, air force 7.9%). **Military expenditure as percentage of GDP** (2005): 2.0%; per capita expenditure US$546.

Background

The Persian Gulf was the location of important trading centers as early as Sumerian times. Its people converted to Islam in Muhammad's lifetime. The Portuguese entered the region in the early 16th century, and the British East India Company arrived about 100 years later. In 1820 the British exacted a peace treaty with local rulers along the coast of the eastern Arabian Peninsula. The area formerly called the Pirate Coast became known as the Trucial Coast. In 1892 the rulers agreed to restrict foreign relations to Britain. Though the British administered the region from 1853, they never assumed sovereignty; each state maintained full internal control. The states formed the Trucial States Council in 1960. In 1971 the sheikhs terminated defense treaties with Britain and established the six-member federation. Ras al-Khaymah joined it in 1972. The UAE aided coalition forces against Iraq in the Persian Gulf War (1991).

Recent Developments

The United Arab Emirates (UAE) unveiled its National Development Strategy in 2007, recognizing the need to develop an infrastructure that was not based on oil revenues. In September Dubai became the largest shareholder in the London Stock Exchange, with 28% ownership, and acquired a 20% stake in the Nasdaq stock market index. Dubai also announced an initial public offering (IPO) of its port-operating company DP World, which at US$4.96 billion was the largest IPO in the Middle East. Abu Dhabi struck a deal with Boeing to become a major supplier of high-tech aerospace components.

Internet resources: <http://uaeinteract.com/travel>.

United Kingdom

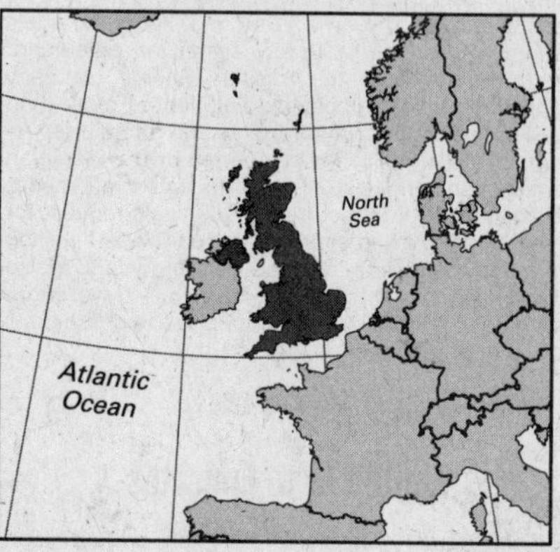

Official name: United Kingdom of Great Britain and Northern Ireland. **Form of government:** constitutional monarchy with two legislative houses (House of Lords [750]; House of Commons [646]). **Chief of state:** British Queen Elizabeth II (from 1952). **Head of government:** Prime Minister Gordon Brown (from 2007). **Capital:**

1 metric ton = about 1.1 short tons; 1 kilometer = 0.6 mi (statute); 1 metric ton-km cargo = about 0.68 short ton-mi cargo; c.i.f.: cost, insurance, and freight; f.o.b.: free on board

London. **Official language:** English. **Official religion:** Churches of England and Scotland "established" (protected by the state but not "official") in their respective countries; no established church in Northern Ireland or Wales. **Monetary unit:** 1 pound sterling (£) = 100 new pence; valuation (1 Jul 2008) US$1 = £0.50.

Demography

Area: 93,628 sq mi, 242,495 sq km, of which England 50,301 sq mi, 130,279 sq km; Wales 8,005 sq mi, 20,733 sq km; Scotland 30,080 sq mi, 77,907 sq km; Northern Ireland 5,242 sq mi, 13,576 sq km. **Population** (2007): 60,863,000. **Density** (2007): persons per sq mi 650.1, persons per sq km 251.0. **Urban** (2005): 89.7%. **Age breakdown** (2005): under 15, 17.9%; 15–29, 19.3%; 30–44, 22.3%; 45–59, 19.3%; 60–74, 13.6%; 75–84, 5.7%; 85 and over, 1.9%. **Ethnic composition** (2002–03): white 89.2%; black 2.0%, of which Caribbean origin 1.0%, African origin 0.9%; Asian Indian 1.7%; Pakistani 1.2%; Bangladeshi 0.5%; Chinese 0.3%; other and not stated 5.1%. **Religious affiliation** (2001): Christian 71.8%, of which Anglican-identified 29%, other Protestant-identified (significantly Presbyterian) 14%, Roman Catholic-identified 10%; Muslim 2.8%; Hindu 1.0%; Sikh 0.6%; Jewish 0.5%; nonreligious 15.0%; other 0.5%; unknown 7.8%. **Sex distribution** (2005): male 48.96%; female 51.04%. **Major cities (urban agglomeration)** (2005): London 7,518,000 (8,505,000); Birmingham 1,001,000 (2,280,000); Manchester 441,000 (2,228,000); Leeds 723,000 (1,519,000); Glasgow 579,000 (1,159,000); Newcastle 276,000 (879,000); Liverpool 448,000 (810,000); Sheffield 521,000; Bradford 485,000; Edinburgh 458,000; Bristol 398,000; Wakefield 321,000; Cardiff 320,000; Coventry 304,000; Doncaster 290,000; Sunderland 284,000; Belfast 268,000. **Location:** western Europe, bordering the North Sea, the English Channel, the Celtic Sea, the Irish Sea, and Ireland. **Mobility** (2001). Population living in the same residence as 2000: 88.6%; different residence, same country/region (of the UK) 8.6%; different residence, different country/region (of the UK) 2.1%; from outside the UK 0.7%. **Households** (2003–04). Average household size 2.4; 1 person 28%, couple 22%, couple with 1–2 children 16%, couple with 3 or more children 3%, single parent with children 6%, other 25%. **Immigration** (2004): permanent residents 518,000; from Bangladesh, India, and Sri Lanka 10.6%; South Africa 5.6%; Australia 5.0%; Pakistan 4.1%; US 2.7%; New Zealand 1.5%; Canada 1.0%; other 69.5%, of which EU 20.8%.

Vital statistics

Birth rate per 1,000 population (2006): 12.4 (world avg. 20.3); within marriage 56.3%. **Death rate** per 1,000 population (2006): 9.5 (world avg. 8.6). **Natural increase rate** per 1,000 population (2005): 2.9 (world avg. 11.7). **Total fertility rate** (avg. births per childbearing woman; 2005): 1.79. **Life expectancy** at birth (2005): male 75.9 years; female 81.0 years.

Social indicators

Educational attainment (2003). Percentage of population ages 25–64 having: up to lower secondary education only 16%; upper secondary 56%; higher 28%, of which at least some university 19%. **Quality of working life** (2004). Average full-time workweek (hours): male 40.8, female 37.5. Annual rate per 100,000 workers (2005; England, Scotland, and Wales only) for: injury or accident 562; death 0.6. Proportion of labor force (employed persons) insured for damages or income loss resulting from: injury 100%; permanent disability 100%; death 100%. Average days lost to labor stoppages per 1,000 employee workdays 34. **Social participation.** Population ages 16 and over participating in voluntary work (2001; England, Scotland, and Wales only) 39%. Trade union membership in total workforce (2003) 27%. Percentage of population attending weekly church services (2001) 8%. **Social deviance** (2004–05; England and Wales only). Offense rate per 100,000 population for: theft and handling stolen goods 3,822.1; criminal damage 2,234.7; violence against the person 1,951.1; burglary 1,281.9; fraud and forgery 525.8; drug offenses 268.3; robbery 167.2. **Material well-being** (2005–06). Households possessing: automobile 74%; telephone 92%; refrigerator/freezer 97%; washing machine 95%; central heating 94%; video recorder 86%; digital, cable, or satellite television receiver 65%.

National economy

Budget (2005–06). *Revenue:* £485,400,000,000 (income tax 26.9%; production and import taxes 24.9%; social security contributions 17.6%). *Expenditures:* £500,700,000,000 (social protection 34.2%; health 17.7%; education 13.9%; defense 6.1%; public order 6.0%). **Gross national income** (at 2006 market prices): US$2,425,690,000,000 (US$40,086 per capita). **Public debt** (2005): US$960,000,000,000. **Production** (metric tons except as noted). *Agriculture, forestry, fishing* (2006): wheat 14,735,000, sugar beets 7,150,000, potatoes 5,684,000, barley 5,239,000, rapeseed 1,870,000, carrots 832,600, oats 728,000, onions 383,400, cabbages 308,200, apples 218,500; livestock (number of live animals) 34,722,000 sheep, 10,159,910 cattle, 4,933,000 pigs; roundwood (2005) 8,589,000 cu m, of which fuelwood 4%; fisheries production (2005) 842,271 (from aquaculture 21%). *Mining and quarrying* (2005): sand and gravel 90,000,000; dolomite 13,000,000; chalk 8,000,000; china clay (kaolin) 2,148,000. *Manufacturing* (value added in £'000,000; 2004): food, beverages, and tobacco 22,570; paper products, printing, and publishing 20,020; transport equipment 18,864; electrical and optical equipment 16,881; chemicals and chemical products 15,645; base metals and fabricated metal products 15,644; machinery and equipment 11,962; rubber and plastic products 8,003. *Energy production (consumption):* electricity (kW-hr; 2004) 395,853,000,000 (403,343,000,000); hard coal (metric tons; 2005–06) 20,600,000 ([2005] 61,800,000); crude petroleum (barrels; 2005–06) 565,400,000 ([2005] 598,900,000); petroleum products (metric tons; 2005) 86,003,000 (80,977,000); natural gas (cu m; 2005–06) 99,037,000,000 ([2004] 115,230,000,000). **Population economically active** (2006): total 30,613,000; activity rate of total population 50.6% (participation rates: ages 16 and over 60.1%; female 45.9%; unemployed [June 2007–August 2007] 5.4%). **Households.** Average household size (2003–04) 2.4; average annual disposable income per household (2004–05) £25,360 (US$46,447); sources of income (2005–06): wages and salaries 67.3%, social security benefits 12.7%, self-employment 8.2%, transfers 7.4%; expenditure (2005–06): food and beverages 18.7%, recreation and culture 18.7%, housing 18.3%, transportation 14.5%, household furnishings 7.6%, clothing and footwear 5.1%. **Selected balance of payments data.** Receipts from (US$'000,000): tourism (2005) 25,959; remittances (2006) 7,339; foreign direct investment (FDI) (2001–05 avg.) 62,835. Disbursements for (US$'000,000): tourism (2005) 58,617; remittances (2006) 3,425; FDI (2001–05 avg.) 73,461. **Land use** as % of total land area (2003): in temporary crops 23.4%, in permanent crops 0.2%, in pasture 46.5%; overall forest area (2005) 11.8%.

Foreign trade

Imports (2005; c.i.f.): £274,828,000,000 (machinery and apparatus 27.2%, of which electrical machinery 19.3%, nonelectrical machinery 7.9%; transport equipment 14.3%, of which motor vehicles and parts 11.4%, aircraft and other transport equipment 2.9%; chemicals and chemical products 10.6%; petroleum and petroleum products 7.4%; food products 6.7%). *Major import sources:* Germany 13.9%; US 7.9%; France 7.9%; The Netherlands 7.3%; Belgium/Luxembourg 5.4%; China 4.7%; Italy 4.5%; Norway 4.4%; Spain 3.8%; Ireland 3.7%; Japan 3.1%. **Exports** (2005; f.o.b.): £209,308,000,000 (machinery and apparatus 29.4%, of which electrical machinery 17.2%, nonelectrical machinery 12.2%; chemicals and chemical products 15.8%, of which pharmaceuticals 5.8%; transport equipment 12.6%, of which motor vehicles and parts 9.2%, aircraft and other transport equipment 3.4%; crude petroleum and petroleum products 9.5%; food products 3.1%). *Major export destinations:* US 14.7%; Germany 11.0%; France 9.4%; Ireland 7.8%; The Netherlands 5.9%; Belgium/Luxembourg 5.3%; Spain 4.8%; Italy 4.1%; Switzerland 2.4%; Sweden 2.2%; Japan 1.9%; Canada 1.6%.

Transport and communications

Transport. *Railroads* (2005–06): length (2005) 17,156 km; passenger-km (England, Scotland, and Wales only) 43,211,000,000; metric ton-km cargo (England, Scotland, and Wales only) 22,000,000,000. *Roads* (2005; England, Scotland, and Wales only): total length 388,008 km (paved 100%). *Vehicles* (2004): passenger cars 27,765,100, trucks and buses 3,522,424. *Air transport* (2006): passenger-km 231,515,000,000; metric ton-km cargo 6,215,000,000. **Communications,** in total units (units per 1,000 persons). Daily newspaper circulation (2004): 17,485,000 (292); televisions (2003): 56,576,000 (950); telephone landlines (2006): 33,603,000 (562); cellular telephone subscribers (2006): 69,657,000 (1,164); personal computers (2005): 45,659,000 (765); total Internet users (2006): 33,534,000 (560); broadband Internet subscribers (2006): 12,995,000 (215).

Education and health

Literacy (2006): virtually 100%. **Health** (2005): physicians 122,345 (1 per 492 persons); hospital beds (2004) 233,223 (1 per 257 persons); infant mortality rate per 1,000 live births (2006) 5.0. **Food** (2005): daily per capita caloric intake 3,449 (vegetable products 72%, animal products 28%).

Military

Total active duty personnel (2006): 191,030 (army 55.0%, navy 21.4%, air force 23.6%); UK troops deployed abroad (2006) 42,900; US troops in the UK (2006) 10,300. **Military expenditure as percentage of GDP** (2005): 2.7%; per capita expenditure US$1,000.

Background

The early pre-Roman inhabitants of Britain were Celtic-speaking peoples, including the Brythonic people of Wales, the Picts of Scotland, and the Britons of Britain. Celts also settled in Ireland c. 500 BC. Julius Caesar invaded and took control of the area in 55–54 BC. The Roman province of Britannia endured until the 5th century and included present-day England and Wales. In the 5th century Nordic tribes of Angles, Saxons, and Jutes invaded Britain. The invasions had little effect on the Celtic peoples of Wales and Scotland.

Christianity began to flourish in the 6th century. During the 8th–9th centuries, Vikings, particularly Danes, raided the coasts of Britain. In the late 9th century Alfred the Great repelled a Danish invasion, which helped bring about the unification of England under Athelstan. The Scots attained dominance in Scotland, which was finally unified under Malcolm II (1005–34).

William of Normandy took England in 1066. The Norman kings established a strong central government and feudal state. The French language of the Norman rulers eventually merged with the Anglo-Saxon of the common people to form the English language. From the 11th century, Scotland came under the influence of the English throne. Henry II conquered Ireland in the late 12th century. His sons, kings Richard I and John, had conflicts with the clergy and nobles, and eventually John was forced to grant the nobles concessions in Magna Carta (1215). The concept of community of the realm developed during the 13th century, providing the foundation for parliamentary government. During the reign of Edward I, statute law developed to supplement English common law, and the first Parliament was convened. In 1314 Robert Bruce won independence for Scotland.

The Tudors became the ruling family of England following the Wars of the Roses (1455–85). Henry VIII established the Church of England and made Wales part of his realm. The reign of Elizabeth I began a period of colonial expansion; 1588 brought the defeat of the Spanish Armada. In 1603 James VI of Scotland ascended to the English throne, becoming James I, and established a personal union of the two kingdoms.

The English Civil Wars erupted in 1642 between Royalists and Parliamentarians, ending in the execution of Charles I (1649). After 11 years of Puritan rule under Oliver Cromwell and his son (1649–60), the monarchy was restored with Charles II. In 1707 England and Scotland assented to the Act of Union, forming the kingdom of Great Britain. The Hanoverians ascended to the English throne in 1714, when George Louis, elector of Hanover, became George I of Great Britain. During the reign of George III, Great Britain's American colonies won independence (1783). This was followed by a period of war with revolutionary France and later with the empire of Napoleon (1789–1815).

In 1801 legislation united Great Britain with Ireland to create the United Kingdom of Great Britain and Ireland. Britain was the birthplace of the Industrial Revo-

1 metric ton = about 1.1 short tons; 1 kilometer = 0.6 mi (statute); 1 metric ton-km cargo = about 0.68 short ton-mi cargo; c.i.f.: cost, insurance, and freight; f.o.b.: free on board

lution in the late 18th century, and it remained the world's foremost economic power until the late 19th century. During the reign of Queen Victoria, Britain's colonial expansion reached its zenith, though the older dominions, including Canada and Australia, were granted independence (1867 and 1901, respectively).

The UK entered World War I allied with France and Russia in 1914. Following the war, revolutionary disorder erupted in Ireland, and in 1921 the Irish Free State was granted dominion status. The six counties of Ulster, however, remained in the UK as Northern Ireland. The UK entered World War II in 1939. Following the war the Irish Free State became the Irish Republic and left the Commonwealth. India gained independence from the UK in 1947.

Throughout the postwar period and into the 1970s, the UK continued to grant independence to its overseas colonies and dependencies. With UN forces, it participated in the Korean War (1950–53). In 1956 it intervened militarily in Egypt during the Suez Crisis. In 1982 it defeated Argentina in the Falkland Islands War. As a result of continuing social strife in Northern Ireland, it joined with Ireland in several peace initiatives, which eventually resulted in an agreement to establish an assembly in Northern Ireland. In 1997 referenda approved in Scotland and Wales devolved power to both countries, though both remained part of the UK.

Recent Developments

After 10 years as prime minister of the UK, Tony Blair stepped down on 27 June 2007. He was succeeded by Gordon Brown, who had served as chancellor of the Exchequer under him. Barely 48 hours after Brown became prime minister two car bombs were discovered and defused in central London and a third vehicle was driven into Glasgow (Scotland) Airport, where it caught fire. A series of floods that had started earlier became more intense in the days immediately after he was sworn in—an estimated one million people were directly affected. He subsequently announced £46 million (about US$92 million) in aid and a £500 million (about US$1 billion) annual increase in spending on flood defenses. One month after becoming prime minister, Brown flew to the US for talks with Pres. George W. Bush. Although both men publicly appeared to be in agreement, the encounter was more strained than previous visits from Blair had been. Brown insisted that decisions about British troops in Iraq would be taken on the advice of the UK's military leaders only. This was evident in September when British troops withdrew from central Basra to Basra Airport, handing over day-to-day control of the city to Iraqi forces and ending the UK's role in patrolling southern Iraq. In October Brown announced that half of the remaining British force would be withdrawn from Iraq by the spring of 2008, leaving 2,500 troops in the country, but in April 2008 this decision was reversed after a spike in violence in Iraq.

Northern Ireland's Assembly was reconvened on 8 May, following almost five years of inactivity, after Sinn Féin, the Roman Catholic nationalist party that had historically been associated with the militant Irish Republican Army, ended its long-standing policy of noncooperation with the province's police service. Ian Paisley, leader of the Protestant Democratic Unionist Party, was sworn in as first minister, with Sinn Féin's Martin McGuinness as his deputy.

The UK's economy grew by 3% in 2007, continuing the steady progress that had begun in the early 1990s. Inflation remained subdued, though in April it was announced that the consumer price index had risen by 3.1% over the previous 12 months. Since this exceeded the 2% target set for the Bank of England (BOE), the bank raised the benchmark repo interest rate. Among other things, this had the effect of cooling the housing market. According to figures released by the Halifax bank (the UK's largest mortgage lender), house prices that had been rising at an annual rate of more than 11% during the first half of 2007 peaked in August and fell in every month after that for the rest of the year. Amid fears that these falls would be accompanied by slower economic growth in 2008, the BOE reduced interest rates again in December.

Internet resources: <www.visitbritain.com>.

United States

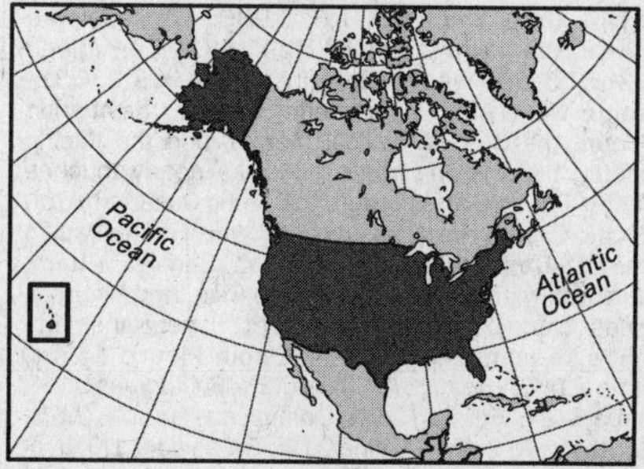

Official name: United States of America. **Form of government:** federal republic with two legislative houses (Senate [100]; House of Representatives [435, excluding 4 nonvoting delegates from the District of Columbia, the US Virgin Islands, American Samoa, and Guam; a nonvoting resident commissioner from Puerto Rico; and a nonvoting resident representative from the Northern Mariana Islands]). **Head of state and government:** President George W. Bush (from 2001). **Capital:** Washington DC. **Official language:** none. **Official religion:** none. **Monetary unit:** 1 dollar (US$) = 100 cents.

Demography

Area: 3,676,486 sq mi, 9,522,055 sq km; inland water area equals 78,797 sq mi [204,083 sq km], and Great Lakes water area equals 60,251 sq mi [156,049 sq km]). **Population** (2007): 302,633,000. **Density** (2006): persons per sq mi 85.6, persons per sq km 33.0. **Urban** (2005): 80.8%. **Sex distribution** (2005): male 49.26%; female 50.74%. **Age breakdown** (2005): under 15, 20.5%; 15–29, 20.9%; 30–44, 21.6%; 45–59, 20.2%; 60–74, 10.7%; 75–84, 4.4%; 85 and over, 1.7%. **Population by race and Hispanic origin** (persons of Hispanic origin may be of any race) (2005): non-Hispanic white 66.9%; Hispanic 14.4%; non-Hispanic black 12.8%; Asian and Pacific Islander 4.5%; American Indian and Eskimo 1.0%; other 0.4%. **Religious affiliation** (2005): Christian 83.3%, of which independent Christian 23.2%, Roman Catholic 19.6%, Protestant (including Anglican) 18.9%, unaffiliated Christian 16.5%, Orthodox 1.8%, other Christian (primarily Mormon and Jehovah's Witness) 3.3%; Jewish 1.9%; Muslim 1.6%; Buddhist 0.9%; New Religionists 0.5%; Hindu 0.4%; traditional beliefs 0.4%; Baha'i 0.3%; Sikh 0.1%; nonreligious 9.8%; atheist 0.5%; other 0.3%. **Mobility** (2005). Reported gross percentage of population living in the same residence as in 2004: 86%; different residence, same county 8%; different county, same state 3%; different state 3%; moved from abroad 1%. **Households** (2006). Total households 116,011,000 (married-couple families 58,945,000 [50.8%]). Average household size 2.6; 1 person 26.6%, 2 persons 33.0%, 3 persons 16.5%, 4 persons 14.0%, 5 or more persons 9.9%. Family households: 78,425,000 (67.6%); nonfamily 37,587,000 (32.4%), of which 1-person 83.1%. **Place of birth** (2005): native-born 255,999,000 (87.9%); foreign-born 35,157,000 (12.1%), of which (2004) Mexico 10,011,000, Philippines 1,222,000, China/Hong Kong 1,067,000, India 1,007,000, Cuba 952,000, Vietnam 863,000, El Salvador 765,000, South Korea 701,000. **Major cities** (2006): New York 8,214,426; Los Angeles 3,849,378; Chicago 2,833,321; Houston 2,144,491; Phoenix 1,512,986; Philadelphia 1,448,394; San Antonio 1,296,682; San Diego 1,256,951; Dallas 1,232,940; San Jose 929,936. **Location:** North America, bordering Canada, the Atlantic Ocean, the Gulf of Mexico, Mexico, and the Pacific Ocean; the outlying state of Alaska nearly touches eastern Russia and borders the Arctic Ocean and the Pacific Ocean; Hawaii is an island group in the Pacific Ocean. **Dependencies:** American Samoa, Guam, Northern Mariana Islands, Puerto Rico, and Virgin Islands (of the US). **Immigration** (2005): permanent immigrants admitted 1,122,400, from Mexico 14.4%, India 7.6%, Africa 7.6%, China 6.2%, Philippines 5.4%, Cuba 3.2%, Vietnam 2.9%, Dominican Republic 2.5%, South Korea 2.4%, Ukraine 2.0%, El Salvador 1.9%, Jamaica 1.6%, Poland 1.4%, Haiti 1.3%, Bosnia and Herzegovina 1.3%, other 38.3%. Refugees (2005) 380,000. Asylum seekers (2000) 386,330.

Vital statistics

Birth rate per 1,000 population (2006): 14.3 (world avg. 20.3); within marriage 64.2%. **Death rate** per 1,000 population (2006): 8.1 (world avg. 8.6). **Natural increase rate** per 1,000 population (2006): 6.2 (world avg. 11.7). **Total fertility rate** (avg. births per childbearing woman; 2006): 2.09. **Life expectancy** at birth (2004): male 75.2 years, of which white male 75.7 years, black male 69.8 years; female 80.4 years, of which white female 80.8 years, black female 76.5 years.

Social indicators

Educational attainment (2005). Percentage of population ages 25 and over having: primary through incomplete secondary 14.8%; secondary 32.2%; some postsecondary 25.4%; 4-year higher degree 18.1%; advanced degree 9.5%. Number of earned degrees (2004): bachelor's degree 1,399,542; master's degree 558,940; doctor's degree 48,378; first-professional degrees (in fields such as medicine, theology, and law) 63,796. **Quality of working life** (2007). Average workweek 41.3 hours. Annual death rate per 100,000 workers (2004) 3.5; leading causes of occupational deaths (2004): transportation incidents 24%, falls 14%, assaults/violent acts 14%, struck by object 10%. Annual occupational injury rate per 100,000 workers (2004) 4.8. Average duration of journey to work (2006) 25.0 minutes (private automobile 86.7%, of which drive alone 76.0%, carpool 10.7%; take public transportation 4.8%; walk 2.5%; work at home 4.0%; other 2.0%). Rate per 1,000 employed workers of discouraged workers (unemployed no longer seeking work; 2005) 3.1. **Access to services** (2005). Proportion of occupied dwellings having access to: electricity 100%; safe public water supply 100%; public sewage collection (1995) 77.0%; septic tanks (1995) 22.8%. **Social participation.** Eligible voters participating in last presidential election (2004) 60.7%. Population ages 16 and over volunteering for an organization (2005): 28.8%; median annual hours 50. Trade-union membership in total workforce (2005) 13.7%. **Social deviance** (2005). Offense rate per 100,000 population for: murder 5.6; rape 31.7; robbery 140.7; aggravated assault 291.1; motor-vehicle theft 416.7; burglary and housebreaking 726.7; larceny-theft 2,286.3; drug-abuse violation 560.1; drunkenness (2003) 149.1. Estimated drug and substance users (population ages 12 and over; 2004): cigarettes 24.9%; binge alcohol 22.8%; marijuana and hashish 6.1%. Rate per 100,000 population of suicide (2005) 10.7. **Leisure** (2002). Favorite leisure activities (percentage of total population ages 18 and over that undertook activity at least once in the previous year): movie 60.0%, exercise program 55.0%, gardening 47.0%, home improvement 42.0%, amusement park 42.0%, sports events 35.0%, charity work 29.0%. **Material well-being** (2003). Occupied dwellings with householder possessing: automobiles, trucks, or vans 91.4%, 1 car with or without trucks or vans 48.1%, 2 cars 23.8%, only trucks and vans 12.1%, no cars, trucks, or vans 8.6%, 3 or more cars 7.4%; telephone 95.5%; television receiver 99.0%; video and DVD players (2002) 91.2%; washing machine (2002) 80.1%; clothes dryer (2002) 75.9%; air conditioner (2002) 75.6%; cable television 77.2%; personal computers 61.8%; Internet connections 54.6%; broadband Internet 19.9%. **Recreational expenditures** (2003): US$660,700,000,000 (television and radio receivers, computers, and video equipment 18.4%; golfing, bowling, and other participatory activities 13.5%; sports supplies 10.3%; nondurable toys and sports equipment 9.1%; books and maps 5.8%; magazines and newspapers 5.5%; spectator amusements 5.4%, of which theater and opera 1.7%, spectator sports 2.1%, movies 1.5%; flowers, seeds, and potted plants 2.8%; other 29.2%).

National economy

Budget (2006). *Revenue:* US$2,285,491,000,000 (income tax 43.6%; social-insurance taxes and contributions 36.8%; corporate taxes 12.1%; excise taxes 3.2%; other 4.3%). *Expenditures:* US$2,708,677,000,000 (social security and medicare 33.1%; defense 18.9%; health 9.9%; interest on debt 8.1%; other 30.0%). **Total outstanding national debt** (September 2007): US$9,027,000,000,000, of which debt held by the public US$5,385,500,000,000, intragovernment holdings US$3,641,500,000,000. **Gross national income** (2006): US$13,150,600,000,000 (US$43,424 per capita). **Production**. *Agriculture, forestry, fishing* (value of production in US$'000,000 except as noted; 2005): corn (maize) 21,859, soybeans 16,928, alfalfa hay 7,320, wheat 7,140, cotton 5,574, grapes 3,013, potatoes 2,903, almonds 2,725, tomatoes 2,260, lettuce 1,982, rice 1,789, apples 1,787, lemons 1,498, strawberries 1,383, sugar beets (2004) 1,107, tobacco 1,053, beans 950, onions 922, mushrooms 908, peanuts (groundnuts) 846, sugarcane (2004) 821, cottonseed 809, sorghum 715, peppers 598, carrots 587, pistachios 574, broccoli 564, cherries 549, peaches 510, barley 506, sunflowers 472, walnuts (2004) 452, watermelons 410, pecans 400, oranges 398, cucumbers 383, blueberries 359, grapefruit 352, cabbage 325, pears 315, sweet potatoes 309, cantaloupe 300, avocados (2004) 293; livestock (number of live animals) 95,838,000 cattle, 61,197,000 pigs, 9,200,000 horses, 6,135,000 sheep, 1,950,000,000 chickens; roundwood 471,862,000 cu m (coniferous 312,700,000 cu m, non-coniferous 159,162,000 cu m), of which fuelwood 9%; fisheries production 5,360,579 metric tons (from aquaculture 9%); aquatic plants production 35,922 (from aquaculture, none). *Metals mining* (metal content in metric tons unless otherwise noted; 2005): molybdenum 56,900 (world rank: 1); beryllium 90 (world rank: 1); copper 1,150,000 (world rank: 2); lead 440,000 (world rank: 3); gold 250,000 kg (world rank: 3); palladium 14,200 kg (world rank: 3); platinum 4,200 kg (world rank: 4); zinc 760,000 (world rank: 5); iron 55,000,000 (world rank: 7); silver 1,300,000 kg (world rank: 7). *Nonmetals mining* (metric tons; 2005): diatomite 635,000 (world rank: 1); bromine 212,000 (world rank: 1); boron 1,230,000 (world rank: 2); perlite 506,000 (world rank: 2); vermiculite 105,000 (world rank: 2); kyanite 90,000 (world rank: 2); barite 500,000 (world rank: 3); feldspar 760,000 (world rank: 4); silicon 276,000 (world rank: 4). *Quarrying* (metric tons; 2005): salt 45,900,000 (world rank: 1); phosphate rock 38,300,000 (world rank: 1); gypsum 17,500,000 (world rank: 1); lime 20,000,000 (world rank: 2). *Manufacturing* (value added in US$'000,000; 2004): chemicals and chemical products 295,328, of which pharmaceuticals and medicine 120,870; transportation equipment 255,974, of which motor vehicle parts 70,796, motor vehicles 84,807, aerospace products and parts 67,594; food and food products 223,433; electronic products 214,650, of which navigational, measuring, medical, and scientific equipment 66,470, communications equipment 30,347, computers and related components 32,344; fabricated metal products 143,899; nonelectrical machinery 133,826; plastic and rubber products 91,517; paper and paper products 74,016; beverages and tobacco products 71,700; refined petroleum and coke 61,830; nonferrous metals 58,800; printing and publishing 57,250; general electrical equipment 52,723; furniture 45,441; wood and wood products 43,662; textiles 32,226; iron and steel 31,445. *Energy production (consumption):* electricity (kW-hr; 2004) 4,174,481,000,000 (4,185,793,000,000); hard coal (metric tons; 2004) 510,918,000 (502,548,000); lignite (metric tons; 2004) 497,961,000 (497,934,000); crude petroleum (barrels; 2004) 1,965,000,000 (5,869,000,000); petroleum products (metric tons; 2004) 814,664,000 (829,104,000); natural gas (cu m; 2004) 529,874,000,000 (622,400,000,000). *Domestic production of energy by source* (2005): coal 33.3%, natural gas 27.2%, crude petroleum 15.7%, nuclear power 11.8%, renewable energy 8.8%, other 3.2%. *Energy consumption by source* (2006): petroleum and petroleum products 40.3%, natural gas 22.4%, coal 22.5%, nuclear electric power 8.2%, hydroelectric and thermal 2.9%; other renewable energy 3.7%; *by end use* (2006): industrial 32.3%, residential and commercial 39.2%, transportation 28.5%. **Households.** Average household size (2006) 2.6; median annual income per household (2006) US$48,201, of which median Asian (including Hispanic) household US$64,238, median white (including Hispanic) household US$50,673, median non-Hispanic household US$52,423, median Hispanic household US$37,781, median black (including Hispanic) household US$31,969; sources of personal income (2004): wages and salaries 68.6%, transfer payments 14.5%, self-employment 9.3%; consumption expenditure (2005): housing 19.0%, transportation 18.0%, insurance and pension 11.2%, food at home 7.1%, fuel and utilities 6.9%, health 5.7%, food away from home 5.7%, recreation 5.1%, wearing apparel 4.1%, alcoholic beverages and tobacco products 1.6%. Average annual expenditure of "consumer units" (households, plus individuals sharing households or budgets; 2005): total US$46,409, of which housing US$15,167, transportation US$8,344, food US$5,931, pensions and social security US$5,204, health care US$2,664, clothing US$1,886, other US$7,213. Selected household characteristics (2006): total number of households 116,011,000, of which (family households by race) white including Hispanic 82.6%, black including Hispanic 12.1%, other 5.3%; Hispanic of any race 14.9%; (by tenure) owned 79,266,000 (68.3%), rented 35,129,000 (30.3%), other 1,616,000 (1.4%); family households 78,425,000, of which married couple 75.2%, female householder 18.4%, male householder 6.4%; nonfamily households 37,587,000, of which female living alone 46.8%, male living alone 36.0%, other 17.2%. **Population economically active** (2007): total 153,231,000 (civilian population only); activity rate of total population 50.6% (participation rates [2004]: ages 16–64, 74.0%; female 46.5%; unemployed [August 2007] 4.6%). **Selected balance of payments data.** Receipts from (US$'000,000): tourism (2005) 102,611; remittances (2006) 2,935; foreign direct investment (FDI) (2001–05 avg.) 101,785. Disbursements for (US$'000,000): tourism (2005) 95,730; remittances (2006) 42,794; FDI (2001–05 avg.) 119,779. Number of foreign visitors (2007) 56,716,277 (17,735,000 from Canada, 15,089,000 from Mexico, 11,406,486 from Europe); number of nationals traveling abroad (2006) 63,662,000 (19,659,000 to Mexico, 13,855,000 to Canada). **Land use** as % of total land area (2003): in temporary crops 19.3%, in permanent crops 0.3%, in pasture 25.9%; overall forest area (2005) 33.1%.

Foreign trade

Imports (2006): US$1,855,400,000,000 ([2005]; motor vehicles and parts 11.7%; crude petroleum 10.9%; chemicals and chemical products 7.7%; computers and office equipment 6.2%; electrical machinery 5.9%; industrial machinery 5.1%; wearing apparel 4.5%; food and beverages 4.1%; iron and steel 1.5%; footwear 1.1%). *Major import sources:* Canada 16.4%; China 15.5%; Mexico 10.7%; Japan 8.0%; Germany 4.8%; UK 2.9%; South Korea 2.5%; Taiwan 2.1%; France 2.0%; Venezuela 2.0%; Malaysia 2.0%; Italy 1.8%; Ireland 1.5%; Nigeria 1.5%. **Exports** (2006): US$1,037,300,000,000 (chemicals and related products 13.3%; electrical machinery 8.2%; motor vehicles 7.9%; agricultural commodities 7.0%; airplanes and parts 5.2%; power-generating machinery 4.6%; general industrial machinery 4.3%; telecommunications equipment 4.2%; computers and office equipment 3.9%; scientific and precision equipment 3.8%; specialized industrial machinery 3.7%). *Major export destinations:* Canada 22.2%; Mexico 12.9%; Japan 5.8%;

China 5.3%; UK 4.4%; Germany 4.0%; South Korea 3.1%; The Netherlands 3.0%; Singapore 2.4%; France 2.3%; Taiwan 2.2%; Belgium 2.1%; Brazil 1.9%.

Transport and communications

Transport. *Railroads* (2004): route length 156,300 km, of which Amtrak operates 35,610 km; passenger-km 41,574,000,000; metric ton-km cargo (2006) 2,835,000,000,000. *Roads* (2004): total length 6,370,400 km (paved 91%). *Vehicles* (2004): passenger cars 136,431,000; trucks and buses 100,811,000. *Navigable channels* (2004) 41,843 km; *oil pipeline* length (2003) 258,892 km; *gas pipeline* length (2004) 2,353,300 km. *Air transport* (2006): passenger-km 1,275,875,000,000; metric ton-km cargo 46,853,000,000. *Certified route passenger/cargo air carriers* (2005) 80; operating revenue (US$'000,000; 2006) 163,824; operating expenses 156,279. **Communications,** in total units (units per 1,000 persons). Daily newspaper circulation (2005): 53,300,000 (180); televisions (2003): 260,000,000 (893); telephone landlines (2006): 172,032,000 (572); cellular telephone subscribers (2006): 233,000,000 (774); personal computers (2005): 223,810,000 (755); total Internet users (2006): 197,800,000 (663); broadband Internet subscribers (2005): 49,391,000 (167).

Education and health

Literacy (2003): percentage of population ages 16 and over: "illiterate" (able to perform no more than the most simple literacy skills) 14%; "basically literate" (able to perform simple and everyday literacy activities) 29%; "intermediately and proficiently literate" (able to perform moderately challenging to complex literacy activities) 57%. **Health:** doctors of medicine (2004) 885,000 (1 per 337 persons), of which office-based practice 538,500; male 74.5%; female 25.5% (including specialties in internal medicine 18.9%, general and family practice 13.6%, pediatrics 9.4%, obstetrics and gynecology 6.3%, anesthesiology 5.6%, psychiatry 4.8%, general surgery 4.7%, emergency medicine 3.5%, orthopedic surgery 3.5%, cardiovascular diseases 3.2%, diagnostic radiology 3.1%, ophthalmology 3.0%, pathology 2.0%); doctors of osteopathy 54,100; nurses 2,421,000 (1 per 824 persons); dentists 167,000 (1 per 1,760 persons); hospital beds (2004) 956,000 (1 per 313 persons), of which nonfederal 95.0% (community hospitals 84.5%, psychiatric 9.0%, long-term general and special 1.6%), federal 5.0%; infant mortality rate per 1,000 live births (2006) 6.4. **Food** (2005): daily per capita caloric intake 3,754 (vegetable products 72.2%, animal products 27.8%); 143% of FAO recommended minimum. Per capita consumption of major food groups (kilograms annually; 2005): milk 256.4; fresh vegetables 125.5; cereal products 177.2; fresh fruits 122.7; red meat 62.7; potatoes 54.7; poultry products 55.8; fats and oil 31.6; sugar 30.2; fish and shellfish 23.4.

Military

Total active duty personnel (2006): 1,547,257 (army 38.5%, navy 24.3%, air force 22.5%, marines 12.1%, coast guard 2.6%). **Total reserve duty personnel** (2006): national guard 464,830 (army 75.6%, air force 24.4%); ready reserves 973,675 (army 55.4%, navy 16.0%, air force 18.3%, marines 9.4%, coast guard 0.9%). **Total special operations forces** (2006): active 31,496; reserve 11,247. **Military expenditure as percentage of GDP** (2005): 4.1%; per capita expenditure US$1,700. **Foreign military sales to the world** (2006): US$18,163,000,000, of which to Pakistan 19.2%, to Australia 13.4%, to Greece 11.7%, to Israel 5.8%, to Japan 5.7%, to Turkey 5.4%.

Background

The territory that is now the US was originally inhabited for several thousand years by numerous American Indian peoples who had probably emigrated from Asia. European exploration and settlement from the 16th century began displacement of the Indians. The first permanent European settlement, by the Spanish, was at St. Augustine FL, in 1565; the British settled Jamestown VA (1607), Plymouth MA (1620), Maryland (1632), and Pennsylvania (1681). They took New York, New Jersey, and Delaware from the Dutch in 1664, a year after the Carolinas had been granted to British noblemen. The British defeat of the French in 1763 ensured British political control over the 13 colonies.

Political unrest caused by British colonial policy culminated in the American Revolution (1775–83) and the Declaration of Independence (1776). The US was first organized under the Articles of Confederation (1781) and then finally under the Constitution (1787) as a federal republic. Boundaries extended west to the Mississippi River, excluding Spanish Florida. Land acquired from France by the Louisiana Purchase (1803) nearly doubled the country's territory. The US fought the War of 1812 with the British and acquired Florida from Spain in 1819. In 1830 it legalized removal of American Indians to lands west of the Mississippi River. Settlement expanded to the West Coast in the mid-19th century, especially after the discovery of gold in California in 1848. Victory in the Mexican War (1846–48) brought the territory of seven more future states (including California and Texas) into US hands. The northwestern boundary was established by treaty with Great Britain in 1846. The US acquired southern Arizona by the Gadsden Purchase (1853). It suffered disunity during the conflict between the slavery-based plantation economy in the South and the free industrial and agricultural economy in the North, culminating in the American Civil War and the abolition of slavery under the 13th Amendment.

After Reconstruction (1865–77), the US experienced rapid growth, urbanization, industrial development, and European immigration. In 1877 it authorized allotment of Indian reservation land to individual tribesmen, resulting in widespread loss of land to whites. By the beginning of the 20th century, it had acquired outlying territories, including Alaska, the Midway Islands, the Hawaiian Islands, the Philippines, Puerto Rico, Guam, Wake Island, American Samoa, the Panama Canal Zone, and the Virgin Islands.

The US participated in World War I during 1917–18. It granted suffrage to women in 1920 and citizenship to American Indians in 1924. The stock market crash of 1929 led to the Great Depression. The US entered World War II after the Japanese bombing of Pearl Harbor (7 Dec 1941). The explosion of the first atomic bomb on Hiroshima, Japan (6 Aug 1945), brought about the end of the war and set the US apart as a military power. After the war the US was involved in the reconstruction of Europe and Japan and embroiled in a rivalry with the Soviet Union that became known as the Cold War. It participated in the Korean War. In 1952 it granted autonomous commonwealth status to Puerto Rico.

Racial segregation in schools was declared unconstitutional in 1954. Alaska and Hawaii were made states in 1959, bringing the total to 50. In 1964 Congress passed the Civil Rights Act and authorized full-scale intervention in the Vietnam War. The mid- to late 1960s were marked by widespread civil disorder, including race riots and antiwar demonstrations. The US accomplished the first manned lunar landing in 1969. All US troops were withdrawn from Vietnam by 1973. The US led a coalition of forces against Iraq in the Persian Gulf War (1991), sent troops to Somalia (1992) to aid starving populations, and participated in NATO air strikes against Serb forces in the former Yugoslavia in 1995 and 1999. Administration of the Panama Canal was turned over to Panama in 1999. The US led another coalition invading Iraq in March 2003 to end the rule of Saddam Hussein.

Recent Developments

Pres. George W. Bush decided in 2007 to increase the US military presence in Iraq with a "surge" of some 30,000 reinforcements. The plan ran counter to majority opinion–from Congress, the Iraq Study Group, and US public-opinion polls. At the surge's peak, some 160,000 US troops were on Iraqi deployment. By year's end it had become obvious that the insurgency had lost some momentum–violent incidents were down by two-thirds and Iraqis had taken over security in many areas. Even so, US military deaths in Iraq reached 899 for the year, the highest number since the 2003 US-led incursion.

Islamic radicals, sheltered in sanctuaries in lawless areas of western Pakistan and financed in part by opium production, escalated armed clashes in Afghanistan, and for the first time, US troop deaths there topped 100. At a NATO summit in Bucharest, Romania, in April 2008, France, the Czech Republic, and Romania, among others, pledged to substantially increase their troop commitments in Afghanistan.

Democrats took control of Congress from Republicans in January 2007, promising major changes. However, Bush and the Republican minority, utilizing vetos and procedural rules, managed to alter or halt many initiatives. In the spring Democrats attached an amendment setting a timeline for withdrawal of US forces to a US$90 billion supplemental Iraq War appropriation. Bush rejected the measure–only his second veto in more than six years in office. Amid GOP warnings that US troops needed resupply, Democrats were forced to pass the appropriation without timeline amendments, part of the US$200 billion that Bush was able to obtain for the war in 2007 with no strings attached. President Bush vetoed five additional bills during the year, including ones that expanded federal funding for embryonic-stem-cell research and doubled expenditures for the State Children's Health Insurance Program, and threatened rejection of some 50 more. Republicans stymied a plan to force pharmaceutical companies to negotiate with the government over Medicare drug prices and a US$50 billion expansion for the Alternative Minimum Tax, a law originally written to ensure that the wealthy paid at least minimal taxes. A threatened veto forced removal of provisions rolling back tax breaks to oil and gas companies. Numerous investigations of past administration actions were launched; one, regarding the firing of eight US attorneys in 2006, led to the resignation of Attorney General Alberto Gonzales. Former vice presidential chief of staff I. Lewis ("Scooter") Libby was convicted in March 2007 of having lied about his involvement in the leak of a covert CIA officer's identity, but Bush quickly commuted his prison sentence. Congress was able to override only one Bush veto in 2007—an appropriations measure that included funding for rebuilding the hurricane-devastated Gulf coast. Congress also succeeded in raising the minimum wage for the first time in a decade, from US$5.15 to US$7.25 per hour by 2009, and passing a law to reduce interest rates on student loans. Congress provided a record funding increase for veterans' health care programs and significantly tightened Washington lobbying and ethics rules. Congress also passed new legislation to expand the use of alternative energy, increase vehicle mileage standards by 40% by 2020, and phase out incandescent light bulbs in favor of fluorescent lighting.

The US economy expanded by almost 3% for the year, though the unemployment rate rose from 4.4% to 5.0%. Of major concern was an overheated real-estate market that brokers had fueled by offering adjustable-rate mortgages at low initial interest rates. By mid-2007, however, a substantial minority of homeowners could not make their payments when their interest rates were adjusted upward, leading to rising delinquency rates and foreclosures. An estimated US$500 billion worth of "subprime" mortgage securities were devalued, reducing the lending capacity of financial institutions. The federal budget deficit declined to US$163 billion by the end of the 2007 fiscal year, but the trade deficit continued at a historic level, and the US dollar lost 10% of its value to the euro in 2007 alone.

An apparent foreign-relations success involved North Korea, which for four years had resisted calls to dismantle its fledgling nuclear-weapons capacity. In September 2007 negotiators announced that North Korea had agreed to catalog and dismantle its nuclear-testing sites in return for a US$300 million aid package. At year's end North Korea failed to honor a disclosure deadline, but in May 2008 the country turned over a large, if incomplete, file of documents relating to its nuclear programs.

US relations with Russia deteriorated during the year. US officials were openly critical of Vladimir Putin's centralization of control over the Russian government, suggesting democracy was being undermined, and this notion was strengthened when Putin, barred from seeking a third consecutive term as president in 2008, accepted the role of prime minister from his hand-picked successor in May 2008. As the US pushed toward installing missile defense shields in Poland and the Czech Republic, Russia suspended its participation in the 1990 Conventional Forces in Europe Treaty, an arms-control agreement, and threatened to aim nuclear missiles at European targets.

Internet resources: <www.seeamerica.org>.

Uruguay

Official name: República Oriental del Uruguay (Oriental Republic of Uruguay). **Form of government:** republic with two legislative houses (Senate [31]; Chamber of Representatives [99]). **Head of state and govern-**

ment: President Tabaré Ramón Vázquez Rosas (from 2005). **Capital:** Montevideo. **Official language:** Spanish. **Official religion:** none. **Monetary unit:** 1 peso uruguayo (UYU) = 100 centesimos; valuation (1 Jul 2008) US$1 = UYU 19.35.

Demography

Area: 68,679 sq mi, 177,879 sq km. **Population** (2007): 3,340,000. **Density** (2007): persons per sq mi 48.6, persons per sq km 18.8. **Urban** (2004): 91.8%. **Sex distribution** (2006): male 48.67%; female 51.33%. **Age breakdown** (2006): under 15, 23.2%; 15–29, 22.8%; 30–44, 20.5%; 45–59, 16.1%; 60–74, 11.4%; 75–84, 4.7%; 85 and over, 1.3%. **Ethnic composition** (2006): white (mostly Spanish, Italian, or mixed Spanish-Italian) 87.4%; black/part-black 8.4%; Amerindian/part-Amerindian 3.0%; other/unknown 1.2%. **Religious affiliation** (2004): Roman Catholic 54.0%; Protestant 11.0%; Mormon 3.0%; Jewish 0.8%; nonreligious/atheist 26.0%; other 5.2%. **Major cities** (2004): Montevideo 1,269,552; Salto 99,072; Paysandú 73,272; Las Piedras 69,222; Rivera 64,426. **Location:** southern South America, bordering Brazil, the South Atlantic Ocean, and Argentina.

Vital statistics

Birth rate per 1,000 population (2006): 14.8 (world avg. 20.3); (2002) within marriage 42.9%. **Death rate** per 1,000 population (2006): 9.4 (world avg. 8.6). **Total fertility rate** (avg. births per childbearing woman; 2006): 1.99. **Life expectancy** at birth (2006): male 72.5 years; female 79.0 years.

National economy

Budget (2005). *Revenue:* UYU 82,343,000,000 (tax revenue 67.9%, of which taxes on goods and services 49.1%; social security contributions 20.5%; nontax revenue 11.6%). *Expenditures:* UYU 89,947,000,000 (general public services 39.3%, of which public debt payments 22.6%; social security and welfare 19.0%; education 14.2%; health 7.9%; defense 5.2%). **Public debt** (external, outstanding; 2005): US$7,866,-000,000. **Production** (metric tons except as noted). *Agriculture, forestry, fishing* (2006): rice 1,300,000, soybeans 632,000, beef 516,000; livestock (number of live animals) 11,956,000 cattle, 9,712,000 sheep; roundwood (2005) 5,702,000 cu m, of which fuelwood 35%; fisheries production (2005) 125,953. *Mining and quarrying* (2005): limestone 1,185,000; clays 64,450; gold 3,151 kg. *Manufacturing* (value added in US$'000,000; 2003): food products 411; refined petroleum products 261; pesticides, soaps, and pharmaceuticals 106. *Energy production (consumption):* electricity (kW-hr; 2004) 8,183,000,000 (8,265,000,000); coal (metric tons; 2004) none (1,000); crude petroleum (barrels; 2004) none (15,437,000); petroleum products (metric tons; 2004) 2,021,000 (1,538,000); natural gas (cu m; 2004) none (111,000,000). **Households.** Average household size (2004) 3.1; average annual income per household (2005) UYU 177,264 (US$7,242). **Population economically active** (2006): total 1,580,400; activity rate 47.7% (participation rates: ages 14–64, 72.7%; female 43.5%; unemployed [June 2006–May 2007] 10.1%). **Gross national income** (at 2006 market prices): US$18,801,000,000 (US$5,640 per capita). **Selected balance of payments data.** Receipts from (US$'000,000): tourism (2005) 594; remittances (2006) 115; foreign direct investment (FDI) (2001–05 avg.) 368; official development assistance (2005) 73 (commitments). Disbursements for (US$'000,000): tourism (2005) 252; remittances (2006) 3.0; FDI (2001–05 avg.) 9.8. **Land use** as % of total land area (2003): in temporary crops 7.8%, in permanent crops 0.2%, in pasture 77.4%; overall forest area (2005) 8.6%.

Foreign trade

Imports (2006; c.i.f.): US$4,775,000,000 (crude and refined petroleum 27.5%; machinery and appliances 16.0%; chemicals and chemical products 12.7%; food, beverages, and tobacco products 8.7%; transport equipment 7.4%). *Major import sources:* Argentina 22.6%; Brazil 22.6%; Venezuela 12.6%; China 7.3%; US 6.8%. **Exports** (2006; f.o.b.): US$3,952,000,000 (beef 23.7%; hides and leather goods 8.6%; dairy products, eggs, and honey 6.9%; textiles and wearing apparel 6.8%; rice 5.5%; plastics and rubber products 5.1%). *Major export destinations:* Brazil 14.7%; US 13.2%; Argentina 7.6%; Russia 5.7%; Germany 4.2%.

Transport and communications

Transport. *Railroads* (2004): route length (2005) 2,073 km; passenger-km 11,000,000; metric ton-km cargo 297,000,000. *Roads* (2006): length 8,696 km (paved 40%). *Vehicles* (2005): passenger cars 523,866; trucks and buses 84,354. *Air transport* (2006; PLUNA only): passenger-km 1,096,000,000. **Communications,** in total units (units per 1,000 persons). Daily newspaper circulation (2004): 264,000 (79); televisions (2003): 838,000 (252); telephone landlines (2006): 987,000 (296); cellular telephone subscribers (2006): 2,330,000 (699); personal computers (2005): 450,000 (135); total Internet users (2006): 756,000 (227); broadband Internet subscribers (2006): 107,000 (32).

1 metric ton = about 1.1 short tons; 1 kilometer = 0.6 mi (statute); 1 metric ton-km cargo = about 0.68 short ton-mi cargo; c.i.f.: cost, insurance, and freight; f.o.b.: free on board

Education and health

Educational attainment (2004). Percentage of population ages 25 and over having: 0–3 years of education 7.7%; 4–6 years 32.1%; 7–9 years 18.4%; 10–12 years 22.7%; incomplete/complete higher 19.1%. **Literacy** (2003): population ages 15 and over literate 98.0%; males literate 97.6%; females literate 98.4%. **Health:** physicians (2006) 13,705 (1 per 243 persons); hospital beds (2003) 6,661 (1 per 499 persons); infant mortality rate per 1,000 live births (2006) 12.4. **Food** (2005): daily per capita caloric intake 3,576 (vegetable products 76%, animal products 24%); 187% of FAO recommended minimum.

Military

Total active duty personnel (2006): 25,100 (army 67.7%, navy/coast guard 19.9%, air force 12.4%). **Military expenditure as percentage of GDP** (2005): 1.3%; per capita expenditure US$67.

Background

The Spanish navigator Juan Díaz de Solís sailed into the Río de la Plata in 1516. The Portuguese established Colonia in 1680. Subsequently, the Spanish established Montevideo in 1726, driving the Portuguese from their settlement; 50 years later Uruguay became part of the Viceroyalty of the Río de la Plata. It gained independence from Spain in 1811. The Portuguese regained it in 1821, incorporating it into Brazil as a province. A revolt against Brazil in 1825 led to its being recognized as an independent state in 1828. It battled Paraguay in 1865–70. For much of World War II Uruguay remained neutral. The presidential office was abolished in 1951 and replaced with a nine-member council. The country adopted a new constitution and restored the presidential system in 1966. A military coup occurred in 1973, but the country returned to civilian rule in 1985. The 1990s brought a general upturn in the economy.

Recent Developments

The year 2007 was another one of steady economic growth for Uruguay, but the political climate was heated. GDP grew by a very solid 5.6%, and unemployment hovered around 9.5%, but inflation, which was running at 8.5%, was considerably above the central bank target range. The tax-reform program that was passed in January to help alleviate poverty and address inequality created an income tax that affected many businesspeople. The government faced increased pressure from public-sector unions demanding higher wages and from students and teachers opposed to the government's educational-reform project. The bitter conflict with Argentina over two pulp paper plants constructed on the Uruguayan side of the Río Uruguay had not been resolved by mid-2008, even as one of the plants was given permission by the Uruguayan government to begin production in November 2007.

Internet resources: <www.turismo.gub.uy>.

Uzbekistan

Official name: Uzbekiston Respublikasi (Republic of Uzbekistan). **Form of government:** republic with two legislative bodies (Senate [100]; Legislative Chamber

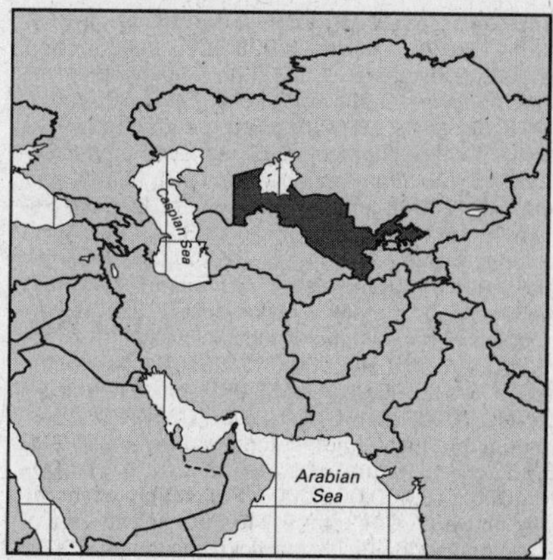

[120]). **Head of state and government:** President Islam Karimov (from 1990), assisted by Prime Minister Shavkat Mirziyayev (from 2003). **Capital:** Tashkent (Toshkent). **Official language:** Uzbek. **Official religion:** none. **Monetary unit:** sum (UZS; plural sumy); valuation (1 Jul 2008) US$1 = UZS 1,310.02.

Demography

Area: 172,700 sq mi, 447,400 sq km. **Population** (2007): 27,372,000. **Density** (2007): persons per sq mi 158.5, persons per sq km 61.2. **Urban** (2006): 35.9%. **Sex distribution** (2006): male 49.56%; female 50.44%. **Age breakdown** (2006): under 15, 32.9%; 15–29, 30.3%; 30–44, 19.6%; 45–59, 11.2%; 60–74, 4.3%; 75 and over, 1.7%. **Ethnic composition** (2000): Uzbek 78.3%; Tajik 4.7%; Kazakh 4.1%; Tatar 3.3%; Russian 2.5%; Karakalpak 2.1%; other 5.0%. **Religious affiliation** (2000): Muslim (mostly Sunni) 76.2%; Russian Orthodox 0.8%; Jewish 0.2%; nonreligious 18.1%; other 4.7%. **Major cities** (2007): Tashkent 1,959,190; Namangan 446,237; Andijon 321,622; Samarqand 312,863; Buxoro 249,037. **Location:** central Asia, bordering Kazakhstan, Kyrgyzstan, Tajikistan, Afghanistan, and Turkmenistan.

Vital statistics

Birth rate per 1,000 population (2006): 20.4 (world avg. 20.3). **Death rate** per 1,000 population (2006): 5.2 (world avg. 8.6). **Total fertility rate** (avg. births per childbearing woman; 2006): 2.91. **Life expectancy** at birth (2006): male 61.2 years; female 68.1 years.

National economy

Budget (2006). *Revenue:* UZS 6,406,000,000,000 (taxes on income and profits 20.2%; VAT 17.3%; taxes on property and resources 12.2%; excise taxes 10.2%). *Expenditures:* UZS 6,331,000,000,000 (health and education 34.4%; social security 27.0%; national economy 9.0%; centralized investments 8.1%). **Households.** Average household size (2004) 5.6; income per household (1995) UZS 35,165 (US$1,040); sources of income (2006): self-employment and rent 55.1%, wages and salaries 29.8%, transfers 15.1%; expenditure (1995): food and beverages 71.0%, clothing and footwear 14.0%, recreation 6.0%. **Public debt** (external, outstanding; 2006): US$3,343,000,000. **Produc-

tion (metric tons except as noted). *Agriculture, forestry, fishing* (2006): wheat 5,996,305, seed cotton 3,600,300, tomatoes 1,583,571; livestock (number of live animals) 10,034,000 sheep, 7,044,600 cattle, 1,973,100 goats, 16,600 camels; roundwood 26,700 cu m, of which fuelwood 69%; fisheries production (2005) 5,425 (from aquaculture 70%). *Mining and quarrying* (2004): copper (metal content) 80,000; uranium (metal content) 2,016; gold 93,000 kg. *Manufacturing* (value of production in UZS '000,000,000; 2006): nonferrous metals 2,705; mineral fuels 2,487; machinery and metalworking products 1,986. *Energy production (consumption):* electricity (kW-hr; 2006) 49,300,000,000 (47,000,000,000); lignite (metric tons; 2004) 2,699,000 (2,633,000); crude petroleum (barrels; 2006) 39,465,000 ([2004] 31,504,000); petroleum products (metric tons; 2004) 6,145,000 (5,852,000); natural gas (cu m; 2006) 62,500,-000,000 (48,400,000,000). **Population economically active** (2004): total 9,945,500; activity rate of total population 38.7% (participation rates [2001]: ages 16–59 [male], 16–54 [female] 70.4%; female 44.0%; unemployed [official rate; 2006] 0.2%). **Gross national income** (2006): US$16,108,000,000 (US$507 per capita). **Selected balance of payments data.** Receipts from (US$'000,000): tourism (2004) 28; remittances (2003) 600; foreign direct investment (2001–05 avg.) 53; official development assistance (2005) 206 (commitments). **Land use** as % of total land area (2003): in temporary crops 11.0%, in permanent crops 0.8%, in pasture 52.2%; overall forest area (2005) 8.0%.

Foreign trade

Imports (2006; c.i.f.): US$4,395,900,000 (machinery and metalworking products 40.3%; chemicals and chemical products 15.0%; base metals 10.4%; food products 8.1%). *Major import sources:* Russia 27.8%; South Korea 15.2%; China 10.4%; Kazakhstan 7.3%; Germany 7.1%. **Exports** (2006; f.o.b.): US$6,389,800,000 (cotton fiber 17.2%; energy products [including natural gas and crude petroleum] 13.1%; base metals [significantly gold] 12.9%; machinery and apparatus 10.1%). *Major export destinations:* Russia 23.7%; Poland 11.7%; China 10.4%; Turkey 7.7%; Kazakhstan 5.9%.

Transport and communications

Transport. *Railroads* (2006): length 3,950 km; passenger-km 2,352,000,000; metric ton-km cargo 19,300,000,000. *Roads* (2005): total length 84,400 km (paved 85%). *Vehicles* (1994): passenger cars 865,300; buses 14,500. *Air transport* (2006): passenger-km 4,700,000,000; metric ton-km cargo 79,400,000. **Communications,** in total units (units per 1,000 persons). Daily newspaper circulation (2004): 50,000 (1.9); televisions (2003): 7,232,000 (280); telephone landlines (2005): 1,794,000 (67); cellular telephone subscribers (2005): 720,000 (27); total Internet users (2006): 1,700,000 (63); broadband Internet subscribers (2005): 8,300 (0.3).

Education and health

Educational attainment (2002). Percentage of population ages 25 and over having: no formal education/unknown 2.5%; incomplete primary education 9.0%; primary 7.3%; secondary 66.0%; higher 15.2%. **Literacy** (2003): total population ages 15 and over literate 99.3%. **Health** (2005): physicians 70,159 (1 per 371 persons); hospital beds 135,143 (1 per 193 persons); infant mortality rate per 1,000 live births (2006) 70.0. **Food** (2005): daily per capita caloric intake 2,201 (vegetable products 81%, animal products 19%); 114% of FAO recommended minimum.

Military

Total active duty personnel (2006): 55,000 (army 73%, air force 27%); German troops 163. **Military expenditure as percentage of GDP** (2005): 0.4%; per capita expenditure US$2.

Background

Genghis Khan's grandson Shibaqan received the territory of Uzbekistan as his inheritance in the 13th century AD. His Mongols ruled over nearly 100 mainly Turkic tribes, who would eventually intermarry with the Mongols to form the Uzbeks and other Turkic peoples of central Asia. In the early 16th century, a federation of Mongol-Uzbeks invaded and occupied settled regions, including an area called Transoxania that would become the Uzbeks' permanent homeland. By the early 19th century the region was dominated by the khanates of Khiva, Bukhara, and Quqon, all of which eventually succumbed to Russian domination. The Uzbek Soviet Socialist Republic was created in 1924. In June 1990 Uzbekistan became the first Central Asian republic to declare sovereignty. It achieved full independence from the USSR in 1991. During the 1990s its economy was considered the strongest in Central Asia, though its political system was deemed harsh.

Recent Developments

Throughout 2007 the Uzbek leadership sought to reverse the country's worsening economy. In February Pres. Islam Karimov told his cabinet that Uzbekistan urgently needed to expand its output of oil and natural gas and to improve the tax-collection rate by fighting the "shadow" economy. The population had been driven to rely on this shadow economy by Karimov's previous restrictions on the import of consumer goods, which the country could not produce for itself. Despite his comments, however, the import restrictions remained. Throughout the year various officials called for increased domestic and foreign investment in the Uzbek economy. In March Foreign Minister Vladimir Norov asserted that the economy was stable and growing and that foreign investment was increasing. Official statistics seemed to bear this out, as the State Committee on Statistics claimed that in 2007 GDP rose by 9.5%, while industrial output rose by 12.1% and agricultural output by 6.1%. As well, official unemployment dropped by 9.0%. In August the Uzbek authorities liquidated the Uzbek-US Zeravshan-Newmont gold-extraction venture and gave its assets to a local firm, sending a discouraging signal to potential foreign investors.

Internet resources: <www.uzbektourism.uz>.

1 metric ton = about 1.1 short tons; 1 kilometer = 0.6 mi (statute); 1 metric ton-km cargo = about 0.68 short ton-mi cargo; c.i.f.: cost, insurance, and freight; f.o.b.: free on board

Vanuatu

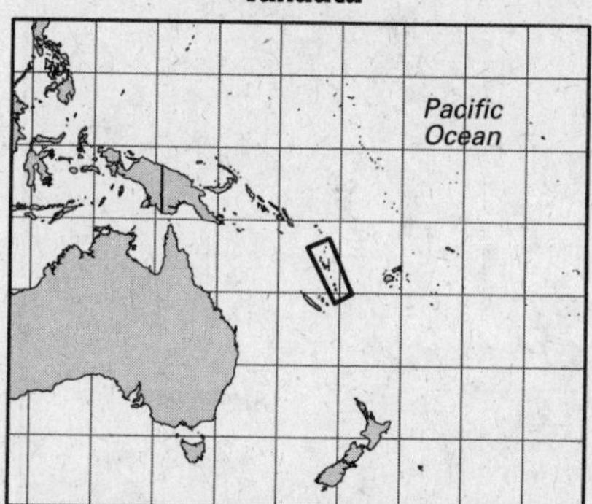

Official name: Ripablik blong Vanuatu (Bislama); République de Vanuatu (French); Republic of Vanuatu (English). **Form of government:** republic with a single legislative house (Parliament [52]). **Chief of state:** President Kalkot Mataskelekele (from 2004). **Head of government:** Prime Minister Ham Lini (from 2004). **Capital:** Port Vila. **Official languages:** Bislama; French; English. **Official religion:** none. **Monetary unit:** vatu (Vt); valuation (1 Jul 2008) US$1 = Vt 96.21.

Demography

Area: 4,707 sq mi, 12,190 sq km. **Population** (2007): 226,000. **Density** (2007): persons per sq mi 48.0, persons per sq km 18.5. **Urban** (2003): 22.8%. **Sex distribution** (2003): male 51.40%; female 48.60%. **Age breakdown** (1999): under 15, 42.2%; 15–29, 26.9%; 30–44, 17.0%; 45–59, 8.8%; 60–74, 3.7%; 75 and over, 1.4%. **Ethnic composition** (1999): Ni-Vanuatu (Melanesian) 98.7%; European and other Pacific Islanders 1.3%. **Religious affiliation** (2005): Protestant 70%, of which Presbyterian 32%, Anglican 13%, Adventist 11%; Roman Catholic 13%; traditional beliefs (John Frum cargo cult) 5%; other 12%. **Major towns** (2004): Port Vila 36,900; Luganville 12,300. **Location:** island group in Oceania, between the South Pacific Ocean and the Coral Sea.

Vital statistics

Birth rate per 1,000 population (2005): 23.1 (world avg. 20.3). **Death rate** per 1,000 population (2005): 7.9 (world avg. 8.6). **Total fertility rate** (avg. births per childbearing woman; 2005): 2.77. **Life expectancy** at birth (2005): male 61.0 years; female 64.1 years.

National economy

Budget (2005). *Revenue:* Vt 8,795,800,000 (tax revenue 83.5%, of which VAT 32.0%, tax on international trade 27.4%; nontax revenue 9.9%; foreign grants 6.6%). *Expenditures:* Vt 7,964,200,000 (wages and salaries 53.0%; goods and services 21.6%; transfers 11.1%; interest payments 4.4%; other [including technical assistance] 9.9%). **Public debt** (external, outstanding; 2004): US$71,900,000. **Production** (metric tons except as noted). *Agriculture, forestry, fishing* (2006): coconuts 315,000, copra 34,500, bananas 14,040; livestock (number of live animals) 152,000 cattle, 62,000 pigs, 12,000 goats; roundwood (2005) 119,000 cu m, of which fuelwood 76%; fisheries production (2005) 151,080. *Mining and quarrying:* small quantities of coral-reef limestone, crushed stone, sand, and gravel. *Manufacturing* (value added in Vt '000,000; 1995): food, beverages, and tobacco 645; wood products 423; fabricated metal products 377. *Energy production (consumption):* electricity (kW-hr; 2004) 44,000,000 (44,000,000); petroleum products (metric tons; 2004) none (29,000). **Land use** as % of total land area (2003): in temporary crops 1.6%, in permanent crops 7.0%, in pasture 3.4%; overall forest area (2005) 36.1%. **Population economically active** (1999): total 76,370; activity rate of total population 40.9% (participation rates: ages 15–64, 75.1%; female 44.9%; unemployed [2000] 1.7%). **Gross national income** (2006): US$344,000,000 (US$1,556 per capita). **Households.** Average household size (2004) 4.7; sources of income (1985): wages and salaries 59.0%, self-employment 33.7%; expenditure (1990; Port Vila and Luganville only): food and nonalcoholic beverages 30.5%, housing and energy 20.7%, transportation 13.2%, health and recreation 12.3%, tobacco and alcohol 10.4%. **Selected balance of payments data.** Receipts from (US$'000,000): tourism (2005) 74; remittances (2006) 11; foreign direct investment (FDI) (2001–05 avg.) 14; official development assistance (2005) 39. Disbursements for (US$'000,000): tourism (2005) 11; remittances (2006) 18; FDI (2001–05 avg.) 0.8.

Foreign trade

Imports (2006; c.i.f.): Vt 17,645,000,000 (machinery and transport equipment 25.9%; food and live animals 18.3%; mineral fuels 11.9%; chemicals and chemical products 9.6%). *Major import sources* (2005): Australia 41.3%; New Zealand 13.9%; Fiji 8.0%; Singapore 7.1%; France 3.4%. **Exports** (2006; f.o.b.): Vt 5,130,000,000 (domestic exports 71.2%, of which kava 13.6%, beef 9.1%, copra 6.3%, timber 6.0%, cocoa 5.4%; reexports 28.8%). *Major export destinations* (2005; domestic exports): EU 34.8%; Australia 14.7%; New Caledonia 7.5%; Japan 5.2%; New Zealand 1.3%.

Transport and communications

Transport. *Roads* (2000): total length 1,070 km (paved 24%). *Vehicles* (2001): passenger cars 2,600; trucks and buses 4,400. *Air transport* (2005; Air Vanuatu only): passenger-km 220,861,000; metric ton-km cargo 1,647,000. **Communications**, in total units (units per 1,000 persons). Daily newspaper circulation (2005): 2,000 (9.5); televisions (2004): 2,700 (13); telephone landlines (2005): 7,000 (32); cellular telephone subscribers (2005): 13,000 (59); personal computers (2005): 3,000 (14); total Internet users (2005): 8,000 (38); broadband Internet subscribers (2004): 20 (0.1).

Education and health

Educational attainment (1999). Percentage of population ages 15 and over having: no formal schooling 18.0%; incomplete primary education 20.6%; completed primary 35.5%; some secondary 12.2%; completed secondary 8.5%; higher 5.2%, of which university 1.3%. **Literacy** (2005): total population ages 15 and over literate 74%. **Health** (2004): physicians 29 (1 per 7,138 persons); hospital beds (2003) 397 (1 per 511 persons); infant mortality rate per 1,000 live births (2005) 55.2. **Food** (2005): daily per capita caloric intake 2,025 (vegetable products 81%, animal products 19%); 113% of FAO recommended minimum.

Military

Total active duty personnel (2006): none; in 2005 Vanuatu had a paramilitary force of about 200.

Background

The islands of Vanuatu were inhabited for at least 3,000 years by Melanesian peoples before being discovered in 1606 by the Portuguese. They were rediscovered by French navigator Louis-Antoine de Bougainville in 1768 and then explored by English mariner Capt. James Cook in 1774 and named the New Hebrides. Sandalwood merchants and European missionaries arrived in the mid-19th century; they were followed by British and French cotton planters. Control of the islands was sought by both the French and British, who agreed in 1906 to form a condominium government. During World War II a major Allied naval base was on Espíritu Santo; the island group escaped Japanese invasion. The New Hebrides became the independent Republic of Vanuatu in 1980. Much of the nation's housing was ravaged by a hurricane in 1987.

Recent Developments

Vanuatu enjoyed continued political stability and a steady 3% rate of economic growth in 2007. The value of primary commodities (coconut oil, kava, copra, and beef), which contributed about 20% to total exports, increased with the resumption of kava exports, and growing demand for copra was expected to generate higher incomes for the 65% of the population that depended on agriculture. The commodities sector was also expected to grow as a result of the government's successful use of coconut-oil-based biofuel for power generation and the planned use of biofuel in the government's vehicle fleet. Vanuatu's tourism was growing rapidly as a result of investment in hotels and increased airline services from major markets.

Internet resources: <www.vanuatutourism.com>.

Vatican City State

Official name: State of the Vatican City (Holy See). **Form of government:** ecclesiastical. **Chief of state:** Pope Benedict XVI (from 2005). **Head of government:** Secretary of State Tarcisio Cardinal Bertone (from 2006). **Capital:** Vatican City. **Languages:** Italian; Latin. **Religion:** Roman Catholic. **Monetary unit:** 1 euro (€) = 100 cents; valuation (1 Jul 2008) US$1 = €0.63.

Demography

Area: 0.17 sq mi, 0.44 sq km. **Population:** (2007): 930. **Density:** (2007): persons per sq mi 5,471, persons per sq km 2,114. **Location:** southern Europe, within the commune of Rome, Italy. **Annual budget:** US$209,000,000. **Industries:** banking and finance; printing; production of a small amount of mosaics and uniforms; tourism.

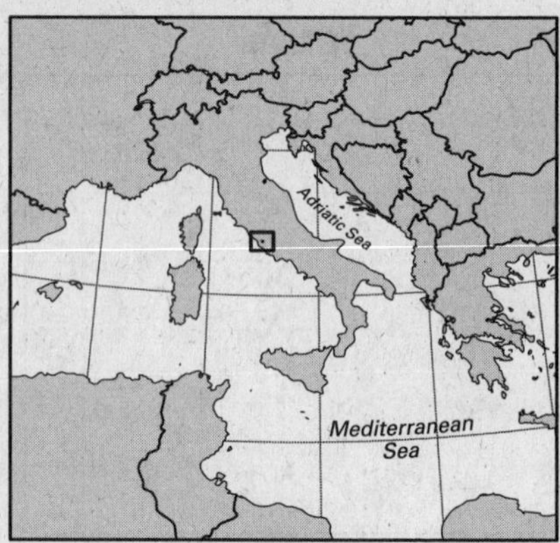

Background

Vatican City, the independent papal state, is the smallest independent state in the world. Its medieval and Renaissance walls form its boundaries except on the southeast, at St. Peter's Square. Within the walls is a miniature nation, with its own diplomatic missions, newspaper, post office, radio station, banking system, army of more than 100 Swiss Guards, and publishing house. Extraterritoriality of the state extends to Castel Gandolfo, summer home of the Pope, and to several churches and palaces in Rome proper. Its independent sovereignty was recognized in the Lateran Treaty of 1929. The pope has absolute executive, legislative, and judicial powers within the city. He appoints the members of the Vatican's government organs, which are separate from those of the Holy See. The state's many imposing buildings include St. Peter's Basilica, the Vatican Palace, and the Vatican Museums. Frescoes by Michelangelo and Pinturicchio in the Sistine Chapel and Raphael's Stanze are also there. The Vatican Library contains a priceless collection of manuscripts from the pre-Christian and Christian eras.

Recent Developments

There was an intense calendar of foreign initiatives in 2007, which included formal visits from US Pres. George W. Bush and British Prime Minister Tony Blair, as well as visits by the presidents of both Israel and the Palestinian Authority to Vatican City. The plight of Roman Catholics in China was also a focus of Vatican attention, with calls for Beijing to restrain action against priests not affiliated with the state-recognized Chinese Patriotic Catholic Association. Finally, stronger ties were pursued with the Muslim faith, adherents of which were announced in March 2008 to outnumber Roman Catholics for the first time in history.

Internet resources:
<www.vatican.va/phome_en.htm>.

Venezuela

Official name: República Bolivariana de Venezuela (Bolivarian Republic of Venezuela). **Form of government:** federal multiparty republic with a unicameral

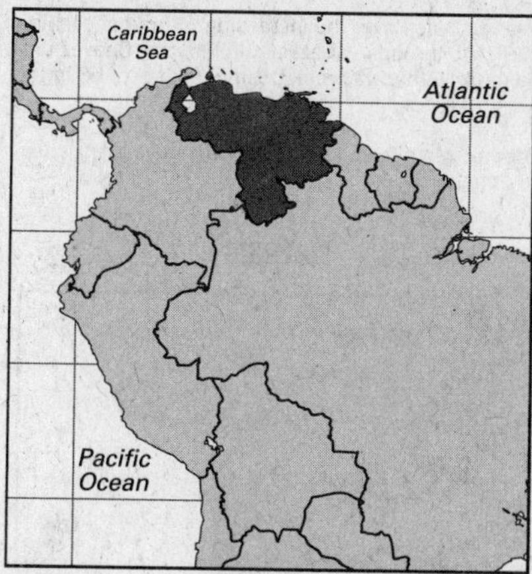

legislature (National Assembly [167]). **Head of state and government:** President Hugo Chávez Frias (from 2002). **Capital:** Caracas. **Official language:** Spanish; 31 indigenous Indian languages were made official in May 2002. **Official religion:** none. **Monetary unit:** 1 bolívar fuerte (BsF) = 100 céntimos; valuation (1 Jul 2008) US$1 = BsF 2,147.30 (the bolívar fuerte replaced the bolívar [Bs] 1 Jan 2008, at the rate of 1 BsF = Bs 1,000).

Demography

Area: 353,841 sq mi, 916,445 sq km. **Population** (2007): 26,024,000. **Density** (2007): persons per sq mi 73.5, persons per sq km 28.4. **Urban** (2005): 93.4%. **Sex distribution** (2006): male 49.52%; female 50.48%. **Age breakdown** (2006): under 15, 32.1%; 15–29, 26.9%; 30–44, 20.5%; 45–59, 13.2%; 60–74, 5.5%; 75–84, 1.5%; 85 and over, 0.3%. **Ethnic composition** (2000): mestizo 63.7%; local white 20.0%; local black 10.0%; other white 3.3%; Amerindian 1.3%; other 1.7%. **Religious affiliation** (2005): Roman Catholic 84.5%; Protestant 4.0%; nonreligious/other 11.5%. **Major cities (urban agglomerations)** (2001/2005): Caracas 1,836,000 (2,913,000); Maracaibo 1,609,000 (2,255,000); Valencia 1,196,000 (2,451,000); Barquisimeto 811,000 (1,029,000); Ciudad Guayana 629,000. **Location:** northern South America, bordering the Caribbean Sea, the North Atlantic Ocean, Guyana, Brazil, and Colombia.

Vital statistics

Birth rate per 1,000 population (2006): 21.8 (world avg. 20.3). **Death rate** per 1,000 population (2006): 5.1 (world avg. 8.6). **Total fertility rate** (avg. births per childbearing woman; 2006): 2.59. **Life expectancy** at birth (2006): male 70.0 years; female 76.3 years.

National economy

Budget (2006). *Revenue:* Bs 117,326,000,000,000 (petroleum income 52.9%, of which royalties 37.5%, taxes 13.0%; nonpetroleum income 47.1%, of which VAT 22.4%). *Expenditures:* Bs 117,255,000,000 (current expenditure 75.0%; development expenditure 22.8%; other 2.2%). **Public debt** (external, outstanding; 2005): US$29,317,000,000. **Production** (metric tons except as noted). *Agriculture, forestry, fishing* (2006): sugarcane 8,895,000, corn (maize) 2,375,000, rice 1,115,000; livestock (number of live animals) 16,615,000 cattle, 110,000,000 chickens; roundwood (2005) 4,906,000 cu m, of which fuelwood 78%; fisheries production (2005) 492,210 (from aquaculture 5%). *Mining and quarrying* (2005): iron ore (metal content) 13,200,000; bauxite 5,900,000; phosphate rock (gross weight) 392,000. *Manufacturing* (value added in Bs '000,000,000; 2004): food products 8,122; iron and steel 3,022; refined petroleum 2,890. *Energy production (consumption):* electricity (kW-hr; 2005) 99,200,000,000 (73,400,000,000); coal (metric tons; 2005) 8,200,000 ([2004] none); crude petroleum (barrels; 2006) 1,175,000,000 ([2004] 373,000,000); petroleum products (metric tons; 2004) 56,645,000 (21,738,000); natural gas (cu m; 2004) 24,975,000,000 (24,975,000,000). **Selected balance of payments data.** Receipts from (US$'000,000): tourism (2005) 641; remittances (2006) 300; foreign direct investment (FDI) (2001–05 avg.) 2,320. Disbursements for (US$'000,000): tourism (2005) 1,281; remittances (2006) 253; FDI (2001–05 avg.) 732. **Households.** Average household size (2005) 4.5; average annual household income (2006) Bs 13,848,000 (US$6,450); expenditure (2002): food and nonalcoholic beverages 27.3%, housing and energy 13.5%, transport 10.5%, expenditures in cafés and hotels 9.0%. **Gross national income** (2006): US$177,866,000,000 (US$6,540 per capita). **Population economically active** (2006): total 12,379,700; activity rate of total population 45.9% (participation rates: ages 15–64, 68.7%; female 38.6%; unemployed [July 2006–June 2007] 9.4%). **Land use** as % of total land area (2003): in temporary crops 2.9%, in permanent crops 0.9%, in pasture 20.7%; overall forest area (2005) 54.1%.

Foreign trade

Imports (2006): US$32,226,000,000 (machinery and apparatus 20.7%; road vehicles and parts 14.5%; chemicals and chemical products 10.4%). *Major import sources* (2005): US 31.6%; Colombia 11.0%; Brazil 9.1%; Mexico 6.9%; Panama 3.9%. **Exports** (2006): US$65,210,000,000 (petroleum [all forms] 89.6%; iron and steel [all forms] 2.7%; aluminum [all forms] 2.1%). *Major export destinations* (2005): US 50.9%; Puerto Rico/US Virgin Islands 7.8%; Netherlands Antilles 7.2%; Canada 2.4%; Colombia 1.8%.

Transport and communications

Transport. *Railroads:* route length (2005) 768 km; metric ton-km cargo (2004) 22,000,000. *Roads* (2004): total length 96,200 km (paved 34%). *Vehicles* (2004): passenger cars 2,466,000; trucks and buses 677,000. *Air transport* (2005): passenger-km 2,578,700,000; metric ton-km cargo 2,100,000. **Communications,** in total units (units per 1,000 persons). Daily newspaper circulation (2003): 1,981,000 (80); televisions (2004): 5,000,000 (201); telephone landlines (2006): 4,217,000 (164); cellular telephone subscribers (2006): 18,790,000 (733); personal computers (2005): 2,475,000 (98); total Internet users (2006): 4,160,000 (162); broadband Internet subscribers (2006): 538,000 (21).

Education and health

Educational attainment (2003). Percentage of head-of-household population having: no formal schooling 10.2%; primary education or less 38.5%; some secondary 36.9%; completed secondary/higher 14.4%. **Literacy** (2003): total population ages 15 and over literate 93.0%; males literate 93.3%; females literate 92.7%. **Health** (2003): physicians 35,756 (1 per 722 persons); hospital beds 74,866 (1 per 345 persons); infant mortality rate (2006) 23.0. **Food** (2005): daily per capita caloric intake 2,417 (vegetable products 82%, animal products 18%); 131% of FAO recommended minimum.

Military

Total active duty personnel (2006): 82,300 (army 41.3%, navy 22.2%, air force 8.5%, national guard 28.0%). **Military expenditure as percentage of GDP** (2005): 1.2%; per capita expenditure US$60.

Background

In 1498 Christopher Columbus sighted Venezuela; in 1499 the navigators Alonso de Ojeda, Amerigo Vespucci, and Juan de la Cosa traced the coast. A Spanish missionary established the first European settlement at Cumaná c. 1520. In 1718 it was included in the Viceroyalty of New Granada and was made a captaincy general in 1731. Venezuelan Creoles led by Francisco de Miranda and Simón Bolívar spearheaded the South American independence movement, and though Venezuela declared independence from Spain in 1811, that status was not assured until 1821. Military dictators generally ruled the country from 1830 until the overthrow of Marcos Pérez Jiménez in 1958. A new constitution adopted in 1961 marked the beginning of democracy. As a founding member of OPEC, it enjoyed relative economic prosperity from oil production during the 1970s, and its economy has remained dependent on the world petroleum market. The leftist president Hugo Chávez promulgated a new constitution in 1999, and he was reelected in 2002; a period of great political and economic tumult ensued.

Recent Developments

In November 2007 Venezuela's National Assembly approved modifications to the 1999 constitution that would increase the power of the national executive and central government. One of the changes would allow for the indefinite reelection of the president, and another would end the central bank's autonomy. Venezuela's GDP grew 23.6% in 2007 and for the first time exceeded US$200 billion. The nonpetroleum sector grew at a rate of 9.5% in 2007, though the petroleum sector contracted by 4.2%. Inflation between the beginning of 2007 and April 2008 reached 32.7%, one of the higher rates among less-developed economies. Petroleum remained central to Venezuela's economy. Over the past decade reserves of sweet crude had declined, and heavy-oil projects in the Orinoco Basin had become more important. In May 2007 Pres. Hugo Chávez unilaterally modified the contracts under which foreign companies exploited four heavy-oil projects. The administration of US Pres. George W. Bush was frustrated over the increasing volume of cocaine trafficked through Venezuela. In Moscow Chávez proclaimed, "Either we break US imperialism or US imperialism will definitely break the world."

Internet resources: <www.venezuelatuya.com/index-eng.htm?>.

Vietnam

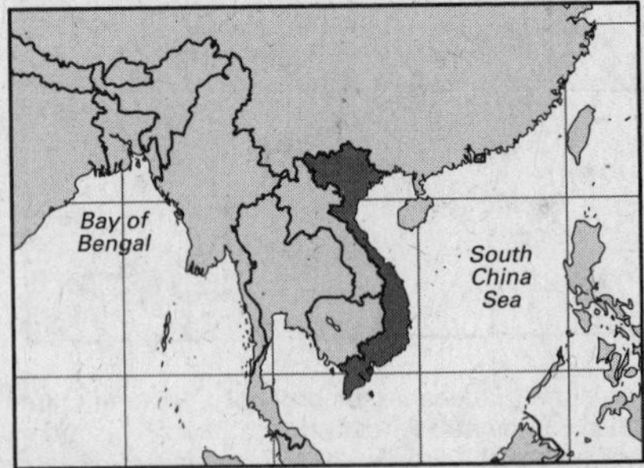

Official name: Cong Hoa Xa Hoi Chu Nghia Viet Nam (Socialist Republic of Vietnam). **Form of government:** socialist republic with one legislative house (National Assembly [493]). **Head of state:** President Nguyen Minh Triet (from 2006). **Head of government:** Prime Minister Nguyen Tan Dung (from 2006). **Capital:** Hanoi. **Official language:** Vietnamese. **Official religion:** none. **Monetary unit:** 1 dong (VND) = 10 hao = 100 xu; valuation (1 Jul 2008) US$1 = VND 16,844.50.

Demography

Area: 127,882 sq mi, 331,212 sq km. **Population** (2007): 87,375,000. **Density** (2007): persons per sq mi 683.2, persons per sq km 263.8. **Urban** (2005): 27.0%. **Sex distribution** (2005): male 49.14%; female 50.86%. **Age breakdown** (2005): under 15, 27.9%; 15–29, 30.1%; 30–44, 22.2%; 45–59, 12.1%; 60–74, 5.4%; 75–84, 1.9%; 85 and over, 0.4%. **Ethnic composition** (1999): Vietnamese 86.2%; Tho (Tay) 1.9%; Montagnards 1.7%; Thai 1.7%; Muong 1.5%; Khmer 1.4%; Nung 1.1%; Miao (Hmong) 1.0%; Dao 0.8%; other 2.7%. **Religious affiliation** (2005): Buddhist 48%; New-Religionist (mostly Cao Dai and Hoa Hao) 11%; traditional beliefs 10%; Roman Catholic 7%; Protestant 1%; nonreligious/atheist 20%; other 3%. **Major cities (urban agglomeration)** (2004/2005): Ho Chi Minh City 3,452,100 (5,065,000); Hanoi 1,420,400 (4,164,000); Haiphong 591,100 (1,873,000); Da Nang 459,400. **Location:** southeastern Asia, bordering China, the Gulf of Tonkin, the South China Sea, the Gulf of Thailand, Cambodia, and Laos.

Vital statistics

Birth rate per 1,000 population (2005): 17.1 (world avg. 20.3). **Death rate** per 1,000 population (2005): 6.2 (world avg. 8.6). **Total fertility rate** (avg. births per childbearing woman; 2005): 1.94. **Life expectancy** at birth (2005): male 67.8 years; female 73.6 years.

National economy

Budget (2004). *Revenue:* VND 166,900,000,000,000 (tax revenue 71.2%, of which VAT 24.6%, corporate taxes 22.3%, taxes on trade 19.8%; nontax revenues 27.6%; grants 1.2%). *Expenditures:* VND 190,200,000,000,000 (current expenditures 61.9%, of which social services 28.3%, economic services 5.5%, interest payment 3.2%; capital expenditures 38.1%). **Public debt** (external, outstanding; 2005): US$16,513,000,000. **Gross national income** (2006): US$56,583,000,000 (US$656 per capita). **Production** (metric tons except as noted). *Agriculture, forestry, fishing* (2006): rice 35,826,000, sugarcane 15,679,000, cassava 7,714,000; livestock (number of live animals) 26,855,300 pigs, 6,510,800 cattle, 2,921,000 buffalo, 64,380,000 ducks; roundwood (2005) 31,587,212 cu m, of which fuelwood 83%; fisheries production (2005) 3,367,200 (from aquaculture 43%); aquatic plants production (2005) 30,000 (from aquaculture 100%). *Mining and quarrying* (2005): phosphate rock 800,000; tin (metal content) 3,500. *Manufacturing* (value added in US$'000,000; 2000): food products 736; cement, bricks, and pottery 418; wearing apparel 376. *Energy production (consumption):* electricity (kW-hr; 2005) 53,320,000,000 ([2004] 46,029,000,000); coal (metric tons; 2005) 32,400,000 (14,900,000); crude petroleum (barrels; 2005) 131,200,000 ([2004] negligible); petroleum products (metric tons; 2004) 335,000,000 (11,358,000); natural gas (cu m; 2005) 6,342,000,000 (6,342,000,000). **Population economically active** (2004): total 43,242,000; activity rate 52.9% (participation rates: ages 15–64, 77.7%; female 49.0%; unemployed [2006] 4.8%). **Households** (2004). Average household size 4.4; average annual income per household (1997–98) VND 15,494,000 (US$1,165); sources of income: wages and salaries 32.7%, self-employment 27.0%, agriculture 22.6%; expenditure: food, beverages, and tobacco 53.5%, transportation and communications 10.8%, household furnishings 9.1%. **Selected balance of payments data.** Receipts from (US$'000,000): tourism (2005) 1,880; remittances (2006) 4,800; foreign direct investment (2001–05 avg.) 1,516; official development assistance (2005) 1,887 (commitments). **Land use** as % of total land area (2003): in temporary crops 21.2%, in permanent crops 7.5%, in pasture 2.1%; overall forest area (2005) 39.7%.

Foreign trade

Imports (2004; c.i.f.): US$31,500,000,000 (machinery equipment [including aircraft] 17.5%; petroleum products 11.5%; iron and steel 8.3%; garments and leather 7.2%; cloth 6.0%). *Major import sources* (2006): China 16.5%; Singapore 14.0%; Taiwan 10.7%; Japan 10.5%; South Korea 8.6%. **Exports** (2004; f.o.b.): US$26,500,000,000 (crude petroleum 22.1%; garments 17.1%; footwear 10.5%; fish, crustaceans, and mollusks 9.4%; electronic products 4.1%). *Major export destinations* (2006): US 19.7%; Japan 13.1%; Australia 9.2%; China 7.6%; Singapore 4.1%.

Transport and communications

Transport. *Railroads* (2005): route length 2,600 km; passenger-km 4,580,000,000; metric ton-km cargo 2,948,400,000. *Roads* (2004): total length 137,359 km (paved 44%). *Vehicles* (2003): passenger cars, trucks, and buses 600,000. *Air transport* (2005–06): passenger-km 11,787,000,000; metric ton-km cargo 251,100,000. **Communications,** in total units (units per 1,000 persons). Daily newspaper circulation (2003): 1,530,000 (19); televisions (2003): 15,938,000 (197); telephone landlines (2005): 15,845,000 (188); cellular telephone subscribers (2005): 9,593,000 (114); personal computers (2005): 1,174,000 (14); total Internet users (2005): 10,711,000 (130); broadband Internet subscribers (2005): 210,000 (2.5).

Education and health

Educational attainment (1999). Percentage of population ages 18 and over having: no formal education 9.0%; primary education 29.2%; lower secondary 32.5%; upper secondary 24.9%; incomplete/complete higher 4.3%; advanced degree 0.1%. **Literacy** (2003): percentage of population ages 15 and over literate 94.0%; males literate 95.8%; females literate 92.3%. **Health** (2006): physicians 52,800 (1 per 1,633 persons); hospital beds 198,400 (1 per 434 persons); infant mortality rate per 1,000 live births (2005) 26.0. **Food** (2005): daily per capita caloric intake 2,892 (vegetable products 87%, animal products 13%); 157% of FAO recommended minimum.

Military

Total active duty personnel (2006): 455,000 (army 90.5%, navy 2.9%, air force 6.6%). **Military expenditure as percentage of GDP** (2005): 6.0%; per capita expenditure US$38.

Background

A distinct Vietnamese group began to emerge c. 200 BC in the independent kingdom of Nam Viet, which was annexed to China in the 1st century BC. The Vietnamese were under continuous Chinese control until the 10th century AD. The southern region was gradually overrun by Vietnamese from the north in the late 15th century. The area was divided into two parts in the early 17th century, with the northern part known as Tonkin and the southern part as Cochin China. In 1802 the northern and southern parts of Vietnam were unified under a single dynasty.

Following several years of attempted French colonial expansion in the region, the French captured Saigon in 1859 and later the rest of the area, controlling it until World War II. The Japanese occupied Vietnam in 1940–45 and declared it independent at the end of World War II, a move the French opposed. The French and Vietnamese fought the First Indochina War until French forces with US financial backing were defeated at Dien Bien Phu in 1954; evacuation of French troops ensued.

Following an international conference at Geneva, Vietnam was partitioned along the 17th parallel, with the northern part under Ho Chi Minh and the southern part under Bao Dai; the partition was to be temporary, but the reunification elections scheduled for 1956 were never held. Bao Dai declared the independence of South Vietnam (Republic of Vietnam), while the Communists established North Vietnam (Democratic Republic of Vietnam). The activities of North Vietnamese guerrillas and pro-communist rebels in South Vietnam led to US intervention and the Vietnam War. A cease-fire agreement was signed in 1973, and US troops were withdrawn. The civil war soon resumed, and in 1975 North Vietnam invaded

South Vietnam and the South Vietnamese government collapsed. In 1976 the two Vietnams were united as the Socialist Republic of Vietnam. From the mid-1980s the government enacted a series of economic reforms and began to open up to Asian and Western nations. During the 1990s the US moved to normalize relations with it.

Recent Developments

In January 2007 Vietnam became the World Trade Organization's 150th member, and in October the country was elected to nonpermanent membership on the UN Security Council. These events set the context for an intense year of diplomacy. Pres. Nguyen Minh Triet visited Beijing in May, resulting in a joint communiqué that stressed long-term trade and economic cooperation and addressed territorial issues. In a speech delivered in California in June, Triet promoted bilateral trade and investment and reached out to the Vietnamese-American community. Prime Minister Nguyen Tan Dung visited India in July to cement a strategic partnership, then focused on trade and investment the following month on trips to Indonesia, the Philippines, Singapore, Myanmar (Burma), and Brunei. In September Dung made stops in Russia, Poland, and the Czech Republic before addressing the UN General Assembly. Meanwhile President Triet attended the Asia-Pacific Economic Cooperation summit in Australia and made a side visit to New Zealand.

Internet resources: <www.vietnamtourism.gov.vn/english>.

Virgin Islands (US)

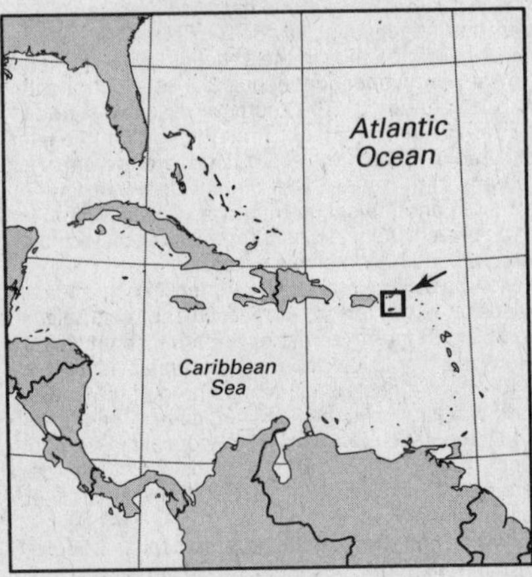

Official name: Virgin Islands of the United States. **Political status:** organized unincorporated territory of the US with one legislative house (Senate [15]). **Chief of state:** US President George W. Bush (from 2001). **Head of government:** Governor John deJongh, Jr. (from 2007). **Capital:** Charlotte Amalie. **Official language:** English. **Official religion:** none. **Monetary unit:** 1 US dollar (US$) = 100 cents.

Demography

Area: 136 sq mi, 353 sq km. **Population** (2007): 113,000. **Density** (2007): persons per sq mi 830.9, persons per sq km 320.1. **Urban** (2006): 94.4%. **Sex distribution** (2006): male 47.71%; female 52.29%. **Age breakdown** (2006): under 15, 22.4%; 15–29, 18.8%; 30–44, 20.0%; 45–59, 21.3%; 60–74, 13.4%; 75 and over, 4.1%. **Ethnic composition** (2000): black 76.2%; white 13.1%; mixed race 3.5%; Asian 1.1%; other 6.1%. **Religious affiliation** (2000): Christian 96.3%, of which Protestant 51.0% (including Anglican 13.0%), Roman Catholic 27.5%, independent Christian 12.2%; nonreligious 2.2%; other 1.5%. **Major towns** (2000): Charlotte Amalie 11,004 (urban agglomeration 18,914); Christiansted 2,637; Frederiksted 732. **Location:** northeastern Caribbean, islands between the Caribbean Sea and the North Atlantic Ocean.

Vital statistics

Birth rate per 1,000 population (2006): 14.0 (world avg. 20.3); (1998) within marriage 30.2%. **Death rate** per 1,000 population (2006): 6.4 (world avg. 8.6). **Total fertility rate** (avg. births per childbearing woman; 2006): 2.17. **Life expectancy** at birth (2006): male 75.2 years; female 83.1 years.

National economy

Budget. Revenue (2006): US$718,700,000 (income tax 54.1%; corporate taxes 25.8%). *Expenditures* (2004): US$592,000,000 (direct federal expenditures 100%). **Public debt** (2005–06): US$1,150,000,000. **Production.** *Agriculture, forestry, fishing* (value of sales in US$'000; 2002): ornamental plants and other nursery products 799, livestock and livestock products 775 (notably cattle and calves and hogs and pigs), vegetables 340 (notably tomatoes and cucumbers); livestock (number of live animals; 2006) 8,000 cattle, 4,000 goats, 3,200 sheep; fisheries production (2005) 1,269 metric tons. *Mining and quarrying:* sand and crushed stone for local use. *Manufacturing* (value of sales in US$'000; 2002): beverages and tobacco products 44,766; stone, clay, and glass products 32,939; computer and electronic products 22,875. *Energy production (consumption):* electricity (kW-hr; 2005) 996,100,000 (926,400,000); coal (metric tons; 2002) none (290,000); crude petroleum (barrels; 2002) none (149,000,000); petroleum products (metric tons; 2002) 18,801,000 (1,588,000). **Households** (2004). Average household size 2.5; average annual income per household US$37,201; sources of income (1999): wages and salaries 73.9%, transfers 10.0%, self-employment 8.8%; expenditures (2001): housing 38.8%, food and beverages 12.5%, transportation 11.1%, education and communications 7.1%. **Population economically active** (2004): total 44,299; activity rate of total population 39.7% (participation rates: ages 16 and over 53.1%; female 52.7%; unemployed [2007] 5.9%). **Gross domestic product** (at 2006 market prices): US$3,080,000,000 (US$27,300 per capita). **Selected balance of payments data.** Receipts from (US$'000,000): tourism (2006) 1,466. **Land use** as % of total land area (2003): in temporary crops 6%, in permanent crops 3%, in pasture 9%; overall forest area (2005) 28%.

1 metric ton = about 1.1 short tons; 1 kilometer = 0.6 mi (statute); 1 metric ton-km cargo = about 0.68 short ton-mi cargo; c.i.f.: cost, insurance, and freight; f.o.b.: free on board

Foreign trade

Imports (2005): US$10,243,300,000 (foreign crude petroleum 85.3%; other [significantly manufactured goods] 14.7%). *Major import sources:* US 11.3%; other countries (mostly Venezuela) 88.7%. **Exports** (2005): US$10,476,300,000 (refined petroleum 89.5%; unspecified [significantly rum and watches] 10.5%). *Major export destinations:* US 95.0%.

Transport and communications

Transport. *Roads* (2004): total length 1,257 km (paved 95%). *Vehicles* (2006): registered vehicles 69,330. Cruise ships (2006–07): passenger arrivals 1,900,253. *Air transport* (2006–07; St. Croix and St. Thomas airports only): passenger arrivals 676,039. **Communications,** in total units (units per 1,000 persons). Daily newspaper circulation (2005): 15,000 (134); televisions (2000): 65,000 (594); telephone landlines (2006): 65,000 (576); cellular telephone subscribers (2005): 80,000 (713); total Internet users (2005): 30,000 (268); broadband Internet subscribers (2005): 3,000 (27).

Education and health

Educational attainment (2004). Percentage of population ages 25 and over having: no formal schooling 0.5%; incomplete primary to incomplete secondary 39.1%; complete secondary 29.8%; some higher 11.9%; undergraduate 13.8%; advanced degree 4.9%. **Health** (2005): physicians 165 (1 per 680 persons); hospital beds (main hospitals on St. Thomas and St. Croix only) 320 (1 per 350 persons); infant mortality rate per 1,000 live births (2006) 7.9.

Military

Total active duty personnel (2006): no domestic military force is maintained; the US is responsible for defense and external security.

Background

The Virgin Islands of the US probably were originally settled by Arawak Indians, but they were inhabited by the Caribs when Christopher Columbus landed on St. Croix in 1493. St. Croix was occupied by the Dutch, English, French, and Spanish and was at one time owned by the Knights of Malta. Denmark occupied St. Thomas, St. John, and St. Croix and established them as a Danish colony in 1754. The US purchased the Danish West Indies in 1917 for US$25 million and changed the name to the Virgin Islands. They were administered by the US Department of the Interior from 1931. In 1954 the Organic Act of the Virgin Islands created the current governmental structure, and in 1970 the first popularly elected governor took office. The area suffered extensive damage by hurricanes in 1995.

Recent Developments

The US Virgin Islands Water and Power Authority in January 2007 presented a US$1.2 billion, 10-year plan designed to break its dependence on oil-fired generation by substituting increasing amounts of renewable energy. Officials called for 20% of the dependency's fuel needs to be met using renewable energy sources, including wind and solar energy and, after a March 2008 government visit to Nevis, geothermal operations.

Internet resources: <www.usvitourism.vi>.

Yemen

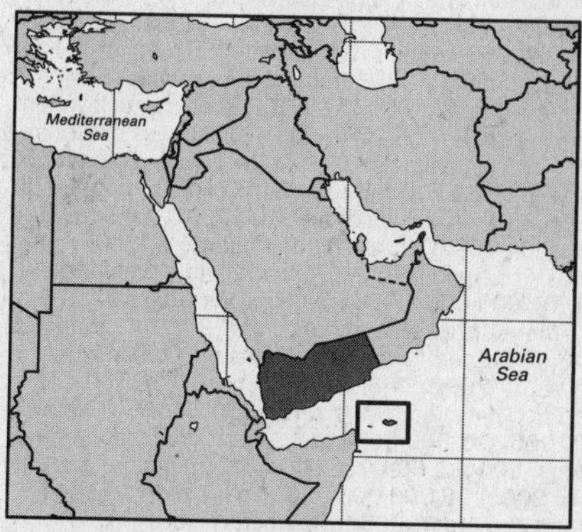

Official name: Al-Jumhuriyah al-Yamaniyah (Republic of Yemen). **Form of government:** multiparty republic with two legislative houses (Consultative Council [111]; House of Representatives [301]). **Head of state:** President Major General ʿAli ʿAbdallah Salih (from 1990). **Head of government:** Prime Minister ʿAli Muhammad Mujawar (from 2007). **Capital:** Sanaa. **Official language:** Arabic. **Official religion:** Islam. **Monetary unit:** 1 Yemeni rial (YR) = 100 fils; valuation (1 Jul 2008): US$1 = YR 198.95.

Demography

Area: 203,891 sq mi, 528,076 sq km. **Population** (2007): 22,231,000. **Density** (2007): persons per sq mi 109.0, persons per sq km 42.1. **Urban** (2006): 28.6%. **Sex distribution** (2004): male 50.99%; female 49.01%. **Age breakdown** (2004): under 15, 45.6%; 15–29, 29.5%; 30–44, 12.8%; 45–59, 6.9%; 60–74, 3.8%; 75–84, 1.0%; 85 and over, 0.4%. **Ethnic composition** (2000): Arab 92.8%; Somali 3.7%; black 1.1%; Indo-Pakistani 1.0%; other 1.4%. **Religious affiliation** (2005): Muslim, nearly 100%, of which Sunni 58%, Shiʿi 42%. **Major cities** (2004): Sanaa 1,707,586; Aden 589,419; Taʿizz (2001) 450,000; Al-Hudaydah (2001) 425,000; Al-Mukalla (2001) 165,000. **Location:** the Middle East, bordering Oman, the Arabian Sea, the Gulf of Aden, the Red Sea, and Saudi Arabia.

Vital statistics

Birth rate per 1,000 population (2006): 42.8 (world avg. 20.3). **Death rate** per 1,000 population (2006): 8.3 (world avg. 8.6). **Natural increase rate** per 1,000 population (2006): 34.5 (world avg. 11.7). **Total fertility rate** (avg. births per childbearing woman; 2006): 6.58. **Life expectancy** at birth (2006): male 60.2 years; female 64.1 years.

National economy

Budget (2006). *Revenue:* YR 1,437,000,000,000 (oil revenue 75.5%; tax revenue 18.5%; nontax revenue

6.0%). *Expenditures:* YR 1,405,000,000,000 (transfers and subsidies 31.2%; wages and salaries 26.0%; interest on debt 6.3%). **Public debt** (external, outstanding; 2005): US$4,717,000,000. **Population economically active** (2004): total 4,244,000; activity rate of total population 21.6% (participation rates: ages 15–64, 41.8%; female 12.1%; unemployed 16.2%). **Production** (metric tons except as noted). *Agriculture, forestry, fishing* (2006): sorghum 401,843, potatoes 226,366, tomatoes 211,734, khat (qat) 147,444 (khat's (qat's) agricultural and nonagricultural contribution is about 10% of total GDP; khat (qat) cultivation employs nearly 15% of the labor force); livestock (number of live animals) 8,197,024 sheep, 8,041,955 goats, 1,463,700 cattle, 347,145 camels; roundwood 366,885 cu m, of which fuelwood 100%; fisheries production 229,660. *Mining and quarrying* (2005): salt 90,000; gypsum 38,000. *Manufacturing* (value added in YR '000,000; 2006): food and beverages 121,761; cement, bricks, and ceramics 34,294; tobacco 26,556. *Energy production (consumption):* electricity (kW-hr; 2006) 5,336,900,000 (3,624,500,000); crude petroleum (barrels; 2006) 133,000,000 ([2005] 31,000,000); petroleum products (metric tons; 2004) 2,804,000 (4,047,000); natural gas (cu m; 2005) 38,000,000,000 (n.a.). **Land use** as % of total land area (2003): in temporary crops 2.9%, in permanent crops 0.2%, in pasture 30.4%; overall forest area (2005) 1.0%. **Gross national income** (2006): US$17,083,000,000 (US$786 per capita). **Households.** Average household size (2004) 7.1; income per household (1998) YR 29,035 (US$217); expenditures (1999): food and nonalcoholic beverages 43.8%, tobacco and khat (qat) 14.8%, housing and energy 13.3%. **Selected balance of payments data.** Receipts from (US$'000,000): tourism (2005) 181; remittances (2005) 1,283; foreign direct investment (2001–05 avg.) 24; official development assistance (2005) 336. Disbursements for (US$'000,000): tourism (2005) 167; remittances (2005) 109.

Foreign trade

Imports (2006; c.i.f.): YR 1,043,119,407,000 (crude and refined petroleum 24.8%; food and live animals 19.2%; machinery and apparatus 13.7%; base and fabricated metals 10.2%; transport equipment 9.7%). *Major import sources:* UAE 22.0%; Saudi Arabia 9.7%; Switzerland 9.1%; China 7.3%; Kuwait 6.7%. **Exports** (2006; f.o.b.): YR 1,316,197,658,000 (crude and refined petroleum 91.7%; food and live animals 3.9%, of which fish 2.0%; machinery and apparatus 1.3%). *Major export destinations:* India 24.0%; China 22.5%; Thailand 14.4%; UK 5.9%; US 5.7%.

Transport and communications

Transport. *Roads* (2006): total length 71,300 km (paved 9%). *Vehicles* (2004): passenger cars 522,437; trucks and buses 506,766. *Air transport* (2002): passenger-km 1,598,000,000; metric ton-km cargo (2005) 67,000,000. **Communications,** in total units (units per 1,000 persons). Daily newspaper circulation (2006): 236,000 (11); televisions (2003): 6,780,000 (359); telephone landlines (2005): 968,000 (47); cellular telephone subscribers (2006): 2,978,000 (139); personal computers (2005): 300,000 (14); total Internet users (2006): 270,000 (13).

Education and health

Educational attainment (2004). Percentage of population ages 10 and over having: no formal schooling 46.0%; reading and writing ability 31.5%; primary education 12.0%; secondary 7.2%; higher 3.3%. **Literacy** (2005): percentage of total population ages 15 and over literate 53.0%; males literate 74.7%; females literate 52.4%. **Health** (2006): physicians 5,980 (1 per 3,495 persons); hospital beds 14,413 (1 per 1,450 persons); infant mortality rate per 1,000 live births 59.5. **Food** (2005): daily per capita caloric intake 1,926 (vegetable products 92%, animal products 8%); 109% of FAO recommended minimum.

Military

Total active duty personnel (2006): 66,700 (army 90.0%, navy 2.5%, air force 7.5%). **Military expenditure as percentage of GDP** (2005): 7.0%; per capita expenditure US$50.

Background

Yemen was the home of ancient Minaean, Sabaean, and Himyarite kingdoms. The Romans invaded the region in the 1st century AD. In the 6th century it was conquered by Ethiopians and Persians. Following conversion to Islam in the 7th century, it was ruled nominally under a caliphate. The Egyptian Ayyubid dynasty ruled there from 1173 to 1229, after which the region passed to the Rasulids. From 1517 through 1918, the Ottoman Empire maintained varying degrees of control, especially in the northwestern section. A boundary agreement was reached in 1934 between the northwestern imam-controlled territory, which subsequently became the Yemen Arab Republic (North Yemen), and the southeastern British-controlled territory, which subsequently became the People's Democratic Republic of Yemen (South Yemen). Relations between the two Yemens remained tense and were marked by conflict throughout the 1970s and 1980s. Reaching an accord, the two officially united as the Republic of Yemen in 1990. Its 1993 elections were the first free, multiparty general elections held in the Arabian Peninsula, and they were the first in which women participated. In 1994, after a two-month civil war, a new constitution was approved.

Recent Developments

According to the UN High Commissioner for Refugees, more than 20,000 people entered Yemen illegally from East Africa in 2007, leaving poverty and war behind, and at least 400 died along the way, with as many missing and feared dead. The number entering in the first two months of 2008 alone topped 8,700. A mosque was firebombed in April 2007 by two unidentified attackers, who doused people with gasoline before lighting them on fire. In July a suicide bomber attacked a convoy of Spanish tourists, killing seven Spaniards and two Yemenis at the Queen of Sheba temple in Marib. Yemen continued to work with US special forces based in Djibouti to fight al-Qaeda, members of which were thought to travel throughout Yemen.

Internet resources: <www.yementourism.com>.

1 metric ton = about 1.1 short tons; 1 kilometer = 0.6 mi (statute); 1 metric ton-km cargo = about 0.68 short ton-mi cargo; c.i.f.: cost, insurance, and freight; f.o.b.: free on board

Zambia

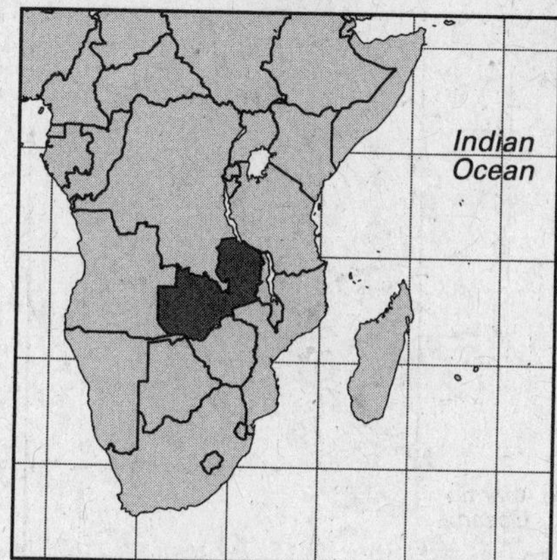

Official name: Republic of Zambia. **Form of government:** multiparty republic with one legislative house (National Assembly [158]). **Head of state and government:** President Rupiah Banda (acting; from 2008). **Capital:** Lusaka. **Official language:** English. **Official religion:** none; however, in 1996 Zambia was declared a Christian nation per the preamble of a constitutional amendment. **Monetary unit:** 1 Zambian kwacha (K) = 100 ngwee; valuation (1 Jul 2008) US$1 = K 3,210.00.

Demography

Area: 290,585 sq mi, 752,612 sq km. **Population** (2007): 11,477,000. **Density** (2007): persons per sq mi 39.5, persons per sq km 15.2. **Urban** (2006): 36.9%. **Sex distribution** (2005): male 49.75%; female 50.25%. **Age breakdown** (2005): under 15, 46.2%; 15–29, 30.6%; 30–44, 13.4%; 45–59, 6.1%; 60–74, 3.0%; 75–84, 0.6%; 85 and over, 0.1%. **Ethnic composition** (2000): Bemba 21.5%; Tonga 11.3%; Lozi 5.2%; Nsenga 5.1%; Tumbuka 4.3%; Ngoni 3.8%; Chewa 2.9%; other 45.9%. **Religious affiliation** (2000): Christian 82.4%, of which Roman Catholic 29.7%, Protestant (including Anglican) 28.2%, independent Christian 15.2%, unaffiliated Christian 5.5%; traditional beliefs 14.3%; Baha'i 1.8%; Muslim 1.1%; other 0.4%. **Major cities** (2000): Lusaka 1,084,703; Ndola 374,757; Kitwe 363,734; Kabwe 176,758; Chingola 147,448. **Location:** southern Africa, bordering Tanzania, Malawi, Mozambique, Zimbabwe, Botswana, Namibia, Angola, and the Democratic Republic of the Congo.

Vital statistics

Birth rate per 1,000 population (2006): 41.0 (world avg. 20.3). **Death rate** per 1,000 population (2006): 21.8 (world avg. 8.6). **Total fertility rate** (avg. births per childbearing woman; 2006): 5.39. **Life expectancy** at birth (2006): male 38.0 years; female 38.2 years.

National economy

Budget (2006). *Revenue:* K 16,635,000,000,000 (grants 60.2%; tax revenue 38.4%, of which income tax 18.0%, VAT 10.9%, excise taxes 5.6%; nontax revenue 1.4%). *Expenditures:* K 9,248,000,000,000 (current expenditures 77.1%; capital expenditures 20.3%; other 2.6%). **Production** (metric tons except as noted). *Agriculture, forestry, fishing* (2006): sugarcane 2,700,000, cassava 950,000, corn (maize) 865,000, fresh-cut flowers (value of sales; 2000) US$21,000,000; livestock (number of live animals) 2,600,000 cattle, 1,270,000 goats, 340,000 pigs; roundwood (2005) 8,053,000 cu m, of which fuelwood 90%; fisheries production (2005) 70,125 (from aquaculture 7%). *Mining and quarrying* (2005): copper (metal content) 447,000; cobalt (metal content) 9,300; amethyst 1,100,000 kg. *Manufacturing* (2005): cement 435,000; refined copper 399,000; vegetable oils (2001) 11,800. *Energy production (consumption):* electricity (kW-hr; 2004) 8,512,000,000 (8,281,000,000); coal (metric tons; 2004) 233,000 (153,000); crude petroleum (barrels; 2004) none (3,938,000); petroleum products (metric tons; 2004) 490,000 (528,000). **Households.** Average household size (2005) 5.1; average annual income per household (2004) K 6,024,360 (US$1,261); expenditure (1993–94): food, beverages, and tobacco 57.1%, transportation and communications 9.6%, housing and energy 8.5%. **Selected balance of payments data.** Receipts from (US$'000,000): tourism (2005) 164; foreign direct investment (2001–05 avg.) 165; official development assistance (2005) 945. Disbursements for (US$'000,000): tourism (2005) 94; remittances (2006) 24. **Population economically active** (2000): total 3,165,200; activity rate of total population 32.0% (participation rates: ages 12–64, 55.8%; female 41.3%; unemployed 12.7%). **Gross national income** (2006): US$10,339,000,000 (US$884 per capita). **Public debt** (external, outstanding; 2005): US$4,085,000,000. **Land use** as % of total land area (2003): in temporary crops 7.1%, in permanent crops 0.04%, in pasture 40.4%; overall forest area (2005) 57.1%.

Foreign trade

Imports (2004): US$2,017,000,000 (chemicals and chemical products 16.4%; nonelectrical machinery and equipment 16.2%; printed matter 11.8%; petroleum [all forms] 9.5%; road vehicles 7.6%). *Major import sources:* South Africa 46.2%; UK 14.2%; Saudi Arabia 7.1%; Zimbabwe 6.0%; France 2.9%. **Exports** (2004): US$1,461,000,000 (copper 43.1%; cobalt 15.9%; food and live animals 9.5%; cotton 8.2%). *Major export destinations:* South Africa 25.6%; UK 17.0%; Switzerland 16.0%; Tanzania 7.4%; Democratic Republic of the Congo 7.0%.

Transport and communications

Transport. *Railroads* (1998): length (2005) 2,173 km; passenger-km 586,000,000; metric ton-km cargo 702,000,000. *Roads* (2001): total length 91,440 km (paved 22%). *Vehicles* (1996): passenger cars 157,000; trucks and buses 81,000. *Air transport* (2006; Zambian Airways Limited only): passenger-km 56,609,000. **Communications,** in total units (units per 1,000 persons). Daily newspaper circulation (2004): 55,000 (5); televisions (2003): 551,000 (51); telephone landlines (2006): 93,000 (7.9); cellular telephone subscribers (2006): 1,663,000 (140); personal computers (2005): 131,000 (11); total Internet users (2006): 500,000

(42); broadband Internet subscribers (2006): 2,300 (0.2).

Education and health

Educational attainment (2001–02). Percentage of population ages 15 and over having: no formal schooling/unknown 14.7%; some primary education 33.4%; completed primary 19.7%; some secondary 22.0%; completed secondary 5.9%; higher 4.3%. **Literacy** (2006): population ages 15 and over literate 68.0%; males literate 76.3%; females literate 59.8%. **Health:** physicians (2004) 1,264 (1 per 8,672 persons); hospital beds (2004) 21,924 (1 per 500 persons); infant mortality rate per 1,000 live births (2006) 100.5. **Food** (2005): daily per capita caloric intake 1,642 (vegetable products 94%, animal products 6%); 90% of FAO recommended minimum.

Military

Total active duty personnel (2006): 15,100 (army 89.4%; air force 10.6%). **Military expenditure as percentage of GDP** (2005): 0.7%; per capita expenditure US$4.

Background

Archaeological evidence suggests that early humans roamed present-day Zambia one to two million years ago. Ancestors of the modern Tonga tribe reached the region early in the 2nd millennium BC, but other modern peoples from Congo and Angola reached the country only in the 17th and 18th centuries. Portuguese trading missions were established early in the 18th century. Emissaries of Cecil Rhodes and the British South Africa Co. concluded treaties with most of the Zambian chiefs during the 1890s. The company administered the region known as Northern Rhodesia until 1924, when it became a British protectorate. It was part of the Central African Federation of Rhodesia and Nyasaland in 1953–63. In 1964 Northern Rhodesia became the independent republic of Zambia. A constitutional amendment was passed in 1990 allowing opposition parties; the following years were filled with political tension.

Recent Developments

In January 2007 Pres. Levy Mwanawasa launched Zambia's Fifth National Development Plan, which focused on improving health, education, and the infrastructure and encouraging foreign investment. In April China made Zambia a loan of US$39 million to repair flood damage, and in May Zambia received US$50 million from Western donors to help clean up pollution created by mining. In June the United Kingdom agreed to provide about US$800 million to relieve poverty over the next decade. The country's decaying railway system received US$250 million from the UK, South Africa, and the US to connect copper mines in Zambia and eventually to link Zambia's railway system with Angola's Benguela Railway, while in October Japan agreed to help further improve Zambia's infrastructure.

Internet resources: <www.zambiatourism.com>.

Zimbabwe

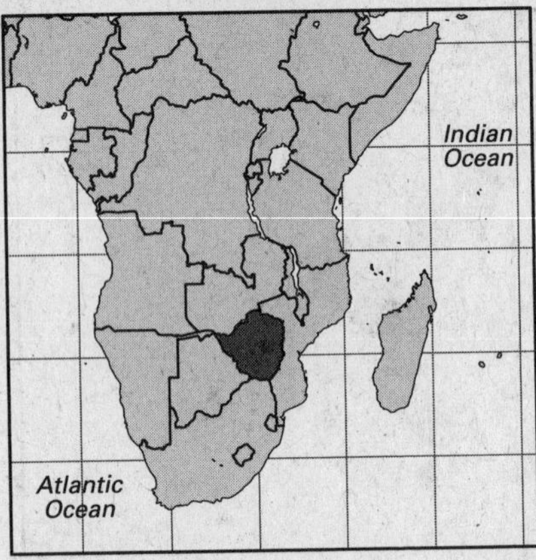

Official name: Republic of Zimbabwe. **Form of government:** multiparty republic with two legislative houses (Senate [93]; House of Assembly [210]). **Head of state and government:** President Robert Mugabe (from 1987). **Capital:** Harare. **Official language:** English. **Official religion:** none. **Monetary unit:** 1 (new third) Zimbabwe dollar (Z$) = 100 cents; valuation (1 Jul 2008) US$1 = Z$1,081,091.75 (the [new third] Z$ replaced the [new second] Z$ 6 Sep 2007, at the rate of 1 [new third] Z$ = [new second] Z$1,200; the [new second] Z$ had replaced the [old] Z$ on 1 Aug 2006, at the rate of 1 [new second] Z$ = [old] Z$1,000; in September 2007 the black-market value was nearly [new third] Z$250,000 = US$1).

Demography

Area: 150,872 sq mi, 390,757 sq km. **Population** (2007): 12,311,000. **Density** (2007): persons per sq mi 81.6, persons per sq km 31.5. **Urban** (2006): 36.4%. **Sex distribution** (2005): male 49.95%; female 50.05%. **Age breakdown** (2005): under 15, 37.6%; 15–29, 35.2%; 30–44, 14.5%; 45–59, 7.7%; 60–74, 3.8%; 75 and over, 1.2%. **Ethnic composition** (2003): Shona 71%; Ndebele 16%; other African 11%; white 1%; mixed race/Asian 1%. **Religious affiliation** (2005): African independent Christian 38%; traditional beliefs 25%; Protestant 14%; Roman Catholic 8%; Muslim 1%; other (mostly unaffiliated Christian) 14%. **Major cities** (2002): Harare 1,444,534; Bulawayo 676,787; Chitungwiza 321,782; Mutare 170,106; Gweru 141,260. **Location:** southern Africa, bordering Mozambique, South Africa, Botswana, Namibia, and Zambia.

Vital statistics

Birth rate per 1,000 population (2005): 28.2 (world avg. 20.3). **Death rate** per 1,000 population (2005): 21.9 (world avg. 8.6). **Total fertility rate** (avg. births per childbearing woman; 2005): 3.18. **Life expectancy** at birth (2005): male 40.2 years; female 38.0 years.

National economy

Budget (2004). *Revenue:* (old) Z$8,071,700,000,000 (tax revenue 96.2%, of which income tax 50.5%, sales tax 29.4%, customs duties 11.5%, excise tax 3.5%; nontax revenue 3.8%). *Expenditures:* (old) Z$9,630,900,000,000 (current expenditures 87.3%, of which goods and services 52.1%, transfer payments 21.7%, interest payments 13.5%; development expenditure 12.7%). **Population economically active** (2003): total 5,542,000; activity rate of total population 43.1% (participation rates: ages 15–64, 74.0%; female 44.0%; unemployed [2006] 70%). **Production** (metric tons except as noted). *Agriculture, forestry, fishing* (2006): sugarcane 3,600,000, corn (maize) 900,000, seed cotton 280,000; livestock (number of live animals) 5,400,000 cattle, 3,000,000 goats, 610,000 sheep; roundwood (2005) 9,107,600 cu m, of which fuelwood 89%; fisheries production (2005) 15,452 (from aquaculture 16%). *Mining and quarrying* (2005): chromite 614,720; asbestos 122,000; nickel (metal content) 8,556. *Manufacturing* (value added in US$'000,000; 1998): beverages 171; foodstuffs 148; textiles 99. *Energy production (consumption):* electricity (kW-hr; 2004) 9,908,000,000 (11,948,000,000); coal (metric tons; 2004) 3,398,000 (3,435,000); petroleum products (metric tons; 2004) none (594,000). **Public debt** (external, outstanding; 2005): US$3,222,-000,000. **Households.** Average household size (2004) 4.5; income per household (1992) (old) Z$1,689 (US$332); expenditure (1995): food 33.6%, housing 17.3%, beverages and tobacco 16.0%, household durable goods 7.5%. **Gross national income** (2006): US$1,734,000,000 (US$131 per capita). **Selected balance of payments data.** Receipts from (US$'000,-000): tourism (2005) 99; remittances (2005) 500–1,300; foreign direct investment (2001–05 avg.) 29; official development assistance (2005) 220 (commitments). Disbursements for (US$'000,000): tourism (1998) 131. **Land use** as % of total land area (2003): in temporary crops 8.3%, in permanent crops 0.3%, in pasture 44.5%; overall forest area (2005) 45.3%.

Foreign trade

Imports (2004): US$1,989,000,000 (fuel and electricity 23.3%; machinery and transport equipment 21.0%; chemicals and chemical products 20.2%; food 8.1%). *Major import sources:* South Africa 50.5%; Botswana 4.3%; UK 4.0%; Zambia 2.5%; US 1.9%. **Exports** (2004): US$1,679,700,000 (gold 15.6%; tobacco 13.5%; ferroalloys 11.0%; platinum 10.4%; cotton lint 7.3%; horticultural products [including cut flowers] 5.0%). *Major export destinations:* South Africa 30.2%; Switzerland 6.0%; UK 5.9%; China 4.8%; Germany 4.0%.

Transport and communications

Transport. *Railroads* (2004): route length 3,077 km; passenger-km (1998) 408,223,000; metric ton-km cargo 1,377,000. *Roads* (2002): total length 97,267 km (paved 19%). *Vehicles* (2002): passenger cars 570,866; trucks and buses 84,456. *Air transport* (2006; Air Zimbabwe only): passenger-km 671,185,-000; metric ton-km cargo 8,547,000. **Communications,** in total units (units per 1,000 persons). Daily newspaper circulation (2004): 166,000 (14); televisions (2004): 610,000 (50); telephone landlines (2006): 332,000 (25); cellular telephone subscribers (2006): 833,000 (64); personal computers (2005): 850,000 (71); total Internet users (2006): 1,220,000 (93); broadband Internet subscribers (2006): 10,000 (0.8).

Education and health

Educational attainment (1992). Percentage of population ages 25 and over having: no formal schooling 22.3%; primary 54.3%; secondary 13.1%; higher 3.4%. **Literacy** (2006): percentage of total population ages 15 and over literate 92.4%; males literate 95.5%; females literate 89.3%. **Health:** physicians (2004) 2,086 (1 per 5,792 persons); hospital beds (1996) 22,975 (1 per 501 persons); infant mortality rate per 1,000 live births (2005) 52.3. **Food** (2005): daily per capita caloric intake 1,794 (vegetable products 93%, animal products 7%); 97% of FAO recommended minimum.

Military

Total active duty personnel (2006): 29,000 (army 86.2%, air force 13.8%). **Military expenditure as percentage of GDP** (2005): 2.3%; per capita expenditure US$11.

Background

Remains of Stone Age cultures dating back 500,000 years have been found in the Zimbabwe area. The first Bantu-speaking peoples reached it during the 5th–10th centuries AD, driving the San (Bushmen) inhabitants into the desert. A second migration of Bantu-speakers began c. 1830. During this period the British and Afrikaners moved up from the south, and the area came under the administration of the British South Africa Co. in 1889–1923. Called Southern Rhodesia (1911–64), it became a self-governing British colony in 1923. The colony united in 1953 with Nyasaland (Malawi) and Northern Rhodesia (Zambia) to form the Central African Federation of Rhodesia and Nyasaland. The federation dissolved in 1963, and Southern Rhodesia reverted to its former colonial status. In 1965 it issued a unilateral declaration of independence considered illegal by the British government, which led to economic sanctions against it. The country proclaimed itself a republic in 1970 and called itself Rhodesia in 1964–79. In 1979 it instituted limited majority rule and changed its name to Zimbabwe Rhodesia. It was granted independence by Britain in 1980 and became Zimbabwe. Robert Mugabe, Zimbabwe's first prime minister, became president in 1987. Although a multiparty system was established in 1990, Mugabe's rule became more and more autocratic.

Recent Developments

After a year in which Morgan Tsvangirai and his opposition Movement for Democratic Change (MDC) had been campaigning for "mass action" to effect regime change, Pres. Robert Mugabe in 2007 banned political rallies across Zimbabwe. Further attempts by the opposition to mount demonstrations were blocked by police, and in March MDC leaders in Harare were arrested. Tsvangirai drove to the police station where his supporters were being held and was himself arrested and savagely beaten. In late March 2008, the presidential election was contested. In the weeks leading up to the poll, there were reports of widespread violence and intimidation by supporters of Mugabe. After delaying the publication of the election results, which MDC supporters insisted showed that Tsvangirai had won the office outright, the electoral commission claimed that a runoff was required. Tsvangirai withdrew, however, after weeks of violence against his supporters. Mugabe won the presidency unopposed, but by September the issue of leadership of the country had not been resolved.

Internet resources: <www.gta.gov.zw>.

Antarctica

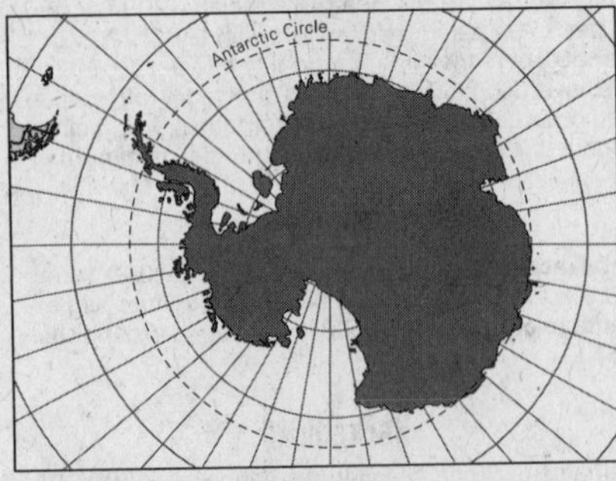

Background

The Russian F.G. von Bellingshausen, the Englishman Edward Bransfield, and the American Nathaniel Palmer all claimed first sightings of the continent in 1820. The period from the 1760s to c. 1900 was dominated by the exploration of Antarctic and subantarctic seas. In the early 20th century, the "heroic era" of Antarctic exploration, Robert Scott and, later, Ernest Shackleton made expeditions deep into the interior. Roald Amundsen reached the South Pole in December 1911, and Scott followed in 1912. The first half of the 20th century was also Antarctica's colonial period. Seven nations claimed sectors of the continent, while many other nations carried out explorations. In 1957–58, 12 nations established over 50 stations on the continent for cooperative study. In 1961 the Antarctic Treaty, which reserved Antarctica for free and nonpolitical scientific study, was enacted. A 1991 agreement imposed a permanent ban on mineral exploitation.

Recent Developments

The International Polar Year began in March 2007, and it brought together polar experts to study the North and South poles in depth with emphasis on their roles in global climate processes. During the 2006–07 austral summer, 37,506 tourists visited Antarctica, and nearly 25,000 landed in the Antarctic Treaty area, a 14% yearly increase. In November the tour ship *Explorer* struck ice near the South Shetland Islands and sank. All of the passengers and crew were rescued, but the incident raised concerns about the potential damage that could result from increased tourism. A German-led research expedition collected samples of creatures living up to 6 km (3.7 mi) below the surface of the Weddell Sea, hundreds of species of which had never before been seen. Using more than 1,000 images, American and British scientists completed the first high-definition map of Antarctica, which was 10 times more detailed than any map previously made.

Internet resources: <www.antarctica.org>.

Arctic Regions

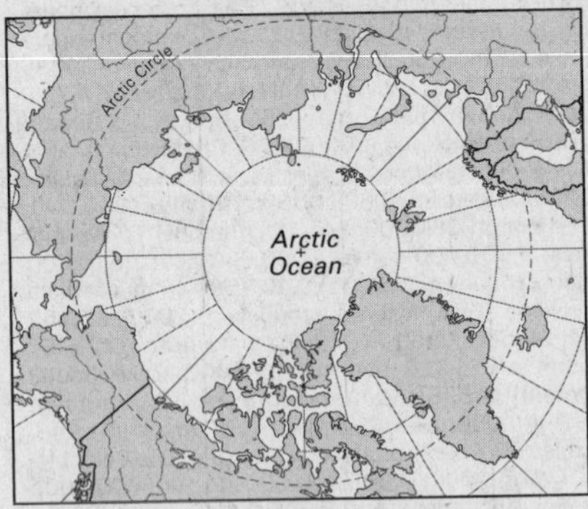

The Arctic regions may be defined in physical terms (astronomical [north of the Arctic Circle], climatic [above the 10 °C (50 °F) July isotherm], or vegetational [above the northern limit of the tree line]) or in human terms (the territory inhabited by the circumpolar cultures). The region includes portions of Canada, the US, Russia, Finland, Sweden, Norway, Iceland, and Greenland (part of Denmark). The Arctic Ocean, 14.09 million sq km (5.44 million sq mi) in area, constitutes about two-thirds of the region. The land area consists of permanent ice cap, tundra, or taiga. The population of peoples belonging to the circumpolar cultures (2007 est.) is about 530,000 (Aleuts [in Russia and Alaska], more than 4,000; Athabascans [in North America], 45,000; Inuits [or Eskimos, in Russian Chukhotka, North America, and Greenland], 160,000; Sami [or Lapps, in Northern Europe], 70,000; and 41 indigenous peoples [in the Russian North], 250,000). International organizations concerned with the Arctic include the Arctic Council, the Inuit Circumpolar Council, and the Indigenous Peoples' Secretariat. In 2007 Arctic sea ice melted dramatically. The new record-low ice extent, set in September, was 4.13 million sq km (1.59 million sq mi). This extent of sea ice was 23% less than that recorded in 2005, when the previous record low was set, and 39% below the long-term average from 1979 to 2000. In August a Russian research team used manned submersibles to place a Russian flag on the seabed at the North Pole. The US, Canada, and Denmark challenged Russia's claim. The US Geological Survey estimated that the Arctic held 25% of the world's undiscovered oil and natural gas reserves. The Northwest Passage became ice free for a short period of time in 2007, the first occurrence in recorded history of a completely open passage. Canada, which maintained that the passage through the Arctic archipelago was a domestic waterway, announced that it was building eight Arctic patrol ships and began work on a deepwater port at the eastern entrance to the Northwest Passage. In 2007 the Intergovernmental Panel on Climate Change released a report confirming that the Arctic had experienced the greatest warming of any region on the planet.

Membership in International Organizations

African Union (AU; formerly [until 2002] Organization for African Unity)
Founded: 1963. **Members:** 52 countries of Africa (all except Morocco), Western Sahara.
Web site: <www.africa-union.org>.

Andean Community
Founded: 1969. **Members:** Bolivia, Colombia, Ecuador, Peru; associate members Argentina, Brazil, Chile, Paraguay, Uruguay; observer states Mexico, Panama.
Web site: <www.comunidadandina.org>.

Asia-Pacific Economic Cooperation (APEC)
Founded: 1989. **Members:** Australia, Brunei, Canada, Chile, China, Hong Kong, Indonesia, Japan, Republic of Korea, Malaysia, Mexico, New Zealand, Papua New Guinea, Peru, Philippines, Singapore, Taiwan, Thailand, US, Vietnam.
Web site: <www.apec.org>.

Association of Southeast Asian Nations (ASEAN)
Founded: 1967. **Members:** Brunei, Cambodia, Indonesia, Laos, Malaysia, Myanmar (Burma), Philippines, Singapore, Thailand, Vietnam.
Web site: <www.aseansec.org>.

Caribbean Community and Common Market (CARICOM)
Founded: 1973. **Members:** Antigua and Barbuda, The Bahamas (Community member only), Barbados, Belize, Dominica, Grenada, Guyana, Haiti, Jamaica, Montserrat, Saint Kitts and Nevis, Saint Lucia, Saint Vincent and the Grenadines, Suriname, Trinidad and Tobago; associate members Anguilla, Bermuda, British Virgin Islands, Cayman Islands, Turks and Caicos Islands.
Web site: <www.caricom.org>.

Common Market for Eastern and Southern Africa (COMESA)
Founded: 1994. **Members:** Burundi, Comoros, Democratic Republic of the Congo, Djibouti, Egypt, Eritrea, Ethiopia, Kenya, Libya, Madagascar, Malawi, Mauritius, Rwanda, Seychelles, The Sudan, Swaziland, Uganda, Zambia, Zimbabwe.
Web site: <www.comesa.int>.

Commonwealth (also called Commonwealth of Nations)
Founded: 1931. **Members:** United Kingdom and 52 other countries, all of which were once under British rule or administratively connected to another member country (Fiji was suspended in December 2006); Nauru is a Special Member.
Web site: <www.thecommonwealth.org>.

Commonwealth of Independent States (CIS)
Founded: 1991. **Members:** Armenia, Azerbaijan, Belarus, Georgia, Kazakhstan, Kyrgyzstan, Moldova, Russia, Tajikistan, Turkmenistan, Uzbekistan, Ukraine.
Web site: <www.cisstat.com>.

Community of Portuguese Language Countries (CPLP)
Founded: 1996. **Members:** Angola, Brazil, Cape Verde, East Timor, Guinea-Bissau, Mozambique, Portugal, São Tomé and Príncipe; observer states Equatorial Guinea, Mauritius.
Web site: <www.cplp.org>.

Council of Europe
Founded: 1949. **Members:** 47 European and former Soviet countries; observer states Canada, Japan, Mexico, US, Vatican City.
Web site: <www.coe.int>.

Economic Community of West African States (ECOWAS)
Founded: 1975. **Members:** Benin, Burkina Faso, Cape Verde, Côte d'Ivoire, The Gambia, Ghana, Guinea, Guinea-Bissau, Liberia, Mali, Niger, Nigeria, Senegal, Sierra Leone, Togo.
Web site: <www.ecowas.int>.

European Free Trade Association (EFTA)
Founded: 1960. **Members:** Iceland, Liechtenstein, Norway, Switzerland.
Web site: <www.efta.int>.

European Union (EU)
Founded: 1950. **Members:** Austria, Belgium, Bulgaria, Cyprus, Czech Republic, Denmark, Estonia, Finland, France, Germany, Greece, Hungary, Ireland, Italy, Latvia, Lithuania, Luxembourg, Malta, The Netherlands, Poland, Portugal, Romania, Slovakia, Slovenia, Spain, Sweden, UK.
Web site: <www.europa.eu.int>.

Group of Eight (G-8)
Founded: 1975. **Members:** Canada, France, Germany, Italy, Japan, Russia, UK, US, EU.
Web site: <www.g8.utoronto.ca>.

Gulf Cooperation Council (GCC)
Founded: 1981. **Members:** Bahrain, Kuwait, Oman, Qatar, Saudi Arabia, UAE.
Web site: <www.gcc-sg.org/eng/index.php>.

Latin American Integration Association (ALADI)
Founded: 1980. **Members:** Argentina, Bolivia, Brazil, Chile, Colombia, Cuba, Ecuador, Mexico, Paraguay, Peru, Uruguay, Venezuela.
Web site: <www.aladi.org>.

League of Arab States (Arab League)
Founded: 1945. **Members:** Algeria, Bahrain, Comoros, Djibouti, Egypt, Iraq, Jordan, Kuwait, Lebanon, Libya, Mauritania, Morocco, Oman, Palestinian Authority, Qatar, Saudi Arabia, Somalia, The Sudan, Syria, Tunisia, UAE, Yemen; observer states Eritrea, Venezuela.
Web site: <www.arableagueonline.org/las/index_en.jsp>.

Nordic Council of Ministers
Founded: 1971. **Members:** Denmark, Finland, Iceland, Norway, Sweden, autonomous regions of Greenland, Faroe Islands, Åland Islands.
Web site: <www.norden.org>.

North Atlantic Treaty Organization (NATO)
Founded: 1949. **Members:** Belgium, Bulgaria, Canada, Czech Republic, Denmark, Estonia, France, Germany, Greece, Hungary, Iceland, Italy, Latvia, Lithuania, Luxembourg, The Netherlands, Norway, Poland, Portugal, Romania, Slovakia, Slovenia, Spain, Turkey, UK, US.
Web site: <www.nato.int>.

Organisation for Economic Co-operation and Development (OECD)
Founded: 1960. **Members:** Australia, Austria, Belgium, Canada, Czech Republic, Denmark, Finland, France, Germany, Greece, Hungary, Iceland, Ireland, Italy, Japan, Republic of Korea, Luxembourg, Mexico, The Netherlands, New Zealand, Norway, Poland, Portugal, Slovakia, Spain, Sweden, Switzerland, Turkey, UK, US.
Web site: <www.oecd.org>.

Organization for Security and Co-operation in Europe (OSCE)
Founded: 1973. **Members:** 54 countries of Europe and Central Asia, plus Canada and the US.
Web site: <www.osce.org>.

Organization of American States (OAS)
Founded: 1948. **Members:** all 35 independent countries of the Western Hemisphere (Cuba's participation has been denied since 1962); 61 permanent observer states (including the EU).
Web site: <www.oas.org>.

Organization of the Petroleum Exporting Countries (OPEC)
Founded: 1960. **Members:** Algeria, Angola, Ecuador, Iran, Iraq, Kuwait, Libya, Nigeria, Qatar, Saudi Arabia, UAE, Venezuela; Indonesia announced in May 2008 that it would withdraw at the end of 2008.
Web site: <www.opec.org>.

Organization of the Islamic Conference (OIC)
Founded: 1969. **Members:** 56 Islamic countries (mainly in Africa and Asia), Palestinian Authority; observer states Bosnia and Herzegovina, Central African Republic, Russia, Thailand, Turkish Republic of Northern Cyprus.
Web site: <www.oic-oci.org>.

Pacific Islands Forum (PIF; formerly [until 2000] South Pacific Forum)
Founded: 1971. **Members:** Australia, Cook Islands, Federated States of Micronesia, Fiji, Kiribati, Marshall Islands, Nauru, New Zealand, Niue, Palau, Papua New Guinea, Samoa, Solomon Islands, Tonga, Tuvalu, Vanuatu.
Web site: <www.forumsec.org>.

Secretariat of the Pacific Community (SPC; formerly South Pacific Commission)
Founded: 1947. **Members:** American Samoa, Australia, Cook Islands, Federated States of Micronesia, Fiji, France, French Polynesia, Guam, Kiribati, Marshall Islands, Nauru, New Caledonia, New Zealand, Niue, Northern Mariana Islands, Palau, Papua New Guinea, Pitcairn Islands, Samoa, Solomon Islands, Tokelau, Tonga, Tuvalu, US, Vanuatu, Wallis and Futuna.
Web site: <www.spc.int>.

Union of South American Nations (UNASUR/UNASUL)
Founded: 2004. **Members:** Argentina, Bolivia, Brazil, Chile, Colombia, Ecuador, Guyana, Paraguay, Peru, Suriname, Uruguay, Venezuela.
Web site: <www.comunidadandina.org>.

South Asian Association for Regional Cooperation (SAARC)
Founded: 1985. **Members:** Afghanistan, Bangladesh, Bhutan, India, Maldives, Nepal, Pakistan, Sri Lanka; observer states Australia, China, EU, Iran, Japan, Republic of Korea, Mauritius, Myanmar (Burma), US.
Web site: <www.saarc-sec.org>.

Southern African Development Community (SADC)
Founded: 1980. **Members:** Angola, Botswana, Democratic Republic of the Congo, Lesotho, Madagascar, Malawi, Mauritius, Mozambique, Namibia, South Africa, Swaziland, Tanzania, Zambia, Zimbabwe.
Web site: <www.sadc.int>.

Southern Common Market (MERCOSUL/MERCOSUR)
Founded: 1991. **Members:** Argentina, Brazil, Paraguay, Uruguay; associate members Bolivia, Chile, Colombia, Ecuador, Peru, Venezuela.
Web site: <www.mercosur.int/msweb>.

United Nations (UN)
Founded: 1945. **Members:** 192 countries.
Web site: <www.un.org>.

World Trade Organization (WTO)
Founded: 1995. **Members:** 152 member countries worldwide; 31 observer states as of May 2008.
Web site: <www.wto.org>.

Secretaries-General of the United Nations

The UN General Assembly appoints the Secretary-General to a five-year term on the recommendation of the 15-member Security Council; permanent members of the Security Council have veto power over nominees. The Secretary-General balances diverse and sometimes conflicting duties in the various roles of diplomat, advocate, administrator, and civil servant. The Secretary-General has a broad mandate, being able to marshal resources and advocacy on issues as various as peace efforts around the globe and disease prevention and treatment. ***Internet resource:*** *<www.un.org>.*

SECRETARY GENERAL	TERM	COMMENTS
Sir Gladwyn Jebb (acting) (UK)	1945–1946	
Trygve Lie (Norway)	1946–1952	resigned in November 1952
Dag Hammarskjöld (Sweden)	1953–1961	died in September 1961
U Thant (Burma, now Myanmar)	1961–1971	acting Secretary-General November 1961; elected 1962
Kurt Waldheim (Austria)	1972–1981	China vetoed a third term
Javier Pérez de Cuéllar (Peru)	1982–1991	
Boutros Boutros-Ghali (Egypt)	1992–1996	US vetoed a second term
Kofi Annan (Ghana)	1997–2006	
Ban Ki-moon (South Korea)	2007–	

The International Criminal Court

The International Criminal Court (ICC) was established by the Rome Statute of the International Criminal Court on 17 Jul 1998. The statute that created the ICC went into force on 1 Jul 2002; the court was fully operational as of July 2003. As of June 2008, the ICC has 106 member countries.

President
Philippe Kirsch (Canada)

First Vice President
Akua Kuenyehia (Ghana)

Second Vice President
René Blattmann (Bolivia)

Chief Prosecutor
Luis Moreno-Ocampo (Argentina)

Judges
List A—elected as experts in criminal law and procedure
Bruno Cotte (France)
Fatoumata Dembele Diarra (Mali)
Adrian Fulford (United Kingdom)
Daniel David Ntanda Nsereko (Uganda)
Elizabeth Odio Benito (Costa Rica)

Judges (continued)
Georghios M. Pikis (Cyprus)
Song Sang-Hyun (Republic of Korea)
Sylvia Steiner (Brazil)
Ekaterina Trendafilova (Bulgaria)

List B—elected as experts in international law and human rights law
René Blattmann (Bolivia)
Hans-Peter Kaul (Germany)
Philippe Kirsch (Canada)
Erkki Kourula (Finland)
Akua Kuenyehia (Ghana)
Navanethem Pillay (South Africa)
Mauro Politi (Italy)
Fumiko Saiga (Japan)
Anita Usacka (Latvia)

Registrar
Silvana Arbia (Italy)

United Nations Membership by Date of Admission

COUNTRY	DATE OF ADMISSION	COUNTRY	DATE OF ADMISSION	COUNTRY	DATE OF ADMISSION
Argentina	24 Oct 1945	Venezuela	15 Nov 1945	Malaysia	17 Sep 1957
Belarus	24 Oct 1945	Guatemala	21 Nov 1945	Guinea	12 Dec 1958
Brazil	24 Oct 1945	Norway	27 Nov 1945	Benin	20 Sep 1960
Chile	24 Oct 1945	The Netherlands	10 Dec 1945	Burkina Faso	20 Sep 1960
China[1]	24 Oct 1945	Honduras	17 Dec 1945	Cameroon	20 Sep 1960
Cuba	24 Oct 1945	Uruguay	18 Dec 1945	Central African Rep.	20 Sep 1960
Denmark	24 Oct 1945	Ecuador	21 Dec 1945	Chad	20 Sep 1960
Dominican Rep.	24 Oct 1945	Iraq	21 Dec 1945	Dem. Rep. of the Congo	20 Sep 1960
Egypt	24 Oct 1945	Belgium	27 Dec 1945		
El Salvador	24 Oct 1945	Afghanistan	19 Nov 1946	Rep. of the Congo	20 Sep 1960
France	24 Oct 1945	Iceland	19 Nov 1946	Côte d'Ivoire	20 Sep 1960
Haiti	24 Oct 1945	Sweden	19 Nov 1946	Cyprus	20 Sep 1960
Iran	24 Oct 1945	Thailand	16 Dec 1946	Gabon	20 Sep 1960
Lebanon	24 Oct 1945	Pakistan	30 Sep 1947	Madagascar	20 Sep 1960
Luxembourg	24 Oct 1945	Yemen	30 Sep 1947	Niger	20 Sep 1960
New Zealand	24 Oct 1945	Myanmar	19 Apr 1948	Somalia	20 Sep 1960
Nicaragua	24 Oct 1945	Israel	11 May 1949	Togo	20 Sep 1960
Paraguay	24 Oct 1945	Indonesia	28 Sep 1950	Mali	28 Sep 1960
Philippines	24 Oct 1945	Albania	14 Dec 1955	Senegal	28 Sep 1960
Poland	24 Oct 1945	Austria	14 Dec 1955	Nigeria	7 Oct 1960
USSR (later Russia)	24 Oct 1945	Bulgaria	14 Dec 1955	Sierra Leone	27 Sep 1961
Saudi Arabia	24 Oct 1945	Cambodia	14 Dec 1955	Mauritania	27 Oct 1961
Syria	24 Oct 1945	Finland	14 Dec 1955	Mongolia	27 Oct 1961
Turkey	24 Oct 1945	Hungary	14 Dec 1955	Tanzania	14 Dec 1961
Ukraine	24 Oct 1945	Ireland	14 Dec 1955	Burundi	18 Sep 1962
UK	24 Oct 1945	Italy	14 Dec 1955	Jamaica	18 Sep 1962
US	24 Oct 1945	Jersey	14 Dec 1955	Rwanda	18 Sep 1962
Greece	25 Oct 1945	Jordan	14 Dec 1955	Trinidad and Tobago	18 Sep 1962
India	30 Oct 1945	Laos	14 Dec 1955	Algeria	8 Oct 1962
Peru	31 Oct 1945	Libya	14 Dec 1955	Uganda	25 Oct 1962
Australia	1 Nov 1945	Nepal	14 Dec 1955	Kuwait	14 May 1963
Costa Rica	2 Nov 1945	Portugal	14 Dec 1955	Kenya	16 Dec 1963
Liberia	2 Nov 1945	Romania	14 Dec 1955	Malawi	1 Dec 1964
Colombia	5 Nov 1945	Spain	14 Dec 1955	Malta	1 Dec 1964
Mexico	7 Nov 1945	Sri Lanka	14 Dec 1955	Zambia	1 Dec 1964
South Africa	7 Nov 1945	Morocco	12 Nov 1956	The Gambia	21 Sep 1965
Canada	9 Nov 1945	The Sudan	12 Nov 1956	Maldives	21 Sep 1965
Ethiopia	13 Nov 1945	Tunisia	12 Nov 1956	Singapore	21 Sep 1965
Panama	13 Nov 1945	Japan	18 Dec 1956	Guyana	20 Sep 1966
Bolivia	14 Nov 1945	Ghana	8 Mar 1957	Lesotho	17 Oct 1966

United Nations Membership by Date of Admission (continued)

COUNTRY	DATE OF ADMISSION	COUNTRY	DATE OF ADMISSION	COUNTRY	DATE OF ADMISSION
Botswana	17 Oct 1966	Djibouti	20 Sep 1977	Kyrgyzstan	2 Mar 1992
Barbados	9 Dec 1966	Vietnam	20 Sep 1977	Moldova	2 Mar 1992
Mauritius	24 Apr 1968	Solomon Islands	19 Sep 1978	San Marino	2 Mar 1992
Swaziland	24 Sep 1968	Dominica	18 Dec 1978	Tajikistan	2 Mar 1992
Equatorial Guinea	12 Nov 1968	St. Lucia	18 Sep 1979	Turkmenistan	2 Mar 1992
Fiji	13 Oct 1970	Zimbabwe	25 Aug 1980	Uzbekistan	2 Mar 1992
Bahrain	21 Sep 1971	St. Vincent and the Grenadines	16 Sep 1980	Bosnia and Herzegovina	22 May 1992
Bhutan	21 Sep 1971	Vanuatu	15 Sep 1981	Croatia	22 May 1992
Qatar	21 Sep 1971	Belize	25 Sep 1981	Slovenia	22 May 1992
Oman	7 Oct 1971	Antigua and Barbuda	11 Nov 1981	Georgia	31 Jul 1992
United Arab Emirates	9 Dec 1971	St. Kitts and Nevis	23 Sep 1983	Czech Republic	19 Jan 1993
The Bahamas	18 Sep 1973	Brunei	21 Sep 1984	Slovakia	19 Jan 1993
Germany	18 Sep 1973	Namibia	23 Apr 1990	Macedonia[2]	8 Apr 1993
Bangladesh	17 Sep 1974	Liechtenstein	18 Sep 1990	Eritrea	28 May 1993
Grenada	17 Sep 1974	Estonia	17 Sep 1991	Monaco	28 May 1993
Guinea-Bissau	17 Sep 1974	North Korea	17 Sep 1991	Andorra	28 Jul 1993
Cape Verde	16 Sep 1975	South Korea	17 Sep 1991	Palau	15 Dec 1994
Mozambique	16 Sep 1975	Latvia	17 Sep 1991	Kiribati	14 Sep 1999
São Tomé and Príncipe	16 Sep 1975	Lithuania	17 Sep 1991	Nauru	14 Sep 1999
Papua New Guinea	10 Oct 1975	Marshall Islands	17 Sep 1991	Tonga	14 Sep 1999
Comoros	12 Nov 1975	Federated States of Micronesia	17 Sep 1991	Tuvalu	5 Sep 2000
Suriname	4 Dec 1975	Armenia	2 Mar 1992	Serbia	1 Nov 2000
Seychelles	21 Sep 1976	Azerbaijan	2 Mar 1992	Switzerland	10 Sep 2002
Angola	1 Dec 1976	Kazakhstan	2 Mar 1992	East Timor (Timor-Leste)	27 Sep 2002
Samoa	15 Dec 1976			Montenegro	28 Jun 2006

[1]The Republic of China (Taiwan) held the seat until 25 Oct 1971, when UN Res. 2758 gave the membership and a seat on the Security Council to the People's Republic of China. [2]Macedonia is known in the UN as The Former Yugoslav Republic of Macedonia.

Rulers and Regimes

Europe

Roman Emperors

Overlapping reigns denote corulers. Diocletian (284–305) laid the foundation for the Byzantine Empire in the East when he appointed Maximian (286–305) to rule over the Western portion of the empire. Rome thus remained a unified state but was divided administratively. Theodosius I (379–395) was the last emperor to rule over a unified Roman Empire. When he died, Rome split into Eastern and Western empires. For a complete list of the Eastern emperors after the fall of Rome, see "Byzantine Empire."

REIGN	BYNAME	FULL NAME
27 BC–AD 14	Augustus	Caesar Augustus
14–37	Tiberius	Tiberius Caesar Augustus
37–41	Caligula	Gaius Caesar Augustus Germanicus
41–54	Claudius	Tiberius Claudius Caesar Augustus Germanicus
54–68	Nero	Nero Claudius Caesar Augustus Germanicus
68–69	Galba	Servius Galba Caesar Augustus
69	Otho	Marcus Otho Caesar Augustus
69	Vitellius	Aulus Vitellius Germanicus
69–79	Vespasian	Caesar Vespasianus Augustus
79–81	Titus	Titus Vespasianus Augustus
81–96	Domitian	Caesar Domitianus Augustus
96–98	Nerva	Nerva Caesar Augustus
98–117	Trajan	Caesar Nerva Traianus Augustus
117–138	Hadrian	Caesar Traianus Hadrianus Augustus
138–161	Antoninus Pius	Caesar Titus Aelius Hadrianus Antoninus Augustus Pius
161–180	Marcus Aurelius	Marcus Aurelius Antoninus
161–169	Lucius Verus	Lucius Aurelius Verus
177–192	Commodus	Lucius Aelius Aurelius Commodus
193	Pertinax	Publius Helvius Pertinax
193	Didius Julianus	Marcus Didius Severus Julianus

Roman Emperors (continued)

REIGN	BYNAME	FULL NAME
193–211	Septimius Severus	Lucius Septimius Severus Pertinax
198–217	Caracalla	Marcus Aurelius Severus Antoninus
209–212	Geta	Publius Septimius Geta
217–218	Macrinus	Marcus Opellius Severus Macrinus
218–222	Elagabalus	Sacerdos dei invicti solis Elagabali Marcus Aurelius Antoninus
222–235	Alexander Severus	Marcus Aurelius Severus Alexander
235–238	Maximin	Gaius Julius Verus Maximinus
238	Gordian I	Marcus Antonius Gordianus Sempronianus Romanus Africanus
238	Gordian II	Marcus Antonius Gordianus Sempronianus Romanus Africanus
238	Maximus	Marcus Clodius Pupienus Maximus
238	Balbinus	Decius Caelius Calvinus Balbinus
238–244	Gordian III	Marcus Antonius Gordianus
244–249	Philip	
249–251	Decius	Galus Messius Quintus Trianus Decius
251	Hostilian	Gaius Valens Hostilianus Messius Quintus
251–253	Gallus	Gaius Vibius Trebonianus Gallus
253	Aemilian	Marcus Aemilius Aemilianus
253–260	Valerian	Publius Licinius Valerianus
253–268	Gallienus	Publius Licinius Egnatius Gallienus
268–270	Claudius II Gothicus	Marcus Aurelius Valerius Claudius
269–270	Quintillus	Marcus Aurelius Claudius Quintillus
270–275	Aurelian	Lucius Domitius Aurelianus
275–276	Tacitus	Marcus Claudius Tacitus
276	Florian	Marcus Annius Florianus
276–282	Probus	Marcus Aurelius Probus
282–283	Carus	Marcus Aurelius Carus
283–285	Carinus	Marcus Aurelius Carinus
283–284	Numerian	Marcus Aurelius Numerius Numerianus
284–305[1]	Diocletian	Gaius Aurelius Valerius Diocletianus
286–305[2]	Maximian	Marcus Aurelius Valerius Maximianus Heraclius
305–311[1]	Galerius	Gaius Galerius Valerius Maximianus
305–306[2]	Constantius I Chlorus	Flavius Valerius Constantius
306–307[2]	Severus	Flavius Valerius Severus
306–312[2]	Maxentius	Marcus Aurelius Valerius Maxentius
308–324[1]	Licinius	Valerius Licinianus Licinius
312–337[2]	Constantine I	Flavius Valerius Constantinus
337–340[2]	Constantine II	Flavius Claudius [or Julius] Constantinus
337–350[2]	Constans I	Flavius Julius Constans
337–361[2]	Constantius II	Flavius Julius [or Valerius] Constantius
350–353[2]	Magnentius	Flavius Magnus Magnentius
361–363[2]	Julian	Flavius Claudius Julianus
363–364[2]	Jovian	Flavius Jovianus
364–375[2]	Valentinian I	Flavius Valentinianus
364–378[1]	Valens	Flavius Valens
365–366[1]	Procopius	
375–383[2]	Gratian	Flavius Gratianus Augustus
375–392[2]	Valentinian II	Flavius Valentinianus
379–395[2]	Theodosius I	Flavius Theodosius
395–408[1]	Arcadius	Flavius Arcadius
395–423[2]	Honorius	Flavius Honorius
408–450[1]	Theodosius II	
421[2]	Constantius III	
425–455[2]	Valentinian III	Flavius Placidius Valentinianus
450–457[1]	Marcian	Marcianus
455[2]	Petronius Maximus	Flavius Ancius Petronius Maximus
455–456[2]	Avitus	Flavius Maccilius Eparchus Avitus
457–474[1]	Leo I	Leo Thrax Magnus
457–461[2]	Majorian	Julius Valerius Majorianus
461–467[2]	Libius Severus	Libius Severianus Severus
467–472[2]	Anthemius	Procopius Anthemius
472[2]	Olybrius	Anicius Olybrius
473–474[2]	Glycerius	
474–475[2]	Julius Nepos	
474[1]	Leo II	
474–491[1]	Zeno	
475–476[2]	Romulus Augustulus	Flavius Momyllus Romulus Augustulus

[1]*Ruled in the East only.* [2]*Ruled in the West only.*

Sovereigns of Britain

SOVEREIGN	DYNASTY OR HOUSE	REIGN
Kings of Wessex (West Saxons)		
Egbert	Saxon	802–839
Aethelwulf (Ethelwulf)	Saxon	839–856/858
Aethelbald (Ethelbald)	Saxon	855/856–860
Aethelberht (Ethelbert)	Saxon	860–865/866
Aethelred I (Ethelred)	Saxon	865/866–871
Alfred the Great	Saxon	871–899
Edward the Elder	Saxon	899–924
Sovereigns of England		
Athelstan[1]	Saxon	925–939
Edmund I	Saxon	939–946
Eadred (Edred)	Saxon	946–955
Eadwig (Edwy)	Saxon	955–959
Edgar	Saxon	959–975
Edward the Martyr	Saxon	975–978
Ethelred II the Unready (Aethelred)	Saxon	978–1013
Sweyn Forkbeard	Danish	1013–14
Ethelred II the Unready (restored)	Saxon	1014–16
Edmund II Ironside	Saxon	1016
Canute	Danish	1016–35
Harold I Harefoot	Danish	1035–40
Hardecanute	Danish	1040–42
Edward the Confessor	Saxon	1042–66
Harold II	Saxon	1066
William I the Conqueror	Norman	1066–87
William II	Norman	1087–1100
Henry I	Norman	1100–35
Stephen	Blois	1135–54
Henry II	Plantagenet	1154–89
Richard I	Plantagenet	1189–99
John	Plantagenet	1199–1216
Henry III	Plantagenet	1216–72
Edward I	Plantagenet	1272–1307
Edward II	Plantagenet	1307–27
Edward III	Plantagenet	1327–77
Richard II	Plantagenet	1377–99
Henry IV	Plantagenet: Lancaster	1399–1413
Henry V	Plantagenet: Lancaster	1413–22
Henry VI	Plantagenet: Lancaster	1422–61
Edward IV	Plantagenet: York	1461–70
Sovereigns of England (continued)		
Henry VI (restored)	Plantagenet: Lancaster	1470–71
Edward IV (restored)	Plantagenet: York	1471–83
Edward V	Plantagenet: York	1483
Richard III	Plantagenet: York	1483–85
Henry VII	Tudor	1483–1509
Henry VIII	Tudor	1509–47
Edward VI	Tudor	1547–53
Mary I	Tudor	1553–58
Elizabeth I	Tudor	1558–1603
Sovereigns of Great Britain and the United Kingdom[2, 3]		
James I (VI of Scotland)[2]	Stuart	1603–25
Charles I	Stuart	1625–49
Commonwealth		
Oliver Cromwell, Lord Protector		1653–58
Richard Cromwell, Lord Protector		1658–59
Sovereigns of Great Britain and the United Kingdom (restored)		
Charles II	Stuart	1660–85
James II	Stuart	1685–88
William III and Mary II[4]	Orange/ Stuart	1689–1702
Anne	Stuart	1702–14
George I	Hanover	1714–27
George II	Hanover	1727–60
George III[3]	Hanover	1760–1820
George IV[5]	Hanover	1820–30
William IV	Hanover	1830–37
Victoria	Hanover	1837–1901
Edward VII	Saxe-Coburg-Gotha	1901–10
George V[6]	Windsor	1910–36
Edward VIII[7]	Windsor	1936
George VI	Windsor	1936–52
Elizabeth II	Windsor	1952–

[1]Athelstan was king of Wessex and the first king of all England. [2]James VI of Scotland became also James I of England in 1603. Upon accession to the English throne he styled himself "King of Great Britain" and was so proclaimed. Legally, however, he and his successors held separate English and Scottish kingships until the Act of Union of 1707, when the two kingdoms were united as the Kingdom of Great Britain. [3]The United Kingdom was formed on 1 Jan 1801, with the union of Great Britain and Ireland. After 1801 George III was styled "King of the United Kingdom of Great Britain and Ireland." [4]William and Mary, as husband and wife, reigned jointly until Mary's death in 1694. William then reigned alone until his own death in 1702. [5]George IV was regent from 5 Feb 1811. [6]In 1917, during World War I, George V changed the name of his house from Saxe-Coburg-Gotha to Windsor. [7]Edward VIII succeeded upon the death of his father, George V, on 20 Jan 1936, but abdicated on 11 Dec 1936, before coronation.

Rulers of Scotland

Knowledge about the early Scottish kings (until Malcolm II) is slim and is partly based on traditional lists. The dating of reigns is thus inexact.

RULER	REIGN
Kenneth I MacAlpin	843–858
Donald I	858–862
Constantine I	862–877
Aed (Aodh)	877–878
Eochaid (Eocha) and Giric (Ciric)[1]	878–889
Donald II	889–900

Rulers of Scotland (continued)

RULER	REIGN
Constantine II	900–943
Malcolm I	943–954
Indulf	954–962
Dub	962–966
Culen	966–971
Kenneth II	971–995
Constantine III	995–997
Kenneth III	997–1005
Malcolm II	1005–34
Duncan I	1034–40
Macbeth	1040–57
Lulach	1057–58
Malcolm III Canmore	1058–93
Donald Bane (Donalbane)	1093–94
Duncan II	1093–94
Donald Bane (restored)	1094–97
Edgar	1097–1107
Alexander I	1107–24
David I	1124–53
Malcolm IV	1153–65
William I the Lion	1165–1214
Alexander II	1214–49
Alexander III	1249–86
Margaret, Maid of Norway	1286–90
Interregnum	1290–92
John de Balliol	1292–96
Interregnum	1296–1306
Robert I the Bruce	1306–29
David II	1329–71
House of Stewart (Stuart)[2]	
Robert II	1371–90
Robert III	1390–1406
James I	1406–37
James II	1437–60
James III	1460–88
James IV	1488–1513
James V	1513–42
Mary, Queen of Scots	1542–67
James VI[3]	1567–1625

[1]Eochaid may have been a minor and Giric his guardian, or Giric may have been a usurper. Both appear in the lists of kings for the period. [2]"Stewart" was the original spelling for the Scottish family, but during the 16th century French influence led to the adoption of the spelling Stuart (or Steuart), owing to the absence of the letter "w" in the French alphabet. [3]James VI of Scotland became also James I of England in 1603. Upon accession to the English throne he styled himself "King of Great Britain" and was so proclaimed. Legally, however, he and his successors held separate English and Scottish kingships until the Act of Union of 1707, when the two kingdoms were united as the Kingdom of Great Britain.

British Prime Ministers

The origin of the term prime minister and the question of to whom it should originally be applied have long been issues of scholarly and political debate. Although the term was used as early as the reign of Queen Anne (1702–14), it acquired wider currency during the reign of George II (1727–60), when it began to be used as a term of reproach toward Robert Walpole. The title prime minister did not become official until 1905, to refer to the leader of a government.

Before the development of the Conservative and Liberal parties in the mid-19th century, parties in Britain were, for the most part, simply alliances of prominent groups or aristocratic families. The designations Whig and Tory tend often to be approximate. In all cases, the party designation is that of the prime minister; he or she might lead a coalition government, as did David Lloyd George and Winston Churchill (in his first term).

PRIME MINISTER	PARTY	TERM
Robert Walpole	Whig	1721–42
Spencer Compton	Whig	1742–43
Henry Pelham	Whig	1743–54
Thomas Pelham-Holles	Whig	1754–56
William Cavendish	Whig	1756–57
Thomas Pelham-Holles	Whig	1757–62
John Stuart		1762–63
George Grenville		1763–65
Charles Watson Wentworth	Whig	1765–66
William Pitt		1766–68
Augustus Henry Fitzroy		1768–70
Frederick North		1770–82
Charles Watson Wentworth	Whig	1782
William Petty-Fitzmaurice		1782–83
William Henry Cavendish-Bentinck	Whig	1783
William Pitt	Tory	1783–1801
Henry Addington	Tory	1801–04
William Pitt	Tory	1804–06
William Wyndham Grenville		1806–07
William Henry Cavendish-Bentinck	Whig	1807–09
Spencer Perceval	Tory	1809–12
Robert Banks Jenkinson	Tory	1812–27
George Canning	Tory	1827
Frederick John Robinson	Tory	1827–28
Arthur Wellesley	Tory	1828–30
Charles Grey	Whig	1830–34
William Lamb	Whig	1834
Arthur Wellesley	Tory	1834
Robert Peel	Tory	1834–35
William Lamb	Whig	1835–41
Robert Peel	Conservative	1841–46
John Russell	Whig-Liberal	1846–52
Edward Geoffrey Stanley	Conservative	1852
George Hamilton-Gordon		1852–55
Henry John Temple	Liberal	1855–58
Edward Geoffrey Stanley	Conservative	1858–59
Henry John Temple	Liberal	1859–65
John Russell	Liberal	1865–66
Edward Geoffrey Stanley	Conservative	1866–68
Benjamin Disraeli	Conservative	1868
William Ewart Gladstone	Liberal	1868–74

British Prime Ministers (continued)

PRIME MINISTER	PARTY	TERM
Benjamin Disraeli	Conservative	1874–80
William Ewart Gladstone	Liberal	1880–85
Robert Cecil	Conservative	1885–86
William Ewart Gladstone	Liberal	1886
Robert Cecil	Conservative	1886–92
William Ewart Gladstone	Liberal	1892–94
Archibald Philip Primrose	Liberal	1894–95
Robert Cecil	Conservative	1895–1902
Arthur James Balfour	Conservative	1902–05
Henry Campbell-Bannerman	Liberal	1905–08
H.H. Asquith	Liberal	1908–16
David Lloyd George	Liberal	1916–22
Bonar Law	Conservative	1922–23
Stanley Baldwin	Conservative	1923–24
Ramsay Macdonald	Labour	1924
Stanley Baldwin	Conservative	1924–29
Ramsay Macdonald	Labour	1929–35
Stanley Baldwin	Conservative	1935–37
Neville Chamberlain	Conservative	1937–40
Winston Churchill	Conservative	1940–45
Clement Attlee	Labour	1945–51
Winston Churchill	Conservative	1951–55
Anthony Eden	Conservative	1955–57
Harold Macmillan	Conservative	1957–63
Alec Douglas-Home	Conservative	1963–64
Harold Wilson	Labour	1964–70
Edward Heath	Conservative	1970–74
Harold Wilson	Labour	1974–76
James Callaghan	Labour	1976–79
Margaret Thatcher	Conservative	1979–90
John Major	Conservative	1990–97
Tony Blair	Labour	1997–2007
Gordon Brown	Labour	2007–

Rulers of France

RULER	REIGN
Carolingian dynasty	
Pippin III the Short	751–768
Charles I (Charlemagne, Kingdom of the Franks)	768–814
Louis I (Kingdom of the Franks)	814–840
civil war	840–843
Charles II (Kingdom of the West Franks)	843–877
Louis II (Kingdom of the West Franks)	877–879
Louis III (Kingdom of the West Franks)	879–882
Carloman (Kingdom of the West Franks)	879–884
Charles (III) (Charles III, Holy Roman Empire)	884–887
Robertian (Capetian) dynasty	
Eudes	888–898
Carolingian dynasty	
Charles III	893/898–923
Robertian (Capetian) dynasty	
Robert I	922–923
Rudolf (Raoul, or Rodolphe)	923–936
Carolingian dynasty	
Louis IV	936–954
Lothair (Lothaire)	954–986
Louis V	986–987
Capetian dynasty	
Hugh Capet (Hugues Capet)	987–996
Robert II	996–1031
Henry I (Henri)	1031–60
Philip I (Philippe)	1060–1108
Louis VI	1108–37
Louis VII	1137–80
Philip II (Philippe)	1180–1223
Louis VIII	1223–26
Louis IX (Saint Louis)	1226–70
Philip III (Philippe)	1270–85
Philip IV (Philippe)	1285–1314
Louis X	1314–16
John I (Jean)	1316
Philip V (Philippe)	1316–22
Charles IV	1322–28
Valois dynasty	
Philip VI (Philippe)	1328–50
John II (Jean)	1350–64
Charles V	1364–80
Charles VI	1380–1422
Charles VII	1422–61
Louis XI	1461–83
Charles VIII	1483–98
Valois dynasty (Orléans branch)	
Louis XII	1498–1515
Valois dynasty (Angoulême branch)	
Francis I (François)	1515–47
Henry II (Henri)	1547–59
Francis II (François)	1559–60
Charles IX	1560–74
Henry III (Henri)	1574–89
House of Bourbon	
Henry IV (Henri)	1589–1610
Louis XIII	1610–43
Louis XIV	1643–1715
Louis XV	1715–74
Louis XVI	1774–92
Louis (XVII)	1793–95
First Republic	
National Convention	1792–95
Directorate	1795–99
Consulate (Napoléon Bonaparte)	1799–1804
First Empire (emperors)	
Napoleon I (Napoléon Bonaparte)	1804–14, 1815
Napoleon (II)	1815
House of Bourbon	
Louis XVIII	1814–24
Charles X	1824–30
House of Orléans	
Louis-Philippe	1830–48
Second Republic (president)	
Louis-Napoléon Bonaparte	1848–52

Rulers of France (continued)

RULER	REIGN
Second Empire (emperor)	
Napoleon III (Louis-Napoléon Bonaparte)	1852–70
Third Republic (presidents)	
Adolphe Thiers	1871–73
Marie-Edmé-Patrice-Maurice, comte de Mac-Mahon, duc de Magenta	1873–79
Jules Grévy	1879–87
Sadi Carnot	1887–94
Jean Casimir-Périer	1894–95
Félix Faure	1895–99
Émile Loubet	1899–1906
Armand Fallières	1906–13
Raymond Poincaré	1913–20
Paul Deschanel	1920
Alexandre Millerand	1920–24
Gaston Doumergue	1924–31
Paul Doumer	1931–32

RULER	REIGN
Third Republic (presidents) (continued)	
Albert Lebrun	1932–40
French State (État Français, or Vichy France)	
Philippe Pétain	1940–44
Provisional government	1944–47
Fourth Republic (presidents)	
Vincent Auriol	1947–54
René Coty	1954–59
Fifth Republic (presidents)	
Charles de Gaulle	1959–69
Georges Pompidou	1969–74
Valéry Giscard d'Estaing	1974–81
François Mitterrand	1981–95
Jacques Chirac	1995–2007
Nicolas Sarkozy	2007–

Rulers of Spain

RULER	REIGN
House of Habsburg	
Charles I (Carlos)	1516–56
Philip II (Felipe)	1556–98
Philip III (Felipe)	1598–1621
Philip IV (Felipe)	1621–65
Charles II (Carlos)	1665–1700
House of Bourbon (Borbón)	
Philip V (Felipe)	1700–24
Louis (Luis)	1724
Philip V (2nd time)	1724–46
Ferdinand VI (Fernando)	1746–59
Charles III (Carlos)	1759–88
Charles IV (Carlos)	1788–1808
Ferdinand VII (Fernando)	1808
House of Bonaparte	
Joseph (José)	1808–13
House of Bourbon (Borbón)	
Ferdinand VII (2nd time)	1814–33

RULER	REIGN
House of Bourbon (Borbón) (continued)	
Isabella II (Isabel)	1833–68
Interregnum	1868–70
House of Savoy	
Amadeus I (Amadeo)	1870–73
Republic	1873–74
House of Bourbon (Borbón)	
Alfonso XII	1874–85
Alfonso XIII	1886–1931
Republic	1931–39
Nationalist Regime	
Francisco Franco	1939–75
House of Bourbon (Borbón)	
Juan Carlos	1975–

Rulers of Germany

On 25 Jul 1806 the Confederation of the Rhine was founded, with Karl Theodor von Dalberg as prince primate (1806–13). After the dissolution of the Rhine Confederation, there was no true central power until 1815, when the German Confederation was founded. In 1867 the governing structure became the North German Confederation, and in 1871 the German Reich. For rulers of Germany before the Confederation of the Rhine, see Holy Roman Emperors.

RULER	REIGN OR TERM
Emperors	
Hohenzollern dynasty	
Wilhelm I	1871–88
Friedrich III	1888
Wilhelm II	1888–1918
Presidents	
Richard Müller	1918
Robert Leinert	1918–19
Wilhelm Pfannkuch	1919
Eduard David	1919
Friedrich Ebert	1919–25

RULER	REIGN OR TERM
Presidents (continued)	
Paul von Hindenburg	1925–34
Adolf Hitler (Führer)	1934–45
Karl Dönitz	1945
Chancellors	
Otto Fürst von Bismarck	1871–90
Leo Graf von Caprivi	1890–94
Chlodwig Fürst zu Hohenlohe-Schillingsfürst	1894–1900
Bernhard Graf Fürst von Bülow	1900–09
Theobald von Bethmann Hollweg	1909–17

Rulers of Germany (continued)

RULER	REIGN OR TERM
Chancellors (continued)	
Georg Michaelis	1917
Georg Graf von Hertling	1917–18
Maximilian Prinz von Baden	1918
Friedrich Ebert	1918
Philipp Scheidemann	1919
Gustav Bauer	1919–20
Wolfgang Kapp (in rebellion)	1920
Hermann Müller	1920
Konstantin Fehrenbach	1920–21
Joseph Wirth	1921–22
Wilhelm Cuno	1922–23
Gustav Stresemann	1923
Wilhelm Marx	1923–24
Hans Luther	1925–26
Wilhelm Marx	1926–28
Hermann Müller	1928–30
Heinrich Brüning	1930–32
Franz von Papen	1932
Kurt von Schleicher	1932–33
Adolf Hitler	1933–45
Joseph Goebbels	1945
Lutz Graf Schwerin von Krosigk (chairman of interim government)	1945

Allied occupation 1945–49

German Democratic Republic (East Germany)[1]

RULER	REIGN OR TERM
Presidents	
Wilhelm Pieck	1949–60
Chairmen of the Council of State	
Walter Ulbricht	1960–73
Willi Stoph	1973–76
Erich Honecker	1976–89
Egon Krenz	1989
Sabine Bergmann-Pohl	1990

Federal Republic of Germany (West Germany)[1]

RULER	REIGN OR TERM
Presidents	
Theodor Heuss	1949–59
Heinrich Lübke	1959–69
Gustav Heinemann	1969–74
Walter Scheel	1974–79
Karl Carstens	1979–84
Richard von Weizsäcker	1984–94
Roman Herzog	1994–99
Johannes Rau	1999–2004
Horst Köhler	2004–
Chancellors	
Konrad Adenauer	1949–63
Ludwig Erhard	1963–66
Kurt Georg Kiesinger	1966–69
Willy Brandt	1969–74
Helmut Schmidt	1974–82
Helmut Kohl	1982–98
Gerhard Schröder	1998–2005
Angela Merkel	2005–

[1]*After World War II, Germany was split into four occupational zones, governed by the French, British, American, and Soviet powers. The Western zones were merged and, on 23 May 1949, became the independent Federal Republic of Germany. On 7 October of the same year, the Soviet zone was proclaimed the German Democratic Republic. On 3 Oct 1990, the latter was incorporated into the Federal Republic of Germany.*

Holy Roman Emperors

The Holy Roman Empire encompassed a varying complex of lands in Western and Central Europe. Ruled over by Frankish and then German kings, the empire officially dissolved on 6 Aug 1806, when Francis II resigned his title.

EMPEROR	REIGN
Carolingian dynasty	
Charlemagne (Charles I)	800–814
Louis I	814–840
Civil War	840–843
Lothair I	843–855
Louis II	855–875
Charles II	875–877
Interregnum	877–881
Charles III	881–887
Interregnum	887–891
House of Spoleto	
Guy	891–894
Lambert	894–898
Carolingian dynasty	
Arnulf	896–899
Louis III	901–905
House of Franconia	
Conrad I	911–918
Carolingian dynasty	
Berengar	915–924
House of Saxony (Liudolfings)	
Henry I	919–936
Otto I	936–973
Otto II	973–983
Otto III	983–1002
Henry II	1002–24
Salian dynasty	
Conrad II	1024–39
Henry III	1039–56

Holy Roman Emperors (continued)

EMPEROR	REIGN
Salian dynasty (continued)	
Henry IV	1056–1106
Rival claimants:	
Rudolf	1077–80
Hermann	1081–93
Conrad	1093–1101
Henry V	1105/06–25
House of Supplinburg	
Lothair II	1125–37
House of Hohenstaufen	
Conrad III	1138–52
Frederick I (Barbarossa)	1152–90
Henry VI	1190–97
Philip	1198–1208
Welf dynasty	
Otto IV	1198–1214
House of Hohenstaufen	
Frederick II	1215–50
Rival claimants:	
Henry (VII)	1220–35
Henry Raspe	1246–47
William of Holland	1247–56
Conrad IV	1250–54
Great Interregnum	1254–73
Richard	1257–72
Alfonso (Alfonso X of Castile)	1257–75
House of Habsburg	
Rudolf I	1273–91
House of Nassau	
Adolf	1292–98
House of Habsburg	
Albert I	1298–1308
House of Luxembourg	
Henry VII	1308–13

EMPEROR	REIGN
House of Habsburg	
Frederick (III)	1314–26
House of Wittelsbach	
Louis IV	1314–46
House of Luxembourg	
Charles IV	1346–78
Wenceslas	1378–1400
House of Wittelsbach	
Rupert	1400–10
House of Luxembourg	
Jobst	1410–11
Sigismund	1410–37
House of Habsburg	
Albert II	1438–39
Frederick III	1440–93
Maximilian I	1493–1519
Charles V	1519–56
Ferdinand I	1556–64
Maximilian II	1564–76
Rudolf II	1576–1612
Matthias	1612–19
Ferdinand II	1619–37
Ferdinand III	1637–57
Leopold I	1658–1705
Joseph I	1705–11
Charles VI	1711–40
House of Wittelsbach	
Charles VII	1742–45
House of Habsburg	
Francis I	1745–65
Joseph II	1765–90
Leopold II	1790–92
Francis II	1792–1806

Rulers of Russia[1]

RULER	REIGN
Princes and Grand Princes of Moscow (Muscovy): Danilovich dynasty[2]	
Daniel (son of Alexander Nevsky)	c. 1276–1303
Yury	1303–25
Ivan I	1325–40
Semyon (Simeon)	1340–53
Ivan II	1353–59
Dmitry Donskoy	1359–89
Vasily I	1389–1425
Vasily II	1425–62
Ivan III	1462–1505
Vasily III	1505–33
Ivan IV	1533–47
Tsars of Russia: Danilovich dynasty	
Ivan IV	1547–84
Fyodor I	1584–98
Tsars of Russia: Time of Troubles	
Boris Godunov	1598–1605
Fyodor II	1605

RULER	REIGN
Tsars of Russia: Time of Troubles (continued)	
False Dmitry	1605–06
Vasily (IV)	1606–10
Interregnum	1610–12
Tsars and Empresses of Russia and the Russian Empire: Romanov dynasty[3]	
Michael III	1613–45
Alexis	1645–76
Fyodor III	1676–82
Peter I (Ivan V coruler 1682–96)	1682–1725
Catherine I	1725–27
Peter II	1727–30
Anna	1730–40
Ivan VI	1740–41
Elizabeth	1741–61 (O.S.)
Peter III[4]	1761–62 (O.S.)
Catherine II	1762–96
Paul	1796–1801
Alexander I	1801–25

Rulers of Russia[1] (continued)

RULER	REIGN
Tsars and Empresses of Russia and the Russian Empire: Romanov dynasty[3] (continued)	
Nicholas I	1825-55
Alexander II	1855-81
Alexander III	1881-94
Nicholas II	1894-1917
Provisional government	1917
Chairmen (or First Secretaries) of the Communist Party of the Soviet Union	
Vladimir Lenin	1917-24
Joseph Stalin	1924-53
Chairmen (or First Secretaries) of the Communist Party of the Soviet Union (continued)	
Georgy Malenkov	1953
Nikita Khrushchev	1953-64
Leonid Brezhnev	1964-82
Yury Andropov	1982-84
Konstantin Chernenko	1984-85
Mikhail Gorbachev	1985-91
Presidents of Russia	
Boris Yeltsin	1990-99
Vladimir Putin	2000-08
Dmitry Medvedev	2008-

[1]This table includes leaders of Muscovy, Russia, the Russian Empire, and the Soviet Union. [2]The Danilovich dynasty is a late branch of the Rurik dynasty, named after its progenitor, Daniel. [3]On 22 Oct (Old Style) 1721, Peter I the Great took the title of "emperor." However, despite the official titling, conventional usage took an odd turn. Every male sovereign continued usually to be called tsar, but every female sovereign was conventionally called empress. [4]The direct line of the Romanov dynasty came to an end in 1761 with the death of Elizabeth, daughter of Peter I, but subsequent rulers of the "Holstein-Gottorp dynasty" (the first, Peter III, was son of Charles Frederick, duke of Holstein-Gottorp, and Anna, daughter of Peter I) took the family name of Romanov.

Middle East

Byzantine Emperors

The Byzantine Empire comprised what was previously the eastern half of the Roman Empire. It survived for nearly 1,000 years after the western half had crumbled into various feudal kingdoms; it finally fell to Ottoman Turkish onslaughts in 1453. For emperors of the Eastern Roman Empire (at Constantinople) before the fall of Rome, see "Roman Emperors."

EMPEROR	REIGN
Zeno	474-491
Anastasius I	491-518
Justin I	518-527
Justinian I	527-565
Justin II	565-578
Tiberius II Constantine	578-582
Maurice Tiberius	582-602
Phocas	602-610
Heraclius	610-641
Heraclius Constantine	641
Heraclonas (or Heraclius)	641
Constans II (Constantine Pogonatus)	641-668
Constantine IV	668-685
Justinian II Rhinotmetus	685-695
Leontius	695-698
Tiberius III	698-705
Justinian II Rhinotmetus (restored)	705-711
Philippicus	711-713
Anastasius II	713-715
Theodosius III	715-717
Leo III	717-741
Constantine V Copronymus	741-775
Leo IV	775-780
Constantine VI	780-797
Irene (empress)	797-802
Nicephorus I	802-811
Stauracius	811
Michael I Rhangabe	811-813
Leo V	813-820
Michael II Balbus	820-829
Theophilus	829-842
Michael III	842-867
Basil I	867-886
Leo VI	886-912
Alexander	912-913
Constantine VII Porphyrogenitus	913-959
Romanus I Lecapenus	920-944
Romanus II	959-963
Nicephorus II Phocas	963-969
John I Tzimisces	969-976
Basil II Bulgaroctonus	976-1025
Constantine VIII	1025-28
Romanus III Argyrus	1028-34
Michael IV	1034-41
Michael V Calaphates	1041-42
Zoe (empress)	1042-56
Constantine IX Monomachus	1042-55
Theodora (empress)	1055-56
Michael VI Stratioticus	1056-57
Isaac I Comnenus	1057-59
Constantine X Ducas	1059-67
Romanus IV Diogenes	1067-71
Michael VII Ducas	1071-78
Nicephorus III Botaniates	1078-81
Alexius I Comnenus	1081-1118
John II Comnenus	1118-43
Manuel I Comnenus	1143-80
Alexius II Comnenus	1180-83
Andronicus I Comnenus	1183-85
Isaac II Angelus	1185-95
Alexius III Angelus	1195-1203
Isaac II Angelus (restored) and Alexius IV Angelus (joint ruler)	1203-04
Alexius V Ducas Murtzuphlus	1204
Latin emperors	
Baldwin I	1204-06
Henry	1206-16

Byzantine Emperors (continued)

EMPEROR	REIGN
Latin emperors (continued)	
Peter	1217
Yolande (empress)	1217–19
Robert	1221–28
Baldwin II	1228–61
John	1231–37
Nicaean emperors	
Constantine (XI) Lascaris	1204–05?
Theodore I Lascaris	1205?–22
John III Ducas Vatatzes	1222–54
Theodore II Lascaris	1254–58
John IV Lascaris	1258–61

EMPEROR	REIGN
Greek emperors restored	
Michael VIII Palaeologus	1261–82
Andronicus II Palaeologus	1282–1328
Andronicus III Palaeologus	1328–41
John V Palaeologus	1341–76
John VI Cantacuzenus	1347–54
Andronicus IV Palaeologus	1376–79
John V Palaeologus (restored)	1379–90
John VII Palaeologus	1390
John V Palaeologus (restored)	1390–91
Manuel II Palaeologus	1391–1425
John VIII Palaeologus	1421–48
Constantine XI Palaeologus	1449–53

Caliphs

When Muhammad died on 8 Jun 632, Abu Bakr, his father-in-law, succeeded to his political and administrative functions. He and his three immediate successors are known as the "perfect" or "rightly guided" caliphs. After them, the title was borne by the 14 Umayyad caliphs of Damascus (from 661–750) and subsequently by the 38 'Abbasid caliphs of Baghdad (both are named after their clans of origin). The empire of the caliphate grew rapidly through conquest during its first two centuries to include most of southwestern Asia, North Africa, and Spain. 'Abbasid power ended in 945, when the Buyids took Baghdad under their rule. They retained the 'Abbasid caliphs as figureheads; other dynasties in Central Asia and the Ganges River basin acknowledged the 'Abbasid caliphs as spiritual leaders. The Fatimids, however, proclaimed a new caliphate in 920 in their capital of al-Mahdiyah in Tunisia; it lasted until 1171, by which time opposition within the sect caused it to disintegrate. 'Abbasid authority was partially restored in the 12th century, but the caliphate ceased to exist with the Mongol destruction of Baghdad in 1258. Some principal caliphs are listed below.

CALIPH	REIGN
"Perfect" caliphs	
Abu Bakr	632–634
'Umar I	634–644
'Uthman ibn 'Affan	644–656
'Ali	656–661
Umayyad caliphs (Damascus)	
Mu'awiyah I	661–680
'Abd al-Malik	685–705
al-Walid	705–715
Hisham	724–743
Marwan II	744–750
'Abbasid caliphs (Baghdad)	
as-Saffah	749–754
Harun	786–809
al-Ma'mun	813–833

CALIPH	REIGN
Fatimid caliphs (al-Mahdiyah)	
al-Mahdi	909–934
al-Qa'im	934–946
al-Mansur	946–953
al-Mu'izz	953–975
al-Hakim	996–1021
al-Mustansir	1036–94
al-Musta'li	1094–1101
'Abbasid caliph (Baghdad)	
al-Nasir	1180–1225

Sultans of the Ottoman Empire

One of the most powerful states in the world during the 15th and 16th centuries, the Ottoman empire was created by Turkish tribes in Anatolia and spanned more than 600 years. It came to an end in 1922, when it was replaced by the Turkish Republic and various successor states in southeastern Europe and the Middle East. At its height the empire included most of southeastern Europe, the Middle East as far east as Iraq, North Africa as far west as Algeria, and most of the Arabian Peninsula. The term Ottoman is a dynastic appellation derived from Osman (Arabic: 'Uthman), the nomadic Turkmen chief who founded both the dynasty and the empire.

SULTAN	REIGN
Osman I	c. 1300–1324
Orhan	1324–1360
Murad I	1360–1389
Bayezid I	1389–1402
Mehmed I	1413–1421
Murad II	1421–1444
Mehmed II	1444–1446

SULTAN	REIGN
Murad II (second reign)	1446–1451
Mehmed II (second reign)	1451–1481
Bayezid II	1481–1512
Selim I	1512–1520
Suleyman I	1520–1566
Selim II	1566–1574
Murad III	1574–1595

Sultans of the Ottoman Empire (continued)

SULTAN	REIGN
Mehmed III	1595–1603
Ahmed I	1603–1617
Mustafa I	1617–1618
Osman II	1618–1622
Mustafa I (second reign)	1622–1623
Murad IV	1623–1640
Ibrahim	1640–1648
Mehmed IV	1648–1687
Suleyman II	1687–1691
Ahmed II	1691–1695
Mustafa II	1695–1703
Ahmed III	1703–1730
Mahmud I	1730–1754
Osman III	1754–1757
Mustafa III	1757–1774
Abdulhamid I	1774–1789
Selim III	1789–1807
Mustafa IV	1807–1808
Mahmud II	1808–1839
Abdulmecid I	1839–1861
Abdulaziz	1861–1876
Murad V	1876
Abdulhamid II	1876–1909
Mehmed V	1909–1918
Mehmed VI	1918–1922

Persian Dynasties

Dates given are approximate and may overlap.

DYNASTY/KINGDOM	PERIOD
Median	728–550 BC
Achaemenian	559–330 BC
Hellenistic period of Alexander and the Seleucids[1]	330 BC–247 BC
Parthian period (Arsacid dynasty)[2]	247 BC–AD 224
Sasanian	224–651
Arab invasion and the advent of Islam	640–829
Iranian intermezzo[3]	821–1055
Seljuqs	1038–1157
Mongols[4]	1220–1335
Timurids and Ottoman Turks	1380–1501
Safavid	1502–1736
Afghan interlude	1723–36
Nader Shah	1736–47
Zand	1750–79
Qajars	1794–1925
Pahlavi	1925–79

[1]Dates from the death of Darius III, the last Achaemenian king, and the invasion of Alexander the Great. [2]Dates from the year in which the Parnian chief Arsaces first battled the Seleucids. [3]Includes the Tahirid, Samanid, Ghaznavids, and Buyid dynasties. [4]Mainly the Il-Khanid dynasty (1256–1353).

Asia

Indian Dynasties

Dates given are approximations.

DYNASTY	LOCATION	DATES
Nanda	Ganges Valley	400 BC
Maurya	India, barring the area south of Mysore (Karnataka)	400–200 BC
Indo-Greeks	northern India	200–100 BC
Sunga	Ganges Valley and parts of central India	200–100 BC
Satavahana	northern Deccan	100 BC–AD 300
Saka	western India	100 BC–AD 400
Kusana	northern India and Central Asia	AD 100–300
Gupta	northern India	400–600
Harsa	northern India	700
Pallava	Tamil Nadu	400–900
Calukya	western and central Deccan	600–800
Pala	Bengal	800–1100
Pratihara	western India and upper Ganges Valley	900–1100
Rastrakuta	western and central Deccan	800–1100
Cola	Tamil Nadu	900–1300
Candella	Bundelkhand	1000–1200
Cauhan	Rajasthan	1000–1200
Caulukya	Gujarat	1000–1300
Paramara	western and central India	1000–1100
Later Calukya	western and central Deccan	1000–1200
Hoysala	central and southern Deccan	1200–1400
Yadava	northern Deccan	1200–1300
Pandya	Tamil Nadu	1300–1400

Japanese Historical Periods and Rulers

PERIOD	DATES
Asuka	552–710
Nara	710–784
Heian	794–1185
Kamakura	1192–1333
Muromachi (or Ashikaga)	1338–1573
Azuchi-Momoyama	1574–1600
Edo (or Tokugawa)	1603–1867
Meiji	1868–1912

Japanese Historical Periods and Rulers (continued)

Reign dates for the first 28 sovereigns (Jimmu through Senka) are taken from the *Nihon shoki* ("Chronicles of Japan"). The first 14 sovereigns are considered legendary, and while the next 14 are known to have existed, their exact reign dates have not been verified historically. When the year of actual accession and year of formal coronation are different, the latter is placed in parentheses after the former. If the two events took place in the same year, no special notation is used. If only the coronation year is known, it is placed in parentheses.

EMPEROR	REIGN
Jimmu	(660)–585 BC
Suizei	(581)–549 BC
Annei	549–511 BC
Itoku	(510)–477 BC
Kosho	(475)–393 BC
Koan	(392)–291 BC
Korei	(290)–215 BC
Kogen	(214)–158 BC
Kaika	158–98 BC
Sujin	(97)–30 BC
Suinin	(29 BC)–AD 70
Keiko	(71)–130
Seimu	(131)–190
Chuai	(192)–200
Jingu Kogo (regent)	201–269
Ojin	(270)–310
Nintoku	(313)–399
Richu	(400)–405
Hanzei	(406)–410
Ingyo	(412)–453
Anko	453–456
Yuryaku	456–479
Seinei	(480)–484
Kenzo	(485)–487
Ninken	(488)–498
Buretsu	498–506
Keitai	(507)–531
Ankan	531 (534)–535
Senka	535–539
Kimmei	539–571
Bidatsu	(572)–585
Yomei	585–587
Sushun	587–592
Suiko (empress regnant)	593–628
Jomei	(629)–641
Kogyoku (empress regnant)	(642)–645
Kotoku	645–654
Saimei (empress regnant: Kogyoku rethroned)	(655)–661
Tenji	661 (668)–672
Kobun	672
Temmu	672 (673)–686
Jito (empress regnant)	686 (690)–697
Mommu	697–707
Gemmei (empress regnant)	707–715
Gensho (empress regnant)	715–724
Shomu	724–749
Koken (empress regnant)	749–758
Junnin	758–764
Shotoku (empress regnant: Koken rethroned)	764 (765)–770
Konin	770–781
Kammu	781–806
Heizei	806–809
Saga	809–823
Junna	823–833
Nimmyo	833–850
Montoku	850–858
Seiwa	858–876
Yozei	876 (877)–884
Koko	884–887

EMPEROR	REIGN
Uda	887–897
Daigo	897–930
Suzaku	930–946
Murakami	946–967
Reizei	967–969
En'yu	969–984
Kazan	984–986
Ichijo	986–1011
Sanjo	1011–16
Go-Ichijo	1016–36
Go-Suzaku	1036–45
Go-Reizei	1045–68
Go-Sanjo	1068–72
Shirakawa	1072–86
Horikawa	1086–1107
Toba	1107–23
Sutoku	1123–41
Konoe	1141–55
Go-Shirakawa	1155–58
Nijo	1158–65
Rokujo	1165–68
Takakura	1168–80
Antoku	1180–85[1]
Go-Toba	1183 (1184)–98
Tsuchimikado	1198–1210
Juntoku	1210 (1211)–21
Chukyo	1221
Goshirakawa	1221 (1222)–32
Shijo	1232 (1233)–42
Go-Saga	1242–46
Go-Fukakusa	1246–59/60
Kameyama	1259/60–74
Gouda	1274–87
Fushimi	1287 (1288)–98
Go-Fushimi	1298–1301
Go-Nijo	1301–08
Hanazono	1308–18
Go-Daigo	1318–39
Go-Murakami	1339–68
Chokei	1368–83
Go-Kameyama	1383–92
The Northern court[2]	
Kogon	1331 (1332)–33
Komyo	1336 (1337/38)–48
Suko	1348 (1349/50)–51
Go-Kogon	1351 (1353/54)–71
Go-Enyu	1371 (1374/75)–82
Go-Komatsu	1382–92
Go-Komatsu	1392–1412
Shoko	1412 (1414)–28
Go-Hanazono	1428 (1429/30)–64
Go-Tsuchimikado	1464 (1465/66)–1500
Go-Kashiwabara	1500 (1521)–26
Go-Nara	1526 (1536)–57
Ogimachi	1557 (1560)–86
Go-Yozei	1586 (1587)–1611
Go-Mizunoo	1611–29
Meisho (empress regnant)	1629 (1630)–43
Go-Komyo	1643–54
Go-Sai	1654/55 (1656)–63

Japanese Historical Periods and Rulers (continued)

EMPEROR	REIGN
The Northern court[2] (continued)	
Reigen	1663–87
Higashiyama	1687–1709
Nakamikado	1709 (1710)–35
Sakuramachi	1735–47
Momozono	1747–62
Go-Sakuramachi (empress regnant)	1762 (1763)–71
Go-Momozono	1771–79
Kokaku	1780–1817
Ninko	1817–46
Komei	1846 (1847)–66
Meiji (personal name: Mutsuhito; era name: Meiji)	1867 (1868)–1912
Taisho (personal name: Yoshihito; era name: Taisho)	1912 (1915)–26
Hirohito (era name: Showa)	1926 (1928)–1989
Akihito (era name: Heisei)	1989 (1990)–

[1]Antoku's reign overlaps that of Go-Toba. Go-Toba was placed on the throne by the Minamoto clan after the rival Taira clan had fled Kyoto with Antoku. [2]From 1336 until 1392 Japan witnessed the spectacle of two contending Imperial courts—the Southern court of Go-Daigo and his descendants, whose sphere of influence was restricted to the immediate vicinity of the Yoshino Mountains, and the Northern court of Kogon and his descendants, which was under the domination of the Ashikaga family.

Chinese Dynasties

Dates given for early dynasties are approximate and may overlap.

DYNASTY	ALTERNATE NAME	DATES
Hsia[1]	Xia	c. 2205–1766 BC
Shang		c. 1760–1030 BC
Western Zhou	Chou	c. 1050–771 BC
Eastern Zhou	Chou	c. 771–255 BC
Qin	Ch'in	221–206 BC
Han		206 BC–AD 220
Western Jin	Chin	265–317
Eastern Jin[2]	Chin	317–420
Six Dynasties[2]		220–589
Wu		222–80
Eastern Jin[2]		317–420
Liusong		420–79
Six Dynasties[2] (continued)		
Southern Qi		479–502
Southern Liang		502–57
Southern Chen		557–89
Sui		581–618
T'ang	Tang	618–907
Five Dynasties[3]	Ten Kingdoms[3]	907–960
Sung	Song	960–1279
Yüan	Yuan, Mongol	1206–1368
Ming		1368–1644
Ch'ing	Qing, Manchu	1644–1911/12

[1]The Hsia Dynasty is mentioned in legends but is of undetermined historicity. [2]Between the fall of the Han and the establishment of the Sui, China was divided into two societies, northern and southern. The Six Dynasties had their capital at Nanjing in the south. The Eastern Jin is considered one of these six dynasties and so is listed twice. [3]Period of time between the fall of the T'ang dynasty and the founding of the Sung dynasty, when five would-be dynasties followed one another in quick succession in North China. The era is also known as the period of the Ten Kingdoms because 10 regimes dominated separate regions of South China during the same period.

Leaders of the People's Republic of China Since 1949

Chinese Communist Party leaders

NAME	TITLE	DATES
Mao Zedong	CCP chairman	1949–1976
Hua Guofeng	CCP chairman	1976–1981
Hu Yaobang	CCP chairman; after September 1982, general secretary of the CCP	1981–1987
Zhao Ziyang	CCP general secretary	1987–1989
Jiang Zemin	CCP general secretary	1989–2002
Hu Jintao	CCP general secretary	2002–

premiers

NAME	DATES
Zhou Enlai	1949–1976
Hua Guofeng	1976–1980
Zhao Ziyang	1980–1987
Li Peng	1987–1998
Zhu Rongji	1998–2003
Wen Jiabao	2003–

Note: although he held no top party or state position, Deng Xiaoping was de facto leader of China from 1977 to 1997.

Dalai Lamas

The Dalai Lama is the head of the dominant Dge-lugs-pa (Yellow Hat) order of Tibetan Buddhists and, until 1959, was both spiritual and temporal ruler of Tibet. In accordance with the belief in reincarnate lamas, which began to develop in the 14th century, the successors of the first Dalai Lama were considered his rebirths and came to be regarded as physical manifestations of the compassionate bodhisattva ("buddha-to-be"), Avalokitesvara.

Dalai Lamas (continued)

DALAI LAMA	NAME	LIVED
first	Dge-'dun-grub-pa	1391–1475
second	Dge-'dun-rgya-mtsho	1475–1542
third	Bsod-nams-rgya-mtsho	1543–1588
fourth	Yon-tan-rgya-mtsho	1589–1617
fifth	Ngag-dbang-rgya-mtsho	1617–1682
sixth	Tshangs-dbyangs-rgya-mtsho	1683–1706
seventh	Bskal-bzang-rgya-mtsho	1708–1757
eighth	'Jam-dpal-rgya-mtsho	1758–1804
ninth	Lung-rtogs-rgya-mtsho	1806–1815[1]
tenth	Tshul-khrims-rgya-mtsho	1816–1837[1]
eleventh	Mkhas-grub-rgya-mtsho	1838–1856[1]
twelfth	'Phrin-las-rgya-mtsho	1856–1875[1]
thirteenth	Thub-bstan-rgya-mtsho	1875–1933[2]
fourteenth	Bstan-'dzin-rgya-mtsho	1935–[3]

[1]*Dalai Lamas 9–12 all died young, and the country was ruled by regencies.* [2]*Reigned as head of a sovereign state from 1912.* [3]*Ruled from exile in Dharmsala, India, from 1960.*

The Americas

Pre-Columbian Civilizations

Various aboriginal American Indian cultures evolved in Meso-America (part of Mexico and Central America) and the Andean region (western South America) prior to Spanish exploration and conquest in the 16th century. These pre-Columbian civilizations were extraordinary developments in human society and culture, characterized by kingdoms and empires, great monuments and cities, and refinements in the arts, metallurgy, and writing. Dates given below are approximations.

CULTURE	LOCATION	DATES
Meso-American civilizations		
Olmec	Gulf coast of southern Mexico	1150 BC–800 BC
Zapotec	Oaxaca, particularly Monte Albán	500 BC–AD 900
Totonac	east-central Mexico	500 BC–AD 900
Teotihuacán	Teotihuacán, in the Valley of Mexico	AD 400–600
Maya	southern Mexico and Guatemala	250–900
Toltec	central Mexico	900–1200
Aztec	central and southern Mexico	1400–early 1500s
Andean civilizations		
Nazca	southern coast of Peru	200 BC–AD 600
Recuay	northern highlands of Peru	200 BC–AD 600
Tiwanaku	Lake Titicaca, Bolivia	200 BC–AD 1000
Moche (Mochica)	northern coast of Peru	AD 1–700
Inca	Pacific coast of South America	1100–1532

Africa

Historic Sub-Saharan African States

STATE	LOCATION IN PRESENT-DAY COUNTRIES	FLOURISHED
Aksumite kingdom	Ethiopia, Sudan	1st–10th centuries
Asante empire	Ghana	18th–19th centuries
Basuto kingdom	Lesotho	19th century
Benin kingdom	Nigeria	12th–19th centuries
kingdom of Buganda	Uganda	14th–20th centuries
kingdom of Bunyoro	Uganda	15th–19th centuries
kingdom of Burundi	Burundi	17th–20th centuries
kingdom of Dahomey	Benin	17th–19th centuries
Darfur	Sudan	17th–19th centuries
kingdom of Dongola	Sudan	7th–14th centuries
Fulani empire	Cameroon, Niger, Nigeria	19th–20th centuries
Ghana empire	Mali, Mauritania	4th–13th centuries
Hausa states	Nigeria	14th–19th centuries
Kanem-Bornu	Nigeria, Chad, Cameroon, Niger, Libya	9th–19th centuries
Kongo kingdom	Angola, Dem. Rep. of Congo	14th–17th centuries
Kuba kingdom	Dem. Rep. of Congo	17th–19th centuries
kingdom of Kush	Egypt, Sudan	c. 850 BC–c. AD 325
Luba empire	Dem Rep. of Congo	16th–19th centuries
Lunda empire	Dem. Rep. of Congo, Angola, Zambia	17th–19th centuries
Mali empire	Mali, Mauritania, Senegal, Gambia, Guinea-Bissau	13th–16th centuries

Historic Sub-Saharan African States (continued)

STATE	LOCATION IN PRESENT-DAY COUNTRIES	FLOURISHED
Ndongo kingdom	Angola	14th–17th centuries
kingdom of Nubia	Egypt, Sudan	4th–7th centuries
Oyo empire	Nigeria	16th–19th centuries
Rozwi empire	Zimbabwe, Botswana	17th–19th centuries
Shewa empire	Ethiopia	15th–19th centuries
Songhai empire	Nigeria, Niger	6th–17th centuries
Tukulor empire	Mali	19th century
Wolof empire	Senegal	14th–19th centuries
Zeng empire	Somalia, Kenya, Tanzania, Mozambique	10th–16th centuries
Zulu kingdom	South Africa	19th century

One of Africa's least-explored regions, the northern part of the Republic of the Congo, an area of huge swamps and nearly impenetrable forests, was traversed by foot in 1999. Dr. Michael Fay, an ecologist with the Wildlife Conservation Society, and a team of 12 others undertook a 1,200-mi (1,900-km) survey of this area as well as similar areas in neighboring Gabon. The team concluded that this wilderness is seriously threatened.

Populations

Largest Urban Agglomerations

Agglomerations include a central city and associated neighboring communities.

Source: United Nations, World Urbanization Prospects: The 2007 Revision.

RANK	AGGLOMERATION	COUNTRY	POPULATION (2007)
1	Tokyo	Japan	35,676,000
2	New York City–Newark	US	19,040,000
3	Mexico City	Mexico	19,028,000
4	Mumbai (Bombay)	India	18,978,000
5	São Paulo	Brazil	18,845,000
6	Delhi	India	15,926,000
7	Shanghai	China	14,987,000
8	Kolkata (Calcutta)	India	14,787,000
9	Dhaka	Bangladesh	13,485,000
10	Buenos Aires	Argentina	12,795,000
11	Los Angeles–Long Beach–Santa Ana	US	12,500,000
12	Karachi	Pakistan	12,130,000
13	Cairo	Egypt	11,893,000
14	Rio de Janeiro	Brazil	11,748,000
15	Osaka-Kobe	Japan	11,294,000
16	Beijing	China	11,106,000
17	Manila	Philippines	11,100,000
18	Moscow	Russia	10,452,000
19	Istanbul	Turkey	10,061,000
20	Paris	France	9,904,000
21	Seoul	Rep. of Korea	9,796,000
22	Lagos	Nigeria	9,466,000
23	Jakarta	Indonesia	9,125,000
24	Chicago	US	8,990,000
25	Guangzhou	China	8,829,000
26	London	UK	8,567,000
27	Lima	Peru	8,012,000
28	Tehran	Iran	7,873,000
29	Kinshasa	Dem. Rep. of the Congo	7,843,000
30	Bogotá	Colombia	7,772,000

Migration of Foreigners into Selected Countries

Percentages of foreign or foreign-born populations in selected Organisation for Economic Co-operation and Development countries. Source: <www.oecd.org>.

COUNTRY	FOREIGNERS AS % OF TOTAL POPULATION 2000	2005
Luxembourg[1]	37.3	39.6
Australia[2]	23.0	23.8
Switzerland[2]	21.9	23.8
New Zealand[2]	17.2	19.4
Canada[2]	18.1	19.1
Austria[2]	10.5	13.5
US[2]	11.0	12.9
Sweden[2]	11.3	12.4
Belgium[2]	10.3	12.1
Ireland[2]	8.7	11.0
The Netherlands[2]	10.1	10.6
UK[2]	7.9	9.7
Germany[1]	8.9	8.8
Norway[2]	6.8	8.2
France[2]	N/A	8.1
Denmark[2]	5.8	6.5
Portugal[2]	5.1	6.3
Spain[1]	2.2	6.2
Greece[1]	2.9	5.2
Czech Republic[2]	4.2	5.1
Italy[1]	2.4	4.6
Finland[2]	2.6	3.4

N/A indicates data not available. [1]*Indicates foreign population.* [2]*Indicates foreign-born population.*

Persons of Concern Worldwide

The Office of the UN High Commissioner for Refugees (UNHCR) attempts to ease the plight of various "persons of concern," including refugees and asylum seekers. Sources: UNHCR 2007 Global Trends: Refugees, Asylum-seekers, Returnees, Internally Displaced and Stateless Persons; *Internal Displacement Monitoring Centre.*

Persons of Concern to UNHCR by Category (estimates as of 1 Jan 2008)

REGION	REFUGEES	ASYLUM SEEKERS	RETURNED REFUGEES	INTERNALLY DISPLACED PERSONS (IDPS)[1]	STATELESS AND OTHER	TOTAL[2]
Asia and Oceania	6,335,663	70,955	421,574	4,285,844	2,255,461	13,762,074
Africa	2,498,329	272,282	302,644	5,888,837	100,547	10,731,653
Europe	1,569,168	234,197	6,356	565,636	649,909	3,033,793
North America	456,960	121,397	—	—	—	578,357
Latin America and the Caribbean	530,550	41,155	28	3,000,000	13	3,571,746
Total	11,390,670	739,986	730,640[3]	13,740,317	3,005,930	31,677,661

Total Number of Refugees (estimates as of 1 January of each year)

YEAR	REFUGEES	YEAR	REFUGEES
1999	11,429,700	2004	9,671,800
2000	11,625,700	2005	9,236,500
2001	12,062,500	2006	8,394,400
2002	12,029,900	2007	9,877,700
2003	10,389,600	2008	11,390,670

Origin of Major Refugee Populations[4] (estimates as of 1 Jan 2008)

COUNTRY OF ORIGIN	TOTAL	COUNTRY OF ORIGIN	TOTAL
Afghanistan	3,057,661	Burundi	375,727
Iraq	2,309,247	Dem. Rep. of the Congo	370,374
Colombia	551,744	Vietnam	327,776
The Sudan	523,032	Turkey	221,939
Somalia	457,357	Eritrea	208,743

Host Country of Major Refugee Populations (estimates as of 1 Jan 2008)

COUNTRY OF ASYLUM	TOTAL	COUNTRY OF ASYLUM	TOTAL
Pakistan	2,035,023	Tanzania	435,630
Syria	1,503,769	China	301,078
Iran	963,546	United Kingdom	299,718
Germany	578,879	Chad	294,017
Jordan	500,281	United States	281,219

Internally Displaced Persons (2007)

COUNTRY	TOTAL	COUNTRY	TOTAL
The Sudan	5,800,000	Georgia	222,000–247,000
Iraq	2,480,000	Ethiopia	200,000
Colombia	2,390,000–4,000,000	Kenya	200,000
Dem. Rep. of the Congo	1,400,000	Central African Republic	197,000
Uganda	1,270,000	Chad	179,000
Somalia	1,000,000	Afghanistan	161,000
Turkey	950,000–1,200,000	Peru	150,000
Côte d'Ivoire	709,000	Israel	150,000–420,000
Azerbaijan	690,000+	Bosnia and Herzegovina	132,000
India	600,000+	Burundi	100,000
Zimbabwe	570,000	East Timor	100,000
Myanmar (Burma)	500,000+	Indonesia	100,000–200,000
Bangladesh	500,000	Lebanon	90,000–390,000
Sri Lanka	460,000	Philippines	20,000–300,000
Syria	430,000	Russia	19,000–159,000
Serbia	247,000		

[1]Data include only those IDPs to whom UNHCR extends protection and/or assistance. [2]Includes unlisted returned IDPs. [3]Includes 38 undefined persons. [4]A separate mandate of the UN Relief and Works Agency for Palestine Refugees in the Near East (UNWRA) covers more than 4,300,000 Palestinans. Palestinians outside of the UNWRA, such as those in Iraq and Libya, numbered 341,237 in 2008. In addition, there were an estimated 1,739,000 refugees in the West Bank and the Gaza Strip in 2007.

Languages of the World

Most Widely Spoken Languages

Listing the languages spoken by more than 1% of humankind, this table enumerates speakers of each tongue as a primary or secondary language. Figures based on data from Linguasphere 2000. For more information visit <www.linguasphere.org>.

LANGUAGE	NUMBER OF SPEAKERS (MILLIONS)	% OF WORLD POPULATION (APPROXIMATE)	LANGUAGE FAMILY
English	1,000	16	Indo-European (Germanic)
Mandarin	1,000	16	Sino-Tibetan (Chinese)
Hindi/Urdu[1]	900	15	Indo-European (Indo-Aryan)
Spanish	450	7	Indo-European (Romance)
Russian/Belarusian	320	5	Indo-European (Slavic)
Arabic	250	4	Afro-Asiatic (Semitic)
Bengali/Sylhetti	250	4	Indo-European (Indo-Aryan)
Malay/Indonesian	200	3	Austronesian (Malayo-Polynesian)
Portuguese	200	3	Indo-European (Romance)
Japanese	130	2	isolated language
French	125	2	Indo-European (Romance)
German	125	2	Indo-European (Germanic)
Thai/Lao	90	1	Tai
Punjabi	85	1	Indo-European (Indo-Aryan)
Wu	85	1	Sino-Tibetan (Chinese)
Javanese	80	1	Austronesian (Malayo-Polynesian)
Marathi	80	1	Indo-European (Indo-Aryan)
Turkish/Azeri/Turkmen	80	1	Altaic (Turkic)
Korean	75	1	isolated language
Vietnamese	75	1	Mon-Khmer (Vietic)
Cantonese	70	1	Sino-Tibetan (Chinese)
Italian	70	1	Indo-European (Romance)
Tamil	70	1	Dravidian
Telugu	70	1	Dravidian
Ukrainian	65	1	Indo-European (Slavic)
Bhojpuri/Maithili	60	1	Indo-European (Indo-Aryan)
Persian/Tajik	60	1	Indo-European (Iranian)
Swahili	60	1	Afro-Asiatic (Niger-Congo)
Tagalog	60	1	Austronesian (Malayo-Polynesian)

[1]Although Hindi and Urdu use different writing systems, these languages are branches of Hindustani and are orally mutually intelligible.

English Neologisms

New entries from Merriam-Webster's Collegiate® Dictionary, *Eleventh Edition (© 2008). The date in parentheses is the date of the word's earliest recorded use in English of the sense given (not necessarily of the word's very earliest meaning in English).*

air quotes (1989): a gesture made by raising and flexing the index and middle fingers of both hands that is used to call attention to a spoken word or expression

dark energy (1998): a hypothetical form of energy that produces a force that opposes gravity and is thought to be the cause of the accelerating expansion of the universe

dirty bomb (1956): a bomb designed to release radioactive material

dwarf planet (1993): a celestial body that orbits the Sun and has a spherical shape but is too small to disturb other objects from its orbit

edamame (1951): immature green soybeans usually in the pod

fanboy (1919): a boy who is an enthusiastic devotee (as of comics or movies)

infinity pool (1992): an outdoor swimming pool having an edge over which water flows into a trough but seems to flow into the horizon

jukebox musical (1993): a musical that features popular songs from the past

kiteboarding (1996): the sport of riding on a small surfboard that is propelled across water by a large kite to which the rider is harnessed

malware (1990): software designed to interfere with a computer's normal functioning

mental health day (1971): a day that an employee takes off from work in order to relieve stress or renew vitality

mondegreen (1954): a word or phrase that results from a mishearing of something said or sung

netroots (2003): the grassroots political activists who communicate via the Internet especially by blogs

norovirus (2002): any of a genus of small round single-stranded RNA viruses; *specifically*: Norwalk Virus

pescatarian (1993): a vegetarian whose diet includes fish

phytonutrient (1994): a bioactive plant-derived compound (as resveratrol) associated with positive health effects

English Neologisms (continued)

pretexting (1992): the practice of presenting oneself as someone else in order to obtain private information
prosecco (1881): a dry Italian sparkling wine
racino (1995): a racetrack at which slot machines are available for gamblers
soju (1978): Korean vodka distilled from rice
subprime (1995): **1:** having or being an interest rate that is higher than a prime rate and is extended especially to low-income borrowers **2:** extending or obtaining a subprime loan
supercross (1983): a motorcycle race held in a stadium on a dirt track having hairpin turns and high jumps
Texas Hold'em (1995): poker in which each player is dealt two cards facedown and all players share five cards dealt faceup
webinar (1998): a live online educational presentation during which participating viewers can submit questions and comments
wing nut (c. 1900): one who advocates extreme measures or changes: radical

Scholarship

National Libraries of the World

The national libraries listed below are generally open to the public. National libraries are usually the primary repository for a nation's printed works. Sources: "National Libraries of the World: An Address List," IFLA Publications; *International Dictionary of Library Histories,* 2001, Fitzroy Dearborn Publishers.

LIBRARY	LOCATION	YEAR FOUNDED[1]	SPECIAL COLLECTIONS, ARCHIVES, PAPERS
Biblioteca Nacional de España	Madrid, Spain	1836	manuscripts, Miguel de Cervantes
Biblioteca Nacional de la República Argentina	Buenos Aires	1810	Arturo Frondizi
Biblioteca Nacional de México	Mexico City	1867	Jesuit works, early Mexican printing
Biblioteca Nacional de Portugal	Lisbon	1796	Luís de Camões, Desiderius Erasmus
Biblioteca Nacional de Venezuela	Caracas	1833	politics and diplomacy, Simón Bolívar
Biblioteca Nazionale Centrale di Firenze	Florence, Italy	1861	Reformation, Galileo Galilei
Biblioteca Nazionale Centrale di Roma	Rome, Italy	1876	Jesuit collections, Gabriele D'Annunzio
Biblioteka Narodowa	Warsaw, Poland	1928	engravings, music
Bibliotheca Alexandrina	Alexandria, Egypt	2002[2]	ancient manuscripts, Egyptian heritage
Bibliothèque et Archives Nationales du Québec	Montreal, QC, Canada	2004	artists' books, maps
Bibliothèque Nationale de France	Paris	1461	Denis Diderot, Jean-Paul Sartre
British Library	London	1973[3]	Charles Dickens, George B. Shaw
Deutsche Nationalbibliothek Frankfurt am Main	Germany	2006	bibliographies, exile literature (1933–45)
Deutsche Nationalbibliothek Leipzig	Germany	2006	socialism, Anne-Frank-Shoah-Bibliothek
Fundação Biblioteca Nacional	Rio de Janeiro, Brazil	1810	botany, Latin American music
Jewish National and University Library	Jerusalem, Israel	1892	world Jewish history, Albert Einstein
Koninklijke Bibliotheek	The Hague, Netherlands	1798	Hugo Grotius, Constantijn Huygens
Library and Archives Canada	Ottawa	2004	hockey, portraits of Canadians
Library of Congress	Washington DC	1800	Americana, folk music, early motion pictures
Milli Kutuphane	Ankara, Turkey	1948	Mustafa Kemal Atatürk
National Agricultural Library	Beltsville MD	1962	research reports
National Diet Library[4]	Tokyo, Japan	1948	Japanese culture, Allied occupation
National Library of Australia	Canberra	1960	Asian and Pacific area
National Library of China[5]	Beijing	1909	art, early communism
National Library of Education	Washington DC	1994	research reports
National Library of Greece[6]	Athens	1866[7]	incunabula
National Library of India	Kolkata (Calcutta)	1903	rare journals of vernacular languages
National Library of Ireland	Dublin	1877	biography, Gaelic manuscripts
National Library of Medicine	Bethesda MD	1956	history of medicine
National Library of New Zealand[8]	Wellington	1965	European exploration, missionary activity
National Library of Pakistan	Islamabad	1993	manuscripts, censuses
National Library of the Philippines	Manila	1901	presidential papers
National Library of Russia[9]	St. Petersburg	1795	rare books, Russian history
National Library of Scotland	Edinburgh	1925	mountaineering, witchcraft

National Libraries of the World (continued)

LIBRARY	LOCATION	YEAR FOUNDED	SPECIAL COLLECTIONS, ARCHIVES, PAPERS
National Library of South Africa	Pretoria; Cape Town	1999	Africana, cookery
National Library of Sweden[10]	Stockholm	1661	Scandinavian cartography and manuscripts
National Library of Wales	Aberystwyth	1907	publications of overseas Welsh settlements

[1]*In present institutional form.* [2]*Originally founded in the 3rd century* BC. [3]*Originally founded in 1753 as the British Museum Library.* [4]*Kokuritsu Kokkai Toshokan.* [5]*Zhongguo Guojia Tushuguan.* [6]*Ethnike Bibliotheke tes Hellados.* [7]*Originally founded in 1832 as the Public Library.* [8]*Te Puna Matauranga o Aotearoa.* [9]*Rossyskaya Natsionalnaya Biblioteka.* [10]*Kungliga Biblioteket.*

World Education Profile

This table provides comparative data about the education systems in 30 selected countries. Definitions as well as information gathering and reporting methods vary widely from country to country, so the statistics presented here are not always exactly comparable.

Compulsory education = the number of years of education and ages of pupils required by the system; **enrollment ratio** = the actual number of children attending primary school or secondary school as a percentage of all children in the primary school or secondary school age group as defined by the country (number may exceed 100%); **enrollment ratio** for higher education = total enrollment in higher education, regardless of age, as a percentage of all persons of school-leaving age to five years thereafter; **student/teacher ratio** = number of pupils or students per teacher at each level; **expenditure** = total public expenditure on education as a percentage of GDP in 2006.

Sources: *Britannica World Data,* 2008; *UNESCO Global Education Digest,* 2007.

	% LITERACY RATE OF THOSE 15 AND OLDER				COMPULSORY EDUCATION		ENROLLMENT RATIO (2006)			STUDENT/TEACHER RATIO (2004)			EXPENDITURE
COUNTRY	YEAR	TOTAL	M	F	# YEARS	AGES	PRI.	SEC.	HIGHER	PRI.	SEC.	HIGHER	
Africa													
Egypt	2007	72.0	83.6	60.7	9	6–14	103	88[1]	35[2]	21.4[3]	13.7[3]	–	4.2
Kenya	2002	84.3	90.0	78.5	8	6–13	106	50	3[1]	32.9[3]	18.6[3]	–	6.9
Senegal	2007	42.6	53.1	32.3	6	7–12	80	24	6[2]	43.2	26.4	24.6[2]	5.0
South Africa	2007	88.0	88.9	87.2	9	7–15	106[1]	95[1]	15	33.8[3]	29.6[3]	16.7[3]	5.4
Asia													
China	2007	93.3	96.5	90.0	9	6–14	111	76	22	20.0	18.6	15.5	1.9[4]
India	2007	66.0	76.9	54.5	9	6–14	112	54[2]	12	41.3	32.0	26.4	3.2[2]
Indonesia	2007	91.4	94.9	88.0	9	7–15	114	64	17	20.3[3]	14.2[3]	14.7[3]	3.6
Iran	2007	84.7	90.0	79.4	5	6–10	118	81[2]	27	22.6	24.2	–	5.1
Israel	2003	95.4	97.3	93.6	11	5–15	110	92	58	12.0[2]	6.2[2]	–	6.9[1]
Japan	2007	100.0	100.0	100.0	10	6–15	100	101	57	17.3[2]	14.5[2]	17.8[2]	3.5[2]
Philippines	2007	93.4	93.1	93.7	7	6–12	110	83	28	35.5	40.8	22.1[3]	2.5[2]
Saudi Arabia	2007	85.0	89.1	79.4	6	6–11	54[3]	53[5]	29	11.3[2]	11.0[2]	48.8[2]	6.8[1]
Thailand	2007	94.1	95.9	92.6	9	6–14	108	78	46	20.5	23.2	34.3	4.2[2]
Turkey	2007	88.7	96.2	81.2	9	6–14	94	79	35	26.9[6]	20.7[6]	25.7[7]	4.0[1]
Europe													
France	1995	98.8	98.9	98.7	11	6–16	110	114	56	10.9[7]	10.3[7]	25.4[7]	5.7[2]
Germany	1998	100.0	100.0	100.0	13	6–18	103	101	51[3]	35.3[7]	23.5[7]	12.1[7]	4.6[1]
Greece	2007	97.1	98.2	96.0	9	6–14	102	103	95	11.0[7]	9.2[7]	13.5[7]	4.4[2]
Italy	2007	98.9	99.1	98.6	9	6–14	103	100	67	10.8[3]	14.5[3]	21.9[3]	4.5[2]
Poland	2007	99.3	99.6	99.0	9	7–15	98	100	66	13.3[6]	14.0[6]	19.4[6]	5.5[2]
Russia	2007	99.5	99.7	99.4	10	6–15	96	84	72	–	–	17.9[6]	3.8[2]
Sweden	2000	100.0	100.0	100.0	10	7–16	96	103	79	9.5[2]	9.2[2]	11.4[3]	7.1[2]
United Kingdom	2006	100.0	100.0	100.0	12	5–16	105	98	59	21.3[7]	16.0[7]	19.7[3]	5.6[2]
Latin America													
Argentina	2007	97.6	97.6	97.7	10	5–14	112[2]	84[2]	64[2]	15.2[8]	18.7[8]	10.2[8]	3.8[1]
Brazil	2007	90.5	90.1	90.9	8	7–14	137[2]	105[2]	25[2]	21.5[3]	18.6[3]	19.6[3]	4.0[1]
Cuba	2007	99.8	99.8	99.8	9	6–14	101	94	88	10.6[6]	10.1[6]	14.6[6]	9.1
Mexico	2007	92.4	94.4	90.6	10	6–15	113	87	26	24.3[5]	16.0[5]	9.9[5]	5.5[2]
Peru	2007	90.5	95.2	85.8	11	6–16	116	94	35	22.2	16.6	–	2.5
North America													
Canada	2005	100.0	100.0	100.0	11	6–16	100[1]	117[1]	62[1]	17.4[5]	18.4	19.8[1]	5.2[5]
United States	1998	95.5	95.7	95.3	12	6–17	98	94	82	–	–	13.5[7]	5.3[2]
Oceania													
Australia	2006	100.0	100.0	100.0	11	5–15	105	150	73	16.0[7]	12.1[7]	10.6[7]	4.5[2]

[1]*2004 data.* [2]*2005 data.* [3]*2003 data.* [4]*1999 data.* [5]*2002 data.* [6]*2007 data.* [7]*2006 data.* [8]*2001 data.*

Religion

World Religions

At the beginning of the 21st century, one-third of the world's population is Christian, another one-fifth is Muslim, about one-eighth is Hindu, and one-eighth is nonreligious. Most people living in Europe and the Americas are Christian, while the vast majority of Muslims and Hindus are found in Asia. The plurality of Christians are Roman Catholics, of Muslims are Sunni, and of Hindus are Vaishnavites. Africa hosts slightly more Christians than Muslims, with much of the rest of the population listed as ethnic religionists, which describes followers of local, tribal, animistic, or shamanistic religions.

In addition to the predominant world religions (Christianity, Islam, Hinduism), there are small but noticeable percentages of Chinese folk religionists, Buddhists, other ethnic religionists, atheists, and new-religionists. Among the remaining distinct religions, Sikhs, Spiritists, Jews, Baha'is, Confucianists, Jains, Shintoists, Taoists, and Zoroastrians each make up less than one-half of one percent of religious adherents.

Christianity

Christianity traces its origins to the 1st century AD and to Jesus of Nazareth, whom it affirms to be the chosen one (Christ) of God. Geographically the most widely diffused of all faiths, it has a constituency of more than two billion people. Its largest groups are the Roman Catholic Church, the Eastern Orthodox churches, and the Protestant churches; in addition, there are several independent churches of Eastern Christianity as well as numerous sects throughout the world.

Christianity's sacred scripture is the Bible, particularly the New Testament. Its principal tenets are that Jesus is the son of God (the second person of the Holy Trinity), that God's love for the world is the essential component of his being, and that Jesus died to redeem humankind.

Christianity was originally a movement of Jews who accepted Jesus as the messiah, but the movement quickly became predominantly Gentile. Nearly all Christian churches have an ordained clergy, which lead group worship services and are viewed as intermediaries between the laity and the divine in some churches. Most Christian churches administer at least two sacraments: baptism and the Lord's Supper.

Islam

Islam is a religion that originated in the Middle East and was promulgated by the Prophet Muhammad in Arabia in the 7th century AD. The Arabic term *islam*, literally "surrender," illuminates the fundamental religious idea of Islam—that the believer (called a Muslim, from the active particle of *islam*) accepts "surrender to the will of Allah" (Arabic: "God"). Allah's will is made known through the sacred scriptures, the Koran, which Allah revealed to his messenger, Muhammad. In Islam, Muhammad is considered the last of a series of prophets (including Adam, Noah, Jesus, and others), and his message simultaneously consummates and abrogates the "revelations" attributed to earlier prophets.

The religious obligations of all Muslims are summed up in the Five Pillars of Islam. The fundamental concept in Islam is the Shari'ah, or Law, which embraces the total way of life commanded by God. Observant Muslims pray five times a day and join in community worship on Fridays at the mosque, where worship is led by an imam. Every believer is required to make a pilgrimage to Mecca, the holiest city, at least once in a lifetime, barring poverty or physical incapacity. The month of Ramadan is set aside for fasting. Jihad, considered a sixth pillar by some sects, is not accepted by most of the Islamic community as a call to wage physical war against unbelievers.

Divisions occurred early in Islam, brought about by disputes over the succession to the caliphate, resulting in various sects (Sunni, Shi'ite, Ismaili, Sufi). From the 19th century, the concept of the Islamic community inspired Muslim peoples to cast off Western colonial rule, and in the late 20th century fundamentalist movements toppled a number of secular Middle Eastern governments. A movement of African American Muslims emerged in the 20th century in the US.

Hinduism

Hinduism is the oldest of the world's major religions, dating back more than 3,000 years, though its present forms are of more recent origin. It evolved from Vedism, the religion of the Indo-European peoples who settled in India at the end of the 2nd millennium BC. The vast majority of the world's Hindus live in India, though significant minorities may be found in Pakistan and Sri Lanka, and smaller numbers live in Myanmar, South Africa, Trinidad, Europe, and the US.

Though the various Hindu sects each rely on their own set of scriptures, they all revere the ancient Vedas, which were brought to India by Aryan invaders after 1200 BC. The philosophical Vedic texts called the Upanishads explored the search for knowledge that would allow mankind to escape the cycle of reincarnation. Fundamental to Hinduism is the belief in a cosmic principle of ultimate reality called brahman, and its identity with the individual soul, or atman. All creatures go through a cycle of rebirth, or samsara, which can be broken only by spiritual self-realization, after which liberation, or moksha, is attained. The principle of karma determines a being's status within the cycle of rebirth.

The greatest Hindu deities are Brahma, Vishnu, and Shiva. The major sources of classical mythology are the Mahabharata (which includes the Bhagavadgita, the most important religious text of Hinduism), the Ramayana, and the Puranas. The hierarchical social structure of the caste system is important in Hinduism; it is supported by the principle of dharma. During the 20th century Hinduism was blended with Indian nationalism to become a potent political force.

Other major religions

Buddhism, a religion concentrated in Asia with some representation in North America, was founded by the Buddha (Siddhartha Gautama, or Gotama) in northeast India in the 5th century BC. By adhering to the Buddha's teachings, the believer can alleviate suffering through an understanding of the transitory nature of existence, in the hopes of achieving enlightenment. Distinct from Buddhism, **Shinto** is the

(continued on page 571)

The 2008 Annual Megacensus of Religions

David B. Barrett, Todd M. Johnson, and Peter F. Crossing

Each year since 1750, churches and religions around the world have generated increasing volumes of new statistical data. Much of this information is uncovered in decennial governmental censuses; half the countries of the world have long asked their populations to state their religions, if any, and they still do today. The other major source of data each year consists of the decentralized censuses undertaken by many religious headquarters. Each year almost all Christian denominations ask and answer

Worldwide Adherents of All Religions, mid-2008

	AFRICA	ASIA	EUROPE	LATIN AMERICA
Christians	465,880,000	364,106,000	583,802,000	536,162,000
Affiliated	439,561,000	359,186,000	559,099,000	530,146,000
Roman Catholics	159,776,000	128,901,000	275,209,000	474,595,000
Independents	92,928,000	179,166,000	21,104,000	42,381,000
Protestants	130,376,000	61,598,000	67,829,000	56,214,000
Orthodox	42,220,000	13,951,000	190,031,000	895,000
Anglicans	47,655,000	838,000	26,241,000	875,000
Marginal Christians	3,377,000	3,062,000	4,127,000	10,825,000
Doubly affiliated	*−36,771,000*	*−28,330,000*	*−25,442,000*	*−55,639,000*
Unaffiliated	26,319,000	4,920,000	24,703,000	6,016,000
Muslims	392,636,100	992,850,000	40,749,000	1,830,000
Hindus	2,813,000	906,190,000	1,681,000	760,000
Chinese universists	38,500	385,861,000	312,000	186,000
Buddhists	165,000	377,515,000	1,792,000	767,000
Ethnoreligionists	116,125,000	147,571,000	1,153,000	3,654,000
Neoreligionists	126,000	104,208,000	393,000	819,000
Sikhs	65,100	22,592,000	475,000	6,500
Jews	130,000	5,750,000	1,850,000	1,046,000
Spiritists	3,500	0	143,000	13,348,000
Baha'is	2,229,000	3,786,000	142,000	910,000
Confucianists	300	6,346,000	18,300	500
Jains	86,600	5,378,000	18,000	0
Taoists	0	3,365,000	0	0
Shintoists	0	2,715,000	0	8,000
Zoroastrians	900	152,000	5,700	0
Other religionists	80,000	217,000	259,000	110,000
Nonreligious	6,012,000	619,845,000	82,658,000	16,958,000
Atheists	614,000	126,914,000	15,676,000	2,839,000
Total population	**987,005,000**	**4,075,361,000**	**731,127,000**	**579,404,000**

Continents. These follow current UN demographic terminology, which now divides the world into the six major areas shown above. See United Nations, *World Population Prospects: The 2006 Revision* (New York: UN, 2007), with populations of all continents, regions, and countries covering the period 1950–2050, with 100 variables for every country each year. Note that "Asia" includes the former Soviet Central Asian states, and "Europe" includes all of Russia eastward to the Pacific.

Change rate. This column documents the annual change in 2008 (calculated as an average change from 2005 to 2010) in worldwide religious and nonreligious adherents.

Countries. The last column enumerates sovereign and nonsovereign countries in which each religion or religious grouping has a numerically significant and organized following.

Adherents. As defined in the 1948 Universal Declaration of Human Rights, a person's religion is what he or she professes, confesses, or states that it is. Totals are enumerated for each of the world's 240 countries following the methodology of the *World Christian Encyclopedia,* 2nd ed. (2001), and *World Christian Trends* (2001), using recent censuses, polls, surveys, yearbooks, reports, Web sites, literature, and other data. See the World Christian Database <www.worldchristiandatabase.org> for more detail. Religions (including nonreligious and atheists) are ranked in order of worldwide size in mid-2008.

Total population. UN medium variant figures for mid-2008, as given in *World Population Prospects: The 2006 Revision*.

Alphabetical listing of religions

Atheists. Persons professing atheism, skepticism, disbelief, or irreligion, including the militantly antireligious (opposed to all religion). In recent years a flurry of books have outlined the Western philosophical and scientific basis for atheism. Ironically, the vast majority of atheists today are found in Asia (primarily Chinese communists).

Buddhists. 56% Mahayana, 38% Theravada (Hinayana), 6% Tantrayana (Lamaism).

Chinese universists. Followers of a unique complex of beliefs and practices that may include universism (yin/yang cosmology with dualities earth/heaven, evil/good, darkness/light), ancestor cult, Confucian ethics, divination, festivals, folk religion, goddess worship, household gods, local deities, mediums, metaphysics, monasteries, neo-Confucianism, popular religion, sacrifices, shamans, spirit writing, and Taoist and Buddhist elements.

statistical questions on major religious subjects. A third annual source is the total of 27,000 new books each on the religious situation in each single country, as well as some 9,000 printed annual yearbooks or official handbooks. Together, these three major sources of data constitute a massive annual megacensus, though decentralized and uncoordinated. The two tables below combine all these data on religious affiliation. The first table summarizes worldwide adherents by religion. The second goes into more detail for the United States of America. This year one column has been added to the worldwide table: annual change as a growth rate. This allows comparisons between religious traditions: this year the world's two largest religious communities, Christians and Muslims, increased by 27,473,000 and 25,350,200, respectively, but Christians grew at 1.23%, while Muslims grew at 1.80%. Detail may not add to total given because of rounding.

NORTHERN AMERICA	OCEANIA	WORLD	%	CHANGE RATE (%)	NUMBER OF COUNTRIES
277,089,400	27,496,000	2,254,535,000	33.4	1.23	240
221,643,000	23,068,000	2,132,703,000	31.6	1.27	240
83,210,000	8,727,000	1,130,418,000	16.7	1.14	237
74,085,000	1,478,000	411,142,000	6.1	1.88	223
61,119,000	8,185,000	385,321,000	5.7	1.48	234
6,679,000	776,000	254,552,000	3.8	0.36	137
2,867,000	5,046,000	83,522,000	1.2	1.63	165
11,577,000	650,000	33,618,000	0.5	1.87	218
−17,894,000	*−1,794,000*	*−165,870,000*	*−2.5*	*1.29*	*174*
55,446,000	4,428,000	121,832,000	1.8	0.64	232
5,556,000	460,000	1,434,081,100	21.2	1.80	211
1,756,000	471,000	913,671,000	13.5	1.46	126
747,000	150,000	387,294,500	5.7	0.65	96
3,504,000	575,000	384,318,000	5.7	0.71	136
1,567,000	343,000	270,413,000	4.0	1.15	145
1,633,000	90,100	107,269,100	1.6	0.70	107
647,000	49,700	23,835,300	0.4	1.52	44
6,212,000	108,000	15,096,000	0.2	0.98	135
168,000	7,400	13,669,900	0.2	1.11	56
660,000	141,000	7,868,000	0.1	1.92	219
0	53,300	6,418,400	0.1	0.22	15
95,700	800	5,579,100	0.1	1.43	13
12,200	0	3,377,200	0.1	−0.04	5
61,500	0	2,784,500	0.0	0.52	8
20,600	1,700	180,900	0.0	−0.33	25
670,000	10,000	1,346,000	0.0	1.31	79
39,847,000	4,294,000	769,614,000	11.4	0.30	239
1,852,000	427,000	148,322,000	2.2	0.05	221
342,098,000	**34,678,000**	**6,749,673,000**	**100.0**	**1.17**	**240**

Christians. Followers of Jesus Christ, enumerated here under **Affiliated**—those affiliated with Christian churches (church members, with names written on church rolls, usually total number of baptized persons including children baptized, dedicated, or undedicated), the total in 2008 being 2,132,703,000, shown above divided among the six standardized ecclesiastical megablocs and with (negative and italicized) figures for those **Doubly affiliated** persons (all who are baptized members of two denominations)—and **Unaffiliated,** who are persons professing or confessing in censuses or polls to be Christians though not so affiliated. **Independents.** This term here denotes members of Christian churches and networks that regard themselves as postdenominationalist and neoapostolic and thus independent of historical, mainstream, organized, institutionalized, confessional, denominationalist Christianity. **Marginal Christians.** Members of denominations who define themselves as Christians but who are on the margins of organized mainstream Christianity (e.g., Unitarians, Mormons, Jehovah's Witnesses, Christian Scientists, and Religious Scientists).

Confucianists. Non-Chinese followers of Confucius and Confucianism, mostly Koreans in Korea.

Ethnoreligionists. Followers of local, tribal, animistic, or shamanistic religions, with members restricted to one ethnic group.

Hindus. 68% Vaishnavites, 27% Shaivites, 2% neo-Hindus and reform Hindus.

Jews. Adherents of Judaism. For detailed data on "core" Jewish population, see the annual "World Jewish Populations" article in the American Jewish Committee's *American Jewish Year Book.*

Muslims. 84% Sunnis, 14% Shi'ites, 2% other schools.

Neoreligionists. Followers of Asian 20th-century neoreligions, neoreligious movements, radical new crisis religions, and non-Christian syncretistic mass religions.

Nonreligious. Persons professing no religion, nonbelievers, agnostics, freethinkers, uninterested, or dereligionized secularists indifferent to all religion but not militantly so.

Other religionists. Including a handful of religions, quasi-religions, pseudoreligions, parareligions, religious or mystic systems, and religious and semireligious brotherhoods of numerous varieties.

Religious Adherents in the United States of America, 1900–2005

For categories not described below, see notes to Worldwide Adherents of All Religions, pp. 568–69.

	1900	%	MID-1970	%	MID-1990	%
Christians	73,260,000	96.4	190,520,000	90.7	218,720,600	85.4
Affiliated	54,425,000	71.6	152,304,000	72.5	175,885,600	68.7
Independents	5,850,000	7.7	35,108,000	16.7	66,900,000	26.1
Roman Catholics	10,775,000	14.2	48,305,000	23.0	56,500,000	22.1
Protestants	35,000,000	46.1	58,568,000	27.9	60,216,000	23.5
Marginal Christians	800,000	1.1	6,114,000	2.9	8,940,000	3.5
Orthodox	400,000	0.5	4,189,000	2.0	5,150,000	2.0
Anglicans	1,600,000	2.1	3,196,000	1.5	2,450,000	1.0
Doubly affiliated	*0*	*0.0*	*−3,176,000*	*−1.5*	*−24,270,400*	*−9.5*
Evangelicals	*32,068,000*	*42.2*	*35,137,000*	*16.7*	*38,400,000*	*15.0*
evangelicals	*11,000,000*	*14.5*	*45,500,000*	*21.7*	*90,656,000*	*35.4*
Unaffiliated	18,835,000	24.8	38,216,000	18.2	42,835,000	16.7
Jews	1,500,000	2.0	6,700,000	3.2	5,535,000	2.2
Muslims	10,000	0.0	800,000	0.4	3,500,000	1.4
Black Muslims	0	0.0	200,000	0.1	1,250,000	0.5
Buddhists	30,000	0.0	200,000	0.1	1,880,000	0.7
Neoreligionists	10,000	0.0	560,000	0.3	1,155,000	0.5
Ethnoreligionists	100,000	0.1	70,000	0.0	780,000	0.3
Hindus	1,000	0.0	100,000	0.0	750,000	0.3
Baha'is	2,800	0.0	138,000	0.1	600,000	0.2
Sikhs	0	0.0	10,000	0.0	160,000	0.1
Spiritists	0	0.0	0	0.0	120,000	0.0
Chinese universists	70,000	0.1	90,000	0.0	76,000	0.0
Jains	0	0.0	3,000	0.0	5,000	0.0
Shintoists	0	0.0	0	0.0	50,000	0.0
Zoroastrians	0	0.0	0	0.0	14,400	0.0
Taoists	0	0.0	0	0.0	10,000	0.0
Other religionists	10,200	0.0	450,000	0.2	530,000	0.2
Nonreligious	1,000,000	1.3	10,270,000	4.9	21,442,000	8.4
Atheists	1,000	0.0	200,000	0.1	770,000	0.3
US population	**75,995,000**	**100.0**	**210,111,000**	**100.0**	**256,098,000**	**100.0**

Methodology. This table extracts and analyzes a microcosm of the world religion table. It depicts the United States, the country with the largest number of adherents to Christianity, the world's largest religion. Statistics at five points in time from 1900 to 2005 are presented. Each religion's **Annual Change** for 2000–05 is also analyzed by **Natural** increase (births minus deaths, plus immigrants minus emigrants) per year and **Conversion** increase (new converts minus new defectors) per year, which together constitute the **Total** increase per year. **Rate** increase is then computed as a percentage per year.

Structure. Vertically the table lists 30 major religious categories. The major categories (including nonreligious) in the US are listed, with the largest (Christians) first. Indented names of groups in the adherents column on the far left are subcategories of the groups above them and are also counted in these unindented totals, so they should not be added twice into the column total. Figures in italics draw adherents from all categories of Christians above and so cannot be added together with them. Figures for Christians are built upon detailed head counts by churches, often to the last digit, and the totals are then rounded to the nearest 1,000. Because of rounding, the corresponding percentage figures may sometimes not total exactly 100%. Religions are ranked in order of size in 2005.

Christians. All persons who profess publicly to follow Jesus Christ as God and Savior. This category is subdivided into **Affiliated** Christians (church members) and **Unaffiliated** (nominal) Christians (professing Christians not affiliated with any church). See also the note on Christians to the world religion table. The first six lines under "Affiliated" Christians are ranked by size in 2005 of each of the 6 megablocs (Anglican, Independent, Marginal Christian, Orthodox, Protestant, and Roman Catholic).

Evangelicals/evangelicals. These two designations—italicized and enumerated separately here—cut across all of the six Christian traditions or ecclesiastical blocs listed above and should be considered separately from them. The **Evangelicals** (capital *E*) are mainly Protestant churches, agencies, and individuals who call themselves by this term (for example, members of the National Association of Evangelicals); they usually emphasize 5 or more of 7, 9, or 21 fundamental doctrines (salvation by faith, personal acceptance, verbal inspiration of Scripture, depravity of man, Virgin Birth, miracles of Christ, atonement, evangelism, Second Advent, et al.). The **evangelicals** (lower-case *e*) are Christians of evangelical conviction from all traditions who are committed to the evangel (gospel) and involved in personal witness and mission in the world.

Jews. Core Jewish population relating to Judaism, excluding Jewish persons professing a different religion.

Other categories. Definitions are as given under the world religion table.

MID-2000	%	MID-2005	%	ANNUAL CHANGE, 2000–05 NATURAL	CONVERSION	TOTAL	RATE (%)
235,268,500	82.6	244,828,200	81.7	2,475,900	−564,000	1,911,900	0.80
188,174,800	66.1	195,982,500	65.4	1,980,300	−418,800	1,561,500	0.82
67,128,000	23.6	70,389,000	23.5	706,400	−54,200	652,200	0.95
62,970,000	22.1	67,902,000	22.6	662,700	323,700	986,400	1.52
57,544,000	20.2	57,105,000	19.0	605,600	−693,400	−87,800	−0.15
10,087,000	3.5	10,680,000	3.6	106,200	12,400	118,600	1.15
5,331,000	1.9	5,677,000	1.9	56,100	13,100	69,200	1.27
2,300,000	0.8	2,248,000	0.7	24,200	−34,600	−10,400	−0.46
−17,185,200	*−6.0*	*−18,018,500*	*−6.0*	*−180,900*	*14,200*	*−166,700*	*0.95*
39,938,000	*14.0*	*40,633,000*	*13.6*	*420,300*	*−281,300*	*139,000*	*0.35*
95,900,000	*33.7*	*101,603,000*	*33.9*	*1,009,200*	*131,400*	*1,140,600*	*1.16*
47,093,700	16.5	48,845,700	16.3	495,600	−145,200	350,400	0.73
5,656,000	2.0	5,761,000	1.9	59,500	−38,500	21,000	0.37
4,322,000	1.5	4,750,200	1.6	45,500	40,100	85,600	1.91
1,650,000	0.6	1,850,000	0.6	17,400	22,600	40,000	2.31
2,594,000	0.9	2,811,000	0.9	27,300	16,100	43,400	1.62
1,418,000	0.5	1,498,000	0.5	14,900	1,100	16,000	1.10
1,336,000	0.5	1,424,000	0.5	14,100	3,500	17,600	1.28
1,238,000	0.4	1,338,000	0.4	13,000	7,000	20,000	1.57
552,000	0.2	593,000	0.2	5,800	2,400	8,200	1.44
239,000	0.1	270,000	0.1	2,500	3,700	6,200	2.47
142,000	0.0	149,000	0.0	1,500	−100	1,400	0.97
80,300	0.0	86,700	0.0	800	500	1,300	1.55
74,100	0.0	79,500	0.0	800	300	1,100	1.42
57,500	0.0	60,600	0.0	600	0	600	1.06
16,200	0.0	17,000	0.0	200	0	200	0.97
11,400	0.0	12,000	0.0	100	0	100	1.03
577,000	0.2	600,000	0.2	6,100	−1,500	4,600	0.78
30,127,000	10.6	34,401,000	11.5	317,100	537,700	854,800	2.69
1,148,000	0.4	1,167,000	0.4	12,100	−8,300	3,800	0.33
284,857,000	**100.0**	**299,846,000**	**100.0**	**2,998,000**	**0**	**2,998,000**	**1.03**

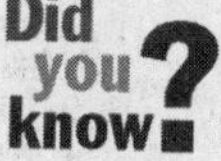

The first sale of a military airplane was made on 8 Feb 1908, when Orville and Wilbur Wright contracted to supply one Wright Model A flyer to the US Army Signal Corps, plus a US$5,000 bonus should it exceed the speed requirement of 40 miles (65 km) per hour. The next year the plane completed its trial flights and met the condition for the bonus.

World Religions (continued)

(continued from page 567)
indigenous religion of Japan and has no founder, sacred scriptures, or fixed dogmas. Also based in Asia, **Chinese folk religionists** are followers of local deities and engage in ancestor worship and divination. They also adhere to Confucian ethics, though statistically **Confucianists** are categorized as non-Chinese (mostly Korean) followers of Confucius, a Chinese philosopher of the 6th century BC. Confucianism is not an organized religion as much as it is a political and social ideology. Also in the Confucian tradition, a **Taoist** seeks the correct path of human conduct and an understanding of the Absolute Tao.

Zoroastrianism is an ancient pre-Islamic religion of Iran that survives there and in India. It was founded by the Iranian prophet Zoroaster in the 6th century BC and has both monotheistic and dualistic features. Also founded in Iran is the **Baha'i** faith, created as a universal religion in the mid-19th century AD for the worship of Baha' Ullah and his forerunner, the Bab; it has no priesthood or formal sacraments and is chiefly concerned with social ethics.

Jainism was founded in India in the 6th century BC by Vardhamana, or Mahavira, a monastic reformer in the Vedic, or early Hindu, tradition. Jainism emphasizes a path to spiritual purity and enlightenment through a disciplined mode of life founded upon the tradition of ahimsa, nonviolence to all living creatures.

Sikhism is a monotheistic religion founded in the late 15th century AD in India, historically associated with the Punjab region, though it includes representation in Europe and North America.

Judaism, like Christianity and Islam, is monotheistic and maintains the manifestation of God in human events, particularly through Moses in the Torah at Mount Sinai in the 13th century BCE. Jews, who come together in both religious and ethnic communities, have worldwide representation, with the greatest concentration in North America and the Middle East.

New-Religionists are followers of New Religious movements and non-Christian syncretistic mass religions.

Chronological List of Popes

According to Roman Catholic doctrine, the pope is the successor of **St. Peter**, who was head of the Apostles. The pope thus is seen to have full and supreme power of jurisdiction over the universal church in matters of faith and morals, as well as in church discipline and government. Until the 4th century, the popes were usually known only as bishops of Rome. From 1309–77, the popes' seat was at Avignon, France. In the table, **antipopes**, who opposed the legitimately elected bishop of Rome and endeavored to secure the papal throne, are listed in italics. The elections of several antipopes are greatly obscured by incomplete or biased records, and at times even their contemporaries could not decide who was the true pope. It is impossible, therefore, to establish an absolutely definitive list of antipopes.

POPE	REIGN
Peter	?–c. 64
Linus	c. 67–76/79
Anacletus	76–88 or 79–91
Clement I	88–97 or 92–101
Evaristus	c. 97–c. 107
Alexander I	105–115 or 109–119
Sixtus I	c. 115–c. 125
Telesphorus	c. 125–c. 136
Hyginus	c. 136–c. 140
Pius I	c. 140–155
Anicetus	c. 155–c. 166
Soter	c. 166–c. 175
Eleutherius	c. 175–189
Victor I	c. 189–199
Zephyrinus	c. 199–217
Calixtus I (Callistus)	217?–222
Hippolytus	217, 218–235
Urban I	222–230
Pontian	230–235
Anterus	235–236
Fabian	236–250
Cornelius	251–253
Novatian	251
Lucius I	253–254
Stephen I	254–257
Sixtus II	257–258
Dionysius	259–268
Felix I	269–274
Eutychian	275–283
Gaius	283–296
Marcellinus	291/296–304
Marcellus I	308–309
Eusebius	309/310
Miltiades (Melchiades)	311–314
Sylvester I	314–335
Mark	336
Julius I	337–352
Liberius	352–366
Felix (II)	355–358
Damasus I	366–384
Ursinus	366–367
Siricius	384–399
Anastasius I	399–401
Innocent I	401–417
Zosimus	417–418
Boniface I	418–422
Eulalius	418–419
Celestine I	422–432
Sixtus III	432–440
Leo I	440–461
Hilary	461–468
Simplicius	468–483
Felix III (or II)[1]	483–492
Gelasius I	492–496

POPE	REIGN
Anastasius II	496–498
Symmachus	498–514
Laurentius	498, 501–c. 505/507
Hormisdas	514–523
John I	523–526
Felix IV (or III)[1]	526–530
Dioscorus	530
Boniface II	530–532
John II	533–535
Agapetus I	535–536
Silverius	536–537
Vigilius	537–555
Pelagius I	556–561
John III	561–574
Benedict I	575–579
Pelagius II	579–590
Gregory I	590–604
Sabinian	604–606
Boniface III	604
Boniface IV	608–615
Deusdedit (Adeodatus I)	615–618
Boniface V	619–625
Honorius I	625–638
Severinus	640
John IV	640–642
Theodore I	642–649
Martin I	649–655
Eugenius I	654–657
Vitalian	657–672
Adeodatus II	672–676
Donus	676–678
Agatho	678–681
Leo II	682–683
Benedict II	684–685
John V	685–686
Conon	686–687
Sergius I	687–701
Theodore	687
Paschal	687
John VI	701–705
John VII	705–707
Sisinnius	708
Constantine	708–715
Gregory II	715–731
Gregory III	731–741
Zacharias (Zachary)	741–752
Stephen (II)[2]	752
Stephen II (or III)[2]	752–757
Paul I	757–767
Constantine (II)	767–768
Philip	768
Stephen III (or IV)[2]	768–772
Adrian I	772–795
Leo III	795–816
Stephen IV (or V)[2]	816–817
Paschal I	817–824
Eugenius II	824–827

POPE	REIGN
Valentine	827
Gregory IV	827–844
John	844
Sergius II	844–847
Leo IV	847–855
Benedict III	855–858
Anastasius (Anastasius the Librarian)	855
Nicholas I	858–867
Adrian II	867–872
John VIII	872–882
Marinus I	882–884
Adrian III	884–885
Stephen V (or VI)[2]	885–891
Formosus	891–896
Boniface VI	896
Stephen VI (or VII)[2]	896
Romanus	897
Theodore II	897
John IX	898–900
Benedict IV	900
Leo V	903
Christopher	903–904
Sergius III	904–911
Anastasius III	911–913
Lando	913–914
John X	914–928
Leo VI	928
Stephen VII (or VIII)[2]	929–931
John XI	931–935
Leo VII	936–939
Stephen VIII (or IX)[2]	939–942
Marinus II	942–946
Agapetus II	946–955
John XII	955–964
Leo VIII[3]	963–965
Benedict V[3]	964–966?
John XIII	965–972
Benedict VI	973–974
Boniface VII (1st time)	974
Benedict VII	974–983
John XIV	983–984
Boniface VII (2nd time)	984–985
John XV (or XVI)[4]	985–996
Gregory V	996–999
John XVI (or XVII)[4]	997–998
Sylvester II	999–1003
John XVII (or XVIII)[4]	1003
John XVIII (or XIX)[4]	1004–09
Sergius IV	1009–12
Gregory (VI)	1012
Benedict VIII	1012–24
John XIX (or XX)[4]	1024–32
Benedict IX (1st time)	1032–44
Sylvester III	1045

Chronological List of Popes (continued)

POPE	REIGN
Benedict IX (2nd time)	1045
Gregory VI	1045–46
Clement II	1046–47
Benedict IX (3rd time)	1047–48
Damasus II	1048
Leo IX	1049–54
Victor II	1055–57
Stephen IX (or X)[2]	1057–58
Benedict X	1058–59
Nicholas II	1059–61
Alexander II	1061–73
Honorius (II)	1061–72
Gregory VII	1073–85
Clement (III)	1080–1100
Victor III	1086–87
Urban II	1088–99
Paschal II	1099–1118
Theodoric	1100–02
Albert (Aleric)	1102
Sylvester (IV)	1105–11
Gelasius II	1118–19
Gregory (VIII)	1118–21
Calixtus II (Callistus)	1119–24
Honorius II	1124–30
Celestine (II)	1124
Innocent II	1130–43
Anacletus (II)	1130–38
Victor (IV)	1138
Celestine II	1143–44
Lucius II	1144–45
Eugenius III	1145–53
Anastasius IV	1153–54
Adrian IV	1154–59
Alexander III	1159–81
Victor (IV)	1159–64
Paschal (III)	1164–68
Calixtus (III)	1168–78
Innocent (III)	1179–80
Lucius III	1181–85
Urban III	1185–87
Gregory VIII	1187
Clement III	1187–91
Celestine III	1191–98
Innocent III	1198–1216
Honorius III	1216–27
Gregory IX	1227–41
Celestine IV	1241
Innocent IV	1243–54
Alexander IV	1254–61
Urban IV	1261–64

POPE	REIGN
Clement IV	1265–68
Gregory X	1271–76
Innocent V	1276
Adrian V	1276
John XXI[4]	1276–77
Nicholas III	1277–80
Martin IV[5]	1281–85
Honorius IV	1285–87
Nicholas IV	1288–92
Celestine V	1294
Boniface VIII	1294–1303
Benedict XI	1303–04
Clement V (at Avignon from 1309)	1305–14
John XXII[4] (at Avignon)	1316–34
Nicholas (V) (at Rome)	1328–30
Benedict XII (at Avignon)	1334–42
Clement VI (at Avignon)	1342–52
Innocent VI (at Avignon)	1352–62
Urban V (at Avignon)	1362–70
Gregory XI (at Avignon, then Rome from 1377)	1370–78
Urban VI	1378–89
Clement (VII) (at Avignon)	1378–94
Boniface IX	1389–1404
Benedict (XIII) (at Avignon)	1394–1423
Innocent VII	1404–06
Gregory XII	1406–15
Alexander (V) (at Bologna)	1409–10
John (XXIII) (at Bologna)	1410–15
Martin V[5]	1417–31
Clement (VIII)	1423–29
Eugenius IV	1431–47
Felix (V) (Amadeus VIII of Savoy)	1439–49
Nicholas V	1447–55
Calixtus III (Callistus)	1455–58
Pius II	1458–64
Paul II	1464–71
Sixtus IV	1471–84

POPE	REIGN
Innocent VIII	1484–92
Alexander VI	1492–1503
Pius III	1503
Julius II	1503–13
Leo X	1513–21
Adrian VI	1522–23
Clement VII	1523–34
Paul III	1534–49
Julius III	1550–55
Marcellus II	1555
Paul IV	1555–59
Pius IV	1559–65
Pius V	1566–72
Gregory XIII	1572–85
Sixtus V	1585–90
Urban VII	1590
Gregory XIV	1590–91
Innocent IX	1591
Clement VIII	1592–1605
Leo XI	1605
Paul V	1605–21
Gregory XV	1621–23
Urban VIII	1623–44
Innocent X	1644–55
Alexander VII	1655–67
Clement IX	1667–69
Clement X	1670–76
Innocent XI	1676–89
Alexander VIII	1689–91
Innocent XII	1691–1700
Clement XI	1700–21
Innocent XIII	1721–24
Benedict XIII	1724–30
Clement XII	1730–40
Benedict XIV	1740–58
Clement XIII	1758–69
Clement XIV	1769–74
Pius VI	1775–99
Pius VII	1800–23
Leo XII	1823–29
Pius VIII	1829–30
Gregory XVI	1831–46
Pius IX	1846–78
Leo XIII	1878–1903
Pius X	1903–14
Benedict XV	1914–22
Pius XI	1922–39
Pius XII	1939–58
John XXIII	1958–63
Paul VI	1963–78
John Paul I	1978
John Paul II	1978–2005
Benedict XVI	2005–

[1]The higher number is used if Felix (II), who reigned from 355 to 358 and is ordinarily classed as an antipope, is counted as a pope. [2]Though elected on 23 Mar 752, Stephen (II) died two days later before he could be consecrated and thus is ordinarily not counted. The issue has made the numbering of subsequent Stephens somewhat irregular. [3]Either Leo VIII or Benedict V may be considered an antipope. [4]A confusion in the numbering of popes named John after John XIV (reigned 983–984) resulted because some 11th-century historians mistakenly believed that there had been a pope named John between antipope Boniface VII and the true John XV (reigned 985–996). Therefore they mistakenly numbered the real popes John XV to XIX as John XVI to XX. These popes have since customarily been renumbered XV to XIX, but John XXI and John XXII continue to bear numbers that they themselves formally adopted on the assumption that there had indeed been 20 Johns before them. In current numbering there thus exists no pope by the name of John XX. [5]In the 13th century the papal chancery misread the names of the two popes Marinus as Martin, and as a result of this error Simon de Brie in 1281 assumed the name of Pope Martin IV instead of Martin II. The enumeration has not been corrected, and thus there exist no Martin II and Martin III.

Law & Crime

International Terrorist Organizations

"Terrorism" is a subjective term. The list of organizations included here is that of the US Department of State, issued on 8 Apr 2008. The list is updated periodically. Translations and acronyms of organizations' names are given in bold parenthetically; names and acronyms by which organizations are also known follow and are not in bold.

Abu Nidal Organization (ANO) (Fatah Revolutionary Council, Arab Revolutionary Brigades, Black September, Revolutionary Organization of Socialist Muslims)
Founded in 1974 as a splinter group from the Palestinian Liberation Organization (PLO); led by Sabri al-Banna.
country or region of operation: Middle East, primarily Iraq and Lebanon; has also operated in Asia and Europe
primary goals: elimination of Israel, establishment of a Palestinian state

Abu Sayyaf Group (ASG)
Founded in the early 1990s as a splinter group from Moro National Liberation Front by Abdurajak Abubakar Janjalani; mainly made up of semiautonomous factions.
country or region of operation: Philippines, Malaysia
primary goals: establishment of an independent Islamic state in the southern Philippines

Ansar al-Islam (Partisans of Islam)
Founded in 2001 as an offshoot of the Islamic Movement in Iraqi Kurdistan; led by Najmeddin Faraj Ahmed, aka Mullah Krekar (currently in custody in Norway awaiting deportation to Iraq).
country or region of operation: Iraq
primary goals: establishment of an Islamic state in the Kurdish areas of northern Iraq, expulsion of Operation Iraqi Freedom (OIF) coalition from Iraq

al-Aqsa Martyrs Brigades
Founded in 2000 as an offshoot of Fatah; diffuse cell-based leadership structure.
country or region of operation: Gaza Strip, West Bank, Israel
primary goals: removal of Israeli forces from the West Bank and Gaza Strip, establishment of a Palestinian state with Jerusalem as its capital

Armed Islamic Group (GIA)
Founded in 1992; leadership uncertain; fewer than 50 active members thought to be at large.
country or region of operation: Algeria
primary goals: replacement of secular Algerian government with an Islamic state

Asbat al-Ansar
Founded in the late 1980s, a splinter faction of Muslim fighters in Lebanon's civil war; led by Abou Mahjan, aka Abdel Karim al-Saadi.
country or region of operation: Lebanon
primary goals: replacement of secular Lebanese government with an Islamic state based on the ancient caliphate system of government

AUM Shinrikyo (AUM Supreme Truth, Aleph)
Founded in 1987 by Shoko Asahara; led by Fumihiro Joyu.
country or region of operation: Japan
primary goals: takeover of Japan and the world

Basque Fatherland and Liberty (Euzkadi Ta Askatasuna, ETA)
Founded in 1959; allegedly led by Mikel Albizu Iriarte, aka Mikel Antza.
country or region of operation: Basque autonomous regions of northern Spain and southwestern France
primary goals: establishment of an independent Basque state based on Marxism

Communist Party of the Philippines/New People's Army (CPP/NPA)
Founded in 1969 as a Maoist successor to the pro-Soviet Partido Komunista Pilipinas; led from exile by José María Sisón.
country or region of operation: Philippines
primary goals: overthrow of the Philippine government

Continuity Irish Republican Army (CIRA)
Founded in 1994 as a splinter group of Irish Republican Army (IRA) after the latter declared its first cease-fire.
country or region of operation: Northern Ireland, Republic of Ireland
primary goals: removal of British forces from Northern Ireland

Hamas (Islamic Resistance Movement)
Founded in 1987 by Sheikh Ahmed Yasin as an offshoot of Muslim Brotherhood; led by Khalid Meshal.
country or region of operation: Gaza Strip, West Bank, Israel; also present throughout the Middle East
primary goals: elimination of Israel, establishment of an Islamic Palestinian state

Harakat ul-Jihad-i-Islami/Bangladesh (HUJI-B)
Founded in the 1990s; affiliated with al-Qaeda.
country or region of operation: Bangladesh
primary goals: establishment of Bangladesh as an Islamic state

Harakat ul-Mujahidin (HUM) (Movement of Holy Warriors)
Founded in the mid-1980s or early 1990s; led by Farooq Kashmiri.
country or region of operation: the Kashmir region of Pakistan and India
primary goals: establishment of Kashmir as part of an Islamic state

International Terrorist Organizations (continued)

Hezbollah (Party of God) (Islamic Jihad, Revolutionary Justice Organization, Organization of the Oppressed on Earth, Islamic Jihad for the Liberation of Palestine)

Founded in 1982; governed by the Majlis al-Shura (Consultative Council) led by Hassan Nasrallah; spiritual leader Sheikh Muhammad Hussein Fadlallah.

country or region of operation: Lebanon; also has cells worldwide

primary goals: establishment of Islamic rule in Lebanon, elimination of Israel, liberation of occupied Arab lands

Islamic Jihad Group (IJG)

Founded in 2004; offshoot of Islamic Movement of Uzbekistan (IMU).

country or region of operation: Central Asia

primary goals: replacement of the secular Uzbekistan government with an Islamic state

Islamic Movement of Uzbekistan (IMU)

Founded in 1996; led by Tohir Yoldashev.

country or region of operation: Central and South Asia, primarily Uzbekistan, Tajikistan, Kyrgyzstan, Afghanistan, Iran, and Pakistan

primary goals: replacement of the secular Uzbekistan government with an Islamic state

Jaish-e-Mohammed (Army of Muhammad)

Founded in 2000 as a spin-off from Harakat ul-Mujahidin; led by Maulana Masood Azhar.

country or region of operation: South Asia, primarily Pakistan and India

primary goals: establishment of Pakistani control over India-administered Kashmir

al-Jama'ah al-Islamiyah (Islamic Group, IG)

Founded in the late 1970s; loosely organized in two factions led by Mustafa Hamza (currently in custody in Egypt) and Rifai Taha Musa; spiritual leader Sheikh Umar Abd al-Rahman.

country or region of operation: Egypt; also operates in several countries worldwide

primary goals: replacement of Egyptian government with an Islamic state

Jemaah Islamiyah (JI)

Founded in the mid-1990s as a successor to Darul Islam; led by Abu Bakar Baasyir.

country or region of operation: Southeast Asia, particularly Indonesia, Singapore, and Malaysia

primary goals: establishment of a pan-Islamic state in Southeast Asia

al-Jihad (Egyptian Islamic Jihad, Jihad Group, Islamic Jihad)

Founded in the late 1970s by Ayman al-Zawahiri; merged with al-Qaeda in 2001.

country or region of operation: Egypt and other countries, including Yemen, Afghanistan, Pakistan, Lebanon, and Great Britain; activities now centered mainly outside Egypt

primary goals: replacement of Egyptian government with an Islamic state, attacks on US and Israeli interests

Kahane Chai (Kach)

Founded in 1971 by Meir Kahane; Kahane Chai founded as follow-up group by Binyamin Kahane after Meir's assassination in 1990; Binyamin Kahane assassinated in 2000.

country or region of operation: Israel, West Bank

primary goals: expansion of Israel, removal of Palestinians

Kongra-Gel (KGK) (formerly Kurdistan Workers Party, PKK, KADEK)

Founded in 1974; led by Abdullah Ocalan (imprisoned since 1999).

country or region of operation: Turkey; also operates in Europe and the Middle East

primary goals: establishment of independent Kurdish state

Lashkar-i Tayyaba (LT, Army of the Righteous)

Founded in 1990 as the military arm of Markaz-ud-Dawa-wal-Irshad (MDI), a Pakistani-based Islamic fundamentalist organization; led by Abdul Wahid Kashmiri.

country or region of operation: South Asia, primarily Pakistan and India

primary goals: establishment of Pakistani control over India-administered Kashmir, creation of a pan-Islamic state in Central Asia

Lashkar I Jhangvi

Founded in 1996 as an offshoot of the Sipah-e Sahaba (the Army of Muhammad's Companions); decentralized leadership structure.

country or region of operation: Pakistan.

primary goals: replacement of the Pakistani government with an Islamic state

Liberation Tigers of Tamil Eelam (LTTE)

Founded in 1976; led by Velupillai Prabhakaran.

country or region of operation: Sri Lanka

primary goals: establishment of an independent Tamil state

Libyan Islamic Fighting Group (LIFG)

Founded in 1995 among Libyans who had fought against Soviet forces in Afghanistan; led by Anas Sebai.

country or region of operation: Libya, various Middle Eastern and European countries

primary goals: overthrow of the government of Libyan leader Muammar al-Qaddafi

Moroccan Islamic Combatant Group (GICM)

Founded in the 1990s as an offshoot of the Moroccan organization Shabiba Islamiya (Islamic Youth).

country or region of operation: Afghanistan, Belgium, Denmark, Egypt, France, Morocco, Spain, Turkey, United Kingdom

primary goals: creation of an Islamic state in Morocco

International Terrorist Organizations (continued)

Mojahedin-e Khalq Organization (MEK) (National Liberation Army of Iran [NLA, the militant wing], People's Mujahidin of Iran [PMOI], National Council of Resistance [NCR], Muslim Iranian Student's Society [front organization to garner financial support])
Founded in the 1960s; led by Maryam and Masud Rajavi.
country or region of operation: Iran, Iraq
primary goals: establishment of a secular government in Iran

National Liberation Army (ELN)
Founded in 1965; led by Nicolas Rodríguez Bautista.
country or region of operation: Colombia
primary goals: replacement of the ruling Colombian government with a Marxist state

Palestine Liberation Front (PLF)
Founded in the mid-1970s as splinter group from PFLP–GC.
country or region of operation: Israel, Iraq
primary goals: elimination of Israel, establishment of a Palestinian state

Palestinian Islamic Jihad (PIJ)
Founded in the 1970s; most active faction led by Ramadan Shallah.
country or region of operation: Israel, West Bank, Gaza Strip; also elsewhere in Middle East, primarily Lebanon and Syria
primary goals: elimination of Israel, establishment of an Islamic Palestinian state

Popular Front for the Liberation of Palestine (PFLP)
Founded in 1967 as part of the PLO by George Habash (discontinued PLO participation in 1993); led by Ahmed Sadat (imprisoned by the Palestinian Authority since 2002).
country or region of operation: Syria, Lebanon, Israel, West Bank, Gaza Strip
primary goals: promotion of national unity and revitalization of the PLO, opposition to peace negotiations with Israel

Popular Front for the Liberation of Palestine–General Command (PFLP–GC)
Founded in 1968 as splinter group from PFLP; led by Ahmad Jabril.
country or region of operation: Syria, Lebanon, Israel, West Bank, Gaza Strip
primary goals: opposition to the PLO and to peace negotiations with Israel

al-Qaeda
Founded in the late 1980s; established and led by Osama bin Laden.
country or region of operation: worldwide
primary goals: establishment of worldwide Islamic rule, overthrow of non-Islamic governments, expulsion of Western influences from Muslim states, killing of US citizens

al-Qaeda Organization in the Islamic Maghreb (formerly Salafist Group for Call and Combat, GSPC)
Founded in 1996 as a splinter of the Armed Islamic Group; led by Abou Mossaab Abdelouadoud.
country or region of operation: primarily Algeria, with significant activity elsewhere in North Africa and in Europe
primary goals: replacement of the Algerian government with an Islamic state

Real IRA (True IRA)
Founded in 1998 as a splinter group of the Irish Republican Army (IRA); led by Michael "Mickey" McKevitt (imprisoned since 2001).
country or region of operation: Northern Ireland; also elsewhere in Great Britain and in Ireland
primary goals: removal of British forces from Northern Ireland, unification of Ireland

Revolutionary Armed Forces of Colombia (FARC)
Founded in 1964 as the military branch of the Colombian Communist Party; governed by a group led by Manuel Marulanda (until his death in March 2008) and including Jorge Briceno and five others.
country or region of operation: Colombia; also some operations in Venezuela, Ecuador, and Panama
primary goals: replacement of the ruling Colombian government with a Marxist state

Revolutionary Nuclei (Revolutionary Cells)
Founded in 1995 as an offshoot of or successor to Revolutionary People's Struggle (ELA).
country or region of operation: Greece, primarily Athens
primary goals: elimination of US military bases in Greece, opposition to capitalism and NATO/EU membership

Revolutionary Organization 17 November
Founded in 1975; relatively small group operating secretly, allegedly led by Alexandros Giotopoulos (imprisoned in Greece since 2002).
country or region of operation: Greece, primarily Athens
primary goals: elimination of US military bases in Greece, removal of Turkish forces from Cyprus, opposition to capitalism and NATO/EU membership

Revolutionary People's Liberation Party/Front (DHKP/C) (Devrimci Sol, Revolutionary Left, Dev Sol)
Founded in 1978 as a splinter group from Turkish People's Liberation Party/Front; led by Dursun Karatas.
country or region of operation: Turkey, primarily Istanbul
primary goals: promotion of Marxism, opposition to US and NATO

al-Shabaab
Founded in 2006 by fighters from the recently ousted Islamic Courts Union.
country or region of operation: Somalia
primary goals: ejection of Ethiopian and other foreign troops from Somalia, reestablishment of an Islamic government in the country

International Terrorist Organizations (continued)

Shining Path (Sendero Luminoso, SL)
Founded in the late 1960s by Abimael Guzman; led by Macario Ala.
country or region of operation: Peru, primarily rural areas
primary goals: replacement of the Peruvian government with a communist state, opposition to influence by foreign governments

Tanzim Qaidat al-Jihad fi Bilad al-Rafidayn (QJBR, al-Qaeda in Iraq) (formerly Jamaat al-Tawhid waal-Jihad, JTJ, al-Zarqawi Network)
Founded in April 2004 by Abu Musab al-Zarqawi shortly after the commencement of OIF; adopted current name in October 2004 after merging with Osama bin Laden's al-Qaeda.
country or region of operation: Iraq
primary goals: explulsion of OIF coalition from Iraq, establishment of Islamic state in Iraq

United Self-Defense Forces of Colombia (Autodefensas Unidas de Colombia, AUC)
Founded in 1997 as an umbrella organization of paramilitary groups; led by Carlos Castaño.
country or region of operation: Colombia
primary goals: opposition to and defense against leftist guerrilla groups

Military Affairs

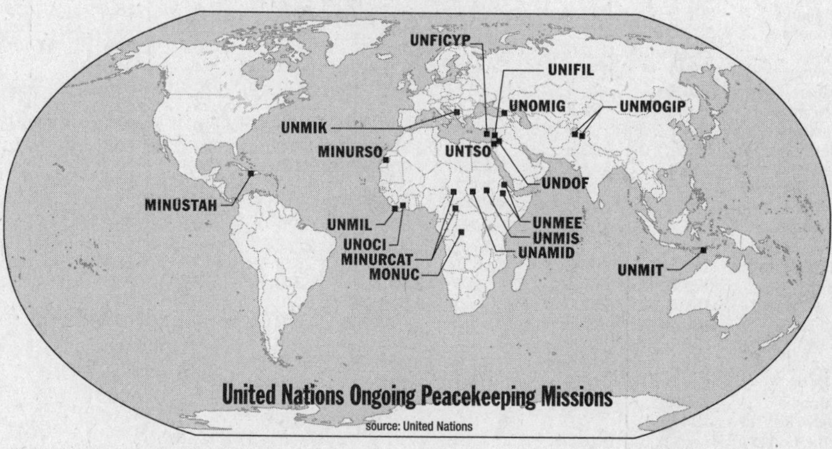

United Nations Ongoing Peacekeeping Missions
source: United Nations

MINURCAT	United Nations Mission in the Central African Republic and Chad—since September 2007 (145)
MINURSO	United Nations Mission for the Referendum in Western Sahara—since April 1991 (230)
MINUSTAH	United Nations Stabilization Mission in Haiti—since June 2004 (9,055)
MONUC	United Nations Organization Mission in the Democratic Republic of the Congo—since November 1999 (18,428)
UNAMID	African Union/United Nations Hybrid Operation in Darfur—since July 2007 (9,563)
UNDOF	United Nations Disengagement Observer Force (in the Golan Heights)—since May 1974 (1,046)
UNFICYP	United Nations Peacekeeping Force in Cyprus—since March 1964 (925)
UNIFIL	United Nations Interim Force in Lebanon—since March 1978 (12,383)
UNMEE	United Nations Mission in Ethiopia and Eritrea—since July 2000 (328)
UNMIK	United Nations Interim Administration Mission in Kosovo—since June 1999 (39[1])
UNMIL	United Nations Mission in Liberia—since September 2003 (13,934)
UNMIS	United Nations Mission in the Sudan—since March 2005 (9,924)
UNMIT	United Nations Integrated Mission in Timor-Leste—since August 2006 (1,550[2])
UNMOGIP	United Nations Military Observer Group in India and Pakistan—since January 1949 (45)
UNOCI	United Nations Operation in Côte d'Ivoire—since April 2004 (9,174)
UNOMIG	United Nations Observer Mission in Georgia—since August 1993 (149)
UNTSO	United Nations Truce Supervision Organization (in Jerusalem)—since May 1948 (153)

Parenthetical figures indicate military personnel as of 31 May 2008. Civilian forces, including police officers, are not included in this table. [1]Data are as of 1 Mar 2008. [2]Data are as of 30 Apr 2008.

Nations with Largest Armed Forces

Countries with a military strength of at least 100,000 active personnel. Personnel numbers are in thousands ('000) and reflect November 2007 data; spending totals are from 2007 budgets except where noted. Source: The International Institute of Strategic Studies, The Military Balance 2008.

COUNTRY	MILITARY PERSONNEL ACTIVE	MILITARY PERSONNEL RESERVES	DEFENSE SPENDING (US$ BILLIONS)	MAIN BATTLE TANKS	MAJOR WARSHIPS/ CARRIERS	SUB-MARINES	COMBAT AIRCRAFT	STRATEGIC NUCLEAR WEAPONS
China	2,105.0	800.0	46.7	8,810+	75/0	62	2,554	yes
United States	1,498.2	1,082.7	622.0	8,023+	113/11	136	4,191	yes
India	1,288.0	1,155.0	28.5	4,249	48/1	16	599	yes
North Korea	1,106.0	4,700.0	2.3[1]	4,060+	8/0	63	590	yes
Russia	1,027.0	20,000.0	33.0	23,669	113/1	136	2,345	yes
South Korea	687.0	4,500.0	26.9	2,390	44/0	12	563	
Pakistan	619.0	304.0[2]	4.5	2,461+	7/0	8	376	yes
Iran	545.0	350.0	7.2	1,613+	5/0	3	319	
Turkey	510.6	378.7	10.9	4,205	24/0	13	435	
Iraq	494.8	0.0	—	77+	0/0	0	0	
Egypt	468.5	479.0	3.4	3,505	11/0	4	489	
Vietnam	455.0	5,000.0	3.7	1,935	11/0	2	219	
Myanmar (Burma)	406.0	107.3[2]	6.9[1]	255	3/0	0	125	
Brazil	367.9	1,340.0	21.6	353	15/1	5	327	
Thailand	306.6	200.0	3.4	848	20/1	0	182	
Indonesia	302.0	400.0	3.6	405	29/0	2	94	
Syria	292.6	314.0	1.5	4,950	2/0	0	583	
Taiwan	290.0	1,657.0	9.6	1,831+	26/0	4	510	
France	254.9	25.4	51.7	996	35/2	10	316	yes
Colombia	254.3	61.9	7.1	0	4/0	4	115	
Mexico	248.7	39.9	4.0	0	7/0	0	86	
Germany	245.7	161.8	43.2	2,035	17/0	12	298	
Japan	240.4	41.8	43.7	900	53/0	16	360	
Saudi Arabia	223.5	15.5[2]	33.3	910	11/0	0	278	
Eritrea	201.8	120.0	0.1[3]	150	0/0	0	18	
Morocco	195.8	150.0	2.5	696	3/0	0	89	
Italy	186.0	41.9	17.8	320	25/2	7	267	
United Kingdom	180.5	199.3	61.1	386	28/3	13	354	yes
Israel	176.5	565.0	9.5	3,501	3/0	3	393	[4]
Greece	156.6	251.0	5.5	1,514	17/0	9	357	
Sri Lanka	150.9	5.5	1.2	62	0/0	0	22	
Bangladesh	150.0	63.9[2]	1.0	220	4/0	0	76+	
Spain	149.2	319.0	11.0	339	12/1	4	197	
Algeria	147.0	150.0	3.7	895	9/0	2	141	
Ethiopia	138.0	0.0	0.3	246+	0/0	0	48	
Dem. Rep. of the Congo	134.5	0.0	0.2	89	0/0	0	5	
Ukraine	129.9	1,000.0	1.8	2,984	5/0	1	221	
Poland	127.3	234.0	7.7	946	8/0	5	103	
Cambodia	124.3	67.0[2]	0.1	170+	0/0	0	24	
Venezuela	115.0	8.0	2.6	190	8/0	2	104	
Peru	114.0	188.0	1.3	336	9/0	6	70	
The Sudan	109.3	85.0[2]	0.6	465	0/0	0	51	
Malaysia	109.0	51.6	4.0	32	11/0	0	68	
Angola	107.0	10.0[2]	2.3	300+	0/0	0	90	
Philippines	106.0	131.0	1.1[1]	65	1/0	0	30	
Jordan	100.5	65.0	1.6	1,145	0/0	0	100	

[1]Spending estimate based on 2006 budget. [2]Paramilitary forces. [3]Spending based on 2005 budget. [4]Although believed by many to possess the world's sixth largest arsenal of nuclear weapons, Israel has never declared a nuclear capability nor has one been proven to exist.

Did you know?

Crafted of laminated birch wood and popularly known as the "Spruce Goose," Howard Hughes's HK-1 Hercules was designed during World War II in an effort to build a troop-and-cargo transport plane that did not rely on precious wartime materials in its construction. On 2 Nov 1947, Hughes piloted the aircraft for its first and only flight, which lasted for roughly a mile. At the time the Spruce Goose was three times larger than any plane ever built, and it still holds the record for the largest wingspan of any aircraft. The plane was put in its hangar and kept in flight-ready condition for nearly 30 years, as per Hughes's orders. It is now on permanent display at the Evergreen Aviation Educational Center in McMinnville OR.

United States

US Presidential Election of 2008

by James Carney (McCain) and Michael Weiskopf (Obama)

On 4 Nov 2008, Democrat Barack Obama defeated Republican John McCain in decisive fashion to win election as the 44th President of the United States by a margin of 349–163 in the electoral college, with 26 electoral votes still undecided as of 5 November. The popular vote was closer than the electoral results, with Obama claiming 52% of the votes to McCain's 46%. "Change has come to America," declared the victorious candidate, a freshman Senator from Illinois who made history as the first African American elected to the nation's highest office. TIME profiled the two candidates before the election.

The Resurrection of John McCain

In war and in politics, John McCain has endured more than his share of near-death experiences. He's been shot out of the sky and held captive, hung from ropes by his two broken arms, and beaten senseless. His 2008 campaign is his second run for president; he lost before, nearly lost again, and was all but disowned by his party. So on 19 January, the night of South Carolina's Republican primary, when the victory he needed to keep his campaign alive seemed as if it might be slipping away, McCain stood silent amid the chaos of his crowded hotel suite, his eyes fixed on the TV screen. Rumors that the primary was about to be called for McCain had fizzled, supplanted by whispers that Mike Huckabee had taken a slim lead. For a moment, it all seemed as though it were going to fall down again.

But the announcement came: "McCain wins South Carolina!" The room erupted in cheers; McCain's wife Cindy dissolved into tears; and the candidate's pale, scarred, 71-year-old face spread into a huge grin. It was the beginning of his resurrection, which culminated in his selection as the Republican Party's presidential nominee at the party's September convention in Minnesota—one year after his once formidable campaign all but collapsed in debt and acrimony in the summer of 2007.

The towering obstacle between McCain and victory was not so much his rivals for the nomination but the suspicion long held by many Republicans, especially rock-ribbed conservatives, that the senator and former war hero was too much the maverick on issues that matter deeply to them to be trusted to occupy the White House.

Conservative fears about McCain are often irrational: through a 25-year career in Congress, first in the House and then in the Senate, McCain proved himself consistently pro-life on abortion and a hawk on defense, a scourge of wasteful government spending and a generally reliable vote in favor of tax cuts. Yet at the 2007 Conservative Political Action Conference, an annual gathering of party power brokers, McCain was booed.

But it is also true that conservatives have a lengthy bill of complaint against McCain. In the past decade he has joined with Democrats on a series of crusades in Congress—with Russ Feingold on campaign-finance reform and Ted Kennedy on immigration reform—that a majority of Republicans have opposed. He voted against President Bush's tax cuts in 2001 and 2003, citing the need for fiscal restraint. And during his 2000 campaign, he labeled Pat Robertson and the Rev. Jerry Falwell "agents of intolerance."

He has seemed to delight in doing battle with members of his own party and creed. All the while—and this may be what galls conservatives most—McCain has been hailed by liberals and lionized in the mainstream news media for being a rebel. This maverick reputation, so prized for its general-election appeal, made it difficult for McCain to pass the primary threshold.

The Right Stuff. Both conservative and independent voters have the same question about McCain: what kind of Republican is he? In 2000, when the US was at peace and the economy was luxuriating in the frothy end days of the first Internet boom, McCain's first campaign was about character and biography much more than issues. McCain was the authentic hero, the fighter pilot who had been shot down over Hanoi and spent more than five years as a prisoner of war. He was the reformer and the straight talker, the rare politician who—perhaps because of his experience as a POW—wasn't going to compromise his principles or hold his tongue to please his party. He was also, at his core, still the rowdy, runty, red-tempered plebe who finished near the bottom of his class at the Naval Academy despite an IQ of 133. McCain became a symbol in 2000 of courage and candor. Few took close looks at his policy positions. It was almost enough to get him the GOP nomination.

In 2008 it is different. Character and authenticity still matter, but McCain's reputation as an expert on defense and foreign affairs carries far greater weight in the post-9/11 world than it did eight years before. On Iraq, McCain supported the invasion and still does. But he was an early critic of the way the Bush administration was prosecuting the war and called for a change in strategy that would include a surge in US troops to gain control of Baghdad. At the time, advocating an increase in US troop levels in Iraq rather than a reduction was unpopular even within the GOP. But McCain stood by Bush when the policy was implemented.

The success of the troop surge gave McCain points for prescience and reaffirmed his political courage. Yet there was a downside too. As violence in Iraq ebbed, economic anxiety rocketed to the top of voters' concerns. The shift exposed one of McCain's weaknesses. He is a conviction politician, passionate about the issues that animate him, dismissive of and uninterested in those that don't. Iraq, foreign policy, the military, and treatment of veterans—these topics get him excited. In the domestic realm, he's fire and energy when he rails against pork-barrel spending. But mention other issues—taxes, health care, education policy—and he briefly resorts to talking points before changing the subject.

What's both refreshing and vaguely masochistic about McCain is that even when he knows it's in his short-term political interest to dodge a question or adjust his message, he often just won't—or can't—do it. If McCain wins the White House, he will be 72 when he takes office, the oldest person ever to ascend to the presidency. He has suffered serious skin cancers over the years, not to mention brutal physical torture as a prisoner of war. His age and health are of legitimate concern to voters. But McCain doesn't downplay his liabilities; he highlights them. "I'm older than dirt, with more scars than Frankenstein," he jokes. Yet there are few who doubt that the aging war hero—because of his appeal beyond his party—could well become the nation's 44th president.

Obama: How He Learned To Win

Barack Obama had not been in politics for long when he got his tail whipped by a veteran Chicago congressman in his own backyard. For a brief period that followed, Obama seemed a bit unsure about what to do with his life. Yet within four years, Obama had won a seat in the US Senate. Less than four years after that, he clinched the Democratic nomination for president.

How did this man come so far so fast? Much of the answer can be traced to the lessons of his first thumping. It was after that brief race in 2000 that Obama learned how to be a politician. He jettisoned his Harvard-tested speaking style for something more down-home. He learned how to cultivate those in power without being defined by them. And he learned how to be different things to different people: a reformer groomed by an old-fashioned machine boss, an African American heavily financed by white liberals, a Harvard lawyer whose bootstrapping life story gained traction with white ethnics.

In the heyday of Chicago's Democratic machine, politics was open only to those with a sponsor. By the time Obama got into the game in the 1990s, it was no longer an exclusive club. Still, old practices died hard; the same virtues of loyalty and familiarity were rewarded by new bosses who expected political newcomers to pay their dues—and wait their turn.

One exception was Hyde Park, a small, integrated, partially gentrified neighborhood of professionals and University of Chicago professors. Obama moved there as a newly minted lawyer specializing in civil rights cases and lecturing at the university's law school. In 1996 he won his first political election to represent Hyde Park in the state senate. But after three years in the state capital of Springfield, a restless Obama turned an eye to the seat for the 1st congressional district of Illinois.

Since 1992, the heavily black 1st had been represented by Bobby Rush, who cofounded the Illinois Black Panther Party before going mainstream as an alderman and ward committeeman. But Rush stumbled badly in early 1999 when he lost to incumbent Richard M. Daley in the Democratic primary for the mayor's job. Obama argued that Rush had failed in leadership and vision. But his delivery was stiff—"more Harvard than Chicago," said an adviser who had watched Obama put a church audience to sleep. He was a cultural outsider, and Rush attacked his Ivy League education: "We're not impressed with these folks with these Eastern elite degrees," he argued. Not growing up on the South Side raised other suspicions about Obama, as did his white mother. When the race was over, Rush piled up 61% of the vote, compared with 30% for Obama.

Once More, with Friends. The campaign left Obama US$60,000 in debt and unsure of his future. At 38, he was a state legislator in a party out of power, a black politician trounced in the black heartland, an outsider in the tribal world of Chicago politics. His long absences from home had angered his wife. Now he saw a way out: a statewide race for the US Senate seat held by Republican Peter Fitzgerald, up for reelection in 2004. But if Obama were to become the Democratic nominee, he would have to win the support of working-class blacks and party regulars. He found a mentor in the unlikely form of Emil Jones, a former sewer inspector in Chicago who had worked his way up the Democratic machine on the Far South Side to become Illinois's senate president in 2003, a pork-barreling, wheeling-and-dealing powerhouse.

By embracing Obama early, Jones stopped pivotal endorsements of rivals and helped Obama line up support from groups that had large black memberships—teachers, government employees, and service workers. In control of the state Senate agenda, Jones picked Obama to steer and ultimately get credit for laws passed late in 2003 that had been long sought by the black community: death-penalty reform, fattening tax credits for the working poor, and a measure to curb racial profiling.

Obama also learned the art of public speaking at the scores of black churches he visited in 2000, absorbing the rhythms of pastors and watching how their congregations reacted. Speaking at their Sunday services, he linked his candidacy to the larger march forward of African Americans. He often mentioned his pastor, Jeremiah Wright (though Wright's strident attacks on racism in the US led Obama to break ties with him in 2008).

Obama's rise from a modest upbringing to the pinnacle of US education drew a connection to the life struggles of ordinary people. Partly as a result, he won the support of some small-town white lawmakers whom he'd gotten to know in legislative battles and occasional poker games in Springfield.

Obama was now politicking at a high level and building a different kind of organization to pay for it. He opened a rich vein of political cash in Chicago's black business elite, a new generation of corporate, banking, and manufacturing executives. With the support of Penny Pritzker of the Hyatt hotel clan, he won over Chicago's biggest political donors, many of them Jewish professionals and business owners.

Obama raised almost US$6 million in the primary. More than half his war chest came from people working for industry groups—legal, securities, real estate, banking, health care, utilities, and insurance among them. His Democratic rivals tore each other up, letting Obama keep to the high road. At a Chicago rally against the US invasion of Iraq, he declared, "I don't oppose all wars. What I'm opposed to is a dumb war." His prophetic words would power his campaign for the presidential nomination four years later.

The Senate race turned into a rout, with Obama taking nearly 53% of the vote in a three-way race. He scored a landslide in the black community, handily won a pair of ethnic-white wards on Chicago's Northwest Side, and earned a third of the downstate vote, backed by college students and farmers.

The seeds of Obama's political future were planted during that Democratic primary campaign. At his primary victory party in May 2004, he noted the improbable triumph of a "skinny guy from the South Side with a funny name like Barack Obama." And then he repeated a line that had capped his campaign commercials:

"Yes, we can. Yes, we can."

United States History

United States Chronology

1492 Christopher Columbus, sailing under the Spanish flag, discovers America, 12 October.
1513 Ponce de León of Spain lands in Florida and gives that region its name.
1534 France sends Jacques Cartier to find a route to the Far East; he explores along the St. Lawrence River, and France lays claim to part of North America.
1541 Hernando de Soto of Spain discovers the Mississippi River near the site of Memphis.
1565 St. Augustine, the oldest permanent settlement in the US, is founded by Spaniards.
1587 A party under John White lands at Roanoke Island (now in North Carolina); when White returns three years later, the entire settlement has disappeared.
1607 The English make the first permanent settlement in the New World at Jamestown; Virginia becomes the first of the 13 English colonies.
1619 The first representative assembly in America, the House of Burgesses, meets in Virginia; the first blacks land in Virginia.
1620 Pilgrims from the ship *Mayflower* found a settlement at Plymouth.
1649 The Act Concerning Religion passed by Maryland's legislature is the first law of religious toleration in the English colonies.
1682 The Sieur de La Salle explores the lower Mississippi valley and claims the entire region for France.
1733 Georgia, the 13th and last of the English colonies in America, is founded.
1754 Both England and the colonies reject the Albany Plan of Union to unite the colonies. The French and Indian War between France and England begins in America.
1763 The Treaty of Paris ends the French and Indian War; Britain wins control of the New World; Louisiana is ceded to Spain, Florida to Britain.
1765 The Quartering Act and the Stamp Act anger Americans; nine colonies are represented at the Stamp Act Congress.
1770 British troops fire on a crowd, killing five people in the so-called Boston Massacre.
1772 Committees of Correspondence are organized in almost all of the colonies.
1773 The Boston Tea Party, the first action in a chain leading to war with Britain, takes place.
1774 The First Continental Congress meets at Philadelphia and protests the five Intolerable Acts.
1775 The battles of Lexington and Concord and Bunker Hill occur; the Second Continental Congress meets.
1776 The Declaration of Independence is adopted. George Washington crosses the Delaware River to fight at Trenton NJ.
1777 Americans capture Gen. John Burgoyne and a large British force at Saratoga NY.
1778–79 Gen. George Rogers Clark leads a victorious expedition into the Northwest Territory.
1781 Washington accepts the surrender of Charles Cornwallis at Yorktown VA. The Articles of Confederation become the government of the US.
1783 A treaty of peace with Great Britain is signed at Paris, formally ending the Revolutionary War.
1786–87 Shays's Rebellion in Massachusetts shows weaknesses of the Confederation government.
1787 The Northwest Territory is organized by Congress. A convention meets to draft a new constitution.
1788 The US Constitution is ratified by the necessary nine states to ensure adoption.
1789 The new US government goes into effect; Washington is inaugurated president; the first Congress meets in New York City.
1791 The Bill of Rights is added to the Constitution. Vermont is the first new state admitted to the Union.
1793 Eli Whitney invents the cotton gin, which leads to large-scale cotton growing in the South.
1800 The national capital is moved from Philadelphia to Washington DC.
1803 Louisiana is purchased from France. The Supreme Court makes its *Marbury* v. *Madison* decision; Congress halts the importation of slaves into the US after 1807.
1804–06 Meriwether Lewis and William Clark blaze an overland trail to the Pacific and return.
1807 Robert Fulton's steamboat makes a successful journey from New York City to Albany NY.
1812–14 The US maintains its independence in a conflict with Britain, the War of 1812.
1818 The US and Canada settle a boundary dispute and agree on an open border between the countries.
1820 The Missouri Compromise settles the problem of slavery in new states for the next 30 years.
1823 The Monroe Doctrine warns European nations that the US will protect the Americas.
1825 The Erie Canal, from the Hudson River to the Great Lakes, becomes a great water highway to the Middle West.
1829 The inauguration of Pres. Andrew Jackson introduces the era of Jacksonian Democracy.
1836 Texas wins its independence from Mexico.
1843 The first migration begins on the Oregon Trail.
1845 Texas is annexed and admitted as a state.
1846 The Oregon boundary dispute is settled with Britain. The Mexican War begins.
1847 Brigham Young leads a party of Mormons into the Salt Lake valley, Utah.
1848 The Mexican War ends; the US gains possession of the California and New Mexico regions.
1849 The gold rush to California begins.
1850 The Compromise of 1850 admits California as a free state and postpones war between the North and South.
1853 The Gadsden Purchase adds 117,935 sq km (45,535 sq mi) to what is now the southwestern US.
1854 The Kansas-Nebraska Act reopens the slavery issue and leads to the organization of the Republican party.
1857 The Dred Scott decision of the Supreme Court declares that the Missouri Compromise is illegal.
1860 Abraham Lincoln is elected president; South Carolina secedes from the Union.
1861 The Confederate States of America is formed; the Civil War begins; Union forces are routed at Bull Run, Virginia. Telegraph links New York City with San Francisco.
1862 Gen. Ulysses S. Grant launches a Union attack in the West; the Confederate invasion of Maryland is halted at Antietam. The Homestead Act grants 160 acres to each settler.
1863 Federal forces win decisive battles at Gettysburg PA, Vicksburg MS, and Chattanooga TN. The Emancipation Proclamation takes effect.

1864 Gen. William Tecumseh Sherman captures Atlanta and marches across Georgia; Grant closes in on Richmond VA.
1865 Gen. Robert E. Lee surrenders to Grant at Appomattox Court House VA, ending the Civil War. Lincoln is assassinated.
1867 Reconstruction acts impose military rule on the South. Alaska is purchased from Russia.
1869 The first transcontinental railroad is completed as two lines meet at Promontory UT.
1876 The telephone is invented. The Centennial Exposition in Philadelphia celebrates the 100th birthday of the US.
1877 The withdrawal of the last federal troops from the South ends the Reconstruction period. Railroad workers begin the first nationwide strike.
1879 The first practical electric light is invented by Thomas A. Edison.
1883 The Pendleton Civil Service Act provides for examinations as the basis of appointment to some government positions.
1884–85 The first skyscraper, the Home Insurance Building, is erected in Chicago.
1886 The American Federation of Labor (AFL) is organized; its first president is Samuel Gompers.
1887 The Interstate Commerce Act is adopted to control railroads that cross state lines.
1889–90 The first pan-American conference is held in Washington DC.
1890 The Sherman Anti-Trust Act is passed in an effort to curb the growth of monopolies.
1896 Henry Ford's first car is driven on the streets of Detroit.
1898 The US wins the Spanish-American War and gains the Philippines, Puerto Rico, and Guam.
1903 The air age begins with the successful airplane flight by the Wright brothers.
1906 The Federal Food and Drug Act is passed to protect the public from impure food and drugs.
1912 New Mexico and Arizona, the 47th and 48th states, are admitted to the Union.
1913 Federal income tax is authorized by the 16th Amendment; the 17th Amendment provides for the popular election of US senators.
1914 The Panama Canal is opened under the control of the US. World War I breaks out in Europe; Pres. Woodrow Wilson appeals for neutrality in the US.
1915 A German submarine sinks the British ship *Lusitania* with the loss of 124 American lives. A telephone line is established coast to coast.
1917 Germany begins open submarine warfare; the US declares war against Germany.
1918 Pres. Wilson proposes "Fourteen Points" as the basis for peace; Americans fight at Chateau-Thierry, Belleau Wood, Saint-Mihiel, and Argonne Forest; an armistice ends the war.
1918–19 Pres. Wilson attends the Paris Peace Conference of victorious nations.
1919 The US Senate rejects the League of Nations. Navy pilots make the first flight across the Atlantic. Prohibition is established by the 18th Amendment.
1920 The right to vote is given to women by the 19th Amendment. KDKA begins broadcasting in Pittsburgh PA, becoming the first commercial radio station.
1921 National immigration quotas are introduced.
1921–22 The Washington Conference restricts warship construction among the chief naval powers.
1924 The army plane *Chicago* makes the first flight around the world.
1927 Charles A. Lindbergh makes the first nonstop solo flight across the Atlantic.
1928 The Kellogg-Briand Pact outlaws war.
1929 The stock market reaches a new high and then crashes; the panic marks the beginning of the Great Depression; millions of workers are unemployed.
1932 Franklin Delano Roosevelt is elected president.
1933 The New Deal is launched; the gold standard is suspended; the National Recovery Act is passed; bank deposits are insured; the Tennessee Valley Authority is organized. The 21st Amendment repeals prohibition.
1934 Congress tightens control over securities, passes the first Reciprocal Trade Agreement Act, and launches the federal housing program.
1935 The National Labor Relations (Wagner) Act guarantees collective bargaining to labor; the Congress of Industrial Organizations (CIO) is founded. The Social Security Act is passed.
1936 The Hoover Dam (Boulder Dam) is completed across the Colorado River.
1938 The Fair Labor Standards Act provides a federal yardstick for wages and hours of workers.
1939 Germany invades Poland to start World War II; the US declares neutrality.
1940 The US begins a huge rearmament program; the first peacetime draft takes effect. Roosevelt defies tradition and accepts the presidential nomination for a third term.
1941 The Lend-Lease Act is passed; the Atlantic Charter is signed; the Japanese attack on Pearl Harbor, Hawaii, brings the US into World War II.
1942 Americans launch a counteroffensive in the Pacific; the Allies invade North Africa.
1943 The Allied invasion of Italy is the first landing on the European continent.
1944 The Allies launch the greatest sea-to-land assault in history in the invasion of France; the Allies invade the Philippines; the GI Bill of Rights is passed.
1945 Germany surrenders, 8 May; the US drops an atomic bomb on Hiroshima, Japan, 6 August; Japan surrenders, 2 September. The Cold War begins between the US and the Soviet Union.
1946 The Philippines is granted independence by the US. The Atomic Energy Commission is created.
1947 The Senate passes the Truman Doctrine. The Taft-Hartley labor law is enacted. The Department of Defense consolidates the army, navy, and air force.
1948 The European Recovery Program is enacted. Harry S. Truman is elected president.
1949 The Fair Deal program is announced. The US and its allies force the Soviet Union to lift the Berlin blockade. The North Atlantic Treaty Organization (NATO) is founded.
1950 The US and several other members of the UN send military forces to the aid of the Republic of Korea; bitter war develops.
1951 A two-term limit is put on the presidency by ratification of the 22nd Amendment to the Constitution.
1952 The US and its allies end the occupation of West Germany. The election of Dwight D. Eisenhower ends 20 years of Democratic governance.
1953 The Korean War ends. The Department of Health, Education, and Welfare becomes the 10th cabinet post.
1954 Racial segregation of public schools is declared illegal by the Supreme Court.
1955 The two largest labor organizations merge into one group—the AFL-CIO. The Salk poliomyelitis vaccine is proved successful.
1956 Eisenhower is reelected president; Democrats win control of Congress.

1957 The Eisenhower Doctrine to strengthen the US position in the Middle East is adopted.
1958 The first US artificial Earth satellite is launched. The US joins the International Atomic Energy Agency.
1959 Alaska becomes the 49th state, Hawaii the 50th.
1960 A US spy plane is downed over the Soviet Union.
1961 The CIA is involved in an unsuccessful invasion of Cuba at the Bay of Pigs. The 23rd Amendment to the Constitution gives Washington DC residents the right to vote in presidential elections. Alan Shepard becomes the first American to make spaceflight. American troops are sent to defend West Berlin.
1962 The Cuban missile crisis erupts; the Soviets remove missiles from Cuba at the urging of the US.
1963 The March on Washington for Jobs and Freedom takes place. Pres. John F. Kennedy is assassinated in Dallas TX. A nuclear test-ban treaty is signed.
1964 The 24th Amendment to the Constitution bans poll taxes in federal elections. A landmark civil rights bill is passed. The Supreme Court allows reapportionment.
1965 US combat forces fight in Vietnam. The voting-rights bill and the Medicare Act are signed. The Department of Housing and Urban Development becomes the 11th cabinet post.
1966 The Department of Transportation becomes the 12th cabinet post.
1967 The 25th Amendment to the Constitution provides for presidential succession.
1968 The assassinations of Martin Luther King, Jr., and Robert F. Kennedy provoke riots.
1969 US astronauts land on the Moon.
1970 Four students at Kent State University in Ohio are killed by National Guard soldiers during anti-Vietnam War protests.
1971 The 26th Amendment to the Constitution gives 18-year-olds the right to vote in all elections.
1972 Pres. Richard M. Nixon visits China and the Soviet Union.
1973 The US withdraws its troops from Vietnam. Vice-Pres. Spiro T. Agnew resigns. Gas prices go up as OPEC raises the price of petroleum 400%.
1974 The Watergate scandal and the threat of impeachment force Nixon to resign.
1977 The Department of Energy becomes a new cabinet post. A treaty is signed to return the Panama Canal to Panama by the year 2000.
1978 Pres. Jimmy Carter hosts the Camp David talks between Israel's Menachem Begin and Egypt's Anwar el-Sadat.
1979 The second Strategic Arms Limitation Talks (SALT II) treaty is signed by the US and the Soviet Union. Militants seize 66 American hostages in a takeover of the US embassy in Iran.
1980 The Department of Health, Education, and Welfare is separated into the Department of Health and Human Services and the Department of Education.
1981 Pres. Ronald Reagan is wounded in an assassination attempt. A major tax cut and increased defense spending pass Congress. Sandra Day O'Connor is appointed the first woman Supreme Court justice.
1983 Reagan announces the Star Wars missile-defense program. The US invades Grenada.
1985 A summit between Reagan and Soviet leader Mikhail Gorbachev is held in Geneva, Switzerland.
1986 The space shuttle *Challenger* explodes shortly after liftoff. The US bombs targets in Libya. The Iran-contra affair is revealed.
1987 The Iran-contra hearings are held. The stock market collapses. Reagan and Gorbachev sign the Intermediate-Range Nuclear Forces (INF) treaty.
1988 The Department of Veterans Affairs is approved as a cabinet post.
1989 The *Exxon Valdez* supertanker spills 10 million gallons of crude oil off the Alaskan coast. The US invades Panama. The Berlin Wall ceases to divide the two Germanys, signaling the end of the Cold War.
1990 US troops are sent to Saudi Arabia in response to Iraq's invasion of Kuwait.
1991 An air and ground war leads to the Iraqi surrender and withdrawal from Kuwait. The Soviet Union comes apart.
1992 The 27th Amendment to the Constitution bars Congress from giving itself a midterm pay raise. Riots erupt in Los Angeles after a jury acquits white policemen accused of beating African American Rodney King. The North American Free Trade Agreement (NAFTA) is signed by the US, Canada, and Mexico.
1993 Janet Reno becomes the first woman attorney general. The World Trade Center in New York City is bombed.
1995 Timothy McVeigh detonates a bomb in a terrorist attack on the Alfred P. Murrah Federal Building in Oklahoma City, killing 168 people.
1998 Pres. Bill Clinton is impeached for perjury and obstruction of justice; he is acquitted by the Senate the following year.
2000 The results of the presidential election are challenged by Vice Pres. Al Gore; the US Supreme Court overrules the Florida Supreme Court's order for a statewide manual recount of ballots; George W. Bush wins the presidency.
2001 On 11 September, two hijacked airplanes demolish the World Trade Center in New York City, another crashes into the Pentagon outside Washington DC, and a fourth crashes in the southern Pennsylvania countryside. Pres. Bush calls for a global "war on terror" and sends US troops into Afghanistan, eventually displacing the Taliban regime.
2002 Republicans take control of both houses of Congress, holding both the legislative and executive branches of government for the first time since 1952.
2003 The US launches a war to depose the Saddam Hussein regime in Iraq and takes control of the country after just weeks of fighting. Congress passes a US$350 billion tax cut.
2004 Scandal erupts with the publication of photos of prisoner abuse at Abu Ghraib prison in Iraq. The independent 9/11 Commission finds no credible evidence of a connection between Iraq and al-Qaeda's attacks of 11 Sep 2001. Bush is reelected president.
2005 The US lags among donor nations in debt forgiveness for developing nations and disaster aid. Hurricane Katrina strikes the Gulf Coast, destroying much of New Orleans and killing 1,833 people.
2006 Conservative lawyer John G. Roberts, Jr., is appointed to the Supreme Court as chief justice. Former vice president Al Gore's film, *An Inconvenient Truth*, convinces many people that global warming is a danger to the environment (it will win an Academy Award in 2007). As the Iraq War continues, Democrats gain control of both houses of Congress.
2007 In an effort to quell a persistent insurrection against the US-backed government of Iraq, Pres. Bush orders a "surge" of 20,000 additional US troops.
2008 A continuing crisis in the suprime mortgage industry, leading to foreclosures, loan defaults, and falling home values, together with record-high prices of petroleum, pushes the US economy to the brink of recession. US troop deaths in Iraq topped 4,100 by July, while deaths in Afghanistan numbered over 475.

Important Documents in US History

Mayflower Compact

On 21 Nov 1620 (11 November, Old Style), 41 male passengers on the Mayflower signed the following compact prior to their landing at Plymouth (now Massachusetts). The compact resulted from the fear that some members of the company might leave the group and settle on their own. The Mayflower Compact bound the signers into a body politic for the purpose of forming a government and pledged them to abide by any laws and regulations that would later by established. The document was not a constitution but rather an adaptation of the usual church covenant to a civil situation. It became the foundation of Plymouth's government.

In the name of God, Amen.

We whose names are underwritten, the loyal subjects of our dread sovereign Lord, King James, by the grace of God, of Great Britain, France and Ireland king, defender of the faith, etc., having undertaken, for the glory of God, and advancement of the Christian faith, and honor of our king and country, a voyage to plant the first colony in the Northern parts of Virginia, do by these presents solemnly and mutually in the presence of God, and one of another, covenant and combine ourselves together into a civil body politic, for our better ordering and preservation and furtherance of the ends aforesaid; and by virtue hereof to enact, constitute, and frame such just and equal laws, ordinances, acts, constitutions, and offices, from time to time, as shall be thought most meet and convenient for the general good of the colony, unto which we promise all due submission and obedience.

In witness whereof we have hereunder subscribed our names at Cape-Cod the 11 of November, in the year of the reign of our sovereign lord, King James, of England, France, and Ireland the eighteenth, and of Scotland the fifty-fourth. Anno Domine 1620.

Declaration of Independence

On 4 Jul 1776 the Continental Congress officially adopted the Declaration of Independence. Two days before, the Congress had "unanimously" voted (with New York abstaining) to be free and independent from Britain. The Declaration of Independence was written largely by Thomas Jefferson. After modifications by the Congress, the document was prepared and voted upon. New York delegates voted to accept it on 15 July, and on 19 July the Congress ordered the document to be engrossed as "The Unanimous Declaration of the Thirteen United States of America." It was accordingly put on parchment, and members of the Congress present on 2 August affixed their signatures to this parchment copy on that day, and others later. The last signer was Thomas McKean of Delaware, whose name was not placed on the document before 1777.

The Unanimous Declaration of the Thirteen United States of America

When in the Course of human events, it becomes necessary for one people to dissolve the political bands which have connected them with another, and to assume among the powers of the earth, the separate and equal station to which the Laws of Nature and of Nature's God entitle them, a decent respect to the opinions of mankind requires that they should declare the causes which impel them to the separation.—We hold these truths to be self-evident, that all men are created equal, that they are endowed by their Creator with certain unalienable Rights, that among these are Life, Liberty and the pursuit of Happiness.—That to secure these rights, Governments are instituted among Men, deriving their just powers from the consent of the governed,—That whenever any Form of Government becomes destructive of these ends, it is the Right of the People to alter or to abolish it, and to institute new Government, laying its foundation on such principles and organizing its powers in such form, as to them shall seem most likely to effect their Safety and Happiness.

Prudence, indeed, will dictate that Governments long established should not be changed for light and transient causes; and accordingly all experience hath shown, that mankind are more disposed to suffer, while evils are sufferable, than to right themselves by abolishing the forms to which they are accustomed. But when a long train of abuses and usurpations, pursuing invariably the same Object evinces a design to reduce them under absolute Despotism, it is their right, it is their duty, to throw off such Government, and to provide new Guards for their future security.—Such has been the patient sufferance of these Colonies; and such is now the necessity which constrains them to alter their former Systems of Government. The history of the present King of Great Britain is a history of repeated injuries and usurpations, all having in direct object the establishment of an absolute Tyranny over these States.

To prove this, let Facts be submitted to a candid world.—He has refused his Assent to Laws, the most wholesome and necessary for the public good.—He has forbidden his Governors to pass Laws of immediate and pressing importance, unless suspended in their operation till his Assent should be obtained; and when so suspended, he has utterly neglected to attend to them.—He has refused to pass other Laws for the accommodation of large districts of people, unless those people would relinquish the right of Representation in the Legislature, a right inestimable to them and formidable to tyrants only.—He has called together legislative bodies at places unusual, uncomfortable, and distant from the depository of their public Records, for the sole purpose of fatiguing them into compliance with his measures.—He has dissolved Representative Houses repeatedly, for opposing with manly firmness his invasions on the rights of the people.—He has refused for a long time, after such dissolutions, to cause others to be elected; whereby the Legislative powers, incapable of Annihilation, have returned to the People at large for their exercise; the State remaining in the mean time exposed to all the dangers of invasion from without, and convulsions within.—He has endeavoured to prevent the population of these States; for that purpose obstructing the Laws for Naturalization of Foreigners; refusing to pass others to encourage their migration hither, and raising the conditions of new Appropriations of Lands.—He has obstructed the Administration of Justice, by refusing his Assent to Laws for establishing Judiciary powers.—He has made judges dependent on his Will alone, for the tenure of their offices, and the amount and payment of their salaries.—He has erected a multitude of New Offices, and sent hither swarms of Officers to harrass our people, and eat out their substance.—He has kept among us, in times of peace, Standing Armies, without the Consent of our legislatures.—He has affected to render the Military independent of and superior to the Civil power.—He has combined with others to subject us to a jurisdiction foreign to our constitution, and unacknowledged by our laws; giving his Assent to their Acts of pretended Legislation:—For quartering large bodies of armed troops among us:—For protecting them, by a mock Trial, from punishment for any Murders which they should commit on the Inhabitants of these States:—For cutting off our Trade with all parts of the world:—For imposing Taxes on us without our Consent:—For depriving us in many cases, of the benefits of Trial by Jury:—For transporting us beyond Seas to be tried for pretended offences:—For abolishing the free System of English Laws in a neighbouring Province, establishing therein an Arbitrary government, and enlarging its Boundaries so as to render it at once an example and fit instrument for introducing the same absolute rule into these Colonies:—For taking away our Charters, abolishing our most valuable Laws, and altering fundamentally the Forms of our Governments:—For suspending our own Legislatures, and declaring themselves invested with power to legislate for us in all cases whatsoever.—He has abdicated Government here, by declaring us out of his Protection and waging War against us.—He has plundered our seas, ravaged our Coasts, burnt our towns, and destroyed the lives of our people.—He is at this time transporting large Armies of foreign Mercenaries to compleat the works of death, desolation and tyranny, already begun with circumstances of Cruelty & perfidy scarcely paralleled in the most barbarous ages, and totally unworthy the Head of a civilized nation.—He has constrained our fellow Citizens taken Captive on the high Seas to bear Arms against their Country, to become the executioners of their friends and Brethren, or to fall themselves by their Hands.—He has excited domestic insurrections amongst us, and has endeavoured to bring on the inhabitants of our frontiers, the merciless Indian Savages, whose known rule of warfare, is an undistinguished destruction of all ages, sexes and conditions. In every stage of these Oppressions We have Petitioned for Redress in the most humble terms: Our repeated Petitions have been answered only by repeated injury. A Prince, whose character is thus marked by every act which may define a Tyrant, is unfit to be the ruler of a free people. Nor have We been wanting in attentions to our Brittish brethren. We have warned them from time to time of attempts by their legislature to extend an unwarrantable jurisdiction over us. We have reminded them of the circumstances of our emigration and settlement here. We have appealed to their native justice and magnanimity, and we have conjured them by the ties of our common kindred to disavow these usurpations, which, would inevitably interrupt our connections and correspondence. They too have been deaf to the voice of justice and of consanguinity. We must, therefore, acquiesce in the necessity, which denounces our Separation, and hold them, as we hold the rest of mankind. Enemies in War, in Peace Friends.—

We, therefore, the Representatives of the United States of America, in General Congress, Assembled, appealing to the Supreme Judge of the world for the rectitude of our intentions, do, in the Name, and by Authority of the good People of these Colonies, solemnly publish and declare, That these United Colonies are, and of Right ought to be Free and Independent States; that they are Absolved from all Allegiance to the British Crown, and that all political connection between them and the State of Great Britain, is and ought to be totally dissolved; and that as Free and Independent States, they have full Power to levy War, conclude Peace, contract Alliances, establish Commerce, and to do all other Acts and Things which Independent States may of right do.—And for the support of this Declaration, with a firm reliance on the protection of Divine Providence, we mutually pledge to each other our Lives, our Fortunes and our sacred Honor.

Signers of the Declaration of Independence

	BIRTHPLACE	OCCUPATION
Connecticut		
Samuel Huntington (1731–1796)	Windham CT	lawyer, judge
Roger Sherman (1721–1793)	Newton MA	cobbler, surveyor, lawyer, judge
William Williams (1731–1811)	Lebanon CT	merchant, judge
Oliver Wolcott (1726–1797)	Windsor CT	soldier, sheriff, judge
Delaware		
Thomas McKean (1734–1817)	New London PA	lawyer, judge
George Read (1733–1798)	North East MD	lawyer, judge
Caesar Rodney (1728–1784)	Dover DE	judge
Georgia		
Button Gwinnett (c. 1735–1777)	bapt. Gloucester, England	merchant
Lyman Hall (1724–1790)	Wallingford CT	physician
George Walton (c. 1741–1804)	Farmville VA	lawyer, judge

Signers of the Declaration of Independence (continued)

	BIRTHPLACE	OCCUPATION
Maryland		
Charles Carroll of Carrollton (1737–1832)	Annapolis MD	lawyer
Samuel Chase (1741–1811)	Somerset county MD	lawyer, judge
William Paca (1740–1799)	Abingdon MD	lawyer, judge
Thomas Stone (1743–1787)	Charles county MD	lawyer
Massachusetts		
John Adams (1735–1826)	Braintree (Quincy) MA	lawyer
Samuel Adams (1722–1803)	Boston MA	politician
Elbridge Gerry (1744–1814)	Marblehead MA	merchant
John Hancock (1737–1793)	Braintree (Quincy) MA	merchant
Robert Treat Paine (1731–1814)	Boston MA	lawyer, judge
New Hampshire		
Josiah Bartlett (1729–1795)	Amesbury MA	physician, judge
Matthew Thornton (c. 1714–1803)	Ireland	physician
William Whipple (1730–1785)	Kittery ME	merchant, soldier, judge
New Jersey		
Abraham Clark (1726–1794)	Elizabethtown NJ	surveyor, lawyer, sheriff
John Hart (c. 1711–1779)	Stonington CT	farmer, judge
Francis Hopkinson (1737–1791)	Philadelphia PA	lawyer, judge, author
Richard Stockton (1730–1781)	near Princeton NJ	lawyer
John Witherspoon (1723–1794)	Gifford, Scotland	clergyman, author, educator
New York		
William Floyd (1734–1821)	Brookhaven NY	soldier
Francis Lewis (1713–1802)	Llandaff, Wales	merchant
Philip Livingston (1716–1778)	Albany NY	merchant
Lewis Morris (1726–1798)	Morrisania (Bronx county) NY	farmer, soldier, judge
North Carolina		
Joseph Hewes (1730–1779)	Kingston NJ	merchant
William Hooper (1742–1790)	Boston MA	lawyer, judge
John Penn (1741–1788)	near Port Royal VA	lawyer
Pennsylvania		
George Clymer (1739–1813)	Philadelphia PA	merchant
Benjamin Franklin (1706–1790)	Boston MA	printer, publisher, author, scientist
Robert Morris (1734–1806)	Lancashire, England	merchant
John Morton (1724–1777)	Ridley PA	judge
George Ross (1730–1779)	New Castle DE	lawyer, judge
Benjamin Rush (1746–1813)	Byberry PA	physician
James Smith (c. 1719–1806)	Dublin, Ireland	lawyer
George Taylor (1716–1781)	Ireland	ironmaster
James Wilson (1742–1798)	Fife, Scotland	lawyer, judge
Rhode Island		
William Ellery (1727–1820)	Newport RI	lawyer, judge
Stephen Hopkins (1707–1785)	Providence RI	judge, educator
South Carolina		
Thomas Heyward, Jr. (1746–1809)	St. Helena's (now St. Luke's) parish SC	lawyer, judge
Thomas Lynch, Jr. (1749–1779)	Winyah SC	lawyer
Arthur Middleton (1742–1787)	near Charleston SC	planter, legislator
Edward Rutledge (1749–1800)	Charleston SC	lawyer
Virginia		
Carter Braxton (1736–1797)	Newington Plantation VA	planter
Thomas Jefferson (1743–1826)	Shadwell VA	lawyer, author, educator
Benjamin Harrison (c. 1726–1791)	Berkeley VA	planter, politician
Francis Lightfoot Lee (1734–1797)	Westmoreland county VA	farmer
Richard Henry Lee (1732–1794)	Westmoreland county VA	planter, judge
Thomas Nelson, Jr. (1738–1789)	Yorktown VA	planter
George Wythe (1726–1806)	Elizabeth City county (Hampton) VA	lawyer, educator

The Constitution of the United States

The Constitution was written during the summer of 1787 in Philadelphia by 55 delegates to a Constitutional Convention that was called ostensibly to amend the Articles of Confederation. It was submitted for ratification to the 13 states on 28 Sep 1787. In June 1788, after the Constitution had been ratified by nine states (as required by Article VII), Congress set 4 Mar 1789 as the date for the new government to commence proceedings.

Preamble

We the People of the United States, in Order to form a more perfect Union, establish Justice, insure domestic Tranquility, provide for common defence, promote the general Welfare, and secure the Blessings of Liberty to ourselves and our Posterity, do ordain and establish this Constitution for the United States of America.

Article I

Section 1—

All legislative Powers herein granted shall be vested in a Congress of the United States, which shall consist of a Senate and House of Representatives.

Section 2—

The House of Representatives shall be composed of Members chosen every second Year by the People of the several States, and the Electors in each State shall have the Qualifications requisite for Electors of the most numerous Branch of the State Legislature.

No Person shall be a Representative who shall not have attained to the Age of twenty five Years, and been seven Years a Citizen of the United States, and who shall not, when elected, be an Inhabitant of that State in which he shall be chosen.

Representatives and direct Taxes shall be apportioned among the several States which may be included within this Union, according to their respective Numbers, which shall be determined by adding to the whole Number of free Persons, including those bound to Service for a Term of Years, and excluding Indians not taxed, three fifths of all other Persons. The actual Enumeration shall be made within three Years after the first Meeting of the Congress of the United States, and within every subsequent Term of ten Years, in such Manner as they shall by Law direct. The Number of Representatives shall not exceed one for every thirty Thousand, but each State shall have at Least one Representative; and until such enumeration shall be made, the State of New Hampshire shall be entitled to chuse three, Massachusetts eight, Rhode-Island and Providence Plantations one, Connecticut five, New-York six, New Jersey four, Pennsylvania eight, Delaware one, Maryland six, Virginia ten, North Carolina five, South Carolina five, and Georgia three.

When vacancies happen in the Representation from any State, the Executive Authority thereof shall issue Writs of Election to fill such Vacancies.

The House of Representatives shall chuse their speaker and other Officers; and shall have the sole Power of Impeachment.

Section 3—

The Senate of the United States shall be composed of two Senators from each State, chosen by the Legislature thereof for six Years; and each Senator shall have one Vote.

Immediately after they shall be assembled in Consequence of the first Election, they shall be divided as equally as may be into three Classes. The Seats of the Senators of the first Class shall be vacated at the Expiration of the second Year, of the second Class at the Expiration of the fourth Year, and of the third Class at the Expiration of the sixth Year, so that one third may be chosen every second Year; and if Vacancies happen by Resignation, or otherwise, during the Recess of the Legislature of any State, the Executive thereof may make temporary Appointments until the next Meeting of the Legislature, which shall then fill such Vacancies.

No Person shall be a Senator who shall not have attained to the Age of thirty Years, and been nine Years a Citizen of the United States, and who shall not, when elected, be an Inhabitant of that State for which he shall be chosen.

The Vice President of the United States shall be President of the Senate, but shall have no Vote, unless they be equally divided.

The Senate shall chuse their other Officers, and also a President pro tempore, in the Absence of the Vice President, or when he shall exercise the Office of President of the United States.

The Senate shall have the sole Power to try all Impeachments. When sitting for that Purpose, they shall be on Oath or Affirmation. When the President of the United States is tried, the Chief Justice shall preside: And no Person shall be convicted without the concurrence of two thirds of the Members present. Judgment in Cases of Impeachment shall not extend further than to removal from Office, and disqualification to hold and enjoy any Office of honor, Trust or Profit under the United States: but the Party convicted shall nevertheless be liable and subject to Indictment, Trial, Judgment and Punishment, according to law.

Section 4—

The Times, Places and Manner of holding Elections for Senators and Representatives, shall be prescribed in each State by the Legislature thereof; but the Congress may at any time by Law make or alter such Regulations, except as to the Places of chusing Senators.

The Congress shall assemble at least once in every Year, and such Meeting shall be on the first Monday in December, unless they shall by Law appoint a different Day.

Section 5—

Each House shall be the Judge of the Elections, Returns and Qualifications of its own Members, and a Majority of each shall constitute a Quorum to do business; but a smaller Number may adjourn from day to day, and may be authorized to compel the Attendance of absent Members, in such Manner, and under such Penalties as each House may provide.

Each House may determine the Rules of its Proceedings, punish its Members for disorderly Behaviour, and, with the Concurrence of two thirds, expel a Member.

Each House shall keep a journal of its Proceedings, and from time to time publish the same, excepting such Parts as may in their Judgment require Secrecy; and the yeas and Nays of the Members of either House on any question shall, at the Desire of one fifth of those Present, be entered on the journal.

Neither House, during the Session of Congress, shall, without the Consent of the other, adjourn for more than three days, nor to any other place than that in which the two Houses shall be sitting.

Section 6—
The Senators and Representatives shall receive a Compensation for their Services, to be ascertained by Law, and paid out of the Treasury of the United States. They shall in all Cases, except Treason, Felony and Breach of the Peace, be privileged from Arrest during their Attendance at the Session of their respective Houses, and in going to and returning from the same; and for any Speech or Debate in either House, they shall not be questioned in any other Place.

No Senator or Representative shall, during the Time for which he was elected, be appointed to any civil Office under the Authority of the United States, which shall have been created, or the Emoluments whereof shall have been encreased during such time; and no Person holding any Office under the United States, shall be a Member of either House during his Continuance in Office.

Section 7—
All Bills for raising Revenue shall originate in the House of Representatives; but the Senate may propose or concur with Amendments as on other Bills.

Every Bill which shall have passed the House of Representatives and the Senate, shall, before it become a Law, be presented to the President of the United States; If he approve he shall sign it, but if not he shall return it, with his Objections to that House in which it shall have originated, who shall enter the Objections at large on their Journal, and proceed to reconsider it. If after such Reconsideration two thirds of that House shall agree to pass the Bill, it shall be sent, together with the Objections, to the other House, by which it shall likewise be reconsidered, and if approved by two thirds of that House, it shall become a Law. But in all such Cases the Votes of both Houses shall be determined by yeas and Nays, and the Names of the Persons voting for and against the Bill shall be entered on the Journal of each House respectively. If any Bill shall not be returned by the President within ten Days (Sundays excepted) after it shall have been presented to him, the Same shall be a Law, in like Manner as if he had signed it, unless the Congress by their Adjournment prevent its Return, in which Case it shall not be a Law.

Every Order, Resolution, or Vote to which the Concurrence of the Senate and House of Representatives may be necessary (except on a question of Adjournment) shall be presented to the President of the United States; and before the Same shall take Effect, shall be approved by him, or being disapproved by him, shall be repassed by two thirds of the Senate and House of Representatives, according to the Rules and Limitations prescribed in the Case of a Bill.

Section 8—
The Congress shall have Power To lay and collect Taxes, Duties, Imposts and Excises, to pay the Debts and provide for the common Defence and general Welfare of the United States; but all Duties, Imposts and Excises shall be uniform throughout the United States;

To borrow Money on the credit of the United States;

To regulate Commerce with foreign Nations, and among the several States, and with the Indian Tribes;

To establish an uniform Rule of Naturalization, and uniform Laws on the subject of Bankruptcies throughout the United States;

To coin Money, regulate the Value thereof, and of foreign Coin, and fix the Standard of Weights and Measures;

To provide for the Punishment of counterfeiting the Securities and current Coin of the United States;

To establish Post Offices and post Roads;

To promote the Progress of Science and useful Arts, by securing for limited Times to Authors and Inventors the exclusive Right to their respective Writings and Discoveries;

To constitute Tribunals inferior to the supreme Court;

To define and punish Piracies and Felonies committed on the high Seas, and Offences against the Law of Nations;

To declare War, grant Letters of Marque and Reprisal, and make rules concerning Captures on Land and Water;

To raise and support Armies, but no Appropriation of Money to that Use shall be for a longer Term than two Years;

To provide and maintain a Navy;

To make Rules for the Government and Regulation of the land and naval Forces;

To provide for calling forth the Militia to execute the Laws of the Union, suppress Insurrections and repel Invasions;

To provide for organizing, arming, and disciplining, the Militia, and for governing such Part of them as may be employed in the Service of the United States, reserving to the States respectively, the Appointment of the Officers, and the Authority of training the Militia according to the discipline prescribed by Congress;

To exercise exclusive Legislation in all Cases whatsoever, over such District (not exceeding ten Miles square), as may, by Cession of particular States, and the Acceptance of Congress, become the Seat of the Government of the United States, and to exercise like Authority over all Places purchased by the Consent of the Legislature of the State in which the Same shall be for the Erection of Forts, Magazines, Arsenals, dock-Yards, and other needful Buildings; — And

To make all Laws which shall be necessary and proper for carying into Execution the foregoing Powers, and all other Powers vested by this Constitution in the Government of the United States, or in any Department or Officer thereof.

Section 9—
The Migration or Importation of such Persons as any of the States now existing shall think proper to admit, shall not be prohibited by the Congress prior to the Year one thousand eight hundred and eight, but a Tax or duty may be imposed on such Importation, not exceeding ten dollars for each Person.

The Privilege of the Writ of Habeas Corpus shall not be suspended, unless when in Cases of Rebellion or Invasion the public Safety may require it.

No Bill of Attainder or ex post facto Law shall be passed.

No Capitation, or other direct, Tax shall be laid, unless in Proportion to the Census or Enumeration herein before directed to be taken.

No Tax or Duty shall be laid on Articles exported from any State.

No Preference shall be given by any Regulation of Commerce or Revenue to the Ports of one State over those of another; nor shall Vessels bound to, or from, one State, be obliged to enter, clear or pay Duties in another.

No money shall be drawn from the Treasury, but in Consequence of Appropriations made by Law; and a regular Statement and Account of the Receipts and Expenditures of all public Money shall be published from time to time.

No Title of Nobility shall be granted by the United States: And no Person holding any Office of Profit or Trust under them, shall, without the Consent of the Congress, accept of any present, Emolument, Office, or Title, of any kind whatever, from any King, Prince, or foreign State.

Section 10—
No State shall enter into any Treaty, Alliance, or Confederation; grant Letters of Marque and Reprisal; coin Money; emit Bills of Credit; make any Thing but gold and silver Coin a Tender in Payment of Debts; pass any Bill of Attainder, ex post facto Law, or Law impairing the Obligation of Contracts, or grant any Title of Nobility.

No State shall, without the Consent of the Congress, lay any Imposts or Duties on Imports or Exports, except what may be absolutely necessary for executing it's inspection Laws: and the net Produce of all Duties and Imposts, laid by any State on Imports or Exports, shall be for the Use of the Treasury of the United States; and all such Laws shall be subject to the Revision and Controul of the Congress.

No State shall, without the Consent of Congress, lay any Duty of Tonnage, keep Troops, or Ships of War in time of Peace, enter into any Agreement or Compact with another State, or with a foreign Power, or engage in War, unless actually invaded, or in such imminent Danger as will not admit of delay.

Article II

Section 1—
The executive Power shall be vested in a President of the United States of America. He shall hold his Office during the Term of four Years, and, together with the Vice President, chosen for the same Term, be elected, as follows

Each State shall appoint, in such Manner as the Legislature thereof may direct, a Number of Electors, equal to the whole Number of Senators and Representatives to which the State may be entitled in the Congress: but no Senator or Representative, or Person holding an Office of Trust or Profit under the United States, shall be appointed an Elector.

The Electors shall meet in their respective States, and vote by Ballot for two Persons, of whom one at least shall not be an Inhabitant of the same State with themselves. And they shall make a List of all the Persons voted for, and of the Number of Votes for each; which List they shall sign and certify, and transmit sealed to the Seat of the Government of the United States, directed to the President of the Senate. The President of the Senate shall, in the Presence of the Senate and House of Representatives, open all the Certificates, and the Votes shall then be counted. The Person having the greatest Number of Votes shall be the President, if such Number be a Majority of the whole Number of Electors appointed; and if there be more than one who have such Majority, and have an equal Number of Votes, then the House of Representatives shall immediately chuse by Ballot one of them for President: and if no Person have a Majority, then from the five highest on the List the said House shall in like Manner chuse the President. But in chusing the President, the Votes shall be taken by States, the Representation from each State having one Vote; A quorum for this Purpose shall consist of a Member or Members from two thirds of the States, and a Majority of all the States shall be necessary to a Choice. In every Case, after the Choice of the President, the Person having the greatest Number of Votes of the Electors shall be the Vice President. But if there should remain two or more who have equal Votes, the Senate shall chuse from them by Ballot the Vice President.

The Congress may determine the Time of chusing the Electors, and the Day on which they shall give their Votes; which Day shall be the same throughout the United States.

No Person except a natural born Citizen, or a Citizen of the United States, at the time of the Adoption of this Constitution, shall be eligible to the Office of President; neither shall any Person be eligible to that Office who shall not have attained to the Age of thirty five Years, and been fourteen Years a Resident within the United States.

In Case of the Removal of the President from Office, or of his Death, Resignation, or Inability to discharge the Powers and Duties of the said Office, the Same shall devolve on the Vice President, and the Congress may by Law provide for the Case of Removal, Death, Resignation or Inability, both of the President and Vice President, declaring what Officer shall then act as President, and such Officer shall act accordingly, until the Disability be removed, or a President shall be elected.

The President shall, at stated Times, receive for his Services, a Compensation, which shall neither be encreased nor diminished during the Period for which he shall have been elected, and he shall not receive within that Period any other Emolument from the United States, or any of them.

Before he enter on the Execution of his Office, he shall take the following Oath or Affirmation: "I do solemnly swear (or affirm) that I will faithfully execute the Office of President of the United States, and will to the best of my Ability, preserve, protect and defend the Constitution of the United States."

Section 2—
The President shall be Commander in Chief of the Army and Navy of the United States, and of the Militia of the several States, when called into the actual Service of the United States; he may require the Opinion, in writing, of the principal Officer in each of the executive Departments, upon any Subject relating to the Duties of their respective Offices, and he shall have Power to grant Reprieves and Pardons for Offences against the United States, except in Cases of Impeachment.

He shall have Power, by and with the Advice and Consent of the Senate, to make Treaties, provided two thirds of the Senators present concur; and he shall nominate, and by and with the Advice and Consent of the Senate, shall appoint Ambassadors, other public Ministers and Consuls, Judges of the supreme Court, and all other Officers of the United States, whose Appointments are not herein otherwise provided for, and which shall be established by Law: but the Congress may by Law vest the Appointment of such inferior Officers, as they think proper, in the President alone, in the Courts of Law, or in the Heads of Departments.

The President shall have Power to fill up all Vacancies that may happen during the Recess of the Senate, by granting Commissions which shall expire at the End of their next Session.

Section 3—
He shall from time to time give to the Congress Information of the State of the Union, and recommend to their Consideration such Measures as he shall judge necessary and expedient; he may, on extraordinary Occasions, convene both Houses, or either of them, and in Case of Disagreement between them, with Respect to the Time of Adjournment, he may adjourn them to such Time as he shall think proper; he shall receive Ambassadors and other public Ministers; he shall take Care that the Laws be faithfully executed, and shall Commission all the Officers of the United States.

Section 4—
The President, Vice President and all civil Officers of the United States, shall be removed from Office on Impeachment for, and Conviction of, Treason, Bribery, or other High Crimes and Misdemeanors.

Article III

Section 1—
The judicial Power of the United States, shall be vested in one supreme Court, and in such inferior Courts as the Congress may from time to time ordain and establish. The Judges, both of the supreme and inferior Courts, shall hold their Offices during good Behaviour, and shall, at stated Times, receive for their Services, a Compensation, which shall not be diminished during their Continuance in Office.

Section 2—
The judicial Power shall extend to all Cases, in Law and Equity, arising under this Constitution, the Laws of the United States, and Treaties made, or which shall be made, under their Authority; — to all Cases affecting Ambassadors, other public Ministers and Consuls; — to all Cases of admiralty and maritime jurisdiction; — to Controversies to which the United States shall be a Party; — to Controversies between two or more States;-between a State and Citizens of another State; — between Citizens of different States; — between Citizens of the same State claiming Lands under Grants of different States, and between a State, or the Citizens thereof, and foreign States, Citizens or Subjects.

In all Cases affecting Ambassadors, other public Ministers and Consuls, and those in which a State shall be Party, the supreme Court shall have original Jurisdiction. In all the other Cases before mentioned, the supreme Court shall have appellate Jurisdiction, both as to Law and Fact, with such Exceptions, and under such Regulations as the Congress shall make.

The Trial of all Crimes, except in Cases of Impeachment, shall be by Jury; and such Trial shall be held in the State where the said Crimes shall have been committed; but when not committed within any State, the Trial shall be at such Place or Places as the Congress may by Law have directed.

Section 3—
Treason against the United States, shall consist only in levying War against them, or in adhering to their Enemies, giving them Aid and Comfort. No Person shall be convicted of Treason unless on the Testimony of two Witnesses to the same overt Act, or on Confession in open Court.

The Congress shall have Power to declare the Punishment of Treason, but no Attainder of Treason shall work Corruption of Blood, or Forfeiture except during the Life of the Person attainted.

Article IV

Section 1—
Full Faith and Credit shall be given in each State to the public Acts, Records, and judicial Proceedings of every other State. And the Congress may by general Laws prescribe the Manner in which such Acts, Records and Proceedings shall be proved, and the Effect thereof.

Section 2—
The Citizens of each State shall be entitled to all Privileges and Immunities of Citizens in the several States.

A person charged in any State with Treason, Felony, or other Crime, who shall flee from justice, and be found in another State, shall on Demand of the executive Authority of the State from which he fled, be delivered up, to be removed to the State having Jurisdiction of the Crime.

No Person held to Service or Labour in one State, under the Laws thereof, escaping into another, shall in Consequence of any Law or Regulation therein, be discharged from such Service or Labour, but shall be delivered upon on Claim of the Party to whom such Service or Labour may be due.

Section 3—
New States may be admitted by the Congress into this Union; but no new State shall be formed or erected within the Jurisdiction of any other State; nor any State be formed by the Junction of two or more States, or Parts of States, without the Consent of the Legislatures of the States concerned as well as of the Congress.

The Congress shall have Power to dispose of and make all needful Rules and Regulations respecting the Territory or other Property belonging to the United States; and nothing in this Constitution shall be so construed as to Prejudice any Claims of the United States, or of any particular State.

Section 4—
The United States shall guarantee to every State in this Union a Republican Form of Government, and shall protect each of them against Invasion; and on Application of the Legislature, or of the Executive (when the Legislature cannot be convened) against domestic Violence.

Article V

The Congress, whenever two thirds of both Houses shall deem it necessary, shall propose Amendments to this Constitution, or, on the Application of the Legislatures of two thirds of the several States, shall call a Convention for proposing Amendments, which, in either Case, shall be valid to all Intents and Purposes, as Part of this Constitution, when ratified by the Legislatures of three fourths of the several States, or by Conventions in three fourths thereof, as the one or the other Mode of Ratification may be proposed by the Congress; Provided that no Amendment which may be made prior to the Year One thousand eight hundred and eight shall in any Manner affect the first and fourth Clauses in the Ninth Section of the first

Article; and that no State, without its Consent, shall be deprived of its equal Suffrage in the Senate.

Article VI

All Debts contracted and Engagements entered into, before the Adoption of this Constitution, shall be as valid against the United States under this Constitution, as under the Confederation.

This Constitution, and the Laws of the United States which shall be made in Pursuance thereof; and all Treaties made, or which shall be made, under the Authority of the United States, shall be the supreme Law of the Land; and the Judges in every State shall be bound thereby, any Thing in the Constitution or Laws of any State to the Contrary notwithstanding.

The Senators and Representatives before mentioned, and the Members of the several State Legislatures, and all executive and judicial Officers, both of the United States and of the several States, shall be bound by Oath or Affirmation, to support this Constitution; but no religious Test shall ever be required as a Qualification to any Office or public Trust under the United States.

Article VII

The Ratification of the Conventions of nine States, shall be sufficient for the Establishment of this Constitution between the States so ratifying the Same.

Done in Convention by the Unanimous Consent of the States present the Seventeenth Day of September in the Year of our Lord one thousand seven hundred and Eighty seven and of the Independence of the United States of America the Twelfth
IN WITNESS whereof We have hereunto subscribed our Names,

G° Washington—
Presid^t. and deputy from Virginia

New Hampshire
John Langdon
Nicholas Gilman

Massachusetts
Nathaniel Gorham
Rufus King

Connecticut
Wm. Saml. Johnson
Roger Sherman

New York
Alexander Hamilton

New Jersey
Wil: Livingston
David Brearley
Wm. Paterson
Jona: Dayton

Pennsylvania
B. Franklin
Thomas Mifflin
Robt Morris
Geo. Clymer
Thos. FitzSimons
Jared Ingersoll
James Wilson
Gouv Morris

Delaware
Geo: Read
Gunning Bedford jun
John Dickinson
Richard Bassett
Jaco: Broom

Maryland
James McHenry
Dan of St Thos. Jenifer
Danl Carroll

Virginia
John Blair—
James Madison Jr.

North Carolina
Wm. Blount
Rich'd Dobbs Spaight
Hu Williamson

South Carolina
J. Rutledge
Charles Cotesworth Pinckney
Charles Pinckney
Pierce Butler

Georgia
William Few
Abr Baldwin

Attest:
William Jackson, *Secretary*

[*Rhode Island and the Providence Plantations*
Rhode Island did not send delegates to the Constitutional Convention.]

Bill of Rights

The first 10 amendments to the Constitution were adopted as a single unit on 15 Dec 1791. Together, they constitute a collection of mutually reinforcing guarantees of individual rights and of limitations on federal and state governments.

Amendment I

Congress shall make no law respecting an establishment of religion, or prohibiting the free exercise thereof; or abridging the freedom of speech, or of the press; or the right of the people peaceably to assemble, and to petition the Government for a redress of grievances.

Amendment II

A well regulated Militia, being necessary to the security of a free State, the right of the people to keep and bear Arms, shall not be infringed.

Amendment III

No Soldier shall, in time of peace be quartered in any house, without the consent of the Owner, nor in time of war, but in a manner to be prescribed by law.

Amendment IV

The right of the People to be secure in their persons,

houses, papers, and effects, against unreasonable searches and seizures, shall not be violated, and no Warrants shall issue, but upon probable cause, supported by Oath or affirmation, and particularity describing the place to be searched, and the persons or things to be seized.

Amendment V

No person shall be held to answer for a capital, or otherwise infamous crime, unless on a presentment or indictment of a Grand Jury, except in cases arising in the land or naval forces, or in the Militia, when in actual service in time of War or public danger; nor shall any person be subject for the same offence to be twice put in jeopardy of life or limb; nor shall be compelled in any criminal case to be a witness against himself, nor be deprived of life, liberty, or property, without due process of law; nor shall private property be taken for public use, without just compensation.

Amendment VI

In all criminal prosecutions, the accused shall enjoy the right to a speedy and public trial, by an impartial jury of the State and district wherein the crime shall have been committed, which district shall have been previously ascertained by law, and to be informed of the nature and cause of the accusation; to be confronted with the witnesses against him; to have compulsory process for obtaining witnesses in his favor, and to have Assistance of Counsel for his defence.

Amendment VII

In Suits at common law, where the value in controversy shall exceed twenty dollars, the right of trial by jury shall be preserved, and no fact tried by a jury, shall be otherwise re-examined in any Court of the United States, than according to the rules of the common law.

Amendment VIII

Excessive bail shall not be required, nor excessive fines imposed, nor cruel and unusual punishments inflicted.

Amendment IX

The enumeration in the Constitution, of certain rights, shall not be construed to deny or disparage others retained by the people.

Amendment X

The powers not delegated to the United States by the Constitution, nor prohibited by it to the States, are reserved to the States respectively, or to the people.

Further Amendments

Amendment XI
(ratified 7 Feb 1795)

The Judicial power of the United States shall not be construed to extend to any suit in law or equity, commenced or prosecuted against one of the United States by Citizens of another State, or by Citizens or Subjects of any Foreign State.

Amendment XII
(ratified 15 Jun 1804)

The Electors shall meet in their respective states and vote by ballot for President and Vice-President, one of whom, at least, shall not be an inhabitant of the same state with themselves; they shall name in their ballots the person voted for as President, and in distinct ballots the person voted for as Vice-President, and they shall make distinct lists of all persons voted for as President, and of all persons voted for as Vice-President, and of the number of votes for each, which lists they shall sign and certify, and transmit sealed to the seat of the government of the United States, directed to the President of the Senate; — The President of the Senate shall, in the presence of the Senate and House of Representatives, open all the certificates and the votes shall then be counted; — The person having the greatest number of votes for President, shall be the President, if such number be a majority of the whole number of Electors appointed; and if no person have such majority, then from the persons having the highest numbers not exceeding three on the list of those voted for as President, the House of Representatives shall choose immediately, by ballot, the President. But in choosing the President, the votes shall be taken by states, the representation from each state having one vote; a quorum for this purpose shall consist of a member or members from two-thirds of the states, and a majority of all the states shall be necessary to a choice. And if the House of Representatives shall not choose a President whenever the right of choice shall devolve upon then, before the fourth day of March next following, then the Vice-President shall act as President, as in the case of the death or other constitutional disability of the President. — The person having the greatest number of votes as Vice-President, shall be the Vice-President, if such number be a majority of the whole number of Electors appointed, and if no person have a majority, then from the two highest numbers on the list, the Senate shall choose the Vice-President; a quorum for the purpose shall consist of two-thirds of the whole number of Senators, and a majority of the whole number shall be necessary to a choice. But no person constitutionally ineligible to the office of President shall be eligible to that of Vice-President of the United States.

Amendment XIII
(ratified 6 Dec 1865)

Section 1—
Neither slavery nor involuntary servitude, except as a punishment for crime whereof the party shall have been duly convicted, shall exist within the United States, or any place subject to their jurisdiction.

Section 2—
Congress shall have power to enforce this article by appropriate legislation.

Amendment XIV
(ratified 9 Jul 1868)

Section 1—
All persons born or naturalized in the United States, and subject to the jurisdiction thereof, are citizens of the United States and of the State wherein they reside. No State shall make or enforce any law which shall abridge the privileges or immunities of citizens of the United States; nor shall any State deprive any person of life, liberty, or property, without due process of law; nor deny to any person within its jurisdiction the equal protection of the laws.

Section 2—
Representatives shall be apportioned among the several States according to their respective numbers, counting the whole number of persons in each State, excluding Indians not taxed. But when the right to vote at any election for the choice of electors for President and Vice President of the United States, Representatives in Congress, the Executive and Judicial officers of a State, or the members of the Legislature thereof, is denied to any of the male inhabitants of such State, being twenty-one years of age, and citizens of the United States, or in any way abridged, except for participation in rebellion, or other crime, the basis of representation therein shall be reduced in the proportion which the number of such male citizens shall bear to the whole number of male citizens twenty-one years of age in such State.

Section 3—
No person shall be a Senator or Representative in Congress, or elector of President and Vice President, or hold any office, civil or military, under the United States, or under any State, who, having previously taken an oath, as a member of Congress, or as an officer of the United States, or as a member of any State legislature, or as an executive or judicial officer of any State, to support the Constitution of the United States, shall have engaged in insurrection or rebellion against the same, or given aid or comfort to the enemies thereof. But Congress may by a vote of two-thirds of each House, remove such disability.

Section 4—
The validity of the public debt of the United States, authorized by law, including debts incurred for payment of pensions and bounties for services in suppressing insurrection or rebellion, shall not be questioned. But neither the United States nor any State shall assume or pay any debt or obligation incurred in aid of insurrection or rebellion against the United States, or any claim for the loss or emancipation of any slave; but all such debts, obligations and claims shall be held illegal and void.

Section 5—
The Congress shall have power to enforce, by appropriate legislation, the provisions of this article.

Amendment XV
(ratified 8 Feb 1870)

Section 1—
The right of citizens of the United States to vote shall not be denied or abridged by the United States or by any State on account of race, color, or previous condition of servitude.

Section 2—
The Congress shall have power to enforce this article by appropriate legislation.

Amendment XVI
(ratified 3 Feb 1913)

The Congress shall have power to lay and collect taxes on incomes, from whatever source derived, without apportionment among the several States, and without regard to any census or enumeration.

Amendment XVII
(ratified 13 Feb 1913)

The Senate of the United States shall be composed of two Senators from each State, elected by the people thereof for six years; and each Senator shall have one vote. The electors in each State shall have the qualifications requisite for electors of the most numerous branch of the State legislatures.

When vacancies happen in the representation of any State in the Senate, the executive authority of such State shall issue writs of election to fill such vacancies: Provided, That the legislature of any State may empower the executive thereof to make temporary appointments until the people fill the vacancies by election as the legislature may direct.

This amendment shall not be so construed as to affect the election or term of any Senator chosen before it becomes valid as part of the Constitution.

Amendment XVIII
(ratified 16 Jan 1919; repealed 5 Dec 1933 by Amendment XXI)

Section 1—
After one year from the ratification of this article the manufacture, sale, or transportation of intoxicating liquors within, the importation thereof into, or the exportation thereof from the United States and all territory subject to the jurisdiction thereof for beverage purposes is hereby prohibited.

Section 2—
The Congress and the several States shall have concurrent power to enforce this article by appropriate legislation.

Section 3—
This article shall be inoperative unless it shall have been ratified as an amendment to the Constitution by the legislatures of the several States as provided in the Constitution, within seven years from the date of the submission hereof to the States by the Congress.

Amendment XIX
(ratified 18 Aug 1920)

The right of citizens of the United States to vote shall not be denied or abridged by the United States or by any State on account of sex.

Congress shall have power to enforce this article by appropriate legislation.

Amendment XX
(ratified 23 Jan 1933)

Section 1—
The terms of the President and Vice President shall end at noon on the 20th day of January, and the terms of Senators and Representatives at noon on the 3d day of January, of the years in which such terms would have ended if this article had not been ratified; and the terms of their successors shall then begin.

Section 2—
The Congress shall assemble at least once in every year, and such meeting shall begin at noon on the 3d day of January, unless they shall by law appoint a different day.

Section 3—
If, at the time fixed for the beginning of the term of the President, the President elect shall have died, the Vice President elect shall become President. If a President shall not have been chosen before the time fixed for the beginning of his term, or if the President elect shall have failed to qualify, then the Vice President elect shall act as President until a President

shall have qualified; and the Congress may by law provide for the case wherein neither a President elect nor a Vice President elect shall have qualified, declaring who shall then act as President, or the manner in which one who is to act shall be selected, and such person shall act accordingly until a President or Vice President shall have qualified.

Section 4—
The Congress may by law provide for the case of the death of any of the persons from whom the House of Representatives may choose a President whenever the right of choice shall have devolved upon them, and for the case of the death of any of the persons from whom the Senate may choose a Vice President whenever the right of choice shall have devolved upon them.

Section 5—
Sections 1 and 2 shall take effect on the 15th day of October following the ratification of this article.

Section 6—
This article shall be inoperative unless it shall have been ratified as an amendment to the Constitution by the legislatures of three-fourths of the several States within seven years from the date of its submission.

Amendment XXI
(ratified 5 Dec 1933)

Section 1—
The eighteenth article of amendment to the Constitution of the United States is hereby repealed.

Section 2—
The transportation or importation into any State, Territory, or possession of the United States for delivery or use therein of intoxicating liquors, in violation of the laws thereof, is hereby prohibited.

Section 3—
This article shall be inoperative unless it shall have been ratified as an amendment to the Constitution by conventions in the several States, as provided in the Constitution, within seven years from the date of the submission hereof to the States by the Congress.

Amendment XXII
(ratified 27 Feb 1951)

Section 1—
No person shall be elected to the office of the President more than twice, and no person who has held the office of President, or acted as President, for more than two years of a term to which some other person was elected President shall be elected to the office of the President more than once. But this Article shall not apply to any person holding the office of President when this Article was proposed by the Congress, and shall not prevent any person who may be holding the office of President, or acting as President, during the term within which this Article becomes operative from holding the office of President or acting as President during the remainder of such term.

Section 2—
This Article shall be inoperative unless it shall have been ratified as an amendment to the Constitution by the legislatures of three-fourths of the several States within seven years from the date of its submission to the States by the Congress.

Amendment XXIII
(ratified 29 Mar 1961)

Section 1—
The District constituting the seat of Government of the United States shall appoint in such manner as the Congress may direct:

A number of electors of President and Vice President equal to the whole number of Senators and Representatives in Congress to which the District would be entitled if it were a State, but in no event more than the least populous State; they shall be in addition to those appointed by the States, but they shall be considered, for the purposes of the election of President and Vice President, to be electors appointed by a State; and they shall meet in the District and perform such duties as provided by the twelfth article of amendment.

Section 2—
The Congress shall have power to enforce this article by appropriate legislation.

Amendment XXIV
(ratified 23 Jan 1964)

Section 1—
The right of citizens of the United States to vote in any primary or other election for President or Vice President, for electors for President or Vice President, or for Senator or Representative in Congress, shall not be denied or abridged by the United States or any State by reason of failure to pay any poll tax or other tax.

Section 2—
The Congress shall have power to enforce this article by appropriate legislation.

Amendment XXV
(ratified 23 Jan 1967)

Section 1—
In case of the removal of the President from office or of his death or resignation, the Vice President shall become President.

Section 2—
Whenever there is a vacancy in the office of the Vice President, the President shall nominate a Vice President who shall take office upon confirmation by a majority vote of both Houses of Congress.

Section 3—
Whenever the President transmits to the President pro tempore of the Senate and the Speaker of the House of Representatives his written declaration that he is unable to discharge the powers and duties of his office, and until he transmits to them a written declaration to the contrary, such powers and duties shall be discharged by the Vice President as Acting President.

Section 4—
Whenever the Vice president and a majority of either the principal officers of the executive departments or of such other body as Congress may by law provide, transmit to the President pro tempore of the Senate and the Speaker of the House of Representatives their written declaration that the President is unable to discharge the powers and duties of his office, the Vice President shall immediately assume the powers and duties of the office as Acting President.

Thereafter, when the President transmits to the President pro tempore of the Senate and the Speaker of the House of Representatives his written declaration that no inability exists, he shall resume the powers and duties of his office unless the Vice President and a majority of either the principal officers of the executive department or of such other body as Congress may by law provide, transmit within four days to the President pro tempore of the Senate and the Speaker of the House of Representatives their written declaration that the President is unable to discharge the powers and duties of his office. Thereupon Congress shall decide the issue, assembling within forty-eight hours for that purpose if not in session. If the Congress, within twenty-one days after receipt of the latter written declaration, or, if Congress is not in session, within twenty-one days after Congress is required to assemble, determines by two-thirds vote of both Houses that the President is unable to discharge the powers and duties of his office, the Vice President shall continue to discharge the same as Acting President; otherwise, the President shall resume the powers and duties of his office.

Amendment XXVI
(ratified 1 Jul 1971)

Section 1—
The right of citizens of the United States, who are eighteen years of age or older, to vote shall not be denied or abridged by the United States or by any State on account of age.

Section 2—
The Congress shall have power to enforce this article by appropriate legislation.

Amendment XXVII
(ratified 7 May 1992)

No law, varying the compensation for the services of the Senators and Representatives, shall take effect, until an election of representatives shall have intervened.

Confederate States and Secession Dates

In the months following Abraham Lincoln's election as president in 1860, seven states of the Deep South held conventions and approved secession, thus precipitating the Civil War. After the attack on Fort Sumter SC on 12 Apr 1861, Virginia, Arkansas, North Carolina, and Tennessee also seceded (Tennessee was the only state to hold a popular referendum without a convention on secession). The Confederacy operated as a separate government, with Jefferson Davis as president and Alexander H. Stephens as vice president. Its principal goals were the preservation of states' rights and the institution of slavery. Although it enjoyed a series of military victories in the first two years of fighting, the surrender at Appomattox VA by Gen. Robert E. Lee on 9 Apr 1865 signaled its dissolution.

STATE	DATE	STATE	DATE	STATE	DATE
South Carolina	20 Dec 1860	Georgia	19 Jan 1861	Arkansas	6 May 1861
Mississippi	9 Jan 1861	Louisiana	26 Jan 1861	North Carolina	20 May 1861
Florida	10 Jan 1861	Texas	1 Feb 1861	Tennessee	8 Jun 1861
Alabama	11 Jan 1861	Virginia	17 Apr 1861		

Emancipation Proclamation

The Emancipation Proclamation was issued by Pres. Abraham Lincoln and freed the slaves of the Confederate states in rebellion against the Union. After the Battle of Antietam (17 Sep 1862), Lincoln issued his proclamation calling on the revolted states to return to their allegiance before the next year, otherwise their slaves would be declared free men. No state returned, and the threatened declaration was issued on 1 Jan 1863.

By the President of the United States of America:

A Proclamation.

Whereas, on the twenty-second day of September, in the year of our Lord one thousand eight hundred and sixty-two, a proclamation was issued by the President of the United States, containing, among other things, the following, to wit:

"That on the first day of January, in the year of our Lord one thousand eight hundred and sixty-three, all persons held as slaves within any State or designated part of a State, the people whereof shall then be in rebellion against the United States, shall be then, thenceforward, and forever free; and the Executive Government of the United States, including the military and naval authority thereof, will recognize and maintain the freedom of such persons, and will do no act or acts to repress such persons, or any of them, in any efforts they may make for their actual freedom.

"That the Executive will, on the first day of January aforesaid, by proclamation, designate the States and parts of States, if any, in which the people thereof, respectively, shall then be in rebellion against the United States; and the fact that any State, or the people thereof, shall on that day be, in good faith, represented in the Congress of the United States by members chosen thereto at elections wherein a majority of the qualified voters of such State shall have participated, shall, in the absence of strong countervailing testimony, be deemed conclusive evidence that such State, and the people thereof, are not then in rebellion against the United States."

Now, therefore I, Abraham Lincoln, President of the United States, by virtue of the power in me vested as Commander-in-Chief, of the Army and Navy of the United States in time of actual armed rebellion against the authority and government of the United States, and as a fit and necessary war measure for suppressing said rebellion, do, on this first day of January, in the year of our Lord one thousand eight hundred and sixty-three, and in accordance with my purpose so to do publicly proclaimed for the full period of one hundred days, from the day first above mentioned, order and designate as the States and parts of States wherein the people thereof respectively, are this day in rebellion against the United States, the following, to wit:

Arkansas, Texas, Louisiana, (except the Parishes of St. Bernard, Plaquemines, Jefferson, St. John, St. Charles, St. James Ascension, Assumption, Terrebonne, Lafourche, St. Mary, St. Martin, and Orleans, including the City of New Orleans) Mississippi, Alabama, Florida, Georgia, South Carolina, North Carolina, and Virginia, (except the forty-eight counties designated as West Virginia, and also the counties of Berkley, Accomac, Northampton, Elizabeth City, York, Princess Ann, and Norfolk, including the cities of Norfolk and Portsmouth[)], and which excepted parts, are for the present, left precisely as if this proclamation were not issued.

And by virtue of the power, and for the purpose aforesaid, I do order and declare that all persons held as slaves within said designated States, and parts of States, are, and henceforward shall be free; and that the Executive government of the United States, including the military and naval authorities thereof, will recognize and maintain the freedom of said persons.

And I hereby enjoin upon the people so declared to be free to abstain from all violence, unless in necessary self-defence; and I recommend to them that, in all cases when allowed, they labor faithfully for reasonable wages.

And I further declare and make known, that such persons of suitable condition, will be received into the armed service of the United States to garrison forts, positions, stations, and other places, and to man vessels of all sorts in said service.

And upon this act, sincerely believed to be an act of justice, warranted by the Constitution, upon military necessity, I invoke the considerate judgment of mankind, and the gracious favor of Almighty God.

In witness whereof, I have hereunto set my hand and caused the seal of the United States to be affixed.

Done at the City of Washington, this first day of January, in the year of our Lord one thousand eight hundred and sixty three, and of the Independence of the United States of America the eighty-seventh.

By the President: Abraham Lincoln.
William H. Seward, Secretary of State.

Gettysburg Address

On 19 Nov 1863, Pres. Abraham Lincoln delivered this speech at the consecration of the National Cemetery at Gettysburg PA, the site of one of the most decisive battles of the American Civil War. The two-hour main address at the dedication ceremony was delivered by Edward Everett, the best-known orator of the time. It is Lincoln's short speech, however, that is remembered, not only as a memorial to those who gave their lives on the battlefield, but as a statement of the ideals on which the nation was founded.

Four score and seven years ago our fathers brought forth on this continent a new nation, conceived in Liberty, and dedicated to the proposition that all men are created equal. Now we are engaged in a great civil war, testing whether that nation or any nation so conceived and so dedicated, can long endure. We are met on a great battle-field of that war. We have come to dedicate a portion of that field, as a final resting place for those who here gave their lives that that nation might live. It is altogether fitting and proper that we should do this. But, in a larger sense, we can not dedicate—we can not consecrate—we can not hallow—this ground. The brave men, living and dead, who struggled here, have consecrated it, far above our poor power to add or detract. The world will little note, nor long remember what we say here, but it can never forget what they did here. It is for us the living, rather, to be dedicated here to the unfinished work which they who fought here have thus far so nobly advanced. It is rather for us to be here dedicated to the great task remaining before us—that from these honored dead we take increased devotion to that cause for which they gave the last full measure of devotion—that we here highly resolve that these dead shall not have died in vain—that this nation, under God, shall have a new birth of freedom—and that government of the people, by the people, for the people, shall not perish from the earth.

United States Government

The Presidency at a Glance

	PRESIDENT	POLITICAL PARTY	TIME IN OFFICE	VICE PRESIDENT
1	George Washington	Federalist	1789–1797	John Adams
2	John Adams	Federalist	1797–1801	Thomas Jefferson
3	Thomas Jefferson	Jeffersonian Republican	1801–1809	Aaron Burr George Clinton
4	James Madison	Jeffersonian Republican	1809–1817	George Clinton Elbridge Gerry
5	James Monroe	Jeffersonian Republican	1817–1825	Daniel D. Tompkins
6	John Quincy Adams	National Republican	1825–1829	John C. Calhoun

The Presidency at a Glance (continued)

	PRESIDENT	POLITICAL PARTY	TIME IN OFFICE	VICE PRESIDENT
7	Andrew Jackson	Democratic	1829–1837	John C. Calhoun Martin Van Buren
8	Martin Van Buren	Democratic	1837–1841	Richard M. Johnson
9	William Henry Harrison*	Whig	4 Mar–4 Apr 1841	John Tyler
10	John Tyler	Whig	1841–1845	none
11	James K. Polk	Democratic	1845–1849	George Mifflin Dallas
12	Zachary Taylor*	Whig	1849–1850	Millard Fillmore
13	Millard Fillmore	Whig	1850–1853	none
14	Franklin Pierce	Democratic	1853–1857	William Rufus de Vane King
15	James Buchanan	Democratic	1857–1861	John C. Breckinridge
16	Abraham Lincoln*†	Republican	1861–1865	Hannibal Hamlin Andrew Johnson
17	Andrew Johnson	Democratic (Union)	1865–1869	none
18	Ulysses S. Grant	Republican	1869–1877	Schuyler Colfax Henry Wilson
19	Rutherford B. Hayes	Republican	1877–1881	William A. Wheeler
20	James A. Garfield*†	Republican	4 Mar–19 Sep 1881	Chester A. Arthur
21	Chester A. Arthur	Republican	1881–1885	none
22	Grover Cleveland	Democratic	1885–1889	Thomas A. Hendricks
23	Benjamin Harrison	Republican	1889–1893	Levi Parons Morton
24	Grover Cleveland	Democratic	1893–1897	Adlai E. Stevenson
25	William McKinley*†	Republican	1897–1901	Garret A. Hobart Theodore Roosevelt
26	Theodore Roosevelt	Republican	1901–1909	Charles Warren Fairbanks
27	William Howard Taft	Republican	1909–1913	James Schoolcraft Sherman
28	Woodrow Wilson	Democratic	1913–1921	Thomas R. Marshall
29	Warren G. Harding*	Republican	1921–1923	Calvin Coolidge
30	Calvin Coolidge	Republican	1923–1929	Charles G. Dawes
31	Herbert Hoover	Republican	1929–1933	Charles Curtis
32	Franklin D. Roosevelt*	Democratic	1933–1945	John Nance Garner Henry A. Wallace Harry S. Truman
33	Harry S. Truman	Democratic	1945–1953	Alben W. Barkley
34	Dwight D. Eisenhower	Republican	1953–1961	Richard M. Nixon
35	John F. Kennedy*†	Democratic	1961–1963	Lyndon B. Johnson
36	Lyndon B. Johnson	Democratic	1963–1969	Hubert H. Humphrey
37	Richard M. Nixon**	Republican	1969–1974	Spiro T. Agnew Gerald R. Ford
38	Gerald R. Ford	Republican	1974–1977	Nelson A. Rockefeller
39	Jimmy Carter	Democratic	1977–1981	Walter F. Mondale
40	Ronald Reagan	Republican	1981–1989	George H.W. Bush
41	George H.W. Bush	Republican	1989–1993	Dan Quayle
42	William J. Clinton	Democratic	1993–2001	Albert Gore
43	George W. Bush	Republican	2001–2009	Richard B. Cheney
44	Barack Obama	Democratic	2009–	Joe Biden

**Died in office.   **Resigned from office.   †Assassinated.*

Presidential Biographies

George Washington (22 Feb [11 Feb, Old Style] 1732, Westmoreland county VA–14 Dec 1799, Mt. Vernon, in Fairfax county VA), American Revolutionary commander-in-chief (1775–83) and first president of the US (1789–97). Born into a wealthy family, he was educated privately and worked as a surveyor from age 14. In 1752 he inherited his brother's estate at Mount Vernon, including 18 slaves whose ranks grew to 49 by 1760, though he disapproved of slavery. In the French and Indian War he was commissioned a colonel and sent to the Ohio Territory. After Edward Braddock was killed, Washington became commander of all Virginia forces, entrusted with defending the western frontier (1755–58). He resigned to manage his estate and in 1759 married Martha Dandridge Custis (1731–1802), a widow. He served in the House of Burgesses 1759–74, where he supported the colonists' cause, and in the Continental Congress 1774–75. In 1775 he was elected to command the Continental Army. In the ensuing American Revolution, he proved a brilliant commander and stalwart leader despite several defeats. With the war effectively ended by the capture of Yorktown (1781), he resigned his commission and returned to Mount Vernon (1783). He was a delegate to and presiding officer of the Constitutional Convention (1787) and helped secure ratification of the Constitution in Virginia. When the state electors met to select the first president

(1789), Washington was the unanimous choice. He formed a cabinet to balance sectional and political differences but was committed to a strong central government. Elected to a second term, he followed a middle course between the political factions that became the Federalist Party and Democratic Party. He proclaimed a policy of neutrality in the war between Britain and France (1793) and sent troops to suppress the Whiskey Rebellion (1794). He declined to serve a third term, setting a 144-year precedent, and retired in 1797 after delivering his "Farewell Address." Known as the "father of his country," he is regarded as one of the greatest figures in US history.

John Adams (30 Oct [19 Oct, Old Style] 1735, Braintree [now in Quincy] MA–4 Jul 1826, Quincy MA), first vice president (1789–97) and second president (1797–1801) of the US. He practiced law in Boston and in 1764 married Abigail Smith. Active in the American independence movement, he was elected to the Massachusetts legislature and served as a delegate to the Continental Congress (1774–78), where he was appointed to several committees, including one with Thomas Jefferson and others to draft the Declaration of Independence. He served as a diplomat in France, The Netherlands, and England (1778–88). In the first US presidential election, he received the second largest number of votes and became vice president under George Washington. Adams's term as president was marked by controversy over his signing the Alien and Sedition Acts in 1798 and by his alliance with the conservative Federalist Party. In 1800 he was defeated for reelection by Jefferson and retired to live a secluded life in Massachusetts. In 1812 he was reconciled with Jefferson, with whom he began an illuminating correspondence. Both men died on 4 Jul 1826, the Declaration's 50th anniversary. Pres. John Quincy Adams was his son.

Thomas Jefferson (13 Apr [2 Apr, Old Style] 1743, Shadwell VA–4 Jul 1826, Monticello VA), third president of the US (1801–9). He was a planter and lawyer from 1767, as well as a slaveholder who opposed slavery. While a member of the House of Burgesses (1769–75), he initiated the Committee of Correspondence (1773) with Richard Henry Lee and Patrick Henry. In 1774 he wrote the influential *Summary View of the Rights of British America*, stating that the British Parliament had no authority to legislate for the colonies. A delegate to the second Continental Congress, he was appointed to the committee to draft the Declaration of Independence and became its primary author. He was elected governor of Virginia (1779–81) but was unable to organize effective opposition when British forces invaded the colony (1780–81). Criticized for his conduct, he retired, vowing to remain a private citizen. Again a member of the Continental Congress (1783–85), he proposed territorial provisions later incorporated in the Northwest Ordinances. He traveled in Europe on diplomatic missions and became minister to France (1785–89). George Washington made him secretary of state (1790–93). He soon became embroiled in conflict with Alexander Hamilton over their opposing interpretations of the Constitution. This led to the rise of factions and political parties, with Jefferson representing the Democratic-Republicans. He served as vice president (1797–1801) but opposed the Alien and Sedition Acts enacted under Pres. John Adams. As part of this opposition, Jefferson drafted one of the Virginia and Kentucky Resolutions. In 1801 he became president after an electoral-vote tie with Aaron Burr was settled by the House of Representatives. Jefferson initiated frugal fiscal policies and simplicity in the ceremonial role of the president. He oversaw the Louisiana Purchase and authorized the Lewis and Clark Expedition. He sought to avoid involvement in the Napoleonic Wars by signing the Embargo Act. He retired to his plantation, Monticello, where he pursued his many interests in science, philosophy, and architecture. He served as president of the American Philosophical Society 1797–1815, and in 1819 he founded and designed the University of Virginia. In January 2000, the Thomas Jefferson Memorial Foundation accepted the conclusion, supported by DNA evidence, that Jefferson had fathered at least one, and perhaps as many as six, children with Sally Hemings, one of his house slaves. After a long estrangement, he and Adams became reconciled in 1813 and exchanged views on national issues. They both died on July 4, 1826, the 50th anniversary of the signing of the Declaration of Independence.

James Madison (16 Mar [5 Mar, Old Style] 1751, Port Conway VA–28 Jun 1836, Montpelier VA), fourth president of the US (1809–17). He served in the state legislature (1776–80, 1784–86). At the Constitutional Convention (1787), his active participation and his careful notes on the debates earned him the title "father of the Constitution." To promote ratification, he collaborated with Alexander Hamilton and John Jay on *The Federalist*. In the House of Representatives (1789–97), he sponsored the Bill of Rights, was a leading Jeffersonian Republican, and split with Hamilton over funding state war debts. In reaction to the Alien and Sedition Acts, he drafted one of the Virginia and Kentucky Resolutions (1798). He was appointed secretary of state (1801–9) by Thomas Jefferson, with whom he developed US foreign policy. Elected president in 1808, he was occupied by the trade and shipping embargo problems caused by France and Britain that led to the War of 1812. He was reelected in 1812; his second term was marked principally by the war, during which he reinvigorated the Army and also saw approval of the charter of the Second Bank of the US and the first US protective tariff. He retired to his Virginia estate, Montpelier, with his wife, Dolley (1768–1849), whose political acumen he had long prized. He continued to write articles and letters and served as rector of the University of Virginia (1826–36).

James Monroe (28 Apr 1758, Westmoreland county VA–4 Jul 1831, New York NY), fifth president of the US (1817–25). He fought in the American Revolution and studied law under Thomas Jefferson. He served in the Congress (1783–86) and Senate (1790–94), where he opposed George Washington's administration. He nevertheless became minister to France (1794–96), where he misled the French about US politics and was recalled. He served as governor of Virginia 1799–1802. President Jefferson sent him to France, where he helped negotiate the Louisiana Purchase (1803), then named him minister to Britain (1803–7). He returned to Virginia and became governor (1811), but he resigned to become US secretary of state (1811–17) and secretary of war (1814–15). He served two terms as president, presiding in a period that became known as the Era of Good Feelings. He oversaw the Seminole War (1817–18) and the acquisition of the Floridas (1819–21) and signed the Missouri Compromise (1820). With secretary of state John Quincy Adams, he developed the principles of US foreign policy later called the Monroe Doctrine.

John Quincy Adams (11 Jul 1767, Braintree [now in Quincy] MA—23 Feb 1848, Washington DC), sixth president of the US (1825–29). He was the eldest son of Pres. John Adams and Abigail. He accompanied his father to Europe on diplomatic missions (1778–80) and was later appointed minister to The Netherlands (1794) and Prussia (1797). In 1801 he returned to Massachusetts and served in the Senate (1803–8). Resuming his diplomatic service, he became minister to Russia (1809–11) and Britain (1815–17). Appointed secretary of state (1817–24), he was instrumental in acquiring Florida from Spain and in drafting the Monroe Doctrine. He was one of three candidates in the 1824 presidential election, in which none received a majority of the electoral votes, though Andrew Jackson received a plurality. The decision went to the House of Representatives, where Adams received crucial support from Henry Clay and the electoral votes necessary to elect him president. He appointed Clay secretary of state, which further angered Jackson. Adams's presidency was unsuccessful; when he ran for reelection, Jackson defeated him. In 1830 he was elected to the House of Representatives, where he served until his death. He was outspoken in his opposition to slavery and in 1839 proposed a constitutional amendment forbidding slavery in any new state admitted to the Union. Southern congressmen prevented discussion of antislavery petitions by passing gag rules (repealed in 1844 as a result of Adams's persistence). In 1841 he successfully defended the slaves in the *Amistad* mutiny case.

Andrew Jackson (15 Mar 1767, Waxhaws region SC—8 Jun 1845, the Hermitage, near Nashville TN), seventh president of the US (1829–37). He fought briefly in the American Revolution near his frontier home, where his family was killed. He studied law and in 1788 was appointed prosecuting attorney for western North Carolina. When the region became the state of Tennessee, he was elected to the House of Representatives (1796–97) and Senate (1797–98). He served on the state supreme court (1798–1804) and in 1802 was elected major general of the Tennessee militia. When the War of 1812 began, he offered the US the services of his 50,000-volunteer militia. He was sent to fight the Creek Indians allied with the British in Mississippi Territory. After a lengthy battle (1813–14), he defeated them at the Battle of Horseshoe Bend. After capturing Pensacola FL from the British-allied Spanish, he marched overland to engage the British in Louisiana. A decisive victory at the Battle of New Orleans made him a national hero, dubbed "Old Hickory" by the press. After US acquisition of Florida, he was named governor of the territory (1821). One of four candidates in the 1824 presidential election, he won an electoral-votes plurality but the House gave the election to John Quincy Adams. In 1828 Jackson defeated Adams after a fierce campaign and became the first president elected from west of the Appalachian Mountains. His election was considered a triumph of political democracy. He replaced many federal officeholders with his supporters, a process that became known as the spoils system. He pursued a policy of moving Native Americans westward with the Indian Removal Acts. He split with his vice president, John C. Calhoun, over the nullification movement. His reelection in 1832 was due in part to support for his anticapitalistic fiscal policies and a controversial veto that affected the Bank of the US. His popularity continued to build throughout his presidency. During his tenure a strong Democratic Party developed that led to a vigorous two-party system.

Martin Van Buren (5 Dec 1782, Kinderhook NY—24 Jul 1862, Kinderhook NY), eighth president of the US (1837–41). He practiced law and served in the NY state senate (1812–20) and as state attorney general (1816–19). He became the leader of an informal group of political supporters, called the Albany Regency because they dominated state politics even while Van Buren was in Washington. He was elected to the US Senate (1821–28), where he supported states' rights and opposed a strong central government. After John Quincy Adams became president, he joined with Andrew Jackson and others to form a group that later became the Democratic Party. He was elected governor of New York (1828) but resigned to become US secretary of state (1829–31). He was nominated for vice president at the first Democratic Party convention (1832) and served under Jackson (1833–37). As Jackson's chosen successor, he defeated William H. Harrison to win the 1836 election. His presidency was marked by an economic depression, the Maine-Canada border dispute, the Seminole War in Florida, and debate over the annexation of Texas. He was defeated in his bid for reelection and failed to win the Democratic nomination in 1844 because of his antislavery views. In 1848 he was nominated for president by the Free Soil Party but failed to win the election and retired.

William Henry Harrison (9 Feb 1773, Charles City county VA—4 Apr 1841, Washington DC), ninth president of the US (1841). Born into a political family, he enlisted in the army at 18 and served under Anthony Wayne at the Battle of Fallen Timbers. In 1798 he became secretary of the Northwest Territories, and in 1800 governor of the new Indiana Territory. In response to pressure from white settlers, he negotiated treaties with the Native Americans that ceded millions of acres of additional land to the US. When Tecumseh organized an uprising in 1811, Harrison led a US force to defeat the Indians at the Battle of Tippecanoe, a victory that largely established his reputation in the public mind. In the War of 1812 he was made a brigadier general and defeated the British and their Indian allies at the Battle of the Thames in Ontario. After the war he moved to Ohio, where he became prominent in the Whig Party. He served in the House of Representatives (1816–19) and Senate (1825–28). As the Whig candidate in the 1836 presidential election, he lost narrowly. In 1840 he and his running mate, John Tyler, won election with a slogan emphasizing Harrison's frontier triumph: "Tippecanoe and Tyler too!" The 68-year-old Harrison delivered his inaugural speech without a hat or overcoat in a cold drizzle, contracted pneumonia, and died one month later, the first president to die in office.

John Tyler (29 Mar 1790, Charles City county VA—18 Jan 1862, Richmond VA), 10th president of the US (1841–45). He practiced law before serving in the state legislature (1811–16, 1823–25, 1839) and as governor of Virginia (1825–27). In the House of Representatives (1817–21) and Senate (1827–36), he was a states-rights supporter. Though a slaveholder, he sought to prohibit the slave trade in the District of Columbia, provided Maryland and Virginia concurred. He resigned from the Senate rather than acquiesce to state instructions to change his vote on a censure of Pres. Andrew Jackson. After breaking with the Democratic Party, he was nominated by the Whig Party for vice president under William H. Harrison. They won the 1840 election, carefully avoiding the issues and stressing party loyalty and the slogan "Tippecanoe and Tyler too!" Harrison died a month after taking office, and Tyler became the first to attain the presidency "by accident." He vetoed a national bank bill supported by the Whigs, and all but one member of the cabinet resigned, leaving him without party support. Nonetheless, he reorganized the navy, settled the second of the Seminole Wars in Florida, and oversaw the annexation of Texas. He was nominated for reelection but withdrew in favor of James Polk and retired to his Virginia plantation. Committed to states' rights but opposed to secession, he organized the Washington Peace Conference (1861) to resolve sectional differences. When the Senate rejected a proposed compromise, Tyler urged Virginia to secede.

James Knox Polk (2 Nov 1795, Mecklenburg county NC—15 Jun 1849, Nashville TN), 11th president of the US (1845–49). He became a lawyer in Tennessee and a friend and supporter of Andrew Jackson, who helped Polk win election to the House of Representatives (1825–39). He left the House to become governor of Tennessee (1839–41). At the deadlocked 1844 Democratic convention Polk was nominated as the compromise candidate; he is considered the first dark-horse presidential candidate. A proponent of western expansion, he campaigned with the slogan "Fifty-four Forty or Fight," to bring a solution to the Oregon Question. Elected at 49, the youngest president to that time, he successfully concluded the Oregon border dispute with Britain (1846) and secured passage of the Walker Tariff Act (1846), which lowered import duties and helped foreign trade. He led the prosecution of the Mexican War, which resulted in large territorial gains but reopened the debate over the extension of slavery. His administration also established the Department of the Interior, the US Naval Academy, and the Smithsonian Institution, oversaw revision of the treasury system, and proclaimed the validity of the Monroe Doctrine. Though an efficient and competent president, deft in his handling of Congress, he was exhausted by his efforts and did not seek reelection; he died three months after leaving office.

Zachary Taylor (24 Nov 1784, Montebello VA—9 Jul 1850, Washington DC), 12th president of the US (1849–50). Born in Virginia, he grew up on the Kentucky frontier. He fought in the War of 1812, the Black Hawk War (1832), and the Seminole War in Florida (1835–42), earning the nickname "Old Rough-and-Ready" for his indifference to hardship. Sent to Texas in anticipation of war with Mexico, he defeated the Mexican invaders at the battles of Palo Alto and Resaca de la Palma (1846). After the Mexican War formally began, he captured Monterrey and granted the Mexican army an eight-week armistice. Displeased, Pres. James Polk moved Taylor's best troops to serve under Winfield Scott in the invasion of Veracruz. Taylor ignored orders to remain in Monterrey and marched south to defeat a large Mexican force at the Battle of Buena Vista (1847). He became a national hero and was nominated as the Whig candidate for president (1848). He defeated Lewis Cass to win the election. His brief term was marked by a controversy over the new territories that produced the Compromise of 1850 as well as by a scandal involving members of his cabinet. He died, probably of cholera, after only 16 months in office and was succeeded by Millard Fillmore.

Millard Fillmore (7 Jan 1800, Locke Township, NY—8 Mar 1874, Buffalo NY), 13th president of the US (1850–53). Born into poverty, he became an indentured apprentice at 15. He studied law with a local judge and began to practice in Buffalo in 1823. Initially identified with the Anti-Masonic Party (1828–34), he followed his political mentor, Thurlow Weed, to the Whigs and was soon a leader of the party's northern wing. He served in the House of Representatives (1833–35, 1837–43), where he became a follower of Henry Clay. In 1848 the Whigs nominated Fillmore as vice president, and he was elected with Zachary Taylor. He became president on Taylor's death in 1850. Though he abhorred slavery, he supported the Compromise of 1850 and insisted on federal enforcement of the Fugitive Slave Act. His stand, which alienated the North, led to his defeat by Winfield Scott at the Whigs' nominating convention in 1852 and effectively led to the death of the party. Throughout his career he advocated US internal development and was an early champion of expansion in the Pacific. In 1853 he sent Matthew Perry with a US fleet to Japan, forcing its isolationist government to enter into trade and diplomatic relations. He returned to Buffalo and was nominated for president by the third-party Know-Nothing Party in 1856, but he was defeated by Democrat James Buchanan.

Franklin Pierce (23 Nov 1804, Hillsboro NH—8 Oct 1869, Concord NH), 14th president of the US (1853–57). He practiced law and served in the House of Representatives (1833–37) and Senate (1837–42). He returned to his law practice, serving briefly in the Mexican War. At the deadlocked Democratic convention of 1852, he was nominated as the compromise candidate; though largely unknown nationally, he unexpectedly trounced Winfield Scott in the general election. For the sake of harmony and business prosperity, he was inclined to oppose antislavery agitation so as to placate Southern opinion. He promoted US territorial expansion, resulting in the diplomatic controversy of the Ostend Manifesto. He reorganized the diplomatic and consular service and created the Court of Claims. He encouraged plans for a transcontinental railroad and approved the Gadsden Purchase. To promote northwestern migration and conciliate sectional demands, he approved the Kansas-Nebraska Act but was unable to settle the resultant problems. Defeated for renomination by James Buchanan in 1856, he retired from politics.

James Buchanan (23 Apr 1791, near Mercersburg PA—1 Jun 1868, near Lancaster PA), 15th president of the US (1857–61). He became a lawyer and member of the Pennsylvania legislature before serving in the House of Representatives (1821–31), as minister to Russia (1832–34), and in the Senate (1834–45). He was secretary of state in James Polk's cabinet (1845–49). As minister to Britain (1853–56), he helped draft the Ostend

Manifesto. In 1856 he secured the Democratic nomination and election as president, defeating John C. Fremont. Though experienced in government and law, he lacked the moral courage to deal effectively with the slavery crisis and equivocated on the question of Kansas's status as a slaveholding state. The ensuing split within his party allowed Abraham Lincoln to win the election of 1860. He denounced the secession of South Carolina following the election and sent reinforcements to Fort Sumter, but he failed to respond further to the mounting crisis.

Abraham Lincoln (12 Feb 1809, near Hodgenville KY—15 Apr 1865, Washington DC), 16th president of the US (1861–65). Born in a Kentucky log cabin, he moved to Indiana in 1816 and to Illinois in 1830. He worked as a storekeeper, rail-splitter, postmaster, and surveyor, then enlisted as a volunteer in the Black Hawk War and became a captain. Though largely self-taught, he practiced law in Springfield IL and served in the state legislature (1834–40). He was elected as a Whig to the House of Representatives (1847–49). As a circuit-riding lawyer from 1849, he became one of the state's most successful lawyers, noted for his shrewdness, common sense, and honesty (earning him the nickname "Honest Abe"). In 1856 he joined the Republican Party, which nominated him as its candidate in the 1858 Senate election. In a series of seven debates with Stephen A. Douglas (the Lincoln-Douglas Debates), he argued against the extension of slavery into the territories, though not against slavery itself. Although morally opposed to slavery, he was not an abolitionist. During the campaign, he attempted to rebut Douglas's charge that he was a dangerous radical by reassuring audiences that he did not favor political equality for blacks. Despite his loss in the election, the debates brought him national attention. He again ran against Douglas in the 1860 presidential election, which he won by a large margin. But the South opposed his position on slavery in the territories, and before his inauguration seven Southern states had seceeded from the Union. The ensuing American Civil War completely consumed Lincoln's administration. He excelled as a wartime leader, creating a high command for directing all the country's energies and resources toward the war effort and combining statecraft and overall command of the armies with what some have called military genius. However, his abrogation of some civil liberties, especially the writ of habeas corpus, and the closing of several newspapers by his generals disturbed both Democrats and Republicans, including some members of his own cabinet. To unite the North and influence foreign opinion, he issued the Emancipation Proclamation (1863); his Gettysburg Address (1863) further ennobled the war's purpose. The continuing war affected some Northerners' resolve and his reelection was not assured, but strategic battle victories turned the tide and he easily defeated George B. McClellan in 1864. His platform included passage of the 13th Amendment outlawing slavery (ratified 1865). At his second inaugural, with victory in sight, he spoke of moderation in reconstructing the South and building a harmonious Union. On 14 Apr, five days after the war ended, he was shot by John Wilkes Booth and soon after died.

Andrew Johnson (29 Dec 1808, Raleigh NC—31 Jul 1875, near Carter Station TN), 17th president of the US (1865–69). Born in North Carolina and reared in Tennessee, he was self-educated and initially worked as a tailor. He organized a workingman's party and was elected to the state legislature (1835–43), where he became a spokesman for small farmers. He served in the House of Representatives (1843–53) and as governor of Tennessee (1853–57). Elected to the Senate (1857–62), he opposed antislavery agitation, but in 1860 he opposed Southern secession, even after Tennessee seceded in 1861, and during the Civil War he was the only Southern senator who refused to join the Confederacy. In 1862 he was appointed military governor of Tennessee, then under Union control. In 1864 he was selected to run for vice president with Pres. Abraham Lincoln; he assumed the presidency after Lincoln's assassination. During Reconstruction he favored a moderate policy that readmitted former Confederate states to the Union with few provisions for reform or civil rights for freedmen. In 1867 the Radical Republicans in Congress passed civil rights legislation and established the Freedmen's Bureau. His veto angered Congress, which passed the Tenure of Office Act. In 1868 in defiance of the act, Johnson dismissed secretary of war Edwin M. Stanton, an ally of the Radicals. The House responded by impeaching the president for the first time in US history. In the subsequent Senate trial, the charges proved weak and the necessary two-thirds vote needed for conviction failed by one vote. Johnson remained in office until 1869, but his effectiveness had ended. He returned to Tennessee, where he won reelection to the Senate shortly before he died.

Ulysses S. Grant (Hiram Ulysses Grant) (27 Apr 1822, Point Pleasant OH—23 Jul 1885, Mount McGregor NY), 18th president of the US (1869–77). He served in the Mexican War under Zachary Taylor; he resigned his commission in 1854 when he could not afford to bring his family west. Allegations that he became a drunkard in the lonely years in the West and in later life, though never proved, would affect his reputation. He worked unsuccessfully at farming in Missouri and at his family's leather business in Illinois. When the Civil War began (1861), he was appointed brigadier general; his 1862 attack on Fort Donelson TN, produced the first major Union victory. He drove off a Confederate attack at Shiloh but was criticized for heavy Union losses. He devised the campaign to take the stronghold of Vicksburg MS, in 1863, cutting the Confederacy in half from east to west. Following his victory at the Battle of Chattanooga in 1864, he was appointed commander of the Union army. While William T. Sherman made his famous march across Georgia, Grant attacked Robert E. Lee's forces in Virginia, bringing the war to an end in 1865. Grant's administrative ability and innovative strategies were largely responsible for the Union victory. His successful Republican presidential campaign made him, at 46, the youngest man yet elected president. His two terms were marred by administrative inaction and political scandal involving members of his cabinet, including the Crédit Mobilier scandal and the Whiskey Ring operation. He was more successful in foreign affairs, in which he was aided by his secretary of state, Hamilton Fish. He supported amnesty for Confederate leaders and protection for black civil rights. His veto of a bill to increase the amount of legal tender (1874) diminished the currency crisis in the next 25 years.

In 1881 he moved to New York; when a partner defrauded an investment firm co-owned by his son, the family was impoverished. His memoirs were published by his friend Mark Twain.

Rutherford Birchard Hayes (4 Oct 1822, Delaware OH—17 Jan 1893, Fremont OH), 19th president of the US (1877–81). He practiced law in Cincinnati, representing defendants in several fugitive-slave cases and becoming associated with the new Republican Party. After fighting in the Union army, he served in the House of Representatives (1865–67). As governor of Ohio (1868–72, 1875–76), he advocated a sound currency backed by gold. In 1876 he won the Republican nomination for president. His opponent, Samuel Tilden, won a larger popular vote, but Hayes's managers contested the electoral-vote returns in four states, and a special Electoral Commission awarded the election to Hayes. As part of a secret compromise reached with Southerners, he withdrew the remaining federal troops from the South, ending Reconstruction, and promised not to interfere with elections there, ensuring the return of white Democratic supremacy. He introduced civil-service reform based on merit, incurring a dispute with Roscoe Conkling and the conservative "stalwart" Republicans. At the request of state governors, he used federal troops against strikers in the railroad strikes of 1877. Declining to run for a second term, he retired to work for humanitarian causes.

James Abram Garfield (19 Nov 1831, near Orange [in Cuyahoga county] OH—19 Sep 1881, Elberon [now in Long Branch] NJ), 20th president of the US (1881). He graduated from Williams College, then returned to Ohio to teach and head an academy that became Hiram College. In the Civil War he led the 42nd Ohio Volunteers and fought at Shiloh and Chickamauga. He resigned as a major general to serve in the House of Representatives (1863–80). A Radical Republican during Reconstruction, he served on the Electoral Commission in the 1876 election and was the House Republican leader from 1876 to 1880, when he was elected to the Senate. At the 1880 Republican nominating convention, the delegates supporting Ulysses S. Grant and James Blaine became deadlocked. On the 36th ballot Garfield was nominated as a compromise presidential candidate, with Chester Arthur as vice president, and won by a narrow margin. His brief term, less than 150 days, was marked by a dispute with Sen. Roscoe Conkling over patronage. On July 2 he was shot at Washington's railroad station by Charles J. Guiteau, an Arthur supporter. He died on September 19 after 11 weeks of public debate over the ambiguous constitutional conditions for presidential succession (later clarified by the 20th and 25th Amendments).

Chester Alan Arthur (5 Oct 1829, North Fairfield VT—18 Nov 1886, New York NY), 21st president of the US (1881–85). He practiced law in New York City from 1854. He became active in local Republican politics and a close associate of party leader Roscoe Conkling, and was appointed customs collector for the port of New York (1871–78), an office long known for its employment of the spoils system. He conducted the business of the office with integrity but continued to pad its payroll with Conkling loyalists. At the Republican national convention in 1880, Arthur became the compromise choice for vice president on the ticket with James Garfield, and he became president upon Garfield's assassination. As president, Arthur displayed unexpected independence by vetoing measures that rewarded political patronage. He also signed the Pendleton Act, which created a civil-service system based on merit. He recommended the appropriations that initiated the rebuilding of the Navy toward the strength it later achieved in the Spanish-American War (1898). He failed to win his party's nomination for a second term.

(Stephen) Grover Cleveland (18 Mar 1837, Caldwell NJ—24 Jun 1908, Princeton NJ), 22nd and 24th president of the US (1885–89, 1893–97). He practiced law in Buffalo NY from 1859, where he entered Democratic Party politics. As mayor of Buffalo (1881–82), he was known as a foe of corruption. As governor of New York (1883–85), he earned the hostility of Tammany Hall with his independence, but in 1884 he won the Democratic nomination for president. The first Democratic president since 1856, he supported civil-service reform and opposed high protective tariffs, which became an issue in the 1888 election, when he was narrowly defeated by Benjamin Harrison. In 1892 he was reelected by a huge popular plurality. In 1893 he attributed the US's severe economic depression to the Sherman Silver Purchase Act of 1890 and strongly urged Congress to repeal the act. The economic unrest resulted in the Pullman Strike in 1894. An isolationist, he opposed territorial expansion. In 1895 he invoked the Monroe Doctrine in the border dispute between Britain and Venezuela. By 1896 supporters of the Free Silver Movement controlled the Democratic Party, which nominated William Jennings Bryan instead of Cleveland for president. He retired to New Jersey, where he lectured at Princeton University.

Benjamin Harrison (20 Aug 1833, North Bend OH—13 Mar 1901, Indianapolis IN), 23rd president of the US (1889–93). The grandson of Pres. William H. Harrison, he practiced law in Indianapolis from the mid-1850s. He served in the Union army in the Civil War, rising to brigadier general. He served a term in the Senate (1881–87) and, even though he lost reelection, was nominated for president by the Republicans. He went on to defeat the incumbent, Grover Cleveland, who lost despite winning more of the popular vote. As president, his domestic policy was marked by passage of the Sherman Antitrust Act. His foreign policy expanded US influence abroad. His secretary of state, James Blaine, presided at the conference that led to the establishment of the Pan-American Union, resisted pressure to abandon US interests in the Samoan Islands (1889), and negotiated a treaty with Britain in the Bering Sea Dispute (1891). Defeated for reelection by Cleveland in 1892, he returned to Indianapolis to practice law. In 1898–99 he was the leading counsel for Venezuela in its boundary dispute with Britain.

William McKinley (29 Jan 1843, Niles OH—14 Sep 1901, Buffalo NY), 25th president of the US (1897–1901). He served in the Civil War as an aide to Col. Rutherford B. Hayes, who later encouraged his political career. He was elected to the House of Representatives (1877–91), where he favored protective tariffs and sponsored the McKinley Tariff of 1890. With the support of Mark Hanna, he was elected governor (1892–96). In 1896 he won the Republican presidential nomination and the general election, defeating William Jennings Bryan. He called a special session of Congress to increase customs duties, but was soon embroiled in events in Cuba and responses to the sinking of the USS *Maine*, which led to the Spanish-American War. At the war's end, he advocated US dependency status for the Philippines, Puerto Rico, and other former Spanish territories. He again defeated Bryan by a large majority in 1900 and began a tour to urge control of trusts and commercial reciprocity to boost foreign trade, issues neglected during the war. In Buffalo NY on 6 Sep 1901, he was fatally shot by an anarchist, Leon Czolgosz. He was succeeded by Theodore Roosevelt.

Theodore Roosevelt (27 Oct 1858, New York NY—6 Jan 1919, Oyster Bay NY), 26th president of the US (1901–9). He was elected to the New York legislature in 1882, where he became a Republican leader opposed to the Democratic political machine. After political defeats and the death of his wife, he went to the Dakota Territory to ranch. He returned to New York to serve on the US Civil Service Commission (1889–95) and as head of the city's board of police commissioners (1895–97). A supporter of William McKinley, he served as assistant secretary of the navy (1897–98). When the Spanish-American War was declared, he resigned to organize a cavalry unit, the Rough Riders. He returned to New York a hero and was elected governor in 1899. As the Republican vice-presidential nominee, he took office when McKinley was reelected, and he became president on McKinley's assassination in 1901. One of his early initiatives was to urge enforcement of the Sherman Antitrust Act against business monopolies. He won election in his own right in 1904, defeating Alton Parker. At his urging, Congress regulated railroad rates and passed the Pure Food and Drug Act and Meat Inspection Act (1906) to provide new consumer protections. He set aside national forests, parks, and mineral, oil, and coal lands for conservation. He and secretary of state Elihu Root announced the Roosevelt corollary to the Monroe Doctrine, which reinforced the US position as defender of the Western Hemisphere. For mediating an end to the Russo-Japanese War, he received the 1906 Nobel Peace Prize. He secured a treaty with Panama for construction of a trans-isthmus canal. Declining to seek reelection, he secured the nomination for William H. Taft. After traveling in Africa and Europe, he tried to win the Republican presidential nomination in 1912; when he was rejected, he organized the Bull Moose Party and ran on a policy of New Nationalism, but he failed to win the election. Throughout his life he continued to write, publishing extensively on history, politics, travel, and nature.

William Howard Taft (15 Sep 1857, Cincinnati OH—8 Mar 1930, Washington DC), 27th president of the US (1909–13). He served on the state superior court (1887–90), as US solicitor general (1890–92), and as US appellate judge (1892–1900). He was appointed head of the Philippine Commission to set up a civilian government in the islands and was its first civilian governor (1901–4). He served as US secretary of war (1904–8) under Pres. Theodore Roosevelt, who supported Taft's nomination for president in 1908. He won the election but became allied with the conservative Republicans, causing a rift with party progressives. He was again the nominee in 1912, but the split with Roosevelt and the Bull Moose Party resulted in the electoral victory of Woodrow Wilson. Taft later taught law at Yale University (1913–21), served on the National War Labor Board (1918), and was a supporter of the League of Nations. As chief justice of the Supreme Court (1921–30), he introduced reforms that made it more efficient. He secured passage of the Judges Act of 1925, which gave the Court wider discretion in accepting cases. His important opinion in *Myers* v. *US* (1926) upheld the president's authority to remove federal officials. In poor health, he resigned in 1930.

(Thomas) Woodrow Wilson (28 Dec 1856, Staunton VA—3 Feb 1924, Washington DC), 28th president of the US (1913–21). He earned a law degree and later received his doctorate from Johns Hopkins University. He taught political science at Princeton University (1890–1902), and as its president (1902–10), he introduced various reforms. With the support of progressives, he was elected governor of New Jersey. His reform measures attracted national attention, and he became the Democratic presidential nominee in 1912. His campaign emphasized the progressive measures of his New Freedom policy, and he defeated Theodore Roosevelt and William H. Taft to win the presidency. As president, he approved legislation that lowered tariffs, created the Federal Reserve System, established the Federal Trade Commission, and strengthened labor unions. In foreign affairs he promoted self-government for the Philippines and sought to contain the Mexican civil war. From 1914 he maintained US neutrality in World War I, offering to mediate a settlement and initiate peace negotiations. After the sinking of the *Lusitania* (1915) and other unarmed ships, he obtained a pledge from Germany to stop its submarine campaign. Campaigning on the theme that he had "kept us out of war," he was narrowly reelected in 1916, defeating Charles Evans Hughes. Germany's renewed submarine attacks on unarmed passenger ships caused Wilson to ask for a declaration of war in April 1917. In a continuing effort to negotiate a peace agreement, he presented the Fourteen Points (1918). He led the US delegation to the Paris Peace Conference, where he attempted to stand on his original principles but was forced to compromise by the demands of various countries. The Treaty of Versailles faced opposition in the Senate from the Republican majority led by Henry C. Lodge. In search of popular support for the treaty and its League of Nations, Wilson began a cross-country speaking tour, but he collapsed and returned to Washington DC (Sep 1919), where a stroke left him partially paralyzed. He rejected any attempts to compromise his version of the League of Nations and urged his Senate followers to vote against ratification of the treaty, which was defeated in 1920. He was awarded the 1919 Nobel Peace Prize for his work on the League of Nations.

Warren Gamaliel Harding (2 Nov 1865, Caledonia (now Blooming Grove) OH—2 Aug 1923, San Francisco CA), 29th president of the US (1921–23). He became a newspaper publisher in Marion OH, where he was allied with the Republican Party's political machine. He served successively as state senator (1899–1902), lieutenant governor (1903–04), and US senator (1915–21), supporting conservative policies. At the deadlocked 1920 Republican presidential convention, he was chosen as the compromise candidate. Pledging a "return to normalcy" after World War I, he defeated James Cox with over 60% of the popular vote, the largest margin to that time. On his recommendation, Congress established a budget system for the federal government, passed a high protective tariff, revised wartime taxes, and restricted immigration. His administration convened the Washington Conference (1921–22). His ill-advised cabinet and patronage appointments, including Albert Fall, led to the Teapot Dome scandal and characterized his administration as corrupt. While in Alaska, he received word of the corruption about to be exposed and headed back. He arrived in San Francisco exhausted, reportedly suffering from food poisoning and other ills, and died there under unclear circumstances. He was succeeded by his vice president, Calvin Coolidge.

(John) Calvin Coolidge (4 Jul 1872, Plymouth VT—5 Jan 1933, Northampton MA), 30th president of the US (1923–29). He practiced law in Massachusetts from 1897 and served as lieutenant governor before being elected governor in 1918. He gained national attention by calling out the state guard during the Boston police strike in 1919. At the 1920 Republican convention, "Silent Cal" was nominated for vice president on Warren G. Harding's winning ticket. When Harding died in office in 1923, Coolidge became president. He restored confidence in an administration discredited by scandals and won the presidential election in 1924, defeating Robert La Follette. He vetoed measures to provide farm relief and bonuses to World War I veterans. His presidency was marked by apparent prosperity. Congress maintained a high protective tariff and instituted tax reductions that favored capital. Coolidge declined to run for a second term. His conservative policies of domestic and international inaction have come to symbolize the era between World War I and the Great Depression.

Herbert Clark Hoover (10 Aug 1874, West Branch IA—20 Oct 1964, New York NY), 31st president of the US (1929–33). As a mining engineer, he administered engineering projects on four continents (1895–1913). He then headed Allied relief operations in England and Belgium prior to World War I, at which time he was appointed national food administrator (1917–19) and instituted programs that furnished food to the Allies and famine-stricken areas of Europe. Appointed secretary of commerce (1921–27), he reorganized the department, creating divisions to regulate broadcasting and aviation. He oversaw commissions to build Boulder (later Hoover) Dam and the St. Lawrence Seaway. In 1928, as the Republican presidential candidate, he soundly defeated Alfred E. Smith. His hopes for a "New Day" program were quickly overwhelmed by the Great Depression. As a believer in individual freedom, he vetoed bills to create a federal unemployment agency and to fund public-works projects, instead favoring private charity. In 1932 he finally allowed relief to farmers through the Reconstruction Finance Corp. He was overwhelmingly defeated in 1932 by Franklin Roosevelt. He continued to speak out against relief measures and criticized New Deal programs. After World War II he participated in famine-relief work in Europe and was appointed head of the Hoover Commission.

Franklin Delano Roosevelt (30 Jan 1882, Hyde Park NY—12 Apr 1945, Warm Springs GA), 32nd president of the US (1933–45). He was attracted to politics as an admirer of his cousin Pres. Theodore Roosevelt and became active in the Democratic Party. In 1905 he married distant cousin Eleanor Roosevelt, who would become a valued adviser in future years. He served in the state senate (1910–13) and as assistant secretary of the navy (1913–20). In 1920 he was nominated for vice president. The next year he was stricken with polio; though unable to walk, he remained active in politics. As governor of New York (1929–33), he set up the first state relief agency in the US. In 1932 he won the Democratic presidential nomination with the help of James Farley and easily defeated Pres. Herbert Hoover. In his inaugural address to a nation of more than 13 million unemployed, he pronounced that "the only thing we have to fear is fear itself." Congress passed most of the changes he sought in his New Deal program in the first hundred days of his term. He was overwhelmingly reelected in 1936 over Alf Landon. To solve legal challenges to the New Deal, he proposed enlarging the Supreme Court, but his "court-packing" plan aroused strong opposition and had to be abandoned. By the late 1930s economic recovery had slowed, but Roosevelt was more concerned with the growing threat of war. In 1940 he was reelected to an unprecedented third term, defeating Wendell Willkie. He maintained US neutrality toward the war in Europe but approved the principle of lend-lease and in 1941 met with Winston Churchill to draft the Atlantic Charter. With US entry into World War II, he mobilized industry for military production and formed an alliance with Britain and the Soviet Union; he met with Churchill and Joseph Stalin to form war policy at Tehran (1943) and Yalta (1945). Despite declining health, he won reelection for a fourth term against Thomas Dewey (1944) but served only briefly before his death. His presidency is well regarded in US history.

Harry S. Truman (8 May 1884, Lamar MO—26 Dec 1972, Kansas City MO), 33rd president of the US (1945–53). He worked at various jobs before serving with distinction in World War I. He became a partner in a Kansas City haberdashery; when the business failed, he entered Democratic Party politics with the help of Thomas Pendergast. He was elected county judge (1922–24), and later became presiding judge of the county court (1926–34). His reputation for honesty and good management gained him bipartisan support. In the Senate (1935–45), he led a committee that exposed fraud in defense production. In 1944 he was chosen to replace the incumbent Henry Wallace as vice-presidential nominee and was elected with Pres. Franklin Roosevelt. After only 82 days as vice president, he became president on Roosevelt's death (April 1945). He quickly made final arrangements for the San Francisco charter-writing meeting of the UN; helped arrange Germany's unconditional surrender on 8 May, which ended World War II in Europe; and in July attended the Potsdam Conference. The Pacific war ended officially on 2 Sep, after he ordered atomic bombs dropped on Hiroshima and Nagasaki; his justification was a report that 500,000 US troops would be lost in a conventional invasion of Japan. He announced the Truman Doctrine to aid Greece and Turkey (1947), established the Central Intelligence Agency, and pressed for passage of the Marshall Plan to aid European countries. In 1948 he defeated Thomas Dewey despite widespread expectation of his own defeat. He initiated a foreign policy of containment to restrict the Soviet Union's sphere of influence, pursued his

Point Four Program, and initiated the Berlin airlift and the NATO pact of 1949. In the Korean War he sent troops under Gen. Douglas MacArthur to head the United Nations forces. Problems of pursuing the war occupied his administration until he retired. Though he was often criticized during his presidency, Truman's reputation grew steadily in later years.

Dwight David Eisenhower (14 Oct 1890, Denison TX—28 Mar 1969, Washington DC), 34th president of the US (1953–61). He graduated from West Point (1915), then served in the Panama Canal Zone (1922–24) and in the Philippines under Douglas MacArthur (1935–39). In World War II Gen. George Marshall appointed him to the army's war-plans division (1941), then chose him to command US forces in Europe (1942). After planning the invasions of North Africa, Sicily, and Italy, he was appointed supreme commander of Allied forces (1943). He planned the Normandy Campaign (1944) and the conduct of the war in Europe until the German surrender (1945). He was promoted to five-star general (1944) and was named army chief of staff in 1945. He served as president of Columbia University from 1948 until being appointed supreme commander of NATO in 1951. Both Democrats and Republicans courted Eisenhower as a presidential candidate; in 1952, as the Republican candidate, he defeated Adlai Stevenson with the largest popular vote up to that time. He defeated Stevenson again in 1956 in an even larger landslide. His achievements included efforts to contain Communism with the Eisenhower Doctrine. He sent federal troops to Little Rock AR to enforce integration of a city high school (1957). When the Soviet Union launched Sputnik I (1957), he was criticized for failing to develop the US space program and responded by creating NASA (1958). In his last weeks in office the US broke diplomatic relations with Cuba.

John Fitzgerald Kennedy (29 May 1917, Brookline MA—22 Nov 1963, Dallas TX), 35th president of the US (1961–63). The son of Joseph P. Kennedy, he graduated from Harvard University and joined the Navy in World War II, where he earned medals for heroism. Elected to the House of Representatives (1947–53) and the Senate (1953–60), he supported social legislation and became increasingly committed to civil rights legislation. He supported the policies of Harry Truman but accused the State Department of trying to force Chiang Kai-shek into a coalition with Mao Zedong. In 1960 he won the Democratic nomination for president; after a vigorous campaign, managed by his brother Robert F. Kennedy and aided financially by his father, he narrowly defeated Richard Nixon. He was the youngest person and the first Roman Catholic elected president. In his inaugural address he called on Americans to "ask not what your country can do for you, ask what you can do for your country." He proposed tax-reform and civil rights legislation but received little congressional support. He established the Peace Corps and the Alliance for Progress. His foreign policy began with the abortive Bay of Pigs invasion (1961), which emboldened the Soviet Union to move missiles to Cuba, sparking the Cuban missile crisis. In 1963 he successfully concluded the Nuclear Test-Ban Treaty. In November 1963 he was assassinated while riding in a motorcade in Dallas by a sniper, allegedly Lee Harvey Oswald. The killing is considered the most notorious political murder of the 20th century. Kennedy's youth, energy, and charming family brought him world adulation and sparked the idealism of a generation, for whom the Kennedy White House became known as "Camelot." Details about his powerful family and personal life, especially concerning his extramarital affairs, tainted his image in later years.

Lyndon Baines Johnson (27 Aug 1908, Gillespie county TX—22 Jan 1973, San Antonio TX), 36th president of the US (1963–69). He taught school in Houston before going to Washington DC in 1932 as a congressional aide. There he was befriended by Sam Rayburn and his political career blossomed. He won a seat in the House of Representatives (1937–49) as the New Deal was under conservative attack. His loyalty impressed Pres. Franklin Roosevelt, who made Johnson a protégé. He won election to the Senate in 1949 in a vicious campaign that saw fraud on both sides. As Democratic whip (1951–55) and majority leader (1955–61), he developed a talent for consensus building among dissident factions with methods both tactful and ruthless. He was largely responsible for passage of the civil rights bills of 1957 and 1960, the first in the 20th century. In 1960 he was elected vice president; he became president after the assassination of John F. Kennedy. In his first few months in office he won from Congress passage of a huge quantity of important civil rights, tax-reduction, antipoverty, and conservation legislation. He defeated Barry Goldwater in the 1964 election by the largest popular majority to that time and announced his Great Society program. He was diverted from overseeing its enactment by the escalation of US involvement in the Vietnam War, beginning with the Gulf of Tonkin Resolution. His approval ratings diminished markedly and led to his decision not to seek reelection in 1968. He retired to his Texas ranch.

Richard Milhous Nixon (9 Jan 1913, Yorba Linda CA—22 Apr 1994, New York NY), 37th president of the US (1969–74). He studied law at Duke University and practiced in California 1937–42. After serving in World War II, he was elected to the House of Representatives in 1947, employing harsh campaign tactics. He came to national attention with the Alger Hiss case and was elected to the Senate in 1951, again following a bitter campaign. He won the vice presidency in 1952 on a ticket with Dwight D. Eisenhower; they were reelected easily in 1956. As presidential candidate in 1960, he lost narrowly to John F. Kennedy. After failing to win the 1962 California gubernatorial race, he retired from politics and moved to New York to practice law. He reentered politics by running for president in 1968, and he defeated Hubert H. Humphrey with his "Southern strategy" of seeking votes from Southern and Western conservatives in both parties. As president, he began to gradually withdraw US military forces in an effort to end the Vietnam War while ordering the secret bombing of North Vietnamese military centers in Laos and Cambodia. Attacks on North Vietnamese sanctuaries in Cambodia drew widespread protest. Economic problems caused by inflation made the US budget deficit the largest to date, and in 1971 Nixon established unprecedented peacetime controls on wages and prices. He won reelection in 1972 with a landslide victory over George McGovern. Assisted by Henry A. Kissinger, he concluded the Vietnam War. He reopened communications with Communist China and made a state visit there. On his visit to the Soviet Union, the first by a US president, he signed the bilateral SALT agreements. The Watergate scandal overshadowed his second term; his complicity in efforts to cover up his involvement and the likelihood of impeachment led to his becoming, in August 1974, the first president to resign from office. Though never convicted of wrongdoing, he was pardoned by his successor, Gerald Ford. He retired to write his memoirs and books on foreign policy.

Gerald Rudolph Ford, Jr. (Leslie Lynch King, Jr.; 14 Jul 1913, Omaha NE—26 Dec 2006, Rancho Mirage CA), 38th president of the US (1974–77). He was an infant when his parents divorced, and his mother later married Gerald R. Ford. He attended the University of Michigan and Yale Law School, and practiced law in Michigan after World War II. He served in the House of Representative 1948–73, becoming minority leader in 1965. After Spiro Agnew resigned as vice president in 1973, Richard Nixon nominated Ford to fill the vacant post. When the Watergate scandal forced Nixon's departure, Ford became the first president who had not been elected to either the vice presidency or the presidency. A month later he pardoned Nixon; to counter widespread outrage, he voluntarily appeared before a House subcommittee to explain his action. His administration gradually lowered the high inflation rate it inherited. Ford's relations with the Democratic-controlled Congress were typified by his more than 50 vetoes, of which more than 40 were sustained. In the final days of the Vietnam War in 1975, he ordered an airlift of 237,000 anti-Communist Vietnamese refugees, most of whom came to the US. Reaction against Watergate contributed to his defeat by James Earl Carter, Jr., in 1976.

James Earl Carter, Jr. (1 Oct 1924, Plains GA), 39th president of the US (1977–81). He graduated from the US Naval Academy and served in the navy until 1953, when he left to manage the family peanut business. He served in the state senate 1962–66. Elected governor (1971–75), he opened Georgia's government offices to blacks and women and introduced stricter budgeting procedures for state agencies. In 1976, though lacking a national political base or major backing, he won the Democratic nomination and the presidency, defeating the sitting president, Gerald Ford. As president, Carter helped negotiate a peace treaty between Egypt and Israel, signed a treaty with Panama to make the Panama Canal a neutral zone after 1999, and established full diplomatic relations with China. In 1979–80 the Iran hostage crisis became a major political liability. He responded more forcefully to the USSR's invasion of Afghanistan in 1979, embargoing the shipment of US grain to that country and leading a boycott of the 1980 Summer Olympics in Moscow. Hampered by high inflation and a recession engineered to tame it, he lost his bid for reelection to Ronald Reagan. He subsequently became involved in international diplomatic negotiations and helped oversee elections in countries with insecure democratic traditions. Carter was awarded the Nobel Peace Prize in 2002.

Ronald Wilson Reagan (6 Feb 1911, Tampico IL—5 Jun 2004, Bel Air CA), 40th president of the US (1981–89). He attended Eureka College and worked as a radio sports announcer before going to Hollywood in 1937. In his career as a movie actor, he had roles in 50 films and was twice president of the Screen Actors Guild (1947–52, 1959–60). Reagan became a spokesman for the General Electric Co. and hosted its television theater program 1954–62. Having gradually changed his political affiliation from liberal Democrat to conservative Republican, he was elected governor of California and served 1967–74. In 1980 he defeated incumbent Pres. James Earl Carter, Jr., to become president. Shortly after taking office, he was wounded in an assassination attempt. Reagan adopted supply-side economics to promote rapid economic growth and reduce the federal deficit. Congress approved most of his proposals (1981), which succeeded in lowering inflation but doubled the national debt by 1986. He began the largest peacetime military buildup in US history and in 1983 proposed construction of the Strategic Defense Initiative. His foreign policy included the INF Treaty to restrict intermediate-range nuclear weapons and the invasion of Grenada. In 1984 Reagan defeated Walter Mondale in a landslide for reelection. Details of his administration's involvement in the Iran-Contra Affair emerged in 1986 and significantly weakened his popularity and authority. Though his intellectual capacity for governing was often disparaged, his artful communication skills enabled him to pursue numerous conservative policies with conspicuous success. In 1994 he revealed that he had Alzheimer disease.

George Herbert Walker Bush (12 Jun 1924, Milton MA), 41st president of the US (1989–93). The son of Prescott Bush, later a Connecticut senator, he served in World War II, graduated from Yale University, and started an oil business in Texas. He served in the House of Representatives 1966–70 as a Republican. He then served as ambassador to the UN (1971–72), chief liaison to China (1974–76), and head of the CIA (1976–77). In 1980 he ran for president but lost the nomination to Ronald Reagan. Bush served as vice president with Reagan (1981–88), whom he succeeded as president, defeating Michael Dukakis. He made no dramatic departures from Reagan's policies. In 1989 he ordered a brief military invasion of Panama, which toppled that country's leader, Gen. Manuel Noriega. He helped impose a UN-approved embargo against Iraq in 1990 to force its withdrawal from Kuwait. When Iraq refused, he authorized a US-led air offensive that began the Persian Gulf War. Despite general approval of his foreign policy, an economic recession led to his defeat by William Jefferson Clinton in 1992. His son George W. Bush was elected president in 2000 and reelected in 2004. In the aftermath of the 26 Dec 2004 tsunami, Bush joined fellow former president Bill Clinton as leader of a fundraising effort to aid victims of the disaster.

William Jefferson Clinton (William Jefferson Blythe III; 19 Aug 1946, Hope AR), 42nd president of the US (1993–2001). He was adopted, after his father's death in a car crash, by his mother's second husband, Roger Clinton. He attended Georgetown University, Oxford University (as a Rhodes Scholar), and Yale Law School, then taught at the University of Arkansas School of Law. He served as state attorney general (1977–79) and served several terms as governor (1979–81, 1983–92), during which he reformed Arkansas's educational system and encouraged the growth of industry through favorable tax policies. He won the Democratic presidential nomination in 1992, after withstanding charges of personal impropriety, and defeated the incumbent, George H.W. Bush. As president, he obtained approval of the North American Free Trade Agreement in 1993. He and his wife, Hillary Rodham Clinton, strongly advocated their plan to overhaul the US health care system, but Congress rejected it. He committed US forces to a peacekeeping initiative in Bosnia and Herzegovina. In 1994 the Democrats lost control of Congress for the first time since 1954. Clinton defeated Robert Dole to win reelection in 1996. He faced renewed charges of personal impropriety, this time involving Monica Lewinsky, and as a result, in 1998 he became the second president in history to be impeached. Charged with perjury and obstruction of justice, he was acquitted at his Senate trial in 1999. His two terms saw sustained economic growth and successive budget surpluses, the first in three decades. In the aftermath of the 26 Dec 2004 tsunami, Clinton joined fellow former president George H.W. Bush as leader of a fundraising effort to aid victims of the disaster.

George Walker Bush (6 Jul 1946, New Haven CT), 43rd president of the US (from 2001). The eldest child of Pres. George H.W. Bush, he attended Yale University and Harvard Business School. After spending a decade in the oil business with mixed success, he served as managing general partner of the Texas Rangers baseball franchise. In 1994 he was elected governor of Texas (1995–2000). Despite losing the national popular vote to Vice President Al Gore by more than 500,000 votes, he gained the presidency when a Supreme Court ruling effectively ended a recount of ballots in Florida. His response to the terrorist attacks on 11 Sep 2001 gave shape to his administration. The invasion of Iraq by US-led forces in March 2003 was followed by a problematic occupation during which a burgeoning insurgency threatened Iraqi efforts to stabilize a democratically elected government. Bush won reelection in 2004. The loss of Republican control of Congress in elections in November 2006 limited his power to steer legislation to passage at the end of his time in the White House.

Vice Presidents

	NAME	DATES OF BIRTH/DEATH	TIME IN OFFICE	PRESIDENT
1	John Adams	30 Oct 1735–4 Jul 1826	1789–97	George Washington
2	Thomas Jefferson	13 Apr 1743–4 Jul 1826	1797–1801	John Adams
3	Aaron Burr	6 Feb 1756–14 Sep 1836	1801–05	Thomas Jefferson
4	George Clinton[1]	26 Jul 1739–20 Apr 1812	1805–09	Thomas Jefferson
			1809–12	James Madison
5	Elbridge Gerry	17 Jul 1744–23 Nov 1814	1813–14	James Madison
6	Daniel D. Tompkins	21 Jun 1774–11 Jun 1825	1817–25	James Monroe
7	John C. Calhoun[2]	18 Mar 1782–31 Mar 1850	1825–29	John Quincy Adams
			1829–32	Andrew Jackson
8	Martin Van Buren	5 Dec 1782–24 Jul 1862	1833–37	Andrew Jackson
9	Richard M. Johnson	17 Oct 1781–19 Nov 1850	1837–41	Martin Van Buren
10	John Tyler	29 Mar 1790–18 Jan 1862	1841	William Henry Harrison[1]
11	George Mifflin Dallas	10 Jul 1792–31 Dec 1864	1845–49	James K. Polk
12	Millard Fillmore	7 Jan 1800–8 Mar 1874	1849–50	Zachary Taylor[1]
13	William Rufus de Vane King[1]	7 Apr 1786–18 Apr 1853	4 Mar–18 Apr 1853	Franklin Pierce
14	John C. Breckinridge	21 Jan 1821–17 May 1875	1857–61	James Buchanan
15	Hannibal Hamlin	27 Aug 1809–4 Jul 1891	1861–65	Abraham Lincoln[1]
16	Andrew Johnson	29 Dec 1808–31 Jul 1875	1865	
17	Schuyler Colfax	23 Mar 1823–13 Jan 1885	1869–73	Ulysses S. Grant
18	Henry Wilson[1]	16 Feb 1812–22 Nov 1875	1873–75	Ulysses S. Grant
19	William A. Wheeler	30 Jun 1819–4 Jun 1887	1877–81	Rutherford B. Hayes
20	Chester A. Arthur	5 Oct 1829–18 Nov 1886	1881	James A. Garfield[1]
21	Thomas A. Hendricks[1]	7 Sep 1819–25 Nov 1885	4 Mar–25 Nov 1885	Grover Cleveland
22	Levi Parsons Morton	16 May 1824–16 May 1920	1889–93	Benjamin Harrison
23	Adlai E. Stevenson	23 Oct 1835–14 Jun 1914	1893–97	Grover Cleveland
24	Garret A. Hobart[1]	3 Jun 1844–21 Nov 1899	1897–99	William McKinley
25	Theodore Roosevelt	27 Oct 1858–6 Jan 1919	1901	William McKinley[1]
26	Charles Warren Fairbanks	11 May 1852–4 Jun 1918	1905–09	Theodore Roosevelt
27	James Schoolcraft Sherman[1]	24 Oct 1855–30 Oct 1912	1909–12	William Howard Taft
28	Thomas R. Marshall	14 Mar 1854–1 Jun 1925	1913–21	Woodrow Wilson

Vice Presidents (continued)

	NAME	DATES OF BIRTH/DEATH	TIME IN OFFICE	PRESIDENT
29	Calvin Coolidge	4 Jul 1872–5 Jan 1933	1921–23	Warren G. Harding[1]
30	Charles G. Dawes	27 Aug 1865–23 Apr 1851	1925–29	Calvin Coolidge
31	Charles Curtis	25 Jan 1860–8 Feb 1936	1929–33	Herbert Hoover
32	John Nance Garner	22 Nov 1868–7 Nov 1967	1933–41	Franklin D. Roosevelt
33	Henry A. Wallace	7 Oct 1888–18 Nov 1965	1941–45	Franklin D. Roosevelt
34	Harry S. Truman	8 May 1884–26 Dec 1972	1945	Franklin D. Roosevelt[1]
35	Alben W. Barkley	24 Nov 1877–30 Apr 1956	1949–53	Harry S. Truman
36	Richard M. Nixon	9 Jan 1913–22 Apr 1994	1953–61	Dwight D. Eisenhower
37	Lyndon B. Johnson	27 Aug 1908–22 Jan 1973	1961–63	John F. Kennedy[1]
38	Hubert H. Humphrey	27 May 1911–13 Jan 1978	1965–69	Lyndon B. Johnson
39	Spiro T. Agnew[2]	9 Nov 1918–17 Sep 1996	1969–73	Richard M. Nixon
40	Gerald R. Ford	14 Jul 1913	1973–74	Richard M. Nixon[2]
41	Nelson A. Rockefeller	8 Jul 1908–26 Jan 1979	1974–77	Gerald R. Ford
42	Walter F. Mondale	5 Jan 1928	1977–81	Jimmy Carter
43	George H.W. Bush	12 Jun 1924	1981–89	Ronald Reagan
44	Dan Quayle	4 Feb 1947	1989–93	George H.W. Bush
45	Albert Gore	31 Mar 1948	1993–2001	William J. Clinton
46	Richard B. Cheney	30 Jan 1941	2001–09	George W. Bush
47	Joe Biden	20 Nov 1942	2009–	Barack Obama

[1]*Died in office.* [2]*Resigned from office.*

Presidents' Spouses and Children

Maiden names of the presidents' wives appear in small capital letters.

DATE OF MARRIAGE	PRESIDENTS, SPOUSES, AND CHILDREN
6 Jan 1759	**George Washington** **Martha DANDRIDGE Custis** (2 Jun 1731–22 May 1802) no children
25 Oct 1764	**John Adams** **Abigail SMITH** (22 Nov 1744–28 Oct 1818) ▸ Abigail Amelia Adams (1765–1813), ▸ John Quincy Adams (1767–1848), ▸ Susanna Adams (1768–1770), ▸ Charles Adams (1770–1800), ▸ Thomas Boylston Adams (1772–1832)
1 Jan 1772	**Thomas Jefferson** **Martha WAYLES Skelton** (30 Oct 1748–6 Sep 1782) ▸ Martha Washington Jefferson (1772–1836), ▸ Jane Randolph Jefferson (1774–1775), ▸ infant son (1777–1777), ▸ Mary Jefferson (1778–1804), ▸ Lucy Elizabeth Jefferson (1780–1781), ▸ Lucy Elizabeth Jefferson (1782–1785)
15 Sep 1794	**James Madison** **Dolley Dandridge PAYNE Todd** (20 May 1768–12 Jul 1849) no children
16 Feb 1786	**James Monroe** **Elizabeth KORTRIGHT** (30 Jun 1768–23 Sep 1830) ▸ Eliza Kortright Monroe (1786–1835?), ▸ James Spence Monroe (1799–1800), ▸ Maria Hester Monroe (1803–1850)
26 Jul 1797	**John Quincy Adams** **Louisa Catherine JOHNSON** (12 Feb 1775–15 May 1852) ▸ George Washington Adams (1801–1829), ▸ John Adams (1803–1834), ▸ Charles Francis Adams (1807–1886), ▸ Louisa Catherine Adams (1811–1812)
Aug 1791	**Andrew Jackson** **Rachel DONELSON Robards** (15? Jun 1767–22 Dec 1828) no children

Presidents' Spouses and Children (continued)

DATE OF MARRIAGE	PRESIDENTS, SPOUSES, AND CHILDREN
	Martin Van Buren
21 Feb 1807	**Hannah Hoes** (8 Mar 1783–5 Feb 1819) ▸ Abraham Van Buren (1807–1873), ▸ John Van Buren (1810–1866), ▸ Martin Van Buren (1812–1855), ▸ Smith Thompson Van Buren (1817–1876)
	William Henry Harrison
25 Nov 1795	**Anna Tuthill Symmes** (25 Jul 1775–25 Feb 1864) ▸ Elizabeth Bassett Harrison (1796–1846), ▸ John Cleves Symmes Harrison (1798–1830), ▸ Lucy Singleton Harrison (1800–1826), ▸ William Henry Harrison (1802–1838), ▸ John Scott Harrison (1804–1878), ▸ Benjamin Harrison (1806–1840), ▸ Mary Symmes Harrison (1809–1842), ▸ Carter Bassett Harrison (1811–1839), ▸ Anna Tuthill Harrison (1813–1865), ▸ James Findlay Harrison (1814–1817)
	John Tyler
29 Mar 1813	**Letitia Christian** (12 Nov 1790–10 Sep 1842) ▸ Mary Tyler (1815–1848), ▸ Robert Tyler (1816–1877), ▸ John Tyler (1819–1896), ▸ Letitia Tyler (1821–1907), ▸ Anne Contesse Tyler (1825–1825), ▸ Alice Tyler (1827–1854), ▸ Tazewell Tyler (1830–1874)
26 Jun 1844	**Julia Gardiner** (4 May 1820–10 Jul 1889) ▸ David Gardiner Tyler (1846–1927), ▸ John Alexander Tyler (1848–1883), ▸ Julia Gardiner Tyler (1849?–1871), ▸ Lachlan Tyler (1851–1902), ▸ Lyon Gardiner Tyler (1853–1935), ▸ Robert Fitzwalter Tyler (1856–1927), ▸ Pearl Tyler (1860–1947)
	James K. Polk
1 Jan 1824	**Sarah Childress** (4 Sep 1803–14 Aug 1891) no children
	Zachary Taylor
21 Jun 1810	**Margaret Mackall Smith** (21 Sep 1788–14 Aug 1852) ▸ Anne Margaret Mackall Taylor (1811–1875), ▸ Sarah Knox Taylor (1814–1835), ▸ Octavia Pannel Taylor (1816–1820), ▸ Margaret Smith Taylor (1819–1820), ▸ Mary Elizabeth Taylor (1824–1909), ▸ Richard Taylor (1826–1879)
	Millard Fillmore
5 Feb 1826	**Abigail Powers** (13 Mar 1798–30 Mar 1853) ▸ Millard Powers Fillmore (1828–1889), ▸ Mary Abigail Fillmore (1832–1854)
10 Feb 1858	**Caroline Carmichael McIntosh** (21 Oct 1813–11 Aug 1881) no children
	Franklin Pierce
10 Nov 1834	**Jane Means Appleton** (12 Mar 1806–2 Dec 1863) ▸ Franklin Pierce (1836–1836), ▸ Frank Robert Pierce (1839–1843), ▸ Benjamin Pierce (1841–1853)
	James Buchanan never married
	Abraham Lincoln
4 Nov 1842	**Mary Ann Todd** (13 Dec 1818–16 Jul 1882) ▸ Robert Todd Lincoln (1843–1926), ▸ Edward Baker Lincoln (1846–1850), ▸ William Wallace Lincoln (1850–1862), ▸ Thomas Lincoln (1853–1871)
	Andrew Johnson
17 May 1827	**Eliza McCardle** (4 Oct 1810–15 Jan 1876) ▸ Martha Johnson (1828–1901), ▸ Charles Johnson (1830–1863), ▸ Mary Johnson (1832–1883), ▸ Robert Johnson (1834–1869), ▸ Andrew Johnson (1852–1879)
	Ulysses S. Grant
22 Aug 1848	**Julia Boggs Dent** (26 Jan 1826–14 Dec 1902) ▸ Frederick Dent Grant (1850–1912), ▸ Ulysses Simpson Grant (1852–1929), ▸ Ellen Wrenshall Grant (1855–1922), ▸ Jesse Root Grant (1858–1934)
	Rutherford B. Hayes
30 Dec 1852	**Lucy Ware Webb** (28 Aug 1831–25 Jun 1889) ▸ Birchard Austin Hayes (1853–1926), ▸ James Webb Cook Hayes (1856–1934), ▸ Rutherford Platt Hayes (1858–1927), ▸ Joseph Thompson Hayes (1861–1863), ▸ George Crook Hayes (1864–1866), ▸ Fanny Hayes (1867–1950), ▸ Scott Russell Hayes (1871–1923), ▸ Manning Force Hayes (1873–1874)

Presidents' Spouses and Children (continued)

DATE OF MARRIAGE	PRESIDENTS, SPOUSES, AND CHILDREN
	James A. Garfield
11 Nov 1858	**Lucretia Rudolph** (19 Apr 1832–13 Mar 1918)
	▸ Eliza Arabella Garfield (1860–1863), ▸ Harry Augustus Garfield (1863–1942), ▸ James Rudolph Garfield (1865–1950), ▸ Mary Garfield (1867–1947), ▸ Irvin McDowell Garfield (1870–1951), ▸ Abram Garfield (1872–1958), ▸ Edward Garfield (1874–1876)
	Chester A. Arthur
25 Oct 1859	**Ellen Lewis Herndon** (30 Aug 1837–12 Jan 1880)
	▸ William Lewis Herndon Arthur (1860–1863), ▸ Chester Alan Arthur (1864–1937), ▸ Ellen Herndon Arthur (1871–1915)
	Grover Cleveland
2 Jun 1886	**Frances Folsom** (21 Jul 1864–29 Oct 1947)
	▸ Ruth Cleveland (1891–1904), ▸ Esther Cleveland (1893–1980), ▸ Marion Cleveland (1895–1977), ▸ Richard Folsom Cleveland (1897–1974), ▸ Francis Grover Cleveland (1903–1995)
	Benjamin Harrison
20 Oct 1853	**Caroline Lavinia Scott** (1 Oct 1832–25 Oct 1892)
	▸ Russell Benjamin Harrison (1854–1936), ▸ Mary Scott Harrison (1858–1930)
6 Apr 1896	**Mary Scott Lord Dimmick** (30 Apr 1858–5 Jan 1948)
	▸ Elizabeth Harrison (1897–1955)
	William McKinley
25 Jan 1871	**Ida Saxton** (8 Jun 1847–26 May 1907)
	▸ Katherine McKinley (1871–1875), ▸ Ida McKinley (1873–1873)
	Theodore Roosevelt
27 Oct 1880	**Alice Hathaway Lee** (29 Jul 1861–14 Feb 1884)
	▸ Alice Lee Roosevelt (1884–1980)
2 Dec 1886	**Edith Kermit Carow** (6 Aug 1861–30 Sep 1948)
	▸ Theodore Roosevelt (1887–1944), ▸ Kermit Roosevelt (1889–1943), ▸ Ethel Carow Roosevelt (1891–1977), ▸ Archibald Bulloch Roosevelt (1894–1979), ▸ Quentin Roosevelt (1897–1918)
	William Howard Taft
19 Jun 1886	**Helen Herron** (2 Jun 1861–22 May 1943)
	▸ Robert Alphonso Taft (1889–1953), ▸ Helen Herron Taft (1891–1987), ▸ Charles Phelps Taft (1897–1983)
	Woodrow Wilson
24 Jun 1885	**Ellen Louise Axson** (15 May 1860–6 Aug 1914)
	▸ Margaret Woodrow Wilson (1886–1944), ▸ Jessie Woodrow Wilson (1887–1933), ▸ Eleanor Randolph Wilson (1889–1967)
18 Dec 1915	**Edith Bolling Galt** (15 Oct 1872–28 Dec 1961)
	no children
	Warren G. Harding
8 Jul 1891	**Florence Mabel Kling De Wolf** (15 Aug 1860–21 Nov 1924)
	no children
	Calvin Coolidge
4 Oct 1905	**Grace Anna Goodhue** (3 Jan 1879–8 Jul 1957)
	▸ John Coolidge (1906–2000), ▸ Calvin Coolidge (1908–1924)
	Herbert Hoover
10 Feb 1899	**Lou Henry** (29 Mar 1874–7 Jan 1944)
	▸ Herbert Clark Hoover (1903–1969), ▸ Allan Henry Hoover (1907–1993)
	Franklin D. Roosevelt
17 Mar 1905	**(Anna) Eleanor Roosevelt** (11 Oct 1884–7 Nov 1962)
	▸ Anna Eleanor Roosevelt (1906–1975), ▸ James Roosevelt (1907–1991), ▸ Franklin Roosevelt (1909–1909), ▸ Elliott Roosevelt (1910–1990), ▸ Franklin Delano Roosevelt (1914–1988), ▸ John Aspinwall Roosevelt (1916–1981)

Presidents' Spouses and Children (continued)

DATE OF MARRIAGE	PRESIDENTS, SPOUSES, AND CHILDREN
	Harry S. Truman
28 Jun 1919	**Elizabeth Virginia (Bess) Wallace** (13 Feb 1885–18 Oct 1982) ▸ Margaret (Mary) Truman (1924–2008)
	Dwight D. Eisenhower
1 Jul 1916	**Marie (Mamie) Geneva Doud** (14 Nov 1896–1 Nov 1979) ▸ Doud Dwight Eisenhower (1917–1921), ▸ John Sheldon Doud Eisenhower (1922–)
	John F. Kennedy
12 Sep 1953	**Jacqueline Lee Bouvier** (28 Jul 1929–19 May 1994) ▸ Caroline Bouvier Kennedy (1957–), ▸ John Fitzgerald Kennedy (1960–1999), Patrick Bouvier Kennedy (1963–1963)
	Lyndon B. Johnson
17 Nov 1934	**Claudia Alta (Lady Bird) Taylor** (22 Dec 1912–11 Jul 2007) ▸ Lynda Bird Johnson (1944–), ▸ Luci Baines Johnson (1947–)
	Richard M. Nixon
21 Jun 1940	**Thelma Catherine (Patricia) Ryan** (16 Mar 1912–22 Jun 1993) ▸ Patricia Nixon (1946–), ▸ Julie Nixon (1948–)
	Gerald R. Ford
15 Oct 1948	**Elizabeth Ann (Betty) Bloomer Warren** (8 Apr 1918–) ▸ Michael Gerald Ford (1950–), ▸ John Gardner Ford (1952–), ▸ Steven Meigs Ford (1956–), ▸ Susan Elizabeth Ford (1957–)
	Jimmy Carter
7 Jul 1946	**(Eleanor) Rosalynn Smith** (18 Aug 1927–) ▸ John William Carter (1947–), ▸ James Earl Carter (1950–), ▸ Donnel Jeffrey Carter (1952–), ▸ Amy Lynn Carter (1967–)
	Ronald Reagan
24 Jan 1940	**Jane Wyman (née Sarah Jane Fulks)** (4 Jan 1914–10 Sep 2007) ▸ Maureen Elizabeth Reagan (1941–2001), ▸ Michael Edward Reagan (1945–), ▸ Christine Reagan (1947–1947)
4 Mar 1952	**Nancy Davis (née Anne Frances Robbins)** (6 Jul 1921–) ▸ Patricia Ann Reagan (1952–), ▸ Ronald Prescott Reagan (1958–)
	George H.W. Bush
6 Jan 1945	**Barbara Pierce** (8 Jun 1925–) ▸ George Walker Bush (1946–), ▸ Robin Bush (1949–1953), ▸ John Ellis (Jeb) Bush (1953–), ▸ Neil Mallon Bush (1955–), ▸ Marvin Pierce Bush (1956–), ▸ Dorothy Walker Bush (1959–)
	William J. Clinton
11 Oct 1975	**Hillary Diane Rodham** (26 Oct 1947–) ▸ Chelsea Clinton (1980–)
	George W. Bush
5 Nov 1977	**Laura Lane Welch** (4 Nov 1946–) ▸ Barbara Bush (1981–), ▸ Jenna Bush (1981–)

Presidential Succession

The president is the chief executive of the US. In contrast to the parliamentary form of government, under which the head of state is mainly ceremonial, the presidential system, such as that in the US, vests the president with great authority. The role of the president—including the process of presidential succession—is outlined in Article II of the Constitution of 1787, the fundamental law of the US federal system of government. Presidential nomination procedures are often recognized as constitutional elements, though they are outside the letter of the Constitution.

The Presidential Succession Act of 1792 established the stages of succession: from the president to the vice president, then to the Senate president pro tempore and next to the speaker of the House of Representatives. In 1886 new legislation removed the latter two from succession, replacing them with cabinet officers. The pattern of presidential succession was again changed in 1947, when the the speaker of the House was placed next in line after the vice president, followed by the Senate president pro tempore, the secretary of state, and finally, the remaining cabinet officers in the order that their departments were first formed.

History

The administration of the first president, George Washington, set the customary precedent of serving only two terms, a tradition maintained until Pres. Franklin D. Roosevelt was elected to a third and fourth term in the 1940s. Congress adopted the 22nd Amendment in 1951, which limits presidents to two terms in office.

In 1841 William Henry Harrison became the first president to die in office and was succeeded by his vice president, John Tyler. In 1850, when Zachary Taylor died after only 16 months in office, he was succeeded by Millard Fillmore. In the same manner, Vice Pres. Andrew Johnson assumed the presidency after Pres. Abraham Lincoln's assassination.

When Pres. James Garfield was shot on 2 Jul 1881, he became incapacitated, raising serious constitutional questions over who should perform the functions of the presidency. For 80 days the president lay ill, and it was generally agreed that in such cases the vice president (Chester Arthur) was empowered by the Constitution to assume the powers and duties of the office of president. But should Arthur be only acting president until Garfield recovered, or would he receive the office itself and thus displace his predecessor? Because of an ambiguity in the Constitution, opinion was divided, and because Congress was not in session, the problem could not be debated there. No further action was taken before the death of the president, the result of slow blood poisoning, on 19 September. This ambiguity over succession was later clarified by the 20th (1933) and 25th (1967) Amendments. Other vice presidents who succeeded upon the death of presidents included Theodore Roosevelt in 1901, Calvin Coolidge in 1923, Harry S. Truman in 1945, and Lyndon B. Johnson in 1963.

Please visit **<www.britannica.com/presidents>** for information about all previous presidencies.

US Presidential Cabinets

The cabinet is composed of the heads of executive departments chosen by the president with the consent of the Senate. Cabinet officials do not hold seats in Congress and are not regulated by the US Constitution, which makes no mention of such a body. The existence of the cabinet is a matter of custom dating back to George Washington, who consulted regularly with his department heads as a group. Original dates of service are given for officials appointed midterm and for newly created posts. Interim officials are not listed. Presidencies and new positions are indicated in bold.

George Washington

30 APR 1789–3 MARCH 1793 (TERM 1)	
State	Thomas Jefferson
Treasury	Alexander Hamilton
War	Henry Knox
Attorney General	Edmund Randolph

4 MAR 1793–3 MAR 1797 (TERM 2)	
State	Thomas Jefferson; Edmund Randolph (2 Jan 1794); Timothy Pickering (20 Aug 1795)
Treasury	Alexander Hamilton; Oliver Wolcott, Jr. (2 Feb 1795)
War	Henry Knox; Timothy Pickering (2 Jan 1795); James McHenry (6 Feb 1796)
Attorney General	Edmund Randolph; William Bradford (29 Jan 1794); Charles Lee (10 Dec 1795)

John Adams

4 MAR 1797–3 MAR 1801	
State	Timothy Pickering; John Marshall (6 Jun 1800)
Treasury	Oliver Wolcott, Jr.; Samuel Dexter (1 Jan 1801)
War	James McHenry; Samuel Dexter (12 Jun 1800)
Navy	Benjamin Stoddert (18 Jun 1798)
Attorney General	Charles Lee

Thomas Jefferson

4 MAR 1801–3 MAR 1805 (TERM 1)	
State	James Madison
Treasury	Samuel Dexter; Albert Gallatin (14 May 1801)
War	Henry Dearborn
Navy	Benjamin Stoddert; Robert Smith (27 Jul 1801)
Attorney General	Levi Lincoln

US Presidential Cabinets (continued)

Thomas Jefferson (continued)

4 MAR 1805–3 MAR 1809 (TERM 2)

State	James Madison
Treasury	Albert Gallatin
War	Henry Dearborn
Navy	Robert Smith
Attorney General	John Breckenridge; Caesar Augustus Rodney (20 Jan 1807)

James Madison

4 MAR 1809–3 MAR 1813 (TERM 1)

State	Robert Smith
Treasury	Albert Gallatin
War	John Smith; William Eustis (8 Apr 1809); John Armstrong (5 Feb 1813)
Navy	Robert Smith; Paul Hamilton (15 May 1809); William Jones (19 Jan 1813)
Attorney General	Caesar Augustus Rodney; William Pinkney (6 Jan 1812)

4 MAR 1813–3 MAR 1817 (TERM 2)

State	James Monroe
Treasury	Albert Gallatin; George Washington Campbell (9 Feb 1814); Alexander James Dallas (14 Oct 1814); William Harris Crawford (22 Oct 1816)
War	John Armstrong; James Monroe (1 Oct 1814); William Harris Crawford (8 Aug 1815)
Navy	William Jones; Benjamin Williams Crowninshield (16 Jan 1815)
Attorney General	William Pinkney; Richard Rush (11 Feb 1814)

James Monroe

4 MAR 1817–3 MAR 1821 (TERM 1)

State	John Quincy Adams
Treasury	William Harris Crawford
War	John C. Calhoun
Navy	Benjamin Williams Crowninshield; Smith Thompson (1 Jan 1819)
Attorney General	Richard Rush; William Wirt (15 Nov 1817)

4 MAR 1821–3 MAR 1825 (TERM 2)

State	John Quincy Adams
Treasury	William Harris Crawford
War	John C. Calhoun
Navy	Smith Thompson; Samuel Lewis Southard (16 Sep 1823)
Attorney General	William Wirt

John Quincy Adams

4 MAR 1825–3 MAR 1829

State	Henry Clay
Treasury	Richard Rush
War	James Barbour; Peter Buell Porter (21 Jun 1828)
Navy	Samuel Lewis Southard
Attorney General	William Wirt

Andrew Jackson

4 MAR 1829–3 MAR 1833 (TERM 1)

State	Martin Van Buren; Edward Livingston (24 May 1831)
Treasury	Samuel Delucenna Ingham; Louis McLane (8 Aug 1831)
War	John Henry Eaton; Lewis Cass (8 Aug 1831)
Navy	John Branch; Levi Woodbury (23 May 1831)
Attorney General	John Macpherson Berrien; Roger Brooke Taney (20 Jul 1831)

4 MAR 1833–3 MAR 1837 (TERM 2)

State	Edward Livingston; Louis McLane (29 May 1833); John Forsyth (1 Jul 1834)
Treasury	Louis McLane; William John Duane (1 Jun 1833); Roger Brooke Taney (23 Sep 1833); Levi Woodbury (1 Jul 1834)
War	Lewis Cass
Navy	Levi Woodbury; Mahlon Dickerson (30 Jun 1834)
Attorney General	Roger Brooke Taney; Benjamin Franklin Butler (18 Nov 1833)

US Presidential Cabinets (continued)

	Martin Van Buren
4 MAR 1837–3 MAR 1841	
State	John Forsyth
Treasury	Levi Woodbury
War	Joel Roberts Poinsett
Navy	Mahlon Dickerson; James Kirke Paulding (1 Jul 1838)
Attorney General	Benjamin Franklin Butler; Felix Grundy (1 Sep 1838); Henry Dilworth Gilpin (11 Jan 1840)
	William Henry Harrison
4 MAR 1841–4 APR 1841	
State	Daniel Webster
Treasury	Thomas Ewing
War	John Bell
Navy	George Edmund Badger
Attorney General	John Jordan Crittenden
	John Tyler
6 APR 1841–3 MAR 1845	
State	Daniel Webster; Abel Parker Upshur (24 Jul 1843); John C. Calhoun (1 Apr 1844)
Treasury	Thomas Ewing; Walter Forward (13 Sep 1841); John Canfield Spencer (8 Mar 1843); George Mortimer Bibb (4 Jul 1844)
War	John Bell; John Canfield Spencer (12 Oct 1841); James Madison Porter (8 Mar 1843); William Wilkins (20 Feb 1844)
Navy	George Edmund Badger; Abel Parker Upshur (11 Oct 1841); David Henshaw (24 Jul 1843); Thomas Walker Gilmer (19 Feb 1844); John Young Mason (26 Mar 1844)
Attorney General	John Jordan Crittenden; Hugh Swinton Legaré (20 Sep 1841); John Nelson (1 Jul 1843)
	James K. Polk
4 MAR 1845–3 MAR 1849	
State	James Buchanan
Treasury	Robert James Walker
War	William Learned Marcy
Navy	George Bancroft; John Young Mason (9 Sep 1846)
Attorney General	John Young Mason; Nathan Clifford (17 Oct 1846); Isaac Toucey (29 Jun 1848)
	Zachary Taylor
4 MAR 1849–9 JUL 1850	
State	John Middleton Clayton
Treasury	William Morris Meredith
War	George Washington Crawford
Navy	William Ballard Preston
Attorney General	Reverdy Johnson
Interior	Thomas Ewing (8 Mar 1849)
	Millard Fillmore
10 JUL 1850–3 MAR 1853	
State	Daniel Webster; Edward Everett (6 Nov 1852)
Treasury	Thomas Corwin
War	George Washington Crawford; Charles Magill Conrad (15 Aug 1850)
Navy	William Alexander Graham; John Pendleton Kennedy (26 Jul 1852)
Attorney General	Reverdy Johnson; John Jordan Crittenden (14 Aug 1850)
Interior	Thomas Ewing; Thomas McKean Thompson McKennan (15 Aug 1850); Alexander Hugh Holmes Stuart (16 Sep 1850)
	Franklin Pierce
4 MAR 1853–3 MAR 1857	
State	William Learned Marcy
Treasury	James Guthrie
War	Jefferson Davis
Navy	James Cochran Dobbin
Attorney General	Caleb Cushing
Interior	Robert McClelland

US Presidential Cabinets (continued)

	James Buchanan
4 MAR 1857–3 MAR 1861	
State	Lewis Cass; Jeremiah Sullivan Black (17 Dec 1860)
Treasury	Howell Cobb; Philip Francis Thomas (12 Dec 1860); John Adams Dix (15 Jan 1861)
War	John Buchanan Floyd
Navy	Isaac Toucey
Attorney General	Jeremiah Sullivan Black; Edwin McMasters Stanton (22 Dec 1860)
Interior	Jacob Thompson
	Abraham Lincoln
4 MAR 1861–3 MAR 1865 (TERM 1)	
State	William Henry Seward
Treasury	Salmon Portland Chase; William Pitt Fessenden (5 Jul 1864)
War	Simon Cameron; Edwin McMasters Stanton (20 Jun 1862)
Navy	Gideon Welles
Attorney General	Edward Bates; James Speed (5 Dec 1864)
Interior	Caleb Blood Smith; John Palmer Usher (8 Jan 1863)
4 MAR 1865–15 APR 1865 (TERM 2)	
State	William Henry Seward
Treasury	Hugh McCulloch
War	Edwin McMasters Stanton
Navy	Gideon Welles
Attorney General	James Speed
Interior	John Palmer Usher
	Andrew Johnson
15 APR 1865–3 MAR 1869	
State	William Henry Seward
Treasury	Hugh McCulloch
War	Edwin McMasters Stanton; John McAllister Schofield (1 Jun 1868)
Navy	Gideon Welles
Attorney General	James Speed; Henry Stanbery (23 Jul 1866); William Maxwell Evarts (20 Jul 1868)
Interior	John Palmer Usher; James Harlan (15 May 1865); Orville Hickman Browning (1 Sep 1866)
	Ulysses S. Grant
4 MAR 1869–3 MAR 1873 (TERM 1)	
State	Elihu Benjamin Washburne; Hamilton Fish (17 Mar 1869)
Treasury	George Sewall Boutwell
War	John Aaron Rawlins; William Tecumseh Sherman (11 Sep 1869); William Worth Belknap (1 Nov 1869)
Navy	Adolph Edward Borie; George Maxwell Robeson (25 Jun 1869)
Attorney General	Ebenezer Rockwood Hoar; Amos Tappan Akerman (8 Jul 1870); George Henry Williams (10 Jan 1872)
Interior	Jacob Dolson Cox; Columbus Delano (1 Nov 1870)
4 MAR 1873–3 MAR 1877 (TERM 2)	
State	Hamilton Fish
Treasury	William Adams Richardson; Benjamin Helm Bristow (4 Jun 1874); Lot Myrick Morrill (7 Jul 1876)
War	William Worth Belknap; Alphonso Taft (11 Mar 1876); James Donald Cameron (1 Jun 1876)
Navy	George Maxwell Robeson
Attorney General	George Henry Williams; Edward Pierrepont (15 May 1875); Alphonso Taft (1 Jun 1876)
Interior	Columbus Delano; Zachariah Chandler (19 Oct 1875)
	Rutherford B. Hayes
4 MAR 1877–3 MAR 1881	
State	William Maxwell Evarts
Treasury	John Sherman
War	George Washington McCrary; Alexander Ramsey (12 Dec 1879)
Navy	Richard Wigginton Thompson; Nathan Goff, Jr. (6 Jan 1881)
Attorney General	Charles Devens
Interior	Carl Schurz

US Presidential Cabinets (continued)

James A. Garfield

4 MAR 1881–19 SEP 1881	
State	James Gillespie Blaine
Treasury	William Windom
War	Robert Todd Lincoln
Attorney General	(Isaac) Wayne MacVeagh
Navy	William Henry Hunt
Interior	Samuel Jordan Kirkwood

Chester A. Arthur

20 SEP 1881–3 MAR 1885	
State	James Gillespie Blaine; Frederick Theodore Frelinghuysen (19 Dec 1881)
Treasury	William Windom; Charles James Folger (14 Nov 1881); Walter Quintin Gresham (24 Sep 1884); Hugh McCulloch (31 Oct 1884)
War	Robert Todd Lincoln
Navy	William Henry Hunt; William Eaton Chandler (17 Apr 1882)
Attorney General	(Isaac) Wayne MacVeagh; Benjamin Harris Brewster (3 Jan 1882)
Interior	Samuel Jordan Kirkwood; Henry Moore Teller (17 Apr 1882)

Grover Cleveland

4 MAR 1885–3 MAR 1889	
State	Thomas Francis Bayard
Treasury	Daniel Manning; Charles Stebbins Fairchild (1 Apr 1887)
War	William Crowninshield Endicott
Navy	William Collins Whitney
Attorney General	Augustus Hill Garland
Interior	Lucius Quintus Cincinnatus Lamar; William Freeman Vilas (16 Jan 1888)
Agriculture	Norman Jay Colman (13 Feb 1889)

Benjamin Harrison

4 MAR 1889–3 MAR 1893	
State	James Gillespie Blaine; John Watson Foster (29 Jun 1892)
Treasury	William Windom; Charles Foster (24 Feb 1891)
War	Redfield Proctor; Stephen Benton Elkins (24 Dec 1891)
Navy	Benjamin Franklin Tracy
Attorney General	William Henry Harrison Miller
Interior	John Willock Noble
Agriculture	Jeremiah McLain Rusk

Grover Cleveland

4 MAR 1893–3 MAR 1897	
State	Walter Quintin Gresham; Richard Olney (10 Jun 1895)
Treasury	John Griffin Carlisle
War	Daniel Scott Lamont
Navy	Hilary Abner Herbert
Attorney General	Richard Olney; Judson Harmon (11 Jun 1895)
Interior	Hoke Smith; David Rowland Francis (4 Sep 1896)
Agriculture	Julius Sterling Morton

William McKinley

4 MAR 1897–3 MAR 1901 (TERM 1)	
State	John Sherman; William Rufus Day (28 Apr 1898); John Hay (30 Sep 1898)
Treasury	Lyman Judson
War	Russell Alexander Alger; Elihu Root (1 Aug 1899)
Navy	John Davis Long
Attorney General	Joseph McKenna; John William Griggs (1 Feb 1898)
Interior	Cornelius Newton Bliss; Ethan Allen Hitchcock (20 Feb 1899)
Agriculture	James Wilson

4 MAR 1901–14 SEP 1901 (TERM 2)	
State	John Hay
Treasury	Lyman Judson Gage
War	Elihu Root
Navy	John Davis Long
Attorney General	John William Griggs; Philander Chase Knox (10 Apr 1901)
Interior	Ethan Allen Hitchcock
Agriculture	James Wilson

US Presidential Cabinets (continued)

	Theodore Roosevelt
14 SEP 1901–3 MAR 1905 (TERM 1)	
State	John Hay
Treasury	Lyman Judson Gage; Leslie Mortier Shaw (1 Feb 1902)
War	Elihu Root; William Howard Taft (1 Feb 1904)
Navy	John Davis Long; William Henry Moody (1 May 1902); Paul Morton (1 Jul 1904)
Attorney General	Philander Chase Knox; William Henry Moody (1 Jul 1904)
Interior	Ethan Allen Hitchcock
Agriculture	James Wilson
Commerce and Labor	George Bruce Cortelyou (16 Feb 1903); Victor Howard Metcalf (1 Jul 1904)
4 MAR 1905–3 MAR 1909 (TERM 2)	
State	John Hay; Elihu Root (19 Jul 1905); Robert Bacon (27 Jan 1909)
Treasury	Leslie Mortier Shaw; George Bruce Cortelyou (4 Mar 1907)
War	William Howard Taft; Luke Edward Wright (1 Jul 1908)
Navy	Paul Morton; Charles Joseph Bonaparte (1 Jul 1905); Victor Howard Metcalf (17 Dec 1906); Truman Handy Newberry (1 Dec 1908)
Attorney General	William Henry Moody; Charles Joseph Bonaparte (17 Dec 1906)
Interior	Ethan Allen Hitchcock; James Rudolph Garfield (4 Mar 1907)
Agriculture	James Wilson
Commerce and Labor	Victor Howard Metcalf; Oscar Solomon Straus (17 Dec 1906)
	William Howard Taft
4 MAR 1909–3 MAR 1913	
State	Philander Chase Knox
Treasury	Franklin MacVeagh
War	Jacob McGavock Dickinson; Henry Lewis Stimson (22 May 1911)
Navy	George von Lengerke Meyer
Attorney General	George Woodward Wickersham
Interior	Richard Achilles Ballinger; Walter Lowrie Fisher (7 Mar 1911)
Agriculture	James Wilson
Commerce and Labor	Charles Nagel
	Woodrow Wilson
4 MAR 1913–3 MAR 1917 (TERM 1)	
State	William Jennings Bryan; Robert Lansing (23 Jun 1915)
Treasury	William Gibbs McAdoo
War	Lindley Miller Garrison; Newton Diehl Baker (9 Mar 1916)
Navy	Josephus Daniels
Attorney General	James Clark McReynolds; Thomas Watt Gregory (3 Sep 1914)
Interior	Franklin Knight Lane
Agriculture	David Franklin Houston
Commerce	William Cox Redfield (5 Mar 1913)
Labor	William Bauchop Wilson (5 Mar 1913)
4 MAR 1917–3 MAR 1921 (TERM 2)	
State	Robert Lansing; Bainbridge Colby (23 Mar 1920)
Treasury	William Gibbs McAdoo; Carter Glass (16 Dec 1918); David Franklin Houston (2 Feb 1920)
War	Newton Diehl Baker
Navy	Josephus Daniels
Attorney General	Thomas Watt Gregory; Alexander Mitchell Palmer (5 Mar 1919)
Interior	Franklin Knight Lane; John Barton Payne (13 Mar 1920)
Agriculture	David Franklin Houston; Edwin Thomas Meredith (2 Feb 1920)
Commerce	William Cox Redfield; Joshua Willis Alexander (16 Dec 1919)
Labor	William Bauchop Wilson
	Warren G. Harding
4 MAR 1921–2 AUG 1923	
State	Charles Evans Hughes
Treasury	Andrew William Mellon
War	John Wingate Weeks
Navy	Edwin Denby
Attorney General	Harry Micajah Daugherty

US Presidential Cabinets (continued)

	Warren G. Harding (continued)
4 MAR 1921–2 AUG 1923 (CONTINUED)	
Interior	Albert Bacon Fall; Hubert Work (5 Mar 1923)
Agriculture	Henry Cantwell Wallace
Commerce	Herbert Hoover
Labor	James John Davis
	Calvin Coolidge
3 AUG 1923–3 MAR 1925 (TERM 1)	
State	Charles Evans Hughes
Treasury	Andrew William Mellon
War	John Wingate Weeks
Navy	Edwin Denby; Curtis Dwight Wilbur (18 Mar 1924)
Attorney General	Harry Micajah Daugherty; Harlan Fiske Stone (9 Apr 1924)
Interior	Hubert Work
Agriculture	Henry Cantwell Wallace; Howard Mason Gore (21 Nov 1924)
Commerce	Herbert Hoover
Labor	James John Davis
4 MAR 1925–3 MAR 1929 (TERM 2)	
State	Frank Billings Kellogg
Treasury	Andrew William Mellon
War	John Wingate Weeks; Dwight Filley Davis (14 Oct 1925)
Navy	Curtis Dwight Wilbur
Attorney General	John Garibaldi Sargent
Interior	Hubert Work; Roy Owen West (21 Jan 1929)
Agriculture	William Marion Jardine
Commerce	Herbert Hoover; William Fairfield Whiting (11 Dec 1928)
Labor	James John Davis
	Herbert Hoover
4 MAR 1929–3 MAR 1933	
State	Henry Lewis Stimson
Treasury	Andrew William Mellon; Ogden Livingston Mills (13 Feb 1932)
War	James William Good; Patrick Jay Hurley (9 Dec 1929)
Navy	Charles Francis Adams
Attorney General	William De Witt Mitchell
Interior	Ray Lyman Wilbur
Agriculture	Arthur Mastick Hyde
Commerce	Robert Patterson Lamont; Roy Dikeman Chapin (14 Dec 1932)
Labor	James John Davis; William Nuckles Doak (9 Dec 1930)
	Franklin D. Roosevelt
4 MAR 1933–20 JAN 1937 (TERM 1)	
State	Cordell Hull
Treasury	William Hartman Woodin; Henry Morgenthau, Jr. (8 Jan 1934)
War	George Henry Dern
Navy	Claude Augustus Swanson
Attorney General	Homer Stille Cummings
Interior	Harold LeClaire Ickes
Agriculture	Henry Agard Wallace
Commerce	Daniel Calhoun Roper
Labor	Frances Perkins
20 JAN 1937–20 JAN 1941 (TERM 2)	
State	Cordell Hull
Treasury	Henry Morgenthau, Jr.
War	Harry Hines Woodring; Henry Lewis Stimson (10 Jul 1940)
Attorney General	Homer Stille Cummings; Frank Murphy (17 Jan 1939); Robert Houghwout Jackson (18 Jan 1940)
Navy	Claude Augustus Swanson; Charles Edison (11 Jan 1940); Frank Knox (10 Jul 1940)
Interior	Harold LeClaire Ickes
Agriculture	Henry Agard Wallace; Claude Raymond Wickard (5 Sep 1940)
Commerce	Daniel Calhoun Roper; Harry Lloyd Hopkins (23 Jan 1939); Jesse Holman Jones (19 Sep 1940)
Labor	Frances Perkins

US Presidential Cabinets (continued)

	Franklin D. Roosevelt (continued)
20 JAN 1941–20 JAN 1945 (TERM 3)	
State	Cordell Hull; Edward Reilly Stettinius (1 Dec 1944)
Treasury	Henry Morgenthau, Jr.
War	Henry Lewis Stimson
Navy	Frank Knox; James Vincent Forrestal (18 May 1944)
Attorney General	Robert Houghwout Jackson; Francis Biddle (5 Sep 1941)
Interior	Harold LeClaire Ickes
Agriculture	Claude Raymond Wickard
Commerce	Jesse Holman Jones
Labor	Frances Perkins
20 JAN 1945–12 APR 1945 (TERM 4)	
State	Edward Reilly Stettinius
Treasury	Henry Morgenthau, Jr.
War	Henry Lewis Stimson
Navy	James Vincent Forrestal
Attorney General	Francis Biddle
Interior	Harold LeClaire Ickes
Agriculture	Claude Raymond Wickard
Commerce	Jesse Holman Jones; Henry Agard Wallace (2 Mar 1945)
Labor	Frances Perkins
	Harry S. Truman
12 APR 1945–20 JAN 1949 (TERM 1)	
State	Edward Reilly Stettinius; James Francis Byrnes (3 Jul 1945); George Catlett Marshall (21 Jan 1947)
Treasury	Henry Morgenthau, Jr.; Frederick Moore (23 Jul 1945); John Wesley Snyder (25 Jun 1946)
War	Henry Lewis Stimson; Robert Porter Patterson (27 Sep 1945); Kenneth Clairborne Royall (25 Jul 1947)
Defense	James Vincent Forrestal (17 Sep 1947)
Navy	James Vincent Forrestal
Attorney General	Francis Biddle; Thomas Campbell Clark (1 Jul 1945)
Interior	Harold LeClaire Ickes; Julius Albert Krug (18 Mar 1946)
Agriculture	Claude Raymond Wickard; Clinton Presba Anderson (30 Jun 1945); Charles Franklin Brannan (2 Jun 1948)
Commerce	Henry Agard Wallace; William Averell Harriman (28 Jan 1947); Charles Sawyer (6 May 1948)
Labor	Frances Perkins; Lewis Baxter Schwellenbach (1 Jul 1945)
20 JAN 1949–20 JAN 1953 (TERM 2)	
State	Dean Gooderham Acheson
Treasury	John Wesley Snyder
Defense	James Vincent Forrestal; Louis Arthur Johnson (28 Mar 1949); George Catlett Marshall (21 Sep 1950); Robert Abercrombie Lovett (17 Sep 1951)
Attorney General	Thomas Campbell Clark; James Howard McGrath (24 Aug 1949)
Interior	Julius Albert Krug; Oscar Littleton Chapman (19 Jan 1950)
Agriculture	Charles Franklin Brannan
Commerce	Charles Sawyer
Labor	Maurice Joseph Tobin
	Dwight D. Eisenhower
20 JAN 1953–20 JAN 1957 (TERM 1)	
State	John Foster Dulles
Treasury	George Magoffin Humphrey
Defense	Charles Erwin Wilson
Attorney General	Herbert Brownell
Interior	Douglas McKay; Frederick Andrew Seaton (8 Jun 1956)
Agriculture	Ezra Taft Benson
Commerce	Sinclair Weeks
Labor	Martin Patrick Durkin; James Paul Mitchell (9 Oct 1953)
Health, Education, and Welfare	Oveta Culp Hobby (11 Apr 1953); Marion Bayard Folson (1 Aug 1955)
20 JAN 1957–20 JAN 1961 (TERM 2)	
State	John Foster Dulles; Christian Archibald Herter (22 Apr 1959)
Treasury	George Magoffin Humphrey; Robert Bernard Anderson (29 Jul 1957)

US Presidential Cabinets (continued)

	Dwight D. Eisenhower (continued)
20 JAN 1957–20 JAN 1961 (TERM 2) (CONTINUED)	
Defense	Charles Erwin Wilson; Neil Hosler McElroy (9 Oct 1957); Thomas Sovereign Gates, Jr. (2 Dec 1959)
Attorney General	Herbert Brownell, Jr.; William Pierce Rogers (27 Jan 1958)
Interior	Frederick Andrew Seaton
Agriculture	Ezra Taft Benson
Commerce	Sinclair Weeks; Frederick Henry Mueller (10 Aug 1959)
Labor	James Paul Mitchell
Health, Education, and Welfare	Marion Bayard Folsom; Arthur Sherwood Flemming (1 Aug 1958)
	John F. Kennedy
20 JAN 1961–22 NOV 1963	
State	David Dean Rusk
Treasury	C. Douglas Dillon
Defense	Robert S. McNamara
Attorney General	Robert F. Kennedy
Interior	Stewart L. Udall
Agriculture	Orville Lothrop Freeman
Commerce	Luther H. Hodges
Labor	Arthur J. Goldberg; W. Willard Wirtz (25 Sep 1962)
Health, Education, and Welfare	Abraham Ribicoff; Anthony J. Celebrezze (31 Jul 1962)
	Lyndon B. Johnson
22 NOV 1963–20 JAN 1965 (TERM 1)	
State	David Dean Rusk
Treasury	C. Douglas Dillon
Defense	Robert S. McNamara
Attorney General	Robert F. Kennedy
Interior	Stewart L. Udall
Agriculture	Orville Lothrop Freeman
Commerce	Luther H. Hodges
Labor	W. Willard Wirtz
Health, Education, and Welfare	Anthony J. Celebrezze
20 JAN 1965–20 JAN 1969 (TERM 2)	
State	David Dean Rusk
Treasury	C. Douglas Dillon; Henry H. Fowler (1 Apr 1965); Joseph W. Barr (21 Dec 1968)
Defense	Robert S. McNamara; Clark M. Clifford (1 Mar 1968)
Attorney General	Nicholas Katzenbach; Ramsey Clark (10 Mar 1967)
Interior	Stewart L. Udall
Agriculture	Orville Lothrop Freeman
Commerce	John T. Connor; Alexander B. Trowbridge (14 Jun 1967); C.R. Smith (6 Mar 1968)
Labor	W. Willard Wirtz
Health, Education, and Welfare	Anthony J. Celebrezze; John W. Gardner (18 Aug 1965); Wilbur J. Cohen (9 May 1968)
Housing and Urban Development	Robert C. Weaver (18 Jan 1966); Robert C. Wood (7 Jan 1969)
Transportation	Alan Stephenson Boyd (16 Jan 1967)
	Richard M. Nixon
20 JAN 1969–20 JAN 1973 (TERM 1)	
State	William Pierce Rogers
Treasury	David M. Kennedy; John B. Connally (11 Feb 1971); George P. Shultz (12 Jun 1972)
Defense	Melvin R. Laird
Attorney General	John N. Mitchell; Richard G. Kleindienst (12 Jun 1972)
Interior	Walter Hickel; Rogers C.B. Morton (29 Jan 1971)
Agriculture	Clifford Morris Hardin; Earl Lauer Butz (2 Dec 1971)
Commerce	Maurice H. Stans; Peter G. Peterson (21 Feb 1972)
Labor	George P. Shultz; James D. Hodgson (2 Jul 1970)
Health, Education, and Welfare	Robert H. Finch; Elliot L. Richardson (24 Jun 1970)
Housing and Urban Development	George W. Romney
Transportation	John Anthony Volpe
20 JAN 1973–9 AUG 1974 (TERM 2)	
State	William Pierce Rogers; Henry Alfred Kissinger (22 Sep 1973)
Treasury	George P. Shultz; William E. Simon (8 May 1974)

US Presidential Cabinets (continued)

Richard M. Nixon (continued)

20 JAN 1973–9 AUG 1974 (TERM 2) (CONTINUED)

Defense	Elliot L. Richardson; James R. Schlesinger (2 Jul 1973)
Attorney General	Richard G. Kleindienst; Elliot L. Richardson (25 May 1973); William B. Saxbe (4 Jan 1974)
Interior	Rogers C.B. Morton
Agriculture	Earl Lauer Butz
Commerce	Frederick B. Dent
Labor	Peter J. Brennan
Health, Education, and Welfare	Caspar W. Weinberger
Housing and Urban Development	James T. Lynn
Transportation	Claude Stout Brinegar

Gerald R. Ford

9 AUG 1974–20 JAN 1977

State	Henry Alfred Kissinger
Treasury	William E. Simon
Defense	James R. Schlesinger; Donald H. Rumsfeld (20 Nov 1975)
Attorney General	William B. Saxbe; Edward H. Levi (7 Feb 1975)
Interior	Rogers C.B. Morton, Jr.; Stanley K. Hathaway (13 Jun 1975); Thomas S. Kleppe (17 Oct 1975)
Agriculture	Earl Lauer Butz; John Albert Knebel (4 Nov 1976)
Commerce	Frederick B. Dent; Rogers C.B. Morton, Jr. (1 May 1975); Elliot L. Richardson (2 Feb 1976)
Labor	Peter J. Brennan; John T. Dunlop (18 Mar 1975); W.J. Usery, Jr. (10 Feb 1976)
Health, Education, and Welfare	Caspar W. Weinberger; David Mathews (8 Aug 1975)
Housing and Urban Development	James T. Lynn; Carla A. Hills (10 Mar 1975)
Transportation	Claude Stout Brinegar; William Thaddeus Coleman, Jr. (7 Mar 1975)

Jimmy Carter

20 JAN 1977–20 JAN 1981

State	Cyrus Roberts Vance; Edmund Sixtus Muskie (8 May 1980)
Treasury	W. Michael Blumenthal; G. William Miller (6 Aug 1979)
Defense	Harold Brown
Attorney General	Griffin B. Bell; Benjamin R. Civiletti (16 Aug 1979)
Interior	Cecil D. Andrus
Agriculture	Robert Selmer Bergland
Commerce	Juanita M. Kreps; Philip M. Klutznick (9 Jan 1980)
Labor	Ray Marshall
Health, Education, and Welfare	Joseph A. Califano, Jr.; Patricia Roberts Harris (3 Aug 1979)
Health and Human Services	Patricia Roberts Harris (27 Sep 1979)
Housing and Urban Development	Patricia Roberts Harris; Moon Landrieu (24 Sep 1979)
Transportation	Brockman Adams; Neil Edward Goldschmidt (24 Sep 1979)
Energy	James R. Schlesinger (1 Oct 1977); Charles W. Duncan, Jr. (24 Aug 1979)
Education	Shirley M. Hufstedler (6 Dec 1979)

Ronald Reagan

20 JAN 1981–20 JAN 1985 (TERM 1)

State	Alexander Meigs Haig, Jr.; George P. Shultz (16 Jul 1982)
Treasury	Donald T. Regan
Defense	Caspar W. Weinberger
Attorney General	William French Smith
Interior	James G. Watt; William P. Clark (21 Nov 1983)
Agriculture	John Rusling Block
Commerce	Malcolm Baldrige
Labor	Raymond J. Donovan
Health and Human Services	Richard S. Schweiker; Margaret M. Heckler (9 Mar 1983)
Housing and Urban Development	Samuel R. Pierce, Jr.
Transportation	Andrew Lindsay Lewis, Jr.; Elizabeth Hanford Dole (7 Feb 1983)
Energy	James B. Edwards; Donald Paul Hodel (8 Dec 1982)
Education	Terrel H. Bell

20 JAN 1985–20 JAN 1989 (TERM 2)

State	George P. Shultz
Treasury	Donald T. Regan; James A. Baker III (25 Feb 1985); Nicholas F. Brady (18 Aug 1988)

US Presidential Cabinets (continued)

	Ronald Reagan (continued)
20 JAN 1985–20 JAN 1989 (TERM 2) (CONTINUED)	
Defense	Caspar W. Weinberger; Frank C. Carlucci (21 Nov 1987)
Attorney General	William French Smith; Edwin Meese III (25 Feb 1985); Richard Thornburgh (11 Aug 1988)
Interior	Donald Paul Hodel
Agriculture	John Rusling Block; Richard Edmund Lyng (7 Mar 1986)
Commerce	Malcolm Baldrige; C. William Verity (19 Oct 1987)
Labor	Raymond J. Donovan; William E. Brock (29 Apr 1985); Ann Dore McLaughlin (17 Dec 1987)
Health and Human Services	Margaret M. Heckler; Otis R. Bowen (13 Dec 1985)
Housing and Urban Development	Samuel R. Pierce, Jr.
Transportation	Elizabeth Hanford Dole; James Horace Burnley IV (3 Dec 1987)
Energy	John S. Herrington
Education	Terrel H. Bell; William J. Bennett (7 Feb 1985); Lauro F. Cavazos, Jr. (20 Sep 1988)
	George H.W. Bush
20 JAN 1989–20 JAN 1993	
State	James A. Baker III; Lawrence Sidney Eagleburger (8 Dec 1992)
Treasury	Nicholas F. Brady
Defense	Richard B. Cheney
Attorney General	Richard Thornburgh; William Barr (20 Nov 1991)
Interior	Manuel Lujan, Jr.
Agriculture	Clayton Keith Yeutter; Edward Rell Madigan (7 Mar 1991)
Commerce	Robert A. Mosbacher; Barbara H. Franklin (27 Feb 1992)
Labor	Elizabeth Hanford Dole; Lynn Morley Martin (7 Feb 1991)
Health and Human Services	Louis W. Sullivan
Housing and Urban Development	Jack F. Kemp
Transportation	Samuel Knox Skinner; Andrew Hill Card, Jr. (22 Jan 1992)
Energy	James D. Watkins
Education	Lauro F. Cavazos, Jr.; Lamar Alexander (14 Mar 1991)
Veterans Affairs	Edward J. Derwinski (15 Mar 1989)
	William J. Clinton
20 JAN 1993–20 JAN 1997 (TERM 1)	
State	Warren Minor Christopher
Treasury	Lloyd M. Bentsen; Robert E. Rubin (10 Jan 1995)
Defense	Les Aspin; William J. Perry (3 Feb 1994)
Attorney General	Janet Reno
Interior	Bruce Babbitt
Agriculture	Alphonso Michael Espy; Daniel Robert Glickman (30 Mar 1995)
Commerce	Ronald H. Brown; Mickey Kantor (12 Apr 1996)
Labor	Robert B. Reich
Health and Human Services	Donna E. Shalala
Housing and Urban Development	Henry G. Cisneros
Transportation	Federico Fabian Peña
Energy	Hazel R. O'Leary
Education	Richard W. Riley
Veterans Affairs	Jesse Brown
20 JAN 1997–20 JAN 2001 (TERM 2)	
State	Madeleine Korbel Albright
Treasury	Robert E. Rubin; Lawrence H. Summers (2 Jul 1999)
Defense	William S. Cohen
Attorney General	Janet Reno
Interior	Bruce Babbitt
Agriculture	Daniel Robert Glickman
Commerce	William M. Daley; Norman Y. Mineta (21 Jul 2000)
Labor	Alexis Herman
Health and Human Services	Donna E. Shalala
Housing and Urban Development	Andrew M. Cuomo
Transportation	Rodney Earl Slater
Energy	Federico Fabian Peña; Bill Richardson (18 Aug 1998)
Education	Richard W. Riley
Veterans Affairs	Togo D. West, Jr.

US Presidential Cabinets (continued)

George W. Bush

20 JAN 2001–20 JAN 2005 (TERM 1)	
State	Colin L. Powell
Treasury	Paul H. O'Neill; John W. Snow (7 Feb 2003)
Defense	Donald H. Rumsfeld
Attorney General	John Ashcroft
Interior	Gale A. Norton
Agriculture	Ann M. Veneman
Commerce	Donald L. Evans
Labor	Elaine L. Chao
Health and Human Services	Tommy G. Thompson
Housing and Urban Development	Mel Martinez; Alphonso Jackson (31 Mar 2004)
Transportation	Norman Y. Mineta
Energy	Spencer Abraham
Education	Rod Paige
Veterans Affairs	Anthony J. Principi
Homeland Security	Tom Ridge (8 Oct 2001)

20 JAN 2005– (TERM 2)		WEB SITE
State	Condoleezza Rice	<www.state.gov>
Treasury	John W. Snow; Henry M. Paulson, Jr. (19 Jun 2006)	<www.ustreas.gov>
Defense	Donald Rumsfeld; Robert M. Gates (18 Dec 2006)	<www.defenselink.mil>
Attorney General	Alberto R. Gonzales; Michael Mukasey (9 Nov 2007)	<www.usdoj.gov>
Interior	Gale A. Norton; Dirk Kempthorne (26 May 2006)	<www.doi.gov>
Agriculture	Mike Johanns; Ed Schafer (28 Jan 2008)	<www.usda.gov>
Commerce	Carlos M. Gutierrez	<www.commerce.gov>
Labor	Elaine L. Chao	<www.dol.gov>
Health and Human Services	Michael O. Leavitt	<www.hhs.gov>
Housing and Urban Development	Alphonso Jackson; Steve Preston (5 Jun 2008)	<www.hud.gov>
Transportation	Norman Y. Mineta; Mary E. Peters (30 Sep 2006)	<www.dot.gov>
Energy	Samuel W. Bodman	<www.energy.gov>
Education	Margaret Spellings	<www.ed.gov>
Veterans Affairs	R. James Nicholson; James B. Peake (20 Dec 2007)	<www.va.gov>
Homeland Security	Michael Chertoff	<www.dhs.gov>

Additionally, the White House lists the following as cabinet-rank members: Vice President Richard B. Cheney, Chief of Staff Joshua B. Bolten, Environmental Protection Agency Administrator Stephen Johnson, US Trade Representative Susan Schwab, Office of Management and Budget Director Jim Nussle, and National Drug Control Policy Director John Walters.

The Great Red Spot, the most conspicuous feature on the planet Jupiter, is an enormous storm system that has been raging for more than 300 years. It is about 26,000 km (16,200 mi) long and 14,000 km (8,700 mi) wide—large enough to engulf two Earth-sized planets side by side.

Impeachment

The American federal impeachment process is rooted in Article II, Section 4, of the US Constitution. Impeachment has rarely been employed, largely because it is such a cumbersome process. It can occupy Congress for a lengthy period of time, fill thousands of pages of testimony, and involve conflicting and troublesome political pressures. Repeated attempts in the US Congress to amend the procedure, however, have been unsuccessful, partly because impeachment is regarded as an integral part of the system of checks and balances in the US government.

Andrew Johnson was the first US president ever impeached. In 1868 he was charged with attempting to remove, contrary to statute, the secretary of war, Edwin M. Stanton, with inducing a general of the army to violate an act of Congress, and with contempt of Congress. Johnson was acquitted by a margin of a single vote. In 1974 the Judiciary Committee of the House of Representatives voted three articles of impeachment against Pres. Richard M. Nixon, but he resigned before impeachment proceedings in the full House could begin. In December 1998 the House of Representatives voted to impeach Pres. William J. Clinton, charging him with perjury and obstruction of justice in investigations of his relationship with a White House intern, Monica Lewinsky. In the trial, the Senate voted not guilty on the perjury charge (55–45) and not guilty on the obstruction of justice charge (50–50); since 67 guilty votes are needed for a conviction, President Clinton was acquitted.

Every US state except Oregon provides for the removal of executive and judicial officers by impeachment. Exact procedures vary somewhat from state to state, but they are all similar to federal impeachment.

Supreme Court

Justices of the Supreme Court of the United States

Listed under presidents who made appointments (bold). Chief justices' names appear in italics.

NAME	TERM OF SERVICE[1]
George Washington	
John Jay	1789–95
James Wilson	1789–98
John Rutledge	1790–91
William Cushing	1790–1810
John Blair	1790–96
James Iredell	1790–99
Thomas Johnson	1792–93
William Paterson	1793–1806
John Rutledge[2]	1795
Samuel Chase	1796–1811
Oliver Ellsworth	1796–1800
John Adams	
Bushrod Washington	1799–1829
Alfred Moore	1800–04
John Marshall	1801–35
Thomas Jefferson	
William Johnson	1804–34
Brockholst Livingston	1807–23
Thomas Todd	1807–26
James Madison	
Gabriel Duvall	1811–35
Joseph Story	1812–45
James Monroe	
Smith Thompson	1823–43
John Quincy Adams	
Robert Trimble	1826–28
Andrew Jackson	
John McLean	1830–61
Henry Baldwin	1830–44
James M. Wayne	1835–67
Roger Brooke Taney	1836–64
Philip P. Barbour	1836–41
Martin Van Buren	
John Catron	1837–65
John McKinley	1838–52
Peter V. Daniel	1842–60
John Tyler	
Samuel Nelson	1845–72
James Polk	
Levi Woodbury	1845–51
Robert C. Grier	1846–70
Millard Fillmore	
Benjamin R. Curtis	1851–57
Franklin Pierce	
John Archibald Campbell	1853–61
James Buchanan	
Nathan Clifford	1858–81
Abraham Lincoln	
Noah H. Swayne	1862–81
Samuel Freeman Miller	1862–90
David Davis	1862–77
Stephen Johnson Field	1863–97
Salmon P. Chase	1864–73
Ulysses S. Grant	
William Strong	1870–80
Joseph P. Bradley	1870–92
Ward Hunt	1873–82
Morrison Remick Waite	1874–88
Rutherford B. Hayes	
John Marshall Harlan	1877–1911
William B. Woods	1881–87
James Garfield	
Stanley Matthews	1881–89
Chester A. Arthur	
Horace Gray	1882–1902
Samuel Blatchford	1882–93
Grover Cleveland	
Lucius Q.C. Lamar	1888–93
Melville Weston Fuller	1888–1910
Benjamin Harrison	
David J. Brewer	1890–1910
Henry B. Brown	1891–1906
George Shiras, Jr.	1892–1903
Howell E. Jackson	1893–95
Grover Cleveland	
Edward Douglass White	1894–1910
Rufus Wheeler Peckham	1896–1909
William McKinley	
Joseph McKenna	1898–1925
Theodore Roosevelt	
Oliver Wendell Holmes	1902–32
William R. Day	1903–22
William H. Moody	1906–10
William H. Taft	
Horace H. Lurton	1910–14
Charles Evans Hughes	1910–16
Willis Van Devanter	1911–37
Joseph R. Lamar	1911–16
Edward Douglass White	1910–21
Mahlon Pitney	1912–22
Woodrow Wilson	
James C. McReynolds	1914–41
Louis Brandeis	1916–39
John H. Clarke	1916–22
Warren G. Harding	
William Howard Taft	1921–30
George Sutherland	1922–38
Pierce Butler	1923–39
Edward T. Sanford	1923–30
Calvin Coolidge	
Harlan Fiske Stone	1925–41
Herbert Hoover	
Charles Evans Hughes	1930–41
Owen Roberts	1930–45
Benjamin N. Cardozo	1932–38
Franklin D. Roosevelt	
Hugo L. Black	1937–71
Stanley F. Reed	1938–57
Felix Frankfurter	1939–62
William O. Douglas	1939–75
Frank Murphy	1940–49
Harlan Fiske Stone	1941–46
James F. Byrnes	1941–42
Robert H. Jackson	1941–54
Wiley B. Rutledge	1943–49
Harry S. Truman	
Harold H. Burton	1945–58
Fred M. Vinson	1946–53
Tom C. Clark	1949–67
Sherman Minton	1949–56
Dwight D. Eisenhower	
Earl Warren	1953–69
John Marshall Harlan	1955–71
William J. Brennan, Jr.	1956–90
Charles E. Whittaker	1957–62
Potter Stewart	1958–81
John F. Kennedy	
Byron R. White	1962–93
Arthur J. Goldberg	1962–65
Lyndon B. Johnson	
Abe Fortas	1965–69
Thurgood Marshall	1967–91
Richard M. Nixon	
Warren E. Burger	1969–86
Harry A. Blackmun	1970–94
Lewis F. Powell, Jr.	1972–87
William H. Rehnquist	1972–86
Gerald Ford	
John Paul Stevens	1975–
Ronald Reagan	
Sandra Day O'Connor	1981–2006
William H. Rehnquist	1986–2005
Antonin Scalia	1986–
Anthony M. Kennedy	1988–
George H.W. Bush	
David H. Souter	1990–
Clarence Thomas	1991–
Bill Clinton	
Ruth Bader Ginsburg	1993–
Stephen G. Breyer	1994–
George W. Bush	
John G. Roberts	2005–
Samuel Anthony Alito, Jr.	2006–

[1] *The year the justice took the judicial oath is here used as the beginning date of service, for until that oath is taken the justice is not vested with the prerogatives of the office. Justices, however, receive their commissions ("letters patent") before taking their oaths—in some instances, in the preceding year.* [2] *John Rutledge was acting chief justice; the US Senate refused to confirm him.*

Milestones of US Supreme Court Jurisprudence

Information includes cases' short names, citation, year of release, and a short description of the Supreme Court's findings and importance for US law.

***Marbury* v. *Madison*, 5 U.S. 137 (1803):** the first instance in which the high court declared an act of Congress (the Judiciary Act of 1789, which in part authorized the court to compel action by the executive branch) to be unconstitutional, thus establishing the doctrine of judicial review.

***Martin* v. *Hunter's Lessee*, 14 U.S. 304 (1816):** asserted the US Supreme Court's power of appellate review of state Supreme Court decisions.

***McCulloch* v. *Maryland*, 17 U.S. 316 (1819):** affirmed the constitutional doctrine of the "implied powers" of Congress, determining that Congress had not only the powers expressly conferred upon it by the Constitution but also all authority "appropriate" to carry out such powers.

***Dred Scott* v. *Sandford*, 60 U.S. 393 (1857):** ruled that blacks, free or enslaved, were not citizens under the Constitution, and further determined that only states, and not Congress or territorial governments, had the power to prohibit slavery, thus overturning the Missouri Compromise of 1820 and legalizing slavery in all US territories. The citizenship of all races was affirmed with the ratification of the Fourteenth Amendment in 1868.

***Santa Clara County* v. *Southern Pacific Railroad Co.*, 118 U.S. 394 (1886):** established that corporations are "persons" within the meaning of the Fourteenth Amendment, extending to them the rights of due process and equal protection.

***Plessy* v. *Ferguson*, 163 U.S. 537 (1896):** permitted racial segregation in "separate but equal" public facilities.

***Lochner* v. *New York*, 198 U.S. 45 (1905):** found that a state labor law limiting the number of hours in the work week violated due process because the "right of contract between the employer and employees" is protected under the Fourteenth Amendment.

***Standard Oil Co. of New Jersey et al.* v. *United States*, 221 U.S. 1 (1911):** ruled that the activities of the Standard Oil Company of New Jersey, a holding company that through its subsidiaries controlled most of the US petroleum industry, constituted an undue restraint of trade and ordered the company's dissolution under the Sherman Antitrust Act.

***Schenck* v. *United States*, 249 U.S. 47 (1919):** found, in the case of an American socialist convicted of espionage for distributing antidraft leaflets during wartime, that First Amendment freedom of expression is limited when there exists a "clear and present danger that [the speech] will bring about the substantive evils that Congress has a right to prevent."

***Brown* v. *Board of Education of Topeka*, 349 U.S. 294 (1954):** ruled that racial segregation in public schools violated the Fourteenth Amendment, overturning the doctrine of "separate but equal" facilities reached in *Plessy* v. *Ferguson*.

***Mapp* v. *Ohio*, 367 U.S. 643 (1961):** found that the Fourth Amendment prohibition of unreasonable search and seizure, and the inadmissibility of evidence obtained in violation of it, applied to state as well as to federal government.

***Baker* v. *Carr*, 369 U.S. 186 (1962):** ruled that, under the equal protection clause of the Fourteenth Amendment, issues relating to the apportionment of congressional districts could be resolved in federal courts.

***Gideon* v. *Wainwright*, 372 U.S. 335 (1963):** declared that the Sixth Amendment right to counsel applies to defendants in state as well as federal courts.

***New York Times Co.* v. *Sullivan*, 376 U.S. 254 (1964):** protected the press from the prospects of large damage awards in libel cases by requiring that "actual malice" be demonstrated; public officials who sue for damages must prove that a falsehood had been issued with knowledge that it was false or in reckless disregard of whether it was false or not.

***Heart of Atlanta Motel* v. *United States*, 379 U.S. 241; *Katzenbach* v. *McClung*, 379 U.S. 294 (1964):** upheld Title II of the Civil Rights Act of 1964 (which prohibits segregation or discrimination in places of public accommodation involved in interstate commerce) in the cases of an Atlanta motel and a Birmingham AL restaurant, both of which discriminated against blacks. The court ruled that both engaged in transactions affecting interstate commerce, and thus were within the purview of congressional regulation, and that the Civil Rights Act itself was constitutional.

***Griswold* v. *Connecticut*, 381 U.S. 479 (1965):** ruled that a state law prohibiting the use of contraceptives (including providing information, advice, or prescriptions for them) violated "the right of marital privacy" implied within the Bill of Rights.

***Miranda* v. *Arizona*, 384 U.S. 436 (1966):** ruled that the prosecution may not use statements made by a person in police custody unless minimum procedural safeguards were followed and established guidelines to guarantee arrested persons' Fifth Amendment right not to be compelled to incriminate themselves. These guidelines included informing arrestees prior to questioning that they have the right to remain silent, that anything they say may be used against them as evidence, and that they have the right to the counsel of an attorney.

***Loving* v. *Virginia*, 388 U.S. 1 (1967):** declared that antimiscegenation laws (prohibitions of interracial marriage) have no legitimate purpose outside of racial discrimination and thus violate the Fourteenth Amendment.

***New York Times Co.* v. *United States*, 403 U.S. 713 (1971):** in what was known as the "Pentagon Papers" case, the court vacated a US Justice Department injunction that restrained the *New York Times* and *Washington Post* from publishing excerpts of a top-secret report on the Vietnam War, ruling that such prior restraint of the press was subject to a "heavy burden of . . . justification," which the government failed to meet.

***Wisconsin* v. *Yoder*, 406 U.S. 205 (1972):** in the case of members of an Old Order Amish community who refused on religious grounds to keep their children in school past the eighth grade, found that the right to free exercise of religion outweighed the state's interest in universal education.

***Roe* v. *Wade*, 410 U.S. 113 (1973):** held that overly restrictive state regulation of abortion is unconstitutional. In balancing the "compelling state interest[s]" in protecting the health of pregnant women and the potential life of fetuses, the court ruled that regulation of abortion could begin no sooner than about the end of the first trimester, with increasing regulation permissible in the second and third trimesters;

the state's interest in protecting the fetus was found to increase with the fetus's "capability for meaningful life outside the mother's womb."

***Gregg* v. *Georgia*, 428 U.S. 153; *Proffitt* v. *Florida*, 428 U.S. 242; *Jurek* v. *Texas*, 428 U.S. 262 (1976):** ruled that the death penalty, in and of itself, does not violate the Eighth Amendment if applied under certain guidelines in first-degree murder cases.

***Cruzan by Cruzan* v. *Director, Missouri Department of Health*, 497 U.S. 261 (1990):** found that, in the absence of "clear and convincing evidence" of a person's desire to refuse medical treatment or not to live on life support, a state could require that such treatment continue. When such evidence exists, however, a patient's wishes must be respected.

***Rust* v. *Sullivan*, 500 U.S. 173 (1991):** ruled that Congress could prohibit recipients of family-planning funds from providing or discussing abortion as a family planning option. The court held that this did not violate the First Amendment because clinics were still free to provide such counseling as a "financially and physically" separate activity.

***Planned Parenthood of Southeastern Pennsylvania* v. *Casey*, 505 U.S. 833 (1992):** softened the ruling in *Roe* v. *Wade* by finding that some state regulation of abortion prior to fetal viability, including a 24-hour waiting period, mandatory counseling, and a parental-consent requirement for minors, is permissible as long as the regulations do not place an "undue burden" on the woman.

***Romer* v. *Evans*, 517 U.S. 620 (1996):** invalidated a Colorado referendum passed by popular vote that prohibited conferral of protected status on the basis of sexual orientation; the court ruled that the referendum was overbroad, bore little relationship to legimate state interests, and violated the Fourteenth Amendment of the US Constitution.

***Oncale* v. *Sundowner Offshore Services, Inc., et al.*, 523 U.S. 75 (1998):** found that Title VII's prohibition of workplace sexual discrimination applied equally in cases when the harasser and victim are of the same sex.

***Boy Scouts of America* v. *Dale*, 530 U.S. 640 (2000):** ruled that the Boy Scouts, because it is a private organization, was within its rights when it dismissed a scoutmaster expressly because of his avowed homosexuality. The court reasoned that a state statute banning discrimination on the basis of sexual orientation in places of public accommodation was outweighed by the Scouts' First Amendment right to freedom of association.

***Stenberg* v. *Carhart*, 530 U.S. 914 (2000):** ruled that a state law criminalizing the performance of dilation and extraction—or "partial-birth"—abortions violated the Constitution (following the same reasoning as in *Roe* v. *Wade*) because it allowed no consideration of the health of the woman in choosing the procedure.

***Bush* v. *Gore*, 531 U.S. 98 (2000):** stopped the manual recounts, then under way in certain Florida counties at the demand of Al Gore, of disputed ballots from the November 2000 presidential election on the grounds that inconsistent vote-counting standards among the several counties involved amounted to a violation of the Fourteenth Amendment's equal protection clause. Because George W. Bush at the time led Al Gore in the number of officially recognized Florida votes, the decision meant that he would win the state and thus the general election, despite having lost the popular vote.

***Atkins* v. *Virginia*, 536 U.S. 304 (2002):** ruled that the death penalty, when applied to mentally retarded individuals, constitutes a "cruel and unusual punishment" prohibited by the Eighth Amendment.

***Eldred* v. *Ashcroft*, 537 U.S. 186 (2003):** upheld a 1998 federal statute that granted a 20-year extension to all existing copyrights.

***Lockyer* v. *Andrade*, 538 U.S. 63; *Ewing* v. *California*, 538 U.S. 11 (2003):** upheld a "three-strikes" law that imposes long prison sentences for a third offense, even nonviolent crimes.

***State Farm Mutual Auto Insurance Co.* v. *Campbell*, 538 U.S. 408 (2003):** placed limits on "irrational and arbitrary" punitive damages and established new guidelines that generally bar consideration of a defendant's wealth or conduct outside the state's borders and lower the ratio of punitive to compensatory damages.

***Brown* v. *Legal Foundation of Washington*, 538 U.S. 216 (2003):** held that channeling interest on short-term deposits by lawyers on accounts held in trust for their clients to legal assistance programs for the poor is not an unconstitutional taking of property.

***Nevada Department of Human Resources* v. *Hibbs*, 538 U.S. 721 (2003):** held that state governments may be sued by their employees for failing to honor the federally guaranteed right to take time off from work for family emergencies.

***United States* v. *American Library Association*, 539 U.S. 194 (2003):** upheld the Children's Internet Protection Act, which conditions access to federal grants and subsidies upon the installation of antipornography filters on all Internet-connected computers.

***Grutter* v. *Bollinger*, 539 U.S. 306 (2003); *Gratz* v. *Bollinger*, 539 U.S. 244 (2003):** in a pair of decisions addressing affirmative action in admissions at the University of Michigan, the court endorsed *Regents of the University of California* v. *Bakke*'s articulation of diversity as a compelling interest, so long as the admissions program's operation is "holistic" and "individualized," and upheld Michigan's law school admissions program. In *Gratz*, the court struck down Michigan's undergraduate admissions program because reserving spaces for underrepresented minorities was the "functional equivalent of a quota."

***Georgia* v. *Ashcroft*, 539 U.S. 461 (2003):** ruled that race-sensitive redistricting could consider more general minority influence in the political process when drawing particular district lines rather than addressing only the actual number of minority voters present.

***Lawrence* v. *Texas*, 539 U.S. 558 (2003):** explicitly overruling *Bowers* v. *Hardwick*, 478 U.S. 186 (1986), the court declared that gay men and lesbians are "entitled to respect for their private lives" under the due process clause of the Fourteenth Amendment and rendered unconstitutional state statutes outlawing sex between adults of the same gender.

***Elk Grove Unified School District* v. *Newdow*, 542 U.S. 1 (2004):** sidestepping the question of whether the inclusion of the phrase "under God" was an unconstitutional endorsement by a public school of a religious viewpoint, the court ruled that Michael Newdow, who filed suit on behalf of his daughter, lacked standing to file on her behalf because he was not the custodial parent.

***Blakely* v. *Washington*, 542 U.S. 296 (2004):** held that the Washington state system permitting judges to make independent findings that increase a convicted defendant's sentence beyond the ordinary range for the crime violated the Sixth Amendment guarantee of a right to trial by jury and to a higher standard of proof.

***Cheney* v. *US District Court*, 542 U.S. 367 (2004):** sent the Sierra Club and Judicial Watch back to the lower court in a dispute over the level of executive privilege the vice president's energy policy task force exercised in the face of discovery orders. The court held that "[s]pecial considerations control when the Executive's interests in maintaining its autonomy and safeguarding its communications' confidentiality are implicated."

***Hamdi* v. *Rumsfeld*, 542 U.S. 507; *Rasul v. Bush*, 542 U.S. 466 (2004):** ruled that while Congress may empower the executive branch to detain even US citizens as enemy combatants, any enemy combatant in US custody may challenge detention as illegal in federal court with the assistance of counsel. The court declared that "a state of war is not a blank check for the president when it comes to the rights of the nation's citizens."

***United States* v. *Booker* and *United States v. Fanfan*, 543 U.S. 220 (2005):** ruled that mandatory federal sentencing guidelines violated defendants' Sixth Amendment right to jury trials because they require judges to make decisions affecting prison time.

***Roper* v. *Simmons*, 543 U.S. 551 (2005):** held that the execution of a felon who had committed a capital crime while a juvenile violates the Eighth Amendment prohibition of cruel and unusual punishment, that "the State cannot extinguish [the juvenile defendant's] life and his potential to attain a mature understanding of his own humanity."

***Gonzales* v. *Raich*, 545 U.S. 1 (2005):** ruled that doctors may not prescribe marijuana to ease the symtoms patients and sufferers of other serious illnesses experience. The Court held that the federal Controlled Substances Act, which bars medical use of marijuana, overrides state legislation allowing such use.

***Kelo* v. *City of New London*, 545 U.S. 469 (2005):** found that governmental entities may exercise the power of eminent domain over private property and cede the property to private developers to promote economic growth, so long as a carefully formulated plan to provide significant benefits to the community provides a rational basis for the taking.

***Gonzales* v. *Oregon*, 546 U.S. 243 (2006):** ruled that an Oregon law permitting physicians to provide lethal drugs to terminally ill patients did not violate the Controlled Substances Act.

***Hamdan* v. *Rumsfeld*, 548 U.S. 557 (2006):** ruled that the government's special military commissions were not lawful courts. The commissions were to have tried some of the prisoners who had been captured in the "global war on terror."

***Gonzales* v. *Carhart*, 550 U.S. ___ (2007):** held that a federal law banning "partial-birth" abortion was not unconstitutional.

***Parents Involved in Community Schools* v. *Seattle School District No. 1*, 551 U.S. ___ (2007):** held that using a student's race in determining the availability of a spot at a desired school, even for the purpose of preventing resegregation, violated the 14th Amendment.

***Hein* v. *Freedom from Religion Foundation*, 551 U.S. __ (2007):** ruled that taxpayers had no standing to challenge the use of federal money to support the Office of Faith-Based and Community Initiatives, despite questions about the separation of church and state.

***Federal Election Commission* v. *Wisconsin Right to Life*, 551 U.S. ___ (2007):** held that a restriction on union- and corporate-sponsored advertising from a 2002 campaign-finance law threatened free speech.

***District of Columbia* v. *Heller*, 554 U.S. ___ (2008):** ruled that citizens have the right to bear arms without the need to be in service to a militia. This decision struck down a Washington DC handgun ban and threatened scores of other such bans nationwide.

***Boumediene* v. *Bush*, 553 U.S. ___ (2008):** ruled that foreign prisoners held at Guantánamo Bay, Cuba, have the right to challenge their detention in US courts.

United States Congress

The Senate, 110th Congress

According to Article I, Section 3, of the US Constitution, a US senator must be at least 30 years old, must reside in the state he or she represents at the time of the election, and must have been a citizen of the United States for 9 years. Voters elect two senators from each state; terms are for 6 years and begin on 3 January. Senators originally made US$6.00 per day; each current senator's salary is US$169,300 per year. The majority and minority leaders and the president pro tempore receive US$181,100 per year.

US Senate Web site: <www.senate.gov>.

Senate leadership

president:	Richard Cheney
president pro tempore:	Robert C. Byrd
majority leader:	Harry Reid
minority leader:	Mitch McConnell
asst. majority leader (majority whip):	Dick Durbin
asst. minority leader (minority whip):	Jon Kyl

STATE	NAME AND PARTY	SERVICE BEGAN	TERM ENDS
Alabama	Richard Shelby (R)	1987	2011
	Jeff Sessions (R)	1997	2009
Alaska	Ted Stevens (R)	1968[1]	2009
	Lisa Murkowski (R)	2002	2011
Arizona	John McCain (R)	1987	2011
	Jon Kyl (R)	1995	2013
Arkansas	Blanche Lincoln (D)	1999	2011
	Mark Pryor (D)	2003	2009
California	Dianne Feinstein (D)	1992[2]	2013
	Barbara Boxer (D)	1993	2011
Colorado	Wayne Allard (R)	1997	2009
	Ken Salazar (D)	2005	2011

The Senate, 110th Congress (continued)

STATE	NAME AND PARTY	SERVICE BEGAN	TERM ENDS
Connecticut	Chris Dodd (D)	1981	2011
	Joe Lieberman (ID)	1989	2013
Delaware	Joseph R. Biden, Jr. (D)	1973	2009
	Tom Carper (D)	2001	2013
Florida	Bill Nelson (D)	2001	2013
	Mel Martinez (R)	2005	2011
Georgia	Saxby Chambliss (R)	2003	2009
	Johnny Isakson (R)	2005	2011
Hawaii	Daniel K. Inouye (D)	1963	2011
	Daniel Kahikina Akaka (D)	1990[3]	2013
Idaho	Larry Craig (R)	1991	2009
	Mike Crapo (R)	1999	2011
Illinois	Dick Durbin (D)	1997	2009
	Barack Obama (D)	2005	2011
Indiana	Richard G. Lugar (R)	1977	2013
	Evan Bayh (D)	1999	2011
Iowa	Chuck Grassley (R)	1981	2011
	Tom Harkin (D)	1985	2009
Kansas	Sam Brownback (R)	1996[4]	2011
	Pat Roberts (R)	1997	2009
Kentucky	Mitch McConnell (R)	1985	2009
	Jim Bunning (R)	1999	2011
Louisiana	Mary L. Landrieu (D)	1997	2009
	David Vitter (R)	2005	2011
Maine	Olympia J. Snowe (R)	1995	2013
	Susan Collins (R)	1997	2009
Maryland	Benjamin L. Cardin (D)	2007	2013
	Barbara Mikulski (D)	1987	2011
Massachusetts	Edward M. Kennedy (D)	1962	2013
	John Kerry (D)	1985	2009
Michigan	Carl Levin (D)	1979	2009
	Debbie Stabenow (D)	2001	2013
Minnesota	Amy Klobuchar (D)	2007	2013
	Norm Coleman (R)	2003	2009
Mississippi	Thad Cochran (R)	1979	2009
	Roger Wicker (R)	2007[5]	2009
Missouri	Kit Bond (R)	1987	2011
	Claire McCaskill (D)	2007	2013
Montana	Max Baucus (D)	1979	2009
	Jon Tester (D)	2007	2013
Nebraska	Chuck Hagel (R)	1997	2009
	Ben Nelson (D)	2001	2013
Nevada	Harry Reid (D)	1987	2011
	John Ensign (R)	2001	2013
New Hampshire	Judd Gregg (R)	1993	2011
	John E. Sununu (R)	2003	2009
New Jersey	Robert Menendez (D)	2006[6]	2013
	Frank R. Lautenberg (D)	2003	2009
New Mexico	Pete V. Domenici (R)	1973	2009
	Jeff Bingaman (D)	1983	2013
New York	Charles E. Schumer (D)	1999	2011
	Hillary Rodham Clinton (D)	2001	2013
North Carolina	Elizabeth Dole (R)	2003	2009
	Richard Burr (R)	2005	2011
North Dakota	Kent Conrad (D)	1987	2013
	Byron L. Dorgan (D)	1993	2011
Ohio	Sherrod Brown (D)	2007	2013
	George V. Voinovich (R)	1999	2011
Oklahoma	James M. Inhofe (R)	1994[7]	2009
	Tom Coburn (R)	2005	2011
Oregon	Ron Wyden (D)	1996[8]	2011
	Gordon Smith (R)	1997	2009
Pennsylvania	Arlen Specter (R)	1981	2011
	Robert P. Casey (D)	2007	2013
Rhode Island	Jack Reed (D)	1997	2009
	Sheldon Whitehouse (D)	2007	2013
South Carolina	Lindsey Graham (R)	2003	2009
	Jim DeMint (R)	2005	2011

The Senate, 110th Congress (continued)

STATE	NAME AND PARTY	SERVICE BEGAN	TERM ENDS
South Dakota	Tim Johnson (D)	1997	2009
	John Thune (R)	2005	2011
Tennessee	Bob Corker (R)	2007	2013
	Lamar Alexander (R)	2003	2009
Texas	Kay Bailey Hutchison (R)	1993[9]	2013
	John Cornyn (R)	2002	2009
Utah	Orrin G. Hatch (R)	1977	2013
	Bob Bennett (R)	1993	2011
Vermont	Patrick Leahy (D)	1975	2011
	Bernie Sanders (I)	2007	2013
Virginia	John Warner (R)	1979	2009
	Jim Webb (D)	2007	2013
Washington	Patty Murray (D)	1993	2011
	Maria Cantwell (D)	2001	2013
West Virginia	Robert C. Byrd (D)	1959	2013
	Jay Rockefeller (D)	1985	2009
Wisconsin	Herb Kohl (D)	1989	2013
	Russ Feingold (D)	1993	2011
Wyoming	John Barrasso (R)	2007[10]	2009
	Mike Enzi (R)	1997	2009

Republicans: 49; Democrats: 49; Independents: 1; Independent Democrats: 1

[1]*Ted Stevens was appointed in December 1968 to fill the vacancy caused by the death of Edward Lewis (Bob) Bartlett.* [2]*Dianne Feinstein was elected in November 1992 to complete the term of Pete Wilson, who resigned in 1991 to become California's governor.* [3]*Daniel Kahikina Akaka was appointed in April 1990 after winning a special election to fill the vacancy caused by the death of Spark M. Matsunaga.* [4]*Sam Brownback was elected in November 1996 to complete the term of Bob Dole, who resigned to campaign for the presidency.* [5]*Roger Wicker was appointed in December 2007 to fill the vacancy caused by the resignation of Trent Lott.* [6]*Robert Menendez was appointed in January 2006 to fill the vacancy caused by the resignation of Jon S. Corzine.* [7]*James M. Inhofe was elected in November 1994 to complete the term of David Boren, who resigned to become president of the University of Oklahoma.* [8]*Ron Wyden was elected in January 1996 to complete the term of Bob Packwood, who resigned in 1995.* [9]*Kay Bailey Hutchison was elected in June 1993 to complete the term of Lloyd Bentsen, Jr., who resigned to become secretary of the treasury.* [10]*John Barrasso was appointed in June 2007 to fill the vacancy caused by the death of Craig Thomas.*

Senate Standing Committees

COMMITTEE	CHAIRMAN (PARTY–STATE)	RANKING MINORITY MEMBER (PARTY–STATE)	NUMBER OF MEMBERS		NUMBER OF SUBCOMMITTEES
			MAJORITY	MINORITY	
Agriculture, Nutrition, and Forestry	Tom Harkin (D-IA)	Saxby Chambliss (R-GA)	11	10	5
Appropriations	Robert C. Byrd (D-WV)	Thad Cochran (R-MS)	15	14	12
Armed Services	Carl Levin (D-MI)	John McCain (R-AZ)	13	12	6
Banking, Housing, and Urban Affairs	Chris Dodd (D-CT)	Richard Shelby (R-AL)	11	10	5
Budget	Kent Conrad (D-ND)	Judd Gregg (R-NH)	12[1]	11	none
Commerce, Science, and Transportation	Daniel K. Inouye (D-HI)	Ted Stevens (R-AK)	12	11	7
Energy and Natural Resources	Jeff Bingaman (D-NM)	Pete V. Domenici (R-NM)	12[1]	11	4
Environment and Public Works	Barbara Boxer (D-CA)	James M. Imhofe (R-OK)	10[1]	9	6
Finance	Max Baucus (D-MT)	Chuck Grassley (R-IA)	11	10	5
Foreign Relations	Joseph R. Biden, Jr. (D-DE)	Richard G. Lugar (R-IN)	11	10	7
Health, Education, Labor, and Pensions	Edward M. Kennedy (D-MA)	Mike Enzi (R-WY)	11[1]	10	3
Homeland Security and Governmental Affairs	Joe Lieberman (ID-CT)	Susan Collins (R-ME)	9	8	3
Judiciary	Patrick Leahy (D-VT)	Arlen Specter (R-PA)	10	9	7
Rules and Administration	Dianne Feinstein (D-CA)	Bob Bennett (R-UT)	10	9	none
Small Business and Entrepreneurship	John Kerry (D-MA)	Olympia J. Snowe (R-ME)	10	9	none
Veterans Affairs	Daniel K. Akaka (D-HI)	Larry Craig (R-ID)	8[1]	7	none

[1]*Bernie Sanders is an Independent but caucuses with the Democratic Party.*

Senate Special, Select, and Other Committees

COMMITTEE	CHAIRMAN (PARTY-STATE)	RANKING MINORITY MEMBER (PARTY-STATE)	NUMBER OF MEMBERS MAJORITY	MINORITY
Special Committee on Aging	Herb Kohl (D-WI)	Gordon Smith (R-OR)	11	10
Select Committee on Ethics	Barbara Boxer (D-CA)	John Cornyn (R-TX)	3	3
Committee on Indian Affairs	Byron L. Dorgan (D-ND)	Lisa Murkowski (R-AK)	8	7
Select Committee on Intelligence	Jay Rockefeller (D-WV)	Kit Bond (R-MO)	8	7

Joint Committees of Congress

The joint committees of Congress include members from both the Senate and the House of Representatives. They function as overseeing entities but do not have the power to approve appropriations or legislation. Chairmanship of the Joint Economic Committee is determined by seniority and alternates between the Senate and the House every Congress. The Joint Committee on the Library of Congress is evenly made up of members from the House Administration Committee and the Senate Rules and Administration Committee. Chairmanship and vice chairmanship of the Joint Committee on Printing alternates between the House and the Senate every Congress. The Joint Committee on Taxation is composed of five members from the Senate Committee on Finance and five members from the House Committee on Ways and Means (three majority and two minority members from each).

COMMITTEE	CHAIRMAN (PARTY-STATE)	VICE CHAIRMAN (PARTY-STATE)	NUMBER OF MEMBERS DEMOCRATS	REPUBLICANS
Economic	Sen. Charles E. Schumer (D-NY)	Rep. Carolyn B. Maloney (D-NY)	12	8
Library	Sen. Dianne Feinstein (D-CA)	Rep. Robert A. Brady (D-PA)	6	4
Printing	Rep. Robert A. Brady (D-PA)	Sen. Dianne Feinstein (D-CA)	6	4
Taxation	Sen. Max Baucus (D-MT)	Rep. Charles B. Rangel (D-NY)	6	4

The House of Representatives, 110th Congress

Parties: Democrat (D); Republican (R); Independent (I).
*Party totals: **Democrats** 236; **Republicans** 199.*

According to Article I, Section 2, of the US Constitution, a US representative must be at least 25 years old, must reside in the state he or she represents at the time of the election, and must have been a citizen of the United States for seven years. Each state is entitled to at least one representative, with additional seats apportioned based on population. Each congressperson originally represented 30,000 people; the range in 2007 was from 522,830 (Wyoming) to 957,861 (Montana) persons per representative. Terms are for 2 years and begin on 3 January (unless otherwise noted). The current representative's salary is US$169,300 per year. The majority and minority leaders receive US$188,100 per year; the speaker of the House receives US$217,400 per year.

American Samoa, the District of Columbia, Guam, and the Virgin Islands elect delegates; Puerto Rico elects a resident commissioner. Their formal duties are the same, but the resident commissioner serves a four-year term. They may participate in debate and serve on committees but are not permitted to vote.

Numbers preceding the names refer to districts. Certain states gained (+) or lost (–) districts by reapportionment since the 107th Congress.

US House Web site: <www.house.gov>.

House leadership

speaker of the House:	Nancy Pelosi (D-CA)
majority leader:	Steny H. Hoyer (D-MD)
minority leader:	John A. Boehner (R-OH)
majority whip:	James E. Clyburn (D-SC)
minority whip:	Roy Blunt (R-MO)

STATE	REPRESENTATIVES	SERVICE BEGAN
Alabama	1. Jo Bonner (R)	Jan 2003
	2. Terry Everett (R)	Jan 1993
	3. Mike Rogers (R)	Jan 2003
	4. Robert B. Aderholt (R)	Jan 1997
	5. Robert E. (Bud) Cramer, Jr. (D)	Jan 1991
	6. Spencer Bachus (R)	Jan 1993
	7. Artur Davis (D)	Jan 2003
Alaska	Don Young (R)	Mar 1973
Arizona (+2)	1. Rick Renzi (R)	Jan 2003
	2. Trent Franks (R)	Jan 2003
	3. John B. Shadegg (R)	Jan 1995
	4. Ed Pastor (D)	Sep 1991
	5. Harry E. Mitchell (D)	Jan 2007
	6. Jeff Flake (R)	Jan 2001
Arizona (cont.)	7. Raúl M. Grijalva (D)	Jan 2003
	8. Gabrielle Giffords (D)	Jan 2007
Arkansas	1. Marion Berry (D)	Jan 1997
	2. Vic Snyder (D)	Jan 1997
	3. John Boozman (R)[1]	Nov 2001
	4. Mike Ross (D)	Jan 2001
California (+1)	1. Mike Thompson (D)	Jan 1999
	2. Wally Herger (R)	Jan 1987
	3. Daniel E. Lungren (R)	Jan 2005
	4. John T. Doolittle (R)	Jan 1991
	5. Doris O. Matsui (D)[2]	Mar 2005
	6. Lynn C. Woolsey (D)	Jan 1993
	7. George Miller (D)	Jan 1975
	8. Nancy Pelosi (D)	Jun 1987

The House of Representatives, 110th Congress (continued)

STATE	REPRESENTATIVES	SERVICE BEGAN
California (cont.)	9. Barbara Lee (D)	Apr 1998
	10. Ellen O. Tauscher (D)	Jan 1997
	11. Jerry McNerney (D)	Jan 2007
	12. Jackie Speier (D)[3]	Apr 2008
	13. Fortney "Pete" Stark (D)	Jan 1973
	14. Anna G. Eshoo (D)	Jan 1993
	15. Michael M. Honda (D)	Jan 2001
	16. Zoe Lofgren (D)	Jan 1995
	17. Sam Farr (D)	Jun 1993
	18. Dennis A. Cardoza (D)	Jan 2003
	19. George Radanovich (R)	Jan 1995
	20. Jim Costa (D)	Jan 2005
	21. Devin Nunes (R)	Jan 2003
	22. Kevin McCarthy (R)	Jan 2007
	23. Lois Capps (D)	Mar 1998
	24. Elton Gallegly (R)	Jan 1987
	25. Howard P. "Buck" McKeon (R)	Jan 1993
	26. David Dreier (R)	Jan 1981
	27. Brad Sherman (D)	Jan 1997
	28. Howard L. Berman (D)	Jan 1983
	29. Adam B. Schiff (D)	Jan 2001
	30. Henry A. Waxman (D)	Jan 1975
	31. Xavier Becerra (D)	Jan 1993
	32. Hilda L. Solis (D)	Jan 2001
	33. Diane E. Watson (D)[4]	Jun 2001
	34. Lucille Roybal-Allard (D)	Jan 1993
	35. Maxine Waters (D)	Jan 1991
	36. Jane F. Harman (D)[5]	Jan 1993
	37. Laura Richardson (D)[6]	Sep 2007
	38. Grace F. Napolitano (D)	Jan 1999
	39. Linda T. Sánchez (D)	Jan 2003
	40. Edward R. Royce (R)	Jan 1993
	41. Jerry Lewis (R)	Jan 1979
	42. Gary G. Miller (R)	Jan 1999
	43. Joe Baca (D)	Nov 1999
	44. Ken Calvert (R)	Jan 1993
	45. Mary Bono Mack (R)	Apr 1998
	46. Dana Rohrabacher (R)	Jan 1989
	47. Loretta Sanchez (D)	Jan 1997
	48. John Campbell (R)[7]	Dec 2005
	49. Darrell E. Issa (R)	Jan 2001
	50. Brian P. Bilbray (R)[8]	Jan 1995
	51. Bob Filner (D)	Jan 1993
	52. Duncan Hunter (R)	Jan 1981
	53. Susan A. Davis (D)	Jan 2001
Colorado (+1)	1. Diana DeGette (D)	Jan 1997
	2. Mark Udall (D)	Jan 1999
	3. John T. Salazar (D)	Jan 2005
	4. Marilyn N. Musgrave (R)	Jan 2003
	5. Doug Lamborn (R)	Jan 2007
	6. Thomas G. Tancredo (R)	Jan 1999
	7. Ed Perlmutter (D)	Jan 2007
Connecticut (−1)	1. John B. Larson (D)	Jan 1999
	2. Joe Courtney (D)	Jan 2007
	3. Rosa L. DeLauro (D)	Jan 1991
	4. Christopher Shays (R)	Aug 1987
	5. Christopher S. Murphy (D)	Jan 2007
Delaware	Michael N. Castle (R)	Jan 1993
Florida (+2)	1. Jeff Miller (R)[9]	Oct 2001
	2. Allen Boyd (D)	Jan 1997
	3. Corrine Brown (D)	Jan 1993
Florida (cont.)	4. Ander Crenshaw (R)	Jan 2001
	5. Ginny Brown-Waite (R)	Jan 2003
	6. Cliff Stearns (R)	Jan 1989
	7. John L. Mica (R)	Jan 1993
	8. Ric Keller (R)	Jan 2001
	9. Gus M. Bilirakis (R)	Jan 2007
	10. C.W. Bill Young (R)	Jan 1971
	11. Kathy Castor (D)	Jan 2007
	12. Adam H. Putnam (R)	Jan 2001
	13. Vern Buchanan (R)	Jan 2007
	14. Connie Mack (R)	Jan 2005
	15. Dave Weldon (R)	Jan 1995
	16. Tim Mahoney (D)	Jan 2007
	17. Kendrick B. Meek (D)	Jan 2003
	18. Ileana Ros-Lehtinen (R)	Aug 1989
	19. Robert Wexler (D)	Jan 1997
	20. Debbie Wasserman Schultz (D)	Jan 2005
	21. Lincoln Diaz-Balart (R)	Jan 1993
	22. Ron Klein (D)	Jan 2007
	23. Alcee L. Hastings (D)	Jan 1993
	24. Tom Feeney (R)	Jan 2003
	25. Mario Diaz-Balart (R)	Jan 2003
Georgia (+2)	1. Jack Kingston (R)	Jan 1993
	2. Sanford D. Bishop, Jr. (D)	Jan 1993
	3. Lynn A. Westmoreland (R)	Jan 2005
	4. Henry C. Johnson (D)	Jan 2007
	5. John Lewis (D)	Jan 1987
	6. Tom Price (R)	Feb 2005
	7. John Linder (R)	Jan 1993
	8. Jim Marshall (D)	Jan 2003
	9. Nathan Deal (R)	Jan 1993
	10. Paul Broun (R)[10]	Jul 2007
	11. Phil Gingrey (R)	Jan 2003
	12. John Barrow (D)	Jan 2005
	13. David Scott (D)	Jan 2003
Hawaii	1. Neil Abercrombie (D)[11]	Sep 1986
	2. Mazie K. Hirono (D)	Jan 2007
Idaho	1. Bill Sali (R)	Jan 2007
	2. Michael K. Simpson (R)	Jan 1999
Illinois (−1)	1. Bobby L. Rush (D)	Jan 1993
	2. Jesse L. Jackson, Jr. (D)	Dec 1995
	3. Daniel Lipinski (D)	Jan 2005
	4. Luis V. Gutierrez (D)	Jan 1993
	5. Rahm Emanuel (D)	Jan 2003
	6. Peter J. Roskam (R)	Jan 2007
	7. Danny K. Davis (D)	Jan 1997
	8. Melissa L. Bean (D)	Jan 2005
	9. Janice D. Schakowsky (D)	Jan 1999
	10. Mark Steven Kirk (R)	Jan 2001
	11. Jerry Weller (R)	Jan 1995
	12. Jerry F. Costello (D)	Aug 1988
	13. Judy Biggert (R)	Jan 1999
	14. Bill Foster (D)[12]	Mar 2008
	15. Timothy V. Johnson (R)	Jan 2001
	16. Donald A. Manzullo (R)	Jan 1993
	17. Phil Hare (D)	Jan 2007
	18. Ray LaHood (R)	Jan 1995
	19. John Shimkus (R)	Jan 1997
Indiana (−1)	1. Peter J. Visclosky (D)	Jan 1985
	2. Joe Donnelly (D)	Jan 2007
	3. Mark E. Souder (R)	Jan 1995

The House of Representatives, 110th Congress (continued)

STATE	REPRESENTATIVES	SERVICE BEGAN
Indiana (cont.)	4. Steve Buyer (R)	Jan 1993
	5. Dan Burton (R)	Jan 1983
	6. Mike Pence (R)	Jan 2001
	7. André Carson (D)[13]	Mar 2008
	8. Brad Ellsworth (D)	Jan 2007
	9. Baron P. Hill (D)[14]	Jan 1999
Iowa	1. Bruce L. Braley (D)	Jan 2007
	2. David Loebsack (D)	Jan 2007
	3. Leonard L. Boswell (D)	Jan 1997
	4. Tom Latham (R)	Jan 1995
	5. Steve King (R)	Jan 2003
Kansas	1. Jerry Moran (R)	Jan 1997
	2. Nancy E. Boyda (D)	Jan 2007
	3. Dennis Moore (D)	Jan 1999
	4. Todd Tiahrt (R)	Jan 1995
Kentucky	1. Ed Whitfield (R)	Jan 1995
	2. Ron Lewis (R)	May 1994
	3. John A. Yarmuth (D)	Jan 2007
	4. Geoff Davis (R)	Jan 2005
	5. Harold Rogers (R)	Jan 1981
	6. Ben Chandler (D)[15]	Feb 2004
Louisiana	1. Steve Scalise (R)[16]	May 2008
	2. William J. Jefferson (D)	Jan 1991
	3. Charlie Melancon (D)	Jan 2005
	4. Jim McCrery (R)	Apr 1988
	5. Rodney Alexander (R)	Jan 2003
	6. Donald J. Cazayoux, Jr. (D)[17]	May 2008
	7. Charles W. Boustany, Jr. (R)	Jan 2005
Maine	1. Thomas H. Allen (D)	Jan 1997
	2. Michael H. Michaud (D)	Jan 2003
Maryland	1. Wayne T. Gilchrest (R)	Jan 1991
	2. C.A. "Dutch" Ruppersberger (D)	Jan 2003
	3. John P. Sarbanes (D)	Jan 2007
	4. Donna F. Edwards (D)[18]	Jun 2008
	5. Steny H. Hoyer (D)	May 1981
	6. Roscoe G. Bartlett (R)	Jan 1993
	7. Elijah E. Cummings (D)	Apr 1996
	8. Chris Van Hollen (D)	Jan 2003
Massachusetts	1. John W. Olver (D)	Jun 1991
	2. Richard E. Neal (D)	Jan 1989
	3. James P. McGovern (D)	Jan 1997
	4. Barney Frank (D)	Jan 1981
	5. Niki Tsongas (D)[19]	Oct 2007
	6. John F. Tierney (D)	Jan 1997
	7. Edward J. Markey (D)	Nov 1976
	8. Michael E. Capuano (D)	Jan 1999
	9. Stephen F. Lynch (D)[20]	Oct 2001
	10. William D. Delahunt (D)	Jan 1997
Michigan (−1)	1. Bart Stupak (D)	Jan 1993
	2. Peter Hoekstra (R)	Jan 1993
	3. Vernon J. Ehlers (R)	Dec 1993
	4. Dave Camp (R)	Jan 1991
	5. Dale E. Kildee (D)	Jan 1977
	6. Fred Upton (R)	Jan 1987
	7. Tim Walberg (R)	Jan 2007
	8. Mike Rogers (R)	Jan 2001
	9. Joe Knollenberg (R)	Jan 1993

STATE	REPRESENTATIVES	SERVICE BEGAN
Michigan (cont.)	10. Candice S. Miller (R)	Jan 2003
	11. Thaddeus G. McCotter (R)	Jan 2003
	12. Sander M. Levin (D)	Jan 1983
	13. Carolyn C. Kilpatrick (D)	Jan 1997
	14. John Conyers, Jr. (D)	Jan 1965
	15. John D. Dingell (D)	Dec 1955
Minnesota	1. Timothy J. Walz (D)	Jan 2007
	2. John Kline (R)	Jan 2003
	3. Jim Ramstad (R)	Jan 1991
	4. Betty McCollum (D)	Jan 2001
	5. Keith Ellison (D)	Jan 2007
	6. Michele Bachmann (R)	Jan 2007
	7. Collin C. Peterson (D)	Jan 1991
	8. James L. Oberstar (D)	Jan 1975
Mississippi (−1)	1. Travis W. Childers (D)[21]	May 2008
	2. Bennie G. Thompson (D)	Apr 1993
	3. Charles W. "Chip" Pickering (R)	Jan 1997
	4. Gene Taylor (D)	Oct 1989
Missouri	1. William Lacy Clay (D)	Jan 2001
	2. W. Todd Akin (R)	Jan 2001
	3. Russ Carnahan (D)	Jan 2005
	4. Ike Skelton (D)	Jan 1977
	5. Emanuel Cleaver (D)	Jan 2005
	6. Sam Graves (R)	Jan 2001
	7. Roy Blunt (R)	Jan 1997
	8. Jo Ann Emerson (R)	Nov 1996
	9. Kenny C. Hulshof (R)	Jan 1997
Montana	Dennis R. Rehberg (R)	Jan 2001
Nebraska	1. Jeff Fortenberry (R)	Jan 2005
	2. Lee Terry (R)	Jan 1999
	3. Adrian Smith (R)	Jan 2007
Nevada (+1)	1. Shelley Berkley (D)	Jan 1999
	2. Dean Heller (R)	Jan 2007
	3. Jon C. Porter (R)	Jan 2003
New Hampshire	1. Carol Shea-Porter (D)	Jan 2007
	2. Paul W. Hodes (D)	Jan 2007
New Jersey	1. Robert E. Andrews (D)	Nov 1990
	2. Frank A. LoBiondo (R)	Jan 1995
	3. Jim Saxton (R)	Nov 1984
	4. Christopher H. Smith (R)	Jan 1981
	5. Scott Garrett (R)	Jan 2003
	6. Frank Pallone, Jr. (D)	Nov 1988
	7. Mike Ferguson (R)	Jan 2001
	8. Bill Pascrell, Jr. (D)	Jan 1997
	9. Steven R. Rothman (D)	Jan 1997
	10. Donald M. Payne (D)	Jan 1989
	11. Rodney P. Frelinghuysen (R)	Jan 1995
	12. Rush D. Holt (D)	Jan 1999
	13. Albio Sires (D)[22]	Nov 2006
New Mexico	1. Heather Wilson (R)	Jun 1998
	2. Steve Pearce (R)	Jan 2003
	3. Tom Udall (D)	Jan 1999
New York (−2)	1. Timothy H. Bishop (D)	Jan 2003
	2. Steve Israel (D)	Jan 2001

The House of Representatives, 110th Congress (continued)

STATE	REPRESENTATIVES	SERVICE BEGAN
New York (cont.)	3. Peter T. King (R)	Jan 1993
	4. Carolyn McCarthy (D)	Jan 1997
	5. Gary L. Ackerman (D)	Mar 1983
	6. Gregory W. Meeks (D)	Feb 1998
	7. Joseph Crowley (D)	Jan 1999
	8. Jerrold Nadler (D)	Nov 1992
	9. Anthony D. Weiner (D)	Jan 1999
	10. Edolphus Towns (D)	Jan 1983
	11. Yvette D. Clarke (D)	Jan 2007
	12. Nydia M. Velázquez (D)	Jan 1993
	13. Vito Fossella (R)	Nov 1997
	14. Carolyn B. Maloney (D)	Jan 1993
	15. Charles B. Rangel (D)	Jan 1971
	16. José E. Serrano (D)	Mar 1990
	17. Eliot L. Engel (D)	Jan 1989
	18. Nita M. Lowey (D)	Jan 1989
	19. John J. Hall (D)	Jan 2007
	20. Kirsten E. Gillibrand (D)	Jan 2007
	21. Michael R. McNulty (D)	Jan 1989
	22. Maurice D. Hinchey (D)	Jan 1993
	23. John M. McHugh (R)	Jan 1993
	24. Michael A. Arcuri (D)	Jan 2007
	25. James T. Walsh (R)	Jan 1989
	26. Thomas M. Reynolds (R)	Jan 1999
	27. Brian Higgins (D)	Jan 2005
	28. Louise McIntosh Slaughter (D)	Jan 1987
	29. John R. "Randy" Kuhl, Jr. (R)	Jan 2005
North Carolina (+1)	1. G.K. Butterfield (D)	Jan 2005
	2. Bob Etheridge (D)	Jan 1997
	3. Walter B. Jones (R)	Jan 1995
	4. David E. Price (D)	Jan 1997
	5. Virginia Foxx (R)	Jan 2005
	6. Howard Coble (R)	Jan 1985
	7. Mike McIntyre (D)	Jan 1997
	8. Robin Hayes (R)	Jan 1999
	9. Sue Wilkins Myrick (R)	Jan 1995
	10. Patrick T. McHenry (R)	Jan 2005
	11. Heath Shuler (D)	Jan 2007
	12. Melvin L. Watt (D)	Jan 1993
	13. Brad Miller (D)	Jan 2003
North Dakota	Earl Pomeroy (D)	Jan 1993
Ohio (−1)	1. Steve Chabot (R)	Jan 1995
	2. Jean Schmidt (R)	Sep 2005
	3. Michael R. Turner (R)	Jan 2003
	4. Jim Jordan (R)	Jan 2007
	5. Robert E. Latta (R)[23]	Dec 2007
	6. Charles A. Wilson (D)	Jan 2007
	7. David L. Hobson (R)	Jan 1991
	8. John A. Boehner (R)	Jan 1991
	9. Marcy Kaptur (D)	Jan 1983
	10. Dennis J. Kucinich (D)	Jan 1997
	11. Stephanie Tubbs Jones (D)	Jan 1999
	12. Patrick J. Tiberi (R)	Jan 2001
	13. Betty Sutton (D)	Jan 2007
	14. Steven C. LaTourette (R)	Jan 1995
	15. Deborah Pryce (R)	Jan 1993
	16. Ralph Regula (R)	Jan 1973
	17. Tim Ryan (D)	Jan 2003
	18. Zachary T. Space (D)	Jan 2007
Oklahoma (−1)	1. John Sullivan (R)[24]	Feb 2002
	2. Dan Boren (D)	Jan 2005
	3. Frank D. Lucas (R)	May 1994
	4. Tom Cole (R)	Jan 2003
	5. Mary Fallin (R)	Jan 2007
Oregon	1. David Wu (D)	Jan 1999
	2. Greg Walden (R)	Jan 1999
	3. Earl Blumenauer (D)	May 1996
	4. Peter A. DeFazio (D)	Jan 1987
	5. Darlene Hooley (D)	Jan 1997
Pennsylvania (−2)	1. Robert A. Brady (D)	May 1998
	2. Chaka Fattah (D)	Jan 1995
	3. Phil English (R)	Jan 1995
	4. Jason Altmire (D)	Jan 2007
	5. John E. Peterson (R)	Jan 1997
	6. Jim Gerlach (R)	Jan 2003
	7. Joe Sestak (D)	Jan 2007
	8. Patrick J. Murphy (D)	Jan 2007
	9. Bill Shuster (R)	May 2001
	10. Christopher P. Carney (D)	Jan 2007
	11. Paul E. Kanjorski (D)	Jan 1985
	12. John P. Murtha (D)	Feb 1974
	13. Allyson Y. Schwartz (D)	Jan 2005
	14. Michael F. Doyle (D)	Jan 1995
	15. Charles W. Dent (R)	Jan 2005
	16. Joseph R. Pitts (R)	Jan 1997
	17. Tim Holden (D)	Jan 1993
	18. Tim Murphy (R)	Jan 2003
	19. Todd Russell Platts (R)	Jan 2001
Rhode Island	1. Patrick J. Kennedy (D)	Jan 1995
	2. James R. Langevin (D)	Jan 2001
South Carolina	1. Henry E. Brown, Jr. (R)	Jan 2001
	2. Joe Wilson (R)[25]	Dec 2001
	3. J. Gresham Barrett (R)	Jan 2003
	4. Bob Inglis (R)	Jan 2005
	5. John M. Spratt, Jr. (D)	Jan 1983
	6. James E. Clyburn (D)	Jan 1993
South Dakota	Stephanie Herseth Sandlin (D)[26]	Jun 2004
Tennessee	1. David Davis (R)	Jan 2007
	2. John J. Duncan, Jr., (R)	Nov 1988
	3. Zach Wamp (R)	Jan 1995
	4. Lincoln Davis (D)	Jan 2003
	5. Jim Cooper (D)[27]	Jan 1983
	6. Bart Gordon (D)	Jan 1985
	7. Marsha Blackburn (R)	Jan 2003
	8. John S. Tanner (D)	Jan 1989
	9. Steve Cohen (D)	Jan 2007
Texas (+2)	1. Louie Gohmert (R)	Jan 2005
	2. Ted Poe (R)	Jan 2005
	3. Sam Johnson (R)	May 1991
	4. Ralph M. Hall (R)[28]	Jan 1981
	5. Jeb Hensarling (R)	Jan 2003
	6. Joe Barton (R)	Jan 1985
	7. John Abney Culberson (R)	Jan 2001
	8. Kevin Brady (R)	Jan 1997
	9. Al Green (D)	Jan 2005
	10. Michael T. McCaul (R)	Jan 2005
	11. K. Michael Conaway (R)	Jan 2005

The House of Representatives, 110th Congress (continued)

STATE	REPRESENTATIVES	SERVICE BEGAN
Texas (cont.)	12. Kay Granger (R)	Jan 1997
	13. Mac Thornberry (R)	Jan 1995
	14. Ron Paul (R)	Jan 1997
	15. Rubén Hinojosa (D)	Jan 1997
	16. Silvestre Reyes (D)	Jan 1997
	17. Chet Edwards (D)	Jan 2005
	18. Sheila Jackson-Lee (D)	Jan 1995
	19. Randy Neugebauer (R)[29]	Jun 2003
	20. Charles A. Gonzalez (D)	Jan 1999
	21. Lamar S. Smith (R)	Jan 1987
	22. Nick Lampson (D)[30]	Jan 1997
	23. Ciro D. Rodriguez (D)[31]	Apr 1997
	24. Kenny Marchant (D)	Jan 2005
	25. Lloyd Doggett (D)	Jan 2005
	26. Michael C. Burgess (R)	Jan 2003
	27. Solomon P. Ortiz (D)	Jan 1983
	28. Henry Cuellar (D)	Jan 2005
	29. Gene Green (D)	Jan 1993
	30. Eddie Bernice Johnson (D)	Jan 1993
	31. John R. Carter (R)	Jan 2003
	32. Pete Sessions (R)	Jan 1997
Utah	1. Rob Bishop (R)	Jan 2003
	2. Jim Matheson (D)	Jan 2001
	3. Chris Cannon (R)	Jan 1997
Vermont	Peter Welch (D)	Jan 2007
Virginia	1. Robert J. Wittman (R)[32]	Dec 2007
	2. Thelma D. Drake (R)	Jan 2005
	3. Robert C. Scott (D)	Jan 1993
	4. J. Randy Forbes (R)[33]	Jun 2001
Virginia (cont.)	5. Virgil H. Goode, Jr. (R)	Jan 1997
	6. Bob Goodlatte (R)	Jan 1993
	7. Eric Cantor (R)	Jan 2001
	8. James P. Moran (D)	Jan 1991
	9. Rick Boucher (D)	Jan 1983
	10. Frank R. Wolf (R)	Jan 1981
	11. Tom Davis (R)	Jan 1995
Washington	1. Jay Inslee (D)[34]	Jan 1993
	2. Rick Larsen (D)	Jan 2001
	3. Brian Baird (D)	Jan 1999
	4. Doc Hastings (R)	Jan 1995
	5. Cathy McMorris Rodgers (R)	Jan 2005
	6. Norman D. Dicks (D)	Jan 1977
	7. Jim McDermott (D)	Jan 1989
	8. David G. Reichert (R)	Jan 2005
	9. Adam Smith (D)	Jan 1997
West Virginia	1. Alan B. Mollohan (D)	Jan 1983
	2. Shelley Moore Capito (R)	Jan 2001
	3. Nick J. Rahall II (D)	Jan 1977
Wisconsin (−1)	1. Paul Ryan (R)	Jan 1999
	2. Tammy Baldwin (D)	Jan 1999
	3. Ron Kind (D)	Jan 1997
	4. Gwen Moore (D)	Jan 2005
	5. F. James Sensenbrenner, Jr. (R)	Jan 1979
	6. Thomas E. Petri (R)	Apr 1979
	7. David R. Obey (D)	Apr 1969
	8. Steve Kagen (D)	Jan 2007
Wyoming	Barbara Cubin (R)	Jan 1995

JURISDICTION	REPRESENTATIVES	SERVICE BEGAN
American Samoa	(Delegate) Eni F.H. Faleomavaega (D)	Jan 1989
District of Columbia	(Delegate) Eleanor Holmes Norton (D)	Jan 1991
Guam	(Delegate) Madeleine Bordallo (D)	Jan 2003
Puerto Rico	(Resident Commissioner) Luis G. Fortuño (R)	Jan 2005
US Virgin Islands	(Delegate) Donna M. Christensen (D)	Jan 1997

[1]John Boozman was elected 20 Nov 2001 following the resignation of Asa Hutchinson. [2]Doris O. Matsui was elected 8 Mar 2005 following the death of Robert T. Matsui. [3]Jackie Speier was elected 8 Apr 2008 following the death of Tom Lantos. [4]Diane E. Watson was elected 5 Jun 2001 following the death of Julian C. Dixon. [5]Jane F. Harman did not serve 3 Jan 1999–3 Jan 2001. [6]Laura Richardson was elected 21 Aug 2007 following the death of Juanita Millender-McDonald. [7]John Campbell was elected 6 Dec 2005 following the resignation of Christopher Cox. [8]Brian P. Bilbray did not serve 3 Jan 2001–6 Jun 2005. He was elected 6 June 2005 following the resignation of Randall (Duke) Cunningham. [9]Jeff Miller was elected 16 Oct 2001 following the resignation of Joe Scarborough. [10]Paul Broun was elected 17 Jul 2007 following the death of Charlie Norwood. [11]Neil Abercrombie did not serve 3 Jan 1987–3 Jan 1991. [12]Bill Foster was elected 8 Mar 2008 following the resignation of J. Dennis Hastert. [13]André Carson was elected 11 Mar 2008 following the death of Julia Carson. [14]Baron P. Hill did not serve 3 Jan 2005–3 Jan 2007. [15]Ben Chandler was elected 17 Feb 2004 following the resignation of Ernie Fletcher. [16]Steve Scalise was elected 3 May 2008 following the resignation of Bobby Jindal. [17]Donald J. Cazayoux, Jr., was elected 3 May 2008 following the resignation of Richard H. Baker. [18]Donna F. Edwards was elected 17 Jun 2007 following the resignation of Albert Russell Wynn. [19]Niki Tsongas was elected 16 Oct 2007 following the resignation of Martin T. Meehan. [20]Stephen F. Lynch was elected 16 Oct 2001 following the death of John Joseph Moakley. [21]Travis W. Childers was elected 13 May 2008 following the resignation of Roger F. Wicker. [22]Albio Sires was elected 7 Nov 2006 following the resignation of Robert Menendez. [23]Robert E. Latta was elected 11 Dec 2007 following the death of Paul E. Gillmor. [24]John Sullivan was elected 8 Jan 2002 following the resignation of Steve Largent. [25]Joe Wilson was elected 18 Dec 2001 following the death of Floyd Spence. [26]Stephanie Herseth Sandlin was elected 1 Jun 2004 following the resignation of William Janklow. [27]Jim Cooper did not serve 3 Jan 1995–3 Jan 2003. [28]Ralph M. Hall defected to the Republican Party on 5 Jan 2004. [29]Randy Neugebauer was elected 3 June 2003 following the resignation of Larry Combest. [30]Nick Lampson did not serve 3 Jan 2005–3 Jan 2007. [31]Ciro D. Rodriguez took office 12 Apr 1997 following the death of Frank Tejada. He did not serve 3 Jan 2005–3 Jan 2007. [32]Robert J. Wittman was elected 11 Dec 2007 following the death of Jo Ann Davis. [33]J. Randy Forbes was elected 19 Jun 2001 following the death of Norman Sisisky. [34]Jay Inslee did not serve 3 Jan 1995–3 Jan 1999.

House of Representatives Standing Committees

COMMITTEE	CHAIRMAN (PARTY-STATE)	RANKING MINORITY MEMBER (PARTY-STATE)	NUMBER OF MEMBERS		NUMBER OF SUBCOM-MITTEES
			MAJORITY	MINORITY	
Agriculture	Collin C. Peterson (D-MN)	Bob Goodlatte (R-VA)	25	20	6
Appropriations	David R. Obey (D-WI)	Jerry Lewis (R-CA)	37	29	12
Armed Services	Ike Skelton (D-MO)	Duncan Hunter (R-CA)	34	28	7
Budget	John M. Spratt, Jr. (D-SC)	Paul Ryan (R-WI)	22	17	none
Education and Labor	George Miller (D-CA)	Howard P. "Buck" McKeon (R-CA)	27	22	5
Energy and Commerce	John D. Dingell (D-MI)	Joe Barton (R-TX)	31	26	6
Financial Services	Barney Frank (D-MA)	Spencer Bachus (R-AL)	37	33	5
Foreign Affairs	Howard L. Berman (D-CA)	Ileana Ros-Lehtinen (R-FL)	27	23	7
Homeland Security	Bennie G. Thompson (D-MS)	Peter T. King (R-NY)	19	15	6
House Administration	Robert A. Brady (D-PA)	Vernon J. Ehlers (R-MI)	6	3	2
Judiciary	John Conyers, Jr. (D-MI)	Lamar S. Smith (R-TX)	23	17	5
Natural Resources	Nick J. Rahall II (D-WV)	Don Young (R-AK)	27	22	5
Oversight and Government Reform	Henry A. Waxman (D-CA)	Tom Davis (R-VA)	23	18	5
Rules	Louise McIntosh Slaughter (D-NY)	David Dreier (R-CA)	9	4	2
Science and Technology	Bart Gordon (D-TN)	Ralph M. Hall (R-TX)	24	20	5
Small Business	Nydia M. Velázquez (D-NY)	Steve Chabot (R-OH)	18	15	5
Standards of Official Conduct	Stephanie Tubbs Jones (D-OH)	Doc Hastings (R-WA)	5	5	none
Transportation and Infrastructure	James L. Oberstar (D-MN)	John L. Mica (R-FL)	41	34	6
Veterans' Affairs	Bob Filner (D-CA)	Steve Buyer (R-IN)	16	13	4
Ways and Means	Charles B. Rangel (D-NY)	Jim McCrery (R-LA)	24	17	6
Permanent Select Committee on Intelligence	Silvestre Reyes (D-TX)	Peter Hoekstra (R-MI)	12	9	4
Select Committee on Energy Independence and Global Warming	Edward J. Markey (D-MA)	F. James Sensenbrenner, Jr. (R-WI)	9	6	none

Henri Matisse's painting *Le Bateau* (*The Boat*) was accidentally hung upside down in New York's Museum of Modern Art for 47 days in 1961. During that time 116,000 visitors saw it, but it wasn't until stockbroker Genevieve Habert called the *New York Times* about the mistake that the director of exhibitions was notified and the work was rehung properly.

Electoral Votes by State

Each state receives one electoral vote for each of its representatives and one for each of its two senators, ensuring at least three votes for each state, as the Constitution guarantees at least one representative regardless of population. Allocations are based on the 2000 census and are applicable for subsequent elections.

Total: 538; Majority needed to elect president and vice president: 270

STATE	NUMBER OF VOTES	STATE	NUMBER OF VOTES	STATE	NUMBER OF VOTES
Alabama	9	Kentucky	8	North Dakota	3
Alaska	3	Louisiana	9	Ohio	20
Arizona	10	Maine	4	Oklahoma	7
Arkansas	6	Maryland	10	Oregon	7
California	55	Massachusetts	12	Pennsylvania	21
Colorado	9	Michigan	17	Rhode Island	4
Connecticut	7	Minnesota	10	South Carolina	8
Delaware	3	Mississippi	6	South Dakota	3
District of Columbia	3	Missouri	11	Tennessee	11
Florida	27	Montana	3	Texas	34
Georgia	15	Nebraska	5	Utah	5
Hawaii	4	Nevada	5	Vermont	3
Idaho	4	New Hampshire	4	Virginia	13
Illinois	21	New Jersey	15	Washington	11
Indiana	11	New Mexico	5	West Virginia	5
Iowa	7	New York	31	Wisconsin	10
Kansas	6	North Carolina	15	Wyoming	3

Congressional Apportionment

The US Constitution requires a decennial census to determine the apportionment of representatives for each state in the House of Representatives. There was no reapportionment based on 1920 census figures.

	representatives										
STATE	**1790**	**1800**	**1810**	**1820**	**1830**	**1840**	**1850**	**1860**	**1870**	**1880**	**1890**
Alabama	NA	NA	1[1]	3	5	7	7	6	8	8	9
Alaska	NA	NA	NA	NA	NA	NA	NA	NA	NA	NA	NA
Arizona	NA	NA	NA	NA	NA	NA	NA	NA	NA	NA	NA
Arkansas	NA	NA	NA	NA	1[1]	1	2	3	4	5	6
California	NA	NA	NA	NA	NA	2[1]	2	3	4	6	7
Colorado	NA	NA	NA	NA	NA	NA	NA	NA	1[1]	1	2
Connecticut	7	7	7	6	6	4	4	4	4	4	4
Delaware	1	1	2	1	1	1	1	1	1	1	1
Florida	NA	NA	NA	NA	NA	1[1]	1	1	2	2	2
Georgia	2	4	6	7	9	8	8	7	9	10	11
Hawaii	NA	NA	NA	NA	NA	NA	NA	NA	NA	NA	NA
Idaho	NA	NA	NA	NA	NA	NA	NA	NA	NA	1[1]	1
Illinois	NA	NA	1[1]	1	3	7	9	14	19	20	22
Indiana	NA	NA	1[1]	3	7	10	11	11	13	13	13
Iowa	NA	NA	NA	NA	NA	2[1]	2	6	9	11	11
Kansas	NA	NA	NA	NA	NA	NA	NA	1	3	7	8
Kentucky	2	6	10	12	13	10	10	9	10	11	11
Louisiana	NA	NA	1[1]	3	3	4	4	5	6	6	6
Maine	NA	NA	NA	7	8	7	6	5	5	4	4
Maryland	8	9	9	9	8	6	6	5	6	6	6
Massachusetts	14	17	20	13	12	10	11	10	11	12	13
Michigan	NA	NA	NA	NA	1[1]	3	4	6	9	11	12
Minnesota	NA	NA	NA	NA	NA	NA	2[1]	2	3	5	7
Mississippi	NA	NA	1[1]	1	2	4	5	5	6	7	7
Missouri	NA	NA	NA	1	2	5	7	9	13	14	15
Montana	NA	NA	NA	NA	NA	NA	NA	NA	NA	1[1]	1
Nebraska	NA	NA	NA	NA	NA	NA	NA	1[1]	1	3	6
Nevada	NA	NA	NA	NA	NA	NA	NA	1[1]	1	1	1
New Hampshire	4	5	6	6	5	4	3	3	3	2	2
New Jersey	5	6	6	6	6	5	5	5	7	7	8
New Mexico	NA	NA	NA	NA	NA	NA	NA	NA	NA	NA	NA
New York	10	17	27	34	40	34	33	31	33	34	34
North Carolina	10	12	13	13	13	9	8	7	8	9	9
North Dakota	NA	NA	NA	NA	NA	NA	NA	NA	NA	1[1]	1
Ohio	NA	1[1]	6	14	19	21	21	19	20	21	21
Oklahoma	NA	NA	NA	NA	NA	NA	NA	NA	NA	NA	NA
Oregon	NA	NA	NA	NA	NA	NA	1[1]	1	1	1	2
Pennsylvania	13	18	23	26	28	24	25	24	27	28	30
Rhode Island	2	2	2	2	2	2	2	2	2	2	2
South Carolina	6	8	9	9	9	7	6	4	5	7	7
South Dakota	NA	NA	NA	NA	NA	NA	NA	NA	NA	2[1]	2
Tennessee	1[1]	3	6	9	13	11	10	8	10	10	10
Texas	NA	NA	NA	NA	NA	2[1]	2	4	6	11	13
Utah	NA	NA	NA	NA	NA	NA	NA	NA	NA	NA	1[1]
Vermont	2	4	6	5	5	4	3	3	3	2	2
Virginia	19	22	23	22	21	15	13	11	9	10	10
Washington	NA	NA	NA	NA	NA	NA	NA	NA	NA	1[1]	2
West Virginia	NA	NA	NA	NA	NA	NA	NA	NA	3	4	4
Wisconsin	NA	NA	NA	NA	NA	2[1]	3	6	8	9	10
Wyoming	NA	NA	NA	NA	NA	NA	NA	NA	NA	1[1]	1
Total	**106**	**142**	**186**	**213**	**242**	**232**	**237**	**243**	**293**	**332**	**357**

Congressional Apportionment (continued)

STATE	representatives									
	1900	1910	1930	1940	1950	1960	1970	1980	1990	2000
Alabama	9	10	9	9	9	8	7	7	7	7
Alaska	NA	NA	NA	NA	1[1]	1	1	1	1	1
Arizona	NA	1[2]	1	2	2	3	4	5	6	8
Arkansas	7	7	7	7	6	4	4	4	4	4
California	8	11	20	23	30	38	43	45	52	53
Colorado	3	4	4	4	4	4	5	6	6	7
Connecticut	5	5	6	6	6	6	6	6	6	5
Delaware	1	1	1	1	1	1	1	1	1	1
Florida	3	4	5	6	8	12	15	19	23	25
Georgia	11	12	10	10	10	10	10	10	11	13
Hawaii	NA	NA	NA	NA	1[1]	2	2	2	2	2
Idaho	1	2	2	2	2	2	2	2	2	2
Illinois	25	27	27	26	25	24	24	22	20	19
Indiana	13	13	12	11	11	11	11	10	10	9
Iowa	11	11	9	8	8	7	6	6	5	5
Kansas	8	8	7	6	6	5	5	5	4	4
Kentucky	11	11	9	9	8	7	7	7	6	6
Louisiana	7	8	8	8	8	8	8	8	7	7
Maine	4	4	3	3	3	2	2	2	2	2
Maryland	6	6	6	6	7	8	8	8	8	8
Massachusetts	14	16	15	14	14	12	12	11	10	10
Michigan	12	13	17	17	18	19	19	18	16	15
Minnesota	9	10	9	9	9	8	8	8	8	8
Mississippi	8	8	7	7	6	5	5	5	5	4
Missouri	16	16	13	13	11	10	10	9	9	9
Montana	1	2	2	2	2	2	2	2	1	1
Nebraska	6	6	5	4	4	3	3	3	3	3
Nevada	1	1	1	1	1	1	1	2	2	3
New Hampshire	2	2	2	2	2	2	2	2	2	2
New Jersey	10	12	14	14	14	15	15	14	13	13
New Mexico	NA	1[2]	1	2	2	2	2	3	3	3
New York	37	43	45	45	43	41	39	34	31	29
North Carolina	10	10	11	12	12	11	11	11	12	13
North Dakota	2	3	2	2	2	2	1	1	1	1
Ohio	21	22	24	23	23	24	23	21	19	18
Oklahoma	5[1]	8	9	8	6	6	6	6	6	5
Oregon	2	3	3	4	4	4	4	5	5	5
Pennsylvania	32	36	34	33	30	27	25	23	21	19
Rhode Island	2	3	2	2	2	2	2	2	2	2
South Carolina	7	7	6	6	6	6	6	6	6	6
South Dakota	2	3	2	2	2	2	2	1	1	1
Tennessee	10	10	9	10	9	9	8	9	9	9
Texas	16	18	21	21	22	23	24	27	30	32
Utah	1	2	2	2	2	2	2	3	3	3
Vermont	2	2	1	1	1	1	1	1	1	1
Virginia	10	10	9	9	10	10	10	10	11	11
Washington	3	5	6	6	7	7	7	8	9	9
West Virginia	5	6	6	6	6	5	4	4	3	3
Wisconsin	11	11	10	10	10	10	9	9	9	8
Wyoming	1	1	1	1	1	1	1	1	1	1
Total	**391**	**435**	**435**	**435**	**437**	**435**	**435**	**435**	**435**	**435**

NA: Not applicable. [1]*Number assigned after apportionment.* [2]*Included in anticipation of statehood.*

Military Affairs

US Military Leadership

President, Commander in Chief:	George W. Bush (20 Jan 2001)
Secretary of Defense:	Robert M. Gates (18 Dec 2006)
Chairman, Joint Chiefs of Staff:	Mike Mullen (1 Oct 2007)
Vice Chairman, Joint Chiefs of Staff:	James E. Cartwright (31 Aug 2007)

RANK/POSITION	NAME (DATE ASSUMED POST)
Army	
Chief of Staff	George W. Casey, Jr. (10 Apr 2007)
Vice Chief of Staff	Peter W. Chiarelli (4 Aug 2008)
Sergeant Major	Kenneth O. Preston (15 Jan 2004)
Sec. of the Army	Pete Geren (16 Jul 2007)
Under Sec. of the Army (acting)	Nelson M. Ford (4 Dec 2007)
Navy	
Chief of Naval Operations	Gary Roughead (29 Sep 2007)
Vice Chief of Naval Operations	Patrick M. Walsh (April 2007)
Master Chief Petty Officer	Joe R. Campa, Jr. (10 Jul 2006)
Sec. of the Navy	Donald C. Winter (3 Jan 2006)
Under Sec. of the Navy	*vacant*
Air Force	
Chief of Staff	Norton A. Schwartz (12 Aug 2008)
Vice Chief of Staff	*vacant*
Chief Master Sergeant	Rodney J. McKinley (30 Jun 2006)
Sec. of the Air Force (acting)	Michael B. Donley (21 Jun 2008)
Under Sec. of the Air Force	*vacant*
Marine Corps	
Commandant	James T. Conway (13 Nov 2006)
Asst. Commandant	James F. Amos (2 Jul 2008)
Sergeant Major	Carlton W. Kent (25 Apr 2007)
Coast Guard	
Commandant	Thad W. Allen (25 May 2006)
Vice Commandant	Vivien S. Crea (5 Jun 2006)
Chief of Staff	Clifford I. Pearson (June 2008)
Master Chief Petty Officer	Charles W. Bowen (14 Jun 2006)

Unified Combatant Commands

The Unified Combatant Commands provide operational control of US combat forces and are organized geographically to a significant extent. Unified Commanders receive orders through the chairman of the Joint Chiefs of Staff. Their structure is flexible, changing to accommodate evolving US security needs. Although the number of commands may vary, each command must be composed of forces from at least two of the armed services. Information is current as of August 2008.

COMMAND	HEADQUARTERS	COMMANDER IN CHIEF
US European Command	Stuttgart-Vaihingen, Germany	Gen. Bantz John Craddock, USA
US Pacific Command	Honolulu HI	Adm. Timothy J. Keating, USN
US Joint Forces Command	Norfolk VA	Gen. James N. Mattis, USMC
US Southern Command	Miami FL	Adm. James Stavridis, USN
US Central Command	MacDill Air Force Base, Florida	Gen. David Petraeus, USA
US Northern Command	Peterson Air Force Base, Colorado	Gen. Victor E. Renuart, Jr., USAF
US Special Operations Command	MacDill Air Force Base, Florida	Adm. Eric T. Olson, USN
US Transportation Command	Scott Air Force Base, Illinois	Gen. Duncan J. McNabb, USAF
US Strategic Command	Offutt Air Force Base, Nebraska	Gen. Kevin P. Chilton, USAF
US Africa Command[1]	Stuttgart-Vaihingen, Germany	Gen. William E. Ward, USA

[1]*The US Africa Command is a sub-unified command under the US European Command.*

North Atlantic Treaty Organization (NATO) International Commands

The NATO military command structure comprises two main strategic commands, Allied Command for Operations (ACO) and Allied Command Transformation (ACT, which works closely with the US Joint Forces Command). Their subordinate centers, also listed, change as their security measures evolve.

ALLIED COMMAND OPERATIONS (ACO)
Headquarters (SHAPE) Casteau, Belgium
Supreme Allied Commander, Europe (SACEUR)
Gen. Bantz John Craddock (USA) (7 Dec 2006–)

SUBORDINATE OPERATIONAL COMMANDS
Joint Force Command Brunssum,
JFC HQ Brunssum, Netherlands
Commander in Chief: Gen. Egon Ramms (Army, Germany) (26 Jan 2007–)

Joint Force Command Naples,
JFC HQ Naples, Italy
Commander in Chief: Adm. Mark Fitzgerald (USN) (30 Nov 2007–)

Joint Command Lisbon,
JC HQ Oeiras, Portugal
Commander in Chief: Vice Adm. James A. Winnefeld, Jr. (USN) (14 Sep 2007–)

NATO International Commands (continued)

ALLIED COMMAND TRANSFORMATION (ACT)
Headquarters Norfolk VA
Supreme Allied Commander, Transformation: Gen. James N. Mattis (USMC) (9 Nov 2007–)

SUBORDINATE CENTERS AND SCHOOLS
Joint Analysis and Lessons Learned Centre (JALLC), Lisbon, Portugal
Joint Force Training Centre (JFTC), Bydgoszcz, Poland

SUBORDINATE CENTERS AND SCHOOLS (CONTINUED)
Joint Warfare Centre (JWC), Stavanger, Norway
NATO Communications and Information Systems School (NCISS), Latina, Italy
NATO Defense College (NDC), Rome, Italy
NATO School, Oberammergau, Germany
NATO Undersea Research Centre (NURC), La Spezia, Italy

Chairmen of the Joint Chiefs of Staff

The 1949 amendments to the National Security Act of 1947 created the position of chairman of the Joint Chiefs of Staff, the principal military adviser to the president, the secretary of defense, and the National Security Council. The president appoints the chairman for a two-year term with the advice and consent of the Senate. In 1986 the chairman's eligibility for service increased from two to three reappointments (there is no limit on reappointment during wartime). The Joint Chiefs of Staff consist of the chairman, a vice chairman, the chief of staff of the Army, the chief of staff of the Air Force, the chief of naval operations, and the commandant of the Marine Corps. Acting chairmen are not included in this table.

NAME	MILITARY BRANCH	DATES OF SERVICE
Gen. of the Army Omar N. Bradley	US Army	16 Aug 1949–14 Aug 1953
Adm. Arthur W. Radford	US Navy	15 Aug 1953–14 Aug 1957
Gen. Nathan F. Twining	US Air Force	15 Aug 1957–30 Sep 1960
Gen. Lyman L. Lemnitzer	US Army	1 Oct 1960–30 Sep 1962
Gen. Maxwell D. Taylor	US Army	1 Oct 1962–1 Jul 1964
Gen. Earle G. Wheeler	US Army	3 Jul 1964–1 Jul 1970
Adm. Thomas H. Moorer	US Navy	2 Jul 1970–30 Jun 1974
Gen. George S. Brown	US Air Force	1 Jul 1974–20 Jun 1978
Gen. David C. Jones	US Air Force	21 Jun 1978–17 Jun 1982
Gen. John W. Vessey, Jr.	US Army	18 Jun 1982–30 Sep 1985
Adm. William J. Crowe, Jr.	US Navy	1 Oct 1985–30 Sep 1989
Gen. Colin L. Powell	US Army	1 Oct 1989–30 Sep 1993
Gen. John M. Shalikashvili	US Army	25 Oct 1993–30 Sep 1997
Gen. Harry Shelton	US Army	1 Oct 1997–30 Sep 2001
Gen. Richard B. Myers	US Air Force	1 Oct 2001–29 Sep 2005
Gen. Peter Pace	US Marine Corps	30 Sep 2005–30 Sep 2007
Adm. Mike Mullen	US Navy	1 Oct 2007–

Worldwide Deployment of the US Military

Deployments of active duty military personnel as of 30 Sep 2007. Regional totals include countries and areas not shown in the table. N/A means not available. Source: US Department of Defense.

COUNTRY/REGIONAL AREA	TOTAL	ARMY	NAVY	MARINE CORPS	AIR FORCE
US and territories					
continental US[1]	882,201	411,546	117,368	98,756	254,531
Alaska	19,408	11,432	44	26	7,906
Hawaii[1]	34,838	19,867	5,595	4,483	4,893
Guam[1]	2,836	39	1,064	3	1,730
Puerto Rico[1]	137	53	41	22	21
transients	52,527	6,625	9,849	31,405	4,648
afloat	92,590	0	92,590	0	0
total ashore and afloat	**1,084,548**	**449,563**	**226,551**	**134,699**	**273,735**
Europe					
Belgium	1,328	730	93	26	479
Bosnia and Herzegovina	209	176	14	7	12
Germany[1]	57,080	41,926	281	290	14,583
Greece	363	12	290	17	44
Greenland	126	0	0	0	126
Italy[1]	9,855	3,176	2,538	58	4,083
The Netherlands	579	298	23	14	244
Portugal	826	25	29	8	764
Spain	1,286	97	726	165	298
Turkey	1,594	66	9	16	1,503

Worldwide Deployment of the US Military (continued)

COUNTRY/REGIONAL AREA	TOTAL	ARMY	NAVY	MARINE CORPS	AIR FORCE
Europe (continued)					
United Kingdom[1]	9,825	355	443	75	8,952
afloat	1,469	0	1,469	0	0
total ashore and afloat	**85,050**	**46,953**	**5,969**	**873**	**31,255**
East Asia and Pacific					
Australia	140	24	28	22	66
Japan[1]	32,803	2,460	3,789	13,736	12,818
South Korea[1]	27,014	18,344	242	380	8,048
afloat	12,278	0	10,858	1,420	0
total ashore and afloat	**72,719**	**20,950**	**15,025**	**15,743**	**21,001**
Africa, Near East, and South Asia					
Afghanistan[2]	25,240	19,200	700	40	5,300
Iraq (Operation Iraqi Freedom)[2]	218,500	138,500	24,900	31,300	23,800
Bahrain	1,495	27	1,248	198	22
Djibouti	2,100	430	860	460	350
Qatar	411	189	5	37	180
Senegal	1,361	1,352	1	8	0
afloat	2,474	0	370	2,104	0
total ashore and afloat (excluding Iraq and Afghanistan)	**9,279**	**2,425**	**2,796**	**3,221**	**837**
Western Hemisphere					
total ashore and afloat	**2,038**	**711**	**593**	**370**	**364**
all foreign countries (excluding Iraq and Afghanistan)					
ashore	272,124	72,454	91,641	48,269	59,760
afloat	22,879	0	19,355	3,524	0
total ashore and afloat	**295,003**	**72,454**	**110,996**	**51,793**	**59,760**
worldwide (excluding Iraq and Afghanistan)					
ashore	1,264,082	522,017	225,602	182,968	333,495
afloat	115,469	0	111,945	3,524	0
total ashore and afloat	**1,379,551**	**522,017**	**337,547**	**186,492**	**333,495**

[1]Service members deployed to Operation Iraqi Freedom are included in these country figures.
[2]Includes deployed Reserve/National Guard.

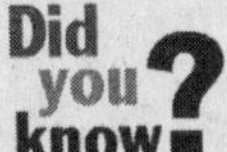

Communications satellites comprising a network or system are nearly always launched to a distance of 35,890 km (22,300 mi) above the Earth. At this altitude the motion of a satellite becomes synchronized with the Earth's rotation, causing the craft to remain fixed over a single location. If properly positioned, three communications satellites traveling in such a synchronous orbit can relay signals between stations around the world.

Military Ranks and Monthly Pay

Pay given in US dollars as of 1 Jan 2008.

Enlisted personnel

	E-1	E-2	E-3	E-4	E-5
Army	private	private	private first class	corporal	sergeant
Navy	seaman recruit	seaman apprentice	seaman	petty officer third class	petty officer second class
Air Force	airman basic	airman	airman first class	senior airman	staff sergeant
Marine Corps	private	private first class	lance corporal	corporal	sergeant
0–6 years	1,240–1,340	1,503	1,580–1,781	1,751–2,038	1,910–2,237
6–12 years				2,125	2,393–2,692
12–18 years					2,709
18–24 years					
over 24 years					

Military Ranks and Monthly Pay (continued)

Enlisted personnel (continued)

	E-6	E-7	E-8	E-9
Army	staff sergeant	sergeant first class	master sergeant, first sergeant	sergeant major
Navy	petty officer first class	chief petty officer	senior chief petty officer	master chief petty officer
Air Force	technical sergeant	master sergeant, first sergeant	senior master sergeant, first sergeant	chief master sergeant
Marine Corps	staff sergeant	gunnery sergeant	master sergeant, first sergeant	master gunnery sergeant, sergeant major
0–6 years	2,084–2,492	2,409–2,864		
6–12 years	2,595–2,916	2,968–3,247	3,466–3,619	4,234
12–18 years	3,090–3,182	3,427–3,677	3,714–3,951	4,330–4,593
18–24 years	3,227	3,785–3,968	4,173–4,478	4,736–5,161
over 24 years		4,043–4,330	4,584–4,943	5,366–6,573

Warrant officers

	W-1	W-2	W-3	W-4	W-5
Army	warrant officer	chief warrant officer	chief warrant officer	chief warrant officer	chief warrant officer
Navy		"	"	"	"
Marine Corps	"	"	"	"	"
	W-1	**W-2**	**W-3**	**W-4**	**W-5**
0–6 years	2,486–2,977	2,832–3,239	3,200–3,515	3,504–3,985	
6–12 years	3,157–3,545	3,422–3,849	3,659–4,234	4,168–4,533	
12–18 years	3,719–4,022	3,989–4,292	4,373–4,697	4,809–5,282	
18–24 years	4,145–4,295	4,412–4,652	4,993–5,313	5,470–5,925	6,231–6,547
over 24 years		4,727	5,441–5,614	6,147–6,528	6,783–8,154

Officers (with more than 4 years served as a warrant or enlisted member of the armed services)

	O-1E	O-2E	O-3E
Army	second lieutenant (lt.)	first lieutenant (lt.)	captain
Navy	ensign	lieutenant, jr. grade	lieutenant
Air Force	second lieutenant	first lieutenant	captain
Marine Corps	second lieutenant	first lieutenant	captain
0–6 years	3,200	3973	4,524
6–12 years	3,417–3,673	4,055–4,402	4,740–5,132
12–18 years	3,800–3,973	4,570–4,696	5,385–5,721
18–24 years			5,888
over 24 years			

Officers

	O-1	O-2	O-3	O-4	O-5
Army	second lieutenant	first lieutenant	captain	major	lieutenant colonel
Navy	ensign	lt., jr. grade	lieutenant	lt. commander	commander
Air Force	second lieutenant	first lieutenant	captain	major	lieutenant colonel
Marine Corps	second lieutenant	first lieutenant	captain	major	lieutenant colonel
0–6 years	2,543–3,200	2,930–3,973	3,391–4,524	3,857–4,829	4,470–5,450
6–12 years		4,055	4,740–5,132	5,106–5,771	5,667–6,084
12–18 years			5,385–5,517	6,059–6,373	6,293–6,980
18–24 years				6,440	7,177–7,594
over 24 years					
	O-6	**O-7**	**O-8**	**O-9**	**O-10**
Army	colonel	brigadier general	major general	lieutenant general	general
Navy	captain	rear admiral (lower half)	rear admiral (upper half)	vice admiral	admiral
Air Force	colonel	brigadier general	major general	lieutenant general	general
Marine Corps	colonel	brigadier general	major general	lieutenant general	general
0–6 years	5,363–6,277	7,235–7,850	8,707–9,234		
6–12 years	6,301–6,607	8,074–8,550	9,470–9,956		
12–18 years	6,607–7,646	8,805–9,865	10,331–10,761		
18–24 years	8,036–8,647	10,543	11,228–11,946	12,305–12,482	14,069–14,138
over 24 years	8,871–9,493	10,543–10,808	11,946–12,551	12,738–15,264	14,432–17,300

Number of Living Veterans[1]

Source: Statistical Abstract of the US: 2008.

AGE IN YEARS	KOREAN CONFLICT	VIETNAM ERA	GULF WAR[2]	TOTAL WARTIME[3,4]	TOTAL PEACETIME	TOTAL VETERANS[4]
under 35	—	—	1,937,000	1,937,000	12,000	1,949,000
35-39	—	—	979,000	979,000	304,000	1,283,000
40-44	—	—	633,000	633,000	985,000	1,618,000
45-49	—	67,000	464,000	526,000	1,340,000	1,866,000
50-54	—	1,188,000	321,000	1,393,000	588,000	1,980,000
55-59	—	2,872,000	201,000	2,938,000	143,000	3,081,000
60-64	—	2,600,000	80,000	2,616,000	384,000	3,000,000
65 and over	3,086,000	1,229,000	32,000	6,813,000	2,387,000	9,200,000
Female, total	74,000	258,000	728,000	1,175,000	557,000	1,731,000
Total[5]	**3,086,000**	**7,956,000**	**4,647,000**	**17,835,000**	**6,142,000**	**23,977,000**

[1]As of 30 Sep 2006. Includes those living outside of the US. Estimated. [2]Service from 2 Aug 1990 to the present. [3]Veterans who served in more than one wartime period are counted only once. [4]Includes an estimate of 3,151,000 veterans of World War II, all 65 or over, of which 149,000 are female. [5]Detail may not add to total given because of rounding.

Veterans Receiving Compensation

Numbers of veterans receiving compensation for service-related disabilities and low-income veterans receiving pensions who have permanent and total mostly non-service-related disabilities or are age 65 or older. N/A means not applicable.

TIME OF SERVICE	1980	1990	2001	2002	2003	2004	2005	2006
World War I	198,000	18,000	—[1]	—[1]	—[1]	—[1]	—[1]	—[1]
World War II	1,849,000	1,294,000	624,000	583,000	546,000	506,000	466,000	430,000
Korean conflict[2]	317,000	305,000	246,000	243,000	241,000	237,000	231,000	226,000
Vietnam era[3]	569,000	685,000	862,000	922,000	983,000	1,028,000	1,068,000	1,104,000
Gulf War[4]	N/A	N/A	368,000	421,000	479,000	540,000	617,000	701,000
peacetime	262,000	444,000	569,000	575,000	583,000	587,000	591,000	596,000
Total	**3,195,000**	**2,746,000**	**2,669,000**	**2,744,000**	**2,832,000**	**2,898,000**	**2,973,000**	**3,056,000**

[1]Fewer than 500. [2]Service from 27 Jun 1950–31 Jan 1955. [3]Service from 5 Aug 1964–7 May 1975. [4]Service from 2 Aug 1990 to the present.

US Casualties of War

Data prior to World War I are based on incomplete records. Casualty data exclude personnel captured or missing in action. N/A means not available or unknown. Sources: US Department of Defense and US Coast Guard.

				CASUALTIES		
WAR	**SERVICE BRANCH**	**NUMBER OF COMBATANTS**	**WOUNDED[1]**	**BATTLE DEATHS**	**OTHER DEATHS**	**TOTAL DEATHS**
Revolutionary War (1775–83)	Army	N/A	6,004	4,044	N/A	N/A
	Navy	N/A	114	342	N/A	N/A
	Marines	N/A	70	49	N/A	N/A
	total	**184,000–250,000[2]**	**6,188**	**4,435**	**20,000[2]**	**24,435**
War of 1812 (1812–15)	Army	N/A	4,000	1,950	N/A	N/A
	Navy	N/A	439	265	N/A	N/A
	Marines	N/A	66	45	N/A	N/A
	Coast Guard	100	N/A	0	N/A	N/A
	total	**286,830**	**4,505**	**2,260**	**N/A**	**N/A**
Indian Wars (about 1817–98)	**total**	**106,000[2]**	**N/A**	**1,000[2]**	**N/A**	**N/A**
Mexican-American War (1846–48)	Army	N/A	4,102	1,721	11,550	13,271
	Navy	N/A	3	1	N/A	N/A
	Marines	N/A	47	11	N/A	N/A
	Coast Guard	71	N/A	N/A	N/A	N/A
	total	**78,789**	**4,152[4]**	**1,733[4]**	**N/A**	**N/A**
Civil War (1861–65) Union	Army	2,128,948	280,040	138,154	221,374	359,528
	Navy	N/A	1,710	2,112	2,411	4,523
	Marines	84,415	131	148	312	460

US Casualties of War (continued)

WAR	SERVICE BRANCH	NUMBER OF COMBATANTS	WOUNDED[1]	CASUALTIES BATTLE DEATHS	OTHER DEATHS	TOTAL DEATHS
Civil War (1861–65)	Coast Guard	219	N/A	1	N/A	N/A
Union (continued)	**total**	**N/A**	**281,881[4]**	**140,415**	**224,097[4]**	**364,512[4]**
Confederate[3]	**total**	**600,000–1,500,000**	**137,000[2]**	**74,524**	**124,000[2]**	**198,524**
Spanish-American War (1898)	Army	280,564	1,594	369	2,061	2,430
	Navy	22,875	47	10	N/A	N/A
	Marines	3,321	21	6	N/A	N/A
	Coast Guard	660	N/A	0	N/A	0
	total	**307,420**	**1,662**	**385**	**2,061**	**N/A**
World War I (1917–18)	Army[4]	4,057,101	193,663	50,510	55,868	106,378
	Navy	599,051	819	431	6,856	7,287
	Marines	78,839	9,520	2,461	390	2,851
	Coast Guard	8,835	N/A	111	81	192
	total	**4,743,826**	**204,002[4]**	**53,513**	**63,195**	**116,708**
World War II (1941–46)	Army[4]	11,260,000	565,861	234,874	83,400	318,274
	Navy	4,183,466	37,778	36,950	25,664	62,614
	Marines	669,100	68,207	19,733	4,778	24,511
	Coast Guard	241,093	N/A	574	1,343	1,917
	total	**16,353,659**	**671,846[4]**	**292,131**	**115,185**	**407,316**
Korean War (1950–53)	Army	2,834,000	77,596	27,731	2,125	29,856
	Navy	1,177,000	1,576	506	154	660
	Marines	424,000	23,744	4,266	242	4,508
	Air Force	1,285,000	368	1,238	314	1,552
	Coast Guard	8,500[5]	0	0	0	0
	total	**5,764,143**	**103,284**	**33,741**	**2,835**	**36,576**
Vietnam War (1964–73)	Army	4,368,000	96,802	30,952	7,261	38,213
	Navy	1,842,000	4,178	1,628	934	2,562
	Marines	794,000	51,392	13,091	1,749	14,840
	Air Force	1,740,000	931	1,744	841	2,585
	Coast Guard	8,000	60	7	N/A	7
	total	**8,752,000**	**153,363[6]**	**47,422**	**10,785[4]**	**58,207[4]**
Persian Gulf War[7] (1990–91)	Army	338,636	354	98	126	224
	Navy	152,419	12[8]	5[8]	50[8]	55[8]
	Marines	97,878	92	24	44	68
	Air Force	76,543	9	20	15	35
	Coast Guard	400	N/A	N/A	N/A	N/A
	total	**665,876**	**467**	**147**	**235**	**382**
War on Terrorism[9] (2001–)	Army	N/A	1,673	249	132	381
	Navy	N/A	18	18	15	33
	Marines	N/A	126	12	28	40
	Air Force	N/A	81	10	18	28
	Coast Guard	N/A	N/A	N/A	N/A	N/A
	total	**N/A**	**1,898**	**289**	**193**	**482**
Iraq War[10] (2003–)	Army	N/A	20,058	2,330	540	2,870
	Navy	N/A	609	63	30	93
	Marines	N/A	8,413	825	150	975
	Air Force	N/A	371	26	18	44
	Coast Guard	N/A	N/A	1	0	1
	total	**N/A**	**29,451**	**3,245**	**738**	**3,983**
other[11]						

[1]Data in this column account for the total number of wounds. Marine Corps data for World War II, the Spanish-American War, and earlier wars represent the number of combatants wounded. [2]Estimate. [3]US service members only. [4]Excluding unavailable Coast Guard data. [5]Number eligible for Korean Service Medal. [6]Excludes 150,332 wounded that did not require hospital care. [7]Data for military personnel serving in the theater of operation. [8]Includes Coast Guard. [9]Operation Enduring Freedom; data for 7 Oct 2001–15 Mar 2008. [10]Operation Iraqi Freedom; data for 20 Mar 2003–15 Mar 2008. [11]US casualties of other recent military operations: in Grenada (1983) 119 wounded, 19 battle deaths; in Panama (1989) 324 wounded, 23 battle deaths; in Somalia (1992–94) 153 wounded, 43 battle deaths.

Ouroboros was the emblematic serpent of ancient Egypt and Greece, represented with its tail in its mouth as continually devouring itself and being reborn. It represented the eternal cycle of destruction and re-creation. In the 19th century, a vision of Ouroboros gave the German chemist Friedrich August Kekule von Stradonitz the idea of linked carbon atoms forming the benzene ring.

Leading Department of Defense Contractors

Top 70 Department of Defense contractors listed according to net value of prime contract awards, fiscal year 2006. Source: <www.fpds.gov>.

RANK	CONTRACTOR	AMOUNT (US$)
1	Lockheed Martin	27,089,418,408
2	Boeing	19,685,209,761
3	Northrop Grumman	16,052,078,855
4	General Dynamics	11,568,473,145
5	Raytheon	9,422,453,632
6	KBR[1]	5,980,228,469
7	BAE Systems	5,925,627,191
8	L-3 Communications Holdings	4,820,846,861
9	United Technologies	4,543,177,267
10	Science Applications International	3,116,435,222
11	Humana	2,645,110,495
12	General Electric	2,409,626,230
13	ITT	2,306,480,820
14	MacAndrews & Forbes Holdings	2,137,695,311
15	Health Net	2,119,299,090
16	TriWest Healthcare Alliance	2,021,460,650
17	Electronic Data Systems	1,977,712,608
18	Computer Sciences	1,900,982,784
19	Honeywell International	1,452,348,447
20	Harris	1,411,116,393
21	URS	1,385,388,617
22	Rockwell Collins	1,353,619,801
23	DRS Technologies	1,323,319,720
24	AmerisourceBergen	1,322,372,832
25	Federal Express Charter Program Team Arrangement	1,292,917,713
26	Booz Allen Hamilton	1,231,221,729
27	Bell Boeing Joint Project Office	1,110,561,993
28	Evergreen International Airlines	1,023,465,614
29	Kuwait Petroleum	1,011,270,194
30	Bechtel Group	998,290,091
31	Environmental Chemical	993,582,490
32	Oshkosh Truck	988,263,557
33	Exxon Mobil	988,105,594
34	Textron	958,725,656
35	Alliant Techsystems	829,395,903
36	CACI International	827,127,742
37	Equilon Enterprises	804,836,908
38	National Agricultural Cooperative Federation	762,328,685
39	Phillips & Jordan	707,759,130
40	General Atomic Technologies	689,466,975
41	BP	677,607,532
42	McKesson	666,104,126
43	Valero Energy	661,171,541
44	Mitre	660,556,094
45	Aerospace	653,969,926
46	Cardinal Health	632,801,796
47	Syracuse Research	615,049,000
48	Dell	582,676,347
49	Refinery Associates of Texas	576,557,185
50	Cerberus Partner	560,047,105
51	United Industrial	559,522,358
52	Chugach Alaska	553,547,112
53	Government of Canada	548,187,636
54	A.P. Møller-Maersk Group	543,540,080
55	Battelle Memorial Institute	536,918,620
56	Johns Hopkins University	524,399,371
57	Jacobs Engineering Group	520,108,952
58	Abu Dhabi National Oil	494,286,000
59	Kraft Foods	466,704,419
60	ARINC Management	459,900,968
61	Ceres Environmental Services	454,718,957
62	AshBritt	445,287,311
63	Hunt Building	438,163,722
64	EDO	437,280,229
65	Ceradyne	436,231,155
66	McDonnell Douglas	435,424,231
67	Afognak Native	423,906,827
68	Tetra Tech	423,280,258
69	Hawker Beechcraft	406,096,563
70	DynCorp Technical Services	405,635,195

[1]*Until April 2007 KBR was a subsidiary of Halliburton.*

CIA Directors

The National Security Act of 26 Jul 1947 established the Central Intelligence Agency (CIA) on 18 Sep 1947. By authority of a presidential directive of 22 Jan 1946, the director of central intelligence served as a member of the National Intelligence Authority and as head of the Central Intelligence Group. When the office of director of national intelligence (DNI) was created in 2005, the title of the head of the CIA, who would report to the DNI, was changed to director of the Central Intelligence Agency. The director coordinates the nation's intelligence activities and informs the president on issues of national security. Acting directors are not included in this table.

NAME	DATES OF SERVICE
Rear Adm. Sidney W. Souers, USNR	23 Jan 1946–9 Jun 1946
Lt. Gen. Hoyt S. Vandenberg, USA	10 Jun 1946–30 Apr 1947
Rear Adm. Roscoe H. Hillenkoetter, USN	1 May 1947–6 Oct 1950
Gen. Walter Bedell Smith, USA	7 Oct 1950–9 Feb 1953
Allen W. Dulles	26 Feb 1953–28 Nov 1961
John A. McCone	29 Nov 1961–27 Apr 1965
Vice Adm. William F. Raborn, Jr., USN	28 Apr 1965–29 Jun 1966
Richard M. Helms	30 Jun 1966–1 Feb 1973
James R. Schlesinger	2 Feb 1973–2 Jul 1973
William E. Colby	4 Sep 1973–29 Jan 1976
George H.W. Bush	30 Jan 1976–20 Jan 1977
Adm. Stansfield Turner, USN	9 Mar 1977–20 Jan 1981
William J. Casey	28 Jan 1981–29 Jan 1987
William H. Webster	26 May 1987–31 Aug 1991
Robert M. Gates	6 Nov 1991–20 Jan 1993
R. James Woolsey	5 Feb 1993–10 Jan 1995
John M. Deutch	10 May 1995–15 Dec 1996
George J. Tenet	11 Jul 1997–11 Jul 2004
Porter J. Goss	24 Sep 2004–29 May 2006
Gen. Michael V. Hayden, USAF	30 May 2006–

The National Security Council (NSC)

The National Security Act of 1947 established the NSC to advise the president on policies relating to national security. In addition to regular attendees, the chief of staff to the president, counsel to the president, and assistant to the president for economic policy are invited to attend all meetings. The attorney general and the director of the Office of Management and Budget are also invited to attend when needed.

chair	George W. Bush (president)
regular attendees	Richard B. Cheney (vice president)
	Condoleezza Rice (secretary of state)
	Henry M. Paulson, Jr. (secretary of the treasury)
	Robert M. Gates (secretary of defense)
	Stephen Hadley (assistant to the president for national security affairs)
military adviser	Mike Mullen (chairman of the Joint Chiefs of Staff)
intelligence adviser	Michael V. Hayden (director of the CIA)
additional participants	Joshua B. Bolten (chief of staff)
	Fred Fielding (counsel to the president)
	Keith Hennessey (assistant to the president for economic policy)
	Michael Mukasey (attorney general)
	Jim Nussle (director of the Office of Management and Budget)

On 23 Mar 1953 Pres. Dwight D. Eisenhower established the office of assistant to the president for national security affairs (commonly referred to as the national security advisor). Holders of this office are listed below.

NAME	DATES OF SERVICE
Robert Cutler	23 Mar 1953–1 Apr 1955
Dillon Anderson	2 Apr 1955–1 Sep 1956
Robert Cutler	7 Jan 1957–23 Jun 1958
Gordon Gray	24 Jun 1958–13 Jan 1961
McGeorge Bundy	20 Jan 1961–28 Feb 1966
Walt W. Rostow	1 Apr 1966–1 Dec 1968
Henry A. Kissinger	2 Dec 1968–2 Nov 1975[1]
Brent Scowcroft	3 Nov 1975–19 Jan 1977
Zbigniew Brzezinski	20 Jan 1977–20 Jan 1981
Richard V. Allen	21 Jan 1981–4 Jan 1982
William P. Clark	4 Jan 1982–16 Oct 1983
Robert C. McFarlane	17 Oct 1983–3 Dec 1985
John M. Poindexter	4 Dec 1985–25 Nov 1986
Frank C. Carlucci	2 Dec 1986–22 Nov 1987
Colin L. Powell	23 Nov 1987–19 Jan 1989
Brent Scrowcroft	20 Jan 1989–19 Jan 1993
W. Anthony Lake	20 Jan 1993–13 Mar 1997
Samuel R. Berger	14 Mar 1997–20 Jan 2001
Condoleezza Rice	22 Jan 2001–25 Jan 2005
Stephen Hadley	26 Jan 2005–

[1]*Henry A. Kissinger served concurrently as secretary of state from 21 Sep 1973.*

United States Population

The Changing Face of America

The population of the United States increased by 32.7 million people between the censuses of 1990 and 2000. That increase represented the largest population growth in census history. Census 2000 revealed a nation with more ethnic and racial diversity. During the 1990s the Hispanic population (Hispanics may be of any race) increased by 58%, the Asian population by 48%. The immigration of these groups accounted for about 13.3 million of the country's total population—a number not equaled in American history. The second largest number of immigrants recorded—10.1 million people—occurred between 1905 and 1914. Of the 281.4 million people residing in the United States on census day, non-Hispanic whites accounted for 69.1% of the population; Hispanics, 12.5%; blacks, 12.3%; and Asians, 3.6%.

The changing face of the United States was reflected in cities, suburbs, and rural areas. For the first time, nearly half of the nation's 100 largest cities were home to more African Americans, Hispanics, Asians, and other minorities than to non-Hispanic whites. While the population of the country's fastest-growing cities, such as Las Vegas and Phoenix, increased in all racial and ethnic categories, 71 of the top 100 cities lost non-Hispanic white residents to the suburbs and beyond. The nation's largest cities gained 3.8 million Hispanic residents, a 43% increase from a decade ago. Many cities, including Boston, Los Angeles, and Dallas, would have lost population in the 1990s were it not for large gains in the number of Hispanics.

Even with the arrival of a record number of immigrants (who tend to be relatively young), the United States continued to age as a nation. The median age of the country's population in 2000 was 35.3—five years older than the median age in 1950. (The median age splits the population in half: 50% are over the median age, 50% under it.) This increase in median age was tied to the graying of the post-World War II "baby boom" generation. Born from 1946 through 1964, baby boomers between 36 and 54 years of age represented 28% of the country's total population. The median age for non-Hispanic whites was 38.6, Asians 32.7, blacks 30.2, and Hispanics 25.8. Census 2000 revealed that the country's population was 50.9% female and 49.1% male. There were 37.1 million males under the age of 18 as compared with 35.2 million females. By the age of 36, however, there were more females than males. Female senior citizens 65 years and older outnumbered males 20.6 million to 14.4 million.

The Northeast and Midwest regions had the country's oldest populations. Median ages for those regions were 36.8 and 35.6, respectively. In contrast, the West had the population with the youngest median age, 33.8.

State Populations, 1790–2007

Resident population of the states and the District of Columbia. Numbers are in thousands ('000)[1].
Source: US Census Bureau.

STATE	1790	1800	1810	1820	1830	1840	1850	1860	1870	1880	1890	1900
AL		1	9	128	310	591	772	964	997	1,263	1,513	1,829
AK										33	32	64
AZ									10	40	88	123
AR			1	14	30	98	210	435	484	803	1,128	1,312
CA							93	380	560	865	1,213	1,485
CO								34	40	194	413	540
CT	238	251	262	275	298	310	371	460	537	623	746	908
DE	59	64	73	73	77	78	92	112	125	147	168	185
DC		8	15	23	30	34	52	75	132	178	230	279
FL					35	54	87	140	188	269	391	529
GA	83	163	252	341	517	691	906	1,057	1,184	1,542	1,837	2,216
HI												154
ID									15	33	89	162
IL			12	55	157	476	851	1,712	2,540	3,078	3,826	4,822
IN		6	25	147	343	686	988	1,350	1,681	1,978	2,192	2,516
IA						43	192	675	1,194	1,625	1,912	2,232
KS								107	364	996	1,428	1,470
KY	74	221	407	564	688	780	982	1,156	1,321	1,649	1,859	2,147
LA			77	153	216	352	518	708	727	940	1,119	1,382
ME	97	152	229	298	399	502	583	628	627	649	661	694
MD	320	342	381	407	447	470	583	687	781	935	1,042	1,188
MA	379	423	472	523	610	738	995	1,231	1,457	1,783	2,239	2,805
MI			5	9	32	212	398	749	1,184	1,637	2,094	2,421
MN							6	172	440	781	1,310	1,751
MS		8	31	75	137	376	607	791	828	1,132	1,290	1,551
MO			20	67	140	384	682	1,182	1,721	2,168	2,679	3,107
MT									21	39	143	243
NE								29	123	452	1,063	1,066
NV								7	42	62	47	42
NH	142	184	214	244	269	285	318	326	318	347	377	412
NJ	184	211	246	278	321	373	490	672	906	1,131	1,445	1,884
NM							62	94	92	120	160	195
NY	340	589	959	1,373	1,919	2,429	3,097	3,881	4,383	5,083	6,003	7,269
NC	394	478	556	639	738	753	869	993	1,071	1,400	1,618	1,894
ND								5	2	37	191	319
OH		45	231	581	938	1,519	1,980	2,340	2,665	3,198	3,672	4,158
OK											259	790
OR							12	52	91	175	318	414
PA	434	602	810	1,049	1,348	1,724	2,312	2,906	3,522	4,283	5,258	6,302
RI	69	69	77	83	97	109	148	175	217	277	346	429
SC	249	346	415	503	581	594	669	704	706	996	1,151	1,340
SD									12	98	349	402
TN	36	106	262	423	682	829	1,003	1,110	1,259	1,542	1,768	2,021
TX							213	604	819	1,592	2,236	3,049
UT							11	40	87	144	211	277
VT	85	154	218	236	281	292	314	315	331	332	332	344
VA	692	808	878	938	1,044	1,025	1,119	1,220	1,225	1,513	1,656	1,854
WA							1	12	24	75	357	518
WV	56	79	105	137	177	225	302	377	442	618	763	959
WI						31	305	776	1,055	1,315	1,693	2,069
WY									9	21	63	93
US total[2]	**3,929**	**5,308**	**7,240**	**9,638**	**12,866**	**17,069**	**23,192**	**31,443**	**39,818[3]**	**50,156**	**62,948**	**75,995**

[1]Detail may not add to total given because of rounding. [2]Alaska and Hawaii are not included in the US total until

State Populations, 1790–2007 (continued)

1910	1920	1930	1940	1950	1960	1970	1980	1990	2000	2007 EST.
2,138	2,348	2,646	2,833	3,062	3,267	3,444	3,894	4,040	4,447	4,628
64	55	59	73	129	226	300	402	550	627	683
204	334	436	499	750	1,302	1,771	2,718	3,665	5,131	6,339
1,574	1,752	1,854	1,949	1,910	1,786	1,923	2,286	2,351	2,673	2,835
2,378	3,427	5,677	6,907	10,586	15,717	19,953	23,668	29,811	33,872	36,553
799	940	1,036	1,123	1,325	1,754	2,207	2,890	3,294	4,302	4,862
1,115	1,381	1,607	1,709	2,007	2,535	3,032	3,108	3,287	3,406	3,502
202	223	238	267	318	446	548	594	666	784	865
331	438	487	663	802	764	757	638	607	572	588
753	968	1,468	1,897	2,771	4,952	6,789	9,746	12,938	15,983	18,251
2,609	2,896	2,909	3,124	3,445	3,943	4,590	5,463	6,478	8,187	9,545
192	256	368	423	500	633	769	965	1,108	1,212	1,283
326	432	445	525	589	667	713	944	1,007	1,294	1,499
5,639	6,485	7,631	7,897	8,712	10,081	11,114	11,427	11,431	12,420	12,853
2,701	2,930	3,239	3,428	3,934	4,662	5,194	5,490	5,544	6,081	6,345
2,225	2,404	2,471	2,538	2,621	2,758	2,824	2,914	2,777	2,926	2,988
1,691	1,769	1,881	1,801	1,905	2,179	2,247	2,364	2,478	2,689	2,776
2,290	2,417	2,615	2,846	2,945	3,038	3,219	3,661	3,687	4,042	4,241
1,656	1,799	2,102	2,364	2,684	3,257	3,641	4,206	4,222	4,469	4,293
742	768	797	847	914	969	992	1,125	1,228	1,275	1,317
1,295	1,450	1,632	1,821	2,343	3,101	3,922	4,217	4,781	5,297	5,618
3,366	3,852	4,250	4,317	4,691	5,149	5,689	5,737	6,016	6,349	6,450
2,810	3,668	4,842	5,256	6,372	7,823	8,875	9,262	9,295	9,938	10,072
2,076	2,387	2,564	2,792	2,982	3,414	3,805	4,076	4,376	4,919	5,198
1,797	1,791	2,010	2,184	2,179	2,178	2,217	2,521	2,575	2,845	2,919
3,293	3,404	3,629	3,785	3,955	4,320	4,677	4,917	5,117	5,597	5,878
376	549	538	559	591	675	694	787	799	902	958
1,192	1,296	1,378	1,316	1,326	1,411	1,483	1,570	1,578	1,711	1,775
82	77	91	110	160	285	489	800	1,202	1,998	2,565
431	443	465	492	533	607	738	921	1,109	1,236	1,316
2,537	3,156	4,041	4,160	4,835	6,067	7,168	7,365	7,748	8,414	8,686
327	360	423	532	681	951	1,016	1,303	1,515	1,819	1,970
9,114	10,385	12,588	13,479	14,830	16,782	18,237	17,558	17,991	18,977	19,298
2,206	2,559	3,170	3,572	4,062	4,556	5,082	5,882	6,632	8,046	9,061
577	647	681	642	620	632	618	653	639	642	640
4,767	5,759	6,647	6,908	7,947	9,706	10,652	10,798	10,847	11,353	11,467
1,657	2,028	2,396	2,336	2,233	2,328	2,559	3,025	3,146	3,451	3,617
673	783	954	1,090	1,521	1,769	2,091	2,633	2,842	3,421	3,747
7,665	8,720	9,631	9,900	10,498	11,319	11,794	11,864	11,883	12,281	12,433
543	604	687	713	792	859	947	947	1,003	1,048	1,058
1,515	1,684	1,739	1,900	2,117	2,383	2,591	3,122	3,486	4,012	4,408
584	637	693	643	653	681	666	691	696	755	796
2,185	2,338	2,617	2,916	3,292	3,567	3,924	4,591	4,877	5,689	6,157
3,897	4,663	5,825	6,415	7,711	9,580	11,197	14,229	16,986	20,852	23,904
373	449	508	550	689	891	1,059	1,461	1,723	2,233	2,645
356	352	360	359	378	390	444	511	563	609	621
2,062	2,309	2,422	2,678	3,319	3,967	4,648	5,347	6,189	7,079	7,712
1,142	1,357	1,563	1,736	2,379	2,853	3,409	4,132	4,867	5,894	6,468
1,221	1,464	1,729	1,902	2,006	1,860	1,744	1,950	1,793	1,808	1,812
2,334	2,632	2,939	3,138	3,435	3,952	4,418	4,706	4,892	5,364	5,602
146	194	226	251	291	330	332	470	454	494	523
91,972	**105,711**	**122,775**	**131,669**	**150,697**	**179,323**	**203,302[3]**	**226,546[3]**	**248,791[3]**	**281,425[3]**	**301,621**

1960, the year after both achieved statehood. [3]Figures were revised by the Census Bureau after the census.

Total US Population and Area, 1790–2007

The total land/water area data from 1790 to 1970 were recalculated for the 1980 census. Information for Alaska and Hawaii is included in all censuses after 1940. N/A means not available. Source: US Census Bureau.

CENSUS	POPULATION	POPULATION GROWTH (%)	TOTAL LAND/WATER AREA (SQ MI)	LAND AREA (SQ MI)	PEOPLE/SQ MI OF LAND AREA
1790	3,929,214	–	891,364	864,746	4.5
1800	5,308,483	35.1	891,364	864,746	6.1
1810	7,239,881	36.4	1,722,685	1,681,828	4.3
1820	9,638,453	33.1	1,792,552	1,749,462	5.5
1830	12,866,020	33.5	1,792,552	1,749,462	7.4
1840	17,069,453	32.7	1,792,552	1,749,462	9.8
1850	23,191,876	35.9	2,991,655	2,940,042	7.9
1860	31,443,321	35.6	3,021,295	2,969,640	10.6
1870	39,818,449	26.6	3,612,299	3,540,705	11.2
1880	50,189,209	26.0	3,612,299	3,540,705	14.2
1890	62,979,766	25.5	3,612,299	3,540,705	17.8
1900	76,212,168	21.0	3,618,770	3,547,314	21.5
1910	92,228,496	21.0	3,618,770	3,547,045	26.0
1920	106,021,537	15.0	3,618,770	3,546,931	29.9
1930	123,202,624	16.2	3,618,770	3,551,608	34.7
1940	132,164,569	7.3	3,618,770	3,551,608	37.2
1950	151,325,798	14.5	3,618,770	3,552,206	42.6
1960	179,323,175	18.5	3,618,770	3,540,911	50.6
1970	203,302,031	13.4	3,618,770	3,536,855	57.5
1980	226,542,199	11.4	3,618,770	3,539,289	64.0
1990	248,718,302	9.8	3,717,796	3,536,278	70.3
2000	281,422,509	13.1	3,794,083	3,537,439	79.6
2007	301,621,157	7.2	N/A	N/A	N/A

US Population by Race, Sex, Median Age, and Residence

Numbers are in thousands ('000) except for the median age figures and the residency percentages. N/A means not available. Source: US Census Bureau.

	RACE			SEX		MEDIAN	RESIDENCE[2]	
YEAR	WHITE	BLACK	OTHER[1]	MALE	FEMALE	AGE	URBAN (%)	RURAL (%)
1790	3,172	757	N/A	N/A	N/A	N/A	5.1	94.9
1800	4,306	1,002	N/A	N/A	N/A	N/A	6.1	93.9
1810	5,862	1,378	N/A	N/A	N/A	N/A	7.3	92.7
1820	7,867	1,772	N/A	4,897	4,742	16.7	7.2	92.8
1830	10,537	2,329	N/A	6,532	6,334	17.2	8.8	91.2
1840	14,196	2,874	N/A	8,689	8,381	17.8	10.8	89.2
1850	19,553	3,639	N/A	11,838	11,354	18.9	15.4	84.6
1860	26,923	4,442	79	16,085	15,358	19.4	19.8	80.2
1870	34,337	5,392	89	19,494	19,065	20.2	25.7	74.3
1880	43,403	6,581	172	25,519	24,637	20.9	28.2	71.8
1890	55,101	7,489	358	32,237	30,711	22.0	35.1	64.9
1900	66,809	8,834	351	38,816	37,178	22.9	39.6	60.4
1910	81,732	9,828	413	47,332	44,640	24.1	45.6	54.4
1920	94,821	10,463	427	53,900	51,810	25.3	51.2	48.8
1930	110,287	11,891	597	62,137	60,638	26.4	56.1	43.9
1940	118,215	12,866	589	66,062	65,608	29.0	56.5	43.5
1950	134,942	15,042	713	74,833	75,864	30.2	64.0	36.0
1960	158,832	18,872	1,620	88,331	90,992	29.5	69.9	30.1
1970	178,098	22,581	2,557	98,926	104,309	28.0	73.6	26.3
1980	194,713	26,683	5,150	110,053	116,493	30.0	73.7	26.3
1990	199,686	29,986	9,233	121,271	127,494	32.8	78.0	22.0
2000	211,461	34,658	13,118	138,054	143,368	35.3	79.0	21.0
2007	241,167	38,756	21,698	148,659	152,962	36.6	N/A	N/A

[1]"Other" refers to Asians, Pacific Islanders, American Indians, Alaska Natives, and those belonging to two or more races. Alaska and Hawaii are excluded from the population numbers until 1960, the first census after they became states in 1959. [2]The census definitions for urban and rural areas have changed through the decades.

US Population by Race and Hispanic Origin

Census 2000 was the first US census in which individuals could report themselves as being of more than one race. For the comparison between these census results and the 2007 data, this table uses the 2000 census information that was revised in April 2000. Hispanic or Latino people may be of any race.

Source: US Census Bureau.

RACE	2000 CENSUS NUMBER[1]	%[1]	2007 NUMBER[1]	%[1]	% INCREASE FROM 2000 TO 2007[1]
White	228,107,000	81.1	241,167,000	80.0	+5.7
Black or African American	35,705,000	12.7	38,756,000	12.8	+8.5
American Indian or Alaska Native	2,664,000	0.9	2,938,000	1.0	+10.3
Asian	10,589,000	3.8	13,366,000	4.4	+26.2
Native Hawaiian/other Pacific Islander	463,000	0.2	537,000	0.2	+16.0
Two or more races	3,898,000	1.4	4,856,000	1.6	+24.6
Total population	**281,425,000**	**100.0**	**301,621,000**	**100.0**	**+7.2**

HISPANIC OR LATINO POPULATION	2000 CENSUS NUMBER[1]	%[1]	2007 NUMBER[1]	%[1]	% DIFFERENCE 2000/2007[1]
Hispanic or Latino (of any race)	35,306,000	12.5	45,504,000	15.1	+28.9
Not Hispanic or Latino	246,118,000	87.5	256,117,000	84.9	+4.1
Total population	**281,425,000**	**100.0**	**301,621,000**	**100.0**	**+7.2**

[1]*Detail may not add to total given because of rounding.*

Foreign-Born Population in the US, 1850–2006

The foreign-born population consists of persons born outside the United States to parents who were not US citizens. Information from 1950 to 2000 was taken from sample data. Populations of Alaska and Hawaii were included starting in 1960. In 1850 and 1860 data, the entire slave population was considered native-born.

Source: *Statistical Abstract of the United States: 2008.*

YEAR	POPULATION TOTAL	FOREIGN-BORN	% OF TOTAL	YEAR	POPULATION TOTAL	FOREIGN-BORN	% OF TOTAL
1850	23,191,876	2,244,602	9.7	1940	131,669,275	11,594,896	8.8
1860	31,443,321	4,138,697	13.2	1950	150,216,110	10,347,395	6.9
1870	38,558,371	5,567,229	14.4	1960	179,325,671	9,738,091	5.4
1880	50,155,783	6,679,943	13.3	1970	203,210,158	9,619,302	4.7
1890	62,622,250	9,249,547	14.8	1980	226,545,805	14,079,906	6.2
1900	75,994,575	10,341,276	13.6	1990	248,709,873	19,767,316	7.9
1910	91,972,266	13,515,886	14.7	2000	281,421,906	31,107,889	11.1
1920	105,710,620	13,920,692	13.2	2005	288,378,000	35,690,000	12.4
1930	122,775,046	14,204,149	11.6	2006[1]	293,834,000	35,659,000	12.1

[1]*As of March.*

Total Immigrants Admitted to the US, 1901–2007

Numbers shown include only immigrant aliens admitted for permanent residence and are for fiscal years. Currently the fiscal year begins 1 October and ends 30 September. Prior to 1976, the fiscal year began 1 July and ended 30 June.

Source: *Yearbook of Immigration Statistics,* 2007.

	YEAR	NUMBER	YEAR	NUMBER	YEAR	NUMBER	YEAR	NUMBER
	1901	487,918	1911	878,587	1921	805,228	1931	97,139
	1902	648,743	1912	838,172	1922	309,556	1932	35,576
	1903	857,046	1913	1,197,892	1923	522,919	1933	23,068
	1904	812,870	1914	1,218,480	1924	706,896	1934	29,470
	1905	1,026,499	1915	326,700	1925	294,314	1935	34,956
	1906	1,100,735	1916	298,826	1926	304,488	1936	36,329
	1907	1,285,349	1917	295,403	1927	335,175	1937	50,244
	1908	782,870	1918	110,618	1928	307,255	1938	67,895
	1909	751,786	1919	141,132	1929	279,678	1939	82,998
	1910	1,041,570	1920	430,001	1930	241,700	1940	70,756
Totals	**1901–10**	**8,795,386**	**1911–20**	**5,735,811**	**1921–30**	**4,107,209**	**1931–40**	**528,431**

Total Immigrants Admitted to the US, 1901–2007 (continued)

	YEAR	NUMBER	YEAR	NUMBER	YEAR	NUMBER	YEAR	NUMBER
	1941	51,776	1951	205,717	1961	271,344	1971	370,478
	1942	28,781	1952	265,520	1962	283,763	1972	384,685
	1943	23,725	1953	170,434	1963	306,260	1973	398,515
	1944	28,551	1954	208,177	1964	292,248	1974	393,919
	1945	38,119	1955	237,790	1965	296,697	1975	385,378
	1946	108,721	1956	321,625	1966	323,040	1976[1]	499,093
	1947	147,292	1957	326,867	1967	361,972	1977	458,755
	1948	170,570	1958	253,265	1968	454,448	1978	589,810
	1949	188,317	1959	260,686	1969	358,579	1979	394,244
	1950	249,187	1960	265,398	1970	373,326	1980	524,295
Totals	**1941-50**	**1,035,039**	**1951-60**	**2,515,479**	**1961-70**	**3,321,677**	**1971-80**	**4,399,172**
	1981	595,014	1991	1,826,595	2001	1,058,902		
	1982	533,624	1992	973,445	2002	1,059,356		
	1983	550,052	1993	903,916	2003	703,542		
	1984	541,811	1994	803,993	2004	957,883		
	1985	568,149	1995	720,177	2005	1,122,257		
	1986	600,027	1996	915,560	2006	1,266,129		
	1987	599,889	1997	797,847	2007	1,052,415		
	1988	641,346	1998	653,206				
	1989	1,090,172	1999	644,787				
	1990	1,535,872	2000	841,002				
Totals	**1981-90**	**7,255,956**	**1991-2000**	**9,080,528**	**2001-07**	**7,220,484**		

Totals 1901-2007: 53,995,172

[1]*Includes the 15 months from 1 Jul 1975 through 30 Sep 1976.*

Immigrants Admitted to the US by Country of Birth and State of Residence

Fiscal year 2006. Korea used to designate both North and South Korea.
Source: <www.dhs.gov>.

STATE OF RESIDENCE	TOTAL IMMIGRANTS	TOP FIVE COUNTRIES OF BIRTH (NUMBER OF IMMIGRANTS)
Alabama	4,278	Mexico (535), Philippines (325), China (301), India (280), Guatemala (180)
Alaska	1,554	Philippines (457), Mexico (102), China (92), Korea (79), Canada (66)
Arizona	21,530	Mexico (10,030), Philippines (871), India (715), China (675), Canada (570)
Arkansas	2,926	Mexico (981), El Salvador (220), Philippines (181), China (170), Vietnam (155)
California	264,677	Mexico (66,744), China (27,305), Philippines (26,982), India (14,110), El Salvador (11,767)
Colorado	12,714	Mexico (3,245), China (783), Ethiopia (602), Vietnam (468), Philippines (341)
Connecticut	18,700	Jamaica (1,365), Poland (1,175), Brazil (1,092), Ecuador (1,017), Colombia (982)
Delaware	2,265	Mexico (252), India (194), China (147), Jamaica (107), Kenya (97)
District of Columbia	3,775	Ethiopia (566), El Salvador (551), Nigeria (143), China (133), Philippines (106)
Florida	155,996	Cuba (37,711), Colombia (19,832), Haiti (12,599), Jamaica (7,207), Venezuela (6,486)
Georgia	32,202	Mexico (3,708), India (2,433), Colombia (1,350), China (1,263), Vietnam (1,183)
Hawaii	7,501	Philippines (3,723), China (815), Japan (742), Korea (361), Vietnam (220)
Idaho	2,377	Mexico (842), China (139), Philippines (131), Canada (94), Bosnia and Herzegovina (84)
Illinois	52,459	Mexico (11,735), Poland (5,496), India (4,479), Philippines (4,125), China (2,456)
Indiana	8,125	Mexico (1,204), China (654), Philippines (515), India (494), Myanmar (Burma) (246)
Iowa	4,086	Mexico (882), Vietnam (268), The Sudan (242), China (215), Guatemala (173)
Kansas	4,280	Mexico (1,187), Vietnam (301), China (245), India (237), Philippines (155)
Kentucky	5,506	Cuba (801), India (391), Mexico (361), Philippines (344), China (312)
Louisiana	2,693	Vietnam (299), Mexico (188), China (182), India (176), Philippines (137)
Maine	1,719	Somalia (198), China (139), Canada (133), The Sudan (122), Philippines (97)

Immigrants Admitted to the US by Country of Birth and State of Residence (continued)

STATE OF RESIDENCE	TOTAL IMMIGRANTS	TOP FIVE COUNTRIES OF BIRTH (NUMBER OF IMMIGRANTS)
Maryland	30,204	El Salvador (2,422), Ethiopia (1,917), China (1,605), Nigeria (1,605), Philippines (1,576)
Massachusetts	35,560	Brazil (3,141), China (2,768), Dominican Republic (2,751), Haiti (1,789), India (1,520)
Michigan	20,911	Iraq (1,541), India (1,526), Mexico (1,354), Albania (1,206), China (1,103)
Minnesota	18,254	Somalia (2,844), Thailand (2,102), Ethiopia (1,516), Mexico (746), Liberia (728)
Mississippi	1,480	Mexico (215), Philippines (193), India (135), China (134), Vietnam (81)
Missouri	6,857	Mexico (489), Bosnia and Herzegovina (431), China (403), Philippines (356), Vietnam (324)
Montana	505	Canada (62), China (62), Philippines (46), Germany (24), United Kingdom (18)
Nebraska	3,795	Mexico (1,041), The Sudan (300), Guatemala (294), Vietnam (213), El Salvador (163)
Nevada	14,714	Mexico (3,759), Philippines (2,400), Cuba (931), China (827), El Salvador (592)
New Hampshire	2,990	China (177), Canada (162), Brazil (155), India (155), Dominican Republic (151)
New Jersey	65,934	India (6,491), Dominican Republic (5,340), Colombia (4,175), Philippines (4,007), Ecuador (3,357)
New Mexico	3,805	Mexico (1,965), Cuba (215), Philippines (173), China (166), Vietnam (87)
New York	180,165	China (23,891), Dominican Republic (19,233), Jamaica (8,983), Ecuador (7,339), Bangladesh (7,180)
North Carolina	18,989	Mexico (2,865), India (1,128), China (878), Vietnam (835), Colombia (737)
North Dakota	649	Canada (71), The Sudan (63), Somalia (45), Bosnia and Herzegovina (36), China (35)
Ohio	16,592	China (1,195), Philippines (1,179), Somalia (1,115), India (1,090), Mexico (608)
Oklahoma	4,591	Mexico (1,182), Vietnam (331), India (282), Philippines (277), China (238)
Oregon	9,192	Mexico (1,636), Ukraine (861), China (786), Vietnam (529), Philippines (383)
Pennsylvania	25,958	China (2,353), India (2,111), Dominican Republic (1,135), Vietnam (983), Mexico (904)
Rhode Island	4,778	Dominican Republic (906), Guatemala (599), Cape Verde (341), Liberia (297), Colombia (288)
South Carolina	5,292	Mexico (643), Colombia (429), Philippines (346), China (260), India (255)
South Dakota	1,013	Ethiopia (93), The Sudan (86), China (54), Mexico (52), Guatemala (51)
Tennessee	10,042	Philippines (1,127), Mexico (1,011), Egypt (646), India (605), China (509)
Texas	89,037	Mexico (35,830), India (4,131), El Salvador (4,125), Philippines (3,937), Vietnam (3,460)
Utah	5,749	Mexico (1,188), Peru (273), China (249), Brazil (203), Philippines (193)
Vermont	895	Canada (92), China (69), Kenya (51), Somalia (40), United Kingdom (36)
Virginia	38,488	El Salvador (3,168), Bolivia (2,050), Ethiopia (1,854), Korea (1,827) India (1,799)
Washington	23,805	Mexico (2,305), Ukraine (1,957), Philippines (1,774), China (1,577), India (1,441)
West Virginia	764	China (77), India (55), Philippines (51), Pakistan (34), Guatemala (30)
Wisconsin	8,341	Mexico (1,400), Thailand (1,190), China (501), India (455), Laos (427)
Wyoming	376	Mexico (62), China (33), Canada (28), Philippines (26), Russia (16)

Americans 65 and Older, 1900–2008

Data for Hawaii and Alaska are included after 1950. Source: US Census Bureau.

CENSUS YEAR	NUMBER OF PEOPLE 65 AND OLDER	% OF TOTAL POPULATION	CENSUS YEAR	NUMBER OF PEOPLE 65 AND OLDER	% OF TOTAL POPULATION
1900	3,080,498	4.1	1960	16,559,580	9.2
1910	3,949,524	4.3	1970	20,065,502	9.8
1920	4,933,215	4.7	1980	25,549,427	11.3
1930	6,633,805	5.4	1990	31,241,831	12.6
1940	9,019,314	6.8	2000	34,991,753	12.4
1950	12,269,537	8.1	2008	38,690,169	12.7

Poverty Level by State, 1980–2006

Source: US Census Bureau. Totals may vary due to rounding.

	% OF PEOPLE IN POVERTY			NUMBER OF PEOPLE IN POVERTY ('000)		
STATE	1980	1990	2006	1980	1990	2006
Alabama	21.2	19.2	14.3	810	779	650
Alaska	9.6	11.4	8.8	36	57	58
Arizona	12.8	13.7	14.4	354	484	902
Arkansas	21.5	19.6	17.7	484	472	487
California	11.0	13.9	12.2	2,619	4,128	4,427
Colorado	8.6	13.7	9.7	247	461	466
Connecticut	8.3	6.0	8.0	255	196	275
Delaware	11.8	6.9	9.3	68	48	80
District of Columbia	20.9	21.1	18.3	131	120	104
Florida	16.7	14.4	11.5	1,692	1,896	2,068
Georgia	13.9	15.8	12.6	727	1,001	1,172
Hawaii	8.5	11.0	9.3	81	121	116
Idaho	14.7	14.9	9.6	138	157	141
Illinois	12.3	13.7	10.6	1,386	1,606	1,338
Indiana	11.8	13.0	10.6	645	714	674
Iowa	10.8	10.4	10.3	311	289	301
Kansas	9.4	10.3	12.8	215	259	349
Kentucky	19.3	17.3	16.8	701	628	690
Louisiana	20.3	23.6	17.0	868	952	713
Maine	14.6	13.1	10.2	158	162	134
Maryland	9.5	9.9	8.4	389	468	469
Massachusetts	9.5	10.7	12.0	542	626	758
Michigan	12.9	14.3	13.3	1,194	1,315	1,323
Minnesota	8.7	12.0	8.2	342	524	422
Mississippi	24.3	25.7	20.6	591	684	596
Missouri	13.0	13.4	11.4	625	700	659
Montana	13.2	16.3	13.4	102	134	125
Nebraska	13.0	10.3	10.2	199	167	180
Nevada	8.3	9.8	9.5	70	119	241
New Hampshire	7.0	6.3	5.4	63	68	71
New Jersey	9.0	9.2	8.8	659	711	762
New Mexico	20.6	20.9	16.9	268	319	328
New York	13.8	14.3	14.0	2,391	2,571	2,668
North Carolina	15.0	13.0	13.8	877	829	1,225
North Dakota	15.5	13.7	11.4	99	87	70
Ohio	9.8	11.5	12.1	1,046	1,256	1,371
Oklahoma	13.9	15.6	15.2	406	481	531
Oregon	11.5	9.2	11.8	309	267	439
Pennsylvania	9.8	11.0	11.3	1,142	1,328	1,397
Rhode Island	10.7	7.5	10.4	97	71	110
South Carolina	16.8	16.2	11.2	534	548	474
South Dakota	18.8	13.3	10.6	127	93	82
Tennessee	19.6	16.9	14.9	884	833	879
Texas	15.7	15.9	16.4	2,247	2,684	3,816
Utah	10.0	8.2	9.3	148	143	235
Vermont	12.0	10.9	7.8	62	61	48
Virginia	12.4	11.1	8.6	647	705	651
Washington	12.7	8.9	8.0	538	434	502
West Virginia	15.2	18.1	15.3	297	328	277
Wisconsin	8.5	9.3	10.1	403	448	555
Wyoming	10.4	11.0	9.9	49	51	51
All US	**13.0**	**13.5**	**12.3**	**29,272**	**33,585**	**36,460**

Population of US Territories

Total midyear population. Source: US Census Bureau.

YEAR	PUERTO RICO	GUAM	VIRGIN ISLANDS	NORTHERN MARIANA ISLANDS	AMERICAN SAMOA
1970	2,721,754	86,470	63,476	12,359	27,267
1975	2,935,124	102,110	94,484	14,938	29,640
1980	3,209,648	106,869	99,636	16,890	32,418
1985	3,382,106	120,615	100,760	21,386	38,633
1990	3,536,910	134,110	104,235	44,037	47,199
1995	3,731,006	143,856	113,896	58,128	56,911
2000	3,915,798	154,623	120,917	71,912	65,446
2008	3,959,450	175,877	108,210	86,616	57,496

States and Other Areas of the United States

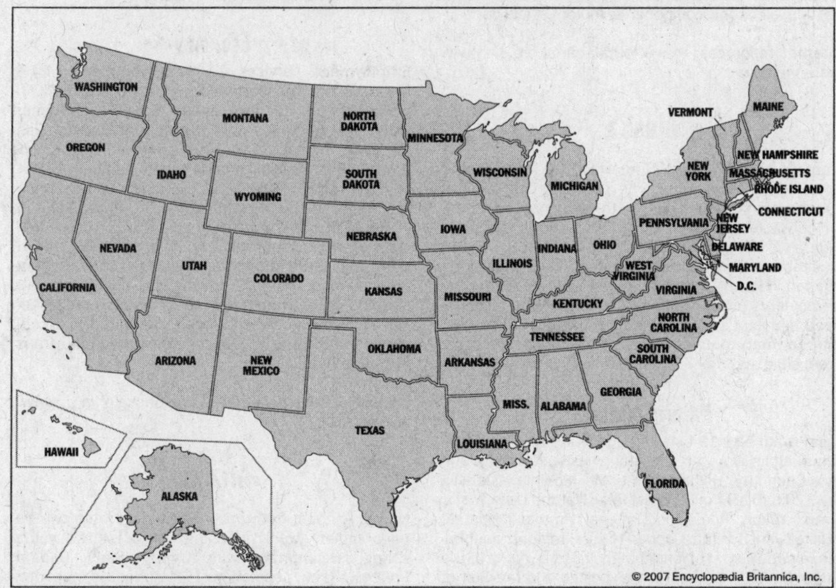

Alabama

Name: Alabama, from the Choctaw language, meaning "thicket clearers." **Nickname:** Heart of Dixie. **Capital:** Montgomery. **Rank:** population: 23rd; area: 30th; pop. density: 25th. **Motto:** *Audemus Jura Nostra Defendere* (We Dare Defend Our Rights). **Song:** "Alabama," words by Julia S. Tutwiler and music by Edna Gockel Gussen. **Amphibian:** Red Hills salamander. **Bird:** yellowhammer. **Fish:** largemouth bass (freshwater); tarpon (saltwater). **Flower:** camellia. **Fossil:** *Basilosaurus cetoides.* **Gemstone:** star blue quartz. **Insect:** monarch butterfly. **Mineral:** hematite. **Reptile:** Alabama red-bellied turtle. **Rock:** marble. **Tree:** southern longleaf pine.

Natural features

Land area: 51,700 sq mi, 133,902 sq km. **Mountain ranges:** Appalachian, Raccoon, Lookout. **Highest point:** Cheaha Mountain, 2,407 ft (734 m). **Largest lake:** Lake Guntersville. **Major rivers:** Mobile, Alabama, Tombigbee, Tennessee, Chattahoochee, Conecuh, Pea, Tensaw, Tallapoosa. **Natural regions:** the Appalachian Plateaus, extending across the north-central region; Interior Low Plateaus, far north; Valley and Ridge Province and small portion of the Piedmont Province, covering the east; Coastal Plain, covering the southern half of the state. **Location:** Southeast, bordering Tennessee, Georgia, Florida, and Mississippi. **Climate:** temperate, with mild winters and hot, humid summers; temperatures mellowed by altitude in the northern counties and relatively higher in the southern counties; summer heat is often alleviated by winds blowing in from the Gulf of Mexico. **Land use:** forest, 64.4%; agricultural, 7.5%; pasture, 0.2%; other, 27.9%.

People

Population (2006): 4,599,030; 89.0 persons per sq mi (34.3 persons per sq km). **Vital statistics** (2005; per 1,000 population): birth rate, 13.3; death rate, 10.4; marriage rate, 9.5; divorce rate, 4.9. **Major cities** (2006): Birmingham 229,424; Montgomery 201,998; Mobile 192,830; Huntsville 168,132; Tuscaloosa 83,052.

Government

Statehood: entered the Union on 14 Dec 1819 as the 22nd state. **State constitution:** adopted 1901. **Representation in US Congress:** 2 senators; 7 representatives. **Electoral college:** 9 votes (based on the 2000 census). **Political divisions:** 67 counties.

Economy

Employment: services 25.2%; trade 21.6%; manufacturing 16.9%; government 16.4%; construction 6.2%; finance, insurance, real estate 4.9%; transportation, public utilities 4.6%; agriculture, forestry, fishing 3.5%; mining 0.5%. **Production:** manufacturing 19.0%; services 16.9%; trade 16.9%; government 15.8%; finance, insurance, real estate 14.7%; transportation, utilities 8.7%; construction 4.7%; agriculture, forestry, fisheries 2.0%; mining 1.3%. **Chief agricultural products:** *Crops:* cotton, corn, soybeans, peanuts (groundnuts), potatoes, sweet potatoes, peaches, pecans, fruits and vegetables, winter wheat, hay, honey. *Livestock:* cattle and calves, poultry, hogs. *Fish catch:* marine fish, including red snapper; freshwater fish, including catfish; marine crustaceans, including shrimp, crab; marine mollusks, including mussels, oysters. **Chief manufactured products:** food products, meat products, poultry processing, textiles, apparel, wood products, mobile homes, paper and paperboard, petroleum products, plastics and rubber products, iron and steel, aluminum products, semiconductors, electronic components, motor vehicle parts.

Internet resources: <www.touralabama.org>; <www.alabama.gov>.

Alaska

Name: Alaska, from the Aleut word *Alyeska,* meaning "great land." **Nickname:** The Last Frontier. **Capital:** Juneau. **Rank:** population: 47th; area: 1st; pop. density: 50th. **Motto:** North to the Future. **Song:** "Alaska's Flag," words by Marie Drake and music by Elinor Dusenbury. **Bird:** willow ptarmigan. **Fish:** giant king salmon. **Flower:** forget-me-not. **Fossil:** *Mammuthus primigenius* (woolly mammoth). **Gemstone:** jade. **Insect:** four-spot skimmer dragonfly. **Mammal:** moose. **Marine mammal:** bowhead whale. **Mineral:** gold. **Tree:** sitka spruce.

Natural features

Land area: 589,194 sq mi, 1,526,005 sq km. **Mountain ranges:** Wrangell, Chugach, Alaska, Brooks, Aleutian, Boundary. **Highest point:** Mt. McKinley (Denali), 20,320 ft (6,194 m). **Largest lake:** Iliamna Lake. **Major rivers:** Yukon, Porcupine, Tanana, Koyukuk, Noatak, Kuskokwim, Susitna, Copper. **Natural regions:** panhandle, a narrow strip of land that includes portions of the Coast Mountains; coastal archipelago and the Gulf of Alaska islands; the Alaska Peninsula and Aleutian island chain that separates the North Pacific from the Bering Sea; the Alaska Range, extending across the south-central region; the Interior Plateau, including the basin of the Yukon River, the central plains and tablelands of the interior, the Seward Peninsula to the west, and the Brooks Range, sometimes called the North Slope, to the north; the Arctic Coastal Plain, a treeless region of tundra lying at the northernmost edge of the state; tundra-covered islands of the Bering Sea. **Location:** international border with Canada. **Climate:** temperate with much regional variation in temperature and precipitation; *southern coastal and southeastern region, Gulf of Alaska and Aleutian Islands:* cool summers and moderate winters, with high precipitation; *interior basin:* moderate summers and very cold winters, with low to moderate precipitation; *islands and coast of the Bering Sea:* cool summers and very cold winters; *central plains and uplands:* moderate summers and frigid winters; *North Slope:* moderate summers and frigid winters, though not as severe as interior regions. **Land use:** forest, 24.1%; pasture, 0.0%; other, 75.9%.

People

Population (2006): 670,053; 1.1 persons per sq mi (0.4 person per sq km). **Vital statistics** (2005; per 1,000 population): birth rate, 15.8; death rate, 4.4; marriage rate, 8.3; divorce rate, 5.8. **Major cities** (2006): Anchorage 278,700; Fairbanks 31,142; Juneau 30,737; College 12,000; Sitka 8,920.

Government

Statehood: entered the Union on 3 Jan 1959 as the 49th state. **State constitution:** adopted 1956. **Representation in US Congress:** 2 senators; 1 representative. **Electoral college:** 3 votes (based on the 2000 census). **Political divisions:** 16 boroughs.

Economy

Employment: services 26.9%; government 24.4%; trade 18.7%; transportation, public utilities 7.7%; finance, insurance, real estate 5.3%; construction 5.1%; manufacturing 4.8%; agriculture, forestry, fishing 4.1%; mining 3.0%. **Production:** mining 20.1%; government 19.4%; transportation, utilities 16.7%; services 13.0%; trade 10.1%; finance, insurance, real estate 10.1%; construction 4.6%; manufacturing 4.2%; agriculture, forestry, fishing 1.7%. **Chief agricultural products:** *Crops:* hay, milk, potatoes, timber. *Livestock:* cattle and calves, pigs. *Fish catch:* marine fish, salmon, herring, groundfish, shellfish, crab, shrimp. **Chief manufactured products:** processed fish and seafood (fresh, frozen, canned, and cured), lumber and wood products, paper products, transportation products.

Internet resources: <www.travelalaska.com>; <www.alaska.gov>.

Arizona

Name: Arizona, from *arizonac,* derived from two Papago Indian words meaning "place of the young spring." **Nickname:** Grand Canyon State. **Capital:** Phoenix. **Rank:** population: 16th; area: 6th; pop. density: 33rd. **Motto:** *Ditat Deus* (God Enriches). **Song:** "Arizona March Song," words by Margaret Rowe Clifford and music by Maurice Blumenthal. **Amphibian:** Arizona treefrog. **Bird:** cactus wren. **Fish:** Arizona trout. **Flower:** saguaro blossom. **Fossil:** petrified wood. **Gemstone:** turquoise. **Mammal:** ringtail. **Reptile:** Arizona ridgenose rattlesnake. **Tree:** palo verde.

Natural features

Land area: 113,999 sq mi, 295,256 sq km. **Mountain ranges:** Black, Gila Bend, Chuska, Hualapai, San Francisco, White. **Highest point:** Humphreys Peak, 12,633 ft (3,851 m). **Largest lake:** Lake Roosevelt. **Major rivers:** Colorado, Little Colorado, Verde, Salt, Gila. **Natural regions:** the Colorado Plateaus, northeast third of the state, include the Grand Canyon and the Painted Desert; the Basin and Range Province, south, east, central, and northwest, includes the Sonoran Desert in the southwest corner and part of the Great Basin Desert to the northwest. **Location:** Southwest, bordering Utah, Colorado, New Mexico, California, and Nevada; international border with Mexico. **Climate:** varies with location; half of Arizona is semiarid, one-third is arid, and the remainder is humid; *basin and range region:* arid and semiarid to subtropical climate; *Colorado Plateaus:* cool to cold winters and a semiarid climate; *Transition Zone:* climate ranges widely, from arid to humid. **Land use:** pasture, 44.2%; forest, 5.7%; agricultural, 1.3%; other, 48.8%.

People

Population (2006): 6,166,318; 54.1 persons per sq mi (20.9 persons per sq km). **Vital statistics** (2005; per 1,000 population): birth rate, 16.2; death rate,

For details about state governments, see pages 682–687; for energy data, see pages 705–706.

7.7; marriage rate, 6.3; divorce rate, 4.1. **Major cities** (2006): Phoenix 1,512,986; Tucson 518,956; Mesa 447,541; Glendale 246,531; Chandler 240,595; Scottsdale 231,127; Gilbert 191,517; Tempe 169,712.

Government

Statehood: entered the Union on 14 Feb 1912 as the 48th state. **State constitution:** adopted 1911. **Representation in US Congress:** 2 senators; 8 representatives. **Electoral college:** 10 votes (based on the 2000 census). **Political divisions:** 15 counties.

Economy

Employment: services 32.5%; trade 22.7%; government 13.4%; manufacturing 8.8%; finance, insurance, real estate 8.3%; construction 6.6%; transportation, public utilities 4.5%; agriculture, forestry, fishing 2.6%; mining 0.6%. **Production:** services 22.0%; finance, insurance, real estate 18.7%; trade 17.4%; manufacturing 14.4%; government 12.1%; transportation, public utilities 10.9%; construction 5.8%; agriculture, forestry, fishing 1.5%; mining 0.8%. **Chief agricultural products:** *Crops:* cotton and cottonseed, wheat, sorghum, hay, barley, corn (maize), potatoes, grapes, apples, vegetables and melons, dairy products, lettuce. *Livestock:* cattle and calves, hogs and pigs, sheep and lambs, angora goats. **Chief manufactured products:** semiconductors, communications equipment, electric and electronic equipment, transportation equipment, soap products, nonferrous metal products.

Internet resources: <www.arizonaguide.com>; <www.az.gov>.

Arkansas

Name: Arkansas, from an unknown Native American word describing the Quapaw tribe (also known as the Arkansaw), meaning "people who live downstream." **Nickname:** Natural State. **Capital:** Little Rock. **Rank:** population: 32nd; area: 27th; pop. density: 35th. **Motto:** *Regnat Populus* (The People Rule). **Songs:** "Arkansas," words and music by Wayland Holyfield; "Oh, Arkansas," words and music by by Terry Rose and Gary Klaff. **Bird:** mockingbird. **Flower:** apple blossom. **Gemstone:** diamond. **Insect:** honeybee. **Mammal:** white-tailed deer. **Mineral:** quartz crystal. **Rock:** bauxite. **Tree:** pine tree.

Natural features

Land area: 53,178 sq mi, 137,730 sq km. **Mountain ranges:** Ozark, Ouachita. **Highest point:** Mt. Magazine, 2,753 ft (839 m). **Largest lake:** Lake Chicot. **Major rivers:** Arkansas, Red, Quachita, White. **Natural regions:** the Ozark Plateaus, including the Boston Mountains, north and northwest regions; the Ouachita Province, including the Arkansas valley and the Ouachita Mountains, central region; the Coastal Plain, extends from southwest to northeast. **Location:** South, bordering Missouri, Tennessee, Mississippi, Louisiana, Texas, and Oklahoma. **Climate:** temperate, with mild winters and hot summers. **Land use:** forest, 44.1%; agricultural, 22.1%; pasture, 0.1%; other, 33.7%.

People

Population (2006): 2,810,872; 52.9 persons per sq mi (20.4 persons per sq km). **Vital statistics** (2005; per 1,000 population): birth rate, 14.1; death rate, 10.2; marriage rate, 12.6; divorce rate, 6.0. **Major cities** (2006): Little Rock 184,422; Fort Smith 83,461; Fayetteville 68,726; Springdale 63,082; Jonesboro 60,489.

Government

Statehood: entered the Union on 15 Jun 1836 as the 25th state. **State constitution:** adopted 1874. **Representation in US Congress:** 2 senators; 4 representatives. **Electoral college:** 6 votes (based on the 2000 census). **Political divisions:** 75 counties.

Economy

Employment: services 24.4%; trade 21.3%; manufacturing 18.3%; government 13.9%; agriculture, forestry, fishing 6.6%; construction 5.8%; transportation, public utilities 5.5%; finance, insurance, real estate 4.8%; mining 0.4%. **Production:** manufacturing 22.5%; trade 18.4%; services 15.6%; government 12.3%; finance, insurance, real estate 11.6%; transportation, public utilities 10.5%; construction 4.6%; agriculture, forestry, fisheries 3.7%; mining 0.8%. **Chief agricultural products:** *Crops:* corn (maize), cotton, hay, rice, sorghum, soybeans, wheat, apples, blueberries, grapes, peaches, pecans, strawberries, tomatoes, watermelon. *Livestock:* cattle and calves, hogs and pigs, poultry. *Aquaculture:* catfish. **Chief manufactured products:** food products, meatpacking, poultry processing, lumber, paper and paper products, refined petroleum, chemical products, plastic and rubber products, iron and steel manufacturing, fabricated metal products, machinery, transportation products.

Internet resources: <www.arkansas.com>; <www.arkansas.gov>.

California

Nickname: Golden State. **Capital:** Sacramento. **Rank:** population: 1st; area: 3rd; pop. density: 11th. **Motto:** *Eureka* (I Have Found It). **Song:** "I Love You, California," words by F.B. Silverwood and music by A.F. Frankenstein. **Bird:** California quail. **Fish:** golden trout (freshwater); garibaldi (saltwater). **Flower:** California poppy. **Fossil:** saber-tooth cat. **Gemstone:** benitoite. **Insect:** California dogface butterfly. **Mammal:** California grizzly bear. **Marine mammal:** California gray whale. **Mineral:** gold. **Reptile:** desert tortoise. **Rock:** serpentine. **Tree:** California redwood.

Natural features

Land area: 158,633 sq mi, 410,858 sq km. **Mountain ranges:** Coast, Sierra Nevada, Santa Lucia, Cascade, Klamath, Tehachapi, San Gabriel, San Bernardino. **Highest point:** Mt. Whitney, 14,494 ft (4,418 m). **Largest lake:** Lake Tahoe. **Major rivers:** Colorado, Sacramento, Pit, San Joaquin. **Natural regions:** Basin and Range Province, northeast corner, also eastern border with Arizona and southern Nevada; Cascade-Sierra Mountains, running from north to south along the east-central region; Pacific Border Province, west, including the Coast Ranges to the west, the Klamath Mountains to the north, the Los Angeles Ranges to the south, and the California Trough (commonly referred to as the Central Valley) to the east; Lower Californian Province, southwestern tip. **Location:** West, bordering Oregon, Nevada, and Arizona; international border with Mexico. **Climate:** Mediterranean climate, with moderate temperatures, warm, dry summers, and cool, rainy winters. **Land use:** pasture, 17.5%; forest, 13.7%; agricultural, 9.3%; other, 59.5%.

People

Population (2006): 36,457,549; 229.8 persons per sq mi (88.7 persons per sq km). **Vital statistics** (2005; per 1,000 population): birth rate, 15.2; death rate, 6.4; marriage rate, 6.3; divorce rate (2001), 6.6. **Major cities** (2006): Los Angeles 3,849,378; San Diego 1,256,951; San Jose 929,936; San Francisco 744,041; Long Beach 472,494; Fresno 466,714; Sacramento 453,781; Oakland 397,067.

Government

Statehood: entered the Union on 9 Sep 1850 as the 31st state. **State constitution:** adopted 1879. **Representation in US Congress:** 2 senators; 53 representatives. **Electoral college:** 55 votes (based on the 2000 census). **Political divisions:** 58 counties.

Economy

Employment: services 33.8%; trade 20.7%; government 13.3%; manufacturing 11.2%; finance, insurance, real estate 8.0%; construction 4.6%; transportation, public utilities 4.5%; agriculture, forestry, fishing 3.7%; mining 0.2%. **Production:** services 23.4%; finance, insurance, real estate 21.7%; trade 15.9%; manufacturing 14.6%; government 10.7%; transportation, utilities 7.3%; construction 3.8%; agriculture, forestry, fishing 1.9%; mining 0.6%. **Chief agricultural products:** *Crops:* wheat, oats, rice, grains, apples, apricots, cherries, grapes, olives, peaches, pears, citrus fruits, strawberries, onions, lima beans, artichokes, broccoli, snap beans, vegetables, dairy products, eggs. *Livestock:* cattle and calves, sheep and lambs. *Fish catch:* bonito, halibut, mackerel, groundfish, rockfish (commonly called Pacific red snapper), sablefish (also called black cod), soles and sand dabs, sardines, white seabass, shark, swordfish, tuna, crab, California spiny lobster, Pacific Ocean (pink) shrimp, prawns, squid. *Extractive products:* timber. **Chief manufactured products:** food products, meat and poultry processing, soft-drink products, beer and wine, textiles, apparel, lumber and wood products, paper and paper products, printing, refined petroleum, asphalt, chemical products, pharmaceuticals, plastic and rubber products, glass and glass products, construction materials, steel products, metal products, machinery, communications equipment, semiconductors and computers, electronics, transportation equipment, furniture, medical equipment, sporting goods.

Internet resources: <www.visitcalifornia.com>; <www.ca.gov>.

Colorado

Name: Colorado, from a Spanish word meaning "red." **Nickname:** Centennial State. **Capital:** Denver. **Rank:** population: 22nd; area: 8th; pop. density: 37th. **Motto:** *Nil sine Numine* (Nothing Without Providence). **Songs:** "Where the Columbines Grow," words and music by A.J. Flynn; "Rocky Mountain High," words and music by John Denver. **Bird:** lark bunting. **Fish:** greenback cutthroat trout. **Flower:** white and lavender columbine. **Fossil:** stegosaurus. **Gemstone:** aquamarine. **Insect:** Colorado hairstreak butterfly. **Mammal:** Rocky Mountain bighorn sheep. **Tree:** Colorado blue spruce.

Natural features

Land area: 104,094 sq mi, 269,602 sq km. **Mountain ranges:** Rocky, Front, Medicine Bow, Park, Rabbit Ears, San Juan, Sangre de Cristo, Sawatch. **Highest point:** Mt. Elbert, 14,433 ft (4,399 m). **Largest lakes:** Blue Mesa Reservoir (man-made); Grand Lake (natural). **Major rivers:** Colorado, Arkansas, South Platte, Rio Grande. **Natural regions:** the Great Plains Province, eastern half of state, includes the High Plains to the east, Colorado Piedmont to the west, and Raton Section to the south; Southern Rocky Mountains, running down the middle of the state; Middle Rocky Mountains and Wyoming Basin, northwest corner; Colorado Plateaus, western and southwestern border, include the Uinta Basin to the north, the Canyon Lands in the middle, and the Navajo Section to the south. **Location:** West, bordering Wyoming, Nebraska, Kansas, Oklahoma, New Mexico, and Utah. **Climate:** *eastern plains:* hot summers and dry, cold, windy, and generally harsh winters; *piedmont:* similar to eastern plains; also experiences the Chinook wind, a dry, descending winter airstream from the high mountains that is warmed by compression as it descends; *mountains and high plateaus:* cool summers, cold winters, and much increased precipitation; snow may fall during any month of the year, with amounts ranging from about 20 to 50 inches. **Land use:** pasture, 37.2%; agricultural, 12.5%; forest, 4.9%; other, 45.4%.

People

Population (2006): 4,753,377; 45.7 persons per sq mi (17.6 persons per sq km). **Vital statistics** (2005; per 1,000 population): birth rate, 14.8; death rate, 6.3; marriage rate, 6.4; divorce rate, 4.4. **Major cities** (2006): Denver 566,974; Colorado Springs 372,437; Aurora 303,582; Lakewood 140,024; Fort Collins 129,467.

Government

Statehood: entered the Union on 1 Aug 1876 as the 38th state. **State constitution:** adopted 1876. **Representation in US Congress:** 2 senators; 7 representatives. **Electoral college:** 9 votes (based on the 2000 census). **Political divisions:** 64 counties.

Economy

Employment: services 32.3%; trade 22.0%; government 13.5%; finance, insurance, real estate 8.4%; manufacturing 8.2%; construction 6.5%; transportation, public utilities 5.4%; agriculture, forestry, fishing

For details about state governments, see pages 682–687; for energy data, see pages 705–706.

2.8%; mining 0.9%. **Production:** services 23.1%; finance, insurance, real estate 17.5%; trade 16.1%; transportation, utilities 12.2%; government 11.9%; manufacturing 10.2%; construction 6.0%; mining 1.6%; agriculture 1.5%. **Chief agricultural products:** *Crops:* millet, corn (maize), hay, potatoes, onions, sugar beets, sunflowers, wheat, dairy products, eggs, greenhouse products. *Livestock:* cattle and calves, hogs and pigs, sheep and lambs. **Chief manufactured products:** meat products, beverages, printing, semiconductors, computer and electronic products.

Internet resources: <www.colorado.com>; <www.colorado.gov>.

Connecticut

Name: Connecticut, from the Mohegan word *Quinnehtukqut,* meaning "long river place" or "beside the long tidal river." **Nickname:** Constitution State. **Capital:** Hartford. **Rank:** population: 29th; area: 48th; pop. density: 4th. **Motto:** *Qui Transtulit Sustinet* (He Who Transplanted Still Sustains). **Song:** "Yankee Doodle," words and music from folk tradition. **Bird:** robin. **Flower:** mountain laurel. **Fossil:** *Eubrontes giganteus.* **Insect:** praying mantis. **Mammal:** sperm whale. **Mineral:** garnet. **Shellfish:** eastern oyster. **Tree:** white oak.

Natural features

Land area: 5,006 sq mi, 12,966 sq km. **Mountain range:** Berkshire Hills. **Highest point:** Mt. Frissell, 2,380 ft (725 m). **Largest lake:** Candlewood Lake. **Major rivers:** Connecticut, Housatonic, Thames. **Natural regions:** the New England Province covers the state, divided into the Western Upland, Central Lowland (Connecticut Valley), and Eastern Upland. **Location:** New England, bordering Massachusetts, Rhode Island, and New York. **Climate:** moderate temperate climate; coastal portions have somewhat warmer winters and cooler summers than does the interior; northwestern uplands have cooler and longer winters with heavier falls of snow; occasional hurricanes cause flooding and damage, particularly along the coastline. **Land use:** forest, 53.4%; agricultural, 5.4%; other, 41.2%.

People

Population (2006): 3,504,809; 700.1 persons per sq mi (270.3 persons per sq km). **Vital statistics** (2005; per 1,000 population): birth rate, 11.9; death rate, 8.4; marriage rate, 5.5; divorce rate, 2.7. **Major cities** (2006): Bridgeport 137,912; Hartford 124,512; New Haven 124,001; Stamford 119,261; Waterbury 107,251.

Government

Statehood: entered the Union on 9 Jan 1788 as the 5th state. **State constitution:** adopted 1965. **Representation in US Congress:** 2 senators; 5 representatives. **Electoral college:** 7 votes (based on the 2000 census). **Political divisions:** 8 counties.

Economy

Employment: services 34.3%; trade 20.2%; manufacturing 14.0%; government 11.2%; finance, insurance, real estate 9.5%; construction 4.8%; transportation, public utilities 4.2%; agriculture, forestry, fishing 1.5%; mining 0.1%. **Production:** finance, insurance, real estate 28.7%; services 22.0%; manufacturing 16.5%; trade 14.5%; government 8.3%; transportation, utilities 5.9%; construction 3.3%; agriculture 0.7%; mining 0.1%. **Chief agricultural products:** *Crops:* corn (maize), silage, hay, tobacco, apples, pears, dairy products, eggs. *Livestock:* poultry, cattle and calves, sheep and lambs, horses. *Fish catch:* lobster, clams, oysters, shad, marine fish. **Chief manufactured products:** printing, pharmaceutical products, soap and cleaning products, plastics, metal products, machinery, communications equipment, electronics, aerospace products, aircraft engines.

Internet resources: <www.ctvisit.com>; <www.ct.gov>.

Delaware

Name: Delaware, from Delaware River and Bay; named in turn for Sir Thomas West, Baron De La Warr. **Nickname:** First State. **Capital:** Dover. **Rank:** population: 45th; area: 49th; pop. density: 6th. **Motto:** Liberty and Independence. **Song:** "Our Delaware," words by George B. Hynson and music by Will M.S. Brown. **Bird:** Blue Hen chicken. **Fish:** weakfish. **Flower:** peach blossom. **Insect:** ladybug. **Mineral:** sillimanite. **Tree:** American holly.

Natural features

Land area: 2,026 sq mi, 5,247 sq km. **Highest point:** Ebright Azimuth, 448 ft (137 m). **Largest lake:** Red Mill Pond. **Major rivers:** Delaware, Nanticoke, Pocomoke. **Natural regions:** the Piedmont Province, including the Piedmont Upland, covers the northernmost tip of the state; the remainder consists of the Coastal Plain. **Location:** East, bordering Pennsylvania, New Jersey, and Maryland. **Climate:** temperate, with high humidity, hot summers, and cold winters. **Land use:** agricultural, 29.8%; forest, 22.2%; other, 48.0%.

People

Population (2006): 853,476; 421.3 persons per sq mi (162.7 persons per sq km). **Vital statistics** (2005; per 1,000 population): birth rate, 13.8; death rate, 8.8; marriage rate, 5.5; divorce rate, 3.9. **Major cities** (2006): Wilmington 72,826; Dover 34,735; Newark 30,014; Pike Creek 20,500; Bear 18,500.

Government

Statehood: entered the Union on 7 Dec 1787 as the 1st state. **State constitution:** adopted 1897. **Representation in US Congress:** 2 senators; 1 representative. **Electoral college:** 3 votes (based on the 2000 census). **Political divisions:** 3 counties.

Economy

Employment: services 28.6%; trade 20.6%; government 13.5%; finance, insurance, real estate 12.8%; manufacturing 12.6%; construction 6.1%; transportation, public utilities 3.8%; agriculture, forestry, fishing 1.9%. **Production:** finance, insurance, real estate 39.8%; services 15.5%; manufacturing 14.2%; trade

11.1%; government 9.2%; transportation, utilities 5.1%; construction 4.3%; agriculture 0.8%. **Chief agricultural products:** *Crops:* corn, soybeans, wheat, barley, peas, vegetables, dairy products. *Livestock:* poultry, cattle and calves, hogs. *Fish catch:* crustaceans, crab, clams. **Chief manufactured products:** chemicals, food products, paper products, rubber and plastics products, metal products, printed materials.

Internet resources: <www.visitdelaware.com>; <www.delaware.gov>.

District of Columbia

Motto: *Justitia Omnibus* (Justice for All). **Bird:** woodthrush. **Flower:** American Beauty rose. **Tree:** scarlet oak.

Natural features

Land area: 68 sq mi, 176 sq km. **Major river:** Potomac. **Location:** East, bordered by Maryland and Virginia. **Climate:** humid, subtropical climate.

People

Population (2006): 581,530; 8,551.9 persons per sq mi (3,304.1 persons per sq km). **Vital statistics:** (2005; per 1,000 population): birth rate, 14.3; death rate, 9.3; marriage rate, 4.2; divorce rate, 2.0.

Government

Representation in US Congress: 1 congressional delegate. **Political divisions:** 8 wards.

Economy

Employment: services 43.5%; government 36.0%; trade 7.3%; finance, insurance, real estate 5.2%; transportation, public utilities 3.0%; manufacturing 1.9%; construction 1.5%; agricultural service, forestry, fishing 1.4%. **Production:** services 38.3%; government 36.6%; finance, insurance, real estate 13.5%; transportation, utilities 5.0%; trade 4.0%; manufacturing 1.4%; construction 1.0%; other 0.2%. **Chief manufactured products:** printing and publishing products.

Internet resources: <www.washington.org>; <www.dc.gov>.

Florida

Name: Florida, in honor of Pascua Florida ("feast of the flowers"), Spain's Easter celebration. **Nickname:** Sunshine State. **Capital:** Tallahassee. **Rank:** population: 4th; area: 24th; pop. density: 8th. **Motto:** In God We Trust. **Song:** "Old Folks at Home" ("Swanee River"), words and music by Stephen Foster. **Bird:** mockingbird. **Butterfly:** zebra longwing. **Fish:** sailfish (saltwater); largemouth bass (freshwater). **Flower:** orange blossom. **Gemstone:** moonstone. **Mammal:** Florida panther. **Marine mammal:** manatee. **Saltwater mammal:** porpoise. **Reptile:** alligator. **Rock:** agatized coral. **Tree:** sabal palm.

Natural features

Land area: 58,599 sq mi, 151,771 sq km. **Highest point:** Britton Hill 345 ft (105 m). **Largest lake:** Lake Okeechobee. **Major rivers:** Kissimmee, Suwannee, St. Johns, Caloosahatchee, Indian, Withlacoochee, Apalachicola, Perdido, St. Marys. **Natural regions:** Western Highlands, a region at the westernmost end of the panhandle; Marianna Lowlands, east of the Western Highlands; Tallahassee Hills, covering the northern border with Georgia; Central Highlands, extending down the middle two-thirds of the peninsula; Coastal Lowlands, curving along the eastern, southern, and western coasts of the peninsula; the Everglades, far southern quarter of the peninsula. **Location:** Southeast, bordering Georgia and Alabama. **Climate:** tropical south of a west–east line drawn from Bradenton along the south shore of Lake Okeechobee to Vero Beach; subtropical north of this line; hot, humid summers and mild, pleasant winters; hurricane season from June to November. **Land use:** forest, 33.9%; agricultural, 7.7%; pasture, 7.2%; other, 51.2%.

People

Population (2006): 18,089,888; 308.7 persons per sq mi (119.2 persons per sq km). **Vital statistics** (2005; per 1,000 population): birth rate, 12.7; death rate, 9.6; marriage rate, 8.9; divorce rate, 4.6. **Major cities** (2006): Jacksonville 794,555; Miami 404,048; Tampa 332,888; St. Petersburg 248,098; Orlando 220,186; Hialeah 217,141; Fort Lauderdale 185,804; Tallahassee 159,012.

Government

Statehood: entered the Union on 3 Mar 1845 as the 27th state. **State constitution:** adopted 1968. **Representation in US Congress:** 2 senators; 25 representatives. **Electoral college:** 27 votes (based on the 2000 census). **Political divisions:** 67 counties.

Economy

Employment: services 35.3%; trade 23.2%; government 13.1%; finance, insurance, real estate 8.2%; manufacturing 6.4%; construction 5.7%; transportation, public utilities 4.8%; agriculture, forestry, fishing 3.0%; mining 0.1%. **Production:** services 24.4%; finance, insurance, real estate 21.5%; trade 19.1%; government 12.2%; transportation, utilities 8.6%; manufacturing 7.2%; construction 5.1%; agriculture 1.8%; mining 0.2%. **Chief agricultural products:** *Crops:* citrus fruit, fruits and vegetables, corn (maize), cotton, peanuts (groundnuts), soybeans, sugarcane, tobacco, honey, dairy products, eggs, nursery plants and flowers. *Livestock:* cattle and calves, poultry, hogs and pigs. *Aquaculture:* catfish. *Fish catch:* marine fish, crab, shrimp, oyster. **Chief manufactured products:** food products, meatpacking, soft drinks, apparel, paper products, pesticides and fertilizers, agricultural chemicals, plastics, construction materials, fabricated metal products, machinery, communications equipment, semiconductors, electronics, aerospace products, airplane engines, ships and boats, medical and surgical equipment.

Internet resources: <www.flausa.com>; <www.myflorida.com>.

For details about state governments, see pages 682–687; for energy data, see pages 705–706.

Georgia

Name: Georgia, named for George II, king of England at the time the colony of Georgia was founded. **Nicknames:** Empire State of the South; Peach State. **Capital:** Atlanta. **Rank:** population: 9th; area: 23rd; pop. density: 17th. **Mottoes:** Wisdom, Justice, and Moderation; Agriculture and Commerce, 1776. **Song:** "Georgia on My Mind," words by Stuart Gorrell and music by Hoagy Carmichael. **Bird:** brown thrasher. **Fish:** largemouth bass. **Flower:** Cherokee rose. **Fossil:** shark tooth. **Gemstone:** quartz. **Insect:** honeybee. **Marine mammal:** right whale. **Mineral:** staurolite. **Reptile:** gopher tortoise. **Tree:** live oak.

Natural features

Land area: 58,922 sq mi, 152,607 sq km. **Mountain range:** Blue Ridge. **Highest point:** Brasstown Bald, 4,784 ft (1,458 m). **Largest lake:** Lanier. **Major rivers:** Chattahoochee, Flint, Apalachicola, Ocmulgee, Oconee, Altamaha, Savannah. **Natural regions:** Blue Ridge Province, north-central edge; Valley and Ridge Province, northwest corner; Piedmont Province, northern half of state; Coastal Plain, southern half of state, divided into the Sea Island Section (southeast) and the East Gulf Coastal Plain (southwest). **Location:** Southeast, bordering North Carolina, South Carolina, Florida, Alabama, and Tennessee. **Climate:** temperate, though maritime tropical air masses dominate the climate in summer; generally hot summers and cool winters; precipitation somewhat evenly distributed throughout the seasons in the north, whereas the southern and coastal areas have more summer rains; snow seldom occurs outside the mountainous northern counties. **Land use:** forest, 58.0%; agricultural, 11.0%; other, 31.0%.

People

Population (2006): 9,363,941; 158.9 persons per sq mi (61.4 persons per sq km). **Vital statistics** (2005; per 1,000 population): birth rate, 15.7; death rate, 7.2; marriage rate, 6.9; divorce rate (2001), 3.8. **Major cities** (2006): Atlanta 486,411; Augusta 189,366; Columbus 188,660; Savannah 127,889; Athens 111,580.

Government

Statehood: entered the Union on 2 Jan 1788 as the 4th state. **State constitution:** adopted 1982. **Representation in US Congress:** 2 senators; 13 representatives. **Electoral college:** 15 votes (based on the 2000 census). **Political divisions:** 159 counties.

Economy

Employment: services 27.7%; trade 23.1%; government 14.9%; manufacturing 13.5%; finance, insurance, real estate 6.7%; transportation, public utilities 5.8%; construction 5.7%; agriculture, forestry, fishing 2.5%; mining 0.2%. **Production:** services 19.2%; trade 18.4%; manufacturing 17.0%; finance, insurance, real estate 15.3%; government 11.9%; transportation, utilities 11.4%; construction 5.0%; agriculture 1.3%; mining 0.5%. **Chief agricultural products:** *Crops:* peanuts (groundnuts), pecans, rye, corn (maize), cotton, cottonseed, hay, oats, sorghum, soybeans, tobacco, wheat, peaches, apples, onions, watermelon, snap beans, cabbage, cucumbers, blueberries, grapes, honey, dairy products. *Livestock:* poultry, pigs, cattle and calves. *Aquaculture:* catfish, trout. *Extractive products:* timber. **Chief manufactured products:** food products, soft drinks, textiles, wood products, paper products, chemical products, transportation equipment.

Internet resources: <www.georgia.org>; <www.georgia.gov>.

Hawaii

Nickname: Aloha State. **Capital:** Honolulu. **Rank:** population: 42nd; area: 47th; pop. density: 13th. **Motto:** *Ua Mau ke Ea o ka Aina i ka Pono* (The Life of the Land Is Perpetuated in Righteousness). **Song:** "Hawai'i Pono'i" ("Our Hawaii"), words by King David Kalakaua and music by Henry Berger. **Bird:** nene, or Hawaiian goose. **Fish:** rectangular triggerfish (in Hawaiian, *humuhumunukunuku 'apua'a*). **Flower:** yellow hibiscus (in Hawaiian, *pua ma'o hau hele*). **Gemstone:** black coral. **Marine mammal:** humpback whale. **Tree:** kukui, or candlenut.

Natural features

Land area: 6,461 sq mi, 16,734 sq km; the eight largest islands: *Hawaii:* 4,028 sq mi, 10,433 sq km; *Maui:* 728 sq mi, 1,886 sq km; *Oahu:* 607 sq mi, 1,574 sq km; *Kauai:* 552 sq mi, 1,430 sq km; *Molokai:* 280 sq mi, 725 sq km; *Lanai:* 140 sq mi, 363 sq km; *Niihau:* 72 sq mi, 186 sq km; *Kahoolawe:* 45 sq mi, 117 sq km. **Mountain ranges:** Koolau, Waianae (both Oahu). **Highest point:** Mauna Kea (Hawaii), 13,796 ft (4,205 m). **Major rivers:** Wailuku (Hawaii); Waimea, Hanalei (Kauai). **Natural regions:** The eight major islands at the eastern end of the 1,500-mile-long chain of islands are, from west to east, Niihau, Kauai, Oahu, Molokai, Lanai, Kahoolawe, Maui, and Hawaii; each island contains regions of mountains, deeps, ridges, and wide beaches; active volcanoes are found on the island of Hawaii. **Location:** islands surrounded by the Pacific Ocean. **Climate:** tropical; rainfall variations throughout the state are dramatic, ranging from 8.7 inches (220 mm) a year at Kawaihae on the island of Hawaii, to roughly 444 inches (11,280 mm) at Mt. Waialeale on the island of Kauai. **Land use:** forest, 28.9%; pasture, 23.4%; agricultural, 7.1%; other, 40.6%.

People

Population (2006): Total, 1,285,498; 199.0 persons per sq mi (76.8 persons per sq km). **Vital statistics** (2005; per 1,000 population): birth rate, 14.1; death rate, 7.2; marriage rate, 22.5; divorce rate (2001), 3.8. **Major cities** (2000): Honolulu (2006) 377,357; Hilo 40,759; Kailua 36,513; Kaneohe 34,970; Waipahu 33,108.

Government

Statehood: entered the Union on 21 Aug 1959 as the 50th state. **State constitution:** adopted 1950. **Representation in US Congress:** 2 senators; 2 representatives. **Electoral college:** 4

votes (based on the 2000 census). **Political divisions:** 4 counties.

Economy

Employment: services 31.3%; government 22.3%; trade 22.0%; finance, insurance, real estate 8.4%; transportation, public utilities 6.3%; construction 4.2%; agriculture, forestry, fishing 2.8%; manufacturing 2.7%; mining 0.1%. **Production:** finance, insurance, real estate 23.2%; services 22.1%; government, 21.8%; trade 14.7%; transportation, utilities 10.4%; construction 4.0%; manufacturing 2.5%; agriculture 1.2%; mining 0.1%. **Chief agricultural products:** *Crops:* pineapples, sugarcane, cut flowers, macadamia nuts, coffee, milk, eggs. *Livestock:* cattle and calves. *Aquaculture:* fish, shellfish. **Chief manufactured products:** food products, processed sugar, canned pineapple, preserved fruits and vegetables, wearing apparel and textile products, printing and publishing.

Internet resources: <www.gohawaii.com>; <www.hawaiitourismauthority.org>.

Idaho

Nickname: Gem State. **Capital:** Boise. **Rank:** population: 39th; area: 14th; pop. density: 44th. **Motto:** *Esto Perpetua* (It Is Forever). **Song:** "Here We Have Idaho," words by McKinley Helm and Albert J. Tompkins and music by Sallie Hume Douglas. **Bird:** mountain bluebird. **Fish:** cutthroat trout. **Flower:** syringa. **Fossil:** Hagerman horse fossil (*Equus simplicidens*). **Gemstone:** star garnet. **Horse:** Appaloosa. **Insect:** monarch butterfly. **Tree:** western white pine.

Natural features

Land area: 83,570 sq mi, 216,445 sq km. **Mountain ranges:** Northern Rocky, Middle Rocky, Sawtooth, Pioneer, Continental Divide, Beaverhead, Clearwater, Bitterroot, Salmon River, Lost River, Lemhi. **Highest point:** Borah Peak, 12,662 ft (3,859 m). **Largest lake:** Lake Pend Oreille. **Major rivers:** Snake, Salmon. **Natural regions:** Northern Rocky Mountains, covering most of the northern half of the state; Columbia Plateau, extending across the south-central and southwestern regions; Great Basin region of the Basin and Range Province, southeast; Middle Rocky Mountains, extreme southeastern tip. **Location:** Northwest, bordering Montana, Wyoming, Utah, Nevada, Oregon, and Washington; international border with Canada. **Climate:** continental, with warm wet summers and cold dry winters, but regionally diverse; in general, precipitation increases and mean temperatures drop with increases in altitude. **Land use:** pasture, 12.0%; agricultural, 10.2%; forest, 7.5%; other, 70.3%.

People

Population (2006): 1,466,465; 17.5 persons per sq mi (6.8 persons per sq km). **Vital statistics** (2005; per 1,000 population): birth rate, 16.1; death rate, 7.5; marriage rate, 10.5; divorce rate, 4.9. **Major cities** (2006): Boise 198,638; Nampa 76,587; Meridian 59,832; Pocatello 53,932; Idaho Falls 52,786.

Government

Statehood: entered the Union on 3 Jul 1890 as the 43rd state. **State constitution:** adopted 1889. **Representation in US Congress:** 2 senators; 2 representatives. **Electoral college:** 4 votes (based on the 2000 census). **Political divisions:** 44 counties.

Economy

Employment: services 26.1%; trade 22.7%; government 15.0%; manufacturing 11.4%; agriculture, forestry, fishing 7.5%; construction 7.1%; finance, insurance, real estate 5.4%; transportation, public utilities 4.4%; mining 0.5%. **Production:** manufacturing 21.6%; trade 16.6%; services 16.3%; government 13.4%; finance, insurance, real estate 11.8%; transportation, utilities 7.8%; construction 6.6%; agriculture 5.2%; mining 0.6%. **Chief agricultural products:** *Crops:* potatoes, wheat, hay, sugar beets, barley, alfalfa seed, Kentucky bluegrass seed, hops, beans, onions, lentils, peas, honey, dairy products. *Livestock:* cattle and calves, sheep and lambs. *Extractive products:* timber, trout. **Chief manufactured products:** food processing, lumber and wood products, paper, printing, chemicals, plastics and rubber products, nonmetallic mineral products, fabricated metal products, machinery, computers and electronic products, transportation equipment, furniture.

Internet resources: <www.visitidaho.org>; <www.idaho.gov>.

Illinois

Name: Illinois, from a Native American word meaning "tribe of superior men." **Nickname:** Prairie State. **Capital:** Springfield. **Rank:** population: 5th; area: 25th; pop. density: 12th. **Motto:** State Sovereignty, National Union. **Slogan:** Land of Lincoln. **Song:** "Illinois," words by Charles H. Chamberlain and music by Archibald Johnston. **Bird:** cardinal. **Fish:** bluegill. **Flower:** violet. **Fossil:** tully monster. **Insect:** monarch butterfly. **Mammal:** white-tailed deer. **Mineral:** fluorite. **Tree:** white oak.

Natural features

Land area: 57,915 sq mi, 149,999 sq km. **Highest point:** Charles Mound, 1,235 ft (376 m). **Largest lake:** Carlyle Lake. **Major rivers:** Mississippi, Ohio, Wabash. **Natural regions:** Central Lowland, a region of sloping hills and broad, shallow river valleys covering almost the entire state; Ozark Plateaus, extreme southwest; Interior Low Plateaus and Coastal Plain, extreme southeastern tip. **Location:** Midwest, bordering Wisconsin, Indiana, Kentucky, Missouri, and Iowa. **Climate:** continental, with hot summers and cold, snowy winters; wide seasonal and regional variations. **Land use:** agricultural, 66.5%; forest, 11.0%; other, 22.5%.

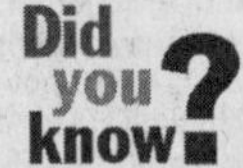

Cairo, Illinois was so named because the site was thought to resemble that of the Egyptian capital.

For details about state governments, see pages 682–687; for energy data, see pages 705–706.

People

Population (2006): 12,831,970; 221.6 persons per sq mi (85.5 persons per sq km). **Vital statistics** (2005; per 1,000 population): birth rate, 14.0; death rate, 8.1; marriage rate, 5.8; divorce rate, 2.5. **Major cities** (2006): Chicago 2,833,321; Aurora 170,617; Rockford 155,138; Naperville 142,901; Joliet 142,702.

Government

Statehood: entered the Union on 3 Dec 1818 as the 21st state. **State constitution:** adopted 1970. **Representation in US Congress:** 2 senators; 20 representatives. **Electoral college:** 21 votes (based on the 2000 census). **Political divisions:** 102 counties.

Economy

Employment: services 30.9%; trade 21.2%; manufacturing 14.0%; government 12.2%; finance, insurance, real estate 9.0%; transportation, public utilities 5.5%; construction 4.7%; agriculture, forestry, fishing 2.3%; mining 0.3%. **Production:** services 22.6%; finance, insurance, real estate 20.4%; manufacturing 16.3%; trade 16.2%; government 9.9%; transportation, utilities 9.2%; construction 4.5%; agriculture 0.8%; mining 0.3%. **Chief agricultural products:** *Crops:* corn (maize), soybeans, wheat, hay, oats, sorghum, apples, peaches, snap beans, sweet corn, potatoes, cabbage, dairy products, eggs. *Livestock:* pigs, cattle and calves, horses, poultry. **Chief manufactured products:** food products, beverages, textiles, leather goods, apparel, wood products, paper products, printing, petroleum and coal products, asphalt paving, chemicals, pharmaceuticals, plastics and rubber products, nonmetallic mineral products, iron and steel products, fabricated metals, machinery, computers and electronics, appliances, and transportation equipment.

Internet resources: <www.enjoyillinois.com>; <www.illinois.gov>.

Indiana

Name: Indiana, generally thought to mean "land of the Indians." **Nickname:** Hoosier State. **Capital:** Indianapolis. **Rank:** population: 15th; area: 38th; pop. density: 15th. **Motto:** The Crossroads of America. **Song:** "On the Banks of the Wabash, Far Away," words and music by Paul Dresser. **Bird:** cardinal. **Flower:** peony. **Rock:** limestone. **Tree:** tulip tree (yellow poplar).

Natural features

Land area: 36,418 sq mi, 94,322 sq km. **Highest point:** Hoosier Hill, 1,257 ft (383 m). **Largest lake:** Lake Monroe. **Major rivers:** Wabash, Ohio. **Natural regions:** Central Lowland comprises most of the state and includes the Eastern Lake Section to the north and the Till Plains in the center; Interior Low Plateaus, including the Highland Rim Section, cover the southern quarter of the state. **Location:** Midwest, bordering Michigan, Ohio, Kentucky, and Illinois. **Climate:** continental, with four distinct seasons; hot summers, cold winters, and mild spring and fall, with increased risk of tornadoes in spring. **Land use:** agricultural, 57.5%; forest, 16.5%; other, 26.0%.

People

Population (2006): 6,313,520; 173.4 persons per sq mi (66.9 persons per sq km). **Vital statistics** (2005; per 1,000 population): birth rate, 13.9; death rate, 8.8; marriage rate, 7.7; divorce rate, N/A. **Major cities** (2006): Indianapolis 785,597; Fort Wayne 248,637; Evansville 115,738; South Bend 104,905; Gary 97,715.

Government

Statehood: entered the Union on 11 Dec 1816 as the 19th state. **State constitution:** adopted 1851. **Representation in US Congress:** 2 senators; 10 representatives. **Electoral college:** 11 votes (based on the 2000 census). **Political divisions:** 92 counties.

Economy

Employment: services 26.2%; trade 22.7%; manufacturing 19.7%; government 11.7%; finance, insurance, real estate 6.0%; construction 5.8%; transportation, public utilities 4.8%; agriculture, forestry, fishing 3.0%; mining 0.3%. **Production:** manufacturing 30.9%; services 16.6%; trade 15.4%; finance, insurance, real estate 13.0%; government 10.0%; transportation, utilities 7.6%; construction 5.1%; agriculture 1.0%; mining 0.4%. **Chief agricultural products:** *Crops:* corn (maize), soybeans, wheat, hay, popcorn, tobacco, tomatoes, peppermint, spearmint, watermelon, blueberries, snap beans, cucumbers, apples, milk, eggs. *Livestock:* pigs, cattle and calves, poultry. **Chief manufactured products:** iron and steel, metal products, motor vehicle parts, machinery, food products, dairy products, soft drinks, wood products, paper products, mobile homes, asphalt.

Internet resources: <www.visitindiana.net>; <www.in.gov>.

Iowa

Name: Iowa, named for the Iowa (or Ioway) Indians who once inhabited the area. **Nickname:** Hawkeye State. **Capital:** Des Moines. **Rank:** population: 30th; area: 26th; pop. density: 34th. **Motto:** Our Liberties We Prize and Our Rights We Will Maintain. **Song:** "The Song of Iowa," words by S.H.M. Byers, to the tune of "O Tannenbaum." **Bird:** eastern goldfinch. **Flower:** wild rose. **Rock:** geode. **Tree:** oak.

Natural features

Land area: 56,271 sq mi, 145,741 sq km. **Highest point:** Hawkeye Point, 1,670 ft (509 m). **Largest lake:** Spirit Lake. **Major rivers:** Des Moines, Mississippi, Missouri, Big Sioux. **Natural regions:** overall, Central Lowland, including the Western Lake Section, north and central regions; Dissected Till Plains, south; Wisconsin Driftless Section, northeast corner. **Location:** Midwest, bordering Minnesota, Wisconsin, Illinois, Missouri, Nebraska, and South Dakota. **Climate:** continental, with hot summers and cold, snowy winters. **Land use:** agricultural, 70.8%; forest, 6.4%; other, 22.8%.

People

Population (2006): 2,982,085; 53.0 persons per sq mi (20.5 persons per sq km). **Vital statistics** (2005;

per 1,000 population): birth rate, 13.3; death rate, 9.4; marriage rate, 6.9; divorce rate, 2.7. **Major cities** (2006): Des Moines 193,886; Cedar Rapids 124,417; Davenport 99,514; Sioux City 83,262; Waterloo 65,998.

Government

Statehood: entered the Union on 28 Dec 1846 as the 29th state. **State constitution:** adopted 1857. **Representation in US Congress:** 2 senators; 5 representatives. **Electoral college:** 7 votes (based on the 2000 census). **Political divisions:** 99 counties.

Economy

Employment: services 26.8%; trade 22.4%; manufacturing 14.0%; government 13.2%; agriculture, forestry, fishing 7.7%; finance, insurance, real estate 6.2%; construction 5.1%; transportation, public utilities 4.4%; mining 0.1%. **Production:** manufacturing 22.4%; services 17.0%; trade 16.9%; finance, insurance, real estate 15.1%; government 12.0%; transportation, utilities 8.5%; construction 4.4%; agriculture 3.5%; mining 0.3%. **Chief agricultural products:** *Crops*: corn (maize), soybeans, hay, oats, grain, milk, eggs, butter, honey, popcorn, sorghum. *Livestock:* poultry, hogs and pigs, beef cattle, sheep and lambs. **Chief manufactured products:** food products, dairy products, meatpacking, pesticide, fertilizer, and other agricultural chemicals, farm machinery, construction machinery, household appliances, motor vehicle parts.

Internet resources: <www.traveliowa.com>; <www.iowa.gov>.

Kansas

Name: Kansas, from the Sioux word *kansa* ("people of the south wind") for the Native Americans who lived in the region. **Nickname:** Sunflower State. **Capital:** Topeka. **Rank:** population: 33rd; area: 15th; pop. density: 40th. **Motto:** *Ad Astra per Aspera* (To the Stars Through Difficulties). **Song:** "Home on the Range," words by Brewster Higley and music by Dan Kelly. **Amphibian:** barred tiger salamander. **Bird:** western meadowlark. **Flower:** wild native sunflower. **Insect:** honeybee. **Mammal:** American buffalo. **Reptile:** ornate box turtle. **Tree:** cottonwood.

Natural features

Land area: 82,277 sq mi, 213,096 sq km. **Highest point:** Mount Sunflower, 4,039 ft (1,231 m). **Largest lake:** Milford Lake. **Major rivers:** Kansas, Arkansas, Big Blue, Republican, Solomon, Saline, Smoky Hill, Cimarron, Verdigris, Neosho (Grand). **Natural regions:** the Great Plains Province, covering the western half of the state, consists of the High Plains to the west and the Plains Border to the east; the Central Lowland covers the eastern half of the state and consists of the Dissected Till Plains to the north and the Osage Plains to the south. **Location:** Central, bordering Nebraska, Missouri, Oklahoma, and Colorado. **Climate:** temperate but continental, with great extremes between summer and winter temperatures but few long periods of extreme hot or cold. **Land use:** agricultural, 50.3%; pasture, 30.1%; forest, 2.9%; other, 16.7%.

People

Population (2006): 2,764,075; 33.6 persons per sq mi (13.0 persons per sq km). **Vital statistics** (2005; per 1,000 population): birth rate, 14.5; death rate, 9.0; marriage rate, 7.0; divorce rate, 3.1. **Major cities** (2006): Wichita 357,698; Overland Park 166,722; Kansas City 143,801; Topeka 122,113; Olathe 114,662.

Government

Statehood: entered the Union on 29 Jan 1861 as the 34th state. **State constitution:** adopted 1859. **Representation in US Congress:** 2 senators; 4 representatives. **Electoral college:** 6 votes (based on the 2000 census). **Political divisions:** 105 counties.

Economy

Employment: services 26.5%; trade 22.2%; government 16.0%; manufacturing 12.6%; agriculture, forestry, fishing 5.9%; finance, insurance, real estate 5.7%; construction 5.2%; transportation, public utilities 4.9%; mining 1.2%. **Production:** trade 18.2%; services 17.4%; manufacturing 16.8%; government 13.5%; finance, insurance, real estate 12.9%; transportation, utilities 12.5%; construction 4.6%; agriculture 2.9%; mining 1.3%. **Chief agricultural products:** *Crops:* wheat, corn (maize), sorghum, hay, soybeans, sunflower seed and oil, apples, peaches, pecans. *Livestock:* beef cattle, dairy cattle, hogs, sheep and lambs, horses and other equines. **Chief manufactured products:** food products, grain and oilseed milling, meat products, printing, refined petroleum, soap and cleaning products, plastic products, aerospace products and parts, aircraft.

Internet resources: <www.travelks.com>; <www.kansas.gov>.

Kentucky

Name: Kentucky, possibly from the Iroquois word for "prairie." **Nickname:** Bluegrass State. **Capital:** Frankfort. **Rank:** population: 26th; area: 37th; pop. density: 22nd. **Motto:** United We Stand, Divided We Fall. **Song:** "My Old Kentucky Home," words and music by Stephen Foster. **Bird:** cardinal. **Butterfly:** viceroy butterfly. **Fish:** Kentucky bass. **Flower:** goldenrod. **Horse:** Thoroughbred. **Tree:** tulip poplar. **Wild animal:** gray squirrel.

Natural features

Land area: 40,409 sq mi, 104,659 sq km. **Mountain ranges:** Cumberland, Pine. **Highest point:** Black Mountain, 4,145 ft (1,263 m). **Largest lake:** Kentucky Lake. **Major rivers:** Mississippi, Ohio, Big Sandy, Licking, Kentucky, Salt, Green, Tradewater, Cumberland, Tennessee. **Natural regions:** Appalachian Plateaus cover the eastern third of the state; Interior Low Plateaus, including the Highland Rim Section and the Lexington Plain, cover the re-

For details about state governments, see pages 682–687; for energy data, see pages 705–706.

mainder, with the exception of the Coastal Plain, which covers the extreme southwestern tip. **Location:** Midwest, bordering Indiana, Ohio, West Virginia, Virginia, Tennessee, Missouri, and Illinois. **Climate:** temperate continental climate, with hot, humid summers and cold winters. **Land use:** forest, 40.6%; agricultural, 21.2%; other, 38.2%.

People

Population (2006): 4,206,074; 104.1 persons per sq mi (40.2 persons per sq km). **Vital statistics** (2005; per 1,000 population): birth rate, 13.5; death rate, 9.7; marriage rate, 8.8; divorce rate, 4.5. **Major cities** (2006): Louisville 554,496; Lexington 270,789; Owensboro 55,525; Bowling Green 53,176; Covington 42,797.

Government

Statehood: entered the Union on 1 Jun 1792 as the 15th state. **State constitution:** adopted 1891. **Representation in US Congress:** 2 senators; 6 representatives. **Electoral college:** 8 (based on the 2000 census). **Political divisions:** 120 counties.

Economy

Employment: services 25.4%; trade 21.7%; government 14.9%; manufacturing 14.9%; agriculture, forestry, fishing 6.4%; construction 5.8%; transportation, public utilities 5.2%; finance, insurance, real estate 4.5%; mining 1.2%. **Production:** manufacturing 27.5%; services 16.0%; trade 15.7%; government 13.5%; finance, insurance, real estate 10.9%; transportation, utilities 8.0%; construction 4.5%; mining 2.1%; agriculture 1.8%. **Chief agricultural products:** *Crops:* tobacco, soybeans, corn (maize), wheat, hay, sorghum, eggs, dairy products. *Livestock:* racing and show horses, beef cattle, dairy cattle, hogs, poultry, sheep and lambs. **Chief manufactured products:** food products, meatpacking, beverages, tobacco, apparel, paper products, printing, chemical products, paint, resin and synthetic rubber products, plastic products, iron and steel, aluminum, fabricated metal products, machinery, appliances, motor vehicles.

Internet resources: <www.kentuckytourism.com>; <www.kentucky.gov>.

Louisiana

Name: Louisiana, named for Louis XIV, king of France. **Nickname:** Pelican State. **Capital:** Baton Rouge. **Rank:** population: 25th; area: 31st; pop. density: 24th. **Motto:** Union, Justice and Confidence. **Songs:** "Give Me Louisiana," words and music by Doralice Fontane; "You Are My Sunshine," words and music by Jimmy H. Davis and Charles Mitchell. **Amphibian:** green tree frog. **Bird:** brown pelican. **Crustacean:** crawfish. **Fish:** white perch (freshwater); spotted sea trout, or speckled trout (saltwater). **Flower:** magnolia. **Fossil:** petrified palmwood. **Gemstone:** agate. **Insect:** honeybee. **Mammal:** black bear. **Reptile:** alligator. **Tree:** bald cypress.

Natural features

Land area: 47,716 sq mi, 123,584 sq km. **Highest point:** Driskill Mountain, 535 ft (163 m). **Largest lake:** Lake Ponchartrain. **Major rivers:** Mississippi, Red, Sabine. **Natural regions:** the entire state consists of the Coastal Plain and is divided into the West Gulf Coastal Plain to the west, the Mississippi Alluvial Plain to the northeast, and the East Gulf Coastal Plain in the southeast. **Location:** South, bordering Arkansas, Mississippi, and Texas. **Climate:** subtropical, with hot, humid summers, tempered by frequent afternoon thunder showers, alternating with mild winters; subject to tropical storms: hurricane season from June through November. **Land use:** forest, 42.5%; agricultural, 17.3%; pasture, 0.9%; other, 39.3%.

People

Population (2006): 4,287,768; 89.9 persons per sq mi (34.7 persons per sq km). **Vital statistics** (2001; per 1,000 population): birth rate, 13.5; death rate, 9.3; marriage rate, 8.1; divorce rate, N/A. **Major cities** (2006): Baton Rouge 229,553; New Orleans 223,388; Shreveport 200,199; Metairie 130,000; Lafayette 114,214.

Government

Statehood: entered the Union on 30 Apr 1812 as the 18th state. **State constitution:** adopted 1974. **Representation in US Congress:** 2 senators; 5 representatives. **Electoral college:** 9 votes (based on the 2000 census). **Political divisions:** 64 parishes.

Economy

Employment: services 29.2%; trade 21.6%; government 17.4%; manufacturing 8.7%; construction 6.8%; transportation, public utilities 5.6%; finance, insurance, real estate 5.3%; agriculture, forestry, fishing 2.8%; mining 2.7%. **Production:** services 17.6%; manufacturing 15.2%; trade 15.1%; finance, insurance, real estate 13.0%; government 12.3%; mining 11.7%; transportation, utilities 9.2%; construction 4.9%; agriculture 1.0%. **Chief agricultural products:** *Crops:* soybeans, cotton, corn (maize), sorghum, hay, sugarcane, rice, wheat, sweet potatoes, pecans, strawberries, peaches, milk, eggs. *Livestock:* cattle and calves, chickens, hogs. *Aquaculture:* catfish, crawfish. *Fish catch:* shrimp, oysters, marine fish, freshwater fish. *Extractive products:* timber. **Chief manufactured products:** industrial chemicals, agricultural chemicals, plastics materials and resins, refined petroleum, cane sugar products, beverages, food and food products, paper and paper products, fabricated metal products, wood and wood products, communications equipment, ships, boats, and nautical equipment.

Internet resources: <www.louisianatravel.com>; <www.louisiana.gov>.

Maine

Name: Maine, possibly named for the former French province of Maine, or used to distinguish the mainland portion of the territory from offshore islands. **Nickname:** Pine Tree State. **Capital: Augusta. **Rank:** population: 40th; area: 39th; pop. density: 38th. **Motto:** *Dirigo* (I Direct). **Song:** "State of Maine Song," words and music by Roger Vinton Snow. **Bird:** chickadee. **Fish:** landlocked salmon. **Flower:** white pine cone and tassel. **Fossil:** *Pertica quadrifaria*. **Gemstone:** tourmaline. **Insect:** honeybee. **Mammal:** moose. **Tree:** white pine.

Natural features

Land area: 33,126 sq mi, 85,795 sq km. **Mountain ranges:** Appalachian, Longfellow. **Highest point:** Mount Katahdin, 5,268 ft (1,606 m). **Largest lake:** Moosehead Lake. **Major rivers:** Saco, Androscoggin, Kennebec, Penobscot, St. John's, St. Croix, Allagash. **Natural regions:** entire state is part of the larger New England Province, subdivided into the White Mountain section (southwest), Seaboard Lowland Section (southeast coastline), and New England Upland Section (north and central regions). **Location:** New England, bordering New Hampshire; international border with Canada. **Climate:** cool maritime climate, with coldest temperatures and greatest snowfall occurring in northern regions. **Land use:** forest, 84.0%; agricultural, 1.8%; other 14.2%.

People

Population (2006): 1,321,574; 39.9 persons per sq mi (15.4 persons per sq km). **Vital statistics** (2005; per 1,000 population): birth rate, 10.7; death rate, 9.7; marriage rate, 7.9; divorce rate, 3.5. **Major cities** (2006): Portland 63,011; Lewiston 35,734; Bangor 31,008; South Portland 23,784; Auburn 23,156.

Government

Statehood: entered the Union on 15 Mar 1820 as the 23rd state. **State constitution:** adopted 1819. **Representation in US Congress:** 2 senators; 2 representatives. **Electoral college:** 4 votes (based on the 2000 census). **Political divisions:** 16 counties.

Economy

Employment: services 30.2%; trade 23.0%; government 13.7%; manufacturing 13.1%; construction 6.3%; finance, insurance, real estate 5.9%; transportation, public utilities 4.1%; agriculture, forestry, fishing 3.7%. **Production:** services 20.1%; finance, insurance, real estate 18.8%; trade 18.0%; manufacturing 15.4%; government 14.0%; transportation, utilities 7.0%; construction 4.6%; agriculture, forestry, fishing 2.0%. **Chief agricultural products:** *Crops:* potatoes, blueberries, hay, apples, cranberries, oats, honey, corn (maize), dairy products, eggs. *Livestock:* poultry, cattle and calves, sheep and lambs. *Aquaculture:* salmon, rainbow trout. *Fish catch:* marine fish, lobster, shrimp, crab, clams, haddock, cod, mackerel. *Extractive industries:* timber. **Chief manufactured products:** paper, leather, lumber and wood products, food products, semiconductors, apparel, printing and publishing, plastic products, ships and boats.

Internet resources: <www.visitmaine.com>; <www.maine.gov>.

Maryland

Name: Maryland, in honor of Henrietta Maria, queen of England at the time the colony of Maryland was founded. **Nickname:** Old Line State. **Capital:** Annapolis. **Rank:** population: 19th; area: 42nd; pop. density: 5th. **Motto:** *Fatti Maschii, Parole Femine* (Manly Deeds, Womanly Words). **Song:** "Maryland, My Maryland," words by James Ryder Randall, to the tune of "O Tannenbaum." **Bird:** Baltimore oriole. **Crustacean:** Maryland blue crab. **Dinosaur:** *Astrodon johnstoni.* **Fish:** rockfish (striped bass). **Flower:** black-eyed Susan. **Insect:** Baltimore checkerspot. **Reptile:** diamondback terrapin. **Tree:** white oak.

Natural features

Land area: 10,454 sq mi, 27,076 sq km. **Mountain ranges:** Allegheny, Appalachian. **Highest point:** Backbone Mountain, 3,360 ft (1,024 m). **Largest lake:** Deep Creek Lake. **Major rivers:** Potomac, Patuxent, Susquehanna. **Natural regions:** Coastal Plain, eastern half of the state, includes the Embayed Section near the southwest corner of the peninsula; Piedmont Province, central, includes the Piedmont Upland to the north and the Piedmont Lowlands to the west; Blue Ridge Province, northwest; Valley and Ridge Province, part of western neck; Appalachian Plateau, extreme western neck. **Location:** East, bordering Pennsylvania, Delaware, District of Columbia, Virginia, and West Virginia. **Climate:** continental in the west, but a humid, subtropical climate prevails in the east; hurricanes often bring much rain to eastern regions. **Land use:** forest, 30.1%; agricultural, 19.3%; other, 50.6%.

People

Population (2006): 5,615,727; 537.2 persons per sq mi (207.4 persons per sq km). **Vital statistics** (2005; per 1,000 population): birth rate, 13.4; death rate, 7.9; marriage rate, 6.7; divorce rate, 3.1. **Major cities** (2006): Baltimore 631,366; Columbia 94,700; Silver Spring 73,000; Rockville 59,114; Frederick 58,882.

Government

Statehood: entered the Union on 28 Apr 1788 as the 7th state. **State constitution:** adopted 1867. **Representation in US Congress:** 2 senators; 8 representatives. **Electoral college:** 10 votes (based on the 2000 census). **Political divisions:** 23 counties.

Economy

Employment: services 34.4%; trade 21.1%; government 17.3%; finance, insurance, real estate 8.3%; manufacturing 6.4%; construction 6.3%; transportation, public utilities 4.4%; agriculture, forestry, fishing 1.8%; mining 0.1%. **Production:** services 24.2%; finance, insurance, real estate 21.3%; government 17.5%; trade 15.2%; manufacturing 8.1%; transportation, utilities 7.5%; construction 5.4%; agriculture 0.8%; mining 0.1%. **Chief agricultural products:** *Crops:* corn (maize), soybeans, wheat, vegetables, potatoes, tobacco, dairy products, eggs. *Livestock:* cattle and calves, pigs, poultry. *Aquaculture:* hybrid striped bass, catfish, tilapia, trout, oysters. *Fish catch:* blue crab, other crustaceans, oysters, mollusks, marine fish. **Chief manufactured products:** primary metals, ships

For details about state governments, see pages 682–687; for energy data, see pages 705–706.

and boats, food products, motor vehicles, chemical products, paper and printing, plastics and rubber, fabricated metal products, machinery, computers and electronics, transportation equipment.

Internet resources: <www.mdisfun.org>; <www.maryland.gov>.

Massachusetts

Name: Massachusetts, named for the Massachusett tribe of Native Americans who lived in the Great Blue Hill region south of Boston; the word *Massachusett* means "at or about the great hill." **Nickname:** Bay State. **Capital:** Boston. **Rank:** population: 13th; area: 45th; pop. density: 3rd. **Motto:** *Ense Petit Placidam sub Libertate Quietem* (By the Sword We Seek Peace, but Peace Only Under Liberty). **Song:** "All Hail to Massachusetts," words and music by Arthur J. Marsh. **Bird:** black-capped chickadee. **Fish:** cod. **Flower:** mayflower. **Fossil:** theropod dinosaur tracks. **Gemstone:** rhodonite. **Insect:** ladybug. **Marine mammal:** right whale. **Mineral:** babingtonite. **Rock:** Roxbury puddingstone. **Tree:** American elm.

Natural features

Land area: 8,263 sq mi, 21,401 sq km. **Mountain ranges:** Berkshire Mountains, Hoosac Range, Taconic Range. **Highest point:** Mount Greylock, 3,491 ft (1,064 m). **Largest lake:** Webster Lake. **Major rivers:** Connecticut, Charles, Merrimack, Housatonic, Taunton. **Natural regions:** the New England Province, comprising most of the state, subdivided into the Taconic Section along the west, the New England Upland Section in the central region, and the Seaboard Lowland Section, covering the eastern third of the state; Coastal Plain, comprising the peninsula region. **Location:** New England, bordering New Hampshire, Rhode Island, Connecticut, New York, and Vermont. **Climate:** temperate continental climate, with cold snowy winters and warm, humid summers; climate is colder but drier in western Massachusetts, although its winter snowfalls may be more severe. **Land use:** forest, 49.9%; agricultural, 4.7%; other, 45.4%.

People

Population (2006): 6,437,193; 779.0 persons per sq mi (300.8 persons per sq km). **Vital statistics** (2005; per 1,000 population): birth rate, 12.0; death rate, 8.3; marriage rate, 6.1; divorce rate, 2.2. **Major cities** (2006): Boston 590,763; Worcester 175,454; Springfield 151,176; Lowell 103,229; Cambridge 101,365.

Government

Statehood: entered the Union on 6 Feb 1788 as the 6th state. **State constitution:** adopted 1780. **Representation in US Congress:** 2 senators; 10 representatives. **Electoral college:** 12 votes (based on the 2000 census). **Political divisions:** 14 counties.

Economy

Employment: services 38.2%; trade 20.6%; manufacturing 11.9%; government 11.2%; finance, insurance, real estate 8.2%; construction 4.6%; transportation, public utilities 4.1%; agriculture, forestry, fishing 1.3%; mining 0.1%. **Production:** services 26.8%; finance, insurance, real estate 24.5%; trade 15.3%; manufacturing 13.9%; government 9.1%; transportation, utilities 5.6%; construction 4.1%; agriculture 0.5%. **Chief agricultural products:** *Crops:* tobacco, cranberries, hay, potatoes, sweet corn, dairy products, eggs. *Livestock:* cattle and calves, poultry. *Fish catch:* marine fish, lobster, crab, mollusks. *Aquaculture:* oysters, quahogs, soft-shelled clams, scallops. **Chief manufactured products:** food products, dairy products, soft drinks, textiles, paper products, printing, pharmaceuticals, plastic products, nonferrous metal products, fabricated metal products, machinery, communications equipment, semiconductors and electronics, electrical equipment, software, aerospace equipment, aircraft engines, surgical and medical equipment.

Internet resources: <www.mass-vacation.com>; <www.mass.gov>.

Michigan

Name: Michigan, from Native American word *Michigana* meaning "great, or, large lake." **Nicknames:** Wolverine State; Great Lake State. **Capital:** Lansing. **Rank:** population: 8th; area: 11th; pop. density: 21st. **Motto:** *Si Quaeris Peninsulam Amoenam, Circumspice* (If You Seek a Pleasant Peninsula, Look Around You). **Song:** "Michigan, My Michigan," words by Giles Kavanagh and music by H.J. O'Reilly Clint. **Bird:** robin. **Fish:** brook trout. **Flower:** apple blossom. **Gemstone:** chlorastrolite. **Mammal:** white-tailed deer (game mammal). **Reptile:** painted turtle. **Rock:** Petoskey stone. **Tree:** white pine.

Natural features

Land area: 96,716 sq mi, 250,493 sq km. **Highest point:** Mount Arvon, 1,979 ft (603 m). **Largest lake:** Houghton Lake. **Major rivers:** Montreal, Brule, Menominee, St. Clair. **Natural regions:** the Central Lowland, Eastern Lake Section, covers all of Lower Michigan and part of the Upper Peninsula region; the western half of the Upper Peninsula consists of Superior Upland, as do two small areas at the eastern end. **Location:** Midwest, bordering Ohio, Indiana, and Wisconsin; international border with Canada. **Climate:** continental; the Great Lakes cool the hot winds of summer and warm the cold winds of winter, giving Michigan a milder climate than some other north-central states, although the Upper Peninsula is relatively cooler; very high snowfall along the coast of Lake Michigan. **Land use:** forest, 44.7%; agricultural, 21.7%; other, 33.6%.

People

Population (2006): 10,095,643; 104.4 persons per sq mi (40.3 persons per sq km). **Vital statistics** (2005; per 1,000 population): birth rate, 12.6; death rate, 8.6; marriage rate, 6.1; divorce rate, 3.4. **Major cities** (2006): Detroit 871,121; Grand Rapids 193,083; Warren 134,589; Sterling Heights 127,991; Flint 117,068.

Government

Statehood: entered the Union on 26 Jan 1837 as the 26th state. **State constitution:** adopted 1963. **Repre-**

sentation in US Congress: 2 senators; 15 representatives. **Electoral college:** 17 votes (based on the 2000 census). **Political divisions:** 83 counties.

Economy

Employment: services 29.2%; trade 22.2%; manufacturing 18.4%; government 12.1%; finance, insurance, real estate 6.9%; construction 4.9%; transportation, public utilities 3.8%; agriculture, forestry, fishing 2.3%; mining 0.2%. **Production:** manufacturing 26.2%; services 19.6%; trade 17.1%; finance, insurance, real estate 14.1%; government 10.3%; transportation, utilities 6.6%; construction 4.8%; agriculture 0.9%; mining 0.3%. **Chief agricultural products:** *Crops:* apples, asparagus, beans, blueberries, carrots, celery, cherries, corn (maize), flowers, grapes and wine, honey, wool, maple syrup, mint, onions, peaches, plums, potatoes, dairy products, eggs, strawberries, sugar, soybeans. *Livestock:* beef and dairy cattle and calves, pigs, poultry, sheep and lambs. *Aquaculture:* Rainbow, brook, and brown trout, yellow perch, catfish. *Extractive industries:* Christmas trees. **Chief manufactured products:** motor vehicles, salt, plastics, pharmaceuticals, soaps, milled grain, dry cereals, agricultural machinery, office furniture, dairy products, preserved fruits and vegetables, printed matter, electrical equipment, measuring and control devices.

Internet resources: <www.michigan.org>; <www.michigan.gov>.

Minnesota

Name: Minnesota, from a Dakota word meaning "sky-tinted water." **Nickname:** North Star State. **Capital:** St. Paul. **Rank:** population: 21st; area: 12th; pop. density: 32nd. **Motto:** *L'Étoile du Nord* (The Star of the North). **Song:** "Hail! Minnesota," first verse and music by Truman E. Rickard, second verse by Arthur E. Upson. **Bird:** common loon. **Fish:** walleye pike. **Flower:** pink and white lady slipper. **Gemstone:** Lake Superior agate. **Insect:** monarch butterfly. **Tree:** Norway pine.

Natural features

Land area: 86,939 sq mi, 225,171 sq km. **Mountain ranges:** Mesabi, Vermillion, Cuyuna. **Highest point:** Eagle Mountain, 2,301 ft (701 m). **Largest lake:** Red Lake. **Major rivers:** Minnesota, St. Croix, Mississippi. **Natural regions:** Superior Upland, northeast corner; Central Lowland, covering most of the state; Western Lake Section, center; Dissected Till Plains, extreme southwest corner and south-central edge; Wisconsin Driftless Section, extreme southeast. **Location:** North central, bordering Wisconsin, Iowa, South Dakota, and North Dakota; international border with Canada. **Climate:** continental, with very cold winters and warm summers. **Land use:** agricultural, 39.1%; forest, 30.3%; other, 30.6%.

People

Population (2006): 5,167,101; 59.4 persons per sq mi (22.9 persons per sq km). **Vital statistics** (2005; per 1,000 population): birth rate, 13.8; death rate, 7.3; marriage rate, 5.9; divorce rate (2004), 2.8. **Major cities** (2006): Minneapolis 372,833; St. Paul 273,535; Rochester 96,975; Duluth 84,167; Bloomington 80,869.

Government

Statehood: entered the Union on 11 May 1858 as the 32nd state. **State constitution:** adopted 1857. **Representation in US Congress:** 2 senators; 8 representatives. **Electoral college:** 10 votes (based on the 2000 census). **Political divisions:** 87 counties.

Economy

Employment: services 30.3%; trade 22.0%; manufacturing 14.3%; government 12.0%; finance, insurance, real estate 7.6%; transportation, public utilities 4.7%; construction 4.6%; agriculture, forestry, fishing 4.2%; mining 0.3%. **Production:** services 20.8%; finance, insurance, real estate 18.5%; manufacturing 18.1%; trade 17.6%; government 10.2%; transportation, utilities 7.6%; construction 5.0%; agriculture 1.7%; mining 0.5%. **Chief agricultural products:** *Crops:* corn (maize), green peas, dry beans, onions, carrots, apples, oats, hay, spring wheat, barley, soybeans, potatoes, sugar beets, flaxseed, dairy products, eggs. *Livestock:* pigs, cattle and calves, poultry, sheep and lambs. **Chief manufactured products:** food and food processing, malt beverages and other alcoholic products, dairy products, meatpacking, industrial machinery, computers and office machines, electronics and electric equipment, precision instruments, printing and publishing, call centers and communications, information technology, forest products, medical manufacturing, plastics and rubber manufacturing.

Internet resources: <www.exploreminnesota.com>; <www.state.mn.us>.

Mississippi

Name: Mississippi, from a Native American word meaning "great waters" or "father of waters." **Nickname:** Magnolia State. **Capital:** Jackson. **Rank:** population: 31st; area: 32nd; pop. density: 31st. **Motto:** *Virtute et Armis* (By Valor and Arms). **Song:** "Go, Mississippi," words and music by Houston Davis. **Bird:** mockingbird. **Fish:** largemouth bass. **Flower:** magnolia. **Fossil:** prehistoric whale. **Insect:** honeybee. **Mammal:** white-tailed deer. **Marine mammal:** bottle-nosed dolphin (porpoise). **Rock:** petrified wood. **Tree:** magnolia tree.

Natural features

Land area: 47,692 sq mi, 123,522 sq km. **Highest point:** Woodall Mountain, 806 ft (246 m). **Major rivers:** Mississippi, Pearl, Big Black, Yazoo, Tombigbee, Pascagoula, Tennessee. **Natural regions:** the entire state consists of the Coastal Plain, subdivided into the Mississippi Alluvial Plain, in the west, and the East Gulf Coastal Plain, comprising the central and eastern regions. **Location:** South, bordering Tennessee, Alabama, Louisiana, and Arkansas. **Climate:**

For details about state governments, see pages 682–687; for energy data, see pages 705–706.

mild, with hot, humid summers and mild winters; coastal area is subject to hurricanes from June to October. **Land use:** forest, 54.9%; agricultural, 16.3%; other, 28.8%.

People

Population (2006): 2,910,540; 61.0 persons per sq mi (23.6 persons per sq km). **Vital statistics** (2005; per 1,000 population): birth rate, 14.5; death rate, 10.1; marriage rate, 5.9; divorce rate, 4.5. **Major cities** (2006): Jackson 176,614; Gulfport 64,316; Hattiesburg 48,012; Biloxi 44,342; Southaven 41,295.

Government

Statehood: entered the Union on 10 Dec 1817 as the 20th state. **State constitution:** adopted 1890. **Representation in US Congress:** 2 senators; 5 representatives. **Electoral college:** 6 votes (based on the 2000 census). **Political divisions:** 82 counties.

Economy

Employment: services 24.5%; trade 19.7%; government 17.8%; manufacturing 17.5%; construction 5.5%; agriculture, forestry, fishing 5.2%; finance, insurance, real estate 4.7%; transportation, public utilities 4.5%; mining 0.6%. **Production:** manufacturing 20.6%; services 17.4%; trade 16.8%; government 16.0%; finance, insurance, real estate 11.4%; transportation, utilities 9.5%; construction 4.7%; agriculture 2.6%; mining 1.0%. **Chief agricultural products:** *Crops:* cotton, soybeans, rice, wheat, corn, greenhouse and nursery plants, sweet potatoes, pecans. *Livestock:* cattle and calves. *Aquaculture:* catfish, pearl farming. *Fish catch:* marine fish, freshwater fish, shrimp, oysters, crustaceans. *Extractive industries:* timber. **Chief manufactured products:** food products, transport equipment, apparel, textiles, electrical equipment, rubber products, metal products.

Internet resources: <www.visitmississippi.org>; <www.mississippi.gov>.

Missouri

Name: Missouri, named for Native American tribe that lived in the region; the name means "town of the large canoes." **Nickname:** Show Me State. **Capital:** Jefferson City. **Rank:** population: 18th; area: 20th; pop. density: 28th. **Motto:** *Salus Populi Suprema Lex Esto* (The Welfare of the People Shall Be the Supreme Law). **Song:** "Missouri Waltz," words by J.R. Shannon and music by John Valentine Eppel. **Aquatic animal:** paddlefish. **Bird:** bluebird. **Fish:** channel catfish. **Flower:** white hawthorn blossom. **Fossil:** crinoid. **Insect:** honeybee. **Mammal:** Missouri mule. **Mineral:** galena. **Rock:** mozarkite. **Tree:** flowering dogwood.

Natural features

Land area: 69,704 sq mi, 180,533 sq km. **Mountain ranges:** Ozark Plateau, St. Francois. **Highest point:** Taum Sauk Mountain, 1,772 ft (540 m). **Largest lake:** Truman Lake. **Major rivers:** Missouri, Mississippi, Des Plaines. **Natural regions:** Central Lowland, northwestern, subdivided into the Dissected Till Plains to the north and the Osage Plains to the west; Ozark Plateaus, including the Springfield-Salem Plateaus, southeast; Coastal Plain, including the Mississippi Alluvial Plain, extreme southeastern tip. **Location:** Midwest, bordering Iowa, Illinois, Kentucky, Tennessee, Arkansas, Oklahoma, Kansas, and Nebraska. **Climate:** continental, with hot, humid summers and cold winters; the state lies in "Tornado Alley," the zone of maximum tornado occurrence, and has an average of 27 tornadoes annually. **Land use:** agricultural, 30.7%; forest, 28.1%; pasture, 0.2%; other, 41.0%.

People

Population (2006): 5,842,713; 83.8 persons per sq mi (32.4 persons per sq km). **Vital statistics** (2005; per 1,000 population): birth rate, 13.6; death rate, 9.4; marriage rate, 8.1; divorce rate, 3.6. **Major cities** (2006): Kansas City 447,306; St. Louis 347,181; Springfield 150,797; Independence 109,400; Columbia 94,428.

Government

Statehood: entered the Union on 10 Aug 1821 as the 24th state. **State constitution:** adopted 1945. **Representation in US Congress:** 2 senators; 9 representatives. **Electoral college:** 11 votes (based on the 2000 census). **Political divisions:** 114 counties.

Economy

Employment: services 29.3%; trade 21.8%; government 13.3%; manufacturing 12.9%; finance, insurance, real estate 6.8%; transportation, public utilities 5.8%; construction 5.5%; agriculture, forestry, fishing 4.5%; mining 0.2%. **Production:** services 20.5%; manufacturing 19.3%; trade 17.1%; finance, insurance, real estate 15.3%; government 11.4%; transportation, utilities 10.1%; construction 4.9%; agriculture 1.1%; mining 0.3%. **Chief agricultural products:** *Crops:* soybeans, corn (maize), cotton, rice, grain sorghum, hay, wheat, fruits and vegetables, dairy products. *Livestock:* cattle and calves, pigs, sheep and lambs, poultry. *Extractive industries:* timber. **Chief manufactured products:** industrial machinery, transportation equipment, food processing, malt beverages, soft drinks, meat and poultry products, preserved fruits and vegetables, soaps and detergents, agricultural chemicals, pharmaceuticals, printing and publishing, primary metals, nonelectrical machinery, fabricated metals, petroleum and coal products, electrical equipment, stone, clay, and glass products.

Internet resources: <www.visitmo.com>; <www.missouri.gov>.

Montana

Name: Montana, from the Spanish word *montaña* ("mountain," or "mountainous region"). **Nickname:** Treasure State. **Capital:** Helena. **Rank:** population: 44th; area: 4th; pop. density: 48th. **Motto:** *Oro y Plata* (Gold and Silver). **Song:** "Montana," words by Charles C. Cohan and music by Joseph E. Howard. **Bird:** western meadowlark. **Fish:** cutthroat trout. **Flower:** bitterroot. **Fossil:** *Maiasaura*. **Gemstones:** agate; sapphire. **Mammal:** grizzly bear. **Tree:** ponderosa pine.

Natural features

Land area: 147,042 sq mi, 380,837 sq km. **Mountain ranges:** Rocky, Grand Teton. **Highest point:** Granite Peak, 12,799 ft (3,901 m). **Largest lake:** Flathead Lake. **Major rivers:** Kootenai, Clark Fork, Flathead, Missouri, Yellowstone. **Natural regions:** Northern Rocky Mountains, western two-fifths of the state; Middle Rocky Mountains, small area along the south-central border; Missouri Plateau region of the Great Plains Province, eastern three-fifths of the state. **Location:** Northwest, bordering North Dakota, South Dakota, Wyoming, and Idaho; international border with Canada. **Climate:** continental; most of the Great Plains region is semiarid, with warm summers and cold winters; west of the Rocky Mountains the climate is milder. **Land use:** pasture, 39.0%; agricultural, 15.4%; forest, 5.7%; other, 39.9%.

People

Population (2006): 944,632; 6.4 persons per sq mi (2.5 persons per sq km). **Vital statistics** (2005; per 1,000 population): birth rate, 12.4; death rate, 9.0; marriage rate, 7.3; divorce rate, 3.8. **Major cities** (2006): Billings 100,148; Missoula 64,081; Great Falls 56,215; Bozeman 35,061; Butte 32,110.

Government

Statehood: entered the Union on 8 Nov 1889 as the 41st state. **State constitution:** adopted 1972. **Representation in US Congress:** 2 senators; 1 representative. **Electoral college:** 3 votes (based on the 2000 census). **Political divisions:** 56 counties.

Economy

Employment: services 30.4%; trade 23.4%; government 15.5%; agriculture, forestry, fishing 6.7%; finance, insurance, real estate 6.1%; construction 6.1%; manufacturing 5.6%; transportation, public utilities 5.0%; mining 1.3%. **Production:** services 20.3%; trade 16.9%; government 16.4%; finance, insurance, real estate 13.7%; transportation, utilities 11.9%; manufacturing 7.5%; construction 5.6%; agriculture 4.0%; mining 3.7%. **Chief agricultural products:** *Crops:* wheat, barley, hay, oats, safflowers, sunflowers, mustard, sugar beets, dry beans, grapes, garlic, oil seeds, corn (maize), potatoes, honey, cherries, dairy products. *Livestock:* beef and dairy cattle and calves, sheep and lambs, poultry, horses, llamas. *Extractive industries:* timber, Christmas trees. **Chief manufactured products:** food processing, lumber and wood products, metal processing, petroleum products, chemical manufacturing, cement and concrete products, fabricated metal products, machinery.

Internet resources: <www.visitmt.com>; <www.mt.gov>.

Nebraska

Name: Nebraska, from a Native American word meaning "flat water," a reference to the Platte River. **Nickname:** Cornhusker State. **Capital:** Lincoln. **Rank:** population: 38th; area: 16th; pop. density: 42nd. **Motto:** Equality Before the Law. **Song:** "Beautiful Nebraska," words by Jim Fras and Guy Gage Miller and music by Jim Fras. **Bird:** western meadowlark. **Fish:** channel catfish. **Flower:** goldenrod. **Fossil:** mammoth. **Gemstone:** blue agate. **Insect:** honeybee. **Mammal:** white-tailed deer. **Rock:** prairie agate. **Tree:** cottonwood.

Natural features

Land area: 77,353 sq mi, 200,343 sq km. **Highest point:** Panorama Point 5,424 ft (1,653 m). **Largest lake:** Lake McConaughy. **Major rivers:** Missouri, Platte, Elkhorn, Loup, Republican, Big Blue, Niobrara. **Natural regions:** Great Plains Province, western three-quarters of the state; Missouri Plateau, at the northern corners; High Plains, central and north central; Plains Border, southern border; Central Lowland, including the Dissected Till Plains, eastern quarter of the state. **Location:** Central, bordering South Dakota, Iowa, Missouri, Kansas, Colorado, and Wyoming. **Climate:** continental, with hot summers and very cold winters; blizzards are not uncommon in winter; western half of state is semiarid. **Land use:** pasture, 46.6%; agricultural, 39.5%; forest, 1.6%; other, 12.3%.

People

Population (2006): 1,768,331; 22.9 persons per sq mi (8.8 persons per sq km). **Vital statistics** (2005; per 1,000 population): birth rate, 14.9; death rate, 8.5; marriage rate, 7.0; divorce rate, 3.4. **Major cities** (2006): Omaha 419,545; Lincoln 241,167; Bellevue 47,594; Grand Island 44,632; Kearney 29,385.

Government

Statehood: entered the Union on 1 Mar 1867 as the 37th state. **State constitution:** adopted 1875. **Representation in US Congress:** 2 senators; 3 representatives. **Electoral college:** 5 votes (based on the 2000 census). **Political divisions:** 93 counties.

Economy

Employment: services 28.1%; trade 22.2%; government 14.1%; manufacturing 10.4%; agriculture, forestry, fishing 7.3%; finance, insurance, real estate 7.2%; transportation, public utilities 5.5%; construction 5.0%; mining 0.2%. **Production:** services 19.1%; trade 16.7%; finance, insurance, real estate 15.5%; government 14.1%; manufacturing 14.0%; transportation, utilities 10.8%; agriculture 4.8%; construction 4.8%; mining 0.1%. **Chief agricultural products:** *Crops:* corn (maize), soybeans, hay, wheat, sorghum, dry edible beans, sugar beets. *Livestock:* beef cattle, dairy cattle, pigs, sheep and lambs, poultry. **Chief manufactured products:** meatpacking, canned and frozen fruits and vegetables, flour, cereal, grain products, beverages, dairy products, livestock feeds, transportation equipment (significantly motorcycles and small commercial vehicles), printing and publishing, rubber and plastic goods, fabricated metal products, primary metals.

Internet resources: <www.visitnebraska.org>; <www.nebraska.gov>.

For details about state governments, see pages 682–687; for energy data, see pages 705–706.

Nevada

Name: Nevada, from the Spanish *nevada* ("snow-clad"), a reference to the high mountain scenery of the Sierra Nevada on the southwestern border with California. **Nicknames:** Sagebrush State; Silver State. **Capital:** Carson City. **Rank:** population: 35th; area: 7th; pop. density: 43rd. **Motto:** All for Our Country. **Song:** "Home Means Nevada," words and music by Bertha Raffeto. **Bird:** mountain bluebird. **Fish:** Lahontan cutthroat trout. **Flower:** sagebrush. **Fossil:** ichthyosaur. **Gemstones:** fire opal; turquoise. **Mammal:** desert bighorn sheep. **Metal:** silver. **Reptile:** desert tortoise. **Rock:** sandstone. **Trees:** single-leaf piñon; bristlecone pine.

Natural features

Land area: 110,561 sq mi, 286,352 sq km. **Mountain ranges:** Snake, Schell Creek, Monitor, Toiyabe, Shoshone, Humboldt, Santa Rosa. **Highest point:** Boundary Peak, 13,143 ft (4,006 m). **Largest lakes:** Pyramid Lake (natural), Lake Mead (man-made). **Major rivers:** Humboldt, Truckee, Carson, Walker, Muddy, Virgin. **Natural regions:** the Basin and Range Province covers all of the state, except for the southwestern corner, which consists of the Cascade-Sierra Mountains, and the northeastern corner, which comprises part of the Columbia Plateau. **Location:** West, bordering Idaho, Utah, Arizona, California, and Oregon. **Climate:** semiarid but with regional variation: northern and eastern areas have long, cold winters and short, relatively hot summers, whereas in southern Nevada the summers are long and hot and the winters brief and mild. **Land use:** pasture, 11.7%; agricultural, 0.9%; forest, 0.4%; other, 87.0%.

People

Population (2006): 2,495,529; 22.6 persons per sq mi (8.7 persons per sq km). **Vital statistics** (2005; per 1,000 population): birth rate, 15.4; death rate, 7.7; marriage rate, 61.0; divorce rate, 7.7. **Major cities** (2006) Las Vegas 552,539; Henderson 240,614; Reno 210,255; North Las Vegas 197,567; Sunrise Manor 191,858; Paradise 186,370; Spring Valley 172,110; Enterprise 119,100.

Government

Statehood: entered the Union on 31 Oct 1864 as the 36th state. **State constitution:** adopted 1864. **Representation in US Congress:** 2 senators; 3 representatives. **Electoral college:** 5 votes (based on the 2000 census). **Political divisions:** 16 counties; 1 independent city.

Economy

Employment: services 42.2%; trade 19.5%; government 10.7%; construction 8.9%; finance, insurance, real estate 7.0%; transportation, public utilities 4.7%; manufacturing 4.1%; agriculture, forestry, fishing 1.5%; mining 1.5%. **Production:** services 32.5%; finance, insurance, real estate 16.9%; trade 15.0%; government 10.3%; construction 10.2%; transportation, utilities 8.0%; manufacturing 4.1%; mining 2.2%; agriculture 0.7%. **Chief agricultural products:** *Crops:* hay, wheat, corn (maize), potatoes, rye, oats, alfalfa, barley, vegetables, dairy products, some fruits. *Livestock*: cattle and calves, horses, sheep and lambs, hogs, poultry. **Chief manufactured products:** food processing, candy, frozen desserts, dairy products, soft drinks, paper products, chemical products, plastics, construction materials, industrial machinery, printing and publishing.

Internet resources: <travelnevada.com>; <www.nevada.gov>.

New Hampshire

Name: New Hampshire, named for Hampshire, England, by Captain John Mason. **Nickname:** Granite State. **Capital:** Concord. **Rank:** population: 41st; area: 44th; pop. density: 19th. **Motto:** Live Free or Die. **Songs:** "Old New Hampshire," words by John F. Holmes and music by Maurice Hoffmann; "New Hampshire, My New Hampshire," words by Julius Richelson and music by Walter P. Smith. **Amphibian:** red-spotted newt. **Bird:** purple finch. **Fish:** brook trout (freshwater); striped bass (saltwater). **Flower:** purple lilac. **Gemstone:** smokey quartz. **Insect:** ladybug. **Mammal:** white-tailed deer. **Mineral:** beryl. **Rock:** granite. **Tree:** white birch.

Natural features

Land area: 9,282 sq mi, 24,040 sq km. **Mountain ranges:** White, Ossipee, Sandwich, Presidential. **Highest point:** Mt. Washington, 6,288 ft (1,917 m). **Largest lake:** Lake Winnipesaukee. **Major rivers:** Merrimack, Salmon Falls, Connecticut, Saco, Piscataqua, Androscoggin. **Natural regions:** the New England Province covers the entire state and is subdivided into the White Mountain Section in the northern third, the New England Upland Section in the south-central region, and the Seaboard Lowland Section in the southeast corner. **Location:** New England, bordering Maine, Massachusetts, and Vermont; international border with Canada. **Climate:** temperate but highly varied: winter temperatures may drop below 0 °F (−18 °C) for days at a time; summers are relatively cool, and precipitation is rather evenly distributed over the four seasons. **Land use:** forest, 65.6%; agricultural, 2.1%; other, 32.3%.

People

Population (2006): 1,314,895; 141.7 persons per sq mi (54.7 persons per sq km). **Vital statistics** (2005; per 1,000 population): birth rate, 11.0; death rate, 7.6; marriage rate, 7.3; divorce rate, 3.3. **Major cities** (2006): Manchester 109,497; Nashua 87,157; Concord 42,378; Rochester 30,117; Dover 28,422.

Government

Statehood: entered the Union on 21 Jun 1788 as the 9th state. **State constitution:** adopted 1784. **Representation in US Congress:** 2 senators; 2 representatives. **Electoral college:** 4 votes (based on the 2000 census). **Political divisions:** 10 counties.

Economy

Employment: services 31.5%; trade 24.0%; manufacturing 15.5%; government 10.9%; finance, insurance, real estate 6.9%; construction 6.0%; transportation, public utilities 3.5%; agriculture, forestry, fishing 1.6%; mining 0.1%. **Production:** finance, insurance, real estate 23.2%; manufacturing 22.1%; services 19.6%; trade 16.5%; government 7.8%; transportation, utilities 5.8%; construction 4.1%; agriculture 0.7%; mining 0.1%. **Chief agricultural products:** *Crops:* apples, honey, fruits and vegetables, ornamental horticulture, Christmas trees, dairy products, eggs, herbs, maple syrup, wool. *Livestock:* horses, dairy cattle, sheep and lambs. *Fish catch:* marine fish, seafood. *Extractive products:* timber. **Chief manufactured products:** industrial machinery, computers and software, electrical equipment, semiconductors, processed foods, precision instruments, medical and surgical instruments, fabricated metal products, rubber and plastic products, printing and publishing, paper and paper products.

Internet resources: <www.visitnh.gov>; <www.nh.gov>.

New Jersey

Name: New Jersey, named for the island of Jersey in the English Channel. **Nickname:** Garden State. **Capital:** Trenton. **Rank:** population: 11th; area: 46th; pop. density: 1st. **Motto:** Liberty and Prosperity. **Bird:** eastern goldfinch. **Fish:** brook trout. **Flower:** violet. **Fossil:** *Hadrosaurus foulkii.* **Insect:** honeybee. **Mammal:** horse. **Tree:** red oak.

Natural features

Land area: 7,813 sq mi, 20,236 sq km. **Mountain range:** Appalachian. **Highest point:** Kittatinny Mountain, 1,803 ft (550 m). **Largest lake:** Lake Hopatcong. **Major rivers:** Delaware, Hudson, Passaic, Hackensack, Raritan. **Natural regions:** the Valley and Ridge Province, Middle Section, northwest corner; the New England Province, consisting of the New England Upland Section, east of the Valley and Ridge area; the Piedmont Province, including the Piedmont Lowlands, extending from the northeast corner to part of the border with Pennsylvania; the Coastal Plain, Embayed Section, southern half of the state. **Location:** Northeast, bordering New York, Delaware, and Pennsylvania. **Climate:** continental; relatively colder winters in northwest, milder conditions in the south, and hot summers throughout the state. **Land use:** forest, 30.8%; agricultural, 10.1%; other, 59.1%.

People

Population (2006): 8,724,560; 1,116.7 persons per sq mi (431.1 persons per sq km). **Vital statistics** (2005; per 1,000 population): birth rate, 13.0; death rate, 8.3; marriage rate, 5.0; divorce rate, 2.9. **Major cities** (2006): Newark 281,402; Jersey City 241,789; Paterson 148,708; Elizabeth 126,179; Edison 99,523.

Government

Statehood: entered the Union on 18 Dec 1787 as the 3rd state. **State constitution:** adopted 1947. **Representation in US Congress:** 2 senators; 13 representatives. **Electoral college:** 15 votes (based on the 2000 census). **Political divisions:** 21 counties.

Economy

Employment: services 32.8%; trade 21.6%; government 13.0%; manufacturing 11.0%; finance, insurance, real estate 9.7%; transportation, public utilities 6.3%; construction 4.3%; agriculture, forestry, fishing 1.2%; mining 0.1%. **Production:** finance, insurance, real estate 23.7%; services 23.5%; trade 17.0%; manufacturing 11.9%; government 10.1%; transportation, utilities 9.5%; construction 3.8%; agriculture 0.5%; mining 0.1%. **Chief agricultural products:** *Crops:* cranberries, blueberries, peaches, asparagus, bell peppers, spinach, lettuce, cucumbers, sweet corn, tomatoes, snap beans, cabbage, escarole and endive, eggplants, nursery and greenhouse products, dairy products, eggs. *Livestock:* horses, cattle, poultry. *Fish catch:* bluefish, tilefish, flounder, hake, shellfish. **Chief manufactured products:** chemical products, pharmaceuticals, electronic and electrical equipment, communications equipment, semiconductors, industrial equipment, petroleum products, fabricated metal products, clay products, food products.

Internet resources: <www.newjersey.gov>; <www.state.nj.us/travel>.

New Mexico

Name: New Mexico, named for the country of Mexico. **Nickname:** Land of Enchantment. **Capital:** Santa Fe. **Rank:** population: 36th; area: 5th; pop. density: 45th. **Motto:** *Crescit Eundo* (It Grows as It Goes). **Songs:** "O, Fair New Mexico," words and music by Elizabeth Garrett; "Así es Nuevo Mexico," words and music by Amadeo Lucero. **Bird:** roadrunner. **Fish:** New Mexico cutthroat trout. **Flower:** yucca. **Fossil:** coelophysis. **Gemstone:** turquoise. **Insect:** tarantula hawk wasp. **Tree:** piñon pine.

Natural features

Land area: 121,590 sq mi, 314,917 sq km. **Mountain ranges:** Rocky, Sangre de Cristo. **Highest point:** Wheeler Peak, 13,161 ft (4,011 m). **Largest lake:** Elephant Butte Reservoir. **Major rivers:** Rio Grande, Pecos, Canadian, San Juan, Gila. **Natural regions:** Great Plains Province, eastern third of the state, subdivided into the Raton Section to the north, the High Plains along the eastern edge, and the Pecos Valley to the west; Southern Rocky Mountains, north-central region; Colorado Plateau, northwest corner, including the Navajo Section and Datil Section; Basin and Range Province, central region and southwest corner, with the Sacramento Section to the east and the Mexican Highland to the south. **Location:** Southwest, bordering Colorado, Oklahoma, Texas, and Arizona; international border with Mexico. **Climate:** arid; moderate temperatures but great variation by altitude; temperatures drop dramatically after dark. **Land use:** pasture, 51.3%; forest, 7.0%; agricultural, 2.0%; other, 39.7%.

People

Population (2006): 1,954,599; 16.1 persons per sq mi (6.2 persons per sq km). **Vital statistics** (2005; per 1,000 population): birth rate, 15.0; death rate, 7.7;

For details about state governments, see pages 682–687; for energy data, see pages 705–706.

marriage rate, 6.7; divorce rate, 4.6. **Major cities** (2006): Albuquerque 504,949; Las Cruces 86,268; Santa Fe 72,056; Rio Rancho 71,607; Roswell 45,582.

Government

Statehood: entered the Union on 6 Jan 1912 as the 47th state. **State constitution:** adopted 1911. **Representation in US Congress:** 2 senators; 3 representatives. **Electoral college:** 5 votes (based on the 2000 census). **Political divisions:** 33 counties.

Economy

Employment: services 29.7%; trade 21.9%; government 20.4%; construction 6.4%; finance, insurance, real estate 6.0%; manufacturing 5.7%; transportation, public utilities 4.2%; agriculture, forestry, fishing 3.6%; mining 2.1%. **Production:** services 18.0%; government 16.8%; manufacturing 16.7%; trade 13.6%; finance, insurance, real estate 13.1%; mining 8.4%; transportation, utilities 7.4%; construction 4.0%; agriculture 2.1%. **Chief agricultural products:** *Crops:* pecans, apples, potatoes, onions, dry beans, chile, peanuts (groundnuts), hay, sorghum, corn (maize), wheat, eggs, dairy products, wool. *Livestock:* dairy cattle, beef cattle, poultry, sheep and lambs. *Extractive industries:* timber. **Chief manufactured products:** electronic equipment, semiconductors, printing and publishing, processed foods.

Internet resources: <www.newmexico.org>; <www.newmexico.gov>.

New York

Name: New York, named in honor of the English duke of York. **Nickname:** Empire State. **Capital:** Albany. **Rank:** population: 3rd; area: 28th; pop. density: 7th. **Motto:** *Excelsior* (Ever Upward). **Song:** "I Love New York," words and music by Steve Karmen. **Bird:** bluebird. **Fish:** brook trout. **Flower:** rose. **Fossil:** *Eurypterus remipes.* **Gemstone:** garnet. **Mammal:** beaver. **Tree:** sugar maple.

Natural features

Land area: 53,097 sq mi, 137,521 sq km. **Mountain ranges:** Adirondack, Catskill, Shawangunk, Taconic. **Highest point:** Mt. Marcy, 5,344 ft (1,629 m). **Largest lake:** Oneida Lake. **Major rivers:** Hudson, Mohawk, Genesee, Oswego, Delaware, Susquehanna, Allegheny. **Natural regions:** Central Lowland, Eastern Lake Section, extends along the northern coast of Lake Ontario; St. Lawrence Valley, Northern Section, extends along the northern border with Canada; Adirondack Province, northeast; Appalachian Plateaus, including the Mohawks, Southern New York, and Catskill Sections, extend along the southern border with Pennsylvania and up halfway through the state; Valley and Ridge Province, southeastern edge bordering Connecticut and Massachusetts; Coastal Plain, Embayed Section, covers the islands of Manhattan and Long Island. **Location:** Northeast, bordering Vermont, Massachusetts, Connecticut, New Jersey, and Pennsylvania; international border with Canada. **Climate:** temperate continental, with hot, humid summers and cold, dry, snowy winters. **Land use:** forest, 56.1%; agricultural, 17.1%; other, 26.8%.

People

Population (2006): 19,306,183; 363.6 persons per sq mi (140.4 persons per sq km). **Vital statistics** (2005; per 1,000 population): birth rate, 12.8; death rate, 8.0; marriage rate, 7.0; divorce rate, 2.8. **Major cities** (2006): New York 8,214,426; Buffalo 276,059; Rochester 208,123; Yonkers 197,852; Syracuse 140,658.

Government

Statehood: entered the Union on 26 Jul 1788 as the 11th state. **State constitution:** adopted 1894. **Representation in US Congress:** 2 senators; 29 representatives. **Electoral college:** 31 votes (based on the 2000 census). **Political divisions:** 62 counties.

Economy

Employment: services 35.9%; trade 19.0%; government 14.1%; finance, insurance, real estate 11.1%; manufacturing 9.7%; transportation, public utilities 4.9%; construction 3.9%; agriculture, forestry, fishing 1.3%; mining 0.1%. **Production:** finance, insurance, real estate 32.8%; services 23.0%; trade 12.9%; manufacturing 10.3%; government 10.2%; transportation, utilities 7.3%; construction 3.0%; agriculture 0.4%; mining 0.1%. **Chief agricultural products:** *Crops:* apples, cabbage, corn (maize), potatoes, onions, grapes, snap beans, dry beans, grain, hay, cherries, strawberries, maple syrup, horticulture products, milk, eggs, other dairy products. *Livestock:* cattle and calves, chickens. **Chief manufactured products:** food processing, chemical products, apparel, primary metals, industrial machinery, computers and software, scientific and measuring instruments, transportation equipment, electric and electronic equipment, industrial machinery, printing and publishing, biotechnology.

Internet resources: <www.iloveny.com>; <www.ny.gov>.

North Carolina

Name: North Carolina, named in honor of Charles I of England. **Nickname:** Old North State. **Capital:** Raleigh. **Rank:** population: 10th; area: 29th; pop. density: 16th. **Motto:** *Esse Quam Videri* (To Be Rather Than To Seem). **Song:** "The Old North State," words by William Gaston, to the tune of a traditional German melody. **Bird:** cardinal. **Fish:** channel bass. **Flower:** dogwood. **Gemstone:** emerald. **Insect:** honeybee. **Mammal:** gray squirrel. **Reptile:** eastern box turtle. **Rock:** granite. **Tree:** pine.

Natural features

Land area: 52,671 sq mi, 136,417 sq km. **Mountain ranges:** Appalachian, Great Smoky, Blue Ridge. **Highest point:** Mt. Mitchell, 6,684 ft (2,037 m). **Largest lake:** Lake Mattamuskeet. **Major rivers:** Roanoke, Yadkin, Pee Dee. **Natural regions:** Valley and Ridge Province, far western edge; Piedmont Province, consisting of the Piedmont Upland, extending in a southwest to northeast direction through the center of the state; Coastal Plain, eastern third, divided into the Sea Island Section to the south and the Embayed Section to the north. **Location:** East, bordering Virginia, South Carolina, Georgia, and Tennessee. **Climate:** ranges from medium continental conditions in the mountain region (though summers are cooler and rainfall heavier) to the subtropical conditions of the state's southeastern corner; hurricanes occasionally occur along the coast, and there have been tornadoes inland. **Land use:** forest, 45.9%; agricultural, 16.4%; other, 37.7%.

People

Population (2006): 8,856,505; 168.1 persons per sq mi (64.9 persons per sq km). **Vital statistics** (2005; per 1,000 population): birth rate, 14.2; death rate, 8.6; marriage rate, 6.8; divorce rate, 3.8. **Major cities** (2006): Charlotte 630,478; Raleigh 356,321; Greensboro 236,865; Durham 209,009; Winston-Salem 196,990; Fayetteville 168,033.

Government

Statehood: entered the Union on 21 Nov 1789 as the 12th state. **State constitution:** adopted 1970. **Representation in US Congress:** 2 senators, 13 representatives. **Electoral college:** 15 votes (based on the 2000 census). **Political divisions:** 100 counties.

Economy

Employment: services 25.1%; trade 21.2%; manufacturing 18.5%; government 15.2%; construction 6.6%; finance, insurance, real estate 5.9%; transportation, public utilities 4.3%; agriculture, forestry, fishing 3.1%; mining 0.1%. **Production:** manufacturing 24.1%; finance, insurance, real estate 18.3%; services 16.4%; trade 15.0%; government 12.5%; transportation, utilities 7.1%; construction 4.9%; agriculture 1.5%; mining 0.2%. **Chief agricultural products:** *Crops:* tobacco, corn (maize), barley, potatoes, peanuts (groundnuts), apples, blueberries, grapes, peaches, pecans, strawberries, tomatoes, cabbages, watermelons, cucumbers, sweet potatoes, horticultural products, Christmas trees, dairy products, eggs. *Livestock:* cattle and calves, chickens, pigs, horses. *Aquaculture:* catfish, trout. *Extractive industries:* timber. **Chief manufactured products:** textiles, cotton and synthetic fibers, yarns, threads, knitted goods, cigarettes and tobacco products, chemical products, pharmaceuticals, electronic and electrical equipment, furniture, lumber, paper products, processed foods.

Internet resources: <www.visitnc.com>; <www.northcarolina.gov>.

North Dakota

Name: North Dakota, from the Dakota division of the Sioux, the Native American tribe that inhabited the plains before the arrival of Europeans; *dakota* is the Sioux word for "friend." **Nickname:** Peace Garden State. **Capital:** Bismarck. **Rank:** population: 48th; area: 18th; pop. density: 47th. **Motto:** Liberty and Union Now and Forever, One and Inseparable. **Song:** "North Dakota Hymn," words by James W. Foley and music by C.S. Putnam. **Bird:** western meadowlark. **Fish:** northern pike. **Flower:** wild prairie rose. **Fossil:** teredo petrified wood. **Tree:** American elm.

Natural features

Land area: 70,700 sq mi, 183,112 sq km. **Highest point:** White Butte, 3,506 ft (1,069 m). **Largest lake:** Devils Lake. **Major rivers:** Red, Souris, Missouri, Little Missouri, James. **Natural regions:** Central Lowland covers eastern half of the state, with the Western Lake Section lying in the east-central region; Great Plains Province covers western half of the state, including sections of the Missouri Plateau to the north and south. **Location:** North central, bordering Minnesota, South Dakota, and Montana; international border with Canada. **Climate:** continental, with hot summers and cold winters, warm days and cool nights in summer, low humidity and low precipitation, and much wind and sunshine. **Land use:** agricultural, 53.6%; pasture, 24.5%; forest, 1.0%; other, 20.9%.

People

Population (2006): 635,867; 9.0 persons per sq mi (3.5 persons per sq km). **Vital statistics** (2005; per 1,000 population): birth rate, 13.2; death rate, 9.1; marriage rate, 6.5; divorce rate, 2.4. **Major cities** (2006) Fargo 90,056; Bismarck 58,333; Grand Forks 50,372; Minot 34,745; West Fargo 21,508.

Government

Statehood: entered the Union on 2 Nov 1889 as the 39th state. **State constitution:** adopted 1889. **Representation in US Congress:** 2 senators; 1 representative. **Electoral college:** 3 votes (based on the 2000 census). **Political divisions:** 53 counties.

Economy

Employment: services 28.5%; trade 22.5%; government 16.4%; agriculture, forestry, fishing 9.7%; manufacturing 5.7%; finance, insurance, real estate 5.6%; transportation, public utilities 5.3%; construction 5.2%; mining 1.1%. **Production:** trade 19.5%; services 19.4%; government 14.4%; finance, insurance, real estate 14.1%; transportation, utilities 10.3%; manufacturing 9.0%; construction 5.5%; agriculture 4.1%; mining 3.6%. **Chief agricultural products:** *Crops*: hard red spring wheat, durum wheat, flaxseed, canola, dry beans, sunflowers, barley, honey, potatoes, dairy products, wool. *Livestock*: cattle and calves, sheep and lambs, pigs. *Extractive industries*: timber. **Chief manufactured products:** food processing, wood products, petroleum products, transportation equipment, machinery and apparatus.

Internet resources: <www.ndtourism.com>; <www.nd.gov>.

Ohio

Name: Ohio, from an Iroquois word meaning "great river." **Nickname:** Buckeye State. **Capital:** Columbus. **Rank:** population: 7th; area: 34th; pop. density: 10th. **Motto:** With God, All Things Are Possible. **Song:** "Beautiful Ohio," words by Ballard MacDonald and music by Mary Earl. **Bird:** cardinal. **Flower:** red carnation. **Fossil:** *Trilobite isotelus*. **Gemstone:** flint. **Insect:**

For details about state governments, see pages 682–687; for energy data, see pages 705–706.

ladybug. **Mammal:** white-tailed deer. **Reptile:** black racer snake. **Tree:** Ohio buckeye.

Natural features

Land area: 44,825 sq mi, 116,096 sq km. **Highest point:** Campbell Hill, 1,549 ft (472 m). **Largest lake:** Grand Lake St. Marys. **Major rivers:** Ohio, Maumee, Cuyahoga, Miami, Scioto, Muskingum. **Natural regions:** the Appalachian Plateau, eastern half of the state, includes the Southern New York Section to the north and the Kanawha Section to the east; the Central Lowlands, western half of the state, includes the Eastern Lake Section in the northwest corner, the Till Plains in the central region, and the Lexington Plain in the southwest. **Location:** Midwest, bordering Michigan, Pennsylvania, West Virginia, Kentucky, and Indiana. **Climate:** continental, with hot, humid summers and cold, dry winters. **Land use:** agricultural, 42.5%; forest, 27.3%; other, 30.2%.

People

Population (2006): 11,478,006; 256.1 persons per sq mi (98.9 persons per sq km). **Vital statistics** (2005; per 1,000 population): birth rate, 13.0; death rate, 9.4; marriage rate, 6.6; divorce rate, 3.6. **Major cities** (2006): Columbus 733,203; Cleveland 444,313; Cincinnati 332,252; Toledo 298,446; Akron 209,704; Dayton 156,771; Youngstown 81,520; Parma 80,009.

Government

Statehood: entered the Union on 1 Mar 1803 as the 17th state. **State constitution:** adopted 1851. **Representation in US Congress:** 2 senators; 18 representatives. **Electoral college:** 20 votes (based on the 2000 census). **Political divisions:** 88 counties.

Economy

Employment: services 29.0%; trade 22.8%; manufacturing 17.0%; government 12.1%; finance, insurance, real estate 7.2%; construction 5.1%; transportation, public utilities 4.3%; agriculture, forestry, fishing 2.3%; mining 0.3%. **Production:** manufacturing 25.8%; services 18.2%; trade 16.8%; finance, insurance, real estate 15.5%; government 10.7%; transportation, utilities 7.4%; construction 4.3%; agriculture 0.8%; mining 0.4%. **Chief agricultural products:** *Crops:* corn (maize), soybeans, grapes, apples, vegetables, tobacco, winter wheat, dairy products, eggs, greenhouse and nursery products. *Livestock:* cattle and calves, hogs, poultry, goats. *Extractive industries:* timber. **Chief manufactured products:** industrial machinery, nonelectrical machinery, food processing, transportation equipment, fabricated metals, iron and steel, chemical products and pharmaceuticals, rubber products.

Internet resources: <consumer.discoverohio.com>; <www. ohio.gov>.

Oklahoma

Name: Oklahoma, from two Choctaw words: *okla*, meaning "people," and *humma*, meaning "red." **Nickname:** Sooner State. **Capital:** Oklahoma City. **Rank:** population: 28th; area: 19th; pop. density: 36th. **Motto:** *Labor Omnia Vincit* (Labor Conquers All Things). **Song:** "Oklahoma," words by Oscar Hammerstein and music by Richard Rodgers. **Bird:** scissor-tailed flycatcher. **Fish:** white, or sand, bass. **Flower:** mistletoe. **Insect:** honeybee. **Mammal:** bison. **Reptile:** collared lizard (also known as the mountain boomer). **Rock:** rose rock. **Tree:** redbud.

Natural features

Land area: 69,898 sq mi, 181,035 sq km. **Mountain ranges:** Ouachita, Arbuckle, Wichita, Sandstone Hills. **Highest point:** Black Mesa, 4,973 ft (1,516 m). **Largest lake:** Lake Eufaula. **Major rivers:** Arkansas, Red, Canadian. **Natural regions:** Great Plains Province, panhandle region, includes the High Plains to the west and the Plains Border to the east; Central Lowland, covering most of the state, includes the Osage Plains in the central region; West Gulf Coastal Plain, southeastern corner; Ouachita Province, east-central region, includes the Arkansas Valley in the center and the Ouachita Mountains to the south; Ozark Plateaus, northeast corner, include the Boston Mountains and Springfield-Salem Plateaus. **Location:** South central, bordering Kansas, Missouri, Arkansas, Texas, New Mexico, and Colorado. **Climate:** variable by region: the southern humid belt merges with a colder northern continental one and humid eastern and dry western zones that cut through the state; no region is free from heavy wind; typical sudden rises and falls in temperature cause many heavy thunderstorms, blizzards, and tornadoes. **Land use:** pasture, 31.6%; agricultural, 20.1%; forest, 16.5%; other, 31.8%.

People

Population (2006): 3,579,212; 51.2 persons per sq mi (19.8 persons per sq km). **Vital statistics** (2005; per 1,000 population): birth rate, 14.6; death rate, 10.2; marriage rate, 7.3; divorce rate, 5.6. **Major cities** (2006): Oklahoma City 537,734; Tulsa 382,872; Norman 102,827; Broken Arrow 88,314; Lawton 87,540.

Government

Statehood: entered the Union on 16 Nov 1907 as the 46th state. **State constitution:** adopted 1907. **Representation in US Congress:** 2 senators; 5 representatives. **Electoral college:** 7 votes (based on the 2000 census). **Political divisions:** 77 counties.

Economy

Employment: services 28.3%; trade 20.9%; government 16.6%; manufacturing 10.0%; finance, insurance, real estate 5.8%; agriculture, forestry, fishing 5.6%; transportation, public utilities 5.1%; construction 4.8%; mining 3.0%. **Production:** services 18.2%; manufacturing 16.9%; trade 16.5%; government 15.9%; finance, insurance, real estate 12.2%; transportation, utilities 9.2%; mining 4.9%; construction 3.8%; agriculture 2.3%. **Chief agricultural products:** *Crops:* wheat, hay, sorghum, soybeans, cotton, dairy products. *Livestock:* cattle and calves, poultry, hogs and pigs. **Chief manufactured products:** electronics and electrical equipment, communications equipment, transportation equipment, food processing, petroleum products.

Internet resources: <www.travelok.com>; <www.ok.gov>.

Oregon

Name: Oregon, of uncertain origin. **Nickname:** Beaver State. **Capital:** Salem. **Rank:** population: 27th; area: 10th; pop. density: 39th. **Motto:** *Alis Volat Propiis* (She Flies with Her Own Wings). **Song:** "Oregon, My Oregon," words by J.A. Buchanan and music by Henry B. Murtagh. **Bird:** western meadowlark. **Fish:** Chinook salmon. **Flower:** Oregon grape. **Gemstone:** Oregon sunstone. **Insect:** Oregon swallowtail. **Mammal:** beaver. **Rock:** thunder egg. **Tree:** Douglas fir.

Natural features

Land area: 97,047 sq mi, 251,351 sq km. **Mountain ranges:** Coast, Klamath, Cascade, Blue, Wallowa. **Highest point:** Mt. Hood, 11,239 ft (3,425 m). **Largest lake:** Upper Klamath Lake. **Major rivers:** Snake, Owyhee, Columbia, Coquille. **Natural regions:** northern Rocky Mountains, northeastern corner, include the Blue Mountain Section; Columbia Plateaus, north and north-central region, include the Walla Walla Plateau in the central region, Harney Section to the south, and Payette Section to the southeast; Basin and Range Province, south-central border, includes the Great Basin; Cascade Sierra Mountains, west central region, include the Middle and Southern Cascades; Pacific Border Province, western coast, includes the Klamath Mountains to the south, the Oregon Coast Range in the center and north, and the Puget Trough to the east. **Location:** Northwest, bordering Washington, Idaho, Nevada, and California. **Climate:** ranges from equable, mild, marine conditions on the coast to continental conditions of dryness and extreme temperature in the interior. **Land use:** forest, 20.5%; pasture, 15.1%; agricultural, 6.0%; other, 58.4%.

People

Population (2006): 3,700,758; 38.1 persons per sq mi (14.7 persons per sq km). **Vital statistics** (2005; per 1,000 population): birth rate, 12.6; death rate, 8.6; marriage rate, 7.4; divorce rate, 4.3. **Major cities** (2006): Portland 537,081; Salem 152,239; Eugene 146,356; Gresham 97,105; Beaverton 89,643.

Government

Statehood: entered the Union on 14 Feb 1859 as the 33rd state. **State constitution:** adopted 1857. **Representation in US Congress:** 2 senators; 5 representatives. **Electoral college:** 7 votes (based on the 2000 census). **Political divisions:** 36 counties.

Economy

Employment: services 29.4%; trade 22.8%; manufacturing 13.1%; government 12.6%; finance, insurance, real estate 6.6%; construction 5.7%; agriculture, forestry, fishing 5.1%; transportation, public utilities 4.5%; mining 0.2%. **Production:** manufacturing 24.8%; services 17.6%; trade 16.1%; finance, insurance, real estate 14.4%; government 11.8%; transportation, utilities 7.1%; construction 5.3%; agriculture 2.8%; mining 0.1%. **Chief agricultural products:** *Crops:* horticulture and nursery products, Christmas trees, berries, pears, cherries, apples, hazelnuts, snap beans, peas, onions, carrots, wheat, hay, potatoes, barley, dry beans, mint, hops, corn (maize), sugar beets. *Livestock*: cattle and calves, horses, mink, poultry, sheep and lambs. *Fish catch:* marine fish, tuna, salmon, shellfish, crab, shrimp. *Extractive industries:* timber. **Chief manufactured products:** lumber and wood products, food processing, aircraft and spacecraft, semiconductors, computers.

Internet resources: <www.traveloregon.com>; <www.oregon.gov>.

Pennsylvania

Name: Pennsylvania, named for Admiral Sir William Penn, father of the territory's founder, William Penn, and also including the Latin term *sylvania* ("woodlands"). **Nickname:** Keystone State. **Capital:** Harrisburg. **Rank:** population: 6th; area: 33rd; pop. density: 9th. **Motto:** Virtue, Liberty, and Independence. **Song:** "Pennsylvania," words and music by Eddie Khoury and Ronnie Bonner. **Bird:** ruffled grouse. **Fish:** brook trout. **Flower:** mountain laurel. **Fossil:** *Phacops rana*. **Insect:** firefly. **Mammal:** white-tailed deer. **Tree:** hemlock.

Natural features

Land area: 46,056 sq mi, 119,284 sq km. **Mountain ranges:** Appalachian, Allegheny. **Highest point:** Mt. Davis, 3,213 ft (979 m). **Largest lake:** Raystown Lake. **Major rivers:** Delaware, Lehigh, Schuylkill, Susquehanna, Ohio. **Natural regions:** Central Lowland, Eastern Lake Section, extreme northwestern edge; Appalachian Plateaus, including the Southern New York, Allegheny Mountain, and Kanawha sections, western half of state; Valley and Ridge Province, central region, including portions of the Appalachian Mountains; Piedmont Province, comprising the Piedmont Lowlands and Upland, southeast corner; Coastal Plain, extreme southeast edge; New England Province, New England Upland Section, east-central border. **Location:** Northeast, bordering New York, New Jersey, Delaware, Maryland, West Virginia, Ohio. **Climate:** continental, with warm humid summers and cold snowy winters in general, but with wide fluctuations in seasonal temperatures. **Land use:** forest, 53.9%; agricultural, 17.7%; other, 28.4%.

People

Population (2006): 12,440,621; 270.1 persons per sq mi (104.3 persons per sq km). **Vital statistics** (2005; per 1,000 population): birth rate, 11.7; death rate, 10.4; marriage rate, 4.7; divorce rate, 2.3. **Major cities** (2006): Philadelphia 1,448,394; Pittsburgh 312,819; Allentown 107,294; Erie 102,036; Reading 81,183.

Government

Statehood: entered the Union on 12 Dec 1787 as the 2nd state. **State constitution:** adopted 1968. **Representation in US Congress:** 2 senators, 19 represen-

For details about state governments, see pages 682–687; for energy data, see pages 705–706.

tatives. **Electoral college:** 21 votes (based on the 2000 census). **Political divisions:** 67 counties.

Economy

Employment: services 32.7%; trade 21.5%; manufacturing 14.5%; government 11.4%; finance, insurance, real estate 7.7%; construction 5.0%; transportation, public utilities 4.9%; agriculture, forestry, fishing 2.0%; mining 0.4%. **Production:** services 22.4%; manufacturing 19.4%; finance, insurance, real estate 18.4%; trade 15.2%; government 10.2%; transportation, utilities 8.6%; construction 4.2%; agriculture 0.9%; mining 0.7%. **Chief agricultural products:** *Crops:* mushrooms, apples, tobacco, grapes, peaches, cut flowers, dairy products. *Livestock:* cattle and calves, poultry, pigs, horses. **Chief manufactured products:** electronic equipment, communications systems, semiconductors, chemical and pharmaceutical products, food processing, iron and steel, industrial machinery, transportation equipment, paper products.

Internet resources: <www.visitpa.com>; <www.pa.gov>.

Rhode Island

Name: Rhode Island, from the Greek island of Rhodes. **Nicknames:** Little Rhody; Ocean State. **Capital:** Providence. **Rank:** population: 43rd; area: 50th; pop. density: 2nd. **Motto:** Hope. **Song:** "Rhode Island's It for Me," words by Charlie Hall and music by Maria Day. **Bird:** Rhode Island Red chicken. **Flower:** violet. **Mineral:** bowenite. **Rock:** cumberlandite.

Natural features

Land area: 1,223 sq mi, 3,168 sq km. **Highest point:** Jerimoth Hill, 812 ft (247 m). **Largest lake:** Scituate Reservoir. **Major rivers:** Blackstone, Pawtuxet, Pawcatuck. **Natural regions:** the entire state is part of the New England Province, subdivided into the New England Upland (western two-thirds) and the Seaboard Lowland (eastern third). **Location:** New England, bordering Connecticut and Massachusetts. **Climate:** humid continental climate; marine influences are discernible in differences between coastal and inland location; extreme weather conditions, including tropical storms, ice storms, and heavy snow. **Land use:** forest, 45.9%; agricultural, 2.5%; other, 51.6%.

People

Population (2006): 1,067,610; 872.9 persons per sq mi (337.0 persons per sq km). **Vital statistics** (2005; per 1,000 population): birth rate, 11.8; death rate, 9.4; marriage rate, 7.0; divorce rate, 2.9. **Major cities** (2006): Providence 175,255; Warwick 85,925; Cranston 81,479; Pawtucket 72,998; East Providence 49,123.

An alternate source for the name of Rhode Island is Roodt Eyland (Red Island), which is what the Dutch called an island in Narragansett Bay because of its red soil.

Government

Statehood: entered the Union on 29 May 1790 as the 13th state. **State constitution:** adopted 1986. **Representation in US Congress:** 2 senators; 2 representatives. **Electoral college:** 4 votes (based on the 2000 census). **Political divisions:** 5 counties.

Economy

Employment: services 34.7%; trade 20.3%; manufacturing 14.8%; government 13.4%; finance, insurance, real estate 7.6%; construction 4.4%; transportation, public utilities 3.4%; agriculture, forestry, fishing 1.3%; mining 0.1%. **Production:** finance, insurance, real estate 26.7%; services 21.7%; trade 14.3%; manufacturing 12.6%; government 12.0%; transportation, utilities 6.7%; construction 5.3%; agriculture 0.7%. **Chief agricultural products:** *Crops:* hay, corn (maize), apples, peaches, dairy products, eggs, potatoes. *Livestock:* poultry, cattle and calves, sheep and lambs. *Fish catch:* marine fish, shellfish. **Chief manufactured products:** jewelry, silverware, textiles, fabricated metals, electrical equipment, machinery, surgical instruments, plastic goods, printing and publishing, primary metals.

Internet resources: <www.visitrhodeisland.com>; <www.ri.gov>.

South Carolina

Name: South Carolina, named in honor of Charles I of England. **Nickname:** Palmetto State. **Capital:** Columbia. **Rank:** population: 24th; area: 40th; pop. density: 20th. **Mottoes:** *Animis Opibusque Parati* (Prepared in Mind and Resources); *Dum Spiro Spero* (While I Breathe, I Hope). **Songs:** "Carolina," words by Henry Timrod and music by Anne Custis Burgess; "South Carolina on My Mind," words and music by Hank Martin and Buzz Arledge. **Amphibian:** spotted salamander. **Bird:** Carolina wren. **Fish:** striped bass. **Flower:** Carolina jessamine. **Gemstone:** amethyst. **Insect:** Carolina mantid. **Mammal:** white-tailed deer. **Reptile:** loggerhead turtle. **Rock:** blue granite. **Tree:** palmetto.

Natural features

Land area: 31,118 sq mi, 80,595 sq km. **Mountain range:** Blue Ridge. **Highest point:** Sassafras Mountain, 3,560 ft (1,085 m). **Largest lake:** Lake Marion. **Major rivers:** Pee Dee, Savannah, Ashley, Combahee, Edisto. **Natural regions:** Coastal Plain covers the eastern two-thirds of the state and includes the Sea Island Section in the central region; Piedmont Province extends across the central and western region and includes the Piedmont Upland; Blue Ridge Province covers the far northwestern corner and includes the Southern Section. **Location:** Southeast, bordering North Carolina and Georgia. **Climate:** subtropical, with hot, humid summers and generally mild winters; an average of 10 tornadoes a year, usually occurring during the spring; hurricanes are less frequent, but they do in some years cause damage to the coast. **Land use:** forest, 56.0%; agricultural, 11.9%; other, 32.1%.

People

Population (2006): 4,321,249; 138.9 persons per sq mi (53.6 persons per sq km). **Vital statistics** (2005;

per 1,000 population): birth rate, 13.6; death rate, 8.8; marriage rate, 8.3; divorce rate, 2.9. **Major cities** (2006): Columbia 119,961; Charleston 107,845; North Charleston 87,482; Rock Hill 61,620; Mount Pleasant 59,113.

Government

Statehood: entered the Union on 23 May 1788 as the 8th state. **State constitution:** adopted 1895. **Representation in US Congress:** 2 senators; 6 representatives. **Electoral college:** 8 votes (based on the 2000 census). **Political divisions:** 46 counties.

Economy

Employment: services 24.7%; trade 22.4%; manufacturing 17.3%; government 16.7%; construction 6.4%; finance, insurance, real estate 5.9%; transportation, public utilities 4.1%; agriculture, forestry, fishing 2.4%; mining 0.1%. **Production:** manufacturing 21.4%; trade 17.4%; services 16.4%; government 15.1%; finance, insurance, real estate 13.7%; transportation, utilities 8.9%; construction 5.9%; agriculture 1.1%; mining 0.2%. **Chief agricultural products:** *Crops:* tobacco, cotton, barley, corn (maize), peanuts (groundnuts), oats, grains, peaches, apples, pecans, watermelons, sweet potatoes, tomatoes, snap beans, cucumbers, dairy products, eggs. *Livestock:* cattle and calves, chickens, pigs. **Chief extractive products:** timber, marine fish, oysters, clams, shrimp. **Chief manufactured products:** Chemical products, industrial chemicals, pharmaceuticals, and agricultural fertilizers, textiles, apparel, industrial machinery, plastic and rubber products, paper and paperboard, electronics and electrical equipment, motor vehicle parts and accessories, lumber.

Internet resources: <www.discoversouthcarolina.com>; <www.sc.gov>.

South Dakota

Name: South Dakota, from the Dakota division of the Sioux, the Native American tribe that inhabited the plains before the arrival of Europeans; *dakota* is the Sioux word for "friend." **Nickname:** Mount Rushmore State. **Capital:** Pierre. **Rank:** population: 46th; area: 17th; pop. density: 46th. **Motto:** Under God the People Rule. **Song:** "Hail! South Dakota," words and music by Deecort Hammitt. **Bird:** Chinese ring-necked pheasant. **Fish:** walleye. **Flower:** pasque. **Fossil:** triceratops. **Gemstone:** Fairburn agate. **Insect:** honeybee. **Mammal:** coyote. **Mineral:** rose quartz. **Tree:** Black Hills spruce.

Natural features

Land area: 77,117 sq mi, 199,732 sq km. **Mountain range:** Black Hills. **Highest point:** Harney Peak, 7,242 ft (2,207 m). **Largest lake:** Lake Thompson. **Major rivers:** Big Sioux, Vermillion, James, Grand, Moreau, Cheyenne, Bad, White. **Natural regions:** the Central Lowland, eastern third of the state, includes the Dissected Till Plains along the eastern edge and the Western Lake Section at the center; the Great Plains Province, western two-thirds of the state; the Black Hills, far west; the High Plains, southern border; the Missouri Plateau, west. **Location:** North central, bordering North Dakota, Minnesota, Iowa, Nebraska, Wyoming, and Montana. **Climate:** characterized by extremes in temperature, low precipitation, and relatively low humidity; cyclonic storms occur frequently in the east-river section during the spring and summer. **Land use:** pasture, 44.7%; agricultural, 34.6%; forest, 1.0%; other, 19.7%.

People

Population (2006): 781,919; 10.1 persons per sq mi (3.9 persons per sq km). **Vital statistics** (2005; per 1,000 population): birth rate, 14.8; death rate, 9.1; marriage rate, 8.4; divorce rate, 3.0. **Major cities** (2006): Sioux Falls 142,396; Rapid City 62,715; Aberdeen 24,071; Watertown 20,526; Brookings 18,802.

Government

Statehood: entered the Union on 2 Nov 1889 as the 40th state. **State constitution:** adopted 1889. **Representation in US Congress:** 2 senators; 1 representative. **Electoral college:** 3 votes (based on the 2000 census). **Political divisions:** 66 counties.

Economy

Employment: services 27.5%; trade 22.3%; government 13.7%; manufacturing 10.3%; agriculture, forestry, fishing 9.1%; finance, insurance, real estate 7.2%; construction 5.0%; transportation, public utilities 4.5%; mining 0.5%. **Production:** finance, insurance, real estate 18.1%; trade 17.7%; services 17.6%; manufacturing 14.0%; government 12.6%; transportation, utilities 8.2%; agriculture 6.9%; construction 4.1%; mining 0.6%. **Chief agricultural products:** *Crops:* corn (maize), hay, wheat, sunflowers, dairy products, eggs, flaxseed, barley, wool, rye. *Livestock:* cattle and calves, pigs, sheep and lambs. **Chief manufactured products:** industrial machinery, office machines, computers, food products, electronics, printing and publishing, lumber mills, fabricated metal products, medical instruments, jewelry.

Internet resources: <www.travelsd.com>; <www.sd.gov>.

Tennessee

Name: Tennessee, from Cherokee village name. **Nickname:** Volunteer State. **Capital:** Nashville. **Rank:** population: 17th; area: 35th; pop. density: 18th. **Motto:** Agriculture and Commerce. **Songs:** "My Homeland, Tennessee," words by Nell Grayson Taylor and music by Roy Lamont Smith; "When It's Iris Time in Tennessee," words and music by Willa Mae Waid; "The Tennessee Waltz," words and music by Redd Stewart and Pee Wee King; "Rocky Top," words and music by Boudleaux and Felice Bryant; "The Pride of Tennessee," words and music by Fred Congdon, Thomas Vaughn, and Carol Elliot. **Amphibian:** cave salamander. **Bird:** mockingbird. **Fish:** largemouth bass; channel catfish. **Flower:** iris. **Gemstone:** river pearl. **Insects:** firefly; ladybug. **Mammal:** raccoon. **Reptile:** box turtle. **Rocks:** limestone; agate. **Tree:** tulip poplar.

Natural features

Land area: 42,143 sq mi, 109,150 sq km. **Mountain ranges:** Unaka, Great Smoky. **Highest point:**

For details about state governments, see pages 682–687; for energy data, see pages 705–706.

Clingmans Dome, 6,643 ft (2,025 m). **Largest lake:** Reelfoot. **Major rivers:** Tennessee, Cumberland, Mississippi. **Natural regions:** Blue Ridge Province, eastern border; Valley and Ridge Province, extending from southwest to northeast; Appalachian Plateau, central, running from south to north, includes the Cumberland Plateau Section in the center and the Cumberland Mountain Section at the northern end; Interior Low Plateau, west central, includes the Nashville Basin and Highland Rim Section. **Location:** South, bordering Kentucky, Virginia, North Carolina, Georgia, Alabama, Mississippi, Arkansas, and Missouri. **Climate:** moderate continental climate, with cool, but not cold, winters and warm summers. **Land use:** forest, 44.3%; agricultural, 17.6%; other, 38.1%.

People

Population (2006): 6,038,803; 143.3 persons per sq mi (55.3 persons per sq km). **Vital statistics** (2005; per 1,000 population): birth rate, 13.7; death rate, 9.6; marriage rate, 10.3; divorce rate, 4.6. **Major cities** (2006): Memphis 670,902; Nashville 552,120; Knoxville 182,337; Chattanooga 155,190; Clarksville 113,175.

Government

Statehood: entered the Union on 1 Jun 1796 as the 16th state. **State constitution:** adopted 1870. **Representation in US Congress:** 2 senators; 9 representatives. **Electoral college:** 11 votes (based on the 2000 census). **Political divisions:** 95 counties.

Economy

Employment: services 27.8%; trade 21.8%; manufacturing 16.2%; government 12.1%; finance, insurance, real estate 6.7%; construction 5.9%; transportation, public utilities 5.4%; agriculture, forestry, fishing 3.8%; mining 0.2%. **Production:** manufacturing 20.8%; services 20.6%; trade 19.1%; finance, insurance, real estate 14.1%; government 11.5%; transportation, utilities 8.3%; construction 4.4%; agriculture 0.9%; mining 0.3%. **Chief agricultural products:** *Crops:* cotton, tobacco, peaches, apples, tomatoes, snap beans, honey, dairy products, eggs, wool, hay, corn (maize), wheat, sorghum. *Livestock:* cattle and calves, poultry, hogs, sheep and lambs. *Aquaculture:* catfish, trout. *Extractive products:* timber. **Chief manufactured products:** transportation equipment, motor vehicles, aircraft parts, boats, chemical and pharmaceutical products, printing and publishing, electronics, lumber, paper, apparel, surgical appliances and supplies.

Internet resources: <www.tnvacation.com>; <www.tn.gov>.

Texas

Name: Texas, from the Caddo Indian word *teysha,* or *tejas,* which means "hello friend." **Nickname:** Lone Star State. **Capital:** Austin. **Rank:** population: 2nd; area: 2nd; pop. density: 26th. **Motto:** Friendship. **Song:** "Texas, Our Texas," words and music by William J. Marsh and Gladys Yoakum Wright. **Bird:** mockingbird. **Fish:** Guadalupe bass. **Flower:** bluebonnet. **Fossil:** pleurocoelus. **Gemstone:** Texas blue topaz. **Insect:** monarch butterfly. **Mammal:** Mexican free-tailed bat (flying); longhorn (large); armadillo (small). **Reptile:** horned lizard. **Rock:** petrified palmwood. **Tree:** pecan.

Natural features

Land area: 266,853 sq mi, 691,146 sq km. **Mountain ranges:** Rocky, Guadalupe. **Highest point:** Guadalupe Peak, 8,749 ft (2,667 m). **Largest lake:** Caddo Lake. **Major rivers:** Red, Trinity, Brazos, Colorado, Rio Grande. **Natural regions:** Coastal Plain, southern and eastern regions, includes the West Gulf Coastal Plain near the east-central coast; Central Lowland, north central, includes the Osage Plains; Great Plains Province, extending from the panhandle across most of central and western Texas, includes the Edwards Plateau to the south, Pecos Valley to the west, High Plains to the north, and Central Texas Section; Basin and Range Province, extreme western region, comprises the Mexican Highland to the south and the Sacramento Section to the north. **Location:** Southwest, bordering Oklahoma, Arkansas, Louisiana, and New Mexico; international border with Mexico. **Climate:** varies by region, though summers are generally very hot and winters are somewhat mild; East Texas is considerably wetter than the very dry West Texas region; tornadoes are a frequent threat between April and November. **Land use:** pasture, 56.2%; agricultural, 14.9%; forest, 6.2%; other, 22.7%.

People

Population (2006): 23,507,783; 88.1 persons per sq mi (34.0 persons per sq km). **Vital statistics** (2005; per 1,000 population): birth rate, 16.9; death rate, 6.8; marriage rate, 7.4; divorce rate, 3.2. **Major cities** (2006): Houston 2,144,491; San Antonio 1,296,682; Dallas 1,232,940; Austin 709,893; Fort Worth 653,320; El Paso 609,415; Arlington 367,197; Corpus Christi 285,267.

Government

Statehood: entered the Union on 29 Dec 1845 as the 28th state. **State constitution:** adopted 1876. **Representation in US Congress:** 2 senators; 32 representatives. **Electoral college:** 34 votes (based on the 2000 census). **Political divisions:** 254 counties.

Economy

Employment: services 29.1%; trade 21.6%; government 14.5%; manufacturing 10.1%; finance, insurance, real estate 7.5%; construction 6.1%; transportation, public utilities 5.4%; agriculture, forestry, fishing 3.5%; mining 2.2%. **Production:** services 19.9%; trade 17.6%; finance, insurance, real estate 14.7%; manufacturing 14.0%; government 11.2%; transportation, utilities 10.9%; mining 5.7%; construction 4.7%; agriculture 1.3%. **Chief agricultural products:** *Crops:* cotton, apples, greenhouse and nursery products, corn (maize), sorghum, wheat, dairy products, eggs, rice. *Livestock:* cattle and calves, pigs, chickens. *Extractive products:* timber, shrimp. **Chief manufactured products:** Refined petroleum, petroleum products, food products, computers and electronics, chemicals and plastics, apparel, wood and paper products, nonelectrical machinery, fabricated metal products, aerospace products and parts, aircraft parts, motor vehicle parts.

Internet resources: <www.traveltex.com>; <www.texas.gov>.

Utah

Name: Utah, named for the Ute tribe; the word *ute* means "people of the mountains." **Nickname:** Beehive State. **Capital:** Salt Lake City. **Rank:** population: 34th; area: 13th; pop. density: 41st. **Motto:** Industry. **Song:** "Utah, This Is the Place," words by Sam and Gary Francis and music by Gary Francis. **Bird:** California seagull. **Fish:** Bonneville cutthroat trout. **Flower:** sego lily. **Fossil:** allosaurus. **Gemstone:** topaz. **Insect:** honeybee. **Mammal:** Rocky Mountain elk. **Mineral:** copper. **Rock:** coal. **Tree:** blue spruce.

Natural features

Land area: 84,899 sq mi, 219,887 sq km. **Mountain ranges:** Uinta, Wasatch, Rocky. **Highest point:** Kings Peak, 13,528 ft (4,123 m). **Largest lake:** Great Salt Lake. **Major rivers:** Colorado, Green, Sevier. **Natural regions:** Basin and Range Province, western half of the state, includes the Great Salt Lake Desert and Bonneville Salt Flats to the north and the Great Basin to the south; Middle Rocky Mountains, northeast; Colorado Plateaus, east-central and southeast regions, include the Grand Canyon Section to the south, the High Plateaus of Utah and Canyon Lands in the center, the Navajo Section in the extreme southeast corner, and the Uinta Basin to the north. **Location:** West, bordering Idaho, Wyoming, Colorado, Arizona, and Nevada. **Climate:** primarily arid; southwest has a warm, almost dry, subtropical climate, while the southern part of the Colorado Plateau has cool, dry winters and wet summers. **Land use:** pasture, 19.6%; forest, 3.5%; agricultural, 3.1%; other, 73.8%.

People

Population (2006): 2,550,063; 30.0 persons per sq mi (11.6 persons per sq km). **Vital statistics** (2005; per 1,000 population): birth rate, 20.9; death rate, 5.4; marriage rate, 8.6; divorce rate, 4.0. **Major cities** (2006): Salt Lake City 178,858; West Valley City 119,841; Provo 113,984; West Jordan 94,309; Sandy 94,203.

Government

Statehood: entered the Union on 4 Jan 1896 as the 45th state. **State constitution:** adopted 1895. **Representation in US Congress:** 2 senators; 3 representatives. **Electoral college:** 5 votes (based on the 2000 census). **Political divisions:** 29 counties.

Economy

Employment: services 29.7%; trade 22.0%; government 14.6%; manufacturing 10.9%; finance, insurance, real estate 7.8%; construction 7.0%; transportation, public utilities 4.9%; agriculture, forestry, fishing 2.4%; mining 0.7%. **Production:** services 20.6%; trade 16.9%; finance, insurance, real estate 16.4%; government 14.4%; manufacturing 13.3%; transportation, utilities 8.8%; construction 6.5%; mining 1.8%; agriculture 1.1%. **Chief agricultural products:** *Crops:* hay, grains, peaches, cherries, onions, dairy products. *Livestock:* cattle and calves, sheep and lambs, mink, poultry. *Aquaculture:* trout. **Chief manufactured products:** industrial machinery, computers, office equipment, transportation equipment, aerospace products, missile parts, motor vehicle parts, surgical tools, electromedical equipment, food processing.

Internet resources: <www.utah.com>; <www. utah.gov>.

Vermont

Name: Vermont, from the French *vert mont*, meaning "green mountain." **Nickname:** Green Mountain State. **Capital:** Montpelier. **Rank:** population: 49th; area: 43rd; pop. density: 30th. **Motto:** Freedom and Unity. **Song:** "These Green Mountains," words and music by Diane Martin. **Bird:** hermit thrush. **Flower:** red clover. **Insect:** honeybee. **Mammal:** Morgan horse. **Tree:** sugar maple.

Natural features

Land area: 9,615 sq mi, 24,903 sq km. **Mountain ranges:** Green, Appalachian, Hoosac, Taconic. **Highest point:** Mt. Mansfield, 4,393 ft (1,339 m). **Largest lake:** Lake Champlain. **Major rivers:** Lamoille, Winooski, Otter Creek, Poultney, White, Missisquoi. **Natural regions:** the New England Province, eastern two-thirds of the state, includes the Taconic Section to the south, the Green Mountain Section in the center, the New England Upland Section along the east-central edge, and the White Mountain Section in the far northeast corner; the St. Lawrence Valley, western edge of the state, includes the Champlain Section in the central portion; the Valley and Ridge Province, small section along the west-central edge, includes the Hudson Valley. **Location:** New England, bordering New Hampshire, Massachusetts, and New York; international border with Canada. **Climate:** cool continental, with very cold, snowy winters and warm, mild summers. **Land use:** forest, 67.1%; agricultural, 9.5%; other, 23.4%.

People

Population (2006): 623,908; 64.9 persons per sq mi (25.1 persons per sq km). **Vital statistics** (2005; per 1,000 population): birth rate, 10.4; death rate, 7.9; marriage rate, 8.9; divorce rate, 3.3. **Major cities** (2006): Burlington 38,358; South Burlington 17,014; Rutland 16,964; Montpelier 7,954.

Government

Statehood: entered the Union on 4 Mar 1791 as the 14th state. **State constitution:** adopted 1793. **Representation in US Congress:** 2 senators; 1 representative. **Electoral college:** 3 votes (based on the 2000 census). **Political divisions:** 14 counties.

Economy

Employment: services 32.4%; trade 21.0%; manufacturing 13.7%; government 12.8%; construction 6.5%; finance, insurance, real estate 5.7%; transportation, public utilities 4.0%; agriculture, forestry, fishing 3.7%; mining 0.2%. **Production:** services 22.3%; finance, insurance, real estate 17.7%; manufacturing 17.5%; trade 15.7%; government 12.4%; transportation, utilities 7.6%; construction

For details about state governments, see pages 682–687; for energy data, see pages 705–706.

4.4%; agriculture 2.2%; mining 0.3%. **Chief agricultural products:** *Crops:* apples, honey, corn (maize), hay, greenhouse and nursery products, Christmas trees, maple syrup, fruits and vegetables, dairy products, eggs, wool. *Livestock:* cattle and calves, chickens, turkeys, sheep and lambs, horses. *Extractive products:* timber. **Chief manufactured products:** electrical and electronic equipment, fabricated metal products, nonelectrical machinery, paper and allied products, printing and publishing, food products, transportation equipment, lumber and wood products.

Internet resources: <www.travel-vermont.com>; <www.vermont.gov>.

Virginia

Name: Virginia, named in honor of Elizabeth I of England, known as the "Virgin Queen." **Nickname:** Old Dominion. **Capital:** Richmond. **Rank:** population: 12th; area: 36th; pop. density: 14th. **Motto:** *Sic Semper Tyrannis* (Thus Ever to Tyrants). **Song:** "Carry Me Back to Old Virginia," words and music by James B. Bland. **Bird:** cardinal. **Fish:** brook trout. **Flower:** dogwood. **Fossil:** *Chesapecten jeffersonius.* **Insect:** tiger swallowtail butterfly. **Tree:** dogwood.

Natural features

Land area: 40,600 sq mi, 105,154 sq km. **Mountain ranges:** Blue Ridge, Appalachian. **Highest point:** Mt. Rogers, 5,729 ft (1,746 m). **Largest lake:** Smith Mountain Lake. **Major rivers:** Potomac, Shenandoah, James, Roanoke. **Natural regions:** Coastal Plain, eastern region below the Potomac River; Piedmont Province, extending from the south-central border up to the border with Maryland, includes the Piedmont Upland and Piedmont Lowlands; Blue Ridge Province, west of the Piedmont Province; Valley and Ridge region, covering most of western Virginia, includes the Shenandoah Valley and Allegheny, Shenandoah, and Appalachian mountains; Appalachian Plateau, extreme western tip of the state, includes the Cumberland Mountain and Kanawha sections. **Location:** East, bordering Maryland, North Carolina, Tennessee, Kentucky, and West Virginia. **Climate:** generally mild and equable but varies according to elevation and proximity to Chesapeake Bay and the Atlantic. **Land use:** forest, 48.7%; agricultural, 10.6%; other, 40.7%.

People

Population (2006): 7,642,884; 188.2 persons per sq mi (72.7 persons per sq km). **Vital statistics** (2005; per 1,000 population): birth rate, 13.8; death rate, 7.6; marriage rate, 8.2; divorce rate, 3.9. **Major cities** (2006): Virginia Beach 435,619; Norfolk 229,112; Chesapeake 220,560; Arlington 199,776; Richmond 192,913; Newport News 178,281; Hampton 145,017; Alexandria 136,974.

Government

Statehood: entered the Union on 26 Jun 1788 as the 10th state. **State constitution:** adopted 1970. **Representation in US Congress:** 2 senators; 11 representatives. **Electoral college:** 13 votes (based on the 2000 census). **Political divisions:** 95 counties.

Economy

Employment: services 30.1%; trade 20.1%; government 18.9%; manufacturing 10.2%; finance, insurance, real estate 6.9%; construction 6.2%; transportation, public utilities 4.7%; agriculture, forestry, fishing 2.5%; mining 0.3%. **Production:** services 22.6%; government 17.8%; finance, insurance, real estate 17.3%; trade 14.4%; manufacturing 13.1%; transportation, utilities 9.0%; construction 4.6%; agriculture 0.8%; mining 0.4%. **Chief agricultural products:** *Crops:* tobacco, soybeans, corn (maize), peanuts (groundnuts), cotton, apples, tomatoes, wheat, hay, potatoes, honey. *Livestock:* chickens, turkeys, pigs, cattle and calves, sheep and lambs. *Aquaculture:* clams, soft-shell crabs, oysters, trout, catfish, hybrid striped bass. *Extractive products:* timber, blue crab. **Chief manufactured products:** electronics and electrical equipment, paper and paper products, tobacco products, plastic and rubber materials, pharmaceuticals and chemical products, food and food products, printing and publishing.

Internet resources: <www.virginia.org>; <www.virginia.gov>.

Washington

Name: Washington, named in honor of George Washington. **Nickname:** Evergreen State. **Capital:** Olympia. **Rank:** population: 14th; area: 21st; pop. density: 23rd. **Motto:** *Alki* (By and By). **Song:** "Washington My Home," words and music by Helen Davis. **Bird:** willow goldfinch. **Fish:** steelhead trout. **Flower:** coast rhododendron. **Fossil:** Columbian mammoth. **Gemstone:** petrified wood. **Insect:** green darner dragonfly. **Tree:** western hemlock.

Natural features

Land area: 68,097 sq mi, 176,370 sq km. **Mountain ranges:** Olympic, Cascade, Blue. **Highest point:** Mt. Rainier, 14,410 ft (4,392 m). **Largest lake:** Moses Lake. **Major rivers:** Columbia, Pend Oreille, Snake, Yakima. **Natural regions:** Pacific Border Province, western quarter of the state, includes the Olympic Mountains to the west and the Puget Trough to the east; Cascade-Sierra Mountains, running north to south down center of state, include the Northern and Middle Cascades; Northern Rocky Mountains, northeast corner; Columbia Plateaus, eastern, central, and southern regions, include the Walla Walla Plateau in the center and the Blue Mountain Section in the southeast corner. **Location:** Northwest, bordering Idaho and Oregon; international border with Canada. **Climate:** moderate winters and cool summers west of the Cascades; east of the Cascade Range seasonal temperature variations are greater, with cold winters and warm, mild summers; throughout the state precipitation is greatest in the cooler months, with frequent cyclonic storms, some with gale-force winds. **Land use:** forest, 28.9%; agricultural, 14.7%; pasture, 13.3%; other, 43.1%.

People

Population (2006): 6,395,798; 93.9 persons per sq mi (36.3 persons per sq km). **Vital statistics** (2005; per 1,000 population): birth rate, 13.2; death rate, 7.3; marriage rate, 6.6; divorce rate, 4.0. **Major cities** (2006): Seattle 582,454; Spokane 198,081; Tacoma 196,532; Vancouver 158,855; Bellevue 118,186.

Government

Statehood: entered the Union on 11 Nov 1889 as the 42nd state. **State constitution:** adopted 1889. **Representation in US Congress:** 2 senators; 9 representatives. **Electoral college:** 11 votes (based on the 2000 census). **Political divisions:** 39 counties.

Economy

Employment: services 28.7%; trade 21.9%; government 15.7%; manufacturing 11.8%; finance, insurance, real estate 7.3%; construction 5.6%; transportation, public utilities 4.6%; agriculture, forestry, fishing 4.2%; mining 0.2%. **Production:** services 25.0%; finance, insurance, real estate 17.4%; trade 16.8%; government 13.2%; manufacturing 12.6%; transportation, utilities 7.9%; construction 4.9%; agriculture 2.1%; mining 0.2%. **Chief agricultural products:** *Crops:* apples, peaches, pears, cherries, grapes, apricots, raspberries, dried peas, lentils, asparagus, carrots, sweet corn, green peas, potatoes, mint oil, hops, wheat, hay. *Livestock:* cattle and calves, chickens, turkeys, horses. *Extractive products:* oysters, clams, mussels, crab, shrimp, geoduck, sea cucumbers, marine fish, salmon, timber. **Chief manufactured products:** aerospace equipment, food processing, forest products, advanced medical and technology products, aluminum products, fish processing.

Internet resources: <www.experiencewa.com>; <www.wa.gov>.

West Virginia

Name: West Virginia, named in honor of Elizabeth I of England, known as the "Virgin Queen." **Nickname:** Mountain State. **Capital:** Charleston. **Rank:** population: 37th; area: 41st; pop. density: 29th. **Motto:** *Montani Semper Liberi* (Mountaineers Are Always Free). **Songs:** "This Is My West Virginia," words and music by Iris Bell; "West Virginia, My Home Sweet Home," words and music by Julian G. Hearne, Jr.; "The West Virginia Hills," words by Ellen King and music by H.E. Engle. **Bird:** cardinal. **Fish:** brook trout. **Flower:** rhododendron. **Gemstone:** West Virginia fossil coral. **Insect:** monarch butterfly. **Mammal:** black bear. **Tree:** sugar maple.

Natural features

Land area: 24,230 sq mi, 62,755 sq km. **Mountain ranges:** Appalachian, Allegheny. **Highest point:** Spruce Knob, 4,863 ft (1,482 m). **Largest lake:** Summersville Lake. **Major rivers:** Ohio, Big Sandy, Guyandotte, Great Kanawha, Little Kanawha, Monongahela, Potomac. **Natural regions:** the Valley and Ridge Province, eastern edge of the state, includes portions of the Shenandoah Mountains; the remainder of the state consists of the Appalachian Plateaus and includes the Kanawha Section to the south, and the Allegheny Mountains in the northeast. **Location:** East, bordering Pennsylvania, Maryland, Virginia, Kentucky, and Ohio. **Climate:** humid continental, except for a marine modification in the lower panhandle. **Land use:** forest, 68.1%; agricultural, 5.3%; other, 26.6%.

People

Population (2006): 1,818,470; 75.1 persons per sq mi (29.0 persons per sq km). **Vital statistics** (2005; per 1,000 population): birth rate, 11.5; death rate, 11.4; marriage rate, 7.4; divorce rate, 5.1. **Major cities** (2006): Charleston 50,846; Huntington 49,007; Parkersburg 31,755; Wheeling 29,330; Morgantown 28,654.

Government

Statehood: entered the Union on 20 Jun 1863 as the 35th state. **State constitution:** adopted 1872. **Representation in US Congress:** 2 senators; 3 representatives. **Electoral college:** 5 votes (based on the 2000 census). **Political divisions:** 55 counties.

Economy

Employment: services 28.1%; trade 22.2%; government 17.1%; manufacturing 9.9%; construction 5.9%; transportation, public utilities 5.2%; finance, insurance, real estate 4.8%; agriculture, forestry, fishing 3.3%; mining 3.3%. **Production:** services 17.9%; manufacturing 16.0%; government 15.5%; trade 15.5%; finance, insurance, real estate 11.3%; transportation, utilities 11.3%; mining 7.3%; construction 4.6%; agriculture 0.6%. **Chief agricultural products:** *Crops:* hay, apples, corn (maize), tobacco, peaches, dairy products. *Livestock:* cattle and calves, sheep and lambs, poultry. *Extractive products:* timber. **Chief manufactured products:** chemical products, automobile parts, primary metal and fabricated metal products, glassware, computer software, wood products, electrical equipment, industrial machinery, pharmaceuticals.

Internet resources: <www.wvtourism.com>; <www.wv.gov>.

Wisconsin

Name: Wisconsin, an anglicized version of a French rendering of a Native American name said to mean "the place where we live." **Nickname:** Badger State. **Capital:** Madison. **Rank:** population: 20th; area: 22nd; pop. density: 27th. **Motto:** Forward. **Song:** "On, Wisconsin," words and music by William T. Purdy. **Bird:** robin. **Fish:** muskellunge (muskie). **Flower:** wood violet. **Fossil:** trilobite. **Insect:** honeybee. **Mammal:** badger. **Mineral:** galena. **Rock:** red granite. **Tree:** sugar maple.

Natural features

Land area: 65,498 sq mi, 169,639 sq km. **Mountain ranges:** Baraboo, Rib, Gogebic. **Highest point:**

For details about state governments, see pages 682–687; for energy data, see pages 705–706.

Timms Hill, 1,952 ft (595 m). **Largest lake:** Lake Winnebago. **Major rivers:** Wisconsin, St. Croix, Rock, Mississippi, Namekagon, Wolf, Pine-Popple, Brule, Pike. **Natural regions:** Superior Upland, northern half of the state, divided into highland and lowland sections; Central Lowland, southern half of the state, divided into the Wisconsin Driftless Section to the west and the Eastern Lake Section to the east, with a section of the Till Plains occupying a small area at the southern border. **Location:** Midwest, bordering Michigan, Illinois, Iowa, and Minnesota. **Climate:** continental, with long, cold winters and warm, but relatively short, summers. **Land use:** forest, 40.4%; agricultural, 28.7%; other, 30.9%.

People

Population (2006): 5,556,506; 84.8 persons per sq mi (32.8 persons per sq km). **Vital statistics** (2005; per 1,000 population): birth rate, 12.8; death rate, 8.4; marriage rate, 6.1; divorce rate, 3.0. **Major cities** (2006): Milwaukee 573,358; Madison 223,389; Green Bay 100,353; Kenosha 96,240; Racine 79,592.

Government

Statehood: entered the Union on 29 May 1848 as the 30th state. **State constitution:** adopted 1848. **Representation in US Congress:** 2 senators; 8 representatives. **Electoral college:** 10 votes (based on the 2000 census). **Political divisions:** 72 counties.

Economy

Employment: services 26.7%; trade 21.8%; manufacturing 19.2%; government 11.9%; finance, insurance, real estate 6.8%; construction 4.8%; transportation, public utilities 4.4%; agriculture, forestry, fishing 4.2%; mining 0.1%. **Production:** manufacturing 26.3%; services 17.8%; trade 15.8%; finance, insurance, real estate 15.6%; government 10.6%; transportation, utilities 7.1%; construction 4.7%; agriculture 1.9%; mining 0.1%. **Chief agricultural products:** *Crops:* dairy products, corn (maize), honey, maple syrup, oats, hay, snap and green beans, potatoes, strawberries, tart cherries, cranberries, Christmas trees, mint for oil, beets, cabbage, carrots, green peas, cucumbers. *Livestock:* cattle and calves, hogs, mink. *Extractive products:* freshwater fish. **Chief manufactured products:** processed foods, beer, industrial machinery, paper and paper products, fabricated metal products, transportation equipment, household appliances.

Internet resources: <www.travelwisconsin.com>; <www.wisconsin.gov>.

Wyoming

Name: Wyoming, from a Delaware Indian word meaning "mountains and valleys alternating." **Nicknames:** Equality State; Cowboy State. **Capital:** Cheyenne. **Rank:** population: 50th; area: 9th; pop. density: 49th. **Motto:** Equal Rights. **Song:** "Wyoming," words by Charles E. Winter and music by George E. Knapp. **Bird:** meadowlark. **Fish:** cutthroat trout. **Flower:** Indian paintbrush. **Fossil:** knightia. **Gemstone:** jade. **Mammal:** bison. **Reptile:** horned toad. **Tree:** plains cottonwood.

Natural features

Land area: 97,813 sq mi, 253,334 sq km. **Mountain ranges:** Rocky, Big Horn, Grand Teton, Wind River, Continental Divide, Sierra Madre, Washakie. **Highest point:** Gannett Peak, 13,804 ft (4,207 m). **Largest lake:** Yellowstone Lake. **Major rivers:** Snake, Colorado, Green, Columbia. **Natural regions:** Great Plains Province, eastern third of the state, includes the Black Hills in the northeast corner, the High Plains in the southwest corner, and the Missouri Plateau in the center; Wyoming Basin, central and southern regions; Southern Rocky Mountains, southern border; Middle Rocky Mountains, northwest third of the state, also cover a small area on the southern border; Northern Rocky Mountains, extreme northwestern tip of the state. **Location:** West, bordering Montana, South Dakota, Nebraska, Colorado, Utah, and Idaho. **Climate:** semiarid continental, with long, cold winters and relatively short, warm summers. **Land use:** pasture, 44.0%; agricultural, 3.5%; forest, 1.5%; other, 51.0%.

People

Population (2006): 515,004; 5.3 persons per sq mi (2.0 persons per sq km). **Vital statistics** (2005; per 1,000 population): birth rate, 14.2; death rate, 8.0; marriage rate, 9.4; divorce rate, 5.3. **Major cities** (2006): Cheyenne 55,314; Casper 52,089; Laramie 25,688; Gillette 23,899; Rock Springs 19,324.

Government

Statehood: entered the Union on 10 Jul 1890 as the 44th state. **State constitution:** adopted 1889. **Representation in US Congress:** 2 senators; 1 representative. **Electoral college:** 3 votes (based on the 2000 census). **Political divisions:** 23 counties.

Economy

Employment: services 25.0%; trade 21.3%; government 19.5%; construction 6.9%; finance, insurance, real estate 6.6%; mining 5.9%; transportation, public utilities 5.4%; agriculture, forestry, fishing 5.3%; manufacturing 4.1%. **Production:** mining 22.0%; transportation, utilities 14.8%; government 14.1%; trade 11.8%; services 11.6%; finance, insurance, real estate 11.3%; manufacturing 6.6%; construction 5.4%; agriculture 2.5%. **Chief agricultural products:** *Crops:* hay, wheat, barley, sugar beets, corn (maize), wool. *Livestock:* cattle and calves, sheep and lambs. **Chief manufactured products:** refined petroleum, lumber and wood products, food products, fabricated metal products.

Internet resources: <www.wyomingtourism.org>; <www.wyoming.gov>.

The United States has the largest known reserves of coal in the world, and roughly half of the coal it produces comes from Wyoming, while one-third of the coal that is consumed in the nation is taken from that state's Powder River Basin.

State Government

Governors of US States and Territories

Governors of New Hampshire and Vermont serve two-year terms; all others serve four-year terms. Parties: Democrat (D); Republican (R); Popular Democrat (PD); Covenant (C). Sources: National Governors Association; Council of State Governments.

STATE	GOVERNOR	IN OFFICE SINCE	PRESENT TERM EXPIRES
Alabama	Bob Riley (R)	January 2003	January 2011
Alaska	Sarah Palin (R)	December 2006	December 2010*
Arizona	Janet Napolitano (D)	January 2003	January 2011
Arkansas	Mike Beebe (D)	January 2007	January 2011*
California	Arnold Schwarzenegger (R)[1]	November 2003	January 2011
Colorado	Bill Ritter (D)	January 2007	January 2011*
Connecticut	M. Jodi Rell (R)[2]	July 2004	January 2011*
Delaware	Ruth Ann Minner (D)	January 2001	January 2009
Florida	Charlie Crist (R)	January 2007	January 2011*
Georgia	Sonny Perdue (R)	January 2003	January 2011
Hawaii	Linda Lingle (R)	December 2002	December 2010
Idaho	C.L. "Butch" Otter (R)	January 2007	January 2011*
Illinois	Rod Blagojevich (D)	January 2003	January 2011*
Indiana	Mitch Daniels (R)	January 2005	January 2009*
Iowa	Chet Culver (D)	January 2007	January 2011*
Kansas	Kathleen Sebelius (D)	January 2003	January 2011
Kentucky	Steve Beshear (D)	December 2007	December 2011*
Louisiana	Bobby Jindal (R)	January 2008	January 2012*
Maine	John Baldacci (D)	January 2003	January 2011
Maryland	Martin O'Malley (D)	January 2007	January 2011*
Massachusetts	Deval Patrick (D)	January 2007	January 2011*
Michigan	Jennifer Granholm (D)	January 2003	January 2011
Minnesota	Tim Pawlenty (R)	January 2003	January 2011*
Mississippi	Haley Barbour (R)	January 2004	January 2012
Missouri	Matt Blunt (R)	January 2005	January 2009*
Montana	Brian Schweitzer (D)	January 2005	January 2009*
Nebraska	Dave Heineman (R)[3]	January 2005	January 2011
Nevada	Jim Gibbons (R)	January 2007	January 2011*
New Hampshire	John Lynch (D)	January 2005	January 2009*
New Jersey	Jon Corzine (D)	January 2006	January 2010*
New Mexico	Bill Richardson (D)	January 2003	January 2011
New York	David A. Paterson (D)[4]	March 2008	January 2011*
North Carolina	Michael F. Easley (D)	January 2001	January 2009
North Dakota	John Hoeven (R)	December 2000	December 2008*
Ohio	Ted Strickland (D)	January 2007	January 2011*
Oklahoma	Brad Henry (D)	January 2003	January 2011
Oregon	Ted Kulongoski (D)	January 2003	January 2011
Pennsylvania	Edward G. Rendell (D)	January 2003	January 2011
Rhode Island	Don Carcieri (R)	January 2003	January 2011
South Carolina	Mark Sanford (R)	January 2003	January 2011
South Dakota	Mike Rounds (R)	January 2003	January 2011
Tennessee	Phil Bredesen (D)	January 2003	January 2011
Texas	Rick Perry (R)[5]	December 2000	January 2011*
Utah	Jon Huntsman, Jr. (R)	January 2005	January 2009*
Vermont	Jim Douglas (R)	January 2003	January 2009*
Virginia	Tim Kaine (D)	January 2006	January 2010
Washington	Chris Gregoire (D)	January 2005	January 2009*
West Virginia	Joe Manchin III (D)	January 2005	January 2009*
Wisconsin	Jim Doyle (D)	January 2003	January 2011*
Wyoming	Dave Freudenthal (D)	January 2003	January 2011

TERRITORY	GOVERNOR	IN OFFICE SINCE	PRESENT TERM EXPIRES
American Samoa	Togiola T.A. Tulafono (D)[6]	April 2003	January 2009
Guam	Felix Perez Camacho (R)	January 2003	January 2011
Northern Mariana Islands	Benígno Fitial (C)	January 2006	January 2010*
Puerto Rico	Aníbal Acevedo Vilá (PD)	January 2005	January 2009*
Virgin Islands	John deJongh, Jr. (D)	January 2007	January 2011*

Governors of US States and Territories (continued)

**Present governor is eligible for reelection. [1]Arnold Schwarzenegger was elected in October 2003 following the recall of former governor Gray Davis. Gov. Schwarzenegger was elected to a full term in November 2006. [2]Lt. Gov. M. Jodi Rell became governor on 1 Jul 2004 following John G. Rowland's resignation. Gov. Rell was elected to a full term in November 2006. [3]Lt. Gov. Dave Heineman became governor on 21 Jan 2005 following Mike Johanns's appointment to the office of US secretary of agriculture. Gov. Heineman was elected to a full term in November 2006. [4]Lt. Gov. David A. Paterson became governor in March 2008 following Eliot Spitzer's resignation. [5]Lt. Gov. Rick Perry became governor in December 2000 following George W. Bush's election as president of the United States. Gov. Perry was elected to a full term in November 2002. [6]Lt. Gov. Togiola T.A. Tulafono became governor in April 2003 following the death of Gov. Tauese Sunia. Gov. Tulafono was elected to a full term in November 2004.*

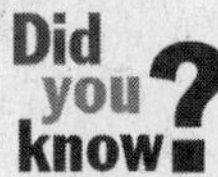

The deepest continental body of water on Earth is Lake Baikal in southern Siberia, Russia. It reaches a maximum depth of 5,314 feet (1,620 meters). Plant and animal life in the lake is rich and varied, and about three-quarters of the species are peculiar to Baikal. Approximately 600 plant species live on or near the surface of the water, and there are more than 1,200 animal species at different depths, including one mammal, the Baikal seal.

State Officers and Legislatures

Sources: Web sites of the individual states; The Book of the States, *vol. 40; and the* CSG State Directory, *published by the Council of State Governments. Legislature figures are as of January 2008.*

STATE/OFFICE	OFFICEHOLDER	PAY[1]
Alabama		
Governor	Bob Riley (R)	US$112,895
Lt. Gov.	Jim Folsom, Jr. (D)	US$61,714
Sec. of State	Beth Chapman (R)	US$79,580
Atty. Gen.	Troy King (R)	US$161,794
Treasurer	Kay Ivey (R)	US$79,580
Legislature		
Senate	Dem: 23; Rep: 12	
House	Dem: 62; Rep: 43	
Alaska		
Governor	Sarah Palin (R)	US$125,000
Lt. Gov.	Sean R. Parnell (R)	US$100,000
Sec. of State[2]		
Atty. Gen.	Talis J. Colberg (R)	US$122,640
Treasurer[3]	Brian Andrews (Deputy Treasury Commissioner)	US$102,480
Legislature		
Senate	Dem: 9; Rep: 11	
House	Dem: 17; Rep: 23	
Arizona		
Governor	Janet Napolitano (D)	US$95,000
Lt. Gov.[4]		
Sec. of State	Jan Brewer (R)	US$70,000
Atty. Gen.	Terry Goddard (D)	US$90,000
Treasurer	Dean Martin (R)	US$70,000
Legislature		
Senate	Dem: 13; Rep: 17	
House	Dem: 27; Rep: 33	
Arkansas		
Governor	Mike Beebe (D)	US$80,848
Lt. Gov.	Bill Halter (D)	US$39,075
Sec. of State	Charlie Daniels (D)	US$50,529
Atty. Gen.	Dustin McDaniel (D)	US$67,373
Treasurer	Martha A. Shoffner (D)	US$50,529
General Assembly		
Senate	Dem: 27; Rep: 8	
House	Dem: 75; Rep: 25	

STATE/OFFICE	OFFICEHOLDER	PAY[1]
California		
Governor	Arnold Schwarzenegger (R)	US$212,179
Lt. Gov.	John Garamendi (D)	US$159,134
Sec. of State	Debra Bowen (D)	US$159,134
Atty. Gen.	Edmund G. Brown, Jr. (D)	US$184,301
Treasurer	Bill Lockyer (D)	US$169,743
Legislature		
Senate	Dem: 25; Rep: 15	
Assembly	Dem: 48; Rep: 32	
Colorado		
Governor	Bill Ritter (D)	US$90,000
Lt. Gov.	Barbara O'Brien (D)	US$68,500
Sec. of State	Mike Coffman (R)	US$68,500
Atty. Gen.	John W. Suthers (R)	US$80,000
Treasurer	Cary Kennedy (D)	US$68,500
General Assembly		
Senate	Dem: 20; Rep: 15	
House	Dem: 40; Rep: 25	
Connecticut		
Governor	M. Jodi Rell (R)	US$150,000
Lt. Gov.	Michael C. Fedele (R)	US$110,000
Sec. of State	Susan Bysiewicz (D)	US$110,000
Atty. Gen.	Richard Blumenthal (D)	US$110,000
Treasurer	Denise L. Nappier (D)	US$110,000
General Assembly		
Senate	Dem: 24; Rep: 12	
House	Dem: 107; Rep: 44	
Delaware		
Governor	Ruth Ann Minner (D)	US$132,500
Lt. Gov.	John Carney, Jr. (D)	US$75,500
Sec. of State	Harriet Smith Windsor (D)	US$123,850
Atty. Gen.	Joseph Biden III (D)	US$140,950
Treasurer	Jack Markell (D)	US$110,050
General Assembly		
Senate	Dem: 13; Rep: 8	
House	Dem: 19; Rep: 22	

State Officers and Legislatures (continued)

STATE/OFFICE	OFFICEHOLDER	PAY[1]
Florida		
Governor	Charlie Crist (R)	US$132,932
Lt. Gov.	Jeffrey D. Kottkamp (R)	US$127,399
Sec. of State	Kurt Browning (R)	US$120,000
Atty. Gen.	Bill McCollum (R)	US$131,604
Treasurer[3]	Alex Sink (Chief Financial Officer)	US$131,604
Legislature		
Senate	Dem: 14; Rep: 26	
House	Dem: 42; Rep: 78	
Georgia		
Governor	Sonny Perdue (R)	US$135,281
Lt. Gov.	Casey Cagle (R)	US$88,941
Sec. of State	Karen Handel (R)	US$120,036
Atty. Gen.	Thurbert E. Baker (D)	US$133,778
Treasurer[3]	W. Daniel Ebersole (Dir., Office of Treasury and Fiscal Services)	US$126,500
General Assembly		
Senate	Dem: 22; Rep: 34	
House	Dem: 72; Rep: 107; vacant: 1	
Hawaii		
Governor	Linda Lingle (R)	US$117,600
Lt. Gov.	James R. Aiona, Jr. (R)	US$105,000
Sec. of State[2]		
Atty. Gen.	Mark J. Bennett (R)	US$114,708
Treasurer[3]	Georgina K. Kawamura (Director of Budget and Finance)	US$109,248
Legislature		
Senate	Dem: 21; Rep: 4	
House	Dem: 44; Rep: 7	
Idaho		
Governor	C.L. "Butch" Otter (R)	US$105,560
Lt. Gov.	Jim Risch (R)	US$27,820
Sec. of State	Ben Ysursa (R)	US$85,800
Atty. Gen.	Lawrence Wasden (R)	US$95,160
Treasurer	Ron G. Crane (R)	US$85,800
Legislature		
Senate	Dem: 7; Rep: 28	
House	Dem: 19; Rep: 51	
Illinois		
Governor	Rod Blagojevich (D)	US$158,000
Lt. Gov.	Pat Quinn (D)	US$120,000
Sec. of State	Jesse White (D)	US$139,400
Atty. Gen.	Lisa Madigan (D)	US$139,400
Treasurer	Alexi Giannoulias (D)	US$120,800
General Assembly		
Senate	Dem: 37; Rep: 22	
House	Dem: 67; Rep: 51	
Indiana		
Governor	Mitch Daniels (R)	US$95,000
Lt. Gov.	Becky Skillman (R)	US$76,000
Sec. of State	Todd Rokita (R)	US$66,000
Atty. Gen.	Steve Carter (R)	US$79,400
Treasurer	Richard E. Mourdock (R)	US$66,000
General Assembly		
Senate	Dem: 17; Rep: 33	
House	Dem: 51; Rep: 49	
Iowa		
Governor	Chet Culver (D)	US$130,000
Lt. Gov.	Patty Judge (D)	US$103,212

STATE/OFFICE	OFFICEHOLDER	PAY[1]
Iowa (continued)		
Sec. of State	Michael A. Mauro (D)	US$103,212
Atty. Gen.	Tom Miller (D)	US$123,669
Treasurer	Michael L. Fitzgerald (D)	US$103,212
General Assembly		
Senate	Dem: 30; Rep: 20	
House	Dem: 53; Rep: 47	
Kansas		
Governor	Kathleen Sebelius (D)	US$108,007
Lt. Gov.	Mark V. Parkinson (D)	US$30,549
Sec. of State	Ron Thornburgh (R)	US$83,905
Atty. Gen.	Stephen Six (D)	US$96,489
Treasurer	Lynn Jenkins (R)	US$83,905
Legislature		
Senate	Dem: 10; Rep: 30	
House	Dem: 47; Rep: 78	
Kentucky		
Governor	Steve Beshear (D)	US$137,506
Lt. Gov.	Daniel Mongiardo (D)	US$101,596
Sec. of State	Trey Grayson (R)	US$101,596
Atty. Gen.	Jack Conway (D)	US$101,596
Treasurer	Todd Hollenbach (D)	US$101,596
General Assembly		
Senate	Dem: 15; Rep: 22; Ind: 1	
House	Dem: 64; Rep: 36	
Louisiana		
Governor	Bobby Jindal (R)	US$130,000
Lt. Gov.	Mitch Landrieu (D)	US$115,000
Sec. of State	Jay Dardenne (R)	US$115,000
Atty. Gen.	James D. Caldwell (D)	US$115,000
Treasurer	John Kennedy (D)	US$115,000
Legislature		
Senate	Dem: 25 Rep: 14	
House	Dem: 52; Rep: 50; Ind: 2; vacant: 1	
Maine		
Governor	John Baldacci (D)	US$70,000
Lt. Gov.[5]		
Sec. of State	Matthew Dunlap (D)	US$71,302
Atty. Gen.	G. Steven Rowe (D)	US$90,438
Treasurer	David G. Lemoine (D)	US$71,032
Legislature		
Senate	Dem: 18; Rep: 17	
House	Dem: 90; Rep: 59; Unenrolled: 2	
Maryland		
Governor	Martin O'Malley (D)	US$150,000
Lt. Gov.	Anthony G. Brown (D)	US$125,000
Sec. of State	John McDonough (D)	US$78,750
Atty. Gen.	Douglas F. Gansler (D)	US$125,000
Treasurer	Nancy K. Kopp (D)	US$125,000
General Assembly		
Senate	Dem: 33; Rep: 14	
House	Dem: 104; Rep: 37	
Massachusetts		
Governor	Deval Patrick (D)	US$140,535
Lt. Gov.	Timothy Murray (D)	US$124,920
Sec. of State	William F. Galvin (D)	US$130,916
Atty. Gen.	Martha Coakley (D)	US$133,644
Treasurer	Timothy Cahill (D)	US$130,916
General Court (legislature)		
Senate	Dem: 35; Rep: 5	
House	Dem: 140; Rep: 19; vacant: 1	

State Officers and Legislatures (continued)

STATE/OFFICE	OFFICEHOLDER	PAY[1]
Michigan		
Governor	Jennifer Granholm (D)	US$177,000
Lt. Gov.	John D. Cherry, Jr. (D)	US$123,900
Sec. of State	Terri Lynn Land (R)	US$124,900
Atty. Gen.	Mike Cox (R)	US$124,900
Treasurer	Robert J. Kleine	US$174,204
Legislature		
Senate	Dem: 17; Rep: 21	
House	Dem: 58; Rep: 52	
Minnesota		
Governor	Tim Pawlenty (R)	US$120,303
Lt. Gov.	Carol Molnau (R)	US$78,197
Sec. of State	Mark Ritchie (D)	US$90,227
Atty. Gen.	Lori Swanson (D)	US$114,288
Treasurer[3]	Tom J. Hanson (Commissioner of Finance)	US$108,388
Legislature		
Senate	Dem: 45; Rep: 22	
House	Dem: 85; Rep: 49	
Mississippi		
Governor	Haley Barbour (R)	US$122,160
Lt. Gov.	Phil Bryant (R)	US$60,000
Sec. of State	C. Delbert Hosemann, Jr. (R)	US$90,000
Atty. Gen.	Jim Hood (D)	US$108,960
Treasurer	Tate Reeves (R)	US$90,000
Legislature		
Senate	Dem: 27; Rep: 25	
House	Dem: 74; Rep: 48	
Missouri		
Governor	Matt Blunt (R)	US$129,923
Lt. Gov.	Peter Kinder (R)	US$83,965
Sec. of State	Robin Carnahan (D)	US$104,608
Atty. Gen.	Jay Nixon (D)	US$113,046
Treasurer	Sarah Steelman (R)	US$104,608
General Assembly		
Senate	Dem: 14; Rep: 20	
House	Dem: 71; Rep: 92	
Montana		
Governor	Brian Schweitzer (D)	US$100,121
Lt. Gov.	John Bohlinger (R)	US$79,007
Sec. of State	Brad Johnson (R)	US$79,123
Atty. Gen.	Mike McGrath (D)	US$89,602
Treasurer[3]	Janet Kelly (Dir., Dept. of Administration)	US$93,597
Legislature		
Senate	Dem: 26; Rep: 24	
House	Dem: 49; Rep: 50; Constitution: 1	
Nebraska		
Governor	Dave Heineman (R)	US$105,000
Lt. Gov.	Rick Sheehy (R)	US$75,000
Sec. of State	John A. Gale (R)	US$85,000
Atty. Gen.	Jon Bruning (R)	US$95,000
Treasurer	Shane Osborn (R)	US$85,000
Legislature (unicameral)		
Senate	49 nonpartisan members	
Nevada		
Governor	Jim Gibbons (R)	US$141,000
Lt. Gov.	Brian K. Krolicki (R)	US$60,000
Sec. of State	Ross Miller (D)	US$97,000
Atty. Gen.	Catherine Cortez Masto (D)	US$133,000

STATE/OFFICE	OFFICEHOLDER	PAY[1]
Nevada (continued)		
Treasurer	Kate Marshall (D)	US$97,000
Legislature		
Senate	Dem: 10; Rep: 11	
Assembly	Dem: 27; Rep: 15	
New Hampshire		
Governor	John Lynch (D)	US$108,990
Lt. Gov.[5]		
Sec. of State	William Gardner (D)	US$94,584
Atty. Gen.	Kelly Ayotte (R)	US$105,396
Treasurer	Catherine Provencher	US$94,584
General Court (legislature)		
Senate	Dem: 14; Rep: 10	
House	Dem: 237; Rep: 158; Ind: 1; vacant: 4	
New Jersey		
Governor	Jon Corzine (D)	US$175,000
Lt. Gov.[5]		
Sec. of State	Nina Mitchell Wells (D)	US$141,000
Atty. Gen.	Anne Milgram (D)	US$141,000
Treasurer	R. David Rousseau	US$141,000
Legislature		
Senate	Dem: 23; Rep: 17	
General Assembly	Dem: 48; Rep: 32	
New Mexico		
Governor	Bill Richardson (D)	US$110,000
Lt. Gov.	Diane Denish (D)	US$85,000
Sec. of State	Mary Herrera (D)	US$85,000
Atty. Gen.	Gary K. King (D)	US$95,000
Treasurer	James B. Lewis (D)	US$85,000
Legislature		
Senate	Dem: 24; Rep: 18	
House	Dem: 42; Rep: 28	
New York		
Governor	David A. Paterson (D)	US$179,000
Lt. Gov.	vacant	US$151,500
Sec. of State	Lorraine Cortés-Vázquez (D)	US$120,800
Atty. Gen.	Andrew M. Cuomo (D)	US$151,500
Treasurer	Aida Brewer	US$124,811
Legislature		
Senate	Dem: 29; Rep: 33	
Assembly	Dem: 108; Rep: 42	
North Carolina		
Governor	Michael F. Easley (D)	US$135,854
Lt. Gov.	Beverly Perdue (D)	US$119,901
Sec. of State	Elaine F. Marshall (D)	US$119,901
Atty. Gen.	Roy Cooper (D)	US$119,901
Treasurer	Richard H. Moore (D)	US$119,901
General Assembly		
Senate	Dem: 31; Rep: 19	
House	Dem: 68; Rep: 52	
North Dakota		
Governor	John Hoeven (R)	US$96,183
Lt. Gov.	Jack Dalrymple (R)	US$74,668
Sec. of State	Alvin A. Jaeger (R)	US$76,511
Atty. Gen.	Wayne Stenehjem (R)	US$83,991
Treasurer	Kelly Schmidt (R)	US$72,256
Legislative Assembly		
Senate	Dem: 21; Rep: 26	
House	Dem: 33; Rep: 61	

State Officers and Legislatures (continued)

STATE/OFFICE	OFFICEHOLDER	PAY[1]
Ohio		
Governor	Ted Strickland (D)	US$144,830
Lt. Gov.	Lee Fisher (D)	US$142,500
Sec. of State	Jennifer Brunner (D)	US$109,986
Atty. Gen.	Nancy H. Rogers (D)	US$109,986
Treasurer	Richard Cordray (D)	US$109,986
General Assembly		
Senate	Dem: 12; Rep: 21	
House	Dem: 46; Rep: 53	
Oklahoma		
Governor	Brad Henry (D)	US$140,000
Lt. Gov.	Jari Askins (D)	US$109,250
Sec. of State	M. Susan Savage (D)	US$94,500
Atty. Gen.	W.A. Drew Edmondson (D)	US$126,500
Treasurer	Scott Meacham (D)	US$109,250
Legislature		
Senate	Dem: 24; Rep: 24	
House	Dem: 44; Rep: 57	
Oregon		
Governor	Ted Kulongoski (D)	US$93,600
Lt. Gov.[4]		
Sec. of State	Bill Bradbury (D)	US$72,000
Atty. Gen.	Hardy Myers (D)	US$77,200
Treasurer	Randall Edwards (D)	US$72,000
Legislative Assembly		
Senate	Dem: 18; Rep: 11; Ind: 1	
House	Dem: 31; Rep: 29	
Pennsylvania		
Governor	Edward G. Rendell (D)	US$170,150
Lt. Gov.	Catherine Baker Knoll (D)	US$142,924
Sec. of State	Pedro A. Cortés (D)	US$122,509
Atty. Gen.	Tom Corbett (R)	US$141,565
Treasurer	Robin L. Wiessmann	US$141,565
General Assembly		
Senate	Dem: 21; Rep: 29	
House	Dem: 102; Rep: 101	
Rhode Island		
Governor	Don Carcieri (R)	US$117,817
Lt. Gov.	Elizabeth H. Roberts (D)	US$99,214
Sec. of State	A. Ralph Mollis (D)	US$99,214
Atty. Gen.	Patrick C. Lynch (D)	US$105,416
Treasurer	Frank T. Caprio (D)	US$99,214
General Assembly		
Senate	Dem: 33; Rep: 5	
House	Dem: 62; Rep: 13	
South Carolina		
Governor	Mark Sanford (R)	US$106,078
Lt. Gov.	André Bauer (R)	US$46,545
Sec. of State	Mark Hammond (R)	US$92,007
Atty. Gen.	Henry McMaster (R)	US$92,007
Treasurer	Converse Chellis (R)	US$92,007
General Assembly		
Senate	Dem: 19; Rep: 27	
House	Dem: 51; Rep: 73	
South Dakota		
Governor	Mike Rounds (R)	US$111,972
Lt. Gov.	Dennis Daugaard (R)	US$16,833
Sec. of State	Chris Nelson (R)	US$76,080
Atty. Gen.	Larry Long (R)	US$95,076
Treasurer	Vernon L. Larson (R)	US$76,080

STATE/OFFICE	OFFICEHOLDER	PAY[1]
South Dakota (continued)		
Legislature		
Senate	Dem: 15; Rep: 20	
House	Dem: 20; Rep: 50	
Tennessee		
Governor	Phil Bredesen (D)	US$159,960
Lt. Gov.[6]	Ron Ramsey (R)	US$54,372
Sec. of State	Riley Darnell (D)	US$180,000
Atty. Gen.	Robert E. Cooper, Jr. (D)	US$154,800
Treasurer	Dale Sims	US$180,000
General Assembly		
Senate	Dem: 16; Rep: 16; Ind: 1	
House	Dem: 53; Rep: 46	
Texas		
Governor	Rick Perry (R)	US$150,000
Lt. Gov.	David Dewhurst (R)	US$7,200
Sec. of State	Phil Wilson (R)	US$117,516
Atty. Gen.	Greg Abbott (R)	US$150,000
Treasurer[3]	Susan Combs (Comptroller) (R)	US$150,000
Legislature		
Senate	Dem: 11; Rep: 20	
House	Dem: 71; Rep: 79	
Utah		
Governor	Jon Huntsman, Jr. (R)	US$107,200
Lt. Gov.	Gary R. Herbert (R)	US$101,840
Sec. of State[2]		
Atty. Gen.	Mark Shurtleff (R)	US$101,840
Treasurer	Edward T. Alter (R)	US$101,840
Legislature		
Senate	Dem: 8; Rep: 21	
House	Dem: 20; Rep: 55	
Vermont		
Governor	Jim Douglas (R)	US$150,051
Lt. Gov.	Brian Dubie (R)	US$63,690
Sec. of State	Deborah L. Markowitz (D)	US$95,139
Atty. Gen.	William H. Sorrell (D)	US$113,901
Treasurer	Jeb Spaulding (D)	US$95,139
General Assembly		
Senate	Dem: 23; Rep: 7	
House	Dem: 93; Rep: 49; Ind: 2; Progressive: 6	
Virginia		
Governor	Tim Kaine (D)	US$175,000
Lt. Gov.	Bill Bolling (R)	US$36,321
Sec. of State	Katherine K. Hanley (D)	US$146,916
Atty. Gen.	Robert F. McDonnell (R)	US$150,000
Treasurer	J. Braxton Powell	US$128,371
General Assembly		
Senate	Dem: 21; Rep: 19	
House	Dem: 45; Rep: 53; Ind: 2	
Washington		
Governor	Chris Gregoire (D)	US$163,618
Lt. Gov.	Brad Owen (D)	US$92,106
Sec. of State	Sam Reed (R)	US$114,657
Atty. Gen.	Rob McKenna (R)	US$148,744
Treasurer	Michael J. Murphy (D)	US$114,657
Legislature		
Senate	Dem: 32; Rep: 17	
House	Dem: 63; Rep: 35	

State Officers and Legislatures (continued)

STATE/OFFICE	OFFICEHOLDER	PAY[1]
West Virginia		
Governor	Joe Manchin III (D)	US$95,000
Lt. Gov.[7]	Earl Ray Tomblin (D)	N/A
Sec. of State	Betty Ireland (R)	US$70,000
Atty. Gen.	Darrell V. McGraw, Jr. (D)	US$85,000
Treasurer	John D. Perdue (D)	US$75,000
Legislature		
Senate	Dem: 23; Rep: 11	
House	Dem: 72; Rep: 28	
Wisconsin		
Governor	Jim Doyle (D)	US$137,092
Lt. Gov.	Barbara Lawton (D)	US$72,394
Sec. of State	Douglas La Follette (D)	US$65,079
Atty. Gen.	J.B. Van Hollen (R)	US$133,033
Wisconsin (continued)		
Treasurer	Dawn Marie Sass (D)	US$65,079
Legislature		
Senate	Dem: 18; Rep: 15	
Assembly	Dem: 47; Rep: 52	
Wyoming		
Governor	Dave Freudenthal (D)	US$105,000
Lt. Gov.[4]		
Sec. of State	Max Maxfield (R)	US$92,000
Atty. Gen.	Bruce A. Salzburg (D)	US$125,000
Treasurer	Joseph B. Meyer (R)	US$92,000
Legislature		
Senate	Dem: 7; Rep: 23	
House	Dem: 17; Rep: 43	

[1]The salary rates are from February 2008. [2]The lieutenant governor serves as secretary of state. [3]No official state treasurer; the official in charge of the general treasury performs duties. [4]The secretary of state assumes duties of lieutenant governor. [5]No official lieutenant governor; the president of the Senate succeeds the governor. [6]In Tennessee the speaker of the Senate and the lieutenant governor are one and the same. [7]In West Virginia the president of the Senate and the lieutenant governor are one and the same.

Cities of the United States

US Urban Growth, 1850–2007

Source: US Census Bureau.

RANK	CITY	1850	1900	1950	1990	2000	2007
1	New York NY[1]	515,547	3,437,202	7,891,957	7,322,564	8,008,278	8,274,527
2	Los Angeles CA	1,610	102,479	1,970,358	3,485,398	3,694,820	3,834,340
3	Chicago IL	29,963	1,698,575	3,620,962	2,783,726	2,896,016	2,836,658
4	Houston TX	2,396	44,633	596,163	1,630,553	1,953,631	2,208,180
5	Phoenix AZ		5,544	106,818	983,403	1,321,045	1,552,259
6	Philadelphia PA[1]	121,376	1,293,697	2,071,605	1,585,577	1,517,550	1,449,634
7	San Antonio TX	3,488	53,321	408,442	935,933	1,144,646	1,328,984
8	San Diego CA		17,700	334,387	1,110,549	1,223,400	1,266,731
9	Dallas TX		42,638	434,462	1,006,877	1,188,580	1,240,499
10	San Jose CA		21,500	95,280	782,248	894,943	939,899
11	Detroit MI	21,019	285,704	1,849,568	1,027,974	951,270	916,952
12	Jacksonville FL	1,045	28,429	204,517	635,230	735,617	805,605
13	Indianapolis IN[1]	8,091	169,164	427,173	731,726[2]	781,870[2]	795,458[2]
14	San Francisco CA[1]	34,776	342,782	775,357	723,959	776,733	764,976
15	Columbus OH	17,882	125,560	375,901	632,910	711,470	747,755
16	Austin TX	629	22,258	132,459	465,622	656,562	743,074
17	Fort Worth TX		26,688	278,778	447,619	534,694	681,818
18	Memphis TN	8,841	102,320	396,000	610,337	650,100	674,028
19	Charlotte NC	1,065	18,091	134,042	395,934	540,828	671,588
20	Baltimore MD	169,054	508,957	949,708	736,014	651,154	637,455
21	El Paso TX		15,906	130,485	515,342	563,662	606,913
22	Milwaukee WI	20,061	285,315	637,392	628,088	596,974	602,191
23	Boston MA	136,881	560,892	801,444	574,283	589,141	599,351
24	Seattle WA		80,671	467,591	516,259	563,374	594,210
25	Nashville TN[1]	10,165	80,865	174,307	488,374[2]	545,524[2]	590,807[2]
26	Denver CO[1]		133,859	415,786	467,610	554,636	588,349
27	Washington DC[1]	40,001	278,718	802,178	606,900	572,059	588,292
28	Las Vegas NV			24,624	258,295	478,434	558,880
29	Louisville KY[1]	43,194	204,731	369,129	269,063	256,231	557,789[2]
30	Portland OR	821	90,426	373,628	437,319	529,121	550,396

[1]Cities with boundaries contiguous with their respective counties (year consolidated): New York (1898), Philadelphia (1854), San Francisco (1856), Denver (1902), Washington (District of Columbia) (1790), Louisville (Jefferson county) (2003), and Nashville (Davidson county) (1963). [2]Figure represents the "balance," or the population of the consolidated city minus any semi-incorporated places located within the consolidated city.

Fifteen Fastest-Growing Cities in the US

Based on a population of 100,000 or more. Source: US Census Bureau.

CITY	POPULATION 1 APR 2000	POPULATION 1 JUL 2007	CHANGE (%)
McKinney TX	54,417	115,620	+112.5
North Las Vegas NV	115,531	212,114	+83.6
Gilbert AZ	113,868	207,550	+82.3
Port St. Lucie FL	88,883	151,391	+70.3
Victorville CA	64,058	107,221	+67.4
Elk Grove CA	81,103	131,212	+61.8
Cape Coral FL	102,468	156,981	+53.2
Miramar FL	72,739	108,240	+48.8
Henderson NV	175,274	249,386	+42.3
Denton TX	82,589	115,506	+39.9
Irvine CA	144,145	201,160	+39.6
Chandler AZ	177,103	246,399	+39.1
Roseville CA	79,961	108,759	+36.0
Thornton CO	82,109	110,880	+35.0
Joliet IL	107,093	144,316	+34.8

Fifteen Cities with the Greatest Population Losses in the US

Based on a population of 100,000 or more. Source: US Census Bureau.

CITY	POPULATION 1 APR 2000	POPULATION 1 JUL 2007	CHANGE (%)
New Orleans LA	484,674	239,124	−50.7
Cleveland OH	477,472	438,042	−8.3
Flint MI	124,943	114,662	−8.2
Pittsburgh PA	334,563	311,218	−7.0
Buffalo NY	292,648	272,632	−6.8
Dayton OH	166,210	155,461	−6.5
Hialeah FL	226,440	212,217	−6.3
Toledo OH	313,782	295,029	−6.0
Rochester NY	219,774	206,759	−5.9
Birmingham AL	242,452	229,800	−5.2
Syracuse NY	146,464	139,079	−5.0
Jackson MS	184,256	175,710	−4.6
Philadelphia PA	1,517,550	1,449,634	−4.5
Evansville IN	121,648	116,253	−4.4
Akron OH	217,094	207,934	−4.2

Racial Makeup of the Fifteen Largest US Cities

Information is given in percent of the total population. The Hispanic or Latino category is listed for comparative purposes even though Hispanic or Latino people may be of any race; thus, the rows of racial percentages will not add up to 100 if the Hispanic or Latino entries are included. Excludes population living in institutions. Data are preliminary.

Source: US Census Bureau, *American Community Survey*, 2006 Data Profiles.

CITY	WHITE	BLACK OR AFRICAN AMERICAN	AMERICAN INDIAN AND ALASKA NATIVE	ASIAN	NATIVE HAWAIIAN AND OTHER PACIFIC ISLANDER	SOME OTHER RACE	TWO OR MORE RACES	HISPANIC OR LATINO	TOTAL POPULATION
New York NY	43.9	25.1	0.3	11.7	—	17.0	2.0	27.6	8,214,426
Los Angeles CA	47.1	9.6	0.6	10.4	0.2	29.3	2.9	48.9	3,773,846
Chicago IL	36.5	35.3	0.2	4.9	—	21.4	1.6	28.2	2,749,283
Houston TX	52.7	24.7	0.4	5.0	0.1	15.9	1.2	41.9	2,074,828
Philadelphia PA	41.8	44.3	0.3	5.3	—	6.6	1.6	10.5	1,448,394
Phoenix AZ	76.6	5.6	1.8	2.3	0.2	11.6	1.9	41.2	1,429,637
San Antonio TX	66.0	6.7	0.5	2.1	0.1	22.5	2.1	61.3	1,273,374
San Diego CA	65.0	6.9	0.6	15.3	0.4	8.4	3.5	27.1	1,261,251
Dallas TX	52.9	24.2	0.4	2.3	0.1	18.9	1.2	43.1	1,192,538
San Jose CA	47.0	2.9	0.5	30.5	0.5	15.1	3.5	32.2	916,220
Detroit MI	10.0	83.1	0.3	1.1	—	4.2	1.3	6.2	834,116
Jacksonville FL	61.7	30.7	0.4	3.4	0.1	1.9	1.9	5.8	799,875
Indianapolis IN	66.3	26.7	0.2	1.5	—	3.4	1.9	6.5	789,306
San Francisco CA	53.0	6.7	0.4	31.8	0.5	4.7	2.9	14.1	744,041
Columbus OH	64.6	27.6	0.2	4.3	—	1.4	2.0	4.1	718,477

— Less than 0.05 percent.
Detail may not add to total given because of rounding.

Area and Zip Codes Web Sites

US telephone area codes and postal codes change frequently to accommodate telecommunications user patterns and expansions and shifts in patterns of business and residential development. With regard to telephone area codes, in some cases, an area receives an entirely new area code; in others, a new area code "overlays" the preceding one. Check local listings to determine whether to dial "1" before dialing outside of the area code or to dial the area code as well as the telephone number when dialing within the area code.

Area codes: <www.nanpa.com>.
Zip codes: <http://zip4.usps.com/zip4/welcome.jsp>.

Law and Crime

US Crime Trends, 2007

The crime trends shown below represent the percent change in crimes reported to police in the 2007 calendar year as compared to the same time period in 2006. A negative number indicates that crime declined. Detail may not add to total given because of rounding.

Source: Federal Bureau of Investigation, *Preliminary Annual Uniform Crime Report, January–December 2007.*

POPULATION GROUP AND AREA	NUMBER OF AGENCIES[1]	POPULATION ('000)	VIOLENT CRIME[2]	PROPERTY CRIME[3]	MURDER
cities					
1,000,000 and over	10	25,220	−3.7	−1.0	−9.8
500,000 to 999,999	23	15,424	+0.3	−2.7	−1.2
250,000 to 499,999	38	13,157	−3.9	−4.2	−3.3
100,000 to 249,999	182	27,451	−0.4	−1.9	+1.9
50,000 to 99,999	394	27,252	−1.7	−2.8	+3.7
25,000 to 49,999	680	23,458	−1.2	−1.4	−2.6
10,000 to 24,999	1,470	23,312	+1.9	−1.2	−0.3
under 10,000	6,001	19,549	−0.5	−2.4	+1.8
counties					
metropolitan[4]	1,302	54,195	−1.7	−1.6	−2.4
nonmetropolitan[5]	1,932	22,981	+1.8	−1.7	−5.9
total	**12,032**	**252,000**	**−1.4**	**−2.1**	**−2.7**

POPULATION GROUP AND AREA	FORCIBLE RAPE	ROBBERY	AGGRAVATED ASSAULT	BURGLARY	LARCENY/ THEFT	MOTOR VEHICLE THEFT	ARSON
cities							
1,000,000 and over	−8.0	−2.9	−4.0	+4.0	−0.1	−9.5	−7.2
500,000 to 999,999	−1.2	+0.2	+0.5	−3.3	[6]	−11.2	−8.9
250,000 to 499,999	−6.5	−3.0	−4.3	−2.4	−3.2	−10.0	−4.2
100,000 to 249,999	−4.3	[6]	−0.2	+0.1	−1.4	−7.8	−2.8
50,000 to 99,999	−4.5	−1.0	−1.9	−1.2	−2.1	−9.8	−11.1
25,000 to 49,999	−3.5	−0.4	−1.3	−0.5	−0.7	−9.2	−5.0
10,000 to 24,999	−4.0	+1.3	+3.0	−1.7	−0.4	−8.0	−3.4
under 10,000	−5.4	−0.7	+0.1	−1.6	−2.2	−6.3	−7.7
counties							
metropolitan[4]	−2.7	−1.0	−1.8	−0.9	−0.7	−7.1	−9.7
nonmetropolitan[5]	−3.7	−0.3	+3.0	−1.4	−1.6	−4.2	−5.0
total	**−4.3**	**−1.2**	**−1.2**	**−0.8**	**−1.2**	**−8.9**	**−7.0**

[1]*Law enforcement agencies.* [2]*Includes murder, forcible rape, robbery, and aggravated assault.* [3]*Includes burglary, larceny/theft, and motor vehicle theft but excludes data for arson.* [4]*Includes crimes reported to sheriffs' departments, county police departments, and state police within Metropolitan Statistical Areas.* [5]*Includes crimes reported to sheriffs' departments, county police departments, and state police outside Metropolitan Statistical Areas.* [6]*Negligible.*

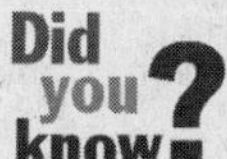

The movement of people from a city to suburbs and the surrounding countryside creates a larger metropolitan area, and the metropolitan areas tend to merge into even larger urban agglomerations, the megalopolises. The biggest in the US is "Boswash," which stretches from Boston MA to Washington DC.

State Crime Rates, 2000–06

Crimes reported to the police per 100,000 population.

STATE	2000 TOTAL	2001[1] TOTAL	2002 TOTAL	2003 TOTAL	2004 TOTAL	2005 TOTAL	2006 TOTAL
AL	4,546	4,319	4,465	4,475	4,452	4,324	4,361
AK	4,249	4,236	4,310	4,360	4,018	4,244	4,293
AZ	5,830	6,077	6,386	6,147	5,845	5,351	5,129
AR	4,115	4,134	4,158	4,088	4,512	4,585	4,519
CA	3,740	3,903	3,944	4,006	3,971	3,849	3,703
CO	3,983	4,219	4,348	4,299	4,293	4,436	3,843
CT	3,233	3,118	2,997	2,984	2,913	2,833	2,785
DE[2]	4,478	4,053	3,939	4,090	3,732	3,744	4,099
DC[3]	7,277	7,710	8,022	7,489	6,230	6,206	6,162
FL	5,695	5,570	5,421	5,188	4,891	4,716	4,698
GA	4,751	4,646	4,507	4,715	4,722	4,621	4,360
HI	5,199	5,386	6,044	5,547	5,047	5,048	4,512
ID	3,186	3,133	3,173	3,175	3,039	2,955	2,666
IL[4]	4,286	4,098	4,016	3,844	3,729	3,632	3,561
IN	3,752	3,831	3,750	3,708	3,723	3,780	3,817
IA	3,234	3,301	3,448	3,254	3,176	3,125	3,086
KS[5]	4,409	4,321	4,087	4,408	4,349	4,174	4,175
KY[6]	2,960	2,938	2,903	2,759	2,783	2,797	2,808
LA	5,423	5,338	5,098	4,948	5,049	4,278	4,691
ME	2,620	2,688	2,656	2,559	2,514	2,525	2,634
MD	4,816	4,867	4,747	4,503	4,341	4,247	4,159
MA	3,026	3,099	3,094	3,036	2,919	2,821	2,838
MI	4,110	4,082	3,874	3,790	3,548	3,643	3,775
MN	3,488	3,584	3,535	3,376	3,309	3,381	3,391
MS	4,004	4,185	4,159	4,031	3,774	3,539	3,507
MO	4,528	4,776	4,602	4,575	4,395	4,453	4,372
MT[5]	3,533	3,689	3,513	3,461	3,230	3,424	2,941
NE	4,096	4,330	4,257	4,046	3,830	3,710	3,623
NV	4,269	4,266	4,498	4,903	4,823	4,848	4,830
NH	2,433	2,322	2,220	2,203	2,207	1,928	2,013
NJ	3,161	3,225	3,024	2,914	2,785	2,688	2,643
NM	5,519	5,324	5,078	4,756	4,885	4,851	4,580
NY	3,100	2,925	2,804	2,715	2,641	2,554	2,488
NC	4,919	4,938	4,721	4,725	4,608	4,543	4,596
ND	2,288	2,418	2,406	2,190	1,996	2,076	2,128
OH	4,042	4,178	4,107	3,984	4,015	4,014	4,029
OK	4,559	4,607	4,743	4,818	4,743	4,551	4,102
OR	4,845	5,044	4,868	5,061	4,929	4,687	3,952
PA	2,995	2,961	2,841	2,828	2,826	2,842	2,883
RI	3,476	3,685	3,589	3,281	3,131	2,970	2,814
SC	5,221	4,753	5,297	5,328	5,289	5,101	5,008
SD	2,320	2,332	2,279	2,177	2,106	1,952	1,791
TN	4,890	5,153	5,019	5,080	5,002	5,028	4,888
TX	4,956	5,153	5,190	5,153	5,035	4,862	4,598
UT	4,476	4,243	4,452	4,505	4,322	4,096	3,741
VT	2,987	2,769	2,530	2,343	2,420	2,400	2,441
VA	3,028	3,178	3,140	3,000	2,953	2,921	2,760
WA	5,106	5,152	5,107	5,102	5,193	5,239	4,826
WV	2,603	2,560	2,515	2,594	2,777	2,898	2,901
WI	3,209	3,321	3,253	3,101	2,873	2,902	3,102
WY	3,298	3,518	3,581	3,578	3,564	3,385	3,220
US	**4,125**	**4,161**	**4,119**	**4,067**	**3,983**	**3,899**	**3,808**

2006 CRIME RATES IN DETAIL

	VIOLENT CRIMES					PROPERTY CRIMES			
STATE	MURDER[7]	FORCIBLE RAPE	AGGRAVATED ASSAULT	ROBBERY	TOTAL	BURGLARY	LARCENY/ THEFT	MOTOR VEHICLE THEFT	TOTAL
AL	8.3	35.9	228	154	425	969	2,644	323	3,936
AK	5.4	76.0	516	90.3	688	617	2,610	377	3,605
AZ	7.5	31.5	313	150	501	925	2,813	890	4,628

State Crime Rates, 2000–06 (continued)

2006 CRIME RATES IN DETAIL (CONTINUED)

	VIOLENT CRIMES					PROPERTY CRIMES			
STATE	MURDER[7]	FORCIBLE RAPE	AGGRAVATED ASSAULT	ROBBERY	TOTAL	BURGLARY	LARCENY/ THEFT	MOTOR VEHICLE THEFT	TOTAL
AR	7.3	46.5	399	98.4	552	1,140	2,562	266	3,968
CA	6.8	25.3	306	195	533	676	1,829	666	3,171
CO	3.3	43.7	264	80.7	392	682	2,332	438	3,451
CT	3.1	18.1	139	121	281	419	1,788	296	2,504
DE	4.9	46.9	427	203	682	725	2,363	330	3,418
DC[3]	29.1	31.8	789	658	1,508	660	2,735	1,259	4,654
FL	6.2	35.8	481	189	712	945	2,619	423	3,986
GA	6.4	23.2	276	166	471	909	2,519	461	3,889
HI	1.6	27.6	163	88.9	281	678	2,949	604	4,230
ID	2.5	40.0	184	20.5	247	513	1,740	166	2,419
IL[4]	6.1	31.8	318	185	542	602	2,124	293	3,020
IN	5.8	29.1	165	115	315	731	2,425	346	3,502
IA	1.8	27.8	210	43.5	284	604	2,031	168	2,803
KS	4.6	44.8	308	67.9	425	723	2,712	315	3,750
KY	4.0	30.8	142	86.2	263	645	1,680	220	2,545
LA	12.4	36.4	515	134	698	1,049	2,580	365	3,994
ME	1.7	25.7	59.0	29.1	116	513	1,904	101	2,519
MD	9.7	21.0	392	256	679	667	2,270	544	3,481
MA	2.9	27.1	292	125	447	547	1,565	279	2,391
MI	7.1	52.2	362	141	562	754	1,964	495	3,213
MN	2.4	31.8	173	105	312	584	2,237	259	3,080
MS	7.7	34.4	150	107	299	936	1,986	287	3,209
MO	6.3	30.2	379	130	546	764	2,627	435	3,827
MT	1.8	28.5	206	17.4	254	311	2,192	185	2,688
NE	2.8	31.0	184	63.8	282	535	2,521	285	3,341
NV	9.0	43.2	408	282	742	995	2,014	1,080	4,089
NH	1.0	26.2	79.4	32.2	139	331	1,435	108	1,874
NJ	4.9	14.2	179	153	352	452	1,557	283	2,292
NM	6.8	56.0	473	108	643	1,070	2,396	472	3,937
NY	4.8	16.4	235	179	435	355	1,531	166	2,053
NC	6.1	28.2	289	152	476	1,213	2,568	340	4,121
ND	1.3	30.4	84.9	11.3	128	376	1,465	159	2,000
OH	4.7	39.6	139	167	350	910	2,443	326	3,679
OK	5.8	41.6	363	87.5	497	961	2,271	373	3,604
OR	2.3	32.3	173	72.7	280	645	2,636	391	3,672
PA	5.9	27.3	238	169	439	463	1,743	237	2,444
RI	2.6	26.7	129	68.8	228	507	1,744	336	2,587
SC	8.3	40.8	580	137	766	990	2,873	380	4,242
SD	1.2	43.0	112	15.2	171	339	1,189	91.8	1,620
TN	6.8	35.5	534	184	760	1,041	2,713	374	4,128
TX	5.9	35.6	316	159	516	917	2,758	406	4,082
UT	1.8	34.1	140	48.8	224	577	2,615	325	3,516
VT	1.9	24.0	93.0	17.6	137	529	1,682	93.9	2,305
VA	5.2	23.4	152	101	282	418	1,867	194	2,478
WA	3.0	42.9	200	100	346	912	2,851	718	4,480
WV	4.1	21.4	207	46.9	280	634	1,772	216	2,622
WI	3.0	20.4	161	100	284	486	2,080	253	2,818
WY	1.7	27.2	197	14.0	240	451	2,379	151	2,981
Total US	**5.7**	**30.9**	**288**	**149**	**474**	**729**	**2,207**	**398**	**3,335**

[1]This table does not include the murder and nonnegligent homicides that occurred because of the terrorist attacks of 11 Sep 2001. [2]Forcible rape count estimated for 2000. [3]Includes reported offenses at the National Zoo and, from 2002, offenses reported by the Metro Transit Police. [4]Data are estimated or incomplete. [5]Crime counts estimated for 2000. [6]Data are limited or estimated between 2000 and 2003. [7]Includes nonnegligent manslaughter.

Sources: US Bureau of Justice Statistics, <http://bjsdata.ojp.usdoj.gov/dataonline>.

Crime in the US, 1984–2006

This table presents the number of crimes reported in the seven categories that, with arson, are known as Part I crimes and are used by the Federal Bureau of Investigation to assess trends in criminality in the country.

Source: Federal Bureau of Investigation.

	VIOLENT CRIME				PROPERTY CRIME		
YEAR	MURDER[1]	FORCIBLE RAPE	ROBBERY	AGGRAVATED ASSAULT	BURGLARY	LARCENY/ THEFT	MOTOR VEHICLE THEFT
1984	18,692	84,233	485,008	685,349	2,984,434	6,591,874	1,032,165
1985	18,976	87,671	497,874	723,246	3,073,348	6,926,380	1,102,862
1986	20,613	91,459	542,775	834,322	3,241,410	7,257,153	1,224,137
1987	20,096	91,111	517,704	855,088	3,236,184	7,499,851	1,288,674
1988	20,675	92,486	542,968	910,092	3,218,077	7,705,872	1,432,916
1989	21,500	94,504	578,326	951,707	3,168,170	7,872,442	1,564,800
1990	23,438	102,555	639,271	1,054,863	3,073,909	7,945,670	1,635,907
1991	24,703	106,593	687,732	1,092,739	3,157,150	8,142,228	1,661,738
1992	23,760	109,062	672,478	1,126,974	2,979,884	7,915,199	1,610,834
1993	24,526	106,014	659,870	1,135,607	2,834,808	7,820,909	1,563,060
1994	23,326	102,216	618,949	1,113,179	2,712,774	7,879,812	1,539,287
1995	21,606	97,470	580,509	1,099,207	2,593,784	7,997,710	1,472,441
1996	19,645	96,252	535,594	1,037,049	2,506,400	7,904,685	1,394,238
1997	18,208	96,153	498,534	1,023,201	2,460,526	7,743,760	1,354,189
1998	16,974	93,144	447,186	976,583	2,332,735	7,376,311	1,242,781
1999	15,522	89,411	409,371	911,740	2,100,739	6,955,520	1,152,075
2000	15,586	90,178	408,016	911,706	2,050,992	6,971,590	1,160,002
2001	16,037	90,863	423,557	909,023	2,116,531	7,092,267	1,228,391
2002	16,204	95,136	420,637	894,348	2,151,875	7,052,922	1,246,096
2003	16,528	93,883	414,235	859,030	2,154,834	7,026,802	1,261,226
2004	16,148	95,089	401,470	847,381	2,144,446	6,937,089	1,237,851
2005	16,692	93,934	417,122	862,947	2,154,126	6,776,807	1,235,226
2006	17,034	92,455	447,403	860,853	2,183,746	6,607,013	1,192,809

Crime trends: percent change in number of offenses[2]

	VIOLENT CRIME				PROPERTY CRIME		
YEARS COMPARED	MURDER[1]	FORCIBLE RAPE	ROBBERY	AGGRAVATED ASSAULT	BURGLARY	LARCENY/ THEFT	MOTOR VEHICLE THEFT
2006/2005	+1.8	−2.0	+7.2	−0.2	+1.3	−2.6	−3.5
2006/2002	+5.0	−2.9	+6.3	−3.4	+1.5	−6.4	−4.3
2006/1997	−6.4	−3.8	−10.3	−15.9	−11.2	−14.7	−11.9

[1]*Includes the crime of nonnegligent manslaughter.* [2]*A minus sign indicates a decrease in crime; a plus sign indicates an increase.*

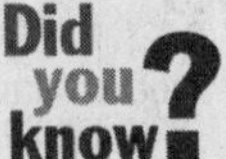

Actual names of US towns: Embarrass, Wisconsin; Goofy Ridge, Illinois; French Lick, Indiana; Intercourse, Alabama; Bumble Bee, Arizona; Toad Suck, Arkansas; Truth or Consequences, New Mexico; Hellhole Palms, California; Uncertain, Texas; and Unalaska, Alaska.

US Cities with Highest and Lowest Crime Rates

This table ranks cities with populations greater than 100,000 by the number of violent crimes reported during 2007.

Source: Federal Bureau of Investigation, *Preliminary Annual Uniform Crime Report, January–December 2007.*

CITIES	VIOLENT CRIME[1]	MURDER	FORCIBLE RAPE	ROBBERY	AGGRAVATED ASSAULT	BURGLARY	LARCENY/ THEFT	CAR THEFT
Highest Crime Rates								
New York NY	50,453	496	875	21,787	27,295	20,914	115,318	13,256
Los Angeles CA	27,801	390	1,004	13,481	12,926	19,629	58,304	23,524
Houston TX	24,564	351	694	11,479	12,040	29,044	74,817	19,465
Philadelphia PA	21,180	392	956	10,258	9,574	11,524	39,167	11,104
Detroit MI	19,683	383	344	6,574	12,382	17,745	20,892	19,604
Las Vegas NV	13,641	119	723	5,251	7,548	15,296	27,156	16,445
Dallas TX	13,248	200	511	7,222	5,315	22,472	47,699	13,791
Memphis TN	13,052	129	451	4,869	7,603	14,607	33,128	6,199
Phoenix AZ	11,159	213	509	4,942	5,495	19,212	49,754	20,859
Baltimore MD	10,182	282	146	3,895	5,859	7,381	16,742	5,816

US Cities with Highest and Lowest Crime Rates (continued)

CITIES	VIOLENT CRIME[1]	MURDER	FORCIBLE RAPE	ROBBERY	AGGRAVATED ASSAULT	BURGLARY	LARCENY/ THEFT	CAR THEFT
Lowest Crime Rates								
Cary NC	134	1	11	58	64	448	1,584	88
Amherst NY	137	2	8	47	80	200	1,558	50
Bellevue WA	138	0	29	61	48	583	3,152	446
Irvine CA	143	4	19	44	76	637	2,404	215
Thousand Oaks CA	146	2	19	38	87	424	1,407	111
Sunnyvale CA	154	2	15	62	75	372	1,896	361
Provo UT	166	0	28	34	104	482	2,477	280
Norman OK	177	4	35	52	86	795	2,549	271
Simi Valley CA	181	2	20	63	96	432	1,729	222
Arvada CO	214	3	29	46	136	423	1,924	238

[1]*Data for overall violent crime rates are composites of murder, forcible rape, robbery, and aggravated assault rates. Data are not available for Chicago IL or Naperville IL, on the list for highest and lowest crime rates, respectively, in recent years.*

Total Arrests in the US

Estimates for the year 2006. Source: Federal Bureau of Investigation, Crime in the United States, 2006.

TYPE OF CRIME	NUMBER OF ARRESTS	TYPE OF CRIME	NUMBER OF ARRESTS
violent crime		**other crime types (continued)**	
aggravated assault	447,948	drunkenness	553,188
robbery	125,605	fraud	280,693
forcible rape	24,535	vandalism	300,679
murder and nonnegligent manslaughter	13,435	weapons (carrying, possessing, etc.)	200,782
violent crime total	**611,523**	curfew and loitering law violations	152,907
		stolen property (buying, receiving, possessing)	122,722
property crime			
larceny/theft	1,081,157	offenses against the family and children	131,491
burglary	304,801	forgery and counterfeiting	108,823
motor vehicle theft	137,757	runaways	114,179
arson	16,582	sex offenses (except forcible rape and prostitution)	87,252
property crime total	**1,540,297**		
		prostitution and commercialized vice	79,673
other crime types		vagrancy	36,471
drug abuse violations	1,889,810	embezzlement	20,012
driving under the influence	1,460,498	gambling	12,307
other assaults	1,305,757	suspicion (not included in total)	2,482
disorderly conduct	703,504	all other offenses (except traffic)	4,022,068
liquor laws	645,734	**total arrests**	**14,380,370**

US State and Federal Prison Population

Source: US Bureau of Justice Statistics.

STATE	NUMBER OF PRISONERS				% CHANGE (31 DEC 2005 TO 31 DEC 2006)
	31 DEC 1980	31 DEC 1990	31 DEC 2005	31 DEC 2006	
Alabama	6,543	15,665	27,888	28,241	+1.3
Alaska[1]	822	2,622	4,812	5,069	+5.3
Arizona[2]	4,372	14,261	33,565	35,892	+6.9
Arkansas	2,911	7,322	13,541	13,729	+1.4
California	24,569	97,309	170,676	175,512	+2.8
Colorado	2,629	7,671	21,456	22,481	+4.8
Connecticut[1]	4,308	10,500	19,442	20,566	+5.8
Delaware[1]	1,474	3,471	6,966	7,206	+3.4
Florida	20,735	44,387	89,768	92,969	+3.6
Georgia[2]	12,178	22,411	48,749	52,792	+8.3
Hawaii[1]	985	2,533	6,146	5,967	−2.9
Idaho	817	1,961	6,818	7,124	+4.5
Illinois	11,899	27,516	44,919	45,106	+0.4
Indiana	6,683	12,736	24,455	26,091	+6.7
Iowa[1]	2,481	3,967	8,737	8,875	+1.6

US State and Federal Prison Population (continued)

STATE	NUMBER OF PRISONERS 31 DEC 1980	31 DEC 1990	31 DEC 2005	31 DEC 2006	% CHANGE (31 DEC 2005 TO 31 DEC 2006)
Kansas	2,494	5,775	9,068	8,816	−2.8
Kentucky	3,588	9,023	19,662	20,000	+1.7
Louisiana	8,889	18,599	36,083	37,012	+2.6
Maine	814	1,523	2,023	2,120	+4.8
Maryland	7,731	17,848	22,737	22,945	+0.9
Massachusetts	3,185	8,345	10,701	11,032	+3.1
Michigan	15,124	34,267	49,546	51,577	+4.1
Minnesota	2,001	3,176	9,281	9,108	−1.9
Mississippi	3,902	8,375	20,515	21,068	+2.7
Missouri	5,726	14,943	30,823	30,167	−2.1
Montana	739	1,425	3,532	3,572	+1.1
Nebraska	1,446	2,403	4,455	4,407	−1.1
Nevada	1,839	5,322	11,782	12,901	+9.5
New Hampshire	326	1,342	2,530	2,805	+10.9
New Jersey	5,884	21,128	27,359	27,371	[3]
New Mexico	1,279	3,187	6,571	6,639	+1.0
New York	21,815	54,895	62,743	63,315	+0.9
North Carolina	15,513	18,411	36,365	37,460	+3.0
North Dakota	253	483	1,385	1,363	−1.6
Ohio	13,489	31,822	45,854	49,166	+7.2
Oklahoma	4,796	12,285	26,676	26,243	−1.6
Oregon	3,177	6,492	13,411	13,707	+2.2
Pennsylvania	8,171	22,290	42,380	44,397	+4.8
Rhode Island[1]	813	2,392	3,654	3,996	+9.4
South Carolina	7,862	17,319	23,160	23,616	+2.0
South Dakota	635	1,341	3,463	3,359	−3.0
Tennessee	7,022	10,388	26,369	25,745	−2.4
Texas	29,892	50,042	169,003	172,116	+1.8
Utah	932	2,496	6,382	6,430	+0.8
Vermont[1]	480	1,049	2,078	2,215	+6.6
Virginia	8,920	17,593	35,344	36,688	+3.8
Washington	4,399	7,995	17,382	17,561	+1.0
West Virginia	1,257	1,565	5,312	5,733	+7.9
Wisconsin	3,980	7,465	22,697	23,431	+3.2
Wyoming	534	1,110	2,047	2,114	+3.3
state	305,458	708,393	1,340,311	1,377,815	+2.8
federal[4]	24,363	65,526	187,618	193,046	+2.9
US total	**329,821**	**773,919**	**1,527,929**	**1,570,861**	**+2.8**

[1]*Jails and prisons are part of an integrated system. Data include total jail and prison population.* [2]*Population figures are based on custody counts.* [3]*Negligible.* [4]*At the end of 2001, the transfer of responsibility for sentenced felons from the District of Columbia to the Federal Bureau of Prisons was completed, so the District of Columbia no longer operates a prison system, and its prisoners are from that date forward included in federal data only.*

Death Penalty Sentences in the US

This table excludes military and federal sentences and executions. Sources: US Bureau of Justice Statistics; Death Penalty Information Center; NAACP Legal Defense and Educational Fund, Inc.

STATE	EXECUTIONS 1976–PRESENT[1]	2007	PRISONERS UNDER DEATH SENTENCE (AS OF 1 JAN 2008)[2]	SOME DEATH-PENALTY CRIMES
Alabama	38	3	201	intentional murder[3]
Alaska	—	—	—	no death penalty
Arizona	23	1	114	1st-degree murder[3]
Arkansas	27	0	38	capital murder[3]; treason
California	13	0	669	1st-degree murder[3]; treason; train wrecking
Colorado	1	0	1	1st-degree murder[3]; treason
Connecticut	1	0	9	capital felony (8 types of aggravated murder)
Delaware	14	0	19	1st-degree murder[3]
District of Columbia	—	—	—	no death penalty
Florida	64	0	388	1st-degree murder; felonious murder; capital drug trafficking; capital sexual battery
Georgia	40	1	107	murder; treason; aircraft hijacking; kidnapping[4]
Hawaii	—	—	—	no death penalty
Idaho	1	0	19	1st-degree murder[3]; aggravated kidnapping
Illinois	12	0	13	1st-degree murder[3]

Death Penalty Sentences in the US (continued)

STATE	EXECUTIONS 1976–PRESENT[1]	EXECUTIONS 2007	PRISONERS UNDER DEATH SENTENCE (AS OF 1 JAN 2008)[2]	SOME DEATH-PENALTY CRIMES
Indiana	19	2	20	murder[3]
Iowa	—	—	—	no death penalty
Kansas	0	0	10	capital murder[3]
Kentucky	2	0	39	murder[3]; aggravated kidnapping
Louisiana	27	0	85	1st-degree murder; treason; rape[5]
Maine	—	—	—	no death penalty
Maryland	5	0	5	1st-degree murder[6]
Massachusetts	—	—	—	no death penalty
Michigan	—	—	—	no death penalty
Minnesota	—	—	—	no death penalty
Mississippi	8	0	65	capital murder; aircraft hijacking
Missouri	66	0	45	1st-degree murder
Montana	3	0	2	capital murder[3]; capital sexual assault
Nebraska	3	0	10	1st-degree murder[3]
Nevada	12	0	83	1st-degree murder[3]
New Hampshire	0	0	0	capital murder (6 types)
New Jersey	—	—	—	no death penalty
New Mexico	1	0	1	1st-degree murder[3]
New York	—	—	—	no death penalty
North Carolina	43	0	166	1st-degree murder
North Dakota	—	—	—	no death penalty
Ohio	26	2	186	murder[3]
Oklahoma	86	3	82	1st-degree murder[3]
Oregon	2	0	35	murder[3]
Pennsylvania	3	0	228	1st-degree murder[3]
Rhode Island	—	—	—	no death penalty
South Carolina	37	1	58	murder[3]
South Dakota	1	1	3	1st-degree murder[3]; aggravated kidnapping
Tennessee	4	2	96	1st-degree murder[3]
Texas	405	26	370	criminal homicide[3]
Utah	6	0	10	murder[3]
Vermont	—	—	—	no death penalty
Virginia	98	0	20	1st-degree murder[3]
Washington	4	0	8	1st-degree murder[3]
West Virginia	—	—	—	no death penalty
Wisconsin	—	—	—	no death penalty
Wyoming	1	0	2	1st-degree murder
totals[7]	**1,099**	**42**	**3,263**	

[1]In 1976 the US Supreme Court ruled that capital punishment was not unconstitutional. [2]In mid-2002 the Supreme Court ruled that juries, not judges, must make decisions determining death penalty cases and that it was unconstitutional to execute mentally retarded offenders. [3]With aggravating factors or circumstances. [4]With bodily injury or ransom when the victim dies. [5]Aggravated rape of a victim under 12. [6]Premeditated or committed during the act of a felony and meeting certain death penalty requirements. [7]Detail may not add to total given because of inclusion of federal and military executions and prisoners.

Directors of the Federal Bureau of Investigation (FBI)

The FBI evolved from an unnamed force appointed by Attorney General Charles J. Bonaparte on 26 Jul 1908. It is the unit of the Department of Justice responsible for investigating foreign intelligence and terrorist activities and violations of federal criminal law. The president appoints the director of the FBI with confirmation from the Senate. Since J. Edgar Hoover's tenure, a director's term may not exceed 10 years. Acting directors are not included in this table.

NAME	DATES OF SERVICE
Stanley Finch	26 Jul 1908–30 Apr 1912
Alexander Bruce Bielaski	30 Apr 1912–10 Feb 1919
William J. Flynn	1 Jul 1919–21 Aug 1921
William J. Burns	22 Aug 1921–14 Jun 1924
J. Edgar Hoover	10 Dec 1924–2 May 1972
Clarence M. Kelley	9 Jul 1973–15 Feb 1978
William H. Webster	23 Feb 1978–25 May 1987
William S. Sessions	2 Nov 1987–19 Jul 1993
Louis J. Freeh	1 Sep 1993–25 Jun 2001
Robert S. Mueller, III	4 Sep 2001–

Society

Family

Average Family Size, 1950–2006

Source: US Census Bureau.

YEAR	NUMBER OF FAMILIES ('000)	PEOPLE PER FAMILY (AVERAGE)	YEAR	NUMBER OF FAMILIES ('000)	PEOPLE PER FAMILY (AVERAGE)	YEAR	NUMBER OF FAMILIES ('000)	PEOPLE PER FAMILY (AVERAGE)
1950	39,303	3.54	1970	51,586	3.58	1990	66,090	3.17
1955	41,951	3.59	1975	55,712	3.42	1995	69,305	3.19
1960	45,111	3.67	1980	59,550	3.29	2000	72,025	3.17
1965	47,956	3.70	1985	62,706	3.23	2006	74,564	3.20

US Population by Age

Numbers are in thousands ('000). Source: US Census Bureau midyear 2008 estimate. Detail may not add to total given because of rounding.

AGE	POPULATION NUMBER	(%)	AGE	POPULATION NUMBER	(%)
under 5 years	21,009,914	6.9	55 to 64 years	33,720,059	11.1
5 to 9 years	20,155,574	6.6	65 to 74 years	20,054,212	6.6
10 to 14 years	19,981,265	6.6	75 years and over	18,635,957	6.1
15 to 19 years	21,728,978	7.2	total population	303,824,646	100.0
20 to 24 years	21,186,421	7.0			
25 to 34 years	40,692,640	13.3	under 20 years	82,875,731	27.3
35 to 44 years	42,338,149	13.9	20 years and over	220,948,915	72.7
45 to 54 years	44,321,477	14.6	65 years and over	38,690,169	12.7

Living Arrangements of Children Under 18 in the US, 2006

Numbers in thousands ('000). Hispanics may be of any race. Detail may not add to total given because of rounding. Source: US Census Bureau.

	RACE			
LIVING IN HOUSEHOLD WITH:	ALL RACES	WHITE	BLACK	HISPANIC
both parents	49,650	41,573	3,884	9,685
mother only	17,164	10,083	5,747	3,674
father only	3,462	2,591	539	603
neither parent	3,389	2,028	1,055	735
totals	73,664	56,332	11,225	14,697

Children Under 18 Living Below the Poverty Level, 1983–2006

Numbers are in thousands ('000). Hispanics may be of any race. N/A means not available. Source: US Census Bureau. For the definition of the poverty level, see <www.census.gov/hhes/poverty/povdef.html>.

	% OF CHILDREN BELOW THE POVERTY LEVEL					NUMBER OF CHILDREN BELOW THE POVERTY LEVEL				
YEAR	ALL[1]	WHITE[2]	BLACK[2]	ASIAN/ PACIFIC ISLANDER[2]	HISPANIC	ALL[1]	WHITE[2]	BLACK[2]	ASIAN/ PACIFIC ISLANDER[2]	HISPANIC
1983	22.3	14.8	46.7	N/A	38.1	13,911	6,649	4,398	N/A	2,312
1984	21.5	13.7	46.6	N/A	39.2	13,420	6,156	4,413	N/A	2,376
1985	20.7	12.8	43.6	N/A	40.3	13,010	5,745	4,157	N/A	2,606
1986	20.5	13.0	43.1	N/A	37.7	12,876	5,789	4,148	N/A	2,507
1987	20.3	11.8	45.1	23.5	39.3	12,843	5,230	4,385	455	2,670
1988	19.5	11.0	43.5	24.1	37.6	12,455	4,888	4,296	474	2,631
1989	19.6	11.5	43.7	19.8	36.2	12,590	5,110	4,375	392	2,603
1990	20.6	12.3	44.8	17.6	38.4	13,431	5,532	4,550	374	2,865
1991	21.8	13.1	45.9	17.5	40.4	14,341	5,918	4,755	360	3,094
1992	22.3	13.2	46.6	16.4	40.0	15,294	6,017	5,106	363	3,637
1993	22.7	13.6	46.1	18.2	40.9	15,727	6,255	5,125	375	3,873
1994	21.8	12.5	43.8	18.3	41.5	15,289	5,823	4,906	318	4,075
1995	20.8	11.2	41.9	19.5	40.0	14,665	5.115	4,761	564	4,080
1996	20.5	11.1	39.9	19.5	40.3	14,463	5,072	4,519	571	4,237
1997	19.9	11.4	37.2	20.3	36.8	14,113	5,204	4,225	628	3,972

Children Under 18 Living Below the Poverty Level, 1983–2006 (continued)

	% OF CHILDREN BELOW THE POVERTY LEVEL					NUMBER OF CHILDREN BELOW THE POVERTY LEVEL				
YEAR	ALL[1]	WHITE[2]	BLACK[2]	ASIAN/ PACIFIC ISLANDER[2]	HISPANIC	ALL[1]	WHITE[2]	BLACK[2]	ASIAN/ PACIFIC ISLANDER[2]	HISPANIC
1998	18.9	10.6	36.7	18.0	34.4	13,467	4,822	4,151	564	3,837
1999	16.9	9.4	33.2	11.9	30.3	12,280	4,155	3,813	381	3,693
2000	16.2	9.1	31.2	12.7	28.4	11,587	4,018	3,581	420	3,522
2001	16.3	9.5	30.2	11.5	28.0	11,733	4,194	3,492	369	3,570
2002	16.7	9.4	32.3	11.7[3]	28.6	12,133	4,090	3,645	315[3]	3,782
2003	17.6	9.8	34.1	12.5[3]	29.7	12,866	4,233	3,877	344[3]	4,077
2004	17.8	10.5	33.7	9.8[3]	28.9	13,041	4,519	3,788	281[3]	4,098
2005	17.6	10.0	34.5	11.0[3]	28.3	12,896	4,254	3,841	317[3]	4,143
2006	17.4	14.1	33.4	12.5	N/A	12,827	7,908	3,777	391	N/A

[1]*Includes other and unclassified.* [2]*Excludes Hispanic population.* [3]*Excludes Pacific Islanders.*

Child Care Arrangements in the US

This table is based on sample surveys of households with children three to five years old who were not yet in kindergarten. Day-care centers, Head Start programs, preschools, prekindergarten, and nursery schools were included as center-based programs. Detail may not add to total given because of rounding and because some children participated in more than one type of nonparental arrangement.

Source: US National Center for Education Statistics.

YEAR OF SURVEY	CHILDREN NUMBER	CHILDREN (%)	UNDER PARENTAL CARE (%)	UNDER A RELATIVE'S CARE (%)	UNDER A NONRELATIVE'S CARE (%)	IN A CENTER-BASED PROGRAM (%)
1999	8,525,000	100.0	23.1	22.8	16.1	59.7
2001[1]	8,551,000	100.0	27.0	21.0	13.0	56.0
2005[1]	9,066,000	100.0	27.0	29.0	15.0	78.0

details from the 2005 survey[1, 2]

FEATURE	CHILDREN NUMBER	CHILDREN (%)	UNDER PARENTAL CARE (%)	UNDER A RELATIVE'S CARE (%)	UNDER A NONRELATIVE'S CARE (%)	IN A CENTER-BASED PROGRAM (%)
total	20,665,000	100.0	40.0	35.0	22.0	60.0
sex						
male	10,598,000	51.3	40.0	33.0	22.0	62.0
female	10,067,000	48.7	41.0	37.0	23.0	58.0
race/ethnic group						
white, non-Hispanic	11,488,000	55.6	38.0	32.0	26.0	61.0
black, non-Hispanic	2,962,000	14.3	31.0	38.0	15.0	63.0
Hispanic	4,283,000	20.7	51.0	41.0	20.0	51.0
other, non-Hispanic	1,933,000	9.4	42.4	38.6	14.7	65.4
household income						
less than US$25,001	5,912,000	28.6	49.0	43.0	16.0	57.0
US$25,001–50,000	5,256,000	25.4	47.0	42.0	19.0	55.0
US$50,001–75,000	4,307,000	20.8	39.0	31.0	27.0	58.0
US$75,001–100,000	2,445,000	11.8	27.0	26.0	26.0	63.0
more than US$100,000	2,746,000	13.3	21.0	26.0	27.0	70.0

[1]*Data for type of care are rounded to whole numbers.* [2]*Data are for ages five and younger.*

Children in the US Living with Nonparents

Children under 18 years of age, 2006. Numbers in thousands ('000). Detail may not add to total given because of rounding. Source: US Census Bureau.

	YEARS OF AGE			
LIVING ARRANGEMENT	UNDER 6	6–11	12–17	UNDER 18
with grandparent	404	489	591	1,484
with other relative	205	201	529	935
in foster home	103	58	81	241
with other nonrelative	205	188	330	723

US Adoptions of Foreign-Born Children

Adoptions of foreign children by US citizens are tracked by the number of immigrant visas issued to orphans entering the US. Source: US Department of State.

TOP 10 COUNTRIES OF ORIGIN	ADOPTIONS FISCAL YEAR 2006	2007
1. China	6,493	5,453
2. Guatemala	4,135	4,728
3. Russia	3,706	2,310
4. Ethiopia	732	1,255
5. South Korea	1,376	939
6. Vietnam	163	828
7. Ukraine	460	606
8. Kazakhstan	587	540
9. India	320	416
10. Liberia	353	314

TOTAL FOREIGN ADOPTIONS FISCAL YEAR	
2002	20,099
2003	21,616
2004	22,884
2005	22,728
2006	20,679
2007	19,613

US Nursing Home Population

The data in these tables were gathered through interviews conducted for the most recent National Nursing Home Survey (2004) and through the publication *Health, United States, 2007.* Only those residents who described themselves as being of one race are included. Data on residents under the age of 65 are not available. Detail may not add to total given because of rounding.

Source: US National Center for Health Statistics.

AGE AT INTERVIEW	TOTAL RESIDENTS	%	GENDER (2004) MALE	%	FEMALE	%
65–74	174,100	13.2	75,400	22.4	98,800	10.1
75–84	468,900	35.6	140,800	41.8	328,000	33.5
85 and older	674,200	51.2	120,600	35.8	553,600	56.5
total	**1,317,200**	**100.0**	**336,800**	**100.0**	**980,400**	**100.0**

	RACE (2004) WHITE	%	BLACK	%
65–74	134,200	11.7	34,500	23.7
75–84	406,000	35.3	54,600	37.6
85 and older	608,600	53.0	56,300	38.7
total	**1,148,800**	**100.0**	**145,400**	**100.0**

	RESIDENT LOCATION (1999) NORTHWEST	%	MIDWEST	%	SOUTH	%	WEST	%
65–74	46,400	12.1	58,900	11.8	63,400	11.9	26,100	12.1
75–84	118,500	30.9	153,200	30.8	179,100	33.7	66,800	31.1
85 and older	184,300	48.1	241,100	48.4	237,700	44.7	94,000	43.7
total	**383,400**	**100.0**	**498,200**	**100.0**	**531,500**	**100.0**	**215,200**	**100.0**

	RESIDENT LOCATION (2006) NORTHEAST	%	MIDWEST	%	SOUTH	%	WEST	%
TOTAL RESIDENTS	336,000	23.4	416,800	29.1	485,200	33.8	195,600	13.6

Unmarried-Couple Households in the US

Data based on Current Population Survey or American Community Survey except for census years of 1960 and 1970. 2005 data shown separately. Numbers in thousands ('000). Source: US Census Bureau.

YEAR	TOTAL US HOUSEHOLDS	UNMARRIED-COUPLE HOUSEHOLDS (OPPOSITE SEX)	% OF TOTAL HOUSEHOLDS	NO CHILDREN UNDER 15	WITH CHILDREN UNDER 15
1960 census	52,799	439	0.8	242	197
1970 census	63,401	523	0.8	327	196
1980	80,776	1,589	2.0	1,159	431
1985	86,789	1,983	2.3	1,380	603
1990	93,347	2,856	3.1	1,966	891
1995	98,990	3,668	3.7	2,349	1,319
2000	104,705	4,736	4.5	3,061	1,675

UNMARRIED-COUPLE HOUSEHOLDS	2005
male householder/female partner	2,660
male householder/male partner	413
female householder/female partner	364
female householder/male partner	2,529
unmarried-couple households	**5,966**
total households	**111,091**

Marital Status of Population by Sex, 1950–2006

The data in this table are taken from surveys of individuals 18 or over conducted by the US Census Bureau and exclude members of the armed forces except those living off post or with their families on post. Data exclude Alaska and Hawaii prior to 1960. Detail may not add to total given because of rounding.
Source: US Census Bureau.

	TOTAL						
	1950	1960	1970	1980	1990	2000	2006
Total individuals surveyed in hundred thousands ('000,000)	111.7	125.5	132.5	159.5	181.8	201.8	219.7
Percentage of individuals never married	22.8	22.0	16.2	20.3	22.2	23.9	25.2
Percentage of individuals married	67.0	67.3	71.7	65.5	61.9	59.5	58.1
Percentage of individuals widowed	8.3	8.4	8.9	8.0	7.6	6.8	6.3
Percentage of individuals divorced	1.9	2.3	3.2	6.2	8.3	9.8	10.4
Percentage of males never married	26.2	25.3	18.9	23.8	25.8	27.0	28.6
Percentage of males married	68.0	69.1	75.3	68.4	64.3	61.5	59.9
Percentage of males widowed	4.2	3.7	3.3	2.6	2.7	2.7	2.5
Percentage of males divorced	1.7	1.9	2.5	5.2	7.2	8.8	9.1
Percentage of females never married	11.1	12.3	13.7	17.1	18.9	21.1	22.0
Percentage of females married	37.6	42.6	68.5	63.0	59.7	57.6	56.5
Percentage of females widowed	7.0	8.3	13.9	12.8	12.1	10.5	9.9
Percentage of females divorced	1.2	1.7	3.9	7.1	9.3	10.8	11.6

United States Education

Educational Attainment by Gender and Race

For people 25 years old and older. Percentage rates for 1960, 1970, and 1980 are based on sample data from the decennial censuses. Rates for 1990, 2000, and 2006 are based on the Current Population Survey.
Source: US Census Bureau.

Percentage who had graduated from high school[1]

	ALL RACES[2]		WHITE		BLACK		HISPANIC[3]		ASIAN/PACIFIC ISLANDER	
CENSUS	MALE	FEMALE	MALE	FEMALE	MALE	FEMALE	MALE	FEMALE	MALE	FEMALE
1960	39.5	42.5	41.6	44.7	18.2	21.8	N/A	N/A	N/A	N/A
1970	51.9	52.8	54.0	55.0	30.1	32.5	37.9	34.2	N/A	N/A
1980	67.3	65.8	69.6	68.1	50.8	51.5	67.3	65.8	N/A	N/A
1990	77.7	77.5	79.1	79.0	65.8	66.5	50.3	51.3	84.0	77.2
2000	84.2	84.0	84.8	85.0	78.7	78.3	56.6	57.5	88.2	83.4
2006	85.0	85.9	85.5	86.7	80.1	81.2	58.5	60.1	89.6	85.5

Percentage who had graduated from college[4]

	ALL RACES[2]		WHITE		BLACK		HISPANIC[3]		ASIAN/PACIFIC ISLANDER	
CENSUS	MALE	FEMALE	MALE	FEMALE	MALE	FEMALE	MALE	FEMALE	MALE	FEMALE
1960	9.7	5.8	10.3	6.0	2.8	3.3	N/A	N/A	N/A	N/A
1970	13.5	8.1	14.4	8.4	4.2	4.6	7.8	4.3	N/A	N/A
1980	20.1	12.8	21.3	13.3	8.4	8.3	9.4	6.0	N/A	N/A
1990	24.4	18.4	25.3	19.0	11.9	10.8	9.8	8.7	44.9	35.4
2000	27.8	23.6	28.5	23.9	16.3	16.7	10.7	10.6	47.6	40.7
2006	29.2	26.9	29.7	27.1	17.2	19.4	11.9	12.9	52.5	47.1

N/A means not available. [1]Through 1990, finished four years or more of high school. [2]Includes races not shown separately in the table. [3]Hispanics may be of any race. [4]Through 1990, finished four years or more of college.

The original color of the US president's residence was the pale grey of the sandstone from which it was built, but it was called the "White House" as early as 1809 because the light sandstone contrasted sharply with the red brick of nearby buildings. It was not until 1902, however, that the building was officially renamed the "White House" by Pres. Theodore Roosevelt.

National Spelling Bee

A spelling bee is a contest or game in which players attempt to spell correctly and aloud words assigned them by an impartial judge. Competition may be individual, with players eliminated when they misspell a word and the last remaining player being the winner, or between teams, the winner being the team with the most players remaining at the close of the contest. The spelling bee is an old custom that was revived in schools in the United States in the late 19th century and enjoyed a great vogue there and in Great Britain. In the US, local, regional, and national competitions continue to be held annually. The US National Spelling Bee was begun by the Louisville *Courier-Journal* newspaper in 1925, and it was taken over by Scripps Howard, Inc., in 1941. To qualify, spellers must meet nine requirements, including that they have neither reached their 16th birthday nor passed beyond the eighth grade.

National Spelling Bee Web site: <www.spellingbee.com>.

YEAR	CHAMPION	WINNING WORD
1925	Frank Neuhauser	gladiolus
1926	Pauline Bell	cerise
1927	Dean Lucas	luxuriance
1928	Betty Robinson	albumen
1929	Virginia Hogan	asceticism
1930	Helen Jensen	fracas
1931	Ward Randall	foulard
1932	Dorothy Greenwald	knack
1933	Alma Roach	torsion
1934	Sarah Wilson	deteriorating
1935	Clara Mohler	intelligible
1936	Jean Trowbridge	interning
1937	Waneeta Beckley	promiscuous
1938	Marian Richardson	sanitarium
1939	Elizabeth Ann Rice	canonical
1940	Laurel Kuykendall	therapy
1941	Louis Edward Sissman	initials
1942	Richard Earnhart	sacrilegious
1943–45		*not held*
1946	John McKinney	semaphore
1947	Mattie Lou Pollard	chlorophyll
1948	Jean Chappelear	psychiatry
1949	Kim Calvin	dulcimer
1950	Diana Reynard; Colquitt Dean (tied)	meticulosity
1951	Irving Belz	insouciant
1952	Doris Ann Hall	vignette
1953	Elizabeth Hess	soubrette
1954	William Cashore	transept
1955	Sandra Sloss	crustaceology
1956	Melody Sachko	condominium
1957	Sandra Owen; Dana Bennett (tied)	schappe
1958	Jolitta Schlehuber	syllepsis
1959	Joel Montgomery	catamaran
1960	Henry Feldman	eudaemonic
1961	John Capehart	smaragdine
1962	Nettie Crawford; Michael Day (tied)	esquamulose
1963	Glen Van Slyke III	equipage
1964	William Kerek	sycophant
1965	Michael Kerpan, Jr.	eczema
1966	Robert A. Wake	ratoon
1967	Jennifer Reinke	chihuahua
1968	Robert L. Walters	abalone
1969	Susan Yoachum	interlocutory
1970	Libby Childress	croissant
1971	Jonathan Knisely	shalloon
1972	Robin Kral	macerate
1973	Barrie Trinkle	vouchsafe
1974	Julie Ann Junkin	hydrophyte
1975	Hugh Tosteson	incisor
1976	Tim Kneale	narcolepsy
1977	John Paola	cambist
1978	Peg McCarthy	deification
1979	Katie Kerwin	maculature
1980	Jacques Bailly	elucubrate
1981	Paige Pipkin	sarcophagus
1982	Molly Dieveney	psoriasis
1983	Blake Giddens	Purim
1984	Daniel Greenblatt	luge
1985	Balu Natarajan	milieu
1986	Jon Pennington	odontalgia
1987	Stephanie Petit	staphylococci
1988	Rageshree Ramachandran	elegiacal
1989	Scott Isaacs	spoliator
1990	Amy Marie Dimak	fibranne
1991	Joanne Lagatta	antipyretic
1992	Amanda Goad	lyceum
1993	Geoff Hooper	kamikaze
1994	Ned G. Andrews	antediluvian
1995	Justin Tyler Carroll	xanthosis
1996	Wendy Guey	vivisepulture
1997	Rebecca Sealfon	euonym
1998	Jody-Anne Maxwell	chiaroscurist
1999	Nupur Lala	logorrhea
2000	George Abraham Thampy	demarche
2001	Sean Conley	succedaneum
2002	Pratyush Buddiga	prospicience
2003	Sai R. Gunturi	pococurante
2004	David Tidmarsh	autochthonous
2005	Anurag Kashyap	appoggiatura
2006	Kerry Close	Ursprache
2007	Evan M. O'Dorney	serrefine
2008	Sameer Mishra	guerdon

Business

The New President's Economy Problem

by Justin Fox, TIME

In the waning minutes of his only TV debate with Democratic incumbent Jimmy Carter in 1980, Ronald Reagan looked straight into the camera and asked, "Are you better off than you were four years ago?" It was a defining question of the campaign—and of late 20th-century American politics. It was also pretty easy to answer. The "misery index," a then-popular measure that added the unemployment rate to the inflation rate, had skyrocketed during Carter's tenure. Taxes had risen sharply. There *were* other issues on voters' minds, like the Iranian hostage crisis and those dang cardigans Carter used to wear. But the economy was crucial to Reagan's victory. After taking office, he responded by ushering in a new era in economic policy—cutting tax rates, slashing regulation, and tirelessly preaching the gospel that individual Americans were better suited to make economic decisions than bureaucrats in Washington were.

This election year, the economy has again been at the forefront of voters' minds.

The misery index is no longer the problem; at 9% and change at midyear, it was miles below the 20% of late 1980. But Americans have a new menu of economic woes—among them a real-estate crash, a credit crisis, a broken health care system, and nagging job insecurity. Poll after poll show a vast majority convinced that the economy and the country are headed in the wrong direction. And that is a problem for the Republican Party: history shows that slow economic growth is among the best predictors of a change in party control of the White House—and in 2008 the economy has barely grown at all.

The bigger issue for voters to wrestle with, though, is not what the economy can do to the presidential race but what the next president can do to the economy. Usually it's not so much. But every once in a while, like when Franklin Delano Roosevelt was elected in 1932 and Reagan in 1980, the effect can be dramatic. Reagan's policies, together with some luck and the inflation-killing zeal of Federal Reserve Chairman Paul Volcker, helped the US economy break out of its 1970s malaise into a new era of flexibility, innovation, and growth. Subsequent presidents, even Democrat Bill Clinton, followed more or less in Reagan's footsteps.

Economic eras don't last forever, though, and there are signs that the current slowdown is a harbinger of something bigger: an end to America's 25-year love affair with tax cuts and deregulation. A lot of the cracks that have emerged during that time have become impossible to ignore—stagnant incomes, a federal budget gone way out of balance, soaring energy prices, a once-in-a-lifetime housing crash, and growing financial risks in retirement and from health care.

What it adds up to is a generalized sense of economic insecurity that has dimmed many Americans' optimism about their future. So there's a chance that the 2008 election could turn out to be a major economic turning point, just like 1980's was. Economic trouble begets economic change. Here's what may be in the offing.

America Needs a Raise. If you feel as if you've been going backward, you haven't been imagining it. According to the US Census Bureau, the median American family made US$58,407 in 2006. That's US$991 less, when you adjust for inflation, than the median in 2000, and indications are that things haven't gotten any better in 2007 or this year.

Recessions—like the one in 2001 and the one we might be in now—always reduce incomes. The problem since 2000 is that even when the economy was growing, the fruits of that growth landed almost exclusively in the pockets of the wealthiest Americans. According to economists Thomas Piketty and Emanuel Saez, 75% of all income gains from 2002 to 2006 went to the top 1%—households making more than US$382,600 a year.

The gap between high and low earners has been growing since the late 1970s, and until recently, economists attributed virtually all of it to technological and demographic changes that increased the premium paid to those with advanced skills and education. If that were true, the only answer would lie along the arduous path of improving the education and skill levels of American workers. And you certainly wouldn't want to discourage people from getting an education by heavily taxing the rewards for it.

But according to Piketty and Saez, the really dramatic gains have all been at the very, very top—not the top 1% but the top 0.01%, who now control 5.46% of all income, their highest share on record. (The data go back to 1913.) Most of these people are well educated, but it's awfully hard to portray their riches purely as rewards for education or skill.

Many economists now believe at least two other factors have contributed to the growth in inequality: globalization and Reagan's big cuts in taxes on the rich. Even as it rewards those at the top of their fields worldwide with spectacular paydays, globalization holds down earnings for millions of Americans who compete with workers overseas—not only lower-skilled factory and phone-center workers but also engineers, lawyers, and doctors. Public opinion has reacted to this with increasing distrust of free trade, a wariness that has been evident during the election campaign. But this is touchy territory: trade may distort the income distribution, but economists remain almost unanimous in warning that restricting trade would slow overall growth.

To the extent they talk about it at all, the two parties take different approaches to closing the income gap. Democrat Barack Obama in particular is explicit about wanting to shift more of the income-tax burden away from the middle class and onto those making more than US$200,000 a year, while Republican John McCain speaks mainly about creating better job-retraining programs for those displaced by globalization. Another potential path, though it hasn't been a major theme in the campaign as of late summer, would be a big effort to repair the country's crumbling infrastructure—which would create lots of jobs that couldn't be outsourced overseas and would also deliver long-term economic benefits. In any case, the income gap is an issue that's been danced around for too long. It's time to address it.

Tax Cuts and Deficits. In general, we levy taxes not to ease income inequality but to fund government. They haven't quite been doing the job lately: for the 2008 fiscal year, which ends in September, it is estimated that the government will spend roughly US$500 billion more than it takes in, a deficit of 3.5% of GDP. That should shrink when the economy starts growing again, but it's not going to disappear without either big cuts in spending or substantial tax increases.

And make no mistake, somebody is going to have to pay those bills someday.

The message many Republicans took from Reagan's successes of the early 1980s, and still preach today, is that tax cuts pay for themselves. That's nonsense—Reagan's rate cuts for the rich may have paid for themselves, but the 1981 tax package as a whole (which included cuts for the poor, the middle class, and corporations) clearly did not. The real lesson of the 1980s was that the US can get away with running far bigger deficits than anyone thought possible while still enjoying strong growth and low inflation.

We've seen a bit more evidence of this in the 2000s, but it can't go on forever. There comes a point at which government debts grow so large that they start to weigh on the economy, through higher interest rates, bigger debt payments, a weaker currency, etc. Reagan and George W. Bush had the advantage of starting out with a relatively small debt as a percentage of GDP. The next president won't be quite so lucky.

The reductions in tax rates on income, capital gains, and corporate dividends that President Bush pushed through in 2001 and 2003 are due to expire in 2010. That could prove a tough blow for a still-wobbly economy to weather, but it would help shrink the deficit over time. The deficit quandary is one for which neither of the candidates have an entirely convincing answer. But the winner in November will be forced to arrive at one once in office.

We Need an Energy Policy. One of the biggest factors in making paychecks seem smaller in recent years has been the sharp increase in energy prices. There's very little a president can do to change this in the short term. Where presidents (and Congress) can have a big impact is in the long-term trajectory of energy prices and their effect on the economy. Elected officials can do this by steering Americans away from oil and toward other energy sources and conservation measures—or by failing to do so, which has been the laissez-faire policy of the past quarter century and has helped land us in our current sorry situation.

What makes doing the right thing on energy difficult is that it would almost inevitably involve raising costs now, with higher taxes on oil, increased subsidies for other energy sources, or higher energy-efficiency standards for vehicles and homes—or all three. Economists tend to prefer the first of these approaches because taxes on gas, oil, or fossil fuels in general tamp demand and allow the market—rather than members of Congress—to sift out the best alternatives.

As a rule, presidential candidates not named Ross Perot don't propose fuel-tax hikes. Interestingly, though, to fight global warming, McCain and Obama favor a carbon-cap-and-trade regimen, which would raise the price of fossil fuels just as surely as a direct tax would. Almost in spite of ourselves, we may end up with a semirational long-term energy policy. It won't make gas cheaper anytime soon—or perhaps ever—but in the long run, it could strengthen the country's economic prospects.

The Costly American Home. Some 1.5 million US homes fell into foreclosure in 2007, and the number is ballooning in 2008. The mess has caused some economists to question why we subsidize housing so heavily to begin with. The tax deduction for home-mortgage interest alone costs the government about US$80 billion a year, and most of that benefit flows to the wealthiest 16% of taxpayers, according to the Tax Foundation. It also means we're subsidizing bigger houses and home-equity loans, possibly at the expense of other investments that might deliver a bigger economic bang.

Several countries have dropped the mortgage-interest deduction in recent years, with no noticeably adverse effects, but there's no indication that any of our presidential candidates are contemplating such a move. What is likely to be on the next administration's agenda are measures to restrain Wall Street—which, by buying and repackaging hundreds of billions of dollars in dodgy home loans, has played a key role in bringing on the housing bubble and bust.

What hasn't really been answered yet is whether we need an entirely new regulatory approach. Ever since Reagan took office, the approach has been to get out of the way and let financial markets work their magic. Now that it's clear just how much of this is black magic, there's a case to be made that financial innovation—especially when it's targeted at consumers—could do with much stricter oversight.

Health Care and Retirement. In the seminal 1980 PBS series *Free to Choose,* which may have helped set the mood for Reagan's victory, economist Milton Friedman argued that economic freedom was just as important as all those freedoms written into the Bill of Rights. This went on to become perhaps the most consistent theme of the Reagan economic era: giving Americans the freedom to succeed or fail on their own economically was a good thing. And it is probably a good thing. But not an unmitigated good. Economic security matters to Americans too.

And finding ways to offer more of it may be the basis of the next big economic-policy revolution.

Economic changes over the past three decades—many the result of government decisions—have "left working families up and down much of the income spectrum living with fewer economic protections, bearing more economic risk, chancing steeper financial falls," writes *Los Angeles Times* reporter Peter Gosselin in his 2008 book *High Wire: The Precarious Financial Lives of American Families.*

That you're-on-your-own ethos is already beginning to change—a little. In 2006 Congress passed a law that has brought positive changes to the 401(k) savings plans that for many Americans have replaced pensions. But the majority of private-sector workers in the country aren't offered a 401(k) or a pension. Both candidates talk of creating a new system of portable retirement accounts for those who don't get one through employers, with Obama's plan the most ambitious.

Then there's health care, which has become perhaps the biggest source of financial worry and occasional disaster among middle-class Americans. It is possible to conceive of a system that brings the 47 million uninsured into the fold, improves medical outcomes, and costs less than what we've got now. It's possible to conceive of because many other wealthy countries already have such systems. If you're looking for big economic change from the next Administration, this is the form it's likely to take.

The key, really, is to accept what works about the existing US economy and attack what doesn't. Reagan never dismantled the core elements of the New Deal, and the new president needs to take care not to thwart the dynamism unleashed by Reagan. But putting off change won't be an option much longer.

US Economy

The US Mint

The US Mint, the world's largest producer of coins and medals, was established by Congress on 2 Apr 1792. It is a bureau of the US Department of the Treasury. The mint manufactures and distributes coins, protects the country's gold and silver assets, and creates medals, commemorative coins, and coin proof sets for purchase by the public. In 2007 it produced 14.5 billion pennies, nickels, dimes, quarters, half dollars, and golden dollars. The director of the mint is appointed by the president and serves a five-year term; in mid-2008 the director was Edmund C. Moy.

From its Washington DC headquarters, the mint operates facilities in Philadelphia PA, Denver CO, San Francisco CA, and West Point NY. All engraving of coins is done at the Philadelphia site (established 1792), where general circulation coins, medals, and coin dies are also produced. Denver (1863) manufactures general circulation coins and coin dies and provides storage for gold and silver bullion. San Francisco (1854) produces only commemorative coins and proof sets; West Point (1937) manufactures uncirculated and proof sets of gold, silver, and platinum coins and stores these metals. The mint is also responsible for the storage and protection of more than 145 million ounces of gold bullion at Fort Knox, Kentucky.

Although general circulation coins were once made from gold, silver, and copper, this is no longer the case. Gold coin production was discontinued in 1933, and in 1966 silver ceased to be used in dimes and quarters. Currently, pennies are composed of copper-plated zinc, golden dollar coins of manganese brass, and all other general circulation coins of cupronickel, an alloy of copper and nickel. In early 2000 the mint began circulating the golden dollar coin, intended to replace the older Susan B. Anthony dollar coin. The new coin featured the image of Sacagawea, the Shoshone Indian woman who traveled as a guide with the Lewis and Clark Expedition in 1804–06. In 1999 the mint began issuing a series of quarters featuring the 50 states. Five quarters were to be issued annually, about 10 weeks apart, each featuring one state's design. State quarters were released in order of the states' ratification of the US Constitution. Introduced in 2007 were Idaho, Montana, Utah, Washington, and Wyoming; in 2008, Alaska, Arizona, Hawaii, New Mexico, and Oklahoma. Nickels commemorating the Lewis and Clark Expedition were released in 2004 and 2005; those issued in 2005 featured a slightly different portrait of Thomas Jefferson. Dollar coins commemorating the US presidents were issued beginning in 2007, with subjects released in the order that they served. The coins are the same size, weight, and metal composition as the Sacagawea golden dollar and have an image of the Statue of Liberty on the back. Only deceased presidents are planned subjects, and currently the schedule of production runs through 2016.

US Mint Web site: <www.usmint.gov>.

Denominations of US Currency

PAPER MONEY

VALUE	PORTRAIT ON FRONT	DESIGN ON BACK	WHEN CIRCULATED
$1	George Washington	Great Seal of US	1929–
$2	Thomas Jefferson	Monticello	1929–75
$2	Thomas Jefferson	John Trumbull's *Signing of the Declaration of Independence*	1976–
$5[1]	Abraham Lincoln	Lincoln Memorial	2000–
$10[1]	Alexander Hamilton	US Treasury	2000–
$20[1]	Andrew Jackson	White House	1998–
$50[1]	Ulysses S. Grant	US Capitol	1997–
$100[1]	Benjamin Franklin	Independence Hall	1996–
$500[2]	William McKinley	ornate figure of value	1929–69
$1,000[2]	Grover Cleveland	ornate figure of value	1929–69
$5,000[2]	James Madison	ornate figure of value	1929–69
$10,000[2]	Salmon P. Chase	ornate figure of value	1929–69
$100,000[3]	Woodrow Wilson	ornate figure of value	—

[1]*Earlier versions issued starting 1929 had same subjects as current version.* [2]*Last printed in 1945.* [3]*Printed 1934–35 but never issued to public.*

COINS

VALUE	PORTRAIT ON FRONT	DESIGN ON BACK	WHEN CIRCULATED
1¢	Abraham Lincoln	"one cent" and wheat	1909–58
1¢	Abraham Lincoln	Lincoln Memorial	1959–
5¢	Thomas Jefferson	Monticello	1938–2003; 2006–
5¢	Thomas Jefferson	"Westward Journey" designs	2004–05
10¢	Franklin D. Roosevelt	torch	1946–
25¢	George Washington	eagle	1932–74; 1977–98
25¢	George Washington	colonial drummer	1975–76[1]
25¢	George Washington	50 state designs	1999–2008

[1]*All 25¢, 50¢, and $1 coins issued in 1975 and 1976 carried the double date 1776–1976.*

Denominations of US Currency (continued)

COINS (CONTINUED)

VALUE	PORTRAIT ON FRONT	DESIGN ON BACK	WHEN CIRCULATED
50¢	John F. Kennedy	presidential seal	1964–74; 1977–
50¢	John F. Kennedy	Independence Hall	1975–76[1]
$1	Dwight D. Eisenhower	eagle	1971–74; 1977–78
$1	Dwight D. Eisenhower	Liberty Bell and Moon	1975–76[1]
$1	Susan B. Anthony	eagle	1979–80; 1999
$1	Sacagawea	eagle	2000–06
$1	presidential portraits	Statue of Liberty	2007–16

[1]*All 25¢, 50¢, and $1 coins issued in 1975 and 1976 carried the double date 1776–1976.*

50 STATE QUARTERS PROGRAM

STATE	WHEN ISSUED	STATE	WHEN ISSUED	STATE	WHEN ISSUED
Alabama	2003	Louisiana	2002	Ohio	2002
Alaska	2008	Maine	2003	Oklahoma	2008
Arizona	2008	Maryland	2000	Oregon	2005
Arkansas	2003	Massachusetts	2000	Pennsylvania	1999
California	2005	Michigan	2004	Rhode Island	2001
Colorado	2006	Minnesota	2005	South Carolina	2000
Connecticut	1999	Mississippi	2002	South Dakota	2006
Delaware	1999	Missouri	2003	Tennessee	2002
Florida	2004	Montana	2007	Texas	2004
Georgia	1999	Nebraska	2006	Utah	2007
Hawaii	2008	Nevada	2006	Vermont	2001
Idaho	2007	New Hampshire	2000	Virginia	2000
Illinois	2003	New Jersey	1999	Washington	2007
Indiana	2002	New Mexico	2008	West Virginia	2005
Iowa	2004	New York	2001	Wisconsin	2004
Kansas	2005	North Carolina	2001	Wyoming	2007
Kentucky	2001	North Dakota	2006		

PRESIDENTIAL $1 COINS PROGRAM

2007	George Washington, John Adams, Thomas Jefferson, James Madison
2008	James Monroe, John Quincy Adams, Andrew Jackson, Martin Van Buren
2009	William Henry Harrison, John Tyler, James K. Polk, Zachary Taylor

US Currency and Coins in Circulation

Currency and coins outstanding and currency in circulation by denomination, 31 Mar 2008. Source: Treasury Bulletin, *June 2008.*

	TOTAL CURRENCY AND COINS	CURRENCY	COINS[1]
amounts in circulation	$815,171,945,937	$778,677,565,847	$36,494,380,090
less amounts held by:			
US Treasury	373,201,702	26,454,367	346,747,335
Federal Reserve Banks	213,186,705,891	211,841,105,413	1,345,600,478
total amounts outstanding	**1,028,731,853,530**	**990,545,125,627**	**38,186,727,903**

DENOMINATION	TOTAL CURRENCY IN CIRCULATION	FEDERAL RESERVE NOTES[2]	US NOTES	CURRENCY NO LONGER ISSUED
$1	$ 9,075,184,311	$ 8,931,966,317	$ 143,503	$143,074,491
$2	1,612,479,116	1,480,316,424	132,150,118	12,574
$5	10,427,897,320	10,291,798,515	108,886,710	27,212,095
$10	15,412,047,510	15,390,959,560	6,300	21,081,650
$20	115,801,058,440	115,780,950,660	3,840	20,103,940
$50	61,052,304,950	61,040,805,150	500	11,499,300
$100	564,983,398,600	564,956,208,300	5,198,100	21,992,200
$500	142,324,000	142,129,500	5,500	189,000
$1,000	165,646,000	165,434,000	5,000	207,000
$5,000	1,765,000	1,710,000	—	55,000
$10,000	3,460,000	3,360,000	—	100,000
fractional notes[3]	600	—	90	510
total currency	**778,677,565,847**	**778,185,638,426**	**246,399,661**	**245,527,760**

[1]*Excludes coins sold to collectors at premium prices.* [2]*Issued on or after 1 Jul 1929.* [3]*Represents value of certain partial denominations not presented for redemption.*

Energy

Energy Consumption by State and Sector

Figures represent '000,000,000,000 BTU for the year 2005. Detail may not add to total given because of rounding. Sources: Energy Information Administration, <www.eia.doe.gov>; US Census Bureau.

	TOTAL	RESIDENTIAL	COMMERCIAL	INDUSTRIAL	TRANS-PORTATION	PER CAPITA ('000,000 BTU)
Alabama	2,119	398	268	961	491	467
Alaska	799	56	62	417	264	1,194
Arizona	1,480	382	336	227	534	249
Arkansas	1,135	229	162	455	290	410
California	8,360	1,516	1,552	2,001	3,291	232
Colorado	1,426	325	290	386	424	305
Connecticut	900	298	213	125	264	258
Delaware	313	71	58	110	73	372
District of Columbia	190	39	125	4	23	327
Florida	4,563	1,333	1,069	566	1,596	257
Georgia	3,173	727	552	925	969	348
Hawaii	333	37	45	72	179	263
Idaho	503	113	79	188	124	353
Illinois	4,122	1,011	765	1,234	1,111	324
Indiana	2,905	550	365	1,344	646	464
Iowa	1,228	239	185	502	302	415
Kansas	1,032	225	192	356	259	376
Kentucky	1,970	370	260	864	477	472
Louisiana	3,613	364	273	2,259	718	804
Maine	482	119	77	156	131	368
Maryland	1,555	442	286	369	459	279
Massachusetts	1,562	474	396	205	487	243
Michigan	3,167	839	640	882	806	313
Minnesota	1,852	407	352	560	534	362
Mississippi	1,182	231	164	429	358	408
Missouri	1,915	514	399	410	593	331
Montana	419	76	68	158	118	448
Nebraska	655	150	128	204	173	373
Nevada	728	166	126	197	239	302
New Hampshire	335	99	79	54	104	257
New Jersey	2,729	636	638	479	977	315
New Mexico	675	108	122	225	220	352
New York	4,180	1,266	1,317	525	1,071	217
North Carolina	2,732	715	563	703	751	315
North Dakota	412	64	61	195	92	648
Ohio	4,082	981	710	1,375	1,015	356
Oklahoma	1,551	305	236	571	440	439
Oregon	1,096	266	204	295	331	302
Pennsylvania	4,050	1,000	717	1,298	1,036	328
Rhode Island	228	80	59	27	62	213
South Carolina	1,694	360	255	651	428	398
South Dakota	274	63	56	66	89	351
Tennessee	2,339	536	383	773	647	391
Texas	11,558	1,618	1,399	5,812	2,730	506
Utah	757	150	143	226	238	302
Vermont	167	50	32	31	54	270
Virginia	2,610	639	593	594	784	345
Washington	2,059	480	372	593	614	328
West Virginia	794	165	113	335	181	440
Wisconsin	1,862	426	356	643	437	336
Wyoming	462	42	55	245	119	912
total	**100,369**	**21,743**	**17,950**	**32,323**	**28,352**	**339**

Energy Consumption by Source

Figures represent '000,000,000,000 BTU for the year 2005.
Source: US Energy Information Administration, <www.eia.doe.gov>.

	PETROLEUM	NATURAL GAS	COAL	HYDROELECTRIC POWER[1]	NUCLEAR ELECTRIC POWER
Alabama	627	364	890	101	330
Alaska	333	434	14	15	0

Energy Consumption by Source (continued)

	PETROLEUM	NATURAL GAS	COAL	HYDROELECTRIC POWER[1]	NUCLEAR ELECTRIC POWER
Arizona	591	328	428	64	269
Arkansas	384	216	247	31	143
California	3,870	2,298	67	396	377
Colorado	494	484	387	14	0
Conneticut	453	172	42	5	162
Delaware	149	49	57	0	0
District of Columbia	29	34	1	0	0
Florida	2,163	814	672	3	300
Georgia	1,159	426	901	40	329
Hawaii	295	3	18	1	0.0
Idaho	161	78	11	85	0.0
Illinois	1,486	984	1,048	1	972
Indiana	880	541	1,594	4	0
Iowa	446	243	430	10	47
Kansas	359	259	380	[2]	92
Kentucky	725	241	986	30	0
Louisiana	1,587	1,367	254	8	163
Maine	264	61	7	41	0
Maryland	604	212	329	17	153
Massachusetts	755	385	119	10	57
Michigan	1,033	928	800	15	343
Minnesota	722	372	379	8	134
Mississippi	463	311	176	0	105
Missouri	747	273	836	12	84
Montana	193	71	200	96	0
Nebraska	232	120	229	9	92
Nevada	280	237	198	17	0
New Hampshire	192	73	44	18	99
New Jersey	1,332	627	125	[2]	327
New Mexico	259	227	318	2	0
New York	1,849	1,108	260	258	442
North Carolina	999	238	812	54	417
North Dakota	138	55	431	13	0
Ohio	1,367	862	1,481	5	154
Oklahoma	567	605	397	26	0
Oregon	393	241	36	310	0
Pennsylvania	1,535	719	1,491	22	795
Rhode Island	98	84	[2]	[2]	0
South Carolina	572	179	431	29	554
South Dakota	120	43	37	31	0
Tennessee	826	238	658	93	290
Texas	5,671	3,625	1,628	13	398
Utah	291	169	406	8	0
Vermont	91	8	[2]	12	42
Virginia	1,037	312	459	15	291
Washington	855	273	112	721	86
West Virginia	273	125	960	15	0
Wisconsin	625	416	523	17	103
Wyoming	161	113	491	8	0
total	**40,733**	**22,645**	**22,795**	**2,703**	**8,149**

[1]*Data do not include results from pumped-storage hydroelectricity.* [2]*Negligible.*

Travel and Tourism

Passports, Visas, and Immunizations

With certain exceptions, a passport is required by law for all US citizens, including infants, to travel outside the United States and its territories. The exceptions of travel without passport to Mexico, Canada, Bermuda, and countries in the Caribbean were eliminated in 2007 by implementation of the Western Hemisphere Travel Initiative. Passports can be applied for at 9,000 passport acceptance facilities nationwide, including most government facilities. State Department passport agencies accept applications only by appointment, usually from those in need of expedited service (two weeks or less). Passport agencies are located in Aurora CO, Boston MA, Chicago IL, Honolulu HI,

Houston TX, Los Angeles CA, Miami FL, New Orleans LA, New York City NY, Norwalk CT, Philadelphia PA, San Francisco CA, Seattle WA, and Washington DC. Everyone must apply in person for his or her first passport; those issued to persons aged 16 and older may be renewed by mail if the person's expiring passport is undamaged and in his or her possession and was issued no more than 15 years previously. Applicants should submit the appropriate paperwork several months in advance of planned travel to allow for processing. New passport fees total US$100 for persons age 16 and up (US$75 application fee, US$25 execution fee) and US$85 for those under 16 (US$60 application fee, US$25 execution fee); expedited service is an additional US$60. Renewal fees are US$75 for all ages. Passports are mailed to applicants in about six weeks or about two weeks for rush service. The status of a passport application may be checked online at <http://travel.state.gov/passport/get/status/status_2567.html> or by contacting the National Passport Information Center at 1-877-487-2778 (toll-free; automated information; representatives available weekdays 6 AM to 12 AM ET, except federal holidays).

To apply in person for a passport requires submission of an application form; proof of US citizenship, such as a certified birth certificate; proof of identity, such as a driver's license; two identical recent 2×2-inch photographs; a social security number; and all applicable fees. Options for proving identity or citizenship are listed on the State Department Web site. A passport is valid for 10 years, or 5 years if issued to a person age 15 or younger. To renew by mail requires submission of an application form, the most recent passport, two identical photographs, and applicable fees. Frequent travelers may request a passport with extra pages. A passport that is lost or stolen in a foreign country must be immediately reported to local police and the nearest US embassy or consulate to allow for the citizen's reentry into the US. Replacing a lost or stolen passport requires completion of a form reporting the loss or theft and an application for a new passport, as well as the usual documentation, photographs, and fees.

Visas. A visa is usually a stamp placed on a US passport by a foreign country's officials allowing the passport owner to visit that country. It is the traveler's responsibility to check visa regulations and obtain visas where necessary before traveling to a foreign country. Visas may be acquired from the embassy or consulate of the intended destination and can be applied for by mail. Processing fees vary among countries.

Immunizations. Under regulations adopted by the World Health Organization, some countries require International Certificates of Vaccination against yellow fever. Other immunizations, such as those for tetanus and polio, should also be up-to-date. Preventive measures for malaria are recommended for some destinations. There are no immunization requirements for returning to the United States. Many countries require HIV/AIDS testing for work, study, or residence permits or for long-term stays.

For passport information, forms, and office locations, access the State Department Web site at <http://travel.state.gov/passport>. Entry requirements for foreign countries, including necessity of visas, immunizations, and HIV testing, are available at <http://travel.state.gov/travel/cis_pa_tw/cis/cis_1765.html>. Additional information on required or recommended health care measures can be obtained from the Centers for Disease Control and Prevention (CDC) at <www.cdc.gov/travel> or by calling 1-877-FYI-TRIP; also helpful are local health departments and the Government Printing Office publication *Health Information for International Travel,* available at the CDC Web site.

Travelers to and from the US

Data for 2002 showed that overseas travel to the US dropped significantly during 2002, primarily as a response to the terrorist attacks of 11 Sep 2001. Since then, however, travel has rebounded at varying levels. 2007 data for all US resident travel to specific overseas countries are not available, but data for air travel to the various regions, as well as Mexico and Canada, are presented below. Source: US Department of Commerce, International Trade Administration, Office of Travel and Tourism Industries.

TOP COUNTRIES OF ORIGIN FOR VISITORS TO THE US (2007)

		% CHANGE FROM 2006
UK	4,497,858	+8
Japan	3,531,489	−4
Germany	1,524,151	+10
France	997,506	+26
South Korea	806,175	+6
Australia	669,536	+11
Brazil	639,431	+22
Italy	634,152	+19
India	567,045	+39
China[1]	539,824	+18
total overseas	**23,892,277**	+10
Canada	17,735,000	+11
Mexico	15,089,000	+13
total worldwide	**56,716,277**	**+11**

REGIONAL DESTINATION OF US AIR TRAVELERS ABROAD (2007)

		% CHANGE FROM 2006
Europe	13,251,785	+3
Caribbean	5,627,545	−2
Asia	5,583,250	+8
Central America	2,541,051	+8
South America	2,451,642	+7
Oceania	820,959	+0.4
Middle East	584,832	+23
Africa	205,173	+24
total overseas	**31,066,237**	**+4**
Mexico	5,762,546	+1
Canada	3,758,128	−3
total worldwide	**40,586,911**	**+3**

Travelers to and from the US (continued)

TOP 10 STATES AND CITIES VISITED BY OVERSEAS VISITORS (2007)[2]

STATE	VISITORS/ IN THOUSANDS ('000)	% CHANGE FROM 2006
New York	7,908	+23
California	5,185	+12
Florida	4,683	+14
Hawaii	1,864	−9
Nevada	1,768	+5
Illinois	1,171	+8
Massachusetts	1,171	+6
Guam[3]	1,099	−6
Texas	1,003	+3
New Jersey	956	+13

CITY	VISITORS/ IN THOUSANDS ('000)	% CHANGE FROM 2006
New York NY	7,646	+23
Los Angeles CA	2,652	+5
Miami FL	2,341	+19
San Francisco CA	2,270	+14
Orlando FL	2,055	+3
Las Vegas NV	1,720	+4
Oahu/Honolulu HI	1,553	−10
Washington DC	1,195	+13
Chicago IL	1,147	+8
Boston MA	1,075	+8

[1]Data for China include Hong Kong. [2]Excludes Canadian and Mexican visitors to the US. [3]Guam is a US territory. If Guam were excluded, Pennsylvania would rank 10th on the list with about 812,000 overseas visitors.

Customs Exemptions

Upon returning to the US from a foreign country, travelers must pay duty on items acquired outside the US. If the value of the items is greater than the allowable exemption, duty must be paid on the excess amount. The general exemption is US$800 per person, but it can also be US$200 or US$1,600 in certain situations. Exemptions apply if the items are in the traveler's possession, are for the traveler's own use, and are declared to US Customs. The traveler must also have been out of the country for at least 48 hours (unless returning from Mexico or the US Virgin Islands) and must not have used any part of the exemption within the past 30 days; if one or both of these requirements does not apply, the allowable exemption drops to US$200 per person and includes additional restrictions. The general exemption of US$800 includes no more than 200 previously exported cigarettes, 100 cigars, and no more than one liter of alcoholic beverages. Cuban tobacco products are prohibited unless purchased in Cuba on authorized travel. Family members may combine their total exemptions in a joint declaration. The US$800 exemption also applies to travelers returning from any of 28 countries and dependencies in the Caribbean Basin or Andean Region but may include two liters of alcoholic beverages, as long as one of the liters was produced in one of these. The 28 countries and dependencies are Antigua and Barbuda, Aruba, The Bahamas, Barbados, Belize, Bolivia, the British Virgin Islands, Colombia, Costa Rica, Dominica, the Dominican Republic, Ecuador, El Salvador, Grenada, Guatemala, Guyana, Haiti, Honduras, Jamaica, Montserrat, the Netherlands Antilles, Nicaragua, Panama, Peru, Saint Kitts and Nevis, Saint Lucia, Saint Vincent and the Grenadines, and Trinidad and Tobago. A US$1,600 exemption applies to travelers returning from a trip that included the US Virgin Islands, American Samoa, or Guam and includes 1,000 cigarettes and five liters of alcoholic beverages; of this amount, 800 cigarettes and one liter of alcohol must be from one of the US islands. The US$1,600 exemption also applies to multi-country travel (such as a cruise) to a US possession and any of the 28 Caribbean Basin and Andean Region countries and dependencies, as long as no more than US$800 worth of goods was purchased in those locations.

Gifts valued at US$100 or less (US$200 or less for gifts sent from American Samoa, Guam, or the US Virgin Islands) may be sent to the US without duty as long as no single person receives more than this value within a single day. Alcoholic beverages may not be sent by mail; tobacco and alcohol-based perfumes worth more than US$5 are not included in the exemption. Travelers may ship goods home for personal use without duty if the value of the goods is US$200 or less and no single person receives more than this value within a single day. This personal exemption increases to US$1,600 for goods purchased and shipped from American Samoa, Guam, or the US Virgin Islands.

Customs information is available from the Customs and Border Protection Web site at <www.cbp.gov/xp/cgov/travel>.

US State Department Travel Warnings

The State Department issues Travel Warnings when it is believed best for Americans to avoid certain countries in the interest of safety. It also releases Travel Alerts of more short-term hazards, such as terrorist threats or political coups, that may endanger American travelers; these include an expiration date when the announcement need no longer be heeded. The department also makes available Consular Information Sheets for all countries, which may discuss safety conditions in that country not severe enough to require a travel warning. Current information can be found at <http://travel.state.gov>.

Travel Warnings were in effect on 3 Jul 2008 for the following: Afghanistan, Algeria, Burundi, the Central African Republic, Chad, Colombia, the Democratic Republic of the Congo, Côte d'Ivoire, East Timor, Eritrea, Haiti, Iran, Iraq, Israel (including the West Bank and the Gaza Strip), Kenya, Lebanon, Nepal, Nigeria, Pakistan, the Philippines, Saudi Arabia, Somalia, Sri Lanka, The Sudan, Syria, Uzbekistan, and Yemen.

Travel Alerts in effect on the same day and set to expire on various dates in July 2008–January 2009 included advisories for Burma (Myanmar), China, Mali, Mexico, Tunisia, and Zimbabwe; the Atlantic and Pacific Oceans, the Caribbean, and the Gulf of Mexico (for hurricane season); and a worldwide caution.

Employment

US Employment by Gender and Occupation

Detail may not add to total given because of rounding. Source: US Bureau of Labor Statistics.

OCCUPATION	WORKERS 16 YEARS AND OLDER (NUMBERS IN '000)					
	TOTAL		MEN		WOMEN	
	2006	2007	2006	2007	2006	2007
management, professional, and related occupations	50,420	51,788	24,928	25,593	25,492	26,195
management, business, and financial-operations occupations	21,233	21,577	12,347	12,375	8,886	9,203
management occupations	15,249	15,486	9,652	9,686	5,597	5,800
business and financial-operations occupations	5,983	6,091	2,694	2,688	3,289	3,403
professional and related occupations	29,187	30,210	12,581	13,218	16,606	16,992
computer and mathematical occupations	3,209	3,441	2,354	2,560	855	881
architecture and engineering occupations	2,830	2,932	2,418	2,511	412	421
life, physical, and social-science occupations	1,434	1,382	813	792	620	591
community and social-services occupations	2,156	2,265	829	890	1,327	1,375
legal occupations	1,637	1,668	791	809	846	858
education, training, and library occupations	8,126	8,485	2,100	2,267	6,026	6,218
arts, design, entertainment, sports, and media occupations	2,735	2,789	1,401	1,476	1,334	1,313
health-care-practitioner and technical occupations	7,060	7,248	1,875	1,913	5,185	5,335
service occupations	23,811	24,137	10,159	10,337	13,653	13,800
health-care-support occupations	3,132	3,138	333	338	2,799	2,800
protective-service occupations	2,939	3,071	2,284	2,380	654	691
food-preparation and serving-related occupations	7,606	7,699	3,297	3,354	4,309	4,345
building- and grounds-cleaning and maintenance occupations	5,381	5,469	3,230	3,280	2,151	2,189
personal-care and service occupations	4,754	4,760	1,014	986	3,740	3,774
sales and office occupations	36,141	36,212	13,275	13,264	22,866	22,948
sales and related occupations	16,641	16,698	8,478	8,424	8,163	8,275
office and administrative-support occupations	19,500	19,513	4,797	4,840	14,703	14,673
natural-resources, construction, and maintenance occupations	15,830	15,740	15,079	15,078	752	662
farming, fishing, and forestry occupations	961	960	750	759	212	201
construction and extraction occupations	9,507	9,535	9,216	9,276	292	258
installation, maintenance, and repair occupations	5,362	5,245	5,114	5,043	248	202
production, transportation, and material-moving occupations	18,224	18,171	14,061	13,983	4,163	4,188
production occupations	9,378	9,395	6,529	6,563	2,850	2,832
transportation and material-moving occupations	8,846	8,776	7,533	7,420	1,313	1,355
total	**144,427**	**146,047**	**77,502**	**78,254**	**66,925**	**67,792**

US Workers Earning the Minimum Wage

This table refers to wage and salary workers who were paid hourly rates in 2007, excluding the incorporated self-employed. The prevailing federal minimum wage was US$5.15/hour until 24 Jul 2007 and US$5.85 thereafter. Workers earning less than minimum wage may have been working in jobs that are exempted from the minimum-wage provision of the Fair Labor Standards Act. Numbers in thousands.

Source: US Bureau of Labor Statistics.

WORKER CHARACTERISTICS	TOTAL NUMBER OF WORKERS	BELOW MINIMUM WAGE	AT MINIMUM WAGE	TOTAL NUMBER OF WORKERS AT OR BELOW MINIMUM WAGE	
				NUMBER	%
age					
16–24 years	16,275	669	145	814	5.0
25 years and over	59,597	793	122	915	1.5
total (16 years and over)	75,873	1,462	267	1,729	2.3
men					
16–24 years	8,314	190	52	242	2.9
25 years and over	29,476	270	34	304	1.0
16 years and over	37,790	460	86	546	1.4
women					
16–24 years	7,961	479	93	572	7.2
25 years and over	30,121	523	88	611	2.0
16 years and over	38,082	1,002	181	1,183	3.1
race and Hispanic or Latino ethnicity[1]					
white (16 years and over)	61,061	1,216	204	1,420	2.3
black (16 years and over)	9,965	150	55	205	2.1
Asian (16 years and over)	2,730	50	1	51	1.9
Hispanic or Latino (16 years and over)	13,168	205	41	246	1.9
full- and part-time workers[2]					
full-time	57,745	658	94	752	1.3
part-time	17,997	799	172	971	5.4

[1]Hispanics may be of any race and are included in both white and black population groups. For these reasons, data for the race/ethnic group category will not add up to total. [2]Full- and part-time workers are distinguished by the number of hours worked. These data do not add up to total because of a small number of multiple jobholders whose status on the principal job is unknown.

Comparative Hourly Compensation Costs

The table shows private-industry employer compensation costs per hour worked by an employee in March 2008. Detail may not add to total given because of rounding. Source: US Bureau of Labor Statistics.

COMPENSATION	ALL WORKERS COST (US$)	(%)	GOODS-PRODUCING WORKERS[1] COST (US$)	(%)	SERVICE WORKERS[2] COST (US$)	(%)
wages and salaries	18.91	70.6	20.93	66.7	9.93	74.8
paid leave	1.80	6.7	1.98	6.3	0.58	4.4
vacation	0.92	3.4	1.06	3.4	0.30	2.2
holiday	0.59	2.2	0.71	2.3	0.18	1.4
sick	0.22	0.8	0.17	0.5	0.08	0.6
other	0.06	0.2	0.04	0.1	0.02	0.1
supplemental pay	0.80	3.0	1.30	4.1	0.24	1.8
premium[3]	0.28	1.0	0.58	1.8	0.14	1.0
shift differentials	0.07	0.3	0.10	0.3	0.04	0.3
nonproduction bonuses	0.46	1.7	0.62	2.0	0.06	0.4
insurance	2.06	7.7	2.88	9.2	0.94	7.1
life	0.04	0.2	0.06	0.2	[4]	[4]
health	1.92	7.2	2.68	8.5	0.90	6.8
short-term disability	0.06	0.2	0.10	0.3	0.02	0.1
long-term disability	0.04	0.1	0.04	0.1	[4]	[4]
retirement and savings	0.96	3.6	1.45	4.6	0.22	1.6
defined benefit	0.43	1.6	0.82	2.6	0.09	0.7
defined contribution	0.53	2.0	0.62	2.0	0.12	0.9

Comparative Hourly Compensation Costs (continued)

COMPENSATION	ALL WORKERS COST (US$)	ALL WORKERS (%)	GOODS-PRODUCING WORKERS[1] COST (US$)	GOODS-PRODUCING WORKERS[1] (%)	SERVICE WORKERS[2] COST (US$)	SERVICE WORKERS[2] (%)
legally required benefits	2.24	8.4	2.85	9.1	1.37	10.3
Social Security[5]	1.58	5.9	1.79	5.7	0.87	6.5
Old-Age, Survivors, and Disability Insurance (OASDI)	1.27	4.7	1.44	4.6	0.70	5.3
Medicare	0.31	1.2	0.35	1.1	0.16	1.2
federal unemployment insurance	0.03	0.1	0.03	0.1	0.04	0.3
state unemployment insurance	0.15	0.6	0.20	0.6	0.12	0.9
workers' compensation	0.47	1.8	0.83	2.7	0.34	2.6
total benefits	**7.86**	**29.4**	**10.45**	**33.3**	**3.34**	**25.2**
total compensation	**26.76**	**100**	**31.38**	**100**	**13.27**	**100**

[1]*Includes mining, construction, and manufacturing.* [2]*Includes public utilities; wholesale and retail trade; transportation and communications; finance, real estate, and insurance; and services.* [3]*Pay for overtime, weekends, and holidays.* [4]*Negligible.* [5]*The total employer cost for Social Security comprises an OASDI portion and a Medicare portion.*

Median Income by Educational and Social Variables

This table refers to people who worked full-time throughout the year and are 15 years and over as of March of the following year. Median income dollar amounts are not adjusted for inflation. N/A means not available. Source: US Census Bureau.

	median income (US$) males				median income (US$) females			
	1980	1990	2000	2006	1980	1990	2000	2006
full-time workers	19,173	28,979	38,891	44,958	11,591	20,591	29,123	34,989
educational level[1]								
less than 9th grade	N/A	10,319	14,131	17,169	N/A	6,268	8,546	10,451
9th to 12th grade (no diploma)	N/A	14,736	18,915	21,184	N/A	7,055	10,063	11,914
high school graduate	N/A	21,546	27,480	31,009	N/A	10,818	15,153	17,546
some college, no degree	N/A	26,591	33,319	37,271	N/A	13,963	20,166	22,709
associate degree	N/A	29,358	38,026	41,807	N/A	17,364	23,124	26,295
bachelor's degree	N/A	36,067	49,080	54,403	N/A	20,967	30,418	35,094
master's degree	N/A	43,125	59,732	67,425	N/A	29,747	40,619	46,250
professional degree	N/A	63,741	83,701	96,926	N/A	34,064	46,084	60,463
doctorate degree	N/A	51,845	71,271	90,511	N/A	37,242	51,460	61,091
race and origin[2,3]								
white	13,328	21,170	29,797	33,843	4,947	10,317	16,079	20,082
white (non-Hispanic)	13,681	21,958	31,508	36,564	4,980	10,581	16,665	20,727
black	8,009	12,868	21,343	25,064	4,580	8,328	15,881	19,103
Hispanic origin	9,659	13,470	19,498	23,452	4,405	7,532	12,248	15,758
age[2]								
15 to 24 years	4,597	6,319	9,546	10,964	3,124	4,902	7,360	8,653
25 to 34 years	15,580	21,393	30,254	32,131	6,973	12,589	21,049	24,179
35 to 44 years	20,037	29,773	37,922	42,637	6,465	14,504	22,077	26,368
45 to 54 years	19,974	31,007	41,039	45,693	6,403	14,230	23,732	27,844
55 to 64 years	15,914	24,804	34,189	41,477	4,926	9,400	16,920	24,186
65 years and over	7,339	14,183	19,411	23,500	4,226	8,044	11,023	13,603
all workers over age 14	12,530	20,293	28,343	32,265	4,920	10,070	16,063	20,014

[1]*The income figures for the various educational levels are for workers 25 years old and over. Before 1991, the level of education categories used by the US Census Bureau differed from the categories presented in this table. Because of this, the 1980 figures for the median income by educational level are not completely comparable with the figures for later years. The figures presented in the 1990 column for educational levels are actually for 1991, the first year the educational categories listed in this table were used by the US Census Bureau.* [2]*Figures for the 1980 sections covering "race and origin" and "age" are for civilian workers only.* [3]*Hispanic people may be of any race.*

The 20 US Metropolitan Areas with the Highest Average Annual Per Capita Incomes

Personal income is income received from all sources, including wages and salaries, property rental, transfers, and interest and dividends. Source: US Bureau of Economic Analysis.

METROPOLITAN AREA	ANNUAL INCOME (US$) 2005	2006	INCOME CHANGE (%)
Bridgeport, CT[1]	67,269	71,901	6.9
San Francisco, CA[2]	52,543	55,801	6.2
San Jose, CA[3]	50,468	53,533	6.1
Naples, FL[4]	49,492	53,265	7.6
Washington, DC, VA, MD, WV[5]	48,697	51,207	5.2
Boston, MA, NH[6]	47,168	50,085	6.2
Sebastian, FL[7]	46,219	49,305	6.7
Trenton-Ewing, NJ	45,923	48,964	6.6
New York, NY, NJ, PA[8]	45,268	48,397	6.9
Boulder, CO	45,849	48,324	5.4
Napa, CA	43,669	46,286	6.0
Barnstable, MA	43,992	46,258	5.2
Santa Cruz–Watsonville, CA	42,643	45,849	7.5
Casper, WY	41,462	45,815	10.5
Midland, TX	40,855	45,274	10.8
Denver-Aurora, CO	42,369	44,299	4.6
Seattle-Tacoma-Bellevue, WA	41,608	44,228	6.3
Hartford, CT[9]	42,369	44,194	4.3
Sarasota-Bradenton-Venice, FL	41,577	44,042	5.9
Minneapolis, MN, WI[10]	42,091	43,696	3.8

[1]*Includes Stamford and Norwalk.* [2]*Includes Oakland and Fremont.* [3]*Includes Sunnyvale and Santa Clara.* [4]*Includes Marco Island.* [5]*Includes Arlington and Alexandria.* [6]*Includes Cambridge and Quincy.* [7]*Includes Vero Beach.* [8]*Includes Long Island.* [9]*Includes West Hartford and East Hartford.* [10]*Includes St. Paul and Bloomington.*

US Federal Minimum Wage Rates, 1952–2008

The table shows the actual minimum wage for the year in question and the value of that minimum wage adjusted for inflation in the year 2008. Source: US Bureau of Labor Statistics.

YEAR	minimum wage US DOLLARS	2008 DOLLARS
1952	0.75	6.13
1953	0.75	6.09
1954	0.75	6.04
1955	0.75	6.06
1956	1.00	7.96
1957	1.00	7.71
1958	1.00	7.50
1959	1.00	7.44
1960	1.00	7.32
1961	1.15	8.33
1962	1.15	8.25
1963	1.25	8.85
1964	1.25	8.74
1965	1.25	8.60
1966	1.25	8.36
1967	1.40	9.08
1968	1.60	9.96
1969	1.60	9.44
1970	1.60	8.93
1971	1.60	8.56
1972	1.60	8.29
1973	1.60	7.81
1974	2.00	8.79
1975	2.10	8.46
1976	2.30	8.76
1977	2.30	8.22
1978	2.65	8.80
1979	2.90	8.65
1980	3.10	8.15
1981	3.35	7.98
1982	3.35	7.52
1983	3.35	7.29
1984	3.35	6.98
1985	3.35	6.74
1986	3.35	6.62
1987	3.35	6.39
1988	3.35	6.13
1989	3.35	5.85
1990	3.80	6.30
1991	4.25	6.76
1992	4.25	6.56
1993	4.25	6.37
1994	4.25	6.21
1995	4.25	6.04
1996	4.75	6.56
1997	5.15	6.95
1998	5.15	6.84
1999	5.15	6.70
2000	5.15	6.48
2001	5.15	6.30
2002	5.15	6.20
2003	5.15	6.06
2004	5.15	5.91
2005	5.15	5.71
2006	5.15	5.53
2007	5.85	6.11
2008	6.55	6.55

US Civilian Federal Employment

Source: Statistical Abstract of the United States: 2008.

AGENCIES[1]	1970	1980	1990	2000	2006
legislative branch	**29,939**	**39,710**	**37,495**	**31,157**	**30,067**
judicial branch	**6,879**	**15,178**	**23,605**	**32,186**	**33,834**
departments of the executive branch	**1,772,363**	**1,716,970**	**2,065,542**	**1,592,200**	**1,689,351**
Executive Office of the President	N/A	N/A	1,731	1,658	1,709
State	40,042	23,497	25,288	27,983	33,968
Treasury	90,683	124,663	158,655	143,508	112,000
Defense	1,169,173	960,116	1,034,152	676,268	676,452
Justice	40,075	56,327	83,932	125,970	106,159
Interior	71,671	77,357	77,679	73,818	71,593
Agriculture	114,309	129,139	122,594	104,466	101,887
Commerce	36,124	48,563	69,920	47,652	40,335
Labor	10,928	23,400	17,727	16,040	15,434
Health and Human Services	110,186	155,662	123,959	62,605	60,756
Housing and Urban Development	15,046	16,964	13,596	10,319	9,814
Transportation	66,970	72,361	67,364	63,598	53,573
Energy	7,156	21,557	17,731	15,692	14,838

US Civilian Federal Employment (continued)

AGENCIES[1]	1970	1980	1990	2000	2006
departments of the executive branch (continued)					
Education	0	7,364	4,771	4,734	4,257
Veterans Affairs	169,241	228,285	248,174	219,547	236,938
Homeland Security	N/A	N/A	N/A	N/A	151,771
independent agencies[2]	N/A	N/A	999,894	1,050,900	945,046
Board of Governors of the Federal Reserve System	N/A	N/A	1,525	2,372	1,869
Environmental Protection Agency	0	14,715	17,123	18,036	18,166
Equal Employment Opportunity Commission	797	3,515	2,880	2,780	2,285
Federal Communications Commission	N/A	N/A	1,778	1,965	1,857
Federal Deposit Insurance Corporation	2,462	3,520	17,641	6,958	4,583
Federal Trade Commission	N/A	N/A	988	1,019	1,027
General Services Administration[3]	37,661	37,654	20,277	14,334	12,460
National Aeronautics and Space Administration	30,674	23,714	24,872	18,819	18,448
National Archives and Records Administration	N/A	N/A	3,120	2,702	3,051
National Labor Relations Board	N/A	N/A	2,263	2,054	1,832
National Science Foundation	N/A	N/A	1,318	1,247	1,325
Nuclear Regulatory Commission	0	3,283	3,353	2,858	3,297
Office of Personnel Management	5,513	8,280	6,636	3,780	4,954
Peace Corps	N/A	N/A	1,178	1,065	1,075
Railroad Retirement Board	N/A	N/A	1,772	1,176	1,004
Securities and Exchange Commission	N/A	N/A	2,302	2,955	3,760
Small Business Administration	4,397	5,804	5,128	4,150	6,148
Smithsonian Institution	2,547	4,403	5,092	5,065	4,953
Social Security Administration	N/A	N/A	N/A	64,474	64,884
Tennessee Valley Authority	23,785	51,714	28,392	13,145	12,624
US Information Agency	10,156	8,138	8,555	2,436	2,144
US International Development Cooperation Agency	N/A	N/A	4,698	2,552	2,723
US Postal Service	721,183	660,014	816,886	860,726	760,039
total, all agencies	**2,866,313**	**2,875,866**	**3,128,267**	**2,708,101**	**2,700,007**

N/A means not available. [1]Includes other branches or agencies not shown separately. [2]The Defense Intelligence Agency was excluded as of November 1984, the National Imagery and Mapping Agency as of October 1996. Entries for 1990, 2000, and 2006 exclude the Central Intelligence Agency and the National Security Agency. [3]Entry for 1980 includes the National Archives and Records Administration, which became an independent agency in 1985.

Older Americans in the Workforce

All numbers are in thousands ('000). Figures are from 2006 and may not add to total given because of rounding. Source: US Census Bureau.

	WORKFORCE BY AGE							
	55 AND OVER		55–59		60–64		65 AND OLDER	
GENDER AND OCCUPATION TYPE	NUMBER	%	NUMBER	%	NUMBER	%	NUMBER	%
men and women								
managerial and professional	9,576	39.3	5,003	40.5	2,738	40.3	1,834	35.4
sales and administrative support	6,418	26.4	3,189	25.8	1,730	25.5	1,499	29.0
service occupations	3,396	14.0	1,539	12.4	957	14.1	900	17.4
construction, extraction, installation, and repair	1,811	7.4	1,027	8.3	498	7.3	286	5.5
production, transportation, and material moving	3,003	12.3	1,543	12.5	841	12.4	619	12.0
farming, fishing, and forestry	132	0.5	59	0.5	33	0.5	40	0.8
total	**24,336**	**100**	**12,361**	**100**	**6,798**	**100**	**5,178**	**100**
men								
managerial and professional	5,252	40.5	2,555	39.7	1,512	42.1	1,185	40.3
sales and administrative support	2,270	17.5	1,068	16.6	657	18.3	546	18.6
service occupations	1,310	10.1	592	9.2	330	9.2	388	13.2
construction, extraction, installation, and repair	1,763	13.6	991	15.4	489	13.6	282	9.6
production, transportation, and material moving	2,269	17.5	1,185	18.4	582	16.2	502	17.1
farming, fishing, and forestry	107	0.8	50	0.8	22	0.6	36	1.2
total	**12,971**	**100**	**6,441**	**100**	**3,592**	**100**	**2,938**	**100**

Older Americans in the Workforce (continued)

GENDER AND OCCUPATION TYPE	WORKFORCE BY AGE: 55 AND OVER NUMBER	55 AND OVER %	55–59 NUMBER	55–59 %	60–64 NUMBER	60–64 %	65 AND OLDER NUMBER	65 AND OLDER %
women								
managerial and professional	4,324	38.0	2,448	41.4	1,227	38.3	649	29.0
sales and administrative support	4,148	36.5	2,122	35.8	1,073	33.5	953	42.6
service occupations	2,086	18.4	947	16.0	627	19.6	512	22.9
construction, extraction, installation, and repair	48	0.4	36	0.6	9	0.3	3	0.2
production, transportation, and material moving	734	6.5	358	6.0	259	8.1	117	5.2
farming, fishing, and forestry	25	0.2	10	0.2	12	0.4	4	0.2
total	**11,365**	**100**	**5,920**	**100**	**3,206**	**100**	**2,239**	**100**

Strikes and Lockouts in the US

Strikes and lockouts are referred to as work stoppages by the Bureau of Labor Statistics. This table covers work stoppages since 1950 involving 1,000 workers or more. The number of workers and stoppages are for stoppages begun during that year. The number of days out from work pertains to all strikes or lockouts in effect during the year, whether they began in that year or not. The heading for estimated working time includes all workers except those employed in private households, forestry, or fisheries. A minus sign (–) indicates a percentage less than .005.
Source: US Bureau of Labor Statistics.

YEAR	strikes and lockouts: NUMBER	WORKERS INVOLVED ('000)	work time lost: DAYS LOST ('000)	% OF WORKING TIME
1950	424	1,698	30,390	0.26
1951	415	1,462	15,070	0.12
1952	470	2,746	48,820	0.38
1953	437	1,623	18,130	0.14
1954	265	1,075	16,630	0.13
1955	363	2,055	21,180	0.16
1956	287	1,370	26,840	0.20
1957	279	887	10,340	0.07
1958	332	1,587	17,900	0.13
1959	245	1,381	60,850	0.43
1960	222	896	13,260	0.09
1961	195	1,031	10,140	0.07
1962	211	793	11,760	0.08
1963	181	512	10,020	0.07
1964	246	1,183	16,220	0.11
1965	268	999	15,140	0.10
1966	321	1,300	16,000	0.10
1967	381	2,192	31,320	0.18
1968	392	1,855	35,367	0.20
1969	412	1,576	29,397	0.16
1970	381	2,468	52,761	0.29
1971	298	2,516	35,538	0.19
1972	250	975	16,764	0.09
1973	317	1,400	16,260	0.08
1974	424	1,796	31,809	0.16
1975	235	965	17,563	0.09
1976	231	1,519	23,962	0.12
1977	298	1,212	21,258	0.10
1978	219	1,006	23,774	0.11
1979	235	1,021	20,409	0.09
1980	187	795	20,844	0.09
1981	145	729	16,908	0.07
1982	96	656	9,061	0.04
1983	81	909	17,461	0.08
1984	62	376	8,499	0.04
1985	54	324	7,079	0.03
1986	69	533	11,861	0.05
1987	46	174	4,481	0.02
1988	40	118	4,381	0.02
1989	51	452	16,996	0.07
1990	44	185	5,926	0.02
1991	40	392	4,584	0.02
1992	35	364	3,989	0.01
1993	35	182	3,981	0.01
1994	45	322	5,021	0.02
1995	31	192	5,771	0.02
1996	37	273	4,889	0.02
1997	29	339	4,497	0.01
1998	34	387	5,116	0.02
1999	17	73	1,996	0.01
2000	39	394	20,419	0.06
2001	29	99	1,151	–
2002	19	46	660	–
2003	14	129	4,091	0.01
2004	17	171	3,344	0.01
2005	22	100	1,736	0.01
2006	20	70	2,688	0.01
2007	21	189	1,265	–

Palm trees are of special interest because of their long fossil record, structural diversity, and economic importance. They have, however, been difficult to study. Their large size and extreme hardness deterred early collectors and led Liberty Hyde Bailey, an eminent American horticulturist of the early 20th century, to call them the big game of the plant world. Few studies of palms were conducted until air travel to remote tropical areas became feasible.

US Trade Union Membership

Numbers are in thousands ('000). N/A means not available. Source: US Bureau of Labor Statistics.

YEAR	NUMBER OF UNION MEMBERS	% OF TOTAL LABOR FORCE	YEAR	NUMBER OF UNION MEMBERS	% OF TOTAL LABOR FORCE	YEAR	NUMBER OF UNION MEMBERS	% OF TOTAL LABOR FORCE
1900[1]	791	N/A	1940	8,717	26.9	1980	20,095	23.0
1905	1,918	N/A	1945	14,322	35.5	1985	16,996	18.0
1910	2,116	N/A	1950	14,300[3]	31.5	1990	16,740	16.1
1915	2,560	N/A	1955	16,802	33.2	1995	16,360	14.9
1920	5,034	N/A	1960	17,049	31.4	2000	16,258	13.5
1925	3,566	N/A	1965	17,299	28.4	2005	15,685	12.5
1930[2]	3,401	11.6	1970	19,381	27.4	2006	15,359	12.0
1935	3,584	13.2	1977[4]	19,335	23.8	2007	15,670	12.1

[1]Data from 1900 to 1925 include Canadian members whose union headquarters were in the US. [2]Agricultural workers were not included as part of the total labor force for the years from 1930 to 1970. [3]Rounded to nearest hundred thousand. [4]Data for 1975 were not available. Data for 1977 on include only employed union members.

US Unemployment Rates

Unemployment rates of the civilian labor force 16 years and older. Source: US Bureau of Labor Statistics.

YEAR	UNEMPLOYMENT RATE (%)	YEAR	UNEMPLOYMENT RATE (%)	YEAR	UNEMPLOYMENT RATE (%)	YEAR	UNEMPLOYMENT RATE (%)
1948	3.8	1963	5.7	1978	6.1	1993	6.9
1949	5.9	1964	5.2	1979	5.8	1994	6.1
1950	5.3	1965	4.5	1980	7.1	1995	5.6
1951	3.3	1966	3.8	1981	7.6	1996	5.4
1952	3.0	1967	3.8	1982	9.7	1997	4.9
1953	2.9	1968	3.6	1983	9.6	1998	4.5
1954	5.5	1969	3.5	1984	7.5	1999	4.2
1955	4.4	1970	4.9	1985	7.2	2000	4.0
1956	4.1	1971	5.9	1986	7.0	2001	4.7
1957	4.3	1972	5.6	1987	6.2	2002	5.8
1958	6.8	1973	4.9	1988	5.5	2003	6.0
1959	5.5	1974	5.6	1989	5.3	2004	5.5
1960	5.5	1975	8.5	1990	5.6	2005	5.1
1961	6.7	1976	7.7	1991	6.8	2006	4.6
1962	5.5	1977	7.1	1992	7.5	2007	4.6

Social Characteristics of the Unemployed in the US

Unemployment as a % of the civilian labor force. N/A means not available. Source: US Bureau of Labor Statistics.

	UNEMPLOYMENT RATES BY YEAR (%)									
SOCIAL CHARACTERISTICS	1975	1980	1985	1990	1995	2000	2004	2005	2006	2007
age (both sexes)										
16 and over[1]	19.9	17.8	18.6	15.5	17.3	13.1	5.5	5.1	4.6	4.6
25–54[2]	6.0	5.1	5.6	4.4	4.3	3.0	4.6	4.1	3.8	3.7
sex (16 years and older)[3]										
men	6.8	5.9	6.2	5.0	4.8	3.3	5.6	5.1	4.6	4.7
women	8.0	6.4	6.6	4.9	4.9	3.6	5.4	5.1	4.6	4.5
race/ethnicity										
white	7.8	6.3	6.2	4.8	4.9	3.5	4.8	4.4	4.0	4.1
black	14.8	14.3	15.1	11.4	10.4	7.6	10.4	10.0	8.9	8.3
Hispanic[4]	12.2	10.1	10.5	8.2	9.3	5.7	7.0	6.0	5.2	5.6
family										
women maintaining families	10.0	9.2	10.4	8.3	8.0	5.9	N/A	N/A	N/A	N/A
married men, spouse present	5.1	4.2	4.3	3.4	3.3	2.0	1.0	0.9	0.8	0.8
overall unemployment	8.5	7.1	7.2	5.6	5.6	4.0	5.5	5.1	4.6	4.6

[1]Data for ages 16–19 until 2004. [2]Data for ages 25 and older until 2004. [3]Data for ages 20 years and older until 2004. [4]Hispanics may be of any race and are included in both the white and black racial categories in this table.

US Unemployment by Occupation

Unemployment rates are for the civilian noninstitutional population aged 16 years and older. Rates represent unemployment as a percent of the labor force for each occupational group. The unemployment rate totals include people without previous work experience and those whose last job was in the military. 2007 data reflect revised population controls used in the survey. Source: US Bureau of Labor Statistics.

OCCUPATION	THOUSANDS OF PERSONS 2006	2007	TOTAL (%) 2006	2007
Management, professional, and related occupations	**1,065**	**1,090**	**2.1**	**2.1**
Management, business, and financial-operations occupations	427	429	2.0	1.9
Management occupations	279	278	1.8	1.8
Business and financial-operations occupations	148	151	2.4	2.4
Professional and related occupations	638	662	2.1	2.1
Computer and mathematical occupations	80	76	2.4	2.1
Architecture and engineering occupations	49	47	1.7	1.6
Life, physical, and social science occupations	27	28	1.8	2.0
Community and social services occupations	50	53	2.3	2.3
Legal occupations	22	40	1.3	2.3
Education, training, and library occupations	196	198	2.4	2.3
Arts, design, entertainment, sports, and media occupations	115	127	4.0	4.4
Health care practitioner and technical occupations	98	93	1.4	1.3
Service occupations	**1,485**	**1,521**	**5.9**	**5.9**
Health care support occupations	152	147	4.6	4.5
Protective-service occupations	105	118	3.4	3.7
Food preparation and serving-related occupations	590	626	7.2	7.5
Building- and grounds-cleaning and maintenance occupations	402	392	7.0	6.7
Personal-care and service occupations	235	238	4.7	4.8
Sales and office occupations	**1,667**	**1,638**	**4.4**	**4.3**
Sales and related occupations	812	835	4.7	4.8
Office and administrative-support occupations	856	804	4.2	4.0
Natural resources, construction, and maintenance occupations	**1,007**	**1,052**	**6.0**	**6.3**
Farming, fishing, and forestry occupations	101	89	9.5	8.5
Construction and extraction occupations	699	781	6.8	7.6
Installation, maintenance, and repair occupations	207	182	3.7	3.4
Production, transportation, and material-moving occupations	**1,127**	**1,128**	**5.8**	**5.8**
Production occupations	544	564	5.5	5.7
Transportation and material-moving occupations	583	564	6.2	6.0
Total, 16 years and over	**7,001**	**7,078**	**4.6**	**4.6**

Occupational Illnesses and Injuries in the US

This table displays the number of nonfatal work injuries and illnesses recorded in 2006. The injuries and illnesses resulted in days away from work in the private industries listed. Detail may not add to total given because of rounding and nonclassifiable responses. Numbers are in thousands ('000). N/A means not available.

Source: US Bureau of Labor Statistics.

CHARACTERISTIC	PRIVATE INDUSTRY[1]	GOODS-PRODUCING INDUSTRIES: NATURAL RESOURCES AND MINING[1,2]	CONSTRUCTION	MANUFACTURING
injury or illness				
sprains and strains	472.7	8.2	52.9	67.8
bruises and contusions	101.3	3.0	9.5	16.8
cuts and lacerations	115.2	2.5	23.9	24.2
carpal tunnel syndrome	13.0	0.1	0.9	5.1
tendinitis	4.8	0.1	0.2	1.7
fractures	94.1	3.4	17.7	16.8
heat burns	17.4	0.4	1.5	3.4
chemical burns	7.5	0.2	1.1	1.8
amputations	8.0	0.3	1.2	3.8
multiple traumatic injuries	45.9	1.1	5.7	7.1
body part affected by injury or illness				
head	82.4	2.7	12.5	15.5
eye	36.0	1.2	7.1	9.6
neck	17.8	0.4	2.2	2.1
trunk	401.9	8.1	44.6	62.7
shoulder	75.8	1.2	7.6	13.5

Occupational Illnesses and Injuries in the US (continued)

CHARACTERISTIC	PRIVATE INDUSTRY[1]	GOODS-PRODUCING INDUSTRIES: NATURAL RESOURCES AND MINING[1,2]	CONSTRUCTION	MANU-FACTURING
body part affected by injury or illness (continued)				
back	250.9	4.7	28.0	35.0
upper extremities	274.2	5.9	38.4	66.2
wrist	48.8	0.8	4.9	11.4
hand, except finger	49.5	1.2	8.0	10.7
finger	106.1	2.5	16.4	30.4
lower extremities	262.2	6.0	40.2	37.4
knee	95.5	2.1	14.6	13.2
foot and toe	57.5	1.2	8.0	9.4
body systems	18.2	0.5	1.7	2.4
multiple parts	115.9	2.3	12.4	13.2
source of injury or illness				
chemicals and chemical products	19.5	0.7	1.7	4.4
containers	147.3	1.5	7.5	23.3
furniture and fixtures	45.3	0.2	2.4	5.8
machinery	77.5	2.3	11.0	26.1
parts and materials	124.6	2.8	34.9	36.5
worker motion or position	163.4	2.4	19.7	33.8
floors, walkways, and ground surfaces	214.6	5.0	28.0	23.8
tools, instruments, and equipment	56.8	1.5	13.8	11.4
vehicles	101.3	2.5	8.4	10.5
health care patient	52.7	—	—	—
exposure or event leading to injury or illness				
contact with objects and equipment	335.5	9.9	58.4	76.4
struck by object	164.7	4.8	30.2	32.6
struck against object	85.7	2.1	14.5	15.1
caught in equipment or object	59.3	2.3	8.4	22.4
fall to lower level	74.3	2.0	18.2	7.8
fall on same level	151.8	3.1	12.2	17.8
slip, trip, or loss of balance—without fall	35.4	0.7	4.2	4.7
overexertion	284.9	3.9	26.7	44.4
overexertion in lifting	151.0	1.7	15.5	23.4
repetitive motion	38.3	0.3	2.6	14.7
exposure to harmful substances	56.5	1.4	5.1	10.7
transportation accidents	56.2	1.5	6.4	4.1
fires and explosions	2.3	0.1	0.5	0.5
assaults and violent acts	22.4	0.9	0.5	0.6
total cases	**1,183.5**	**26.3**	**153.2**	**201.0**

CHARACTERISTIC	SERVICE-PRODUCING INDUSTRIES: TRADE, TRANSPORTATION, AND UTILITIES[2]	FINANCIAL SERVICES	LEISURE AND HOSPITALITY	OTHER SERVICES
injury or illness				
sprains and strains	157.4	13.2	31.9	10.7
bruises and contusions	33.8	3.1	8.4	1.8
cuts and lacerations	28.2	1.7	15.9	3.1
carpal tunnel syndrome	2.8	0.8	0.7	0.4
tendinitis	1.1	0.1	0.3	0.2
fractures	26.8	2.3	6.5	2.1
heat burns	2.4	0.2	6.1	0.5
chemical burns	1.9	0.1	0.9	0.1
amputations	1.3	0.3	0.5	0.1
multiple traumatic injuries	13.3	2.2	3.0	1.0
body part affected by injury or illness				
head	23.2	2.4	6.4	1.9
eye	8.1	0.7	1.9	0.9
neck	6.1	0.6	1.2	0.3
trunk	131.4	10.9	27.1	9.5
shoulder	27.0	1.6	4.8	2.2

Occupational Illnesses and Injuries in the US (continued)

CHARACTERISTIC	SERVICE-PRODUCING INDUSTRIES: TRADE, TRANSPORTATION, AND UTILITIES[2]	FINANCIAL SERVICES	LEISURE AND HOSPITALITY	OTHER SERVICES
body part affected by injury or illness (continued)				
back	80.5	7.2	17.3	5.3
upper extremities	69.5	5.1	31.3	7.0
wrist	13.6	1.6	4.2	1.2
hand, except finger	12.2	0.6	7.3	1.0
finger	24.4	1.6	12.7	2.5
lower extremities	83.9	8.6	19.5	5.6
knee	30.1	2.7	7.0	2.0
foot and toe	21.3	2.3	3.3	1.2
body systems	3.9	1.1	1.6	0.5
multiple parts	33.1	4.4	9.1	2.7
source of injury or illness				
chemicals and chemical products	4.5	0.8	1.7	0.3
containers	73.2	3.0	14.2	2.4
furniture and fixtures	14.3	2.6	6.1	1.1
machinery	17.7	1.8	6.5	1.9
parts and materials	33.3	1.7	2.7	3.5
worker motion or position	48.2	5.6	11.4	4.0
floors, walkways, and ground surfaces	59.2	8.6	24.1	4.7
tools, instruments, and equipment	13.0	1.2	7.5	2.2
vehicles	48.7	3.2	4.4	2.7
health care patient	0.1	0.1	—	0.2
exposure or event leading to injury or illness				
contact with objects and equipment	93.5	7.7	28.8	8.0
struck by object	48.0	3.6	15.2	4.7
struck against object	24.4	2.6	9.0	1.6
caught in equipment or object	14.4	0.8	3.2	0.9
fall to lower level	22.6	2.7	4.2	1.2
fall on same level	41.3	5.7	20.8	3.7
slip, trip, or loss of balance—without fall	10.1	1.2	4.5	0.7
overexertion	100.0	5.8	14.9	6.8
overexertion in lifting	56.7	3.1	8.9	3.2
repetitive motion	8.9	1.6	1.8	0.8
exposure to harmful substances	10.3	1.7	9.7	1.1
transportation accidents	24.0	2.2	2.5	1.4
fires and explosions	0.5	—	0.2	—
assaults and violent acts	3.0	0.9	1.7	0.6
total cases	**354.5**	**33.3**	**96.9**	**27.6**

[1]*Excludes farms with fewer than 11 employees.* [2]*The Mine Safety and Health Administration provided data for mining; the Federal Railroad Administration provided railroad transportation data. The mining category excludes independent mining contractors.*

US Work-Related Fatalities by Cause

Totals for major categories may include some subcategories not listed in the table. Detail may not add to total given because of rounding. Source: US Bureau of Labor Statistics.

CAUSE OF FATALITY	2001–05 NUMBER (AVG.)	2006 NUMBER	2006 (%)
transportation incidents	**2,451**	**2,413**	**42**
highway	1,394	1,329	23
collision between vehicles, mobile equipment	686	644	11
moving in same direction	151	152	3
moving in opposite directions, oncoming	254	234	4
moving in intersection	137	138	2
vehicle struck stationary object or equipment	337	356	6
noncollision	335	297	5
jackknifed or overturned—no collision	274	248	4
nonhighway (farm, industrial premises)	335	342	6
overturned	175	165	3

US Work-Related Fatalities by Cause (continued)

CAUSE OF FATALITY	2001–05 NUMBER (AVG.)	2006 NUMBER	2006 (%)
transportation incidents (continued)			
worker struck by a vehicle	369	372	7
rail vehicle	60	65	1
water vehicle	82	89	2
aircraft	206	215	4
assaults and violent acts	**850**	**754**	**13**
homicides	602	516	9
shooting	465	417	7
stabbing	60	38	1
self-inflicted injury	207	199	3
contact with objects and equipment	**952**	**983**	**17**
struck by object	560	583	10
struck by falling object	345	378	7
struck by flying object	50	69	1
caught in or compressed by equipment or objects	256	281	5
caught in running equipment or machinery	128	148	3
caught in or crushed in collapsing materials	118	107	2
falls	**763**	**809**	**14**
fall to lower level	669	728	13
fall from ladder	125	129	2
fall from roof	154	184	3
fall from scaffold, staging	87	88	2
fall on same level	73	59	1
exposure to harmful substances or environments	**498**	**525**	**9**
contact with electric current	265	247	4
contact with overhead power lines	118	108	2
contact with temperature extremes	44	53	1
exposure to caustic, noxious, or allergenic substances	114	153	3
inhalation of substance	56	58	1
oxygen deficiency	74	64	1
drowning, submersion	54	50	1
fires and explosions	**174**	**201**	**4**
total	**5,704**	**5,703**	**100**

Consumer Prices

US Consumer Price Index, 1913–2007

This table presents the annual change in the Consumer Price Index (CPI) since 1913. The CPI is used as an indicator of price changes in the goods and services purchased by US consumers. The information provided is based on the purchases of a specific group of urban consumers who serve as a sample population representing more than 80% of the total US population. Each annual CPI is compared with the average index level of 100, which is a base number that represents the average price level for the 36-month period covering the years 1982, 1983, and 1984. A minus sign indicates a decrease.

Source: US Bureau of Labor Statistics.

YEAR	ANNUAL CPI	% ANNUAL CHANGE IN CPI	YEAR	ANNUAL CPI	% ANNUAL CHANGE IN CPI	YEAR	ANNUAL CPI	% ANNUAL CHANGE IN CPI
1913	9.9		1921	17.9	−10.5	1929	17.1	0.0
1914	10.0	1.0	1922	16.8	−6.1	1930	16.7	−2.3
1915	10.1	1.0	1923	17.1	1.8	1931	15.2	−9.0
1916	10.9	7.9	1924	17.1	0.0	1932	13.7	−9.9
1917	12.8	17.4	1925	17.5	2.3	1933	13.0	−5.1
1918	15.1	18.0	1926	17.7	1.1	1934	13.4	3.1
1919	17.3	14.6	1927	17.4	−1.7	1935	13.7	2.2
1920	20.0	15.6	1928	17.1	−1.7	1936	13.9	1.5

US Consumer Price Index, 1913–2007 (continued)

YEAR	ANNUAL CPI	% ANNUAL CHANGE IN CPI	YEAR	ANNUAL CPI	% ANNUAL CHANGE IN CPI	YEAR	ANNUAL CPI	% ANNUAL CHANGE IN CPI
1937	14.4	3.6	1961	29.9	1.0	1985	107.6	3.6
1939	13.9	−1.4	1962	30.2	1.0	1986	109.6	1.9
1938	14.1	−2.1	1963	30.6	1.3	1987	113.6	3.6
1940	14.0	0.7	1964	31.0	1.3	1988	118.3	4.1
1941	14.7	5.0	1965	31.5	1.6	1989	124.0	4.8
1942	16.3	10.9	1966	32.4	2.9	1990	130.7	5.4
1943	17.3	6.1	1967	33.4	3.1	1991	136.2	4.2
1944	17.6	1.7	1968	34.8	4.2	1992	140.3	3.0
1945	18.0	2.3	1969	36.7	5.5	1993	144.5	3.0
1946	19.5	8.3	1970	38.8	5.7	1994	148.2	2.6
1947	22.3	14.4	1971	40.5	4.4	1995	152.4	2.8
1948	24.1	8.1	1972	41.8	3.2	1996	156.9	3.0
1949	23.8	−1.2	1973	44.4	6.2	1997	160.5	2.3
1950	24.1	1.3	1974	49.3	11.0	1998	163.0	1.6
1951	26.0	7.9	1975	53.8	9.1	1999	166.6	2.2
1952	26.5	1.9	1976	56.9	5.8	2000	172.2	3.4
1953	26.7	0.8	1977	60.6	6.5	2001	177.1	2.8
1954	26.9	0.7	1978	65.2	7.6	2002	179.9	1.6
1955	26.8	−0.4	1979	72.6	11.3	2003	184.0	2.3
1956	27.2	1.5	1980	82.4	13.5	2004	188.9	2.7
1957	28.1	3.3	1981	90.9	10.3	2005	195.3	3.4
1958	28.9	2.8	1982	96.5	6.2	2006	201.6	3.0
1959	29.1	0.7	1983	99.6	3.2	2007	207.3	2.8
1960	29.6	1.7	1984	103.9	4.3			

US Consumer Price Indexes by Item Group, 1975–2007

The information provided is based on the purchases of a specific group of urban consumers who serve as a sample population representing more than 80% of the total US population. Each annual CPI is compared with the average index level of 100, which is a base number that represents the average price level for the 36-month period covering the years 1982, 1983, and 1984. Source: US Bureau of Labor Statistics.

	CONSUMER PRICE INDEX								
ITEM GROUP	1975	1980	1985	1990	1995	2000	2005	2006	2007
all items	53.8	82.4	107.6	130.7	152.4	172.2	195.3	201.6	207.3
commodities	58.2	86.0	105.4	122.8	136.4	149.2	160.2	164.0	167.5
energy	42.1	86.0	101.6	102.1	105.2	124.6	177.1	196.9	207.7
food	59.8	86.8	105.6	132.4	148.4	167.8	190.7	195.2	202.9
shelter	48.8	81.0	109.8	140.0	165.7	193.4	224.4	232.1	240.6
transportation	50.1	83.1	106.4	120.5	139.1	153.3	173.9	180.9	184.7
medical care	47.5	74.9	113.5	162.8	220.5	260.8	323.2	336.2	351.1
apparel	72.5	90.9	105.0	124.1	132.0	129.6	119.5	119.5	119.0

	% CHANGE IN CPI[1]								
ITEM GROUP	1975	1980	1985	1990	1995	2000	2005	2006	2007
all items	9.1	13.5	3.6	5.4	2.8	3.4	3.4	3.2	2.8
commodities	8.8	12.3	2.1	5.2	1.9	3.3	3.6	2.4	2.1
energy	10.5	30.9	0.7	8.3	0.6	16.9	17.0	11.2	5.5
food	8.5	8.6	2.3	5.8	2.8	2.3	2.4	2.4	4.0
shelter	9.9	17.6	5.6	5.4	3.2	3.3	2.6	3.4	3.7
transportation	9.4	17.9	2.6	5.6	3.6	6.2	6.6	4.0	2.1
medical care	12.0	11.0	6.3	9.0	4.5	4.1	4.2	4.0	4.4
apparel	4.5	7.1	2.8	4.6	−1.0	−1.3	−0.7	0.0	−0.4

[1]*Annual percent change from the preceding year.*

Sample US Consumer Price Indexes by Region, 2006–2007

This table presents the regional annual averages of the CPI for 2007 and the percent change of those averages from 2006 to 2007. The information provided is based on the purchases of a specific group of urban consumers who serve as a sample population representing more than 80% of the total US population. Each annual CPI is compared with the average index level of 100, which is a base number that represents the average price level for the 36-month period covering the years 1982, 1983, and 1984. A minus sign indicates a decrease in price from 2006.

Source: US Bureau of Labor Statistics.

Sample US Consumer Price Indexes by Region, 2006–2007 (continued)

ITEM GROUP	NORTHEAST 2007 CPI	NORTHEAST % CHANGE FROM 2006	MIDWEST 2007 CPI	MIDWEST % CHANGE FROM 2006	SOUTH 2007 CPI	SOUTH % CHANGE FROM 2006	WEST 2007 CPI	WEST % CHANGE FROM 2006
all items	220.5	2.6	198.1	2.7	200.4	2.9	212.2	3.2
food	207.2	4.1	195.9	3.7	200.7	3.8	208.3	4.2
shelter	279.2	3.4	221.3	2.3	214.0	4.1	247.6	4.4
energy	193.4	4.3	171.8	4.4	174.1	0.8	205.6	2.0
apparel	117.6	−1.5	110.2	0.0	132.0	−0.2	112.2	0.1
transportation	182.7	1.2	186.2	2.9	182.7	2.1	187.1	2.1
medical care	374.2	4.8	351.5	4.6	333.9	3.6	354.3	5.1
commodities	171.0	1.9	163.3	2.5	168.4	2.1	167.4	2.1

US Budget

US Public Debt

In order to fund governmental operations, the Department of the Treasury borrows money by selling Treasury bills, US savings bonds, and other securities to the public. The money borrowed by the Treasury is referred to as the public debt. A broader measure of the federal debt is known as the gross federal debt. It consists of the public debt plus money borrowed by federal agencies. The GDP is the gross domestic product.

Source: US Office of Management and Budget.

END OF FISCAL YEAR	PUBLIC DEBT (IN US$ MILLIONS)	% OF GDP	GROSS FEDERAL DEBT (IN US$ MILLIONS)	% OF GDP
1940	42,772	44.2	50,696	52.4
1950	219,023	80.1	256,853	93.9
1960	236,840	45.6	290,525	56.0
1970	283,198	28.0	380,921	37.6
1980	711,923	26.1	909,041	33.3
1990	2,411,558	42.0	3,206,290	55.9
2000	3,409,804	35.1	5,628,700	58.0
2005	4,592,213	37.4	7,905,300	64.4
2006	4,828,973	37.0	8,451,351	64.7
2007	5,049,306	36.7	9,007,653	65.5

US Governmental Spending, 1800–2007

Entries for the years prior to 1933 are based on the administrative budget concept rather than on the unified budget concept. For a discussion of the unified budget concept and related topics, see <www.fms.treas.gov/bulletin/b2008-2ffotxt.doc>. The figures are in thousands ('000). A minus sign indicates a deficit.

Source: US Office of Management and Budget.

YEAR[1]	FEDERAL INCOME	FEDERAL SPENDING	SURPLUS OR DEFICIT
1800	10,849	10,786	63
1801	12,935	9,395	3,541
1802	14,996	7,862	7,134
1803	11,064	7,852	3,212
1804	11,826	8,719	3,107
1805	13,561	10,506	3,054
1806	15,560	9,804	5,756
1807	16,398	8,354	8,044
1808	17,061	9,932	7,128
1809	7,773	10,281	−2,507
1810	9,384	8,157	1,228
1811	14,424	8,058	6,365
1812	9,801	20,281	−10,480
1813	14,340	31,682	−17,341
1814	11,182	34,721	−23,539
1815	15,729	32,708	−16,979
1816	47,678	30,587	17,091
1817	33,099	21,844	11,255
1818	21,585	19,825	1,760
1819	24,603	21,464	3,140
1820	17,881	18,261	−380
1821	14,573	15,811	−1,237
1822	20,232	15,000	5,232
1823	20,541	14,707	5,834
1824	19,381	20,327	−945
1825	21,841	15,857	5,984
1826	25,260	17,036	8,225
1827	22,966	16,139	6,827
1828	24,764	16,395	8,369
1829	24,828	15,203	9,624
1830	24,844	15,143	9,701
1831	28,527	15,248	13,279
1832	31,866	17,289	14,577
1833	33,948	23,018	10,931
1834	21,792	18,628	3,164
1835	35,430	17,573	17,857
1836	50,827	30,868	19,959
1837	24,954	37,243	−12,289
1838	26,303	33,865	−7,562
1839	31,483	26,899	4,584
1840	19,480	24,318	−4,837
1841	16,860	26,566	−9,706
1842	19,976	25,206	−5,230
1843	8,303	11,858	−3,555
1844	29,321	22,338	6,984
1845	29,970	22,937	7,033
1846	29,700	27,767	1,933
1847	26,496	57,281	−30,786

US Governmental Spending, 1800–2007 (continued)

YEAR[1]	FEDERAL INCOME	FEDERAL SPENDING	SURPLUS OR DEFICIT	YEAR[1]	FEDERAL INCOME	FEDERAL SPENDING	SURPLUS OR DEFICIT
1848	35,736	45,377	−9,641	1914	725,117	725,525	−408
1849	31,208	45,052	−13,844	1915	683,417	746,093	−62,676
1850	43,603	39,543	4,060	1916	761,445	712,967	48,478
1851	52,559	47,709	4,850	1917	1,100,500	1,953,857	−853,357
1852	49,847	44,195	5,652	1918	3,645,240	12,677,359	−9,032,120
1853	61,587	48,184	13,403	1919	5,130,042	18,492,665	−13,362,623
1854	73,800	58,045	15,755	1920	6,648,898	6,357,677	291,222
1855	65,351	59,743	5,608	1921	5,570,790	5,061,785	509,005
1856	74,057	69,571	4,486	1922	4,025,901	3,289,404	736,496
1857	68,965	67,796	1,170	1923	3,852,795	3,140,287	712,508
1858	46,655	74,185	−27,530	1924	3,871,214	2,907,847	963,367
1859	53,486	69,071	−15,585	1925	3,640,805	2,923,762	717,043
1860	56,065	63,131	−7,066	1926	3,795,108	2,929,964	865,144
1861	41,510	66,547	−25,037	1927	4,012,794	2,857,429	1,155,365
1862	51,987	474,762	−422,774	1928	3,900,329	2,961,245	939,083
1863	112,697	714,741	−602,043	1929	3,861,589	3,127,199	734,391
1864	264,627	865,323	−600,696	1930	4,057,884	3,320,211	737,673
1865	333,715	1,297,555	−963,841	1931	3,115,557	3,577,434	−461,877
1866	558,033	520,809	37,223	1932	1,923,892	4,659,182	−2,735,290
1867	490,634	357,543	133,091	1933	1,996,844	4,598,496	−2,601,652
1868	405,638	377,340	28,298	1934	2,955,000	6,541,000	−3,586,000
1869	370,944	322,865	48,078	1935	3,609,000	6,412,000	−2,803,000
1870	411,255	309,654	101,602	1936	3,923,000	8,228,000	−4,304,000
1871	383,324	292,177	91,147	1937	5,387,000	7,580,000	−2,193,000
1872	374,107	277,518	96,589	1938	6,751,000	6,840,000	−89,000
1873	333,738	290,345	43,393	1939	6,295,000	9,141,000	−2,846,000
1874	304,979	302,634	2,345	1940	6,548,000	9,468,000	−2,920,000
1875	288,000	274,623	13,377	1941	8,712,000	13,653,000	−4,941,000
1876	294,096	265,101	28,995	1942	14,634,000	35,137,000	−20,503,000
1877	281,406	241,334	40,072	1943	24,001,000	78,555,000	−54,554,000
1878	257,764	236,964	20,800	1944	43,747,000	91,304,000	−47,557,000
1879	273,827	266,948	6,879	1945	45,159,000	92,712,000	−47,553,000
1880	333,527	267,643	65,884	1946	39,296,000	55,232,000	−15,936,000
1881	360,782	260,713	100,069	1947	38,514,000	34,496,000	4,018,000
1882	403,525	257,981	145,544	1948	41,560,000	29,764,000	11,796,000
1883	398,288	265,408	132,879	1949	39,415,000	38,835,000	580,000
1884	348,520	244,126	104,394	1950	39,443,000	42,562,000	−3,119,000
1885	323,691	260,227	63,464	1951	51,616,000	45,514,000	6,102,000
1886	336,440	242,483	93,957	1952	66,167,000	67,686,000	−1,519,000
1887	371,403	267,932	103,471	1953	69,608,000	76,101,000	−6,493,000
1888	379,266	267,925	111,341	1954	69,701,000	70,855,000	−1,154,000
1889	387,050	299,289	87,761	1955	65,451,000	68,444,000	−2,993,000
1890	403,081	318,041	85,040	1956	74,587,000	70,640,000	3,947,000
1891	392,612	365,774	26,839	1957	79,990,000	76,578,000	3,412,000
1892	354,938	345,023	9,914	1958	79,636,000	82,405,000	−2,769,000
1893	385,820	383,478	2,342	1959	79,249,000	92,098,000	−12,849,000
1894	306,355	367,525	−61,170	1960	92,492,000	92,191,000	301,000
1895	324,729	356,195	−31,466	1961	94,388,000	97,723,000	−3,335,000
1896	338,142	352,179	−14,037	1962	99,676,000	106,821,000	−7,146,000
1897	347,722	365,774	−18,052	1963	106,560,000	111,316,000	−4,756,000
1898	405,321	443,369	−38,047	1964	112,613,000	118,528,000	−5,915,000
1899	515,961	605,072	−89,112	1965	116,817,000	118,228,000	−1,411,000
1900	567,241	520,861	46,380	1966	130,835,000	134,532,000	−3,698,000
1901	587,685	524,617	63,068	1967	148,822,000	157,464,000	−8,643,000
1902	562,478	485,234	77,244	1968	152,973,000	178,134,000	−25,161,000
1903	561,881	517,006	44,875	1969	186,882,000	183,640,000	3,242,000
1904	541,087	583,660	−42,573	1970	192,807,000	195,649,000	−2,842,000
1905	544,275	567,279	−23,004	1971	187,139,000	210,172,000	−23,033,000
1906	594,984	570,202	24,782	1972	207,309,000	230,681,000	−23,373,000
1907	665,860	579,129	86,732	1973	230,799,000	245,707,000	−14,908,000
1908	601,862	659,196	−57,334	1974	263,224,000	269,359,000	−6,135,000
1909	604,320	693,744	−89,423	1975	279,090,000	332,332,000	−53,242,000
1910	675,512	693,617	−18,105	1976	298,060,000	371,792,000	−73,732,000
1911	701,833	691,202	10,631	TQ	81,232,000	95,975,000	−14,744,000
1912	692,609	689,881	2,728	1977	355,559,000	409,218,000	−53,659,000
1913	714,463	714,864	−401	1978	399,561,000	458,746,000	−59,185,000

US Governmental Spending, 1800–2007 (continued)

YEAR[1]	FEDERAL INCOME	FEDERAL SPENDING	SURPLUS OR DEFICIT
1979	463,302,000	504,028,000	−40,726,000
1980	517,112,000	590,941,000	−73,830,000
1981	599,272,000	678,241,000	−78,968,000
1982	617,766,000	745,743,000	−127,977,000
1983	600,562,000	808,364,000	−207,802,000
1984	666,486,000	851,853,000	−185,367,000
1985	734,088,000	946,396,000	−212,308,000
1986	769,215,000	990,430,000	−221,215,000
1987	854,353,000	1,004,082,000	−149,728,000
1988	909,303,000	1,064,455,000	−155,152,000
1989	991,190,000	1,143,646,000	−152,456,000
1990	1,031,969,000	1,253,165,000	−221,195,000
1991	1,055,041,000	1,324,369,000	−269,328,000
1992	1,091,279,000	1,381,655,000	−290,376,000
1993	1,154,401,000	1,409,489,000	−255,087,000
1994	1,258,627,000	1,461,877,000	−203,250,000
1995	1,351,830,000	1,515,802,000	−163,972,000
1996	1,453,062,000	1,560,535,000	−107,473,000
1997	1,579,292,000	1,601,250,000	−21,958,000
1998	1,721,798,000	1,652,585,000	69,213,000
1999	1,827,454,000	1,701,891,000	125,563,000
2000	2,025,218,000	1,788,773,000	236,445,000
2001	1,991,194,000	1,863,770,000	127,424,000
2002	1,853,173,000	2,010,970,000	−157,797,000
2003	1,782,342,000	2,157,637,000	−375,295,000
2004	1,880,071,000	2,292,215,000	−412,144,000
2005	2,153,859,000	2,472,205,000	−318,346,000
2006	2,407,254,000	2,655,435,000	−248,181,000
2007	2,568,239,000	2,730,241,000	−162,002,000

[1]The fiscal year ended on 31 December for the budgets from 1800 to 1842. It ended on 30 June for the budgets from 1844 through 1976 and on 30 September from fiscal year 1977. The budget figures for 1843 are for the period from 1 January to 30 June. The third quarter of 1976 was budgeted separately because of the change in the fiscal year calendar. It is referred to as the Transition Quarter (TQ).

Annual National Average Terms on Conventional Single-Family Mortgages, 1977–2006

Source: Federal Housing Finance Board Monthly Interest Rate Survey.

YEAR	CONTRACT INTEREST RATE (%)	INITIAL FEES AND CHARGES (%)	EFFECTIVE INTEREST RATE (%)	TERM TO MATURITY (YEARS)	MORTGAGE AMOUNT (US$'000)	PURCHASE PRICE (US$'000)	LOAN TO PRICE RATIO (%)
1977	8.82	1.22	9.02	26.3	36.3	49.6	75.0
1978	9.37	1.30	9.59	26.7	41.4	57.1	74.6
1979	10.59	1.50	10.85	27.4	48.2	67.7	73.5
1980	12.46	1.97	12.84	27.2	51.7	73.4	72.9
1981	14.39	2.39	14.91	26.4	53.7	76.3	73.1
1982	14.73	2.65	15.31	25.6	55.0	78.4	72.9
1983	12.26	2.39	12.73	26.0	59.9	83.1	74.5
1984	11.99	2.57	12.48	26.8	64.5	86.6	77.0
1985	11.17	2.51	11.64	25.9	70.2	96.1	75.8
1986	9.79	2.21	10.18	25.6	79.3	110.6	74.1
1987	8.95	2.08	9.30	26.8	89.1	121.8	75.2
1988	8.98	1.96	9.30	27.7	97.4	131.6	76.0
1989	9.81	1.87	10.13	27.7	104.5	142.8	74.8
1990	9.74	1.79	10.05	27.0	104.0	142.6	74.7
1991	9.07	1.58	9.34	26.5	106.3	146.7	74.4
1992	7.83	1.58	8.11	25.4	108.7	146.4	76.6
1993	6.93	1.20	7.13	25.5	107.0	143.1	77.2
1994	7.31	1.10	7.49	27.1	109.9	142.0	79.9
1995	7.69	0.97	7.85	27.4	110.4	142.8	79.9
1996	7.58	0.97	7.74	26.9	118.7	155.1	79.0
1997	7.52	0.98	7.68	27.5	126.6	164.5	79.4
1998	6.97	0.85	7.10	27.8	131.8	173.4	78.9
1999	7.14	0.74	7.25	28.2	139.3	184.2	78.5
2000	7.86	0.67	7.96	28.7	148.3	198.9	77.8

Annual National Average Terms on Conventional Single-Family Mortgages, 1977–2006 (cont.)

YEAR	CONTRACT INTEREST RATE (%)	INITIAL FEES AND CHARGES (%)	EFFECTIVE INTEREST RATE (%)	TERM TO MATURITY (YEARS)	MORTGAGE AMOUNT (US$'000)	PURCHASE PRICE (US$'000)	LOAN TO PRICE RATIO (%)
2001	6.94	0.53	7.03	27.6	155.7	215.5	76.2
2002	6.44	0.46	6.51	27.3	163.4	231.2	75.1
2003	5.67	0.37	5.73	26.8	167.9	243.4	73.5
2004	5.68	0.40	5.74	27.9	185.5	262.0	74.9
2005	5.85	0.38	5.90	28.5	211.9	299.8	74.7
2006	6.52	0.41	6.58	29.0	222.3	306.4	76.5

US Bankruptcy Filings, 1980–2007

This table shows the number of business and nonbusiness (consumer) bankruptcy filings in the US since 1980. Bankruptcy is intended to give debtors a fresh start in managing their resources by cancelling many of their debts through a court order called a "discharge." It is also meant to give creditors a fair share of the money that the debtors can afford to pay back.

Businesses may file for bankruptcy under chapter 11 of the IRS Code. Chapter 11 offers protection from creditor demands to a business in debt so that its officers and managers have time to reorganize in order to fulfill obligations to creditors. In some instances, creditors may receive dollar-for-dollar what the business owes them, plus interest. In others, the creditor may only receive pennies on the owed dollar.

Individuals may file for bankruptcy under either chapter 7 of the IRS Code (under which debtors may liquidate assets with the supervision of a trustee in order to receive a nearly immediate discharge of debts) or chapter 13 (under which the debtor enters into a payment plan to repay debt out of future earnings over a three-to-five-year period, with the oversight of a trustee).

Source: American Bankruptcy Institute.

YEAR	TOTAL FILINGS	BUSINESS FILINGS	NONBUSINESS FILINGS	CONSUMER FILINGS AS A PERCENTAGE OF TOTAL FILINGS
1980	331,264	43,694	287,570	86.81%
1981	363,943	48,125	315,818	86.78%
1982	380,251	69,300	310,951	81.78%
1983	348,880	62,436	286,444	82.10%
1984	348,521	64,004	284,517	81.64%
1985	412,510	71,277	341,233	82.72%
1986	530,438	81,235	449,203	84.69%
1987	577,999	82,446	495,553	85.74%
1988	613,465	63,853	549,612	89.59%
1989	679,461	63,235	616,226	90.69%
1990	782,960	64,853	718,107	91.72%
1991	943,987	71,549	872,438	92.42%
1992	971,517	70,643	900,874	92.73%
1993	875,202	62,304	812,898	92.88%
1994	832,829	52,374	780,455	93.71%
1995	926,601	51,959	874,642	94.39%
1996	1,178,555	53,549	1,125,006	95.46%
1997	1,404,145	54,027	1,350,118	96.15%
1998	1,442,549	44,367	1,398,182	96.92%
1999	1,319,465	37,884	1,281,581	97.12%
2000	1,253,444	35,472	1,217,972	97.17%
2001	1,492,129	40,099	1,452,030	97.31%
2002	1,577,651	38,540	1,539,111	97.56%
2003	1,660,245	35,037	1,625,208	97.89%
2004	1,597,462	34,317	1,563,145	97.85%
2005	2,078,415	39,201	2,039,214	98.11%
2006	617,660	19,695	597,965	96.81%
2007	850,912	28,322	822,590	96.67%

US Taxes

US Federal Taxation Structure

This table shows the range of income taxes for various types of households in each tax bracket. In 2008 the standard deductions for most filers are US$5,450 for those submitting returns under status "single" and status "married filing separately," US$8,000 for those filing under status "head of household," and US$10,900 for those submitting returns under status "married filing jointly" or "qualifying widows and widowers with a dependent child." Source: US Department of the Treasury, Internal Revenue Service.

US Federal Taxation Structure (continued)

Single — Schedule X

IF TAXABLE INCOME IS OVER	BUT NOT OVER	THEN THE TAX IS	PLUS	OF THE AMOUNT OVER
US$0	US$8,025	—	10%	US$0
US$8,025	US$32,550	US$802.50	15%	US$8,025
US$32,550	US$78,850	US$4,481.25	25%	US$32,550
US$78,850	US$164,550	US$16,056.25	28%	US$78,850
US$164,550	US$357,700	US$40,052.25	33%	US$164,550
US$357,700	—	US$103,795.75	35%	US$357,700

Married Filing Jointly or Qualifying Widow(er) — Schedule Y-1

IF TAXABLE INCOME IS OVER	BUT NOT OVER	THEN THE TAX IS	PLUS	OF THE AMOUNT OVER
US$0	US$16,050	—	10%	US$0
US$16,050	US$65,100	US$1,605.00	15%	US$16,050
US$65,100	US$131,450	US$8,962.50	25%	US$65,100
US$131,450	US$200,300	US$25,550.00	28%	US$131,450
US$200,300	US$357,700	US$44,828.00	33%	US$200,300
US$357,700	—	US$96,770.00	35%	US$357,700

Married Filing Separately — Schedule Y-2

IF TAXABLE INCOME IS OVER	BUT NOT OVER	THEN THE TAX IS	PLUS	OF THE AMOUNT OVER
US$0	US$8,025	—	10%	US$0
US$8,025	US$32,550	US$802.50	15%	US$8,025
US$32,550	US$65,725	US$4,481.25	25%	US$32,550
US$65,725	US$100,150	US$12,775.00	28%	US$65,725
US$100,150	US$178,850	US$22,414.00	33%	US$100,150
US$178,850	—	US$48,385.00	35%	US$178,850

Head of Household — Schedule Z

IF TAXABLE INCOME IS OVER	BUT NOT OVER	THEN THE TAX IS	PLUS	OF THE AMOUNT OVER
US$0	US$11,450	—	10%	US$0
US$11,450	US$43,650	US$1,145.00	15%	US$11,450
US$43,650	US$112,650	US$5,975.00	25%	US$43,650
US$112,650	US$182,400	US$23,225.00	28%	US$112,650
US$182,400	US$357,700	US$42,755.00	33%	US$182,400
US$357,700	—	US$100,604.00	35%	US$357,700

Individual Income Taxes by US State

This table shows tax rates as of 1 Jan 2008 for tax year 2008. Source: The Federation of Tax Administrators, <www.taxadmin.org/fta/rate/ind_inc.html>.

	TAX RATES		NUMBER OF	INCOME BRACKETS		PERSONAL EXEMPTION			FEDERAL TAX
STATE	LOW	HIGH	BRACKETS	LOW	HIGH	SINGLE	MARRIED	CHILDREN	DEDUCTIBLE
AL	2.0	5.0	3	500[1]	3,000[1]	1,500	3,000	300	yes
AK	no state income tax								
AZ	2.59	4.54	5	10,000[1]	150,000[1]	2,100	4,200	2,300	
AR[2]	1.0	7.0[3]	6	3,699[1]	31,000[1]	23[4]	46[4]	23[4]	
CA[2]	1.0	9.3[5]	6	6,827[1]	44,815[1]	94[4]	188[4]	294[4]	
CO	4.63		1	—flat rate—		—none—			
CT	3.0	5.0	2	10,000[1]	10,000[1]	12,750[6]	24,500[6]	0	
DE	2.2	5.95	6	5,000	60,000	110[4]	220[4]	110[4]	
DC	4.0	8.5	3	10,000	40,000	1,675	3,350	1,675	
FL	no state income tax								
GA	1.0	6.0	6	750[7]	7,000[7]	2,700	5,400	3,000	
HI	1.4	8.25	9	2,400[1]	48,000[1]	1,040	2,080	1,040	
ID[2]	1.6	7.8	8	1,237[8]	24,736[8]	3,500[9]	7,000[9]	3,500[9]	
IL	3.0		1	—flat rate—		2,000	4,000	2,000	
IN	3.4		1	—flat rate—		1,000	2,000	1,000	
IA[2]	0.36	8.98	9	1,379	62,055	40[4]	80[4]	40[4]	yes
KS	3.5	6.45	3	15,000[1]	30,000[1]	2,250	4,500	2,250	
KY	2.0	6.0	6	3,000	75,000	20[4]	40[4]	20[4]	
LA	2.0	6.0	3	12,500[1]	25,000[1]	4,500[10]	9,000[10]	1,000[10]	yes
ME[2]	2.0	8.5	4	4,849[1]	19,450[1]	2,850	5,700	2,850	
MD	2.0	5.5	7	1,000	500,000	2,400	4,800	2,400	
MA[2]	5.3		1	—flat rate—		4,125	8,250	1,000	

Individual Income Taxes by US State (continued)

STATE	TAX RATES LOW	TAX RATES HIGH	NUMBER OF BRACKETS	INCOME BRACKETS LOW	INCOME BRACKETS HIGH	PERSONAL EXEMPTION SINGLE	PERSONAL EXEMPTION MARRIED	PERSONAL EXEMPTION CHILDREN	FEDERAL TAX DEDUCTIBLE
MI[2]	4.35		1	flat rate		3,300	6,600	3,300	
MN[2]	5.35	7.85	3	21,800[11]	71,591[11]	3,500[9]	7,000[9]	3,500[9]	
MS	3.0	5.0	3	5,000	10,000	6,000	12,000	1,500	
MO	1.5	6.0	10	1,000	9,000	2,100	4,200	1,200	yes[12]
MT[2]	1.0	6.9	7	2,500	14,900	2,040	4,080	2,040	yes[12]
NE[2]	2.56	6.84	4	2,400[13]	27,001[13]	113[4]	226[4]	113[4]	
NV	no state income tax								
NH	state income tax is limited to dividends and interest income only								
NJ	1.4	8.97	6	20,000[14]	500,000[14]	1,000	2,000	1,500	
NM	1.7	5.3	4	5,500[15]	16,000[15]	3,500[9]	7,000[9]	3,500[9]	
NY	4.0	6.85	5	8,000[1]	20,000[1]	0	0	1,000	
NC[16]	6.0	7.75	3	12,750[16]	60,000[16]	2,000	4,000	2,000	
ND[2]	2.1	5.54[17]	5	31,850[17]	349,701[17]	3,500[9]	7,000[9]	3,500[9]	
OH[2]	0.618	6.24	9	5,000	200,000	1,450[18]	2,900[18]	1,450[18]	
OK	0.5	5.5[19]	7	1,000[19]	8,701[19]	1,000	2,000	1,000	
OR[2]	5.0	9.0	3	2,900[1]	7,300[1]	169[4]	338[4]	169[4]	yes[12]
PA	3.07		1	flat rate		none			
RI	25.0% federal tax liability[20]								
SC[2]		7.0	6	2,670	13,350	3,500[9]	7,000[9]	3,500[9]	
SD	no state income tax								
TN	state income tax is limited to dividends and interest income only								
TX	no state income tax								
UT	5.0		1	flat rate		[21]	[21]	[21]	
VT[2]	3.6	9.5	5	32,550[22]	357,700[22]	3,500[9]	7,000[9]	3,500[9]	
VA	2.0	5.75	4	3,000	17,000	930	1,860	930	
WA	no state income tax								
WV	3.0	6.5	5	10,000	60,000	2,000	4,000	2,000	
WI[2]	4.6	6.75	4	9,700[23]	145,460[23]	700	1,400	700	
WY	no state income tax								

[1]For joint returns, the taxes are twice the tax imposed on half the income. [2]Sixteen states have statutory provision for automatic adjustment of tax brackets, personal exemption, or standard deductions to the rate of inflation. Massachusetts, Michigan, Nebraska, and Ohio index the personal exemption amounts only. [3]A special tax table is available for low-income taxpayers reducing their tax payments. [4]Tax credits. [5]An additional 1.0% tax is imposed on taxable income over US$1 million. [6]Combined personal exemptions and standard deduction. An additional tax credit is allowed ranging from 75% to 0% based on state adjusted gross income. Exemption amounts are phased out for higher-income taxpayers until they are eliminated for households earning over US$56,500. [7]The tax brackets reported are for single individuals. For married households, the same rates apply to income brackets ranging from US$1,000 to US$10,000. [8]For joint returns, the tax is twice the tax imposed on half the income. A US$10 filing tax is charged for each return, and a US$15 credit is allowed for each exemption. [9]These states allow personal exemption or standard deductions as provided in the Internal Revenue Code. [10]Combined personal exemption and standard deduction. [11]The tax brackets reported are for single individuals. For married couples filing jointly, the same rates apply for income under US$31,860 to over US$126,581. A 6.4% alternative minimum tax rate is also applicable. [12]Deduction is limited to US$10,000 for joint returns and US$5,000 for individuals in Missouri and Montana and to US$5,600 in Oregon. [13]The tax brackets reported are for single individuals. For married couples filing jointly, the same rates apply for income under US$4,800 to over US$54,000. [14]The tax brackets reported are for single individuals. For married couples filing jointly, the tax rates range from 1.4% to 8.97%, applying to seven income brackets from US$20,000 to over US$500,000. [15]The tax brackets reported are for single individuals. For married couples filing jointly, the same rates apply for income under US$8,000 to over US$24,000. Married households filing separately pay the tax imposed on half the income. [16]The tax brackets reported are for single individuals. For married taxpayers, the same rates apply to income brackets ranging from US$21,250 to US$100,000. Lower exemption amounts are allowed for high-income taxpayers. [17]The tax brackets reported are for single individuals. For married taxpayers, the same rates apply to income brackets ranging from US$53,200 to US$349,701. An additional US$300 personal exemption is allowed for joint returns or unmarried heads of households. [18]Plus an additional US$20 per exemption tax credit. [19]The rate range reported is for single persons. For married persons filing jointly, the same rates apply to income brackets ranging from US$2,000 to US$15,000. The top tax rate is scheduled to fall to 5.25% for tax years after 2008. [20]Federal tax liability prior to the enactment of the Economic Growth and Tax Relief Act of 2001. Or, taxpayers have the option of computing tax liability based on a flat 7.0% (6.5% in 2009) of gross income. [21]Tax credits are equal to 6.0% of federal standard/itemized deductions (without state taxes paid) and 75.0% of federal personal exemption amounts. The credit amount is phased out above US$12,000 in income (US$24,000 for joint returns). [22]The tax brackets reported are for single individuals. For married couples filing jointly, the same rates apply for income under US$54,400 to over US$357,700. [23]The tax brackets reported are for single individuals. For married taxpayers, the same rates apply to income brackets ranging from US$12,930 to US$193,950. An additional US$250 exemption is provided for each taxpayer or spouse age 65 or over.

Arts, Entertainment, & Leisure

Hollywood's 800-lb. Golden Gorilla

by Richard Corliss, TIME

It is the magic phrase that brings luster to any career, sells tickets at the box office, moves millions of DVDs. It's the gold standard for the film industry, pop culture's equivalent of the Nobel Prize. Get one, and when you die, the headline on your obit will proclaim OSCAR WINNER.

Every year, the movie industry's glamourati assemble in all their red-carpet glory at the Kodak Theatre in Los Angeles for the annual awards bash of the Academy of Motion Picture Arts and Sciences. Hundreds of millions of people around the world tune in as prizes are doled out to films most of the TV viewers haven't seen. They watch in part because the laying on of statuettes is meant to signify the designation of supreme cinematic quality. The best-picture winner will be able to claim parity with such enduring masterworks as *The Greatest Show on Earth, Around the World in 80 Days, Marty, Oliver!, Ordinary People*...Wait a minute. Those stuffed turkeys and middling domestic dramas won best picture? Yes, they did. All right, we'll try again...with such enduring masterpieces as *King Kong, The Wizard of Oz, Citizen Kane, Psycho, 2001: A Space Odyssey, Raging Bull*...Oops, sorry again. None of those films won the top Oscar, and half weren't even nominated for best picture.

But what about the acting categories? Surely Hollywood has recognized its most potent performers. Not always. If 2009's nominated actors want to join the exalted ranks of Charlie Chaplin, Greta Garbo, Cary Grant, Peter O'Toole, and Barbara Stanwyck, they'd better hope they lose, since none of these luminaries received a competitive Oscar.

So is the Academy Award a long-term guarantee of a film's quality, a leading indicator of acting excellence? Not really.

Sometimes Oscar's taste is validated by history. There are five best-picture winners among the top 10 honorees on the American Film Institute's list of the all-time best movies: *Gone with the Wind, Casablanca, Lawrence of Arabia, The Godfather,* and *Schindler's List*. It's also true that the world's best-grossing film of any decade has usually won best picture: *Gone with the Wind* in the '30s, *The Best Years of Our Lives* in the '40s, *Ben-Hur* in the '50s, *The Sound of Music* in the '60s, *Titanic* in the '90s, and the final *Lord of the Rings* film this decade.

Too often, though, the Academy has rewarded films at the high end of mediocrity, operating within a narrow band of reassuring realism. They're called "movies of quality," which really means movies of piety—stories of cozy spiritual uplift (*Mrs. Miniver, Going My Way*) or, more recently, of superior damaged creatures (*Rain Man, A Beautiful Mind*). And they're often chosen over edgier fare. Thus, in 1977 the softhearted *Rocky* beat four superior films (*All the President's Men, Bound for Glory, Network,* and *Taxi Driver*), and in 1982 another inspirational sports movie, *Chariots of Fire,* won out over *Reds* and *Raiders of the Lost Ark.* Oscar also ignores pictures deemed too weird (i.e., modern) or infra dig (i.e., genre films). In judging movie acting, the Academy is often slow to notice the arrival of talent ready to shake up or reshape a staid industry.

Citizen Kane is the definitive litmus test, and Oscar failed it. At the top of nearly every critics' poll as the best film of all time, Orson Welles's debut movie was praised to the skies when it opened in 1941. But the resemblance of Charles Foster Kane to publisher William Randolph Hearst cued a campaign to suppress the movie, and *Kane* flopped in its initial release. In addition, many in the industry rankled at Welles's boy-genius rep and may have resented the freedom this first-timer was given by his studio, RKO. Under these circumstances, it's probably a miracle that the film received nine Oscar nominations, including three for Welles as actor, director, and coscreenwriter. In the end, it won only for the screenplay, and John Ford's *How Green Was My Valley* took best picture. That study of Welsh family values is a film of intelligent sentiment, but, as has been said about many a movie since—it's no *Citizen Kane*.

No Business Like Show Business. The *Kane* quandary illustrates some of the problems with the Academy Awards: political pressure, suspicion of outsiders, resistance to innovation. But the main and abiding limitation is the people who pick the Oscars. We're not saying that the Academy members are ignorant, that they don't know their business. That's the problem: they all know that movies are a business. And they're a part of it. The people whose names are on the ballot may be their friends or their enemies or their potential employers. In addition, lobbying in Hollywood at Oscar time is as pervasive as it is in Washington anytime. Harvey Weinstein was so expert at campaigning when he and his brother Bob ran Miramax Films that, the prevailing wisdom has it, he cajoled his way to a best-picture prize for the modest *Shakespeare in Love* over Steven Spielberg's odds-on favorite, *Saving Private Ryan.*

Since the great majority of the voters live or work in the Los Angeles area, there is little motive to reward foreign-language films. Few movie lovers would deny that some of the medium's greatest works have been in tongues other than English. Yet no foreign-language film has ever won the top Oscar; only eight have been nominated—and one of them was directed by Clint Eastwood. That's less than 2% for the best films from the rest of the world.

The Academy membership, which now numbers about 5,800, is by definition insular and aging. It takes a while to build a career, in the movie business like anywhere else, and by the time film folk become members of the Academy, they are usually much older than the people they are making their movies for. The advanced average age of the voters—and the gradual conservatizing of their tastes—is one explanation for the films they give prizes to. They not only wouldn't give an Oscar to, say, a Judd Apatow film, but probably haven't seen one.

An Apatow movie like *The 40 Year-Old Virgin* or *Knocked Up* would labor under another handicap: it's designed to make people laugh. The top Oscar has gone to a handful of comedies (including *It Happened One Night* and *Annie Hall*), but generally the Academy prefers to be edified.

The year of *Citizen Kane*, 1941, was also the year of Preston Sturges's *The Lady Eve*, today regarded as one of the great American comedies, with Stanwyck and Henry Fonda brilliant as a cardsharp predator and her millionaire prey. None of them got even a nomination for this supreme farce.

Heroes and Villains. If one actor could encapsulate the limitations of the Oscar mind-set, it would be Stanwyck, who in the early '30s all but created the movies' image of the tough broad, surviving and thriving in the Depression through a wily, earthy cynicism. Stanwyck was sensational in grimy melodramas, from *Illicit* and *Night Nurse* to the immoral, immortal *Baby Face*. But she didn't get an Oscar nomination until 1938, when she broke from her normal screen character to play the nobly sacrificing mother in *Stella Dallas*. Seven years later, when she was a finalist as the rotten femme fatale of *Double Indemnity*, she lost to Ingrid Bergman, whose husband is trying to kill her in *Gaslight*. Oscar chose the wanly victimized wife over the fabulously victimizing one.

Time and again, given the choice between an actor who does great work as a meanie and another who does good work as a cutie or victim, Oscar went for the latter. Marlon Brando's Stanley Kowalski in the 1951 *A Streetcar Named Desire* is one of the major revolutionary performances in movies; it announced the arrival of the Method actor and the sexy brute in one galvanizing package. Yet Brando lost to Humphrey Bogart in *The African Queen*. The Academy went for old style over new, as it did in withholding Oscars from Brando's more sensitive brethren, Montgomery Clift and James Dean. Both were multiple nominees; neither won. And like the late Heath Ledger—who in *Brokeback Mountain* gave a bold, pioneering performance—neither Clift nor Dean lived long enough to be given an honorary award.

At least Clift, Dean, and Ledger had the luck to be making serious dramas from Oscar-winning directors. Anyone who worked in other kinds of movies ran into the wall of the Academy's genre snobbery. Crime movies (later known as film noir) had a dark glory, a stinging postwar fatalism, but flew under the Academy's radar and beneath its contempt. Of the hundreds of westerns in the '50s, some were superb, like Ford's *The Searchers* and Howard Hawks' *Rio Bravo*, but even those A-list directors could not interest Oscar in their oaters—zero nominations for those two great films—or in John Wayne's towering performances in them.

Wayne, of course, was an old-fashioned star. Today we may be in Hollywood's first poststar era. If you judge movie stardom by the actors who headline the biggest hits, then the top stars of 2007 include Tobey Maguire (*Spider-Man 3*), Shia LaBeouf (*Transformers*), Daniel Radcliffe (*Harry Potter and the Order of the Phoenix*) and Gerard Butler (*300*). Each of these films took in more than US$200 million at the domestic box office, or more than three times as much as the political comedy *Charlie Wilson's War*, with a cast headed by Tom Hanks and Julia Roberts. Among actresses in the year's releases, the big star was Ellen Page, whose low-budget *Juno* made US$138 million domestically. Doesn't she deserve an eight-figure contract for her next film? No, because even studio bosses know that, appealing as Page may have been, what drew crowds to *Juno* was story and attitude.

Meanwhile, star vehicles keep tanking. Hollywood still has a guy whose movies are sure-shot smashes: Will Smith. But Oscar voters have usually dismissed his sort of vehicles, science fiction and horror films, as candidates for best picture—from the 1933 *King Kong* (just a trick movie) to *Psycho* (just an exercise in sadism from a director, Alfred Hitchcock, who should know better) to *2001* (what was that about?). *Jaws* and *Star Wars* did get best-picture nominations but didn't take the top prize. See, these weren't people movies; they were simply the sum of their monster or sci-fi special effects.

The '70s brought a new breed of director, steeped in movie lore and movie love, making smart films that were huge hits—and for the longest time, Oscar ignored them too. *The Godfather* won best picture, but its auteur, Francis Ford Coppola, was not named best director. (He won for *The Godfather, Part II*.) Nor did the Academy give Spielberg an Oscar for *Jaws, Close Encounters of the Third Kind, Raiders of the Lost Ark*, or *E.T.* (He had to wait till 1994, when *Schindler's List* took best picture and best director.) Martin Scorsese, by general acclamation the most intense and gifted director of this talented bunch, wasn't even nominated for *Taxi Driver*, then suffered a generation of indignity as his work on *Raging Bull, The Last Temptation of Christ, Goodfellas, Gangs of New York*, and *The Aviator* lost out to that of other, lesser directors. (He finally copped the Oscar in 2007, at 64, for *The Departed*.) And yet they all have the edge on Hitchcock and Hawks, who never won a competitive Oscar.

Now the kids with beards—as Billy Wilder called them—are graybeards, and a younger generation is getting its turn. Look at the directors of the movies nominated for best picture of 2007. Paul Thomas Anderson, writer-director of *There Will Be Blood*, was nominated at 37. Jason Reitman, whose *Juno* was the only US$100 million box-office hit of the five 2007 best-picture finalists, was just 30. That left those two sassy outsiders—Joel Coen, 53, and his brother Ethan, 50—in the mainstream, though their entry, *No Country for Old Men*, carried the double-whammy genre curse of being a kind of western-horror movie. The other competitors were *Michael Clayton*, with George Clooney agonizing handsomely in a story about nasty business ethics (a favorite Academy theme, which explains why it was nominated), and *Atonement*, which fit the old tradition of quality, as a period romance in which beautiful people get horribly victimized.

All five films had their charms, or their poignancy, or their political message, or their steely fury, elements Oscar had often rewarded. None would have shamed the Academy by winning. The winner, *No Country for Old Men*, returned the Coen brothers to their best emotional territory of *Fargo* and *Miller's Crossing*, a place where comic innocence and unmediated violence explosively coexist.

It was among the worthiest winners of the best-picture award in the 80 years of Oscar.

But it was no *Citizen Kane*.

Motion Pictures

Academy Awards (Oscars), 2007

The Academy of Motion Picture Arts and Sciences was formed in 1927 and first awarded the Academy Awards of Merit in May 1929. The honored categories have varied over the years, but best picture, actor, actress, and director have been awarded since the beginning. Awards for supporting actor and actress were added for the films of 1936 and best foreign-language film for 1947. The ceremony is generally held in the early spring of the year following the release of films under consideration; the latest Oscars were awarded 24 Feb 2008 in Los Angeles. Award: gold-plated statuette of a man with a sword.

Academy of Motion Picture Arts and Sciences Web site: <www.oscars.org>.

CATEGORY	WINNER
Motion picture of the year	*No Country for Old Men* (US; Scott Rudin, Ethan Coen, and Joel Coen, producers)
Director	Joel Coen and Ethan Coen (*No Country for Old Men,* US)
Actor	Daniel Day-Lewis (*There Will Be Blood,* US)
Actress	Marion Cotillard (*La Vie en rose,* France/UK/Czech Republic)
Supporting actor	Javier Bardem (*No Country for Old Men,* US)
Supporting actress	Tilda Swinton (*Michael Clayton,* US)
Foreign-language film	*The Counterfeiters* (Austria/Germany; Stefan Ruzowitzky, director)
Animated feature	*Ratatouille* (US; Brad Bird and Jan Pinkava, directors)
Animated short	*Peter & the Wolf* (UK/Poland/Norway; Suzie Templeton, director)
Live-action short	*The Mozart of Pickpockets* (France; Philippe Pollet-Villard, director)
Documentary feature	*Taxi to the Dark Side* (US; Alex Gibney, director)
Documentary short	*Freeheld* (US; Cynthia Wade, director)
Cinematography	Robert Elswit (*There Will Be Blood,* US)
Art direction	Dante Ferretti, art direction; Francesca Lo Schiavo, set decoration (*Sweeney Todd: The Demon Barber of Fleet Street,* US/UK)
Film editing	Christopher Rouse (*The Bourne Ultimatum,* US/Germany)
Costume design	Alexandra Byrne (*Elizabeth: The Golden Age,* UK/France/Germany)
Makeup	Didier Lavergne and Jan Archibald (*La Vie en rose,* France/UK/Czech Republic)
Original score	Dario Marianelli (*Atonement,* UK/France)
Original song	"Falling Slowly," Glen Hansard and Marketa Irglova (*Once,* Ireland)
Sound mixing	Scott Millan, David Parker, and Kirk Francis (*The Bourne Ultimatum,* US/Germany)
Sound editing	Karen Baker Landers and Per Hallberg (*The Bourne Ultimatum,* US/Germany)
Visual effects	Michael Fink, Bill Westenhofer, Ben Morris, and Trevor Wood (*The Golden Compass,* US/UK)
Screenplay, adaptation	Joel Coen and Ethan Coen (*No Country for Old Men,* US)
Screenplay, original	Diablo Cody (*Juno,* US/Canada/Hungary)

Academy Awards (Oscars), 1928–2007

BEST PICTURE

1928 *Wings*
1929 *The Broadway Melody*
1930 *All Quiet on the Western Front*
1931 *Cimarron*
1932 *Grand Hotel*
1933 *Cavalcade*
1934 *It Happened One Night*
1935 *Mutiny on the Bounty*
1936 *The Great Ziegfeld*
1937 *The Life of Emile Zola*
1938 *You Can't Take It with You*
1939 *Gone with the Wind*
1940 *Rebecca*
1941 *How Green Was My Valley*
1942 *Mrs. Miniver*
1943 *Casablanca*
1944 *Going My Way*
1945 *The Lost Weekend*
1946 *The Best Years of Our Lives*
1947 *Gentleman's Agreement*
1948 *Hamlet*
1949 *All the King's Men*
1950 *All About Eve*
1951 *An American in Paris*

BEST PICTURE (CONTINUED)

1952 *The Greatest Show on Earth*
1953 *From Here to Eternity*
1954 *On the Waterfront*
1955 *Marty*
1956 *Around the World in 80 Days*
1957 *The Bridge on the River Kwai*
1958 *Gigi*
1959 *Ben-Hur*
1960 *The Apartment*
1961 *West Side Story*
1962 *Lawrence of Arabia*
1963 *Tom Jones*
1964 *My Fair Lady*
1965 *The Sound of Music*
1966 *A Man for All Seasons*
1967 *In the Heat of the Night*
1968 *Oliver!*
1969 *Midnight Cowboy*
1970 *Patton*
1971 *The French Connection*
1972 *The Godfather*
1973 *The Sting*

BEST PICTURE (CONTINUED)

1974 *The Godfather Part II*
1975 *One Flew Over the Cuckoo's Nest*
1976 *Rocky*
1977 *Annie Hall*
1978 *The Deer Hunter*
1979 *Kramer vs. Kramer*
1980 *Ordinary People*
1981 *Chariots of Fire*
1982 *Gandhi*
1983 *Terms of Endearment*
1984 *Amadeus*
1985 *Out of Africa*
1986 *Platoon*
1987 *The Last Emperor*
1988 *Rain Man*
1989 *Driving Miss Daisy*
1990 *Dances with Wolves*
1991 *The Silence of the Lambs*
1992 *Unforgiven*
1993 *Schindler's List*
1994 *Forrest Gump*
1995 *Braveheart*
1996 *The English Patient*
1997 *Titanic*

Academy Awards (Oscars), 1928–2007 (continued)

BEST PICTURE (CONTINUED)

1998 *Shakespeare in Love*
1999 *American Beauty*
2000 *Gladiator*
2001 *A Beautiful Mind*
2002 *Chicago*
2003 *The Lord of the Rings: The Return of the King*
2004 *Million Dollar Baby*
2005 *Crash*
2006 *The Departed*
2007 *No Country for Old Men*

BEST ACTOR

1928 Emil Jannings (*The Last Command; The Way of All Flesh*)
1929 Warner Baxter (*In Old Arizona*)
1930 George Arliss (*Disraeli*)
1931 Lionel Barrymore (*A Free Soul*)
1932 Wallace Beery (*The Champ*); Fredric March (*Dr. Jekyll and Mr. Hyde*) (tied)
1933 Charles Laughton (*The Private Life of Henry VIII*)
1934 Clark Gable (*It Happened One Night*)
1935 Victor McLaglen (*The Informer*)
1936 Paul Muni (*The Story of Louis Pasteur*)
1937 Spencer Tracy (*Captains Courageous*)
1938 Spencer Tracy (*Boys Town*)
1939 Robert Donat (*Goodbye, Mr. Chips*)
1940 James Stewart (*The Philadelphia Story*)
1941 Gary Cooper (*Sergeant York*)
1942 James Cagney (*Yankee Doodle Dandy*)
1943 Paul Lukas (*Watch on the Rhine*)
1944 Bing Crosby (*Going My Way*)
1945 Ray Milland (*The Lost Weekend*)
1946 Fredric March (*The Best Years of Our Lives*)
1947 Ronald Colman (*A Double Life*)
1948 Laurence Olivier (*Hamlet*)
1949 Broderick Crawford (*All the King's Men*)
1950 José Ferrer (*Cyrano de Bergerac*)
1951 Humphrey Bogart (*The African Queen*)
1952 Gary Cooper (*High Noon*)
1953 William Holden (*Stalag 17*)
1954 Marlon Brando (*On the Waterfront*)
1955 Ernest Borgnine (*Marty*)
1956 Yul Brynner (*The King and I*)
1957 Alec Guinness (*The Bridge on the River Kwai*)
1958 David Niven (*Separate Tables*)
1959 Charlton Heston (*Ben-Hur*)
1960 Burt Lancaster (*Elmer Gantry*)
1961 Maximilian Schell (*Judgment at Nuremberg*)
1962 Gregory Peck (*To Kill a Mockingbird*)
1963 Sidney Poitier (*Lilies of the Field*)
1964 Rex Harrison (*My Fair Lady*)
1965 Lee Marvin (*Cat Ballou*)
1966 Pául Scofield (*A Man for All Seasons*)
1967 Rod Steiger (*In the Heat of the Night*)
1968 Cliff Robertson (*Charly*)
1969 John Wayne (*True Grit*)
1970 George C. Scott (*Patton*) (declined)
1971 Gene Hackman (*The French Connection*)
1972 Marlon Brando (*The Godfather*) (declined)
1973 Jack Lemmon (*Save the Tiger*)
1974 Art Carney (*Harry and Tonto*)
1975 Jack Nicholson (*One Flew Over the Cuckoo's Nest*)
1976 Peter Finch (*Network*) (posthumously)
1977 Richard Dreyfuss (*The Goodbye Girl*)
1978 Jon Voight (*Coming Home*)
1979 Dustin Hoffman (*Kramer vs. Kramer*)
1980 Robert De Niro (*Raging Bull*)
1981 Henry Fonda (*On Golden Pond*)
1982 Ben Kingsley (*Gandhi*)
1983 Robert Duvall (*Tender Mercies*)
1984 F. Murray Abraham (*Amadeus*)
1985 William Hurt (*Kiss of the Spider Woman*)

BEST ACTOR (CONTINUED)

1986 Paul Newman (*The Color of Money*)
1987 Michael Douglas (*Wall Street*)
1988 Dustin Hoffman (*Rain Man*)
1989 Daniel Day-Lewis (*My Left Foot*)
1990 Jeremy Irons (*Reversal of Fortune*)
1991 Anthony Hopkins (*The Silence of the Lambs*)
1992 Al Pacino (*Scent of a Woman*)
1993 Tom Hanks (*Philadelphia*)
1994 Tom Hanks (*Forrest Gump*)
1995 Nicolas Cage (*Leaving Las Vegas*)
1996 Geoffrey Rush (*Shine*)
1997 Jack Nicholson (*As Good as It Gets*)
1998 Roberto Benigni (*Life Is Beautiful*)
1999 Kevin Spacey (*American Beauty*)
2000 Russell Crowe (*Gladiator*)
2001 Denzel Washington (*Training Day*)
2002 Adrien Brody (*The Pianist*)
2003 Sean Penn (*Mystic River*)
2004 Jamie Foxx (*Ray*)
2005 Philip Seymour Hoffman (*Capote*)
2006 Forest Whitaker (*The Last King of Scotland*)
2007 Daniel Day-Lewis (*There Will Be Blood*)

BEST ACTRESS

1928 Janet Gaynor (*7th Heaven; Street Angel; Sunrise*)
1929 Mary Pickford (*Coquette*)
1930 Norma Shearer (*The Divorcee*)
1931 Marie Dressler (*Min and Bill*)
1932 Helen Hayes (*The Sin of Madelon Claudet*)
1933 Katharine Hepburn (*Morning Glory*)
1934 Claudette Colbert (*It Happened One Night*)
1935 Bette Davis (*Dangerous*)
1936 Luise Rainer (*The Great Ziegfeld*)
1937 Luise Rainer (*The Good Earth*)
1938 Bette Davis (*Jezebel*)
1939 Vivien Leigh (*Gone with the Wind*)
1940 Ginger Rogers (*Kitty Foyle*)
1941 Joan Fontaine (*Suspicion*)
1942 Greer Garson (*Mrs. Miniver*)
1943 Jennifer Jones (*The Song of Bernadette*)
1944 Ingrid Bergman (*Gaslight*)
1945 Joan Crawford (*Mildred Pierce*)
1946 Olivia de Havilland (*To Each His Own*)
1947 Loretta Young (*The Farmer's Daughter*)
1948 Jane Wyman (*Johnny Belinda*)
1949 Olivia de Havilland (*The Heiress*)
1950 Judy Holliday (*Born Yesterday*)
1951 Vivien Leigh (*A Streetcar Named Desire*)
1952 Shirley Booth (*Come Back, Little Sheba*)
1953 Audrey Hepburn (*Roman Holiday*)
1954 Grace Kelly (*The Country Girl*)
1955 Anna Magnani (*The Rose Tattoo*)
1956 Ingrid Bergman (*Anastasia*)
1957 Joanne Woodward (*The Three Faces of Eve*)
1958 Susan Hayward (*I Want to Live!*)
1959 Simone Signoret (*Room at the Top*)
1960 Elizabeth Taylor (*Butterfield 8*)
1961 Sophia Loren (*Two Women*)
1962 Anne Bancroft (*The Miracle Worker*)
1963 Patricia Neal (*Hud*)
1964 Julie Andrews (*Mary Poppins*)

Academy Awards (Oscars), 1928–2007 (continued)

BEST ACTRESS (CONTINUED)

1965 Julie Christie (*Darling*)
1966 Elizabeth Taylor (*Who's Afraid of Virginia Woolf?*)
1967 Katharine Hepburn (*Guess Who's Coming to Dinner*)
1968 Katharine Hepburn (*The Lion in Winter*); Barbra Streisand (*Funny Girl*) (tied)
1969 Maggie Smith (*The Prime of Miss Jean Brodie*)
1970 Glenda Jackson (*Women in Love*)
1971 Jane Fonda (*Klute*)
1972 Liza Minnelli (*Cabaret*)
1973 Glenda Jackson (*A Touch of Class*)
1974 Ellen Burstyn (*Alice Doesn't Live Here Anymore*)
1975 Louise Fletcher (*One Flew Over the Cuckoo's Nest*)
1976 Faye Dunaway (*Network*)
1977 Diane Keaton (*Annie Hall*)
1978 Jane Fonda (*Coming Home*)
1979 Sally Field (*Norma Rae*)
1980 Sissy Spacek (*Coal Miner's Daughter*)
1981 Katharine Hepburn (*On Golden Pond*)
1982 Meryl Streep (*Sophie's Choice*)
1983 Shirley MacLaine (*Terms of Endearment*)
1984 Sally Field (*Places in the Heart*)
1985 Geraldine Page (*The Trip to Bountiful*)
1986 Marlee Matlin (*Children of a Lesser God*)
1987 Cher (*Moonstruck*)
1988 Jodie Foster (*The Accused*)
1989 Jessica Tandy (*Driving Miss Daisy*)
1990 Kathy Bates (*Misery*)
1991 Jodie Foster (*The Silence of the Lambs*)
1992 Emma Thompson (*Howards End*)
1993 Holly Hunter (*The Piano*)
1994 Jessica Lange (*Blue Sky*)
1995 Susan Sarandon (*Dead Man Walking*)
1996 Frances McDormand (*Fargo*)
1997 Helen Hunt (*As Good as It Gets*)
1998 Gwyneth Paltrow (*Shakespeare in Love*)
1999 Hilary Swank (*Boys Don't Cry*)
2000 Julia Roberts (*Erin Brockovich*)
2001 Halle Berry (*Monster's Ball*)
2002 Nicole Kidman (*The Hours*)
2003 Charlize Theron (*Monster*)
2004 Hilary Swank (*Million Dollar Baby*)
2005 Reese Witherspoon (*Walk the Line*)
2006 Helen Mirren (*The Queen*)
2007 Marion Cotillard (*La Vie en Rose*)

BEST SUPPORTING ACTOR

1936 Walter Brennan (*Come and Get It*)
1937 Joseph Schildkraut (*The Life of Emile Zola*)
1938 Walter Brennan (*Kentucky*)
1939 Thomas Mitchell (*Stagecoach*)
1940 Walter Brennan (*The Westerner*)
1941 Donald Crisp (*How Green Was My Valley*)
1942 Van Heflin (*Johnny Eager*)
1943 Charles Coburn (*The More the Merrier*)
1944 Barry Fitzgerald (*Going My Way*)
1945 James Dunn (*A Tree Grows in Brooklyn*)
1946 Harold Russell (*The Best Years of Our Lives*)
1947 Edmund Gwenn (*Miracle on 34th Street*)
1948 Walter Huston (*The Treasure of the Sierra Madre*)
1949 Dean Jagger (*Twelve O'Clock High*)
1950 George Sanders (*All About Eve*)
1951 Karl Malden (*A Streetcar Named Desire*)
1952 Anthony Quinn (*Viva Zapata!*)

BEST SUPPORTING ACTOR (CONTINUED)

1953 Frank Sinatra (*From Here to Eternity*)
1954 Edmond O'Brien (*The Barefoot Contessa*)
1955 Jack Lemmon (*Mister Roberts*)
1956 Anthony Quinn (*Lust for Life*)
1957 Red Buttons (*Sayonara*)
1958 Burl Ives (*The Big Country*)
1959 Hugh Griffith (*Ben-Hur*)
1960 Peter Ustinov (*Spartacus*)
1961 George Chakiris (*West Side Story*)
1962 Ed Begley (*Sweet Bird of Youth*)
1963 Melvyn Douglas (*Hud*)
1964 Peter Ustinov (*Topkapi*)
1965 Martin Balsam (*A Thousand Clowns*)
1966 Walter Matthau (*The Fortune Cookie*)
1967 George Kennedy (*Cool Hand Luke*)
1968 Jack Albertson (*The Subject Was Roses*)
1969 Gig Young (*They Shoot Horses, Don't They?*)
1970 John Mills (*Ryan's Daughter*)
1971 Ben Johnson (*The Last Picture Show*)
1972 Joel Grey (*Cabaret*)
1973 John Houseman (*The Paper Chase*)
1974 Robert De Niro (*The Godfather Part II*)
1975 George Burns (*The Sunshine Boys*)
1976 Jason Robards (*All the President's Men*)
1977 Jason Robards (*Julia*)
1978 Christopher Walken (*The Deer Hunter*)
1979 Melvyn Douglas (*Being There*)
1980 Timothy Hutton (*Ordinary People*)
1981 John Gielgud (*Arthur*)
1982 Louis Gossett, Jr. (*An Officer and a Gentleman*)
1983 Jack Nicholson (*Terms of Endearment*)
1984 Haing S. Ngor (*The Killing Fields*)
1985 Don Ameche (*Cocoon*)
1986 Michael Caine (*Hannah and Her Sisters*)
1987 Sean Connery (*The Untouchables*)
1988 Kevin Kline (*A Fish Called Wanda*)
1989 Denzel Washington (*Glory*)
1990 Joe Pesci (*Goodfellas*)
1991 Jack Palance (*City Slickers*)
1992 Gene Hackman (*Unforgiven*)
1993 Tommy Lee Jones (*The Fugitive*)
1994 Martin Landau (*Ed Wood*)
1995 Kevin Spacey (*The Usual Suspects*)
1996 Cuba Gooding, Jr. (*Jerry Maguire*)
1997 Robin Williams (*Good Will Hunting*)
1998 James Coburn (*Affliction*)
1999 Michael Caine (*The Cider House Rules*)
2000 Benicio Del Toro (*Traffic*)
2001 Jim Broadbent (*Iris*)
2002 Chris Cooper (*Adaptation*)
2003 Tim Robbins (*Mystic River*)
2004 Morgan Freeman (*Million Dollar Baby*)
2005 George Clooney (*Syriana*)
2006 Alan Arkin (*Little Miss Sunshine*)
2007 Javier Bardem (*No Country for Old Men*)

BEST SUPPORTING ACTRESS

1936 Gale Sondergaard (*Anthony Adverse*)
1937 Alice Brady (*In Old Chicago*)
1938 Fay Bainter (*Jezebel*)
1939 Hattie McDaniel (*Gone with the Wind*)
1940 Jane Darwell (*The Grapes of Wrath*)
1941 Mary Astor (*The Great Lie*)
1942 Teresa Wright (*Mrs. Miniver*)
1943 Katina Paxinou (*For Whom the Bell Tolls*)
1944 Ethel Barrymore (*None but the Lonely Heart*)
1945 Anne Revere (*National Velvet*)

Academy Awards (Oscars), 1928–2007 (continued)

BEST SUPPORTING ACTRESS (CONTINUED)

1946 Anne Baxter (*The Razor's Edge*)
1947 Celeste Holm (*Gentleman's Agreement*)
1948 Claire Trevor (*Key Largo*)
1949 Mercedes McCambridge (*All the King's Men*)
1950 Josephine Hull (*Harvey*)
1951 Kim Hunter (*A Streetcar Named Desire*)
1952 Gloria Grahame (*The Bad and the Beautiful*)
1953 Donna Reed (*From Here to Eternity*)
1954 Eva Marie Saint (*On the Waterfront*)
1955 Jo Van Fleet (*East of Eden*)
1956 Dorothy Malone (*Written on the Wind*)
1957 Miyoshi Umeki (*Sayonara*)
1958 Wendy Hiller (*Separate Tables*)
1959 Shelley Winters (*The Diary of Anne Frank*)
1960 Shirley Jones (*Elmer Gantry*)
1961 Rita Moreno (*West Side Story*)
1962 Patty Duke (*The Miracle Worker*)
1963 Margaret Rutherford (*The V.I.P.s*)
1964 Lila Kedrova (*Zorba the Greek*)
1965 Shelley Winters (*A Patch of Blue*)
1966 Sandy Dennis (*Who's Afraid of Virginia Woolf?*)
1967 Estelle Parsons (*Bonnie and Clyde*)
1968 Ruth Gordon (*Rosemary's Baby*)
1969 Goldie Hawn (*Cactus Flower*)
1970 Helen Hayes (*Airport*)
1971 Cloris Leachman (*The Last Picture Show*)
1972 Eileen Heckart (*Butterflies Are Free*)
1973 Tatum O'Neal (*Paper Moon*)
1974 Ingrid Bergman (*Murder on the Orient Express*)
1975 Lee Grant (*Shampoo*)
1976 Beatrice Straight (*Network*)
1977 Vanessa Redgrave (*Julia*)
1978 Maggie Smith (*California Suite*)
1979 Meryl Streep (*Kramer vs. Kramer*)
1980 Mary Steenburgen (*Melvin and Howard*)
1981 Maureen Stapleton (*Reds*)
1982 Jessica Lange (*Tootsie*)
1983 Linda Hunt (*The Year of Living Dangerously*)
1984 Peggy Ashcroft (*A Passage to India*)
1985 Anjelica Huston (*Prizzi's Honor*)
1986 Dianne Wiest (*Hannah and Her Sisters*)
1987 Olympia Dukakis (*Moonstruck*)
1988 Geena Davis (*The Accidental Tourist*)
1989 Brenda Fricker (*My Left Foot*)
1990 Whoopi Goldberg (*Ghost*)
1991 Mercedes Ruehl (*The Fisher King*)
1992 Marisa Tomei (*My Cousin Vinny*)
1993 Anna Paquin (*The Piano*)
1994 Dianne Wiest (*Bullets over Broadway*)
1995 Mira Sorvino (*Mighty Aphrodite*)
1996 Juliette Binoche (*The English Patient*)
1997 Kim Basinger (*L.A. Confidential*)
1998 Judi Dench (*Shakespeare in Love*)
1999 Angelina Jolie (*Girl, Interrupted*)
2000 Marcia Gay Harden (*Pollock*)
2001 Jennifer Connelly (*A Beautiful Mind*)
2002 Catherine Zeta-Jones (*Chicago*)
2003 Renée Zellweger (*Cold Mountain*)
2004 Cate Blanchett (*The Aviator*)
2005 Rachel Weisz (*The Constant Gardener*)
2006 Jennifer Hudson (*Dreamgirls*)
2007 Tilda Swinton (*Michael Clayton*)

FOREIGN LANGUAGE FILM (AMERICAN TITLES)

1947 *Shoe-Shine* (Italy)
1948 *Monsieur Vincent* (France)
1949 *The Bicycle Thief* (Italy)
1950 *The Walls of Malapaga* (France/Italy)

FOREIGN LANGUAGE FILM (AMERICAN TITLES) (CONTINUED)

1951 *Rashomon* (Japan)
1952 *Forbidden Games* (France)
1953 not awarded
1954 *Gate of Hell* (Japan)
1955 *Samurai, the Legend of Musashi* (Japan)
1956 *La Strada* (Italy)
1957 *The Nights of Cabiria* (Italy)
1958 *My Uncle* (France)
1959 *Black Orpheus* (France)
1960 *The Virgin Spring* (Sweden)
1961 *Through a Glass Darkly* (Sweden)
1962 *Sundays and Cybele* (France)
1963 *Federico Fellini's 8½* (Italy)
1964 *Yesterday, Today, and Tomorrow* (Italy)
1965 *The Shop on Main Street* (Czechoslovakia)
1966 *A Man and a Woman* (France)
1967 *Closely Watched Trains* (Czechoslovakia)
1968 *War and Peace* (USSR)
1969 *Z* (Algeria)
1970 *Investigation of a Citizen Above Suspicion* (Italy)
1971 *The Garden of the Finzi-Continis* (Italy)
1972 *The Discreet Charm of the Bourgeoisie* (France)
1973 *Day for Night* (France)
1974 *Amarcord* (Italy)
1975 *Dersu Uzala* (USSR)
1976 *Black and White in Color* (Ivory Coast)
1977 *Madame Rosa* (France)
1978 *Get Out Your Handkerchiefs* (France)
1979 *The Tin Drum* (West Germany)
1980 *Moscow Does Not Believe in Tears* (USSR)
1981 *Mephisto* (Hungary)
1982 *To Begin Again* (Spain)
1983 *Fanny & Alexander* (Sweden)
1984 *Dangerous Moves* (Switzerland)
1985 *The Official Story* (Argentina)
1986 *The Assault* (The Netherlands)
1987 *Babette's Feast* (Denmark)
1988 *Pelle the Conqueror* (Denmark)
1989 *Cinema Paradiso* (Italy)
1990 *Journey of Hope* (Switzerland)
1991 *Mediterraneo* (Italy)
1992 *Indochine* (France)
1993 *Belle Epoque* (Spain)
1994 *Burnt by the Sun* (Russia)
1995 *Antonia's Line* (The Netherlands)
1996 *Kolya* (Czech Republic)
1997 *Character* (The Netherlands)
1998 *Life Is Beautiful* (Italy)
1999 *All About My Mother* (Spain)
2000 *Crouching Tiger, Hidden Dragon* (Taiwan)
2001 *No Man's Land* (Bosnia and Herzegovina)
2002 *Nowhere in Africa* (Germany)
2003 *The Barbarian Invasions* (Canada)
2004 *The Sea Inside* (Spain)
2005 *Tsotsi* (South Africa)
2006 *The Lives of Others* (Germany)
2007 *The Counterfeiters* (Austria)

DIRECTING

1928 Lewis Milestone (*Two Arabian Knights*); Frank Borzage (*7th Heaven*)
1929 Frank Lloyd (*The Divine Lady*)
1930 Lewis Milestone (*All Quiet on the Western Front*)
1931 Norman Taurog (*Skippy*)
1932 Frank Borzage (*Bad Girl*)

Academy Awards (Oscars), 1928–2007 (continued)

DIRECTING (CONTINUED)

1933 Frank Lloyd (*Cavalcade*)
1934 Frank Capra (*It Happened One Night*)
1935 John Ford (*The Informer*)
1936 Frank Capra (*Mr. Deeds Goes to Town*)
1937 Leo McCarey (*The Awful Truth*)
1938 Frank Capra (*You Can't Take It with You*)
1939 Victor Fleming (*Gone with the Wind*)
1940 John Ford (*The Grapes of Wrath*)
1941 John Ford (*How Green Was My Valley*)
1942 William Wyler (*Mrs. Miniver*)
1943 Michael Curtiz (*Casablanca*)
1944 Leo McCarey (*Going My Way*)
1945 Billy Wilder (*The Lost Weekend*)
1946 William Wyler (*The Best Years of Our Lives*)
1947 Elia Kazan (*Gentleman's Agreement*)
1948 John Huston (*The Treasure of the Sierra Madre*)
1949 Joseph L. Mankiewicz (*A Letter to Three Wives*)
1950 Joseph L. Mankiewicz (*All About Eve*)
1951 George Stevens (*A Place in the Sun*)
1952 John Ford (*The Quiet Man*)
1953 Fred Zinnemann (*From Here to Eternity*)
1954 Elia Kazan (*On the Waterfront*)
1955 Delbert Mann (*Marty*)
1956 George Stevens (*Giant*)
1957 David Lean (*The Bridge on the River Kwai*)
1958 Vincente Minnelli (*Gigi*)
1959 William Wyler (*Ben-Hur*)
1960 Billy Wilder (*The Apartment*)
1961 Robert Wise, Jerome Robbins (*West Side Story*)
1962 David Lean (*Lawrence of Arabia*)
1963 Tony Richardson (*Tom Jones*)
1964 George Cukor (*My Fair Lady*)
1965 Robert Wise (*The Sound of Music*)
1966 Fred Zinnemann (*A Man for All Seasons*)
1967 Mike Nichols (*The Graduate*)
1968 Carol Reed (*Oliver!*)
1969 John Schlesinger (*Midnight Cowboy*)
1970 Franklin J. Schaffner (*Patton*)
1971 William Friedkin (*The French Connection*)
1972 Bob Fosse (*Cabaret*)
1973 George Roy Hill (*The Sting*)
1974 Francis Ford Coppola (*The Godfather Part II*)
1975 Milos Forman (*One Flew Over the Cuckoo's Nest*)
1976 John G. Avildsen (*Rocky*)
1977 Woody Allen (*Annie Hall*)
1978 Michael Cimino (*The Deer Hunter*)
1979 Robert Benton (*Kramer vs. Kramer*)
1980 Robert Redford (*Ordinary People*)
1981 Warren Beatty (*Reds*)
1982 Richard Attenborough (*Gandhi*)
1983 James L. Brooks (*Terms of Endearment*)
1984 Milos Forman (*Amadeus*)
1985 Sydney Pollack (*Out of Africa*)
1986 Oliver Stone (*Platoon*)
1987 Bernardo Bertolucci (*The Last Emperor*)
1988 Barry Levinson (*Rain Man*)
1989 Oliver Stone (*Born on the Fourth of July*)
1990 Kevin Costner (*Dances with Wolves*)
1991 Jonathan Demme (*The Silence of the Lambs*)
1992 Clint Eastwood (*Unforgiven*)
1993 Steven Spielberg (*Schindler's List*)
1994 Robert Zemeckis (*Forrest Gump*)
1995 Mel Gibson (*Braveheart*)
1996 Anthony Minghella (*The English Patient*)

DIRECTING (CONTINUED)

1997 James Cameron (*Titanic*)
1998 Steven Spielberg (*Saving Private Ryan*)
1999 Sam Mendes (*American Beauty*)
2000 Steven Soderbergh (*Traffic*)
2001 Ron Howard (*A Beautiful Mind*)
2002 Roman Polanski (*The Pianist*)
2003 Peter Jackson (*The Lord of the Rings: The Return of the King*)
2004 Clint Eastwood (*Million Dollar Baby*)
2005 Ang Lee (*Brokeback Mountain*)
2006 Martin Scorsese (*The Departed*)
2007 Joel Coen, Ethan Coen (*No Country for Old Men*)

SCREENPLAY, ADAPTATION[1]

1928 Benjamin Glazer (*7th Heaven*)
1929 Hans Kraly (*The Patriot*)
1931 Howard Estabrook (*Cimarron*)
1932 Edwin Burke (*Bad Girl*)
1933 Victor Heerman, Sarah Y. Mason (*Little Women*)
1934 Robert Riskin (*It Happened One Night*)
1935 Dudley Nichols (*The Informer*)[2] (declined)
1936 Pierre Collings, Sheridan Gibney (*The Story of Louis Pasteur*)[2]
1937 Norman Reilly Raine, Heinz Herald, Geza Herczeg (*The Life of Emile Zola*)[2]
1938 George Bernard Shaw, W.P. Lipscomb, Cecil Lewis, Ian Dalrymple (*Pygmalion*)[2]
1939 Sidney Howard (*Gone with the Wind*)[2]
1940 Donald Ogden Stewart (*The Philadelphia Story*)[2]
1941 Sidney Buchman, Seton I. Miller (*Here Comes Mr. Jordan*)[2]
1942 George Froeschel, James Hilton, Claudine West, Arthur Wimperis (*Mrs. Miniver*)[2]
1943 Julius J. Epstein, Philip G. Epstein, Howard Koch (*Casablanca*)[2]
1944 Frank Butler, Frank Cavett (*Going My Way*)[2]
1945 Charles Brackett, Billy Wilder (*The Lost Weekend*)[2]
1946 Robert E. Sherwood (*The Best Years of Our Lives*)[2]
1947 George Seaton (*Miracle on 34th Street*)[2]
1948 John Huston (*The Treasure of the Sierra Madre*)[2]
1949 Joseph L. Mankiewicz (*A Letter to Three Wives*)[2]
1950 Joseph L. Mankiewicz (*All About Eve*)[2]
1951 Michael Wilson, Harry Brown (*A Place in the Sun*)[2]
1952 Charles Schnee (*The Bad and the Beautiful*)[2]
1953 Daniel Taradash (*From Here to Eternity*)[2]
1954 George Seaton (*The Country Girl*)[2]
1955 Paddy Chayefsky (*Marty*)[2]
1956 James Poe, John Farrow, S.J. Perelman (*Around the World in 80 Days*)
1957 Pierre Boulle, Michael Wilson, Carl Foreman (*The Bridge on the River Kwai*)
1958 Alan Jay Lerner (*Gigi*)
1959 Neil Paterson (*Room at the Top*)
1960 Richard Brooks (*Elmer Gantry*)
1961 Abby Mann (*Judgment at Nuremberg*)
1962 Horton Foote (*To Kill a Mockingbird*)
1963 John Osborne (*Tom Jones*)
1964 Edward Anhalt (*Becket*)
1965 Robert Bolt (*Doctor Zhivago*)
1966 Robert Bolt (*A Man for All Seasons*)

Academy Awards (Oscars), 1928–2007 (continued)

SCREENPLAY, ADAPTATION[1] (CONTINUED)

1967 Stirling Silliphant (*In the Heat of the Night*)
1968 James Goldman (*The Lion in Winter*)
1969 Waldo Salt (*Midnight Cowboy*)
1970 Ring Lardner, Jr. (*M*A*S*H*)
1971 Ernest Tidyman (*The French Connection*)
1972 Mario Puzo, Francis Ford Coppola (*The Godfather*)
1973 William Peter Blatty (*The Exorcist*)
1974 Francis Ford Coppola, Mario Puzo (*The Godfather Part II*)
1975 Lawrence Hauben, Bo Goldman (*One Flew Over the Cuckoo's Nest*)
1976 William Goldman (*All the President's Men*)
1977 Alvin Sargent (*Julia*)
1978 Oliver Stone (*Midnight Express*)
1979 Robert Benton (*Kramer vs. Kramer*)
1980 Alvin Sargent (*Ordinary People*)
1981 Ernest Thompson (*On Golden Pond*)
1982 Costa-Gavras, Donald Stewart (*Missing*)
1983 James L. Brooks (*Terms of Endearment*)
1984 Peter Shaffer (*Amadeus*)
1985 Kurt Luedtke (*Out of Africa*)
1986 Ruth Prawer Jhabvala (*A Room with a View*)
1987 Mark Peploe, Bernardo Bertolucci (*The Last Emperor*)
1988 Christopher Hampton (*Dangerous Liaisons*)
1989 Alfred Uhry (*Driving Miss Daisy*)
1990 Michael Blake (*Dances with Wolves*)
1991 Ted Tally (*The Silence of the Lambs*)
1992 Ruth Prawer Jhabvala (*Howards End*)
1993 Steven Zaillian (*Schindler's List*)
1994 Eric Roth (*Forrest Gump*)
1995 Emma Thompson (*Sense and Sensibility*)
1996 Billy Bob Thornton (*Sling Blade*)
1997 Brian Helgeland, Curtis Hanson (*L.A. Confidential*)
1998 Bill Condon (*Gods and Monsters*)
1999 John Irving (*The Cider House Rules*)
2000 Stephen Gaghan (*Traffic*)
2001 Akiva Goldsman (*A Beautiful Mind*)
2002 Ronald Harwood (*The Pianist*)
2003 Fran Walsh, Philippa Boyens, Peter Jackson (*The Lord of the Rings: The Return of the King*)
2004 Alexander Payne, Jim Taylor (*Sideways*)
2005 Larry McMurtry, Diana Ossana (*Brokeback Mountain*)
2006 William Monahan (*The Departed*)
2007 Joel Coen, Ethan Coen (*No Country for Old Men*)

SCREENPLAY, ORIGINAL[1]

1928 Ben Hecht (*Underworld*)[3]; Joseph Farnham (*The Fair Co-Ed; Laugh, Clown, Laugh; Telling the World*)[4]
1930 Frances Marion (*The Big House*)
1931 John Monk Saunders (*The Dawn Patrol*)[3]
1932 Frances Marion (*The Champ*)[3]
1933 Robert Lord (*One Way Passage*)[3]
1934 Arthur Caesar (*Manhattan Melodrama*)[3]
1935 Ben Hecht, Charles MacArthur (*The Scoundrel*)[3]
1936 Pierre Collings, Sheridan Gibney (*The Story of Louis Pasteur*)[3]
1937 William A. Wellman, Robert Carson (*A Star Is Born*)[3]
1938 Eleanore Griffin, Dore Schary (*Boys Town*)[3]

SCREENPLAY, ORIGINAL[1] (CONTINUED)

1939 Lewis R. Foster (*Mr. Smith Goes to Washington*)[3]
1940 Benjamin Glazer, John S. Toldy (*Arise, My Love*)[3]; Preston Sturges (*The Great McGinty*)[5]
1941 Harry Segall (*Here Comes Mr. Jordan*)[3]; Herman J. Mankiewicz, Orson Welles (*Citizen Kane*)[5]
1942 Emeric Pressburger (*Forty-Ninth Parallel*)[3]; Michael Kanin, Ring Lardner, Jr. (*Woman of the Year*)[5]
1943 William Saroyan (*The Human Comedy*)[3]; Norman Krasna (*Princess O'Rourke*)[5]
1944 Leo McCarey (*Going My Way*)[3]; Lamar Trotti (*Wilson*)[5]
1945 Charles G. Booth (*The House on 92nd Street*)[3]; Richard Schweizer (*Marie-Louise*)[5]
1946 Clemence Dane (*Vacation from Marriage*)[3]; Muriel Box, Sydney Box (*The Seventh Veil*)[5]
1947 Valentine Davies (*Miracle on 34th Street*)[3]; Sidney Sheldon (*The Bachelor and the Bobby-Soxer*)[5]
1948 Richard Schweizer, David Wechsler (*The Search*)[5]
1949 Douglas Morrow (*The Stratton Story*)[3]; Robert Pirosh (*Battleground*)[5]
1950 Edna Anhalt, Edward Anhalt (*Panic in the Streets*)[3]; Charles Brackett, Billy Wilder, D.M. Marshman, Jr. (*Sunset Blvd.*)[5]
1951 Paul Dehn, James Bernard (*Seven Days to Noon*)[3]; Alan Jay Lerner (*An American in Paris*)[5]
1952 Fredric M. Frank, Theodore St. John, Frank Cavett (*The Greatest Show on Earth*)[3]; T.E.B. Clarke (*The Lavender Hill Mob*)[5]
1953 Dalton Trumbo[6] (as Ian McLellan Hunter, *Roman Holiday*)[3]; Charles Brackett, Walter Reisch, Richard L. Breen (*Titanic*)[5]
1954 Philip Yordan (*Broken Lance*)[3]; Budd Schulberg (*On the Waterfront*)[5],
1955 Daniel Fuchs (*Love Me or Leave Me*)[3]; William Ludwig, Sonya Levien (*Interrupted Melody*)[5]
1956 Dalton Trumbo[6] (as Robert Rich, *The Brave One*)[3]; Albert Lamorisse (*The Red Balloon*)[5]
1957 George Wells (*Designing Woman*)
1958 Nedrick Young[6] (as Nathan E. Douglas), Harold Jacob Smith (*The Defiant Ones*)
1959 Russell Rouse, Clarence Greene, Stanley Shapiro, Maurice Richlin (*Pillow Talk*)
1960 Billy Wilder, I.A.L. Diamond (*The Apartment*)
1961 William Inge (*Splendor in the Grass*)
1962 Ennio de Concini, Alfredo Giannetti, Pietro Germi (*Divorce—Italian Style*)
1963 James R. Webb (*How the West Was Won*)
1964 S.H. Barnett, Peter Stone, Frank Tarloff (*Father Goose*)
1965 Frederic Raphael (*Darling*)
1966 Claude Lelouch, Pierre Uytterhoeven (*A Man and a Woman*)
1967 William Rose (*Guess Who's Coming to Dinner*)
1968 Mel Brooks (*The Producers*)
1969 William Goldman (*Butch Cassidy and the Sundance Kid*)
1970 Francis Ford Coppola, Edmund H. North (*Patton*)
1971 Paddy Chayefsky (*The Hospital*)
1972 Jeremy Larner (*The Candidate*)
1973 David S. Ward (*The Sting*)

Academy Awards (Oscars), 1928–2007 (continued)

SCREENPLAY, ORIGINAL[1] (CONTINUED)

1974 Robert Towne (*Chinatown*)
1975 Frank Pierson (*Dog Day Afternoon*)
1976 Paddy Chayefsky (*Network*)
1977 Woody Allen, Marshall Brickman (*Annie Hall*)
1978 Nancy Dowd, Waldo Salt, Robert C. Jones (*Coming Home*)
1979 Steve Tesich (*Breaking Away*)
1980 Bo Goldman (*Melvin and Howard*)
1981 Colin Welland (*Chariots of Fire*)
1982 John Briley (*Gandhi*)
1983 Horton Foote (*Tender Mercies*)
1984 Robert Benton (*Places in the Heart*)
1985 Earl W. Wallace, William Kelley, Pamela Wallace (*Witness*)
1986 Woody Allen (*Hannah and Her Sisters*)
1987 John Patrick Shanley (*Moonstruck*)
1988 Ronald Bass, Barry Morrow (*Rain Man*)
1989 Tom Schulman (*Dead Poets Society*)
1990 Bruce Joel Rubin (*Ghost*)
1991 Callie Khouri (*Thelma & Louise*)
1992 Neil Jordan (*The Crying Game*)
1993 Jane Campion (*The Piano*)
1994 Quentin Tarantino, Roger Avary (*Pulp Fiction*)
1995 Christopher McQuarrie (*The Usual Suspects*)
1996 Joel Coen, Ethan Coen (*Fargo*)
1997 Ben Affleck, Matt Damon (*Good Will Hunting*)
1998 Marc Norman, Tom Stoppard (*Shakespeare in Love*)
1999 Alan Ball (*American Beauty*)
2000 Cameron Crowe (*Almost Famous*)
2001 Julian Fellowes (*Gosford Park*)
2002 Pedro Almodóvar (*Talk to Her*)
2003 Sofia Coppola (*Lost in Translation*)
2004 Charlie Kaufman (*Eternal Sunshine of the Spotless Mind*)
2005 Paul Haggis, Bobby Moresco (*Crash*)
2006 Michael Arndt (*Little Miss Sunshine*)
2007 Diablo Cody (*Juno*)

CINEMATOGRAPHY

1928 Charles Rosher, Karl Struss (*Sunrise*)
1929 Clyde De Vinna (*White Shadows in the South Seas*)
1930 Joseph T. Rucker, Willard Van Der Veer (*With Byrd at the South Pole*)
1931 Floyd Crosby (*Tabu*)
1932 Lee Garmes (*Shanghai Express*)
1933 Charles Bryant Lang, Jr. (*A Farewell to Arms*)
1934 Victor Milner (*Cleopatra*)
1935 Hal Mohr (*A Midsummer Night's Dream*)
1936 Gaetano Gaudio (*Anthony Adverse*)
1937 Karl Freund (*The Good Earth*)
1938 Joseph Ruttenberg (*The Great Waltz*)
1939 Gregg Toland (*Wuthering Heights*)[7]; Ernest Haller, Ray Rennahan (*Gone with the Wind*)[8]
1940 George Barnes (*Rebecca*)[7]; Georges Perinal (*The Thief of Bagdad*)[8]
1941 Arthur Miller (*How Green Was My Valley*)[7]; Ernest Palmer, Ray Rennahan (*Blood and Sand*)[8]
1942 Joseph Ruttenberg (*Mrs. Miniver*)[7]; Leon Shamroy (*The Black Swan*)[8]
1943 Arthur Miller (*The Song of Bernadette*)[7]; Hal Mohr, W. Howard Greene (*The Phantom of the Opera*)[8]
1944 Joseph LaShelle (*Laura*)[7]; Leon Shamroy (*Wilson*)[8]

CINEMATOGRAPHY (CONTINUED)

1945 Harry Stradling (*The Picture of Dorian Gray*)[7]; Leon Shamroy (*Leave Her to Heaven*)[8]
1946 Arthur Miller (*Anna and the King of Siam*)[7]; Charles Rosher, Leonard Smith, Arthur Arling (*The Yearling*)[8]
1947 Guy Green (*Great Expectations*)[7]; Jack Cardiff (*Black Narcissus*)[8]
1948 William Daniels (*The Naked City*)[7]; Joseph Valentine, William V. Skall, Winton Hoch (*Joan of Arc*)[8]
1949 Paul C. Vogel (*Battleground*)[7]; Winton Hoch (*She Wore a Yellow Ribbon*)[8]
1950 Robert Krasker (*The Third Man*)[7]; Robert Surtees (*King Solomon's Mines*)[8]
1951 William C. Mellor (*A Place in the Sun*)[7]; Alfred Gilks, John Alton (*An American in Paris*)[8]
1952 Robert Surtees (*The Bad and the Beautiful*)[7]; Winton C. Hoch, Archie Stout (*The Quiet Man*)[8]
1953 Burnett Guffey (*From Here to Eternity*)[7]; Loyal Griggs (*Shane*)[8]
1954 Boris Kaufman (*On the Waterfront*)[7]; Milton Krasner (*Three Coins in the Fountain*)[8]
1955 James Wong Howe (*The Rose Tattoo*)[7]; Robert Burks (*To Catch a Thief*)[8]
1956 Joseph Ruttenberg (*Somebody Up There Likes Me*)[7]; Lionel Lindon (*Around the World in 80 Days*)[8]
1957 Jack Hildyard (*The Bridge on the River Kwai*)
1958 Sam Leavitt (*The Defiant Ones*)[7]; Joseph Ruttenberg (*Gigi*)[8]
1959 William C. Mellor (*The Diary of Anne Frank*)[7]; Robert L. Surtees (*Ben-Hur*)[8]
1960 Freddie Francis (*Sons and Lovers*)[7]; Russell Metty (*Spartacus*)[8]
1961 Eugen Shuftan (*The Hustler*)[7]; Daniel L. Fapp (*West Side Story*)[8]
1962 Jean Bourgoin, Walter Wottitz (*The Longest Day*)[7]; Fred A. Young (*Lawrence of Arabia*)[8]
1963 James Wong Howe (*Hud*)[7]; Leon Shamroy (*Cleopatra*)[8]
1964 Walter Lassally (*Zorba the Greek*)[7]; Harry Stradling (*My Fair Lady*)[8]
1965 Ernest Laszlo (*Ship of Fools*)[7]; Freddie Young (*Doctor Zhivago*)[8]
1966 Haskell Wexler (*Who's Afraid of Virginia Woolf?*)[7]; Ted Moore (*A Man for All Seasons*)[8]
1967 Burnett Guffey (*Bonnie and Clyde*)
1968 Pasqualino De Santis (*Romeo and Juliet*)
1969 Conrad Hall (*Butch Cassidy and the Sundance Kid*)
1970 Freddie Young (*Ryan's Daughter*)
1971 Oswald Morris (*Fiddler on the Roof*)
1972 Geoffrey Unsworth (*Cabaret*)
1973 Sven Nykvist (*Cries and Whispers*)
1974 Fred Koenekamp, Joseph Biroc (*The Towering Inferno*)
1975 John Alcott (*Barry Lyndon*)
1976 Haskell Wexler (*Bound for Glory*)
1977 Vilmos Zsigmond (*Close Encounters of the Third Kind*)
1978 Nestor Almendros (*Days of Heaven*)
1979 Vittorio Storaro (*Apocalypse Now*)
1980 Geoffrey Unsworth, Ghislain Cloquet (*Tess*)
1981 Vittorio Storaro (*Reds*)
1982 Billy Williams, Ronnie Taylor (*Gandhi*)
1983 Sven Nykvist (*Fanny & Alexander*)
1984 Chris Menges (*The Killing Fields*)
1985 David Watkin (*Out of Africa*)

Academy Awards (Oscars), 1928–2007 (continued)

CINEMATOGRAPHY (CONTINUED)

1986 Chris Menges (*The Mission*)
1987 Vittorio Storaro (*The Last Emperor*)
1988 Peter Biziou (*Mississippi Burning*)
1989 Freddie Francis (*Glory*)
1990 Dean Semler (*Dances with Wolves*)
1991 Robert Richardson (*JFK*)
1992 Philippe Rousselot (*A River Runs Through It*)
1993 Janusz Kaminski (*Schindler's List*)
1994 John Toll (*Legends of the Fall*)
1995 John Toll (*Braveheart*)
1996 John Seale (*The English Patient*)
1997 Russell Carpenter (*Titanic*)
1998 Janusz Kaminski (*Saving Private Ryan*)
1999 Conrad L. Hall (*American Beauty*)
2000 Peter Pau (*Crouching Tiger, Hidden Dragon*)
2001 Andrew Lesnie (*The Lord of the Rings: The Fellowship of the Ring*)
2002 Conrad L. Hall (*Road to Perdition*)
2003 Russell Boyd (*Master and Commander: The Far Side of the World*)
2004 Robert Richardson (*The Aviator*)
2005 Dion Beebe (*Memoirs of a Geisha*)
2006 Guillermo Navarro (*Pan's Labyrinth*)
2007 Robert Elswit (*There Will Be Blood*)

VISUAL EFFECTS[9]

1939 Fred Sersen (*The Rains Came*)
1940 Lawrence Butler (*The Thief of Bagdad*)
1941 Farciot Edouart, Gordon Jennings (*I Wanted Wings*)
1942 Farciot Edouart, Gordon Jennings, William L. Pereira (*Reap the Wild Wind*)
1943 Fred Sersen (*Crash Dive*)
1944 A. Arnold Gillespie, Donald Jahraus, Warren Newcombe (*Thirty Seconds Over Tokyo*)
1945 John P. Fulton (*Wonder Man*)
1946 Thomas Howard (*Blithe Spirit*)
1947 A. Arnold Gillespie, Warren Newcombe (*Green Dolphin Street*)
1948 Paul Eagler, J. McMillan Johnson, Russell Shearman, Clarence Slifer (*Portrait of Jennie*)
1949 *Mighty Joe Young*
1950 *Destination Moon*
1951 *When Worlds Collide*
1952 *Plymouth Adventure*
1953 *The War of the Worlds*
1954 *20,000 Leagues Under the Sea*
1955 *The Bridges at Toko-Ri*
1956 John Fulton (*The Ten Commandments*)
1958 Tom Howard (*tom thumb*)
1959 A. Arnold Gillespie, Robert MacDonald (*Ben-Hur*)
1960 Gene Warren, Tim Baar (*The Time Machine*)
1961 Bill Warrington (*The Guns of Navarone*)
1962 Robert MacDonald (*The Longest Day*)
1963 Emil Kosa, Jr. (*Cleopatra*)
1964 Peter Ellenshaw, Hamilton Luske, Eustace Lycett (*Mary Poppins*)
1965 John Stears (*Thunderball*)
1966 Art Cruickshank (*Fantastic Voyage*)
1967 L.B. Abbott (*Doctor Dolittle*)
1968 Stanley Kubrick (*2001: A Space Odyssey*)
1969 Robbie Robertson (*Marooned*)
1970 A.D. Flowers, L.B. Abbott (*Tora! Tora! Tora!*)
1971 Alan Maley, Eustace Lycett, Danny Lee (*Bedknobs and Broomsticks*)

VISUAL EFFECTS[8] (CONTINUED)

1972 L.B. Abbott, A.D. Flowers (*The Poseidon Adventure*)
1974 Frank Brendel, Glen Robinson, Albert Whitlock (*Earthquake*)
1975 Albert Whitlock, Glen Robinson (*The Hindenburg*)
1976 Carlo Rambaldi, Glen Robinson, Frank Van der Veer (*King Kong*); L.B. Abbott, Glen Robinson, Matthew Yuricich (*Logan's Run*)
1977 John Stears, John Dykstra, Richard Edlund, Grant McCune, Robert Blalack (*Star Wars*)
1978 Les Bowie, Colin Chilvers, Denys Coop, Roy Field, Derek Meddings, Zoran Perisic (*Superman*)
1979 H.R. Giger, Carlo Rambaldi, Brian Johnson, Nick Allder, Denys Ayling (*Alien*)
1980 Brian Johnson, Richard Edlund, Dennis Muren, Bruce Nicholson (*The Empire Strikes Back*)
1981 Richard Edlund, Kit West, Bruce Nicholson, Joe Johnston (*Raiders of the Lost Ark*)
1982 Carlo Rambaldi, Dennis Muren, Kenneth F. Smith (*E.T.: The Extra-Terrestrial*)
1983 Richard Edlund, Dennis Muren, Ken Ralston, Phil Tippet (*Return of the Jedi*)
1984 Dennis Muren, Michael McAlister, Lorne Peterson, George Gibbs (*Indiana Jones and the Temple of Doom*)
1985 Ken Ralston, Ralph McQuarrie, Scott Farrar, David Berry (*Cocoon*)
1986 Robert Skotak, Stan Winston, John Richardson, Suzanne Benson (*Aliens*)
1987 Dennis Muren, William George, Harley Jessup, Kenneth Smith (*Innerspace*)
1988 Ken Ralston, Richard Williams, Edward Jones, George Gibbs (*Who Framed Roger Rabbit*)
1989 John Bruno, Dennis Muren, Hoyt Yeatman, Dennis Skotak (*The Abyss*)
1990 Eric Brevig, Rob Bottin, Tim McGovern, Alex Funke (*Total Recall*)
1991 Robert Skotak (*Terminator 2: Judgment Day*)
1992 Ken Ralston, Doug Chiang, Doug Smythe, Tom Woodruff, Jr. (*Death Becomes Her*)
1993 Dennis Muren, Stan Winston, Phil Tippett, Michael Lantieri (*Jurassic Park*)
1994 Ken Ralston, George Murphy, Stephen Rosenbaum, Allen Hall (*Forrest Gump*)
1995 Scott E. Anderson, Charles Gibson, Neal Scanlan, John Cox (*Babe*)
1996 Volker Engel, Douglas Smith, Clay Pinney, Joseph Viskocil (*Independence Day*)
1997 Robert Legato, Mark Lasoff, Thomas L. Fisher, Michael Kanfer (*Titanic*)
1998 Joel Hynek, Nicholas Brooks, Stuart Robertson, Kevin Mack (*What Dreams May Come*)
1999 John Gaeta, Janek Sirrs, Steve Courtley, Jon Thum (*The Matrix*)
2000 John Nelson, Neil Corbould, Tim Burke, Rob Harvey (*Gladiator*)
2001 Jim Rygiel, Randall William Cook, Richard Taylor, Mark Stetson (*The Lord of the Rings: The Fellowship of the Ring*)
2002 Jim Rygiel, Joe Letteri, Randall William Cook, Alex Funke (*The Lord of the Rings: The Two Towers*)

Academy Awards (Oscars), 1928–2007 (continued)

VISUAL EFFECTS[8] (CONTINUED)

2003 Jim Rygiel, Joe Letteri, Randall William Cook, Alex Funke (*The Lord of the Rings: The Return of the King*)
2004 John Dykstra, Scott Stokdyk, Anthony LaMolinara, John Frazier (*Spider-Man 2*)
2005 Joe Letteri, Brian Van't Hul, Christian Rivers, Richard Taylor (*King Kong*)
2006 John Knoll, Hal Hickel, Charles Gibson, Allen Hall (*Pirates of the Caribbean: Dead Man's Chest*)
2007 Michael Fink, Bill Westenhofer, Ben Morris, Trevor Wood (*The Golden Compass*)

MAKEUP

1981 Rick Baker (*An American Werewolf in London)*
1982 Sarah Monzani, Michele Burke (*Quest for Fire*)
1984 Paul LeBlanc, Dick Smith (*Amadeus*)
1985 Michael Westmore, Zoltan Elek (*Mask*)
1986 Chris Walas, Stephan Dupuis (*The Fly*)
1987 Rick Baker (*Harry and the Hendersons*)
1988 Ve Neill, Steve La Porte, Robert Short (*Beetlejuice*)
1989 Manlio Rocchetti, Lynn Barber, Kevin Haney (*Driving Miss Daisy*)
1990 John Caglione, Jr., Doug Drexler (*Dick Tracy*)
1991 Stan Winston, Jeff Dawn (*Terminator 2: Judgment Day*)
1992 Greg Cannom, Michele Burke, Matthew W. Mungle (*Bram Stoker's Dracula*)
1993 Greg Cannom, Ve Neill, Yolanda Toussieng (*Mrs. Doubtfire*)
1994 Rick Baker, Ve Neill, Yolanda Toussieng (*Ed Wood*)
1995 Peter Frampton, Paul Pattison, Lois Burwell (*Braveheart*)
1996 Rick Baker, David LeRoy Anderson (*The Nutty Professor*)
1997 Rick Baker, David LeRoy Anderson (*Men in Black*)
1998 Jenny Shircore (*Elizabeth*)
1999 Christine Blundell, Trefor Proud (*Topsy-Turvy*)
2000 Rick Baker, Gail Ryan (*Dr. Seuss' How the Grinch Stole Christmas*)
2001 Peter Owen, Richard Taylor (*The Lord of the Rings: The Fellowship of the Ring*)
2002 John Jackson, Beatrice Alba (*Frida*)
2003 Richard Taylor, Peter King (*The Lord of the Rings: The Return of the King*)
2004 Valli O'Reilly, Bill Corso (*Lemony Snicket's A Series of Unfortunate Events*)
2005 Howard Berger, Tami Lane (*The Chronicles of Narnia: The Lion, the Witch, and the Wardrobe)*
2006 David Martí, Montse Ribé (*Pan's Labyrinth*)
2007 Didier Lavergne, Jan Archibald (*La Vie en Rose*)

ORIGINAL SCORE

1938 Erich Wolfgang Korngold (*The Adventures of Robin Hood*)
1939 Herbert Stothart (*The Wizard of Oz*)
1940 Leigh Harline, Paul J. Smith, Ned Washington (*Pinocchio*)
1941 Bernard Herrmann (*All That Money Can Buy*)
1942 Max Steiner (*Now, Voyager*)
1943 Alfred Newman (*The Song of Bernadette*)
1944 Max Steiner (*Since You Went Away*)
1945 Miklós Rózsa (*Spellbound*)
1946 Hugo Friedhofer (*The Best Years of Our Lives*)
1947 Miklós Rózsa (*A Double Life*)

ORIGINAL SCORE (CONTINUED)

1948 Brian Easdale (*The Red Shoes*)
1949 Aaron Copland (*The Heiress*)
1950 Franz Waxman (*Sunset Blvd.*)
1951 Franz Waxman (*A Place in the Sun*)
1952 Dimitri Tiomkin (*High Noon*)
1953 Bronislau Kaper (*Lili*)
1954 Dimitri Tiomkin (*The High and Mighty*)
1955 Alfred Newman (*Love Is a Many-Splendored Thing*)
1956 Victor Young (*Around the World in 80 Days*)
1957 Malcolm Arnold (*The Bridge on the River Kwai*)[10]
1958 Dimitri Tiomkin (*The Old Man and The Sea*)
1959 Miklós Rózsa (*Ben-Hur*)
1960 Ernest Gold (*Exodus*)
1961 Henry Mancini (*Breakfast at Tiffany's*)
1962 Maurice Jarre (*Lawrence of Arabia*)
1963 John Addison (*Tom Jones*)
1964 Richard M. Sherman, Robert B. Sherman (*Mary Poppins*)
1965 Maurice Jarre (*Doctor Zhivago*)
1966 John Barry (*Born Free*)
1967 Elmer Bernstein (*Thoroughly Modern Millie*)
1968 John Barry (*The Lion in Winter*)[11]; John Green (*Oliver!*)[12]
1969 Burt Bacharach (*Butch Cassidy and the Sundance Kid*)[11]; Lennie Hayton, Lionel Newman (*Hello, Dolly!*)[12]
1970 Francis Lai (*Love Story*); The Beatles (*Let It Be*)[13]
1971 Michel Legrand (*Summer of '42*)
1972 Charles Chaplin, Raymond Rasch, Larry Russell (*Limelight*)
1973 Marvin Hamlisch (*The Way We Were*)
1974 Nino Rota, Carmine Coppola (*The Godfather Part II*)
1975 John Williams (*Jaws*)
1976 Jerry Goldsmith (*The Omen*)
1977 John Williams (*Star Wars*)
1978 Giorgio Moroder (*Midnight Express*)
1979 Georges Delerue (*A Little Romance*)
1980 Michael Gore (*Fame*)
1981 Vangelis (*Chariots of Fire*)
1982 John Williams (*E.T.: The Extra-Terrestrial*); Henry Mancini, Leslie Bricusse (*Victor/Victoria*)[13]
1983 Bill Conti (*The Right Stuff*); Michel Legrand, Alan Bergman, Marilyn Bergman (*Yentl*)[13]
1984 Maurice Jarre (*A Passage to India*); Prince (*Purple Rain*)[13]
1985 John Barry (*Out of Africa*)
1986 Herbie Hancock (*'Round Midnight*)
1987 Ryuichi Sakamoto, David Byrne, Cong Su (*The Last Emperor*)
1988 Dave Grusin (*The Milagro Beanfield War*)
1989 Alan Menken (*The Little Mermaid*)
1990 John Barry (*Dances with Wolves*)
1991 Alan Menken (*Beauty and the Beast*)
1992 Alan Menken (*Aladdin*)
1993 John Williams (*Schindler's List*)
1994 Hans Zimmer (*The Lion King*)
1995 Luis Enrique Bacalov (*The Postman* [*Il Postino*])[11]; Alan Menken, Stephen Schwartz (*Pocahontas*)[14]
1996 Gabriel Yared (*The English Patient*)[11]; Rachel Portman (*Emma*)[14]
1997 James Horner (*Titanic*)[11]; Anne Dudley (*The Full Monty*)[14]

Academy Awards (Oscars), 1928–2007 (continued)

ORIGINAL SCORE (CONTINUED)

1998 Nicola Piovani (*Life Is Beautiful*)[11]; Stephen Warbeck (*Shakespeare in Love*)[14]
1999 John Corigliano (*The Red Violin*)
2000 Tan Dun (*Crouching Tiger, Hidden Dragon*)
2001 Howard Shore (*The Lord of the Rings: The Fellowship of the Ring*)
2002 Elliot Goldenthal (*Frida*)
2003 Howard Shore (*The Lord of the Rings: The Return of the King*)
2004 Jan A.P. Kaczmarek (*Finding Neverland*)
2005 Gustavo Santaolalla (*Brokeback Mountain*)
2006 Gustavo Santaolalla (*Babel*)
2007 Dario Marianelli (*Atonement*)

ORIGINAL SONG

1934 Con Conrad, Herb Magidson, "The Continental" (*The Gay Divorcee*)
1935 Harry Warren, Al Dubin, "Lullaby of Broadway" (*Gold Diggers of 1935*)
1936 Jerome Kern, Dorothy Fields, "The Way You Look Tonight" (*Swing Time*)
1937 Harry Owens, "Sweet Leilani" (*Waikiki Wedding*)
1938 Ralph Rainger, Leo Robin, "Thanks for the Memory" (*The Big Broadcast of 1938*)
1939 Harold Arlen, E.Y. Harburg, "Over the Rainbow" (*The Wizard of Oz*)
1940 Leigh Harline, Ned Washington, "When You Wish Upon a Star" (*Pinocchio*)
1941 Jerome Kern, Oscar Hammerstein II, "The Last Time I Saw Paris" (*Lady Be Good*)
1942 Irving Berlin, "White Christmas" (*Holiday Inn*)
1943 Harry Warren, Mack Gordon, "You'll Never Know" (*Hello, Frisco, Hello*)
1944 James Van Heusen, Johnny Burke, "Swinging on a Star" (*Going My Way*)
1945 Richard Rodgers, Oscar Hammerstein II, "It Might As Well Be Spring" (*State Fair*)
1946 Harry Warren, Johnny Mercer, "On the Atchison, Topeka, and the Santa Fe" (*The Harvey Girls*)
1947 Allie Wrubel, Ray Gilbert, "Zip-a-dee-doo-dah" (*Song of the South*)
1948 Jay Livingston, Ray Evans, "Buttons and Bows" (*The Paleface*)
1949 Frank Loesser, "Baby, It's Cold Outside" (*Neptune's Daughter*)
1950 Ray Evans, Jay Livingston, "Mona Lisa" (*Captain Carey, U.S.A.*)
1951 Hoagy Carmichael, Johnny Mercer, "In The Cool, Cool, Cool of the Evening" (*Here Comes the Groom*)
1952 Dimitri Tiomkin, Ned Washington, "High Noon (Do Not Forsake Me, Oh My Darlin')" (*High Noon*)
1953 Sammy Fain, Paul Francis Webster, "Secret Love" (*Calamity Jane*)
1954 Jule Styne, Sammy Cahn, "Three Coins in the Fountain" (*Three Coins in the Fountain*)
1955 Sammy Fain, Paul Francis Webster, "Love Is a Many-Splendored Thing" (*Love Is a Many-Splendored Thing*)
1956 Jay Livingston, Ray Evans, "Whatever Will Be, Will Be (Que Sera, Sera)" (*The Man Who Knew Too Much*)
1957 James Van Heusen, Sammy Cahn, "All the Way" (*The Joker Is Wild*)

ORIGINAL SONG (CONTINUED)

1958 Frederick Loewe, Alan Jay Lerner, "Gigi" (*Gigi*)
1959 James Van Heusen, Sammy Cahn, "High Hopes" (*A Hole in the Head*)
1960 Manos Hadjidakis, "Never on Sunday" (*Never on Sunday*)
1961 Henry Mancini, Johnny Mercer, "Moon River" (*Breakfast at Tiffany's*)
1962 Henry Mancini, Johnny Mercer, "Days of Wine and Roses" (*Days of Wine and Roses*)
1963 James Van Heusen, Sammy Cahn, "Call Me Irresponsible" (*Papa's Delicate Condition*)
1964 Richard M. Sherman, Robert B. Sherman, "Chim Chim Cher-ee" (*Mary Poppins*)
1965 Johnny Mandel, Paul Francis Webster, "The Shadow of Your Smile" (*The Sandpiper*)
1966 John Barry, Don Black, "Born Free" (*Born Free*)
1967 Leslie Bricusse, "Talk to the Animals" (*Doctor Dolittle*)
1968 Michel Legrand, Alan Bergman, Marilyn Bergman, "The Windmills of Your Mind" (*The Thomas Crown Affair*)
1969 Burt Bacharach, Hal David, "Raindrops Keep Fallin' On My Head" (*Butch Cassidy and the Sundance Kid*)
1970 Fred Karlin, Robb Royer (as Robb Wilson), James Griffin (as Arthur James), "For All We Know" (*Lovers and Other Strangers*)
1971 Isaac Hayes, "Theme from *Shaft*" (*Shaft*)
1972 Al Kasha, Joel Hirschhorn, "The Morning After" (*The Poseidon Adventure*)
1973 Marvin Hamlisch, Alan Bergman, Marilyn Bergman, "The Way We Were" (*The Way We Were*)
1974 Al Kasha, Joel Hirschhorn, "We May Never Love Like This Again" (*The Towering Inferno*)
1975 Keith Carradine, "I'm Easy" (*Nashville*)
1976 Barbra Streisand, Paul Williams, "Evergreen (Love Theme from *A Star is Born*)" (*A Star Is Born*)
1977 Joseph Brooks, "You Light Up My Life" (*You Light Up My Life*)
1978 Paul Jabara, "Last Dance" (*Thank God It's Friday*)
1979 David Shire, Norman Gimbel, "It Goes Like It Goes" (*Norma Rae*)
1980 Michael Gore, Dean Pitchford, "Fame" (*Fame*)
1981 Burt Bacharach, Carole Bayer Sager, Christopher Cross, Peter Allen, "Arthur's Theme (Best That You Can Do)" (*Arthur*)
1982 Jack Nitzsche, Buffy Sainte-Marie, Will Jennings, "Up Where We Belong" (*An Officer and a Gentleman*)
1983 Giorgio Moroder, Keith Forsey, Irene Cara, "Flashdance...What a Feeling" (*Flashdance*)
1984 Stevie Wonder, "I Just Called To Say I Love You" (*The Woman in Red*)
1985 Lionel Richie, "Say You, Say Me" (*White Nights*)
1986 Giorgio Moroder, Tom Whitlock, "Take My Breath Away" (*Top Gun*)
1987 Franke Previte, John DeNicola, Donald Markowitz, "(I've Had) The Time of My Life" (*Dirty Dancing*)

Academy Awards (Oscars), 1928–2007 (continued)

ORIGINAL SONG (CONTINUED)

1988 Carly Simon, "Let the River Run" (*Working Girl*)
1989 Alan Menken, Howard Ashman, "Under the Sea" (*The Little Mermaid*)
1990 Stephen Sondheim, "Sooner or Later (I Always Get My Man)" (*Dick Tracy*)
1991 Alan Menken, Howard Ashman, "Beauty and the Beast" (*Beauty and the Beast*)
1992 Alan Menken, Tim Rice, "A Whole New World" (*Aladdin*)
1993 Bruce Springsteen, "Streets of Philadelphia" (*Philadelphia*)
1994 Elton John, Tim Rice, "Can You Feel the Love Tonight" (*The Lion King*)
1995 Alan Menken, Stephen Schwartz, "Colors of the Wind" (*Pocahantas*)
1996 Andrew Lloyd Webber, Tim Rice, "You Must Love Me" (*Evita*)
1997 James Horner, Will Jennings, "My Heart Will Go On" (*Titanic*)
1998 Stephen Schwartz, "When You Believe" (*The Prince of Egypt*)

ORIGINAL SONG (CONTINUED)

1999 Phil Collins, "You'll Be in My Heart" (*Tarzan*)
2000 Bob Dylan, "Things Have Changed" (*Wonder Boys*)
2001 Randy Newman, "If I Didn't Have You" (*Monsters, Inc.*)
2002 Eminem, Jeff Bass, Luis Resto, "Lose Yourself" (*8 Mile*)
2003 Fran Walsh, Howard Shore, Annie Lennox, "Into the West" (*The Lord of the Rings: The Return of the King*)
2004 Jorge Drexler, "Al otro lado del río" (*The Motorcycle Diaries*)
2005 Jordan Houston, Cedric Coleman, Paul Beauregard, "It's Hard Out Here for a Pimp" (*Hustle & Flow*)
2006 Melissa Etheridge, "I Need To Wake Up" (*An Inconvenient Truth*)
2007 Glen Hansard, Marketa Irglova, "Falling Slowly" (*Once*)

[1]The current screenplay categories were adopted for the 1957 awards. Until then, various separate writing awards were given for silent-film title writing, screenplay, story and screenplay, and motion picture story. [2]Screenplay (for script only). [3]Motion picture story (for narrative only; also called original story). [4]Title writing. [5]Story and screenplay (for narrative and script; also called original screenplay). [6]Actual winner was blacklisted at the time of the award and the honored work was attributed to another name or person; pseudonym or nominal winner is listed in parentheses. [7]Black and white. [8]Color. [9]Until 1963, both visual and sound effects were honored as special effects. Only those recipients honored for visual effects are listed here. [10]Scoring. [11]Drama or not a musical. [12]Musical [13]Song score. [14]Musical or comedy.

Sundance Film Festival, 2008

Founded as the Utah/US Film Festival in Salt Lake City in 1978, the exhibition has traditionally focused on documentary and dramatic works from outside the Hollywood mainstream. It came under the auspices of actor Robert Redford's Sundance Institute in 1985 and is held every January in Park City UT.

Sundance Institute Web site: <www.sundance.org>.

American Grand Jury Prize, drama	*Frozen River* (US; director, Courtney Hunt)
American Grand Jury Prize, documentary	*Trouble the Water* (US; directors, Tia Lessin and Carl Deal)
World Cinema Jury Prize, drama	*Ping-pongkingen* (*King of Ping Pong*) (Sweden; director, Jens Jonsson)
World Cinema Jury Prize, documentary	*Man on Wire* (UK; director, James Marsh)
Audience Award, drama	*The Wackness* (US; director, Jonathan Levine)
Audience Award, documentary	*Fields of Fuel* (US; director, Josh Tickell)
World Cinema Audience Award, drama	*Captain Abu Raed* (Jordan; director, Amin Matalqa)
World Cinema Audience Award, documentary	*Man on Wire* (UK; director, James Marsh)
Directing Award, drama	Lance Hammer (*Ballast*, US)
Directing Award, documentary	Nanette Burstein (*American Teen*, US)
World Cinema Directing Award, drama	Anna Melikyan (*Rusalka* [*Mermaid*], Russia)
World Cinema Directing Award, documentary	Nino Kirtadze (*Durakovo: Le Village des fous* [*Durakovo: Village of Fools*], France)
Cinematography Award, drama	Lol Crawley (*Ballast*, US)
Cinematography Award, documentary	Phillip Hunt and Steven Sebring (*Patti Smith: Dream of Life*, US)
Waldo Salt Screenwriting Award	Alex Rivera and David Riker (*Sleep Dealer*, US/Mexico)
Special Jury Prize, documentary	*The Greatest Silence: Rape in the Congo* (US; director, Lisa F. Jackson)
Special Jury Prize, drama (ensemble)	Sam Rockwell, Anjelica Huston, Kelly Macdonald, and Brad Henke (*Choke*, US)
Special Jury Prize, drama (the spirit of independence)	Chusy Haney-Jardine (*Anywhere, USA*, US)
World Cinema Special Jury Prize, drama	*Párpados Azules* (*Blue Eyelids*) (Mexico; director, Ernesto Contreras)

Sundance Film Festival, 2008 (continued)

Jury Prize, short filmmaking	*My Olympic Summer* (US; director, Daniel Robin); *Sikumi* (*On the Ice*), (US; director, Andrew Okpeaha MacLean)
Sundance/NHK International Filmmakers Award	*Huacho* (Chile; director, Alejandro Fernández Almendras); *Here* (US; director, Braden King); *Apoptosis* (Japan; director, Aiko Nagatsu); *The Happiest Girl in the World* (Romania; director, Radu Jude)
Alfred P. Sloan Prize	*Sleep Dealer* (US/Mexico; director, Alex Rivera)

Golden Globes, 2008

The Hollywood Foreign Press Association, a group of non-US film critics working in Hollywood, began awarding prizes for outstanding American motion pictures and acting in 1944 and created the Golden Globe Award in 1945. Over the years the prizes have expanded from recognizing only motion pictures and acting to include directing (1946), screenwriting and film music scoring (1947), foreign-language films (1950), and television (1955), as well as a number of other categories of achievement. Prize: globe encircled by a strip of motion picture film, in gold.

Golden Globes/Hollywood Foreign Press Association Web site: <www.hfpa.org>.

Film	
Drama	*Atonement* (director, Joe Wright)
Musical/comedy	*Sweeney Todd: The Demon Barber of Fleet Street* (director, Tim Burton)
Director	Julian Schnabel (*Le Scaphandre et le papillon* [*The Diving Bell and the Butterfly*])
Actress, drama	Julie Christie (*Away from Her*)
Actor, drama	Daniel Day-Lewis (*There Will Be Blood*)
Actress, musical/comedy	Marion Cotillard (*La Vie en rose*)
Actor, musical/comedy	Johnny Depp (*Sweeney Todd: The Demon Barber of Fleet Street*)
Animated feature film	*Ratatouille* (directors, Brad Bird and Jan Pinkava)
Foreign-language film	*Le Scaphandre et le papillon* (*The Diving Bell and the Butterfly*) (France/US; director, Julian Schnabel)
Supporting actress	Cate Blanchett (*I'm Not There*)
Supporting actor	Javier Bardem (*No Country for Old Men*)
Screenplay	Ethan Coen and Joel Coen (*No Country for Old Men*)
Original score	Dario Marianelli (*Atonement*)
Original song	"Guaranteed" (*Into the Wild*); music and lyrics, Eddie Vedder
Television	
Drama series	*Mad Men*, Lionsgate/AMC
Actress, drama series	Glenn Close (*Damages*)
Actor, drama series	Jon Hamm (*Mad Men*)
Musical/comedy series	*Extras*, BBC/HBO
Actress, musical/comedy series	Tina Fey (*30 Rock*)
Actor, musical/comedy series	David Duchovny (*Californication*)
Miniseries/movie made for TV	*Longford*, Granada/Channel 4/HBO Films
Actress, miniseries/movie made for TV	Queen Latifah (*Life Support*)
Actor, miniseries/movie made for TV	Jim Broadbent (*Longford*)
Supporting actress, series/miniseries/movie	Samantha Morton (*Longford*)
Supporting actor, series/miniseries/movie	Jeremy Piven (*Entourage*)

Toronto International Film Festival, 2007

Founded in 1976, the Toronto International Film Festival is one of North America's best-attended exhibitions and a frequent forum for the premiere of major feature films. The festival, held in September, awards seven prizes, three of which are for Canadian films.

Toronto International Film Festival Web site: <http://tiff07.ca/>.

Canadian feature film	*My Winnipeg* (director, Guy Maddin)
Canadian first feature	*Continental, un film sans fusil* (director, Stéphane LaFleur)
Canadian short	*Pool* (director, Christopher Chan Fui Chong)
FIPRESCI Prize	*La zona* (Mexico; director, Rodrigo Plá)
People's Choice Award	*Eastern Promises* (UK/Canada/US; director, David Cronenberg)
Discovery Award	*Cochochi* (Mexico/UK/Canada; directors, Israel Cárdenas and Laura Amelia Guzmán)
Artistic Innovation Award	*Encarnación* (Argentina; director, Anahí Berneri)

Cannes International Film Festival, 2008

Established in 1946, the Cannes International Film Festival is among the best known and most influential film exhibitions in the world. A nine-member feature-film jury and a four-member short-film and Cinéfondation jury give awards to the best film (Palme d'Or) and other outstanding films (special jury prizes) in their respective categories. The Grand Prix goes to the feature film judged the most original, and the feature jury also chooses the winners of the performance, direction, and screenplay awards. The Caméra d'Or, for best first film, is awarded by a jury comprising film industry professionals and members of the moviegoing public. The Cinéfondation awards are for works of one hour or less by film-school students.

Cannes International Film Festival Web site: <www.festival-cannes.com>.

feature films ▸ **Palme d'Or:** *Entre les murs* (France; director, Laurent Cantet); ▸ **Grand Prix:** *Gomorra* (Italy; director, Matteo Garrone); ▸ **Best actress:** Sandra Corveloni (*Linha de passe*, Brazil); ▸ **Best actor:** Benicio Del Toro (*Che*, US/France/Spain); ▸ **Best director:** Nuri Bilge Ceylan (*Uc maymun* [*Three Monkeys*], France/Italy/Turkey); ▸ **Best screenplay:** Jean-Pierre Dardenne and Luc Dardenne (*Le Silence de Lorna* [*The Silence of Lorna*], Belgium/UK/France/Italy); ▸ **Jury prize:** *Il Divo* (Italy/France; director, Paolo Sorrentino); ▸ **Caméra d'Or:** *Hunger* (UK; director, Steve McQueen)

short films ▸ **Palme d'Or:** *Megatron* (Romania; director, Marian Crisan); ▸ **Jury prize:** *Jerrycan* (Australia; director, Julius Avery)

Cinéfondation ▸ **1st prize:** *Himnon* (*Anthem*) (Israel; director, Elad Keidan); ▸ **2nd prize:** *Forbach* (France; director, Claire Burger); ▸ **3rd prize:** *Stop* (South Korea; director, Park Jae-ok); *Kestomerkitsijät* (*Roadmarkers*) (Finland; director, Juho Kuosmanen)

Berlin International Film Festival, 2008

The Berlin International Film Festival (Internationale Filmfestspiele Berlin), held annually since its founding in West Berlin in 1951, comprises some 20 separate competitions and juries emphasizing aspects of both worldwide and German cinema, each with their own prizes. The International Jury, made up of film-industry figures from across the globe, selects the winners of the Golden and Silver Bears, the festival's top awards.

Berlin International Film Festival Web site: <www.berlinale.de>.

Golden Bear	*Tropa de elite* (*The Elite Squad*) (Brazil; director, José Padilha)
Jury Grand Prize (Silver Bear)	*Standard Operating Procedure* (US; director, Errol Morris)
Silver Bear, director	Paul Thomas Anderson (*There Will Be Blood*, US)
Silver Bear, actress	Sally Hawkins (*Happy-Go-Lucky*, UK)
Silver Bear, actor	Reza Najie (*Avaze gonjeshk-ha* [*The Song of the Sparrows*], Iran)
Silver Bear, script	Wang Xiaoshuai (*Zuo you* [*In Love We Trust*], China)
Silver Bear, film music	Jonny Greenwood (*There Will Be Blood*, US)
Alfred Bauer Prize for a work of particular innovation	*Te acuerdas de Lake Tahoe?* (*Lake Tahoe*) (Mexico; director, Fernando Eimbcke)
Ecumenical Jury Prizes	Competition: *Il y a longtemps que je t'aime* (*I've Loved You So Long*) (France; director, Philippe Claudel); Panorama: *Boy A* (UK; director, John Crowley); Forum: *Corridor #8* (Bulgaria; director, Boris Despodov)
FIPRESCI Awards	Competition: *Te acuerdas de Lake Tahoe?* (*Lake Tahoe*) (Mexico; director, Fernando Eimbcke); Panorama: *Rusalka* (*Mermaid*), (Russia; director, Anna Melikyan); Forum: *Shahida–Brides of Allah* (Israel; director, Natalie Assouline)

US National Film Registry

The US Library of Congress established the National Film Preservation Board in 1988 with the goal of identifying "culturally, historically, or aesthetically important" American films. The board selects 25 films to add to the National Film Registry every year.

National Film Registry Web site: <www.loc.gov/film/filmnfr.html>.

Abbott and Costello Meet Frankenstein (1948)
Adam's Rib (1949)
The Adventures of Robin Hood (1938)
The African Queen (1951)
Alien (1979)
All About Eve (1950)
All My Babies (1953)
All Quiet on the Western Front (1930)
All That Heaven Allows (1955)
All That Jazz (1979)
All the King's Men (1949)
America, America (1963)
American Graffiti (1973)
An American in Paris (1951)
Annie Hall (1977)
Antonia: A Portrait of the Woman (1974)
The Apartment (1960)
Apocalypse Now (1979)
Applause (1929)
Atlantic City (1980)

US National Film Registry (continued)

The Awful Truth (1937)
Baby Face (1933)
Back to the Future (1985)
The Bad and the Beautiful (1953)
Badlands (1973)
The Band Wagon (1953)
The Bank Dick (1940)
The Battle of San Pietro (1945)
Beauty and the Beast (1991)
Ben-Hur (1926)
Ben-Hur (1959)
The Best Years of Our Lives (1946)
Big Business (1929)
The Big Parade (1925)
The Big Trail (1930)
The Big Sleep (1946)
The Birth of a Nation (1915)
The Black Pirate (1926)
The Black Stallion (1979)
Blacksmith Scene (1893)
Blade Runner (1982)
Blazing Saddles (1974)
The Blood of Jesus (1941)
The Blue Bird (1918)
Bonnie and Clyde (1967)
Boyz n the Hood (1991)
Bride of Frankenstein (1935)
The Bridge on the River Kwai (1957)
Bringing Up Baby (1938)
Broken Blossoms (1919)
A Bronx Morning (1931)
The Buffalo Creek Flood: An Act of Man (1975)
Bullitt (1968)
Butch Cassidy and the Sundance Kid (1969)
Cabaret (1972)
The Cameraman (1928)
Carmen Jones (1954)
Casablanca (1942)
Castro Street (1966)
Cat People (1942)
Chan Is Missing (1982)
The Cheat (1915)
The Chechahcos (1924)
Chinatown (1974)
Chulas Fronteras (1976)
Citizen Kane (1941)
The City (1939)
City Lights (1931)
Civilization (1916)
Clash of the Wolves (1925)
Close Encounters of the Third Kind (1977)
Cologne: From the Diary of Ray and Esther (1939)
Commandment Keeper Church, Beaufort, South Carolina, May 1940 (1940)
The Conversation (1974)
Cool Hand Luke (1967)
The Cool World (1963)
Cops (1922)
A Corner in Wheat (1909)
The Court Jester (1956)
The Crowd (1928)
The Curse of Quon Gwon (1916–17)
Czechoslovakia 1968 (1969)
Dance, Girl, Dance (1940)
Dances with Wolves (1990)
Daughter of Shanghai (1937)
Daughters of the Dust (1991)
David Holzman's Diary (1968)
The Day the Earth Stood Still (1951)
Days of Heaven (1978)
Dead Birds (1964)
The Deer Hunter (1978)
Destry Rides Again (1939)
Detour (1946)
Dickson Experimental Sound Film (1894–95)
D.O.A. (1950)
Do the Right Thing (1989)
The Docks of New York (1928)
Dodsworth (1936)
Dog Star Man: Part IV (1964)
Don't Look Back (1967)
Double Indemnity (1944)
Dr. Strangelove or: How I Learned To Stop Worrying and Love the Bomb (1964)
Dracula (1931)
Drums of Winter (1988)
Duck Amuck (1953)
Duck and Cover (1951)
Duck Soup (1933)
E.T.: The Extra-Terrestrial (1982)
Early Abstractions #1–5, 7, 10 (1939–56)
Easy Rider (1969)
Eaux d'Artifice (1953)
El Norte (1983)
Empire (1964)
The Emperor Jones (1933)
The Endless Summer (1966)
Enter the Dragon (1973)
Eraserhead (1977)
Evidence of the Film (1913)
The Exploits of Elaine (1914)
The Fall of the House of Usher (1928)
Fantasia (1940)
Fargo (1996)
Fast Times at Ridgemont High (1982)
Fatty's Tintype Tangle (1915)
Film Portrait (1970)
Five Easy Pieces (1970)
Flash Gordon (series) (1936)
Flesh and the Devil (1927)
Footlight Parade (1933)
Force of Evil (1948)
The Forgotten Frontier (1931)
42nd Street (1933)
The Four Horsemen of the Apocalypse (1921)
Fox Movietone News: Jenkins Orphanage Band (1928)
Frank Film (1973)
Frankenstein (1931)
Freaks (1932)
The French Connection (1971)
The Freshman (1925)
From Here to Eternity (1953)
From Stump to Ship (1930)
From the Manger to the Cross (1912)
Fuji (1974)
Fury (1936)
Garlic Is As Good As Ten Mothers (1980)
The General (1927)
Gerald McBoing-Boing (1950)
Gertie the Dinosaur (1914)
Giant (1956)
Gigi (1958)
Glimpse of the Garden (1957)
The Godfather (1972)
The Godfather, Part II (1974)
Going My Way (1944)
Gold Diggers of 1933 (1933)
The Gold Rush (1925)
Gone with the Wind (1939)
Goodfellas (1990)
The Graduate (1967)
Grand Hotel (1932)
The Grapes of Wrath (1940)
Grass: A Nation's Battle for Life (1925)
The Great Dictator (1940)
The Great Train Robbery (1903)
Greed (1924)
Groundhog Day (1993)
Gun Crazy (1949)
Gunga Din (1939)
H2O (1929)
Halloween (1978)
Hands Up (1929)
Harlan County, U.S.A. (1976)
Harold and Maude (1971)
The Heiress (1949)
Hell's Hinges (1916)
High Noon (1952)
High School (1968)
Hindenburg Disaster Newsreel Footage (1937)
His Girl Friday (1940)
The Hitch-Hiker (1953)
Hoop Dreams (1994)
Hoosiers (1986)
Hospital (1970)
The Hospital (1971)
The House I Live In (1945)
The House in the Middle (1954)
House of Usher (1960)
How Green Was My Valley (1941)
How the West Was Won (1962)
The Hunters (1957)
The Hustler (1961)
I Am a Fugitive from a Chain Gang (1932)
The Immigrant (1917)
Imitation of Life (1934)
In a Lonely Place (1950)
In the Heat of the Night (1967)
In the Land of the Head Hunters (1914)
In the Street (1948–52)
Intolerance (1916)
Invasion of the Body Snatchers (1956)
It (1927)
It Happened One Night (1934)
The Italian (1915)

US National Film Registry (continued)

It's a Wonderful Life (1946)
Jailhouse Rock (1957)
Jam Session (1942)
Jammin' the Blues (1944)
Jaws (1975)
Jazz on a Summer's Day (1959)
The Jazz Singer (1927)
Jeffries-Johnson World's Championship Boxing Contest (1910)
Kannapolis, NC (1941)
Killer of Sheep (1977)
King: A Filmed Record... Montgomery to Memphis (1970)
King Kong (1933)
The Kiss (1896)
Kiss Me Deadly (1955)
Knute Rockne, All American (1940)
Koyaanisqatsi (1983)
The Lady Eve (1941)
Lady Helen's Escapade (1909)
Lady Windermere's Fan (1925)
Lambchops (1929)
The Land Beyond the Sunset (1912)
Lassie Come Home (1943)
The Last Command (1928)
The Last of the Mohicans (1920)
The Last Picture Show (1971)
Laura (1944)
Lawrence of Arabia (1962)
The Learning Tree (1969)
Let's All Go to the Lobby (1957)
Letter from an Unknown Woman (1948)
The Life and Death of 9413: A Hollywood Extra (1928)
The Life and Times of Rosie the Riveter (1980)
The Life of Emile Zola (1937)
Little Caesar (1930)
Little Fugitive (1953)
Little Miss Marker (1934)
The Living Desert (1953)
The Lost World (1925)
Louisiana Story (1948)
Love Finds Andy Hardy (1938)
Love Me Tonight (1932)
Magical Maestro (1952)
The Magnificent Ambersons (1942)
The Making of an American (1920)
The Maltese Falcon (1941)
The Man Who Shot Liberty Valance (1962)
The Manchurian Candidate (1962)
Manhatta (1921)
Manhattan (1979)
March of Time: Inside Nazi Germany (1938)
Marian Anderson: The Lincoln Memorial Concert (1939)
Marty (1955)
*M*A*S*H* (1970)
Master Hands (1936)
Matrimony's Speed Limit (1913)
Mean Streets (1973)
Medium Cool (1969)
Meet Me in St. Louis (1944)
Melody Ranch (1940)
The Memphis Belle: A Story of a Flying Fortress (1944)
Meshes of the Afternoon (1943)
Midnight Cowboy (1969)
Mighty Like a Moose (1926)
Mildred Pierce (1945)
The Miracle of Morgan's Creek (1944)
Miracle on 34th Street (1947)
Miss Lulu Bett (1921)
Modern Times (1936)
Modesta (1956)
Mom and Dad (1944)
Morocco (1930)
Motion Painting No. 1 (1947)
A Movie (1958)
Mr. Smith Goes to Washington (1939)
Multiple Sidosis (1970)
The Music Box (1932)
The Music Man (1962)
My Darling Clementine (1946)
My Man Godfrey (1936)
The Naked City (1948)
The Naked Spur (1953)
Nanook of the North (1922)
Nashville (1975)
National Lampoon's Animal House (1978)
National Velvet (1944)
Naughty Marietta (1935)
Network (1976)
A Night at the Opera (1935)
The Night of the Hunter (1955)
Night of the Living Dead (1968)
Ninotchka (1939)
North by Northwest (1959)
Nostalgia (1971)
Nothing but a Man (1964)
Notorious (1946)
Now, Voyager (1942)
The Nutty Professor (1963)
OffOn (1968)
Oklahoma! (1955)
On the Waterfront (1954)
One Flew over the Cuckoo's Nest (1975)
One Froggy Evening (1955)
Our Day (1938)
Out of the Past (1947)
The Outlaw Josey Wales (1976)
The Ox-Bow Incident (1943)
Pass the Gravy (1928)
Paths of Glory (1957)
Patton (1970)
The Pearl (1948)
Peege (1972)
Peter Pan (1924)
The Phantom of the Opera (1925)
The Philadelphia Story (1940)
Pinocchio (1940)
A Place in the Sun (1951)
Planet of the Apes (1968)
The Plow That Broke the Plains (1936)
Point of Order (1964)
The Poor Little Rich Girl (1917)
Popeye the Sailor Meets Sindbad the Sailor (1936)
Porky in Wackyland (1938)
Power of the Press (1928)
Powers of Ten (1978)
President McKinley Inauguration Footage (1901)
Primary (1960)
Princess Nicotine; or, The Smoke Fairy (1909)
The Prisoner of Zenda (1937)
The Producers (1968)
Psycho (1960)
The Public Enemy (1931)
Pull My Daisy (1958)
Punch Drunks (1934)
Pups Is Pups (Our Gang) (1930)
Raging Bull (1980)
Raiders of the Lost Ark (1981)
A Raisin in the Sun (1961)
Rear Window (1954)
Rebel Without a Cause (1955)
Red Dust (1932)
Red River (1948)
Regeneration (1915)
Reminiscences of a Journey to Lithuania (1971–72)
Republic Steel Strike Riot Newsreel Footage (1937)
Return of the Secaucus 7 (1980)
Ride the High Country (1962)
Rip Van Winkle (1896)
The River (1937)
Road to Morocco (1942)
Rocky (1976)
The Rocky Horror Picture Show (1975)
Roman Holiday (1953)
Rose Hobart (1936)
Sabrina (1954)
Safety Last (1923)
Salesman (1969)
Salome (1922)
Salt of the Earth (1954)
San Francisco Earthquake and Fire, April 18, 1906 (1906)
Scarface (1932)
Schindler's List (1993)
The Searchers (1956)
Serene Velocity (1970)
Sex, Lies, and Videotape (1989)
The Sex Life of the Polyp (1928)
Seven Brides for Seven Brothers (1954)
Seventh Heaven (1927)
Shadow of a Doubt (1943)
Shadows (1959)
Shaft (1971)
Shane (1953)
She Done Him Wrong (1933)
Sherlock, Jr. (1924)
Sherman's March (1986)
Shock Corridor (1963)
The Shop Around the Corner (1940)
Show Boat (1936)
Show People (1928)
Siege (1940)
Singin' in the Rain (1952)

US National Film Registry (continued)

Sky High (1922)
Snow White (1933)
Snow White and the Seven Dwarfs (1937)
Some Like It Hot (1959)
The Son of the Sheik (1926)
The Sound of Music (1965)
St. Louis Blues (1929)
Stagecoach (1939)
A Star Is Born (1954)
Star Theatre (1901)
Star Wars (1977)
Steamboat Willie (1928)
The Sting (1973)
Stormy Weather (1943)
Stranger Than Paradise (1984)
A Streetcar Named Desire (1951)
The Strong Man (1926)
Sullivan's Travels (1941)
Sunrise (1927)
Sunset Boulevard (1950)
Sweet Smell of Success (1957)
Swing Time (1936)
The T.A.M.I. Show (1964)
Tabu (1931)
Tacoma Narrows Bridge Collapse (1940)
The Tall T (1957)
Tarzan and His Mate (1934)
Taxi Driver (1976)
The Tell-Tale Heart (1953)
The Ten Commandments (1956)
Tess of the Storm Country (1914)
Tevye (1939)
Theodore Case Sound Test: Gus Visser and His Singing Duck (1925)
There It Is (1928)
The Thief of Bagdad (1924)
The Thin Blue Line (1988)
The Thin Man (1934)
The Thing from Another World (1951)
Think of Me First as a Person (1960–75)
This Is Cinerama (1952)
This Is Spinal Tap (1984)
Three Little Pigs (1933)
Through Navajo Eyes (series) (1966)
A Time for Burning (1966)
A Time out of War (1954)
Tin Toy (1988)
To Be or Not To Be (1942)
To Fly (1976)
To Kill a Mockingbird (1962)
Tol'able David (1921)
Tom, Tom, the Piper's Son (1969–71)
Tootsie (1982)
Top Hat (1935)
Topaz (1945)
Touch of Evil (1958)
Toy Story (1995)
Traffic in Souls (1913)
Trance and Dance in Bali (1952)
The Treasure of the Sierra Madre (1948)
Trouble in Paradise (1932)
Tulips Shall Grow (1942)
12 Angry Men (1957)
Twelve O'Clock High (1949)
2001: A Space Odyssey (1968)
Unforgiven (1992)
Verbena Tragica (1939)
Vertigo (1958)
The Wedding March (1928)
West Side Story (1961)
Westinghouse Works (1904)
What's Opera, Doc? (1957)
Where Are My Children? (1916)
White Heat (1949)
Why Man Creates (1968)
Why We Fight (series) (1943–45)
Wild and Woolly (1917)
The Wild Bunch (1969)
Wild River (1960)
Will Success Spoil Rock Hunter? (1957)
The Wind (1928)
Wings (1927)
Within Our Gates (1920)
The Wizard of Oz (1939)
Woman of the Year (1942)
A Woman Under the Influence (1974)
The Women (1939)
Woodstock (1970)
Wuthering Heights (1939)
Yankee Doodle Dandy (1942)
Young Frankenstein (1974)
Young Mr. Lincoln (1939)
Zapruder Film of Kennedy Assassination (1963)

Worldwide Top-Grossing Films (Actual US Dollars)

As of 30 Jul 2008. Includes reissues. Source: Exhibitor Relations Co., Inc.

	Film	Year
1	*Titanic*	1997
2	*The Lord of the Rings: The Return of the King*	2003
3	*Pirates of the Caribbean: Dead Man's Chest*	2006
4	*Harry Potter and the Sorcerer's Stone*	2001
5	*Pirates of the Caribbean: At World's End*	2007
6	*Harry Potter and the Order of the Phoenix*	2007
7	*The Lord of the Rings: The Two Towers*	2002
8	*Star Wars: Episode I—The Phantom Menace*	1999
9	*Shrek 2*	2004
10	*Jurassic Park*	1993
11	*Harry Potter and the Goblet of Fire*	2005
12	*Spider-Man 3*	2007
13	*Harry Potter and the Chamber of Secrets*	2002
14	*The Lord of the Rings: The Fellowship of the Ring*	2001
15	*Finding Nemo*	2003
16	*Star Wars: Episode III—Revenge of the Sith*	2005
17	*Spider-Man*	2002
18	*Independence Day*	1996
19	*Shrek the Third*	2007
20	*E.T.: The Extra-Terrestrial*	1982

Top US Video Rentals and Sales, 2007

Data reflect DVD rentals and sales.

Source: Video Business. ***Web site:*** <www.videobusiness.com>.

	RENTALS	SALES
1	*The Departed*	*Transformers*
2	*The Pursuit of Happyness*	*Pirates of the Caribbean: At World's End*
3	*Blood Diamond*	*Happy Feet*
4	*Shooter*	*Shrek the Third*
5	*Wild Hogs*	*Harry Potter and the Order of the Phoenix*
6	*Night at the Museum*	*300*

Top US Video Rentals and Sales, 2007 (continued)

	RENTALS	SALES
7	*Déjà Vu*	*Ratatouille*
8	*The Guardian*	*Night at the Museum*
9	*Premonition*	*Spider-Man 3*
10	*The Illusionist*	*The Departed*
11	*Casino Royale*	*The Bourne Ultimatum*
12	*The Holiday*	*Wild Hogs*
13	*Ghost Rider*	*Planet Earth* (The Complete Series)
14	*Knocked Up*	*Open Season*
15	*The Good Shepherd*	*The Simpsons Movie*
16	*The Prestige*	*Live Free or Die Hard*
17	*Norbit*	*Superbad*
18	*Because I Said So*	*Casino Royale*
19	*Stranger than Fiction*	*Knocked Up*
20	*Man of the Year*	*The Pursuit of Happyness*

US Top-Grossing Films in Constant US Dollars (Estimated)

Admissions—the number of tickets sold to a movie—tell a different story from the raw dollars earned. While recent films have made hundreds of millions of dollars, only 2 of the top 10 films in terms of attendance were released after 1980. Includes reissues. Source: Exhibitor Relations Co., Inc.

		ADMISSIONS	2008 US DOLLARS	ACTUAL US DOLLARS
1	*Gone with the Wind* (1939)	202,044,600	1,430,476,000	198,676,459
2	*Star Wars* (1977)	178,119,600	1,261,086,000	460,998,007
3	*The Sound of Music* (1965)	142,415,400	1,008,300,000	158,671,368
4	*E.T.: The Extra-Terrestrial* (1982)	141,854,300	1,004,328,000	434,949,459
5	*The Ten Commandments* (1956)	131,000,000	927,480,000	65,500,000
6	*Titanic* (1997)	128,345,900	908,688,000	600,788,188
7	*Jaws* (1975)	128,078,800	906,798,000	260,000,000
8	*Doctor Zhivago* (1965)	124,135,500	878,879,000	111,721,910
9	*The Exorcist* (1973)	110,568,700	782,826,000	232,671,011
10	*Snow White and the Seven Dwarfs* (1937)	109,000,000	771,720,000	178,028,683

US Top-Grossing Film Openings

As of 20 Jul 2008. Table lists the largest box-office receipts over the first three days of theatrical release in the United States. Source: Exhibitor Relations Co., Inc.

		ACTUAL US DOLLARS
1	*The Dark Knight* (2008)	158,411,483
2	*Spider-Man 3* (2007)	151,116,516
3	*Pirates of the Caribbean: Dead Man's Chest* (2006)	135,634,554
4	*Shrek the Third* (2007)	121,629,270
5	*Spider-Man* (2002)	114,844,116
6	*Pirates of the Caribbean: At World's End* (2007)	114,732,820
7	*Star Wars: Episode III—Revenge of the Sith* (2005)	108,435,841
8	*Shrek 2* (2004)	108,037,878
9	*X-Men: The Last Stand* (2006)	102,750,665
10	*Harry Potter and the Goblet of Fire* (2005)	102,335,066
11	*Indiana Jones and the Kingdom of the Crystal Skull* (2008)	100,137,835
12	*Iron Man* (2008)	98,618,668
13	*Harry Potter and the Prisoner of Azkaban* (2004)	93,687,367
14	*The Matrix Reloaded* (2003)	91,774,413
15	*Harry Potter and the Sorcerer's Stone* (2001)	90,294,621
16	*Harry Potter and the Chamber of Secrets* (2002)	88,357,488
17	*Spider-Man 2* (2004)	88,156,227
18	*X2: X-Men United* (2003)	85,558,731
19	*The Passion of the Christ* (2004)	83,848,082
20	*Star Wars: Episode II—Attack of the Clones* (2002)	80,027,814

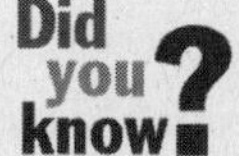

In 2007 Dhaka, Bangladesh, was the fastest-growing megacity in the world. Rural inhabitants of the country, one of the poorest in the world, flock to Dhaka to find jobs, and it is estimated that between 300,000 and 400,000 people move there annually. Bangladesh also has one of the world's highest population densities, and the problems caused by overcrowding are worsened by this migration to the cities.

Television

Emmy Award-winning Television Series, 1948–2007

1948
Most popular program: *Pantomime Quiz*, KTLA
TV film: *Your Show Time: The Necklace*

1949
Live show: *The Ed Wynn Show*, KTTV
Kinescope show: *The Texaco Star Theater*, KNBH (NBC)
TV film: *The Life of Riley*, KNBH
Pub. svc./cultural/educ.: *Crusade in Europe*, KECA-TV/KTTV (ABC)
Children's: *Time for Beany*, KTLA

1950
Variety: *The Alan Young Show*, KTTV (CBS)
Drama: *Pulitzer Prize Playhouse*, KECA-TV (ABC)
Game/audience particip.: *Truth or Consequences*, KTTV (CBS)
Children's: *Time for Beany*, KTLA
Educational: *KFI-TV University*, KFI-TV
Cultural: *Campus Chorus and Orchestra*, KTSL

1951
Variety: *Your Show of Shows* (NBC)
Comedy: *The Red Skelton Show* (NBC)
Drama: *Studio One* (CBS)

1952
Variety: *Your Show of Shows* (NBC)
Comedy: *I Love Lucy* (CBS)
Drama: *Robert Montgomery Presents* (NBC)
Mystery/action/adventure: *Dragnet* (NBC)
Public affairs: *See It Now* (CBS)
Aud. particip./quiz/panel: *What's My Line?* (CBS)
Children's: *Time for Beany* (syndicated)

1953
Variety: *Omnibus* (CBS)
Comedy: *I Love Lucy* (CBS)
Drama: *The U.S. Steel Hour* (ABC)
Mystery/action/adventure: *Dragnet* (NBC)
Public affairs: *Victory at Sea* (NBC)
Aud. particip./quiz/panel: *This Is Your Life* (NBC); *What's My Line?* (CBS)
Children's: *Kukla, Fran, and Ollie* (NBC)

1954
Variety: *Disneyland* (ABC)
Comedy: *Make Room for Daddy* (ABC)
Drama: *The United States Steel Hour* (ABC)
Mystery/intrigue: *Dragnet* (NBC)
Western/adventure: *Stories of the Century* (syndicated)
Cultural/relig./educ.: *Omnibus* (CBS)
Aud. particip./quiz/panel: *This Is Your Life* (NBC)
Children's: *Lassie* (CBS)

1955
Variety: *The Ed Sullivan Show* (CBS)
Comedy: *The Phil Silvers Show: You'll Never Get Rich* (CBS)
Drama: *Producers' Showcase* (NBC)
Action/adventure: *Disneyland* (ABC)
Music: *Your Hit Parade* (NBC)
Documentary: *Omnibus* (CBS)
Aud. particip.: *The $64,000 Question* (CBS)
Children's: *Lassie* (CBS)

1956
Series (½ hr. or less): *The Phil Silvers Show: You'll Never Get Rich* (CBS)
Series (1 hr. or more): *Caesar's Hour* (NBC)
New series: *Playhouse 90* (CBS)

1957
Mus./var./aud. par./quiz: *The Dinah Shore Chevy Show* (NBC)
Comedy: *The Phil Silvers Show: You'll Never Get Rich* (CBS)
Drama, continuing: *Gunsmoke* (CBS)
Drama, anthology: *Playhouse 90* (CBS)
New series: *The Seven Lively Arts* (CBS)
Public service: *Omnibus* (ABC/NBC)

1959[1]
Musical/variety: *The Dinah Shore Chevy Show* (NBC)
Comedy: *The Jack Benny Show* (CBS)
Drama (<1 hr.): *Alcoa-Goodyear Playhouse* (NBC)
Drama (1 hr.+): *Playhouse 90* (CBS)
Western: *Maverick* (ABC)
News reporting: *The Huntley-Brinkley Report* (NBC)
Public service: *Omnibus* (NBC)
Panel/quiz/aud. particip.: *What's My Line?* (CBS)

1960
Variety: *The Fabulous Fifties* (CBS)
Humor: *Art Carney Special* (NBC)
Drama: *Playhouse 90* (CBS)
News: *The Huntley-Brinkley Report* (NBC)
Public affairs/education: *The Twentieth Century* (CBS)
Children's: *Huckleberry Hound* (syndicated)

1961
Variety: *Astaire Time* (NBC)
Humor: *The Jack Benny Show* (CBS)
Drama: *Hallmark Hall of Fame: Macbeth* (NBC)
News: *The Huntley-Brinkley Report* (NBC)
Public affairs/education: *The Twentieth Century* (CBS)
Children's: "Aaron Copland's Birthday Party," *Young People's Concert* (CBS)
Program of the year: *Hallmark Hall of Fame: Macbeth* (NBC)

1962
Variety: *The Garry Moore Show* (CBS)
Humor: *The Bob Newhart Show* (NBC)
Drama: *The Defenders* (CBS)
News: *The Huntley-Brinkley Report* (NBC)
Educational/public affairs: *David Brinkley's Journal* (NBC)
Children's: *New York Philharmonic Young People's Concerts with Leonard Bernstein* (CBS)
Program of the year: *Hallmark Hall of Fame: Victoria Regina* (NBC)

1963
Variety: *The Andy Williams Show* (NBC)
Humor: *The Dick Van Dyke Show* (CBS)
Drama: *The Defenders* (CBS)
News: *The Huntley-Brinkley Report* (NBC)
Commentary/public affairs: *David Brinkley's Journal* (NBC)
Documentary: *The Tunnel* (NBC)
Panel/quiz/aud. particip.: *The G.E. College Bowl* (CBS)

Emmy Award-winning Television Series, 1948–2007 (continued)

1963 (continued)
Children's: *Walt Disney's Wonderful World of Color* (NBC)
Program of the year: *The Tunnel* (NBC)

1964
Variety: *The Danny Kaye Show* (CBS)
Comedy: *The Dick Van Dyke Show* (CBS)
Drama: *The Defenders* (CBS)
News reports: *The Huntley-Brinkley Report* (NBC)
Commentary/public affairs: "Cuba—Part I: The Bay of Pigs" and "Cuba—Part II: The Missile Crisis," *NBC White Paper* (NBC)
Documentary: *The Making of the President 1960* (ABC)
Children's: *Discovery '63–'64* (ABC)
Program of the year: *The Making of the President 1960* (ABC)

1965
Entertainment: *The Dick Van Dyke Show* (CBS); *Hallmark Hall of Fame: The Magnificent Yankee* (NBC); *My Name Is Barbra* (CBS); "What Is Sonata Form?," *New York Philharmonic Young People's Concerts with Leonard Bernstein* (CBS)
News/docu./info./sports: "I, Leonardo da Vinci," *Saga of Western Man* (ABC); *The Louvre* (NBC)

1966
Variety: *The Andy Williams Show* (NBC)
Comedy: *The Dick Van Dyke Show* (CBS)
Drama: *The Fugitive* (ABC)

1967
Variety: *The Andy Williams Show* (NBC)
Comedy: *The Monkees* (NBC)
Drama: *Mission: Impossible* (CBS)

1968
Musical/variety: *Rowan and Martin's Laugh-In* (NBC)
Comedy: *Get Smart* (NBC)
Drama: *Mission: Impossible* (CBS)

1969
Musical/variety: *Rowan and Martin's Laugh-In* (NBC)
Comedy: *Get Smart* (NBC)
Drama: *NET Playhouse* (NET)

1970
Variety/musical: *The David Frost Show* (syndicated)
Comedy: *My World and Welcome to It* (NBC)
Drama: *Marcus Welby, M.D.* (ABC)

1971
Comedy: *All in the Family* (CBS)
Drama: *The Bold Ones: The Senator* (NBC)
Variety, musical: *The Flip Wilson Show* (NBC)
Variety, talk: *The David Frost Show* (syndicated)
New series: *All in the Family* (CBS)

1972
Comedy: *All in the Family* (CBS)
Drama: *Masterpiece Theatre: Elizabeth R* (PBS)
Variety, musical: *The Carol Burnett Show* (CBS)
Variety, talk: *The Dick Cavett Show* (ABC)
New series: *Masterpiece Theatre: Elizabeth R* (PBS)

1973
Comedy: *All in the Family* (CBS)
Drama (continuing): *The Waltons* (CBS)
Drama/comedy (limited): *Masterpiece Theatre: Tom Brown's Schooldays* (PBS)
Variety, musical: *The Julie Andrews Hour* (ABC)
New series: *America* (NBC)

1974
Comedy: *M*A*S*H* (CBS)
Drama: *Masterpiece Theatre: Upstairs, Downstairs* (PBS)
Limited series: *Columbo* (NBC)
Music/variety: *The Carol Burnett Show* (CBS)

1975
Comedy: *The Mary Tyler Moore Show* (CBS)
Drama: *Masterpiece Theatre: Upstairs, Downstairs* (PBS)
Limited series: *Benjamin Franklin* (CBS)
Comedy-variety/music: *The Carol Burnett Show* (CBS)

1976
Comedy: *The Mary Tyler Moore Show* (CBS)
Drama: *Police Story* (NBC)
Limited series: *Masterpiece Theatre: Upstairs, Downstairs* (PBS)
Comedy-variety/music: *NBC's Saturday Night* (NBC)

1977
Comedy: *The Mary Tyler Moore Show* (CBS)
Drama: *Masterpiece Theatre: Upstairs, Downstairs* (PBS)
Limited series: *Roots* (ABC)
Comedy-variety/music: *Van Dyke and Company* (NBC)

1978
Comedy: *All in the Family* (CBS)
Drama: *The Rockford Files* (NBC)
Limited series: *Holocaust* (NBC)
Comedy-variety/music: *The Muppet Show* (syndicated)
Informational: *The Body Human* (CBS)

1979
Comedy: *Taxi* (ABC)
Drama: *Lou Grant* (CBS)
Limited series: *Roots: The Next Generations* (ABC)
Comedy-variety/music: "Steve & Eydie Celebrate Irving Berlin" (NBC)

1980
Comedy: *Taxi* (ABC)
Drama: *Lou Grant* (CBS)
Limited series: *Edward & Mrs. Simpson* (syndicated)
Variety/music: *IBM Presents Baryshnikov on Broadway* (ABC)

1981
Comedy: *Taxi* (ABC)
Drama: *Hill Street Blues* (NBC)
Limited series: *Shogun* (NBC)
Informational: *Steve Allen's Meeting of Minds* (PBS)

1982
Comedy: *Barney Miller* (ABC)
Drama: *Hill Street Blues* (NBC)
Limited series: *Marco Polo* (NBC)
Informational: *Creativity with Bill Moyers* (PBS)

Emmy Award-winning Television Series, 1948–2007 (continued)

1983
Comedy: *Cheers* (NBC)
Drama: *Hill Street Blues* (NBC)
Limited series: *Nicholas Nickleby* (syndicated)
Informational: *The Barbara Walters Specials* (ABC)

1984
Comedy: *Cheers* (NBC)
Drama: *Hill Street Blues* (NBC)
Limited series: *American Playhouse: Concealed Enemies* (PBS)
Informational: *A Walk Through the 20th Century with Bill Moyers* (PBS)

1985
Comedy: *The Cosby Show* (NBC)
Drama: *Cagney & Lacey* (CBS)
Limited series: *Masterpiece Theatre: The Jewel in the Crown* (PBS)
Informational: *The Living Planet: A Portrait of the Earth* (PBS)

1986
Comedy: *The Golden Girls* (NBC)
Drama: *Cagney & Lacey* (CBS)
Miniseries: *Peter the Great* (NBC)
Informational: *Great Performances: Laurence Olivier—A Life* (PBS); *Planet Earth* (PBS)

1987
Comedy: *The Golden Girls* (NBC)
Drama: *L.A. Law* (NBC)
Miniseries: *A Year in the Life* (NBC)
Informational: *Smithsonian World* (PBS); *American Masters: Unknown Chaplin* (PBS)

1988
Comedy: *The Wonder Years* (ABC)
Drama: *thirtysomething* (ABC)
Miniseries: *The Murder of Mary Phagan* (NBC)
Informational: *American Masters: Buster Keaton: A Hard Act To Follow* (PBS); *Nature* (PBS)

1989
Comedy: *Cheers* (NBC)
Drama: *L.A. Law* (NBC)
Miniseries: *War and Remembrance* (ABC)
Variety/music/comedy: *The Tracy Ullman Show* (Fox)
Informational: *Nature* (PBS)

1990
Comedy: *Murphy Brown* (CBS)
Drama: *L.A. Law* (NBC)
Miniseries: *Drug Wars: The Camarena Story* (NBC)
Variety/music/comedy: *In Living Color* (Fox)
Informational: *Smithsonian World* (PBS)

1991
Comedy: *Cheers* (NBC)
Drama: *L.A. Law* (NBC)
Miniseries: *Separate but Equal* (ABC)
Informational: *The Civil War* (PBS)

1992
Comedy: *Murphy Brown* (CBS)
Drama: *Northern Exposure* (CBS)
Miniseries: *A Woman Named Jackie* (NBC)
Variety/music/comedy: *The Tonight Show Starring Johnny Carson* (NBC)

1992 (continued)
Informational: *MGM: When the Lion Roars* (TNT)

1993
Comedy: *Seinfeld* (NBC)
Drama: *Picket Fences* (CBS)
Miniseries: *Prime Suspect 2* (PBS)
Variety/music/comedy: *Saturday Night Live* (NBC)
Informational: *Healing and the Mind with Bill Moyers* (PBS)

1994
Comedy: *Frasier* (NBC)
Drama: *Picket Fences* (CBS)
Miniseries: *Prime Suspect 3* (PBS)
Variety/music/comedy: *Late Show with David Letterman* (CBS)
Informational: *Later with Bob Costas* (NBC)

1995
Comedy: *Frasier* (NBC)
Drama: *NYPD Blue* (ABC)
Miniseries: *Joseph* (TNT)
Variety/music/comedy: *The Tonight Show with Jay Leno* (NBC)
Informational: *Baseball* (PBS); *TV Nation* (NBC)

1996
Comedy: *Frasier* (NBC)
Drama: *ER* (NBC)
Miniseries: *Gulliver's Travels* (NBC)
Variety/music/comedy: *Dennis Miller Live* (HBO)
Informational: *Lost Civilizations* (NBC)

1997
Comedy: *Frasier* (NBC)
Drama: *Law & Order* (NBC)
Miniseries: *Prime Suspect 5: Errors of Judgment* (PBS)
Variety/music/comedy: *Tracey Takes On...* (HBO)
Informational: *Biography* (A&E); *The Great War and the Shaping of the 20th Century* (PBS)

1998
Comedy: *Frasier* (NBC)
Drama: *The Practice* (ABC)
Miniseries: *From the Earth to the Moon* (HBO)
Variety/music/comedy: *Late Show with David Letterman* (CBS)
Nonfiction: *The American Experience* (PBS)

1999
Comedy: *Ally McBeal* (Fox)
Drama: *The Practice* (ABC)
Miniseries: *Horatio Hornblower: The Even Chance* (A&E)
Variety/music/comedy: *Late Show with David Letterman* (CBS)
Nonfiction: *The American Experience* (PBS); *American Masters* (PBS)

2000
Comedy: *Will & Grace* (NBC)
Drama: *The West Wing* (NBC)
Miniseries: *The Corner* (HBO)
Variety/music/comedy: *Late Show with David Letterman* (CBS)
Nonfiction: *American Masters* (PBS)

Emmy Award-winning Television Series, 1948–2007 (continued)

2001
Comedy: *Sex and the City* (HBO)
Drama: *The West Wing* (NBC)
Miniseries: *Anne Frank* (ABC)
Variety/music/comedy: *Late Show with David Letterman* (CBS)
Nonfiction: *American Masters* (PBS)

2002
Comedy: *Friends* (NBC)
Drama: *The West Wing* (NBC)
Miniseries: *Band of Brothers* (HBO)
Variety/music/comedy: *Late Show with David Letterman* (CBS)
Nonfiction: *Biography* (A&E)

2003
Comedy: *Everybody Loves Raymond* (CBS)
Drama: *The West Wing* (NBC)
Miniseries: *Steven Spielberg Presents Taken* (Sci Fi)
Variety/music/comedy: *The Daily Show with Jon Stewart* (Comedy Central)
Nonfiction: *American Masters* (PBS)

2004
Comedy: *Arrested Development* (Fox)
Drama: *The Sopranos* (HBO)
Miniseries: *Angels in America* (HBO)
Variety/music/comedy: *The Daily Show with Jon Stewart* (Comedy Central)

2004 (continued)
Nonfiction: *American Masters* (PBS)

2005
Comedy: *Everybody Loves Raymond* (CBS)
Drama: *Lost* (ABC)
Miniseries: *Masterpiece Theatre: The Lost Prince* (PBS)
Variety/music/comedy: *The Daily Show with Jon Stewart* (Comedy Central)
Nonfiction: *Broadway: The American Musical* (PBS)

2006
Comedy: *The Office* (NBC)
Drama: *24* (Fox)
Miniseries: *Elizabeth I* (HBO)
Variety/music/comedy: *The Daily Show with Jon Stewart* (Comedy Central)
Nonfiction: *10 Days That Unexpectedly Changed America* (The History Channel)

2007
Comedy: *30 Rock* (NBC)
Drama: *The Sopranos* (HBO)
Miniseries: *Broken Trail* (AMC)
Variety/music/comedy: *The Daily Show with Jon Stewart* (Comedy Central)
Nonfiction: *Planet Earth* (Discovery Channel)

[1]*No awards were given in 1958; the 1959 awards included all of calendar year 1958 and part of 1959.*

Theater

Tony Award Winners, 2008

The American Theatre Wing (ATW), established in 1939, created the Tony Awards in 1947 to recognize distinguished achievement in the theater arts as presented on Broadway. The award is named for Antoinette Perry, a former ATW director; since 1967 it has been presented in conjunction with the League of American Theatres and Producers, a Broadway trade association. Nominees are selected each May from among the year's new or newly revived Broadway shows; a body of some 750 current and former theater professionals, critics, and agents votes for the winners. The awards are presented in New York City in June. Prize: silver medallion, set in a base, depicting on one face the masks of tragedy and comedy and on the other the profile of Antoinette Perry.

Tony Awards Web site: <www.tonyawards.com>.

▸ **musical:** *In the Heights* (book, Quiara Alegría Hudes; music and lyrics, Lin-Manuel Miranda); ▸ **play:** *August: Osage County* (playwright, Tracy Letts); ▸ **revival of a musical:** *South Pacific* (book, Oscar Hammerstein II and Joshua Logan; music, Richard Rodgers; lyrics, Oscar Hammerstein II); ▸ **revival of a play:** *Boeing-Boeing* (playwright, Marc Camoletti); ▸ **book, musical:** Stew (*Passing Strange*); ▸ **score:** Lin-Manuel Miranda (*In the Heights*); ▸ **leading actress, musical:** Patti LuPone (*Gypsy*); ▸ **leading actor, musical:** Paulo Szot (*South Pacific*); ▸ **leading actress, play:** Deanna Dunagan (*August: Osage County*); ▸ **leading actor, play:** Mark Rylance (*Boeing-Boeing*); ▸ **featured actress, musical:** Laura Benanti (*Gypsy*); ▸ **featured actor, musical:** Boyd Gaines (*Gypsy*); ▸ **featured actress, play:** Rondi Reed (*August: Osage County*); ▸ **featured actor, play:** Jim Norton (*The Seafarer*); ▸ **direction, musical:** Bartlett Sher (*South Pacific*); ▸ **direction, play:** Anna D. Shapiro (*August: Osage County*); ▸ **costume design, musical:** Catherine Zuber (*South Pacific*); ▸ **costume design, play:** Katrina Lindsay (*Les Liasons dangereuses*); ▸ **lighting design, musical:** Donald Holder (*South Pacific*); ▸ **lighting design, play:** Kevin Adams (*The 39 Steps*); ▸ **scenic design, musical:** Michael Yeargan (*South Pacific*); ▸ **scenic design, play:** Todd Rosenthal (*August: Osage County*); ▸ **sound design, musical:** Scott Lehrer (*South Pacific*); ▸ **sound design, play:** Mic Pool (*The 39 Steps*); ▸ **orchestrations:** Alex Lacamoire and Bill Sherman (*In the Heights*); ▸ **choreography:** Andy Blankenbuehler (*In the Heights*); ▸ **regional theater award:** Chicago Shakespeare Theater, Chicago IL; ▸ **special award:** Robert Russell Bennett.

Tony Awards, 1947–2008

YEAR	BEST MUSICAL	BEST PLAY
1947	*not awarded*	*All My Sons* (Arthur Miller)[1]
1948	*not awarded*	*Mister Roberts* (Thomas Heggen and Joshua Logan)
1949	*Kiss Me, Kate* (book, Bella Spewack and Samuel Spewack; music and lyrics, Cole Porter)	*Death of a Salesman* (Arthur Miller)
1950	*South Pacific* (book, Oscar Hammerstein II and Joshua Logan; music, Richard Rodgers; lyrics, Oscar Hammerstein II)	*The Cocktail Party* (T.S. Eliot)
1951	*Guys and Dolls* (book, Jo Swerling and Abe Burrows; music and lyrics, Frank Loesser)	*The Rose Tattoo* (Tennessee Williams)
1952	*The King and I* (book and lyrics, Oscar Hammerstein II; music, Richard Rodgers)	*The Fourposter* (Jan de Hartog)
1953	*Wonderful Town* (book, Joseph Fields and Jerome Chodorov; music, Leonard Bernstein; lyrics, Betty Comden and Adolph Green)	*The Crucible* (Arthur Miller)
1954	*Kismet* (book, Charles Lederer and Luther Davis; music, Alexander Borodin; adaptation and lyrics, Robert Wright and George Forrest)	*The Teahouse of the August Moon* (John Patrick)
1955	*The Pajama Game* (book, George Abbott and Richard Bissell; music and lyrics, Richard Adler and Jerry Ross)	*The Desperate Hours* (Joseph Hayes)
1956	*Damn Yankees* (book, George Abbott and Douglass Wallop; music and lyrics, Richard Adler and Jerry Ross)	*The Diary of Anne Frank* (Frances Goodrich and Albert Hackett)
1957	*My Fair Lady* (book and lyrics, Alan Jay Lerner; music, Frederick Loewe)	*Long Day's Journey into Night* (Eugene O'Neill)
1958	*The Music Man* (book, Meredith Willson and Franklin Lacey; music and lyrics, Meredith Willson)	*Sunrise at Campobello* (Dore Schary)
1959	*Redhead* (book, Herbert Fields, Dorothy Fields, Sidney Sheldon, and David Shaw; music, Albert Hague; lyrics, Dorothy Fields)	*J.B.* (Archibald MacLeish)
1960	*The Sound of Music* (book, Howard Lindsay and Russel Crouse; music, Richard Rodgers; lyrics, Oscar Hammerstein II); *Fiorello!* (book, Jerome Weidman and George Abbott; music, Jerry Brock; lyrics, Sheldon Harnick) (tied)	*The Miracle Worker* (William Gibson)
1961	*Bye Bye Birdie* (book, Michael Stewart; music, Charles Strouse; lyrics, Lee Adams)	*Beckett* (Jean Anouilh, translated by Lucienne Hill)
1962	*How To Succeed in Business Without Really Trying* (book, Abe Burrows, Jack Weinstock, and Willie Gilbert; music and lyrics, Frank Loesser)	*A Man for All Seasons* (Robert Bolt)
1963	*A Funny Thing Happened on the Way to the Forum* (book, Burt Shevelove and Larry Gelbart; music and lyrics, Stephen Sondheim)	*Who's Afraid of Virginia Woolf?* (Edward Albee)
1964	*Hello, Dolly!* (book, Michael Stewart; music and lyrics, Jerry Herman)	*Luther* (John Osborne)
1965	*Fiddler on the Roof* (book, Joseph Stein; music, Jerry Bock; lyrics, Sheldon Harnick)	*The Subject Was Roses* (Frank Gilroy)
1966	*Man of La Mancha* (book, Dale Wasserman; music, Mitch Leigh; lyrics, Joe Darion)	*Marat/Sade* (Peter Weiss, translated by Geoffrey Skelton)
1967	*Cabaret* (book, Joe Masteroff; music, John Kander; lyrics, Fred Ebb)	*The Homecoming* (Harold Pinter)
1968	*Hallelujah, Baby!* (book, Arthur Laurents; music, Jule Styne; lyrics, Betty Comden and Adolph Green)	*Rosencrantz and Guildenstern Are Dead* (Tom Stoppard)
1969	*1776* (book, Peter Stone; music and lyrics, Sherman Edwards)	*The Great White Hope* (Howard Sackler)
1970	*Applause* (book, Betty Comden and Adolph Greene; music, Charles Strouse; lyrics, Lee Adams)	*Borstal Boy* (Frank McMahon)
1971	*Company* (book, George Furth; music and lyrics, Stephen Sondheim)	*Sleuth* (Anthony Shaffer)
1972	*Two Gentlemen of Verona* (book, John Guare and Mel Shapiro; music, Galt MacDermot; lyrics, John Guare)	*Sticks and Bones* (David Rabe)
1973	*A Little Night Music* (book, Hugh Wheeler; music and lyrics, Stephen Sondheim)	*That Championship Season* (Jason Miller)
1974	*Raisin* (book, Robert Nemiroff and Charlotte Zaltzberg; music, Judd Woldin; lyrics, Robert Brittan)	*The River Niger* (Joseph A. Walker)
1975	*The Wiz* (book, William F. Brown; music and lyrics, Charlie Smalls)	*Equus* (Peter Shaffer)
1976	*A Chorus Line* (book, James Kirkwood and Nicholas Dante; music, Marvin Hamlisch; lyrics, Edward Kleban)	*Travesties* (Tom Stoppard)
1977	*Annie* (book, Thomas Meehan; music, Charles Strouse; lyrics, Martin Charnin)	*The Shadow Box* (Michael Christofer)
1978	*Ain't Misbehavin'* (book, Murray Horwitz and Richard Maltby, Jr.; music, Fats Waller; lyrics, Fats Waller and many others)	*Da* (Hugh Leonard)
1979	*Sweeney Todd* (book, Hugh Wheeler; music and lyrics, Stephen Sondheim)	*The Elephant Man* (Bernard Pomerance)
1980	*Evita* (book and lyrics, Tim Rice; music, Andrew Lloyd Webber)	*Children of a Lesser God* (Mark Medoff)
1981	*42nd Street* (book, Michael Stewart and Mark Bramble; music, Harry Warren; lyrics, Al Dubin)	*Amadeus* (Peter Shaffer)

Tony Awards, 1947–2008 (continued)

YEAR	BEST MUSICAL	BEST PLAY
1982	*Nine* (book, Arthur Kopit; music and lyrics, Maury Yeston)	*The Life and Adventures of Nicholas Nickleby* (David Edgar)
1983	*Cats* (book and lyrics, T.S. Eliot; music, Andrew Lloyd Webber)	*Torch Song Trilogy* (Harvey Fierstein)
1984	*La Cage aux folles* (book, Harvey Fierstein; music and lyrics, Jerry Herman)	*The Real Thing* (Tom Stoppard)
1985	*Big River* (book, William Hauptman; music and lyrics, Roger Miller)	*Biloxi Blues* (Neil Simon)
1986	*The Mystery of Edwin Drood* (book, music, and lyrics, Rupert Holmes)	*I'm Not Rappaport* (Herb Gardner)
1987	*Les Misérables* (book, Alain Boublil and Claude-Michel Schönberg; music, Claude-Michel Schönberg; lyrics, Herbert Kretzmer and Alain Boublil)	*Fences* (August Wilson)
1988	*The Phantom of the Opera* (book, Richard Stilgoe and Andrew Lloyd Webber; music, Andrew Lloyd Webber; lyrics, Charles Hart and Richard Stilgoe)	*M. Butterfly* (David Henry Hwang)
1989	*Jerome Robbins' Broadway* (compilation)	*The Heidi Chronicles* (Wendy Wasserstein)
1990	*City of Angels* (book, Larry Gelbart; music, Cy Coleman; lyrics, David Zippel)	*The Grapes of Wrath* (Frank Galati)
1991	*The Will Rogers Follies* (book, Peter Stone; music, Cy Coleman; lyrics, Betty Comden and Adolph Green)	*Lost in Yonkers* (Neil Simon)
1992	*Crazy for You* (book, Ken Ludwig; music and lyrics, George Gershwin and Ira Gershwin)	*Dancing at Lughnasa* (Brian Friel)
1993	*Kiss of the Spider Woman* (book, Terrence McNally; music, John Kander; lyrics, Fred Ebb)	*Angels in America: Millennium Approaches* (Tony Kushner)
1994	*Passion* (book, James Lapine; music and lyrics, Stephen Sondheim)	*Angels in America: Perestroika* (Tony Kushner)
1995	*Sunset Boulevard* (book and lyrics, Don Black and Christopher Hampton; music, Andrew Lloyd Webber)	*Love! Valour! Compassion!* (Terrence McNally)
1996	*Rent* (book, music, and lyrics, Jonathan Larson)	*Master Class* (Terrence McNally)
1997	*Titanic* (book, Peter Stone; music and lyrics, Maury Yeston)	*The Last Night of Ballyhoo* (Alfred Uhry)
1998	*The Lion King* (book, Roger Allers and Irene Mecchi; music and lyrics, Elton John, Tim Rice, and others)	*Art* (Yasmina Reza)
1999	*Fosse* (compilation)	*Side Man* (Warren Leight)
2000	*Contact* (book, John Weidman; music and lyrics, various artists)	*Copenhagen* (Michael Frayn)
2001	*The Producers* (book, Mel Brooks and Thomas Meehan; music and lyrics, Mel Brooks)	*Proof* (David Auburn)
2002	*Thoroughly Modern Millie* (book, Richard Morris and Dick Scanlan; music, Jeanine Tesori; lyrics, Dick Scanlan)	*The Goat, or Who Is Sylvia?* (Edward Albee)
2003	*Hairspray* (book, Mark O'Donnell and Thomas Meehan; music, Marc Shaiman; lyrics, Scott Wittman and Marc Shaiman)	*Take Me Out* (Richard Greenberg)
2004	*Avenue Q* (book, Jeff Whitty; music and lyrics, Robert Lopez and Jeff Marx)	*I Am My Own Wife* (Doug Wright)
2005	*Monty Python's Spamalot* (book, Eric Idle; music and lyrics, John Du Prez and Eric Idle)	*Doubt* (John Patrick Shanley)
2006	*Jersey Boys* (book, Marshall Brickman and Rick Elice; music, Bob Gaudio; lyrics, Bob Crewe)	*The History Boys* (Alan Bennett)
2007	*Spring Awakening* (book and lyrics, Steven Sater; music, Duncan Sheik)	*The Coast of Utopia* (Tom Stoppard)
2008	*In the Heights* (book, Quiara Alegría Hudes; music and lyrics, Lin-Manuel Miranda)	*August: Osage County* (Tracy Letts)

[1]*Awarded to playwright for Best Author.*

Longest-Running Broadway Shows

As of 6 Aug 2008. Source: Internet Broadway Database, <www.ibdb.com>.

	SHOW	RUN	TOTAL PERFORMANCES
1	*The Phantom of the Opera*	1988–	8,535
2	*Cats*	1982–2000	7,485
3	*Les Misérables*	1987–2003	6,680
4	*A Chorus Line*	1975–90	6,137
5	*Oh! Calcutta!* (revival)	1976–89	5,959
6	*Beauty and the Beast*	1994–2007	5,461
7	*Rent*	1996–	5,083
8	*Chicago* (revival)	1996–	4,860
9	*The Lion King*	1997–	4,445
10	*Miss Saigon*	1991–2001	4,092
11	*42nd Street*	1980–89	3,486
12	*Grease*	1972–80	3,388
13	*Fiddler on the Roof*	1964–72	3,242

Longest-Running Broadway Shows (continued)

SHOW	RUN	TOTAL PERFORMANCES	SHOW	RUN	TOTAL PERFORMANCES
14 *Life with Father*	1939–47	3,224	18 *My Fair Lady*	1956–62	2,717
15 *Tobacco Road*	1933–41	3,182	19 *Threepenny Opera* (revival)	1955–61	2,611
16 *Hello, Dolly!*	1964–70	2,844	20 *The Producers*	2001–07	2,502
17 *Mamma Mia!*	2001–	2,808			

Encyclopædia Britannica's 25 Notable US Theater Companies

COMPANY	LOCATION	ARTISTIC DIRECTOR (2008)
The Acting Company	New York NY	Margot Harley[1]
Actors Theatre of Louisville	Louisville KY	Marc Masterson
Alley Theatre	Houston TX	Gregory Boyd
American Conservatory Theater	San Francisco CA	Carey Perloff
American Repertory Theatre	Cambridge MA	Gideon Lester
Arena Stage	Washington DC	Molly Smith
Center Theatre Group	Los Angeles CA	Michael Ritchie
Chicago Shakespeare Theater	Chicago IL	Barbara Gaines
Cincinnati Playhouse in the Park	Cincinnati OH	Edward Stern[1]
Cleveland Public Theatre	Cleveland OH	Raymond Bobgan[2]
Colony Theatre Company	Burbank CA	Barbara Beckley
El Teatro Campesino	San Juan Bautista CA	Luis Valdez
Folger Theatre	Washington DC	Janet Alexander Griffin[3]
Goodman Theatre	Chicago IL	Robert Falls
Guthrie Theater	Minneapolis MN	Joe Dowling[4]
La Jolla Playhouse	La Jolla CA	Christopher Ashley
Long Wharf Theatre	New Haven CT	Gordon Edelstein
Oregon Shakespeare Festival	Ashland OR	Bill Rauch
Pasadena Playhouse	Pasadena CA	Sheldon Epps
The Public Theater	New York NY	Oskar Eustis
Seattle Repertory Theatre	Seattle WA	David Esbjornson
SITI Company	New York NY	Anne Bogart
Steppenwolf Theatre Company	Chicago IL	Martha Lavey
Victory Gardens Theater	Chicago IL	Dennis Zacek
Yale Repertory Theatre	New Haven CT	James Bundy

[1]*Producing artistic director.* [2]*Executive artistic director.* [3]*Artistic producer.* [4]*Director.*

Music

Grammy Awards 2007

The National Academy of Recording Arts and Sciences was established in 1957 as a professional organization for musicians, producers, technicians, and executives in the US recording industry. The Grammys, first awarded in 1958, recognize excellence in the recording industry without regard to record sales or chart position. Nominees and winners are selected by the Academy's individual members according to the members' areas of expertise. In addition to the four general categories (record, album, and song of the year and best new artist) for which all members are eligible to vote, for 2007 there were 110 categories in 31 fields, of which Academy members were permitted to vote in no more than 8 fields. Prizes for works released 1 Oct 2006–30 Sep 2007 were awarded in Los Angeles on 10 Feb 2008. Prize: gold miniature phonograph.

Grammy Award Web site: <www.grammy.com>.

category: winner (performer in parentheses for songwriting/production awards)

▸ **record (single) of the year:** "Rehab," Amy Winehouse; ▸ **album of the year:** *River: The Joni Letters,* Herbie Hancock; ▸ **song of the year:** "Rehab," Amy Winehouse, songwriter (Amy Winehouse); ▸ **new artist:** Amy Winehouse; ▸ **pop vocal performance, female:** "Rehab," Amy Winehouse; ▸ **pop vocal performance, male:** "What Goes Around...Comes Around," Justin Timberlake; ▸ **pop vocal performance, duo/group:** "Makes Me Wonder," Maroon 5; ▸ **pop vocal album:** *Back to Black,* Amy Winehouse; ▸ **pop vocal album, traditional:** *Call Me Irresponsible,* Michael Bublé; ▸ **rock vocal performance, solo:** "Radio Nowhere," Bruce Springsteen; ▸ **rock vocal performance, duo/group:** "Icky Thump," The White Stripes; ▸ **hard rock performance:** "The Pretender," Foo Fighters; ▸ **metal performance:** "Final Six," Slayer; ▸ **rock song:** "Radio Nowhere," Bruce Springsteen, songwriter (Bruce Springsteen); ▸ **rock album:** *Echoes, Silence, Patience & Grace,* Foo Fighters; ▸ **alternative music album:** *Icky Thump,* The White Stripes; ▸ **R&B vocal performance, female:** "No One," Alicia Keys; ▸ **R&B vocal performance, male:** "Future Baby Mama," Prince; ▸ **R&B vocal**

Grammy Awards 2007 (continued)

performance, duo/group: "Disrespectful," Chaka Khan featuring Mary J. Blige; ▸ **R&B song:** "No One," Dirty Harry, Kerry Brothers, and Alicia Keys, songwriters (Alicia Keys); ▸ **R&B album:** *Funk This,* Chaka Khan; ▸ **R&B album, contemporary:** *Because of You,* Ne-Yo ▸ **rap performance, solo:** "Stronger," Kanye West; ▸ **rap performance, duo/group:** "Southside," Common featuring Kanye West; ▸ **rap song:** "Good Life," Aldrin Davis, Mike Dean, Faheem Najm, and Kanye West, songwriters (Kanye West featuring T-Pain); ▸ **rap album:** *Graduation,* Kanye West; ▸ **country vocal performance, female:** "Before He Cheats," Carrie Underwood; ▸ **country vocal performance, male:** "Stupid Boy," Keith Urban; ▸ **country vocal performance, duo/group:** "How Long," Eagles; ▸ **country song:** "Before He Cheats," Josh Kear and Chris Tompkins, songwriters (Carrie Underwood); ▸ **country album:** *These Days,* Vince Gill; ▸ **bluegrass album:** *The Bluegrass Diaries,* Jim Lauderdale; ▸ **new age album:** *Crestone,* Paul Winter Consort; ▸ **jazz album, contemporary:** *River: The Joni Letters,* Herbie Hancock; ▸ **jazz album, vocal:** *Avant Gershwin,* Patti Austin; ▸ **jazz instrumental solo:** Michael Brecker ("Anagram"); ▸ **jazz album, instrumental:** *Pilgrimage,* Michael Brecker; ▸ **jazz album, large ensemble:** *A Tale of God's Will (A Requiem for Katrina),* Terence Blanchard; ▸ **jazz album, Latin:** *Funk Tango,* Paquito D'Rivera Quintet; ▸ **gospel song:** "Blessed and Highly Favored," Karen Clark-Sheard, songwriter (The Clark Sisters); ▸ **gospel album, rock/rap:** *Before the Daylight's Shot,* Ashley Cleveland; ▸ **gospel album, pop/contemporary:** *A Deeper Level,* Israel and New Breed; ▸ **gospel album, Southern/country/bluegrass:** *Salt of the Earth,* Ricky Skaggs and the Whites; ▸ **gospel album, traditional:** *Live—One Last Time,* The Clark Sisters; ▸ **gospel album, contemporary R&B:** *Free to Worship,* Fred Hammond; ▸ **Latin album, pop:** *El tren de los momentos,* Alejandro Sanz; ▸ **Latin album, rock/alternative:** *No hay espacio,* Black: Guayaba; ▸ **Latin album, urban:** *Residente o visitante,* Calle 13 ▸ **Latin album, tropical:** *La llave de mi corazón,* Juan Luis Guerra ▸ **Mexican/Mexican-American album:** *100% Mexicano,* Pepe Aguilar; ▸ **Tejano album:** *Before the Next Teardrop Falls,* Little Joe y La Familia; ▸ **blues album, traditional:** *Last of the Great Mississippi Delta Bluesmen: Live in Dallas,* Henry James Townsend, Joe Willie "Pinetop" Perkins, Robert Lockwood, Jr., and David "Honeyboy" Edwards; ▸ **blues album, contemporary:** *The Road to Escondido,* J.J. Cale and Eric Clapton; ▸ **folk album, traditional:** *Dirt Farmer,* Levon Helm; ▸ **folk album, contemporary/Americana:** *Washington Square Serenade,* Steve Earle; ▸ **Native American music album:** *Totemic Flute Chants,* Johnny Whitehorse; ▸ **Hawaiian music album:** *Treasures of Hawaiian Slack Key Guitar,* Daniel Ho, George Kahumoku, Jr., Paul Konwiser, and Wayne Wong, producers (various artists); ▸ **reggae album:** *Mind Control,* Stephen Marley; ▸ **world music album, traditional:** *African Spirit,* Soweto Gospel Choir; ▸ **world music album, contemporary:** *Djin djin,* Angelique Kidjo; ▸ **polka album:** *Come Share the Wine,* Jimmy Sturr and His Orchestra; ▸ **spoken word album:** *The Audacity of Hope: Thoughts on Reclaiming the American Dream,* Barack Obama; ▸ **comedy album:** *The Distant Future,* Flight of the Conchords; ▸ **producer, nonclassical:** Mark Ronson; ▸ **producer, classical:** Judith Sherman; ▸ **classical album:** *Made in America,* Leonard Slatkin, conductor; Tim Handley, producer (Nashville Symphony); ▸ **orchestral performance:** *Made in America,* Nashville Symphony; Leonard Slatkin, conductor; ▸ **opera recording:** *Hansel and Gretel,* Charles Mackerras, conductor; Rebecca Evans, Jane Henschel, Jennifer Larmore, Sarah Coppen, Diana Montague, and Sarah Tynan, soloists; Brian Couzens, producer; (Philharmonic Orchestra and New London Children's Choir); ▸ **chamber music performance:** *Strange Imaginary Animals,* Eighth Blackbird; ▸ **classical vocal performance:** *Lorraine Hunt Lieberson Sings Peter Lieberson: Neruda Songs,* Lorraine Hunt Lieberson, soloist; ▸ **contemporary classical composition:** *Made in America,* Joan Tower, composer; ▸ **short-form music video:** "God's Gonna Cut You Down," Johnny Cash; Tony Kaye, director; Rachel Curl, producer

Grammy Awards, 1958–2007

The year denotes the period (from the fall of the previous year to the fall of the year named) for which the winning work or artist was recognized; the prizes are generally awarded during the following year.

YEAR	RECORD (SINGLE) OF THE YEAR	ALBUM OF THE YEAR	BEST NEW ARTIST
1958	"Nel Blu Dipinto Di Blu (Volare)," Domenico Modugno	*The Music from Peter Gunn,* Henry Mancini	*not awarded*
1959	"Mack the Knife," Bobby Darin	*Come Dance with Me,* Frank Sinatra	Bobby Darin
1960	"Theme from A Summer Place," Percy Faith	*The Button-Down Mind of Bob Newhart,* Bob Newhart	Bob Newhart
1961	"Moon River," Henry Mancini	*Judy at Carnegie Hall,* Judy Garland	Peter Nero
1962	"I Left My Heart in San Francisco," Tony Bennett	*The First Family,* Vaughn Meader	Robert Goulet
1963	"The Days of Wine and Roses," Henry Mancini	*The Barbra Streisand Album,* Barbra Streisand	Ward Swingle (The Swingle Singers)
1964	"The Girl from Ipanema," Stan Getz and Astrud Gilberto	*Getz/Gilberto,* Stan Getz and João Gilberto	The Beatles
1965	"A Taste of Honey," Herb Alpert	*September of My Years,* Frank Sinatra	Tom Jones
1966	"Strangers in the Night," Frank Sinatra	*A Man and His Music,* Frank Sinatra	*not awarded*

Grammy Awards, 1958–2007 (continued)

YEAR	RECORD (SINGLE) OF THE YEAR	ALBUM OF THE YEAR	BEST NEW ARTIST
1967	"Up, Up, and Away," The 5th Dimension	*Sgt. Pepper's Lonely Hearts Club Band,* The Beatles	Bobbie Gentry
1968	"Mrs. Robinson," Simon & Garfunkel	*By the Time I Get to Phoenix,* Glen Campbell	José Feliciano
1969	"Aquarius/Let the Sunshine In," The 5th Dimension	*Blood, Sweat & Tears,* Blood, Sweat & Tears	Crosby, Stills & Nash
1970	"Bridge over Troubled Water," Simon & Garfunkel	*Bridge over Troubled Water,* Simon & Garfunkel	The Carpenters
1971	"It's Too Late," Carole King	*Tapestry,* Carole King	Carly Simon
1972	"The First Time Ever I Saw Your Face," Roberta Flack	*The Concert for Bangla Desh,* George Harrison and Friends	America
1973	"Killing Me Softly with His Song," Roberta Flack	*Innervisions,* Stevie Wonder	Bette Midler
1974	"I Honestly Love You," Olivia Newton-John	*Fulfillingness' First Finale,* Stevie Wonder	Marvin Hamlisch
1975	"Love Will Keep Us Together," Captain & Tennille	*Still Crazy After All These Years,* Paul Simon	Natalie Cole
1976	"This Masquerade," George Benson	*Songs in the Key of Life,* Stevie Wonder	Starland Vocal Band
1977	"Hotel California," The Eagles	*Rumours,* Fleetwood Mac	Debby Boone
1978	"Just the Way You Are," Billy Joel	*Saturday Night Fever,* The Bee Gees	A Taste of Honey
1979	"What a Fool Believes," The Doobie Brothers	*52nd Steet,* Billy Joel	Rickie Lee Jones
1980	"Sailing," Christopher Cross	*Christopher Cross,* Christopher Cross	Christopher Cross
1981	"Bette Davis Eyes," Kim Carnes	*Double Fantasy,* John Lennon and Yoko Ono	Sheena Easton
1982	"Rosanna," Toto	*Toto IV,* Toto	Men at Work
1983	"Beat It," Michael Jackson	*Thriller,* Michael Jackson	Culture Club
1984	"What's Love Got To Do with It," Tina Turner	*Can't Slow Down,* Lionel Richie	Cyndi Lauper
1985	"We Are the World," USA for Africa	*No Jacket Required,* Phil Collins	Sade
1986	"Higher Love," Steve Winwood	*Graceland,* Paul Simon	Bruce Hornsby and the Range
1987	"Graceland," Paul Simon	*The Joshua Tree,* U2	Jody Watley
1988	"Don't Worry, Be Happy," Bobby McFerrin	*Faith,* George Michael	Tracy Chapman
1989	"Wind Beneath My Wings," Bette Midler	*Nick of Time,* Bonnie Raitt	Milli Vanilli (revoked)
1990	"Another Day in Paradise," Phil Collins	*Back on the Block,* Quincy Jones	Mariah Carey
1991	"Unforgettable," Natalie Cole with Nat King Cole	*Unforgettable: With Love,* Natalie Cole	Marc Cohn
1992	"Tears in Heaven," Eric Clapton	*Unplugged,* Eric Clapton	Arrested Development
1993	"I Will Always Love You," Whitney Houston	*The Bodyguard,* Whitney Houston	Toni Braxton
1994	"All I Wanna Do," Sheryl Crow	*MTV Unplugged,* Tony Bennett	Sheryl Crow
1995	"Kiss from a Rose," Seal	*Jagged Little Pill,* Alanis Morissette	Hootie and the Blowfish
1996	"Change the World," Eric Clapton	*Falling into You,* Celine Dion	LeAnn Rimes
1997	"Sunny Came Home," Shawn Colvin	*Time Out of Mind,* Bob Dylan	Paula Cole
1998	"My Heart Will Go On," Celine Dion	*The Miseducation of Lauryn Hill,* Lauryn Hill	Lauryn Hill
1999	"Smooth," Santana featuring Rob Thomas	*Supernatural,* Santana	Christina Aguilera
2000	"Beautiful Day," U2	*Two Against Nature,* Steely Dan	Shelby Lynne
2001	"Walk On," U2	*O Brother, Where Art Thou?,* various artists	Alicia Keys
2002	"Don't Know Why," Norah Jones	*Come Away with Me,* Norah Jones	Norah Jones
2003	"Clocks," Coldplay	*Speakerboxxx/The Love Below,* OutKast	Evanescence
2004	"Here We Go Again," Ray Charles and Norah Jones	*Genius Loves Company,* Ray Charles and various artists	Maroon 5
2005	"Boulevard of Broken Dreams," Green Day	*How To Dismantle an Atomic Bomb,* U2	John Legend
2006	"Not Ready To Make Nice," Dixie Chicks	*Taking the Long Way,* Dixie Chicks	Carrie Underwood
2007	"Rehab," Amy Winehouse	*River: The Joni Letters,* Herbie Hancock	Amy Winehouse

Eurovision Song Contest

The European Broadcasting Union (EBU), an association of television and radio companies from Europe and the Mediterranean, began the Eurovision Song Contest in 1956 to promote pop music. Each EBU member country, along with several provisional participants, can nominate one original song per year, with a maximum length of three minutes. The winner is selected based on call-in votes from fans and juries in each participating country. **Eurovision Song Contest Web site:** <www.eurovision.tv>.

YEAR	SONG, SONGWRITER(S) (PERFORMER, COUNTRY)
1956	"Refrain," Emile Gardaz, Géo Voumard (Lys Assia, Switzerland)
1957	"Net als toen," Willy van Hemert, Guus Jansen (Corry Brokken, The Netherlands)
1958	"Dors mon amour," Pierre Delanoe, Hubert Giraud (André Clavaeu, France)
1959	"Een beetje," Willy van Hemert, Dick Schallies (Teddy Scholten, The Netherlands)
1960	"Tom Pillibi," Pierre Cour, André Popp (Jacqueline Boyer, France)
1961	"Nous les amoureux," Jacques Datin, Maurice Vidalin (Jean-Claude Pascal, Luxembourg)
1962	"Un Premier amour," Rolande Valade, Claude Henri Vic (Isabelle Aubret, France)
1963	"Dansevise," Sejr Volmer Sorensen, Otto Francker (Grethe and Jorgen Ingmann, Denmark)
1964	"Non ho l'étà," Nicola Salerno (Gigliola Cinquetti, Italy)
1965	"Poupée de cire, poupée de son," Serge Gainsbourg (France Gall, Luxembourg)
1966	"Merci chérie," Udo Jürgens, Thomas Horbiger (Udo Jürgens, Austria)
1967	"Puppet on a String," Bill Martin, Phil Coulter (Sandie Shaw, United Kingdom)
1968	"La, la, la," Ramon Arcusa, Manuel de la Calva (Massiel, Spain)
1969	"Vivo cantando," Aniano Alcalde, Maria José de Cerato (Salomé, Spain); "Boom Bang-a-Bang," Peter Warne, Alan Moorhouse (Lulu, United Kingdom); "De troubadour," Lennie Kuhr, David Hartsena (Lennie Kuhr, The Netherlands); "Un Jour, un enfant," Eddy Marnay, Emile Stern (Frida Boccara, France) (four-way tie)
1970	"All Kinds of Everything," Derry Lindsay, Jackie Smith (Dana, Ireland)
1971	"Un Banc, un arbre, une rue," Yves Dessca, Jean-Pierre Bourtayre (Séverine, Monaco)
1972	"Après toi," Klaus Munro, Yves Dessca, Mario Panas (Vicky Leandros, Luxembourg)
1973	"Tu te reconnaîtras," Vline Buggy, Claude Morgan (Anne-Marie David, Luxembourg)
1974	"Waterloo," Stikkan Anderson, Benny Andersson, Björn Ulvaeus (ABBA, Sweden)
1975	"Ding-a-Dong," Wil Luikinga, Eddy Owens, Dick Bakker (Teach-In, The Netherlands)
1976	"Save Your Kisses for Me," Tony Hiller, Lee Sheriden, Martin Lee (Brotherhood of Man, United Kingdom)
1977	"L'Oiseau et l'enfant," José Gracy, Jean-Paul Cara (Marie Myriam, France)
1978	"A-Ba-Ni-Bi," Ehud Manor, Nurit Hirsh (Izhar Cohen and the Alphabeta, Israel)
1979	"Hallelujah," Shimrit Orr, Kobi Oshrat (Gali Atari and Milk and Honey, Israel)
1980	"What's Another Year," Shay Healy (Johnny Logan, Ireland)
1981	"Making Your Mind Up," Andy Hill, John Danter (Bucks Fizz, United Kingdom)
1982	"Ein bisschen Frieden," Bernd Meinunger, Ralph Siegel (Nicole, West Germany)
1983	"Si la vie est cadeau," Alain Garcia, Jean-Pierre Millers (Corinne Hermes, Luxembourg)
1984	"Diggi-loo diggi-ley," Britt Lindeborg, Torgny Soederberg (Herrey's, Sweden)
1985	"La det swinge," Rolg Loevland (Bobbysocks, Norway)
1986	"J'aime la vie," Marino Atria, Jean-Pierre Furnémont, Angelo Crisci (Sandra Kim, Belgium)
1987	"Hold Me Now," Sean Sherrard (Johnny Logan, Ireland)
1988	"Ne partez pas sans moi," Nella Martinetti, Atilla Sereftug (Céline Dion, Switzerland)
1989	"Rock Me," Stevo Cvikich, Rajko Dujmich (Riva, Yugoslavia)
1990	"Insieme: 1992," Toto Cutugno (Toto Cutugno, Italy)
1991	"Fångad av en stormvind," Stephan Berg (Carola, Sweden)
1992	"Why Me," Sean Sherrard (Linda Martin, Ireland)
1993	"In Your Eyes," Jimmy Walsh (Niamh Kavanagh, Ireland)
1994	"Rock 'n' Roll Kids," Brendan Graham (Paul Harrington and Charlie McGettigan, Ireland)
1995	"Nocturne," Petter Skavlan, Rolf Lovland (Secret Garden, Norway)
1996	"The Voice," Brendan Graham (Eimear Quinn, Ireland)
1997	"Love Shine a Light," Kimberley Rew (Katrina and the Waves, United Kingdom)
1998	"Diva," Yoav Ginay (Dana International, Israel)
1999	"Take Me to Your Heaven," Gert Lengstrand (Charlotte Nilsson, Sweden)
2000	"Fly on the Wings of Love," Jørgen Olsen (Olsen Brothers, Denmark)
2001	"Everybody," Maian-Anna Kärmas, Ivar Must (Tanel Padar, Dave Benton, and 2XL, Estonia)
2002	"I Wanna," Marija Naumova, Marats Samauskis (Marie N, Latvia)
2003	"Every Way That I Can," Demir Demirkan, Sertab Erener (Sertab Erener, Turkey)
2004	"Wild Dances," Ruslana Lyzhichko, Aleksandr Ksenofontov (Ruslana, Ukraine)
2005	"My Number One," Christos Dantis, Natalia Germanou (Helena Paparizou, Greece)
2006	"Hard Rock Hallelujah," LORDI (LORDI, Finland)
2007	"Molitva," Sasa Milosevic Mare (Marija Serifovic, Serbia)
2008	"Believe," Dima Bilan, Jim Beanz (Dima Bilan, Russia)

Archery is the national sport in Bhutan, where it is a team event, rather than an Olympic-style contest between individuals. Tournaments, often held during holidays, are festive occasions at which entire villages enjoy, food, drink, and merrymaking.

Brit Awards, 2008

The British Phonographic Industry, a trade association of record companies, established the Brit Awards In 1977 to recognize pop acts from Great Britain and abroad. Prize: statuette. **Web site:** *<www.brits.co.uk>.*

BRITISH CATEGORIES
Male solo artist: Mark Ronson
Female solo artist: Kate Nash
Group: Arctic Monkeys
MasterCard Album: Arctic Monkeys, *Favourite Worst Nightmare*
Breakthrough artist: Mika
Single: Take That, "Shine"
Live act: Take That

INTERNATIONAL CATEGORIES
Male solo artist: Kanye West
Female solo artist: Kylie Minogue
Group: Foo Fighters
Album: Foo Fighters, *Echoes, Silence, Patience & Grace*
Critics' choice: Adele.

ADDITIONAL CATEGORY
Outstanding contribution: Paul McCartney

Country Music Association Awards, 2007

The Country Music Association, founded in 1958 as a trade organization for the country and western music industry, began its annual awards ceremony in 1967 and made it the first nationally televised music awards show the following year. Ceremonies are held in November. Prize: hand-blown crystal statuette. **Country Music Association Awards Web site:** <www.cmaawards.com>.

▸ **entertainer of the year:** Kenny Chesney; ▸ **female vocalist of the year:** Carrie Underwood; ▸ **male vocalist of the year:** Brad Paisley; ▸ **Horizon Award:** Taylor Swift; ▸ **vocal duo of the year:** Sugarland; ▸ **vocal group of the year:** Rascal Flatts; ▸ **album of the year:** *It Just Comes Natural,* George Strait; Tony Brown and George Strait, producers; ▸ **song of the year:** "Give It Away" (George Strait), Bill Anderson, Buddy Cannon, and Jamey Johnson, songwriters; ▸ **single of the year:** "Before He Cheats," Carrie Underwood; Mark Bright, producer; ▸ **music video of the year:** "Online," Brad Paisley; Jason Alexander, director; ▸ **musical event of the year:** "Find Out Who Your Friends Are," Tracy Lawrence featuring Tim McGraw and Kenny Chesney; ▸ **musician of the year:** Jerry Douglas (dobro)

The All-Time Top 50 Best-Selling Albums in the United States

As of July 2008. Album sales are given only to the nearest million copies, and in the case of a tie albums are listed alphabetically by artist. Source: Recording Industry Association of America (RIAA), <www.riaa.com>.

	ALBUM	ARTIST	YEAR
1	*Their Greatest Hits (1971–1975)*	Eagles	1976
2	*Thriller*	Michael Jackson	1982
3	*Untitled* ("Led Zeppelin IV")	Led Zeppelin	1971
4	*The Wall*	Pink Floyd	1979
5	*Back in Black*	AC/DC	1980
6	*Greatest Hits, Volume I & Volume II*	Billy Joel	1985
7	*Double Live*	Garth Brooks	1998
8	*Come on Over*	Shania Twain	1997
9	*The Beatles* ("The White Album")	The Beatles	1968
10	*Rumours*	Fleetwood Mac	1977
11	*Boston*	Boston	1976
12	*No Fences*	Garth Brooks	1990
13	*The Bodyguard* (soundtrack)	Whitney Houston and various artists	1992
14	*Jagged Little Pill*	Alanis Morissette	1995
15	*1967–70*	The Beatles	1973
16	*Hotel California*	Eagles	1976
17	*Greatest Hits*	Elton John	1974
18	*Cracked Rear View*	Hootie & the Blowfish	1994
19	*Physical Graffiti*	Led Zeppelin	1975
20	*1962–66*	The Beatles	1973
21	*Saturday Night Fever* (soundtrack)	The Bee Gees and various artists	1977
22	*Born in the U.S.A.*	Bruce Springsteen	1984
23	*Appetite for Destruction*	Guns N' Roses	1987
24	*Greatest Hits*	Journey	1988
25	*Dark Side of the Moon*	Pink Floyd	1973
26	*Supernatural*	Santana	1999
27	*Backstreet Boys*	Backstreet Boys	1997
28	*...Baby One More Time*	Britney Spears	1999
29	*Ropin' the Wind*	Garth Brooks	1991
30	*Bat out of Hell*	Meat Loaf	1977
31	*Metallica*	Metallica	1991
32	*Simon & Garfunkel's Greatest Hits*	Simon & Garfunkel	1972
33	*Millennium*	Backstreet Boys	1999
34	*Live/1975–85*	Bruce Springsteen & the E Street Band	1986
35	*Purple Rain* (soundtrack)	Prince and the Revolution	1984
36	*Greatest Hits 1974–1978*	Steve Miller Band	1978
37	*Whitney Houston*	Whitney Houston	1985
38	*Abbey Road*	The Beatles	1969
39	*Slippery When Wet*	Bon Jovi	1986
40	*II*	Boyz II Men	1994
41	*Hysteria*	Def Leppard	1987
42	*Wide Open Spaces*	Dixie Chicks	1998
43	*Pieces of You*	Jewel	1995
44	*Breathless*	Kenny G	1992
45	*Kenny Rogers' Greatest Hits*	Kenny Rogers	1980
46	*Led Zeppelin II*	Led Zeppelin	1969
47	*Yourself or Someone Like You*	Matchbox 20	1996
48	*Ten*	Pearl Jam	1991
49	*No Jacket Required*	Phil Collins	1985
50	*Hot Rocks 1964–1971*	The Rolling Stones	1972

Rock and Roll Hall of Fame

Music-industry professionals established the Rock and Roll Hall of Fame Foundation in 1983 in order to "recognize the contributions of those who have had a significant impact on the evolution, development, and perpetuation of rock and roll." Performers are eligible for induction 25 years after the release of their first record. The foundation's nominating committee compiles an annual list of eligible artists and distributes this list to about 1,000 rock experts throughout the world. Those performers receiving the highest number of votes, as well as at least 50% of the vote, are inducted. Special committees select inductees in other categories. Those elected to membership receive a statuette depicting an abstract human figure holding aloft a gold record. Inductees for 2008 appear in **boldface.**

Rock and Roll Hall of Fame and Museum Web site: <www.rockhall.com>.

NAME (YEAR OF INDUCTION)
AC/DC (2003)
Paul Ackerman[1] (1995)
Aerosmith (2001)
The Allman Brothers Band (1995)
Herb Alpert and Jerry Moss[2] (2006)
The Animals (1994)
Louis Armstrong[3] (1990)
Chet Atkins[4] (2002)
LaVern Baker (1991)
Hank Ballard (1990)
The Band (1994)
Dave Bartholomew[1] (1991)
Frank Barsalona[2] (2005)
Ralph Bass[1] (1991)
The Beach Boys (1988)
The Beatles (1988)
The Bee Gees (1997)
Benny Benjamin[4] (2003)
Chuck Berry (1986)
Black Sabbath (2006)
Chris Blackwell[1] (2001)
Hal Blaine[4] (2000)
Bobby "Blue" Bland (1992)
Blondie (2006)
Booker T. and the MG's (1992)
David Bowie (1996)
Charles Brown[3] (1999)
James Brown (1986)
Ruth Brown (1993)
Jackson Browne (2004)
Buffalo Springfield (1997)
Solomon Burke (2001)
James Burton[4] (2001)
The Byrds (1991)
Johnny Cash (1992)
Ray Charles (1986)
Leonard Chess[1] (1987)
Charlie Christian[3] (1990)
Eric Clapton (2000)
Dick Clark[1] (1993)
The Clash (2003)
The Coasters (1987)
Eddie Cochran (1987)
Leonard Cohen (2008)
Nat King Cole[3] (2000)
Sam Cooke (1986)
Elvis Costello and the Attractions (2003)
Floyd Cramer[4] (2003)
Cream (1993)
Creedence Clearwater Revival (1993)
Crosby, Stills & Nash (1997)
Bobby Darin (1990)
The Dave Clark Five (2008)
Clive Davis[1] (2000)

NAME (YEAR OF INDUCTION)
Miles Davis (2006)
The Dells (2004)
Bo Diddley (1987)
Dion (1989)
Willie Dixon[3] (1994)
Fats Domino (1986)
Tom Donahue[1] (1996)
The Doors (1993)
Steve Douglas[4] (2003)
The Drifters (1988)
Bob Dylan (1988)
Eagles (1998)
Earth, Wind & Fire (2000)
Duane Eddy (1994)
Ahmet Ertegun[1] (1987)
Nesuhi Ertegun[2] (1991)
The Everly Brothers (1986)
Leo Fender[1] (1992)
The Flamingos (2001)
Fleetwood Mac (1998)
The Four Seasons (1990)
The Four Tops (1990)
Aretha Franklin (1987)
Alan Freed[1] (1986)
Milt Gabler[1] (1993)
Kevin Gamble and Leon Huff[1] (2008)
Marvin Gaye (1987)
Gerry Goffin and Carole King[1] (1990)
Berry Gordy, Jr.[1] (1988)
Bill Graham[1] (1992)
Grandmaster Flash and the Furious Five (2007)
Grateful Dead (1994)
Al Green (1995)
Woody Guthrie[3] (1988)
Buddy Guy (2005)
Bill Haley (1987)
John Hammond[2] (1986)
George Harrison (2004)
Isaac Hayes (2002)
The Jimi Hendrix Experience (1992)
Billie Holiday[3] (2000)
Holland, Dozier, and Holland[1] (1990)
Buddy Holly (1986)
John Lee Hooker (1991)
Howlin' Wolf[3] (1991)
The Impressions (1991)
The Inkspots[3] (1989)
The Isley Brothers (1992)
Mahalia Jackson[3] (1997)
Michael Jackson (2001)
The Jackson 5 (1997)
James Jamerson[4] (2000)

NAME (YEAR OF INDUCTION)
Elmore James[3] (1992)
Etta James (1993)
Jefferson Airplane (1996)
Billy Joel (1999)
Elton John (1994)
Little Willie John (1996)
Johnnie Johnson[4] (2001)
Robert Johnson[3] (1986)
Janis Joplin (1995)
Louis Jordan[3] (1987)
B.B. King (1987)
King Curtis[4] (2000)
The Kinks (1990)
Gladys Knight and the Pips (1996)
Leadbelly[3] (1988)
Led Zeppelin (1995)
Brenda Lee (2002)
Jerry Leiber and Mike Stoller[1] (1987)
John Lennon (1994)
Jerry Lee Lewis (1986)
Little Richard (1986)
Little Walter[4] (2008)
The Lovin' Spoonful (2000)
Frankie Lymon and the Teenagers (1993)
Lynyrd Skynyrd (2006)
Madonna (2008)
The Mamas and the Papas (1998)
Bob Marley (1994)
Martha and the Vandellas (1995)
George Martin[1] (1999)
Curtis Mayfield (1999)
Paul McCartney (1999)
Clyde McPhatter (1987)
John Mellencamp (2008)
Joni Mitchell (1997)
Bill Monroe[3] (1997)
The Moonglows (2000)
Scotty Moore[4] (2000)
Van Morrison (1993)
Jelly Roll Morton[3] (1998)
Syd Nathan[1] (1997)
Ricky Nelson (1987)
The O'Jays (2005)
Roy Orbison (1987)
The Orioles[3] (1995)
Mo Ostin[1] (2003)
Johnny Otis[1] (1994)
Earl Palmer[4] (2000)
Parliament-Funkadelic (1997)
Les Paul[3] (1988)
Carl Perkins (1987)
Tom Petty and the Heartbreakers (2002)

Rock and Roll Hall of Fame (continued)

NAME (YEAR OF INDUCTION)

Sam Phillips[1] (1986)
Wilson Pickett (1991)
Pink Floyd (1996)
Gene Pitney (2002)
The Platters (1990)
The Police (2003)
Doc Pomus[1] (1992)
Elvis Presley (1986)
The Pretenders (2005)
Lloyd Price (1998)
Prince (2004)
Professor Longhair[3] (1992)
Queen (2001)
R.E.M. (2007)
Ma Rainey[3] (1990)
Bonnie Raitt (2000)
The Ramones (2002)
Otis Redding (1989)
Jimmy Reed (1991)
The Righteous Brothers (2003)
Smokey Robinson (1987)
Jimmie Rodgers[3] (1986)
The Rolling Stones (1989)
The Ronettes (2007)
Sam and Dave (1992)
Santana (1998)
Pete Seeger[3] (1996)
Bob Seger (2004)

NAME (YEAR OF INDUCTION)

The Sex Pistols (2006)
Del Shannon (1999)
The Shirelles (1996)
Paul Simon (2001)
Simon & Garfunkel (1990)
Percy Sledge (2005)
Sly and the Family Stone (1993)
Bessie Smith[3] (1989)
Patti Smith (2007)
The Soul Stirrers[3] (1989)
Phil Spector[1] (1989)
Dusty Springfield (1999)
Bruce Springsteen (1999)
The Staple Singers (1999)
Steely Dan (2001)
Seymour Stein[2] (2005)
Jim Stewart[1] (2002)
Rod Stewart (1994)
The Supremes (1988)
Talking Heads (2002)
James Taylor (2000)
The Temptations (1989)
Allen Toussaint[1] (1998)
Traffic (2004)
Big Joe Turner (1987)
Ike and Tina Turner (1991)
U2 (2005)

NAME (YEAR OF INDUCTION)

Ritchie Valens (2001)
Van Halen (2007)
The Velvet Underground (1996)
The Ventures (2008)
Gene Vincent (1998)
T-Bone Walker[3] (1987)
Dinah Washington[3] (1993)
Muddy Waters (1987)
Jann S. Wenner[2] (2004)
Jerry Wexler[1] (1987)
The Who (1990)
Hank Williams[3] (1987)
Bob Wills and His Texas Playboys[3] (1999)
Jackie Wilson (1987)
Stevie Wonder (1989)
Jimmy Yancey[3] (1986)
The Yardbirds (1992)
Neil Young (1995)
The (Young) Rascals (1997)
Frank Zappa (1995)
ZZ Top (2004)

[1]*Ahmet Ertegun Award (nonperformers).* [2]*Lifetime Achievement.* [3]*Early Influences.* [4]*Sidemen.*

Encyclopædia Britannica's 25 World-Class Orchestras

ORCHESTRA	LOCATION	FOUNDED	MUSIC DIRECTOR OR CONDUCTOR (2008)
Berlin Philharmonic Orchestra	Berlin, Germany	1882	Simon Rattle
Boston Symphony Orchestra	Boston MA	1881	James Levine
Chicago Symphony Orchestra	Chicago IL	1891	Bernard Haitink[1]
Cleveland Orchestra	Cleveland OH	1918	Franz Welser-Möst
Gewandhaus Orchestra	Leipzig, Germany	1743	Riccardo Chailly
Israel Philharmonic Orchestra	Tel Aviv, Israel	1936	Zubin Mehta
London Philharmonic Orchestra	London, England	1932	Vladimir Jurowski
London Symphony Orchestra	London, England	1904	Valery Gergiev
Los Angeles Philharmonic	Los Angeles CA	1919	Esa-Pekka Salonen[2]
New York Philharmonic	New York NY	1842	Lorin Maazel[3]
NHK Symphony Orchestra	Tokyo, Japan	1926	Vladimir Ashkenazy
Orchestre de la Suisse Romande	Geneva, Switzerland	1918	Marek Janowski
Orchestre de Paris	Paris, France	1967	Christoph Eschenbach[4]
Orchestre National de France	Paris, France	1934	Daniele Gatti
Orchestre Symphonique de Montréal	Montreal, QC, Canada	1934	Kent Nagano
Oslo Philharmonic Orchestra	Oslo, Norway	1919	Jukka-Pekka Saraste
Philadelphia Orchestra	Philadelphia PA	1900	Charles Dutoit[5]
Philharmonia Orchestra	London, England	1945	Esa-Pekka Salonen
Pittsburgh Symphony Orchestra	Pittsburgh PA	1896	Manfred Honeck
Royal Concertgebouw Orchestra	Amsterdam, Netherlands	1888	Mariss Jansons
Royal Philharmonic Orchestra	London, England	1946	Daniele Gatti[6]
Russian National Orchestra	Moscow, Russia	1990	Mikhail Pletnev
Saint Louis Symphony Orchestra	St. Louis MO	1880	David Robertson
San Francisco Symphony	San Francisco CA	1911	Michael Tilson Thomas
Vienna Philharmonic Orchestra	Vienna, Austria	1842	*guest conductors*

[1]*Principal conductor. Riccardo Muti will assume the musical directorship of the Chicago Symphony Orchestra in September 2010.* [2]*Gustavo Dudamel will assume the musical directorship of the Los Angeles Philharmonic in September 2009.* [3]*Alan Gilbert will assume the musical directorship of the New York Philharmonic in September 2009.* [4]*Paavo Järvi will assume the musical directorship of the Orchestre de Paris in September 2010.* [5]*Chief conductor and artistic adviser. The search for a music director is ongoing in 2008.* [6]*Charles Dutoit will assume the artistic directorship of the Royal Philharmonic Orchestra in 2009.*

Encyclopædia Britannica's Top 25 Opera Companies

COMPANY	LOCATION	FOUNDED	GENERAL OR ARTISTIC DIRECTOR (2008)
Arena di Verona[1]	Verona, Italy	1913	Francesco Girondini
Bayerische Staatsoper (Bavarian State Opera)	Munich, Germany	1653	Nikolaus Bachler
Bolshoi Opera	Moscow, Russia	1776	Makvala Kasrashvili
Canadian Opera Company	Toronto, ON, Canada	1950	Alexander Neef
Grand Théâtre de Genève	Geneva, Switzerland	1962	Jean-Marie Blanchard
Los Angeles Opera	Los Angeles CA	1986	Plácido Domingo
Lyric Opera of Chicago	Chicago IL	1954	William Mason
Magyar Állami Opera (Hungarian State Opera)	Budapest, Hungary	1884	Lajos Vass
Mariinsky Opera Company	St. Petersburg, Russia	1783	Valery Gergiev
Metropolitan Opera	New York NY	1883	Peter Gelb
Opera Australia	Sydney, NSW, and Melbourne, VIC, Australia	1956	Richard Hickox[2]
Opera Cleveland	Cleveland OH	2007	Dean Williamson
Opéra National de Paris	Paris, France	1669	Gerard Mortier
Royal Opera	London, England	1732	Antonio Pappano[2]
San Francisco Opera	San Francisco CA	1923	David Gockley
Staatsoper Unter den Linden (Berlin State Opera)	Berlin, Germany	1742	Daniel Barenboim
Suomen Kansallisooppera (Finnish National Opera)	Helsinki, Finland	1873	Mikko Franck
Teatro alla Scala (La Scala)	Milan, Italy	1778	Stéphane Lissner
Teatro dell'Opera di Roma	Rome, Italy	1880	Mauro Trombetta
Teatro di San Carlo	Naples, Italy	1737	Alessio Vlad
Teatro Massimo	Palermo, Italy	1897	Lorenzo Mariani
Théâtre du Châtelet	Paris, France	1862	Jean-Luc Choplin
Vancouver Opera	Vancouver, BC, Canada	1958	James W. Wright
Washington National Opera	Washington DC	1956	Plácido Domingo
Wiener Staatsoper (Vienna State Opera)	Vienna, Austria	1869	Ioan Holender

[1]The Arena di Verona was built in the 1st century AD; it has been primarily an opera venue since 1913. [2]Music director. The position of general or artistic director does not exist.

It has been speculated that when King James I of England hired 54 of the best writers and scholars in the country for a new English version of the Bible in 1611, William Shakespeare might have been among them. Although there is no conclusive evidence for the Bard's participation in the project, it is nevertheless intriguing that the 46th word of the 46th Psalm is "shake," and the 46th word from the end of the Psalm is "spear." Shakespeare, who was fond of cryptograms, was 46 years old at the time.

Pageants

Miss America

The Miss America Pageant was founded in 1921 as an Atlantic City NJ tourist attraction. Purely a beauty contest in its early years, the competition added a talent category in 1935 and began awarding scholarships a decade later. After 1989 the pageant required evidence of community service, and by 2001 contestants were judged on the basis of talent, community service, leadership, knowledge and understanding, and appearance in swimsuits and eveningwear. Prize: US$50,000 college scholarship. **Miss America contest Web site:** <www.missamerica.org>.

YEAR	WINNER (HOMETOWN)
1921	Margaret Gorman (Washington DC)
1922	Mary Katherine Campbell (Columbus OH)
1923	Mary Katherine Campbell (Columbus OH)
1924	Ruth Malcomson (Philadelphia PA)
1925	Fay Lanphier (Oakland CA)
1926	Norma Smallwood (Tulsa OK)
1927	Lois Delander (Joliet IL)
1928–32	*not held*
1933	Marian Bergeron (West Haven CT)
1934	*not held*
1935	Henrietta Leaver (Pittsburgh PA)
1936	Rose Coyle (Philadelphia PA)
1937	Bette Cooper (Bertrand Island NJ)
1938	Marilyn Meseke (Marion OH)
1939	Patricia Donnelly (Detroit MI)
1940	Frances Burke (Philadelphia PA)
1941	Rosemary LaPlanche (Los Angeles CA)
1942	Jo-Carroll Dennison (Tyler TX)

Miss America (continued)

YEAR	WINNER (HOMETOWN)	YEAR	WINNER (HOMETOWN)
1943	Jean Bartel (Los Angeles CA)	1976	Tawny Godin (Saratoga Springs NY)
1944	Venus Ramey (Washington DC)	1977	Dorothy Benham (Edina MN)
1945	Bess Myerson (New York NY)	1978	Susan Perkins (Columbus OH)
1946	Marilyn Buferd (Los Angeles CA)	1979	Kylene Barker (Roanoke VA)
1947	Barbara Walker (Memphis TN)	1980	Cheryl Prewitt (Ackerman MS)
1948	BeBe Shopp (Hopkins MN)	1981	Susan Powell (Elk City OK)
1949	Jacque Mercer (Litchfield AZ)	1982	Elizabeth Ward (Russellville AR)
1950[1]		1983	Debra Maffett (Anaheim CA)
1951	Yolande Betbeze (Mobile AL)	1984	Suzette Charles (Mays Landing NJ)[2]
1952	Colleen Hutchins (Salt Lake City UT)	1985	Sharlene Wells (Salt Lake City UT)
1953	Neva Langley (Macon GA)	1986	Susan Akin (Meridian MS)
1954	Evelyn Ay (Ephrata PA)	1987	Kellye Cash (Memphis TN)
1955	Lee Meriwether (San Francisco CA)	1988	Kaye Lani Rae Rafko (Monroe MI)
1956	Sharon Ritchie (Denver CO)	1989	Gretchen Carlson (Anoka MN)
1957	Marian McKnight (Manning SC)	1990	Debbye Turner (Columbia MO)
1958	Marilyn Van Derbur (Denver CO)	1991	Marjorie Vincent (Oak Park IL)
1959	Mary Ann Mobley (Brandon MS)	1992	Carolyn Sapp (Honolulu HI)
1960	Lynda Mead (Natchez MS)	1993	Leanza Cornett (Jacksonville FL)
1961	Nancy Fleming (Montague MI)	1994	Kimberly Aiken (Columbia SC)
1962	Maria Fletcher (Asheville NC)	1995	Heather Whitestone (Birmingham AL)
1963	Jacquelyn Mayer (Sandusky OH)	1996	Shawntel Smith (Muldrow OK)
1964	Donna Axum (El Dorado AR)	1997	Tara Dawn Holland (Overland Park KS)
1965	Vonda Van Dyke (Phoenix AZ)	1998	Kate Shindle (Evanston IL)
1966	Deborah Bryant (Overland Park KS)	1999	Nicole Johnson (Virginia Beach VA)
1967	Jane Jayroe (Laverne OK)	2000	Heather French (Maysville KY)
1968	Debra Barnes (Pittsburg KS)	2001	Angela Perez Baraquio (Honolulu HI)
1969	Judith Ford (Belvidere IL)	2002	Katie Harman (Gresham OR)
1970	Pam Eldred (Bloomfield MI)	2003	Erika Harold (Urbana IL)
1971	Phyllis George (Denton TX)	2004	Ericka Dunlap (Orlando FL)
1972	Laurel Schaefer (Bexley OH)	2005	Deirdre Downs (Birmingham AL)
1973	Terry Meeuwsen (De Pere WI)	2006	Jennifer Berry (Tulsa OK)
1974	Rebecca King (Denver CO)	2007	Lauren Nelson (Lawton OK)
1975	Shirley Cothran (Denton TX)	2008	Kirsten Haglund (Farmington Hills MI)

[1]Until the 1950 competition, winners were given the title for the year in which they won; thereafter, they were given the title for the following year, during which most of their reign took place. As a result no Miss America 1950 was named. [2]Runner-up, crowned after resignation of Vanessa Williams (Millwood NY).

Miss Universe

The Miss Universe contest originated in 1952 as a swimwear competition in Long Beach CA in conjunction with the Miss USA pageant. The two pageants were held concurrently until 1965. Women aged 18–27 from some 80 countries and dependencies participate in the competition annually, and the contest is broadcast across the globe. Judging is based on an interview and appearances in swimwear and evening wear. Though it remains primarily a beauty contest, the competition's organizers emphasize a message of cross-cultural harmony and opportunity for women, and winners work with the UN and other organizations to promote HIV/AIDS awareness and women's health and reproductive initiatives. Prize: one-year employment contract, cash, products, and services.

Miss Universe contest Web site: <www.missuniverse.com>.

YEAR	WINNER (COUNTRY)	YEAR	WINNER (COUNTRY)
1952	Armi Kuusela (Finland)	1967	Sylvia Louise Hitchcock (US)
1953	Christiane Martel (France)	1968	Martha Vasconcellos (Brazil)
1954	Miriam Stevenson (US)	1969	Gloria Diaz (Philippines)
1955	Hillevi Rombin (Sweden)	1970	Marisol Malaret (Puerto Rico)
1956	Carol Morris (US)	1971	Georgina Rizk (Lebanon)
1957	Gladys Zender (Peru)	1972	Kerry Anne Wells (Australia)
1958	Luz Marina Zuluaga (Colombia)	1973	Margarita Moran (Philippines)
1959	Akiko Kojima (Japan)	1974	Amparo Muñoz (Spain)
1960	Linda Bement (US)	1975	Anne Marie Pohtamo (Finland)
1961	Marlene Schmidt (West Germany)	1976	Rina Messinger (Israel)
1962	Norma Nolan (Argentina)	1977	Janelle Commissiong (Trinidad and Tobago)
1963	Ieda Maria Vargas (Brazil)	1978	Margaret Gardiner (South Africa)
1964	Kiriaki Corinna Tsopei (Greece)	1979	Maritza Sayalero (Venezuela)
1965	Apasra Hongsakula (Thailand)	1980	Shawn Nichols Weatherly (US)
1966	Margareta Arvidsson (Sweden)	1981	Mona Irene Lailan Sáez Conde (Venezuela)

Miss Universe (continued)

YEAR	WINNER (COUNTRY)	YEAR	WINNER (COUNTRY)
1982	Karen Diane Baldwin (Canada)	1996	Joseph Alicia Machado Fajardo (Venezuela)
1983	Lorraine Downes (New Zealand)	1997	Brook Antoinette Mahealani Lee (US)
1984	Yvonne Ryding (Sweden)	1998	Wendy Fitzwilliam (Trinidad and Tobago)
1985	Deborah Carthy-Deu (Puerto Rico)	1999	Mpule Kwelagobe (Botswana)
1986	Bárbara Palacios Teyde (Venezuela)	2000	Lara Dutta (India)
1987	Cecilia Carolina Bolocco Fonck (Chile)	2001	Denise M. Quiñones August (Puerto Rico)
1988	Porntip Nakhirunkanok (Thailand)	2002	Justine Pasek (Panama)[1]
1989	Angela Visser (The Netherlands)	2003	Amelia Vega (Dominican Republic)
1990	Mona Grudt (Norway)	2004	Jennifer Hawkins (Australia)
1991	Lupita Jones (Mexico)	2005	Natalie Glebova (Canada)
1992	Michelle McLean (Namibia)	2006	Zuleyka Rivera (Puerto Rico)
1993	Dayanara Torres (Puerto Rico)	2007	Riyo Mori (Japan)
1994	Sushmita Sen (India)	2008	Dayana Mendoza (Venezuela)
1995	Chelsi Smith (US)		

[1]*Runner-up, crowned after dismissal of Oksana Fyodorova (Russia) for breach of contract.*

Arts and Letters Awards

Pulitzer Prizes

The Pulitzer Prizes are awarded annually by Columbia University, New York City, based on recommendations from the Pulitzer Prize Board, for works published or produced in the previous calendar year (for music, works must be performed or released between 16 January of the previous year and 15 January of the award year). The prizes, originally endowed by newspaper editor Joseph Pulitzer, were first awarded in 1917. Over the years categories have been added, and 21 prizes are now presented. Most prizes include a US$10,000 cash award; the exception is the prize for public service in journalism, which is a gold medal.

Pulitzer Prize Web site: <www.pulitzer.org>.

Journalism, 2008

CATEGORY AND DESCRIPTION	WINNER	PUBLICATION	SUBJECT
Public Service: awarded to a newspaper for notable public service	staff	*Washington Post*	investigation into the mistreatment of wounded US soldiers at Walter Reed Hospital
Breaking News Reporting: awarded for local reporting of breaking news	staff	*Washington Post*	coverage of the Virginia Tech massacre, the worst mass shooting in US history
Investigative Reporting: awarded to an individual or team for an investigative article or series	Walt Bogdanich and Jake Hooker	*New York Times*	investigation of toxic ingredients in Chinese products
	staff	*Chicago Tribune*	exposure of poor government regulation of children's products
Explanatory Reporting: awarded for clarification of a difficult subject through clear communication of in-depth knowledge	Amy Harmon	*New York Times*	examination of the scientific issues and ethical dilemmas involved in DNA testing
Local Reporting: awarded for consistent, intelligent coverage of a particular topic	David Umhoefer	*Milwaukee Journal Sentinel*	reports on the illegal enrichment of county employees' pensions
National Reporting: awarded for coverage of national news	Jo Becker and Barton Gellman	*Washington Post*	study of US Vice Pres. Dick Cheney and exploration of his influence on national policy
International Reporting: awarded for coverage of international news	Steve Fainaru	*Washington Post*	coverage of the controversial and widespread use of private security contractors in Iraq
Feature Writing	Gene Weingarten	*Washington Post*	portrait of a concert violinist busking in a subway
Commentary	Steven Pearlstein	*Washington Post*	columns that skillfully and clearly explain the nation's complex economic problems
Criticism	Mark Feeney	*Boston Globe*	visual-arts criticism
Editorial Writing: awarded for ability to sway public opinion through solid reasoning, clear style, and "moral purpose"	*no award*		

Journalism (continued)

CATEGORY AND DESCRIPTION	WINNER	PUBLICATION	SUBJECT
Editorial Cartooning: awarded for a cartoon or group of cartoons displaying creativity, superior drawing, and editorial effectiveness	Michael Ramirez	*Investor's Business Daily*	
Breaking News Photography: awarded for color or black-and-white photographs of breaking news, individually or as a group	Adrees Latif	Reuters	depiction of a Japanese videographer who was killed while covering a street demonstration in Myanmar (Burma)
Feature Photography: awarded for color or black-and-white feature photographs, individually or as a group	Preston Gannaway	*Concord* (NH) *Monitor*	photographic chronicle of a family dealing with a parent's terminal illness

Letters, Drama, and Music

Fiction

Awarded for a work of fiction, preferably about American life, by an American author.

YEAR	TITLE	AUTHOR
1917	no award	
1918	*His Family*	Ernest Poole
1919	*The Magnificent Ambersons*	Booth Tarkington
1920	no award	
1921	*The Age of Innocence*	Edith Wharton
1922	*Alice Adams*	Booth Tarkington
1923	*One of Ours*	Willa Cather
1924	*The Able McLaughlins*	Margaret Wilson
1925	*So Big*	Edna Ferber
1926	*Arrowsmith*	Sinclair Lewis
1927	*Early Autumn*	Louis Bromfield
1928	*The Bridge of San Luis Rey*	Thornton Wilder
1929	*Scarlet Sister Mary*	Julia Peterkin
1930	*Laughing Boy*	Oliver Lafarge
1931	*Years of Grace*	Margaret Ayer Barnes
1932	*The Good Earth*	Pearl S. Buck
1933	*The Store*	T.S. Stribling
1934	*Lamb in His Bosom*	Caroline Miller
1935	*Now in November*	Josephine Winslow Johnson
1936	*Honey in the Horn*	Harold L. Davis
1937	*Gone with the Wind*	Margaret Mitchell
1938	*The Late George Apley*	John Phillips Marquand
1939	*The Yearling*	Marjorie Kinnan Rawlings
1940	*The Grapes of Wrath*	John Steinbeck
1941	no award	
1942	*In This Our Life*	Ellen Glasgow
1943	*Dragon's Teeth*	Upton Sinclair
1944	*Journey in the Dark*	Martin Flavin
1945	*A Bell for Adano*	John Hersey
1946	no award	
1947	*All the King's Men*	Robert Penn Warren
1948	*Tales of the South Pacific*	James A. Michener
1949	*Guard of Honor*	James Gould Cozzens
1950	*The Way West*	A.B. Guthrie, Jr.
1951	*The Town*	Conrad Richter
1952	*The Caine Mutiny*	Herman Wouk
1953	*The Old Man and the Sea*	Ernest Hemingway
1954	no award	
1955	*A Fable*	William Faulkner
1956	*Andersonville*	MacKinlay Kantor
1957	no award	
1958	*A Death in the Family*[1]	James Agee
1959	*The Travels of Jaimie McPheeters*	Robert Lewis Taylor
1960	*Advise and Consent*	Allen Drury
1961	*To Kill a Mockingbird*	Harper Lee
1962	*The Edge of Sadness*	Edwin O'Connor
1963	*The Reivers*	William Faulkner
1964	no award	
1965	*The Keepers of the House*	Shirley Ann Grau
1966	*Collected Stories*	Katherine Anne Porter
1967	*The Fixer*	Bernard Malamud
1968	*The Confessions of Nat Turner*	William Styron
1969	*House Made of Dawn*	N. Scott Momaday
1970	*Collected Stories*	Jean Stafford
1971	no award	
1972	*Angle of Repose*	Wallace Stegner
1973	*The Optimist's Daughter*	Eudora Welty
1974	no award	
1975	*The Killer Angels*	Michael Shaara
1976	*Humboldt's Gift*	Saul Bellow
1977	no award	
1978	*Elbow Room*	James Alan McPherson
1979	*The Stories of John Cheever*	John Cheever
1980	*The Executioner's Song*	Norman Mailer
1981	*A Confederacy of Dunces*[1]	John Kennedy Toole
1982	*Rabbit Is Rich*	John Updike
1983	*The Color Purple*	Alice Walker
1984	*Ironweed*	William Kennedy
1985	*Foreign Affairs*	Alison Lurie
1986	*Lonesome Dove*	Larry McMurtry
1987	*A Summons to Memphis*	Peter Taylor

Letters, Drama, and Music (continued)

Fiction (continued)

YEAR	TITLE	AUTHOR
1988	*Beloved*	Toni Morrison
1989	*Breathing Lessons*	Anne Tyler
1990	*The Mambo Kings Play Songs of Love*	Oscar Hijuelos
1991	*Rabbit at Rest*	John Updike
1992	*A Thousand Acres*	Jane Smiley
1993	*A Good Scent from a Strange Mountain*	Robert Olen Butler
1994	*The Shipping News*	E. Annie Proulx
1995	*The Stone Diaries*	Carol Shields
1996	*Independence Day*	Richard Ford
1997	*Martin Dressler: The Tale of an American Dreamer*	Steven Millhauser
1998	*American Pastoral*	Philip Roth
1999	*The Hours*	Michael Cunningham
2000	*Interpreter of Maladies*	Jhumpa Lahiri
2001	*The Amazing Adventures of Kavalier and Clay*	Michael Chabon
2002	*Empire Falls*	Richard Russo
2003	*Middlesex*	Jeffrey Eugenides
2004	*The Known World*	Edward P. Jones
2005	*Gilead*	Marilynne Robinson
2006	*March*	Geraldine Brooks
2007	*The Road*	Cormac McCarthy
2008	*The Brief Wondrous Life of Oscar Wao*	Junot Díaz

[1]*Work published and prize awarded posthumously.*

Drama

Awarded for a play, preferably about American life, by an American author.

YEAR	TITLE	AUTHOR
1917	no award	
1918	*Why Marry?*	Jesse Lynch Williams
1919	no award	
1920	*Beyond the Horizon*	Eugene O'Neill
1921	*Miss Lulu Bett*	Zona Gale
1922	*Anna Christie*	Eugene O'Neill
1923	*Icebound*	Owen Davis
1924	*Hell-Bent fer Heaven*	Hatcher Hughes
1925	*They Knew What They Wanted*	Sidney Howard
1926	*Craig's Wife*	George Kelly
1927	*In Abraham's Bosom*	Paul Green
1928	*Strange Interlude*	Eugene O'Neill
1929	*Street Scene*	Elmer L. Rice
1930	*The Green Pastures*	Marc Connelly
1931	*Alison's House*	Susan Glaspell
1932	*Of Thee I Sing*	George S. Kaufman, Morrie Ryskind, and Ira Gershwin
1933	*Both Your Houses*	Maxwell Anderson
1934	*Men in White*	Sidney Kingsley
1935	*The Old Maid*	Zoe Akins
1936	*Idiot's Delight*	Robert E. Sherwood
1937	*You Can't Take It with You*	Moss Hart and George S. Kaufman
1938	*Our Town*	Thornton Wilder
1939	*Abe Lincoln in Illinois*	Robert E. Sherwood
1940	*The Time of Your Life*	William Saroyan
1941	*There Shall Be No Night*	Robert E. Sherwood
1942	no award	
1943	*The Skin of Our Teeth*	Thornton Wilder
1944	no award	
1945	*Harvey*	Mary Chase
1946	*State of the Union*	Russel Crouse and Howard Lindsay
1947	no award	
1948	*A Streetcar Named Desire*	Tennessee Williams
1949	*Death of a Salesman*	Arthur Miller
1950	*South Pacific*	Richard Rodgers, Oscar Hammerstein II, and Joshua Logan
1951	no award	
1952	*The Shrike*	Joseph Kramm
1953	*Picnic*	William Inge
1954	*The Teahouse of the August Moon*	John Patrick
1955	*Cat on a Hot Tin Roof*	Tennessee Williams
1956	*The Diary of Anne Frank*	Albert Hackett and Frances Goodrich
1957	*Long Day's Journey into Night*[1]	Eugene O'Neill
1958	*Look Homeward, Angel*	Ketti Frings
1959	*J.B.*	Archibald MacLeish
1960	*Fiorello!*	Jerome Weidman, George Abbott, Jerry Bock, and Sheldon Harnick
1961	*All the Way Home*	Tad Mosel
1962	*How To Succeed in Business Without Really Trying*	Frank Loesser and Abe Burrows
1963	no award	
1964	no award	
1965	*The Subject Was Roses*	Frank D. Gilroy
1966	no award	
1967	*A Delicate Balance*	Edward Albee
1968	no award	
1969	*The Great White Hope*	Howard Sackler
1970	*No Place To Be Somebody*	Charles Gordone
1971	*The Effect of Gamma Rays on Man-in-the-Moon Marigolds*	Paul Zindel
1972	no award	
1973	*That Championship Season*	Jason Miller
1974	no award	
1975	*Seascape*	Edward Albee
1976	*A Chorus Line*	Michael Bennett, James Kirkwood, Nicholas Dante, Marvin Hamlisch, and Edward Kleban

Letters, Drama, and Music (continued)

Drama (continued)

YEAR	TITLE	AUTHOR
1977	*The Shadow Box*	Michael Cristofer
1978	*The Gin Game*	Donald L. Coburn
1979	*Buried Child*	Sam Shepard
1980	*Talley's Folly*	Lanford Wilson
1981	*Crimes of the Heart*	Beth Henley
1982	*A Soldier's Play*	Charles Fuller
1983	*'Night, Mother*	Marsha Norman
1984	*Glengarry Glen Ross*	David Mamet
1985	*Sunday in the Park with George*	Stephen Sondheim and James Lapine
1986	no award	
1987	*Fences*	August Wilson
1988	*Driving Miss Daisy*	Alfred Uhry
1989	*The Heidi Chronicles*	Wendy Wasserstein
1990	*The Piano Lesson*	August Wilson
1991	*Lost in Yonkers*	Neil Simon
1992	*The Kentucky Cycle*	Robert Schenkkan
1993	*Angels in America: Millennium Approaches*	Tony Kushner
1994	*Three Tall Women*	Edward Albee
1995	*The Young Man from Atlanta*	Horton Foote
1996	*Rent*[1]	Jonathan Larson
1997	no award	
1998	*How I Learned To Drive*	Paula Vogel
1999	*Wit*	Margaret Edson
2000	*Dinner with Friends*	Donald Margulies
2001	*Proof*	David Auburn
2002	*Topdog/Underdog*	Suzan-Lori Parks
2003	*Anna in the Tropics*	Nilo Cruz
2004	*I Am My Own Wife*	Doug Wright
2005	*Doubt: A Parable*	John Patrick Shanley
2006	no award	
2007	*Rabbit Hole*	David Lindsay-Abaire
2008	*August: Osage County*	Tracy Letts

[1]*Awarded posthumously*

History

Awarded for a work on the subject of American history.

YEAR	TITLE	AUTHOR
1917	*With Americans of Past and Present Days*	J.J. Jusserand
1918	*A History of the Civil War, 1861–1865*	James Ford Rhodes
1919	no award	
1920	*The War with Mexico,* 2 vols.	Justin H. Smith
1921	*The Victory at Sea*	William Sowden Sims and Burton Jesse Hendrick
1922	*The Founding of New England*	James Truslow Adams
1923	*The Supreme Court in United States History*	Charles Warren
1924	*The American Revolution: A Constitutional Interpretation*	Charles Howard McIlwain
1925	*History of the American Frontier*	Frederic L. Paxson
1926	*A History of the United States*	Edward Channing
1927	*Pinckney's Treaty*	Samuel Flagg Bemis
1928	*Main Currents in American Thought,* 2 vols.	Vernon Louis Parrington
1929	*The Organization and Administration of the Union Army, 1861–1865*	Fred Albert Shannon
1930	*The War of Independence*	Claude H. Van Tyne
1931	*The Coming of the War, 1914*	Bernadotte E. Schmitt
1932	*My Experiences in the World War*	John J. Pershing
1933	*The Significance of Sections in American History*[1]	Frederick J. Turner
1934	*The People's Choice*	Herbert Agar
1935	*The Colonial Period of American History*	Charles McLean Andrews
1936	*A Constitutional History of the United States*	Andrew C. McLaughlin
1937	*The Flowering of New England, 1815–1865*	Van Wyck Brooks
1938	*The Road to Reunion, 1865–1900*	Paul Herman Buck
1939	*A History of American Magazines*	Frank Luther Mott
1940	*Abraham Lincoln: The War Years*	Carl Sandburg
1941	*The Atlantic Migration, 1607–1860*	Marcus Lee Hansen
1942	*Reveille in Washington, 1860–1865*	Margaret Leech
1943	*Paul Revere and the World He Lived In*	Esther Forbes
1944	*The Growth of American Thought*	Merle Curti
1945	*Unfinished Business*	Stephen Bonsal
1946	*The Age of Jackson*	Arthur M. Schlesinger, Jr.
1947	*Scientists Against Time*	James Phinney Baxter III
1948	*Across the Wide Missouri*	Bernard De Voto
1949	*The Disruption of American Democracy*	Roy Franklin Nichols
1950	*Art and Life in America*	Oliver W. Larkin
1951	*The Old Northwest: Pioneer Period, 1815–1840*	R. Carlyle Buley

Letters, Drama, and Music (continued)

History (continued)

YEAR	TITLE	AUTHOR
1952	*The Uprooted*	Oscar Handlin
1953	*The Era of Good Feelings*	George Dangerfield
1954	*A Stillness at Appomattox*	Bruce Catton
1955	*Great River: The Rio Grande in North American History*	Paul Horgan
1956	*The Age of Reform*	Richard Hofstadter
1957	*Russia Leaves the War: Soviet-American Relations, 1917–1920*	George F. Kennan
1958	*Banks and Politics in America*	Bray Hammond
1959	*The Republican Era: 1869–1901*	Leonard D. White and Jean Schneider
1960	*In the Days of McKinley*	Margaret Leech
1961	*Between War and Peace: The Potsdam Conference*	Herbert Feis
1962	*The Triumphant Empire: Thunder-Clouds Gather in the West, 1763–1766*	Lawrence H. Gipson
1963	*Washington, Village and Capital, 1800–1878*	Constance McLaughlin Green
1964	*Puritan Village: The Formation of a New England Town*	Sumner Chilton Powell
1965	*The Greenback Era*	Irwin Unger
1966	*The Life of the Mind in America*[1]	Perry Miller
1967	*Exploration and Empire: The Explorer and the Scientist in the Winning of the American West*	William H. Goetzmann
1968	*The Ideological Origins of the American Revolution*	Bernard Bailyn
1969	*Origins of the Fifth Amendment*	Leonard W. Levy
1970	*Present at the Creation: My Years in the State Department*	Dean Acheson
1971	*Roosevelt: The Soldier of Freedom*	James MacGregor Burns
1972	*Neither Black nor White*	Carl N. Degler
1973	*People of Paradox: An Inquiry Concerning the Origins of American Civilization*	Michael Kammen
1974	*The Americans: The Democratic Experience*	Daniel J. Boorstin
1975	*Jefferson and His Time, vols. 1–5*	Dumas Malone
1976	*Lamy of Santa Fe*	Paul Horgan
1977	*The Impending Crisis, 1841–1867*[2]	David M. Potter and Don E. Fehrenbacher
1978	*The Visible Hand: The Managerial Revolution in American Business*	Alfred D. Chandler, Jr.
1979	*The Dred Scott Case*	Don E. Fehrenbacher
1980	*Been in the Storm So Long*	Leon F. Litwack
1981	*American Education: The National Experience, 1783–1876*	Lawrence A. Cremin
1982	*Mary Chesnut's Civil War*	C. Vann Woodward[3]
1983	*The Transformation of Virginia, 1740–1790*	Rhys L. Isaac
1984	no award	
1985	*Prophets of Regulation*	Thomas K. McCraw
1986	*The Heavens and the Earth: A Political History of the Space Age*	Walter A. McDougall
1987	*Voyagers to the West: A Passage in the Peopling of America on the Eve of the Revolution*	Bernard Bailyn
1988	*The Launching of Modern American Science, 1846–1876*	Robert V. Bruce
1989	*Battle Cry of Freedom: The Civil War Era*	James M. McPherson
	Parting the Waters: America in the King Years, 1954–1963	Taylor Branch
1990	*In Our Image: America's Empire in the Philippines*	Stanley Karnow
1991	*A Midwife's Tale*	Laurel Thatcher Ulrich
1992	*The Fate of Liberty: Abraham Lincoln and Civil Liberties*	Mark E. Neely, Jr.
1993	*The Radicalism of the American Revolution*	Gordon S. Wood
1994	no award	
1995	*No Ordinary Time: Franklin and Eleanor Roosevelt: The Home Front in World War II*	Doris Kearns Goodwin
1996	*William Cooper's Town: Power and Persuasion on the Frontier of the Early American Republic*	Alan Taylor
1997	*Original Meanings: Politics and Ideas in the Making of the Constitution*	Jack N. Rakove
1998	*Summer for the Gods: The Scopes Trial and America's Continuing Debate over Science and Religion*	Edward J. Larson
1999	*Gotham: A History of New York City to 1898*	Edwin G. Burrows and Mike Wallace
2000	*Freedom from Fear: The American People in Depression and War, 1929–1945*	David M. Kennedy
2001	*Founding Brothers: The Revolutionary Generation*	Joseph J. Ellis

Letters, Drama, and Music (continued)

History (continued)

YEAR	TITLE	AUTHOR
2002	*The Metaphysical Club: A Story of Ideas in America*	Louis Menand
2003	*An Army at Dawn: The War in North Africa, 1942–1943*	Rick Atkinson
2004	*A Nation Under Our Feet: Black Political Struggles in the Rural South from Slavery to the Great Migration*	Steven Hahn
2005	*Washington's Crossing*	David Hackett Fischer
2006	*Polio: An American Story*	David M. Oshinsky
2007	*The Race Beat: The Press, the Civil Rights Struggle, and the Awakening of a Nation*	Gene Roberts and Hank Klibanoff
2008	*What Hath God Wrought: The Transformation of America, 1815–1848*	Daniel Walker Howe

[1]Awarded posthumously. [2]Potter died before completing the work; Fehrenbacher wrote the final chapters and edited it. [3]Editor.

Biography or Autobiography

Awarded for a biography or autobiography by an American author.

YEAR	TITLE	AUTHOR
1917	*Julia Ward Howe*	Laura Elizabeth Howe Richards and Maude Howe Elliott; assisted by Florence Howe Hall
1918	*Benjamin Franklin, Self-Revealed*	William Cabell Bruce
1919	*The Education of Henry Adams*[1]	Henry Adams
1920	*The Life of John Marshall*, 4 vols.	Albert J. Beveridge
1921	*The Americanization of Edward Bok*	Edward Bok
1922	*A Daughter of the Middle Border*	Hamlin Garland
1923	*The Life and Letters of Walter H. Page*	Burton J. Hendrick
1924	*From Immigrant to Inventor*	Michael Idvorsky Pupin
1925	*Barrett Wendell and His Letters*	M.A. De Wolfe Howe
1926	*The Life of Sir William Osler*, 2 vols.	Harvey Cushing
1927	*Whitman*	Emory Holloway
1928	*The American Orchestra and Theodore Thomas*	Charles Edward Russell
1929	*The Training of an American: The Earlier Life and Letters of Walter H. Page*	Burton J. Hendrick
1930	*The Raven*	Marquis James
1931	*Charles W. Eliot*	Henry James
1932	*Theodore Roosevelt*	Henry F. Pringle
1933	*Grover Cleveland*	Allan Nevins
1934	*John Hay*	Tyler Dennett
1935	*R.E. Lee*	Douglas S. Freeman
1936	*The Thought and Character of William James*	Ralph Barton Perry
1937	*Hamilton Fish*	Allan Nevins
1938	*Andrew Jackson*, 2 vols.	Marquis James
	Pedlar's Progress	Odell Shepard
1939	*Benjamin Franklin*	Carl Van Doren
1940	*Woodrow Wilson, Life and Letters*, vols. 7 and 8	Ray Stannard Baker
1941	*Jonathan Edward*	Ola Elizabeth Winslow
1942	*Crusader in Crinoline*	Forrest Wilson
1943	*Admiral of the Ocean Sea*	Samuel Eliot Morison
1944	*The American Leonardo: The Life of Samuel F.B. Morse*	Carleton Mabee
1945	*George Bancroft: Brahmin Rebel*	Russell Blaine Nye
1946	*Son of the Wilderness*	Linnie Marsh Wolfe
1947	*The Autobiography of William Allen White*	William Allen White
1948	*Forgotten First Citizen: John Bigelow*	Margaret Clapp
1949	*Roosevelt and Hopkins*	Robert E. Sherwood
1950	*John Quincy Adams and the Foundations of American Foreign Policy*	Samuel Flagg Bemis
1951	*John C. Calhoun: American Portrait*	Margaret Louise Coit
1952	*Charles Evans Hughes*	Merlo J. Pusey
1953	*Edmund Pendleton, 1721–1803*	David J. Mays
1954	*The Spirit of St. Louis*	Charles A. Lindbergh
1955	*The Taft Story*	William S. White
1956	*Benjamin Henry Latrobe*	Talbot Faulkner Hamlin
1957	*Profiles in Courage*	John F. Kennedy
1958	*George Washington*, vols. 1–7[2]	Douglas Southall Freeman, John Alexander Carroll, and Mary Wells Ashworth
1959	*Woodrow Wilson, American Prophet*	Arthur Walworth
1960	*John Paul Jones*	Samuel Eliot Morison

Letters, Drama, and Music (continued)

Biography or Autobiography (continued)

YEAR	TITLE	AUTHOR
1961	*Charles Sumner and the Coming of the Civil War*	David Donald
1962	no award	
1963	*Henry James*	Leon Edel
1964	*John Keats*	Walter Jackson Bate
1965	*Henry Adams*, 3 vols.	Ernest Samuels
1966	*A Thousand Days*	Arthur M. Schlesinger, Jr.
1967	*Mr. Clemens and Mark Twain*	Justin Kaplan
1968	*Memoirs*	George E. Kennan
1969	*The Man from New York: John Quinn and His Friends*	Benjamin Lawrence Reid
1970	*Huey Long*	T. Harry Williams
1971	*Robert Frost: The Years of Triumph, 1915–1938*	Lawrance Thompson
1972	*Eleanor and Franklin*	Joseph P. Lash
1973	*Luce and His Empire*	W.A. Swanberg
1974	*O'Neill, Son and Artist*	Louis Sheaffer
1975	*The Power Broker: Robert Moses and the Fall of New York*	Robert A. Caro
1976	*Edith Wharton: A Biography*	R.W.B. Lewis
1977	*A Prince of Our Disorder: The Life of T.E. Lawrence*	John E. Mack
1978	*Samuel Johnson*	Walter Jackson Bate
1979	*Days of Sorrow and Pain: Leo Baeck and the Berlin Jews*	Leonard Baker
1980	*The Rise of Theodore Roosevelt*	Edmund Morris
1981	*Peter the Great: His Life and World*	Robert K. Massie
1982	*Grant: A Biography*	William McFeely
1983	*Growing Up*	Russell Baker
1984	*Booker T. Washington: The Wizard of Tuskegee, 1901–1915*	Louis R. Harlan
1985	*The Life and Times of Cotton Mather*	Kenneth Silverman
1986	*Louise Bogan: A Portrait*	Elizabeth Frank
1987	*Bearing the Cross: Martin Luther King, Jr., and the Southern Christian Leadership Conference*	David J. Garrow
1988	*Look Homeward: A Life of Thomas Wolfe*	David Herbert Donald
1989	*Oscar Wilde*[1]	Richard Ellmann
1990	*Machiavelli in Hell*	Sebastian de Grazia
1991	*Jackson Pollock*	Steven Naifeh and Gregory White Smith
1992	*Fortunate Son: The Healing of a Vietnam Vet*	Lewis B. Puller, Jr.
1993	*Truman*	David McCullough
1994	*W.E.B. Du Bois: Biography of a Race, 1868–1919*	David Levering Lewis
1995	*Harriet Beecher Stowe: A Life*	Joan D. Hedrick
1996	*God: A Biography*	Jack Miles
1997	*Angela's Ashes: A Memoir*	Frank McCourt
1998	*Personal History*	Katharine Graham
1999	*Lindbergh*	A. Scott Berg
2000	*Vera (Mrs. Vladimir Nabokov)*	Stacy Schiff
2001	*W.E.B. Du Bois: The Fight for Equality and the American Century, 1919–1963*	David Levering Lewis
2002	*John Adams*	David McCullough
2003	*Master of the Senate*	Robert A. Caro
2004	*Khrushchev: The Man and His Era*	William Taubman
2005	*De Kooning: An American Master*	Mark Stevens and Annalyn Swan
2006	*American Prometheus: The Triumph and Tragedy*	Kai Bird and Martin J. Sherwin
2007	*The Most Famous Man in America: The Biography of Henry Ward Beecher*	Debby Applegate
2008	*Eden's Outcasts: The Story of Louisa May Alcott and Her Father*	John Matteson

[1]*Awarded posthumously.* [2]*Freeman died in 1953 after completing vols. 1–6; Carroll and Ashworth continued his work with vol. 7.*

Poetry

Awarded for a collection of original verse by an American author.

YEAR	TITLE	AUTHOR
1922	*Collected Poems*	Edwin Arlington Robinson
1923	*The Ballad of the Harp-Weaver; A Few Figs from Thistles;* eight sonnets in *American Poetry, 1922: A Miscellany*	Edna St. Vincent Millay
1924	*New Hampshire: A Poem with Notes and Grace Notes*	Robert Frost
1925	*The Man Who Died Twice*	Edwin Arlington Robinson
1926	*What's O'Clock*[1]	Amy Lowell
1927	*Fiddler's Farewell*	Leonora Speyer

Letters, Drama, and Music (continued)

Poetry (continued)

YEAR	TITLE	AUTHOR
1928	*Tristram*	Edwin Arlington Robinson
1929	*John Brown's Body*	Stephen Vincent Benét
1930	*Selected Poems*	Conrad Aiken
1931	*Collected Poems*	Robert Frost
1932	*The Flowering Stone*	George Dillon
1933	*Conquistador*	Archibald MacLeish
1934	*Collected Verse*	Robert Hillyer
1935	*Bright Ambush*	Audrey Wurdemann
1936	*Strange Holiness*	Robert P. Tristram Coffin
1937	*A Further Range*	Robert Frost
1938	*Cold Morning Sky*	Marya Zaturenska
1939	*Selected Poems*	John Gould Fletcher
1940	*Collected Poems*	Mark Van Doren
1941	*Sunderland Capture*	Leonard Bacon
1942	*The Dust Which Is God*	William Rose Benét
1943	*A Witness Tree*	Robert Frost
1944	*Western Star*[1]	Stephen Vincent Benét
1945	*V-Letter and Other Poems*	Karl Shapiro
1946	no award	
1947	*Lord Weary's Castle*	Robert Lowell
1948	*The Age of Anxiety*	W.H. Auden
1949	*Terror and Decorum*	Peter Viereck
1950	*Annie Allen*	Gwendolyn Brooks
1951	*Complete Poems*	Carl Sandburg
1952	*Collected Poems*	Marianne Moore
1953	*Collected Poems, 1917–1952*	Archibald MacLeish
1954	*The Waking*	Theodore Roethke
1955	*Collected Poems*	Wallace Stevens
1956	*Poems: North & South*	Elizabeth Bishop
1957	*Things of This World*	Richard Wilbur
1958	*Promises: Poems 1954–1956*	Robert Penn Warren
1959	*Selected Poems, 1928–1958*	Stanley Kunitz
1960	*Heart's Needle*	W.D. Snodgrass
1961	*Times Three: Selected Verse from Three Decades*	Phyllis McGinley
1962	*Poems*	Alan Dugan
1963	*Pictures from Breughel*[1]	William Carlos Williams
1964	*At the End of the Open Road*	Louis Simpson
1965	*77 Dream Songs*	John Berryman
1966	*Selected Poems*	Richard Eberhart
1967	*Live or Die*	Anne Sexton
1968	*The Hard Hours*	Anthony Hecht
1969	*Of Being Numerous*	George Oppen
1970	*Untitled Subjects*	Richard Howard
1971	*The Carrier of Ladders*	William S. Merwin
1972	*Collected Poems*	James Wright
1973	*Up Country*	Maxine Kumin
1974	*The Dolphin*	Robert Lowell
1975	*Turtle Island*	Gary Snyder
1976	*Self-Portrait in a Convex Mirror*	John Ashbery
1977	*Divine Comedies*	James Merrill
1978	*Collected Poems*	Howard Nemerov
1979	*Now and Then*	Robert Penn Warren
1980	*Selected Poems*	Donald Justice
1981	*The Morning of the Poem*	James Schuyler
1982	*The Collected Poems*[2]	Sylvia Plath
1983	*Selected Poems*	Galway Kinnell
1984	*American Primitive*	Mary Oliver
1985	*Yin*	Carolyn Kizer
1986	*The Flying Change*	Henry Taylor
1987	*Thomas and Beulah*	Rita Dove
1988	*Partial Accounts: New and Selected Poems*	William Meredith
1989	*New and Collected Poems*	Richard Wilbur
1990	*The World Doesn't End*	Charles Simic
1991	*Near Changes*	Mona Van Duyn
1992	*Selected Poems*	James Tate
1993	*The Wild Iris*	Louise Gluck
1994	*Neon Vernacular: New and Selected Poems*	Yusef Komunyakaa
1995	*The Simple Truth*	Philip Levine
1996	*The Dream of the Unified Field*	Jorie Graham
1997	*Alive Together: New and Selected Poems*	Lisel Mueller
1998	*Black Zodiac*	Charles Wright
1999	*Blizzard of One*	Mark Strand
2000	*Repair*	C.K. Williams
2001	*Different Hours*	Stephen Dunn
2002	*Practical Gods*	Carl Dennis
2003	*Moy Sand and Gravel*	Paul Muldoon
2004	*Walking to Martha's Vineyard*	Franz Wright
2005	*Delights & Shadows*	Ted Kooser
2006	*Late Wife*	Claudia Emerson
2007	*Native Guard*	Natasha Trethewey
2008	*Time and Materials*	Robert Hass
	Failure	Philip Schultz

[1]*Awarded posthumously.* [2]*Work published and prize awarded posthumously.*

General Nonfiction

Awarded for a work of nonfiction, ineligible for any other category, by an American author.

YEAR	TITLE	AUTHOR
1962	*The Making of the President, 1960*	Theodore H. White
1963	*The Guns of August*	Barbara W. Tuchman
1964	*Anti-intellectualism in American Life*	Richard Hofstadter
1965	*O Strange New World*	Howard Mumford Jones
1966	*Wandering Through Winter*	Edwin Way Teale
1967	*The Problem of Slavery in Western Culture*	David Brion Davis

Letters, Drama, and Music (continued)

General nonfiction (continued)

YEAR	TITLE	AUTHOR
1968	*Rousseau and Revolution: A History of Civilization in France, England, and Germany from 1756 and in the Remainder of Europe from 1715 to 1789*	Will and Ariel Durant
1969	*The Armies of the Night*	Norman Mailer
	So Human an Animal	Rene Jules Dubos
1970	*Gandhi's Truth*	Erik H. Erikson
1971	*The Rising Sun*	John Toland
1972	*Stilwell and the American Experience in China, 1911–1945*	Barbara W. Tuchman
1973	*Fire in the Lake: The Vietnamese and the Americans in Vietnam*	Frances Fitzgerald
	Children of Crisis, vols. 2 and 3	Robert Coles
1974	*The Denial of Death*[1]	Ernest Becker
1975	*Pilgrim at Tinker Creek*	Annie Dillard
1976	*Why Survive?: Being Old in America*	Robert N. Butler
1977	*Beautiful Swimmers*	William W. Warner
1978	*The Dragons of Eden*	Carl Sagan
1979	*On Human Nature*	Edward O. Wilson
1980	*Gödel, Escher, Bach: An Eternal Golden Braid*	Douglas R. Hofstadter
1981	*Fin-de-Siècle Vienna: Politics and Culture*	Carl E. Schorske
1982	*The Soul of a New Machine*	Tracy Kidder
1983	*Is There No Place on Earth for Me?*	Susan Sheehan
1984	*The Social Transformation of American Medicine*	Paul Starr
1985	*The Good War: An Oral History of World War Two*	Studs Terkel
1986	*Common Ground: A Turbulent Decade in the Lives of Three American Families*	J. Anthony Lukas
	Move Your Shadow: South Africa, Black and White	Joseph Lelyveld
1987	*Arab and Jew: Wounded Spirits in a Promised Land*	David K. Shipler
1988	*The Making of the Atomic Bomb*	Richard Rhodes
1989	*A Bright Shining Lie: John Paul Vann and America in Vietnam*	Neil Sheehan
1990	*And Their Children After Them*	Dale Maharidge and Michael Williamson
1991	*The Ants*	Bert Holldobler and Edward O. Wilson
1992	*The Prize: The Epic Quest for Oil, Money, and Power*	Daniel Yergin
1993	*Lincoln at Gettysburg: The Words That Remade America*	Garry Wills
1994	*Lenin's Tomb: The Last Days of the Soviet Empire*	David Remnick
1995	*The Beak of the Finch: A Story of Evolution in Our Time*	Jonathan Weiner
1996	*The Haunted Land: Facing Europe's Ghosts After Communism*	Tina Rosenberg
1997	*Ashes to Ashes: America's Hundred-Year Cigarette War, the Public Health, and the Unabashed Triumph of Philip Morris*	Richard Kluger
1998	*Guns, Germs, and Steel: The Fates of Human Societies*	Jared Diamond
1999	*Annals of the Former World*	John McPhee
2000	*Embracing Defeat: Japan in the Wake of World War II*	John W. Dower
2001	*Hirohito and the Making of Modern Japan*	Herbert P. Bix
2002	*Carry Me Home: Birmingham, Alabama, the Climactic Battle of the Civil Rights Revolution*	Diane McWhorter
2003	*"A Problem from Hell": America and the Age of Genocide*	Samantha Power
2004	*Gulag: A History*	Anne Applebaum
2005	*Ghost Wars*	Steve Coll
2006	*Imperial Reckoning: The Untold Story of Britain's Gulag in Kenya*	Caroline Elkins
2007	*The Looming Tower: Al-Qaeda and the Road to 9/11*	Lawrence Wright
2008	*The Years of Extermination: Nazi Germany and the Jews, 1939–1945*	Saul Friedländer

[1]*Awarded posthumously.*

Music

Awarded for a musical piece of "significant dimension" composed by an American and first performed or recorded in the United States between 16 January of the previous year and 15 January of the year of the award.

YEAR	TITLE	COMPOSER
1943	*Secular Cantata No. 2: A Free Song*	William Schuman
1944	*Symphony No. 4, Opus 34*	Howard Hanson
1945	*Appalachian Spring*	Aaron Copland

Letters, Drama, and Music (continued)

Music (continued)

YEAR	TITLE	COMPOSER
1946	*The Canticle of the Sun*	Leo Sowerby
1947	*Symphony No. 3*	Charles Ives
1948	*Symphony No. 3*	Walter Piston
1949	Music for the film *Louisiana Story*	Virgil Thomson
1950	*The Consul*	Gian Carlo Menotti
1951	*Giants in the Earth*	Douglas S. Moore
1952	*Symphony Concertante*	Gail Kubik
1953	no award	
1954	*Concerto for Two Pianos and Orchestra*	Quincy Porter
1955	*The Saint of Bleecker Street*	Gian Carlo Menotti
1956	*Symphony No. 3*	Ernst Toch
1957	*Meditation on Ecclesiastics*	Norman Dello Joio
1958	*Vanessa*	Samuel Barber
1959	*Concerto for Piano and Orchestra*	John LaMontaine
1960	*Second String Quartet*	Elliott Carter
1961	*Symphony No. 7*	Walter Piston
1962	*The Crucible*	Robert Ward
1963	*Piano Concerto No. 1*	Samuel Barber
1964	no award	
1965	no award	
1966	*Variations for Orchestra*	Leslie Bassett
1967	*Quartet No. 3*	Leon Kirchner
1968	*Echoes of Time and the River*	George Crumb
1969	*String Quartet No. 3*	Karel Husa
1970	*Time's Encomium*	Charles Wuorinen
1971	*Synchronisms No. 6 for Piano and Electronic Sound*	Mario Davidovsky
1972	*Windows*	Jacob Druckman
1973	*String Quartet No. 3*	Elliott Carter
1974	*Notturno*	Donald Martino
1975	*From the Diary of Virginia Woolf*	Dominick Argento
1976	*Air Music*	Ned Rorem
1977	*Visions of Terror and Wonder*	Richard Wernick
1978	*Deja Vu for Percussion Quartet and Orchestra*	Michael Colgrass
1979	*Aftertones of Infinity*	Joseph Schwantner
1980	*In Memory of a Summer Day*	David Del Tredici
1981	no award	
1982	*Concerto for Orchestra*	Roger Sessions
1983	*Symphony No. 1 (Three Movements for Orchestra)*	Ellen Taaffe Zwilich
1984	*"Canti del sole" for Tenor and Orchestra*	Bernard Rands
1985	*Symphony RiverRun*	Stephen Albert
1986	*Wind Quintet IV*	George Perle
1987	*The Flight into Egypt*	John Harbison
1988	*12 New Etudes for Piano*	William Bolcom
1989	*Whispers out of Time*	Roger Reynolds
1990	*"Duplicates": A Concerto for Two Pianos and Orchestra*	Mel Powell
1991	*Symphony*	Shulamit Ran
1992	*The Face of the Night, The Heart of the Dark*	Wayne Peterson
1993	*Trombone Concerto*	Christopher Rouse
1994	*Of Reminiscences and Reflections*	Gunther Schuller
1995	*Stringmusic*	Morton Gould
1996	*Lilacs, for Voice and Orchestra*	George Walker
1997	*Blood on the Fields*	Wynton Marsalis
1998	*String Quartet No. 2 (Musica Instrumentalis)*	Aaron Jay Kernis
1999	*Concerto for Flute, Strings, and Percussion*	Melinda Wagner
2000	*Life Is a Dream, Opera in Three Acts: Act II, Concert Version*	Lewis Spratlan
2001	*Symphony No. 2 for String Orchestra*	John Corigliano
2002	*Ice Field*	Henry Brant
2003	*On the Transmigration of Souls*	John Adams
2004	*Tempest Fantasy*	Paul Moravec
2005	*Second Concerto for Orchestra*	Steven Stucky
2006	*Piano Concerto: "Chiavi in mano"*	Yehudi Wyner
2007	*Sound Grammar*	Ornette Coleman
2008	*The Little Match Girl Passion*	David Lang

Special Awards and Citations[1]

YEAR	RECIPIENT	FOR
1992	Art Spiegelman	graphic novel *Maus*
1996	Herb Caen	contributions as a voice of San Francisco
1998	George Gershwin[2]	centennial commemoration of his birth, celebrating his life's work in music
1999	Duke Ellington[2]	centennial commemoration of his birth, celebrating his life's work in music
2006	Edmund S. Morgan	his life's work as an American historian
2006 (cont.)	Thelonious Monk[2]	his contributions to jazz
2007	Ray Bradbury	his contributions to science fiction and fantasy
	John Coltrane[2]	his contributions to jazz
2008	Bob Dylan	his profound influence on pop culture and American music

[1]*For the past 20 years.* [2]*Awarded posthumously.*

National Book Awards

In 1950 a consortium of publishing groups established the National Book Awards. The goals were to bring exceptional books written by Americans to the public's attention and to encourage reading in general. Award categories have varied from the inaugural 3 to as many as 28 in 1980. Today, the awards recognize achievements in four genres: fiction, nonfiction, poetry, and young people's literature. A five-member, independent judging panel chooses a winner for each genre. Award: US$10,000 cash and a bronze sculpture.

Fiction

YEAR	TITLE	AUTHOR
1950	*The Man with the Golden Arm*	Nelson Algren
1951	*The Collected Stories of William Faulkner*	William Faulkner
1952	*From Here to Eternity*	James Jones
1953	*Invisible Man*	Ralph Ellison
1954	*The Adventures of Augie March*	Saul Bellow
1955	*A Fable*	William Faulkner
1956	*Ten North Frederick*	John O'Hara
1957	*The Field of Vision*	Wright Morris
1958	*The Wapshot Chronicle*	John Cheever
1959	*The Magic Barrel*	Bernard Malamud
1960	*Goodbye, Columbus*	Philip Roth
1961	*The Waters of Kronos*	Conrad Richter
1962	*The Moviegoer*	Walker Percy
1963	*Morte d'Urban*	J.F. Powers
1964	*The Centaur*	John Updike
1965	*Herzog*	Saul Bellow
1966	*The Collected Stories of Katherine Anne Porter*	Katherine Anne Porter
1967	*The Fixer*	Bernard Malamud
1968	*The Eighth Day*	Thornton Wilder
1969	*Steps*	Jerzy Kosinski
1970	*Them*	Joyce Carol Oates
1971	*Mr. Sammler's Planet*	Saul Bellow
1972	*The Complete Stories*	Flannery O'Connor
1973	*Augustus*	John Williams
	Chimera	John Barth
1974	*A Crown of Feathers and Other Stories*	Isaac Bashevis Singer
	Gravity's Rainbow	Thomas Pynchon
1975	*Dog Soldiers: A Novel*	Robert Stone
	The Hair of Harold Roux	Thomas Williams
1976	*J.R.*	William Gaddis

Fiction (continued)

YEAR	TITLE	AUTHOR
1977	*The Spectator Bird*	Wallace Stegner
1978	*Blood Tie*	Mary Lee Settle
1979	*Going After Cacciato*	Tim O'Brien
1980	*Sophie's Choice*[1]	William Styron
1981	*Plains Song*[1]	Wright Morris
1982	*Rabbit Is Rich*[1]	John Updike
1983	*The Color Purple*[1]	Alice Walker
1984	*Victory over Japan: A Book of Stories*	Ellen Gilchrist
1985	*White Noise*	Don DeLillo
1986	*World's Fair*	E.L. Doctorow
1987	*Paco's Story*	Larry Heinemann
1988	*Paris Trout*	Pete Dexter
1989	*Spartina*	John Casey
1990	*Middle Passage*	Charles Johnson
1991	*Mating*	Norman Rush
1992	*All the Pretty Horses*	Cormac McCarthy
1993	*The Shipping News*	E. Annie Proulx
1994	*A Frolic of His Own*	William Gaddis
1995	*Sabbath's Theater*	Philip Roth
1996	*Ship Fever*	Andrea Barrett
1997	*Cold Mountain*	Charles Frazier
1998	*Charming Billy*	Alice McDermott
1999	*Waiting*	Ha Jin
2000	*In America*	Susan Sontag
2001	*The Corrections*	Jonathan Franzen
2002	*Three Junes*	Julia Glass
2003	*The Great Fire*	Shirley Hazzard
2004	*The News From Paraguay*	Lily Tuck
2005	*Europe Central*	William T. Vollmann
2006	*The Echo Maker*	Richard Powers
2007	*Tree of Smoke*	Denis Johnson

Nonfiction

YEAR	TITLE	AUTHOR
1950	*The Life of Ralph Waldo Emerson*	Ralph L. Rusk
1951	*Herman Melville*	Newton Arvin
1952	*The Sea Around Us*	Rachel Carson
1953	*The Course of Empire*	Bernard A. De Voto
1954	*A Stillness at Appomattox*	Bruce Catton
1955	*The Measure of Man: On Freedom, Human Values, Survival, and the Modern Temper*	Joseph Wood Krutch
1956	*American in Italy*	Herbert Kubly
1957	*Russia Leaves the War*	George F. Kennan
1958	*The Lion and the Throne: The Life and Times of Sir Edward Coke (1552–1634)*	Catherine Drinker Bowen
1959	*Mistress to an Age: A Life of Madame de Staël*	J. Christopher Herold
1960	*James Joyce*	Richard Ellmann
1961	*The Rise and Fall of the Third Reich: A History of Nazi Germany*	William L. Shirer
1962	*The City in History: Its Origins, Its Transformations, and Its Prospects*	Lewis Mumford
1963	*Henry James, Vol. II: The Conquest of London (1870–1881); Vol. III: The Middle Years (1882–1895)*	Leon Edel
1964	*The Rise of the West: A History of the Human Community*[2]	William H. McNeill
1965	*The Life of Lenin*[2]	Louis Fischer
1966	*A Thousand Days: John F. Kennedy in the White House*[2]	Arthur M. Schlesinger, Jr.
1967	*The Enlightenment: An Interpretation, Vol. I*[2]	Peter Gay
1968	*Memoirs: 1925–1950*[2]	George F. Kennan
1969	*White over Black: American Attitudes Toward the Negro, 1550–1812*[2]	Winthrop D. Jordan
1970	*Huey Long*[2]	T. Harry Williams
1971	*Roosevelt: The Soldier of Freedom*[2]	James MacGregor Burns

National Book Awards (continued)

Nonfiction (continued)

YEAR	TITLE	AUTHOR
1972	*Eleanor and Franklin: The Story of Their Relationship, Based on Eleanor Roosevelt's Private Papers*[3]	Joseph P. Lash
1973	*George Washington, Vol. IV: Anguish and Farewell, 1793–1799*[3]	James Thomas Flexner
1974	*Macaulay: The Shaping of the Historian*[4]	John Clive
1975	*The Life of Emily Dickinson*[3]	Richard B. Sewall
1976	*The Problem of Slavery in the Age of Revolution, 1770–1823*[2]	David Brion Davis
1977	*Norman Thomas: The Last Idealist*[5]	W.A. Swanberg
1978	*Samuel Johnson*[5]	W. Jackson Bate
1979	*Robert Kennedy and His Times*[5]	Arthur M. Schlesinger, Jr.
1980	*The Right Stuff*[6]	Tom Wolfe
1981	*China Men*[6]	Maxine Hong Kingston
1982	*The Soul of a New Machine*[6]	Tracy Kidder
1983	*China: Alive in the Bitter Sea*[6]	Fox Butterfield
1984	*Andrew Jackson and the Course of American Democracy, 1833–1845*	Robert V. Remini
1985	*Common Ground: A Turbulent Decade in the Lives of Three American Families*	J. Anthony Lukas
1986	*Arctic Dreams*	Barry Lopez
1987	*The Making of the Atomic Bomb*	Richard Rhodes
1988	*A Bright Shining Lie: John Paul Vann and America in Vietnam*	Neil Sheehan
1989	*From Beirut to Jerusalem*	Thomas L. Friedman
1990	*The House of Morgan: An American Banking Dynasty and the Rise of Modern Finance*	Ron Chernow
1991	*Freedom*	Orlando Patterson
1992	*Becoming a Man: Half a Life Story*	Paul Monette
1993	*United States: Essays, 1952–1992*	Gore Vidal
1994	*How We Die: Reflections on Life's Final Chapter*	Sherwin B. Nuland
1995	*The Haunted Land: Facing Europe's Ghosts After Communism*	Tina Rosenberg
1996	*An American Requiem: God, My Father, and the War That Came Between Us*	James Carroll
1997	*American Sphinx: The Character of Thomas Jefferson*	Joseph J. Ellis
1998	*Slaves in the Family*	Edward Ball
1999	*Embracing Defeat: Japan in the Wake of World War II*	John W. Dower
2000	*In the Heart of the Sea: The Tragedy of the Whaleship Essex*	Nathaniel Philbrick
2001	*The Noonday Demon: An Atlas of Depression*	Andrew Solomon
2002	*Master of the Senate: The Years of Lyndon Johnson*	Robert A. Caro
2003	*Waiting for Snow in Havana*	Carlos Eire
2004	*Arc of Justice: A Saga of Race, Civil Rights, and Murder in the Jazz Age*	Kevin Boyle
2005	*The Year of Magical Thinking*	Joan Didion
2006	*The Worst Hard Time: The Untold Story of Those Who Survived the Great American Dust Bowl*	Timothy Egan
2007	*Legacy of Ashes: The History of the CIA*	Tim Weiner

Poetry

YEAR	TITLE	AUTHOR
1950	*Paterson: Book III and Selected Poems*	William Carlos Williams
1951	*The Auroras of Autumn*	Wallace Stevens
1952	*Collected Poems*	Marianne Moore
1953	*Collected Poems, 1917–1952*	Archibald MacLeish
1954	*Collected Poems*	Conrad Aiken
1955	*The Collected Poems of Wallace Stevens*	Wallace Stevens
1956	*The Shield of Achilles*	W.H. Auden
1957	*Things of This World: Poems*	Richard Wilbur
1958	*Promises: Poems, 1954–1956*	Robert Penn Warren
1959	*Words for the Wind: The Collected Verse of Theodore Roethke*	Theodore Roethke
1960	*Life Studies*	Robert Lowell
1961	*The Woman at the Washington Zoo*	Randall Jarrell
1962	*Poems*	Alan Dugan
1963	*Traveling Through the Dark*	William Stafford
1964	*Selected Poems*	John Crowe Ransom
1965	*The Far Field*	Theodore Roethke
1966	*Buckdancer's Choice: Poems*	James Dickey
1967	*Nights and Days*	James Merrill
1968	*The Light Around the Body: Poems*	Robert Bly
1969	*His Toy, His Dream, His Rest: 308 Dream Songs*	John Berryman
1970	*The Complete Poems*	Elizabeth Bishop
1971	*To See, To Take: Poems*	Mona Van Duyn
1972	*The Collected Poems of Frank O'Hara*	Frank O'Hara
	Selected Poems	Howard Moss
1973	*Collected Poems, 1951–1971*	A.R. Ammons
1974	*Diving into the Wreck: Poems, 1971–1972*	Adrienne Rich

National Book Awards (continued)

Poetry (continued)

YEAR	TITLE	AUTHOR
1974	*The Fall of America: Poems of These States*	Allen Ginsberg
1975	*Presentation Piece*	Marilyn Hacker
1976	*Self-Portrait in a Convex Mirror: Poems*	John Ashbery
1977	*Collected Poems, 1930–1976*	Richard Eberhart
1978	*The Collected Poems of Howard Nemerov*	Howard Nemerov
1979	*Mirabell: Books of Number*	James Merrill
1980	*Ashes: Poems New & Old*	Philip Levine
1981	*The Need to Hold Still*	Lisel Mueller
1982	*Life Supports: New and Collected Poems*	William Bronk
1983	*Country Music: Selected Early Poems*	Charles Wright
1984	*Selected Poems*	Galway Kinnell
1985	*Yin*	Carolyn Kizer
1986	*The Flying Change*	Henry Taylor
1987	*Thomas and Beulah*	Rita Dove
1988	*Partial Accounts: New and Selected Poems*	William Meredith
1989	*New and Collected Poems*	Richard Wilbur
1990	*The World Doesn't End*	Charles Simic
1991	*What Work Is: Poems*	Philip Levine
1992	*New and Selected Poems*	Mary Oliver
1993	*Garbage*	A.R. Ammons
1994	*Worshipful Company of Fletchers: Poems*	James Tate
1995	*Passing Through: The Later Poems, New and Selected*	Stanley Kunitz
1996	*Scrambled Eggs & Whiskey: Poems, 1991–1995*	Hayden Carruth
1997	*Effort at Speech: New and Selected Poems*	William Meredith
1998	*This Time: New and Selected Poems*	Gerald Stern
1999	*Vice: New and Selected Poems*	Ai
2000	*Blessing the Boats: New and Selected Poems, 1988–2000*	Lucille Clifton
2001	*Poems Seven: New and Complete Poetry*	Alan Dugan
2002	*In the Next Galaxy*	Ruth Stone
2003	*The Singing*	C.K. Williams
2004	*Door in the Mountain: New and Collected Poems, 1965–2003*	Jean Valentine
2005	*Migration: New and Selected Poems*	W.S. Merwin
2006	*Splay Anthem*	Nathaniel Mackey
2007	*Time and Materials*	Robert Hass

Young People's Literature

YEAR	TITLE	AUTHOR
1969	*Journey from Peppermint Street*	Meindert De Jong
1970	*A Day of Pleasure: Stories of a Boy Growing Up in Warsaw*[7]	Isaac Bashevis Singer
1971	*The Marvelous Misadventures of Sebastian*[7]	Lloyd Alexander
1972	*The Slightly Irregular Fire Engine; or, The Hithering Thithering Djinn*[7]	Donald Barthelme
1973	*The Farthest Shore*[7]	Ursula Le Guin
1974	*The Court of the Stone Children*[7]	Eleanor Cameron
1975	*M.C. Higgins, the Great*[7]	Virginia Hamilton
1976	*Bert Breen's Barn*	Walter D. Edmonds
1977	*The Master Puppeteer*	Katherine Paterson
1978	*The View from the Oak: The Private Worlds of Other Creatures*	Judith Kohl and Herbert Kohl
1979	*The Great Gilly Hopkins*	Katherine Paterson
1980	*A Gathering of Days: A New England Girl's Journal, 1830–32*[8]	Joan Blos
1981	*The Night Swimmers*[9]	Betsy Byars
1982	*Westmark*[9]	Lloyd Alexander
1983	*Homesick: My Own Story*[9]	Jean Fritz
1996	*Parrot in the Oven: Mi Vida*	Victor Martinez
1997	*Dancing on the Edge*	Han Nolan
1998	*Holes*	Louis Sachar
1999	*When Zachary Beaver Came to Town*	Kimberly Willis Holt
2000	*Homeless Bird*	Gloria Whelan
2001	*True Believer*	Virginia Euwer Wolff
2002	*The House of the Scorpion*	Nancy Farmer
2003	*The Canning Season*	Polly Horvath
2004	*The Godless*	Pete Hautman
2005	*The Penderwicks*	Jeanne Birdsall
2006	*The Astonishing Life of Octavian Nothing, Traitor to the Nation, Vol. 1: The Pox Party*	M.T. Anderson
2007	*The Absolutely True Diary of a Part-Time Indian*	Sherman Alexie

[1]*Fiction (Hardcover).* [2]*History and Biography (Nonfiction).* [3]*Biography.* [4]*History.* [5]*Biography and Autobiography.* [6]*General Nonfiction (Hardcover).* [7]*Children's Books.* [8]*Children's Books (Hardcover).* [9]*Children's Books, Fiction (Hardcover).*

The PEN/Faulkner Award for Fiction

Named for William Faulkner and affiliated with the writers' organization International PEN (Poets, Playwrights, Editors, Essayists, and Novelists), the PEN/Faulkner Award was founded by writers in 1980 to honor their peers. A panel of fiction writers selects a winning novel or short-story collection and four runners-up. The winning author receives US$15,000, and each of the others receives US$5,000.

PEN/Faulkner Web site: <www.penfaulkner.org>.

YEAR	TITLE	AUTHOR
1981	*How German Is It?*	Walter Abish
1982	*The Chaneysville Incident*	David Bradley
1983	*Seaview*	Toby Olson
1984	*Sent for You Yesterday*	John Edgar Wideman
1985	*The Barracks Thief*	Tobias Wolff
1986	*The Old Forest and Other Stories*	Peter Taylor
1987	*Soldiers in Hiding*	Richard Wiley
1988	*World's End*	T. Coraghessan Boyle
1989	*Dusk and Other Stories*	James Salter
1990	*Billy Bathgate*	E.L. Doctorow
1991	*Philadelphia Fire*	John Edgar Wideman
1992	*Mao II*	Don DeLillo
1993	*Postcards*	E. Annie Proulx
1994	*Operation Shylock*	Philip Roth
1995	*Snow Falling on Cedars*	David Guterson
1996	*Independence Day*	Richard Ford
1997	*Women in Their Beds*	Gina Berriault
1998	*The Bear Comes Home*	Rafi Zabor
1999	*The Hours*	Michael Cunningham
2000	*Waiting*	Ha Jin
2001	*The Human Stain*	Philip Roth
2002	*Bel Canto*	Ann Patchett
2003	*The Caprices*	Sabina Murray
2004	*The Early Stories*	John Updike
2005	*War Trash*	Ha Jin
2006	*The March*	E.L. Doctorow
2007	*Everyman*	Philip Roth
2008	*The Great Man*	Kate Christensen

Newbery Medal

The American Library Association (ALA) began awarding the John Newbery Medal in 1922 to the author of the most distinguished American children's book of the previous year, as judged by the ALA's Children's Librarians' Section (now called the Association for Library Service to Children). Established at the suggestion of Frederic G. Melcher of the R.R. Bowker Publishing Company, the award is named for John Newbery, the 18th-century English publisher who was among the first to publish books exclusively for children. Prize: inscribed bronze medal.

ALA Newbery Medal Web site: <www.ala.org/alsc/newbery.html>.

YEAR	TITLE	AUTHOR
1922	*The Story of Mankind*	Hendrik Willem van Loon
1923	*The Voyages of Doctor Dolittle*	Hugh Lofting
1924	*The Dark Frigate*	Charles Hawes
1925	*Tales from Silver Lands*	Charles Finger
1926	*Shen of the Sea*	Arthur Bowie Chrisman
1927	*Smoky, the Cowhorse*	Will James
1928	*Gay Neck, the Story of a Pigeon*	Dhan Gopal Mukerji
1929	*The Trumpeter of Krakow*	Eric P. Kelly
1930	*Hitty, Her First Hundred Years*	Rachel Field
1931	*The Cat Who Went to Heaven*	Elizabeth Coatsworth
1932	*Waterless Mountain*	Laura Adams Armer
1933	*Young Fu of the Upper Yangtze*	Elizabeth Lewis
1934	*Invincible Louisa: The Story of the Author of Little Women*	Cornelia Meigs
1935	*Dobry*	Monica Shannon
1936	*Caddie Woodlawn*	Carol Ryrie Brink
1937	*Roller Skates*	Ruth Sawyer
1938	*The White Stag*	Kate Seredy
1939	*Thimble Summer*	Elizabeth Enright
1940	*Daniel Boone*	James Daugherty
1941	*Call It Courage*	Armstrong Sperry
1942	*The Matchlock Gun*	Walter Edmonds
1943	*Adam of the Road*	Elizabeth Janet Gray
1944	*Johnny Tremain*	Esther Forbes
1945	*Rabbit Hill*	Robert Lawson
1946	*Strawberry Girl*	Lois Lenski
1947	*Miss Hickory*	Carolyn Sherwin Bailey
1948	*The Twenty-One Balloons*	William Pène du Bois
1949	*King of the Wind*	Marguerite Henry
1950	*The Door in the Wall*	Marguerite de Angeli
1951	*Amos Fortune, Free Man*	Elizabeth Yates
1952	*Ginger Pye*	Eleanor Estes
1953	*Secret of the Andes*	Ann Nolan Clark
1954	*...And Now Miguel*	Joseph Krumgold
1955	*The Wheel on the School*	Meindert De Jong
1956	*Carry On, Mr. Bowditch*	Jean Lee Latham
1957	*Miracles on Maple Hill*	Virginia Sorenson
1958	*Rifles for Watie*	Harold Keith
1959	*The Witch of Blackbird Pond*	Elizabeth George Speare
1960	*Onion John*	Joseph Krumgold
1961	*Island of the Blue Dolphins*	Scott O'Dell
1962	*The Bronze Bow*	Elizabeth George Speare
1963	*A Wrinkle in Time*	Madeleine L'Engle
1964	*It's Like This, Cat*	Emily Neville
1965	*Shadow of a Bull*	Maia Wojciechowska
1966	*I, Juan de Pareja*	Elizabeth Borton de Treviño
1967	*Up a Road Slowly*	Irene Hunt

Newbery Medal (continued)

YEAR	TITLE	AUTHOR
1968	*From the Mixed-Up Files of Mrs. Basil E. Frankweiler*	E.L. Konigsburg
1969	*The High King*	Lloyd Alexander
1970	*Sounder*	William H. Armstrong
1971	*Summer of the Swans*	Betsy Byars
1972	*Mrs. Frisby and the Rats of NIMH*	Robert C. O'Brien
1973	*Julie of the Wolves*	Jean Craighead George
1974	*The Slave Dancer*	Paula Fox
1975	*M.C. Higgins, the Great*	Virginia Hamilton
1976	*The Grey King*	Susan Cooper
1977	*Roll of Thunder, Hear My Cry*	Mildred D. Taylor
1978	*Bridge to Terabithia*	Katherine Paterson
1979	*The Westing Game*	Ellen Raskin
1980	*A Gathering of Days: A New England Girl's Journal, 1830–1832*	Joan W. Blos
1981	*Jacob Have I Loved*	Katherine Paterson
1982	*A Visit to William Blake's Inn: Poems for Innocent and Experienced Travelers*	Nancy Willard
1983	*Dicey's Song*	Cynthia Voigt
1984	*Dear Mr. Henshaw*	Beverly Cleary
1985	*The Hero and the Crown*	Robin McKinley
1986	*Sarah, Plain and Tall*	Patricia MacLachlan
1987	*The Whipping Boy*	Sid Fleischman
1988	*Lincoln: A Photobiography*	Russell Freedman
1989	*Joyful Noise: Poems for Two Voices*	Paul Fleischman
1990	*Number the Stars*	Lois Lowry
1991	*Maniac Magee*	Jerry Spinelli
1992	*Shiloh*	Phyllis Reynolds Naylor
1993	*Missing May*	Cynthia Rylant
1994	*The Giver*	Lois Lowry
1995	*Walk Two Moons*	Sharon Creech
1996	*The Midwife's Apprentice*	Karen Cushman
1997	*The View from Saturday*	E.L. Konigsburg
1998	*Out of the Dust*	Karen Hesse
1999	*Holes*	Louis Sachar
2000	*Bud, Not Buddy*	Christopher Paul Curtis
2001	*A Year Down Yonder*	Richard Peck
2002	*A Single Shard*	Linda Sue Park
2003	*Crispin: The Cross of Lead*	Avi
2004	*The Tale of Despereaux: Being the Story of a Mouse, a Princess, Some Soup, and a Spool of Thread*	Kate DiCamillo
2005	*Kira-Kira*	Cynthia Kadohata
2006	*Criss Cross*	Lynne Rae Perkins
2007	*The Higher Power of Lucky*	Susan Patron
2008	*Good Masters! Sweet Ladies! Voices from a Medieval Village*	Laura Amy Schlitz

Caldecott Medal

The American Library Association (ALA) awards the Caldecott Medal annually to "the artist of the most distinguished American picture book for children." It was established by the ALA in 1938 on the suggestion of Frederic G. Melcher, chairman of the board of the R.R. Bowker Publishing Company, and named for the 19th-century English illustrator Randolph Caldecott. If the author/reteller/translator/editor is someone other than the illustrator, that person's name appears in parentheses after that of the illustrator. Prize: inscribed bronze medal.

Web site: <www.ala.org/alsc/caldecott.html>.

YEAR	TITLE	ILLUSTRATOR
1938	*Animals of the Bible: A Picture Book*	Dorothy P. Lathrop (Helen Dean Fish)
1939	*Mei Li*	Thomas Handforth
1940	*Abraham Lincoln*	Ingri and Edgar Parin d'Aulaire
1941	*They Were Strong and Good*	Robert Lawson
1942	*Make Way for Ducklings*	Robert McCloskey
1943	*The Little House*	Virginia Lee Burton
1944	*Many Moons*	Louis Slobodkin (James Thurber)
1945	*Prayer for a Child*	Elizabeth Orton Jones (Rachel Field)
1946	*The Rooster Crows*	Maude and Miska Petersham
1947	*The Little Island*	Leonard Weisgard (Golden MacDonald, pseud. [Margaret Wise Brown])
1948	*White Snow, Bright Snow*	Roger Duvoisin (Alvin Tresselt)
1949	*The Big Snow*	Berta and Elmer Hader
1950	*Song of the Swallows*	Leo Politi
1951	*The Egg Tree*	Katherine Milhous
1952	*Finders Keepers*	Nicolas, pseud. (Nicholas Mordvinoff) (Will, pseud. [William Lipkind])
1953	*The Biggest Bear*	Lynd Ward
1954	*Madeline's Rescue*	Ludwig Bemelmans
1955	*Cinderella, or the Little Glass Slipper*	Marcia Brown (translated from Charles Perrault by Marcia Brown)
1956	*Frog Went A-Courtin'*	Feodor Rojankovsky (John Langstaff)

Caldecott Medal (continued)

YEAR	TITLE	ILLUSTRATOR
1957	*A Tree Is Nice*	Marc Simont (Janice Udry)
1958	*Time of Wonder*	Robert McCloskey
1959	*Chanticleer and the Fox*	Barbara Cooney (adapted from Chaucer's *The Canterbury Tales* by Barbara Cooney)
1960	*Nine Days to Christmas*	Marie Hall Ets (Marie Hall Ets and Aurora Labastida)
1961	*Baboushka and the Three Kings*	Nicolas Sidjakov (Ruth Robbins)
1962	*Once a Mouse*	Marcia Brown
1963	*The Snowy Day*	Ezra Jack Keats
1964	*Where the Wild Things Are*	Maurice Sendak
1965	*May I Bring a Friend?*	Beni Montresor (Beatrice Schenk de Regniers)
1966	*Always Room for One More*	Nonny Hogrogian (Sorche Nic Leodhas, pseud. [Leclair Alger])
1967	*Sam, Bangs & Moonshine*	Evaline Ness
1968	*Drummer Hoff*	Ed Emberley (Barbara Emberley)
1969	*The Fool of the World and the Flying Ship*	Uri Shulevitz (Arthur Ransome)
1970	*Sylvester and the Magic Pebble*	William Steig
1971	*A Story A Story*	Gail E. Haley
1972	*One Fine Day*	Nonny Hogrogian
1973	*The Funny Little Woman*	Blair Lent (Arlene Mosel)
1974	*Duffy and the Devil*	Margot Zemach (Harve Zemach)
1975	*Arrow to the Sun*	Gerald McDermott
1976	*Why Mosquitoes Buzz in People's Ears*	Leo and Diane Dillon (Verna Aardema)
1977	*Ashanti to Zulu: African Traditions*	Leo and Diane Dillon (Margaret Musgrove)
1978	*Noah's Ark*	Peter Spier
1979	*The Girl Who Loved Wild Horses*	Paul Goble
1980	*Ox-Cart Man*	Barbara Cooney (Donald Hall)
1981	*Fables*	Arnold Lobel
1982	*Jumanji*	Chris Van Allsburg
1983	*Shadow*	Marcia Brown (also translator of original French text by Blaise Cendrars)
1984	*The Glorious Flight: Across the Channel with Louis Blériot*	Alice and Martin Provensen
1985	*Saint George and the Dragon*	Trina Schart Hyman (Margaret Hodges)
1986	*The Polar Express*	Chris Van Allsburg
1987	*Hey, Al*	Richard Egielski (Arthur Yorinks)
1988	*Owl Moon*	John Schoenherr (Jane Yolen)
1989	*Song and Dance Man*	Stephen Gammell (Karen Ackerman)
1990	*Lon Po Po: A Red-Riding Hood Story from China*	Ed Young
1991	*Black and White*	David Macaulay
1992	*Tuesday*	David Wiesner
1993	*Mirette on the High Wire*	Emily Arnold McCully
1994	*Grandfather's Journey*	Allen Say (Walter Lorraine)
1995	*Smoky Night*	David Diaz (Eve Bunting)
1996	*Officer Buckle and Gloria*	Peggy Rathmann
1997	*Golem*	David Wisniewski
1998	*Rapunzel*	Paul O. Zelinsky
1999	*Snowflake Bentley*	Mary Azarian (Jacqueline Briggs Martin)
2000	*Joseph Had a Little Overcoat*	Simms Taback
2001	*So You Want To Be President?*	David Small (Judith St. George)
2002	*The Three Pigs*	David Wiesner
2003	*My Friend Rabbit*	Eric Rohmann
2004	*The Man Who Walked Between the Towers*	Mordicai Gerstein
2005	*Kitten's First Full Moon*	Kevin Henkes
2006	*The Hello, Goodbye Window*	Chris Raschka (Norton Juster)
2007	*Flotsam*	David Wiesner
2008	*The Invention of Hugo Cabret*	Brian Selznick

Coretta Scott King Award

Established in 1970, the Coretta Scott King Award honors outstanding African American authors and illustrators of books for young people. The books, which may be fiction or nonfiction, must be original works that portray some aspect of the black experience. In 1982 the award came under the aegis of the American Library Association. Only authors were eligible for the award until 1974, and no illustrator awards were given in 1975–1977 and 1985. Prize: citation, honorarium, and encyclopedia set.

Coretta Scott King Award Web site: <www.ala.org/ala/emiert/corettascottkingbookaward/corettascott.htm>.

Coretta Scott King Award (continued)

1970 Lillie Patterson, *Martin Luther King, Jr.: Man of Peace*
1971 Charlemae Rollins, *Black Troubador: Langston Hughes*
1972 Elton C. Fax, *17 Black Artists*
1973 *I Never Had It Made: The Autobiography of Jackie Robinson,* as told to Alfred Duckett
1974 author: Sharon Bell Mathis, *Ray Charles;* illustrator: George Ford, *Ray Charles*
1975 author: Dorothy Robinson, *The Legend of Africana*
1976 author: Pearl Bailey, *Duey's Tale*
1977 author: James Haskins, *The Story of Stevie Wonder*
1978 author: Eloise Greenfield, *Africa Dream;* illustrator: Carole Byard, *Africa Dream*
1979 author: Ossie Davis, *Escape to Freedom;* illustrator: Tom Feelings, *Something on My Mind*
1980 author: Walter Dean Myers, *The Young Landlords;* illustrator: Carole Byard, *Cornrows*
1981 author: Sidney Poitier, *This Life;* illustrator: Ashley Bryan, *Beat the Story Drum, Pum-Pum*
1982 author: Mildred D. Taylor, *Let the Circle Be Unbroken;* illustrator: John Steptoe, *Mother Crocodile*
1983 author: Virginia Hamilton, *Sweet Whispers, Brother Rush;* illustrator: Peter Mugabane, *Black Child*
1984 author: Lucille Clifton, *Everett Anderson's Goodbye;* illustrator: Pat Cummings, *My Mama Needs Me*
1985 author: Walter Dean Myers, *Motown and Didi*
1986 author: Virginia Hamilton, *The People Could Fly: American Black Folktales;* illustrator: Jerry Pinkney, *The Patchwork Quilt*
1987 author: Mildred Pitts Walter, *Justin and the Best Biscuits in the World;* illustrator: Jerry Pinkney, *Half a Moon and One Whole Star*
1988 author: Mildred L. Taylor, *The Friendship;* illustrator: John Steptoe, *Mufaro's Beautiful Daughters: An African Tale*
1989 author: Walter Dean Myers, *Fallen Angels;* illustrator: Jerry Pinkney, *Mirandy and Brother Wind*
1990 author: Patricia C. and Frederick L. McKissack, *A Long Hard Journey: The Story of the Pullman Porter;* illustrator: Jan Spivey Gilchrist, *Nathaniel Talking*
1991 author: Mildred D. Taylor, *The Road to Memphis;* illustrator: Leo and Diane Dillon, *Aida*
1992 author: Walter Dean Myers, *Now Is Your Time: The African American Struggle for Freedom;* illustrator: Faith Ringgold, *Tar Beach*
1993 author: Patricia C. McKissack, *Dark Thirty: Southern Tales of the Supernatural;* illustrator: Kathleen Atkins Wilson, *The Origin of Life on Earth: An African Creation Myth*
1994 author: Angela Johnson, *Toning the Sweep;* illustrator: Tom Feelings, *Soul Looks Back in Wonder*
1995 author: Patricia C. and Frederick L. McKissack, *Christmas in the Big House, Christmas in the Quarters;* illustrator: James Ransome, *The Creation*
1996 author: Virginia Hamilton, *Her Stories;* illustrator: Tom Feelings, *The Middle Passage: White Ships/Black Cargo*
1997 author: Walter Dean Myers, *Slam;* illustrator: Jerry Pinkney, *Minty: A Story of Young Harriet Tubman*
1998 author: Sharon M. Draper, *Forged by Fire;* illustrator: Javaka Steptoe, *In Daddy's Arms I Am Tall: African Americans Celebrating Fathers*
1999 author: Angela Johnson, *Heaven;* illustrator: Michele Wood, *i see the rhythm*
2000 author: Christopher Paul Curtis, *Bud, Not Buddy;* illustrator: Brian Pinkney, *In the Time of the Drums*
2001 author: Jacqueline Woodson, *Miracle's Boys;* illustrator: Bryan Collier, *Uptown*
2002 author: Mildred Taylor, *The Land;* illustrator: Jerry Pinkney, *Goin' Someplace Special*
2003 author: Nikki Grimes, *Bronx Masquerade;* illustrator: E.B. Lewis, *Talkin' About Bessie: The Story of Aviator Elizabeth Coleman*
2004 author: Angela Johnson, *The First Part Last;* illustrator: Ashley Bryan, *Beautiful Blackbird*
2005 author: Toni Morrison, *Remember: The Journey to School Integration;* illustrator: Kadir Nelson, *Ellington Was Not a Street*
2006 author: Julius Lester, *Day of Tears: A Novel in Dialogue;* illustrator: Bryan Collier, *Rosa*
2007 author: Sharon Draper, *Copper Sun;* illustrator: Kadir Nelson, *Moses: When Harriet Tubman Led Her People to Freedom*
2008 author: Christopher Paul Curtis, *Elijah of Buxton;* illustrator: Ashley Bryan, *Let It Shine*

The Man Booker Prize

Awarded to the best full-length novel of the year written by a citizen of the Commonwealth or the Republic of Ireland and published in the UK between 1 October and 30 September. Prize: £50,000 (about US$99,000); each shortlisted author receives £1,000 (about US$1,985). In 1993 Salman Rushdie was awarded the Booker of Bookers, a special award to mark 25 years of the Booker Prize, for *Midnight's Children.* In 2008 the Best of Bookers prize, to mark 40 years, was also won by Salman Rushdie's *Midnight's Children.* In 2005 the Man Booker International Prize was created, to be awarded biennially to a living writer for outstanding lifetime achievement. Prize: £60,000 (about US$119,000). Albanian novelist Ismail Kadare won the first Man Booker International Prize in 2005. Nigerian author Chinua Achebe won the second in 2007.

Web site: <www.themanbookerprize.com>.

The Man Booker Prize (continued)

YEAR	TITLE	AUTHOR
1969	*Something to Answer For*	P.H. Newby
1970	*The Elected Member*	Bernice Rubens
1971	*In a Free State*	V.S. Naipaul
1972	*G.*	John Berger
1973	*The Siege of Krishnapur*	J.G. Farrell
1974	*The Conservationist*	Nadine Gordimer
1974	*Holiday*	Stanley Middleton
1975	*Heat and Dust*	Ruth Prawer Jhabvala
1976	*Saville*	David Storey
1977	*Staying On*	Paul Scott
1978	*The Sea, The Sea*	Iris Murdoch
1979	*Offshore*	Penelope Fitzgerald
1980	*Rites of Passage*	William Golding
1981	*Midnight's Children*	Salman Rushdie
1982	*Schindler's Ark*	Thomas Keneally
1983	*Life and Times of Michael K*	J.M. Coetzee
1984	*Hotel du Lac*	Anita Brookner
1985	*The Bone People*	Keri Hulme
1986	*The Old Devils*	Kingsley Amis
1987	*Moon Tiger*	Penelope Lively
1988	*Oscar and Lucinda*	Peter Carey
1989	*The Remains of the Day*	Kazuo Ishiguro
1990	*Possession*	A.S. Byatt
1991	*The Famished Road*	Ben Okri
1992	*The English Patient*	Michael Ondaatje
1992	*Sacred Hunger*	Barry Unsworth
1993	*Paddy Clarke Ha Ha Ha*	Roddy Doyle
1994	*How Late It Was, How Late*	James Kelman
1995	*The Ghost Road*	Pat Barker
1996	*Last Orders*	Graham Swift
1997	*The God of Small Things*	Arundhati Roy
1998	*Amsterdam*	Ian McEwan
1999	*Disgrace*	J.M. Coetzee
2000	*The Blind Assassin*	Margaret Atwood
2001	*True History of the Kelly Gang*	Peter Carey
2002	*Life of Pi*	Yann Martel
2003	*Vernon God Little*	DBC Pierre
2004	*The Line of Beauty*	Alan Hollinghurst
2005	*The Sea*	John Banville
2006	*The Inheritance of Loss*	Kiran Desai
2007	*The Gathering*	Anne Enright

The Costa Book Awards

The Whitbread Book Awards were inaugurated in 1971, and in 2006 Britain's Costa chain of coffee shops took over the prize. Since 1985, awards have been given in five categories: Novel, First Novel, Biography, Poetry, and Children's. From these a panel of judges chooses one overall winner—the Costa Book of the Year. The total prize fund is £50,000 (about US$99,000): each of the category award winners receives £5,000 (about US$9,900), and the Book of the Year winner receives an additional £25,000 (about US$49,700).

This list includes Novel award winners from 1971 to 1984 and Book of the Year winners from 1985 to 2007.

Costa Book Awards Web site: <www.costabookawards.com>.

YEAR	TITLE	AUTHOR
1971	*The Destiny Waltz*	Gerda Charles
1972	*The Bird of Night*	Susan Hill
1973	*The Chip-Chip Gatherers*	Shiva Naipaul
1974	*The Sacred and Profane Love Machine*	Iris Murdoch
1975	*Docherty*	William McIlvanney
1976	*The Children of Dynmouth*	William Trevor
1977	*Injury Time*	Beryl Bainbridge
1978	*Picture Palace*	Paul Theroux
1979	*The Old Jest*	Jennifer Johnston
1980	*How Far Can You Go?*	David Lodge
1981	*Silver's City*	Maurice Leitch
1982	*Young Shoulders*	John Wain
1983	*Fools of Fortune*	William Trevor
1984	*Kruger's Alp*	Christopher Hope
1985	*Elegies*	Douglas Dunn
1986	*An Artist of the Floating World*	Kazuo Ishiguro
1987	*Under the Eye of the Clock*	Christopher Nolan
1988	*The Comforts of Madness*	Paul Sayer
1989	*Coleridge: Early Visions*	Richard Holmes
1990	*Hopeful Monsters*	Nicholas Mosley
1991	*A Life of Picasso*	John Richardson
1992	*Swing Hammer Swing!*	Jeff Torrington
1993	*Theory of War*	Joan Brady
1994	*Felicia's Journey*	William Trevor
1995	*Behind the Scenes at the Museum*	Kate Atkinson
1996	*The Spirit Level*	Seamus Heaney
1997	*Tales from Ovid*	Ted Hughes
1998	*Birthday Letters*	Ted Hughes
1999	*Beowulf*	Seamus Heaney
2000	*English Passengers*	Matthew Kneale
2001	*The Amber Spyglass*	Philip Pullman
2002	*Samuel Pepys: The Unequalled Self*	Claire Tomalin
2003	*The Curious Incident of the Dog in the Night-Time*	Mark Haddon
2004	*Small Island*	Andrea Levy
2005	*Matisse: The Master*	Hilary Spurling
2006	*The Tenderness of Wolves*	Stef Penney
2007	*Day*	A.L. Kennedy

The Orange Broadband Prize

Awarded to a work of published fiction written in English by a woman and published in the United Kingdom or Ireland. Prize: £30,000 (about US$59,000) and a bronze figurine called the "Bessie."

Orange Broadband Prize Web site: <www.orangeprize.co.uk>.

The Orange Broadband Prize (continued)

YEAR	TITLE	AUTHOR
1996	*A Spell of Winter*	Helen Dunmore
1997	*Fugitive Pieces*	Anne Michaels
1998	*Larry's Party*	Carol Shields
1999	*A Crime in the Neighbourhood*	Suzanne Berne
2000	*When I Lived in Modern Times*	Linda Grant
2001	*The Idea of Perfection*	Kate Grenville
2002	*Bel Canto*	Ann Patchett
2003	*Property*	Valerie Martin
2004	*Small Island*	Andrea Levy
2005	*We Need To Talk About Kevin*	Lionel Shriver
2006	*On Beauty*	Zadie Smith
2007	*Half of a Yellow Sun*	Chimamanda Ngozi Adichie
2008	*The Road Home*	Rose Tremain

Prix Goncourt

The Prix de l'Académie Goncourt was first awarded in 1903 from the estate of the brothers and French literary figures Edmond Huot de Goncourt (1822–1896) and Jules Huot de Goncourt (1830–1870) for a work of contemporary prose in French.

Prize: €10 (about US$15). An additional prize is awarded for the best work of new fiction.

YEAR	TITLE	AUTHOR
1903	*Force ennemie*	John-Antoine Nau
1904	*La Maternelle*	Léon Frapié
1905	*Les Civilisés*	Claude Farrère
1906	*Dingley, l'illustre écrivain*	Jérôme and Jean Tharaud
1907	*Terres lorraines*	Emile Moselly
1908	*Ecrit sur l'eau*	Francis de Miomandre
1909	*En France*	Marius-Ary Leblond
1910	*De Goupil à Margot*	Louis Pergaud
1911	*Monsieur des Lourdines*	Alphonse de Chateaubriant
1912	*Les Filles de la pluie*	André Savignon
1913	*Le Peuple de la mer*	Marc Elder
1914	*L'Appel du sol*	Adrien Bertrand
1915	*Gaspard*	René Benjamin
1916	*Le Feu*	Henri Barbusse
1917	*La Flamme au poing*	Henri Malherbe
1918	*Civilisation*	Georges Duhamel
1919	*A l'ombre des jeunes filles en fleur*	Marcel Proust
1920	*Nene*	Ernest Pérochon
1921	*Batouala*	René Maran
1922	*Le Vitriol de la lune; Le Martyre de l'obèse*	Henri Béraud
1923	*Rabevel; ou, le mal des ardents*	Lucien Fabre
1924	*Le Chèvrefeuille; Le Purgatoire; Le Chapitre treize d'Athénée*	Thierry Sandre
1925	*Raboliot*	Maurice Genevoix
1926	*Le Supplice de Phèdre*	Henry Deberly
1927	*Jérôme, 60° latitude nord*	Maurice Bedel
1928	*Un Homme se penche sur son passé*	Maurice Constantin-Weyer
1929	*L'Ordre*	Marcel Arland
1930	*Malaisie*	Henri Fauconnier
1931	*Mal d'amour*	Jean Fayard
1932	*Les Loups*	Guy Mazeline
1933	*La Condition humaine*	André Malraux
1934	*Capitaine Conan*	Roger Vercel
1935	*Sang et lumières*	Joseph Peyré
1936	*L'Empreinte de Dieu*	Maxence van der Meersch
1937	*Faux passeports*	Charles Plisnier
1938	*L'Araigne*	Henri Troyat
1939	*Les Enfants gâtés*	Philippe Hériat
1940	*Les Grandes Vacances*	Francis Ambrière
1941	*Vent de Mars*	Henri Pourrat
1942	*Pareil à des enfants*	Bernard Marc
1943	*Passage de l'homme*	Marius Grout
1944	*Le Premier Accroc coûte 200 francs*	Elsa Triolet
1945	*Mon village à l'heure allemande*	Jean-Louis Bory
1946	*Histoire d'un fait divers*	Jean-Jacques Gautier
1947	*Les Forêts de la nuit*	Jean-Louis Curtis
1948	*Les Grandes Familles*	Maurice Druon
1949	*Week-end à Zuydcoote*	Robert Merle
1950	*Les Jeux sauvages*	Paul Colin
1951	*Le Rivage des Syrtes*	Julien Gracq (declined)
1952	*Léon Morin, prêtre*	Béatrice Beck
1953	*Les Bêtes; Le Temps des morts*	Pierre Gascar
1954	*Mandarins*	Simone de Beauvoir
1955	*Les Eaux mêlées*	Roger Ikor
1956	*Les Racines du ciel*	Romain Gary
1957	*La Loi*	Roger Vailland
1958	*Saint Germain; ou, la négociation*	Francis Walder
1959	*Le Dernier des justes*	André Schwartz-Bart
1960	*Dieu est né en exil*	Vintila Horia
1961	*La Pitié de Dieu*	Jean Cau
1962	*Les Bagages de sable*	Anna Langfus
1963	*Quand la mer se retire*	Armand Lanoux
1964	*L'État sauvage*	Georges Conchon
1965	*L'Adoration*	Jacques Borel
1966	*Oublier Palerme*	Edmonde Charles-Roux
1967	*La Marge*	André Pieyre de Mandiargues
1968	*Les Fruits de l'hiver*	Bernard Clavel
1969	*Creezy*	Félicien Marceau
1970	*Le Roi des Aulnes*	Michel Tournier
1971	*Les Bêtises*	Jacques Laurent
1972	*L'Épervier de Maheux*	Jean Carrière
1973	*L'Ogre*	Jacques Chessex
1974	*La Dentellière*	Pascal Lainé
1975	*La Vie devant soi*	Emile Ajar (declined)
1976	*Les Flamboyants*	Patrick Grainville
1977	*John l'enfer*	Didier Decoin
1978	*Rue des boutiques obscures*	Patrick Modiano
1979	*Pélagie-la-charrette*	Antonine Maillet
1980	*Le Jardin d'acclimatation*	Yves Navarre
1981	*Anne Marie*	Lucien Bodard
1982	*Dans la main de l'ange*	Dominique Fernandez

Prix Goncourt (continued)

YEAR	TITLE	AUTHOR
1983	*Les Égarés*	Frédérick Tristan
1984	*L'Amant*	Marguerite Duras
1985	*Les Noces barbares*	Yann Queffélec
1986	*Valet de nuit*	Michel Host
1987	*La Nuit sacrée*	Tahar Ben Jelloun
1988	*L'Exposition coloniale*	Erik Orsenna
1989	*Un Grand Pas vers le Bon Dieu*	Jean Vautrin
1990	*Les Champs d'honneur*	Jean Rouaud
1991	*Les Filles du calvaire*	Pierre Combescot
1992	*Texaco*	Patrick Chamoiseau
1993	*La Rocher de Tanios*	Amin Maalouf
1994	*Un Aller simple*	Didier van Cauwelaert
1995	*Le Testament français*	Andreï Makine
1996	*Le Chasseur zéro*	Pascale Roze
1997	*La Bataille*	Patrick Rambaud
1998	*Confidence pour confidence*	Paule Constant
1999	*Je m'en vais*	Jean Echenoz
2000	*Ingrid Caven*	Jean-Jacques Schuhl
2001	*Rouge Brésil*	Jean-Christophe Rufin
2002	*Les Ombres errantes*	Pascal Quignard
2003	*La Maîtresse de Brecht*	Jacques-Pierre Amette
2004	*Le Soleil des Scorta*	Laurent Gaudé
2005	*Trois jours chez ma mère*	François Weyergans
2006	*Les Bienveillantes*	Jonathan Littell
2007	*Alabama Song*	Gilles Leroy

Premio Cervantes, the Cervantes Prize for Hispanic Literature

The Spanish Ministry of Culture sponsors the annual prize, which carries an award of €90,450 (about US$135,600). ***Cervantes Prize Web site:*** *<www.mcu.es/premios/CervantesPresentacion.html>.*

YEAR	AUTHOR
1976	Jorge Guillén
1977	Alejo Carpentier
1978	Dámaso Alonso
1979	Jorge Luis Borges; Gerardo Diego
1980	Juan Carlos Onetti
1981	Octavio Paz
1982	Luis Rosales
1983	Rafael Alberti
1984	Ernesto Sábato
1985	Gonzalo Torrente Ballester
1986	Antonio Buero Vallejo
1987	Carlos Fuentes
1988	María Zambrano
1989	Augusto Roa Bastos
1990	Adolfo Bioy Casares
1991	Francisco Ayala
1992	Dulce María Loynaz
1993	Miguel Delibes
1994	Mario Vargas Llosa
1995	Camilo José Cela
1996	José García Nieto
1997	Guillermo Cabrera Infante
1998	José Hierro
1999	Jorge Edwards
2000	Francisco Umbral
2001	Álvaro Mutis
2002	José Jiménez Lozano
2003	Gonzalo Rojas
2004	Rafael Sánchez Ferlosio
2005	Sergio Pitol
2006	Antonio Gamoneda
2007	Juan Gelman

The Jerusalem Prize

The municipality of Jerusalem awards this prize at the biennial Jerusalem International Book Fair to a writer whose work explores the freedom of the individual in society. Prize: US$10,000.

Jerusalem Prize Web site: <www.jerusalembookfair.com>.

YEAR	AUTHOR	COUNTRY
1963	Bertrand Russell	United Kingdom
1965	Max Frisch	Switzerland
1967	André Schwarz-Bart	France
1969	Ignazio Silone	Italy
1971	Jorge Luis Borges	Argentina
1973	Eugène Ionesco	France
1975	Simone de Beauvoir	France
1977	Octavio Paz	Mexico
1979	Sir Isaiah Berlin	United Kingdom
1981	Graham Greene	United Kingdom
1983	V.S. Naipaul	United Kingdom
1985	Milan Kundera	France
1987	J.M. Coetzee	South Africa
1989	Ernesto Sábato	Argentina
1991	Zbigniew Herbert	France
1993	Stefan Heym	Germany
1995	Mario Vargas Llosa	Peru
1997	Jorge Semprun	Spain
1999	Don DeLillo	United States
2001	Susan Sontag	United States
2003	Arthur Miller	United States
2005	António Lobo Antunes	Portugal
2007	Leszek Kolakowski	Poland

T.S. Eliot Prize

Great Britain's Poetry Book Society awards the T.S. Eliot Prize to the best new collection of poetry published in the UK or the Republic of Ireland during the preceding year. The prize is £15,000 (about US$29,800).

T.S. Eliot Prize (continued)

YEAR	WORK	AUTHOR	COUNTRY
1993	*First Language*	Ciaran Carson	Ireland
1994	*The Annals of Chile*	Paul Muldoon	Northern Ireland
1995	*My Alexandria*	Mark Doty	United States
1996	*Subhuman Redneck Poems*	Les Murray	Australia
1997	*God's Gift to Women*	Don Paterson	United Kingdom
1998	*Birthday Letters*	Ted Hughes	United Kingdom
1999	*Billy's Rain*	Hugo Williams	United Kingdom
2000	*The Weather in Japan*	Michael Longley	Northern Ireland
2001	*The Beauty of the Husband*	Anne Carson	Canada
2002	*Dart*	Alice Oswald	United Kingdom
2003	*Landing Light*	Don Paterson	United Kingdom
2004	*Reel*	George Szirtes	United Kingdom
2005	*Rapture*	Carol Ann Duffy	United Kingdom
2006	*District and Circle*	Seamus Heaney	Ireland
2007	*The Drowned Book*	Sean O'Brien	United Kingdom

The Bollingen Prize in Poetry

The Bollingen Prize in Poetry is awarded biennially to the American poet whose work represents the highest achievement in the field of American poetry during the preceding two-year period. The committee considers published work, particularly work published during that preceding two-year period. Former winners of the prize are not eligible.
Award amount: US$100,000.

YEAR	POET	YEAR	POET	YEAR	POET
1948	Ezra Pound	1961	Richard Eberhart	1983	Anthony Hecht
1949	Wallace Stevens		John Hall Wheelock		John Hollander
1950	John Crowe Ransom	1963	Robert Frost	1985	John Ashbery
1951	Marianne Moore	1965	Horace Gregory		Fred Chappell
1952	Archibald MacLeish	1967	Robert Penn Warren	1987	Stanley Kunitz
	William Carlos Williams	1969	John Berryman	1989	Edgar Bowers
1953	W.H. Auden		Karl Shapiro	1991	Laura Riding Jackson
1954	Léonie Adams	1971	Richard Wilbur		Donald Justice
	Louise Bogan		Mona Van Duyn	1993	Mark Strand
1955	Conrad Aiken	1973	James Merrill	1995	Kenneth Koch
1956	Allen Tate	1975	A.R. Ammons	1997	Gary Snyder
1957	E.E. Cummings	1977	David Ignatow	1999	Robert Creeley
1958	Theodore Roethke	1979	W.S. Merwin	2001	Louise Glück
1959	Delmore Schwartz	1981	May Swenson	2003	Adrienne Rich
1960	Yvor Winters		Howard Nemerov	2005	Jay Wright
				2007	Frank Bidart

Architecture Awards

Pritzker Architecture Prize

The Pritzker Prize, awarded by the Hyatt Foundation since 1979, is given to an outstanding living architect for built work. Prize: US$100,000 and a bronze medallion. ***Web site:*** *<www.pritzkerprize.com>.*

YEAR	NAME	COUNTRY	YEAR	NAME	COUNTRY
1979	Philip Johnson	United States	1994	Christian de Portzamparc	France
1980	Luis Barragán	Mexico	1995	Tadao Ando	Japan
1981	James Stirling	Great Britain	1996	Rafael Moneo	Spain
1982	Kevin Roche	United States	1997	Sverre Fehn	Norway
1983	Ieoh Ming Pei	United States	1998	Renzo Piano	Italy
1984	Richard Meier	United States	1999	Sir Norman Foster	Great Britain
1985	Hans Hollein	Austria	2000	Rem Koolhaas	The Netherlands
1986	Gottfried Böhm	West Germany	2001	Jacques Herzog	Switzerland
1987	Kenzo Tange	Japan		Pierre de Meuron	Switzerland
1988	Gordon Bunshaft	United States	2002	Glenn Murcutt	Australia
	Oscar Niemeyer	Brazil	2003	Jørn Utzon	Denmark
1989	Frank O. Gehry	United States	2004	Zaha Hadid	Great Britain
1990	Aldo Rossi	Italy	2005	Thom Mayne	United States
1991	Robert Venturi	United States	2006	Paulo Mendes da Rocha	Brazil
1992	Alvaro Siza	Portugal	2007	Richard Rogers	Great Britain
1993	Fumihiko Maki	Japan	2008	Jean Nouvel	France

AIA Gold Medal

The American Institute of Architects awards the gold medal for an outstanding body of work.

YEAR	NAME
1907	Aston Webb
1909	Charles Follen McKim[1]
1911	George Browne Post
1914	Jean Louis Pascal
1922	Victor Laloux
1923	Henry Bacon
1925	Edwin L. Lutyens
	Bertram Grosvenor Goodhue[1]
1927	Howard Van Doren Shaw
1929	Milton Bennett Medary
1933	Ragnar Östberg
1938	Paul Philippe Cret
1944	Louis Henry Sullivan[1]
1947	Eliel Saarinen
1948	Charles Donagh Maginnis
1949	Frank Lloyd Wright
1950	Patrick Abercrombie
1951	Bernard Ralph Maybeck
1952	Auguste Perret
1953	William Adams Delano
1955	Willem Marinus Dudok
1956	Clarence S. Stein
1957	Ralph Walker
	Louis Skidmore
1958	John Wellborn Root[1]
1959	Walter Gropius
1960	Ludwig Mies van der Rohe
1961	Le Corbusier (Charles Édouard Jeanneret)
1962	Eero Saarinen[1]
1963	Alvar Aalto
1964	Pier Luigi Nervi
1966	Kenzo Tange
1967	Wallace K. Harrison
1968	Marcel Breuer
1969	William Wilson Wurster
1970	Richard Buckminster Fuller
1971	Louis I. Kahn
1972	Pietro Belluschi
1977	Richard Joseph Neutra[1]
1978	Philip C. Johnson
1979	Ieoh Ming Pei
1981	José Luis Sert
1982	Romaldo Giurgola
1983	Nathaniel A. Owings
1985	William Wayne Caudill[1]
1986	Arthur Erickson
1989	Joseph Esherick
1990	E. Fay Jones
1991	Charles W. Moore
1992	Benjamin Thompson
1993	Thomas Jefferson[1]
	Kevin Roche
1994	Norman Foster
1995	César Pelli
1997	Richard Meier
1999	Frank O. Gehry
2000	Ricardo Legorreta
2001	Michael Graves
2002	Tadao Ando
2004	Samuel Mockbee[1]
2005	Santiago Calatrava
2006	Antoine Predock
2007	Edward Larrabee Barnes[1]
2008	Renzo Piano

[1]*Awarded posthumously.*

Special Honors

Hasty Pudding Theatricals Woman of the Year and Man of the Year

The Hasty Pudding Theatricals of Harvard University, an organization of undergraduates, has presented the Woman of the Year award since 1951 and the Man of the Year award since 1967 to performers who have made a "lasting and impressive contribution to the world of entertainment."

YEAR	NAME
1951	Gertrude Lawrence
1952	Barbara Bel Geddes
1953	Mamie Eisenhower
1954	Shirley Booth
1955	Debbie Reynolds
1956	Peggy Ann Garner
1957	Carroll Baker
1958	Katharine Hepburn
1959	Joanne Woodward
1960	Carol Lawrence
1961	Jane Fonda
1962	Piper Laurie
1963	Shirley MacLaine
1964	Rosalind Russell
1965	Lee Remick
1966	Ethel Merman
1967	Lauren Bacall and Bob Hope
1968	Angela Lansbury and Paul Newman
1969	Carol Burnett and Bill Cosby
1970	Dionne Warwick and Robert Redford
1971	Carol Channing and James Stewart
1972	Ruby Keeler and Dustin Hoffman
1973	Liza Minnelli and Jack Lemmon
1974	Faye Dunaway and Peter Falk
1975	Valerie Harper and Warren Beatty
1976	Bette Midler and Robert Blake
1977	Elizabeth Taylor and Johnny Carson
1978	Beverly Sills and Richard Dreyfuss
1979	Candice Bergen and Robert De Niro
1980	Meryl Streep and Alan Alda
1981	Mary Tyler Moore and John Travolta
1982	Ella Fitzgerald and James Cagney
1983	Julie Andrews and Steven Spielberg
1984	Joan Rivers and Sean Connery
1985	Cher and Bill Murray
1986	Sally Field and Sylvester Stallone
1987	Bernadette Peters and Mikhail Baryshnikov
1988	Lucille Ball and Steve Martin
1989	Kathleen Turner and Robin Williams
1990	Glenn Close and Kevin Costner
1991	Diane Keaton and Clint Eastwood
1992	Jodie Foster and Michael Douglas
1993	Whoopi Goldberg and Chevy Chase
1994	Meg Ryan and Tom Cruise
1995	Michelle Pfeiffer and Tom Hanks
1996	Susan Sarandon and Harrison Ford
1997	Julia Roberts and Mel Gibson
1998	Sigourney Weaver and Kevin Kline
1999	Goldie Hawn and Samuel L. Jackson
2000	Jamie Lee Curtis and Billy Crystal
2001	Drew Barrymore and Anthony Hopkins
2002	Sarah Jessica Parker and Bruce Willis
2003	Anjelica Huston and Martin Scorsese
2004	Sandra Bullock and Robert Downey, Jr.
2005	Catherine Zeta-Jones and Tim Robbins
2006	Halle Berry and Richard Gere
2007	Scarlett Johansson and Ben Stiller
2008	Charlize Theron and Christopher Walken

Sport

Sport Coverage

The tables that follow contain the significant information about the top contests of all the major sports that are international in character, as well as some professional and amateur sports that attract a huge national following—such as baseball in the United States and cricket in the United Kingdom, Australia, India, and the other Test Match countries—and some sports, such as rowing, in which national competition overshadows international events. In many sports the Olympic Games held every four years constitute the world championships; they are included in the listings below.

Sporting Codes for Countries

These codes are used to identify countries in the Sport section of the Britannica Almanac.

Codes of the International Olympic Committee (IOC)

AFG	Afghanistan
AHO	Netherlands Antilles
ALB	Albania
ALG	Algeria
AND	Andorra
ANG	Angola
ANT	Antigua and Barbuda
ARG	Argentina
ARM	Armenia
ARU	Aruba
ASA	American Samoa
AUS	Australia
AUT	Austria
AZE	Azerbaijan
BAH	Bahamas, The
BAN	Bangladesh
BAR	Barbados
BDI	Burundi
BEL	Belgium
BEN	Benin
BER	Bermuda
BHU	Bhutan
BIH	Bosnia and Herzegovina
BIZ	Belize
BLR	Belarus
BOL	Bolivia
BOT	Botswana
BRA	Brazil
BRN	Bahrain
BRU	Brunei
BUL	Bulgaria
BUR	Burkina Faso
CAF	Central African Republic
CAM	Cambodia
CAN	Canada
CAY	Cayman Islands
CGO	Congo, Republic of the
CHA	Chad
CHI	Chile
CHN	China
CIV	Côte d'Ivoire
CMR	Cameroon
COD	Congo, Democratic Republic of the
COK	Cook Islands
COL	Colombia
COM	Comoros
CPV	Cape Verde
CRC	Costa Rica
CRO	Croatia
CUB	Cuba
CYP	Cyprus
CZE	Czech Republic
DEN	Denmark
DJI	Djibouti
DMA	Dominica
DOM	Dominican Republic
ECU	Ecuador
EGY	Egypt
ERI	Eritrea
ESA	El Salvador
ESP	Spain
EST	Estonia
ETH	Ethiopia
FIJ	Fiji
FIN	Finland
FRA	France
FSM	Micronesia
GAB	Gabon
GAM	Gambia, The
GBR	Great Britain
GBS	Guinea-Bissau
GEO	Georgia
GEQ	Equatorial Guinea
GER	Germany
GHA	Ghana
GRE	Greece
GRN	Grenada
GUA	Guatemala
GUI	Guinea
GUM	Guam
GUY	Guyana
HAI	Haiti
HKG	Hong Kong
HON	Honduras
HUN	Hungary
INA	Indonesia
IND	India
IRI	Iran
IRL	Ireland
IRQ	Iraq
ISL	Iceland
ISR	Israel
ISV	US Virgin Islands
ITA	Italy
IVB	British Virgin Islands
JAM	Jamaica
JOR	Jordan
JPN	Japan
KAZ	Kazakhstan
KEN	Kenya
KGZ	Kyrgyzstan
KIR	Kiribati
KOR	South Korea
KSA	Saudi Arabia
KUW	Kuwait
LAO	Laos
LAT	Latvia
LBA	Libya
LBR	Liberia
LCA	Saint Lucia
LES	Lesotho
LIB	Lebanon
LIE	Liechtenstein
LTU	Lithuania
LUX	Luxembourg
MAD	Madagascar
MAR	Morocco
MAS	Malaysia
MAW	Malawi
MDA	Moldova
MDV	Maldives
MEX	Mexico
MGL	Mongolia
MHL	Marshall Islands
MKD	Macedonia[1]
MLI	Mali
MLT	Malta
MNE	Montenegro
MON	Monaco
MOZ	Mozambique
MRI	Mauritius
MTN	Mauritania
MYA	Myanmar (Burma)
NAM	Namibia
NCA	Nicaragua
NED	Netherlands, The
NEP	Nepal
NGR	Nigeria
NIG	Niger
NOR	Norway
NRU	Nauru
NZL	New Zealand
OMA	Oman
PAK	Pakistan
PAN	Panama
PAR	Paraguay
PER	Peru
PHI	Philippines

Sporting Codes for Countries (continued)

Codes of the International Olympic Committee (IOC) (continued)

PLE	Palestine
PLW	Palau
PNG	Papua New Guinea
POL	Poland
POR	Portugal
PRK	North Korea
PUR	Puerto Rico
QAT	Qatar
ROU	Romania
RSA	South Africa
RUS	Russia
RWA	Rwanda
SAM	Samoa
SEN	Senegal
SEY	Seychelles
SIN	Singapore
SKN	Saint Kitts and Nevis
SLE	Sierra Leone
SLO	Slovenia
SMR	San Marino
SOL	Solomon Islands
SOM	Somalia
SRB	Serbia
SRI	Sri Lanka
STP	São Tomé and Príncipe
SUD	Sudan, The
SUI	Switzerland
SUR	Suriname
SVK	Slovakia
SWE	Sweden
SWZ	Swaziland
SYR	Syria
TAN	Tanzania
TGA	Tonga
THA	Thailand
TJK	Tajikistan
TKM	Turkmenistan
TLS	East Timor (Timor Leste)
TOG	Togo
TPE	Taiwan
TRI	Trinidad and Tobago
TUN	Tunisia
TUR	Turkey
TUV	Tuvalu
UAE	United Arab Emirates
UGA	Uganda
UKR	Ukraine
URU	Uruguay
USA	United States
UZB	Uzbekistan
VAN	Vanuatu
VEN	Venezuela
VIE	Vietnam
VIN	Saint Vincent and the Grenadines
YEM	Yemen
ZAM	Zambia
ZIM	Zimbabwe

Continental, Historical, and Other Country Codes

AFR	Africa
AIA	Anguilla
AME	The Americas
ARS	Saudi Arabia
ASI	Asia
BIR	Burma (Myanmar)
BLS	Belarus
BOH	Bohemia
BOS	Bosnia and Herzegovina
BUR	Burma
BWI	British West Indies
CEY	Ceylon
CIS	Commonwealth of Indep. States
CKN	Congo-Kinshasa
COB	Congo-Brazzaville
CSV	Czechoslovakia
CUR	Curaçao
DAH	Dahomey
DMN	Dominica
ENG	England
EUR	Europe
FRG	Germany, Federal Republic of
FRO	Faroe Islands
GDR	German Demo-cratic Republic
HBR	British Honduras
HEB	New Hebrides
HOL	Holland/The Netherlands
IOA	International Olympic Athlete
ICE	Iceland
IHO	Netherlands India
IVC	Côte d'Ivoire/Ivory Coast
JAP	Japan
KZK	Kazakhstan
LIT	Lithuania
MAC	Macao
MAU	Mauritius
MOL	Moldova
MOR	Morocco
MSR	Montserrat
NIC	Nicaragua
NIR	Northern Ireland
NKO	Korea, Dem. People's Rep. of (North Korea)
OCE	Oceania
PAL	Palestine
PDR	Korea, Dem. People's Rep. of
PNG	Papua New Guinea
RHO	Rhodesia
SAA	Saarland
SCO	Scotland
SKR	Korea, Rep. of (South Korea)
SWZ	Switzerland
TAH	Tahiti
TAI	Taiwan
TCA	Turks and Caicos Islands
TCH	Czechoslovakia
UAR	United Arab Rep.
UCS	Union of the Czech Rep. and Slovakia
UNT	Unified Team[2]
UPV	Upper Volta
URS	USSR
UVI	US Virgin Islands
WAL	Wales
YUG	Yugoslavia
ZAI	Zaire

[1]*Macedonia is known in the IOC as the Former Yugoslav Republic of Macedonia.* [2]*The Unified Team consisted of athletes from the Commonwealth of Independent States plus Georgia.*

The James E. Sullivan Memorial Trophy

The trophy has been awarded by the Amateur Athletic Union (AAU) since 1930 to honor an athlete who, "by his or her performance, example, and influence as an amateur, has done the most during the year to advance the cause of sportsmanship." The award, named for a past president of the AAU, is usually announced in April. Winners receive a replica in bronze of the original trophy. "Track" refers to track and field.

Web site: <www.aausports.org>.

YEAR	WINNER	SPORT
1930	Bobby Jones	golf
1931	Barney Berlinger	track (decathlon)
1932	Jim Bausch	track (decathlon)
1933	Glenn Cunningham	track (distance running)
1934	Bill Bonthron	track (middle-distance running)
1935	Lawson Little	golf
1936	Glenn Morris	track (decathlon)
1937	Don Budge	tennis
1938	Don Lash	track (distance running)
1939	Joe Burk	rowing
1940	Greg Rice	track (distance running)
1941	Leslie MacMitchell	track (middle-distance running)
1942	Cornelius "Dutch" Warmerdam	track (pole vault)
1943	Gilbert Dodds	track (middle-distance running)

The James E. Sullivan Memorial Trophy (continued)

YEAR	WINNER	SPORT
1944	Ann Curtis	swimming
1945	Doc Blanchard	football
1946	Arnold Tucker	football
1947	John B. Kelly, Jr.	rowing
1948	Bob Mathias	track (decathlon)
1949	Dick Button	figure skating
1950	Fred Wilt	track (distance running)
1951	Bob Richards	track (pole vault/ decathlon)
1952	Horace Ashenfelter	track (distance running)
1953	Sammy Lee	diving
1954	Mal Whitfield	track (middle-distance running)
1955	Harrison Dillard	track (sprints/hurdles)
1956	Pat McCormick	diving
1957	Bobby Morrow	track (sprints)
1958	Glenn Davis	track (hurdles)
1959	Parry O'Brien	track (shot put)
1960	Rafer Johnson	track (decathlon)
1961	Wilma Rudolph	track (sprints)
1962	Jim Beatty	track (distance running)
1963	John Pennel	track (pole vault)
1964	Don Schollander	swimming
1965	Bill Bradley	basketball
1966	Jim Ryun	track (middle-distance running)
1967	Randy Matson	track (shot put/discus)
1968	Debbie Meyer	swimming
1969	Bill Toomey	track (decathlon)
1970	John Kinsella	swimming
1971	Mark Spitz	swimming
1972	Frank Shorter	track (distance running)
1973	Bill Walton	basketball
1974	Rick Wohlhuter	track (middle-distance running)
1975	Tim Shaw	swimming
1976	Bruce Jenner	track (decathlon)
1977	John Naber	swimming
1978	Tracy Caulkins	swimming
1979	Kurt Thomas	gymnastics
1980	Eric Heiden	speed skating
1981	Carl Lewis	track (sprints/long jump)
1982	Mary Decker	track (distance running)
1983	Edwin Moses	track (hurdles)
1984	Greg Louganis	diving
1985	Joan Benoit Samuelson	track (marathon)
1986	Jackie Joyner-Kersee	track (heptathlon)
1987	Jim Abbott	baseball
1988	Florence Griffith Joyner	track (sprints)
1989	Janet Evans	swimming
1990	John Smith	freestyle wrestling
1991	Mike Powell	track (long jump)
1992	Bonnie Blair	speed skating
1993	Charlie Ward	football
1994	Dan Jansen	speed skating
1995	Bruce Baumgartner	freestyle wrestling
1996	Michael Johnson	track (middle-distance running)
1997	Peyton Manning	football
1998	Chamique Holdsclaw	basketball
1999	Coco and Kelly Miller	basketball
2000	Rulon Gardner	Greco-Roman wrestling
2001	Michelle Kwan	figure skating
2002	Sarah Hughes	figure skating
2003	Michael Phelps	swimming
2004	Paul Hamm	gymnastics
2005	J.J. Redick	basketball
2006	Jessica Long	swimming
2007	Tim Tebow	football

The Olympic Games

By the 6th century BC several sporting festivals had achieved cultural importance in the Greek world. The most prominent among them were the Olympic Games at the city of Olympia, first recorded in 776 BC and held at four-year intervals thereafter. Those games, comprising many of the sports now included in the Summer Games, were abolished in AD 393 by the Roman emperor Theodosius I, probably because of their pagan associations.

In 1887 the 24-year-old French aristocrat and educator Pierre, baron de Coubertin, conceived the idea of reviving the Olympic Games and spent seven years gathering support for his plan. At a international congress in 1894, his plan was accepted and the International Olympic Committee (IOC) was founded. The first modern Olympic Games were held in Athens in April 1896, with some 300 representatives from 13 nations competing. The revival led to the formation of international amateur sports organizations and national Olympic committees throughout the world.

The IOC is responsible for maintaining the regular celebration of the games, seeing that the games are carried out in a spirit of peace and intercultural communication, and promoting amateur sport throughout the world. IOC members may not accept from the government of their country, or from any other entity, instructions that compromise their independence.

The Olympic Games have come to be regarded as the world's foremost sports competition. Before the 1970s the Games were officially limited to amateurs, but since that time many events have been opened to professional athletes. In 1924 the Winter Games were created, and in 1986 the IOC voted to alternate the Winter and Summer Games every two years, beginning in 1994.

The games were canceled during the two world wars (1916, 1940, and 1944) and have frequently served as venues for the expression of political dissent. China refused to participate in the Summer Games from 1956 until 1984 because of Taiwan's participation; 26 nations boycotted the games in 1976 over the participation of New Zealand, some of whose athletes had competed in apartheid-era South Africa; the United States and some 60 other countries boycotted the 1980 games in Moscow to protest the Soviet invasion of Afghanistan, and the Communist bloc and Cuba in turn boycotted the 1984 Los Angeles games.

In light of the IOC's declared independence from political and financial interests, in 1998 the world was shocked by allegations of widespread corruption within the committee. Several committee members, it

The Olympic Games (continued)

was found, had accepted bribes to approve the bid of Salt Lake City UT as the site for the 2002 Winter Games. Impropriety was also alleged for several previous bid committees. The IOC responded by expelling six members and in 1999 announced a number of wide-ranging reforms.

IOC Web site: <www.olympic.org>.

Sites of the Modern Olympic Games

Summer Games

YEAR	LOCATION
1896	Athens, Greece
1900	Paris, France
1904	St. Louis MO
1908	London, England
1912	Stockholm, Sweden
1916	*not held*
1920	Antwerp, Belgium
1924	Paris, France
1928	Amsterdam, Netherlands
1932	Los Angeles CA
1936	Berlin, Germany
1940–44	*not held*
1948	London, England
1952	Helsinki, Finland
1956	Melbourne, VIC, Australia
1960	Rome, Italy
1964	Tokyo, Japan
1968	Mexico City, Mexico
1972	Munich, West Germany
1976	Montreal, QC, Canada
1980	Moscow, USSR
1984	Los Angeles CA
1988	Seoul, Republic of Korea
1992	Barcelona, Spain
1996	Atlanta GA
2000	Sydney, NSW, Australia
2004	Athens, Greece
2008	Beijing, China
2012	*scheduled to be held 27 July–12 August, London, England*

Winter Games

YEAR	LOCATION
1924	Chamonix, France
1928	St. Moritz, Switzerland
1932	Lake Placid NY
1936	Garmisch-Partenkirchen, Germany
1940–44	*not held*
1948	St. Moritz, Switzerland
1952	Oslo, Norway
1956	Cortina d'Ampezzo, Italy
1960	Squaw Valley CA
1964	Innsbruck, Austria
1968	Grenoble, France
1972	Sapporo, Japan
1976	Innsbruck, Austria
1980	Lake Placid NY
1984	Sarajevo, Yugoslavia
1988	Calgary, AB, Canada
1992	Albertville, France
1994	Lillehammer, Norway
1998	Nagano, Japan
2002	Salt Lake City UT
2006	Turin, Italy
2010	*scheduled to be held 12–28 February, Vancouver, BC, Canada*
2014	*scheduled to be held 7–23 February, Sochi, Russia*

Summer Olympic Games Champions

Gold-medal winners in all Summer Olympic contests since 1896. Note: East and West Germany fielded a joint all-Germany team in 1956, 1960, and 1964, abbreviated here as GER. The Unified Team in 1992 consisted of the Commonwealth of Independent States plus Georgia, and is abbreviated here as UNT.

Archery

MEN'S INDIVIDUAL

1972 John Williams (USA)
1976 Darrell Pace (USA)
1980 Tomi Poikolainen (FIN)
1984 Darrell Pace (USA)
1988 Jay Barrs (USA)
1992 Sebastien Flute (FRA)
1996 Justin Huish (USA)
2000 Simon Fairweather (AUS)
2004 Marco Galiazzo (ITA)
2008 Viktor Ruban (UKR)

AU CORDON DORE (50 METERS)

1900 Henri Herouin (FRA)

AU CORDON DORE (33 METERS)

1900 Hubert van Innis (BEL)

AU CHAPELET (50 METERS)

1900 Eugène Mougin (FRA)

Archery (continued)

SUR LA PERCHE A LA HERSE

1900 Emmanuel Foulon (FRA)

AU CHAPELET (33 METERS)

1900 Hubert van Innis (BEL)

SUR LA PERCHE A LA PYRAMIDE

1900 Émile Grumiaux (FRA)

DOUBLE AMERICAN ROUND

1904 George Philipp Bryant (USA)

(DOUBLE) YORK ROUND

1904 George Philipp Bryant (USA)
1908 William Dod (GBR)

CONTINENTAL STYLE

1908 Eugène G. Grizot (FRA)

FIXED BIRD TARGET (SMALL)

1920 Edmond van Moer (BEL)

Summer Olympic Games Champions (continued)

Archery (continued)

FIXED BIRD TARGET (LARGE)
1920 Édouard Cloetens (BEL)

MOVING BIRD TARGET (28 M)
1920 Hubert van Innis (BEL)

MOVING BIRD TARGET (33 M)
1920 Hubert van Innis (BEL)

MOVING BIRD TARGET (50 M)
1920 Julien Brulé (FRA)

WOMEN'S INDIVIDUAL
1972 Doreen Wilber (USA)
1976 Luann Ryon (USA)
1980 Ketevan Losaberidze (URS)
1984 Seo Hyang Soon (KOR)
1988 Kim Soo Nyung (KOR)
1992 Cho Youn Jeong (KOR)
1996 Kim Kyung-Wook (KOR)
2000 Yun Mi-Jin (KOR)
2004 Park Sung Hyun (KOR)
2008 Zhang Juan Juan (CHN)

DOUBLE COLUMBIA ROUND
1904 Matilda Scott Howell (USA)

(DOUBLE) NATIONAL ROUND
1904 Matilda Scott Howell (USA)
1908 Sybil Fenton "Queenie" Newall (GBR)

MEN'S TEAM
1904 United States
1988 South Korea
1992 Spain
1996 United States
2000 South Korea
2004 South Korea
2008 South Korea

WOMEN'S TEAM
1904 United States
1988 South Korea
1992 South Korea
1996 South Korea
2000 South Korea
2004 South Korea
2008 South Korea

FIXED TARGET (2 EVENTS)
1920 Belgium

MOVING TARGET (28 M)
1920 The Netherlands

MOVING TARGET (33 M)
1920 Belgium

MOVING TARGET (50 M)
1920 Belgium

Association football (soccer)[1]

MEN
1900 Great Britain
1904 Canada
1908 Great Britain
1912 Great Britain
1920 Belgium

Association football (soccer)[1] (continued)

MEN (CONTINUED)
1924 Uruguay
1928 Uruguay
1936 Italy
1948 Sweden
1952 Hungary
1956 USSR
1960 Yugoslavia
1964 Hungary
1968 Hungary
1972 Poland
1976 East Germany
1980 Czechoslovakia
1984 France
1988 USSR
1992 Spain
1996 Nigeria
2000 Cameroon
2004 Argentina
2008 Argentina

WOMEN
1996 United States
2000 Norway
2004 United States
2008 United States

Athletics (track-and-field) (men)

60 METERS		SEC
1900	Alvin Kraenzlein (USA)	7
1904	Archie Hahn (USA)	7

100 METERS		SEC
1896	Thomas Burke (USA)	12.0
1900	Francis Jarvis (USA)	11.0
1904	Archie Hahn (USA)	11.0
1908	Reginald Walker (RSA)	10.8
1912	Ralph Craig (USA)	10.8
1920	Charles Paddock (USA)	10.8
1924	Harold Abrahams (GBR)	10.6
1928	Percy Williams (CAN)	10.8
1932	Eddie Tolan (USA)	10.3
1936	Jesse Owens (USA)	10.3
1948	Harrison Dillard (USA)	10.3
1952	Lindy Remigino (USA)	10.4
1956	Robert Morrow (USA)	10.5
1960	Armin Hary (GER)	10.2
1964	Robert Hayes (USA)	10.0
1968	James Hines (USA)	9.9
1972	Valery Borzov (URS)	10.14
1976	Hasely Crawford (TRI)	10.06
1980	Allan Wells (GBR)	10.25
1984	Carl Lewis (USA)	9.99
1988	Carl Lewis (USA)	9.92
1992	Linford Christie (GBR)	9.96
1996	Donovan Bailey (CAN)	9.84
2000	Maurice Greene (USA)	9.87
2004	Justin Gatlin (USA)	9.85
2008	Usain Bolt (JAM)	9.69

200 METERS		SEC
1900	Walter Tewksbury (USA)	22.2
1904	Archie Hahn (USA)	21.6
1908	Robert Kerr (CAN)	22.6
1912	Ralph Craig (USA)	21.7
1920	Allen Woodring (USA)	22.0
1924	Jackson Scholz (USA)	21.6
1928	Percy Williams (CAN)	21.8

Athletics (track-and-field) (men) (continued)

200 METERS (CONTINUED)		SEC
1932	Eddie Tolan (USA)	21.2
1936	Jesse Owens (USA)	20.7
1948	Melvin Patton (USA)	21.1
1952	Andy Stanfield (USA)	20.7
1956	Robert Morrow (USA)	20.6
1960	Livio Berruti (ITA)	20.5
1964	Henry Carr (USA)	20.3
1968	Tommie Smith (USA)	19.8
1972	Valery Borzov (URS)	20.00
1976	Donald Quarrie (JAM)	20.23
1980	Pietro Mennea (ITA)	20.19
1984	Carl Lewis (USA)	19.80
1988	Joe DeLoach (USA)	19.75
1992	Mike Marsh (USA)	20.01
1996	Michael Johnson (USA)	19.32
2000	Konstantinos Kenteris (GRE)	20.09
2004	Shawn Crawford (USA)	19.79
2008	Usain Bolt (JAM)	19.30

400 METERS		SEC
1896	Thomas Burke (USA)	54.2
1900	Maxwell Long (USA)	49.4
1904	Harry Hillman (USA)	49.2
1908	Wyndham Halswelle (GBR)	50.0
1912	Charles Reidpath (USA)	48.2
1920	Bevil Rudd (RSA)	49.6
1924	Eric Liddell (GBR)	47.6
1928	Raymond Barbuti (USA)	47.8
1932	William Carr (USA)	46.2
1936	Archie Williams (USA)	46.5
1948	Arthur Wint (JAM)	46.2
1952	Vincent George Rhoden (JAM)	45.9
1956	Charles Jenkins (USA)	46.7
1960	Otis Davis (USA)	44.9
1964	Michael Larrabee (USA)	45.1
1968	Lee Evans (USA)	43.8
1972	Vincent Matthews (USA)	44.66
1976	Alberto Juantorena (CUB)	44.26
1980	Viktor Markin (URS)	44.60
1984	Alonzo Babers (USA)	44.27
1988	Steven Lewis (USA)	43.87
1992	Quincy Watts (USA)	43.50
1996	Michael Johnson (USA)	43.49
2000	Michael Johnson (USA)	43.84
2004	Jeremy Wariner (USA)	44.00
2008	LaShawn Merritt (USA)	43.75

800 METERS		MIN:SEC
1896	Edwin Flack (AUS)	2:11.0
1900	Alfred Tysoe (GBR)	2:01.2
1904	James Lightbody (USA)	1:56.0
1908	Melvin Sheppard (USA)	1:52.8
1912	James Edward Meredith (USA)	1:51.9
1920	Albert Hill (GBR)	1:53.4
1924	Douglas Lowe (GBR)	1:52.4
1928	Douglas Lowe (GBR)	1:51.8
1932	Thomas Hampson (GBR)	1:49.7
1936	John Woodruff (USA)	1:52.9
1948	Malvin Whitfield (USA)	1:49.2
1952	Malvin Whitfield (USA)	1:49.2
1956	Thomas Courtney (USA)	1:47.7
1960	Peter Snell (NZL)	1:46.3
1964	Peter Snell (NZL)	1:45.1
1968	Ralph Doubell (AUS)	1:44.3
1972	David Wottle (USA)	1:45.9
1976	Alberto Juantorena (CUB)	1:43.50
1980	Steven Ovett (GBR)	1:45.40
1984	Joaquim Cruz (BRA)	1:43.00
1988	Paul Ereng (KEN)	1:43.45

Athletics (track-and-field) (men) (continued)

800 METERS (CONTINUED)		MIN:SEC
1992	William Tanui (KEN)	1:43.66
1996	Vebjoern Rodal (NOR)	1:42.58
2000	Nils Schumann (GER)	1:45.08
2004	Yury Borzakovsky (RUS)	1:44.45
2008	Wilfred Bungei (KEN)	1:44.65

1,500 METERS		MIN:SEC
1896	Edwin Flack (AUS)	4:33.2
1900	Charles Bennett (GBR)	4:06.2
1904	James Lightbody (USA)	4:05.4
1908	Melvin Sheppard (USA)	4:03.4
1912	Arnold Jackson (GBR)	3:56.8
1920	Albert Hill (GBR)	4:01.8
1924	Paavo Nurmi (FIN)	3:53.6
1928	Harry Larva (FIN)	3:53.2
1932	Luigi Beccali (ITA)	3:51.2
1936	John Lovelock (NZL)	3:47.8
1948	Henry Eriksson (SWE)	3:49.8
1952	Joseph Barthel (LUX)	3:45.1
1956	Ronald Delany (IRE)	3:41.2
1960	Herbert Elliott (AUS)	3:35.6
1964	Peter Snell (NZL)	3:38.1
1968	Hezekiah Kipchoge ("Kip") Keino (KEN)	3:34.9
1972	Pekka Vasala (FIN)	3:36.3
1976	John Walker (NZL)	3:39.17
1980	Sebastian Coe (GBR)	3:38.40
1984	Sebastian Coe (GBR)	3:32.53
1988	Peter Rono (KEN)	3:35.96
1992	Fermin Cacho Ruiz (ESP)	3:40.12
1996	Noureddine Morceli (ALG)	3:35.78
2000	Noah Ngeny (KEN)	3:32.07
2004	Hicham El Guerrouj (MAR)	3:34.18
2008	Rashid Ramzi (BRN)	3:32.94

5,000 METERS		MIN:SEC
1912	Hannes Kolehmainen (FIN)	14:36.6
1920	Joseph Guillemot (FRA)	14:55.6
1924	Paavo Nurmi (FIN)	14:31.2
1928	Vilho Ritola (FIN)	14:38.0
1932	Lauri Lehtinen (FIN)	14:30.0
1936	Gunnar Höckert (FIN)	14:22.2
1948	Gaston Reiff (BEL)	14:17.6
1952	Emil Zatopek (TCH)	14:06.6
1956	Vladimir Kuts (URS)	13:39.6
1960	Murray Halberg (NZL)	13:43.4
1964	Robert Keyser Schul (USA)	13:48.8
1968	Mohamed Gammoudi (TUN)	14:05.0
1972	Lasse Viren (FIN)	13:26.4
1976	Lasse Viren (FIN)	13:24.76
1980	Miruts Yifter (ETH)	13:21.00
1984	Said Aouita (MAR)	13:05.59
1988	John Ngugi (KEN)	13:11.70
1992	Dieter Baumann (GER)	13:12.52
1996	Venuste Niyongabo (BDI)	13:07.97
2000	Millon Wolde (ETH)	13:35.49
2004	Hicham El Guerrouj (MAR)	13:14.39
2008	Kenenisa Bekele (ETH)	12:57.82

5 MILES		MIN:SEC
1908	Emil Voigt (GBR)	25:11.2

10,000 METERS		MIN:SEC
1912	Hannes Kolehmainen (FIN)	31:20.8
1920	Paavo Nurmi (FIN)	31:45.8
1924	Vilho Ritola (FIN)	30:23.2
1928	Paavo Nurmi (FIN)	30:18.8
1932	Janusz Kusocinski (POL)	30:11.4
1936	Ilmari Salminen (FIN)	30:15.4
1948	Emil Zatopek (TCH)	29:59.6

Summer Olympic Games Champions (continued)

Athletics (track-and-field) (men) (continued)

10,000 METERS (CONTINUED)		MIN:SEC
1952	Emil Zatopek (TCH)	29:17.0
1956	Vladimir Kuts (URS)	28:45.6
1960	Pyotr Bolotnikov (URS)	28:32.2
1964	William Mills (USA)	28:24.4
1968	Nabiba Temu (KEN)	29:27.4
1972	Lasse Viren (FIN)	27:38.4
1976	Lasse Viren (FIN)	27:40.38
1980	Miruts Yifter (ETH)	27:42.70
1984	Alberto Cova (ITA)	27:47.54
1988	Brahim Boutaib (MAR)	27:21.46
1992	Khalid Skah (MAR)	27:46.70
1996	Haile Gebrselassie (ETH)	27:07.34
2000	Haile Gebrselassie (ETH)	27:18.20
2004	Kenenisa Bekele (ETH)	27:05.10
2008	Kenenisa Bekele (ETH)	27:01.17

MARATHON		HR:MIN:SEC
1896	Spiridon Louis (GRE)	2:58:50.0
1900	Michel Theato (FRA)	2:59:45.0
1904	Thomas Hicks (USA)	3:28:53.0
1908	John Hayes (USA)	2:55:18.4
1912	Kenneth McArthur (RSA)	2:36:54.8
1920	Hannes Kolehmainen (FIN)	2:32:35.8
1924	Albin Stenroos (FIN)	2:41:22.6
1928	Boughèra El Ouafi (FRA)	2:32:57.0
1932	Juan Carlos Zabala (ARG)	2:31:36.0
1936	Kitei Son (JPN)	2:29:19.2
1948	Delfo Cabrera (ARG)	2:34:51.6
1952	Emil Zatopek (TCH)	2:23:03.2
1956	Alain Mimoun-O-Kacha (FRA)	2:25:00.0
1960	Abebe Bikila (ETH)	2:15:16.2
1964	Abebe Bikila (ETH)	2:12:11.2
1968	Mamo Wolde (ETH)	2:20:26.4
1972	Frank Shorter (USA)	2:12:19.8
1976	Waldemar Cierpinski (GDR)	2:09:55.0
1980	Waldemar Cierpinski (GDR)	2:11:03.0
1984	Carlos Lopes (POR)	2:09:21.0
1988	Gelindo Bordin (ITA)	2:10:32.0
1992	Hwang Young-Cho (KOR)	2:13:23.0
1996	Josia Thugwane (RSA)	2:12:36.0
2000	Gezahgne Abera (ETH)	2:10:11.0
2004	Stefano Baldini (ITA)	2:10:55.0
2008	Samuel Kamau Wansiru (KEN)	2:06:32.0

110-METER HURDLES		SEC
1896[2]	Thomas Curtis (USA)	17.6
1900	Alvin Kraenzlein (USA)	15.4
1904	Frederick Schule (USA)	16.0
1908	Forrest Smithson (USA)	15.0
1912	Frederick Kelly (USA)	15.1
1920	Earl Thomson (CAN)	14.8
1924	Daniel Kinsey (USA)	15.0
1928	Sydney Atkinson (RSA)	14.8
1932	George Saling (USA)	14.6
1936	Forrest Towns (USA)	14.2
1948	William Porter (USA)	13.9
1952	Harrison Dillard (USA)	13.7
1956	Lee Calhoun (USA)	13.5
1960	Lee Calhoun (USA)	13.8
1964	Hayes Wendell Jones (USA)	13.6
1968	Willie Davenport (USA)	13.3
1972	Rodney Milburn (USA)	13.24
1976	Guy Drut (FRA)	13.30
1980	Thomas Munkelt (GDR)	13.39
1984	Roger Kingdom (USA)	13.20
1988	Roger Kingdom (USA)	12.98
1992	Mark McKoy (CAN)	13.12

Athletics (track-and-field) (men) (continued)

110-METER HURDLES (CONTINUED)		SEC
1996	Allen Johnson (USA)	12.95
2000	Anier Garcia (CUB)	13.00
2004	Liu Xiang (CHN)	12.91
2008	Dayron Robles (CUB)	12.93

200-METER HURDLES		SEC
1900	Alvin Kraenzlein (USA)	25.4
1904	Harry Hillman (USA)	24.6

400-METER HURDLES		SEC
1900	Walter Tewksbury (USA)	57.6
1904[3]	Harry Hillman (USA)	53.0
1908	Charles Bacon (USA)	55.0
1920	Frank Loomis (USA)	54.0
1924	Frederick Morgan Taylor (USA)	52.6
1928	David George Burghley (GBR)	53.4
1932	Robert Tisdall (IRL)	51.7
1936	Glenn Hardin (USA)	52.4
1948	Roy Cochran (USA)	51.1
1952	Charles Moore (USA)	50.8
1956	Glenn Davis (USA)	50.1
1960	Glenn Davis (USA)	49.3
1964	Warren Cawley (USA)	49.6
1968	David Hemery (GBR)	48.1
1972	John Akii-Bua (UGA)	47.82
1976	Edwin Moses (USA)	47.64
1980	Volker Beck (GDR)	48.70
1984	Edwin Moses (USA)	47.75
1988	Andre Phillips (USA)	47.19
1992	Kevin Young (USA)	46.78
1996	Derrick Adkins (USA)	47.54
2000	Angelo Taylor (USA)	47.50
2004	Felix Sánchez (DOM)	47.63
2008	Angelo Taylor (USA)	47.25

2,500-METER STEEPLECHASE		MIN:SEC
1900	George Orton (USA)	7:34.4

2,590-METER STEEPLECHASE		MIN:SEC
1904	James Lightbody (USA)	7:39.6

3,000-METER STEEPLECHASE		MIN:SEC
1920	Percy Hodge (GBR)	10:00.4
1924	Vilho Ritola (FIN)	9:33.6
1928	Toivo Loukola (FIN)	9:21.8
1932	Volmari Iso-Hollo (FIN)	10:33.4[4]
1936	Volmari Iso-Hollo (FIN)	9:03.8
1948	Thore Sjöstrand (SWE)	9:04.6
1952	Horace Ashenfelter (USA)	8:45.4
1956	Christopher Brasher (GBR)	8:41.2
1960	Zdislaw Krzyszkowiak (POL)	8:34.2
1964	Gaston Roelants (BEL)	8:30.8
1968	Amos Biwott (KEN)	8:51.0
1972	Kipchoge Keino (KEN)	8:23.6
1976	Anders Gärderud (SWE)	8:08.02
1980	Bronislaw Malinowski (POL)	8:09.70
1984	Julius Korir (KEN)	8:11.80
1988	Julius Kariuki (KEN)	8:05.51
1992	Mathew Birir (KEN)	8:08.84
1996	Joseph Keter (KEN)	8:07.12
2000	Reuben Kosgei (KEN)	8:21.43
2004	Ezekiel Kemboi (KEN)	8:05.81
2008	Brimin Kiprop Kipruto (KEN)	8:10.34

3,200-METER STEEPLECHASE		MIN:SEC
1908	Arthur Russell (GBR)	10:47.8

Summer Olympic Games Champions (continued)

Athletics (track-and-field) (men) (continued)

3,000 METERS (TEAM) (TEAM/INDIVIDUAL WINNER)		MIN:SEC
1912	United States/Tell Berna	8:44.6
1920	United States/Horace Brown	8:45.4
1924	Finland/Paavo Nurmi	8:32

3 MILES (TEAM) (TEAM/INDIVIDUAL WINNER)		MIN:SEC
1908	Great Britain/Joseph Deakin	14:39.6

5,000 METERS (TEAM) (TEAM/INDIVIDUAL WINNER)		MIN:SEC
1900	Great Britain-Australia/Charles Bennett	15:20

4 MILES (TEAM) (TEAM/INDIVIDUAL WINNER)		MIN:SEC
1904	United States/Arthur Newton (USA)	21:17.8

4 × 100 METER RELAY		SEC
1912	Great Britain	42.4
1920	United States	42.2
1924	United States	41.0
1928	United States	41.0
1932	United States	40.0
1936	United States	39.8
1948	United States	40.6
1952	United States	40.1
1956	United States	39.5
1960	Germany	39.5
1964	United States	39.0
1968	United States	38.2
1972	United States	38.19
1976	United States	38.33
1980	USSR	38.26
1984	United States	37.83
1988	USSR	38.19
1992	United States	37.40
1996	Canada	37.69
2000	winner stripped; undecided by press time	
2004	Great Britain	38.07
2008	Jamaica	37.10

4 × 400 METER RELAY		MIN:SEC
1912	United States	3:16.6
1920	Great Britain	3:22.2
1924	United States	3:16.0
1928	United States	3:14.2
1932	United States	3:08.2
1936	Great Britain	3:09.0
1948	United States	3:10.4
1952	Jamaica	3:03.9
1956	United States	3:04.8
1960	United States	3:02.2
1964	United States	3:00.7
1968	United States	2:56.1
1972	Kenya	2:59.8
1976	United States	2:58.65
1980	USSR	3:01.1
1984	United States	2:57.91
1988	United States	2:56.16
1992	United States	2:55.74
1996	United States	2:55.99
2000	winner stripped; undecided by press time	
2004	United States	2:55.91
2008	United States	2:55.39

1,600-METER RELAY (200 × 200 × 400 × 800 METERS)		MIN:SEC
1908	United States	3:29.4

Athletics (track-and-field) (men) (continued)

8,000 M CROSS-COUNTRY		MIN:SEC
1920	Paavo Nurmi (FIN)	27:15

10,000 M CROSS-COUNTRY		MIN:SEC
1924	Paavo Nurmi (FIN)	32:54.8

12,000 M CROSS-COUNTRY		MIN:SEC
1912	Hannes Kolehmainen (FIN)	45:11.6

3,000-METER WALK		MIN:SEC
1920	Ugo Frigerio (ITA)	13:14.2

3,500-METER WALK		MIN:SEC
1908	George Larner (GBR)	14:55

10,000-METER WALK		MIN:SEC
1912	George Goulding (CAN)	46:28.4
1920	Ugo Frigerio (ITA)	48:06.2
1924	Ugo Frigerio (ITA)	47:49
1948	John Mikaelsson (SWE)	45:13.2
1952	John Mikaelsson (SWE)	45:02.8

10-MILE WALK		HR:MIN:SEC
1908	George Larner (GBR)	1:15:57.4

20,000-METER WALK		HR:MIN:SEC
1956	Leonid Spirin (URS)	1:31:27.4
1960	Vladimir Golubnichy (URS)	1:34:07.2
1964	Kenneth Matthews (GBR)	1:29:34.0
1968	Vladimir Golubnichy (URS)	1:33:58.4
1972	Peter Frenkel (GDR)	1:26:42.6
1976	Daniel Bautista (MEX)	1:24:40.6
1980	Maurizio Damilano (ITA)	1:23:35.5
1984	Ernesto Canto (MEX)	1:23:13.0
1988	Jozef Pribilinec (TCH)	1:19:57.0
1992	Daniel Plaza Montero (ESP)	1:21:45.0
1996	Jefferson Pérez (ECU)	1:20:07.0
2000	Robert Korzeniowski (POL)	1:18:59.0
2004	Ivano Brugnetti (ITA)	1:19:40.0
2008	Valeriy Borchin (RUS)	1:19:01.0

50,000-METER WALK		HR:MIN:SEC
1932	Thomas Green (GBR)	4:50:10.0
1936	Harold Whitlock (GBR)	4:30:41.4
1948	John Ljunggren (SWE)	4:41:52.0
1952	Giuseppe Dordoni (ITA)	4:28:07.8
1956	Norman Read (NZL)	4:30:42.8
1960	Donald Thompson (GBR)	4:25:30.0
1964	Abdon Pamich (ITA)	4:11:12.4
1968	Christophe Höhne (GDR)	4:20:13.6
1972	Bernd Kannenberg (FRG)	3:56:11.6
1980	Hartwig Gauder (GDR)	3:49:24.0
1984	Raúl Gonzáles (MEX)	3:47:26.0
1988	Vyacheslav Ivanenko (URS)	3:38:29.0
1992	Andrey Perlov (UNT)	3:50:13.0
1996	Robert Korzeniowski (POL)	3:43:03.0
2000	Robert Korzeniowski (POL)	3:42:22.0
2004	Robert Korzeniowski (POL)	3:38:46.0
2008	Alex Schwazer (ITA)	3:37:09.0

HIGH JUMP		METERS
1896	Ellery Clark (USA)	1.81
1900	Irving Baxter (USA)	1.90
1904	Samuel Jones (USA)	1.80
1908	Harry Porter (USA)	1.90
1912	Alma Richards (USA)	1.93
1920	Richmond Landon (USA)	1.93
1924	Harold Osborn (USA)	1.98

Summer Olympic Games Champions (continued)

Athletics (track-and-field) (men) (continued)

HIGH JUMP (CONTINUED)		METERS
1928	Robert King (USA)	1.94
1932	Duncan McNaughton (CAN)	1.97
1936	Cornelius Johnson (USA)	2.03
1948	John Winter (AUS)	1.98
1952	Walter Davis (USA)	2.04
1956	Charles Dumas (USA)	2.12
1960	Robert Shavlakadze (URS)	2.16
1964	Valery Brumel (URS)	2.18
1968	Richard Fosbury (USA)	2.24
1972	Yury Tarmak (URS)	2.23
1976	Jacek Wszola (POL)	2.25
1980	Gerd Wessig (GDR)	2.36
1984	Dietmar Mögenburg (FRG)	2.35
1988	Gennady Avdeyenko (URS)	2.38
1992	Javier Sotomayor (CUB)	2.34
1996	Charles Austin (USA)	2.39
2000	Sergey Klyugin (RUS)	2.35
2004	Stefan Holm (SWE)	2.36
2008	Andrey Silnov (RUS)	2.36

STANDING HIGH JUMP		METERS
1900	Ray Ewry (USA)	1.65
1904	Ray Ewry (USA)	1.6
1908	Ray Ewry (USA)	1.57
1912	Platt Adams (USA)	1.63

POLE VAULT		METERS
1896	William Welles Hoyt (USA)	3.30
1900	Irving Baxter (USA)	3.30
1904	Charles Dvorak (USA)	3.50
1908	Edward Cooke (USA); Alfred Gilbert (USA) (*tied*)	3.71
1912	Harry Babcock (USA)	3.95
1920	Frank Foss (USA)	4.09
1924	Lee Barnes (USA)	3.95
1928	Sabin Carr (USA)	4.20
1932	William Miller (USA)	4.31
1936	Earle Meadows (USA)	4.35
1948	Owen Guinn Smith (USA)	4.30
1952	Robert Richards (USA)	4.55
1956	Robert Richards (USA)	4.56
1960	Donald Bragg (USA)	4.70
1964	Fred Hansen (USA)	5.10
1968	Robert Seagren (USA)	5.40
1972	Wolfgang Nordwig (GDR)	5.50
1976	Tadeusz Slusarski (POL)	5.50
1980	Wladyslaw Kozakiewicz (POL)	5.78
1984	Pierre Quinon (FRA)	5.75
1988	Sergey Bubka (URS)	5.90
1992	Maksim Tarasov (UNT)	5.80
1996	Jean Galfione (FRA)	5.92
2000	Nick Hysong (USA)	5.90
2004	Timothy Mack (USA)	5.95
2008	Steve Hooker (AUS)	5.96

LONG JUMP		METERS
1896	Ellery Clark (USA)	6.35
1900	Alvin Kraenzlein (USA)	7.18
1904	Meyer Prinstein (USA)	7.34
1908	Francis Irons (USA)	7.48
1912	Albert Gutterson (USA)	7.60
1920	William Pettersson (SWE)	7.15
1924	William de Hart-Hubbard (USA)	7.44
1928	Edward Hamm (USA)	7.73
1932	Edward Gordon (USA)	7.64
1936	Jesse Owens (USA)	8.06
1948	Willie Steele (USA)	7.82

Athletics (track-and-field) (men) (continued)

LONG JUMP (CONTINUED)		METERS
1952	Jerome Biffle (USA)	7.57
1956	Gregory Bell (USA)	7.83
1960	Ralph Boston (USA)	8.12
1964	Lynn Davies (GBR)	8.07
1968	Robert Beamon (USA)	8.90
1972	Randy Williams (USA)	8.24
1976	Arnie Robinson (USA)	8.35
1980	Lutz Dombrowski (GDR)	8.54
1984	Carl Lewis (USA)	8.54
1988	Carl Lewis (USA)	8.72
1992	Carl Lewis (USA)	8.67
1996	Carl Lewis (USA)	8.50
2000	Ivan Pedroso (CUB)	8.55
2004	Dwight Phillips (USA)	8.59
2008	Irving Jahir Saladino Aranda (PAN)	8.34

STANDING LONG JUMP		METERS
1900	Ray Ewry (USA)	3.21
1904	Ray Ewry (USA)	3.47
1908	Ray Ewry (USA)	3.33
1912	Constantinos Tsiklitiras (GRE)	3.37

TRIPLE JUMP		METERS
1896	James Connolly (USA)	13.71
1900	Myer Prinstein (USA)	14.47
1904	Myer Prinstein (USA)	14.35
1908	Timothy Ahearne (GBR)	14.91
1912	Gustaf Lindblom (SWE)	14.76
1920	Vilho Tuulos (FIN)	14.50
1924	Anthony Winter (AUS)	15.53
1928	Mikio Oda (JPN)	15.21
1932	Chuhei Nambu (JPN)	15.72
1936	Naoto Tajima (JPN)	16.00
1948	Arne Åhman (SWE)	15.40
1952	Adhemar Ferreira da Silva (BRA)	16.22
1956	Adhemar Ferreira da Silva (BRA)	16.35
1960	Josef Szmidt (POL)	16.81
1964	Josef Szmidt (POL)	16.85
1968	Viktor Saneyev (URS)	17.39
1972	Viktor Saneyev (URS)	17.35
1976	Viktor Saneyev (URS)	17.29
1980	Jaak Uudmae (URS)	17.35
1984	Al Joyner (USA)	17.26
1988	Khristo Markov (BUL)	17.61
1992	Michael Conley (USA)	17.63
1996	Kenny Harrison (USA)	18.09
2000	Jonathan Edwards (GBR)	17.71
2004	Christian Olsson (SWE)	17.79
2008	Nelson Évora (POR)	17.67

STANDING TRIPLE JUMP		METERS
1900	Ray Ewry (USA)	10.58
1904	Ray Ewry (USA)	10.54

SHOT PUT		METERS
1896	Robert Garrett (USA)	11.22
1900	Richard Sheldon (USA)	14.10
1904	Ralph Rose (USA)	14.81
1908	Ralph Rose (USA)	14.21
1912	Patrick McDonald (USA)	15.34
1920	Frans Pörhölä (FIN)	14.81
1924	Lemuel Clarence Houser (USA)	14.99
1928	John Kuck (USA)	15.87
1932	Leo Sexton (USA)	16.00
1936	Hans Woellke (GER)	16.20
1948	Wilbur Thompson (USA)	17.12
1952	William Parry O'Brien (USA)	17.41

Summer Olympic Games Champions (continued)

Athletics (track-and-field) (men) (continued)

SHOT PUT (CONTINUED)		METERS
1956	William Parry O'Brien (USA)	18.57
1960	William Nieder (USA)	19.68
1964	Dallas Long (USA)	20.33
1968	Randy Matson (USA)	20.54
1972	Wladislaw Komar (POL)	21.18
1976	Udo Beyer (GDR)	21.05
1980	Vladimir Kiselyov (URS)	21.35
1984	Alessandro Andrei (ITA)	21.26
1988	Ulf Timmermann (GDR)	22.47
1992	Michael Stulce (USA)	21.70
1996	Randy Barnes (USA)	21.62
2000	Arsi Harju (FIN)	21.29
2004	Yury Bilonog (UKR)	21.16
2008	Tomasz Majewski (POL)	21.51

SHOT PUT (TWO HANDS)		METERS
1912	Ralph Rose (USA)	27.7

DISCUS THROW		METERS
1896	Robert Garrett (USA)	29.15
1900	Rezso Bauer (HUN)	36.04
1904	Martin Sheridan (USA)	39.28
1908	Martin Sheridan (USA)	40.89
1912	Armas Taipale (FIN)	45.21
1920	Elmer Niklander (FIN)	44.68
1924	Lemuel Clarence Houser (USA)	46.15
1928	Lemuel Clarence Houser (USA)	47.32
1932	John Anderson (USA)	49.49
1936	Kenneth Carpenter (USA)	50.48
1948	Adolfo Consolini (ITA)	52.78
1952	Sim Iness (USA)	55.03
1956	Alfred Oerter (USA)	56.36
1960	Alfred Oerter (USA)	59.18
1964	Alfred Oerter (USA)	61.00
1968	Alfred Oerter (USA)	64.78
1972	Ludvig Danek (TCH)	64.40
1976	Mac Wilkins (USA)	67.50
1980	Viktor Rashchupkin (URS)	66.64
1984	Rolf Danneberg (FRG)	66.60
1988	Jürgen Schult (GDR)	68.82
1992	Romas Ubartas (LTU)	65.12
1996	Lars Riedel (GER)	69.40
2000	Virgilijus Alekna (LTU)	69.30
2004	Virgilijus Alekna (LTU)	69.89
2008	Gerd Kanter (EST)	68.82

DISCUS (GREEK STYLE)		METERS
1908	Martin Sheridan (USA)	37.99

DISCUS (TWO HANDS)		METERS
1912	Armas Taipale (FIN)	82.86

HAMMER THROW		METERS
1900	John Flanagan (USA)	49.73
1904	John Flanagan (USA)	51.23
1908	John Flanagan (USA)	51.92
1912	Matthew McGrath (USA)	54.74
1920	Patrick Ryan (USA)	52.87
1924	Frederick Tootell (USA)	53.30
1928	Patrick O'Callaghan (IRL)	51.39
1932	Patrick O'Callaghan (IRL)	53.92
1936	Karl Hein (GER)	56.49
1948	Imre Nemeth (HUN)	56.07
1952	Jozsef Csermak (HUN)	60.34
1956	Harold Connolly (USA)	63.19
1960	Vasily Rudenkov (URS)	67.10
1964	Romuald Klim (URS)	69.74

Athletics (track-and-field) (men) (continued)

HAMMER THROW (CONTINUED)		METERS
1968	Gyula Zsivotzky (HUN)	73.36
1972	Anatoly Bondarchuk (URS)	75.50
1976	Yury Sedykh (URS)	77.52
1980	Yury Sedykh (URS)	81.80
1984	Juha Tiainen (FIN)	78.08
1988	Sergey Litvinov (URS)	84.80
1992	Andrey Abduvaliyev (UNT)	82.53
1996	Balazs Kiss (HUN)	81.24
2000	Szymon Ziolkowski (POL)	80.02
2004	Koji Murofushi (JPN)	82.91
2008	Primoz Kozmus (SLO)	82.02

JAVELIN THROW		METERS
1908	Eric Lemming (SWE)	54.83
1912	Eric Lemming (SWE)	60.64
1920	Jonni Myyrä (FIN)	65.78
1924	Jonni Myyrä (FIN)	62.96
1928	Erik Lundkvist (SWE)	66.60
1932	Matti Järvinen (FIN)	72.71
1936	Gerhard Stöck (GER)	71.84
1948	Kai Rautavaara (FIN)	69.77
1952	Cy Young (USA)	73.78
1956	Egil Danielson (NOR)	85.71
1960	Viktor Tsybulenko (URS)	84.64
1964	Pauli Nevala (FIN)	82.66
1968	Janis Lusis (URS)	90.10
1972	Klaus Wolfermann (FRG)	90.48
1976	Miklos Nemeth (HUN)	94.58
1980	Dainis Kula (URS)	91.20
1984	Arto Härkönen (FIN)	86.76
1988	Tapio Korjus (FIN)	84.28
1992	Jan Zelezny (TCH)	89.66
1996	Jan Zelezny (CZE)	88.16
2000	Jan Zelezny (CZE)	90.17
2004	Andreas Thorkildsen (NOR)	86.50
2008	Andreas Thorkildsen (NOR)	90.57

JAVELIN (FREESTYLE)		METERS
1908	Eric Lemming (SWE)	54.45

JAVELIN (TWO HANDS)		METERS
1912	Juho Saaristo (FIN)	109.42

THROWING THE 56 LB WEIGHT		METERS
1904	Étienne Desmarteau (CAN)	10.46
1920	Patrick McDonald (USA)	11.26

TUG-OF-WAR

1900 Sweden-Denmark
1904 United States
1908 Great Britain
1912 Sweden
1920 Great Britain

TRIATHLON (LONG JUMP/SHOT PUT/100 YARDS)

1904 Max Emmerich (USA)

PENTATHLON

1912 Jim Thorpe (USA)[5]; Ferdinand Bie (NOR) (*cowinners*)
1920 Eero Lehtonen (FIN)
1924 Eero Lehtonen (FIN)

DECATHLON

1904 Thomas Kiely (IRL)
1912 Jim Thorpe (USA)[5]; Hugo Wieslander (SWE) (*cowinners*)

Summer Olympic Games Champions (continued)

Athletics (track-and-field) (men) (continued)

DECATHLON (CONTINUED)

1920	Helge Lövland (NOR)
1924	Harold Osborn (USA)
1928	Paavo Yrjölä (FIN)
1932	James Bausch (USA)
1936	Glenn Morris (USA)
1948	Robert Mathias (USA)
1952	Robert Mathias (USA)
1956	Milton Campbell (USA)
1960	Rafer Johnson (USA)
1964	Willi Holdorf (GER)
1968	William Toomey (USA)
1972	Nikolay Avilov (URS)
1976	Bruce Jenner (USA)
1980	Daley Thompson (GBR)
1984	Daley Thompson (GBR)
1988	Christian Schenk (GDR)
1992	Robert Zmelik (TCH)
1996	Dan O'Brien (USA)
2000	Erki Nool (EST)
2004	Roman Sebrle (CZE)
2008	Bryan Clay (USA)

Athletics (track-and-field) (women)

100 METERS		SEC
1928	Elizabeth Robinson (USA)	12.2
1932	Stanislawa Walasiewicz (POL)	11.9
1936	Helen Stephens (USA)	11.5
1948	Francina Blankers-Koen (NED)	11.9
1952	Marjorie Jackson (AUS)	11.5
1956	Elizabeth Cuthbert (AUS)	11.5
1960	Wilma Rudolph (USA)	11.0
1964	Wyomia Tyus (USA)	11.4
1968	Wyomia Tyus (USA)	11.0
1972	Renate Stecher (GDR)	11.07
1976	Annegret Richter (FRG)	11.08
1980	Lyudmila Kondratyeva (URS)	11.06
1984	Evelyn Ashford (USA)	10.97
1988	Florence Griffith Joyner (USA)	10.54
1992	Gail Devers (USA)	10.82
1996	Gail Devers (USA)	10.94
2000	winner stripped; undecided by press time	
2004	Yuliya Nesterenko (BLR)	10.93
2008	Shelly-Ann Fraser (JAM)	10.78

200 METERS		SEC
1948	Francina Blankers-Koen (NED)	24.4
1952	Marjorie Jackson (AUS)	23.7
1956	Elizabeth Cuthbert (AUS)	23.4
1960	Wilma Rudolph (USA)	24.0
1964	Edith Marie McGuire (USA)	23.0
1968	Irena Szewinska (POL)	22.5
1972	Renate Stecher (GDR)	22.40
1976	Bärbel Eckert (GDR)	22.37
1980	Bärbel Eckert-Wöckel (GDR)	22.03
1984	Valerie Brisco-Hooks (USA)	21.81
1988	Florence Griffith Joyner (USA)	21.34
1992	Gwen Torrence (USA)	21.81
1996	Marie-Jose Perec (FRA)	22.12
2000	winner stripped; undecided by press time	
2004	Veronica Campbell (JAM)	22.05
2008	Veronica Campbell-Brown (JAM)	21.74

400 METERS		SEC
1964	Elizabeth Cuthbert (AUS)	52.0
1968	Colette Besson (FRA)	52.0
1972	Monika Zehrt (GDR)	51.08
1976	Irena Szewinska (POL)	49.29

Athletics (track-and-field) (women) (continued)

400 METERS (CONTINUED)		SEC
1980	Marita Koch (GDR)	48.88
1984	Valerie Brisco-Hooks (USA)	48.83
1988	Olga Bryzgina (URS)	48.65
1992	Marie-Jose Perec (FRA)	48.83
1996	Marie-Jose Perec (FRA)	48.25
2000	Cathy Freeman (AUS)	49.11
2004	Tonique Williams-Darling (BAH)	49.41
2008	Christine Ohuruogu (GBR)	49.62

800 METERS		MIN:SEC
1928	Lina Radke-Batschauer (GER)	2:16.8
1960	Lyudmila Lysenko-Shevtsova (URS)	2:04.3
1964	Ann Packer (GBR)	2:01.1
1968	Madeline Manning (USA)	2:00.9
1972	Hildegard Falck (FRG)	1:58.6
1976	Tatyana Kazankina (URS)	1:54.94
1980	Nadezhda Olizarenko (URS)	1:53.50
1984	Doina Melinte (ROM)	1:57.6
1988	Sigrun Wodars (GDR)	1:56.10
1992	Ellen van Langen (NED)	1:55.54
1996	Svetlana Masterkova (RUS)	1:57.73
2000	Maria Mutola (MOZ)	1:56.15
2004	Kelly Holmes (GBR)	1:56.38
2008	Pamela Jelimo (KEN)	1:54.87

1,500 METERS		MIN:SEC
1972	Lyudmila Bragina (URS)	4:01.4
1976	Tatyana Kazankina (URS)	4:05.48
1980	Tatyana Kazankina (URS)	3:56.6
1984	Gabriella Dorio (ITA)	4:03.25
1988	Paula Ivan (ROM)	3:53.96
1992	Hassiba Boulmerka (ALG)	3:55.30
1996	Svetlana Masterkova (RUS)	4:00.83
2000	Nouria Merah-Benida (ALG)	4:05.10
2004	Kelly Holmes (GBR)	3:57.90
2008	Nancy Jebet Langat (KEN)	4:00.23

3,000 METERS		MIN:SEC
1984	Maricica Puica (ROM)	8:35.96
1988	Tatyana Samolenko (URS)	8:26.53
1992	Yelena Romanova (UNT)	8:46.04

3,000-METER STEEPLECHASE		MIN:SEC
2008	Gulnara Samitova-Galkina (RUS)	8:58.81

5,000 METERS		MIN:SEC
1996	Wang Jungxia (CHN)	14:59.88
2000	Gabriela Szabo (ROM)	14:40.79
2004	Meseret Defar (ETH)	14:45.65
2008	Tirunesh Dibaba (ETH)	15:41.40

10,000 METERS		MIN:SEC
1988	Olga Bondarenko (URS)	31:05.21
1992	Derartu Tulu (ETH)	31:06.02
1996	Fernanda Ribeiro (POR)	31:01.63
2000	Derartu Tulu (ETH)	30:17.49
2004	Xing Huina (CHN)	30:24.36
2008	Tirunesh Dibaba (ETH)	29:54.66

MARATHON		HR:MIN:SEC
1984	Joan Benoit (USA)	2:24:52
1988	Rosa Mota (POR)	2:25:40
1992	Valentina Yegorova (UNT)	2:32:41
1996	Fatuma Roba (ETH)	2:26:05
2000	Naoko Takahashi (JPN)	2:23:14
2004	Mizuki Noguchi (JPN)	2:26:20
2008	Constantina Tomescu (ROM)	2:26:44

Summer Olympic Games Champions (continued)

Athletics (track-and-field) (women) (continued)

80-METER HURDLES (100 METERS FROM 1972)		SEC
1932	Mildred "Babe" Didrikson (USA)	11.7
1936	Trebisonda Valla (ITA)	11.7
1948	Francina Blankers-Koen (NED)	11.2
1952	Shirley Strickland de La Hunty (AUS)	10.9
1956	Shirley Strickland de La Hunty (AUS)	10.7
1960	Irina Press (URS)	10.8
1964	Karin Balzer (GER)	10.5
1968	Maureen Caird (AUS)	10.3
1972	Annelie Ehrhardt (GDR)	12.59
1976	Johanna Schaller (GDR)	12.77
1980	Vera Komisova (URS)	12.56
1984	Benita Fitzgerald-Brown (USA)	12.84
1988	Iordanka Donkova (BUL)	12.38
1992	Paraskevi Patoulidou (GRE)	12.64
1996	Ludmila Engquist (SWE)	12.58
2000	Olga Shishigina (KAZ)	12.65
2004	Joanna Hayes (USA)	12.37
2008	Dawn Harper (USA)	12.54

400-METER HURDLES		SEC
1984	Nawal el Moutawakel (MAR)	54.61
1988	Debra Flintoff-King (AUS)	53.17
1992	Sally Gunnell (GBR)	53.23
1996	Deon Hemmings (JAM)	52.82
2000	Irina Privalova (RUS)	53.02
2004	Fani Halkia (GRE)	52.82
2008	Melaine Walker (JAM)	52.64

4 × 100-METER RELAY		SEC
1928	Canada	48.4
1932	United States	47.0
1936	United States	46.9
1948	The Netherlands	47.5
1952	United States	45.9
1956	Australia	44.5
1960	United States	44.5
1964	Poland	43.6
1968	United States	42.8
1972	West Germany	42.81
1976	East Germany	42.55
1980	East Germany	41.60
1984	United States	41.65
1988	United States	41.98
1992	United States	42.11
1996	United States	41.95
2000	The Bahamas	41.95
2004	Jamaica	41.73
2008	Russia	42.31

4 × 400-METER RELAY		MIN:SEC
1972	East Germany	3:23.0
1976	East Germany	3:19.23
1980	USSR	3:20.2
1984	United States	3:18.29
1988	USSR	3:15.18
1992	Unified Team	3:20.20
1996	United States	3:20.91
2000	winner stripped; undecided by press time	
2004	United States	3:19.01
2008	United States	3:18.54

10,000-METER WALK		MIN:SEC
1992	Chen Yueling (CHN)	44:32
1996	Yelena Nikolayeva (RUS)	41:49

Athletics (track-and-field) (women) (continued)

20,000-METER WALK		HR:MIN:SEC
2000	Wang Liping (CHN)	1:29:05
2004	Athanasia Tsoumeleka (GRE)	1:29:12
2008	Olga Kaniskina (RUS)	1:26:31

HIGH JUMP		METERS
1928	Ethel Catherwood (CAN)	1.59
1932	Jean Shiley (USA)	1.66
1936	Ibolya Csak (HUN)	1.60
1948	Alice Coachman (USA)	1.68
1952	Esther Brand (RSA)	1.67
1956	Mildred Louise McDaniel (USA)	1.76
1960	Iolanda Balas (ROM)	1.85
1964	Iolanda Balas (ROM)	1.90
1968	Miloslava Rezkova (TCH)	1.82
1972	Ulrike Meyfarth (FRG)	1.92
1976	Rosemarie Ackermann (GDR)	1.93
1980	Sara Simeoni (ITA)	1.97
1984	Ulrike Meyfarth (FRG)	2.02
1988	Louise Ritter (USA)	2.03
1992	Heike Henkel (GER)	2.02
1996	Stefka Kostadinova (BUL)	2.05
2000	Yelena Yelesina (RUS)	2.01
2004	Yelena Slesarenko (RUS)	2.06
2008	Tia Hellebaut (BEL)	2.05

POLE VAULT		METERS
2000	Stacy Dragila (USA)	4.60
2004	Yelena Isinbayeva (RUS)	4.91
2008	Yelena Isinbayeva (RUS)	5.05

LONG JUMP		METERS
1948	Olga Gyarmati (HUN)	5.69
1952	Yvette Williams (NZL)	6.24
1956	Elzbieta Krzesinska (POL)	6.35
1960	Vera Krepkina (URS)	6.37
1964	Mary Rand (GBR)	6.76
1968	Viorica Viscopoleanu (ROM)	6.82
1972	Heidemarie Rosendahl (FRG)	6.78
1976	Angela Voigt (GDR)	6.72
1980	Tatyana Kolpakova (URS)	7.06
1984	Anisoara Stanciu (ROM)	6.96
1988	Jackie Joyner-Kersee (USA)	7.40
1992	Heike Drechsler (GER)	7.14
1996	Chioma Ajunwa (NGR)	7.12
2000	Heike Drechsler (GER)	6.99
2004	Tatyana Lebedeva (RUS)	7.07
2008	Maurren Higa Maggi (BRA)	7.04

TRIPLE JUMP		METERS
1996	Inessa Kravets (UKR)	15.33
2000	Tereza Marinova (BUL)	15.20
2004	Françoise Mbango Etone (CMR)	15.30
2008	Françoise Mbango Etone (CMR)	15.39

SHOT PUT		METERS
1948	Micheline Ostermeyer (FRA)	13.75
1952	Galina Zybina (URS)	15.28
1956	Tamara Tyshkevich (URS)	16.59
1960	Tamara Press (URS)	17.32
1964	Tamara Press (URS)	18.14
1968	Margitta Gummel (GDR)	19.61
1972	Nadezhda Chizhova (URS)	21.03
1976	Ivanka Khristova (BUL)	21.16
1980	Ilona Slupianek (GDR)	22.41
1984	Claudia Losch (FRG)	20.48
1988	Natalya Lisovskaya (URS)	22.24
1992	Svetlana Krivalyova (UNT)	21.06

Summer Olympic Games Champions (continued)

Athletics (track-and-field) (women) (continued)

SHOT PUT (CONTINUED)		METERS
1996	Astrid Kumbernuss (GER)	20.56
2000	Yanina Korolchik (BLR)	20.56
2004	Yumileidi Cumba (CUB)	19.59
2008	Valerie Vili (NZL)	20.56

DISCUS THROW		METERS
1928	Halina Konopacka (POL)	39.62
1932	Lillian Copeland (USA)	40.58
1936	Gisela Mauermayer (GER)	47.63
1948	Micheline Ostermeyer (FRA)	41.92
1952	Nina Romashkova (URS)	51.42
1956	Olga Fikotova (TCH)	53.69
1960	Nina Ponomaryova-Romashkova (URS)	55.10
1964	Tamara Press (URS)	57.27
1968	Lia Manoliu (ROM)	58.28
1972	Faina Melnik (URS)	66.62
1976	Evelin Schlaak (GDR)	69.00
1980	Evelin Schlaak Jahl (GDR)	69.96
1984	Ria Stalman (NED)	65.36
1988	Martina Hellmann (GDR)	72.30
1992	Maritza Marten (CUB)	70.06
1996	Ilke Wyludda (GER)	69.66
2000	Ellina Zvereva (BLR)	68.40
2004	Natalya Sadova (RUS)	67.02
2008	Stephanie Brown Trafton (USA)	64.74

HAMMER THROW		METERS
2000	Kamila Skolimowska (POL)	71.16
2004	Olga Kuzenkova (RUS)	75.02
2008	Aksana Miankova (BLR)	76.34

JAVELIN THROW		METERS
1932	Mildred "Babe" Didrikson (USA)	43.68
1936	Tilly Fleischer (GER)	45.18
1948	Hermine Bauma (AUT)	45.57
1952	Dana Zatopkova (TCH)	50.47
1956	Inese Jaunzeme (URS)	53.86
1960	Elvira Ozolina (URS)	55.98
1964	Mihaela Penes (ROM)	60.54
1968	Angela Nemeth (HUN)	60.36
1972	Ruth Fuchs (GDR)	63.88
1976	Ruth Fuchs (GDR)	65.94
1980	María Colón (CUB)	68.40
1984	Tessa Sanderson (GBR)	69.56
1988	Petra Felke (GDR)	74.68
1992	Silke Renk (GER)	68.34
1996	Heli Rantanen (FIN)	67.94
2000	Trine Hattestad (NOR)	68.91
2004	Osleidys Menéndez (CUB)	71.53
2008	Barbora Spotakova (CZE)	71.42

PENTATHLON (HEPTATHLON FROM 1984)

1964 Irina Press (URS)
1968 Ingrid Becker (FRG)
1972 Mary Peters (GBR)
1976 Siegrun Siegl (GDR)
1980 Nadezhda Tkachenko (URS)
1984 Glynis Nunn (AUS)
1988 Jackie Joyner-Kersee (USA)
1992 Jackie Joyner-Kersee (USA)
1996 Ghada Shouaa (SYR)
2000 Denise Lewis (GBR)
2004 Carolina Klüft (SWE)
2008 Nataliya Dobrynska (UKR)

Badminton

MEN'S SINGLES

1992 Allan Budi Kusuma (INA)
1996 Poul-Erik Hoyer-Larsen (DEN)
2000 Ji Xinpeng (CHN)
2004 Taufik Hidayat (INA)
2008 Lin Dan (CHN)

MEN'S DOUBLES

1992 South Korea
1996 Indonesia
2000 Indonesia
2004 South Korea
2008 Indonesia

WOMEN'S SINGLES

1992 Susi Susanti (INA)
1996 Bang Soo-Hyun (KOR)
2000 Gong Zhichao (CHN)
2004 Zhang Ning (CHN)
2008 Zhang Ning (CHN)

WOMEN'S DOUBLES

1992 South Korea
1996 China
2000 China
2004 China
2008 China

MIXED DOUBLES

1996 South Korea
2000 China
2004 China
2008 South Korea

Baseball

1992 Cuba
1996 Cuba
2000 United States
2004 Cuba
2008 South Korea

Basketball

MEN

1936 United States
1948 United States
1952 United States
1956 United States
1960 United States
1964 United States
1968 United States
1972 USSR
1976 United States
1980 Yugoslavia
1984 United States
1988 USSR
1992 United States
1996 United States
2000 United States
2004 Argentina
2008 United States

WOMEN

1976 USSR
1980 USSR
1984 United States
1988 United States
1992 Unified Team
1996 United States

Summer Olympic Games Champions (continued)

Basketball (continued)

WOMEN (CONTINUED)

2000 United States
2004 United States
2008 United States

Boxing

48 KG (105.6 LB)

1968 Francisco Rodríguez (VEN)
1972 Gyorgy Gedo (HUN)
1976 Jorge Hernández (CUB)
1980 Shamil Sabyrov (URS)
1984 Paul Gonzales (USA)
1988 Ivailo Khristov (BUL)
1992 Rogelio Marcelo (CUB)
1996 Daniel Petrov Bojilov (BUL)
2000 Brahim Asloum (FRA)
2004 Yan Bhartelemy Varela (CUB)
2008 Zou Shiming (CHN)

51 KG (112 LB)

1904 George Finnegan (USA)
1920 Frank di Genaro (USA)
1924 Fidel La Barba (USA)
1928 Antal Kocsis (HUN)
1932 Istvan Enekes (HUN)
1936 Willi Kaiser (GER)
1948 Pascual Pérez (ARG)
1952 Nate Brooks (USA)
1956 Terence Spinks (GBR)
1960 Gyula Torok (HUN)
1964 Fernando Atzori (ITA)
1968 Ricardo Delgado (MEX)
1972 Georgi Kostadinov (BUL)
1976 Leo Randolph (USA)
1980 Petar Lesov (BUL)
1984 Steven McCrory (USA)
1988 Kim Kwang Sun (KOR)
1992 Chol Choi Su (PRK)
1996 Maikro Romero (CUB)
2000 Wijan Ponlid (THA)
2004 Yuriorkis Gamboa Toledano (CUB)
2008 Somjit Jongjohor (THA)

54 KG (118.8 LB)

1904 Oliver Kirk (USA)
1908 Henry Thomas (GBR)
1920 Clarence Walker (RSA)
1924 William Smith (RSA)
1928 Vittorio Tamagnini (ITA)
1932 Horace Gwynne (CAN)
1936 Ulderico Sergo (ITA)
1948 Tibor Csik (HUN)
1952 Pentti Hämäläinen (FIN)
1956 Wolfgang Behrendt (GER)
1960 Oleg Grigoryev (URS)
1964 Takao Sakurai (JPN)
1968 Valery Sokolov (URS)
1972 Orlando Martínez (CUB)
1976 Gu Yong Jo (PRK)
1980 Juan Hernández (CUB)
1984 Maurizio Stecca (ITA)
1988 Kennedy McKinney (USA)
1992 Joel Casamayor (CUB)
1996 Istvan Kovacs (HUN)
2000 Guillermo Rigondeaux Ortiz (CUB)
2004 Guillermo Rigondeaux Ortiz (CUB)
2008 Badar-Uugan Enkhbat (MGL)

Boxing (continued)

57 KG (125.4 LB)

1904 Oliver Kirk (USA)
1908 Richard Gunn (GBR)
1920 Paul Fritsch (FRA)
1924 John Fields (USA)
1928 Lambertus van Kleveren (NED)
1932 Carmelo Robledo (ARG)
1936 Oscar Casanovas (ARG)
1948 Ernesto Formenti (ITA)
1952 Jan Zachara (TCH)
1956 Vladimir Safronov (URS)
1960 Francesco Musso (ITA)
1964 Stanislav Stepashkin (URS)
1968 Antonio Roldan (MEX)
1972 Boris Kuznetsov (URS)
1976 Angel Herrera (CUB)
1980 Rudi Fink (GDR)
1984 Meldrick Taylor (USA)
1988 Giovanni Parisi (ITA)
1992 Andreas Tews (GER)
1996 Somluck Kamsing (THA)
2000 Bekzat Sattarkhanov (KAZ)
2004 Aleksey Tishchenko (RUS)
2008 Vasyl Lomachenko (UKR)

60 KG (132 LB)

1904 Harry Spanger (USA)
1908 Frederick Grace (GBR)
1920 Samuel Mosberg (USA)
1924 Hans Nielsen (DEN)
1928 Carlo Orlandi (ITA)
1932 Lawrence Stevens (RSA)
1936 Imre Harangi (HUN)
1948 Gerald Dreyer (RSA)
1952 Aureliano Bolognesi (ITA)
1956 Richard McTaggart (GBR)
1960 Kazimierz Pazdzior (POL)
1964 Jozef Grudzien (POL)
1968 Ronnie Harris (USA)
1972 Jan Szczepanski (POL)
1976 Howard Davis (USA)
1980 Angel Herrera (CUB)
1984 Pernell Whitaker (USA)
1988 Andreas Zuelow (GDR)
1992 Oscar De La Hoya (USA)
1996 Hocine Soltani (ALG)
2000 Mario Kindelan (CUB)
2004 Mario César Kindelan Mesa (CUB)
2008 Aleksey Tishchenko (RUS)

64 KG (140.8 LB)

1952 Charles Adkins (USA)
1956 Vladimir Engibaryan (URS)
1960 Bohumil Nemecek (TCH)
1964 Jerzy Kulej (POL)
1968 Jerzy Kulej (POL)
1972 Ray Seales (USA)
1976 Ray Leonard (USA)
1980 Patrizio Oliva (ITA)
1984 Jerry Page (USA)
1988 Vyacheslav Yanovsky (URS)
1992 Héctor Vinent (CUB)
1996 Héctor Vinent (CUB)
2000 Mahamadkadyz Abdullayev (UZB)
2004 Manus Boonjumnong (THA)
2008 Félix Díaz (DOM)

Summer Olympic Games Champions (continued)

Boxing (continued)

69 KG (151.8 LB)
1904 Albert Young (USA)
1920 Julius Schneider (CAN)
1924 Jean Delarge (BEL)
1928 Edward Morgan (NZL)
1932 Edward Flynn (USA)
1936 Sten Suvio (FIN)
1948 Julius Torma (TCH)
1952 Zygmunt Chychla (POL)
1956 Nicolae Linca (ROM)
1960 Giovanni Benvenuti (ITA)
1964 Marian Kasprzyk (POL)
1968 Manfred Wolke (GDR)
1972 Emilio Correa (CUB)
1976 Jochen Bachfeld (GDR)
1980 Andres Aldama (CUB)
1984 Mark Breland (USA)
1988 Robert Wangila (KEN)
1992 Michael Carruth (IRL)
1996 Oleg Saytov (RUS)
2000 Oleg Saytov (RUS)
2004 Bakhtiyar Artayev (KAZ)
2008 Bakhyt Sarsekbayev (KAZ)

71 KG (156.2 LB)
1952 Laszlo Papp (HUN)
1956 Laszlo Papp (HUN)
1960 Wilbert McClure (USA)
1964 Boris Lagutin (URS)
1968 Boris Lagutin (URS)
1972 Dieter Kottysch (FRG)
1976 Jerzy Rybicki (POL)
1980 Armando Martínez (CUB)
1984 Frank Tate (USA)
1988 Park Si Hun (KOR)
1992 Juan Lemus (CUB)
1996 David Reid (USA)
2000 Yermakhan Ibraimov (KAZ)

75 KG (165 LB)
1904 Charles Mayer (USA)
1908 John Douglas (GBR)
1920 Harry Mallin (GBR)
1924 Harry Mallin (GBR)
1928 Piero Toscani (ITA)
1932 Carmen Barth (USA)
1936 Jean Despeaux (FRA)
1948 Laszlo Papp (HUN)
1952 Floyd Patterson (USA)
1956 Gennady Shatkov (URS)
1960 Edward Crook (USA)
1964 Valery Popenchenko (URS)
1968 Christopher Finnegan (GBR)
1972 Vyatcheslav Lemeshev (URS)
1976 Michael Spinks (USA)
1980 Jose Gómez (CUB)
1984 Shin Joon Sup (KOR)
1988 Henry Maske (GDR)
1992 Ariel Hernández (CUB)
1996 Ariel Hernández (CUB)
2000 Jorge Gutiérrez (CUB)
2004 Gaydarbek Gaydarbekov (RUS)
2008 James Degale (GBR)

81 KG (178.2 LB)
1920 Edward Eagan (USA)
1924 Harry Mitchell (GBR)
1928 Viktor Avendano (ARG)

Boxing (continued)

81 KG (178.2 LB) (CONTINUED)
1932 David Carstens (RSA)
1936 Roger Michelot (FRA)
1948 George Hunter (RSA)
1952 Norvel Lee (USA)
1956 James Boyd (USA)
1960 Cassius Clay (USA)
1964 Cosimo Pinto (ITA)
1968 Dan Poznyak (URS)
1972 Mate Parlov (YUG)
1976 Leon Spinks (USA)
1980 Slobodan Kacar (YUG)
1984 Anton Josipovic (YUG)
1988 Andrew Maynard (USA)
1992 Torsten May (GER)
1996 Vasily Zhirov (KAZ)
2000 Aleksandr Lebzyak (RUS)
2004 Andre Ward (USA)
2008 Zhang Xiaoping (CHN)

OVER 81 KG (178.2 LB) (91 KG; 200.2 LB FROM 1984)
1904 Samuel Berger (USA)
1908 Albert Oldman (GBR)
1920 Ronald Rawson (GBR)
1924 Otto Von Porat (NOR)
1928 Arturo Rodriguez (ARG)
1932 Alberto Santiago Lovell (ARG)
1936 Herbert Runge (GER)
1948 Rafael Iglesias (ARG)
1952 Edward Sanders (USA)
1956 Peter Rademacher (USA)
1960 Franco de Piccoli (ITA)
1964 Joseph Frazier (USA)
1968 George Foreman (USA)
1972 Teofilo Stevenson (CUB)
1976 Teofilo Stevenson (CUB)
1980 Teofilo Stevenson (CUB)
1984 Henry Tillman (USA)
1988 Ray Mercer (USA)
1992 Félix Savon (CUB)
1996 Félix Savon (CUB)
2000 Félix Savon (CUB)
2004 Odlanier Solis Fonte (CUB)
2008 Rakhim Chakhkiyev (RUS)

OVER 91 KG (200.2 LB)
1984 Tyrell Biggs (USA)
1988 Lennox Lewis (CAN)
1992 Roberto Balado (CUB)
1996 Vladimir Klichko (UKR)
2000 Audley Harrison (GBR)
2004 Aleksandr Povetkin (RUS)
2008 Roberto Cammarelle (ITA)

Canoeing (men)

KAYAK SINGLES (500 METERS)		MIN:SEC
1976	Vasile Diba (ROM)	1:46.41
1980	Vladimir Parfenovich (URS)	1:43.43
1984	Ian Ferguson (NZL)	1:47.84
1988	Zsolt Gyulay (HUN)	1:44.82
1992	Mikko Kolehmainen (FIN)	1:40.34
1996	Antonio Rossi (ITA)	1:37.423
2000	Knut Holmann (NOR)	1:57.84
2004	Adam van Koeverden (CAN)	1:37.919
2008	Ken Wallace (AUS)	1:37.252

Summer Olympic Games Champions (continued)

Canoeing (men) (continued)

KAYAK PAIRS (500 METERS)		MIN:SEC
1976	East Germany	1:35.87
1980	USSR	1:32.38
1984	New Zealand	1:34.21
1988	New Zealand	1:33.98
1992	Germany	1:29.84
1996	Germany	1:28.697
2000	Hungary	1:47.050
2004	Germany	1:27.040
2008	Spain	1:28.736

KAYAK SINGLES (1,000 METERS)		MIN:SEC
1936	Gregor Hradetzky (AUT)	4:22.90
1948	Gert Fredriksson (SWE)	4:33.20
1952	Gert Fredriksson (SWE)	4:07.90
1956	Gert Fredriksson (SWE)	4:12.80
1960	Erik Hansen (DEN)	3:53.00
1964	Rolf Peterson (SWE)	3:57.13
1968	Mihaly Hesz (HUN)	4:03.58
1972	Aleksandr Shaparenko (URS)	3:48.06
1976	Rüdiger Helm (GDR)	3:48.20
1980	Rüdiger Helm (GDR)	3:48.77
1984	Alan Thompson (NZL)	3:45.73
1988	Gregory Barton (USA)	3:55.27
1992	Clint Robinson (AUS)	3:37.26
1996	Knut Holmann (NOR)	3:25.785
2000	Knut Holmann (NOR)	3:33.26
2004	Eirik Veraas Larsen (NOR)	3:25.897
2008	Tim Brabants (GBR)	3:26.323

KAYAK PAIRS (1,000 METERS)		MIN:SEC
1936	Austria	4:03.80
1948	Sweden	4:07.30
1952	Finland	3:51.10
1956	Germany	3:49.60
1960	Sweden	3:34.70
1964	Sweden	3:38.54
1968	USSR	3:37.54
1972	USSR	3:31.23
1976	USSR	3:29.01
1980	USSR	3:26.72
1984	Canada	3:24.22
1988	United States	3:32.42
1992	Germany	3:16.10
1996	Italy	3:09.190
2000	Italy	3:14.46
2004	Sweden	3:18.420
2008	Germany	3:11.809

KAYAK FOURS (1,000 METERS)		MIN:SEC
1964	USSR	3:14.67
1968	Norway	3:14.38
1972	USSR	3:14.02
1976	USSR	3:08.69
1980	East Germany	3:13.76
1984	New Zealand	3:02.28
1988	Hungary	3:00.20
1992	Germany	2:54.18
1996	Germany	2:51.528
2000	Hungary	2:55.18
2004	Hungary	2:56.919
2008	Belarus	2:55.714

KAYAK SINGLES (10,000 METERS)		MIN:SEC
1936	Ernst Krebs (GER)	46:01.6
1948	Gert Fredriksson (SWE)	50:47.7
1952	Thorvald Strömberg (FIN)	47:22.8
1956	Gert Fredriksson (SWE)	47:43.4

Canoeing (men) (continued)

KAYAK PAIRS (10,000 METERS)		MIN:SEC
1936	Germany	41:45
1948	Sweden	46:09.4
1952	Finland	44:21.3
1956	Hungary	43:37

COLLAPSIBLE KAYAK SINGLES (10,000 METERS)		MIN:SEC
1936	Gregor Hradetzky (AUT)	50:01.2

COLLAPSIBLE KAYAK PAIRS (10,000 METERS)		MIN:SEC
1936	Sweden	45:48.9

KAYAK SINGLES RELAY (1,500 METERS)		MIN:SEC
1960	Germany	7:39.43

SLALOM KAYAK SINGLES	
1972	Siegbert Horn (GDR)
1992	Pierpaolo Ferrazzi (ITA)
1996	Oliver Fix (GER)
2000	Thomas Schmidt (GER)
2004	Benoit Peschier (FRA)
2008	Alexander Grimm (GER)

CANADIAN SINGLES (500 METERS)		MIN:SEC
1976	Aleksandr Rogov (URS)	1:59.23
1980	Sergey Postrekin (URS)	1:53.37
1984	Larry Cain (CAN)	1:57.01
1988	Olaf Heukrodt (GDR)	1:56.42
1992	Nikolay Bukhalov (BUL)	1:51.15
1996	Martin Doktor (CZE)	1:49.934
2000	Gyorgy Kolonics (HUN)	2:24.81
2004	Andreas Dittmer (GER)	1:46.383
2008	Maksim Opalev (RUS)	1:47.140

CANADIAN PAIRS (500 METERS)		MIN:SEC
1976	USSR	1:45.81
1980	Hungary	1:43.39
1984	Yugoslavia	1:43.67
1988	USSR	1:41.77
1992	Unified Team	1:41.54
1996	Hungary	1:40.420
2000	Hungary	1:51.28
2004	China	1:40.278
2008	China	1:41.025

CANADIAN SINGLES (1,000 METERS)		MIN:SEC
1936	Francis Amyot (CAN)	5:32.10
1948	Josef Holecek (TCH)	5:42.00
1952	Josef Holecek (TCH)	4:56.30
1956	Leon Rottman (ROM)	5:05.30
1960	Janos Parti (HUN)	4:33.03
1964	Jürgen Eschert (GER)	4:35.14
1968	Tibor Tatai (HUN)	4:36.14
1972	Ivan Patzaichin (ROM)	4:08.94
1976	Matija Ljubek (YUG)	4:09.51
1980	Lyubomir Lyubenov (BUL)	4:12.38
1984	Ulrich Eicke (FRG)	4:06.32
1988	Ivans Klementyev (URS)	4:12.78
1992	Nikolay Bukhalov (BUL)	4:05.92
1996	Martin Doktor (CZE)	3:54.418
2000	Andreas Dittmer (GER)	3:54.37
2004	David Cal (ESP)	3:46.201
2008	Attila Sándor Vajda (HUN)	3:50.467

CANADIAN PAIRS (1,000 METERS)		MIN:SEC
1936	Czechoslovakia	4:50.10
1948	Czechoslovakia	5:07.10
1952	Denmark	4:38.30

Summer Olympic Games Champions (continued)

Canoeing (men) (continued)

CANADIAN PAIRS (1,000 METERS) (CONTINUED)

		MIN:SEC
1956	Romania	4:47.40
1960	USSR	4:17.04
1964	USSR	4:04.65
1968	Romania	4:07.18
1972	USSR	3:52.60
1976	USSR	3:52.76
1980	Romania	3:47.65
1984	Romania	3:40.60
1988	USSR	3:48.36
1992	Germany	3:37.42
1996	Germany	3:31.870
2000	Romania	3:37.35
2004	Germany	3:41.802
2008	Belarus	3:36.365

CANADIAN SINGLES (10,000 METERS)

		MIN:SEC
1948	Frantisek Capek (TCH)	62:05.2
1952	Frank Havens (USA)	57:41.1
1956	Leon Rottman (ROM)	56:41.0

CANADIAN PAIRS (10,000 METERS)

		MIN:SEC
1936	Czechoslovakia	50:35.5
1948	United States	55:55.4
1952	France	54:08.3
1956	USSR	54:02.4

SLALOM CANADIAN SINGLES

1972	Reinhard Eiben (GDR)
1992	Lukas Pollert (TCH)
1996	Michal Martikan (SVK)
2000	Tony Estanguet (FRA)
2004	Tony Estanguet (FRA)
2008	Michal Martikan (SVK)

SLALOM CANADIAN PAIRS

1972	East Germany
1992	United States
1996	France
2000	Slovakia
2004	Slovakia
2008	Slovakia

Canoeing (women)

KAYAK SINGLES (500 METERS)

		MIN:SEC
1948	Karen Hoff (DEN)	2:31.90
1952	Sylvi Saimo (FIN)	2:18.40
1956	Yelizaveta Dementyeva (URS)	2:18.90
1960	Antonina Seredina (URS)	2:08.08
1964	Lyudmila Khvedosyuk (URS)	2:12.87
1968	Lyudmila Pinayeva-Khvedosyuk (URS)	2:11.09
1972	Yuliya Ryabchinskaya (URS)	2:03.17
1976	Carola Zirzow (GDR)	2:01.05
1980	Birgit Fischer (GDR)	1:57.96
1984	Agneta Andersson (SWE)	1:58.72
1988	Vanya Gecheva (BUL)	1:55.19
1992	Birgit Fischer Schmidt (GER)	1:51.60
1996	Rita Koban (HUN)	1:47.655
2000	Josefa Idem Guerrini (ITA)	2:13.84
2004	Natasa Janics (HUN)	1:47.741
2008	Inna Osypenko-Radomska (UKR)	1:50.673

KAYAK PAIRS (500 METERS)

		MIN:SEC
1960	USSR	1:54.76
1964	Germany	1:56.95
1968	West Germany	1:56.44
1972	USSR	1:53.50
1976	USSR	1:51.15

Canoeing (women) (continued)

KAYAK PAIRS (500 METERS) (CONTINUED)

		MIN:SEC
1980	East Germany	1:43.88
1984	Sweden	1:45.25
1988	East Germany	1:43.46
1992	Germany	1:40.29
1996	Sweden	1:39.329
2000	Germany	1:56.99
2004	Hungary	1:38.101
2008	Hungary	1:41.308

KAYAK FOURS (500 METERS)

		MIN:SEC
1984	Romania	1:38.34
1988	East Germany	1:40.78
1992	Hungary	1:38.32
1996	Germany	1:31.077
2000	Germany	1:34.53
2004	Germany	1:34.340
2008	Germany	1:32.231

SLALOM KAYAK SINGLES

1972	Angelika Bahmann (GDR)
1992	Elisabeth Micheler (GER)
1996	Stepanka Hilgertova (CZE)
2000	Stepanka Hilgertova (CZE)
2004	Elena Kaliska (SVK)
2008	Elena Kaliska (SVK)

Cricket

1900 Great Britain

Croquet

SINGLES (ONE BALL)

1900 Aumoitte (FRA)

SINGLES (TWO BALLS)

1900 Waydelick (FRA)

DOUBLES

1900 France

Cycling (men)

INDIVIDUAL SPRINT

1896[6]	Paul Masson (FRA)
1900[6]	Georges Taillandier (FRA)
1920	Mauritius Peeters (NED)
1924	Lucien Michard (FRA)
1928	Roger Beaufrand (FRA)
1932	Jacobus Van Egmond (NED)
1936	Toni Merkens (GER)
1948	Mario Ghella (ITA)
1952	Enzo Sacchi (ITA)
1956	Michel Rousseau (FRA)
1960	Sante Gaiardoni (ITA)
1964	Giovanni Pettenella (ITA)
1968	Daniel Morelon (FRA)
1972	Daniel Morelon (FRA)
1976	Anton Tkac (TCH)
1980	Lutz Hesslich (GDR)
1984	Mark Gorski (USA)
1988	Lutz Hesslich (GDR)
1992	Jens Fiedler (GER)
1996	Jens Fiedler (GER)
2000	Marty Nothstein (USA)
2004	Ryan Bayley (AUS)
2008	Chris Hoy (GBR)

Summer Olympic Games Champions (continued)

Cycling (men) (continued)

1,000-METER TIME TRIAL		MIN:SEC
1896[7]	Paul Masson (FRA)	24.0
1928	Willy Falck-Hansen (DEN)	1:14.4
1932	Edgar Gray (AUS)	1:13.0
1936	Arie van Vliet (NED)	1:12.0
1948	Jacques Dupont (FRA)	1:13.5
1952	Russell Mockridge (AUS)	1:11.1
1956	Leandro Faggin (ITA)	1:09.8
1960	Sante Gaiardoni (ITA)	1:07.27
1964	Patrick Sercu (BEL)	1:09.59
1968	Pierre Trentin (FRA)	1:03.91
1972	Niels Fredborg (DEN)	1:06.44
1976	Klaus-Jürgen Grünke (GDR)	1:05.927
1980	Lothar Thoms (GDR)	1:02.955
1984	Fredy Schmidtke (FRG)	1:06.104
1988	Aleksandr Kirichenko (URS)	1:04.499
1992	José Moreno (ESP)	1:03.342
1996	Florian Rousseau (FRA)	1:02.712
2000	Jason Queally (GBR)	1:01.609
2004	Chris Hoy (GBR)	1:00.711

1,500-METER TEAM PURSUIT
1900 United States

2,000 METERS
1904 Marcus Hurley (USA)

2,000-METER TANDEM
1908 France
1920 Great Britain
1924 France
1928 The Netherlands
1932 France
1936 Germany
1948 Italy
1952 Australia
1956 Australia
1960 Italy
1964 Italy
1968 France
1972 USSR

INDIVIDUAL PURSUIT
1964 Jiri Daler (TCH)
1968 Daniel Rebillard (FRA)
1972 Knut Knudsen (NOR)
1976 Gregor Braun (FRG)
1980 Robert Dill-Bondi (SUI)
1984 Steve Hegg (USA)
1988 Gintautas Umaras (URS)
1992 Christopher Boardman (GBR)
1996 Andrea Collinelli (ITA)
2000 Robert Bartko (GER)
2004 Bradley Wiggins (GBR)
2008 Bradley Wiggins (GBR)

TEAM PURSUIT
1908 Great Britain
1920 Italy
1924 Italy
1928 Italy
1932 Italy
1936 France
1948 France
1952 Italy
1956 Italy
1960 Italy
1964 Germany

Cycling (men) (continued)

TEAM PURSUIT (CONTINUED)
1968 Denmark
1972 West Germany
1976 West Germany
1980 USSR
1984 Australia
1988 USSR
1992 Germany
1996 France
2000 Germany
2004 Australia
2008 Great Britain

5,000 METERS		MIN:SEC
1908	Benjamin Jones (GBR)	8:36.2

10,000 METERS		MIN:SEC
1896	Paul Masson (FRA)	17:54.2

20,000 METERS		MIN:SEC
1908	Charles Kingsbury (GBR)	34:13.6

50,000 METERS		HR:MIN:SEC
1920	Henry George (BEL)	1:16:43.2
1924	Jacobus Willems (NED)	1:18:24.0

100,000 METERS		HR:MIN:SEC
1896	Léon Flameng (FRA)	3:08:19.2
1908	Charles Bartlett (GBR)	2:41:48.6

ONE-QUARTER MILE (440 YARDS)		SEC
1904	Marcus Hurley (USA)	31.8

ONE-THIRD MILE (586⅔ YARDS)		SEC
1904	Marcus Hurley (USA)	43.8

ONE-LAP TIME TRIAL (660 YARDS)		SEC
1908	Victor Johnson (GBR)	51.2

ONE-HALF MILE (880 YARDS)		MIN:SEC
1904	Marcus Hurley (USA)	1:09.0

1 MILE		MIN:SEC
1904	Marcus Hurley (USA)	2:41.6

1 MILE 1 FURLONG (1,980 YARDS) TEAM PURSUIT
1908 Great Britain

2 MILES		MIN:SEC
1904	Burton Downing (USA)	4:58.0

5 MILES		MIN:SEC
1904	Charles Schlee (USA)	13:08.2

25 MILES
1904 Burton Downing (USA)

12 HOURS
1896 Adolf Schmal (AUT)

INDIVIDUAL POINTS RACE
1984 Roger Ilegems (BEL)
1988 Dan Frost (DEN)
1992 Giovanni Lombardi (ITA)
1996 Silvio Martinello (ITA)
2000 Juan Llaneras (ESP)
2004 Mikhail Ignatyev (RUS)
2008 Joan Llaneras (ESP)

Summer Olympic Games Champions (continued)

Cycling (men) (continued)

KEIRIN		SEC
2000	Florian Rousseau (FRA)	11.020
2004	Ryan Bayley (AUS)	10.601
2008	Chris Hoy (GBR)	10.450

MADISON	
2000	Australia
2004	Australia
2008	Argentina

TEAM SPRINT		SEC
2000	France	44.233
2004	Germany	43.980
2008	Great Britain	43.128

ROAD RACE (INDIVIDUAL)[8]		HR:MIN:SEC
1896	Aristidis Konstantinidis (GRE)	3:22:31.0
1912	Rudolph Lewis (RSA)	10:42:39.0
1920	Harry Stenqvist (SWE)	4:40:01.8
1924	Armand Blanchonnet (FRA)	6:20:48.0
1928	Henry Hansen (DEN)	4:47:18.0
1932	Attilio Pavesi (ITA)	2:28:05.6
1936	Robert Charpentier (FRA)	2:33:05.0
1948	Jose Beyaert (FRA)	5:18:12.6
1952	Andre Noyelle (BEL)	5:06:03.4
1956	Ercole Baldini (ITA)	5:21:17.0
1960	Viktor Kapitonov (URS)	4:20:37.0
1964	Mario Zanin (ITA)	4:39:51.63
1968	Pierfranco Vianelli (ITA)	4:41:25.24
1972	Hennie Kuiper (NED)	4:14:37.0
1976	Bernt Johansson (SWE)	4:46:52.0
1980	Sergey Sukhoruchenkov (URS)	4:48:28.90
1984	Alexei Grewal (USA)	4:59:57.0
1988	Olaf Ludwig (GDR)	4:32:22.0
1992	Fabio Casartelli (ITA)	4:35:21.0
1996	Pascal Richard (SUI)	4:53:56.0
2000	Jan Ullrich (GER)	5:29:08.0
2004	Paolo Bettini (ITA)	5:41:44.0
2008	Samuel Sánchez (ESP)	6:23:49.0

ROAD RACE (TEAM)		HR:MIN:SEC
1912	Sweden	44:35:33.6
1920	France	19:16:43.2
1924	France	19:30:14
1928	Denmark	15:09:14
1932	Italy	7:27:15.2
1936	France	7:39:16.2
1948	Belgium	15:58:17.4
1952	Belgium	15:20:46.6
1956	France	5:21:17

ROAD TIME TRIAL (INDIVIDUAL)		HR:MIN:SEC
1996	Miguel Indurain (ESP)	1:04:05
2000	Vyacheslav Yekimov (RUS)	57:40.42
2004	Tyler Hamilton (USA)	57.31.74
2008	Fabian Cancellara (SUI)	1:02:11.43

ROAD TIME TRIAL (TEAM)		HR:MIN:SEC
1960	Italy	2:14:33.53
1964	The Netherlands	2:26:31.19
1968	The Netherlands	2:07:49.06
1972	USSR	2:11:17.8
1976	USSR	2:08:53
1980	USSR	2:01:21.7
1984	Italy	1:58:28
1988	East Germany	1:57:47.7
1992	Germany	2:01:39

Cycling (men) (continued)

MOUNTAIN BIKE		HR:MIN:SEC
1996	Bart Jan Brentjens (NED)	2:17:38
2000	Miguel Martinez (FRA)	2:09:2.50
2004	Julien Absalon (FRA)	2:15:02
2008	Julien Absalon (FRA)	1:55:59

MOTOCROSS/BMX		MIN:SEC
2008	Maris Strombergs (LAT)	36.190

Cycling (women)

500-METER TIME TRIAL		SEC
2000	Felicia Ballanger (FRA)	34.140
2004	Anna Meares (AUS)	53.016

INDIVIDUAL SPRINT	
1988	Erika Salumae (URS)
1992	Erika Salumae (EST)
1996	Felicia Ballanger (FRA)
2000	Felicia Ballanger (FRA)
2004	Lori-Ann Muenzer (CAN)
2008	Victoria Pendleton (GBR)

INDIVIDUAL PURSUIT	
1992	Petra Rossner (GER)
1996	Antonella Bellutti (ITA)
2000	Leontien Zijlaard-van Moorsel (NED)
2004	Sarah Ulmer (NZL)
2008	Rebecca Romero (GBR)

INDIVIDUAL POINTS RACE	
1996	Nathalie Lancien (FRA)
2000	Antonella Bellutti (ITA)
2004	Olga Slyusareva (RUS)
2008	Marianne Vos (NED)

ROAD RACE (INDIVIDUAL)		HR:MIN:SEC
1984	Connie Carpenter-Phinney (USA)	2:11:14.0
1988	Monique Knol (NED)	2:00:52.0
1992	Kathryn Watt (AUS)	2:04:42.0
1996	Jeannie Longo-Ciprelli (FRA)	2:36:13.0
2000	Leontien Zijlaard-van Moorsel (NED)	3:06:31
2004	Sara Carrigan (AUS)	3:24:24
2008	Nicole Cooke (GBR)	3:32:24

ROAD TIME TRIAL (INDIVIDUAL)		MIN:SEC
1996	Zulfiya Zabirova (RUS)	36:40
2000	Leontien Zijlaard-van Moorsel (NED)	42:00.781
2004	Leontien Zijlaard-van Moorsel (NED)	31:11.53
2008	Kristin Armstrong (USA)	34:51.72

MOUNTAIN BIKE		HR:MIN:SEC
1996	Paola Pezzo (ITA)	1:50:51
2000	Paola Pezzo (ITA)	1:49:24.38
2004	Gunn-Rita Dahle (NOR)	1:56:51
2008	Sabine Spitz (GER)	1:45:11

MOTOCROSS/BMX		MIN:SEC
2008	Anne-Caroline Chausson (FRA)	35.976

Diving (men)

3-METER SPRINGBOARD DIVING	
1908	Albert Zürner (GER)
1912	Paul Günther (GER)
1920	Louis Kuehn (USA)
1924	Albert White (USA)

Summer Olympic Games Champions (continued)

Diving (men) (continued)

3-METER SPRINGBOARD DIVING (CONTINUED)

1928 Peter Desjardins (USA)
1932 Michael Galitzen (USA)
1936 Richard Degener (USA)
1948 Bruce Harlan (USA)
1952 David Browning (USA)
1956 Robert Clotworthy (USA)
1960 Gary Tobian (USA)
1964 Kenneth Sitzberger (USA)
1968 Bernie Wrightson (USA)
1972 Vladimir Vasin (URS)
1976 Philip Boggs (USA)
1980 Aleksandr Portnov (URS)
1984 Gregory Louganis (USA)
1988 Gregory Louganis (USA)
1992 Mark Edward Lenzi (USA)
1996 Xiong Ni (CHN)
2000 Xiong Ni (CHN)
2004 Peng Bo (CHN)
2008 He Chong (CHN)

10-METER PLATFORM (HIGH) DIVING

1904 George Sheldon (USA)
1908 Hjalmar Johansson (SWE)
1912 Erik Adlerz (SWE)
1920 Clarence Pinkston (USA)
1924 Albert White (USA)
1928 Peter Desjardins (USA)
1932 Harold Smith (USA)
1936 Marshall Wayne (USA)
1948 Samuel Lee (USA)
1952 Samuel Lee (USA)
1956 Joaquin Capilla Perez (MEX)
1960 Robert Webster (USA)
1964 Robert Webster (USA)
1968 Klaus DiBiasi (ITA)
1972 Klaus DiBiasi (ITA)
1976 Klaus DiBiasi (ITA)
1980 Falk Hoffman (GDR)
1984 Gregory Louganis (USA)
1988 Gregory Louganis (USA)
1992 Sun Shuwei (CHN)
1996 Dmitry Sautin (RUS)
2000 Tian Liang (CHN)
2004 Hu Jia (CHN)
2008 Matt Mitcham (AUS)

3-METER SYNCHRONIZED SPRINGBOARD DIVING

2000 China
2004 Greece
2008 China

10-METER SYNCHRONIZED PLATFORM (HIGH) DIVING

2000 Russia
2004 China
2008 China

PLUNGE FOR DISTANCE

1904 William Paul Dickey (USA)

PLAIN HIGH DIVING

1912 Erik Adlerz (SWE)
1920 Arvid Wallman (SWE)
1924 Richmond Eve (AUS)

Diving (women)

3-METER SPRINGBOARD DIVING

1920 Aileen Riggin (USA)
1924 Elizabeth Becker-Pinkton (USA)
1928 Helen Meany (USA)
1932 Georgia Coleman (USA)
1936 Marjorie Gestring (USA)
1948 Victoria Draves (USA)
1952 Patricia McCormick (USA)
1956 Patricia McCormick (USA)
1960 Ingrid Krämer-Engel-Gulbin (GER)
1964 Ingrid Krämer-Engel-Gulbin (GER)
1968 Sue Gossick (USA)
1972 Micki King (USA)
1976 Jennifer Chandler (USA)
1980 Irina Kalinina (URS)
1984 Sylvie Bernier (CAN)
1988 Gao Min (CHN)
1992 Gao Min (CHN)
1996 Fu Mingxia (CHN)
2000 Fu Mingxia (CHN)
2004 Guo Jingjing (CHN)
2008 Guo Jingjing (CHN)

10-METER PLATFORM (HIGH) DIVING

1912 Greta Johansson (SWE)
1920 Stefani Fryland Clausen (DEN)
1924 Caroline Smith (USA)
1928 Elizabeth Anna Becker-Pinkston (USA)
1932 Dorothy Poynton (USA)
1936 Dorothy Poynton-Hill (USA)
1948 Victoria Draves (USA)
1952 Patricia McCormick (USA)
1956 Patricia McCormick (USA)
1960 Ingrid Krämer-Engel-Gulbin (GER)
1964 Lesley Leigh Bush (USA)
1968 Milena Duchkova (TCH)
1972 Ulrika Knape (SWE)
1976 Yelena Vaytsekhovskaya (URS)
1980 Martina Jäschke (GDR)
1984 Zhou Ji-Hong (CHN)
1988 Xu Yan-Mei (CHN)
1992 Fu Mingxia (CHN)
1996 Fu Mingxia (CHN)
2000 Laura Wilkinson (USA)
2004 Chantelle Newbery (AUS)
2008 Chen Ruolin (CHN)

3-METER SYNCHRONIZED SPRINGBOARD DIVING

2000 Russia
2004 China
2008 China

10-METER SYNCHRONIZED PLATFORM (HIGH) DIVING

2000 China
2004 China
2008 China

Equestrian sports

GRAND PRIX (DRESSAGE) INDIVIDUAL		MOUNT
1912	Carl Bonde (SWE)	Emperor
1920	Janne Lundblad (SWE)	Uno
1924	Ernst Linder (SWE)	Piccolomini
1928	Carl Friedrich Freiherr von Langen-Parow (GER)	Draufgänger
1932	Xavier Lesage (FRA)	Taine
1936	Heinz Pollay (GER)	Kronos
1948	Hans Moser (SUI)	Hummer
1952	Henri St. Cyr (SWE)	Master Rufus

Summer Olympic Games Champions (continued)

Equestrian sports (continued)

GRAND PRIX (DRESSAGE) INDIVIDUAL (CONTINUED)

		MOUNT
1956	Henri St. Cyr (SWE)	Juli
1960	Sergey Filatov (URS)	Absent
1964	Henri Chammartin (SUI)	Woermann
1968	Ivan Kizimov (URS)	Ikhor
1972	Liselott Linsenhoff (FRG)	Piaff
1976	Christine Stückelberger (SUI)	Granat
1980	Elisabeth Theurer (AUT)	Mon Cherie
1984	Reiner Klimke (FRG)	Ahlerich
1988	Nicole Uphoff (FRG)	Rembrandt 24
1992	Nicole Uphoff (GER)	Rembrandt 24
1996	Isabell Werth (GER)	Gigolo
2000	Anky van Grunsven (NED)	Bonfire
2004	Anky van Grunsven (NED)	Salinero
2008	Anky van Grunsven (NED)	Keltec Salinero

GRAND PRIX (DRESSAGE) TEAM

1928	Germany
1932	France
1936	Germany
1948	France
1952	Sweden
1956	Sweden
1964	Germany
1968	West Germany
1972	USSR
1976	West Germany
1980	USSR
1984	West Germany
1988	West Germany
1992	Germany
1996	Germany
2000	Germany
2004	Germany
2008	Germany

GRAND PRIX (JUMPING) INDIVIDUAL

		MOUNT
1900	Aimé Haegeman (BEL)	Benton II
1912	Jean Cariou (FRA)	Mignon
1920	Tommaso Lequio di Assaba (ITA)	Trebecco
1924	Alphonse Gemuseus (SUI)	Lucette
1928	Frantisek Ventura (TCH)	Eliot
1932	Takeichi Nishi (JPN)	Uranus
1936	Kurt Hasse (GER)	Tora
1948	Humberto Mariles Cortés (MEX)	Arete
1952	Pierre Jonquères d'Oriola (FRA)	Ali Baba
1956	Hans-Günter Winkler (GER)	Halla
1960	Raimondo d'Inzeo (ITA)	Posillipo
1964	Pierre Jonquères d'Oriola (FRA)	Lutteur
1968	William Steinkraus (USA)	Snowbound
1972	Graziano Mancinelli (ITA)	Ambassador
1976	Alwin Schockemöhle (FRG)	Warwick Rex
1980	Jan Kowalczyk (POL)	Artemor
1984	Joe Fargis (USA)	Touch of Class
1988	Pierre Durand (FRA)	Jappeloup
1992	Ludger Beerbaum (GER)	Classic Touch
1996	Ulrich Kirchhoff (GER)	Jus des Pommes
2000	Jeroen Dubbeldam (NED)	Sjiem
2004	Rodrigo Pessoa (BRA)	Baloubet du Rouet
2008	Eric Lamaze (CAN)	Hickstead

GRAND PRIX (JUMPING) TEAM

1912	Sweden
1920	Sweden
1924	Sweden
1928	Spain
1936	Germany
1948	Mexico

Equestrian sports (continued)

GRAND PRIX (JUMPING) TEAM (CONTINUED)

1952	Great Britain
1956	Germany
1960	Germany
1964	Germany
1968	Canada
1972	West Germany
1976	France
1980	USSR
1984	United States
1988	West Germany
1992	The Netherlands
1996	Germany
2000	Germany
2004	Germany
2008	United States

THREE-DAY EVENT (INDIVIDUAL)

		MOUNT
1912	Axel Nordlander (SWE)	Lady Artist
1920	Helmer Mörner (SWE)	Germania
1924	Adolph van der Voort van Zijp (NED)	Silver Piece
1928	Charles Pahud de Mortanges (NED)	Marcroix
1932	Charles Pahud de Mortanges (NED)	Marcroix
1936	Ludwig Stubbendorff (GER)	Nurmi
1948	Bernard Chevallier (FRA)	Aiglonne
1952	Hans von Blixen-Finecke, Jr. (SWE)	Jubal
1956	Petrus Kastenman (SWE)	Iluster
1960	Lawrence Morgan (AUS)	Salad Days
1964	Mauro Checcoli (ITA)	Surbean
1968	Jean-Jacques Goyon (FRA)	Pitou
1972	Richard Meade (GBR)	Laurieston
1976	Edmund Coffin (USA)	Bally-Cor
1980	Federico Euro Roman (ITA)	Rossinan
1984	Mark Todd (NZL)	Charisma
1988	Mark Todd (NZL)	Charisma
1992	Matthew Ryan (AUS)	Kibah Tic Toc
1996	Robert Blyth Tait (NZL)	Ready Teddy
2000	David O'Connor (USA)	Custom Made
2004	Leslie Law (GBR)	Shear L'Eau
2008	Hinrich Romeike (GER)	Marius

THREE-DAY EVENT (TEAM)

1912	Sweden
1920	Sweden
1924	The Netherlands
1928	The Netherlands
1932	United States
1936	Germany
1948	United States
1952	Sweden
1956	Great Britain
1960	Australia
1964	Italy
1968	Great Britain
1972	Great Britain
1976	United States
1980	USSR
1984	United States
1988	West Germany
1992	Australia
1996	Australia
2000	Australia
2004	France
2008	Germany

Summer Olympic Games Champions (continued)

Equestrian sports (continued)

HIGH JUMP		MOUNT
1900	Dominique Maximien Gardéres (FRA); Gian Giorgio Trissino (ITA) (*tied*)	Canela; Oreste

LONG JUMP		MOUNT
1900	Constant van Langhendonck (BEL)	Extra Dry

FIGURE RIDING (INDIVIDUAL)
1920 T. Bouckaert (BEL)

FIGURE RIDING (TEAM)
1920 Belgium

Fencing (men)

FOIL (INDIVIDUAL)
1896 Eugène-Henri Gravelotte (FRA)
1900 Émile Coste (FRA)
1904 Ramón Fonst (CUB)
1912 Nedo Nadi (ITA)
1920 Nedo Nadi (ITA)
1924 Roger Ducret (FRA)
1928 Lucien Gaudin (FRA)
1932 Gustavo Marzi (ITA)
1936 Giulio Gaudini (ITA)
1948 Jehan Buhan (FRA)
1952 Christian d'Oriola (FRA)
1956 Christian d'Oriola (FRA)
1960 Viktor Zhdanovich (URS)
1964 Egon Franke (POL)
1968 Ion Drimba (ROM)
1972 Witold Woyda (POL)
1976 Fabio dal Zotto (ITA)
1980 Vladimir Smirnov (URS)
1984 Mauro Numa (ITA)
1988 Stefano Cerioni (ITA)
1992 Philippe Omnes (FRA)
1996 Alessandro Puccini (ITA)
2000 Kim Young Ho (KOR)
2004 Brice Guyart (FRA)
2008 Benjamin Philip Kleibrink (GER)

FOIL (TEAM)
1904 Cuba
1920 Italy
1924 France
1928 Italy
1932 France
1936 Italy
1948 France
1952 France
1956 Italy
1960 USSR
1964 USSR
1968 France
1972 Poland
1976 West Germany
1980 France
1984 Italy
1988 USSR
1992 Germany
1996 Russia
2000 France
2004 Italy

INDIVIDUAL FOIL, PROFESSIONAL (MASTERS)
1896 Leon Pyrgos (GRE)
1900 Lucien Mérignac (FRA)

Fencing (men) (continued)

INDIVIDUAL FOIL, JUNIOR
1904 Arthur Fox (USA)

EPEE (INDIVIDUAL)
1900 Ramón Fonst (CUB)
1904 Ramón Fonst (CUB)
1908 Gaston Alibert (FRA)
1912 Paul Anspach (BEL)
1920 Armand Massard (FRA)
1924 Charles Delporte (BEL)
1928 Lucien Gaudin (FRA)
1932 Giancarlo Cornaggia-Medici (ITA)
1936 Franco Riccardi (ITA)
1948 Luigi Cantone (ITA)
1952 Edoardo Mangiarotti (ITA)
1956 Carlo Pavesi (ITA)
1960 Giuseppe Delfino (ITA)
1964 Grigory Kriss (URS)
1968 Gyoso Kulcsar (HUN)
1972 Csaba Fenyvesi (HUN)
1976 Alexander Pusch (FRG)
1980 Johan Harmenberg (SWE)
1984 Philippe Boisse (FRA)
1988 Arnd Schmitt (FRG)
1992 Eric Srecki (FRA)
1996 Aleksandr Beketov (RUS)
2000 Pavel Kolobkov (RUS)
2004 Marcel Fischer (SUI)
2008 Matteo Tagliariol (ITA)

EPEE (TEAM)
1908 France
1912 Belgium
1920 Italy
1924 France
1928 Italy
1932 France
1936 Italy
1948 France
1952 Italy
1956 Italy
1960 Italy
1964 Hungary
1968 Hungary
1972 Hungary
1976 Sweden
1980 France
1984 West Germany
1988 France
1992 Germany
1996 Italy
2000 Italy
2004 France
2008 France

INDIVIDUAL EPEE, PROFESSIONAL (MASTERS)
1900 Albert Ayat (FRA)

INDIVIDUAL EPEE, OPEN (AMATEUR AND MASTERS)
1900 Albert Ayat (FRA)

SABRE (INDIVIDUAL)
1896 Ioannis Georgiadis (GRE)
1900 Georges de la Falaise (FRA)
1904 Manuel Díaz (CUB)
1908 Jeno Fuchs (HUN)
1912 Jeno Fuchs (HUN)
1920 Nedo Nadi (ITA)

Summer Olympic Games Champions (continued)

Fencing (men) (continued)

SABRE (INDIVIDUAL) (CONTINUED)

1924 Sandor Posta (HUN)
1928 Odon Vitez Tersztyanszky (HUN)
1932 Gyorgy Piller (HUN)
1936 Endre Kabos (HUN)
1948 Aladar Gerevich (HUN)
1952 Pal Kovacs (HUN)
1956 Rudolph Karpati (HUN)
1960 Rudolph Karpati (HUN)
1964 Tibor Pezsa (HUN)
1968 Jerzy Pawlowski (POL)
1972 Viktor Sidyak (URS)
1976 Viktor Krovopuskov (URS)
1980 Viktor Krovopuskov (URS)
1984 Jean-François Lamour (FRA)
1988 Jean-François Lamour (FRA)
1992 Bence Szabo (HUN)
1996 Stanislav Pozdnyakov (RUS)
2000 Mihai Claudiu Covaliu (ROM)
2004 Aldo Montano (ITA)
2008 Zhong Man (CHN)

SABRE (TEAM)

1908 Hungary
1912 Hungary
1920 Italy
1924 Italy
1928 Hungary
1932 Hungary
1936 Hungary
1948 Hungary
1952 Hungary
1956 Hungary
1960 Hungary
1964 USSR
1968 USSR
1972 Italy
1976 USSR
1980 USSR
1984 Italy
1988 Hungary
1992 Unified Team
1996 Russia
2000 Russia
2004 France
2008 France

INDIVIDUAL SABRE, PROFESSIONAL (MASTERS)

1900 Antonio Conte (ITA)

THREE-CORNERED SABRE

1906 Gustav Casmir (GER)

SINGLE STICK

1904 Albertson Van Zo Post (CUB)

Fencing (women)

FOIL (INDIVIDUAL)

1924 Ellen Osiier (DEN)
1928 Helene Mayer (GER)
1932 Ellen Preis (AUT)
1936 Ilona Schacherer-Elek (HUN)
1948 Ilona Elek (HUN)
1952 Irene Camber (ITA)
1956 Gillian Sheen (GBR)
1960 Adelheid Schmid (GER)
1964 Ildiko Ujlaki-Rejto (HUN)
1968 Yelena Novikova (URS)

Fencing (women) (continued)

FOIL (INDIVIDUAL) (CONTINUED)

1972 Antonella Ragno Lonzi (ITA)
1976 Ildiko Schwarczenberger (HUN)
1980 Pascale Trinquet (FRA)
1984 Jujie Luan (CHN)
1988 Anja Fichtel (FRG)
1992 Giovanna Trillini (ITA)
1996 Laura Gabriela Badea (ROM)
2000 Valentina Vezzali (ITA)
2004 Valentina Vezzali (ITA)
2008 Maria Valentina Vezzali (ITA)

FOIL (TEAM)

1960 USSR
1964 Hungary
1968 USSR
1972 USSR
1976 USSR
1980 France
1984 West Germany
1988 West Germany
1992 Italy
1996 Italy
2000 Italy
2004 *not held*
2008 Russia

EPEE (INDIVIDUAL)

1996 Laura Flessel (FRA)
2000 Timea Nagy (HUN)
2004 Timea Nagy (HUN)
2008 Britta Heidemann (GER)

EPEE (TEAM)

1996 France
2000 Russia
2004 Russia

SABRE (INDIVIDUAL)

2004 Mariel Zagunis (USA)
2008 Mariel Zagunis (USA)

SABRE (TEAM)

2008 Ukraine

Field hockey

MEN

1908 Great Britain
1920 Great Britain
1928 India
1932 India
1936 India
1948 India
1952 India
1956 India
1960 Pakistan
1964 India
1968 Pakistan
1972 West Germany
1976 New Zealand
1980 India
1984 Pakistan
1988 Great Britain
1992 Germany
1996 The Netherlands
2000 The Netherlands
2004 Australia
2008 Germany

Summer Olympic Games Champions (continued)

Field hockey (continued)

WOMEN

1980 Zimbabwe
1984 The Netherlands
1988 Australia
1992 Spain
1996 Australia
2000 Australia
2004 Germany
2008 The Netherlands

Golf

MEN, INDIVIDUAL

1900 Charles Sands (USA)
1904 George Lyon (CAN)

MEN, TEAM

1904 United States

WOMEN

1900 Margaret Abbott (USA)

Gymnastics (men)

COMBINED, OR ALL-AROUND (INDIVIDUAL)

1900 Gustave Sandras (FRA)
1904 Julius Lenhardt (USA)
1908 G. Alberto Braglia (ITA)
1912 G. Alberto Braglia (ITA)
1920 Giorgio Zampori (ITA)
1924 Leon Stukelj (YUG)
1928 Georges Miez (SUI)
1932 Romeo Neri (ITA)
1936 Karl-Alfred Schwarzmann (GER)
1948 Veikko Huhtanen (FIN)
1952 Viktor Chukarin (URS)
1956 Viktor Chukarin (URS)
1960 Boris Shakhlin (URS)
1964 Yukio Endo (JPN)
1968 Sawao Kato (JPN)
1972 Sawao Kato (JPN)
1976 Nikolay Andrianov (URS)
1980 Aleksandr Dityatin (URS)
1984 Koji Gushiken (JPN)
1988 Vladimir Artyomov (URS)
1992 Vitaly Shcherbo (UNT)
1996 Li Xiaosahuang (CHN)
2000 Aleksey Nemov (RUS)
2004 Paul Hamm (USA)
2008 Yang Wei (CHN)

COMBINED, OR ALL-AROUND (TEAM)

1920 Italy
1924 Italy
1928 Switzerland
1932 Italy
1936 Germany
1948 Finland
1952 USSR
1956 USSR
1960 Japan
1964 Japan
1968 Japan
1972 Japan
1976 Japan
1980 USSR
1984 United States
1988 USSR
1992 Unified Team
1996 Russia

Gymnastics (men) (continued)

COMBINED, OR ALL-AROUND (TEAM) (CONTINUED)

2000 China
2004 Japan
2008 China

FLOOR EXERCISE

1932 Istvan Pelle (HUN)
1936 Georges Miez (SUI)
1948 Ferenc Pataki (HUN)
1952 William Thoresson (SWE)
1956 Valentin Muratov (URS)
1960 Nobuyuki Aihara (JPN)
1964 Franco Menichelli (ITA)
1968 Sawao Kato (JPN)
1972 Nikolay Andrianov (URS)
1976 Nikolay Andrianov (URS)
1980 Roland Brückner (GDR)
1984 Li Ning (CHN)
1988 Sergey Kharikov (URS)
1992 Li Xiaosahuang (CHN)
1996 Ioannis Melissanidis (GRE)
2000 Igors Vihrovs (LAT)
2004 Kyle Shewfelt (CAN)
2008 Zou Kai (CHN)

HORIZONTAL BAR

1896 Hermann Weingärtner (GER)
1904 Anton Heida (USA); Edward Henning (USA) (*tied*)
1924 Leon Stukelj (YUG)
1928 Georges Miez (SUI)
1932 Dallas Bixler (USA)
1936 Aleksanteri Saarvala (FIN)
1948 Josef Stalder (SUI)
1952 Jack Günthard (SUI)
1956 Takashi Ono (JPN)
1960 Takashi Ono (JPN)
1964 Boris Shakhlin (URS)
1968 Mikhail Voronin (URS); Akinori Nakayama (JPN) (*tied*)
1972 Mitsuo Tsukahara (JPN)
1976 Mitsuo Tsukahara (JPN)
1980 Stoyan Delchev (BUL)
1984 Shinji Morisue (JPN)
1988 Vladimir Artyomov (URS); Valery Lyukin (URS) (*tied*)
1992 Trent Dimas (USA)
1996 Andreas Wecker (GER)
2000 Aleksey Nemov (RUS)
2004 Igor Cassina (ITA)
2008 Zou Kai (CHN)

PARALLEL BARS

1896 Alfred Flatow (GER)
1904 George Eyser (USA)
1924 August Güttinger (SUI)
1928 Ladislav Vacha (TCH)
1932 Romeo Neri (ITA)
1936 Konrad Frey (GER)
1948 Michael Reusch (SUI)
1952 Hans Eugster (SUI)
1956 Viktor Chukarin (URS)
1960 Boris Shakhlin (URS)
1964 Yukio Endo (JPN)
1968 Akinori Nakayama (JPN)
1972 Sawao Kato (JPN)
1976 Sawao Kato (JPN)
1980 Aleksandr Tkachyov (URS)

Summer Olympic Games Champions (continued)

Gymnastics (men) (continued)

PARALLEL BARS (CONTINUED)
1984 Bart Conner (USA)
1988 Vladimir Artyomov (URS)
1992 Vitaly Shcherbo (UNT)
1996 Rustam Sharipov (UKR)
2000 Li Xiaopeng (CHN)
2004 Valery Goncharov (UKR)
2008 Li Xiaopeng (CHN)

SIDE, OR POMMEL, HORSE
1896 Louis Zutter (SUI)
1904 Anton Heida (USA)
1924 Josef Wilhelm (SUI)
1928 Hermann Hänggi (SUI)
1932 Istvan Pelle (HUN)
1936 Konrad Frey (GER)
1948 Paavo Aaltonen (FIN); Veikko Huhtanen (FIN); Heikki Savolainen (FIN) (*tied*)
1952 Viktor Chukarin (URS)
1956 Boris Shakhlin (URS)
1960 Boris Shakhlin (URS); Eugen Ekman (FIN) (*tied*)
1964 Miroslav Cerar (YUG)
1968 Miroslav Cerar (YUG)
1972 Viktor Klimenko (URS)
1976 Zoltan Magyar (HUN)
1980 Zoltan Magyar (HUN)
1984 Li Ning (CHN); Peter Vidmar (USA) (*tied*)
1988 Lyubomir Geraskov (BUL); Zsolt Borkai (HUN); Dmitry Bilozerchev (URS) (*tied*)
1992 Vitaly Shcherbo (UNT); Pae Gil-su (PRK) (*tied*)
1996 Li Donghua (SUI)
2000 Marius Urzica (ROM)
2004 Teng Haibin (CHN)
2008 Xiao Qin (CHN)

LONG, OR VAULTING, HORSE
1896 Karl Schuhmann (GER)
1904 Anton Heida (USA); George Eyser (USA) (*tied*)
1924 Frank Kriz (USA)
1928 Eugen Mack (SUI)
1932 Savino Guglielmetti (ITA)
1936 Karl-Alfred Schnorzmann (GER)
1948 Paavo Johannes Aaltonen (FIN)
1952 Viktor Chukarin (URS)
1956 Valentin Muratov (URS); Helmut Bantz (GER) (*tied*)
1960 Takashi Ono (JPN); Boris Shakhlin (URS) (*tied*)
1964 Haruhiro Yamashita (JPN)
1968 Mikhail Voronin (URS)
1972 Klaus Köste (GDR)
1976 Nikolay Andrianov (URS)
1980 Nikolay Andrianov (URS)
1984 Lou Yun (CHN)
1988 Lou Yun (CHN)
1992 Vitaly Shcherbo (UNT)
1996 Aleksey Nemov (RUS)
2000 Gervasio Deferr (ESP)
2004 Gervasio Deferr (ESP)
2008 Leszek Blanik (POL)

RINGS
1896 Ioannis Mitropoulos (GRE)
1904 Hermann Glass (USA)
1924 Francesco Martino (ITA)
1928 Leon Stukelj (YUG)
1932 George Gulack (USA)

Gymnastics (men) (continued)

RINGS (CONTINUED)
1936 Alois Hudec (TCH)
1948 Karl Frei (SUI)
1952 Grant Shaginyan (URS)
1956 Albert Azaryan (URS)
1960 Albert Azaryan (URS)
1964 Takuji Hayata (JPN)
1968 Akinori Nakayama (JPN)
1972 Akinori Nakayama (JPN)
1976 Nikolay Andrianov (URS)
1980 Aleksandr Dityatin (URS)
1984 Li Ning (CHN); Koji Gushiken (JPN) (*tied*)
1988 Holger Behrendt (GDR); Dmitry Bilozerchev (URS) (*tied*)
1992 Vitaly Shcherbo (UNT)
1996 Yury Chechi (ITA)
2000 Szilveszter Csollany (HUN)
2004 Dimosthenis Tampakos (GRE)
2008 Chen Yibing (CHN)

TRAMPOLINE
2000 Aleksandr Moskalenko (RUS)
2004 Yury Nikitin (UKR)
2008 Lu Chunlong (CHN)

ROPE CLIMBING
1896 Nicolaos Andriakopoulos (GRE)
1904 George Eyser (USA)
1924 Bedrich Supcik (TCH)
1932 Raymond Bass (USA)

SWEDISH EXERCISES (TEAM)
1912 Sweden
1920 Sweden

OPTIONAL EXERCISES (TEAM)
1912 Norway
1920 Denmark
1932 United States

PARALLEL BARS (TEAM)
1896 Germany

HORIZONTAL BARS (TEAM)
1896 Germany

CLUB SWINGING
1904 Edward Hennig (USA)
1932 George Roth (USA)

TUMBLING
1932 Rowland Wolfe (USA)

COMBINED COMPETITION (7 APPARATUS)
1904 Anton Heida (USA)

COMBINED COMPETITION (9 EVENTS)
1904 Adolf Spinnler (SUI)

PRESCRIBED APPARATUS (TEAM)
1904 United States
1908 Sweden
1912 Italy
1952 Sweden
1956 Hungary

MASS EXERCISES (TEAM)
1952 Finland

Summer Olympic Games Champions (continued)

Gymnastics (men) (continued)

SIDE HORSE (VAULTS)

1924 Albert Séguin (FRA)

Gymnastics (women)

COMBINED, OR ALL-AROUND (INDIVIDUAL)

1952 Mariya Gorokhovskaya (URS)
1956 Larisa Latynina (URS)
1960 Larisa Latynina (URS)
1964 Vera Caslavska (TCH)
1968 Vera Caslavska (TCH)
1972 Lyudmila Turishcheva (URS)
1976 Nadia Comaneci (ROM)
1980 Yelena Davydova (URS)
1984 Mary-Lou Retton (USA)
1988 Yelena Shushunova (URS)
1992 Tatyana Gutsu (UNT)
1996 Liliya Podkopayeva (UKR)
2000 Simona Amanar (ROM)
2004 Carly Patterson (USA)
2008 Nastia Liukin (USA)

COMBINED, OR ALL-AROUND (TEAM)

1928 The Netherlands
1936 Germany
1948 Czechoslovakia
1952 USSR
1956 USSR
1960 USSR
1964 USSR
1968 USSR
1972 USSR
1976 USSR
1980 USSR
1984 Romania
1988 USSR
1992 Unified Team
1996 United States
2000 Romania
2004 Romania
2008 China

BALANCE BEAM

1952 Nina Bocharova (URS)
1956 Agnes Keleti (HUN)
1960 Eva Bosakova (TCH)
1964 Vera Caslavska (TCH)
1968 Natalya Kuchinskaya (URS)
1972 Olga Korbut (URS)
1976 Nadia Comaneci (ROM)
1980 Nadia Comaneci (ROM)
1984 Ecaterina Szabo (ROM); Simona Pauca (ROM) (*tied*)
1988 Daniela Silivas (ROM)
1992 Tatyana Lysenko (UNT)
1996 Shannon Miller (USA)
2000 Liu Xuan (CHN)
2004 Catalina Ponor (ROM)
2008 Shawn Johnson (USA)

UNEVEN PARALLEL BARS

1952 Margit Korondi (HUN)
1956 Agnes Keleti (HUN)
1960 Polina Astakhova (URS)
1964 Polina Astakhova (URS)
1968 Vera Caslavska (TCH)
1972 Karin Janz (GDR)
1976 Nadia Comaneci (ROM)

Gymnastics (women) (continued)

UNEVEN PARALLEL BARS (CONTINUED)

1980 Maxi Gnauck (GDR)
1984 Julianne McNamara (USA); Ma Yanhong (CHN) (*tied*)
1988 Daniela Silivas (ROM)
1992 Li Lu (CHN)
1996 Svetlana Khorkina (RUS)
2000 Svetlana Khorkina (RUS)
2004 Emilie Lepennec (FRA)
2008 He Kexin (CHN)

VAULT

1952 Yekaterina Kalinchuk (URS)
1956 Larisa Latynina (URS)
1960 Margarita Nikolayeva (URS)
1964 Vera Caslavska (TCH)
1968 Vera Caslavska (TCH)
1972 Karin Janz (GDR)
1976 Nelli Kim (URS)
1980 Natalya Shaposhnikova (URS)
1984 Ecaterina Szabo (ROM)
1988 Svetlana Boginskaya (URS)
1992 Henrietta Onodi (HUN); Lavinia Milosovici (ROM) (*tied*)
1996 Simona Amanar (ROM)
2000 Yelena Zamolodchikova (RUS)
2004 Monica Rosu (ROM)
2008 Hong Un Jong (PRK)

FLOOR EXERCISE

1952 Agnes Keleti (HUN)
1956 Larisa Latynina (URS); Agnes Keleti (HUN) (*tied*)
1960 Larisa Latynina (URS)
1964 Larisa Latynina (URS)
1968 Vera Caslavska (TCH); Larissa Petrik (URS) (*tied*)
1972 Olga Korbut (URS)
1976 Nelli Kim (URS)
1980 Nadia Comaneci (ROM); Nelli Kim (URS) (*tied*)
1984 Ecaterina Szabo (ROM)
1988 Daniela Silivas (ROM)
1992 Lavinia Milosovici (ROM)
1996 Liliya Podkopayeva (UKR)
2000 Yelena Zamolodchikova (RUS)
2004 Catalina Ponor (ROM)
2008 Sandra Izbasa (ROM)

RHYTHMIC GYMNASTICS (INDIVIDUAL)

1984 Lori Fung (CAN)
1988 Marina Lobatch (URS)
1992 Aleksandra Timoshenko (UNT)
1996 Yekaterina Serebryanskaya (UKR)
2000 Yuliya Barsukova (RUS)
2004 Alina Kabayeva (RUS)
2008 Yevgeniya Kanayeva (RUS)

RHYTHMIC GYMNASTICS (TEAM)

1996 Spain
2000 Russia
2004 Russia
2008 Russia

TRAMPOLINE

2000 Irina Karavayeva (RUS)
2004 Anna Dogonadze (GER)
2008 He Wenna (CHN)

Summer Olympic Games Champions (continued)

Gymnastics (women) (continued)

HAND APPARATUS (TEAM)

1952 Sweden
1956 Hungary

Handball (team) (outdoors to 1972)

MEN

1936 Germany
1952 Sweden (demonstration)
1972 Yugoslavia
1976 USSR
1980 East Germany
1984 Yugoslavia
1988 USSR
1992 Unified Team
1996 Croatia
2000 Russia
2004 Croatia
2008 France

WOMEN

1976 USSR
1980 USSR
1984 Yugoslavia
1988 South Korea
1992 South Korea
1996 Denmark
2000 Denmark
2004 Denmark
2008 Norway

JEU DE PAUME (ROYAL TENNIS)

1908 Jay Gould (USA)

Judo (men)[9]

60 KG (132 LB)

1964 Takehide Nakatani (JPN)
1972 Takao Kawaguchi (JPN)
1976 Héctor Rodríguez (CUB)
1980 Thierry Rey (FRA)
1984 Shinji Hosokawa (JPN)
1988 Kim Jae-Yup (KOR)
1992 Nazim Guseynov (UNT)
1996 Tadahiro Nomura (JPN)
2000 Tadahiro Nomura (JPN)
2004 Tadahiro Nomura (JPN)
2008 Choi Min Ho (KOR)

66 KG (145.2 LB)

1980 Nikolay Solodukhin (URS)
1984 Yoshiyuki Matsuoka (JPN)
1988 Lee Kyung Ken (KOR)
1992 Rogerio Sampaio Cardoso (BRA)
1996 Udo Quellmalz (GER)
2000 Huseyin Ozkan (TUR)
2004 Masato Uchishiba (JPN)
2008 Masato Uchishiba (JPN)

73 KG (160.6 LB)

1972 Takao Kawaguchi (JPN)
1976 Héctor Rodríguez Torres (CUB)
1980 Ezio Gamba (ITA)
1984 Ahn Byeong Keun (KOR)
1988 Marc Alexandre (FRA)
1992 Toshihiko Koga (JPN)
1996 Kenzo Nakamura (JPN)
2000 Giuseppe Maddaloni (ITA)
2004 Lee Won Hee (KOR)
2008 Elnur Mammadli (AZE)

Judo (men)[9] (continued)

81 KG (178.2 LB)

1972 Toyojazu Nomura (JPN)
1976 Vladimir Nevzorov (URS)
1980 Shota Khabareli (URS)
1984 Frank Wieneke (FRG)
1988 Waldemar Legien (POL)
1992 Hidehiko Yoshida (JPN)
1996 Djamel Bouras (FRA)
2000 Makoto Takimoto (JPN)
2004 Ilias Iliadis (GRE)
2008 Ole Bischof (GER)

90 KG (198 LB)

1964 Isao Okano (JPN)
1972 Shinobu Sekine (JPN)
1976 Isamu Sonoda (JPN)
1980 Jürg Röthlisberger (SUI)
1984 Peter Seisenbacher (AUT)
1988 Peter Seisenbacher (AUT)
1992 Waldemar Legien (POL)
1996 Jeon Ki-Young (KOR)
2000 Mark Huizinga (NED)
2004 Zurab Zviadauri (GEO)
2008 Irakli Tsirekidze (GEO)

100 KG (220 LB)

1972 Shota Chochoshvili (URS)
1976 Kazuhiro Ninomiya (JPN)
1980 Robert van de Walle (BEL)
1984 Ha Young Zoo (KOR)
1988 Aurelio Miguel (BRA)
1992 Antal Kovacs (HUN)
1996 Pawel Nastula (POL)
2000 Kosei Inoue (JPN)
2004 Ihar Makarau (BLR)
2008 Tuvshinbayar Naidan (MGL)

OVER 100 KG (220+ LB)

1964 Isao Inokuma (JPN)
1972 Willem Ruska (NED)
1976 Sergey Novikov (URS)
1980 Angelo Parisi (FRA)
1984 Hitoshi Saito (JPN)
1988 Hitoshi Saito (JPN)
1992 David Khakhaleishvili (UNT)
1996 David Douillet (FRA)
2000 David Douillet (FRA)
2004 Keiji Suzuki (JPN)
2008 Satoshi Ishii (JPN)

OPEN (NO WEIGHT LIMIT)

1964 Antonius Johannes Geesink (NED)
1972 Willem Ruska (NED)
1976 Haruki Uemura (JPN)
1980 Dietmar Lorenz (GDR)
1984 Yasuhiro Yamashita (JPN)

Judo (women)

48 KG (105.6 LB)

1992 Cecile Nowak (FRA)
1996 Kye Sun-Hi (PRK)
2000 Ryoko Tamura (JPN)
2004 Ryoko Tani (JPN)
2008 Alina Alexandra Dumitru (ROM)

52 KG (114.4 LB)

1992 Almudena Muñoz Martínez (ESP)
1996 Marie-Claire Restoux (FRA)

Summer Olympic Games Champions (continued)

Judo (women) (continued)

52 KG (114.4 LB) (CONTINUED)

2000 Legna Verdecia (CUB)
2004 Xian Dongmei (CHN)
2008 Xian Dongmei (CHN)

57 KG (125.4 LB)

1992 Miriam Blasco Soto (ESP)
1996 Driulis González Morales (CUB)
2000 Isabel Fernández (ESP)
2004 Yvonne Bönisch (GER)
2008 Giulia Quintavalle (ITA)

63 KG (138.6 LB)

1992 Catherine Fleury-Vachon (FRA)
1996 Yuko Emoto (JPN)
2000 Severine Vandenhende (FRA)
2004 Ayumi Tanimoto (JPN)
2008 Ayumi Tanimoto (JPN)

70 KG (154 LB)

1992 Odalis Reve Jiménez (CUB)
1996 Cho Min-Sun (KOR)
2000 Sibelis Veranes (CUB)
2004 Masae Ueno (JPN)
2008 Masae Ueno (JPN)

78 KG (171.6 LB)

1992 Kim Mi-Jung (KOR)
1996 Ulla Werbrouck (BEL)
2000 Tang Lin (CHN)
2004 Noriko Anno (JPN)
2008 Yang Xiuli (CHN)

OVER 78 KG (171.6+ LB)

1992 Zhuang Xiaoyan (CHN)
1996 Sun Fuming (CHN)
2000 Yuan Hua (CHN)
2004 Maki Tsukada (JPN)
2008 Tong Wen (CHN)

Lacrosse

1904 Canada
1908 Canada

Modern pentathlon

INDIVIDUAL (MEN)

1912 Gösta Lilliehöök (SWE)
1920 Gustaf Dyrssen (SWE)
1924 Bo Lindman (SWE)
1928 Sven Thofelt (SWE)
1932 Johan Oxenstierna (SWE)
1936 Gotthardt Handrick (GER)
1948 William Grut (SWE)
1952 Lars-Goran Hall (SWE)
1956 Lars-Goran Hall (SWE)
1960 Ferenc Nemeth (HUN)
1964 Ferenc Torok (HUN)
1968 Björn Ferm (SWE)
1972 Andras Balczo (HUN)
1976 Janusz Pyciak-Peciak (POL)
1980 Anatoly Starostin (URS)
1984 Daniele Masala (ITA)
1988 Janos Martinek (HUN)
1992 Arkadiusz Skrzypaszek (POL)
1996 Aleksandr Parygin (KAZ)
2000 Dmitry Svatkovsky (RUS)
2004 Andrey Moiseyev (RUS)
2008 Andrey Moiseyev (RUS)

Modern pentathlon (continued)

INDIVIDUAL (WOMEN)

2000 Stephanie Cook (GBR)
2004 Zsuzsanna Voros (HUN)
2008 Lena Schöneborn (GER)

TEAM (MEN)

1952 Hungary
1956 USSR
1960 Hungary
1964 USSR
1968 Hungary
1972 USSR
1976 Great Britain
1980 USSR
1984 Italy
1988 Hungary
1992 Poland

Motorboat racing

OPEN CLASS, 40 NAUTICAL MILES		BOAT
1908	Émile Thubron (FRA)	*Camille*

8-METER CLASS, 40 NAUTICAL MILES		
1908	Thomas Thornycroft, Bernard Redwood (GBR)	*Cyrinus*

UNDER 60-FOOT CLASS, 40 NAUTICAL MILES		
1908	Thomas Thornycroft, Bernard Redwood (GBR)	*Cyrinus*

Polo

1900 team comprising members from Great Britain and the United States
1908 Great Britain
1920 Great Britain
1924 Argentina
1936 Argentina

Rackets

SINGLES

1908 Evan Noel (GBR)

DOUBLES

1908 Vane Pennell, John Jacob Astor (GBR)

Roque

1904 Charles Jacobus (USA)

Rowing (men)[11]

SINGLE SCULLS		MIN:SEC
1900	Henri Barrelet (FRA)	7:35.6
1904	Frank Greer (USA)	10:08.5
1908	Harry Blackstaffe (GBR)	9:26.0
1912	William Kinnear (GBR)	7:47.6
1920	John Kelly, Sr. (USA)	7:35.0
1924	Jack Beresford (GBR)	7:49.2
1928	Henry Pearce (AUS)	7:11.0
1932	Henry Pearce (AUS)	7:44.4
1936	Gustav Schäfer (GER)	8:21.5
1948	Mervyn Wood (AUS)	7:24.4
1952	Yury Tyukalov (URS)	8:12.8
1956	Vyacheslav Ivanov (URS)	8:02.5
1960	Vyacheslav Ivanov (URS)	7:13.96
1964	Vyacheslav Ivanov (URS)	8:22.51
1968	Henri-Jan Wienese (NED)	7:47.80
1972	Yury Malyshev (URS)	7:10.12
1976	Pertti Karppinen (FIN)	7:29.03
1980	Pertti Karppinen (FIN)	7:09.61

Summer Olympic Games Champions (continued)

Rowing (men)[11] (continued)

SINGLE SCULLS (CONTINUED)		MIN:SEC
1984	Pertti Karppinen (FIN)	7:00.24
1988	Thomas Lange (GDR)	6:49.86
1992	Thomas Lange (GER)	6:51.40
1996	Xeno Mueller (SUI)	6:44.85
2000	Robert Waddell (NZL)	6:48.90
2004	Olaf Tufte (NOR)	6:49.30
2008	Olaf Tufte (NOR)	6:59.83

DOUBLE SCULLS		MIN:SEC
1904	United States	10:03.2
1920	United States	7:09.0
1924	United States	6:34.0
1928	United States	6:41.4
1932	United States	7:17.4
1936	Great Britain	7:20.8
1948	Great Britain	6:51.3
1952	Argentina	7:32.2
1956	USSR	7:24.0
1960	Czechoslovakia	6:47.50
1964	USSR	7:10.66
1968	USSR	6:51.82
1972	USSR	7:01.77
1976	Norway	7:13.20
1980	East Germany	6:24.33
1984	United States	6:36.87
1988	The Netherlands	6:21.13
1992	Australia	6:17.32
1996	Italy	6:16.98
2000	Slovenia	6:16.63
2004	France	6:29.00
2008	Australia	6:27.77

FOUR SCULLS		MIN:SEC
1976	East Germany	6:18.65
1980	East Germany	5:49.81
1984	West Germany	5:57.55
1988	Italy	5:53.37
1992	Germany	5:45.17
1996	Germany	5:56.93
2000	Italy	5:45.56
2004	Russia	5:56.85
2008	Poland	5:41.33

LIGHTWEIGHT DOUBLE SCULLS		MIN:SEC
1996	Switzerland	6:23.47
2000	Poland	6:21.75
2004	Poland	6:20.93
2008	Great Britain	6:10.99

PAIRS (WITHOUT COXSWAIN)		MIN:SEC
1904	United States	10:57.0
1908	Great Britain	9:41.0
1924	The Netherlands	8:19.4
1928	Germany	7:06.4
1932	Great Britain	8:00.0
1936	Germany	8:16.1
1948	Great Britain	7:21.1
1952	United States	8:20.7
1956	United States	7:55.4
1960	USSR	7:02.01
1964	Canada	7:32.94
1968	East Germany	7:26.56
1972	East Germany	6:53.16
1976	East Germany	7:23.31
1980	East Germany	6:48.01
1984	Romania	6:45.39
1988	Great Britain	6:36.84

Rowing (men)[11] (continued)

PAIRS (WITHOUT COXSWAIN) (CONTINUED)		MIN:SEC
1992	Great Britain	6:27.72
1996	Great Britain	6:20.09
2000	France	6:32.97
2004	Australia	6:30.76
2008	Australia	6:37.44

PAIRS (WITH COXSWAIN)		MIN:SEC
1900	The Netherlands/France	7:34.2
1920	Italy	7:56.0
1924	Switzerland	8:39.0
1928	Switzerland	7:42.6
1932	United States	8:25.8
1936	Germany	8:36.9
1948	Denmark	8:00.5
1952	France	8:28.6
1956	United States	8:26.1
1960	Germany	7:29.14
1964	United States	8:21.23
1968	Italy	8:04.81
1972	East Germany	7:17.25
1976	East Germany	7:58.99
1980	East Germany	7:02.54
1984	Italy	7:05.99
1988	Italy	6:58.79
1992	Great Britain	6:49.83

LIGHTWEIGHT FOURS (WITHOUT COXSWAIN)		MIN:SEC
1996	Denmark	6:09.58
2000	France	6:01.68
2004	Denmark	6:01.39
2008	Denmark	5:47.76

FOURS (WITHOUT COXSWAIN)		MIN:SEC
1900	France	7:11.0
1904	United States	9:53.8
1908	Great Britain	8:34.0
1920	Great Britain	7:08.6
1928	Great Britain	6:36.0
1932	Great Britain	6:58.2
1936	Germany	7:01.8
1948	Italy	6:39.0
1952	Yugoslavia	7:16.0
1956	Canada	7:08.8
1960	United States	6:26.26
1964	Denmark	6:59.30
1968	East Germany	6:39.18
1972	East Germany	6:24.27
1976	East Germany	6:37.42
1980	East Germany	6:08.17
1984	New Zealand	6:03.48
1988	East Germany	6:03.11
1992	Australia	5:55.04
1996	Australia	6:06.37
2000	Great Britain	5:56.24
2004	Great Britain	6:06.98
2008	Great Britain	6:06.57

FOURS (WITH COXSWAIN)		MIN:SEC
1900	Germany	5:59.0
1912	Germany	6:59.4
1920	Switzerland	6:54.0
1924	Switzerland	7:18.4
1928	Italy	6:47.8
1932	Germany	7:19.0
1936	Germany	7:16.2
1948	United States	6:50.3
1952	Czechoslovakia	7:33.4

Summer Olympic Games Champions (continued)

Rowing (men)[11] (continued)

FOURS (WITH COXSWAIN) (CONTINUED)		MIN:SEC
1956	Italy	7:19.4
1960	Germany	6:39.12
1964	Germany	7:00.44
1968	New Zealand	6:45.62
1972	West Germany	6:31.85
1976	USSR	6:40.22
1980	East Germany	6:14.51
1984	Great Britain	6:18.64
1988	East Germany	6:10.74
1992	Romania	5:59.37

FOURS, INRIGGERS (WITH COXSWAIN)		MIN:SEC
1912	Denmark	7:47.0

EIGHTS (WITH COXSWAIN)		MIN:SEC
1900	United States	6:09.8
1904	United States	7:50.0
1908	Great Britain	7:52.0
1912	Great Britain	6:15.0
1920	United States	6:02.6
1924	United States	6:33.4
1928	United States	6:03.2
1932	United States	6:37.6
1936	United States	6:25.4
1948	United States	5:56.7
1952	United States	6:25.9
1956	United States	6:35.2
1960	Germany	5:57.18
1964	United States	6:18.23
1968	West Germany	6:07.00
1972	New Zealand	6:08.94
1976	East Germany	5:58.29
1980	East Germany	5:49.05
1984	Canada	5:41.32
1988	West Germany	5:46.05
1992	Canada	5:29.53
1996	The Netherlands	5:42.74
2000	Great Britain	5:33.08
2004	United States	5:42.48
2008	Canada	5:23.89

SIX-MAN NAVAL ROWING BOATS (2,000 METERS)		MIN:SEC
1906	Italy	10:45.0

SIXTEEN-MAN NAVAL ROWING BOATS (3,000 METERS)		MIN:SEC
1906	Greece	16:35.0

Rowing (women)[12]

SINGLE SCULLS		MIN:SEC
1976	Christine Scheiblich (GDR)	4:05.56
1980	Sanda Toma (ROM)	3:40.69
1984	Valeria Racila (ROM)	3:40.68
1988	Jutta Behrendt (GDR)	7:47.19
1992	Elisabeta Lipa (ROM)	7:25.54
1996	Yekaterina Khodotovich (BLR)	7:32.21
2000	Yekaterina Khodotovich Karsten (BLR)	7:28.14
2004	Katrin Rutschow-Stomporowski (GER)	7:18.12
2008	Rumyana Neykova (BUL)	7:22.34

DOUBLE SCULLS		MIN:SEC
1976	Bulgaria	3:44.36
1980	USSR	3:16.27
1984	Romania	3:26.75
1988	East Germany	7:00.48

Rowing (women)[11] (continued)

DOUBLE SCULLS (CONTINUED)		MIN:SEC
1992	Germany	6:49.00
1996	Canada	6:56.84
2000	Germany	6:55.44
2004	New Zealand	7:01.79
2008	New Zealand	7:07.32

LIGHTWEIGHT DOUBLE SCULLS		MIN:SEC
1996	Romania	7:12.78
2000	Romania	7:02.64
2004	Romania	6:56.05
2008	The Netherlands	6:54.74

FOUR SCULLS		MIN:SEC
1976	East Germany	3:29.99
1980	East Germany	3:15.32
1984	Romania	3:14.11
1988	East Germany	6:21.06
1992	Germany	6:20.18
1996	Germany	6:27.44
2000	Germany	6:19.58
2004	Germany	6:29.29
2008	China	6:16.06

PAIRS (WITHOUT COXSWAIN)		MIN:SEC
1976	Bulgaria	4:01.22
1980	East Germany	3:30.49
1984	Romania	3:32.60
1988	Romania	7:28.13
1992	Canada	7:06.22
1996	Australia	7:01.39
2000	Romania	7:11.00
2004	Romania	7:06.55
2008	Romania	7:20.60

FOURS (WITH COXSWAIN [WITHOUT IN 1992])		MIN:SEC
1976	East Germany	3:45.08
1980	East Germany	3:19.27
1984	Romania	3:19.3
1988	East Germany	6:56.0
1992	Canada	6:30.85

EIGHTS (WITH COXSWAIN)		MIN:SEC
1976	East Germany	3:33.32
1980	East Germany	3:03.32
1984	United States	2:59.80
1988	East Germany	6:15.17
1992	Canada	6:02.62
1996	Romania	6:19.73
2000	Romania	6:06.44
2004	Romania	6:17.70
2008	United States	6:05.34

Rugby football

1900	France
1908	Australia
1920	United States
1924	United States

Sailing (yachting)

BOARDSAILING (WINDGLIDER/DIVISION II) (OPEN)	
1984	Stephan van den Berg (NED)
1988	Anthony Bruce Kendall (NZL)

BOARDSAILING (RS:X FROM 2004) (MEN)	
1992	Franck David (FRA)
1996	Nikolaos Kaklamanakis (GRE)
2000	Christoph Sieber (AUT)

Summer Olympic Games Champions (continued)

Sailing (yachting) (continued)

BOARDSAILING (RS:X FROM 2004) (MEN) (CONTINUED)
2004 Gal Fridman (ISR)
2008 Tom Ashley (NZL)

BOARDSAILING (RS:X FROM 2004) (WOMEN)
1992 Barbara Anne Kendall (NZL)
1996 Lee Lai Shan (HKG)
2000 Alessandra Sensini (ITA)
2004 Faustine Merret (FRA)
2008 Yin Jian (CHN)

SINGLE-HANDED DINGHY (LASER RADIAL) (WOMEN)
1992 Linda Andersen (NOR)
1996 Kristine Roug (DEN)
2000 Shirley Anne Robertson (GBR)
2004 Siren Sundby (NOR)
2008 Anna Tunnicliffe (USA)

SINGLE-HANDED DINGHY (LASER) (MEN; OPEN UNTIL 2008)
1996 Robert Scheidt (BRA)
2000 Ben Ainslie (GBR)
2004 Robert Scheidt (BRA)
2008 Paul Goodison (GBR)

SINGLE-HANDED DINGHY (FINN FROM 1952) (OPEN; MEN UNTIL 2008)
1924 Léon Huybrechts (BEL)
1928 Sven Thorell (SWE)
1932 Jacques Lebrun (FRA)
1936 Daniel Kagchelland (NED)
1948 Paul Elvström (DEN)
1952 Paul Elvström (DEN)
1956 Paul Elvström (DEN)
1960 Paul Elvström (DEN)
1964 Wilhelm Kuhweide (GER)
1968 Valentin Mankin (URS)
1972 Serge Maury (FRA)
1976 Jochen Schümann (GDR)
1980 Esko Rechardt (FIN)
1984 Russell Coutts (NZL)
1988 José Luis Doreste (ESP)
1992 José van der Ploeg (ESP)
1996 Mateusz Kusznierewicz (POL)
2000 Iain Percy (GBR)
2004 Ben Ainslie (GBR)
2008 Ben Ainslie (GBR)

DOUBLE-HANDED DINGHY (470) (MEN)
1976 West Germany
1980 Brazil
1984 Spain
1988 France
1992 Spain
1996 Ukraine
2000 Australia
2004 United States
2008 Australia

DOUBLE-HANDED DINGHY (470) (WOMEN)
1988 United States
1992 Spain
1996 Spain
2000 Australia
2004 Greece
2008 Australia

Sailing (yachting) (continued)

YNGLING (WOMEN)
2004 Great Britain
2008 Great Britain

HIGH-PERFORMANCE DINGHY (49ER) (OPEN)
2000 Finland
2004 Spain
2008 Denmark

MULTIHULL (TORNADO) (OPEN)
1976 Great Britain
1980 Brazil
1984 New Zealand
1988 France
1992 France
1996 Spain
2000 Austria
2004 Austria
2008 Spain

FLEET/MATCH RACE KEELBOAT (SOLING) (OPEN)
1972 United States
1976 Denmark
1980 Denmark
1984 United States
1988 East Germany
1992 Denmark
1996 Germany
2000 Denmark

TWO-PERSON KEELBOAT (STAR) (MEN; OPEN UNTIL 2008)
1932 United States
1936 Germany
1948 United States
1952 Italy
1956 United States
1960 USSR
1964 The Bahamas
1968 United States
1972 Australia
1980 USSR
1984 United States
1988 Great Britain
1992 United States
1996 Brazil
2000 United States
2004 Brazil
2008 Great Britain

40-METER CLASS
1920 Sweden

30-METER CLASS
1920 Sweden

12-METER CLASS
1920 (old) Norway
1920 (new) Norway

OVER-10-METER CLASS
1900 France
1908 Great Britain
1912 Norway

Summer Olympic Games Champions (continued)

Sailing (yachting) (continued)

10-METER CLASS
1900 Germany
1912 Sweden
1920 (old) Norway
1920 (new) Norway

8-METER CLASS
1900 Great Britain
1908 Great Britain
1912 Norway
1920 (old) Norway
1920 (new) Norway
1924 Norway
1928 France
1932 United States
1936 Italy

7-METER CLASS
1908 Great Britain
1920 (old) Great Britain

6.5-METER CLASS
1920 (new) The Netherlands

6-METER CLASS
1900 Switzerland
1908 Great Britain
1912 France
1920 (old) Belgium
1920 (new) Norway
1924 Norway
1928 Norway
1932 Sweden
1936 Great Britain
1948 United States
1952 United States

5.5-METER CLASS
1952 United States
1956 Sweden
1960 United States
1964 Australia
1968 Sweden

18-FOOT CENTERBOARD BOAT
1920 Great Britain

12-FOOT CENTERBOARD BOAT
1920 The Netherlands
1924 Belgium

12-FOOT DINGHY
1928 Sweden

MONOTYPE CLASS
1932 France

MONOTYPE CLASS "NURNBERG"
1936 The Netherlands

SWALLOW
1948 Great Britain

FIREFLY
1948 Denmark

SHARPIE
1956 New Zealand

Sailing (yachting) (continued)

DRAGON
1948 Norway
1952 Norway
1956 Sweden
1960 Greece
1964 Denmark
1968 United States
1972 Australia

TEMPEST
1972 USSR
1976 Sweden

FLYING DUTCHMAN
1960 Norway
1964 New Zealand
1968 Great Britain
1972 Great Britain
1976 West Germany
1980 Spain
1984 United States
1988 Denmark
1992 Spain

Shooting (men)

individual

TRAP (CLAY PIGEON) (OPEN 1968–92)
1900 Roger de Barbarin (FRA)
1908 Walter Ewing (CAN)
1912 James Graham (USA)
1920 Mark Arie (USA)
1924 Gyula Halasy (HUN)
1952 George Généreux (CAN)
1956 Galliano Rossini (ITA)
1960 Ion Dumitrescu (ROM)
1964 Ennio Mattarelli (ITA)
1968 John Braithwaite (GBR)
1972 Angelo Scalzone (ITA)
1976 Donald Haldeman (USA)
1980 Luciano Giovannetti (ITA)
1984 Luciano Giovannetti (ITA)
1988 Donald Monakov (URS)
1992 Petr Hrdlicka (TCH)
1996 Michael Constantine Diamond (AUS)
2000 Michael Constantine Diamond (AUS)
2004 Aleksey Alipov (RUS)
2008 David Kostelecky (CZE)

DOUBLE TRAP
1996 Russell Andrew Mark (AUS)
2000 Richard Faulds (GBR)
2004 Ahmed Almaktoum (UAE)
2008 Walton Eller (USA)

SKEET (OPEN UNTIL 1996)
1968 Yevgeny Petrov (URS)
1972 Konrad Wirnhier (FRG)
1976 Josef Panacek (TCH)
1980 Hans Kjeld Rasmussen (DEN)
1984 Matthew Dryke (USA)
1988 Axel Wegner (GDR)
1992 Zhang Shan (CHN)
1996 Ennio Falco (ITA)
2000 Mykola Milchev (UKR)
2004 Andrea Benelli (ITA)
2008 Vincent Hancock (USA)

Summer Olympic Games Champions (continued)

Shooting (men) (continued)

individual (continued)

FREE PISTOL

1896 Sumner Paine (USA)
1900 Karl Konrad Röderer (SUI)
1912 Alfred Lane (USA)
1920 Carl Frederick (USA)
1936 Torsten Ullmann (SWE)
1948 Edwin Vásquez Cam (PER)
1952 Huelet Benner (USA)
1956 Pentti Tapio Linnosvuo (FIN)
1960 Aleksey Gushchin (URS)
1964 Väinö Johannes Markkanen (FIN)
1968 Grigory Kosykh (URS)
1976 Uwe Potteck (GDR)
1980 Aleksandr Melentev (URS)
1984 Xu Haifeng (CHN)
1988 Sorin Babii (ROM)
1992 Konstantin Lukachik (UNT)
1996 Boris Kokorev (RUS)
2000 Tanyu Kiryakov (BUL)
2004 Mikhail Nestruyev (RUS)
2008 Jin Jong Oh (KOR)

RAPID-FIRE PISTOL

1896 Joannis Phrangudis (GRE)
1900 Maurice Larrouy (FRA)
1908 Paul van Asbrock (BEL)
1912 Alfred Lane (USA)
1920 Guilherme Paraense (BRA)
1924 Henry Bailey (USA)
1932 Renzo Morigi (ITA)
1936 Cornelius van Oyen (GER)
1948 Karoly Takacs (HUN)
1952 Karoly Takacs (HUN)
1956 Stefan Petrescu (ROM)
1960 William McMillan (USA)
1964 Pentti Tapio Linnosvuo (FIN)
1968 Jozef Zapedzki (POL)
1972 Jozef Zapedzki (POL)
1976 Norbert Klaar (GDR)
1980 Corneliu Ion (ROM)
1984 Takeo Kamachi (JPN)
1988 Afanasy Kuzmin (URS)
1992 Ralf Schumann (GER)
1996 Ralf Schumann (GER)
2000 Sergey Alifirenko (RUS)
2004 Ralf Schumann (GER)
2008 Oleksandr Petriv (UKR)

SMALL-BORE RIFLE (PRONE)

1908 Arthur Ashton Carnell (GBR)
1912 Frederick Hird (USA)
1920 Lawrence Nuesslein (USA)
1924 Pierre Coquelin de Lisle (FRA)
1932 Bertil Rönnmark (SWE)
1936 Willy Røgeberg (NOR)
1948 Arthur Cook (USA)
1952 Iosif Sarbu (ROM)
1956 Gerald Ouellette (CAN)
1960 Peter Kohnke (GER)
1964 Laszlo Hammerl (HUN)
1968 Jan Kurka (TCH)
1972 Ho Jun Li (PRK)
1976 Karlheinz Smieszek (FRG)
1980 Karoly Varga (HUN)
1984 Edward Etzel (USA)
1988 Miroslav Varga (TCH)
1992 Lee Eun Chul (KOR)

Shooting (men) (continued)

individual (continued)

SMALL-BORE RIFLE (PRONE) (CONTINUED)

1996 Christian Klees (GER)
2000 Jonas Edman (SWE)
2004 Matthew Emmons (USA)
2008 Artur Ayvazian (UKR)

SMALL-BORE RIFLE (3 POSITIONS)

1952 Erling Kongshaug (NOR)
1956 Anatoly Bogdanov (URS)
1960 Viktor Shamburkin (URS)
1964 Lones Wesley Wigger (USA)
1968 Bernd Klingner (FRG)
1972 John Writer (USA)
1976 Lanny Bassham (USA)
1980 Viktor Vlasov (URS)
1984 Malcolm Cooper (GBR)
1988 Malcolm Cooper (GBR)
1992 Gratchia Petikian (UNT)
1996 Jean-Pierre Amat (FRA)
2000 Rajmond Debevec (SLO)
2004 Jia Zhanbo (CHN)
2008 Qiu Jian (CHN)

10-METER RUNNING (GAME) TARGET

1900 Louis Debray (FRA)
1972 Yakov Zheleznyak (URS)
1976 Aleksandr Gazov (URS)
1980 Igor Sokolov (URS)
1984 Li Yuwei (CHN)
1988 Tor Heiestad (NOR)
1992 Michael Jakosits (GER)
1996 Yang Ling (CHN)
2000 Yang Ling (CHN)
2004 Manfred Kurzer (GER)

AIR RIFLE

1984 Philippe Heberle (FRA)
1988 Goran Maksimovic (YUG)
1992 Yury Fedkin (UNT)
1996 Artyom Khadzhibekov (RUS)
2000 Cai Yalin (CHN)
2004 Zhu Quinan (CHN)
2008 Abhinav Bindra (IND)

AIR PISTOL

1988 Tanyu Kiryakov (BUL)
1992 Wang Yifu (CHN)
1996 Roberto di Donna (ITA)
2000 Franck Dumoulin (FRA)
2004 Wang Yifu (CHN)
2008 Pang Wei (CHN)

FREE RIFLE (300 M, 3 POSITIONS)

1908 Albert Helgerud (NOR)
1912 Paul René Colas (FRA)
1920 Morris Fisher (USA)
1924 Morris Fisher (USA)
1948 Emil Grünig (SUI)
1952 Anatoly Bogdanov (URS)
1956 Vasily Borisov (URS)
1960 Hubert Hammerer (AUT)
1964 Gary Lee Anderson (USA)
1968 Gary Lee Anderson (USA)
1972 Lones Wesley Wigger (USA)

Summer Olympic Games Champions (continued)

Shooting (men) (continued)

individual (continued)

ARMY RIFLE (300 M, 3 POSITIONS)
1896 Georgios Orphanidis (GRE)
1900 Emil Kellenberger (SUI)
1912 Sandor Prokop (HUN)

ARMY RIFLE (200 M)
1896 Pantelis Karasevdas (GRE)

FREE RIFLE (1,000 YD PRONE)
1908 Joshua Millner (GBR)

FULL-BORE RIFLE (300 M STANDING)
1900 Lars Madsen (DEN)

FULL-BORE RIFLE (300 M KNEELING)
1900 Konrad Staeheli (SUI)

FULL-BORE RIFLE (300 M PRONE)
1900 Achille Paroche (FRA)

FULL-BORE RIFLE (300 M)
1900 Emil Kellenberger (SUI)

RIFLE (300 M, 2 POSITIONS)
1920 Morris Fisher (USA)

RIFLE (300 M STANDING)
1920 Carl Osburn (USA)

RIFLE (300 M PRONE)
1920 Otto Olsen (NOR)

RIFLE (600 M PRONE)
1920 Hugo Johansson (SWE)

6-MILLIMETER SMALL GUN (OPEN REAR SIGHT)
1900 C. Grosett (FRA)

SMALL-BORE RIFLE (VANISHING TARGET)
1908 William Styles (GBR)
1912 Wilhelm Carlberg (SWE)

SMALL-BORE RIFLE (MOVING TARGET)
1908 John Francis Fleming (GBR)

RUNNING DEER (100 M SINGLE SHOT)
1908 Oscar Swahn (SWE)
1912 Alfred Swahn (SWE)
1920 Otto Olsen (NOR)
1924 John Boles (USA)

RUNNING DEER (100 M DOUBLE SHOT)
1908 Walter Winans (USA)
1912 Ake Lundeberg (SWE)
1920 Ole Andreas Lilloe-Olsen (NOR)
1924 Ole Andreas Lilloe-Olsen (NOR)

RUNNING DEER (100 M SINGLE AND DOUBLE SHOT)
1952 John Larsen (NOR)
1956 Vitaly Romanenko (URS)

LIVE PIGEON
1900 Léon de Lunden (BEL)

GAME SHOOTING
1900 Donald Mackintosh (AUS)

Shooting (men) (continued)

individual (continued)

MILITARY REVOLVER (25 M)
1896 John Paine (USA)

MILITARY REVOLVER (20 M)
1906 Louis Richardet (SUI)
1906 (model 1873–74) Jean Fouconnier (FRA)

REVOLVER AND PISTOL
1900 Paul van Asbrock (BEL)
1908 Paul van Asbrock (BEL)
1912 Alfred Lane (USA)

DUELING PISTOL
1906 (20 m) Léon Moreaux (FRA)
1906 (25 m) Konstantinos Skarlatos (GRE)
1912 Alfred Lane (USA)

team

FREE RIFLE (300 M)
1908 Norway
1912 Sweden

ARMY RIFLE (300 M)
1900 Norway

ARMY RIFLE (ALL-AROUND)
1900 United States
1908 United States
1912 United States

FULL-BORE RIFLE (300 M)
1900 Switzerland

SMALL-BORE RIFLE
1900 Great Britain
1908 Great Britain
1920 United States
1924 France

SMALL-BORE RIFLE (VANISHING TARGET)
1912 Sweden

RIFLE (600 M PRONE)
1920 United States

RIFLE (300 M, 2 POSITIONS)
1920 United States

RIFLE (300 M STANDING)
1920 Denmark

RIFLE (300 M PRONE)
1920 United States

RIFLE (ALL-AROUND)
1920 United States
1924 United States

RUNNING DEER (SINGLE SHOT)
1908 Sweden
1912 Sweden
1920 Norway
1924 Norway

RUNNING DEER (DOUBLE SHOT)
1920 Norway
1924 Great Britain

Summer Olympic Games Champions (continued)

Shooting (men) (continued)

team (continued)

CLAY PIGEON

1900 Great Britain
1908 Great Britain
1912 United States
1920 United States
1924 United States

REVOLVER

1900 Switzerland

PISTOL

1920 United States
1924 United States

REVOLVER AND PISTOL

1900 United States
1908 United States
1912 United States
1920 United States

DUELING PISTOL

1912 Sweden

Shooting (women)

TRAP (CLAY PIGEON)

2000 Daina Gudzineviciute (LTU)
2004 Suzanne Balogh (AUS)
2008 Satu Mäkelä-Nummela (FIN)

DOUBLE TRAP

1996 Kim Rhode (USA)
2000 Pia Hansen (SWE)
2004 Kimberly Rhode (USA)

SKEET

2000 Zemfira Meftakhetdinova (AZE)
2004 Diana Igaly (HUN)
2008 Chiara Cainero (ITA)

PISTOL

1984 Linda Thom (CAN)
1988 Nino Salukvadze (URS)
1992 Marina Logvinenko (UNT)
1996 Li Duihong (CHN)
2000 Mariya Zdravkova Grozdeva (BUL)
2004 Mariya Zdravkova Grozdeva (BUL)
2008 Chen Ying (CHN)

SMALL-BORE RIFLE (3 POSITIONS)

1984 Wu Xiao-Xuan (CHN)
1988 Silvia Sperber (FRG)
1992 Launi Meili (USA)
1996 Aleksandra Ivosev (YUG)
2000 Renata Mauer (POL)
2004 Lyubov Galkina (RUS)
2008 Du Li (CHN)

AIR RIFLE

1984 Pat Spurgin (USA)
1988 Irina Chilova (URS)
1992 Yeo Kab Soon (KOR)
1996 Renata Mauer (POL)
2000 Nancy Johnson (USA)
2004 Du Li (CHN)
2008 Katerina Emmons (CZE)

Shooting (women) (continued)

AIR PISTOL

1988 Jasna Sekaric (YUG)
1992 Marina Logvinenko (UNT)
1996 Olga Klochneva (RUS)
2000 Tao Luna (CHN)
2004 Olena Kostevych (UKR)
2008 Guo Wenjun (CHN)

Softball

1996 United States
2000 United States
2004 United States
2008 Japan

Swimming (men)

50-METER FREESTYLE		SEC
1988	Matthew Biondi (USA)	22.14
1992	Aleksandr Popov (UNT)	21.91
1996	Aleksandr Popov (RUS)	22.13
2000	Anthony Ervin (USA); Gary Hall, Jr. (USA) (*tied*)	21.98
2004	Gary Hall (USA)	21.93
2008	César Cielo Filho (BRA)	21.30

100-METER FREESTYLE		MIN:SEC
1896	Alfred Hajos (HUN)	1:22.2
1904	Zoltan Halmay (HUN)	1:02.8[13]
1908	Charles Daniels (USA)	1:05.6
1912	Duke Paoa Kahanamoku (USA)	1:03.4
1920	Duke Paoa Kahanamoku (USA)	1:00.4
1924	Johnny Weissmuller (USA)	59.0
1928	Johnny Weissmuller (USA)	58.6
1932	Yasuji Miyazaki (JPN)	58.2
1936	Ferenc Csik (HUN)	57.6
1948	Walter Ris (USA)	57.3
1952	Clark Scholes (USA)	57.4
1956	Jon Henricks (AUS)	55.4
1960	John Devitt (AUS)	55.2
1964	Donald Schollander (USA)	53.4
1968	Michael Wenden (AUS)	52.2
1972	Mark Spitz (USA)	51.22
1976	Jim Montgomery (USA)	49.99
1980	Jörg Wöithe (GDR)	50.40
1984	Ambrose Gaines (USA)	49.80
1988	Matthew Biondi (USA)	48.63
1992	Aleksandr Popov (UNT)	49.02
1996	Aleksandr Popov (RUS)	48.74
2000	Pieter Van den Hoogenband (NED)	48.30
2004	Pieter Van den Hoogenband (NED)	48.17
2008	Alain Bernard (FRA)	47.21

100 METER FREESTYLE FOR SAILORS		MIN:SEC
1896	Ioannis Malokinis (GRE)	2:20.4

200-METER FREESTYLE		MIN:SEC
1900	Fred Lane (AUS)	2:25.2
1904	Charles Daniels (USA)	2:44.2[14]
1968	Michael Wenden (AUS)	1:55.2
1972	Mark Spitz (USA)	1:52.78
1976	Bruce Furniss (USA)	1:50.29
1980	Sergey Koplyakov (URS)	1:49.81
1984	Michael Gross (FRG)	1:47.44
1988	Duncan Armstrong (AUS)	1:47.25
1992	Yevgeny Sadovy (UNT)	1:46.70
1996	Danyon Loader (NZL)	1:47.63
2000	Pieter Van den Hoogenband (NED)	1:45.35
2004	Ian Thorpe (AUS)	1:44.71
2008	Michael Phelps (USA)	1:42.96

Summer Olympic Games Champions (continued)

Swimming (men) (continued)

400-METER FREESTYLE — MIN:SEC

Year	Champion	Time
1896	Paul Neumann (AUT)	8:12.6[15]
1904	Charles Daniels (USA)	6:16.2[16]
1908	Henry Taylor (GBR)	5:36.8
1912	George Hodgson (CAN)	5:24.4
1920	Norman Ross (USA)	5:26.8
1924	Johnny Weissmuller (USA)	5:04.2
1928	Victoriano Zorilla (ARG)	5:01.6
1932	Clarence Crabbe (USA)	4:48.4
1936	Jack Medica (USA)	4:44.5
1948	William Smith (USA)	4:41.0
1952	Jean Boiteux (FRA)	4:30.7
1956	Murray Rose (AUS)	4:27.3
1960	Murray Rose (AUS)	4:18.3
1964	Donald Schollander (USA)	4:12.2
1968	Michael Burton (USA)	4:09.0
1972	Bradford Cooper (AUS)	4:00.27
1976	Brian Goodell (USA)	3:51.93
1980	Vladimir Salnikov (URS)	3:51.31
1984	George DiCarlo (USA)	3:51.23
1988	Uwe Dassler (GDR)	3:46.95
1992	Yevgeny Sadovy (UNT)	3:45.00
1996	Danyon Loader (NZL)	3:47.97
2000	Ian Thorpe (AUS)	3:40.59
2004	Ian Thorpe (AUS)	3:43.10
2008	Park Tae Hwan (KOR)	3:41.86

1,500-METER FREESTYLE — MIN:SEC

Year	Champion	Time
1896	Alfred Hajos (HUN)	18:22.2[17]
1900	Johnny Arthur Jarvis (GBR)	13:40.2[18]
1904	Emil Rausch (GER)	27:18.2[19]
1908	Henry Taylor (GBR)	22:48.4
1912	George Hodgson (CAN)	22:00.0
1920	Norman Ross (USA)	22:23.2
1924	Andrew Charlton (AUS)	20:06.6
1928	Arne Borg (SWE)	19:51.8
1932	Kusuo Kitamura (JPN)	19:12.4
1936	Noburu Terada (JPN)	19:13.7
1948	James McLane (USA)	19:18.5
1952	Ford Konno (USA)	18:30.0
1956	Murray Rose (AUS)	17:58.9
1960	John Konrads (AUS)	17:19.6
1964	Robert Windle (AUS)	17:01.7
1968	Michael Burton (USA)	16:38.9
1972	Michael Burton (USA)	15:52.58
1976	Brian Goodell (USA)	15:02.40
1980	Vladimir Salnikov (URS)	14:58.27
1984	Michael O'Brien (USA)	15:05.20
1988	Vladimir Salnikov (URS)	15:00.40
1992	Kieren Perkins (AUS)	14:43.48
1996	Kieren Perkins (AUS)	14:56.40
2000	Grant Hackett (AUS)	14:48.33
2004	Grant Hackett (AUS)	14:43.40
2008	Oussama Mellouli (TUN)	14:40.84

4,000-METER FREESTYLE — MIN:SEC

Year	Champion	Time
1900	Johnny Arthur Jarvis (GBR)	58:24

880-YARD FREESTYLE — MIN:SEC

Year	Champion	Time
1904	Emil Rausch (GER)	13:11.4

1-MILE FREESTYLE — MIN:SEC

Year	Champion	Time
1904	Emil Rausch (GER)	27:18.2

100-METER BUTTERFLY — SEC

Year	Champion	Time
1968	Douglas Russell (USA)	55.9
1972	Mark Spitz (USA)	54.27
1976	Matt Vogel (USA)	54.35

Swimming (men) (continued)

100-METER BUTTERFLY (CONTINUED) — SEC

Year	Champion	Time
1980	Pär Arvidsson (SWE)	54.92
1984	Michael Gross (FRG)	53.08
1988	Anthony Nesty (SUR)	53.00
1992	Pablo Morales (USA)	53.32
1996	Denis Pankratov (RUS)	52.27
2000	Lars Frölander (SWE)	52.00
2004	Michael Phelps (USA)	51.25
2008	Michael Phelps (USA)	50.58

200-METER BUTTERFLY — MIN

Year	Champion	Time
1956	William Yorzyk (USA)	2:19.3
1960	Michael Troy (USA)	2:12.8
1964	Kevin Berry (AUS)	2:06.6
1968	Carl Robie (USA)	2:08.7
1972	Mark Spitz (USA)	2:00.70
1976	Mike Bruner (USA)	1:59.23
1980	Sergey Fesenko (URS)	1:59.76
1984	Jonathan Sieben (AUS)	1:57.04
1988	Michael Gross (FRG)	1:56.94
1992	Mel Stewart (USA)	1:56.26
1996	Denis Pankratov (RUS)	1:56.51
2000	Tom Malchow (USA)	1:55.35
2004	Michael Phelps (USA)	1:54.04
2008	Michael Phelps (USA)	1:52.03

100-METER BACKSTROKE — MIN:SEC

Year	Champion	Time
1904	Walter Brack (GER)	1:16.8[20]
1908	Arno Bieberstein (GER)	1:24.6
1912	Harry Hebner (USA)	1:21.2
1920	Warren Paoa Kealoha (USA)	1:15.2
1924	Warren Paoa Kealoha (USA)	1:13.2
1928	George Kojac (USA)	1:08.2
1932	Masaji Kiyokawa (JPN)	1:08.6
1936	Adolph Kiefer (USA)	1:05.9
1948	Allen Stack (USA)	1:06.4
1952	Yoshinobu Oyakawa (JPN)	1:05.4
1956	David Theile (AUS)	1:02.2
1960	David Theile (AUS)	1:01.9
1968	Roland Matthes (GDR)	58.7
1972	Roland Matthes (GDR)	56.58
1976	John Naber (USA)	55.49
1980	Bengt Baron (SWE)	56.53
1984	Richard Carey (USA)	55.79
1988	Daichi Suzuki (JPN)	55.05
1992	Mark Tewksbury (CAN)	53.98
1996	Jeff Rouse (USA)	54.10
2000	Lenny Krayzelburg (USA)	53.72
2004	Aaron Peirsol (USA)	54.06
2008	Aaron Peirsol (USA)	52.54

200-METER BACKSTROKE — MIN:SEC

Year	Champion	Time
1900	Ernst Hoppenberg (GER)	2:47.0
1964	Jed Graef (USA)	2:10.3
1968	Roland Matthes (GDR)	2:09.6
1972	Roland Matthes (GDR)	2:02.82
1976	John Naber (USA)	1:59.19
1980	Sandor Wladar (HUN)	2:01.93
1984	Richard Carey (USA)	2:00.23
1988	Igor Polyansky (URS)	1:59.37
1992	Martin López-Zubero (ESP)	1:58.47
1996	Brad Bridgewater (USA)	1:58.54
2000	Lenny Krayzelburg (USA)	1:56.76
2004	Aaron Peirsol (USA)	1:54.95
2008	Ryan Lochte (USA)	1:53.94

Summer Olympic Games Champions (continued)

Swimming (men) (continued)

100-METER BREASTSTROKE		MIN:SEC
1968	Donald McKenzie (USA)	1:07.7
1972	Nobutaka Tagushi (JPN)	1:04.94
1976	John Hencken (USA)	1:03.11
1980	Duncan Goodhew (GBR)	1:03.34
1984	Steve Lundquist (USA)	1:01.65
1988	Adrian Moorhouse (GBR)	1:02.04
1992	Nelson Diebel (USA)	1:01.50
1996	Frederick Deburghgraeve (BEL)	1:00.65
2000	Domenico Fioravanti (ITA)	1:00.46
2004	Kosuke Kitajima (JPN)	1:00.08
2008	Kosuke Kitajima (JPN)	0:58.91

200-METER BREASTSTROKE		MIN:SEC
1908	Frederick Holman (GBR)	3:09.2
1912	Walter Bathe (GER)	3:01.8
1920	Hakan Malmroth (SWE)	3:04.4
1924	Robert Skelton (USA)	2:56.6
1928	Yoshiyuki Tsuruta (JPN)	2:48.8
1932	Yoshiyuki Tsuruta (JPN)	2:45.4
1936	Tetsuo Hamuro (JPN)	2:42.5
1948	Joseph Verdeur (USA)	2:39.3
1952	John Davies (AUS)	2:34.4
1956	Masaru Furukawa (JPN)	2:34.7
1960	William Mulliken (USA)	2:37.4
1964	Ian O'Brien (AUS)	2:27.8
1968	Felipe Muñoz (MEX)	2:28.7
1972	John Hencken (USA)	2:21.55
1976	David Wilkie (GBR)	2:15.11
1980	Robertas Zulpa (URS)	2:15.85
1984	Victor Davis (CAN)	2:13.34
1988	Jozsef Szabo (HUN)	2:13.52
1992	Mike Barrowman (USA)	2:10.16
1996	Norbert Rozsa (HUN)	2:12.57
2000	Domenico Fioravanti (ITA)	2:10.87
2004	Kosuke Kitajima (JPN)	2:09.44
2008	Kosuke Kitajima (JPN)	2:07.64

400-METER BREASTSTROKE		MIN:SEC
1904	Georg Zacharias (GER)	7:23.6[21]
1912	Walter Bathe (GER)	6:29.6
1920	Hakan Malmroth (SWE)	6:31.8

200-YARD RELAY		MIN:SEC
1904	United States	2:04.6

200-METER MEDLEY		MIN:SEC
1968	Charles Hickcox (USA)	2:12.0
1972	Gunnar Larsson (SWE)	2:07.17
1984	Alex Baumann (CAN)	2:01.42
1988	Tamas Darnyi (HUN)	2:00.17
1992	Tamas Darnyi (HUN)	2:00.76
1996	Attila Czene (HUN)	1:59.91
2000	Massimiliano Rosolino (ITA)	1:58.98
2004	Michael Phelps (USA)	1:57.14
2008	Michael Phelps (USA)	1:54.23

400-METER MEDLEY		MIN:SEC
1964	Richard William Roth (USA)	4:45.4
1968	Charles Hickcox (USA)	4:48.4
1972	Gunnar Larsson (SWE)	4:31.98
1976	Rod Strachan (USA)	4:23.68
1980	Aleksandr Sidorenko (URS)	4:22.89
1984	Alex Baumann (CAN)	4:17.41
1988	Tamas Darnyi (HUN)	4:14.75
1992	Tamas Darnyi (HUN)	4:14.23
1996	Tom Dolan (USA)	4:14.90
2000	Tom Dolan (USA)	4:11.76

Swimming (men) (continued)

400-METER MEDLEY (CONTINUED)		MIN:SEC
2004	Michael Phelps (USA)	4:08.26
2008	Michael Phelps (USA)	4:03.84

4 × 100-METER MEDLEY RELAY		MIN:SEC
1960	United States	4:05.4
1964	United States	3:58.4
1968	United States	3:54.9
1972	United States	3:48.16
1976	United States	3:42.22
1980	Australia	3:45.70
1984	United States	3:39.30
1988	United States	3:36.93
1992	United States	3:36.93
1996	United States	3:34.84
2000	United States	3:33.73
2004	United States	3:30.68
2008	United States	3:29.34

4 × 100-METER FREESTYLE RELAY		MIN:SEC
1964	United States	3:33.2
1968	United States	3:31.7
1972	United States	3:26.42
1984	United States	3:19.03
1988	United States	3:16.53
1992	United States	3:16.74
1996	United States	3:15.41
2000	Australia	3:13.67
2004	South Africa	3:13.17
2008	United States	3:08.24

4 × 200-METER FREESTYLE RELAY		MIN:SEC
1908	Great Britain	10:55.6
1912	Australia	10:11.2
1920	United States	10:04.4
1924	United States	9:53.4
1928	United States	9:36.2
1932	Japan	8:58.4
1936	Japan	8:51.5
1948	United States	8:46.0
1952	United States	8:31.1
1956	Australia	8:23.6
1960	United States	8:10.2
1964	United States	7:52.1
1968	United States	7:52.3
1972	United States	7:35.78
1976	United States	7:23.22
1980	USSR	7:23.50
1984	United States	7:15.69
1988	United States	7:12.51
1992	Unified Team	7:11.95
1996	United States	7:14.84
2000	Australia	7:07.05
2004	United States	7:07.33
2008	United States	6:58.56

60-METER UNDERWATER		MIN:SEC (UNDERWATER)
1900	Charles de Vendeville (FRA)	1:08.4

200-METER OBSTACLE		MIN:SEC
1900	Frederick Lane (AUS)	2:38.4

10-KM OPEN-WATER MARATHON		HR:MIN:SEC
2008	Maarten van der Weijden (NED)	1:51:51.6

Summer Olympic Games Champions (continued)

Swimming (women)

50-METER FREESTYLE		SEC
1988	Kristin Otto (GDR)	25.49
1992	Yang Wenyi (CHN)	24.79
1996	Amy Van Dyken (USA)	24.87
2000	Inge de Bruijn (NED)	24.32
2004	Inge de Bruijn (NED)	24.58
2008	Britta Steffen (GER)	24.06

100-METER FREESTYLE		MIN:SEC
1912	Fanny Durack (AUS)	1:22.2
1920	Ethelda Bleibtrey (USA)	1:13.6
1924	Ethel Lackie (USA)	1:12.4
1928	Albina Osipowich (USA)	1:11.0
1932	Helene Madison (USA)	1:06.8
1936	Hendrika Mastenbroek (NED)	1:05.9
1948	Greta Andersen (DEN)	1:06.3
1952	Katalin Szoke (HUN)	1:06.8
1956	Dawn Fraser (AUS)	1:02.0
1960	Dawn Fraser (AUS)	1:01.2
1964	Dawn Fraser (AUS)	59.5
1968	Jan Henne (USA)	1:00.0
1972	Sandra Neilson (USA)	58.59
1976	Kornelia Ender (GDR)	55.65
1980	Barbara Krause (GDR)	54.79
1984	Carrie Steinseifer (USA); Nancy Hogshead (USA) (*tied*)	55.92
1988	Kristin Otto (GDR)	54.93
1992	Zhuang Yong (CHN)	54.64
1996	Le Jingyi (CHN)	54.50
2000	Inge de Bruijn (NED)	53.83
2004	Jodie Henry (AUS)	53.84
2008	Britta Steffen (GER)	53.12

200-METER FREESTYLE		MIN:SEC
1968	Debbie Meyer (USA)	2:10.5
1972	Shane Gould (AUS)	2:03.56
1976	Kornelia Ender (GDR)	1:59.26
1980	Barbara Krause (GDR)	1:58.33
1984	Mary Wayte (USA)	1:59.23
1988	Heike Friedrich (GDR)	1:57.65
1992	Nicole Haislett (USA)	1:57.90
1996	Claudia Poll (CRC)	1:58.16
2000	Susie O'Neill (AUS)	1:58.24
2004	Camelia Potec (ROM)	1:58.03
2008	Federica Pellegrini (ITA)	1:54.82

400-METER FREESTYLE		MIN:SEC
1920	Ethelda Bleibtrey (USA)	4:34.0[22]
1924	Martha Norelius (USA)	6:02.2
1928	Martha Norelius (USA)	5:42.8
1932	Helene Madison (USA)	5:28.5
1936	Hendrika Mastenbroek (NED)	5:26.4
1948	Ann Curtis (USA)	5:17.8
1952	Valeria Gyenge (HUN)	5:12.1
1956	Lorraine Crapp (AUS)	4:54.6
1960	Susan Christina von Saltza (USA)	4:50.6
1964	Virginia Duenkel (USA)	4:43.3
1968	Debbie Meyer (USA)	4:31.8
1972	Shane Gould (AUS)	4:19.04
1976	Petra Thümer (GDR)	4:09.89
1980	Ines Diers (GDR)	4:08.76
1984	Tiffany Cohen (USA)	4:07.10
1988	Janet Evans (USA)	4:03.85
1992	Dagmar Hase (GER)	4:07.18
1996	Michelle Smith (IRE)	4:07.25
2000	Brooke Bennett (USA)	4:05.80
2004	Laure Manaudou (FRA)	4:05.34
2008	Rebecca Adlington (GBR)	4:03.22

Swimming (women) (continued)

800-METER FREESTYLE		MIN:SEC
1968	Debbie Meyer (USA)	9:24.0
1972	Keena Rothhammer (USA)	8:53.68
1976	Petra Thümer (GDR)	8:37.14
1980	Michelle Ford (AUS)	8:28.90
1984	Tiffany Cohen (USA)	8:24.95
1988	Janet Evans (USA)	8:20.20
1992	Janet Evans (USA)	8:25.52
1996	Brooke Bennett (USA)	8:27.89
2000	Brooke Bennett (USA)	8:19.67
2004	Ai Shibata (JPN)	8:24.54
2008	Rebecca Adlington (GBR)	8:14.10

100-METER BUTTERFLY		MIN:SEC
1956	Shelley Mann (USA)	1:11.0
1960	Carolyn Schuler (USA)	1:09.5
1964	Sharon Stouder (USA)	1:04.7
1968	Lynette McClements (AUS)	1:05.5
1972	Mayumi Aoki (JPN)	1:03.34
1976	Kornelia Ender (GDR)	1:00.13
1980	Caren Metschuck (GDR)	1:00.42
1984	Mary Meagher (USA)	59.26
1988	Kristin Otto (GDR)	59.00
1992	Qian Hong (CHN)	58.62
1996	Amy Van Dyken (USA)	59.13
2000	Inge de Bruijn (NED)	56.61
2004	Petria Thomas (AUS)	57.72
2008	Lisbeth Lenton Trickett (AUS)	56.73

200-METER BUTTERFLY		MIN:SEC
1968	Aagje Kok (NED)	2:24.7
1972	Karen Moe (USA)	2:15.57
1976	Andrea Pollack (GDR)	2:11.41
1980	Ines Geissler (GDR)	2:10.44
1984	Mary Meagher (USA)	2:06.90
1988	Kathleen Nord (GDR)	2:09.51
1992	Summer Sanders (USA)	2:08.67
1996	Susie O'Neill (AUS)	2:07.76
2000	Misty Hyman (USA)	2:05.88
2004	Otylia Jedrzejczak (POL)	2:06.05
2008	Liu Zige (CHN)	2:04.18

100-METER BACKSTROKE		MIN:SEC
1924	Sybil Bauer (USA)	1:23.2
1928	Maria Braun (NED)	1:22.0
1932	Eleanor Holm (USA)	1:19.4
1936	Dina Senff (NED)	1:18.9
1948	Karen-Margrete Harup (DEN)	1:14.4
1952	Joan Harrison (RSA)	1:14.3
1956	Judith Grinham (GBR)	1:12.9
1960	Lynn Burke (USA)	1:09.3
1964	Cathy Ferguson (USA)	1:07.7
1968	Kaye Hall (USA)	1:06.2
1972	Melissa Belote (USA)	1:05.78
1976	Urike Richter (GDR)	1:01.83
1980	Rica Reinisch (GDR)	1:00.86
1984	Theresa Andrews (USA)	1:02.55
1988	Kristin Otto (GDR)	1:00.89
1992	Krisztina Egerszegi (HUN)	1:00.68
1996	Beth Botsford (USA)	1:01.19
2000	Diana Mocanu (ROM)	1:00.21
2004	Natalie Coughlin (USA)	1:00.37
2008	Natalie Coughlin (USA)	0:58.96

200-METER BACKSTROKE		MIN:SEC
1968	Pokey Watson (USA)	2:24.8
1972	Melissa Belote (USA)	2:19.19
1976	Ulrike Richter (GDR)	2:13.43

Summer Olympic Games Champions (continued)

Swimming (women) (continued)

200-METER BACKSTROKE (CONTINUED)		MIN:SEC
1980	Rica Reinisch (GDR)	2:11.77
1984	Jolanda De Rover (NED)	2:12.38
1988	Krisztina Egerszegi (HUN)	2:09.29
1992	Krisztina Egerszegi (HUN)	2:07.06
1996	Krisztina Egerszegi (HUN)	2:07.83
2000	Diana Mocanu (ROM)	2:08.16
2004	Kirsty Coventry (ZIM)	2:09.19
2008	Kirsty Coventry (ZIM)	2:05.24

100-METER BREASTSTROKE		MIN:SEC
1968	Djurdjica Bjedov (YUG)	1:15.8
1972	Cathy Carr (USA)	1:13.58
1976	Hannelore Anke (GDR)	1:11.16
1980	Ute Geveniger (GDR)	1:10.22
1984	Petra van Staveren (NED)	1:09.88
1988	Tanya Dangalakova (BUL)	1:07.95
1992	Yelena Rudkovskaya (UNT)	1:08.00
1996	Penelope Heyns (RSA)	1:07.73
2000	Megan Quann (USA)	1:07.05
2004	Luo Xuejuan (CHN)	1:06.64
2008	Leisel Jones (AUS)	1:05.17

200-METER BREASTSTROKE		MIN:SEC
1924	Lucy Morton (GBR)	3:33.2
1928	Hilde Schrader (GER)	3:12.6
1932	Claire Dennis (AUS)	3:06.3
1936	Hideko Maehata (JPN)	3:03.6
1948	Petronella van Vliet (NED)	2:57.2
1952	Eva Szekely (HUN)	2:51.7
1956	Ursula Happe (GER)	2:53.1
1960	Anita Lonsbrough (GBR)	2:49.5
1964	Galina Prozumenshchikova-Stepanova (URS)	2:46.4
1968	Sharon Wichman (USA)	2:44.4
1972	Beverley Whitfield (AUS)	2:41.71
1976	Marina Koshevaya (URS)	2:33.35
1980	Lina Kachushite (URS)	2:29.54
1984	Anne Ottenbrite (CAN)	2:30.38
1988	Silke Hörner (GDR)	2:26.71
1992	Kyoko Iwasaki (JPN)	2:26.65
1996	Penelope Heyns (RSA)	2:25.41
2000	Agnes Kovacs (HUN)	2:24.35
2004	Amanda Beard (USA)	2:23.37
2008	Rebecca Soni (USA)	2:20.22

200-METER MEDLEY		MIN:SEC
1968	Claudia Kolb (USA)	2:24.7
1972	Shane Gould (AUS)	2:23.07
1984	Tracy Caulkins (USA)	2:12.64
1988	Daniela Hunger (GDR)	2:12.59
1992	Li Lin (CHN)	2:11.65
1996	Michelle Smith (IRL)	2:13.93
2000	Yana Klochkova (UKR)	2:10.68
2004	Yana Klochkova (UKR)	2:11.14
2008	Stephanie Rice (AUS)	2:08.45

400-METER MEDLEY		MIN:SEC
1964	Donna De Varona (USA)	5:18.7
1968	Claudia Kolb (USA)	5:08.5
1972	Gail Neall (AUS)	5:02.97
1976	Ulrike Tauber (GDR)	4:42.77
1980	Petra Schneider (GDR)	4:36.29
1984	Tracy Caulkins (USA)	4:39.24
1988	Janet Evans (USA)	4:37.76
1992	Krisztina Egerszegi (HUN)	4:36.54
1996	Michelle Smith (IRL)	4:39.18
2000	Yana Klochkova (UKR)	4:33.59

Swimming (women) (continued)

400-METER MEDLEY (CONTINUED)		MIN:SEC
2004	Yana Klochkova (UKR)	4:34.83
2008	Stephanie Rice (AUS)	4:29.45

4 × 100-METER MEDLEY RELAY		MIN:SEC
1960	United States	4:41.1
1964	United States	4:33.9
1968	United States	4:28.3
1972	United States	4:20.75
1976	East Germany	4:07.95
1980	East Germany	4:06.67
1984	United States	4:08.34
1988	East Germany	4:03.74
1992	United States	4:02.54
1996	United States	4:02.88
2000	United States	3:58.30
2004	Australia	3:57.32
2008	Australia	3:52.69

4 × 100-METER FREESTYLE RELAY		MIN:SEC
1912	Great Britain	5:52.8
1920	United States	5:11.6
1924	United States	4:58.8
1928	United States	4:47.6
1932	United States	4:38.0
1936	The Netherlands	4:36.0
1948	United States	4:29.2
1952	Hungary	4:24.4
1956	Australia	4:17.1
1960	United States	4:08.9
1964	United States	4:03.8
1968	United States	4:02.5
1972	United States	3:55.19
1976	United States	3:44.82
1980	East Germany	3:42.71
1984	United States	3:43.43
1988	East Germany	3:40.63
1992	United States	3:39.46
1996	United States	3:39.29
2000	United States	3:36.61
2004	Australia	3:35.94
2008	The Netherlands	3:33.76

4 × 200-METER FREESTYLE RELAY		MIN:SEC
1996	United States	7:59.87
2000	United States	7:57.80
2004	United States	7:53.42
2008	Australia	7:44.31

10-KM OPEN-WATER MARATHON		HR:MIN:SEC
2008	Larisa Ilchenko (RUS)	1:59:27.7

SYNCHRONIZED SWIMMING (INDIVIDUAL)	
1984	Tracie Ruiz (USA)
1988	Carolyn Waldo (CAN)
1992	Kristen Babb-Sprague (USA); Sylvie Fréchette (CAN)[23]

SYNCHRONIZED SWIMMING (DUET)	
1984	United States
1988	Canada
1992	United States
2000	Russia
2004	Russia
2008	Russia

Summer Olympic Games Champions (continued)

Swimming (women) (continued)

SYNCHRONIZED SWIMMING (TEAM)

1996 United States
2000 Russia
2004 Russia
2008 Russia

Table tennis (men)

SINGLES

1988 Yoo Nam Kyu (KOR)
1992 Jan-Ove Waldner (SWE)
1996 Liu Guoliang (CHN)
2000 Kong Linghui (CHN)
2004 Ryu Seung Min (KOR)
2008 Ma Lin (CHN)

TEAM

1988 China
1992 China
1996 China
2000 China
2004 China
2008 China

Table tennis (women)

SINGLES

1988 Chen Jing (CHN)
1992 Deng Yaping (CHN)
1996 Deng Yaping (CHN)
2000 Wang Nan (CHN)
2004 Zhang Yining (CHN)
2008 Zhang Yining (CHN)

TEAM

1988 South Korea
1992 China
1996 China
2000 China
2004 China
2008 China

Taekwondo (men)

58 KG (127.6 LB)

2000 Michail Mouroutsos (GRE)
2004 Chu Mu Yen (TPE)
2008 Guillermo Pérez (MEX)

68 KG (149.6 LB)

2000 Steven Lopez (USA)
2004 Hadi Saei Bonehkohal (IRI)
2008 Son Tae Jin (KOR)

80 KG (176 LB)

2000 Angel Valodia Matos (CUB)
2004 Steven Lopez (USA)
2008 Hadi Saei (IRI)

OVER 80 KG (176+ LB)

2000 Kim Kyong-Hun (KOR)
2004 Moon Sung Dae (KOR)
2008 Cha Dong Min (KOR)

Taekwondo (women)

49 KG (107.8 LB)

2000 Lauren Burns (AUS)
2004 Chen Shih Hsin (TPE)
2008 Wu Jingyu (CHN)

Taekwondo (women) (continued)

57 KG (125.4 LB)

2000 Jung Jae-Eun (KOR)
2004 Jang Ji Won (KOR)
2008 Lim Su Jeong (KOR)

67 KG (147.4 LB)

2000 Lee Sun-Hee (KOR)
2004 Luo Wei (CHN)
2008 Hwang Kyung Seon (KOR)

OVER 67 KG (147.4+ LB)

2000 Chen Zhong (CHN)
2004 Chen Zhong (CHN)
2008 María del Rosario Espinoza (MEX)

Tennis (men)

SINGLES

1896 John Pius Boland (GBR)
1900 Hugh (Laurie) Doherty (GBR)
1904 Beals Wright (USA)
1908 Josiah Ritchie (GBR)
1912 Charles Winslow (RSA)
1920 Louis Raymond (RSA)
1924 Vincent Richards (USA)
1988 Miloslav Mecir (TCH)
1992 Marc Rosset (SUI)
1996 Andre Agassi (USA)
2000 Yevgeny Kafelnikov (RUS)
2004 Nicolas Massu (CHI)
2008 Rafael Nadal (ESP)

DOUBLES

1896 John Pius Boland (GBR), Friedrich Thraun (GER)
1900 Hugh (Laurie) Doherty, Reginald Doherty (GBR)
1904 Edgar Leonard, Beals Wright (USA)
1908 George Hillyard, Reginald Doherty (GBR)
1912 Harold Kitson, Charles Winslow (RSA)
1920 Oswald Noel Turnbull, Maxwell Woosnam (GBR)
1924 Francis Hunter, Vincent Richards (USA)
1988 Kenneth Flach, Robert Seguso (USA)
1992 Boris Becker, Michael Stich (GER)
1996 Todd Woodbridge, Mark Woodforde (AUS)
2000 Sebastien Lareau, Daniel Nestor (CAN)
2004 Fernando Gonzalez, Nicolas Massu (CHI)
2008 Roger Federer, Stanislas Wawrinka (SUI)

MIXED DOUBLES

1900 Charlotte Cooper, Reginald Doherty (GBR)
1912 Dora Köring, Heinrich Schomburgk (GER)
1920 Suzanne Lenglen, Max Décugis (FRA)
1924 Hazel Wightman, R. Norris Williams (USA)

Tennis (women)

SINGLES

1900 Charlotte Cooper (GBR)
1908 Dorothy Chambers-Lambert (GBR)
1912 Marguerite Broquedis (FRA)
1920 Suzanne Lenglen (FRA)
1924 Helen Wills-Moody (USA)
1988 Steffi Graf (FRG)
1992 Jennifer Capriati (USA)
1996 Lindsay Davenport (USA)
2000 Venus Williams (USA)
2004 Justine Henin-Hardenne (BEL)
2008 Yelena Dementyeva (RUS)

Summer Olympic Games Champions (continued)

Tennis (women) (continued)

DOUBLES

1920 Winifred Margaret McNair, Kathleen McKane (GBR)
1924 Helen Wills-Moody, Hazel Wightman (USA)
1988 Zina Garrison, Pamela Shriver (USA)
1992 Gigi Fernandez, Mary Joe Fernandez (USA)
1996 Gigi Fernandez, Mary Joe Fernandez (USA)
2000 Serena Williams, Venus Williams (USA)
2004 Li Ting, Sun Tian Tian (CHN)
2008 Serena Williams, Venus Williams (USA)

Tennis—Covered Courts (indoor tennis)

MEN'S SINGLES

1908 Arthur Gore (GBR)
1912 André Gobert (FRA)

MEN'S DOUBLES

1908 Arthur Gore, Herbert Roper-Barrett (GBR)
1912 Maurice Germot, André Gobert (FRA)

WOMEN'S SINGLES

1908 Gladys Eastlake-Smith (GBR)
1912 Edith Hannam (GBR)

MIXED DOUBLES

1912 Edith Hannam, Charles Dixon (GBR)

Triathlon (swim/bike/run) (men)

2000 Simon Whitfield (CAN)
2004 Hamish Carter (NZL)
2008 Jan Frodeno (GER)

Triathlon (swim/bike/run) (women)

2000 Brigitte McMahon (SUI)
2004 Kate Allen (AUT)
2008 Emma Snowsill (AUS)

Volleyball (men)

INDOOR

1964 USSR
1968 USSR
1972 Japan
1976 Poland
1980 USSR
1984 United States
1988 United States
1992 Brazil
1996 The Netherlands
2000 Yugoslavia
2004 Brazil
2008 United States

BEACH

1996 United States
2000 United States
2004 Brazil
2008 United States

Volleyball (women)

INDOOR

1964 Japan
1968 USSR
1972 USSR
1976 Japan
1980 USSR
1984 China
1988 USSR
1992 Cuba

Volleyball (women) (continued)

INDOOR (CONTINUED)

1996 Cuba
2000 Cuba
2004 China
2008 Brazil

BEACH

1996 Brazil
2000 Australia
2004 United States
2008 United States

Water polo (men)

1900 Great Britain
1904 United States
1908 Great Britain
1912 Great Britain
1920 Great Britain
1924 France
1928 Germany
1932 Hungary
1936 Hungary
1948 Italy
1952 Hungary
1956 Hungary
1960 Italy
1964 Hungary
1968 Yugoslavia
1972 USSR
1976 Hungary
1980 USSR
1984 Yugoslavia
1988 Yugoslavia
1992 Italy
1996 Spain
2000 Hungary
2004 Hungary
2008 Hungary

Water polo (women)

2000 Australia
2004 Italy
2008 The Netherlands

Weight lifting (men)[24, 25]

56 KG (123.2 LB)		KG
1972	Zygmunt Smalcerz (POL)	337.5
1976	Aleksandr Varonin (URS)	242.5
1980	Kanybek Osmanaliyev (URS)	245.0
1984	Zeng Guoqiang (CHN)	235.0
1988	Sevdalin Marinov (BUL)	270.0
1992	Ivan Ivanov (BUL)	265.0
1996	Halil Mutlu (TUR)	287.5
2000	Halil Mutlu (TUR)	305.0
2004	Halil Mutlu (TUR)	295.0
2008	Long Qingquan (CHN)	292.0

62 KG (136.4 LB)		KG
1948	Joseph de Pietro (USA)	307.5
1952	Ivan Udodov (URS)	315.0
1956	Charles Vinci (USA)	342.5
1960	Charles Vinci (USA)	345.0
1964	Aleksey Vakhonin (URS)	357.5
1968	Mohammad Nassiri (IRI)	367.5
1972	Imre Foldi (HUN)	377.5
1976	Norair Nurikian (BUL)	262.5
1980	Daniel Núñez (CUB)	275.0
1984	Wu Shude (CHN)	267.5

Summer Olympic Games Champions (continued)

Weight lifting (men)[24, 25] (continued)

62 KG (136.4 LB) (CONTINUED)		KG
1988	Oksen Mirzoyan (URS)	292.5
1992	Chun Byung Kwan (KOR)	287.5
1996	Tang Ningsheng (CHN)	307.5
2000	Nikolay Pechalov (CRO)	325.0
2004	Shi Zhiyong (CHN)	325.0
2008	Zhang Xiangxiang (CHN)	319.0

69 KG (151.8 LB)		KG
1920	Frans de Haes (BEL)	220.0
1924	Pierino Gabetti (ITA)	402.5[26]
1928	Franz Andrysek (AUT)	287.5
1932	Raymond Suvigny (FRA)	287.5
1936	Anthony Terlazzo (USA)	312.5
1948	Mahmoud Fayad (EGY)	332.5
1952	Rafael Chimishkyan (URS)	337.5
1956	Isaac Berger (USA)	352.5
1960	Yevgeny Minayev (URS)	372.5
1964	Yoshinobu Miyake (JPN)	397.5
1968	Yoshinobu Miyake (JPN)	392.5
1972	Norair Nurikian (BUL)	402.5
1976	Nikolay Kolesnikov (URS)	285.0
1980	Viktor Mazin (URS)	290.0
1984	Chen Weiqiang (CHN)	282.5
1988	Naim Suleymanoglu (TUR)	342.5
1992	Naim Suleymanoglu (TUR)	320.0
1996	Naim Suleymanoglu (TUR)	335.0
2000	Galabin Boevski (BUL)	357.5
2004	Zhang Guozheng (CHN)	347.5
2008	Liao Hui (CHN)	348.0

70 KG (154 LB)		KG
1920	Alfred Neyland (EST)	257.5
1924	Edmond Décottignies (FRA)	440.0[26]
1928	Kurt Helbig (GER); Hans Haas (AUT) (*tied*)	322.5
1932	René Duverger (FRA)	325.0
1936	Mohamed Ahmed Mesbah (EGY); Robert Fein (AUT) (*tied*)	342.5
1948	Ibrahim Shams (EGY)	360.0
1952	Tommy Kono (USA)	362.5
1956	Igor Rybak (URS)	380.0
1960	Viktor Bushuyev (URS)	397.5
1964	Waldemar Baszanowski (POL)	432.5
1968	Waldemar Baszanowski (POL)	437.5
1972	Mukharbi Kirzhinov (URS)	460.0
1976	Pyotr Korol (URS)	305.0
1980	Yanko Rusev (BUL)	342.5
1984	Yao Jingyuan (CHN)	320.0
1988	Joachim Kunz (GDR)	340.0
1992	Israil Militosyan (UNT)	337.5
1996	Zhan Xugang (CHN)	357.5

77 KG (169.4 LB)		KG
1920	Henri Gance (FRA)	245.0
1924	Carlo Galimberti (ITA)	492.5[26]
1928	François Roger (FRA)	335.0
1932	Rudolf Ismayr (GER)	345.0
1936	Khadr el Thouni (EGY)	387.5
1948	Frank Spellman (USA)	390.0
1952	Peter George (USA)	400.0
1956	Fyodor Bogdanovsky (URS)	420.0
1960	Aleksandr Kurynov (URS)	437.5
1964	Hans Zdrazila (TCH)	445.0
1968	Viktor Kurentsov (URS)	475.0
1972	Iordan Bikov (BUL)	485.0
1976	Iordan Mitkov (BUL)	335.0
1980	Asen Zlatev (BUL)	360.0

Weight lifting (men)[24, 25] (continued)

77 KG (169.4 LB) (CONTINUED)		KG
1984	Karl-Heinz Radschinsky (FRG)	340.0
1988	Borislav Gidikov (BUL)	375.0
1992	Fyodor Kassapu (UNT)	357.5
1996	Pablo Lara (CUB)	367.5
2000	Zhan Xugang (CHN)	367.5
2004	Taner Sagir (TUR)	375.0
2008	Sa Jae Hyouk (KOR)	366.0

85 KG (187 LB)		KG
1920	Ernest Cadine (FRA)	290.0
1924	Charles Rigoulot (FRA)	502.5[26]
1928	El Sayed Nosseir (EGY)	355.0
1932	Louis Hostin (FRA)	365.0
1936	Louis Hostin (FRA)	372.5
1948	Stanley Stanczyk (USA)	417.5
1952	Trofim Lomakin (URS)	417.5
1956	Tommy Kono (USA)	447.5
1960	Ireneusz Palinski (POL)	442.5
1964	Rudolph Plyukfelder (URS)	475.0
1968	Boris Selitsky (URS)	485.0
1972	Leif Jenssen (NOR)	507.5
1976	Valery Shary (URS)	365.0
1980	Yury Vardanyan (URS)	400.0
1984	Petre Becheru (ROM)	355.0
1988	Israil Arsamakov (URS)	377.5
1992	Pyrros Dimas (GRE)	370.0
1996	Pyrros Dimas (GRE)	392.5
2000	Pyrros Dimas (GRE)	390.0
2004	George Asanidze (GEO)	382.5
2008	Lu Yong (CHN)	394.0

94 KG (206.8 LB)		KG
1952	Norbert Schemansky (USA)	445.0
1956	Arkady Vorobyev (URS)	462.5
1960	Arkady Vorobyev (URS)	472.5
1964	Vladimir Golovanov (URS)	487.5
1968	Kaarlo Kangasniemi (FIN)	517.5
1972	Andon Nikolov (BUL)	525.0
1976	David Rigert (URS)	382.5
1980	Peter Baczako (HUN)	377.5
1984	Nicu Vlad (ROM)	392.5
1988	Anatoly Khrapaty (URS)	412.5
1992	Kakhi Kakhiashvili (UNT)	412.5
1996	Aleksey Petrov (RUS)	402.5
2000	Akakios Kakhiashvilis (GRE)	405.0
2004	Milen Dobrev (BUL)	407.5
2008	Ilya Ilin (KAZ)	406.0

99 KG (217.8 LB)		KG
1980	Ota Zaremba (TCH)	395.0
1984	Rolf Milser (FRG)	385.0
1988	Pavel Kuznetsov (URS)	425.0
1992	Viktor Tregubov (UNT)	410.0
1996	Akakios Kakhiashvilis (GRE)	420.0

105 KG (231 LB)		KG
1972	Jan Talts (URS)	580.0
1976	Yury Zaytsev (URS)	385.0
1980	Leonid Taranenko (URS)	422.5
1984	Norberto Oberburger (ITA)	390.0
1988	Yury Zakharevitch (URS)	455.0
1992	Ronny Weller (GER)	432.5
1996	Timur Taymazov (UKR)	430.0
2000	Hossein Tavakoli (IRI)	425.0
2004	Dmitry Berestov (RUS)	425.0
2008	Andrei Aramnau (BLR)	436.0

Summer Olympic Games Champions (continued)

Weight lifting (men)[24, 25] (continued)

OVER 105 KG (231+ LB)

		KG
1920	Filippo Bottino (ITA)	265.5
1924	Giuseppe Tonani (ITA)	517.5[26]
1928	Josef Strassberger (GER)	372.5
1932	Jaroslav Skobia (TCH)	380.0
1936	Josef Manger (GER)	410.0
1948	John Davis (USA)	452.5
1952	John Davis (USA)	460.0
1956	Paul Anderson (USA)	500.0
1960	Yury Vlasov (URS)	537.5
1964	Leonid Zhabotinsky (URS)	572.5
1968	Leonid Zhabotinsky (URS)	572.5
1972	Vasily Alekseyev (URS)	640.0
1976	Vasily Alekseyev (URS)	440.0
1980	Sultan Rakhmanov (URS)	440.0
1984	Dinko Lukin (AUS)	412.5
1988	Aleksandr Kurlovich (URS)	462.5
1992	Aleksandr Kurlovich (UNT)	450.0
1996	Andrey Chemerkin (RUS)	457.5
2000	Hossein Reza Zadeh (IRI)	472.5
2004	Hossein Reza Zadeh (IRI)	472.5
2008	Matthias Steiner (GER)	461.0

ONE-HAND LIFT (UNLIMITED CLASS)

		KG
1896	Launceston Elliot (GBR)	71.0
1906	Josef Steinbach (AUT)	76.55

TWO-HAND LIFT (UNLIMITED CLASS)

		KG
1896	Viggo Jensen (DEN)	111.5
1904	Perikles Kakousis (GRE)	111.7
1906	Dimitrios Tofalos (GRE)	142.4

ALL-AROUND DUMBBELLS (UNLIMITED CLASS)

1904 Oscar Osthoff (USA)

Weight lifting (women)

48 KG (105.6 LB)

		KG
2000	Tara Nott (USA)	185.0
2004	Nurcan Taylan (TUR)	210.0
2008	Chen Xiexia (CHN)	212.0

53 KG (116.6 LB)

		KG
2000	Yang Xia (CHN)	225.0
2004	Udomporn Polsak (THA)	222.5
2008	Prapawadee Jaroenrattanatarakoon (THA)	221.0

58 KG (127.6 LB)

		KG
2000	Soraya Jiménez Mendívil (MEX)	222.5
2004	Chen Yanqing (CHN)	237.5
2008	Chen Yanqing (CHN)	244.0

63 KG (138.6 LB)

		KG
2000	Chen Xiaomin (CHN)	242.5
2004	Natalya Skakun (UKR)	242.5
2008	Pak Hyon Suk (PRK)	241.0

69 KG (151.8 LB)

		KG
2000	Lin Weining (CHN)	242.5
2004	Liu Chunhong (CHN)	275.0
2008	Liu Chunhong (CHN)	286.0

75 KG (165 LB)

		KG
2000	Maria Isabel Urrutia (COL)	245.0
2004	Pawina Thongsuk (THA)	272.5
2008	Cao Lei (CHN)	282.0

Weight lifting (women) (continued)

OVER 75 KG (165+ LB)

		KG
2000	Ding Meiyuan (CHN)	300.0
2004	Tang Gonghong (CHN)	305.0
2008	Jang Mi Ran (KOR)	326.0

Wrestling—Freestyle (men)[24]

48 KG (105.6 LB)

1904 Robert Curry (USA)
1972 Roman Dmitriyev (URS)
1976 Khassan Issaev (BUL)
1980 Claudio Pollio (ITA)
1984 Robert Weaver (USA)
1988 Takashi Kobayashi (JPN)
1992 Kim Il (PRK)
1996 Kim Il (PRK)

55 KG (121 LB)

1904 George Mehnert (USA)
1948 Lennart Viitala (FIN)
1952 Hasan Gemici (TUR)
1956 Mirian Tsalkalamanidze (URS)
1960 Ahmet Bilek (TUR)
1964 Yoshikatsu Yoshida (JPN)
1968 Shigeo Nakata (JPN)
1972 Kiyomi Kato (JPN)
1976 Yuji Takada (JPN)
1980 Anatoly Beloglazov (URS)
1984 Saban Trstena (YUG)
1988 Mitsuru Sato (JPN)
1992 Li Hak-son (PRK)
1996 Valentin Iordanov (BUL)
2000 Namig Amdullayev (AZE)
2004 Mavlet Batirov (RUS)
2008 Henry Cejudo (USA)

60 KG (132 LB)

1904 Isidor "Jack" Niflot (USA)
1908 George Mehnert (USA)
1924 Kustaa Pihlajamäki (FIN)
1928 Kaarlo Maakinen (FIN)
1932 Robert Pearce (USA)
1936 Odon Zombory (HUN)
1948 Nasuh Akar (TUR)
1952 Shohachi Ishii (JPN)
1956 Mustafa Dagistanli (TUR)
1960 Terence McCann (USA)
1964 Yojiro Uetake (JPN)
1968 Yojiro Uetake (JPN)
1972 Hideaki Yanagida (JPN)
1976 Vladimir Yumin (URS)
1980 Sergey Beloglazov (URS)
1984 Hideaki Tomiyama (JPN)
1988 Sergey Beloglazov (URS)
1992 Alejandro Puerto Diaz (CUB)
1996 Kendall Cross (USA)
2000 Alireza Dabir (IRI)
2004 Yandro Miguel Quintana (CUB)
2008 Mavlet Batirov (RUS)

63 KG (138.6 LB)

1904 Benjamin Bradshaw (USA)
1908 George Dole (USA)
1920 Charles Ackerly (USA)
1924 Robin Reed (USA)
1928 Allie Morrison (USA)
1932 Hermanni Pihlajamäki (FIN)
1936 Kustaa Pihlajamäki (FIN)
1948 Gazanfer Bilge (TUR)

Summer Olympic Games Champions (continued)

Wrestling—Freestyle (men)[24] (continued)

63 KG (138.6 LB) (CONTINUED)

1952 Bayram Sit (TUR)
1956 Shozo Sasahara (JPN)
1960 Mustafa Dagistanli (TUR)
1964 Osamu Watanabe (JPN)
1968 Masaaki Kaneko (JPN)
1972 Zagalav Abdulbekov (URS)
1976 Yang Jung Mo (KOR)
1980 Magomedgasan Abushev (URS)
1984 Randy Lewis (USA)
1988 John Smith (USA)
1992 John Smith (USA)
1996 Tom Brands (USA)
2000 Murad Umakhanov (RUS)

66 KG (145.2 LB)

1904 Otto Roehm (USA)
1908 George de Relwyskow (GBR)
1920 Kaarlo "Kalle" Anttila (FIN)
1924 Russell Vis (USA)
1928 Osvald Käpp (EST)
1932 Charles Pacome (FRA)
1936 Karoly Karpati (HUN)
1948 Celal Atik (TUR)
1952 Olle Anderberg (SWE)
1956 Emamali Habibi (IRI)
1960 Shelby Wilson (USA)
1964 Enio Valchev Dimov (BUL)
1968 Abdollah Movahed (IRI)
1972 Dan Gable (USA)
1976 Pavel Pinigin (URS)
1980 Saipulla Absaldov (URS)
1984 You In Tak (KOR)
1988 Arsen Fadzayev (URS)
1992 Arsen Fadzayev (UNT)
1996 Vadim Bogiyev (RUS)
2000 Daniel Igali (CAN)
2004 Elbrus Tedeyev (UKR)
2008 Ramazan Sahin (TUR)

74 KG (162.8 LB)

1904 Charles Eriksen (USA)
1924 Hermann Gehri (SUI)
1928 Arvo Haavisto (FIN)
1932 Jack van Bebber (USA)
1936 Frank Lewis (USA)
1948 Yasar Dogu (TUR)
1952 William Smith (USA)
1956 Mitsuo Ikeda (JPN)
1960 Douglas Blubaugh (USA)
1964 Ismail Ogan (TUR)
1968 Mahmut Atalay (TUR)
1972 Wayne Wells (USA)
1976 Jiichiro Date (JPN)
1980 Valentin Raychev (BUL)
1984 David Schultz (USA)
1988 Kenneth Monday (USA)
1992 Park Jang Soon (KOR)
1996 Buvayasa Saytiyev (RUS)
2000 Brandon Slay (USA)
2004 Buvayasa Saytiyev (RUS)
2008 Buvayasa Saytiyev (RUS)

84 KG (184.8 LB)

1908 Stanley Bacon (GBR)
1920 Eino Leino (FIN)
1924 Fritz Haggmann (SUI)
1928 Ernst Kyburz (SUI)

Wrestling—Freestyle (men)[24] (continued)

84 KG (184.8 LB) (CONTINUED)

1932 Ivar Johansson (SWE)
1936 Émile Poilvé (FRA)
1948 Glen Brand (USA)
1952 David Tsimakurdze (URS)
1956 Nikola Stanchev (BUL)
1960 Hasan Gungor (TUR)
1964 Prodan Stoyanov Gardchev (BUL)
1968 Boris Gurevich (URS)
1972 Levan Tediashvili (URS)
1976 John Peterson (USA)
1980 Ismail Abilov (BUL)
1984 Mark Schultz (USA)
1988 Han Myung Woo (KOR)
1992 Kevin Jackson (USA)
1996 Khadshimurad Magomedov (RUS)
2000 Adam Saytev (RUS)
2004 Cael Sanderson (USA)
2008 Revazi Mindorashvili (GEO)

90 KG (198.5 LB)

1920 Anders Larsson (SWE)
1924 John Franklin Spellman (USA)
1928 Thure Sjöstedt (SWE)
1932 Peter Mehringer (USA)
1936 Knut Fridell (SWE)
1948 Henry Wittenberg (USA)
1952 Bror Wiking Palm (SWE)
1956 Gholam-Reza Takhti (IRI)
1960 Ismet Atli (TUR)
1964 Aleksandr Medved (URS)
1968 Ahmet Ayuk (TUR)
1972 Ben Peterson (USA)
1976 Levan Tediashvili (URS)
1980 Sanasar Oganesyan (URS)
1984 Ed Banach (USA)
1988 Macharbek Khadartsev (URS)
1992 Macharbek Khadartsev (UNT)
1996 Rasul Khadem Azghadi (IRI)

96 KG (211.2 LB)

1896 Karl Schumann (GER)
1904 Bernhuff Hansen (USA)
1908 George O'Kelly (GBR)
1920 Robert Rothe (SUI)
1924 Harry Steele (USA)
1928 Johan Richthoff (SWE)
1932 Johan Richthoff (SWE)
1936 Kristjan Palusalu (EST)
1948 Gyula Bobis (HUN)
1952 Arsen Mekokishvili (URS)
1956 Hamit Kaplan (TUR)
1960 Wilfried Dietrich (GER)
1964 Aleksandr Ivanitsky (URS)
1968 Aleksandr Medved (URS)
1972 Ivan Yarygin (URS)
1976 Ivan Yarygin (URS)
1980 Ilya Mate (URS)
1984 Lou Banach (USA)
1988 Vasile Puscasu (ROM)
1992 Leri Khabelov (UNT)
1996 Kurt Angle (USA)
2000 Sagid Murtasaliyev (RUS)
2004 Khajimurat Gatsalov (RUS)
2008 Shirvani Muradov (RUS)

Summer Olympic Games Champions (continued)

Wrestling—Freestyle (men)[24] (continued)

120 KG (264 LB)
1972 Aleksandr Medved (URS)
1976 Soslan Andiyev (URS)
1980 Soslan Andiyev (URS)
1984 Bruce Baumgartner (USA)
1988 David Gobedishvili (URS)
1992 Bruce Baumgartner (USA)
1996 Mahmut Demir (TUR)
2000 David Musulbes (RUS)
2004 Artur Taymazov (UZB)
2008 Artur Taymazov (UZB)

Wrestling—Freestyle (women)

48 KG (105.6 LB)
2004 Irini Merleni (UKR)
2008 Carol Huynh (CAN)

55 KG (121 LB)
2004 Saori Yoshida (JPN)
2008 Saori Yoshida (JPN)

63 KG (138.6 LB)
2004 Kaori Icho (JPN)
2008 Kaori Icho (JPN)

72 KG (158 LB)
2004 Wang Xu (CHN)
2008 Wang Jiao (CHN)

Wrestling—Greco-Roman[24]

48 KG (105.6 LB)
1972 Gheorghe Berceanu (ROM)
1976 Aleksey Shumakov (URS)
1980 Zhaksylyk Ushkempirov (URS)
1984 Vincenzo Maenza (ITA)
1988 Vincenzo Maenza (ITA)
1992 Oleg Kucherenko (UNT)
1996 Sim Kwon-Ho (KOR)

55 KG (121 LB)
1948 Pietro Lombardi (ITA)
1952 Boris Gurevich (URS)
1956 Nikolay Solovyev (URS)
1960 Dumitru Pirvulescu (ROM)
1964 Tsutomu Hanahara (JPN)
1968 Petar Kirov (BUL)
1972 Petar Kirov (BUL)
1976 Vitaly Konstantinov (URS)
1980 Vakhtang Blagidze (URS)
1984 Atsuji Miyahara (JPN)
1988 Jon Ronningen (NOR)
1992 Jon Ronningen (NOR)
1996 Armen Nazaryan (ARM)
2000 Sim Kwon-Ho (KOR)
2004 Istvan Majoros (HUN)
2008 Nazyr Mankiyev (RUS)

60 KG (132 LB)
1924 Eduard Pütsep (EST)
1928 Kurt Leucht (GER)
1932 Jakob Brendel (GER)
1936 Marton Lorincz (HUN)
1948 Kurt Pettersen (SWE)
1952 Imre Hodos (HUN)
1956 Konstantin Vyrupayev (URS)
1960 Oleg Karavayev (URS)
1964 Masamitsu Ichiguchi (JPN)
1968 Janos Varga (HUN)

Wrestling—Greco-Roman[24] (continued)

60 KG (132 LB) (CONTINUED)
1972 Rustem Kazakov (URS)
1976 Pertti Ukkola (FIN)
1980 Shamil Serikov (URS)
1984 Pasquale Passarelli (FRG)
1988 Andras Sike (HUN)
1992 An Han Bong (KOR)
1996 Yury Melnichenko (KAZ)
2000 Armen Nazarian (BUL)
2004 Jung Ji Hyun (KOR)
2008 Islam-Beka Albiyev (RUS)

63 KG (138.6 LB)
1912 Kaarlo Koskelo (FIN)
1920 Oskar Friman (FIN)
1924 Kalle Anttila (FIN)
1928 Voldemar Väli (EST)
1932 Giovanni Gozzi (ITA)
1936 Yasar Erkan (TUR)
1948 Mehmet Oktav (TUR)
1952 Yakov Punkin (URS)
1956 Rauno Leonard Mäkinen (FIN)
1960 Muzahir Sille (TUR)
1964 Imre Polyak (HUN)
1968 Roman Rurua (URS)
1972 Georgi Markov (BUL)
1976 Kazimierz Lipien (POL)
1980 Stilianos Migiakis (GRE)
1984 Kim Weon Kee (KOR)
1988 Kamandar Madzhidov (URS)
1992 Akif Pirim (TUR)
1996 Wlodzimierz Zawadzki (POL)
2000 Varteres Samurgashev (RUS)

66 KG (145.2 LB)
1908 Enrico Porro (ITA)
1912 Eemil Väre (FIN)
1920 Eemil Väre (FIN)
1924 Oskar Friman (FIN)
1928 Lajos Keresztes (HUN)
1932 Erik Malmberg (SWE)
1936 Lauri Koskela (FIN)
1948 Karl Freij (SWE)
1952 Shazam Safin (URS)
1956 Kyösti Emil Lehtonen (FIN)
1960 Avtandil Koridze (URS)
1964 Kazim Ayvaz (TUR)
1968 Munji Mumemura (JPN)
1972 Shamil Khisamutdinov (URS)
1976 Suren Nalbandyan (URS)
1980 Stefan Rusu (ROM)
1984 Vlado Lisjak (YUG)
1988 Levon Dzhulfalakyan (URS)
1992 Attila Repka (HUN)
1996 Ryszard Wolny (POL)
2000 Filiberto Ascuy Aguilera (CUB)
2004 Farid Mansurov (AZE)
2008 Steeve Guénot (FRA)

74 KG (162.8 LB)
1932 Ivar Johansson (SWE)
1936 Rudolf Svedberg (SWE)
1948 Erik Gösta Andersson (SWE)
1952 Miklos Szilvasi (HUN)
1956 Mithat Bayrak (TUR)
1960 Mithat Bayrak (TUR)
1964 Anatoly Kolesov (URS)
1968 Rudolf Vesper (GDR)

Summer Olympic Games Champions (continued)

Wrestling—Greco-Roman[24] (continued)

74 KG (162.8 LB) (CONTINUED)

1972 Viteslav Macha (TCH)
1976 Anatoly Bykov (URS)
1980 Ferenc Kocsis (HUN)
1984 Jouko Salomaki (FIN)
1988 Kim Young Nam (KOR)
1992 Mnatsakan Iskandaryan (UNT)
1996 Filiberto Ascuy Aguilera (CUB)
2000 Murat Kardanov (URS)
2004 Aleksandr Dokturishivili (UZB)
2008 Manuchar Kvirkelia (GEO)

84 KG (184.8 LB)

1908 Frithiof Martenson (SWE)
1912 Claes Johansson (SWE)
1920 Carl Westergren (SWE)
1924 Edward Westerlund (FIN)
1928 Väinö Kokkinen (FIN)
1932 Väinö Kokkinen (FIN)
1936 Ivar Johansson (SWE)
1948 Axel Grönberg (SWE)
1952 Axel Grönberg (SWE)
1956 Givi Kartoziya (URS)
1960 Dimitar Dobrev (BUL)
1964 Branislav Simic (YUG)
1968 Lothar Metz (GDR)
1972 Csaba Hegedus (HUN)
1976 Momir Petkovic (YUG)
1980 Gennady Korban (URS)
1984 Ion Draica (ROM)
1988 Mikhail Mamiashvili (URS)
1992 Peter Farkas (HUN)
1996 Hamza Yerlikaya (TUR)
2000 Hamza Yerlikaya (TUR)
2004 Aleksey Mishin (RUS)
2008 Andrea Minguzzi (ITA)

90 KG (198.5 LB)

1908 Verner Weckman (FIN)
1912 Anders Ahlgren (SWE)
1920 Claes Johansson (SWE)
1924 Carl Westergren (SWE)
1928 Ibrahim Moustafa (EGY)
1932 Rudolf Svensson (SWE)
1936 Axel Cadier (SWE)
1948 Karl-Erik Nilsson (SWE)
1952 Kelpo Olavi Gröndahl (FIN)
1956 Valentin Nikolayev (URS)
1960 Tevfik Kis (TUR)

Wrestling—Greco-Roman[24] (continued)

90 KG (198.5 LB) (CONTINUED)

1964 Boyan Radev (BUL)
1968 Boyan Radev (BUL)
1972 Valery Rezantsev (URS)
1976 Valery Rezantsev (URS)
1980 Norbert Nottny (HUN)
1984 Steven Fraser (USA)
1988 Atanas Komchev (BUL)
1992 Maik Bullmann (GER)
1996 Vyacheslav Oleynyk (UKR)

96 KG (211.2 LB)

1896 Karl Schumann (GER)
1908 Richard Weisz (HUN)
1912 Yrjö Saarela (FIN)
1920 Adolf Lindfors (FIN)
1924 Henri Deglane (FRA)
1928 Rudolf Svensson (SWE)
1932 Carl Westergren (SWE)
1936 Kristjan Palusalu (EST)
1948 Ahmet Kirecci (TUR)
1952 Johannes Kotkas (URS)
1956 Anatoly Parfenov (URS)
1960 Ivan Bogdan (URS)
1964 Istvan Kozma (HUN)
1968 Istvan Kozma (HUN)
1972 Nicolae Martinescu (ROM)
1976 Nikolay Balboshin (URS)
1980 Georgi Raikov-Petkov (BUL)
1984 Vasile Andrei (ROM)
1988 Andrzej Wronski (POL)
1992 Héctor Milian (CUB)
1996 Andrzej Wronski (POL)
2000 Mikael Ljungberg (SWE)
2004 Karam Ibrahim (EGY)
2008 Aslanbek Khushtov (RUS)

120 KG (264 LB)

1972 Anatoly Roshchin (URS)
1976 Aleksandr Kolchinsky (URS)
1980 Aleksandr Kolchinsky (URS)
1984 Jeffrey Blatnick (USA)
1988 Aleksandr Karelin (URS)
1992 Aleksandr Karelin (UNT)
1996 Aleksandr Karelin (RUS)
2000 Rulon Gardner (USA)
2004 Khasan Baroyev (RUS)
2008 Mijain López (CUB)

[1]The competitions in 1900 and 1904 are said to be unofficial. [2]100-meter event. [3]Hurdles were 2′ 6″ high, not 3′. [4]An extra lap of 460 meters was run in error. [5]Jim Thorpe was stripped of his gold medals in 1913 when it was discovered he had briefly competed as a professional athlete; in 1982 his gold medals were restored, and he was declared "cowinner" of the events. [6]2,000-meter event. [7]333.3-meter event. [8]Distance varied from 87 to 320 km. [9]Weight classifications were changed in 1980 and 1996. [10]Weight classifications were changed in 2000. [11]The distances in men's rowing events have varied from time to time. In 1904 it was 2 miles; in 1908, 1.5 miles; from 1912 to 1936, 2,000 m; in 1948, 1 mile 350 yards; and since 1952, 2,000 m (1 mile 427 yards). [12]The distance in women's rowing events was 1,000 m until 1988, at which time it became 2,000 m. [13]100 yards. [14]220 yards. [15]500 meters. [16]440 yards. [17]1,200 meters. [18]1,000 meters. [19]One mile. [20]100 yards. [21]440 yards. [22]300 meters. [23]Fréchette's gold medal awarded in 1993 on basis of error in scoring. [24]Weight classifications have been revised numerous times, most recently after the 1996 Games. [25]In 1976 the press lift was removed, weights given thereafter being the total for the clean and jerk and the snatch. [26]Total of five lifts.

Winter Olympic Games Champions

Gold medalists in all events, 1908–2006 (separate Winter Games were not held until 1924). Since the 2002 Salt Lake City Games, several athletes have been stripped of medals for having failed drug tests. New medalists are shown in this table.

Biathlon (men)

10 KILOMETERS

		MIN:SEC
1980	Frank Ullrich (GDR)	32:10.69
1984	Eirik Kvalfoss (NOR)	30:53.8
1988	Frank-Peter Rötsch (GDR)	25:08.1
1992	Mark Kirchner (GER)	26:02.3
1994	Sergey Chepikov (RUS)	28:07.0
1998	Ole Einar Bjørndalen (NOR)	27:16.2
2002	Ole Einar Bjørndalen (NOR)	24:51.3
2006	Sven Fischer (GER)	26:11.6

12.5-KILOMETER PURSUIT

		MIN:SEC
2002	Ole Einar Bjørndalen (NOR)	32:34.6
2006	Vincent Defrasne (FRA)	35:20.2

15-KILOMETER MASS START

		MIN:SEC
2006	Michael Greis (GER)	47:20.0

20 KILOMETERS

		HR:MIN:SEC
1960	Klas Lestander (SWE)	1:33:21.6
1964	Vladimir Melanin (URS)	1:20:26.8
1968	Magnar Solberg (NOR)	1:13:45.9
1972	Magnar Solberg (NOR)	1:15:55.50[1]
1976	Nikolay Kruglov (URS)	1:14:12.26
1980	Anatoly Alyabyev (URS)	1:08:16.31
1984	Peter Angerer (FRG)	1:11:52.70
1988	Frank-Peter Rötsch (GDR)	56:33.3
1992	Yevgeny Redkin (UNT)[2]	57:34.4
1994	Sergey Tarasov (RUS)	57:25.3
1998	Halvard Hanevold (NOR)	56:16.4
2002	Ole Einar Bjørndalen (NOR)	51:03.3
2006	Michael Greis (GER)	54:23.0

4 × 7.5-KILOMETER RELAY

		HR:MIN:SEC
1968	USSR	2:13:02.4
1972	USSR	1:51:44.92[1]
1976	USSR	1:57:55.64
1980	USSR	1:34:03.27
1984	USSR	1:38:51.70
1988	USSR	1:22:30.00
1992	Germany	1:24:43.5
1994	Germany	1:30:22.1
1998	Germany	1:19:43.3
2002	Norway	1:23:42.3
2006	Germany	1:21:51.5

MILITARY SKI PATROL

1924	Switzerland
1928	Norway
1936	Italy
1948	Switzerland

DISTANCE SHOOTING

1936	Georg Edenhauser (AUT)

ICE SHOOTING (TEAM)

1936	Austria

TARGET SHOOTING

1936	Ignaz Reiterer (AUT)

Biathlon (women)

7.5 KILOMETERS

		MIN:SEC
1992	Anfisa Restsova (UNT)[2]	24:29.2
1994	Myriam Bédard (CAN)	26:08.8
1998	Galina Kukleva (RUS)	23:08.0
2002	Kati Wilhelm (GER)	20:41.4
2006	Florence Baverel-Robert (FRA)	22:31.4

10-KILOMETER PURSUIT

		MIN:SEC
2002	Olga Pyleva (RUS)	31:07.7
2006	Kati Wilhelm (GER)	36:43.6

12.5-KILOMETER MASS START

		MIN:SEC
2006	Anna Carin Olofsson (SWE)	40:36.5

15 KILOMETERS

		MIN:SEC
1992	Antje Misersky (GER)	51:47.2
1994	Myriam Bédard (CAN)	52:06.6
1998	Ekaterina Dafovska (BUL)	54:52.0
2002	Andrea Henkel (GER)	47:29.1
2006	Svetlana Ishmuratova (RUS)	49:24.1

4 × 6-KILOMETER RELAY[3]

		HR:MIN:SEC
1992	France	1:15:55.6
1994	Russia	1:47:19.5
1998	Germany	1:40:13.6
2002	Germany	1:27:55.0
2006	Russia	1:16:12.5

Bobsled

TWO-MAN BOBSLED

		MIN:SEC
1932	United States	8:14.74
1936	United States	5:29.29
1948	Switzerland	5:29.2
1952	West Germany	5:24.54
1956	Italy	5:30.14
1964	Great Britain	4:21.90
1968	Italy	4:41.54
1972	West Germany	4:57.07
1976	East Germany	3:44.42
1980	Switzerland	4:09.36
1984	East Germany	3:25.56
1988	USSR	3:53.48
1992	Switzerland	4:03.26
1994	Switzerland	3:30.81
1998	Canada; Italy (*tied*)	3:37.24
2002	Germany	3:10.11
2006	Germany	3:43.38

FOUR-MAN BOBSLED

		MIN:SEC
1924	Switzerland	5:45.54
1928	United States[4]	3:20.5
1932	United States	7:53.68
1936	Switzerland	5:19.85
1948	United States	5:20.1
1952	West Germany	5:07.84
1956	Switzerland	5:10.44
1964	Canada	4:14.46
1968	Italy	2:17.39
1972	Switzerland	4:43.07
1976	East Germany	3:40.43
1980	East Germany	3:59.92
1984	East Germany	3:20.22
1988	Switzerland	3:47.51
1992	Austria	3:53.90

Winter Olympic Games Champions (continued)

Bobsled (continued)

FOUR-MAN BOBSLED (CONTINUED)	MIN:SEC
1994 Germany	3:27.78
1998 Germany	2:39.41
2002 Germany	3:07.51
2006 Germany	3:40.42

TWO-WOMAN BOBSLED	MIN:SEC
2002 United States	1:37.76
2006 Germany	3:49.98

Curling

MEN

1924 Great Britain
1998 Switzerland
2002 Norway
2006 Canada

WOMEN

1998 Canada
2002 Great Britain
2006 Sweden

Figure Skating

MEN'S SINGLES

1908 Ulrich Salchow (SWE)
1920 Gillis Gräfström (SWE)
1924 Gillis Gräfström (SWE)
1928 Gillis Gräfström (SWE)
1932 Karl Schäfer (AUT)
1936 Karl Schäfer (AUT)
1948 Richard Button (USA)
1952 Richard Button (USA)
1956 Hayes Alan Jenkins (USA)
1960 David Jenkins (USA)
1964 Manfred Schnelldorfer (GER)[5]
1968 Wolfgang Schwarz (AUT)
1972 Ondrej Nepela (TCH)
1976 John Curry (GBR)
1980 Robin Cousins (GBR)
1984 Scott Hamilton (USA)
1988 Brian Boitano (USA)
1992 Viktor Petrenko (UNT)[2]
1994 Aleksey Urmanov (RUS)
1998 Ilia Kulik (RUS)
2002 Aleksey Yagudin (RUS)
2006 Yevgeny Plushchenko (RUS)

WOMEN'S SINGLES

1908 Madge Syers (GBR)
1920 Magda Julin-Mauroy (SWE)
1924 Herma Planck-Szabo (AUT)
1928 Sonja Henie (NOR)
1932 Sonja Henie (NOR)
1936 Sonja Henie (NOR)
1948 Barbara Ann Scott (CAN)
1952 Jeanette Altwegg (GBR)
1956 Tenley Albright (USA)
1964 Sjoukje Dijkstra (NED)
1968 Peggy Fleming (USA)
1972 Beatrix Schuba (AUT)
1976 Dorothy Hamill (USA)
1980 Annett Potzsch (GDR)
1984 Katarina Witt (GDR)
1988 Katarina Witt (GDR)
1992 Kristi Yamaguchi (USA)
1994 Oksana Bayul (UKR)
1998 Tara Lipinski (USA)

Figure Skating (continued)

WOMEN'S SINGLES (CONTINUED)

2002 Sarah Hughes (USA)
2006 Shizuka Arakawa (JPN)

PAIRS

1908 Anna Hübler, Heinrich Burger (GER)
1920 Ludoviga Jakobsson-Eilers, Walter Jakobsson (FIN)
1924 Helene Engelmann, Alfred Berger (AUT)
1928 Andrée Joly, Pierre Brunet (FRA)
1932 Andrée Brunet-Joly, Pierre Brunet (FRA)
1936 Maxi Herber, Ernst Baier (GER)
1948 Micheline Lannoy, Pierre Baugniet (BEL)
1952 Ria Falk, Paul Falk (FRG)
1956 Elisabeth Schwarz, Kurt Oppelt (AUT)
1960 Barbara Wagner, Robert Paul (CAN)
1964 Lyudmila Belousova, Oleg Protopopov (URS)
1968 Lyudmila Belousova, Oleg Protopopov (URS)
1972 Irina Rodnina, Aleksey Ulanov (URS)
1976 Irina Rodnina, Aleksandr Zaytsev (URS)
1980 Irina Rodnina, Aleksandr Zaytsev (URS)
1984 Yelena Valova, Oleg Vasilyev (URS)
1988 Yekaterina Gordeyeva, Sergey Grinkov (URS)
1992 Natalya Mishkutyonok, Artur Dmitriyev (UNT)[2]
1994 Yekaterina Gordeyeva, Sergey Grinkov (RUS)
1998 Oksana Kazakova, Artur Dmitriyev (RUS)
2002 Yelena Berezhnaya, Anton Sikharulidze (RUS); Jamie Sale, David Pelletier (CAN) (*shared*)
2006 Tatyana Totmyanin, Maksim Marinin (RUS)

ICE DANCING

1976 Lyudmila Pakhomova, Aleksandr Gorshkov (URS)
1980 Natalya Linichuk, Gennady Karponosov (URS)
1984 Jayne Torvill, Christopher Dean (GBR)
1988 Natalya Bestemyanova, Andrey Bukin (URS)
1992 Marina Klimova, Sergey Ponomarenko (UNT)[2]
1994 Oksana Grishchuk, Yevgeny Platov (RUS)
1998 Oksana Grishchuk, Yevgeny Platov (RUS)
2002 Marina Anissina, Gwendal Peizerat (FRA)
2006 Tatyana Navka, Roman Kostomarov (RUS)

Ice Hockey

MEN

1920 Canada
1924 Canada
1928 Canada
1932 Canada
1936 Great Britain
1948 Canada
1952 Canada
1956 USSR
1960 United States
1964 USSR
1968 USSR
1972 USSR
1976 USSR
1980 United States
1984 USSR
1988 USSR
1992 Unified Team[2]
1994 Sweden
1998 Czech Republic
2002 Canada
2006 Sweden

Winter Olympic Games Champions (continued)

Ice Hockey (continued)

WOMEN

1998	United States
2002	Canada
2006	Canada

Luge

MEN'S SINGLES

		MIN:SEC
1964	Thomas Köhler (GER)[5]	3:26.77
1968	Manfred Schmid (AUT)	2:52.48
1972	Wolfgang Scheidel (GDR)	3:27.58
1976	Detlef Guenther (GDR)	3:27.688[6]
1980	Bernhard Glass (GDR)	2:54.796
1984	Paul Hildgartner (ITA)	3:04.258
1988	Jens Müller (GDR)	3:05.548
1992	Georg Hackl (GER)	3:02.363
1994	Georg Hackl (GER)	3:21.571
1998	Georg Hackl (GER)	3:18.436
2002	Armin Zöggeler (ITA)	2:57.941
2006	Armin Zöggeler (ITA)	3:26.088

MEN'S PAIRS

		MIN:SEC
1964	Austria	1:41.62
1968	East Germany	1:35.85
1972	Italy; East Germany (*tied*)	1:28.35
1976	East Germany	1:25.604[6]
1980	East Germany	1:19.331
1984	West Germany	1:23.620
1988	East Germany	1:31.940
1992	Germany	1:32.053
1994	Italy	1:36.720
1998	Germany	1:41.105
2002	Germany	1:26.082
2006	Austria	1:34.497

WOMEN'S SINGLES

		MIN:SEC
1964	Ortrun Enderlein (GER)[5]	3:24.67
1968	Erica Lechner (ITA)	2:29.37
1972	Anna-Maria Müller (GDR)	2:59.18
1976	Margit Schumann (GDR)	2:50.621[6]
1980	Vera Zozulya (URS)	2:36.537
1984	Steffi Martin (GDR)	2:46.570
1988	Steffi Walter-Martin (GDR)	3:03.973
1992	Doris Neuner (AUT)	3:06.696
1994	Gerda Weissensteiner (ITA)	3:15.517
1998	Silke Kraushaar (GER)	3:23.779
2002	Sylke Otto (GER)	2:52.464
2006	Sylke Otto (GER)	3:07.979

Skeleton

MEN

		MIN:SEC
1928	Jennison Heaton (USA)	3:01.8
1948	Nino Bibbia (ITA)	5:23.2
2002	Jim Shea (USA)	1:41.96
2006	Duff Gibson (CAN)	1:55.88

WOMEN

		MIN:SEC
2002	Tristan Gale (USA)	1:45.11
2006	Maya Pedersen (SUI)	1:59.83

Alpine Skiing (men)

DOWNHILL

		MIN:SEC
1948	Henri Oreiller (FRA)	2:55.0
1952	Zeno Colò (ITA)	2:30.8
1956	Toni Sailer (AUT)	2:52.2
1960	Jean Vuarnet (FRA)	2:06.0
1964	Egon Zimmermann (AUT)	2:18.16[1]
1968	Jean-Claude Killy (FRA)	1:59.85
1972	Bernhard Russi (SUI)	1:51.43

Alpine Skiing (men) (continued)

DOWNHILL (CONTINUED)

		MIN:SEC
1976	Franz Klammer (AUT)	1:45.73
1980	Leonhard Stock (AUT)	1:45.50
1984	Bill Johnson (USA)	1:45.59
1988	Pirmin Zurbriggen (SUI)	1:59.63
1992	Patrick Ortlieb (AUT)	1:50.37
1994	Tommy Moe (USA)	1:45.75
1998	Jean-Luc Cretier (FRA)	1:50.11
2002	Fritz Strobl (AUT)	1:39.13
2006	Antoine Dénériaz (FRA)	1:48.80

SLALOM

		MIN:SEC
1948	Edy Reinalter (SUI)	2:10.3
1952	Othmar Schneider (AUT)	2:00.0
1956	Toni Sailer (AUT)	3:14.7
1960	Ernst Hinterseer (AUT)	2:08.9
1964	Josef Stiegler (AUT)	2:21.13[1]
1968	Jean-Claude Killy (FRA)	1:39.73
1972	Francisco Ochoa (ESP)	1:49.27
1976	Piero Gros (ITA)	2:03.29
1980	Ingemar Stenmark (SWE)	1:44.26
1984	Phil Mahre (USA)	1:39.41
1988	Alberto Tomba (ITA)	1:39.47
1992	Finn Christian Jagge (NOR)	1:44.39
1994	Thomas Stangassinger (AUT)	2:02.02
1998	Hans-Petter Buraas (NOR)	1:49.31
2002	Jean-Pierre Vidal (FRA)	1:41.06
2006	Benjamin Raich (AUT)	1:43.14

GIANT SLALOM

		MIN:SEC
1952	Stein Eriksen (NOR)	2:25.0
1956	Toni Sailer (AUT)	3:00.1
1960	Roger Staub (SUI)	1:48.3
1964	François Bonlieu (FRA)	1:46.71[1]
1968	Jean-Claude Killy (FRA)	3:29.28
1972	Gustavo Thöni (ITA)	3:09.62
1976	Heini Hemmi (SUI)	3:26.97
1980	Ingemar Stenmark (SWE)	2:40.74
1984	Max Julen (SUI)	2:41.18
1988	Alberto Tomba (ITA)	2:06.37
1992	Alberto Tomba (ITA)	2:06.98
1994	Markus Wasmeier (GER)	2:52.46
1998	Hermann Maier (AUT)	2:38.51
2002	Stephan Eberharter (AUT)	2:23.28
2006	Benjamin Raich (AUT)	2:35.00

SUPERGIANT SLALOM

		MIN:SEC
1988	Franck Piccard (FRA)	1:39.66
1992	Kjetil Andre Aamodt (NOR)	1:13.04
1994	Markus Wasmeier (GER)	1:32.53
1998	Hermann Maier (AUT)	1:34.82
2002	Kjetil André Aamodt (NOR)	1:21.58
2006	Kjetil André Aamodt (NOR)	1:30.65

ALPINE COMBINED

		MIN:SEC
1936	Franz Pfnür (GER)	
1948	Henri Oreiller (FRA)	
1972	Gustavo Thöni (ITA)	
1976	Gustavo Thöni (ITA)	
1988	Hubert Strolz (AUT)	
1992	Josef Polig (ITA)	
1994	Lasse Kjus (NOR)	3:17.53[7]
1998	Mario Reiter (AUT)	3:08.06
2002	Kjetil André Aamodt (NOR)	3:17.56
2006	Ted Ligety (USA)	3:09.35

Winter Olympic Games Champions (continued)

Alpine Skiing (women)

DOWNHILL		MIN:SEC
1948	Hedy Schlunegger (SUI)	2:28.3
1952	Trude Jochom-Beiser (AUT)	1:47.1
1956	Madeleine Berthod (SUI)	1:40.7
1960	Heidi Beibl (GER)[5]	1:37.6
1964	Christl Haas (AUT)	1:55.39[1]
1968	Olga Pall (AUT)	1:40.87
1972	Marie-Thérèse Nadig (SUI)	1:36.68
1976	Rosi Mittermaier (FRG)	1:46.16
1980	Annemarie Moser-Pröll (AUT)	1:37.52
1984	Michael Figini (SUI)	1:13.36
1988	Marina Kiehl (FRG)	1:25.86
1992	Kerrin Lee-Gartner (CAN)	1:52.55
1994	Katja Seizinger (GER)	1:35.93
1998	Katja Seizinger (GER)	1:28.29
2002	Carole Montillet (FRA)	1:39.56
2006	Michaela Dorfmeister (AUT)	1:32.47

SLALOM		MIN:SEC
1948	Gretchen Fraser (USA)	1:57.2
1952	Andrea Lawrence-Mead (USA)	2:10.6
1956	Renée Colliard (SUI)	1:52.3
1960	Anne Heggtveit (CAN)	1:49.6
1964	Christine Goitschel (FRA)	1:29.86[1]
1968	Marielle Goitschel (FRA)	1:59.85
1972	Barbara Cochran (USA)	1:31.24
1976	Rosi Mittermaier (FRG)	1:30.54
1980	Hanni Wenzel (LIE)	1:25.09
1984	Paoletta Magoni (ITA)	1:36.47
1988	Vreni Schneider (SUI)	1:36.69
1992	Petra Kronberger (AUT)	1:32.68
1994	Vreni Schneider (SUI)	1:56.01
1998	Hilde Gerg (GER)	1:32.40
2002	Janica Kostelic (CRO)	1:46.10
2006	Anja Pärson (SWE)	1:29.04

GIANT SLALOM		MIN:SEC
1952	Andrea Lawrence-Mead (USA)	2:06.8
1956	Ossi Reichert (GER)[5]	1:56.5
1960	Yvonne Rüegg (SUI)	1:39.9
1964	Marielle Goitschel (FRA)	1:52.24[1]
1968	Nancy Greene (CAN)	1:51.97
1972	Marie-Therèse Nadig (SUI)	1:29.90
1976	Kathy Kreiner (CAN)	1:29.13
1980	Hanni Wenzel (LIE)	2:41.66
1984	Debbie Armstrong (USA)	2:20.98
1988	Vreni Schneider (SUI)	2:06.49
1992	Pernilla Wiberg (SWE)	2:12.74
1994	Deborah Compagnoni (ITA)	2:30.97
1998	Deborah Compagnoni (ITA)	2:50.59
2002	Janica Kostelic (CRO)	2:30.01
2006	Julia Mancuso (USA)	2:09.19

SUPERGIANT SLALOM		MIN:SEC
1988	Sigrid Wolf (AUT)	1:19.03
1992	Deborah Compagnoni (ITA)	1:21.22
1994	Diann Roffe-Steinrotter (USA)	1:22.15
1998	Picabo Street (USA)	1:18.02
2002	Daniela Ceccarelli (ITA)	1:13.59
2006	Michaela Dorfmeister (AUT)	1:32.47

ALPINE COMBINED		MIN:SEC
1936	Chrislt Cranz (GER)	
1948	Trude Beiser (AUT)	
1972	Annemarie Pröll (AUT)	
1976	Rosi Mittermaier (FRG)	
1988	Anita Wachter (AUT)	
1992	Petra Kronberger (AUT)	

Alpine Skiing (women) (continued)

ALPINE COMBINED (CONTINUED)		MIN:SEC
1994	Pernilla Wiberg (SWE)	3:05.16[7]
1998	Katja Seizinger (GER)	2:40.74
2002	Janica Kostelic (CRO)	2:43.28
2006	Janica Kostelic (CRO)	2:51.08

Freestyle Skiing

MEN'S MOGULS	
1992	Edgar Grospiron (FRA)
1994	Jean-Luc Brassard (CAN)
1998	Jonny Moseley (USA)
2002	Janne Lahtela (FIN)
2006	Dale Begg-Smith (AUS)

MEN'S AERIALS	
1994	Andreas Schönbächler (SUI)
1998	Eric Bergoust (USA)
2002	Ales Valenta (CZE)
2006	Han Xiaopeng (CHN)

WOMEN'S MOGULS	
1992	Donna Weinbrecht (USA)
1994	Stine Lise Hattestad (NOR)
1998	Tae Satoya (JPN)
2002	Kari Traa (NOR)
2006	Jennifer Heil (CAN)

WOMEN'S AERIALS	
1994	Lina Cheryazova (UZB)
1998	Nikki Stone (USA)
2002	Alisa Camplin (AUS)
2006	Evelyne Leu (SUI)

Nordic Skiing (men)

1.5-KILOMETER CROSS-COUNTRY SPRINT		MIN:SEC
2002	Tor Arne Hetland (NOR)	2:56.9
2006	Björn Lind (SWE)	2:26.5

10-KILOMETER CROSS-COUNTRY		MIN:SEC
1992	Vegard Ulvang (NOR)	27:36.0
1994	Bjørn Daehlie (NOR)	24:20.1
1998	Bjørn Daehlie (NOR)	27:24.5

15-KILOMETER CROSS-COUNTRY[8]		HR:MIN:SEC
1924	Thorleif Haug (NOR)	1:14:31.0
1928	Johan Gröttumsbraaten (NOR)	1:37:01.0
1932	Sven Utterström (SWE)	1:23:07.0
1936	Erik-August Larsson (SWE)	1:14:38.0
1948	Martin Lundström (SWE)	1:13:50.0
1952	Hallgeir Brenden (NOR)	1:01:34.0
1956	Hallgeir Brenden (NOR)	49:39.0
1960	Hakkon Brusveen (NOR)	51:55.5
1964	Eero Mäntyranta (FIN)	50:54.1
1968	Harald Grönningen (NOR)	47:54.2
1972	Sven-Ake Lundbäck (SWE)	45:28.24[1]
1976	Nikolay Bazhukov (URS)	43:58.47
1980	Thomas Wassberg (SWE)	41:57.63
1984	Gunde Svan (SWE)	41:25.60
1988	Mikhail Devyatyarov (URS)	41:18.9
1998	Thomas Alsgaard (NOR)	39:13.7
2002	Andrus Veerpalu (EST)	37:07.4
2006	Andrus Veerpalu (EST)	38:01.3

COMBINED PURSUIT[9]		HR:MIN:SEC
1992	Bjørn Daehlie (NOR)	1:05:37.9
1994	Bjørn Daehlie (NOR)	1:00:08.8
1998	Thomas Alsgaard (NOR)	1:07:01.7

Winter Olympic Games Champions (continued)

Nordic Skiing (men) (continued)

COMBINED PURSUIT[9] (CONTINUED)

Year	Champion	HR:MIN:SEC
2002	Thomas Alsgaard (NOR); Frode Estil (NOR) (*tied*)[10]	49:48.9
2006	Yevgeny Dementyev (RUS)	1:17:00.8

30-KILOMETER CROSS-COUNTRY

Year	Champion	HR:MIN:SEC
1956	Veikko Hakulinen (FIN)	1:44:06.0
1960	Sixten Jernberg (SWE)	1:51:03.9
1964	Eero Mäntyranta (FIN)	1:30:50.7
1968	Franco Nones (ITA)	1:35:39.2
1972	Vyacheslav Vedenin (URS)	1:36:31.15[1]
1976	Sergey Savelyev (URS)	1:30:29.38
1980	Nikolay Zimyatov (URS)	1:27:02.80
1984	Nikolay Zimyatov (URS)	1:28:56.30
1988	Aleksey Prokourorov (URS)	1:24:26.3
1992	Vegard Ulvang (NOR)	1:22:27.8
1994	Thomas Alsgaard (NOR)	1:12:26.4
1998	Mika Myllylä (FIN)	1:33:56.0
2002	Christian Hoffmann (AUT)[10]	1:11:31.0

50-KILOMETER CROSS-COUNTRY

Year	Champion	HR:MIN:SEC
1924	Thorleif Haug (NOR)	3:44:32.0
1928	Per Erik Hedlund (SWE)	4:52:03.3
1932	Veli Saarinen (FIN)	4:28:00.0
1936	Elis Viklund (SWE)	3:30:11.0
1948	Nils Karlsson (SWE)	3:47:48.0
1952	Veikko Hakulinen (FIN)	3:33:33.0
1956	Sixten Jernberg (SWE)	2:50:27.0
1960	Kalevi Hämäläinen (FIN)	2:59:06.3
1964	Sixten Jernberg (SWE)	2:43:52.6
1968	Olle Ellefsäter (NOR)	2:28:45.8
1972	Pål Tyldum (NOR)	2:43:14.75[1]
1976	Ivar Formo (NOR)	2:37:30.05
1980	Nikolay Zimyatov (URS)	2:27:24.60
1984	Thomas Wassberg (SWE)	2:15:55.80
1988	Gunde Svan (SWE)	2:04:30.9
1992	Bjørn Daehlie (NOR)	2:03:41.5
1994	Vladimir Smirnov (KAZ)	2:07:20.3
1998	Bjørn Daehlie (NOR)	2:05:08.2
2002	Mikhail Ivanov (RUS)[10]	2:06:20.8
2006	Giorgio Di Centa (ITA)	2:06:11.8

4 × 10-KILOMETER RELAY

Year	Champion	HR:MIN:SEC
1936	Finland	2:41:33.0
1948	Sweden	2:32:08.0
1952	Finland	2:20:16.0
1956	USSR	2:15:30.0
1960	Finland	2:18:45.6
1964	Sweden	2:18:34.6
1968	Norway	2:08:33.5
1972	USSR	2:04:47.94[1]
1976	Finland	2:07:59.72
1980	USSR	1:57:03.46
1984	Sweden	1:55:06.30
1988	Sweden	1:43:58.6
1992	Norway	1:39:26.0
1994	Italy	1:41:15.0
1998	Norway	1:40:55.7
2002	Norway	1:32:45.5
2006	Italy	1:43:45.7

SKI JUMPING (70 METERS)[11]

1924 Jacob Tullin Thams (NOR)
1928 Alf Andersen (NOR)
1932 Birger Ruud (NOR)
1936 Birger Ruud (NOR)
1948 Petter Hugsted (NOR)
1952 Arnfinn Bergmann (NOR)

Nordic Skiing (men) (continued)

SKI JUMPING (70 METERS)[11] (CONTINUED)

1956 Antti Hyvärinen (FIN)
1960 Helmut Recknagel (GER)[5]
1964 Veikko Kankkonen (FIN)
1968 Jiri Raska (TCH)
1972 Yukio Kasaya (JPN)
1976 Hans-Georg Aschenbach (GDR)
1980 Toni Innauer (AUT)
1984 Jens Weissflog (GDR)
1988 Matti Nykänen (FIN)

SKI JUMPING (90 METERS)[11]

1964 Toralf Engan (NOR)
1968 Vladimir Belousov (URS)
1972 Wojciech Fortuna (POL)
1976 Karl Schnabl (AUT)
1980 Jens Tormanen (FIN)
1984 Matti Nykänen (FIN)
1988 Matti Nykänen (FIN)
1992 Ernst Vettori (AUT)
1994 Espen Bredesen (NOR)
1998 Jani Soininen (FIN)
2002 Simon Ammann (SUI)
2006 Lars Bystøl (NOR)

SKI JUMPING (120 METERS)[11]

1992 Toni Nieminen (FIN)
1994 Jens Weissflog (GER)
1998 Kazuyoshi Funaki (JPN)
2002 Simon Ammann (SUI)
2006 Thomas Morganstern (AUT)

NORDIC COMBINED SPRINT (7.5 KILOMETERS)

2002 Samppa Lajunen (FIN)
2006 Felix Gottwald (AUT)

NORDIC COMBINED (15 KILOMETERS)

1924 Thorleif Haug (NOR)
1928 Johan Gröttumsbraaten (NOR)
1932 Johan Gröttumsbraaten (NOR)
1936 Oddbjörn Hagen (NOR)
1948 Heikki Hasu (NOR)
1952 Simon Slåttvik (NOR)
1956 Sverre Stenersen (NOR)
1960 Georg Thoma (GER)[5]
1964 Tormod Knutsen (NOR)
1968 Franz Keller (FRG)
1972 Ulrich Wehling (GDR)
1976 Ulrich Wehling (GDR)
1980 Ulrich Wehling (GDR)
1984 Tom Sandberg (NOR)
1988 Hippolyt Kempf (SUI)
1992 Fabrice Guy (FRA)
1994 Fred Börre Lundberg (NOR)
1998 Bjarte Engen Vik (NOR)
2002 Samppa Lajunen (FIN)
2006 Georg Hettich (GER)

TEAM SKI JUMPING (120 METERS)

1988 Finland (90-m event)
1992 Finland
1994 Germany
1998 Japan
2002 Germany
2006 Austria

Winter Olympic Games Champions (continued)

Nordic Skiing (men) (continued)

NORDIC COMBINED TEAM RELAY

1988	West Germany
1992	Japan
1994	Japan
1998	Norway
2002	Finland
2006	Austria

Nordic Skiing (women)

1.5-KILOMETER CROSS-COUNTRY SPRINT		MIN:SEC
2002	Yuliya Chepalova (RUS)	3:10.6
2006	Chandra Crawford (CAN)	2:12.3

5-KILOMETER CROSS-COUNTRY		MIN:SEC
1964	Klavdiya Boyarskikh (URS)	17:50.5
1968	Toini Gustafsson (SWE)	16:45.2
1972	Galina Kulakova (URS)	17:00.50[1]
1976	Helena Takalo (FIN)	15:48.69
1980	Raisa Smetanina (URS)	15:06.92
1984	Marja-Liisa Hämäläinen (FIN)	17:04.00
1988	Marjo Matikainen (FIN)	15:04.00
1992	Marjut Lukkarinen (FIN)	14:13.8
1994	Lyubov Yegorova (RUS)	14:08.8
1998	Larisa Lazutina (RUS)	17:39.9

10-KILOMETER CROSS-COUNTRY		MIN:SEC
1952	Lydia Wideman (FIN)	41:40.0
1956	Lyubov Kozyreva (URS)	38:11.0
1960	Mariya Gusakova (URS)	39:46.6
1964	Klavdiya Boyarskikh (URS)	40:24.3
1968	Toini Gustafsson (SWE)	36:46.5
1972	Galina Kulakova (URS)	34:17.82[1]
1976	Raisa Smetanina (URS)	30:13.41
1980	Barbara Petzold (GDR)	30:31.54
1984	Marja-Liisa Hämäläinen (FIN)	31:44.20
1988	Vida Ventsene (URS)	30:08.30
1998	Larisa Lazutina (RUS)	46:06.9
2002	Bente Skari (NOR)	28:05.6
2006	Kristina Smigun (EST)	27:51.4

COMBINED PURSUIT[12]		MIN:SEC
1992	Lyubov Yegorova (UNT)[2]	40:08.4
1994	Lyubov Yegorova (RUS)	41:38.1
1998	Larisa Lazutina (RUS)	46:06.9
2002	Beckie Scott (CAN)[10]	25.09:9
2006	Kristina Smigun (EST)	42:48.7

15-KILOMETER CROSS-COUNTRY		MIN:SEC
1992	Lyubov Yegorova (UNT)[2]	42:20.8
1994	Manuela di Centa (ITA)	39:44.5
1998	Olga Danilova (RUS)	46:55.40
2002	Stefania Belmondo (ITA)	39:54.4

20-KILOMETER CROSS-COUNTRY		HR:MIN:SEC
1984	Marja-Liisa Hämäläinen (FIN)	1:01:45.0
1988	Tamara Tikhonova (URS)	55:53.6

30-KILOMETER CROSS-COUNTRY		HR:MIN:SEC
1992	Stefania Belmondo (ITA)	1:22:30.1
1994	Manuela di Centa (ITA)	1:25:41.6
1998	Yuliya Chepalova (RUS)	1:22:01.5
2002	Gabriella Paruzzi (ITA)[10]	1:30:57.1
2006	Katerina Neumannova (CZE)	1:22:25.4

4 × 5-KILOMETER RELAY		HR:MIN:SEC
2002	Germany	49:30.6
2006	Russia	54:47.7

Sled-dog Race

1932	Emile St. Goddard (CAN)

Snowboarding (men)

GIANT SLALOM

1998	Ross Rebagliati (CAN)
2002	Philipp Schoch (SUI)
2006	Philipp Schoch (SUI)

HALFPIPE

1998	Gian Simmen (SUI)
2002	Ross Powers (USA)
2006	Shaun White (USA)

SNOWBOARDCROSS

2006	Seth Wescott (USA)

Snowboarding (women)

GIANT SLALOM

1998	Karine Ruby (FRA)
2002	Isabelle Blanc (FRA)
2006	Daniela Meuli (SUI)

HALFPIPE

1998	Nicola Thost (GER)
2002	Kelly Clark (USA)
2006	Hannah Teter (USA)

SNOWBOARDCROSS

2006	Tanja Frieden (SUI)

Speed Skating (men)

4 × 5-KILOMETER RELAY[13]		HR:MIN:SEC
1956	Finland	1:09:01.0
1960	Sweden	1:04:21.4
1964	USSR	59:20.2
1968	Norway	57:30.0
1972	USSR	48:46.15[1]
1976	USSR	1:07:49.75
1980	East Germany	1:02:11.10
1984	Norway	1:06:49.70
1988	USSR	59:51.10
1992	Unified Team[2]	59:34.8
1994	Russia	57:12.5

500 METERS		SEC
1924	Charles Jewtraw (USA)	44.0
1928	Clas Thunberg (FIN); Bernt Evensen (NOR) (*tied*)	43.4
1932	John Shea (USA)	43.4
1936	Ivar Ballangrud (NOR)	43.4
1948	Finn Helgesen (NOR)	43.1
1952	Kenneth Henry (USA)	43.2
1956	Yevgeny Grishin (URS)	40.2
1960	Yevgeny Grishin (URS)	40.2
1964	Richard McDermott (USA)	40.1
1968	Erhard Keller (FRG)	40.3
1972	Erhard Keller (FRG)	39.44[1]
1976	Yevgeny Kulikov (URS)	39.17
1980	Eric Heiden (USA)	38.03
1984	Sergey Fokichev (URS)	38.19
1988	Uew-Jens Mey (GDR)	36.45
1992	Uew-Jens Mey (GER)	37.14
1994	Aleksandr Golubyov (RUS)	36.33
1998	Hiroyasu Shimizu (JPN)	71.35[14]
2002	Casey Fitzrandolph (USA)	69.23[14]
2006	Joey Cheek (USA)	69.76[14]

Winter Olympic Games Champions (continued)

Speed Skating (men) (continued)

1,000 METERS		MIN:SEC
1976	Peter Mueller (USA)	1:19.32[1]
1980	Eric Heiden (USA)	1:15.18
1984	Gaetan Boucher (CAN)	1:15.80
1988	Nikolay Gulyayev (URS)	1:13.03
1992	Olaf Zinke (GER)	1:14.85
1994	Dan Jansen (USA)	1:12.43
1998	Ids Postma (NED)	1:10.71
2002	Gerard van Velde (NED)	1:07.18
2006	Shani Davis (USA)	1:08.89

1,500 METERS		MIN:SEC
1924	Clas Thunberg (FIN)	2:20.8
1928	Clas Thunberg (FIN)	2:21.1
1932	John Shea (USA)	2:57.5
1936	Charles Mathisen (NOR)	2:19.2
1948	Sverre Farstad (NOR)	2:17.6
1952	Hjalmar Andersen (NOR)	2:20.4
1956	Yury Mikhaylov (URS); Yevgeny Grishin (URS) (*tied*)	2:08.6
1960	Yevegeny Grishin (URS); Roald Aas (NOR) (*tied*)	2:10.4
1964	Ants Antson (URS)	2:10.3
1968	Cornelis Verkerk (NED)	2:03.4
1972	Ard Schenk (NED)	2:02.96[1]
1976	Jan Egil Storholt (NOR)	1:59.38
1980	Eric Heiden (USA)	1:55.44
1984	Gaetan Boucher (CAN)	1:58.36
1988	André Hoffmann (GDR)	1:52.06
1992	Johann Olav Koss (NOR)	1:54.81
1994	Johann Olav Koss (NOR)	1:51.29
1998	Aadne Sondral (NOR)	1:47.87
2002	Derek Parra (USA)	1:43.95
2006	Enrico Fabris (ITA)	1:45.97

5,000 METERS		MIN:SEC
1924	Clas Thunberg (FIN)	8:39.0
1928	Ivar Ballangrud (NOR)	8:50.5
1932	Irving Jaffee (USA)	9:40.8
1936	Ivar Ballangrud (NOR)	8:19.6
1948	Reidar Liaklev (NOR)	8:29.4
1952	Hjalmar Andersen (NOR)	8:10.6
1956	Boris Shilkov (URS)	7:48.7
1960	Viktor Kosichkin (URS)	7:51.3
1964	Knut Johannesen (NOR)	7:38.4
1968	Fred Anton Maier (NOR)	7:22.4
1972	Ard Schenk (NED)	7:23.61[1]
1976	Sten Stensen (NOR)	7:24.48
1980	Eric Heiden (USA)	7:02.29
1984	Thomas Gustafson (SWE)	7:12.28
1988	Thomas Gustafson (SWE)	6:44.63
1992	Geir Karlstad (NOR)	6:59.97
1994	Johann Olav Koss (NOR)	6:34.96
1998	Gianni Romme (NED)	6:22.20
2002	Jochem Uytdehaage (NED)	6:14.66
2006	Chad Hedrick (USA)	6:14.68

10,000 METERS		MIN:SEC
1924	Julius Skutnabb (FIN)	18:04.8
1932	Irving Jaffee (USA)	19:13.6
1936	Ivar Ballangrud (NOR)	17:24.3
1948	Ake Seyffarth (SWE)	17:26.3
1952	Hjalmar Andersen (NOR)	16:45.8
1956	Sigvard Ericsson (SWE)	16:35.9
1960	Knut Johannesen (NOR)	15:46.6
1964	Jonny Nilsson (SWE)	15:50.1
1968	Johnny Höglin (SWE)	15:23.6
1972	Ard Schenk (NED)	15:01.35[1]

Speed Skating (men) (continued)

10,000 METERS (CONTINUED)		MIN:SEC
1976	Piet Kleine (NED)	14:50.59
1980	Eric Heiden (USA)	14:28.13
1984	Igor Malkov (URS)	14:39.90
1988	Thomas Gustafson (SWE)	13:48.20
1992	Bart Veldkamp (NED)	14:12.12
1994	Johann Olav Koss (NOR)	13:30.55
1998	Gianni Romme (NED)	13:15.33
2002	Jochem Uytdehaage (NED)	12:58.92
2006	Bob de Jong (NED)	13:01.57

COMBINED SPEED SKATING	
1924	Clas Thunberg (FIN)

TEAM PURSUIT		MIN:SEC
2006	Italy	3:44.46

Speed Skating (women)

500 METERS		SEC
1960	Helga Haase (GER)[5]	45.9
1964	Lidiya Skoblikova (URS)	45.0
1972	Anne Henning (USA)	43.33[1]
1976	Sheila Young (USA)	42.76
1980	Karin Enke (GDR)	41.78
1984	Christa Rothenburger (GDR)	41.02
1988	Bonnie Blair (USA)	39.10
1992	Bonnie Blair (USA)	40.33
1994	Bonnie Blair (USA)	39.25
1998	Catriona LeMay Doan (CAN)	76.60[14]
2002	Catriona LeMay Doan (CAN)	74.75[14]
2006	Svetlana Zhurova (RUS)	76.57[14]

1,000 METERS		MIN:SEC
1960	Klara Guseva (URS)	1:34.1
1964	Lidiya Skoblikova (URS)	1:32.6
1968	Carolina Geijssen (NED)	1:32.6
1972	Monika Pflug (FRG)	1:31.40[1]
1976	Tatyana Averina (URS)	1:28.43
1980	Natalya Petruseva (URS)	1:24.10
1984	Karin Enke (GDR)	1:21.61
1988	Christa Rothenburger (GDR)	1:17.65
1992	Bonnie Blair (USA)	1:21.90
1994	Bonnie Blair (USA)	1:18.74
1998	Marianne Timmer (NED)	1:16.51
2002	Chris Witty (USA)	1:13.83
2006	Marianne Timmer (NED)	1:16.05

1,500 METERS		MIN:SEC
1960	Lidiya Skoblikova (URS)	2:25.2
1964	Lidiya Skoblikova (URS)	2:22.6
1968	Kaija Mustonen (FIN)	2:22.4
1972	Dianne Holum (USA)	2:20.85[1]
1976	Galina Stepanskaya (URS)	2:16.58
1980	Annie Borckink (NED)	2:10.95
1984	Karin Enke (GDR)	2:03.42
1988	Yvonne van Gennip (NED)	2:00.68
1992	Jacqueline Börner (GER)	2:05.87
1994	Emese Hunyady (AUT)	2:02.19
1998	Marianne Timmer (NED)	1:57.58
2002	Anni Friesinger (GER)	1:54.02
2006	Cindy Klassen (CAN)	1:55.27

3,000 METERS		MIN:SEC
1960	Lidiya Skoblikova (URS)	5:14.3
1964	Lidiya Skoblikova (URS)	5:14.9
1968	Johanna Schut (NED)	4:56.2
1972	Christina Baas-Kaiser (NED)	4:52.14[1]
1976	Tatyana Averina (URS)	4:45.19

Winter Olympic Games Champions (continued)

Speed Skating (women) (continued)

3,000 METERS (CONTINUED)		MIN:SEC
1980	Björg Eva Jensen (NOR)	4:32.13
1984	Andrea Schöne (GDR)	4:24.79
1988	Yvonne van Gennip (NED)	4:11.94
1992	Gunda Niemann (GER)	4:19.90
1994	Svetlana Bazhanova (RUS)	4:17.43
1998	Gunda Niemann-Stirnemann (GER)	4:07.29
2002	Claudia Pechstein (GER)	3:57.70
2006	Ireen Wüst (NED)	4:02.43

5,000 METERS		MIN:SEC
1988	Yvonne van Gennip (NED)	7:14.13
1992	Gunda Niemann (GER)	7:31.57
1994	Claudia Pechstein (GER)	7:14.37
1998	Claudia Pechstein (GER)	6:59.61
2002	Claudia Pechstein (GER)	6:46.91
2006	Clara Hughes (CAN)	6:59.07

TEAM PURSUIT		MIN:SEC
2006	Germany	3:01.25

Short-Track Speed Skating (men)

500 METERS		SEC
1994	Chae Ji-Hoon (KOR)	43.45
1998	Takafumi Nishitani (JPN)	42.862[6]
2002	Marc Gagnon (CAN)	41.802
2006	Apolo Anton Ohno (USA)	41.935

1,000 METERS		MIN:SEC
1992	Kim Ki-Hoon (KOR)	1:30.76
1994	Kim Ki-Hoon (KOR)	1:34.57
1998	Kim Dong Sung (KOR)	1:32.428[6]
2002	Steven Bradbury (AUS)	1:29.109
2006	Ahn Hyun Soo (KOR)	1:26.739

1,500 METERS		MIN:SEC
2002	Apolo Anton Ohno (USA)	2:18.541
2006	Ahn Hyun Soo (KOR)	2:25.341

Short-Track Speed Skating (men) (continued)

5,000-METER RELAY		MIN:SEC
1992	South Korea	7:14.02
1994	Italy	7:11.74
1998	Canada	7:06.075[6]
2002	Canada	6:51.579
2006	South Korea	6:43.376

Short-Track Speed Skating (women)

500 METERS		SEC
1992	Cathy Turner (USA)	47.04
1994	Cathy Turner (USA)	45.98
1998	Annie Perreault (CAN)	46.568[6]
2002	Yang Yang (A) (CHN)	44.187
2006	Wang Meng (CHN)	44.345

1,000 METERS		MIN:SEC
1994	Chun Lee-Kyung (KOR)	1:36.87
1998	Chun Lee-Kyung (KOR)	1:42.776[6]
2002	Yang Yang (A) (CHN)	1:36.391
2006	Jin Sun Yu (KOR)	1:32.859

1,500 METERS		MIN:SEC
2002	Ko Gi-Hyun (KOR)	2:31.581
2006	Jin Sun Yu (KOR)	2:23.494

3,000-METER RELAY		MIN:SEC
1992	Canada	4:36.62
1994	South Korea	4:26.64
1998	South Korea	4:16.260[6]
2002	South Korea	4:12.793
2006	South Korea	4:17.040

Winter Pentathlon[15]

1948 Gustav Lindh (SWE)

[1]Race first timed in hundredths of a second. [2]Unified Team, consisting of athletes from the Commonwealth of Independent States plus Georgia. [3]In 1992 the relay was 3 × 7.5 km; from 1994–2002 it was 4 × 7.5 km. [4]Five men. [5]Joint East-West German team. [6]Race first timed in thousandths of a second. [7]Competition scored on points until 1994. [8]1924–52, 18 km. [9]Results of a 10- or 15-km classical leg determine the starting order of a 10- or 15-km freestyle leg, the first finisher of which is the overall winner; each leg was 15 km in the 2006 Games. [10]Winner after disqualification of top finisher for drug use. [11]From 1924 to 1960 the jumping was held on one hill. In 1964 there were two events, one on a 70-m and the other on an 80-m hill; from 1968 to 1988 there were 70-m and 90-m events. From 1992 to 2002 there were 90-m and 120-m events. In 2006 there were 95-m and 125-m events. [12]Results of a 5- or 7.5-km classical leg determine the starting order of a 5-, 7.5-, or 10-km freestyle leg, the first finisher of which is the overall winner; each leg was 7.5 km in the 2006 Games. [13]3 × 5-km relay until 1976. [14]Combined time for two runs. [15]Includes elements of cross-country skiing, downhill skiing, shooting, fencing, and horse riding.

Olympic Medal Winners—XXIX Summer Games (2008)

The XXIX Summer Games were held in Beijing, China, 8–24 Aug 2008.

EVENT	GOLD MEDALIST	PERFORMANCE	SILVER MEDALIST	BRONZE MEDALIST
Archery				
Men's individual	Viktor Ruban (UKR)	113–112	Park Kyung Mo (KOR)	Bair Badenov (RUS)
Men's team	South Korea	227–225	Italy	China
Women's individual	Zhang Juan Juan (CHN)	110–109	Park Sung Hyun (KOR)	Yun Ok Hee (KOR)
Women's team	South Korea	224–215	China	France
Badminton				
Men's singles	Lin Dan (CHN)	21–12, 21–8	Chong Wei Lee (MAS)	Chen Lin (CHN
Men's doubles	Indonesia	12–21, 21–11, 21–16	China	South Korea

Olympic Medal Winners—XXIX Summer Games (2008) (continued)

EVENT	GOLD MEDALIST	PERFORMANCE	SILVER MEDALIST	BRONZE MEDALIST
Badminton (continued)				
Women's singles	Zhang Ning (CHN)	21-12, 10-21, 21-18	Xia Xingfang (CHN)	Maria Kristin Yulianti (INA)
Women's doubles	China	21-15, 21-13	South Korea	China
Mixed doubles	South Korea	21-11, 21-17	Indonesia	China
Baseball				
	South Korea	3-2	Cuba	United States
Basketball				
Men	United States	118-107	Spain	Argentina
Women	United States	92-65	Australia	Russia
Boxing[1]				
48 kg (105.6 lb)	Zou Shiming (CHN)		Serdamba Purevdorj (MGL)	Paddy Barnes (IRL); Yampier Hernández (CUB)
51 kg (112.2 lb)	Somjit Jongjohor (THA)		Andris Laffita Hernández (CUB)	Vincenzo Picardi (ITA); Georgy Balakshin (RUS)
54 kg (118.8 lb)	Badar-Uugan Enkhbat (MGL)		Yankiel León Alarcón (CUB)	Veaceslav Gojan (MDA); Bruno Julie (MRI)
57 kg (125.4 lb)	Vasyl Lomachenko (UKR)		Khedafi Djelkhir (FRA)	Yakup Kilic (TUR); Shahin Imranov (AZE)
60 kg (132 lb)	Aleksey Tishchenko (RUS)		Daouda Sow (FRA)	Hrachik Javakhyan (ARM); Yordenis Ugás (CUB)
64 kg (140.8)	Félix Díaz (DOM)		Manus Boonjumnong (THA)	Alexis Vastine (FRA); Roniel Iglesias Sotolongo (CUB)
69 kg (151.8 lb)	Bakhyt Sarsekbayev (KAZ)		Carlos Banteaux Suárez (CUB)	Kim Jung Joo (KOR); Hanati Silamu (CHN)
75 kg (165 lb)	James Degale (GBR)		Emilio Correa Bayeaux (CUB)	Darren John Sutherland (IRL); Vijender Kumar (IND)
81 kg (178.2 lb)	Zhang Xiaoping (CHN)		Kenny Egan (IRL)	Yerkebulan Shynaliyev (KAZ); Tony Jeffries (GBR)
91 kg (200.2 lb)	Rakhim Chakhkiyev (RUS)		Clemente Russo (ITA)	Osmay Acosta Duarte (CUB); Deontay Wilder (USA)
91+ kg (200.2+ lb)	Roberto Cammarelle (ITA)		Zhang Zhilei (CHN)	David Price (GBR); Vyacheslav Glazkov (UKR)
Canoeing				
Men				
500-m kayak singles	Ken Wallace (AUS)	1 min 37.252 sec	Adam van Koeverden (CAN)	Tim Brabants (GBR)
1,000-m kayak singles	Tim Brabants (GBR)	3 min 26.323 sec	Eirik Verås Larsen (NOR)	Ken Wallace (AUS)
500-m kayak pairs	Spain	1 min 28.736 sec	Germany	Belarus
1,000-m kayak pairs	Germany	3 min 11.809 sec	Denmark	Italy
1,000-m kayak fours	Belarus	2 min 55.714 sec	Slovakia	Germany
Slalom kayak singles	Alexander Grimm (GER)	171.70 pt	Fabien Lefèvre (FRA)	Benjamin Boukpeti (TOG)
500-m Canadian singles	Maksim Opalev (RUS)	1 min 47.140 sec	David Cal (ESP)	Iurii Cheban (UKR)
1,000-m Canadian singles	Attila Sándor Vajda (HUN)	3 min 50.467 sec	David Cal (ESP)	Thomas Hall (CAN)
500-m Canadian pairs	China	1 min 41.025 sec	Russia	Germany
1,000-m Canadian pairs	Belarus	3 min 36.365 sec	Germany	Hungary
Slalom Canadian singles	Michal Martikan (SVK)	176.65 pt	David Florence (GBR)	Robin Bell (AUS)
Slalom Canadian pairs	Slovakia	190.82 pt	Czech Republic	Russia

Olympic Medal Winners—XXIX Summer Games (2008) (continued)

EVENT	GOLD MEDALIST	PERFORMANCE	SILVER MEDALIST	BRONZE MEDALIST
Canoeing (continued)				
Women				
500-m kayak singles	Inna Osypenko-Radomska (UKR)	1 min 50.673 sec	Josefa Idem (ITA)	Katrin Wagner-Augustin (GER)
500-m kayak pairs	Hungary	1 min 41.308 sec	Poland	France
500-m kayak fours	Germany	1 min 32.231 sec	Hungary	Australia
Slalom kayak singles	Elena Kaliska (SVK)	192.64 pt	Jacqueline Lawrence (AUS)	Violetta Oblinger Peters (AUT)
Cycling				
Men				
Road race	Samuel Sánchez (ESP)	6 hr 23 min 49 sec	Davide Rebellin (ITA)	Fabian Cancellara (SUI)
Individual road time trial	Fabian Cancellara (SUI)	1 hr 2 min 11.43 sec	Gustav Larsson (SWE)	Levi Leipheimer (USA)
Individual pursuit	Bradley Wiggins (GBR)	4 min 16.977 sec	Hayden Roulston (NZL)	Steven Burke (GBR)
Team pursuit	Great Britain	3 min 53.314 sec[2]	Denmark	New Zealand
Individual sprint	Chris Hoy (GBR)		Jason Kenny (GBR)	Mickaël Bourgain (FRA)
Team sprint	Great Britain	43.128 sec	France	Germany
Individual points race	Joan Llaneras (ESP)	60 pt	Roger Kluge (GER)	Chris Newton (GBR)
Madison	Argentina		Spain	Russia
Keirin	Chris Hoy (GBR)		Ross Edgar (GBR)	Kiyofumi Nagai (JPN)
Mountain bike	Julien Absalon (FRA)	1 hr 55 min 59 sec	Jean-Christophe Péraud (FRA)	Nino Schurter (SUI)
Motocross/BMX	Maris Strombergs (LAT)	36.190 sec	Mike Day (USA)	Donny Robinson (USA)
Women				
Road race	Nicole Cooke (GBR)	3 hr 32 min 24 sec	Emma Johansson (SWE)	Tatiana Guderzo (ITA)
Individual road time trial	Kristin Armstrong (USA)	34 min 51.72 sec	Emma Pooley (GBR)	Karin Thürig (SUI)
Individual pursuit	Rebecca Romero (GBR)	3 min 28.321 sec	Wendy Houvenaghel (GBR)	Lesya Kalitovska (UKR)
Individual sprint	Victoria Pendleton (GBR)		Anna Meares (AUS)	Guo Shuang (CHN)
Individual points race	Marianne Vos (NED)	30 pt	Yoanka González (CUB)	Leire Olaberria (ESP)
Mountain bike	Sabine Spitz (GER)	1 hr 45 min 11 sec	Maja Wloszczowska (POL)	Irina Kalentiyeva (RUS)
Motocross/BMX	Anne-Caroline Chausson (FRA)	35.976 sec	Laëtitia Le Corguillé (FRA)	Jill Kintner (USA)
Diving				
Men				
3-m springboard	He Chong (CHN)	572.90 pt	Alexandre Despatie (CAN)	Qin Kai (CHN)
10-m platform	Matt Mitcham (AUS)	537.95 pt	Zhou Luxin (CHN)	Gleb Galperin (RUS)
3-m synchronized springboard	China	469.08 pt	Russia	Ukraine
10-m synchronized platform	China	468.18 pt	Germany	Russia
Women				
3-m springboard	Guo Jingjing (CHN)	415.35 pt	Yuliya Pakhalina (RUS)	Wu Minxia (CHN)
10-m platform	Chen Ruolin (CHN)	447.70 pt	Émilie Heymans (CAN)	Wang Xin (CHN)
3-m synchronized springboard	China	343.50 pt	Russia	Germany
10-m synchronized platform	China	363.54 pt	Australia	Mexico
Equestrian				
Individual 3-day event	Hinrich Romeike (GER)		Gina Miles (USA)	Kristina Cook (GBR)
Team 3-day event	Germany		Australia	Great Britain
Individual dressage	Anky van Grunsven (NED)		Isabell Werth (GER)	Heike Kemmer (GER)
Team dressage	Germany		Netherlands	Denmark
Individual jumping	Eric Lamaze (CAN)		Rolf-Göran Bengtsson (SWE)	Beezie Madden (USA)
Team jumping	United States		Canada	Norway

Olympic Medal Winners—XXIX Summer Games (2008) (continued)

EVENT	GOLD MEDALIST	PERFORMANCE	SILVER MEDALIST	BRONZE MEDALIST
Fencing				
Men				
Individual foil	Benjamin Philip Kleibrink (GER)		Yuki Ota (JPN)	Salvatore Sanzo (ITA)
Individual épée	Matteo Tagliariol (ITA)		Fabrice Jeannet (FRA)	José Luis Abajo (ESP
Team épée	France		Poland	Italy
Individual sabre	Zhong Man (CHN)		Nicolas Lopez (FRA)	Mihai Cavaliu (ROM)
Team sabre	France		United States	Italy
Women				
Individual foil	Maria Valentina Vezzali (ITA)		Nam Hyun Hee (KOR)	Margherita Granbassi (ITA)
Team foil	Russia		United States	Italy
Individual épée	Britta Heidemann (GER)		Ana Maria Branza (ROM)	Ildikó Mincza-Nébald (HUN)
Individual sabre	Mariel Zagunis (USA)		Sada Jacobson (USA)	Becca Ward (USA)
Team sabre	Ukraine		China	United States
Field Hockey				
Men	Germany	1–0	Spain	Australia
Women	The Netherlands	2–0	China	Argentina
Gymnastics				
Men				
Team	China	286.125 pt	Japan	United States
All-around	Yang Wei (CHN)	94.575 pt	Kohei Uchimura (JPN)	Benoît Caranobe (FRA)
Floor exercise	Zou Kai (CHN)	16.050 pt	Gervasio Deferr (ESP)	Anton Golotsutskov (RUS)
Vault	Leszek Blanik (POL)	16.537 pt	Thomas Bouhail (FRA)	Anton Golotsutskov (RUS)
Pommel horse	Xiao Qin (CHN)	15.875 pt	Filip Ude (CRO)	Louis Smith (GBR)
Rings	Chen Yibing (CHN)	16.600 pt	Yang Wei (CHN)	Oleksandr Vorobiov (UKR)
Parallel bars	Li Xiaopeng (CHN)	16.450 pt	Yoo Won Chul (KOR)	Anton Fokin (UZB)
Horizontal bar	Zou Kai (CHN)	16.200 pt	Jonathan Horton (USA)	Fabian Hambüchen (GER)
Trampoline	Lu Chunlong (CHN)	41.00 pt	Jason Burnett (CAN)	Dong Dong (CHN)
Women				
Team	China	188.900 pt	United States	Romania
All-around	Nastia Liukin (USA)	63.325 pt	Shawn Johnson (USA)	Yang Yilin (CHN)
Floor exercise	Sandra Izbasa (ROM)	15.650 pt	Shawn Johnson (USA)	Nastia Liukin (USA)
Vault	Hong Un Jong (PRK)	15.650 pt	Oksana Chusovitina (GER)	Cheng Fei (CHN)
Uneven bars	He Kexin (CHN)	16.725 pt	Nastia Liukin (USA)	Yang Yilin (CHN)
Balance beam	Shawn Johnson (USA)	16.225 pt	Nastia Liukin (USA)	Cheng Fei (CHN)
Trampoline	He Wenna (CHN)	37.80 pt	Karen Cockburn (CAN)	Ekaterina Khilko (UZB)
Individual rhythmic	Yevgeniya Kanayeva (RUS)	75.500 pt	Inna Zhukova (BLR)	Anna Bessonova (UKR)
Team rhythmic	Russia	35.550 pt	China	Belarus
Handball (Team)				
Men	France	15–10, 13–13	Iceland	Spain
Women	Norway	18–13, 16–14	Russia	South Korea
Judo[1]				
Men				
60 kg (132 lb)	Choi Min Ho (KOR)		Ludwig Paischer (AUT)	Rishod Sobirov (UZB); Ruben Houkes (NED)
66 kg (145.2 lb)	Masato Uchishiba (JPN)		Benjamin Darbelet (FRA)	Yordanis Arencibia (CUB); Pak Chol Min (PRK)
73 kg (160.6 lb)	Elnur Mammadli (AZE)		Wang Ki Chun (KOR)	Rasul Boqiev (TJK); Leandro Guilheiro (BRA)

Olympic Medal Winners—XXIX Summer Games (2008) (continued)

EVENT	GOLD MEDALIST	PERFORMANCE	SILVER MEDALIST	BRONZE MEDALIST
Judo (continued)[1]				
Men				
81 kg (178.2 lb)	Ole Bischof (GER)		Kim Jae Bum (KOR)	Tiago Camilo (BRA); Roman Gontiuk (UKR)
90 kg (198 lb)	Irakli Tsirekidze (GEO)		Amar Benikhlef (ALG)	Hesham Mesbah (EGY); Sergei Aschwanden (SUI)
100 kg (220 lb)	Tuvshinbayar Naidan (MGL)		Askhat Zhitkeyev (KAZ)	Movlud Miraliyev (AZE); Henk Grol (NED)
100+ kg (220+ lb)	Satoshi Ishii (JPN)		Abdullo Tangriev (UZB)	Oscar Brayson (CUB); Teddy Riner (FRA)
Women				
48 kg (105.6 lb)	Alina Alexandra Dumitru (ROM)		Yanet Bermoy (CUB)	Paula Belén Pareto (ARG); Ryoko Tani (JPN)
52 kg (114.4 lb)	Xian Dongmei (CHN)		An Kum Ae (PRK)	Soraya Haddad (ALG); Misato Nakamura (JPN)
57 kg (125.4 lb)	Giulia Quintavalle (ITA)		Deborah Gravenstijn (NED)	Ketleyn Quadros (BRA); Xu Yan (CHN)
63 kg (138.6 lb)	Ayumi Tanimoto (JPN)		Lucie Décosse (FRA)	Elisabeth Willeboordse (NED); Won Ok Im (PRK)
70 kg (154 lb)	Masae Ueno (JPN)		Anaysi Hernández (CUB)	Ronda Rousey (USA); Edith Bosch (NED)
78 kg (171.6 lb)	Yang Xiuli (CHN)		Yalennis Castillo (CUB)	Jeong Gyeong Mi (KOR); Stéphanie Possamaï (FRA)
78+ kg (171.6 lb)	Tong Wen (CHN)		Maki Tsukada (JPN)	Lucija Polavder (SLO); Idalys Ortiz (CUB)
Modern Pentathlon				
Men	Andrey Moiseyev (RUS)		Edvinas Krungolcas (LTU)	Andrejus Zadneprovskis (LTU)
Women	Lena Schöneborn (GER)		Heather Fell (GBR)	Victoria Tereshuk (UKR)
Rowing				
Men				
Single sculls	Olaf Tufte (NOR)	6 min 59.83 sec	Ondrej Synek (CZE)	Mahe Drysdale (NZL)
Double sculls	Australia	6 min 27.77 sec	Estonia	Great Britain
Quadruple sculls	Poland	5 min 41.33 sec	Italy	France
Coxless pairs (oars)	Australia	6 min 37.44 sec	Canada	New Zealand
Coxless fours (oars)	Great Britain	6 min 06.57 sec	Australia	France
Eights	Canada	5 min 23.89 sec	Great Britain	United States
Lightweight double sculls	Great Britain	6 min 10.99 sec	Greece	Denmark
Lightweight fours	Denmark	5 min 47.76 sec	Poland	Canada
Women				
Single sculls	Rumyana Neykova (BUL)	7 min 22.34 sec	Michelle Guerette (USA)	Yekaterina Karsten (BLR)
Double sculls	New Zealand	7 min 07.32 sec	Germany	Great Britain
Quadruple sculls	China	6 min 16.06 sec	Great Britain	Germany
Coxless pairs (oars)	Romania	7 min 20.60 sec	China	Belarus
Eights	United States	6 min 05.34 sec	The Netherlands	Romania
Lightweight double sculls	The Netherlands	6 min 54.74 sec	Finland	Canada
Sailing				
Men's 470	Australia		Great Britain	France
Women's 470	Australia		The Netherlands	Brazil
Men's RS:X	Tom Ashley (NZL)		Julien Bontemps (FRA)	Shahar Zubari (ISR)
Women's RS:X	Yin Jian (CHN)		Alessandra Sensini (ITA)	Bryony Shaw (GBR)

Olympic Medal Winners—XXIX Summer Games (2008) (continued)

EVENT	GOLD MEDALIST	PERFORMANCE	SILVER MEDALIST	BRONZE MEDALIST
Sailing (continued)				
Mixed Finn	Ben Ainslie (GBR)		Zach Railey (USA)	Guillaume Florent (FRA)
Women's Yngling	Great Britain		The Netherlands	Greece
Mixed 49er	Denmark		Spain	Germany
Men's Laser	Paul Goodison (GBR)		Vasilij Zbogar (SLO)	Diego Romero (ITA)
Women's Laser	Anna Tunnicliffe (USA)		Gintare Volungeviciute (LTU)	Xu Lijia (CHN)
Men's Star	Great Britain		Brazil	Sweden
Mixed Tornado	Spain		Australia	Argentina
Shooting				
Men				
Rapid-fire pistol	Oleksandr Petriv (UKR)	780.2 pt[3]	Ralf Schumann (GER)	Christian Reitz (GER)
Free pistol	Jin Jong Oh (KOR)	660.4 pt	Tan Zongliang (CHN)	Vladimir Isakov (RUS)
Air pistol	Pang Wei (CHN)	688.2 pt	Jin Jong Oh (KOR)	Jason Turner (USA)
Small-bore (sport) rifle, 3 positions	Qiu Jian (CHN)	1272.5 pt	Jury Sukhorukov (UKR)	Rajmond Debevec (SLO)
Small-bore (sport) rifle, prone	Artur Ayvazian (UKR)	702.7 pt	Matthew Emmons (USA)	Warren Potent (AUS)
Air rifle	Abhinav Bindra (IND)	700.5 pt	Zhu Qinan (CHN)	Henri Häkkinen (FIN)
Trap	David Kostelecky (CZE)	146.0 pt[3]	Giovanni Pellielo (ITA)	Aleksey Alipov (RUS)
Double trap	Walton Eller (USA)	190.0 pt[3]	Francesco D'Aniello (ITA)	Hu Binyuan (CHN)
Skeet	Vincent Hancock (USA)	145.0 pt[3]	Tore Brovold (NOR)	Anthony Terras (FRA)
Women				
Pistol	Chen Ying (CHN)	793.4 pt[3]	Gundegmaa Otryad (MGL)	Munkhbayar Dorjsuren (GER)
Air pistol	Guo Wenjun (CHN)	492.3 pt[3]	Natalya Paderina (RUS)	Nino Salukvadze (GEO)
Small-bore (sport) rifle, 3 positions	Du Li (CHN)	690.3 pt[3]	Katerina Emmons (CZE)	Eglis Yaima Cruz (CUB)
Air rifle	Katerina Emmons (CZE)	503.5 pt[3]	Lyubov Galkina (RUS)	Snjezana Pejcic (CRO)
Trap	Satu Mäkelä-Nummela (FIN)	91.0 pt[3]	Zuzana Stefecekova (SVK)	Corey Cogdell (USA)
Skeet	Chiara Cainero (ITA)	93.0 pt[3]	Kimberley Rhode (USA)	Christina Brinker (GER)
Soccer (Association Football)				
Men	Argentina	1–0	Nigeria	Brazil
Women	United States	1–0	Brazil	Germany
Softball				
	Japan	3–1	United States	Australia
Swimming				
Men				
50-m freestyle	César Cielo Filho (BRA)	21.30 sec[3]	Amaury Leveaux (FRA)	Alain Bernard (FRA)
100-m freestyle	Alain Bernard (FRA)	47.21 sec	Eamon Sullivan (AUS)	César Cielo Filho (BRA); Jason Lezak (USA)[4]
200-m freestyle	Michael Phelps (USA)	1 min 42.96 sec[2]	Park Tae Hwan (KOR)	Peter Vanderkaay (USA)
400-m freestyle	Park Tae Hwan (KOR)	3 min 41.86 sec	Zhang Lin (CHN)	Larsen Jensen (USA)
1,500-m freestyle	Oussama Mellouli (TUN)	14 min 40.84 sec	Grant Hackett (AUS)	Ryan Cochrane (CAN)
100-m backstroke	Aaron Peirsol (USA)	52.54 sec[2]	Matt Grevers (USA)	Hayden Stoeckel (AUS); Arkady Vyatchanin (RUS)[4]
200-m backstroke	Ryan Lochte (USA)	1 min 53.94 sec[2]	Aaron Peirsol (USA)	Arkady Vyatchanin (RUS)
100-m breaststroke	Kosuke Kitajima (JPN)	58.91 sec[2]	Alexander Dale Oen (NOR)	Hugues Duboscq (FRA)
200-m breaststroke	Kosuke Kitajima (JPN)	2 min 07.64 sec[3]	Brenton Rickard (AUS)	Hugues Duboscq (FRA)
100-m butterfly	Michael Phelps (USA)	50.58 sec[3]	Milorad Cavic (SRB)	Andrew Lauterstein (AUS)

Olympic Medal Winners—XXIX Summer Games (2008) (continued)

EVENT	GOLD MEDALIST	PERFORMANCE	SILVER MEDALIST	BRONZE MEDALIST
Swimming (continued)				
Men (continued)				
200-m butterfly	Michael Phelps (USA)	1 min 52.03 sec[2]	László Cseh (HUN)	Takeshi Matsuda (JPN)
200-m individual medley	Michael Phelps (USA)	1 min 54.23 sec[2]	László Cseh (HUN)	Ryan Lochte (USA)
400-m individual medley	Michael Phelps (USA)	4 min 03.84 sec[2]	László Cseh (HUN)	Ryan Lochte (USA)
10-km open-water marathon	Maarten van der Weijden (NED)	1 hr 51 min 51.60 sec	David Davies (GBR)	Thomas Lurz (GER)
4 x 100-m freestyle relay	United States	3 min 08.24 sec[2]	France	Australia
4 x 200-m freestyle relay	United States	6 min 58.56 sec[2]	Russia	Australia
4 x 100-m medley relay	United States	3 min 29.34 sec[2]	Australia	Japan
Women				
50-m freestyle	Britta Steffen (GER)	24.06 sec[3]	Dara Torres (USA	Cate Campbell (AUS)
100-m freestyle	Britta Steffen (GER)	53.12 sec[3]	Lisbeth Lenton Trickett (AUS)	Natalie Coughlin (USA)
200-m freestyle	Federica Pelligrini (ITA)	1 min 54.82 sec[2]	Sara Isakovic (SLO)	Pang Jiaying (CHN)
400-m freestyle	Rebecca Adlington (GBR)	4 min 03.22 sec	Katie Hoff (USA)	Joanne Jackson (GBR)
800-m freestyle	Rebecca Adlington (GBR)	8 min 14.10 sec[2]	Alessia Filippi (ITA)	Lotte Friis (DEN)
100-m backstroke	Natalie Coughlin (USA)	58.96 sec	Kirsty Coventry (ZIM)	Margaret Hoelzer (USA)
200-m backstroke	Kirsty Coventry (ZIM)	2 min 05.24 sec[2]	Margaret Hoelzer (USA)	Reiko Nakamura (JPN)
100-m breaststroke	Leisel Jones (AUS)	1 min 05.17 sec[3]	Rebecca Soni (USA)	Mirna Jukic (AUT)
200-m breaststroke	Rebecca Soni (USA)	2 min 20.22 sec[2]	Leisel Jones (AUS)	Sara Nordenstam (NOR)
100-m butterfly	Lisbeth Lenton Trickett (AUS)	56.73 sec	Christine Magnuson (USA)	Jessicah Schipper (AUS)
200-m butterfly	Liu Zige (CHN)	2 min 04.18 sec[2]	Jiao Liuyang (CHN)	Jessicah Schipper (AUS)
200-m individual medley	Stephanie Rice (AUS)	2 min 08.45 sec[2]	Kirsty Coventry (ZIM)	Natalie Coughlin (USA)
400-m individual medley	Stephanie Rice (AUS)	4 min 29.45 sec[2]	Kirsty Coventry (ZIM)	Katie Hoff (USA)
10-km open-water marathon	Larisa Ilchenko (RUS)	1 hr 59 min 27.70 sec	Keri-Anne Payne (GBR)	Cassandra Patten (GBR)
4 x 100-m freestyle relay	The Netherlands	3 min 33.76 sec[3]	United States	Australia
4 x 200-m freestyle relay	Australia	7 min 44.31 sec[2]	China	United States
4 x 100-m medley relay	Australia	3 min 52.69 sec[2]	United States	China
Synchronized Swimming				
Duet	Russia	99.251 pt	Spain	Japan
Team	Russia	99.500 pt	Spain	China
Table Tennis				
Men's singles	Ma Lin (CHN)	11–9, 11–9, 6–11, 11–7, 11–9	Wang Hao (CHN)	Wang Liqin (CHN)
Men's team	China	3–0	Germany	South Korea
Women's singles	Zhang Yining (CHN)	8–11, 13–11, 11–8, 11–8, 11–3	Wang Nan (CHN)	Guo Yue (CHN)
Women's team	China	3–0	Singapore	South Korea
Taekwondo[1]				
Men				
58 kg (127.6 lb)	Guillermo Pérez (MEX)		Yulis Gabriel Mercedes (DOM)	Chu Mu-yen (TPE); Rohullah Nikpai (AFG)
68 kg (149.6 lb)	Son Tae Jin (KOR)		Mark Lopez (USA)	Sung Yu-chi (TPE); Servet Tazegul (TUR)

Olympic Medal Winners—XXIX Summer Games (2008) (continued)

EVENT	GOLD MEDALIST	PERFORMANCE	SILVER MEDALIST	BRONZE MEDALIST
Taekwondo[1]				
80 kg (176 lb)	Hadi Saei (IRI)		Mauro Sarmiento (ITA)	Steven Lopez (USA); Zhu Guo (CHN)
80+ kg (176+ lb)	Cha Dong Min (KOR)		Alexandros Nikolaidis (GRE)	Arman Chilmanov (KAZ); Chika Yagazie Chukwumerije (NGR)
Women				
49 kg (107.8 lb)	Wu Jingyu (CHN)		Buttree Puedpong (THA)	Dalia Contreras Rivero (VEN); Daynellis Montejo (CUB)
57 kg (125.4 lb)	Lim Su Jeong (KOR)		Azize Tanrikulu (TUR)	Diana Lopez (USA); Martina Zubcic (CRO)
67 kg (147.4 lb)	Hwang Kyung Seon (KOR)		Karine Sergerie (CAN)	Gwladys Patience Epangue (FRA); Sandra Saric (CRO)
67+ kg (147.4+ lb)	María del Rosario Espinoza (MEX)		Nina Solheim (NOR)	Natalia Falavigna (BRA); Sarah Stevenson (GBR)
Tennis				
Men's singles	Rafael Nadal (ESP)	6–3, 7–6, 6–3	Fernando González (CHI)	Novak Djokovic (SRB)
Men's doubles	Switzerland	6–3, 6–4, 6–7, 6–3	Sweden	United States
Women's singles	Yelena Dementyeva (RUS)	3–6, 7–5, 6–3	Dinara Safina (RUS)	Vera Zvonareva (RUS)
Women's doubles	United States	6–2, 6–0	Spain	China
Track and Field (Athletics)				
Men				
100 m	Usain Bolt (JAM)	9.69 sec[2]	Richard Thompson (TRI)	Walter Dix (USA)
200 m	Usain Bolt (JAM)	19.30 sec[2]	Shawn Crawford (USA)	Walter Dix (USA)
400 m	LaShawn Merritt (USA)	43.75 sec	Jeremy Wariner (USA)	David Neville (USA)
4 x 100-m relay	Jamaica	37.10 sec[2]	Trinidad and Tobago	Japan
4 x 400-m relay	United States	2 min 55.39 sec[3]	The Bahamas	Russia
800 m	Wilfred Bungei (KEN)	1 min 44.65 sec	Ismail Ahmed Ismail (SUD)	Alfred Kirwa Yego (KEN)
1,500 m	Rashid Ramzi (BRN)	3 min 32.94 sec	Asbel Kipruto Kiprop (KEN)	Nicholas Willis (NZL)
5,000 m	Kenenisa Bekele (ETH)	12 min 57.82 sec[3]	Eliud Kipchoge (KEN)	Edwin Cheruiyot Soi (KEN)
10,000 m	Kenenisa Bekele (ETH)	27 min 01.17 sec[3]	Sileshi Sihine (ETH)	Micah Kogo (KEN)
Marathon	Samuel Kamau Wansiru (KEN)	2 hr 06 min 32 sec[3]	Jaouad Gharib (MAR	Tsegay Kedebe (ETH)
110-m hurdles	Dayron Robles (CUB)	12.93 sec	David Payne (USA)	David Oliver (USA)
400-m hurdles	Angelo Taylor (USA)	47.25 sec	Kerron Clement (USA)	Bershawn Jackson (USA)
3,000-m steeplechase	Brimin Kiprop Kipruto (KEN)	8 min 10.34 sec	Mahiedine Mekhissi-Benabbad (FRA)	Richard Kipkemboi Mateelong (KEN)
20-km walk	Valeriy Borchin (RUS)	1 hour 19 min 01 sec	Jefferson Pérez (ECU)	Jared Tallent (AUS)
50-km walk	Alex Schwazer (ITA)	3 hr 37 min 09 sec[3]	Jared Tallent (AUS)	Denis Nizhegorodov (RUS)
High jump	Andrey Silnov (RUS)	2.36 m	Germaine Mason (GBR)	Yaroslav Rybakov (RUS)
Long jump	Irving Jahir Saladino Aranda (PAN)	8.34 m	Khotso Mokoena (RSA)	Ibrahim Camejo (CUB)
Triple jump	Nelson Évora (POR)	17.67 m	Phillips Idowu (GBR)	Leevan Sands (BAH)
Pole vault	Steve Hooker (AUS)	5.96 m[3]	Yevgeny Lukyanenko (RUS)	Denys Yurchenko (UKR)
Shot put	Tomasz Majewski (POL)	21.51 m	Christian Cantwell (USA)	Andrei Mikhnevich (BLR)
Discus throw	Gerd Kanter (EST)	68.82 m	Piotr Malachowski (POL)	Virgilijus Alekna (LTU)
Javelin throw	Andreas Thorkildsen (NOR)	90.57 m[3]	Ainars Kovals (LAT)	Tero Pitkämäki (FIN)
Hammer throw	Primoz Kozmus (SLO)	82.02 m	Vadim Devyatovskiy (BLR)	Ivan Tsikhan (BLR)
Decathlon	Bryan Clay (USA)	8,791 pt	Andrei Krauchanka (BLR)	Leonel Suárez (CUB)

Olympic Medal Winners—XXIX Summer Games (2008) (continued)

EVENT	GOLD MEDALIST	PERFORMANCE	SILVER MEDALIST	BRONZE MEDALIST
Track and Field (Athletics) (continued)				
Women				
100 m	Shelly-Ann Fraser (JAM)	10.78 sec	Sherone Simpson (JAM); Kerron Stewart (JAM)[4]	
200 m	Veronica Campbell-Brown (JAM)	21.74 sec	Allyson Felix (USA)	Kerron Stewart (JAM)
400 m	Christine Ohuruogu (GBR)	49.62 sec	Shericka Williams (JAM)	Sanya Richards (USA)
4 x 100-m relay	Russia	42.31 sec	Belgium	Nigeria
4 x 400-m relay	United States	3 min 18.54 sec	Russia	Jamaica
800 m	Pamela Jelimo (KEN)	1 min 54.87 sec	Janeth Jepkosgei Busienei (KEN)	Hasna Benhassi (MAR)
1,500 m	Nancy Jebet Langat (KEN)	4 min 00.23 sec	Iryna Lishchynska (UKR)	Nataliya Tobias (UKR)
5,000 m	Tirunesh Dibaba (ETH)	15 min 41.40 sec	Elvan Abeylegesse (TUR)	Meseret Defar (ETH)
10,000 m	Tirunesh Dibaba (ETH)	29 min 54.66 sec[3]	Elvan Abeylegesse (TUR)	Shalane Flanagan (USA)
Marathon	Constantina Tomescu (ROM)	2 hr 26 min 44 sec	Catherine Ndereba (KEN)	Zhou Chunxiu (CHN)
100-m hurdles	Dawn Harper (USA)	12.54 sec	Sally McLellan (AUS)	Priscilla Lopes-Schliep (CAN))
400-m hurdles	Melaine Walker (JAM)	52.64 sec[3]	Sheena Tosta (USA)	Tasha Danvers (GBR)
3,000-m steeplechase	Gulnara Samitova-Galkina (RUS)	8 min 58.81 sec[2]	Eunice Jepkorir (ETH)	Yekaterina Volkova (RUS)
20-km walk	Olga Kaniskina (RUS)	1 hr 26 min 31 sec[3]	Kjersti Tysse Plätzer (NOR)	Elisa Rigaudo (ITA)
High jump	Tia Hellebaut (BEL)	2.05 m	Blanka Vlasic (CRO)	Anna Chicherova (RUS)
Long jump	Maurren Higa Maggi (BRA)	7.04 m	Tatyana Lebedeva (RUS)	Blessing Okagbare (NGR)
Triple jump	Françoise Mbango Etone (CMR)	15.39 m[3]	Tatyana Lebedeva (RUS)	Hrysopiyi Devetzi (GRE)
Pole vault	Yelena Isinbayeva (RUS)	5.05 m[2]	Jennifer Stuczynski (USA)	Svetlana Feofanova (RUS)
Shot put	Valerie Vili (NZL)	20.56 m	Natallia Mikhnevich (BLR)	Nadzeya Ostapchuk (BLR)
Discus throw	Stephanie Brown Trafton (USA)	64.74 m	Yarelys Barrios (CUB)	Olena Antonova (UKR)
Javelin throw	Barbora Spotakova (CZE)	71.42 m	Mariya Abakumova (RUS)	Christina Obergfoll (GER)
Hammer throw	Aksana Miankova (BLR)	76.34 m[3]	Yipsi Moreno (CUB)	Zhang Wenxiu (CHN)
Heptathlon	Nataliya Dobrynska (UKR)	6,733 pt	Hyleas Fountain (USA)	Tatyana Chernova (RUS)
Triathlon				
Men	Jan Frodeno (GER)	1 hr 48 min 53.28 sec	Simon Whitfield (CAN)	Bevan Docherty (NZL)
Women	Emma Snowsill (AUS)	1 hr 58 min 27.66 sec	Vanessa Fernandes (POR)	Emma Moffatt (AUS)
Volleyball				
Men's indoor	United States	20–25, 25–22, 25–21, 25–23, 25–23	Brazil	Russia
Women's indoor	Brazil	25–15, 18–25, 25–13, 25–21	United States	China
Men's beach	United States	23–21, 17–21, 15–4	Brazil	Brazil
Women's beach	United States	21–18, 21–18	China	China
Water Polo				
Men	Hungary	14–10	United States	Serbia
Women	The Netherlands	9–8	United States	Australia
Weightlifting				
Men				
56 kg (123.2 lb)	Long Qingquan (CHN)	292.0	Hoang Anh Tuan (VIE)	Eko Yuli Irawan (INA)
62 kg (136.4 lb)	Zhang Xiangxiang (CHN)	319.0 kg	Diego Salazar (COL)	Triyatno (INA)
69 kg (151.8 lb)	Liao Hui (CHN)	348.0 kg	Vencelas Dabaya-Tientcheu (FRA)	Tigran Gevorg Martirosyan (ARM)
77 kg (169.4 lb)	Sa Jae Hyouk (KOR)	366.0 kg	Li Hongli (CHN)	Gevorg Davtyan (ARM)

Olympic Medal Winners—XXIX Summer Games (2008) (continued)

EVENT	GOLD MEDALIST	PERFORMANCE	SILVER MEDALIST	BRONZE MEDALIST
Weightlifting (continued)				
Men (continued)				
85 kg (187 lb)	Lu Yong (CHN)	394.0 kg	Andrei Rybakou (BLR)	Tigran Varban Martirosyan (ARM)
94 kg (206.8 lb)	Ilya Ilin (KAZ)	406.0 kg	Szymon Kolecki (POL)	Khadzhimurat Akkayev (RUS)
105 kg (231 lb)	Andrei Aramnau (BLR)	436.0 kg[2]	Dmitry Klokov (RUS)	Dmitry Lapikov (RUS)
105+ kg (231+ lb)	Matthias Steiner (GER)	461.0 kg	Yevgeny Chigishev (RUS)	Viktors Scerbatihs (LAT)
Women				
48 kg (105.6 lb)	Chen Xiexia (CHN)	212.0 kg[3]	Sibel Ozkan (TUR)	Chen Wei-ling (TPE)
53 kg (116.6 lb)	Prapawadee Jaroenrattanatarakoon (THA)	221.0 kg	Yoon Jinhee (KOR)	Nastassia Novikava (BLR)
58 kg (127.6 lb)	Chen Yanqing (CHN)	244.0 kg[3]	Marina Shainova (RUS)	O Jong Ae (PRK)
63 kg (138.6 lb)	Pak Hyon Suk (PRK)	241.0 kg	Irina Nekrassova (KAZ)	Lu Ying-chi (TPE)
69 kg (151.8 lb)	Liu Chunhong (CHN)	286.0 kg[2]	Oksana Slivenko (RUS)	Natalya Davydova (UKR)
75 kg (165 lb)	Cao Lei (CHN)	282.0 kg[3]	Alla Vazhenina (KAZ)	Nadezda Yevstyukhina (RUS)
75+ kg (165 lb)	Jang Mi Ran (KOR)	326.0 kg[2]	Olha Korobka (UKR)	Mariya Grabovetskaya (KAZ)
Wrestling[1]				
Freestyle				
Men				
55 kg (121 lb)	Henry Cejudo (USA)		Tomohiro Matsunaga (JPN)	Besik Kudukhov (RUS); Radoslav Velikov (BUL)
60 kg (132 lb)	Mavlet Batirov (RUS)		Vasyl Fedoryshyn (UKR)	Seyedmorad Mohammadi (IRI); Kenichi Yumoto (JPN)
66 kg (145.2 lb)	Ramazan Sahin (TUR)		Andriy Stadnik (UKR)	Sushil Kumar (IND); Otar Tushishvili (GEO)
74 kg (162.8 lb)	Buvayasa Saytiyev (RUS)		Soslan Tigiev (UZB)	Murad Gaidarov (BLR); Kiril Terziev (BUL)
84 kg (184.8 lb)	Revazi Mindorashvili (GEO)		Yusup Abdusalomov (TJK)	Taras Danko (UKR); Georgy Ketoyev (RUS)
96 kg (211.2 lb)	Shirvani Muradov (RUS)		Taimuraz Tigiyev (KAZ)	Khetag Gazyumov (AZE); George Gogshelidze (GEO)
120+ kg (264 lb)	Artur Taymazov (UZB)		Bakhtiyar Akhmedov (RUS)	David Musulbes (SVK); Marid Mutalimov (KAZ)
Women				
48 kg (105.6 lb)	Carol Huynh (CAN)		Chiharu Icho (JPN)	Irini Merleni (UKR); Mariya Stadnik (AZE)
55 kg (121 lb)	Saori Yoshida (JPN)		Xu Li (CHN)	Jackeline Rentería (COL); Tonya Verbeek (CAN)
63 kg (138.6 lb)	Kaori Icho (JPN)		Alena Kartashova (RUS)	Randi Miller (USA); Yelena Shalygina (KAZ)
72 kg (158.4 lb)	Wang Jiao (CHN)		Stanka Zlateva (BUL)	Kyoko Hamaguchi (JPN); Agnieszka Wieszczek (POL)
Greco-Roman				
55 kg (121 lb)	Nazyr Mankiyev (RUS)		Rovshan Bayramov (AZE)	Roman Amoyan (ARM); Park Eun Chul (KOR)
60 kg (132 lb)	Islam-Beka Albiyev (RUS)		Vitaliy Rahimov (AZE)	Nurbakyt Tengizbayev (KAZ); Ruslan Tiumenbaev (KGZ)
66 kg (145.2 lb)	Steeve Guénot (FRA)		Kanatbek Begaliev (KGZ)	Mikhail Siamonau (BLR); Armen Vardanyan (UKR)

Olympic Medal Winners—XXIX Summer Games (2008) (continued)

EVENT	GOLD MEDALIST	PERFORMANCE	SILVER MEDALIST	BRONZE MEDALIST
Wrestling (continued)				
Greco-Roman (continued)				
74 kg (162.8 lb)	Manuchar Kvirkelia (GEO)		Chang Yongxiang (CHN)	Christophe Guénot (FRA); Yavor Yanakiev (BUL)
96 kg (211.2 lb)	Aslanbek Khushtov (RUS)		Mirko Englich (GER)	Asset Mambetov (KAZ); Adam Wheeler (USA)
120+ kg (264 lb)	Mijain López (CUB)		Khasan Baroyev (RUS)	Mindaugas Mizgaitis (LTU); Yuri Patrikeev (ARM)

[1]*Two bronze medals awarded in each weight division.* [2]*World record.* [3]*Olympic record.* [4]*Tie.*

Olympic Medal Winners—XX Winter Games (2006)

The XX Winter Games were held in Turin, Italy, 10–26 Feb 2006. Since the games, several athletes have been stripped of medals for having failed drug tests. New medalists are shown in this table.

EVENT	GOLD MEDALIST	PERFORMANCE	SILVER MEDALIST	BRONZE MEDALIST
Alpine Skiing				
Men				
Downhill	Antoine Dénériaz (FRA)	1 min 48.80 sec	Michael Walchhofer (AUT)	Bruno Kernen (SUI)
Slalom	Benjamin Raich (AUT)	1 min 43.14 sec	Reinfried Herbst (AUT)	Rainier Schönfelder (AUT)
Giant slalom	Benjamin Raich (AUT)	2 min 35.00 sec	Joël Chenal (FRA)	Hermann Maier (AUT)
Super G	Kjetil André Aamodt (NOR)	1 min 30.65 sec	Hermann Maier (AUT)	Ambrosi Hoffmann (SUI)
Combined event	Ted Ligety (USA)	3 min 09.35 sec	Ivica Kostelic (CRO)	Rainier Schönfelder (AUT)
Women				
Downhill	Michaela Dorfmeister (AUT)	1 min 56.49 sec	Martina Schild (SUI)	Anja Pärson (SWE)
Slalom	Anja Pärson (SWE)	1 min 29.04 sec	Nicole Hosp (AUT)	Marlies Schild (AUT)
Giant slalom	Julia Mancuso (USA)	2 min 09.19 sec	Tanja Poutiainen (FIN)	Anna Ottosson (SWE)
Super G	Michaela Dorfmeister (AUT)	1 min 32.47 sec	Janica Kostelic (CRO)	Alexandra Meissnitzer (AUT)
Combined event	Janica Kostelic (CRO)	2 min 51.08 sec	Marlies Schild (AUT)	Anja Pärson (SWE)
Nordic Skiing				
Men				
1.5-km sprint	Björn Lind (SWE)	2 min 26.5 sec	Roddy Darragon (FRA)	Thobias Fredriksson (SWE)
Team sprint	Thobias Fredriksson, Björn Lind (SWE)	17 min 02.9 sec	Jens Arne Svartedal, Tor Arne Hetland (NOR)	Ivan Alypov, Vasily Rochev (RUS)
15-km classical	Andrus Veerpalu (EST)	38 min 01.3 sec	Lukas Bauer (CZE)	Tobias Angerer (GER)
30-km pursuit	Yevgeny Dementyev (RUS)	1 hr 17 min 0.8 sec	Frode Estil (NOR)	Pietro Piller Cottrer (ITA)
50-km freestyle, mass start	Giorgio Di Centa (ITA)	2 hr 6 min 11.8 sec	Yevgeny Dementyev (RUS)	Mikhail Botwinov (AUT)
4 x 10-km relay	Italy	1 hr 43 min 45.7 sec	Germany	Sweden
95-m ski jump	Lars Bystøl (NOR)	266.5 pt	Matti Hautamäki (FIN)	Roar Ljøkelsøy (NOR)
125-m ski jump	Thomas Morgenstern (AUT)	276.9 pt	Andreas Kofler (AUT)	Lars Bystøl (NOR)
125-m team ski jump	Austria	984.0 pt	Finland	Norway
Nordic combined sprint (7.5-km)	Felix Gottwald (AUT)	17 min 35.0 sec	Magnus Moan (NOR)	Georg Hettich (GER)
Nordic combined 15-km	Georg Hettich (GER)	39 min 44.6 sec	Felix Gottwald (AUT)	Magnus Moan (NOR)
Nordic combined team relay	Austria	49 min 42.6 sec	Germany	Finland
Women				
1.5-km sprint	Chandra Crawford (CAN)	2 min 12.3 sec	Claudia Künzel (GER)	Alena Sidko (RUS)
Team sprint	Anna Dahlberg, Lina Andersson (SWE)	16 min 36.9 sec	Sara Renner, Beckie Scott (CAN)	Aino Kaisa Saarinen, Virpi Kuitunen (FIN)

Olympic Medal Winners—XX Winter Games (2006) (continued)

EVENT	GOLD MEDALIST	PERFORMANCE	SILVER MEDALIST	BRONZE MEDALIST
Nordic Skiing (continued)				
Women (continued)				
10-km classical	Kristina Smigun (EST)	27 min 51.4 sec	Marit Bjørgen (NOR)	Hilde G. Pedersen (NOR)
15-km pursuit	Kristina Smigun (EST)	42 min 48.7 sec	Katerina Neumannova (CZE)	Yevgeniya Medvedeva-Abruzova (RUS)
30-freestyle, mass start	Katerina Neumannova (CZE)	1 hr 22 min 25.4 sec	Yuliya Chepalova (RUS)	Justyna Kowalczyk (POL)
4 x 5-km relay	Russia	54 min 47.7 sec	Germany	Italy
Biathlon				
Men				
10-km sprint	Sven Fischer (GER)	26 min 11.6 sec	Halvard Hanevold (NOR)	Frode Andresen (NOR)
12.5-km pursuit	Vincent Defrasne (FRA)	35 min 20.2 sec	Ole Einar Bjørndalen (NOR)	Sven Fischer (GER)
20 km	Michael Greis (GER)	54 min 23.0 sec	Ole Einar Bjørndalen (NOR)	Halvard Hanevold (NOR)
4 x 6-km relay	Germany	1 hr 21 min 51.5 sec	Russia	France
15-km mass start	Michael Greis (GER)	47 min 20.0 sec	Tomasz Sikora (POL)	Ole Einar Bjørndalen (NOR)
Women				
7.5-km sprint	Florence Baverel-Robert (FRA)	22 min 31.4 sec	Anna Carin Olofsson (SWE)	Liliya Yefremova (UKR)
10-km pursuit	Kali Wilhelm (GER)	36 min 43.6 sec	Martina Glagow (GER)	Albina Akhatova (RUS)
15 km	Svetlana Ishmuratova (RUS)	49 min 24.1 sec	Martina Glagow (GER)	Albina Akhatova (RUS)
4 x 6-km relay	Russia	1 hr 16 min 12.5 sec	Germany	France
12.5-km mass start	Anna Carin Olofsson (SWE)	40 min 36.5 sec	Kati Wilhelm (GER)	Uschi Disl (GER)
Freestyle Skiing				
Men				
Moguls	Dale Begg-Smith (AUS)	26.77 pt	Mikko Rönkainen (FIN)	Toby Dawson (USA)
Aerials	Han Xiaopeng (CHN)	250.77 pt	Dmitry Dashinsky (BLR)	Vladimir Lebedev (RUS)
Women				
Moguls	Jennifer Heil (CAN)	26.50 pt	Kari Traa (NOR)	Sandra Laoura (FRA)
Aerials	Evelyne Leu (SUI)	202.55 pt	Li Nina (CHN)	Alisa Camplin (AUS)
Snowboarding				
Men				
Parallel giant slalom	Philipp Schoch (SUI)		Simon Schoch (SUI)	Siegfried Grabner (AUT)
Halfpipe	Shaun White (USA)	46.8 pt	Danny Kass (USA)	Markku Koski (FIN)
Snowboardcross (SBX)	Seth Wescott (USA)		Radoslav Zidek (SVK)	Paul-Henri Delerue (FRA)
Women				
Parallel giant slalom	Daniela Meuli (SUI)		Amelie Kober (GER)	Doris Günther (AUT)
Halfpipe	Hannah Teter (USA)	46.4 pt	Gretchen Bleiler (USA)	Kjersti Buaas (NOR)
Snowboardcross (SBX)	Tanja Frieden (SUI)		Lindsey Jacobellis (USA)	Dominique Maltais (CAN)
Figure Skating				
Men	Yevgeny Plushchenko (RUS)	167.67 pt	Jeffrey Buttle (CAN)	Evan Lysacek (USA)
Women	Shizuka Arakawa (JPN)	191.34 pt	Sasha Cohen (USA)	Irina Slutskaya (RUS)

Olympic Medal Winners—XX Winter Games (2006) (continued)

EVENT	GOLD MEDALIST	PERFORMANCE	SILVER MEDALIST	BRONZE MEDALIST
Figure Skating (continued)				
Pairs	Tatyana Totmyanina, Maksim Marinin (RUS)	135.84 pt	Zhang Dan, Zang Hao (CHN)	Shen Xue, Zhao Hongbo (CHN)
Ice dancing	Tatyana Navka, Roman Kostomarov (RUS)	200.64 pt	Tanith Belbin, Benjamin Agosto (USA)	Yelena Grushina, Ruslan Goncharov (RUS)
Speed Skating				
Men				
500 m	Joey Cheek (USA)	69.76 sec[1]	Dmitry Dorofeyev (RUS)	Lee Kang Seok (KOR)
1,000 m	Shani Davis (USA)	1 min 08.89 sec	Joey Cheek (USA)	Erben Wennemars (NED)
1,500 m	Enrico Fabris (ITA)	1 min 45.97 sec	Shani Davis (USA)	Chad Hedrick (USA)
5,000 m	Chad Hedrick (USA)	6 min 14.68 sec	Sven Kramer (NED)	Enrico Fabris (ITA)
10,000 m	Bob de Jong (NED)	13 min 01.57 sec	Chad Hedrick (USA)	Carl Verheijen (NED)
Team pursuit	Italy	3 min 44.46 sec	Canada	The Netherlands
Women				
500 m	Svetlana Zhurova (RUS)	76.57 sec[1]	Wang Manli (CHN)	Ren Hui (CHN)
1,000 m	Marianne Timmer (NED)	1 min 16.05 sec	Cindy Klassen (CAN)	Anni Friesinger (GER)
1,500 m	Cindy Klassen (CAN)	1 min 55.27 sec	Kristina Groves (CAN)	Ireen Wüst (NED)
3,000 m	Ireen Wüst (NED)	4 min 02.43 sec	Renate Groenewold (NED)	Cindy Klassen (CAN)
5,000 m	Clara Hughes (CAN)	6 min 59.07 sec	Claudia Pechstein (GER)	Cindy Klassen (CAN)
Team pursuit	Germany	3 min 01.25 sec	Canada	Russia
Short-Track Speed Skating				
Men				
500 m	Apolo Anton Ohno (USA)	41.935 sec	François-Louis Tremblay (FRA)	Ahn Hyun Soo (Kor)
1,000 m	Ahn Hyun Soo (KOR)	1 min 26.739 sec[2]	Lee Ho Suk (KOR)	Apolo Anton Ohno (USA)
1,500 m	Ahn Hyun Soo (KOR)	2 min 25.351 sec	Lee Ho Suk (KOR)	Li Jiajun (CHN)
5,000-m relay	South Korea	6 min 43.376 sec[2]	Canada	United States
Women				
500 m	Wang Meng (CHN)	44.345 sec	Evgeniya Radanova (BUL)	Anouk Leblanc-Boucher (CAN)
1,000 m	Jin Sun Yu (KOR)	1 min 32.859 sec	Wang Meng (CHN)	Yang Yang (A) (CHN)
1,500 m	Jin Sun Yu (KOR)	2 min 23.494 sec	Choi Eun Kyung (KOR)	Wang Meng (CHN)
3,000-m relay	South Korea	4 min 17.040 sec	Canada	Italy
Ice Hockey				
Men (winning team)	Sweden	6–2–0	Finland	Czech Republic
Women (winning team)	Canada	5–0–0	Sweden	United States
Curling				
Men (winning team)	Canada	8–3–0	Finland	United States
Women (winning team)	Sweden	9–2–0	Switzerland	Canada
Bobsled				
Two man	André Lange, Kevin Kuske (GER 1)	3 min 43.38 sec	Pierre Lueders, Lascelles Brown (CAN 1)	Martin Annen, Beat Hefti (SUI 1)
Four man	André Lange, Rene Hoppe, Kevin Kuske, Martin Putze (GER 1)	3 min 40.42 sec	Aleksandr Zoubkov, Filipp Yegorov, Aleksey Seliverstov, Aleksey Voyevoda (RUS 1)	Martin Annen, Thomas Lamparter, Beat Hefti, Cedric Grand (SUI 1)

Olympic Medal Winners—XX Winter Games (2006) (continued)

EVENT	GOLD MEDALIST	PERFORMANCE	SILVER MEDALIST	BRONZE MEDALIST
Bobsled (continued)				
Women	Sandra Kiriasis, Anja Schneiderheinze (GER 1)	3 min 49.98 sec	Shauna Rohbock, Valerie Fleming (USA 1)	Gerda Weissensteiner, Jennifer Isacco (ITA 1)
Luge				
Men (singles)	Armin Zöggeler (ITA)	3 min 26.088 sec	Albert Demchenko (RUS)	Martins Rubenis (LAT)
Men (doubles)	Andreas Linger, Wolfgang Linger (AUT)	1 min 34.497 sec	Andre Florschütz, Torsten Wustlich (GER)	Gerhard Plankensteiner, Oswald Haselrieder
Women (singles)	Sylke Otto (GER)	3 min 07.979 sec	Sylke Kraushaar (GER)	Tatjana Hüfner (GER)
Skeleton				
Men	Duff Gibson (CAN)	1 min 55.88 sec	Jeff Pain (CAN)	Gregor Stähli (SUI)
Women	Maya Pedersen (SUI)	1 min 59.83 sec	Shelley Rudman (GBR)	Mellisa Holllingsworth-Richards (CAN)

[1]*Time is combined total of two heats.* [2]*Olympic record.*

Special Olympics

The Special Olympics is an international program to provide individuals who have intellectual disabilities and are eight years of age or older with year-round sports training and athletic competition in a variety of Olympic-type summer and winter sports. Inaugurated in 1968, the Special Olympics was officially recognized by the International Olympic Committee on 15 Feb 1988. **International headquarters** are in Washington DC.

In June 1963, with support from the Joseph P. Kennedy, Jr., Foundation, **Eunice Kennedy Shriver** (sister of Pres. John F. Kennedy) started a summer day camp at her home in Rockville MD for children with mental retardation. Between 1963 and 1968, the Kennedy Foundation promoted the creation of dozens of similar camps in the United States and Canada. Special awards were developed for physical achievements, and by 1968 Shriver had persuaded the Chicago Park District to join with the Kennedy Foundation in sponsoring a "Special Olympics," held at Soldier Field on 20 July. About 1,000 athletes from 26 US states and Canada participated. The games were such a success that, in December, Special Olympics, Inc. (now **Special Olympics International**), was founded, with chapters in the United States, Canada, and France. The first International Winter Special Olympics Games were held on 5–11 Feb 1977 (in Steamboat Springs CO). The number of participating countries proliferated so that by 2008 there were chapters in some 180 countries. Over 30,000 meets and tournaments are held worldwide each year, culminating in the International Special Olympics Games every two years, alternating between winter and summer sports and each lasting for eight or nine days.

Special Olympics Web site: <www.specialolympics.org>.

Automobile Racing

Of the various types of automobile races, the closed-circuit, or speedway, course was developed largely in the United States. The Indianapolis 500—now the premier Indy car event—was first run in 1911. A low-slung, fenderless (open-wheel) car—called an Indy car—is essential for this race; its suspension (i.e., its ability to hold the track) is as important to a car's performance as its turbocharged engine. Often the chassis manufacturer is different from the engine manufacturer, resulting in cars identified, for example, as a Brabham/Repco. In such cases the chassis maker is listed first, and the chassis maker receives any money or awards that the car may win.

Indy car racing began in 1909, when the American Automobile Association (AAA) began sponsoring a 24-race championship series, including three races at the newly opened Indianapolis Motor Speedway (IMS). In 1956 the AAA gave up its involvement with auto racing, and the United States Auto Club (**USAC**) was organized as the sport's governing body. In 1978 two race-car owners broke away from USAC to form a new organization, Championship Auto Racing Teams, Inc. (**CART**), which sponsored its own series of races. In 1980 CART and USAC joined to form the Championship Racing League, which dissolved after five races. In 1994 the IMS announced a new Indy Racing League (**IRL**) to oversee the Indianapolis 500 beginning in 1996 and a new series of IRL races (leading to an annual drivers' championship) separate from those sponsored by CART.

The standard cars used for Grand Prix road (i.e., closed-highway) racing are known as Formula One (or F-1) cars because they are built according to an evolving formula that was established after World War I by the Fédération Internationale de l'Automobile

Automobile Racing (continued)

(**FIA**). Like the Indy car, the Formula One racer is open-wheeled and low-slung, but the F-1 is slightly smaller and more maneuverable.

There are approximately 18 Grand Prix events held worldwide throughout the year. Drivers compete for the **World Championship of Drivers** (inaugurated in 1950), receiving a total number of points based on their placement in each of the official Grand Prix events.

Many Grand Prix drivers participate in various endurance races, the most famous of which is the **Le Mans Grand Prix d'Endurance**, held on the 13.4-km (8.3-mi) Sarthe circuit, Le Mans, France.

Another type of popular racing event is the rally, which was established in 1907. More than 35 such competitions, raced over a specified route on public roads, take place yearly throughout the world. The classic occasion for rally racing is the **Rallye Automobile Monte-Carlo**, now started in various European cities with Monaco as its terminal point.

Stock-car racing, which began in the United States in the first half of the 20th century, involves the racing of commercial cars that have been altered to increase their speed and maneuverability. The National Association for Stock Car Auto Racing (**NASCAR**) was founded in 1947, and until 2004 it awarded the Winston Cup to the driver who had earned the greatest number of points in a series of official NASCAR Winston Cup events over the stock-car racing season. In 2004 the competition was renamed the Nextel Cup, and from 2008 it is known as the Sprint Cup. The **Daytona 500** is the premiere stock-car event.

Related Web sites: Champ Car: <www.champcar-worldseries.com>; USAC: <www.usacracing.com>; IRL: <www.indycar.com>; FIA: <www.fia.com>; Automobile Club de Monaco <www.acm.mc>; NASCAR: <www.nascar.com>.

Formula One Grand Prix Race Results, 2007–08

The season for the Formula One Grand Prix circuit is March–October. If a race occurs twice in the year covered because of scheduling changes, only the most recent race result is given in the table below.

RACE	DATE	LOCALE	DRIVER (COUNTRY)	WINNER'S TIME (HR:MIN:SEC)
European Grand Prix	22 Jul 2007	Nürburgring, Germany	Fernando Alonso (ESP)	2:06:26.358
Italian Grand Prix	9 Sep 2007	Monza	Fernando Alonso (ESP)	1:18:37.806
Belgian Grand Prix	16 Sep 2007	Spa-Francorchamps	Kimi Räikkönen (FIN)	1:20:39.066
Japanese Grand Prix	30 Sep 2007	Oyama	Lewis Hamilton (GBR)	2:00:34.579
Chinese Grand Prix	7 Oct 2007	Shanghai	Kimi Räikkönen (FIN)	1:37:58.395
Brazilian Grand Prix	21 Oct 2007	São Paulo	Kimi Räikkönen (FIN)	1:28:15.270
Australian Grand Prix	16 Mar 2008	Melbourne	Lewis Hamilton (GBR)	1:34:50.616
Malaysian Grand Prix	23 Mar 2008	Kuala Lumpur	Kimi Räikkönen (FIN)	1:31:18.555
Bahrain Grand Prix	6 Apr 2008	Bahrain	Felipe Massa (BRA)	1:31:06.970
Spanish Grand Prix	27 Apr 2008	Catalonia	Kimi Räikkönen (FIN)	1:38:19.051
Turkish Grand Prix	11 May 2008	Istanbul	Felipe Massa (BRA)	1:26:49.451
Monaco Grand Prix	25 May 2008	Monte-Carlo	Lewis Hamilton (GBR)	2:00:42.742
Canadian Grand Prix	8 Jun 2008	Montreal	Robert Kubica (POL)	1:36:24:447
French Grand Prix	22 Jun 2008	Magny-Cours	Felipe Massa (BRA)	1:31:50.245
British Grand Prix	6 Jul 2008	Silverstone	Lewis Hamilton (GBR)	1:39:09.440
German Grand Prix	20 Jul 2008	Hockenheim	Lewis Hamilton (GBR)	1:31:20.874
Hungarian Grand Prix	3 Aug 2008	Budapest	Heikki Kovalainen (FIN)	1:37:27.067

Indianapolis 500

There was no competition in 1917–18 and 1942–45. Won by an American racer except as indicated.

YEAR	WINNER	AVG. SPEED (MPH)
1911	Ray Harroun	74.602
1912	Joe Dawson	78.719
1913	Jules Goux (FRA)	75.933
1914	René Thomas (FRA)	82.474
1915	Ralph DePalma	89.840
1916[1]	Dario Resta (FRA)	84.001
1919	Howdy Wilcox	88.050
1920	Gaston Chevrolet	88.618
1921	Tommy Milton	89.621
1922	Jimmy Murphy	94.484
1923	Tommy Milton	90.954
1924[2]	L.L. Corum, Joe Boyer	98.234
1925	Peter DePaolo	101.127
1926[3]	Frank Lockhart	95.904
1927	George Souders	97.545
1928	Louie Meyer	99.482
1929	Ray Keech	97.585
1930	Billy Arnold	100.448
1931	Louis Schneider	96.629
1932	Fred Frame	104.144
1933	Louie Meyer	104.162
1934	Bill Cummings	104.863
1935	Kelly Petillo	106.240
1936	Louie Meyer	109.069
1937	Wilbur Shaw	113.580
1938	Floyd Roberts	117.200
1939	Wilbur Shaw	115.035
1940	Wilbur Shaw	114.277
1941[2]	Floyd Davis, Mauri Rose	115.117
1946	George Robson	114.820
1947	Mauri Rose	116.338
1948	Mauri Rose	119.814
1949	Bill Holland	121.327
1950[3]	Johnnie Parsons	124.002
1951	Lee Wallard	126.244
1952	Troy Ruttman	128.922
1953	Bill Vukovich	128.740
1954	Bill Vukovich	130.840
1955	Robert Sweikert	128.209
1956	Pat Flaherty	128.490
1957	Sam Hanks	135.601
1958	Jimmy Bryan	133.791
1959	Rodger Ward	135.857
1960	Jim Rathmann	138.767
1961	A.J. Foyt, Jr.	139.131
1962	Rodger Ward	140.293
1963	Parnelli Jones	143.137
1964	A.J. Foyt, Jr.	147.350
1965	Jim Clark (GBR)	150.686
1966	Graham Hill (GBR)	144.317

Indianapolis 500 (continued)

YEAR	WINNER	AVG. SPEED (MPH)	YEAR	WINNER	AVG. SPEED (MPH)	YEAR	WINNER	AVG. SPEED (MPH)
1967	A.J. Foyt, Jr.	151.207	1982	Gordon Johncock	162.029	1997	Arie Luyendyk (NED)	145.827
1968	Bobby Unser	152.882	1983	Tom Sneva	162.117	1998	Eddie Cheever, Jr.	145.155
1969	Mario Andretti	156.867	1984	Rick Mears	163.612	1999	Kenny Brack (SWE)	153.176
1970	Al Unser	155.749	1985	Danny Sullivan	152.982	2000	Juan Montoya (COL)	167.607
1971	Al Unser	157.735	1986	Bobby Rahal	170.722	2001	Helio Castroneves (BRA)	153.601
1972	Mark Donohue	162.962	1987	Al Unser	162.175	2002	Helio Castroneves (BRA)	166.499
1973[3]	Gordon Johncock	159.036	1988	Rick Mears	144.809	2003	Gil de Ferran (BRA)	156.291
1974	Johnny Rutherford	158.589	1989	Emerson Fittipaldi (BRA)	167.581	2004[3]	Buddy Rice	138.518
1975[3]	Bobby Unser	149.213	1990	Arie Luyendyk (NED)	185.984	2005	Dan Wheldon (GBR)	157.603
1976[3]	Johnny Rutherford	148.725	1991	Rick Mears	176.457	2006	Sam Hornish, Jr.	157.085
1977	A.J. Foyt, Jr.	161.331	1992	Al Unser, Jr.	134.479	2007	Dario Franchitti (GBR)	151.774
1978	Al Unser	161.363	1993	Emerson Fittipaldi (BRA)	157.207	2008	Scott Dixon (NZL)	143.567
1979	Rick Mears	158.899	1994	Al Unser, Jr.	160.872			
1980	Johnny Rutherford	142.862	1995	Jacques Villeneuve (CAN)	153.616			
1981	Bobby Unser	139.084	1996	Buddy Lazier	147.956			

[1]*Scheduled 300-mile race.* [2]*First driver started the race but was replaced during the race by the second driver named.* [3]*Race stopped because of rain (in 1926 after 400 miles, in 1950 after 345 miles, in 1973 after 332.5 miles, in 1975 after 435 miles, in 1976 after 255 miles, and in 2004 after 450 miles).*

NASCAR Nextel Cup Champions

YEAR	WINNER	YEAR	WINNER	YEAR	WINNER	YEAR	WINNER
1949	Red Byron	1964	Richard Petty	1979	Richard Petty	1994	Dale Earnhardt
1950	Bill Rexford	1965	Ned Jarrett	1980	Dale Earnhardt	1995	Jeff Gordon
1951	Herb Thomas	1966	David Pearson	1981	Darrell Waltrip	1996	Terry Labonte
1952	Tim Flock	1967	Richard Petty	1982	Darrell Waltrip	1997	Jeff Gordon
1953	Herb Thomas	1968	David Pearson	1983	Bobby Allison	1998	Jeff Gordon
1954	Lee Petty	1969	David Pearson	1984	Terry Labonte	1999	Dale Jarrett
1955	Tim Flock	1970	Bobby Isaac	1985	Darrell Waltrip	2000	Bobby Labonte
1956	Buck Baker	1971	Richard Petty	1986	Dale Earnhardt	2001	Jeff Gordon
1957	Buck Baker	1972	Richard Petty	1987	Dale Earnhardt	2002	Tony Stewart
1958	Lee Petty	1973	Benny Parsons	1988	Bill Elliott	2003	Matt Kenseth
1959	Lee Petty	1974	Richard Petty	1989	Rusty Wallace	2004	Kurt Busch
1960	Rex White	1975	Richard Petty	1990	Dale Earnhardt	2005	Tony Stewart
1961	Ned Jarrett	1976	Cale Yarborough	1991	Dale Earnhardt	2006	Jimmie Johnson
1962	Joe Weatherly	1977	Cale Yarborough	1992	Alan Kulwicki	2007	Jimmie Johnson
1963	Joe Weatherly	1978	Cale Yarborough	1993	Dale Earnhardt		

Baseball

The sport of baseball—given its definitive form in the United States in the late 19th century—is popular throughout the world, though until 2006 it was organized internationally only for **Little League** players (children ages 5–18). Little League Baseball was founded in Pennsylvania in 1939. The first Little League World Series was in 1947, and the first Little League outside the US was organized in British Columbia in 1951. Baseball is especially popular in Japan and Latin America; it is also one of the national sports of the US.

On a **professional** level, the premier event of baseball in the US is the **World Series** of **Major League Baseball**, in which the first team to win four games wins the Series. In fact, the Series is not contested on an international level, but rather it is played between the leading team of the **National League** (NL; formed 1876) and the leading team of the **American League** (AL; formed 1900 and including, from 1977, one Canadian team). In 2006 the inaugural World Baseball Classic, a competition featuring national teams, was held in Japan, Puerto Rico, and the US. The team from Japan beat Cuba's team in the finals. The second competition is scheduled for early 2009.

Professional baseball began in Japan in 1936. Teams are organized into two leagues of six teams each. The seven-game **Japan Series**, first played in 1950, is contested between the leading team of the Central League (CL) and the leading team of the Pacific League (PL). The modern **Caribbean Series** began in 1970 with the winning team from each league in the Dominican Republic, Mexico, Puerto Rico, and Venezuela.

Related Web sites:
Major League: <http://mlb.mlb.com/index.jsp>;
Little League: <www.littleleague.org>.

Major League Baseball Final Standings, 2007

American League

East Division

CLUB	WON	LOST	GAMES BACK
Boston[1]	96	66	—
New York[1]	94	68	2
Toronto	83	79	13
Baltimore	69	93	27
Tampa Bay	66	96	30

Central Division

CLUB	WON	LOST	GAMES BACK
Cleveland[1]	96	66	—
Detroit	88	74	8
Minnesota	79	83	17
Chicago	72	90	24
Kansas City	69	93	27

West Division

CLUB	WON	LOST	GAMES BACK
Los Angeles[1]	94	68	—
Seattle	88	74	6
Oakland	76	86	18
Texas	75	87	19

National League

East Division

CLUB	WON	LOST	GAMES BACK
Philadelphia[1]	89	73	—
New York	88	74	1
Atlanta	84	78	5
Washington	73	89	16
Florida	71	91	18

Central Division

CLUB	WON	LOST	GAMES BACK
Chicago[1]	85	77	—
Milwaukee	83	79	2
St. Louis	78	84	7
Houston	73	89	12
Cincinnati	72	90	13
Pittsburgh	68	94	17

West Division

CLUB	WON	LOST	GAMES BACK
Arizona[1]	90	72	—
Colorado[1]	90	73	½
San Diego	89	74	1½
Los Angeles	82	80	8
San Francisco	71	91	19

[1]*Gained play-off berth.*

World Series

YEAR	WINNING TEAM	LOSING TEAM	RESULTS
1903	Boston Americans (AL)	Pittsburgh Pirates (NL)	5–3
1904	*not held*		
1905	New York Giants (NL)	Philadelphia Athletics (AL)	4–1
1906	Chicago White Sox (AL)	Chicago Cubs (NL)	4–2
1907	Chicago Cubs (NL)	Detroit Tigers (AL)	4–0[1]
1908	Chicago Cubs (NL)	Detroit Tigers (AL)	4–1
1909	Pittsburgh Pirates (NL)	Detroit Tigers (AL)	4–3
1910	Philadelphia Athletics (AL)	Chicago Cubs (NL)	4–1
1911	Philadelphia Athletics (AL)	New York Giants (NL)	4–2
1912	Boston Red Sox (AL)	New York Giants (NL)	4–3[1]
1913	Philadelphia Athletics (AL)	New York Giants (NL)	4–1
1914	Boston Braves (NL)	Philadelphia Athletics (AL)	4–0
1915	Boston Red Sox (AL)	Philadelphia Phillies (NL)	4–1
1916	Boston Red Sox (AL)	Brooklyn Robins (NL)	4–1
1917	Chicago White Sox (AL)	New York Giants (NL)	4–2
1918	Boston Red Sox (AL)	Chicago Cubs (NL)	4–2
1919	Cincinnati Reds (NL)	Chicago White Sox (AL)	5–3
1920	Cleveland Indians (AL)	Brooklyn Robins (NL)	5–2
1921	New York Giants (NL)	New York Yankees (AL)	5–3
1922	New York Giants (NL)	New York Yankees (AL)	4–0[1]
1923	New York Yankees (AL)	New York Giants (NL)	4–2
1924	Washington Senators (AL)	New York Giants (NL)	4–3
1925	Pittsburgh Pirates (NL)	Washington Senators (AL)	4–3
1926	St. Louis Cardinals (NL)	New York Yankees (AL)	4–3
1927	New York Yankees (AL)	Pittsburgh Pirates (NL)	4–0
1928	New York Yankees (AL)	St. Louis Cardinals (NL)	4–0
1929	Philadelphia Athletics (AL)	Chicago Cubs (NL)	4–1
1930	Philadelphia Athletics (AL)	St. Louis Cardinals (NL)	4–2
1931	St. Louis Cardinals (NL)	Philadelphia Athletics (AL)	4–3
1932	New York Yankees (AL)	Chicago Cubs (NL)	4–0
1933	New York Giants (NL)	Washington Senators (AL)	4–1
1934	St. Louis Cardinals (NL)	Detroit Tigers (AL)	4–3
1935	Detroit Tigers (AL)	Chicago Cubs (NL)	4–2
1936	New York Yankees (AL)	New York Giants (NL)	4–2
1937	New York Yankees (AL)	New York Giants (NL)	4–1
1938	New York Yankees (AL)	Chicago Cubs (NL)	4–0
1939	New York Yankees (AL)	Cincinnati Reds (NL)	4–0
1940	Cincinnati Reds (NL)	Detroit Tigers (AL)	4–3
1941	New York Yankees (AL)	Brooklyn Dodgers (NL)	4–1
1942	St. Louis Cardinals (NL)	New York Yankees (AL)	4–1
1943	New York Yankees (AL)	St. Louis Cardinals (NL)	4–1

World Series (continued)

YEAR	WINNING TEAM	LOSING TEAM	RESULTS
1944	St. Louis Cardinals (NL)	St. Louis Browns (AL)	4–2
1945	Detroit Tigers (AL)	Chicago Cubs (NL)	4–3
1946	St. Louis Cardinals (NL)	Boston Red Sox (AL)	4–3
1947	New York Yankees (AL)	Brooklyn Dodgers (NL)	4–3
1948	Cleveland Indians (AL)	Boston Braves (NL)	4–2
1949	New York Yankees (AL)	Brooklyn Dodgers (NL)	4–1
1950	New York Yankees (AL)	Philadelphia Phillies (NL)	4–0
1951	New York Yankees (AL)	New York Giants (NL)	4–2
1952	New York Yankees (AL)	Brooklyn Dodgers (NL)	4–3
1953	New York Yankees (AL)	Brooklyn Dodgers (NL)	4–2
1954	New York Giants (NL)	Cleveland Indians (AL)	4–0
1955	Brooklyn Dodgers (NL)	New York Yankees (AL)	4–3
1956	New York Yankees (AL)	Brooklyn Dodgers (NL)	4–3
1957	Milwaukee Braves (NL)	New York Yankees (AL)	4–3
1958	New York Yankees (AL)	Milwaukee Braves (NL)	4–3
1959	Los Angeles Dodgers (NL)	Chicago White Sox (AL)	4–2
1960	Pittsburgh Pirates (NL)	New York Yankees (AL)	4–3
1961	New York Yankees (AL)	Cincinnati Reds (NL)	4–1
1962	New York Yankees (AL)	San Francisco Giants (NL)	4–3
1963	Los Angeles Dodgers (NL)	New York Yankees (AL)	4–0
1964	St. Louis Cardinals (NL)	New York Yankees (AL)	4–3
1965	Los Angeles Dodgers (NL)	Minnesota Twins (AL)	4–3
1966	Baltimore Orioles (AL)	Los Angeles Dodgers (NL)	4–0
1967	St. Louis Cardinals (NL)	Boston Red Sox (AL)	4–3
1968	Detroit Tigers (AL)	St. Louis Cardinals (NL)	4–3
1969	New York Mets (NL)	Baltimore Orioles (AL)	4–1
1970	Baltimore Orioles (AL)	Cincinnati Reds (NL)	4–1
1971	Pittsburgh Pirates (NL)	Baltimore Orioles (AL)	4–3
1972	Oakland Athletics (AL)	Cincinnati Reds (NL)	4–3
1973	Oakland Athletics (AL)	New York Mets (NL)	4–3
1974	Oakland Athletics (AL)	Los Angeles Dodgers (NL)	4–1
1975	Cincinnati Reds (NL)	Boston Red Sox (AL)	4–3
1976	Cincinnati Reds (NL)	New York Yankees (AL)	4–0
1977	New York Yankees (AL)	Los Angeles Dodgers (NL)	4–2
1978	New York Yankees (AL)	Los Angeles Dodgers (NL)	4–2
1979	Pittsburgh Pirates (NL)	Baltimore Orioles (AL)	4–3
1980	Philadelphia Phillies (NL)	Kansas City Royals (AL)	4–2
1981	Los Angeles Dodgers (NL)	New York Yankees (AL)	4–2
1982	St. Louis Cardinals (NL)	Milwaukee Brewers (AL)	4–3
1983	Baltimore Orioles (AL)	Philadelphia Phillies (NL)	4–1
1984	Detroit Tigers (AL)	San Diego Padres (NL)	4–1
1985	Kansas City Royals (AL)	St. Louis Cardinals (NL)	4–3
1986	New York Mets (NL)	Boston Red Sox (AL)	4–3
1987	Minnesota Twins (AL)	St. Louis Cardinals (NL)	4–3
1988	Los Angeles Dodgers (NL)	Oakland Athletics (AL)	4–1
1989	Oakland Athletics (AL)	San Francisco Giants (NL)	4–0
1990	Cincinnati Reds (NL)	Oakland Athletics (AL)	4–0
1991	Minnesota Twins (AL)	Atlanta Braves (NL)	4–3
1992	Toronto Blue Jays (AL)	Atlanta Braves (NL)	4–2
1993	Toronto Blue Jays (AL)	Philadelphia Phillies (NL)	4–2
1994	*not held*		
1995	Atlanta Braves (NL)	Cleveland Indians (AL)	4–2
1996	New York Yankees (AL)	Atlanta Braves (NL)	4–2
1997	Florida Marlins (NL)	Cleveland Indians (AL)	4–3
1998	New York Yankees (AL)	San Diego Padres (NL)	4–0
1999	New York Yankees (AL)	Atlanta Braves (NL)	4–0
2000	New York Yankees (AL)	New York Mets (NL)	4–1
2001	Arizona Diamondbacks (NL)	New York Yankees (AL)	4–3
2002	Anaheim Angels (AL)	San Francisco Giants (NL)	4–3
2003	Florida Marlins (NL)	New York Yankees (AL)	4–2
2004	Boston Red Sox (AL)	St. Louis Cardinals (NL)	4–0
2005	Chicago White Sox (AL)	Houston Astros (NL)	4–0
2006	St. Louis Cardinals (NL)	Detroit Tigers (AL)	4–1
2007	Boston Red Sox (AL)	Colorado Rockies (NL)	4–0

[1]*Plus one tied game.*

Major League Baseball All-Time Records[1]

Research courtesy of Baseball Almanac, <www.baseball-almanac.com>.

	PLAYERS/TEAMS	NUMBER	SEASON/DATE
Individual career records			
Games played	Pete Rose	3,562	1963–86
Consecutive games played	Cal Ripken, Jr.	2,632	1982–98
Batting average[2]	Ty Cobb	.366	1905–28
Hits	Pete Rose	4,256	1963–86
Doubles	Tris Speaker	792	1907–28
Triples	Sam Crawford	309	1899–17
Home runs	Barry Bonds	762	1986–2007
Runs	Rickey Henderson	2,295	1979–2003
Runs batted in	Hank Aaron	2,297	1954–76
Walks (batting)	Barry Bonds	2,558	1986–2007
Stolen bases	Rickey Henderson	1,406	1979–2003
Wins (pitching)	Cy Young	511	1890–1911
Earned run average[3]	Ed Walsh	1.82	1904–17
Strikeouts (pitching)	Nolan Ryan	5,714	1966–93
Saves	Trevor Hoffman[4]	524	1993–2007
No-hitters	Nolan Ryan	7	1966–93
Shutouts	Walter Johnson	110	1907–27
Wins (managing)	Connie Mack	3,731	1894–96; 1901–50
Individual season records			
Batting average[5]	Hugh Duffy	.440	1894
Hits	Ichiro Suzuki[4]	262	2004
Doubles	Earl Webb	67	1931
Triples	Chief Wilson	36	1912
Home runs	Barry Bonds	73	2001
Runs	Billy Hamilton	192	1894
Runs batted in	Hack Wilson	191	1930
Walks (batting)	Barry Bonds	232	2004
Stolen bases	Hugh Nicol	138	1887
Wins	Charley Radbourn	59	1884
Earned run average[6]	Tim Keefe	0.86	1880
Strikeouts (pitching)	Matt Kilroy	513	1886
No-hitters	*4 players hold record*	2	
Saves	Bobby Thigpen	57	1990
Shutouts	George Bradley; Grover Alexander	16	1876; 1916
Individual game records[7]			
Hits	Wilbert Robinson; Rennie Stennett	7	10 Jun 1892; 16 Sep 1975
Doubles	*47 players hold record*	4	
Triples	George Strief; Bill Joyce	4	25 Jun 1885; 18 May 1897
Home runs	*12 players hold record*	4	
Runs	Guy Hecker	7	15 Aug 1886
Runs batted in	Jim Bottomley; Mark Whiten	12	16 Sep 1924; 7 Sep 1993
Walks (batting)	Walt Wilmot; Jimmie Foxx	6	22 Aug 1891; 16 Jun 1938
Stolen bases	George Gore; Billy Hamilton	7	25 Jun 1881; 31 Aug 1894
Strikeouts (pitching)	Roger Clemens (twice); Kerry Wood[4]	20	29 Apr 1986 and 18 Sep 1996; 6 May 1998
Team season records			
World Series titles	New York Yankees	26	
Consecutive World Series titles	New York Yankees	5	1949–53
Games won	Chicago Cubs; Seattle Mariners	116	1906; 2001
Highest winning percentage	St. Louis Maroons	.832 (94–19)	1884
Batting average	Philadelphia Phillies	.349	1894
Doubles	St. Louis Cardinals; Boston Red Sox	373	1930; 1997
Triples	Baltimore Orioles	153	1894
Home runs	Seattle Mariners	264	1997
Runs	Boston Beaneaters	1,220	1894
Runs batted in	Boston Beaneaters	1,043	1894
Walks (batting)	Boston Red Sox	835	1949
Stolen bases	Philadelphia Athletics	638	1887

Major League Baseball All-Time Records[1] (continued)

Game records	PLAYERS/TEAMS	NUMBER	SEASON/DATE
Highest total score	Chicago Cubs versus Philadelphia Phillies	26 to 23 (total 49)	25 Aug 1922
Longest nine-inning game	New York Yankees versus Boston Red Sox	4 hr 45 min	18 Aug 2006
Longest extra-inning game (time)	Chicago White Sox versus Milwaukee Brewers	8 hr 6 min	9 May 1984
Longest extra-inning game (innings)	Brooklyn Dodgers versus Boston Braves	26 innings	1 May 1920

[1]Through the end of the 2007 season. [2]Minimum of 1,000 games played and 1,000 at-bats. [3]Minimum of 2,000 innings pitched. [4]Active in 2008. [5]Minimum of 3.1 plate appearances per game played. [6]Minimum of one inning pitched per game played. [7]Nine-inning games only.

Caribbean Series

Held since 1949. Table shows results for past 40 years.

YEAR	WINNING TEAM	COUNTRY	YEAR	WINNING TEAM	COUNTRY
1969	*not held*		1989	Zulia Eagles	VEN
1970	Magallanes Navigators	VEN	1990	Escogido Lions	DOM
1971	Licey Tigers	DOM	1991	Licey Tigers	DOM
1972	Ponce Lions	PUR	1992	Mayagüez Indians	PUR
1973	Licey Tigers	DOM	1993	Santurce Crabbers	PUR
1974	Caguas Creoles	PUR	1994	Licey Tigers	DOM
1975	Bayamón Cowboys	PUR	1995	San Juan Senators	PUR
1976	Hermosillo Orange Growers	MEX	1996	Culiacán Tomato Growers	MEX
1977	Licey Tigers	DOM	1997	Northern Eagles	DOM
1978	Mayagüez Indians	PUR	1998	Northern Eagles	DOM
1979	Magallanes Navigators	VEN	1999	Licey Tigers	DOM
1980	Licey Tigers	DOM	2000	Santurce Crabbers	PUR
1981	*not held*		2001	Cibao Eagles	DOM
1982	Caracas Lions	VEN	2002	Culiacán Tomato Growers	MEX
1983	Arecibo Wolves	PUR	2003	Cibao Eagles	DOM
1984	Zulia Eagles	VEN	2004	Licey Tigers	DOM
1985	Licey Tigers	DOM	2005	Mazatlán Deer	MEX
1986	Mexicali Eagles	MEX	2006	Caracas Lions	VEN
1987	Caguas Creoles	PUR	2007	Cibao Eagles	DOM
1988	Escogido Lions	DOM	2008	Licey Tigers	DOM

Japan Series

Held since 1950. Table shows results for past 10 years.

YEAR	WINNING TEAM	LOSING TEAM	RESULTS
1998	Yokohama BayStars (CL)	Seibu Lions (PL)	4–2
1999	Fukuoka Daiei Hawks (PL)	Chunichi Dragons (CL)	4–1
2000	Yomiuri Giants (CL)	Fukuoka Daiei Hawks (PL)	4–2
2001	Yakult Swallows (CL)	Osaka Kintetsu Buffaloes (PL)	4–1
2002	Yomiuri Giants (CL)	Seibu Lions (PL)	4–0
2003	Fukuoka Daiei Hawks (PL)	Hanshin Tigers (CL)	4–3
2004	Seibu Lions (PL)	Chunichi Dragons (CL)	4–3
2005	Chiba Lotte Marines (PL)	Hanshin Tigers (CL)	4–0
2006	Hokkaido Nippon Ham Fighters (PL)	Chunichi Dragons (CL)	4–1
2007	Chunichi Dragons (CL)	Hokkaido Nippon Ham Fighters (PL)	4–1

Little League World Series

The Little League World Series, first called the National Little League Tournament, was established in 1947. Table shows results for past 10 years.

YEAR	WINNING TEAM/HOME	RUNNER-UP	SCORE
1999	Hirakata/Osaka (JPN)	Phenix City National/Phenix City AL	5–0
2000	Sierra Maestra/Maracaibo (VEN)	Bellaire/Bellaire TX	3–2
2001	Kitasuna/Tokyo (JPN)	Apopka National/Apopka FL	2–1
2002	Valley Sports American/Louisville KY	Sendai Higashi/Sendai (JPN)	1–0
2003	Musashi-Fuchu/Tokyo (JPN)	East Boynton Beach/Boynton Beach FL	10–1
2004	Pabao/Willemstad (AHO)	Conejo Valley/Thousand Oaks CA	5–2

Little League World Series (continued)

YEAR	WINNING TEAM/HOME	RUNNER-UP	SCORE
2005	West Oahu/Ewa Beach HI	Pabao/Willemstad (AHO)	7-6
2006	Columbus Northern/Columbus GA	Kawaguchi/Kawaguchi City (JPN)	2-1
2007	Warner Robins American/Warner Robins GA	Tokyo Kitasuna/Tokyo (JPN)	3-2
2008	Waipio/Waipahu HI	Matamoros/Matamoros (MEX)	12-3

Basketball

American professional basketball is directed by the **National Basketball Association** (NBA; formed 1949). The NBA is divided into the Eastern and Western conferences (EC and WC), the top-ranking teams of which compete yearly for the championship. The NBA began the **Women's Professional Basketball Association** (WNBA), which is also divided into an Eastern and a Western conference, in 1997.

Since the inclusion of basketball as an **Olympic sport** in 1936, the winners of the Olympic tournament have been considered the world champions. The **Fédération Internationale de Basketball** (FIBA; founded 1932) instituted world championships in 1950 for men and in 1953 for women. (Women's basketball was not admitted to the Olympics until 1976.) Amateur basketball in the United States is most closely followed at the **collegiate** level, where the most important event of the season is the **National Collegiate Athletic Association (NCAA) Championship.** The NCAA tournament was first contested in 1939 (by men's teams only). Women's college basketball was first played on a national level in 1972, under the auspices of the Association for Intercollegiate Athletics for Women (AIAW), which gave way in 1982 to the NCAA's first tournament for women.

Related Web sites: NBA: <www.nba.com>; WNBA: <www.wnba.com>; NCAA: <www.ncaa.org>; FIBA: <www.fiba.com>.

National Basketball Association Final Standings, 2007–08

EASTERN CONFERENCE

Atlantic Division

TEAM	WON	LOST	GAMES BACK
Boston[1]	66	16	—
Toronto[1]	41	41	25
Philadelphia[1]	40	42	26
New Jersey	34	48	32
New York	23	59	43

Central Division

TEAM	WON	LOST	GAMES BACK
Detroit[1]	59	23	—
Cleveland[1]	45	37	14
Indiana	36	46	23
Chicago	33	49	26
Milwaukee	26	56	33

Southeast Division

TEAM	WON	LOST	GAMES BACK
Orlando[1]	52	30	—
Washington[1]	43	39	9
Atlanta[1]	37	45	15
Charlotte	32	50	20
Miami	15	67	37

WESTERN CONFERENCE

Northwest Division

TEAM	WON	LOST	GAMES BACK
Utah[1]	54	28	—
Denver[1]	50	32	4
Portland	41	41	13
Minnesota	22	60	32
Seattle	20	62	34

Pacific Division

TEAM	WON	LOST	GAMES BACK
L.A. Lakers[1]	57	25	—
Phoenix[1]	55	27	2
Golden State	48	34	9
Sacramento	38	44	19
L.A. Clippers	23	59	34

Southwest Division

TEAM	WON	LOST	GAMES BACK
New Orleans[1]	56	26	—
San Antonio[1]	56	26	—
Houston[1]	55	27	1
Dallas[1]	51	31	5
Memphis	22	60	34

[1]*Gained play-off berth.*

National Basketball Association All-Time Records[1]

	PLAYERS/TEAMS	NUMBER	SEASON/DATE
Individual career records			
Games played	Robert Parish	1,611	1976-77–1996-97
Points scored	Kareem Abdul-Jabbar	38,387	1969-70–1988-89
Most games, 50 or more points	Wilt Chamberlain	118	1959-60–1972-73
Most consecutive games, 10 or more points	Michael Jordan	866	25 Mar 1986–26 Dec 2001
Field goals attempted	Kareem Abdul-Jabbar	28,307	1969-70–1988-89
Field goals made	Kareem Abdul-Jabbar	15,837	1969-70–1988-89
Field-goal percentage[2]	Artis Gilmore	.599	1976-77–1987-88
Three-point field goals attempted	Reggie Miller	6,486	1987-88–2004-05

National Basketball Association All-Time Records (continued)

	PLAYERS/TEAMS	NUMBER	SEASON/DATE
Individual career records (continued)			
Three-point field goals made	Reggie Miller	2,560	1987-88–2004-05
Three-point field-goal percentage[3]	Jason Kapono	.464	2003-04–2007-08
Free throws attempted	Karl Malone	13,188	1985-86–2003-04
Free throws made	Karl Malone	9,787	1985-86–2003-04
Free-throw percentage[4]	Mark Price	.904	1986-87–1997-98
Assists	John Stockton	15,806	1984-85–2002-03
Rebounds	Wilt Chamberlain	23,924	1959-60–1972-73
Steals[5]	John Stockton	3,265	1984-85–2002-03
Blocked shots[5]	Hakeem Olajuwon	3,830	1984-85–2001-02
Personal fouls	Kareem Abdul-Jabbar	4,657	1969-70–1988-89
Wins (coaching)	Lenny Wilkens	1,332	1969-70–2004-05, except 1972-1974
Individual season records			
Points scored	Wilt Chamberlain	4,029	1961-62
Field goals attempted	Wilt Chamberlain	3,159	1961-62
Field goals made	Wilt Chamberlain	1,597	1961-62
Field-goal percentage	Wilt Chamberlain	.727	1972-73
Three-point field goals attempted	George McCloud	678	1995-96
Three-point field goals made	Ray Allen	269	2005-06
Three-point field-goal percentage	Steve Kerr	.524	1994-95
Free throws attempted	Wilt Chamberlain	1,363	1961-62
Free throws made	Jerry West	840	1965-66
Free-throw percentage	Calvin Murphy	.958	1980-81
Assists	John Stockton	1,164	1990-91
Rebounds	Wilt Chamberlain	2,149	1960-61
Steals[5]	Alvin Robertson	301	1985-86
Blocked shots[5]	Mark Eaton	456	1984-85
Personal fouls	Darryl Dawkins	386	1983-84
Individual game records			
Points scored	Wilt Chamberlain	100	2 Mar 1962
Field goals attempted	Wilt Chamberlain	63	2 Mar 1962
Field goals made	Wilt Chamberlain	36	2 Mar 1962
Three-point field goals attempted	Damon Stoudamire	21	15 Apr 2005
Three-point field goals made	Kobe Bryant; Donyell Marshall	12	7 Jan 2003; 13 Mar 2005
Free throws attempted	Wilt Chamberlain	34	22 Feb 1962
Free throws made	Wilt Chamberlain; Adrian Dantley	28	2 Mar 1962; 4 Jan 1984
Assists	Scott Skiles	30	30 Dec 1990
Rebounds	Wilt Chamberlain	55	24 Nov 1960
Steals[5]	Larry Kenon; Kendall Gill	11	26 Dec 1976; 3 Apr 1999
Blocked shots[5]	Elmore Smith	17	28 Oct 1973
Team records			
Highest winning percentage (season)	Chicago Bulls	.878 (72-10)	1995-96
Consecutive games won	Los Angeles Lakers	33	5 Nov 1971–7 Jan 1972
Championships	Boston Celtics	17	
Consecutive championships	Boston Celtics	8	1959-66
Game records			
Highest combined score	Detroit Pistons versus Denver Nuggets	370 (186-184)	13 Dec 1983
Longest game (overtime periods)	Indianapolis Olympians versus Rochester Royals	6	6 Jan 1951

[1]*Through the end of the 2007-08 season.* [2]*Minimum 2,000 made.* [3]*Minimum 250 made.* [4]*Minimum 1,200 made.* [5]*Since 1973-74; before that season steals and blocked shots were not officially recorded by the NBA.*

Hall-of-famer Willie Stargell was almost 40 when he won the National League Most Valuable Player award (shared with Keith Hernandez) in 1979. Stargell also won the MVP awards for the NL championship series and the World Series, making him the only player in history to win all three awards in the same season.

National Basketball Association (NBA) Championship

SEASON	WINNER	RUNNER-UP	RESULTS
1946–47	Philadelphia Warriors	Chicago Stags	4–1
1947–48	Baltimore Bullets	Philadelphia Warriors	4–2
1948–49	Minneapolis Lakers	Washington Capitols	4–2
1949–50	Minneapolis Lakers	Syracuse Nationals	4–2
1950–51	Rochester Royals	New York Knickerbockers	4–3
1951–52	Minneapolis Lakers	New York Knickerbockers	4–3
1952–53	Minneapolis Lakers	New York Knickerbockers	4–1
1953–54	Minneapolis Lakers	Syracuse Nationals	4–3
1954–55	Syracuse Nationals	Fort Wayne Pistons	4–3
1955–56	Philadelphia Warriors	Fort Wayne Pistons	4–1
1956–57	Boston Celtics	St. Louis Hawks	4–3
1957–58	St. Louis Hawks	Boston Celtics	4–2
1958–59	Boston Celtics	Minneapolis Lakers	4–0
1959–60	Boston Celtics	St. Louis Hawks	4–3
1960–61	Boston Celtics	St. Louis Hawks	4–1
1961–62	Boston Celtics	Los Angeles Lakers	4–3
1962–63	Boston Celtics	Los Angeles Lakers	4–2
1963–64	Boston Celtics	San Francisco Warriors	4–1
1964–65	Boston Celtics	Los Angeles Lakers	4–1
1965–66	Boston Celtics	Los Angeles Lakers	4–3
1966–67	Philadelphia 76ers	San Francisco Warriors	4–2
1967–68	Boston Celtics	Los Angeles Lakers	4–2
1968–69	Boston Celtics	Los Angeles Lakers	4–3
1969–70	New York Knickerbockers	Los Angeles Lakers	4–3
1970–71	Milwaukee Bucks	Baltimore Bullets	4–0
1971–72	Los Angeles Lakers	New York Knickerbockers	4–1
1972–73	New York Knickerbockers	Los Angeles Lakers	4–1
1973–74	Boston Celtics	Milwaukee Bucks	4–3
1974–75	Golden State Warriors	Washington Bullets	4–0
1975–76	Boston Celtics	Phoenix Suns	4–2
1976–77	Portland Trail Blazers	Philadelphia 76ers	4–2
1977–78	Washington Bullets	Seattle SuperSonics	4–3
1978–79	Seattle SuperSonics	Washington Bullets	4–1
1979–80	Los Angeles Lakers	Philadelphia 76ers	4–2
1980–81	Boston Celtics	Houston Rockets	4–2
1981–82	Los Angeles Lakers	Philadelphia 76ers	4–2
1982–83	Philadelphia 76ers	Los Angeles Lakers	4–0
1983–84	Boston Celtics	Los Angeles Lakers	4–3
1984–85	Los Angeles Lakers	Boston Celtics	4–2
1985–86	Boston Celtics	Houston Rockets	4–2
1986–87	Los Angeles Lakers	Boston Celtics	4–2
1987–88	Los Angeles Lakers	Detroit Pistons	4–3
1988–89	Detroit Pistons	Los Angeles Lakers	4–0
1989–90	Detroit Pistons	Portland Trail Blazers	4–1
1990–91	Chicago Bulls	Los Angeles Lakers	4–1
1991–92	Chicago Bulls	Portland Trail Blazers	4–2
1992–93	Chicago Bulls	Phoenix Suns	4–2
1993–94	Houston Rockets	New York Knickerbockers	4–3
1994–95	Houston Rockets	Orlando Magic	4–0
1995–96	Chicago Bulls	Seattle SuperSonics	4–2
1996–97	Chicago Bulls	Utah Jazz	4–2
1997–98	Chicago Bulls	Utah Jazz	4–2
1998–99	San Antonio Spurs	New York Knickerbockers	4–1
1999–2000	Los Angeles Lakers	Indiana Pacers	4–2
2000–01	Los Angeles Lakers	Philadelphia 76ers	4–1
2001–02	Los Angeles Lakers	New Jersey Nets	4–0
2002–03	San Antonio Spurs	New Jersey Nets	4–2
2003–04	Detroit Pistons	Los Angeles Lakers	4–1
2004–05	San Antonio Spurs	Detroit Pistons	4–3
2005–06	Miami Heat	Dallas Mavericks	4–2
2006–07	San Antonio Spurs	Cleveland Cavaliers	4–0
2007–08	Boston Celtics	Los Angeles Lakers	4–2

Women's National Basketball Association (WNBA) Championship

SEASON	WINNER	RUNNER-UP	RESULTS
1997	Houston Comets (EC)	New York Liberty (EC)	1-0
1998	Houston Comets (WC)	Phoenix Mercury (WC)	2-1
1999	Houston Comets (WC)	New York Liberty (EC)	2-1
2000	Houston Comets (WC)	New York Liberty (EC)	2-0
2001	Los Angeles Sparks (WC)	Charlotte Sting (EC)	2-0
2002	Los Angeles Sparks (WC)	New York Liberty (EC)	2-0
2003	Detroit Shock (EC)	Los Angeles Sparks (WC)	2-1
2004	Seattle Storm (WC)	Connecticut Sun (EC)	2-1
2005	Sacramento Monarchs (WC)	Connecticut Sun (EC)	3-1
2006	Detroit Shock (EC)	Sacramento Monarchs (WC)	3-2
2007	Phoenix Mercury (WC)	Detroit Shock (EC)	3-2

Division I National Collegiate Athletic Association (NCAA) Championship—Men

YEAR	WINNER	RUNNER-UP	SCORE
1939	Oregon	Ohio State	46-43
1940	Indiana	Kansas	60-42
1941	Wisconsin	Washington State	39-34
1942	Stanford	Dartmouth	53-38
1943	Wyoming	Georgetown	46-34
1944	Utah	Dartmouth	42-40
1945	Oklahoma A&M	New York	49-45
1946	Oklahoma A&M	North Carolina	43-40
1947	Holy Cross (MA)	Oklahoma	58-47
1948	Kentucky	Baylor	58-42
1949	Kentucky	Oklahoma State	46-36
1950	City College of New York	Bradley	71-68
1951	Kentucky	Kansas State	68-58
1952	Kansas	St. John's (NY)	80-63
1953	Indiana	Kansas	69-68
1954	La Salle	Bradley	92-76
1955	San Francisco	La Salle	77-63
1956	San Francisco	Iowa	83-71
1957	North Carolina	Kansas	54-53
1958	Kentucky	Seattle	84-72
1959	California (Berkeley)	West Virginia	71-70
1960	Ohio State	California (Berkeley)	75-55
1961	Cincinnati	Ohio State	70-65
1962	Cincinnati	Ohio State	71-59
1963	Loyola (IL)	Cincinnati	60-58
1964	UCLA	Duke	98-83
1965	UCLA	Michigan	91-80
1966	Texas Western	Kentucky	72-65
1967	UCLA	Dayton	79-64
1968	UCLA	North Carolina	78-55
1969	UCLA	Purdue	92-72
1970	UCLA	Jacksonville	80-69
1971	UCLA	Villanova	68-62
1972	UCLA	Florida State	81-76
1973	UCLA	Memphis State	87-66
1974	North Carolina State	Marquette	76-64
1975	UCLA	Kentucky	92-85
1976	Indiana	Michigan	86-68
1977	Marquette	North Carolina	67-59
1978	Kentucky	Duke	94-88
1979	Michigan State	Indiana State	75-64
1980	Louisville	UCLA	59-54
1981	Indiana	North Carolina	63-50
1982	North Carolina	Georgetown	63-62
1983	North Carolina State	Houston	54-52
1984	Georgetown	Houston	84-75
1985	Villanova	Georgetown	66-64
1986	Louisville	Duke	72-69
1987	Indiana	Syracuse	74-73
1988	Kansas	Oklahoma	83-79
1989	Michigan	Seton Hall	80-79
1990	UNLV	Duke	103-73
1991	Duke	Kansas	72-65
1992	Duke	Michigan	71-51
1993	North Carolina	Michigan	77-71
1994	Arkansas	Duke	76-72
1995	UCLA	Arkansas	89-78
1996	Kentucky	Syracuse	76-67
1997	Arizona	Kentucky	84-79
1998	Kentucky	Utah	78-69
1999	Connecticut	Duke	77-74
2000	Michigan State	Florida	89-76
2001	Duke	Arizona	82-72
2002	Maryland	Indiana	64-52
2003	Syracuse	Kansas	81-78
2004	Connecticut	Georgia Tech	82-73
2005	North Carolina	Illinois	75-70
2006	Florida	UCLA	73-57
2007	Florida	Ohio State	84-75
2008	Kansas	Memphis	75-68

Division I National Collegiate Athletic Association (NCAA) Championship—Women

YEAR	WINNER	RUNNER-UP	SCORE
1982	Louisiana Tech	Cheyney	76-62
1983	USC	Louisiana Tech	69-67
1984	USC	Tennessee	72-61
1985	Old Dominion	Georgia	70-65
1986	Texas	USC	97-81
1987	Tennessee	Louisiana Tech	67-44
1988	Louisiana Tech	Auburn	56-54
1989	Tennessee	Auburn	76-60
1990	Stanford	Auburn	88-81
1991	Tennessee	Virginia	70-67
1992	Stanford	Western Kentucky	78-62
1993	Texas Tech	Ohio State	84-82
1994	North Carolina	Louisiana Tech	60-59
1995	Connecticut	Tennessee	70-64
1996	Tennessee	Georgia	83-65
1997	Tennessee	Old Dominion	68-59
1998	Tennessee	Louisiana Tech	93-75
1999	Purdue	Duke	62-45

Division I National Collegiate Athletic Association (NCAA) Championship—Women (continued)

YEAR	WINNER	RUNNER-UP	SCORE
2000	Connecticut	Tennessee	71–52
2001	Notre Dame	Purdue	68–66
2002	Connecticut	Oklahoma	82–70
2003	Connecticut	Tennessee	73–68
2004	Connecticut	Tennessee	70–61
2005	Baylor	Michigan State	84–62
2006	Maryland	Duke	78–75
2007	Tennessee	Rutgers	59–46
2008	Tennessee	Stanford	64–48

FIBA World Championship—Men

YEAR	WINNER	RUNNER-UP
1936[1]	United States	Canada
1948[1]	United States	France
1950	Argentina	United States
1952[1]	United States	USSR
1954	United States	Brazil
1956[1]	United States	USSR
1959	Brazil[2]	United States
1960[1]	United States	USSR
1963	Brazil	Yugoslavia
1964[1]	United States	USSR
1967	USSR	Yugoslavia
1968[1]	United States	Yugoslavia
1970	Yugoslavia	Brazil
1972[1]	USSR	United States
1974	USSR	Yugoslavia
1976[1]	United States	Yugoslavia
1978	Yugoslavia	USSR
1980[1]	Yugoslavia	Italy
1982	USSR	United States
1984[1]	United States	Spain
1986	United States	USSR
1988[1]	USSR	Yugoslavia
1990	Yugoslavia	USSR
1992[1]	United States	Croatia
1994	United States	Russia
1996[1]	United States	Yugoslavia
1998	Yugoslavia	Russia
2000[1]	United States	France
2002	Yugoslavia	Argentina
2004[1]	Argentina	Italy
2006	Spain	Greece
2008[1]	United States	Spain

[1]*Olympic championships, recognized as world championships.* [2]*By default.*

FIBA World Championship—Women

YEAR	WINNER	RUNNER-UP
1953	United States	Chile
1957	United States	USSR
1959	USSR	Bulgaria
1964	USSR	Czechoslovakia
1967	USSR	South Korea
1971	USSR	Czechoslovakia
1975	USSR	Japan
1976[1]	USSR	United States
1979	United States	South Korea
1980[1]	USSR	Bulgaria
1983	USSR	United States
1984[1]	United States	South Korea
1986	United States	USSR
1988[1]	United States	Yugoslavia
1990	United States	Yugoslavia
1992[1]	Unified Team[2]	China
1994	Brazil	China
1996[1]	United States	Brazil
1998	United States	Russia
2000[1]	United States	Australia
2002	United States	Russia
2004[1]	United States	Australia
2006	Australia	Russia
2008[1]	United States	Australia

[1]*Olympic championships, recognized as world championships.* [2]*Athletes from the Commonwealth of Independent States plus Georgia.*

Billiard Games

The game of billiards has a surprising number of **varieties** throughout the world. Factors in that variety include the number and appearance of the billiard balls, the size of the table, the existence of side and corner pockets, and the object of play. The classic form of the game—**three-cushion billiards**—is played on a pocketless table with one red ball and two white balls, one of which is marked with a spot; it is often known as French billiards, carom billiards, or (simply) billiards.

Pocket billiards, which embraces both **snooker** and the game sometimes known as **English billiards,** is the prevalent form of billiards in the United Kingdom. The world professional snooker championship was first held in 1927; until 1947 it was won every year by Joe Davis (championships were not held during World War II). The championship was discontinued during the 1950s, was revived during the 1960s, and became a knockout event in 1969.

The American form of pocket billiards, usually known as **pool,** differs markedly from the British game. Its most popular variations are **eight-ball, nine-ball,** and **straight (or 14.1) pool.** Though earlier straight pool tournaments were held with regularity, since the 1970s nine-ball and eight-ball pool have surpassed straight pool in popularity in the United States, and nine-ball has gained some prominence internationally. In 1990 the **World Pool-Billiard Association** (WPA; founded 1987) inaugurated the nine-ball world championship.

WPA Web site: <www.wpa-pool.com>.

World Three-Cushion Championship

Competition has been held since 1928; table shows champions for the past 10 years.

YEAR	WINNER	YEAR	WINNER	YEAR	WINNER
1998	Torbjörn Blomdahl (SWE)	2001	Raymond Ceulemans (BEL)	2004	Dick Jaspers (NED)
1999	Dick Jaspers (NED)	2002	Marco Zanetti (ITA)	2005	Daniel Sánchez (ESP)
2000	Dick Jaspers (NED)	2003	Semih Sayginer (TUR)	2006	Eddy Merckx (BEL)
				2007	Ryuuji Umeda (JPN)

World Professional Snooker Championship

Competition has been held since 1927; table shows champions for the past 10 years.
Won by a British player unless otherwise indicated.

YEAR	WINNER	YEAR	WINNER	YEAR	WINNER
1999	Stephen Hendry	2002	Peter Ebdon	2005	Shaun Murphy
2000	Mark Williams	2003	Mark Williams	2006	Graeme Dott
2001	Ronnie O'Sullivan	2004	Ronnie O'Sullivan	2007	John Higgins
				2008	Ronnie O'Sullivan

WPA World Nine-Ball Championships

Competition has been held since 1990; table shows champions for the past 10 years.

YEAR	MEN'S CHAMPION	WOMEN'S CHAMPION	YEAR	MEN'S CHAMPION	WOMEN'S CHAMPION
1999	Nick Varner (USA)	Liu Shin-Mei (TPE)	2004	Alex Pagulayan (CAN)	Kim Ga Young (KOR)
2000	Chao Fong-Pang (TPE)	Julie Kelly (IRL)	2005	Wu Chia-Ching (TPE)	*not held*
2001	Mika Immonen (FIN)	Allison Fisher (GBR)	2006	Ronnie Alcano (PHI)	Kim Ga Young (KOR)
2002	Earl Strickland (USA)	Liu Shin-Mei (TPE)	2007	Daryl Peach (GBR)	Pan Xiaoting (CHN)
2003	Thorsten Hohmann (GER)	*not held*	2008	*not held by publication date*	Lin Yuan-Chun (TPE)

Bowling

The world governing body for bowling is the **Fédération Internationale des Quilleurs (FIQ).** Since 1954 it has sponsored world bowling championships.

In the **United States,** men's bowling is governed by the **American Bowling Congress (ABC),** which was founded in 1895 but became a constituent of the **United States Bowling Congress (USBC)** in 2004. In 1901 the first national championship was organized; in 1961 the yearly competition was split into two divisions—regular (for those with a combined average score of 851 or higher) and classic (for professionals). The classic division was discontinued in 1980. The **Women's International Bowling Congress (WIBC)** was organized in 1916 and sponsored an annual women's championship until 2004, when organizational mergers created the USBC. Competition takes place between teams, doubles, and singles. The all-events category is won by the individual who has the best score of nine games—three team, three doubles, and three singles scores. The **Professional Bowlers Association (PBA)** was established in 1958. One of its major tournaments is the annual Tournament of Champions.

Related Web sites: FIQ: <www.fiq.org>; USBC: <www.bowl.com>; PBA: <www.pba.com>.

Professional Bowlers Association (PBA) Tournament of Champions

The annual tournament has been held since 1960. This table shows results for the past 40 years.

YEAR	CHAMPION	YEAR	CHAMPION	YEAR	CHAMPION
1968	Dave Davis	1982	Mike Durbin	1996	Dave D'Entremont
1969	Jim Godman	1983	Joe Berardi	1997	John Gant
1970	Don Johnson	1984	Mike Durbin	1998	Bryan Goebel
1971	Johnny Petraglia	1985	Mark Williams	1999	Jason Couch
1972	Mike Durbin	1986	Marshall Holman	2000	Jason Couch
1973	Jim Godman	1987	Pete Weber	2001–02	*not held*
1974	Earl Anthony	1988	Mark Williams	2002–03	Jason Couch
1975	Dave Davis	1989	Del Ballard, Jr.	2003–04	Patrick Healey, Jr.
1976	Marshall Holman	1990	Dave Ferraro	2004–05	Steve Jaros
1977	Mike Berlin	1991	David Ozio	2005–06	Chris Barnes
1978	Earl Anthony	1992	Marc McDowell	2006–07	Tommy Jones
1979	George Pappas	1993	George Branham III	2007–08	Michael Haugen, Jr.
1980	Wayne Webb	1994	Norm Duke		
1981	Steve Cook	1995	Mike Aulby		

United States Bowling Congress (USBC) Bowling Championships—Regular Division

The championships have been held since 1901. This table shows results for the past 20 years.

YEAR	SINGLES	SCORE	ALL-EVENTS	SCORE
1989	Paul Tetreault	813	George Hall	2,227
1990	Robert Hochrein	791	Mike Neumann	2,168
1991	Ed Deines	826	Tom Howery	2,216
1992	Gary Blatchford; Bob Youker, Jr. (tied)	801	Mike Tucker	2,158
1993	Dan Bock	798	Jeff Nimke	2,254
1994	John Weltzien	810	Thomas Holt	2,190
1995	Matt Surina	826	Jeff Kwiatkowski	2,191
1996	Don Scudder, Jr.	823	Scott Kurtz	2,224
1997	John Socha	847	Jeff Richgels	2,241
1998	John Gaines	814	Chris Barnes	2,151
1999	Dan Winter	825	Thomas Jones	2,158
2000	Garran Hein	811	Roy Daniels	2,181
2001	Nicholas Hoagland	798	D.J. Archer	2,219
2002	Mark Millsap	823	Stephen A. Hardy	2,279
2003	Ron Bahr	837	Steve Kloempken	2,215
2004[1]	John Janawicz	858	John Janawicz	2,224
2005	David Adam	791	Scott Craddock	2,131
2006	Wendy Macpherson	812	Dave A. Mitchell	2,189
2007	Frederick Aki	814	Mike Rose, Jr.	2,198
2008	Bryan Young	832	Jay Futrell	2,183

[1]*Table shows American Bowling Congress winners through 2004 and USBC winners thereafter.*

United States Bowling Congress (USBC) Women's Bowling Championships—Classic Division

The championships have been held since 1916. The table shows results for the past 20 years.

YEAR	SINGLES	SCORE	ALL-EVENTS	SCORE
1989	Laura Anderson	683	Nancy Fehr	1,911
1990	Paula Carter; Dana Miller-Mackie (tied)	705	Carol Norman	1,984
1991	Debbie Kuhn	773	Debbie Kuhn	2,036
1992	Patty Ann	680	Mitsuko Tokimoto	1,928
1993	Karen Collura; Kari Murph (tied)	747	Anne Marie Duggan	1,990
1994	Vicki Fifield	716	Wendy Macpherson-Papanos	1,940
1995	Beth Owen	749	Beth Owen	1,983
1996	Cindy Berlanga	723	Lorrie Nichols	1,985
1997	Jan Schmidt	765	Kendra Cameron	2,039
1998	Nellie Glandon	714	Liz Johnson	1,989
1999	Nikki Gianulias	746	Hidemi Mizobuchi	2,065
2000	Cathy Krasner	729	Carolyn Dorin-Ballard	2,147
2001	Lisa Wagner	756	Jonquay Armon	2,044
2002	Theresa Smith	752	Cara Honeychurch	2,150
2003	Michelle Feldman	764	Michelle Feldman	2,048
2004[1]	Sharon Smith	754	Kim Adler	2,133
2005	Leanne Barrette	774	Leanne Barrette	2,231
2006	Karen Stroud	771	Karen Stroud	2,159
2007	Tiffany Stanbrough	745	Wendy Macpherson	2,161
2008	Corrine Ham	736	Liz Johnson	2,113

[1]*Table shows Women's International Bowling Congress winners through 2004 and USBC winners thereafter.*

World Tenpin Bowling Championships—Men

In 1979 the singles category was added; previously, the masters had been the only individual event. Also in that year, eights were discontinued and trios were introduced.

YEAR	SINGLES	MASTERS	DOUBLES	TRIOS	TEAM	EIGHTS
1954		Gösta Algeskog (SWE)	FIN		SWE	SWE
1955		Nisse Backstrom (SWE)	SWE		FRG	FIN
1958		Kalle Asukas (FIN)	SWE		FIN	SWE
1960		Tito Reynolds (MEX)	MEX		VEN	MEX
1963		Les Zikes (USA)	USA		USA	USA
1967		David Pond (GBR)	GBR		FIN	USA
1971		Ed Luther (USA)	PUR		USA	USA
1975		Bud Stoudt (USA)	GBR		FIN	FRG
1979	Ollie Ongtawco (PHI)	Gary Bugden (GBR)	AUS	MAS	AUS	
1983	Armando Marino (COL)	Tony Cariello (USA)	AUS	SWE	FIN	

World Tenpin Bowling Championships—Men (continued)

YEAR	SINGLES	MASTERS	DOUBLES	TRIOS	TEAM	EIGHTS
1987	Patrick Rolland (FRA)	Roger Pieters (BEL)	SWE	USA	SWE	
1991	Ying Chieh Ma (TPE)	Mika Koivuniemi (FIN)	USA	USA	TPE	
1995	Marc Doi (CAN)	Chen-Min Yang (TPE)	SWE	NED	NED	
1999	Gery Verbruggen (BEL)	Ahmed Shaheen (QAT)	SWE	FIN	SWE	
2003	Mika Luoto (FIN)	Michael Little (AUS)	SWE	USA	SWE	
2006	Remy Ong (SIN)	Biboy Rivera (PHI)	SWE	KOR	USA	
2008	Walter Ray Williams, Jr. (USA)	Walter Ray Williams, Jr. (USA)	USA	KOR	USA	

World Tenpin Bowling Championships—Women

In 1963 teams consisted of four women and were played European style (either the entire game on one lane or half of the game on one lane, balance on accompanying lane). In 1979 fours were discontinued and trios were introduced. Also in that year, the singles category was added; previously, the masters had been the only individual event.

YEAR	SINGLES	MASTERS	DOUBLES	TRIOS	FOURS	TEAM
1963		Helen Shablis (USA)	USA		MEX	USA
1967		Helen Weston (USA)	MEX		FIN	FIN
1971		Ashie Gonzalez (PUR)	JPN		USA	USA
1975		Anne Haefker (FRG)	SWE		JPN	JPN
1979	Lita de la Rosa (PHI)	Lita de la Rosa (PHI)	PHI	USA		USA
1983	Lena Sulkanen (SWE)	Lena Sulkanen (SWE)	DEN	FRG		SWE
1987	Edda Piccini (MEX)	Annette Hägre (SWE)	USA	USA		USA
1991	Martina Beckel (GER)	Catherine Willis (CAN)	JPN	CAN		KOR
1995	Debby Ship (CAN)	Celia Flores (MEX)	THA	AUS		FIN
1999	Kelly Kulick (USA)	Ann-Maree Putney (AUS)	AUS	KOR		KOR
2003	Zara Glover (GBR)	Diandra Hyman (USA)	GBR	PHI		MAS
2007	Shannon O'Keefe (USA)	Diandra Asbaty (USA)	KOR	SWE		MAS

Chess

Wilhelm Steinitz is generally recognized as the first official chess world champion, although dates for his 19th-century reign vary. With a few notable exceptions, each successive champion defeated his predecessor in match play. The first exception followed the death of the incumbent **Alexander Alekhine** in 1946. The **Fédération Internationale des Échecs** (FIDE; founded 1924) stepped in and arranged a tournament among leading contenders to determine a new champion in 1948. FIDE continued to oversee regular tournaments and matches to determine challengers—although another exception occurred in 1975, when **Robert (Bobby) Fischer** refused to defend his crown and retired. In 1993 **Garry Kasparov** pulled out of FIDE to defend his title under rival organizations (Professional Chess Association and later Braingames). Without a universally recognized champion, FIDE struggled to obtain funding for its multiyear system of tournaments and matches leading to a title match. So, in 1999 FIDE began to hold annual **knockout tournaments,** with very fast game play, to determine its champion. In a move to unify the championship, in 2006 a competition was held that pitted the FIDE champion (Veselin Topalov) against the rival classical chess champion (Vladimir Kramnik). Kramnik won the controversial match in an overtime period and was named the undisputed world chess champion.

FIDE began organizing the **women's chess championship** in 1953. Controversy has also afflicted this title, as **Zsuzsa Polgar** refused to accept FIDE's terms for her title defense in 1999. In 2000 FIDE adopted a knockout tournament format for the women's championship similar to that of the open tournament.

Competitions called Olympiads are also held biennially. Competition is open to both men and women, but since 1957 there has been a separate Olympiad that is restricted to women.

FIDE Web site: <www.fide.com>.

World Chess Champions—Men

Generally recognized (see Chess above).

REIGN	NAME	NATIONALITY
1866–94	Wilhelm Steinitz	Austrian American
1894–1921	Emanuel Lasker	German
1921–27	José Raúl Capablanca	Cuban
1927–35	Alexander Alekhine	Russian-born French
1935–37	Max Euwe	Dutch
1937–46	Alexander Alekhine	Russian-born French
1948–57	Mikhail Botvinnik	Soviet Russian
1957–58	Vasily Smyslov	Soviet Russian
1958–60	Mikhail Botvinnik	Soviet Russian
1960–61	Mikhail Tal	Soviet Russian
1961–63	Mikhail Botvinnik	Soviet Russian
1963–69	Tigran Petrosyan	Soviet Georgian-born Armenian
1969–72	Boris Spassky	Soviet Russian

World Chess Champions—Men (continued)

REIGN	NAME	NATIONALITY	REIGN	NAME	NATIONALITY
1972–75	Robert (Bobby) Fischer	American	1985–2000	Garry Kasparov	Azerbaijani-born Russian
1975–85	Anatoly Karpov	Soviet Russian	2000–	Vladimir Kramnik	Russian

World Chess Champions—Women

REIGN	NAME	NATIONALITY	REIGN	NAME	NATIONALITY
1927–44	Vera Menchik[1]	Soviet Russian	1991–96	Xie Jun	Chinese
1949–53	Lyudmila Rudenko	Soviet Russian	1996–99	Zsuzsa Polgar	Hungarian
1953–56	Yelizaveta Bykova	Soviet Russian	1999–2001	Xie Jun	Chinese
1956–58	Olga Rubtsova	Soviet Russian	2001–04	Zhu Chen	Chinese
1958–62	Yelizaveta Bykova	Soviet Russian	2004–06	Antoaneta Stefanova	Bulgarian
1962–78	Nona Gaprindashvili	Soviet Georgian	2006–	Xu Yuhua	Chinese
1978–91	Maya Chiburdanidze	Soviet Georgian			

[1]*Killed in an air raid on London in 1944; title left vacant.*

Cricket

Cricket is one of the **national sports** of England, and consequently it is played in nearly all the countries with which England has been associated. The world governing body is the **International Cricket Council** (ICC; founded as the Imperial Cricket Conference in 1909). The most important international cricket matches are the **Test matches**, which have been played since 1877. The Test-playing countries are England, Australia, South Africa (banned from international competition between about 1970 and 1992), West Indies (representing Barbados, Guyana, Jamaica, Trinidad and Tobago, and the Leeward and Windward islands), New Zealand, India, Pakistan, Sri Lanka, Zimbabwe (since 1992), and Bangladesh (since 2000).

The Test table is designed to be read from left to right across the columns. This will indicate, for example, that in Test match play against England, South Africa has won 26 games, has had 50 drawn matches, and has lost 54 games.

The **World Cup** is a quadrennial series of one-day, limited-overs competitions. It was first held in 1975.

International Cricket Council Web site: <www.icc-cricket.com>.

All-Time First-Class Test Cricket Standings (as of 30 Sep 2007)

	England			Australia			South Africa			West Indies			New Zealand		
	WINS	DRAWS	LOSSES	W	D	L	W	D	L	W	D	L	W	D	L
England v.	—	—	—	97	88	131	54	50	26	41	45*	52	41	40	7
Australia v.	131	88	97	—	—	—	44	18	15	48	22†	32	22	16	7
South Africa v.	26	50	54	15	18	44	—	—	—	12	5	2	18	11	4
West Indies v.	52	45*	41	32	22†	48	2	5	12	—	—	—	10	16*	9
New Zealand v.	7	40	41	7	16	22	4	11	18	9	16*	10	—	—	—
India v.	18	45	34	15	21†	32	4	6	10	11	41	30	14	22*	9
Pakistan v.	12	36	19‡	11	17	24	3	2	6	15	15	14	21	18	6
Sri Lanka v.	5	5	8	1	6	11	4	5	8	5	3	2	5	10	9
Zimbabwe v.	0	3	3	0	0	3	0	1	6	0	2	4	0	6	7
Bangladesh v.	0	0	4	0	0	4	0	0	4	0	1	3	0	0	4

	India			Pakistan			Sri Lanka			Zimbabwe			Bangladesh		
	WINS	DRAWS	LOSSES	W	D	L	W	D	L	W	D	L	W	D	L
England v.	34	45	18	19‡	36	12	8	5	5	3	3	0	4	0	0
Australia v.	32	21†	15	24	17	11	11	6	1	3	0	0	4	0	0
South Africa v.	10	6	4	6	2	3	8	5	4	6	1	0	4	0	0
West Indies v.	30	41	11	14	15	15	2	3	5	4	2	0	3	1	0
New Zealand v.	9	22*	14	6	18	21	9	10	5	7	6	0	4	0	0
India v.	—	—	—	8	36	12	10	13	3	7	2	2	4	1	0
Pakistan v.	12	36	8	—	—	—	15	10*	7	8	5*	2	6	0	0
Sri Lanka v.	3	13	10	7	10*	15	—	—	—	10	5	0	10	0	0
Zimbabwe v.	2	2	7	2	5*	8	0	5	10	—	—	—	4	3	1
Bangladesh v.	0	1	4	0	0	6	0	0	10	1	3	4	—	—	—

**Including one match abandoned.* *†Including one tie.* *‡Including one forfeit.*

Curling

The game of curling, played on ice and somewhat akin to bowls or shuffleboard, varies little from country to country. The maximum permitted weight of the curling stones is 44 lb (19.96 kg). The top international **men's competition** was instituted in 1959 (called the Scotch Whisky Cup from 1959 to 1967; the Silver Broom from 1968 to 1985; and the **World Curling Championship** since 1986). Although curling has been played among women of many countries since at least the mid-20th century, the first **women's world curling championship** was not held until 1979.

World Curling Federation Web site: <www.worldcurling.org>.

World Curling Championships—Men

YEAR	WINNER	RUNNER-UP	YEAR	WINNER	RUNNER-UP
1959	Canada	Scotland	1984	Norway	Switzerland
1960	Canada	Scotland	1985	Canada	Sweden
1961	Canada	Scotland	1986	Canada	Scotland
1962	Canada	Scotland	1987	Canada	West Germany
1963	Canada	Scotland	1988	Norway	Canada
1964	Canada	Scotland	1989	Canada	Switzerland
1965	United States	Canada	1990	Canada	Scotland
1966	Canada	Scotland	1991	Scotland	Canada
1967	Scotland	Canada	1992	Switzerland	Scotland
1968	Canada	Scotland	1993	Canada	Scotland
1969	Canada	Scotland	1994	Canada	Sweden
1970	Canada	Scotland	1995	Canada	Scotland
1971	Canada	Scotland	1996	Canada	Scotland
1972	Canada	United States	1997	Sweden	Germany
1973	Sweden	Canada	1998	Canada	Sweden
1974	United States	Canada	1999	Scotland	Canada
1975	Switzerland	Canada	2000	Canada	Sweden
1976	United States	Scotland	2001	Sweden	Switzerland
1977	Sweden	Canada	2002	Canada	Norway
1978	United States	Canada	2003	Canada	Switzerland
1979	Norway	Switzerland	2004	Sweden	Germany
1980	Canada	Norway	2005	Canada	Scotland
1981	Switzerland	United States	2006	Scotland	Canada
1982	Canada	Switzerland	2007	Canada	Germany
1983	Canada	West Germany	2008	Canada	Scotland

World Curling Championships—Women

YEAR	WINNER	RUNNER-UP	YEAR	WINNER	RUNNER-UP
1979	Switzerland	Sweden	1994	Canada	Scotland
1980	Canada	Sweden	1995	Sweden	Canada
1981	Sweden	Canada	1996	Canada	United States
1982	Denmark	Sweden	1997	Canada	Norway
1983	Switzerland	Norway	1998	Sweden	Denmark
1984	Canada	Switzerland	1999	Sweden	United States
1985	Canada	Scotland	2000	Canada	Switzerland
1986	Canada	West Germany	2001	Canada	Sweden
1987	Canada	West Germany	2002	Scotland	Sweden
1988	West Germany	Canada	2003	United States	Canada
1989	Canada	Norway	2004	Canada	Norway
1990	Norway	Scotland	2005	Sweden	United States
1991	Norway	Canada	2006	Sweden	United States
1992	Sweden	United States	2007	Canada	Denmark
1993	Canada	Germany	2008	Canada	China

Cycling

By all accounts, the greatest cycling event of all is the annual **Tour de France** road race (founded 1903). It is raced in several stages over a distance usually exceeding 3,500 km (2,175 mi). From 1911 to 1929 distances exceeded 5,300 km (3,290 mi). A Tour de France for women was first held in 1984, over an 18-stage course of 991 km (616 mi). In addition to this and a great number of other road races held yearly, there are yearly **road racing world championships.**

Track racing championships are also held. The oldest events of track racing are the **sprint** (in which only the last part of the race can actually be considered sprinting) and the **pursuit** (both a team and an

Cycling (continued)

individual event in which contestants start the race on opposite sides of the track and attempt to catch each other). **Mountain bike racing** and **cyclo-cross,** a cross-country bicycle race that requires cyclists to carry their bikes over parts of the course, developed in the latter part of the 20th century. World championships were established for these sports in 1997.

International Cycling Union (Union Cycliste Internationale—UCI) Web site: <www.uci.ch>.

Cycling Champions, 2007–08

In the case of multiday events, the concluding date is given.

EVENT	WINNER (COUNTRY)	DATE
world champions—mountain bikes		**9 Sep 2007**
men		
Cross-country	Julien Absalon (FRA)	
Downhill	Samuel Hill (AUS)	
women		
Cross-country	Irina Kalentiyeva (RUS)	
Downhill	Sabrina Jonnier (FRA)	
world champions—road		**30 Sep 2007**
men		
Individual road race	Paolo Bettini (ITA)	
Individual time trial	Fabian Cancellara (SUI)	
women		
Individual road race	Marta Bastianelli (ITA)	
Individual time trial	Hanka Kupfernagel (GER)	
world champions—cyclo-cross		**27 Jan 2008**
Men	Lars Boom (NED)	
Women	Hanka Kupfernagel (GER)	
world champions—track		**30 Mar 2008**
men		
Individual pursuit	Bradley Wiggins (GBR)	
Individual sprint	Chris Hoy (GBR)	
1-km time trial	Teun Mulder (NED)	
Points	Vasili Kiryienka (BLR)	
Team pursuit	Great Britain	
Team sprint	France	
Keirin	Chris Hoy (GBR)	
Madison	Bradley Wiggins, Mark Cavendish (GBR)	
Scratch	Aliaksandr Lisouski (BLR)	
women		
Individual pursuit	Rebecca Romero (GBR)	
Individual sprint	Victoria Pendleton (GBR)	
500-m time trial	Lisandra Guerra Rodriguez (CUB)	
Points	Marianne Vos (NED)	
Team pursuit	Great Britain	
Team sprint	Great Britain	
Keirin	Jennie Reed (USA)	
Scratch	Eleonora Van Dijk (NED)	
major elite road-race winners		
San Sebastian Classic (Clasica Ciclista San Sebastian)	Leonardo Bertagnolli (ITA)	4 Aug 2007
Vattenfall Cyclassics	Alessandro Ballan (ITA)	19 Aug 2007
Tour of Spain (Vuelta a España)	Denis Menchov (RUS)	1 Sep 2007
Paris–Tours	Alessandro Petacchi (ITA)	14 Oct 2007
Tour of Lombardy (Giro di Lombardia)	Damiano Cunego (ITA)	20 Oct 2007
Paris–Nice	Davide Rebellin (ITA)	16 Mar 2008
Tirreno–Adriatico	Fabian Cancellara (SUI)	18 Mar 2008
Milan–San Remo	Fabian Cancellara (SUI)	22 Mar 2008
Tour of Flanders (Ronde van Vlaanderen)	Stijn Devolder (BEL)	6 Apr 2008
Ghent–Wevelgem	Óscar Freire (ESP)	9 Apr 2008
Paris–Roubaix	Tom Boonen (BEL)	13 Apr 2008
Amstel Gold	Damiano Cunego (ITA)	20 Apr 2008
La Flèche Wallonne	Kim Kirchen (LUX)	23 Apr 2008

Cycling Champions, 2007–08 (continued)

major elite road-race winners (continued)		
Liège-Bastogne-Liège	Alejandro Valverde (ESP)	26 Apr 2008
Tour of Romandie (Tour de Romandie)	Andreas Klöden (GER)	29 Apr 2008
Tour of Italy (Giro d'Italia)	Alberto Contador (ESP)	1 Jun 2008
Critérium du Dauphiné Libéré	Alejandro Valverde (ESP)	8 Jun 2008
Tour of Switzerland (Tour de Suisse)	Roman Kreuziger (CZE)	14 Jun 2008
Tour de France	Carlos Sastre (ESP)	27 Jul 2008

Tour de France

YEAR	WINNER (COUNTRY)	LENGTH OF ROUTE (KM)	YEAR	WINNER (COUNTRY)	LENGTH OF ROUTE (KM)
1903	Maurice Garin (FRA)	2,428	1961	Jacques Anquetil (FRA)	4,397
1904	Henri Cornet (FRA)	2,388	1962	Jacques Anquetil (FRA)	4,274
1905	Louis Trousselier (FRA)	2,975	1963	Jacques Anquetil (FRA)	4,137
1906	René Pottier (FRA)	4,637	1964	Jacques Anquetil (FRA)	4,504
1907	Lucien Petit-Breton (FRA)	4,488	1965	Felice Gimondi (ITA)	4,183
1908	Lucien Petit-Breton (FRA)	4,487	1966	Lucien Aimar (FRA)	4,303
1909	François Faber (LUX)	4,507	1967	Roger Pingeon (FRA)	4,780
1910	Octave Lapize (FRA)	4,474	1968	Jan Janssen (NED)	4,662
1911	Gustave Garrigou (FRA)	5,344	1969	Eddy Merckx (BEL)	4,110
1912	Odile Defraye (BEL)	5,319	1970	Eddy Merckx (BEL)	4,366
1913	Philippe Thys (BEL)	5,387	1971	Eddy Merckx (BEL)	3,689
1914	Philippe Thys (BEL)	5,405	1972	Eddy Merckx (BEL)	3,846
1915–18	*not held*		1973	Luis Ocaña (ESP)	4,140
1919	Firmin Lambot (BEL)	5,560	1974	Eddy Merckx (BEL)	4,098
1920	Philippe Thys (BEL)	5,519	1975	Bernard Thévenet (FRA)	4,000
1921	Léon Scieur (BEL)	5,484	1976	Lucien Van Impe (BEL)	4,050
1922	Firmin Lambot (BEL)	5,375	1977	Bernard Thévenet (FRA)	4,098
1923	Henri Pélissier (FRA)	5,386	1978	Bernard Hinault (FRA)	3,920
1924	Ottavio Bottecchia (ITA)	5,425	1979	Bernard Hinault (FRA)	3,719
1925	Ottavio Bottecchia (ITA)	5,430	1980	Joop Zoetemelk (NED)	3,948
1926	Lucien Buysse (BEL)	5,745	1981	Bernard Hinault (FRA)	3,765
1927	Nicolas Frantz (LUX)	5,341	1982	Bernard Hinault (FRA)	3,489
1928	Nicolas Frantz (LUX)	5,377	1983	Laurent Fignon (FRA)	3,568
1929	Maurice De Waele (BEL)	5,286	1984	Laurent Fignon (FRA)	3,880
1930	André Leducq (FRA)	4,818	1985	Bernard Hinault (FRA)	4,100
1931	Antonin Magne (FRA)	5,095	1986	Greg LeMond (USA)	4,091
1932	André Leducq (FRA)	4,520	1987	Stephen Roche (IRL)	4,100
1933	Georges Speicher (FRA)	4,395	1988	Pedro Delgado (ESP)	3,300
1934	Antonin Magne (FRA)	4,363	1989	Greg LeMond (USA)	3,215
1935	Romain Maes (BEL)	4,338	1990	Greg LeMond (USA)	3,399
1936	Romain Maes (BEL)	4,442	1991	Miguel Indurain (ESP)	3,935
1937	Roger Lapébie (FRA)	4,415	1992	Miguel Indurain (ESP)	3,983
1938	Gino Bartali (ITA)	4,694	1993	Miguel Indurain (ESP)	3,700
1939	Sylvere Maes (BEL)	4,224	1994	Miguel Indurain (ESP)	3,978
1940–46	*not held*		1995	Miguel Indurain (ESP)	3,635
1947	Jean Robic (FRA)	4,640	1996	*no winner*[1]	3,764
1948	Gino Bartali (ITA)	4,922	1997	Jan Ullrich (GER)	3,944
1949	Fausto Coppi (ITA)	4,808	1998	Marco Pantani (ITA)	3,831
1950	Ferdi Kubler (SUI)	4,775	1999	Lance Armstrong (USA)	3,687
1951	Hugo Koblet (SUI)	4,697	2000	Lance Armstrong (USA)	3,663
1952	Fausto Coppi (ITA)	4,807	2001	Lance Armstrong (USA)	3,454
1953	Louison Bobet (FRA)	4,479	2002	Lance Armstrong (USA)	3,272
1954	Louison Bobet (FRA)	4,469	2003	Lance Armstrong (USA)	3,428
1955	Louison Bobet (FRA)	4,855	2004	Lance Armstrong (USA)	3,391
1956	Roger Walkowiak (FRA)	4,496	2005	Lance Armstrong (USA)	3,608
1957	Jacques Anquetil (FRA)	4,686	2006	Óscar Pereiro (ESP)[2]	3,657
1958	Charly Gaul (LUX)	4,319	2007	Alberto Contador (ESP)	3,550
1959	Federico Bahamontes (ESP)	4,355	2008	Carlos Sastre (ESP)	3,554
1960	Gastone Nencini (ITA)	4,173			

[1]*The victory for Bjarne Riis (DEN) was invalidated after he admitted to using illegal performance-enhancing drugs.* [2]*Floyd Landis (USA) was stripped of the title after he was found to have illegal performance-enhancing drugs in his system. His last appeal against the ruling was rejected in June 2008.*

Football

Many types of games are known as football, among them association football (also called soccer), gridiron football (also called American football and known in the United States as, simply, football), Canadian football (also called rugby football), Australian Rules Football (also called footy), and rugby union and rugby league football (also known as rugby, or rugger). Each of these games is unique, though some—such as US football and Canadian football—bear more than a little resemblance, and each has its own distinct following.

American football—professional. The National Football League (NFL) championship play-offs were organized in 1933. The American Football League (founded 1959) was a rival organization until 1970, when it merged with the NFL. The resulting reorganization added a few new teams (1976) and divided the reconstituted NFL into two conferences, the American Football Conference and the National Football Conference. The play-off winner in each conference becomes that conference's representative in the Super Bowl, the final game of the professional football season.

American football—college. Historically the national champion of college football has been informally selected by two rival opinion polls—one based on a survey of collegiate football coaches (currently conducted by *USA Today*) and the other on a survey of sportswriters (conducted by the Associated Press [AP]). The AP sportswriters' poll began in 1936. The coaches' poll was begun in 1950 by the United Press (now United Press International [UPI]). Where polls designated different teams, both are listed. Desire for a clear-cut national champion led to the creation of the Bowl Championship Series (BCS) in 1999. The BCS uses a formula involving team records, strength of schedule, and rankings to determine the top two teams, who then meet in a national championship game. The site of the game annually shifts between the four major Bowls—Fiesta, Orange, Rose, and Sugar. The first of the Bowl games, the Rose Bowl, had its inaugural game in 1902 during the 12th annual Tournament of Roses festival in Pasadena CA. In 1935 the Sugar Bowl (played in New Orleans LA) and the Orange Bowl (played in Miami FL) were inaugurated. The Fiesta Bowl (played in Phoenix AZ) began play in 1971.

Canadian football—professional. The rules and organization of professional football in Canada have evolved gradually for well over 100 years based on the Canadian Rugby Union (formed in 1891). Until 1936 the game included intercollegiate teams. In 1958 the Canadian Football League was formed, dividing into two conferences, Eastern and Western. In 1981 these were renamed divisions. The two teams that win the division championships meet for the championship of the League, the Grey Cup (instituted in 1909). The intercollegiate teams withdrew from the Grey Cup competition in 1936, but the league did not become strictly professional until the mid-1950s.

Australian football—professional. Australian Rules Football, originally called Melbourne Rules Football, emerged in the state of Victoria in the late 1850s as a sporting alternative during the southern winter, when cricket was not played. The Victorian Football Association (formed in 1877) was supplanted by the Victorian Football League (formed in 1896), which was renamed the Australian Football League (AFL) in 1990 after two teams from outside Victoria were admitted in 1987. Currently, the eight AFL teams with the best records at the end of a 22-week season qualify for the play-offs. The first premiership Grand Final was played in 1886.

Association football. The game of association football is governed by the Fédération Internationale de Football Association (FIFA; founded 1904). The quadrennial FIFA World Cup (organized as the World Cup in 1930) was the first official internationally contested association football match. The popularity of the World Cup and, even earlier, the Copa América (1916) in South America led to the development of several regional cup competitions, including the European Champion Clubs' Cup (1955; discontinued after the 1992–93 season and superseded by the UEFA Champions League), the Asian Cup (1956), the African Cup of Nations (1957), and the Libertadores de América Cup (1960). Competition for the FIFA Women's World Cup began in 1991. The Major League Soccer Cup in the US was launched in 1996.

Rugby union football. Rugby union football was open to amateurs only until 1995. The Six Nations Championship was first played in 1882 (as the Four Nations) and is now contested by England, Scotland, Wales, Ireland, France (since 1910), and Italy (since 2000). The international Test matches further include South Africa, New Zealand, and Australia. The International Rugby Football League (FIRA; now FIRA-AER) oversees rugby in 39 other (i.e., non-Test) countries. The chief international competition between rugby union clubs in the Southern Hemisphere is the tri-nation Super 14 (Super 10 from 1993 to 1995 and Super 12 from 1996 to 2005). Teams from Australia (four), South Africa (five), and New Zealand (five) play in a round-robin tournament; the four teams with the best records qualify for the semifinals. The World Cup, sponsored by the International Rugby Board (founded 1886), was inaugurated in 1987. The competition is held every four years.

Rugby league football. Rugby league World Cup competition began in 1954 between professionals from Australia, France, Great Britain, and New Zealand. In 1975 it was renamed the International Championship. Competition was discontinued after 1977 but revived during the 1980s. The match has been held irregularly every few years.

Related Web sites: National Football League (NFL): <www.nfl.com>; Canadian Football League (CFL): <www.cfl.ca>; Australian Football League (AFL): <www.afl.com.au>; Fédération Internationale de Football Association (FIFA): <www.fifa.com>; Union of European Football Associations (UEFA): <www. uefa.com>; Major League Soccer (MLS): <www. majorleaguesoccer.com>; International Rugby Board (Rugby Union): <www.irb.com>; Rugby League International Federation: <www.rlif.org>; Super 12: <www.super12.rugby.com.au>.

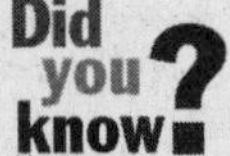

Barry Bonds's 73 home runs in 2001 broke the major-league record of 70 hit by the St. Louis Cardinals' Mark McGwire only three years earlier. But the previous record for home runs by a professional ballplayer was 72, hit by Joe Bauman for the minor-league Roswell Rockets in 1954. Bauman hit .400 with 224 RBIs that season, yet he never made it to the major leagues.

National Football League Final Standings, 2007–08

American Football Conference

TEAM	WON	LOST	TIED	TEAM	WON	LOST	TIED
East Division				**South Division**			
New England[1]	16	0	0	Indianapolis[1]	13	3	0
Buffalo	7	9	0	Jacksonville[1]	11	5	0
New York Jets	4	12	0	Tennessee[1]	10	6	0
Miami	1	15	0	Houston	8	8	0
North Division				**West Division**			
Pittsburgh[1]	10	6	0	San Diego[1]	11	5	0
Cleveland	10	6	0	Denver	7	9	0
Cincinnati	7	9	0	Kansas City	4	12	0
Baltimore	5	11	0	Oakland	4	12	0

National Football Conference

TEAM	WON	LOST	TIED	TEAM	WON	LOST	TIED
East Division				**South Division**			
Dallas[1]	13	3	0	Tampa Bay[1]	9	7	0
New York Giants[1]	10	6	0	Carolina	7	9	0
Washington[1]	9	7	0	New Orleans	7	9	0
Philadelphia	8	8	0	Atlanta	4	12	0
North Division				**West Division**			
Green Bay[1]	13	3	0	Seattle[1]	10	6	0
Minnesota	8	8	0	Arizona	8	8	0
Detroit	7	9	0	San Francisco	5	11	0
Chicago	7	9	0	St. Louis	3	13	0

[1]*Gained play-off berth.*

American Pro Football All-Time Records[1]

	PLAYERS/TEAMS	NUMBER	SEASON/DATE
Individual career records			
Total games	Morten Andersen	382	1982–2007, except 2005
Total points	Morten Andersen	2,544	1982–2007, except 2005
Touchdowns, total	Jerry Rice	208	1985–2004
Touchdowns, passing	Brett Favre	442	1991–2007
Touchdowns, receiving	Jerry Rice	197	1985–2004
Touchdowns, rushing	Emmitt Smith	164	1990–2004
Field goals made	Morten Andersen	565	1982–2007, except 2005
Extra points made (kicked)	George Blanda	943	1949–75, except 1959
Passing yardage	Brett Favre	61,655	1991–2007
Passing completions	Brett Favre	5,377	1991–2007
Receiving yardage	Jerry Rice	22,895	1985–2004
Rushing yardage	Emmitt Smith	18,355	1990–2004
Interceptions (defense)	Paul Krause	81	1964–79
Sacks (defense)[2]	Bruce Smith	200	1985–2003
Coaching, total wins	Don Shula	328	1963–95
Individual season records			
Total points	LaDainian Tomlinson	186	2006
Touchdowns, total	LaDainian Tomlinson	31	2006
Touchdowns, passing	Tom Brady	50	2007
Touchdowns, receiving	Randy Moss	23	2007
Touchdowns, rushing	LaDainian Tomlinson	28	2006
Field goals made	Neil Rackers	40	2005
Extra points made (kicked)	Stephen Gostkowski	74	2007
Passing yardage	Dan Marino	5,084	1984
Receiving yardage	Jerry Rice	1,848	1995
Rushing yardage	Eric Dickerson	2,105	1984

American Pro Football All-Time Records[1] (continued)

	PLAYERS/TEAMS	NUMBER	SEASON/DATE
Individual season records (continued)			
Interceptions (defense)	Dick Lane	14	1952
Sacks (defense)[2]	Michael Strahan	22.5	2001
Individual game records			
Total points	Ernie Nevers	40	28 Nov 1929
Touchdowns, total	Ernie Nevers; Dub Jones; Gale Sayers	6	28 Nov 1929; 25 Nov 1951; 12 Dec 1965
Touchdowns, passing	Sid Luckman; Adrian Burk; George Blanda; Y.A. Tittle; Joe Kapp	7	14 Nov 1943; 17 Oct 1954; 19 Nov 1961; 28 Oct 1962; 28 Sep 1969
Touchdowns, receiving	Bob Shaw; Kellen Winslow; Jerry Rice	5	2 Oct 1950; 22 Nov 1981; 14 Oct 1990
Touchdowns, rushing	Ernie Nevers	6	28 Nov 1929
Field goals made	Rob Bironas	8	21 Oct 2007
Longest field goal	Tom Dempsey; Jason Elam	63 yd	8 Nov 1970; 25 Oct 1998
Extra points made (kicked)	Pat Harder; Bob Waterfield; Charlie Gogolak	9	17 Oct 1948; 22 Oct 1950; 27 Nov 1966
Passing yardage	Norm Van Brocklin	554	28 Sep 1951
Receiving yardage	Willie Anderson	336	11 Nov 1989 (overtime)
Rushing yardage	Adrian Peterson	296	4 Nov 2007
Longest run from scrimmage	Tony Dorsett	99 yd	3 Jan 1983
Interceptions (defense)	*18 players hold record*	4	
Sacks (defense)[2]	Derrick Thomas	7	11 Nov 1990
Team season records			
League championships (including Super Bowls)	Green Bay Packers	12	
Super Bowl titles	Dallas Cowboys; San Francisco 49ers; Pittsburgh Steelers	5	
Consecutive Super Bowl titles	*7 teams hold record*	2	
Undefeated regular season	New England Patriots; Miami Dolphins; Chicago Bears	16 wins; 14 wins; 13 wins	2007; 1972; 1934
Total points scored	New England Patriots	589	2007
Touchdowns, total	New England Patriots	75	2007
Touchdowns, passing	Indianapolis Colts	51	2004
Touchdowns, rushing	Green Bay Packers	36	1962
Field goals made	Arizona Cardinals	43	2005
Passing yardage	St. Louis Rams	5,232	2000
Rushing yardage	New England Patriots	3,165	1978
Game records			
Highest score, one team	Washington Redskins	72	27 Nov 1966
Highest total score	Washington Redskins versus New York Giants	113 (72–41)	27 Nov 1966
Longest game	Miami Dolphins versus Kansas City Chiefs	82:40 (two overtimes)	25 Dec 1971

[1]*Through the 2007–08 season.* [2]*Since 1982; before that year sacks were not officially recorded by the NFL.*

Super Bowl

NFL-AFL championship 1966–70; NFL championship from 1970–71 season.

	SEASON	WINNER	RUNNER-UP	SCORE
I	1966–67	Green Bay Packers (NFL)	Kansas City Chiefs (AFL)	35–10
II	1967–68	Green Bay Packers (NFL)	Oakland Raiders (AFL)	33–14
III	1968–69	New York Jets (AFL)	Baltimore Colts (NFL)	16–7
IV	1969–70	Kansas City Chiefs (AFL)	Minnesota Vikings (NFL)	23–7

Super Bowl (continued)

V	1970–71	Baltimore Colts (AFC)	Dallas Cowboys (NFC)	16–13
VI	1971–72	Dallas Cowboys (NFC)	Miami Dolphins (AFC)	24–3
VII	1972–73	Miami Dolphins (AFC)	Washington Redskins (NFC)	14–7
VIII	1973–74	Miami Dolphins (AFC)	Minnesota Vikings (NFC)	24–7
IX	1974–75	Pittsburgh Steelers (AFC)	Minnesota Vikings (NFC)	16–6
X	1975–76	Pittsburgh Steelers (AFC)	Dallas Cowboys (NFC)	21–17
XI	1976–77	Oakland Raiders (AFC)	Minnesota Vikings (NFC)	32–14
XII	1977–78	Dallas Cowboys (NFC)	Denver Broncos (AFC)	27–10
XIII	1978–79	Pittsburgh Steelers (AFC)	Dallas Cowboys (NFC)	35–31
XIV	1979–80	Pittsburgh Steelers (AFC)	Los Angeles Rams (NFC)	31–19
XV	1980–81	Oakland Raiders (AFC)	Philadelphia Eagles (NFC)	27–10
XVI	1981–82	San Francisco 49ers (NFC)	Cincinnati Bengals (AFC)	26–21
XVII	1982–83	Washington Redskins (NFC)	Miami Dolphins (AFC)	27–17
XVIII	1983–84	Los Angeles Raiders (AFC)	Washington Redskins (NFC)	38–9
XIX	1984–85	San Francisco 49ers (NFC)	Miami Dolphins (AFC)	38–16
XX	1985–86	Chicago Bears (NFC)	New England Patriots (AFC)	46–10
XXI	1986–87	New York Giants (NFC)	Denver Broncos (AFC)	39–20
XXII	1987–88	Washington Redskins (NFC)	Denver Broncos (AFC)	42–10
XXIII	1988–89	San Francisco 49ers (NFC)	Cincinnati Bengals (AFC)	20–16
XXIV	1989–90	San Francisco 49ers (NFC)	Denver Broncos (AFC)	55–10
XXV	1990–91	New York Giants (NFC)	Buffalo Bills (AFC)	20–19
XXVI	1991–92	Washington Redskins (NFC)	Buffalo Bills (AFC)	37–24
XXVII	1992–93	Dallas Cowboys (NFC)	Buffalo Bills (AFC)	52–17
XXVIII	1993–94	Dallas Cowboys (NFC)	Buffalo Bills (AFC)	30–13
XXIX	1994–95	San Francisco 49ers (NFC)	San Diego Chargers (AFC)	49–26
XXX	1995–96	Dallas Cowboys (NFC)	Pittsburgh Steelers (AFC)	27–17
XXXI	1996–97	Green Bay Packers (NFC)	New England Patriots (AFC)	35–21
XXXII	1997–98	Denver Broncos (AFC)	Green Bay Packers (NFC)	31–24
XXXIII	1998–99	Denver Broncos (AFC)	Atlanta Falcons (NFC)	34–19
XXXIV	1999–2000	St. Louis Rams (NFC)	Tennessee Titans (AFC)	23–16
XXXV	2000–01	Baltimore Ravens (AFC)	New York Giants (NFC)	34–7
XXXVI	2001–02	New England Patriots (AFC)	St. Louis Rams (NFC)	20–17
XXXVII	2002–03	Tampa Bay Buccaneers (NFC)	Oakland Raiders (AFC)	48–21
XXXVIII	2003–04	New England Patriots (AFC)	Carolina Panthers (NFC)	32–29
XXXIX	2004–05	New England Patriots (AFC)	Philadelphia Eagles (NFC)	24–21
XL	2005–06	Pittsburgh Steelers (AFC)	Seattle Seahawks (NFC)	21–10
LXI	2006–07	Indianapolis Colts (AFC)	Chicago Bears (NFC)	29–17
LXII	2007–08	New York Giants (NFC)	New England Patriots (AFC)	17–14

College Football National Champions

SEASON	CHAMPION
1924–25	Notre Dame
1925–26	Dartmouth
1926–27	Stanford
1927–28	Illinois
1928–29	USC
1929–30	Notre Dame
1930–31	Notre Dame
1931–32	USC
1932–33	Michigan
1933–34	Michigan
1934–35	Minnesota
1935–36	Southern Methodist
1936–37	Minnesota
1937–38	Pittsburgh
1938–39	Texas Christian
1939–40	Texas A&M
1940–41	Minnesota
1941–42	Minnesota
1942–43	Ohio State
1943–44	Notre Dame
1944–45	Army
1945–46	Army
1946–47	Notre Dame
1947–48	Notre Dame
1948–49	Michigan
1949–50	Notre Dame

SEASON	CHAMPION
1950–51	Oklahoma
1951–52	Tennessee
1952–53	Michigan State
1953–54	Maryland
1954–55	Ohio State (AP); UCLA (UP)
1955–56	Oklahoma
1956–57	Oklahoma
1957–58	Auburn (AP); Ohio State (UP)
1958–59	Louisiana State
1959–60	Syracuse
1960–61	Minnesota
1961–62	Alabama
1962–63	USC
1963–64	Texas
1964–65	Alabama
1965–66	Alabama (AP); Michigan State (UPI)
1966–67	Notre Dame
1967–68	USC
1968–69	Ohio State
1969–70	Texas
1970–71	Nebraska (AP); Texas (UPI)
1971–72	Nebraska

SEASON	CHAMPION
1972–73	USC
1973–74	Notre Dame (AP); Alabama (UPI)
1974–75	Oklahoma (AP); USC (UPI)
1975–76	Oklahoma
1976–77	Pittsburgh
1977–78	Notre Dame
1978–79	Alabama (AP); USC (UPI)
1979–80	Alabama
1980–81	Georgia
1981–82	Clemson
1982–83	Penn State
1983–84	Miami (FL)
1984–85	Brigham Young
1985–86	Oklahoma
1986–87	Penn State
1987–88	Miami (FL)
1988–89	Notre Dame
1989–90	Miami (FL)
1990–91	Colorado (AP); Georgia Tech (UPI)
1991–92	Miami (FL) (AP); Washington (UPI)
1992–93	Alabama

College Football National Champions (continued)

SEASON	CHAMPION	SEASON	CHAMPION	SEASON	CHAMPION
1993–94	Florida State	1998–99	Tennessee	2004–05	USC
1994–95	Nebraska	1999–2000	Florida State	2005–06	Texas
1995–96	Nebraska	2000–01	Oklahoma	2006–07	Florida
1996–97	Florida	2001–02	Miami (FL)	2007–08	Louisiana State
1997–98	Michigan (AP); Nebraska (*USA Today*/ESPN)	2002–03	Ohio State		
		2003–04	Louisiana State (BCS); USC (AP)		

Rose Bowl

SEASON	WINNER	RUNNER-UP	SCORE	SEASON	WINNER	RUNNER-UP	SCORE
1901–02	Michigan	Stanford	49–0	1961–62	Minnesota	UCLA	21–3
1915–16	Washington State	Brown	14–0	1962–63	USC	Wisconsin	42–37
				1963–64	Illinois	Washington	17–7
1916–17	Oregon	Pennsylvania	14–0	1964–65	Michigan	Oregon State	34–7
1917–18	Mare Island[1]	Camp Lewis[2]	19–7	1965–66	UCLA	Michigan State	14–12
1918–19	Great Lakes[3]	Mare Island[1]	17–0				
1919–20	Harvard	Oregon	7–6	1966–67	Purdue	USC	14–13
1920–21	California	Ohio State	28–0	1967–68	USC	Indiana	14–3
1921–22	California	Washington and Jefferson	0–0	1968–69	Ohio State	USC	27–16
				1969–70	USC	Michigan	10–3
1922–23	USC	Penn State	14–3	1970–71	Stanford	Ohio State	27–17
1923–24	Washington	Navy	14–14	1971–72	Stanford	Michigan	13–12
1924–25	Notre Dame	Stanford	27–10	1972–73	USC	Ohio State	42–17
1925–26	Alabama	Washington	20–19	1973–74	Ohio State	USC	42–21
1926–27	Alabama	Stanford	7–7	1974–75	USC	Ohio State	18–17
1927–28	Stanford	Pittsburgh	7–6	1975–76	UCLA	Ohio State	23–10
1928–29	Georgia Tech	California	8–7	1976–77	USC	Michigan	14–6
1929–30	USC	Pittsburgh	47–14	1977–78	Washington	Michigan	27–20
1930–31	Alabama	Washington State	24–0	1978–79	USC	Michigan	17–10
				1979–80	USC	Ohio State	17–16
1931–32	USC	Tulane	21–12	1980–81	Michigan	Washington	23–6
1932–33	USC	Pittsburgh	35–0	1981–82	Washington	Iowa	28–0
1933–34	Columbia	Stanford	7–0	1982–83	UCLA	Michigan	24–14
1934–35	Alabama	Stanford	29–13	1983–84	UCLA	Illinois	45–9
1935–36	Stanford	Southern Methodist	7–0	1984–85	USC	Ohio State	20–17
				1985–86	UCLA	Iowa	45–28
1936–37	Pittsburgh	Washington	21–0	1986–87	Arizona State	Michigan	22–15
1937–38	California	Alabama	13–0	1987–88	Michigan State	USC	20–17
1938–39	USC	Duke	7–3				
1939–40	USC	Tennessee	14–0	1988–89	Michigan	USC	22–14
1940–41	Stanford	Nebraska	21–13	1989–90	USC	Michigan	17–10
1941–42	Oregon State	Duke	20–16	1990–91	Washington	Iowa	46–34
1942–43	Georgia	UCLA	9–0	1991–92	Washington	Michigan	34–14
1943–44	USC	Washington	29–0	1992–93	Michigan	Washington	38–31
1944–45	USC	Tennessee	25–0	1993–94	Wisconsin	UCLA	21–16
1945–46	Alabama	USC	34–14	1994–95	Penn State	Oregon	38–20
1946–47	Illinois	UCLA	45–14	1995–96	USC	Northwestern	41–32
1947–48	Michigan	USC	49–0	1996–97	Ohio State	Arizona State	20–17
1948–49	Northwestern	California	20–14	1997–98	Michigan	Washington State	21–16
1949–50	Ohio State	California	17–14				
1950–51	Michigan	California	14–6	1998–99	Wisconsin	UCLA	38–31
1951–52	Illinois	Stanford	40–7	1999–2000	Wisconsin	Stanford	17–9
1952–53	USC	Wisconsin	7–0	2000–01	Washington	Purdue	34–24
1953–54	Michigan State	UCLA	28–20	2001–02	Miami (FL)	Nebraska	37–14
1954–55	Ohio State	USC	20–7	2002–03	Oklahoma	Washington State	34–14
1955–56	Michigan State	UCLA	17–14				
1956–57	Iowa	Oregon State	35–19	2003–04	USC	Michigan	28–14
1957–58	Ohio State	Oregon	10–7	2004–05	Texas	Michigan	38–37
1958–59	Iowa	California	38–12	2005–06	Texas	USC	41–38
1959–60	Washington	Wisconsin	44–8	2006–07	USC	Michigan	32–18
1960–61	Washington	Minnesota	17–7	2007–08	USC	Illinois	49–17

[1]*US Marine Corps team.* [2]*US Army team.* [3]*US Navy team.*

Orange Bowl

SEASON	WINNER	RUNNER-UP	SCORE
1934–35	Bucknell	Miami (FL)	26–0
1935–36	Catholic	Mississippi	20–19
1936–37	Duquesne	Mississippi State	13–12
1937–38	Auburn	Michigan State	6–0
1938–39	Tennessee	Oklahoma	17–0
1939–40	Georgia Tech	Missouri	21–7
1940–41	Mississippi State	Georgetown	14–7
1941–42	Georgia	Texas Christian	40–26
1942–43	Alabama	Boston College	37–21
1943–44	Louisiana State	Texas A&M	19–14
1944–45	Tulsa	Georgia Tech	26–12
1945–46	Miami (FL)	Holy Cross	13–6
1946–47	Rice	Tennessee	8–0
1947–48	Georgia Tech	Kansas	20–14
1948–49	Texas	Georgia	41–28
1949–50	Santa Clara	Kentucky	21–13
1950–51	Clemson	Miami (FL)	15–14
1951–52	Georgia Tech	Baylor	17–14
1952–53	Alabama	Syracuse	61–6
1953–54	Oklahoma	Maryland	7–0
1954–55	Duke	Nebraska	34–7
1955–56	Oklahoma	Maryland	20–6
1956–57	Colorado	Clemson	27–21
1957–58	Oklahoma	Duke	48–21
1958–59	Oklahoma	Syracuse	21–6
1959–60	Georgia	Missouri	14–0
1960–61	Missouri	Navy	21–14
1961–62	Louisiana State	Colorado	25–7
1962–63	Alabama	Oklahoma	17–0
1963–64	Nebraska	Auburn	13–7
1964–65	Texas	Alabama	21–17
1965–66	Alabama	Nebraska	39–28
1966–67	Florida	Georgia Tech	27–12
1967–68	Oklahoma	Tennessee	26–24
1968–69	Penn State	Kansas	15–14
1969–70	Penn State	Missouri	10–3
1970–71	Nebraska	Louisiana State	17–12
1971–72	Nebraska	Alabama	38–6
1972–73	Nebraska	Notre Dame	40–6
1973–74	Penn State	Louisiana State	16–9
1974–75	Notre Dame	Alabama	13–11
1975–76	Oklahoma	Michigan	14–6
1976–77	Ohio State	Colorado	27–10
1977–78	Arkansas	Oklahoma	31–6
1978–79	Oklahoma	Nebraska	31–24
1979–80	Oklahoma	Florida State	24–7
1980–81	Oklahoma	Florida State	18–17
1981–82	Clemson	Nebraska	22–15
1982–83	Nebraska	Louisiana State	21–20
1983–84	Miami (FL)	Nebraska	31–30
1984–85	Washington	Oklahoma	28–17
1985–86	Oklahoma	Penn State	25–10
1986–87	Oklahoma	Arkansas	42–8
1987–88	Miami (FL)	Oklahoma	20–14
1988–89	Miami (FL)	Nebraska	23–3
1989–90	Notre Dame	Colorado	21–6
1990–91	Colorado	Notre Dame	10–9
1991–92	Miami (FL)	Nebraska	22–0
1992–93	Florida State	Nebraska	27–14
1993–94	Florida State	Nebraska	18–16
1994–95	Nebraska	Miami	24–17
1995–96	Florida State	Notre Dame	31–26
1996–97	Nebraska	Virginia Tech	41–21
1997–98	Nebraska	Tennessee	42–17
1998–99	Florida	Syracuse	31–10
1999–2000	Michigan	Alabama	35–34
2000–01	Oklahoma	Florida State	13–2
2001–02	Florida	Maryland	56–23
2002–03	USC	Iowa	38–17
2003–04	Miami (FL)	Florida State	16–14
2004–05	USC	Oklahoma	55–19
2005–06	Penn State	Florida State	26–23
2006–07	Louisville	Wake Forest	24–13
2007–08	Kansas	Virginia Tech	24–21

Sugar Bowl

SEASON	WINNER	RUNNER-UP	SCORE
1934–35	Tulane	Temple	20–14
1935–36	Texas Christian	Louisiana State	3–2
1936–37	Santa Clara	Louisiana State	21–14
1937–38	Santa Clara	Louisiana State	6–0
1938–39	Texas Christian	Carnegie Tech	15–7
1939–40	Texas A&M	Tulane	14–13
1940–41	Boston College	Tennessee	19–13
1941–42	Fordham	Missouri	2–0
1942–43	Tennessee	Tulsa	14–7
1943–44	Georgia Tech	Tulsa	20–18
1944–45	Duke	Alabama	29–26
1945–46	Oklahoma A&M	St. Mary's (CA)	33–13
1946–47	Georgia	North Carolina	20–10
1947–48	Texas	Alabama	27–7
1948–49	Oklahoma	North Carolina	14–6
1949–50	Oklahoma	Louisiana State	35–0
1950–51	Kentucky	Oklahoma	13–7
1951–52	Maryland	Tennessee	28–13
1952–53	Georgia Tech	Mississippi	24–7
1953–54	Georgia Tech	West Virginia	42–19
1954–55	Navy	Mississippi	21–0
1955–56	Georgia Tech	Pittsburgh	7–0
1956–57	Baylor	Tennessee	13–7
1957–58	Mississippi	Texas	39–7
1958–59	Louisiana State	Clemson	7–0
1959–60	Mississippi	Louisiana State	21–0
1960–61	Mississippi	Rice	14–6
1961–62	Alabama	Arkansas	10–3
1962–63	Mississippi	Arkansas	17–13
1963–64	Alabama	Mississippi	12–7
1964–65	Louisiana State	Syracuse	13–10
1965–66	Missouri	Florida	20–18
1966–67	Alabama	Nebraska	34–7
1967–68	Louisiana State	Wyoming	20–13
1968–69	Arkansas	Georgia	16–2
1969–70	Mississippi	Arkansas	27–22
1970–71	Tennessee	Air Force	34–13
1971–72	Oklahoma	Auburn	40–22
1972–73	Oklahoma	Penn State	14–0
1973–74	Notre Dame	Alabama	24–23
1974–75	Nebraska	Florida	13–10
1975–76	Alabama	Penn State	13–6
1976–77	Pittsburgh	Georgia	27–3
1977–78	Alabama	Ohio State	35–6
1978–79	Alabama	Penn State	14–7
1979–80	Alabama	Arkansas	24–9
1980–81	Georgia	Notre Dame	17–10
1981–82	Pittsburgh	Georgia	24–20

Sugar Bowl (continued)

SEASON	WINNER	RUNNER-UP	SCORE
1982–83	Penn State	Georgia	27–23
1983–84	Auburn	Michigan	9–7
1984–85	Nebraska	Louisiana State	28–10
1985–86	Tennessee	Miami (FL)	35–7
1986–87	Nebraska	Louisiana State	30–15
1987–88	Auburn	Syracuse	16–16
1988–89	Florida State	Auburn	13–7
1989–90	Miami (FL)	Alabama	33–25
1990–91	Tennessee	Virginia	23–22
1991–92	Notre Dame	Florida	39–28
1992–93	Alabama	Miami (FL)	34–13
1993–94	Florida	West Virginia	41–7
1994–95	Florida State	Florida	23–17
1995–96	Virginia Tech	Texas	28–10
1996–97	Florida	Florida State	52–20
1997–98	Florida State	Ohio State	31–14
1998–99	Ohio State	Texas A&M	24–14
1999–2000	Florida State	Virginia Tech	46–29
2000–01	Miami (FL)	Florida	37–20
2001–02	Louisiana State	Illinois	47–34
2002–03	Georgia	Florida State	26–13
2003–04	Louisiana State	Oklahoma	21–14
2004–05	Auburn	Virginia Tech	16–13
2005–06	West Virginia	Georgia	38–35
2006–07	Louisiana State	Notre Dame	41–14
2007–08	Georgia	Hawaii	41–10

Fiesta Bowl

SEASON	WINNER	RUNNER-UP	SCORE
1971–72	Arizona State	Florida State	45–38
1972–73	Arizona State	Missouri	49–35
1973–74	Arizona State	Pittsburgh	28–7
1974–75	Oklahoma State	Brigham Young	16–6
1975–76	Arizona State	Nebraska	17–14
1976–77	Oklahoma	Wyoming	41–7
1977–78	Penn State	Arizona State	42–30
1978–79	Arkansas	UCLA	10–10
1979–80	Pittsburgh	Arizona	16–10
1980–81	Penn State	Ohio State	31–19
1981–82	Penn State	USC	26–10
1982–83	Arizona State	Oklahoma	32–21
1983–84	Ohio State	Pittsburgh	28–23
1984–85	UCLA	Miami (FL)	39–37
1985–86	Michigan	Nebraska	27–23
1986–87	Penn State	Miami (FL)	14–10
1987–88	Florida State	Nebraska	31–28
1988–89	Notre Dame	West Virginia	34–21
1989–90	Florida State	Nebraska	41–17
1990–91	Louisville	Alabama	34–7
1991–92	Penn State	Tennessee	42–17
1992–93	Syracuse	Colorado	26–22
1993–94	Arizona	Miami (FL)	29–0
1994–95	Colorado	Notre Dame	41–24
1995–96	Nebraska	Florida	62–24
1996–97	Penn State	Texas	38–15
1997–98	Kansas State	Syracuse	35–18
1998–99	Tennessee	Florida State	23–16
1999–2000	Nebraska	Tennessee	31–21
2000–01	Oregon State	Notre Dame	41–9
2001–02	Oregon	Colorado	38–16
2002–03	Ohio State	Miami (FL)	31–24
2003–04	Ohio State	Kansas State	35–28
2004–05	Utah	Pittsburgh	35–7
2005–06	Ohio State	Notre Dame	34–20
2006–07	Boise State	Oklahoma	43–42
2007–08	West Virginia	Oklahoma	48–28

Heisman Trophy Winners

The Heisman Trophy is named for John Heisman, a director of the Downtown Athletic Club (DAC) in New York City who died in 1936. The trophy goes to an outstanding college football player at the end of the football season each year. A committee composed of DAC members, members of the media, and representatives from each of the 50 states cast ballots to determine the winner. Web site: <www.heisman.com>.

YEAR	WINNER	COLLEGE	POSITION
1935	Jay Berwanger	Chicago	HB
1936	Larry Kelley	Yale	E
1937	Clint Frank	Yale	HB
1938	Davey O'Brien	Texas Christian	QB
1939	Nile Kinnick	Iowa	HB
1940	Tom Harmon	Michigan	HB
1941	Bruce Smith	Minnesota	HB
1942	Frank Sinkwich	Georgia	HB
1943	Angelo Bertelli	Notre Dame	HB
1944	Les Horvath	Ohio State	QB
1945	Felix Blanchard	Army	FB
1946	Glenn Davis	Army	HB
1947	John Lujack	Notre Dame	QB
1948	Doak Walker	Southern Methodist	HB
1949	Leon Hart	Notre Dame	E
1950	Vic Janowicz	Ohio State	HB
1951	Dick Kazmaier	Princeton	HB
1952	Billy Vessels	Oklahoma	HB
1953	John Lattner	Notre Dame	HB
1954	Alan Ameche	Wisconsin	FB
1955	Howard Cassady	Ohio State	HB
1956	Paul Hornung	Notre Dame	QB
1957	John David Crow	Texas A&M	HB
1958	Pete Dawkins	Army	HB
1959	Billy Cannon	Louisiana State	HB
1960	Joe Bellino	Navy	HB
1961	Ernie Davis	Syracuse	HB
1962	Terry Baker	Oregon State	QB
1963	Roger Staubach	Navy	QB
1964	John Huarte	Notre Dame	QB
1965	Mike Garrett	USC	HB
1966	Steve Spurrier	Florida	QB
1967	Gary Beban	UCLA	QB
1968	O.J. Simpson	USC	HB
1969	Steve Owens	Oklahoma	HB
1970	Jim Plunkett	Stanford	QB
1971	Pat Sullivan	Auburn	QB
1972	Johnny Rodgers	Nebraska	WR

Heisman Trophy Winners (continued)

YEAR	WINNER	COLLEGE	POSITION
1973	John Cappelletti	Penn State	HB
1974	Archie Griffin	Ohio State	HB
1975	Archie Griffin	Ohio State	HB
1976	Tony Dorsett	Pittsburgh	HB
1977	Earl Campbell	Texas	HB
1978	Billy Sims	Oklahoma	HB
1979	Charles White	USC	HB
1980	George Rogers	South Carolina	HB
1981	Marcus Allen	USC	HB
1982	Herschel Walker	Georgia	HB
1983	Mike Rozier	Nebraska	HB
1984	Doug Flutie	Boston College	QB
1985	Bo Jackson	Auburn	HB
1986	Vinny Testaverde	Miami (FL)	QB
1987	Tim Brown	Notre Dame	WR
1988	Barry Sanders	Oklahoma State	RB
1989	Andre Ware	Houston	QB
1990	Ty Detmer	Brigham Young	QB
1991	Desmond Howard	Michigan	WR
1992	Gino Torretta	Miami	QB
1993	Charlie Ward	Florida State	QB
1994	Rashaan Salaam	Colorado	TB
1995	Eddie George	Ohio State	RB
1996	Danny Wuerffel	Florida	QB
1997	Charles Woodson	Michigan	DB
1998	Ricky Williams	Texas	RB
1999	Ron Dayne	Wisconsin	RB
2000	Chris Weinke	Florida State	QB
2001	Eric Crouch	Nebraska	QB
2002	Carson Palmer	USC	QB
2003	Jason White	Oklahoma	QB
2004	Matt Leinart	USC	QB
2005	Reggie Bush	USC	RB
2006	Troy Smith	Ohio State	QB
2007	Tim Tebow	Florida	QB

Canadian Football League Grey Cup

Held since 1909. Table shows results for past 20 years.

YEAR	WINNER	RUNNER-UP	SCORE
1988	Winnipeg Blue Bombers (ED)	British Columbia Lions (WD)	22–21
1989	Saskatchewan Roughriders (WD)	Hamilton Tiger-Cats (ED)	43–40
1990	Winnipeg Blue Bombers (ED)	Edmonton Eskimos (WD)	50–11
1991	Toronto Argonauts (ED)	Calgary Stampeders (WD)	36–21
1992	Calgary Stampeders (WD)	Winnipeg Blue Bombers (ED)	24–10
1993	Edmonton Eskimos (WD)	Winnipeg Blue Bombers (ED)	33–23
1994	British Columbia Lions (WD)	Baltimore Stallions (ED)	26–23
1995[1]	Baltimore Stallions (SD)	Calgary Stampeders (ND)	37–20
1996	Toronto Argonauts (ED)	Edmonton Eskimos (WD)	43–37
1997	Toronto Argonauts (ED)	Saskatchewan Roughriders (WD)	47–23
1998	Calgary Stampeders (WD)	Hamilton Tiger-Cats (ED)	26–24
1999	Hamilton Tiger-Cats (ED)	Calgary Stampeders (WD)	32–21
2000	British Columbia Lions (WD)	Montreal Alouettes (ED)	28–26
2001	Calgary Stampeders (WD)	Winnipeg Blue Bombers (ED)	27–19
2002	Montreal Alouettes (ED)	Edmonton Eskimos (WD)	25–16
2003	Edmonton Eskimos (WD)	Montreal Alouettes (ED)	34–22
2004	Toronto Argonauts (ED)	British Columbia Lions (WD)	27–19
2005	Edmonton Eskimos (WD)	Montreal Alouettes (ED)	38–35
2006	British Columbia Lions (WD)	Montreal Alouettes (ED)	25–14
2007	Saskatchewan Roughriders (WD)	Winnipeg Blue Bombers (ED)	23–19

[1]*In 1995 only, the divisions were reconfigured and renamed Northern and Southern in response to the inclusion of American teams in the CFL (1993–96).*

Australian Football League Final Standings, 2007[1]

Teams that qualified for play-offs only.

TEAM	WON	LOST	TIED	POINTS
Geelong Cats	18	4	0	72
Port Adelaide Power	15	7	0	60
West Coast Eagles	15	7	0	60
North Melbourne Kangaroos	14	8	0	56
Hawthorn Hawks	13	9	0	52
Collingwood Magpies	13	9	0	52
Sydney Swans	12	9	1	50
Adelaide Crows	12	10	0	48

[1]*The Geelong Cats were the 2007 champions.*

Rugby World Cup

YEAR	WINNER	RUNNER-UP	SCORE
1987	New Zealand	France	29–9
1991	Australia	England	12–6
1995	South Africa	New Zealand	15–12
1999	Australia	France	35–12
2003	England	Australia	20–17
2007	South Africa	England	15–6

Rugby League World Cup

YEAR	WINNER	RUNNER-UP	SCORE
1954	Great Britain	France	16–12
1957	Australia	Great Britain	29–21
1960	Great Britain	Australia	66–37
1968	Australia	France	20–2
1970	Australia	Great Britain	12–7
1972	Great Britain	Australia	10–10[1]
1975[2]	Australia[3]		
1977[2]	Australia	Great Britain	13–12
1988	Australia	New Zealand	25–12
1992	Australia	Great Britain	10–6
1995	Australia	England	16–8
2000	Australia	New Zealand	40–12

[1]Great Britain won on match points. [2]Called International Championship from 1975 to 1977. [3]Championships played without a grand final match; England was the runner-up.

Super 14 Rugby Final Standings, 2008[1]

Super 12 until 2006. Four points are awarded for a win and two for a draw; one bonus point is given for a loss by seven points or fewer and one for a team that scores four or more tries.

TEAMS (COUNTRY)	POINTS	W	L	D	BONUS
Crusaders (NZL)	52	11	2	0	8
New South Wales Waratahs (AUS)	43	9	3	1	5
Sharks (RSA)	42	9	3	1	4
Hurricanes (NZL)	41	8	4	1	7
Stormers (RSA)	41	8	4	1	7
Blues (NZL)	40	8	5	0	8
Chiefs (NZL)	34	7	6	0	6
Western Force (AUS)	33	7	6	0	5
Brumbies (AUS)	30	6	7	0	6
Bulls (RSA)	28	6	7	0	4
Highlanders (NZL)	19	3	10	0	7
Queensland Reds (AUS)	18	3	9	1	4
Central Cheetahs (RSA)	13	1	12	0	9
Lions (RSA)	12	2	10	1	2

[1]The Bulls were the 2008 champions.

Six Nations Championship

Five Nations until 2000. Round-robin tournament, usually ending in April.

YEAR	WINNER
1947	England, Ireland[1]
1948	Ireland[2,3]
1949	Ireland[2]
1950	Wales[2,3]
1951	France, Ireland, Wales
1952	Wales[2,3]
1953	England
1954	England[2], France, Wales[1]
1955	France, Wales[1]
1956	Wales
1957	England[2,3]
1958	England
1959	France
1960	England[2], France[1]
1961	France
1962	France
1963	England
1964	Wales
1965	France, Ireland
1966	France
1967	France
1968	France[3]
1969	Wales[2]
1970	France, Wales[1]
1971	Wales[2,3]
1972	*not completed*
1973	*quintuple tie*
1974	Ireland
1975	Wales
1976	Wales[2,3]
1977	France[3,4]
1978	Wales[2,3]
1979	Wales[2]
1980	England[2,3]
1981	France[3]
1982	Ireland[2]
1983	France, Ireland[1]
1984	Scotland[2,3]
1985	Ireland[2]
1986	France, Scotland[1]
1987	France[3]
1988	France, Wales[1,2]
1989	France
1990	Scotland[2,3]
1991	England[2,3]
1992	England[2,3]
1993	France
1994	Wales
1995	England[2,3]
1996	England[2]
1997	France[3,5]
1998	France[3,5]
1999	Scotland
2000	England
2001	England
2002	France[3,5]
2003	England[2,3]
2004	France[3,6]
2005	Wales[2,3]
2006	France[6]
2007	France[6]
2008	Wales[2,3]

[1]Tied. [2]Triple Crown (all three matches, excluding France and Italy) winner. [3]Grand Slam (all matches) winner. [4]Triple Crown won by Wales. [5]Triple Crown won by England. [6]Triple Crown won by Ireland.

FIFA World Cup—Men

YEAR	WINNER	RUNNER-UP	SCORE
1930	Uruguay	Argentina	4–2
1934	Italy	Czechoslovakia	2–1
1938	Italy	Hungary	4–2
1950	Uruguay	Brazil	2–1
1954	West Germany	Hungary	3–2
1958	Brazil	Sweden	5–2
1962	Brazil	Czechoslovakia	3–1
1966	England	West Germany	4–2
1970	Brazil	Italy	4–1
1974	West Germany	The Netherlands	2–1
1978	Argentina	The Netherlands	3–1
1982	Italy	West Germany	3–1

FIFA World Cup—Men (continued)

YEAR	WINNER	RUNNER-UP	SCORE	YEAR	WINNER	RUNNER-UP	SCORE
1986	Argentina	West Germany	3–2	1998	France	Brazil	3–0
1990	West Germany	Argentina	1–0	2002	Brazil	Germany	2–0
1994	Brazil	Italy	0–0 (3–2[1])	2006	Italy	France	1–1 (5–3[1])

[1]*Won in a penalty kick shoot-out.*

FIFA World Cup—Women

YEAR	WINNER	RUNNER-UP	SCORE	YEAR	WINNER	RUNNER-UP	SCORE
1991	United States	Norway	2–1	2003	Germany	Sweden	2–1
1995	Norway	Germany	2–0	2007	Germany	Brazil	2–0
1999	United States	China	0–0 (5–4[1])				

[1]*Won in a penalty kick shoot-out.*

UEFA Champions League

Known until 1992–93 as the European Champion Clubs' Cup; played on a knockout basis until 1992–93 and as a combination of group and knockout rounds since then. The competition has been held since 1955; table shows results for the past 20 years.

SEASON	WINNING TEAM (COUNTRY)	RUNNER-UP (COUNTRY)	SCORE
1988–89	AC Milan (ITA)	FC Steaua Bucuresti (ROM)	4–0
1989–90	AC Milan (ITA)	SL Benfica (POR)	1–0
1990–91	FK Crvena Zvezda Beograd (YUG)	Olympique de Marseille (FRA)	0–0 (5–3[1])
1991–92	FC Barcelona (ESP)	Sampdoria UC (ITA)	1–0
1992–93	Olympique de Marseille (FRA)	AC Milan (ITA)	1–0
1993–94	AC Milan (ITA)	FC Barcelona (ESP)	4–0
1994–95	AFC Ajax (NED)	AC Milan (ITA)	1–0
1995–96	Juventus FC (ITA)	AFC Ajax (NED)	1–1 (4–2[1])
1996–97	BV Borussia Dortmund (GER)	Juventus FC (ITA)	3–1
1997–98	Real Madrid CF (ESP)	Juventus FC (ITA)	1–0
1998–99	Manchester United (ENG)	FC Bayern München (GER)	2–1
1999–2000	Real Madrid CF (ESP)	Valencia CF (ESP)	3–0
2000–01	FC Bayern München (GER)	Valencia CF (ESP)	1–1 (5–4[1])
2001–02	Real Madrid CF (ESP)	Bayer 04 Leverkusen (GER)	2–1
2002–03	AC Milan (ITA)	Juventus FC (ITA)	0–0 (3–2[1])
2003–04	FC Porto (POR)	AS Monaco (FRA)	3–0
2004–05	Liverpool FC (ENG)	AC Milan (ITA)	3–3 (3–2[1])
2005–06	FC Barcelona (ESP)	Arsenal FC (ENG)	2–1
2006–07	AC Milan (ITA)	Liverpool FC (ENG)	2–1
2007–08	Manchester United (ENG)	Chelsea FC (ENG)	1–1 (6–5[1])

[1]*Won in a penalty kick shoot-out.*

UEFA European Championship

YEAR	WINNING TEAM	RUNNER-UP	SCORE
1960	USSR	Yugoslavia	2–1
1964	Spain	USSR	2–1
1968	Italy	Yugoslavia	2–0
1972	West Germany	USSR	3–0
1976	Czechoslovakia	West Germany	2–2
1980	West Germany	Belgium	2–1
1984	France	Spain	2–0
1988	The Netherlands	USSR	2–0
1992	Denmark	Germany	2–0
1996	Germany	Czech Republic	2–1
2000	France	Italy	2–1
2004	Greece	Portugal	1–0
2008	Spain	Germany	1–0

UEFA Cup

The UEFA Cup is considered Europe's second most important football competition. Established in the 1971–72 season, the Cup was restructured after the UEFA Cup Winners' Cup was abolished in 1998–99. Originally played on an entirely two-legged basis, since 1998 the competition has concluded with a single match. The Cup competition is open to top- and second-ranked teams in each country's league as well as winners of domestic cups.

SEASON	WINNING TEAM (COUNTRY)	RUNNER-UP (COUNTRY)	SCORE
1971–72	Tottenham Hotspur FC (ENG)	Wolverhampton Wanderers FC (ENG)	2–1, 1–1
1972–73	Liverpool FC (ENG)	VfL Borussia Mönchengladbach (FRG)	3–0, 0–2
1973–74	Feyenoord (NED)	Tottenham Hotspur FC (ENG)	2–2, 2–0
1974–75	VfL Borussia Mönchengladbach (FRG)	FC Twente (NED)	0–0, 5–1
1975–76	Liverpool FC (ENG)	Club Brugge KV (BEL)	3–2, 1–1
1976–77	Juventus FC (ITA)	Athletic Club Bilbao (ESP)	1–0, 1–2
1977–78	PSV Eindhoven (NED)	SC Bastia (FRA)	0–0, 3–0
1978–79	VfL Borussia Mönchengladbach (FRG)	FK Crvena Zvezda Beograd (YUG)	1–1, 1–0
1979–80	Eintracht Frankfurt (FRG)	VfL Borussia Mönchengladbach (FRG)	2–3, 1–0
1980–81	Ipswich Town FC (ENG)	AZ Alkmaar (NED)	3–0, 2–4
1981–82	IFK Göteborg (SWE)	Hamburger SV (FRG)	1–0, 3–0
1982–83	RSC Anderlecht (BEL)	SL Benfica (POR)	1–0, 1–1
1983–84	Tottenham Hotspur FC (ENG)	RSC Anderlecht (BEL)	1–1, 1–1 (4–3[1])
1984–85	Real Madrid CF (ESP)	Videoton FCF (HUN)	3–0, 0–1
1985–86	Real Madrid CF (ESP)	1. FC Köln (FRG)	5–1, 0–2
1986–87	IFK Göteborg (SWE)	Dundee United FC (SCO)	1–0, 1–1
1987–88	Bayer 04 Leverkusen (FRG)	RCD Espanyol (ESP)	0–3, 3–0 (3–2[1])
1988–89	SSC Napoli (ITA)	VfB Stuttgart (FRG)	2–1, 3–3
1989–90	Juventus FC (ITA)	AC Fiorentina (ITA)	3–1, 0–0
1990–91	Internazionale FC (ITA)	AS Roma (ITA)	2–0, 0–1
1991–92	AFC Ajax (NED)	Torino Calcio (ITA)	2–2, 0–0
1992–93	Juventus FC (ITA)	BV Borussia Dortmund (GER)	3–1, 3–0
1993–94	Internazionale FC (ITA)	SV Austria Salzburg (AUT)	1–0, 1–0
1994–95	Parma AC (ITA)	Juventus FC (ITA)	1–0, 1–1
1995–96	FC Bayern München (GER)	FC Girondins de Bordeaux (FRA)	2–0, 3–1
1996–97	FC Schalke 04 (GER)	Internazionale FC (ITA)	1–0, 0–1 (4–1[1])
1997–98	Internazionale FC (ITA)	SS Lazio (ITA)	3–0
1998–99	Parma AC (ITA)	Olympique de Marseille (FRA)	3–0
1999–2000	Galatasaray SK (TUR)	Arsenal FC (ENG)	0–0 (4–1[1])
2000–01	Liverpool FC (ENG)	Deportivo Alavés (ESP)	5–4
2001–02	Feyenoord (NED)	BV Borussia Dortmund (GER)	3–2
2002–03	FC Porto (POR)	Celtic FC (SCO)	3–2[2]
2003–04	Valencia CF (ESP)	Olympique de Marseille (FRA)	2–0
2004–05	CSKA Moscow (RUS)	Sporting (POR)	3–1
2005–06	Sevilla FC (ESP)	Middlesbrough FC (ENG)	4–0
2006–07	Sevilla FC (ESP)	RCD Espanyol (ESP)	2–2 (3–1[1])
2007–08	FC Zenit St. Petersburg (RUS)	Rangers FC (SCO)	2–0

[1]*Won in a penalty kick shoot-out.* [2]*Won on "silver goal" in overtime.*

Copa Libertadores de América

Held since 1960. Table shows results for the past 20 years.

YEAR	WINNER (COUNTRY)	RUNNER-UP (COUNTRY)	SCORES
1989	Atlético Nacional (COL)	Olímpia (PAR)	0–2, 2–0 (5–4[1])
1990	Olímpia (PAR)	Barcelona (ECU)	2–0, 1–1
1991	Colo Colo (CHI)	Olímpia (PAR)	0–0, 3–0
1992	São Paulo (BRA)	Newell's Old Boys (ARG)	0–1, 1–0 (3–2[1])
1993	São Paulo (BRA)	Universidad Católica (CHI)	5–1, 0–2
1994	Vélez Sársfield (ARG)	São Paulo (BRA)	1–0, 0–1 (5–4[1])
1995	Grêmio (BRA)	Atlético Nacional (COL)	3–1, 1–1
1996	River Plate (ARG)	América de Cali (COL)	0–1, 2–0
1997	Cruzeiro (BRA)	Sporting Cristal (PER)	0–0, 1–0
1998	Vasco da Gama (BRA)	Barcelona (ECU)	2–0, 2–1
1999	Palmeiras (BRA)	Deportiva Cali (COL)	0–1, 2–1 (4–3[1])
2000	Boca Juniors (ARG)	Palmeiras (BRA)	2–2, 0–0 (4–2[1])
2001	Boca Juniors (ARG)	Cruz Azul (MEX)	1–0, 0–1 (3–1[1])
2002	Olímpia (PAR)	São Caetano (BRA)	0–1, 2–1 (4–2[1])

Copa Libertadores de América (continued)

YEAR	WINNER (COUNTRY)	RUNNER-UP (COUNTRY)	SCORES
2003	Boca Juniors (ARG)	Santos (BRA)	2–0, 3–1
2004	Once Caldas (COL)	Boca Juniors (ARG)	0–0, 1–1 (2–0[1])
2005	São Paulo (BRA)	Atlético Paranaense (BRA)	1–1, 4–0
2006	Internacional (BRA)	São Paulo (BRA)	2–1, 2–2
2007	Boca Juniors (ARG)	Grêmio (BRA)	3–0, 2–0
2008	Liga de Quito (ECU)	Fluminense (BRA)	4–2, 1–3 (3–1[1])

[1]*Won in a penalty kick shoot-out.*

Copa América

Held since 1916. Table shows results for past 20 years. The cup was contested by rounds in 1989 and 1991 (scores are shown here as winner's wins/losses/draws in final round) and by a final championship match from 1993.

YEAR	WINNER	RUNNER-UP	SCORE
1989	Brazil	Uruguay	3/0/0
1991	Argentina	Brazil	4/0/0
1993	Argentina	Mexico	2–1
1995	Uruguay	Brazil	1–1 (4–2[1])
1997	Brazil	Bolivia	3–1
1999	Brazil	Uruguay	3–0
2001	Colombia	Mexico	1–0
2003	*postponed until 2004*		
2004	Brazil	Argentina	2–2 (2–0[1])
2007	Brazil	Argentina	3–0

[1]*Won in a penalty kick shoot-out.*

Asian Cup

Scored on a points (percentage of wins) system until 1972.

YEAR	WINNER	RUNNER-UP	SCORE
1956	South Korea	Israel	83.3
1960	South Korea	Israel	100
1964	Israel	India	100
1968	Iran	Burma	100
1972	Iran	South Korea	2–1
1976	Iran	Kuwait	1–0
1980	Kuwait	South Korea	3–0
1984	Saudi Arabia	China	2–0
1988	Saudi Arabia	South Korea	0–0 (4–3[1])
1992	Japan	Saudi Arabia	1–0
1996	Saudi Arabia	United Arab Emirates	0–0 (4–2[1])
2000	Japan	Saudi Arabia	1–0
2004	Japan	China	3–1
2007	Iraq	Saudi Arabia	1–0

[1]*Won in a penalty kick shoot-out.*

African Cup of Nations

YEAR	WINNER	RUNNER-UP	SCORE
1957	Egypt	Ethiopia	4–0
1959	Egypt	The Sudan	2–1
1962	Ethiopia	Egypt	4–2
1963	Ghana	The Sudan	3–0
1965	Ghana	Tunisia	3–2
1968	Dem. Rep. of the Congo	Ghana	1–0
1970	The Sudan	Ghana	1–0
1972	Rep. of the Congo	Mali	3–2
1974	Zaire	Zambia	2–2, 2–0[1]
1976	Morocco	Guinea	1–1[2]
1978	Ghana	Uganda	2–0
1980	Nigeria	Algeria	3–0
1982	Ghana	Libya	1–1 (7–6[3])
1984	Cameroon	Nigeria	3–1
1986	Egypt	Cameroon	0–0 (5–4[3])
1988	Cameroon	Nigeria	1–0
1990	Algeria	Nigeria	1–0
1992	Côte d'Ivoire	Ghana	0–0 (11-10[3])
1994	Nigeria	Zambia	2–1
1996	South Africa	Tunisia	2–0
1998	Egypt	South Africa	2–0
2000	Cameroon	Nigeria	2–2 (4–3[3])
2002	Cameroon	Senegal	0–0 (3–2[3])
2004	Tunisia	Morocco	2–1
2006	Egypt	Côte d'Ivoire	0–0 (4–2[3])
2008	Egypt	Cameroon	1–0

[1]*Game replayed.* [2]*Won via group format.* [3]*Won in a penalty kick shoot-out.*

Major League Soccer Cup

YEAR	WINNER	RUNNER-UP	SCORE
1996	DC United	Los Angeles Galaxy	3–2 (OT)
1997	DC United	Colorado Rapids	2–1
1998	Chicago Fire	DC United	2–0
1999	DC United	Los Angeles Galaxy	2–0
2000	Kansas City Wizards	Chicago Fire	1–0
2001	San Jose Earthquakes	Los Angeles Galaxy	2–1 (OT)

Major League Soccer Cup (continued)

YEAR	WINNER	RUNNER-UP	SCORE
2002	Los Angeles Galaxy	New England Revolution	1–0
2003	San Jose Earthquakes	Chicago Fire	4–2
2004	DC United	Kansas City Wizards	3–2
2005	Los Angeles Galaxy	New England Revolution	1–0 (OT)
2006	Houston Dynamo	New England Revolution	4–3 (OT)
2007	Houston Dynamo	New England Revolution	2–1

Golf

In **individual events**, three of the four major men's golf championships, the **British and US Open tournaments** and the **Professional Golfers' Association Championship**, are played annually at a variety of golf courses in their respective countries. Each is played over 72 holes, and each is preceded by qualifying rounds. The fourth major, the invitational **Masters Tournament**, is held annually at the Augusta [GA] National Golf Course. Events for amateurs include the **US and British Amateur championships.** In 2007 the **Professional Golf Association** (PGA) inaugurated the **FedExCup**, a season-long competition in which players accumulate points based on their performances in various PGA events (including the major tournaments, which are weighted more heavily), participate in a four-week play-off, and determine the FedExCup champion at a final Tour Championship.

Women's golf has been around nearly as long as men's golf, but until the late 1940s, it was limited to amateurs. Thus, for women, the **British and US Amateur championships** were the major tournaments. The **US Women's Open Championship** was started in 1946, and the **Ladies Professional Golf Association** (LPGA) was formed in 1950. Since that time women's professional golf has flourished. In 1976 the **Women's British Open Championship** was added to the golf calendar.

In **team events**, the **Ryder Cup** was originally a biennial match between the US and Great Britain, but beginning in 1979 it was expanded into a biennial match between the United States and Europe. The **World Cup**, formerly known as the Canada Cup, is a men's tournament for two-man professional teams. Teams of British and US women golfers compete every two years for the **Curtis Cup**, which since 1964 has involved two days' play of three 18-hole foursomes and six 18-hole singles. The **Solheim Cup**, the women's professional team tournament, had been played in even-numbered years since 1990 but was moved to odd-numbered years (beginning in 2003) following the rescheduling of the Ryder Cup because of the events of 11 Sep 2001.

Related Web sites: United States Golf Association: <www.usga.org>; Professional Golf Association: <www.pgatour.com>; Ladies Professional Golf Association: <www.lpga.com>.

FedExCup

In 2007 the PGA inaugurated the FedExCup, a season-long competition in which players accumulate points based on their performances in various PGA events throughout the year. In a standard (non-major) tournament, for instance, 25,000 points are awarded, with the winner receiving 4,500 points, a runner-up receiving 2,700 points, and so on. The four major tournaments award 27,500 points, with 4,950 going to the winner. The cumulative total of points each player has received during the regular season determines that player's seed going into a four-tournament play-off at the end of the year, for which the top 144 players are eligible. The points are reset for this play-off, with the regular-season leader starting with 100,000 points, the second-place finisher receiving 99,500, and so on. A progressive cut through the first three of these play-off events determines the players who qualify for the final competition, the Tour Championship, which determines the FedExCup champion. The first play-off tournament has a field of 144, the second 120, and the third 70. The winner of each of the first three receives 11,000 points, the second-place finisher 7,400, and so on. The winner of the Tour Championship receives 12,500 points, and each position receives slightly more than corresponding finishes in the other events. The player with the most cumulative play-off points at the end of the Tour Championship becomes the FedExCup champion and is awarded US$10 million, US$1 million of which is deferred into a retirement fund, making this the largest single bonus payout in professional sports. (In 2007 the entire US$10 million awarded to the winner was deferred.) Tiger Woods was the inaugural FedExCup champion.

Masters Tournament

Won by an American golfer except as indicated.

YEAR	WINNER
1934	Horton Smith
1935	Gene Sarazen
1936	Horton Smith
1937	Byron Nelson
1938	Henry Picard
1939	Ralph Guldahl
1940	Jimmy Demaret
1941	Craig Wood
1942	Byron Nelson
1943–45	*not held*
1946	Herman Keiser
1947	Jimmy Demaret
1948	Claude Harmon
1949	Sam Snead
1950	Jimmy Demaret
1951	Ben Hogan
1952	Sam Snead
1953	Ben Hogan

Masters Tournament (continued)

YEAR	WINNER
1954	Sam Snead
1955	Cary Middlecoff
1956	Jack Burke
1957	Doug Ford
1958	Arnold Palmer
1959	Art Wall
1960	Arnold Palmer
1961	Gary Player (RSA)
1962	Arnold Palmer
1963	Jack Nicklaus
1964	Arnold Palmer
1965	Jack Nicklaus
1966	Jack Nicklaus
1967	Gay Brewer
1968	Bob Goalby
1969	George Archer
1970	Billy Casper
1971	Charles Coody
1972	Jack Nicklaus
1973	Tommy Aaron
1974	Gary Player (RSA)
1975	Jack Nicklaus
1976	Raymond Floyd
1977	Tom Watson
1978	Gary Player (RSA)
1979	Fuzzy Zoeller
1980	Seve Ballesteros (ESP)
1981	Tom Watson
1982	Craig Stadler
1983	Seve Ballesteros (ESP)
1984	Ben Crenshaw
1985	Bernhard Langer (FRG)
1986	Jack Nicklaus
1987	Larry Mize
1988	Sandy Lyle (SCO)
1989	Nick Faldo (ENG)
1990	Nick Faldo (ENG)
1991	Ian Woosnam (WAL)
1992	Fred Couples
1993	Bernhard Langer (GER)
1994	José María Olazábal (ESP)
1995	Ben Crenshaw
1996	Nick Faldo (ENG)
1997	Tiger Woods
1998	Mark O'Meara
1999	José María Olazábal (ESP)
2000	Vijay Singh (FIJ)
2001	Tiger Woods
2002	Tiger Woods
2003	Mike Weir (CAN)
2004	Phil Mickelson
2005	Tiger Woods
2006	Phil Mickelson
2007	Zach Johnson
2008	Trevor Immelman (RSA)

United States Open Championship—Men

Won by an American golfer except as indicated.

YEAR	WINNER
1895	Horace Rawlins
1896	James Foulis
1897	Joe Lloyd
1898	Fred Herd
1899	Willie Smith
1900	Harry Vardon (GBR)
1901	Willie Anderson
1902	Laurence Auchterlonie
1903	Willie Anderson
1904	Willie Anderson
1905	Willie Anderson
1906	Alex Smith
1907	Alex Ross
1908	Fred McLeod
1909	George Sargent
1910	Alex Smith
1911	John J. McDermott
1912	John J. McDermott
1913	Francis Ouimet
1914	Walter Hagen
1915	Jerome D. Travers
1916	Chick Evans
1917–18	*not held*
1919	Walter Hagen
1920	Edward Ray (GBR)
1921	James M. Barnes
1922	Gene Sarazen
1923	Bobby Jones
1924	Cyril Walker
1925	Willie MacFarlane, Jr.
1926	Bobby Jones
1927	Tommy Armour
1928	Johnny Farrell
1929	Bobby Jones
1930	Bobby Jones
1931	Billy Burke
1932	Gene Sarazen
1933	John Goodman
1934	Olin Dutra
1935	Sam Parks, Jr.
1936	Tony Manero
1937	Ralph Guldahl
1938	Ralph Guldahl
1939	Byron Nelson
1940	Lawson Little
1941	Craig Wood
1942–45	*not held*
1946	Lloyd Mangrum
1947	Lew Worsham
1948	Ben Hogan
1949	Cary Middlecoff
1950	Ben Hogan
1951	Ben Hogan
1952	Julius Boros
1953	Ben Hogan
1954	Ed Furgol
1955	Jack Fleck
1956	Cary Middlecoff
1957	Dick Mayer
1958	Tommy Bolt
1959	Billy Casper
1960	Arnold Palmer
1961	Gene Littler
1962	Jack Nicklaus
1963	Julius Boros
1964	Ken Venturi
1965	Gary Player (RSA)
1966	Billy Casper
1967	Jack Nicklaus
1968	Lee Trevino
1969	Orville Moody
1970	Tony Jacklin (GBR)
1971	Lee Trevino
1972	Jack Nicklaus
1973	Johnny Miller
1974	Hale Irwin
1975	Lou Graham
1976	Jerry Pate
1977	Hubert Green
1978	Andy North
1979	Hale Irwin
1980	Jack Nicklaus
1981	David Graham (AUS)
1982	Tom Watson
1983	Larry Nelson
1984	Fuzzy Zoeller
1985	Andy North
1986	Raymond Floyd
1987	Scott Simpson
1988	Curtis Strange
1989	Curtis Strange
1990	Hale Irwin
1991	Payne Stewart
1992	Tom Kite
1993	Lee Janzen
1994	Ernie Els (RSA)
1995	Corey Pavin
1996	Steve Jones
1997	Ernie Els (RSA)
1998	Lee Janzen
1999	Payne Stewart
2000	Tiger Woods
2001	Retief Goosen (RSA)
2002	Tiger Woods
2003	Jim Furyk
2004	Retief Goosen (RSA)
2005	Michael Campbell (NZL)
2006	Geoff Ogilvy (AUS)
2007	Angel Cabrera (ARG)
2008	Tiger Woods

British Open Tournament—Men

Won by a British golfer unless otherwise indicated.

YEAR	WINNER	YEAR	WINNER	YEAR	WINNER
1860	Willie Park, Sr.	1907	Arnaud Massy (FRA)	1963	Bob Charles (NZL)
1861	Tom Morris, Sr.	1908	James Braid	1964	Tony Lema (USA)
1862	Tom Morris, Sr.	1909	John H. Taylor	1965	Peter Thomson (AUS)
1863	Willie Park, Sr.	1910	James Braid	1966	Jack Nicklaus (USA)
1864	Tom Morris, Sr.	1911	Harry Vardon	1967	Roberto de Vicenzo (ARG)
1865	Andrew Strath	1912	Ted Ray	1968	Gary Player (RSA)
1866	Willie Park, Sr.	1913	John H. Taylor	1969	Tony Jacklin
1867	Tom Morris, Sr.	1914	Harry Vardon	1970	Jack Nicklaus (USA)
1868	Tom Morris, Jr.	1915–19	*not held*	1971	Lee Trevino (USA)
1869	Tom Morris, Jr.	1920	George Duncan	1972	Lee Trevino (USA)
1870	Tom Morris, Jr.	1921	Jock Hutchison (USA)	1973	Tom Weiskopf (USA)
1871	*not held*	1922	Walter Hagen (USA)	1974	Gary Player (RSA)
1872	Tom Morris, Jr.	1923	Arthur Havers	1975	Tom Watson (USA)
1873	Tom Kidd	1924	Walter Hagen (USA)	1976	Johnny Miller (USA)
1874	Mungo Park	1925	James Barnes (USA)	1977	Tom Watson (USA)
1875	Willie Park, Jr.	1926	Bobby Jones (USA)	1978	Jack Nicklaus (USA)
1876	Bob Martin	1927	Bobby Jones (USA)	1979	Seve Ballesteros (ESP)
1877	Jamie Anderson	1928	Walter Hagen (USA)	1980	Tom Watson (USA)
1878	Jamie Anderson	1929	Walter Hagen (USA)	1981	Bill Rogers (USA)
1879	Jamie Anderson	1930	Bobby Jones (USA)	1982	Tom Watson (USA)
1880	Robert Ferguson	1931	Tommy Armour (USA)	1983	Tom Watson (USA)
1881	Robert Ferguson	1932	Gene Sarazen (USA)	1984	Seve Ballesteros (ESP)
1882	Robert Ferguson	1933	Denny Shute (USA)	1985	Sandy Lyle (SCO)
1883	Willie Fernie	1934	Henry Cotton	1986	Greg Norman (AUS)
1884	Jack Simpson	1935	Alfred Perry	1987	Nick Faldo
1885	Bob Martin	1936	Alfred Padgham	1988	Seve Ballesteros (ESP)
1886	David Brown	1937	Henry Cotton	1989	Mark Calcavecchia (USA)
1887	Willie Park, Jr.	1938	Reg A. Whitcombe	1990	Nick Faldo
1888	Jack Burns	1939	Richard Burton	1991	Ian Baker-Finch (AUS)
1889	Willie Park, Jr.	1940–45	*not held*	1992	Nick Faldo
1890	John Ball	1946	Sam Snead (USA)	1993	Greg Norman (AUS)
1891	Hugh Kirkaldy	1947	Fred Daly (IRE)	1994	Nick Price (ZIM)
1892	Harold Hilton	1948	Henry Cotton	1995	John Daly (USA)
1893	William Auchterlonie	1949	Bobby Locke (RSA)	1996	Tom Lehman (USA)
1894	John H. Taylor	1950	Bobby Locke (RSA)	1997	Justin Leonard (USA)
1895	John H. Taylor	1951	Max Faulkner	1998	Mark O'Meara (USA)
1896	Harry Vardon	1952	Bobby Locke (RSA)	1999	Paul Lawrie (SCO)
1897	Harold Hilton	1953	Ben Hogan (USA)	2000	Tiger Woods (USA)
1898	Harry Vardon	1954	Peter Thomson (AUS)	2001	David Duval (USA)
1899	Harry Vardon	1955	Peter Thomson (AUS)	2002	Ernie Els (RSA)
1900	John H. Taylor	1956	Peter Thomson (AUS)	2003	Ben Curtis (USA)
1901	James Braid	1957	Bobby Locke (RSA)	2004	Todd Hamilton (USA)
1902	Sandy Herd	1958	Peter Thomson (AUS)	2005	Tiger Woods (USA)
1903	Harry Vardon	1959	Gary Player (RSA)	2006	Tiger Woods (USA)
1904	Jack White	1960	Kel Nagle (AUS)	2007	Padraig Harrington (IRL)
1905	James Braid	1961	Arnold Palmer (USA)	2008	Padraig Harrington (IRL)
1906	James Braid	1962	Arnold Palmer (USA)		

US Professional Golfers' Association (PGA) Championship

Won by an American golfer except as indicated.

YEAR	WINNER	YEAR	WINNER	YEAR	WINNER
1916	James M. Barnes	1931	Tom Creavy	1945	Byron Nelson
1917–18	*not held*	1932	Olin Dutra	1946	Ben Hogan
1919	James M. Barnes	1933	Gene Sarazen	1947	Jim Ferrier
1920	Jock Hutchison	1934	Paul Runyan	1948	Ben Hogan
1921	Walter Hagen	1935	Johnny Revolta	1949	Sam Snead
1922	Gene Sarazen	1936	Denny Shute	1950	Chandler Harper
1923	Gene Sarazen	1937	Denny Shute	1951	Sam Snead
1924	Walter Hagen	1938	Paul Runyan	1952	Jim Turnesa
1925	Walter Hagen	1939	Henry Picard	1953	Walter Burkemo
1926	Walter Hagen	1940	Byron Nelson	1954	Chick Harbert
1927	Walter Hagen	1941	Vic Ghezzi	1955	Doug Ford
1928	Leo Diegel	1942	Sam Snead	1956	Jack Burke
1929	Leo Diegel	1943	*not held*	1957	Lionel Hebert
1930	Tommy Armour	1944	Bob Hamilton	1958	Dow Finsterwald

US Professional Golfers' Association (PGA) Championship (continued)

YEAR	WINNER	YEAR	WINNER	YEAR	WINNER
1959	Bob Rosburg	1976	Dave Stockton	1993	Paul Azinger
1960	Jay Hebert	1977	Lanny Wadkins	1994	Nick Price (ZIM)
1961	Jerry Barber	1978	John Mahaffey	1995	Steve Elkington (AUS)
1962	Gary Player (RSA)	1979	David Graham (AUS)	1996	Mark Brooks
1963	Jack Nicklaus	1980	Jack Nicklaus	1997	Davis Love III
1964	Bobby Nichols	1981	Larry Nelson	1998	Vijay Singh (FIJ)
1965	Dave Marr	1982	Raymond Floyd	1999	Tiger Woods
1966	Al Geiberger	1983	Hal Sutton	2000	Tiger Woods
1967	Don January	1984	Lee Trevino	2001	David Toms
1968	Julius Boros	1985	Hubert Green	2002	Rich Beems
1969	Raymond Floyd	1986	Bob Tway	2003	Shaun Micheel
1970	Dave Stockton	1987	Larry Nelson	2004	Vijay Singh (FIJ)
1971	Jack Nicklaus	1988	Jeff Sluman	2005	Phil Mickelson
1972	Gary Player (RSA)	1989	Payne Stewart	2006	Tiger Woods
1973	Jack Nicklaus	1990	Wayne Grady (AUS)	2007	Tiger Woods
1974	Lee Trevino	1991	John Daly	2008	Padraig Harrington (IRL)
1975	Jack Nicklaus	1992	Nick Price (ZIM)		

Ladies Professional Golf Association (LPGA) Championship

Won by an American golfer except as indicated.

YEAR	WINNER	YEAR	WINNER	YEAR	WINNER
1955	Beverly Hanson	1973	Mary Mills	1991	Meg Mallon
1956	Marlene Hagge	1974	Sandra Haynie	1992	Betsy King
1957	Louise Suggs	1975	Kathy Whitworth	1993	Patty Sheehan
1958	Mickey Wright	1976	Betty Burfeindt	1994	Laura Davies (GBR)
1959	Betsy Rawls	1977	Chako Higuchi	1995	Kelly Robbins
1960	Mickey Wright	1978	Nancy Lopez	1996	Laura Davies (GBR)
1961	Mickey Wright	1979	Donna Caponi	1997	Chris Johnson
1962	Judy Kimball	1980	Sally Little	1998	Se Ri Pak (KOR)
1963	Mickey Wright	1981	Donna Caponi	1999	Juli Inkster
1964	Mary Mills	1982	Jan Stephenson (AUS)	2000	Juli Inkster
1965	Sandra Haynie	1983	Patty Sheehan	2001	Karrie Webb (AUS)
1966	Gloria Ehret	1984	Patty Sheehan	2002	Se Ri Pak (KOR)
1967	Kathy Whitworth	1985	Nancy Lopez	2003	Annika Sörenstam (SWE)
1968	Sandra Post	1986	Pat Bradley	2004	Annika Sörenstam (SWE)
1969	Betsy Rawls	1987	Jane Geddes	2005	Annika Sörenstam (SWE)
1970	Shirley Englehorn	1988	Sherri Turner	2006	Se Ri Pak (KOR)
1971	Kathy Whitworth	1989	Nancy Lopez	2007	Suzann Pettersen (NOR)
1972	Kathy Ahern	1990	Beth Daniel	2008	Yani Tseng (TPE)

United States Women's Open Championship

Won by an American golfer except as indicated.

YEAR	WINNER	YEAR	WINNER	YEAR	WINNER
1946	Patty Berg	1962	Murle Breer	1980	Amy Alcott
1947	Betty Jameson	1963	Mary Mills	1981	Pat Bradley
1948	Babe Didrikson Zaharias	1964	Mickey Wright	1982	Janet Anderson
1949	Louise Suggs	1965	Carol Mann	1983	Jan Stephenson (AUS)
1950	Babe Didrikson Zaharias	1966	Sandra Spuzich	1984	Hollis Stacy
1951	Betsy Rawls	1967	Catherine Lacoste (FRA)[1]	1985	Kathy Baker
1952	Louise Suggs	1968	Susie Berning	1986	Jane Geddes
1953	Betsy Rawls	1969	Donna Caponi	1987	Laura Davies (GBR)
1954	Babe Didrikson Zaharias	1970	Donna Caponi	1988	Liselotte Neumann (SWE)
1955	Fay Crocker	1971	JoAnne Carner	1989	Betsy King
1956	Kathy Cornelius	1972	Susie Berning	1990	Betsy King
1957	Betsy Rawls	1973	Susie Berning	1991	Meg Mallon
1958	Mickey Wright	1974	Sandra Haynie	1992	Patty Sheehan
1959	Mickey Wright	1975	Sandra Palmer	1993	Lauri Merten
1960	Betsy Rawls	1976	JoAnne Carner	1994	Patty Sheehan
1961	Mickey Wright	1977	Hollis Stacy	1995	Annika Sörenstam (SWE)
		1978	Hollis Stacy	1996	Annika Sörenstam (SWE)
		1979	Jerilyn Britz	1997	Alison Nicholas (GBR)
				1998	Pak Se Ri (KOR)

United States Women's Open Championship (continued)

YEAR	WINNER	YEAR	WINNER	YEAR	WINNER
1999	Juli Inkster	2003	Hilary Lunke	2006	Annika Sörenstam (SWE)
2000	Karrie Webb (AUS)	2004	Meg Mallon	2007	Cristie Kerr
2001	Karrie Webb (AUS)	2005	Birdie Kim (KOR)	2008	Inbee Park (KOR)
2002	Juli Inkster				

[1]*Amateur.*

Women's British Open Championship

Won by a British golfer unless otherwise indicated.

YEAR	WINNER	YEAR	WINNER	YEAR	WINNER
1976	J. Lee Smith	1987	Alison Nicholas	1998	Sherri Steinhauer (USA)
1977	Vivien Saunders	1988	Corinne Dibnah (AUS)	1999	Sherri Steinhauer (USA)
1978	Janet Melville	1989	Jane Geddes (USA)	2000	Sophie Gustafson (SWE)
1979	Alison Sheard (RSA)	1990	Helen Alfredsson (SWE)	2001	Pak Se Ri (KOR)
1980	Debbie Massey (USA)	1991	Penny Grice-Whittaker	2002	Karrie Webb (AUS)
1981	Debbie Massey (USA)	1992	Patty Sheehan (USA)	2003	Annika Sörenstam (SWE)
1982	Marta Figueras-Dotti (SPA)	1993	Mardi Lunn (AUS)	2004	Karen Stupples
1983	*not held*	1994	Liselotte Neumann (SWE)	2005	Jang Jeong (KOR)
1984	Okamoto Ayako (JAP)	1995	Karrie Webb (AUS)	2006	Sherri Steinhauer (USA)
1985	Betsy King (USA)	1996	Emilee Klein (USA)	2007	Lorena Ochoa (MEX)
1986	Laura Davies	1997	Karrie Webb (AUS)	2008	Ji Yai Shin (KOR)

Ryder Cup

YEAR	RESULT	YEAR	RESULT
1927	United States 9½, Great Britain 2½	1971	United States 18½, Great Britain 13½
1929	Great Britain 7, United States 5	1973	United States 19, Great Britain 13
1931	United States 9, Great Britain 3	1975	United States 21, Great Britain 11
1933	Great Britain 6½, United States 5½	1977	United States 12½, Great Britain 7½
1935	United States 9, Great Britain 3	1979	United States 17, Europe 11
1937	United States 8, Great Britain 4	1981	United States 18½, Europe 9½
1939–45	*not held*	1983	United States 14½, Europe 13½
1947	United States 11, Great Britain 1	1985	Europe 16½, United States 11½
1949	United States 7, Great Britain 5	1987	Europe 15, United States 13
1951	United States 9½, Great Britain 2½	1989	Europe 14, United States 14
1953	United States 6½, Great Britain 5½	1991	United States 14½, Europe 13½
1955	United States 8, Great Britain 4	1993	United States 15, Europe 13
1957	Great Britain 7½, United States 4½	1995	Europe 14½, United States 13½
1959	United States 8½, Great Britain 3½	1997	Europe 14½, United States 13½
1961	United States 14½, Great Britain 9½	1999	United States 14½, Europe 13½
1963	United States 23, Great Britain 9	2001	*postponed until 2002*
1965	United States 19½, Great Britain 12½	2002	Europe 15½, United States 12½
1967	United States 23½, Great Britain 8½	2004	Europe 18½, United States 9½
1969	United States 16, Great Britain 16	2006	Europe 18½, United States 9½

Curtis Cup

YEAR	RESULT	YEAR	RESULT
1932	United States 5½, Britain and Ireland 3½	1970	United States 11½, Britain and Ireland 6½
1934	United States 6½, Britain and Ireland 2½	1972	United States 10, Britain and Ireland 8
1936	United States[1] 4½, Britain and Ireland 4½	1974	United States 13, Britain and Ireland 5
1938	United States 5½, Britain and Ireland 3½	1976	United States 11½, Britain and Ireland 6½
1940–46	*not held*	1978	United States 12, Britain and Ireland 6
1948	United States 6½, Britain and Ireland 2½	1980	United States 13, Britain and Ireland 5
1950	United States 7½, Britain and Ireland 2½	1982	United States 14½, Britain and Ireland 3½
1952	Britain and Ireland 5, United States 4	1984	United States 9½, Britain and Ireland 8½
1954	United States 6, Britain and Ireland 3	1986	Britain and Ireland 13, United States 5
1956	Britain and Ireland 5, United States 4	1988	Britain and Ireland 11, United States 7
1958	Britain and Ireland[1] 4½, United States 4½	1990	United States 14, Britain and Ireland 4
1960	United States 6½, Britain and Ireland 2½	1992	Britain and Ireland 10, United States 8
1962	United States 8, Britain and Ireland 1	1994	Britain and Ireland[1] 9, United States 9
1964	United States 10½, Britain and Ireland 7½	1996	Britain and Ireland 11½, United States 6½
1966	United States 13, Britain and Ireland 5	1998	United States 10, Britain and Ireland 8
1968	United States 10½, Britain and Ireland 7½	2000	United States 10, Britain and Ireland 8

Curtis Cup (continued)

YEAR	RESULT	YEAR	RESULT
2002	United States 11, Britain and Ireland 7	2006	United States 11½, Britain and Ireland 6½
2004	United States 10, Britain and Ireland 8	2008	United States 13, Britain and Ireland 7

[1]*In case of a tie the defenders retain the cup.*

United States Amateur Championship—Men

Won by an American golfer except as indicated. Table shows results for the past 20 years.

YEAR	WINNER	YEAR	WINNER	YEAR	WINNER
1989	Chris Patton	1996	Tiger Woods	2003	Nick Flanagan (AUS)
1990	Phil Mickelson	1997	Matt Kuchar	2004	Ryan Moore
1991	Mitch Voges	1998	Hank Kuehne	2005	Edoardo Molinari (ITA)
1992	Justin Leonard	1999	David Gossett	2006	Richie Ramsay (SCO)
1993	John Harris	2000	Jeff Quinney	2007	Colt Knost
1994	Tiger Woods	2001	Ben Dickerson	2008	Danny Lee (NZL)
1995	Tiger Woods	2002	Ricky Barnes		

British Amateur Championship—Men

Won by a British golfer except as indicated. Table shows results for the past 20 years.

YEAR	WINNER	YEAR	WINNER	YEAR	WINNER
1989	Stephen Dodd	1996	Warren Bledon	2003	Gary Wolstenholme
1990	Rolf Muntz (NED)	1997	Craig Watson	2004	Stuart Wilson
1991	Gary Wolstenholme	1998	Sergio García (ESP)	2005	Brian McElhinney (IRL)
1992	Stephen Dundas	1999	Graeme Storm	2006	Julien Guerrier (FRA)
1993	Ian Pyman	2000	Mikko Ilonen (FIN)	2007	Drew Weaver (USA)
1994	Lee James	2001	Michael Hoey (IRL)	2008	Reinier Saxton (NED)
1995	Gordon Sherry	2002	Alejandro Larrazábal (ESP)		

United States Women's Amateur Championship

Won by an American golfer except as indicated. Table shows results for the past 20 years.

YEAR	WINNER	YEAR	WINNER	YEAR	WINNER
1989	Vicki Goetze	1996	Kelli Kuehne	2003	Virada Nirapathpongporn (THA)
1990	Pat Hurst	1997	Silvia Cavalleri (ITA)	2004	Jane Park
1991	Amy Fruhwirth	1998	Grace Park	2005	Morgan Pressel
1992	Vicki Goetze	1999	Dorothy Delasin	2006	Kimberly Kim
1993	Jill McGill	2000	Marcy Newton	2007	María José Uribe (COL)
1994	Wendy Ward	2001	Meredith Duncan	2008	Amanda Blumenherst
1995	Kelli Kuehne	2002	Becky Lucidi		

Ladies' British Amateur Championship

Won by a British golfer except as indicated. Table shows results for the past 20 years.

YEAR	WINNER	YEAR	WINNER	YEAR	WINNER
1989	Helen Dobson	1996	Kelli Kuehne (USA)	2003	Elisa Serramia (ESP)
1990	Julie Wade Hall	1997	Alison Rose	2004	Louise Stahle (SWE)
1991	Valerie Michaud	1998	Kim Rostron	2005	Louise Stahle (SWE)
1992	Bernille Pedersen (DEN)	1999	Marine Monnet (FRA)	2006	Belén Mozo (ESP)
1993	Catriona Lambert	2000	Rebecca Hudson	2007	Carlota Ciganda (ESP)
1994	Emma Duggleby	2001	Marta Prieto (ESP)	2008	Anna Nordqvist (SWE)
1995	Julie Wade Hall	2002	Rebecca Hudson		

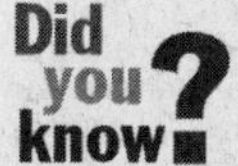

The oldest stadium in continuous use in professional football is Soldier Field in Chicago. It officially opened in 1924 as Municipal Grant Park Stadium. It was renamed Soldier Field the next year, though construction was not completed until 1928. A section that enclosed the north end of the stadium was completed in 1939, and a controversial upgrade, which added a futuristic shell compared by some to a flying saucer, was added in 2002.

World Cup

YEAR	WINNER
1953	Argentina (Antonio Cerdá and Roberto de Vicenzo)
1954	Australia (Peter Thomson and Kel Nagle)
1955	United States (Chick Harbert and Ed Furgol)
1956	United States (Ben Hogan and Sam Snead)
1957	Japan (Torakichi Nakamura and Koichi Ono)
1958	Ireland (Harry Bradshaw and Christy O'Connor)
1959	Australia (Peter Thomson and Kel Nagle)
1960	United States (Sam Snead and Arnold Palmer)
1961	United States (Sam Snead and Jimmy Demaret)
1962	United States (Sam Snead and Arnold Palmer)
1963	United States (Arnold Palmer and Jack Nicklaus)
1964	United States (Arnold Palmer and Jack Nicklaus)
1965	South Africa (Gary Player and Harold Henning)
1966	United States (Arnold Palmer and Jack Nicklaus)
1967	United States (Arnold Palmer and Jack Nicklaus)
1968	Canada (Al Balding and George Knudson)
1969	United States (Orville Moody and Lee Trevino)
1970	Australia (David Graham and Bruce Devlin)
1971	United States (Jack Nicklaus and Lee Trevino)
1972	Taiwan (Hsieh Min-nan and Lu Liang-huan)
1973	United States (Johnny Miller and Jack Nicklaus)
1974	South Africa (Bobby Cole and Dale Hayes)
1975	United States (Johnny Miller and Lou Graham)
1976	Spain (Seve Ballesteros and Manuel Piñero)
1977	Spain (Seve Ballesteros and Antonio Garrido)
1978	United States (John Mahaffey and Andy North)
1979	United States (Hale Irwin and John Mahaffey)
1980	Canada (Dan Halldorson and Jim Nelford)
1981	*not held*
1982	Spain (Manuel Piñero and José Maria Cañizares)
1983	United States (Rex Caldwell and John Cook)
1984	Spain (José Maria Cañizares and José Rivero)
1985	Canada (Dan Halldorson and Dave Barr)
1986	*not held*
1987	Wales (Ian Woosnam and David Llewellyn)
1988	United States (Ben Crenshaw and Mark McCumber)
1989	Australia (Peter Fowler and Wayne Grady)
1990	Germany (Bernhard Langer and Torsten Giedeon)
1991	Sweden (Anders Forsbrand and Per-Ulrik Johansson)
1992	United States (Fred Couples and Davis Love III)
1993	United States (Fred Couples and Davis Love III)
1994	United States (Fred Couples and Davis Love III)
1995	United States (Fred Couples and Davis Love III)
1996	South Africa (Ernie Els and Wayne Westner)
1997	Ireland (Padraig Harrington and Paul McGinley)
1998	England (Nick Faldo and David Carter)
1999	United States (Tiger Woods and Mark O'Meara)
2000	United States (Tiger Woods and David Duval)
2001	South Africa (Ernie Els and Retief Goosen)
2002	Japan (Shigeki Maruyama and Toshi Izawa)
2003	South Africa (Trevor Immelman and Rory Sabbatini)
2004	England (Paul Casey and Luke Donald)
2005	Wales (Bradley Dredge and Stephen Dodd)
2006	Germany (Marcel Siem and Bernhard Langer)
2007	Scotland (Colin Montgomerie and Marc Warren)

Horse Racing

In the **oldest type** of horse racing, the rider sits astride the horse; in the other type of race, best known as **harness racing,** the driver sits in a sulky—a two-wheeled vehicle attached by shafts and traces to the horse. In the former type, a **Thoroughbred** horse is raced over either a track or a course of jumps and turns (**steeplechase**). Harness horses can be trotters or pacers and are Standardbred horses raced on a track.

The English Thoroughbred classics. The races are run by 3-year-old colts and fillies. **The Derby,** first run in 1780, is run at Epsom Downs, Surrey, over 1½ miles. **The Oaks** (for fillies only), also run at Epsom Downs, was first run in 1779; the oldest of the English races, however, is the **St. Leger** (1776). It is run over 1 mile 6½ furlongs at Doncaster, South Yorkshire. The **2,000 Guineas** (1809) is run over 1 mile at Newmarket, Suffolk. A horse that wins the Derby, the St. Leger, and the 2,000 Guineas all in one year is said to have won the **British Triple Crown.**

The American Thoroughbred classics. The **Kentucky Derby,** a **Triple Crown** event first run in 1875 and perhaps the best known of American horse races, is raced at Churchill Downs in Louisville KY, over a 10-furlong (1¼-mile) track. Another of the Triple Crown classics, the **Preakness Stakes,** was instituted in 1873; it is run over 9½ furlongs (1³⁄₁₆ miles) at Pimlico Race Track in Baltimore MD. The third Triple Crown event is the 12-furlong (1½-mile) **Belmont Stakes,** established in 1867. It is run at Belmont Park Race Track, Long Island NY. All three events are for 3-year-old horses.

Australian Thoroughbred racing. The Victoria Racing Club's **Melbourne Cup,** first run in 1861, is one of the world's great handicap races. The day on which it is held (the first Tuesday in November) is a public holiday in Melbourne, VIC.

Dubai World Cup, first run in 1996, is the world's richest horse race ($6 million in 2007). The 2,000-m (about 1¼-mi) race is held on the dirt track at the Nad Al Sheba Racecourse in Dubai, United Arab Emirates, and is open to four-year-old and older Thoroughbred horses.

The **Grand National,** the world's most significant and widely followed **steeplechase** race, has been run annually at Aintree Racecourse near Liverpool, England, since 1839. The race, which includes 30 jumps, is run over a traditional distance of 4 miles 4 furlongs.

Horse Racing (continued)

Harness racing. In the United States, the **Hambletonian Trot** is probably the most prestigious of harness races. It was established in 1926, was raced in New York, Kentucky, and Illinois, and is now run at the Meadowlands in New Jersey.

Related Web sites: US National Thoroughbred Racing Association: <www.ntra.com>; Fédération Equestre Internationale: <www.horsesport.org>; *Thoroughbred Times:* <www.thoroughbredtimes.com>; and *Racing Post*: <www.racingpost.co.uk>.

Major Thoroughbred Race Winners 2007–08

United States

DATE	RACE	WINNER	JOCKEY
4 Aug 2007	John C. Mabee Handicap	Precious Kitten	Rafael Bejarano
5 Aug 2007	Haskell Invitational Handicap	Any Given Saturday	Garrett Gomez
11 Aug 2007	Arlington Million Stakes	Jambalaya	Robby Albarado
11 Aug 2007	Beverly D. Stakes	Royal Highness	Rene Douglas
11 Aug 2007	Secretariat Stakes	Shamdinan	Julien Leparoux
11 Aug 2007	Sword Dancer Invitational Stakes	Grand Couturier	Calvin Borel
18 Aug 2007	Alabama Stakes	Lady Joanne	Calvin Borel
18 Aug 2007	Del Mar Oaks	Rutherienne	Corey Nakatani
19 Aug 2007	Pacific Classic Stakes	Student Council	Richard Migliore
24 Aug 2007	Personal Ensign Handicap	Miss Shop	Javier Castellano
25 Aug 2007	Travers Stakes	Street Sense	Calvin Borel
1 Sep 2007	Woodward Stakes	Lawyer Ron	John Velazquez
8 Sep 2007	Man o' War Stakes	Doctor Dino	Olivier Peslier
8 Sep 2007	Ruffian Handicap	Ginger Punch	Rafael Bejarano
29 Sep 2007	Flower Bowl Invitational	Lahudood	Alan Garcia
29 Sep 2007	Goodwood Handicap	Tiago	Mike Smith
29 Sep 2007	Yellow Ribbon Stakes	Nashoba's Key	Joseph Talamo
30 Sep 2007	Beldame Stakes	Unbridled Belle	Ramon Dominguez
30 Sep 2007	Jockey Club Gold Cup Stakes	Curlin	Robby Albarado
30 Sep 2007	Joe Hirsch Turf Classic Invitational Stakes	English Channel	John Velazquez
30 Sep 2007	Vosburgh Stakes	Fabulous Strike	Ramon Dominguez
5 Oct 2007	Alcibiades Stakes	Country Star	Rafael Bejarano
6 Oct 2007	Champagne Stakes	War Pass	Cornelio Velasquez
6 Oct 2007	Frizette Stakes	Indian Blessing	Garrett Gomez
6 Oct 2007	Lane's End Breeders' Futurity	Wicked Style	Robby Albarado
6 Oct 2007	Shadwell Turf Mile Stakes	Purim	Jamie Theriot
7 Oct 2007	Ancient Title Stakes	Idiot Proof	David Romero Flores
7 Oct 2007	Spinster Stakes	Panty Raid	Garrett Gomez
13 Oct 2007	Queen Elizabeth II Challenge Cup Stakes	Bit of Whimsy	Javier Castellano
27 Oct 2007	Breeders' Cup Classic	Curlin	Robby Albarado
27 Oct 2007	Breeders' Cup Distaff	Ginger Punch	Rafael Bejarano
27 Oct 2007	Breeders' Cup Filly and Mare Turf	Lahudood	Alan Garcia
27 Oct 2007	Breeders' Cup Juvenile	War Pass	Cornelio Velasquez
27 Oct 2007	Breeders' Cup Juvenile Fillies	Indian Blessing	Garrett Gomez
27 Oct 2007	Breeders' Cup Mile	Kip Deville	Cornelio Velasquez
27 Oct 2007	Breeders' Cup Sprint	Midnight Lute	Garrett Gomez
27 Oct 2007	Breeders' Cup Turf	English Channel	John Velazquez
23 Nov 2007	Citation Handicap	Lang Field	Jon Court
24 Nov 2007	Cigar Mile Handicap	Daaher	Michael Luzzi
25 Nov 2007	Hollywood Derby	Daytona	Mike Smith
25 Nov 2007	Matriarch Stakes	Precious Kitten	Rafael Bejarano
22 Dec 2007	CashCall Futurity	Into Mischief	Victor Espinoza
2 Feb 2008	Donn Handicap	Spring At Last	Eibar Coa
1 Mar 2008	Frank E. Kilroe Mile Handicap	Ever a Friend	Tyler Baze
1 Mar 2008	Santa Anita Handicap	Heatseeker	Rafael Bejarano
8 Mar 2008	Santa Anita Oaks	Ariege	Corey Nakatani
9 Mar 2008	Santa Margarita Invitational Handicap	Nashoba's Key	Garrett Gomez
29 Mar 2008	Florida Derby	Big Brown	Kent Desormeaux
5 Apr 2008	Apple Blossom Handicap	Zenyatta	Mike Smith
5 Apr 2008	Ashland Stakes	Little Belle	Rajiv Maragh
5 Apr 2008	Carter Handicap	Bustin Stones	Edgar Prado
5 Apr 2008	Santa Anita Derby	Colonel John	Corey Nakatani
5 Apr 2008	Wood Memorial Stakes	Tale of Ekati	Edgar Prado
11 Apr 2008	Maker's Mark Mile Stakes	Kip Deville	Cornelio Velasquez
12 Apr 2008	Blue Grass Stakes	Monba	Edgar Prado
2 May 2008	Kentucky Oaks	Proud Spell	Gabriel Saez
3 May 2008	Humana Distaff Stakes	Intangaroo	Alonso Quinonez

Major Thoroughbred Race Winners 2007–08 (continued)

United States (continued)

DATE	RACE	WINNER	JOCKEY
3 May 2008	Kentucky Derby[1]	Big Brown	Kent Desormeaux
3 May 2008	Turf Classic Stakes	Einstein	Robby Albarado
17 May 2008	Preakness Stakes[1]	Big Brown	Kent Desormeaux
26 May 2008	Gamely Stakes	Precious Kitten	Rafael Bejarano
26 May 2008	Metropolitan Handicap	Devine Park	Alan Garcia
26 May 2008	Shoemaker Mile Stakes	Daytona	Alex Solis
7 Jun 2008	Belmont Stakes[1]	Da' Tara	Alan Garcia
7 Jun 2008	Charles Whittingham Memorial Handicap	Artiste Royal	David Romero Flores
7 Jun 2008	Just a Game Stakes	Ventura	Garrett Gomez
7 Jun 2008	Manhattan Handicap	Dancing Forever	Rene Douglas
14 Jun 2008	Ogden Phipps Handicap	Ginger Punch	Rafael Bejarano
14 Jun 2008	Stephen Foster Handicap	Curlin	Robby Albarado
28 Jun 2008	Hollywood Gold Cup Stakes	Mast Track	Tyler Baze
28 Jun 2008	Suburban Handicap	Frost Giant	Rudy Rodriguez
5 Jul 2008	American Oaks Invitational Stakes	Pure Clan	Julien Leparoux
5 Jul 2008	Triple Bend Invitational Handicap	Street Boss	David Romero Flores
5 Jul 2008	United Nations Stakes	Presious Passion	Eddie Castro
5 Jul 2008	Vanity Handicap	Zenyatta	Mike Smith
12 Jul 2008	Man o' War Stakes	Red Rocks	Javier Castellano
12 Jul 2008	Princess Rooney Handicap	Mistical Plan	Corey Nakatani
19 Jul 2008	Coaching Club American Oaks	Music Note	Javier Castellano
20 Jul 2008	Eddie Read Handicap	Monzante	Rafael Bejarano
26 Jul 2008	Diana Stakes	Forever Together	Julien Leparoux
26 Jul 2008	Whitney Handicap	Commentator	John Velazquez
27 Jul 2008	Bing Crosby Handicap	Street Boss	David Romero Flores

Canada

DATE	RACE	WINNER	JOCKEY
5 Aug 2007	Breeders' Stakes	Marchfield	Patrick Husbands
16 Sep 2007	Woodbine Mile Stakes	Shakespeare	Garrett Gomez
21 Oct 2007	Canadian International Stakes	Cloudy's Knight	Ramsey Zimmerman
21 Oct 2007	E.P. Taylor Stakes	Mrs. Lindsay	Johnny Murtagh
22 Jun 2008	Queen's Plate Stakes	Not Bourbon	Jono Jones
13 Jul 2008	Prince of Wales Stakes	Harlem Rocker	Eibar Coa

England

DATE	RACE	WINNER	JOCKEY
21 Aug 2007	Juddmonte International Stakes	Authorized	Frankie Dettori
23 Aug 2007	Nunthorpe Stakes	Kingsgate Native	Jimmy Quinn
15 Sep 2007	St. Leger Stakes[2]	Lucarno	Jimmy Fortune
29 Sep 2007	Queen Elizabeth II Stakes	Ramonti	Frankie Dettori
3 May 2008	2,000 Guineas[2]	Henrythenavigator	Johnny Murtagh
4 May 2008	1,000 Guineas	Natagora	Christophe Lemaire
7 Jun 2008	The Derby[2]	New Approach	Kevin Manning
19 Jun 2008	Ascot Gold Cup	Yeats	Johnny Murtagh
5 Jul 2008	Coral-Eclipse Stakes	Mount Nelson	Johnny Murtagh
26 Jul 2008	King George VI and Queen Elizabeth Stakes	Duke of Marmalade	Johnny Murtagh
30 Jul 2008	Sussex Stakes	Henrythenavigator	Johnny Murtagh

Ireland

DATE	RACE	WINNER	JOCKEY
8 Sep 2007	Irish Champion Stakes	Dylan Thomas	Kieren Fallon
15 Sep 2007	Irish St. Leger	Yeats	Kieren Fallon
24 May 2008	Irish 2,000 Guineas	Henrythenavigator	Johnny Murtagh
25 May 2008	Irish 1,000 Guineas	Halfway to Heaven	Seamus Heffernan
29 Jun 2008	Irish Derby	Frozen Fire	Seamus Heffernan
13 Jul 2008	Irish Oaks	Moonstone	Johnny Murtagh

France

DATE	RACE	WINNER	JOCKEY
12 Aug 2007	Prix du Haras de Fresnay-le-Buffard	Manduro	Stéphane Pasquier
7 Oct 2007	Prix de l'Arc de Triomphe	Dylan Thomas	Kieren Fallon
7 Oct 2007	Prix Jean-Luc Lagardère (Grand Critérium)	Rio de la Plata	Frankie Dettori
28 Oct 2007	Prix Royal-Oak	Allegretto	Ryan Moore

Major Thoroughbred Race Winners 2007–08 (continued)

	France (continued)		
27 Apr 2008	Prix Ganay	Duke of Marmalade	Johnny Murtagh
11 May 2008	Poule d'Essai des Poulains	Falco	Olivier Peslier
11 May 2008	Poule d'Essai des Pouliches	Zarkava	Christophe Soumillon
18 May 2008	Prix Saint-Alary	Belle et Celebre	Christophe Lemaire
1 Jun 2008	Prix du Jockey Club	Vision d'Etat	Ioritz Mendizabal
8 Jun 2008	Prix de Diane	Zarkava	Christophe Soumillon
29 Jun 2008	Grand Prix de Saint-Cloud	Youmzain	Richard Hughes
14 Jul 2008	Grand Prix de Paris	Montmartre	Christophe Soumillon
	Germany		
2 Sep 2007	Grosser Preis von Baden	Quijano	Andrasch Starke
23 Sep 2007	Preis von Europa	Schiaparelli	Andrasch Starke
6 Jul 2008	Deutsches Derby	Kamsin	Andrasch Starke
	Italy		
14 Oct 2007	Gran Premio del Jockey Club	Schiaparelli	Andrasch Starke
11 May 2008	Derby Italiano	Cima de Triomphe	Silvano Mulas
	Australia		
20 Oct 2007	Caulfield Cup	Master O'Reilly	Vlad Duric
27 Oct 2007	Cox Plate	El Segundo	Luke Nolen
6 Nov 2007	Melbourne Cup	Efficient	Michael Rodd
	United Arab Emirates		
29 Mar 2008	Dubai Duty Free	Jay Peg	Anton Marcus
29 Mar 2008	Dubai Golden Shaheen	Benny the Bull	Edgar Prado
29 Mar 2008	Dubai Sheema Classic	Sun Classique	Kevin Shea
29 Mar 2008	Dubai World Cup	Curlin	Robby Albarado
29 Mar 2008	Godolphin Mile	Diamond Stripes	Edgar Prado
29 Mar 2008	UAE Derby	Honour Devil	Johnny Murtagh
	Japan		
25 Nov 2007	Japan Cup	Admire Moon	Yasunari Iwata
	Hong Kong		
9 Dec 2007	Hong Kong Cup	Ramonti	Frankie Dettori
23 Feb 2008	Hong Kong Gold Cup	Viva Pataca	Darren Beadman
27 Apr 2008	Queen Elizabeth II Cup	Archipenko	Kevin Shea
	Singapore		
18 May 2008	International Cup	Jay Peg	Anton Marcus

[1]*American Triple Crown race.* [2]*British Triple Crown race.*

Triple Crown Champions—United States

YEAR	HORSE	YEAR	HORSE	YEAR	HORSE	YEAR	HORSE
1919	Sir Barton	1937	War Admiral	1946	Assault	1977	Seattle Slew
1930	Gallant Fox	1941	Whirlaway	1948	Citation	1978	Affirmed
1935	Omaha	1943	Count Fleet	1973	Secretariat		

The Kentucky Derby

YEAR	HORSE	JOCKEY	YEAR	HORSE	JOCKEY
1875	Aristides	Oliver Lewis	1886	Ben Ali	Paul Duffy
1876	Vagrant	Bobby Swim	1887	Montrose	Isaac Lewis
1877	Baden-Baden	William Walker	1888	Macbeth II	George Covington
1878	Day Star	Jimmy Carter	1889	Spokane	Thomas Kiley
1879	Lord Murphy	Charlie Shauer	1890	Riley	Isaac Murphy
1880	Fonso	George Garret Lewis	1891	Kingman	Isaac Murphy
1881	Hindoo	James McLaughlin	1892	Azra	Alonzo Clayton
1882	Apollo	Babe Hurd	1893	Lookout	Eddie Kunze
1883	Leonatus	William Donohue	1894	Chant	Frank Goodale
1884	Buchanan	Isaac Murphy	1895	Halma	James Perkins
1885	Joe Cotton	Erskine Henderson	1896	Ben Brush	Willie Simms

The Kentucky Derby (continued)

YEAR	HORSE	JOCKEY
1897	Typhoon II	Fred Garner
1898	Plaudit	Willie Simms
1899	Manuel	Fred Taral
1900	Lieut. Gibson	Jimmy Boland
1901	His Eminence	James Winkfield
1902	Alan-a-Dale	James Winkfield
1903	Judge Himes	Harold Booker
1904	Elwood	Frank Prior
1905	Agile	Jack Martin
1906	Sir Huon	Roscoe Troxler
1907	Pink Star	Andy Minder
1908	Stone Street	Arthur Pickens
1909	Wintergreen	Vincent Powers
1910	Donau	Fred Herbert
1911	Meridian	George Archibald
1912	Worth	Carroll Hugh Shilling
1913	Donerail	Roscoe Goose
1914	Old Rosebud	John McCabe
1915	Regret	Joe Notter
1916	George Smith	John Loftus
1917	Omar Khayyam	Charles Borel
1918	Exterminator	William Knapp
1919	Sir Barton	John Loftus
1920	Paul Jones	Ted Rice
1921	Behave Yourself	Charles Thompson
1922	Morvich	Albert Johnson
1923	Zev	Earl Sande
1924	Black Gold	John D. Mooney
1925	Flying Ebony	Earl Sande
1926	Bubbling Over	Albert Johnson
1927	Whiskery	Linus McAtee
1928	Reigh Count	Charles Lang
1929	Clyde Van Dusen	Linus McAtee
1930	Gallant Fox	Earl Sande
1931	Twenty Grand	Charles Kurtsinger
1932	Burgoo King	Eugene James
1933	Brokers Tip	Don Meade
1934	Cavalcade	Mack Garner
1935	Omaha	William Saunders
1936	Bold Venture	Ira Hanford
1937	War Admiral	Charles Kurtsinger
1938	Lawrin	Eddie Arcaro
1939	Johnstown	James Stout
1940	Gallahadion	Carroll Bierman
1941	Whirlaway	Eddie Arcaro
1942	Shut Out	Wayne D. Wright
1943	Count Fleet	John Longden
1944	Pensive	Conn McCreary
1945	Hoop Jr.	Eddie Arcaro
1946	Assault	Warren Mehrtens
1947	Jet Pilot	Eric Guerin
1948	Citation	Eddie Arcaro
1949	Ponder	Steve Brooks
1950	Middleground	William Boland
1951	Count Turf	Conn McCreary
1952	Hill Gail	Eddie Arcaro
1953	Dark Star	Henry Moreno
1954	Determine	Raymond York
1955	Swaps	William Shoemaker
1956	Needles	David Erb
1957	Iron Liege	William Hartack
1958	Tim Tam	Ismael Valenzuela
1959	Tomy Lee	William Shoemaker
1960	Venetian Way	William Hartack
1961	Carry Back	John Sellers
1962	Decidedly	William Hartack
1963	Chateaugay	Braulio Baeza
1964	Northern Dancer	William Hartack
1965	Lucky Debonair	William Shoemaker
1966	Kauai King	Don Brumfield
1967	Proud Clarion	Robert Ussery
1968	Forward Pass	Ismael Valenzuela
1969	Majestic Prince	William Hartack
1970	Dust Commander	Mike Manganello
1971	Canonero II	Gustavo Avila
1972	Riva Ridge	Ron Turcotte
1973	Secretariat[1]	Ron Turcotte
1974	Cannonade	Angel Cordero, Jr.
1975	Foolish Pleasure	Jacinto Vasquez
1976	Bold Forbes	Angel Cordero, Jr.
1977	Seattle Slew	Jean Cruguet
1978	Affirmed	Steve Cauthen
1979	Spectacular Bid	Ronnie Franklin
1980	Genuine Risk	Jacinto Vasquez
1981	Pleasant Colony	Jorge Velasquez
1982	Gato del Sol	Eddie Delahoussaye
1983	Sunny's Halo	Eddie Delahoussaye
1984	Swale	Laffit Pincay, Jr.
1985	Spend a Buck	Angel Cordero, Jr.
1986	Ferdinand	William Shoemaker
1987	Alysheba	Chris McCarron
1988	Winning Colors	Gary Stevens
1989	Sunday Silence	Patrick Valenzuela
1990	Unbridled	Craig Perret
1991	Strike the Gold	Chris Antley
1992	Lil E. Tee	Pat Day
1993	Sea Hero	Jerry Bailey
1994	Go for Gin	Chris McCarron
1995	Thunder Gulch	Gary Stevens
1996	Grindstone	Jerry Bailey
1997	Silver Charm	Gary Stevens
1998	Real Quiet	Kent Desormeaux
1999	Charismatic	Chris Antley
2000	Fusaichi Pegasus	Kent Desormeaux
2001	Monarchos	Jorge Chávez
2002	War Emblem	Victor Espinoza
2003	Funny Cide	José Santos
2004	Smarty Jones	Stewart Elliott
2005	Giacomo	Mike Smith
2006	Barbaro	Edgar Prado
2007	Street Sense	Calvin Borel
2008	Big Brown	Kent Desormeaux

[1]*Fastest time—1 min $59\frac{2}{5}$ sec.*

The Preakness Stakes

YEAR	HORSE	JOCKEY
1873	Survivor	George Barbee
1874	Culpepper	William Donohue
1875	Tom Ochiltree	Lloyd Hughes
1876	Shirley	George Barbee
1877	Cloverbrook	Cyrus Holloway
1878	Duke of Magenta	Cyrus Holloway
1879	Harold	Lloyd Hughes
1880	Grenada	Lloyd Hughes
1881	Saunterer	T. Costello
1882	Vanguard	T. Costello

The Preakness Stakes (continued)

YEAR	HORSE	JOCKEY
1883	Jacobus	George Barbee
1884	Knight of Ellerslie	S. Fisher
1885	Tecumseh	James McLaughlin
1886	The Bard	S. Fisher
1887	Dunboyne	William Donohue
1888	Refund	Fred Littlefield
1889	Buddhist	George Anderson
1890	Montague	W. Martin
1894[1]	Assignee	Fred Taral
1895	Belmar	Fred Taral
1896	Margrave	Henry Griffin
1897	Paul Kauvar	T. Thorpe
1898	Sly Fox	Willie Simms
1899	Half Time	R. Clawson
1900	Hindus	H. Spencer
1901	The Parader	Fred Landry
1902	Old England	L. Jackson
1903	Flocarline	W. Gannon
1904	Bryn Mawr	Eugene Hildebrand
1905	Cairngorm	W. Davis
1906	Whimsical	Walter Miller
1907	Don Enrique	G. Mountain
1908	Royal Tourist	Eddie Dugan
1909	Effendi	Willie Doyle
1910	Layminster	Roy Estep
1911	Watervale	Eddie Dugan
1912	Colonel Holloway	Clarence Turner
1913	Buskin	James Butwell
1914	Holiday	Andy Schuttinger
1915	Rhine Maiden	Douglas Hoffman
1916	Damrosch	Linus McAtee
1917	Kalitan	Everett Haynes
1918[2]	War Cloud	John Loftus
	Jack Hare, Jr.	Charles Peak
1919	Sir Barton	John Loftus
1920	Man o' War	Clarence Kummer
1921	Broomspun	Frank Coltiletti
1922	Pillory	Louis Morris
1923	Vigil	Benny Marinelli
1924	Nellie Morse	John Merimee
1925	Coventry	Clarence Kummer
1926	Display	John Maiben
1927	Bostonian	Alf J. "Whitey" Abel
1928	Victorian	Raymond Workman
1929	Dr. Freeland	Louis Schaefer
1930	Gallant Fox	Earl Sande
1931	Mate	George Ellis
1932	Burgoo King	Eugene James
1933	Head Play	Charles Kurtsinger
1934	High Quest	Robert Jones
1935	Omaha	Willie Saunders
1936	Bold Venture	George Woolf
1937	War Admiral	Charles Kurtsinger
1938	Dauber	Maurice Peters
1939	Challedon	George Seabo
1940	Bimelech	Fred A. Smith
1941	Whirlaway	Eddie Arcaro
1942	Alsab	Basil James
1943	Count Fleet	John Longden
1944	Pensive	Conn McCreary
1945	Polynesian	Wayne D. Wright
1946	Assault	Warren Mehrtens
1947	Faultless	Doug Dodson
1948	Citation	Eddie Arcaro
1949	Capot	Ted Atkinson
1950	Hill Prince	Eddie Arcaro
1951	Bold	Eddie Arcaro
1952	Blue Man	Conn McCreary
1953	Native Dancer	Eric Guerin
1954	Hasty Road	Johnny Adams
1955	Nashua	Eddie Arcaro
1956	Fabius	William Hartack
1957	Bold Ruler	Eddie Arcaro
1958	Tim Tam	Ismael Valenzuela
1959	Royal Orbit	William Harmatz
1960	Bally Ache	Robert Ussery
1961	Carry Back	John Sellers
1962	Greek Money	John L. Rotz
1963	Candy Spots	William Shoemaker
1964	Northern Dancer	William Hartack
1965	Tom Rolfe	Ron Turcotte
1966	Kauai King	Don Brumfield
1967	Damascus	William Shoemaker
1968	Forward Pass	Ismael Valenzuela
1969	Majestic Prince	William Hartack
1970	Personality	Eddie Belmonte
1971	Canonero II	Gustavo Avila
1972	Bee Bee Bee	Eldon Nelson
1973	Secretariat	Ron Turcotte
1974	Little Current	Miguel Rivera
1975	Master Derby	Darrel McHague
1976	Elocutionist	John Lively
1977	Seattle Slew	Jean Cruguet
1978	Affirmed	Steve Cauthen
1979	Spectacular Bid	Ron Franklin
1980	Codex	Angel Cordero, Jr.
1981	Pleasant Colony	Jorge Velasquez
1982	Aloma's Ruler	Jack Kaenel
1983	Deputed Testamony	Donald Miller
1984	Gate Dancer	Angel Cordero, Jr.
1985	Tank's Prospect[3]	Pat Day
1986	Snow Chief	Alex Solis
1987	Alysheba	Chris McCarron
1988	Risen Star	Eddie Delahoussaye
1989	Sunday Silence	Patrick Valenzuela
1990	Summer Squall	Pat Day
1991	Hansel	Jerry Bailey
1992	Pine Bluff	Chris McCarron
1993	Prairie Bayou	Mike Smith
1994	Tabasco Cat	Pat Day
1995	Timber Country	Pat Day
1996	Louis Quatorze	Pat Day
1997	Silver Charm	Gary Stevens
1998	Real Quiet	Kent Desormeaux
1999	Charismatic	Chris Antley
2000	Red Bullet	Jerry Bailey
2001	Point Given	Gary Stevens
2002	War Emblem	Victor Espinoza
2003	Funny Cide	José Santos
2004	Smarty Jones	Stewart Elliott
2005	Afleet Alex	Jeremy Rose
2006	Bernardini	Javier Castellano
2007	Curlin	Robby Albarado
2008	Big Brown	Kent Desormeaux

[1]No competition in 1891–93. *[2]Run in two divisions in 1918 because of the large number of starters.*
[3]Fastest time—1 min 53⅖ sec.

The Belmont Stakes

YEAR	HORSE	JOCKEY
1867	Ruthless	Gilbert Patrick
1868	General Duke	Bobby Swim
1869	Fenian	Charley Miller
1870	Kingfisher	Edward Brown
1871	Harry Bassett	W. Miller
1872	Joe Daniels	James Rowe
1873	Springbok	James Rowe
1874	Saxon	George Barbee
1875	Calvin	Bobby Swim
1876	Algerine	Billy Donohue
1877	Cloverbrook	Cyrus Holloway
1878	Duke of Magenta	Lloyd Hughes
1879	Spendthrift	George Evans
1880	Grenada	Lloyd Hughes
1881	Saunterer	T. Costello
1882	Forester	James McLaughlin
1883	George Kinney	James McLaughlin
1884	Panique	James McLaughlin
1885	Tyrant	Paul Duffy
1886	Inspector B	James McLaughlin
1887	Hanover	James McLaughlin
1888	Sir Dixon	James McLaughlin
1889	Eric	W. Hayward
1890	Burlington	Shelby Barnes
1891	Foxford	Edward Garrison
1892	Patron	W. Hayward
1893	Comanche	Willie Simms
1894	Henry of Navarre	Willie Simms
1895	Belmar	Fred Taral
1896	Hastings	Henry Griffin
1897	Scottish Chieftain	J. Scherrer
1898	Bowling Brook	Fred Littlefield
1899	Jean Bereaud	R. Clawson
1900	Ildrim	Nash Turner
1901	Commando	H. Spencer
1902	Masterman	John Bullman
1903	Africander	John Bullman
1904	Delhi	George Odom
1905	Tanya	Eugene Hildebrand
1906	Burgomaster	Lucien Lyne
1907	Peter Pan	G. Mountain
1908	Colin	Joe Notter
1909	Joe Madden	Eddie Dugan
1910	Sweep	James Butwell
1913[1]	Prince Eugene	Roscoe Troxler
1914	Luke McLuke	Merritt Buxton
1915	The Finn	George Byrne
1916	Friar Rock	Everett Haynes
1917	Hourless	James Butwell
1918	Johren	Frank Robinson
1919	Sir Barton	John Loftus
1920	Man o' War	Clarence Kummer
1921	Grey Lag	Earl Sande
1922	Pillory	C.H. Miller
1923	Zev	Earl Sande
1924	Mad Play	Earl Sande
1925	American Flag	Albert Johnson
1926	Crusader	Albert Johnson
1927	Chance Shot	Earl Sande
1928	Vito	Clarence Kummer
1929	Blue Larkspur	Mack Garner
1930	Gallant Fox	Earl Sande
1931	Twenty Grand	Charles Kurtsinger
1932	Faireno	Tom Malley
1933	Hurryoff	Mack Garner
1934	Peace Chance	Wayne D. Wright
1935	Omaha	Willie Saunders
1936	Granville	James Stout
1937	War Admiral	Charles Kurtsinger
1938	Pasteurized	James Stout
1939	Johnstown	James Stout
1940	Bimelech	Fred A. Smith
1941	Whirlaway	Eddie Arcaro
1942	Shut Out	Eddie Arcaro
1943	Count Fleet	John Longden
1944	Bounding Home	Gayle L. Smith
1945	Pavot	Eddie Arcaro
1946	Assault	Warren Mehrtens
1947	Phalanx	Ruperto Donoso
1948	Citation	Eddie Arcaro
1949	Capot	Ted Atkinson
1950	Middleground	William Boland
1951	Counterpoint	David Gorman
1952	One Count	Eddie Arcaro
1953	Native Dancer	Eric Guerin
1954	High Gun	Eric Guerin
1955	Nashua	Eddie Arcaro
1956	Needles	David Erb
1957	Gallant Man	William Shoemaker
1958	Cavan	Pete Anderson
1959	Sword Dancer	William Shoemaker
1960	Celtic Ash	William Hartack
1961	Sherluck	Braulio Baeza
1962	Jaipur	William Shoemaker
1963	Chateaugay	Braulio Baeza
1964	Quadrangle	Manuel Ycaza
1965	Hail to All	John Sellers
1966	Amberoid	William Boland
1967	Damascus	William Shoemaker
1968	Stage Door Johnny	Heliodoro Gustines
1969	Arts and Letters	Braulio Baeza
1970	High Echelon	John Rotz
1971	Pass Catcher	Walter Blum
1972	Riva Ridge	Ron Turcotte
1973[2]	Secretariat	Ron Turcotte
1974	Little Current	Miguel Rivera
1975	Avatar	William Shoemaker
1976	Bold Forbes	Angel Cordero, Jr.
1977	Seattle Slew	Jean Cruguet
1978	Affirmed	Steve Cauthen
1979	Coastal	Ruben Hernandez
1980	Temperence Hill	Eddie Maple
1981	Summing	George Martens
1982	Conquistador Cielo	Laffit Pincay, Jr.
1983	Caveat	Laffit Pincay, Jr.
1984	Swale	Laffit Pincay, Jr.
1985	Creme Fraiche	Eddie Maple
1986	Danzig Connection	Chris McCarron
1987	Bet Twice	Craig Perret
1988	Risen Star	Eddie Delahoussaye
1989	Easy Goer	Pat Day
1990	Go and Go	Mick Kinane
1991	Hansel	Jerry Bailey
1992	A.P. Indy	Eddie Delahoussaye
1993	Colonial Affair	Julie Krone
1994	Tabasco Cat	Pat Day
1995	Thunder Gulch	Gary Stevens
1996	Editor's Note	Rene Douglas
1997	Touch Gold	Chris McCarron
1998	Victory Gallop	Gary Stevens
1999	Lemon Drop Kid	José Santos
2000	Commendable	Pat Day
2001	Point Given	Gary Stevens
2002	Sarava	Edgar Prado

The Belmont Stakes (continued)

YEAR	HORSE	JOCKEY	YEAR	HORSE	JOCKEY
2003	Empire Maker	Jerry Bailey	2006	Jazil	Fernando Jara
2004	Birdstone	Edgar Prado	2007	Rags to Riches	John Velazquez
2005	Afleet Alex	Jeremy Rose	2008	Da' Tara	Alan Garcia

[1]*No competition in 1911–1912.* [2]*Fastest time—2 min 24 sec.*

Horse of the Year

A Horse of the Year was selected by the *Daily Racing Form* from 1936 to 1970 and independently by the Thoroughbred Racing Association beginning in 1950. From 1971 these two organizations, plus the National Turf Writers Association, founded the Eclipse Awards, of which the Horse of the Year is the top among the 22 American prizes.

YEAR	HORSE	YEAR	HORSE	YEAR	HORSE	YEAR	HORSE
1936	Granville	1954	Native Dancer	1971	Ack Ack	1989	Sunday Silence
1937	War Admiral	1955	Nashua	1972	Seçretariat	1990	Criminal Type
1938	Seabiscuit	1956	Swaps	1973	Secretariat	1991	Black Tie Affair
1939	Challedon	1957	Bold Ruler[1]; Dedicate[2]	1974	Forego	1992	A.P. Indy
1940	Challedon	1958	Round Table	1975	Forego	1993	Kotashaan
1941	Whirlaway	1959	Sword Dancer	1976	Forego	1994	Holy Bull
1942	Whirlaway	1960	Kelso	1977	Seattle Slew	1995	Cigar
1943	Count Fleet	1961	Kelso	1978	Affirmed	1996	Cigar
1944	Twilight Tear	1962	Kelso	1979	Affirmed	1997	Favorite Trick
1945	Busher	1963	Kelso	1980	Spectacular Bid	1998	Skip Away
1946	Assault	1964	Kelso	1981	John Henry	1999	Charismatic
1947	Armed	1965	Roman Brother[1]; Moccasin[2]	1982	Conquistador Cielo	2000	Tiznow
1948	Citation	1966	Buckpasser	1983	All Along	2001	Point Given
1949	Capot[1]; Coaltown[2]	1967	Damascus	1984	John Henry	2002	Azeri
1950	Hill Prince	1968	Dr. Fager	1985	Spend a Buck	2003	Mineshaft
1951	Counterpoint	1969	Arts and Letters	1986	Lady's Secret	2004	Ghostzapper
1952	One Count[1]; Native Dancer[2]	1970	Fort Marcy[1]; Personality[2]	1987	Ferdinand	2005	Saint Liam
1953	Tom Fool			1988	Alysheba	2006	Invasor
						2007	Curlin

[1]*Daily Racing Form.* [2]Thoroughbred Racing Association.

2,000 Guineas

England's 2,000 Guineas race has been run since 1809. The table shows the winners for the past 20 years.

YEAR	HORSE	JOCKEY	YEAR	HORSE	JOCKEY
1989	Nashwan	Willie Carson	1999	Island Sands	Frankie Dettori
1990	Tirol	Mick Kinane	2000	King's Best	Kieren Fallon
1991	Mystiko	Michael Roberts	2001	Golan	Kieren Fallon
1992	Rodrigo de Triano	Lester Piggot	2002	Rock of Gibraltar	Johnny Murtagh
1993	Zafonic	Pat Eddery	2003	Refuse To Bend	Pat Smullen
1994	Mister Baileys	Jason Weaver	2004	Haafhd	Richard Hills
1995	Pennekamp	Thierry Jarnet	2005	Footstepsinthesand	Kieren Fallon
1996	Mark of Esteem	Frankie Dettori	2006	George Washington	Kieren Fallon
1997	Entrepreneur	Mick Kinane	2007	Cockney Rebel	Olivier Peslier
1998	King of Kings	Mick Kinane	2008	Henrythenavigator	Johnny Murtagh

The Derby

The Derby has been run since 1780. The table shows the winners for the past 20 years.

YEAR	HORSE	JOCKEY	YEAR	HORSE	JOCKEY
1989	Nashwan	Willie Carson	1997	Benny the Dip	Willie Ryan
1990	Quest for Fame	Pat Eddery	1998	High Rise	Olivier Peslier
1991	Generous	Alan Munro	1999	Oath	Kieren Fallon
1992	Dr Devious	John Reid	2000	Sinndar	Johnny Murtagh
1993	Commander in Chief	Mick Kinane	2001	Galileo	Mick Kinane
1994	Erhaab	Willie Carson	2002	High Chaparral	Johnny Murtagh
1995	Lammtarra	Walter R. Swinburn	2003	Kris Kin	Kieren Fallon
1996	Shaamit	Michael Hills	2004	North Light	Kieren Fallon

The Derby (continued)

YEAR	HORSE	JOCKEY	YEAR	HORSE	JOCKEY
2005	Motivator	Johnny Murtagh	2007	Authorized	Frankie Dettori
2006	Sir Percy	Martin Dwyer	2008	New Approach	Kevin Manning

The St. Leger

The St. Leger has been run since 1776. The table shows the winners for the past 20 years.

YEAR	HORSE	JOCKEY	YEAR	HORSE	JOCKEY
1988	Minster Son	Willie Carson	1998	Nedawi	John Reid
1989	Michelozzo	Steve Cauthen	1999	Mutafaweq	Richard Hills
1990	Snurge	Richard Quinn	2000	Millenary	Richard Quinn
1991	Toulon	Pat Eddery	2001	Milan	Mick Kinane
1992	User Friendly	George Duffield	2002	Bollin Eric	Kevin Darley
1993	Bob's Return	Philip Robinson	2003	Brian Boru	Jamie Spencer
1994	Moonax	Pat Eddery	2004	Rule of Law	Kerrin McEvoy
1995	Classic Cliché	Frankie Dettori	2005	Scorpion	Frankie Dettori
1996	Shantou	Frankie Dettori	2006	Sixties Icon	Frankie Dettori
1997	Silver Patriarch	Pat Eddery	2007	Lucarno	Jimmy Fortune

Triple Crown Champions—British

YEAR	WINNER	YEAR	WINNER	YEAR	WINNER	YEAR	WINNER
1853	West Australian	1891	Common	1900	Diamond Jubilee	1918	Gainsborough
1865	Gladiateur	1893	Isinglass	1903	Rock Sand	1935	Bahram
1866	Lord Lyon	1897	Galtee More	1915	Pommern	1970	Nijinsky
1886	Ormonde	1899	Flying Fox	1917	Gay Crusader		

Melbourne Cup

The Melbourne Cup race has been run since 1861. The table shows the winners for the past 20 years.

YEAR	HORSE	JOCKEY	YEAR	HORSE	JOCKEY
1988	Empire Rose	Tony Allan	1998	Jezabeel	Chris Munce
1989	Tawrrific	Shane Dye	1999	Rogan Josh	John Marshall
1990	Kingston Rule	Darren Beadman	2000	Brew	Kerrin McEvoy
1991	Let's Elope	Steven King	2001	Ethereal	Scott Seamer
1992	Subzero	Greg Hall	2002	Media Puzzle	Damien Oliver
1993	Vintage Crop	Mick Kinane	2003	Makybe Diva	Glen Boss
1994	Jeune	Wayne Harris	2004	Makybe Diva	Glen Boss
1995	Doriemus	Damien Oliver	2005	Makybe Diva	Glen Boss
1996	Saintly	Darren Beadman	2006	Delta Blues	Yasunari Iwata
1997	Might and Power	Jim Cassidy	2007	Efficient	Michael Rodd

The Dubai World Cup

YEAR	HORSE	JOCKEY	YEAR	HORSE	JOCKEY
1996	Cigar	Jerry Bailey	2003	Moon Ballad	Frankie Dettori
1997	Singspiel	Jerry Bailey	2004	Pleasantly Perfect	Alex Solis
1998	Silver Charm	Gary Stevens	2005	Roses in May	John Velazquez
1999	Almutawakel	Richard Hills	2006	Electrocutionist	Frankie Dettori
2000	Dubai Millennium	Frankie Dettori	2007	Invasor	Fernando Jara
2001	Captain Steve	Jerry Bailey	2008	Curlin	Robby Albarado
2002	Street Cry	Jerry Bailey			

The Hambletonian Trot

YEAR	HORSE	DRIVER	YEAR	HORSE	DRIVER
1926	Guy McKinney	Nat Ray	1934	Lord Jim	Hugh M. Parshall
1927	Iosola's Worthy	Marvin Childs	1935	Greyhound	Scepter F. Palin
1928	Spencer	William H. Leese	1936	Rosalind	Ben White
1929	Walter Dear	Walter Cox	1937	Shirley Hanover	Henry Thomas
1930	Hanover's Bertha	Thomas Berry	1938	McLin Hanover	Henry Thomas
1931	Calumet Butler	Richard D. McMahon	1939	Peter Astra	Hugh M. Parshall
1932	The Marchioness	William Caton	1940	Spencer Scott	Fred Egan
1933	Mary Reynolds	Ben White	1941	Bill Gallon	Lee Smith

The Hambletonian Trot (continued)

YEAR	HORSE	DRIVER
1942	The Ambassador	Ben White
1943	Volo Song	Ben White
1944	Yankee Maid	Henry Thomas
1945	Titan Hanover	Harry Pownall, Sr.
1946	Chestertown	Thomas Berry
1947	Hoot Mon	Scepter F. Palin
1948	Demon Hanover	Harrison Hoyt
1949	Miss Tilly	Fred Egan
1950	Lusty Song	Delvin Miller
1951	Mainliner	Guy Crippen
1952	Sharp Note	Bion Shively
1953	Helicopter	Harry Harvey
1954	Newport Dream	Adelbert Cameron
1955	Scott Frost	Joseph O'Brien
1956	The Intruder	Ned Bower
1957	Hickory Smoke	John Simpson, Sr.
1958	Emily's Pride	Flave Nipe
1959	Diller Hanover	Frank Ervin
1960	Blaze Hanover	Joseph O'Brien
1961	Harlan Dean	James Arthur
1962	A.C.'s Viking	Sanders Russell
1963	Speedy Scot	Ralph Baldwin
1964	Ayres	John Simpson, Sr.
1965	Egyptian Candor	Adelbert Cameron
1966	Kerry Way	Frank Ervin
1967	Speedy Streak	Adelbert Cameron
1968	Nevele Pride	Stanley Dancer
1969	Lindy's Pride	Howard Beissinger
1970	Timothy T.	John Simpson, Sr.
1971	Speedy Crown	Howard Beissinger
1972	Super Bowl	Stanley Dancer
1973	Flirth	Ralph Baldwin
1974	Christopher T.	William Haughton
1975	Bonefish	Stanley Dancer
1976	Steve Lobell	William Haughton
1977	Green Speed	William Haughton
1978	Speedy Somolli	Howard Beissinger
1979	Legend Hanover	George Sholty
1980	Burgomeister	William Haughton
1981	Shiaway St. Pat	Ray Remmen
1982	Speed Bowl	Tom Haughton
1983	Duenna	Stanley Dancer
1984	Historic Freight	Ben Webster
1985	Prakas	William O'Donnell
1986	Nuclear Kosmos	Ulf Thoresen
1987	Mack Lobell	John Campbell
1988	Armbro Goal	John Campbell
1989	Park Avenue Joe; Probe (tied)	Ronald Waples; William Fahy
1990	Harmonious	John Campbell
1991	Giant Victory	Jack Moiseyev
1992	Alf Palema	Mickey McNichol
1993	American Winner	Ron Pierce
1994	Victory Dream	Michel Lachance
1995	Tagliabue	John Campbell
1996	Continentalvictory	Michel Lachance
1997	Malabar Man	Malvern Burroughs
1998	Muscles Yankee	John Campbell
1999	Self Possessed	Michel Lachance
2000	Yankee Paco	Trevor Ritchie
2001	Scarlet Knight	Stefan Melander
2002	Chip Chip Hooray	Eric Ledford
2003	Amigo Hall	Michel Lachance
2004	Windsong's Legacy	Trond Smedshammer
2005	Vivid Photo	Roger Hammer
2006	Glidemaster	John Campbell
2007	Donato Hanover	Ron Pierce
2008	Deweycheatumnhowe	Ray Schnittker

Ice Hockey

The **National Hockey League** (NHL), which was organized in Canada in 1917 with five professional teams, welcomed the first US team, the Boston Bruins, in 1924. Since 1926 the symbol of supremacy in professional hockey has been the **Stanley Cup,** which is awarded to the winner of a play-off that concludes the NHL season. The Stanley Cup was presented to amateur champions from 1893 to 1925.

The **World Hockey Championships,** contested by national teams and sponsored by the **International Ice Hockey Federation** (IIHF; founded 1908), have been held since 1930 for men and since 1990 for women.

Related Web sites: National Hockey League: <www.nhl.com>; International Ice Hockey Federation: <www.iihf.com>.

World Hockey Championship—Men

YEAR	WINNER
1930	Canada
1931	Canada
1932[1]	Canada
1933	United States
1934	Canada
1935	Canada
1936[1]	Great Britain
1937	Canada
1938	Canada
1939	Canada
1940–46	*not held*
1947	Czechoslovakia
1948[1]	Canada
1949	Czechoslovakia
1950	Canada
1951	Canada
1952[1]	Canada
1953	Sweden
1954	USSR
1955	Canada
1956[1]	USSR
1957	Sweden
1958	Canada
1959	Canada
1960[1]	United States
1961	Canada
1962	Sweden
1963	USSR
1964[1]	USSR
1965	USSR
1966	USSR
1967	USSR
1968[1]	USSR
1969	USSR
1970	USSR
1971	USSR
1972[2]	Czechoslovakia
1973	USSR
1974	USSR
1975	USSR
1976	Czechoslovakia
1977	Czechoslovakia
1978	USSR
1979	USSR
1980[1]	United States
1981	USSR
1982	USSR
1983	USSR
1984[1]	USSR
1985	Czechoslovakia
1986	USSR
1987	Sweden

World Hockey Championship—Men (continued)

YEAR	WINNER	YEAR	WINNER	YEAR	WINNER	YEAR	WINNER
1988[1]	USSR	1994	Canada	2000	Czech Republic	2006	Sweden
1989	USSR	1995	Finland	2001	Czech Republic	2007	Canada
1990	Sweden	1996	Czech Republic	2002	Slovakia	2008	Russia
1991	Sweden	1997	Canada	2003	Canada		
1992	Sweden	1998	Sweden	2004	Canada		
1993	Russia	1999	Czech Republic	2005	Czech Republic		

[1]*Olympic champions, recognized as world champions in this table (for earlier Olympics, see Olympic Games).*
[2]*In 1972 a separate world championship was held for the first time in an Olympic year.*

World Hockey Championship—Women

YEAR	WINNER	YEAR	WINNER	YEAR	WINNER
1990	Canada	1999	Canada	2004	Canada
1992	Canada	2000	Canada	2005	United States
1994	Canada	2001	Canada	2006[1]	Canada
1997	Canada	2002[1]	Canada	2007	Canada
1998[1]	United States	2003	*not held*	2008	United States

[1]*Olympic champions; separate world championships are not held in Olympic years. Olympic gold medalists are sometimes considered world champions.*

National Hockey League Final Standings, 2008

EASTERN CONFERENCE

Northeast Division

	WON	LOST	OTL[1]
Montreal[2]	47	25	10
Ottawa[2]	43	31	8
Boston[2]	41	29	12
Buffalo	39	31	12
Toronto	36	35	11

Atlantic Division

	WON	LOST	OTL[1]
Pittsburgh[2]	47	27	8
New Jersey[2]	46	29	7
New York Rangers[2]	42	27	13
Philadelphia[2]	42	29	11
New York Islanders	35	38	9

Southeast Division

	WON	LOST	OTL[1]
Washington[2]	43	31	8
Carolina	43	33	6
Florida	38	35	9
Atlanta	34	40	8
Tampa Bay	31	42	9

WESTERN CONFERENCE

Central Division

	WON	LOST	OTL[1]
Detroit[2]	54	21	7
Nashville[2]	41	32	9
Chicago	40	34	8
Columbus	34	36	12
St. Louis	33	36	13

Northwest Division

	WON	LOST	OTL[1]
Minnesota[2]	44	28	10
Colorado[2]	44	31	7
Calgary[2]	42	30	10
Edmonton	41	35	6
Vancouver	39	33	10

Pacific Division

	WON	LOST	OTL[1]
San Jose[2]	49	23	10
Anaheim[2]	47	27	8
Dallas[2]	45	30	7
Phoenix	38	37	7
Los Angeles	32	43	7

[1]*Overtime losses, worth one point.* [2]*Gained play-off berth.*

The Stanley Cup

YEAR	WINNER	RUNNER-UP	RESULTS
1893	Montreal Amateur Athletic Association	*no challengers*	
1894	Montreal Amateur Athletic Association	Ottawa Generals	2-0
1895	Montreal Victorias	*no challengers*	
1896	Winnipeg Victorias (Feb.); Montreal Victorias (Dec.)	Montreal Victorias (Feb.); Winnipeg Victorias (Dec.)	1-0; 1-0
1897	Montreal Victorias	Ottawa Capitals	1-0
1898	Montreal Victorias	*no challengers*	
1899	Montreal Victorias (Feb.); Montreal Shamrocks (March)	Winnipeg Victorias (Feb.); Queen's University (March)	2-0; 1-0
1900	Montreal Shamrocks	Winnipeg Victorias; Halifax Crescents	2-1; 2-0
1901	Winnipeg Victorias	Montreal Shamrocks	2-0
1902	Winnipeg Victorias (Jan.); Montreal Amateur Athletic Association (March)	Toronto Wellingtons (Jan.); Winnipeg Victorias (March)	2-0; 2-1

The Stanley Cup (continued)

YEAR	WINNER	RUNNER-UP	RESULTS
1903	Montreal Amateur Athletic Association (Feb.); Ottawa Silver Seven (March)	Winnipeg Victorias (Feb.); Montreal Victorias (March); Rat Portage Thistles (March)	2–1; 1–0; 2–0
1904	Ottawa Silver Seven	Winnipeg Rowing Club; Toronto Marlboros; Montreal Wanderers; Brandon Wheat Kings	2–1; 2–0; 0–0 (tie); 2–0
1905	Ottawa Silver Seven	Dawson City Nuggets; Rat Portage Thistles	2–0; 2–1
1906	Ottawa Silver Seven (Feb., March); Montreal Wanderers (March, Dec.)	Queen's University (Feb.); Smiths Falls (March); Ottawa Silver Seven (March); New Glasgow Cubs (Dec.)	2–0; 2–0; 1–1; 2–0
1907	Kenora Thistles (Jan.); Montreal Wanderers (March)	Montreal Wanderers (Jan.); Kenora Thistles (March)	2–0; 1–1
1908	Montreal Wanderers	Ottawa Victorias; Winnipeg Maple Leafs; Toronto Trolley Leaguers; Edmonton Eskimos	2–0; 2–0; 1–0; 1–1
1909	Ottawa Senators	*no challengers*	
1910	Ottawa Senators (Jan.); Montreal Wanderers (March)	Edmonton Eskimos (Jan.); Galt (Jan.); Berlin Union Jacks (March)	1–0; 2–0; 2–0
1911	Ottawa Senators	Port Arthur Bearcats; Galt	1–0; 1–0
1912	Quebec Bulldogs	Moncton Victories	2–0
1913	Quebec Bulldogs[1]	Sydney Miners	2–0
1914	Toronto Blueshirts	Victoria Cougars; Montreal Canadiens	3–0; 1–1
1915	Vancouver Millionaires	Ottawa Senators	3–0
1916	Montreal Canadiens	Portland Rosebuds	3–2
1917	Seattle Metropolitans	Montreal Canadiens	3–1
1918	Toronto Arenas	Vancouver Millionaires	3–2
1919	*no decision*[2]		
1920	Ottawa Senators	Seattle Metropolitans	3–2
1921	Ottawa Senators	Vancouver Millionaires	3–2
1922	Toronto St. Pats	Vancouver Millionaires	3–2
1923	Ottawa Senators	Edmonton Eskimos; Vancouver Maroons	2–0; 3–1
1924	Montreal Canadiens	Calgary Tigers; Vancouver Maroons	2–0; 2–0
1925	Victoria Cougars	Montreal Canadiens	3–1
1926	Montreal Maroons	Victoria Cougars	3–1
1927	Ottawa Senators	Boston Bruins	2–0
1928	New York Rangers	Montreal Maroons	3–2
1929	Boston Bruins	New York Rangers	2–0
1930	Montreal Canadiens	Boston Bruins	2–0
1931	Montreal Canadiens	Chicago Black Hawks	3–2
1932	Toronto Maple Leafs	New York Rangers	3–0
1933	New York Rangers	Toronto Maple Leafs	3–1
1934	Chicago Black Hawks	Detroit Red Wings	3–1
1935	Montreal Maroons	Toronto Maple Leafs	3–0
1936	Detroit Red Wings	Toronto Maple Leafs	3–1
1937	Detroit Red Wings	New York Rangers	3–2
1938	Chicago Black Hawks	Toronto Maple Leafs	3–1
1939	Boston Bruins	Toronto Maple Leafs	4–1
1940	New York Rangers	Toronto Maple Leafs	4–2
1941	Boston Bruins	Detroit Red Wings	4–0
1942	Toronto Maple Leafs	Detroit Red Wings	4–3
1943	Detroit Red Wings	Boston Bruins	4–0
1944	Montreal Canadiens	Chicago Black Hawks	4–0
1945	Toronto Maple Leafs	Detroit Red Wings	4–3
1946	Montreal Canadiens	Boston Bruins	4–1
1947	Toronto Maple Leafs	Montreal Canadiens	4–2
1948	Toronto Maple Leafs	Detroit Red Wings	4–0
1949	Toronto Maple Leafs	Detroit Red Wings	4–0
1950	Detroit Red Wings	New York Rangers	4–3
1951	Toronto Maple Leafs	Montreal Canadiens	4–1
1952	Detroit Red Wings	Montreal Canadiens	4–0
1953	Montreal Canadiens	Boston Bruins	4–1
1954	Detroit Red Wings	Montreal Canadiens	4–3
1955	Detroit Red Wings	Montreal Canadiens	4–3
1956	Montreal Canadiens	Detroit Red Wings	4–1
1957	Montreal Canadiens	Boston Bruins	4–1
1958	Montreal Canadiens	Boston Bruins	4–2
1959	Montreal Canadiens	Toronto Maple Leafs	4–1

The Stanley Cup (continued)

YEAR	WINNER	RUNNER-UP	RESULTS
1960	Montreal Canadiens	Toronto Maple Leafs	4-0
1961	Chicago Black Hawks	Detroit Red Wings	4-2
1962	Toronto Maple Leafs	Chicago Black Hawks	4-2
1963	Toronto Maple Leafs	Detroit Red Wings	4-1
1964	Toronto Maple Leafs	Detroit Red Wings	4-3
1965	Montreal Canadiens	Chicago Black Hawks	4-3
1966	Montreal Canadiens	Detroit Red Wings	4-2
1967	Toronto Maple Leafs	Montreal Canadiens	4-2
1968	Montreal Canadiens	St. Louis Blues	4-0
1969	Montreal Canadiens	St. Louis Blues	4-0
1970	Boston Bruins	St. Louis Blues	4-0
1971	Montreal Canadiens	Chicago Black Hawks	4-3
1972	Boston Bruins	New York Rangers	4-2
1973	Montreal Canadiens	Chicago Black Hawks	4-2
1974	Philadelphia Flyers	Boston Bruins	4-2
1975	Philadelphia Flyers	Buffalo Sabres	4-2
1976	Montreal Canadiens	Philadelphia Flyers	4-0
1977	Montreal Canadiens	Boston Bruins	4-0
1978	Montreal Canadiens	Boston Bruins	4-2
1979	Montreal Canadiens	New York Rangers	4-1
1980	New York Islanders	Philadelphia Flyers	4-2
1981	New York Islanders	Minnesota North Stars	4-1
1982	New York Islanders	Vancouver Canucks	4-0
1983	New York Islanders	Edmonton Oilers	4-0
1984	Edmonton Oilers	New York Islanders	4-1
1985	Edmonton Oilers	Philadelphia Flyers	4-1
1986	Montreal Canadiens	Calgary Flames	4-1
1987	Edmonton Oilers	Philadelphia Flyers	4-3
1988	Edmonton Oilers	Boston Bruins	4-0
1989	Calgary Flames	Montreal Canadiens	4-2
1990	Edmonton Oilers	Boston Bruins	4-1
1991	Pittsburgh Penguins	Minnesota North Stars	4-2
1992	Pittsburgh Penguins	Chicago Blackhawks	4-0
1993	Montreal Canadiens	Los Angeles Kings	4-1
1994	New York Rangers	Vancouver Canucks	4-3
1995	New Jersey Devils	Detroit Red Wings	4-0
1996	Colorado Avalanche	Florida Panthers	4-0
1997	Detroit Red Wings	Philadelphia Flyers	4-0
1998	Detroit Red Wings	Washington Capitals	4-0
1999	Dallas Stars	Buffalo Sabres	4-2
2000	New Jersey Devils	Dallas Stars	4-2
2001	Colorado Avalanche	New Jersey Devils	4-3
2002	Detroit Red Wings	Carolina Hurricanes	4-1
2003	New Jersey Devils	Mighty Ducks of Anaheim	4-3
2004	Tampa Bay Lightning	Calgary Flames	4-3
2005	*not held due to players' strike and season cancellation*		
2006	Carolina Hurricanes	Edmonton Oilers	4-3
2007	Anaheim Ducks	Ottawa Senators	4-1
2008	Detroit Red Wings	Pittsburgh Penguins	4-2

[1]*Though Victoria defeated Quebec in challenge games, Victoria's win was not officially recognized.* [2]*Series between Montreal Canadiens and Seattle Metropolitans called off because of flu epidemic.*

Marathon

The marathon is a long-distance footrace first held at the revival of the Olympic Games at Athens in 1896. It commemorates the legendary feat of a Greek soldier who, in 490 BC, is supposed to have run from Marathon to Athens, a distance of about 40 km (25 mi), to bring news of the Athenian victory over the Persians. Appropriately, the first modern marathon winner in 1896 was a Greek, Spyridon Louis. In 1924 the **Olympic marathon distance** was standardized at 42,195 m, or 26 mi 385 yd. This was based on a decision of the British Olympic Committee to start the 1908 Olympic race from Windsor Castle and finish it in front of the royal box in the stadium at London. The marathon was added to the **women's Olympic program** in 1984. Because marathon courses are not of equal difficulty, the **International Association of Athletics Federations** (IAAF) does not list a world record for the event. After the Olympic Games championship, one of the most coveted honors in marathon running is

Marathon (continued)

victory in the **Boston Marathon**, held annually since 1897. It draws athletes from all parts of the world and in 1972 became the first marathon officially to allow women to compete. The **New York City Marathon** also attracts participants from many countries, as does the **Chicago Marathon.** Other popular marathons are held in London, Berlin, Dublin, and Rotterdam (The Netherlands).

Related Web sites:
Boston Marathon: <www.bostonmarathon.org>;
New York City Marathon: <www.ingnycmarathon.org>;
Chicago Marathon: <www.chicagomarathon.com>.

Boston Marathon

Won by an American runner except as indicated. Times are given in hours:minutes:seconds.

men

YEAR	WINNER	TIME	YEAR	WINNER	TIME
1897	John J. McDermott	2:55:10	1950	Ham Kee Yong (KOR)	2:32:39
1898	Ronald J. McDonald (CAN)	2:42:00	1951	Tanaka Shigeki (JPN)	2:27:45
1899	Lawrence J. Brignoli	2:54:38	1952	Doroteo Flores (GUA)	2:31:53
1900	John J. Caffrey (CAN)	2:39:44	1953	Yamada Keizo (JPN)	2:18:51
1901	John J. Caffrey (CAN)	2:29:23	1954	Veikko L. Karanen (FIN)	2:20:39
1902	Sammy A. Mellor	2:43:12	1955	Hamamura Hideo (JPN)	2:18:22
1903	John C. Lorden	2:41:29	1956	Antti Viskari (FIN)	2:14:14
1904	Michael Spring	2:39:04	1957	John J. Kelley	2:20:05
1905	Frederick Lorz	2:38:25	1958	Franjo Mihalic (YUG)	2:25:54
1906	Tim Ford	2:45:45	1959	Eino Oksanen (FIN)	2:22:42
1907	Thomas Longboat (CAN)	2:24:24	1960	Paavo Kotila (FIN)	2:20:54
1908	Thomas P. Morrissey	2:25:43	1961	Eino Oksanen (FIN)	2:23:39
1909	Henri Renaud	2:53:36	1962	Eino Oksanen (FIN)	2:23:48
1910	Fred L. Cameron (CAN)	2:28:52	1963	Aurele Vandendriessche (BEL)	2:18:58
1911	Clarence H. DeMar	2:21:39	1964	Aurele Vandendriessche (BEL)	2:19:59
1912	Michael J. Ryan	2:21:18	1965	Shigematsu Morio (JPN)	2:16:33
1913	Fritz Carlson	2:25:14	1966	Kimihara Kenji (JPN)	2:17:11
1914	James Duffy (CAN)	2:25:01	1967	David McKenzie (NZL)	2:15:45
1915	Edouard Fabre (CAN)	2:31:41	1968	Amby Burfoot	2:22:17
1916	Arthur V. Roth	2:27:16	1969	Unetani Yoshiaki (JPN)	2:13:49
1917	William K. Kennedy	2:28:37	1970	Ron Hill (GBR)	2:10:30
1918	*not held*		1971	Alvaro Mejia (COL)	2:18:45
1919	Carl W.A. Linder	2:29:13	1972	Olavi Suomalainen (FIN)	2:15:30
1920	Peter Trivoulides	2:29:31	1973	Jon Anderson	2:16:03
1921	Frank Zuna	2:18:57	1974	Neil Cusack	2:13:39
1922	Clarence H. DeMar	2:18:10	1975	Bill Rodgers	2:09:55
1923	Clarence H. DeMar	2:23:47	1976	Jack Fultz	2:20:19
1924	Clarence H. DeMar	2:29:40	1977	Jerome Drayton (CAN)	2:14:46
1925	Charles L. Mellor	2:33:06	1978	Bill Rodgers	2:10:13
1926	John C. Miles (CAN)	2:25:40	1979	Bill Rodgers	2:09:27
1927	Clarence H. DeMar	2:40:22	1980	Bill Rodgers	2:12:11
1928	Clarence H. DeMar	2:37:07	1981	Seko Toshihiko (JPN)	2:09:26
1929	John C. Miles (CAN)	2:33:08	1982	Alberto Salazar	2:08:51
1930	Clarence H. DeMar	2:34:48	1983	Greg A. Meyer	2:09:00
1931	James P. Hennigan	2:46:45	1984	Geoff Smith (GBR)	2:10:34
1932	Paul DeBruyn (GER)	2:33:36	1985	Geoff Smith (GBR)	2:14:05
1933	Leslie S. Pawson	2:31:01	1986	Robert de Castella (AUS)	2:07:51
1934	Dave Komonen (CAN)	2:32:53	1987	Seko Toshihiko (JPN)	2:11:50
1935	John A. Kelley	2:32:07	1988	Ibrahim Hussein (KEN)	2:08:43
1936	Ellison M. Brown	2:33:40	1989	Abebe Mekonnen (ETH)	2:09:06
1937	Walter Young (CAN)	2:33:20	1990	Gelindo Bordin (ITA)	2:08:19
1938	Leslie S. Pawson	2:35:34	1991	Ibrahim Hussein (KEN)	2:11:06
1939	Ellison M. Brown	2:28:51	1992	Ibrahim Hussein (KEN)	2:08:14
1940	Gerard Cote (CAN)	2:28:28	1993	Cosmas N'Deti (KEN)	2:09:33
1941	Leslie S. Pawson	2:30:38	1994	Cosmas N'Deti (KEN)	2:07:15
1942	Joe Smith	2:26:51	1995	Cosmas N'Deti (KEN)	2:09:22
1943	Gerard Cote (CAN)	2:28:25	1996	Moses Tanui (KEN)	2:09:16
1944	Gerard Cote (CAN)	2:31:50	1997	Lameck Aguta (KEN)	2:10:34
1945	John A. Kelley	2:30:40	1998	Moses Tanui (KEN)	2:07:34
1946	Stylianos Kyriakides (GRE)	2:29:27	1999	Joseph Chebet (KEN)	2:09:52
1947	Suh Yun Bok (KOR)	2:25:39	2000	Elijah Lagat (KEN)	2:09:47
1948	Gerard Cote (CAN)	2:31:02	2001	Lee Bong Ju (KOR)	2:09:43
1949	Karl G. Leandersson (SWE)	2:31:50	2002	Rodgers Rop (KEN)	2:09:02

Boston Marathon (continued)

men (continued)

YEAR	WINNER	TIME	YEAR	WINNER	TIME
2003	Robert Kipkoech Cheruiyot (KEN)	2:10:11	2006	Robert Kipkoech Cheruiyot (KEN)	2:07:14
2004	Timothy Cherigat (KEN)	2:10:37	2007	Robert Kipkoech Cheruiyot (KEN)	2:14:13
2005	Hailu Negussie (ETH)	2:11:45	2008	Robert Kipkoech Cheruiyot (KEN)	2:07:46

women

YEAR	WINNER	TIME	YEAR	WINNER	TIME
1972	Nina Kuscsik	3:10:26	1991	Wanda Panfil (POL)	2:24:18
1973	Jacqueline Hansen	3:05:59	1992	Olga Markova (RUS)	2:23:43
1974	Michiko Gorman	2:47:11	1993	Olga Markova (RUS)	2:25:27
1975	Liane Winter (FRG)	2:42:24	1994	Uta Pippig (GER)	2:21:45
1976	Kim Merritt	2:47:10	1995	Uta Pippig (GER)	2:25:11
1977	Michiko Gorman	2:46:22	1996	Uta Pippig (GER)	2:27:12
1978	Gayle S. Barron	2:44:52	1997	Fatuma Roba (ETH)	2:26:23
1979	Joan Benoit	2:35:15	1998	Fatuma Roba (ETH)	2:23:21
1980	Jacqueline Gareau (CAN)	2:34:28	1999	Fatuma Roba (ETH)	2:23:25
1981	Allison Roe (NZL)	2:26:46	2000	Catherine Ndereba (KEN)	2:26:11
1982	Charlotte Teske (FRG)	2:29:33	2001	Catherine Ndereba (KEN)	2:23:53
1983	Joan Benoit	2:22:42	2002	Margaret Okayo (KEN)	2:20:43
1984	Lorraine Moller (NZL)	2:29:28	2003	Svetlana Zakharova (RUS)	2:25:20
1985	Lisa Larsen	2:34:06	2004	Catherine Ndereba (KEN)	2:24:27
1986	Ingrid Kristiansen (NOR)	2:24:55	2005	Catherine Ndereba (KEN)	2:25:13
1987	Rosa Mota (POR)	2:25:21	2006	Rita Jeptoo (KEN)	2:23:38
1988	Rosa Mota (POR)	2:24:30	2007	Lidiya Grigoryeva (RUS)	2:29:18
1989	Ingrid Kristiansen (NOR)	2:24:33	2008	Dire Tune (ETH)	2:25:25
1990	Rosa Mota (POR)	2:25:23			

New York City Marathon

Won by an American runner except as indicated. Times are given in hours:minutes:seconds.

YEAR	MEN	TIME	WOMEN	TIME
1970	Gary Muhrcke	2:31:38	*no finisher*	
1971	Norm Higgins	2:22:54	Beth Bonner	2:55:22
1972	Robert Karlin	2:27:52	Nina Kuscsik	3:08:41
1973	Tom Fleming	2:21:54	Nina Kuscsik	2:57:07
1974	Norbert Sander	2:26:30	Katherine Switzer	3:07:29
1975	Tom Fleming	2:19:27	Kim Merritt	2:46:14
1976	Bill Rodgers	2:10:09	Michiko Gorman	2:39:11
1977	Bill Rodgers	2:11:28	Michiko Gorman	2:43:10
1978	Bill Rodgers	2:12:12	Grete Waitz (NOR)	2:32:30
1979	Bill Rodgers	2:11:42	Grete Waitz (NOR)	2:27:33
1980	Alberto Salazar	2:09:41	Grete Waitz (NOR)	2:25:41
1981	Alberto Salazar	2:08:13	Allison Roe (NZL)	2:25:29
1982	Alberto Salazar	2:09:29	Grete Waitz (NOR)	2:27:14
1983	Rod Dixon	2:08:59	Grete Waitz (NOR)	2:27:00
1984	Orlando Pizzolato	2:14:53	Grete Waitz (NOR)	2:29:30
1985	Orlando Pizzolato	2:11:34	Grete Waitz (NOR)	2:28:34
1986	Gianni Poli (ITA)	2:11:06	Grete Waitz (NOR)	2:28:06
1987	Ibrahim Hussein (KEN)	2:11:01	Priscilla Welch (GBR)	2:30:17
1988	Steve Jones (WAL)	2:08:20	Grete Waitz (NOR)	2:28:07
1989	Juma Ikangaa (TAN)	2:08:01	Ingrid Kristiansen (NOR)	2:25:30
1990	Douglas Wakiihuri (KEN)	2:12:39	Wanda Panfil (POL)	2:30:45
1991	Salvador Garcia (MEX)	2:09:28	Liz McColgan (GBR)	2:27:23
1992	Willie Mtolo (RSA)	2:09:29	Lisa Ondieki (AUS)	2:24:40
1993	Andrés Espinosa (MEX)	2:10:04	Uta Pippig (GER)	2:26:24
1994	German Silva (MEX)	2:11:21	Tegla Loroupe (KEN)	2:27:37
1995	German Silva (MEX)	2:11:00	Tegla Loroupe (KEN)	2:28:06
1996	Giacomo Leone (ITA)	2:09:54	Anuta Catuna (ROM)	2:28:18
1997	John Kagwe (KEN)	2:08:12	Franziska Rochat-Moser (SUI)	2:28:43
1998	John Kagwe (KEN)	2:08:45	Franca Fiacconi (ITA)	2:25:17
1999	Joseph Chebet (KEN)	2:09:14	Adriana Fernández (MEX)	2:25:06
2000	Abdelkhader El Mouaziz (MAR)	2:10:09	Lyudmila Petrova (RUS)	2:25:45
2001	Tesfaye Jifar (ETH)	2:07:43	Margaret Okayo (KEN)	2:24:21
2002	Rodgers Rop (KEN)	2:08:07	Joyce Chepchumba (KEN)	2:25:56

New York City Marathon (continued)

YEAR	MEN	TIME	WOMEN	TIME
2003	Martin Lel (KEN)	2:10:30	Margaret Okayo (KEN)	2:22:31
2004	Hendrik Ramaala (RSA)	2:09:28	Paula Radcliffe (GBR)	2:23:10
2005	Paul Tergat (KEN)	2:09:30	Jelena Prokopcuka (LAT)	2:24:41
2006	Marîlson Gomes dos Santos (BRA)	2:09:58	Jelena Prokopcuka (LAT)	2:25:05
2007	Martin Lel (KEN)	2:09:04	Paula Radcliffe (GBR)	2:23:09

Chicago Marathon

Won by an American runner except as indicated. Times are given in hours:minutes:seconds.

YEAR	MEN	TIME	WOMEN	TIME
1977	Dan Cloeter	2:17:52	Dorothy Doolittle	2:50:47
1978	Mark Stanforth	2:19:20	Lynae Larson	2:59:25
1979	Dan Cloeter	2:23:20	Laura Michalek	3:15:45
1980	Frank Richardson	2:14:04	Sue Petersen	2:45:03
1981	Philip Coppess	2:16:13	Tina Gandy	2:49:39
1982	Greg Meyer	2:10:59	Nancy Conz	2:33:23
1983	Joseph Nzau (KEN)	2:09:44	Rosa Mota (POR)	2:31:12
1984	Steve Jones (GBR)	2:08:05	Rosa Mota (POR)	2:26:01
1985	Steve Jones (GBR)	2:07:13	Joan Benoit Samuelson	2:21:21
1986	Toshihiko Seko (JPN)	2:08:27	Ingrid Kristiansen (NOR)	2:27:08
1987	*not held*			
1988	Alejandro Cruz (MEX)	2:08:57	Lisa Weidenbach	2:29:17
1989	Paul Davis-Hale (GBR)	2:11:25	Lisa Weidenbach	2:28:15
1990	Martín Pitayo (MEX)	2:09:41	Aurora Cunha (POR)	2:30:11
1991	Joseildo Rocha (BRA)	2:14:33	Midde Hamrin-Senorski (SWE)	2:36:21
1992	José César de Souza (BRA)	2:16:14	Linda Somers	2:37:41
1993	Luiz Antônio dos Santos (BRA)	2:13:15	Ritva Lemettinen (FIN)	2:33:18
1994	Luiz Antônio dos Santos (BRA)	2:11:16	Kristy Johnston	2:31:34
1995	Eamonn Martin (GBR)	2:11:18	Ritva Lemettinen (FIN)	2:28:27
1996	Paul Evans (GBR)	2:08:52	Marian Sutton (GBR)	2:30:41
1997	Khalid Khannouchi (MAR)	2:07:10	Marian Sutton (GBR)	2:29:03
1998	Ondoro Osoro (KEN)	2:06:54	Joyce Chepchumba (KEN)	2:23:57
1999	Khalid Khannouchi (MAR)	2:05:42	Joyce Chepchumba (KEN)	2:25:59
2000	Khalid Khannouchi (USA)	2:07:01	Catherine Ndereba (KEN)	2:21:33
2001	Ben Kimondiu (KEN)	2:08:52	Catherine Ndereba (KEN)	2:18:47
2002	Khalid Khannouchi (USA)	2:05:56	Paula Radcliffe (GBR)	2:17:18
2003	Evans Rutto (KEN)	2:05:50	Svetlana Zakharova (RUS)	2:23:07
2004	Evans Rutto (KEN)	2:06:16	Constantina Tomescu-Dita (ROM)	2:23:45
2005	Felix Limo (KEN)	2:07:02	Deena Kastor	2:21:25
2006	Robert K. Cheruiyot (KEN)	2:07:35	Berhane Adere (ETH)	2:20:42
2007	Patrick Ivuti (KEN)	2:11:11	Berhane Adere (ETH)	2:33:49

Rodeo

A uniquely **North American** competition, the rodeo has been held on a more-or-less formal basis since the late 1920s. From 1929 to 1944 the **men's world all-around rodeo champion** was named by the **Rodeo Association of America.** Since 1944 the all-around champion has been the leading money winner of the year—with the exception of the years 1976–78, when the champion was the cowboy who won the most money at the **National Finals Rodeo.** The Rodeo Association of America changed its name several times but has been known as the **Professional Rodeo Cowboys Association** (PRCA) since 1975. Among other rodeo sanctioning activities, the PRCA qualifies cowboys for the National Finals Rodeo, currently held in early December in Las Vegas NV. There competitions are held in each of several events, including bronc riding (bareback and saddle), bull riding, calf roping, and steer wrestling (individual and team). Women compete in one event only, barrel racing.

Professional Rodeo Cowboys Association Web site: <www.prorodeo.com>.

Men's World All-Around Rodeo Champions

Awarded since 1929. Table shows champions for the past 20 years.

YEAR	WINNER	YEAR	WINNER	YEAR	WINNER	YEAR	WINNER
1988	Dave Appleton	1990	Ty Murray	1992	Ty Murray	1994	Ty Murray
1989	Ty Murray	1991	Ty Murray	1993	Ty Murray	1995	Joe Beaver

Men's World All-Around Rodeo Champions (continued)

YEAR	WINNER	YEAR	WINNER	YEAR	WINNER	YEAR	WINNER
1996	Joe Beaver	1999	Fred Whitfield	2002	Trevor Brazile	2005	Ryan Jarrett
1997	Dan Mortensen	2000	Joe Beaver	2003	Trevor Brazile	2006	Trevor Brazile
1998	Ty Murray	2001	Cody Ohl	2004	Trevor Brazile	2007	Trevor Brazile

Skiing

Although most of the events had been contested at the regional level since the mid-19th century, the first internationally organized **skiing championships** did not take place until 1924. From 1924 to 1931 only **Nordic** competition was involved; **Alpine** championship events were added to world competition in 1931 and to the Olympics in 1936. Except in Olympic years, the Nordic and Alpine championships are held separately and at different locations. **Events** include cross-country races, ski jumping, biathlon, and relay races (Nordic) and downhill and slalom skiing (Alpine). Since 1967, an **Alpine World Cup** has been presented to the competitor with the best combined downhill, slalom, giant slalom, and supergiant slalom (super-G) performance over a series of major contests. A **Nordic World Cup** for cross-country events has been awarded since 1979.

International Ski Federation Web site: <www.fis-ski.com>.

Alpine Skiing World Championships—Men

The table shows results for the past 20 years.

DOWNHILL

1988[1]	Permin Zurbriggen (SUI)
1989	Hansjorg Tauscher (FRG)
1991	Franz Heinzer (SUI)
1992[1]	Patrick Ortlieb (AUS)
1993	Urs Lehmann (SUI)
1994[1]	Tommy Moe (USA)
1995	*not held*
1996	Patrick Ortlieb (AUS)
1997	Bruno Kernen (SUI)
1998[1]	Jean-Luc Cretier (FRA)
1999	Hermann Maier (AUT)
2001	Hannes Trinkl (AUT)
2002[1]	Fritz Strobl (AUT)
2003	Michael Walchhofer (AUT)
2005	Bode Miller (USA)
2006[1]	Antoine Dénériaz (FRA)
2007	Aksel Lund Svindal (NOR)

COMBINED

1988[1]	Hubert Strolz (AUT)
1989	Marc Girardelli (LUX)
1991	Stefan Eberharter (AUT)
1992[1]	Josef Polig (ITA)
1993	Lasse Kjus (NOR)
1994[1]	Lasse Kjus (NOR)
1995	*not held*
1996	Marc Girardelli (LUX)
1997	Kjetil André Aamodt (NOR)
1998[1]	Mario Reiter (AUT)
1999	Kjetil André Aamodt (NOR)
2001	Kjetil André Aamodt (NOR)
2002[1]	Kjetil André Aamodt (NOR)
2003	Bode Miller (USA)
2005	Benjamin Raich (AUT)
2006[1]	Ted Ligety (USA)
2007	Daniel Albrecht (SUI)

SLALOM

1989	Rudolf Nierlich (AUT)
1991	Marc Girardelli (LUX)
1992[1]	Finn Christian Jagge (NOR)
1993	Kjetil André Aamodt (NOR)
1994[1]	Thomas Stangassinger (AUT)
1995	*not held*
1996	Alberto Tomba (ITA)
1997	Tom Stiansen (NOR)
1998[1]	Hans-Petter Buraas (NOR)
1999	Kalle Palander (FIN)
2001	Mario Matt (AUT)
2002[1]	Jean-Pierre Vidal (FRA)
2003	Ivica Kostelic (CRO)
2005	Benjamin Raich (AUT)
2006[1]	Benjamin Raich (AUT)
2007	Mario Matt (AUT)

GIANT SLALOM

1988[1]	Alberto Tomba (ITA)
1989	Rudolf Nierlich (AUT)
1991	Rudolf Nierlich (AUT)
1992[1]	Alberto Tomba (ITA)
1993	Kjetil André Aamodt (NOR)
1994[1]	Markus Wasmeier (GER)
1995	*not held*
1996	Alberto Tomba (ITA)
1997	Michael von Grünigen (SUI)
1998[1]	Hermann Maier (AUT)
1999	Lasse Kjus (NOR)
2001	Michael von Grünigen (SUI)
2002[1]	Stephan Eberharter (AUT)
2003	Bode Miller (USA)
2005	Hermann Maier (AUT)
2006[1]	Benjamin Raich (AUT)
2007	Aksel Lund Svindal (NOR)

SUPERGIANT SLALOM

1988[1]	Franck Piccard (FRA)
1989	Martin Hangl (SUI)
1991	Stephan Eberharter (AUT)
1992[1]	Kjetil André Aamodt (NOR)
1993	*not held*
1994[1]	Markus Wasmeier (GER)
1995	*not held*
1996	Atle Skaardal (NOR)
1997	Atle Skaardal (NOR)
1998[1]	Hermann Maier (AUT)
1999	Lasse Kjus (NOR), Hermann Maier (AUT) (*tied*)
2001	Daron Rahlves (USA)
2002[1]	Kjetil André Aamodt (NOR)
2003	Stephan Eberharter (AUT)
2005	Bode Miller (USA)
2006[1]	Kjetil André Aamodt (NOR)
2007	Patrick Staudacher (ITA)

[1]*Olympic champions, recognized as world champions.*

Alpine Skiing World Championships—Women

The table shows results for the past 20 years.

DOWNHILL

1988[1]	Marina Kiehl (FRG)
1989	Maria Walliser (SUI)
1991	Petra Kronberger (AUT)
1992[1]	Kerrin Lee-Gartner (CAN)
1993	Kate Pace (CAN)
1994[1]	Katja Seizinger (GER)
1995	*not held*
1996	Picabo Street (USA)
1997	Hilary Lindh (USA)
1998[1]	Katja Seizinger (GER)
1999	Renate Götschl (AUT)

Alpine Skiing World Championships—Women (continued)

DOWNHILL (CONTINUED)

2001 Michaela Dorfmeister (AUT)
2002[1] Carole Montillet (FRA)
2003 Mélanie Turgeon (CAN)
2005 Janica Kostelic (CRO)
2006[1] Michaela Dorfmeister (AUT)
2007 Anja Pärson (SWE)

COMBINED

1988[1] Anita Wachter (AUT)
1989 Tamara McKinney (USA)
1991 Chantal Bournissen (SUI)
1992[1] Petra Kronberger (AUT)
1993 Miriam Vogt (GER)
1994[1] Pernilla Wiberg (SWE)
1995 *not held*
1996 Pernilla Wiberg (SWE)
1997 Renate Götschl (AUT)
1998[1] Katja Seizinger (GER)
1999 Pernilla Wiberg (SWE)
2001 Martina Ertl (GER)
2002[1] Janica Kostelic (CRO)
2003 Janica Kostelic (CRO)
2005 Janica Kostelic (CRO)
2006[1] Janica Kostelic (CRO)
2007 Anja Pärson (SWE)

SLALOM

1988[1] Vreni Schneider (SUI)
1989 Mateja Svet (YUG)
1991 Vreni Schneider (SUI)

SLALOM (CONTINUED)

1992[1] Petra Kronberger (AUT)
1993 Karin Buder (AUT)
1994[1] Vreni Schneider (SUI)
1995 *not held*
1996 Pernilla Wiberg (SWE)
1997 Deborah Compagnoni (ITA)
1998[1] Hilde Gerg (GER)
1999 Zali Steggall (AUS)
2001 Anja Paerson (SWE)
2002[1] Janica Kostelic (CRO)
2003 Janica Kostelic (CRO)
2005 Janica Kostelic (CRO)
2006[1] Anja Pärson (SWE)
2007 Sarka Zahrobska (CZE)

GIANT SLALOM

1988[1] Vreni Schneider (SUI)
1989 Vreni Schneider (SUI)
1991 Pernilla Wiberg (SWE)
1992[1] Pernilla Wiberg (SWE)
1993 Carole Merle (FRA)
1994[1] Deborah Compagnoni (ITA)
1995 *not held*
1996 Deborah Compagnoni (ITA)
1997 Deborah Compagnoni (ITA)
1998[1] Deborah Compagnoni (ITA)

GIANT SLALOM (CONTINUED)

1999 Alexandra Meissnitzer (AUT)
2001 Sonja Nef (SUI)
2002[1] Janica Kostelic (CRO)
2003 Anja Pärson (SWE)
2005 Anja Pärson (SWE)
2006[1] Julia Mancuso (USA)
2007 Nicole Hosp (AUT)

SUPERGIANT SLALOM

1988[1] Sigrid Wolf (AUT)
1989 Ulrike Maier (AUT)
1991 Ulrike Maier (AUT)
1992[1] Deborah Compagnoni (ITA)
1993 Katja Seizinger (GER)
1994[1] Diann Roffe-Steinrotter (USA)
1995 *not held*
1996 Isolde Kostner (ITA)
1997 Isolde Kostner (ITA)
1998[1] Picabo Street (USA)
1999 Alexandra Meissnitzer (AUT)
2001 Régine Cavagnoud (FRA)
2002[1] Daniela Ceccarelli (ITA)
2003 Michaela Dorfmeister (AUT)
2005 Anja Pärson (SWE)
2006[1] Michaela Dorfmeister (AUT)
2007 Anja Pärson (SWE)

[1]*Olympic champions, recognized as world champions.*

Alpine World Cup

The winner is determined by the number of points awarded for finishes in various competitions during the season.

YEAR	MEN	WOMEN
1967	Jean-Claude Killy (FRA)	Nancy Greene (CAN)
1968	Jean-Claude Killy (FRA)	Nancy Greene (CAN)
1969	Karl Schranz (AUT)	Gertrude Gabl (AUT)
1970	Karl Schranz (AUT)	Michele Jacot (FRA)
1971	Gustavo Thöni (ITA)	Annemarie Pröll (AUT)
1972	Gustavo Thöni (ITA)	Annemarie Pröll (AUT)
1973	Gustavo Thöni (ITA)	Annemarie Pröll (AUT)
1974	Piero Gros (ITA)	Annemarie Moser-Pröll (AUT)
1975	Gustavo Thöni (ITA)	Annemarie Moser-Pröll (AUT)
1976	Ingemar Stenmark (SWE)	Rosi Mittermaier (FRG)
1977	Ingemar Stenmark (SWE)	Lise-Marie Morerod (SUI)
1978	Ingemar Stenmark (SWE)	Hanni Wenzel (LIE)
1979	Peter Luescher (SUI)	Annemarie Moser-Pröll (AUT)
1980	Andreas Wenzel (LIE)	Hanni Wenzel (LIE)
1981	Phil Mahre (USA)	Marie-Thérèse Nadig (SUI)
1982	Phil Mahre (USA)	Erika Hess (SUI)
1983	Phil Mahre (USA)	Tamara McKinney (USA)
1984	Pirmin Zurbriggen (SUI)	Erika Hess (SUI)
1985	Marc Girardelli (LUX)	Michela Figini (SUI)
1986	Marc Girardelli (LUX)	Maria Walliser (SUI)
1987	Pirmin Zurbriggen (SUI)	Maria Walliser (SUI)
1988	Pirmin Zurbriggen (SUI)	Michela Figini (SUI)
1989	Marc Girardelli (LUX)	Vreni Schneider (SUI)
1990	Pirmin Zurbriggen (SUI)	Petra Kronberger (AUT)
1991	Marc Girardelli (LUX)	Petra Kronberger (AUT)
1992	Paul Accola (SUI)	Petra Kronberger (AUT)
1993	Marc Girardelli (LUX)	Anita Wachter (AUT)
1994	Kjetil André Aamodt (NOR)	Vreni Schneider (SUI)
1995	Alberto Tomba (ITA)	Vreni Schneider (SUI)
1996	Lasse Kjus (NOR)	Katja Seizinger (GER)
1997	Luc Alphand (FRA)	Pernilla Wiberg (SWE)
1998	Hermann Maier (AUT)	Katja Seizinger (GER)

Alpine World Cup (continued)

YEAR	MEN	WOMEN
1999	Lasse Kjus (NOR)	Alexandra Meissnitzer (AUT)
2000	Hermann Maier (AUT)	Renate Götschl (AUT)
2001	Hermann Maier (AUT)	Janica Kostelic (CRO)
2002	Stephan Eberharter (AUT)	Michaela Dorfmeister (AUT)
2003	Stephan Eberharter (AUT)	Janica Kostelic (CRO)
2004	Hermann Maier (AUT)	Anja Pärson (SWE)
2005	Bode Miller (USA)	Anja Pärson (SWE)
2006	Benjamin Raich (AUT)	Janica Kostelic (CRO)
2007	Aksel Lund Svindal (NOR)	Nicole Hosp (AUT)
2008	Bode Miller (USA)	Lindsey Vonn (USA)

Nordic Skiing World Championships—Men

The table shows results for the past 20 years.

SPRINT

2001	Tor Arne Hetland (NOR)
2002[1]	Tor Arne Hetland (NOR)
2003	Thobias Fredriksson (SWE)
2005	Vassily Rochev (RUS)
2006[1]	Bjørn Lind (SWE)
2007	Jens Arne Svartedal (NOR)

10-KILOMETER CROSS-COUNTRY[2]

1991	Terje Langli (NOR)
1992[1]	Vegard Ulvang (NOR)
1993	Sture Sivertsen (NOR)
1994[1]	Bjørn Daehlie NOR)
1995	Vladimir Smirnov (KAZ)
1997	Bjørn Daehlie (NOR)
1998[1]	Bjørn Daehlie (NOR)
1999	Mika Myllyla (FIN)

15-KILOMETER CROSS-COUNTRY[2, 3]

1988[1]	Mikhail Devyatyarov (URS)
1989	Harri Kirvesniemi (FIN–classical), Gunde Svan (SWE–freestyle)
1991	Bjørn Daehlie (NOR)
1992[1]	Bjørn Daehlie (NOR)
1993	Bjørn Daehlie (NOR)
1994[1]	Bjørn Daehlie (NOR)
1995	Vladimir Smirnov (KAZ)
1997	Bjørn Daehlie (NOR)
1998[1]	Thomas Alsgaard (NOR)
1999	Thomas Alsgaard (NOR)
2001	Per Elofsson (SWE)
2002[1]	Andrus Veerpalu (EST)

15-KM CROSS-COUNTRY[2, 3] (CONT.)

2003	Axel Teichmann (GER)
2005	Pietro Piller Cottrer (ITA)
2006[1]	Andrus Veerpalu (EST)
2007	Lars Berger (NOR)

COMBINED PURSUIT[2]

2001	Per Elofsson (SWE)
2002[1]	Thomas Alsgaard (NOR), Frode Estil (NOR) (*tied*)
2003	Per Elofsson (SWE)
2005	Vincent Vittoz (FRA)
2006[1]	Yevgeny Dementyev (RUS)

30-KILOMETER CROSS-COUNTRY

1988[1]	Aleksey Prokurorov (URS)
1989	Vladimir Smirnov (URS)
1991	Gunde Svan (SWE)
1992[1]	Vegard Ulvang (NOR)
1993	Bjørn Daehlie (NOR)
1994[1]	Thomas Alsgaard (NOR)
1995	Vladimir Smirnov (KAZ)
1997	Aleksey Prokurorov (RUS)
1998[1]	Mika Myllyla (FIN)
1999	Mika Myllyla (FIN)
2001	Andrus Veerpalu (EST)
2002[1]	Christian Hoffmann (AUT)
2003	Thomas Alsgaard (NOR)
2005	*not held*
2006[1]	Yevgeny Dementyev (RUS)
2007	*not held*

50-KILOMETER CROSS-COUNTRY

1988[1]	Gunde Svan (SWE)
1989	Gunde Svan (SWE)
1991	Torgny Mogren (SWE)
1992[1]	Bjørn Daehlie (NOR)
1993	Torgny Mogren (SWE)
1994	Vladimir Smirnov (KAZ)
1995	Silvio Fauner (ITA)
1997	Mika Myllyla (FIN)
1998[1]	Bjørn Daehlie (NOR)
1999	Mika Myllyla (FIN)
2001	Johann Mühlegg (ESP)
2002[1]	Mikhail Ivanov (RUS)
2003	Martin Koukal (CZE)
2005	Frode Estil (NOR)
2006[1]	Giorgio Di Centa (ITA)
2007	Odd-Bjørn Hjelmeset

RELAY[4]

1988[1]	Sweden
1989	Sweden
1991	Norway
1992[1]	Norway
1993	Norway
1994[1]	Italy
1995	Norway
1997	Norway
1998[1]	Norway
1999	Austria
2001	Norway
2002[1]	Norway
2003	Norway
2005	Norway
2006[1]	Italy
2007	Norway

[1]Olympic champions, recognized as world champions. [2]From 1991 to 1999, the 10-km event was held in tandem with the 15-km event; one event featured classical and the other freestyle technique. Medals were awarded for both races. Beginning in 2001 this pursuit race (skiers competing directly against each other rather than against the clock) led to one medal being awarded upon winning. The 10-km was discontinued, and the 15-km became a stand-alone event featuring classical technique. In 2001–03 the pursuit race featured two 10-km races; since then, two 15-km races. [3]18-km cross-country until 1952; 15-km in 1954 and thereafter. [4]Military relay until 1939; 40-km relay in 1948 and thereafter.

Nordic Skiing World Championships—Women

The table shows results for the past 20 years.

SPRINT

2001	Pirjo Manninen (FIN)
2002[1]	Yuliya Chepalova (RUS)
2003	Marit Bjørgen (NOR)
2005	Emilie Öhrstig (SWE)
2006[1]	Chandra Crawford (CAN)
2007	Astrid Jacobsen (NOR)

5-KILOMETER CROSS-COUNTRY[2]

1988[1]	Marjo Matikainen (FIN)
1989	*not held*
1991	Trude Dybendahl (NOR)
1992[1]	Marjut Lukkarinen (FIN)
1993	Larisa Lazutina (RUS)
1994[1]	Lyubov Yegorova (RUS)
1995	Larisa Lazutina (RUS)
1997	Yelena Vyalbe (RUS)
1998[1]	Larisa Lazutina (RUS)
1999	Bente Martinsen (NOR)

Nordic Skiing World Championships—Women (continued)

10-KILOMETER CROSS-COUNTRY[2]

1988[1]	Vida Ventsene (URS)
1989	Marja-Liisa Kirvesniemi (FIN–classical); Yelena Vyalbe (URS–freestyle)
1991	Yelena Vyalbe (URS)
1992[1]	Lyubov Yegorova (UNT[3])
1993	Stefania Belmondo (ITA)
1994[1]	Lyubov Yegorova (RUS)
1995	Larisa Lazutina (RUS)
1997	Stefania Belmondo (ITA)
1998[1]	Larisa Lazutina (RUS)
1999	Stefania Belmondo (ITA)
2001	Bente Skari-Martinsen (NOR)
2002[1]	Bente Skari (NOR)
2003	Bente Skari (NOR)
2005	Katerina Neumannova (CZE)
2006[1]	Kristina Smigun (EST)
2007	Katerina Neumannova (CZE)

COMBINED PURSUIT[2]

2001	Virpi Kuitunen (FIN)
2002[1]	Beckie Scott (CAN)
2003	Kristina Smigun (EST)
2005	Yuliya Chepalova (RUS)

COMBINED PURSUIT[2] (CONTINUED)

2006[1]	Kristina Smigun (EST)
2007	Olga Zavyalova (RUS)

15-KILOMETER CROSS-COUNTRY

1989	Marjo Matikainen (FIN)
1991	Yelena Vyalbe (URS)
1992[1]	Lyubov Yegorova (URS)
1993	Yelena Vyalbe (RUS)
1994[1]	Manuela Di Centa (ITA)
1995	Larissa Lazutina (RUS)
1997	Yelena Vyalbe (RUS)
1998[1]	Olga Danilova (RUS)
1999	Stefania Belmondo (ITA)
2001	Bente Skari-Martinsen (NOR)
2002[1]	Stefania Belmondo (ITA)
2003	Bente Skari (NOR)

20-KILOMETER CROSS-COUNTRY

1988[1]	Tamara Tikhonova (URS)

30-KILOMETER CROSS-COUNTRY

1989	Yelena Vyalbe (URS)
1991	Lyubov Yegorova (URS)
1992[1]	Stefania Belmondo (ITA)
1993	Stefania Belmondo (ITA)

30-KM CROSS-COUNTRY (CONT.)

1994[1]	Manuela Di Centa (ITA)
1995	Yelena Vyalbe (RUS)
1997	Yelena Vyalbe (RUS)
1998[1]	Yulia Chepalova (RUS)
1999	Larisa Lazutina (RUS)
2001	*canceled*
2002[1]	Gabriella Paruzzi (ITA)
2003	Olga Savyalova (RUS)
2005	Marit Bjørgen (NOR)
2006[1]	Katerina Neumannova (CZE)
2007	Virpi Kuitunen (FIN)

RELAY[4]

1988[1]	USSR
1989	Finland
1991	USSR
1992[1]	Unified Team
1993	Russia
1994[1]	Russia
1995	Russia
1997	Russia
1998[1]	Russia
1999	Russia
2001	Russia
2002[1]	Germany
2003	Germany
2005	Norway
2006[1]	Russia
2007	Finland

[1]Olympic champions, recognized as world champions. [2]From 1991 to 1999, the 5-km event was held in tandem with the 10-km event; one event featured classical and the other freestyle technique. Medals were awarded for both races. Beginning in 2001 this pursuit race (skiers competing directly against each other rather than against the clock) led to one medal being awarded upon winning. The 5-km was discontinued, and the 10-km became a stand-alone event featuring classical technique. In 2001–03 the pursuit race featured two 5-km races; since then, two 7.5-km races. [3]Unified Team, consisting of athletes from the Commonwealth of Independent States plus Georgia. [4]15-km relay until 1974; 20-km in 1976 and thereafter.

Nordic Skiing World Championships—Nordic Combined

The Nordic combined involves a 15-km cross-country race and ski jumping; the combined sprint is a 7.5-km race plus ski jumping. The table shows results for the past 20 years.

YEAR	COMBINED
1988[1]	Hippolyt Kempf (SUI)
1989	Trond Einar Elden (NOR)
1990	*not held*
1991	Fred Børre Lundberg (NOR)
1992[1]	Fabrice Guy (FRA)
1993	Kenji Ogiwara (JPN)
1994[1]	Fred Børre Lundberg (NOR)
1995	Fred Børre Lundberg (NOR)
1996	*not held*
1997	Kenji Ogiwara (JPN)
1998[1]	Bjarte Engen Vik (NOR)
1999	Bjarte Engen Vik (NOR)
2000	*not held*
2001	Bjarte Engen Vik (NOR)
2002[1]	Samppa Lajunen (FIN)
2003	Ronny Ackermann (GER)

YEAR	COMBINED (CONT.)
2004	*not held*
2005	Ronny Ackermann (GER)
2006[1]	Georg Hettich (GER)
2007	Ronny Ackermann (GER)

YEAR	COMBINED SPRINT
1999	Bjarte Engen Vik (NOR)
2000	*not held*
2001	Marco Baacke (GER)
2002[1]	Samppa Lajunen (FIN)
2003	Johnny Spillane (USA)
2004	*not held*
2005	Ronny Ackermann (GER)
2006[1]	Felix Gottwald (AUT)
2007	Hannu Manninen (FIN)

YEAR	TEAM
1988[1]	West Germany
1989	Norway

YEAR	TEAM (CONT.)
1990	*not held*
1991	Austria
1992[1]	Japan
1993	Japan
1994[1]	Japan
1995	Japan
1996	*not held*
1997	Norway
1998[1]	Norway
1999	Finland
2000	*not held*
2001	Norway
2002[1]	Finland
2003	Austria
2004	*not held*
2005	Norway
2006[1]	Austria
2007	Finland

[1]Olympic champions, recognized as world champions.

Nordic Skiing World Championships—Ski Jump

The table shows results for the past 20 years.

YEAR	NORMAL HILL[1]
1988[2]	Matti Nykänen (FIN)
1989	Jens Weissflog (GDR)
1991	Heinz Kuttin (AUT)
1992[2]	Ernst Vettori (AUT)
1993	Masahiko Harada (JPN)
1994[2]	Espen Bredesen (NOR)
1995	Takanobu Okabe (JPN)
1997	Janne Ahonen (FIN)
1998[2]	Jani Soininen (FIN)
1999	Kazuyoshi Funaki (JPN)
2001	Adam Malysz (POL)
2002[2]	Simon Ammann (SUI)
2003	Adam Malysz (POL)
2005	Rok Benkovic (SLO)
2006[2]	Lars Bystøl (NOR)
2007	Adam Malysz (POL)

YEAR	LARGE HILL[3]
1988[2]	Matti Nykänen (FIN)
1989	Jari Puikkonen (FIN)
1991	Franci Petek (YUG)
1992[2]	Toni Nieminen (FIN)
1993	Espen Bredesen (NOR)
1994[2]	Jens Weissflog (GER)
1995	Tommy Ingebrigtsen (NOR)
1997	Masahiko Harada (JPN)
1998[2]	Kazuyoshi Funaki (JPN)
1999	Martin Schmitt (GER)
2001	Martin Schmitt (GER)
2002[2]	Simon Ammann (SUI)
2003	Adam Malysz (POL)
2005	Janne Ahonen (FIN)
2006[2]	Thomas Morgenstern (AUT)
2007	Simon Ammann (SUI)

YEAR	TEAM JUMP (NORMAL HILL[1])
2001	Austria
2002	*not held*
2003	*not held*
2005	Austria
2006	*not held*
2007	*not held*

YEAR	TEAM JUMP (LARGE HILL[3])
1988[2]	Finland
1989	Finland
1991	Austria
1992[2]	Finland
1993	Norway
1994[2]	Germany
1995	Finland
1997	Finland
1998[2]	Japan
1999	Germany
2001	Germany
2002[2]	Germany
2003	Finland
2005	Austria
2006[2]	Austria
2007	Austria

[1]The distance of the jump in the normal hill competition has varied over time; since 1992 it has been set at either 90 or 95 meters. [2]Olympic champions, recognized as world champions. [3]The distance of the jump in the large hill competition has varied over time; since 1992 it has been set at either 120 or 125 meters.

Nordic World Cup

The winner is determined by the number of points awarded for finishes in various competitions during the season.

YEAR	MEN	WOMEN
1979	Oddvar Braa (NOR)	Galina Kulakova (URS)
1980	*not held*	
1981	Aleksandr Zavyalov (URS)	Raisa Smetanina (URS)
1982	Bill Koch (USA)	Berit Aunli (NOR)
1983	Aleksandr Zavyalov (URS)	Marja-Liisa Hämälainen (FIN)
1984	Gunde Svan (SWE)	Marja-Liisa Hämälainen (FIN)
1985	Gunde Svan (SWE)	Anette Boe (NOR)
1986	Gunde Svan (SWE)	Marjo Matikainen (FIN)
1987	Torgny Mogren (SWE)	Marjo Matikainen (FIN)
1988	Gunde Svan (SWE)	Marjo Matikainen (FIN)
1989	Gunde Svan (SWE)	Yelena Vyalbe (URS)
1990	Vegard Ulvang (NOR)	Larisa Lazutina (URS)
1991	Vladimir Smirnov (URS)	Yelena Vyalbe (URS)
1992	Bjørn Daehlie (NOR)	Yelena Vyalbe (URS)
1993	Bjørn Daehlie (NOR)	Lyudmila Yegorova (RUS)
1994	Vladimir Smirnov (KAZ)	Manuela Di Centa (ITA)
1995	Bjørn Daehlie (NOR)	Yelena Vyalbe (RUS)
1996	Bjørn Daehlie (NOR)	Manuela Di Centa (ITA)
1997	Bjørn Daehlie (NOR)	Yelena Vyalbe (RUS)
1998	Thomas Alsgaard (NOR)	Larisa Lazutina (RUS)
1999	Bjørn Daehlie (NOR)	Bente Martinsen (NOR)
2000	Johann Mühlegg (ESP)	Bente Skari-Martinsen (NOR)
2001	Per Elofsson (SWE)	Yuliya Chepalova (RUS)
2002	Per Elofsson (SWE)	Bente Skari (NOR)
2003	Mathias Fredriksson (SWE)	Bente Skari (NOR)
2004	Rene Sommerfeldt (GER)	Gabriella Paruzzi (ITA)
2005	Axel Teichmann (GER)	Marit Bjørgen (NOR)
2006	Tobias Angerer (GER)	Marit Bjørgen (NOR)
2007	Tobias Angerer (GER)	Virpi Kuitunen (FIN)
2008	Lukas Bauer (CZE)	Virpi Kuitunen (FIN)

Sled Dog Racing

Sled dog racing (or dogsled racing) is the sport of racing sleds pulled by sled dogs over snow-covered cross-country courses; it was developed from a principal **Eskimo** method of transportation. Dogsleds are still used for transportation and working purposes in some northern areas, although they largely have been replaced by aircraft and snowmobiles. The modern **racing sled** weighs about 30 lb (13.5 kg). Its frame (traditionally of ash) is lashed together with leather and its runners sheathed with steel or aluminum. **Dogs** usually are specially bred and trained Eskimo dogs, Siberian huskies, Samoyeds, or Alaskan Malamutes. The **teams** typically consist of 4–10 dogs, with more being used for longer races. They are driven in pairs in a gang hitch. Control of the team is by voice, though drivers may

Sled Dog Racing (continued)

carry whips as well. In open country, point-to-point races are held. In more populated areas, back roads form the course, with races usually varying in **length** from 12–30 mi (19–48 km). A team of dogs can pull the sled and its driver, called a **musher**, at speeds of more than 20 mph (32 km/hr). Teams start at intervals and race for time. Usually, all dogs must finish in the hitch order in which they started, and an injured dog must be carried on the sled.

A dogsled-racing event was included in the 1932 **Winter Olympics** program. The sport is popular in Norway, Canada, Alaska, and the northern states of the contiguous United States. The **Iditarod Trail Sled Dog Race** has been held in Alaska since 1973.

Iditarod Trail Sled Dog Race

Men and women compete together in this annual race held in March between Anchorage and Nome AK. A short race of 56 mi (90 km) organized in 1967 evolved in 1973 into the current race. The course, roughly 1,100 mi (1,770 km) long, partially follows the old Iditarod Trail dogsled mail route blazed from Knik to Nome in 1910. The course length and route vary slightly from year to year, and the middle third takes alternate routes in odd and even years. In 1976 the US Congress designated the original Iditarod Trail as a National Historic Trail.

Iditarod Web site: <www.iditarod.com>.

YEAR	WINNER	TIME
1973	Dick Wilmarth	20 days 49 min 41 sec
1974	Carl Huntington	20 days 15 hr 2 min 7 sec
1975	Emmitt Peters	14 days 14 hr 43 min 45 sec
1976	Gerald Riley	18 days 22 hr 58 min 17 sec
1977	Rick Swenson	16 days 16 hr 27 min 13 sec
1978	Dick Mackey	14 days 18 hr 52 min 24 sec
1979	Rick Swenson	15 days 10 hr 37 min 47 sec
1980	Joe May	14 days 7 hr 11 min 51 sec
1981	Rick Swenson	12 days 8 hr 45 min 2 sec
1982	Rick Swenson	16 days 4 hr 40 min 10 sec
1983	Rick Mackey	12 days 14 hr 10 min 44 sec
1984	Dean Osmar	12 days 15 hr 7 min 33 sec
1985	Libby Riddles	18 days 20 min 17 sec
1986	Susan Butcher	11 days 15 hr 6 min 0 sec
1987	Susan Butcher	11 days 2 hr 5 min 13 sec
1988	Susan Butcher	11 days 11 hr 41 min 40 sec
1989	Joe Runyan	11 days 5 hr 24 min 34 sec
1990	Susan Butcher	11 days 1 hr 53 min 23 sec
1991	Rick Swenson	12 days 16 hr 34 min 39 sec
1992	Martin Buser	10 days 19 hr 17 min 15 sec
1993	Jeff King	10 days 15 hr 38 min 15 sec
1994	Martin Buser	10 days 13 hr 5 min 39 sec
1995	Doug Swingley	10 days 13 hr 2 min 39 sec
1996	Jeff King	9 days 5 hr 43 min 13 sec
1997	Martin Buser	9 days 8 hr 30 min 45 sec
1998	Jeff King	9 days 5 hr 52 min 26 sec
1999	Doug Swingley	9 days 14 hr 31 min 7 sec
2000	Doug Swingley	9 days 58 min 6 sec
2001	Doug Swingley	9 days 19 hr 55 min 50 sec
2002	Martin Buser	8 days 22 hr 46 min 2 sec
2003	Robert Sørlie	9 days 15 hr 47 min 36 sec
2004	Mitch Seavey	9 days 12 hr 20 min 22 sec
2005	Robert Sørlie	9 days 18 hr 39 min 31 sec
2006	Jeff King	9 days 11 hr 11 min 36 sec
2007	Lance Mackey	9 days 5 hr 8 min 41 sec
2008	Lance Mackey	9 days 11 hr 46 min 48 sec

Swimming

The **Fédération Internationale de Natation** (International Swimming Federation, FINA, still known by its French acronym that includes an "a" for "Amateur"; founded 1908) is the world governing body for amateur swimming. It held the first world swimming championships in 1973. After 1975 the FINA championships were held in non-Olympic, even-numbered years. (An exception was the 1991 championship that took place in Australia during the summer month of January.) Diving, synchronized (or synchro) swimming, and water polo events are included in the competition.

A distinction is made between **long-course** (50-m) and **short-course** (25-m) pools for purposes of record setting; world championships and other major contests were long held in 50-m pools, but now a separate World Championship and World Cup take place for 25-m pools.

International Swimming Federation Web site: <www.fina.org>.

World Swimming and Diving Championships—Men

swimming

50-M FREESTYLE

1986	Tom Jager (USA)
1991	Tom Jager (USA)
1994	Aleksandr Popov (RUS)
1998	Bill Pilczuk (USA)
2001	Anthony Ervin (USA)
2003	Aleksandr Popov (RUS)
2005	Roland Schoeman (RSA)
2007	Benjamin Wildman-Tobriner (USA)

100-M FREESTYLE

1973	Jim Montgomery (USA)
1975	Andy Coan (USA)
1978	David McCagg (USA)
1982	Jorg Woithe (GDR)
1986	Matt Biondi (USA)
1991	Matt Biondi (USA)
1994	Aleksandr Popov (RUS)
1998	Aleksandr Popov (RUS)
2001	Anthony Ervin (USA)
2003	Aleksandr Popov (RUS)
2005	Filippo Magnini (ITA)
2007	Filippo Magnini (ITA)

200-M FREESTYLE

1973	Jim Montgomery (USA)
1975	Tim Shaw (USA)
1978	Bill Forrester (USA)
1982	Michael Gross (FRG)

World Swimming and Diving Championships—Men (continued)

swimming (continued)

200-M FREESTYLE (CONTINUED)
1986 Michael Gross (FRG)
1991 Giorgio Lamberti (ITA)
1994 Antti Kasvio (FIN)
1998 Michael Klim (AUS)
2001 Ian Thorpe (AUS)
2003 Ian Thorpe (AUS)
2005 Michael Phelps (USA)
2007 Michael Phelps (USA)

400-M FREESTYLE
1973 Rick DeMont (USA)
1975 Tim Shaw (USA)
1978 Vladimir Salnikov (URS)
1982 Vladimir Salnikov (URS)
1986 Rainer Henkel (FRG)
1991 Jörg Hoffmann (GER)
1994 Kieren Perkins (AUS)
1998 Ian Thorpe (AUS)
2001 Ian Thorpe (AUS)
2003 Ian Thorpe (AUS)
2005 Grant Hackett (AUS)
2007 Park Tae Hwan (KOR)

800-M FREESTYLE
2001 Ian Thorpe (AUS)
2003 Grant Hackett (AUS)
2005 Grant Hackett (AUS)
2007 Przemyslaw Stanczyk (POL)

1,500-M FREESTYLE
1973 Steve Holland (AUS)
1975 Tim Shaw (USA)
1978 Vladimir Salnikov (URS)
1982 Vladimir Salnikov (URS)
1986 Rainer Henkel (FRG)
1991 Jörg Hoffmann (GER)
1994 Kieren Perkins (AUS)
1998 Grant Hackett (AUS)
2001 Grant Hackett (AUS)
2003 Grant Hackett (AUS)
2005 Grant Hackett (AUS)
2007 Mateusz Sawrymowicz (POL)

50-M BACKSTROKE
2001 Randall Bal (USA)
2003 Thomas Rupprath (GER)
2005 Aristeidis Grigoriadis (GRE)
2007 Gerhard Zandberg (RSA)

100-M BACKSTROKE
1973 Roland Matthes (GDR)
1975 Roland Matthes (GDR)
1978 Bob Jackson (USA)
1982 Dirk Richter (GDR)
1986 Igor Polyansky (URS)
1991 Jeff Rouse (USA)
1994 Martín Lopez-Zubero (ESP)
1998 Lenny Krayzelburg (USA)
2001 Matt Welsh (AUS)
2003 Aaron Peirsol (USA)
2005 Aaron Peirsol (USA)
2007 Aaron Peirsol (USA)

200-M BACKSTROKE
1973 Roland Matthes (GDR)
1975 Zoltan Verraszto (HUN)
1978 Jesse Vassallo (USA)
1982 Rick Carey (USA)
1986 Igor Polyansky (URS)
1991 Martín Lopez-Zubero (ESP)
1994 Vladimir Selkov (RUS)
1998 Lenny Krayzelburg (USA)
2001 Aaron Peirsol (USA)
2003 Aaron Peirsol (USA)
2005 Aaron Peirsol (USA)
2007 Ryan Lochte (USA)

50-M BREASTSTROKE
2001 Oleg Lisogor (UKR)
2003 James Gibson (GBR)
2005 Mark Warnecke (GER)
2007 Oleg Lisogor (UKR)

100-M BREASTSTROKE
1973 John Hencken (USA)
1975 David Wilkie (GBR)
1978 Walter Kusch (FRG)
1982 Steve Lundquist (USA)
1986 Victor Davis (CAN)
1991 Norbert Rozsa (HUN)
1994 Norbert Rozsa (HUN)
1998 Fred De Burghgraeve (BEL)
2001 Roman Sloudnov (RUS)
2003 Kosuke Kitajima (JPN)
2005 Brendan Hansen (USA)
2007 Brendan Hansen (USA)

200-M BREASTSTROKE
1973 David Wilkie (GBR)
1975 David Wilkie (GBR)
1978 Nick Nevid (USA)
1982 Victor Davis (CAN)
1986 Joszef Szabo (HUN)
1991 Mike Barrowman (USA)
1994 Norbert Rozsa (HUN)
1998 Kurt Grote (USA)
2001 Brendan Hansen (USA)
2003 Kosuke Kitajima (JPN)
2005 Brendan Hansen (USA)
2007 Kosuke Kitajima (JPN)

50-M BUTTERFLY
2001 Geoff Huegill (AUS)
2003 Matt Welsh (AUS)
2005 Roland Schoeman (RSA)
2007 Roland Schoeman (RSA)

100-M BUTTERFLY
1973 Bruce Robertson (CAN)
1975 Greg Jagenburg (USA)
1978 Joseph Bottom (USA)
1982 Matt Gribble (USA)
1986 Pablo Morales (USA)
1991 Anthony Nesty (SUR)
1994 Rafal Szukala (POL)
1998 Michael Klim (AUS)
2001 Lars Frolander (SWE)
2003 Ian Crocker (USA)

100-M BUTTERFLY (CONTINUED)
2005 Ian Crocker (USA)
2007 Michael Phelps (USA)

200-M BUTTERFLY
1973 Robin Backhaus (USA)
1975 Bill Forrester (USA)
1978 Mike Bruner (USA)
1982 Michael Gross (FRG)
1986 Michael Gross (FRG)
1991 Melvin Stewart (USA)
1994 Denis Pankratov (RUS)
1998 Denys Silantyev (UKR)
2001 Michael Phelps (USA)
2003 Michael Phelps (USA)
2005 Pawel Korzeniowski (POL)
2007 Michael Phelps (USA)

200-M INDIVIDUAL MEDLEY
1973 Gunnar Larsson (SWE)
1975 Andras Hargitay (HUN)
1978 Graham Smith (CAN)
1982 A. Sidorenko (URS)
1986 Tamas Darnyi (HUN)
1991 Tamas Darnyi (HUN)
1994 Jani Sievinen (FIN)
1998 Marcel Wouda (NED)
2001 M. Rosolino (ITA)
2003 Michael Phelps (USA)
2005 Michael Phelps (USA)
2007 Michael Phelps (USA)

400-M INDIVIDUAL MEDLEY
1973 Andras Hargitay (HUN)
1975 Andras Hargitay (HUN)
1978 Jesse Vassallo (USA)
1982 Ricardo Prado (BRA)
1986 Tamas Darnyi (HUN)
1991 Tamas Darnyi (HUN)
1994 Tom Dolan (USA)
1998 Tom Dolan (USA)
2001 Alessio Boggiatto (ITA)
2003 Michael Phelps (USA)
2005 Laszlo Cseh (HUN)
2007 Michael Phelps (USA)

4 × 100-M FREESTYLE RELAY
1973 United States
1975 United States
1978 United States
1982 United States
1986 United States
1991 United States
1994 United States
1998 United States
2001 Australia
2003 Russia
2005 United States
2007 United States

4 × 200-M FREESTYLE RELAY
1973 United States
1975 West Germany
1978 United States
1982 United States
1986 East Germany

World Swimming and Diving Championships—Men (continued)

swimming (continued)

4 × 200-M FREESTYLE RELAY (CONT.)
1991 Germany
1994 Sweden
1998 Australia
2001 Australia
2003 Australia
2005 United States
2007 United States

4 × 100-M MEDLEY RELAY
1973 United States
1975 United States
1978 United States
1982 United States
1986 United States
1991 United States
1994 United States

4 × 100-M MEDLEY RELAY (CONT.)
1998 Australia
2001 Australia
2003 United States
2005 United States
2007 Australia

diving

1-M SPRINGBOARD
1991 Edwin Jongejans (NED)
1994 Evan Stewart (ZIM)
1998 Yu Zhuocheng (CHN)
2001 Wang Feng (CHN)
2003 Xu Xiang (CHN)
2005 Alexandre Despatie (CAN)
2007 Luo Yutong (CHN)

3-M SPRINGBOARD
1973 Phil Boggs (USA)
1975 Phil Boggs (USA)

3-M SPRINGBOARD (CONTINUED)
1978 Phil Boggs (USA)
1982 Greg Louganis (USA)
1986 Greg Louganis (USA)
1991 Kent Ferguson (USA)
1994 Yu Zhuocheng (CHN)
1998 Dmitry Sautin (RUS)
2001 Dmitry Sautin (RUS)
2003 Aleksandr Dobrosok (RUS)
2005 Alexandre Despatie (CAN)
2007 Qin Kai (CHN)

PLATFORM
1973 Klaus Dibiasi (ITA)
1975 Klaus Dibiasi (ITA)
1978 Greg Louganis (USA)
1982 Greg Louganis (USA)
1986 Greg Louganis (USA)
1991 Sun Shuwei (CHN)
1994 Dmitry Sautin (RUS)
1998 Dmitry Sautin (RUS)
2001 Tian Liang (CHN)
2003 Alexandre Despatie (CAN)
2005 Hu Jia (CHN)
2007 Gleb Galperin (RUS)

World Swimming and Diving Championships—Women

swimming

50-M FREESTYLE
1986 Tamara Costache (ROM)
1991 Zhuang Yong (CHN)
1994 Le Jingyi (CHN)
1998 Amy Van Dyken (USA)
2001 Inge De Bruijn (NED)
2003 Inge De Bruijn (NED)
2005 Lisbeth Lenton (AUS)
2007 Lisbeth Lenton (AUS)

100-M FREESTYLE
1973 Kornelia Ender (GDR)
1975 Kornelia Ender (GDR)
1978 Barbara Krause (GDR)
1982 Birgit Meineke (GDR)
1986 Kristin Otto (GDR)
1991 Nicole Haislett (USA)
1994 Le Jingyi (CHN)
1998 Jenny Thompson (USA)
2001 Inge De Bruijn (NED)
2003 Hanna-Maria Seppälä (FIN)
2005 Jodie Henry (AUS)
2007 Lisbeth Lenton (AUS)

200-M FREESTYLE
1973 Keena Rothhammer (USA)
1975 Shirley Babashoff (USA)
1978 Cynthia Woodhead (USA)
1982 Annemarie Verstappen (NED)
1986 Heike Friedrich (GDR)
1991 Hayley Lewis (AUS)
1994 Franziska van Almsick (GER)

200-M FREESTYLE (CONTINUED)
1998 Claudia Poll (CRC)
2001 Giaan Rooney (AUS)
2003 Alena Popchanka (BLR)
2005 Solenne Figues (FRA)
2007 Laure Manaudou (FRA)

400-M FREESTYLE
1973 Heather Greenwood (USA)
1975 Shirley Babashoff (USA)
1978 Tracey Wickham (AUS)
1982 Carmela Schmidt (GDR)
1986 Heike Friedrich (GDR)
1991 Janet Evans (USA)
1994 Yang Aihua (CHN)
1998 Chen Yan (CHN)
2001 Yana Klochkova (UKR)
2003 Hannah Stockbauer (GER)
2005 Laure Manaudou (FRA)
2007 Laure Manaudou (FRA)

800-M FREESTYLE
1973 Novella Calligaris (ITA)
1975 Jenny Turrall (AUS)
1978 Tracey Wickham (AUS)
1982 Kim Linehan (USA)
1986 Astrid Strauss (GDR)
1991 Janet Evans (USA)
1994 Janet Evans (USA)
1998 Brooke Bennett (USA)
2001 Hannah Stockbauer (GER)
2003 Hannah Stockbauer (GER)
2005 Kate Ziegler (USA)
2007 Kate Ziegler (USA)

1,500-M FREESTYLE
2001 Hannah Stockbauer (GER)
2003 Hannah Stockbauer (GER)
2005 Kate Ziegler (USA)
2007 Kate Ziegler (USA)

50-M BREASTSTROKE
2001 Luo Xuejuan (CHN)
2003 Luo Xuejuan (CHN)
2005 Jade Edmistone (AUS)
2007 Jessica Hardy (USA)

100-M BREASTSTROKE
1973 Renate Vogel (GDR)
1975 Hannelore Anke (GDR)
1978 Yuliya Bogdanova (URS)
1982 Ute Geweniger (GDR)
1986 Sylvia Gerasch (GDR)
1991 Linley Frame (AUS)
1994 Samantha Riley (AUS)
1998 Kristy Kowal (USA)
2001 Luo Xuejuan (CHN)
2003 Luo Xuejuan (CHN)
2005 Leisel Jones (AUS)
2007 Leisel Jones (AUS)

200-M BREASTSTROKE
1973 Renate Vogel (GDR)
1975 Hannelore Anke (GDR)
1978 Lina Kachushite (URS)
1982 Svetlana Varganova (URS)
1986 Silke Hörner (GDR)
1991 Yelena Volkova (URS)

World Swimming and Diving Championships—Women (continued)

swimming (continued)

200-M BREASTSTROKE (CONTINUED)
1994 Samantha Riley (AUS)
1998 Agnes Kovacs (HUN)
2001 Agnes Kovacs (HUN)
2003 Amanda Beard (USA)
2005 Leisel Jones (AUS)
2007 Leisel Jones (AUS)

50-M BUTTERFLY
2001 Inge De Bruijn (NED)
2003 Inge De Bruijn (NED)
2005 Danni Miatke (AUS)
2007 Therese Alshammar (SWE)

100-M BUTTERFLY
1973 Kornelia Ender (GDR)
1975 Kornelia Ender (GDR)
1978 Joan Pennington (USA)
1982 Mary T. Meagher (USA)
1986 Kornelia Gressler (GDR)
1991 Qian Hong (CHN)
1994 Liu Limin (CHN)
1998 Jenny Thompson (USA)
2001 Petria Thomas (AUS)
2003 Jenny Thompson (USA)
2005 Jessicah Schipper (AUS)
2007 Lisbeth Lenton (AUS)

200-M BUTTERFLY
1973 Rosemarie Kother (GDR)
1975 Rosemarie Kother (GDR)
1978 Tracy Caulkins (USA)
1982 Ines Geissler (GDR)
1986 Mary T. Meagher (USA)
1991 Summer Sanders (USA)
1994 Liu Limin (CHN)
1998 Susie O'Neill (AUS)
2001 Petria Thomas (AUS)
2003 Otylia Jedrzejczak (POL)
2005 Otylia Jedrzejczak (POL)
2007 Jessicah Schipper (AUS)

50-M BACKSTROKE
2001 Haley Cope (USA)
2003 Nina Zhivanevskaya (ESP)
2005 Giaan Rooney (AUS)
2007 Leila Vaziri (USA)

100-M BACKSTROKE
1973 Ulrike Richter (GDR)
1975 Ulrike Richter (GDR)
1978 Linda Jezek (USA)
1982 Kristin Otto (GDR)
1986 Betsy Mitchell (USA)
1991 Krisztina Egerszegi (HUN)
1994 He Cihong (CHN)
1998 Lea Maurer (USA)
2001 Natalie Coughlin (USA)
2003 Antje Buschschulte (GER)
2005 Kirsty Coventry (ZIM)
2007 Natalie Coughlin (USA)

200-M BACKSTROKE
1973 Melissa Belote (USA)
1975 Birgit Treiber (GDR)
1978 Linda Jezek (USA)
1982 Cornelia Sirch (GDR)
1986 Cornelia Sirch (GDR)
1991 Krisztina Egerszegi (HUN)
1994 He Cihong (CHN)
1998 Roxana Maracineanu (FRA)
2001 Diana Mocanu (ROM)
2003 Katy Sexton (GBR)
2005 Kirsty Coventry (ZIM)
2007 Margaret Hoelzer (USA)

200-M INDIVIDUAL MEDLEY
1973 Andrea Hubner (GDR)
1975 Kathy Heddy (USA)
1978 Tracy Caulkins (USA)
1982 Petra Schneider (GDR)
1986 Kristin Otto (GDR)
1991 Lin Li (CHN)
1994 Lu Bin (CHN)
1998 Wu Yanyan (CHN)
2001 Martha Bowen (USA)
2003 Yana Klochkova (UKR)
2005 Katie Hoff (USA)
2007 Katie Hoff (USA)

400-M INDIVIDUAL MEDLEY
1973 Gudrun Wegner (GDR)
1975 Ulrika Tauber (GDR)
1978 Tracy Caulkins (USA)
1982 Petra Schneider (GDR)

400-M INDIVIDUAL MEDLEY (CONT.)
1986 Kathleen Nord (GDR)
1991 Lin Li (CHN)
1994 Dai Guohong (CHN)
1998 Chen Yan (CHN)
2001 Yana Klochkova (UKR)
2003 Yana Klochkova (UKR)
2005 Katie Hoff (USA)
2007 Katie Hoff (USA)

4 × 100-M FREESTYLE RELAY
1973 East Germany
1975 East Germany
1978 United States
1982 East Germany
1986 East Germany
1991 United States
1994 China
1998 United States
2001 Germany
2003 United States
2005 Australia
2007 Australia

4 × 200-M FREESTYLE RELAY
1986 East Germany
1991 Germany
1994 China
1998 Germany
2001 Great Britain
2003 United States
2005 United States
2007 United States

4 × 100-M MEDLEY RELAY
1973 East Germany
1975 East Germany
1978 United States
1982 East Germany
1986 East Germany
1991 United States
1994 China
1998 United States
2001 Australia
2003 China
2005 Australia
2007 Australia

diving

1-M SPRINGBOARD
1991 Gao Min (CHN)
1994 Chen Lixia (CHN)
1998 Irina Lashko (RUS)
2001 Blythe Hartley (CAN)
2003 Irina Lashko (AUS)
2005 Blythe Hartley (CAN)
2007 He Zi (CHN)

3-M SPRINGBOARD
1973 Christa Kohler (GDR)
1975 Irina Kalinina (URS)
1978 Irina Kalinina (URS)
1982 Megan Neyer (USA)

3-M SPRINGBOARD (CONT.)
1986 Gao Min (CHN)
1991 Gao Min (CHN)
1994 Tan Shuping (CHN)
1998 Yulia Pakhalina (RUS)
2001 Guo Jingjing (CHN)
2003 Guo Jingjing (CHN)
2005 Guo Jingjing (CHN)
2007 Guo Jingjing (CHN)

PLATFORM
1973 Ulrika Knape (SWE)
1975 Janet Ely (USA)
1978 Irina Kalinina (URS)

PLATFORM (CONT.)
1982 Wendy Wyland (USA)
1986 Chen Lin (CHN)
1991 Fu Mingxia (CHN)
1994 Fu Mingxia (CHN)
1998 Olena Zhupina (UKR)
2001 Xu Mian (CHN)
2003 Emilie Heymans (CAN)
2005 Laura Wilkinson (USA)
2007 Wang Xin (CHN)

Swimming World Records—Long Course (50 m)

men

EVENT	RECORD HOLDER (COUNTRY)	PERFORMANCE	DATE
50-m freestyle	Eamon Sullivan (AUS)	21.28 sec	28 Mar 2008
100-m freestyle	Eamon Sullivan (AUS)	47.05 sec	13 Aug 2008
200-m freestyle	Michael Phelps (USA)	1 min 42.96 sec	12 Aug 2008
400-m freestyle	Ian Thorpe (AUS)	3 min 40.08 sec	30 Jul 2002
800-m freestyle	Grant Hackett (AUS)	7 min 38.65 sec	27 Jul 2005
1;500-m freestyle	Grant Hackett (AUS)	14 min 34.56 sec	29 Jul 2001
50-m backstroke	Liam Tancock (GBR)	24.47 sec	2 Apr 2008
100-m backstroke	Aaron Peirsol (USA)	52.54 sec	12 Aug 2008
200-m backstroke	Ryan Lochte (USA)	1 min 53.94 sec	15 Aug 2008
50-m breaststroke	Oleg Lisogor (UKR)	27.18 sec	2 Aug 2002
100-m breaststroke	Kosuke Kitajima (JPN)	58.91 sec	11 Aug 2008
200-m breaststroke	Kosuke Kitajima (JPN)	2 min 07.51 sec	8 Jun 2008
50-m butterfly	Roland Schoeman (RSA)	22.96 sec	25 Jul 2005
100-m butterfly	Ian Crocker (USA)	50.40 sec	30 Jul 2005
200-m butterfly	Michael Phelps (USA)	1 min 52.03 sec	13 Aug 2008
200-m individual medley	Michael Phelps (USA)	1 min 54.23 sec	15 Aug 2008
400-m individual medley	Michael Phelps (USA)	4 min 03.84 sec	10 Aug 2008
4 × 100-m freestyle relay	United States (Jason Lezak, Michael Phelps, Garrett Weber-Gale, Cullen Jones)	3 min 08.24 sec	11 Aug 2008
4 × 200-m freestyle relay	United States (Ryan Lochte, Michael Phelps, Peter Vanderkaay, Ricky Berens)	6 min 58.56 sec	13 Aug 2008
4 × 100-m medley relay	United States (Brendan Hansen, Jason Lezak, Michael Phelps, Aaron Peirsol)	3 min 29.34 sec	17 Aug 2008

women

EVENT	RECORD HOLDER (COUNTRY)	PERFORMANCE	DATE
50-m freestyle	Lisbeth Lenton Trickett (AUS)	23.97 sec	29 Mar 2008
100-m freestyle	Lisbeth Lenton Trickett (AUS)	52.88 sec	27 Mar 2008
200-m freestyle	Federica Pellegrini (ITA)	1 min 54.82 sec	13 Aug 2008
400-m freestyle	Federica Pellegrini (ITA)	4 min 01.53 sec	24 Mar 2008
800-m freestyle	Rebecca Adlington (GBR)	8 min 14.10 sec	16 Aug 2008
1,500-m freestyle	Kate Ziegler (USA)	15 min 42.54 sec	17 Jun 2007
50-m backstroke	Sophie Edington (AUS)	27.67 sec	23 Mar 2008
100-m backstroke	Kirsty Coventry (ZIM)	58.77 sec	11 Aug 2008
200-m backstroke	Kirsty Coventry (ZIM)	2 min 05.24 sec	16 Aug 2008
50-m breaststroke	Jade Edmistone (AUS)	30.31 sec	30 Jan 2006
100-m breaststroke	Leisel Jones (AUS)	1 min 05.09 sec	20 Mar 2006
200-m breaststroke	Rebecca Soni (USA)	2 min 20.22 sec	15 Aug 2008
50-m butterfly	Therese Alshammar (SWE)	25.46 sec	13 Jun 2007
100-m butterfly	Inge de Bruijn (NED)	56.61 sec	17 Sep 2000
200-m butterfly	Liu Zige (CHN)	2 min 04.18 sec	14 Aug 2008
200-m individual medley	Stephanie Rice (AUS)	2 min 08.45 sec	13 Aug 2008
400-m individual medley	Stephanie Rice (AUS)	4 min 29.45 sec	10 Aug 2008
4 × 100-m freestyle relay	The Netherlands (Inge Dekker, Femke Heemskerk, Ranomi Kromowidjojo, Marleen Veldhuis)	3 min 33.62 sec	18 Mar 2008
4 × 200-m freestyle relay	Australia (Linda Mackenzie, Stephanie Rice, Bronte Barratt, Kylie Palmer)	7 min 44.31 sec	14 Aug 2008
4 × 100-m medley relay	Australia (Leisel Jones, Jessicah Schipper, Emily Seebohm, Lisbeth Lenton Trickett)	3 min 52.69 sec	17 Aug 2008

Swimming World Records—Short Course (25 m)

men

EVENT	RECORD HOLDER (COUNTRY)	PERFORMANCE	DATE
50-m freestyle	Duje Draganja (CRO)	20.81 sec	11 Apr 2008
100-m freestyle	Stefan Nystrand (SWE)	45.83 sec	17 Nov 2007
200-m freestyle	Ian Thorpe (AUS)	1 min 41.10 sec	6 Feb 2000
400-m freestyle	Grant Hackett (AUS)	3 min 34.58 sec	18 Jul 2002
800-m freestyle	Grant Hackett (AUS)	7 min 23.42 sec	19 Jul 2008
1,500-m freestyle	Grant Hackett (AUS)	14 min 10.10 sec	7 Aug 2001
50-m backstroke	Thomas Rupprath (GER)	23.27 sec	10 Dec 2004

Swimming World Records—Short Course (25 m) (continued)

men (continued)

EVENT	RECORD HOLDER (COUNTRY)	PERFORMANCE	DATE
100-m backstroke	Ryan Lochte (USA)	49.99 sec	9 Apr 2006
200-m backstroke	Markus Rogan (AUT)	1 min 47.84 sec	13 Apr 2008
50-m breaststroke	Oleg Lisogor (UKR)	26.17 sec	21 Jan 2006
100-m breaststroke	Ed Moses (USA)	57.47 sec	23 Jan 2002
200-m breaststroke	Ed Moses (USA)	2 min 02.92 sec	17 Jan 2004
50-m butterfly	Kaio Almeida (BRA)	22.60 sec	17 Dec 2005
100-m butterfly	Ian Crocker (USA)	49.07 sec	26 Mar 2004
200-m butterfly	Franck Esposito (FRA)	1 min 50.73 sec	8 Dec 2002
100-m individual medley	Ryan Lochte (USA)	51.15 sec	13 Apr 2008
200-m individual medley	Ryan Lochte (USA)	1 min 51.56 sec	11 Apr 2008
400-m individual medley	László Cseh (HUN)	3 min 59.33 sec	14 Dec 2007
4 × 100-m freestyle relay	United States (Ryan Lochte, Bryan Lundquist, Nathan Adrian, Doug Van Wie)	3 min 08.44 sec	9 Apr 2008
4 × 200-m freestyle relay	Australia (Kirk Palmer, Grant Hackett, Grant Brits, Kenrick Monk)	6 min 52.66 sec	31 Aug 2007
4 × 100-m medley relay	Russia (Stanislav Donets, Sergey Geybel, Yevgeny Korotyshkin, Aleksandr Sukhorukov)	3 min 24.29 sec	13 Apr 2008

women

EVENT	RECORD HOLDER (COUNTRY)	PERFORMANCE	DATE
50-m freestyle	Marleen Veldhuis (NED)	23.25 sec	13 Apr 2008
100-m freestyle	Lisbeth Lenton (AUS)	51.70 sec	9 Aug 2005
200-m freestyle	Lisbeth Lenton (AUS)	1 min 53.29 sec	19 Nov 2005
400-m freestyle	Laure Manaudou (FRA)	3 min 56.09 sec	9 Dec 2006
800-m freestyle	Kate Ziegler (USA)	8 min 08.00 sec	14 Oct 2007
1,500-m freestyle	Kate Ziegler (USA)	15 min 32.90 sec	12 Oct 2007
50-m backstroke	Sanja Jovanovic (CRO)	26.37 sec	13 Apr 2008
100-m backstroke	Natalie Coughlin (USA)	56.51 sec	28 Oct 2007
200-m backstroke	Kirsty Coventry (ZIM)	2 min 00.91 sec	11 Apr 2008
50-m breaststroke	Jessica Hardy (USA)	29.58 sec	10 Apr 2008
100-m breaststroke	Leisel Jones (AUS)	1 min 03.72 sec	25 Apr 2008
200-m breaststroke	Leisel Jones (AUS)	2 min 17.75 sec	29 Nov 2003
50-m butterfly	Felicity Galvez (AUS)	25.32 sec	11 Apr 2008
100-m butterfly	Lisbeth Lenton Trickett (AUS)	55.74 sec	25 Apr 2008
200-m butterfly	Yuko Nakanishi (JPN)	2 min 03.12 sec	23 Feb 2008
100-m individual medley	Natalie Coughlin (USA)	58.80 sec	23 Nov 2002
200-m individual medley	Kirsty Coventry (ZIM)	2 min 06.13 sec	12 Apr 2008
400-m individual medley	Kirsty Coventry (ZIM)	4 min 26.52 sec	9 Apr 2008
4 × 100-m freestyle relay	The Netherlands (Hinkelien Schreuder, Femke Heemskerk, Inge Dekker, Marleen Veldhuis)	3 min 29.42 sec	12 Apr 2008
4 × 200-m freestyle relay	The Netherlands (Inge Dekker, Femke Heemskerk, Marleen Veldhuis, Ranomi Kromowidjojo)	7 min 38.90 sec	9 Apr 2008
4 × 100-m medley relay	United States (Margaret Hoelzer, Jessica Hardy, Rachel Komisarz, Kara Denby)	3 min 51.36 sec	11 Apr 2008

Tennis

Four events dominate world championship tennis. The first of the traditional **"Big Four,"** or **"Grand Slam,"** events was the **All-England Lawn Tennis Championships** (better known as the **Wimbledon** Championships), founded in 1877. Its only event the first year was the men's singles championships; women first competed in 1884. Major tennis tournaments also sprang up in the **United States** (1881 for men; women's singles competition first officially added 1889), **France** (1891 for men; women's singles competition added 1897), and **Australia** (1905 for men; women's singles competition added 1922). Open tennis (open, that is, to both professionals and amateurs) became the rule in the Big Four tournaments in 1968. International team tennis was organized in 1900 with the institution of the **Davis Cup.** Men's teams competing for the Davis Cup play four singles matches and one doubles match in elimination rounds. The **Wightman Cup** was contested yearly between British and American women's teams from 1923 to 1989. The **International Tennis Federation** (ITF, formerly the International Lawn Tennis Federation; founded 1913) established the **Federation Cup** in 1963 (called the Fed Cup since 1994) for international women's team competition. It is decided by elimination rounds of two singles and one doubles contest.

Related Web sites: International Tennis Federation: <www.itftennis.com>; ATP (formerly Association of Tennis Professionals): <www.atptennis.com>; Women's Tennis Association: <www.wtatour.com>.

Australian Open Tennis Championships—Singles

YEAR	MEN	WOMEN
1905	Rodney Heath (AUS)	
1906	Tony Wilding (NZL)	
1907	Horace Rice (AUS)	
1908	Fred Alexander (USA)	
1909	Tony Wilding (NZL)	
1910	Rodney Heath (AUS)	
1911	Norman Brookes (AUS)	
1912	J. Cecil Parke (GBR)	
1913	E.F. Parker (AUS)	
1914	Pat O'Hara Wood (AUS)	
1915	Francis Lowe (GBR)	
1916–18	*not held*	
1919	A.R.F. Kingscote (GBR)	
1920	Pat O'Hara Wood (AUS)	
1921	Rhys Gemmell (AUS)	
1922	James Anderson (AUS)	Margaret Molesworth (AUS)
1923	Pat O'Hara Wood (AUS)	Margaret Molesworth (AUS)
1924	James Anderson (AUS)	Sylvia Lance (AUS)
1925	James Anderson (AUS)	Daphne Akhurst (AUS)
1926	John Hawkes (AUS)	Daphne Akhurst (AUS)
1927	Gerald Patterson (AUS)	Esna Boyd (AUS)
1928	Jean Borotra (FRA)	Daphne Akhurst (AUS)
1929	John Gregory (GBR)	Daphne Akhurst (AUS)
1930	Gar Moon (AUS)	Daphne Akhurst (AUS)
1931	Jack Crawford (AUS)	Coral Buttsworth (AUS)
1932	Jack Crawford (AUS)	Coral Buttsworth (AUS)
1933	Jack Crawford (AUS)	Joan Hartigan (AUS)
1934	Fred Perry (GBR)	Joan Hartigan (AUS)
1935	Jack Crawford (AUS)	Dorothy Round (GBR)
1936	Adrian Quist (AUS)	Joan Hartigan (AUS)
1937	Vivian McGrath (AUS)	Nancye Wynne (AUS)
1938	Don Budge (USA)	Dorothy Bundy (USA)
1939	John Bromwich (AUS)	Emily Westacott (AUS)
1940	Adrian Quist (AUS)	Nancye Wynne (AUS)
1941–45	*not held*	
1946	John Bromwich (AUS)	Nancye Wynne Bolton (AUS)
1947	Dinny Pails (AUS)	Nancye Wynne Bolton (AUS)
1948	Adrian Quist (AUS)	Nancye Wynne Bolton (AUS)
1949	Frank Sedgman (AUS)	Doris Hart (USA)
1950	Frank Sedgman (AUS)	Louise Brough (USA)
1951	Dick Savitt (USA)	Nancye Wynne Bolton (AUS)
1952	Ken McGregor (AUS)	Thelma Long (AUS)
1953	Ken Rosewall (AUS)	Maureen Connolly (USA)
1954	Mervyn Rose (AUS)	Thelma Long (AUS)
1955	Ken Rosewall (AUS)	Beryl Penrose (AUS)
1956	Lew Hoad (AUS)	Mary Carter (AUS)
1957	Ashley Cooper (AUS)	Shirley Fry (USA)
1958	Ashley Cooper (AUS)	Angela Mortimer (GBR)
1959	Alex Olmedo (PER)	Mary Carter-Reitano (AUS)
1960	Rod Laver (AUS)	Margaret Smith (AUS)
1961	Roy Emerson (AUS)	Margaret Smith (AUS)
1962	Rod Laver (AUS)	Margaret Smith (AUS)
1963	Roy Emerson (AUS)	Margaret Smith (AUS)
1964	Roy Emerson (AUS)	Margaret Smith (AUS)
1965	Roy Emerson (AUS)	Margaret Smith (AUS)
1966	Roy Emerson (AUS)	Margaret Smith (AUS)
1967	Roy Emerson (AUS)	Nancy Richey (USA)
1968	Bill Bowrey (AUS)	Billie Jean King (USA)
1969	Rod Laver (AUS)	Margaret Smith Court (AUS)
1970	Arthur Ashe (USA)	Margaret Smith Court (AUS)
1971	Ken Rosewall (AUS)	Margaret Smith Court (AUS)
1972	Ken Rosewall (AUS)	Virginia Wade (GBR)
1973	John Newcombe (AUS)	Margaret Smith Court (AUS)
1974	Jimmy Connors (USA)	Evonne Goolagong (AUS)
1975	John Newcombe (AUS)	Evonne Goolagong (AUS)
1976	Mark Edmondson (AUS)	Evonne Goolagong Cawley (AUS)
1977	Roscoe Tanner (USA)	Kerry Reid (AUS)
1977[1]	Vitas Gerulaitis (USA)	Evonne Goolagong Cawley (AUS)

Australian Open Tennis Championships—Singles (continued)

YEAR	MEN	WOMEN
1978[1]	Guillermo Vilas (ARG)	Chris O'Neill (AUS)
1979[1]	Guillermo Vilas (ARG)	Barbara Jordan (USA)
1980[1]	Brian Teacher (USA)	Hana Mandlikova (TCH)
1981[1]	Johan Kriek (RSA)	Martina Navratilova (USA)
1982[1]	Johan Kriek (RSA)	Chris Evert Lloyd (USA)
1983[1]	Mats Wilander (SWE)	Martina Navratilova (USA)
1984[1]	Mats Wilander (SWE)	Chris Evert Lloyd (USA)
1985[1]	Stefan Edberg (SWE)	Martina Navratilova (USA)
1987[2]	Stefan Edberg (SWE)	Hana Mandlikova (TCH)
1988	Mats Wilander (SWE)	Steffi Graf (FRG)
1989	Ivan Lendl (TCH)	Steffi Graf (FRG)
1990	Ivan Lendl (TCH)	Steffi Graf (FRG)
1991	Boris Becker (GER)	Monica Seles (YUG)
1992	Jim Courier (USA)	Monica Seles (YUG)
1993	Jim Courier (USA)	Monica Seles (YUG)
1994	Pete Sampras (USA)	Steffi Graf (GER)
1995	Andre Agassi (USA)	Mary Pierce (FRA)
1996	Boris Becker (GER)	Monica Seles (USA)
1997	Pete Sampras (USA)	Martina Hingis (SUI)
1998	Petr Korda (CZE)	Martina Hingis (SUI)
1999	Yevgeny Kafelnikov (RUS)	Martina Hingis (SUI)
2000	Andre Agassi (USA)	Lindsay Davenport (USA)
2001	Andre Agassi (USA)	Jennifer Capriati (USA)
2002	Thomas Johansson (SWE)	Jennifer Capriati (USA)
2003	Andre Agassi (USA)	Serena Williams (USA)
2004	Roger Federer (SUI)	Justine Henin-Hardenne (BEL)
2005	Marat Safin (RUS)	Serena Williams (USA)
2006	Roger Federer (SUI)	Amélie Mauresmo (FRA)
2007	Roger Federer (SUI)	Serena Williams (USA)
2008	Novak Djokovic (SER)	Mariya Sharapova (RUS)

[1]*Tournament held in December rather than January.* [2]*1986 not held.*

Australian Open Tennis Championships—Doubles

YEAR	MEN	WOMEN
1905	Tom Tachell, Randolph Lycett	
1906	Tony Wilding, Rodney Heath	
1907	Harry Parker, William Gregg	
1908	Fred Alexander, Alfred Dunlop	
1909	Ernie F. Parker, J.P. Keane	
1910	Horace Rice, Ashley Campbell	
1911	Rodney Heath, Randolph Lycett	
1912	J. Cecil Parke, Charles Dixon	
1913	Ernie F. Parker, Alf Hedemann	
1914	Ashley Campbell, Gerald Patterson	
1915	Horace Rice, Clarrie Todd	
1916–18	*not held*	
1919	Pat O'Hara Wood, Ron Thomas	
1920	Pat O'Hara Wood, Ron Thomas	
1921	S.H. Eaton-Rice, Rhys Gemmell	
1922	Gerald Patterson, John Hawkes	Esne Boyd, Marjorie Mountain
1923	Pat O'Hara Wood, Bert St. John	Esne Boyd, Sylvia Lance
1924	Norman Brookes, James Anderson	Daphne Akhurst, Sylvia Lance
1925	Gerald Patterson, Pat O'Hara Wood	Daphne Akhurst, Sylvia Lance Harper
1926	Gerald Patterson, John Hawkes	Meryl O'Hara Wood, Esne Boyd
1927	Gerald Patterson, John Hawkes	Meryl O'Hara Wood, Louise Bickerton
1928	Jean Borotra, Jacques Brugnon	Daphne Akhurst, Esne Boyd
1929	Jack Crawford, Harry Hopman	Daphne Akhurst, Louise Bickerton
1930	Jack Crawford, Harry Hopman	Margaret Molesworth, Emily Hood
1931	Charles Donohoe, Ray Dunlop	Daphne Akhurst Cozens, Louise Bickerton
1932	Jack Crawford, Gar Moon	Coral Buttsworth, Marjorie Cox Crawford
1933	Ellsworth Vines, Keith Gledhill	Margaret Molesworth, Emily Hood Westacott
1934	Fred Perry, George Hughes	Margaret Molesworth, Emily Hood Westacott
1935	Jack Crawford, Vivian McGrath	Evelyn Dearman, Nancy Lyle
1936	Adrian Quist, D.P. Turnbull	Thelma Coyne, Nancye Wynne
1937	Adrian Quist, D.P. Turnbull	Thelma Coyne, Nancye Wynne

Australian Open Tennis Championships—Doubles (continued)

YEAR	MEN	WOMEN
1938	Adrian Quist, John Bromwich	Thelma Coyne, Nancye Wynne
1939	Adrian Quist, John Bromwich	Thelma Coyne, Nancye Wynne
1940	Adrian Quist, John Bromwich	Thelma Coyne, Nancye Wynne Bolton
1941-45	*not held*	
1946	Adrian Quist, John Bromwich	Joyce Fitch, Mary Bevis
1947	Adrian Quist, John Bromwich	Thelma Coyne Long, Nancye Wynne Bolton
1948	Adrian Quist, John Bromwich	Thelma Coyne Long, Nancye Wynne Bolton
1949	Adrian Quist, John Bromwich	Thelma Coyne Long, Nancye Wynne Bolton
1950	Adrian Quist, John Bromwich	Louise Brough, Doris Hart
1951	Ken McGregor, Frank Sedgman	Thelma Coyne Long, Nancye Wynne Bolton
1952	Ken McGregor, Frank Sedgman	Thelma Coyne Long, Nancye Wynne Bolton
1953	Lew Hoad, Ken Rosewall	Maureen Connolly, Julia Sampson
1954	Rex Hartwig, Mervyn Rose	Mary Bevis Hawton, Beryl Penrose
1955	Vic Seixas, Tony Trabert	Mary Bevis Hawton, Beryl Penrose
1956	Lew Hoad, Ken Rosewall	Mary Bevis Hawton, Thelma Coyne Long
1957	Lew Hoad, Neale Fraser	Althea Gibson, Shirley Fry
1958	Ashley Cooper, Neale Fraser	Mary Bevis Hawton, Thelma Coyne Long
1959	Rod Laver, Robert Mark	Sandra Reynolds, Renee Schuurman
1960	Rod Laver, Robert Mark	Maria Bueno, Christine Truman
1961	Rod Laver, Robert Mark	Mary Reitano, Margaret Smith
1962	Roy Emerson, Neale Fraser	Robyn Ebbern, Margaret Smith
1963	Bob Hewitt, Fred Stolle	Robyn Ebbern, Margaret Smith
1964	Bob Hewitt, Fred Stolle	Judy Tegart, Lesley Turner
1965	John Newcombe, Tony Roche	Margaret Smith, Lesley Turner
1966	Roy Emerson, Fred Stolle	Carole Graebner, Nancy Richey
1967	John Newcombe, Tony Roche	Judy Tegart, Lesley Turner
1968	Dick Crealy, Allan Stone	Karen Krantzcke, Karrie Melville
1969	Roy Emerson, Rod Laver	Margaret Smith Court, Judy Tegart
1970	Bob Lutz, Stan Smith	Margaret Smith Court, Judy Tegart Dalton
1971	John Newcombe, Tony Roche	Margaret Smith Court, Evonne Goolagong
1972	Owen Davidson, Ken Rosewall	Kerry Harris, Helen Gourlay
1973	Mal Anderson, John Newcombe	Margaret Smith Court, Virginia Wade
1974	Ross Case, Geoff Masters	Evonne Goolagong, Peggy Michel
1975	John Alexander, Phil Dent	Evonne Goolagong, Peggy Michel
1976	John Newcombe, Tony Roche	Evonne Goolagong Cawley, Helen Gourlay
1977	Arthur Ashe, Tony Roche	Dianne Fromholtz, Helen Gourlay
1977[1]	Allan Stone, Ray Ruffels	Evonne Goolagong Cawley, Helen Gourlay Cawley; Mona Guerrant, Kerry Reid[2]
1978[1]	Wojtek Fibak, Kim Warwick	Renata Tomanova, Betsy Nagelsen
1979[1]	Peter McNamara, Paul McNamee	Judy Chaloner, Dianne Evers
1980[1]	Kim Warwick, Mark Edmondson	Martina Navratilova, Betsy Nagelsen
1981[1]	Kim Warwick, Mark Edmondson	Kathy Jordan, Anne Smith
1982[1]	John Alexander, John Fitzgerald	Martina Navratilova, Pam Shriver
1983[1]	Mark Edmondson, Paul McNamee	Martina Navratilova, Pam Shriver
1984[1]	Mark Edmondson, Sherwood Stewart	Martina Navratilova, Pam Shriver
1985[1]	Paul Annacone, Christo van Rensburg	Martina Navratilova, Pam Shriver
1987[3]	Stefan Edberg, Anders Järryd	Martina Navratilova, Pam Shriver
1988	Rick Leach, Jim Pugh	Martina Navratilova, Pam Shriver
1989	Rick Leach, Jim Pugh	Martina Navratilova, Pam Shriver
1990	Pieter Aldrich, Danie Visser	Jana Novotna, Helena Sukova
1991	Scott Davis, David Pate	Patty Fendick, Mary Joe Fernández
1992	Todd Woodbridge, Mark Woodforde	Arantxa Sánchez Vicario, Helena Sukova
1993	Danie Visser, Laurie Warder	Gigi Fernández, Natasha Zvereva
1994	Jacco Eltingh, Paul Haarhuis	Gigi Fernández, Natasha Zvereva
1995	Jared Palmer, Richey Reneberg	Arantxa Sánchez Vicario, Jana Novotna
1996	Stefan Edberg, Petr Korda	Arantxa Sánchez Vicario, Chanda Rubin
1997	Todd Woodbridge, Mark Woodforde	Martina Hingis, Natasha Zvereva
1998	Jonas Björkman, Jacco Eltingh	Martina Hingis, Mirjana Lucic
1999	Jonas Björkman, Patrick Rafter	Martina Hingis, Anna Kournikova
2000	Ellis Ferreira, Rick Leach	Lisa Raymond, Rennae Stubbs
2001	Jonas Björkman, Todd Woodbridge	Venus Williams, Serena Williams
2002	Mark Knowles, Daniel Nestor	Martina Hingis, Anna Kournikova
2003	Michaël Llodra, Fabrice Santoro	Venus Williams, Serena Williams
2004	Michaël Llodra, Fabrice Santoro	Virginia Ruano Pascual, Paola Suárez

Australian Open Tennis Championships—Doubles (continued)

YEAR	MEN	WOMEN
2005	Wayne Black, Kevin Ullyett	Alicia Molik, Svetlana Kuznetsova
2006	Bob Bryan, Mike Bryan	Yan Zi, Zheng Jie
2007	Bob Bryan, Mike Bryan	Cara Black, Liezel Huber
2008	Jonathan Erlich, Andy Ram	Alona Bondarenko, Kateryna Bondarenko

[1]Tournament held in December rather than January. *[2]Tie; finals rained out.* *[3]1986 not held.*

French Open Tennis Championships—Singles

From 1891 to 1924, only members of French tennis clubs were eligible to play in the French Open. The table shows the winners only since 1925, when the tournament was opened to international competition.

YEAR	MEN	WOMEN
1925	René Lacoste (FRA)	Suzanne Lenglen (FRA)
1926	Henri Cochet (FRA)	Suzanne Lenglen (FRA)
1927	René Lacoste (FRA)	Kornelia Bouman (NED)
1928	Henri Cochet (FRA)	Helen Wills (USA)
1929	René Lacoste (FRA)	Helen Wills (USA)
1930	Henri Cochet (FRA)	Helen Wills Moody (USA)
1931	Jean Borotra (FRA)	Cilly Aussem (GER)
1932	Henri Cochet (FRA)	Helen Wills Moody (USA)
1933	John Crawford (AUS)	Margaret Scriven (GBR)
1934	Gottfried von Cramm (GER)	Margaret Scriven (GBR)
1935	Fred Perry (GBR)	Hilde Sperling (DEN)
1936	Gottfried von Cramm (GER)	Hilde Sperling (DEN)
1937	Henner Henkel (GER)	Hilde Sperling (DEN)
1938	Don Budge (USA)	Simone Mathieu (FRA)
1939	Don McNeill (USA)	Simone Mathieu (FRA)
1940	*not held*	*not held*
1941	Bernard Destremau (FRA)	*not held*
1942	Bernard Destremau (FRA)	*not held*
1943	Yvon Petra (FRA)	*not held*
1944	Yvon Petra (FRA)	*not held*
1945	Yvon Petra (FRA)	*not held*
1946	Marcel Bernard (FRA)	Margaret Osborne (USA)
1947	Joseph Asboth (HUN)	Patricia Todd (USA)
1948	Frank Parker (USA)	Nelly Landry (BEL)
1949	Frank Parker (USA)	Margaret Osborne du Pont (USA)
1950	Budge Patty (USA)	Doris Hart (USA)
1951	Jaroslav Drobny (TCH)	Shirley Fry (USA)
1952	Jaroslav Drobny (TCH)	Doris Hart (USA)
1953	Ken Rosewall (AUS)	Maureen Connolly (USA)
1954	Tony Trabert (USA)	Maureen Connolly (USA)
1955	Tony Trabert (USA)	Angela Mortimer (GBR)
1956	Lew Hoad (AUS)	Althea Gibson (USA)
1957	Sven Davidson (SWE)	Shirley Bloomer (GBR)
1958	Mervyn Rose (AUS)	Zsuzsi Kormoczi (HUN)
1959	Nicola Pietrangeli (ITA)	Christine Truman (GBR)
1960	Nicola Pietrangeli (ITA)	Darlene Hard (USA)
1961	Manuel Santana (ESP)	Ann Haydon (GBR)
1962	Rod Laver (AUS)	Margaret Smith (AUS)
1963	Roy Emerson (AUS)	Lesley Turner (AUS)
1964	Manuel Santana (ESP)	Margaret Smith (AUS)
1965	Fred Stolle (AUS)	Lesley Turner (AUS)
1966	Tony Roche (AUS)	Ann Haydon Jones (GBR)
1967	Roy Emerson (AUS)	Françoise Durr (FRA)
1968	Ken Rosewall (AUS)	Nancy Richey (USA)
1969	Rod Laver (AUS)	Margaret Smith Court (AUS)
1970	Jan Kodes (TCH)	Margaret Smith Court (AUS)
1971	Jan Kodes (TCH)	Evonne Goolagong (AUS)
1972	Andres Gimeno (ESP)	Billie Jean King (USA)
1973	Ilie Nastase (ROM)	Margaret Smith Court (AUS)
1974	Björn Borg (SWE)	Chris Evert (USA)
1975	Björn Borg (SWE)	Chris Evert (USA)
1976	Adriano Panatta (ITA)	Sue Barker (USA)
1977	Guillermo Vilas (ARG)	Mima Jausovec (YUG)
1978	Björn Borg (SWE)	Virginia Ruzici (ROM)
1979	Björn Borg (SWE)	Chris Evert Lloyd (USA)

French Open Tennis Championships—Singles (continued)

YEAR	MEN	WOMEN
1980	Björn Borg (SWE)	Chris Evert Lloyd (USA)
1981	Björn Borg (SWE)	Hana Mandlikova (TCH)
1982	Mats Wilander (SWE)	Martina Navratilova (USA)
1983	Yannick Noah (FRA)	Chris Evert Lloyd (USA)
1984	Ivan Lendl (TCH)	Martina Navratilova (USA)
1985	Mats Wilander (SWE)	Chris Evert Lloyd (USA)
1986	Ivan Lendl (TCH)	Chris Evert Lloyd (USA)
1987	Ivan Lendl (TCH)	Steffi Graf (FRG)
1988	Mats Wilander (SWE)	Steffi Graf (FRG)
1989	Michael Chang (USA)	Arantxa Sánchez Vicario (ESP)
1990	Andres Gómez (ECU)	Monica Seles (YUG)
1991	Jim Courier (USA)	Monica Seles (YUG)
1992	Jim Courier (USA)	Monica Seles (YUG)
1993	Sergi Bruguera (ESP)	Steffi Graf (GER)
1994	Sergi Bruguera (ESP)	Arantxa Sánchez Vicario (ESP)
1995	Thomas Muster (AUT)	Steffi Graf (GER)
1996	Yevgeny Kafelnikov (RUS)	Steffi Graf (GER)
1997	Gustavo Kuerten (BRA)	Iva Majoli (CRO)
1998	Carlos Moya (ESP)	Arantxa Sánchez Vicario (ESP)
1999	Andre Agassi (USA)	Steffi Graf (GER)
2000	Gustavo Kuerten (BRA)	Mary Pierce (FRA)
2001	Gustavo Kuerten (BRA)	Jennifer Capriati (USA)
2002	Albert Costa (ESP)	Serena Williams (USA)
2003	Juan Carlos Ferrero (ESP)	Justine Henin-Hardenne (BEL)
2004	Gastón Gaudio (ARG)	Anastasiya Myskina (RUS)
2005	Rafael Nadal (ESP)	Justine Henin-Hardenne (BEL)
2006	Rafael Nadal (ESP)	Justine Henin-Hardenne (BEL)
2007	Rafael Nadal (ESP)	Justine Henin (BEL)
2008	Rafael Nadal (ESP)	Ana Ivanovic (SRB)

French Open Tennis Championships—Doubles

YEAR	MEN	WOMEN
1925	Jean Borotra, René Lacoste	Suzanne Lenglen, Didi Vlasto
1926	Vinnie Richards, Howard Kinsey	Suzanne Lenglen, Didi Vlasto
1927	Henri Cochet, Jacques Brugnon	Irene Peacock, Bobby Heine
1928	Jean Borotra, Jacques Brugnon	Phoebe Watson, Eileen Bennett
1929	Jean Borotra, René Lacoste	Lili de Alvarez, Kea Bouman
1930	Henri Cochet, Jacques Brugnon	Helen Wills Moody, Elizabeth Ryan
1931	George Lott, John Van Ryn	Eileen Whittingstall, Betty Nuthall
1932	Henri Cochet, Jacques Brugnon	Helen Wills Moody, Elizabeth Ryan
1933	Pat Hughes, Fred Perry	Simone Mathieu, Elizabeth Ryan
1934	Jean Borotra, Jacques Brugnon	Simone Mathieu, Elizabeth Ryan
1935	Jack Crawford, Adrian Quist	Margaret Scriven, Kay Stammers
1936	Jean Borotra, Marcel Bernard	Simone Mathieu, Billie Yorke
1937	Gottfried von Cramm, Henner Henkel	Simone Mathieu, Billie Yorke
1938	Bernard Destremau, Yvon Petra	Simone Mathieu, Billie Yorke
1939	Don McNeill, Charles Harris	Simone Mathieu, Jadwiga Jedrzejowska
1940–45	*not held*	
1946	Marcel Bernard, Yvon Petra	Louise Brough, Margaret Osborne
1947	Eustace Fannin, Eric Sturgess	Louise Brough, Margaret Osborne
1948	Lennart Bergelin, Jaroslav Drobny	Doris Hart, Patricia Todd
1949	Pancho Gonzáles, Frank Parker	Louise Brough, Margaret Osborne du Pont
1950	Billy Talbert, Tony Trabert	Doris Hart, Shirley Fry
1951	Ken McGregor, Frank Sedgman	Doris Hart, Shirley Fry
1952	Ken McGregor, Frank Sedgman	Doris Hart, Shirley Fry
1953	Lew Hoad, Ken Rosewall	Doris Hart, Shirley Fry
1954	Vic Seixas, Tony Trabert	Maureen Connolly, Nell Hopman
1955	Vic Seixas, Tony Trabert	Beverly Fleitz, Darlene Hard
1956	Don Candy, Robert Perry	Angela Buxton, Althea Gibson
1957	Mal Anderson, Ashley Cooper	Shirley Bloomer, Darlene Hard
1958	Ashley Cooper, Neale Fraser	Rosie Reyes, Yola Ramirez
1959	Nicola Pietrangeli, Orlando Sirola	Sandra Reynolds, Renee Schuurman
1960	Roy Emerson, Neale Fraser	Maria Bueno, Darlene Hard
1961	Roy Emerson, Rod Laver	Sandra Reynolds, Renee Schuurman
1962	Roy Emerson, Neale Fraser	Sandra Reynolds Price, Renee Schuurman
1963	Roy Emerson, Manuel Santana	Ann Haydon Jones, Renee Schuurman

French Open Tennis Championships—Doubles (continued)

YEAR	MEN	WOMEN
1964	Roy Emerson, Ken Fletcher	Margaret Smith, Lesley Turner
1965	Roy Emerson, Fred Stolle	Margaret Smith, Lesley Turner
1966	Clark Graebner, Dennis Ralston	Margaret Smith, Judy Tegart
1967	John Newcombe, Tony Roche	Françoise Durr, Gail Sheriff
1968	Ken Rosewall, Fred Stolle	Françoise Durr, Ann Haydon Jones
1969	John Newcombe, Tony Roche	Françoise Durr, Ann Haydon Jones
1970	Ilie Nastase, Ion Tiriac	Françoise Durr, Gail Chanfreau
1971	Arthur Ashe, Marty Riessen	Françoise Durr, Gail Chanfreau
1972	Bob Hewitt, Frew McMillan	Billie Jean King, Betty Stove
1973	John Newcombe, Tom Okker	Margaret Smith Court, Virginia Wade
1974	Dick Crealy, Onny Parun	Chris Evert, Olga Morozova
1975	Brian Gottfried, Raúl Ramírez	Chris Evert, Martina Navratilova
1976	Fred McNair, Sherwood Stewart	Fiorella Bonicelli, Gail Chanfreau Lovera
1977	Brian Gottfried, Raúl Ramírez	Regina Marsikova, Pam Teeguarden
1978	Hank Pfister, Gene Mayer	Mimi Jausovec, Virginia Ruzici
1979	Sandy Mayer, Gene Mayer	Wendy Turnbull, Betty Stove
1980	Victor Amaya, Hank Pfister	Kathy Jordan, Anne Smith
1981	Heinz Günthardt, Balázs Taróczy	Rosalyn Fairbank, Tanya Harford
1982	Sherwood Stewart, Ferdi Taygan	Martina Navratilova, Anne Smith
1983	Anders Järryd, Hans Simonsson	Rosalyn Fairbank, Candy Reynolds
1984	Henri Leconte, Yannick Noah	Martina Navratilova, Pam Shriver
1985	Kim Warwick, Mark Edmondson	Martina Navratilova, Pam Shriver
1986	John Fitzgerald, Tomas Smid	Martina Navratilova, Andrea Temesvari
1987	Robert Seguso, Anders Järryd	Martina Navratilova, Pam Shriver
1988	Emilio Sánchez, Andres Gómez	Martina Navratilova, Pam Shriver
1989	Jim Grabb, Patrick McEnroe	Larisa Savchenko, Natasha Zvereva
1990	Sergio Casal, Emilio Sánchez	Jana Novotna, Helena Sukova
1991	John Fitzgerald, Anders Järryd	Gigi Fernández, Jana Novotna
1992	Jacob Hlasek, Marc Rosset	Gigi Fernández, Natasha Zvereva
1993	Luke Jensen, Murphy Jensen	Gigi Fernández, Natasha Zvereva
1994	Byron Black, Jonathan Stark	Gigi Fernández, Natasha Zvereva
1995	Jacco Eltingh, Paul Haarhuis	Gigi Fernández, Natasha Zvereva
1996	Yevgeny Kafelnikov, Daniel Vacek	Lindsay Davenport, Mary Joe Fernández
1997	Yevgeny Kafelnikov, Daniel Vacek	Gigi Fernández, Natasha Zvereva
1998	Jacco Eltingh, Paul Haarhuis	Martina Hingis, Jana Novotna
1999	Mahesh Bhupathi, Leander Paes	Venus Williams, Serena Williams
2000	Todd Woodbridge, Mark Woodforde	Martina Hingis, Mary Pierce
2001	Mahesh Bhupathi, Leander Paes	Virginia Ruano Pascual, Paola Suárez
2002	Yevgeny Kafelnikov, Paul Haarhuis	Virginia Ruano Pascual, Paola Suárez
2003	Bob Bryan, Mike Bryan	Kim Clijsters, Ai Sugiyama
2004	Xavier Malisse, Olivier Rochus	Virginia Ruano Pascual, Paola Suárez
2005	Jonas Björkman, Max Mirnyi	Virginia Ruano Pascual, Paola Suárez
2006	Jonas Björkman, Max Mirnyi	Lisa Raymond, Samantha Stosur
2007	Mark Knowles, Daniel Nestor	Alicia Molik, Mara Santangelo
2008	Pablo Cuevas, Luis Horna	Anabel Medina Garrigues, Virginia Ruano Pascual

All-England (Wimbledon) Tennis Championships—Singles

YEAR	MEN	WOMEN
1877	Spencer Gore (GBR)	
1878	Frank Hadow (GBR)	
1879	John Hartley (GBR)	
1880	John Hartley (GBR)	
1881	Willie Renshaw (GBR)	
1882	Willie Renshaw (GBR)	
1883	Willie Renshaw (GBR)	
1884	Willie Renshaw (GBR)	Maud Watson (GBR)
1885	Willie Renshaw (GBR)	Maud Watson (GBR)
1886	Willie Renshaw (GBR)	Blanche Bingley (GBR)
1887	Herbert Lawford (GBR)	Lottie Dod (GBR)
1888	Ernest Renshaw (GBR)	Lottie Dod (GBR)
1889	Willie Renshaw (GBR)	Blanche Bingley Hillyard (GBR)
1890	William Hamilton (GBR)	Lena Rice (GBR)
1891	Wilfred Baddeley (GBR)	Lottie Dod (GBR)
1892	Wilfred Baddeley (GBR)	Lottie Dod (GBR)
1893	Joshua Pim (GBR)	Lottie Dod (GBR)
1894	Joshua Pim (GBR)	Blanche Bingley Hillyard (GBR)

All-England (Wimbledon) Tennis Championships—Singles (continued)

YEAR	MEN	WOMEN
1895	Wilfred Baddeley (GBR)	Charlotte Cooper (GBR)
1896	Harold Mahony (GBR)	Charlotte Cooper (GBR)
1897	Reggie Doherty (GBR)	Blanche Bingley Hillyard (GBR)
1898	Reggie Doherty (GBR)	Charlotte Cooper (GBR)
1899	Reggie Doherty (GBR)	Blanche Bingley Hillyard (GBR)
1900	Reggie Doherty (GBR)	Blanche Bingley Hillyard (GBR)
1901	Arthur Gore (GBR)	Charlotte Cooper Sterry (GBR)
1902	Laurie Doherty (GBR)	Muriel Robb (GBR)
1903	Laurie Doherty (GBR)	Dorothea Douglass (GBR)
1904	Laurie Doherty (GBR)	Dorothea Douglass (GBR)
1905	Laurie Doherty (GBR)	May Sutton (USA)
1906	Laurie Doherty (GBR)	Dorothea Douglass (GBR)
1907	Norman Brookes (AUS)	May Sutton (USA)
1908	Arthur Gore (GBR)	Charlotte Cooper Sterry (GBR)
1909	Arthur Gore (GBR)	Dora Boothby (GBR)
1910	Tony Wilding (NZL)	Dorothea Douglass Lambert Chambers (GBR)
1911	Tony Wilding (NZL)	Dorothea Douglass Lambert Chambers (GBR)
1912	Tony Wilding (NZL)	Ethel Larcombe (GBR)
1913	Tony Wilding (NZL)	Dorothea Douglass Lambert Chambers (GBR)
1914	Norman Brookes (AUS)	Dorothea Douglass Lambert Chambers (GBR)
1915–18	*not held*	
1919	Gerald Patterson (AUS)	Suzanne Lenglen (FRA)
1920	Bill Tilden (USA)	Suzanne Lenglen (FRA)
1921	Bill Tilden (USA)	Suzanne Lenglen (FRA)
1922	Gerald Patterson (AUS)	Suzanne Lenglen (FRA)
1923	Bill Johnston (USA)	Suzanne Lenglen (FRA)
1924	Jean Borotra (FRA)	Kathleen McKane (GBR)
1925	René Lacoste (FRA)	Suzanne Lenglen (FRA)
1926	Jean Borotra (FRA)	Kathleen McKane Godfree (GBR)
1927	Henri Cochet (FRA)	Helen Wills (USA)
1928	René Lacoste (FRA)	Helen Wills (USA)
1929	Henri Cochet (FRA)	Helen Wills (USA)
1930	Bill Tilden (USA)	Helen Wills Moody (USA)
1931	Sidney Wood (USA)	Cilly Aussem (GER)
1932	Ellsworth Vines (USA)	Helen Wills Moody (USA)
1933	Jack Crawford (AUS)	Helen Wills Moody (USA)
1934	Fred Perry (GBR)	Dorothy Round (GBR)
1935	Fred Perry (GBR)	Helen Wills Moody (USA)
1936	Fred Perry (GBR)	Helen Jacobs (USA)
1937	Don Budge (USA)	Dorothy Round (GBR)
1938	Don Budge (USA)	Helen Wills Moody (USA)
1939	Bobby Riggs (USA)	Alice Marble (USA)
1940–45	*not held*	
1946	Yvon Petra (FRA)	Pauline Betz (USA)
1947	Jack Kramer (USA)	Margaret Osborne (USA)
1948	Bob Falkenburg (USA)	Louise Brough (USA)
1949	Ted Schroeder (USA)	Louise Brough (USA)
1950	Budge Patty (USA)	Louise Brough (USA)
1951	Dick Savitt (USA)	Doris Hart (USA)
1952	Frank Sedgman (AUS)	Maureen Connolly (USA)
1953	Vic Seixas (USA)	Maureen Connolly (USA)
1954	Jaroslav Drobny (TCH)	Maureen Connolly (USA)
1955	Tony Trabert (USA)	Louise Brough (USA)
1956	Lew Hoad (AUS)	Shirley Fry (USA)
1957	Lew Hoad (AUS)	Althea Gibson (USA)
1958	Ashley Cooper (AUS)	Althea Gibson (USA)
1959	Alex Olmedo (PER)	Maria Bueno (BRA)
1960	Neale Fraser (AUS)	Maria Bueno (BRA)
1961	Rod Laver (AUS)	Angela Mortimer (GBR)
1962	Rod Laver (AUS)	Karen Susman (USA)
1963	Chuck McKinley (USA)	Margaret Smith (AUS)
1964	Roy Emerson (AUS)	Maria Bueno (BRA)
1965	Roy Emerson (AUS)	Margaret Smith (AUS)
1966	Manuel Santana (ESP)	Billie Jean King (USA)
1967	John Newcombe (AUS)	Billie Jean King (USA)
1968[1]	Rod Laver (AUS)	Billie Jean King (USA)
1969	Rod Laver (AUS)	Ann Jones (GBR)
1970	John Newcombe (AUS)	Margaret Smith Court (AUS)

All-England (Wimbledon) Tennis Championships—Singles (continued)

YEAR	MEN	WOMEN
1971	John Newcombe (AUS)	Evonne Goolagong (AUS)
1972	Stan Smith (USA)	Billie Jean King (USA)
1973	Jan Kodes (TCH)	Billie Jean King (USA)
1974	Jimmy Connors (USA)	Chris Evert (USA)
1975	Arthur Ashe (USA)	Billie Jean King (USA)
1976	Björn Borg (SWE)	Chris Evert (USA)
1977	Björn Borg (SWE)	Virginia Wade (GBR)
1978	Björn Borg (SWE)	Martina Navratilova (TCH)
1979	Björn Borg (SWE)	Martina Navratilova (USA)
1980	Björn Borg (SWE)	Evonne Goolagong Cawley (AUS)
1981	John McEnroe (USA)	Chris Evert Lloyd (USA)
1982	Jimmy Connors (USA)	Martina Navratilova (USA)
1983	John McEnroe (USA)	Martina Navratilova (USA)
1984	John McEnroe (USA)	Martina Navratilova (USA)
1985	Boris Becker (FRG)	Martina Navratilova (USA)
1986	Boris Becker (FRG)	Martina Navratilova (USA)
1987	Pat Cash (AUS)	Martina Navratilova (USA)
1988	Stefan Edberg (SWE)	Steffi Graf (GDR)
1989	Boris Becker (FRG)	Steffi Graf (GDR)
1990	Stefan Edberg (SWE)	Martina Navratilova (USA)
1991	Michael Stich (GER)	Steffi Graf (GER)
1992	Andre Agassi (USA)	Steffi Graf (GER)
1993	Pete Sampras (USA)	Steffi Graf (GER)
1994	Pete Sampras (USA)	Conchita Martínez (ESP)
1995	Pete Sampras (USA)	Steffi Graf (GER)
1996	Richard Krajicek (NED)	Steffi Graf (GER)
1997	Pete Sampras (USA)	Martina Hingis (SUI)
1998	Pete Sampras (USA)	Jana Novotna (CZE)
1999	Pete Sampras (USA)	Lindsay Davenport (USA)
2000	Pete Sampras (USA)	Venus Williams (USA)
2001	Goran Ivanisevic (CRO)	Venus Williams (USA)
2002	Lleyton Hewitt (AUS)	Serena Williams (USA)
2003	Roger Federer (SUI)	Serena Williams (USA)
2004	Roger Federer (SUI)	Mariya Sharapova (RUS)
2005	Roger Federer (SUI)	Venus Williams (USA)
2006	Roger Federer (SUI)	Amélie Mauresmo (FRA)
2007	Roger Federer (SUI)	Venus Williams (USA)
2008	Rafael Nadal (ESP)	Venus WIlliams (USA)

[1]*Open since 1968.*

All-England (Wimbledon) Tennis Championships—Doubles

YEAR	MEN	WOMEN
1879	L.R. Erskine, H. Lawford	
1880	William Renshaw, Ernest Renshaw	
1881	William Renshaw, Ernest Renshaw	
1882	J.T. Hartley, R.T. Richardson	
1883	C.W. Grinstead, C.E. Welldon	
1884	William Renshaw, Ernest Renshaw	
1885	William Renshaw, Ernest Renshaw	
1886	William Renshaw, Ernest Renshaw	
1887	Herbert Wilberforce, P.B. Lyon	
1888	William Renshaw, Ernest Renshaw	
1889	William Renshaw, Ernest Renshaw	
1890	Joshua Pim, F.O. Stoker	
1891	Wilfred Baddeley, Herbert Baddeley	
1892	E.W. Lewis, H.S. Barlow	
1893	Joshua Pim, F.O. Stoker	
1894	Wilfred Baddeley, Herbert Baddeley	
1895	Wilfred Baddeley, Herbert Baddeley	
1896	Wilfred Baddeley, Herbert Baddeley	
1897	Reggie Doherty, Laurie Doherty	
1898	Reggie Doherty, Laurie Doherty	
1899	Reggie Doherty, Laurie Doherty	
1900	Reggie Doherty, Laurie Doherty	
1901	Reggie Doherty, Laurie Doherty	

All-England (Wimbledon) Tennis Championships—Doubles (continued)

YEAR	MEN	WOMEN
1902	Sidney Smith, Frank Riseley	
1903	Reggie Doherty, Laurie Doherty	
1904	Reggie Doherty, Laurie Doherty	
1905	Reggie Doherty, Laurie Doherty	
1906	Sidney Smith, Frank Riseley	
1907	Norman Brookes, Anthony Wilding	
1908	Anthony Wilding, M.J.G. Ritchie	
1909	Arthur Gore, H. Roper Barrett	
1910	Anthony Wilding, M.J.G. Ritchie	
1911	Andre Gobert, Max Decugis	
1912	H. Roper Barrett, Charles Dixon	
1913	H. Roper Barrett, Charles Dixon	Winifred McNair, Dora Boothby
1914	Norman Brookes, Anthony Wilding	Elizabeth Ryan, Agatha Morton
1915–18	*not held*	
1919	R.V. Thomas, Pat O'Hara Wood	Suzanne Lenglen, Elizabeth Ryan
1920	Richard Williams, Chuck Garland	Suzanne Lenglen, Elizabeth Ryan
1921	Randolph Lycett, Max Woosnam	Suzanne Lenglen, Elizabeth Ryan
1922	James Anderson, Randolph Lycett	Suzanne Lenglen, Elizabeth Ryan
1923	Leslie Godfree, Randolph Lycett	Suzanne Lenglen, Elizabeth Ryan
1924	Frank Hunter, Vinnie Richards	Hazel Wightman, Helen Wills
1925	Jean Borotra, René Lacoste	Suzanne Lenglen, Elizabeth Ryan
1926	Henri Cochet, Jacques Brugnon	Mary Browne, Elizabeth Ryan
1927	Bill Tilden, Frank Hunter	Helen Wills, Elizabeth Ryan
1928	Henri Cochet, Jacques Brugnon	Peggy Saunders, Phoebe Watson
1929	Wilmer Allison, John Van Ryn	Peggy Saunders Michell, Phoebe Watson
1930	Wilmer Allison, John Van Ryn	Helen Wills Moody, Elizabeth Ryan
1931	George Lott, John Van Ryn	Phyllis Mudford, Dorothy Barron
1932	Jean Borotra, Jacques Brugnon	Doris Metaxa, Josane Sigart
1933	Jean Borotra, Jacques Brugnon	Simone Mathieu, Elizabeth Ryan
1934	George Lott, Lester Stoefen	Simone Mathieu, Elizabeth Ryan
1935	Adrian Quist, Jack Crawford	Freda James, Kay Stammers
1936	Pat Hughes, Raymond Tuckey	Freda James, Kay Stammers
1937	Don Budge, Gene Mako	Simone Mathieu, Billie Yorke
1938	Don Budge, Gene Mako	Sarah Palfrey Fabyan, Alice Marble
1939	Bobby Riggs, Elwood Cooke	Sarah Palfrey Fabyan, Alice Marble
1940–45	*not held*	
1946	Jack Kramer, Tom Brown	Louise Brough, Margaret Osborne
1947	Jack Kramer, Bob Falkenburg	Patricia Todd, Doris Hart
1948	John Bromwich, Frank Sedgman	Louise Brough, Margaret Osborne du Pont
1949	Pancho Gonzáles, Frank Parker	Louise Brough, Margaret Osborne du Pont
1950	Adrian Quist, John Bromwich	Louise Brough, Margaret Osborne du Pont
1951	Ken McGregor, Frank Sedgman	Doris Hart, Shirley Fry
1952	Ken McGregor, Frank Sedgman	Doris Hart, Shirley Fry
1953	Lew Hoad, Ken Rosewall	Doris Hart, Shirley Fry
1954	Rex Hartwig, Mervyn Rose	Louise Brough, Margaret Osborne du Pont
1955	Rex Hartwig, Lew Hoad	Angela Mortimer, Anne Shilcock
1956	Lew Hoad, Ken Rosewall	Angela Buxton, Althea Gibson
1957	Budge Patty, Gardnar Mulloy	Althea Gibson, Darlene Hard
1958	Sven Davidson, Ulf Schmidt	Maria Bueno, Althea Gibson
1959	Roy Emerson, Neale Fraser	Jeanne Arth, Darlene Hard
1960	Rafael Osuna, Dennis Ralston	Maria Bueno, Darlene Hard
1961	Roy Emerson, Neale Fraser	Karen Hantze, Billie Jean Moffitt
1962	Bob Hewitt, Fred Stolle	Karen Hantze Susman, Billie Jean Moffitt
1963	Rafael Osuna, Antonio Palafox	Maria Bueno, Darlene Hard
1964	Bob Hewitt, Fred Stolle	Margaret Smith, Leslie Turner
1965	John Newcombe, Tony Roche	Maria Bueno, Billie Jean Moffitt
1966	John Newcombe, Ken Fletcher	Maria Bueno, Nancy Richey
1967	Bob Hewitt, Frew McMillan	Billie Jean Moffitt King, Rosemary Casals
1968[1]	John Newcombe, Tony Roche	Billie Jean King, Rosemary Casals
1969	John Newcombe, Tony Roche	Margaret Smith Court, Judy Tegart
1970	John Newcombe, Tony Roche	Billie Jean King, Rosemary Casals
1971	Roy Emerson, Rod Laver	Billie Jean King, Rosemary Casals
1972	Bob Hewitt, Frew McMillan	Billie Jean King, Betty Stove
1973	Jimmy Connors, Ilie Nastase	Billie Jean King, Rosemary Casals
1974	John Newcombe, Tony Roche	Evonne Goolagong, Peggy Michel
1975	Vitas Gerulaitis, Sandy Mayer	Ann Kiyomura, Kazuko Sawamatsu
1976	Brian Gottfried, Raúl Ramírez	Chris Evert, Martina Navratilova
1977	Ross Case, Geoff Masters	Helen Gourlay Cawley, Joanne Russell

All-England (Wimbledon) Tennis Championships—Doubles (continued)

YEAR	MEN	WOMEN
1978	Bob Hewitt, Frew McMillan	Kerry Reid, Wendy Turnbull
1979	John McEnroe, Peter Fleming	Billie Jean King, Martina Navratilova
1980	Peter McNamara, Paul McNamee	Kathy Jordan, Anne Smith
1981	John McEnroe, Peter Fleming	Martina Navratilova, Pam Shriver
1982	Peter McNamara, Paul McNamee	Martina Navratilova, Pam Shriver
1983	John McEnroe, Peter Fleming	Martina Navratilova, Pam Shriver
1984	John McEnroe, Peter Fleming	Martina Navratilova, Pam Shriver
1985	Heinz Günthardt, Balázs Taróczy	Kathy Jordan, Elizabeth Smylie
1986	Joakim Nyström, Mats Wilander	Martina Navratilova, Pam Shriver
1987	Robert Seguso, Ken Flach	Claudia Kohde-Kilsch, Helena Sukova
1988	Robert Seguso, Ken Flach	Steffi Graf, Gabriela Sabatini
1989	John Fitzgerald, Anders Järryd	Jana Novotna, Helena Sukova
1990	Rick Leach, Jim Pugh	Jana Novotna, Helena Sukova
1991	John Fitzgerald, Anders Järryd	Larisa Savchenko, Natasha Zvereva
1992	John McEnroe, Michael Stich	Gigi Fernández, Natasha Zvereva
1993	Todd Woodbridge, Mark Woodforde	Gigi Fernández, Natasha Zvereva
1994	Todd Woodbridge, Mark Woodforde	Gigi Fernández, Natasha Zvereva
1995	Todd Woodbridge, Mark Woodforde	Arantxa Sánchez Vicario, Jana Novotna
1996	Todd Woodbridge, Mark Woodforde	Helena Sukova, Martina Hingis
1997	Todd Woodbridge, Mark Woodforde	Gigi Fernández, Natasha Zvereva
1998	Jacco Eltingh, Paul Haarhuis	Martina Hingis, Jana Novotna
1999	Mahesh Bhupathi, Leander Paes	Lindsay Davenport, Corina Morariu
2000	Todd Woodbridge, Mark Woodforde	Venus Williams, Serena Williams
2001	Donald Johnson, Jared Palmer	Lisa Raymond, Rennae Stubbs
2002	Jonas Björkman, Todd Woodbridge	Venus Williams, Serena Williams
2003	Jonas Björkman, Todd Woodbridge	Kim Clijsters, Ai Sugiyama
2004	Jonas Björkman, Todd Woodbridge	Cara Black, Rennae Stubbs
2005	Stephen Huss, Wesley Moodie	Cara Black, Liezel Huber
2006	Bob Bryan, Mike Bryan	Yan Zi, Zheng Jie
2007	Arnaud Clément, Michaël Llodra	Cara Black, Liezel Huber
2008	Daniel Nestor, Nenad Zimonjic	Venus Williams, Serena Williams

[1]*Open since 1968.*

United States Open Tennis Championships—Singles

YEAR	MEN	WOMEN
1881	Richard Sears (USA)	
1882	Richard Sears (USA)	
1883	Richard Sears (USA)	
1884	Richard Sears (USA)	
1885	Richard Sears (USA)	
1886	Richard Sears (USA)	
1887	Richard Sears (USA)	Ellen Hansell (USA)
1888	Henry Slocum, Jr. (USA)	Bertha Townsend (USA)
1889	Henry Slocum, Jr. (USA)	Bertha Townsend (USA)
1890	Oliver Campbell (USA)	Ellen Roosevelt (USA)
1891	Oliver Campbell (USA)	Mabel Cahill (USA)
1892	Oliver Campbell (USA)	Mabel Cahill (USA)
1893	Robert Wrenn (USA)	Aline Terry (USA)
1894	Robert Wrenn (USA)	Helen Helwig (USA)
1895	Fred Hovey (USA)	Juliette Atkinson (USA)
1896	Robert Wrenn (USA)	Elisabeth Moore (USA)
1897	Robert Wrenn (USA)	Juliette Atkinson (USA)
1898	Malcom Whitman (USA)	Juliette Atkinson (USA)
1899	Malcom Whitman (USA)	Marion Jones (USA)
1900	Malcom Whitman (USA)	Myrtle McAteer (USA)
1901	William Larned (USA)	Elisabeth Moore (USA)
1902	William Larned (USA)	Marion Jones (USA)
1903	Laurie Doherty (GBR)	Elisabeth Moore (USA)
1904	Holcombe Ward (USA)	May Sutton (USA)
1905	Beals Wright (USA)	Elisabeth Moore (USA)
1906	Bill Clothier (USA)	Helen Homans (USA)
1907	William Larned (USA)	Evelyn Sears (USA)
1908	William Larned (USA)	Maud Barger-Wallach (USA)
1909	William Larned (USA)	Hazel Hotchkiss (USA)
1910	William Larned (USA)	Hazel Hotchkiss (USA)

United States Open Tennis Championships—Singles (continued)

YEAR	MEN	WOMEN
1911	William Larned (USA)	Hazel Hotchkiss (USA)
1912	Maurice McLoughlin (USA)	Mary Browne (USA)
1913	Maurice McLoughlin (USA)	Mary Browne (USA)
1914	R. Norris Williams (USA)	Mary Browne (USA)
1915	Bill Johnston (USA)	Molla Bjurstedt (NOR)
1916	R. Norris Williams (USA)	Molla Bjurstedt (NOR)
1917	Lindley Murray (USA)	Molla Bjurstedt (NOR)
1918	Lindley Murray (USA)	Molla Bjurstedt (NOR)
1919	Bill Johnston (USA)	Hazel Hotchkiss Wightman (USA)
1920	Bill Tilden (USA)	Molla Bjurstedt Mallory (USA)
1921	Bill Tilden (USA)	Molla Bjurstedt Mallory (USA)
1922	Bill Tilden (USA)	Molla Bjurstedt Mallory (USA)
1923	Bill Tilden (USA)	Helen Wills (USA)
1924	Bill Tilden (USA)	Helen Wills (USA)
1925	Bill Tilden (USA)	Helen Wills (USA)
1926	René Lacoste (FRA)	Molla Bjurstedt Mallory (USA)
1927	René Lacoste (FRA)	Helen Wills (USA)
1928	Henri Cochet (FRA)	Helen Wills (USA)
1929	Bill Tilden (USA)	Helen Wills (USA)
1930	John Doeg (USA)	Betty Nuthall (GBR)
1931	Ellsworth Vines (USA)	Helen Wills Moody (USA)
1932	Ellsworth Vines (USA)	Helen Jacobs (USA)
1933	Fred Perry (GBR)	Helen Jacobs (USA)
1934	Fred Perry (GBR)	Helen Jacobs (USA)
1935	Wilmer Allison (USA)	Helen Jacobs (USA)
1936	Fred Perry (GBR)	Alice Marble (USA)
1937	Don Budge (USA)	Anita Lizana (CHI)
1938	Don Budge (USA)	Alice Marble (USA)
1939	Bobby Riggs (USA)	Alice Marble (USA)
1940	Don McNeill (USA)	Alice Marble (USA)
1941	Bobby Riggs (USA)	Sarah Palfrey Cooke (USA)
1942	Ted Schroeder (USA)	Pauline Betz (USA)
1943	Joe Hunt (USA)	Pauline Betz (USA)
1944	Frank Parker (USA)	Pauline Betz (USA)
1945	Frank Parker (USA)	Sarah Palfrey Cooke (USA)
1946	Jack Kramer (USA)	Pauline Betz (USA)
1947	Jack Kramer (USA)	Louise Brough (USA)
1948	Pancho Gonzáles (USA)	Margaret du Pont (USA)
1949	Pancho Gonzáles (USA)	Margaret du Pont (USA)
1950	Arthur Larsen (USA)	Margaret du Pont (USA)
1951	Frank Sedgman (AUS)	Maureen Connolly (USA)
1952	Frank Sedgman (AUS)	Maureen Connolly (USA)
1953	Tony Trabert (USA)	Maureen Connolly (USA)
1954	Vic Seixas (USA)	Doris Hart (USA)
1955	Tony Trabert (USA)	Doris Hart (USA)
1956	Ken Rosewall (AUS)	Shirley Fry (USA)
1957	Mal Anderson (AUS)	Althea Gibson (USA)
1958	Ashley Cooper (AUS)	Althea Gibson (USA)
1959	Neale Fraser (AUS)	Maria Bueno (BRA)
1960	Neale Fraser (AUS)	Darlene Hard (USA)
1961	Roy Emerson (AUS)	Darlene Hard (USA)
1962	Rod Laver (AUS)	Margaret Smith (AUS)
1963	Rafael Osuna (MEX)	Maria Bueno (BRA)
1964	Roy Emerson (AUS)	Maria Bueno (BRA)
1965	Manuel Santana (ESP)	Margaret Smith (AUS)
1966	Fred Stolle (AUS)	Maria Bueno (BRA)
1967	John Newcombe (AUS)	Billie Jean King (USA)
1968[1]	Arthur Ashe (USA)	Virginia Wade (GBR); Margaret Smith Court (AUS)
1969[1]	Rod Laver (AUS); Stan Smith (USA)	Margaret Smith Court (AUS)
1970	Ken Rosewall (AUS)	Margaret Smith Court (AUS)
1971	Stan Smith (USA)	Billie Jean King (USA)
1972	Ilie Nastase (ROM)	Billie Jean King (USA)
1973	John Newcombe (AUS)	Margaret Smith Court (AUS)
1974	Jimmy Connors (USA)	Billie Jean King (USA)
1975	Manuel Orantes (ESP)	Chris Evert (USA)
1976	Jimmy Connors (USA)	Chris Evert (USA)
1977	Guillermo Vilas (ARG)	Chris Evert (USA)
1978	Jimmy Connors (USA)	Chris Evert (USA)

United States Open Tennis Championships—Singles (continued)

YEAR	MEN	WOMEN
1979	John McEnroe (USA)	Tracy Austin (USA)
1980	John McEnroe (USA)	Chris Evert Lloyd (USA)
1981	John McEnroe (USA)	Tracy Austin (USA)
1982	Jimmy Connors (USA)	Chris Evert Lloyd (USA)
1983	Jimmy Connors (USA)	Martina Navratilova (USA)
1984	John McEnroe (USA)	Martina Navratilova (USA)
1985	Ivan Lendl (TCH)	Hana Mandlikova (TCH)
1986	Ivan Lendl (TCH)	Martina Navratilova (USA)
1987	Ivan Lendl (TCH)	Martina Navratilova (USA)
1988	Mats Wilander (SWE)	Steffi Graf (FRG)
1989	Boris Becker (FRG)	Steffi Graf (FRG)
1990	Pete Sampras (USA)	Gabriela Sabatini (ARG)
1991	Stefan Edberg (SWE)	Monica Seles (YUG)
1992	Stefan Edberg (SWE)	Monica Seles (YUG)
1993	Pete Sampras (USA)	Steffi Graf (GER)
1994	Andre Agassi (USA)	Arantxa Sánchez Vicario (SPA)
1995	Pete Sampras (USA)	Steffi Graf (GER)
1996	Pete Sampras (USA)	Steffi Graf (GER)
1997	Patrick Rafter (AUS)	Martina Hingis (SUI)
1998	Patrick Rafter (AUS)	Lindsay Davenport (USA)
1999	Andre Agassi (USA)	Serena Williams (USA)
2000	Marat Safin (RUS)	Venus Williams (USA)
2001	Lleyton Hewitt (AUS)	Venus Williams (USA)
2002	Pete Sampras (USA)	Serena Williams (USA)
2003	Andy Roddick (USA)	Justine Henin-Hardenne (BEL)
2004	Roger Federer (SUI)	Svetlana Kuznetsova (RUS)
2005	Roger Federer (SUI)	Kim Clijsters (BEL)
2006	Roger Federer (SUI)	Mariya Sharapova (RUS)
2007	Roger Federer (SUI)	Justine Henin (BEL)
2008	Roger Federer (SUI)	Serena Williams (USA)

[1]In 1968 and 1969 both amateur and open championships were held. Ashe won both men's competitions in 1968; Smith won the amateur championship in 1969. Court won the women's amateur competition in 1968 and both championships in 1969. Thereafter the championships were open.

United States Open Tennis Championships—Doubles

YEAR	MEN	WOMEN
1881	Clarence Clark, Fred Taylor	
1882	Richard Sears, James Dwight	
1883	Richard Sears, James Dwight	
1884	Richard Sears, James Dwight	
1885	Richard Sears, Joseph Clark	
1886	Richard Sears, James Dwight	
1887	Richard Sears, James Dwight	
1888	Oliver Campbell, Valentine Hall	
1889	Henry Slocum, Howard Taylor	Bertha Townsend, Margarette Ballard
1890	Valentine Hall, Clarence Hobart	Ellen Roosevelt, Grace Roosevelt
1891	Oliver Campbell, Robert Huntington	Mabel Cahill, Mrs. W. Fellowes Morgan
1892	Oliver Campbell, Robert Huntington	Mabel Cahill, Adeline McKinley
1893	Clarence Hobart, Fred Hovey	Aline Terry, Hattie Butler
1894	Clarence Hobart, Fred Hovey	Helen Helwig, Juliette Atkinson
1895	Malcom Chace, Robert Wrenn	Helen Helwig, Juliette Atkinson
1896	Carr Neel, Samuel Neel	Elisabeth Moore, Juliette Atkinson
1897	Leo Ware, George Sheldon	Juliette Atkinson, Kathleen Atkinson
1898	Leo Ware, George Sheldon	Juliette Atkinson, Kathleen Atkinson
1899	Holcombe Ward, Dwight Davis	Jane Craven, Myrtle McAteer
1900	Holcombe Ward, Dwight Davis	Edith Parker, Hallie Champlin
1901	Holcombe Ward, Dwight Davis	Juliette Atkinson, Myrtle McAteer
1902	Reggie Doherty, Laurie Doherty	Juliette Atkinson, Marion Jones
1903	Reggie Doherty, Laurie Doherty	Elisabeth Moore, Carrie Neely
1904	Holcombe Ward, Beals Wright	Mary Sutton, Miriam Hall
1905	Holcombe Ward, Beals Wright	Helen Homans, Carrie Neely
1906	Holcombe Ward, Beals Wright	Mrs. L.S. Coe, Mrs. D.S. Platt
1907	Fred Alexander, Harold Hackett	Marie Weimer, Carrie Neely
1908	Fred Alexander, Harold Hackett	Evelyn Sears, Margaret Curtis
1909	Fred Alexander, Harold Hackett	Hazel Hotchkiss, Edith Rotch

United States Open Tennis Championships—Doubles (continued)

YEAR	MEN	WOMEN
1910	Fred Alexander, Harold Hackett	Hazel Hotchkiss, Edith Rotch
1911	Raymond Little, Gustave Touchard	Hazel Hotchkiss, Eleanora Sears
1912	Maurice McLoughlin, Thomas Bundy	Dorothy Green, Mary Browne
1913	Maurice McLoughlin, Thomas Bundy	Mary Browne, Mrs. R.H. Williams
1914	Maurice McLoughlin, Thomas Bundy	Mary Browne, Mrs. R.H. Williams
1915	William Johnston, Clarence Griffin	Hazel Hotchkiss Wightman, Eleanora Sears
1916	William Johnston, Clarence Griffin	Molla Bjurstedt, Eleanora Sears
1917	Fred Alexander, Harold Throckmorton	Molla Bjurstedt, Eleanora Sears
1918	Bill Tilden, Vinnie Richards	Marion Zinderstein, Eleanor Goss
1919	Norman Brookes, Gerald Patterson	Marion Zinderstein, Eleanor Goss
1920	William Johnston, Clarence Griffin	Marion Zinderstein, Eleanor Goss
1921	Bill Tilden, Vinnie Richards	Mary Browne, Mrs. R.H. Williams
1922	Bill Tilden, Vinnie Richards	Marion Zinderstein Jessup, Helen Wills
1923	Bill Tilden, Brian Norton	Kathleen McKane, Phyllis Covell
1924	Howard Kinsey, Robert Kinsey	Hazel Hotchkiss Wightman, Helen Wills
1925	Richard Williams, Vinnie Richards	Mary Browne, Helen Wills
1926	Richard Williams, Vinnie Richards	Elizabeth Ryan, Eleanor Goss
1927	Bill Tilden, Frank Hunter	Kathleen McKane Godfree, Ermyntrude Harvey
1928	George Lott, John Hennessey	Hazel Hotchkiss Wightman, Helen Wills
1929	George Lott, John Doeg	Phoebe Watson, Peggy Michell
1930	George Lott, John Doeg	Betty Nuthall, Sarah Palfrey
1931	Wilmer Allison, John Van Ryn	Betty Nuthall, Eileen Whittingstall
1932	Ellsworth Vines, Keith Gledhill	Helen Jacobs, Sarah Palfrey
1933	George Lott, Lester Stoefen	Betty Nuthall, Freda James
1934	George Lott, Lester Stoefen	Helen Jacobs, Sarah Palfrey
1935	Wilmer Allison, John Van Ryn	Helen Jacobs, Sarah Palfrey Fabyan
1936	Don Budge, Gene Mako	Marjorie Van Ryn, Carolin Babcock
1937	Gottfried von Cramm, Henner Henkel	Sarah Palfrey Fabyan, Alice Marble
1938	Don Budge, Gene Mako	Sarah Palfrey Fabyan, Alice Marble
1939	Adrian Quist, John Bromwich	Sarah Palfrey Fabyan, Alice Marble
1940	Jack Kramer, Ted Schroeder	Sarah Palfrey Fabyan, Alice Marble
1941	Jack Kramer, Ted Schroeder	Sarah Palfrey Cooke, Margaret Osborne
1942	Gardnar Mulloy, Billy Talbert	Louise Brough, Margaret Osborne
1943	Jack Kramer, Frank Parker	Louise Brough, Margaret Osborne
1944	Don McNeill, Bob Falkenburg	Louise Brough, Margaret Osborne
1945	Gardnar Mulloy, Billy Talbert	Louise Brough, Margaret Osborne
1946	Gardnar Mulloy, Billy Talbert	Louise Brough, Margaret Osborne
1947	Jack Kramer, Ted Schroeder	Louise Brough, Margaret Osborne
1948	Gardnar Mulloy, Billy Talbert	Louise Brough, Margaret Osborne du Pont
1949	John Bromwich, Billy Sidwell	Louise Brough, Margaret Osborne du Pont
1950	John Bromwich, Frank Sedgman	Louise Brough, Margaret Osborne du Pont
1951	Ken McGregor, Frank Sedgman	Doris Hart, Shirley Fry
1952	Mervyn Rose, Vic Seixas	Doris Hart, Shirley Fry
1953	Rex Hartwig, Mervyn Rose	Doris Hart, Shirley Fry
1954	Vic Seixas, Tony Trabert	Doris Hart, Shirley Fry
1955	Kosei Kamo, Atushi Miyagi	Louise Brough, Margaret Osborne du Pont
1956	Lew Hoad, Ken Rosewall	Louise Brough, Margaret Osborne du Pont
1957	Ashley Cooper, Neale Fraser	Louise Brough, Margaret Osborne du Pont
1958	Alex Olmedo, Hamilton Richardson	Jeanne Arth, Darlene Hard
1959	Roy Emerson, Neale Fraser	Jeanne Arth, Darlene Hard
1960	Roy Emerson, Neale Fraser	Maria Bueno, Darlene Hard
1961	Charles McKinley, Dennis Ralston	Darlene Hard, Lesley Turner
1962	Rafael Osuna, Antonio Palafox	Maria Bueno, Darlene Hard
1963	Charles McKinley, Dennis Ralston	Robyn Ebbern, Margaret Smith
1964	Charles McKinley, Dennis Ralston	Karen Susman, Billie Jean Moffitt
1965	Roy Emerson, Fred Stolle	Carole Caldwell Graebner, Nancy Richey
1966	Roy Emerson, Fred Stolle	Maria Bueno, Nancy Richey
1967	John Newcombe, Tony Roche	Billie Jean Moffitt King, Rosemary Casals
1968[1]	Robert Lutz, Stan Smith	Maria Bueno, Margaret Smith Court
1969[1]	Ken Rosewall, Fred Stolle; Dick Crealy, Allan Stone	Françoise Durr, Darlene Hard; Margaret Smith Court, Virginia Wade
1970	Pierre Barthes, Niki Pilic	Margaret Smith Court, Judy Dalton
1971	John Newcombe, Roger Taylor	Rosemary Casals, Judy Dalton
1972	Cliff Drysdale, Roger Taylor	Françoise Durr, Betty Stove
1973	Owen Davidson, John Newcombe	Margaret Smith Court, Virginia Wade
1974	Robert Lutz, Stan Smith	Billie Jean King, Rosemary Casals
1975	Jimmy Connors, Ilie Nastase	Margaret Smith Court, Virginia Wade
1976	Tom Okker, Marty Riessen	Delina Boshoff, Ilana Kloss

United States Open Tennis Championships—Doubles (continued)

YEAR	MEN	WOMEN
1977	Bob Hewitt, Frew McMillan	Martina Navratilova, Betty Stove
1978	Robert Lutz, Stan Smith	Billie Jean King, Martina Navratilova
1979	John McEnroe, Peter Fleming	Wendy Turnbull, Betty Stove
1980	Robert Lutz, Stan Smith	Billie Jean King, Martina Navratilova
1981	John McEnroe, Peter Fleming	Kathy Jordan, Anne Smith
1982	Kevin Curren, Steve Denton	Rosemary Casals, Wendy Turnbull
1983	John McEnroe, Peter Fleming	Martina Navratilova, Pam Shriver
1984	John Fitzgerald, Tomas Smid	Martina Navratilova, Pam Shriver
1985	Robert Seguso, Ken Flach	Claudia Kohde-Kilsch, Helena Sukova
1986	Andres Gómez, Slobodan Zivojinovic	Martina Navratilova, Pam Shriver
1987	Stefan Edberg, Anders Järryd	Martina Navratilova, Pam Shriver
1988	Sergio Casal, Emilio Sánchez	Gigi Fernández, Robin White
1989	John McEnroe, Mark Woodforde	Martina Navratilova, Hana Mandlikova
1990	Pieter Aldrich, Danie Visser	Martina Navratilova, Gigi Fernández
1991	John Fitzgerald, Anders Järryd	Pam Shriver, Natasha Zvereva
1992	Jim Grabb, Richey Reneberg	Gigi Fernández, Natasha Zvereva
1993	Ken Flach, Rick Leach	Arantxa Sánchez Vicario, Helena Sukova
1994	Jacco Eltingh, Paul Haarhuis	Arantxa Sánchez Vicario, Jana Novotna
1995	Todd Woodbridge, Mark Woodforde	Gigi Fernández, Natasha Zvereva
1996	Todd Woodbridge, Mark Woodforde	Gigi Fernández, Natasha Zvereva
1997	Yevgeny Kafelnikov, Daniel Vacek	Lindsay Davenport, Jana Novotna
1998	Sandon Stolle, Cyril Suk	Martina Hingis, Jana Novotna
1999	Sébastien Lareau, Alex O'Brien	Venus Williams, Serena Williams
2000	Lleyton Hewitt, Max Mirnyi	Julie Halard-Decugis, Ai Sugiyama
2001	Wayne Black, Kevin Ullyet	Lisa Raymond, Rennae Stubbs
2002	Mahesh Bhupathi, Max Mirnyi	Virginia Ruano Pascual, Paola Suárez
2003	Jonas Björkman, Todd Woodbridge	Virginia Ruano Pascual, Paola Suárez
2004	Mark Knowles, Daniel Nestor	Virginia Ruano Pascual, Paola Suárez
2005	Bob Bryan, Mike Bryan	Lisa Raymond, Samantha Stosur
2006	Martin Damm, Leander Paes	Nathalie Dechy, Vera Zvonareva
2007	Simon Aspelin, Julian Knowle	Nathalie Dechy, Dinara Safina
2008	Bob Bryan, Mike Bryan	Cara Black, Liezel Huber

[1]In 1968 and 1969 both amateur and open championships were held. Lutz and Smith won both men's competitions in 1968; Crealy and Stone took the men's amateur championships in 1969. Bueno and Court won both women's competitions in 1968; Court and Wade took the women's amateur championships in 1969. Thereafter the championships were open.

Davis Cup

YEAR	WINNER	RUNNER-UP	RESULTS
1900	United States	British Isles	3–0
1901	*not held*		
1902	United States	British Isles	3–2
1903	British Isles[1]	United States	4–1
1904	British Isles	Belgium	5–0
1905	British Isles	United States	5–0
1906	British Isles	United States	5–0
1907	Australasia[2]	British Isles	3–2
1908	Australasia	United States	3–2
1909	Australasia	United States	5–0
1910	*not held*		
1911	Australasia	United States	5–0
1912	British Isles	Australasia	3–2
1913	United States	Great Britain	3–2
1914	Australia	United States	3–2
1915–18	*not held*		
1919	Australia	Great Britain	4–1
1920	United States	Australia	5–0
1921	United States	Japan	5–0
1922	United States	Australia	4–1
1923	United States	Australia	4–1
1924	United States	Australia	5–0
1925	United States	France	5–0
1926	United States	France	4–1
1927	France	United States	3–2
1928	France	United States	4–1
1929	France	United States	3–2
1930	France	United States	4–1
1931	France	United Kingdom	3–2
1932	France	United States	3–2
1933	United Kingdom	France	3–2
1934	United Kingdom	United States	4–1
1935	United Kingdom	United States	5–0
1936	United Kingdom	Australia	3–2
1937	United States	United Kingdom	4–1
1938	United States	Australia	3–2
1939	Australia	United States	3–2
1940–45	*not held*		
1946	United States	Australia	5–0
1947	United States	Australia	4–1
1948	United States	Australia	5–0
1949	United States	Australia	4–1
1950	Australia	United States	4–1
1951	Australia	United States	3–2
1952	Australia	United States	4–1
1953	Australia	United States	3–2
1954	United States	Australia	3–2
1955	Australia	United States	5–0
1956	Australia	United States	5–0
1957	Australia	United States	3–2
1958	United States	Australia	3–2
1959	Australia	United States	3–2

Davis Cup (continued)

YEAR	WINNER	RUNNER-UP	RESULTS	YEAR	WINNER	RUNNER-UP	RESULTS
1960	Australia	Italy	4–1	1984	Sweden	United States	4–1
1961	Australia	Italy	5–0	1985	Sweden	West Germany	3–2
1962	Australia	Mexico	5–0	1986	Australia	Sweden	3–2
1963	United States	Australia	3–2	1987	Sweden	India	5–0
1964	Australia	United States	3–2	1988	West Germany	Sweden	4–1
1965	Australia	Spain	4–1	1989	West Germany	Sweden	3–2
1966	Australia	India	4–1	1990	United States	Australia	3–2
1967	Australia	Spain	4–1	1991	France	United States	3–1
1968	United States	Australia	4–1	1992	United States	Switzerland	3–1
1969	United States	Romania	5–0	1993	Germany	Australia	4–1
1970	United States	West Germany	5–0	1994	Sweden	Russia	4–1
1971	United States	Romania	3–2	1995	United States	Russia	3–2
1972	United States	Romania	3–2	1996	France	Sweden	3–2
1973	Australia	United States	5–0	1997	Sweden	United States	5–0
1974	South Africa[3]	India		1998	Sweden	Italy	4–1
1975	Sweden	Czechoslovakia	3–2	1999	Australia	France	3–2
1976	Italy	Chile	4–1	2000	Spain	Australia	3–1
1977	Australia	Italy	3–1	2001	France	Australia	3–2
1978	United States	United Kingdom	4–1	2002	Russia	France	3–2
1979	United States	Italy	5–0	2003	Australia	Spain	3–1
1980	Czecho-slovakia	Italy	4–1	2004	Spain	United States	3–2
				2005	Croatia	Slovak Republic	3–2
1981	United States	Argentina	3–1	2006	Russia	Argentina	3–2
1982	United States	France	4–1	2007	United States	Russia	4–1
1983	Australia	Sweden	3–2				

[1]Included Ireland up to 1922. [2]Included Australia and New Zealand up to 1923. [3]Forfeit; India withdrew from the final.

Fed Cup

YEAR	WINNER	RUNNER-UP	RESULTS	YEAR	WINNER	RUNNER-UP	RESULTS
1963	United States	Australia	2–1	1986	United States	Czechoslovakia	3–0
1964	Australia	United States	2–1	1987	West Germany	United States	2–1
1965	Australia	United States	2–1	1988	Czechoslovakia	USSR	2–1
1966	United States	West Germany	3–0	1989	United States	Spain	3–0
1967	United States	United Kingdom	2–0	1990	United States	USSR	2–1
1968	Australia	The Netherlands	3–0	1991	Spain	United States	2–1
1969	United States	Australia	2–1	1992	Germany	Spain	2–1
1970	Australia	West Germany	3–0	1993	Spain	Australia	3–0
1971	Australia	United Kingdom	3–0	1994	Spain	United States	3–0
1972	South Africa	United Kingdom	2–1	1995	Spain	United States	3–2
1973	Australia	South Africa	3–0	1996	United States	Spain	5–0
1974	Australia	United States	2–1	1997	France	The Netherlands	4–1
1975	Czechoslovakia	Australia	3–0	1998	Spain	Switzerland	3–2
1976	United States	Australia	2–1	1999	United States	Russia	4–1
1977	United States	Australia	2–1	2000	United States	Spain	5–0
1978	United States	Australia	2–1	2001	Belgium	Russia	2–1
1979	United States	Australia	3–0	2002	Slovakia	Spain	3–1
1980	United States	Australia	3–0	2003	France	United States	4–1
1981	United States	United Kingdom	3–0	2004	Russia	France	3–2
1982	United States	West Germany	3–0	2005	Russia	France	3–2
1983	Czechoslovakia	West Germany	2–1	2006	Italy	Belgium	3–2
1984	Czechoslovakia	Australia	2–1	2007	Russia	Italy	4–0
1985	Czechoslovakia	United States	2–1				

Track & Field

The world governing body for track and field, or athletics, is the **International Association of Athletics Federations** (IAAF), founded in 1912. The sport includes relay running, a number of individual running, jumping, and throwing events, and one event (the decathlon for men and the heptathlon for women) that includes all three activities. The best-known competition for most track-and-field athletics is the **Olympic Games** held every four years. The **World Cup** (inaugurated 1977) is a finals-only competition

Track & Field (continued)

for national, hemispheric, and continental teams. In 1983, however, the first officially recognized non-Olympic world athletics championships were held.

A long-distance event that has special status is the **marathon race**, the standard distance for which is 42,195 m (26 mi 385 yd).

IAAF Web site: <www.iaaf.org>.

Outdoor Track & Field World Records

men

EVENT	RECORD HOLDER (NATIONALITY)	PERFORMANCE	DATE
100 m	Usain Bolt (JAM)[1]	9.69 sec	16 Aug 2008
200 m	Usain Bolt (JAM)[1]	19.30 sec	20 Aug 2008
400 m	Michael Johnson (USA)	43.18 sec	26 Aug 1999
800 m	Wilson Kipketer (DEN)	1 min 41.11 sec	24 Aug 1997
1,000 m	Noah Ngeny (KEN)	2 min 11.96 sec	5 Sep 1999
1,500 m	Hicham El Guerrouj (MAR)	3 min 26.00 sec	14 Jul 1998
1 mile	Hicham El Guerrouj (MAR)	3 min 43.13 sec	7 Jul 1999
3,000 m	Daniel Komen (KEN)	7 min 20.67 sec	1 Sep 1996
5,000 m	Kenenisa Bekele (ETH)	12 min 37.35 sec	31 May 2004
10,000 m	Kenenisa Bekele (ETH)	26 min 17.53 sec	26 Aug 2005
marathon[2]	Haile Gebrselassie (ETH)	2 hr 4 min 26 sec	30 Sep 2007
110-m hurdles	Dayron Robles (CUB)	12.87 sec	12 Jun 2008
400-m hurdles	Kevin Young (USA)	46.78 sec	6 Aug 1992
20-km walk	Sergey Morozov (RUS)[1]	1 hr 16 min 43 sec	8 Jun 2008
50-km walk	Denis Nizhegorodov (RUS)[1]	3 hr 34 min 14 sec	11 May 2008
steeplechase	Saif Saaeed Shaheen (QAT)	7 min 53.63 sec	3 Sep 2004
4 × 100-m relay	Jamaica[1]	37.10 sec	22 Aug 2008
4 × 400-m relay	United States	2 min 54.20 sec	22 Aug 1993
high jump	Javier Sotomayor (CUB)	2.45 m (8 ft ½ in)	27 Jul 1993
long jump	Mike Powell (USA)	8.95 m (29 ft 4½ in)	30 Aug 1991
triple jump	Jonathan Edwards (GBR)	18.29 m (60 ft ¼ in)	7 Aug 1995
pole vault	Sergey Bubka (UKR)	6.14 m (20 ft 1¾ in)	31 Jul 1994
shot put	Randy Barnes (USA)	23.12 m (75 ft 10¼ in)	20 May 1990
discus throw	Jürgen Schult (GDR)	74.08 m (243 ft)	6 Jun 1986
hammer throw	Yury Sedykh (URS)	86.74 m (284 ft 7 in)	30 Aug 1986
javelin throw	Jan Zelezny (CZE)	98.48 m (323 ft 1 in)	25 May 1996
decathlon	Roman Sebrle (CZE)	9,026 pt	27 May 2001

women

EVENT	RECORD HOLDER (NATIONALITY)	PERFORMANCE	DATE
100 m	Florence Griffith-Joyner (USA)	10.49 sec	16 Jul 1988
200 m	Florence Griffith-Joyner (USA)	21.34 sec	29 Sep 1988
400 m	Marita Koch (GDR)	47.60 sec	6 Oct 1985
800 m	Jarmila Kratochvilova (TCH)	1 min 53.28 sec	26 Jul 1983
1,000 m	Svetlana Masterkova (RUS)	2 min 28.98 sec	23 Aug 1996
1,500 m	Qu Yunxia (CHN)	3 min 50.46 sec	11 Sep 1993
1 mile	Svetlana Masterkova (RUS)	4 min 12.56 sec	14 Aug 1996
3,000 m	Wang Junxia (CHN)	8 min 6.11 sec	13 Sep 1993
5,000 m	Tirunesh Dibaba (ETH)[1]	14 min 11.15 sec	6 Jun 2008
10,000 m	Wang Junxia (CHN)	29 min 31.78 sec	8 Sep 1993
marathon[2]	Paula Radcliffe (GBR)	2 hr 15 min 25 sec	13 Apr 2003
100-m hurdles	Yordanka Donkova (BUL)	12.21 sec	20 Aug 1988
400-m hurdles	Yuliya Pechonkina (RUS)	52.34 sec	8 Aug 2003
20-km walk	Olimpiada Ivanova (RUS)	1 hr 25 min 41 sec	7 Aug 2005
steeplechase	Gulnara Samitova-Galkina (RUS)[1]	8 min 58.81 sec	17 Aug 2008
4 × 100-m relay	East Germany	41.37 sec	6 Oct 1985
4 × 400-m relay	USSR	3 min 15.17 sec	1 Oct 1988
high jump	Stefka Kostadinova (BUL)	2.09 m (6 ft 10¼ in)	30 Aug 1987
long jump	Galina Chistyakova (URS)	7.52 m (24 ft 8¼ in)	11 Jun 1988
triple jump	Inessa Kravets (UKR)	15.50 m (50 ft 10¼ in)	10 Aug 1995
pole vault	Yelena Isinbayeva (RUS)[1]	5.05 m (16 ft 6¾ in)	18 Aug 2008
shot put	Natalya Lisovskaya (URS)	22.63 m (74 ft 3 in)	7 Jun 1987
discus throw	Gabriele Reinsch (GDR)	76.80 m (252 ft)	9 Jul 1988
hammer throw	Tatyana Lysenko (RUS)	77.80 m (255 ft)	15 Aug 2006
javelin throw	Osleidys Menéndez (CUB)	71.70 m (235 ft 3 in)	14 Aug 2005
heptathlon	Jackie Joyner-Kersee (USA)	7,291 pt	24 Sep 1988
decathlon	Austra Skujyte (LTU)	8,358 points	15 Apr 2005

[1]*Pending ratification.* [2]*Not an officially ratified event; best performance on record.*

Indoor Track & Field World Records

men

EVENT	RECORD HOLDER (NATIONALITY)	PERFORMANCE	DATE
50 m	Donovan Bailey (CAN)	5.56 sec	9 Feb 1996
60 m	Maurice Greene (USA)	6.39 sec	3 Feb 1998
200 m	Frank Fredericks (NAM)	19.92 sec	18 Feb 1996
400 m	Kerron Clement (USA)	44.57 sec	12 Mar 2005
800 m	Wilson Kipketer (DEN)	1 min 42.67 sec	9 Mar 1997
1,000 m	Wilson Kipketer (DEN)	2 min 14.96 sec	20 Feb 2000
1,500 m	Hicham El Guerrouj (MAR)	3 min 31.18 sec	2 Feb 1997
1 mile	Hicham El Guerrouj (MAR)	3 min 48.45 sec	12 Feb 1997
3,000 m	Daniel Komen (KEN)	7 min 24.90 sec	6 Feb 1998
5,000 m	Kenenisa Bekele (ETH)	12 min 49.60 sec	20 Feb 2004
50-m hurdles	Mark McKoy (CAN)	6.25 sec	5 Mar 1986
60-m hurdles	Colin Jackson (GBR)	7.30 sec	6 Mar 1994
5,000-m walk	Mikhail Shchennikov (RUS)	18 min 07.08 sec	14 Feb 1995
4 × 200-m relay	Great Britain and Northern Ireland	1 min 22.11 sec	3 Mar 1991
4 × 400-m relay	United States	3 min 02.83 sec	7 Mar 1999
4 × 800-m relay	United States	7 min 13.94 sec	6 Feb 2000
High jump	Javier Sotomayor (CUB)	2.43 m (7 ft 11½ in)	4 Mar 1989
Long jump	Carl Lewis (USA)	8.79 m (28 ft 10 in)	27 Jan 1984
Triple jump	Aliecer Urrutia (CUB); Christian Olsson (SWE)	17.83 m (58 ft 6 in)	1 Mar 1997; 7 Mar 2004
Pole vault	Sergey Bubka (UKR)	6.15 m (20 ft 2¼ in)	21 Feb 1993
Shot put	Randy Barnes (USA)	22.66 m (74 ft 4¼ in)	20 Jan 1989
Heptathlon	Dan O'Brien (USA)	6,476 pt	14 Mar 1993

women

EVENT	RECORD HOLDER (NATIONALITY)	PERFORMANCE	DATE
50 m	Irina Privalova (RUS)	5.96 sec	9 Feb 1995
60 m	Irina Privalova (RUS)	6.92 sec	11 Feb 1993
200 m	Merlene Ottey (JAM)	21.87 sec	13 Feb 1993
400 m	Jarmila Kratochvilova (TCH)	49.59 sec	7 Mar 1982
800 m	Jolanda Ceplak (SLO)	1 min 55.82 sec	3 Mar 2002
1,000 m	Maria Mutola (MOZ)	2 min 30.94 sec	25 Feb 1999
1,500 m	Yelena Soboleva (RUS)	3 min 57.71 sec	9 Mar 2008
1 mile	Doina Melinte (ROM)	4 min 17.14 sec	9 Feb 1990
3,000 m	Meseret Defar (ETH)	8 min 23.72 sec	3 Feb 2007
5,000 m	Tirunesh Dibaba (ETH)	14 min 27.42 sec	27 Jan 2007
50-m hurdles	Cornelia Oschkenat (GDR)	6.58 sec	20 Feb 1988
60-m hurdles	Susanna Kallur (SWE)	7.68 sec	10 Feb 2008
3,000-m walk	Claudia Stef (ROM)	11 min 40.33 sec	30 Jan 1999
4 × 200-m relay	Russia	1 min 32.41 sec	29 Jan 2005
4 × 400-m relay	Russia	3 min 23.37 sec	28 Jan 2006
4 × 800-m relay	Russia	8 min 18.54 sec	11 Feb 2007
High jump	Kajsa Bergqvist (SWE)	2.08 m (6 ft 10 in)	4 Feb 2006
Long jump	Heike Drechsler (GDR)	7.37 m (24 ft 2¼ in)	13 Feb 1988
Triple jump	Tatyana Lebedeva (RUS)	15.36 m (50 ft 4¾ in)	6 Mar 2004
Pole vault	Yelena Isinbayeva (RUS)	4.95 m (16 ft 2¾ in)	16 Feb 2008
Shot put	Helena Fibingerova (TCH)	22.50 m (73 ft 9¾ in)	19 Feb 1977
Pentathlon	Irina Belova (UNT)	4,991 pt	15 Feb 1992

World Track & Field Championships—Men

YEAR	WINNER
100 M	
1983	Carl Lewis (USA)
1987	Carl Lewis (USA)
1991	Carl Lewis (USA)
1993	Linford Christie (GBR)
1995	Donovan Bailey (CAN)
1997	Maurice Greene (USA)
1999	Maurice Greene (USA)
2001	Maurice Greene (USA)
2003	Kim Collins (SKN)
2005	Justin Gatlin (USA)
2007	Tyson Gay (USA)

YEAR	WINNER
200 M	
1983	Calvin Smith (USA)
1987	Calvin Smith (USA)
1991	Michael Johnson (USA)
1993	Frank Fredericks (NAM)
1995	Michael Johnson (USA)
1997	Ato Boldon (TRI)
1999	Maurice Greene (USA)
2001	Konstadinos Kederis (GRE)
2003	John Capel (USA)
2005	Justin Gatlin (USA)
2007	Tyson Gay (USA)

YEAR	WINNER
400 M	
1983	Bert Cameron (JAM)
1987	Thomas Schoenlebe (GDR)
1991	Antonio Pettigrew (USA)
1993	Michael Johnson (USA)
1995	Michael Johnson (USA)
1997	Michael Johnson (USA)
1999	Michael Johnson (USA)
2001	Avard Moncur (BAH)
2003	Jerome Young (USA)
2005	Jeremy Wariner (USA)
2007	Jeremy Wariner (USA)

World Track & Field Championships—Men (continued)

YEAR	WINNER
800 M	
1983	Willi Wülbeck (FRG)
1987	Billy Konchellah (KEN)
1991	Billy Konchellah (KEN)
1993	Paul Ruto (KEN)
1995	Wilson Kipketer (DEN)
1997	Wilson Kipketer (DEN)
1999	Wilson Kipketer (DEN)
2001	André Bucher (SUI)
2003	Djabir Saïd-Guerni (ALG)
2005	Rashid Ramzi (BRN)
2007	Alfred Kirwa Yego (KEN)
1,500 M	
1983	Steve Cram (GBR)
1987	Abdi Bile (SOM)
1991	Noureddine Morceli (ALG)
1993	Noureddine Morceli (ALG)
1995	Noureddine Morceli (ALG)
1997	Hicham El Guerrouj (MAR)
1999	Hicham El Guerrouj (MAR)
2001	Hicham El Guerrouj (MAR)
2003	Hicham El Guerrouj (MAR)
2005	Rashid Ramzi (BRN)
2007	Bernard Lagat (USA)
5,000 M	
1983	Eamonn Coghlan (IRL)
1987	Said Aouita (MAR)
1991	Yobes Ondieki (KEN)
1993	Ismael Kirui (KEN)
1995	Ismael Kirui (KEN)
1997	Daniel Komen (KEN)
1999	Salah Hissou (MAR)
2001	Richard Limo (KEN)
2003	Eliud Kipchoge (KEN)
2005	Benjamin Limo (KEN)
2007	Bernard Lagat (USA)
10,000 M	
1983	Alberto Cova (ITA)
1987	Paul Kipkoech (KEN)
1991	Moses Tanui (KEN)
1993	Haile Gebrselassie (ETH)
1995	Haile Gebrselassie (ETH)
1997	Haile Gebrselassie (ETH)
1999	Haile Gebrselassie (ETH)
2001	Charles Kamathi (KEN)
2003	Kenenisa Bekele (ETH)
2005	Kenenisa Bekele (ETH)
2007	Kenenisa Bekele (ETH)
STEEPLECHASE	
1983	Patriz Ilg (FRG)
1987	Francesco Panetta (ITA)
1991	Moses Kiptanui (KEN)
1993	Moses Kiptanui (KEN)
1995	Moses Kiptanui (KEN)
1997	Wilson Boit Kipketer (KEN)
1999	Christopher Koskei (KEN)
2001	Reuben Kosgei (KEN)
2003	Saif Saaeed Shaheen (QAT)
2005	Saif Saaeed Shaheen (QAT)
2007	Brimin Kiprop Kipruto (KEN)
110-M HURDLES	
1983	Greg Foster (USA)
1987	Greg Foster (USA)

YEAR	WINNER
110-M HURDLES (CONTINUED)	
1991	Greg Foster (USA)
1993	Colin Jackson (GBR)
1995	Allen Johnson (USA)
1997	Allen Johnson (USA)
1999	Colin Jackson (GBR)
2001	Allen Johnson (USA)
2003	Allen Johnson (USA)
2005	Ladji Doucouré (FRA)
2007	Liu Xiang (CHN)
400-M HURDLES	
1983	Edwin Moses (USA)
1987	Edwin Moses (USA)
1991	Samuel Matete (ZAM)
1993	Kevin Young (USA)
1995	Derrick Adkins (USA)
1997	Stéphane Diagana (FRA)
1999	Fabrizio Mori (ITA)
2001	Felix Sánchez (DOM)
2003	Felix Sánchez (DOM)
2005	Bershawn Jackson (USA)
2007	Kerron Clement (USA)
MARATHON	
1983	Robert de Castella (AUS)
1987	Douglas Wakiihuri (KEN)
1991	Hiromi Taniguchi (JPN)
1993	Mark Plaatjes (USA)
1995	Martín Fiz (ESP)
1997	Abel Antón (ESP)
1999	Abel Antón (ESP)
2001	Gezahegne Abera (ETH)
2003	Jaouad Gharib (MAR)
2005	Jaouad Gharib (MAR)
2007	Luke Kibet (KEN)
20-KM WALK	
1983	Ernesto Canto (MEX)
1987	Maurizio Damilano (ITA)
1991	Maurizio Damilano (ITA)
1993	Valentí Massana (ESP)
1995	Michele Didoni (ITA)
1997	Daniel García (MEX)
1999	Ilya Markov (RUS)
2001	Roman Rasskazov (RUS)
2003	Jefferson Pérez (ECU)
2005	Jefferson Pérez (ECU)
2007	Jefferson Pérez (ECU)
50-KM WALK	
1983	Ronald Weigel (GDR)
1987	Hartwig Gauder (GDR)
1991	Aleksandr Potashov (URS)
1993	Jesús Angel García (ESP)
1995	Valentin Kononen (FIN)
1997	Robert Korzeniowski (POL)
1999	Ivano Brugnetti (ITA)
2001	Robert Korzeniowski (POL)
2003	Robert Korzeniowski (POL)
2005	Sergey Kirdyapkin (RUS)
2007	Nathan Deakes (AUS)
4 × 100-M RELAY	
1983	United States
1987	United States
1991	United States
1993	United States

YEAR	WINNER
4 × 100-M RELAY (CONTINUED)	
1995	Canada
1997	Canada
1999	United States
2001	United States
2003	United States
2005	France
2007	United States
4 × 400-M RELAY	
1983	USSR
1987	United States
1991	United Kingdom
1993	United States
1995	United States
1997	United States
1999	United States
2001	United States
2003	France
2005	United States
2007	United States
HIGH JUMP	
1983	Gennady Avdeyenko (URS)
1987	Patrik Sjöberg (SWE)
1991	Charles Austin (USA)
1993	Javier Sotomayor (CUB)
1995	Troy Kemp (BAH)
1997	Javier Sotomayor (CUB)
1999	Vyacheslav Voronin (RUS)
2001	Martin Buss (GER)
2003	Jacques Freitag (RSA)
2005	Yuri Krymarenko (UKR)
2007	Donald Thomas (BAH)
POLE VAULT	
1983	Sergey Bubka (URS)
1987	Sergey Bubka (URS)
1991	Sergey Bubka (URS)
1993	Sergey Bubka (UKR)
1995	Sergey Bubka (UKR)
1997	Sergey Bubka (UKR)
1999	Maksim Tarasov (RUS)
2001	Dmitri Markov (AUS)
2003	Giuseppe Gibilisco (ITA)
2005	Rens Blom (NED)
2007	Brad Walker (USA)
LONG JUMP	
1983	Carl Lewis (USA)
1987	Carl Lewis (USA)
1991	Mike Powell (USA)
1993	Mike Powell (USA)
1995	Iván Pedroso (CUB)
1997	Iván Pedroso (CUB)
1999	Iván Pedroso (CUB)
2001	Iván Pedroso (CUB)
2003	Dwight Phillips (USA)
2005	Dwight Phillips (USA)
2007	Irving Saladino (PAN)
TRIPLE JUMP	
1983	Zdzislaw Hoffman (POL)
1987	Khristo Markov (BUL)
1991	Kenny Harrison (USA)
1993	Mike Conley (USA)
1995	Jonathan Edwards (GBR)
1997	Yoelbi Quesada (CUB)

World Track & Field Championships—Men (continued)

YEAR	WINNER
TRIPLE JUMP (CONTINUED)	
1999	Charles Michael Friedek (GER)
2001	Jonathan Edwards (GBR)
2003	Christian Olsson (SWE)
2005	Walter Davis (USA)
2007	Nelson Évora (POR)
SHOT PUT	
1983	Edward Sarul (POL)
1987	Werner Günthör (SUI)
1991	Werner Günthör (SUI)
1993	Werner Günthör (SUI)
1995	John Godina (USA)
1997	John Godina (USA)
1999	C.J. Hunter (USA)
2001	John Godina (USA)
2003	Andrey Mikhnevich (BLR)
2005	Adam Nelson (USA)
2007	Reese Hoffa (USA)
DISCUS THROW	
1983	Imrich Bugar (TCH)
1987	Jürgen Schult (GDR)
1991	Lars Riedel (GER)
1993	Lars Riedel (GER)

YEAR	WINNER
DISCUS THROW (CONTINUED)	
1995	Lars Riedel (GER)
1997	Lars Riedel (GER)
1999	Anthony Washington (USA)
2001	Lars Riedel (GER)
2003	Virgilijus Alekna (LTU)
2005	Virgilijus Alekna (LTU)
2007	Gerd Kanter (EST)
HAMMER THROW	
1983	Sergey Litvinov (URS)
1987	Sergey Litvinov (URS)
1991	Yury Sedykh (URS)
1993	Andrey Abduvaliyev (TJK)
1995	Andrey Abduvaliyev (TJK)
1997	Heinz Weis (GER)
1999	Karsten Kobs (GER)
2001	Szymon Ziolkowski (POL)
2003	Ivan Tikhon (BLR)
2005	Ivan Tikhon (BLR)
2007	Ivan Tikhon (BLR)
JAVELIN THROW	
1983	Detlef Michel (GDR)
1987	Seppo Räty (FIN)
1991	Kimmo Kinnunen (FIN)

YEAR	WINNER
JAVELIN THROW (CONTINUED)	
1993	Jan Zelezny (CZE)
1995	Jan Zelezny (CZE)
1997	Marius Corbett (RSA)
1999	Aki Parviainen (FIN)
2001	Jan Zelezny (CZE)
2003	Sergey Makarov (RUS)
2005	Andrus Varnik (EST)
2007	Tero Pitkämäki (FIN)
DECATHLON	
1983	Daley Thompson (GBR)
1987	Torsten Voss (GDR)
1991	Dan O'Brien (USA)
1993	Dan O'Brien (USA)
1995	Dan O'Brien (USA)
1997	Tomas Dvorak (CZE)
1999	Tomas Dvorak (CZE)
2001	Tomas Dvorak (CZE)
2003	Tom Pappas (USA)
2005	Bryan Clay (USA)
2007	Roman Sebrle (CZE)

World Track & Field Championships—Women

YEAR	WINNER
100 M	
1983	Marlies Göhr (GDR)
1987	Silke Gladisch (GDR)
1991	Katrin Krabbe (GER)
1993	Gail Devers (USA)
1995	Gwen Torrence (USA)
1997	Marion Jones (USA)
1999	Marion Jones (USA)
2001	Zhanna Pintusevich (UKR)
2003	Torri Edwards (USA)
2005	Lauryn Williams (USA)
2007	Veronica Campbell (JAM)
200 M	
1983	Marita Koch (GDR)
1987	Silke Gladisch (GDR)
1991	Katrin Krabbe (GER)
1993	Merlene Ottey (JAM)
1995	Merlene Ottey (JAM)
1997	Zhanna Pintusevich (UKR)
1999	Inger Miller (USA)
2001	Marion Jones (USA)
2003	Anastasiya Kapachinskaya (RUS)
2005	Allyson Felix (USA)
2007	Allyson Felix (USA)
400 M	
1983	Jarmila Kratochvilova (TCH)
1987	Olga Bryzgina (URS)
1991	Marie-José Pérec (FRA)
1993	Jearl Miles (USA)
1995	Marie-José Pérec (FRA)
1997	Cathy Freeman (AUS)
1999	Cathy Freeman (AUS)
2001	Amy Mbacke Thiam (SEN)
2003	Ana Guevara (MEX)

YEAR	WINNER
400 M (CONTINUED)	
2005	Tonique Williams-Darling (BAH)
2007	Christine Ohuruogu (GBR)
800 M	
1983	Jarmila Kratochvilova (TCH)
1987	Sigrun Wodars (GDR)
1991	Liliya Nurutdinova (URS)
1993	Maria Mutola (MOZ)
1995	Ana Quirot (CUB)
1997	Ana Quirot (CUB)
1999	Ludmila Formanova (CZE)
2001	Maria Mutola (MOZ)
2003	Maria Mutola (MOZ)
2005	Zulia Calatayud (CUB)
2007	Janeth Jepkosgei (KEN)
1,500 M	
1983	Mary Decker (USA)
1987	Tatyana Samolenko (URS)
1991	Hassiba Boulmerka (ALG)
1993	Liu Dong (CHN)
1995	Hassiba Boulmerka (ALG)
1997	Carla Sacramento (POR)
1999	Svetlana Masterkova (RUS)
2001	Gabriela Szabo (ROM)
2003	Tatyana Tomashova (RUS)
2005	Tatyana Tomashova (RUS)
2007	Maryam Yusuf Jamal (BRN)
3,000 M[1]	
1983	Mary Decker (USA)
1987	Tatyana Samolenko (URS)
1991	Tatyana Dorovskikh (URS)
1993	Qu Yunxia (CHN)
1995	Sonia O'Sullivan (IRL)

YEAR	WINNER
3,000 M[1] (CONTINUED)	
1997	Gabriela Szabo (ROM)
1999	Gabriela Szabo (ROM)
2001	Olga Yegorova (RUS)
2003	Tirunesh Dibaba (ETH)
2005	Tirunesh Dibaba (ETH)
2007	Meseret Defar (ETH)
10,000 M[2]	
1987	Ingrid Kristiansen (NOR)
1991	Liz McColgan (GBR)
1993	Wang Junxia (CHN)
1995	Fernanda Ribeiro (POR)
1997	Sally Barsosio (KEN)
1999	Gete Wami (ETH)
2001	Derartu Tulu (ETH)
2003	Berhane Adere (ETH)
2005	Tirunesh Dibaba (ETH)
2007	Tirunesh Dibaba (ETH)
STEEPLECHASE	
2005	Dorcus Inzikuru (UGA)
2007	Yekaterina Volkova (RUS)
100-M HURDLES	
1983	Bettine Jahn (GDR)
1987	Ginka Zagorcheva (BUL)
1991	Ludmila Narozhilenko (URS)
1993	Gail Devers (USA)
1995	Gail Devers (USA)
1997	Ludmila Engquist (SWE)
1999	Gail Devers (USA)
2001	Anjanette Kirkland (USA)
2003	Perdita Felicien (CAN)
2005	Michelle Perry (USA)
2007	Michelle Perry (USA)

World Track & Field Championships—Women (continued)

YEAR	WINNER
400-M HURDLES	
1983	Yekaterina Fesenko (URS)
1987	Sabine Busch (GDR)
1991	Tatyana Ledovskaya (URS)
1993	Sally Gunnell (GBR)
1995	Kim Batten (USA)
1997	Nezha Bidouane (MAR)
1999	Daimí Pernía (CUB)
2001	Nezha Bidouane (MAR)
2003	Jana Pittman (AUS)
2005	Yuliya Pechonkina (RUS)
2007	Jana Rawlinson (AUS)
MARATHON	
1983	Grete Waitz (NOR)
1987	Rosa Mota (POR)
1991	Wanda Panfil (POL)
1993	Asari Junko (JPN)
1995	Maria Machado (POR)
1997	Hiromi Suzuki (JPN)
1999	Jong Song Ok (PRK)
2001	Lidia Simon (ROM)
2003	Catherine Ndereba (KEN)
2005	Paula Radcliffe (GBR)
2007	Catherine Ndereba (KEN)
10-KM WALK[2]	
1987	Irina Strakhova (URS)
1991	Alina Ivanova (URS)
1993	Sari Essayeh (FIN)
1995	Irina Stankina (RUS)
1997	Annarita Sidoti (ITA)
20-KM RACE WALK[3]	
1999	Liu Hongyu (CHN)
2001	Olimpiada Ivanova (RUS)
2003	Yelena Nikolayeva (RUS)
2005	Olimpiada Ivanova (RUS)
2007	Olga Kaniskina (RUS)
4 × 100-M RELAY	
1983	East Germany
1987	United States
1991	Jamaica
1993	Russia
1995	United States
1997	United States
1999	Bahamas
2001	Germany
2003	France
2005	United States
2007	United States
4 × 400-M RELAY	
1983	East Germany
1987	East Germany
1991	USSR

YEAR	WINNER
4 × 400-M RELAY (CONTINUED)	
1993	United States
1995	United States
1997	Germany
1999	Russia
2001	Jamaica
2003	United States
2005	Russia
2007	United States
HIGH JUMP	
1983	Tamara Bykova (URS)
1987	Stefka Kostadinova (BUL)
1991	Heike Henkel (GER)
1993	Ioamnet Quintero (CUB)
1995	Stefka Kostadinova (BUL)
1997	Hanne Haugland (NOR)
1999	Inga Babakova (UKR)
2001	Hestrie Cloete (RSA)
2003	Hestrie Cloete (RSA)
2005	Kajsa Bergqvist (SWE)
2007	Blanka Vlasic (CRO)
POLE VAULT[3]	
1999	Stacy Dragila (USA)
2001	Stacy Dragila (USA)
2003	Svetlana Feofanova (RUS)
2005	Yelena Isinbayeva (RUS)
2007	Yelena Isinbayeva (RUS)
LONG JUMP	
1983	Heike Daute (GDR)
1987	Jackie Joyner-Kersee (USA)
1991	Jackie Joyner-Kersee (USA)
1993	Heike Drechsler (GER)
1995	Fiona May (ITA)
1997	Ludmila Galkina (RUS)
1999	Niurka Montalvo (ESP)
2001	Fiona May (ITA)
2003	Eunice Barber (FRA)
2005	Tianna Madison (USA)
2007	Tatyana Lebedeva (RUS)
TRIPLE JUMP[4]	
1993	Anna Biryukova (RUS)
1995	Inessa Kravets (UKR)
1997	Sarka Kasparkova (CZE)
1999	Paraskevi Tsiamita (GRE)
2001	Tatyana Lebedeva (RUS)
2003	Tatyana Lebedeva (RUS)
2005	Trecia Smith (JAM)
2007	Yargelis Savigne (CUB)
SHOT PUT	
1983	Helena Fibingerova (TCH)
1987	Natalya Lisovskaya (URS)
1991	Huang Zhihong (CHN)

YEAR	WINNER
SHOT PUT (CONTINUED)	
1993	Huang Zhihong (CHN)
1995	Astrid Kumbernuss (GER)
1997	Astrid Kumbernuss (GER)
1999	Astrid Kumbernuss (GER)
2001	Yanina Korolchik (BLR)
2003	Svetlana Krivelyova (RUS)
2005	Nadezhda Ostapchuk (BLR)
2007	Valerie Vili (NZL)
DISCUS THROW	
1983	Martina Opitz (GDR)
1987	Martina Hellmann (GDR)
1991	Tsvetanka Khristova (BUL)
1993	Olga Burova (RUS)
1995	Ellina Zvereva (BLR)
1997	Beatrice Faumuina (NZL)
1999	Franka Dietzsch (GER)
2001	Ellina Zvereva (BLR)
2003	Irina Yachenko (BLR)
2005	Franka Dietzsch (GER)
2007	Franka Dietzsch (GER)
HAMMER THROW[3]	
1999	Mihaela Melinte (ROM)
2001	Yipsi Moreno (CUB)
2003	Yipsi Moreno (CUB)
2005	Olga Kuzenkova (RUS)
2007	Betty Heidler (GER)
JAVELIN THROW	
1983	Tiina Lillak (FIN)
1987	Fatima Whitbread (GBR)
1991	Xu Demei (CHN)
1993	Trine Hattestad (NOR)
1995	Natalya Shikolenko (BLR)
1997	Trine Hattestad (NOR)
1999	Mirela Tzelili (GRE)
2001	Osleidys Menéndez (CUB)
2003	Mirela Manjani (GRE)
2005	Osleidys Menéndez (CUB)
2007	Barbora Spotáková (CZE)
HEPTATHLON	
1983	Ramona Neubert (GDR)
1987	Jackie Joyner-Kersee (USA)
1991	Sabine Braun (GER)
1993	Jackie Joyner-Kersee (USA)
1995	Ghada Shouaa (SYR)
1997	Sabine Braun (GER)
1999	Eunice Barber (FRA)
2001	Yelena Prokhorova (RUS)
2003	Carolina Klüft (SWE)
2005	Carolina Klüft (SWE)
2007	Carolina Klüft (SWE)

[1]*Became 5,000 m in 1995.* [2]*Event added in 1987.* [3]*Event added in 1999.* [4]*Event added in 1993.*

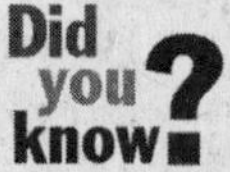

In Japan, sumo wrestling was under Imperial patronage between 710 and 1185 and was a popular spectator sport, but during the shogunate, public matches were banned. Professional sumo wrestling in Japan dates from the revival of public matches after 1600. Exceptionally agile men weighing 300 pounds or more are common in this sport. Lengthy rituals and elaborate posturings accompany the bouts, which are, by contrast, quite brief, often lasting only a few seconds.

IAAF World Cup—Men

YEAR	WINNER
100 M	
1977	Steve Williams (USA)
1979	James Sanford (USA)
1981	Allan Wells (GBR)
1985	Ben Johnson (CAN)
1989	Linford Christie (GBR)
1992	Linford Christie (GBR)
1994	Linford Christie (GBR)
1998	Obadele Thompson (BAR)
2002	Uchenna Emedolu (NGR)
2006	Tyson Gay (USA)
200 M	
1977	Clancy Edwards (USA)
1979	Silvio Leonard (CUB)
1981	Melvin Lattany (USA)
1985	Robson Caetano da Silva (BRA)
1989	Robson Caetano da Silva (BRA)
1992	Robson Caetano da Silva (BRA)
1994	John Regis (GBR)
1998	Frank Fredericks (NAM)
2002	Francis Obikwelu (POR)
2006	Wallace Spearmon (USA)
400 M	
1977	Alberto Juantorena (CUB)
1979	Kashief Hassan (SUD)
1981	Cliff Wiley (USA)
1985	Mike Franks (USA)
1989	Roberto Hernández (CUB)
1992	Sunday Bada (NGR)
1994	Antonio Pettigrew (USA)
1998	Iwan Thomas (GBR)
2002	Michael Blackwood (JAM)
2006	LaShawn Merritt (USA)
800 M	
1977	Alberto Juantorena (CUB)
1979	James Maina (KEN)
1981	Sebastian Coe (GBR)
1985	Sammy Koskei (KEN)
1989	Tom McKean (GBR)
1992	David Sharpe (GBR)
1994	Mark Everett (USA)
1998	Nils Schumann (GER)
2002	Antonio Manuel Reina (ESP)
2006	Youssef Saad Kamel (BRN)
1,500 M	
1977	Steve Ovett (GBR)
1979	Thomas Wessinghage (FRG)
1981	Steve Ovett (GBR)
1985	Omer Khalifa (SUD)
1989	Abdi Bile (SOM)
1992	Mohammed Suleiman (QAT)
1994	Noureddine Morceli (ALG)
1998	Laban Rotich (KEN)
2002	Bernard Lagat (KEN)
2006	Alex Kipchirchir (KEN)
3,000 M	
1998	Dieter Baumann (GER)
2002	Craig Mottram (AUS)
2006	Craig Mottram (AUS)
5,000 M	
1977	Miruts Yifter (ETH)
1979	Miruts Yifter (ETH)
1981	Eamonn Coghlan (IRL)
1985	Doug Padilla (USA)
1989	Said Aouita (MAR)
1992	Fita Bayesa (ETH)
1994	Brahim Lahlafi (MAR)
1998	Daniel Komen (KEN)
2002	Alberto García (ESP)
2006	Saif Saaeed Shaheen (QAT)
10,000 M	
1977	Miruts Yifter (ETH)
1979	Miruts Yifter (ETH)
1981	Werner Schildhauer (GDR)
1985	Wodajo Bulti (ETH)
1989	Salvatore Antibo (ITA)
1992	Addis Abebe (ETH)
1994	Khalid Skah (MAR)
STEEPLECHASE	
1977	Michael Karst (FRG)
1979	Henry Rono (KEN)
1981	Boguslaw Maminski (POL)
1985	Julius Kariuki (KEN)
1989	Julius Kariuki (KEN)
1992	Philip Barkutwo (KEN)
1994	Moses Kiptanui (KEN)
1998	Damian Kallabis (GER)
2002	Wilson Boit Kipketer (KEN)
2006	Saif Saaeed Shaheen (QAT)
110-M HURDLES	
1977	Thomas Munkelt (GDR)
1979	Reynaldo Nehemiah (USA)
1981	Greg Foster (USA)
1985	Tony Campbell (USA)
1989	Roger Kingdom (USA)
1992	Colin Jackson (GBR)
1994	Tony Jarrett (GBR)
1998	Falk Balzer (GER)
2002	Anier García (CUB)
2006	Allen Johnson (USA)
400-M HURDLES	
1977	Edwin Moses (USA)
1979	Edwin Moses (USA)
1981	Edwin Moses (USA)
1985	Andre Phillips (USA)
1989	David Patrick (USA)
1992	Samuel Matete (ZAM)
1994	Samuel Matete (ZAM)
1998	Samuel Matete (ZAM)
2002	James Carter (USA)
2006	Kerron Clement (USA)
4 × 100-M RELAYS	
1977	United States
1979	Americas
1981	Europe
1985	United States
1989	United States
1992	United States
1994	Great Britain
1998	Great Britain
4 × 100-M RELAYS (CONTINUED)	
2002	United States
2006	United States
4 × 400-M RELAYS	
1977	West Germany
1979	United States
1981	United States
1985	United States
1989	Americas
1992	Africa
1994	Great Britain
1998	United States
2002	Americas
2006	United States
TRIPLE JUMP	
1977	João de Oliveira (BRA)
1979	João de Oliveira (BRA)
1981	João de Oliveira (BRA)
1985	Willie Banks (USA)
1989	Mike Conley (USA)
1992	Jonathan Edwards (GBR)
1994	Yoelbi Quesada (CUB)
1998	Charles Friedek (GER)
2002	Jonathan Edwards (GBR)
2006	Walter Davis (USA)
HIGH JUMP	
1977	Rolf Beilschmidt (GDR)
1979	Franklin Jacobs (USA)
1981	Tyke Peacock (USA)
1985	Patrik Sjöberg (SWE)
1989	Patrik Sjöberg (SWE)
1992	Yury Sergeyenko (UNT[1])
1994	Javier Sotomayor (CUB)
1998	Charles Austin (USA)
2002	Yaroslav Rybakov (RUS)
2006	Tomas Janku (CZE)
POLE VAULT	
1977	Mike Tully (USA)
1979	Mike Tully (USA)
1981	Konstantin Volkov (URS)
1985	Sergey Bubka (URS)
1989	Philippe Collet (FRA)
1992	Igor Potapovich (UNT[1])
1994	Okkert Brits (RSA)
1998	Maksim Tarasov (RUS)
2002	Okkert Brits (RSA)
2006	Steven Hooker (AUS)
LONG JUMP	
1977	Arnie Robinson (USA)
1979	Larry Myricks (USA)
1981	Carl Lewis (USA)
1985	Mike Conley (USA)
1989	Larry Myricks (USA)
1992	Iván Pedroso (CUB)
1994	Fred Salle (GBR)
1998	Iván Pedroso (CUB)
2002	Savanté Stringfellow (USA)
2006	Irving Saladino (PAN)
SHOT PUT	
1977	Udo Beyer (GDR)
1979	Udo Beyer (GDR)

IAAF World Cup—Men (continued)

YEAR	WINNER
SHOT PUT (CONTINUED)	
1981	Udo Beyer (GDR)
1985	Ulf Timmermann (GDR)
1989	Ulf Timmermann (GDR)
1992	Mike Stulce (USA)
1994	C.J. Hunter (USA)
1998	John Godina (USA)
2002	Adam Nelson (USA)
2006	Ralf Bartels (GER)
DISCUS THROW	
1977	Wolfgang Schmidt (GDR)
1979	Wolfgang Schmidt (GDR)
1981	Armin Lemme (GDR)
1985	Georgy Kolnoochenko (URS)
1989	Jürgen Schult (GDR)
1992	Anthony Washington (USA)
1994	Vladimir Dubrovshchik (BLR)
1998	Virgilijus Alekna (LTU)
2002	Róbert Fazekas (HUN)
2006	Virgilijus Alekna (LTU)
JAVELIN THROW	
1977	Michael Wessing (FRG)
1979	Wolfgang Hanisch (GDR)
1981	Dainis Kula (URS)
1985	Uwe Hohn (GDR)
1989	Steve Backley (GBR)
1992	Jan Zelezny (TCH)
1994	Steve Backley (GBR)
1998	Steve Backley (GBR)
2002	Sergey Makarov (RUS)
2006	Andreas Thorkildsen (NOR)
HAMMER THROW	
1977	Karl-Hans Riehm (FRG)
1979	Sergey Litvinov (URS)
1981	Yuriy Sedykh (URS)
1985	Jüri Tamm (URS)
1989	Heinz Weis (FRG)
1992	Tibor Gécsek (HUN)
1994	Andrey Abduvaliyev (TJK)
1998	Tibor Gécsek (HUN)
2002	Adrián Annus (HUN)
2006	Murofushi Koji (JPN)
TEAM	
1977	East Germany
1979	United States
1981	Europe
1985	United States
1989	United States
1992	Africa
1994	Africa
1998	Africa
2002	Africa
2006	Europe

[1]*Unified Team, consisting of athletes from the Commonwealth of Independent States plus Georgia.*

IAAF World Cup—Women

YEAR	WINNER
100 M	
1981	Evelyn Ashford (USA)
1985	Marlies Göhr (GDR)
1977	Marlies Oelsner (GDR)
1979	Evelyn Ashford (USA)
1981	Evelyn Ashford (USA)
1985	Marlies Göhr (GDR)
1989	Sheila Echols (USA)
1992	Natalya Voronova (UNT[1])
1994	Irina Privalova (RUS)
1998	Marion Jones (USA)
2002	Marion Jones (USA)
2006	Sherone Simpson (JAM)
200 M	
1977	Irina Szewinska (POL)
1979	Evelyn Ashford (USA)
1981	Evelyn Ashford (USA)
1985	Marita Koch (GDR)
1989	Silke Möller (GDR)
1992	Marie-José Pérec (FRA)
1994	Merlene Ottey (JAM)
1998	Marion Jones (USA)
2002	Debbie Ferguson (BAH)
2006	Sanya Richards (USA)
400 M	
1977	Irina Szewinska (POL)
1979	Marita Koch (GDR)
1981	Jarmila Kratochvilova (TCH)
1985	Marita Koch (GDR)
1989	Ana Quirot (CUB)
1992	Jearl Miles (USA)
1994	Irina Privalova (RUS)
1998	Falilat Ogunkoya (NGR)
2002	Ana Guevara (MEX)
2006	Sanya Richards (USA)
800 M	
1977	Totka Petrova (BUL)
1979	Nikolina Shtereva (BUL)
1981	Lyudmila Veselkova (URS)
1985	Christine Wachtel (GDR)
1989	Ana Quirot (CUB)
1992	Maria Mutola (MOZ)
1994	Maria Mutola (MOZ)
1998	Maria Mutola (MOZ)
2002	Maria Mutola (MOZ)
2006	Zulia Calatayud (CUB)
1,500 M	
1977	Tatyana Kazankina (URS)
1979	Christiane Wartenburg (GDR)
1981	Tamara Sorokina (URS)
1985	Hildegard Körner (GDR)
1989	Paula Ivan (ROM)
1992	Yekaterina Podkopayeva (UNT[1])
1994	Hassiba Boulmerka (ALG)
1998	Svetlana Masterkova (RUS)
2002	Süreyya Ayhan (TUR)
2006	Maryam Yusuf Jamal (BRN)
3,000 M	
1977	Grete Waitz (NOR)
1979	Svetlana Ulmasova (URS)
1981	Angelika Zauber (GDR)
1985	Ulrike Bruns (GDR)
1989	Yvonne Murray (GBR)
1992	Derartu Tulu (ETH)
1994	Yvonne Murray (GBR)
1998	Gabriela Szabo (ROM)
2002	Berhane Adere (ETH)
2006	Tirunesh Dibaba (ETH)
5,000 M	
1998	Sonia O'Sullivan (IRL)
2002	Olga Yegorova (RUS)
2006	Meseret Defar (ETH)
10,000 M	
1985	Aurora Cunha (POR)
1989	Kathrin Ullrich (GDR)
1992	Derartu Tulu (ETH)
1994	Elana Meyer (RSA)
STEEPLECHASE	
2006	Alesia Turava (BLR)
100-M HURDLES	
1977	Grazyna Rabsztyn (POL)
1979	Grazyna Rabsztyn (POL)
1981	Tatyana Anisimova (URS)
1985	Cornelia Oschkenat (GDR)
1989	Cornelia Oschkenat (GDR)
1992	Aliuska López (CUB)
1994	Aliuska López (CUB)
1998	Glory Alozie (NGR)
2002	Gail Devers (USA)
2006	Brigitte Foster-Hylton (JAM)
400-M HURDLES	
1979	Bärbel Klepp (GDR)
1981	Ellen Neumann (GDR)
1985	Sabine Busch (GDR)
1989	Sandra Farmer-Patrick (USA)
1992	Sandra Farmer-Patrick (USA)
1994	Sally Gunnell (GBR)
1998	Nezha Bidouane (MAR)
2002	Yuliya Pechonkina (RUS)
2006	Yuliya Pechonkina (RUS)
4 × 100-M RELAYS	
1977	Europe Select
1979	Europe Select
1981	East Germany
1985	East Germany
1989	East Germany
1992	Asia

IAAF World Cup—Women (continued)

YEAR	WINNER
4 × 100-M RELAYS (CONTINUED)	
1994	Africa
1998	United States
2002	Americas
2006	Americas
4 × 400-M RELAYS	
1977	East Germany
1979	East Germany
1981	East Germany
1985	East Germany
1989	Americas
1992	Americas
1994	Great Britain
1998	Germany
2002	Americas
2006	Americas
TRIPLE JUMP	
1992	Li Huirong (CHN)
1994	Anna Biryukova (RUS)
1998	Olga Vasdeki (GRE)
2002	Françoise Mbango Etone (CMR)
2006	Tatyana Lebedeva (RUS)
HIGH JUMP	
1977	Rosemarie Ackermann (GDR)
1979	Debbie Brill (CAN)
1981	Ulrike Meyfarth (FRG)
1985	Stefka Kostadinova (BUL)
1989	Silvia Costa (CUB)
1992	Ioamnet Quintero (CUB)
1994	Britta Bilac (SLO)
1998	Monica Iagar-Dinescu (ROM)
HIGH JUMP (CONTINUED)	
2002	Hestrie Cloete (RSA)
2006	Yelena Slesarenko (RUS)
POLE VAULT	
2002	Annika Becker (GER)
2006	Yelena Isinbaeva (RUS)
LONG JUMP	
1977	Lyn Jacenko (AUS)
1979	Anita Stukane (URS)
1981	Sigrid Ulbricht (GDR)
1985	Heike Daute Drechsler (GDR)
1989	Galina Chistyakova (URS)
1992	Heike Drechsler (GER)
1994	Inessa Kravets (UKR)
1998	Heike Drechsler (GER)
2002	Tatyana Kotova (RUS)
2006	Lyudmila Kolchanova (RUS)
SHOT PUT	
1977	Ilona Slupianek (GDR)
1979	Ilona Slupianek (GDR)
1981	Ilona Slupianek (GDR)
1985	Natalya Lisovskaya (URS)
1989	Huang Zhihong (CHN)
1992	Belsis Laza (CUB)
1994	Zhihong Huang (CHN)
1998	Vita Pavlysh (UKR)
2002	Irina Korzhanenko (RUS)
2006	Valerie Vili (NZL)
DISCUS THROW	
1977	Faina Melnik (URS)
1979	Evelin Jahl (GDR)
1981	Evelin Jahl (GDR)
DISCUS THROW (CONTINUED)	
1985	Martina Optiz (GDR)
1989	Ilke Wyludda (GDR)
1992	Maritza Marten (CUB)
1994	Ilke Wyludda (GER)
1998	Franka Dietzsch (GER)
2002	Beatrice Faumuina (NZL)
2006	Franka Dietzsch (GER)
JAVELIN THROW	
1977	Ruth Fuchs (GDR)
1979	Ruth Fuchs (GDR)
1981	Antoaneta Todorova (BUL)
1985	Olga Gavrilova (URS)
1989	Petra Felke (GDR)
1992	Tessa Sanderson (GBR)
1994	Trine Hattestad (NOR)
1998	Joanna Stone (AUS)
2002	Osleidys Menéndez CUB)
2006	Steffi Nerius (GER)
HAMMER THROW	
2002	Gu Yuan (CHN)
2006	Kamila Skolimowska (POL)
TEAM	
1977	Europe Select
1979	East Germany
1981	East Germany
1985	East Germany
1989	East Germany
1992	Unified Team[1]
1994	Europe
1998	United States
2002	Russia
2006	Russia

[1]*Unified Team, consisting of athletes from the Commonwealth of Independent States plus Georgia.*

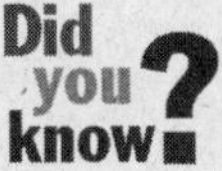

In 1920, major league baseball outlawed the spitball, a pitch that, with the aid of saliva or some other lubricant, dips sharply as it nears the batter. It was determined that the spitball gave pitchers an unfair advantage. Those pitchers who were then using it, however, were allowed to continue with it until they retired.

World Cross Country Championships

Competition has been held since 1973; table shows results from the past 20 years.

men (12,000 meters)

YEAR	INDIVIDUAL (NATIONALITY)	TEAM
1989	John Ngugi (KEN)	Kenya
1990	Khalid Skah (MAR)	Kenya
1991	Khalid Skah (MAR)	Kenya
1992	John Ngugi (KEN)	Kenya
1993	William Sigei (KEN)	Kenya
1994	William Sigei (KEN)	Kenya
1995	Paul Tergat (KEN)	Kenya
1996	Paul Tergat (KEN)	Kenya
1997	Paul Tergat (KEN)	Kenya
1998	Paul Tergat (KEN)	Kenya
1999	Paul Tergat (KEN)	Kenya
2000	Mohammed Mourhit (BEL)	Kenya
2001	Mohammed Mourhit (BEL)	Kenya
2002	Kenenisa Bekele (ETH)	Kenya
2003	Kenenisa Bekele (ETH)	Kenya
2004	Kenenisa Bekele (ETH)	Ethiopia
2005	Kenenisa Bekele (ETH)	Ethiopia
2006	Kenenisa Bekele (ETH)	Kenya
2007	Zersenay Tadesse (ERI)	Kenya
2008	Kenenisa Bekele (ETH)	Kenya

World Cross Country Championships (continued)

women (8,000 meters)

YEAR	INDIVIDUAL (NATIONALITY)	TEAM
1989	Annette Sargent (FRA)	USSR
1990	Lynn Jennings (USA)	USSR
1991	Lynn Jennings (USA)	Kenya
1992	Lynn Jennings (USA)	Kenya
1993	Albertina Dias (POR)	Kenya
1994	Hellen Chepngeno (KEN)	Portugal
1995	Derartu Tulu (ETH)	Kenya
1996	Gete Wami (ETH)	Kenya
1997	Derartu Tulu (ETH)	Ethiopia
1998	Sonia O'Sullivan (IRE)	Kenya
1999	Gete Wami (ETH)	Ethiopia
2000	Derartu Tulu (ETH)	Ethiopia
2001	Paula Radcliffe (GBR)	Kenya
2002	Paula Radcliffe (GBR)	Ethiopia
2003	Werknesh Kidane (ETH)	Ethiopia
2004	Benita Johnson (AUS)	Ethiopia
2005	Tirunesh Dibaba (ETH)	Ethiopia
2006	Tirunesh Dibaba (ETH)	Ethiopia
2007	Lornah Kiplagat (NED)	Ethiopia
2008	Tirunesh Dibaba (ETH)	Ethiopia

Volleyball

World **volleyball championships** for men were inaugurated in 1949. **Women's** competition began in 1952. These biennial championships are organized by the **Fédération Internationale de Volleyball** (FIVB; founded 1947). Indoor volleyball has been included in the Olympic Games since 1964 and beach volleyball since 1996.

FIVB Web site: <www.fivb.org>.

World Volleyball Championships

YEAR	MEN	WOMEN
1949	USSR	
1952	USSR	USSR
1956	Czechoslovakia	USSR
1960	USSR	USSR
1962	USSR	Japan
1964[1]	USSR	Japan
1966	Czechoslovakia	Japan
1967	*not held*	Japan
1968[1]	USSR	USSR
1970	East Germany	USSR
1972[1]	Japan	USSR
1974	Poland	Japan
1976[1]	Poland	Japan
1978	USSR	Cuba
1980[1]	USSR	USSR
1982	USSR	China
1984[1]	United States	China
1986	United States	China
1988[1]	United States	USSR
1990	Italy	USSR
1992[1]	Brazil	Cuba
1994	Italy	Cuba
1996[1]	The Netherlands	Cuba
1998	Italy	Cuba
2000[1]	Yugoslavia	Cuba
2002	Brazil	Italy
2004[1]	Brazil	China
2006	Brazil	Russia
2008[1]	United States	Brazil

[1]*Olympic champions, considered world champions.*

Weight Lifting

World weight lifting is overseen by the **International Weightlifting Federation** (IWF; founded 1905). The first **men's international weight lifting competition** was held in London in 1891; the sport was also included in the first modern Olympic Games, in Athens in 1896. By the 1930s championship events consisted of the snatch, clean and jerk, and press (which was eliminated in 1972). **Women's world championships** have been held since 1987, and women's competition was added to the Olympics in 2000. In 1998 the IWF established **new weight classes** (eight for men and seven for women) as well as a new world standard for each class in determining world records.

IWF Web site: <www.iwf.net>.

Weight Lifting World Records

Total weight for snatch and clean-and-jerk lifts.

men

WEIGHT CLASS	RECORD HOLDER (COUNTRY)	PERFORMANCE	DATE
56 kg (123 lb)	Halil Mutlu (TUR)	305 kg (672 lb)	16 Sep 2000
62 kg (137 lb)	Zhang Jie (CHN)	326 kg (719 lb)	28 Apr 2008
69 kg (152 lb)	Galabin Boevski (BUL)	357 kg (787 lb)	24 Nov 1999

Weight Lifting World Records (continued)

men (continued)

WEIGHT CLASS	RECORD HOLDER (COUNTRY)	PERFORMANCE	DATE
77 kg (170 lb)	Plamen Zhelyazkov (BUL)	377 kg (831 lb)	27 Mar 2002
85 kg (187 lb)	Lu Yong (CHN); Andrei Rybakov (BLR)	394 kg (869 lb)	15 Aug 2008; 15 Aug 2008
94 kg (207 lb)	Akakios Kakiasvilis (GRE)	412 kg (908 lb)	27 Nov 1999
105 kg (231.5 lb)	Andrei Aramnau (BLR)	436 kg (961 lb)	18 Aug 2008
105+ kg (231.5+ lb)	Hossein Rezazadeh (IRI)	472 kg (1041 lb)	26 Sep 2000

women

WEIGHT CLASS	RECORD HOLDER (COUNTRY)	PERFORMANCE	DATE
48kg (106 lb)	Yang Lian (CHN)	217 kg (478 lb)	1 Oct 2006
53 kg (117 lb)	Qiu Hongxia (CHN)	226 kg (498 lb)	2 Oct 2006
58 kg (128 lb)	Chen Yanqing (CHN)	251 kg (553 lb)	3 Dec 2006
63 kg (139 lb)	Liu Haixia (CHN)	257 kg (567 lb)	23 Sep 2007
69 kg (152 lb)	Liu Chunhong (CHN)	286 kg (631 lb)	13 Aug 2008
75 kg (165 lb)	Svetlana Podobedova (RUS)	286 kg (631 lb)	2 Jun 2006
75+ kg (165+ lb)	Jang Mi Ran (KOR)	326 kg (719 lb)	16 Aug 2008

World Weight Lifting Champions, 2008

men

WEIGHT CLASS	WINNER (COUNTRY)	PERFORMANCE
56 kg (123 lb)	Long Qinquan (CHN)	292 kg (644 lb)
62 kg (137 lb)	Zhang Xiangxiang (CHN)	319 kg (703 lb)
69 kg (152 lb)	Liao Hui (CHN)	348 kg (767 lb)
77 kg (170 lb)	Sa Jae Hyouk (KOR)	366 kg (807 lb)
85 kg (187 lb)	Lu Yong (CHN)	394 kg (869 lb)
94 kg (207 lb)	Ilya Ilin (KAZ)	406 kg (895 lb)
105 kg (231 lb)	Andrei Aramnau (BLR)	436 kg (961 lb)
105+ kg (231+ lb)	Matthias Steiner (GER)	461 kg (1,016 lb)

women

WEIGHT CLASS	WINNER (COUNTRY)	PERFORMANCE
48 kg (106 lb)	Chen Xiexia (CHN)	212 kg (467 lb)
53 kg (117 lb)	Prapawadee Jaroenrattanatarakoon (THA)	221 kg (487 lb)
58 kg (128 lb)	Chen Yanqing (CHN)	244 kg (538 lb)
63 kg (139 lb)	Pak Hyon Suk (KOR)	241 kg (531 lb)
69 kg (152 lb)	Liu Chunhong (CHN)	286 kg (631 lb)
75 kg (165 lb)	Cao Lei (CHN)	282 kg (622 lb)
75+ kg (165+ lb)	Jang Mi Ran (KOR)	326 kg (719 lb)

Cycling as a sport officially began on 31 May 1868, with a 1,200-metre (1,312-yard) race between the fountains and the entrance of Saint-Cloud Park (near Paris). The winner was James Moore, an 18-year-old expatriate Englishman from Paris. On 7 Nov 1869, the first city-to-city race was held between Paris and Rouen, France; again Moore was the winner, covering the 135 km (84 miles) in 10 hours 25 minutes, including time spent walking his bicycle up the steeper hills.

INDEX

Page numbers in **boldface** indicate main subject references; references in *italics* indicate illustrations. Photographs are on plates 1–16 after page 480, flags of the world are on plates 17–22, and maps of the world are on plates 23–32.

A

Abdel Shafi, Haidar 76
abstinence 205
Academy Award, *or* Oscar 23, **727**, 729
  photographs Plate 15
accident
  causes of death, US 203, 204
  causes of death, worldwide 202
  US occupational injuries 716
  US work-related fatalities 718
  see also disaster
Achernar (star) 134
acquired immunodeficiency syndrome: *see* AIDS
Acrux (star) 134
Adams, Gerry 37
Adams, John 596, **598**, 608, 612, 624
Adams, John Quincy 596, **599**, 608, 613, 624
Adelson, Jay 36
adoption
  US adoptions of foreign-born children 698
aerospace technology 167
Afghanistan 218
  chronology 11, 14, 17, 18, 26, 29
  disasters 32, 33
  flags of the world Plate 17
  internally displaced persons 563
  refugees 563
Africa
  causes of death 200
  caves 195
  continents 191
  deserts 196
  disasters 32, 33
  education 566
  forests 190
  historic states 561
  mountains 194
  refugees 563
  religions 568
  rivers 198
  temperature extremes 174
  US deployment 640
  volcanoes 196
  world maps Plate 26
  worldwide health indicators 200
  see also individual nations by name
African Cup of Nations 22, **879**
African Union, *or* AU, *or* Organization for African Unity 15, 25, 545
Agassi, Andre 35
Agee, Philip Burnett Franklin 76
agriculture
  Svalbard Global Seed Vault 23, 187
AIA Gold Medal 782
AIDS, *or* acquired immunodeficiency syndrome 13, **204**
  see also HIV
air force
  armed forces 578
  US casualties 643
  US deployment 639
  US military leadership 638
  US pay scale 640
air quotes 564
air travel, *or* aviation **172**, 571, 578
  chronology 11
  disasters 30, 31, 32, 33
airport
  engineering projects 186
  world's busiest 173
al-Qaeda: *see* Qaeda, al-
al-Walid ibn Talal ibn Abdulaziz al-Saud, Prince 36
Alabama 653
  crime rates 690
  currency: quarters 704
  death penalty sentences 694
  disasters 33
  electoral votes 635
  energy consumption 705
  government 682, 683
  immigration 650
  income taxes 725
  poverty level 652
  prison population 693
  state population 646
  US Congress 627, 630, 636
ALADI: *see* Latin American Integration Association
Alaska 654
  crime rates 690
  currency: quarters 704
  electoral votes 635
  energy consumption 705
  government 682, 683
  immigration 650
  poverty level 652
  prison population 693
  state population 646
  US Congress 627, 630, 636
Albania 220
  disasters 33
  flags of the world Plate 17
album (music) 756
Aldebaran (star) 134
Algeria 221
  chronology 14, 19
  flags of the world Plate 17
All-England Tennis Championships, *or* Wimbledon **918**, **920**
  photographs Plates 12, 13
Allen, Paul 35
Allen, Ray
  photographs Plate 13
alloy 165
Alpha Centauri (star) 133
alpine skiing 902
  Alpine World Cup 903
  Olympic Games 831, 846
  world championships 902
Altair (star) 134
amendment (US Constitution) **591, 592**
American Academy of Arts and Letters Awards 109
American Civil War 595, 642
American football: *see* football
American Indian, *or* Native American 561
American Samoa 223
  flags of the world Plate 17
  US governors 682
  US House 634
  US population 652
Americas, the
  death causes 202
  pre-Columbian civilizations 561
  worldwide health indicators 200
  see also North America; South America; *and* individual nations by name
ampere 154, 155, 158
Amte, Baba 76
Anaya, Jorge Isaac 76
Andean Community 545
Andorra 224
  flags of the world Plate 17
Anglicanism 568, 570
Angola 225
  disasters 33
  flags of the world Plate 17
animal 188
Antarctica 25, **544**
  continents 191
  mountains 194
  temperature extremes 174
  volcanoes 196
  world maps Plate 25
Antares (star) 134
Anthony, John Duke 9
Antigua and Barbuda 226
  flags of the world Plate 17
Antonioni, Michelangelo 76
Apatow, Judd 36
APEC: *see* Asia-Pacific Economic Cooperation
apogee (astronomy)
  Moon 145
applied science 165
April
  astronomical phenomena 135
Aquarius 130, 132

Arab League: *see* League of Arab States
archery 755, 786, 836
architecture
awards 25, 781
civil engineering 180
Seven Wonders of the Ancient World 180
tallest buildings 181
Arctic Ocean 197
Arctic Regions 544
chronology 12, 13, 28
Arcturus (star) 133
area (mathematics) 157, 162
area code (US) 689
Arfons, Art Eugene 76
Argentina 228
cell phone subscribers 166
disasters 32
education 566
flags of the world Plate 17
Aries 130, 132
'Arif, 'Abd al-Rahman 76
Arizona 654
crime rates 690
currency: quarters 704
death penalty sentences 694
electoral votes 635
energy consumption 705, 706
government 682, 683
immigration 650
income taxes 725
poverty level 652
prison population 693
state population 646
US Congress 627, 630, 636
Arkansas 655
crime rates 690, 691
currency: quarters 704
death penalty sentences 694
disasters 33
electoral votes 635
energy consumption 705, 706
government 682, 683
immigration 650
income taxes 725
poverty level 652
prison population 693
state population 646
US Congress 627, 630, 636
armed force: see military
Armenia 229
flags of the world Plate 17
Armstrong, Lance 35
army
armed forces 578
US casualties 642
US deployment 639
US military leadership 638
US pay scale 640
Arnold, Eddy 76
Arrington, Michael 36
Arthur, Chester A. 597, **602,** 610, 616, 624
artificial limb
chronology 29
arts, the 727
awards and honors 105, 106, 109, 729, 761
best-selling albums 756
chronology 18, 20, 26
influential people of 2008 36
photographs Plate 14
see also film; literature; music; theater
Aruba 231
flags of the world Plate 17
ASEAN: *see* Association of Southeast Asian Nations
Asia
causes of death 202
caves 195
continents 191
deserts 196
education 566
forests 190
health indicators 200
mountains 194
refugees 563
religions 568
rivers 198
rulers and regimes 558
temperature extremes 174
US deployment 640
volcanoes 196
world maps Plate 27
see also individual nations by name
Asia-Pacific Economic Cooperation, *or* APEC 545
Asian Cup 879
Aspinall, Neil Stanley 76
association football, *or* soccer 868
chronology 11, 12, 18, 28, 30
major cups 876, 877, 878, 879
Olympic Games 787, 841
photographs Plate 13
Association of Southeast Asian Nations, *or* ASEAN 545
asteroid 140, **146**
asteroid belt 146
Astor, Brooke Russell 76
astrology 132
astronomical unit, *or* AU 128
astronomy
astronomical constants 128
astronomical phenomena, 2009 135
astronomical positions 129
celestial bodies 139
constellations 129
cosmogony 127
morning and evening stars 137
stars 132, 133
see also solar system; space exploration
asylum
refugees 563
atheism 568, 570
athlete: *see* sport
athletics: *see* track and field
Atlantic Ocean 197
disasters 32
atmosphere *192*
chronology 26
atomic number *164*
atomic weight *164*
AU: *see* African Union
AUC: *see* United Self-Defense Forces of Colombia
August
astronomical phenomena 136
Aung San Suu Kyi, Daw 35
aurora 138
Australia 232
chronology 18, 19, 22
continents 191
deserts 196
education 566
flags of the world Plate 17
rivers 199
temperature extremes 174
Thoroughbred racing 889, 894
world maps Plate 31
Australian Aborigine 23
Australian football 16, 868, **875**
Australian Open (tennis) **913**
Austria 235
flags of the world Plate 17
autobiography 766
automobile industry 12, 15, 20, 28, 29
automobile racing 849
chronology 14, 17, 18, 23, 28, 29
avalanche 33
aviation: *see* air travel
award 89, 729, 746, 753, 761
see also specific awards by name
Azcona, Rafael 76
Azerbaijan 16, 18, **236**
disasters 31
flags of the world Plate 17
internally displaced persons 563
refugee population 563
Aztec (people) 20

B

Babylonia 161
Bachelet, Michelle 35
badminton 795, 836
Baghdad
photographs Plate 3
Baha'ism 124, 568, 570
Bahamas, The 238
disasters 34
flags of the world Plate 17
Bahrain 239
construction 9
flags of the world Plate 17
baiji, *or* Chinese river dolphin, *or* Yangtze River dolphin 13
Baikal, Lake 683
Bailey, Liberty Hyde 714
Balkanization 217
Ballmer, Steve 36
Ban Ki-moon 39
Bangladesh 240
cell phone subscribers 166
chronology 13, 14, 18, 19
disasters 32, 33, 34
flags of the world Plate 17
banking 8
chronology 19, 21, 24
photographs Plate 9
bankruptcy 724
Barbados 242
flags of the world Plate 17

Bardem, Javier
photographs Plate 15
Barre, Raymond-Octave-Joseph 76
Bartholomew I 35
Bartsch, Constellations of 131
baseball 851, 852, 935
chronology 13, 14, 17, 18, 19, 22
Major League All-Time Records 854
Olympic Games 795, 837
basketball 15, 29, **856**
NBA All-Time Records 856, 857
NBA championships 858
Olympic Games 795, 837
photographs Plate 13
WNBA championships 859
"Bateau, Le" 635
beach volleyball 12
Beadle, Jeremy James Anthony Gibson 76
Bear Stearns 9
beauty pageant 759
Beckham, David 39
Becrux (star) 134
bee (insect) 14
Beijing Olympic Games 836
photographs Plates 1, 11
Beirut
photographs Plate 3
Belarus 243
flags of the world Plate 17
Belgium 18, 20, 23, 24, **245**
flags of the world Plate 17
Belize 246
chronology 22
flags of the world Plate 17
Belmont Stakes 29, 886, **892**
Benedict XVI, *or* Joseph Alois Ratzinger 39
Bengal, Bay of 33
Benin 248
flags of the world Plate 17
Bergman, Ingmar 76
Berlin International Film Festival 741
Berlusconi, Silvio 39
Bermuda 249
flags of the world Plate 17
Bernanke, Ben 35
Berzin, Isaac 35
Beta Centauri (star) 134
Betancourt, Ingrid
photographs Plate 4
Betelgeuse (star) 134
beverage 160, 211
Bezos, Jeff 36
Bhutan 250, 755
chronology 24
flags of the world Plate 17
Bhutto, Benazir 76
chronology 17, 20
photographs Plate 16
biathlon 829, 847
Bible 759
Biden, Joseph Robinette 40
photographs Plate 6
Big Brown (racehorse) 28
Bill of Rights (US) **591**
billiard games 860
bin Laden, Osama 40
biodiesel 7
biofuel 7
biography 766
biomass 7
birth control 206
Bishop, Joey 77
Black Sea 18, 34
blackjack 161
Blackwater USA 15
Blair, Tony 35, 40
Blankfein, Lloyd 36
blizzard 33
Bloomberg, Michael 35
Blu-ray disc (technology) 20, 23
Blunt, Ray 630
BMI: see body mass index
boat accident
disasters 31, 32, 33
boating: *see* motorboat racing; sailing
bobsleigh, *or* bobsled 829, 848
body mass index, *or* BMI 216
Boehner, John A. 630
Bolin, Bert Richard Johannes 77
Bolivia 17, 27, **251**
flags of the world Plate 17
Bollingen Prize 781
Bonds, Barry 18
Booker Prize: *see* Man Booker Prize
Böselager, Philipp von 77
Bosnia and Herzegovina 19, **253**
flags of the world Plate 17
internally displaced persons 563
refugee population 563
Boston Celtics (basketball) 29
photographs Plate 13
Boston Marathon 26, 899
Boston Red Sox (baseball) 17
"Boswash" 689
Botswana 255
flags of the world Plate 17
Boumediene v. Bush 627
bowling 861
Bowman, Christopher 77
boxing 796, 837
Bradshaw, Richard James 77
Brant, Henry Dreyfuss 77
Brazil 256
armed forces 578
cell phone subscribers 166
chronology 13, 18, 23, 28
disasters 31, 32, 33, 34
education 566
flags of the world Plate 17
bridge 184
chronology 12, 13, 28
civil engineering projects 186
disasters 32
longest-span structures 182
Brilliant, Larry 35
Brinker, Nancy 36
Brit Awards 756
British Amateur Championship (golf) **885**
British Broadcasting Company 23
British Open (golf) **882**
photographs Plate 13
British/US measurement system 155, **157**
Broadway 29, 751
Brooklyn Bridge
photographs Plate 14
Brooks-Randolph, Angie Elisabeth 77
Brown, Bill 77
Brown, Gordon 41
Brunei 258
flags of the world Plate 17
Bruni, Carla
photographs Plate 5
Buchanan, James 597, **600**, 615, 624
Buckley, William F., Jr. 77
Buddhism 567, 568, 570
chronology 15
Dalai Lamas 560
holidays 124
budget, government (US) 721
building
civil engineering projects 186
disasters 31, 34
Gulf States' construction boom 9
tallest in the world 181
see also architecture
Bulgaria 260
chronology 12
flags of the world Plate 17
Burkina Faso 262
flags of the world Plate 17
Burma: *see* Myanmar
Burundi 14, **263**
flags of the world Plate 17
internally displaced persons 563
refugees 563
bus accident 33
Bush, George H. W. 597, **606**, 611, 622, 624
Bush, George W. 35, 41, 597, **607**, 611, 623, 624
chronology 11, 22
business 701
chronology 15, 16, 22
influential people of 2008 36
photographs Plate 9
Byrd, Robert C. 627
Byzantine Empire 556

C

cabinet, presidential (US) **612**
Cachao 77
calcium 210, 211
Caldecott Medal 19, **775**
Calderón, Felipe 41
calendar 119
holidays 123
perpetual calendar 125
California 655
chronology 17
crime rates 690, 691
currency: quarters 704
death penalty sentences 694
disasters 31
electoral votes 635
energy consumption 705, 706
government 682, 683

immigration 650
income taxes 725
poverty level 652
prison population 693
state population 646
US Congress 627, 630, 636
caliph 557
Callisto (moon) 142
calorie
food label 214
meeting dietary guidelines 210
nutritional values 211, 212
ways to burn calories 215
Calvo Sotelo y Bustelo, Leopoldo 77
Cambodia 264
flags of the world Plate 17
Cameroon 266
flags of the world Plate 17
Canada 267
chronology 11, 13, 29
education 566
flags of the world Plate 17
Thoroughbred racing 888
Canadian football 18, 868, 875
canal 187
Canary Islands 31
Cancer (astronomy) 130, 132
candela 154, 155
Cannes International Film Festival 741
canoeing 797, 837
Canopus (star) 133
Cape Verde 270
flags of the world Plate 17
Capella (star) 133
Capricornus, *or* Capricorn 130, 132
carbohydrate 210, 211, 214
Carey, Mariah 36
Caribbean Community and Common Market, *or* CARICOM 545
Caribbean region 32
world maps Plate 24
Caribbean Series (baseball) 22, **855**
Carlin, George 77
photographs Plate 16
Carney, James 579
carom billiards: *see* three-cushion billiards
Carroll, Cynthia 36
Carter, Jimmy 597, **606**, 611, 621
Casillas, Iker
photographs Plate 13
Cassini-Huygens (spacecraft) 170
casualty 642
catch-as-catch-can wrestling: *see* freestyle wrestling
Caucasus 194
causeway 183
cave 195
Cedar Rapids (Iowa) 29
photographs Plate 8
celestial bodies 139, 146
cellular telephone 166, 167
Celsius 158, 159
Central African Republic 272
flags of the world Plate 17
internally displaced persons 563
Central Intelligence Agency, *or* CIA 19, 644
Cervantes Prize 780
Chad 273
chronology 11, 17, 22
flags of the world Plate 18
refugee population 563
Chambers, John 36
Chandra X-Ray Observatory 170
Charisse, Cyd 77
Charles Frankel Prize: *see* National Humanities Medal
Charon (moon) 140, 153
Chávez Frías, Hugo 42
chemical element
applied science 165
periodic table 164
chemistry 165
chronology 16
Nobel Prize winners 94
periodic table 164
Cheney, Richard 627
chess 863
Chicago Marathon 16, **901**
children
chronology 15, 17
education profile 566
infant mortality rates 200
United States
adoptions 698
causes of death 203
child care arrangements 697
dietary guidelines 210
food guide pyramid 209
living arrangements 696
obesity concerns 117
population 696
poverty 696
presidents' families 608
children's literature
awards 773, 774, 775, 776
chronology 20, 21
Chile 275
chronology 15, 27
flags of the world Plate 18
China 276
ancient units of measurement 162
armed forces of the world 578
cell phone subscribers 166
chronology 11, 14, 17, 18, 20, 23, 24, 26, 27, 28, 29
disasters 30, 31, 32, 33, 34
dynasties and leaders 560
education 566
flags of the world Plate 18
holidays 124
photographs Plates 1, 10, 11
refugee population 563
US adoptions 698
Chinese calendar 122
Chinese river dolphin: *see* baiji
Chinese universist 568, 570
Chissano, Joaquim 17
Chivian, Eric 36
cholesterol 210, 214
Christianity 567, 568, 570, 572
holidays 123
see also Roman Catholicism
Christodoulos 77
chronology 11
disasters 30
United States 581
CIA: *see* Central Intelligence Agency
cinema: *see* motion picture
circumference (mathematics) 162
CIS: *see* Commonwealth of Independent States
city: *see* urban area
civil engineering 180, 186
civil holiday 126
Civil War, American: *see* American Civil War
Cizik, Richard 36
Clarke, Arthur C. 77
Clarke, Janet H. 8
Cleveland, Grover 597, **602,** 610, 616, 624
climate
global temperatures and precipitation 174
normal temperatures and precipitation, US 175
world extremes 174
see also meteorology
climate change: *see* global warming
Clinton, Hillary Rodham 35, 43
photographs Plate 7
Clinton, William J. 597, **606,** 611, 622, 624
clock 119
Clooney, George 36
Clyburn, James E. 630
coal
US energy consumption 703
coast guard
US casualties 642
US military leadership 638
cocaine (drug) **19**
Coen, Ethan 36
Coen, Joel 36
coin (US) 703, 704
Colledge, Cecilia 77
college football 868, 871
chronology 14, 21
Colombia 279
armed forces 578
cell phone subscribers 166
chronology 18, 21, 23, 24
flags of the world Plate 18
internally displaced persons 563
photographs Plate 4
Colorado 656
crime rates 690, 691
currency: quarters 704
death penalty sentences 694
electoral votes 635
energy consumption 705, 706
government 682, 683
immigration 650
income taxes 725
poverty level 652

prison population 693
state population 646
US Congress 627, 631, 636
COMESA: *see* Common Market for Eastern and Southern Africa
comet 141, **154**
Comet 2P: *see* Encke's Comet
Comet 9P: *see* Temple 1 Comet
Common Market for Eastern and Southern Africa, *or* COMESA 545
Commonwealth, *or* Commonwealth of Nations 545, 777
Commonwealth of Independent States, *or* CIS 545
communications 166
see also individual nations by name
Community of Portuguese Language Countries, *or* CPLP 545
Comoros 25, **281**
flags of the world Plate 18
compensation: *see* wage
Compton, Sir John George Melvin 78
computer 21, 22
see also Internet
condom 205
Confederacy (US history) **595**
Confucianism 568, 569, 571
Congo, Democratic Republic of the (Kinshasa) **282**
disasters 31, 32, 33, 34
flags of the world Plate 18
internally displaced persons 563
refugee population 563
Congo, Republic of the (Brazzaville) **284**, 562
flags of the world Plate 18
Congress (US) **627**
apportionment 636
electoral votes 635
House of Representatives 630
House of Representatives standing committees 635
joint committees 630
Senate 627
Senate standing committees 629
Congressional Gold Medal 105
Connecticut 657
crime rates 690, 691
currency: quarters 704
death penalty sentences 694
electoral votes 635
energy consumption 705, 706
government 682, 683
immigration 650
income taxes 725
poverty level 652
prison population 693
state population 646
US Congress 628, 631, 636
conservation 199
constellation 129
constitution (US) **587**
Bill of Rights 591
further amendments 592
Consumer Price Index, *or* CPI
United States 719, 720
continent 191
see also individual continents by name
contraception 206
cooking 159
Coolidge, Calvin 597, **604**, 610, 618, 624
Coordinated Universal Time 119
Copa América 879
Coretta Scott King Award 776
Corliss, Richard 727
corn 7
Cornioley, Pearl 78
cosmogony 127
Costa Book of the Year Award 778
Costa Rica 285
flags of the world Plate 18
Côte d'Ivoire 286
flags of the world Plate 18
internally displaced persons 563
Cotillard, Marion
photographs Plate 15
coulomb 158
Council of Europe 545
country: *see* nation
Country Music Association Awards 756
court
International Criminal Court 547
US Supreme Court 624
CPI: *see* Consumer Price Index
CPLP: *see* Community of Portuguese Language Countries
Craig, Larry 14
cricket 799, **864**
crime 574
arrests in the US 692
causes of death 202, 203
chronology 19, 20, 23
crime in the US 692
death penalty in the US 694
terrorist organizations 574
US crime trends 689
US nationwide crime statistics 692
US prison populations 693
US state crime rates 690
US work-related fatalities 719
Croatia 288
flags of the world Plate 18
croquet 799
cross country 935
Cuba 289
chronology 23, 24, 26
disasters 32
education 566
flags of the world Plate 18
curling 865
Olympic Games 830, 848
currency
United States 703, 704
Curtis Cup 880, **884**
customs 708
cycling 865, 866, 937
chronology 12, 15, 23
Olympic Games 799, 838
cyclone 18, 19, 27
Cyprus 20, 24, **291**
flags of the world Plate 18
Cyrus, Miley 36
Czech Republic 293
flags of the world Plate 18

D

dairy *208, 209,* 211
Dakar Rally 21
Dalai Lama 16, 35, **560**
dam 185, 186
Darfur 12, 15
dark energy 564
"Dark Knight, The" (film)
photographs Plate 14
Darman, Richard Gordon 78
Davis Cup 926
day 125, 128
Day-Lewis, Daniel
photographs Plate 15
daylight saving time, *or* summer time **121**
Daytona 500 23
Dean (hurricane) 13
disasters 31
death: *see* mortality
death penalty (US) 694
DeBakey, Michael Ellis 78, 105
decathlon 928
December
astronomical phenomena 137
eclipses 138
decimal 163
Declaration of Independence (US) **584**, 585
Deep Impact (spacecraft) 170
Defense, Department of (US)
leading contractors 644
military affairs 638
defense contractor 644
Delaware 657
crime rates 690, 691
currency: quarters 704
death penalty sentences 694
electoral votes 635
energy consumption 705, 706
government 682, 683
immigration 650
income taxes 725
poverty level 652
prison population 693
state population 646
US Congress 628, 631, 636
Dello Joio, Norman 78
demography: *see under* individual nations by name
Deneb (star) 134
Denmark 294
chronology 13
flags of the world Plate 18
density 165
DeOssie, Zak
photographs Plate 13
Derby, The 29, **893**
desert 196
Detroit Red Wings (ice hockey) 29
Dhaka (Bangladesh) 745

Di Stefano, Giuseppe 78
dice 161
Diddley, Bo 78
diet, *or* nutrition **207**, 210, 211
  nutrition, children, and obesity 117
  see also health; physical activity
Dimon, Jamie 36
dirty bomb 564
disaster 30
  geologic disasters 178
  photographs Plates 8, 10
discus (sports) 792, 795, 928
disease and disorder 204
  causes of death 201, 202, 203
  work-related in US 719
District of Columbia: *see* Washington, DC
District of Columbia v. **Heller** 627
Dith Pran 78
diving 907
  championships 909, 910
  Olympic Games 801, 802, 838
divorce 699
Djibouti 29, **296**
  flags of the world Plate 18
dogsled racing: *see* sled dog racing
Dominica 297
  flags of the world Plate 18
Dominican Republic 299
  disasters 32
  flags of the world Plate 18
Downey, Robert, Jr. 36
drama: *see* theater
driving under the influence 693
Drnovsek, Janez 78
drowning
  causes of death worldwide 202
drug: *see* medicine
Dubai World Cup 886, **894**
Dubailand 9
Durbin, Dick 627
DVD (technology) 20, 23
dwarf planet
  neologisms 564
  Pluto 153

E

Earth 143
  astronomical constants 128
  atmosphere structure *192*
  caves 195
  celestial bodies 139, 175
  forests 189, 190
  geology 191
  life 188
  meteorology 174
  natural disasters 178
  superlatives 142
  see also world and specific topics by name
earthquake
  chronology 11, 13, 15, 27, 28
  disasters 31, 33, 34, 178
  historical earthquakes 179
  measurement 178
  photographs Plate 10
  tsunami 180
East Africa Submarine Cable System 187
East Timor 300
  chronology 13, 22
  flags of the world Plate 18
  internally displaced persons 563
eclipse 138
ecology: *see* environment
Economic Community of West African States, *or* ECOWAS 545
economics
  Nobel Prize winners 103
  subprime mortgages 8
  United States 701, 703
  see also individual nations and other subjects by name
Ecuador 23, **301**
  flags of the world Plate 18
edamame 564
education
  science scholarship award 116
  United States
    attainment by gender and race, US 699
    median income 711
  world profile 566
  see also individual nations by name
EFTA: *see* European Free Trade Association
Egozy, Eran 36
Egypt 303
  ancient units of measurement 161
  armed forces of the world 578
  cell phone subscribers 166
  chronology 17
  disasters 33
  education 566
  flags of the world Plate 18
1812, War of 642
Eisenhower, Dwight D. 597, **605**, 611, 619, 624
El Salvador 304
  flags of the world Plate 18
Elder, Will 78
elderly: *see* senior citizen
Eldorado (Texas)
  photographs Plate 8
election
  electoral votes 635
  US presidency 579
  see also individual nations by name
electrical unit 158
element, chemical 164, 165
Eliasson, Olafur
  photographs Plate 14
Ellis, Albert 78
Emancipation Proclamation (US) **595**
emigration 562
Emmy Awards 15, **746**
employment 709
  see also unemployment
Encke's Comet, *or* Comet 2P 141
endangered species 13, 22, 28
energy 705
  biofuel 7
  food consumption 210, 211
  US consumption 702, 705
England 12
  sovereigns 550
  Thoroughbred racing 893
English billiards 860
English language 564
entertainment 727
  photographs Plates 14, 15, 16
  see also performing arts and specific types of entertainment by name
environment
  chronology 16, 18, 24
  national parks, US 199
  see also conservation; global warming
Equatorial Guinea 306
  flags of the world Plate 18
equestrian sports 802, 838
  see also horse racing
Eritrea 29, **307**
  armed forces 578
  flags of the world Plate 18
ESA: *see* European Space Agency
Estonia 309
  flags of the world Plate 18
ethanol 7
Ethiopia 310
  armed forces of the world 578
  flags of the world Plate 18
  internally displaced persons 563
  US adoptions 698
ethnoreligionist 568, 569, 570
EU: *see* European Union
euro (currency) 20
Euro 2008 (association football) 30
  photographs Plate 13
Europe
  causes of death 202
  caves 195
  chronology 25
  continents 191
  education 566
  forests 190
  health indicators 201
  mountains 194
  refugees 563
  religions 568
  rivers 198
  rulers 548
  temperature extremes 174
  US deployment 639
  volcanoes 197
  world maps Plate 28
  see also individual nations by name
European Champion Clubs' Cup: *see* UEFA Champions League
European Free Trade Association, *or* EFTA 545
European Space Agency, *or* ESA 167
European Union, *or* EU 545
  chronology 19, 20
Eurovision Song Contest 755

evening star 137
exercise: *see* physical activity
exploration: *see* space exploration
explosion
disasters 30, 31, 32, 33, 34
US work-related fatalities 719
extinction: *see* endangered species
Exxon Mobil Corporation 21
Exxon Valdez oil spill 30

F

F-1 racing: *see* Formula One racing
F-Scale: *see* Fujita scale
Fahrenheit 158, 159
Fairhurst, Angus 78
falling star: *see* meteor
family 696
fanboy, *or* fangirl
neologisms 564
farad 158
Faroe Islands 312
flags of the world Plate 18
Farrow, Mia 35
fat
food labels 214
food pyramid *209*
intake in US diet *208*
nutritional values 210, 211
fat-soluble vitamin 208
Fay, Michael 562
FDA: see Food and Drug Administration
February
astronomical phenomena 135
Fed Cup, *or* Federation Cup **927**
Federal Bureau of Investigation, *or* FBI 695
federal deficit: see public debt
Federal Election Commission v. Wisconsin Right to Life 627
federal tax (US) **724**
Federation Cup: see Fed Cup
Federer, Roger 29
photographs Plate 12
FedEx Cup 880
Felix (hurricane) 31
Felker, Clay Schuette 78
female: see women
fencing 804, 839
Fengshen (typhoon) 30, 34
fiber 210, 214
fiber-optic cable
East Africa Submarine Cable System 187
fiction
awards 771, 774, 777, 778
Pulitzer Prize 762
field hockey 805, 839
Fields Medal 110
Fiesta Bowl 874
FIFA World Cup 876, 877
figure skating 830, 847
Fiji 313
flags of the world Plate 18
Fillmore, Millard 597, **600,** 609, 614, 624
film: *see* motion picture
finance: *see* banking; business; economics
Finland 314
flags of the world Plate 18
fire
disasters 32, 34
US work-related fatalities 719
first lady (US) 608
Fischer, Bobby 78
fish
fat intake in US diet *208*
food guide pyramid *209*
nutritional value 212
fitness: see physical activity
flag
flags of the world Plates 17–22
flight 172
space exploration 167
flood 29
disasters 31, 32, 33, 34
photographs Plate 8
flora: see plant
Florida 658
chronology 30
crime rates 690, 691
currency: quarters 704
death penalty sentences 694
electoral votes 635
energy consumption 705, 706
government 682, 684
immigration 650
poverty level 652
prison population 693
state population 646
US Congress 628, 631, 636
flowering plant, *or* angiosperm
oldest plants 189
Fogelberg, Dan 78
Fomalhaut (star) 134
food
chronology 23, 26, 27, 29
cooking measurements 159
food label 214
food pyramid *209*
health indicators 200
nutritional value 210, 211
see also diet
Food and Drug Administration, The, *or* FDA 207
food pyramid ***209***
football 868, 869
chronology 12, 13, 19, 20,22
photographs Plate 13
see also association football; rugby
foreclosure
photographs Plate 9
Ford, Gerald R. 597, **606,** 611, 621, 624
foreign trade: *see under* individual nations by name
forest 189
Formula One racing, *or* F-1 racing, *or* Grand Prix racing 850
Fossett, Steve 14, 78
fossil 24
Fox, Justin 701
fraction (mathematics) 163
France 316
armed forces of the world 578
cell phone subscribers 166
chronology 18
disasters 31
education 566
flags of the world Plate 18
photographs Plate 5
Prix Goncourt 779
rulers 552
Thoroughbred racing 888
freedom
Jerusalem Prize 780
freestyle skiing 832, 847
freestyle wrestling, *or* catch-as-catch-can wrestling 845
French billiards: see three-cushion billiards
French Guiana 318
French Open (tennis) 29, **916, 917**
photographs Plate 12
French Polynesia 320
disasters 31
flags of the world Plate 18
Frontiere, Georgia Irwin 79
fruit
fat intake in US diet *208*
food guide pyramid *209*
nutrition 210, 212
fuel 7
fuel-cell car 29
Fujita scale, *or* F-Scale 177

G

G-8: *see* Group of Eight
Gabon 321
flags of the world Plate 18
Gabriel, Peter 35
Galilean satellite 148
Gambia, The 322
flags of the world Plate 18
game (recreation) 161
Gamma-ray Large Area Space Telescope: *see* GLAST
Gandhi, Sonia 35
Ganymede (satellite) 141
Garfield, James A. 597, **602,** 610, 616, 624
Garnett, Kevin
photographs Plate 13
Gates, Robert 35
Gaza Strip 15, 30
photographs Plate 3
GCC: *see* Gulf Cooperation Council
Gebrselassie, Haile 16
Gelb, Peter 36
Gemini (astronomy) 130, 132
General Motors 15
genetics 21, 28
genital herpes 205
geology 191
disasters 178
geologic time scale 193
Georgia 324
chronology 13, 18, 21, 26, 29
flags of the world Plate 18
internally displaced persons 563
photographs Plate 2

Georgia (US) **659**
crime rates 690, 691
currency: quarters 704
death penalty sentences 694
disasters 24
electoral votes 635
energy consumption 705, 706
government 682, 684
immigration 650
income taxes 725
poverty level 652
prison population 693
state population 646
US Congress 628, 631, 636
Germany 325
armed forces of the world 578
cell phone subscribers 166
chronology 14
education 566
flags of the world Plate 18
refugee population 563
rulers 553
Thoroughbred racing 889
gestation 188
Getty, Estelle 79
Gettysburg Address 596
Ghana 328
flags of the world Plate 18
Ghazi, Abdul Rashid 79
Gilbert, Elizabeth 36
GLAST (telescope) 29
global warming
chronology 11, 13, 18, 25
Golden Globes 740
golf 880
chronology 11, 12, 13, 15, 16, 29
Olympic champions 806
photographs Plates 12, 13
World Cup 880, 886
gonorrhea 205
González, Ángel 79
Gore, Al 49
Goulet, Robert 79
government
influential people of 2008 35
United States 596, 682
see also individual nations and states by name
Gracq, Julien 79
grain
fat intake in US diet *208*
food guide pyramid *209*
nutritional value 212
Grammy Awards 22, **752**
Grand National, The 886
Grand Prix racing: *see* Formula One racing
Grant, Ulysses S. 597, **601**, 609, 615, 624
Gray, Simon 79
Great Britain: *see* United Kingdom
Great Wall of China 14
Greco-Roman wrestling
Olympic Games 827, 845
Greece 329
ancient units of measurement 162
armed forces 578
chronology 14, 18, 21
disasters 31
education 566
flags of the world Plate 18
Greenland 331
chronology 13, 28
flags of the world Plate 18
Gregorian calendar, *or* New Style calendar **121**
Grenada 332
flags of the world Plate 19
Grey Cup 875
Griffin, Merv 79
Griffin, Michael 36
Group of Eight, *or* G-8 545
Guadeloupe 334
Guam 335
flags of the world Plate 19
US governors 682
US House 634
US population 652
Guatemala 33, **336**
flags of the world Plate 19
US adoptions 698
Guernsey 337
flags of the world Plate 19
Guinea 338
flags of the world Plate 19
Guinea-Bissau 340
flags of the world Plate 19
Gulf Cooperation Council, *or* GCC 9, 545
Gulf States 9
Gulf War 642, 643
Guyana 15, **341**
flags of the world Plate 19
Gygax, Ernest Gary 79
gymnastics 806, 808, 839
photographs Plate 11

H

Habash, George 79
Hagen, Earle 79
Haiti 342
flags of the world Plate 19
Hale-Bopp, Comet 141
Hall, Oakley Maxwell 79
Halley's Comet 141
Hamas, *or* Islamic Resistance Movement 574
chronology 30
Hambletonian Trot 894
hammer throw 928
Olympic Games 792, 795
Han, Jeff 36
Hancock, Herbie 36
handball 809, 839
Harding, Warren 597, **610**, 617, 624, 635
Hardwick, Elizabeth 79
Harel, Yossi 79
harness racing 12, 886, 894
Harper, Stephen 13, 51
Harrington, Padraig
photographs Plate 13
Harris, René Reynaldo 79
Harrison, Benjamin 597, **602**, 610, 616, 624
Harrison, William Henry 597, **599**, 609, 614
"Harry Potter and the Deathly Hallows" 12
"Harry Potter and the Order of the Phoenix" 11
Hartack, Bill 79
Harvard University 782
Hasty Pudding Theatricals Man and Woman of the Year Awards 782
Hawaii 659
crime rates 690, 691
currency: quarters 704
electoral votes 635
energy consumption 705, 706
government 682, 684
immigration 650
income taxes 725
poverty level 652
prison population 693
state population 646
US Congress 628, 631, 636
Hayes, Isaac 79
Hayes, Rutherford B. 597, **602**, 609, 615, 624
Hazlewood, Lee 80
Healey, Jeff 80
health 200
body mass index 216
chronology 16, 18, 22
contraceptive use by US women 206
heat disorders 176
nutrition, children, and obesity 117
safer sex defined 205
Ultraviolet Index 176
US health expenditures *206*
see also diet; physical activity; and individual nations by name
health care 702
heart
target training zones *216*
heat index 176
heat wave
disasters 31
Heinz, W. C. 80
Heisman Trophy 874
Helms, Jesse 80
photographs Plate 16
Helmsley, Leona 80
Hevelius, Constellations of 131
heptathlon 928, 929
Herrera Campíns, Luis 80
Heston, Charlton 80
Hezbollah, *or* Party of God 30, 575
photographs Plate 3
high jump 928, 929
Olympic champions 790, 794
highway 186
Hill, Oliver 80
Hillary, Edmund Percival 80
Hillery, Patrick John 80
Hinduism 567, 568, 569, 570
holidays 124
Hipparchus 119
Hispanic literature 780
history
ancient units of measurement 161

Pulitzer Prize 764
recent disasters 30
recent events 11
rulers, regimes, and dynasties 548
US chronology 581
see also individual nations and other subjects by name
HIV, *or* human immunodeficiency virus **204**
causes of death 201, 203
chronology 11, 12
safer sex defined 205
hockey: *see* field hockey; ice hockey
Hofmann, Albert 80
holiday
civil 126
religious and traditional 123
Hollywood Foreign Press Association 740
Holy Roman Empire 554
Honda Motor Company, Ltd. 29
Honduras 344
disasters 33
flags of the world Plate 19
honeybee 14
Hong Kong 345
chronology 20
disasters 33
flags of the world Plate 19
Thoroughbred racing 889
Hoover, Herbert 597, **604**, 610, 618, 624
Horse of the Year 893
horse racing 886
chronology 17, 21, 25, 28, 29
see also thoroughbred racing
Hosseini, Khaled 36
House of Representatives (US) **630**
congressional apportionment 630
joint committees 630
standing committees 635
housing market 8, 702
photographs Plate 9
Hoyer, Steny H. 630
Hu Jintao 35, 52
Huckabee, Mike
photographs Plate 7
Hughes, Brendan 80
human being
body mass index 216
male/female/young/group 189
see also children; men; women
human immunodeficiency virus: *see* HIV
Humbard, Rex 80
Hungary 347
flags of the world Plate 19
hurdles 928, 929
Olympic Games 789, 794
hurricane
chronology 13
classifications 177
costliest in the US 178
deadliest in the US 177
names 177
Hurwicz, Leonid 80
Huygens: *see* Cassini-Huygens
Hyakutake Comet 141
Hyde, Henry 81
hydroelectricity
US energy consumption 705
hydrologic project 186
Hyperion 149

I

i-LIMB (artificial limb) 29
IAAF World Cup 933, 934
Ibrahim, Anwar 35
Ibrahim, Mo 36
ICC: *see* International Criminal Court
ice dancing 830, 848
ice hockey 26, 29, 830, 848, **895**, 896
ice skating 834, 847
Iceland 348
flags of the world Plate 19
Idaho 14, **660**
crime rates 690, 691
currency: quarters 704
death penalty sentences 694
electoral votes 635
energy consumption 705
government 682, 684
immigration 650
income taxes 725
poverty level 652
prison population 693
state population 646
US Congress 628, 631, 636
Iditarod Trail Sled Dog Race 24, **907**
Illinois 660
chronology 23
crime rates 690, 691
currency: quarters 704
death penalty sentences 694
electoral votes 635
energy consumption 705
government 682, 684
immigration 650
income taxes 725
poverty level 652
prison population 693
state population 646
US Congress 628, 631
Immelt, Jeffrey 36
immigration
foreign-born population in the US 649, 698
immigrants admitted to the US 649, 650
migration of foreigners 562
immunization 706
impeachment 623
income: see wage
income tax (US)
federal 724
state 725
India 350
armed forces of the world 578
cell phone subscribers 166
chronology 11, 12, 14, 17, 24
disasters 30, 31, 33, 34
dynasties 558
education 566
flags of the world Plate 19
internally displaced persons 563
photographs Plate 3
US adoptions 698
Indian Ocean 197
Indian Wars (N.Am.) 642
Indiana 661
crime rates 690, 691
currency: quarters 704
death penalty sentences 695
electoral votes 635
energy consumption 705, 706
government 682, 684
immigration 650
income taxes 725
poverty level 652
prison population 693
state population 646
US Congress 628, 631, 636
Indianapolis 500 28, **850**
Indonesia 352
armed forces of the world 578
cell phone subscribers 166
chronology 15, 22
disasters 31, 32
education 566
flags of the world Plate 19
internally displaced persons 563
Indy car racing 850
IndyMac Bank
photographs Plate 9
infant
causes of death, U.S. 203
worldwide health indicators 200
infinity pool 564
injury 202, 716
insurance
comparative hourly compensation costs 710
US health care expenditure *206*
Intel Science Talent Search 116
internally displaced persons 563
International Criminal Court, *or* ICC **547**
International Medal for Outstanding Discoveries in Mathematics: see Fields Medal
international organization 545
terrorist organizations 574
International Space Station, *or* ISS 167, 170
International System of Units, *or* SI **154**
international trade: *see under* individual nations by name
Internet 166
chronology 18, 30
see also individual subjects for relevant Web sites
invention
National Inventor of the Year Award 116
Iowa 29, **661**
crime rates 690, 691
currency: quarters 704
electoral votes 635
energy consumption 705, 706
government 682, 684

immigration 650
income taxes 725
poverty level 652
prison population 693
state population 646
US Congress 628, 632, 636

Iran 354
armed forces of the world 578
cell phone subscribers 166
chronology 11, 14, 16, 19, 27, 28
disasters 33
education 566
flags of the world Plate 19
Persian dynasties 558
refugee population 563

Iraq 355
chronology 11, 12, 13, 14, 15, 16, 19, 20, 21, 23, 29, 30
flags of the world Plate 19
internally displaced persons 563
photographs Plates 3, 4
refugee population 563

Iraq War, *or* Second Persian Gulf War 13, 15, 16, 21, 23, 29
US casualties 643

Ireland 25, **357**
flags of the world Plate 19
Thoroughbred racing 888

iron
nutrition 210, 211

Islam 567, 568, 570
calendar 122
caliphs 557
holidays 124

Islamic Resistance Movement: see Hamas

island 194

Isle of Man 359
flags of the world Plate 19

Israel 360
armed forces 578
chronology 11, 13, 14, 15, 18, 21, 24, 28, 29, 30
education 566
flags of the world Plate 19
internally displaced persons 563
photographs Plates 3, 4

ISS: *see* International Space Station

Istanbul 33

Italy 361
armed forces of the world 578
cell phone subscribers 166
chronology 13, 14
education 566
flags of the world Plate 19
Roman emperors 548
Thoroughbred racing 889

Ivan (cyclone) 33

J

Jackson, Andrew 597, **599**, 608, 613, 624

Jainism 568, 570, 571

Jamaica 363
flags of the world Plate 19

James E. Sullivan Memorial Trophy 784

January
astronomical phenomena 135
eclipses 138

Japan 365
armed forces of the world 578
cell phone subscribers 166
chronology 11, 15, 18, 29
education 566
flags of the world Plate 19
holidays 124
rulers and regimes 558
sumo wrestling 932
Thoroughbred racing 889

Japan Prize 111

Japan Series 17, **855**

javelin (sports) 792, 795, 928

Jefferson, Thomas 584, 596, **598**, 608, 612, 624

Jepsen, Mary Lou 36

Jersey 367
flags of the world Plate 19

Jerusalem Prize 780

Jesus Christ: *see* Christianity

Jew: *see* Judaism

Jiwei, Lou 36

Jigme Khesar Namgyal Wangchuk 25

Jobs, Steve 36

Johnson, Andrew 597, **601**, 609, 615

Johnson, Lady Bird 81

Johnson, Lyndon B. 597, **605**, 611, 620, 624

Johnson, Tom 81

Joint Chiefs of Staff, chairman of (US) **639**

Jolie, Angelina 35

Jordan 368
disasters 33
flags of the world Plate 19

Jordan, Hamilton 81

journalism
Pulitzer Prize 761
photographs Plate 16

Judaism 568, 570, 571
calendar 121
holidays 123

judo 809, 839

jukebox musical 564

Julian calendar, *or* Old Style calendar **121**

July
astronomical phenomena 136
eclipses 138

June
astronomical phenomena 135

Jupiter 147
celestial bodies 140
Great Red Spot 623
moons 141, 148
morning and evening stars 137
rings 149
superlatives 141, 142

K

Kabul (Afghanistan)
photographs Plate 3

Kaká 35

Kansas 662
crime rates 690, 691
currency: quarters 704
death penalty sentences 695
electoral votes 635
energy consumption 705, 706
government 682, 684
immigration 650
income taxes 725
poverty level 652
prison population 693
state population 646
US Congress 628, 632, 636

Karadzic, Radovan
photographs Plate 5

Kashmir 31, 33

kayaking 797, 798, 837

Kayani, Ashfaq 35

Kazakhstan 370
chronology 16
disasters 33
flags of the world Plate 19
US adoptions 698

Kekule, Friedrich August von 643

Kelvin 154, 155, 159

Kennedy, John F. 597, **605**, 611, 620, 624

Kennedy, Ted
photographs Plate 7

Kennedy Center Honors 105

Kentucky 662
crime rates 690, 691
currency: quarters 704
death penalty sentences 695
disasters 33
electoral votes 635
energy consumption 705, 706
government 682, 684
immigration 650
income taxes 725
poverty level 652
prison population 694
state population 646
US Congress 628, 632, 636

Kentucky Derby 28, 886, **889**

Kenya 371
chronology 20, 21, 22, 26
education 566
flags of the world Plate 19
internally displaced persons 563

Kerr, Deborah 81

Khalil, Mustafa 81

Kidd, Michael 81

Kiet, Vo Van 87

kilogram 154, 155

Kim Jong Il 55

King James Bible 759

Kiribati 22, **373**
flags of the world Plate 19

Kirkwood gaps 146

kiteboarding 564

Kluger, Jeffrey 117

Knievel, Evel 81

Koolhaas, Rem 36

Kopp, Wendy 36

Korea, North 374
armed forces of the world 578
chronology 11, 15, 16, 25, 30
disasters 31

flags of the world Plate 19
photographs Plate 2, 15
Korea, South 376
armed forces of the world 578
cell phone subscribers 166
chronology 16, 18, 19, 20
disasters 33
flags of the world Plate 19
US adoptions 698
Korean Conflict 642, 643
Korman, Harvey 81
Kornberg, Arthur 81
Kosovo 377
Balkanization 217
chronology 20, 21, 23, 24, 26, 29
photographs Plate 2
Kovács, László 81
Kroes, Neelie 36
Kuiper Belt 141, 146
Kurd, Ali Ahmed 12
Kyoto Prize 29
Kuwait 379
construction 9
flags of the world Plate 19
Kwanzaa 124
Kyl, John 627
Kyrgyzstan 380
flags of the world Plate 19

L

labor
civilian federal employment 712
comparative hourly compensation costs 710
highest average salary 712
median income 711
minimum wage 712
occupational illnesses and injuries 716
older Americans 713
strikes and lockouts 714
trade union membership 715
US employment 709
work-related fatalities by cause 718
see also employment; unemployment
Lacaille, Southern constellations of 131
lacrosse 810
Ladies' British Amateur Championship (golf) **885**
Ladies' Professional Golf Association Championship: *see* LPGA Championship
Lagerfeld, Karl 36
lake 198
Lamb, Willis Eugene, Jr. 81
land reclamation 187
landslide
disasters 31, 32
language 564
Laos 382
flags of the world Plate 19
large number 163
Latin America
chronology 19
education 566
refugees 563
religions 568
Latin American Integration Association, *or* ALADI 545
Latvia 383
flags of the world Plate 19
Laurus, Metropolitan 81
law 574
chronology 19, 23
international court 547
United States 689
death penalty 694
FBI directors 695
landmark rulings 625
prison population 693
Supreme Court 5, 624
see also crime
law case (US) **625**
League of Arab States, *or* Arab League 545
Lebanon 385
chronology 14, 21, 27, 29, 30
flags of the world Plate 19
internally displaced persons 563
LED: *see* light emitting diode system
Lederberg, Joshua 81
Ledger, Heath 82
photographs Plate 14
Lee, Sherman Emery 82
legume 213
Lehman, Clarence 7
leisure 727
Lekima (typhoon) 32
L'Engle, Madeleine 82
Leo (astronomy) 130, 132
Lesotho 386
flags of the world Plate 19
Levin, Ira Marvin 82
Libby, Lewis "Scooter" 11
Liberation Tigers of Tamil Eelam, *or* LTTE 575
Liberia 388
flags of the world Plate 19
US adoptions 698
Libertadores de América Cup 878
libertarianism 6
Libra (constellation) 130, 132
library 565
Libya 12, **389**
disasters 34
flags of the world Plate 20
Liechtenstein 391
flags of the world Plate 20
life 23, **188**
life expectancy 200
light 128
light bulb 30
light emitting diode system, *or* LED 116
light rail: *see* subway
light-year 128
Lincoln, Abraham 595, 596, 597, **601**, 609, 615, 624
liquid measure 160
liquor 160
Lisbon Treaty 19
literacy
world profile 566
literature
awards 771, 774, 776, 777, 779, 780
Nobel Prize 100
Pulitzer Prize 762
chronology 16, 24, 29
photographs Plate 16
Lithuania 30, **392**
flags of the world Plate 20
Little League World Series 14, **855**
lockout (US) **714**
London Marathon 26
longevity
mammals 188
oldest plants 189
worldwide health indicators 200
long jump
Olympic Games 791
López, Michelsen, Alfonso 82
López Trujillo, Alfonso Cardinal 82
Louisiana 15, **663**
crime rates 690, 691
currency: quarters 704
death penalty sentences 695
electoral votes 635
energy consumption 705, 706
government 682, 684
immigration 650
income taxes 725
poverty level 652
prison population 694
state population 646
US Congress 628, 632, 636
Love, Kermit 82
Loving, Mildred 82
LPGA Championship 29, **883**
LTTE: *see* Liberation Tigers of Tamil Eelam
luge 831, 849
luminosity class 133
lunar eclipse 138
lunar month 122
lunar parallax 128
Lustiger, Jean-Marie Cardinal 82
Luxembourg 393
flags of the world Plate 20
Lys, Ihor 116

M

Ma Ying-jeou 35
Mac, Bernie 82
Macau 395
flags of the world Plate 20
Macedonia 396
flags of the world Plate 20
Madagascar 397
disasters 33
flags of the world Plate 20
Madison, James 596, **598**, 608, 613, 624
Mahesh Yogi, Maharishi 82
Mailer, Norman 82
main-belt asteroid 147
Maine 663
crime rates 690, 691
currency: quarters 704
electoral votes 635

energy consumption 705, 706
government 682, 684
immigration 650
income taxes 725
poverty level 652
prison population 694
state population 646
US Congress 628, 632, 636
Mainwaring, Chris 82
Major League Soccer Cup 879
Maktum, Sheikh Mohammed ibn Rashid al- 35
Malawi 399
flags of the world Plate 20
Malaysia 400
flags of the world Plate 20
Maldives 13, **402**
flags of the world Plate 20
male: *see* men
Mali 403
flags of the world Plate 20
malnutrition
causes of death worldwide 202
Malta 404
chronology 20
flags of the world Plate 20
malware 564
mammal 188
Mamo, Anthony Joseph 82
Man Booker Prize 777
Mann, Abby 82
Mann, Delbert 82
Manulis, Martin Ellyot 83
map
UN peacekeeping missions *577*
world maps Plates 23–32
marathon 898, 928, 930, 932
chronology 16, 17, 26
Olympic Games 789, 793
Marceau, Marcel 83
March
astronomical phenomena 135
Marine Corps (US)
US casualties 642
US deployment 639
US military leadership 638
US pay scale 640
marriage
statistics 699
unmarried-couple households 698
Mars 145
celestial bodies 139
morning and evening stars 137
photographs Plate 10
superlatives 142
Mars Exploration Rover Mission 170
Mars Express (space program) 170
Mars Global Surveyor, *or* MGS 170
Mars Odyssey 170
Mars Pathfinder 170
Mars Reconnaissance Orbiter 170
Marshall Islands 406
flags of the world Plate 20
Martin, Dick 83
Martinique 407
Marulanda Vélez, Manuel 83
Maryland 664
crime rates 690, 691
currency: quarters 704
death penalty sentences 695
electoral votes 635
energy consumption 705, 706
government 682, 684
immigration 651
income taxes 725
poverty level 652
prison population 694
state population 646
US Congress 628, 632, 636
mass 165
Massachusetts 665
crime rates 690, 691
currency: quarters 704
electoral votes 635
energy consumption 705, 706
government 682, 684
immigration 651
income taxes 725
Mayflower Compact 584
poverty level 652
prison population 694
state population 646
US Congress 628, 632, 636
Masters Tournament 880
mathematics
decimal equivalents of common fractions 163
Fields Medal 110
large numbers 163
mathematical formulas 162
playing cards and dice chances 161
Roman numerals 162
Matisse, Henri 635
Mauritania 408
chronology 20
flags of the world Plate 20
Mauritius 410
flags of the world Plate 20
May
astronomical phenomena 135
Mayflower Compact 584
Mayotte 411
McCain, John 35, 59, **579**
photographs Plate 6
McConnell, Mitch 627
McGee, Harold 36
McKay, Jim 83
McKinley, William 597, **602**, 610, 616, 624
measurement 154
earthquakes 178
time 119
meat *208, 209,* 213
Mediate, Rocco 29
photographs Plate 12
Medicaid (US) *206*
Medicare (US) *206*
medicine
chronology 15, 16, 22, 23, 29
Nobel Prize winners 97
see also health
Mediterranean region
death causes 202
Medvedev, Dmitry 59
photographs Plate 5
megalopolis 689
Mehsud, Baitullah 35
Melbourne Cup 886
men
mortality
causes of death 201
life expectancy 200
United States
dietary guidelines 210
education 699
employment 709
food guide pyramid *209*
income 710, 711
marriage statistics 699
nursing home population 698
older Americans in the workforce 713
physical activity 215
population 648
unemployment 715
mental health day 564
MERCOSUR: *see* Southern Common Market
Mercury (planet) 21, 139, 141, **142**
morning and evening stars 137
Merkel, Angela 59
Messenger (spacecraft) 21
Messmer, Pierre August Joseph 83
Messner, Tammy Faye 83
metal 165
meteor, *or* falling star, *or* shooting star **137**
meteor shower 137
meteorite 137, 175
meteoroid 137, 146
meteorology 174
meter 154, 155
meter-kilogram-second system, *or* MKS system 156
methane gas 7
methicillin-resistant Staphylococcus aureus, *or* MRSA (bacterium) 16
metric system
conversion table 155
cooking 159
spirits 160
tables of equivalents 156
weight, mass, density 165
metro: *see* subway
metropolitan area: *see* urban area
Mexican-American War 642
Mexico 412
armed forces 578
cell phone subscribers 166
chronology 14, 20, 27, 28
disasters 30, 31, 32
education 566
flags of the world Plate 20
photographs Plate 7
Meyer, Stephenie 36
MGS: *see* Mars Global Surveyor
Mianzhu City (China)
photographs Plate 10

Michaels, James Walker 83
Michaels, Lorne 36
Michigan 665
crime rates 690, 691
currency: quarters 704
electoral votes 635
energy consumption 705, 706
government 682, 685
immigration 651
income taxes 726
poverty level 652
prison population 694
state population 646
US Congress 628, 632, 636
Micronesia 415
flags of the world Plate 20
Middle East 12
rulers 556
world maps Plate 25
Miles, Buddy 83
military 577
chronology 12, 29
armed forces 638, 578
NATO commands 638
United States 200, 638, 640
see also individual nations by name
milk
food guide pyramid *209*
Milongo, André 83
Minghella, Anthony 83
minimum wage 12, 710, 712
mining
disasters 31
Minnesota 666
chronology 12
crime rates 690, 691
currency: quarters 704
electoral votes 635
energy consumption 705, 706
government 682, 685
immigration 651
income taxes 726
poverty level 652
prison population 694
state population 646
US Congress 628, 632, 636
Mint (US) **703**
Miss America 759
Miss Universe 760
Mississippi 666
crime rates 690, 691
currency: quarters 704
death penalty sentences 695
electoral votes 635
energy consumption 705, 706
government 682, 685
immigration 651
income taxes 726
poverty level 652
prison population 694
state population 646
US Congress 628, 632, 636
Missouri 635
crime rates 690, 691
currency: quarters 704
death penalty sentences 695
disasters 34
electoral votes 635
energy consumption 705, 706
government 682, 685
immigration 651
income taxes 726
poverty level 652
prison population 694
state population 646
US Congress 628, 632, 636
Mitchell, George 35
MKS system: *see* meter-kilogram-second system
modern pentathlon 810, 840
Moldova 416
flags of the world Plate 20
mole (measurement) 154, 155
Monaco 417
flags of the world Plate 20
Mondavi, Robert 83
mondegreen 564
money: see currency
Mongolia 418
flags of the world Plate 20
monogamy 205
Monroe, James 596, **598**, 608, 613, 624
monsoon 30
Montana 667
crime rates 690, 691
currency: quarters 704
death penalty sentences 695
electoral votes 635
energy consumption 705, 706
government 682, 685
immigration 651
income taxes 726
poverty level 652
prison population 694
state population 646
US Congress 628, 632, 636
Montenegro 420
flags of the world Plate 20
month
astronomical phenomena 135
astronomy 128
calendars 122
Moon (Earth) **144**
astronomical constants 128
celestial bodies 139
chronology 17
eclipses 138
perigee and apogee 145
phases 144, 145
moon (satellite)
Earth 144
eclipse 138
Jupiter 148
Neptune 152
Saturn 149
superlatives 141
Uranus 151
Morales, Evo 35
Mormon fundamentalist community
photographs Plate 8
morning star 137
Morocco 421
armed forces 578
disasters 33, 34
flags of the world Plate 20
Morrice, Norman 83
Morse, Barry 83
mortality
causes of death, US 203, 204
causes of death, worldwide 201, 202
war casualties, US 642
work-related fatalities, US 718
mortgage 8, **723**
motion picture, *or* cinema, *or* film, *or* movie **729**
awards 739, 740, 741
Academy Awards 727, 729
chronology 12, 20, 22, 23
photographs Plates 14, 15
top-grossing films 744, 745
top 100 films 89
US National Film Registry 741
video rental and sales 744
motorboat racing 810
mountain 194
movie: see motion picture
Mozambique 423
chronology 17
flags of the world Plate 20
MRSA (bacterium): see methicillin-resistant Staphylococcus aureus
mud slide
disasters 31
Mugabe, Robert 29
photographs Plate 4
Muhammad: *see* Islam
Muli, Koki 20
Murakami, Takashi 36
Murcer, Bobby Ray 83
murder: see crime
Murdoch, Rupert 36
Musharraf, Pervez 19
photographs Plate 4
music 752
awards 752, 753, 755, 756, 757
Academy Awards 737, 738
Pulitzer Prizes 769
chronology 18, 19, 22, 24, 28
opera companies 759
orchestras 758
photographs Plate 15
musical 749
Muslim: see Islam
Myanmar, *or* Burma **425**
armed forces of the world 578
chronology 15, 27, 28, 29
disasters 34
flags of the world Plate 20
internally displaced persons 563

N

Nadal, Rafael
photographs Plate 12
Naimi, Ali al- 36
name 177, 188, 692
Namibia 426
flags of the world Plate 20
Nargis (cyclone) 27, 34
NASA, *or* National Aeronautics and Space Administration 22, 167
NASCAR 18, 851

nation, *or* country **218**
sporting codes 783
see also individual nations by name
National Aeronautics and Space Administration*: see* NASA
National Basketball Association: *see* basketball
National Book Award 771
National Collegiate Athletic Association, *or* NCAA
basketball 859
National Film Registry 741
National Football League, *or* NFL 868, 869
chronology 13, 20, 22
National Hockey League, *or* NHL **895**, 896
National Humanities Medal, *or* Charles Frankel Prize **109**
National Inventor of the Year Award 116
national library: *see* library
National Magazine Awards 27
National Medal of Arts 106
National Medal of Science 112
national park (US) **199**
National Security Council, *or* NSC **645**
National Spelling Bee (US) **700**
Native American: see American Indian
NATO: *see* North Atlantic Treaty Organization
natural gas
chronology 18, 21, 30
US energy consumption 705
nature 117, 199
see also individual subjects by name
Nauru 427
flags of the world Plate 20
navy
armed forces 578
US casualties 642
US deployment 639
US military leadership 638
US pay scale 640
NBA: *see* basketball
NCAA: *see* National Collegiate Athletic Association
near-Earth asteroid 146, 147
Nebraska 19, **668**
crime rates 690, 691
currency: quarters 704
death penalty sentences 695
electoral votes 635
energy consumption 705, 706
government 682, 685
immigration 651
income taxes 726
poverty level 652
prison population 695
state population 646
US Congress 628, 632, 636
Nelson, Ken 83
neologism 564
neoreligionist 568, 570
Nepal 428
chronology 20, 26, 28, 29, 30
flags of the world Plate 20
Neptune 152
celestial bodies 140
moons and rings 152
morning and evening stars 137
superlatives 141
Netherlands, The 430
flags of the world Plate 20
Netherlands Antilles 432
flags of the world Plate 20
netroots 564
Nevada 669
crime rates 690, 691
currency: quarters 704
death penalty sentences 695
electoral votes 635
energy consumption 705, 706
government 682, 685
immigration 651
poverty level 652
prison population 694
state population 646
US Congress 628, 632, 636
New Caledonia 433
New Hampshire 669
crime rates 690, 691
currency: quarters 704
death penalty sentences 695
electoral votes 635
energy consumption 705, 706
government 682, 685
immigration 651
income taxes 726
poverty level 652
prison population 694
state population 646
US Congress 628, 632, 636
"New Horizons" (spacecraft) 153
New Jersey 670
crime rates 690, 691
currency: quarters 704
death penalty sentences 694
electoral votes 635
energy consumption 705, 706
government 682, 685
immigration 651
income taxes 726
poverty level 652
prison population 695
state population 646
US Congress 628, 632, 636
New Mexico 670
crime rates 690, 691
currency: quarters 704
death penalty sentences 695
electoral votes 635
energy consumption 705, 706
government 682, 685
immigration 651
income taxes 726
poverty level 652
prison population 694
state population 646
US Congress 628, 632, 636
New Style calendar: *see* Gregorian calendar
New York 671
crime rates 690, 691
currency: quarters 704
death penalty sentences 695
electoral votes 635
energy consumption 705, 706
government 682, 685
immigration 651
income taxes 726
poverty level 652
prison population 694
state population 646
US Congress 628, 632, 636
New York City (NY, US) 24
New York City Marathon 17, **900**
New York Giants 22
photographs Plate 13
New York Philharmonic (orchestra)
photographs Plate 15
New Zealand 434
flags of the world Plate 20
Newbery Medal 774
Nextel Cup 851
NFL: *see* National Football League
NHL: *see* National Hockey League
Nicaragua 436
disasters 31
flags of the world Plate 20
Niger 437
flags of the world Plate 20
Nigeria 438
cell phone subscribers 166
chronology 15, 23
disasters 32, 33, 34
flags of the world Plate 20
nine-ball 861
Nixon, Richard M. 597, **605**, 611, 620, 624
Nobel Prize 16, **91**
Noel (tropical storm)
disasters 32
nonfiction
awards 768, 771
Nooyi, Indra 36
Nordic Combined 905
Nordic Council of Ministers 545
Nordic skiing
Nordic World Cup 906
Olympic Games 832, 846
world championships 904, 905
Norman, Larry David 84
norovirus 564
North America
caves 195
continents 191
deserts 196
education 566
forests 190
mountains 195
refugees 563
religions 569
rivers 198
temperature extremes 174
volcanoes 197
world maps Plate 29
worldwide health indicators 200
see also individual nations by name
North Atlantic Treaty Organization, *or* NATO 545
chronology 11, 17
North Carolina 671
crime rates 690, 691
currency: quarters 704

death penalty sentences 695
electoral votes 635
energy consumption 705, 706
government 682, 685
immigration 651
income taxes 726
poverty level 652
prison population 694
state population 646
US Congress 628, 633, 636
North Dakota 672
crime rates 690, 691
currency: quarters 704
electoral votes 635
energy consumption 705, 706
government 682, 685
immigration 651
income taxes 726
poverty level 652
prison population 694
state population 646
US Congress 628, 633, 636
North Korea: see Korea, North
Northern Ireland
chronology 11, 23
Northern Mariana Islands
US governors 682
US population 652
Northwest Passage 15
Norway 440
chronology 15
flags of the world Plate 20
novel: *see* fiction
November
astronomical phenomena 136
NSC: *see* National Security Council
nuclear energy
chronology 17, 19
US consumption 705
photographs Plate 2
nuclear weapon
armed forces 578
chronology 19
number 154
fractions to decimals 163
large numbers 163
Roman numerals 162
nursing home
US population 698
nut
nutritional value 213
nutrition: *see* diet
Nuxhall, Joe 84

O

OAS: *see* Organization of American States
Obama, Barack 35, 62, **580**
photographs Plate 6
obesity 117
body mass index 216
obituary 76
photographs Plate 16
ocean 197
tsunami 180
Oceania, *or* Tropical Pacific
causes of death 202
caves 195
continents 191
education 566
forests 190
health indicators 201
mountains 195
refugees 563
religions 569
rivers 199
temperature extremes 174
US deployment 640
volcanoes 196
world maps Plate 32
see also individual countries by name
Ochoa, Lorena 35
October
astronomical phenomena 136
odds (game) 161
Odhaib, Madeeha Hasan 35
Odinga, Raila 26
O'Donnell, Joe 84
OECD: *see* Organisation for Economic Co-operation and Development
Oerter, Al 84
O'Hara, Kelli
photographs Plate 15
Ohio 672
crime rates 690, 691
currency: quarters 704
death penalty sentences 695
electoral votes 635
energy consumption 705, 706
government 682, 686
immigration 651
income taxes 726
poverty level 652
prison population 694
state population628
US Congress 628, 633, 636
ohm 158
OIC: see Organization of the Islamic Conference
oil (food) *208*, 211
oil (fuel): see petroleum
oil spill 19
Oklahoma 673
crime rates 690, 691
currency: quarters 704
death penalty sentences 695
electoral votes 635
energy consumption 705, 706
government 682, 686
immigration 651
income taxes 726
poverty level 652
prison population 694
state population 646
US Congress 628, 633, 636
Old Style calendar: see Julian calendar
Olga (tropical storm) 32
Olmert, Ehud
photographs Plate 4
Olympic Games 785
champions
Summer Games 786
Winter Games 829
chronology 11, 25
photographs Plates 1, 11
recent medal winners
2008 Summer Games 836
2006 Winter Games 846
sites of modern games 786
see also Special Olympics; *and* individual sports by name
Olympus Mons 142
Oman 442
construction 9
flags of the world Plate 20
O'Neill, Norm 84
Oort cloud 141
OPEC: see Organization of Petroleum Exporting Countries
opera company 759
Orange Bowl 873
Orange Broadband Prize, *or* Orange Prize 29, **778**
orchestra 758
Oregon 674
crime rates 690, 691
currency: quarters 704
death penalty sentences 695
electoral votes 635
energy consumption 705, 706
government 682, 686
immigration 651
income taxes 726
poverty level 652
prison population 694
state population 646
US Congress 628, 633, 636
Organisation for Economic Co-operation and Development, *or* OECD 546
organization, international: *see* international organization
Organization for African Unity: *see* African Union
Organization for Security and Co-operation in Europe, *or* OSCE 546
Organization of American States, *or* OAS 546
Organization of Petroleum Exporting Countries, *or* OPEC 546
Organization of the Islamic Conference, *or* OIC 546
Orman, Suze 36
Orthodox Christianity 568, 570
Oscar: *see* Academy Award
OSCE: *see* Organization for Security and Co-operation in Europe
Ottoman Empire 557
see also Turkey
Ouroboros 643
outer-belt asteroid 147
oven 159
Oz, Mehmet 36

P

Pacific Islands: see Oceania
Pacific Islands Forum, *or* South Pacific Forum 546
Pacific Ocean 197
volcanoes 196
pageant: *see* beauty pageant

paid leave
comparative hourly compensation costs 710
Paisley, Ian 63
Pakistan 443
armed forces of the world 578
cell phone subscribers 166
chronology 11, 12, 14, 15, 16, 17, 18, 19, 20, 22, 25, 26, 27, 29, 30
disasters 31, 32
flags of the world Plate 20
photographs Plates 4, 16
refugee population 563
Palau 445
flags of the world Plate 21
Palestinian Authority 13, 19
Palestinians 11, 12
Palin, Sarah 63
photographs Plate 6
palm tree 714
Panama 446
chronology 14
disasters 34
flags of the world Plate 21
Panama Canal 14
paper money (US) 703
Papua New Guinea 447
chronology 27
flags of the world Plate 21
Paraguay 449
chronology 26
flags of the world Plate 21
park
national parks in US 199
parsec 128
Party of God: *see* Hezbollah
passport 706
Pausch, Randy 35, 84
Pavarotti, Luciano 84
PBA Tournament of Champions 861
peace
Nobel Prize winners 16, 101
peacekeeping mission (UN) 577
Pelosi, Nancy 630
PEN/Faulkner Award 24, **774**
Pennsylvania 674
crime rates 690, 691
currency: quarters 704
death penalty sentences 695
electoral votes 635
energy consumption 705, 706
government 682, 686
immigration 651
income taxes 726
poverty level 652
prison population 694
state population 646
US Congress 628, 633, 636
pentathlon 792, 795, 929
see also modern pentathlon; winter pentathlon
people 35
obituaries 76
influential people of 2008, 35
Person of the Year, 1927–2007, 90
rulers 548
UN persons of concern 563
US presidents 596, 597
see also award; chronology; religion; sports
performing arts
Kennedy Center Honors 105
see also individual arts by name
perigee (astronomy)
Moon 145
periodic table 164
perpetual calendar 125
Perry, Tyler 36
Persia 558
see also Iran
Persian Gulf War (1990–91) 643
Persian Gulf War, Second: see Iraq War
persons of concern 563
Peru 450
chronology 13, 15, 29
disasters 31
education 566
flags of the world Plate 21
internally displaced persons 563
pescatarian 564
Petraeus, David H.
photographs Plate 4
petroleum
chronology 17, 20, 23, 25, 28
photographs Plate 9
US energy consumption 705
PGA Championship (golf) **882**
Phelps, Michael 64
photographs Plate 11
Phoenix (spacecraft) 12, 170
photographs Plate 10
Philippines 452
cell phone subscribers 166
disasters 34
education 566
flags of the world Plate 21
internally displaced persons 563
physical activity, *or* exercise **207**
Americans and physical activity 215
burn calories 215
target heart rate *216*
see also diet; health
physics 165
Nobel Prize winners 16, 91
physiology
Nobel Prize winners 97
phytonutrient 564
Pierce, Franklin 597, **600**, 609, 614, 624
Pierce, Paul
photographs Plate 13
PIF: *see* Pacific Islands Forum
Pisces 130, 132
Pistorius, Oscar 35
Pitt, Brad 35
planet 142
morning and evening stars 137
superlatives 141
see also solar system; individual planets by name
planetary ring: see ring
plant 189
taxonomy 188
play: see theater
playing cards 161
Pleshette, Suzanne 84
Pluto 153
celestial bodies 140
superlatives 141
pocket billiards 860
poetry 12
awards 28, 767, 772, 781
poison
causes of death worldwide 202
disasters 32
see also venom
poker 11, 161
Poland 453
cell phone subscribers 166
chronology 18
disasters 33
education 566
flags of the world Plate 21
polar bear 28
pole vault 928, 929
Olympic champions 791, 794
Polites, Geoffrey Paul 84
politics: *see* individual political entities by name
Polk, James K. 597, **600**, 609, 614, 624
Pollack, Sydney 84
Pollux (star) 134
polo 810
pool (sport) 860, 861
pope 572
population
largest cities 562
refugees 563
United States 645, 648, 649
territories 652
urban areas 687, 688
see also specific nations and states by name
Portugal 455
chronology 14, 28
flags of the world Plate 21
postal system
US zip code web site 689
potassium 214
poultry *208*, 213
poverty
children 696
state levels 652
Power, Samantha 217
Powercore (LED system device) 116
pre-Columbian civilization 561
Preakness Stakes 886, **890**
precipitation
global temperatures and precipitation 174
US cities 175
Premio Cervantes: *see* Cervantes Prize
preservation (nature) **199**
president (US) **596**
biographies 597
cabinets 612
election 2008 579
photographs Plates 6, 7

impeachment 623
National Medal of Arts 106
succession 611
vice presidents 607
wives and children 608
Presidential Medal of Freedom 17
pretexting 565
price: *see* Consumer Price Index
prime minister (UK) **551**
prison 13
US state and federal population 693
Pritzker Architecture Prize 25, **781**
Prix Goncourt 779
Procyon (star) 134
Professional Bowlers Association Tournament of Champions: *see* PBA Tournament of Champions
Professional Golfers' Association Championship: *see* PGA Championship
Pronovost, Peter 36
property crime
arrests in the US 693
US crime rates 690, 692
US crime trends 689
prosecco 565
protein 210, 211, 214
Protestantism 568, 570
Ptolemy 130
public debt (US) 702, 721
publishing 21
Puerto Rico 456
chronology 25
flags of the world Plate 21
US governors 682
US House 634
US population 652
Pulitzer Prize 25, **761**
Putin, Vladimir 35, 65
Person of the Year 2007 90
photographs Plate 5

Q

Qaeda, al- 20, 576
Qatar 458
construction 9
flags of the world Plate 21
quarter
US states coin program 704

R

Rabinowitz, Victor 84
race
children 696, 697
education 699
median income 711
minimum wage 710
nursing home population 698
US cities 688
US population 648, 649
US unemployment rates 715
racino 565
rackets (sport) 810
Radiohead 36
railway
civil engineering projects 187
Rambo, Dottie 84
Rankine (temperature) 159
Raymond, Paul 84
RDA: *see* recommended daily allowance
Reagan, Ronald 597, **606**, 611, 621, 624
Réaumur scale format 159
recommended daily allowance, *or* RDA 207
refugee 563
Reid, Harry 627
relay (sports)
Olympic Games 790, 794
religion 567
Dalai Lamas 560
holidays 123
popes 572
Templeton Prize winners 104
world map Plate 23
renewable energy 7
retirement
compensation costs 710
US economy 702
Réunion 459
Revolutionary War (US) 642
Rhode Island 675
crime rates 690, 691
currency: quarters 704
electoral votes 635
energy consumption 705, 706
government 682, 686
immigration 651
income taxes 726
poverty level 652
prison population 694
state population 646
US Congress 628, 633, 636
Rice, Condoleezza 66
Richter scale 178
Rigel (star) 133
Right Livelihood Awards 19
Rigopulos, Alex 36
ring, *or* planetary ring
Jupiter 149
Neptune 152
Saturn 150
Uranus 151
river 198
Rizzuto, Phil 84
Roberto, Holden Álvaro 85
Roberts, John G. 66
Rock, Chris 36
rock and roll
Hall of Fame inductees 757
Roddick, Dame Anita 85
rodeo 20, **901**
Roderick, John 85
Roitfeld, Carine 36
Roman Catholicism 568, 570
chronology 11
popes 572
Roman Empire 548
ancient units of measurement 162
see also Italy
Roman numeral 162
Romania 460
disasters 31
flags of the world Plate 21
Romanov, Grigory Vasilyevich 85
Romney, Mitt
photographs Plate 7
Roosevelt, Franklin D. 597, **604**, 610, 618, 624
Roosevelt, Theodore 597, **603**, 610, 617, 624
roque (sport) 810
Rose Bowl 872
Rosen, Jeffrey 5
Rothschild, Baron Elie Robert de 85
rowing
Olympic Games 810, 840
Rudd, Kevin 22, 35
rugby 868, 875, 876
chronology 12, 17, 24
Olympic champions 812
Rugby league football 868, **876**
World Cup 875, 876
Rugby union football 868, **876**
runaway 693
running: *see* marathon; track and field
rural area
US population 648
Russert, Tim 36, 85
photographs Plate 16
Russia 462
armed forces of the world 578
cell phone subscribers 166
chronology 11, 12, 13, 14, 16, 17, 19, 23, 26, 27, 29
education 566
flags of the world Plate 21
internally displaced persons 563
photographs Plates 2, 5, 16
rulers 555
US adoptions 698
see also Union of Soviet Socialist Republics
Rwanda 464
disasters 33
flags of the world Plate 21
Ryan, Tony 85
Ryder Cup 880, **884**

S

Saad al-Abdullah al-Salim al-Sabah, Sheikh 85
Saakashvili, Mikhail 67
SAARC: *see* South Asian Association for Regional Cooperation
SADC: *see* Southern African Development Community
Sadr, Muqtada al- 35
safer sex 205
safety
aviation 173
heat index 176
ultraviolet index 176
wind chill 176
Saffir, Herbert Seymour 85
Saffir/Simpson Hurricane Scale 177
Sagittarius 130, 132
sailing, *or* yachting 11
Olympic Games 812, 840

Saint Kitts and Nevis 466
flags of the world Plate 21
Saint Laurent, Yves 85
St. Leger, The 886, **894**
Saint Lucia 467
flags of the world Plate 21
Saint Vincent and the Grenadines 468
flags of the world Plate 21
salary: *see* wage
Samoa 470
flags of the world Plate 21
San Marino 471
flags of the world Plate 21
Sánchez, Yoani 35
sandstorm 14
São Tomé and Príncipe 472
flags of the world Plate 21
Sarkozy, Nicolas 67
photographs Plate 5
satellite, artificial 167
saturated fat
dietary guidelines 210
fat intake in US diet *208*
food label 214
nutrition 211
Saturn 149
celestial bodies 140
moons 149
morning and evening stars 137
rings 150
superlatives 142
Saud, Prince al-Walid ibn Talal ibn Abdulaziz al- 36
Saudi Arabia 473
construction 9
disasters 32
education 566
flags of the world Plate 21
savings
comparative hourly compensation costs 710
Savoy, Gene 85
Scheider, Roy 85
Schengen zone (Europe) 20
Schiff, Nicholas 36
scholarship 565
see also education
schooling: *see* education
science 117
awards 110, 112
chronology 18, 21
influential people of 2008, 35
see also specific subjects by name
Scofield, Paul 85
scorpion 147
Scorpius 130, 132
Scotland 550
sea: *see* ocean
sea ice 13, 15
secession (Confederacy) 595
second (time) 119, 154, 155
Second Amendment (US Constitution) 30
Secretariat of the Pacific Community, *or* SPC, *or* South Pacific Commission 546
seed
nutritional values 213
Svalbard Global Seed Vault 23, 187
Senate (US) **627**
joint committees with House of Representatives 630
standing committees 629
Sendler, Irena 85
Senegal 475
disasters 32
education system 566
flags of the world Plate 21
senior citizen
Americans 65 and older 651
causes of death in US 203
median income in US 711
US nursing home population 698
US physical activity 215
US population 651
US workforce 713
September
astronomical phenomena 136
Serbia 476
Balkanization 217
chronology 20, 23, 24
flags of the world Plate 21
photographs Plate 5
refugee population 563
Serrault, Michel 85
Sethi, P. K. 86
Seven Wonders of the Ancient World 180
sex
safer sex defined 205
sexually transmitted diseases 205
sex offense, *or* sexual assault
US crime statistics 692, 693
sexually transmitted disease, *or* STD **205**
HIV and AIDS 204
safer sex defined 205
Seychelles 478
flags of the world Plate 21
Shakespeare, William 759
Shakhlin, Boris 86
Shekhar, Chandra 86
Shintoism 568, 570
ship
disasters 31, 32
Shomron, Dan 86
shooting
Olympic Games 814, 841
shooting star: *see* meteor
short-track speed skating
Olympic Games 836, 848
shot put 928, 929
Olympic Games 791, 794
SI: see International System of Units
Sidr (cyclone) 18, 19
disasters 32
Siegbahn, Kai Manne Börje 86
Sierra Leone 14, **479**
disasters 31, 32
flags of the world Plate 21
Sikhism 568, 570, 571
holidays 124
Sills, Beverly 86
Sills, Paul 86
Sinduhije, Alexis 35
Singapore 481
flags of the world Plate 21
Thoroughbred racing 889
Sippy, G. P. 86
Sirius (star) 133, 142
Six Nations Championship 876
skating: *see* ice skating
skeleton (sport)
Olympic Games 831, 849
ski jump 833, 906
skiing 902
see also specific types of skiing
sled dog racing 24, **906**, 907
Olympic champions 834
Slim Helú, Carlos 36
Slovakia 482
flags of the world Plate 21
Slovenia 484
flags of the world Plate 21
small body (astronomy) **146**
Smith, Ian Douglas 86
Smith, Mike 86
Smith, Roger Bonham 86
snooker 861
Snow, Tony 86
snowboarding 834, 847
Snyder, Tom 86
soccer: see association football
Social Security
comparative hourly compensation costs 711
society
family statistics, US 696
see also individual nations by name
sodium
food labels 214
meeting dietary guidelines 210
nutritional values 211
Soe Win 86
softball
Olympic Games 817, 841
soju 565
solar eclipse 138
solar parallax 128
solar system 139
celestial bodies 139
morning and evening stars 137
solar system entities
asteroid belt 146
comets 154
meteors 137
planets and satellites 142
Sun 142
superlatives 141
see also specific entities by name
Soldier Field (Chicago, Ill.) 917
Solheim Cup 880
Sollie, Tom 17
Solomon, Susan 36
Solomon Islands 485
flags of the world Plate 21
Solzhenitsyn, Aleksandr 86
photographs Plate 16
Somalia 486
chronology 17
flags of the world Plate 21
refugee population 563

song 755
South Africa 488
cell phone subscribers 166
chronology 13, 26, 28
disasters 34
education system 566
flags of the world Plate 21
South America 28
causes of death 202
caves 196
continents 191
deserts 196
forests 190
mountains 195
rivers 199
temperature extremes 174
volcanoes 197
world maps Plate 30
worldwide health indicators 200
see also individual nations by name
South Asian Association for Regional Cooperation, *or* SAARC 546
South Carolina 675
crime rates 690, 691
currency: quarters 704
death penalty sentences 694
electoral votes 635
energy consumption 705, 706
government 682, 686
immigration 651
income taxes 726
poverty level 652
prison population 695
state population 646
US Congress 628, 633, 636
South Dakota 676
crime rates 690, 691
currency: quarters 704
death penalty sentences 695
electoral votes 635
energy consumption 705, 706
government 682, 686
immigration 651
poverty level 652
prison population 694
state population 646
US Congress 629, 633, 636
South Korea: *see* Korea, South
South Pacific Commission: *see* Secretariat of the Pacific Community
South Pacific Forum: *see* Pacific Islands Forum
Southern African Development Community, *or* SADC 546
Southern Common Market, *or* MERCOSUR 546
southern constellations 131
Soviet Union: *see* Union of Soviet Socialist Republics
soybean 7
Soyuz (space program) 168
space exploration 167
chronology 16, 21, 25, 26, 28, 29
firsts 171
photographs Plate 10
space shuttle, *or* Space Transportation System, *or* STS 169
Spain 489
armed forces 578
cell phone subscribers 166
Cervantes Prize 780
chronology 14, 21, 26
flags of the world Plate 21
rulers 553
Spanish-American War 643
SPC: *see* Secretariat of the Pacific Community
Special Olympics 849
spectral class 132
speed of light 128
speed skating 834, 848
spelling bee 700
Spica (star) 134
Spingarn Medal 109
spiritism 568, 570
spirits: *see* liquor
spitball (baseball) 935
Spitzer, Eliot
photographs Plate 7
sport 783
photographs Plates 11, 12, 13
see also Olympic Games; *and* individual sports by name
Springsteen, Bruce 36
"Spruce Goose" (airplane) 578
Sri Lanka 491
armed forces 578
chronology 17, 20, 26
flags of the world Plate 21
internally displaced persons 563
stadium 885
Stanley Cup 29, **896**
star 129, 132, 133, 137
see also Sun
Stargell, Willie 857
state (US) **653**
Confederacy 595
crime rates 690
electoral votes 635
government officers and legislatures 683
governors 682
population 646
poverty level 652
prison population 693
quarters program 704
signers of the Declaration of Independence 585
see also individual states by name
State, Department of (US)
travel warnings 708
stateless person 563
STD: *see* sexually transmitted disease
steeplechase (horse racing) 886
steeplechase (track) 928, 929
Olympic Games 789
Stewart, John Coburn 87
Stewart, William Huffman 87
Stoppard, Tom 36
storm 33
strike (US) 15, 18, 19, 22, **714**
STS: *see* space shuttle
subprime 565
subprime mortgage 8
subway, *or* metro, *or* light rail
civil engineering projects 187
succession
US presidents 611
Sud, Shivani 116
Sudan, The 493
chronology 12, 16, 18, 21
disasters 34
flags of the world Plate 21
internally displaced persons 563
refugees 563
Sugar Bowl 873
Suharto 87
suicide
causes of death, worldwide 202
US work-related fatalities 719
suicide bombing 13, 20
sultan 557
Summer Olympic Games
champions 786
sites 786
2008 medal winners 836
summer time: *see* daylight saving time
sumo wrestling 932
Sun 142
astronomical constants 128
brightness 133
celestial bodies 139
classification of stars 132
eclipses 138
Ultraviolet Index 176
see also solar system
Sundance Film Festival 739
Super 14 Rugby Championship 876
Super Bowl 870
photographs Plate 13
supercross 565
supplemental pay
comparative hourly compensation costs 710
Supreme Court (US) **5, 624**
chronology 29, 30
justices 624
legal milestones 625
Suriname 15, **494**
disasters 34
flags of the world Plate 21
Sutong Bridge (China) 28
Svalbard Global Seed Vault 23, 187
Swaziland 495
flags of the world Plate 21
Sweden 497
education 566
flags of the world Plate 21
sweets
nutritional value 213
swimming 907
Olympic Games 817, 841
photographs Plate 11
world records 911
Swinton, Tilda
photographs Plate 15
Switzerland 498
flags of the world Plate 22

synchronized swimming
Olympic Games 821, 842
syphilis 205
Syria 500
armed forces of the world 578
chronology 14, 15, 16, 28
disasters 31
flags of the world Plate 22
internally displaced persons 563

T

T. S. Eliot Prize 780
table tennis 822, 842
taekwondo 822, 842
Taft, William Howard 597, **603**, 610, 617, 624
Taiwan 502
armed forces of the world 578
chronology 21, 29
flags of the world Plate 22
Tajikistan 503
flags of the world Plate 22
Takarli, Fu'ad al- 87
Taliban
photographs Plate 3
Tanzania 505
flags of the world Plate 22
refugee population 563
Taoism 568, 570
Tata, Ratan 36
Taurus 130, 132
tax
US economic problems 702
US federal structure 724
US state individual income taxes 725
taxonomy 188
Taylor, Jill Bolte 36
Taylor, Zachary 597, **600**, 609, 614
Tebow, Tim 19
technology 117
awards 111, 116
see also individual subjects by name
telephone
cell phones 166, 167
US area code web site 689
telescope 29
television
chronology 15, 22
Emmy Awards 746
temperature
equivalents 158
extremes 174
global temperatures and precipitation 174
heat index 176
normal temperatures and precipitation in US cities 175
wind chill 176
Temple 1 Comet, *or* Comet 9P 141
Templeton, John Marks 87
Templeton Prize 24, **104**
Tennessee 676
crime rates 690, 691
currency: quarters 704
death penalty sentences 695
disasters 33
electoral votes 635
energy consumption 705, 706
government 682, 686
immigration 651
income taxes 726
poverty level 652
prison population 694
state population 646
US Congress 629, 633, 636
tennis 912
chronology 11, 14, 21, 29
Olympic Games 822, 843
tenpin bowling 862
Teoctist 87
terrorism
chronology 13, 14, 30
organizations 574
Terrorism, War on
US casualties 643
Tethys 141
Texas 677
chronology 25, 28
crime rates 690, 691
currency: quarters 704
death penalty sentences 695
electoral votes 635
energy consumption 705, 706
government 682, 686
immigration 651
poverty level 652
prison population 694
state population 646
US Congress 629, 633, 636
Texas Hold'em 565
Thailand 506
armed forces of the world 578
cell phone subscribers 166
chronology 13, 16, 22, 23
disasters 32, 34
education 566
flags of the world Plate 22
theater 749, 751, 752
chronology 24, 29
Pulitzer Prize 763
theater company 752
theft: *see* property crime
Thompson, Hank 87
Thomson, James 36
Thorn, Gaston Egmond 87
Thornburgh, Nathan 6
Thoroughbred racing 886, **887**, 889, 890, 892, 893, 894
three-cushion billiards, *or* carom billiards, or French billiards 860, 861
Tibbets, Paul Warfield, Jr. 87
Tibet 24
Dalai Lamas 560
photographs Plate 3
tiger 22
time 119
geologic time scale *193*
"Time" (magazine)
Balkanization 217
Hollywood and the Academy Awards 727
libertarianism 6
obesity and children 117
influential people of 2008 35
Person of the Year, 1927–2007, 90
top 100 films 89
US economy 701
US Supreme Court 5
time zone
map 120
Titan (satellite) 149
Togo 508
flags of the world Plate 22
Tonga 509
flags of the world Plate 22
Tony Awards 29, **749**
photographs Plate 15
tornado 24, 33, **177**
Toronto Film Festival 740
Tour de France 867
tourism 706
toy
chronology 12, 18
track and field, *or* athletics **927**
chronology 14, 16
Olympic Games 787, 843
see also marathon
trade union (US) 715
traffic accident
disasters 31
train
disasters 30, 32, 33
trans fat 214
transportation
air travel 172
US work-related fatalities 718
see also individual nations by name
travel 706
customs exemptions 708
passports, visas, and immunizations 706
travelers to and from the US 707
US State Department travel warnings 708
tree 189
triathlon
Olympic Games 792, 823, 844
Trinidad and Tobago 510
flags of the world Plate 22
Triple Crown (horse racing) **889**, **894**
triple jump 928, 929
Olympic champions 791, 794, 844
Triton (satellite) 152
Truman, Harry S. 597, **604**, 611, 619, 624
Truman, Margaret 87
tsunami 180
Tsvangirai, Morgan 30
tug-of-war (sports) 792
tulip mania 190
Tunguska event 137
Tunisia 512
flags of the world Plate 22
tunnel
civil engineering projects 187
world's longest tunnels 184
Turin Olympic Games 846
Turkey 513
armed forces of the world 578

cell phone subscribers 166
chronology 14, 17, 18, 21, 23, 27
disasters 32
education 566
flags of the world Plate 22
internally displaced persons 563
Ottoman sultans 557
refugee populations 563
Turkmenistan 515
chronology 16
flags of the world Plate 22
Turner, Ike 87
Tuvalu 516
flags of the world Plate 22
2,000 Guineas 886, **893**
2001 Mars Odyssey 170
Tyler, John 597, **599**, 609, 614, 624
typhoon 30

U

UEFA Champions League 877
UEFA Cup 878
UEFA European Championship 877
Uganda 518
chronology 23
disasters 31, 34
flags of the world Plate 22
internally displaced persons 563
refugees 563
Ukraine 519
armed forces of the world 578
cell phone subscribers 166
chronology 16, 20
disasters 30, 32
flags of the world Plate 22
US adoptions 698
Ultraviolet Index, *or* UV Index **176**
UN: *see* United Nations
unemployment (US) 715, **716**
Unified Combatant Commands 638
Union of South American Nations, *or* UNASUR/UNASUL 28, 546
Union of Soviet Socialist Republics, *or* USSR
rulers 556
space exploration 167
see also Russia
United Arab Emirates 521
construction 9
flags of the world Plate 22
Thoroughbred racing 889, 894
United Kingdom 522
armed forces of the world 578
awards 756, 777, 778, 780
cell phone subscribers 166
chronology 12, 14, 16, 18, 25, 27
education 566
flags of the world Plate 22
large numbers 163
measurement system 157
prime ministers 551
refugee population 563
rulers of Scotland 550
sovereigns of Britain 550
Thoroughbred racing 888, 893
United Nations, *or* UN
chronology 13, 16, 17, 29
international organizations 546
membership 547
peacekeeping missions *577*
persons of concern 563
secretaries general 546
United Self-Defense Forces of Colombia, *or* Autodefensas Unidas de Colombia, *or* AUC 577
United States 525, 579
area code Web sites 689
arts and entertainment
awards 105, 106
films 741, 745
literature 761, 771, 781
music 756, 769
television 746
theater 749
video rentals 744
budget 721
chronology 11, 12, 13, 14, 18, 21, 22, 23, 29
cities 687, 688, 689
crime rates in US 692
disasters 31, 33, 34
economics and business
bankruptcy filings 724
consumer price indexes 719, 720
currency 703, 704
governmental spending 721
mortgages 723
photographs Plate 9
public debt 721
US economic problems 701
US Mint 703
education 699
National Spelling Bee 700
world education profile 566
elections
congressional apportionment 636
electoral votes by state 635
photographs Plates 6, 7
presidency 2008 579
employment 709
civilian federal employment 712
employment by gender and occupation 709
occupational hazards 717, 718
senior citizens 651, 713
strikes and lockouts 714
unemployment 714, 715, 716
union membership 715
wages 710, 711, 712
energy 705, 706
flags of the world Plate 22
government - executive branch
CIA directors 644
FBI directors 695
impeachment 623
National Security Council 645
presidents 596, 597, 608, 611, 623
vice presidents 607
government - judicial branch
legal milestones 625
Supreme Court decisions 5
Supreme Court justices 624
government - legislative branch 627
health
contraceptive use 206
food pyramid *209*
dietary guidelines 210
fat intake *208*
health care expenditure *206*
leading causes of death 203, 204
obesity and children 117
physical activity 215
history
chronology 581
major documents 584, 587, 591, 595, 596
history - recent events
chronology 11
law and crime 689
map 653
military 638
armed forces of the world 578
defense contractor 644
joint chiefs of staff 639
veterans 642
nature
costliest hurricanes 178
deadliest hurricanes 177
national parks 199
temperature and precipitation 175
population 645, 648, 652, 699
by age 696
by religion 570
nursing homes 698
poverty level 652
refugees 563
unmarried-couple households 698
science and technology
awards 112, 116
British/US measurement system 157
cell phone use 166, 167
Internet use 166
large numbers 163
society 696
children 696, 697, 698
education 699
poverty 652, 696
religion 570
space exploration 167
sports
photographs Plates 11, 12, 13
Thoroughbred racing 886, 887, 889, 890, 892
see also specific sports by name
states 653
Confederacy 595
crime rates 690

electoral votes 635
governors 682
officers and legislatures 683
populations 646
prison population 693
see also individual states by name
taxation structure 724
travel and tourism 706, 707
aviation 172, 173
customs 708
zip code Web sites 689
see also people and states by name
United States Amateur Golf Championship 885
United States Bowling Congress Bowling Championships 862
United States Open (golf) 29, **881**
photographs Plate 12
United States Open (tennis) **922, 924**
United States Women's Amateur Championship (golf) **885**
United States Women's Open (golf) **883**
universe 127
unmarried-couple households 698
Upshaw, Gene 87
Uranus 151
celestial bodies 140
moons and rings 151, 152
morning and evening stars 137
superlatives 141
urban area
US cities 687
crime 689, 692
fastest growing 688
population losses 688
racial makeup 688
salaries, highest 712
temperatures and precipitation 175
urban growth 687
US population 648
urban agglomerations 562
Uruguay 21, **529**
flags of the world Plate 22
USSR: *see* Union of Soviet Socialist Republics
Utah 678
crime rates 690, 691
currency: quarters 704
death penalty sentences 695
electoral votes 635
energy consumption 705, 706
government 682, 686
immigration 651
income taxes 726
poverty levels 652
prison population 694
state population 646
US Congress 629, 634, 636
US prison population 694
UV Index: *see* Ultraviolet Index
Uzbekistan 14, **531**
flags of the world Plate 22

V

vagrancy 693
Valhalla 142
Van Buren, Martin 624, 597, **599**, 609, 614
Van Schalk, Graham William Wakefield 116
vandalism 693
Vanuatu 533
flags of the world Plate 22
Vatican City State 534
flags of the world Plate 22
Vega (star) 133
vegetable 210, 213
fat intake in US diet *208*
food guide pyramid *209*
Venezuela 534
chronology 18, 19
flags of the world Plate 22
venom 147
Venter, J. Craig 36
Venus 139, 141, **143**
morning and evening stars 137
Vermont 678
crime rates 690, 691
currency: quarters 704
electoral votes 635
energy consumption 705, 706
government 682, 686
immigration 651
income taxes 726
poverty level 652
prison population 694
state population 646
US Congress 629, 634, 636
veteran 642
vice president (US) **607**
video 744
video game 27
Vietnam 536
armed forces of the world 578
disasters 32
flags of the world Plate 22
refugee population 563
Vietnam War 642, 643
violence
causes of death, worldwide 202
violent crime
arrests in the US 693
US crime rates 690, 692
US crime trends 689
Virgin Islands (US) **538**
flags of the world Plate 22
US governors 682
US House 634
US population 652
Virginia 679
crime rates 690, 691
currency: quarters 704
death penalty sentences 695
electoral votes 635
energy consumption 705, 706
government 682, 686
immigration 651
income taxes 726
poverty level 652
prison population 694
state population 646
US Congress 629, 634, 636
Virgo 130, 132
virus (biology) 14
visa 706
vital statistics: *see under* individual nations by name
vitamin 207, 210
Vo Van Kiet 87
volcano 196
chronology 27
eruptions 180
volleyball 936
Olympic Games 823, 844
volt 158
volume
British/US measurement system 157
mathematical formulas 162
voting: *see* election
Voyager (spacecraft) 169

W

wage 711, 712
comparative hourly compensation costs 710
minimum wage, US 712
US economy 701
US military pay scale 640
Wagoner, Porter 88
walk (sports) 928, 929
Olympic Games 790, 794
Walsh, Bill 88
Walsh, Brian 117
Wangchuk, Jigme Khesar Namgyal 25
war
causes of death, worldwide 202
US casualties 642
see also individual nations by name
Washington 679
crime rates 690, 691
currency: quarters 704
death penalty sentences 694
electoral votes 635
energy consumption 705, 706
government 682, 686
immigration 651
poverty level 652
prison population 695
state population 646
US Congress 629, 634, 636
Washington, George 596, **597**, 608, 612, 624
Washington, DC, *or* District of Columbia **658**
crime rates 690, 691
electoral votes 635
energy consumption 705, 706
immigration 650
income taxes 725
poverty level 652
state population 646
US House 634
water
fruits and vegetables 210
oceans and seas 197

worldwide health indicators 200
water polo
Olympic Games 823, 844
water-soluble vitamin 207
watt 158
Wearne, Eileen 88
weather: *see* climate; meteorology
Web site: see Internet
webinar 565
weight 155, 157, **165**
body mass index 216
weightlifting 936
current world champions 937
Olympic Games 823, 844
Weiskopf, Michael 579
Wessex, kings of 550
West Virginia 680
crime rates 690, 691
currency: quarters 704
electoral votes 635
energy consumption 705, 706
government 682, 687
immigration 651
income taxes 726
poverty level 652
prison population 694
state population 646
US Congress 629, 634, 636
Wexler, Jerry 88
Wheeler, John Archibald 88
Whitbread Book Awards see Costa Book of the Year Awards
"White House" 699
Whiteley, Frank Yewell, Jr. 88
Whitney, Phyllis A. 88
WHO: *see* World Health Organization
Wild 2 Comet, *or* 81P Wild 141
wildfire 11, 17, 31
Williams, Serena
photographs Plate 13
Williams, Venus
photographs Plate 13
Willis, Bill 88
Wilson, Woodrow 597, **603**, 610, 617, 624
Wimbledon: see All-England Tennis Championships
wind chill 176
Winfrey, Oprah 35
wing nut 565
Winston, Stan 88
Winter Olympic Games
champions 829
sites 786
2006 medal winners 846
winter pentathlon 836
Wisconsin 29, **680**
crime rates 690, 691
currency: quarters 704
electoral votes 635
energy consumption 705, 706
government 682, 687
immigration 651
income taxes 726
poverty level 652
prison population 694
state population 646
US Congress 629, 634, 636
WNBA: *see* basketball
women 778
basketball 859, 860
mortality
causes of death 201
life expectancy 200
physical activity 215
United States
contraceptive use 206
dietary guidelines 210
education 699
employment 709, 711
food guide pyramid *209*
income 710, 711
marriage statistics 699
nursing home population 698
older Americans in the work-force 714
population 648
unemployment 715
Women's British Open Championship 884
Women's National Basketball Association: *see* basket-ball
Woodiwiss, Kathleen 88
Woodruff, John Youie 88
Woods, Tiger 29, 75
photographs Plate 12
work stoppage 714
workers' compensation
comparative hourly 711
world 217
cellular phone subscribers 166
flags of the world Plates 17–22
health 200
Internet use 166
largest dams 185
longest tunnels 184
religions 569
world maps Plate 23
seven wonders of the ancient world 180
tallest buildings 181
temperature extremes 174
time zones *120*
world maps Plates 24–25
see also Earth and other spe-cific subjects by name
World Bank 19
World Cross Country Championships 935
world cup: *see under* specific sport
World Health Organization, *or* WHO 21, 22
World Hockey Championship 895
World Series 17, **852**
World Trade Organization, *or* WTO 546
World Volleyball Championships 936
World War I 642, 643
World War II 642, 643
World Wide Web, *or* WWW
Internet 166
see also individual subjects for more Internet resources
wrestling
Olympic Games 826, 845
Wright, Bob 35
Wright, Suzanne 35
WTO: see World Trade Organization
WWW: *see* World Wide Web
Wyman, Jane 88
Wyoming 681
crime rates 690, 691
currency: quarters 704
death penalty sentences 695
electoral votes 635
energy consumption 705, 706
government 682, 687
immigration 651
poverty level 652
prison population 694
state population 646
US Congress 629, 634, 636

Y

yachting: *see* sailing
Yamanaka, Shinya 36
Yangtze River dolphin: *see* baiji
year
astronomical constants 128
astronomical phenomena for 2009, 135
measuring time 119
see also calendar
Yearning for Zion Ranch (Texas)
photographs Plate 8
Yemen 539
disasters 32
flags of the world Plate 22
Yongbyon (North Korea)
photographs Plate 2
young adult literature: see children's literature
Youth Olympics 11
Yugoslavia: *see* Montenegro; Serbia

Z

Zahir Shah, Mohammad 88
Zambia 541
flags of the world Plate 22
Zaret, Hy 88
Zhang Hanzhi 88
Zimbabwe 542
chronology 14, 15, 26, 27, 28, 29, 30
flags of the world Plate 22
internally displaced persons 563
photographs Plate 4
zip code
US Web sites 689
Zodiac 132
constellations 130
Zoroastrianism 568, 570, 571
holidays 124
Zuckerberg, Mark 36
Zuma, Jacob 35